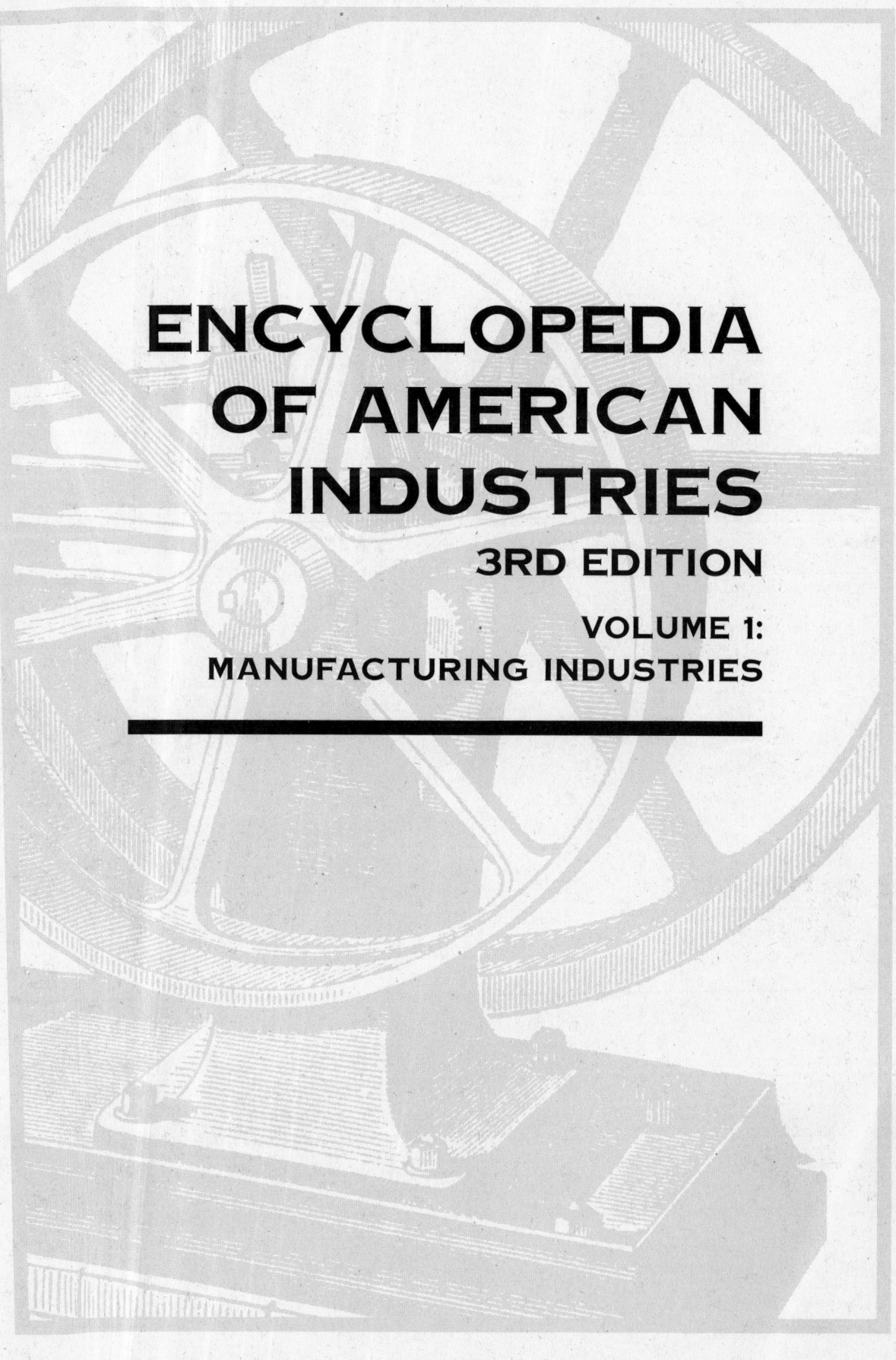

ENCYCLOPEDIA OF AMERICAN INDUSTRIES

3RD EDITION

VOLUME 1: MANUFACTURING INDUSTRIES

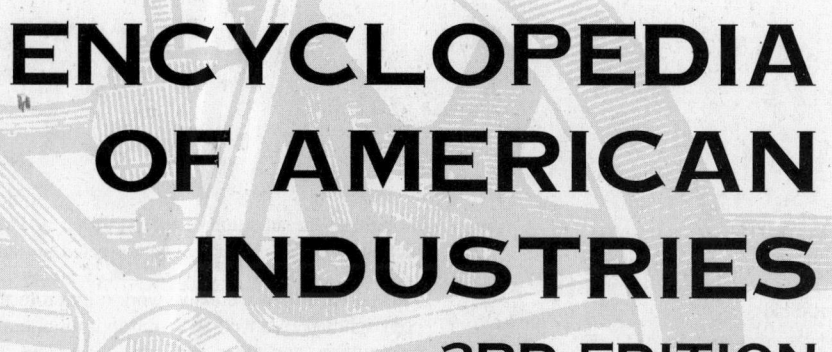

ENCYCLOPEDIA
OF AMERICAN
INDUSTRIES

3RD EDITION

VOLUME 1:
MANUFACTURING INDUSTRIES

REBECCA MARLOW-FERGUSON,
EDITOR

GALE GROUP

Detroit
New York
San Francisco
London
Boston
Woodbridge, CT

ENCYCLOPEDIA OF AMERICAN INDUSTRIES

THIRD EDITION

GALE GROUP STAFF

Editor: Rebecca Marlow-Ferguson

Associate Editor: Brian Rabold

Associate Editor: Chris Lopez

Contributing Editors: Alex Alviar, Caryn Anders, Donna Craft, Sheila Dow, Eric Hoss, Kathleen E. Maki Potts, Jaime E. Noce, Amanda C. Quick

Managing Editor Erin E. Braun

Electronic and Prepress Composition Manager: Mary Beth Trimper

Assistant Manager, Composition Purchasing and Electronic Prepress: Evi Seoud

Buyer: NeKita McKee

Production Design Manager: Kenn Zorn

Art Director: Pamela A. E. Galbreath

Technical Support Services: Wayne Z. Fong, Venus Little

Library of Congress Card Number: 00-106822

ISBN 0-7876-4273-8 (Set)
ISBN 0-7876-4274-6 (Volume One)
ISBN 0-7876-4275-4 (Volume Two)

Printed in the United States of America

CONTENTS

LUMBER & WOOD PRODUCTS, EXCEPT FURNITURE

FURNITURE AND FIXTURES

PAPER & ALLIED PRODUCTS

PRINTING, PUBLISHING & ALLIED INDUSTRIES

CHEMICALS & ALLIED PRODUCTS

PETROLEUM REFINING & RELATED INDUSTRIES

RUBBER & MISCELLANEOUS PLASTICS PRODUCTS

ELECTRONIC & OTHER ELECTRICAL EQUIPMENT & COMPONENTS, EXCEPT COMPUTER EQUIPMENT

MINING INDUSTRIES

CONSTRUCTION INDUSTRIES

TRANSPORTATION, COMMUNICATIONS, ELECTRIC, GAS, & SANITARY SERVICES

WHOLESALE TRADE

RETAIL TRADE

FINANCE, INSURANCE, & REAL ESTATE

PUBLIC ADMINISTRATION

INTRODUCTION

The *Encyclopedia of American Industries (EAI)* is a major business reference tool that provides detailed, comprehensive information on a wide range of industries in every realm of American business. Volume one provides separate coverage of 459 manufacturing industries. Volume two presents 545 essays covering the vast array of service and other non-manufacturing industries in the United States. Combined, these two volumes provide individual essays on every industry recognized by the U.S. Standard Industrial Classification (SIC) system. Both volumes of *EAI* are arranged numerically by SIC code for easy use. Additionally, each entry in the third edition includes the corresponding North American Industry Classification System (NAICS) code(s).

CONTENT AND ARRANGEMENT

Industry Essays. The *Encyclopedia*'s business coverage includes information on historical events of consequence, as well as relevant trends and statistics entering the twenty-first century. Sections of coverage in an essay may include the following:

- Industry Snapshot: Provides an overview of the industry and identifies key trends, issues, and statistics.
- Organization and Structure: Discusses the configuration and functional aspects of the industry, including government regulation, sub-industry divisions, and interaction with other industries.
- Background and Development: Relates the industry's genesis and historical development, including major technological advances, scandals, pioneering companies, major products, important legislation, and other factors that shaped the industry.
- Current Conditions: Provides information on the status of the industry in the late 1990s to early 2000s, with an eye to industry challenges on the horizon.

- Industry Leaders: Profiles major companies within the industry and includes discussion of financial performance.
- Workforce: Contains information on the size, diversity, and characteristics of the industry's workforce.
- America and the World: Discusses the global marketplace for the U.S. industry, as well as international participation in U.S. markets.
- Research and Technology: Furnishes information on major technological advances, areas of research, and their potential impact on the industry.
- Further Reading: Provides users with suggested further reading on the industry. These sources, many of which were also used to compile the essays, are publicly accessible materials such as magazines, general and academic periodicals, books, annual reports, and government sources, as well as material supplied by industry associations. This edition also includes references to numerous Internet sources. When available, the URL address and updated or visited date of these resources is included, although such addresses are apt to change frequently.

Graphs. The *Encyclopedia of American Industries* includes more than 350 informative, easy-to-read graphs detailing a wide range of key economic and business information. Graphs without source information have been compiled from the research material used to write the essay or from original research.

Conversion Tables. Two industry classification tables allow cross-referencing of SIC categories with the NAICS industry codes. (Please see below for additional information.)

Indexes. The *Encyclopedia of American Industries'* index contains alphabetic references from both volumes to companies, trade associations, significant business trends, government agencies, historical figures, and key legislation. It also includes cross-references for acronyms and variant names.

ABOUT INDUSTRY CLASSIFICATION

Encyclopedia of American Industries offers tools to analyze industries using two industry classification systems. The primary system, the Standard Industrial Classification (SIC) system, was established by the U.S. government to provide a uniform means for collecting, presenting, and analyzing economic data. SIC codes are still widely used by federal, state, and local government agencies; trade associations; private research organizations; and business professionals to promote comparability in the presentation of statistical data. In addition, *EAI* includes reference tables for the 1997 North American Industry Classification System (NAICS), which has been adopted by the U.S. government as its new standard for economic data. Each essay includes the corresponding NAICS code(s) as well.

1987 Standard Industrial Classification (SIC). Each SIC code classifies business and nonprofit establishments by the types of activities in which they are engaged; in other words, it is "industry-oriented." An establishment is an economic unit where a service is performed or a product is manufactured or sold (generally at a single physical location). To be recognized as a separate industry within the SIC system, a set of establishments must be statistically significant according to criteria such as the number of persons employed and the volume of business conducted. Each establishment is placed in an SIC category according to its primary activity, which is determined by the industry from which it derives the most revenue. Many large companies, however, operate multiple establishments and may participate in several industries, thus it is possible for a company to be a leading force in SIC categories outside of its primary industry.

The SIC system comprises four levels of classification, as described below:

- Divisions: The broadest SIC categories are divisions that define an activity in very general terms: Agriculture, Forestry, and Fishing; Mining; Construction; Manufacturing; Transportation, Communications, Electric, Gas, and Sanitary Services; Wholesale Trade; Retail Trade; Finance, Insurance, and Real Estate; and Public Administration, for example.
- Major Groups: Within these broad categories are major groups. Each begins with a unique two-digit code that makes up the first two numbers of the complete four-digit SIC code. In the case of Manufacturing, the major group codes range between 20 and 39. Examples of two-digit groups in Manufacturing are:

Food & Kindred Products (20); Tobacco Products (21); Furniture & Fixtures (25); Printing, Publishing, & Allied Industries (27); and Industrial & Commercial Machinery & Computer Equipment (35).
- Industry Groups: Major groups are further subdivided into three-digit industry groups. Each is assigned a three-digit code based on the two-digit code for its major group. For example, Printing, Publishing & Allied Industries is broken down into 271 for Newspapers, 272 for Periodicals, and 273 for Books.
- Industries: Industry Groups are divided still further into specific classifications that are assigned complete, four-digit codes based on the Industry Group. These four-digit classifications are the basis for the industries detailed in *EAI*.

1997 North American Industry Classification System (NAICS). Although NAICS has officially replaced the SIC system, industry information is still maintained in SIC categories for this edition. The *Encyclopedia of American Industries* provides conversion tables to compare SIC data with NAICS data, which the governments of Canada, Mexico, and the United States jointly adopted. It includes broad classifications that are common among the three nations as well as unique national-level classifications. Industries are specified within NAICS by up to six digits, however in some cases the most specific category is only five digits. The conversion tables provided in this book reflect the U.S. version of NAICS, which contains six digits.

NAICS is similar in principle to the SIC system but differs in industry specificity and grouping; NAICS is "production-oriented," or dependent on the activity of the industry. Also, although the U.S. Census Bureau calls NAICS a hierarchical numbering system, it does not have broad terms broken down into narrower terms, broken down into sub-classifications, then sub-sub-classifications—as with the SIC system.

Unfortunately, total reliance on NAICS data means the loss of historical information for some industries. To help combat this, in 2001 the Census Bureau is slated to release its information in both SIC and NAICS formats.

COMMENTS AND SUGGESTIONS

Questions, comments, and suggestions regarding the *Encyclopedia of American Industries* are welcomed. Please contact:

The Editor
Encyclopedia of American Industries
Gale Group
27500 Drake Rd.
Farmington Hills, MI 48331-3535
Telephone: 248-699-4253
Toll-Free: 800-347-GALE
URL: http://www.galegroup.com

FOREWORD

EXPANSION SUSTAINED: A MACRO VIEW OF U.S. ECONOMIC ACTIVITY AND INDUSTRY TRENDS

A multitude of events, most perhaps coincidental, converged to produce the thriving U.S. economy of the 1990s and early 2000s. By most measures, the period of expansion has been the longest in U.S. history, as well as one marked by a particularly elusive mix of favorable conditions. Vigorous macroeconomic growth, low price inflation, high labor participation rates, rising personal incomes and wealth, and a sharply rising stock market are only some of the auspicious hallmarks of the vibrant, world-leading economy.

To keep everything in perspective, though, it's useful to consider the unlikely convergence of events that intensified and prolonged the expansion. To take only a few examples, such diverse influences as very inexpensive oil prices (until late 1998); economic troubles in Asia, Russia, and Latin America; and the commercialization of a communications network known as the Internet all worked to the U.S. economic benefit. Cheap oil, for instance, helped keep price inflation down and, in doing so, probably helped forestall the Federal Reserve's raising of interest rates. Meanwhile, currency slumps and economic problems elsewhere in the world helped funnel capital into U.S. markets, fueling price growth in the stock markets and, at least temporarily, providing capital to U.S. businesses. And for its part, the Internet's mainstream emergence triggered a deluge of spending on computer hardware, software, and services extending to nearly every sector of the economy. Had the timing been different, and had there not been such a convergence, the economy might have puttered out years earlier.

But far from puttering out, the U.S. economy barreled forward, breaking records with surprising ease and causing some economists to rethink their theories about sustainable growth. In 1999 the U.S. gross domestic product approached $9.26 trillion in current dollars, marking a robust 4.2 percent gain after inflation is factored out.

That came on the heels of two previous years of 4-plus percent growth in real terms. All the while, inflation remained largely at bay, and the U.S. unemployment rate hovered at 30-year lows.

Both companies and individuals benefited from the 1990s expansion. Corporate earnings at U.S. firms advanced decisively throughout the decade, with before-tax profits more than doubling between 1990 and 1999. In the meantime, real disposable personal income grew by about 26 percent in total over the period, or by about 15 percent on a per capita basis.

INTERNET AND E-COMMERCE INCREASINGLY PERVASIVE

Moving on to events that have contributed to economic growth, an obvious question is, what is the impact of the Internet on traditional industries and the economy as a whole? Clearly, any attempt at a comprehensive answer could fill an entire book, and on just one industry at that. With that in mind, there are several broad implications to consider.

Online Marketplaces. Whereas in the mid- and late 1990s most Internet activity was confined to individual companies and trade organizations establishing a presence, since the late 1990s a new crop of sites has been recreating industries and vertical supply chains online. A few examples of these electronic marketplaces:

- The metals industries have multiple sites devoted to trading metals online.
- Three top paper companies in 2000 announced a global online marketplace that allows businesses to buy and sell forest products in a multi-vendor environment and do so seamlessly by integrating their purchasing and logistics systems with the site.

pete on price—potentially cutting into profits—and find it necessary to justify their mark-ups if they're not the low-cost producer.

Ultimately, as well, winners and losers will emerge in the e-commerce field. Developing and maintaining sophisticated e-commerce sites requires considerable skill and resources, and for some companies the investment will exceed the revenue potential. This is already apparent in several of the online retail categories, where competition for consumer mind share and market share is intense and even the leaders have had a tough time turning a profit, let alone the lower-tier players. This dynamic is widely expected to result in retail consolidation as the less able competitors are bought out, refocused, or simply go out of business, all this while online sales continue to grow in the aggregate at phenomenal rates. Observers see this weeding out as a necessary stage in the evolution of e-commerce.

- A large truck-parts manufacturer has launched a site to enable online purchases of parts and trucking-related services from a variety of providers.

These sites and a multitude of others aim to offer a competitive, usually neutral exchange that lets companies and consumers quickly determine a range of prices and options available and complete a transaction on the spot. The emphasis in the future, moreover, will be on providing value-added information and services via the online marketplace beyond simply quoting prices and entering transactions.

The trend toward industry marketplaces online, most pronounced in the lucrative business-to-business e-commerce category, is likely to get much bigger. Forrester Research, a market research firm, predicted that by 2003 the business-to-business online market would be worth $2.7 trillion—and more than half of those sales would be conducted through online marketplaces. In perhaps a less rigorous survey of business-to-business conference attendees, Forrester found that fully 71 percent of corporate leaders expected their companies to participate in such marketplaces by 2001.

Competitive Impact. Aside from shifting business and consumer transactions to an electronic medium, e-commerce promises to upset the competitive status quo in some industries. One reason is rising cost transparency associated with the Internet. As buyers gain access to fuller information about how much competing products cost and how much components of those products sell for, they'll enjoy a stronger negotiating position with suppliers. This means many suppliers will increasingly com-

ROBUST CAPITAL FLOWS AND INVESTMENT

Investment is a means of generating new growth opportunities by funding promising economic endeavors. By most measures, the U.S. economic investment climate was markedly robust in the 1990s. This includes not only the celebrated gains in the stock markets, which were awash with capital from both domestic and international sources, but also strong advances in corporate fixed investment and research and development (R&D). Expansion in these areas is usually seen as a platform for future economic growth.

Overall, Federal Reserve statistics pinpointed growth in gross private domestic investment at nearly 47 percent between 1995 and 1999. Private investment in equipment and software, a major component of corporate fixed investment, grew in the late 1990s at a torrid 8 to 12 percent a year, two to three times the rate of growth in the broader U.S. economy. Spending on information technology hardware and software contributed heavily to the increase.

Meanwhile, R&D spending trailed somewhat because of cutbacks in federal grants for research. R&D is responsible for, among other things, breakthrough technologies that can greatly impact entire industries and, potentially, the economy as a whole. Spending in this area grew at a more modest average of 6.6 percent annually from 1995 to 1999, according to a report compiled by the National Science Foundation (NSF), yet that rate still outpaced GDP growth. While federal support has diminished since the early 1990s, corporate R&D funding has more than picked up the slack, and now accounts for almost three-quarters of R&D spending in the United States. The NSF estimated total R&D outlays in 1999 at $247 billion.

Venture Capital. Venture capital has also become a key source of financing for new, innovative companies. The use of venture capital, privately placed equity (and sometimes debt) funding for start-up companies, burgeoned in the 1990s with the influx of new Internet-related companies, and more importantly, the boom in Internet stocks. Venture capital firms take massive stakes in risky albeit promising companies in hopes of cashing out handsomely months or years later when the companies go public. In 1999 venture capital in the United States soared to $36.5 billion, almost three times the 1998 level and a sixfold increase from 1995.

Despite its dramatic rise, venture capital directly impacts only a narrow portion of the economy—primarily Internet and health-care technology concerns. In the late 1990s between 1,000 and 2,000 companies a year, only a fraction all new start-ups, received venture backing. Total funding through venture capital also pales in comparison to other modes of investment, which measure in the hundreds of billions of dollars and even trillions.

Soaring Stocks. The buoyant stock markets represent a different kind of investment—that of capital—and often a more speculative kind. Nonetheless, they have been an increasingly important source of operations funding for start-ups and acquisitive companies. Increasing reliance on market equity has fed into so-called New Economy theories, which hold that, among other things, new technology companies—especially Internet firms—aren't as burdened by higher interest rates as traditional companies because they hold less debt. However, this assertion has been hotly contested and the evidence for it is spotty.

Still, the price growth of technology shares, in particular, has been staggering. From mid-1990 to mid-2000, the NASDAQ Composite Index, a broadly based stock gauge with heavy technology weighting, skyrocketed 600 percent. And that's even after a precipitous decline in early 2000, when the index peaked above the 5,000 mark, but soon tumbled back to the 3,500 range. A handful of computer and Internet firm shares grew by even greater multiples, although there was also no shortage of also-rans that failed to deliver exponential investment growth.

Other leading indexes such as the New York Stock Exchange Composite Index and the Standard & Poor's 500 also recorded sharp gains in the 1990s, although not nearly as big as the NASDAQ's. All told, the NYSE Composite, a broad measure of established, large-capitalization stocks, rose 220 percent from mid-1990 to mid-2000, while the narrower S&P 500, another large-cap metric, climbed 282 percent.

Reasons Behind the Rally. A few trends have contributed to the prolonged stock rally. For one, an ongo-

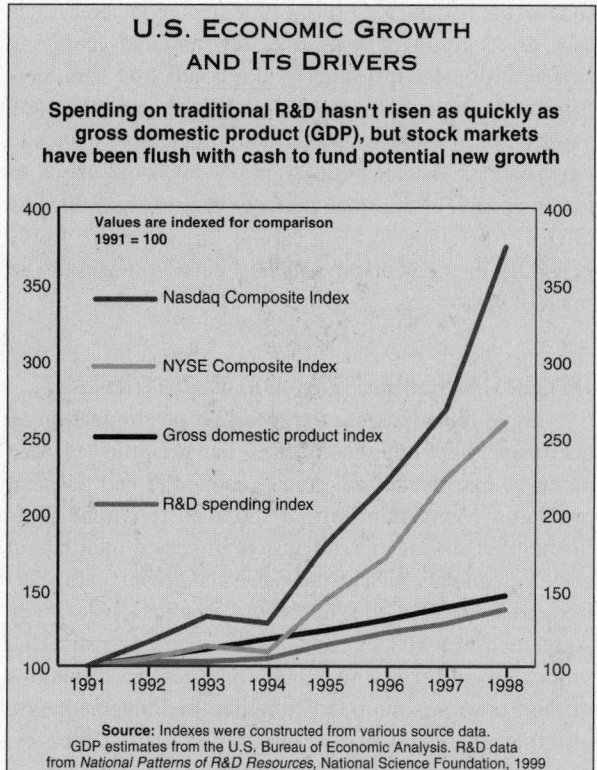

U.S. ECONOMIC GROWTH AND ITS DRIVERS

Spending on traditional R&D hasn't risen as quickly as gross domestic product (GDP), but stock markets have been flush with cash to fund potential new growth

Values are indexed for comparison
1991 = 100

- Nasdaq Composite Index
- NYSE Composite Index
- Gross domestic product index
- R&D spending index

Source: Indexes were constructed from various source data. GDP estimates from the U.S. Bureau of Economic Analysis. R&D data from *National Patterns of R&D Resources*, National Science Foundation, 1999

ing trend toward self-managed 401(k) retirement plans has funneled vast sums of cash into the market, particularly into mutual funds. U.S. assets held in mutual funds more than doubled from $1.9 trillion in 1995 to more than $4.5 trillion by the end of 1999, based on statistics published by the Federal Reserve. Estimates by industry groups placed the 1999 value at closer to a whopping $6 trillion. While either figure includes asset appreciation in the general stock market and other sources, to give an indication of how much new money has been flowing into funds, one estimate valued new inflows into mutual funds at $165 billion in 1999 alone.

Another event that helped ignite the U.S. stock markets was, oddly enough, economic crisis elsewhere in the world. In the wake of the Asian currency crisis of the late 1990s, when fiscal vagaries in up-and-coming Southeast Asian countries triggered a debilitating withdrawal of international capital from several of the region's emerging markets. Global investors effected a so-called flight to quality by pumping their money into U.S.-based assets. A similar story unfolded in Russia in 1998, when the country's currency collapsed amid foreign investors' jitters over ineffective reforms and political corruption in that beleaguered country.

Back at home, continued low interest rates helped stimulate demand for stocks over bonds and other more rate-sensitive investment vehicles in the United States.

Indeed, the Federal Reserve in 1998 lowered interest rates as a direct result of fears over international economic strife. With safer instruments like bonds and bank certificates of deposit offering underwhelming returns—and some U.S. Treasury securities in shorter supply thanks to the balanced federal budget—many investors chose to test their luck in the stock markets instead. As well, low interest rates tend to keep capital flowing more freely generally in the economy, fueling economic activity in myriad ways.

INTERNATIONAL TRADE PATTERNS

Trade liberalization, the lowering or elimination of tariffs and other trade restrictions, has been the keystone of many free-market advocates' economic and political programs. Momentum toward so-called free trade grew in the 1990s with the conclusion of major multilateral trade agreements such as the General Agreement on Tariffs and Trade (GATT), the North American Free Trade Agreement (NAFTA), and a series of accords that brought about greater integration between the 15 nations of the European Union (EU). While the implementation of these agreements hasn't always lived up to the theory, overall they've been the main policy thrust behind what's known to many as globalization, or the expansion of corporate enterprises and their supply chains across international boundaries.

According to World Trade Organization (WTO) figures, in 1999 countries exported a collective $5.6 trillion in merchandise (including some double counting from re-exports) and $1.3 trillion in commercial services. Western Europe, including both EU and non-EU countries, is the world's largest exporting region, supplying about 42 percent of global exports in 1999. Asia and North America followed, with 27 percent and 17 percent, respectively. The regional rank order was the same for imports, although North America occupied a larger share.

U.S. Trade Performance.   Despite perennial worries about the trade deficit, the United States remains the world's largest single-nation exporter of merchandise, shipping nearly $700 billion worth in 1999. It leads the next-largest exporter, Germany, by a comfortable margin, and for the most part, U.S. exports have been growing faster than either Germany's or those of Japan, the third-largest exporter. Top U.S. export sectors in terms of dollar value include aerospace, electronic and mechanical components (especially semiconductors), motor vehicle parts, computer equipment, and telecommunications equipment. Those five industry groups accounted for 20 to 25 percent of all U.S. exports in the late 1990s. Canada, Mexico, and Japan were the largest destination countries, and the EU ranked number two (behind Canada) when treated as a single market.

Meanwhile, the sectors most dependent on foreign-made goods include some of the same: motor vehicles, computer equipment, oil, electronic and mechanical components, and parts and accessories for office equipment. Altogether, the United States imported $1.059 trillion worth of products in 1999, leaving a yawning merchandise trade gap of $364 billion. In descending order, the largest suppliers of imports into the United States include Canada, Japan, Mexico, China, and Germany. Thus, the United States maintains trade deficits with most of its biggest trading partners, but it does have country-level surpluses with a number of smaller partners, including the Netherlands, Australia, Belgium, Egypt, Argentina, and Hong Kong.

Trade in services remains a bright spot for observers who lament the merchandise trade deficit, although there are some indications that the services trade has been losing a bit of its luster. In 1999 the United States exported $252 billion worth of services, including foreign tourism, royalties, and professional services rendered abroad. That compares with $182 billion in imports. However, the trade surplus in services has been narrowing since its 1997 peak at $82 billion; it fell to $74 billion in 1998 and to just below $70 billion in 1999. Economic softness in parts of Asia and Latin America contributed to the declines. But some economists believe services are an inherently shallow base on which to build an export program, and thus weren't swayed even when the surplus was mounting.

Interpreting the Trade Deficit.   The U.S. trade deficit widened significantly throughout the 1990s in the face of a strong U.S. dollar, substantial wealth creation domestically, and economic troubles in some parts of the world. These and other circumstances conspired to create heightened demand for foreign-made goods, and only moderate demand for U.S. goods abroad. The problem isn't that U.S. exports haven't been growing, but that imports have climbed consistently at a faster pace.

All of this feeds into the continuing debate over whether a massive trade deficit is really a problem when most of the other economic ducks are in a row, so to speak. Mainstream economic theory holds that trade deficits are harmful over the long term because they usually lead to current account deficits for a country, where the current account is an economic concept encompassing the net national income from international transactions. The current account deficit, in turn, demonstrates that foreign entities are getting an increasing share of U.S. dollars and assets.

And here's where the damage might be done: as emerging economies regain their steam after the late-1990s setbacks, foreign holders of U.S. currency could begin to rid themselves of dollars and dollar-denominated assets in favor of assets based elsewhere. The resulting

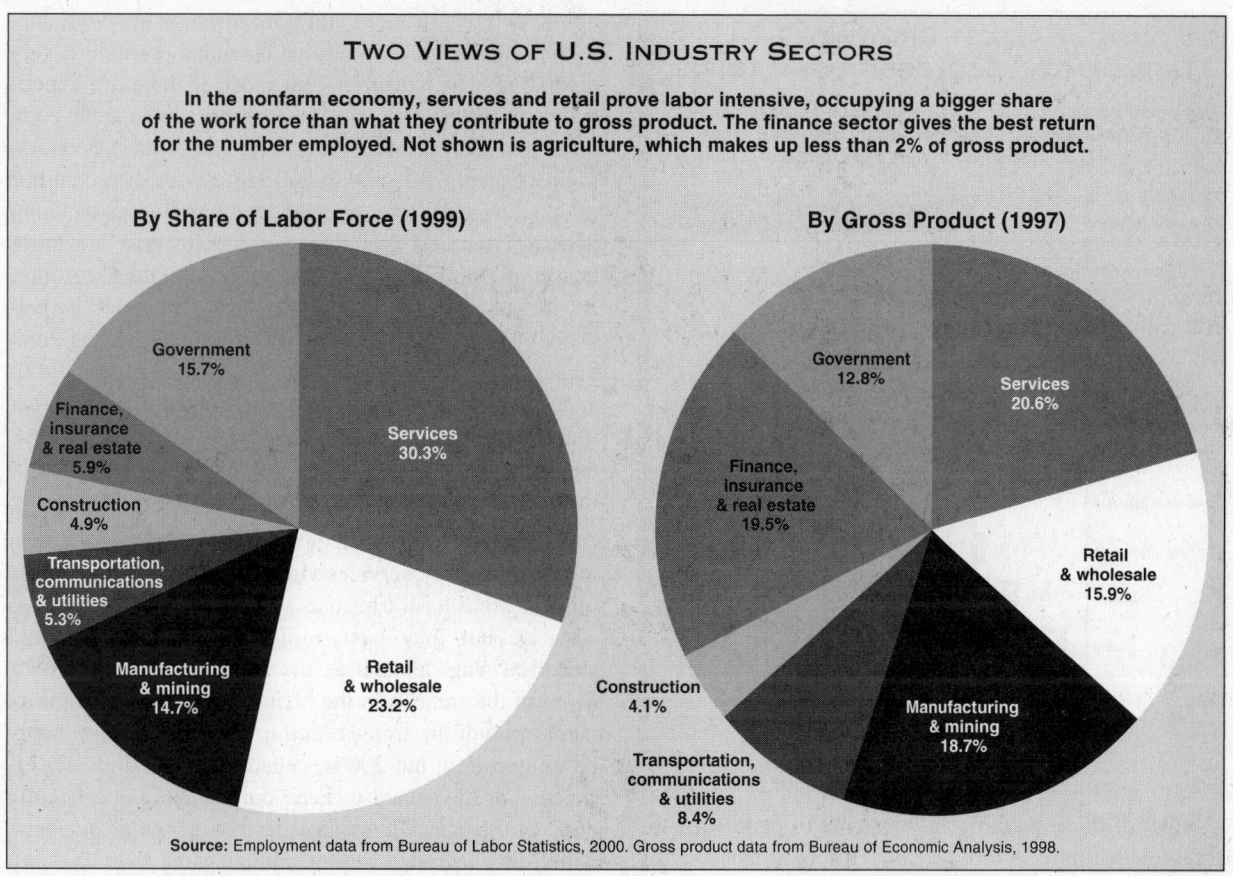

Two Views of U.S. Industry Sectors

In the nonfarm economy, services and retail prove labor intensive, occupying a bigger share of the work force than what they contribute to gross product. The finance sector gives the best return for the number employed. Not shown is agriculture, which makes up less than 2% of gross product.

By Share of Labor Force (1999)

Government 15.7%
Finance, insurance & real estate 5.9%
Construction 4.9%
Transportation, communications & utilities 5.3%
Manufacturing & mining 14.7%
Services 30.3%
Retail & wholesale 23.2%

By Gross Product (1997)

Government 12.8%
Services 20.6%
Finance, insurance & real estate 19.5%
Retail & wholesale 15.9%
Construction 4.1%
Transportation, communications & utilities 8.4%
Manufacturing & mining 18.7%

Source: Employment data from Bureau of Labor Statistics, 2000. Gross product data from Bureau of Economic Analysis, 1998.

influx of dollars in the foreign exchange markets would likely drive the dollar's value down, particularly if the transition is sudden. A weak dollar would, over time, tend to improve the trade balance by making imports into the United States less attractive on price and exports out of the United States more attractive on price. But correcting the balance that way, according to many economists, would probably be an unpleasant process to say the least. A declining dollar would tend to cause price inflation, and as a result, interest rates would creep upward. Further into the vicious cycle, tighter control on capital flows would tend to slow purchases, and ultimately, economic growth. The dismal outcomes could include rising unemployment, stagnant or bearish financial markets, and in the worst case, recession.

Each step in the pernicious cycle has been observed in recent times. Indeed, the late-1990s Asian financial crisis stemmed in large part from capital flight and currency sell-offs in otherwise economically dynamic countries. However, the question is, at what point is a current account shortfall bad enough to cause such an adverse chain of events? Clearly that threshold is harder to reach with an economy as large and as stable as that of the United States. Even clearer is the plain fact that the United States has been running current account deficits

for the better of two decades, through bad economic times and good.

SECTOR TRENDS

Macroeconomic forces aside, a host of industry- and sector-specific trends add texture to the U.S. economic mosaic. The most important of these trends are already rooted firmly in the economy:

- Widespread investment in information technology and communications infrastructure continues to stimulate brisk demand for products and services in those areas.
- Electronic transactions increasingly alter and supplant physical transactions in sectors as diverse as entertainment, consumer retailing, wholesaling, and banking, to name a few.
- Manufacturers cope with declining profitability on sales of physical products by bundling them with value-adding services.
- Commoditized, low-value-added manufactures and services are being sought more and more from foreign providers with lower overhead costs.
- Seemingly contradictory binges of outsourcing and mergers/acquisitions continue at large corporations as they try to optimize their economies of scope and scale.

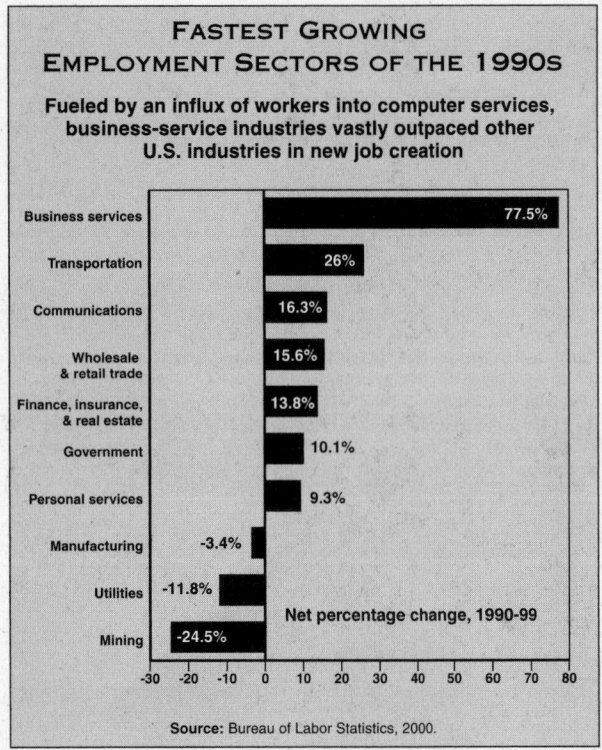

FASTEST GROWING EMPLOYMENT SECTORS OF THE 1990S

Fueled by an influx of workers into computer services, business-service industries vastly outpaced other U.S. industries in new job creation

Sector	Net percentage change, 1990-99
Business services	77.5%
Transportation	26%
Communications	16.3%
Wholesale & retail trade	15.6%
Finance, insurance, & real estate	13.8%
Government	10.1%
Personal services	9.3%
Manufacturing	-3.4%
Utilities	-11.8%
Mining	-24.5%

Source: Bureau of Labor Statistics, 2000.

All of those patterns are expected to persist for the foreseeable future. A more detailed discussion of specific sectors follows.

Manufacturing. It's well documented that manufacturing industries as a whole are in the midst of a long-term decline as a proportion of the U.S. economy. A few manufacturing industries have suffered real setbacks because of changing technology and market forces, foreign competition, and other factors, but in general the decline is the result of simply a slower rate of growth than other sectors of the economy, notably service industries.

U.S. employment in manufacturing has diminished slightly since the 1980s, and a forecast by the Bureau of Labor Statistics anticipates a very minor further decrease in the early 2000s. Manufacturers of nondurable goods like apparel, food, and chemicals are expected to deliver the weakest performance within the sector, both in terms of employment declines and the value of industry sales.

By contrast, makers of durable goods such as industrial machinery, computers and communications devices, semiconductors and electronic components, and medical goods are predicted to fare better. Some will actually boost their employment levels modestly, and overall they're likely to continue increasing productivity and output at vibrant rates throughout the first decade of the twenty-first century.

Business and Transportation Services. Services of all sorts are expected to occupy a growing share of U.S. economic output. Business and transportation services, subsectors of the broader service economy, contain a very diverse mix of industries, but most of them are experiencing robust growth. Business services include the computer and data service industries, which have been enjoying exceptional growth and are expected to continue to do so over the long term. Indeed, the Bureau of Labor Statistics forecast computer services to post the third-fastest growth rate in gross output of all industry groups. Business services also contain such specialties as personnel and recruiting firms and equipment leasing companies. All combined, business services in the 1990s added more new employees to their ranks than any other industry sector, and while the rate is expected to slow, the sector's growth is apt to continue outpacing that of the broader economy well into the 2000s.

Transportation services range from passenger transit to cargo delivery services via air, land, and sea. Growth in these areas hasn't been as swift as in general business services, but they have turned in solid results amid steadily rising demand as the broader economy grows. More of the same is in the offing. Although net employment growth in transportation services will probably be miniscule in the 2000s, consolidation and greater efficiency are expected to keep output rising at a healthy clip. Worth special mention is the car-rental business, which has recorded strong annual gains over the past decade and is projected to continue that trend in coming years.

Communications Services. The communications sector is one of the pillars of the information economy, and indeed, the world economy. The sector's prominence has risen considerably as its infrastructure has grown ever more vital to modern lifestyles and economic activities. Whether it's traditional wireline phone service, wireless communications, high-speed data networks, or entertainment and rich-content electronic media, demand for communications services has swelled in recent years as technological change and deregulation have helped usher in new forms of service at increasingly affordable rates.

The communications industries are undergoing tremendous consolidation, as witnessed by an array of once unthinkable mergers in the late 1990s and early 2000s among local-service carriers, long-distance providers, wireless services, Internet access providers, cable TV system operators, and content providers. Many expect the momentum toward consolidation to continue. As a result, job growth in most communications businesses will be subdued. But industry revenues on the whole will remain on a steady upward track, even as service prices continue to drop.

Retail and Wholesale Trade. With a few exceptions, the retail and wholesale sectors aren't known for dramatic growth. Rather, they tend to eke out a modest existence by sheer volume of transactions, benefiting from the fact most personal consumption spending is channeled through retail firms. In essence, retailers are logistics and marketing specialists who take a vast, disorganized universe of products and render them accessible and possibly more attractive to potential buyers. Meanwhile, wholesalers work behind the scenes, supplying retailers and other businesses with a preordained assortment of goods.

Thus, because their main function is in aggregating merchandise for sale, retailing and wholesaling face more than most sectors a potentially drastic paradigm shift with the onset of electronic commerce. Some prognosticators have gone so far as to say the customary wholesale business could be eliminated entirely by a combination of e-commerce and powerful chain retailers that can negotiate directly with manufacturers. Retailers, too, must contend with unfavorable economics versus virtual storefronts—the infrastructure of a retail chain is costly and inefficient compared to a high-tech inventory and outsourced logistics system. It's precisely with such a system that some electronic challengers hope to wrest market share from traditional retailers.

Still, retailers have several things going for them. In some cases, such as with food purchases, many observers believe that consumers will be reluctant to give up the tactile and visual experiences of shopping in a store, and they'll hesitate to give up the spontaneity of deciding what to buy just minutes before they consume it. Retailers' existing physical infrastructure and market share also provide a powerful platform from which to launch integrated e-commerce/traditional retail ventures. As for conventional wholesalers, they have some infrastructure and market advantages as well, but are probably more vulnerable in the long run.

Whatever the impact of e-commerce, traditional wholesalers and retailers aren't likely to be extinct anytime soon. But their tepid growth rates are expected to slow further in the early 2000s, including both the rate of new job creation and the rate of sales growth. Restaurants, especially, are predicted to lag. Retail and wholesale saw substantial consolidation during the 1990s, and more of the same is anticipated in the 2000s.

FOOD & KINDRED PRODUCTS

MEAT PACKING PLANTS

This industry includes establishments primarily engaged in the slaughtering (for their own account or on a contract basis for the trade) of cattle, hogs, sheep, lambs, and calves for meat to be sold or to be used on the same premises in canning, cooking, curing, freezing, and in making sausage, lard, and other products. The industry also includes establishments primarily engaged in slaughtering horses for human consumption. Businesses primarily engaged in slaughtering, dressing, and packing poultry, rabbits, and other small game are classified in **SIC 2015: Poultry Slaughtering and Processing.** Those primarily engaged in slaughtering and processing animals not for human consumption are classified in **SIC 2048: Prepared Feeds and Feed Ingredients for Animals and Fowls, Except Dogs and Cats.** Businesses primarily involved in manufacturing sausages and meat specialties from purchased meats are classified in **SIC 2013: Sausages and Other Prepared Meat Products.**

NAICS CODE(S)

311611 (Animal (Except Poultry) Slaughtering)

INDUSTRY SNAPSHOT

With annual sales in the $90 billion range, meat packing was one of the largest agriculture-based industries in the United States in the 1990s. However, in recent years changing consumer eating habits have impacted the beef and pork industries which are by far the largest sectors in this industry category. As Americans ate less beef, the beef industry retrenched, eliminating smaller and inefficient plants and expanding their operations to incorporate poultry products. At the same time, the pork industry was striving to reposition pork as "the meat of choice." Although technically a "red" meat, it was gaining acceptance as an alternative to the other white meat, chicken.

In the mid-1990s there were 1,312 establishments in the industry, a 1 percent increase from 1990. By 1998 this number had dropped to 930. In 1998, the industry shipped $44 billion worth of products, down 12 percent from 1997.

ORGANIZATION AND STRUCTURE

The American Meat Institute (AMI) reported that there were more than 1.25 million livestock operations, raising beef cattle, hogs, and sheep destined for human consumption in the United States in the 1990s. According to statistics from the U.S. Department of Agriculture (USDA), in 1998 cash receipts from livestock totaled $43.6 billion: $483 million for sheep and lambs, $9.4 billion for hogs and pigs, and $33.7 billion for cattle and calves. This was approximately $6 billion less than receipts in 1997, despite record high production.

The meat packing plants that processed these animals into food and non-food products ranged in size from those handling small numbers of livestock to operations processing millions of animals a year. According to the USDA, federally inspected slaughter and processing plants numbered 930 in 1998. The dominance of a few major companies is demonstrated by the fact that four packers processed approximately 82 percent of the beef, and three packers processed close to 35 percent of the pork. The USDA reports that in 1998, nearly 35.5 million commercial cattle were slaughtered, representing a 2 percent decrease from 1997. Also in 1998, 101.0 million commercial hogs (an increase of 10 percent) and 3.8 million sheep and lambs (a decrease of 3 percent) were slaughtered.

According to the USDA, the U.S. meat and poultry industry is spread among all 50 states. Industry sources indicate that the midwestern states raised about 46 percent of the cattle and over 15 percent of the hogs in the 1990s, while south central states raised more than 15 percent of the cattle and nearly 70 percent of the hogs. The top five cattle slaughtering states were Kansas, Nebraska, Texas, Colorado, and Iowa. Iowa, Illinois, Minnesota, North Carolina, and South Dakota led in the slaughter of hogs, according to the USDA. Pennsylvania, which had the largest number of federally inspected plants, representing almost 14 percent of all plants in the United States, ranked only eleventh in production.

BACKGROUND AND DEVELOPMENT

The colonial farmers of New England, who were the first meat packers in the United States, used salt to preserve meat. As the nation expanded westward, slaughterhouses were built near population centers so meat could reach the table before it spoiled. The livestock herds were driven overland or barged to these early packing plants. So many hogs were slaughtered in Cincinnati, Ohio, that the city was called "Porkopolis."

For sanitary reasons, meat packing operations could only be carried out during the cold winter months, with ice used for refrigeration. The development of mechanical refrigeration and refrigerated railroad cars in the second half of the nineteenth century changed this. From late 1865 until the 1920s, Chicago, a hub city for the railroads, became renowned for its array of stockyards that collected and slaughtered livestock, often under harrowing working conditions.

With the turn of the century came mechanized disassembly and conveyor procedures in the plants, and the 1950s saw major improvements in plant sanitation and packaging. By the 1980s, the meat packing industry had again dispersed. Slaughterhouses moved closer to the feedlots where the animals were raised. Not having to ship them long distances reduced the stress, weight loss, and injury to the animals that was the inevitable effect of long journeys in crowded cattle cars and trucks.

Regulations. Under the 1906 Meat Inspection Act, U.S. pre- and post-mortem inspection of meat entering interstate and foreign commerce became mandatory. Meat to be used entirely within a single state may be inspected by that state's agriculture department. The Federal program was conducted by the Food Safety and Inspection Service (FSIS) of the USDA. During the late 1980s and throughout the 1990s, unfavorable media criticism of the inspection system spurred an overhaul of FSIS procedures.

Outbreaks of *E. coli* bacteria and lysteria resulted in several deaths and millions of dollars in meat recalls during the 1990s. This lead to increased scrutiny of the federal meat inspection program and fostered the Pathogen Reduction and Hazard Analysis and Critical Control Points (HACCP) rule instituted in 1996. This required the industry to update its inspection methods, which had changed little in the previous 50 years. From 1996 to 1999 new inspection plans were initiated, with all raw meat and poultry products being inspected using methods capable of detecting invisible pathogens by January 2000. The meat industry also continues to promote safe meat handling practices in the home through consumer education programs, labeling, and advertising.

Slaughter. The desirability of stunning animals prior to slaughter was recognized in both Europe and the United States before the end of the nineteenth century. The practice became mandatory in the United States in 1960 with the passage of the Humane Slaughter Act. The Act requires that before being slaughtered, animals must be rendered unconscious by mechanical, electrical, or chemical means in order to cause the animal a minimum of excitement or discomfort. Captive-bolt pistols or pneumatic guns may be used on cattle. Pistols, electric shock or anesthetization in a carbon dioxide chamber is allowed for sheep and pigs. Compressed-air stunners and gas chambers for smaller animals came into use after World War II. Exceptions to federal requirements are made for ritual slaughters that satisfy the requirements of a particular faith. In kosher inspection, for example, a member of the Jewish faith cuts the throat and bleeds the animal without first stunning it and then examines it for abnormalities before approving it for food use.

After stunning, cattle are suspended by one or both hindlegs while the carotid arteries and jugular veins are cut. Hides are then removed by an automated process. A straight cut opens the center of the belly to remove the viscera. Next, the carcasses are split down the center of the backbone. Beef carcasses might then be shrouded, a procedure in which the carcasses are cooled for 24 hours after being tightly wrapped in muslin that has been soaked in warm water. The carcass fat is smooth and trim when the shroud is removed. Specialty meat items like the brains, kidneys, tail, tongue, and sweetbreads do not accompany the carcass but are an important income source for packers. The procedures for veal carcasses are similar except that the hides are left on during chilling. Veal carcasses have very little fat and would shrink during chilling if the hides were removed.

In hog slaughter, the animals are bled after stunning by severing a large vein. The carcasses are then submerged in hot water to loosen the hair. After the removal of the hair, the carcass is eviscerated, split, and chilled.

Grading. While meat inspection is mandatory, grading is a voluntary program. Funded by fees paid by the packers, the service is offered by the USDA's Agricultural and Marketing Service. Grading establishes uniform trading standards and helps to determine the value of various meat cuts. Meat carcasses are graded by both quality and yield.

The quality grades for beef are prime, choice, good, standard, commercial, utility, cutter, and canner. Carcass characteristics that determine the grade include marbling (the streaks of fat in the lean portions), the color and texture of the meat, and maturity. Consumers tend to interpret grading as an indication of taste and tenderness, although it was not designed for this purpose. Growing consumer perceptions that lean meat is healthier have increased the demand for lower-fat grades. The ratio of usable meat to bone and fat determines a carcass' yield grade. Combined with the quality grade it is used to establish the monetary value of a carcass.

Working Conditions. The slaughterhouses of the United States in the early twentieth century were grim and dangerous places to work. Low wages coupled with unsafe conditions made the stockyards of Chicago and other cities hazardous work sites. But it was not until reports on conditions there grew widespread—thanks in part to Upton Sinclair's novel *The Jungle,* which depicted in chilling detail the deplorable environment of the stockyards of Chicago—that the government turned its attention to the industry. Slaughterhouse conditions furthered the cause of fledgling unions, which grew in strength over the ensuing years.

At the end of the twentieth century, automation had not replaced manual labor and the extensive use of sharp knives and other hand tools. Workers were still lifting and lugging heavy carcasses, abattoir floors were slippery, and workers suffered from exposure due to the need for continuous refrigeration systems. Despite AMI and Occupational Safety and Health Administration (OSHA) guidelines, 36 percent of meatpacking employees are injured on the job each year. The meatpacking industry still has the highest injury rate of any U.S. industry. As long as there is no economical and reliable cutting machinery that can accommodate the physical variety of animal carcasses, processing will continue to be a manual operation.

In the early 1990s, the industry's rate of cumulative trauma disorders (CTDs) was higher than all other manufacturing industries. The illness usually took the form of carpal tunnel syndrome, in which repeated, rapid, and forceful motions pinch and compress the nerve that runs through the wrist to the hand. Lower back and various tendon disorders were also reported. Under-reporting of injury and illness still remains a chronic problem, as the majority of the meatpacking workforce is comprised of illegal aliens.

Two of the nation's largest meat packers, IBP, Inc. and John Morrell, were cited in 1987 by OSHA for under-reporting or failing to record injuries and illnesses. Both companies contested the OSHA fines, which were greatly reduced. More importantly, OSHA recognized that the CTDs plaguing meat industry workers needed new solutions. In 1990 OSHA issued its first ergonomic guidelines after consultation with the AMI and labor groups. The guidelines emphasized worker training in proper techniques, strengthened by refresher courses, and the importance of reporting CTD symptoms early to prevent permanent injury. Medical management by trained health care providers was another program component.

OSHA offered special incentives to meat packers who entered into voluntary agreements with the agency to lessen their ergonomic hazards. While they would still be subject to OSHA inspections, they would not be cited or penalized on ergonomic grounds. Opinions on OSHA's voluntary guidelines were mixed. Jim Marsden, AMI vice-president for scientific and technical affairs, said in *Occupational Hazards,* that they were "especially effective because they're geared toward hazard prevention." Industry critics did not always agree. Phillip L. Immesote, president of the United Food and Commercial Workers Union, testified at a hearing of the House Employment and Housing Subcommittee that OSHA was about to repeat earlier disastrous experiences with "a new program of exemptions and voluntary compliance in the nation's packing houses."

By the end of the decade injuries were slightly lower in the major plants, though the industry was still plagued by the problem. In November 1999, OSHA proposed new guidelines to address repetitive stress injuries in the workplace. These guidelines again focused heavily on ergonomic accommodations in the workplace. While not specifically aimed at the meat packing industry, they could have an impact. Industry opposition to the guidelines was high, and it remains to be seen if the guidelines will be enacted by Congress.

CURRENT CONDITIONS

Per capita meat consumption (red meat and poultry) increased from 209.3 pounds in retail weight in 1996 to 220.6 pounds in 1999. Red meat consumption remained stable throughout the 1990s, ranging between 65 and 68 pounds per year, down from a high of 79.2 pounds in 1985. The USDA has forecast larger meat supplies at lower wholesale prices, with resulting competition for consumer dollars at the retail level.

Beef. Meat processors have sought to improve their business outlook by expanding into the fast-growing poultry market. The number of major meat producers also engaged in production of poultry products rose dramati-

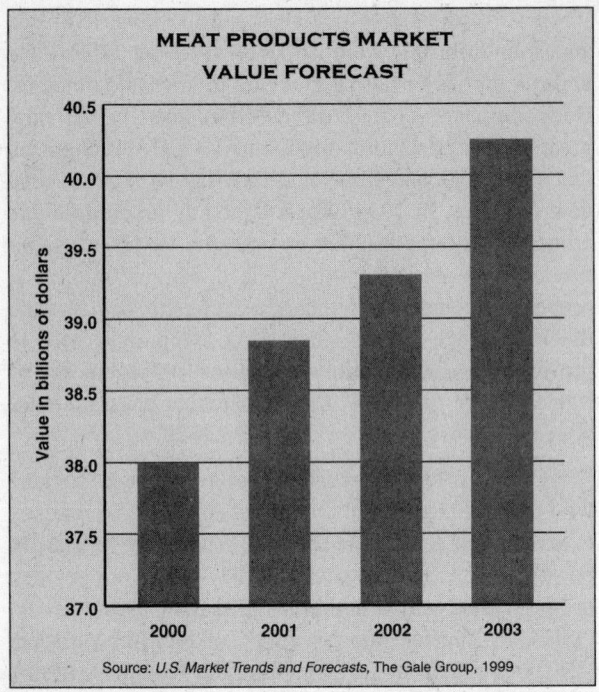

MEAT PRODUCTS MARKET VALUE FORECAST

Source: *U.S. Market Trends and Forecasts*, The Gale Group, 1999

section, and hundreds of producers. Goals included building demand for pork by creating new products and expanding current uses; ensuring that pork met or surpassed consumer expectations of safety, quality, and value; and positioning the industry as socially responsible.

Whether the potential for larger herds and increased production could be parlayed into industry growth was dependent on other factors, such as cost competitiveness, exports, and the continued popularity of pork products. During the late 1990s the industry experienced record high production, consumption, exports, and record low prices for live hogs. Pork producers were the most severely impacted, suffering $2.5 billion in loses in 1998 and $1 billion in loses in 1999. The pork industry continues to consolidate and move South and West away from the traditional Midwest hog states. Efforts are being made to align production and packing facilities to avoid the problems suffered in the late 1990s due to a lack of capacity at slaughter facilities during peak production times. Demand for pork both nationally and internationally continues to rise at record rates.

cally throughout the 1990s. The beef industry has also been heavily advertising beef as a healthy, easy to prepare dinner meat, as in their ''Beef Made Easy'' campaign which features low-fat, easy to prepare menu options. The beef industry has also been trying to market beef as a brand, rather than a generic meat, in order to boost demand.

Enhanced genetics, the introduction of new feed additives and growth stimulants, and nutritional advances all played a part in the improvements in cattle growth rate during the last quarter of the twentieth century. Consumer demand for lean beef, as well as environmental concerns, are expected to continue to have an impact on the beef industry into the 21st century.

Pork. Nationwide, the number of hog enterprises has dwindled in recent years, as has the number of slaughtering facilities. Many of the smaller operations have dropped out, while the larger outfits expanded. For pig-slaughtering operations, this reduction and consolidation of sources adversely impacted the industry in 1998 and 1999, despite a 10 percent increase in production.

According to the *Statistical Abstract of the United States: 1997,* Iowa had the largest number of hogs and pigs on farms, with 13,400. North Carolina and Illinois were the next two largest, with 8,200 and 4,800 hogs and pigs respectively.

In the mid-1990s, the National Pork Producers Council announced a comprehensive plan to promote pork as the meat of choice both domestically and worldwide. The plan was the joint output of the National Pork Board, the National Live Stock and Meat Board's pork

INDUSTRY LEADERS

Industry sources report that IBP, Inc., ConAgra, Inc., and Cargill Incorporated are the top three beef slaughterers, while IBP, ConAgra, and John Morrell operated the country's top three pork slaughter operations.

IBP, Inc. Competition for the number one spot in the meat packing industry was strong, but Nebraska-based IBP, Inc., a subsidiary of Occidental Petroleum Corp., held on with sales of $12.85 billion in 1998. These posted earnings continued the company's growth pattern. IBP, Inc. touts itself as the world's largest producer of fresh beef and pork and operates 24 plants in North America. Archer Daniels Midland owns approximately 14 percent of IBP.

With the acquisition of Foodbrands America, Inc. in early 1997, IBP enjoyed an increased workforce. Foreign exports accounted for a small percentage of sales, most of them to the Far East (Japan, Korea, and Taiwan). IBP continues to concentrate on beef and pork slaughter and processing, leaving the diversification into poultry products to competitors like ConAgra, Inc. and Cargill Meat Sector in Minneapolis. During the late 1990s IBP also continued to grow its value-added meat products (deli meats, pizza toppings, frozen appetizers, etc.) and acquired Russer Foods, H&M Food Systems, and Thorn Apple Valley, all smaller players in the meat market.

By relocating its slaughterhouses in 1961 to where the beef was, near Nebraska's and Iowa's cattle farms, IBP changed the meat-packing industry. At the company's plant in Dakota City, Nebraska, animal carcasses were carried over 20 miles of conveyor systems. Within

48 hours, a 650-pound carcass could be broken, cut, and packed into 65- to 80-pound boxes for shipment to supermarkets. Pork became an important part of IBP's success starting in 1976, and by the late 1980s the company planned six plants in Iowa and Nebraska, all within a 100-mile radius of the nation's largest hog-producing area. IBP continues to shift plants and production to areas offering the most strategic advantage to the meat markets. IBP now has operations in the United States and eight foreign countries.

ConAgra, Inc. Originally known as Nebraska Consolidated Mills, ConAgra's expansion to its present status as a leading food producer began in earnest with its development of Duncan Hines cake mix in the 1950s. The company became a multifaceted food provider in the 1960s and 1970s, establishing a number of poultry processing plants to complement its growing flour mill business. In 1971 the company changed its name to ConAgra and continued its expansion into a variety of manufacturing industries. The company's purchases in recent years have included United Agri Products (1978), Banquet Frozen Foods (1980), Armour Food Company (1983), Beatrice (1990), and Van Camp (1995), as well as purchasing assets and numerous other related businesses. ConAgra offers over 50 brands, including Hunt's, Wesson, Armour, and Butterball, and operates more than 200 retail outlets. In 1998 sales were reported as $23.8 billion, and the company had 82,000 employees in 35 countries.

Cargill. Founded in 1865, Cargill built its reputation in commodity trading, but by 1993 was one of the country's largest suppliers of raw foods and ingredients, with sales reaching $11 to $13 billion from diversified activities ranging from corn and flour milling to oilseed processing.

In 1993, although Cargill still regarded itself primarily as an ingredient supplier, it had become the nation's third largest meat packer. Cargill had acquired Excel Corp., a leading name in boxed beef and pork, in 1979. When Cargill formed its Meat Sector in the early 1990s, it included the Excel Corp. and Cargill Meat Products (which further processed beef and pork). In 1993, Cargill announced that it would sell its meat processing business in Japan, although it continues to export beef to Japan. Excel distributed most of its products under private label. Cargill handles approximately 20 percent of cattle slaughter in the country. In 1997 it acquired the North American salt assets of Akzo Salt Inc. and became the second largest salt production company in the nation. 1999 sales were estimated at $45.71 billion dollars, making Cargill the third largest food company in the United States, behind Philip Morris and ConAgra.

WORKFORCE

The number of employees in the meat packing and processing industry began registering modest increases in the early 1990s, up to 467,800 in 1995, according to the AMI. In the food industry as a whole, meat packing and processing is the largest employer. According to U.S. Department of Labor statistics, slaughterers' and butchers' earnings averaged $8.64 an hour in 1997.

Meat packing is also a highly labor-intensive industry, and a large majority of the total employees (84 percent) were production workers, compared to 72 percent in all food preparation sectors and 67 percent in all manufacturing industries.

Because of the low wages of the industry, employee turnover remains high. The industry employs a large number of immigrants, which may contribute to the turnover, along with the demanding working conditions. Although no large scale labor disturbances have occurred recently, there have been isolated strikes at plants, such as the 1999 strike against IBC in Pasco, Washington.

AMERICA AND THE WORLD

The domestic meat industry continues to thrive, with annual red meat consumption estimated at 123.9 pounds per person in 1998. The industry has been fighting hard to maintain meat's image as a safe and nutritious food choice, and has recently instituted inspections which can detect invisible pathogens. The industry has also begun to explore irradiation as a way to increase safety and shelf life. Ad campaigns (including "Beef Made Easy" and "Pork. The other white meat.") are part of the industry's attempt to brand their products in order to increase demand. At the same time, it is also focusing on new technologies for creating leaner meats in response to consumer demand.

International Trade. The United States enjoyed a favorable trade balance in red meat products, with exports of meat and related products valued at approximately $4.44 billion in 1998. However, the weakened Asian markets continued to impact exports. In 1997, the United States became the largest pork exporter in the world, exporting 474,000 metric tons in carcass weight. The major destinations for beef exports were Japan, Mexico, Canada, Republic of Korea, and Hong Kong. Japan, Canada, and Mexico were the top importers of U.S. pork. Trade with the European Union was still restricted due to bans on meat treated with hormones.

For the late 1990s and into 2000, the USDA predicted a slight decline in meat trade, improving as the Asian economies continue to recover, and improved meat inspections reassure markets of meat safety. Although the United States had a favorable trade balance, it still imported $3.21 billion in beef and related products in 1998, and was the world's third largest importer of pork, at 287,000 metric tons.

The top five countries from which the U.S. imported red meat were: Australia, Canada, New Zealand, Denmark, and Argentina. Pork imports came primarily from Canada and Denmark.

FURTHER READING

"Finance and Economics: Big Beef." *The Economist,* 24 January 1998.

National Pork Board. *U.S. Pork.* Available from http://www.uspork.org/.

National Pork Producers Council. *1998-99 Pork Facts.* Available from http://www.nppc.org/PorkFacts/98PORKFA.pdf.

Tank, Al. *Perspective of the U.S. Pork Industry.* Available from http://www.nppc.org/PROD/tankperspective.html.

United States Department of Agriculture. *Foreign Agricultural Service.* Available from http://www.fas.usda.gov/.

United States Department of Agriculture. *Livestock Slaughter 1998 Summary.* Available from http://usda.mannlib.cornell.edu/reports/nassr/livestock/pls-bban/lsan0399.txt.

United States Department of Agriculture. *Meat Animals Production, Disposition, and Income 1998 Summary.* Available from http://usda.mannlib.cornell.edu/reports/nassr/livestock/zma-bb/meat0599.txt.

United States Department of Labor. *Bureau of Labor Statistics.* Available from http://stats.bls.gov.

"Workers Strike over Labor Contract at Pasco, Wash., Meat Plant." *Omaha World - Herald,* 11 June 1999.

SIC 2013

SAUSAGES AND OTHER PREPARED MEAT PRODUCTS

Establishments in this category are primarily engaged in manufacturing sausages, cured meats, smoked meats, canned meats, frozen meats and other prepared meats and meat specialties, from purchased carcasses and other materials. Products include bologna, bacon, corned beef, frankfurters (except poultry), headcheese, luncheon meat, pigs' feet, sandwich spreads, stew, pastrami, and hams (except poultry). Prepared meat plants operated by packinghouses as separate establishments are also included in this industry.

Establishments primarily engaged in canning or otherwise processing poultry, rabbits, and other small game are classified in **SIC 2015: Poultry Slaughtering and Processing.** Establishments primarily engaged in canning meat for baby food are classified in **SIC 2032: Canned Specialties.** Establishments primarily engaged in the cutting up and resale of purchased fresh carcasses,

for the trade, are classified in **SIC 5147: Meats and Meat Products,** a wholesale trade industry.

NAICS CODE(S)

311612 (Meat Processed from Carcasses)

INDUSTRY SNAPSHOT

There were 1,200 establishments in the industry in the mid-1990s, up 2 percent since 1990. In 1996 U.S. companies in this industry shipped products worth $21 billion; the value of shipments for all meat products was $102 billion. Retail value of beef consumed in 1998 exceeded $51 billion, according to the U.S. Department of Agriculture (USDA). Imports of red meat in 1998 were valued at $3.2 billion, while red meat exports were worth an estimated $4.4 billion. Prepared meats also found a niche among the salty snack category, evinced by recent sales increases in this market.

In 1998 the red meat industry, which included meat-packing plants and establishments that produced processed pork and beef products, accounted for only 58 percent of the entire meat industry, which included poultry and poultry products, compared to 80 percent in 1988. The consensus among analysts is that this shifting market share is due to increasing consumer demand for healthier foods. The shift does not appear to be away from meat, according to USDA data, as red meat production hit an all-time high of 45.1 million pounds in 1998. The prepared food industry continues to formulate new products to meet consumer demands for lighter, leaner, and easier to prepare foods. In 1998 the industry introduced no less than 728 new products in the processed meat and poultry category.

Per capita consumption of red meat continued to increase throughout 1998, and studies done by both the USDA and the American Meat Institute (AMI) show that 99 percent of Americans eat meat, and 94 percent eat red meat. Total meat, poultry, and fish consumption has risen by 15 pounds per person over the past decade. The USDA estimates that the average American ate 124 pounds of red meat and 93.6 pounds of poultry in 1998.

ORGANIZATION AND STRUCTURE

Prepared meat products are marketed to supermarkets and wholesale clubs, and oftentimes the "store brand" purchased was produced by a large company and labeled locally. The pizza industry (for toppings), food services, and in-store delicatessens make up the rest of the market share. Companies in this category also manufacture private label meats for restaurants.

Meat processors often work closely with vendors from other industries to develop innovative new packaging ideas, mindful of the importance of packaging from a marketing and a practical point of view. Because meat is a highly perishable item, packaging must ensure that the food inside will not spoil and that it will retain its flavor for long periods of time. The packaging must also be convenient and attractive to the consumer. The concept of meeting consumer demands through marketing is reflected in packaging, which presents each product's traits, i.e. low-fat, low-sodium, etc.

In addition to the large national brands, many regional brands of hams, sausages, hot dogs, lunch meats, and other prepared meats are available for family-run companies. A proliferation of processed meat products has put shelf and cooler space at a premium, forcing producers to create niches in major markets and design more convenient and tastier products. The prepared meat industry's practice of creating products and the demand for them that had not previously existed among consumers is part of a larger food industry trend called differentiation. With differentiation, similar foods are altered enough to appear different either in preparation, flavor, or packaging, and are then marketed as new products.

Prepared meat businesses owe much of their growth to the creation of variations, such as premium, economy, flavored, low-salt, low-fat, high-protein, or more convenient versions of a basic meat product. The industry devised creations such as microwaveable bacon and sausages, shelf-staple stews and dinners, low-fat deli meats, frozen microwaveable hamburgers, or cheese-filled hot dogs. Reduced fat products are among the fastest growing markets of all processed meats. Changes in the production of such "healthier" versions to improve their taste and texture have appealed to consumers and have spawned a devoted following.

Costs and prices in this industry are greatly affected by the hog commodities market. Some companies not only operate their own packinghouses, but they also raise hogs in order to avoid the price swings that often occur in the commodities market. When hog supplies increase, manufacturers' profit margins generally expand because only a small part of that savings is passed on to the consumer. When hog supplies decrease, forcing prices up, the manufacturers' profit margin narrows. Another factor affecting price is the strict guidelines aimed at safer meat processing. Techniques required to prevent bacteria and disease have increased the cost of production.

Package Labeling. Nutrition labeling laws designed to enforce the 1990 Nutrition Labeling and Education Act were announced in 1992. The regulations required food processors to provide consumers with additional nutrition information on labels. The rules went into effect in 1995, but most companies voluntarily switched their labels before the deadline.

The new labels require the manufacturer to list the total fat content, amount of saturated fat, number of calories derived from fat, and cholesterol, sodium, carbohydrates, and protein content in its products. According to the regulations, meat processors may use the term "light in sodium" if the meat product's sodium levels have been reduced 50 percent. In addition, the rules defined terms such as "lite or light," "low fat," "fat-free," "reduced calories," "low in saturated fat," "high fiber," and other terms that manufacturers have been using to tout the "healthiness" of products. In order to use any of those terms on the label, food must meet the requirements of the definition. For example, a "low-fat" product must have only three grams of fat or less in a serving. The government also established standard serving sizes for many foods so that food manufacturers could no longer decrease serving sizes in order to meet claims that products were low-calorie or low-sodium.

The regulations were designed to eliminate much of the hype routinely utilized by food manufacturers. Companies that bring in less than $500,000 in annual sales were exempt from the laws. However, it was expected that the entire food industry, including prepared meat businesses, would spend about $2.8 billion on new labels and other related expenses. In addition to the nutrition labels, preparation guidelines on how to safely prepare meat products became prevalent after several prominent cases of E. coli infections occurred during the 1990s.

Environmental Concerns. Many highly processed or packaged meat products provided convenience to consumers, but at a price to the environment. Disposable microwaveable packages free up consumers from dirty dishes, but create more waste. Because of increasing public concern about the problem of garbage disposal, products packaged in disposable containers face growing criticism. Laws that require recyclable packaging could have an impact on the companies that produce some processed meat products. Environmentalists and relief workers also continue to voice their criticism of the meat industry and its use of immense amounts of grain crops, water, energy, grazing areas, and other natural resources in the development of its product.

BACKGROUND AND DEVELOPMENT

Many of the companies in this industry began as meat-packing companies and sold nonbranded meat to stores, food services, and meat product manufacturers. They diversified, however, as it became clear that the food processing business was more profitable and less susceptible to swings in commodity prices and that the nature of the fresh pork business was cyclical. A company that processed pork earned 10 times as much on every dollar of sales as a company that derived most of its income from slaughtering.

Many of the establishments that produce prepared meat products also own and run the packinghouses that supply them with meat. Hormel, once a large meatpacking concern, severely limited its packing operations and concentrated most of its resources on processing hot dogs, cold cuts, sausages, and other prepared meats. In some cases meat manufacturing establishments have leased packing services or have exclusive contracts from meatpackers to supply only that manufacturer. Hormel leased one of its slaughter plants to a pork processing company to operate, but it provided the hogs and purchased all of the plant's prime cuts and processed product output.

Establishments that pack or process red meat suffered in the 1990s, as a result of increased consumer demand for poultry products, which were perceived to be a healthier choice. In 1992 there were 1,264 companies in the prepared meat industry, according to the *1992 Census of Manufacturers. The 1997 Census of Manufacturers* has split the industry into two six-digit NAICS categories, 311613 and 311612, making some comparisons difficult. In addition, the number of red meat processors also producing poultry products continues to rise.

Furthermore, companies closed inefficient plants and introduced innovative new products. Companies processing red meat expanded into other product areas, especially poultry, through acquisitions or mergers. Meat packers diversified, shifting attention from meat packing to processing of low-fat cold cuts and other meat products.

CURRENT CONDITIONS

As a result of consumer demands for healthier prepared-meats, meat processing companies introduced many "light" or "low-fat" versions of popular products. Chicken or turkey cold cuts and hot dogs stole market share from beef and pork products. According to Marketing Intelligence Service, Ltd. and reported by AMI, "more than 50 percent of the product lines in the lunch meat and hot dog categories contain a reduced fat or nutritional claim. The extra low-fat (97 percent fat-free) hot dog and bologna market has grown by more than 21 percent."

It is likely that processors will continue to diversify their product offerings. Additions of low-fat and flavor enhanced products along with faster, easier, and healthier prepared meats helped the industry grow despite slowdowns in other meat markets in the late 1990s. Also quick "grab and go" meat snacks represented the largest growth in the salty snacks category in 1995 with sales up 16.5 percent over the year before.

Sales of bacon have declined, in all probability because of bacon's fat and cholesterol content; sales of bacon in restaurants remained steady, however, suggesting that consumers allow themselves some leeway in their quest for a healthier diet. The introduction of "lower salt," "reduced fat," and "fat-free" bacon should help compensate for this trend.

In any event, the increased emphasis on healthy nutrition has revolutionized the prepared meat product industry. Philip Morris's Oscar Mayer Foods Corp. cut nearly 300 slow-selling products, dropped prices on bacon, hot dogs, and bologna, and added light bologna and turkey bacon as part of an ambitious low-fat lunch meat line. ConAgra's Armour Swift-Eckrich Inc. subsidiary continues to enhance its line of Healthy Choice brand lunch meats and hot dogs to compete against Oscar Mayer's Healthy Favorites and a Weight Watchers lunch meat line, produced by Hillshire Farms, which is owned by Sara Lee Corporation.

In 1999 sales of refrigerated dinner sausage exceeded $1.03 billion, up 6.7 percent. Frozen sausage sales were $260 million, up 16.8 percent over the previous year. Breakfast sausage sales rose to $678 million, up 3 percent. Eight hundred thirty-four million pounds of hot dogs were sold in 1998, along with more than 100 million pounds of poultry hot dogs. Fat-free and light hot dogs added 150 million pounds to the market. Hot dog sales contributed $1.5 billion to the market, according to the National Hot Dog and Sausage Council.

ConAgra's Healthy Choice line of products has grown steadily since its introduction in 1988. As of 1999 there were 300 products in the line, with sales of $1.5 billion. The Healthy Choice products include beef, pork, and poultry-based meats. It is sold in prepackaged form as well as at supermarket deli counters; the company also plans to market it to food services. Company officials from Armour Swift-Eckrich predicted that its new line of 97-percent fat-free lunch meats would expand the existing market by turning light users of lunch meats into medium and heavy users, possibly reversing a trend away from lunchmeat sandwiches that confronted the industry and sent processors looking for convenient substitutes to entice "brown baggers."

Lunch Preferences. Volume sales for lean sliced luncheon meats were up 7.2 percent in 1995, far exceeding the 1.6 percent increase for the overall luncheon meat category, according to Information Resources Inc. statistics. Consumers are making healthier choices, opting for the light, lean, and fat-free products. However, the market for full fat brand names still has a significant following. Oscar Mayer continues to be the industry leader in lunch meat sales, with 24 percent of the market share in 1995 and still holding the leader position at the end of the decade.

INDUSTRY LEADERS

A majority of widely recognized processed meat brands are now owned by large conglomerates, and many of them started out as small, regional, independent meatpacking and meat processing companies. Three national industry leaders are Sara Lee Corporation, Hormel Foods

Corporation, and Oscar Mayer Foods Corporation, a subsidiary of Philip Morris Companies, Inc. There are still many localized companies, but their sales only account for a small percentage of total industry sales.

Sara Lee Corporation (known as Consolidated Foods until 1985) was one of the largest meat processing establishments in the United States. Sara Lee held the number one position in sales in three of the major categories of packaged and processed meats. The company's Hillshire Farm smoked sausage product commanded a 38 percent share of the $1 billion retail market. Its Jimmy Dean breakfast sausage and Ball Park hot dog brands each owned a 22 percent share of their respective billion-dollar markets. Sara Lee also boasts a number of very strong regional brands, such as Bryan, Kahn, and others. Sara Lee had total sales of $20.012 billion in 1999.

With the purchase of Kraft General Foods in 1988 for $12.9 billion, Philip Morris acquired Oscar Mayer and Louis Rich meat products. In 1998 the Oscar Mayer division of Philip Morris had revenues of $17.3 billion, and 99 percent of North Americans consumed a Kraft Food product, according to the Kraft Foods Web site. One of Oscar Mayer's products, Lunchables, a prepackaged lunch in a box, was marketed toward parents. Containing lunch meat, crackers, cheese, etc., it was to be the ideal "take along" lunch for school children. In 1996 and 1997 various consumer advocate groups claimed that Lunchables were too high in fat to be considered a nutritious lunch. In response to consumer demand for lower fat products, Oscar Mayer is phasing out its line of Healthy Favorites low-fat luncheon meats and replacing them with a fat-free lineup.

Conglomerate agribusiness ConAgra had total annual sales of more than $24.5 billion in 1999 and employed more than 82,000 people in 35 countries. ConAgra acquired Armour from Greyhound in 1983, and Swift-Eckrich from the Beatrice Co. in 1990. Armour and Swift-Eckrich became a single subsidiary of ConAgra, which manufactures Sizzlean, Swift Premium Brown 'N Serve Sausage, and Eckrich sausages, as well as other Armour and Swift products. Before the acquisition, Swift had been the third-largest manufacturer of processed meat after Oscar Mayer and Sara Lee. ConAgra also owns meatpacking companies Swift Independent Packing and Monfort, and continues to acquire smaller companies, such as Gilardi Foods in 1998.

George A. Hormel & Company was founded in Austin, Minnesota, in 1891 as a slaughterhouse and retail meat products shop. Its earnings for the first year were $220,000. About 100 years later, the company name was changed to Hormel Foods Corporation, reflecting its change in focus from a packing and meat company to a food processing company offering meat products, frozen foods, and microwaveable products, as well as branded fresh pork and beef. One of the most widely recognized products from the line is SPAM, a pork-based luncheon meat in a can. Hormel was one of the few older meat companies that remained independent after a wave of takeovers in the 1980s. It had sales of $3.35 billion in 1999.

Hormel became known as the industry's innovator in the late 1980s. It was one of the largest meatpackers in the country, but its president, Richard Knowlton, closed many of its slaughtering facilities in the 1980s and began focusing on producing processed and branded meat products. Since the early 1980s, Hormel's hog slaughter capacity has been cut 75 percent. The portion of its revenues generated by prepared meat and other food products rose to between 65 and 75 percent.

In the first half of the 1980s Hormel introduced two or three new products annually. In one 18-month period during the second half of the decade, however, it introduced 134 new products, including those made from chicken, turkey, and fish. In 1986 Hormel acquired Jennie-O Foods, the nation's largest privately owned turkey processor. New products to enter the market in the 1990s included *JENNIE-O* spiced and marinated turkey fillets, *HORMEL ALWAYS TENDER* fresh pork, microwave bacon, turkey pepperoni, turkey chili, and fat-free hot dogs.

Like Hormel, Smithfield Foods was an independent company, but on a smaller scale. It initially produced only pork products, and it spent a fraction of the more than $70 million on advertising that Hormel spent. In 1999 it has become the world's largest hog producer and fresh pork processor, with sales totaling over $3.7 billion.

The name recognition of Smithfield canned hams enabled it to diversify into production of hot dogs, bacon, sausages, and lunch meats from its main pork-packing operations. Smithfield continued to grow and expand its operations throughout the 1990s both nationally and internationally. In 1999 it bought Tyson Foods' pork operations for $80 million.

Thorn Apple Valley, Inc. was one of the largest producers of customer-owned private label meat products, as well as one of the largest regional producers of bacon, hot dogs, lunch meats, and smoked sausages. Due to difficulties in the pork market, Thorn Apple Valley declared Chapter 11 bankruptcy in 1999 and was acquired by IBP Inc., which has become one of the nation's largest producers of meat products. IBP Inc. sales for 1999 exceeded $12.8 billion.

AMERICA AND THE WORLD

For many foreign companies, the new label laws created by the 1990 Nutrition Labeling and Education Act were difficult to comply with because businesses were not accustomed to providing such complete product content analyses. Although the labels could be considered a barrier to trade and therefore incompatible with the General Agreement on Tariffs and Trade (GATT), it was unlikely that any challenge would hold up, as both foreign and domestic companies had to observe the same regulations.

Meat exports in the 1990s have been strongest to Japan, Mexico, Republic of Korea, Canada, and the Middle East. Difficulties have arisen with economic downturns in Asia and Russia, and a European Union ban on meat treated with growth hormones. Despite these issues, exports continue to be strong, though the USDA Foreign Agricultural Service predicts the markets to be in decline rather than growth, while the Asian markets appear to be recovering at the end of the decade.

FURTHER READING

American Meat Institute. *Cattle and Beef Industry Statistics.* Washington, 1999. Available from http://www.beef.org.

Hoover's Online, 2000. Available from http://www.hoovers.com/.

Hormel Foods Web Site, 1999. Available from http://www.hormel.com.

International Natural Sausage Casing Association Web Site, August 1999. Available from http://www.insca.org/.

Kraft Foods Web Site, 1999. Available from http://www.kraftfoods.com.

National Hot Dog and Sausage Council Web Site, 1998. Available from http://www.hot-dog.org/.

Prepared Foods Magazine, 1997-2000. Available from http://www.preparedfoods.com.

United States Census Bureau. *1997 Economic Census.* "Manufacturing-Industry Series," February 2000. Available from http://www.census.gov.

United States Department of Agriculture. Foreign Agricultural Service. *Status of U.S. Meat Product Exports in 1998.* Available from http://www.fas.usda.gov.

SIC 2015

POULTRY SLAUGHTERING AND PROCESSING

This industry includes establishments primarily engaged in slaughtering, dressing, packing, freezing, and canning poultry, rabbits, and other small game, or in manufacturing products from such meats, for their own account or on a contract basis for the trade. This industry also includes the drying, freezing, and breaking of eggs.

NAICS CODE(S)

311615 (Poultry Processing)
311999 (All Other Miscellaneous Food Processing)

INDUSTRY SNAPSHOT

Beginning in the early 1930s, the poultry industry was dominated by many small growers and processors. The U.S. poultry business evolved into a vertically integrated industry in the mid-1930s, in which a few top companies accounted for most of the country's broiler (chicken) and turkey production. Vertical integration combined the previously independent and fragmented operations of feedmills, hatcheries, farms, slaughterers, and processors into giant conglomerates that managed all stages of production.

Broilers, which are chickens raised specifically for table consumption, represented by far the largest component of the industry, with the value of production exceeding $14.1 billion in 1997, compared to $2.8 billion for turkey. Broiler production was concentrated in 17 southeastern states on the eastern seaboard and Gulf of Mexico. This so-called "broiler belt" was the source of 90 percent of production. No such regional concentration existed in the turkey sector. The top four turkey producing states were North Carolina, Minnesota, Virginia, and Arkansas. Broilers averaged 39.3 cents per pound (live weight equivalent) in 1998, compared to 37.7 cents in 1997. There were 7.76 billion broilers produced in 1997 alone, the equivalent of 37.5 billion pounds of broiler meat. It is anticipated that the amount of broilers produced per year will continue to rise. The value of egg production decreased 4 percent in 1998.

ORGANIZATION AND STRUCTURE

According to the U.S. 1992 Census of Manufacturers, there were 593 establishments in the poultry and egg processing business. Additionally, many red meat processing plants also slaughter poultry. In 1998 there were 6,500 federally-inspected and 2,550 state-inspected slaughtering and processing plants in the United States.

Most broilers (99 percent) in the 1990s were produced under contractual arrangements in which the broiler company provided a grower with day-old chicks, and the grower then raised the birds in the carefully controlled environment of the grow-out house. Protected from disease and predators in an enclosed system, the birds would be fed mostly a diet of vitamin- and mineral-fortified corn and soybean meal during the six-and-a-half week period it took to bring them to market weight of about four pounds. Prior to being sent to the processing plant, the birds might be tested for traces of pesticides, toxins, or antibiotics in the ongoing United States Department of Agriculture (USDA) residue monitoring program. In 1935 it took approximately 16 weeks for a 3.5 to

4.5 pound broiler to be fully produced. In the 1990s, with advanced technology, that time has been reduced to six to seven weeks.

The five primary product categories handled within the poultry processing industry were: chicken, turkeys, ducks, geese, and egg products. Available chicken types included young broilers/fryers weighing an average of 3 pounds; specially grown, 6- to 8- pound young roasters; capons, surgically desexed male birds weighing more than 9 pounds; heavy hens (often called stewing hens), over a year old and weighing 4 to 6 pounds; and Rock Cornish or Cornish game hens, young chickens weighing about 1 to 2 pounds. About 18 percent of ready-to-cook chickens were sold as whole birds; the rest were sold as broiler parts or as boneless chicken breasts or thighs.

Annual per capita consumption of turkey stabilized in 1997 to about 17.6 pounds per person. Total annual turkey production for 1998 was 2.83 billion turkeys. The methods used in breeding, raising, slaughtering, and processing turkeys were almost identical with those used for chicken. Turkey hens reached maturity at about 16 weeks, with a market weight of 16 to 18 pounds. Toms took 19 weeks to reach market weight of 28 to 30 pounds. Most turkeys were sold whole, either fresh or frozen. The USDA ranked North Carolina as the number one state for turkey production in 1998.

The White Pekin was the most popular duck breed for mass production in the 1990s. Annual production was about 21 million ducks, which were generally packaged and sold whole and frozen. Duck feathers and down used by bedding manufacturers were valuable by-products. According to the Duckling Council, consumption of White Pekin increased 11.5 percent between 1995 and 1998. The total population of geese in the United States rarely exceeded 5 million; most were raised in Minnesota and Iowa.

Egg production in the United States during 1998 was over 79.9 billion, and was valued at $4.35 billion dollars. The average cost of a dozen eggs was 65.5 cents. Egg consumption increased in the late 1990s, to 255 eggs per person in 1999.

In 1998 egg exports were 2.62 million, a 4 percent decrease from 1997. This represented 33 percent of the global trade, down from 36 percent in 1997 and 48 percent in 1996. This was due in part to low EU egg prices, and a downturn in the Asian economy decreasing demand. Hong Kong and Canada were the largest importers of U.S. egg products.

BACKGROUND AND DEVELOPMENT

History. Poultry processing was one of the nation's first agribusinesses, characterized by many small farms. In the early days, raising meat and poultry was secondary to egg production. One of the first stages in the mechanization of poultry processing was the accelerated development in the 1920s of incubators that could hold thousands of eggs. Farmers could start with 500 chicks and no longer depended on hens to hatch them.

Prior to World War II, home cooks were likely to buy chickens live. After the war, more and more consumers purchased either "New York dressed" chickens—with only the blood and feathers removed—or in some areas, "dressed and drawn" birds—with head, feet, and intestines removed. The change had far-reaching effects, transferring the preparation of poultry to the processing plant, which consumers trusted to be as clean as their own kitchens.

Starting in the 1940s, the poultry industry went through three major changes: an increasing rate of vertical integration, which was largely completed by the mid-1950s; the phasing out of small operations and the concentration of production among a few large firms; and the movement of processing operations to the southeastern states to be closer to the broiler supply.

Regulations. Since mandatory federal inspection began in 1957, all commercially produced chickens were inspected by the USDA for wholesomeness before going to market. Traditionally, inspection took place in the processing plant, conducted by a USDA inspector who relied on sight, touch, and smell to determine the wholesomeness of each bird as it passed by on a swiftly moving conveyer line. In 1978, USDA introduced a faster, modified system in which three inspectors divided the task. One inspected the bird's exterior, another its viscera, and a third made a final inspection of the bird. A more scientific system, Pathogen Reduction and Hazard Analysis and Critical Control Points (HACCP), was imposed in 1996 by the Food Safety and Inspection Service (FSIS). Under this program, inspectors identify hazards, determine the points at which they can be controlled, and recommend corrective action. In December 1996 the USDA's FSIS completed its ruling on the validity of labeling poultry as "fresh." Starting in December 1997, poultry could only carry the "fresh" label if the chicken had not been chilled below 26 degrees Fahrenheit. These rulings were part of the truth in labeling issues that changed food labeling throughout all industries.

In terms of processing, USDA regulations required that washed and eviscerated chickens be submerged in a water-filled chill tank that quickly reduced the birds' body temperatures to 40 degrees or lower to prevent multiplication of salmonella and other microorganisms commonly found on chicken skin. The regulations further required that the water in continuous chill systems be replaced at a rate of one-half gallon per chicken as birds were added to the system.

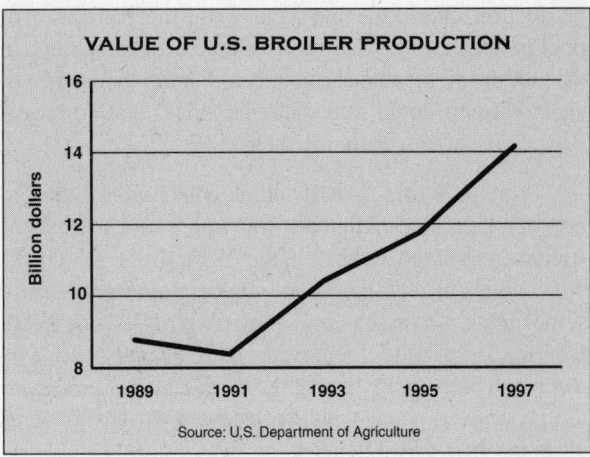

VALUE OF U.S. BROILER PRODUCTION

Source: U.S. Department of Agriculture

Food safety continued to be an issue for poultry processors in the 1990s. Following an outbreak of foodborne illnesses, the USDA required a new labeling policy under which safe-handling instructions explain the need to refrigerate poultry until it is cooked, cook it thoroughly, refrigerate or discard leftovers immediately, and keep work areas clean. In issuing the new labeling recommendations, the USDA cited surveys that revealed consumer ignorance of such basic food safety procedures. The government also cited data from the Centers for Disease Control (CDC) in Atlanta, Georgia, which showed that one-third of at-home food poisoning incidents were caused by undercooking, and another 12 percent resulted from holding precooked food at unsafe temperatures. Safe-handling instructions were publicized by the leading industry associations, the National Broiler Council and the National Turkey Federation. The USDA has also instituted a new ad campaign entitled "Fight Bac" to instruct consumers in safe handling of meat products.

In 1992, the USDA ruled that fresh or frozen uncooked whole carcasses or parts could be treated by irradiation. In 1993 irradiated, packaged poultry became commercially available, albeit in only four independently owned retail stores. Irradiation eliminated up to 99.9 percent of salmonella and 100 percent of campylobacter organisms, and probably any listeria bacteria as well. Irradiation of food continues to be controversial in the public. In 1999 the USDA proposed extending ionizing irradiation to refrigerated and frozen meats. The proposed rule required labeling of irradiated meat and meat products sold at retail.

CURRENT CONDITIONS

In 1998 broiler production increased 7 percent from 1997, to $15.1 billion dollars. The average price per pound was 39.9 cents, and the industry produced 38.6 billion pounds in live weight equivalent.

In 1999, America's annual per capita consumption (PCC) of chicken increased to 78.9 pounds and turkey

consumption was 17.8 pounds per person. In the same period, red meat PCC, which included beef, pork, veal, and lamb, dropped to 123.4 pounds, down from a high of 136.7 pounds in 1980. Starting in 1992, chicken consumption for the first time surpassed that of beef, America's former top meat choice, and this trend continued throughout the decade.

A survey by the National Broiler Council in 1998 cited that 50 percent of consumers eat chicken at least twice a week. The survey cited taste, healthfulness and versatility as the top three reasons consumers choose chicken. The USDA predicts that pork and poultry per capita consumption will continue to increase.

Industry leaders continue to grow and acquire vertically related businesses. For example, Tyson Foods, the world's largest single producer of chicken products, boasts its vertical integration to be "from the egg to the finished product on your table," including genetics, hatchery, growing, and processing facilities. Tyson chickens, like most of the nation's poultry, are primarily produced on small, family-owned farms, and in 1999 Tyson also began an incentive program to small growers to maintain environmentally friendly farms.

In the 1990s chicken parts markets became increasingly segmented, with separate destinations for white and dark meat. Nearly all of the white meat remained in the United States, while the dark meat was much more likely to be exported.

INDUSTRY LEADERS

The nation's leading producer, processor, and marketer of poultry and poultry products throughout the 1990s was Arkansas-based Tyson Foods, Inc. Sales in fiscal 1998 reached $7.36 billion, up from $6.45 billion in fiscal 1996. In 1998 approximately 85 percent of sales came from chicken products. Predictions estimate that by the year 2005, annual sales for Tyson will reach $10 billion.

In 1995 Tyson acquired McCarty Farms' and Cargill's broiler-chicken processing operations. In 1998 they acquired the large-scale poultry operations of Hudson Foods, formerly one of its largest competitors in the chicken business. In 1999, Tyson had 83 plants in 20 U.S. states, exported products to over 55 countries, and was the United States' number one poultry exporter. In a 1999 press release, Tyson stated that it believed "cold pasteurization (irradiation) has been scientifically proven to be a safe process, which dramatically reduces harmful bacteria in food products including poultry," and intended to offer clearly labeled irradiated products as long as there is consumer demand.

Started in 1933 as a cotton cooperative, Georgia-based Gold Kist Inc. was the second-ranked poultry processor in 1998 with annual sales of $1.65 billion dollars, processing 14 million broilers per week. It is a leading exporter, with about 8 percent of its production sold in international markets throughout the world. Total employment exceeded 16,500 people in 1998. The cooperative operated 11 processing plants in Georgia, Alabama, Florida, and the Carolinas.

Yet another leading broiler company in the United States was Perdue Farms Incorporated, producing 42 million pounds of chicken products and 3.5 million pounds of turkey products each week. Annual sales in 1999 were $2.2 billion dollars.

Another Arkansas-based company, ConAgra, ranks third in broiler production. Annual sales in 1999 exceeded $24.5 million dollars. ConAgra reorganized in the late 1990s, closing more than 20 production plants. ConAgra has operations in 35 countries and employs over 82,000 people. Products included Country Pride Roasted Chicken and a line of 20 premium boneless and bone-in Butterball products.

The largest turkey producers in 1997 were Butterball Turkey Corp., owned by ConAgra, producing 900 million pounds of product; Jennie-O Foods, owned by Hormel, producing 766 million pounds of product; and Wampler, owned by WLR Foods, Inc., producing 685 million pounds.

WORKFORCE

The poultry processing industry has become increasingly automated, yet still employs a large number of cutters, trimmers and packers. This is repetitive work, and the industry is notorious for its high rate of repetitive motion injuries. OSHA announced new ergonomic guidelines in 1999 in an attempt to address the situation. The industry is also prone to high rates of injury in the processing plants.

Low wages were characteristic of the poultry industry, with meat cutters' median weekly earnings of $370 in 1998. While the industry employs a high proportion of low-wage production workers, it also requires highly skilled personnel in research and development and to manage and maintain the increasingly efficient and technologically advanced processing operations.

AMERICA AND THE WORLD

Year 2000 was projected to be a better year for world trade than the mid to late 1990s. At the time the global economy appeared to be recovering after economic slowdowns in both Asia and Russia.

Despite difficult economies in Asia and Russia, broiler exports for 2000 were projected at 4.68 billion, a slight increase over 1999. Exports of other chicken totaled 270 million pounds in 1999, down 4 percent from

1998. However, strong foreign competition, weak demand in Russia due to the devalued ruble, and competition from pork depressed prices. As Asian markets recovered somewhat at the end of the 1990s, exports to Hong Kong and China increased. In 1999, exports continued to be highest to Japan, Mexico, Canada and Hong Kong.

Turkey exports in 2000 were expected to be up from 1999, but still far below mid 1990 levels. Mexico was the largest importer of U.S. turkey in 1999, having a large effect on the overall export totals.

Egg exports appeared to be suffering greatly from decreases in the markets to Mexico and Hong Kong. Exports to Mexico fell 72 percent during the first 8 months of 1999. However, exports were expected to rise in 2000, and were projected at 170 million dozen.

RESEARCH AND TECHNOLOGY

New processing and packaging technologies facilitated the poultry industry's rapid growth in the last half of the twentieth century. Over the years, numerous automated processes have taken the place of manual labor at various stages of production. For example, mechanized killing machines capable of killing five birds per second, five times more than a skilled worker could accomplish with a sharp knife, were introduced in the 1960s. Defeathering operations were also automated.

Mechanical eviscerating machines came into use in the 1970s. At about the same time, mechanized cutting of the birds into parts was increasingly performed in processing plants rather than by meatcutters in retail outlets. The late 1970s also saw the introduction of automatic deboning machines capable of processing up to 800 pieces of chicken a minute and separating edible meat from bonier parts. The machines also collected meat scraps from partially defleshed carcasses; the scraps were used in the further processing of patties, soups, luncheon meats, and other products.

By the 1990s, as consumers began to expect the ready-to-cook convenience of portioned chicken, ultra-thin, high-pressure waterjet cutting and shaping delivered it. Video cameras sensed the changing pattern from a light projected on a partially prepared carcass. A computer received the information, calculated the best cutting patterns, and sent directions to waterjet nozzles, which then made precise cuts, trimming and portioning the chicken at the same time. Another machine used pistons to force chopped chicken through molds that created three-dimensional formed products. The possibilities included geometric shapes, concave patties, and pieces that looked like boneless breasts.

Since sanitation has always been a concern, the poultry processing industry continued research into chemical cleansers and new dispensing techniques in the 1990s.

For example, some firms experimented with low-cost robots that could transfer a variety of poultry products from conveyer belts to other processing areas. Also, improved inspection methods instated in 1996 and the use of irradiation have increased poultry safety.

FURTHER READING

Hoovers Online, 2000. Available from http://www.hoovers .com.

Hyatt, Dale. "The U.S. Poultry Industry." Available from http://gallus.tamu.edu/fsis/fsman1.html.

Meat & Poultry: Business Journal of the Meat and Poultry Industry Available from http://www.meatpoultry.com.

National Cattlemen's Association. *Cattle and Beef Industry Statistics,* 1999. Available from http://www.beef.org.

United States Bureau of Labor Statistics. Occupational Outlook Handbook. *Butchers and Meat, Poultry, and Fish Cutters,* 1999. Available from http://www.bls.gov.

United States Department of Agriculture. *National Agricultural Statistics Service Publications,* 1999. Available from http://www.usda.gov.

USA Poultry and Egg Export Council. *Industry Web Site,* 1999. Available from http://www.usapeec.org.

SIC 2021

CREAMERY BUTTER

This industry consists of establishments primarily engaged in manufacturing creamery butter.

NAICS CODE(S)

311512 (Creamery Butter Manufacturing)

INDUSTRY SNAPSHOT

Despite modern sanitary production methods, entering the twenty-first century, butter is not much different from that enjoyed centuries ago by people who churned milk in animal skins slung from the backs of camels and horses. Butter manufacturing and marketing, a sector of the dairy industry, is extremely regionalized and competitive. The industry's quality standards and farm pricing are highly regulated by the U.S. government. Government price support programs were reduced throughout the 1990s, which in turn led to a more competitive marketplace and more volatility in the prices of dairy products, including butter.

BACKGROUND AND DEVELOPMENT

Commercial production of butter is a relatively recent development. In 1870 nearly all of the 514 million pounds of U.S. butter was produced on farms. The spreading effects of the Industrial Era and the invention of machinery changed all that. In 1864, a Bavarian brewmaster applied the process of centrifugation to butter making. A cream batching machine was introduced in 1877, followed two years later by the continuous cream separator.

Other innovations helped to advance the industry. The Babcock test, perfected in 1890, accurately measured the percentage of fat in milk and cream. Pasteurization insured a high quality of both milk and cream. Additionally, the use of pure cultures of lactic acid bacteria and the invention of refrigeration aided the preservation of quality.

The first U.S. butter manufacturing creamery was built in Manchester, Iowa, in 1871. By 1991, commercial production exceeded 1.3 billion Pounds, and Wisconsin and California were the leading butter producers, accounting for 654 million pounds. According to the U.S. Census Bureau, in 1997 there were 34 establishments whose primary purpose was the manufacture of creamery butter. Wisconsin and California were still primary butter-producing states. Also, the largest U.S. single-site dairy complex was the Land O'Lakes plant in Tulare, California.

Under federal regulations, butter sold in the United States is made exclusively from milk or cream, or both, and must contain at least 80 percent milkfat by weight. Coloring or salt may be added. Butter is labeled by the U.S. Department of Agriculture (USDA) as Grade AA, A, or B, according to flavor intensity, texture, color, and salt taste.

Throughout the 1990s butter producers sold their butter products in supermarkets, club stores, and other retail outlets. In addition to individual consumers, butter producers served the foodservice industry (restaurants and fastfood operations), institutions (hospitals and schools), and industrial customers (bakeries). At the retail level, Grade A butter was typically packaged in quarter pound sticks packed four to a cardboard carton, while whipped butter, developed for easier spreadability, was packaged in tubs. Industrial and foodservice packaging ranged from 68-pound blocks to individually wrapped, single-serve pats. Butteroil, the anhydrous form of butter developed to use up surpluses during a period of lowered public consumption, has been used by the confectionery and baking industries and as a cooking oil.

During the 1980s butter consumption slowed as health and calorie-conscious consumers switched to margarine and other spreads. From 1981 to 1991, annual per capita butter consumption increased only slightly from 3.7 to 3.9 pounds. In 1995 supermarket sales of butter were $689 million, down from the 1991 figure of $917.5 million. Total U.S. butter sales in 1995 were $1.3 billion, virtually unchanged from 1991.

To offset the decrease in butter consumption, the industry researched alternate ways to market its product. One way was the use of butteroil (produced by heating butter until its emulsion breaks down then removing the milk serum through centrifugation) as a substitute for other oils in cooking and baking. Butter producers also introduced flavored butters such as honey, garlic, and herb butter, hoping to increase consumer interest.

CURRENT CONDITIONS

The value of product shipments has fluctuated slightly from 1992 to 1997. In 1992, shipments were valued at $1.2 billion; 1993, $1.1 billion; 1994, $1.0 billion; 1995, $1.2 billion; 1996, $1.5 billion; and 1997, $1.4 billion. In the late 1990s, America actually experienced a shortage of butter and record prices for milk butterfat. In turn, the retail price of butter also increased. According to the *Wall Street Journal,* "Part of the reason butter supplies [were] so low is that milk production in California, which produces about 20 percent of the nation's milk, slipped earlier [in 1998] when El Nino-fueled storms turned dairy farms to mud. Industry officials say the production shortfall was compounded when U.S. exporter continued to use federal subsidies to arrange for the shipment of millions of pounds of butter overseas." Demand for butterfat continued increasing into the 2000s.

INDUSTRY LEADERS

The largest butter producers in the United States were also among the largest of the Midwest dairy cooperatives, Land O'Lakes and MidAmerica Dairymen, Inc. These co-ops, which had originated to represent farmers in obtaining the best milk prices, grew to become manufacturers and marketers of butter and other dairy products. The Land O'Lakes cooperative, established in 1921, led the retail butter industry in the 1990s with a 35 percent market share. Headquartered in Arden Hills, Minneapolis, Land O'Lakes had the number one brand of butter in the United States and marketed more than 600 dairy products. Net sales in 1999 were $5.6 billion. MidAmerica Dairymen, Inc. sold its butter products to retailers under its Mid-Am name and to private label customers. Associated Milk Producers, Inc. (AMPI) was another major cooperative with strong butter manufacturing operations. Formed in 1969, AMPI churned out approximately 5 billion pounds of butter, cheese, and other solid milk products each year. The company operated the largest butter-packaging plant in the United States. Sales in 1998 reached $1.1 billion.

By the late 1990s, the West Coast was replacing the Midwest as the leading producer of dairy products. Many distributors blamed Midwest farmers' reluctance to modernize.

RESEARCH AND TECHNOLOGY

At the close of the century, the use of recombinant bovine growth hormone (rBGH) to stimulate cows' milk production was the dominant issue in the dairy industry. Manufactured by Monsanto and approved for use by the U.S. Food and Drug Administration (FDA) in 1993 (in use since 1994), rBGH was criticized for its tendency to create udder infections in cows. Antibiotics administered to the cows passed into their milk and, subsequently, into consumers. Critics charged that humans were in danger of developing a resistance to antibiotics, which could prove fatal when needed for disease control. There was also concern that rBGH could cause cancer. Land O' Lakes, a vocal supporter of rBGH, was often targeted by protestors. In early 1997, a Vermont campaign to require labeling of all dairy products containing rBGH milk was struck down by the courts. In the late 1990s, many groups still wanted the use of rBGH stopped; in 1998, for example, the Sierra Club of Canada was protesting its use in the United States, hoping to stall Canadian approval. They were trying to urge Monsanto to conduct more extensive testing.

FURTHER READING

"And Why Shouldn' We Like Butter." *Philadelphia Inquirer,* 12 July 1998.

"BGH Label Law Struck Down." *Vegetarian Times,* January 1997.

Butter Facts. California Manufacturing Milk Advisory Board, 1991.

"Consumer Expenditures Study." *Supermarket News,* September 1996.

"Europe Bans rBGH." *Health News & Review,* Spring 1995.

Hoover's Online. Hoover's Inc., 2000. Available from http://www.hoovers.com.

Kilman, Scott, and Rekha Balu. "Butter Shortage Is Lifting Dairy Prices." *Wall Street Journal,* 23 June 1998.

Milk Facts. Washington: Milk Industry Foundation, 1992.

"Robocow." *Village Voice,* 14 March 1995.

U.S. Census Bureau. "Creamery Butter Manufacturing." *1997 Economic Census,* 4 June 1999.

"U.S. Food Consumption." *Food Review,* May 1996.

SIC 2022

NATURAL, PROCESSED AND IMITATION CHEESE

This industry encompasses establishments primarily engaged in manufacturing natural cheese (except cottage cheese), cheese foods, cheese spreads, and cheese analogues (imitations and substitutes). These establishments also produce byproducts, such as raw liquid whey.

NAICS CODE(S)

311513 (Cheese Manufacturing)

INDUSTRY SNAPSHOT

Cheese is one of the principal product groups in the dairy industry and has become increasingly important to the growth of the entire dairy industry in the United States. Wisconsin has been the leading cheese producer of the 21 major cheese-producing states in the nation; its shipment value was approximately $4.3 billion. California was the number-two cheese producer in the late 1990s, following an aggressive promotional campaign. Annual per capita consumption of cheese increased yearly during the 1990s (to 28.9 pounds in 1998), with projections at more than 35 pounds per person by 2005. The total value of industry shipments increased from $11 billion in the mid-1980s to approximately $18 billion by the mid-1990s. In 1997 the value of shipments was more than $20 billion.

The United States has developed very few cheeses of its own. Processors have instead replicated European cheeses and used their European names, except for Roquefort, which is a protected name. Some of the cheeses created in this country are monterey jack, brick, colby, and herkimer. All of these cheeses are firm, ripened cheddar-type cheeses.

ORGANIZATION AND STRUCTURE

Kraft, the leading cheese producer, is part of a diversified conglomerate. In 1988, Kraft was purchased by the tobacco producer, Philip Morris Companies Inc., for $12.9 billion. Philip Morris combined Kraft with an 1985 acquisition to form Kraft General Foods, the largest coffee and cheese producer in the United States. Its strongest competition in the cheese area of its operations came from large dairy companies and dairy cooperatives like Beatrice, Sargento, Inc., and Tillamook.

As Americans' cheese palate became more adventurous in the 1990s, there were growing numbers of small, regional cheese makers sending their specialty products to market. U.S. cheese producers obtain the raw milk from which their products are made from thousands of commercial dairy farms. The number of farms has been dwindling steadily for decades, but they have grown larger in size and milk production efficiency has been vastly improved. Many of the farmers are members of one of the several hundred regional dairy co-ops. These co-ops, formed to represent milk producers in price setting, are beginning to take over other dairy operations, including the manufacture and marketing of a broad range of cheese products and ingredients. Large food processors either own their own farms or purchase raw milk from the co-ops and independent farmers. Approximately one-third of the 157,483 million pounds of raw milk produced by the country's 9.4 million dairy cows in 1996 was used to make cheese.

The dairy industry has been heavily regulated by the government. Cheese manufactured in the United States must meet Standards of Identity, which define such product characteristics as content levels of milkfat and manufacturing methods. Either Class I milk or milk of manufacturing grade may be used to make cheese. Class I fluid milk meets stricter standards, which include regular inspections of the herd, herd housing facilities, and dairy equipment and milk storage units to ensure that they satisfy health and sanitation requirements. It is used for human consumption as a beverage or in manufactured products such as cheese. Milk of manufacturing grade meets less stringent standards and may only be used for manufactured products.

The government has regulated milk pricing through the Federal Milk Marketing Orders authorized by the Agricultural Marketing Act of 1937, or the Agricultural Act of 1949, which established the ongoing dairy price support program. The complex pricing system affected all segments of the dairy industry.

BACKGROUND AND DEVELOPMENT

Although there is no record of when cheese was first used as a food, its origins have been estimated to date back to 6000-7000 B.C. Its lasting quality made it a source of nourishment both at home and on journeys, and armies often carried cheese among their provisions. The first U.S. cheese plant was built in 1851 in Rome, New York, and the area remained the center of American cheesemaking for the next 50 years. The U.S. cheesemaking industry began shifting westward toward Wisconsin in the early 1900s.

There are hundreds of varieties of cheese worldwide and numerous ways of classifying them, usually according to the coagulating agent (rennet or acid) or texture (very hard, hard, semisoft, soft, or acid). Natural cheeses are made directly from milk (or sometimes whey) by pressing the curd that forms when milk has been coagulated (or curdled), then heated and stirred, and then finally draining off the whey (the remaining liquid part of the milk). Processed cheeses are made from a combination of one or more batches of natural cheeses, heated to pasteurization temperatures. They were developed in the 1920s to extend shelf life, ensure product uniformity, and make slicing easier, while simulating natural cheese. The first U.S. patent for processed cheese was issued to J.L. Kraft in 1916; it described a method of emulsifying the heated cheese mixture using alkaline salts.

Cheese analogues are made without butterfat and are designed to resemble natural or processed cheese in appearance, taste, texture, and nutrition. The cost savings of using less expensive fats, such as vegetable oils instead of butterfat, provided the incentive to produce cheese analogues. Early examples were produced in the early 1900s by skimming butterfat from whole milk, replacing it with another fat, and then following regular cheesemaking procedures. Technology using dried milk protein, hydrogenated vegetable oil, emulsifiers, and other ingredients was developed in the early 1970s to simulate processed american and mozzarella cheeses.

Some of the principal cheese products are: cheddar and swiss (hard); parmesan and romano (very hard); mozzarella, brick, havarti, and blue (semisoft); brie, bel paese, and camembert (soft); powders and blends; and reduced-fat.

The economic health of the cheese industry was varied at the start of the 1990s. Both sales and production of cheese hit record highs in the early 1990s as indicated by the following statistics: $18 billion in sales; 6.1 billion pounds of natural cheese; and 2.2 billion pounds of processed cheese. Overall industry growth, however, was flat, and in 1992, supermarket sales of $5.36 billion had dipped 3.06 percent from 1991. Sales were fairly evenly divided among three major markets: retail, foodservice (restaurants, fast-food outlets, institutions), and industrial (ingredients used by other food processors).

The biggest supermarket sellers were unshredded american and other natural cheeses. The biggest gains, however, were registered in natural (11.28 percent) and processed (72.6 percent) shredded cheeses. Sales of Italian cheeses in particular were projected to continue their upward curve in all areas. Although per capita consumption of cheese had hovered at a fairly steady amount of 11-12 pounds since the mid-1980s, annual Italian cheese consumption had surged by 50 percent, from 6.5 to 9.4 pounds per person in that period. Most of this increase was in mozzarella, with consumption exceeding 7 pounds per capita in 1991.

Pre-sliced, packaged process cheeses represented a healthy chunk of cheese sales, and processors followed up with packaged shredded cheese in such flavored varieties as "taco" and "pizza." Retailers also found that pre-sliced cheeses were popular among consumers at the deli counter as well. Vacuum-packed, pre-sliced cheese allowed deli counter staff to deal with other tasks instead of slicing cheese to order and reduced the time that customers spent waiting in line.

Industrial sales of cheese ingredients continued to grow. They accounted for about 28 percent of the industry's $18 billion sales figure for the early 1990s. Here, too, much of the growth was in Italian-style cheeses, but processed cheeses, powders, and other natural cheeses were also big sellers. Industrial uses of cheese expanded as the country's changing demographics resulted in increased popularity of prepared and frozen foods.

Pizza's continuing popularity contributed to the strength of the foodservice market, which is the third largest market for cheese makers. Italian cheese sales increased approximately 10 percent from 1987 to 1991, a period during which the segment as a whole grew 6.6 percent. The biggest increase was in hospitals and schools. The most significant change during the period was the waning popularity of cheddar compared to processed cheese.

Portions of the cheese industry were suffering in the early 1990s. Declining cheese production in Minnesota was costing the state economy nearly $831 million annually and more than 12,000 jobs, according to a University of Minnesota study. Milk product sales of cheese (and ice cream) were down 10 percent from 1985. As production and sales dropped, so did dairy farm purchases from related industries. The milk production declines were triggered in part by sell-outs due to lower milk pricing and a relatively low per-cow production.

The size of the cheese market was $4 billion in the fiscal year ended September 1996. The wholesale price of cheese was expected to increase in 1996 to $1.34 per pound, one cent above the 1994 level. Retail price averaged $3.09 per pound.

Of the 7.9 billion pounds of cheese produced in 1996, 123 million pounds were sent abroad, while domestic use accounted for 7.5 billion pounds. Per capita consumption in the United States was 27.9 pounds.

Lowfat. Of the 7.5 billion pounds of cheese sold in the United States in 1996, some 15.3 percent consisted of low-fat products, but their flavor and texture could not match that of full-fat standard cheeses. A prime research effort of the cheese industry in the 1990s was to develop ways to improve the flavor of low-fat and fat-free products. Some success was achieved by using new adjunct cultures to enhance flavor. The development of new starter cultures created especially for low-fat cheeses also allowed for greater flavor with lower acidity.

By mid-decade, one of every four dollars consumers spent on cheese went toward the purchase of reduced-fat or no-fat cheeses. Improved technology continued to enhance taste and texture of these products. The Wisconsin Center for Dairy Research patented a manufacturing protocol that used a firmer milk coagulum to increase flavor and moisture of reduced- and no-fat products. It was projected that sales of reduced- and no-fat cheese would represent 50 percent of all cheese purchases after 2000.

CURRENT CONDITIONS

Approximately 524 companies were engaged in the cheese industry in the late 1990s. The total value of shipments exceeded $20 billion in 1997. The product breakdown was as follows (in terms of shipment values): natural cheese, except cottage cheese ($15.0 billion); processed cheese and related products ($4.7 billion); cheese substitutes (185.5 million); and raw liquid whey ($54.1 million).

In 2000 the American Dairy Association, the National Dairy Council, and the U.S. Dairy Export Council were working with regional dairy promotion organizations to increase advertising. One successful campaign ''Behold . . . The Power of Cheese'' was running a timely spot in January 2000 called ''Election,'' which was about a political candidate who essentially loses the race as soon as he declares that he doesn't like cheese.

INDUSTRY LEADERS

Kraft, long the country's top cheese producer, held 26.8 percent of the $1.6 billion natural cheese market and 61.3 percent of the processed cheese market in 1995. The cheese giant suffered from the recession of the early 1990s, and consolidated two cheese plants into one in Illinois and closed another in Michigan. Kraft reported 1998 sales of $17.3 billion, a 2.8 percent sales growth over the previous year.

Kraft's Specialty Products Division planned strong promotional activity for its Italian and specialty cheeses in foodservice, in-store deli, and institutional markets. In the industrial market, Kraft Food Ingredients (KFI) sold a wide range of natural and processed cheeses and cheese substitutes to other food processors for use as food ingredients. The company that built its reputation on the pasteurized processed cheese it patented in 1916 continued to add to its consumer product line. ''Marketers like Kraft are facing more competition than they ever have before,'' according to Robert Eckert, of Kraft USA's Retail Division, in *Dairy Field* magazine.

Some of Kraft's competition was coming from Sargento Cheese Company Inc., which nearly knocked the giant from its number-one-in-the-market perch in the shredded cheese area in the late 1990s. With its $320 million in sales versus Kraft's $2 billion, Wisconsin-based Sargento Cheese Co. wouldn't displace Kraft, but it was a company to watch. Kraft sales had also dropped in the $1.5 billion processed cheese slices section of the dairy case as consumers opted for regional brand names or lower-priced private label brands. ConAgra's Beatrice Cheese unit also planned to do battle with Kraft's long-standing dominance with a line of 30 new fat-free cheeses under its Healthy Choice label.

Co-ops that processed the raw milk from their dairy farm membership were also strong contenders in the competitive cheese industry. Mid-America Dairymen, Inc. (Mid-Am), the country's second-largest dairy co-op in the early 1990s, produced cheese from the milk of its member farms. Mid-Am used both milk of manufacturing grade and Class I (Grade A) milk that was not bottled for beverage use. It was one of the largest manufacturers of natural cheese in the country and also produced a range of specialty cheeses. Its output of mozzarella alone, largely destined for its fresh pizza customers, came to 180 million pounds a year. Under its Mid-America Farms label, it sold its cheese products to consumers, institutional and foodservice markets, and to food manufacturers for use as food ingredients.

RESEARCH AND TECHNOLOGY

New technologies in the industry focused on product safety, automation, and quality controls. An increasing number of large cheddar cheese plants operate non-stop, seven days a week, using sophisticated computer control systems that are able to pump 50,000 pounds of milk per hour. Many of these systems allow a single operator to oversee the following processes: pasteurizing the milk, adding the starter culture, making the cheese, draining the whey, cheddaring, and milling and salting.

FURTHER READING

Friend, Janin. ''Reduced-Fat Cheese Sales Expected to Gain.'' *Supermarket News,* 14 October 1996.

Hoover's Company Profiles. Hoover's Online, 2000.

Lazich, Robert S. *Market Share Reporter 1997.* Detroit: Gale Research, 1997.

Williams, Mina. ''Cheese Campaign Expands in Second Year,'' *Supermarket News,* 29 July 1996.

U.S. Census Bureau. ''Manufacturing-Industry Series.'' *1997 Economic Census.* Washington, D.C.: GPO, 24 June 1999.

SIC 2023

DRY, CONDENSED, AND EVAPORATED DAIRY PRODUCTS

This classification covers establishments primarily engaged in manufacturing dry, condensed, and evaporated dairy products. Included in this industry are establishments primarily engaged in manufacturing mixes for the preparation of frozen ice cream and ice milk and dairy and non-dairy base cream substitutes and dietary supplements.

NAICS CODE(S)

311514 (Dry, Condensed, and Evaporated Dairy Product
      Manufacturing)

INDUSTRY SNAPSHOT

The dry, condensed, and evaporated dairy products sector of the highly regionalized dairy industry embraces both small family operations and multinational giants, reporting sales in the billions of dollars. The spectrum of products produced by this industry is just as broad, ranging from retail staples like canned, evaporated milks, which have been familiar on market shelves for more than a century, to sophisticated milk protein ingredients that are constantly being refined in research laboratories for new food uses. With products as comforting as mother's milk and as baffling to consumers as the sodium caseinates that appear on the labels of the latest sports drinks, it was a $9.36 billion industry by the 1990s.

ORGANIZATION AND STRUCTURE

From World War II, a dwindling number of dairy farms have supplied the raw milk from which dry, condensed, and evaporated milk products are processed, but the farms have become much larger. Huge dairy farm cooperatives combined with operations that processed the raw milk to produce branded consumer products and milk ingredients marketed to food and animal feed processors. Darigold Inc. was the largest Pacific Northwest cooperative in the early 1990s.

The small companies that had pioneered condensed and evaporated milk technology and production in the nineteenth century were still in business more than 100 years later, producing the same products with which they had started out—and many, many others. Borden, Inc. and Pet, Inc. had grown into diversified giants ranked in the top 50 food companies nationwide. Pharmaceutical companies also reached into this dairy food category with their infant formulas. There was always room, though, for smaller companies, often specializing in milk ingredients like whey proteins and ice cream/yogurt/milkshake mixes.

BACKGROUND AND DEVELOPMENT

Removal of all or part of the water from milk not only reduces transportation costs and makes handling easier, but it also allows unrefrigerated storage of sterilized or dried products for prolonged periods. Such products may be intended for consumer use or as ingredients in diverse processed foods.

The Federal Drug & Cosmetic Act has established Standards of Identity (SID) for milk products which define what can be packaged under a given product name. The Food and Drug Administration (FDA) designates food ingredients to be generally recognized as safe (GRAS) when extensive past use has not shown any harmful effects.

Dry Milk. Marco Polo, it is said, encountered sun-dried milk in his travels through Mongolia in the thirteenth century. It remained for later scientists to develop commercial production processes. An early patent for a commercial process to manufacture dried milk was granted in 1855. Technological advances since then have enabled a wide variety of manufactured milk products with applications in frozen dairy desserts, ice cream, frozen soft and hard yogurt, bakery goods, confectionery products, dry mixes, soups, animal feeds, and countless other nutritional and functional uses.

Nonfat dry milk (NDM) results when both fat and water are removed from milk. Lactose (milk sugar), milk proteins, and milk minerals are present in the same relative proportions as in fresh milk. Moisture is not more than 5 percent by weight, and fat content is not more than 1.5 percent by weight unless otherwise indicated. In the 1990s, nearly a billion pounds of NDM were being produced every year.

Dry whole milk results from the removal of water from milk. It contains not less than 26 percent milk fat and not more than 4 percent moisture. Dry buttermilk is made by removing the water from buttermilk derived from butter manufacture. It has not less than 4.5 percent milk fat content and not more than 5 percent moisture.

Milk Proteins. Derived through various processing steps from skim milk, milk proteins are used as ingredients in a wide range of food products both for their nutritional value and for their functionality. Casein, milk's principal protein, has been commercially isolated from skim milk since 1900. There are two basic types, depending on the coagulating agent used to precipitate the casein from the milk: lactic (acid) casein and rennet casein. Most acid caseins intended for food applications were converted to caseinates by dissolving the acid casein curd with water and dilute alkali and then drying the solution. Sodium caseinate is generally recognized as safe (GRAS).

Casein has a higher Protein Efficiency Ratio (PER) than vegetable proteins. Under the *Code of Federal Regulations,* "if the protein efficiency ratio of protein is equal to or better than that of casein, the U.S. Recommended Daily Allowance (RDA) is 45 grams." However, if the PER is lower than that of casein (2.5), then 65 grams of protein are required to meet the U.S. RDA. Because of its high protein quality and content, low lactose, and bland flavor, casein is used in nutritional supplements. Nutritional foods commonly formulated with casein include high-protein beverage powders, fortified cereals, infant formulas, and nutrition bars. Products incorporating casein for its functional properties of imparting texture, viscosity, emulsification, and opacity included coffee creamers, soups, sauces, ice cream, whipped toppings, yogurt, and salad dressings.

Whey seemed to have been the "forgotten" milk protein until April 1971, when representatives of 56 firms gathered to consider the potential of these milk solids that remain after cheese manufacture. Warren S. Clark, Jr., executive director of the American Dairy Products Institute, wrote in the *Encyclopedia of Food Science and Technology,* "In no area of the modern dairy industry have changes of a technical nature been as innovative and rapid as in the whey products segment." The Food and Drug Administration affirmed the safety of whey products and their manufacture in 1984 with a declaration of common and usual names for diverse whey products ("Whey," "Reduced Minerals Whey," and "Whey Protein Concentrate") and by granting them GRAS status.

Evaporated Milk. When Gail Borden returned to the United States from England in 1851, it was on a ship that had to carry cows to provide milk for the immigrant children on board. There was no way to carry fresh milk on a long sea voyage without it spoiling. Five years later, in 1856, Borden was granted patents in the United States and England for the preservation of milk after it had been evaporated in a vacuum. The method used no added sugar, but sweetened condensed milk was to be Borden's first commercial product in 1861.

Thirty years later, the Helvetia Milk Condensing Company began production of the world's first unsweetened evaporated milk in 1885, calling it Highland Evaporated Cream after the plant's home in Highland, Illinois. The company was later to change its name to Pet, Inc.

Evaporated milk is a canned whole milk concentrate with a specified quantity of added vitamin D. Vitamin A may also be added. Related products are evaporated skimmed milk, evaporated low fat milk, evaporated filled milk, and evaporated goat milk.

Dairy and Non-Dairy Creamers. Health-conscious consumers in the 1990s regarded non-dairy creamers as cholesterol free and, therefore, better for you than milk-based products. Nestle's Carnation, which introduced Coffee-Mate in 1961, added Coffee-Mate Lite in 1989 and again extended this top-selling non-dairy creamer line in 1992 with Hazelnut, Irish Creme, and Amaretto flavored powders. Pet, Inc. also marketed a non-dairy creamer.

Infant Formulas. Infant formulas that approximate human milk are fed to infants all over the world, sometimes as their sole source of nutrients during the first months of life. Such products were unknown until the twentieth century, when they became a reliable alternative to breast-feeding. In the London of the early 1800s, only about 10 percent of infants not breast-fed lived past their first birthdays.

In the United States, the Infant Formula Act of 1980 and its 1986 amendments very specifically govern the manufacture of commercial infant formulas. The Act authorized the FDA to implement quality control regulations and recall procedures, labeling and nutrient requirements, and requirements for exempt infant formulas. Additionally, infant formulas must satisfy Federal Food, Drug and Cosmetic Act regulations dealing with foods for special dietary use, good manufacturing practices, and canned foods (for liquid infant formulas only).

The stringent regulations governing infant formulas have included setting maximum levels for 29 nutrients and minimum levels for 10. Labels were required to include a nutrient declaration; "use by" date information; a statement such as "use as directed by a physician"; a warning statement of the consequences of improper preparation; preparation and use directions that included pictograms if appropriate; and more. All of these requirements had long been standard practices of its member manufacturers, according to the Infant Formula Council.

Infant formulas were a $1.9 billion business in the 1990s, presenting their products as the best substitute for mother's milk. Yet, the industry was mired in federal and state price-fixing investigations. Antitrust inquiries were directed at contracts awarded to the three top producers under the Special Supplemental Food Program for Women, Infants and Children (WIC), designed for low-income families. Although federally funded, WIC was administered by the states, which were paying full retail prices for formula because there was no competitive bidding.

In the early 1990s, Abbott Laboratories, which marketed infant formulas through its Ross Laboratories unit, and Bristol-Myers Squibb, whose infant formulas were sold through its Mead Johnson Nutritional Group, shared 85 percent of the market. American Home Products accounted for about 9 percent of the market, selling through Wyeth-Ayerst Laboratories. The other major producers were Nestle's Carnation unit and Gerber, which marketed a Bristol-Myers product.

In June 1992, after a two-year investigation into the three biggest producers, the Federal Trade Commission charged them with price-rigging, contending that they had rigged contracts awarded under the federally-funded Special Supplemental Food Program for Women, Infants and Children. This program accounts for approximately one of every three cans of formula sold. The cost to the government was estimated at $25 million. Mead-Johnson and American Home, while admitting no wrongdoing, agreed to settle. Abbott Laboratories initially planned to fight the charges in federal court. The *Wall Street Journal* quoted Duane Burnham, Abbott's chairman and chief executive officer: "We have competed responsibly, aggressively, and completely within the law." In May 1993, however, Abbott Laboratories agreed to pay more than $140 million to settle a number of suits filed against the company nationwide and consolidated in Florida to simplify proceedings. The Federal Trade Commission's actions against Abbott remain in place.

Value of shipments in this industry was expected to increase to $8.1 billion in 1997, over 1996 shipments of an estimated $7.9 billion. Value of imports dropped from $345 million in 1989 to $247 million (forecast) in 1993, but increased to $383 million by 1995. Exports jumped from $519 million in 1994 to $583 million in 1995.

In the mid-1990s the dairy industry was witnessing the highest raw milk and milkfat prices in history due to low grain yields, high feed costs, and high demand for dairy products. According to *Dairy Foods,* despite a subsequent increase in retail dairy prices, however, most dairy categories posted good growth for 1996 as consumers continued to eagerly patronize dairy products.

Dry whole milk production during March 1996 totaled 10.6 million pounds, down 39 percent from 1995. Production of nonfat dry milk during March 1996 was 110 million pounds, down 7 percent from March 1995. Canned milk production during March 1996 totaled 35 million pounds, down 27 percent from March 1995.

CURRENT CONDITIONS

In the late 1990s, 213 establishments participated in this industry. More than 15,000 people were employed, helping contribute to the $9.02 billion value of shipments. The majority of the value was derived from dry milk products and mixtures, including infant formulas. The second largest sector was dairy product substitutes, followed closely by canned milk products, including condensed and evaporated milk.

RESEARCH AND TECHNOLOGY

Evaporation and Drying. Water is removed from milk either by evaporation, in which heat is applied under a vacuum, or by drying. Spray drying has been the more widely used method for preparing dried milk products. In this process, the condensed fluid milk is pumped from the vacuum pan while it is still hot and atomized in the heated air of the spray dryer either by the centrifugal force of being discharged from a rapidly turning disk or by being forced through a narrow nozzle. Drying is almost instantaneous.

Roller drying has rarely been used to dry milk for human use. In this process, condensed milk is fed between a pair of heated rollers and adheres to them in a thin film. The dried milk is scraped off by a sharp blade and hammered into uniform, fine particles. In addition to roller and spray drying, these products could be made by foam or freeze drying. It was also possible to make them more readily soluble; such products were called ''instantized.''

Ultra-High Temperature Processing. Ultra-high temperature processing, which produced liquid soft-serve ice cream and yogurt mixes with a 90-day shelf life, six to nine times that of standard processing, enabled food service distributors in the 1990s to compete with local and regional dairies with a full line of dairy products. Until then, the dairies had a tight hold on this lucrative segment of the dairy industry, selling to giant fast food outlets like McDonald's as well as mom-and-pop stores.

FURTHER READING

Cremeans, John E., ed. *Handbook of North American Industry.* Washington: Bernan Press, 1999.

''Dairy Speaks': The Big Picture: Higher Prices, But Higher Demand,'' *Dairy Foods,* 15 October 1996.

O'Donnell, Claudia, D. ''The Right Mix: At Rich Products, R&D Is Incorporated Into Every Phase of the Business,'' *Prepared Foods,* March 1996.

Rice, Judy. ''Conquering a Critical Control Point.'' *Prepared Foods,* October 1996.

Rickard, Leah. ''Price Hikes, Baby Boom Nurture Formula Sales.'' *Advertising Age,* 10 April 1995.

U.S. Census Bureau. ''Manufacturing-Industry Series.'' *1997 Economic Census.* Washington, D.C.: GPO, 24 August 1999.

SIC 2024

ICE CREAM AND FROZEN DESSERTS

This industry classification encompasses establishments primarily engaged in manufacturing ice cream and other frozen desserts: frozen yogurt, ice milk, ices and sherbets, frozen custard, mellorine, frozen tofu, and pops (frozen desserts on sticks).

NAICS CODE(S)

311520 (Ice Cream and Frozen Dessert Manufacturing)

INDUSTRY SNAPSHOT

The ice cream and frozen desserts industry is an important sector of the American dairy industry. Ice cream was an $11 billion industry in the late 1990s; worldwide consumption of frozen desserts rose steadily throughout the decade. Premium and super premium ice cream desserts, which contained higher amounts of butterfat than regular ice cream, gained popularity in the late 1990s, while frozen yogurt, a $585 million market in the mid-1990s, declined in consumption. According to a report issued by Euromonitor, a London-based market research firm, worldwide consumption of ice cream grew through the 1990s, increasing 17 percent between 1993 and 1997.

ORGANIZATION AND STRUCTURE

The production of ice cream begins with the milk produced by America's dairy farmers, many of whom belong to large dairy cooperatives that market their milk to processors or, in some cases, operate their own processing facilities for the manufacture of ice cream and other dairy products. In the early 1990s, America's 10 million dairy cows produced 148,526 million pounds of milk; approximately 8.6 percent of this milk, or 12.8 million pounds, was used to make frozen dairy products.

Manufacturers of ice cream and other frozen desserts range in size from small operations with sales under $1 million a year to subsidiaries or divisions of giant, diversified companies with annual sales in the billions of dollars and for which frozen desserts are only a portion of their total product lines. In the early 1990s, there were approximately 675 establishments making ice cream, 305 making ice milk, and 175 making water ice. Most of these plants made more than one type of frozen dessert product.

Traditionally a highly regionalized industry, the frozen desserts and ice cream segment began to consolidate in the late 1990s as distribution became more advanced and national firms were formed. Still, many top producers' brand names were known only in the geographic areas in which they were distributed. Distribution to sales outlets was vital to the success of the frozen desserts, and competition for distributors remained keen.

BACKGROUND AND DEVELOPMENT

Whether ice cream originated in China or Rome is a matter of debate, but there was little debate in the 1990s that ice cream and other frozen desserts had regained their position as one of America's favorite treats. Ice cream as we know it—smooth and creamy—was introduced in the United States early in the twentieth century as a result of two technological advances: homogenization, which reduced the fat particle size in milk; and a continuous freezing process that enabled a consistent ice crystal structure. Production and manufacturing advancements that have since been implemented have centered primarily on formulation refinements and stabilizer and process systems.

Ice cream is a frozen, pasteurized mixture of milk, cream, nonfat milk solids, sugars, and stabilizers. Its contents and manufacture are regulated by the government and must meet Standards of Identity. To be called ice cream, a product must contain a minimum of 10 percent butterfat, which is dispersed throughout the mix to impart smooth texture. Fresh sweet cream is the best source of butterfat; unsalted butter, which is about 83 percent fat, can replace 50 to 75 percent of sweet cream fat. Other fat sources that can be used include anhydrous butter oil, concentrated sweet cream, and dried cream. French ice cream, or frozen custard, also contains more than 1.4 percent of egg yolk solid. Consumer concerns about the negative health effects of fat in the diet, however, led to the popularity of lower-fat products such as ice milk, which contained between 2 percent and 7 percent butterfat. "Ice milk" as a product name, however, was headed for extinction with passage of the Nutrition Labeling and Education Act.

Other standard ice cream ingredients include sugars and sweeteners, milk proteins, stabilizers, and emulsifiers. Sweetening agents can be natural (using corn sweeteners, sucrose processed from cane and beet sugars, or fructose) or artificial (using aspartame). The milk proteins used are whey proteins and casein. Milk and milk products themselves have some natural stabilizing and emulsifying properties that often eliminate the need for additional stabilizers and emulsifiers. Stabilizers help to prevent texture deterioration caused by inevitable temperature fluctuations that occur during distribution, which cause ice crystals to melt and then reform into larger crystals. Emulsifiers enhance the whipping qualities of the ice cream mix by creating a smoother texture and body.

Flavorings may be added before or after pasteurization, and may be pure flavor extracts, pure extracts with some synthetic or artificial components, or artificial flavors. As a general rule, premium ice creams use pure extracts and fruits, nuts, candies, and syrups to add flavor. In the 1990s, mix-in flavors like Chocolate Chip Cookie Dough, Carrot Cake Passion, and Cappuccino Commotion were very popular.

The luxury, or super premium, ice creams that were regaining popularity in the 1990s were pioneered by Reuben Mattus in the early 1960s. Using all top-quality, natural ingredients, and no artificial stabilizers or other additives, Mattus created Haagen-Dazs, a highly successful product that set the pattern for rich, clean-tasting ice creams. In the 1980s, such ice cream novelties as ice pops, fudgesicles, and ice cream sandwiches, which had been originally marketed at children, were becoming popular with adults. Haagen-Dazs entered this market with such products as Dove bars and Haagen-Dazs frozen yogurt bars.

Sherbets were defined by the Federal Code of Regulations to contain between 1 and 2 percent butterfat and between 2 and 5 percent total milk-derived solids. Ices contain no milk-derived ingredients or egg ingredients other than egg white; they can be made with nonpasteurized mixes because of their typically high acidity formulation. Mellorine products, although similar to ice cream, contain a combination of vegetable and animal fat in place of butterfat. Federal Standards of Identity require mellorine products to contain at least 6.0 percent fat and no less than 3.5 percent protein.

Frozen yogurts are made using the bacteria cultures *streptococcus thermophilus* and/or *lactobacillus bulgaricus*. Because most refrigerated yogurts were lowfat and had a healthy image with consumers, frozen yogurt was assumed to have the same health benefits as the refrigerated product. The Code of Federal Regulations, however, which required specific starting cultures and acidity levels for refrigerated yogurt, set no such product characteristic requirements for frozen yogurt. The National Yogurt Association (NYA) endorsed a 1991 International Ice Cream Association petition to the government that would standardize manufacturing procedures and require frozen yogurt to be made with specific characterizing yogurt cultures.

Nutrition Labeling and Education Act. By defining terms that had been unclear, the U.S. Food and Drug Administration's (FDA) Nutrition Labeling and Education Act (NLEA), with its May 1994 compliance deadline, enabled many frozen food processors to call their products "lowfat ice cream." The act also separated the link between calories and fat, so that desserts getting more than half their calories from fat could be labeled "light" if their fat content had been reduced 50 percent from their reference product. The "light" label was also permitted on products getting less than half their calories from fat if the products had either a 50 percent fat reduction or a one-third reduction in calories.

A significant change in the new labeling did away with the term "ice milk." Lower-fat ice creams, which previously had to be called "ice milk," are now labeled as "reduced fat," "light," "lowfat," "nonfat," or "fat-free," depending on the product's fat content.

Although the definitions of the terms were clear, the actual fat content percentages were not, because they were tied to the indefinite term, "reference food." Thus, "reduced fat" meant that a product had 25 percent less fat than its "reference food." "Light" referred to a product that had a 50 percent fat reduction from the reference food, and a "lowfat" product was defined as having not more than 3 grams of total fat in a half-cup serving. "Nonfat" and "fat-free" were defined as products having less than 0.5 grams total fat per reference amount. The reference amount was a half-cup for ice cream and frozen yogurt products and 85 grams for flavored ices and juice bars.

To determine the reference food, processors first had to find the marketplace average fat or calorie content by looking at the leading brands in the area where the product was to be sold. For example, a processor would have to compare its "light" Fudge Ripple with leading brands of Fudge Ripple to calculate how much of a reduction in fat or calories would satisfy the "50 percent less" requirement. If, on average, the leading brands contained

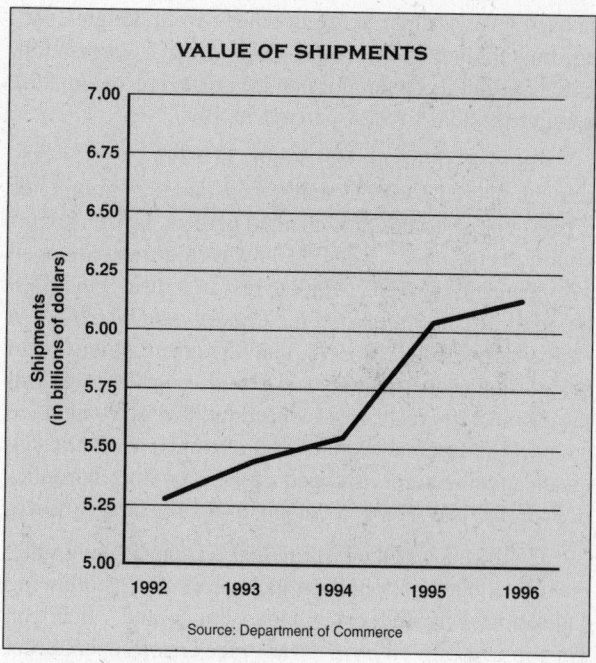

VALUE OF SHIPMENTS

Shipments (in billions of dollars)

Source: Department of Commerce

16 grams of fat, then a product containing 8 grams of fat could be labeled "light."

In 1991, ice cream and frozen dessert sales ranked third behind the fluid milk and cheese sectors of the dairy industry, exceeding $9.0 billion and representing over 15 percent of the dairy industry's overall sales of $62.8 billion. Measured by consumption, frozen desserts led the entire dairy industry segment in 1992. Consumption of frozen yogurt, a lowfat alternative to ice cream, rose by 17 percent, and ice cream's 7 percent gain was attributed largely to reduced-fat products.

With sales of $3.2 billion in 1991, ice cream was making a comeback as America's favorite dessert. Sales of other frozen desserts (ice milk, frozen yogurt nonfat/lowfat products, novelties, sherbets and sorbets, tofu-based products, and mellorine and miscellaneous products) brought the industry total to $9.5 billion for the year. Overall, production increased 4 percent from 1990, with full-fat ice creams still leading the market at 61 percent. Frozen yogurt production, however, increased by 25 percent. In 1992, the number of reduced-fat ice creams, which represented 54 percent of all reduced-fat product introductions in 1990, dropped from 311 to only 94, or 23 percent of the market segment.

CURRENT CONDITIONS

Americans spent more than $11 billion on ice cream and other frozen desserts in the late 1990s, and in 1998 Americans ate about 1.6 billion gallons of ice cream. U.S. citizens were the leading consumers of frozen treats worldwide, eating 20 liters per capita, versus an average of 2.3 liters per individual globally. Not only were Americans consuming the most ice cream, but more American households were partaking in other frozen delights. According to the International Dairy Foods Association, U.S. household consumption of ice cream grew from 86.1 percent in 1996 to 91.8 percent in 1997.

Sales of premium ice creams in 1998 grew 13 percent compared to 1997 sales, and super premium ice creams enjoyed sales growth of 15 percent. Frozen yogurt continued its downward slide, however, as sales dropped 19.3 percent in 1998. Market research firm Find/SVP reported in *The Market for Ice Cream and Other Frozen Desserts,* published in 1998, that 83 percent of ice cream sold through supermarkets and groceries in 1997 was full fat. About 12 percent was reduced fat, lowfat, or light ice cream. The remainder consisted of nonfat varieties. Ice cream manufacturers stepped up new product introductions in the late 1990s, reversing a three-year slowdown.

California was the leading ice cream producing state, making about 172.5 million gallons in 1997. Following California were Indiana, Ohio, Illinois, and Michigan. The top five U.S. cities in terms of ice cream supermarket sales in the late 1990s were Portland, Oregon; Omaha, Nebraska; Seattle, Washington; St. Louis, Missouri; and Buffalo/Rochester, New York. The most popular flavors included vanilla, nut varieties, chocolate, Neapolitan, and candy mix-in varieties, but coffee and caramel flavors showed strong growth in the gourmet ice cream segment.

Australia trailed the United States in worldwide consumption of ice cream and frozen desserts, eating about 18.5 liters per head. Those in Western Europe enjoyed ice cream as well, with Sweden accounting for about 15.8 liters per capita, Italy 9.1 liters, and the Netherlands, Israel, Belgium, and the United Kingdom all consuming between 8 and 9 liters per head. Canada was next, consuming about 9.2 liters per capita. The fastest growing market, however, was Asia, where sales more than doubled in the 1990s, according to Euromonitor.

INDUSTRY LEADERS

The leading ice cream brands in 1998, according to Information Resources, Inc., were as follows: private label brands ($855.2 million in sales); Breyer's ($443.9 million); Dreyer's/Edy's ($374.9 million); Blue Bell ($199.2 million); Haagen-Dazs ($167.9 million), and Ben & Jerry's ($137.8 million). All experienced increases in sales compared to 1997.

Haagen-Dazs Co., whose parent company, Pillsbury Company, was in turn owned by European-based Diageo PLC, set a course in the 1990s that aimed at leaving the competition trailing. The company offered something for everyone in the frozen dessert segment: premium ice creams, frozen yogurt novelties on a stick, 98 percent fat-free frozen yogurts, and a new super premium line of mix-in flavored frozen yogurts and ice creams. One of the leaders of the super premium segment, Haagen-Dazs

announced plans in 1999 to form a joint venture with Nestle USA, the second-largest novelty ice cream company in the United States. The new company, tentatively named Ice Cream Partners USA, hoped to combine the strengths of Haagen-Dazs and Nestle to satiate American palates. James Dintaman, CEO and president of Nestle's ice cream group, said in *Supermarket News* in August 1999: "We conclude that the United States is the strongest ice cream market, and there is no question that this is a highly fragmented industry—nearly $11 billion dollars in retail sales. . . . We will now be a stronger player, and [the joint venture] allows us to capture all of the trends in terms of impulse and indulgence."

Hot on the heels of Haagen-Dazs was Ben & Jerry's Homemade, Inc., a leading manufacturer of super premium ice cream. Ben & Jerry's is known for both its social action programs—the company typically donates about 8 percent of pretax profits to charitable and political programs—and its unusual ice cream flavors. The company had 1998 sales of $209.2 million, up more than 20 percent from 1997. Ben & Jerry's ice cream was sold in Europe, Canada, and Japan in a variety of forms, including frozen yogurt, lowfat ice cream, sorbet, and smoothies. The company started each year with a list of up to 200 potential new flavors, and in 1999 Ben & Jerry's introduced four new premium flavors, including Southern Pecan Pie and Triple Caramel Chunk.

Dreyer's Grand Ice Cream of Oakland, California, with 1998 sales of $1.02 billion, was the leading U.S. ice-cream manufacturer. The company produced and distributed ice cream under its Dreyer's brand in 14 states in the West as well as overseas. Dreyer's also made ice cream under the Edy's brand, which was sold in eastern states and in markets where Dreyer's was not available. In 1998 the company launched its premium line of ice cream, named Dreyer's Homemade Ice Cream. Dreyer's offered a number of frozen dessert items spanning each frozen treat category such as lowfat, sugar-free, and fat-free ice creams, ice cream pies, and frozen novelties. The diversified company had numerous partnerships with other ice cream manufacturers and handled distribution for Ben & Jerry's ice cream, Nestle, and Healthy Choice. In addition, Dreyer's manufactured ice cream for Starbucks, the gourmet coffee company, and Godiva Chocolatier, Inc., the maker of gourmet chocolates and coffees. Godiva ice creams were introduced to supermarkets in 1999 and were labeled ultra-premium. The Godiva offerings included such fat-filled flavors as Belgian Dark Chocolate, Chocolate Raspberry Truffle, Pecan Caramel Truffle, and White Chocolate Raspberry.

Another leader in the ice cream and frozen dessert industry was Good Humor-Breyers Ice Cream Company, a subsidiary of Unilever United States, Inc. Unilever's parent company, Unilever PLC, was the global leader in the ice cream industry and spent the late 1990s acquiring numerous ice cream companies, including firms in Mexico, China, and the Philippines. In the United States, Good Humor-Breyers made and sold a number of brands, including the industry-leading Breyers; Klondike, which made ice cream sandwiches and bars; Minute Maid, which offered sorbets and bars; and Popsicle. In August 1999 Unilever published *Licks, Sticks and Bricks: A World History of Ice Cream,* which offered a detailed look at the development of ice cream. Breyers and Dreyer's together accounted for about 31 percent of the U.S. ice cream market in 1997.

FURTHER READING

"Americans Put Taste at a Premium." *Harrisburg Patriot,* 21 July 1999.

Billings, Alvin. "Sweet Statistical Trends in United States Ice Cream Market." *Quick Frozen Foods International,* 1 July 1999.

Clark, Gerry. "High-fat heaven." *Dairy Foods,* 1 March 1999.

Smyth, William. "Nestle and Haagen Dazs to Join Forces." *Supermarket News,* 30 August 1999.

Wellman, David. "Butterfat City." *Supermarket Business,* January 1999.

"With Unilever and Nestle leading the pack, ice cream intake approaches 13 billion liters." *Quick Frozen Foods International,* April 1998.

SIC 2026

FLUID MILK

This industry encompasses establishments primarily engaged in processing fluid milk, cream, and related products that included cottage cheese, yogurt (except frozen), and other cultured milk products.

NAICS CODE(S)

311511 (Fluid Milk Manufacturing)

INDUSTRY SNAPSHOT

The fluid milk industry is an important subsector of the nation's dairy business. Fluid milk producers are often huge, sophisticated, diversified operations with product lines crossing industry boundaries. They manufacture and market a mix of fluid milk products, cheeses, ice creams, butter, dairy ingredients, and sometimes extensive lines of non-dairy products as well.

The 1990s brought a variety of changes and challenges for the industry. The pace of consolidation quickened. The number of dairy farms and dairy farm cooperatives was shrinking, and the federal government passed the Federal Agricultural Improvement and Reform (FAIR) Act, which started the phasing out of dairy price supports starting in 1996. In addition, although production was increasing, controversy concerning the introduction of scientific methodologies responsible for these increases, such as the use of Bovine Growth Hormone (BST), was considerable.

The biggest issue still facing dairy farmers is stabilizing the price of milk. Congress has before it several proposals, all with severe critics and ardent supporters. The industry also must combat the image that milk has as a high nutrient, but high fat product.

ORGANIZATION AND STRUCTURE

The highly regionalized fluid milk industry started on the dairy farm—where the raw milk was produced—and extended out to processors and manufacturing plants owned by dairy farm cooperatives, general food processors, and even by supermarket chains marketing private label product lines. These processing plants made a variety of milk products destined for retail outlets, food service and institutional markets, and, to a lesser degree, other countries. Milk is an extremely perishable commodity, and supply and demand can fluctuate unpredictably, depending on such variables as the output of individual cows, weather conditions, and even road conditions met by tank trucks.

In the 1990s, changes in the dairy industry transformed the complex relationships between cooperatives and processors. Dairy cooperatives traditionally helped to reduce the impact of such fluctuations on milk handlers by more efficiently coordinating supply arrangements and routing raw milk supplies not needed for fluid milk. Dairy cooperatives assisting the producers in price setting have in many cases taken over all stages of dairy operations, including herd management and milking; management of fluid milk supplies and surpluses; development of competitive new products; fluid milk processing; and the manufacture and marketing of a broad range of dairy products and ingredients.

Government pricing regulations were another means of insuring market stability. The government regulated milk pricing to farmers through Federal Milk Marketing Orders authorized by the Agricultural Marketing Act of 1937 or the Agricultural Act of 1949, which established the ongoing dairy price support program for areas where producers had agreed to abide by it. Supervised regionally by the U.S. Department of Agriculture (USDA), prices were established geographically and according to the milk supply, fat content, weight, and the end use of the milk. From its inception, the support price fluctuated according to market conditions. In addition to the federal pricing structure, almost one-third of milk producing states also regulated milk pricing to farmers.

Milk Processing. Cow milk is the principal source of America's fluid milk supply. It contains about 87 percent water and 13 percent solids, which are composed of solids-not-fat (SNF) and milk fat. Components of SNF are mostly protein (caseins and whey), lactose, and minerals important to human nutrition. An excellent source of calcium, phosphorous, and vitamins A and B-2, and a good source of vitamins A, B-1 and B-12, milk's nutritional components earned it the label of "most perfect food." It is, however, a poor source for iron, copper, manganese, nicotinic acid, and vitamins C and D. Since the 1920s, most milk sold in the United States has been fortified with vitamin D.

Class I fluid milk meets strict standards, which include regular inspections of the herd and herd housing facilities, dairy equipment, and milk storage units to insure that they satisfy health and sanitation requirements. Class I milk is used for human consumption or in manufactured milk products. Milk of manufacturing grade does not meet such strict standards and is priced lower.

In most dairy operations, raw milk is piped from a milking machine to a refrigerated bulk storage tank before it is transferred to a tank truck for delivery to a plant. There it undergoes the following processing operations:

- Separation: The milk is split into cream (fat) and skim milk. The cream is then added back to the milk stream to achieve the desired fat content.
- Pasteurization: The milk is heated to destroy pathogenic bacteria and other undesirable organisms that might lead to spoilage. In continuous high-temperature-short-time pasteurization (HTST), milk is heated to 161 degrees Fahrenheit (72 degrees Celsius) for a minimum of 15 seconds. Since about 1970, ultrahigh temperature pasteurization (UHT), through which milk is heated at temperatures as high as 265 degrees Fahrenheit (130 degrees Celsius) for three seconds, has been used with products such as heavy and light cream and half-and-half. This process has extended shelf life for several months.
- Homogenization: This process breaks up the fat globules in milk, forming a stable emulsion that does not separate. Most fluid milk is homogenized.

Fresh Milk. The following products are included in the fresh milk category: whole milk, lowfat milk, skim or nonfat milk, cream, half-and-half, and buttermilk.

Whole milk contains not less than 3.25 percent milkfat and 8.25 percent SNF. Vitamins A and D may be added at levels of at least 2,000 International Units (IU) per quart for vitamin A and 400 IU for vitamin D. Flavoring ingredients may also be added.

Lowfat milk contains milkfat at levels of 0.5, 1.5, or 2 percent, not less than 8.25 percent SNF, and at least 2,000 IU of vitamin A per quart. If vitamin D is added, it must be present at a level of 400 IU per quart. Flavoring ingredients are also permitted.

Skim or nonfat milk contains less than 0.5 percent milkfat and not less than 8.25 percent SNF. It must contain 2,000 IU of vitamin A per quart. If vitamin D is added, it must be present at a level of 400 IU per quart. Flavoring ingredients are permitted.

Cream is made by separating out most of the skim milk and is rich in milkfat. Light (coffee) cream contains at least 18 percent and no more than 30 percent milk fat. Heavy (whipping) cream contains at least 36 percent milkfat. Half-and-half, a mixture of milk and cream, contains between 10.5 percent and 18 percent milkfat. It was often preferred over coffee cream for its lower fat and calorie content and lower cost.

Buttermilk is a byproduct of churning cream into butter. Similar in composition to skim milk, it is condensed and dried for commercial use in baking and packaged cake mixes; it is not sold for consumption.

Cultured Milk Products. For centuries, people have known how to preserve the nutritional values of fresh milk for weeks or months by using bacterial cultures. Lactic-acid producing bacteria and certain characterizing ingredients may be added to fresh milk products and, depending on the level of milkfat, they may be labeled "cultured buttermilk," "cultured lowfat buttermilk," or "cultured skim milk (or nonfat) buttermilk." Yogurt, sour cream, dry curd cottage cheese, and cottage cheese are included in the cultured milk products category.

Yogurt is made by culturing a mixture of milk and cream with lactic acid-producing bacteria, *Lactobacillus bulgaricus* and *Streptococcus thermophilus,* and contains not less than 3.25 percent milkfat and 8.25 percent SNF. Often sweeteners, flavorings, and other ingredients are added. Lowfat yogurt contains no more than 2 percent milkfat, and nonfat yogurt contains less than 0.5 percent milkfat. Sour cream results from the addition of lactic acid-producing bacteria to pasteurized cream containing not less than 18 percent milkfat.

Dry curd cottage cheese is made by adding either lactic-acid producing bacteria or acidifiers to skim milk and/or reconstituted nonfat dry milk. Rennet and/or other enzymes may also be added to help curd formation. The soft, unripened cheese contains less than 0.5 percent milkfat and no more than 80 percent moisture. Cottage cheese is made by the addition of a creaming mixture to dry curd cottage cheese. It contains at least 4 percent milkfat and no more than 80 percent moisture. Lowfat cottage cheese contains 2 percent or less milkfat and no more than 82.5 percent moisture.

BACKGROUND AND DEVELOPMENT

History. The first cows landed at the Jamestown Colony in North America in 1611, and 13 years later, in 1624, cows were brought to Plymouth Colony. At that time, dairying was a family affair, and it was not until urbanization that dairy farms were established to supply nearby cities. In the industry's infancy, a large number of small, local producers provided the milk for their immediate areas. With the introduction of milk preservation and sanitation methods, it became possible for large dairy processors, often far removed from raw milk sources, to supply ever more distant markets.

A creamery built in Goshen, Connecticut, in 1810, was one of the first formal business units established as a cooperative venture. Cooperative cheese rings and dairy cooperatives in eastern states soon followed, and the movement spread to Wisconsin and other Midwestern states. It did not gain momentum, however, until after the Civil War, when the Grange and other farm organizations sponsored a number of experimental cooperatives. By 1900 there were approximately 1,000 farmer cooperatives. A period of dynamic growth occurred from 1915 to 1930 when cooperatives were placed under statute laws rather than common law. Passage of the Capper-Volstead Act in 1992 established the right of agricultural producers to band together in voluntary associations for mutual benefit in collective processing, handling, and marketing of agricultural products in interstate and foreign commerce.

Some milestones along the way include: Louis Pasteur's experiments using heat to kill microorganisms in milk (1856); Gail Borden's first successful milk condensery in Burrville, Connecticut (1857); development of the milk bottle by Dr. Hervey D. Thatcher of Potsdam, New York (1884); introduction of tuberculin testing for dairy herds and Dr. S. M. Babcock's perfection of a fat content test for milk and cream (1890); introduction of commercial pasteurizing machinery (1895); perfection of the automatic bottle filler and capper (1911); the first use of tank trucks for milk transport (1914); successful sale of homogenized milk in Torrington, Connecticut (1919); introduction of vitamin D-fortified milk (1932); perfection of a vacuum pasteurization process (1946); introduction of ultra-high temperature (UHT) pasteurization (1948); the start of nutrition labeling for fluid milk products (1974); widespread acceptance of UHT milks (1981); increased popularity of low fat and skim milk, with sales surpassing whole milk for the first time (1988); mandatory nutrition labeling under the Nutrition Labeling and Education Act (1991).

In 1991 nearly 10 million dairy cows were on cooperative farms or on the increasingly rare small and independent dairy farms in the United States. They yielded an annual average of 14,867 pounds of milk per cow, for a total of 148,526 million pounds. Breeding efficiency, the ability to improve the herds rapidly using artificial insemination techniques introduced in the 1940s, and the selection of superior sires brought milk production a long way from the mid-1800s, when cows produced an average of only 322 gallons annually.

Also by 1991, fluid milk accounted for 39.3 percent of all dairy industry sales—$24.7 billion out of a total of $62.8 billion for the entire dairy industry. By the mid-1990s, however, per-capita milk sales had experienced a decline of 15 percent since 1975.

Record-breaking floods and drenching rains left tens of thousands of acres in the Mississippi River valley under water in the summer of 1993. Despite damage measured in tens of billions of dollars, it looked as if dairy farmers would be spared the worst of it. Minnesota farmers, for example, were unable to plant vast portions of acreage, but the cows responded to cooler-than-usual temperatures by giving more milk. A Land O'Lakes spokesman expected this to offset higher feed cost and increased risk of udder infections from the sloppy conditions.

Scandal in the Dairy Industry. Computerized bid-analysis techniques uncovered conspiracies in Florida in the mid-1980s, where the court said that illegal bid-rigging had raised the price of milk by as much as 14 percent. The U.S. Department of Justice and some other states began their own investigations, and by mid-1987 signs of illegal bid-rigging extended into Georgia, Alabama, and Mississippi. Said Gina Talomona of the Justice Department in *The American School Board Journal,* these federal and state bid-rigging probes constituted the country's "biggest antitrust case in at least the last 10 years." The dollars involved were considerable. According to the Milk Industry Foundation, from 1981 to 1991 a steady 7 percent of fluid milk sales had been to schools. Fines and settlements had come to more than $100 million by 1993.

Even as investigations and prosecutions proceeded, a report from the General Accounting Office (GAO) criticized the government for its share of responsibility for the schemes. Once bid-rigging had been discovered, said the GAO, the USDA had the authority to halt federal funding to companies found guilty of bid-rigging and to bar their future participation in the federally financed programs. Under federal marketing and price-support programs, moreover, dairies were aware of competitors' minimum prices, creating a situation that provided opportunities for collusion.

The USDA countered that debarment of private companies was inappropriate if the companies paid the penalties imposed and satisfied the federal agency's requirements.

Controversy. Monopolistic practices and political contributions have been the main controversies attached to dairy co-ops. Consumer advocate Ralph Nader accused the three largest dairy co-ops—Associated Milk Producers, Inc. (AMPI); Dairymen, Inc.; and Mid-America Dairymen, Inc. (Mid-Am)—of illegal contributions totaling $422,000 to President Richard Nixon's re-election campaign in order to influence the administration to enact higher price supports (enacted in 1971) and to drop antitrust suits against the three co-ops.

Eventually, AMPI pleaded guilty to having made illegal contributions in 1968, 1970, and 1971. This, however, was not the end of AMPI's legal battles; in 1989 the U.S. Supreme Court upheld an appeals court ruling, filed in 1971 by the National Farmers' Organization (NFO), which determined that AMPI had conspired to eliminate competitive milk producers.

Meanwhile, after decades of backing the industry through price support programs and the purchase of surpluses, the federal government was gradually reducing its role, although no one was predicting the elimination of supports in the near future. As with many issues in the dairy industry, opinions were divided as to whether supports protected the dairy farmers or whether a free market would serve them better.

In the early 1990s, industry analysts forecasted that fluid milk sales were likely to drop between 1 and 1.5 percent annually. In 1992 sales declined in every major milk product except yogurt, which posted a 5.8 percent gain. The figures illustrated the trend reported by the Milk Industry Foundation (MIF), which said that from 1974 to 1991, total fluid milk product sales (plain whole milk, lowfat milk, skim milk, flavored milk and drinks, and buttermilk) had risen a scant 0.05 percent, from 52,476 million pounds to 55,227 pounds. Sales of whole milk had plummeted 43.7 percent in that period, from 36,765 million pounds to 20,680 pounds, while lowfat milk sales had jumped from 9,763 to 25,221 million pounds.

Consumers' health concerns about fat in their diets presented opportunities for the introduction of flavorful low-fat and skim milk products, and dairy companies were working to improve the taste of these products in order to compete with non-dairy beverages like soft drinks, bottled waters, beer, juices, and sports drinks.

Per capita sales from 1974 to 1991 dropped 10.6 percent, from 245.9 pounds to 219.0 for all milk products, and from 172.3 to 82.0 for whole milk. During the same period, lowfat milk sales more than doubled, from 45.8 to 100.0 pounds per capita.

A report by Bozell Worldwide consultants detailed a 23 percent drop in per capita milk consumption reported for the 35 years from 1955 to 1990, and it noted a dramatic drop in milk drinking after age 17; at the time, 64 percent of the U.S. population was 25 or older. Still,

nearly 95 percent of American households purchased milk, usually from supermarkets, where milk posted 1991 sales of nearly $6.8 billion and accounted for 31.06 percent of dairy case sales. It was the most frequently purchased supermarket item for the year ending March 1992, just ahead of bread.

Nevertheless, milk's image as the most perfect and nutritionally complete food was slipping. Studies linked it to diabetes and certain infant allergies. Consumers also expressed concern about the fat in milk, although a 1990 Pennsylvania State University study found that more than half of the survey's respondents didn't know the fat content of whole and skim milks, and 40 percent didn't know the fat content of lowfat milk. Even those who thought they knew milk's fat content tended to overstate it. A National Dairy Board study found that many Americans believed, erroneously, that reducing fat content also depleted milk's nutrients.

Facing slow sales growth and virtually no increase in consumption, fluid milk producers began to take aggressive steps to improve the industry's outlook. A combination of consumer education, advertising and promotion, and consumer-responsive new products was seen as imperative to restoring consumer demand for and confidence in fluid milk and fluid milk products.

In 1993, the Milk Industry Foundation (MIF) took steps to set up a fund for a $55-million national consumer education program, the only strategy on which the fragmented industry was likely to unite. The money was to come from an assessment on Class I fluid milk sales. Said Bill Tinklepaugh, MIF vice president, in *Dairy Field* magazine, "Although the 1990 Farm Bill authorized a national advertising program, here we are in 1992 still trying to build a coalition of support for any program. That's because milk processors have so many divergent points of view." Howard Dean, chairman and chief executive officer of Dean Foods Co. and 1991-92 MIF chairman, said in the same article, "we've never been able to get our act together and coordinate the industry."

As sales of fluid milk flattened out and cottage cheese sales plunged in the 1980s, sales of cultured milk products increased. Yogurt sales soared by 88 percent—from 583 to 1,098 million pounds—from 1980 to 1991, and sour cream and dips jumped 61 percent, from 408 to 657 million pounds. Growing popularity of ethnic foods, especially Mexican, in the late 1980s and early 1990s, spurred growth in the $750-million sour cream and dip market. Combined sales of cultured products reached $4 billion in 1991.

In the last decade of the twentieth century, the industry appeared poised to tackle changes in the fluid milk market in united fashion and form a probable position of financial strength. A major development was the passage of the Federal Agricultural Improvement and Reform Act of 1996 (FAIR), which called for a phased elimination of government supports for dairy products. In 1996, the support price was $10.35 per cwt level. This was expected to move to $9.90 by 1999. Price supports were to be eliminated altogether by 2000.

In 1996, Bovine Growth Hormone (BST) was in its second year, and the industry saw increasing rates of adoption. It was estimated that one-third of dairy cows received BST in 1996. Usage of hormonal injections was expected to increase steadily each year through the end of the decade, leveling off at 50 percent by 2002.

Milk prices were unusually high by mid-decade, due to rising production costs and weather-related feed grain shortages that drove up farmers' costs of feeding dairy cows. With the higher costs, milk production was down 1.16 billion pounds in 1996.

In an effort to counteract these trends by boosting consumption of milk, the industry introduced national advertising campaigns, such as the "milk mustache" series of ads that featured well-known athletes and celebrities. The industry also petitioned the Food & Drug Administration (FDA) to eliminate strict labeling standards for milk and other products. In late 1996, the FDA announced a new policy that would make labeling of dairy products consistent with that of other lowfat and nonfat foods. For example, under the new policy, 2 percent milk was to be renamed "reduced fat," 1 percent relabeled as "lowfat," and skim milk as "fat free" or "nonfat." The new rules were applauded by the International Dairy Foods Association as opening the way for the industry to formulate more lower-fat products.

CURRENT CONDITIONS

In 1999 the Beverage Marketing Corporation (BMC) issued its first report on the overall conditions of the top nine beverages in the United States. The categories included beer, bottled water, fruit beverages, soft drinks, spirits and wine, coffee, tea, and milk. These beverages had an overall volume growth of 2.4 percent from 1997 to 1998. Milk was the only one of the nine with lower volume—.04 percent. However, milk was second in terms of wholesale dollars, with 16.8 percent, and second in per capita consumption, at 23.6 gallons, with soft drinks first in both categories.

With so many new products on the market in the beverage category, competition is fierce. The challenge is making consumers aware that milk has no more calories than a can of regular cola and is far more nutritious. Consumers tend to save milk for breakfast products, such as cereal. The per capita consumption rate is actually lower—closer to 20 gallons—when the milk used on cereal and in cooking is taken into account.

Milk is not something consumers buy or order with restaurant or take out meals. Most people perceive eating out as a treat and tend to order "treat" drinks for themselves and their children, not milk. Consumers are very aware of how much milk they have in their house and how fresh it is. However, if running low on milk at dinnertime, most consumers will switch to something else, saving the milk for breakfast, instead of running to the store to buy more.

Milk production continues to rise. In the first three quarters of 1999, U.S. dairy farms produced 122.3 million pounds—up from 118.5 million pounds in the first three quarters of 1998, a 3.2 percent increase. There were 27.5 million milk cows, about the same as in 1998. The amount of milk per cow in the first three quarters of 1999 was 13,366 pounds, up 3.4 percent from the same time in 1998. The states with the largest production of milk in 1999 were California, Wisconsin, New York, Pennsylvania, and Minnesota. California, Indiana, Arizona, Florida, and Virginia recorded the greatest increases in production.

Government, both federal and local, has a heavy hand in the dairy industry. California enacted legislation in 1962 requiring lowfat milk sold in that state to have added calcium and protein. The regulations, which supporters said were needed to protect children's and older peoples' health, effectively prevented out of state producers from selling milk in the state. In 1999 a California state appeals court ruled the state could not fine out of state milk producers for selling milk in California that meets federal nutritional guidelines.

As part of the Farm Bill of 1996, the Northeast Interstate Dairy Compact (NIDC) was to have been a transitional system of dairy price supports to help dairy farmers in the northeastern United States. The NIDC was to have been phased out by April 1999, but Congress extended it until October of that year while they tried to come to a consensus regarding milk pricing. The dairy compact (and new ones, if passed) provide a floor to milk prices and guarantee regionality of milk supplies. This leaves the heavily milk producing states of the Midwest with a smaller market to sell to. The compacts are limited to continuous states. The USDA countered with a proposal to reduce the number of federal marketing orders from 31 to 11. The orders would still be responsible for setting milk prices.

Critics of the dairy compacts charge that it is a price-fixing scheme and eliminates all pretense of market forces in the industry. Some claim it would favor farms in the compact and encourage overproduction, thereby reducing milk prices for all producers. The International Dairy Foods Association has stated the continuation of the compacts would cost consumers and taxpayers (who foot the bill for Women, Infant, and Children (WIC) programs) from $571 million to $1.64 billion.

The biggest problem to dairy reform is that the legislators themselves often don't understand the complexities of the industry. The U.S. senators from the upper Midwest oppose continuing the NIDC or creating new compacts, claiming that Wisconsin dairy farmers would lose $64 million in sales a year. Even a senator from Massachusetts, a beneficiary of the NIDC, opposes its continuation. The compact has resulted in higher prices to consumers to the tune of $74,000 per dairy farmer, yet on average the farmer in Massachusetts received only $3,000. The charge is that most of the money goes to large farms in Vermont to protect them from competition. The smaller farmer is being bought out by the larger ones; they are going out of business even faster—by 25 percent—than before the so-called protections.

INDUSTRY LEADERS

Dean Foods. With 14 percent of the total market and sales of $2.1 billion in 1998, Dean Foods was the leader of the fluid milk industry since Borden, Inc. sold off their dairy segment. Dairy products accounted for 75 percent of the company's $2.7 billion in 1998 sales. Dean's milk processing plants bought raw milk directly from farmers and processed it into skim milk, half-and-half, whipping cream, yogurt, sour cream, buttermilk, and cottage cheese. Typically, some 75 percent of plant output was marketed to supermarkets and other retail food outlets. The rest was supplied to restaurants, hotels, schools, hospitals, military installations, and fast food chains. Industrial sales accounted for a relatively small portion of Dean's business.

For decades the company's strategy had been growth through acquisition, a policy Dean planned to continue through the 1990s as milk consumption flattened. Typically, Dean sought to purchase larger dairies with sales in the $25-million to $80-million range, often retaining their strong regional brand names. In 1993 the company entered into negotiations to purchase the Flav-O-Rich, Inc. fluid milk and ice cream business. Flav-O-Rich, which operated nine fluid milk plants in the southeastern United States, was the milk-processing subsidiary of Dairymen, Inc., one of the country's largest dairy cooperatives. Dean was also looking to Mexico for growth. With half of the country's population under 18, the prime age group for drinking milk, and a chronic shortage of fresh milk, Mexico was an attractive new market for expansion.

In 1999 Dean Foods continued its buying spree, acquiring Berkeley Farms and the Lucky Stores dairy operations in California. Dean now has farms and processing plants across the country. The strategy is to buy well-established family farms, with good brand recognition and a loyal customer base. Dean Foods also acquired farms in Alabama, Kentucky, and Ohio in 1999.

Cooperatives. By 1998 the Dairy Farmers of America (DFA) was the largest dairy cooperative, with 20 percent of the nation's farmers as members. DFA produces about 32.5 million pounds of milk from 22,000 farmers in 42 states. Four cooperatives had joined DFA to make America's largest cooperative—Milk Marketing, Inc.; Mid-America Dairymen; Associated Milk Producers, Inc.; and Western Dairymen Cooperative.

Suiza Foods. Suiza Foods of Dallas, Texas, was a market leader in fluid milk production and distribution. The company markets under several national and regional brands, including International Delight, Second Nature, Naturally Yours, Lehigh Valley Farms, and Velda Farms. Suiza had sales of $3.4 billion in the first three quarters of 1999, up from $2.3 billion in the same time period of 1998. Suiza is competing heavily against Dean Foods in the race to acquire dairy farms. In 1998 the company bought 13 farms and in 1999 entered into several joint ventures with the DFA cooperative. In the fall of 1999, Suiza announced the acquisition of Southern Foods Group, which it hoped would be completed by the end of the year. The addition of Southern Foods would give Suiza 81 plants with a retail reach of 140,000 stores and a total of 17,500 employees.

WORKFORCE

According to the Bureau of Labor Statistics, farm workers made a median hourly wage of $7.13 in 1997. That year, there were 8,600 farm workers in the United States whose mean annual earnings were $15,780.

Jobs in the dairy industry requiring a college degree included farm and processing plant management, quality control, and research. Training for herd management, milk production, processing, distribution, and sales could be obtained from secondary and vocational schools.

AMERICA AND THE WORLD

NAFTA. The North American Free Trade Agreement (NAFTA) will do away with existing tariffs and other trade barriers among the United States, Canada, and Mexico until 2018, creating the world's largest consumer market with a combined economy of nearly $6.5 trillion. Negotiations for the agreement concluded in 1992, and U.S. Congress passed the legislation late in 1993.

The International Dairy Foods Association predicted that the treaty would be an overall benefit to the U.S. dairy industry, including the fluid milk sector. With or without NAFTA, Mexico was seen as a potential growth area by the dairy industry. Mexico, which had been a major importer of dry milk and cheese products, had also increased its imports of such fresh dairy products as fluid milk and yogurt. The impact of the treaty on dairymen was likely to be less in Canadian trade.

The opportunities NAFTA would create for fluid milk products in Mexico in the 1990s also presented many challenges for U.S. companies. Only about one-half of Mexico's households had refrigerators. Moreover, Mexican consumers often bought food at small neighborhood stores, also with little refrigeration; even some of the better-equipped supermarkets turned off electricity overnight. Quality controls for dairy products in Mexico were also much less stringent than those in the United States. As much as 40 percent of Mexican-produced milk went straight from the cow to the consumer, without being pasteurized.

Europe. The introduction of milk quotas in 1984 to curtail surplus milk production under the European Commission's Common Agriculture Policy (CAP), had apparently backfired by the 1990s. Production efficiency was suffering and competition was down. The industry was becoming polarized, as large producers were growing in size and smaller companies found it increasingly difficult to survive. Restrictive quotas also had an impact on available milk volumes in the domestic market. Processors, if strong enough, could purchase dairies in new markets to assure raw milk supply. Those unable to do this were threatened with takeover. Buying power, too, was becoming concentrated in a small number of powerful and aggressive retailing groups. The large, well-established international dairy suppliers were able to stand up to their demands, but smaller, national producers were at risk.

World Milk Production. There was very little international trade of fluid milk in the early 1990s. According to a National Dairy Board (NDB) market development plan for 1993, there was no change in the average rate of worldwide milk production from 1987 to 1991, but there was a significant drop in production in the former Soviet Union and Eastern Europe after the disintegration of communist rule. Much of the NDB data was drawn from the Foreign Agricultural Service (FAS) Dairy Livestock, Dairy and Poultry Division (DLP), so it does not include data from non-reporting countries.

The world's largest milk producer was the European Community, with an estimated production of 119.9 million tons in 1999. The former Soviet Union, which includes Russia and the Ukraine, was expected to have a decline in milk production for 1999 over 1998, as a census of milk cows in March showed the number of milk cows had declined by 7 percent. Australia and New Zealand combined to produce 21.3 million tons of milk in 1999, Mexico and Japan produced 8.5 million pounds, and Canada produced 8.3 million pounds. Worldwide, production rose about one percent from 1998 to 1999 to 386.5 million pounds. Long-range trends indicated that large, populous developing nations like Mexico, India, and China would increase production capabilities.

RESEARCH AND TECHNOLOGY

Bovine Growth Hormone (BST). There was consternation and divided opinion among dairy farmers and processors in the late 1980s and early 1990s on how, and whether, they would make use of bovine somatotropin (BST), even though it had been found safe for human consumption by the National Institutes of Health. This genetically engineered version of a hormone that occurs naturally in cows increases milk production by as much as 15 percent. Marketed by its producer, Monsanto, under the trade name Posilac, proponents argue that milk from BST-treated cows is indistinguishable from those produced by ordinary cows. Critics, however, note that cows that have been treated with BST (or BGH-bovine growth hormone, as it is also known) are more likely to contract mastitis, an udder infection.

Approved by the FDA, the hormone was the subject of labeling debate as well. If milk products produced from BST-treated cows were required to be labeled as such, it would open the door to similar requirements for other undisclosed substances in foods, such as pesticides and antibiotic residues.

FURTHER READING

"Appeals Court Overturns Calif. Milk Producer Ban." *Nation's Restaurant News,* 6 September 1999.

Blamey, Pamela. "Rising Production Costs Continue to Milk High Dairy Prices." *Supermarket News,* 14 October 1996.

Clark, Gerry. "Border Wars: The Dairy Compact Concept is Poised to Either Realize a New Dawn or Face a Final Sunset." *Dairy Foods,* June 1999.

"Dairy-Admendment Supporters Rally for Compacts." *Supermarket News,* 27 September 1999.

"Dairy Production and Trade Developments." *Foreign Agriculture Service,* July 1999. Available from http://www.fas.usda.gov.

"Dean Foods 1999 Annual Report." *Dean Foods Company,* 23 November 1999. Available from http://www.prnewswire.com.

"Dean Foods Company Profile." *Dean Foods Company,* 23 November 1999. Available from http://www.prnewswire.com.

"Farmworkers, Farm and Ranch Animals." *1997 National Occupational Employment and Wage Estimates,* 24 November 1999. Available from http://stats.bls.gov.

Gill, Kathy E. "Farmers Form Largest Cooperative." *About.com,* 8 January 1998. Available from http://agriculture.about.com.

Juday, Dave. "Sour, Curdled, and Gross." *National Review,* 12 July 1999.

"Milk Production." *National Agricultural Statistics Service,* 14 October 1999. Available from http://www.usda.mannlib.cornell.edu.

"New BMC Report Surveys Drinkscape, Including Where Coffee, Tea, Milk Fit." *Beverage World,* 15 August 1999.

"New Labeling Rules for Dairy Products are Planned by FDA." *Wall Street Journal,* 20 November 1996.

Quail, Jennifer. "Milk Not Flowing With Meals To Go." *Supermarket News,* 11 October 1999.

"Suiza Foods 3rd Quarter Earnings Rise 19.0 Percent." *Suiza Foods,* 4 November 1999. Available from http://www.suizafoods.com/press.

"Suiza Foods Enters Joint Venture with Dairy Farmers of America." *Suiza Foods,* 18 December 1998. Available from http://www.suizafoods.com/press.

Vosburgh, Robert. "California Ruling May Cut Milk Prices in State." *Supermarket News,* 16 August 1999.

SIC 2032

CANNED SPECIALTIES

This category covers establishments primarily engaged in canning specialty products, such as baby foods, nationality specialty foods, and soups, except seafood.

NAICS CODE(S)

311422 (Specialty Canning)
311999 (All Other Miscellaneous Food Manufacturing)

INDUSTRY SNAPSHOT

Canned foods suffered a decline at the beginning of the 1990s as consumers turned to fresh and frozen products in a search of healthier foods. However, thanks to new nutritional labeling and canned products that featured lower salt and lighter syrups, that trend showed signs of reversing in the latter part of the decade. Soup led the category in sales, with condensed soup as the best-selling canned food item on the shelf. Ethnic foods were the fastest growing aspect of the industry.

BACKGROUND AND DEVELOPMENT

Cans have unquestioned advantages as food containers. Hermetically sealed, they protect their contents from contamination as well as prevent undesirable fluctuations in moisture content; the absorption of oxygen, gases, and undesirable odors; and exposure to light. In addition, they allow for high-speed filling, sealing, and casing, and retailers can display them easily and attractively.

Compared to other methods of food preservation, canning is a recent development. Freezing goes back to the ice ages, and even smoking and drying were used before recorded history. Canning did not come along until the first quarter of the nineteenth century.

Nicholas Appert, a French confectioner and chef, theorized in 1795 that if food is heated in a container with no air in it, the food will keep. He worked on his theorem for 14 years, cooking foods in cork-stopped bottles in boiling water. Sent around the world on sailing ships, Appert's preserved fruits and vegetables remained wholesome. Eventually an English merchant, Peter Durand, would develop the use of tin canisters in 1810.

The first U.S. patent for tin containers was granted in 1825. At first, cans were made by hand; even an expert in the process could turn out only five or six an hour. The term canning came to mean sterilizing food by heat and sealing it in airtight containers, either metal or glass, at an individual's home or in a processing plant.

The Civil War accelerated the need for canned foods and, by the war's end, production of canned foods had increased six times—and Americans had learned to trust them. The importance of canned foods to the military was underscored again during World War II, when two-thirds of the food supplies for the U.S. and Allied forces came in cans. When the Japanese capture of Malaya cut off important sources of tin, conservation of the metal in the United States became critical. At the same time, glass containers, which had always been used for some foods, were used to replace tin cans.

Technological advances in the canning industry accelerated after the Civil War. The invention of the retort, or pressure cooker, in 1874 made it possible to control cooking temperatures for the sealed cans. The invention of the so-called sanitary can in 1900 was a cylindrical can that had an open top, enabling canners to deposit larger food pieces without the damage that occurred when filling the old hole-and-cap can. The lid for the new can could be attached mechanically, without the solder seal coming into contact with the food.

Near the end of the twentieth century, when consumers were concerned about lead in food, tin replaced lead in soldering. Other packaging developments included the flexible pouch for low-acid foods and cans made of aluminum and of steel.

Canned Soups. Sales of canned soup totaled $2.6 billion in 1995, with condensed versions accounting for more than $1.8 billion. Sales of single-serving cans were just over $800 million. The canned soup market was huge, with sales coming from commercial outlets, such as restaurants, cafeterias, fast-food chains, and non-commercial institutions, such as schools, hospitals, and the military.

"Healthy" was the hot word in canned soups in the 1990s. Campbell Soup Company, long the industry leader, started the decade by launching 11 new soups under its Healthy Request label.

ConAgra, Inc. entered the arena with its Healthy Choice line of soups. Even with no experience in soups,

ConAgra, the second-largest food company in the country, was optimistic about its low-sodium, low-fat, low-cholesterol product.

Pet, Inc., maker of Progresso soups, lowered salt in its Sodium Watch Soups, while Pritikin Systems, a division of Quaker Oats, put out a line of Healthy Soups. Pet's Progresso brand continued to capitalize on eating trends in the 1990s with six new ready-to-serve canned soups, containing pasta combined with a flavorful broth and plenty of vegetables.

In the latter part of the 1990s, Campbell's introduced ready-to-serve soup in glass jars and embarked on a $15-million advertising campaign to promote the new line. Soups with an emphasis on fresh appearance and flavor, as well as healthier formulations (low-sodium, low-fat, no-MSG) were put on the market; they were more appealing than ever. Vegetable broths also increased in popularity as a result of consumers' focus on healthy eating.

Baby Foods. By 1995 baby food sales in the United States reached $1 billion. The major manufacturers spent much of the 1990s cutting prices to win back customers who had switched over to value-price store brands. Additional customers were lost when the Center for Science in the Public Interest admonished several top brands for having excessive water and fillers in their baby foods.

In response to the criticism, Gerber Products Company, the leader in the category, introduced new versions of its core foods without added starch or sugar. The company also produced a line of Tropical Baby Foods targeting the Hispanic market. Beech-Nut, a division of St. Louis, Missouri-based Ralston-Purina, introduced its chemical and pesticide-free Special Harvest line of fruits, vegetables, cereals, dinners, and juices from organic sources in 1991, but poor sales caused the company to abandon the line two years later.

Several independent companies marketing organic baby foods appeared in the 1990s—notably Earth's Best and Growing Healthy, Inc. In spite of the popularity of so-called health foods among the general public, the market for infant health foods was slow to catch on. One reason was fierce brand loyalty among consumers for Gerber and Heinz. That outlook could change, however. In March 1996, H.J. Heinz Company acquired Earth's Best, and Gerber introduced four new vegetarian products with pasta and increased protein.

Ethnic Foods. The market for ethnic foods grew an average of 9.4 percent annually in the 1990s. As discounted and private label products, as well as new products geared toward niche markets, crowded supermarket shelves in the 1990s, many famous old brands began to disappear. La Choy and Chun King were typical of threatened brands, with competition coming from the increasing availability of fresh Chinese food.

Mexican specialties and southern soul food were the top sellers in the 1990s. Their growth spurred the growth of minority-owned businesses such as Goya Foods, Glory Foods, and Garcia Canning Co.

Canned pasta faced tough competition from the dried and fresh pasta industries. The Chef Boyardee brand of canned spaghetti was the industry leader with a 59 percent share of the market by mid-decade. Acquired by International Home Foods in 1996 from long-time parent American Home Food Products, Chef Boyardee launched its ABCs and 123s pasta shapes with an aggressive media campaign. Campbell Soup's Franco-American brand was second with a 36 percent share. In the late 1990s, Franco-American promoted its Superiore variety in an effort to attract more adult consumers.

CURRENT CONDITIONS

In 1997 the industry's 140 establishments employed more than 19,000 people. The 1997 value of shipments reached $8.1 billion. Canned soups and stews had a shipment value of nearly $4.1 billion; canned baby foods' value was $1.4 billion. Canned ethnic foods had shipments valued at $769.0 million.

INDUSTRY LEADERS

Campbell Soup Company. The undisputed leader of the industry in the 1990s and indeed throughout its long history, Campbell Soup Company was selling 5 billion cans of soup a year, or close to half of all soup sales in the market. Founded in 1869 by Joseph Campbell, a fruit merchant, and Abram Anderson, an ice box manufacturer, the company reported sales of $6.4 billion for 1999 (nearly 66 percent from soup sales).

Perhaps no event in the Campbell Soup Company's long history was more momentous than the arrival in 1897 of a 24 year-old chemist, Dr. John T. Dorrance, who signed on at a salary of $7.50. When he died 33 years later, he was sole owner of the Campbell Soup Company and amassed a personal fortune of $115 million, an amount equal to $850 million in the 1990s. Dorrance's descendants own about 50 percent of the company.

Young Dorrance was a man with an idea: condensed soup. When he joined Campbell Soup Company, soup was sold in 32-ounce cans for about 30 cents. Since soup was made mostly of water, Dorrance reasoned, the removal of water would save on shipping, cans, and weight. Dorrance introduced condensed soups in ten and a half ounce cans selling for 10 cents. To win over consumers who tended not to trust the quality of such a low-cost product, he spent heavily on advertising and promotion. In 1990 Campbell produced its 20-billionth can of condensed tomato soup.

Campbell Soup Company's marketing high points include the 1904 introduction of the enduring image of the Campbell kids, created by Philadelphia artist Grace Gebbie Drayton. In the 1930s, the slogan ''M'm! M'm! Good!'' entered the nation's consciousness when Campbell sponsored the ''Amos 'n' Andy'' and the George Burns and Gracie Allen radio shows.

One more momentous event may be on the horizon. In March 2000 the company's president departed, which raised the odds for a merger. Wall Street analysts even saw a hostile takeover in the company's future.

Gerber Products Company. A symbol of quality and trust, the Gerber baby was adopted as an official trademark in 1931, three years after Fremont Canning Company of Fremont, Michigan, began pureeing foods for babies. Commercial artist Dorothy Hope Smith created the unfinished charcoal sketch of a neighbor's child, who was the first Gerber baby. Gerber has a selection of more than 190 foods.

FURTHER READING

''Baby Foods.'' *Supermarket Business,* September 1996.

Pawlosky, Mark. ''Health Food for Babies is Slow to Grow.'' *Wall Street Journal,* 14 June 1995.

Pollack, Judann. ''Franco-American Ads Go Comparative.'' *Advertising Age,* 21 October 1996.

U.S. Census Bureau. ''Manufacturing-Industry Series.'' *1997 Economic Census.* Washington, D.C.: GPO, 24 January 2000.

SIC 2033

CANNED FRUITS, VEGETABLES, PRESERVES, JAMS, AND JELLIES

This industry includes establishments primarily engaged in canning fruits, vegetables, and fruit and vegetable juices; and in manufacturing ketchup and similar tomato sauces, or natural and imitation preserves, jams, and jellies. Establishments primarily engaged in canning seafood are classified in **SIC 2091: Canned and Cured Fish and Seafoods;** and those manufacturing canned specialties, such as baby foods and soups, except seafood, are classified in **SIC 2032: Canned Specialties.**

NAICS CODE(S)

311421 (Fruit and Vegetable Canning)

INDUSTRY SNAPSHOT

The canned foods industry generated more than $14.5 billion in sales in the late 1990s. Canned food processors were the primary market for many of the nation's farmers. By contracting and paying in advance for a large part of the harvest, the industry guaranteed farmers and growers a cash income, helping to absorb the risks of marketing produce on the fresh market.

According to the U.S. Department of Agriculture, tomatoes, sweet corn, snap beans, and green peas were the four most-processed vegetables in the industry. Domestic demand for processed tomato products grew throughout the 1990s, while consumption of canned green peas declined. Production costs of canned goods consisted of payments to farmers, container and label costs, labor, and fuel for transportation. Insurance, rental payments, and machinery costs also contributed to production costs.

BACKGROUND AND DEVELOPMENT

Napoleon has been credited with saying, ''An army marches on its stomach.'' Whether he did or not, he knew the importance of supplying his troops with adequate, wholesome food during a successful military campaign. When the governing French Directorate offered a prize in 1795 to the citizen who found a way to keep food fresh during campaigns, Napoleon supported the project. Fourteen years later, in 1810, Emperor Napoleon would award the prize to Nicholas Appert, an obscure French confectioner and chef, whose accomplishment secured his place in history.

Appert theorized that when food is heated in a container with no air in it, the food would keep. He cooked foods in cork-stoppered bottles in boiling water, perfecting his methods. Proof of his success came when Appert's preserved fruits and vegetables were sent around the world on sailing ships and remained edible. Two months after Appert published his procedures, an English merchant, Peter Durand, applied to King George III for a patent for a ''Method of Preserving Animal Food, Vegetable Food, or Other Perishable Articles a Long Time from Perishing or Becoming Useless.'' Durand's use of tin canisters in his process revolutionized food packaging and launched the canning industry as we know it. Captain Edward Perry took tinned foods on his Arctic expeditions in the first quarter of the nineteenth century. Tinned pea soup and beef left behind by his party were recovered and eaten in 1911, and tins of veal and carrots from Perry's 1824 expedition were found to have been safely preserved when they were opened more than 100 years later, in 1939.

Around 1822, tinned foods came to the United States, and the first American patent for tin containers was granted three years later. By the mid-1800s, vegetable processing in steel canisters coated with tin to protect against rust and erosion was becoming widespread, and the words ''tin can'' and ''canning'' entered the language. Canning came to mean sterilizing food by heat and sealing it in airtight containers, either metal or glass.

Canning activities were undertaken both in food processing plants and in households across the country.

In 1861, canners began adding calcium chloride to the water in which they cooked their closed cans. This enabled canners to use higher temperatures; production time was thus shortened, and production volume increased. The improved technology came just in time for the Civil War, which spurred a demand for canned products. By the time the war was over, production of canned foods had grown six times over, and Americans had learned to trust the quality of the products contained therein.

The importance of canned foods to the military was emphasized during World War II, when two-thirds of the food supplies for the United States and allied forces came in cans. When the Japanese capture of Malaya cut off important sources of tin, conservation of the metal on the home front became critical. At the same time, glass containers, which had previously been used for some foods, were often used in place of tin cans.

The advent of a wide variety of food package choices in the 1980s led to a decline in the sales of canned food in metal cans. Microwave-safe plastic containers, high-barrier film pouches, and form-fill and seal cups were some of the choices offered to consumers. Furthermore, some advertisers claimed superior freshness for foods packed in glass jars. In 1986 the Can Manufacturers Institute, the National Food Processors Association, and the American Steel Institute formed the Canned Food Information Council (CFIC) to restore canned foods' former level of acceptance and popularity, while disseminating positive information about the nutritional quality and appetizing nature of foods in metal cans.

Regulations. The U.S. Department of Agriculture (USDA) grades canned vegetables on a point system, rating them on such characteristics as texture, size, variety, maturity, taste, odor, and absence of defects. Three more standards were applied to canned foods by the Food and Drug Administration (FDA): Standard of Quality referred to the permitted number of defects or foreign materials; Standard of Fill specified the minimum content for a particular size can or jar; and Standard of Identity regulated what was in the container.

Nutritional Quality of Canned Foods. Because canned foods are heat sterilized in a sealed steel can, there is no need at all for preservatives. As consumer tastes changed, the levels of salt and sugar, which were commonly added for flavor, were reduced to satisfy consumer demand for low-salt and low-sugar products. As for their nutrition, the CFIC reported a National Food Processors Association study conducted for the USDA. Because canned foods are already cooked, home-cooked fresh lima beans, peas, spinach, sweet potatoes, carrots, and

squash were compared with frozen vegetables that were boiled or microwaved. Vitamin, mineral, and fiber content were found to be similar and, in some cases, the canned product exceeded even its fresh counterpart in vitamin content. Studies comparing canned fruits to those fresh and frozen yielded similar results. Canning actually protects foods from oxygen that can destroy vitamins A, B, C, D, and carotene. The process can also eliminate up to 99 percent of pesticide residues and destroy the bacteria that leads to spoilage.

Vegetables and Fruits. Most produce destined for canning goes directly from the growing fields to a nearby processing plant. Production methods allow vegetables to be canned within hours of harvest. It is in the plant that vegetables and fruit are chopped, sliced, peeled, or otherwise prepared for packing in cans. Blanching helps to preserve texture and flavor. Once they are in vacuum-packed cans and sealed, they are sent into the retort, or cooker, to be heat-processed. Cooling is the final step before the cans are labeled and prepared for distribution.

Canned vegetables and fruits lost shelf space in grocery stores in the late 1990s, while fresh produce gained popularity. Production of tomatoes, sweet corn, snap beans, and green peas declined 2 percent in 1998, but the tomato industry fared well a year later, harvesting a record crop. The tomato was the second most popular vegetable in the United States and had grown in consumption—the annual use of tomatoes per head in the United States grew almost 30 percent from the late 1970s to the late 1990s. Of the total consumed, about 81 percent was in the form of processed tomato goods, such as sauces, ketchup, salsa, juice, and pastes.

Though canned corn was long the top seller among canned vegetables, U.S. demand declined in the late 1990s, keeping prices of canned sweet corn low. In 1999, acreage of corn destined for canning markets declined 6 percent over 1998 figures. Canned green peas suffered more severely in terms of consumption, and per capita use of green peas in both canned and frozen form dropped 5 percent in the late 1990s as compared to the same period a decade earlier. According to the U.S. Department of Agriculture, consumption of canned green peas in the late 1990s was less than half of what it had been in the early 1970s.

Juices. Traditionally, children have been the nation's juice drinkers. The 1990s, however, brought a decline in adult consumption of alcoholic beverages and a rise in adult juice consumption. Makers of bottled waters, soft drinks, and juices entered into spirited competition for these adult consumers. All-natural juices and cranberry juices enjoyed increased demand in the late 1990s, and manufacturers continued to introduce new products. According to market research firm Information Resources, Inc., sales of 100 percent juice in food, drug, and mass merchant stores increased 9 percent in 1998, while overall sales of bottled juice products rose 3 percent. Cranberry juice sales were indicative of the trend toward all-natural juices: Information Resources reported that sales of 100 percent cranberry juices for the year ended July 1999 had grown 72 percent over sales from the previous year. Sales of the standard cranberry-cocktail drinks, on the other hand, declined around 1 percent.

Some juice manufacturers came under fire in the late 1980s and early 1990s for misleading product labeling, and concerns regarding safe production of juices persisted throughout the decade. A $2 million fine was levied by the federal government in 1987 on Beech-Nut Nutrition Corporation for selling a mix of sweetened water and chemicals as "apple juice." Investigators estimated that as much as 10 percent of juice sold, most of it orange juice, was adulterated, usually with sugar or watery orange byproducts. Manufacturers cited in cases from 1987-1993 were mostly major wholesalers to important producers and grocery chains, not companies familiar to the public.

Jams, Jellies, and Preserves. This category is comprised of several distinct products. Jellies, a mixture of fruit juice, sugar, and pectin, are clear and bright with a tender but firm texture. Jams and preserves are thicker, made by cooking fruit, pectin, and sugar until the texture is almost a puree. In preserves, the fruit chunks are larger. Conserves, similar to jam, mix more than one kind of fruit and perhaps nuts. Marmalade contains citrus fruit rind, most often Seville oranges. Fruit butter is made by stewing fruit, sugar, and spices to a thick, smooth, spreadable consistency. Under federal guidelines, in order for a product to be called a jam or jelly it had to contain 55 percent sugar and be so labeled. Reduced-sugar products that catered to a health-conscious consumer were sweetened with fruit juice and had to be called something other than "jam" or "jelly."

Despite a more weight-conscious population, the jam and jellies category experienced flat growth during the early 1990s. Throughout the 1990s, the category battled innovative breakfast foods that competed with the traditional jam and toast breakfast. The introduction of specialty products in the late 1990s, however, helped to somewhat reinvigorate the slow-growing segment. While the $671.9 million jellies and jams industry declined by 2 percent in terms of sales in 1998, it rose 2 percent in terms of units sold, reported Information Resources. The category experienced the strongest sales in the fall, back-to-school season. New products such as peanut butter and jam mixed together in a jar, jams in squeeze bottles, and packages of peanut butter, jelly, and crackers, were among the new items targeted toward jam consumers.

Spaghetti Sauces. Americans spent more than $2 billion on pasta products in the mid- to late 1990s, and sales of spaghetti sauces kept pace at $2 billion as well. Leaders in the field were Van den Bergh Food Co.'s Ragu, Campbell Soup Co.'s Prego, and ConAgra's Hunt's label. These ranged from traditional, meat- and mushroom-flavored sauces to a no-fat, no-cholesterol line of "light" sauces. In the latter part of the 1990s, Van Den Bergh and Campbell's were embroiled in a three-year legal battle over Campbell's advertisement that claimed its Prego sauce was thicker than Van Den Bergh's Prego Old World Style. In the fall of 1996, a judge ruled in Campbell's favor. At the decade's end, Van Den Bergh, now merged with the Thomas J. Lipton Company to become the Lipton Company (a wholly owned subsidiary of Unilever), planned new packaging, new flavors, and a new aggressive advertising campaign. Also in the late 1990s, companies introduced a host of gourmet pasta sauces, such as alfredo and pesto, to meet demand for Italian cuisine, which was growing increasingly popular.

Salsa. Salsa includes an array of sauces that includes picante, enchilada, taco, and other chili-based sauces. Salsa grew in consumption during the late 1980s and early 1990s, and in 1991 salsa outsold ketchup in retail stores by $40 million. By 1999, however, ketchup was back on top. Nonetheless, the popularity of Mexican-style foods was undeniable, growing stronger through the 1990s. Large manufacturers such as Hormel, Nabisco, Frito-Lay, and PET Inc. all introduced Mexican-style products, and national Mexican food restaurant chains such as Taco Bell and El Torito introduced packaged versions of their products for the retail industry.

CURRENT CONDITIONS

Cost-conscious consumers and strong competition took a toll in the food industry overall in the 1990s. The canning industry faced continued competition from the fresh and frozen food industries. Some canners focused on the so-called value-added segment, such as asparagus, specialty corn, glass jar mushrooms, and tomatoes, to boost sales. Recognizing and serving regional preferences, along with the sale of larger-sized packaging, were two other marketing tactics used by the canning industry.

By the late 1990s, innovation was the trend among canned goods manufacturers. Because the shelf space dedicated to canned goods in supermarkets was shrinking, companies attempted to create demand by offering innovative products, such as convenience items— products that demanded little preparation on the part of the consumer. Private-label brands increased in popularity as well, and, at the turn of the century, private-label canned vegetables enjoyed a U.S. market share of about 44 percent, while private-label canned fruits had a share of about 40 percent.

Legislation. In the first half of the 1990s, the Nutritional Labeling Education Act (NLEA) mandated sweeping changes in labeling, with the emphasis more on the relationship between nutrition and chronic disease than on vitamin/mineral content. Intended to reduce consumer confusion and end the chaos of individual manufacturers' label definitions, the act called for standardized serving sizes (reference amounts) and established rules for health claims and relating them to U.S. Recommended Daily Intakes (RDIs) and U.S. Recommended Daily Allowances (RDAs) for vitamin/mineral percentages. Because this legislation called for dramatic changes in the packaging for canned foods, some manufacturers complained that meeting the requirements of the NLEA legislation would substantially increase their production costs.

INDUSTRY LEADERS

A number of large canners of fruits and vegetables fought for market share in the late 1990s. Among the leaders were H.J. Heinz Company, Del Monte Foods Company, Campbell Soup Company, and Ocean Spray Cranberries, Inc. Heinz, with 1999 sales of $9.3 billion, had a diverse product line of more than 5,700 items. The top manufacturer of private-label soup, Heinz was also the leader of the ketchup segment. The company struggled in the late 1990s, however, and Heinz suffered from flat sales and declining market share in the ketchup arena. In 1998, Heinz ketchup's market share dropped to a low of 44 percent. Ketchup, which accounted for 11 percent of total company revenues, was Heinz's crown jewel. To ignite sales, Heinz launched an aggressive marketing campaign and introduced new products and new packaging. By late 1999, Heinz's share of the ketchup market had increased to more than 50 percent.

Del Monte was the largest producer and distributor of canned fruit and vegetables in the United States, but the company suffered from financial problems during the 1990s. In the late 1990s, however, the company sought to revitalize sales and its image, and the company embarked on a strategy of growth through acquisitions, new product launches, and hard-hitting marketing and advertising. In addition, Del Monte went public in 1999. In 1997 Del Monte's share of the canned fruit segment was an impressive 42 percent. Its share of the canned vegetable industry was about 20 percent. The company then acquired Contadina from Nestle in 1997, greatly adding to its offerings in the canned tomato and pasta sauce categories. Del Monte reported 1999 sales of $1.5 billion, up nearly 15 percent from 1998. Its net income increased 180 percent.

Campbell Soup was the leader of the domestic soup market, holding a share of 75 percent. The company was also the maker of Prego spaghetti sauces and Pace salsa products. Despite its command of the soup segment, Campbell's suffered from sluggish sales in the late 1990s. To stimulate sales, the company attempted to diversify its product line, introducing such new soup items as ready-to-serve soups in resealable plastic containers and soups in individual-sized microwave cans. Despite this aggressive marketing, Campbell's sales for fiscal 1999 reached $6.4 billion, a drop of 4 percent from 1998 sales.

Massachusetts-based Ocean Spray Cranberries remained the leading producer of canned and bottled juices in North America. A cooperative of 900 cranberry and citrus growers in the United States and Canada, Ocean Spray posted sales of about $1.5 billion in fiscal 1998. Due to the increased popularity of cranberry drinks, Ocean Spray enjoyed strong sales and commanded about 75 percent of the cranberry market. The company introduced a number of new beverages in the late 1990s, including blended drinks that combined cranberry with such fruits as tangerines and apples. Perhaps the company's greatest innovation in the late 1990s was its introduction of 100 percent juice drinks, which Ocean Spray launched in 1998 under the name Wellfleet Farms. The company began selling the juice under its own Ocean Spray name in 1999, and sales grew. Despite the success of Ocean Spray's 100 percent juice drinks, the market leader was Northland Farms Inc., which had a share of 34.5 percent in 1999. Northland was recognized as being the company responsible for reinvigorating the then-sluggish 100 percent juice category.

AMERICA AND THE WORLD

The United States exported $25 billion worth of processed food in the mid-1990s. Canned fruits and vegetables were among the top five industries in foreign trade. Heinz, for instance, received about half of its total sales from overseas operations in the late 1990s. In the burgeoning processed tomato segment, exports enjoyed growing sales. Exports of sauces rose 2 percent in 1999, ketchup was up 4 percent, and whole peeled tomato goods increased 14 percent. Tomato juice exports also rose slightly, but exports of tomato paste declined. Canada was the largest market for U.S. tomato product exports. Japan and Mexico also imported U.S. tomato products; exports to Mexico, in fact, rose 24 percent in 1999. Canned sweet corn was also a major U.S. export, but in 1999 export volume declined 1 percent compared to 1998 figures. Exports to Japan, Taiwan, and Germany declined, but exports to the Netherlands, Norway, and South Korea increased.

RESEARCH AND TECHNOLOGY

The 1990s saw the installation of new retort systems at a number of plants. Some automated systems were flexible enough to process food in glass jars, flexible pouches, plastic tubs, or irregular shapes. In batch retorting, a single operator can handle a system that automatically stacks cans in trays, conveys them into the retort, removes them after sterilization and cooling, and carries them back to a destacker.

Packaging Advances. The 1990s also saw the development of new, upscale cans to rival glass containers in style and sophistication. Not unlike the innovative changes in plastic packaging that had marked the 1980s, the new cans were designed to enhance the containers' appeal and convenience to consumers. Campbell, for example, launched Cianto pasta sauce in the United Kingdom in a Quantum can. Produced by the Foodcan Group of CarnaudMetalbox (CMB), the distinctive, vertically fluted can with labeling graphics lithographed directly onto the metal won a 1992 Worldstar Award from the World Packaging Organization. CMB has also licensed the technology for its Ferrolite can to North American can makers. The Ferruled can, a plastic-laminated, microwaveable, recyclable, fully retortable steel can, was another Worldstar winner for CMB.

FURTHER READING

"52nd Annual Consumer Expenditures Study." *Supermarket News,* September 1999.

"Annual Report on American Industry" *Forbes,* 13 January 1997.

Barron, Kelly. "Breathing New Life into a Tired Old Brand." *Forbes,* 30 November 1998.

Buss, Dale. "Cranberry Juice is Sweet." *Supermarket News,* 15 November 1999.

"Canned Goods." *Supermarket Business,* September 1996.

"Del Monte Cooking up Pasta Sauce." *Advertising Age,* March 1996.

"Del Monte to Be Purchased by Texas Pacific Group." *The New York Times,* 1 March 1997.

Howell, Debbie. "All-Natural Juice Products Squeeze Into the Lead." *Discount Store News,* 22 March 1999.

Murray, Barbara. "Jammin' With Jellies." *Supermarket News,* 30 August 1999.

"New Labels for Ketchup's Real Fans." *The New York Times,* 12 June 1996.

Pollack, Judann. "Prego Prevails in Battle Over Comparative Ad." *Advertising Age,* 16 September 1996.

"Unilever's New Lipton Recasts, Repackages Ragu." *Brandweek,* 13 January 1997.

SIC 2034

DRIED AND DEHYDRATED FRUITS, VEGETABLES, AND SOUP MIXES

This category covers establishments primarily engaged in sun drying or artificially dehydrating fruits and vegetables, or in manufacturing packaged soup mixes from dehydrated ingredients. Establishments primarily engaged in the grading and marketing of farm dried fruits, such as prunes and raisins, are classified in **SIC 5149: Groceries and Related Products, Not Elsewhere Classified.**

NAICS CODE(S)

311423 (Dried and Dehydrated Food Manufacturing)
311211 (Flour Milling)

Dried and dehydrated fruits, vegetables, and soups generated a shipment value of $3.04 billion in 1997, according to the U.S. Census Bureau. Dried and dehydrated fruits and vegetables made up nearly $2.11 billion of this total, while soup mixes accounted for nearly $842 million. The most popular dried products in 1997 were potatoes and raisins.

Sun drying, one of the oldest known methods of fruit preservation, originated thousands of years ago. Dehydration preserved foods by removing the moisture that microorganisms needed to thrive. Although the technique remained in use in the 1990s, mechanical drying methods increased beginning in the late nineteenth century. Besides preservation, reduction in bulk and weight were considerations in the drying of fruits and vegetables.

As consumer interest in healthy eating continued to rise during the 1990s, processors of dates, raisins, dried apricots, apples, cherries, and other fruits promoted their products as nutritious snacks, as well as ingredients for home baking and cooking. Processors used dried fruits in a wide variety of food products. Dates—popular with retail shoppers—lent texture, flavor, and sweetness to processed cereals, baked goods, snack bars, and frozen desserts. Along with dates, raisins enjoyed a variety of uses in food processing. Products introduced in the 1990s included donuts with raisins, fat-free raisin cookies and fruit bars, and even raisin salami. Dried cranberries were also gaining popularity among American consumers.

The industry also witnessed the introduction of sophisticated processing technology, such as quality-monitoring computer programs and lasers. New dehydration processes, such as a three-stage vegetable dehydrator employed by Breedlove Dehydration Foods of Lubbock, Texas, were used to save surplus food for later distribution to a national network of food banks to feed the homeless.

Some 154 establishments (most in California or Idaho) employing 14,263 people made up this industry in the late 1990s. Two strong performers were Dole Food Company Inc. and Blue Diamond Growers, both of California. Dole's 1999 sales were nearly $5.1 billion, while Blue Diamond's 1999 sales were $404 million. Of course,

Dole is more diversified than Blue Diamond, and neither of these figures solely represent this industry's sales.

FURTHER READING

U.S. Census Bureau. "Manufacturing-Industry Series." *1997 Economic Census.* Washington, D.C.: GPO, 22 October 1999.

SIC 2035

PICKLED FRUITS AND VEGETABLES, VEGETABLE SAUCES AND SEASONINGS, AND SALAD DRESSINGS

This category covers establishments primarily engaged in pickling and brining fruits and vegetables and in manufacturing salad dressings, vegetable relishes, sauces, and seasonings. Establishments primarily engaged in manufacturing catsup and similar tomato sauces are classified in **SIC 2033: Canned Fruits, Vegetables, Preserves, Jams, and Jellies,** and those packing purchased pickles and olives are classified in wholesale or retail trade. Establishments primarily engaged in manufacturing dry salad dressing and dry sauce mixes are classified in **SIC 2099: Food Preparations, Not Elsewhere Classified.**

NAICS CODE(S)

311421 (Fruit and Vegetable Canning)

311941 (Mayonnaise, Dressing, and Other Prepared Sauce Manufacturing)

Diversified multibillion dollar companies such as H.J. Heinz Company, Kraft General Foods, Inc., and Best Foods Division of CPC International, Inc. were the major producers of pickles, sauces and seasonings, and salad dressings in the 1990s. However, small, regional independents often accounted for many familiar products.

The industry reflected the trends that were influencing other food processors—consumers were concerned with healthier eating and developed the taste for exotic flavors and ethnic cuisine. Retail sales of sauces and dressings well exceeded $3 billion in 1997. Pourable salad dressings outstripped all other products in the category with sales of more than $1.3 billion, closely followed by mayonnaise and other sandwich spreads, and gravy and sauce mixes. Pickles accounted for $1 billion of the $1.5 billion relish market at mid-decade. According to the Calorie Control Council, low-fat salad dressings, sauces, and mayonnaise were one of the top choices of adults who reported using so-called lite products. The proliferation of pre-made salad kits were also seen as a

reason for the boost in salad dressing sales. This industry had a shipment value of $1.47 billion in 1997.

In 1950, the Food and Drug Administration (FDA) established standards of identity, which regulated the ingredients and manufacturing of mayonnaise, salad dressing, and French dressing. Other dressings, though not regulated, had predictable flavors and characteristics. Italian, ranch, thousand island, French, and bleu cheese were America's favorite salad dressings in the 1990s according to an Association for Dressings and Sauces (ADS) survey reported in *Institutional Distribution* magazine. Steady growth in the sector was in line with the findings of the same ADS survey that three out of four people ate a tossed salad every other day.

Low-fat, low-calorie dressings were introduced to meet consumers' dietary concerns, but achieving the flavor and texture to which people were accustomed was a challenge. Indeed, by the end of the twentieth century, the food additives industry was growing faster than the food industry as consumers demanded improved flavor, texture, color, and nutritional benefits.

Pickle Packers International, Inc., reported that consumption of pickles had more than doubled from the mid-1940s to the early 1990s to an estimated nine pounds per person annually. According to the May 1996 issue of *Food Review,* this figure decreased markedly by mid-decade to 4.7 pounds. Pickle and other pickled product producers comprised 64 of the 129 establishments in this industry in the late 1990s.

FURTHER READING

Boehning, Julie C. "Dressing Up." *Supermarket News,* 3 June 1996.

"Food Producers Appeal to Fat-Free Crowd." *Marketing News,* 14 August 1995.

U.S. Census Bureau. "Manufacturing-Industry Series." *1997 Economic Census.* Washington, D.C.: GPO, 24 January 2000.

"U.S. Food Consumption." *Food Review,* May 1996.

SIC 2037

FROZEN FRUITS, FRUIT JUICES, VEGETABLES

This classification covers establishments primarily engaged in freezing fruits, fruit juices, and vegetables. These establishments also produce important byproducts such as fresh or dried citrus pulp.

NAICS CODE(S)

311411 (Frozen Fruit, Juice, and Vegetable Processing)

INDUSTRY SNAPSHOT

Frozen foods became available commercially beginning in 1930, making this category a comparative newcomer to the U.S. food industry. By 1998 overall retail sales of frozen foods in the United States reached about $25.7 billion. Of this total, supermarket sales of frozen fruit accounted for $178 million, frozen juices for $1.1 billion, frozen plain vegetables for $1.7 billion, frozen prepared vegetables for $109 million, and frozen potatoes and onions for $842 million.

Consumers receive frozen fruits, fruit juices, and vegetables through two main sales outlets: grocery stores and foodservice. Grocery stores include supermarkets, other retail stores, and the emerging warehouse clubs; foodservice is a highly fragmented market including restaurants, lodging and recreation outlets, separate eating and drinking establishments, health care institutions, colleges and universities, primary and secondary schools, airlines, business and industry, the military, and more. Foodservice sales, according to Technomic, Inc., reached $38.6 billion in 1998 and accounted for about 60 percent of total frozen food sales in the United States.

The frozen fruits, fruit juices, and vegetables industry has been greatly influenced by changes in the needs of the American consumer. Single-parent families, two-income families, and growing numbers of women in the workforce fueled the demand for convenience foods in convenient packaging. To compete in this changing marketplace, processors of commodity frozen vegetables extended their product lines with value-added items such as prepared meals, sauced vegetables, frozen entrees, pasta, and vegetable mixes; although changing demographics affected more than new product introductions. Single-serving frozen vegetables were an example of packaging that targeted changing demographic patterns, but they sold well only in stores with a high proportion of singles, or younger and elderly couples for customers.

ORGANIZATION AND STRUCTURE

The major producers of frozen fruits, fruit juices, and vegetables were subsidiaries or divisions of diversified, multinational, multibillion-dollar conglomerates. Ore-Ida, a leading producer of frozen potato products in the 1990s, was, for most of the decade, a subsidiary of H.J. Heinz. Minute-Maid, the top frozen orange juice concentrate, was produced by a division of Coca-Cola. Birds Eye, named for Clarence Birdseye, the "father" of the frozen food industry in the United States, was a Kraft General Foods (KGF) brand; KGF belonged to the Philip Morris family of companies. Green Giant was a subsidiary of Pillsbury Co. J.R. Simplot and its Food Group division were the lone privately held companies among the major ones. Alongside these industry giants, smaller newcomers and regional processors carved out significant markets for themselves. McCain Foods USA, for example, laid claim to being the fastest growing frozen food company in the United States in the late 1990s and made a significant step in that direction when it purchased Ore-Ida from Heinz in 1997.

BACKGROUND AND DEVELOPMENT

History. Humans have been using cold to preserve food quality for as long as they have been eating. More than 100,000 years ago food was stored in caves, where the temperatures were naturally low. Ice and snow were used to preserve food when they were available. It was not until the twentieth century, however, that scientific research into freezing foods really began. The ability to deliver frozen food to consumers is generally dated from October 14, 1924, when Clarence Birdseye received a patent for his revolutionary new apparatus called a plate freezer. A few more years passed before M.A. Joslyn and W.V. Cruess reported the necessity of blanching vegetables prior to freezing.

The industry has advanced steadily since. In 1930 June peas and spinach were the first commercially available frozen vegetables, making their debut in Massachusetts supermarkets. A shortage of tin for cans during World War II spurred the growth of frozen foods. Mechanically refrigerated railroad cars came into use in 1949, and the early 1960s saw the development of individually quick frozen (IQF) foods.

All food preservation systems are designed to prevent deterioration and spoilage during storage. Lowering food temperature decreases or inhibits the speed of chemical and physical reactions that result in spoilage. Microorganisms are a factor in the deterioration of food quality, but microbiologic growth stops when food temperature is reduced to less than negative 10 degrees Celsius. Foods frozen at temperatures as low as negative 40 degrees Celsius were not unusual towards the end of the twentieth century.

Manufacturing. Processors used several methods of freezing foods. High quality could be achieved with individual quick freezing. Its advantages were rapid freezing rates, and the fact that, because food pieces did not cohere into a solid block, individual portions could be stored in large containers. This made it particularly suitable for foodservice. In blast freezing, fans passed cold air over the food. Food could also be frozen between plates containing freezing coils, or by immersion into freezing liquid such as salt solutions, liquid nitrogen, and liquid carbon dioxide.

After a period of steady growth since 1986, the frozen food market dropped in the recessionary 1990s. Even though poundage production was up slightly, production value was down for the first time since 1947, as a surplus of vegetables had lowered prices. Sales in the frozen fruit and juice concentrate sectors were also down.

CURRENT CONDITIONS

Vegetables. The most popular frozen vegetable in both supermarket and foodservice markets has long been the potato. According to the American Frozen Food Institute, frozen food processors handled 8 billion pounds of potatoes on a yearly basis. Of that 8 billion pounds, about 80 percent was used for the beloved french fry. Between 1990 and 1996, supermarket sales of potatoes rose 13.2 percent and accounted for 41.1 percent of supermarket sales. Other frozen vegetables did not fare as well in the late 1990s, however, as the trend toward fresh produce gained in strength. According to Nielsen Marketing Research, sales of frozen mixed vegetables and sweet corn rose 40.7 percent and 8.2 percent, respectively, from 1990 and 1996, but frozen carrots, green beans, broccoli, and peas all suffered from declines.

Sales of organic frozen vegetables climbed in the late 1990s as organic foods gained in popularity. Organic frozen food sales in natural-product outlets were estimated to have reached $198.5 million in 1997. Nielsen reported that sales of organic frozen french fries rose from $25,300 to $94,800 in 1996, and sales of frozen organic vegetables, organic peas, organic corn, organic broccoli, and organic green beans also rose.

In the late 1990s frozen vegetable manufacturers sought to boost sales and to attract consumers by focusing on the healthful aspects of eating sufficient amounts of vegetables and fruits. In 1998 the U.S. Food and Drug Administration declared that frozen fruits and vegetables were just as beneficial as their fresh counterparts. Since most frozen vegetables were individually quick frozen within hours of harvest, they offered home cooks and foodservice operations the advantages of labor-saving convenience plus nutrient value, no waste, speed and ease of preparation, and year-round availability. The federal government also launched a campaign to motivate citizens to consume at least five servings of fruits and vegetables a day.

Fruits. The U.S. Department of Agriculture (USDA) provides voluntary grade standards for fruits and vegetables to help processors achieve uniform product quality. The best quality fruit is usually either sold as fresh produce or individually quick frozen, which results in a product close to fresh fruit. In the latter process, no sugar is added, and the speed of freezing minimizes ice crystal damage. Factors affecting fruit quality are color, size, blemishes, flavor, firmness, and unwanted portions such as skin, pits, or leaves. In bulk freezing, the fruit is filled into containers and then frozen. Such fruit can be frozen alone or with sugar or syrups added; sometimes fruit is frozen in its own juice.

Supermarket sales of frozen fruit in 1998 were $178 million. Among the most popular fruits were strawberries, raspberries, and blueberries. Blueberries significantly grew in popularity in the late 1990s as its antioxidant properties were heavily promoted.

Fruit Juices. The frozen juice segment suffered through the late 1990s as consumers opted for chilled and shelf-stable container juices, which both provided greater convenience to the time-constrained shopper of the 1990s. Juices became available in a variety of nonfrozen capacities, such as in individual boxes, in concentrate form in plastic containers, and in large cans. According to Information Resources, Inc., a market research firm, domestic supermarket sales of frozen juices during the 52-week period that ended May 24, 1998, reached $1.15 billion, a drop of 11.1 percent from the year-earlier period. Even frozen orange juice, a perennial favorite that accounted for about half of the entire frozen drink segment, suffered from declining sales; frozen orange juice sales also fell 11.1 percent during the same period, while sales of chilled orange juice increased 6.9 percent, to $2.45 billion.

To reinvigorate slow frozen juice sales, manufacturers turned toward such strategies as cross merchandising, new packaging, new products, and marketing. Some juice companies attempted to boost the convenience factor of frozen juices in order to lure consumers. Welch's, the grape juice leader, marketed a new frozen juice container that could be thawed in a microwave, thereby decreasing the time needed to mix a container of juice. Other manufacturers focused on one of the strongest selling points of frozen juice—price—and also introduced new flavors. Cross merchandising, such as pairing frozen juices with such items as frozen breakfast items, was also a tactic employed by frozen juice manufacturers.

INDUSTRY LEADERS

J.R. Simplot Company was one of the largest processors of frozen potatoes in the late 1990s. Best known as a major supplier of french fries to the McDonald's restaurant chain, Simplot also processed fruits and vegetables at plants in California, Washington, Iowa, and Mexico, with more than half of them destined for foodservice use. The privately held Simplot had 1999 sales of $2.73 billion. McCain Foods was also a major processor of frozen potatoes. McCain supplied french fries to Burger King restaurants. McCain, which also sold frozen vegetables through its Ore-Ida subsidiary, had 1998 sales of $3.48 billion.

Another frozen vegetables and fruits leader in the late 1990s included ConAgra, one of the largest and most diversified frozen food manufacturers in the United States. ConAgra offered frozen potato items as well as frozen prepared foods. Its family of brands included Healthy Choice, Banquet, Kid Cuisine, and Marie Callender's. Another giant, Agrilink Foods Vegetable Co., became larger with the acquisition in 1998 of the vegetable operations of Dean Foods. The purchase included the Birds Eye brand, a top frozen vegetable brand. Agrilink also acquired Agripac, Inc., a private-label frozen vegetable manufacturer and exporter. Pillsbury Company subsidiary, Green Giant USA, was another frozen vegetable leader.

AMERICA AND THE WORLD

In the 1990s manufacturers of frozen fruits, fruit juices, and vegetables looked overseas for opportunities to expand. As the U.S. market for orange juice matured in the 1990s, the three leading producers, Minute Maid, Citrus Hill, and Tropicana, were looking to Europe and Japan for increased sales. Exports of frozen vegetables doubled between 1990 and 1996. Frozen potatoes especially enjoyed growing popularity overseas, with exports doubling in the late 1990s. The leading market for frozen french fries was Japan, which accounted for about half of total frozen potato exports. Other countries that imported frozen potatoes from the U.S. included Hong Kong, Korea, Singapore, Mexico, and Brazil. Another popular frozen vegetable export was sweet corn, though export volume fell 1 percent during the first 9 months of 1999. Exports to Japan, the largest market for frozen sweet corn, declined 5 percent, but exports to Canada and China increased.

RESEARCH AND TECHNOLOGY

In 1989 the Chicago-based Institute of Food Technologists (IFT) named the ten most significant food science innovations to have taken place during its 50-year history. Third on their list was the development of frozen concentrated citrus juices at the U.S. Department of Agriculture research laboratories in the mid-1940s. The addition of approximately 7 percent fresh juice to the concentrate was the key to the product's success. Since that time, processors have further refined the process with the addition of essential oils and natural flavors to the concentrate before it is packaged and frozen. Also making IFT's top ten list was the development of new freezing methods that enabled the prediction of optimal freezing and storage conditions, an important advance because nutrient loss is negligible when foods are properly frozen and stored.

Another breakthrough in the twentieth century was the development of plastic packaging. Among plastic's advantages: it is heat sealable, microwavable, resistant to corrosion, and easily made. More than 80 percent of American households had microwave ovens by the early 1990s, and makers of frozen vegetables and fruits used dual-purpose plastics in packaging that enabled consumers to use either traditional top-of-the-stove cooking methods or the popular microwave ovens.

Agriculturalists in the field of plant breeding were focusing on improving the taste and nutritional value of vegetables used in frozen products, particularly onions, carrots, cucumbers, and garlic.

FURTHER READING

''Annual Consumer Expenditures Study.'' *Supermarket News,* September 1999.

Breyer, R. Michelle. ''Juice War.'' *Supermarket News,* 3 August 1998.

''Business Linked to Berries Is Not New to Controversy.'' *New York Times,* 3 April 1997.

Friedman, Michael. ''A Fresh Challenge.'' *Progressive Grocer,* 1 October 1998.

''Frozen Foods, Potato & Seafood Sales Figure Prominently in ConAgra Growth.'' *Quick Frozen Foods International,* 1 January 1999.

Glaser, Lawrence, et al. ''Demand For Frozen Vegetables: A Comparison of Organic and Conventional Products.'' *Frozen Food Digest,* 1 February 1999.

''Heinz Cutting 2500 Jobs in Revamping.'' *New York Times,* 15 March 1997.

''J.R. Simplot.'' *Nation's Restaurant News,* 2 February 1996.

Murray, Barbara. ''Promotional Tour will Promote Fruits and Vegetables.'' *Supermarket News,* 5 April 1999.

Pierce, J.J. ''Frozen Vegetables Bring in the Green While Improving Consumers' Health.'' *Quick Frozen Foods International,* 1 April 1999.

''U.S. Food Consumption.'' *Food Review,* May 1996.

SIC 2038

FROZEN SPECIALTIES NOT ELSEWHERE CLASSIFIED

This industry comprises establishments primarily engaged in manufacturing frozen food specialties, not elsewhere classified, such as frozen dinners and frozen pizza. The manufacture of some important frozen foods and specialties is classified elsewhere. For example, establishments primarily engaged in manufacturing frozen dairy specialties are classified in **SIC 2024: Ice Cream and Frozen Desserts;** those manufacturing frozen bakery products are classified in **SIC 2051: Bread and Other Bakery Products** and **SIC 2053: Frozen Bakery Products, Except Bread;** those manufacturing frozen fruits and vegetables are classified in **SIC 2037: Frozen Fruits, Fruit Juices, and Vegetables;** and those manufacturing frozen fish and seafood specialties are classified in **SIC 2092: Prepared Fresh or Frozen Fish and Seafood.**

NAICS CODE(S)

311412 (Frozen Specialty Food Manufacturing)

INDUSTRY SNAPSHOT

Companies in the industry shipped $8.6 billion worth of products in 1995, an increase of 12 percent since 1990; this amount rose to $10.2 billion in 1997. There were 333 establishments in the industry in the mid-1990s, an increase of 20 percent since 1990, and in 1997 there were 412 establishments. In the mid-1990s, the industry employed 44,429 people, an increase of 10 percent since 1990. The industry employed 48,029 in 1997.

BACKGROUND AND DEVELOPMENT

Clarence Birdseye is considered the father of the frozen food industry. He created the freezing process so that preserved foods did not need to be cooked immediately. Birdseye formed Birds Eye Foods Ltd. in London in 1954; it later became a subsidiary of Unilever. According to *Quick Frozen Foods International,* Birds Eye ''virtually held an umbrella over the industry during the squalls of its infancy.''

The frozen food industry evolved during the early 1960s as the proliferation of supermarkets and self-service stores made mass marketing of frozen food products profitable. At the same time, refrigerator-freezers and stand-alone freezers gained in popularity. The first frozen food products were vegetables, poultry, fish, and fruit in boilable pouches. Items such as frozen juice concentrate, ice cream novelties, baked goods, variety dinners, seafood, breakfast items, and pizza gradually entered the industry from the mid-1960s through the 1990s.

Beginning in the 1980s, standard TV dinners gave way to a variety of meals and frozen specialty items that offered more choices and met specific dietary requirements. Frozen food manufacturers targeted their products at the needs of busy families who desired quick meal preparation and a large variety. They also developed new frozen entrees for children.

The rapid growth in the industry is also attributable to the introduction of the microwave oven. In fact, *Quick Frozen Foods International* called the combination of the microwave oven and frozen food a ''marriage of convenience: Frozen food performs better in a microwave oven.'' The magazine reported that microwave oven owners spent 34 percent more on pizza, 29 percent more on breakfast foods, 19 percent more on entrees, and 16 percent more on dinners than non-microwave owners. Improvements in taste over the past 40 years also made frozen food specialties increasingly attractive to busy families.

Leading frozen food manufacturers engaged in damaging price wars and expensive trade promotions in the early 1990s. As a result, many companies began shifting their focus toward generating profits from existing products instead of launching new brands and line extensions.

CURRENT CONDITIONS

The frozen food industry grew from a $250 million retail business in 1947 to more than $20 billion by the 1990s, according to the National Frozen Food Association. Total retail sales in 1997 reached $24 billion. The dinner and entree category was the largest—with sales of more than $4.5 billion. Also, the foodservice market accounted for nearly 60 percent of the industry's sales, and frozen products equaled 32 percent of total foodservice sales.

In the 1990s, dual-income households and the convenience of microwave ovens contributed to annual growth in the frozen food category. However, consumers also complained about the poor texture and inferior browning effect of microwaveable foods. Cognizant of this concern, technicians in the food additives field increased research into methods to improve the flavor, texture, color, shelf-life, and nutritional benefits of frozen foods.

Convenience in preparation is the primary appeal of frozen foods. Americans used fewer and fewer ingredients to prepare their meals in the late 1990s and often substituted frozen foods for fresh produce. Concerns about health and nutrition also led consumers to reduce their intake of foods containing fat and sodium. The specialty frozen food industry responded by offering low-cholesterol and low-fat products. H.J. Heinz, for example, introduced a 98 percent fat-free frozen dinner for its Budget Gourmet brand.

According to *Supermarket News,* ''frozen Mexican and Tex-Mex foods have outgrown their purely regional appeal to gain acceptance in the diets of many Americans.'' Double-digit dollar gains for frozen ethnic foods are expected to continue into the twenty-first century. Less well-known companies, including Tai Pan and Yu Sing, were also increasing sales of ethnic foods (specifically oriental) in the 1990s.

At the close of the 1990s, industry analysts were urging the frozen food industry to develop new prepared foods in order to avoid losing additional market share to ready-to-eat meals, including microwavable shelf-stable and refrigerated items. Sales of such products could erode the market share held by frozen foods from 66 percent in the mid-1990s to 34 percent by the year 2000. According to Techtronic, Inc. frozen food held 18 percent of total supermarket sales in 1999.

In 1998 the American Frozen Food Institute released a report detailing a consumer research study. One finding was that frozen food has gained 20 percent more store space over the last ten years. An additional finding was that the Great Lakes and the Plains regions of the United States have had the greatest growth in frozen food sales.

FURTHER READING

American Frozen Food Institute Web Site, 2000. Available from http://www.affi.com/facts/decafood.htm.

"The Decline and Fall of the Microwave." *Futurist,* March/April 1995.

Friedman, Michael. "International Foods Growing." *Frozen Food Age,* February 1997.

U.S. Census Bureau. "Manufacturing-Industry Series." *1997 Economic Census.* Washington, D.C.: GPO, 3 November 1999.

SIC 2041

FLOUR AND OTHER GRAIN MILL PRODUCTS

This industry comprises establishments primarily engaged in milling flour from wheat, rye, and other grains except rice. Rice millers are categorized in **SIC 2044: Rice Milling.** Establishments involved in corn milling by the wet process are categorized in **SIC 2046: Wet Corn Milling.**

Products of this industry include plain flour or mixes and doughs prepared from milled ingredients. Establishments that supply mixes and doughs prepared from purchased ingredients are categorized in **SIC 2045: Prepared Flour Mixes and Doughs.**

NAICS CODE(S)

311211 (Flour Milling)

INDUSTRY SNAPSHOT

Explosive growth and a bright future, tempered by growing environmental and health concerns, characterized this industry in 2000. Shipments of flour and other grain mill products reached a record $8.045 billion in 1997, according to the U.S. Census of Manufacturers, while mill construction and modernization programs flourished, indicating that industry players felt the market was ripe for large-scale investment. There were 385 mills in the United States in the late 1990s, slightly reversing the trend of the past few decades toward fewer mills, and highlighting milling companies' optimistic investment patterns. Most of the industry's value ($6.1 billion) was derived from wheat flour, while corn mill products accounted for $696.0 million in shipments. Flour production increased as well, to a record 18.3 million tons in 1997, up 14 percent from 1990, aided by an increase in per capita flour consumption. A healthy economy favorable to the baking industry, especially marked in the wild proliferation of specialty baking stores like bagel shops, has further fueled robust growth.

While the industry has expanded, its customer base and marketing focus have changed radically. Especially after World War II and accelerating rapidly beginning in the 1970s, domestic flour-consumption patterns shifted away from household consumers and toward commercial bakers, including fast-food outlets. Due to general lifestyle changes and economic expansion, household baking has declined considerably; individual consumers increasingly tend to purchase their bread, dough, and mixes prepared from grocery stores and bakeries. Flour use, then, has become more and more institutionalized. At the same time, the domestic market overall has flourished, much to the industry's benefit; the United States was, for much of the twentieth century, by far the world's leading exporter of flour and grain mill products, and exports were the industry's lifeline. By 2000, exports accounted for only 3 percent of all flour. The fading international presence of the United States in the flour industry has, moreover, coincided with a growing worldwide demand for flour and grain mill products. Nonetheless, the bulk of the flour industry has contented itself to focus on the domestic market, which promises attractive returns in coming years.

ORGANIZATION AND STRUCTURE

Although any grain (rice, oats, barley, corn, millet, sorghum, and wheat) can be ground into flour, most of the world's flour was produced from wheat; the industry consumed more than 790 million bushels of wheat in 1998. Using standard milling procedures, 100 pounds of wheat yielded approximately 72 pounds of white flour. In addition to flour, the milling process produced millfeeds, which were made from pieces of bran and other portions of the wheat kernel. Millfeeds were used as ingredients in livestock food.

Flour could be packaged for sale to the household or bakery markets or used as an ingredient in bakery mixes, breads or doughs, or pastas. Different bread varieties were made with varying recipes but, on average, 100 pounds of flour could make about 150 one-pound loaves of bread. The bread and cake industry consumed approximately 75 percent of the flour milled in the United States. Other flour products included cookies, cereals, gravies, soups, whiskeys, and beers. Flour products were also used in nonfood applications such as the manufacture of plywood adhesives, industrial starches, fertilizers, paving mixes, polishes, and cosmetics. Approximately 85 percent of the flour used by industrial users was milled from hard and durum wheat varieties.

Furthermore, mills used a process called fractionation to separate the flour according to the fineness of its particles. Course fractions were reground. Intermediate fractions were used in applications requiring low amounts of protein, and fine fraction flour was blended with other flours or used alone in applications where high protein content was necessary. White flour was often bleached with agents such as potassium bromide, methyl bromide, methyl iodide, iodate, acetone peroxide, azodicarbonamide, ascorbic acid, and chlorine dioxide. In addition to providing consistent coloring, bleaching improved the condition of the flour gluten, which in turn improved its baking quality. These chemicals were often also used as fumigants to defend stored flour and grains against rodents and insects, an increasing concern as storage capacity continued to increase; total commercial grain storage totaled about 220 million tons in 1999.

White flour is made only with the endosperm portion of the wheat kernel. Farina is also made from the endosperm, but it is ground to produce a granular product. The term "wheat germ" refers to the part of the wheat kernel from which a seed sprouts. It contains oil that is sometimes extracted for separate processing. Wheat germ is also used in breakfast cereals, breads, and other bakery products. Whole wheat flour, also called graham flour, is made from the endosperm, bran, and germ combined; it has a higher protein content than regular white flour. Pastas such as spaghetti, macaroni, and noodles are made from durum wheat. A popular pasta ingredient, semolina, is a granular grind of durum endosperm, comparable to farina.

The diverse end uses of flours require a wide variety of milled grain products produced from different types of wheat. In the late 1990s, approximately 14 different wheat species were grown. The three most frequently used varieties are common wheat (*Triticum aestivum*), club wheat (*Triticum compactum*), and durum wheat (*Triticum durum*). Together, these three accounted for 90 percent of the wheat grown in the United States.

Different wheats are classified as hard, soft, or durum. Hard wheats are used to make flours for breads and rolls. Soft wheats are used primarily in cakes, cookies, crackers, and prepared mixes. Durum wheat is almost exclusively used to make pasta products. Although a single modern flour mill might offer more than one product, it typically grinds only one class of wheat. Approximately 70 percent of the U.S. milling capacity during the late 1980s was devoted to hard wheat. Soft wheat mills accounted for 20 percent, durum wheat accounted for 8 percent, and mills dedicated to whole wheat production represented 2 percent of the nation's milling capacity.

BACKGROUND AND DEVELOPMENT

Milled grains have been used as principal food staples for thousands of years. Corn has been the predominant grain used by people in Latin America and the sub-Saharan regions of Africa, while many Asian nations have depended on rice. Inhabitants of Europe and North America relied primarily on wheat products.

The origins of wheat farming and milling are obscure. Historians estimate that wheat cultivation began between 10,000 and 15,000 years ago, marking the beginning of civilization. Because they could be stored, stocked, and transported, grains led to the evolution of trading practices. Documents in the form of artistic depictions and early writings chronicled the development of wheat grinding technologies and baking methods in ancient Egypt, Assyria, Greece, and China.

One of the oldest types of wheat known is bulgur wheat, and the earliest means employed to separate the parts of the wheat kernel involved rubbing the grain between the hands. Another method used the action of hoofed animals walking over grains that had been spread on hard ground. Winnowing was a process in which grains were tossed in the air so that the chaff would blow away. Removing the individual grains from the rest of the plant was necessary before milling could take place.

Wheat kernels are made up of three components: endosperm, bran, and germ. The endosperm represents about 83.0 percent of the kernel and contains the starchy portion used to make white flour. The bran accounts for about 14.5 percent of the wheat kernel and is used in whole wheat flour and animal feeds. The smallest portion of the kernel, the germ, represents only about 2.5 percent of the kernel. The most common uses of wheat germ are in human food products and in animal feeds. Historically, the germ was separated from the rest of the wheat kernel because it contained fat and did not keep well in long term storage.

Grain milling practices were developed to separate the kernel components and make flour. The first types of milling procedures involved the use of rubbing stones, mortar and pestles, or querns. Querns were devices made from two stacked, disk-shaped stones. Wheat grains were poured into the quern through a hole in the top stone. As the two stones turned against each other, the abrasive movement separated the parts of the wheat kernels and ground the endosperm into flour. The flour was then discharged between the stones.

More efficient methods of grinding grain progressed along with the development of alternative power supplies. Horses and oxen could turn millstones better than humans. Wind- and water-operated mills supplanted animal power. As the United States was settled, mills were constructed in almost every town. Typically the mill relied on water power and was, therefore, located near a source of running water.

The first continuous system for milling wheat into flour was developed during the last part of the eighteenth century by an American, Oliver Evans. Evans' mill design utilized steam technology and employed conveyors and bucket elevators to move the grain through a multi-phase milling process. Further advances in milling technology occurred during the nineteenth century. In 1865, Edmund La Croix developed a middlings purifier that separated the granular endosperm from the bran so that it could be reground to produce a better grade of flour. During the 1870s, the first roller mills in the United States were constructed. Roller mills possessed several advantages: they eliminated the need of dressing millstones; they were able to produce flour through a more gradual extraction process, which enabled millers to yield a larger percentage of better grade flour; and they lent themselves to greater efficiency, thereby making the construction of larger mills more feasible.

As U.S. citizens moved westward, milling centers moved with them. Mills became larger in size but fewer in number. In 1870, an estimated 22,000 mills served the nation's population of about 30 million. One hundred and ten years later, the nation's population of 220 million was served by an estimated 150 to 250 mills. In Michigan, for instance, the number of mills fell from 534 at the turn of the century to 6 in 1990. The consolidation of mills and the trend toward facilities with greater capacities led to the creation of giant corporations such as Pillsbury Co. and General Mills, Inc. Millers began offering a wider variety of products during the early 1900s. Self-rising flour, biscuit and cake mixes, and prepared doughs were introduced during the 1920s and 1930s but failed to gain widespread popularity until after World War II.

During the middle of the twentieth century, fundamental changes occurred in the primary location of mills. Prior to the 1950s, the cost of shipping wheat and the cost of shipping flour were approximately equal, and mills were frequently built close to wheat fields. During the early 1960s, the cost of shipping grain decreased following the introduction of hopper rail cars. At the same time, costs surrounding sanitation requirements increased the price of shipping flour. As a result, mills were constructed in close proximity to end markets rather than near the wheat fields.

Granular flour, a product made with particles of a uniform size with carefully controlled amounts of atomized moisture to reduce clumping, was introduced during the 1960s. Although granular flour was more expensive than regular flour, it offered several advantages. It had less dust, was easier to pour, did not require sifting, and it dispersed in cold liquids.

During the 1970s, sales of household flour declined as society moved away from home baking and homemakers demonstrated a preference for the convenience and consistency of prepared mixes. In addition, many mixes were less expensive than individual ingredients. Baking from ''scratch'' ceased to be an activity of necessity and was relegated to hobby status. Demographic information revealed that households with higher incomes were more likely to use flour than lower income households. Flour volume losses within the household sector were partially offset by increases of flour sales to commercial bakers.

CURRENT CONDITIONS

Although overall flour consumption dipped somewhat during the early 1970s, annual per capita flour consumption underwent dramatic growth in the final three decades of the twentieth century, from 49.5 kilograms in 1972 to 67.5 kilograms in 1997. Such skyrocketing consumption was unprecedented in U.S. history. Several factors contributed to this phenomenon, including the surge in consumption of fast-foods and other flour-based convenience foods such as sandwiches and pizzas and, perhaps conversely, increased nutrition consciousness and the corresponding growth in demand for fine breads, especially fiber, bran, and whole grain products.

Consolidation was perhaps the most consistent trend in flour milling. Beginning especially in the 1980s, the number of mills have declined, while market shares of the top companies have escalated rapidly. In 1973, the top four milling companies controlled 34 percent of the nation's capacity, while the top ten accounted for 61 percent. One of the most radical ownership restructurings occurred in 1989, when Pillsbury Company, one of the largest flour millers in the United States, sold its mills to Archer Daniels Midland Company and Cargill Flour Milling and became one of the nation's largest purchasers of flour for its mixes and refrigerated doughs. In 1999, six of those former top-ten companies were no longer in business. The largest flour miller, Archer Daniels Midland Milling, held nearly a quarter of total capacity, and the top four firms controlled two-thirds of the market; the top ten accounted for 83 percent.

Average milling capacity, meanwhile, has expanded enormously, increasing about 80 percent between 1973 and 1998. In 2000, most mills held a capacity of more than 45 tons. Most of the mills that were shut down over the last two decades were those with smaller capacity. The trend toward corporate mills was driven by the goals of reducing labor and transportation costs and increasing profits, favoring those companies with large production facilities that can create economies of scale. The number of mills with capacity above 227 tons exceeded, in 1994, the number of mills with capacity below that benchmark. The efficiency of the mills in place has escalated along with consolidation, evidenced by the 90 percent capacity at which most mills in the United States now operate. Finally, the pace of this expansion continues to grow; new capacity additions in 1997 amounted to 7 percent of existing capacity.

The trend toward fewer, yet larger, firms has further resulted in a heightened willingness of and need for companies to invest heavily in technological innovation.

Whereas the flour milling industry was once characterized by the drive for low-cost operations as its basis of competition, firms in the late 1990s were pouring money into modernization schemes aimed at streamlining their larger facilities. Most analysts expect these investments to pay off, as forecasts offer no hint that the expansion of the flour industry will be mitigated in the near future.

Other effects of the industry's consolidation have generated uncertainties. A by-product of increased capacity and centralization of production is the dual needs of increased quality-control measures and more efficient production. Biotechnology, generally agreed, especially among the larger players, to be a practical and feasible solution to these problems, is hailed by some as an integral and welcome aspect of flour milling's future. Critics, however, tend to view this trend as dubious or worse. The research and application of processes aimed at improving flour quality, maximizing production, and staving off pests via gene manipulation is one of the most contentious and crucial issues the flour and grain mill products industry is poised to face in the twenty-first century, as environmentalists, consumer advocates, and many scientists and other critics question the safety to humans and the environment of genetically modified foods.

A number of environmental concerns topped the industry's challenges in the early 2000s. Global environmental accords, such as those reached at the Kyoto Conference in Japan, have aimed at completely phasing out the use of chemicals with an ozone-depletion level of 0.2 or higher; this includes methyl bromide, the most popular fumigant in U.S. flour mills. The United States, the largest producer of methyl bromide, agreed to reduce emissions by 2012 seven percent from their 1990 levels. Not all millers have accepted the news graciously; many are concerned about the costs involved in continuing to meet governmental standards regarding cleanliness and pest control without their staple fumigant. One existing alternative is methyl iodide, which carries an ozone-depletion level of 0.016, compared with methyl bromide's 0.6. However, the price for methyl iodide in 1999 was $12 per kilogram, about three times that of methyl bromide.

The Environmental Protection Agency (EPA) implemented regulations in 1999 aimed at reducing levels of phosphine, another fumigant typically used in grain and similar agricultural storage facilities, including flour mills to control insects and rodents. Commonly used in the form of an aluminum or magnesium tablet, phosphide, like methyl bromide, actually penetrates the kernel or grain mass. In forty years, twelve deaths have been attributed to the chemical; the particular separate incidences that spurred the EPA into action involved two women, one elderly and the other pregnant, who died from organophosphate poisoning after storage facilities near their homes were fumigated. While some industry players hold that such tragedies could be avoided with proper application procedures, the industry must adopt to the new regulations.

Potassium bromate has also attracted the ire of environmentalists and health monitors. The additive, for decades a staple of the baking industry used to improve dough texture, has been found to cause cancer in laboratory animals. Moreover, potassium bromate is an oxidation material; oxidation has generated concerns over insect infestation. The U.S. Food and Drug Administration (FDA) has urged millers and bakers to cease the use of potassium bromate since the early 1990s, though so far there is no mandate against its use. The American Bakers Association, meanwhile, maintains that potassium bromate residues can and should be eliminated with proper handling and baking techniques, without necessitating the banning of potassium bromate altogether.

Another major challenge facing the grain mill industry was the charge that flour performance was diminishing. Industry researchers speculated that one cause of deteriorating quality was a grain breeding program that had emphasized increasing yield per acre without paying sufficient attention to the quality of the end products produced with the grain. Other possible causes included a drop in the amount of protein, a declining protein quality, an ever-increasing number of wheat varieties, the impact of agricultural practices such as irrigation and fertilizers, and milling practices that improved efficiency but with potentially inferior results.

Various flour-treatment procedures exist to improve the appearance, nutritional content, and baking quality of flour during the milling process. Flour enrichment, for example, adds iron and B vitamins to stave off vitamin deficiencies; enrichment is credited with eliminating diseases such as beriberi and pellagra in the United States. Today, about 95 percent of bread in the United States uses enriched flour.

INDUSTRY LEADERS

The largest miller in the United States in 1999, ranked by milling capacity, was Archer Daniels Midland Company, a diversified food producer, at 46.8 million pounds. Established in 1923 via an acquisition that made it the world's largest linseed oil producer, the firm has continually expanded its operations, covering the gamut of agribusiness, including wheat milling and cereal grains. ADM's milling products include dry and wet milling corn, wheat flour, durum flour, and bulgur for both retail and institutional customers worldwide. The firm posted sales of $13.7 billion in 1999 and employed 23,600 people.

ConAgra Inc. was second-largest, with capacity of 29.67 million pounds. Another diversified food products organization, ConAgra classified its businesses into three areas: Grocery and Diversified Products, Refrigerated Foods, and Food Inputs and Ingredients, whose combined sales reached $24.9 billion in 1999. In addition to its wheat flour production mills, ConAgra operated oat, dry corn, and barley processing facilities. ConAgra operated 30 mills in the United States, with others in Canada and the United Kingdom.

Cargill Foods, which began as a grain elevator in the mid-nineteenth century, occupied the number three position in milling capacity, at 24.98 million tons. One of the largest food companies in the world, with operations in 65 countries worldwide, Cargill maintained 80,600 employees and generated $45.7 billion in revenue in 1999. In 1998, Cargill acquired Continental Grain Company, a top industry player. In 1997, Cargill reorganized its milling operations along Eastern and Western regional lines. Cargill Foods' Flour Mills produce bulk and packaged flours and mixes.

Once the nation's largest flour miller, General Mills' milling capacity has shrunk to 7.6 million tons. Its milling and baking products, however, continue to position it as an industry leader, with 10,000 employees and 1999 revenue of $6.49 billion. The company produces leading household flours, sold under the Gold Medal and Robin Hood labels, and mixes, such as Bisquick and Betty Crocker.

WORKFORCE

Employment in the flour and grain mill products industry registered a slight upswing in the late 1990s, to 12,800 workers, after years of incremental declines; in 1993 the figure stood at 12,400, and dipped below that in the interim. In 1997, industry employees earned an average of about $14.53 per hour. Out of the 380 active mills, 172 maintained a staff of 20 or more workers, while 75 had more than 50 workers.

Safety issues within the industry included dust control, noise abatement, and controlling hazards that presented risks for fire and explosions. Concentrations of grain dust above certain limits were susceptible to burning rapidly if ignited. Dust control was also necessary to limit possible worker exposure to microorganisms, pesticide residues, toxins, insect parts, and animal hairs. Some studies suggested that workers with high levels of exposure to grain dust might be susceptible to respiratory diseases such as chronic bronchitis. Noise in mills was primarily attributed to pneumatic blowers and vehicles. Finally, complications relating from fumigants, a major concern to the industry as a whole as regulatory scrutiny clamps down, was of acute concern to employees.

To control potential work place hazards, modern mills reduced dust generation by minimizing grain handling, reducing the velocity of grain movement, and installing enclosed conveyor systems. Protection from excessive noise was achieved by isolating work stations and limiting exposure.

FURTHER READING

"Methyl Bromide Update." *World Grain,* February 1998. Available from http://www.sosland.com.

Posner, Elieser S., and Arthur N. Hibbs. *Wheat Flour Milling.* St. Paul, MN: American Association of Cereal Chemists, 1997.

Sosland, Morton I. "Project Apollo: Milling Technology Enhanced by Human Milling Skills." *Milling & Baking News,* 15 June 1999.

Sudgen, David. "Defining Flour Strength." *World Grain,* June 1998. Available from http://www.sosland.com.

Trood, Ian S.V. "Flour Power." *World Grain,* September 1999. Available from http://www.sosland.com.

U.S. Census Bureau. *1997 Census of Manufacturers.* Washington, D.C.: Department of Commerce, 1999.

Wheat Flour Institute. *From Wheat to Flour.* Washington, D.C.: Wheat Flour Institute, 1981.

Wylie, Stormy. "Battle Over Phosphine." *World Grain,* February 1999. Available from http://www.sosland.com.

SIC 2043

CEREAL BREAKFAST FOODS

This industry is comprised of establishments that manufacture cereal breakfast foods. Establishments that primarily manufacture granola and other types of breakfast bars are categorized in **SIC 2064: Candy and Other Confectionary Products.**

NAICS CODE(S)

311920 (Coffee and Tea Manufacturing)
311230 (Breakfast Cereal Manufacturing)

INDUSTRY SNAPSHOT

In the mid-1990s breakfast cereal makers underwent major repositioning, rethinking their product development procedures. Cereal manufacturers were confronted with changing consumer habits when it came to eating breakfast. Statistics for 1999 showed that cereal consumption fell by 1 percent in a $7.52-billion market. Despite the quickened pace of American lives, 85 percent of Americans claimed to eat breakfast in 1999. However, *how* Americans chose to eat breakfast became a concern for cereal manufacturers. *Progressive Grocer* reported that 57 percent of individuals eat breakfast away from home. Quick serve restaurants like McDonald's, ready-to-eat breakfast bars, bagels, and muffins offered consumers on-the-go alternatives to cereal.

Consumer awareness of health and nutrition also played a major part in shaping the industry during the mid- to late 1990s. Cereal manufacturers began to tout the benefits of eating breakfast cereal right on the package—vitamin-fortified, low in fat, and a good source of fiber. According to *Supermarket News,* when the Food and Drug Administration (FDA) said that eating oats may help prevent heart disease, over the 12 months ending in March 1998, volume sales for Cheerios increased 5.5 percent, Fiber One volume increased by 9 percent, and Total Raisin Bran volume increased by 6 percent.

BACKGROUND AND DEVELOPMENT

Ready-to-eat cereals first appeared during the late 1800s. According to one account, John Kellogg, a doctor who belonged to a vegetarian group, developed wheat and corn flakes to extend the group's dietary choices. John's brother, Will Kellogg, saw potential in the innovative grain products and initiated commercial production and marketing. Patients at a Battle Creek, Michigan, sanitarium were among Kellogg's first customers.

Another cereal producer with roots in the nineteenth century was the Quaker Oats Company. In 1873, the North Star Oatmeal Mill built an oatmeal plant in Cedar Rapids, Iowa. North Star reorganized with other enterprises and together they formed Quaker Oats in 1901.

The Washburn Crosby Company, a predecessor to General Mills, entered the market during the 1920s. The company's first ready-to-eat cereal, Wheaties, was introduced to the American public in 1924. According to General Mills, Wheaties was developed when a Minneapolis clinician spilled a mixture of gruel that he was making for his patients on a hot stove. The clinician approached the Washburn Crosby Company with his product and, following many tests and refinements, Wheaties was born. Other General Mills cereals followed in rapid succession. In 1937 Crispy Corn Kix was introduced. The company also launched the world's first ready-to-eat oat cereal in 1941. Originally named Cheerioats, the product later became "Cheerios."

During the 1940s cereal makers benefited from improved methods of puffing cereal products. Puffing methods employed a principle somewhat analogous to popping corn. Cereal ingredients were cooked and formed into pellets with precisely monitored amounts of water. The product was heated in an enclosed container called a "gun." As the heat increased, the water within the pellets turned to steam. The steam expanded and built up pressure within the gun until the intensity of the pressure caused the end of the gun to open. When the gun opened, the force of the escaping steam propelled the pellets out of the gun into a receiving bin and, as the steam erupted from the pellets, it left them permeated with thousands of air holes. These air holes caused the

pellet to become larger and less dense. For example, one type of puffed product made with a pellet measuring 0.156 inches in diameter measured 0.5 inches after puffing. During the first decade of the 1900s, before the development of modern puffing procedures, puffed products were actually shot from cannons.

Many kinds of cereal were manufactured with a device called a food extruder. The extruder mixed and cooked cereal ingredients in a process that also shaped and colored the mixture. Ingredients were added at one end of the extruder and conveyed through its inner mechanisms by spiraling screws. A die at the other end of the extruder squeezed out cereal shapes and a blade cut the pieces at a predetermined size.

These food extruders were similar in operation to meat grinders. The first extruders, used during the 1930s, had only a single screw and often had problems caused by dried pieces of food. The machines were improved by the development of twin screws. Twin-screw extruders had two screws that intermeshed and cleaned each other as they propelled the cereal mixture.

The second half of the twentieth century brought rapid increases in brand offerings and growing national interest in ready-to-eat cereals. Many popular presweetened cereals aimed at the children's market were introduced during the 1950s. Trix and Lucky Charms were launched in 1954. Cocoa Puffs made its first appearance in 1958. Adult cereals made an impact during the 1960s. Total, touted as a product containing 100 percent of the officially established U.S. recommended daily allowance (RDA) of vitamins and iron, was introduced in 1961. In 1970, the ready-to-eat cereal market was valued at $659 million, and it had reached $1.9 billion by 1979.

In the 1980s and on into the 1990s, U.S. consumers became increasingly interested in health issues and, consequently, in improving their diets. In response, Kellogg introduced Nutri-Grain, the first line of flaked, whole grain ready-to-eat cereals with no sugar or preservatives. Other Kellogg offerings aimed at the health-conscious market included Crispix in 1983, Just Right in 1985, and Smart Start in 1998.

In 1985, Kellogg held a 40 percent share of the total ready-to-eat cereal market, which had grown to $4.35 billion. General Mills held a 22 percent share, followed by Post (14 percent), Quaker Oats (8 percent) and Ralston Purina (6 percent). All other cereal manufacturers combined held the remaining 10 percent. According to a report published by *Prepared Foods,* 92.4 percent of U.S. households used ready-to-eat cereal. The average household had four packages, and the country consumed more than 20 billion bowls annually.

According to figures published by the U.S. Department of Commerce, the cereal breakfast foods industry shipped $6.6 billion worth of products in 1987. The total included $5 billion of products considered primary to the industry and $1.3 billion of secondary products. Miscellaneous transactions accounted for $319 million. These figures yielded a specialization ratio of 79 percent, an increase from the 77 percent specialization ratio recorded in 1982.

The largest and most rapidly growing segment within the industry consisted of ready-to-eat (RTE) cereals. By the end of the 1980s, the RTE market was estimated at $4.8 billion. By 1992, industry analysts valued it at $7.3 billion.

A much smaller segment, hot cereals, experienced virtually no growth between 1982 and 1987. In 1988, however, the hot cereal market garnered sales of $600 million, a 20 percent increase over figures for the previous year. The sudden surge was attributed to a national focus on the reported health benefits of oat bran.

Much of the growth within the ready-to-eat cereal segment during the later part of the 1980s was attributed to interest in oat bran. Products specifically labeled "oat bran" were valued at $34.9 million in 1987, $105.2 million in 1988, and $328.2 million in 1989. Oat bran's popularity, however, was short-lived. A study published in the *New England Journal of Medicine* debunked advertising claims that oat bran possessed the ability to lower cholesterol levels. The study led to consumer skepticism and a downturn in the success of new products based on key ingredients. In 1990 ready-to-eat cereal sales increased only 0.2 percent.

Another ingredient to suffer from health controversies was psyllium. Psyllium, a grain grown mainly in India, was said to help reduce cholesterol and thereby reduce risks of heart disease. A study done by the University of Minnesota, reporting a 9 percent reduction in cholesterol levels among people who ate a cereal containing psyllium, was used to document the claims. Subsequently, General Mills incorporated it in "Benefit" and Kellogg used it in "Heartwise."

The Food and Drug Administration (FDA) had previously approved psyllium for use as a laxative, but its use as a food had not been certified. The FDA expressed concern that it could result in damaging health consequences to the intestinal tract such as constipation, fecal impaction, depletion of necessary colon bacteria, and shifts in the body's ability to absorb nutrients. Allergic reaction posed another problem related to psyllium use. Consequently, General Mills discontinued Benefit in January 1990, and Kellogg encountered problems with regulatory challenges to its advertising. Six states—Iowa, California, Florida, Minnesota, Texas, and Wisconsin— brought suit against the company regarding the health benefit claims for Heartwise and other products including

Special K, 40+; Bran Flakes, and Frosted Flakes. In addition, Texas banned Heartwise. The suits were settled in 1991 when Kellogg agreed to pay each of the six states $30,000 to use for consumer or nutritional education and changed the name from "Heartwise" to "Fiberwise."

The 1990s were notable for shifts in traditionally held markets. Kellogg's Frosted Flakes had lost its top position to General Mills' Cheerios, and the cereal giant's previous 40 percent market share slipped to 32 percent in 1998. At the same time, General Mills' market share increased to 31.4 percent. *Fortune* magazine estimated each percentage point was worth about $75 million dollars per year.

In addition, many of the country's major cereal manufacturers faced problems because of changing patterns regarding brand loyalty. Customers preferred purchasing a variety of cereals rather than one favorite. Another challenge was the growing percentage of market share being captured by private labels marketed by a supermarket or grocer. Private labels accounted for 7.8 percent of the ready-to-eat cereal market.

Another change noted during the early 1990s was a shift away from products promoted solely on the basis of health benefits. Although consumers continued to look at nutritional content, other factors such as taste, variety, convenience, and price were also important. The "all-family" cereal segment held almost half of the ready-to-eat market. All-family cereals were not as sweet as children's cereals but had more sugar than traditional adult cereals. Examples included General Mills' Wheaties Honey Gold and Kellogg's Frosted Bran.

The snack market, which was estimated to be more than three times larger than the ready-to-eat cereal market, represented an emerging growth area for cereal makers. Following the U.S. Department of Agriculture's (USDA) release of its recommendation that Americans eat 6-11 servings of grain per day, cereal makers began promotions touting their products as tasty treats with positive health benefits. An estimated 7 percent of ready-to-eat cereals were consumed as snacks throughout the day. For example, Cheerios was promoted as a snack for toddlers, and an estimated one-third of all Chex cereal was purchased for use as an ingredient in snack mixes rather than for breakfast consumption. Two new products aimed directly at the snack market were Kellogg's Rice Krispies Treats and General Mills' Fingos.

CURRENT CONDITIONS

Although cereal sales grew by 7 percent a year throughout the 1980s, growth came largely from price hikes. A price war erupted in the U.S. breakfast cereal market in 1996 following a long period of high cereal prices. According to *The Financial Times,* analysts said that producers had been greedy and continued to raise prices in the belief that their brands were so strong that consumers would pay inflated prices. When cereal prices were as high as $5 per box, consumers balked and began looking at alternatives to the brand names cereals such as the private label offered by the supermarket or bagged cereals. As a result, according to *Supermarket Business,* private cereal brand name products have seen market share grow by 60 percent since 1990, to total 7.8 percent in 1998. According to John McMillin, Prudential industry analyst, "Consumers are buying more bagged and boxed private label cereals. And alternative breakfast foods, like bagels and bakery products, clearly have had an impact on cereal sales."

At the end of the century, cereal makers were looking at new ways to market and advertise products, particularly towards adults who eat cereal in the morning, at lunch, and for snacks. New products and marketing campaigns aimed at adults seemed to pay off. New products made up for 11 percent of the $7-billion cereal market in 1997, up from 4.6 percent in 1996. Kellogg's introduced Honey Crunch Corn Flakes as the sponsor of a NASCAR auto race in 1996. In 1997, it was a $72-million brand with a 1 percent market share, which is respectable for a new brand. Kellogg's also promoted their cereal by partnering with Microsoft to offer software for both kids and adults. General Mills' Cinnamon Grahams and Old Navy paired up to offer coupons for Old Navy on the back of the cereal boxes and featured Cinnamon Grahams in Old Navy stores. "The old way of launching a new product, through promotions and coupons, is not sufficient anymore," noted Debbie Scott, a marketing manager for General Mills. Patrick Schumann, a food industry analyst for Edward Jones Investments in St. Louis, said "the ready-to-eat cereal segment in the United States is going to remain very challenging in 1999 and into 2000."

INDUSTRY LEADERS

Kellogg Company was the leader among national cereal makers with 1998 sales revenue of $6.8 billion. Established in 1906, Kellogg Company was the world's market leader in ready-to-eat cereals throughout most of the twentieth century. In 1998, Kellogg had 45 percent of the world market share for cereal. Canada, the United Kingdom, and Australia represented Kellogg's three largest overseas markets. Kellogg's cereals hold eight of the top ten spots on the "Top Cereal Brands in Great Britain," based on sales, according to *Business Rankings Annual 1999.*

A few well-known Kellogg products were Corn Flakes, Frosted Mini-Wheats, Corn Pops, and Fruit Loops. In addition to its ready-to-eat cereal division, Kellogg also operated Mrs. Smith's Frozen Foods. The Mrs. Smith's division manufactured Eggo waffles and frozen pies. In 1996 Kellogg purchased Lenders Bagels

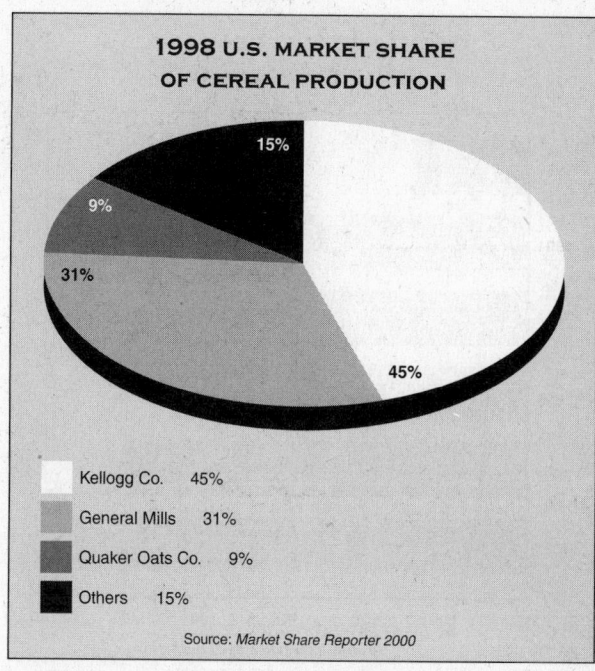

1998 U.S. MARKET SHARE OF CEREAL PRODUCTION

- 15%
- 9%
- 31%
- 45%

Kellogg Co.   45%

General Mills   31%

Quaker Oats Co.   9%

Others   15%

Source: *Market Share Reporter 2000*

for $466 million, from Kraft Foods Inc. However, Kellogg's sold the underperforming line to Aurora Foods Inc. in September 1999 for $275 million. Attempting to appeal to changing consumer tastes, Kellogg's launched the K-Sentials line in 1999 and Snack-a-longs, a "carry pack that includes a package of either Fruit Loops or Corn Pops, a sip-carton of Minute Maid fruit punch, a Nutri-Grain bar, a napkin, and a finger puppet." Originally, Snack-a-longs were positioned in the breakfast aisle near the cereals, but it did not sell very well. According to *Progressive Grocer,* Kellogg's found through test marketing that "most people were buying Snack-a-longs for a snack after breakfast. When Kellogg's moved the product into the deli section, sales took off."

In April 1999 Kellogg's announced that its first quarter profits fell 30 percent as a result of spending more on product development and advertising. Soon after this announcement, Arnold Langbo was replaced by Carlos Gutierrez as the new CEO.

General Mills, with 1998 sales revenue of $5.6 billion, was the second largest cereal manufacturer, closing in on Kellogg's heels with 31.4 percent of the market share. Big G cereals included flaked products such as Total, Raisin Bran, and Country Corn Flakes; the company's puffed varieties included Kix, Trix, and Cocoa Puffs. In May 1999 General Mills introduced Sunrise, the first-ever certified organic cereal from a major manufacturer. Its consumer foods division included its line of Big G cereals, Gold Medal Flour, Betty Crocker mixes, and Hamburger Helper. Outside its consumer foods division, the company also owned the Red Lobster and Olive Garden Restaurants. The restaurants accounted for approximately one-third of General Mills' total revenues.

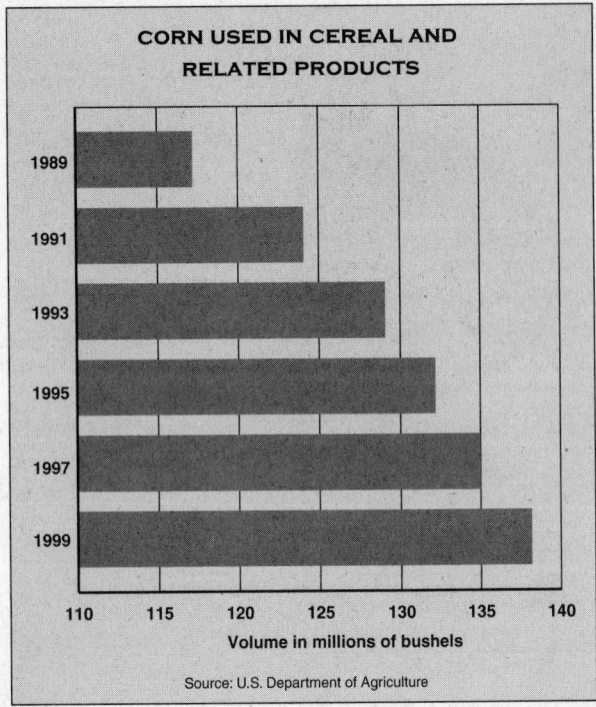

CORN USED IN CEREAL AND RELATED PRODUCTS

Volume in millions of bushels

Source: U.S. Department of Agriculture

Another leading cereal maker, ranked third with $4.8 billion in 1998 sales revenues, was the Quaker Oats Company. The company's first puffed product, "Puffed Rice," was introduced in 1905. In 1992, Quaker Oats held an 8.9 percent share of the ready-to-eat cereal market, and its principal product was Cap'n Crunch. Within the smaller hot cereal segment, however, the company held approximately 60 percent of the market. In addition to cereal products, Quaker Oats produced Aunt Jemima Pancake mix and Gatorade sports drinks.

AMERICA AND THE WORLD

Kellogg was the first American company to enter the foreign market for ready-to-eat cereals. In 1914 the company began distribution in Ontario, Canada, and ten years later the company began operations in Australia. Kellogg opened its first plant in England in 1938 and began operations on the European continent in the 1950s. By the early 1990s, Kellogg distributed its products to 150 nations and in some of these markets held a market share as large as 80 percent.

English-speaking nations represented the largest cereal markets. Consumption in non-English markets was estimated at only one-fourth the amount consumed by English speakers. For example, during the early 1990s per capita consumption of ready-to-eat cereal in England was 13.3 pounds per person, but in France it was only 1.8 pounds. On the European continent, consumption averaged 3.0 pounds per year. Shifting attention away from traditional breakfasts and focusing interest on low-cholesterol, convenient snack alternatives, cereal makers

viewed low per capita consumption areas as potential growth fields. In Spain sales were growing at a rate of 20 percent per year; in Portugal they were growing at an annual rate of 50 percent. Some industry forecasters estimated that by the year 2000 the European cereal market would experience more than a four-fold increase and reach $6.5 billion.

General Mills was also active in expanding overseas operations. In Europe General Mills and Nestle formed a joint venture called Cereal Partners Worldwide (CPW). In 1992, CPW claimed a 15 percent share of the United Kingdom market and planned an aggressive expansion campaign on the European continent. CPW also planned to enter the Mexican market and expand into Malaysia, Thailand, Philippines, Singapore, Indonesia, and Brunei.

FURTHER READING

Benezra, Karen. "Cereal Giants Call Truce in Price War that Failed to Appetize." *Campaign,* 26 September 1997.

Brooklyn Public Library. *Business Rankings Annual 1999.* Farmington Hills, MI: Gale Group, 1999.

Canedy, Dana. "Is the Box Half-Full or Half-Empty? Top Cereal Maker Fights to Retain Eroding Share." *New York Times,* 28 November 1999.

———. "Can Kellogg Break Out of the Box?" *New York Times,* 24 January 1999.

Dwyer, Steve. "Breakfast Choices Rise & Shine." *Prepared Foods,* February 1999.

Hawn, Carleen. "General Mills Tests the Limits." *Forbes,* 6 April 1998.

Janoff, Barry. "Bowling for Dollars." *Progressive Grocer,* July 1999.

Kelley, B.G. "Breakfast Foods." *Supermarket Business,* September 1998.

"Kellogg to Sell Bagel Unit to Aurora for $275 Million." *New York Times,* 28 September 1999.

Kelly, Jane. "It's a Whole New Bowl Game." *Grocer,* 14 February 1998.

Lach, Jennifer. "What's For Breakfast?" *American Demographics,* May 1999.

Miller, James P. "Kellogg Earnings, Excluding Items, Decline by 41 Percent." *Wall Street Journal,* 1 February 1999.

Neuborne, Ellen. "Mmm! Cereal for Dinner." *Business Week,* 24 November 1997.

"Not Just For Breakfast." *ID: The Voice of Foodservice Distribution,* 15 May 1995.

Thompson, Stephanie. "Breakfast Rush." *Brandweek,* 27 January 1997.

Turcsik, Richard. "Breakfast Cereal Sales are Gaining Crisply, Powered by More Vitamins, More Fiber and Heartfelt Ad Campaigns." *Supermarket News,* 15 May 1998.

"U.S. Cereal Producers-1998." *Market Share Reporter 2000.* Farmington Hills, MI: Gale Group, 1999.

SIC 2044

RICE MILLING

This industry comprises establishments that clean, polish, or process rice. Principal products include rice flour, rice meal, white rice, brown rice, and rice bran. The growing of rice is discussed under **SIC 0112: Rice.**

NAICS CODE(S)

311212 (Rice Milling)

One of the smaller segments of U.S. grain milling, rice milling was worth $1.723 billion in 1995, according to the U.S. Census Bureau, a 6 percent drop from the previous year. Industry sales were expected to recover slowly to the $1.8 billion level between 1996 and 1998. In 1997, the value of shipments was reported at nearly $2.4 billion. At 5.8 million metric tons, the United States produced just 1.7 percent of the world's milled rice in 1995, however its 2.9 million tons of exports commanded an 18 percent share of world exports for the same year. Because rice growing is concentrated heavily in the southern and western United States, most of the U.S. rice mills operate in these regions. In 1997 of the 68 industry establishments, 14 were in Arkansas and 9 were in Texas. Actually, six states produce 99 percent of all rice grown in the United States: Arkansas, California, Louisiana, Mississippi, Missouri, and Texas.

At an average of 26.29 pounds per person in 1999, U.S. per capita rice consumption has nearly tripled since 1970. The USA Rice Federation estimated that more than 90 percent of this consumption was domestic rice. Increases reflect the product's nutritional merits, low cost, and consumer appeal. Marketed as a healthy food, rice contains only trace amounts of fat and naturally provides protein, thiamin, riboflavin, niacin, phosphorous, iron, and potassium. It is also cholesterol free, gluten free, and low in sodium.

Rice grows to maturity in 100 to 120 days. When rice is harvested, it is first dried for stable storage and then sold to a rice mill. At this stage, the rice is referred to as "paddy" or "rough" rice. Using high-tech machinery, millers shell the rice by removing the inedible hull surrounding each individual grain. Beneath the hull, rice grains still possess seven natural bran layers. In this state, the rice is sold as brown rice, or "polished" to remove the bran and produce white rice kernels. Discarded bran may be used to extract oils or as a food ingredient.

Because polishing rice removes some of the grain's natural ingredients, some millers employ a procedure called "parboiling" to ameliorate nutrient losses. Parboiled rice is soaked in pressurized water, steamed, and dried before milling. In addition to helping grains preserve their nutrients, parboiling helps produce grains that fluff better and are less sticky when cooked. Parboiled grains, however, take longer to cook.

Other rice mill products include brewers rice, enriched rice, and precooked rice. Brewers rice is made of small, broken rice fragments leftover after shelling and polishing and is primarily used by pet food manufacturers and brewers. Enriched rice contains artificially replaced nutrients. Precooked rice is cooked and dehydrated after it is milled.

Direct food use rice accounted for more than 50 percent of all rice sold in the United States. According to the USA Rice Federation, direct food use (grocery, food service, and warehouse clubs) each saw increases in 1999 as compared to 1998—56.8 percent (increase of 3.5 percent); 37.5 percent (increase of 4.6 percent) and 4.9 percent (increase of 28.6 percent), respectively.

The industry is dominated by Riceland Foods, Inc., of Stuttgart, Arkansas. Riceland is the largest rice miller and marketer in the world. In 1998 the company reported sales of nearly $804 million and employed 1,850 people. Riviana Foods, with 1999 sales of $462 million and 2,767 employees, was the top U.S. seller of rice, according to *Hoover's Company Profiles.* Another large U.S. miller was American Rice, Inc. The company emerged from bankruptcy in late 1999.

On February 18, 2000, the U.S. Department of Agriculture (USDA) informed the USA Rice Federation that they would allocate rice for the first time in the Section 416(b) food aid program. This news was significant for U.S. rice producers and millers since it increased exports by more than 150,000 metric tons after a year of record supply.

FURTHER READING

Riceland Foods, Inc. "About Riceland." Stuttgart, AR: 1996.

U.S. Census Bureau. "Manufacturing-Industry Series." *1997 Economic Census.* Washington, D.C.: GPO, 15 November 1999.

———. "Value of Product Shipments." *1996 Annual Survey of Manufactures.* Washington, D.C.: GPO, 1998.

USA Rice Federation. *About USA Rice.* Washington: 1996. Available from http://www.usarice.com/rice.html.

———. "Rice Consumption in the United States at a Record High," 21 January 1999.

———. "Increased Food Aid Benefits Entire U.S. Rice Industry," 18 February 2000.

SIC 2045

PREPARED FLOUR MIXES AND DOUGHS

This industry classification comprises establishments primarily involved in manufacturing prepared mixes and doughs from purchased flours. Establishments primarily involved in milling flour from grain and manufacturing grain mill products, including prepared mixes and doughs, are classified in **SIC 2041: Flour and Other Grain Mill Products.**

NAICS CODE(S)

311822 (Flour Mixes and Dough Manufacturing from Purchased Flour)

In 1995 establishments classified in this industry shipped products totaling $4.8 billion. This represented a 17 percent increase over the $4.1 billion total for 1994, and a 23 percent increase over 1992 figures. Total costs of material for the industry amounted to $2.0 billion in 1992, but by 1994, this had risen to $2.2 billion, an increase of 8 percent, and in 1995 the costs were at $2.4 billion, an increase of 20 percent over the 1992 figure.

The value of product shipments was $4.8 billion in 1997, with cake and cookie mixes accounting for the majority. The cost of materials reached $2.4 billion in 1997. Three of the leading companies were Dean Food Products, Inc.; Cereal Food Processors, Inc.; and Continental Mills Inc.

The concept of commercial mixes first developed when millers began adding a leavening agent and salt to flour products to make "self-rising" formulations. Self-rising flours became popular in the southeastern portion of the United States because traditional leavening agents, such as baking powder, had limited shelf life in hot, humid climates.

The development of a stable shortening led to the introduction of the nation's first biscuit mix in the 1920s. Cake mixes tentatively appeared during the 1930s after the industry learned how to dehydrate eggs. Because mixes were convenience products rather than necessities, further commercial development was hampered by the economic hardships and product shortages associated with the Depression and World War II. Following World War II, however, the country embraced convenience. Cake mixes reappeared and began to find increasing popularity not only with homemakers but also among restaurants and institutional users.

During the early 1990s, mixes continued to enjoy widespread popularity. Many bakers preferred mixes to traditional "from scratch" recipes because in addition to offering convenience, they provided consistently favorable results, even for inexperienced cooks. Prepared mixes were available for a wide variety of products including breads, rolls, cakes, cookies, and pancakes. Mixes were generally one of two kinds. One type required only the addition of a specified amount of liquid. Another type required the addition of other ingredients such as eggs and shortening.

According to a report published by *Institutional Distribution,* the best selling cake mixes to food service establishments were chocolate, white, devil's food, spice, and pound cakes. In addition, carrot, crumb, gingerbread, lemon, sponge, angel food, applesauce, banana, and brownie mixes were also popular.

According to government statistics, this industry employed 15,100 workers in 1995, a 25 percent increase over 1987 figures; approximately 15,400 people were employed in 1997. The leading states in employment in 1987 were Illinois, Tennessee, Indiana, and Missouri. By the mid-1990s, California displaced Indiana. In 1997 Georgia, Illinois, and Missouri employed the greatest number of workers.

FURTHER READING

From Wheat to Flour. Washington: Wheat Flour Institute, 1981.

U.S. Census Bureau. "Manufacturing-Industry Series." *1997 Economic Census.* Washington, D.C.: GPO, 15 November 1999.

SIC 2046

WET CORN MILLING

This industry comprises establishments primarily engaged in milling corn or sorghum grain (milo) by the wet process, and producing starch, syrup, oil, sugar, and by-products, such as gluten feed and meal. Also included in this industry are establishments primarily engaged in manufacturing starch from other vegetable sources, such as potatoes and wheat. Establishments primarily engaged in manufacturing table syrups from corn syrup and other ingredients and those manufacturing starch base dessert powders, are classified in **SIC 2099: Food Preparations, Not Elsewhere Classified.**

NAICS CODE(S)

311221 (Wet Corn Milling)

Also known as corn refining, wet corn milling in the United States grew by more than 50 percent from 1987 to 1995, expanding shipments from $4.8 billion in 1987 to $7.5 billion in 1995. Performance in 1995 showed a 17 percent increase in value over shipments in 1992, when the industry totaled $6.4 billion in shipments. Growth in the 1990s was not steady, however, with 1993 actually showing a decrease of 3.8 percent in the value of wet corn milling shipments from 1992. Shipment values were expected to continue to rise in the late 1990s; it was nearly $8.5 billion in 1997.

The industry processed an estimated 1.5 billion bushels of corn in 1996, or roughly 20 percent of the U.S. corn crop in that year. In 1998 the United States produced 1.7 billion bushels of corn; this was a decrease from 1995's 2.2 billion bushels.

Use of the corn kernel differs by product. Corn starch is used in a variety of industries, including food products, paper, adhesives, textiles, and pharmaceuticals. Starch can also be converted to ethanol. Wet corn millers advocated using ethanol as part of an overall national energy policy. Between 1981 and 1991 drivers around the world traveled almost one trillion miles on fuels made with ethanol blends. Also produced from starch, corn sweeteners—corn syrup, dextrose, and high fructose corn syrup (HFCS)—accounted for more than 55 percent of U.S. sweetener consumption in the late 1990s, according to the Corn Refiners Association. An estimated 400 million bushels of corn were used annually to make HFCS, which since 1980 has been the sweetener of choice for the major U.S. soft drink manufacturers.

Germ is the portion of the kernel from which a seed would sprout. The germ contains oils used to make margarine, mayonnaise, salad dressings, and shortening. Other portions of the corn kernel are made up of protein and are used to produce corn gluten feed and corn gluten meal for animals and poultry.

According to the U.S. Census Bureau, the industry's product share in 1995 was divided among corn sweeteners, which accounted for 48.7 percent of industry shipments by value, followed by wet process corn by-products at 19.9 percent, manufactured starch at 18.6 percent, corn oil at 12.5 percent, and miscellaneous products at 0.3 percent. In 1997 corn sweeteners and manufactured starch were the most profitable industry segments.

Approximately 58 establishments were in the industry in the mid-1990s. Such multibillion dollar agribusiness concerns as Archer Daniels Midland Company (ADM) of Decatur, Illinois; Cargill, Incorporated of Minneapolis, Minnesota; and Corn Products International Inc. of Bedford Park, Illinois, were among the leading producers. ADM, which operated four wet corn milling facilities, employed 23,603 workers and generated sales of $14.3 billion in 1999. Cargill, Inc., the largest privately owned company in the United States, employed more than 84,000 people worldwide and topped $50.0 billion in sales in 1999. Corn Products International posted sales of $1.7 billion in 1999, approximately 15 percent of

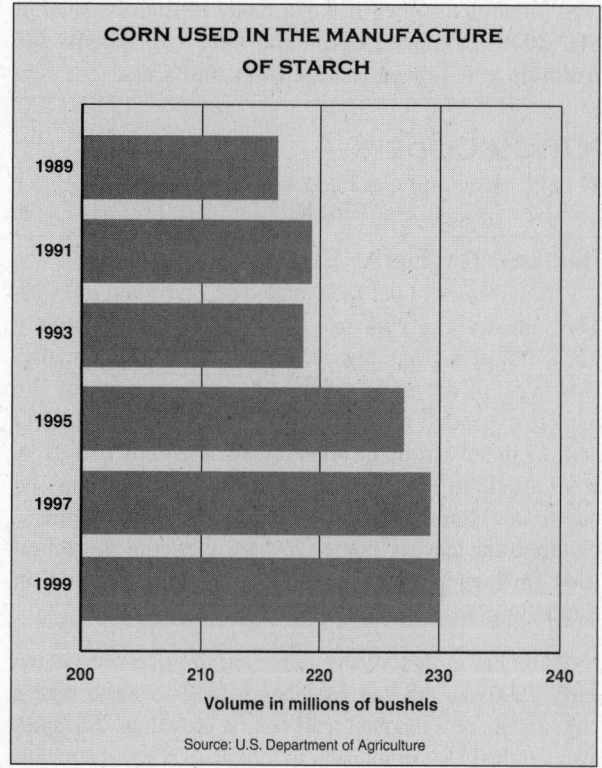

CORN USED IN THE MANUFACTURE OF STARCH

Volume in millions of bushels

Source: U.S. Department of Agriculture

which was attributed to its corn refining business. Corn Products is a spinoff of CPC International.

Employment fluctuated considerably during the 1980s and 1990s, varying from a low of 8,300 in 1989 to a high of 9,700 in 1991. The industry's workforce was 9,217 people in 1997, with Iowa, Illinois, and Indiana providing more than 70 percent of the industry's labor.

FURTHER READING

Corn Refiners Association. *Welcome to the Corn Refiners Association, Inc. Home Page,* 1997. Available from http://www.corn.org.

U.S. Census Bureau. "Manufacturing-Industry Series." *1997 Economic Census.* Washington, D.C.: GPO, 27 November 1999.

U.S. Department of Agriculture. National Agricultural Statistics Service. *Statistical Highlights 1998-1999: Farm Economics,* 2000. Available from http://www.usda.gov/nass.

SIC 2047

DOG AND CAT FOOD

This industry consists of establishments primarily engaged in manufacturing dog and cat food from cereal, meat, and other ingredients. These preparations may be canned, frozen, or dry. Establishments manufacturing feed for animals other than dogs and cats are classified in **SIC 2048: Prepared Feeds and Feed Ingredients for Animals and Fowls, Except Dogs and Cats.**

NAICS CODE(S)

311111 (Dog and Cat Food Manufacturing)

INDUSTRY SNAPSHOT

Retail sales of pet food totaled $11.2 billion in 1999. The industry's growth rate in the 1980s was relatively flat, with an average growth of 1 or 2 percent annually. However, in the mid- to late 1990s, the growth of the market expanded approximately 4 percent, with growth coming mainly from the premium and specialty brands. A 1999 article in *Progressive Grocer* suggests this may be due to the booming economy and that as baby boomers' children are leaving home they are spending more lavishly on their pets. In 1998 cat food sales were up an astounding 8.8 percent.

The flat growth of the 1980s led to price wars in the early 1990s as the various manufacturers vied to take a larger share of a stagnant market. Flat growth in U.S. sales also led the U.S. pet industry to look to exports as a means of expanding the market. At the same time, the Pet Food Institute—the association to which 95 percent of all U.S. pet food manufacturers belong—tried to expand the number of U.S. pet owners by targeting groups not usually associated with pet ownership, such as singles. Their success in increasing ownership was primarily through promoting cat ownership since cats need less attention and are more adaptable to the lifestyle of the single person.

Another 1990s effort to overcome flat sales was the development of "upscale" healthy and gourmet pet food products. This paralleled a similar trend in the larger food industry. Established specialists in this area of the pet food market benefited greatly. By the end of the decade, grocery stores, which were losing sales to superstores such as Petco and PETsMART, began to compete in the specialty food market and redesigned their pet food aisles to include a wider variety of specialty items from cat snacks and party packs to grooming other supplies. Sales growth in pet supplies ranges between 4 to 15 percent, far surpassing the growth in food sales. The industry also continued to advertise heavily on television, spending 126 million on network television advertisements in 1997.

Beginning in the mid-1990s, pet owners began following the general food trend toward healthy diets, leaving behind traditional pet foods for those with more protein and fewer chemical additives and preservatives. According to *Supermarket Business* the largest growth in the pet food market was in the super-premium brand segment. These often were veterinarian recommended diets focusing on the needs of older or overweight pets.

ORGANIZATION AND STRUCTURE

The dog and cat food segment of the pet food industry comprises primarily two types of firms. One is the large, general manufacturer producing a variety of dog and cat foods along with other types of feed and/or food for humans in other divisions or subsidiaries. These manufacturers sell their products primarily through grocery stores. The other type is the specialty firm that exclusively produces pet food, which is usually health-related or other specialized type. Traditionally, the general firms sell their product in grocery stores while the specialty firms sell their products through veterinary offices or specialty stores.

The pet food industry is subject to regulation at the federal and state levels. In 1958 the manufacturers of pet food formed the Pet Food Institute (PFI), a national trade association. PFI acts as a spokesman for the industry before the various regulatory agencies and bodies, sponsors research, represents the U.S. industry in international meetings, and works on uniform standards for pet food. PFI worked with the American Association of Feed Control Officials (AAFCO) to develop a uniform law on pet food standards that states may use as a model whenever they consider changes to their laws and regulations on the topic. Each state has its own set of laws and regulations that apply to pet food.

Regulation of the Pet Food Industry. At the federal level, pet food labeling and advertising claims are regulated by the Food and Drug Administration (FDA), the Federal Trade Commission (FTC), and the Department of Agriculture. All pet food plants are subject to FDA inspection, and many of the FDA's canned food regulations apply to pet foods. Many manufacturers produce and/or sell products in more than one state, which means their product and its labels much also meet each state's regulations. In August 1996, the AAFCO passed new regulations, which went into effect in January 1998. These regulations govern the use of the terms "lite" and "less fat" on the U.S. pet foods' labels. In January 2000 the AAFCO published rules regulating the use of the label "Animal feeding tests using AAFCO procedures substantiate that [the product] provides complete and balanced nutrition for all life stages." Before 2000, this label could be used on products that had not been tested but were in the same family of products. The new regulations more strictly and narrowly define the term "family;" producers have until 2005 to comply.

Sales Outlets/Product Distribution. Dog and cat food has traditionally been sold in grocery stores, pet stores, and by veterinarians. Veterinarian sales are especially prevalent for those brands that are marketed as a health specialty. Health consciousness for pets paralleled the general trend toward health consciousness for humans in recent years. This movement led to increased attention to labeling and awareness of obesity in pets and the development of more specialized pet foods, with greater emphasis on health in the marketing of the product. Grocery stores, however, still remained the largest outlet for sales of pet food.

In the 1980s and early 1990s, the advent of the discount retailer as a major economic force in America began to change that trend. The biggest loser was the grocery store. The interest in health foods allowed those brands traditionally marketed through veterinarians and breeders to retain market share while the share of the grocery store fell to the discount chain. According to a 1999 article in *Progressive Grocer,* supermarket chains saw their share of the total pet food market fall to 50 percent. Efforts to stem the flow with cheaper, in-house brands had only moderate success since people continued to prefer national brands, but they wanted them at a lower price. Grocery stores began to market more premium brands and expand their pet offerings in an effort to lure pet owners back to their shelves.

The downward trend in supermarket sales was also due to the proliferation of pet megastores such as PETsMART and Petco, which sell premium brands at discount prices, undercutting supermarkets by 10 to 30 percent. By the end of the 1990s, online Internet shops such as Pets.com and Petopia.com had also entered the market but had yet to show a profit.

BACKGROUND AND DEVELOPMENT

The first commercially prepared dog food was a biscuit product introduced in England in about 1860, according to the Pet Food Institute. Dry dog foods were subsequently developed with formulas based on the nutritional knowledge of the day. After World War I, canned horse meat for dog food was introduced into the United States. In the late 1920s, the first commercial pet food diet was developed by the Ralston Purina Company. In the 1930s canned cat food and dry meat meal dog foods came into use. These were succeeded by dry expanded type pet foods, which came onto the market during the 1950s. The 1960s, notes the Institute, "were marked with great diversification in the types of food available to the pet owner including dry cat food, many more varieties of canned products, and new soft-moist products. With the growth of the industry has come a greatly expanded use of by-products from the meat, poultry, and seafood processing industry. Approximately 1.1 million tons of these by-products are now used annually in pet foods."

According to *Prepared Foods* there were 121 new pet food product introductions in 1996 versus 174 in 1995, including flavors such as salmon filets and pate. New specialty products included "Wheat Grass for Cats" to help with their digestive tracts, and fancy dog treats such as "Canine Cookies". In general new products offered each year total more than 100, with 105 new products offered in 1998, and an astounding 251 new pet food products introduced in 1997.

CURRENT CONDITIONS

In 1999, the pet market continued to experience growth, with retail pet food sales of more than $11 billion, up from $10.6 billion in 1998. The number of dogs in the United States in 1999 was 58.2 million, representing 37.9 percent of U.S. households, and cats numbered 72 million, representing 34.5 percent of U.S. households. Cat ownership is increasing faster than dog ownership, and the majority of the growth in the food market is in the specialty food category.

INDUSTRY LEADERS

Leading companies involved in the manufacture of dog and cat food in the United States include the Ralston Purina Company of St. Louis, with 1999 sales of $4.7 billion and brand names such as Cat Chow and Meow Mix; Nestle USA, Inc., a subsidiary of Nestle S.A., which had 1999 international sales of more than $5.2 billion and brand names of Friskies, Alpo, Fancy Feast, and Mighty Dog; H.J. Heinz Company of Pittsburgh, with 1998 sales of $9.3 billion, and brand names such as 9 Lives, Ken-L-Ration, and Gravy Train; and Mars, Inc. with 1998 sales of more than $1.5 billion and brand names of Kal Kan, Pedigree, Sheba, and Whiskas. Specialty stores such as PETsMART and Petco also held significant market shares. Pet superstores accounted for 15 percent of pet food sales.

According to *Supermarket Business,* in 1999 canned cat food sales were led by Heinz's 9 Lives, with $188.7 million in sales, while the leading brand of canned dog food was Nestle's Prime Cuts, with sales of $118.8 million. The leading semi-moist dog food that year were private labels, with $24.3 million in sales, while the leading semi-moist cat food was Ralston Purina's Happy Cat brand, with $8.1 million in sales. Kal Kan Pedigree Mealtime led in the dry dog food category with $331.3 million in sales, and Purina Cat Chow led the dry cat food category with $133.7 million in sales.

AMERICA AND THE WORLD

According to *Pet Food Industry,* the United States has managed to maintain a favorable trade balance in the pet food industry. Exports amounted to $821 million in 1998, while imports were at $184 million, according to the United Nations Food and Agriculture Organization. Canada, Japan, and the European Community are the three biggest markets for U.S. dog and cat food product exports.

FURTHER READING
Brooker, Katrina. "Amazon vs. Everybody." *Fortune,* 8 November 1999.

Brumback, Nancy. "Bark Gets Louder." *Progressive Grocer.* October 1999.

Campbell, Lisa. "P&G Acquisition Heralds International Pet Project." *Campaign,* 1 October 1999.

Dauber, Don. "Shake-up in Pet Food Industry Belts Petco Stock." *San Diego Union-Tribune,* 12 August 1999.

Health Benefits Included. *Prepared Foods,* April 1999.

McLuhan, Robert. "Whiskas Ad Offers a Whole New Perspective on Cat Food." *Marketing,* 22 July 1999.

People Pleasin' Pet Food. *Prepared Foods,* 15 April 1997.

"The Pet Food Report." *Pet Food Industry,* September 1999.

A Welcome Pet-Food Labeling Change. *Consumer Reports,* November 1998.

Wellman, David. "Fighting Like Cats and Dogs." *Supermarket Business,* November 1998.

SIC 2048

PREPARED FEEDS AND FEED INGREDIENTS FOR ANIMALS AND FOWLS, EXCEPT DOGS AND CATS

This classification covers establishments primarily engaged in manufacturing prepared feeds, feed ingredients, and adjuncts for animals and fowls, except dogs and cats. Included in this industry are poultry and livestock feed and feed ingredients such as alfalfa meal, feed supplements, and feed concentrates and pre-mixes. Also included are establishments primarily engaged in slaughtering animals for animal feed. Establishments primarily engaged in slaughtering animals for human consumption are classified in **SIC 2011: Meat Packing Plants, SIC 2013: Sausages and Other Prepared Meat Products,** and **SIC 2015: Poultry Slaughtering and Processing.** Establishments primarily engaged in manufacturing cat and dog foods are classified in **SIC 2047: Dog and Cat Food.**

NAICS CODE(S)

311611 (Animal (except Poultry) Slaughtering)
311119 (Other Animal Food Manufacturing)

INDUSTRY SNAPSHOT

Feed is by far the largest input cost of producing food and fiber of animal origin, exceeding even the initial cost of the animals themselves. The cost of feed represents 50 to 70 percent of the cost of producing meat, milk, and eggs at the farm level. For instance, the United States Department of Agriculture (USDA) calculates that it requires 88 pounds of feed to produce 100 pounds of milk; 9,523 pounds of feed to produce a steer; 1,273 pounds to produce a lamb; 50 pounds of feed for 100 eggs; 261 pounds of feed to produce 100 pounds of poultry; and 629 pounds of feed for 100 pounds of pork. In the case of grass-eating livestock such as cattle and sheep, a great deal of their nutrition may come from foraging pasture land, but the latter stages of their lives often require significant portions of prepared feeds. With poultry and hogs, however, nourishment is supplied primarily through prepared feed mixes.

According to the American Feed Industry Association, as much as $18 billion worth of feed ingredients are purchased each year. These products range from grain mixes to orange rinds to beet pulps. The feed industry is one of the most competitive businesses in the agricultural sector and is by far the largest purchaser of U.S. corn, feed grains, and soybean meal. Tens of thousands of farmers with feed mills on their own farms are able to compete with huge conglomerates with national distribution.

ORGANIZATION AND STRUCTURE

Owning a feed mill is a capital intensive operation. Many modern feed mills increasingly rely on computer technology; human hands rarely touch the feed ingredients. Not only can the feed mill itself be a multimillion dollar investment—with attendant costs associated with maintaining a competitive position regarding machinery—but the feed manufacturer must also have an expensive commodity inventory on hand at all times. Mill managers attempt to purchase their ingredients up front, often contracting for goods months in advance. To hedge the risks associated with fluctuating grain and commodity prices, many feed manufacturers utilize the option of futures trading. Most feed manufacturers also have a sizable investment in a truck fleet used to deliver bulk feed to dairies, poultry, and swine operations. Virtually all cattle feedlots in the United States, however, prepare their feed on the premises in bulk form. Many poultry processing companies own their own feed mills and sell the feed to contracting poultry producers who in turn sell their broilers back to the processor.

Retail outlets often will carry only one brand of feed. In return, the feed companies do extensive advertising in the rural press, usually on a regional basis. Another important aspect of the feed industry is the production of sacked feed, which is sold through farm supply stores and feed dealers. This feed is often used for 4-H and Future Farmers of America projects, backyard poultry projects, and for feeding horses and small animals like rabbits and guinea pigs. Although the sacked feed sold in farm supply stores is prepared in the same manner as the feed delivered in bulk form, it is more expensive because of the extra packaging.

Nutritional Experts. More than 150 micro- and macro-ingredients are covered in a guide prepared by the Nutrition Council, which has become the authoritative source for the feed industry. Nutritionists are commonly employed in the feed manufacturing industry to determine the needs of domestic livestock. Animal nutritionists rely heavily on university research and industry publications for information on the chemical properties of various feed ingredients and their use and availability.

The role of the nutritionist is to calculate a ration that fits the nutritional requirements for the least cost. This is known as a "least-cost ration," and is the ultimate goal of all livestock nutritionists. There are thousands of professional nutritionists working for livestock feed suppliers, poultry feed manufacturers, feedlots, and poultry raising operations who spend a great deal of their time determining the needs of each animal during different phases of its productive life cycle. Nutritionists use the most sophisticated computer hardware and software to make these calculations on a daily basis. Nutritionists either are employed in-house or work as consultants.

The job of the feed manufacturer is to buy the commodities and blend them in the feed mill according to the specifications outlined by the nutritionist. There is little room for error because, if the ration is not apportioned correctly, lowered animal production and diminished outward appearance can occur.

Associations. The 1992 merger between the National Feed Ingredients Association (NFIA) and the American Feed Industry Association (AFIA) under the AFIA name brought the entire feed industry under representation by a single organization for the first time since 1909. The membership of the American Feed Industry Association includes companies that manufacture feed to sell, firms that manufacture feed for their own animals, and those that provide equipment, ingredients, services and supplies to feed manufacturers. AFIA headquarters are located in Arlington, Virginia.

One of the primary goals of the AFIA is to represent the interests of the feed industry on federal legislation and regulation. The AFIA meets often with U.S. Food and Drug Administration officials to coordinate such things as mill inspections, manufacturing practices, labeling requirements, feed additives, and the administration of laws and regulations. The AFAI played a leading role in the development of the Uniform State Feed Law and other regulations mandating uniform feed labels.

CURRENT CONDITIONS

According to the USDA, one of the largest expenditures for U.S. farmers in 1998 was feed, accounting for 13.6 percent of total farm production expenditures, which reached $183.6 billion. Of the $83,987 average spent per domestic farm in 1998, about $11,439 was allotted for feed purchases. Overall feed prices dropped from 1997 to 1998, however. In 1997 feed expenditures reached $26.3 billion, while in 1998 feed costs dropped to $25.0 million.

The main ingredients used in commercially prepared feed were the feed grains, which included corn, soybeans, sorghum, oats, and barley. The USDA reported that 1999 U.S. feed grain production was forecast to reach 266 million metric tons. The number of cattle on feed increased in 1999, keeping the outlook for feed sales positive. The use of corn in the 1999-2000 marketing year rose due to growing feed usage. Sorghum and barley usage fell, but exports of sorghum were forecast to increase as a result of declining exports of corn to Mexico. In the 1990s, shipment value increased from about $1.6 billion in 1995 to about $1.7 billion in 1997. According to the delivered cost, field corn and soybean cake and meat were by far the most profitable ingredients of prepared feeds at $4.25 million.

The sale and manufacture of pre-mixes is an industry within an industry. Pre-mixes are comprised of micro-ingredients such as vitamins, minerals, chemical preservatives, antibiotics, fermentation products, and other essential ingredients that are purchased from pre-mix companies, usually in sacked form, for blending into commercial rations. Because of the availability of these products, a farmer who uses his own grain can formulate his own rations and be assured that his animals are getting the recommended levels of minerals and vitamins.

INDUSTRY LEADERS

Leading companies involved in prepared feeds production in the late 1990s included ConAgra Inc., an Omaha, Nebraska-based firm; and Cargill, Incorporated, a diversified company that was the nation's top exporter of grain. In 1998 Ralston Purina Company, based in St. Louis, Missouri, formed Agribrands International, Inc. to control its international animal feed and agricultural products division. Agribrands produced feed and other products for livestock in markets outside of the United States and had about 75 facilities operating in 16 countries. Other significant industry players included ContiGroup Companies, Inc., the world's leading cattle feeder; Cenex Harvest States Cooperative, which was primarily involved in grain trading; and Farmland Industries, Inc., the leading agricultural cooperative in the United States. Farmland was a worldwide exporter of products, such as grain. The company had 1999 sales of more than $10 billion. A proposed 1999 merger with Cenex Harvest States fell through.

FURTHER READING

Hoover's Online, 2000. Available from http://www.hoovers.com.

Leake, Linda L. "Sign of the Times." *Farm Journal*, February 2000. Available from http://www.farmjournal.com.

U.S. Department of Agriculture. "Feed Outlook." Economic Research Service, 14 December 1999. Available from http://usdamannlib.cornell.edu.

U.S. Department of Agriculture. National Agricultural Statistics Service. "Farm Production Expenditures Summary." Economic Research Service, July 1999. Available from http://usda.mannlib.cornell.edu.

SIC 2051

BREAD, CAKE, AND RELATED PRODUCTS

This industry is comprised of establishments that make fresh or frozen breads or rolls and perishable bakery products such as cakes, pies, and pastries. Manufacturers of dry bakery products such as cookies and crackers are classified in **SIC 2052: Cookies and Crackers.** Establishments involved in manufacturing frozen bakery products other than bread are classified in **SIC 2053: Frozen Bakery Products, Except Bread.** On-premises, retail bakeries are classified in **SIC 5461: Retail Bakeries.**

NAICS CODE(S)

311812 (Commercial Bakeries)

INDUSTRY SNAPSHOT

As the baked goods industry faced the new century, consolidation of regional bakeries was continuing, taking regional names national. The major players were also continuing to look for good buying opportunities to strengthen their positions in the market. As supermarkets expand their fresh bakery departments, they are feared to impose on regional bakeries' markets. The fear hadn't been realized in 1999, though, as commercially baked pies and cakes had $686 million in sales at supermarkets. Some analysts feel that continued good quality and new product introduction will allow the commercially prepared products to survive and grow.

ORGANIZATION AND STRUCTURE

Historically, the baking industry established itself close to population centers. Because bread and cake products were perishable, proximity to a customer base was a primary concern. One way growing bakeries overcame this geographic constraint was through the purchase of companies in other areas. Many acquisitions and mergers within the industry during the last decades of the twentieth century transformed baking establishments with regional shipping systems into large conglomerates with national distribution networks. In addition, large baking establishments often attracted the attention of other investors. Since 1960 many of the nation's top wholesale bakeries were purchased by food processing companies.

The practice of buying or merging with existing firms had benefits in addition to overcoming problems related to delivering fresh products to the marketplace. Buying and refurbishing existing facilities was often less expensive than building new plants. Buying also helped avoid problems associated with creating excess capacity in specific geographic areas. Despite the trend toward building large corporations, many independent family-owned bakeries remained successful. In 1987 an estimated 56.3 percent of all wholesale bread and cake plants operated with fewer than 20 employees. These small establishments, however, captured only 2.3 percent of the industry's total sales.

The baking industry was monitored and regulated by several governmental agencies. For example, the U.S. Department of Health, Education and Welfare set the definitions and standards used to identify wheat and related products. The Food and Drug Administration (FDA) regulated product quality and mandated procedures by which food additives were to be approved prior to use. And, the National Research Council's Food and Nutritional Board (along with the American Medical Association's Council on Foods and Nutrition) published guidelines for enriching bread products with nutrients.

BACKGROUND AND DEVELOPMENT

The oldest existing written record of a baked grain product dates back to about 2600 B.C. The earliest known breads were flat and were baked on smooth stones or clay plates. According to a theory held by some historians, the ancient Egyptians created the world's first leavened breads. Leavened bread was made with ingredients possessing the chemical properties necessary to make dough rise. By contrast, unleavened breads were made from doughs that did not rise.

The ability to bake leavened breads may have been developed along with the ability to brew beer, as both processes relied on fermentation. Fermentation refers to a complex chemical process in which organic compounds are broken down into simpler substances. In alcoholic fermentation, the yeast converts a mixture's sugar or starch into carbon dioxide and alcohol. Recipes with sufficient liquid produced beer-like beverages. In mixtures with less liquid, the carbon dioxide produced by the fermentation process made the dough rise.

Fermentation of wheat and water mixtures was accomplished through the incorporation of yeast. Yeast is a member of the fungus family. Although an individual "yeast" is a single-celled organism, it lives and grows by multiplying into cultures consisting of thousands of cells. In order to grow, the cells eat the sugar and starch in dough mixtures. Early yeasts were incorporated into recipes by letting doughs sit out for a period of time to ''sour.'' These wild yeast cultures, once established in a dough mixture, were carefully maintained through a process whereby some dough from each batch was saved to incorporate into the next batch. Before the development of commercial yeast, all leavened bread was made from sourdoughs. Sourdough breads are still made from flour, water, yeast, and bacteria.

Although many grains and other products could be fermented, wheat flours were the only ones to exhibit leavening. Wheat possessed a type of gluten (plant protein) unlike the gluten of other grains. Wheat gluten, when kneaded, formed an elastic structure that had the unique ability to trap the carbon dioxide given off by the yeast and to stretch and expand as more gas was created. When leavened doughs were baked, the heat killed the yeast but the dough's expanded structure remained. As a result, leavened breads were lighter and more airy than their unleavened counterparts.

The ancient Egyptians are also sometimes credited with inventing ovens. According to one theory, the first ''ovens'' were earthen pots. Early bakers discovered that when dough was placed inside preheated pots, it cooked more evenly than it did when placed on top of a heat source. The construction of permanent oven structures soon followed. Along with the development of ovens came the development of bread varieties as bakers experimented with different shapes and different ingredients. Sweet cakes first appeared in the twelfth century B.C. During the classical era, the Greeks modified oven designs and introduced the use of more innovative ingredients including milk, oil, wine, cheese, and honey.

Commercial bakeries first appeared in the Roman Empire. Under early Roman rule, baking progressed to an art form. As the Empire began to crumble, however, bakeries were taken over by the government, and commercial baking became virtually nonexistent. White flour was a luxury available only to royalty. During the Middle Ages, only monasteries and manor houses baked large quantities of leavened products. Monasteries were also credited with the development of pie crusts, an early pastry product. Although pie crusts were originally used only with meat dishes, they gained popularity for dessert items when sweetening ingredients were used. Early sweeteners in baked goods consisted of honey, raisins, and other types of dried fruits. The use of sugar was introduced during the 1500s. Innovative bakers using sugared batters and doughs developed cakes and pastries.

Commercial baking as a trade began to rise again during the urbanization that accompanied the early Industrial Revolution. Innovations of the late nineteenth and early twentieth century enabled the mass-production of baked goods. As a result, large baking facilities began to supplant small local establishments. One of the most important innovations was the development of ''tame'' yeast because these yeast cultures produced uniform, predictable results. Wild yeast cultures were too time consuming and too unpredictable to make automatic production feasible. The first yeasts used by commercial bakers were obtained from brewers and, in 1868, Charles Fleischmann made a compressed, distiller's yeast. The selective breeding of pure yeast cultures began in 1883 and, by the early 1900s, fast acting yeasts were well established.

Another innovation that helped shorten the time required to make bread was the mechanization of dough kneading. Kneading was necessary to develop gluten elasticity. The introduction of harder wheat hybrids that produced stronger flours enabled bakers to formulate doughs capable of withstanding the stress of mechanical kneading. The practice was introduced in the 1920s and had gained widespread acceptance by the 1950s.

The automation of milling and baking practices, however, did not produce uniformly beneficial results. In the 1930s, the U.S. Department of Agriculture (USDA) conducted nutritional surveys and found extensive thiamine and riboflavin deficiencies in some segments of the population. The deficiencies were attributed to milling methods that yielded finer white flours with diminished nutritional value. For example, stone-ground white flour contained 60 percent of the grain's original thiamine content, and roller-milled white flour contained only 12-20 percent of the wheat's original thiamine content. Concomitant with the surveys that identified these nutritional deficiencies, researchers developed the ability to synthesize vitamins.

During the 1940s efforts were made to restore the vitamins lost by milling practices. In 1941, the National Research Council recommended enriching white flour and white bread. Within a year, an estimated 75-80 percent of the nation's white bread was enriched on a voluntary basis. During World War II, bread enrichment was mandated by the federal government and, to ensure continuation after the war, 27 individual states passed enrichment regulations. The Food, Drug, and Cosmetic Act, which became law in 1952, defined minimum and maximum levels for thiamine, riboflavin, and niacin enrichment.

Congress gave the Food and Drug Administration (FDA) the responsibility of establishing guidelines concerning the practice of adding nutrients to food products. According to recognized standards, the word ''enriched'' meant adding B-vitamins, iron, and optionally calcium to flour or cereal grain products. ''Restored'' referred to the practice of replacing natural nutrients that were lost during processing. ''Fortification'' involved the addition of nutrients not naturally present in a food. A few well known examples were the addition of vitamin D to milk or iodine to salt. During the early 1980s, an estimated 90 percent of all standard commercial white bread was enriched.

Three bread-making techniques produced most of the commercial bread in the United States. These were called the straight dough process, the sponge method, and continuous production. In the straight dough process, all ingredients, including the yeast, were combined. The resulting dough rested during the fermentation process. Following fermentation, mechanical means were used to form loaves, and the loaves were permitted to rise again before baking.

The sponge method was based on traditional bread making techniques but employed highly mechanized procedures. Recipes were based on ingredient weight rather than volume measurements. Flour was mixed with yeast and water to make a dough or "sponge," which was then permitted to ferment for several hours. After fermentation, other ingredients and additional flour were added and the dough was remixed. Following a time of rest, the dough was cut into pieces and placed in pans. After placement in pans, the dough was allowed to rise and was then moved to an oven for baking. Typical fermentation resulted in a five-fold volume increase. Resting times averaged 20-30 minutes, and rising times were approximately one hour.

The continuous production method was also highly automated. Flour and other ingredients were fed into a production line under carefully monitored conditions. The resulting dough was extruded through dies, pressed (or cut), and placed in pans. The pans moved by conveyor through a large oven. Slicing machines cut finished loaves and packaging machines blew wrappers open with a puff of air to receive the finished product.

The commercial baking industry produced two basic types of breads—yeast breads and quick breads. Yeast breads were leavened with yeast. Quick breads used other leavening agents such as baking powder. Baking powder, which also worked by producing carbon dioxide, produced results more quickly than yeast. Quick breads included such products as muffins, loaves, and biscuits.

According to Ed Wood, a researcher of the history of bread making, 75 percent of the bread consumed in industrialized nations is produced by large commercial bakeries. The Wheat Flour Institute calculated that during the early 1980s, U.S. bakers produced approximately 250 million pounds of bread every week. Bread products were available in many varieties; some individual bakers' lines exceeded 200 different products.

The most popular kind of bread is white bread made from white flour. French breads are made without milk, sugar, and shortening. Their characteristic texture is created by injecting steam into the oven during baking, and

the flavor comes from the wheat itself. "Whole wheat breads" are made from whole wheat flour, and "wheat bread" is made from a blend of white flour and whole wheat flour. Cracked wheat breads are made from white flour and crushed wheat meal. Other bread varieties are made with white flours of varying coarseness. Rye breads are made with a mixture of rye flour and wheat flour because rye flour by itself does not possess the chemical properties necessary to produce a leavened product. Two types of rye flours are used to produce different rye breads. Light rye is made from the grain's endosperm; dark rye is made from the entire kernel.

In addition to its bread products, the baking industry also produces cakes. Cakes are typically made from pourable batters. The basic ingredients are flour, liquid, eggs, and leavening agents—plus flavorings and sometimes fat. The rising action of a baking cake is similar to the leavening action of bread. When a cake bakes, steam and gases cause the batter to expand. Different types of cakes are classified according to how they are leavened and whether they contain fat.

Two broad cake classifications are foam cakes and butter cakes. Foam cakes, typically airy and mild, are primarily leavened with air. One way in which this is accomplished is by beating egg whites and folding them into the mixture. Examples of foam cakes include angel food cake and sponge cake. Butter cakes rely on leavening agents such as baking powder, baking soda, or yeast. Butter cakes are typically more tender and possess a smoother texture than foam cakes. Examples include layer cakes and pound cakes. Other types of cakes do not easily fit these traditional distinctions. Chiffon cakes use egg whites and baking powder for leavening. Tortes are similar to sponge cakes but rely on ground nuts or crumbs to replace some or all of their flour.

According to figures for 1990, annual per capita consumption of bread products was increasing slightly. The average U.S. citizen consumed 28 pounds of white bread, 23 pounds of variety breads, 23 pounds of rolls, 15 pounds of cake, and four pounds of doughnuts and other sweet yeast products. Between 1991 and 1992 the value of the industry's shipments increased by 3.1 percent to $18.4 billion. Projections for 1993 anticipated that production would reach $19.2 billion. Forecasters predicted that annual per capita bread consumption would reach 60 pounds by the end of the century. One factor expected to drive the increase was the release of the Department of Agriculture's new four-tiered Food Guide Pyramid. The updated Food Guide Pyramid recommended 6-11 daily servings from the bread and grain food group.

Consumption increases varied by product, however, and overall industry growth was expected to be less than 1 percent in 1993 and only about 1.5 percent annually between 1993 and 1997. Industry watchers expected white bread to capture 58 percent of the total bread market. Demand for snack cakes was expected to increase 2-2.5 percent annually as manufacturers improved quality and offered new packaging options such as individually wrapped, single-servings within larger boxes. Sales of sweet yeast doughnuts were expected to increase 2.5 percent per year. With the continuing emphasis on healthy, low-fat foods, the consumption of fresh bagels exceeded $500 million in 1992, with sales growing at more than 30 percent annually.

A number of products, however, experienced declining consumption. Dinner roll consumption tapered off when pasta products gained popularity as bread substitutes. Sales of large pies, snack pies, full-size cakes, and cake-type doughnuts slackened as part of a national trend toward health consciousness. Some analysts noted that the increased consumption of sweet yeast doughnuts and snack cakes was contrary to the general trend toward more healthy products. They attributed the continuing popularity of these items to convenience.

Recessionary conditions prevalent in the United States during the early 1990s also impacted the bread and cake products industry. Lower priced products, particularly white breads, attracted renewed interest. In 1992, white bread averaged $0.75 per pound. Whole wheat bread sold for $1.02 per pound, and French breads averaged $1.26 per pound.

As the bread and cake industry entered the 1990s, its products were available virtually everywhere within the United States. Most of the products produced by commercial bakers were sold through grocery stores where breads and rolls represented the fifth largest selling category of grocery items. Additionally, the baking industry was the nation's largest consumer of nonfat dried milk. One industry analyst stated that 9 million tons of bread, rolls, and buns were sold annually. Another report pointed out that U.S. commercial bakeries consumed 73 percent of the nation's milled flour in 1980.

Despite its ubiquitous presence, however, the bread and cake industry faced several challenges in the early 1990s. One challenge was increased competition from in-store bakeries. Supermarkets with large numbers of in-store bakeries in 1990 included Winn-Dixie (with 1,117), Kroger (946), and A&P (716). Although goods baked on the premises were often priced higher than prepackaged goods, they held several advantages. Customers perceived them as fresher, and on-premises bakeries could offer specialty cakes and breads that were not available from mass producers. In-store bakeries often promoted products as impulse items, placing them near the front of the store to take advantage of baking aromas.

To meet the competition from in-store bakeries, commercial wholesalers began offering more variety in single-serving packages and increasing the assortment of specialty products. Industry analysts disagreed about the long-term effect in-store bakeries would have on traditional distribution networks. Although sales from in-store bakeries increased from $4.9 billion in 1986 to $8 billion in 1990, the rate at which they were being developed slowed during the early 1990s.

In addition to competition from in-store bakeries, wholesalers faced increased competition from prepared mixes. Prepared mixes were marketed to customers who wanted the convenience of purchased items and the freshness of newly baked goods. Competition from prepared mixes came not only within the household market, but also in the institutional market as users such as restaurants turned increasingly toward mixes.

Private label manufacturers also captured a growing portion of the bread and cake market. As the nation endured recessionary times during the early 1990s, consumers paid more attention to food prices. In order to retain market share, major manufacturers increased use of couponing and discounting.

Another challenge facing the industry during the early 1990s was increased concern about the environment. During the leavening process, ethyl alcohol was released into the atmosphere. As a result, Southern California's South Coast Air Quality Management District Board ordered smog controls on the ovens of 24 large commercial bakeries. In addition, some environmental groups criticized the industry for its use of excess packaging. Officials countered the charges with claims that the packaging was necessary to prevent spoilage. To ameliorate the criticism, bakery wrapper recycling programs were instituted in some areas.

The bread and cake industry also faced the challenge of producing products for a nation caught up in a conflict between health consciousness and a desire for taste gratification. In 1989 many items were reformulated to eliminate ingredients viewed as unhealthy. These included such ingredients as tropical oils and other fat, sugar, and salt. The elimination of fat from many classes of bakery items was a difficult accomplishment because the fat incorporated in batters and doughs served many technical and aesthetic functions. Technically, it assisted the leavening process by incorporating air into mixtures, enabling the even transfer of heat during baking and giving moisture to the final product. Aesthetically, the fat produced a favorable texture and added flavor.

To reformulate recipes without fat, different types of fat replacers were studied. Entenmann's Bakery, a subsidiary of CPC Baking, Inc., was the first national company to offer a line of fat-free products. It began test marketing them in 1989 and reported sales of $200 million during the first full year of production. To honor

Entenmann's achievement, the American Marketing Association awarded the company with the 1990 Edison Award for New Product Marketer of the Year. Entenmann's also received the grand prize from the Gorman's New Product Contest. The introduction of fat-free items helped increase consumption among consumers who traditionally skipped dessert items.

Following the launch of fat-free products during the early 1990s, many consumers reported that cholesterol and overall fat content were important in purchasing decisions. As the trend expanded and many companies began bringing fat-free products to the marketplace, Campbell Taggart introduced an enriched bread with the name IronKids in 1989. The bread was made with the same fiber content as the company's whole wheat bread; therefore, the FDA challenged the product's name and marketing methods. Campbell Taggart and the FDA reached a compromise in 1992. Under the terms of the compromise, Campbell Taggart printed a disclaimer under the IronKids logo stating that the name "refers only to a children's fitness program, and has no reference to either extra iron in this bread or to the bread resulting in superior strength or performance."

Interest in healthy products, however, appeared to be waning in 1992. A study conducted by the NPD Group of Port Washington, New York, documented a shift toward snacking and diminished concern about calorie content. Consumers were also less likely to read labels. More emphasis was placed on upscale, indulgent products than on products aimed at health-conscious consumers. A similar trend was revealed by the results of a Gallup Poll in which consumer statements about health concerns contradicted consumer spending habits. Industry analysts theorized that low fat sweet goods were of an inferior quality and priced higher than traditional formulas. One exception was noted within the bread category where multigrain items with high fiber and low fat contents were doing well.

In the mid-1990s, increased costs of raw materials cut into the profit margins of large and small players in the industry. In 1996 bread and cake products constituted an $18.4-billion industry that employed 183,000 workers. Shipments by mid-decade were valued at $16.1 billion, with bread accounting for almost one-third of that total.

CURRENT CONDITIONS

In the late 1990s, more fresh bakeries opened for business and more supermarkets expanded their fresh bakeries. Despite this, commercially prepared bakery items were gaining sales overall. Information Resources Inc. of Chicago found that commercially baked pie sales in supermarkets were up 12.5 percent and baked cake sales were up 14.5 percent from April 1998 through March 1999 (compared to the previous year). Private-

label cakes rose 21 percent and private-label pies climbed 7.1 percent in sales, while Entenmann's pies fell 9 percent. Some industry observers feel that the quality of commercially baked goods has improved and the number of offerings has grown, thus keeping the commercial bakers in close competition with fresh-baked products.

The entire commercially baked products industry remained flat in 1999, as analysts pointed out that the food sector was not doing well as a whole on Wall Street, with their stocks behind the market by 34 percent. Some investors are looking for the food industry to consolidate more, as regional companies buy others and become national names.

INDUSTRY LEADERS

Interstate Bakeries Corporation was the nation's largest baker and distributor of fresh bread and cake products. In 1996 Interstate reported sales of $3.5 billion and more than 50 percent of that came from the sales of snack cakes. That year the company operated 63 bread and cake bakeries throughout the United States.

Interstate was formed in 1937 following the consolidation of two baking companies in Kansas City. Interstate operated two major divisions—the Bread Division and the Cake Division. Its major brands included Dolly Madison, Butternut, and Holsum. Interstate distributed products through more than 100,000 food outlets located along 4,200 routes. The distribution network covered all regions of the United States except the Northeast. Interstate's thrift store network, which had 780 operating stores, was the industry's most extensive.

Flowers Industries was another major player in the industry through co-ownership of the second-largest cookie and cracker business in the United States—the newly combined Keebler & Sunshine Biscuit Company. Flowers, which was founded in 1919, operated in 16 states by 1996. The company's products included white and variety breads, buns, rolls, snack cakes, pastries, pies, doughnuts, and brownies. Its major brands were Nature's Own, Cobblestone Mill, Bluebird, Country Hearth, and Mrs. Smith's Frozen Pies, which had been acquired in a merger with Shipley Baking Co. of Fort Smith, Arkansas. In addition, the company manufactured products under regional brands and private labels.

Flowers continued to acquire other companies to maintain its number one status in the industry. The company bought Home Baking Co. in May 1999, which added $15 million in sales to Flowers and gave it a stronger presence in the foodservice industry in the southeastern United States and Caribbean. At the end of 1999, Flowers bought a bakery from retailer The Kroger Co., agreeing to make and distribute Kroger brand baked goods to 210 Kroger stores. By the beginning of 2000, Flowers expected to buy a small bakery—with about $15 million in sales a year—and a larger firm—with $100 million in sales a year.

In November 1999 Earthgrains Co. announced the acquisition of Metz Baking Co. The move put Earthgrains in the number two position in the baked goods industry. Metz was a regional player, with the number one brands of bread in Chicago, Milwaukee, and Minneapolis, while Earthgrains' brands could be found in the South. The company had annual sales of $2.5 billion, taking second place from Best Foods.

Entenmann's was established in 1898 by William Entenmann. The company made its deliveries with a horse and buggy but, in 1957, a decision was made to switch from delivery routes to wholesale distribution through supermarkets. In 1978 the company was purchased by Warner-Lambert Company and was then sold, in 1982, to General Foods Corporation. After General Foods was acquired by Philip Morris and its operations merged with Philip Morris' Kraft subsidiary, the bakery line was considered outside of the company's core business and was sold in 1995 to Kraft competitor Best Foods. Entenmann's reported 1998 sales of $113 million. The Entenmann's line included more than 200 different products in 8 categories: danish, sweet cakes, pastry, cakes, cupcakes, pies, cookies, and doughnuts.

RESEARCH AND TECHNOLOGY

One of the most extensive areas of ongoing research within the industry involved investigating methods of extending shelf life and preserving product freshness. One method, modified atmosphere packaging (MAP), involved introducing a predetermined atmosphere inside special barrier packaging materials at the time products were sealed for shipping. Nitrogen and carbon dioxide were the most frequently used gases in MAP. The technique was used to replace oxygen, a primary contributor to product staleness. According to published reports, MAP extended shelf life up to 30 days and increased freezer life up to 6 months.

Another, more advanced method of controlling the atmosphere within a product package was called controlled atmosphere packaging (CAP). CAP relied on active means of manipulating the gas in a package's "headspace." Products were packed with chemical inserts to actively manipulate the environment within the package. For example, oxygen scavengers, frequently composed of iron compounds, would absorb any oxygen remaining after a package was sealed. Eliminating oxygen from packaging was important because it inhibited mold growth. Studies indicated that CAP extended the time period in which a product would remain mold-free by 300 percent.

MAP and CAP technologies presented many benefits. They eliminated the need for preservatives and reduced distribution costs by eliminating the need for freezing and chilling during transportation. They also increased customer convenience because products did not require freezing following purchase. They also helped maintain appropriate moisture levels so products did not dry out. Two of the biggest problems surrounding MAP and CAP usage were customer perception and price. Customers did not view bakery products with extended shelf life as fresh, and products packaged with MAP and CAP were more expensive than those packaged with traditional methods. One industry analyst suggested that CAP and MAP technologies were best suited for wholesalers with large geographic distribution networks, rather than local baking operations.

A new form of lecithin was developed by Riceland Foods in 1998. Bakers had used liquid lecithin for years, but it contained about 35 percent oil. The new powdered lecithin contained only 2 percent oil, making it useful for low-fat baking. Lecithin supplies the good taste and moistness to low-fat bakery products, making them taste more like the full-fat varieties. The product also reduces the amount of egg yolks bakers need to use, without adding any cholesterol.

FURTHER READING

"Flowers Industries Announces Agreement to Acquire Home Baking Company." *Flowers Industries,* 21 May 1999. Available from http://www.flowersindustries.com/new/current/21051999a.html.

"Flowers Industries Announces Agreement to Acquire Memphis Bakery from Kroger." *Floers Industries,* 28 September 1999. Available from http://www.flowersindustries.com/news/current/09281999.htm.

"Flowers Industries Announces Record Sales for Fiscal 1996," 1997. Available from http://www.prnewswire.com/cgi-bin/.

"Flowers Industries to Acquire Bakery from Kroger." *Nation's Restaurant News,* 25 October 1999.

LaBell, Fran. "Dry Lecithin Benefits Cakes, Mixes." *Prepared Foods,* May 1998.

Mann, Jennifer. "Kansas City, Mo.-Based Firm Reports Increased Revenue for Quarter." *Knight-Ridder/Tribune Business News,* 14 September 1999.

———. "Kansas City, Mo.-Based Bakery Tries to Ward Off Takeover Attempts." *Knight-Ridder/Tribune Business News,* 11 October 1999.

Nicklaus, David. "Clayton, Mo.-Based Bread Firm to Purchase Rival." *Knight-Ridder/Tribune Business News,* 15 November 1999.

Smyth, William. "Half-Baked? With Fresh Bakeries Spring Up in More and More Supermarkets, Retailers Weigh in on the Effect Upon Sales of Commercial Baked Goods and Their Merchandising Strategies to Maximize the Category." *Supermarket News,* 19 July 1999.

U.S. Bureau of the Census. *1995 Annual Survey of Manufactures.* Washington, D.C.: GPO, 1997.

Wood, Ed. *World Sourdoughs from Antiquity.* Cascade, ID: Sinclair Publishing, 1989.

SIC 2052

COOKIES AND CRACKERS

This category includes establishments primarily engaged in manufacturing fresh cookies, crackers, pretzels, and similar "dry" bakery products. Secondary products that are part of this industry include biscuits, graham crackers, saltines, cracker meal and crumbs, cracker sandwiches made from crackers, wafers, and ice cream cones and cups.

NAICS CODE(S)

311821 (Cookie and Cracker Manufacturing)
311919 (Other Snack Food Manufacturing)
311812 (Commercial Bakeries)

INDUSTRY SNAPSHOT

Although Mom is still America's favorite cookie maker, the bakeries that attempt to make cookies and crackers as good as Mom's have become a huge industry. Total sales of cookies and crackers was estimated at approximately $9.8 billion in 1998. While major players are dominant, 27 percent of the 8,900 nationally distributed brands in 1999 were not under one of the major labels.

Adult consumers have turned their backs on low-fat and no-fat items and begun returning to better tasting products. While sales of expensive national brand cookies have declined somewhat, sales of lower-priced private labels have risen.

Keebler, which went public in 1998, has sought to acquire other baking companies to supplant Nabisco as the number one player in the industry. Keebler had a 28 percent share of the cookie and cracker market in 1998, to Nabisco's 34 percent. Every fourth cookie or cracker bought in the United States today is sold by Keebler. Every third is sold by Nabisco.

ORGANIZATION AND STRUCTURE

In the major bakery companies, the cookies and crackers segment of business often operates as a separate division. Many bakery companies are divisions of holding companies that are also involved with other consumer products that include food, beverages, and, in the case with RJR Nabisco, Inc., tobacco.

Other manufacturers of cookies and crackers operate strictly under the bakery goods heading. Companies such as Mrs. Field's Cookies and Famous Amos at one time operated exclusively out of their own retail outlets. They later expanded to supermarkets and specialty stores. A number of these private label companies work through distributors that can handle a number of varied products. Many of the larger companies handle their own distribution, working directly with supermarkets and retailers.

BACKGROUND AND DEVELOPMENT

The U.S. Chamber of Commerce noted that cookie and cracker manufacturing was the fastest growing segment of the bakery industry in 1992. Shipments of all bakery products rose an average of 1.3 percent per year from the years 1987 to 1992. Sales of cookies and crackers for the same years, however, increased by rates of 2.3 percent. The primary reason given for the projected increase in sales was the recent introduction of low-fat, low-calorie, low-cholesterol cookies and crackers.

Well into the late 1980s, bakery goods showed a consistent increase in sales. But consumption of sweet baked goods began to decline around 1992. Consumers were changing their buying habits and sought out bakery products that were lower in calories. Cookie and cracker sales also slowed by 1992, but showed signs of growth due to the availability of the new low-fat varieties.

An important reason for declines in Nabisco's cookie and cracker business is that, during the 1980s, Nabisco aggressively increased its prices until consumers started buying less. Nabisco still holds the lion's share of the business; however, private labels have begun to cut heavily into Nabisco's market share. Nabisco is said to be working overtime to undercut its private label competition. In an effort to bolster its market, Nabisco is making an effort to gain market space in discount outlets and convenience stores. Nonetheless, private labels are slowly making inroads in all the major cookie and cracker markets.

Because it is still the leader in the cookie and cracker industry, the private labels appear to be pointing their big guns at Nabisco. There are a number of upscale private lines available, including Sam's Choice, a line being sold at Wal-Mart stores, and Master Choice, sold at A & P stores. One of the front-runners, and a leader of the upscale private label pack, is President's Choice. Produced by Canada's Loblaw Companies, the chocolate chip entry is beginning to close the lead that Nabisco's Chips Ahoy! brand enjoys.

A number of companies introduced products to suit a changing market of health-conscious consumers. Nabisco introduced a new line of fat-free cookies and crackers called Snackwells. As reported in *Advertising Age,* Nabisco management insists that "The company is placing substantial corporate emphasis behind product categories that health-wise consumers are increasingly demanding." The company added that Snackwell cookies have one gram of fat compared with three grams in traditional cookies on the market.

By 1997, Snackwells was the top-selling brand of cookie and cracker in the country. The brand's popularity reflected the fact that 173 million Americans were eating reduced-fat and fat-free foods, representing an 81 percent increase from 1993.

Food and Drug Administration (FDA) approval in 1996 of a new fat substitute, Olestra, promised to change the low-fat cookie and cracker market even further. Olestra, which was developed by Procter & Gamble, added no fat or calories to foods and was expected to appear in new formulations of crackers, tortilla chips and other snacks.

Bakery companies have been making changes in the ingredients they have been using for years in efforts to minimize the use of chemical agents. Companies are phasing out potassium bromate, which had always been a integral part of their recipes. Health-conscious, label-reading consumers are turning from products with potassium bromate to products that contain acceptable alternatives, such as barley malt. The *U.S. Industrial Outlook* reported that the per capita consumption of crackers edged up mainly due to bakery companies changing ingredients to satisfy consumer demands and tastes. The increase, it was believed, was due to cracker manufacturers eliminating questionable ingredients like tropical oils and white flour, and using canola oil and whole wheat flour in their place. This combination is preferred by health-conscious adults who purchase crackers and examine ingredient labels.

CURRENT CONDITIONS

The consumer segment most responsible for boosting the sales of baked goods is the 35- to 54-year-old age group, according to a survey compiled by the U.S. Bureau of Labor Statistics. The survey showed that people in this age group regularly spend more for bakery products. Happily for cookie and cracker manufacturers, this consumer segment was growing at a rate of 2.7 percent yearly, and by 1997, it was expected to represent 29.3 percent of the total U.S. population. One explanation for heightened consumption was that this group was at the peak of their earning potential, and therefore had more disposable income.

In 1998 cookies and crackers became the second largest segment of the dry grocery category in supermarkets, with carbonated beverages coming in first. Almost 98 percent of all households purchase cookies and crackers, yet sales continue to climb, up 4 percent in the first half of 1999.

Manufacturers of cookies and crackers are working harder at expanding their sources of sales. They are exploring non-traditional outlets such as toy retailers,

drug stores, and children's stores to sell their products. They are incorporating the use of licensed characters for their cookies, hoping to increase consumption of cookies among children aged 5 to 14. Nabisco led the way, by introducing the Rugrats Frosted Cookie, based on the television series, in August of 1999.

The biggest turnaround in the industry in the late 1990s was the sudden and swift rejection of the manufacturers' no-fat and low-fat cookie and cracker lines. Calling it a return to indulgence, the industry has scrambled to present its products, both current and new, as full-flavored. While consumers continued to worry about the amount of fat in their diets, it seems that cookies and crackers were not the place they were looking to cut it.

Many industry leaders are introducing new products and reformulating old ones. Nabisco's Snackwell line will no longer be advertised as no-fat, but rather reduced fat. The company will add fat to its cracker lines, but still be about 40 percent less fat than regular cracker lines.

Keebler, seeing consumers would buy new products, provided they tasted good, rolled out several new products in 1999. In May 1999 the company introduced Keebler's Double Fudge 'n Caramel Cookies, to great success. Where the cookies were launched, Keebler saw its entire Fudge Shoppe Cookie line sales increase 56 percent. Targeting the adult market, Keebler also concentrated on its Soft Batch Brand, introducing a new product, Homestyle Soft Batch Cookies, in 1999.

One of the brands Keebler inherited when it bought Sunshine Biscuits was Hydrox. Hydrox was introduced in 1908, four years before Oreo. Nabisco had the superior distribution lines and marketing dollars and soon overtook Hydrox, leading customers, even today, to believe Oreo hit the market first. Keebler plans on aggressively challenging Oreo's market share. Keebler changed the name of the cookie to Droxies, redesigned the cookie, and planned to reformulate the recipe in the spring of 2000. Some analysts fear the new Droxies would be seen as a rip-off of a rip-off and warned that Keebler has a big hill to climb.

Nabisco is aggressively marketing its cornerstone brand, Oreo. In 1999 the company held the third annual Oreo stacking contest and rolled out a new contest—Don't Eat the Winning Oreo. Nabisco created a special cookie mold that allows the company to stamp a prize directly on the cookie. When a customer got an Oreo with "Car", for example, they won a car.

The inflation-adjusted prices of agricultural commodities are not expected to represent a factor in the cookies and crackers manufacturing industry. Although there have been periodic price increases, the average index of real prices of ingredients has actually shown a decline. This pattern should continue. Also, with the use of computers and better telecommunications, bakery companies today are more sophisticated and more easily able to protect themselves against sudden price increases of agricultural commodities.

INDUSTRY LEADERS

Nabisco has consistently been the leader in the industry. The Nabisco Company produces, distributes, and markets a broad range of cookies, crackers, and snacks. Nabisco Biscuit Company sells nine of the top 10 cookies and crackers worldwide, including Chips Ahoy! and Oreo chocolate sandwich cookies, the world's largest-selling cookie brands; Ritz crackers; and Snackwell cookies and crackers. Nabisco reported sales of $1.8 billion in the first half of 1999 in their biscuit division, up from $1.7 billion in the first six months of 1998.

Nabisco markets its products through a direct store delivery system. To boost its share of the cookie market, Nabisco signed a licensing agreement with ConAgra in 1997 to market cookies and bread crisps under the Healthy Choice brand name.

Majority shareholders of RJR Nabisco fought the board of directors to spin off its tobacco holdings. The shareholders feared increasing lawsuits and government intervention would put a large strain on the company, draining assets from the profitable food divisions. In June of 1999 RJR Nabisco Holdings Corp was renamed Nabisco Group Holdings Corp, reflecting that the corporation separated its food and tobacco businesses.

The second largest cookie manufacturer in terms of market share is Keebler, a public company, with Flowers Industries, Inc. owning a 55 percent share. Like Nabisco's, Keebler's products are represented in major supermarkets throughout the country. Keebler also produces and distributes a wide range of crackers and snacks. Keebler acquired Sunshine Biscuit in 1996, went public in 1998, and bought President Baking Co, bringing Famous Amos cookies and Girl Scout cookies under the Keebler umbrella. Due to these acquisitions and strong brand showings, Keebler posted a 20.1 percent gain in sales in the first half of 1999 over 1998, to $185 million.

WORKFORCE

In 1995 the cookies and cracker industry employed approximately 49,200 people, 38,700 of whom fall into the category of production workers. The average hourly wages for those workers came to about $12.57 per hour. The states with the most employees in the cookies and crackers industry are North Carolina, Illinois, Pennsylvania, and Georgia. In 1999 the reported wages for bakers was $11,960-$40,039 and route drivers was $11,960-$27,559.

AMERICA AND THE WORLD

The export trade of bakery goods has amounted to a small portion of the total bakery production in the United States, because of the problem of perishability and consumer preference in other countries. Nevertheless, bakery exports are growing. Exports consist mainly of cookies, crackers, and specialty cakes that have adequate shelf life, attractive packaging, and competitive prices.

The real value of U.S. export shipments for all bakery items was not likely to grow more than 1.5-2.0 percent annually from 1993 to 1997. The fastest growth was expected to be from cookies and crackers exports, which is expected to grow about 2 percent yearly. International competitiveness of bakery products is still a long way off.

It is conceivable, however, that in the coming years exports and imports of bakery products, with cookies and crackers leading the way, will become more of a viable international fixture. According to *U.S. Industrial Outlook,* international trade in bakery products will continue to increase.

RESEARCH AND TECHNOLOGY

Concern for the environment has affected the operations of bakery companies. Most are now spending more of their dollars on environmental protection. Many companies are introducing pollution abatement equipment, especially for their ovens, and will be introducing other pollution control measures. Many are converting their delivery vans so they can operate on cleaner-burning propane instead of gasoline. It is expected that environmental control efforts will eventually increase operating costs by as much as 10 percent.

Some manufacturers are employing extrusion used in other food industries. This engineering process permits continuous blending of ingredients. It results in a greater variety of products being made available to the consumer, and it results in less waste during production time, and also consumes less energy. Changes in ingredients and procedures are monitored carefully by the Food and Drug Administration.

Nabisco has implemented an engineering information management software system, called WorkPlace ActiveAsset. This enables its 11 bakeries and headquarters to easily share information, such as engineering drawings. This software will allow everyone, including consultants, suppliers, and local bakeries, to access the complex engineering information. Nabisco has also created an online analytical processing (OLAP) data mart. With more than 8,000 products, the OLAP allows Nabisco to accurately track sales and consumer preferences, with the largest data mart holding sales, price discount, spoilage, transportation, and promotional information for two years. Management, financial analysts, and salespeople use this information. Using this information led to the dropping of the LifeSaver holiday candy packs at Christmas. The product wasn't selling, and the move saved Nabisco $1 million.

Not to be outdone, Keebler rolled out its IDEA Wizard (Instant Data Evaluation Access) in 1999. Since the cookie market and cracker market are distinct, with its own customers and loyalties, the IDEA Wizard allows Keebler to collect information on each segment of its markets, then develop plans for specific retailers regarding self space and merchandising. The IDEA Wizard stores information from several sources, including scanners. Retailers access the information, along with audio and video clips about new products, focus groups, and marketing messages from Keebler.

One problem facing all makers of cookies is uniformity of product, so the right number fit in the packaging. Scientists, underwritten in part by Nabisco, have discovered a way to break down pentosans in flour. Pentosans are large sugar molecules that slow the rise and fall of dough. With fewer pentosans in flour, the cookie dough rises, then falls with a burst, making a flatter cookie. While the enzyme needed to break down pentosans cost about $2.50 for every 1,000 pounds of flour, the result of fewer pentosans is a quicker baking time.

FURTHER READING

Beil, Laura. "Science Unlocks Key to Better Cookie." *The Dallas Morning News,* 2 April 1999.

"Cookies and Crackers." *Progressive Grocer,* September 1999.

"Cookie and Cracker Statistics." *American Institute of Baking,* 18 November 1999. Available from http://www.aibonline.org/Services/Online/StatisticsAndTrends/Cookie.htm.

"Elves Team Up With Girl Scouts." *The Washington Post,* 27 August 1998.

"FDA Approves Fat Substitute, Olestra," 1999. Available from http://vm.cfsan.fda.gov/.

Hays, Constance L. "Nabisco Brings Back Some of the Fat in Snackwell's." *The Dallas Morning News,* 6 May 1998.

"Keebler Completes Acquisition of President Baking Company." *Business Wire,* 27 September 1998.

"Keebler Foods company Announces Public Offering." *The Hollow Treebune,* 21 January 1999. Available from http://www.keebler.com/newsroom/press_releases/pr_199/pr012199.htm.

"Keebler Foods Company Announces Record Earnings for Fourth Quarter and 1998." *The Hollow Treebune,* 3 February 1999. Available from http://www.keebler.com/newsroom/press_releases/pr_1999/pr-020399.htm.

"Keebler Profits Rise, Cookie and Cracker Sales Up." *Reuters Business Report,* 4 November 1999.

Lazich, Robert S., ed. *Market Share Reporter, 1997.* Detroit: Gale Research, 1997.

Lukas, Paul. "Oreos to Hydrox: Resistance is Futile." *Fortune,* 15 March 1999.

"Nabisco: Company Profile." *Town Hall: Nabisco Headquarters,* 18 November 1999. Available from http://www.nabisco.com/townhall/PR_IR/CompanyProfile.html.

"Nabisco Implements WorkPlace ActiveAsset System for Engineering Information Management." *Business Wire,* 2 June 1998.

"Nabisco Reports Second quarter Results." *Business Wire,* 21 July 1999.

Schroeder, Eric. "Cookies-A Full Flavor Phenomenon." *Milling & Baking News,* 31 August 1999.

"State of the Industry Report." *American Institute of Baking.* 18 November 1999. Available from http://www.aibonline.org/Services/Online/StatisticsAndTrends/Cookie.htm.

Ward's Business Directory of U.S. Private and Public Companies. Detroit: Gale Research, 1997.

Zerega, Blaise. "Nabisco Ekes Surprise Savings Out of OLAP Data mats." *InfoWorld,* 21 September 1999.

SIC 2053

FROZEN BAKERY PRODUCTS, EXCEPT BREAD

This industry comprises establishments primarily involved in manufacturing frozen bakery products other than bread and bread-type rolls. Products include frozen cakes, croissants, doughnuts, pies, and sweet yeast goods. Manufacturers of frozen bread and bread-type rolls are classified in **SIC 2051: Bread, Cake, and Related Products.**

NAICS CODE(S)

311813 (Frozen Bakery Product Manufacturing)

Twenty-four companies were primarily involved in the manufacture of frozen bakery products with total sales of $848.0 million in 1995, down from $1.0 billion in 1987. Industry employment was also down in 1995 to 6,100 people, from 9,900 in 1987.

In 1997 nearly 240 establishments were engaged in this industry, employing more than 15,000 people—a dramatic increase from 1995. The total value of shipments was $2.5 billion in 1997. In terms of shipment value, the largest segment of the industry was frozen pies. Frozen cakes and pastries were also major components. The smallest segment was frozen cookie and cracker products.

According to the January 27, 1997 issue of *Brandweek,* 82 percent of American consumers were eating breakfast at home, thus creating a $16-billion market. Manufacturers targeted those consumers who were looking for convenience, as well as attempting to woo those who were purchasing breakfast at fast-food restaurants and convenience stores.

The late 1990s saw the beginnings of a breakfast foods war among manufacturers of frozen and fresh products. Kellogg's added more flavors of waffles, while Pillsbury introduced Toaster Scrambles in three varieties: cheese and egg; cheese, egg, and bacon; and cheese, egg, and ham. Sara Lee planned to redirect its marketing efforts to its new fresh division in an attempt to tap into the $300-million supermarket bagel business.

One of the first companies to offer frozen bakery products to the American marketplace was Sara Lee. Sara Lee Bakery was founded in 1949 by Charles Lubin. Originally the company offered a line of premium, fresh-baked products and made shipments within a 200-mile radius of its Chicago location. In 1953, in order to accommodate the needs of long-distance clients, the company pioneered freezing methods and nine years later made the decision to switch its production exclusively to frozen products.

Chicago-based Sara Lee is not only the leader among manufacturers of frozen baked goods, but one of the top ten public food and beverage companies in the United States and Canada. Initially, Sara Lee's more than 200 different items were sold in supermarkets and in 40 nations around the globe. Sales figures for 1999 topped $20 billion.

Another industry leader was Kellogg Company with Mrs. Smith's and Eggo products. Both brands were market leaders within their categories and sold predominantly to convenience-conscious customers.

Mrs. Smith's expanded its market territory throughout the 1990s by offering products in Canada. In addition to being promoted for their convenience, Eggo Waffles were also marketed at the health market. Kellogg had overall sales of nearly $7 billion in 1999.

FURTHER READING

Hoover's Company Profiles. Hoover's Online, 2000. Available from http://www.hoovers.com.

U.S. Census Bureau. ''Manufacturing-Industry Series.'' *1997 Economic Census.* Washington, D.C.: GPO, 15 November 1999.

SIC 2061

CANE SUGAR, EXCEPT REFINING

This classification includes establishments primarily engaged in manufacturing raw sugar, syrup, or finished (granulated or clarified) sugar from sugar cane. Establish-

ments primarily engaged in refining sugar from purchased raw sugar or sugar syrup are classified in **SIC 2062: Cane Sugar Refining.** Plantations primarily involved in production of sugarcane and sugar beets are classified in **SIC 0133: Sugarcane and Sugar Beets.**

NAICS CODE(S)

311311 (Sugarcane Mills)

INDUSTRY SNAPSHOT

The sugar cane industry is confined by the crop's growing conditions and the logistics of transporting sugar cane. Production in the United States is limited to Florida, Hawaii, Louisiana, and Texas and the commonwealth of Puerto Rico. Florida alone accounts for more than 50 percent of total U.S. cane sugar production. For the 1999-2000 harvest, cane sugar production is projected at almost 3.9 million short tons, raw value (STRV), of which slightly more 2 million STRV are expected to come from Florida. Mills that process the sugar cane into raw sugar must be located near cane plantations since cut sugar cane is too bulky and heavy to ship. Mills in this category process cane into crystals of raw sugar that can be transported in bulk, like grain, aboard ships or by land.

A tropical grass that reaches a maximum height of 10 to 20 feet, sugar cane contains a relatively high level of sucrose. Sugar mills begin the process of extracting sucrose from the sugar cane by washing the stalks of cane and cutting them into shreds with rotating knives. The shredded cane is then run between giant rollers to extract the sugary juice. This juice is then clarified and crystallized into golden raw sugar. The raw sugar that emerges from the sugar mills is more than 95 percent sucrose.

U.S. sugar cane milling profitability depends on federal government subsidies and import controls. Since the late 1700s, producing raw sugar has been a lucrative business for growers and millers. Domestic sugar prices have been government controlled, and foreign imports have been severely limited. Some members of Congress, as well as numerous American agricultural policy critics, have been advocating less government involvement. They have been pushing for decreased price supports for domestic sugar cane as well as the lifting or easing of foreign sugar quotas. Critics claim import controls hurt small sugar-producing Caribbean nations—as well as the Philippines.

ORGANIZATION AND STRUCTURE

Sugar mills are located near the plantations on which sugarcane is grown and harvested. In many cases, these are operated by the plantations or as cooperatives by the owners of several sugarcane plantations. United States Sugar Corporation in Clewiston, Florida, for example, is both a grower and manufacturer of raw cane sugar.

Mills run continuously, day and night, from fall until spring, when the last cane is harvested. To facilitate the constant milling, growers cultivate a variety of sugar cane that they can harvest throughout the season. The variety of cane available, however, depends on the soil and climate on a particular plantation.

Government Supports. The U.S. government has supported sugar prices for more than 200 years. In 1789, the federal government imposed an import tariff to raise revenue and, for the next 100 years, this sugar tariff yielded almost 20 percent of all import duties, the main source of government money before the Civil War. The Sugar Act of 1934 regulated domestic sugar production, imports, and prices. Import quotas were assigned to foreign sugar-growing countries.

Price supports were applied sporadically during the 1970s, depending upon the price of sugar on the world market. Temporary suspensions of price controls in 1974 and 1980 resulted in increased sugar prices. Shortages soon followed and, with that, sugar prices plummeted.

As a result, in the Agriculture and Food Act of 1981 the government agreed to purchase raw cane sugar and refined beet sugar for a specific price per pound if commercial prices were not high enough. In order to avoid payments, the government imposed tariffs to discourage imports, limit the supply of sugar and, therefore, keep sugar prices level at or above the government's minimum price. Farmers claim to get no benefit from the subsidies. Industry claims are that U.S. consumers pay 28 percent less for sugar than consumers anywhere else worldwide; however, the U.S. price for sugar in 1995 was more than double the world's price. Subsequent agricultural acts continued to provide price supports for sugar, keeping quotas low and prices high in the domestic market.

In recent decades, the United States has imposed strict quotas on import of foreign sugar, cutting imports 80 percent since 1975. The tariff on sugar imports in excess of the quota was also high enough to discourage imports. This quota has created great controversy regarding U.S. trade with developing nations. More than 110 countries grow sugar cane or sugar beets, and many of the developing nations have become dependent on sugar as a source of employment and income. In the early 1990s, the United States imported less than 1.5 million tons of sugar to make up the difference between the sugar cane produced domestically and the approximately 9 million tons used.

Some critics of U.S. foreign trade policy have blamed the federal sugar support program for the rise in cocaine traffic into the United States. These critics claimed that not only did the sugar program hurt other countries financially, but the loss of sugar trade with the United States contributed to increased coca (from which cocaine is derived) production in Bolivia and Peru. U.S.

sugar producers disputed this claim, maintaining a primary factor in the decline was nationalization of Peru's sugar industry, not cuts in U.S. sugar imports.

Price supports for sugar in the United States are provided in the form of nonrecourse loans so that sugar growers can borrow money with the crop as collateral. The government sets the value of the crop collateral at a minimum price per pound, guaranteeing that the sugar producer will receive at least that price, even if the commodity price drops. Loans are made to the processor because the raw sugarcane must be milled before being sold or stored. When the raw sugar is sold, the growers reportedly receive payment as well. In many cases the processor and the grower are the same concern. In 1996, to protest U.S. policies surrounding subsidies, the Sugar Cane Growers Cooperative of Florida said it would decline $28,000 in government payments.

Processing. The harvesting of sugar cane poses many challenges to producers. Harvesting is either carried out by hand cutting or machine cutting. While harvesting by machine costs half as much as harvesting by hand, mills complain that machine-harvested sugar includes too much debris—such as roots, dirt, leaves, and dead animals—according to Alec Wilkinson in his book *Big Sugar, Seasons in the Cane Fields of Florida*. He notes that mill owners estimate machine-harvested sugar cane includes 7 to 10 percent trash, while hand-cut cane includes only about 2 percent. Mill owners complain that trash costs them money because it clogs the machines and absorbs juice during milling. According to Wilkinson, mill owners claim machines leave too much cane in the field; machines cannot cut as close to the ground as the hand cutters. Owners claim that every acre left with half-inch cane stubble would have made another half ton of cane to be milled.

Sugar cane stalks are transported to nearby mills in trucks or railroad cars to be washed and shredded then placed in crushing machines or vats of hot water to dissolve the sugar. Crushing machines break open the cane and squeeze out the sugary juice. Water dissolves more of the sugar in the stalk, creating a sugary mixture called cane juice. The cane juice is heated, and lime is added to settle impurities; next, carbon dioxide is used to remove the lime. The clear juice moves on to giant evaporator tanks. After removing most of the water, the thickened mixture is transferred to a vacuum pan where the mixture is heated to remove still more water. When crystals form in the syrup, the mixture is transferred to a centrifuge. The mixture is spun at high speeds to separate large sugar crystals from the thick syrup. The crystals, 97 to 99 percent sucrose, are called raw sugar. Producers may package the raw sugar, as turbinado, for consumer use or sell it to cane sugar refiners for the manufacture of granulated or powdered sugar. Any foreign sugar shipped to the United States is also transported in raw form.

CURRENT CONDITIONS

The late 1990s saw a sharp decline in U.S. sugar prices, blamed by cane sugar producers on increased sugar imports from Mexico under the North American Free Trade Agreement (NAFTA). As sugar cane harvesting for the 1999-2000 crop year got under way in October 1999, the U.S. sugar price had fallen below 19 cents a pound, its lowest level in decades. U.S. Sugar Corporation, a major player in the industry, reported that although the crop size outlook was good, price prospects were gloomy. "The good economy in the United States has bypassed farmers," said Robert H. Buker Jr., senior vice president at U.S. Sugar. "Even worse, though farmers are suffering, the prices in grocery stores haven't gone down. Sugar is at some of its lowest prices even, but Snickers haven't gotten any cheaper."

Sugar and other agricultural supports continue to be criticized by certain members of Congress and other government officials. Although cuts in price supports are likely, the government is unlikely to remove all supports. Sugar producers claimed that the federal sugar program protected U.S. consumers from wild swings in world prices. Critics say U.S. consumers spend an extra $1.4 billion annually because of the government program. The industry contends that figure should be about $200 million.

U.S. companies (including Coca-Cola; Mars, Inc.; and Kraft) are among the critics of sugar tariffs. In 1991, E. J. Brach's, a candy manufacturer, asked that a part of Chicago be declared a free trade zone so the company could import sugar at the world price. Brach's officials said that if the company had to continue to pay inflated U.S. sugar prices, it would be forced to move its operations out of the country. The sugar industry successfully blocked the company's application for free trade status.

The U.S. sugar industry and its very powerful lobby claimed that 80 percent of the sugar in the United States is consumed by food processors who did not pass drops in sugar prices on to consumers. They cited government reports that said, from 1982 to 1992, the average cost of sweeteners (cane sugar, beet sugar, and high fructose corn syrup) rose only about 9 percent, which was less than the rate of inflation; however, prices for products containing sugar rose 54 percent. The chairman of the American Sugar Alliance also claimed that U.S. consumers pay 25 percent less for sugar than consumers in other developed nations and that the U.S. price for sugar was 10 percent less than the world average retail price. The American Sugar Alliance asserted that since the United States was not self-sufficient in sugar production—it imported 27 percent of its sugar in 1991—exporters of sugar to the United States received the same level of price supports as U.S. sugar cane producers.

NAFTA promised to open up the sugar market to Mexico; however, rather than increasing overall import of sugar, it would probably reduce U.S. purchases from the Philippines and Caribbean nations. According to a 1988 *Monthly Review* article, "the industry is confronted with virtual extinction over the next decade," attributing the move to "policy decisions adopted in the boardrooms of a minuscule number of beverage companies with no consideration whatsoever for the millions of sugar workers and their families around the world." In other words, a shift to corn sweeteners and other sugar substitutes was to blame.

The shift to high fructose corn syrup use by the U.S. beverage industry began in the 1980s. Its price in 1985 was approximately seven U.S. cents per pound less than sugar, and the savings to the industry megaliths the previous year had been $90 million. This move by the beverage industry was assisted, contended *Monthly Review,* by the push of corn conglomerates such as Archer-Daniels-Midland Company and Cargill. That same year the U.S. sugar market declined by about 8 percent.

The U.S. Department of Agriculture's (USDA) National Agricultural Statistics Service (NASS) projected 1999-2000 cane sugar production of 3.87 million short tons, raw value (STRV), up slightly from its projection of 3.85 million STRV for the 1998-1999 crop year. Florida, according to NASS projections, was expected to produce 2.03 million STRV, while Louisiana was expected to account for output of 1.40 million STRV. Hawaii's cane sugar production was projected at 330,000 STRV; Texas and Puerto Rico were expected to follow with output of 100,000 STRV and 15,000 STRV, respectively.

At 430,000 acres, the total Florida sugar cane acreage harvested for sugar in the 1999-2000 crop year was expected to be slightly above the level farmed in 1998-1999. Florida's yield per acre, according to NASS, was expected to be about 4.7 tons, down slightly from the previous crop year. In Louisiana, sugar cane acreage was projected to increase to a total of 420,000 acres, up about 20,000 acres from the previous crop year.

On the price front, world raw sugar prices hit a fourteen-year low on April 28, 1999, when the July contract traded as low as 3.93 cents per pound. The cut-rate sugar prices at the world level attracted buyers from Iran and Bangladesh as well as buying interest from Russia. As April ended, however, the July contract price firmed to 4.33 cents per pound. For the month as a whole, world raw sugar prices averaged 5.44 cents per pound, nearly half the 10.22 cents per pound of a year earlier. During the same period, U.S. nearby futures prices for raw sugar averaged 22.57 cents per pound, while the July contract traded in a range between 22.27 and 22.70 cents per pound. However, by the fall of 1999, U.S. sugar prices had fallen below 19 cents per pound, their lowest level in decades. U.S. sugar producers said the sharp drop in prices could be traced to increased imports of Mexican sugar under NAFTA.

Pollution in the Everglades. According to environmentalists, agricultural run-off from sugar plantations and milling processes in southern Florida have been responsible for damage to the Everglades. In 1991, United States Sugar Corporation was fined $3.75 million for improper disposal of hazardous materials from one of its Clewiston mills in the Everglades. The company pleaded guilty to knowingly allowing hazardous wastes into local landfills during three harvest years. Environmentalists continue to raise concerns about the impact of the sugar industry on the fragile ecosystem of the Everglades.

INDUSTRY LEADERS

The undisputed leader in the domestic cane sugar industry is U.S. Sugar Corp. of Clewiston, Florida, which produces nearly 10 percent of all American sugar. A privately held company, U.S. Sugar is not required to reveal its financial results, but its 1997 sales were estimated at $430 million. Another major player in the industry is Alexander and Baldwin Inc., headquartered in Hawaii. A widely diversified company with holdings in transportation, real estate, and other agricultural commodities, Alexander and Baldwin posted revenue of nearly $1.3 billion in 1998, up about 5 percent from the previous year. Another major producer in the cane sugar industry is St. Joe Co., which is also widely diversified. In 1998, St. Joe posted revenue of $322 million.

Another major player in the Florida cane sugar business is the Fanjul family which, through its network of family-owned sugar plantations, is said to supply the domestic market with more than 15 percent of its cane sugar. Members of the Fanjul family, which emigrated to this country from Cuba after Fidel Castro took power in 1959, control a number of cane sugar companies, including Flo-Sun Sugar, Okeelanta Corp., Osceola Farms, New Hope Sugar, and Kendall Sugar Cane.

In Louisiana and Texas, major sugar producers include Rio Grande Valley Sugar, Cora-Texas Manufacturing, Sterling Sugars Inc., Cajun Sugar Cooperative Inc., Alma Plantation Ltd., Louisiana Sugar Cane, M.A. Patout and Son Ltd., Iberia Sugar Coop Inc., and LaFourche Sugars Corp.

WORKFORCE

Although cutters are employed by the sugar growers, they are discussed here because many southern Florida plantations are owned by the large sugar mills and are therefore part of this industry in the country's leading sugar-producing state. Sugar harvesters, called cane cutters, face one of the most grueling jobs imaginable. For decades, the Florida sugar cane industry came under fire for the severe, even slave-like conditions in which the

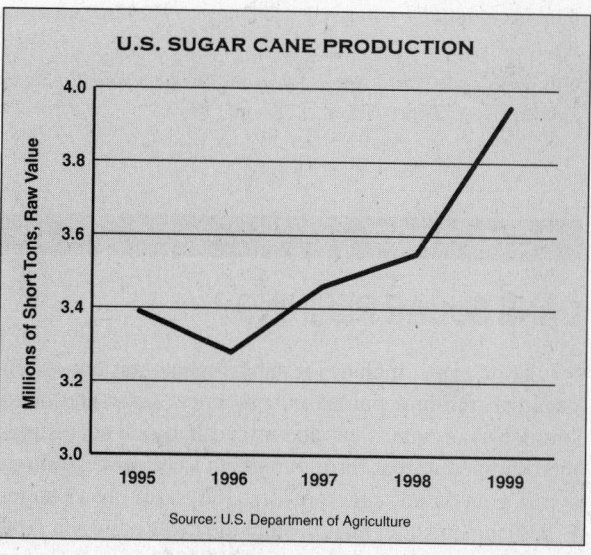

U.S. SUGAR CANE PRODUCTION

Source: U.S. Department of Agriculture

cutters lived and for illegal practices concerning wages. Most Florida cane cutters were seasonal workers migrating from the Caribbean for the harvest.

A 1991 congressional report accused the sugar cane industry of violating labor laws. In 1992, U.S. Sugar Corp., one of the largest sugar concerns in Florida, agreed to a wage increase and other improvements. Farm-worker advocacy groups were hoping to win reforms for cane cutters working at other sugar companies. However, southern Florida producers were increasingly turning to machine cutting because of the historical controversy about the treatment of immigrant labor by the industry.

Employment in the fields and in the mills is seasonal, peaking between fall and spring. According to the Bureau of Labor Statistics, in 1990 total employment of production workers in the industry was 3,500 in July and 6,400 in November. One cooperative based in a single county in Florida reported employing about 900 people in 1996 on a payroll exceeding $26 million.

FURTHER READING

Bacon, Kenneth H. "U.S., Mexico Have Tentative Pact on Sugar Trade." *Wall Street Journal,* 29 July 1992.

Barry, Robert D. "The U.S. Sugar Program in the 1980s." *National Food Review,* January-March 1990.

Egan, Jack. "A New Battle for the Sultans of Sugar." *U.S. News & World Report,* 17 July 1995.

Lawrence, Richard. "Bitter Aftertaste for 'Big Sugar.'" *Journal of Commerce and Commercial,* 5 October 1995.

"Sugar Cane Growers Cooperative of Florida Rejects Payment from Federal Government." *PR Newswire,* 3 July 1996.

U.S. Bureau of the Census. *Current Industrial Reports.* Washington, D.C.: GPO, 1998.

U.S. Sugar Corp. "U.S. Sugar Corporation Begins 1999-2000 Sugar Harvest Season as Sugar Prices Collapse," 1999. Avail-

able from http://www.ussugar.com/news/991011sugarharvest
.html.

Wilkinson, Alec. *Big Sugar, Seasons in the Cane Fields of Florida.* New York: Alfred A. Knopf, 1989.

SIC 2062

CANE SUGAR REFINING

This entry includes establishments primarily engaged in refining purchased raw cane sugar and sugar syrup. Sugar cane is cut and milled into raw cane sugar, then shipped in that form to refiners to be processed into syrup, granulated sugar, powdered sugar, or brown sugar. Establishments that manufacture the raw cane sugar from sugar cane are included under **SIC 2061: Cane Sugar, Except Refining.** Other products of the cane sugar refining process include blackstrap molasses and invert sugar.

NAICS CODE(S)

311312 (Cane Sugar Refining)

The U.S. cane sugar refining industry has been facing heavy competition and increased economic challenges over the past two decades. However, the resulting shakeout and rationalization within the sector has managed to stabilize the situation, ensuring, at least in the short term, a viable future for a significantly streamlined industry. Manufacturers of beet sugar, high fructose corn syrup (HFCS), and artificial sweeteners have all taken a large share of the market away from cane sugar refiners.

From 1982 through 1996, the last year for which industry-wide employment statistics are available, the workforce in the U.S. cane sugar refining business plummeted from 173,000 to 65,000. Surprisingly, however, the value of shipments has not shown nearly so precipitous a drop as has been seen in industry employment. Shipments in 1982 were valued at about $3 billion and had dropped by 1996 to about $2.7 billion. Shipments for the year 2000 were projected to run about $2.5 billion.

Soft drink manufacturers switched to HFCS from liquid cane sugar in the 1980s, striking a severe blow to the sugar industry. To compensate for the losses, cane sugar refiners diversified, adding sugar beet processing operations and/or wet-milling operations to produce HFCS and other corn sweeteners. Beet sugar's share of the sugar market increased from 30 percent in the 1970s to 40 percent in the 1980s, and its market share continued to rise in the 1990s and into the 2000s.

In addition to the rise in HFCS, there were other problems for cane sugar refiners. Domestic production of

sugar cane dropped, and a strict quota on imported raw cane sugar was imposed by the federal government. The drop in availability of imported raw sugar was especially serious to the industry since sugar refineries in the United States processed more imported raw sugar than domestically-milled raw sugar.

Price, in addition to new product competition, plagued the cane sugar refining industry in the 1990s. Federal programs kept the price of domestic sugar higher than world market prices. In 1992, for example, when the world price of sugar was 10 cents a pound, the price in the United States was 21 cents a pound. The government also imposed a quota to prevent cheaper imported sugar from flooding the U.S. market. The United States continued to import some raw sugar because it did not grow enough to meet U.S. demand. Additional problems with crops—drought years in Texas, storms in Florida, and freezing temperatures in Louisiana—in the mid-1990s further depressed yields.

High fructose corn syrup producers have been able to undercut the sugar market—both beet sugar and cane sugar—make HFCS a cheaper alternative sweetening agent for processed foods. Americans consumed more corn syrup than refined sugar in the early 1990s, particularly in soft drinks. The beverage industry is said to be a primary force behind the demise of cane sugar production. Coca-Cola was the largest sugar buyer in the United States in the 1980s, accounting for 10 percent of the market.

At least one market continued to prefer cane sugar to its competitors. Candy and pastry makers were not impressed with substitutes for refined cane sugar. They insisted that beet sugar was not suitable for their purposes and that they achieved better results with pure cane sugar. According to the U.S. government, cane sugar and beet sugar have the same chemical formula so refiners cannot claim any difference between them.

To produce refined sugar from raw sugar, the raw sugar crystals are transported, aboard ships or trains to refineries where first the yellow-brown film is rinsed off. The sugar crystals are dissolved in water and poured through a series of filters until the liquid is clear. The syrup is heated so the liquid evaporates leaving crystals again. The crystals are spun in a centrifuge, and then the white sugar is separated into a drying drum where any remaining moisture is eliminated. Syrup that does not form crystals is used to make brown sugar. Molasses is another by-product of the refining process.

One of the most significant developments in cane sugar refining business came in late 1997 when Imperial Holly Corp. and Savannah Foods and Industries Inc. merged to create the largest domestic refiner and processor of sugar. The resulting company was renamed Imperial

Sugar Co. The company operates four cane sugar refineries, as well as a number of beet sugar facilities. The company markets sugar products under a variety of brand names, including Imperial, Dixie Crystals, Pioneer Sugar, Holly Sugar, Spreckels Sugar, and Diamond Crystal. Tate and Lyle North American Sugars, a subsidiary of London-based Tate and Lyle PLC, accounts for about 20 percent of the U.S. sugar market, marketing the best-selling Domino brand sugar products. In addition to refining cane sugar, Tate and Lyle processes beet sugar as well.

FURTHER READING

Bacon, Kenneth. ''Politics & Policy: U.S., Mexico Have Tentative Pact on Sugar Trade.'' *Wall Street Journal,* 29 July 1992.

Clairmonte, Frederick, and John Cavanagh. ''Destruction of the Sugar Industry.'' *Monthly Review,* May 1988.

Lawrence, Richard. ''Bitter Aftertaste for 'Big Sugar.''' *Journal of Commerce and Commercial,* 5 October 1995.

U.S. Bureau of the Census. *Current Industrial Reports.* Washington, D.C.: GPO, 1998.

SIC 2063

BEET SUGAR

This entry includes establishments primarily engaged in manufacturing sugar from sugar beets.

NAICS CODE(S)

311313 (Beet Sugar Manufacturing)

Sugar beets are one of the world's main sugar sources and an important source of sugar for the United States—more than 1.4 million acres of sugar beets are grown in 14 states. Reduced raw cane sugar imports hurt U.S. refiners in the 1980s, and the sugar industry turned to sugar beets to make up the difference. The United States processes more sugar from domestically-grown sugar beets than from domestically-grown sugar cane. Many cane refiners also invested in sugar beet processing firms in the 1980s as the sugar beet market share (including imports) climbed from 30 percent in the 1970s to 40 percent in 1988.

The beet sugar industry traces its origins to ancient Babylon, Egypt, and Greece, where sugar beets were grown. In 1744, a German chemist discovered that sugar from sugar beets was the same as sugar from sugar cane. About 50 years later, another German chemist developed a method for extracting sugar from the beets. Sugar mills were soon built in Europe and Russia. In 1838, sugar beets were being processed in the United States as well. The first successful commercial beet sugar mill was built in Alvarado, California, by American businessman E.H. Dyer.

Unlike sugarcane, which is processed into raw sugar (see **SIC 2061: Cane Sugar, except Refining**) to be marketed to cane refiners (see **SIC 2062: Cane Sugar Refining**), beets are processed directly into refined sugar. Beet sugar is produced from the root of the sugar beet plant, which is shipped to factories to be washed and cut into thin slices called cossettes. These cossettes are soaked in diffusers to remove the sugar. The resulting pulp is dried and mixed with molasses to make cattle feed. The sugar-water mixture goes through a series of purification processes in which lime, carbon dioxide, and filtration are used to remove impurities. Finally, the liquid is reheated until evaporation leaves a crystallized sugar product. Sugar products manufactured from sugar beets include dried beet pulp, beet sugar, molasses, granulated sugar, liquid sugar, invert sugar, powdered sugar, and syrup.

The federal government has provided price supports to the U.S. sugar industry for almost 200 years. Many consumer groups and commentators are critical of the U.S. program that protects the sugar industry. In 1990, James Bovard, a policy analyst, wrote in *USA Today* that the sugar program results in American sugar prices that are double or triple world prices, keeps out foreign sugar to create ''artificial shortages,'' and costs sugar-cane-producing allies such as the Philippines hundreds of millions of dollars in lost trade. When market conditions became bad in 1993 and 1994—reportedly the second time in history—industry leaders asked the U.S. Department of Agriculture (USDA) to help stimulate prices by imposing an allotment system, to balance beet sugar supply and demand.

California's sugar beet industry best exemplifies the results of these problems of the mid-1990s. Plagued by drought, disease and other problems, the state's once vibrant sugar beet industry, for the most part, never recovered. Crop yields in 1993 were down significantly. Between 1990 and 1996, the land devoted to sugar beet cultivation was cut by about 50 percent to about 90,000 acres. Two of California's eight sugar beet processing plants closed between the 1993 and 1994 harvests.

In the 1994 season, growers for Spreckels Sugar Co.—founded in 1898, once California's leading beet refiner—began reporting yields more than 20 percent lower than the previous year. Coupled with rock bottom prices and an over-abundance of beets in other states for the second year running, it was a disaster. Spreckels didn't survive; its assets and debts were purchased in 1996 by Imperial Holly.

According to the U.S. Census Bureau, in 1997 the beet sugar industry had 36 establishments, most with 100 employees or more, employing a total of 7,718 people. Statistics released in late 1999 show the value of shipments at $2.73 billion, up from $2.19 billion in 1992.

The main producers of sugar beets worldwide are Canada, France, Germany, Poland, Russia, Ukraine, and the United States. Traditional sugar beet producing states are California, Idaho, Michigan, North Dakota, and Wyoming. Leading beet sugar producing companies include American Crystal Sugar Company, Imperial Sugar Company, and Tate & Lyle North American Sugars Inc. American Crystal is owned by more than 2900 growers in North Dakota and Minnesota. The company, formed in 1899 and converted to a co-op in 1973, saw sales of $844.0 million. Imperial (formerly Imperial Holly Corp.) is the largest refined sugar supplier in the United States; it had 1999 sales of $1.9 billion. Tate & Lyle accounts for more than 20 percent of the sugar market with its Domino brand and also operates Western Sugar.

FURTHER READING

Barry, Robert D. "The U.S. Sugar Program in the 1980s." *National Food Review,* January-March 1990.

Graebner, Lynn. "Sugar Beet Industry Falls on Tough Times." *The Business Journal Serving Greater Sacramento,* 26 August 1996.

"Holly Sugar Corp. to Acquire Spreckels Sugar Operation." *Milling & Baking News,* 16 January 1996.

U.S. Census Bureau. "Manufacturing-Industry Series." *1997 Economic Census.* Washington, D.C.: GPO, 9 September 1999.

SIC 2064

CANDY AND OTHER CONFECTIONERY PRODUCTS

This category includes establishments primarily engaged in manufacturing candy, including chocolate candy, other confections, and related products, including chocolate-covered candy bars; breakfast bars; candy, except solid chocolate; chocolate bars made from purchased chocolate; chocolate candy, except solid chocolate; confectionery cake ornaments; fudge; granola bars; marshmallows; candy-covered nuts; candied, glazed, or crystallized fruits; and popcorn balls and candy-covered popcorn products. Establishments engaged primarily in manufacturing solid chocolate bars from cacao beans are classified under **SIC 2066: Chocolate and Cocoa Products.** Establishments manufacturing chewing gum are included under **SIC 2067: Chewing Gum,** while those primarily engaged in roasting and salting nuts are classified in **SIC 2068: Salted and Roasted Nuts and Seeds.** Establishments primarily engaged in manufacturing confectionery for direct sale on the premises to household consumers are classified in **SIC 5441: Candy, Nut, and Confectionery Stores.**

NAICS CODE(S)

311330 (Confectionery Manufacturing from Purchased Chocolate)

311340 (Non-Chocolate Confectionery Manufacturing)

INDUSTRY SNAPSHOT

Americans—and for that matter just about everybody else—have an insatiable appetite for candy. The U.S. population as a whole consumes more than 7 billion pounds of the stuff each year. Only about half of that is chocolate, with gummy bears and all sorts of other non-chocolate confections accounting for roughly 3.5 billion pounds. According to an August 1999 report in *USA Today,* "candy accounts for only about one-sixth of the whopping 152 pounds of sugar the average American eats in a year."

Market growth was exceptional through the late 1990s. In keeping with the health conscious consumers, low-fat/low-calorie candies gained prominence in the industry. However, the level of new product introductions in the industry was low during the mid-1990s. With sales of more than $22 billion, candy and other confections made the third biggest consumer-food category in late 1999, trailing only soft drinks and milk.

As the new millennium started, the U.S. candy and confectionery industry was expected to experience continued slow but steady growth, spurred by a robust U.S. economy and consumer demand for new candy products. The global market was also expected to see continued growth and prosperity. Despite the generally bright outlook for the industry worldwide, there are a number of challenges that will be faced by the industry's equipment and ingredient suppliers. These challenges include the shift in technical knowledge from the manufacturer to the supplier, increased new product development, new distribution channels, continued plant and company consolidation, and the introduction of so-called nutraceuticals into confectionery products.

Many members of the U.S. candy industry continue to be family-owned, especially the gourmet candy and confectionery manufacturers. Even leading candy maker Mars, Inc. is privately held by the Mars family.

BACKGROUND AND DEVELOPMENT

Many of the most popular candy bars sold today were developed between the 1890s and 1920 by various candy makers around the country. Rights to many of these candies have been bought and sold many times since they were developed and now are owned by large corporations such as Mars, Hershey Foods, Warner-Lambert, and RJR Nabisco.

Milton S. Hershey manufactured the first chocolate bar in the United States in 1894. Hershey Kisses were introduced in 1907. The Bunte Brothers are credited with manufacturing the first chocolate-covered candy bars in 1911. During World War I, Hershey and other candy makers shipped large blocks of chocolate to army training camps, where the blocks were cut into smaller chunks for distribution. This task became too time-consuming for military personnel, and the manufacturers started wrapping individual chocolate bars before shipping them. After the war, the candy makers continued to sell candy commercially in this form, and this method of selling candy became popular and convenient.

Many lines of candy bars were first sold for a dime, but sales did not catch on since consumers could buy a pound of loose candy for that same dime. Immediately after World War I, however, sugar and chocolate prices dropped and the price of most candy bars was dropped to a nickel. The price remained fairly constant until the late 1960s, when the price went back to a dime because of rising costs. Since then, prices have steadily climbed.

The forerunners of Canada Mints and NECCO wafers were first produced in 1847 by Chase and Company, with Canada Mints themselves introduced in Canada in the late 1880s and brought to the United States in 1908. NECCO wafers were introduced in 1912 by New England Confectionery Company, a company formed by Chase and two other candy companies; the NECCO brand name is derived from the company's initials.

LifeSavers first rolled into production in 1912 in a small factory in Cleveland, Ohio, when Cornelius Crane, a chocolate maker, developed mint tablets as a summertime product to compensate for the drop-off in sales of chocolate during the hot summer months. Crane went to a pill manufacturer to produce the mints and a malfunctioning machine produced mints with a hole in the center, thus creating the first LifeSavers product.

The first part of the twentieth century marked an explosive period of growth for the industry. Dozens of new candy products were introduced during this period, and many have endured. Ferrara Pan, a candy company formed in 1919 in Illinois, produced Jaw Breakers, Atomic Fireballs, and Boston Baked Beans. In 1919 the Oh Henry! bar was first manufactured by the Williamson Candy Company of Chicago. Charleston Chews were first sold in 1922 by the Fox-Cross Candy Company near San Francisco. Goobers were first made by the Blumenthal Chocolate Company in 1925. Holloway Milk Duds were introduced in 1926 by the Holloway Company. During the 1920s and 1930s, the James O. Welch Company introduced several favorites that are still around today, including Sugar Daddy, Sugar Babies, Pom Poms, and Junior Mints. Heath Bars, manufactured by the L.S. Heath Company, went on the market in 1932. Chunky was developed in the mid-1930s by Philip Silverstein, a New York candy maker.

In 1930 the most popular candy bar in America was created—Snickers. Snickers is one of the few candy bars still produced by its Originator—Mars, Inc., which today is one of the largest private companies in the United States. Mars introduced the Milky Way bar in 1923, 3 Musketeers and the Mars Bar in the 1930s, and M&M's in 1941.

Peter Paul Candies was formed in 1919 and introduced its first candy bar, the Konabar. Three years later, the company introduced the dark chocolate-covered coconut bar that served as the cornerstone of the company's product line—Mounds. The first Mounds was a single bar for a nickel, but during the Depression, Peter Paul doubled the size of the package by adding a second bar without increasing the price. This two-for-one tactic increased sales, despite the hard times. Peter Paul replaced hand wrapping with machine wrapping by converting a machine designed to wrap soap bars. The company also became one of the first to venture into broadcast advertising. In 1948 the company combined almonds with coconut to launch Almond Joy. Peter Paul acquired York Peppermint Patty in 1972. Several years later, Cadbury Schweppes PLC acquired the company for $58 million.

The candy industry has gone through a period of consolidation during the past 20 to 30 years. In the 1960s Hershey acquired Reese's, maker of Reese's Peanut Butter Cups since 1923; in 1977 Hershey acquired Y&S Candies, which had marketed licorice Twizzlers and Nibs since the 1920s. Hershey's acquisition of Cadbury Schweppes' U.S. division in 1988 propelled Hershey past Mars to become the leading U.S. candy maker. The purchase gave Hershey the rights to Peter Paul Almond Joy and Mounds, as well as Cadbury and Caramello products, to buttress its already impressive product line.

Despite the presence of such corporate giants as Mars, Inc. and Hershey Foods Corporation, several independent companies have maintained a significant presence in the industry. Tootsie Roll Industries has remained an independent company since its founding in 1896. It markets a line of Tootsie Roll products, as well as several products including Mason Dots and Bonomo Turkish Taffy, it acquired through the purchase of smaller companies.

Another company that remained independent since its beginnings is PEZ Candy Inc., with its flavored rectangular sugar tablets and vast array of plastic, flip-top dispensers. PEZ was founded in 1952 and is based in Orange, Connecticut. The first PEZ tablets were invented in 1927 as a peppermint tablet and cigarette substitute. PEZ was an abbreviation for *pfefferminz*, the German word for peppermint.

Sales for candy rose in 1992, after steep declines in 1990 and 1991. Manufacturers launched aggressive new product campaigns in 1992 and maintained the recent trend towards products with reduced fat and sugar content.

Candy exports were strong, especially with Mexico and Canada, and were expected to improve further with the passage of the North American Free Trade Agreement (NAFTA). Candy makers, though, are also concerned about the ramifications of new environmental regulations that might require them to provide recyclable packaging.

The industry has grown steadily in the 1990s. By 1992, shipments were valued at $8.9 billion. Adjusted for inflation, the value of candy and confectionery shipments rose an estimated 3.2 percent in that year. Between 1987 and 1991, the inflation-adjusted value of industry shipments rose 2.2 percent annually.

Although sales of regular candy have been substantial, the candy makers have increasingly taken notice of the relatively recent nutritional health emphasis and used it as a source of growth. In 1992 sugar-free and other ''healthier'' candies accounted for only one percent of the confectionery market, but industry members anticipate the market will grow, especially as new low-fat or low-calorie ingredients improve the taste of the so-called ''healthier'' chocolate candies.

Caprenin, developed by The Procter & Gamble Company, combined the taste and consistency of ordinary fat, but contained half the calories. Mars used it in its reduced-fat, reduced-calorie Milky Way II, which contained half the calories of the original Milky Way and eight grams of fat. Smaller companies were also trying to capitalize on the health market. In 1992, 92 percent of supermarkets and other stores sold some kind of sugar-free candy. Although most retail outlets said that sugar-free candy sales represented a very small market share, 87 percent of the store buyers surveyed expected demand for sugar-free items to continue to increase well into the 1990s. At the beginning of 1993, all ten candy bars on the top-selling candy list in the United States were manufactured by Mars, Hershey, or Nestle. Snickers remained the number one candy bar with sales of more than $61 million annually; Hershey products were second and third on the list, with Reese's Peanut Butter Cups (sales of $41 million) and Kit Kat ($36 million). The rest of the list included M&M's Plain (Mars, almost $32 million); Butterfinger (Nestle, almost $32 million); M&M's Peanut (Mars, almost $30 million); Crunch (Nestle, $26 million); Hershey Milk Chocolate ($24 million); Hershey Almond (24 million); and 3 Musketeers (Mars, $20 million).

CURRENT CONDITIONS

The late 1990s saw slow but steady growth in U.S. candy shipments. Total shipments in 1997, excluding gum products, were 6.45 million pounds, up a modest 1.4 percent from 6.36 million pounds in 1996. The quantity of chocolate candy shipped increased 0.8 percent, while non-chocolate candy shipments rose by 2.0 percent. The increase in dollar value of these shipments was more pronounced, probably a reflection of inflation. In dollar terms, total shipments of candy, excluding gum products, were valued at $13.17 billion, up 7.8 percent from 1996 shipments valued at $12.21 billion. The value of chocolate candy shipped increased 7.0 percent, and non-chocolate shipments showed an increase in value of 9.6 percent.

Candy makers are also cashing in on the holiday markets. The seasonal candy market posted overall respective dollar and unit volume gains of 10.4 percent and 9.7 percent in 1995, according to the *Candy Industry* overview of this industry.

Mars, Hershey, and Nestle had traditionally stayed away from the holiday candy market, but when candy consumption and sales remained flat, the candy giants saw great opportunity to capture a major share of the holiday sales. The three companies repackaged many of their most famous goodies in pastel colors for Easter. Their entry into the holiday market shoved aside many of the usual holiday candy manufacturers.

Many other confectioners are looking to the kids' market for growth. Industry experts and retailers note that more than 50 percent of children in the United States between the ages of four and twelve possess an average of $4 a week to spend. Many candy makers were thus pitching their products directly to this market segment.

The adult health conscious market was seen as a major growth market for this industry. Nabisco's Snackwell's brand of products pioneered a new era in this industry. The resounding success of Snackwell's motivated many manufacturers to join this era of new comparable products designed to placate consumers worried about the fat and calorie content in existing products. Hershey and Mars offered their new alternatives with the launch of Sweet Escapes and Milky Way Lite respectively. Other smaller companies were quick to join the growing fray as well. The market for sugar-free candies was valued at more than $50 million in the mid-1990s.

The holiday market and Americans' increasing preoccupation with healthier eating were not the only marketing opportunities being exploited by candy manufacturers. The coming of the new millennium provided many candy manufacturers with a new vehicle. At the industry's annual All Candy Expo, held in Chicago in June 1999, a number of candy makers introduced confections boxed and branded with the words ''Year 2000.'' Others offered more elaborate Y2K gimmicks, including the Countdown Millennium Watch offered by Gallerie Au Chocolat. A digital clock, it is shaped like a stopwatch and emits a buzzing sound and dispenses candy when one of its side buttons is pushed.

INDUSTRY LEADERS

Hershey Foods Corp. and Mars Inc. rank number one and number two, respectively, in the U.S. candy market. Privately held, Mars Inc. is secretive about its financial performance, but analysts estimated its 1998 revenues at about $15 billion. Although this dwarfed Hershey's 1998 sales of $4.4 billion, much of the Mars revenue is generated by its non-candy operations, including Uncle Ben's rice products and a full product line of pet foods. In candy sales alone, Hershey is the leader.

Hershey Foods Corp., based in the Pennsylvania town that bears its name, produces a full line of candy products bearing the Hershey brand name as well as such other leading candy brands as Reese's, Twizzler, Almond Joy, Jolly Rancher, and Kit Kat. Hershey's workforce numbers more than 16,000 employees. The company's net income in 1998 hit nearly $341 million, an increase of 1.4 percent from the previous year.

Mars Inc., headquartered in McLean, Virginia, was founded in 1911 by candy salesman Frank C. Mars, and it was still in the hands of the Mars family in the early 2000s. The company's co-presidents are John F. Mars and Forest E. Mars Jr., who also serves as the company's chief executive officer. Although it is a major candy manufacturer, the company has diversified into a number of non-candy product lines, including Uncle Ben's rice products and pet foods sold under the brand names of Kal Kan, Pedigree, Sheba, and Whiskas. Among its leading candy products are M&Ms, Snickers, Milky Way, and 3 Musketeers. The company employs 30,000 people worldwide.

Nabisco Holdings Corp. of New York, a highly diversified company, also has a significant presence in the confectionery industry, primarily through its Nabisco subsidiary. Nabisco Holdings' 1998 sales toped $8 billion; its workforce totaled more than 50,000 employees. Among the factors in Nabisco's success are the continuing popularity of its Oreo and Chips Ahoy! Cookie brands, as well as the more recent success of its low-fat Snackwell's brand cookies and snacks.

Other leading U.S. candy makers include Leaf Inc., Lance Inc., Russell Stover Candies Inc., E.J. Brach Corp., Sathers Inc., Archibald Candy Corp., Farley Foods U.S.A., and Tootsie Roll Industries Inc.

AMERICA AND THE WORLD

The international confectionery market, valued at nearly $80 billion, is growing at a compound annual rate of 0.7 percent, according to *Candy Industry,* a monthly trade journal. The U.S. market for candy and other confectionery products is estimated at $23.8 billion, while the market for all of North America is valued at about $36.0 billion. The North American market was growing at a compound annual rate of 2.7 percent, as of mid-1999.

Leading growth markets, in terms of per capita consumption, are the countries of Vietnam, Brazil, Ireland, China, and the Czech Republic. All are experiencing consumption increases ranging from 11 to 25 percent.

Although Europeans consume a great amount of candy, Europe continues to be a relatively poor market for U.S. candy. High duties have kept U.S. candy out of the European Union (EU), although some American companies have invested in European candy companies and avoided the duties. U.S. companies face stiff competition from European confectioners, particularly Swiss chocolate producers, which are typically considered to market finer quality confections than American companies. Hershey purchased its first European company in 1991 with the $31 million acquisition of Gubor Schokoladen, a chocolate company that manufactures pralines and chocolates. Warner-Lambert, a large pharmaceutical and consumer products manufacturer that also produces cough drops and other confectionery products, entered into a joint venture with Alivar S.p.A to sell cough drops and candies in Italy, a large confectionery market.

FURTHER READING

"Annual Update Unveils Industry's Fortune." *Candy Industry,* January 1995.

"Champions a Gold Medal Year." *Candy Industry,* July 1996.

Dornblaser, Lynn. "Candy Is More than Dandy." *Prepared Foods,* 15 April 1996.

"The Expanding Market for Bulk Candy." *Candy Industry,* July 1996.

Fishman, Ted C. "We're Killing Ourselves with Sweetness." *USA Today,* 23 August 1999.

Henry, Jim. "Keeping it in the Family: and Industry Discussion." *Candy Industry,* January 1996.

U.S. Bureau of the Census. *Current Industrial Reports.* Washington, D.C.: GPO, 1998.

"U.S. Candy Industry Looking to Cash In on Y2K." *Reuters,* 23 June 1999.

SIC 2066

CHOCOLATE AND COCOA PRODUCTS

Included in this industry classification are establishments primarily engaged in shelling, roasting, and grinding cocoa beans for the purpose of making chocolate liquor—from which cocoa powder and cocoa butter are derived—and in the further manufacture of solid chocolate bars, chocolate coatings, and other chocolate and cocoa products. Also included is the manufacture of similar products, except candy, from purchased chocolate or cocoa. Establishments primarily engaged in manufacturing candy from purchased cocoa products are classified in **SIC 2064: Candy and Other Confectionery Products.**

NAICS CODE(S)

311320 (Chocolate and Confectionery Manufacturing from Cacao Beans)

INDUSTRY SNAPSHOT

The chocolate and cocoa products industry has traditionally been subject to significant fluctuations in demand. Chocolate products tend to be seasonal in nature, with demand increasing sharply during the holidays. Typically the third and fourth quarters reflect the highest sales. In addition, several consumer trends have had an impact on demand. These include rising sales of premium-priced chocolates and the growing concern about the health risks associated with the consumption of such high-fat foods like chocolate.

The number of establishments producing chocolate and cocoa products in the United States was 398 in 1997. Estimated retail sales of chocolate products for 1998 was $13 billion.

ORGANIZATION AND STRUCTURE

All cocoa beans processed by U.S. manufacturers must be imported, by direct purchase or through the services of a broker, as cacao trees require a tropical climate to flourish. Growers are paid for the beans at market price, which is determined primarily by the quality and availability of the crop worldwide. A testament to cocoa's importance as a commodity is the existence of cocoa exchanges, similar to standard stock exchanges, in New York City, London, Hamburg, and Amsterdam. The beans are then processed to make chocolate liquor, which is in turn used to further manufacture such products as cocoa, chocolate syrup, and solid chocolate chips and baking bars. The chocolate liquor is also often sold to other manufacturers that combine it with additional ingredients to produce confections, bakery items, and dairy products.

Manufacturers roast, shell, and grind the beans to produce unsweetened chocolate, the chocolate liquor that is the basic ingredient of all chocolate products. Further processing of chocolate liquor falls into two categories: cocoa manufacture and chocolate manufacture.

In cocoa production the fat is pressed from chocolate liquor, leaving cocoa cake that is crushed to form cocoa powder. The powder may be sweetened and sold as a cocoa beverage or left unsweetened for use in bakery and dairy products and for home cooking use. Cocoa butter, the fat removed from the chocolate liquor, is used mainly in sweetened chocolate, but is also used as a moisturizer in soaps, creams, and medications.

The production of chocolate requires the addition of sugar or other sweeteners and cocoa butter to chocolate liquor. Milk solids are also added in the manufacture of milk chocolate. Bulk quantities of sweetened chocolate (blocks of at least 4.5 kilograms) are considered chocolate coating and are used for candy coverings and baked goods. Chocolate coating is generally more expensive than the confectioners' coatings, which are made from cocoa powder.

Chocolate manufacturers sell these semi-processed cocoa products to other firms that use the items in the production of confectionery, baked goods, and dairy products such as chocolate milk. In addition, some producers also manufacture their own confectionery. Exports of chocolate products consist mainly of confectionery items rather than semi-processed chocolate.

BACKGROUND AND DEVELOPMENT

The history of the chocolate and cocoa products industry in the United States dates from 1765. In that year, supplied by cocoa beans from the West Indies, the first chocolate factory was established in New England. Physician James Baker funded the venture, whose brand (Baker's) continue to be produced today by Kraft General Foods, Incorporated.

During World War I, the U.S. government recognized chocolate's worth as both nourishment and a morale booster to those in the armed forces. Space was made on cargo planes coming into the country so a sufficient supply of cocoa beans would be available to manufacture chocolate products. The U.S. Army D-rations still include 4-ounce chocolate bars, and cocoa bean products are part of the rarified rations of NASA space travelers.

The chocolate industry did not escape the effects of the recession of early 1990s. Few cocoa-based companies in North America have not experienced layoffs, mergers and consolidations, plant closings, shift cutbacks, advertising budget slashes, and operational streamlining, reflected in poor sales figures and fiscal restraint. Between 1989 and 1991, the industry experienced 50 acquisitions, mergers, licensing agreements, or joint ventures, and companies have been intent on expanding and diversifying their product base.

The decline in world output of cocoa and the increase in demand for chocolates in new markets such as China, Russia, and other emerging economies indicate the arrival of a long-awaited bull market in cocoa. Another area in which the demand for cocoa increased was the beverage industry. Of the 2,894 new product introductions in 1995, approximately one-half of the beverage products consisted of either cocoa, coffee, or tea.

In the mid-1990s, more producers began catering to health conscious consumers. Popularity of lite (low-fat) candy and lite desserts increased dramatically. Bakers also began offering reduced fat and fat-free chocolate items.

CURRENT CONDITIONS

By 1998, American chocolate consumption reached 3.3 billion pounds annually, or 12.2 pounds per person. Despite denials by the Chocolate Manufacturers Association and the National Confectioners Association, reports continued to circulate about a coming chocolate shortage and an increase in prices. Unfavorable weather and plant a disease were cited as the primary reason for possible shortages. El Nino was blamed for dry conditions in cacao-growing regions. Witches' broom, a fungus that rots the cocoa pod, caused irreparable harm to Brazil's cocoa production; the company dropped from the world's number-one grower in the 1970s to fifth place by the end of the century. Growers feared that the fungus would spread to neighboring countries.

Additionally, the depletion of the tropical rainforest in the primary cacao producing countries of Brazil, Costa Rica, Ghana, Trinidad, Malaysia, Cote d'Ivoire, and Indonesia was of great concern to American Cocoa Research Institute (ACRI). A continuing demand for cocoa products led to an increase in cocoa farming acreage to 16.3 million, much of it in cleared areas. According to the Institute, the cacao tree's natural habitat is in the shade of the rainforest where pollination and pest control occur naturally. The transfer of trees to open areas results in increased use of fertilizers and pesticides.

In response to this concern, the ACRI established the Sustainable Cocoa Program to assist farmers in increasing or maintaining productivity at levels that are "economically viable, ecologically sound, and culturally acceptable." The program's goal is to establish a sustainable and geographically diverse supply of cocoa by 2010.

INDUSTRY LEADERS

Industry leaders at the end of the twentieth century included Hershey Foods Corporation, Farley Candy Company, World's Finest Chocolate, Inc., Merckens Chocolate Company, and Ghirardelli Chocolate Company.

Hershey Foods Corporation is a multinational corporation that grew from the company founded by Milton S. Hershey in 1894. Hershey has two divisions—one domestic and the other international. Hershey Chocolate North American is the domestic producer of chocolate, confectionery products, and chocolate-related grocery products. Hershey International oversees the corporation's international operations and exports to more than 90 countries. In 1998, the corporation posted net sales of $4.4 billion and employed 15,000 workers. In July 1999, citing rising production costs, Hershey announced that it would no longer process its own cocoa.

RESEARCH AND TECHNOLOGY

In an effort to compensate for lagging sales, a number of chocolate and cocoa-based companies have adopted technological solutions to increase efficiency and lower production costs. Grace Cocoa's new Chocolate Americas Division headquarters, for example, built a $95-million plant with 335,000 square feet of computer-integrated manufacturing constructed on a barren site in a Milwaukee, Wisconsin, industrial park. According to a *Candy Industry* interview with Dave Pollock, director of manufacturing at the new factory, "this really is the future."

Part of the new technology in the plant includes the computerization of a number of production processes. While this has helped facilitate more efficient productivity, it also has engendered a number of challenges. One of these was retraining employees who were familiar with only rudimentary chocolate making procedures. The state of Wisconsin helped offset some of the retraining costs by contributing 50 percent of the cost of employees' tuition at local technical colleges.

Cocoa has become such an intrinsic and valuable part of the U.S. economy that efforts by industry and science are underway to better understand the bean itself. The American Cocoa Research Institute contributed $1.5 million to Penn State University's Molecular Biology of Cocoa program. The main objective of the program is to increase understanding of the biology, botany, and genetics of the cocoa plant. The objectives of the study include the study of disease resistance, quality, plant delivery, and tools.

FURTHER READING

American Cocoa Research Institute. "ACRI Sustainable Cocoa Program Overview," 5 November 1999. Available from http://www.acri-cocoa.org/ac_scpo.html.

"Charlie and the Chocolate Plantation." *E*, July 1999.

"Chocoholics' Plight: Bad Weather, Disease, Force Coca Prices Up." *St. Louis Post-Dispatch*, 27 October 1997.

Chocolate Manufacturers Association. "No Need To Panic: Chocolate Supplies Are Ample," 9 July 1999. Available from http://www.candyusa.org/panic.html.

Dornblaser, Lynn. "Adult Drinks Lead the Beverage Pack." *Prepared Foods*, 15 April 1996.

Ingram, Molly. "Glaze, Drizzle, Dip and Chip—Chocolate Does It All." *Bakery Production and Marketing*, 15 February 1996.

Lemonick, Michael D. "No Wonder You Can't Resist: Chocolate and Marijuana Share the Same Chemistry." *Time*, 2 September 1996.

Sanik, Sholom. "How 'Bout a Nice Hot Cocoa Contract." *Futures*, December 1996.

Sulon, Bill. "Hershey Foods to End Cocoa Processing." *The Patriot News*, 14 July 1999.

SIC 2067

CHEWING GUM

This industry consists of establishments primarily engaged in manufacturing chewing gum or chewing gum base.

NAICS CODE(S)

311340 (Non-Chocolate Confectionery Manufacturing)

INDUSTRY SNAPSHOT

The American chewing gum industry has been marked by strong periods of growth and decline throughout the twentieth century. Since the 1970s this industry has been growing at a faster pace overseas than within the United States. The industry's overall success has been the result of low manufacturing costs and aggressive marketing campaigns. In 1997 there were 10 U.S. manufacturers in this industry, employing about 3,521 workers.

As one of the best performers in the candy industry, chewing gum continues to be a favorite among American consumers. Overall domestic gum sales, however, were flat in the late 1990s, though sales of sugar and sugar-free gum continued to rise steadily. Consumers, adults, seniors, and children alike continue chewing various types of gum for a variety of reasons, thereby adding to the market demand in this industry. Innovations such as smoking-cessation gums and dental gums, which offered promises to clean teeth, entered the industry in the late 1990s.

ORGANIZATION AND STRUCTURE

Chewing gum companies use two main channels of distribution: one channel is through wholesalers, who supply retail stores in the areas they serve; the other channel is the delivery of boxes of chewing gum directly to large retail outlets from the manufacturers' warehouses and factories. The retail distribution chain includes food, drug, variety, and convenience stores, gas stations, newsstands, and restaurants. Another important channel for these manufacturers has been distributors who stock vending machines.

BACKGROUND AND DEVELOPMENT

History. Though chewing gum bases are primarily synthetic today, gum was originally derived from natural sources such as tree resins and saps. The use of chewing gum made from tree resin dates back to ancient Greek and Mayan civilizations. In North America, Wampanoag Indians introduced chewing gum to European settlers. The gum was made from the resin of spruce trees.

Americans began manufacturing gum in the mid-1800s, adding paraffin wax, which was used to make the gum softer and last longer. At about this time flavors such as mint were added to the gum, helping to increase the product's popularity. In 1848 John Curtis of Maine started producing the first commercial spruce gum.

American settlers traveling west learned about chewing chicle, the hardened sap of sapodilla trees, from the Osage Indians. The sapodilla tree is found mainly in the tropical rain forests of the Yucatan Peninsula of Mexico and Guatemala. By 1869 the first commercial chicle was manufactured, and in 1906 paraffin was added to chicle.

During the late 1800s, companies that would become the industry leaders entered this business, making valuable contributions to the industry as a whole. William Wrigley Jr. was a baking soda salesman who started offering two packages of chewing gum with each can of baking soda. When this promotion proved successful, Mr. Wrigley decided to enter the relatively undeveloped chewing gum business. His first two brands were Lotta and Vassar; later in 1893 he introduced Juicy Fruit and Wrigley's Spearmint. In the early days Wrigley used premiums to encourage merchants to stock his chewing gum. The success of this method of marketing led to a published catalog of premiums for retailers. Wrigley was also one of the pioneers in the use of advertising to promote brand-name merchandise. Advertisements for Wrigley's gum ran in newspapers, magazines, and on outdoor posters. Even during industry slumps, Wrigley continued advertising.

By 1910 Wrigley's Spearmint gum was the largest selling chewing gum in the United States. Later that year the company expanded by opening a factory in Canada. By 1927 Wrigley plants were being built in Great Britain and Australia. The different preferences in international markets led to new types of products and flavors. Perhaps the most successful product for the company outside the United States was the pellet-shaped chewing gum sold under the PK brand.

Another industry leader, Franklin Channing, invented the first dental gum, Dentyne, in 1899. About the same time, Henry Fleer created Chiclets, the first candy-coated chewing gum.

Bubble gum was first developed in 1906, but early batches were too sticky to sell, and it was not until 1928 that bubble gum was first marketed. Another important development in this industry was the first sugarless gum, which was created in the late 1940s (but not marketed until the 1950s). LifeSavers' CareFree and American Chicle's Trident appeared in the mid-1960s and dominated the sugarless gum market early on. In the 1980s Wrigley's Extra gum was launched, and by 1990 it controlled 40 percent of the $480 million sugar-free gum market.

Sugar-free gums began using xylitol, an artificial sweetener, in the late 1970s. However, in 1978, the U.S. Food and Drug Administration began investigating possible links between xylitol and cancer; though no link was ever established, products made with xylitol were reformulated using other artificial sweeteners. In the early 1990s xylitol was reintroduced by Leaf Specialty Products, who manufactured XyliFresh, a chewing gum intended for fighting plaque.

Chewing gum manufacturers have also enjoyed heightened success during war times. The Wm. Wrigley Jr. Company recorded an increase in chewing gum demand during World War I and II and during the 1990-91 conflict in the Persian Gulf. In fact, during World War II, when top-grade ingredients were scarce, production was limited to the armed forces, and civilians were sold a lesser quality gum under the brand name Orbit.

Marketing and Product Trends. Since it was first sold in America, gum has been packaged with novelties, such as sports cards, toys, and comic strips. In the twentieth century, companies launched novelty bubble gums, which were packaged in a variety of shapes and unusual forms, such as school lockers and toothpaste tubes.

In the early 1990s sour gum became popular with children. These chewing gums have an extremely sour taste that becomes sweet and eventually has a neutral or tangy taste. Children often used these gums to play jokes on friends or to prove their mettle. In 1992 sour gum brought in an estimated $70 million in retail sales. Moreover, as the demand for sour gum caught suppliers by surprise, a "black market" for the product emerged.

In the 1980s chewing gum sales were boosted by campaigns that promoted chewing gum as an alternative to smoking. Other advertisements have endorsed sugar-free gums as being good for teeth. In addition to advertisements on television, radio, and in newspapers, companies in this industry use sales representatives to market their products. These representatives regularly visit retailers and assist them with display designs and layouts.

In 1993 LifeSavers made industry news with its innovative approach to selling bubble gum. Its Bubble Yum product was promoted through a traveling virtual reality arcade game, and LifeSavers was the first company to use the game as a marketing tool. The game, called Planet Bubble Yum, featured chunks of bubble gum flying around in three-dimensional animation. Bubble Yum charged proof of purchase seals for admission. The tour traveled to shopping malls in major U.S. cities, with an average attendance of 1,100 people per location.

After a slump during the 1970s and early 1980s, chewing gum manufacturers entered the 1990s on a slight upswing. A new interest in chewing gum emerged in the United States since gum was promoted as an alternative to smoking when more public places began to prohibit smoking. Domestic per capita consumption of chewing gum

increased from 168 sticks in 1986 to 183 in 1992, resulting in a 1.3 percent average annual rise in gum sales.

Production. The cost of producing chewing gum has always been low. High demand for chewing gum, allowing for high volume production, and advances in automation have helped to reduce costs further. The price of ingredients, such as corn syrup and gum base, has also declined since the 1970s, thus reducing costs and increasing profit margins.

Modern methods and new materials have changed the character of chewing gum. Natural ingredients have become scarce due to changing climatic conditions, demand, and development in regions where the ingredients were harvested. Chicle and other products from trees are now used in conjunction with synthetic materials. Most chewing gums are made with five basic ingredients: chewing gum base, sugar, corn syrup, softeners (such as glycerin and other vegetable oils), and flavors (mostly extracted from mint plants). In sugar-free gums, sugar and corn syrup are usually replaced with aspartame, mannitol, and/or sorbitol.

Manufacturers typically employ food chemists to inspect and test all ingredients and materials. The Wm. Wrigley Jr. Company maintains a central quality assurance laboratory where samples from each factory are tested regularly so that flavor and texture are consistent in their products throughout the world.

CURRENT CONDITIONS

According to the U.S. Census Bureau, Americans ate about 1.8 pounds of gum per capita each year. The growth rate of gum fell 5.2 percent in 1997, and the $1 billion U.S. gum market showed little signs of growth. To blame were increasing sales of mints, including new intensely flavored mints. Mint sales skyrocketed by 40 percent in the second half of the decade. To combat declining sales, gum manufacturers introduced new, intensely flavored products. Wrigley launched a brand called Everest Powerful Mint Gum through subsidiary Amurol Confections Co. The strong mint gum was targeted toward adults hooked on strong mints. Wrigley also launched Eclipse gum in the summer of 1999, its first new product in five years. Eclipse, a mint gum, was marketed as a breath-deodorizing gum.

Total retail sales of gum in the U.S. in 1997 reached $2.2 billion, according to the National Confectioners Association. In terms of retail sales at food stores, sales of gum for the year ended April 17, 1999, broke down as follows: bubble gum had sales of $79.1 million, a decline of 3.8 percent compared to the previous year; sugar-free bubble gum had sales of $40.2 million, down 4.1 percent; chewing gum enjoyed sales of $237.6 million, down 1.7 percent; and sugar-free chewing gum had sales of

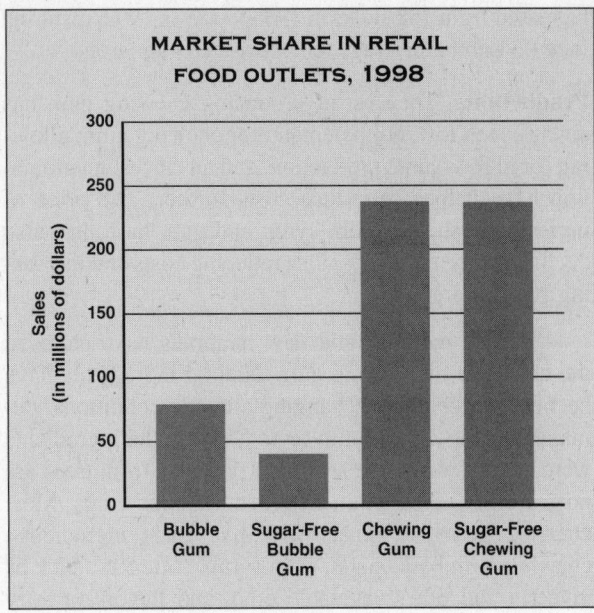

MARKET SHARE IN RETAIL FOOD OUTLETS, 1998

INDUSTRY LEADERS

Wm. Wrigley Jr. Company was the world's leading manufacturer of chewing gum. The company commanded about 50 percent of the U.S. gum market and had strong operations overseas as well, with about 60 percent of revenues coming from international operations. Wrigley sold its gum products in more than 140 countries. Wrigley's subsidiaries produced chewing gum base and manufactured novelty gums. The company suffered through the late 1990s as it faced increased competition, particularly from the mints category, and profits were stagnant. In late 1999, however, Wrigley showed indications of recovery. Wrigley's 1998 sales were $2 billion.

Warner-Lambert Company was the second-ranked industry leader, with more than $10.2 billion in overall sales revenues and 41,000 employees in 1999. Its American Chicle Company, maker of Chiclets, was founded in 1856. The company also manufactured breath mints and other confectioneries. In addition to Chiclets, the company's chewing gum brands included Trident and Dentyne.

Other industry leaders included Nabisco Group Holdings Corp., maker of the Carefree and Bubble Yum brands, and the Topps Company, Inc., with 1999 sales of $229.4 million. Topps Company, was also a leader in commercial printing (see **SIC 2759: Commercial Printing, Gravure**) for their bubble gum sports cards. This company has been most noted in the gum industry for producing Bazooka Bubble Gum.

AMERICA AND THE WORLD

Much of American-produced chewing gum is sold overseas. Wrigley has operated in Europe since the 1910s and has had 80 percent of the chewing gum market in Britain and Germany. A growing market was Russia, where gum chewing had once been forbidden. Wrigley, according to ACNielsen, commanded about 60 percent of the $180 million Russian chewing gum market in the late 1990s. Its main competitor was a Danish company named Dandy.

Though Wrigley's international sales grew significantly through the 1990s, the company did not position itself in Latin America, where many governments required joint ventures. In the mid-1990s Wrigley's business abroad was rising over 10 percent annually; during that time the company opened a factory in China, where people had already been introduced to chewing gum through shipments from Singapore.

Warner-Lambert also fared well in overseas markets. In the late 1990s about 60 percent of its overall sales were from overseas. The company's markets included Canada, Europe, Asia, the Middle East, and Latin America. In the mid-1990s Warner-Lambert launched an aggressive ad-

$237 million, up 15.4 percent. Overall gum sales in retail food outlets were $594 million, up 4 percent, according to ACNielsen. Of all confectionery items, gum placed second. Sugar-free chewing gum also sold well in drug stores, increasing an impressive 23.2 percent. Though other gum types suffered from declines in sales, the strong performance by sugar-free chewing gum boosted overall gum sales in drug stores by 6.6 percent.

The top gum brands in terms of dollar share, according to Management Science Associates, Inc., were Extra, Trident, Winterfresh, Doublemint, Big Red, Bubblicious, Ice Breakers, Juicy Fruit, Dentyne Ice, and Carefree. Other types of gum gaining popularity in the late 1990s included smoking-cessation gum, dental gum, and breath-refreshing gum. According to sales figures from Chicago-based Information Resources, Inc., in *Supermarket News,* food stores held 12 percent of the smoking-cessation market, mass merchandisers held 20 percent of the market, and drug stores held a whopping 68 percent of the market in 1996.

Gum manufacturers continued to introduce new products, especially to cater to one of their biggest groups of consumers—kids. It was found that kids make 270 visits to stores a year averaging 5.2 purchases a week. Therefore, gum manufacturers spent a lot of money and time researching new products that would appeal to kids. Packaging played an important role in gum purchases. Innovative products like gum squeezed out of a tube, Roller Racer Bubble Gum, Bubble Cube, a 3-D puzzle toy filled with bubble bits, and gum rolled up like ribbon several feet long were some of the hot gum products on the market. Increasingly popular in the late 1990s were sour and intensely flavored gums.

vertising campaign in Latin America, which included materials to help their products stand out in crowded street kiosks.

RESEARCH AND TECHNOLOGY

Companies in this industry are continually seeking ingredients and processes that can improve product quality and packaging. In the 1980s new synthetic gum bases were developed to overcome the limitations of previously used natural ingredients. These new materials are aimed at increasing gum flavor, improving texture, and reducing stickiness.

The environmental impact of the packaging used for chewing gum has been of considerable concern for companies in this industry. These companies rely on the wrappers and plastic packaging to keep gum fresh, yet these materials result in considerable waste. Scientists at gum companies have been evaluating and making changes to packaging and researching materials to meet future disposal and recycling requirements.

FURTHER READING

"Champions a Gold Medal Year." *Candy Industry,* July 1996.

"Eschew It? Russians Now Enjoy Their Gum." *Grand Rapids Press,* 3 October 1999.

Kaplan, Andrew. "Gum and Mints: Categories with Pop." *U.S. Distribution Journal,* 15 July 1995.

Malbin, Peter. "Butting Out: Retailers Are Caught in Swirl of Potential—and problems—in Merchandising High-Priced Smoking Cessation Products." *Supermarket News,* 4 November 1996.

Naughton, Keith. "Chewed Out by Mints." *Newsweek,* 1 November 1999.

Peltz, James F. "Investors See Room for Growth by Gum-Maker." *New Orleans Times-Picayune,* 26 December 1999.

Smyth, William. "New Intense Gums, Mint are Chewing Up Volume." *Supermarket News,* 25 October 1999.

Tiffany, Susan. "Candy Booms in Robust Economy." *Candy Industry,* 1 July 1999.

U.S. Census Bureau. "Nonchocolate Confectionery Manufacturing." *1997 Economic Census.* Washington, D.C.: GPO, 15 December 1999.

SIC 2068

SALTED AND ROASTED NUTS AND SEEDS

This category includes establishments primarily engaged in manufacturing salted, roasted, dried, cooked, or canned nuts or in processing grains or seeds in a similar manner for snack purposes. Establishments primarily engaged in manufacturing confectionery-coated nuts are classified under **SIC 2064: Candy and Confectionery Products** and those manufacturing peanut butter are classified under **SIC 2099: Food Preparations, Not Elsewhere Classified.**

NAICS CODE(S)

311911 (Roasted Nuts and Peanut Butter Manufacturing)

In the late 1990s, salted or dried peanuts accounted for about 53 percent of the snack-nut market. The rest of the snack-nut market was split among mixed nuts, cashews, walnuts, almonds, pistachios, and macadamia nuts. Salted or roasted sunflower seeds, pumpkin seeds, and other seeds are also included in this category. Nuts and seeds are sold both packaged and as bulk food in grocery stores.

The industry shipped $2.8 billion worth of goods in 1995, up from $2.3 billion in 1990. Industry exports totaled 983 million tons in 1995. The number of establishments in the industry has increased 13 percent since 1990, from 87 to 98 in 1995. In 1997 the value of shipments, as reported by the U.S. Census Bureau, was nearly $3.1 billion. The number of industry players increased as well; approximately 125 establishments were operating in 1997.

The market for snack nuts has remained fairly level for a decade. Snack-food nuts have strong competition from potato chips, tortilla chips, pretzels, and microwave popcorn for the nation's snack dollars. The snack-nut and seed industry has handled its competition by introducing new flavors of seeds and nuts. For example, Blue Diamond introduced lemon-chili and ranch-flavored almonds in some parts of the country, and Planters introduced hot and mild versions of spicy peanuts, as well as low-fat honey roasted peanuts.

Manufacturers have also tried more creative packaging to expand their markets. Planters brought out a line of snacks in small, narrow bags and called them Munch-and-Go Tube Nuts. Merchandising efforts for nut and seed snacks are minimal compared to those for potato chips, though. Manufacturers have also been pushing for more shelf space and displays in grocery stores. Nut and seed snacks are often placed in the "impulse" area—near registers. While salted snack nuts and seeds showed flat sales, many producers and distributors were optimistic about sales of dried nuts because of their nutritional value.

Price has been another factor working against the industry. About 20 to 25 percent of domestic peanuts are used for snack nuts. With peanut prices kept high by government quotas, restrictions against imports, and support prices, peanut snack manufacturers are somewhat restricted in their supplies and prices. While almond processors and processors of other nuts can buy foreign nuts, peanut processors must buy domestically-grown peanuts. A drought in 1990 sent peanut prices soaring, resulting in deep profit losses for peanut processors. Prices were lowered by the 2000s.

Peanuts for snack nuts are usually purchased raw by a nut sheller. Processors, such as Planters, purchase the shelled nuts and send them on to blanchers to have the skins removed. (Commercial processors used 161 million pounds of shelled peanuts during January 2000.) Finally, the processing company receives them for roasting. Some snack nut companies, however, do the shelling and blanching themselves.

Many non-peanut nuts are sold through grower-owned co-operatives such as Blue Diamond Almonds and Diamond Walnuts. In 1992 Blue Diamond marketed 40 percent of the almonds grown in California, the only state in which almonds are grown commercially. Ten years earlier, Blue Diamond was handling 55 percent of the crop, but some growers dropped out to sell their almonds to other California and out-of-state processors. California far surpasses other states in terms of 1997 product shipments with $1.2 billion. The closest followers were Georgia ($362.0 million), Massachusetts ($44.5 million), Illinois ($24.6 million), and Michigan ($20.4 million).

The industry sales leader was Nabisco Foods Group (Planters brand), with overall 1999 sales of $8.3 billion and 50,700 employees. Dole Food Company was second, with overall 1999 sales of $5.1 billion and 53,500 employees. Other industry leaders included Lance Inc. (1999 sales of $531.0 million and 4,878 employees); Blue Diamond Growers (1999 sales of $404.0 million and 1,150 employees); John B. Sanfilippo & Son Inc. (1999 sales of $319.2 million and 1,430 employees); and ML Macadamia Orchards, L.P. (1999 sales of $16.0 million and 3 employees).

FURTHER READING

Dorn, Chad A. "Nut Market Going Nutty in 1996." *Candy Industry,* October 1996.

Hoover's Company Profiles. Hoover's Online, 2000. Available from http://www.hoovers.com.

"Processed Nuts." *Retail Business: Market Surveys,* September 1995.

Saxton, Lisa. "Health Nuts: Buyers Are Hoping Reduced-fat Peanuts Will Whip the Category into Better Shape." *Supermarket News,* 25 September 1995.

U.S. Census Bureau. "Manufacturing-Industry Series." *1997 Economic Census.* Washington, D.C.: GPO, 27 July 1999.

SIC 2074

COTTONSEED OIL MILLS

This category covers establishments primarily engaged in manufacturing cottonseed oil, cake, meal, and linters, or in processing purchased cottonseed oil into forms other than edible cooking oils. Businesses primarily involved in refining cottonseed oil into edible cooking oils are covered in **SIC 2079: Shortening, Table Oils, Margarine, and Other Edible Fats and Oils, Not Elsewhere Classified.**

NAICS CODE(S)

311223 (Other Oilseed Processing)
311225 (Fats and Oils Refining and Blending)

The first successful cottonseed oil mill began production in Natchez, Mississippi, in 1833. Up to that point, cottonseed left over from planting had been regarded as a health hazard and a source of pollution. The cottonseed industry grew swiftly after the Civil War, making the United States the largest consumer of cottonseed in the world. Total U.S. cottonseed production reached 7.6 million tons in 1996. In 1997 production fell to 6.9 million tons, according to the National Agricultural Statistics Service (NASS). NASS also estimated 1998 production at 5.2 million tons. The value of shipments reached $844 million in 1997, as reported by the U.S. Census Bureau.

The milling of raw cottonseed yields three products: hulls, linters, and kernels. The hull is typically used as livestock feed, the linters are used for the manufacturing of various products, and the kernels are crushed for oil and meal production. Cottonseed meal typically represents 60-80 percent of total crushed production. Aside from its role in the production of salad dressings, margarine, and shortening, the chief use for the oil is in the manufacture of lubricants, paint, and soap. The principal use for cottonseed meal is as a high-protein feed supplement for cattle, swine, and poultry, and it is also used as a fertilizer. In 1996, U.S. meal production reached 1.73 million tons, and oil production reached 635,500 tons. In 997 approximately 3.9 million tons of cottonseed was crushed.

Before the crushing of cottonseeds, but after the removal of the longer fibers processed in the manufacture of fabrics, the linters—shorter cotton fibers—are removed by a range of methods suited to their various uses in the production of sterile absorbent cotton, felt, and padding; in the manufacture of paper, film, explosives, plastics, and rayon; and as a source of essentially pure cellulose for the chemical industry.

Mill-run processing of linters is a one-step procedure used for smaller quantities than are handled in alternative processing methods. Various production approaches yield both longer and shorter linters for use either in the chemical industry or for other purposes. A two-step processing method yields, at the first stage, the longer and softer first-cut linters well suited to the production of absorbent cotton, felt, and padding. At the second stage (the portion of the production process that generally represents the bulk of total linter production), the shorter and tougher second-cut linters usually reserved for use in the chemicals industry are garnered.

Any part of cottonseed intended for consumption by humans or by nonruminant (not hoofed) animals must be processed in such a way as to extract the gossypol, a pigment toxic to all nonruminants. Because this pigment is located in the tiny glands of cottonseed, the development of a glandless strain of cottonseed was seen as holding potentially great promise for the future of the cottonseed industry. In the mid-1990s a new cottonseed variety with a ''healthier'' high-oleic acid profile was developed, which could increase market share for cotton in the cooking and salad oil industries traditionally dominated by soybean oil.

U.S. exports of cottonseed oil in 1996-1997 were highest to Canada (34,997 metric tons) and El Salvador (21,461 metric tons). Mexico and Japan followed with 7,206 metric tons and 6,969 metric tons, respectively. Korea received the most cottonseed meal and cake at 17,067 metric tons. The only country with higher cottonseed production than the United States in 1998 was China with 8.3 million metric tons.

FURTHER READING

Food and Agriculture Policy Research Institute. *FAPRI 1996 Agricultural Outlook.* Columbia, MO: 1996. Available from http://ssu.agri.missouri.edu.

U.S. Census Bureau. ''Manufacturing-Industry Series.'' *1997 Economic Census.* Washington, D.C.: GPO, 14 October 1999.

U.S. Dept of Agriculture. National Agricultural Statistics Service. *1997 Agricultural Outlook.* Washington, D.C.: Economic Research Service, 1997. Available from http://usda.mannlib.cornell.edu/reports.

———. ''Statistics of Oilseeds, Fats, and Oils.'' *Agricultural Statistics 1999.* Washington, D.C.: Economic Research Service, 1999.

SIC 2075

SOYBEAN OIL MILLS

This category covers establishments primarily engaged in manufacturing soybean oil, cake, and meal, and soybean protein isolates and concentrates, or in processing purchased soybean oil into forms other than edible cooking oils. Businesses primarily engaged in refining soybean oil into edible cooking oils are classified in **SIC 2079: Shortening, Table Oils, Margarine, and Other Edible Fats and Oils, Not Elsewhere Classified.**

NAICS CODE(S)

311222 (Soybean Processing)
311225 (Fats and Oils Refining and Blending)

Traditionally one of the largest U.S. crops, soybeans are especially valuable because the same automated presses yield two important products with closely linked markets—soybean oil and, representing more than 80 percent of the total, soybean meal.

In the 1950s and 1960s, the largest food market for soybean meal was in meat processing, which used soy flour as a protein filler. This product eventually became outmoded as improved refining techniques yielded isolated soy proteins and concentrates having a wider range of applications and little or no independent flavor. These ingredients grew in popularity after legislation was passed that freed meat product manufacturers from regulations that insisted on prominent package labeling of the presence of such ingredients. In the 1970s and 1980s, increasing desirability of high-protein animal feeds, and soy's enhanced status as a healthy ingredient in food, led to increased demand for meal. Soybean meal and oil production volume increased proportionally.

A record U.S. soybean crop in 1994 resulted in lower prices, as the farm price dropped from $6.40 in 1994 to $5.35 per bushel in 1995. Domestic use of soybean oil increased in 1995, reaching almost 13 billion pounds and was projected to increase through 2004, while slow growth was projected for many competing fats and oils. Total U.S. production of soybeans totaled 2.38 billion bushels in 1996, up 9 percent from 1995, ranking second behind the bumper crop of 1994 (2.51 billion bushels). As a result of 1994 volume, soybean oil production in 1994 rose 8 percent from 1993, to 6.8 million metric tons.

Total U.S. production reached a record 2.76 billion bushels in 1998, but the average price per bushel was only $5.35 as compared to 1994's $5.48 or 1996's $7.35. The price of soybean oil per pound has fluctuated from 27.71 cents in 1994, to 21.60 cents in 1996, to 25.08 cents in 1997, according to the U.S. Department of Agriculture. The price of soybean meal per short ton has fluctuated as well, from $162.60 in 1994, to $270.90 in 1996, to $185.54 in 1997.

The top four states, in terms of soybean production in 1998, were Iowa, Illinois, Indiana, and Minnesota. The number of soybeans crushed in 1997 reached 1.6 billion bushels, producing 18.1 billion pounds of soybean oil and

38 million tons of soybean cake and meal, according to the U.S. Department of Agriculture.

The *1996 USDA Agricultural Outlook* predicted that world grain and oilseed markets would face tight supplies and strong prices through the rest of the century, due primarily to stronger economic and population growth in developing countries, such as Asia and Latin America. U.S. exports of soybeans and soybean meal—dominant in the global meal market—were expected to account for the bulk of the growth in world soybean output, as the United States was projected to increase its share of world output from 48 percent in 1995 to 50 percent by 2000, with Asia importing half of all U.S. grain shipments. Europe was another strong market for U.S. exports.

The trend in the United States appeared to be in favor of greater acceptance and more widespread use of soybean products, especially in the form of isolated soy proteins and concentrates. Isolated soy proteins (ISPs) have been shown to equal the protein quality of milk and egg protein, to make logical substitutes for dairy protein because of their lack of fiber and 90 percent protein content, and to have uses in coffee creamers, protein-fortified beverages, weight-loss products and body-building supplements, certain medical foods, and milk-free infant formulas.

According to the U.S. Census Bureau, 93 establishments were engaged in soybean oil processing. One leading company in the industry in 1999 was AG Processing Inc. of Omaha, Nebraska. The company is one of the largest soybean processors in the United States, with an average of 15,000 acres of soybeans processed each day. Ag reported 1998 sales of $2.6 billion and 2,550 employees.

Another leader was Archer Daniels Midland Company of Decatur, Illinois. Nearly two-thirds of the company's sales come from oilseed products. Archer reported 1999 sales of $14.3 billion and 23,603 employees.

In the mid-1990s, there were significant technological advances in the production of biodiesel, a biodegradable, nontoxic, lower-emitting alternative to petroleum diesel fuel. Biodiesel is a fuel and edible oil blend for use in diesel engines and was expected to boost demand for soybean oil. The Chicago Biodiesel Plant, operated by Columbus Foods Company, which began production in 1997, was the first plant in the United States to produce biodiesel from combinations of used vegetable oils and fresh soybean oil, and it is expected to act as a model for future biodiesel production. In the late 1990s, Ag Processing was also promoting its soybean oil-based biofuels.

FURTHER READING

Food and Agriculture Policy Research Institute. *FAPRI 1996 Agricultural Outlook.* Columbia, MO: 1996. Available from http://ssu.agri.missouri.edu.

U.S. Census Bureau. ''Manufacturing-Industry Series.'' *1997 Economic Census.* Washington, D.C.: GPO, 12 October 1999.

U.S. Dept of Agriculture. National Agricultural Statistics Service. *1997 Agricultural Outlook.* Washington: Economic Research Service, 1997. Available from http://usda.mannlib.cornell.edu.

————. *Agricultural Statistics 1999.* ''Statistics of Oilseeds, Fats, and Oils.'' Washington, D.C.: Economic Research Service, 1999.

SIC 2076

VEGETABLE OIL MILLS, EXCEPT CORN, COTTONSEED, AND SOYBEAN

This category covers establishments primarily engaged in manufacturing vegetable oils, cake, and meal, with the exception of corn, cottonseed, and soybean, or in processing such vegetable oils into forms other than edible cooking oils. Businesses primarily engaged in manufacturing corn oil and its byproducts are classified in **SIC 2046: Wet Corn Milling;** those refining vegetable oils into edible cooking oils are covered in **SIC 2079: Shortening, Table Oils, Margarine, and Other Edible Fats and Oils, Not Elsewhere Classified;** and those primarily refining these oils for medicinal purposes are discussed in **SIC 2833: Medicinal Chemicals and Botanical Products.**

NAICS CODE(S)

311223 (Other Oilseed Processing)
311225 (Fats and Oils Refining and Blending)

High vegetable oil prices in 1994-95 increased oil's contribution to the value of seeds. This stimulated production of high-oil-content seeds such as rapeseed and sunflower seed in 1995-96. However, U.S. oilseed production was estimated at 70.2 million tons, down 9.5 million tons from 1994-95. In that same year, production of palm oil rose 6 percent, and rapeseed continued to increase its market share, with 12 percent of world protein meal consumption in 1996. Industry analysts paid particular attention to sunflowers (along with soybeans and corn, one of the biggest U.S. crops) and to rapeseed, due to a significant boost in production levels in the mid-1990s, up nearly 37 percent from 1993 to 1996. In 1998 the most expensive refined oil per pound was rapeseed (at 90 cents).

Sunflowers can be processed using the same automated presses as corn and soybeans, but they use less water and are drought resistant. These advantages, together with the Sunflower seed Oil Assistance Program (SOAP), which helps to offset the competitiveness of highly subsidized European Community vegetable oils, helped overcome reduced levels of production and the loss of two major export markets in the early 1990s—Egypt and Russia—and boost U.S. sunflower seed oil exports in 1992 and 1993. Total U.S. sunflower seed production reached 5.2 billion pounds in 1998—an increase from 1997's 3.7 billion pounds. The value of production increased as well, from $426.7 million in 1997 to $524.6 million in 1998. The value of sunflower oil production was $420.1 million in 1998.

Canola is the name for a group of rapeseed varieties, and accounts for the majority of rapeseed grown in the United States and Canada. As a relatively new contender in the United States, canola in the early 1990s faced an uncertain future, when the product was seen as one that might join the so-called specialty oils market—alongside such products as linseed oil, coconut oil, and walnut oil. However, in the late 1990s canola was sought after by increasingly health-conscious food and edible oil industries because of its low saturated fat content, which is the lowest among major vegetable oils. Most of the canola oil consumed in the United States is imported from Canada, and domestic use increased 10 percent in 1996, as U.S. rapeseed consumption reached 316 million pounds. Canola meal (originally known as rapeseed meal) has similar nutritional qualities to soybean meal, and it is often used as a cattle feed supplement. Canola was also likely to see increased industrial use, as a genetically-engineered variety of canola called high-lauric acid canola was being produced. Lauric acid, previously only available from coconut or palm kernel oil, is a key ingredient in soaps, detergents, lubricants, cosmetics, and confections.

The U.S. typically produces less than 10 percent of world sunflower seeds. Among international producers in 1996 and 1997, Argentina and the Former Soviet Union were the largest producers and exporters, producing 5.40 and 5.46 million metric tons, respectively. Canada was the principal producer and exporter of canola, and palm oil was the most heavily traded oil in the world.

In 1998 world production of palm oil was 16.9 million metric tons. Rapeseed oil followed with 11.6 million metric tons. Sunflower oil and coconut oil were 8.2 million metric tons and 3.5 million metric tons, respectively. According to the U.S. Department of Agriculture, U.S. imports of coconut oil, rapeseed oil, palm oil, and linseed oil were 589,192 metric tons; 491,083 metric tons; 134,516 metric tons; and 3,103 metric tons, respectively.

FURTHER READING

Food and Agriculture Policy Research Institute. *FAPRI 1996 Agricultural Outlook*. Columbia, MO: 1996. Available from http://ssu.agri.missouri.edu.

Good, Darrel, and George Flaskerud. "Oilseeds Policy." College Station, TX: Texas A&M University, 1996. Available from http://ianrwww.unl.edu/farmbill/oilseed.htm.

U.S. Census Bureau. *Current Industrial Report Series, Fats and Oils: Oilseed Crushing*. Washington, D.C.: GPO, 1996. Available from http://www.census.gov/industry/.

U.S. Census Bureau. "Manufacturing-Industry Series." *1997 Economic Census*. Washington, D.C.: GPO, 12 October 1999.

U.S. Dept of Agriculture. National Agricultural Statistics Service. *1997 Agricultural Outlook*. Washington, D.C.: Economic Research Service, 1997. Available from http://usda.mannlib.cornell.edu/reports.

———. "Statistics of Oilseeds, Fats, and Oils." *Agricultural Statistics 1999*. Washington, D.C.: Economic Research Service, 1999.

SIC 2077

ANIMAL AND MARINE FATS AND OILS

This category covers establishments primarily engaged in manufacturing animal oils (including fish oil and other marine animal oils) and fish and animal meal, together with those rendering inedible stearin, grease, and tallow from animal fat, bones, and meat scraps. Establishments primarily engaged in manufacturing lard and edible tallow and stearin are classified in meat-producing industries; those that refine marine animal oils for medicinal purposes are classified in **SIC 2833: Medicinal Chemicals and Botanical Products;** and those manufacturing fatty acids are classified in **SIC 2899: Chemicals and Chemical Preparations, Not Elsewhere Classified.**

NAICS CODE(S)

311613 (Rendering and Meat By-Product Processing)
311711 (Seafood Canning)
311712 (Fresh and Frozen Seafood Processing)
311225 (Fats and Oils Refining and Blending)

The majority of the industry in the late 1990s was engaged in the manufacture of feed and fertilizer byproducts. Grease and inedible tallow accounted for 40 percent of industry shipments, and other animal and marine oil mill products made up the remaining 8 percent. The total value of shipments for this industry in 1995 was $3.13 billion. The total value of shipments for animal and marine fats was not available for 1997, but total fats and oils refining and blending was $7.14 billion, according to the U.S. Census Bureau. Total world production of fish oils decreased in 1997-1998 to 889,000 metric tons (from 1.2 million metric tons in 1996-1997).

Though the output quantities for meat meal and tankage were much larger than those for fish meal and oil in this industry in the 1990s, and though fish meal typically constituted a small portion of the feeds given to poultry, pigs, and cattle (among such other ingredients as feather meal, meat meal, bone meal, and soybean meal), fish meal could make up more than 50 percent of the content of feeds manufactured for pond-raised salmon and trout.

In addition, fish meal represented a uniquely valuable source of nutrition because of its especially rich crude protein content and prominence of essential amino acids and because its consumption was linked to faster growth and reproduction in livestock and larger quantities of eggs and milk. Moreover, fish oil—a natural by-product of fish meal manufacturing, released when steam-cooked fish are passed through large screw presses—had significant value in the domestic food industry.

There were several companies of significant size engaged in this industry in the late 1990s. Darling International Inc., based in Irving, Texas, had 1998 sales of $337 million and employed around 1,400 workers. Other leading members of the industry included National By-Products Inc., of Des Moines, Iowa, and American Proteins Inc., based in Roswell, Georgia.

The outlook for employment in the industry was bleak in the late 1990s. The total number of employees in 1995 was 8,600, down nearly 20 percent from 1988, and jobs for production workers were expected to decline steadily through 2000.

FURTHER READING

U.S. Census Bureau. "Manufacturing-Industry Series." *1997 Economic Census.* Washington, D.C.: GPO, 12 October 1999.

U.S. Dept of Agriculture. National Agricultural Statistics Service. *1997 Agricultural Outlook.* Washington, D.C.: Economic Research Service, 1997. Available from http://usda.mannlib.cornell.edu/reports.

———. "Statistics of Oilseeds, Fats, and Oils." *Agricultural Statistics 1999.* Washington, D.C.: GPO, 2000.

SIC 2079

SHORTENING, TABLE OILS, MARGARINE, AND OTHER EDIBLE FATS AND OILS, NOT ELSEWHERE CLASSIFIED

This category covers establishments primarily involved in manufacturing shortening, table oils, margarine, and other edible fats and oils that are not elsewhere classified. Companies primarily engaged in producing corn oil are discussed in **SIC 2046: Wet Corn Milling.**

NAICS CODE(S)

311225 (Fats and Oils Refining and Blending)
311222 (Soybean Processing)
311223 (Other Oilseed Processing)

Many of the goods classified in this industry are long-time staples of the American kitchen. Commonly utilized for cooking and baking purposes, products such as shortening, vegetable oil, and margarine have become established presences in the marketplace. The market in the late 1990s was dominated by shortenings and cooking oils. The industry shipped $5.75 billion in goods in 1995. In 1997 the value of shipments was $6.16 billion.

Margarine is a key product in this industry. Invented in France in 1869, margarine's introduction to the United States was initially impeded by low quality and the efforts of a powerful butter lobby, which led to discriminatory taxes. With technical improvements and altered legislation, margarine enjoyed increased acceptance. It came to be largely regarded as a healthier and cheaper alternative to butter. By the early 1990s, however, the $1.5-billion margarine industry began to falter while butter, which offered bargain prices, increased its market share. Now, many consumers who switched from butter to margarine for health reasons have become disillusioned after learning that vegetable shortenings may also raise the risk of cardiovascular disease. Production of margarine was slowly declining—from 2.8 billion pounds in 1992, to 2.5 billion pounds in 1995, to 2.4 billion pounds in 1997. Margarine remained a major moneymaker for its producers, however. Per capita consumption was 8.6 pounds in 1997—a substantial decrease from 1993's high of 11.1 pounds.

The fastest growing segment of the industry in the late 1990s was the specialty oils market, which included blended oils such as canola/corn oil, corn/palm oil, olive/canola oil, and peanut/sesame oil, as well as flavored cooking oils that infuse herbs and other seasonings, including garlic. The specialty oils market averaged 50 percent annual gains in the mid-1990s and was worth more than $100 million in 1995. In addition, newer contenders like canola and olive oil grabbed the attention of increasingly health-conscious consumers in the mid- to late 1990s. Physicians were impressed by reports that stated that the rate of heart disease in certain regions of the Mediterranean—where olive is the principal oil consumed—was relatively low, and that dietary monounsaturated fat was capable of lowering total cholesterol. U.S. imports of olive oil during 1996 totaled 118,000 tons, an 18 percent increase from 1991 figures. Spain was the leader in world olive oil production in 1996 (with 1.06 million metric tons); they were followed by Italy (with 578,000 metric tons).

The industry employed approximately 7,425 people in 1997. The average annual salary for production workers was $29,700 in the mid-1990s. Due to increased productivity and increased automation, gradual reductions in the workforce were projected through 2000.

FURTHER READING

Spethmann, Betsy. "Flavors Fuel Run on Oils." *Brandweek,* 27 November 1995.

U.S. Census Bureau. "Manufacturing-Industry Series." *1997 Economic Census.* Washington, D.C.: GPO, 12 October 1999.

U.S. Department of Agriculture. National Agricultural Statistics Service. *Agricultural Statistics 1999.* "Statistics of Oilseeds, Fats, and Oils." Washington, D.C.: Economic Research Service, 1999.

SIC 2082

MALT BEVERAGES

This category includes establishments primarily engaged in the manufacturing of malt beverages, including ale, beer, malt liquor, nonalcoholic beer, porter, and stout.

NAICS CODE(S)

312120 (Breweries)

INDUSTRY SNAPSHOT

Beer has been a part of the American lifestyle since the birth of the country. Beer was brewed in colonial America and was made by American Indians. Through the years, beer has served cultural, spiritual, and even medicinal purposes. With nearly 80 million American beer drinkers, beer has become one of the most popular beverages, second only to water and tea.

Each year, the U.S. malt beverage industry produces and sells more than 2.6 billion cases of beer, or about 193.3 million barrels. A barrel of beer is equal to two kegs or 31 gallons, which is roughly 13.8 24-unit cases of 12-ounce cans or bottles. The wholesale value of malt beverage shipments averages approximately $15 billion annually. According to the Beer Institute, the trade association for the malt beverage industry, the United States is the world's largest producer of beer, brewing more than 20 percent of the world's volume.

Three major companies hold nearly 78 percent of the market share in the United States. These breweries are Anheuser-Busch, located in St. Louis, Missouri; Miller Brewing Company in Milwaukee, Wisconsin; and Coors Brewing Company in Golden, Colorado.

The two top-selling brands, Budweiser and Bud Light, both belonged to Anheuser-Busch, along with almost 48 percent of the market share and 75 percent of

the industry profits. Ranking second was Miller with the third-best selling product, Miller Light. Ranked third was Coors Brewing Company with the fourth most-popular beer, Coors Light.

Although light beer continued to dominate the market with a 37 percent share, the consumption rate of micro brews or specialty beer also continued to grow in popularity. Since the industry-leader Boston Beer Company was founded in 1984, the microbrew business has grown into a $1 billion industry. And while the market for craft beer was flat from 1997 to 1998, the segment was projected to grow through 2000, capturing 6 percent of the total domestic beer market.

Another good sign for the U.S. beer industry was its strong showing overseas. Various markets grew more accessible, especially the most eagerly sought Asian market. Japan continued to be the largest market for U.S. beer, but export rates also climbed in Hong Kong, Brazil, Taiwan, Canada, and Russia.

ORGANIZATION AND STRUCTURE

This industry includes only those companies that manufacture beer. The industry has consistently been dominated by three major U.S. breweries, yet, regardless of size, all breweries have to sell their products through wholesalers and retailers. This distribution channel is the result of accommodating the variety of federal, state, and local regulations regarding the sale of alcoholic beverages.

Federal and State Regulation. The Federal Alcohol Administration Act (FAA) was put into place at the end of Prohibition in 1933. Since that time, the Bureau of Alcohol, Tobacco and Firearms (ATF) has been responsible for administering and enforcing the FAA, including qualifying brewers, collecting brewer and wholesaler occupational taxes, and regulating trade practices, advertising, and labeling.

Beyond the uniformity of the FAA, regulations varied greatly among the 50 states, as the Beer Institute reported in their testimony to the U.S. Senate regarding the Malt Beverage Interbrand Competition Act. Probably the most dramatic example of regulatory diversity is the way that states sell beer. "Open" states license retailers and wholesalers to handle the distribution and sale of alcoholic beverages. Thirty-two states and the District of Columbia are considered "open" states. The other 18 states operate under the control method, in which each state government buys and sells alcoholic beverages at the wholesale and retail levels.

In addition to federal regulations, some states have set up independent agencies responsible for the administration, licensing, and enforcement of state laws and the collection of state revenues. Additionally, some state legislatures created their own Alcoholic Beverage Control (ABC) agencies with rule-making power, and 32 states have allowed citizens to vote for or against the sale of liquor in various cities or counties.

BACKGROUND AND DEVELOPMENT

The foundation of the U.S. beer industry can be traced to the ancient times of kings and pharaohs. Babylonian clay tablets more than 8,000 years old depicted beer being brewed and gave detailed recipes. Other writings indicated that beer was brewed by the Egyptians as early as 3000 B.C. and by the Chinese in the 23rd century B.C. One of the world's oldest breweries still in existence is Brauerei Beck in Germany, where Beck's beer was first brewed in 1533.

Beer was first brewed in America in 1587 at Sir Walter Raleigh's colony in Roanoke, Virginia, and Puritan settlers brewed beer in Boston as early as 1620. In 1791, Congress levied the first tax on alcohol. By 1870, Adolphus Busch had pioneered the use of refrigerated railroad cars to ship beer over long distances. Following the steady development of temperance groups, the Pure Food and Drug Act, more commonly known as the Volstead Act, went into effect on January 16, 1920. This act ushered in the era of Prohibition, which banned the sale of alcoholic beverages. During this 13 year period, production and distribution of millions of gallons of alcohol fell into the hands of "bootleggers."

After Prohibition was repealed in 1933, federal and state governments tightened regulations under the Federal Alcohol Act (FAA) and various state regulations. Brewers also adopted policies of self-regulation, such as the Distilled Spirits Council of the United States's (DISCUS) voluntary "code of good practice." Following Prohibition, beer was produced in 750 locations throughout the country. It was distributed to wholesalers and retailers in limited geographic regions that seem extremely small when compared to current distribution areas. By the 1930s, the primary way to sell beer was in draft form and in refillable bottles.

In order for breweries to continue expanding, however, less costly containers were needed. The beer can, introduced in 1935, filled those needs perfectly. By the end of World War II, the beer can had become such a popular container that glass companies soon created the one-way bottle to keep up with the competition. Both of these less-expensive containers allowed brewers to ship more beer and expand markets. By 1946, breweries served markets that were at one time only accessible to local and regional companies, and this expansion soon created the nationwide market of the major breweries.

Total sales volume for the domestic beer market rose 1 percent in 1996, a small but symbolic gesture breaking a decade-long stagnation in consumption rates. Although incremental, this industry growth can be attributed to the rise in microbrews, which has posted double-digit growth since 1995, and to imported beers. Both segments are significant but small; microbrews made up only two percent of the market and imports just five percent in 1998.

Companies began to consolidate with others to save operating expenses. In 1995 fourth-ranked Stroh Brewery Company acquired G. Heileman, makers of Colt 45, Old Style, and Henry Weinhard, among other labels.

Causes for the stagnant market were attributed to the effects of the federal excise tax hike in 1991, unfavorable demographics (not enough 21-year-olds), and continuing health concerns regarding alcohol consumption. A bit of good news for the beer industry was that the mini baby-boom generation was about to come of age, so the flat market of 21-year-olds would soon grow.

Attempting to boost incremental sales and expand the beer market, companies continued to introduce new products—often creating entirely new segments such as light beer, nonalcoholic beer, ice beer, bottled draft beer, and clear malt liquor drinks such as *Zima.*

In 1996 light beer became the largest segment of the beer market with 37.25 percent—more than 70 million barrels. Nonalcoholic beer also has helped the beer business. Although small compared to total beer consumption, volume of nonalcoholic beer has more than doubled since its 1989 level and remained steady since 1991.

In an industry of mature brands, companies were looking at the future of microbrews. Sales in this segment grew an average of 40 percent from 1987 to 1997. Specialty brewing in the United States grew from a $600 million industry in 1992 to a $1 billion industry in 1994. Even the big names were offering craft brews. In 1994, Anheuser-Busch (A-B), bought a stake in Seattle's Redhook Ale Brewery, while Coors Brewing Company landed Killian's Irish Red.

The undisputed leader of the microbrew segment has been the Boston Beer Company (BBC) and its product Samuel Adams. The tenth largest beer producer in the country, BBC manufactured 700 barrels in 1994, only about three one-thousandths of the beer sold in the U.S. that year. However small, this volume was still greater than the total of the next six microbrewers combined. When the BBC was founded in 1984, fewer than 40 micro-breweries existed. Since then, an estimated 500 small breweries and brew pubs have opened, with an additional 50 added each year from 1985 on.

According to the U.S. Department of Commerce, Japan was the largest market for U.S. beer in the mid-1990s, although sales were actually down 16.6 percent in the country in 1995. Sales came in 62 percent higher in 1995 than in 1994 in Hong Kong, 214.5 percent higher in Brazil, 108.6 percent higher in Taiwan, 33.6 percent higher in Canada, and 78.9 percent higher in

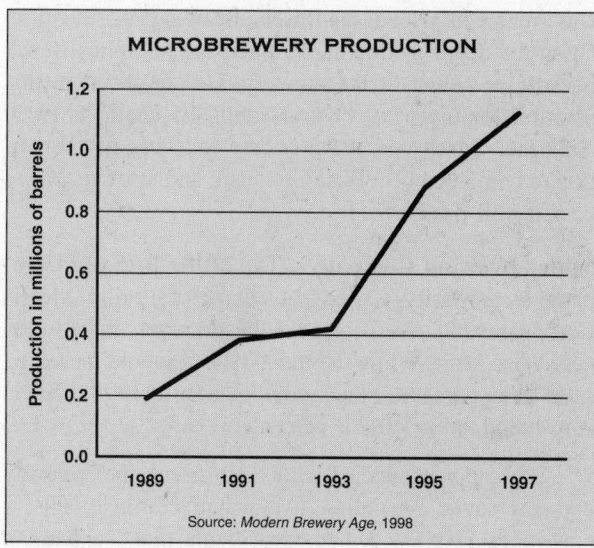

MICROBREWERY PRODUCTION

Production in millions of barrels

1989 1991 1993 1995 1997

Source: *Modern Brewery Age*, 1998

Russia. The total U.S. imported beer market hit an all-time high in 1995, with volume topping out at an estimated 343.5 million gallons. This growth represented a 5.5 percent jump in volume from 1994 and was almost a 40 percent improvement over a ten year period.

The surge in imports to the United States was attributed to the American consumer's desire for high quality, full-bodied brews; lower total alcohol consumption; and becoming accustomed to higher prices for both domestic craft brews and imported brands. Among the world's best-selling beers, only Heineken, the Danish Carlsberg, and Guinness may be regarded as truly international.

North America and the Caribbean countries (Mexico, Canada, Jamaica) led exports in 1995, with 165.8 million gallons of beer shipped to the United States, up from 160 million gallons in 1994. The Europeans exported a record 161.8 million gallons of beer to the United States, up almost 8 percent from 1994. The Asian/Pacific region exported 7.4 million gallons to the United States—virtually the same figure as in 1994.

CURRENT CONDITIONS

The stagnate beer market seemed to improve by 1999 when sales for the industry grew about 1.5 percent. Annual U.S. sales was 193.3 million barrels in 1998 and were projected to reach 203.9 million barrels by 2003. The average per capita consumption of beer in the United States was 22 gallons in 1998, with Nevada leading the nation with 34 gallons and Utah drinking the least, with 13 gallons per capita.

The three big leaders in the beer industry continued to be Anheuser-Busch, Miller, and Coors. With the two top-selling brands, Budweiser and Bud Light, A-B dominated the domestic beer market in 1998. Anheuser-Busch, with 47.9 percent of the market, shipped more than twice as much beer as second-place Miller, who had

20.6 percent of the market (declining for the third straight year) and the third best-selling product, Miller Light. Coors Brewing Company, with its fourth-place Coors Light, rose slightly in market share to 11 percent in 1998.

Some of the growth in the beer industry is attributable to rising prices and the taste for super-premium products. To cash in on that taste and to secure more and better shelf space, the industry is constantly introducing new products. In 1999 A-B unveiled Tequiza, which is beer with a touch of tequila. At the end of 1999 the company was test marketing Devon's Original Shandy, a combination of beer and lemonade.

No longer an industry in its infancy, the craft brewing segment of the beer market had some growing pains in the late 1990s. Sales were flat for 1998, with craft brews selling about 5.6 million barrels in both 1997 and 1998. Consumers became choosier about their craft beers, no longer assuming—or buying into the notion—that craft beers are automatically better than those of national or international companies.

Some specialty beer firms reacted by merging, closing, reformulating their brew, or making a conscious effort to stay small. While many companies jumped on the specialty brew bandwagon, many also went out of business. Industry-wide sales may have been flat in 1998, but 21 of the top 50 specialty beer companies reported a 10 percent or more growth rate in 1998.

"The microbrewery segment is expected to grow to a six percent domestic market share by 2000 from 2.5 percent now, but not every brewer in business today will be around then," said Mike Gerend, president of Wisconsin Brewing Co. Gerend suggested that a true microbrew would be most successful in its hometown market and would survive on consumer loyalty.

"I think that the issue that the major brewers have to deal with is that the combination of microbrews and imports are skimming the cream off the top," said Emanuel Goldman, a leading drink analyst for Paine Webber. "It's an industry that is basically not growing. The beer per cap is undergoing a very gradual decline, and so what you have is what has existed for some time in the distilled spirits business, people drinking less but drinking better," said Goldman.

For the larger companies, especially Miller, consolidation was the way to maintain or grow market share. In 1999 Stroh Brewery formally shut its doors, selling their Weinhard's and Mickey's brands to Miller. The rest of the Stroh brands and a brewery in Pennsylvania were sold to Pabst. The brands included Stroh's, Old Milwaukee, Schlitz, Schaefer, and Schlitz Malt Liquor.

In late 1999 Miller completed its acquisition of the only remaining brewery in the Northwest, Olympia Brewing Co. Miller planned to sink $20 million into the aging facility to bring production up to two million barrels by the end of 2000, doubling 1999 production levels.

Miller was also rethinking its exclusivity arrangements with wholesalers. Miller wholesalers quietly added other beer brands to their stable making them, and Miller, more profitable. Some Miller distributors even bought or merged with Coors wholesalers. Some industry observers said this may be the only way to compete in markets with a heavy A-B presence. In the summer of 1999 Miller also signed a distribution agreement with Heineken.

INDUSTRY LEADERS

Anheuser-Busch, Inc.   Anheuser-Busch, Inc. is the world's largest brewer and the main subsidiary of the Anheuser-Busch Companies, based in St. Louis, Missouri. With 13 breweries, Anheuser-Busch produces 15 naturally brewed beers, two non-alcoholic beers, and imports three beers for distribution in the United States. By 1998, Anheuser-Busch sold an all-time industry record of 93.9 million barrels of beer in one year. In the third quarter of 1999 A-B had profits of $461.5 million, up 13 percent from the same time the previous year. Sales were $3.8 billion in 1999's third quarter, boosted by a three percent increase in sales. During this time, A-B announced they would raise prices again by three percent.

Anheuser-Busch brands are exported to more than 40 countries and brewed under the company's supervision in five countries. Anheuser-Busch employs over 44,000 people and works with approximately 900 independent wholesale distributors. Anheuser-Busch also operates 11 company-owned distributorships. Other beer-related Anheuser-Busch subsidiaries are Anheuser-Busch International, Inc.; Busch Agricultural Resources, Inc.; Metal Container Corporation; Anheuser-Busch Recycling Corporation; Busch Media Group, Inc.; Busch Creative Services Corporation; St. Louis Refrigerator Car Company; Manufacturers Railway Company; and the International Label Company. Anheuser-Busch brands are Budweiser, Bud Light, Bud Dry Draft, Michelob, Michelob Light, Michelob Classic Dark, Michelob Dry, Michelob Golden Draft, Michelob Golden Draft Light, Busch, Busch Light, Natural Light, Natural Pilsner, O'Doul's, King Cobra, Carlsberg, Carlsberg Light, and Elephant Malt Liquor.

Adolphus Busch, founder of the Anheuser-Busch Brewing Company, immigrated to the United States in 1857, arriving in St. Louis via New Orleans. In 1861, Adolphus married Lilly Anheuser, and after serving a short time in the Union Army, he returned home and joined the management of his father-in-law's brewery. In 1869, Adolphus purchased half ownership of another brewery, called the Bavarian Brewery, which was restructured with his father-in-law, Eberhard Anheuser, as president and Busch as secretary. In 1879, the company

was renamed Anheuser-Busch Brewing Association. Upon the death of Eberhard Anheuser, Adolphus Busch became president of the brewery. He continued in this position for the next 33 years until his death in 1913. Anheuser-Busch was the first brewer to use pasteurization to help keep beer fresh in transit, and most packaged beer is still pasteurized today.

Miller Brewing Company.   The Miller Brewing Company is a wholly owned subsidiary of Phillip Morris Companies Inc., with corporate headquarters in Milwaukee, Wisconsin. While the industry as a whole increased sales three percent in the second quarter of 1999, Miller' core-brand sales fell 2.2 percent.

With approximately 10,000 employees, the company operates seven breweries, five manufacturing plants, a glass-bottling plant, a hops processing plant, a malting factory, and a packaging/printing plant. The Miller Brewing Company produces over 40 million barrels of beer each year. The company's major brands are Miller High Life, Miller Lite, Lowenbrau, Miller Genuine Draft, Meister Brau, Milwaukee's Best, Magnum Malt Liquor, Leinenkugal, and Sharp's nonalcoholic beer. Miller products are distributed to retailers in the United States, Puerto Rico, and the Virgin Islands by a network of approximately 690 distributors. The company's products are also sold in approximately 50 foreign markets in Europe, Asia, and the Caribbean, including U.S. military bases.

The Miller Brewing Company was founded by German immigrant Frederick Miller, who settled in Milwaukee after a brief stay in New York City. He bought the Plank Road Brewery in 1855, and soon after opened a 20-acre park or "sommer-garten." After Frederick's death, the Milwaukee Brewery was passed on to Miller's children. The W.R. Grace Co. purchased most of the children's stock in the Miller Brewing Company in 1966. Phillip Morris Inc. purchased the company in 1969 and the rest of the family's stock in 1970.

Coors Brewing Company.   The Adolph Coors Company, founded in 1873, is America's third-largest brewer. Headquartered in Golden, Colorado, Coors sells approximately 17 million barrels of beer annually in 49 states and the District of Columbia. The Coors Brewing Company employs 7,100 people, works with 597 independent distributors, and has seven company-owned distributorships. The Adolph Coors Company has three autonomous business units that are operated by fourth-generation Coors family members. These are the Coors Brewing Company, the Coors Ceramics Company, and the Coors Technology Companies. The Coors Brewing Company is the only brewery that does not pasteurize any of its beer. Instead, it uses a sterile filtration process that the company developed in the late 1950s. Coors is the only company with a complete line of draft or non-pasteurized beers.

The Coors Brewing Company operates three breweries, including the world's largest single-site brewery. Coors products are exported to 12 foreign markets and to U.S. military bases in 16 countries worldwide. The company also has licensing agreements to brew and distribute Coors products in Japan, Canada, Scotland, and Korea. Coors brands include original Coors, Coors Light, Coors Extra Gold, George Killian's Irish Red, Keystone and Keystone Light, Coors Winterfest (a seasonal beer), and Coors Cutter (a nonalcoholic beer).

German immigrant Adolph Coors founded the Coors Brewing Company. Upon his arrival in the United States in 1868, Adolph spent many years as a laborer and saved his money to fulfill his dream of owning a brewery. One day Adolph Coors found an abandoned tannery in the town of Golden at the base of Table Mountain. He and other investors remodeled the tannery and soon began brewing Coors beer. By 1880, Adolph was able to buy out his investors. The company was sustained during Prohibition by divesting into other industries, including a cement manufacturing facility and a porcelain plant. The Coors Ceramics Company has been one of the world's largest producers of industrial technical ceramics, and the sole supplier of chemical porcelain used in the United States, Mexico, and Canada.

WORKFORCE

The U.S. beer industry consisted of 54 leading breweries that employ approximately 97,000 people in all areas of the industry (including non-manufacturing areas). According to the Beer Institute, "Brewery workers' wages are among the highest of more than 350 industries annually surveyed by the U.S. Department of Labor. These men and women take home approximately $2.2 billion a year in salaries and wages with additional millions paid in the form of fringe benefits and retirement programs." Bureau of Labor Statistics data indicate, however, that the number of employees directly involved in the industry has dropped over the past several decades, from more than 71,000 workers in 1960 to less than 40,000 in the late 1990s.

The top five states that were home to the largest number of brewery employees are New York, Wisconsin, Pennsylvania, California, and Washington. The largest numbers of employees worked as packaging and filling machine operators, driver-sales workers, salespeople, truck drivers, tractor operators, supervisors, and laborers. Estimates by the Bureau of Labor Statistics showed that virtually all occupations within the beer industry would decline in the percentage of total employed by the year 2000. Those jobs that include "hands-on" involvement, such as freight, stock and material movers, hand packers, and testers, were predicted to decline by at least 25 percent.

AMERICA AND THE WORLD

Faced with domestic consumption rates at a stand still, U.S. companies turned to the international arena to expand their markets. A-B was considering opportunities from Latin America to Europe and the Far East. Competitors feared that the company would eventually work with French company Kronenbourg (part of the Danone group), which would give A-B a strong distribution network in Europe.

In keeping with its strategic plan, A-B reworked its agreement with Kirin, the number one brewer in Japan. Instead of brewing 65 percent of their beer in Japan, Kirin would brew 100 percent of A-B's beer under a licensing agreement. Kirin would also sell A-B's products and A-B would discontinue it's separate sales force in Japan. A-B currently makes and markets Kirin's beer in the United States.

The countries that spend the most per capita on beer in 1998 were Japan, the United Kingdom, the United States, Germany, and France. The countries with the highest growth rate in 1998 were Spain, up 6.3 percent; Italy, up 4.2 percent; and the United Kingdom, up 3.7 percent. International increases in beer consumption have largely been attributable to Western influences and culture.

U.S. companies were looking for markets with financial strength and disposable income, such as Latin America and the Asian marketplace. In fact, it seemed that beer companies throughout the world were rushing into the exploding markets of Thailand, Vietnam, and most importantly China—which many predicted would be the largest beer market in the world by the end of the decade.

FURTHER READING

"Alcoholic Beverages." *U.S. Industry & Trade Outlook '99*, New York: McGraw-Hill, 1999.

"Anheuser-Busch Reports Record Year." *Supermarket News,* 10 March 1997.

"Beer Industry Economic Contribution Study." *Beer Institute Online,* 20 November 1999. Available from http://www .beerinst.org/economics/summary.htm.

"Beer Sales Flat But Malt News Abounds." *Beverage Industry,* July 1999.

Buck, Howard. "Tumwater, Wash., Brewery Merges with Miller Brewing Company." *Knight-Ridder/Tribune Business News,* 20 October 1999.

"Buzz about Beer." *Beverage World,* 15 February 1997.

Causey, James. "Miller, Pabst Beverages Shipments Fall as Anheuser-Busch's Rise." *Knight-Ridder/Tribune Business News,* 15 January 1997.

———. "Only Icehouse, Lite Sell More for Miller in 1996." *Knight-Ridder/Tribune Business News,* 20 January 1997.

Chura, Hillary. "Beer: Positioning Takes on Greater Value." *Advertising Age,* 11 October 1999.

Chura, Hillary, and Beth Synder. "Crying in Their Beer: Miller Brewing Co. Sales Remain Stagnant, with the Only Significant Growth Attributed to High Life." *Advertising Age,* 2 August 1999.

Dawson, Havis. "Something for Everyone." *Beverage World,* February 1996.

Holleran, Joan. "Craft Brews, a Beer Rabbit?" *Beverage Industry,* January 1997.

"Indicators." *Time,* 22 November 1999.

"It's a Small World for US Brewers." *Beverage Industry,* May 1996.

Khermouch, Gerry. "Miller Seen Easing Other-Brand Policy." *Brandweek,* 9 August 1999.

"Miller History." Milwaukee, WI: Miller Brewing Company.

Mullins, Robert. "Microbrewers See Slower Growth, Shake-out." *The Business Journal-Milwaukee,* 4 January 1997.

Olgeirson, Ian. "Is the Microbrewing Industry Tapped Out?" *Denver Business Journal,* 18 September 1998.

Prince, Greg W. "Shut Up and Drink." *Beverage World,* February 1996.

————. "This seat is taken." *Beverage World,* March 1996.

Sfiligoj, Eric. "The Europeans strike back." *Beverage World,* February 1996.

Smit, Barbara. "Global Beer War Set to Explode." *The European,* 25 July 1996.

Stamborski, Al. "Sales, Price Increase Buoy Anheuser-Busch's Quarterly Profits." *Knight-Ridder/Tribune Business News,* 27 October 1999.

SIC 2083

MALT

This classification covers establishments primarily engaged in manufacturing malt or malt by-products from barley or other grains.

NAICS CODE(S)

311213 (Malt Manufacturing)

Malt is a barley kernel that has been allowed to sprout and is used primarily for brewing and distilling. It has long been a central element in beer production. Anywhere from 25 to 50 pounds of malt are used to make one barrel of beer.

In September 1999 the U.S. Department of Agriculture (USDA) estimated barley production to be 284 million bushels, down 19 percent from the previous year's estimate and the lowest production since 1953. North Dakota was the leading producer of barley in the United States, though the state's yields declined 6 bushels from 1998 to 49 bushels per acre. Other leading barley produc-

ing states were Montana, Idaho, Washington, and Colorado. The top five states produced almost three-fourths of the nation's 1999 barley crop. Montana yields grew 2 bushels from the previous season, and record high yields were produced in Kentucky, New Jersey, North Carolina, and Pennsylvania.

Malt is created by germinating moistened barley under controlled conditions for a short period of time, usually four days. The germination process activates the enzyme systems, specialized proteins that break down the barley's starch and protein. Once germinated, the "green malt" must be kilned, or dried with heat. Essentially, the malt is cooked to stop its growth, although the enzyme activity continues. Prior to kilning, the rootlets that appear during germination are removed and discarded. What is left after kilning is considered to be malt.

About 90 percent of all malting barley grown is used by brewers, with the remainder used as feedstock. Brewers create a mash with the malt by mixing it with water and heating it under controlled conditions. During the mashing process, the enzymes break down the starch into sugars and proteins, creating a soluble mixture or extract. The soluble product is filtered, and yeast is added. Other starches such as corn or rice are added at this time, along with hops for flavor.

All beer has some malt content. Budget beers usually are 50 percent malt and 50 percent corn or rice, while premium beer composition may be as high as 70 percent malt. Brewers generally specify to barley growers the variety of malt needed for particular brands.

A number of the major American beer producers maintained in-house malt operations in the late 1990s. Examples included Busch Agricultural Resources, Inc., a subsidiary of Anheuser-Busch Inc., which operated several malt plants that supplied the company with approximately one-third of Anheuser-Busch's malt needs. Miller Brewing Company, the second largest brewery in the U.S., had its own malt plant as well, located in Waterloo, Wisconsin.

Great Western Malting Company was another leading malt producer. Great Western was a subsidiary of the ConAgra Malt network, which consisted of Canada Malting Company, Hugh Baird & Sons, and Argentine company Malteria Pampa S.A. ADM Malting Division, a division of Archer Daniels Midland, was one of the largest malting companies in the world. Another U.S. industry leader was Froedtert Malt Corp., the U.S. arm of the International Malting Company, a joint venture between Archer Daniels Midland and Lesaffre et Compagnie. Other malt producers included Schreier Malting Co., which produced about 123,000 metric tons of malt a year, Rahr Malting Co., and Minnesota Malting Co.

Both feed and malting barley averaged $2.35 per bushel in 1997. The price dropped to $1.98 per bushel in the 1998-99 growing season, according to the USDA. Farmers were expected to receive between $1.90 and $2.20 per bushel in the 1999-2000 season.

A major issue for maltsters and brewers has been vomitoxin levels and growing scab-resistant barley. Growing malting-grade barley has been difficult over the past years due to a vomitoxin-producing scab that affects the malting of barley. Although it does not affect humans, barley affected with vomitoxin disturbs the malting process. Another issue concerning barley growers was the need for higher yielding malt barley varieties. The American Malting Barley Association, working in conjunction with Busch Agricultural Resources, Inc., and the breeding programs at North Dakota State University and University of Minnesota, sought to develop new barley varieties. In the late 1990s, North Dakota State University developed ND15477, a six-row barley, University of Minnesota worked on M98, a six-row barley, and Busch Agricultural Resources developed B2978, another six-row variety.

FURTHER READING

Bailey, Ann. "Agweek Magazine Malting Barley Outlook Column." *Knight-Ridder/Tribune Business News*, 24 September 1995.

Campbell, Erin. "Red River Valley Awaits Experimental Scab-Resistant Barley." *Knight-Ridder/Tribune Business News*, 6 March 1997.

"ConAgra Bids on Malting Concern." *Nation's Restaurant News*, 2 October 1995.

Flaskerud, George. "U.S. Barley Production Estimates Increase." *Knight-Ridder/Tribune Business News*, 28 October 1996.

Menke, Jayson. "Barley Growers at North Dakota Conference Want Worldwide Identity, Farm Bill." *Knight-Ridder/Tribune Business News*, 10 January 1996.

———. "Demand Drives Barley Acres Higher." *Knight-Ridder/Tribune Business News*, 30 December 1996.

"Tiger Oats to Buy 50 percent of ConAgra's Malting Business" *Feedstuffs*, 6 May 1996.

U.S. Department of Agriculture. "Feed Outlook." Washington, D.C.: Economic Research Service, 14 December 1999. Available from http://usda.mannlib.cornell.edu/reports.

U.S. Department of Agriculture. National Agricultural Statistics Service. "Small Grains Summary." Washington, D.C.: Agricultural Statistics Board, 30 September 1999.

SIC 2084

WINES, BRANDY, AND BRANDY SPIRITS

This category includes establishments primarily engaged in manufacturing wines, brandy, and brandy spirits. This industry also includes bonded wine cellars that are engaged in blending wines. Establishments that primarily bottle purchased wines, brandy, and brandy spirits but do not manufacture wines and brandy are classified in **SIC 5182: Wine and Distilled Alcoholic Beverages.**

NAICS CODE(S)
312130 (Wineries)

INDUSTRY SNAPSHOT

Although the first commercial wine venture in the United States was in Pennsylvania in 1793, the majority of modern American wineries have been located in California, with Washington and New York coming in a distant second and third, respectively. California has accounted for more than 90 percent of all U.S. wine production and more than 70 percent of all wine sold in the United States. According to the Wine Institute, "If viewed as a nation, California would rank sixth in worldwide wine production, following Spain but bigger than Germany. The dominant wine producer in California continues to be the Gallo family, controlling nearly 40 percent of the wine market."

Table wine has been the most popular kind of wine sold in the United States. Varietals, table wines made predominately of one kind of grape, have continued to grow in popularity, following the trend that consumers are drinking fewer, but better wines. One reason for the increase of premium wine sales is the growing number of consumers over the age of 55.

Retail wine sales in the United States rose steadily in the 1990s, reaching $17 billion in 1998. Per capita consumption rates also rose from 1.80 gallons in 1995 to 1.96 gallons in 1998. Strong consumer demand for wine weakened the availablity of grapes in mid-decade, driving up the price of grapes to an all-time high in 1995. However, a bumper crop in 1998 (the United States crushed 2.2 million tons of grapes that year) led to lower prices in 1999.

Fueling this increase in wine consumption has been the improved U.S. economy and the publicity of reports touting the benefits of moderate wine consumption. In 1996, the U.S. government, for the first time, acknowledged moderate wine consumption to be a part of a heart-healthy diet. This statement of public policy should only further fuel the growth of wine sales in the United States in the years to come.

Imported wine also has seen tremendous growth in the United States, and many California wine companies have established relationships with producers in Chile and Argentina to sell their wine. For example, the Canandaigua Wine Company, the second-largest wine seller in the United States, has established a relationship with Vino

Santa Carolina Chilean wines to become that company's sole agent and exclusive importer for the United States.

ORGANIZATION AND STRUCTURE

All winemakers must sell their products through wholesalers and retailers to accommodate various federal, state, and local regulations regarding the sale of alcoholic beverages. The Federal Alcohol Administration Act (FAA) was established after the 13-year Prohibition Era ended in 1933. The Bureau of Alcohol, Tobacco and Firearms (ATF) is responsible for administering and enforcing the FAA, including qualifying wine makers, collecting producer and wholesaler occupational taxes, and regulating trade practices, advertising, and labeling. Beyond the uniformity of the FAA, regulations vary greatly among the 50 states.

States can sell wine in one of two ways, either in a controlled environment or using an open, licensed method. "Open" states have licensed retailers and wholesalers that handle the distribution and sale of alcoholic beverages. Thirty-two states and the District of Columbia are "open" states. The other 18 states operate under the control method, in which each state government buys and sells alcoholic beverages at the wholesale and retail levels. In addition to federal regulations, some states have set up their own independent agencies that are responsible for the administration, licensing, and enforcement of state laws and the collection of state revenues. Some state legislatures even have created their own Alcoholic Beverage Control (ABC) agencies with rule-making power, and 32 states allow their citizens to vote for or against the sale of liquor on a city or county-wide basis.

BACKGROUND AND DEVELOPMENT

California wine making began in 1769 when Father Junipero Serra planted vines at Mission San Diego. In September 1772, the grapes were harvested and pressed, creating California's first vintage. These early wines were produced for sacramental purposes and personal consumption at the missions.

The commercial era of wine production began in 1830 with the efforts of Frenchman Jean Louis Vignes from Bordeaux, France. His vineyard was located in what is now downtown Los Angeles. The wine industry boomed as an ancillary result of the discovery of gold in California in 1848. A surge of Europeans came to the state seeking their fortune. Immigrants from Italy, France, and Germany who had no luck finding gold turned to a trade they already knew—winemaking.

Between 1860 and 1880, the industry grew rapidly as numerous wineries were established. By 1890, several of the state's famous wine regions already had taken shape and the industry was producing 25 million gallons of wine per year. After suffering losses from a vine pest called phylloxera, the industry virtually disappeared with the passage of Prohibition in 1919. The repeal of Prohibition in 1933, however, prompted the industry to rebuild. Growth was steady between 1949 and 1960, with annual output increasing from 117 million gallons to 129 million gallons. By the 1970s, the demand for California table wines had doubled.

As the industry evolved, so did consumer preferences. From 1933 to 1967, dessert wine was the most popular kind of wine in the United States. During the 1970s, generic table wines, like California Chablis and California Burgundy, dominated sales. By the late 1980s, varietal wines, those labeled with the name of the grape, had taken over; these wines were expected to remain prominent throughout the 1990s.

After posting a 6.5 percent loss in 1993, wine sales in the United States continued to rise, while per capita consumption remained steady at 1.8 gallons. According to the San Francisco-based Wine Institute, consumer demand for premium varietal wines spurred a 5 percent increase in California table wine sales in 1994—the strongest performance in more than a decade.

While most of the largest wine producers reported record sales, and consumer tastes moved upscale to more expensive wines, 1994 was noted as the best year for the wine industry since the late 1980s. "The end of the drought, the waning of phylloxera root louse problems and increased consumer demand all have wine makers singing a new tune," reported Clifford Carlsen of *The San Francisco Business Times.*

Total U.S. production again rose in 1995, up 10.3 percent at 437 million gallons. According to wine industry analyst Jon Frederickson of Gomberg, Fredrickson and Associates of San Francisco, California, saw wine sales increase 8 percent in 1995 to a record $4.4 billion. Increased consumer demand and a relatively strong supply of fruit contributed to the industry's continued strong growth.

Following record wine sales and all-time high prices for grapes in 1995, the industry experienced another banner year in 1996. In fact, many North Coast wineries, with sales increases of 30 to 40 percent, did not have enough wine to meet the staggering demand.

The improved economy and continuing news reports about the health benefits of moderate wine consumption has fueled the continued growth of the industry. A 1991 broadcast of *60 Minutes* reported a link between moderate wine consumption and a reduced risk of heart attack. Called the French Paradox, two scientists found that despite similar fat intake, France's heart attack rate was one-third that of the United States. A key factor they attributed to this was the French custom of drinking wine with meals. Red wine sales increased more than 75 percent since that 1991 report.

Champagne sales continued to drop despite increases of specific brands. From a peak of 18.2 million 9-liter cases of sparkling wine and champagne in the United States in 1986, consumption fell to 12.3 million 9-liter cases in 1995. Causes for the decline were high prices for champagne, high taxes, high cost of shipping, and lack of consistent, high-profile marketing programs.

Production. The making of wine begins with the grape harvest, which generally occurs from August through November, depending upon the grape variety and the weather. The grapes are placed in a crusher that separates the stems from the fruit and breaks up the berries. The stems are then discarded, leaving a combination of juice, seeds, pulp, and skins, called ''must.'' Juice from red or white wine grapes is colorless.

To make white wine, the skins and seeds usually are removed from the must after a few hours. The remaining juice is called ''free-run.'' The discarded skins also are pressed to extract the ''press juice.'' Both juices then are filtered, placed in storage, and given yeast to facilitate the fermentation process. White wine fermentation can last anywhere from three days to three weeks. Upon completion, the wine is filtered for solids or remaining yeast. The wine then is aged for a period of one week to a year in stainless steel, oak, or redwood containers. It also can be aged in the bottle. After aging, the wine can be blended with other wines to create a desired style or can be sent to be finished, a process that stabilizes and filters the wine before bottling.

Production of red wine is slightly different than the process of making white wine. Red wine is fermented at warmer temperatures than white wine. For red wine production, the skins are fermented with the crushed juice to give it color and flavor. The skins float to the top and are moistened regularly with juice to extract color and flavor. Red wine usually is fermented for 5 to 10 days and then is filtered, clarified, and preserved with sulfites. Red wine commonly is aged in oak barrels for one to two years.

Champagne is made in one of two ways: method champenoise and charmat process. In method champenoise, still wine is blended with a mixture (called triage) of still wine, yeast, and a sugar substance. This blend is resealed in bottles where it is fermented for a second time and aged. Carbon dioxide collects in the bottles, which is released in a rush of bubbles when the bottles are uncorked. In the charmat, or bulk, process, the still wine, yeast, and sugar are fermented in a pressurized tank rather than in bottles.

Types of Wines. Wines sold in the United States generally are divided into the following categories: champagne, aperitifs, dessert wines, table wines, and varietal wines. Also included in this classification are brandy and other fortified wines. Wines can be named one of four ways: by variety, which tells the predominant type of grape; by a generic name describing the color, such as blush; by the region that originally inspired the wine, such as Chablis; or by a proprietary name, which is a label created by the winery.

Champagne and sparkling wines are names used interchangeably in the United States for wines with effervescence. These wines range from very dry (natural), to dry (brut), to slightly sweet (extra dry), to sweet (sec and demi-sec). Aperitifs are appetizer wines usually served prior to a meal and can include champagnes and sherries. Dessert wines are officially classified as those with an alcohol content of 17 percent to 21 percent. They can be sweet or dry and include sherries and ports.

Table wine is a term commonly used to describe all red, white, blush, and rose wines that contain 7 to 14 percent alcohol. These wines are still rather effervescent and are served mainly with meals. Table wines can be made from any grape or combination of grapes and in any style that the winemaker chooses. Varietal wines are table wines that are made from a minimum of 75 percent of a particular grape variety; they carry the name of the grape variety from which they are produced, such as Chardonnay or Merlot.

The red table wine category has been led by Cabernet Sauvignon, a full-bodied, rich, intense wine with noticeable tannins. A leading prestigious varietal, Cabernet Sauvignon has been one of the most widely available wines from California. Other red varietals include Merlot, Petite Sirah, and Zinfandel. Merlot is a medium- to full-bodied wine that originally was made for the sole purpose of blending with Cabernet Sauvignon. Petite Sirah is a wine with deep color, full body, and a fresh-berry taste. Zinfandel, known as the classic California wine, is known for its versatility, range of style, and its raspberry-spicy aroma and flavor.

White table wines have been dominated by Chardonnay, which is the most widely planted variety of grape in California, making up more than 56,000 acres. It is a dry wine that has a balance of fruit, acidity, and texture. Depending upon what the winemaker uses for storage, Chardonnay can range from clean and crisp wines to rich, complex, oak-aged wines.

Other white varietals include French Columbard, Sauvignon Blanc, Johannisberg Reisling, Gewurztraminer, and Pinot Blanc. French Columbard is generally fresh and fruity, ranging from light to medium in body. Sauvignon Blanc has been one of the fastest growing varietals in California; sometimes called Fume Blanc, it is best known for its grassy, herbal flavors and is often consumed with fish and shellfish. Johannisberg Riesling, from the German Riesling grape, is aromatic, delicate, and slightly sweet. Late Harvest Rieslings are good accompaniments for dessert. Gewurztraminer offers spicy aromas and flavors and a slight wisp of residual sweetness. Often this wine goes well with Asian food. Pinot Blanc is a unique, dry white wine, with styles ranging from bold, oak-aged to crisp and medium-bodied.

Brandy is "burnt wine" or fruit wine that is boiled and aged in wood. Virtually any type of fruit can be used to make brandy, although grapes have been the most common. Brandy has been produced primarily in Spain, Italy, and France and most recently in the United States. Cognac has been considered to be the best of all brandies. Cognac's discerning characteristic has been its blending. "While other brandies . . . are sometimes unblended or vintage-dated, cognacs, from the most basic V.S. to the rarest X.O., are almost always the final product of tens of cognacs, which have been married to achieve the proper balance, flavor and style," according to the *New York Times Magazine*.

Fortified wines were the creation of the Spanish and Portuguese and included port, sherry, and Madeira. Sherry is made by blending younger sherries with older sherries in oak casks. It varies in dryness levels and in hues. Harvey's Bristol Cream, imported by Hiram Walker & Sons, has been the top selling sherry in the United States, with a nearly 41 percent market share. The best seller is a blend of aged oloroso, a fortified full-bodied sherry, and Pedro Ximines grapes, which sweetens the mixture.

Port is red wine fortified with grape brandy. It was created unintentionally in the seventeenth century when Portugal tried to ship its table wine to England. In order to stabilize the wine during its voyage across the Atlantic, the wine needed the addition of grape brandy. England has remained the most popular market for port.

Madeira comes from a tropical island of the same name and is a raisiny, sweet wine. Madeira has been closely linked with the history of the United States, according to the *New York Times Magazine*. It was considered to be the wine of choice for American Revolutionary notables such as Thomas Jefferson, George Washington, and Ben Franklin. Unlike other wines that soured during the long, hot voyage across the Atlantic, Madeira was the only wine known to improve dramatically with the introduction of heat.

CURRENT CONDITIONS

Wine sales were expected to continue their increase as the federal government took an unprecedented step in advocating moderate consumption. When the U.S. government issued new dietary guidelines in 1996, it Acknowledged, for the first time, the benefits of moderate wine consumption. Previously, the government had warned that even small amounts of alcohol had "no net health benefit."

"Writing that language into the dietary guidelines was an extraordinary statement of public policy change in the United States. It's a foundation we can build on into the next century," said John De Luca, president of the Wine Institute, the trade association for the wine industry. He added that the revised guidelines culminated five years of work to redefine the image of wine, "putting it back on the dining room table where it's been for 2,000 years."

Leading the pack in wine sales have been the varietals. Relatively new to the industry, a "fighting" varietal has been defined as a value-priced, cork-finished, 750 ml varietal wine. The leader in fighting varietals has been Glen Ellen, followed by Fetzer's Bel Arbors, Sebastiani's Country Wines and Swan Cellar label, Beringer's Napa Valley, and Robert Mondavi's Woodbridge. Tim Wallace, a Glen Ellen executive, told *Beverage Dynamics* that "fighting varietals are the foundation for the American wine industry in the future."

In the late 1990s, fruit flavored varietal wines became popular. Canadaigua introduced Arbor Mist in 1998 in flavors such as peach and tropical fruits chardonnay and exotic fruits and sangria zinfandel. Other producers followed suit including Sutter Home's Portico, Earnest & Julio Gallo's Wild Vines, and the Wine Group's Lyrica.

The introduction of fruit flavored varietals caused a minor uproar among wine purists in the industry. Because these wines contain less than 7 percent alcohol, they are regulated for the Federal Drug Administration (FDA), which does not issue designation requirements for varietals.

At the end of the twentieth century, U.S. producers of champagne and sparkling wine commanded a 70 percent share of the domestic market. Growth continued to be slow. In 1997, shipments of champagne rose 1 percent for the first time since the 1980s, but they fell by 3 percent the following year. These losses were attributed to consumers' abandonment of the less expensive charmat producers in favor of the higher-end method champenoise varieties.

The good news is that the quality of champagne, both domestic and imported, has been rising. "Champagne producers have begun to make a lighter, more elegant non-vintage brut, one that better suits the American palate. Dramatic improvements in taste and technique all have been pioneered in California's best sparkling wine regions—Carneros, Mendocino County, and the central coast." In return, these domestic producers have seen consumers move to brands that offer high quality at affordable prices.

The sale of wine over the Internet stirred a heated debate between the U.S. Congress and the wine industry. Spurred by a rash of student-led violence in the nation's schools, legislators created a bill on youth crime and gun control. An amendment to the bill gave states the power to use federal courts to enforce local laws governing the interstate alcohol trade. Proponents said that the amendment's purpose was to prevent underage drinking. Many in the wine industry believed that it would restrict their business. A survey of 176 California vintners, conducted by the Wine Institute, found that 9 out of 10 ship their products to out-of-state customers and 50 percent use Web sites to sell their products.

INDUSTRY LEADERS

As dominant as the state of California is in the wine industry, so too are the wineries of California winemakers Ernest & Julio Gallo (E & J Gallo). Controlling nearly 40 percent of the U.S. wine market, E & J Gallo Wineries lead every wine category in which they compete. According to the *Wine Spectator,* one out of every three bottles of wine made in America is a Gallo product. The world's largest wine maker, E & J Gallo Wineries had annual sales of more than $1 billion.

In 1933, the original Ernest and Julio Gallo brothers winery was founded in Modesto, California. Unable to obtain bank financing, they bought crushing and fermenting equipment on 90-day terms and rented a warehouse to make their first commercial wine. Using pamphlets on winemaking from the local library and grapes bought on a promise to pay from eventual sales, the two brothers made their first batch of wine. By 1993, Gallo owned five separate vineyards totaling more than 2,000 acres. The company has remained a private, family-owned business (two of Julio Gallo's great-grandchildren, Matt and Gina, are actively involved in the company's wine-making operations) and is one of the largest organic farms in the United States.

The company's success has been due in part to the partnership of the Gallo brothers; Ernest marketed the wine that Julio made. Another part of Gallo's success has been its quest for improving the quality of the wine it produced. To this end, Gallo replanted its vineyard in Livingston in 1946 using grape varieties that had not been previously grown in the area. Various viticultural techniques were experimented with, and in 1947 a formal research program was established to evaluate the results. Specific standards were developed for wine making and have been used ever since.

In 1965, Julio Gallo established the first Growers Relations Department and shared research findings with area growers. In 1967, Gallo offered long-term contracts to selected growers, giving economic security and incentive to replant vineyards with the better grapes varieties

recommended by Gallo. During the 1970s, the winery shifted to producing premium varietal wines, and in 1991 it introduced its first ultra-premium wine, 1991 Sonoma Estate Chardonnay. Leading brands for E & J Gallo Wineries have been Gallo, Andre, Bartles & James, and Carlo Rossi.

Recent newcomer, Canadaigua Wine Company, became the number two seller in the U.S. wine market in 1995 with the acquisition of the Almaden and Inglenook wine labels (in 1994) from Heublein for $130.5 million. Although the company name may not be well known, its products such as Almaden, Inglenook, Taylor California Wines, and Paul Masson Wines are household names.

The company is a father-and-son operation located in upstate New York, started in 1945 by Marvin Sands, who bought a sauerkraut factory and turned it into a winery for $60,000. For 10 years, Canandaigua Industries sold fruit wines in bulk to local bottlers who would then sell them under their own brand names. In 1954, Sands turned away from bulk wines and created a brand for himself—Richards Wild Irish Rose, a blended red dessert wine. During the 1960s, Wild Irish Rose represented nearly all of the company's sales.

Working from that base, Sands slowly expanded, acquiring 11 small wineries through 1984. Then the company jumped on the wine cooler bandwagon with their Sun Country Wine Coolers. Although they suffered an operating loss of $20 million in 1987 and 1988 due to expensive advertising, Sands realized the power of the company's distribution network and began looking for established brands.

In 1991, Canadaigua made its first major purchase with Cook's Champagne for $60 million. Then came additional purchases in 1993, 1994, 1998, and 1999. By the end of the twentieth century, Canadaigua was posting annual sales of $740 million.

The Seagram Company, Ltd. has been one of the world's leading producers and marketers of distilled spirits and wines. Originally, Seagram divided its wine collection into two specialized divisions: The Seagram Classics Wine Company and Seagram Chateau & Estates Wine Company.

Based in San Mateo, California, the Seagram Classics Wine Company has produced, marketed, and exported the wines of Sterling Vineyards, the Monterey Vineyard, and Mumm Napa Valley. The division also has imported and marketed Mumm Champagnes and Barton & Guestier Wines from France and has acted as sales agent for select California and overseas wines.

Based in New York, the Seagram Chateau & Estates Wine Company has imported many European wines, including 35 percent of all classified Bordeaux. The company also has imported Seagram-owned Perrier-jouet

Champagnes (the third best-selling champagne in the United States), Sandeman Ports and Sherries, and Janneau Armagnacs.

In an effort to improve customer service, Seagram merged these two U.S. based wine companies in 1996. Sam Bronfman II, president of The Seagram Classic Wine Company, was selected to head this new operation, to be called the Seagram Chateau and Estate Wines company.

Kentucky-based Brown-Forman has been well known for its collection of distilled spirits, especially bourbon. During the 1960s and 1970s, the company expanded into the wine industry with the acquisition of Korbel champagne and brandy in 1965, and Bolla and Cella wines in 1968. By the early 1990s, Brown-Forman established a separate division for its wine operations and embarked on an aggressive plan to expand its business through long-term marketing and distribution contracts. Its base of wine products by 1991 included Bolla, Fontana, Candida, Brolio, Korbel, and Noilly Prat.

Aiming to expand in the wine market, Brown-Forman acquired Californian Fetzer in 1995. The Fetzer line sells 2.2 million cases in the United States, and with the help of Brown-Forman, the brand was expected to make significant progress in export markets.

WORKFORCE
In total, the winemaking industry employs more than 17,000 workers. The majority of wineries were family-owned, were located predominately in California, and have created a tremendous impact on that state's economy. Los Angeles-based Recon Research Corporation reported that the California wine industry has contributed nearly $1.5 billion annually to the Sonoma County economy, employing more than 3,600 people and creating secondary industrial employment of an additional 2,500 jobs.

AMERICA AND THE WORLD
Overseas planting of premium varietals have been growing at a fast pace and will be a significant new source of wine for U.S. consumers. In fact, California wineries bought unprecedented amounts of overseas wine to meet consumer demand for low-priced everyday wine and to expand their existing line of products in the mid-1990s.

For example, in 1996 Robert Mondavi began importing a Chilean line of wines, the Caletara brand, priced in the $6 to $9 range. A second brand, Edwardo Chadwick, was introduced in the $12 to $15 range, followed by a brand in an even higher price range. In 1995, the winery also launched a line of Italian varietals.

Another emerging wine growing country has been Australia. Demand for Australian wine skyrocketed as American consumers enjoyed the Australian style of wine. Its worldwide trademark of generous flavors, soft tannins, and accessible fruit made this wine easier to like when young, a perfect style of wine for Americans. In 1990, the Australians shipped only 578,000 cases of wine to the United States. By the decade's end, the Australian Wine Bureau reported that more than 4 million cases of Australian wine would be shipped to the United States by 2001, and by 2026, shipments should total more than 10 million cases with an estimated value of $440 million.

According to the Department of Commerce, U.S. wine exports totaled $537 million in 1998. The largest markets were the United Kingdom, Japan, and Canada. Mexico was expected to be an important market in the twenty-first century because, according to the North American Free Trade Agreement (NAFTA), the 16 percent tariff on American wine sales to that country would be lifted around the year 2004.

FURTHER READING
Anderson, Nick. "Battle Brews Over Online Sales of Alcohol." *Los Angeles Times,* 1999.

Bellamy, Gail. "Wine Update." *Restaurant Hospitality,* October 1995.

Berger, Dan. "Australian Wines." *Beverage & Food Dynamics,* January/February 1997.

———. "The Hottest-Selling Wines in America Are the Latest Fruit-Flavored Varietals." *Beverage Dynamics,* November 1999.

"Brown-Forman Puts Weight Behind Fetzer." *Grocer,* 12 August 1995.

Carlsen, Clifford. "Full-bodied Sales Make 1994 Vintage Year for Wineries." *San Francisco Business Times,* 4 August 1995.

Carlsen, Clifford. "Robust Year of Sales Gives Wine Makers a Healthy Glow." *San Francisco Business Times,* 15 November 1996.

"Chile is Hot." *Beverage World,* September 1996.

Lane, Randall. "Who's Afraid of Big, Bad Gallo?" *Forbes,* 13 February 1995.

"Quality Across the Board." *Beverage and Food Dynamics,* November 1996.

"Seagram Puts it All Together." *Beverage World,* October 1996.

Wine Institute. "U.S. Champagne & Sparkling Wine." San Francisco: March 1998. Available from http://www.wineinstitute.org.

SIC 2085

DISTILLED AND BLENDED LIQUORS

This category includes establishments primarily engaged in manufacturing alcoholic liquors by distillation and in manufacturing cordials and alcoholic cocktails by blending, processing, or mixing liquors and other ingredients. Establishments primarily engaged in manufacturing industrial alcohol are classified in **SIC 2869: Industrial Organic Chemicals, Not Elsewhere Classified,** and those bottling purchased liquors are classified in **SIC 5182: Wine and Distilled Alcoholic Beverages.**

NAICS CODE(S)

312140 (Distilleries)

INDUSTRY SNAPSHOT

In 1997, American consumption of distilled spirits totaled 138.7 million cases, a very slight 0.01 percent decrease from 1996. While American consumers drank less frequently, they chose higher quality or specialty products. The resurgence of classic cocktails such as Martinis and Manhattans helped the sale of premium dark spirits, although white spirits such as vodka and gin remained more popular.

The liquor industry, which consisted of large, multinational corporations, was trying to counter a 23 percent decline in U.S. consumption rates, which had peaked in 1981. Citing the need to compete with marketers of beer and wine, the liquor industry made a controversial decision to lift a 48-year-old voluntary ban on television advertising.

Response to this decision was swift and came from a variety of sources, including President Clinton and various public interest organizations. Congress held hearings regarding all advertising for alcoholic beverages on radio and television. The outcome of these hearings also affected the growing presence of liquor companies on the World Wide Web.

On a brighter note, American liquor marketers continued to make inroads with product exportation. Claiming a banner year in 1997, U.S. exports of distilled spirits rose 15.3 percent over 1996. Volumes of whiskey, rum, and neutral grain spirits exported continued to increase. Industry-wide shipments totaled $3.96 billion in 1997.

All the major liquor companies had their eye on the international arena, especially the Asian market. Japan was already at the top of the U.S. export list, and had been a favorite home for American whiskey. Latin America was also noted for its tremendous growth opportunity, especially for premium-priced products.

ORGANIZATION AND STRUCTURE

A few large companies that offer a variety of alcoholic beverages dominated the distilled spirits industry. Most started with a flagship brand, such as Jim Beam Bourbon, and have diversified into a family of products that includes whiskey and non-whiskey items, such as gin, vodka, rum, tequila, cordials, mixed cocktails, and even fruit juices and other non-alcoholic or low-alcohol beverages. Many, such as Seagram's, Diageo, and Allied Domecq are subsidiaries of large multinational conglomerates with very diverse portfolios.

This category includes only those companies that produce distilled spirits. All distillers have to sell their products through wholesalers and retailers, in order to accommodate various federal, state, and local regulations regarding the sale of alcoholic beverages. The Federal Alcohol Administration Act (FAA) was established at the end of the 13-year Prohibition Era in 1933. The FAA, which is enforced by the Bureau of Alcohol, Tobacco and Firearms (ATF), qualifies distillers, collects producer and wholesaler occupational taxes, and regulates trade practices, advertising, and labeling. Beyond the uniformity of the FAA, regulations vary greatly among the 50 states.

States can sell distilled spirits either with an "open," licensed method or in a controlled environment. Open states have licensed retailers and wholesalers that handle the distribution and sale of alcoholic beverages. Thirty-two states and the District of Columbia are open market. The other 18 states operate under the control method, in which each state government buys and sells alcoholic beverages at the wholesale and retail levels.

In addition to federal regulations, some states have set up their own independent agencies that are responsible for the administration, licensing, and enforcement of state laws, and the collection of state revenues. Some state legislatures have created their own Alcoholic Beverage Control (ABC) agencies with rule-making power, and 32 states allow their citizens to vote for or against the sale of liquor on a city or county-wide basis.

BACKGROUND AND DEVELOPMENT

All forms of alcoholic beverages—beer, wine and liquor—are based on fermentation, the natural process of decomposition of organic materials containing carbohydrates. Liquor production involves the extra step of distillation, which reduces the original water content and greatly increases the alcoholic strength. While beer averages 2 to 8 percent alcohol content, and wine averages from 8 to 14 percent, distilled spirits range from 35 to 50 percent alcohol. Two types of raw materials are used to make a distilled spirit: sugar and carbohydrates. Sugary materials include grapes, sugarcane, agave, molasses, and sugar. Those materials with high levels of carbohydrates are corn, rye, rice, barley, wheat, and potatoes.

Civilizations in almost every part of the world have developed some type of alcoholic beverage. The Chinese distilled a beverage from rice beer before 800 B.C. The Arabs developed a method used to produce a distilled beverage. A reference to distillation appears in the writings of the Greek philosopher Aristotle, and the Romans produced distilled beverages, although no written references can be found prior to 100 A.D. Liquor production was reported in Britain before the Roman conquest. However, production of distilled spirits in Western Europe was limited until the eighth century, after contact with the Arabs.

Distilled spirits can be classified into two categories: brown goods and white goods. Brown goods include all whiskies, bourbons, and scotches. White goods include vodka, gin, rum, and tequila. Other major segments in the distilled spirits market are the cordial or liquor category and the assortment of ready-to-drink cocktails.

Whiskey. Whiskey is an all-encompassing term for any distilled liquor made from a fermented mash of grain. While all whiskey is distilled in a similar manner, each can taste very different. The four primary steps to make whiskey are mashing, fermenting, distilling, and aging. The grains of corn, barley, rye, and/or wheat are ground into a fine meal, mixed with water, and cooked until the starches have been converted into sugars. This creates a "mash" that is mixed with yeast, converting the sugars into alcohol. The fermented mixture is then pumped into a still where steam condensation allows the alcohol to separate from the water and by-products. Fresh from the still, the whiskey is colorless, harsh, and in need of aging. It is the aging process that enhances the spirit and refines the whiskey, giving it an amber color.

Federal regulations specify that whiskey must be "produced at less than 190 proof and bottled at not less than 80 proof." American-distilled whiskeys include Tennessee, rye, and blended. Tennessee whiskey, such as Jack Daniel's and George Dickel, is a distinct product due to the filtering of the whiskey through charcoal prior to aging. Rye whiskey is made from at least 51 percent rye and distilled at no more than 160 proof. The whiskey then is stored at no more than 125 proof in new oak barrels. Blended whiskey, such as Seagram's Seven Crown, comes from at least 20 percent straight whiskey mixed with other whiskey grain neutral spirits. Blended whiskey became popular during World War II when whiskey was in short supply and distillers stretched its availability by adding grain neutral spirits.

Scotland remains the international leader in high-quality whiskey making. Blessed with natural resources and the ideal climate for making whiskey, Scotland boasts a long and rich history of distillation and a devotion to creating distinctly individual malts. By law, all scotch whiskey must be aged at least three years, al-though few brands enter the United States without being aged at least four. Scotch can be bottled in the country of origin or it can be shipped in bulk to the United States for bottling, which can be more cost effective.

More than 95 percent of scotch consumed worldwide is blended whiskey. Blends are the result of mixing both single malts and grain whiskies and are created to "soften" the harsher characteristics of individual malt whiskies. Although they are still a small percentage of the overall scotch consumption in the United States, single-malt whiskies have been made by Scottish distillers for more than 500 years. Single malts, the original scotch whiskies, are derived from sprouted barley that has been dried in kilns fired by peat and coal, which imparts a distinctive smoky character to the spirit. Produced by more than 100 scotch distilleries, each single malt has a style and flavor all its own.

Canadian whiskey is a blend of mostly rye with corn, wheat, and barley malt. By Canadian law, no more than 9.09 percent of a Canadian label may include whiskey from other countries. It must be blended from cereal grains, and it has to age in wood at least three years. As a rule, Canadian whiskies are light-bodied and slightly pale, with a reputation for having a mellow quality.

Irish whiskey is made from a fermented mash of malted and unmalted barley, corn, rye, and lesser amounts of other cereal grains. Unlike the Scots, who dry malt over an open peat fire to give it a smoky flavor, the Irish dry malt in closed kilns. Irish whiskies are full-bodied and possess a smooth malt flavor. All Irish whiskies are triple-distilled in copper pot stills and are aged three to nine years in reused sherry, brandy, bourbon, or rum oak casks. Irish whiskey remains the smallest of all the distilled spirits categories in the United States, accounting for less than 1 percent of all distilled spirits consumption.

Bourbon. Part of the whiskey group, bourbon is a uniquely American product, as corn is its main raw material. The drink was created unintentionally in 1789 when a Bourbon County, Kentucky, farmer sealed his whiskey in a charred barrel. This aging process picked up the mellow smoky flavor of the wood, giving bourbon its distinctive taste. In 1964, the U.S. Congress officially named bourbon America's "Native Spirit," and has tightly regulated bourbon's production to ensure a consistent, quality product. Straight bourbon whiskey is required by law to contain at least 51 percent corn; to be distilled at no more than 160 proof; and to be aged a minimum of two years in new, charred oak containers. Jim Beam Kentucky Straight Bourbon Whiskey continues to be the best-selling bourbon in the United States.

Vodka. Vodka continues to be the most popular liquor in America, accounting for more than one out of every five bottles of distilled spirits sold. According to U.S.

federal regulations, vodka lacks aroma, taste, and color. It is distilled at a high proof, extracting all of the congeners, or the natural compounds in the distillate that give the product its taste and aroma. Because vodka is highly neutral, it is possible to make it from a mash of the cheapest and most readily available raw ingredients. Although traditionally made from potatoes, vodka is now generally produced from cereal grains, including rye, wheat, and barley, but mostly corn.

Vodka originated in Russia during the 14th century and has remained commonplace in Russia, Poland, and the Baltic States. It became popular in the United States after World War II with the introduction of a drink called the Moscow Mule. In the land of its origin, vodka is usually consumed chilled, straight up in small glasses and accompanied by appetizers. In the United States, vodka is the base ingredient in a variety of popular cocktails.

Gin. Gin is the distilled product of juniper berries mixed with a clear grain-based spirit. First distilled by a 17th-century professor of medicine in Holland to produce an inexpensive medicine, gin quickly became a popular drink in Britain and later in the United States. Government regulations require that gin be bottled at 80 proof or higher, have a juniper berry flavor, and be made either by distillation or compounding. Compound gin, a less costly method, is the combination of neutral spirits with the oil and extracts of the botanicals.

Aging is not a factor with gin, although U.S. producers sometimes age their gins, imparting a pale, golden color. Instead, each gin achieves its distinct taste through the distiller's specific combination of gin botanicals, such as cassia, anise, coriander, angelica, and juniper. Gin is a flavored spirit. Without the flavoring, it would be vodka.

Rum. A favorite American spirit long before bourbon whiskey, rum is a sweet, distilled spirit made from sugar cane. Although debate continues as to where rum was first produced, by the late 17th century the liquor was being distilled in the American colonies using molasses from the West Indies. In fact, the first distillery in what is now called the United States was built on Staten Island and was already producing rum when the English seized the Dutch colony in 1664.

By federal law, rum must be distilled from the fermented juice of sugar cane, sugar cane syrup, sugar cane molasses, or other sugar cane by-products at less than 190 proof. It can be made anywhere, although more than 80 percent of rum is produced in Puerto Rico. The two main types of rum are light-bodied rums, which have a dry, subtle flavor, and full-bodied rums, a more aromatic variety.

Tequila. Made from the heart of the agave plant, Tequila is produced in its namesake town located in the central Mexican state of Jalisco. The core of the plant, which resembles a large pineapple, is harvested, cut into chunks, and baked in steam ovens. The juice is extracted by steaming and compressing the core. After fermenting for several days, the juice is distilled at a low proof. The tequila then is double distilled to a powerful 110 proof and reduced to 80 proof with water before bottling.

Although tequila can be bottled as a clear product, the gold and "anejo" products are aged in wood. Gold tequila is kept in large oak vats for about nine months to a year, acquiring its pale gold color. By law, tequila designated anejo must be aged in a wood container for at least one year, although most anejo products are aged for three to seven years.

Cordial. The cordial or liqueur category is the largest and most diverse in terms of the number of brands, flavors, and alcohol content. It also is one of the largest in total case sales. Products in this category encompass all flavors, and are used as after-dinner drinks, aperitifs, components of classic cocktails or popular shooters, or as flavorful enhancements to foods.

Originating in Europe, cordials and liqueurs are alcoholic beverages that are prepared by mixing or compounding various spirits with flavorings. The cordial category includes schnapps, liqueurs, cremes, and brandies. Cordials must contain at least 2.5 percent sugar by weight, although most are considerably higher in their sugar content and may contain up to 35 percent of a sweetening agent.

Cordials are produced by one of the following methods: percolation, maceration, or distillation. The percolation process starts with pouring the spirits in the bottom of a large tank with a basket-like container filled with fruit and spices near the top. The sprits then are "percolated" up through the basket, extracting the flavors of the fruit. With maceration, the fruit and other ingredients are mixed with the spirit and allowed to steep until all the flavors have been extracted. In the distillation process, all the ingredients are placed in the still with grain neutral spirits and gently heated.

CURRENT CONDITIONS

American consumption of distilled spirits decreased slightly in 1997 by 0.1 percent. This decrease was expected to continue in the long run; spirit sales were forecast to slip to 136.6 million cases by 2002, down from 138.7 million in 1997.

The top sellers in 1997 were Bacardi's Rum (6.5 million cases, up 1.1 percent from 1996), Smirnoff's Vodka (5.7 million cases, down 2.8 percent), and Absolut Vodka (3.4 million cases, up 3.0 percent). Vodka continued to surpass all other types of distilled spirits, holding 23.7 percent of the distilled market, although this was a

DOMESTIC CONSUMPTION OF DISTILLED LIQUOR

slight decrease of 0.3 percent from 1996. More than 32.9 million cases of Vodka were sold in the U.S. in 1997. In the past, vodka was popular because American consumers wanted lighter, less flavorful beverages. But as classic cocktails were revived in the 1990s, many were resurrected with a vodka base. Moreover, premium vodkas such as Ketel One, Absolut, and Skyy, were growing in popularity, as well as infused vodkas such as Absolut Citron, Absolut Kurrant, Finlandia Cranberry, Finlandia Pineapple, and Tanqueray Sterling Citrus.

In 1997, the sales breakdown of other distilled spirits was as follows: Canadian whiskey, 16.0 million cases; cordials, 15.9 million cases; rum, 13.5 million cases; bourbon (including blended and straight), 13.0 million cases; gin, 11.3 million cases; scotch, 9.6 million cases; tequila, 5.9 million cases; blended whiskey, 6.3 million cases; and Irish whiskey, 310,000 cases.

Rum usage rose by 3.8 percent in 1997. Following in the footsteps of infused vodka, rum flavored with spices or citrus also gained popularity with American consumers. Captain Morgan Original Spiced Rum from Seagram's captured the number two spot in the rum category with sales of 1.67 million cases in 1997.

Gin also posted a slight loss in 1997, The loss was largely on the part of the domestic brands, while usage of imported gin grew. This was attributed to the more sophisticated and upscale image of the imports, which are attempting to take the greatest advantage of America's resurgent love affair with the return of classic cocktails and martini bars.

While white goods declined slightly in sales, the decline of dark goods was much higher, despite the renewed popularity of classic cocktails such as Manhattans and Rob Roys. The only category of whiskey to increase sales was Irish whiskey, which increased for the sixth straight year in 1997. And while this category remained the smallest of all distilled spirits, its 1997 volume rose

6.9 percent. Despite the overall decrease in dark spirits, most suppliers have introduced higher-priced, higher-proofed products in recent years and this activity showed no signs of stopping.

While the decreased consumption of spirits in America is a trend which won't likely be reversed in the near future, Impact's Global Alcoholic Beverage Drinks Study forecast a 21 million-liter consumption gain worldwide by 2005, with distilled spirits at 18.33 billion liters, all growing from 1998 levels. The projected average annual compound growth rate for spirits was 0.1 percent between 2000 and 2005. Distilled spirits were expected to hold 9.7 percent of the global market in 2005, dropping from 10.6 percent in 1998.

Industry Regulations. After a peak consumption year in 1981, the industry saw consumption decrease slowly nearly every year. Seagram Americas became the first spirits marketer to break the 48-year-old voluntary ban on television advertising in June 1996 with its ad for Crown Royal Canadian whiskey on KRIS-TV in Corpus Christi, Texas. Major TV networks, however, refused to take liquor ads, and cable and local stations were left as the only outlet for spirits advertising.

The issue of liquor advertising opened a floodgate of controversy, including admonishments from President Clinton, Mothers Against Drunk Drivers, and Reed Hundt, chairman of the Federal Trade Commission. All of these parties said the ban should remain to protect children. George Hacker, of the advocacy group Center for Science in the Public Interest, said the repeal of the broadcast ad ban "marks the beginning of an open liquor-marketing season on America's children and teens."

The Federal Communications Commission (FCC) began a formal inquiry into the placement and content of Seagram's ads, while the Federal Trade Commission (FTC) followed with its own investigation. Congress took up this issue with the Senate Commerce Committee telecommunications subcommittee hearings in March 1997. Witnesses included the FTC Chairman Robert Pitofsky, FCC Chairman Reed Hundt, industry critics including former Senator George McGovern and representatives of the beer, liquor, broadcast, and cable industries.

In September of 1999, the Federal Trade Commission released their report on industry efforts to avoid promoting alcohol to underage consumers. The report, "Self-Regulation in the Alcohol Industry," recommended that industry improve enforcement of their "Code of Good Practice" by adopting a third-party review of compliance, and reduce underage exposure to alcohol ads by changing the current placement standards. The report also recommended that all industry members adopt and build upon the industry's current best practices, and go beyond the minimum code requirements. The report also urged companies to give special attention to restricting access to web sites that advertise alcohol. It noted that some companies had already made an attempt to address concerns by discontinuing the use of content that would appeal to underage users. Dr. Peter H. Cressy, president and CEO of the Distilled Spirits Council of the United States (DISCUS), issued a statement confirming that the distillers were willing to review the "Best Practices" identified in the report and consider any new provisions recommended.

Other legislative action of the late 1990s included the BAC amendment. Approved by the senate in 1998 by a wide margin, the amendment, which set a 0.08 blood-alcohol content level, brought a lobbying blitz from the liquor industry. About 15 states passed the BAC laws and legislation was introduced in 25 state legislatures.

The passage of the so-called "21st Amendment Enforcement Act," restricting the sale of alcohol over the Internet was passed by the U.S. House of Representatives in August 1999. The legislation originated with Mothers Against Drunk Driving (MADD), which had concerns with the sale of alcohol to minors over the Internet. Bob Shearouse, MADD's director of public policy, said, "We don't want a total ban, but just proper safeguards." The legislation was welcomed by anti-alcohol crusaders and by wine wholesalers, who considered themselves vulnerable to online vintners. Those opposing the legislation included the wine industry and e-commerce advocates, who believed the restrictions posed a threat to a free Internet marketplace.

The legislation provided state attorneys general in 20 states the power to seek a federal injunction against any company who may be in violation of state alcohol laws. In the other 30 states direct shipments are illegal, and in Florida, Georgia, Indiana, Kentucky, North Carolina, and Tennessee, direct shipments are a felony. Since most states require alcoholic beverages to be sold only through a state-licensed wholesaler, under the Enforcement Act, states can prosecute out-of-state companies if they make shipments violating the state's law.

As of 2000, alcohol was the most heavily taxed consumer product in the United States; more than half the money consumers spent on a bottle of distilled spirits went for taxes. Federal, state, and local governments received more than $7.5 billion per year in tax revenue from the distilled spirits industry and $18 billion from the entire alcoholic beverage industry. According to DISCUS, the federal beverage alcohol tax structure was particularly biased against distilled spirits.

INDUSTRY LEADERS

A subsidiary of Diageo PLC, United Distillers & Vintners (UDV) was the world's leading and most profitable wine and spirits company in 1998, with sales of 109 million nine-liter cases and operating profits of $1.8 billion. UDV was the result of a merger between Grand Metropolitan and Guinness. The creation of UDV was a strategic breakthrough in the spirits industry, bringing together leading brands in most spirit categories and access to customers in more than 200 countries. UDV's brands included Baileys liqueur, Gordon's, Gilbey and Tanqueray gin, Johnnie Walker, J&B Rare and Bell's whiskeys, and Smirnoff vodka. UDV had also formed trading partnerships with Moët Hennessy and José Cuervo.

Allied Domecq PLC is the world's number two distiller, recording annual brand shipments of 49 million nine-liter cases in 1998. Allied Domecq owned 12 of the top 100 international premium spirit brands, including Ballantine's scotch whiskey, Beefeater gin, Kahlua, Sauza tequila, Canadian Club whiskey, Courvoisier, and Tia Maria.

Joseph Seagram & Sons Inc. is one of the world's leading producers and marketers of distilled spirits and wine, with 1998 revenues of over $4.8 billion, an increase of 6 percent over 1997. The business was organized on a global basis and conducted through subsidiaries and affiliates in 30 countries. Known as the Seagram Spirits and Wine Group, this division has been responsible for the production, brand management, business development, marketing, sales, and distribution of nearly all of Seagram's beverage alcohol business. The only exceptions have been Seagram's U.S. cooler business and the U.S.-based, specialized, premium wine operations.

Seagram's brands included Chivas Regal scotch whiskey, Crown Royal Canadian whiskey, Captain Morgan Original Spiced Rum, Absolut Vodka, Martell Cognac, Don Julio Tequila, Glenlivet single malt scotch whiskey, and Seagram's gin. Seagram's acquired Don Julio Tequila in May of 1999.

Kentucky-based Brown-Forman Corporation was created in 1870 when George C. Brown and John Forman opened their distillery in Louisville to producer Old Forester bourbon. In 1902, Forman sold his interest in the company to the Brown family, which has remained in control of the business ever since. 1999 revenues were over $2 billion, and the company employed 7,600 people. Well-known brands included Jack Daniel's, Gentleman Jack, Old Forester, Early Times, Canadian Mist, Southern Comfort, Korbel, Jack Daniel's Country Cocktails, Finlandia Vodkas, Bushmills Irish Whiskeys, and Glenmorangie Single Highland Malts.

Fortune Brands Inc.'s subsidiary Jim Beam Brands Worldwide is one of the largest distilled spirits companies in the United States, with $1.3 billion in 1998 sales. Jim Beam Bourbon has been the company's flagship brand and the best-selling bourbon in the United States and world-

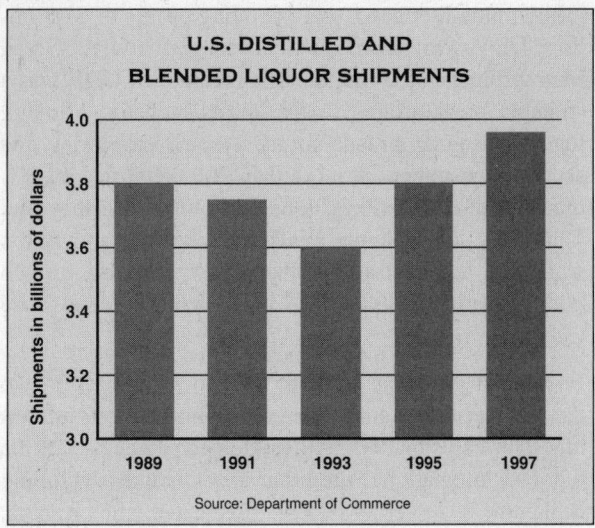

U.S. DISTILLED AND BLENDED LIQUOR SHIPMENTS

Source: Department of Commerce

wide. The company started in 1795 when Jacob Beam, a Kentucky farmer, developed his recipe for Kentucky bourbon whiskey. His son, David, joined the business, and with the assistance of new roads the distillery business grew as distribution broadened into the surrounding counties. In the following years, the distillery was moved twice, first to take advantage of an abundance of spring water and again to be closer to the railroad lines. The company's distillery is located on 430 acres in Clermont, 30 miles south of Louisville. Booker Noe, grandson of Jim Beam, is the Master Distiller at Clermont. In addition to Jim Beam Bourbon, the company produces a number of other bourbons, cordials, liqueurs and whiskeys.

WORKFORCE

In 1997, this industry's 60 establishments employed 6,545 people, over 4,000 of whom worked in production. These production workers earned an average hourly wage of $16.26.

AMERICA AND THE WORLD

U.S. exports of distilled spirits reached a record high in 1997, according to *Adams 1998 Liquor Handbook*. Since 1995, U.S. distilled spirits exports have more than doubled both in value and volume. In 1991, U.S. distilled spirits exports totaled 10 percent of industry sales; by 1997, they totaled over half of industry sales. From 1995 to 1996, exports rose over 200 percent. Volume exports of U.S. whiskey, rum, and neutral grain spirits categories all increased in 1997, while U.S. whiskey, brandy, gin, cordials, and neutral grain spirits increased in value. Approximately 62 percent of U.S. distilled spirit exports in 1997 consisted of branded items, such as whiskey (51.0 percent), rum (6.0 percent), liqueurs and cordials (3.0 percent), vodka (2.0 percent) and gin (0.3 percent).

"International expansion represents a great opportunity for distillers. Leading spirit brands already enjoy worldwide cachet, especially within the whiskey and cognac categories," reported Jim Barrett in the *Value Line Investment Survey*. Export opportunities could be found in the fast-growing markets of the Asia Pacific region, Latin America, and the former Soviet Bloc. "Not only are these expanding markets, but the growth is generally occurring among higher-margin, deluxe brands. What's more, trade barriers were lifted in a number of countries, such as India and Taiwan," added Barrett. *Impact* projected that by 2000, the consumption of distilled spirits globally would stand at 18.33 billion liters, and by 2005 it would reach 18.44 billion liters.

The Asia Pacific area has included some of the largest whiskey markets in world, with Japan at the top of the U.S. export list. The rapid ascent of a middle class in these countries was a positive indicator for the future of beverage alcohol marketers. "Export is the hot spot," Barry M. Berish, president of Jim Beam Brands Co., noted in *Business Week*. The *U.S. Industry & Trade Outlook '99* forecasted that U.S. exports would increase 3 to 8 percent annually in the five years following 1999.

In 1997, U.S. whiskey exports led product categories with an 8.2 percent increase over 1996 for a total of over 8 million cases. Japan, Germany, and Australia were significant growth markets for exported U.S. whiskey in 1997, with the improved Japanese economy showing an increase of 50 percent. Japan accounted for 20 percent of the total value of U.S. exports of whiskey, followed by Germany with 19 percent, Australia with 14 percent, the United Kingdom with 11 percent, and Spain and France with 4 percent apiece.

Beverage alcohol marketers also were beginning to focus on growth in other countries. After successful penetration of the Japanese market, whiskey advertising could be found in Britain and other affluent markets. Latin America, for example, has become the second greatest growth opportunity, particularly for premium-priced scotch marketers like Seagram. Sales of scotch grew over 50 percent in 1991 in Venezuela, with much of the growth occurring among higher-priced brands, such as Chivas Regal Scotch. Scotch whiskey has remained the most popular distilled spirit in the world and has been sold in 190 countries. In 1999, tequila had become the fastest growing distilled spirit, and companies increasingly produced new and unique tequila varieties in an effort to attract consumers.

FURTHER READING

Adams 1998 Liquor Handbook. Adams Business Media Inc., 1998.

"Allied Domecq: Sprits and Wines: Introduction," 1999. Available from http://www.allieddomecqplc.com/about/.

"Brown-Forman Corporation Products," 1999. Available from http://www.brown-forman.com/.

"Developing Countries Expected to Lead Alcoholic Beverage Growth." *The Premier Just-Drinks: Surveys and Stats 1999.* Available from http://www.just-drinks.com/.

"Diageo: Who we are," 1999. Available from http://www .diageo.com/.

"Discus Announces Record Year for U.S. Distilled Spirits Exports." Washington, D.C.: Distilled Spirits Council of the United States, 24 April 1996.

Distilled Sprits Council of the United States. "Distillers Spirits Advertising in Perspective," 1999. Available from http://www .discus.health.org.

———. "Distilled Spirits. Responsible Industry. Responsible Consumers. Overview," 1999. Available from http://www .discus.health.org/factsabout.htm/.

"The Dow Lifts Some Spirits" *Time,* 17 February 1997.

Federal Trade Commission. "FTC Reports on Industry Efforts to Avoid Promoting Alcohol to Underage Consumers," September 1999. Available from http://www.ftc.gov.

———. "Self-Regulation in the Alcohol Industry." September 1999. Available from http://www.ftc.gov/.

Fried, Eunice. "High-Powered Drinks: Cost Aside, Ultra Premium Vodka is Surging in Popularity." *Black Enterprise,* March 1996.

"Year in Review 1998: business-and-industrial-review." *Encyclopaedia Britannica.* Available from http://search.britannica .com/.

SIC 2086

BOTTLED AND CANNED SOFT DRINKS AND CARBONATED WATERS

This category includes establishments primarily engaged in manufacturing soft drinks and carbonated waters. Establishments primarily engaged in manufacturing fruit and vegetable juices are classified in various canned, frozen, and preserved food classifications. Those manufacturing fruit syrups for flavoring are classified in **SIC 2087: Flavoring Extracts and Flavoring Syrups, Not Elsewhere Classified;** those manufacturing nonalcoholic cider are classified in **SIC 2099: Food Preparations, Not Elsewhere Classified.** Establishments primarily engaged in bottling natural water are classified in **SIC 5149: Groceries and Related Products, Not Elsewhere Classified.**

NAICS CODE(S)

312111 (Soft Drink Manufacturing)
312112 (Bottled Water Manufacturing)

INDUSTRY SNAPSHOT

Soft drinks have become intrinsically tied to the "American way of life," and the leading soft drink, Coca-Cola, is a virtual icon of American culture. Close to 500 soft drinks manufacturers and bottling companies operate in the United States. Americans consume more soft drinks than any other beverage—more than twice the second beverage, coffee. Soft drinks accounted for more than 29 percent of American beverage consumption. The U.S. market included nearly 450 different soft drinks.

Soft drinks is a $56 billion a year industry. Two companies, Coca-Cola and Pepsi-Cola, controlled nearly three-quarters of the U.S. soft drink market, with each company producing four of the top ten best-selling brands. Approximately 500 bottlers operate across the United States. Modern bottling plants produce more than 2,000 soft drinks per minute on each line of operation.

There is more to America's soft drink industry than just the companies that provide consumers with their favorite refreshments, according to the National Soft Drinks Association (NSDA). It's also a big part of the U.S. economy, buying products and services from many different industries, creating thousands of jobs, and contributing to worthwhile causes in local communities.

Soft drink flavorings are the number one product purchased, followed by metal cans in second place, and plastics used for packaging in third place. The soft drink industry also is a big buyer of corn syrup, advertising services, glass containers, boxes for shipping bottle caps, warehousing, fruits and vegetables, motor freight, carbonated water, sugar, and many other products and services that contribute to the manufacture of soft drinks.

ORGANIZATION AND STRUCTURE

Soft drink companies manufacture and sell beverage syrups and bases to bottling operations that add sweeteners and/or carbonated water to produce the final product. Independent bottlers work under contract with various soft drink manufacturers and are allotted specific territories to serve. The manufacturers provide the bottlers not only with syrups and bases, but also with a variety of business services, including product quality control, marketing, advertising, engineering, and financial and personnel training. In turn, the bottlers supply the required capital investment for land, buildings, machinery, equipment, trucks, bottles, and cases.

The soft drink industry sells its product in two forms, packaged and fountain service. With fountain service, the soft drink product is dispensed and served in cups, typically in a restaurant or any location with a food service station. The industry as a whole sold 15.2 billion gallons of soft drinks in 1997.

BACKGROUND AND DEVELOPMENT

The soft drink industry began in the mid-1880s with the creation of a syrup that was mixed with carbonated water and served at drug store lunch counters. During the early years, soft drinks were sold only in stores that could provide fountain service. Increasing distribution was tied to building additional syrup manufacturing plants.

With the advent of bottling machinery, soft drinks began to be distributed beyond the town drug store. The first merchant to bottle Coca-Cola was Joseph A. Biedenharn of Vicksburg, Mississippi, who installed a bottling machine in his candy store in 1894. The development of large-scale bottling assisted the proliferation of Coca-Cola, and by 1895 the drink was sold in nearly every part of the United States. An infrastructure of independent bottlers working under contract with Coca-Cola, producing the drink to exact specifications, and distributing it within a specific region, soon became the model distribution method for Coke and was emulated by others.

The 1960s and 1970s brought acquisitions and diversification for Coca-Cola and Pepsi-Cola. In 1960, Coke purchased Minute Maid and later acquired Duncan Foods. The Coca-Cola Company Foods Division was created in 1967 and was later renamed Coca-Cola Foods. Meanwhile, Pepsi-Cola merged with Frito-Lay in 1965, changing its name to PepsiCo but maintaining its beverage division under the name Pepsi-Cola. PepsiCo soon ventured into food service and snack foods with the acquisition of Pizza Hut, Taco Bell, and Kentucky Fried Chicken restaurants.

During the 1980s, as consumers became more interested in health and fitness, the soft drink industry faced stiff competition from the makers of bottled water. In response, soft drink manufacturers developed low-calorie and caffeine-free beverages, such as Diet Coke and Diet Pepsi. The start of the 1990s ushered in a new kind of competition focused on ''New Age'' beverages such as ready-to-drink teas, fruit juice beverages, and flavored waters. Gatorade, the perennial leader among sports drinks, saw new competition during the 1990s.

From the simple beginnings of one cola, the soft drink industry exploded into a kaleidoscope of traditional sodas, natural sodas, fruit juice drinks, and various kinds of bottled water. Coca-Cola Classic was the best selling soft drink in the United States and around the world in 1992, controlling nearly 20 percent of the domestic market and 46 percent of the worldwide market. Coke Classic controlled 19.3 percent of the soft drink market and posted a sales increase of 1.5 percent for the year. Pepsi-Cola was the second best-selling soft drink for the year, with a 16.1 percent market share, down 0.8 percent over 1991. Diet Coke, Diet Pepsi, and Dr Pepper completed the list of the top five soft drink brands for 1992.

Some industry leaders contend that the U.S. soft drink market has begun a slow, steady decline, citing its failure to post double-digit growth since the end of the 1980s. Pointing to an aging U.S. population and changing consumer tastes, industry analysts predicted that per capita consumption and the total consumption rate would not increase significantly in the near future. To combat a weak U.S. market, soft drink manufacturers aggressively pursued overseas markets. Although no other country has a soft drink consumption rate as high as the United States, many areas have been targeted as potential for expansion, especially the underdeveloped and highly populated areas of China and India. The Coca-Cola Company has been the clear leader in overseas expansion with nearly 75 percent of its operating profits coming from areas outside the United States.

Traditional cola producers were caught off-guard by the rise of generic store brands during the early 1990s as the recession drove consumers to experiment with these lower-priced drinks. These colas were not expected to create a significant amount of brand loyalty, so they did not appear to pose a substantial threat to the major soft drink manufacturers.

Despite market dominance, traditional cola products continued to lose market share. Total soft drink consumption grew roughly 5.0 percent annually between 1983 and 1989, but slowed to 3.0 percent in 1990 and only 1.6 percent by 1991. Even the diet cola market has faltered since 1990, losing ground to new drinks commonly called ''New Age'' beverages. In a category that enjoyed a 10 to 20 percent growth rate during the 1980s, sales growth for diet colas decreased to approximately 3 percent per year. Industry analysts suggest that new drinks, including sodas and bottled water, are the most formidable opponents to traditional colas. This market segment began with the rise of the bottled water industry in the United States and expanded into the creation of the New Age category.

Strongest during the 1980s, bottled water remained a vibrant and growing segment of the beverage market into the 1990s. This industry can be divided into two segments, bulk water and refreshment beverages. Bulk water is nonsparkling water that is consumed instead of tap water, and it represented about 80 percent of the market. Refreshment beverages ranged from water such as Evian to flavored, vitamin-enriched sparkling mineral water from Crystal Geyser. While bulk water usually is bought through a delivery service in five-gallon containers or larger, refreshment beverages are premium, image-driven brands, prepared in smaller containers and sold for both on- and off-premise consumption. These products compete directly with sodas and mixers.

Since 1980, the U.S. bottled water market has grown to nearly 3 billion gallons in annual consumption. After a decade of double-digit growth, the market faltered in

1991, showing only a 0.5 percent gain in volume. Analysts blamed the recession and concerns about safety, prompted by the Perrier recall in 1990, for the downturn. The industry began to rebound in 1992 with a 3.7 percent increase in volume and a 3.2 percent increase in sales. By 1993, more than 700 brands of bottled water were produced in the United States at 430 bottling facilities. Another 75 brands of water were imported.

The Perrier Group was the largest bottled water company in the United States. Acquired in 1992 by Nestle, the Perrier Group includes a collection of strong regional domestic waters plus its flagship brand. The second largest bottled water company in the United States has been McKesson Water Products, with most of its business centered around home and office delivery. More than 80 percent of the company's sales have been in California with its Sparkletts brand.

Beyond bottled water, an entirely new market segment appeared, answering Americas' call for flavored drinks that are lighter, less filling, less sweet, "healthier," and more sophisticated than traditional soda. New Age beverages have covered everything from flavored sparkling waters to natural sodas to fruit juice drinks to flavored teas and bottled coffee products. A beverage fits in the New Age category if it is "relatively new to the market, considered by the consumer as 'good for me' and containing natural and/or healthy ingredients without preservatives," industry analyst Michael Bellas told *Beverage World.*

The all-natural soda division has been the most active New Age segment. Although sales slumped in 1990, "all-natural sodas stormed back to reach $309.8 million in sales in 1991, up a whopping 51 percent," reported Eric Sfiligoj in *Beverage World.* Consumption of all-natural sodas reached 81.3 million gallons annually by 1991, second in the category only to flavored waters. The healthy growth of all-natural sodas has been in direct response to the success of Vancouver-based Clearly Canadian. Launched in 1987, Clearly Canadian is Canadian water pumped from deep artesian wells and mixed with fruit flavors. The product is sweetened with fructose and contains preservatives.

Sales of New Age beverages were projected to grow at 8 percent annually through 1995, with growth rates hitting 11 percent by 1996, according to *Beverage Dynamics.* With projections such as these, it was only a matter of time before the national cola brands added their own products to the plethora of New Age drinks. In early 1992, Pepsi introduced Crystal Pepsi, a clear, cola-flavored beverage that was 100 percent naturally flavored and contained no preservatives or caffeine. During its first year of national distribution in 1993, Crystal Pepsi captured more than 2 percent of the soft drink market or roughly $1 billion in sales.

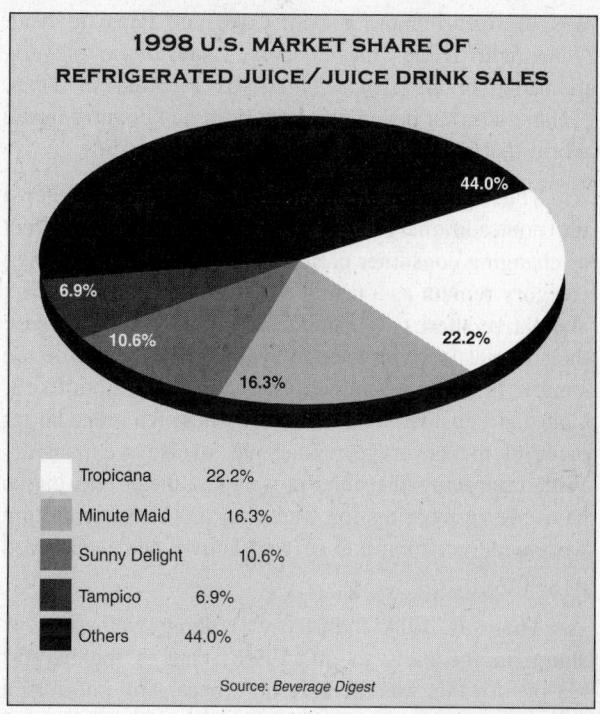

1998 U.S. MARKET SHARE OF REFRIGERATED JUICE/JUICE DRINK SALES

44.0%
22.2%
16.3%
10.6%
6.9%

Tropicana		22.2%
Minute Maid		16.3%
Sunny Delight		10.6%
Tampico		6.9%
Others		44.0%

Source: *Beverage Digest*

Coca-Cola also launched its New Age soda, Nordic Mist, in 1992. The Coke product is a mixture of sparkling water, high fructose corn syrup, citric acid, potassium, and one of five natural fruit flavors. "New Age isn't our bread and butter," said Bob Bertini of Coca-Cola USA in *Beverage Dynamics,* "but it deserves a place at the table. We want to be fully represented in every category that makes sense for us. We're trying to respond to changes in the market, but our priority is still colas and traditional soft drinks."

In the face of rising competition from all fronts of the beverage market, both Coke and Pepsi turned to joint ventures with other beverage companies. Pepsi-Cola has been working with Ocean Spray to provide all of their ready-to-drink beverages, including Ocean Spray Splash, a five-flavor line of fruit sparklers, and Ocean Spray Lemonade. In this alliance, Pepsi has become the exclusive distributor of all Ocean Spray single-serve products.

In a joint venture with Nestle, Coca-Cola created the Coca-Cola Nestle Refreshment Company (CCNR) in 1991 to market ready-to-drink coffee, tea, and chocolate beverages. Nestea Iced Tea, CCNR's first project, was introduced in the United States in March 1992. The bottled tea has no preservatives, artificial flavors or colors, and comes in regular and diet versions.

Both cola manufacturers also introduced sports drinks, such as All Sport by Pepsi and PowerAde by Coke. Sports drinks replenish fluids, minerals, and energy lost during exercise, and the market for these drinks has grown into a billion-dollar retail segment. Gatorade accounted for nearly 90 percent of nationwide sales and was the one brand for both Coke and Pepsi to beat. "Gatorade defines the category," says Jesse Meyers, publisher of *Beverage Digest,* as reported in *Time.* "There is not a beverage category in any country in the world that is so dominated by one producer."

The movement of major players like Coke and Pepsi into nontraditional beverage markets has shown the affect of changing consumer preferences. Should the New Age category remain as a firmly established and viable drink alternative, these two manufacturers are likely to increase their domestic rivalry, possibly to the detriment of the smaller firms in the marketplace. Moreover, both Coca-Cola and Pepsi-Cola have set their sites on a much larger piece of the beverage market pie, overseas expansion. With improving distribution systems, these two giants have been preparing for what they do best, promoting worldwide consumption of well-known and well-loved products.

The soft drink industry was doing well after its slump in the early to mid-1990s. One of the biggest reasons for this was the industry's expansion into fertile overseas markets. Innovative marketing strategies and timely new product introductions caused U.S. consumption of soft drinks to improve. According to *Beverage World,* carbonated soft drink consumption increased to 13.3 billion gallons in 1994, an increase of 4.3 percent from 1993. Fruit beverages consumption was 3.3 billion gallons in 1994, an increase of 3.8 percent from 1993.

New Age drinks were the best performers in the mid-1990s. Bottled water consumption reached 2.5 billion gallons in 1994, an increase of 10.4 percent from 1993. Sports drinks performed even better, with the consumption reaching 391.1 million gallons in 1994, an increase of 11.4 percent over consumption in 1993.

Bottled water was seen as the best performing star of the soft drinks industry in the mid- to late 1990s. Its success was attributed to many factors including, "A perception of a healthy, natural, good-for-you product," according to *Beverage World.* Given the concerns over municipal water, it was considered the only beverage category that was driven because it was a tap water replacement. The bottled water industry saw many "firsts" in the mid-1990s. It was the first time that this industry "topped 2.5 billion gallons, measured more than 10 gallons per capita, and totaled more than 3 billion in wholesale receipts," according to *Beverage World.* The sparkling water segment, however, was the only down spot in the industry, with dollar sales going down almost 10 percent according to *Beverage World.*

Packaging and Recycling. Since 1989, soft drink container recycling has risen from 48.7 percent to more than 60.0 percent—a 23 percent increase. Nearly 48 billion soft drink containers were recycled in 1995, and soft drink containers accounted for less than 1 percent of the U.S. solid waste stream. Although beverage containers account for less than 20 percent of materials collected in most curbside programs, they generate up to 73 percent of total scrap revenue. Packaging innovations lightened the weight of soft drink containers by an average of 30 percent since 1972. Nearly 78 percent of soft drinks are packaged, while the remaining 22 percent are dispensed from fountains. In 1995, 62.6 billion soft drinks were packaged in cans, 16.8 billion were packaged in PET plastic bottles, and 3.6 billion were packaged in glass bottles.

CURRENT CONDITIONS

Soft drinks are an integral part of American life and culture. In 1997 Americans consumed an average of 2.4 eight-ounce servings of soft drinks per day. While there are hundreds of brands, the big two of the industry—Coke and Pepsi—have been busy buying smaller soft drink companies in order to increase market share. Competition is fierce, with battles fought daily over shelf space, fountain rights, and pricing. To meet the needs of staying on top, companies need to accumulate large amounts of capital and equipment and react to the constantly changing retail markets.

During the past few years the number of independent bottlers declined as major soft drink manufacturers consolidated bottling operations by acquiring independent companies and combining them into one large operation. By early 1999 the number of Coca-Cola bottlers in the United States dropped to 96, from 353 in 1980. Some analysts say the number of bottlers will drop to 50 or fewer by 2004. The mergers of the independent bottlers began as the amount of capital and equipment needed to continue modernization increased rapidly.

Coca-Cola Enterprises (CCE) was formed in 1986, and in 1999 it distributed 74 percent of Coca-Cola's volume. CCE spent more than $2 billion in acquiring other Coca-Cola bottlers and has become the world's largest soft drink bottler. The company's production accounted for 55 percent of all the bottled and canned Coke products sold in the United States, and it operated in 37 states, Washington, D.C., and the U.S. Virgin Islands. By 2004, it is expected that CCE will control 80 percent of the distribution of Coca-Cola products. The parent company of Coca-Cola owns about 40 percent of CCE and in 1999 increased its spending on the subsidiary by 54 percent—up to $1.2 billion on marketing and sales-related equipment.

Meanwhile, Pepsi's company-owned bottling operations have been responsible for 52 percent of its bottling volume. Seeing the success of CCE, Pepsi plans in 1999-2000 to spin off its bottling operations into a separate company.

The leaders of the soft drink industry market products heavily, constantly vying for brand loyalty. As the coffee industry went after the middle-age market, the soft drink industry promoted heavily to the younger set. It paid off—marketing research shows that coffee is now below milk, soft drinks, tea, fruit drinks, juices, and alcoholic beverages as the drink of choice during at home dinners. Pepsi developed hip new ads aimed at the younger crowd, including a young girl who adopts celebrity voices such as Marlon Brando's to intimidate those who would dare serve her a Coke.

Marketing and market share also include plans for new products. But, as Pepsi recently found out, there may not be room for new products in consumers' hearts. In a move reminiscent of Coke's disastrous New Coke campaign, Pepsi rolled out a new diet cola called Pepsi One in October 1998. Hyped by the company as a better tasting diet cola, sales started strong, with Pepsi One capturing 2 percent of the market. It soon faltered as consumers decided it didn't taste all that different from Diet Pepsi. Pepsi One's share soon fell to 1.4 percent of the market.

A battleground for the big two is the sports arena market. Coke has a huge advantage over Pepsi in pouring rights for sports arenas, but in recent years Pepsi has made some headway, capturing some sought-after accounts. Coke is the leader in sports marketing with pouring rights to 23 of 30 football stadiums in the NFL and exclusive marketing rights to seven teams. Pepsi pours at six stadiums and markets exclusively to four NFL teams. Dr Pepper pours at one stadium, the Cowboys' Texas Stadium, and RC Cola is the exclusive drink at the Green Bay Packers' Lambeau Field. From 1997 to 1998 Pepsi acquired the rights to pour at Denver's Mile High Stadium, yet Coke retained the marketing rights with the team.

Coke dominates in other sport venues, as well. Coke pours at 22 Major League Baseball (MLB) stadiums, 24 National Basketball Association (NBA) arenas, and 21 National Hockey League (NHL) arenas. Pepsi has the rights to eight MLB stadiums, five NBA arenas, and six NHL areas. Dr Pepper shares pouring rights at MLB's Texas Rangers' The Ballpark.

Both companies are also fighting to win fans in NASCAR, the fastest growing sport in the United States. Both sponsor races (the Coca-Cola 600 and the Pepsi 500) and Pepsi is the primary sponsor of Jeff Gordon in the Busch series and a secondary sponsor of Jeff Gordon's Winston Cup car. Coke is a secondary sponsor of several Winston Cup drivers, including Bill Elliot, Dale Earnhardt, and Kyle Petty.

The aggressive marketing has paid off—in 1999 American teenagers drank twice as much soda as milk. In 1979 those figures were reversed. Alarmed at the trends, educators and legislators in Washington enacted laws

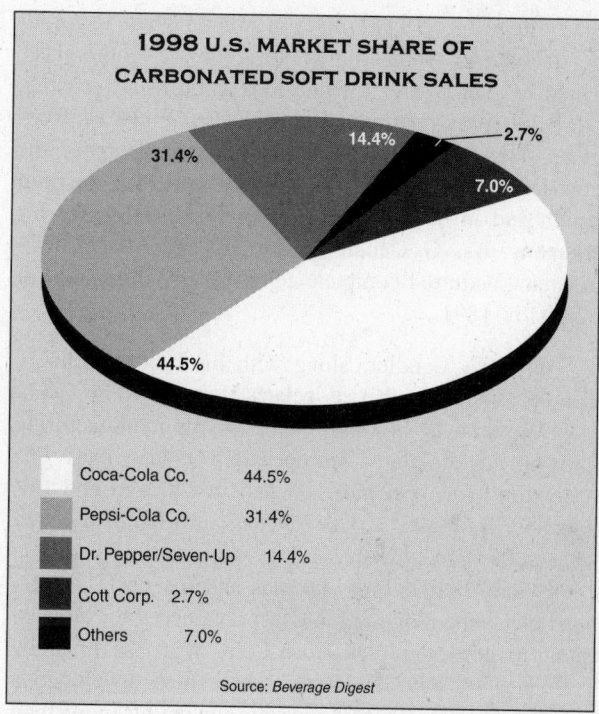

1998 U.S. MARKET SHARE OF CARBONATED SOFT DRINK SALES

☐	Coca-Cola Co.	44.5%
☐	Pepsi-Cola Co.	31.4%
☐	Dr. Pepper/Seven-Up	14.4%
☐	Cott Corp.	2.7%
■	Others	7.0%

Source: *Beverage Digest*

keeping soft drink manufacturers from selling products in the nations' schools before and during lunch. Principals at some schools began allowing companies to offer free drinks at lunch, thereby getting around the law. Congress introduced the Better Nutrition for School Children Act of 1999 banning the giveaways. Industry spokesmen said the industry remained neutral on the legislation, saying they were for school choice on the matter. They pointed out that some principals were in favor of the free soft drinks as it kept some students on school grounds eating nutritional lunches, instead of leaving campus to eat at fast-food establishments.

Pouring rights are also fought over in a wide spectrum of places—fast food establishments, college campuses, convenience stores, hotels, and others. In 1999 Pepsi signed an agreement with Orion Food systems, which operated franchises in more than 2000 locations in the world. These locations include office buildings, college campuses, shopping malls, supermarkets, and more.

INDUSTRY LEADERS

Coca-Cola has been the world's most popular soft drink, holding as high as 51 percent global market share in 1998. Using a franchise system for distribution, the company and its subsidiaries sold the flagship brand and other brands in the Sprite, Tab, and Diet Coke families in more than 195 countries and territories. Coke reported third quarter 1999 sales of $5.2 billion.

Coca-Cola originated in Atlanta, Georgia, on May 8, 1886, when pharmacist Dr. John Styth Pemberton created a caramel-colored syrup in his backyard. He took a jug of the syrup to Jacob's Pharmacy in Atlanta where the product debuted as a soda fountain drink for five cents a glass. Thinking that two C's would look good in advertising, Dr. Pemberton's partner and bookkeeper Frank M. Robinson suggested the name Coca-Cola and designed the now-famous script trademark. Dr. Pemberton, in poor health and in need of funds, soon sold portions of his company. Asa G. Candler, a druggist and Atlanta businessman, acquired complete control of the company for $2,300 in 1891.

In 1892, Candler, along with his brother John S. Candler and two other associates, formed "The Coca-Cola Company." In 1894, the first syrup manufacturing plant outside of Atlanta was opened in Dallas, Texas. The following year, two more opened in Chicago and Los Angeles. By 1895, Coca-Cola was available in every state in the United States. Large-scale bottling began in 1899 when Benjamin F. Thomas and Joseph B. Whitehead of Chattanooga, Tennessee, obtained the exclusive rights to bottle and sell Coca-Cola. With the financial assistance of John T. Lupton, these men developed a regional franchise bottling system, engaging more than 1,000 bottlers in 20 years.

In 1919, The Coca-Cola Company was sold to Atlanta banker Ernest Woodruff for $25 million. Ernest's son Robert was elected president of The Coca-Cola Company in 1923, when the business was reincorporated in Delaware and 500,000 shares of common stock were sold publicly for $40 per share. The new president led the company for six decades.

Coca-Cola's diversification into the food industry began with the purchase of Minute Maid Corporation in 1960, and the Minute Maid and Hi-C trademarks joined Coke's family of beverages. The company acquired Duncan Foods and formed The Coca-Cola Company Foods Division in 1967, now known as Coca-Cola Foods. In 1986, the company consolidated its U.S. bottling operations, creating Coca-Cola Enterprises (CCE), 51 percent of which was sold to the public. In late 1999 Coca-Cola finished its acquisition of Cadbury Schweppes' non-North American businesses. The transaction added Schweppes, Canada Dry, Dr Pepper, Crush, and regional brands in 161 countries to Coke's international business.

To sell its products throughout the world, The Coca-Cola Company divided its operations into two sectors, the North America Soft Drink Business Sector and the International Soft Drink Business Sector. The North American division covers Coca-Cola USA, which operates in the United States, and Coca-Cola, Ltd., which operates in Canada. The International division has been divided into five operating units: EC Group, Northeast Europe/Middle East Group, Latin America Group, Pacific Group, and the Africa Group.

Pepsi-Cola, the beverage division of PepsiCo, Inc., a worldwide consumer products company, was the second leader with third quarter 1999 sales of $1.3 billion and a global market share of 20.8 percent in 1998. The Pepsi brand, in addition to Diet Pepsi, Slice, Mountain Dew, and Mug Root Beer, accounted for as much as one-third of the soft drink market in the United States. Pepsi, a leading soft drink with nearly $17 billion in worldwide retail sales, was first created in 1898. Caleb D. Bradham, a druggist in New Bern, North Carolina, invented the drink and named it Pepsi-Cola, claiming it cured dyspepsia or indigestion. Various owners operated the Pepsi-Cola Company from 1923 through 1963. Under the direction of Donald M. Kendall, who became company president in 1963, Pepsi acquired Frito-Lay, the largest snack chip company in the United States, and became PepsiCo, Inc. Additional acquisitions have included Pizza Hut (1977), Taco Bell (1978), and Kentucky Fried Chicken (1986).

Pepsi-Cola North America manufactures and sells soft drink concentrate to company-owned and independent franchised bottlers operating facilities throughout the United States and Canada. The company also provides fountain beverage syrups to restaurants, including Taco Bell, KFC (formerly Kentucky Fried Chicken), and Pizza Hut. Pepsi-Cola International (PCI) controls the company's international soft drink operations. Through this division, Pepsi-Cola products are sold in 155 countries and territories throughout the world.

The top brands of soft drinks for 1999 were: Coke Classic, Pepsi-Cola, Diet Coke, Mountain Dew, Sprite, Dr Pepper, Diet Pepsi, 7UP, Caffeine Free Diet Coke, and Minute Maid.

The Dr Pepper/Seven-Up Companies operates one of the industry's most modern manufacturing plants near St. Louis, Missouri, which produces all of the company's concentrates, extracts, and syrups. The plant also makes most of Cadbury's concentrate sold in North America. Dr Pepper/Seven-Up Companies' administrative headquarters are located in Dallas. Operating divisions are Dr Pepper USA, Seven-Up USA, Premier Beverages, Dr Pepper/Seven-Up Foodservice, and International.

WORKFORCE

According to the U.S. Department of Labor, overall employment in food processing (including beverages) has been projected to decline 6 percent by the year 2005. Like other manufacturing industries, food processing has become less labor intensive, and occupational projections reflected this predicted decline. According to *Manufacturing USA,* by the year 2000, employment for packaging and filling machine operations will drop 26.9 percent; industrial truck and tractor operators, 23.4 percent; freight stock and materials movers (by hand), 23.8 percent; and hand packers and packagers, 32.3 percent. Professional specialty occupations, such as engineers and computer scientists, have been expected to grow, reflecting the industry's continued emphasis on scientific research to improve food products and production processes. However, these jobs have comprised a very small proportion of industry employment.

AMERICA AND THE WORLD

Soft drinks have been produced or consumed in nearly every corner of the world. Growing consumption trends can be attributed to rising disposable incomes, falling trade barriers, universal product acceptance, and a rising demand for American consumer goods. Both Pepsi-Cola and Coca-Cola have company-owned franchised bottling plants in more than 120 countries that produce their respective brands within each country rather than exporting them from the United States.

Beverages that are exported from the United States include unsweetened bottled water, but these figures have remained relatively low as the worldwide market for bottled water has been dominated by a few well-established European producers. However, U.S. producers of sweetened water or New Age beverages have fared better in the export market. The international beverage market has seen the dominance and continued development of Coke and Pepsi in all parts of the world. These companies have taken the rivalry overseas and have been spending millions to develop new markets for their products. One market that Pepsi-Cola dominated has been Russia, controlling twice the market share of Coke. Establishing its presence in Russia during the Nixon Administration, Pepsi gained entry into the country through a barter deal involving the exportation of vodka. By 1993, Pepsi-Cola controlled 4 percent of the market compared to Coke's 2 percent. The obvious market growth potential has made this former Soviet state a prime target for an American invasion of the cola wars.

In April 1993, Coke announced the construction of a $15-million production plant and training facility near Moscow. These facilities will serve the kiosks that have been installed in various Russian communities. Coca-Cola owns these kiosks, which are shaped like giant Coke cans, and rents them to a wholesaler, who in turns employs local citizens to operate the small soda stands. The acceptance of Russian rubles instead of American dollars differentiates this enterprise from the other American operations in Russia. "The idea," reported Laurie Hays in the *Wall Street Journal*, "is that such transactions will help the economy firm up and ultimately put more money into the pockets of citizens—more money they can use to buy Coke."

In the latter half of 1999, Coke reported record sales in every operating group around the world, including Japan, Mexico, and Brazil. Strong overseas sales were expected to continue in the year 2000 due to economic stability

around the world, responding aggressively to problems in Belgium, and currency stabilization. In June 1999, coke suffered a public relations nightmare when it was reported that many Belgium children were sick after drinking Coca-Cola products. The reports of symptoms spread to other countries and, by mid-summer 1999, Coke sales were restricted or banned in Belgium, France, Spain, Switzerland, Luxembourg, and the Netherlands. Coke stepped in quickly, determining that the problems stemmed from a lack of quality at some independent bottlers in France and Belgium. The bans were lifted fairly quickly, and Coke recovered with rising sales by the end of 1999.

Coke continues to market aggressively around the world, mainly with sports themes and events. The company has promotional giveaways of movie tickets and music, and in Australia it will have several market tie-ins with the 2000 Olympic Games held in Sydney.

In August 1993, PepsiCo announced its plans to invest $500 million in Poland over the next five years, with $200 million expressly for the development of a Pepsi market among the country's 38 million consumers. This investment was the third such announcement made by Pepsi. The company previously revealed a $115-million, five-year investment plan for Hungary and a $750-million plan for Mexico.

With per-capita consumption second only to the United States, Mexico has been set up as another major battleground for the cola wars. The largest Pepsi bottler outside of the United States has been Grupo Embotellador de Mexico SA, or Gemex, located in Mexico City. Meanwhile, Fomento Economico Mexicano SA, or Femsa, owns the largest Coke franchise in the world and is located in Monterrey. Needless to say, Pepsi dominated Mexico City while Coke covered the southern Mexico markets. With the assistance of market reforms enacted by Mexico's President Carlos Salinas de Gortari, both Coke and Pepsi have been working to compete in each other's established territories.

In the United States, imported unsweetened bottled waters, both still and carbonated, have continued to dominate their segment of the U.S. water and soft drink market. In 1991, France was responsible for 60 percent of unsweetened water imports and 34 percent of all water and soft drink imports. Canada had 24 percent of the unsweetened water imports, mainly with Clearly Canadian, and 42 percent of carbonated soft drinks. Due to the cost of shipping and distribution, imported products generally have been more expensive than domestically produced drinks and can be found at the luxury end of the U.S. market.

RESEARCH AND TECHNOLOGY

Advances in computer technology and automation improved all aspects of the soft drink manufacturing industry from inventory control to "smart" vending machines. Those companies with computerized operations have found both increased profitability and improved product quality. One example of a computerized system is a plant-wide automated measurement system used in some syrup manufacturing plants. Working with a personal computer, the automated system can measure nearly every important segment of beverage production, including syrup usage, Brix count (percent sugar), and beverage carbonation. Other system checks include monitoring the purification system for failures and checking the warehouse temperature for the precise dew point. "By keeping much closer control on all critical process variables, we [Abex Beverage Corporation] have been able over time to significantly improve yields, while also increasing the quality and consistency of our product," reported Randy Mostert, Abex production manager, in *Beverage World.*

Another technological advancement can be found on the user-end of the soft drink industry with the "smart" vending machines. These products use computerized components that keep track of stock supplies, sales patterns, breakdowns, and other conditions. "Bottlers are looking for ways to increase revenues and reduce costs," Bill Astin, senior vice-president of sales and marketing at the Vendo Co., told *Beverage Industry.* Astin continued, "This improved technology allows them to do just that."

The media ran several stories in 1999 saying that Coke was planning to use smart vending machines to charge more for soft drinks in hotter weather and during intermissions at stadium events. In October 1999 the company, through a press release, stated that it had no intention of raising the cost of a can of Coke depending on the weather. The company stated that the technology would be used for interactive experiences for the consumer and would allow the company to better place machines.

General Programming Inc. introduced a wireless communications package called Vending Manager; this program allows vending machines to place orders as they are required, rather than have someone manually check the stock level. "Loss of sales from a stock-out situation or out-of-order situations will be eliminated, as machines will immediately notify the dispatcher of their status," said H.O. Bransom, president of General Programming Inc., in *Beverage Industry.*

Claiming that it could be the wave of the future, Coca-Cola USA already has started to test market a version of the smart vending machine called the Generation II (GII), manufactured by Royal Vendors. "With the GII, it—collecting data—is as simple as plugging a hand-held computer into the vendor controller, or keying the LED readout to deliver the information for the route person," said Ray Steeley, president of Royal Vendors, in *Beverage Industry.*

The final outcome of computerized operations eventually will be the paperless warehouse, where computers, robotics, and electronic information transmission will control all operations. "Computer control gives instant information on the whereabouts of any material within the system," said Jim Larsen, vice-president of Eaton-Kenway, the company that installed a real-time management system (along with Operations Management Inc.) in Coca-Cola Enterprises Market Service Center in Cincinnati, Ohio, in 1991. "Those who use a real-time communications system in the warehouse also report better inventory control, faster truck check-in and check-out, better stock rotation in the distribution center and elimination of truck load errors," added Norand Corporation executive Tom Miller in *Beverage Industry.*

FURTHER READING

"The 49th Annual Report on the American Industry." *Forbes,* 13 January 1997.

"1998 Top-10 Soft Drink Companies and Brands." *Beverage Digest,* 12 February 1999.

Ackerman, Elise. "A Coke Scare in Europe." *U.S. News & World Report,* 28 June 1999.

"The Board of Directors of the Coca-Cola Company Declares Regular Quarterly Dividend." *Coca-Cola Press Release,* 21 October 1999. Available from http://www.thecoca-colacompany.com/news.

"Earnings Releases Third Quarter 1999." *PepsiCo Press Release,* 6 October 1999. Available from http://www.pepsico.com.

"Global CSD Market at 31 Bil Cases. Coke Holds 51 Share. Pepsi at 20.8." *Beverage Digest,* 24 September 1999.

Kelly, Erin. "Dairy-State Senators Take Aim at Soft Drinks in Schools." *Gannett News Service,* 10 May 1999.

"Liquid Stats." *Beverage World,* 18 November 1999. Available from http://www.beverageworld.com/liquidstats.html.

Messenger, Bob. "Did Pepsi Try ONE Too Many Times?" *Food Processing,* August 1999.

"Orion Foods and Pepsi-Cola Form Global Partnership." *PepsiCo Press Release,* 6 October 1999. Available from http://www.pepsico.com/press.

Sfiligoj, Eric. "The Big Get Smaller." *Beverage World,* January 1996.

"Soft Drinks Give Coffee the Shakes." *Prepared Foods,* August 1999.

"Sports Arena Pouring Rights: Coke Holds Wide Lead. Pepsi Gains." *Beverage Digest,* 9 October 1998.

"Statement on Vending Machine Technology." *Coca-Cola Press Release,* 28 October 1999. Available from http://www.thecoca-colacompany.com/news.

Unger, Henry. "Consolidation Sweeping Coca-Cola Bottlers." *The Atlanta Constitution,* 23 March 1999.

FLAVORING EXTRACTS AND FLAVORING SYRUPS, NOT ELSEWHERE CLASSIFIED

This category includes establishments primarily engaged in manufacturing flavoring extracts, syrups, powders, and related products, not elsewhere classified. The products are generally used at soda fountains or during the manufacture of soft drinks, as well as for adding color to baked products and confectioneries. Establishments primarily engaged in manufacturing chocolate syrup are classified in **SIC 2066: Chocolate and Cocoa Products.**

NAICS CODE(S)

311930 (Flavoring Syrup and Concentrate Manufacturing)

311942 (Spice and Extract Manufacturing)

311999 (All Other Miscellaneous Food Manufacturing)

INDUSTRY SNAPSHOT

While most foods have some flavor, certain agents can enhance the taste of these foods. These products encompass a wide range of materials that can be used alone or mixed into a blend. Substances used for flavoring "are those predominately purchased for flavoring contributions rather than functional characteristics," Kraft Food Ingredients marketing director Russ Williams told *Food Product Design.*

The approximately $4.8-billion global flavors market grew at a yearly clip of about 7.3 percent from 1992 to 1997. Worldwide sales dropped off somewhat in the late 1990s as financial troubles affected numerous economies, such as those in Asia, Brazil, and Russia.

In the late 1990s consumer trends continued to focus on natural ingredients and products that were perceived as "healthy." Medicinal ingredients such as ginseng and garlic became more commonplace. Tropical and exotic flavors also regained popularity and were often paired with more established fruit flavors. The results were such flavors as kiwi-strawberry and cranberry-mango.

Approximately 175 U.S. companies were involved in the production of flavoring extracts and syrups under the flavoring syrup and concentrate manufacturing umbrella. A total of 6,243 workers were employed in the flavoring extracts and syrups industry in 1997. In the mid-1990s about a dozen companies accounted for almost two-thirds of the flavor industry's sales to beverage and food processors.

Colorants continued to be one of the smallest segments of the food additives industry. The natural colo-

rants, mainly caramel color used in cola drinks, dominated the industry with $155 million in sales annually in the early and mid-1990s. Synthetic colorants also have been used largely by the beverage industry, followed by usage in pet food, confections and gums, and dry mixes.

ORGANIZATION AND STRUCTURE

Flavoring manufacturers, sometimes called "flavor houses," create extracts, syrups, powders, and other forms of flavoring materials. These manufacturers work with natural base ingredients purchased from suppliers throughout the world. The manufacturers' dependence on natural sources leaves the flavor chemicals open to price fluctuation due to the availability and cost of the raw materials. Once processed, flavoring ingredients are sold to soft drink companies and other makers of processed foods.

Flavor manufacturers and food producers cooperated increasingly in research and development efforts to create new food products. Flavor producers also provide technical support on flavor issues, especially with the beverage industry. Flavor houses custom tailor flavors, relying heavily on work in application laboratories. "Each flavor is so application-specific that flavor companies and product developers must work closely together with flavor chemists to make it work," Marcia Sprague, vice-president of Merlin Development, told *Prepared Foods.*

Although the starting materials may be of natural origin, all flavoring materials are processed in some manner. The distillation process uses hot water or steam to extract the aromatic materials from the flavoring materials. The quality of the flavor depends on the raw materials and the process. The product derived from this process is called a volatile or essential oil.

Extraction is used to obtain characteristic flavoring attributes provided by nonvolatiles. Organic solvents are used to dissolve volatile and nonvolatile compounds from the natural starting material. After removing the solvent, usually with a high vacuum process, the flavoring compounds remain. An extracted flavor often is fractionated into many parts and only certain ones are selected for the final flavor.

Extraction and distillation remain important methods for obtaining natural flavor components. Types of extracted/distilled flavor components are essential oils, aromatic fractions of the plant, oleoresins (which are extracts without volatiles), standardized oleoresins (added with extra essential oils), and concentrated oils (which are essential oils fractionated to a specific degree of concentration).

The flavoring industry worked closely with the Food and Drug Administration (FDA), primarily through the efforts of industry trade association Flavor Extract Manufacturers Association (FEMA). FEMA has been participating in the development of the Nutritional Labeling and Education Act of 1990. This legislation mandated that producers detail the ingredients used in processed food formulations. This act was implemented in May 1993.

BACKGROUND AND DEVELOPMENT

Development of the modern flavor industry occurred when some of the earliest flavors were manufactured by extraction during the 1940s. By the 1950s and 1960s the industry moved toward the use of synthetic flavor compounds as flavoring agents. By the 1970s "natural" began to be a selling point, and methods were sought to develop pure, natural chemicals. One problem with these natural extracts was that the raw materials varied in taste and intensity. However, the modern flavor industry resolved this issue by compounding natural flavor chemicals rather than using the extracts as final flavors. This procedure provided food manufacturers with consistent flavors.

CURRENT CONDITIONS

Though the flavors market grew steadily throughout the 1990s, the industry experienced flat growth in the late 1990s, particularly in 1998. North America and Europe accounted for the majority of sales in the international flavors market, with sales of about $2.7 billion out of a total of $4.8 billion in 1997. The market experienced signs of recovery in 1999, though several major flavors manufacturers continued to suffer from slumping revenues.

According to the 1999 Flavor Usage Survey conducted by *Beverage Industry,* which polled individuals in nearly every segment of the beverage industry, including soft drinks, juices, flavored waters, and specialty drinks, the flavor considered to be the top flavor of 1999 was cola. Cola was selected by 31 percent of those surveyed. Second most popular was orange, with 15 percent of the vote. The top flavors used by beverage makers, according to the respondents, were orange, lemon, grape, strawberry, lime, cherry, apple, cola, cranberry, and grapefruit, respectively. Almost half of those polled indicated that they would be using and introducing new flavors in the late 1990s and early 2000s. Many named such flavors as grapefruit, lemon-lime, and orange as the flavors that would be used in new drinks.

Other flavors that enjoyed increasing popularity in the late 1990s were exotic flavors, including passion fruit, mango, and guarana, as well as flavored coffee and tea drinks. Coffeehouses around the world began adding flavors, such as hazelnut, raspberry, Irish Cream, and vanilla to espresso drinks, regular coffee, hot chocolate, and tea. Health drinks and energy drinks, which relied heavily on natural and fruit flavors, also enjoyed increased consumption.

INDUSTRY LEADERS

The flavor producing companies became larger and were based more multinationally in the late 1990s. The trend was toward continued globalization, and flavors companies carried on with expansion plans. The top ten flavors and fragrance companies in terms of 1998 sales, according to *Chemical Market Reporter,* were International Flavors & Fragrances Inc. (IFF) with total sales of $1.41 billion in 1998; Givaudan-Roure Corporation; Firmenich; Universal Foods Corporation; Takasago; Bush Boake Allen Inc.; T. Hasegawa; Dragoco; Haarmann & Reimer; and Quest.

IFF's flavors were marketed primarily to manufacturers of prepared foods, beverages, confections, dairy foods, and pharmaceuticals. International sales accounted for about 70 percent of revenues. The company's flavors division accounted for 42 percent of its total sales in 1998. IFF planned to expand its Latin American presence and had a flavor manufacturing plant under construction in Brazil in the late 1990s. The company also updated facilities in the United Kingdom, Holland, and France, and constructed a new powder production facility in Australia. Though IFF's Latin American sales were down in early 1999, its sales of flavors in Asia rose 10 percent.

Universal Foods manufactured flavors and aromas, which accounted for 40 percent of revenues, as well as colors, cosmetics, yeasts, and pharmaceuticals. Universal, which had 1999 sales of $920 million, grew its flavors and colors businesses in the 1990s through acquisitions. Universal acquired Sundi GmbH, a German-based flavors maker, DC Flavours Ltd. of England, and Arancia Ingredientes Especiales SA de CV of Mexico.

A growing company was Danish company Danisco A/S. Danisco bought Borthwicks, a British flavors manufacturer, Cultor, and U.S. company Beck Flavors, a natural extracts maker. Beck made more than 2,000 flavorings and was the third largest producer of vanilla in the U.S. in the late 1990s. Beck was also the largest manufacturer of coffee flavors in the nation. The acquisition of Beck doubled Danisco's flavorings revenues in the United States.

AMERICA AND THE WORLD

Despite the economic crises affecting Asia, Asian countries continued to be targets for flavors manufacturers. Studies showed that consumption of flavored products is directly proportional to per-capita income. As the middle class grows in Asian countries, demand for Western-style beverages was likely to gain ground. Growth in Asia was projected to have the ability to drive flavor growth higher well into the next century. Expansion into Asia also would allow companies easier access to newer, more exotic flavors.

Other global markets that appealed to the flavors industry included Latin America and Germany, which represented the largest flavors market in Europe. Most of the leading flavors companies, including IFF, Givaudan Roure, and Bush Boake Allen, had operations in Latin America.

RESEARCH AND TECHNOLOGY

New technologies, particularly in extraction techniques and applications of biotechnology were being applied in the flavors industry, which was expected to post dramatic results in the coming years. Biotechnology is the most advanced of the new flavor technologies and will be used to create "natural flavors of the future."

The flavors industry claims that commercially growing an entire plant for a single flavor molecule is unnecessary and wasteful. Plant cell culture technology allows scientists to grow only the part of the plant that contains the desired flavor molecule.

Cost advantages of this type of cell manufacture are numerous. According to Decision Resources, yields would be increased per unit mass of plant tissue; processing costs would be reduced since very little plant tissue needs to be removed; and the quality of the extracted oil would be higher. This technology should also save time because it should be possible to grow or generate exotic plants in a short time span compared with traditional plant growing methods.

FURTHER READING

Brown, Suzanne J. "Flavored Syrups Continue to Pour into International Markets." *Tea & Coffee Trade Journal,* 1 January 1999.

Carroll, Susan. "Flavors Market is Poised for Recovery This Year." *Chemical Market Reporter,* 19 July 1999.

"Danisco Inches Up Flavor Ladder with its Acquisition of Beck." *Chemical Market Reporter,* 19 October 1998.

"First Quarter F&F Earnings In Line with Low Expectations." *Chemical Market Reporter,* 3 May 1999.

Floreno, Anthony. "Flavors Taste Brave New World: Expansion into Asia and Beverage are Driving Growth and New Product Development, While Biotechnology Holds Promise for the Future. (Food Additives '96)." *Chemical Marketing Reporter,* 24 June 1996.

Holleran, Joan. "1999 Flavor Survey Reveals Many Facets of Flavors." *Beverage Industry,* 1 February 1999.

"Title Wave of Trends: No Single Flavor Trend Dominates the Beverage Industry." *Beverage Industry,* November 1996.

U.S. Census Bureau. "Flavoring Syrup and Concentrate Manufacturing." *1997 Economic Census.* Washington, D.C.: 6 December 1999. Available from http://www.census.gov.

CANNED AND CURED FISH AND SEAFOODS

This category covers establishments primarily engaged in cooking and canning seafood products such as fish, shrimp, oysters, clams, and crab or in curing seafood products by means such as smoking, salting or drying. It also includes manufacturers of seafood soups, chowders, stews, broths, and juices. Establishments primarily engaged in preparing fresh fish or shucking and packing fresh oysters in nonsealed containers are classified in **SIC 2092: Prepared Fresh or Frozen Fish and Seafoods.**

NAICS CODE(S)
311711 (Seafood Canning)

INDUSTRY SNAPSHOT

Production and retail sales of canned fishery products remained relatively flat through the 1990s. In 1998 canned fishery products in the U.S. were valued at $1.8 billion, which reflected an increase of $172.5 million over the pack of canned fishery products in 1997. The pack, which was 1.5 billion pounds, was down 34.1 million pounds. Total salmon production in 1998 was 162 million pounds, up only slightly from 1997. Total tuna production reached 680 million pounds, up from 627 million pounds in 1997.

Other products included six different species of clam in East Coast production centers located in Maine, Maryland, Massachusetts, and Florida; and on the West Coast areas in Oregon, Washington, and Alaska. East Coast canners principally packed hard and soft shell clams, while most West Coast production involved razor clams, which were most often sold as minced clam meat. Other types of mollusks (soft-bodied shellfish) canned in the United States included oysters, mussels, abalone, cockles, donax (coquina, or small, clams), snails, and squid.

Of the approximately $46 billion spent on fish and shellfish products in the United States, about $15 billion was attributed to retail store sales. Overall annual consumption of seafood was up from 12.5 pounds per capita in 1980 to about 14.6 pounds per head in 1997. Of total seafood products consumed in the United States, about 61 percent was imported.

BACKGROUND AND DEVELOPMENT

Fish curing is one of the oldest industries in North America. Even before permanent European settlements had been established, fishermen were harvesting cod and other species off the northeastern coastline of the American continent. Fish were preserved and prepared for marketing by salting. According to Roy E. Martin of the National Fisheries Institute, "As early as 1580 more than three hundred ships from Europe were salting cod in this area."

New England colonists depended on salted cod and smoked herring for food and as trade items. During the seventeenth and eighteenth centuries, cured fish products made major contributions to the economies of New England and eastern Canada. Disputes over fishing rights and restraints on trade contributed to the political climate leading up to the Revolutionary War. Martin, writing in *The Seafood Industry,* stated, "The English Parliament in 1775 prohibited the New England colonies from trading directly with foreign countries and prevented New England vessels from fishing on the banks off Newfoundland, in the Gulf of St. Lawrence, and on the coasts of Labrador and Nova Scotia where they had been accustomed to fishing. This restriction meant ruin to the New England fish-curing industry, and the edict was one cause of the Revolutionary War."

Another type of preservation, pickling, was also used commercially with fish and mollusk products through the 1800s. Pickled and cured fish products continued to be major industries until the processes were gradually supplanted by canning technology and by innovations enabling fresh and frozen seafood products to be delivered to inland markets.

During the early years of the nineteenth century, the first canned seafood products appeared in the United States. Initial offerings included salmon, lobsters, and oysters. Of these three, the most popular, and first to be canned on an industrial scale, was the Chesapeake Bay oyster. Canning technology enabled the sale of oysters to inland people who had previously been unable to purchase them. As canning technology improved, other products were added to the menu. Sardines, for example, were first successfully canned in Maine around the middle of the nineteenth century. As more products became available, consumer acceptance increased. The Civil War also helped the new industry gain favor by introducing many soldiers to canned products.

The 1860s saw the beginning and rapid expansion of canning operations for Pacific salmon. From a small beginning in California, salmon canners spread north into Washington and Canada. The first canneries opened in Alaska in 1878. The 1870s also brought the first menhaden (a type of fish from the herring family) cannery. It opened on Long Island in 1872. Canned fish cakes (cod and haddock products) were introduced in 1878. By 1880, other canned items included mackerel, clams, and crabs. U.S. production of canned products in 1880 was valued at $15 million. Finnan haddie (smoked haddock) was first offered commercially in 1890. "Salad Fish," canned flaked meat from cod and haddock, was

introduced in 1898. Other turn-of-the-century products included pickled sturgeon, carp, and shark meat.

During the early years of the twentieth century, the sardine canning industry moved from the East Coast to the West Coast. Canneries sprang up in the Monterey Bay area of California. As sardine canning operations expanded, demand for fish exceeded availability. To help increase catches, new fishing methods were developed using a special type of net, called a lampara net. Lampara nets encircled entire schools of fish and yielded large harvests. Canners also continued bringing new products to American consumers. Items added during the early years of the twentieth century included shad, alewives (another member of the herring family), and tuna. The first commercial offering of tuna was made in 1909 by the Southern California Fish Company. Only albacore tuna was used, and the first year's production equaled 2,000 cases.

In the following decade many major participants in the U.S. canned and cured seafood industry were founded. Ocean Beauty Seafoods was founded in 1910, Ward's Cove Packing Company in 1912, and in 1914 Peter Pan Seafoods and Van Camp Seafoods were established. By 1915, only six years after the first commercial offering of albacore, California processors packed 237,265 cases. In the Monterey Bay area, the sardine cannery industry was well established and continued growing. In 1918 nine sardine canning plants in Monterey packed a total of 1.4 million cases.

The 1920s saw expansion of Pacific mackerel canneries and increased activity in the Alaskan salmon industry. By the end of the decade, 159 canneries were operating in Alaska. Improvements in cold storage technology enabled canners to receive and process larger quantities of fish. Refined fishing techniques developed during the 1920s helped fishermen meet ever-growing demand. Purse seines, a type of large net closed by a drawstring-like apparatus, were capable of dropping to a depth of 100 feet and enclosing an area 100 feet across. Newer boats were built to operate hundreds of miles offshore and carry up to 150 tons of fish.

Catches of albacore, however, began decreasing during the 1920s and tuna canners consolidated. In 1926 albacore catches plummeted. As a substitute, Van Camp Seafood Company offered yellowfin tuna and marketed it as "Fancy Light Meat Tuna." Sardine catches continued in large numbers and canneries prospered through the 1930s and early 1940s. Owners expanded operations by adding fish by-products such as poultry and livestock feed, fertilizer, and fish oil to their product lines.

During World War II the canning industry faced several challenges. Tuna boats were requisitioned by the Maritime Commission and by the U.S. Navy, primarily for use in delivering supplies. Fish harvests were reduced, as fishermen enlisted or were drafted into armed service. Antisubmarine efforts along the Pacific coast restricted fleet movement. And inside the canneries, labor shortages persisted, intensified by a governmental policy of moving Japanese workers to internment camps. Despite the problems, however, the war years proved to be profitable ones for tuna and other fish packers because of the heavy demand spurred by government requisitions for canned products to feed troops.

During the second half of the 1940s, sardine catches began declining and forced canneries, one after another, to close. By 1952 Monterey's sardine era had ended. Industry analysts have attributed the declining sardine catches to various causes including pollution, climate and current changes, natural fish cycles, and fished-out stocks. Although the 1950s saw the demise of many sardine canners, other segments of the industry prospered. Larger fishing boats traveled greater distances from shore, and some companies opened canneries in more distant locations. For example, in 1954, the Van Camp Seafood Company opened canning facilities in Pago Pago (Samoan Islands). The plant received fish from Japan, Korea, and Taiwan. It employed 600 people and averaged 145 tons of production daily. The modernization of fishing techniques continued to improve catches. By 1961 most commercial fishing vessels shifted from hook-and-line gear to mechanized purse seining. By the 1980s tuna fishermen were using seines measuring up to 4,800 feet by 702 feet that were capable of hauling 200-ton catches.

These large nets, however, drew criticism because the seines indiscriminately captured all fish swimming in a school. For reasons not completely understood, dolphins often schooled with yellowfin tuna, and reports of dolphin mortality increased. To help alleviate problems associated with dolphin mortality, the Marine Mammal Protection Act of 1972 banned the importation of fish and fish products caught in ways that posed excessive risks to ocean mammals. Another piece of legislation, the Boxer-Biden Dolphin Protection Consumer Information Act of 1991 was passed to govern the conditions under which fishing operations could operate if their products carried a "dolphin-safe" label. In 1990 three major U.S. tuna canners, Star-Kist (owned by H. J. Heinz), Bumble Bee Seafoods, and Van Camp Seafood ("Chicken of the Sea" brand) promised to provide dolphin-safe tuna.

At the close of the twentieth century, the U.S. government, backed by several mainstream environmental groups, was poised to rescind the embargo on tuna caught by boats not adhering to the Marine Mammal Protection Act.

CURRENT CONDITIONS

U.S. sales of canned fish and seafood were largely on the decline in the late 1990s. The lower consumption of canned tuna and canned salmon affected the overall consumption level of seafood, and per capita seafood consumption fell 4.5 percent in 1997 to 14.6 pounds per head. Overall consumption rose to 14.9 pounds per person in 1998 due to increased consumption of fresh and frozen fish and shellfish. Per capita consumption of cured fish products remained steady at 0.3 pounds per person annually, but consumption of canned fish and shellfish dropped to 4.4 pounds per person in 1998, down from 5.1 pounds per person in 1990. Canned tuna consumption rose slightly in 1998 compared to 1997 figures, but canned salmon consumption fell, from 0.4 pounds per person to 0.3 pounds per capita. Record consumption levels for canned fish occurred in 1936, when consumption reached 5.8 pounds per person. Cured fish had a record year in 1909, when per capita consumption was 4.0 pounds.

Sales of canned tuna rebounded in 1998 after declines in the mid-1990s. According to Information Resources, Inc., a market research firm, sales of canned tuna for the 52-week period ending January 3, 1999, reached $1.2 billion, up 4.1 percent over the year-earlier period. U.S. per capita consumption of canned tuna reached 3.4 pounds per person in 1998. The best year for canned tuna in the 1990s was 1990, when per capita consumption was 3.7 pounds.

In 1997 Congress passed the International Dolphin Conservation Program Act. The Act sought to regulate the tuna industry so as to protect dolphins, which were often injured or killed when ensnared in tuna nets. In January 2000 the U.S. government announced plans to enact new regulations to meet international standards for protecting dolphins in Pacific Ocean waters. The regulations put into practice a new dolphin-safe labeling system. The special labels could be applied to tuna products if no dolphins were harmed or killed when the tuna were caught. In addition, the regulations allowed for the import of tuna products into the United States if the tuna had been harvested within the confines of the Dolphin Conservation Program Act.

INDUSTRY LEADERS

One of the largest companies involved in canning and curing fish and seafood products was Trident Seafoods Corp. Trident, a privately owned company headquartered in Seattle, Washington, was founded in 1973. Trident operated as a vertically integrated harvesting, processing, and marketing company. Trident employed about 2,800 employees in the late 1990s and had five processing plants in Alaska and three in Washington State. A company spokesman estimated that the company's product mix in the 1990s was 80 percent frozen products and 20 percent canned. Trident's canned salmon was offered under several brands: Faust, Lily, Prelate,

Rubinstein's, Sea-Alaska, Tulip, and Whitney's. In the late 1990s the company acquired Tyson Seafoods from Tyson Foods Inc.

Another leader in the canned fish and seafood industry was International Home Foods, Inc., the maker of Bumble Bee tuna, the second-ranked tuna in the U.S. The diversified company also produced other canned goods, including meat products and vegetables. In 1999 International Home Foods acquired the canned seafood operations of British Columbia Packers from George Weston Ltd., a Canadian company. The purchase included such brands as Clover Leaf and Paramount. Paramount was the leading canned tuna and canned salmon brand in Canada. International Home Foods had 1998 sales of $1.7 billion, up 39 percent from the previous year.

Other significant participants in the seafood canning industry were H.J. Heinz Co., which had the leading canned tuna brand in the U.S.—Star-Kist, Icicle Seafood International Inc., and Chicken of the Sea International. During the 1960s Chicken of the Sea was the largest canner of an advertised brand of tuna in the United States. In addition to its tuna line, the ''Chicken of the Sea'' brand included canned salmon products. ''Chicken of the Sea'' was the first to offer skinless/boneless canned salmon.

FURTHER READING

''Consumers Expenditures Survey.'' *Supermarket News,* September 1996.

''International Home Foods, Inc.'' *Food Institute Report,* 11 January 1999.

Martin, Roy E., and George J. Flick, eds. *The Seafood Industry.* New York: Van Nostrand Reinhold, 1990.

Murray, Barbara. ''Lent Events Heat Sales of Fish, Canned and Frozen.'' *Supermarket News,* 15 March 1999.

National Marine Fisheries Service. Office of Science & Technology. ''Fisheries of the United States—1998.'' Washington, D.C.: Fisheries Statistics & Economics Division. Available from http://www.nmfs.gov.

National Oceanic and Atmospheric Administration. ''Americans Ate More Shrimp, Less Canned Fish in 1997.'' Available from http://www.noaa.gov/public-affairs.

Warren, Brad. ''Salmon Glut May Force Changes.'' *National Fisherman,* March 1996.

SIC 2092

PREPARED FRESH OR FROZEN FISH AND SEAFOODS

This category covers establishments that prepare seafoods, including shrimpcakes, crabcakes, fishcakes, chowders, and stews in raw or cooked frozen form. Prepared fresh fish are eviscerated or processed by removal of heads, fins, and scales. This industry also includes establishments primarily engaged in the shucking and packing of fresh oysters in nonsealed containers.

NAICS CODE(S)

311712 (Fresh and Frozen Seafood Processing)

INDUSTRY SNAPSHOT

During the 1980s, health and diet concerns led American consumers to add more fish and seafood to their diets; this marked a significant trend toward higher levels of consumption of poultry, fish, and seafoods at the expense of red meat. The perennial worries about the quality of fish and seafoods, which swiftly lose their taste and freshness, were compounded by growing consumer knowledge about the potential harmful effects of pollution and the consequences of improper handling and storage. A *Consumer Reports* analysis in early 1992 found that much of the seafood consumed by Americans was often of poor quality.

In the late 1990s, the National Fisheries Institute (NFI) commissioned a study that found that less than 30 percent of the younger generation—those 35 to 50—called themselves moderate seafood users. In an effort to boost per capital consumption, the NFI turned its attention to seafood marketing. The institute launched an ''Eat Seafood Twice a Week for Better Health'' campaign, similar to the catchy ''5-a-day'' program used by the produce industry. Marketing plans for 2001 included a program promoting seafood as ''the protein next door,'' according to a report in *ID: The Voice of Foodservice Distribution.*

One reason for the stagnant per capita consumption rates includes negative images of the fishing industry, which came under attack from recreational fishers and environmental groups who charged that certain waters were being over-fished. The Gulf Coast Conservation Association has been successful in pushing through legislation in Texas, Florida, Alabama, and Louisiana to prevent commercial fishers from destroying wetlands and endangering certain fish species. According to a 1998 report by the National Academy of Sciences, over-exploitation is causing a 30 percent decline of fish stocks worldwide, from orange roughy and shark to swordfish and tuna. The report also said that an additional 44 percent are nearing over-exploitation. It was also noted that in U.S. waters, 80 percent of commercial fish stocks, from Atlantic halibut to red snapper to Pacific ocean perch, were disappearing.

ORGANIZATION AND STRUCTURE

In general, small-scale processing plants are tied to local fleets that are in turn tied to specific stocks of fish that in many cases fluctuate dramatically, discouraging processors from expanding operations, developing new products, or adopting new technology. Those fleets not equipped for processing at sea are obliged to return to land at short intervals, rather than when full, so that their harvest can be processed while the fish is still fresh. In addition to an expansion of at-sea processing operations and a greater use of fish and shellfish raised by aquacultural means, vertical integration was seen as the key to a profitable restructuring of the American fish and seafoods processing industry. Some industry observers felt restructuring was necessary to bring about large-scale, sustained investment in underutilized species, greater speed to market, and the ability to respond to shortages and gluts.

In an effort to boost consumption, a better program of inspection was regarded as a necessity for the future of the industry. While there was no mandatory inspection of fish and seafood by the federal government, processors, retailers, and wholesalers could pay for a U.S. Department of Commerce inspection. Approximately 10 percent of processors were participating in such voluntary inspection programs in 1992. But even in this restricted form there was no uniformity; three different seals were available, designating different levels of inspection. Regulations at the state level differed from region to region but in general gave little protection to consumers.

By the mid-1990s, the rising incidence of seafood poisoning, estimated at 20,000 to 60,000 cases per year, prompted the Food and Drug Administration (FDA) to apply the Hazard Analysis and Critical Control Points (HACCP) program to the seafood industry.

Followed on a voluntary basis by other food industries since 1959, HACCP is a scientific and systematic method used to monitor the microbiological, chemical, and physical safety of prepared foods. Under the plan, seafood distributors must identify any critical points at which their product's quality is endangered and then install safeguards. Although the regulations do not apply to fishing vessels or transporters, the processors are responsible for ensuring that the product reaches them in the purest form. For example, distributors are expected to only accept fish from government-approved waters.

Compliance with the HACCP program is expensive for the industry—$70 to $160 million to institute and $40 to $80 million per year thereafter. However, the FDA says the cost will be offset by the reduced incidence of food poisoning, the nutritional benefits of more people eating seafood, and increased export income.

BACKGROUND AND DEVELOPMENT

Soon after World War II, American consumers began to rely increasingly on the convenience of fully or partially prepared fish and seafoods, often available in frozen form. These fish products were available with or without coatings of breading; batter coatings were intro-

duced in the 1960s. Batter-fried fish and seafood reached the consumer only after an extensive preparation in which the product was dusted with flour, encased in batter, and then lightly fried to fix the batter and achieve specified standards of texture and quality.

Fish and seafood constituted about half of the frozen battered and breaded products consumed in the United States, the largest consumer of breaded fish and seafood in the world. The most frequently consumed type of coated seafood was precooked and raw portions of fish, followed by shrimp, fishcakes, and scallops. Among the breaded products most typically sold in frozen form were scallops, oysters, clam strips, clamcakes, and squid rings (calamari).

Freezing technology permitted great advances in an industry dependent on a product subject to rapid spoilage. However, not all species of fish and seafood responded well to freezing, and often delicacies of texture and flavor could be lost. For instance, whereas crabmeat generally was found to freeze less well and have a briefer shelf life than many other types of fish and seafoods, king crab was discovered to lend itself rather well to freezing. Well-suited to shrimp, catfish, and halibut, the technique of rapid freezing proved especially effective because it minimized losses of texture and flavor by guaranteeing uniformity of freezing. The ''I.Q.F.'' marking, which referred to individually quick frozen products, thus became a selling point for the American consumer.

The United States was for a long period the world leader in terms of its versatility in processing, handling, distributing, and marketing frozen fish and seafoods. It was also an early leader in deploying techniques for freezing catches aboard ships, yet lost its edge in the commercial application of this technology, which allowed fishing vessels to remain at sea for greater periods of time. Ships could remain at sea until their load was full instead of frequently returning to shore to ensure the freshness of their catch.

CURRENT CONDITIONS

Despite the healthful attributes of fish and seafood and the convenience of prepared fish and seafoods, per capita seafood consumption peaked in 1987 with 16.2 pounds per person, hovered around 15.0 to 15.2 pounds in the mid-1990s and stood at 14.9 pounds in 1998. Although per capital consumption remained somewhat stagnant, U.S. production of uncooked, raw fish fillets and steaks, including blocks, reached 438.7 million pounds in 1998, up 29 million pounds from 409.7 million pounds in 1997.

A summary of a National Fisheries Institute report published in *Prepared Foods* noted that annual per capita consumption of fish and seafoods in America was forecast to reach 20 pounds in the year 2000, with total consumption of shrimp alone increasing to one billion pounds (from 567 million pounds in 1989). In addition, the National Restaurant Association predicted that by the year 2000 fish and seafood would constitute about 8 percent of total meat and poultry consumption in America, compared to 7 percent in 1964.

Per capital consumption may indeed be on the rise. Frozen seafood sales were up 11.3 percent in the 52 weeks ending June 20, 1999, up more than two and a half times 1998's 4.3 percent increase. Gorton's Seafood, an industry leader in the prepared frozen fish and seafoods industry, is using its Web site to try to increase consumption. The site includes everything from information on how to select fish at the store to cooking tips, nutritional facts, and recipes. Gorton's also promotes the Web site on its product packaging.

The value of shipments produced by the industry has increased through the 1990s, hitting 6.7 billion in 1996 and was expected to rise to 8.4 billion in 2000, according to projections in *Manufacturing USA*.

While the number of establishments involved in the processing was decreasing, the number of employees in the industry continued to rise each year. In 1996, there were 32,400 production workers; that number is expected to hit 34,100 in 2000, an increase of 1,700 workers.

INDUSTRY LEADERS

The number of establishments involved in the processing of fish and seafoods declined during the 1990s and was expected to continue declining. In 1993, 690 establishments were involved in processing fresh and frozen prepared fish, while the number slipped to 658 in 1995 and was expected to drop to 603 by 2000. These companies ranged in size from tiny operations, employing a handful of workers and concentrating on a single species or type of preparation, to large businesses engaged in many other areas.

The industry is concentrated along the coasts, with the Pacific Coast dominating. In the 1990s, the state of Washington had the most establishments, with 87, employing 7,200 workers and shipping $1.4 billion worth of product. Alaska followed with 84 establishments employing 8,000 workers and shipping $1.2 billion in product. Massachusetts was next with $967 million in shipments and 2,200 workers.

Major companies in this industry include Gorton's Seafood, based in Gloucester, Massachusetts (1,000 employees and $400 million in sales); Rich-SeaPak Corp., based in St. Simons Island, Georgia (1,100 employees and $250 million in sales); and Icicle Seafoods Inc., based in Seattle, Washington (2,500 employees and $240 million in sales).

WORKFORCE

According to the U.S. Department of Labor, little change in employment in the American fish and seafoods processing industry is expected through the year 2005, though there is likely to be a shift in the distribution of the work performed, with an increase of semiskilled workers for processing plants and a decrease in skilled workers for markets and other retail centers.

The skills most important to processors include good eye-hand coordination, manual dexterity, depth perception, and color discrimination. These skills were usually acquired in apprenticeship programs or on the job, rather than in any formal educational settings. Work environments often require extended periods of standing for employees, as well as low temperatures needed to keep product fresh.

Aside from promotion to a supervisory position, employment in processing of fish and seafoods offers few career prospects. In this area, as in other areas of the fishing industry, wages are typically low, although there are some variances in salary scales based on geographic location. While the average wage stood at $7.94 per hour in 1996, *Manufacturing USA* predicted wages to increase to $9.16 in 2000.

AMERICA AND THE WORLD

The United States is the third largest consumer of seafood worldwide and relies on imports to meet demand. Imports of processed fishery products reached $5.3 billion in 1992, while exports reached $3.2 billion. In 1998, U.S. imports of edible fishery products reached 3.6 billion pounds, 308.2 million pounds more than 1997. Those imports were valued at $8.2 billion, up $418.9 million from 1997. Fresh and frozen products accounted for 3.1 billion pounds of the imports and were valued at $7.4 billion.

In 1998, U.S. exports of fresh and frozen items were 1.4 billion pounds, a decrease of 331.6 million pounds from 1997. Principal exports included 153.4 million pounds of salmon, 255.3 million pounds of surimi, and 43 million pounds of lobsters, valued at $255.1 million, $284.4 million, and $187.8 million, respectively.

RESEARCH AND TECHNOLOGY

According to *Frozen Food Digest,* between 1980 and 1990 the quantity of farm-raised processed catfish in the United States rose from 46 million pounds to 377 million pounds, and production of surimi also increased between 1987 and 1989 from 67 million pounds to 300 million pounds. Processing of both continued to rise during the 1990s. The growth of catfish consumption partly reflected a substantial increase in aquaculture, which *Frozen Food Digest* noted was "outpacing all other types of farming'' in the United States. The trend toward aquaculture was a significant one, not only because of the growing proportion of the U.S. supply of fish and seafood to which it contributed, but also because it brought harvesting and processing into closer conjunction and thereby assured a higher and more consistent quality of product.

''Species such as catfish, salmon, shrimp and oysters, which are grown in aquaculture farms, are becoming increasingly important,'' Richard Gutting Jr., executive vice president of the National Fisheries Instate, told *Frozen Food Digest*. ''We are growing more and more seafood each year.'' The Minaqua fish farm in Beckley, West Virginia, has devised a method for raising trout and arctic char in abandoned coal mines. The pure mine water remains a steady 55 degrees Fahrenheit year-round, which the company claims is perfect for breeding. The venture makes a landlocked state a competitor in the fishing industry.

New processing and packaging technologies that extend the shelf life of fresh and prepared fish and seafoods are keys to growth in the processing industry. Other challenges facing this industry include developing seafood products that can be microwaved without any loss of crispness and improving the overall quality of such products. Another focus will be creating new products to catch new customers.

FURTHER READING

''Around the Coasts.'' *National Fisherman,* October 1996.

''Foreign Trade.'' *National Marine Fisheries Service,* 14 December 1999. Available from http://www.nmfs.gov/trade/default.html.

Haltaman, Carol. ''National Fisheries Institute: What We Can Do For You.'' *ID: The Voice of Foodservice Distribution,* September 1999.

Harrison, Dan. ''Frozen Seafood Marketing Missing the Boat.'' *Frozen Food Age,* September 1999.

Hunter, Beatrice Trum. ''Food for Thought.'' *Consumers' Research,* July 1996.

''Per Capita U.S. Consumption.'' *National Marine Fisheries Service,* 14 December 1999. Available from http://www.nmfs.gov/trade/default.html.

''Processed Fishery Products.'' *National Marine Fisheries Service,* 14 December 1999. Available from http://www.nmfs.gov/trade/default.html.

''Seafood.'' *Frozen Food Digest,* October 1999.

''Struggling to Stay Afloat.'' *U.S. News and World Report,* 5 August 1996.

Warren, Brad. ''Salmon Glut May Force Changes.'' *National Fisherman,* March 1996.

ROASTED COFFEE

This category covers establishments primarily engaged in roasting coffee and in manufacturing coffee concentrates and extracts in powdered, liquid, or frozen form, including freeze-dried. Coffee roasting by wholesale grocers is covered in **SIC 5149: Groceries and Related Products, Not Elsewhere Classified.**

NAICS CODE(S)
311920 (Coffee and Tea Manufacturing)

INDUSTRY SNAPSHOT
In the early 1990s, coffee consumption continued to remain strong, with coffee shops maintaining their presence throughout the country. Roasters, small and large, continued to enjoy strong markets. Starbucks continues to expand with plans to add 2,000 stores by the year 2000. Other players moved to enter the specialty coffee market—Procter & Gamble acquired Millstone Coffee, a privately held firm that roasts and distributes gourmet, whole-bean coffee products to supermarkets in December 1995.

Coffee hasn't always enjoyed this popularity. Between 1970 and 1980, U.S. per capita consumption of coffee in gallons had dropped from 33.4 to 26.7, although it held steady at that approximate rate throughout the 1980s. At an estimated 1.75 cups, daily per capita consumption of coffee in 1991 was a far cry from that of the all-time high of 3.1 cups reached in 1962. The advent of specialty coffees seemed to signal a turnaround in the coffee industry. Having in past decades exported a taste for instant coffee, the United States began importing a demand for specialty coffees.

A nationwide rediscovery of coffee led to increased growth in this industry beginning in the late 1980s, with production growing from a level of $96 billion in 1986 to more than $110 billion in 1994. In early 1997 coffee futures soared due to heavy roaster buying—the biggest one-day gain since July 1994.

Production of coffee beans rose sharply in 1998-99, with Brazil having the greatest increase. The increased supply led to a drop in prices that, combined with exchange rates unfavorable to coffee-producing countries, led to lower earnings. In 1999-2000 it is expected that Brazil will have had smaller yields, leading to higher prices and profits for coffee producing countries and roasters.

ORGANIZATION AND STRUCTURE
Due to a climate that cannot support coffee trees in areas other than Hawaii and Puerto Rico, U. S. production of coffee beans has been negligible. Instead the

United States has become the largest importer of the beans, purchased from producing nations through traders. For this reason traders play an important role in the U.S. coffee industry, albeit one constrained by their obligation to serve the requirements of roasters. Thus the National Coffee Association (NCA), formed in the early 1970s, is dominated by the roasters.

Processing of coffee beans is performed by manufacturers that roast the beans for packaging. Also, roasters often further process the beans to be sold for brewing and instant coffee. At least until the mid-1980s, coffee produced in the United States was thought to be less superior than that of other countries. According to Michael Sivetz and Norman W. Desrosier in *Coffee Technology,* this was explained by the fact that many of the leading manufacturers were owned by multinational conglomerates: "Most of the bad features in handling coffee in the United States (and elsewhere too) are due to mass production and centralized marketing and sales. The indicated particular treatment of green, roast ground coffees and their brewing is in conflict with corporate mass production and selling policies. . . . Commercial aspects, that is profit-making, invariably override technical considerations and process technology."

BACKGROUND AND DEVELOPMENT

The U.S. coffee industry can be traced back to the seventeenth century, when coffeehouses, already quite popular in Europe, began to open in the colonies. Indeed, Revolutionary War strategy was often plotted in these establishments. At that point in time, only whole coffee beans were available, and these were sold from a barrel to be blended and ground in the home for boiling.

This method of preparing coffee proved its inconvenience during the Civil War, when transporting beans and grinders was quickly found to be unwieldy. As an alternative, coffee was made into a sort of concentrate by grinding it into a pulp that was fashioned into bricks and allowed to harden. This allowed soldiers to slice off an appropriate amount for boiling. In the meantime, however, entrepreneurs saw an opportunity. By roasting, blending, grinding, and packaging the coffee for sale, they offered consumers a welcome convenience.

Coffee beans are mainly categorized into two major varieties: arabica and robusta. Arabica beans are the most flavorful, and gourmet coffees are made with this type. Robusta beans are used in commercially packaged and instant coffees. Roasters store the purchased beans in silos until they are blended, which occurs immediately prior to roasting. Control of the blending process is usually done electronically, with preset percentages of the different varieties to go into the blend. In addition to the type of bean used in a blend, roasting plays an important role in the resulting coffee's taste. Roasting eliminates the moisture from the bean, releasing the flavor. The color of the roasted beans determines the flavor, and consistency of color throughout a bean produces a high-quality brew. The beans should be dark enough to give the maximum amount of flavor, though not so dark that the coffee tastes scorched.

Until the end of World War II, robusta beans commanded a significantly lower price than arabica, not only because they are less flavorful, but also because they can be harvested more easily. Thereafter, the price differential was reduced by two developments: demand for robusta was boosted by coffee-consuming nations' shift toward blends that combined both kinds of beans and, on an even larger scale, the introduction and great success of soluble coffee (or "instant" as it would later be known) derived largely, though not exclusively, from robusta.

According to Richard L. Lucier, author of *The International Political Economy of Coffee,* "Only 8 percent of world production was of robusta coffee in the late 1940s, but robusta's share more than tripled by the early 1970s. Over the same time period, soluble coffee's share of world consumption grew from virtually zero (i.e. consumption was of regular coffee) to nearly 25 percent." Key points in the rapid development of the U.S. coffee industry during the decades after World War II included the pioneering of a soluble process by Hills Brothers in 1953, Nestle's introduction in the same year of decaffeinated instant coffee, the emergence of freeze-dried coffee in 1965, and the creation of continuous freeze-drying systems in 1975.

The increasing demand for robusta had a sharp impact on the coffee-producing nations. Central and South America, where much of the world's arabica is grown, dominated coffee production before the 1950s. By the late 1980s, however, more than a third of world coffee production took place in the robusta-growing countries of Africa and Southeast Asia.

Latin America also suffered when the coffee boom, occurring from 1955 to 1962, was followed by a slump in prices triggered by over-production, a crisis that led in 1962 to the first of several International Coffee Agreements intended to stabilize prices. As M. Th. A. Pieterse and H. J. Silvis explained in *The World Coffee Market* and the International Coffee Agreement, "The instrument used is a system of export quotas, which—depending on price developments—limits producing members' exports to consuming members' markets. The role of consuming members is to police producing members' adherence to the quota provisions." According to Richard Lucier's analysis, the swift and concerted response by the U.S. coffee industry to the slump-induced crisis in Latin America reflected the political climate of the time (fear of Communist inroads into countries with deteriorating economies) as well as concern about the possible overall disruption of world coffee production and an attachment to neighbors and long-term trading partners.

Despite numerous reports linking various health problems with coffee consumption, the results of such studies have been inconclusive and ambiguous. There is no definitive proof that coffee drinkers are at higher risk for high cholesterol, heart disease, birth defects, cancer of the bladder or pancreas, or high blood pressure. Though the drop in coffee consumption through the 1960s and 1970s may have reflected anxiety induced by the sheer number of these reports, it may also have been prompted in part by dissatisfaction with the quality of the product.

The increasing demand for specialty coffees suggested that consumers were attracted to higher quality brews, especially when accompanied by lower levels of caffeine—arabica beans are not only less bitter than robusta but also contain about half as much caffeine, the component of coffee most frequently cited in connection with potentially harmful side effects.

Coffee shops continued to enjoy prominence throughout American culture during the mid-1990s, with Starbucks the unchallenged leader. Numerous smaller roasters, however, had also entered the market, enjoying measured success on a less dominant basis.

The industry showed strong signs in early 1997, with coffee markets showing record levels as roasters took advantage of favorable prices and rising inventories. Speculation about the amount of coffee that Brazil, the world's leading producer, would harvest in late spring, 1997, indicated some uncertainty about whether these strong levels could be maintained.

CURRENT CONDITIONS

The growing supply of coffee—about 107 million bags in 1998-99, up 9 percent over 1997-98 production levels—caused prices to spiral down, leaving the value of coffee exports 10 percent lower, to $11 billion in 1998-99. While the robusta beans increased about 5 percent in price primarily due to drought conditions in Asia, arabica beans saw prices plunge around 30 percent in 1999. The prices at the wholesale level have affected prices at the U.S. retail level; instant coffee prices in 1999 are slightly higher than in 1998 and 1999 roasted coffee prices are about 10-15 percent below the 1998 level.

The same cannot be said for the turn of the century. Analysts are predicting a worldwide production of coffee at 104.5 million bags in 1999-2000. Although Cote d'Ivoire, Columbia, Ecuador, and India, among others, are expected to increase their coffee crop production, Brazil—the leader worldwide in coffee—is expected to have a smaller crop, mainly due to lack of rain.

Other coffee producing countries look to Brazil's output to gauge where the market will go. In 1998-99 the U.S. Department of Agriculture estimated that Brazil's coffee crop came to 35.6 million bags. Both the Brazilian government and private analysts feel the 1999-2000 crop will have come in much lower—around 25.5 million bags or 30 percent less.

Coffee prices have begun to fluctuate greatly at the wholesale level as importers move away from stocking the commodity. Instead of having reserves handy when coffee is scarce, thereby taking advantage of rising prices, the importers are avoiding storage and associated costs of keeping a ready supply of coffee beans.

In the specialty coffee market, the number of coffeehouses in the United States will continue to grow. The Specialty Coffee Association of America (SCAA) predicts the number of coffeehouses to rise from 12,000 in 1999 to 18,000 in 2015. Before that rise, however, the SCAA feels the industry will consolidate, as companies purchase one another, thereby closing some stores. As a result, the trade group predicts the number of stores to drop to around 10,000, before rebounding to the 2015 figure.

As popularity of coffee grows and the coffeehouses add food to their menus, restaurants are beginning to re-evaluate what they serve to their customers. Some restaurants are beginning to treat coffee as they would wine; offering their customers a wide range of choices and matching different types to different foods. The SCAA feels this will introduce more people to specialty coffees, leading to greater sales at coffeehouses and at the grocery store.

The independent coffeehouses and roasters that do not get bought in the consolidation frenzy will emerge stronger than ever. They will boast freshness, homemade quality, and endure with higher profits, as the public perceives their product to be better.

INDUSTRY LEADERS

In a 1995 ranking in *Advertising Age,* year-to-date leaders in sales of ground coffee were Folgers with 27.4 percent of the market, followed by a 19.5 percent share for Kraft's Maxwell House. These two brands strongly dominate the market with private label brands showing the next highest share of market at only 7.6 percent.

According to an analysis by Bill Saporito that appeared in *Fortune,* Kraft General Foods became more aggressive in its promotion of Maxwell House when Philip Morris acquired the company in 1988, introducing a risk-taking mood. Saporito noted several reasons why such aggressiveness in the battle for market share in the ground and soluble coffee markets seemed ill advised: with a profit of less than a penny per cup of coffee at stake, such coffee manufacturers had been competing against each other in expensive advertising campaigns, together with costly promotions aimed at supermarkets (in the form of incentives) and consumers (in the form of coupons), all the while neglecting opportunities to take advantage of a burgeoning taste for the more profitable specialty coffees, except by cautiously introducing upscale versions of already popular brands.

Because the giants in the U.S. coffee business imported in pre-roasted or even ready-soluble form so much of the coffee they used, much of the coffee processing actually done in this country was performed by smaller concerns, including those companies marketing the increasingly popular specialty coffees.

Among coffee manufacturers Starbucks Corporation led the way. Starbucks is the leading retailer, roaster, and brand of specialty coffee in North America. The company opened its first store in Seattle in 1971 and by October 1999 had nearly 2,500 coffee shops throughout the United States in office buildings, shopping centers, airport terminals, cruise ships and supermarkets. Starbucks has aggressively marketing its whole beans through the Internet, direct marketing, grocery stores, and coffee-houses.

Starbucks went public in 1992, with continued success well into the late 1990s as Americans continued their obsession with gourmet coffee and related products. Starbucks has also introduced coffee-flavored ice cream and beer and launched a cold coffee drink called Frappuccino with Pepsico. The company expanded outside the United States in 1996 with its first international stores in Tokyo and Toronto. Starbucks reported consolidated net revenues of $1.7 billion for fiscal 1999, compared to $1.3 billion in fiscal 1998, a 28 percent increase.

Diedrich Coffee, which operates Diedrich coffee-houses and Gloria Jean's Coffee, is the number two specialty coffee retailer in the United States. In September 1999 Diedrich Coffee had 355 retail locations, up from 43 in October 1998, due mainly to the acquisition of Coffee People, Inc., a larger competitor. The company plans to move aggressively, adding up to 1,500 new franchised outlets by 2007.

Gloria Jean's same store sales rose 4 percent in its first quarter (ending September 22, 1999) compared to the same period in 1998. A 6.1 percent increase of same store sales from the first quarter of 1998 to the first quarter of 1998 at Diedrich coffeehouses was attributed to customers visiting more frequently. The company reported a loss of $389,000 in the first quarter of 1999, compared to a loss of $609,000 in the same quarter of 1998. Due to the acquisition of Coffee People, Diedrich was able to post a 169 percent gain in sales, to $16.3 million, in the first quarter of 1999, compared to $6.0 million in the same period of 1998.

In September 1999 New World Coffee-Manhattan Bagel Inc. announced it had purchased New York Bagel Enterprises, Inc. New World owns Seattle's Best Coffee and in 1999 owned or franchised stores in 28 states under its three brand names. The company had revenues of $7.6 million in the first six months of 1999 and $520,000 in store opening profits. The Seattle Coffee Company (SCC) was founded in 1969 and is one of the United States' oldest specialty roasters. SCC markets two very different coffees—Seattle's Best and Torrefazione Italia. SCC counts restaurants, food services, and airlines among its more than 7500 wholesale customers; additionally, each brand has its own retail operations, totaling 100 stores by the end of 1999.

AMERICA AND THE WORLD

Coffee is produced in only a few areas around the world, yet is consumed by people all over the world. The largest coffee-consuming countries produce very little coffee. Coffee production occurs in warm climates, such as those in South and Central America, the Caribbean, and parts of Africa and Asia. The United States, France, Germany, and Japan account for about one-half of all coffee consumption, with the United States leading the way, importing $3.6 billion in coffee in 1998. Although the consumption of coffee has been rising at the same rate as population growth, new markets in Russia and Eastern Europe have fueled the demand for coffee.

Brazil produces about one-third of all coffee in the world, yet coffee accounted for only 5 percent of Brazil's export earnings in 1999. In Columbia, coffee accounted for 20 percent of export earnings; in the Central American coffee-producing countries, it was 20-30 percent; in African countries, 5 percent; and minimal in Asia, except for Vietnam. Vietnamese coffee exports accounted for about 15 percent of export earnings in 1999, up from 2 percent in 1993.

The top 10 coffee-producing countries in the first six months of 1999 were (in order): Mexico, Brazil, Columbia, Guatemala, Costa Rica, Vietnam, Honduras, El Salvador, Venezuela, and Indonesia.

Since coffee accounts for high export earnings in Central America, the weather is a big factor—from freezes, to drought, to too much rain. Hurricane George and Tropical Storm Mitch blew through Central America in 1998, causing widespread damage. It was estimated that those storms caused a loss in coffee crops of around one million bags of coffee, with a value of $100 million.

Unlike other coffee-consuming nations, the United States imposed no import duty on this particular commodity. Another unique feature of the U.S. market is the nation's close cultural, geographical, political, and economic ties to Latin America, and thus to such major coffee producers as Brazil, Columbia, and Mexico. Although Mexico has been by far the least important of these in terms of output, its close proximity to roasters in the southern United States and its consequent ability to transport coffee overland have been advantageous.

RESEARCH AND TECHNOLOGY

For several reasons, the leading manufacturers of coffee in the United States, despite their dependence on imported beans, managed to resist any competition from among the coffee-producing nations. One key advantage was that of patented technology, and consequently automated production on a huge (and therefore highly economical) scale. Eliminating much repetitive labor in loading and unloading, the introduction of the continuous roaster enabled a single person to operate two units continuously producing 5000 kilograms per hour, thereby doubling productivity to the level of 1600 bags per person-day. The developing coffee-producing nations could neither match this technological advantage nor afford to compete with U.S. manufacturers in a field characterized by heavy promotional and advertising costs.

Another obstacle preventing coffee-producing nations from manufacturing coffee for the U.S. market was that the industry leaders had used their technological advantage to shape local tastes to specific blends manufactured with great consistency. A single coffee-producing nation could not possibly draw on a sufficient variety of coffees to match these exact blends.

With the shift in national taste towards specialty coffees, quality of beans became a paramount concern for new producers entering the developing gourmet market. In response, the established American manufacturers began experimenting with refined versions of popular lines and researching possible new products, such as iced coffee. Based on its success in Japan, and given its potential appeal to younger consumers, iced coffee was regarded by a number of analysts as a probable strong seller in the American market during the 1990s. Others, however, remained skeptical of this product's ability to reproduce the success achieved by iced teas, diet sodas, or health drinks.

FURTHER READING

"Coffee Exporters Count on Higher Earnings." *Agricultural Outlook Magazine,* March 1999. Available from http://www.econ.ag.gov/epubs/pdf/agout/mar99/index.htm.

"Daily Coffee Newsletter." *Best Investments,* 5 November 1999. Available from http://www.binews.com/news.htm.

Ferguson, Mike. "The Next 15 Years of Retail." *Specialty Coffee Association of America,* November 1999. Available from http://www.scaa.com.

"Irvine, Calif.-Based Coffee Retailer Stems Losses with Boost in Sales." *The Orange County Register,* 4 November 1999.

POTATO CHIPS, CORN CHIPS, AND SIMILAR SNACKS

This classification consists of establishments primarily engaged in manufacturing potato chips, corn chips, and similar snacks. Establishments primarily engaged in manufacturing pretzels and crackers are classified in **SIC 2052: Cookies and Crackers;** those manufacturing candy covered popcorn are classified in **SIC 2064: Candy and Other Confectionery Products;** those manufacturing salted, roasted, cooked, or canned nuts and seeds are classified in **SIC 2068: Salted and Roasted Nuts and Seeds;** and those manufacturing packaged unpopped popcorn are classified in **SIC 2099: Food Preparations, Not Elsewhere Classified.**

NAICS CODE(S)

311919 (Other Snack Food Manufacturing)

INDUSTRY SNAPSHOT

The "salty snack" industry includes potato chips, corn chips, tortilla chips, ready-to-eat popcorn (except candy-coated), pork rinds, potato sticks, and extruded snacks such as cheese puffs. Overall, retail dollar sales for snacks during 1998 totaled $18 billion, an increase of 7.3 percent from 1997. Potato chips and tortilla chips controlled the snack foods market.

In the mid-1990s, private label brands of salty snacks grew at unprecedented rates. According to the Private Label Manufacturers Association, store brands reported a 15.4 percent increase compared to an 11 percent increase in sales of national brands.

Even though the salty snacks industry experienced an almost flat overall growth rate in the mid-1990s, low fat and no fat salty snacks experienced tremendous growth. Low fat and no fat potato chip sales grew 48 percent in 1995, as compared to 1994; also, low fat and no fat tortilla chips grew 67 percent in 1995, again compared to 1994. However, by 1999 the craze for low fat and no fat snacks seemed to be on the decline.

ORGANIZATION AND STRUCTURE

The salty snack foods industry had a unique structure, since Frito-Lay controlled roughly 50 percent of the total market share with retail sales of about $10.98 billion in 1998. Its nearest competitor, Borden Snacks Group, regularly had retail sales of just more than $1 billion. Eagle Snacks, a unit of Anheuser-Busch breweries, was the third-largest maker of salty snacks at the century's close, with $600 million in retail sales. Although the industry had some elements of a monopoly (aggressive pricing and distribution policies among chip makers, along with the regional presence of many large and small manufacturers) kept it highly competitive.

Numerous companies of descending size made up the snack industry. Many competed only on a regional level, and some found it difficult to price their products competitively with the larger manufacturers. Others, however, created a market niche, sometimes with a specialty product such as kettle style potato chips or baked chips sold through health food stores. If their product met with success among customers, the smaller makers could often charge higher prices than the biggest manufacturers. Larger manufacturers were generally full-service snack companies—those offering a full range of products, including potato chips, tortilla chips, and other salty snacks. The smaller producers were more likely to specialize.

One such small manufacturer was Cape Cod Potato Chip Co., a Massachusetts-based firm that began frying chips over a kitchen stove before purchasing a storefront potato chip shop in 1980. The hand-operated frying kettles produced only 120 pounds of chips per hour, in contrast with the industry standard commercial cookers that produced 4,000 pounds. A decade after opening, Cape Cod employed 200 people—although the operation was purchased in 1985 by Eagle Snacks.

BACKGROUND AND DEVELOPMENT

The potato chip was born accidentally in 1853, when railroad magnate and naval commodore Cornelius Vanderbilt was vacationing in a popular East Coast inn. He ordered fried potatoes but disliked them and returned the fries to the kitchen, complaining that they were "too thick." The cook, a Native American named George Crumm, reacted with indignation. He sliced a potato into slivers as thin as he could, fried them, and served them to Vanderbilt.

The newly invented snack gained popularity among other customers, but remained primarily a restaurant item for several decades. This style of potatoes became known as Saratoga chips, named after the town in which they were first consumed. In 1895, William Tappenden of Cleveland began manufacturing potato chips for home consumption. Snack food innovations included the introduction of ridged potato chips in 1966 and fabricated potato chips in the 1970s.

Popcorn is perhaps the oldest salty snack food still widely consumed. Indigenous peoples in what became Peru were known to toast corn kernels over flames until they burst. This tradition was recorded as early as the fifteenth century. North American Indians also prepared popcorn, and it was believed to have been shared at the first Thanksgiving dinner in Plymouth, Massachusetts. The term popcorn became accepted around 1820. Early American settlers may have eaten it—sprinkled with sugar and doused in cream—as the first breakfast cereal. It was also used decoratively from the beginning of its history, having been strung and draped on Christmas trees during the 1800s.

In 1885 the snack food received a boost from the invention of the first popping machine by a Chicago inventor named Charles Cretors. His machine used oil to pop the corn and was used for about a century until the development of the hot air popper. In the mid-1960s, the snack began to be manufactured on a mass scale by Orville Redenbacher—who then promoted his brand as a gourmet hybrid popcorn. The next major innovation came in 1986, when Pillsbury introduced microwavable popcorn.

Industry analysts reported that the snack food industry fared well in the early 1990s, given the economic downturn. In fact, over time the industry developed a reputation for being recession proof. However, stiff competition required increasingly aggressive promotions to grab the consumer dollar, so some viewed salty snacks as a no-growth industry.

Dollar sales of savory snacks—in a broad category including pretzels and snack nuts—grew from $10.6 billion in 1987 to $13.8 billion in 1992, an increase of 30 percent. Per capita consumption jumped from 17.49 pounds in 1987 to 20.55 pounds in 1992. The field was dominated by Frito-Lay, a subsidiary of Pepsi Co., which claimed nearly half of the overall salty snack food market in 1992. But Americans' appetite for specialty and relatively "healthy" snacks kept the industry competitive. More than 400 new products were introduced in both 1991 and 1992, including several varieties of multigrain chips, flavored ready-to-eat popcorn, and diet cheese puffs.

The industry experienced steady sales growth, even during the recession of the early 1990s. But pound sales volume rose faster than dollar sales volume in both 1991 and 1992 due to the keen competition that characterized the industry. The decline in price per pound was also consistent with falling retail grocery prices nationwide. The issues described by snack food companies as posing the biggest challenges to profitability in the mid-1990s included: competitive pricing, government mandated nutritional labeling, changing distribution patterns, and rising supermarket shelf fees.

Profits for salty snack manufacturers were 7.5 percent in 1992, representing a slight drop from the previous year. These figures included additional snacks, such as pretzels and packaged nuts, which were made by "full-service" salty snack companies such as Frito-Lay and Borden. Pre-tax profit margins for this broad category of snacks slipped from 6.8 percent in 1991 to 4.2 percent in 1992. Domestic dollar sales in 1992 were $9.6 billion—up overall from 1991 sales. Consumers bought approximately 3.6 billion pounds of salty snacks, or nearly 18 pounds per capita consumption.

Potato chips led the way in salty snack consumption in 1992, with a retail sales volume of $4.41 billion. This dollar amount represented the sale of more than 1.66 billion pounds of potato chips, which claimed 32 percent of the market for all savory snacks—including popcorn, meat snacks, pretzels, and snack nuts. Tortilla chips were the second most consumed salty snack. More than $2.57 billion worth were sold in 1992—a volume of 1.06 billion pounds. This represented a 20.5 percent market share by pound volume, or 18.6 percent by dollar sales. Potato chips and tortilla chips combined accounted for about 50 percent of the savory snack market.

More than 40 percent of all purchases of salty snacks were made in supermarkets—food stores that reported annual sales of at least $2 million. Grocery stores—food stores with sales of less than $2 million annually—accounted for between 10 and 20 percent of salty snack sales in 1992, depending on the product. The remaining salty snacks were sold in convenience stores, mass merchandisers—large general merchandise stores that also carried grocery items—warehouse club stores, drug stores, vending machines, and other retail outlets such as delicatessens, liquor stores, and sports stadiums.

Shifting Distribution Patterns. A market research study found that consumers paid an average price of $2.66 per pound of savory snacks in 1992, down 2.6 percent from $2.73 per pound the previous year. This was attributed to several factors—including the recession and the competitive nature of retail products—but another major factor was a shift in distribution patterns. Large warehouse club stores and mass merchandisers charged lower prices for snacks in order to attract customers from smaller supermarkets and grocery stores. While supermarkets accounted for nearly 50 percent of salty snack sales, sales by dollar volume rose only about 1 percent. In contrast, warehouse clubs saw an increase of more than 50 percent in savory snack sales, and mass merchandisers also saw double digit growth. Since these larger outlets charged less per pound for snacks than supermarkets, the increased sales represented a decline in profitability.

Convenience stores charged the highest prices for both potato chips and corn chips. In 1992, average potato chip prices were $3.06 per pound—the only outlet where prices passed the $3.00 mark. In contrast, potato chips sold for $2.49 per pound in supermarkets and $2.44 at mass merchandisers. In that same year, corn chips sold for $2.74 per pound in convenience stores, compared with $2.44 in supermarkets and $2.00 in warehouse clubs.

Prices began a trend toward equalization in the early 1990s, however. Convenience store prices of tortilla chips, for instance, were $2.61 per pound in 1992—the

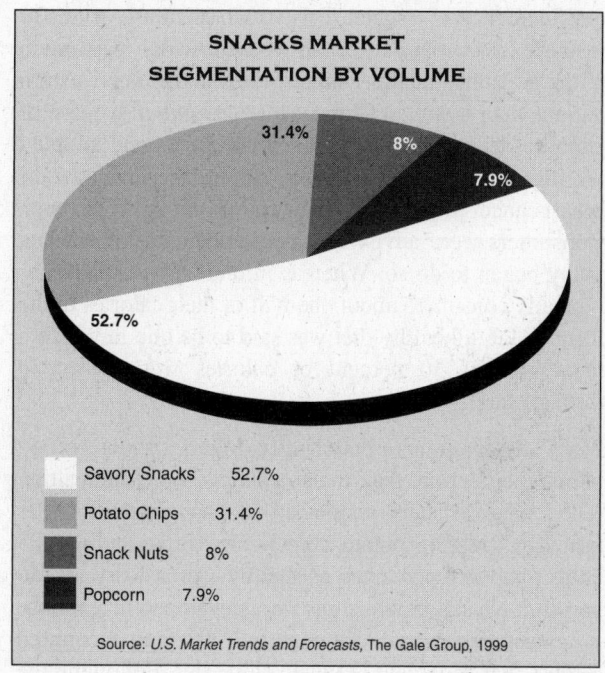

SNACKS MARKET SEGMENTATION BY VOLUME

Savory Snacks	52.7%
Potato Chips	31.4%
Snack Nuts	8%
Popcorn	7.9%

Source: *U.S. Market Trends and Forecasts*, The Gale Group, 1999

highest of any outlet, though 10 percent lower than the previous year. Supermarkets, grocery stores, mass merchandisers, and drug stores saw only a modest shift in tortilla chip prices. However, the price at warehouse clubs jumped almost 30 percent to $2.27 per pound. This trend also reflected the fierce competition that kept profits low throughout the recession.

Moreover, savory snacks experienced intensely competitive pricing in supermarkets. Full-line snack companies reported spending 52 cents of each promotional dollar on price reductions. Another 25 percent of promotional expenses went toward advertising and 16 percent was used for in-store promotions. On the whole, 72 percent of full-line manufacturers reported spending more money for advertising and other promotional endeavors in 1992 than in 1991. In addition, retail shelf space increased in price during the early 1990s. The average cost per section foot per store paid by salty snack manufacturers leaped from $283.33 in 1991 to $342.86 in 1992.

Health Implications. The salty snack industry adapted to shifting consumer demands and perceptions throughout the last several decades. During the late 1960s and 1970s, Americans learned from health experts that they were consuming salt in greater quantities than was necessary or healthy. The average individual needed about one-third teaspoon of salt per day. High consumption of salty snacks and other prepared or processed foods resulted in more than double the recommended intake.

In more recent years, university studies linked low fat diets to reduced rates of cancer and heart disease. Research showed that low fat diets, typical of those in the Far East, were associated with low or virtually nonexistent incidence of cancer. This was particularly true, for instance, in breast cancer for women, which was much more prevalent in the United States and other western nations than it was in China. Moreover, when women of Chinese descent lived in the United States and adopted the high fat diet typical of Americans, the incidence of breast cancer jumped to the rate found among westerners. Consumers were advised to reduce their fat intake, and many began to do so. Whereas in the 1960s, Americans typically consumed about one-half of their calories in the form of fat, a healthy diet was said to be one in which a maximum of 30 percent of calories was consumed through fats.

Thus, manufacturers of salty, high fat foods battled public perception that their products were unhealthy. Salty snack makers responded to changing consumer tastes by creating potato chips, corn chips, and tortilla chips that were perceived as healthy—or at least not too harmful. No salt potato chips were developed in response to consumer demand, although in 1992 they accounted for less than 1 percent of potato chip sales. Following the unspectacular success of no salt chips, low salt varieties were introduced and proved more successful, showing double digit market share growth in the early 1990s.

Low oil potato chips proved more successful, making up 3.7 percent of chip sales by volume. From 1991 to 1992 alone, this category of potato chip jumped by 24.3 percent. Other specialty chips were baked rather than fried, and another manufacturer sold chips that were cooked in the potato's own juices, resulting in a fat-free chip. Similar innovations were found in the tortilla chip industry in the early 1990s. Low salt and low oil tortilla chips combined to make up about 9 percent of overall volume.

Despite manufacturers' responsiveness to consumer demand for healthier products, the desire to eat foods lower in fat nevertheless affected the salty snack industry. Among industry products, popcorn consumption virtually exploded in the late 1980s and early 1990s. Multigrain snacks also showed remarkable growth for the first few years after their introduction. Other foods that competed with potato chips and similar snacks included pretzels and snack nuts, both of which gained market share much more rapidly than potato chips and tortilla chips in the early 1990s. Double digit growth was observed in both ready-to-eat popcorn and in pretzels from 1991 to 1992—12 percent and 15.5 percent, respectively. This was due at least in part to consumer perception of pretzels and nuts as having more nutritive value than potato chips. Even low oil chips contained more fat than pretzels, for instance, which were baked rather than fried. Snack nuts contained relatively little salt and oil and featured nutrients such as protein and minerals not found in potato or tortilla chips.

Flavor Variety. The development of flavored chips and snacks throughout the 1980s and 1990s was generally successful in keeping snack consumption on the rise. Small manufacturers introduced kettle-style potato chips—cooked in kettles as done previously. Many larger manufacturers followed suit, either developing their own versions of kettle chips or buying smaller companies that developed them for regional markets. In 1992, kettle style chips made up 5.5 percent of pound volume consumed.

Regularly shaped chips made up 46.2 percent of pound volume, and ridged chips of all flavors accounted for 34.4 percent in 1992. Fabricated chips represented 13.9 percent of the market for potato chips in that same year. Flavored potato and corn chips also multiplied, accounting for many of the new product introductions during the late 1980s and early 1990s. In addition to barbecue flavored potato chips, consumers purchased sour cream and onion, ranch, and other flavors.

Tortilla chips experienced the most success of any salty snack food with the introduction of flavor varieties. Regular flavored chips made up 61.4 percent of the tortilla chip market in 1992, while cheese flavored tortilla chips accounted for 26.3 percent of the market. The third most popular flavor that year was ranch, which represented just under 8 percent of the market. Other varieties included salsa, spicy hot, jalapeno, chili, and oat bran flavors. In addition, white corn tortilla chips were introduced in the early 1990s and found favor with consumers.

Ready-to-Eat Popcorn. Ready-to-eat (RTE) popcorn grew in popularity during the late 1980s and early 1990s. Dollar sales jumped from $248 million in 1987 (including caramel coated) to more than half a billion dollars in 1992. This was in contrast to more sluggish growth in the microwavable popcorn category, in which sales remained flat from 1990 to 1992 after booming during the 1980s. Analysts attributed this slowdown to market maturation—almost 90 percent of consumers owned a microwave oven by 1990.

While caramel coated RTE popcorn made up the largest market share of any individual type—39.2 percent in 1992—non-coated popcorn accounted for 60.8 percent of total RTE popcorn consumption. Regular flavor had the largest share of sales after caramel, with nearly 20 percent of the market. White cheddar and cheese combined made up more than 17 percent of the market, with butter flavor accounting for nearly 12 percent, and cinnamon and other flavors combining to total about 2 percent. Sales of all varieties grew in double digits from 1991 to 1992, except for white cheddar flavored popcorn, which dropped 13.2 percent in the latter year. Low salt RTE popcorn sold well, claiming 6.3 percent of pound volume in supermarkets.

Whereas total popcorn sales slid downward 4.2 percent to $1.4 billion in 1992, RTE popcorn sales (including caramel flavored) increased 12 percent to $510.0 million that same year. Measured in pound volume, sales grew 15.4 percent between 1991 and 1992, with 154.2 million pounds consumed. Many RTE brands were air popped, making them virtually fat free. Moreover, RTE popcorn could be purchased and eaten immediately, making it even more convenient than its microwavable competitors. RTE varieties appeared to be causing the demise of a second competitor, unpopped popcorn, for which dollar sales slumped 11.3 percent to $117.4 million in 1992. This trend suggested that RTE popcorn would eventually split the market with microwavable brands, while unpopped popcorn would become a supermarket dinosaur.

Showing similar pricing and distribution patterns to potato and tortilla chips, RTE popcorn commanded the highest price in convenience stores in 1992—$3.46 per pound. The lowest price, $2.28 per pound, was found in the warehouse club stores, which nevertheless saw an 11.8 percent price increase over the previous year. As of the early 1990s, RTE popcorn was produced by only a few manufacturers, but as others took note of its popularity and profitability, new companies began marketing their own products.

Extruded Snacks. Extruded snacks is the industry term for cheese puffs, corn puffs, and onion rings. The largest segment of this snack category—about 96 percent—was controlled by cheese flavored products. Sales of extruded snacks remained flat relative to other salty snacks from 1987 to 1992. Dollar volume was $694.3 million in 1987 and $774.0 in 1992, having dropped from its peak of $813.0 million in 1991. Like other savory snacks, extruded snacks were characterized by the introduction, in the late 1980s and early 1990s, of many flavor varieties. A diet company even introduced individual-serving size, low-calorie cheese curls. But the new varieties failed to bring as much growth as expected to the industry overall.

Extruded cheese snacks, although no higher in fat content than potato chips and corn chips, suffered from a consumer perception that they were highly processed and not as healthful as related snack foods. Throughout the last decade, consumers showed a preference for more natural, less processed foods—including snack foods. Although consumers wanted convenience, there was nevertheless a trend toward the use of whole foods rather than refined foods, which might have implications for the extruded snack industry.

Pork Rinds. The pork rind segment of the salty snack industry grew steadily from $163.4 million in 1987 to $236 million in 1992. Double-digit sales growth in the late 1980s slowed to about 5 percent annually in the early 1990s. One reason for growth in this segment was that the industry leader, Frito-Lay, increased its focus on pork rinds in its promotions—particularly in the southern United States. The South represented more than 50 percent of total pork rind consumption, with Pacific states totaling another 20 percent. The New England and mid-Atlantic states had virtually no market, with only 4 percent of national pork rind sales.

Supermarkets sold only 18 percent of pork rinds in 1992, while grocery stores—the smaller volume of the two types—saw 27 percent of the snack's sales. Convenience stores, which charged the highest price for pork rinds—$6.12 per pound—accounted for 18 percent of sales. Boosting this snack's popularity was the introduction of microwavable brands in 1992. The new product offered a 60 to 70 percent reduction in fat—undoubtedly a source of appeal to consumers. In addition, pork rinds, like other salty snacks, appeared in flavor varieties including Cajun, jalapeno, barbecue, and chili.

Multigrain Chips. Of all the salty snacks manufactured and sold in the early 1990s, the type that demonstrated the greatest growth was the multigrain chip. Although only a $198-million industry in 1992, this sales volume represented a growth of 76.5 percent from the previous year. The first-year sales of Frito-Lay's multigrain product, Sunchips, totaled $115 million.

Introduced in 1990 by Frito-Lay, multigrain chips grew quickly enough that industry observers expected the product to become a substantial segment of the salty snack industry. Two competitors introduced their own versions of multigrain chips, but Frito-Lay still cornered the market in 1992 with $192 million in sales—nearly all of the product's volume. The success of multigrain chips was attributed to the perceived health value of the snack, which was made of grains and was relatively low in salt and oil.

By contrast, the decline in sales for four straight years signaled a maturing market for corn chips. In 1987, the corn chip industry saw $560 million in sales, but by 1992 that figure had grown to only $598 million. The introduction of flavor varieties did not boost sales—which peaked in 1989 at $668 million and slid each year thereafter. Efforts by Frito-Lay to bolster sales through redesigned packaging and new marketing campaigns met with consumer apathy. Nevertheless, corn chips represented 4.3 percent of the overall snack market.

Industry Challenges. In a 1993 survey of salty snack manufacturers, increased government regulations were cited most often as the biggest challenge facing the industry in the mid-1990s. This concern arose from the passage of the Nutrition Labeling and Education Act of 1990 (NLEA), which required that all food manufacturers list nutrients in greater detail beginning in May 1994. In addition, the NLEA required manufacturers to list nutritional components of foods by serving sizes determined at the discretion of the government. Previously, food makers determined portion size and listed vitamins, protein, minerals, fat, and calorie content accordingly.

The trend mentioned second most frequently in the survey was the increasing consolidation of the industry. Growing consumer emphasis on the health value of foods was cited as the third most important trend in the mid-1990s. Other trends noted were increasing retail shelf space fees, continued intense pricing competition with other manufacturers, demographic changes, and rising environmental concerns.

CURRENT CONDITIONS

Sales for the snack food industry reached $18.0 billion in 1998, up 7.3 percent from 1997. Sales in all markets—food, drug, and mass merchant—rose in 1998.

Potato Chips. Potato chips increased 15.1 percent in sales from 1997 to 1998, with pound volume increasing 6.5 percent. The low fat and no fat lines of potato chips were behind the surge in sales, and by 1999 it looked as though the category would shrink considerably.

Tortilla and Corn Chips. Tortilla chips were bought overwhelmingly in supermarkets—44.8 percent of all tortilla sales. Corn chips saw sales of almost $750 million, with 49 percent of that going to supermarkets. Dorito's led the way in tortillas with $693 million in sales, followed by Tostito's with $526 million in sales. Frito's was the corn chip leader with $208 million in sales, followed by Frito's Scoops with $98 million. Manufactures were beginning to combine sales of tortilla and corn chips with dips and salsa, thus appealing to customers' desired convenience.

Extruded Snacks. In 1998 extruded snacks had sales of $810.0 million, up just 1.4 percent from 1997. The leaders for this category are Chee-tos with $228 million in sales, followed by private-label brands with $45 million. Extruded snack manufacturers continued to try to pump up the segment, experimenting with urban and ethnic lines. The top flavors for extruded snacks were cheese and hot.

Reduced Fat and Fat-Free Products. When Frito-Lay introduced their Wow! fat-free potato chips, they were well received, and the industry recognized the fat-free line as the best selling new product in 1998. That year sales of Wow! chips were $350 million, and some analysts had predicted future sales of about $500 million a year. By 1999 the company said it expected only about $250 million in annual sales from the fat-free line. While the fat-free line of potato chips had been heavily anticipated, by the time Frito-Lay got them to the market, interest in fat-free snacks, cakes, and cookies had dropped considerably among consumers. Nutrition experts hurt sales when they appealed to the Food and Drug Administration (FDA) for labels on the products warning consumers of possible gastrointestinal side effects of olean—a fat substitute—and that the chips had been fortified with vitamins A, D, E, and K since olean prevented their absorption.

Regional Competitors. Frito-Lay is the undisputed leader in the salty snack category, with 62 percent of the sales in the industry. The company has a firm grip on premium shelf space, outspends every other company in marketing and merchandising, and has a superior distribution system. Independent companies in the industry continued to consolidate or go out of business and, by 1998, there were 111 snack companies.

INDUSTRY LEADERS

The Frito-Lay Company reported snack sales of $11 billion worldwide in 1998. The Frito-Lay Company was based in Plano, Texas, and had 30,000 employees. Because of its 62 percent market share, Frito-Lay's activities and innovations reverberated throughout the salty snack food industry. Sales from the manufacturer accounted for 60 percent of the total of its parent company—Pepsi Co. A competitive battle for market share during the early 1990s prompted Frito-Lay to carry out a reorganization, which included repricing products and laying off 1,800 executives. In addition, 2,000 employees were shifted from administrative positions into sales jobs.

For years large corporations tried to challenge Frito-Lay's dominance in the snack business. Anheuser-Busch, Keebler, and Borden all tried and, after battling the giant in advertising and merchandising dollars, all decided to get out of the salty snack business. The closest brand to competing nationally against Frito-Lay was Eagle, a brand owned by Anheuser-Busch for 20 years. After losing about $75 million on the brand, Anheuser-Busch sold the division to Proctor and Gamble (P&G).

P&G, a leader in packaged goods, has the money and the stamina to take on Frito-Lay, a fight analysts will be watching closer. Some analysts look to P&G's development of Pringles as a sign they're in for the long haul. P&G stuck with Pringles, a relatively new type of chip, and in the late 1990s—30 years after its introduction—Pringles generates $1 billion in sales each year and sales were growing at about 20 percent a year.

P&G bought the Eagle brand in 1996 and waited until 1998 to begin test marketing the brand, beginning in Portland, Maine. Frito-Lay has cause for concern. Before the Eagle brand began its testing, P&G's share of the snack market had started climbing—from 5.8 percent to 7.4 percent.

FURTHER READING

"Financial Review." *Pepsico,* 18 November 1999. Available from http://www.pepsico.com/1998/.

Freeman, Laurie. "Hot Categories Prove Americans Make the Healthy Choice when Possible." *Advertising Age,* 27 February 1995.

Horovitz, Bruce. "P&G Stages Snack Attack Eagle Goes Head-To-Head vs. Chip Champ Frito-Lay." *USA Today,* 16 September 1998.

Kuhn, Mary Ellen. "The Skinny on Snacks: Healthy Is Hot." *Food Processing,* March 1995.

LeDuc Doug. "Snack Food Makers Foresee Less Price Pressure After Eagle Brands Demise." *Knight Ridder/Tribune Business News,* 19 March 1996.

Smyth, William. "SFA: Salty-Snack Sales are Soaring in 1999." *Supermarket News,* 27 September 1999.

Snack Foods Association. "1996 State of the Industry Report." *Snack World,* June 1996.

Thompson, Stephanie. "Frito-Lay Brand Dominance Breeds P-L Snack Upstarts." *Brandweek,* 25 November 1996.

Yung, Katherine. "An Expanding Palate: Frito-Lay Focusing on Expansion in Non-Salty Snack Markets." *The Dallas Morning News,* 15 October 1999.

———. "Chipping Away at Competition Bob's Texas Style Makes Gutsy Move into Home Turf of Frito-Lay." *The Dallas Morning News,* 8 August 1999.

———. "Frito-Lay's Profits Boost Pepsi's Revenues as Soft-Drink Price Rises." *Knight-Ridder/Tibune Business News,* 7 October 1999.

———. "Sales of Frito-Lay's Fat-Free Chips Fall Short of Expectations." *Knight-Ridder/Tribune Business News,* 12 October 1999.

SIC 2097

MANUFACTURED ICE

This category covers ice plants operated by public utilities and establishments manufacturing artificial ice for sale in the form of blocks or cubes; it excludes makers of dry ice, which are categorized in **SIC 2813: Industrial Gases.**

NAICS CODE(S)

312113 (Ice Manufacturing)

Technological advances freed consumers from their long dependence on the harvest of local, naturally occurring sources of ice by permitting first its export and then its manufacture. This production, whether by private companies or by public utilities, was based on developments that also heralded the era of domestic refrigeration, and the ice trays found in most American kitchens became the major rival of commercial ice manufacturers. In terms of volume, however, domestic refrigerators could not compete with ice plants, and manufactured ice has sold well in outlets where goods for parties, receptions, and other events are routinely purchased.

In 2000, ice manufacturers' products ranged from pound bags of ice cubes in varying quantities, to blocks of ice in weights of 10 to 300 pounds. The larger blocks were particularly popular for ice carvings at outdoor festivals and banquet buffets.

Much of the industry's annual revenues depends on the weather. The warmer the temperature, the more ice consumers buy. Logically, sales of manufactured ice are highest during the summer months of June, July, and August. Due to the ever-increasing efficiency of ice-making machinery and delivery, the wholesale price of ice has increased only by five cents since the late 1970s, to between 45 cents and 50 cents per pound in the late 1990s.

Purity is a primary issue among ice suppliers. As Michael R. Enright explained in *Nation's Business,* many ice suppliers have learned to enhance the purity of their product by creating a hole in the center of each cube and then flushing it, rinsing away the sulfur, iron, and other impurities in water that had concentrated there during the formation of the cube. Such purity concerned not only consumers but also businesses that required large quantities of ice to keep food cool and fresh. Despite the convenience and cheapness of ice produced in-house by such businesses, ice manufacturing specialists had the potential to create a product with greater purity.

Both the continuing quest for purity and a heightened consciousness about ecological issues on the part of consumers have made a promising development in the 1990s—the marketing of gourmet ice, as harvested from glaciers, springs, and other sources pre-dating or little affected by human pollution. This illustrates a return to the very origins of the ice industry, though with the probable addition of innovative packaging this time around.

Since the late 1980s, legislation at various levels of government led to tightened controls on sanitation and an improved standard of quality in the ice industry. Mandating drug testing of truck drivers further regulated the industry.

According to the *1997 Economic Census,* 582 establishments (the majority with 1 to 4 employees) were engaged in ice manufacturing. The value of 1997 shipments was approximately $431 million.

FURTHER READING

Bryan, Dave. "Ice Company Has Stood the Heat for 20 Years." *Triangle Business Journal,* 14 July 1995.

U.S. Census Bureau. "Manufacturing-Industry Series." *1997 Economic Census.* Washington, D.C.: GPO, 14 May 1999.

SIC 2098

MACARONI, SPAGHETTI, VERMICELLI, AND NOODLES

This category covers establishments primarily engaged in manufacturing dry macaroni, spaghetti, vermicelli, and noodles. Establishments primarily engaged in manufacturing canned macaroni and spaghetti are classified in **SIC 2032: Canned Specialties,** and those manufacturing fried noodles, such as Chinese noodles, are classified in **SIC 2099: Food Preparations, Not Elsewhere Classified.**

NAICS CODE(S)

311823 (Pasta Manufacturing)

INDUSTRY SNAPSHOT

In the two decades from 1975 to 1995, Americans increased their pasta consumption by 90 percent. Pasta was manufactured almost exclusively in the United States from durum semolina wheat. A growing consumer preference for nutritious, low-fat foods boosted the health of the industry, nearly doubling mean annual per capita consumption in the last 20 years to 24 pounds. In 1995, the typical consumer ate pasta an average of 2.7 times a week. The increased consumption was also due to a shift in consumer perceptions: it gained popularity among middle class and affluent adults and seniors, rather than being viewed as a meal for children or the working poor, as was the case during the 1960s.

Industry shipments in 1997 totaled nearly $1.8 billion, up from $1.3 billion in 1992. Slightly more than 6,000 people were employed by the nation's approximately 226 pasta manufacturing establishments.

ORGANIZATION AND STRUCTURE

Approximately fifty companies produce virtually all the pasta made in the United States through 266 establishments. Half of those firms were divisions or subsidiaries of larger companies. The bulk of dried pasta and noodles was sold through retail outlets such as supermarkets, convenience stores, and gourmet shops, for personal consumption. A scant 5 percent was sold to the food service industry.

Pasta Manufacturing. Dried pasta was manufactured from coarsely ground durum wheat, or "semolina." Durum was a hard, winter wheat, known for its high level of gluten, which made a stiff dough appropriate for pasta. Farina, a softer wheat, was sometimes added, as were powdered flavorings such as tomato or spinach. Gluten was also sometimes added to the dough, and "enriched" pasta received nutritional supplements such as thiamin,

niacin, riboflavin, and iron. Most pasta was made without eggs, but noodles were formed by adding eggs to the dough before processing.

Prior to the formation of pasta into its characteristic shape, the wheat was harvested and tested for moisture content, volume, color, insects, chaff, and bran. Once the wheat was determined to meet sufficient standards, the process of milling began. Wheat was first "tempered," or soaked in water, to separate the bran from the berry. Tempering also gave the berry enough moisture to prevent shattering when it was ground—the next part of the process. Once ground, the wheat was sifted numerous times to create semolina—coarsely ground flour, with particles about the size of sugar crystals. A byproduct of this repeated sifting was durum flour, which was sold for other uses. The semolina was added to water and any other ingredients, such as dyes, to create dough, which was then extruded through machines that formed the pasta into its ultimate shape. The pasta was then dried, packaged, and distributed.

In 1996, the United States produced 1.65 billion pounds of dry pasta for retail purposes, 0.64 billion pounds for industrial purposes, and 0.34 pounds for food service use.

BACKGROUND AND DEVELOPMENT

Although pasta was generally associated with Italy, and indeed many of the varied shapes originated from that country, the first pasta was actually Chinese. The development of an agricultural civilization led to pasta, possibly around 3000 B.C. Ancient Greeks considered pasta "marcus"—meaning "divine food." An Etruscan tomb created around 400 B.C. depicted the making of the grain product. Horace, a poet who lived in the first century B.C., described lasagna as one course of a Roman banquet.

Pasta was also a part of the cuisine of the Middle East. The Jewish and Arabic cultures, as well as that of Persia, discussed pasta as well as noodles. Germans consumed it, and the Genoese ate it in the thirteenth century. All of this took place before Marco Polo's legendary expedition to China, which led to the widespread consumption by Italians, who added red tomatoes to the recipe.

Noodles were consumed in the New World, prepared in the manner popular among the British—accompanied with a cream sauce and cheese. Thomas Jefferson was the first prominent American to embrace pasta, when he purchased a "macaroni" machine in Italy and shipped it to the United States. An Italian restaurateur in Richmond, Virginia, served pasta to his influential clientele, which included Jefferson.

By 1848, French miller Antoine Zerega opened the first macaroni factory. He followed both Chinese and

Italian traditions, drying strands of spaghetti on the rooftop of his Brooklyn factory. The subsequent immigration of large numbers of Italians to New York helped bring pasta into the mainstream of American cuisine.

A subtle wheat flavor was considered the ideal taste for pasta, since blandness prevented the pasta noodle from competing with the flavor of the sauce. The ideal texture of pasta was obtained when it was cooked ''al dente.'' This translated from Italian literally as ''to the tooth,'' but it described a noodle that was firm when chewed.

Regulatory Challenges. Like much of the food industry, pasta manufacturers faced increased regulation under new federal laws. The Nutrition Labeling and Education Act (NLEA) of 1990, which took effect in May 1994, required that pasta packaging list nutrients in greater detail than in the past. In addition, the NLEA provided for the Food and Drug Administration to determine the serving size on which nutritional information was based— something that had previously been determined by the manufacturers themselves.

Another trend in regulation in the early 1990s was based on concern over the effects of fumigants on the ozone layer. Many pasta manufacturers employed methyl bromide to rid storage areas of weevils and other pests that consumed wheat. One bill considered in 1993 declared methyl bromide a class one ozone-depleter and called for its production to be discontinued by the year 2000.

Competitive Challenges. The greatest challenge to the dry pasta and noodle industry was expected to come from competition with other types of pasta. For example, the sales volume of frozen pasta grew at an annual rate of 19.1 percent from 1980 to 1985 and 13.4 percent from 1986 to 1991. Although growth was expected to slow to about 6.7 percent per year in the latter part of the 1990s, the popularity of frozen pasta was expected to continue throughout the remainder of the decade, with consumption estimated at 62 billion pounds in 1995.

This growth was attributable to the convenience of frozen pasta, which came with a variety of sauces and required nothing more than heating in the microwave or the conventional oven. While cooking dry pasta was simple and required little time, preparation of the sauce could be more complex, and working individuals were increasingly reluctant to create meals from intricate or lengthy recipes.

Shelf-stable pasta was yet another product that eroded market share of dry pasta, and was expected to continue to do so. The shelf-stable category included dry packages like macaroni and cheese, pasta and noodle side dish mixes, add-meat dinner mixes, and soups or other meals that came in microwaveable containers. Shelf-stable pasta sales grew 6.7 percent annually in the early

1980s, but its popularity grew during the latter part of the decade by about 10 percent. Sales of this product were expected to grow at an annual rate of better than 10 percent through the remainder of the 1990s.

Fresh pasta, which showed an increase in sales volume of 60 percent annually from 1988 to 1991, experienced a decrease in the latter half of the 1990s. Initially, fresh pasta gained market share among the affluent at the expense of its dry counterpart, as it was perceived to be more flavorful and nutritious. It was sold in gourmet shops, as well as restaurants and supermarkets. The drawback of fresh pasta was its perishability, a result of its high moisture content. The greater ease of distribution enjoyed by dry pasta manufacturers was believed to be a primary reason that dry pasta held its own in market share.

Canned pasta posed no competitive threat to dry pasta and noodles. Despite attempts to upgrade its image to a premium food product, canned pasta was still perceived to be most appropriate for children or for lower income individuals. Canned food was also viewed as having depleted nutritional value, and the health value that drove much of the rise in pasta consumption was perceived to be lacking in canned dishes. Moreover, canned spaghetti with sauce was not believed by consumers to be as flavorful as that of either fresh, frozen, or dry pasta.

New Jersey-based Campbell Soup Company, a leader in the canned pasta market under the name Franco-American, continued to introduce new children's dishes—including teddy bear shaped pasta and sporty shapes, like bicycles, in sauces—and an upscale variety called Superiors targeted at adults. Despite such innovations, canned pasta market analysts did not anticipate that this product would pose a threat to dry pasta's market share. After sales volume of this product grew 3.3 percent annually from 1980 to 1985, and 5.3 percent per year from 1986 to 1991, it was projected to increase less than 1.0 percent annually through the mid- and late 1990s.

The industry faced challenges entering the mid-1990s, however, as foreign producers flooded the market and the nation's durum wheat was attacked by Karnal Bunt disease. Additionally, tougher labeling requirements, made effective in 1994, affected pasta industry profit levels, as did environmental protection and laws designed to protect employees, such as mandatory health care provisions.

CURRENT CONDITIONS

Industry shipments of dried pasta were $1.8 billion in 1997, a 38 percent increase from 1992. One reason for this dramatic trend was research about cancer and heart disease prevention combined with the nutritional qualities of pasta. Numerous public and private studies during the 1970s and 1980s linked diets high in fat content with various types of cancers and heart disease. During this same time period, separate research of individuals in developing countries demonstrated the benefits of a diet high in fiber—a non-nutritional substance found in whole grains, vegetables, and fruits. In addition, studies revealed the importance of complex carbohydrates, which were also found in grains such as durum wheat. Consuming complex carbohydrates helped to provide a steady flow of energy because they took longer to digest than simple carbohydrates.

All of these findings rippled throughout the food industry, causing consumer preference to shift away from meals high in fat toward foods low in fat. Americans reduced their consumption of meat and dairy products as part of a healthier overall diet. Simultaneously, consumers embraced diets with a higher percentage of whole grain foods—including pasta. In fact, the popularity of pasta among athletes led to the term "carbo-loading," which was frequently accomplished through the ingestion of pasta or other grains. The consumption of foods high in complex carbohydrates prior to a marathon or other athletic endurance event was widely believed to boost performance.

In addition to being high in carbohydrates, pasta products became widely recognized for their nutritional value and relatively low levels of fat. A 10-ounce serving of cooked pasta contained 420 calories, 14 grams of protein (although wheat protein was considered incomplete), and only 1 gram of fat. It also provided one-fifth of the iron, niacin, and riboflavin, and one-third of the thiamin, needed for one day.

The general perception of pasta also evolved over the last three decades. In the 1960s, consumers thought of meatballs and spaghetti as a child's meal, too unsophisticated for adults. With the introduction of pasta varieties—lasagna, fettuccini, manicotti, linguine, ravioli, cannelloni, tortellini, and angel hair pasta—the age-old grain food gained acceptance among affluent adults, for both dining out and eating in. Moreover, the typical marinara, or tomato-based, sauce served with ground beef or meatballs gave way to a multitude of flavored toppings—ranging from basil and pine nuts to Alfredo or cream sauces. Another popular accompaniment to the noodle was a mixture of vegetables, often in a marinara sauce, known as "pasta primavera."

As the popularity of pasta grew, so did the market for value-added, or flavored, varieties. At the end of the 1990s, popular flavors included smoked salmon, porcini mushroom, tomato basil, lemon pepper, and chili pepper.

Other factors contributing to pasta's popularity included its convenience, durability, and economy. A box of dried pasta lasted up to seven years on the shelf. It was a relatively good food value, at a cost of about a quarter

per 10-ounce serving. The nationwide availability of prepared sauces added to the ease with which a pasta meal could be prepared. Pasta could be cooked on the stove top in about 10 to 15 minutes. It could be reheated—along with the accompanying sauce—in a microwave oven in half of that time. These factors had significant appeal to the increasing numbers of dual-income and single-parent households in the United States.

Most pasta was served for dinner (approximately 75 percent in the mid-1990s), but the trend went toward more frequent pasta lunches, with a 20-percent increase in consumption at this meal. The most popular shapes were macaroni, which saw a 33-percent increase in consumption, and lasagna, which showed 31-percent growth. Pasta products also dominated the side dish market, with 669 varieties offered in 1995, far exceeding the amount of rice dishes (137), salads (41), potato products (17), and stuffing mixes (14).

Retail sales of dried pasta were $2.3 billion in 1995, a 50 percent increase from 1991. This trend continued through the close of the century.

INDUSTRY LEADERS

Hershey Foods Corporation, a $3 billion company located in Hershey, Pennsylvania, was the largest pasta manufacturer. The company's Pasta Division produced approximately 600 pounds of pasta in 1995 through such brands as Ronzini, Skinner, American Beauty, and Delmonico. In 1999, the company divested itself of New World Pasta, a product line that generated $400 million in sales for 1997, choosing to focus more on its confectionery and grocery products. Hershey Foods made $450 million on the deal.

Minneapolis-based Borden Incorporated's Pasta Division, also manufactured 600 pounds of pasta in 1995, primarily through its Creamette and Prince lines. That same year, Borden Incorporated, which posted sales of $5.9 billion, became a privately owned company when it was purchased by partners of the investment firm Kohlberg, Kravis, Roberts, and Co. In 1998, Borden Foods Inc. generated $706 million in sales and employed 1,800 people.

The America Italian pasta Company (AIPC) had 1999 sales of $220.1 million and employed 562 people. With the leading pasta brand, Muellers, and several other private and branded labels, AIPC was able to control 25 percent of the market. Its major customers included Wal-Mart, Sam's Club, SYSCO, and a number of major food processors and grocery stores.

WORKFORCE

Due to technological advances in the pasta industry, including the use of computers in the manufacturing process, the number of workers declined from the early

1980s to the mid-1990s. About 8,400 people were employed in the manufacture of dry pasta in 1982; by 1997, that figure dropped to 6,300. Production workers accounted for 77 percent of the workforce and earned an average hourly income of $12.36. New Jersey led the country in employment with 662 people, and California was second with 576.

AMERICA AND THE WORLD

Until the 1990s, the United States imported a negligible volume of manufactured pasta. That situation changed drastically as foreign producers moved to take advantage of the expanding U.S. pasta market. U.S. pasta distributors complained about the inferior quality of some pastas from Italy and Turkey, charging that those countries were purposely dumping inferior products on the U.S. market at lower-than-market prices. The outcry prompted the International Trade Commission and the Commerce Department to impose stiff tariffs on the imported products. The targeted importers were expected to appeal the tariffs.

The durum wheat from which pasta was made grew steadily as an export beginning with the 1959-60 growing season. Exports of this wheat variety were zero that year, but climbed to peak annual levels of 80 million bushels during the 1980s. By the 1990s, the United States was exporting 50 percent of its annual production. Algeria was the largest importer of U.S. durum wheat, with Tunisia second. Trade with those countries was part of the Export Enhancement Program, an incentive program to facilitate U.S. exports to North African nations.

As domestic pasta consumption skyrocketed, durum farmers were hard-pressed to meet the demand. In 11 of the 15 years from 1981 to 1996, domestic use of durum for pasta production combined with export sales exceeded domestic production. The shortage of durum wheat drove prices up to $7.50 per bushel, a substantial increase from the $4.50 price of the late 1980s.

After the passage of the Canada/United States Free Trade Agreement (CUSTA), in 1988 U.S. farmers in Minnesota, North Dakota, and Montana voiced concern over the growing volume of Canadian wheat sold in the U.S. By the 1990s, Canadian wheat accounted for 14 percent of U.S. durum production. The situation was exacerbated when U.S. durum wheat fields were hit by Karnal Bunt disease, which reduced the wheat to a powdery soot. Canada banned imports of all U.S. durum and many U.S. producers refused to accept durum from states where infected wheat was reported.

The United States ranked fourth in the world in mean annual per capita pasta consumption. Italians consumed over 59 pounds per capita annually and Venezuelans nearly 28 pounds, while Americans ate 19 pounds apiece annually. With popularity of pasta on the increase due to its perceived convenience and nutritional value, however, per capita consumption in the United States was predicted to surpass that of every nation in the world except Italy by the year 2000.

In 1997, the United States imported 583.7 million pounds, up nearly 11-fold from 1975.

FURTHER READING
"Annual Consumer Expenditures Survey." *Supermarket News,* September 1996.

"The Bunt Bonanza." *Alberta Report/Western Report,* 16 April 1996.

Darnay, Arsen, J., ed. *Manufacturing USA.* 5th ed. Detroit: Gale Research, 1996.

Dornblaser, Lynn. "Pasta Garnishes More Meals." *Prepared Foods,* Mid-April 1996.

"Hershey Foods Announces Agreement to Sell U.S. Pasta Business." Hershey Foods News Release, 15 December 1998.

Hoover's Company Capsules, 20 March 2000. Available from http://www.hoovers.com.

"Industry Statistics," 20 March 2000. Available from http://www.ilovepasta.org.

"Making Tons of Pasta Helps to Form Northland's Economic Foundation." *Kansas City Business Journal,* 1 March 1996.

"Milling & Baking News," 27 October 1998.

Tagliabue, John. "Pasta Makers of the World Unite." *The New York Times,* 28 October 1995.

Turcsik, Richard. "Stiff Tariffs Expected on Imports of Pasta." *Supermarket News,* 7 August 1995.

"The United States-Canada Durum Wheat War." *Choices: The Magazine of Food, Farm & Resource Issues,* 1995.

U.S. Census Bureau. *1997 Economic Census—Manufacturing.* Washington, D.C.: GPO 1999.

"U.S. Food Consumption." *Food Review,* May-August 1995.

SIC 2099

FOOD PREPARATIONS, NOT ELSEWHERE CLASSIFIED

This classification includes establishments primarily engaged in manufacturing food preparations not classified under another category. It includes manufacturers of items such as syrups, leavening agents, dry mixes (for sauces and gravies), packaged mixes (made from pasta, rice, and potatoes), seasonings and spices, and ready-to-eat meals and salads. Also included are manufacturers of miscellaneous food specialties, such as fried Chinese noodles, sorghum, tortillas, honey, marshmallow creme, peanut butter, popcorn, tea, tofu, and vinegar.

Miscellaneous food preparations with separate classifications include: **SIC 2091: Canned and Cured Fish and Seafoods**; **SIC 2092: Fresh or Frozen Prepared Fish and Seafoods**; **SIC 2095: Roasted Coffee**; **SIC 2096: Potato Chips and Similar Snacks**; **SIC 2097: Manufactured Ice**; and **SIC 2098: Macaroni and Spaghetti.** Manufacturers of flour mixes are classified in Industry Group 204.

NAICS CODE(S)

311423 (Dried and Dehydrated Food Manufacturing)
111998 (All Other Miscellaneous Crop Farming)
311340 (Non-Chocolate Confectionery Manufacturing)
311911 (Roasted Nuts and Peanut Butter Manufacturing)
311991 (Perishable Prepared Food Manufacturing)
311830 (Tortilla Manufacturing)
311920 (Coffee and Tea Manufacturing)
311941 (Mayonnaise, Dressing, and Other Prepared Sauce Manufacturing)
311942 (Spice and Extract Manufacturing)
311999 (All Other Miscellaneous Food Manufacturing)

INDUSTRY SNAPSHOT

By 1995, miscellaneous food preparations had grown to a $14 billion industry in current dollars. According to government statistics, the total value of goods shipped by establishments classified in SIC 2099 totaled $14.9 billion in 1996. Value of good shipped was projected to total $17 billion by the year 2000. In addition, some businesses with other classifications manufactured products considered primary to the industry.

In 1995 1,738 establishments comprised the industry represented by SIC 2099; 674 of these establishments employed 20 or more people. Total establishments in the industry were projected at 1,895 for the year 2000, with 675 of these employing 20 or more people. Statewide, California led the industry. According to 1992 census data, the state housed 337 establishments with $1.9 billion in shipments and a total of 12,400 employees.

BACKGROUND AND DEVELOPMENT

Vinegar. One of oldest products classified within SIC 2099 is vinegar. Records of vinegar use date back 5,000 years, and some historians estimate it was known as long ago as 10,000 years. During the Civil War, vinegar was used to prevent scurvy, a disease caused by vitamin C deficiency. Throughout vinegar's long history, it has had a wide variety of applications, including use as a preservative and as a cleaning agent.

Vinegar, derived from two French words meaning "sour wine," is a product of fermentation. When natural sugars ferment they produce alcohol, which after undergoing further acetic fermentation becomes vinegar. One of the best known types is wine vinegar, but throughout history many other types of vinegar have been produced. These include vinegars made from naturally sweet products like molasses, sorghum, honey, and syrup, and vinegars made from fruits, potatoes, and grains.

Four different methods have evolved to control the fermentation process by which vinegars are made. Under the most labor-intensive method, called the solera system, vinegar is aged in different types of wood, a process that can take decades. Another technique, termed the Orleans method, uses a starter culture in a manner similar to the process by which bakers ferment bread dough in sourdough preparation. The Orleans method is implemented to produce vinegar in wooden barrels and takes up to six months. A faster method, termed the "quick process," involves the aeration of wine along with organic materials to produce vinegar in about a week. The quickest vinegar production, however, occurs in a process called continuous production, which requires holding wine in a pressurized tank under carefully controlled conditions. Air is forced through the liquid to aid the fermentation process. Wine is continually added and finished vinegar taken off the top of the tank. Converting wine into vinegar using this process takes approximately one day.

In the United States, the vinegar industry formed alongside the apple industry. As a result, it was concentrated in areas with large harvests of apples. Cider vinegar was made from apples or apple juice. As the U.S. vinegar industry developed, it offered a variety of products to perform different functions. White vinegar, also called distilled vinegar, is primarily used in home canning and for making pickles, salsa, and relishes. Wine vinegar is an integral ingredient in vinaigrettes. Malt vinegar, a mildly sweet product, complements salads and fish and chips. Rice vinegar, a particularly strong variety, is added to sushi rice. A rich, dark product, balsamic vinegar is used for vinaigrettes and as a condiment. Sherry vinegar, another variety with a strong flavor, is a cooking vinegar. In addition to the types of vinegar produced by using varying sources, infused vinegars are made by adding flavorings such as berries, garlic, or herbs.

Tofu. A product with a long history, tofu is a white, gelatinous substance made from soybean curd. It bears a slight resemblance to cream cheese but has a softer texture that has sometimes been described as "squishy." Although tofu by itself is considered bland, when cooked in a recipe it picks up flavors from other ingredients. To make tofu, manufacturers begin by soaking soybeans for 12 to 18 hours. After soaking, the beans are mashed and strained. The retained juice solidifies, is cut into portions, and packaged for sale.

Originating in China approximately 1,000 years ago, tofu was a staple in Oriental cooking for centuries. Tofu began gaining popularity in the United States following World War II when returning servicemen, accustomed to eating it abroad, began eating tofu at home.

Sales of tofu experienced rapid growth in the early 1990s. Because it is a good protein source naturally low in saturated fat, with no cholesterol, its popularity was increasing particularly among vegetarians and health-conscious consumers. Tofu also benefited from a growing interest in ethnic cooking. The tofu expansion could be attributed in part to improvements in packaging technology, giving products a longer shelf life. Most tofu was sold in packages of water and had a short shelf life of only about 10 days. In 1990 one producer, Mori-Nu, reported the development of innovative packaging enabling its product to have a 10-month shelf life without refrigeration.

One of the nation's largest tofu producers, Azumaya, Inc., of San Francisco, began producing tofu in 1927. In 1991 the company reported daily production of 3.5 tons of tofu. Some industry analysts predicted that tofu would become as popular as yogurt.

Tea. Another food product with historic ties to China is tea. Tea was originally made from the dried, processed leaves of an Asian shrub. One of the oldest companies in the U.S. tea industry was founded by Sir Thomas Lipton, a Scotsman, who began importing tea into the United States in 1890. The first instant tea was marketed by the Nestle Beverage Company in 1948.

Sales of tea products experienced growth the United States during the 1990s. According to Information Resources Inc. of Chicago, the sales of loose teas and tea in bags grew 1.0 percent to $640 million; ready-to-drink teas sold in the United States increased 1.8 percent to $421 million in 1995. The market is no longer relegated to a simple hot drink served with lemon and honey; it has married tea—black, green, or herbal—to all sorts of flavor permutations.

Herbal teas in supermarkets passed the $100 million sales mark in 1991. The top three companies in herbal tea sales were Celestial Seasonings, Inc. with 49.1 percent of the market (and with a new line of herbal "remedy" teas in 1995), Lipton with 23.1 percent, and Bigelow with 14.6 percent. In 1992 enough herbal tea was sold in the United States to brew 58 million gallons. Sales represented a 5 percent increase over the previous year. According to a report in *Brandweek,* one of every eight cups of tea consumed in the United States is either decaffeinated or herbal, and approximately 80 percent is consumed as iced tea. In 1993 *Beverage World* estimated that iced tea sales would continue growing at an annual rate of 50 percent.

Product expansions in the tea category, according to *Prepared Foods* are attributable to introductions of green teas and chai. Green teas purportedly provide healing

benefits, which is why numerous companies now provide green tea products, including John Wagner & Sons and AFC. Chai is a rich, milky tea-based drink often used as part of Indian ceremonial meals and tastes of vanilla, honey, and spices. Oregon Chai introduced its chai liquid concentrates to consumers in 1995.

Tea-juice hybrids increased in popularity through 1995, with a great number of product introductions that year—and not only from Snapple. Nestle added numerous products to its Nestea line in 1995, including an instant Lemonade Tea, and Suntea Style mix, and several fruit-flavored beverage mixes. Snapple Cider Tea—a combination of black tea and apple cider that may be served hot or cold—was introduced by The Quaker Oats Company. (Snapple was sold to Triarc Companies in 1997.)

Peanut Butter. One product native to the Americas is peanut butter. While not indigenous to North America, peanuts were grown by South Americans at least 1,000 years ago. Although the circumstances of their introduction to North America is unknown, historians believe peanuts were grown by early European settlers, who used them as food for hogs. George Washington Carver is credited with developing more than 300 uses for peanuts and helping establish them as an important crop. Improvements made between the 1930s and the 1990s helped peanut farmers experience a fivefold increase in per acre yields. During the early 1990s, most U.S. peanut production came from Georgia. Other leading peanut cultivation states were Alabama, Texas, North Carolina, and Virginia.

Approximately half the peanuts eaten in the United States are consumed in the form of peanut butter. *Consumer Reports* calculated that on any given day peanut butter is consumed by one out of every six Americans. Although peanut butter is considered a good source of protein, dietary fiber, and B vitamins, it contains a high percentage of fat. To make peanut butter, manufacturers remove peanut skins and grind the nuts into a thick, pasty substance. Frequently, hydrogenated vegetable oil is added as a stabilizer, and salt and sugar are added to improve flavor. Chunky varieties, containing pieces of peanuts, were also developed.

One of the problems associated with peanut butter is the presence of aflatoxin. Aflatoxin is a carcinogenic poison produced by *aspergillus flavus,* a mold that grows on peanuts when they are not properly stored. Aflatoxin problems first appeared in the 1960s and led U.S. officials to establish limits on the amount of the substance allowable in peanut products. A 1990 *Consumer Reports* study noted that some peanut butter exceeded allowable levels of aflatoxin.

During the early 1990s, the top U.S. peanut butter brands—Jif, Skippy, and Peter Pan—accounted for two-thirds of all peanut butter sales. Specialty and health food stores offered ''natural'' peanut butters that lacked sweeteners and stabilizers and some featured ''grind your own'' peanut butter options.

In 1993 industry watchers noted a decline in peanut butter sales. The drop was attributed to calorie-consciousness. Consumers also turned away from name brands in favor of private labels. According to a September 1993 report in the *Wall Street Journal,* peanut butter sales declined 12.2 percent during the 13-week period ending July 4, 1993. Chunky peanut butter sales fell the most, declining 15.7 percent, while creamy sales dropped 10.9 percent.

Spices. According to the U.S. Department of Agriculture, the average U.S. spice consumption was an estimated 815 million pounds between 1990 and 1994, compared with 541 million for the period between 1980 and 1984. Per capita consumption rose a point from a period a decade ago. Domestic production increased to meet the demand.

Total sales of spices, domestic and imported, in the United States were about $2 billion in 1994, double that of a decade ago, and compared to sales of between $400 and 450 million in the mid-1970s. Dehydrated garlic and onions accounted for about two-thirds of national spice production in 1994, with cayenne or red peppers representing an estimated 30 percent, and then mustard seed and various herbs account for the balance.

Sales are anticipated to continue unabated. ''If the current rate of per capita consumption continues and the U.S. population reaches the forecasted 274.8 million by the year 2000,'' predicted analysts Peter J. Buzzanell and Kathryn L. Lipton, ''total domestic use of spices would increase 8 percent from 1990-94 to an estimated 877 million pounds. But all indications are that the growth likely will be even higher. The trend toward less salt in foods will likely continue to stimulate more spice use to compensate for flavor loss.''

An estimated 60 percent of spices sold in the United States are to add flavor to the food processing and food service industries. Population growth (particularly census figures noting increased Asian and Hispanic populations), increased popularity of ethnic foods and prepared meals, and increased consumption of food outside the home can be attributed to the continued growth in spice sales. Major spice users include fast-food outlets such as Kentucky Fried Chicken and McDonald's, which not only spice their foods, but provide prepackaged condiments to customers.

CURRENT CONDITIONS

Initiatives within the food industry affected SIC 2099 during the late 1990s. The President's Council on

Food Safety was established in August 1998 in order to review the results of a national study (by the National Academy of Sciences) of the federal food safety structure. The study had concluded that food safety decision should be based mainly on scientific premises, and that Congress should establish unified cohesion among food safety programs. The vice president of the Grocery Managers of America (GMA) noted that the study was a step in the right direction, and advocated efficient use of resources to respond to priority food safety problems. At the same time, the GMA warned against creating an immense government bureaucracy that would deal with food safety issues. GMA represented more than 2.5 million workers with sales of over $450 billion. A spokesperson from the National Food Processors Association (NFPA) echoed the sentiments of the GMA, but expressed the additional concern that the report focused too much on the potential enforcement authority of the government rather than making use of effective safety enforcement already in place in the industry.

Smaller trends within the industry were indicative of larger societal impetus. A rising interest in health among consumers continued during the 1990s. Several companies in the food industry pioneered nutraceutical foods, or products with a health benefit. Industry companies that patented nutraceutical products during 1998 included Kellogg's (seven patents) and Nabisco (one patent).

INDUSTRY LEADERS

A leader within the tea segment of SIC 2099 is the Thomas J. Lipton Company, a wholly owned subsidiary of Unilever PLC. Lipton, headquartered in Englewood Cliffs, New Jersey, reported sales of $3 billion in fiscal 1996. This represented a substantial increase over the $1.4 billion in sales posted in 1992, which was a 4.3 percent increase over 1991 sales. According to one report, Lipton controlled about half of the black tea market, estimated at $423 million in 1992.

Lipton, a pioneer in the development of naturally decaffeinated teas, was founded in 1915 by Sir Thomas Lipton, who had been selling his teas in the United States since 1890. In 1992 Lipton reported that its Suffolk, Virginia, production facility blended more than 36 million pounds of tea. Lipton's tea products include tea bags, instant iced tea, and ready-to-drink iced tea. In 1991 the company established the Pepsi Lipton Tea Partnership, a venture undertaken to bring together expertise from Lipton's tea producers and Pepsi's bottling and distribution system. In addition to tea products, Lipton also marketed Lipton Soup Mixes, Recipe Secrets, Lipton Side Dishes, and Cup-a-Soup. The company's Lawry's division offered spice and seasoning blends, sauces, and Mexican food products.

Another major participant in this market segment was Nestle USA, Inc., which had 15 food and beverage companies. Products of the Nestle Beverage Company include Nestea, Carnation hot cocoa, and Nestle Quick, while the Nestle Refrigerated Food Company produces Contadina refrigerated pizza kits and sauces. Other major Nestle divisions include Nestle Food Company, Nestle Frozen Food Company, and Nestle Brands Foodservice. In 1992 the Nestle organization reported net sales of $7 billion and a staff of 43,000. Nestle USA Inc., which is the segment of the corporation that manufactures products including chocolate, frozen dinners under the Stouffer's brand, ice cream and chocolate milk, posted sales in excess of $3.5 billion in 1994.

At the helm of the spice segment within this industry classification is McCormick & Company, Inc., founded in 1889 and—according to company literature—the largest spice company in the world. Its product line, sold in the United States on the East Coast under the McCormick label and on the West Coast under the Schilling label, features a wide variety of spices from 18 areas around the world. The company's other primary business involves plastic bottle and tube manufacturing.

McCormick/Schilling had a 45 percent share in the U.S. retail spice market in 1999. McCormick's industrial and food service divisions provide flavors, seasonings, and specialty food products to more than 80 of the top 100 food manufacturers in the United States as well as to many major restaurant chains. In addition to the United States, McCormick sold products globally; in 1993 the company announced intentions to develop markets in China and the Pacific Rim. In the retail spice market, Burns Philip held the second largest market share during 1999 at 12 percent.

Universal Foods Corporation, a major producer in several of this industry's segments, is an international company involved in manufacturing and marketing a wide variety of food products, including flavors and colors, dehydrated vegetables, frozen french fried potatoes, and yeast products. The company posted sales of $806.4 million in 1996. The company's yeast products are marketed under the Red Star label.

Red Star yeast production began during the latter part of the 1800s. In the 1920s the company perfected an aeration process that enabled it to make an improved compressed yeast product. Further work led to the development of a less perishable yeast. In the early 1990s Universal Foods claimed it was the largest and most diversified manufacturer and distributor of yeast products within the United States. Red Star reported sales of $160.0 million in 1995.

In 1993 Universal Foods reported a 7 percent increase in yeast revenue, a significant portion of which

was attributable to trends within the pizza industry toward producing extra large pizzas. Within the consumer baking market, a rise in yeast sales was attributed to the growing popularity of bread machines. According to company statistics, U.S. households owned an estimated three million bread machines in 1993.

During the late 1990s, general industry leaders included SUPERVALU Inc., with 1999 sales of $17.4 billion; Kraft Foods Inc. with 1998 sales of $17.3 billion; RJR Nabisco Corp. with 1998 sales of $17 billion; American Home Products Corporation with 1998 sales of $13.4 billion; and Abbott Laboratories with 1999 sales of $13.1 billion. Kellogg Company and General Mills, Inc. are among the other leading companies in this industry segment whose brand names are immediately recognizable to American consumers; these companies followed closely behind industry leaders in annual sales amounts. In 1998 Kellogg had sales of $6.76 billion and General Mills had sales of $6.24 billion.

Kellogg maintained its philanthropic visibility in the industry after the Y2K crisis at the turn of the millennium failed to materialize. The company partnered with America's Second Harvest (a hunger relief organization) to sponsor a month long food drive beginning in mid January 2000. The drive encouraged people to donate unused stockpiled Y2K food for the hungry or underprivileged. Kellogg had participated in initiatives to fight hunger for over 20 years. In 1999 the company donated 19 million pounds of food to the food bank of America's Second harvest. The company included the W. K. Kellogg Foundation, one of the largest private charities in the world. Kellogg had sales in over 160 worldwide countries during the late 1990s.

Nabisco, another industry leader, changed its name from RJR Nabisco Holdings in order to distance itself from its increasingly unpopular tobacco products. The offshoot company (R.J. Reynolds Tobacco) faced lawsuits from all 50 states at the end of the 1990s. Nabisco Company remained possibly liable for tobacco-related lawsuits, even after splitting from R.J. Reynolds.

WORKFORCE

According to the U.S. Department of Commerce, industry employment totaled 57,900 in 1987. The industry's combined payroll topped $1.1 billion. The leading states in employment were California, Illinois, New York, and Texas. By 1996 the leading states that employed people in the industry were California, Illinois, Texas, and New York, respectively. In the broader industry classification that includes SIC 2099 (SIC 209, Miscellaneous Foods), the majority of employees (10.6 percent) worked as hand packers and packagers, followed closely (at 9.3 percent) by cannery workers. In 1996 the average establishment in the industry totaled 49 employees, maintained a payroll of $1,574,035, and paid $12.68 per hour.

FURTHER READING

"America's Second Harvest and Kellogg's Announce National Millennium Food Drive: 'Y Go 2 Waste,'" 3 January 2000. Available from http://www.prnewswire.com.

"Background on Thomas J. Lipton Company." Englewood Cliffs, NJ: Thomas J. Lipton Co., 1996.

Buzzanell, Peter J.; Lipton, Kathryn L. "Whether a Pinch or a Dash, It Adds up to a Growing U.S. Spice Market." *Food Review,* September-December 1995.

Dornblaser, Lynn. "Adult Drinks Lead the Beverage Pack." *Prepared Foods,* 15 April 1996.

"Estimated Retail Pasta Consumption." National Pasta Association, 1996.

"GMA: Food Safety Report Shows Need for Better Coordination, Planning: But No Reason Shown to Create Single Food Safety Bureaucracy," 15 March 1999. Available from http://www.prnewswire.com.

"Largest Spice Makers, 1999." *Investext* Thompson Financial Services, 5 January 1999.

Meeting the Growing Demand for Diversified Yeast Products. Milwaukee: Universal Foods, 1996.

"Nutraceutical Pioneers A Among Food Companies." *Food Processing,* May 1998.

"President's Council on Food Safety Outlines Bold Strategic Plan," 19 January 1999. Available from http://www.prnewswire.com.

TOBACCO PRODUCTS

CIGARETTES

This category covers establishments primarily engaged in manufacturing cigarettes from tobacco or other materials.

NAICS CODE(S)

312221 (Cigarette Manufacturing)

INDUSTRY SNAPSHOT

Battered by multibillion-dollar lawsuits and anti-smoking campaigns, the U.S. tobacco industry confronts a shrinking yet resilient market at home and widening demand abroad. In 1999 U.S. cigarette shipments fell 9-10 percent as tax-induced price hikes and antismoking sentiment cut into demand. Price increases, however, have helped prop up sales and profits. Nonetheless, financial markets, originally encouraged by the industry's large government settlements, lost confidence in 1999 and caused tobacco stocks to tumble by as much as 60 percent.

Tobacco companies have been so besieged with lawsuits that investment reports on the industry, normally flush with statistics and commentary on short-term profits, have found it necessary to delve into arguments, proceedings, and other minutia of individual cases at trial. The biggest legal initiative, brought collectively by the attorneys general of 46 states, resulted in a massive 25-year, $206-billion settlement by cigarette manufacturers. Hundreds of other lawsuits, most from private individuals, have inundated tobacco companies as well, but few have gone to trial. Meanwhile, lawyers on the cases were collectively taking in hundreds of millions of dollars a year—and will continue to do so for decades to come.

The industry remains highly concentrated. The top three cigarette makers—Philip Morris, R.J. Reynolds, and Brown & Williamson—controlled about 87 percent of the U.S. market as of 1999. Indeed, Census Bureau reports show that only nine cigarette companies operate in the United States. Market share evidence suggests that the larger producers, especially Philip Morris, which alone makes up half of all U.S. production, could continue to crowd out smaller producers.

ORGANIZATION AND STRUCTURE

From the industry's nascence in the mid-nineteenth century, when many cigarette manufacturers began as tobacco farmers, to the 1990s, the number of participants has been limited. Early cigarette producers were located in proximity to the tobacco fields of the southern United States, typically operating in the same region as their competition. Nearly a century and a half later, the cigarette industry still consisted of a small, almost fraternal group of manufacturers, several of whom had been in competition with one another since the nineteenth century.

Cigarette manufacturers are still clustered in just a few southeastern states. Production of cigarettes is confined to the four-state region of North Carolina, Virginia, Georgia, and Kentucky. The bulk of these manufacturing facilities are located in North Carolina.

BACKGROUND AND DEVELOPMENT

The origins of tobacco in the United States date back to before the formation of the nation itself, and the growth and sale of this product represented one of the key agricultural crops that spurred the country's growth in the eighteenth and nineteenth centuries. The use of tobacco to produce cigarettes in any widespread fashion did not occur, however, until the dawn of the twentieth century. Other uses for tobacco precluded the popularity of cigarettes, as Americans in the early nineteenth century enjoyed plug and twist tobacco, then smoking tobacco, and finally cigars, all of which overshadowed cigarette production in terms of volume for most of the century. Even in the mid-1800s, the use of tobacco had its detractors, and cigarette smokers, many of whom were women, suffered from a somewhat ignoble image. As a social commentator in 1854 wrote in reference to New York: "Some of the *ladies* of this refined and fashion-forming metropolis are aping the silly ways of some pseudo-accomplished foreigners in smoking Tobacco through a weaker and more *feminine* article which has been most delicately denominated *cigarette*."

A decade later, however, the production volume of cigarettes had increased enough to become the object of special federal taxation, which, according to the Internal Revenue Law promulgated in June 1864, levied one dollar per one hundred packages not exceeding five dollars in aggregate value. The following year, 19.7 million cigarettes were produced, and manufacturers were buffeted by a series of tax hikes, first to two dollars per thousand and then to five dollars per thousand. This arrested the growth of the industry just as sales were beginning to elevate cigarette manufacturers' importance in the tobacco industry. In 1868 tax rates were cut back to $1.50 per thousand and growth resumed, marking the beginning of 20-year period that would witness the most rapid percentage growth rate in the production of cigarettes in the history of the industry.

Cigarette production reached 500 million in 1880 and eclipsed the one billion mark five years later. By the 1880s, there were five principal manufacturers of cigarettes: Washington Duke Sons & Co., Allen & Ginter, Kinney Tobacco Co., William S. Kimball & Co., and Goodwin & Co. Together these companies produced 2.18 billion cigarettes annually by the end of the decade, 91.7 percent of the national output of 2.41 billion. These companies, referred to as the "Tobacco Trust," essentially controlled the cigarette market, enjoying a virtually unassailable lead over other, smaller manufacturers. This monopolistic trait would characterize the industry throughout much of its existence.

The ability of these companies to secure such a wide advantage over their competition was partly due to significant technological innovations achieved during the 1880s that ended the time-consuming chore of rolling cigarettes by hand. On a good day, a skilled laborer could roll 3,000 cigarettes during a ten-hour workday—a production rate that threatened to place a ceiling on the industry's growth. But beginning in 1872, the age of mechanization in the cigarette industry was initiated. The first cigarette manufacturing machine, patented by Albert H. Hook, earned a modicum of success, but did not prove to be commercially viable. By 1881, however, significant

improvements had been made in a design patented by James A. Bonsack. This machine could churn out 200 to 220 cigarettes per minute, accomplishing in 15 minutes what it took an experienced production worker ten hours to complete.

Bolstered by the ability to produce more cigarettes with lower labor costs, the five companies that occupied the industry's leading positions grew quickly by moving into untapped markets and securing their overwhelming lead in the U.S. market. In 1890 the composition of the industry's manufacturers became more homogeneous when the five leading companies, at the urging of James Duke of Washington Duke & Sons Co., merged to form the American Tobacco Co., which initially focused primarily on the production of cigarettes. Over the next 20 years, the American Tobacco Co. acquired an interest in roughly 250 companies. This cigarette giant expanded into other tobacco products, securing commanding leads in every product branch of the tobacco industry with the exception of cigars. In the manufacture of cigarettes, plug, smoking tobacco, fine cut tobacco, snuff, and little cigars, the conglomerate's production output in the first decade of the twentieth century represented no less than 76 percent of the country's total volume, giving smaller manufacturers little hope of wresting market share away from the industry's predominant leader.

If the five leading manufacturers in the 1880s justly earned the moniker "Tobacco Trust" when operating as separate companies, then their union certainly deserved the same label. The U.S. Supreme Court said as much in May 1911, when it found the American Tobacco Co. in violation of the Sherman Act. Six months after the ruling, the court issued a decree stipulating that the enormously powerful tobacco company be divided into 16 independent corporations, none of which could wield monopolistic control over any one product branch within the tobacco industry.

Post-Breakup Growth. Although certainly a significant chapter in the history of the cigarette industry, the parceling of the American Tobacco Co.'s sundry divisions and subsidiaries did not affect the cigarette industry as greatly as the cigar industry, primarily because cigarettes still did not represent a major branch of the tobacco industry. The cigarette industry was burgeoning, however, and stood on the brink of catapulting past all other branches of the tobacco industry. The first step toward this end came six years after the restructuring of the industry, when the United States entered World War I and cigarettes were issued to soldiers in the U.S. Army and Navy.

Once the habit of smoking cigarettes had extended to women, thereby doubling the potential customer base, sales began to mushroom, and the cigarette branch of the industry at last overtook all other branches. Over the ensuing 20 years, during which time many of the widely popular brands—Chesterfield, Lucky Strike, Old Gold, Camel, Raleigh, and Marlboro—emerged, the consumption of cigarettes grew rapidly. Domestic tobacco leaf consumption increased 42.5 percent between 1910 and 1930, while the production of cigarettes increased from 8.64 billion to 125.20 billion, a 1,339 percent increase. In these first two decades following the dissolution decree, there were approximately 15 to 20 manufacturers deriving the bulk of their revenue from the production of cigarettes. Only four of these manufacturers, commonly referred to as the "Big Four," held any appreciable share of the market. Indeed, these manufacturers—the restructured American Tobacco Co., R.J. Reynolds Tobacco Co., P. Lorillard Co., and Liggett & Meyers Tobacco Co.—held as firm a grip on the U.S. cigarette market as American Tobacco had before the U.S. Supreme Court's ruling; they controlled more than 95 percent of the market.

Clearly, the dissolution of American Tobacco had not produced the U.S. Supreme Court's intended effects; a monarchy had merely been replaced with an oligarchy. Smaller, independent cigarette manufacturers were able to record enviable profits during this period, largely because of the bountiful market itself, but none could challenge the "Big Four" in magnitude. Accordingly, as the cigarette industry continued to grow, these powerful manufacturers became more formidable, further widening the gulf separating the industry's upper echelon and the rest of the competition.

The next two decades of business brought continued success to the industry's four largest manufacturers and witnessed the rise of an additional member to the industry's elite, Philip Morris & Company Ltd., Inc. Philip Morris introduced its mainstay Marlboro brand in 1925, which reached an annual production total of approximately 500 million cigarettes. But the industry's leading brands during these years, Camel and Lucky Strike, each sold 25 billion cigarettes a year, by far outpacing Philip Morris's production volume and providing little room for the future ascension of the smaller, formerly British-based manufacturer. Instead, Philip Morris was able to climb the industry's ranking list due to a strong relationship with cigarette jobbers throughout its distribution network and by virtue of prudent management. By the end of the 1940s, after Philip Morris had already unseated Lorillard to occupy the industry's fourth place position, the "Tobacco Trust" now included five members, generating an aggregate sales total of $357.3 million.

Postwar Unease. The 1950s heralded a new era for cigarette manufacturers, one in which it became necessary to defend growing criticism of the product being sold. Since the industry's emergence, anti-cigarette and anti-tobacco factions from both the federal and consumer

sector had railed against the sale and use of tobacco. Manufacturers had fared fairly well, effectively beating back the rising tide of protest against their business. While industry manufacturers had suffered run-ins with the Federal Trade Commission (FTC) concerning misleading advertising, the federal government had subsidized a large portion of the industry before World War II, which helped to allay the fears of manufacturers.

During the 1950s, however, medical reports linking health problems to smoking began to surface. In 1953 the Sloan-Kettering Cancer Institute's report showed a relationship between cancer and tobacco, and manufacturers consequently found themselves fighting against an entirely new and much more formidable foe—scientific evidence.

In 1964 the U.S. Surgeon General issued a landmark report linking smoking with lung cancer and heart disease. A year later, the U.S. Congress promulgated the Cigarette Advertising and Labeling Act, which stipulated that health warnings be placed on each cigarette package. In 1971 cigarette advertisements on radio and television were banned. Although these announcements and restrictions did not cause the industry to collapse, the rate of smoking in the United States began to spiral downward.

Cigarette manufacturers had already begun creating different types of cigarettes—filter tips during the 1950s, then low-tar cigarettes during the 1960s and 1970s—and marketed these products not to create more customers, but to capture their competitor's customers. By the 1970s, however, Philip Morris and R.J. Reynolds had gained considerable ground on their competition, making the industry essentially a battle between the two behemoths. Philip Morris gained the upper hand in 1976 when its Marlboro brand passed R.J. Reynolds' Winston.

During the 1980s, lower-priced, discount cigarettes began to enter the market with increasing frequency. This enabled smaller cigarette manufacturers to thrive for a short time, until the industry's preeminent leaders dropped their own prices and set about capturing the low-end market. By this time, the reams of medical reports delineating the hazardous effects of smoking had firmly grabbed the attention of the American populace, transforming anti-tobacco factions into a powerful nationwide movement. Cigarette taxation doubled in 1983 and continued to rise, particularly during the late 1980s, increasing the popularity of lower-priced cigarettes. Consequently, cigarette manufacturers diversified their operations with unprecedented fervor, while casting an eye to international business opportunities.

Decade of Legal Skirmishes. As the U.S. economy recovered from recession in the early 1990s, cigarette makers were saddled with much larger problems. These difficulties had always confronted the industry, but they intensified in the early and mid-1990s.

In June 1992 the Supreme Court reversed an appeals court ruling concerning the product liability of cigarette manufacturers. Earlier, two lower courts had ruled that the family of a woman who had died of lung cancer could not sue cigarette manufacturers on the grounds they had withheld information about potential health dangers. The Court's reversal sent cigarette manufacturers' stock prices cascading downward, as industry participants braced for a rash of lawsuits.

Around the same period, cigarette manufacturers suffered diminishing influence over federal lawmakers. In the past, through the combined efforts of the tobacco lobby and elected representatives from tobacco-growing states, manufacturers had been able to slow the rate of federally imposed cigarette taxes and to mitigate federal legislation aimed at curbing cigarette use. Tobacco companies' diminished clout left them ever more vulnerable to legal attacks.

Restrictions on smoking in public areas grew increasingly common as well. This was in part a result of a 1993 Environmental Protection Agency (EPA) report that classified environmental tobacco smoke as a class-A carcinogen and alleged that 3,000 nonsmokers die annually from second-hand smoke. Many communities instituted strict rules regarding cigarette use, and even the U.S. Department of Defense issued restrictions that banned smoking in all military work spaces, including military bases. Businesses, too, banned smoking in response to state laws and public outcry.

Another threat to the cigarette industry was repeated attempts at regulatory oversight under the Clinton administration, particularly the zealous efforts of Commissioner David Kessler, head of the Food and Drug Administration (FDA). In a campaign that was part politics and part science, Kessler testified before Congress that he believed nicotine was a highly addictive drug being manipulated by tobacco companies. He argued that if tobacco functioned as a drug, it should be regulated as one, too, pleading the case for FDA jurisdiction over tobacco products. Ultimately this controversial assertion was heard in 1999 before the Supreme Court, and the Court decided in March 2000 that tobacco does not fall under the FDA's purview as defined by Congress.

In the meantime, a flood of lawsuits deluged tobacco companies. Emanating from the Supreme Court's 1992 ruling, the suits were brought by individuals and groups who sought damages from cigarette manufacturers for smoking-related illnesses and by government agencies that wished to recover the costs to the public health system for treating such ailments. In total, according to one report, more than 800 individual and class-action suits were brought against tobacco companies between 1990 and mid-1998. However, only a handful made it to trial, and even fewer produced verdicts against the industry.

Government Settlements. In early 1997 the anti-tobacco forces gained new ground. They successfully split the tobacco companies' united front by pressuring the Liggett Company to settle a class-action lawsuit. Liggett's move was not entirely unexpected—with only a 2 percent share of the U.S. market, the company lacked the resources to fight an extended court battle. Liggett broke with long-established industry policy and admitted that cigarettes cause cancer and that nicotine is addictive.

By 1997 tobacco companies were in extended negotiations with state attorneys general and began to test the waters for a large national settlement that would spare the industry some or all of the seemingly endless litigation before it. In a mammoth $370-billion proposal, the companies even contemplated submitting to limited FDA regulation as well as significant measures to curb underage smoking. In return, they hoped to gain at least partial immunity from the barrage of litigation coming at them.

Some attorneys general were receptive, but the focus shifted to Congress and a plan to pass the settlement and immunity framework as federal law rather than as agreements approved separately by each state. In Washington, however, the settlement became mired in politics and competing proposals. A number of lawmakers called for a steeper payout, as much as $500 billion, and debated the merits and legality of the proposed immunity. Meanwhile, the Clinton administration, deeply divided over the matter, was slow to weigh in on what terms it would support.

In March 1998 Senate leaders tried to revive the federal tobacco settlement with a bipartisan bill negotiated by Senator John McCain. Tougher on the industry than the companies' own proposal, the bill was supported by President Clinton and a diverse mix of senators. The legislation was to include annual liability caps for punitive damages paid by tobacco companies. However, after weeks of bruising debate and a fistful of conflicting amendments put forth, in June the Republican leadership withdrew its support for the bill and it never went before the full Senate. The House failed to produce anything even close to being viable, and the federal initiative lost nearly all of its steam.

Meanwhile, state attorneys general renewed their attack, aided in some states by specially crafted laws that made it easier for them to prove their cases and collect damages. Settlement talks also restarted in June after the McCain bill died. The companies appeared more hesitant now, and some may have sensed rising political clout with Congress' failure to act. But the attorneys general, led by Washington Attorney General Christine Gregoire, pressed ahead with negotiations, attempting to unite their conflicting demands and reach a consensus the industry was likely to accept.

In November 1998 both sides finally reached an agreement. Ultimately 46 states and the country's five largest cigarette makers were party to a deal that would pay states $206 billion over 25 years, funded by new cigarette taxes. What's more, the settlement was somewhat more lenient on tobacco companies than the defunct 1997 proposal. It required less money for the states, fewer restrictions on marketing and advertising, and no stipulation that the industry be regulated by the FDA. The remaining four states, Florida, Minnesota, Mississippi, and Texas, had previously obtained settlements worth $40 billion.

Just as government litigation seemed to be winding down, however, the Clinton Justice Department in 1999 announced its intentions to sue tobacco companies on similar grounds to the state suits. Preliminary hearings on the federal suit began in 2000. Separately, in 2000 a pair of cigarette wholesalers filed suit in federal court accusing major cigarette makers of price fixing.

CURRENT CONDITIONS

Rising tobacco taxes and widening antismoking policies have resulted in a diminished U.S. market for cigarettes. The industry raised cigarette prices by 45 cents in 1998 and by another 22 cents in 1999 in order to finance the state settlements. In 1999 U.S. tobacco companies shipped 419.3 billion cigarettes, a 9 percent drop from a year earlier and 13.5 percent below 1997's 485 billion. Totaling about 76 packs of cigarettes for every person in the United States, industry shipments in 1999 were valued at $52 billion. In 2000 between 45 million and 50 million U.S. adults were smokers, equal to an adult smoking rate of about 23 percent.

Market Share. Philip Morris continues to lead the industry by a huge margin. In 1999 it supplied 49.6 percent of all U.S. cigarette shipments. This was up slightly from the year before in part because Philip Morris acquired three minor brands from Liggett. The company's market-leading Marlboro brand alone represented 36.4 percent of shipments. R.J. Reynolds is second, with a 23.2 percent share in 1999, followed by Brown & Williamson (13.5 percent), Lorillard (9.3 percent), and Liggett (1.2 percent).

Purchase Trends. Although discount cigarettes had for years eroded market share of the premium brands, in the late 1990s premium labels regained ground. As of 1999, premium brands accounted for 73.4 percent of all domestic cigarette sales by volume, up slightly from the year before. Earlier in the decade, premium volume had sunk as low as 68.6 percent due to the popularity of discount

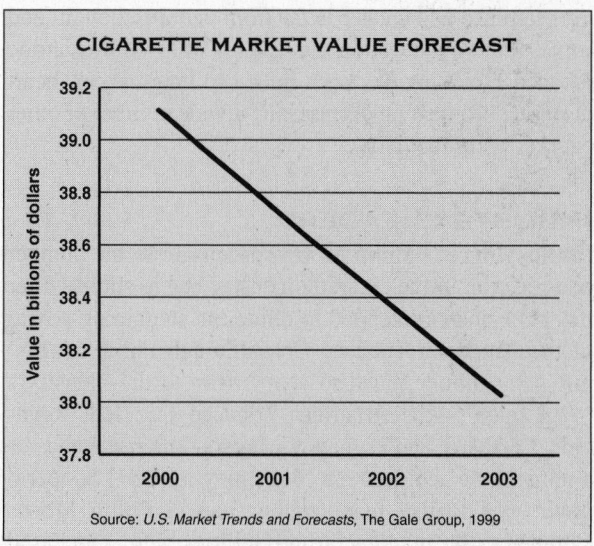

CIGARETTE MARKET VALUE FORECAST

Value in billions of dollars

Source: *U.S. Market Trends and Forecasts,* The Gale Group, 1999

brands, which gained favor rapidly during the 1980s. Interestingly, premium's share rebounded just as tax increases and litigation caused cigarette prices to soar.

In another surprising trend, as cigarette prices rise, according to some research, smokers tend to consume fewer but stronger cigarettes. With young smokers, this pattern can actually increase a smoker's intake of tar and nicotine.

Other ways of mitigating tobacco taxes—some with questionable legality—have also gained attention. E-commerce has emerged as one way to beat high state taxes. When the tobacco store is based in a low-tax state or on a Native American reservation, shoppers anywhere in the country can purchase cigarettes over the Internet with little or no tax added. In high-tax states the savings could add up to more than 40 percent off local prices. However, in some states cigarette buyers are required to report their purchases from out-of-state sources and pay tax accordingly. Another cost-cutting strategy on the rise is to import cigarettes that were previously exported for foreign sale. Known as gray marketing, and often considered illegal, this practice doesn't circumvent all taxes but provides cigarettes at significant mark-down compared to normal domestic prices.

New Products. The industry regularly develops new products, many targeted at special niches of the cigarette market. One area under active development by several companies has been cigarettes made from low-nitrosamine tobacco. By altering the tobacco-curing process, manufacturers are able to reduce or even eliminate nitrosamines, chemicals that some scientists have identified as a key carcinogen in tobacco products. Low-nitrosamine tobacco could be used in a special line of products for health-conscious smokers or could one day become the standard in all cigarettes. Test marketing of a few products was expected to begin in 2000. The link between nitrosamines and cancer is far from certain, though, and some observers question the benefits of low-nitrosamine tobacco. Smoking has been linked to lung cancer, heart disease, chronic lung disease, and a wide number of other cancers and disorders.

INDUSTRY LEADERS

Philip Morris. Philip Morris' ascension to the number one position in the cigarette industry began shortly after the 1911 decree intended to dilute the staggering power of the American Tobacco Co. Although Philip Morris' initial magnitude paled in comparison to the industry's ''Big Four''—the American Tobacco Co., R.J. Reynolds, Lorillard, and Liggett & Meyers—its rise stands as a remarkable achievement. Beginning as the U.S. operations of a British manufacturer named Philip Morris Company, the manufacturing facilities were purchased by U.S. financier George J. Whelan, who acquired several of the small manufacturing concerns left for sale after the break up of American Tobacco. Formed as a U.S. company in 1919 and renamed Philip Morris & Company Ltd., Inc., the company introduced the brand of cigarette that would eventually catapult the fledgling manufacturing concern toward the top of its market in 1925. That brand, Marlboro, did not begin its meteoric rise until the ubiquitous Marlboro Man, the rough-hewn American cowboy, first appeared on cigarette packages in 1955. In the interim, Philip Morris slowly climbed the industry's ladder through effective marketing and a strong relationship with cigarette jobbers on the East Coast, ensuring that the company's products received preferential treatment during the all-important journey from manufacturing site to retail stores.

By 1936, Philip Morris maintained a firm grip on the industry's fourth position through its widely popular English Blend cigarettes introduced three years earlier. Following World War II, several poor management decisions, including an overestimation of the nation's consumption capacity and a belated entry into the filter segment of the industry sent the company's sales spiraling downward. By 1960, Philip Morris had fallen to sixth place in the U.S. cigarette market—last among the major U.S. manufacturers.

The introduction of the Marlboro Man in 1955, however, strengthened Philip Morris' domestic sales, while an early move into foreign markets underpinned the company's domestic resurgence. By 1973, Marlboro cigarettes were the second most popular brand in the United States, ranking only behind RJR's Winston brand. Three years later, Marlboro eclipsed Winston, and Philip Morris became the second-largest seller of tobacco in the world. As Marlboro became the nation's preferred cigarette, Philip Morris branched into the production of low-tar cigarettes with its Merit brand, then intensified its efforts

toward overseas expansion. As a result of these two marketing strategies, plus the growing popularity of Marlboro cigarettes, Philip Morris surpassed RJR in 1983 to become the world's largest cigarette manufacturer. In the 1990s the company consolidated its lead, with market share just shy of 50 percent by 1999 and plans to capture a half point a year thereafter.

R.J. Reynolds. Incorporated in 1879 as R.J. Reynolds Tobacco Company, RJR garnered initial success through the efforts of the company's founder, Richard Joshua Reynolds, and by virtue of its association with the American Tobacco Co. during the lucrative ''trust years'' in the tobacco industry. Operating as a subsidiary of American Tobacco from 1899 until the dissolution decree of 1911, Reynolds' company thrived, earning a majority of its profits through the sale of chewing and smoking tobacco under the respective Schnapps and Prince Albert brands. The company did not manufacture cigarettes until 1913—shortly after Reynolds had resumed control of the company following the U.S. Supreme Court's ruling—but once it did, the company's success came quickly with its widely popular Camel brand of cigarettes.

For the next 20 years, the company's success was primarily predicated on the popularity of Camel cigarettes, but by the late 1930s and throughout the 1940s, the company's exponential growth began to slow due to labor problems, antitrust suits, and one particular product flop, Cavalier cigarettes. By the 1950s, however, R.J. Reynolds began to effect a turnaround by selling its new filter tip brand of cigarettes, Winston, which first appeared in 1954. Two years later, the company introduced its Salem brand, the industry's first king-size filter-tipped menthol cigarette. This, combined with the continuing success of the Camel and Winston brands, elevated the company's standing in the market above all others.

When Philip Morris' Marlboro surpassed Winston in 1976, the company countered with the introduction of a ''back-to-nature'' brand of cigarettes called Real, but the effort failed miserably and the product was discontinued in 1980. In that same year, the company's management sought to ameliorate its position by expanding overseas, leading to an agreement with China to manufacture and sell cigarettes there, the first U.S. company to reach an accord with that country.

However, this historic move abroad was not enough to stop the company's slide to the industry's number two position three years later, when Philip Morris ascended to the industry's number one position. In 1985, to stave off further losses, R.J. Reynolds purchased Nabisco Brands, Inc. for $4.9 billion (the same year in which Philip Morris acquired General Foods Corporation). Three years after the Nabisco purchase, Kohlberg Kravis Roberts & Co., an investment firm, purchased RJR Nabisco for $24.88

billion in what was then the biggest leveraged buyout in U.S. history.

Though heralded as a success in its first years, tensions between its food and tobacco businesses dogged RJR Nabisco throughout the 1990s. Investors clamored for the company to issue a separate stock for the tobacco business, hoping to avoid the volatility and risks associated with the tobacco litigation. In 1999 R.J. Reynolds sold its international tobacco unit to Japan Tobacco and was spun off as a separate company. The reorganized R.J. Reynolds Tobacco Company, owned by a holding company called R.J. Reynolds Tobacco Holdings, Inc., competes only in the United States.

AMERICA AND THE WORLD

As legislation, litigation, and other anti-smoking initiatives have dampened the cigarette business at home, U.S. tobacco companies have made aggressive overtures to foreign markets. Despite its attacks on domestic tobacco, the U.S. government has lent considerable support to U.S. tobacco interests abroad, prompting some comparisons to the narcotics trade U.S. officials have chided other nations about. Philip Morris, through its Philip Morris International unit, has been perhaps the most ardent expansionist among U.S. companies. This was particularly the case after RJR sold its international operations in 1999. That year Philip Morris International shipped 667.9 billion units, or about one-seventh of global non-U.S. production.

Nonetheless, U.S. cigarette makers must surmount a variety of obstacles in foreign markets. They contend with government-licensed monopolies, different tastes, and in some cases, more established competitors. Increasingly they also face the same health concerns and activism that has saddled their U.S. operations. Finally, although faster growth has been common in international markets, economic slowdowns and turmoil in areas like Asia, Russia, and South America doused market growth in the late 1990s, highlighting the risks of international expansion.

Only one major U.S. tobacco concern, Brown & Williamson, is held by a non-U.S. company. Its parent, British American Tobacco plc, commonly known as B.A.T., is based in the United Kingdom.

FURTHER READING

"All the Tar and None of the Taxes." *Business Week,* 13 December 1999.

Centers for Disease Control and Prevention. "Targeting Tobacco Use." *Tobacco Information and Prevention Source.* Washington, 1999. Available from www.cdc.gov/tobacco.

"Cigarettes with Low-Nitrosamine Tobacco an Exciting Prospect." *World Tobacco,* May 1999.

Curriden, Mark. "Despite Settlements, Tobacco Industry Still Battles Individual Suits." *Dallas Morning News,* 27 July 1998.

Egan, Cathleen. "Tobacco Cos. 4Q Profits Soft as Volume Continues to Drop." *Wall Street Journal,* 11 January 2000.

Fromson, Brett D. "Slugfest in the Smoke Ring." *Washington Post,* 1 March 1998.

Geyelin, Milo. "Fat Legal Fees in Tobacco Cases Face Challenge as Honeymoon Ends." *Wall Street Journal,* 16 June 1999.

———. "Group of 46 States Agree to Accept $206 Billion Tobacco Settlement." *Wall Street Journal,* 23 November 1998.

Gibbs, Nancy. "Up In Smoke." *Time,* 29 June 1998.

"Grey Market Attacked." *World Tobacco,* September 1999.

"Still Hooked on the Evil Weed." *Business Week,* 5 July 1999.

SIC 2121

CIGARS

This industry consists of establishments that primarily are engaged in the manufacture of cigars. Manufacturers of other tobacco items are treated in **SIC 2111: Cigarettes**; **SIC 2131: Chewing and Smoking Tobacco and Snuff**; and **SIC 2141: Tobacco Stemming and Redrying.**

NAICS CODE(S)

312229 (Other Tobacco Product Manufacturing)

INDUSTRY SNAPSHOT

The cigar industry has experienced dramatic growth in recent years thanks to increasing acceptance of cigar smoking among the "Generation X" population, a resurgence in "cigar evenings," and the popularity of the Internet where cigars are being sold in record numbers. The magazine *Cigar Aficionado,* introduced in 1992, is generally credited with the upturn in the cigar industry. No longer a passion for older men alone, changing demographics find "twentysomethings," both men and women, participating in cigar evenings and joining the traditional 35- to 65-year-old traditionalists in the purchase of premium cigars. Celebrities have also helped add to the allure, adorning the cover of *Cigar Aficionado* and showing up frequently at soirees boasting "stogies."

The cigar industry was enjoying this continued rebirth in the late 1990s. The United States had about 1 million premium cigar smokers. The number of cigars smoked in the United States increased about 50 percent between 1993 and 1996. However, the anti-smoking trend among consumers and the government will continue to impact cigar sales in the 2000s. Industry insiders predict that cigar sales will taper off but still remain at a high level.

ORGANIZATION AND STRUCTURE

Serving the industry, The Cigar Association of America, established more than 50 years ago, consists of regular members (the cigar makers headquartered in the United States) and associate members (including foreign cigar manufacturers, importers, leaf dealers, and other suppliers.) The organization's principle activities involve maintaining cigar industry statistics, public relations efforts, and lobbying federal and state governments on issues of import to the industry, especially taxation of their products.

BACKGROUND AND DEVELOPMENT

Like other tobacco products, the sale of cigars had dropped off as Americans became increasingly concerned about the effects of tobacco smoking on health and fitness. In the mid-1970s, volume was more than 5.5 billion, and at the industry's peak in 1964, unit sales reached 9 billion cigars. The volume of cigar sales fell about five percent a year during a 15-year period, dropping to 2.2 billion units sold in 1991.

While the upswing in the cigar market was strong, consumption still doesn't match the record highs of the mid-1960s. Cigar smokers have traded quantity for quality. They smoke fewer cigars, but when they do smoke, they often smoke cigars of a high quality. Declines in volume have been offset by increases in prices and a growing market for premium cigars. Sales in dollars have risen to about $700 million in the early 1990s. In 1995 imports of premium cigars rose to 176.3 million units, an increase from 1994's level of 132.4 million. In 1996 imports increased to $294 million.

Changes in distribution systems also helped the industry, as more discount stores and supermarkets began carrying a wider variety of cigars, especially the higher-priced cigars. The Internet has also played a role in cigar sales, with companies like J.R. Cigar finding it difficult to match demand. In late 1996, J.R. Cigar even began turning down orders from new customers as it struggled to fill orders. Mike's Cigars, Famous Smoke Shop, and J.R. Tobacco make up the "big three" of the discount cigar mail-order business. All were enjoying a renaissance in the late 1990s. Manufacturers were sitting on back orders in the 5 to 6 million unit range in 1996.

Laws prohibiting smoking in public places, increased taxes on tobacco products, and medical findings that cigars cause mouth, throat, and pancreatic cancer have had an impact on the U.S. cigar industry. According to an American Cancer Society study published in November 1999, "cigar smokers [also] experience a 30 percent increased death rate from heart disease before age 75." Cigar manufacturers have been combating these obstacles by increasing promotional activities with wholesalers and by introducing new products in various sizes. Their efforts were working—cigar smoking was still high, even among high school students.

CURRENT CONDITIONS

The cigar industry also continues to deal with the sale of both authentic and counterfeit Cuban cigars in the United States. The Cigar Association of America has been trying to halt the sale of these illegal products, estimating that they cost U.S. cigar makers $28 million a year. Approximately 6 million Cuban cigars are smuggled into the United States every year. In August 1996, government officials found over $50,000 of contraband cigars on one boat in Florida. The sale of Cuban cigars has been illegal in the U.S. since 1962, when President Kennedy signed the Cuban trade embargo.

Habanos, a Cuban cigar seller, "has signed a contract with China's state tobacco monopoly to sell hand-rolled premium Havanas to the tightly regulated internal Chinese market," according to the March 12, 2000 edition of the *San Jose Mercury News*. After China, the only large, unconquered market is the United States.

The U.S. Census Bureau reported in late 1999 that there were 38 U.S. establishments in the cigar industry, employing 3,845 people. Additionally, the 1997 value of product shipments reached $3.5 billion.

INDUSTRY LEADERS

Many U.S. companies are involved in this industry. Some of the majors include Swisher International Group Inc.; Consolidated Cigar Holdings Inc.; 800-JR Cigar, Inc.; and General Cigar Holdings, Inc. Swisher, based in Darien Connecticut, produces mass-market cigars such as Swisher Sweets and King Edward and premiums such as Bering and La Primadora. Sales in 1998 were $267 million. Swisher went private in 1999.

Consolidated Cigar Holdings is the largest U.S. cigar maker with brands such as Antonio y Cleopatra, Don Diego, Dutch Masters, El Producto. Its revenue in 1997 was $299 million. In 1999, Consolidated Cigar was bought by France's SEITA, since merged with Spain's Tabacalera to create Atladis (the world's fourth-largest tobacco company).

A leading distributor and retailer of premium cigars, 800-JR Cigar had 1999 sales of $317 million. In March 1999, the company announced that it is in the position to receive the first legal shipment of Cuban cigars if and when the embargo ends.

General Cigar Holdings markets premium cigars including Macanudo and Temple Hall, as well as mass-market cigars such as Garcia y Vega and Tiparillo. The company saw sales of $182 million in 1999.

WORKFORCE

Still, the industry has needed to respond to change. While cigars were once handmade products, technology has taken over in most companies. In Miami, however, Cuban and Central American immigrants in a half dozen small cigar factories have continued to make hand-rolled cigars. With a decline of qualified cigar rollers, cigar-rolling is becoming a lost craft.

The making of a hand-rolled cigar is a complicated, slow process. The tobacco reaches the factory and is then baled so that it can age for 18 months to 2 years. The tobacco is then blended and rolled by a master blender. After bunching, pressing, and wrapping, cigars are individually inspected, then they are sent to the aging room where they remain for 21 to 180 days.

FURTHER READING

''800-JR CIGAR, Inc. Supplies Havanas.'' *PR Newswire,* 14 March 2000.

''Chinese Market Opening to Cigars.'' *San Jose Mercury News,* 12 March 2000.

''Cigar Smoking Increases Early Death From Heart Disease.'' *PR Newswire,* 7 November 1999.

Edelman, Vladimir. ''Blowing Smoke: The Cigar Renaissance.'' *Inc. Online,* 1 July 1996.

Flanagan, William G. ''Cigar Madness.'' *Forbes,* 21 April 1997.

U.S. Census Bureau. ''Manufacturing-Industry Series.'' *1997 Economic Census.* Washington, D.C.: GPO, 18 May 1999.

SIC 2131

CHEWING AND SMOKING TOBACCO AND SNUFF

This industry consists of establishments primarily engaged in manufacturing chewing and smoking tobacco and snuff. Other tobacco product industries are discussed in **SIC 2111: Cigarettes; SIC 2121: Cigars;** and **SIC 2141: Tobacco and Redrying.**

NAICS CODE(S)

312229 (Other Tobacco Product Manufacturing)

In the early 2000s the $1.8-billion U.S. smokeless tobacco industry continued to be dominated by U.S. Tobacco, Conwood, and Swedish Match (formerly Pinkerton). Several others including National Tobacco,

Swisher, and Brown and Williamson also compete for a small percent of this industry.

U.S. Tobacco, with its Skoal and Copenhagen brands, consistently accounts for more than 80 percent of sales in the moist snuff category and is the overall sales leader for smokeless tobacco. The popularity of its Kodiak brand enables Conwood to control 13 percent of the moist snuff market. Swedish Match (Red Man and Granger brands) is the market leader in the loose-leaf category and is a strong competitor with U.S. Tobacco and Conwood for total sales of smokeless tobacco.

The snuff business enjoyed an upsurge in the mid-1970s after nearly half a century of lackluster sales. The hardcore market remained in the South among the older population. However in the mid-1970s, snuff began to regain some popularity, especially as young men turned to it because they thought it was a safe alternative to cigarettes. Labels warning of dangers and a ban on television and radio advertising of smokeless tobacco were not required until 1986, when the U.S. Surgeon General proclaimed it a cause of mouth cancer and other oral diseases.

Demand for smokeless tobacco rose sharply during the 1980s and early 1990s. Among smokeless products, moist snuff was the leader with total U.S. output rising 83 percent—from 30 million pounds in 1981 to 55 million pounds in 1993. In the early 1990s, as cigarette and cigar volume dropped, smokeless tobacco products grew 3-5 percent in sales volume annually. By the mid-1990s moist snuff had become the largest segment in terms of both total sales and volume produced. The increase was due to a number of factors: increased smoking restrictions, promotions and advertising, and the waning impact of tax hikes, negative publicity, and health warnings. Manufacturers of loose-leaf, plug, and dry snuff experienced a slow slide in volume sales but maintained profits through price increases.

So far smokeless tobacco companies have found creative alternatives to counter governmental restrictions. Advertising in magazines, at auto races and rodeos, as well as through direct mail campaigns, has been crucial in boosting sale and developing brand loyalty. These well-organized promotions and the introduction of new flavors strengthened sales of both loose-leaf tobacco and moist snuff in the late 1990s.

The industry faced many challenges in the 1990s as the public became more concerned about tobacco-related health issues. The mid- to late 1990s saw a flurry of legal activity as states sued companies to compensate state health-care providers for the cost of treating tobacco-related illnesses. In addition to the suits for smoking tobacco, U.S. Tobacco and other smokeless tobacco producers were sued for injuries that plaintiffs claimed were caused by chewing tobacco. However, industry leaders such as U.S. Tobacco enjoy high profit margins and smokeless tobacco sales continue to rise as consumers associate more health risks with cigarettes.

The future of growth of the smokeless tobacco industry will depend not only on public opinion of tobacco products but also on governmental regulation that could affect advertising and raise prices.

FURTHER READING

American Cancer Society. *Cancer Facts & Figures—1997.* Available from www.cancer.org/97tobacc.html.

Federal Trade Commission. ''Report to Congress.'' Washington, 12 January 1999. Available from www.ftc.gov/opa/1999/9901.htm.

Frank, Allan Dodds. ''Tobacco Under Fire.'' *CNNfn Archives,* Atlanta: Cable News Network, 15 May 1996. Available from www.cnnfn.com/news/9605/15/tobacco_attack_pkg/index.htm.

Forbes Annual Report on American Industry, 13 January 1997. Available from www.forbes.com.

Greising, David, and Catherine Yang. ''Peace Talks in the Tobacco Wars?'' *Business Week,* 10 February 1997.

''Smokeless Tobacco.'' *U.S. Distribution Journal,* June 1999.

''Smokeless Tobacco Producers Come Under Fire.'' *CNN Archives.* Cable News Network, 28 December 1995.

U.S. Census Bureau. ''Manufacturing-Industry Series.'' *1997 Economic Census.* Washington, 18 August 1999. Available from www.census.gov.

White, Larry C. *Merchants of Death: The American Tobacco Industry.* New York: William Morrow, 1988.

SIC 2141

TOBACCO STEMMING AND REDRYING

Establishments in this industry classification are primarily engaged in the stemming and redrying of tobacco or in manufacturing reconstituted tobacco. Establishments that sell leaf tobacco as merchants, wholesalers, agents, or brokers, and which may also be engaged in stemming tobacco, are classified in **SIC 5159: Farm Product Raw Materials, Not Elsewhere Classified.** Leaf tobacco warehouses that also may be engaged in stemming tobacco are classified in **SIC 4221: Farm Product Warehousing and Storage.**

NAICS CODE(S)

312229 (Other Tobacco Product Manufacturing)
312210 (Tobacco Stemming and Redrying)

INDUSTRY SNAPSHOT

According to the U.S. Census Bureau, 25 establishments were engaged in the stemming and redrying of tobacco in 1997. They employed 5,085 people, including 3,698 production workers who were paid an average hourly wage of $8.39. Shipments in this industry were valued at $3.46 billion. The cost of materials was $2.8 billion, and capital expenditures totaled $26.6 million. All but two of the companies in this industry had at least 20 employees.

In 1997 tobacco processors, like the tobacco industry as a whole, faced an uncertain outlook in the United States. Domestic cigarette consumption was down, owing to higher prices, tougher restrictions on smoking in public places, greater awareness of the health risks of tobacco use, and declining social acceptance. Cigarette companies were roundly criticized for promoting smoking among teenagers and, in March 1997, tough rules went into effect to reduce teen smoking. Thousands of tobacco farmers, whose families had often been in the business for generations, were shifting out of the product and into other crops, such as cotton.

Tobacco processing is truly an international business, however, and all of the major companies in the segment have extensive growing, processing, and sales operations overseas. Foreign markets expanded during the first half of the decade but had flattened by 1999.

ORGANIZATION AND STRUCTURE

The global processing and distribution of tobacco is dominated by three companies—Universal Corp., DIMON Inc., and Standard Commercial Corp.—which have large operations in the important tobacco-growing regions of the world. These companies buy the farmers' tobacco at auction (common in the United States) or contract to buy tobacco from the farmer. In certain overseas markets where the firms have contracted to buy the farmers' entire crop, they will often provide financial and technical assistance as well to ensure the tobacco's quality. In the United States most of the processors' tobacco purchases at auction are made to fill specific orders from the major domestic and overseas cigarette producers, with whom they often have relationships extending over many years.

After purchase, the tobacco is processed to meet the specific needs of the cigarette manufacturer, whose representatives are frequently at the processor's facilities to monitor the work on their orders. At the factory the tobacco is reclassified according to grade; blended to meet customer requirements regarding color, body, and chemistry; and threshed to remove the stem from the leaf (although some tobacco is processed in whole leaf form). The processed tobacco is redried to remove excess moisture so it can be held in storage for a long time. The companies also perform most of the processing of tobacco that is not bought at auction and thus enters the U.S. stabilization pool, under the auspices of the U.S. Department of Agriculture (USDA). The companies generally do not make cigarettes or other consumer tobacco products.

In the United States two major types of tobacco are grown: flue-cured and burley. Flue-cured is one of the most widely grown tobaccos in the world. It is cured by the grower, usually with gas- or oil-generated heat, and it serves as the basic ingredient in light blended or ''American type'' cigarettes. In the United States flue-cured tobacco is grown on the east coast from Virginia to Florida and especially in North Carolina. Burley tobacco, on the other hand, is air cured and is grown primarily in Kentucky and Tennessee. Mature tobacco is a perishable commodity that must be processed quickly to prevent fermentation or deterioration. Tobacco processors thus locate their facilities near the principal sources of the crop.

BACKGROUND AND DEVELOPMENT

While domestic consumption of tobacco products continued to slow in the early to mid-1990s, the major processors remained relatively unscathed. One reason was that the manufacturers imported more foreign tobacco, which was inexpensive but more profitable than domestic tobacco. Between 1989 and 1992 U.S. tobacco imports—the bulk of which were from Brazil, Zimbabwe, Argentina, Thailand, and Malawi—had more than doubled, while domestic output had risen 26 percent.

Moreover, primarily because of increased smoking in Asia, worldwide tobacco consumption had jumped 75 percent in the 1970s and 1980s and was continuing to rise by 1 to 2 percent a year. Demand for American-blend cigarettes, which tasted milder compared with the stronger and harsher cigarettes smoked in most of the world, was increasing, even in countries where overall demand was flat or down. Overseas demand for milder cigarettes, coupled with reduced trade barriers in important markets such as Japan, helped U.S. exports surge to 260 billion cigarettes in 1995, compared to 100 billion in 1987 and 59 billion in 1985. U.S. processors were well positioned to supply the flue-cured and burley tobaccos that are used to make the relatively low-tar, low-nicotine American-blend cigarette.

The industry experienced temporary downturns in 1993 and 1994 due to new legislation that required U.S.-produced cigarettes to contain at least 75 percent domestically grown tobacco (the ''75/25 Rule''), lower-than-expected initial demand for imported tobacco products in Central and Eastern Europe and the former Soviet Union, and an oversupply attributable to record foreign tobacco crops.

By the mid-1990s the demand and supply imbalance in world tobacco markets improved. Leaf tobacco production outside the United States was curtailed, the 75/25 Rule was replaced by a string of less stringent import quotas, and U.S. cigarette manufacturers began to buy more tobacco from outside the United States.

Nevertheless, U.S. tobacco farmers remained wary and uncertain. As Kentucky Farm Bureau president William Sprague told the *Lexington Herald Leader* in 1996, ''It's a paradox: we have an increasing world demand for something we can produce in this state very well. But all farmers are seeing and reading about is the ill effects of tobacco. It has our farmers gun shy.'' The long-term downward trend in domestic consumption had forced some growers to switch to alternative crops such as cotton. The number of tobacco farms in North Carolina, which grows about two-thirds of the country's flue-cured tobacco, dropped from about 100,000 in the mid-1980s to 42,000 in 1991.

While their own segment remained profitable, the processors, like other industry participants, were concerned about the increasingly strong steps being taken to limit tobacco use. Dozens of localities around the country had passed measures that curtailed smoking in offices, restaurants, and other public places, and nationwide restrictions were being suggested in Congress. Studies that determined secondhand cigarette smoke could cause lung cancer gained credence. States sued the cigarette manufacturers to pick up their health-care costs and gained significant court victories. In March 1997 bipartisan legislation was unveiled that would hike Federal cigarette taxes 43 cents per pack to pay for health insurance costs for children and reduce the deficit. The outlook for the domestic tobacco industry was bleak.

CURRENT CONDITIONS

The U.S. tobacco industry continued to suffer setbacks into the late 1990s, and hundreds of workers lost their jobs as processing facilities closed or reduced production. Hurricane Floyd caused widespread crop damage in 1999. Tobacco companies were sued in court for marketing products that were considered to be health hazards. The federal government and other groups continued their campaigns to discourage tobacco use. Cigarette consumption dropped 7 percent to 465 billion pieces in 1998, while production dropped 6 percent to 680 billion pieces.

Some types of tobacco products became more popular, however. Output of large cigars and cigarillos reached an estimated 2.9 billion in 1998, an increase of almost 500 million cigars in one year. The average adult male consumer bought 37.8 cigars that year, up from 36.9 in 1997. Cigarette makers launched line extensions and repositioned established brands, emphasizing ''ultra-light'' varieties that contained less tar and nicotine. A new method of curing tobacco was devised to reduce or eliminate the formation of nitrosamines, which were thought to be the substances in tobacco smoke that were most apt to cause cancer.

INDUSTRY LEADERS

Some of the largest firms that stemmed and redried tobacco were also involved in endeavors as diverse as the manufacturing of cigarettes, the bottling of soft drinks, highway construction, and the sale of groceries and flowers. These companies included Philip Morris Inc., of New York, with 1998 sales of $11.5 billion; Universal Corp., of Richmond, Virginia, with sales of $4.3 billion; DIMON Inc., of Danville, Virginia, with sales of $2.2 billion; Brown and Williamson Tobacco Corp., of Louisville, Kentucky, with sales of $1.7 billion; Standard Commercial Corp. of Wilson, North Carolina, with sales of $1.5 billion; UST Inc., of Greenwich, Connecticut, with sales of $1.4 billion; and Brown and Root International Inc., of Louisville, Kentucky, with sales of $675 million.

Many companies whose primary business was the stemming and redrying of tobacco were subsidiaries of the larger firms. They included Dibrell Brothers Inc., of Danville, Virginia; Monk-Austin Inc., of Farmville, North Carolina; Standard Commercial Tobacco Co., of Wilson, North Carolina; Universal Leaf Tobacco Company Inc., of Richmond, Virginia; and K.R. Edwards Leaf Tobacco Company Inc., of Smithfield, North Carolina. One of the largest independent companies in the industry was Flue-Cured Tobacco Cooperative Stabilization Corp., of Raleigh, North Carolina, with sales of $100 million.

WORKFORCE

In the United States, tobacco processors buy flue-cured tobacco from July through November and burley tobacco from late November until January or February. Processing takes place throughout the buying season and is usually finished within two to three months after purchase. During these periods, the industry's work force swells. Some seasonal employees are covered by union collective bargaining agreements. Seasonal labor is also used extensively in overseas operations.

AMERICA AND THE WORLD

In terms of supply and demand, in the 1990s the U.S. tobacco processing industry was increasingly looking abroad. The elimination of trade barriers and the rising popularity of lighter, American-blend cigarettes expanded overseas markets. Following the fall of the Berlin Wall in 1989, new markets for U.S. exports sprang up in the former Soviet republics and in Eastern Europe. Demand in some countries grew enormously. Cigarette consumption in China, for example, was more than five times greater than in 1965. U.S. cigarette exports tripled between 1985 and 1992, owing to the popularity of American tobacco products and reduced trade barriers in countries such as Japan. The trend continued into the mid-1990s. Exports of domestically produced cigarettes in 1995 totaled 35.1 percent of production, up from 31.8 percent in 1994 and 30.9 percent in 1993.

As international suppliers of tobacco, the processors were also selling tobacco grown overseas for cigarette manufacture in non-U.S. factories. The large processors had major operations in Brazil, Zimbabwe, Malawi, and other tobacco-growing countries. In several countries the processor will contract directly with tobacco farmers, in some cases before harvest, and thus take the risk that the delivered product will meet the market's quality requirements. In some countries the major processors also provide agronomy services and advances for fertilizers and supplies.

FURTHER READING

Bickers, Christopher. ''Quotas Go Begging, But Imports Rise.'' *World Tobacco,* November 1996.

''Cigarettes with Low-Nitrosamine Tobacco an Exciting Prospect.'' *World Tobacco,* May 1999.

Bridges, Roger. ''Record Exports Set to Continue.'' *World Tobacco,* September 1995.

''DIMON Announces Acquisition of Intabex.'' *PR Newswire,* 14 February 1997.

Frazier, Shirley. ''Tobacco.'' *U.S. Distribution Journal,* May 1999.

Lucke, James. ''Kentucky Farmers Fear Tobacco Shortage May Harm State in World Markets.'' *Knight-Ridder/Tribune Business News,* 15 July 1996.

U.S. Department of Agriculture, Economic Research Service. ''U.S. Tobacco Crop Down 11 Percent in 1999.'' Washington, D.C.: GPO, 1999. Available from http://www.usda.gov/nass/pubs/estindx3.htm#tobacco.

U.S. Department of Commerce, U.S. Census Bureau. *1997 Economic Census.* Washington, D.C.: GPO, 1999. Available from http://www.census.gov/prod/ec97/97m3122a.pdf.

''Zimbabwe.'' *World Tobacco,* November 1996.

TEXTILE MILL PRODUCTS

BROADWOVEN FABRIC MILLS, COTTON

This category covers establishments primarily engaged in the production of woven fabrics more than 12 inches (30.48 centimeters) in width, wholly or chiefly by weight of cotton. Broadwoven fabrics primarily of cotton are utilized in three general end-product categories: apparel, home furnishings, and industrial products. Most of the broadwoven cotton apparel fabrics serve the outerwear market—men's, ladies', and children's shirts, blouses, pants, and dresses. Some lightweight jackets and boxer shorts are also produced from broadwoven cotton fabric. The home-furnishings market includes terry towels; sheets, pillowcases, blankets, bedspreads, and other bedding accessories; table linens, dish towels, and dish rags; draperies; and upholstery fabrics and wall coverings. Carpet and rug manufacturers are classified in **SIC 2273: Carpets and Rugs.** Establishments involved in tire cord and fabric production are classified in **SIC 2296: Tire Cords and Fabrics.** Those establishments engaged in finishing cotton broadwoven fabrics are classified in **SIC 2261: Finishers of Broadwoven Fabrics of Cotton.**

INDUSTRY SNAPSHOT

Manufacturing of cotton broadwovens—like most segments of textiles—is a mature industry. Since the mid-1980s major U.S. firms in the industry have pursued growth largely through mergers, acquisitions, and foreign markets; they have maximized profits typically through cost cutting and sourcing low-cost labor from foreign countries. The industry faces formidable competition on price from imported textiles, particularly those from Asian nations and Mexico. Nonetheless, the value of U.S. industry shipments rose modestly throughout the first half of the 1990s and totaled more than $7 billion by the year 2000.

ORGANIZATION AND STRUCTURE

Fabric weavers generally are vertically integrated companies that produce their own yarn. The primary reason for integrated weaving plants is that despite fashion changes that occur in the woven segment, yarn counts—the size of the yarn—as well as fabric constructions remain fairly stable. Fabric knitters, on the other hand, are faced with constant changes in yarn size and construction. Therefore, most knitters find it more economical to purchase yarn from sales yarn companies.

CURRENT CONDITIONS

Cotton remains a viable material for the textile market despite predictions in the 1960s and 1970s that manmade products would completely replace natural fiber. Cotton's inherent qualities, such as absorbency and breathability, and new fabric finishes have kept the fiber's market share strong. Cotton's competitiveness can be partially attributed to improvements such as the all-cotton, wrinkle resistant fabrics that are particularly popular for making men's pants, softer finishes, and flame-retardant treatments. Researchers are also developing antibacterial finishes and temperature responsive treatments for cottons.

The general state of the economy, coupled with the level of consumer confidence, has a great impact on operations engaged in the manufacture of broadwoven cotton fabrics for apparel products. High consumer confidence coupled with a strong economy helped companies producing fabrics for apparel enjoy success at the close of the twentieth century.

New housing starts, which remained strong at the end of the 1990s, were the chief factor outside of trade matters affecting manufacturers of broadwoven cotton fabrics for home furnishings. Although a large market exists for replacement sheets, pillow cases, and towels, nothing spurs this segment of the industry as much as new housing starts.

Several factors affect the demand for broadwoven cotton fabrics for industrial use. These include the success of the automotive industry, the activity in new highways and bridges, and the nature of the agriculture industry. A significant section of the agriculture industry—cotton farming—also has a tremendous influence. Costs of raw materials have a direct effect on the annual success of producers of broadwoven cotton fabrics, no matter what the application. The price of raw materials are affected by weather and other natural factors. In the spring of 1995 the price of cotton escalated to more than $1 per pound due to shortages of foreign crops cause by the boll worm in China and by the leaf curl virus in Pakistan. As crop production increased through the late 1990s, stocks of cotton grew to be larger than historical averages. The surplus helped ease some of the squeeze on profit margins of this segment of the textile industry as the manufacturers of cotton broadwoven fabric mills saw the price of cotton decline to approximately 50 cents per pound in July 1999.

WORKFORCE

In 1997 the U.S. Census Bureau reported total employment by cotton fabric mills to be 48,428 people. Production workers accounted for 87 percent of that total. Although the long-term downward trend in employment continued through the end of the 1990s, the higher-skilled and higher-paying jobs in this industry remained relatively constant.

AMERICA AND THE WORLD

A number of factors influence the success of companies engaged in the manufacturing of broadwoven cotton fabrics, but none has the impact equal to that of international trade. For a number of years, imports—particularly in the apparel fabrics sector—rose steadily, severely affecting operation of U.S. manufacturers of broadwoven cotton fabrics. Manufacturers of broadwoven cotton fabrics were affected by imported garments—which are usually cut and sewn from fabrics manufactured in the same country as the garments—as well as fabrics.

The U.S. textile industry continued to feel the effects of the Asian financial crisis throughout the late 1990s. Low-cost Asian imports affected domestic sales, business in the Caribbean, and exports to overseas markets in Asia.

The North American Free Trade Agreement (NAFTA), which became official January 1, 1994, proved to be a boon to manufacturers of broadwoven cotton fabrics throughout the late 1990s. In 1997 NAFTA countries accounted for more than 45 percent of the market for exports of U.S. textiles with a value of almost

$4.4 billion. Growth in this market continued in 1998 and 1999, reaching almost 60 percent.

While the signing of NAFTA proved beneficial to manufacturers of broadwoven cotton fabrics, the signing in 1993 of what is known as the Uruguay Round of the General Agreement on Tariffs and Trade (GATT), had just the opposite effect. The Uruguay Round agreement was signed by 117 nations following seven years of negotiations. This agreement phased out tariffs on textiles set by the Multifiber Arrangement (MFA) by 2005. In January 1995 the administration and enforcement of GATT was assumed by the newly formed World Trade Organization.

As noted by Doug Ellis, president of the American Textile Manufacturers Institute (ATMI) and chief executive officer of Southern Mills, Inc. in Atlanta, Georgia, the foreign market openings promised in the Uruguay Round did not materialize. Countries such as India, Pakistan, Brazil, Argentina, and Egypt kept their markets closed to U.S. exports while increasing their exports to the United States by billions of dollars.

In late November 1999, the ATMI urged Congress to pass the Senate version of the Caribbean Basin Initiative bill. The Senate version of the bill would allow apparel imports from the Caribbean to qualify for both duty-free and quota-free treatment if U.S. fabric made from U.S. yarn and U.S. thread was used. Two independent studies regarding this were cited by ATMI president Doug Ellis that indicated U.S. employment in textile and textile related fields would increase substantially, while textile shipments would grow between $7 billion to $9 billion. This would benefit both the U.S. textile industry and its workers, noted Ellis.

RESEARCH AND TECHNOLOGY

Manufacturers of broadwoven cotton fabrics replaced shuttle looms with shuttleless weaving machines as rapidly as economically feasible. These machines offered geometrically higher weaving speeds than those of shuttle systems. Use of electronics in the broadwoven manufacturing process permitted even higher increases in speeds. Speeds on any filling insertion system vary depending on type and width of fabric being woven.

When first developed, each shuttleless filling insertion system was designed specifically for a somewhat narrow fabric application range. As systems were improved, modified, and computerized, the application ranges broadened considerably. Projectile, flexible rapier, and rigid rapier systems were more versatile and could handle heavier, more complicated styles such as plaid upholstery. Modifications to air-jet systems, however, broadened the application range to include more than just simple, lightweight styles such as printcloth and sheeting. Burlington Industries and Swift Textiles both produced heavyweight denim on air-jet machines, and a few companies began experimenting with heavyweight upholstery fabrics on air jets as well.

Electronic technology contributed greatly to the operation of shuttleless weaving machines in the broadwoven cotton sector. Systems provided more control in the air bursts from the series of nozzles on air-jet machines, permitting greater manufacturing speeds and production of a broader range of fabric weights. Jacquard machines—which control multicolored, extremely complicated patterns—incorporated electronics that permitted higher speeds in the production of fancy upholstery fabrics on flexible and rigid rapiers. Electronic advances also paved the way for the installation of automation features on shuttleless weaving machines, such as automatic filling break repair, automatic cloth removal at specified lengths, and automatic filling supply cone replenishment.

The biggest contribution made by electronic technology to broadwoven cotton manufacturing was in monitoring and control of the operation. Microprocessor-driven systems monitored and provided real-time data on efficiency, production, and quality. The data could be provided for any time period the manufacturer wished to designate. This data could also be supplied for an individual machine or several machines grouped by style and job assignment. Such information permitted the evaluation of styles and fabrics and gave the broadwoven fabrics manufacturer the ability to select those materials most suited for the production machinery available.

As electronic systems become more advanced, they not only permitted monitoring of the operation, but controlled of many of the functions as well. Modern systems can detect many mechanical and electrical problems. Depending on the sophistication of the system and the severity of the problem, the system can correct the problem, signal technicians as to the nature of the problem, or stop the machine until the problem is corrected. Totally automated systems (known as ''lights out'' operations) have been created for spinning machines, while complete automation of the weaving process is still far from being cost-effective.

Computerization of the textile industry has been a critical part of the quick response (QR) programs that are being adopted by companies in an attempt to shorten the time between the placement of retail orders and the delivery of textile goods to stores. The companies coordinating such programs communicate using bar codes and electronic data interchange. With the ability to pinpoint production times and quantities, mills can direct production according to individual orders. The mills, as well as apparel manufacturers and retailers, benefit from the resulting reduction in inventory costs. QR programs also reduce forced markdowns and stockouts on the retail

level, while providing a smoother flow of production that significantly improves textile mills' operating margins.

At the end of 1999, the Internet was introduced into the textile world as an additional means of product distribution. The e-commerce for fabrics allowed buyers to search a large database of fabrics and place orders for them online. The database contained digital images of sample yardage sent by the manufacturers with detailed product specifications included at the Web site.

The market for business-to-business e-commerce was expected to be larger than that of business-to-consumer. The use of the Internet allowed the manufacturers of broadwoven cotton fabrics to reach a worldwide market of prospective buyers.

FURTHER READING

Cotton Incorporated. ''Cotton Perspective,'' April 1996.

Jablonski, Mary. ''Multifactor Productivity: Cotton and Synthetic Broadwoven Fabrics.'' *Monthly Labor Review,* July 1995.

Lee, Jill. ''Textile Advances Enhance Cotton Markets.'' *Agricultural Research,* May 1996.

McClenahen, John S. ''A Yarn That's No Tall Tale.'' *Industry Week,* 1 July 1996.

National Cotton Council of America. ''Cotton Supply and Demand.'' *EconCentral,* 1999. Available from http://www.econcentral.org/wasde1.htm.

———. ''U.S. and World Cotton Economic Outlook,'' November 1999. Available from http://www.onlinetextilenews.com.

Nelson, Cotton. ''Crop Estimate Increases by 300,000 Bales.'' *National Cotton Council of America,* 10 December 1999. Available from http://www.cotton.org/ncc/news/1999.

Reichard, Robert S. ''Do Positive Signs Point to Prosperity?'' *Textile World,* January 1997.

Rozelle, Walter N. ''Business Outlook.'' *Textile World,* January 1997.

———. ''Parras Cone: A Product of a NAFTA Partnership.'' *Textile World,* February 1996.

Standard & Poor's Industry Surveys. New York: Standard & Poor's Corp., 1999.

U.S. Census Bureau. ''Broadwoven Fabrics.'' *Current Industrial Reports,* 1997. Available from http://www.census.gov.

SIC 2221

BROADWOVEN FABRIC MILLS, MANMADE FIBER AND SILK

This category covers establishments primarily engaged in the production of woven fabrics more than 12 inches (30.48 centimeters) in width, wholly or chiefly by weight of manmade fiber and/or silk. Broadwoven fabrics primarily of manmade fiber are utilized in three general end-product categories: apparel, home furnishings, and industrials. Broadwoven fabrics primarily of silk are for the most part utilized in apparel products. Occasionally, broadwoven silk fabrics serve the home furnishings market.

Production of broadwoven fabrics with content wholly or primarily by weight of cotton is included in **SIC 2211: Broadwoven Fabric Mills, Cotton.** Production of broadwoven fabrics with content wholly or chiefly by weight of wool, mohair, or other similar animal fiber is included in **SIC 2231: Broadwoven Fabric Mills, Wool (Including Dyeing and Finishing).** Production of narrow fabric, generally 12 inches or less in width, of cotton, wool, silk, and manmade fiber is included in **SIC 2241: Narrow Fabric and Other Smallwares Mills: Cotton, Wool, Silk, and Manmade Fiber.**

NAICS CODE(S)

313210 (Broadwoven Fabric Mills)

INDUSTRY SNAPSHOT

According to the U.S. Census Bureau, 452 establishments were engaged in the production of manmade fiber and/or silk broadwoven fabrics in the United States in 1997. These establishments had total employment of 77,129 people. More than 85 percent (or a total of 65,687 people) were involved directly with the production of these broadwoven fabrics. Total payroll was more than $2.0 billion, and the value of shipments exceeded $10.6 billion.

Principal fibers used in broadwoven manmade fiber fabrics for apparel are polyester, rayon, and nylon with occasional use of polypropylene or olefin fiber. These fabrics are generally used for men's, ladies', and children's outerwear including shirts, blouses, pants, and dresses; leisure and activewear; heavy and lightweight jackets and coats; suits; and sleepwear and lingerie.

The home furnishings market for manmade broadwoven fabrics includes sheets, pillowcases, blankets, bedspreads, and other bedding accessories; table linens or napery products; draperies; upholstery fabrics; and wall coverings. The principal manmade fibers used in home furnishings are polyester, rayon, polypropylene, acrylic, and occasionally nylon. Carpet and rug manufacturers are discussed in **SIC 2273: Carpets and Rugs.**

Industrial applications for broadwoven manmade fibers include materials used in the automotive, agricultural, geotextile, medical, recreational, and transportation industries. Broadwoven manmade fiber fabrics also find use in conveyor and other industrial belting products as well as in specialized applications such as soft-sided luggage and protective clothing. Tire cord and fabric production is included in **SIC 2296: Tire Cord and Fabrics.**

Broadwoven fabrics of manmade fiber for industrial applications are made from the widest variety of fiber types. Traditional manmade fibers such as nylon, polyester, acrylic, polypropylene or olefin, and rayon find numerous uses in the area of industrial fabrics. A number of industrial applications products, however, require the characteristics of some specialized manmade fibers. Some of these fibers include the aramid family with such fibers as Nomex and Kevlar, both manufactured by DuPont. Nomex is highly flame resistant, and fabrics manufactured from this fiber are used in such products as protective clothing for firefighting, space exploration, and racing. Kevlar, with strength characteristics superior to steel, can be found in fabrics manufactured for bulletproof vests and other protective devices.

Other manmade fibers with high-performance characteristics for use in specialized applications and their major producers include carbon fiber (BASF and Courtaulds); glass fiber (Owens-Corning Fiberglass Corp. and PPG Industries Inc.); polybenzimidazole (Hoechst Celanese); polyetheretherketone (Albany International and Shakespeare Monofilament); and sulfur (Albany International and Phillips Fibers Corp.).

Of the numerous producers of traditional manmade fibers that are used in broadwoven fabrics, some of the principal U.S. producers are Eastman Chemical Products Inc. (acetate); Mann Industries and Monsanto (acrylic); Albany International, Allied Fibers, BASF Corp., Hercules Inc., and Phillips Fibers Corp. (olefin polypropylene); Courtaulds Fibers Inc. and North American Rayon Corp. (rayon); and Globe Mfg. Co. (spandex).

ORGANIZATION AND STRUCTURE

Producers of broadwoven fabrics of manmade fiber and silk, like the producers of other broadwoven fabrics, are for the most part vertically integrated textile manufacturing companies; that is, most broadwoven companies manufacture their own yarn requirements. Many of them also dye and finish their own fabrics.

Aside from the many different generic types of manmade fiber—including polyester, nylon, and rayon—and the different brands within each generic type—including Du Pont's Dacron, Eastman's Kodel, and Hoechst Celanese's Trevira—fabrics may be woven from two forms of manmade fiber yarn: filament or staple. Filament yarn is a continuous strand of manmade fiber. Staple manmade fiber yarn consists of many individual fibers cut to a specific length. These fibers measure approximately one to one-and-a-half inches in length if they are to be spun into yarn on a cotton system spinning process. If they are to be spun on a woolen or worsted system spinning process, the fibers are cut up to six or eight inches in length. The form of manmade fiber yarn to be woven depends on the end-use application of the fabric. Staple fiber arrives at the textile plant in bales, just like cotton or wool. It is processed just like cotton or wool on the same machinery.

Of the billions of square yards of manmade fiber and silk broadwoven fabric woven in the mid- through late 1990s, more than half was produced using 85 percent or more of continuous filament yarn. The percentage of manmade fiber broadwoven fabrics produced from continuous filament yarn has trended upward since 1980, when this type represented 37 percent of the 10.7 billion square yards produced. In 1988 the amount of the manmade fiber broadwoven fabric produced from continuous filament yarn reached 50 percent for the first time. Consumption of filament fiber by broadwoven manmade fabric producers has remained at or above this level since that time.

BACKGROUND AND DEVELOPMENT

A discussion of weaving systems types and the emergence of shuttleless weaving as the most efficient, productive, and quality producing system can be found in **SIC 2211: Broadwoven Fabric Mills, Cotton.** All of the shuttleless weaving systems—projectile, rigid and flexible rapier, and air-jet—described in the broadwoven cotton fabrics section are in use in weaving broadwoven fabrics from manmade fiber and silk. Producers of many of the styles of broadwoven manmade fiber fabrics can also use the water-jet system of weaving as well. This requires the yarn to be hydrophobic—the fiber must not absorb moisture, the styles must be relatively simple in construction, and the material must be relatively light in weight so that a stream of water can carry the yarn across the weaving machine. Most manmade fibers are hydrophobic, with rayon and its variants being the notable exceptions.

Water-jet weaving machines are manufactured by Nissan Motor Co. Ltd., Tsudakoma Corp. of Japan, and Zbrojovka-Vsetin of the Czech Republic. Water-jet weaving machines operate at a production rate of more than 1,000 ppm, which is more than 500 percent faster than conventional shuttle weaving systems, approximately 200 percent faster than projectile and both rapier systems, and at least 25 percent faster than the average air-jet weaving machine.

CURRENT CONDITIONS

As a group (and aside from competition within the group) producers of broadwoven fabrics of manmade fiber and silk faced two types of competition for market share, especially in the apparel sector and, to a lesser extent, in the home furnishings market. The two types of competition are fabrics and garments imported from developing countries and a trend toward increasing consumer preference for products made from natural fibers.

Increasing consumer preference for products made from natural fibers, including cotton and wool, stems from several factors. The first of these is marketing and promotional campaigns conducted by Cotton Incorporated, an organization sponsored and paid for by the cotton growers of the United States. Formed in 1971 in an attempt to offset the huge gains in market share being made by polyester, the organization's purpose is to promote the use of cotton in fabrics. Since its formation, cotton has increased its U.S. market share at the expense of manmade fiber in production of broadwoven fabrics every year. With headquarters and marketing offices in New York and research facilities in Raleigh, North Carolina, Cotton Incorporated's principal means of promoting cotton as a fiber of choice in broadwoven fabrics are massive television commercials: "The Fabric of Our Lives" and the use of the cotton bowl logo in products made of 100 percent cotton or the cotton-blend logo in products made of at least 60 percent cotton. In a recognition survey of 12 leading product logos among consumers in 1993, the cotton logo was deemed the second most recognizable logo, behind the Shell Oil Co. logo. The survey found that the cotton logo was more recognizable than such logos as those of CBS, Chrysler, Dutch Boy, Merrill Lynch, Prudential, Maxwell House, Kodak, and Wrigley's.

The second factor playing a part in decreasing market share among manmade fiber broadwovens compared to natural fiber broadwovens has to do with increasing environmental concerns among consumers. Most manmade fibers are produced in chemical plants from a variety of chemicals with inherent potential for environmental problems. Few, if any, fiber producers violated any environmental regulations, but the perception of potential problems is a factor producers of manmade fiber fabrics must overcome.

The third factor playing a part in decreasing market share among manmade fiber broadwovens is the minimization, if not elimination, of what has historically been the major objection to broadwoven fabrics of cotton. With current capabilities that reduce wrinkles in cotton fabrics and make the products more in the line of "easy care" or "wash-and-wear" polyester products, cotton fabric producers have taken a giant step toward attracting additional consumers. The makers of manmade fabrics have responded by improving existing fabrics and creating new products. Lycra has been adapted to include some cotton-like attributes—breathability and washability—while providing excellent stretchability. Lycra was especially important in the marketing of garments constructed of manmade fibers, when manufacturers promoted the "high-tech" look of stretch twills and suitings. The relatively new microdernier fabrics, although they were initially very expensive, are also expected to become popular for their easy care, breathability, and dense, soft characteristics. Specialty fabrics such as DuPont's CoolMax polyester and Cordura Plus nylon were being introduced into apparel manufacturing.

Production of broadwoven fabric reached 16.4 billion square yards in 1997, up almost 4 percent over 1996 levels. Man-made fiber fabrics increased nearly 2 percent. Although production gains in cotton and wool broadwoven fabrics were realized, man-made fibers and silk broadwoven fabric remained the leader in the market.

Mergers, acquisitions, divestitures, and joint ventures were avenues manufacturers of broadwoven fabrics took to become more productive, efficient, and profitable. Companies continued to modernize and expand their facilities, spending $2 billion a year for capital investments.

Manufacturers targeted 3 to 4 percent of corporate sales for capital expenditures. One new piece of equipment replaced 5 or 10, or more, older machines performing similar tasks. Evolving technology in equipment and production techniques, along with development and improvement of end-use applications, were a key focus for manufacturers of broadwoven fabric, man-made fiber, and silk through the end of the 1990s and into the twenty-first century.

Three agreements that affected producers of man-made fiber and silk broadwoven fabrics were the General Agreement of Tariffs and Trade (GATT), the North American Free Trade Agreement (NAFTA), and the American Textile Partnership (AMTEX). The first two are agreements between the United States government and governments of other countries, while the third is an agreement between the United States government and the United States textile/apparel complex.

The third agreement—AMTEX—is between the United States Department of Energy (DOE) and the U.S. textile/apparel complex to provide research and existing government technologies to boost U.S. competitiveness. In 1997 several projects were in progress as joint industry-DOE efforts:

- Computer-Aided Fabric Evaluation (CAFE): This technology is used for computer vision target recognition systems that can tell the difference between military and civilian aircraft or vehicles. It is also used for high-speed inspection systems that detect pattern and color defects in U.S. currency and postage stamps. Through AMTEX, this technology will be used to detect and classify defects, as hundreds of square yards of fabric per minute "fly by" an inspection system.
- Cotton Biotechnology: Researchers sought to improve cotton fiber performance and plant yield, with the result of developing longer, stronger, and more uniform plant fibers.

- Electronic Embedded Fingerprints: Tiny electronic microchips and radio transponders were developed by the DOE to permanently identify or tag missiles or items that were to be controlled under international treaties. While current devices are about the size of a penny, AMTEX proposes to develop a smaller version about the size of a grain of rice. It will include a small radio transmitter and will be packaged for permanent encasement in apparel or other products counterfeited in foreign markets.
- On-Line Process Control (OPCon): AMTEX was working to identify and develop technologies that would allow for faster transitions between products, cost effective production of small lots, and eliminate off-quality productions and off-line testing.
- Rapid Cutting: The government invested in developing high-power lasers for the Strategic Defense Initiative program, isotope separation, and scientific investigations. The new use of these technologies will be to create a new generation of high-speed cutting machines ten to twenty times faster than current machines. This will allow both small and large companies to enter the era of demand-activated-manufacturing and custom apparel manufacturing.
- Sensors for Agile Manufacturing (SFAM): The AMTEX partnership was developing sensors and feedback control methods to increase the industry's productivity, flexibility, and sewing safety.
- Textile Resource Conservation (TReC): Methods were being developed for eliminating the discharge of waste into the environment. Manufacturing processes were being revised to use less energy and natural resources.

AMERICA AND THE WORLD

The Asian financial crisis continued to adversely affect the textile industry through the late 1990s with the manmade fabric segment being hit particularly hard. From 1997 through 1998, overall imports of fabrics from Asia increased 35 percent. During that same period man-made fiber fabric imports from Asia increased by 51 percent. In 1999 the U.S. Commerce Department reported that prices for imports from Asia continued to fall with imports of Asian fabrics dropping 6.5 percent in price.

In 1998 overall textile imports from Asia increased to 6.6 billion square meter equivalents (sme). Three of the countries showing large gains in textile imports to the United States were Thailand, at an increase of 37 percent; Pakistan, at 36 percent; and Japan, at 30 percent. Conversely, U.S. exports to these regions fell 30 percent, 35 percent, and 25 percent respectively. Total U.S. exports to the region were down 24 percent to $853 million.

The signing of the General Agreement of Tariffs and Trade (GATT) proved an obstacle for manufacturers of broadwoven, manmade, and silk fabrics. Known as the Uruguay Round of GATT, the agreement was signed in 1993 by 117 nations following seven years of negotiations. This agreement phased out tariffs on textiles set by the Multi Fiber Arrangement (MFA) by 2005. In January 1995 the administration and enforcement of GATT was assumed by the World Trade Organization. Representatives from the American Textile Manufacturers Institute (ATMI) and the American Apparel Manufacturers Association (AAMA) in 1999, urged government action to eliminate large imbalances in market accessibility by getting all countries to fully implement their commitments to the agreement reached in the Uruguay Round.

The North American Free Trade Agreement (NAFTA) went into effect January 1, 1994 and proved beneficial to manufacturers of manmade and silk broadwoven fabrics. In 1998 Mexico was the largest exporter of apparel to the United States. Mexican export levels rose to 2 billion square meter equivalents (sme) and because more than two-thirds of Mexican apparel exports contained U.S. yarn and fabric, U.S. textile exports to Mexico reached a record $4.5 billion.

Representatives from ATMI urged Congress in late November 1999 to pass the Senate version of the Caribbean Basin Initiative bill. The Senate version of the bill would allow apparel imports to qualify for both duty-free and quota-free treatment if U.S. fabric made from U.S. yarn and U.S. thread was used. According to the ATMI, U.S. textile exports to the Caribbean were expected to increase by $11 billion over five years.

RESEARCH AND TECHNOLOGY

Textile mills used computerization of the industry to develop quick response programs (QR) that shortened the time between the placement of retail orders and the delivery of textile goods to stores. Communicating through the use of bar codes and electronics data interchange enabled companies to use the information to direct production. Reduction in inventory costs benefited the textile mills along with apparel manufacturers and retailers.

October 1998 saw the introduction of a new electronic database designed as an information gathering center between the U.S. textile industry and its suppliers. The Voluntary Product Environmental Profile (VPEP) is an effort to make the exchange of important information relating to the environment, health, and safety more efficient. In addition to facilitating a more efficient exchange of data between manufacturers and their suppliers, it provides information required for regulatory compliance and aids them in making better environmental decisions about their operations.

Textile companies were concentrating efforts to deliver the right designs at the right time, so they purchased new and expanded CAD equipment in 1999. The design computers were up to ten times faster than the old systems. Manufacturers saw the digital printing system, which included a wide-format printer capable of printing rolls of fabric up to 60 inches wide, and specially formulated inks and software as a means to cost reduction.

The Internet was introduced into the textile world as an additional means of product distribution at the close of 1999. The e-commerce for fabrics allowed buyers to search a large database of fabrics and place orders for them online. The database contained digital images of sample yardage sent by the manufacturers with detailed product specifications included at the Web site.

The manufacturers of broadwoven manmade and silk fabrics would be able to reach a worldwide market of prospective buyers through the use of the Internet. Marketing experts expected business-to-business e-commerce to be 10 to 20 times greater than that of the business-to-consumer market.

FURTHER READING

Addis, Karen K. "ATMI Unveils Electronic Environmental Product Profile," 14 October 1998. Available from http://www.atmi.org/newsroom.

——. "U.S. and European Textile and Apparel Industries Urge Government Action to Gain Market Access to Address Trade Imbalances," 14 July 1999. Available from http://www.atmi.org/newsroom/releases/.

American Textile Manufacturers Institute. "Study Shows 'Yarn-Forward' Caribbean Basin Initiative Trade Legislation Would Benefit Industry," 20 September 1999. Available from http://www.onlinetextilenews.com/news/.

"Broadwoven Goods Production, 1997." Washington, D.C.: U.S. Census Bureau.

Grudier, Alison. "CAD Developers Gear up for Y2K," 27 December 1999. Available from http://www.textileworld.com.

Jablonski, Mary. "Multifactor Productivity: Cotton and Synthetic Broadwoven Fabrics." *Monthly Labor Review,* July 1995.

Luther, Michael. "Dupont's Fall 1996 Vision: Wardrobe of High-Tech Versatility." *Textile World,* January 1996.

McClenahen, John S. "A Yarn That's No Tall Tale." *Industry Week,* 1 July 1996.

Raiman, Gail. "U.S. Textile Industry Hit Hard by Flood of Low-cost Asian Imports," 23 February 1999. Available from http://www.atmi.org/newsroom/releases/.

Smith, William C. "Industrial Textiles Thrive Through Technology," 6 May 1999. Available from http://www.textileworld.com.

Standard & Poor's Industry Surveys. New York: Standard & Poor's Corporation, 1999.

U.S. Bureau of the Census. "Broadwoven Fabrics." *Current Industrial Reports.* Washington, D.C.: GPO, 1997.

"Washington Outlook." *Textile World,* January 1996.

SIC 2231

BROADWOVEN FABRIC MILLS, WOOL (INCLUDING DYEING AND FINISHING)

This category covers establishments primarily engaged in the production of woven fabrics more than 12 inches (30.48 centimeters) in width, wholly or chiefly by weight of wool, mohair or similar animal fibers; dyeing and finishing of woven wool fabrics; and those shrinking and sponging wool goods for the trade. These fabrics are used primarily for production of apparel (especially outerwear), home furnishings (especially blankets), and specialty items, such as billiard table cloth.

Establishments primarily engaged in weaving or tufting wool carpets and rugs are classified in **SIC 2273: Carpets and Rugs.** Production of broadwoven fabrics with content wholly or primarily by weight of cotton is included in **SIC 2211: Broadwoven Fabric Mills, Cotton.** Production of broadwoven fabrics with content wholly or chiefly by weight of manmade fiber and silk is included in **SIC 2221: Broadwoven Fabric Mills, Manmade Fiber and Silk.** Production of narrow fabric, generally 12 inches or less in width, of cotton, wool, silk, and manmade fiber is included in **SIC 2241: Narrow Fabric and Other Smallwares Mills: Cotton, Wool, Silk, and Manmade Fiber.**

NAICS Code(s)

313210 (Broadwoven Fabric Mills)
313311 (Broadwoven Fabric Finishing Mills)
313312 (Textile and Fabric Finishing (except Broadwoven Fabric) Mills)

Industry Snapshot

There are fewer than 100 establishments producing broadwoven fabrics of wool, mohair, or similar animal fiber, according to the U.S. Department of Commerce, Bureau of the Census. Of all fibers in this classification, the greatest production is in wool fiber. According to the Department of Commerce, the value of production shipments in 1997 for these fabrics exceeded $1.3 billion. The vast majority of fabrics was produced for the apparel industry.

U.S. mill use in 1996 was 164.4 million pounds, an increase from 1995 of 2.6 million pounds. The 1997 levels stayed steady at 164.3 million pounds before dropping substantially in 1998 to 123.6 million pounds. This represented a 0.7 percent of total fibers consumed, a drop of 0.3 percent from 1995 through 1997. With U.S. mills producing some 132.2 million square yards of broadwoven gray, chiefly wool fabric in 1998, the wool segment of this industry continued to produce just a fraction of the quantities produced of cotton and manmade/silk broadwoven fabrics.

The U.S. Census Bureau reported total industry employment at 9,227 workers in 1997. Of this, 7,063 workers were directly involved with production. Total payroll was $234.2 million. Employment declined in 1997, falling by 4,473 workers from 1992. Strides in technology, along with international competition, consolidations, and increasing productivity, contributed to the downward trend. However, the technology also increased the need for higher-skilled workers, resulting in higher payroll costs.

The two largest producers of wool fabrics were Burlington Industries and Forstmann & Co., formerly the wool division of J.P. Stevens. In 1998 Burlington posted net income at $31.5 million and employed 18,500 people. Forstmann & Co. reported 1998 sales at $149.6 million, a 24.8 percent sales growth since 1997. In 1998 the companies employed 1,375 people, up 44.7 percent from 1997.

Organization and Structure

Producing woolen broadwoven fabrics is similar in principle to making broadwoven fabrics in the cotton and manmade sectors. However, wool and other animal fibers must be scoured before being processed into yarn to remove animal greases and other debris that become entangled in the wool before shearing.

The processes required to make yarns—opening, carding, drafting, roving, and spinning—use machines that are larger and designed to process long-staple fibers. These fibers are four to eight inches long, compared to seven-eighths to one-and-three-eighths inches for cotton. Most manmade fiber is cut to process on the cotton system of yarn manufacturing and is thus approximately the same length as the cotton fibers. Some manmade fibers are designed to go into products that replace woolen fabrics—suitings and blankets—that will be blended with wool fibers (polyester-wool blends, which are cut to process on woolen machinery).

Like makers of broadwoven cotton and manmade fabrics, producers of woolen fabrics are generally fully integrated; they produce, weave, then dye the yarn, and finish the woven fabric. Some companies maintain yarn manufacturing and weaving operations in one manufacturing plant and dyeing and finishing in another. Frequently, however, producers of woolen yarn and fabrics buy wool that has already been scoured. The scoured wool purchased by producers of woolen fabrics is generally known as "woolen tops."

There are three categories of manufacturing machinery for production of wool yarns: woolen, worsted, and semiworsted. The category used is determined by the intended fabric's end use. Mohair and other animal fibers were processed on standard woolen, worsted, and semiworsted yarn manufacturing machines with occasional modifications to adjust for variations in fiber length.

Most woolen and other animal fiber broadwoven fabrics were produced on projectile, rigid, and flexible rapier weaving machines. Air-jet weaving machines were not suitable for production of heavyweight woolen fabrics but are used occasionally if the woolen fabric is a very lightweight worsted product. Water jet weaving machines cannot be used to produce broadwoven fabrics of wool and similar animal fibers.

In the early 1990s, only Japan's Tsudakoma Corp. and Toyoda Automatic Loom Works Ltd. manufactured air-jet weaving machines for making worsted fabrics. Sulzer Ruti of Switzerland manufactured projectile machines that were widely used to produce broadwoven fabrics of wool and similar animal fibers. A number of weaving machine manufacturers produced flexible and rigid rapier looms that were used for weaving broadwoven fabrics from woolen and other animal fiber yarns. Flexible rapier weaving machines were available from a small number of Italian and Belgian companies. Rigid rapier weaving machines were available through several European woolen broadwoven fabric makers.

Dyeing and finishing of woolen fabrics was performed on machinery similar to that found in the processing of cotton and manmade fibers. However, chemicals designed specifically for woolen and other animal fibers were used. Frequently, and more often in woolen fabrics than in other types, dyeing was done prior to the manufacture of the fabric. This was done by dyeing the raw wool after scouring or by dyeing the wool yarn. Dyeing the wool before it was made into fabric was absolutely necessary if the finished product was going to contain a plaid, stripe, or any multicolored pattern (unless the fabric was going to be printed with the design). Since many of the wool fabrics that were woven would be printed with multicolored patterns, stripes, or plaids, predyeing of the raw material or yarn was more common in woolen operations than in those processing cotton and/or manmade fiber.

Most wool is raised in Australia, New Zealand, and the United Kingdom, increasing its cost to textile plants in the United States (where wool production is insignificant). The added cost of scouring plus the increased cost of wool processing machinery further increase the price of woolen products. Mohair is even more expensive than that wool. Subsequently, wool, mohair, and similar animal fibers used to produce broadwoven fabrics have been more expensive (as raw materials) than cotton and most

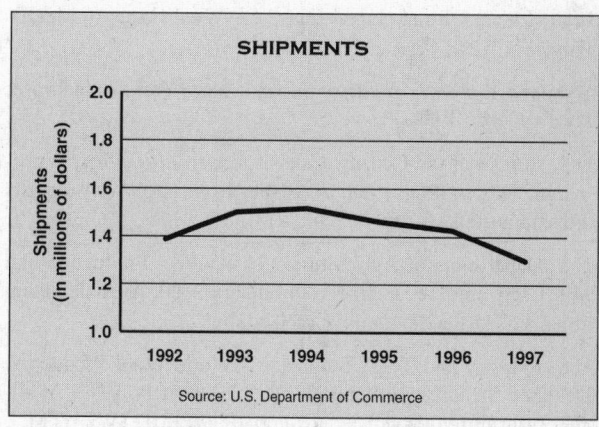

SHIPMENTS

Shipments (in millions of dollars)

Source: U.S. Department of Commerce

manmade fibers. For this reason, apparel, blankets, and other common applications for wool and animal fibers are often considered luxury items. The most expensive fibers used in textile applications include certain manmade fibers and those with special applications for high strength or resistance to heat.

CURRENT CONDITIONS

Wool consumption continued to decrease as retail sales of wool apparel declined in the late 1990s. Weaker mill demand was a direct result of the drop in wool consumption in 1997 and 1998. End-use fiber consumption of wool in the United States in 1998 was less than one percent.

In 1999, mill consumption of raw wool was expected to be nearly 30 million pounds less than in 1998. During the first nine months of 1999, apparel wool consumption was 36 percent less than the previous year. In the same period, nearly 25 million pounds were used in the woolen system and 27 million in the worsted system. Top production of wool was 25 million pounds, compared with 39 million in 1998.

At the end of the century, slower economic activity abroad, importation of low-priced wool coats, and weak retail sales of wool apparel were contributing to reduced mill use, according to the U.S. Bureau of the Census. Reductions also were attributed to the weather, as milder winter conditions prevailed and casual attire became more acceptable in the workplace.

Manufacturers began to address the problems of consumer perception of wool as old-fashioned and problematic. Creating comfortable, easy-care fabrics to gain consumers' attention became a priority. Manufacturers hoped that investment in new technology, innovation, research, and advertising would increase output.

FURTHER READING

Hoover's Inc. *Hoover's Company Capsules*, 1999. Available from http://www.hoovers.com.

Muir, Lucie. "Rejuvenated Image for Wool Focus to Meet." *Women's Wear Daily,* 15 June 1999.

Standard & Poor's Industry Surveys. New York: Standard & Poor's Corp., 1999.

U.S. Bureau of the Census. *Current Industrial Reports.* Washington, D.C.: GPO, 1998. Available from http://www.census.gov/ftp/pub/industry/.

U.S. Department of Agriculture. "U.W. Wool Production and Mill Use Continue Decline," 17 January 2000. Available from http://www.usda2.mannlib.cornell.edu.

U.S. Industry and Trade Summary. "World Wool Production Declined Steadily During 1993-97," 11 January 1999. Available from http://www.usitc.gov/er/nl1999/ER0111W2.HTM.

University of Texas. "U.S. Fibers End Use Summary, Excluding Glass Fiber, 1989-1998," 15 January 2000. Available from http://www.utexas.edu/depts/bbr/natfiber/natstat/data/3t012.htm.

University of Texas. "U.S. (1982-1998) and other North American (1992-1998) Mill Fiber Consumption," 15 January 2000. Available from http://www.utexas.edu/depts/bbr/natfiber/natstat/data/.

SIC 2241

NARROW FABRIC AND OTHER SMALLWARES MILLS: COTTON, WOOL, SILK AND MANMADE FIBER

This category covers establishments primarily engaged in weaving or braiding narrow fabrics of cotton, wool, silk, and manmade fibers, including glass fibers. These fabrics are generally 12 inches or less in width in their final form but may be made initially in wider widths that are specially constructed for cutting to narrower widths. Also included in this industry are establishments primarily engaged in producing fabric-covered elastic yarn or thread.

Weavers of broadwoven fabrics, those that are generally greater than 12 inches in width, are covered in **SIC 2211: Broadwoven Fabric Mills, Cotton; SIC 2221: Broadwoven Fabric Mills, Manmade Fiber and Silk; and SIC 2231: Broadwoven Fabric Mills, Wool (Including Dyeing and Finishing).**

Products that fall into the narrow fabrics category include webbing for military use, industrial belting, automotive seat belts; narrow apparel products such as waistbands and straps; tapes for venetian blinds, insulating, zippers, and fasteners; ribbons, laces, fringe, and other trimmings; and labels, strapping, and shoelaces.

NAICS CODE(S)

313221 (Narrow Fabric Mills)

In 1997 some 273 U.S. operations engaged in the production of narrow fabrics, according to the U.S. Census Bureau. These companies produced and shipped $1.39 billion worth of narrow fabric products and employed more than 16,000 people. Wages for the industry's 13,438 production workers totaled $251 million, with the average employee earning $9 per hour. The industry spent $605 million on materials.

Narrow fabrics are usually divided into two categories: elastic and rigid (or nonelastic). Narrow fabrics that, when stretched, will then return to the original shape and size fall into the elastic group. Elastic narrow fabrics include waistbands and some straps.

Narrow fabrics weaving machines differ from broadwoven weaving machines in more ways than the width of fabrics produced. Narrow fabrics weaving machines produce more than one fabric at a time. Generally speaking, the wider the fabric, the fewer multiples of fabric pieces are woven. Some narrow fabrics are produced on broadwoven weaving machines, and the fabric is slit into the narrow widths after it is woven.

Electronic machinery has become increasingly important to this industry, largely because of the need to be versatile. For example, a company that supplies labels for apparel has to be able to respond quickly when a garment manufacturer suddenly needs to change the labels on its products.

While demand for some other textiles often fluctuates with the economy, the market for narrow fabrics tends to remain fairly stable. This is especially true for webbings for industrial and military use and tapes, bandages, and gauze for the medical trade.

During the mid-1990s, products made for cargo and transport, such as cargo lifting straps and automotive tow straps, remained a primary source of income. Sporting goods products, such as golf-bag straps, came in second, followed by automotive seat belts. Sling devices, including many products for use in the medical field, and pet products, such as leashes and collars, rounded out the field.

In 1997 North Carolina had 35 of the nation's 273 narrow fabric mills, California had 22, Massachusetts and New York each had 18, and New Jersey had 15. The 128 establishments with at least 20 employees generated $738 million (53 percent) of the $1.4 billion worth of merchandise shipped by this industry.

Like many other textile manufacturers, some companies in this category were merging to form larger corporations, shutting down their less profitable plants, and reducing production at other plants. This trend toward consolidation and greater efficiency was triggered in part by changes in international trade agreements, which opened the industry to global competition. The price of raw materials, decreased demand for certain textiles, and technological advances were also factors.

Spartan Mills Inc., of Spartanburg, South Carolina, was one of the largest firms in this industry in 1998, with 4,800 employees and annual sales of $400 million. Other leading companies included Worldtex Inc., of Hickory, North Carolina; BGF Industries Inc., of Greensboro, North Carolina; Conso International Corp., of Union, South Carolina; and C.M. Offray and Son Inc., of Chester, New Jersey.

FURTHER READING

Malone, Scott. "Wordtex Acquires Elastic Fabric Facility from FTL." *WWD*, 5 January 1999.

U.S. Department of Commerce, Bureau of the Census. *1996 Annual Survey of Manufactures*. Washington, D.C.: GPO, 1998.

U.S. Department of Commerce, Bureau of the Census. *1997 Economic Census*. Washington, D.C.: GPO, 1999. Available from http://www.census.gov/prod/ec97/97m3132b.pdf.

SIC 2251

WOMEN'S FULL-LENGTH AND KNEE-LENGTH HOSIERY, EXCEPT SOCKS

This industry category includes establishments primarily engaged in knitting, dyeing, or finishing women's and misses' full-length and knee-length hosiery (except socks), both seamless and full-fashion, and pantyhose. Those establishments primarily engaged in knitting, dyeing, or finishing women's and misses' knee-length socks and anklets can be found in **SIC 2252: Hosiery, Not Elsewhere Classified.** Establishments primarily engaged in manufacturing elastic (orthopedic) hosiery are classified in **SIC 3842: Orthopedic, Prosthetic, and Surgical Appliances and Supplies.**

NAICS CODE(S)

315111 (Sheer Hosiery Mills)

According to the U.S. Census Bureau, there were 153 establishments engaged in the production of women's full-length and knee-length hosiery in 1997, a decrease from 161 establishments in 1991. The industry shipped $1.6 billion worth of goods, spent $818.0 million on materials, and paid $35.0 million for capital expenditures. It employed 17,579 people, including 15,690 production workers who earned an average hourly wage of $8.69. About half of the establishments in this category had at least 20 employees.

About 56 percent of the establishments in this category were located in North Carolina, home to 70 percent of the largest companies producing women's hosiery (except socks). Alabama and California also had relatively large concentrations of businesses in this industry.

Most women's hosiery products are made of textured nylon and produced on small-diameter knitting machines. The processes involved in production of the goods covered by this category include: production of POY (partially oriented yarn) nylon filament by fiber producers; texturizing (or texturing) the nylon filament; knitting the filament nylon into the hosiery product; boarding the hosiery to obtain proper size and shape; and finishing the hosiery products and packaging them. Texturing of the nylon hosiery yarn is covered in **SIC 2282: Yarn Texturizing, Throwing, Twisting, and Winding Mills.**

The biggest event in the development of hosiery manufacturing was DuPont's invention of nylon, which was introduced to the public in 1938, replacing the baggier cotton or more expensive silk stockings. Finding a commercially palatable name for what was officially polyhexamethyleneadipamide took more than two years. Nylon, the word, is a derivative of nylon stockings' widely rumored "no-run" feature.

Sales growth in the women's hosiery industry slowed in 1993 and 1994 and remained sluggish in 1995. Women's sheer hosiery sales were $2.7 billion, up 2 percent from 1994, and tights and opaques sales dropped by almost 2 percent. In 1996, however, tights and opaques sales rose 16 percent to $681.0 million and Spandex Leg sales climbed 12 percent, while sheer hosiery sales dropped nearly 1 percent due in large part to the 19 percent drop in all-nylon, non-control top hosiery sales.

The market for sheer hosiery declined during the late 1990s because "the barelegged look" (wearing no stockings) became fashionable, and because a trend toward more casual clothes encouraged women to wear slacks and socks instead of short dresses and nylon stockings. Manufacturers responded by conducting consumer research to help them launch new products and improve old ones to meet women's needs. For example, some lines of hosiery provided the barelegged look but covered imperfections in women's legs. Comfort, durability, body contouring, and overall high quality became increasingly important factors in hosiery. Nevertheless, demand for sheer hosiery and tights dropped for the fifth consecutive year in 1998, down 8 percent since 1997, according to *Supermarket Business.*

One of the largest companies producing goods in this category was Sara Lee Corp. (Chicago, Illinois), a diversified firm with 139,000 employees and total sales of $20 billion in 1998. Its hosiery subsidiary L'eggs Brands Inc. (Winston-Salem, North Carolina) had estimated sales of

$660 million. Another subsidiary, Hanes Hosiery Inc. (Winston-Salem, North Carolina), had sales of $260 million. Other leading companies included Ithaca Industries Inc. (Wilkesboro, North Carolina) with estimated sales of $333 million, Glen Raven Mills Inc. (Burlington, North Carolina) with estimated sales of $291 million, Hampshire Group Ltd. (Anderson, South Carolina) with sales of $169 million, and Americal Corp. (Henderson, North Carolina) with estimated sales of $123 million.

Trade negotiations during the 1990s opened up opportunities for a potential export market. In 1994 trade barriers were reduced in Japan, Canada, and Mexico as a result of the North American Free Trade Agreement (NAFTA). In the third quarter of 1996 U.S. total hosiery exports dropped 5 percent from 1995 figures, with most of the decrease attributed to the 77 percent decline in women's full- and knee-length hosiery. Pantyhose and tights exports grew 15 percent to 7.8 million dozens of pairs, with 1.8 million dozens of pairs exported to El Salvador and another 1.5 million dozens of pairs to Mexico. A new World Trade Organization (WTO) was established in 1995, and the Multifiber Arrangement (MFA)—which allowed importing countries to limit the flow of imports from lower cost, developing countries— was replaced by the Agreement on Textiles and Clothing (ATC), which required phasing out MFA quotas over a 10-year period. According to Linda Shelton in an *Industry, Trade, and Technology Review* report, "The elimination of MFA quotas likely will have a significant impact on the U.S. textile and apparel sector given the level of protection that such restrictions have provided domestic producers over the past two decades." Since the United States had until 2005 to implement the ATC, the legislation's impact on the hosiery industry might not be realized for several years.

FURTHER READING

Brady, Jennifer L. "Sara Lee Reports 12.8 Percent Profit Hike in Second Quarter." *Women's Wear Daily,* 26 January 1996. Available from http://207.51.71.250/samples/archive/1996/000/497.htm.

Feitelberg, Rosemary. "Vendors Deal with Consolidation." *Women's Wear Daily,* 14 June 1999.

National Association of Hosiery Manufacturers. *Annual Summary.* Charlotte, NC: National Association of Hosiery Manufacturers, 1995. Available from http://www.nahm.com/601c.htm.

———. *Imports of Tights from Mexico Increase.* Charlotte, NC: National Association of Hosiery Manufacturers, 1995. Available from http://www.nahm.com/601f.htm.

———. *1996 Hosiery Sales Leap Ahead.* Charlotte, NC: National Association of Hosiery Manufacturers, 1996. Available from http://www.nahm.com/601d.htm.

Schwartz, Ela. "Sheer Strategy." *Supermarket Business,* 15 September 1999.

Shelton, Linda, and Robert Wallace. "World Textile and Apparel Trade: A New Era." *Industry, Trade, and Technology Review,* October 1996.

U.S. Census Bureau. *1997 Economic Census.* Washington, D.C.: GPO, 1999. Available from http://www.census.gov/prod/ec97/97m3151a.pdf.

Wilson, Eric. "Sara Lee's Game Plan: More Spandex." *Women's Wear Daily,* 3 March 1997.

SIC 2252

HOSIERY, NOT ELSEWHERE CLASSIFIED

This category covers establishments primarily engaged in knitting, dyeing, or finishing hosiery, not elsewhere classified. Establishments engaged in the knitting, dyeing, or finishing of anklets, boys' hosiery, children's hosiery, leg warmers, men's hosiery, socks, slipper socks, and men's and children's tights are included in this category. Establishments engaged in the production of women's full-length and knee-length hosiery and panty hose are classified in **SIC 2251: Women's Full-Length and Knee-Length Hosiery, Except Socks.** Establishments engaged in manufacturing elastic (orthopedic) hosiery are classified in **SIC 3842: Orthopedic, Prosthetic, and Surgical Appliances and Supplies.**

NAICS CODE(S)

315111 (Sheer Hosiery Mills)
315119 (Other Hosiery and Sock Mills)

The U.S. Census Bureau reported that in 1997 there were 401 companies operating in this category. They shipped $3 billion worth of goods, spent $1.57 billion on materials, and paid out $96 million for capital expenditures. They employed 35,647 people, including 31,628 production workers who earned an average hourly wage of $8.46.

Of the 439 plants in operation, 254 (58 percent) had at least 20 employees. Most establishments in the segment were concentrated in the Southeast; 208 were in North Carolina, and 132 were in Alabama.

Unlike most companies that weave fabric, establishments in this segment usually purchase yarn instead of making their own because it would be too costly and inefficient for each facility to manufacture the many types of yarn used to make hosiery. After buying the yarn, most companies in this category complete their own dyeing, finishing, and packaging. At that point, their merchandise is ready for retail sale.

Products in this category range from heavy woolen socks used by hunters to lightweight anklets worn by small children. They can be made from cotton, wool, nylon, polyester, polypropylene, rayon, mohair, and other fibers, as well as blends of two or more fibers. The fabric is produced on small-diameter knitting machines.

This category grew during the early 1990s, due in large part to the increasing popularity of casual clothing and a strong movement toward active wear throughout most of the United States. Men's finished seamless hosiery and anklets made of natural fibers made up slightly more than 60 percent of sales within this category at that time.

According to the National Association of Hosiery Manufacturers Annual Report 1996, there were 334 hosiery production companies operating 440 plants around the United States in 1996. Eighty-five of these plants were in the women's sheer hosiery business. The other 355 were in the sock industry.

During the late 1990s, hosiery manufacturers tried to operate more efficiently—and some companies merged—to compete more effectively in the global marketplace. Kayser-Roth Corp. was acquired by an Italian hosiery firm named Golden Lady. (It had previously been owned by a Mexican company.) Renfro Corp. and Ridgeview Inc. were two leading hosiery makers that closed factories to reduce their expenses.

The leading company in this category was Kayser-Roth Corp. (Greensboro, North Carolina) with sales estimated at $500 million in 1998 and approximately 6,000 employees. Other leaders in the industry were Renfro Corp. (Mount Airy, North Carolina) with estimated sales of $169 million; Adams-Millis Div. (a subsidiary of Sara Lee Corp. based in High Point, North Carolina) with estimated sales of $140 million; Ridgeview Inc. (Newton, North Carolina) with sales of $98 million; Chipman-Union Inc. (Union Point, Georgia) with estimated sales of $90 million; and DeSoto Mills Inc. (Fort Payne, Alabama) with sales of $88 million. Diversified hosiery makers also competed in this industry, including Fruit of the Loom Inc. (Chicago, Illinois), Jockey International Inc. (Kenosha, Wisconsin), Americal Corp. (Henderson, North Carolina), Kentucky Derby Hosiery Company Inc. (Hopkinsville, Kentucky), and Danskin Inc. (New York, New York).

In 1996 about 30 percent of hosiery imports were "9802" transactions (hosiery partially made in the United States, then shipped out of the country for further work, then brought back into the United States to be sold). The hosiery imported that year was 42 percent socks, 13 percent tights/opaques, 41 percent pantyhose, and 4 percent women's full-length hosiery.

FURTHER READING

1996 Annual Report of the National Association of Hosiery Manufacturers, 1997.

"A Legwear Megadeal: Italy's Golden Lady to Buy Kayser-Roth." *WWD,* 30 December 1998.

Calnan, Christopher. "Sock-Maker Renfro to Close Plant in Western Virginia and Reopen Another." *Knight-Ridder/Tribune Business News,* 19 November 1999.

Feitelberg, Rosemary. "Vendors Deal with Consolidation." *WWD,* 14 June 1999.

Hopkins, Stella M. "Firms Line Up to Buy Greensboro, N.C., No Nonsense Hosiery Maker." *Knight-Ridder/Tribune Business News,* 25 September 1998.

"Ridgeview to Close Seneca Falls, N.Y., Knitting Plant." *Daily News Record,* 20 January 1999.

U.S. Department of Commerce. Census Bureau. *1997 Economic Census.* Washington, D.C.: GPO, 1999. Available from http://www.census.gov/prod/ec97/97m3151b.pdf.

SIC 2253

KNIT OUTERWEAR MILLS

Manufacturers in this category are primarily engaged in knitting outerwear from yarn or in the production of outerwear from knit fabrics produced in the same establishment. Establishments that are primarily engaged in hand knitting outerwear for the trade are included in this industry. Establishments primarily engaged in knitting gloves and mittens are classified in **SIC 2259: Knitting Mills, Not Elsewhere Classified.** Those manufacturing outerwear from purchased knit fabrics are classified in the major group for apparel and other finished products made from fabrics and similar materials.

Products manufactured under this category include such diverse products as bathing suits, bathrobes, beachwear, blouses, body stockings, caps, collar and cuff sets, dresses, hats, headwear, housecoats, jackets, jerseys and sweaters, jogging suits, leotards, lounging robes, mufflers, neckties, pants, scarves, shawls, shirts, outerwear, shoulderettes, ski suits, skirts, slacks, suits, sweat bands, sweat pants, sweat shirts, sweaters and sweater coats, T-shirts, tank tops, ties, trousers, warm-up suits, and wristlets.

NAICS CODE(S)

315191 (Outerwear Knitting Mills)

INDUSTRY SNAPSHOT

This category in 1997 contained more establishments, 679, than any other category classified in Industry Group 225 (knitting mills). In 1997, according to the U.S. Economic Census, the value of shipments from this industry was $5.69 billion, virtually unchanged from 1995 shipments of $5.68 billion. There were a reported 45,954 employees working in the knit outerwear industry in 1997.

The industry's major players in the late 1990s ranged from large, widely diversified Sara Lee Corp. to a number of somewhat smaller companies more narrowly focused on the production of apparel. In the latter category were VF Corp., Russell Corp., Tultex Corp., and Dyersburg Corp.

In addition to its involvement in knitwear and other apparel, Sara Lee, headquartered in Chicago, has a major stake in food products, jewelry, and cosmetics. With more than 138,000 employees worldwide, Sara Lee reported sales of $20 billion in fiscal 1999, the twelve months ending June 30, 1999.

VF Corp., based in Greensboro, North Carolina, employs 70,000 people and manufactures a broad range apparel, of which knitted outerwear is only one segment. The company reported 1998 sales of $5.48 billion, up 4.9 percent from 1997. Russell, headquartered in Atlanta, posted 1998 revenue of $1.18 billion, down 3.9 percent from its performance in 1997. Russell employs a workforce of more than 15,500.

Tultex, a major producer of active wear and college-licensed sports clothing, is headquartered in Martinsville, Virginia. With a workforce of more than 5,000 people, Tultex reported 1998 sales of $469 million. Based in Dyersburg, Tennessee, Dyersburg Corp. reported revenue of $312 million in fiscal 1999, the 12 months ending September 30, 1999. Dyersburg boasted a workforce of more than 2,200 people as of late 1999.

Most of these companies have capitalized on one of the fastest growing product areas in the textile industry and the fastest growing section of apparel textile products: leisure and active wear. Popular products in this market segment include T-shirts and golf shirts (knit shirts with collars) for men, women, and children. The T-shirt business has been one of the fastest growing in the textile industry, especially with the trend toward putting messages and company names on them.

ORGANIZATION AND STRUCTURE

Two broad categories of knitting machines produced the products in this classification—circular and flat. Circular machines are much more prominent in this category because flat machines generally are used in the production of sweaters. Major producers of circular knitting machines were Camber International of Leicester, England; Fukuhara Ltd. of Osaka, Japan; Mayer & Cie of Albstadt, Germany; Monarch Knitting Machine Corp. of St. Glendale, New York; Terrot Strickmaschen GmbH of Stuttgart, Germany; Tritex International Ltd. of Leicester, England; and Vanguard-Supreme of Monroe, North Carolina. Monarch and Mayer were among the major

producers of flat knitting machines as well as Liba Maschinenfabrik GmbH of Naila/Bavaria, Germany, and Karl Mayer of Obertshauesen, Germany.

While it is a generally accepted practice that companies in the weaving business are fully integrated (they produce their own yarn requirements), it is also a general rule that knitting companies are not fully integrated (they buy their required yarn). Most manufacturers of knit products require so many different types of yarn that it is not economically feasible for them to produce their own. Notable exceptions to this practice in the knitting sector were the largest companies in the industry, including Sara Lee. Larger companies can produce their own yarn because they can confine specific products to certain plants and they can invest in modern yarn manufacturing machinery and equipment. Also, while producing more than most other knitting companies, larger companies do not produce as many types of products.

One similarity between large companies such as Sara Lee to the other knitting companies that are not integrated is that knitting operations are not housed in the same buildings as yarn manufacturing operations. Dyeing and finishing the knit fabrics is, however, usually located in the same plant with the knitting operation.

Each week, Sara Lee's Mountain City plant produced more than 1 million pounds of 100 percent cotton yarn for the company's Hanes Beefy-T T-shirt products. The plant was modern not only in its machinery and equipment, but it also employed state-of-the-art electronic information systems technology and the latest in management techniques. At the fully automated plant, bales of cotton were manually unloaded from the delivery trucks, but no one touched any part of the product after that until palletized cartons of yarn were ready to be put back on the same trucks for shipment to Sara Lee's knitting plants.

The Mountain City plant also was fully computer-integrated. A computerized network system monitored each machine for quality, production, and efficiency. A series of alarms and shut-down capabilities alerted teams if problems occurred.

The unique management technique at Mountain City broke industry norms. There were no supervisors except the plant manager. The plant operated 24 hours a day, seven days a week, with two 12-hour shifts. Each shift had two 20-person teams that were responsible for each half of the plant. These teams patrolled operations, monitored electronic information systems, and controlled the manufacturing facility. Teams hired and fired team members and participated in extensive training in such areas as problem solving and consensus decision-making. All employees were salaried and were given business cards. As a symbol of ownership, a tree was planted on the plant's property with each employee's name recorded on a plaque displayed by the tree. In addition, all employees were paid an incentive bonus based on plant production and quality evaluated at the knitting plant.

BACKGROUND AND DEVELOPMENT

While the basic principles of knitting have not changed over the years, the recent use of electronic technology has tremendously enhanced the process. The most prominent infusion of electronics has been use of CAD/CAM (computer-aided design/computer-aided manufacturing) systems. The best known system was manufactured by Monarch Design Systems, which produced a system that increased creativity, productivity, and versatility. Products designed to be knitted on an electronic knitting machine were transferred onto a 3.5 inch disk and then loaded on a Macintosh computer. The disc was then transferred to the knitting machine by a loading device on the knitting floor. This innovation, like new electronic processes in weaving, reduced to hours (in some cases minutes) processes that once took weeks.

Another form of electronics used in the knitting industry was a program for monitoring performance of the process as well as production of the product. One such system was STARFISH (start as you intend to finish), developed by Cotton Technology International, of Manchester, England. STARFISH was a set of computer programs that related the properties and dimensions of a knitted cotton fabric to the knitting parameters and the finishing route. By the using such programs, manufacturers and buyers could quickly calculate the performance of the most popular fabric constructions after dyeing and finishing. Thus, major savings in development time and money were achieved and decision making enhanced.

The knitting industry also took advantage of the textile industry's advancements in using technology to control costs. The American Textile Partnership (AMTEX) collaborated on many projects to increase efficiency, including fostering research and development between the integrated U.S. textile industry and national laboratories. The Demand Activated Manufacturing Architecture (DAMA) project was developing a communications system between the textile industry and the consumer. The rapid communication allowed the industry to quickly respond to changes in the marketplace with appropriate manufacturing processes and inventories—thereby cutting overall costs.

CURRENT CONDITIONS

With increased use of leisure and active wear, business in the industry continued to improve. Passage of the North American Free Trade Agreement (NAFTA) also augured well for manufacturers of products in this classification. North American countries made up the U.S. textile industry's most important export markets, and demand for U.S. made and U.S. style products in Mexico was expected to increase, especially for affordable T-shirts, sweat suits, and jogging suits.

FURTHER READING

Brookstein, David. "U.S. Textiles Has Global Opportunities." *Textile World,* February 1997.

"DAMA Pilot Project Under Way." *Textile World,* October 1996.

Hoover's Online. *Hoover's Company Capsules,* 1999. Available from http://www.hoovers.com.

Morrissey, James A. "Textile Firms Turn Trash to Treasure." *Textile World,* February 1997.

"NAFTA Boosts U.S. Textiles." *Textile World,* January 1997.

Richard, Robert. "Market Outlook." *Textile World,* March 1996.

Rozelle, Walter. "Business Outlook." *Textile World,* March 1996.

Textile Highlights. Washington, D.C.: American Textile Manufacturers Institute, March 1994.

U.S. Census Bureau. *1997 Economic Census.* Washington, D.C.: GPO, 1999.

U.S. Department of Commerce. *U.S. Industry and Trade Outlook '99.* Washington, D.C.: GPO, 1999.

SIC 2254

KNIT UNDERWEAR AND NIGHTWEAR MILLS

This category covers those establishments primarily engaged in knitting underwear and nightwear from yarn or in manufacturing underwear and nightwear from knit fabrics produced in the same establishment. Companies primarily engaged in manufacturing underwear and nightwear from purchased knit fabrics are classified in the Major Industry Group 23 (apparel and other finished products made from fabrics and similar materials). Those establishments that produce knitted robes are classified in **SIC 2253: Knit Outerwear Mills.**

NAICS CODE(S)

315192 (Underwear and Nightwear Knitting Mills)

Products manufactured by companies in this classification include underwear briefs and knitted underwear drawers, night gowns, negligees, knit pajamas, ladies' and girls' panties, undershirts, T-shirts used as undershirts (both V-neck and regular neck), slips, and union suits or long (winter) underwear.

There were 56 establishments engaged in the production of underwear and nightwear in 1997, according to the U.S. Department of Commerce, Bureau of the Census. Those establishments shipped $686.0 million worth of products, down from $1.48 billion in 1995. Total employees in 1997 numbered 6,941, a 40 percent drop from 11,400 in 1995. Average hourly wages among the industry's 5,967 production workers dropped from $8.84 in 1995 to $8.77 in 1997.

Almost all products in this category are made on circular knitting machines. Most men's and boys' underwear is made from 100 percent cotton or cotton-polyester blends. Until recently, most women's and girls' underwear was produced from nylon, with silk used as somewhat of a luxury item. By the 1990s the trend in women's underwear was to use cotton. During the late 1980s and early 1990s some companies began modeling women's lines after men's cotton briefs. Such products were successful.

According to the Census Bureau's 1995 Current Industrial Report on Apparel, underwear and nightwear accounted for the bulk of all women's and men's apparel production. There were 1.1 billion units of men's underwear and nightwear produced and 1.3 billion units of women's; however, the value of the underwear was far below that of all other apparel.

The early 1990s saw a healthy growth in underwear and nightwear exports. This trend was expected to continue, in part because trade restrictions were reduced by the 1994 passage of the North American Free Trade Agreement (NAFTA).

The Census Bureau reported that in 1997, North Carolina accounted for $138 million worth of the nation's $898 million total production of men's and junior boys' knit underwear and nightwear. North Carolina also led in the manufacture of women's, misses', juniors', girls', little boys', and infants' knit underwear and nightwear, producing $143 million of the nation's total of $325 million. Georgia produced $11 million in that category, and Pennsylvania produced $43 million. Of the nation's 56 underwear and nightwear knitting mills, 12 were located in North Carolina. The 33 establishments with 20 or more employees generated $398 million (58 percent) of the nation's $686 million worth of products in this industry.

Among the leading underwear companies, Jockey International Inc., of Kenosha, Wisconsin, had revenues of approximately $340 million in 1998. Fruit Of The Loom Inc. of Lexington, South Carolina, had revenues of $2.2 billion; and Maidenform Worldwide, Inc., headquartered in New York, had revenues of $400 million. Other industry leaders included VF Corp. of Greensboro, North Carolina; Sara Lee Knit Products of Winston Salem, North Carolina; Hampton Industries Inc. of Kinston,

North Carolina; Spring City Knitting Company Inc. of Cartersville, Georgia; and Cinderella Knitting Mills Inc., of New York.

FURTHER READING

"Forbes 500 Largest Private Companies." Forbes Inc., 1997. Available from http://www.forbes.com.

U.S. Department of Commerce. Bureau of the Census. *1996 Annual Survey of Manufactures.* Washington, D.C.: GPO, 1998.

U.S. Department of Commerce. Bureau of the Census. *1997 Economic Census.* Washington, D.C.: GPO, 1999. Available from http://www.census.gov/prod/ec97/97m3151d.pdf.

U.S. Department of Labor. Bureau of Labor Statistics. *1998-99 Occupational Outlook Handbook.* Washington, D.C.: GPO, 1998. Available from http://stats/bls.gov/oco/ocos235.htm.

SIC 2257

WEFT KNIT FABRIC MILLS

Establishments in this classification are primarily engaged in knitting weft, or circular, fabrics or in the dyeing or finishing of weft, or circular, fabrics. These companies may sell their fabrics to manufacturers of outerwear, underwear, or other products in the apparel or home furnishings industries. Companies engaged in knitting weft outerwear fabrics and subsequently producing outerwear in the same establishment are discussed in **SIC 2253: Knit Outerwear Mills.** Also, establishments engaged in knitting circular underwear and nightwear products and that manufacture the end-product at the same site are discussed in **SIC 2254: Knit Underwear and Nightwear Mills.** Overall, those companies who buy knit fabrics for the production of outerwear and underwear are described in the major group for apparel and other finished products made from fabrics and similar materials.

NAICS CODE(S)

313241 (Weft Knit Fabric Mills)
313312 (Textile and Fabric Finishing (except Broadwoven Fabric) Mills)

The U.S. Census Bureau reported that 256 establishments produced weft knit fabrics in 1997. These companies shipped $3.1 billion worth of fabric that year, down from $5.2 billion in 1995. This category employed approximately 24,903 workers in 1997 (20,765 of whom were production workers), with a total payroll estimated at $579 million. The average wage for production workers was $9.69 per hour.

Fabrics produced in this category are used across the spectrum of finished goods, from leisure and active wear to more expensive evening wear. The handling of circular knit fabrics is a more delicate process than the handling of woven goods, because the fabrics are not as stable in the finished state. Extreme care must be taken and special containers must be used when shipping circular knit fabrics.

One industry trend during 1997 was the rise of micro-denier fabrics. These densely woven textiles mimic soft silk because they are woven from fabrics containing less than one denier per filament; this creates a fabric that feels like silk and costs considerably less.

In 1997 Dyersburg Corp. of Dyersburg, Tennessee, paid $123.0 million for Almanac Knits and became the nation's largest circular knitting company. The corporation employed 3,160 people and had sales of $417.5 million in 1998. The Fashion Apparel Division of Guilford Mills Inc., had 3,000 employees and sales of $415.0 million. Other industry leaders included Collins and Aikman Textile Group of Charlotte, North Carolina; Malden Mills Industries Inc. of Lawrence, Massachusetts; and Spartan Mills Inc. of Spartanburg, South Carolina.

Guilford Mills' acquisition of Hofmann Laces Ltd. in 1996 was one of the largest in its history, part of a series of takeovers designed to help the company expand globally. In 1999 Guilford Mills began work on a huge textile and garment manufacturing park in Altamira, Mexico, to expand its foreign operations. Meanwhile, Dyersburg Corp., Spartan Mills, and other companies closed some of their U.S. plants and reduced production in others.

The merging of many small- and mid-size companies into giant conglomerates during the late 1990s helped the U.S. textile industry buy and sell merchandise worldwide. This consolidation was largely due to changes in international trade agreements.

FURTHER READING

"Annual Report on American Industry." *Forbes Magazine,* 13 January 1997, 90.

Gridley, Clark. "Guilford Mills Mulls Acquisition on a Global Basis, Says Hays." *Daily News Record,* 11 January 1996, 13.

Malone, Scott. "Guildford, Cone Plan Joint Venture in Mexico." *WWD,* 3 May 1999, 15.

Maycumber, S. Gray. "Dyersburg Buying Almanac: Will Be Largest U.S. Circular." *Daily News Record,* 18 July 1997, 4.

Textile Highlights. Washington, D.C.: American Textile Manufacturers Institute, March 1997.

U.S. Department of Commerce. U.S. Census Bureau. *1996 Annual Survey of Manufactures.* Washington, D.C.: GPO, 1998.

U.S. Department of Commerce. U.S. Census Bureau. *1997 Economic Census.* Washington, D.C.: GPO, 1999. Available from http://www.census.gov/prod/ec97/97m3132e.pdf.

LACE AND WARP KNIT FABRIC MILLS

Establishments in this category are primarily engaged in knitting, dyeing, or finishing warp (flat) knit fabrics; or in manufacturing, dyeing, or finishing lace goods. Products in this category include lace bed sets; lace covers for chairs, dressers, pianos, and tables; curtains and lace curtain fabrics; lace edgings; knit netting; warp knit pile fabrics; and tricot fabrics.

NAICS CODE(S)

313249 (Other Knit Fabric and Lace Mills)
313312 (Textile and Fabric Finishing (except Broadwoven Fabric) Mills)

There were an estimated 196 establishments engaged in the production of warp knit goods or lace products in 1997. Of these, 120 employed 20 or more people. Employment slipped from a high in 1982 of 21,100 employees working within this classification to 20,500 in 1988, a trend that continued into the 1990s, decreasing to an estimated 18,377 by 1997. The industry's 15,277 production workers earned $328 million that year at an average hourly wage of $10.46. North Carolina had 45 mills, the most in this category. Other states with high concentrations of companies in this industry included New York, New Jersey, Rhode Island, Florida, California, and Pennsylvania.

Employees worked as sewing machine operators, textile draw-out and winding machine workers, hand packers and packagers, inspectors, laborers, industrial machinery mechanics, textile bleaching and dyeing machine workers, hand workers, textile machine setters and set-up operators, blue collar worker supervisors, general managers, top executives, and freight and stock handlers.

Warp, or flat, knitting machines look like weaving machines but produce fabrics more like those produced on circular knitting machines. Warp knit is a specialized fabric made by a process in which nylon, acetate, and polyester yarns are run lengthwise in the fabric, forming interlocking loops. The cost, compared to that of circular knit techniques, is relatively low.

During the 1980s a slump in clothing sales and a growing flood of inexpensive imports slowed growth in this industry considerably. Throughout the early to mid-1990s domestic manufacturers remained competitive by introducing new specialty fabrics, such as microdeniers and spandex blends. Microdenier fabrics are stretchy and have a high filament count that gives them a silky feel. Introduced by Guilford Mills Inc. in 1991, this fabric quickly gained a niche market in the warp knit industry. By early 1997 the market for spandex blends had grown markedly. Spandex was being used in a wide range of warp knit fabrics: foundation garments, swimwear, active wear, lace, hosiery, and medical supplies/clothing. Other popular products included woven fabrics with two-way stretch; sheer fabrics in the 15-, 20-, and 30-den range; high-denier fabrics for foundation and control garments, blends with Tencel microdenier and acrylic, and performance fabrics with u-v resistance and thermal and antimicrobal properties.

In 1999 Malden Mills Industries Inc. and Patagonia Inc. introduced Polartech Regulator, a high-performance fleece designed for people to use in the back country. One variety of the new fabric featured polyester yarns in a warp knit design. The two companies had also cooperated 13 years earlier to introduce the first polar fleece fabrics for outdoor enthusiasts.

In 1998 the largest company in this category was Guilford Mills Inc. of Greensboro, North Carolina, a public firm with sales of $900 million and 7,000 employees. Other industry leaders were Liberty Fabrics Inc. of New York; FAB Industries Inc. of New York; Lida Inc. of Charlotte, North Carolina; Mohican Mills Inc. of Lincolnton, North Carolina; and H. Warshow and Sons Inc. of New York. Additional large textile manufacturers involved in this industry included CMI Industries Inc. of Clinton, South Carolina; Malden Mills Industries Inc. of Lawrence, Massachusetts; and Texfi Industries Inc. of Rocky Mount, North Carolina.

During the mid-1990s the North American Free Trade Agreement (NAFTA) and the General Agreement on Tariffs and Trade (GATT) opened new markets for the textile industry, but also increased foreign competition. Some U.S. textile companies began opening facilities in other countries. For example, in 1994 Guilford Mills had production plants in the United Kingdom and part-ownership in the largest warp knitting company in Mexico. In 1998 Guilford Mills bought land for another Mexican operation, a textile manufacturing complex that would later supply fabric for an apparel assembly enterprise on the same site.

FURTHER READING

Balin, Kim Thuy. "Patagonia and Malden Regulate the Backcountry." *Sporting Goods Business,* 25 January 1999, 16.

Ostroff, Jim. "Guilford to Build Textile Plant in Mexico." *WWD,* 13 October 1998, 27.

Rozelle, Walter N. "Miracle Fiber Now Coming Into Its Own." *Textile World,* January 1997.

U.S. Department of Commerce. U.S. Census Bureau. *1997 Economic Census.* Washington, D.C.: GPO, 1999. Available from http://www.census.gov/prod/ec97/97m3132f.pdf.

SIC 2259

KNITTING MILLS, NOT ELSEWHERE CLASSIFIED

Companies in this classification are primarily engaged in knitting gloves and other articles not elsewhere classified. Establishments primarily making woven or knit fabric gloves and mittens from purchased fabrics are classified in **SIC 2381: Yarn Spinning Mills.**

NAICS CODE(S)
315191 (Outerwear Knitting Mills)
315192 (Underwear and Nightwear Knitting Mills)
313241 (Weft Knit Fabric Mills)
313249 (Other Knit Fabric and Lace Mills)

Products manufactured by companies in this category include bags and bagging, bedspreads, curtains, dishcloths, elastic girdle blanks, girdles and other foundation garments, gloves, shoe linings, mittens, stockinettes, towels, and washcloths.

Many companies in this category were small, family-owned businesses serving niche markets. In 1997 there were 24 establishments classified in this industry category, down from 90 establishments operating in 1995. These companies shipped $96.3 million worth of fabric in 1997, compared to $308.1 million in 1995.

Employees of this industry worked as sewing machine operators, textile draw-out and winding machine workers, hand packers and packagers, inspectors, industrial machinery mechanics, textile bleaching and dyeing machine workers, testers, hand workers, textile machine setters and set-up operators, blue collar worker supervisors, general managers, and material movers and handlers.

Like many companies in the knitting business, firms in this category tend to buy yarn that is customized to suit their requirements instead of running their own dyeing and finishing operations. When dyeing and finishing is required, the companies either have the work done on a commission basis or, in some cases, sell goods to dyers and finishers who in turn deliver the finished fabric. For some types of knit work gloves, dyeing and finishing is not necessary; the gloves are made from greige fabric and left the natural color.

Technological advances during the 1990s occurred in three areas throughout the entire textile industry: computer-aided design (CAD), production, and communications; new modular manufacturing systems; and ergonomics (work place instruments designed to improve the safety, health, and efficiency of workers). Smaller firms were often the least efficient. Miscellaneous knitting mills usually had only a few knitting machines, which were either circular or flat machines depending on the product made.

Many of the newer machines were quieter, easier to operate, and designed to reduce workers' stress and injury. Particular emphasis was placed on reducing the repetitive-motion injuries typical of apparel workers that had led to more government regulations, higher workers' compensation costs, and rising health care costs.

Between 1987 and 1995 the number of people employed in this category increased to 3,700, but by 1997 it had plummeted to 935. Total payroll in the segment was $26.25 million. The industry's 796 production workers were paid an average hourly wage of $11.46 that year.

In 1997, of the 196 companies involved in this industry, 120 (61 percent) had at least 20 employees. These larger firms accounted for 67 percent of the merchandise shipped in the category, and they paid 68 percent of the total wages. North Carolina had the largest number of companies in this segment, followed by New York and New Jersey.

Various diversified textile companies produced goods in this category, but among those who made it their primary business, Beacon Looms Inc. (New York) was the largest, with 500 employees and sales of $25.0 million in 1998. Dorothy's Ruffled Originals Inc. (Wilmington, North Carolina) had 350 employees and sales of $18.0 million. Scott Mills Inc. (Plymouth Meeting, Pennsylvania) had 43 employees and sales of $14.8 million, and Arlington Hat Company Inc. (Long Island City, New York) had 95 employees and sales of $6.0 million.

FURTHER READING

"Annual Report on American Industry." *Forbes Magazine,* 13 January 1997.

Chirls, Stuart. "Knit Sales Strong, but Snags Loom." *WWD,* 4 November 1997.

U.S. Department of Commerce. *1996 Annual Survey of Manufactures: Statistics for Industry Groups and Industries.* Washington, D.C.: GPO, 1998.

U.S. Department of Commerce. U.S. Census Bureau. *1997 Economic Census.* Washington, D.C.: GPO, 1999. Available from http://www.census.gov/prod/ec97/97m3132f.pdf.

SIC 2261

FINISHERS OF BROADWOVEN FABRICS OF COTTON

This category covers establishments primarily engaged in finishing purchased broadwoven cotton fabrics or finishing such fabrics on a commission basis. These finishing operations include bleaching, dyeing, printing (roller, screen, flock, plisse), and other mechanical finishing, such as preshrinking, calendering, and napping. Also included in this industry are establishments primarily engaged in shrinking and sponging of cotton broadwoven fabrics for the trade and chemical finishing for water repellency, fire resistance, and mildew proofing. Establishments primarily engaged in finishing wool broadwoven fabrics are classified in **SIC 2231: Broadwoven Fabric Mills, Wool (Including Dyeing and Finishing);** those finishing knit goods are classified in knitting mill industries; and those coating or impregnating fabrics are classified in **SIC 2295: Coated Fabrics, Not Rubberized.**

NAICS CODE(S)

313311 (Broadwoven Fabric Finishing Mills)

INDUSTRY SNAPSHOT

In 1995 there were approximately 349 U.S. establishments engaged in dyeing and/or finishing of broadwoven cotton fabrics. Of these establishments, 126 employed 20 or more workers. The vast majority of these are located in the southeastern United States, particularly in North Carolina (24) and South Carolina (15). Some establishments, such as Burlington Industries Inc., Cone Mills Corp., and Thomaston Mills Inc., are engaged in both manufacturing and finishing of broadwoven cotton fabrics. Some companies, such as Cranston Print Works, are engaged only in the dyeing and finishing of broadwoven cotton fabrics. Total establishments in the industry for the year 2000 were projected at 319.

More than 95 percent of manufactured broadwoven cotton fabrics receive some form of dyeing and/or finishing treatment. Even industrial products that require no coloration still require some type of finishing process to render the fabric useful in its intended application. In the early 1990s, environmentally conscious products began attracting consumer attention. Sheets and pillowcases that were produced without dyeing or chemical processing became popular in department stores. But even these products necessitate a finishing process, albeit one without chemicals, to become useful bedding products.

ORGANIZATION AND STRUCTURE

The finishing of broadwoven fabrics is subdivided into three general processing categories: fabric preparation, fabric coloration, and fabric finishing. Fabric preparation consists primarily of bleaching and preparing fabrics with chemical agents to aid in subsequent processing. Such processes, depending on the end result desired, may be performed in open-width fabric form or in fabric rope form.

Coloration of fabrics consists of a variety of dyeing methods executed via batch or continuous process procedures and printing. Printing of broadwovens may be performed by screen printing machines, roller printing machines, roller-screen printing machines, or by a process known as transfer printing.

Fabric finishing is accomplished either through surface (dry) finishing or wet finishing. Surface or dry finishing consists of such processes as sueding, sanding, and napping and imparts a certain texture or feel to the fabric. Wet finishing consists of preshrinking or sanforizing, mercerization, or heat-setting. Chemical finishes for water repellency, flame retardancy, mildew proofing, and wash-and-wear characteristics are applied during finishing processes. Fabric straightening (elimination of bow and bias) and width setting is also performed during finishing.

Virtually all establishments engaged in dyeing and finishing of broadwoven cotton fabrics have at least part of their operations involved in commission work—dyeing and finishing services performed on fabrics owned by other companies. Dyeing and finishing facilities generally utilize much more complicated production processes than do facilities designed for other textile processes. This is due both to the volume of water used in dyeing and finishing operations and the amount of chemicals used in each dyeing and finishing process. Dyeing and finishing machines and equipment are generally custom-designed to meet specific applications and needs. Piping requirements for water, steam, and chemicals will vary from one installation to another as well. Therefore, building facilities used for dyeing and finishing operations are usually custom-designed. While buildings for other textile processes, such as yarn manufacturing, knitting, and weaving, carry structural specifications due to the weight and vibration potential of the machines, dyeing and finishing building specifications must consider machine weight plus machine and piping design and configuration.

Establishments engaged in dyeing and finishing of broadwoven cotton fabrics generally serve three market categories: apparel, home furnishings, and industrials. In the United States, apparel and home furnishings account for 75 to 80 percent of the broadwoven cotton fabric production. Imports are eroding those markets, however, at a time when industrial fabrics are growing in end uses. Some industry observers expect industrial fabrics to account for approximately 35 percent of production by the end of the 1990s.

In the apparel area, companies dye and finish broadwoven cotton fabrics for men's and ladies' shirts and blouses, children's wear, men's trousers and ladies' pants, leisure and sports wear, and other clothing. Because of some advances developed by Cotton Incorpo-

rated, the research arm of the Cotton Growers' Association, companies can now produce water repellent broadwoven cotton rain wear. Cotton Incorporated has also developed some finishes that allow production of wash-and-wear (easy care, no-iron) cotton fabrics.

In home furnishings, dyers and finishers of broadwoven cotton fabrics supply bedding products (sheets, pillowcases and shams, light comforters and blankets, and dust ruffles); bath products (bath towels, hand towels, and wash cloths); and other household items such as draperies and curtains, napery products (napkins and tablecloths), kitchen towels, upholstery fabrics, and cushion covers. In the industrial area, broadwoven cotton fabrics are dyed and/or finished toward production of medical and hospital goods, abrasive fabrics such as sanding belt fabrics, conveyor belts, tents, awnings, luggage, and other products.

BACKGROUND AND DEVELOPMENT

Along with immense technology advancements, trade agreements during the 1990s had a significant impact on finishers of cotton broadwoven fabrics. Trade agreements enacted in the early 1990s gave the industry the opportunity to compete in the global marketplace through effective brand recognition and marketing together with capital investments in systems such as Demand Activated Manufacturing Architecture (DAMA) that increase efficiency.

The General Agreement on Tariffs and Trade (GATT), which reduced or eliminated tariffs among 117 nations throughout the 1990s, will not, according to American Textile Manufacturers Institute (ATMI) officials, have a positive impact on U.S. producers of dyed and finished broadwoven cotton fabrics. However, since global textile usage could grow dramatically in the future due to developing economies and increasing populations, how much of a negative impact this agreement will have on U.S. dyers and finishers remains to be seen.

The North American Free Trade Agreement (NAFTA), enacted in 1993, which essentially removes all trade restrictions among Canadian, American, and Mexican businesses, had a positive economic effect for U.S. dyers and finishers of broadwoven cotton fabrics. North American countries were the U.S. textile industry's most important export markets throughout the 1990s, and Mexico was expected to continue to be a growing market.

CURRENT CONDITIONS

By the end of 1999, the textile industry as a whole continued to be influenced by global trade conditions and the demands of certain markets. The ATMI reported at the end of 1999 that textile shipments had decreased in 1998 and 1999 as a result of competition from low-priced Asian textiles. Asian textile prices fell by 6.5 percent, negatively impacting the American textile market. On the other hand, American textile imports to Mexico continued to grow and had increased 19 percent during the first ten months of 1999. By the end of 1999, Mexico and the Caribbean Basin Initiative (CBI) region remained the two largest American textile export markets. Textile shipments in 1999 decreased, continuing a trend from 1998. American textile shipments during 1999 fell three percent to total $78 billion.

INDUSTRY LEADERS

The largest company engaged only in finishing broadwoven cotton fabrics is Cranston Print Works headquartered in Cranston, Rhode Island. In 1996 Cranston Print Works had approximately 1,700 employees and $253 million in sales. According to *Hoover's Online,* in the year 2000 Cranston Print Works had sales that ranged from $100 million to $250 million. The next two largest companies in this industry, both with an estimated $55 million in sales, are Santee Print Works headquartered in Sumter, South Carolina, and Cecil Saydah Co. headquartered in Los Angeles, California.

WORKFORCE

Pressure from low-priced Asian textiles had its impact on the American textile industry work force. According to the ATMI, textile industry employment continued to decline in 1999 to an average of 562,000 workers. This represented a 6 percent decrease in the textile work force from 1998. The work week in the industry also changed, with the average hours worked decreasing 7 percent during 1999. Economic census data from 1996 showed an average of 65 employees per establishment for SIC 2261, with an average wage of $9.37 per hour. For the broader industry classification SIC 226, textile draw-out and winding machine operators comprised the largest percentage (30.6 percent) of occupations in the industry.

RESEARCH AND TECHNOLOGY

As a part of industry-wide efforts to remain competitive in the international arena, cotton broadwoven fabric finishers have explored several new operating systems. One such system, called Quick Response, demonstrated throughout the 1990s that as a communications process it could boost production of U.S. made broadwoven cotton products. The Quick Response system requires partnerships throughout the softgoods pipeline—fiber producers, textile manufacturers, apparel manufacturers and retail establishments—and makes use of electronic technology, especially bar coding and Electronic Data Interchange (EDI), to receive up-to-date information. This immediate market feedback enables every member of the pipeline to reduce inventories, shorten delivery times between each pipeline partner, and eliminate processing steps at some partner members' operations without adding them at others.

The system also permits orders from retail establishments that are smaller than season requirements and enables these retail establishments to reorder in mid-season after buying trends and patterns have been established. This process, when all elements are in place, reduces costs at all pipeline partner establishments and reduces the number of necessary markdowns at the end of the season in the retail establishments.

The American Textile Partnership (AMTEX) also aided U.S. producers of dyed and finished broadwoven cotton fabrics throughout the mid-1990s. AMTEX enacted a pact in 1993 in which national laboratories, in conjunction with the U.S. Department of Energy, work on selected projects with the U.S. textile industry and its research facilities to develop systems to make the industry more competitive.

The AMTEX project with the most immediate results is Demand Activated Manufacturing Architecture (DAMA), which expands on the Quick Response system. Under the DAMA system, electronics inform pipeline partners of each garment sold by making use of point-of-sale data generated during scanning of bar-coded hang tags. The DAMA pilot project began in September of 1996, and results have shown that the creation of an electronic marketplace will improve operations and reduce costs through controlling warehouse costs and inventory size and reducing wastes, while improving customer responsiveness and product development. The years of preparation with the Quick Response system have allowed the industry to quickly realize the competitive advantages of capitalizing on the national information super highway.

In 1995 Cotton Inc. cooperated with the Textile/ Clothing Technology Corporation to create a new spray technique for finishing broadwoven cotton. The new technique, called "metered addition of chemicals" used some of the machinery already in operation to dip and dye cotton and garments. According to a representative of Cotton Inc., the new process equaled the quality of garment finishing using dipping or dying methods. Other benefits to the new process included a short time to carry out the spraying (20 minutes to complete a cycle of spraying), the complete use of all chemicals (which are absorbed by the material and not left as waster to be disposed of), and the accessibility of the process to smaller finishing establishments. The spraying process was particularly appealing to companies dealing in smaller finishing volumes, since chemicals could be premixed, eliminating the need for staff chemists. In 1995 a machine that could carry out the spraying process and handle up to 100 pounds of fabric was estimated to cost $21,000.

During the late 1990s, the industry also explored advances in drying finished textiles. Watlow Electric Manufacturing Company found that radiant panel heaters worked better than ceramic radiant heaters for drying silk screening on fabrics. The radiant panel heating process accomplished drying of finished fabric in half the time needed for the ceramic radiant heating process. According to Watlow Company, the manufacturers of the radiant panels, one finisher of textiles was able to reduce inventory with the new heating process.

FURTHER READING

Clune, Ray. "High Performance WR Fabrics—Let Us Spray." *Daily News Record,* 1995.

Dun & Bradstreet Million Dollar Directory: America's Leading Public & Private Companies. New York: Dun & Bradstreet, 1996.

Morrissey, James A. "Textile Firms Turn Trash to Treasure." *Textile World,* February 1997.

"NAFTA Boosts U.S. Textiles." *Textile World,* January 1997.

"Radiant Heater Case History #8," 1996. Available from http://www.watlow.com/casemenu/cases/radi002.htm.

Richard, Robert. "Market Outlook." *Textile World,* March 1996.

Rozelle, Walter. "Business Outlook." *Textile World,* March 1996.

"Textile Year-End Trade and Economic Report." *American Textile Manufacturers Institute,* 22 December 1999. Available from http://www.atmi.org/NewsRoom/releases/pr199941.html.

SIC 2262

FINISHERS OF BROADWOVEN FABRICS OF MANMADE FIBER AND SILK

Establishments in this category are primarily engaged in finishing purchased manmade fiber and silk broadwoven fabrics or finishing such fabrics on a commission basis. Those companies engaged in the dyeing and finishing of broadwoven cotton fabrics are discussed in **SIC 2261: Finishers of Broadwoven Fabrics of Cotton.** Establishments primarily engaged in finishing wool broadwoven fabrics are classified in **SIC 2231: Broadwoven Fabric Mills, Wool (Including Dyeing and Finishing);** those finishing knit goods are classified in knitting mills industry group; and those coating or impregnating fabrics are classified in **SIC 2295: Coated Fabrics, Not Rubberized.** Finishing operations found in **SIC 2262: Finishing Plants, Manmade** include bleaching, dyeing, printing, preshrinking, calendering, and napping.

NAICS CODE(S)

313311 (Broadwoven Fabric Finishing Mills)

INDUSTRY SNAPSHOT

In 1995 there were 215 establishments engaged in the finishing of broadwoven manmade and silk fabrics, according to the U.S. Bureau of the Census. The census projected a decrease to 170 establishments by the year 2000, with 100 of them employing 20 or more people. The great majority of these companies were engaged in finishing polyester fabrics. In 1996, the industry employed 22,500 people and shipped $3.9 billion worth of fabrics. These companies were projected to have 17,600 employees by the year 2000 with shipments of $3.7 billion.

ORGANIZATION AND STRUCTURE

Finishing of broadwoven fabrics is subdivided into three general processing categories: fabric preparation, fabric coloration, and fabric finishing. Fabric preparation consists primarily of bleaching and preparing fabrics with chemical agents to aid in subsequent processing. Such processes, depending on the end result desired, may be performed in open-width fabric form or in fabric-rope form. Severe bleaching of fabrics of manmade fibers isn't necessary to the extent broadwoven cotton fabric bleaching is required, because impurities from the cotton plant are found in broadwoven cotton fabrics. Machines most commonly used in the preparation process include kiers, J-boxes, roller steamers, conveyor steamers, semi-J-box steamers, and high-temperature pressure steamers. The most common chemical agent used is hydrogen peroxide.

Coloration of fabrics consists of a variety of dyeing methods, either in batch or continuous process procedures and printing. The continuous process is by far the most popular in the United States as it is based on high-volume, low-cost-per-unit operations. However, as more and more companies begin articipating in Quick Response or Demand Activated Manufacturing Architecture (DAMA) partnerships, it may become necessary to increase the number of batch perations, which are generally geared toward shorter-run, lower-volume products. Printing of broadwovens may be performed by screen printing machines, roller printing machines, roller-screen printing machines, or by a process known as transfer printing.

The subcategory of finishing divides again into surface or dry finishing and wet finishing. Surface or dry finishing consists of such processes as sueding, sanding, and napping and imparts a certain texture or feel to the fabric. Wet finishing consists of preshrinking or sanforizing, mercerization, or heat-setting. Chemical finishes for water repellency, flame retardancy, mildew proofing, and wash-and-wear characteristics, are applied during finishing processes.

The practice of treating fabrics with resins or other agents to impart shrinkage stabilization, creaseproofing, and shape retention has become extremely important. Collectively, these properties are now known as durable press. Compressive shrinking, generally known as sanforizing, takes place during finishing and prevents shrinking of finished garments. In finishing, widths are set, while fabrics are straightened and given particular feels or hands. It is the final process in textile manufacturing of broadwoven fabrics.

Establishments engaged in dyeing and finishing of broadwoven manmade fiber and silk fabrics generally serve three market categories: apparel, homefurnishings, and industrials. In the United States, apparel and home-furnishings account for 75 to 80 percent of broadwoven fabric production. Because imports are eroding those markets and industrial fabrics are growing in end uses, however, industrials are expected to account for approximately 35 percent of production by the year 2000.

BACKGROUND AND DEVELOPMENT

The 1992 census data showed that a majority of establishments in the industry were located in New Jersey (29), followed closely by North Carolina (25), and South Carolina (20). South Carolina shipped the highest dollar amount in 1992 ($9.1 billion) and employed the greatest number of people (7,300).

Two trade agreements enacted at the end of 1993 have had an effect on the future of this industry. The General Agreement on Tariffs and Trade (GATT), which reduces or eliminates tariffs among 117 nations through 2005 will not, according to American Textile Manufacturers Institute (ATMI) officials, have a positive impact on U.S. producers of dyed and finished broadwoven manmade fiber and silk fabrics. How much of a negative impact this agreement will have on U.S. dyers and finishers remains to be seen. In part, it will depend on the results of efforts put into cooperative systems such as the Quick Response and DAMA systems. The North American Free Trade Agreement (NAFTA), which essentially removes all trade restrictions among Canadian, U.S., and Mexican businesses, has shown short-term positive impacts on the U.S. textile industry since North American countries were the U.S. textile industry's most important export markets throughout the 1990s, and Mexico is expected to continue to be a growing market. The agreement should continue to have a long-range positive effect on U.S. dyers and finishers of broadwoven manmade fiber and silk fabrics, according to officials at the ATMI.

CURRENT CONDITIONS

By the end of 1999, the textile industry as a whole continued to be influenced by global trade conditions. The ATMI reported at the end of 1999 that textile ship-ments had decreased in 1998 and 1999 as a result of competition from low priced Asian textiles. Asian textile prices fell by 6.5 percent, negatively impacting the American textile market. On the other hand, American textile imports to Mexico continued to grow and had increased 19 percent during the first ten months of 1999. By the end of 1999, Mexico and the Caribbean Basin Initiative (CBI) region remained the two largest American textile export markets. American textile shipments during 1999 totaled $78 billion.

Declining demand for home furnishing fabrics impacted at least one American company during 1999. North Carolina based Cone Mills Corp. eliminated 250 jobs in late 1999, citing declining demand as the reason. Cone had struggled to improve its earnings with some success; two of its plants lost $3.6 million during the second quarter of 1998 and had decreased losses to $1.7 million during the second quarter of 1999. But company spokespeople blamed the sluggish industry conditions in part on slow international sales, caused by the Asian economic crisis which lowered the price of foreign products and hurt the industry as a whole. Cone Mills reported that sluggish earnings were not caused by competition from cheaper imported materials.

INDUSTRY LEADERS

Kenyon Industries Inc., headquartered in Kenyon, Rhode Island, and founded in 1989, had 400 employees and $25 million in sales in 1996. Kenyon had 359 employees by the end of 1998 and 1998 sales of $45 million. The second largest company in the industry, Amerbelle Corporation of Vernon, Connecticut, also had an estimated $25 million in sales. The third largest company, J&J Flock Products Inc. of Easton, Pennsylvania, had $17 million in sales in 1996.

RESEARCH AND TECHNOLOGY

Research and technological developments have played a vital role in keeping the U.S. textile industry competitive, and as a part of this industry-wide effort to remain competitive in the international arena, cotton broadwoven fabric finishers have explored several new operating systems. One such system, called Quick Response, demonstrated throughout the 1990s that as a communications process it could boost production of U.S.-made broadwoven cotton products. The Quick Response system requires partnerships throughout the softgoods pipeline—fiber producers, textile manufacturers, apparel manufacturers, and retail establishments—and makes use of electronic technology, especially bar coding and Electronic Data Interchange (EDI), to receive up-to-date information. This process, when all elements are in place, reduces costs at all pipeline partner establishments and reduces the number of necessary markdowns at the end of the season in the retail establishments. The system also overcomes some of the advantages held by establishments exporting products from low-wage, developing countries into the United States.

The American Textile Partnership (AMTEX) enacted a pact in 1993 in which national laboratories, in conjunction with the United States Department of Energy, work on selected projects with the U.S. textile industry and its research facilities to develop systems to make the industry more competitive. The AMTEX project with the most immediate and far-reaching results is Demand Activated Manufacturing Architecture (DAMA), which expands on the Quick Response system. Under the DAMA system, electronics inform each pipeline partner of each garment sold by making use of point-of-sale data generated during scanning of bar-coded hang tags. The DAMA pilot project, begun in September 1996, has shown that the creation of an electronic marketplace will improve operations and reduce costs through controlling warehouse costs and inventory size and reducing waste, while improving customer responsiveness and product development. The Quick Response system has allowed the textile industry to realize the competitive advantages of capitalizing on the national information superhighway.

In 1997, the industry journal *Textile World* announced an innovation produced by Kleinewefer Texilmaschinen—a finishing system known as the Nipco-L-Flex Calendaring System. The innovation incorporated a roller system that would reduce wear to material during processing and would allow high operating temperatures without damage. Other anticipated benefits included reduced downtime of machinery and the elimination of temperature variations.

FURTHER READING
Brookstein, David. "U.S. Textiles Has Global Opportunities." *Textile World,* February 1997.

"DAMA Pilot Project Under Way." *Textile World,* October 1996.

Doering, I. "Kleinewefers: Nipco-L-Flex Calendaring." *Textile World,* April 1997.

Dun & Bradstreet Million Dollar Directory: America's Leading Public & Private Companies Series 1996. New York: Dun & Bradstreet, 1996.

Gresock, Sam. "Cone Mills to Cut 250 Jobs at Fabric Finishing Plant in Carlisle, S.C." *Kinght-Ridder/Tribune Business News,* 19 August 1999.

Morrissey, James A. "Textile Firms Turn Trash to Treasure." *Textile World,* February 1997.

"NAFTA Boosts U.S. Textiles." *Textile World,* January 1997.

Richard, Robert. "Market Outlook." *Textile World,* March 1996.

Rozelle, Walter. "Business Outlook." *Textile World,* March 1996.

Standard & Poor's Industry Surveys. New York: Standard & Poor's Corporation, 1996.

SIC 2269

FINISHERS OF TEXTILES, NOT ELSEWHERE CLASSIFIED

Companies included in this category are those that dye and finish textiles, not elsewhere classified, such as bleaching, dyeing, printing, and finishing of raw stock, yarn, braided goods, and narrow fabrics, except wool and knit fabrics. These establishments perform finishing operations on purchased textiles or on a commission basis.

NAICS CODE(S)
313311 (Broadwoven Fabric Finishing Mills)
313312 (Textile and Fabric Finishing (Except Broadwoven Fabric) Mills)

Most companies in this category dye raw stock or yarn. (Any fiber may be dyed in the raw stock or yarn form.) In the late 1990s, there were approximately 450 U.S. companies engaged in finishing textiles, not elsewhere classified. This represented a substantial increase from the 178 firms reported in 1991. In 1996, these businesses shipped $956.7 million worth of goods, which was less than the $1.2 billion shipped in this category in 1991. Textile finishers employed 9,700 people in 1995, with a total annual payroll of $222.5 million.

Business grew steadily throughout the 1990s for companies engaged in raw stock or package dyeing. Analysts expected business to keep rising because "fancy" fabrics, such as plaids, stripes, and various patterns, require that yarn be colored prior to weaving or knitting. This may be done in either the raw stock form or the yarn form. As of early 1997, the North American Free Trade Agreement (NAFTA) brought increased exports from this and most other textile categories to Canada and Mexico.

Industry leader Knoll Inc. of East Greenville, Pennsylvania, which focused more of its attention on its office furniture business, generated 1998 sales of $948 million while employing 4,050 workers. In 1999 Warburg Pincus Ventures LP, which had purchased 60-percent ownership of Knoll from Westinghouse Electric in 1996 for $565 million, sought to buyout the remaining 40 percent of the stock that Knoll offered at $17 a share when going public in 1997. When Warburg initially offered $25 per share, shareholders (some of whom had paid as much as $40 per share) countered with a lawsuit contending that Warburg's majority ownership prevented competitive bidding. Shareholders agreed on a selling price of $28 per share, which Warburg agreed to pay in cash amounting to $495 million. After acquiring complete ownership of Knoll, Warburg planned on making the company private.

Rounding out the top three industry leaders were Milwaukee-based Meridian Industries, which generated 1998 sales of $220 million with 1,500 employees, and Coats Industrial North America of Charlotte, North Carolina, which garnered $200 million in 1998 sales while employing 2,100 workers.

FURTHER READING

McCalla, John. "Knoll Stockholders to Vote on Buyout." *Philadelphia Business Journal,* 3 September 1999.

Textile Highlights. Washington, D.C.: American Textile Manufacturers Institute, March 1997.

U.S. Department of Commerce. *1995 Annual Survey of Manufactures: Statistics for Industry Groups and Industries.* Washington, D.C.: GPO, 1997.

SIC 2273

CARPETS AND RUGS

This industry includes establishments primarily engaged in manufacturing woven, tufted, and other carpets and rugs such as art squares, floor mattings, needle punch carpeting, and doormats and mattings from textile materials or from twisted paper, grasses, reeds, coir, sisal, jute, or rags. Coverage includes aircraft and automobile floor coverings, except rubber or plastics; bathmats and sets; dyeing and finishing of rugs and carpets; and Wilton carpets.

NAICS CODE(S)

314110 (Carpet and Rug Mills)

INDUSTRY SNAPSHOT

After a ten-year span of steady sales in the 1980s, the carpet industry's primary residential and commercial clients were faced with decreased buying power and constrained budgets and thereby placed carpet buying as a low priority. Higher interest rates, slower starts in new home construction, and sluggish real estate further reduced residential interest in new carpet. Industrywide sales plunged from $8.5 billion in 1990 to less than $7 billion in 1991. Burgeoning consumer confidence and new home construction helped drive a recovery mid-decade, and gross carpet and rug sales increased to more than $9.5 billion on volume of 1.6 billion square yards in 1995. The vast majority—more than 90 percent—of those sales came from tufted carpet and rugs, while woven and other floorcoverings constituted the remainder.

Corporate consolidation was one of the industry's biggest issues in the late 1980s and early 1990s. Mergers and acquisitions reduced the number of participating companies from more than 300 in 1980 to 100 by the mid-1990s, with vertically-integrated "mega-mills" emerging at the top of the heap. The top three players commanded an estimated 64 percent of industry sales volume in 1997. In the industry, Cone Mills returned the most on equity (28.3 percent) of all public textile companies during 1995. Mohawk Industries returned the most on equity (26.5 percent) among public home furnishing companies in 1995.

ORGANIZATION AND STRUCTURE

In the mid-1990s, 238 of America's 383 manufacturing plants were located in the state of Georgia. Carpet mills specialize in producing carpet backing as well as carpets and rugs. Intense competition in the 1980s led forward-looking companies to acquire both manufacturing and retailing operations in an effort to cut costs.

Tradition, profits, and consumer preferences, more than a specific management approach, have historically dictated the organization of the carpet industry. The product flows to residential and contract clients primarily via the following two methods: directly from mill to client or from mill to dealer or wholesale distributor, then to a retailer who sells to a client. If manufacturers in the industry continue to follow the lead of Shaw Industries, Inc., the contemporary industry leader, the industry's organizational mode may be revamped. According to analysts, Shaw's acquisition-based growth coincided with the company's novel management approach. First the company hired aggressive, no commission, straight salary sales representatives. Next, in another cost savings move, Shaw signed shorter, more flexible agreements with retailers and in the process eliminated distributors, a long standing entity in carpet promotion. Whether this strategy is adaptable industry wide remains to be seen; however, carpet manufacturers foresee several outcomes. For example, retailers are expected to begin buying most carpet directly from the mills. Second, total industry recovery will require the development of strategies to create more unified partnerships between manufacturers, retailers, and cleaners that would allow them to serve and sustain customer confidence.

BACKGROUND AND DEVELOPMENT

The first carpet mill opened in Philadelphia in 1791. Until the mid-1800s, carpet manufacturing in the United States was a tedious process using hand operated machines. High quality, artful appeal, and high cost described the carpets of this period. However, during this period and continuing over the next century, several events changed the manufacturing and utility of rugs and carpets. Much of the impetus for industrialization of the

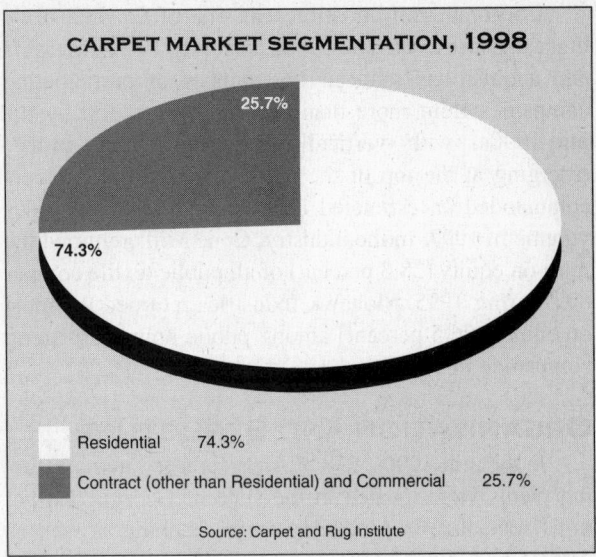

CARPET MARKET SEGMENTATION, 1998

25.7%

74.3%

Residential   74.3%

Contract (other than Residential) and Commercial   25.7%

Source: Carpet and Rug Institute

carpet industry began when Erastus B. Bigelow, known as the "Father of the Modern Carpet Industry," obtained a patent for his invention of a power driven loom. As power looms became more refined and functional, carpet manufacturing became a profitable venture.

The next milestone in the carpet industry came with changes in the composition of carpet. Originally all carpets were made entirely of wool because it insulated against cold and repelled water. Because of these characteristics, wool was declared an essential commodity during World War II and, consequently, carpet production was severely curtailed in favor of war goods production. This setback served as an incentive for researching wool substitutes, which in turn led to the development and upgrade of new natural and synthetic carpet fabrics. By the 1960s, E.I. DuPont de Nemours and Co.'s man-made continuous filament carpet nylon and Chemstrand's acrylic fibers were supplying most of the fibers for broadloom carpets in the industry. Today, nylon accounts for 67.8 percent of the fibers used in carpet manufacturing, followed by 22.2 percent polypropylene, and 9.4 percent polyester, with wool constituting a little more than 0.6 percent of the total.

Weaving, needle-punch, and bonding and tufting are the principle carpet manufacturing processes, with the tufting method accounting for 95 percent of all carpets currently produced and sold in the United States. Tufting differs from weaving and other processes in that yarn is pushed through a previously manufactured backing material, while weaving produces the carpet backing simultaneously as the carpet is being manufactured. As tufting became popularized as a faster and more economical alternative to the traditional weaving process, carpet manufacturers discovered several other cost and labor advantages. Utilization of the tufting process produced broadloom eight to ten times faster, required less fined-tuned weaving skills, and ultimately lowered prices suffi-

ciently to attract lower and middle income groups. Nearly 63 percent of the industry's tufting mills were located in the South due the area's abundance of low-cost labor and excellent water supply.

The impact of these milestones solidified the "homing" of the carpet industry. Between 1950 and 1968, U.S. production of residential and commercial broadloom carpet and rugs rose from 85.7 to 435.0 million square yards, with tufted carpet shipments topping woven Axminster, Wilton, velvet, chenille, and knitted carpets by more than 81 percent in 1968. Price, aesthetics, and utility changed the image of carpet from a luxury item to an essential accessory for every home. By the 1980s, consumer carpet selections included an enormous variety of colors and patterns suitable as indoor/outdoor floor or wall coverings. Moisture repellents and stain resistant treatments increased the life spans of some carpets by as much as ten years and allowed manufacturers to extend carpet warranties. Residential or "home use" carpet, one of the industry's major markets, comprised 76 percent of all floor coverings, 55 percent of which was used for remodeling and replacement purposes, and 45 percent in new home construction in the early 1990s. Carpets for commercial or contract use formed the next primary market and represented the preferred floor covering for 73 percent of all commercial space in offices, schools, hotels, hospitals, airplanes, and other heavily trafficked public areas.

Ironically, just as the "homing phase" of the carpet appeal became entrenched in American living, both residential and commercial users began voicing concerns regarding health and environmental hazards attributed to carpet. In 1987, the Consumer Product Safety Commission received more than 130 complaints about carpeting, mostly focusing on eye and throat irritation beginning after installation of new carpet. One such incident occurred at the Environmental Protection Agency (EPA), where employees complained of flu-like symptoms within days after a new carpet was installed. Specific causes of the illnesses were never identified, but several areas were investigated. No toxic chemicals were found in the carpet, but questions remained regarding toxic ingredients in the carpet adhesives. Another theory postulated that noxious fumes resulted from carpet deterioration. Later tests, so named the Anderson tests after the testing company, Anderson Laboratories Inc., introduced the possibility that carpet emissions capable of killing mice could also produce adverse effects on human life.

Despite disclaiming some of the hazards, the carpet industry vowed to reassess its overall manufacturing process, including the type and quality of raw materials used, the use of pesticides, microbiological contamination, and carpet installation and maintenance processes. Consistent with the industry's objectives to improve consumer confidence, the Carpet and Rug Institute, the industry's trade association, launched a labeling program listing various characteristics of carpet. The Institute is also collaborating with the EPA in the development of indoor air quality guidelines for carpet.

Because consumers remained unconvinced of the carpet industry's intent to alleviate the health hazards of carpet, a consumer lawsuit was filed in 1993 against several carpet manufacturers. Consumers involved in the suit were seeking monetary compensation and other rewards from manufacturers accused of promoting misleading claims regarding carpet air emissions hazards and so-called environmentally friendly carpets.

In the early 1990s, many homeowners took advantage of falling interest rates and refinanced their mortgages. This allowed homeowners to spend more money on remodeling expenditures and new carpeting. A stabilized real estate market with increased new housing starts and greater turnover in home sales would also have a positive impact on carpet sales. As businesses recovered from the recession, contract carpet dealers sought increased business with hospital, health care, and retail facilities. Schools were also seen by many in the industry as a potential growth market.

Carpet and rug sales totaled $9.5 billion in 1995 on volume of 1.6 billion square yards. As they had throughout the postwar era, tufted carpet and rugs continued to dominate, with 87 percent of volume and more than 90 percent of revenues. More than 85 percent of tufted carpet yardage sold was in roll goods. More than two-thirds of all tufted floorcovering yardage was made with nylon face yarn, while about 20 percent were made from polypropylene and another 6 percent was constituted of polyester.

Over the last twenty years, one consistent indicator of this industry's condition has come from tracking real disposable income—as it rose or decreased, so did carpet and rug sales. The 1996 edition of *Manufacturing USA: Industry Analyses, Statistics, and Leading Companies* forecast total U.S. carpet and rug production to grow to $12.5 billion by 1998. Some observers expected the industry's consolidation to bring increased prosperity by eliminating overcapacity. Increases in residential construction and consumer confidence also seemed to bode well for the industry.

CURRENT CONDITIONS

During the 1990s, the majority of industry establishments were located in Georgia, which shipped a total of $7.17 million worth of goods, according to Census data, and employed 31,600 people. By 1996, the industry as a whole shipped $11.18 million, and it was projected to ship $12.74 billion by the year 2000. The majority of U.S. carpet imports in 1997 came from India (45 percent), followed by China (25 percent); imports totaled $961 million. Exports

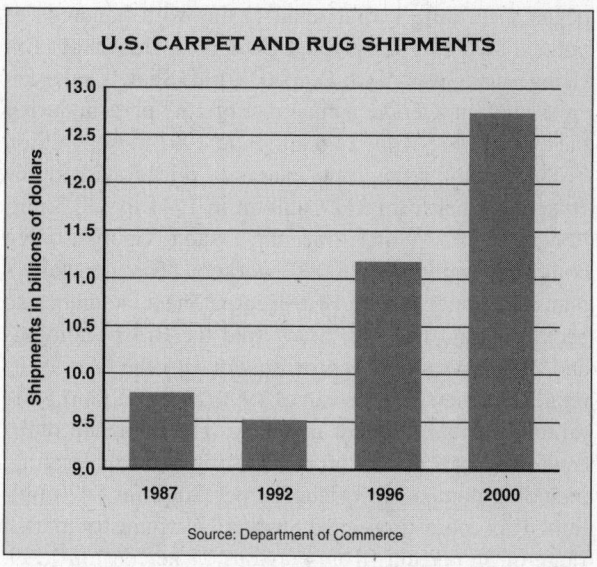

U.S. CARPET AND RUG SHIPMENTS

Source: Department of Commerce

totaled $858 million and the largest markets included Canada, Mexico, Japan, and the United Kingdom.

The Carpet and Rug Institute, an industry organization, also maintained 1997 industry data. Shipments in 1997 totaled $10.3 billion with a $15.7 billion retail value. Worldwide, the U.S. occupied 45 percent of the carpet market. Among all floor coverings, carpet occupied 65 to 70 percent of the marketshare. Marketshare of fibers used in the industry in 1997 included nylon (59.3 percent), Olefin (33.7 percent), polyester (6.6 percent), and wool (0.4 percent).

INDUSTRY LEADERS

Certainly bigger is not always better, yet it appeared to be very helpful for several manufacturers in the carpet industry. Companies undergoing a consolidation or merger found that infusion of capital frequently meant new equipment and expansion of research and development. Such organizational changes represented the norm for the carpet and rug industry in the early and mid-1990s. Acquisitions within the industry created a new crop of mega-mills with Shaw Industries, Inc. topping the list.

Founded in 1967 by brothers Robert Shaw and J.C. Shaw, Shaw Industries, Inc. has long utilized acquisitions to carve out a profitable niche in the carpet industry. In fact, it entered the market via the acquisition of a Georgia carpet mill. The 1987 purchase of West Point-Pepperell Inc. pushed Shaw's revenues over the $1-billion mark and made it the world's largest carpet manufacturer in 1987. Growth via acquisition merely accelerated from that point. By 1995, the company had garnered more than one-fourth of wholesale carpet sales.

Having achieved its goal of establishing a worldwide niche in each important aspect of carpet manufacturing, it began to acquire carpet retail chains with hundreds of outlets, including Carpetland USA Inc., The Carpet Exchange, and New York Carpet World. Shaw's sales increased at an average annual rate of 15.3 percent during the early 1990s, from $1.6 billion in 1991 to $2.9 billion by 1995. But rising raw materials prices slashed the company's net from $127 million in 1994 to $52.3 million in 1995. At that time, the Dalton, Georgia-based company employed 25,000 workers. The company's plans to acquire several British carpet manufacturers also backfired, and in 1999, Shaw sold the British holdings and 275 carpet stores in order to win back the favor of its retail customers. By the end of 1999, Shaw had lost $200 million on its efforts to diversify. The company redirected its focus toward manufacturing and wholesaling; including purchasing Queen Carpet Corp. for $470 million. This acquisition gave Shaw a U.S. industry market share of 35 percent (from previous 27 percent) in 1999. Claimed Robert Shaw, "We are better for having learned more about our customers and the retail business." Shaw's 1998 sales were $3.54 million.

Calhoun, Georgia's Mohawk Industries, Inc. placed a distant second to Shaw, with 18,200 employees and sales of $2,63 million in 1998. Founded in 1878, Mohawk found itself scrambling to keep up with its much younger, but larger, competitor in the early 1990s. Following a public stock offering in 1992, the company made four acquisitions in two years, including Horizon Industries Inc., Karastan-Bigelow Inc., and American Rug Craftsmen Inc. In 1994, Mohawk merged with highly profitable Aladdin Mills Inc. The purchases catapulted Mohawk from eleventh in the industry to number two, increased its sales from $761.0 million in 1992 to $1.6 billion in 1995, and multiplied its market share from less than 4 percent to 19 percent in 1997. The company boasts three of the industry's most recognizable brands: Mohawk, Karastan, and Bigelow. Notwithstanding its impressive growth, Mohawk Industries struggled to cut costs and thereby raise its profitability. By 1998, net income for the year had increased 58.2 percent for a total of $107.6 million. Mohawk continued to focus on its niche markets—household rugs, laminated and tiled flooring, and office carpet.

While high-level mergers raised eyebrows regarding anti-trust issues, many analysts noted the negative impact of these mergers on smaller companies. Smaller companies have more limited pricing options. Therefore, attempts by small manufacturers to duplicate the cost cutting strategies of the mega-mills generally threaten their profitability and ultimately their survival.

WORKFORCE

Having risen to 55,000 in the late 1980s, carpet and rug industry employment declined to less than 50,000 in the early 1990s before rebounding to 55,200 in 1994. More than half of those workers were employed in Georgia, "The Carpet Capitol of the World." Production workers made up approximately 78 percent of the workforce.

While machine operators constituted the industry's largest employment category, computerization of carpet manufacturing was changing job functions and requirements. Machines for tufting, shearing, and many other functions connected to computers were expected to eliminate many low-skilled jobs. The industry was expected to require higher skilled laborers to operate the sophisticated machinery.

By and large, the majority of the industry's production employees had low literacy levels and were unable to interpret computer feedback. Without upgrading the literacy skills of their production workers, manufacturers stood to lose the potentially high returns from converting to a high-tech environment. With more than one-third of their 560 employees deficient in these literacy skills, Collins & Aikman Corp., a Georgia-based carpet mill, developed programs combining remedial education and computer training on company time.

AMERICA AND THE WORLD

In the early 1990s, the United States accounted for more than half of the world's carpet consumption. According to the *U.S. Census of Manufactures,* imports to the United States constituted less than 6 percent of the quantity of carpeting purchased and less than 10 percent of the value in 1995. As Shaw Industries CEO Robert Shaw noted in a 1996 interview for *Textile World,* "We have no foreign competition for all practical purposes." China and Iran were historically the largest importers, but with an embargo against Iran since 1979 and China's Most Favored Nation status under question in the 1990s, carpet and rug importers turned to India, the Philippines and Vietnam (after the Clinton Administration lifted an embargo against that nation in 1994) for supplies. Exports from the U.S. made up slightly more than 7 percent of the quantity and value that year. Several factors constrain international carpet and rug trade, among them quotas and duties, high shipping costs, and the influence of America's leading carpet makers, who are often able to price imports out of the market. Most of America's carpet exports go to Canada. While Americans attributed their spectacular performance in this neighboring market to Canada's lack of competitiveness, Canadians viewed the growth as unfair competition. American carpet companies were accused of "dumping" their goods in Canada at unfairly low prices. The resulting failure of scores of Canadian carpet businesses prompted the Canadian government to institute recovery measures by imposing a permanent duty averaging 12 percent on all American carpets. Although the "dumping" issue had strained relations between the Canada and the United States, Canada was expected to remain an important export market.

In the future, outcomes of other trade issues may well expand or reduce opportunities for U.S. manufacturers to create a global presence. Carpet mills downplayed the impact of the North American Free Trade Agreement (NAFTA), which merged Canada, Mexico, and the United States into one market. The European Community Agreement (EC), another international trade agreement affecting the textile industry, was also expected to enhance international opportunities in textile production.

In the early 1990s industry leaders were aggressively pursuing international trade, though not necessarily through export. Shaw Industries entered both the Australian and Mexican markets via joint ventures. If finding an international niche meant physically relocating to a lucrative market, more companies could be expected to follow the example of Belgium's Beaulieu Group, which established a facility in Georgia as part of its objective to diversify and penetrate the American market.

RESEARCH AND TECHNOLOGY

Research and technology for the carpet industry has focused on producing high quality and environmentally-friendly products, and responding to contemporary customer needs. To these ends, several innovations were in progress in the early 1990s. New backing materials were being developed to replace the environmentally-unfriendly latex. As a secondary backing bond to tufted and needle punched carpets, hot melt adhesive films produced no fumes inside or outside the mills, offered between 70 percent and 80 percent energy savings, and resulted in a 50 percent reduction in backing application time. Waste reduction and reclamation were also key issues under study. Some in the industry campaigned to reduce carpet trim waste, which not only cost U.S. carpet companies an estimated $25 million per year, but also generated tons of useless material destined for landfills. Other ideas being studied for waste reduction included reducing widths of backings and developing pure synthetic backings to match face fibers which would allow burning or recycling of the whole carpet. Many, including industry leader Shaw Industries, adopted the goal of "zero manufacturing waste."

Recycling programs focused on recycling or converting packaging materials like PET bottles and used carpet into everything from floor tiles to concrete reinforcement material and highway guard rails, to like-new carpet fiber. While these solutions required a concerted industry-wide effort, a few company initiatives showed some merit. DuPont maintained a joint program with Sonoco Products Co., which involved reclaiming cardboard drums used to deliver its fluorochemical products.

Hoechst Celanese Corp.'s introduction of a new environmentally friendly carpet not only eliminated latex and the usual odor connected with indoor air quality problems, but it also totally eliminated carpet waste because it was made of 100 percent recyclable polyester.

Another area of research addressed utilization of carpet to reduce physical stress, injuries, and fatigue in a variety of environments. While carpet's nonslip, pliant properties remain favorable, biomechanical studies could lift the carpet industry's sales by measuring how the human body reacts to subtle differences in floor surface properties. Research at the University of Pittsburgh's Medical and Engineering Schools is currently studying body reactions to different carpet and cushion combinations in different facilities, such as high and low-impact aerobic exercise settings.

One industry company took the challenge seriously to work toward making carpet manufacturing more environmentally friendly. Owner Ray Anderson of Interface Inc., a billion dollar carpet company, began changing his operations after he read *The Ecology of Commerce*, by Paul Hawken in 1994. Since then, Anderson reduced scrap (and saved $67 million), reduced operations energy by using less nylon in carpet tiles, and introduced plans to lease carpeting so that old carpet didn't end up in landfills. Interface converted one of its plants to solar energy in 1999 and introduced a product that looked like carpet but could be mopped like vinyl. Anderson also planned to host an environmental summit in mid-1999.

FURTHER READING

Cohen, Warren. "4 Ray Anderson." *U.S News and World Report,* 28 December 1998.

"Most Profitable Public Textiles Companies by Return on Equity, 1996." "Annual Report on American Industry." *Forbes,* 1 January 1996.

Ghosh, Chandrani. "Floored." *Forbes,* 15 November 1999.

Macdonald, Julie. "Carpet Magic." *Hotel & Motel Management,* 6 February 1995.

McCurry, John W. "Shaw Industries Near $3-Billion Sales Plateau." *Textile World,* May 1996.

Schut, Jan H. "'Impossible' Carpet Compound Makes Good." *Plastics World,* February 1996.

"Top Carpet Makers, 1997." *Wall Street Journal,* 19 August 1998.

"U.S. Carpet Imports, 1998." *India Abroad,* 2 January 1998.

Wilson, Frank C. "Carpet Trim Waste: Money Down the Drain." *Textile World,* September 1996.

Wyman, Lissa. "The China Syndrome: Rug Import Options." *HFN: The Weekly Newspaper for the Home Furnishing Network,* 8 July 1996.

YARN SPINNING MILLS

This industry is made up of establishments primarily engaged in spinning yarn wholly or chiefly by weight of cotton, manmade fibers, silk, wool, mohair, or similar animal fibers. Products include acetate and acrylic yarn, made from purchased staple; carded, carpet, combed, and cordage yarn (all of cotton); crochet yarn; and cotton, silk, wood, and manmade staple.

NAICS Code(s)
313111 (Yarn Spinning Mills)

There were approximately 400,000 establishments involved in the yarn spinning mills industry in 1994. This number was estimated to have increased to 411,000 in 1997. The value of industry shipments increased approximately 12.5 percent from 1994 ($8.01 billion) to 1997 ($9.42 billion).

An average two-piece suit currently includes about 67,000 yards of yarn composed of roughly 350 million manmade fibers, textured and colored to produce a natural look. These characteristics basically describe the product flow of yarn spinning mills—from fiber, to yarn, to apparel and home accessories. The actual yarn spinning process entails first cleaning of cotton, wool, silk, or other fibers and then a combing or carding process which turns tangled fibers into straight, even rolls that resemble loose ropes of soft cotton yarn. Depending on the specifications, machines are set to spin yarn of multiple lengths and textures.

Consumers with active lifestyles have called for more livable fabric combining fashion with rough-ready, easy care qualities, and stretchable wear. "Casual Fridays" in the United States, a move toward casual business dress, supports a trend that has been particularly good for cotton. The volume of cotton increased more than 30 percent since 1990, compared to 8 percent for all other fibers. All but 5 percent of spun yarn in the United States was made from cotton and other man-made fibers as of the late 1990s.

During the early establishment of the industry in the eighteenth century, most spinning mills operated as independent entities. Later, mergers and consolidations in the yarn spinning industry opened diversification opportunities, and many spinning mills became subsidiaries or integrated components of larger carpet or textile mills, or they combined with specialized dyeing facilities. In the 1990s, these mills increasingly used high technology in order to meet the demands of efficient production and improved fiber quality—at the same time protecting the environment and conserving resources.

Protecting the health of textile workers became an issue in the 1980s. The Occupational Safety and Health Administration (OSHA), formed in 1970, set out to minimize illness and death resulting from cotton dust in textile mills. Referred to as "brown lung" disease, 1988 statistics estimated that 35,000 current and former textile employees had severe cases of "brown lung," and another 100,000 workers had symptoms that indicated early stages of the disease. As unions worked to improve hazardous mill conditions, textile manufacturers often opposed strict sanitation measures imposed by OSHA. In the early 1990s, questions remained as to the legality of some of the restrictions and how best to provide safer factory conditions.

Yarn spinning mills shared the textile industry's apprehension regarding the impact of the North American Free Trade Agreement (NAFTA). Some yarn spinners foresaw a negative impact based on claims that NAFTA would benefit Canada and Mexico more than the United States. Other spinners envisioned more positive results for the United States, particularly if NAFTA required Canada and Mexico to use yarns produced in North America. The threat of mills closing or a possible mass exodus of plants to Mexico was not perceived as an immediate threat; however, the president of the American Yarn Spinners Association did envision possible long term drawbacks resulting from NAFTA. In his opinion, the more imminent threat on American yarn spinning mills was posed by the General Agreement on Tariffs and Trade (GATT), another trade agreement, which in draft form, proposed to cut U.S. textile apparel import duties. In 1998, U.S. exports were valued at more than $400 million.

In contrast to other industries, growth in technological advances allowed a clear vision for twenty-first century yarn spinning mills. Industry literature referred to spinning systems rather than spinning mills. By the year 2000, *Textile World* predicted that daytime operations of spinning departments would be staffed with maintenance technicians, monitoring personnel, and a single supervisor. Night operations were expected to be staffless and monitored by sophisticated computers.

Changes in yarn, speed, styles, and other functions would become electronic functions or increasingly programmable. One certain outcome of computerization would be severely reduced manpower needs. In preparing for the coming high tech environment, industry research and development focused on refining and developing new equipment in the mid-1990s. Air-jet spinning machines, long recognized for evenness and minimal defects, were expected to achieve increased acceptance because of their ability to spin cotton-polyester blend yarn. If slippage problems could be overcome, the friction spinning machine would be used for medium and fine yarn count range, especially for cotton, due to the high quality and evenness of its output.

Yarn spinners continued to develop new more colorful and functional yarns. In the 1990s, three variations on DuPont's Cordura nylon went on the market. Originally introduced as a tire cord fiber, Cordura has been introduced as a fabric for outdoor recreational apparel. In addition to its light weight qualities, the Cordura/acrylic blend offered twice the abrasion resistance of ballistic nylon, three times that of vinyl or standard nylon, and four times that of cotton. Previous applications included luggage, backpacks, boots, and rugged ski apparel.

Industry leaders in 1999 were Dixie Group Inc. of Chattanooga, Tennessee, with revenues of $662 million; Parkdale Mills, Inc. of Gastonia, North Carolina, with revenues of $342 million; and Pharr Yarns Inc. of McAdenville, North Carolina, with revenues of $300 million.

As of late 1999, yarn spinning mills employed 58,800 workers, of which 53,600 labored in production. Employees worked slightly more than 42 hours a week, averaging 5 hours of overtime, and were paid $10.45 an hour. Most mills were located in North Carolina. Job growth was expected to continue a decline into the year 2006.

FURTHER READING

''Occupational Outlook Handbook 1998-99.'' *Bureau of Labor Statistics.* Washington, D.C.: GPO, 1999. Available from http://stats.bls.gov.

U.S. Census Bureau. ''Economic Census 1997.'' Washington, D.C.: GPO, 1999. Available from http://www.census.gov.

U.S. Industry and Trade Outlook '99. The McGraw-Hill Companies, 1999.

''What's New in Cotton Research.'' *Cotton Incorporated,* July 1996.

SIC 2282

YARN TEXTURIZING, THROWING, TWISTING, AND WINDING MILLS

Establishments included in this classification are those that are primarily engaged in texturizing (or texturing), throwing (another name for texturizing), twisting, winding, or spooling purchased yarns or manmade fiber filaments wholly or chiefly by weight of cotton, manmade fibers, silk, or wool, mohair, or similar animal fibers, or in performing such activities on a commission basis. Establishments primarily engaged in dyeing or finishing purchased yarns or finishing yarns on a commission basis are classified in **SIC 2231: Broadwoven Fabric Mills, Wool (Including Dyeing and Finishing)** if the

yarns are of wool, and in **SIC 2269: Finishers of Textiles, Not Elsewhere Classified** if they are of other fibers. Establishments primarily engaged in producing and texturizing manmade fiber filaments and yarns in the same plant are classified in **SIC 2823: Cellulosic Manmade Fibers.**

NAICS CODE(S)

313112 (Yarn Texturing, Throwing and Twisting Mills)
313312 (Textile and Fabric Finishing (except Broadwoven Fabric) Mills)

INDUSTRY SNAPSHOT

According to the U.S. Bureau of the Census, there were 134 establishments operating in this classification in 1997. Those businesses shipped $4.2 billion worth of products, spent $3.1 billion on materials, and paid $240.0 million for capital expenditures. North Carolina had by far the largest concentration of establishments in this industry, followed by Pennsylvania, Alabama, California, and New Jersey. Unifi Inc. of Greensboro, North Carolina, was the world's largest texturizing company and held about 70 percent of the U.S. texturizing market in 1999, according to *Fortune* magazine.

Texturizing is a process whereby partially oriented filament yarn (POY) is stabilized through heating and drawing. This produces a crimped continuous filament yarn. Generally speaking, two types of manmade POY are texturized: nylon and polyester. Texturized nylon is used primarily in the manufacturing of ladies' hosiery. Texturized polyester is used in various apparel and home-furnishings products and, to a lesser extent, in industrial fabric. There are two types of texturizing machines; most POY products are texturized on false-twist texturizing machines, but some are made with air-jet texturizing machines.

ORGANIZATION AND STRUCTURE

POY comes to the texturizing plant wound on tubes, which serve as the supply packages for the texturizing machines. These are purchased from manmade fiber producers such as Du Pont, Eastman Chemical Co., Hoechst Celanese, Tollaram Fibers, American Micrell, and Wellman. These packages contain anywhere from 10 to 100 pounds of POY. To receive the more economical, larger packages, a texturizing plant must be equipped with automated package-handling equipment, which has been available since 1990. Some older plants, especially those involved in small niche markets, opted not to purchase the automated equipment and must order the smaller package size.

Most texturized yarn is produced by companies such as Unifi for sale to weaving and knitting establishments. Some weaving plants, such as Burlington Industries and

Milliken & Co., produce yarn for their own consumption. Texturizing machines are not manufactured in the United States; instead, false-twist and air-jet texturizing machines are made by companies in Europe and Japan.

BACKGROUND AND DEVELOPMENT

Texturizing is relatively new compared to other segments of the textile industry, most of which have been around for centuries. The beginnings of texturizing go back to the invention of nylon more than 50 years ago when texturizing was used to process nylon yarn for hosiery. The new industry blossomed in the 1970s as the system to produce polyester filament yarns for use during the doubleknit polyester craze. As rapidly as doubleknit polyester leisure suits grew in popularity, texturizing grew as a necessary process. Unfortunately for the more than one hundred polyester texturizing plants that sprang up overnight, polyester texturizing died with doubleknit polyester leisure suits.

Despite its relatively young age, texturizing enjoyed more technological advances throughout the last two decades than any other textile process. The Textured Yarn Association of America (TYAA) formed in 1972 to establish quality standards for the fledgling industry. TYAA members learned at the association's twentieth anniversary meeting in July 1992 that since 1972, texturizing speeds had more than quadrupled and package sizes had tripled. Electronics now controlled operations, temperatures, speeds, and twists and monitored quality, temperature, and efficiency. Nearly every machine maker offered at least one model with automated features such as doffing, package handling, and creeling.

At the first organizational meeting, TYAA hosted more than one hundred texturizing companies. Most of these were supplying yarn for the doubleknit polyester trade. At TYAA's 1993 annual meeting, ten texturizing companies were represented. By the mid-1990s membership in TYAA included suppliers to the industry, users of texturized yarn, and companies who performed the texturizing process. Annual poundage for texturizing at TYAA's beginning was in the neighborhood of 1.6 billion. During the mid-1990s the figure was something less than 1.0 billion, but the dollar value had increased substantially. Those companies who divorced themselves from the doubleknit disaster were making products that required high-tech specifications and much higher quality.

CURRENT CONDITIONS

The U.S. Census Bureau reported that in 1997 this industry employed 20,244 people, including 18,036 production workers who earned an average hourly wage of $10.19. Of the 134 establishments in the category, 100 had at least 20 employees, and 66 had at least 100 employees. Establishments with fewer than 20 employees accounted for about 1 percent of all shipments.

The primary product of 45 establishments was textured, crimped, or bulked filament yarns, including stretch yarn made from purchased filament yarn. This segment shipped $2.96 billion worth of goods, spent $2.19 billion on materials, and paid $217 million for capital expenditures.

The primary product of 36 establishments was thrown filament yarns, except textured yarns. This segment shipped $962.0 million worth of goods, spent $728.0 million on materials, and paid $16.6 million for capital expenditures.

The primary product of 11 establishments was novelty and plied yarns other than wool, not spun or thrown at the same establishment. This segment shipped $128.7 million worth of goods, spent $81.0 million on materials, and paid $3.0 million for capital expenditures.

The primary product of seven establishments was commission receipts for throwing or texturing of filament yarns. This segment shipped $53.0 million worth of goods, spent $30.0 million on materials, and paid $1.9 million for capital expenditures.

INDUSTRY LEADERS

Unifi Inc. (Greensboro, North Carolina) has long been the industry leader in texturizing in the United States. Unifi had 6,400 employees and sales of $1.38 billion in 1998. Its Yadkinville Div. subsidiary (Yadkinville, North Carolina) had estimated sales of $430 million, its Norlina Div. subsidiary (Glen Raven, North Carolina) had estimated sales of $47 million, and its Unifi Spun Yarn Inc. subsidiary (Sanford, North Carolina) had estimated sales of $41 million.

Among other companies whose primary business was within this segment of the textile industry, Jefferson Mills Inc. (Pulaski, Virginia) had 300 employees and sales of $46 million; Burke Mills Inc. (Valdese, North Carolina) had 307 employees and sales of $42.2 million; Modern Fibers Inc. (Fitzgerald, Georgia) had 240 employees and estimated sales of $36 million; and Brunswick Worsted Mills (Pickens, South Carolina) had 220 employees and sales of $15 million.

AMERICA AND THE WORLD

Yarn texturizing, along with the rest of the U.S. textile industry, increasingly competed in the global marketplace during the 1990s. The world's growing population, developing world economies, the technical advantages of systems such as Quick Response and DAMA, and new trade agreements worked together to positively affect this segment of the industry. The North American Free Trade Agreement (NAFTA), which essentially removed all trade restrictions among Canadian, U.S., and Mexican businesses, helped the U.S. textile industry in some ways, but it also contributed to the closure of some U.S. textile mills and the reduction of operations at others.

RESEARCH AND TECHNOLOGY

Research and technology have provided several new operating systems that have helped the U.S. textile industry remain competitive. One such system, Quick Response, creates partnerships up and down the softgoods pipeline—fiber producers, textile manufacturers, apparel manufacturers, and retail establishments—and uses electronic technology, especially bar coding and Electronic Data Interchange (EDI), to receive up-to-date information. When the process works as it should, the system overcomes some of the advantages held by establishments that export products from low-wage, developing countries into the United States.

In 1993 the American Textile Partnership (AMTEX) enacted a pact in which national laboratories, the U.S. Department of Energy (DOE), and the textile industry develop systems to make the industry more competitive. One AMTEX project, Demand Activated Manufacturing Architecture (DAMA), expands on the Quick Response system. Under the DAMA system, electronics inform pipeline partners of each garment sold by analyzing point-of-sale data generated when bar-coded hang tags are scanned. The DAMA pilot project, begun in 1996, has shown that an electronic marketplace will improve operations and reduce expenses by controlling warehouse costs and inventory size and reducing wastes. It will also improve customer responsiveness and product development.

FURTHER READING

Brookstein, David. "U.S. Textiles Has Global Opportunities." *Textile World,* February 1997.

"DAMA Pilot Project Under Way." *Textile World,* October 1996.

Maycumber, S. Gray. "Unifi in Joint Venture with Burlington Industries: Deal Involves Burlington Madison Yarn Co.'s Texturing Operations." *Daily News Record,* 27 April 1998.

McCurry, John. "Technology Underscores Unifi's Success." *Textile World,* January 1997.

Morrissey, James A. "Textile Firms Turn Trash to Treasure." *Textile World,* February 1997.

"Nafta Boosts U.S. Textiles." *Textile World,* January 1997.

Richard, Robert. "Market Outlook." *Textile World,* March 1996.

Rozelle, Walter. "Business Outlook." *Textile World,* March 1996.

"Unifi: Tightening Starts at Home." *Fortune,* 8 November 1999.

U.S. Department of Commerce. Census Bureau. *1997 Economic Census.* Washington, D.C.: GPO, 1999. Available from http://www.census.gov/prod/ec97/97m3131b.pdf.

SIC 2284

THREAD MILLS

Establishments in this classification are primarily engaged in manufacturing thread from cotton, silk, manmade fibers, wool, or similar animal fibers. Important products in this category include sewing, crochet, darning, embroidery, tatting, hand-knitting, and other handicraft threads. Establishments primarily engaged in manufacturing thread from flax, hemp, and ramie are included in **SIC 2299: Textile Goods, Not Elsewhere Classified.**

NAICS CODE(S)

313113 (Thread Mills)
313312 (Textile and Fabric Finishing (except Broadwoven Fabric) Mills)

The thread industry has enjoyed continued growth in sales throughout the 1990s, with an estimated $986.6 million worth of products shipped in 1997, up from $799.3 million in 1991. The largest component of this category is sewing thread, purchased mainly by the apparel industry. American & Efird, Inc. of Mount Holly, North Carolina, with 1999 sales of $369.0 million, and Coats Industrial North America of Charlotte, North Carolina, with 1999 sales of $200.0 million, were the largest manufacturers of thread.

While sales were up, total thread industry employment figures dropped from 6,200 in 1992 to an estimated 4,900 in 1997. Employment of machinery operators in the textile industry as a whole was expected to decline through the year 2006 because of changing trade regulations and labor saving machinery. Hourly production workers in thread mills earned less, on average, than many of their counterparts in other industries, with pay scales increasing slightly from $7.34 in 1992 to $8.19 in 1997. States with the most thread mills and the highest number of employees in this industry included North Carolina, Massachusetts, and Georgia.

The future for thread sales appeared to be good, with natural fibers outselling manmade fibers because of strong demand by the carpet, apparel, and household furnishing markets.

FURTHER READING

Davison's Textile Blue Book. Atlanta, GA: Apparel Exchange, 1997. Available from http://apparelex.com/bluebok/thr_573.htm.

U.S. Census Bureau. *Economic Census 1997*. Washington, D.C.: GPO, 1999. Available from http://www.census.gov.

Occupational Outlook Handbook 1998-99. Bureau of Labor Statistics, 2000. Available from http://www.bls.gov.

SIC 2295

COATED FABRICS, NOT RUBBERIZED

This industry includes establishments primarily engaged in manufacturing coated, impregnated, or laminated textiles and in the special finishing of textiles, such as varnishing and waxing. Establishments primarily engaged in rubberizing purchase fabrics are classified in **SIC 3069: Fabricated Rubber Products, Not Elsewhere Classified,** and those establishments engaged in dyeing and finishing textiles are classified in various textile industries or **SIC 2231: Broadwoven Fabric Mills, Wool (Including Dyeing and Finishing).**

NAICS CODE(S)

313320 (Fabric Coating Mills)

The coated fabrics (not rubberized) manufacturing industry is regarded as a part of the larger miscellaneous textile goods business sector. While the textile goods industry as a whole has seen its employment figures gradually drop over the past decade, employment figures for the coated fabrics industry increased. In 1992, the total number of workers in the coated fabrics (not rubberized) industry was 9,200, with 1997 figures reaching more than 9,935. The total 1997 payroll for this industry was almost $336 million. The workforce was composed primarily of hourly production workers (7,069 in 1997), who earned an average of $14.90 per hour in 1997; this was a 24 percent increase from the $12.00 hourly wage of 1992.

During the nineties, the industry saw significant growth in the value of products shipped—with 1997 figures reaching almost $1.9 billion, up from $1.5 billion in 1992. A large percentage of companies engaged in coated fabrics manufacturing post annual sales in excess of 20 million. There were 227 establishments operating in this category for some or all of 1997.

Industry leaders include Collins and Aikman Corp. of Charlotte, North Carolina, with 1998 sales of more than $1.8 billion and 15,900 employees; Hexcel Corp. of Stamford, Connecticut, with 1998 sales of just less than $1.1 billion and 6,875 employees; and Cytec Fiberite Inc. of Tempe, Arizona, with 1998 sales of $450.0 million and 1,400 employees. Other significant companies in this industry include Ludlow Corp. of Exeter, New Hampshire;

Reeves Brothers Inc. of Spartanburg, South Carolina; and Hart Holding Company Inc. of Darien, Connecticut.

High demand for non-rubberized coated fabrics is in the area of furniture and wall coverings. Non-rubberized coated fabrics are also used in the manufacture of children's toys, nonwoven shoes, soft luggage, awnings and canopies, tents, sports equipment, industrial and marine supplies, and protective clothing. Strong specialty markets include vehicle air bags used by the automotive industry.

FURTHER READING

Manufacturing USA: Industry Analyses, Statistics, and Leading Companies. Detroit: Gale Research, 1996.

U.S. Census Bureau. "Fabric Coating Mills." *1997 Economic Census-Manufacturing*, 10 February 2000. Available from http://www.census.gov/prod/ec97/97m3133c.pdf.

SIC 2296

TIRE CORD AND FABRICS

This category covers establishments that produce cord and fabric of manmade fibers, cotton, glass, steel, or other materials used for reinforcing rubber tires, industrial belting, fuel cells, and similar applications. Manufacturers of coated fabrics that are not rubberized are covered under **SIC 2295: Coated Fabrics, Not Rubberized.** For discussion of weaving systems, refer to **SIC 2211: Broadwoven Fabric Mills, Cotton.**

NAICS CODE(S)

314992 (Tire Cord and Tire Fabric Mills)

The U.S. Department of Commerce's 1997 Economic Census reported that 15 U.S. companies produced tire cord and fabrics for the rubber tire industry. Only three of those companies had fewer than 20 employees, and all but five had at least 100 employees. This industry employed 5,699 people in 1997—including 4,711 production workers who earned an average hourly wage of $12.31. The industry shipped $1.2 billion worth of goods, spent $791.0 million on materials, and paid $70.0 million in capital expenditures.

While some tire cord was made with steel in the 1990s, most tire reinforcement came from such synthetic materials as nylon, polyester, and rayon fiber. Of the 744 million tons of manmade fiber used as tire reinforcement worldwide in 1993, 57 percent was nylon, nearly 24 percent was polyester, and approximately 19 percent was rayon. In North America the 165 million tons of manmade fiber used in 1993 was 55 percent polyester, nearly 43 percent nylon, and nearly 2 percent rayon.

Specifications for tire cord were generally dictated by the type of tire made. The three most common types of tires were radial, bias, and high performance. In the United States radial tires held about 90 percent of the market in the early 1990s, but high-performance tires were becoming increasingly popular. Production demands for tire cord fabric were directly related to the number of new cars and trucks sold, as well as the need for replacement tires on existing automobiles and trucks.

The manufacture of tire cord fabrics involved two general processing steps: twisting and weaving. In the twisting process, two or three ends of the tire cord material are twisted together to form a two- or three-ply yarn. The plied yarn then goes through a second round of twisting called cabling, in which two or three strands of the plied yarn are twisted together to form 2/2, 2/3, 3/2, or 3/3 cabled yarn. During weaving, the cabled tire cord serves as the warp or lengthwise yarn in the tire cord fabric. Tire cord makers use a light cotton thread to form the filling or crosswise yarn in the fabric. This light-weight yarn, which holds the cabled tire cord in place, dissolves during the rubberizing process, leaving only lengthwise strands of tire cord in the fabric.

Traditionally, all tire cord fabrics were produced on shuttle system weaving machines. By the end of the 1980s, however, two companies—Draper Corp. of Spartanburg, South Carolina, and Gunne GmbH of Moehnesse-Gunne, Germany—began making air-jet weaving machines for production of tire cord fabrics. Air-jet weaving machines produced tire cord fabric about 3.5 times faster than shuttle system weaving machines, increasing tire cord fabric production tremendously. However, few companies produced the air-jet weaving machine for tire cord in the 1990s, as few companies were engaged in that business.

Among companies whose primary products were tire cord and tire cord fabrics, Amercord Inc. (Lumber City, Georgia) was one of the largest, with 850 employees and estimated sales of $69 million in 1998. WesTeck Inc. (Thomaston, Georgia) had 1,100 employees and sales of $69 million; Richmond Converters (Laurel Hill, North Carolina) had 200 employees and estimated sales of $21 million. Clemson Fabrics Inc. (LaGrange, Georgia) had 200 employees and estimated sales of $17 million, and Utica Converters Inc. (Utica, New York) had 225 employees and sales of $15.7 million.

FURTHER READING

"Associated Materials Reports Sale of Amercord." *PR Newswire,* 19 November 1999.

U.S. Department of Commerce. *1996 Annual Survey of Manufactures.* Washington, D.C.: GPO, 1998.

U.S. Department of Commerce. Census Bureau. *1997 Economic Census.* Washington, D.C.: GPO, 1999. Available from http://www.census.gov/prod/ec97/97m3149d.pdf.

SIC 2297

NONWOVEN FABRICS

Included in this category are establishments that are primarily engaged in manufacturing nonwoven fabrics by mechanical, chemical, thermal, or solvent means, or by combinations thereof. Establishments that are primarily engaged in producing woven felts are classified in **SIC 2231: Broadwoven Fabric Mills, Wool (Including Dyeing and Finishing).** Those producing other felts are classified in **SIC 2299: Textile Goods, Not Elsewhere Classified.**

A wide variety of products are made using the nonwoven process. They are generated by textile-, paper-, and/or extrusion-type processes. Nonwovens produced from textile-type processes include filtration fabrics, shoe furnishings, insulation padding, apparel components, wipes, medical dressing, medical apparel, coverstock, foodservice wipes, and automotive headliner. Nonwovens from paper-type processes include tea bags, surgical drape, apparel components, air filters, premoistened towelettes, and wet wipes. Those nonwovens produced from extrusion-type processes include geotextiles (fabrics used as road beds and erosion prevention systems), protective clothing, reinforcement fabrics, coverstock, filtration fabrics, roofing, automobile carpet backing, laundry aids, homefurnishings, and regular carpet backing. Some nonwoven products are made from a combination or hybrid of processes; these include surgical drape, wound dressing, sorbent media, medical apparel, and disposable components.

NAICS CODE(S)

313230 (Nonwoven Fabric Mills)

INDUSTRY SNAPSHOT

The nonwoven fabrics industry is one of the fastest growing sectors of the textile business. New end uses, replacing those in the woven and knitted sector, are being developed every day. It is generally immune from import competition. The production of nonwoven fabrics requires a substantial capital investment and a relatively small workforce; therefore, it is not an attractive industry for developing countries where finding employment for numerous people is a prime objective.

This category requires sophisticated, electronically controlled machinery and highly trained fabric engineers.

In almost all cases where nonwoven fabrics can be substituted for woven and knitted fabrics, the result is a less expensive product. The U.S. Bureau of the Census reported that in 1997 there were 193 establishments producing nonwoven fabrics. They shipped $3.8 billion worth of merchandise, spent $2.3 billion on materials, and invested $272 million in new and used buildings and other structures, machinery, equipment, and other capital expenditures.

ORGANIZATION AND STRUCTURE

Nonwoven is a generic term used to describe a fabric that is produced differently from a fabric made by weaving or, more broadly, a fabric that is different from traditional woven or knitted fabrics. Like all fabrics, nonwovens are planar structures that are relatively flat, flexible, and porous. Unlike traditional fabrics that are made by mechanically interlacing (weaving) or interlooping (knitting) yarns composed of fibers or filaments, nonwoven fabrics are made by mechanically, chemically, or thermally interlocking layers or networks of fibers, filaments, or yarns; interlocking fibers or filaments concurrent with their extrusion; perforating films; or forming porous films concurrent with their extrusion.

Terminology used in the trade to describe nonwoven fabrics has been coined from the method used to form the web, the technology used to bond the web into a fabric, the forming/bonding combination, and the end-use application. Web formation jargon includes dry laid, carded, crosslapped, garnetted, air laid, wet laid, cylinder formed, extruded, meltblown, cast film, coformed, and flashspun. Terms associated with bonding include mechanically bonded, stitchbonded, needlefelted, needlepunched, spunlaced, jetlaced hydroentangled, apertured, chemically bonded, resin bonded, latex bonded, powder bonded, print bonded, saturated, spray bonded, foam bonded, frothed, thermal bonded, point bonded, and ultrasonically welded. Examples of forming/bonding terms for nonwovens are card/bond and spunbond. Examples of end-use application terminology are disposables, durables, semidurables, coverstock, geotextiles, filter fabric, sorbers, medical dressing, premoistened towellete, and wipe. Also, nonwovens are often described according to their fiber content such as polyester nonwoven, rayon nonwoven, polypropylene nonwoven, cotton/polyester nonwoven, pulp/polyester nonwoven or polypropylene/pulp nonwoven. Other nonwoven terms frequently encountered include film laminate, composite, SMS, and hybrid.

BACKGROUND AND DEVELOPMENT

The nonwoven fabrics industry is international in scope. The concept of making fabrics directly from fibers on needlepunch machinery achieved commercial viability in North America and Europe more than 75 years ago.

Facilities for producing commercial quantities of fabrics using wet-laid technology were established in the United States during the 1930s. Large-scale commercial production facilities for chemically bonded nonwovens were placed in operation in the United States during the early 1940s and in Europe and Japan following World War II.

The first extrusion operations dedicated to making fabrics directly from polymer melts were opened in the United States and Europe during the mid- to late 1960s. By the mid-1990s about half of the worldwide nonwoven fabric production capacity was located in North America, a third in Europe, and an eighth in Japan. Capacities in these areas were expanding at annual growth rates ranging 6 to 10 percent through both productivity improvements and the installation of new facilities. In addition, new nonwoven enterprises were being launched throughout Asia and South America. At that time about two-thirds of all nonwovens were made directly from fibers, and one-third were made directly from polymers.

An interesting history of technical, market, and product emphasis has occurred during the relatively short period of nonwoven industrialization. The early thrust in nonwoven usage emphasized replacing traditional woven and knitted fabrics. During this initial phase, proprietary technology was used not only to produce fabric structures that performed better than the items they were designed to replace, but it also was used when traditional fabrics could not be used. As a result, new applications and markets were established and the industry expanded.

As the industry matured and technology became publicly available, emphasis in the various sectors of the industry changed. By the mid-1990s some portions of the nonwovens industry were technology driven while others were market driven. A number of firms were proprietary technology-based while others were turn-key plant operations. Some were commodity roll-goods producers while others were more oriented to niche markets with high value-added products. Many nonwovens producers continued the quest for new markets and more opportunities to compete with traditional textiles, papers, and plastics.

Production of nonwoven roll goods in the United States climbed over the 2.5 billion pound level for the first time in 1992. By nonwoven type, application distribution was as follows: The majority of card/resinbond and card/thermalbond fabrics went into coverstock, while interlinings, wipes, and carrier sheets accounted for most of the remainder. Interlinings were one of the largest growing markets for nonwoven fabrics with 40 million pounds of fiber going to meet interlinings demand in 1995, according to Dlemson's School of Textiles, Giber & Polymer Science.

More than half of the highloft volume was used in furniture and sleeping applications. Filtration, apparel, insulation, healthcare, and geotextile products accounted for most of the remainder. Stitchbond fabrics were used in bedding, shoes, and a variety of coated products. Automotive trim and geotextiles accounted for 50 to 60 percent of needlepunch fabrics.

As much as two-thirds of spunlace fabrics were used in medical products. Medical product applications also accounted for about one-third of wet laid nonwovens.

Most bonded pulp fabrics were used as wipes or absorbent components. The largest yardage applications for spunbonds was coverstock. About half of meltblown nonwoven roll goods were used in filtration and medical applications. Porous film applications included coverstock, medical products, and laminating media. Nonwoven hybrids were used in absorbent products, wipes, filtration, and barrier applications.

CURRENT CONDITIONS

In 1997 the greatest amounts of goods shipped in this category were manufactured in North Carolina ($635 million), South Carolina ($433 million), and Tennessee ($337 million). Georgia, Wisconsin, and Virginia were also major producers.

The U.S. Census Bureau reported that 83 establishments made goods in this category as their primary products in 1997. Those businesses shipped $2.8 billion worth of merchandise and employed 11,097 people, including 7,970 production workers who earned an average hourly wage of $14.61.

INDUSTRY LEADERS

One of the largest companies whose primary product was nonwoven fabrics was Polymer Group Inc. (North Charleston, South Carolina) with 3,800 employees and sales of $802.9 million in 1998. Other industry leaders included Reemay Inc. (Old Hickory, Tennessee) with 600 employees and sales of $180 million; Veratec (Walpole, Massachusetts) with 1,200 employees and sales of $140 million; FiberTech Group Inc. (Landisville, New Jersey) with 220 employees and sales of $70 million; and National Nonwovens (Easthampton, Massachusetts) with 350 employees and sales of $32 million.

FURTHER READING

Brookstein, David. "U.S. Textiles Has Global Opportunities." *Textile World,* February 1997.

"DAMA Pilot Project Under Way." *Textile World,* October 1996.

Morrissey, James A. "Textile Firms Turn Trash to Treasure." *Textile World,* February 1997.

"Nafta Boosts U.S. Textiles." *Textile World,* January 1997.

Richard, Robert. "Market Outlook." *Textile World,* March 1996.

Rozelle, Walter. "Business Outlook." *Textile World,* March 1996.

———. "Nonwovens: Growth in New and Established Markets." *Textile World,* August 1996.

U.S. Department of Commerce. Census Bureau. *1997 Economic Census.* Washington, D.C.: GPO, 1999. Available from http://www.census.gov/prod/ec97/97m3132d.pdf.

SIC 2298

CORDAGE AND TWINE

This classification covers businesses that make rope, cable, cordage, twine, and related products from abaca (Manila) sisal, henquen, hemp, cotton, paper, jute, flax, manmade fibers including glass, and other fibers. Products include binder and baler twine, blasting mats and rope, fiber cable, camouflage nets not made in weaving mills, cargo nets, braided cord, fish nets and seines, fishing lines, insulator pads, rope nets, rope, rope slings, and wire ropes.

NAICS CODE(S)

314991 (Rope, Cordage and Twine Mills)

In 1997 there were 189 companies producing rope, cordage, and twine products, according to the U.S. Department of Commerce, Bureau of the Census. These businesses shipped $777 million worth of products, down from $817 million in 1995. They employed 6,417 people and had a total estimated payroll of $159 million. Their 4,866 production workers earned an average hourly wage of $9.77. The industry spent $411 million on materials and paid $25 million for capital expenditures. States with the largest concentrations of businesses in this category included Texas, California, Florida, Washington, and Georgia.

Generally, cordage and twine plants are not as modern as other textile producers. Most serve niche markets with closely controlled product specifications. The marine industry constitutes one of the largest markets for this category. During the mid-1990s though, that market declined when boat sales dropped because of a new luxury tax that was levied on that industry.

Almost all cordage and twine makers buy their yarn from sales yarn mills. Two or more strands of yarn are then twisted (plied) a certain number of turns per inch. Depending on the intended use for the product, cabling follows the twisting process. Cabling is similar to twisting except that where twisting involves wrapping several single strands of yarn together, cabling wraps several strands of plied yarns together. The cabling continues until the proper size of twine, cord, or rope is developed.

Of the 201 establishments in this industry in 1997, 130 (65 percent) had fewer than 20 employees. Among the largest was Wire Rope Corporation of America Inc. of St. Joseph, Missouri, with 500 employees and sales of approximately $77 million in 1998. Sackner Products (a division of Jason Inc. based in Grand Rapids, Michigan) had 300 employees and estimated sales of $52.5 million. Other leaders included Lehigh Group of Macungie, Pennsylvania, with 250 employees and estimated sales of $44 million; Mitchellace Inc. of Portsmouth, Ohio, with 250 employees and estimated sales of $39 million; Columbian Rope Co. of Guntown, Mississippi, with 300 employees and sales of $35 million; Fitec International Inc. of Memphis, Tennessee, with 570 employees and sales of $35 million; Tolaram Fibers Inc. of Ansonville, North Carolina, with 225 employees and estimated sales of $34 million; and Blue Mountain Industries of Anniston, Alabama, with 550 employees and sales of $32 million.

FURTHER READING

Hoover's Company Capsules. Austin, TX: Hoover's, Inc., 1997. Available from http://www.hoovers.com.

U.S. Department of Commerce. *1995 Annual Survey of Manufactures.* Washington, D.C.: GPO, 1997.

U.S. Department of Commerce. Census Bureau. *1997 Economic Census.* Washington, D.C.: GPO, 1999. Available from http://www.census.gov/prod/ec97/97m3149c.pdf.

U.S. Department of Labor. Bureau of Labor Statistics. *Career Guide to Industries, 1998-99 Edition. Bulletin 2503.* Washington, D.C.: GPO, 1998.

SIC 2299

TEXTILE GOODS, NOT ELSEWHERE CLASSIFIED

This category covers companies making textile products not included in other industry classifications. These include linen, jute, and felt goods; padding and upholstery filling; and processed waste and recovered fibers and flock. Establishments that prepare textile fibers for spinning, such as wool scouring and carbonizing, and combing and converting tow to top, are also grouped here.

Companies that primarily weave wool felts and wool haircloth are classified in **SIC 2231: Broadwoven Fabric Mills, Wool (Including Dyeing and Finishing).** Those that primarily make needle punch carpeting are classified in **SIC 2273: Carpets and Rugs.** Businesses that primarily make lace goods are classified in **SIC 2258: Lace and Warp Knit Fabric Mills,** and those that primarily sort wiping rags or waste are classified in **SIC 5093: Wholesale Trade.**

NAICS CODE(S)

313210 (Broadwoven Fabric Mills)

313230 (Nonwoven Fabric Mills)

313312 (Textile and Fabric Finishing (except Broadwoven Fabric) Mills)

313221 (Narrow Fabric Mills)

313113 (Thread Mills)

313111 (Yarn Spinning Mills)

314999 (All Other Miscellaneous Textile Product Mills)

Approximately 1,900 companies were grouped in this category in 1995, up from 591 listed in 1991. The U.S. Department of Commerce, Bureau of the Census reports that companies in this category shipped $2.34 billion worth of goods in 1996, up substantially from $1.61 billion in 1991. In 1995, this category employed 19,900 workers (15,500 in production), with a total estimated payroll of $450 million.

The top three industry leaders for this category in 1998 were Milliken and Co. of Spartanburg, South Carolina, with $3.2 billion in sales; WestPoint Stevens Inc. of West Point, Georgia, with 1998 sales of almost $1.8 billion; and Atlanta-based Interface Inc., with 1998 sales of almost $1.3 billion. Other significant companies in the industry included Russell Corp. Knit Apparel Division of Alexander City, Alabama; Carpenter Co. of Richmond, Virginia; Ply Gem Industries Inc. of Providence, Rhode Island; and Albany International Corp. of Albany, New York.

In the 1990s, environmental concerns affected business in this category, especially those using textiles by-products. Taking by-products to the landfill used to be common practice among all textile plants. Now that this is neither economically feasible nor environmentally acceptable, plants must find other outlets for their by-products. This opened up new opportunities for companies in this classification. In the late 1990s, the North American Free Trade Agreement (NAFTA) had little effect on this industry segment.

FURTHER READING

U.S. Department of Commerce. *1995 Annual Survey of Manufactures.* Washington, D.C.: GPO, 1997.

U.S. Department of Commerce. *1996 Annual Survey of Manufactures.* Washington, D.C.: GPO, 1998.

APPAREL & OTHER FINISHED PRODUCTS MADE FROM FABRICS & SIMILAR MATERIALS

MEN'S AND BOYS' SUITS, COATS, AND OVERCOATS

This category covers establishments primarily engaged in manufacturing men's and boy's tailored suits, coats, and overcoats from purchased woven or knit fabrics. Establishments primarily engaged in manufacturing uniforms (except athletic and work uniforms) are also included in this industry. Establishments primarily engaged in manufacturing men's work uniforms and clothing are classified in **SIC 2326: Men's and Boys' Work Clothing,** and those manufacturing men's and boys' athletic uniforms are classified in **SIC 2329: Men's and Boys' Clothing, Not Elsewhere Classified.** Knitting mills primarily engaged in manufacturing suits and coats are classified in **SIC 2253: Knit Outerwear Mills.**

NAICS CODE(S)

315211 (Men's and Boys' Cut and Sew Apparel Contractors)
315222 (Men's and Boys' Cut and Sew Suit, Coat, and Overcoat Manufacturing)

INDUSTRY SNAPSHOT

Throughout the 1990s, output and employment in the men's and boys' suit and coat industry continued the long-term pattern of contraction that had begun over two decades earlier. In 1979, industry sources estimated that, of the 25 million suits sold in the United States, approximately 80 percent were U.S. made; in 1994, by contrast, according to Department of Commerce figures, U.S. manufacturers accounted for a much smaller share—55 percent—of the many fewer suits, just 13 million, sold in this country. The

number of people employed making suits and coats had fallen from more than 100,000 in the late 1960s to 21,400 in 1997. The outlook of this branch of production was being shaped by a number of processes—a changing retail structure, the impact of imports produced with cheap labor—that were having similar effects across the entire apparel industry. Of all the factors affecting the suit and coat industry, however, probably the single most significant was a steady change in dress habits among American men.

ORGANIZATION AND STRUCTURE

About 222 U.S. companies produced men's and boys' suits and coats in 1998, down from more than 443 in 1982. Most were small enterprises, with fewer than 250 employees. The industry consisted of three major types of companies: manufacturers, contractors, and jobbers. Manufacturers cut and sew finished products entirely within their own facilities. Jobbers specialize in cutting the fabric, which they then supply to contractors for sewing. The major suppliers of these manufacturers are textile mills, which produce the broad-woven fabrics accounting for roughly three-quarters of the materials consumed by the industry.

Manufacturers sell their goods primarily to three types of retailers: small specialty clothing stores, department stores, and large menswear discount chains. During the 1990s, manufacturers became more dependent on the large discounters—such as Men's Wearhouse, Today's Man, and S&K Famous Brands—which expanded their operations often at the expense of the small stores, some 4,000 of which closed by 1996. Some of these discounters expanded so quickly that they overreached and suffered the consequences, at least temporarily.

BACKGROUND AND DEVELOPMENT

The clothing industry in the United States began to develop in the eighteenth century, but most clothing was still being made in homes until the Civil War. Quality menswear was long the province of skilled tailors, while most ready-to-wear clothing was imported. In the nineteenth century, however, urban migration, the sewing machine, and a demand for war uniforms changed the industry.

Urban Migration. As more and more people began moving to cities in the nineteenth century, they became more concerned with their clothing. As Claudia B. Kidwell and Margaret C. Christman pointed out in *Suiting Everyone: The Democratization of Clothing in America,* "For the most part factory workers could not afford the services of a good tailor, but they still wanted clothing that looked in no way appreciably different from the mainstream fashion. Consequently, the demand was there—not for the inferior or specialized clothing that had previously distinguished 'ready-made,' but rather for 'equal clothing' for anyone, which anyone could afford to buy."

Tailors began to develop "scientific principles" and "proportional systems" for making clothing that would fit almost anyone. In 1848, Oliver Hudson, a men's clothier in Boston, advertised that "sizes are indicated by number and a printed tag is attached to each article, so that anyone after becoming familiar with the size will seldom find it necessary to try a second garment." Tailors also began hiring workers, usually women who worked in the home, for many of the less skilled tasks, such as sewing straight seams.

Brooks Brothers, the famous New York clothier, is thought to have introduced the first ready-to-wear men's suits in the United States in 1845 and pioneered the "sack suit" around the turn of the century. The comfortable, boxy-looking sack suit was a stark departure from the tight-fitting suits with padded shoulders and pleated trousers that were then popular in Europe, and it was considered the first genuinely American business attire. The sack suit evolved into the Ivy League look of the 1950s and the celebrated gray flannel suit of the 1960s.

Sewing Machine. Although many people contributed to the invention of the sewing machine, Elias Howe Jr., an American machinist, demonstrated a working model in 1845 and received a patent the following year. Isaac Merritt Singer, another American, made improvements to Howe's machine and introduced "the Perpetual Action Belay Stitch Machine" in 1850. Singer's was considered the first practical sewing machine. Although the two inventors squabbled over patent rights for years, I.M. Singer & Co. was formed in 1851 and garment manufacturers began placing their orders.

By some estimates, sewing machines reduced the cost of manufacturing simple ready-to-wear clothes by as much as 80 percent. In the mid-1860s, Brooks Brothers noted that a top-quality overcoat that took six days to sew by hand could be made in three using a sewing machine. A foot treadle was added in 1871, which further increased productivity, and Singer Sewing Machine Co., renamed after Singer's death in 1875, introduced the first electric sewing machine in 1889.

Civil War. Most clothing in the United States was made in homes before the Civil War, except military uniforms. At first, the U.S. government hired outside contractors to produce uniforms that were somewhat consistent in color and style. In 1812, however, the United States Army Clothing Establishment—perhaps the first true clothing factory in the United States—was created in Philadelphia. Fabric was cut to a standard pattern and then packaged along with padding, facing cloth, thread, and buttons. The materials were then delivered to "widows and other meritorious females" who sewed them into uniforms working at home. As private clothing factories appeared, they copied the same structure.

The demand for uniforms during the Civil War had several consequences. Because the Army's Establishment could not supply enough uniforms by itself, the government awarded contracts to other clothiers, many of whom received their first exposure to mass production. Second, military demand stimulated improvements in technology, including development of better cutting machines, pressers, and buttonholers. The Establishment also kept the first detailed records on measurements, which helped manufacturers develop regular ready-to-wear sizes after the war. In 1879, Albert S. Bolles wrote in the *Industrial History of the United States* that "the home manufacture of men's garments has virtually ceased, and every one, from ploughman to railroad president, goes to the store for his goods, and can be suited, if he chooses, from the shelves of the store at once."

Immigration. Many people who worked in the early clothing industry, both as inside cutters and contract seamstresses, were immigrants, primarily Irish in the 1840s and Germans in the 1850s. Many of the Jews who emigrated from Germany after 1860 also entered the clothing trade (although more often as retailers). The industry continued to provide thousands of low-paying jobs to later immigrants, including thousands of Italians and Russian Jews who arrived between 1880 and 1910. Many of these immigrants worked long hours in overcrowded, poorly ventilated buildings that became known as sweatshops.

Immigrants not only provided labor for the menswear industry, they fueled demands for its products. One of the first purchases a new arrival made was a new American-made suit, which, according to Kidwell and Christman, could instantly transform him "from 'greenhorn' to 'someone who belonged.'" In the cities, men began wearing suits to work no matter what their occupations, even if they wore aprons or other work garments over the suits to keep them clean.

In 1869, garment workers in Philadelphia, led by Uriah Stephens, formed the Noble Order of the Knights of Labor—one of the first labor unions in the United States. Among its goals were an eight-hour workday and the abolition of child labor. The Knights of Labor remained a secretive, fraternal organization until 1879, when members elected Terence V. Powderly as Grand Master Workman. Powderly called for ''one big union'' and welcomed workers from other industries, including Catholics, whom Stephens had excluded. Membership in the Knights of Labor rose from about 10,000 in 1879 to more than 100,000 in 1885. In 1885, the Knights of Labor led an unsuccessful strike against the Texas and Pacific Railroad, and its influence waned. Eventually, it was supplanted by the American Federation of Labor (AFL) as the most powerful union in the United States. In the early 1900s, the United States passed laws outlawing sweatshops and regulating child labor.

Hart, Schaffner & Marx. The first men's clothing manufacturer to eliminate outside contract labor was Hart, Schaffner & Marx in 1911. Originally known as Harry Hart & Brother, the company was started in 1871 as a retail outlet in Chicago by Harry and Max Hart. In 1897, Hart, Schaffner & Marx became the first clothing manufacturer to advertise nationally, and within a few years, was the leading men's clothing label in the United States. Hart, Schaffner & Marx also promoted standards for the clothing industry, such as insisting that an ''all-wool'' suit should be made of 100 percent wool (although the federal Wool Products Labeling Act was not passed until 1939). In 1906, Hart, Schaffner & Marx announced that its ready-to-wear men's clothing came in 14 basic body types so customers could get a more tailored look. The company boasted: ''We design models especially for men who call themselves hard to fit. Stouts, slims, short stout men, big and little men, men who are built 'close to the ground,' long bodies and short legs, men with slightly stooping shoulders; all the odd sizes have their special models, made to fit.''

Fashion. Men's fashions were never as changeable as women's, except perhaps during the leisure-suit phenomenon of the 1970s. Leisure suits were an urban adaptation of the safari jacket and accounted for more than half of all men's and boy's suits produced in the United States in 1975—when more than 12 million were sold. But sales of leisure suits were less than half that in 1976, and by 1983 the leisure suit had disappeared. Similarly, knit fabrics were used in nearly 75 percent of suits and coats made in the 1970s, but they virtually disappeared by the mid-1980s.

CURRENT CONDITIONS

The persistent downward trend in U.S. production of suits and coats that began in the 1970s continued through the 1990s. For example, U.S. manufacturers produced 9.6 million suits in 1995, valued at $930 million, and 11.6 million tailored coats, valued at $737 million. These figures represented a significant drop in quantity and value from just a year earlier, when 11.2 million suits and 13.5 million tailored coats were made. Industry analysts explained the contraction as resulting from two major factors: competition from inexpensive imported clothes and acceptance of more casual dress. Central to this trend were relaxed dress codes at large corporations, most notably IBM, which instituted ''dress down'' days on which employees wear casual clothes. (One Boston mortician reported that formal attire was no longer universal—even on corpses.)

Office attire became ''dress casual,'' a hybrid that was less formal than suits but more presentable than T-shirts and jeans. American men were still buying clothing because many had to furnish entire wardrobes more appropriate to the new standard. But sales of suits—once, with coats, the bread and butter of the men's apparel industry—continued declining. The trend was accelerated in the mid- to late 1990s when the predominance of the personal computer made it possible for many people to work from home. More and more men didn't need to appear in public every work day and found that they could easily make do with one or two suits. It's always possible that the formal suit could make a comeback, of course, but as long as the new millionaires choose to announce their initial public offerings wearing open shirts and khakis, a suit resurgence is probably unlikely.

INDUSTRY LEADERS

Oxford Industries Inc. and Hartmarx Corp. are the two largest manufacturers of men's and boys' suits and coats throughout the 1990s. Both companies manufacture other apparel but have an established presence in those markets. Oxford posted 1999 total sales of $862.4 million, while Hartmarx's total sales in 1998 were $725.0 million.

Hartmarx was in dire financial straits in the early 1990s, but by the mid-1990s, they had engineered a major reorganization and financial comeback. With more than $300 million in debt and annual net losses reaching $220 million in fiscal 1992, the company was surrounded by bankruptcy rumors; its stock price plunged to $3.00 a share from $34.75 a share in 1987. The company responded by closing unprofitable retail stores, including selling the Kuppenheimer unit, downsizing from 35 to 22 factories, developing casual menswear lines, and establishing new ties with retailers. The newly downsized company was again profitable in 1993 and 1994, and had shed a large portion of its debt.

WORKFORCE

The suit and coat industry employed 21,402 people in 1997, 17,317 of whom were production workers. At Hartmarx, the largest producer, most production workers are covered by contracts with the Union of Needletrades, Industrial and Textile Employees (UNITE). Sewing machine operators, mostly women, are the largest group in the workforce (55.5 percent). The assembly of suits and coats is organized largely according to the bundle system, in which each operator performs one task on a bundle of pieces, which is then taken to the next operator and so on until the piece is finished. Production of a typical men's suit is broken down, in this way, into as many as 100 different operations.

AMERICA AND THE WORLD

Imported goods met a substantial share of U.S. consumers' demand for suits and coats in the mid-1990s. In 1994, for example, 70 percent of tailored coats and 45 percent of suits bought by U.S. consumers were imports. The value of imported suits and coats rose rapidly in the first half of the 1990s. Between 1991 and 1994, for example, imports of men's and boys' wool suits rose from $258 to $354 million.

International trade treaties ratified in the mid-1990s are expected to substantially affect domestic apparel industries, including production of suits and coats. The Agreement on Textiles and Clothing (ATC), which took effect January 1, 1995, called for the phaseout over 10 years of the bilateral import quotas that the United States had negotiated with textile- and apparel-exporting countries under the Multifiber Agreement (MFA). The terms of the ATC, however, preserve import quotas on most apparel items, including suits and coats, until 2005, while accelerating the rise of quota limits up until that year.

RESEARCH AND TECHNOLOGY

After World War II, improvements in the sewing machine eliminated the need to stitch button holes, pockets, belt loops, and lapels by hand. New technology since the 1960s also increased productivity, although some technologies that seemed promising had to be abandoned. In the 1960s, some manufacturers replaced reciprocating blade cutting machinery with lasers, but the lasers tended to fuse layers of synthetic fabrics. Computer-controlled spreading, marking, and cutting systems were introduced in the late 1970s and early 1980s. Sewing machines also became more sophisticated beginning in the late 1960s, eliminating much of the manual labor involved in handling and positioning garments as they moved from one sewing-machine operator to another. Such advances led to significant increases in productivity, and employment dropped significantly faster than the value of output since the early 1980s.

FURTHER READING

Cleary, David Powers. *Great American Brands.* New York: Fairchild Publications, 1981.

Kidwell, Claudia B., and Margaret C. Christman. *Suiting Everyone: The Democratization of Clothing in America.* Washington, D.C.: Smithsonian Institution Press, 1974.

Patterson, Gregory. "Hartmarx, Having Restyled Itself, Sees Robust Profits." *Wall Street Journal,* 31 May 1995.

Shelton, Linda, and Robert Wallace. "World Textile and Apparel Trade: A New Era." *Industry, Trade, and Technology Review,* October 1996. Available from http://www.usitc.gov/ittr .htm.

Sieling, Mark Scott, and Daniel Curtin. "Patterns of Productivity Change in Men's and Boys' Suits and Coats." *Monthly Labor Review,* November 1988.

U.S. Bureau of the Census. *1997 Economic Census.* Washington, D.C.: GPO, 1999.

SIC 2321

MEN'S AND BOYS' SHIRTS

This category includes establishments primarily engaged in manufacturing men's and boys' shirts (including polo and sport shirts) from purchased woven or knit fabrics. Establishments primarily engaged in manufacturing work shirts are classified in **SIC 2326.** Knitting mills primarily engaged in manufacturing outerwear are classified in **SIC 2253.**

NAICS CODE(S)

315211 (Men's and Boys' Cut and Sew Apparel Contractors)
315223 (Men's and Boys' Cut and Sew Shirt (except Work Shirt) Manufacturing)

INDUSTRY SNAPSHOT

Slow and steady growth in production and declines in employment characterized the men's and boys' shirt industry as it entered the second half of the 1990s. From 1982 to 1994 the value of shipments by firms in the industry climbed from roughly $3.5 to $5.1 billion dollars; at the same time, total employment dropped from 88,700 to 73,600 thousand people. Meanwhile, the two major branches of the industry—woven shirts and knit shirts—were moving in opposite directions. Production of woven shirts, including dress and sport shirts, declined for most of the 1990s, while production of knit shirts, especially T-shirts, increased rapidly.

Conditions in the men's and boys' shirt industry reflected the impact of a number of broader forces, including domestic market conditions, economic globalization, and new technological possibilities. Slow overall growth in this branch of the apparel industry was partly attributable to the declining share of personal income that Americans were spending on clothing, which kept demand in check even though the economy was growing at a steady pace. Cost-conscious consumers increasingly turned to "non-traditional" retailers, such as discount menswear stores, factory outlets, and direct-mail catalogs. U.S. manufacturers had to compete for space on retail shelves with shirtmakers from foreign countries, and this competition became more intense with the passage of new international trade treaties in the mid-1990s. U.S. firms attempted to stay competitive by taking advantage of opportunities to "outsource" work abroad, shipping cut cloth to contractors in the Caribbean Basin or Mexico and then importing the sewn products at preferential duties. New technologies and communication systems provided domestic shirt manufacturers with a potential competitive advantage vis-a-vis foreign producers on the basis of flexibility, rather than cost alone.

ORGANIZATION AND STRUCTURE

U.S. shirt production is heavily concentrated in the southeastern states, especially North Carolina, Alabama, Kentucky, South Carolina, and Georgia, which together account for about 55 percent of total shipments. North Carolina and Georgia account for one-quarter of the almost 2 million U.S. jobs in textile production, apparel manufacture, and production of synthetic fibers and cotton. California also commands a huge percentage of the jobs, about 181,000 in various textile-related industries, three times more than all of New England.

The two most important supplies for men's and boys' shirt establishments are knit fabrics and broadwoven cloths. For most of the twentieth century, knit and woven shirts have been assembled from cut pieces of fabric according to the "bundle system." Sewing a dress shirt requires anywhere from 20 to 40 operations under this system. Each operation is the specialty of a certain sewing-machine operator, who performs his or her single task on a large bundle of cut pieces, reties the pieces in the bundle, and then sends them along to the next operator.

At any moment there are thousands of garment-pieces lying on the factory floor, a huge "work-in-process that represents the manufacturer's inventory." It takes less than 20 minutes of actual labor to assemble a shirt in this system. But those 20 minutes are spread over a production cycle that lasts as long as six weeks, from the time separate pieces are cut to the time they are packaged for distribution. The bundle system maximizes the productivity of individual operators but also results in

a costly build-up of in-process inventory and hinders manufacturers' flexibility to respond to changing consumer demand. The industry's largest manufacturers report that department stores and mass merchandisers are the biggest consumers of their products. In addition, a number of firms are expanding sales through their own retail divisions, especially factory stores at outlet malls.

BACKGROUND AND DEVELOPMENT

The historical development of the men's and boys' shirt industry can be divided into two basic periods: the eras before and after the 1918 introduction of the soft-collar-attached shirt. The current state of the men's and boys' shirt industry is the result of a range of influences, including wars; political, industrial, and technological revolutions; government policies; apparel construction and design changes; introductions of new natural and synthetic fibers and/or improvements in their resiliency; and the fleeting nature of fashion preferences.

The American Revolution of 1776 gave birth to the U.S. apparel industry. It created a climate in which the activities of urban-based industrialists, bankers, merchants, and other professions and crafts could flourish. Progressing in step with this newly emergent and triumphant political/economic class of white males were styles of dress reflective of their own particular preferences. These tastes were largely utilitarian in design and style. Early uniformity in fashion tastes facilitated mass production of ready-made shirts.

From its infancy at the end of the American Revolution to the outbreak of the Civil War in 1861, the U.S. apparel industry was nurtured by a highly protectionist trade policy. Between 1816 and 1829 tariffs on imported clothing rose from 25 to 50 percent, where they remained until 1860. Additional duties were imposed if the imported clothing arrived in the United States on board a ship of foreign origin.

The introduction of sewing-machine technology in the 1850s precipitated the downfall of these tariffs and allowed U.S. shirt manufacturers to compete in international markets. The increased productivity generated by sewing machines propelled the U.S. apparel industry to a world-status second to none. The industry's main advantage lay in its ability to reduce the cost of labor per shirt, which led to a sharp decrease in the selling price of its product. The sewing machine had a profound structural impact on the organization of the workplace. It ultimately led to greater divisions of labor based on outinization and specialization. Highly paid, skilled tailors were replaced by low-wage, semi-skilled, or unskilled laborers who arrived from Europe to work in U.S. factories.

Another milestone in the shirt industry occurred with the outbreak of the Civil War. Prior to the war, manufacturers and retailers of ready-made apparel had been hampered by the absence of standard clothing sizes. To facilitate its clothing orders for private manufacturers, the Union Army's Philadelphia Quartermaster collected body measurements from more than one million recruits and conscripts. These measurements were organized into tables of standardized body proportions that could be easily applied to the manufacture of civilian garments.

In the early twentieth century fashion began to have a greater influence on the direction of the men's and boys' shirt industry. Affluent, well-dressed men eschewed the soft shirts being offered by Sears, Roebuck and Co. in favor of the "stiff-bosom" shirt, a marker of mental, as opposed to manual, labor. Cluett, Peabody's "Arrow" line of stiff-bosom shirts came in 20 starch collar styles of the "poke" type: a plain standing collar without tabs. By 1906 fashion tastes had shifted from the poke-type detached collar to embrace the fold or turned-down collar style. Arrow promoted this new collar through the creation of the "Arrow collar man," whose sex appeal over the next dozen or so years managed to drive the sales of Arrow's 400-plus detached-collar styles to the $32 million mark. In 1911 the notched detached-collar shirt was all the rage. Accompanying advertisements told consumers that this new type of collar saved time, money, and temper since it prevented buttonholes from ripping, did not tear fingernails, and bypassed the use of metal collar boutonnieres.

A new fashion wave swept across the United States in 1918: the soft-collar-attached shirt. During their tour of duty in World War I, many American men became impressed with the relative comfort of the soft-collar-attached khaki army shirt, especially when compared to its more irritating starched, collar-detached civilian counterpart. In fact, just prior to the widespread circulation of the collar-attached shirt in its various civilian guises, the market was booming with sales of military shirts, replete with regulation army cuffs and pocket, collar, and sleeve insignias.

In 1920 John M. Van Heusen introduced a three-ply collar constructed in a one-piece arc. It incorporated the advantage of the starch collar's crisp appearance with the comfort of the soft collar. It also had the advantage of retaining its shape longer than other collars due to its construction. By 1925 the Van Heusen Shirt Company ran advertisements declaring it the "collar of the century," while incorporating the new collar into the design of their entire line of shirts. Van Heusen also pioneered a patented weaving process that introduced the one-piece collar, which would become an industry standard. The collar's novel quality lay in its uniform thickness, designed and constructed without any lining so that, even after repeated wearings, it proved to be wrinkle-, blister-, and buckle-resistant.

World War II also spawned important changes in shirt production. First, the war-effort contributed to the economic integration of the southern- and northern-based apparel industries, whose prior operations had been largely conducted on a regional basis. The war also introduced new synthetic materials that eventually found their way to the apparel industry. Immediately following World War II, some shirt manufacturers began using nylon and other synthetic fibers. Though receiving enthusiastic support from the public, not all major shirt producers were willing to plunge into the nylon shirt fad. Cluett, Peabody announced that no Arrow-label shirts would be produced from nylon. Along with other traditional shirt producers, Cluett, Peabody questioned the propriety of using synthetic fibers as a "shirting fabric."

During the 1950s three major technological changes occurred that had a great impact on the shirt industry. Concerns about the longevity of synthetic fibers were silenced when Du Pont became the first U.S. commercial producer of the manmade fiber polyester, marketed under the brand name Dacron. Consumers prized polyester for its wrinkle resistance and iron-free maintenance, its ability to maintain shape after repeated washing, and its permanent heat-setting treatment process that helped maintain pleats and guard against shrinkage and sagging. The ease with which polyester could be blended with other fibers was also a boon to manufacturers.

The year 1956 witnessed the introduction of wash-and-wear, all-cotton shirts. Thanks to a special resin treatment, apparel made of natural fibers was now able to withstand repeated laundering without losing its original shape or appearance. Three years later manufacturers began treating apparel with special finishing processes that allowed stains to be washed out with plain cold water. Minnesota Mining and Manufacturing (3M), of St. Paul, Minnesota, introduced the revolutionary "Scotchgard" process during the 1950s as well. The oil-based spray proved resistant against the harshest of conditions and could be used in a wide range of products to prevent penetration of moisture, dust particles, and oil staining.

CURRENT CONDITIONS

The two major segments of the men's and boys' shirt industry were moving in opposite directions in the 1990s. In 1995 U.S. manufacturers shipped 1.13 billion knit shirts (including T-shirts, sweatshirts, and polo shirts), valued at $5.84 billion, up from $4.89 billion in 1992 and $3.92 billion in 1991. These gains were entirely due to a jump in shipments of T-shirts and tank tops, which climbed from 565 million shirts at $2.09 billion in 1991, to 833 million shirts at $3.99 billion in 1995. Earnings from boys' knit shirts showed the most growth, with 1998 sales doubling those from the previous year. The merchandising bonanza offered by the 1996 summer Olympics in Atlanta, Georgia, spurred further growth in knit shirt sales. By contrast, shipments of woven shirts (including dress, business, and sports shirts) declined steadily over the same period, from 105 million shirts at $1.11 billion in 1992, to 88.4 million shirts at $990 million in 1995. But woven shirts made a slight recovery near the end of the decade, at least in discount clothing stores. Total sales of men's woven sport shirts in discount stores during the first half of 1998 rose 3.8 percent compared to the same period in 1997, from $355.0 million to $368.7 million. Total sales of men's knit sport shirts in discount stores rose only 1.3 percent over the same period, to $712.7 million.

The very different fortunes of these two segments of the industry were attributable in part to the "casualization" of American clothing tastes, expressed in the trend toward corporate dressing-down, which hurt sales of dress and business shirts. By the mid-1990s dress-shirt manufacturers were responding to this trend by developing new lines of casual woven shirts, sometimes known as "Friday wear." T-shirt sales not only gained from this trend but also benefited from the synergy between corporate merchandising campaigns and the desire of millions of Americans to wear clothing expressing their loyalties to sports teams, rock groups, and other popular icons. Sports apparel by itself generated almost $1.5 billion in sales during 1998.

While these trends had markedly different impacts on the various branches of the U.S. men's and boys' shirt industry in the 1990s, both knit and woven shirt producers felt the effect of competition from overseas manufacturers, who were producing cheap goods with cheap labor. Additional long-term uncertainties were thrown into the mix by the passage of the 1993 North American Free Trade Agreement (NAFTA), the 1994 General Agreement on Tariffs and Trade (GATT), and the 1995 Agreement on Textiles and Clothing (ATC).

The apparel industry has been extremely susceptible to import competition over the last 50 years and has frequently lobbied the U.S. government to impose tariffs and quotas. The share of imports in U.S. consumption of both knit and woven shirts rose substantially from the 1970s to the 1990s, although import penetration was much higher for woven shirts. The Multifiber Agreement (MFA) had regulated U.S. imports of textiles and apparel since 1974. On the basis of bilateral agreements with individual countries, the MFA established import quotas on most apparel items, including suits. NAFTA, GATT, and ATC dismantled many of those protections. For example, ACT increased the number of items allowed into the United States under the apparel quotas and will phase out quotas on shirts altogether by 2005.

How did shirt manufacturers respond to the challenges posed by foreign competition? One strategy involved a combination of downsizing U.S. operations by closing plants and laying off production workers, while outsourcing an increasingly large portion of work to company-owned plants or contractors in Mexico or the Caribbean Basin. Many U.S. companies manufacture shirts with cheap foreign labor by sending cut fabric to these foreign plants, where they are sewn and finished. The finished items are then shipped back to the United States at preferential duties. Between 1991 and 1995 the value of such "807" imported shirts (a figure that included the value added in both the United States and abroad) rose from $183 million to $1.03 billion.

If offshore production gave U.S. companies a chance to produce their goods with cheap labor, domestic production entailed its own set of advantages, especially proximity to the huge U.S. consumer market and the opportunity to respond rapidly to shifting consumer demands. One major shirt manufacturer, Hampton Industries Inc., has estimated that the production cycle (the time from cutting the fabric to the product's arrival at the company's distribution center) for shirts produced in the Far East lasts as long as six months. For shirts produced in the Caribbean Basin, Hampton estimated that the production cycle lasts about ten weeks, and for shirts produced in the United States it lasts just five weeks.

Leading U.S shirt manufacturers have also capitalized on domestic production advantages by pursuing a consumer-driven "quick response" strategy. This strategy integrates numerous dimensions of the production cycle with an eye toward shortening a cycle's duration, implementing productivity improvements, and shrinking inventory levels through the immediate transmission of consumer taste to manufacturers. The quick response strategy depends on a manufacturer's investment in state-of-the-art communications systems, known as electronic data interchange (EDI). EDI systems link manufacturers to retailers' computer-recorded sales information, allowing them to track changes in consumer preferences as they happen.

Quick response strategies also attempt to reduce inventories and accelerate production cycles so that changing consumer preferences can be quickly translated into modified products. The most far-reaching attempt to accomplish these goals involves the replacement of the bundle system of assembly with "modular" production. In modular systems teams of multi-skilled operators work together to produce a single garment or a single part of a garment, such as a collar. Pay is based on an entire team's output, giving incentive for team-members to shift tasks when backlogs develop. Workers focus on maximizing the number of finished pieces produced by the whole team, rather than on the number of individual operations performed. Individual worker productivity in a modular system is not normally as high as that of specialized workers in the progressive bundle system. But modular systems reduce inventory and accelerate the production cycle for assembly of an entire garment. Although modular systems have received strong backing from industry analysts, industry leaders, and unions, manufacturers have been slow to change their management and human resource practices.

INDUSTRY LEADERS

Discount stores, national chains, and department stores dominated sales of men's and boys' shirts. Discount stores owned an 18.9 percent share of the market in 1997, with earnings of approximately $9.6 billion. Major chains owned about an 18.7 share of the market in the same year, with earnings of approximately $9.5 billion. Department stores owned a 17.7 percent share of the market, with earnings of approximately $9.0 billion. But specialty chains such as Gap are rapidly gaining ground. In 1997 specialty chains had a 10.6 market share, with earnings of $5.4 billion, an increase of more than 17 percent.

The largest producers of men's dress shirts were Phillips Van Heusen Corp. (''Van Heusen,'' ''Geoffrey Beane,'' ''Izod,'' and ''Gant'' brand names), Cluett, Peabody Inc. (''Arrow''), and Salant Corp., (''Manhattan'' and ''John Henry''). In 1999 Supreme International of Miami, Florida, purchased the John Henry and Manhattan brands from Salant for $27 million. Supreme International then licensed its entire dress shirt inventory to Phillips-Van Heusen for $44 million. The deal helped Phillips Van Heusen maintain its stranglehold share of the U.S. dress shirt and designer dress shirt markets.

Another leading producer of men's dress shirts was C.F. Hathaway Shirts, a division of Warnaco Group Inc. Founded in Waterville, Maine, in 1837, Hathaway is the nation's oldest shirtmaker. However, the company lost $5 million in 1995. In November of the next year a group of investors purchased the Waterville factory and hired industry veteran Don Sappington as CEO. The deal was supported domestically by the federal government, state and city agencies, and a $1-million grant from the Economic Development Administration. Within two years of the purchase, factory production was back at full capacity. In 1998 the new management decided to advertise the brand name again for the first time in 15 years. The ads concentrated on marketing cotton shirts in the $45 to $65 range, with blends selling at $40 to $45.

Another venerable name in the shirt-making industry did not fare as well. Founded in St. Louis, Missouri, in 1876, Boyd's filed for Chapter 11 bankruptcy in 1994. Jack Culian attempted to rescue the store in July 1996, buying the Boyd's brand name for $3,500 and raising $200,000 from investors. In October 1996 Boyd's reopened its doors with the motto ''a new era with an old friend.'' But the seller of traditional dress shirts and formal attire could not turn the corner. With four salespeople, less than a thousand customers, and industry trends heading toward more casual business attire, Boyd's closed its doors for the final time in September 1999.

WORKFORCE

Total employment in the men's and boys' shirt industry in 1994 was 73,600, among whom 66,800 were production workers. These figures represented the results of the industry's long-term downsizing, as employment had been dropping more-or-less steadily since the early 1980s. While total employment was declining, the average hours worked by production employees exhibited a modest but steady rise, going from 36 hours per week in 1981 to 37.1 hours per week in 1992. For the same period, these workers' average wage rose from $4.55 to $6.56 per hour. By 1994 average wages had reached $6.95. Women annually accounted for more than 50 percent of the workforce during the 1990s, while racial minorities accounted for more than one-third.

Occupational categories in the men's and boys' shirt industry fell within four production-related classifications: cutting, sewing, finishing, and miscellaneous departments. The Bureau of Labor Statistics forecast that the number of workers in each of these categories would undergo a continuous decline through the year 2005. Assuming a continuation of the more-or-less forward momentum of the industry's productivity, employment of sewing machines operators was projected to experience the steepest decrease. In 1999 management took care of its workers, entering into a three-year contract that included wage increases, an additional paid holiday, and better health care benefits.

RESEARCH AND TECHNOLOGY

Reducing the large number of sewing machine, assembly, and packaging operations necessary in the manufacture of a single dress shirt has been a hurdle that the industry has been struggling to clear. According to Ernest Schramyr, president of Jet Sew, one key variable factoring into the production cycle of a shirt batch— generally 1,500 shirts—has been the length of time it takes to move from one operation to the next. In an article in *Bobbin,* Schramyr discussed an alternative shirt production system, which called for the installation of already available robotic units as a means of expediting many assembly operations. If implemented, Schramyr said that a typical shirt would require only 27 (instead of 40) total operations.

Manufacturers have also been exploring the unit production system (UPS) as an alternative to existing assembly-operations. Under the UPS garments are manufactured one unit at a time rather than as parts of a series or bundle. An overhead conveyor whisks garment pieces to sewing operators, who quickly stitch a collar, button, or pocket before the machine shoots the clothing to another worker. Some manufacturers that have experimented with the UPS report increases in productivity, but no statistics are available for the industry as a whole. The most notable drawbacks associated with the UPS are its relatively high start-up costs and, according to traditional investment criteria, its tendency to generate a marginal return on investment.

FURTHER READING

Abernathy, Frederick H., et al. ''The Information-Integrated Channel: A Study of the U.S. Apparel Industry in Transition.'' *Brooking Institute Papers on Economic Activity. Microeconomics,* 1995.

Darnay, Arsen, ed. *Manufacturing USA.* Detroit: Gale Research, 1996.

Dunlop, John T., and David Weil. ''Diffusion and Performance of Modular Production in the U.S. Apparel Industry.'' *Industrial Relations,* July 1996.

McGraw, Dan. ''Dressing Down for Dollars.'' *U.S. News & World Report,* 13 May 1996.

Rublin, Lauren. ''Time To Go Short? Despite Casual Friday, Demand for Men's Clothing Is Showing Signs of Flagging,'' *Barron's,* 17 August 1998.

Schramyr, Ernst. ''Jets-In-Time: 13 Operation Can Go.'' *Bobbin,* May 1987.

Shelton, Linda, and Robert Wallace. ''World Textile and Apparel Trade: A New Era.'' *Industry, Trade, and Technology Review,* October 1996. Available from http://www.usitc.gov/ittr.htm.

U.S. Bureau of the Census Web Site, December 1999. Available from http://www.census.gov.

Zagorin, Adam. ''Short-shirted in Maine.'' *Time,* 3 June 1996.

SIC 2322

MEN'S AND BOYS' UNDERWEAR AND NIGHTWEAR

This category includes establishments primarily engaged in manufacturing men's and boys' underwear and nightwear from purchased woven or knit fabrics. Knitting mills primarily engaged in manufacturing underwear and nightwear are classified in **SIC 2254: Knit Underwear and Nightwear Mills;** and those manufacturing men's and boys' robes are classified in **SIC 2384: Robes and Dressing Gowns.**

NAICS CODE(S)

315211 (Men's and Boys' Cut and Sew Apparel Contractors)

315221 (Men's and Boys' Cut and Sew Underwear and Nightwear Manufacturing)

INDUSTRY SNAPSHOT

Starting in the early to mid-1980s the economic fortunes of the men's and boys' underwear and nightwear industry entered a period of sharp decline. By the late 1980s and then extending well into the 1990s, both the retail and wholesale levels of distribution had undergone a period of widespread shakeout and structural change. This led to the breakup of many established lines of distribution and sent producers scrambling in search of new outlet sources. Even in instances where these links were not severed, they were considerably transformed, which typically led to the implementation of quick response systems.

Also, as the U.S. economy began to experience a period of economic recovery in the mid-1990s, the upward movement of apparel prices historically associated with upturns in economic activity failed to materialize. The expected price rises were held in check due to stiff price competition from both U.S. and foreign producers. As a result, some firms in the industry found themselves burdened with levels of excess capacity that were never before encountered during previous periods of economic recovery. Finally, the lingering overhang of takeover debt piled up to defend against hostile takeover threats—a frenzy that peaked in the late 1980s and subsided in the early 1990s—continued to exert a dampening effect on company profits and growth.

By the 1990s, a particularly important force shaping the U.S. nightwear and underwear industry was economic globalization. As foreign competitors' share of the domestic market expanded throughout the first part of the decade, U.S. firms adapted by basing an increasing share of their own production outside of the United States. The passage of the North American Free Trade Agreement (NAFTA) and the Agreement on Textiles and Clothing (ATC) seemed likely to provide further stimulus to both trends in the near future.

In addition, while the industry was staggering under economic difficulties, its larger firms continued to gain market share and were well positioned to invest internally generated funds in state-of-art technologies. These new technology investments were expected to result in a boost in productivity and lower unit costs of production. Under the prevailing economic circumstances, if the middle and lower tier firms in the industry failed to keep pace, some industry observers expected the gap related to productivity and unit cost differentials to widen, placing the continued existence of the less competitive firms in serious jeopardy.

ORGANIZATION AND STRUCTURE

In the 1990s, approximately 90 U.S. establishments were involved in the manufacture of men's and boys' underwear and nightwear. Of these, about 70 operated with 20 or more employees. The industry was heavily concentrated in the southeastern United States, with Georgia, Tennessee, South Carolina, and Kentucky accounting for nearly three-quarters of all employment in the industry.

BACKGROUND AND DEVELOPMENT

Underwear. At the turn of the twentieth century, underwear was designed with one purpose in mind—as apparel to be worn underneath more stylistic outer garments for the simple purpose of protecting the wearer against seasonal elements. During severe weather, a man could choose from several different styles and weights of either one- or two-piece long-sleeved and long-legged knitted wool underwear. For the summer months, the wearer changed to underwear that was lighter and cooler, though it was also designed in a long-sleeved and long-legged style. A popular two-piece outfit was made of French knitted balbriggan. It featured an undershirt complete with a fancy collarette neck, pearl buttons, ribbed close fitting cuffs and a fine silk-like finish. The matching drawers came with a sateen band and pearl buttons. It was available in the colors of either ecru or camel hair. Though interest in silk underwear was growing on the margin, due not so much to its aesthetic or status-symbol value as to its superior drying quality, underwear made of knitted wool dominated throughout the first two decades of the twentieth century.

The early twenties witnessed the arrival of the one-piece union suit. The union suit featured an athletically tapered look and came with long or short sleeves. Made from knit of long staple combed cotton yarn and sewn with smooth flat locked seams, the union suit was especially designed to eliminate the feeling of tightness around the crotch area. The union suit was also tailored to fit different body lengths and was available in long, medium, and short sizes.

The next innovation was athletic underwear, which was cut very brief and was available in a variety of staple and fancy woven cloths. It came with a trouser seat designed so that when opened it made no contact with the body. The sleeveless athletic shirt, popular throughout the 1930s, was adapted from the top half of the tank swimsuit worn by U.S. men during the early years of the twentieth century. It was supplanted in the 1940s by the short-sleeve T-shirt worn by World War II servicemen. The soldiers found these garments so comfortable, that they continued to wear them on reentering civilian life. By the 1950s, the T-shirt had been transformed into a popular outerwear garment. It was propelled into the national consciousness by rebellious movie idols such as James Dean and Marlon Brando, who wore T-shirts, as opposed to the more traditional sportshirt, with their blue jeans.

Perhaps the biggest sensation to hit the men's underwear scene was the 1934 arrival of jock-type underwear shorts. Advertisements proclaimed their virtues, noting that jock-type shorts, designed with the male figure in mind, featured a No-gap opening with gentle support, elastic fabric, no buttons, no bulk, and no binding. By 1936 lightweight jock-type underwear was available in open weave and netlike fabric, with very high porosity. During the early 1940s, boxer shorts, some of them made with grippers, continued to gain in popularity but never supplanted jock-type knitted underwear, which by 1946 were available with an inverted Y-front construction accompanied by advertisements that proclaimed them to be scientifically perfected for correct male support.

Synthetic fabrics appeared in the 1950s. Nylon underwear took the spotlight and was soon followed by polyester and cotton blends in a variety of colors. Men's fashion critics dubbed the 1960s and early 1970s the Peacock Revolution. During this period men's underwear fashions showed regard for style and color that had been historically reserved for outerwear apparel. Undershirts and shorts, for instance, were color coordinated and could be found in a broad assortment of colors, patterns, and fabrics.

Sleepwear. Until the 1920s, when central heating became more widespread, the standard boys' sleep apparel consisted of a one-piece body suit with attached feet. As for men, a muslin nightshirt designed as a collarless pullover with long sleeves and side vents was standard. It usually extended below the calf, had three buttons in the front, and a chest pocket.

By 1925, as central heat became increasingly commonplace, the switch from men's nightshirts to pajamas gathered full force as the warmth factor was no longer quite as paramount. Men's Wear magazine noted that the tendency to discard nightshirts in order to take up the wearing of pajamas was everywhere in evidence, and pajama manufacturers sought to portray the new product as a vastly preferable alternative to the staid old nightshirt.

At the close of the 1920s and into the early 1930s, broadcloth competed with sateen for the number one position among sleepwear fabrics. Large bold striped pajamas were the style of choice. By 1936 pajamas designed with extended waistbands and pleats for added comfort were, for the first time, promoted not just for sleepwear but also for at-home leisure activities.

In the early 1960s the distinction between sleepwear and men's leisure-wear grew even more blurred. Men's pajamas regularly incorporated fashions and designs from sportswear and dress shirts. By the 1970s the transformation of sleepwear into sporty leisure or lounge wear was complete. The leading sleepwear manufacturers were busy putting together mix-match coordinate packages of either similar or contrasting fabrics. Even the once-maligned nightshirt made a comeback as Pierre Cardin marketed a lightweight floral-striped version design especially for the holiday season. Marketing buzzwords such as Unjamas and Kimojamas were created to emphasize a pajamas dual loungewear and sleepwear characteristics. During this time, the prevailing wisdom appeared to be that whatever proved popular in sportswear was to be immediately adapted to sleepwear.

CURRENT CONDITIONS

Downsizing domestic production and increased offshore production were prevalent trends in this industry in the latter half of the 1990s. Fruit of the Loom, for example, closed six U.S. plants in 1995 and laid off 3,200 workers, about 12 percent of its U.S. workforce. By 1999, they had laid off 95 percent of their U.S. workforce, with the bulk of the jobs moving to the Caribbean. Packaging operations followed in order to expedite delivery.

One reason for the move overseas was that underwear manufacturers were not enjoying the price increases occurring in other segments of the apparel industry. Cost control became a primary concern.

Manufacturers also faced a shrinking customer base due to the consolidation of department stores. As a result, many companies developed Web sites so that customers could order online without visiting a retail outlet. Web sites were also introduced so that distributors could use them for ordering and inventory.

INDUSTRY LEADERS

Two firms, Fruit of the Loom Inc. and Sara Lee Corp., dominated the U.S. men's and boys' underwear industry in the 1990s. Sara Lee sold underwear under the Hanes brand, and in 1997 introduced products under a license agreement with Polo/Ralph Lauren.

Fruit of the Loom brands included Fruit of the Loom, BVD, Munsingwear, Botany 500, and John Henry. Fruit of the Loom posted $2.2 billion in sales in 1998. However, by the end of the century, the company and its CEO, William Farley, were in serious trouble. After a hasty move of its headquarters to the Cayman Islands and most of its workforce to Mexico, the Caribbean, and Central America to save money and avoid taxes, the company suffered a severe inventory shortage. The largely untrained workers made inferior products, forcing Fruit of the Loom to hire subcontractors and to pay its employees overtime to meet the shortfall. In August 1999 Farley was relieved of his responsibilities as CEO. In December 1999 Fruit of the Loom filed for bankruptcy. A month later, Farley was ousted from his position as chairman of the board. He was replaced by Sir Brian Wolfson, a businessman and eight-year Fruit of the Loom board member from Great Britain.

Joe Boxer Corp., a popular producer of boxer shorts, designed its products in the United States, but subcontracted all manufacturing to firms in the Far East. Calvin Klein was also a force in the industry by the end of the century, with $141 million in sales.

WORKFORCE

Industry employment data from the last two decades of the twentieth century reflected a trend of steady job losses. Underlying this trend were automation in the industry and the tendency of U.S. producers to relocate apparel establishments abroad or to outsource to foreign locations work formerly performed within U.S. borders. When compared to the measures of employment by gender and race for the U.S. manufacturing sector as a whole, women and minority workers were a greater presence in the apparel workforce than in most other manufacturing industries.

In 1996, the Amalgamated Clothing and Textile Workers Union and the International Ladies Garment Union merged to form the Union of Needletrades, Industrial and Textile Employees (UNITE). UNITE's primary focus at the turn of the new century were the elimination of sweatshop working conditions and increased safety for workers. The American Apparel Manufacturers Association instituted a Worldwide Responsible Apparel Production (WRAP) certification program in December 1999 in an effort to enforce bans on forced labor, child labor, and workplace discrimination.

AMERICA AND THE WORLD

Import penetration of the U.S. underwear market has traditionally been relatively low compared to other apparel sectors. One explanation that analysts have offered for this pattern is that underwear production by U.S. firms is highly automated and efficient, reducing the importance of the difference in hourly wages between U.S. establishments and foreign competitors. However, imports in the apparel industry as a whole increased by at least 10 percent per year in the latter half of the 1990s. As barriers to imports continued to fall in the wake of the implementation of NAFTA and ATC in the middle of the decade, all signs indicated that competition with foreign manufacturers would continue to shape the U.S. nightwear and underwear industry.

RESEARCH AND TECHNOLOGY

By the mid-1990s, the most aggressive industry response to its economic condition was to step up its investment in state-of-the-art communication systems that facilitated the rapid transmission of sales information back to the producers, so as to immediately adjust production to consumer preferences. Referred to as the quick response system, this consumer-driven process more finely integrated various phases of the production cycle, shortening the duration of various production steps and reducing inventory levels to a bare minimum.

In addition to the quick response system, firms active in this industry directed major investments at computer-controlled machinery. Such purchases were undertaken in an effort to increase productivity, to minimize waste, and to secure efficiencies in traditional apparel areas such as design, cutting, embroidery, sewing, finishing, ticketing, and distribution operations. Independent of the particular area of operation, the overall investment goal was intended to reduce the amount of labor-time per task, which remained high when compared to other nonapparel group industry standards.

FURTHER READING

Crowley, Aileen. "Underwear, Activewear, Now Web-ware." *PC Week,* 10 February 1997.

Franklin, Stephen. "Fruit of the Loom Ousts Farley." *Chicago Tribune,* 11 January 2000.

Guilford, Roxanna. "Understanding the Challenges of Underwear." *Apparel Industry Magazine,* November 1999.

U.S. Bureau of the Census. *Current Industrial Reports.* Washington, D.C.: GPO, 1996. Available from http://www.census.gov/cir/www/mq23a.html.

U.S. International Trade Commission. *Industry and Trade Summary.* Washington, D.C.: GPO, 1995. Available from http://www.usitc.gov/wais/reports/rptindex.htm?apparel.

SIC 2323

MEN'S AND BOYS' NECKWEAR

This category includes establishments primarily engaged in manufacturing men's and boys' neckties, scarves, and mufflers from purchased woven or knit fabrics. Knitting mills primarily engaged in manufacturing neckties, scarves, and mufflers are classified under **SIC 2253: Knit Outerwear Mills.**

NAICS CODE(S)

315993 (Men's and Boys' Neckwear Manufacturing)

INDUSTRY SNAPSHOT

About 122 establishments were engaged in the manufacture of men's and boys' neckwear in the United States in 1997, according to the U.S. Census Bureau. Shipments of neckwear from these businesses were $597 million, compared to $700 million in 1994 and $500 million in 1990. The industry spent $269 million for materials and paid $3.6 million for new and used buildings and other structures, machinery, and equipment.

A climate of uncertainty had surrounded the industry in the mid-1990s in large part due to changing conditions of international trade after the implementation of the North American Free Trade Agreement (NAFTA) and the Agreement on Textiles and Clothing (ATC). The progressive growth of the import share of the U.S. neckwear market during the 1980s and early 1990s generated considerable alarm and prompted calls for protectionism among members of the Neckwear Association of America (NAA), the principal trade association representing U.S. neckwear manufacturers.

ORGANIZATION AND STRUCTURE

According to U.S. Census Bureau figures, nearly half of the establishments that manufactured neckwear in 1997 were small operations with fewer than 20 employees. Neckwear production was not heavily concentrated in any particular region. The states with the most neckwear operations were New York, California, North Carolina, and New Jersey.

BACKGROUND AND DEVELOPMENT

To a large extent, even before the advent of the "quick response" system, the emergence and eventual growth of the twentieth-century neckwear industry was predicated on consumer trends. An ability to stay abreast of fashion and changes in design construction proved critical in determining whether a company survived as an industry leader. Other growth-related influences of comparable importance were: changing fashions and construction of shirts, for which neckwear apparel served as a complementary article of clothing; utilization of breakthrough technological processes, which usually emerged first in non-neckwear apparel industries and led to the progressive marginalization of handmade neckwear in favor of machine-made methods; and the development of a professional/managerial strata in the U.S. workforce.

Fashion-Related Growth. At the turn of the century the two most prominent styles worn with the popular wing collar shirt were the sailor's knot Teck and Joinville ready-tied neckwear. The Teck was available with both straight and pointed ends, while Joinville was a straight-end only model. According to a 1900 Sears, Roebuck & Co. catalog, Teck and Joinville ties 6 inches wide and 34 inches long were "the most popular and swellest gentleman's scarf ever produced" and were made from the purest of specially imported woven silk. Such ties were available in an assortment of more than 300 designs and in almost every color and shade.

During the 1910s, the last decade before the appearance of the collar-attached shirt, the white, starched-collar, high-band Belmont shirt was an instant hit. It was worn with a narrow tie whose small knot was conspicuously located at the bottom of the shirt's collar. Also meeting with wide acceptance was the Henley detached collar shirt worn with a wide-body necktie covering much of the shirt's front. Two other new forms of ties were introduced during this period: the butterfly bow and the long tie formed in a sailor's knot.

Around 1920, the civilian collar-attached shirt hit the scene and became an instant success, largely due to demobilized World War I veterans who had worn a version of the shirt in the military and found it noticeably more comfortable than its collar-detached alternative. At about the same time, a highly significant design breakthrough also occurred in the neckwear industry. A technique that incorporated a loose stitch method to sew a bias-cut wool interlining (a line cutting diagonally across a fabric's grain) made possible the development of ties that retained their original shape after being knotted and unknotted. These relatively resilient ties went on to become an industry standard.

In the mid-1920s, marked changes in neckwear colors and fabrics were introduced. Ties were designed to capture the attention of women shoppers, who made up the largest component of consumers responsible for the purchase of men's neckwear items. By the late 1920s, the silk-and-wool tie rose to prominence thanks to its ripple weave design, which imparted a three dimensional effect. Among the growing number of college students, ties had taken hold and become an everyday part of dress, even though fashions differed across geographic regions.

The Great Depression of the 1930s ushered in the first appearance of woolen ties, whose growing popularity threatened the reign of silk fabric ties. During this time, the influence of British fashion was at its greatest in the United States, as witnessed by the rise in popularity of two British formal evening wear bow ties: the straight club bow and the satin butterfly bow tied in a narrow knot.

In 1936, improvements in the design and construction of the wash tie led to its gaining widespread acceptance. Wash neckwear worn in a sailor's knot tie or bow tie was now available in a twin-ply design that fortified fabric strength and wrinkle resistance. Other significant advances in the design and construction of wash ties came from the introduction of spiral seams, which increased durability; improvements in bias cut shapes, which permitted a more perfect-looking knot; and hand bar tacking, which eliminated the unraveling of loose stitching during laundering. Due to the popularity of the widespread collar shirt, the wash bow tie and the large knot tie, known as the Windsor knot, rose to prominence.

World War II diverted silk fabric into the manufacture of parachutes, and rayon quickly became the number one tie fabric while wool maintained its solid hold on second. Wool's persistence in the marketplace was a result of its relatively wrinkle-resistant qualities, along with the fact that it was fashionable to sport a wool tie with button-down shirt and single-breasted three-button suit. During the same period of the silkless tie, the highly idiosyncratic hand-painted tie, usually with sporting motifs, was introduced and proceeded to become a mainstay for the whole decade.

From 1950 to 1960, three significant design and construction breakthroughs reverberated through the neckwear industry. Washable, nonwrinkle, and no-stretch Dacron knit ties hit the scene in the early 1950s. Next came wash-and-wear all-cotton ties, which, due to a special resin treatment process, retained their original shape and appearance after washing. Around 1957, a more opulent line of what fashion critics referred to as "elegant air" ties became popular. The trouble with these rather expensive ties was their inability to withstand stains. The solution arrived in 1959, when ties were treated with a special finish named Scotchgard, which permitted stains to be washed out with plain cold water.

Major Technological Manufacturing Changes. While the neckwear industry has probably never been in the forefront of major technological innovations, it has proven adept at integrating other non-neckwear apparel industry technologies into its production processes.

The introduction of the sewing machine in 1846 prompted a reorganization of the apparel industry in general and helped transform the neckwear industry from a handicraft to a form of machine-based mass production. The sewing machine's introduction quickened the division of labor and job specialization trends spreading through the apparel industry. The productivity gains made from these changes were staggering.

Other technological innovations were soon introduced throughout the apparel industry. For example, electric-powered portable cutting knives, motor-driven cloth spreading machines, and gas-powered pressing machines displaced such devices as smaller hand-held irons.

Later manufacturing developments included a cloth cutting process directed by laser beams and the integration of computers used for pattern making, grading, and fabric utilization. In addition, the application of computers to other areas of manufacturing operations continued. Consequently, the value added per production worker increased from $10,000 in 1940 to $44,857 in 1989.

Rise of the Managerial/Professional Strata. As the economic situation in the United States changed, a managerial and professional strata emerged. The shirt-and-tie style of dress that was practically mandatory for white collar workers for much of the twentieth century provided a substantial market for the neckwear industry. New trends at the end of the century, however, were casting doubt on the stability of this demand.

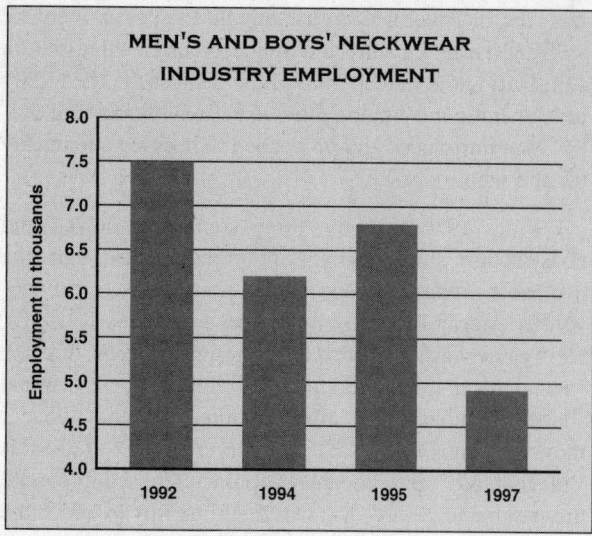

MEN'S AND BOYS' NECKWEAR INDUSTRY EMPLOYMENT

While neckwear shipments increased in the first half of the 1990s, there were two signs of trouble ahead for U.S. businesses in this industry. First, new international trade treaties promised to increase the pressure from imported goods on an industry that had historically been vulnerable to foreign competition. Second, relaxed dress codes in U.S. corporations and a more casual approach to dressing in general meant that American men were wearing ties less often.

Tie fashions shifted significantly during the first half of the 1990s. Conservatively patterned yellow and red power ties, which had set the tone in the 1980s, were suddenly out of fashion. The new ties tended to be wider and more brightly colored, and they had bolder abstract patterns.

CURRENT CONDITIONS

In 1997 the two most important material inputs in this industry were broadwoven fabrics and narrow fabrics. The industry shipped $440 million worth of woven silk ties, $57 million worth of woven polyester ties, $10 million worth of woven ties made from other fabrics, and $10 million worth of other neckwear such as leather neckties and knit or woven mufflers and scarves.

By 1998 woven neckwear had been popular for several years, largely because it was eye-catching and unusual. Although demand for woven neckwear remained high, some industry insiders were predicting that consumer preferences would soon begin to shift toward prints. The neckwear market in general did not grow quickly during the late 1990s because fewer consumers were wearing neckties.

INDUSTRY LEADERS

One of the leading U.S. neckwear manufacturers in the late 1990s was Wemco Inc., based in New Orleans,

Louisiana. At the beginning of the decade, the company had fallen behind fashion trends and began to lose orders from major department stores. A move to revamp the company in the early 1990s led to new orders from Wal-Mart, as well as a comeback in department-store purchases. Wemco had a workforce of about 350 people in 1998 and estimated sales of $55 million.

Other companies that made men's and boy's neckwear as a primary business included Superba Inc. (Los Angeles, California) with 600 employees and sales of $95 million, Castle Neckwear Inc. (Los Angeles, California) with 150 employees and sales of $20 million, and Remington Apparel Company Inc. (a subsidiary of Remington Equities Corp. based in Graham, Texas) with 200 employees and sales of $15 million.

Superba, one of the largest firms in the industry, had been in business since 1873. In 1999 the company obtained the license to use the famous Wilke-Rodriguez name on a new line of ties. Designer Eddie Rodriguez told *Daily News Record* that his goal was "to make men want to wear ties again." Rodriguez was known for his ability to design modern fashions that appealed to young consumers.

WORKFORCE

Employment in the men's and boys' neckwear industry, despite annual fluctuations, remained relatively flat for the period from 1982 to 1994. By 1997 the Census Bureau estimated that 4,914 people were employed in the neckwear industry, including 3,801 production workers who earned an average hourly wage of $9.75. These figures were down considerably from 1992, when total employment stood at 7,500 workers.

AMERICA AND THE WORLD

International trade has long been a contentious issue for the U.S. neckwear industry. From 1974 until 1995, world trade in textiles and apparel was regulated under the Multifiber Arrangement (MFA). Yet only a portion of neckwear category types—not including most silk neckwear categories—were covered by this agreement, and no specific quota structures had been put into effect. Therefore, neckwear producers successfully lobbied the U.S. government to impose tariff or import duties.

A trade agreement put into effect from 1981 through 1987, which specified a staged reduction in neckwear tariff duties, highlighted the industry's import vulnerability. The overall results of a report prepared for the NAA by Economic Consulting Services Inc. were less than favorable. The U.S. neckwear industry experienced a sustained decline in domestic profits; production employment fell from 5,300 to 4,800 workers; and these negative trends occurred during a period when U.S. demand for neckwear was on the increase. During the same period, neckwear imports increased by 356 percent, going from approximately 373 thousand dozen to 1,698 thousand dozen units. The report indicated that Korean and Chinese neckwear manufacturers gained the most market share throughout the period.

The 1993 passage of the Uruguay Round of the General Agreement on Tariffs and Trade (GATT) meant that the provisions contained in the MFA were to be supplanted and phased out gradually from 1995 to 2005. Much to the displeasure of the NAA, the terms of the GATT called for a significant reduction in worldwide tariff duties.

To compete with lower-priced imports, U.S. neckwear manufacturers took advantage of tariff provision 9802 (formerly 807), as set forth by the Harmonized Tariff Schedule of the United States (HTSUS). The provision allowed companies to export components made in the United States, assemble them into finished neckwear in foreign factories, and return them to the United States for sale with duty charged only on the foreign value added. In the past, Mexico and Caribbean countries were the largest recipients of HTSUS 9802 trade. With the passage of NAFTA, Caribbean countries expressed concern that 9802 economic activity in their region would shift eventually to Mexico's advantage.

RESEARCH AND TECHNOLOGY

Beginning in the late 1980s, neckwear establishments, like all segments of the apparel industry, invested heavily in state-of-the-art communications systems that rapidly transmit and respond to information about consumer preferences in the marketplace. These information technology systems, together with attempts to shorten the production cycle and reduce in-process inventories, formed a consumer-driven strategy called "quick response." Manufacturers often adopted "quick response" systems because of pressure from wholesalers and retailers who were determined to accelerate shipments of hot-selling items and shorten the time required to respond to changing consumer preferences.

Neckwear firms also invested in computer-controlled automated machines to increase productivity and improve the efficiency of their design, cutting, embroidery, sewing, finishing, ticketing, and distribution operations. Most investment projects were undertaken to reduce the labor-time component per task, which remained excessively high compared to other nonapparel industry group standards. Typically, larger neckwear firms, because of their economies of scale and access to internal financing, were better positioned to implement high-cost technological advances. As a result, the pattern of technological change was anything but uniform across all neckwear establishments.

FURTHER READING

Brodsky, Renatt. "Not Your Ordinary Knot: Designer Eddie Rodriguez Pledges to Bring Fresh Perspective to Newly Licensed Neckwear Line." *Daily News Record,* 30 April 1999.

Button, Graham. "Tieing One On." *Forbes,* 23 October 1995.

Mckinney, Melonee. "Neckwear Industry Begins to Look Beyond Wovens: Some Execs Feel It's Time to Again Emphasize Prints." *Daily News Record,* 2 January 1998.

U.S. Department of Commerce. Census Bureau. *1997 Economic Census.* Washington, D.C.: GPO, 1999. Available from http://www.census.gov/prod/ec97/97m3159c.pdf.

SIC 2325

MEN'S AND BOYS' SEPARATE TROUSERS AND SLACKS

This category includes establishments primarily engaged in manufacturing men's and boys' separate trousers and slacks from purchased woven or knit fabrics, including jeans, dungarees, and jean-cut casual slacks. Establishments primarily engaged in manufacturing complete suits are classified in **SIC 2311: Men's and Boys' Suits, Coats, and Overcoats;** those manufacturing workpants (excluding jeans and dungarees) are classified in **SIC 2326: Men's and Boys' Work Clothing.** Knitting mills primarily engaged in manufacturing men's and boys' separate trousers and slacks are classified in **SIC 2253: Knit Outerwear Mills.**

NAICS CODE(S)

315211 (Men's and Boys' Cut and Sew Apparel Contractors)

315224 (Men's and Boys' Cut and Sew Trouser, Slack, and Jean Manufacturing)

INDUSTRY SNAPSHOT

During the 1990s, the value of shipments by U.S. companies making men's and boys' trousers and slacks rose steadily, while employment levels remained flat. If aggregate statistics suggested stable conditions, these years were in fact a period of substantial transformation in this industry.

Pressures for change came from a number of different sources. First, shifts in the nature of consumer demand, especially a growing preference for casual clothes, led manufacturers to introduce new lines and new products in the early 1990s. By the end of the decade, however, the marketplace was overrun with men's casual pants and it appeared that American men had completed their casual work wardrobes.

Second, concentration in the U.S. retail industry meant that manufacturers of pants had fewer potential retailers with whom to deal, and this process, consequently, gave greater leverage to those powerful chains that remained. In response to retailers' demands for cheaper goods and faster replenishment, manufacturers invested in new communications technologies and developed new methods of production. Finally, U.S. manufacturers had to compete for space on retailers' shelves with cheaply produced imported pants—a trend that was likely to intensify in the aftermath of the implementation of new international trade agreements in the mid-1990s. One response to pressure from foreign competitors was to downsize domestic production and base an increasing share of production offshore.

ORGANIZATION AND STRUCTURE

In the 1990s some 400 establishments owned by 278 companies were engaged in the production of men's and boys' trousers and slacks. Despite the large number of enterprises, this was a relatively highly concentrated industry, as the four largest manufacturers produced 60 percent of industry shipments. The industry was concentrated geographically in the south and southeast of the United States. Texas led the way with almost 20 percent of all industry employment, followed by Tennessee, Georgia, and Alabama, each with just more than 10 percent.

Men's and boys' jeans (including jean-cut casual slacks) was the most important major product class for this industry, accounting for 64 percent of the value of industry shipments; men's and boys' separate dress and sport trousers, pants, and slacks accounted for 26 percent; and about 10 percent was accounted for by contract or commission work on various product categories. By far the most important material used in this industry was broadwoven fabric; this fabric made up 78 percent ($1.539 billion) of total material costs for the industry.

Establishments in this industry sold their goods to department stores, specialty clothing shops, mass merchandisers, and discount chains. In addition, a number of leading pants manufacturers were expanding their own network of brand-name retail outlets. In the last two decades of the twentieth century, there was substantial concentration among U.S. apparel retailers as a result of bankruptcies and consolidation. These remaining retail chains controlled a larger share of the market and enjoyed greater leverage in their relationships with manufacturers.

BACKGROUND AND DEVELOPMENT

In colonial America, the trousers worn by members of the elite classes were, in part, a means of denoting social status and wealth. Typically, these trousers, or breeches, as they were then called, were produced by highly skilled craftsmen. Although they had utilitarian function, no effort was spared in trying to embellish these slacks, which were made from the finest of fabrics and decorated with ornaments of distinction.

The outcome of the American Revolution thrust an emergent and growing middle class, composed of industrialists, merchants, storekeepers, and their various assistants or professionals, to the forefront of political and economic activity and had a profound impact on men's fashion. The fashions of the European nobility were quickly discarded because they symbolized the garb of counterrevolutionaries. Gone were ornately designed trousers. Garments manufactured by U.S. producers gained prominence, while those woven from imported fabrics were looked upon with political disfavor. Simplicity and utility were central to what was regarded as good taste in dress. The day George Washington was inaugurated as the first president of the United States, he wore a suit coat and pants of fine dark brown broadcloth woven in one of the regional hotbeds of the American Revolution—Worcester, Massachusetts.

The taste among American men for utilitarian design contributed to new production and commercial methods in the industry. Tailors began to cut pants in batches and, after sewing them, stored them as inventory on demand or displayed them on retailers' shelves. Advertisers attempted to drum up demand for these ready-made goods. In Boston, George W. Simmons made extensive use of newspaper advertising when, in 1842, he began to promote slacks using enclosed window displays rather than simply hanging or stacking trousers outside his shop. Simmons was also reported to have launched balloons announcing sales and to have established a successful mail order department. Similar efforts, using various novel forms of advertising meant to enhance brand recognition, were undertaken by Jacob Reed and Brooks Brothers.

Almost from the end of the American Revolution until 1860, the embryonic U.S. apparel industry, including the trouser business, was nurtured by a highly protectionist government policy. Until 1816, the duty for imported slacks stood at 25 percent. By 1828 it had reached 50 percent, where it remained until 1860. During the same period, an additional tariff was applied when imported trousers arrived on U.S. shores in foreign ships.

After 1860 U.S. producers believed they could hold their own against foreign competitors. More than one-half a century of protection had provided the industry with the necessary breathing space to mature and eventually enter the global marketplace with a world-class level of productivity. Confidence in the industry's second-to-none productivity level was warranted, due primarily to the introduction and diffusion of sewing machine technology by the late 1850s, which decreased labor time and, consequently, costs of finished garments.

From the standpoint of the workers, however, the sewing machines' productivity-enhancing virtues were anything but a benefit. The widespread diffusion of the sewing machine quickly eliminated the need for highly paid skilled laborers performing hand sewing operations. At the same time it permitted the employment of semi-skilled employees, whose wages gravitated towards a bare subsistence level. Whether employed in domestic tenement quarters or in factory sweatshops, working conditions were abysmal, health hazards went unchecked, and child labor was common. For the next couple of decades, the ranks of semiskilled workers grew, and working conditions became more miserable with each successive wave of immigration. It was not until the formation of apparel-based trade unions that such conditions began to be combated.

Until the outbreak of the Civil War, manufacturers and retailers of ready-made pants confronted a persistent problem—the absence of any reliable sizing standards to assure that mass-produced clothing would fit properly. The solution arrived from a study performed by the U.S. Army's Philadelphia Quartermaster Depot, which had collected body size measurement data on over a million recruits and conscripts. The depot organized these measurements into tables of standard body proportions and thus created a set of data that could be readily applied to the standardization of manufactured civilian garments.

Body sizing standards, coupled with the diffusion of sewing machine technology, radically transformed the clothing industry by increasing the division of labor. By 1895 these changes resulted in what came to be known as the bundle system of production, where one or more workers performed a single operation on a repetitive basis. Once the bundle limit was reached, the work in process was passed on to the next station of workers performing another distinct operation. This process would continue until the entire trouser garment was completed. The bundle system proved to be an enduring and flexible method of production, capable of undergoing refinement, modification, and integration with new technologies. It was still in widespread use throughout the apparel industry in the mid-1990s.

The 1880s witnessed the first major improvement in the nonsewing processes, when the sword knife and slotted table were introduced into cutting rooms. Later came the electrically operated knife, which, though immobile, proved to be the forerunner of the more modern, portable, electrically driven assortment of cutting tools. In turn, the widespread application of portable rotary and reciprocating electric knives would not have been possible without earlier advances in the construction of electric motors. In the late 1890s, pressing operations were transformed. Operations reliant upon gas- and coal-heated irons were replaced first by the steam pressing iron and later the steam pressing machine.

New technological developments late in the twentieth century featured a laser beam-directed cloth-cutting process along with the integration of computers utilized for pattern making, grading, and fabric selection. The extension of computer-aided job processes to most areas of trouser production was expected to continue. Such efforts were in step with the industry's drive to raise the level of productivity, a measure usually achieved by changes in the value added per production worker.

These changes were the results of attempts by American pants manufacturers to adapt to the shifting clothing habits of American men, in a society where informal dress was increasingly common in both business and leisure contexts. This was a trend that showed every sign of continuing—a Levi Strauss survey showed that by the year 2000, one-half of all U.S. corporations would no longer require formal dress at all and that 75 percent of U.S. workers would be wearing casual clothes to the office. In order to capitalize, major manufacturers like Levi Strauss and Haggar Corp. introduced new lines of pants in the mid-1990s that would straddle the division between casual and formal wear.

Another important product innovation in the early 1990s was the introduction of wrinkle-free cotton pants. These pants, treated with a chemical finish to prevent wrinkling, were first marketed in 1989 by Farah Inc. By the mid-1990s all other major manufacturers had introduced their own wrinkle-free products that represented the fastest growing segment of the domestic men's apparel market.

U.S. manufacturers strived to maintain their share of this market in the face of competition from foreign manufacturers by taking advantage of tariff provision 9802 (formerly 807), of the Harmonized Tariff Schedule of the United States (HTSUS). This provision allowed U.S manufacturers to ship cut pieces offshore to Caribbean Basin countries, where they are sewn, either by outside contractors or in company-owned factories, and then reimported to the United States with duty assessed only upon the value added outside the United States. The other side of this process, of course, was the downsizing of U.S. manufacturing, involving closure of assembly plants and layoffs of workers. This trend was more pronounced for manufacturing of formal pants, which require considerably more labor than jeans. One major manufacturer, Farah Inc., had shifted all sewing and finishing operations offshore by 1996.

Some of the same manufacturers, however, also developed strategies that pointed in the direction of increasing the competitiveness of domestic manufacturing operations. Known as quick response, these strategies were aimed at enhancing the flexibility of manufacturers in responding to changing buying habits of consumers and changing demands of retailers. The most widely adopted quick response strategy was the development of state-of-the-art communications networks, known as electronic

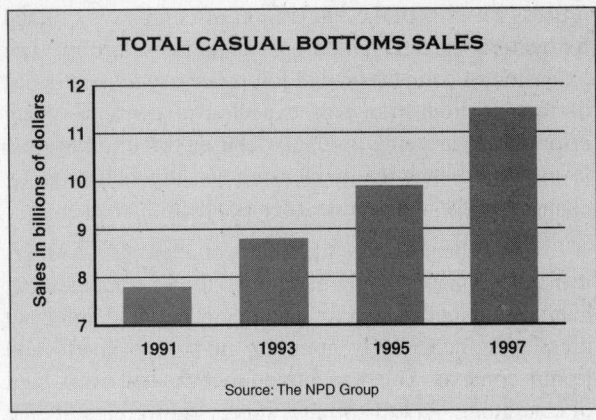

TOTAL CASUAL BOTTOMS SALES

Source: The NPD Group

data interchange (EDI), which link the computer systems of manufacturers to retailers and allow manufacturers almost instant access to information about retail sales of their items. Manufacturers could immediately adjust production schedules and shipments according to this data.

Manufacturers also attempted to speed up the production cycle in order to take full advantage of their access to data about market conditions. A far-reaching, but not very widely implemented, strategy for meeting this goal was the replacement of the long-standing bundle system with modular systems of production. In modular systems, teams of multiskilled operators work together to sew an entire pair of pants. Pay is based on the entire team's output, rather than an individual piece-rate, giving incentive for team members to shift tasks when backlogs develop and to focus on maximizing the number of finished pieces produced by the whole team, rather than the number of individual operations performed. While individual labor productivity may not be quite as high as in the progressive bundle system, where each operator performs just one specialized task, in-process inventory levels are reduced, and the production cycle for assembly of an entire garment is greatly accelerated. Although industry analysts, industry leaders, and unions began to advocate for adoption of modular production as a key part of quick response strategies as far back as the 1980s, manufacturers were slow to undertake such a dramatic overhaul of their management and human resources practices. A study of firms from a number of different branches of the apparel industry in early 1992 revealed that less than 10 percent of all garments were produced according to the modular system. However, at least one major company in the trousers and slacks industry, Levi Strauss, adopted the modular production with enthusiasm in the mid-1990s.

CURRENT CONDITIONS

The sales of casual pants and jeans rose steadily through the last decade of the twentieth century. Jeans sales were $3.6 billion in 1991; by 1997, sales reached $5.2 billion. Sales of casual pants increased from $2.2 billion in 1991 to $3.4 billion in 1997. A leveling off began at the start of the new century. Industry analysts credited this with a glut on the khaki market as well as the beginning of a backlash against the so-called Casual Friday phenomenon. Discount stores, national chains, and department stores were the top three outlets for the purchase of men's apparel.

INDUSTRY LEADERS

The leading U.S. manufacturers of men's and boys' trousers and slacks in the mid-1990s were Levi Strauss Associates (with its Levis and Dockers brand names), V.F. Corporation (Wrangler, Rustler, and Lee), Haggar Corp. (Haggar and St. James), and Farah Inc. (Savane, Farah, and John Henry). V.F. Corp. had the largest share of the domestic jeans market, with 30 percent. Levi Strauss was second overall in jeans, although its Levis brand was the best-selling individual brand. Levi Strauss led in casual pants, with its Dockers brand, followed by Haggar, which led in domestic sales of formal pants.

Levi Strauss, still owned by the descendants of its founder, was the largest brand-name apparel manufacturer in the world in the 1990s. The company complemented its extremely successful Levis and Dockers brand names by introducing a third major line of pants in late 1996, Slates, designed to compete in the corporate casual market. Levi Strauss was clearly in a position to benefit from the turn towards more casual business clothing in the 1990s and successfully pressed its advantage by aggressively marketing its products via fashion shows, seminars, and videotapes targeted at thousands of corporate employers. Another strong aspect of the company was the prestige of its Levis brand name among foreign consumers, which enabled it to sell blue jeans as a fashion item at considerably higher prices than domestically. As a result of these factors, Levi Strauss' sales were strong throughout the 1990s, posting between $6.6 and $6.7 billion in sales worldwide in each of the last five years of the decade. Sales in the Americas alone were $3.9 billion in 1998.

Levi Strauss also earned notoriety in the 1990s for its values-based approach to management, based on encouraging employee input in decision-making, diversifying management personnel, and applying ethical standards in foreign sourcing operations.

In January of 1999, Levi's president, Peter Jacobi, retired after 28 years with the company. The following month, Levi Strauss closed 11 North American plants, laying off 5,900 of its 19,900 U.S. workers.

Both V.F. and Haggar also enjoyed strong sales in the 1990s. A key to V.F.'s success was the performance of its quick response computer links to major retailers, such as J.C. Penney and Wal-Mart. V.F.'s computer center received nightly data from these retailers about the days sales and immediately set the process in motion to replenish the sold products. Replacements for a pair of jeans sold on a Tuesday were thus often on the retailers shelf by Thursday. The effectiveness of this system was seen by some analysts as the cause of V.F.'s growing edge in domestic jeans sales over Levi Strauss, which had begun implementing plans to emulate its competitor by the mid-1990s. Haggar's success in the first half of the 1990s was at least partly due to its aggressive marketing of wrinkle-free cotton pants. Both V.F. and Haggar, despite their strong sales, were in the process of downsizing domestic production in the 1990s.

WORKFORCE

The vast majority of the employees in the men's and boys' trousers and slacks industry were production workers. Wages were slightly under $8 per hour by the end of the 1990s. Major employers in this industry reported that only small minorities of their workers were covered by collective bargaining agreements. However, in 1996, the Amalgamated Clothing and Textile Workers Union merged with the International Ladies Garment Union to form the Union of Needletrades, Industrial and Textile Employees (UNITE). UNITE's strong organizing efforts caused Guess jeans to move 40 percent of its manufacturing operations to Mexico and South America by 1997.

AMERICA AND THE WORLD

With the passage of the North American Free Trade Agreement (NAFTA) and the Agreement on Textiles and Clothing (ATC) in the mid-1990s, competition from foreign manufacturers and pressures to downsize domestic operations were likely to increase. The former lifted quotas and removed some tariffs on apparel imports from Mexico. The latter called for accelerated growth in quota levels for apparel imports from other countries and for the eventual elimination of quotas by the year 2005.

RESEARCH AND TECHNOLOGY

In addition to the quick response system, men's and boys' trousers and slacks firms directed major investments at computer-controlled automated machinery in an effort to increase productivity and secure production efficiencies in the areas of design, cutting, embroidery, sewing, finishing, ticketing, and various distribution operations. Independent of the particular area of operation, most investment projects were undertaken with the intention of reducing the labor-time component per task, which remained excessively high relative to other nonapparel industry group standards. Because of their economies of scale and access to internally generated funds, the larger trousers and slacks firms have been better positioned to implement technological advances. This has resulted in a pattern of technological change that

is highly uneven across the entire men's and boys' slacks industry.

FURTHER READING

Canedy, Dana. "Struggling to Duplicate a Success." *New York Times,* 9 October 1996.

Dunlop, John T., and David Weil. "Diffusion and Performance of Modular Production in the U.S. Apparel Industry." *Industrial Relations,* July 1996.

Himmelstein, Linda, and Nancy Walser. "Levi's Versus the Dress Code." *Business Week,* 1 April 1996.

Hornblower, Margot. "Guess Gets Out." *Time,* 27 January 1997.

Lenzner, Robert, and Stephen S. Johnson. "A Few Yards of Denim and Five Copper Rivets." *Forbes,* 26 February 1996.

Rublin, Lauren R. "Go Short." *Barron's,* 17 August 1998.

U.S. Bureau of the Census. *Current Industrial Reports: Apparel.* Available from http://www.census.gov/cir/www/mq23a .html.

U.S. International Trade Commission. *Industry and Trade Summary.* Washington, D.C.: GPO, 1995. Available from http:// www.usitc.gov/ittr.htm.

SIC 2326

MEN'S AND BOYS' WORK CLOTHING

This category includes establishments primarily engaged in manufacturing men's and boys' work shirts, workpants (excluding jeans and dungarees), other work clothing, and washable service apparel. Establishments primarily engaged in manufacturing separate trousers and slacks (including jeans and dungarees) are classified in **SIC 2325: Men's and Boys' Separate Trousers and Slacks.**

NAICS CODE(S)

315211 (Men's and Boys' Cut and Sew Apparel Contractors)
315225 (Men's and Boys' Cut and Sew Work Clothing Manufacturing)

INDUSTRY SNAPSHOT

About 225 establishments active in the manufacture of men's and boys' work clothing accounted for an inflation-adjusted value of total product shipments of $1.2 billion in 1992. This figure, though up by 6.1 percent from 1991, remained in line with the five year declining trend, which peaked during 1987 and 1988 and was some 13.2 percent below the peak period's level of performance. This decline leveled through the mid-1990s, and moderate growth was forecast for the industry at the end of the twentieth century. Total product shipments reached $1.7 billion in 1994; by 1999, shipments were forecast to reach nearly $2.1 billion. But as production showed steady recovery through the 1990s, employment in the industry declined. In 1996, the industry employed roughly 23,400 individuals, down from 28,500 in 1994, and down even further from 30,000 in 1993.

In 1987, the U.S. Census Bureau rearranged some of the apparel industry's categories, making it more difficult to determine some of the statistical trends after 1987. Prior to 1987, the men's and boys' work clothing was classified as SIC 2328 and included jeans and dungarees among its product classifications. In 1987 jeans and dungarees were excluded from men's and boys' work clothes and assigned to **SIC 2325: Men's and Boys' Separate Trousers and Slacks.**

Unlike other apparel industries, which are variously categorized within the apparel industry group according to gender, age, and body part specific garments, the men's and boys' work clothes industry produced apparel garments extending from the neck down to the feet. These included: work aprons, coveralls, work jackets and laboratory coats, institutionalized medical uniforms, work overalls and overall jackets, work pants, washable service industry apparel, work shirts, and nontailored uniforms.

Following years of consecutive growth, the men's and boys' work clothing industry garnered a reputation for being the only recession-proof industry. This was in stark contrast to other industries within the apparel group who were highly susceptible to business cycle swings. Things changed when the work wear industry entered a protracted period of stagnant to falling growth beginning with the recession of 1981 to 1982. Through the early 1990s, industry statistics lagged behind those achieved during its former years of prosperity.

To a great extent the industry's woes were precipitated from its demand side. A steady and prolonged falloff of its once core industrial and agricultural customer base left the industry in shambles. This resulted in considerable intraindustry price competition and a run-up in unused manufacturing capacity. These same economic forces were also responsible for the industry's downsizing and served to explain why the total number of manufacturing establishments went down from 255 in 1987 to approximately 225 in 1992, to a decline of 11.8 percent. In 1993, there were a total of 275 establishments engaged in some aspect the of men's and boys' work clothing industry, most of which had over 50 employees.

A glance at the movement of some of the industry's more dominant product categories for the period of 1981 to 1990 provided further evidence of stagnation and decline. In terms of consumer purchases of men's work pants, for 1986 to 1990 the average annual volume fell to 16.4 million units, declining by about 13.5 percent from the previous five years. For the category of men's overalls, during 1986 to 1990 the annual volume of consumer purchases averaged 6.7 million units, a decline of 18.3 percent from the previous five years. Finally, for the category of men's work shirts, for 1986 to 1990 the average annual volume of consumer purchases was 31.6 million units, a decline of 11.5 percent from the previous five years. In fact, it was not until 1992 that shipment value of men's and boys' work clothing began to reach levels comparable to those in 1987 and 1988. In 1994, the industry shipments surpassed $1.7 billion; in 1995 the value of shipments rose to $1.8 billion, and in 1996 shipments reached nearly $1.8 billion. Estimates of 1997 and 1998 shipments topped the $2 billion mark, and forecasts for 1999 pointed to a 1.5 percent increase in shipments over the previous year, continuing the trend of modest growth.

Unlike other apparel industries, the men's and boys' work clothing industry remained relatively immune from the deluge of imports wreaking havoc on the domestic markets of their apparel counterparts. On the work wear industry's input side, however, imports were playing an important role as more companies were turning to inputs to lower labor and material costs so as to reverse the long-term slide in profit margins. To this end the ''outsourcing'' of work formerly performed within establishments to contractors outside U.S. borders had become an established trend.

One major demand-side development, anticipated to fill the void left by the falloff in industrial and agricultural markets, was the ongoing structural shift toward a service-based economy. Such a movement carried with it the potential for opening up vast areas of untapped demand for washable nontailored uniforms in health care facilities, personal care services, fast food chains, and other food preparation and service institutions. Viewed as a strategy to build customer recognition and loyalty, the wearing of corporate uniforms had already become an established trend among some airlines, banks, fitness centers, retail chain stores, and major hotels by 1999.

The men's and boys' work clothing industry also got a boost in the mid- to late 1990s with a growing interest in work wear as fashion. Brands such as Carhartt and Dickie's picked up on this trend and began marketing overalls, jackets, shirts, and workpants to the public as fashion wear. Industry leader V.F. Corp. was also expanding in the fashion/work wear market.

ORGANIZATION AND STRUCTURE

In 1993 approximately 275 establishments were active in the production and/or sales of men's and boys' work clothing. The largest concentrations of the industry's establishments were located in the East South Central, West South Central, and South Atlantic regions of the United States.

In 1996, the industry's dominant companies were: V.F. Corp.'s Tennessee-based Red Kap Industries, with $420 million in sales and 6,000 employees; Missouri-based Angelica Uniform Group, with $170 million in sales and 3,000 employees; Georgia-based Riverside Manufacturing Co., with $240 million in sales and 2,400 employees; Florida-based Superior Surgical Mfg. Co. Inc., with $135 million in sales and 1,900 employees; and Missouri-based Unitog Co., with $214 million in sales and 3,100 employees. Founded in 1932, Unitog has experienced 66 years of consecutive growth.

Input data available from 1982 and 1987 indicated that the primary materials consumed by the men's and boys' work clothing industry when ranked by cost were: materials, parts, containers, and supplies; broadwoven fabrics; and knit fabrics. The primary sources of input supply were from imports, broadwoven fabric mills, apparel made from purchased materials, and knit fabric mills. For the same two years, the share of the industry's total output disaggregated by its major product category indicated that men's and boys' work shirts accounted for 23.5 percent; men's and boys' work clothing and washable service apparel registered 58.3 percent; contract and commission work on men's and boys' work clothing in general was 9.5 percent; and men's and boys' work clothing not specified by any kind accounted for 8.7 percent.

During the late 1980s and into the 1990s, the distribution network servicing the men's and boys' work clothing industry was undergoing a fundamental transformation. For articles like washable uniforms and service related apparel, laundry rental companies had historically been the major source of distribution to large companies. But when corporate demand for a more customized look requiring a greater assortment of new fabrics, styles, and colors started to reverberate through the industry, many of the industry's larger firms bypassed the traditional laundry rental channel and opened their own corporate accounts, through which they sold directly to the wearing customer. As a result, domestic fabric mills that supplied materials to the work clothing industry also began closer working relationships with work wear manufacturers in a joint effort to better serve the industry's developing corporate accounts.

For individual purchases of work clothes, mass merchandisers and discount outlets accounted for the largest share of sales, followed by smaller specialty stores located outside of major urban areas. A development of a more recent kind featured the appearance of farm/fleet stores. These were large stores located in rural areas that carried a wide assortment of work related items ranging from work clothes to farm equipment. The stores' core customer base consisted of farmers and truckers who

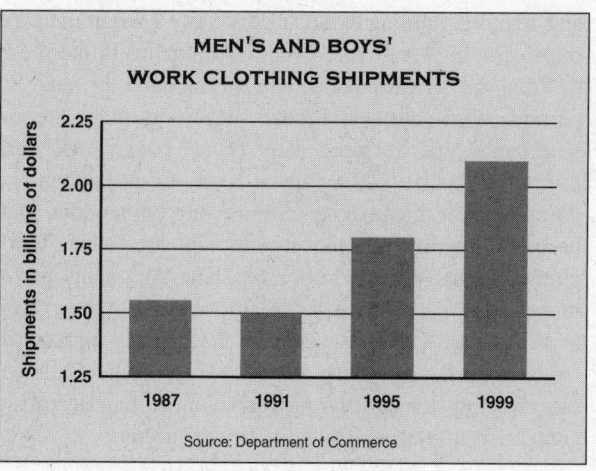

MEN'S AND BOYS' WORK CLOTHING SHIPMENTS

Source: Department of Commerce

wore functional work clothes for occupational reasons. Two major operators active throughout the Midwest were Blain Farm & Fleet and Mills Farm & Fleet.

Catalog sales picked up noticeably during the late 1980s and throughout the 1990s, and were expected to show continued strength into the future. Internet sales increased with the advent of e-commerce at the end of the twentieth century.

BACKGROUND AND DEVELOPMENT

In a less spectacular manner, the ready-to-wear work clothes industry followed the historical trajectory of the more colorful men's apparel industry. With the onset of the industrial era in the early nineteenth century spurring the transformation from rural to urban life, the demand for working apparel soon surpassed the production of custom tailors and housewives. To meet the increased demand, manufacturers began mass producing work clothes; these early efforts were of inferior quality to the earlier handmade clothing and were avoided because they were uncomfortable. As improved fabrics were introduced to the men's apparel industry, mass-produced work clothing became widely accepted. During the same period, improved and expanded sewing machine technology provided added impetus to the industry's emergence and boosted its output to unprecedented levels. Further fueling the industry was an extensive survey compiled during the Civil War on the height and chest measurements of more than one million soldiers, providing the first mass statistical data on the form and build of U.S. men. Immediately after the war these results were made available to producers of men's ready-made work clothes, forming a scientific basis for better-fitting clothing.

A milestone event that dramatically accelerated the need for ready-made work clothes was the Gold Rush of 1848. The prospect of getting rich drew thousands of men westward to pan or mine for gold. Figuring that these adventurers would need tents for shelter, Levi Strauss journeyed to California with a supply of heavy fabrics for tent making. Among these fabrics was a French material referred to as "de Nime," which Americans pronounced as "denim." Aware that no one was meeting the need for durable work clothes, Strauss began to make denim workpants that featured large back pockets to hold mining tools. By adding metal rivets to strengthen the durability of the pockets, Strauss hit on an idea that brought him almost instant success—and the men's work clothes industry started booming. The continued settlement of the West, not just in California but in the prairie and mountain states as well, created a steady market for ready-made work clothes for decades to come. To meet the growing demand, large work clothes manufacturing centers sprung up in Chicago and St. Louis.

Beginning in the early twentieth century, the steady growth of a work force comprised of semiskilled and unskilled laborers, engaged in various mass production-related occupations across the entire range of manufacturing and agricultural industries, proved a boon to work clothes producers. After World War II, an unprecedented rise in the consumption of consumer durables was matched by the growth of a repair industry whose workers, more often than not, were outfitted with nontailored work uniforms. To the envy of the nonwork clothes apparel industries that regularly incurred the economic vicissitudes of the traditional business cycle, the work clothes industry proceeded along its expansionary path in a steady manner until the onset of its stagnation period beginning in the early 1980s.

CURRENT CONDITIONS

The stabilization of the men's and boys' work clothing industry was due in part to the U.S. economy's structural shift to service-providing industries and occupations where career/work apparel tended to be the norm. According to Bureau of Labor Statistics (BLS) employment estimates, approximately 9 out of every 10 new jobs in the 1990s were added in service-providing industries such as transportation, communications, public utilities, trade, health care, finance, insurance, real estate, food handling and production, sanitation, and government. At the same time, the increasing trend towards a cultural climate of corporate uniformed-employees—as a means to foster brand recognition and customer loyalty—breathed new life into the industry and held out the promise of future growth.

With the shift in the focus of the economy from manufacturing to service industries, the men's and boys' work clothing industry had to make adjustments in their product lines. Being the first to invest in the latest apparel technologies, the larger firms were best positioned to seize the day and offer a greater volume of high quality garments at lower cost than their smaller rivals. These largest manufacturers led the industry's regrowth, but it remained unclear whether the big companies would totally eclipse the smaller competitors.

While dollar value of shipments of work clothing showed modest increases through the mid-1990s, third quarter 1996 figures revealed a decline in the productions of all segments of the men's and boys' work clothing industry. Production of work jackets fell 21 percent from third quarter 1995; work shirts dropped 7 percent; work pants declined 4 percent; and washable service apparel tumbled 10 percent.

A new World Trade Organization (WTO) was established in 1995, and the Multifiber Arrangement (MFA) which allowed importing countries to limit the flow of imports from lower cost developing countries was replaced by the Agreement on Textiles and Clothing (ATC), which required the phasing out of MFA quotas over a ten-year period. According to Linda Shelton in an *Industry, Trade, and Technology Review* report, "The elimination of MFA quotas likely will have a significant impact on the U.S. textile and apparel sector given the level of protection that such restrictions have provided domestic producers over the past two decades." The U.S. has until 2005 to implement the ATC, and the legislation's impact on the men's and boys' work clothing industry will be felt at the beginning of the 2000s.

Agreements such as the North American Free Trade Agreement (NAFTA) and General Agreement on Trade and Tariffs (GATT) will also likely increase the flow of imported goods to the United States. Trade with Southeast Asia was also very important to the apparel industry, with a 16.5 percent increase in imports from countries in that region in 1997, up from a more moderate 7 percent increase between 1992 and 1996.

WORKFORCE

In 1990, the dominant occupational categories for the work clothes industry were: sewing machine operators; inspectors, precision inspectors, and testers; blue collar work supervisors; pressing machine operators; hand packers and packagers; and hand cutters and trimmers. Close to 56 percent of the work force was engaged in sewing operations, while the remaining categories individually fell within the 3 to 2 percent range. According to an occupational survey undertaken by the BLS, all of the major occupational categories within the work clothes industry would experience significant declines by the year 2005. Given the more or less forward trajectory of the industry's productivity trend, the decline in sewing machine operators was expected to encounter the steepest decline.

Total employment in the men's and boys' work clothing industry continued to decline through the 1990s, reflecting the apparel industry's increased use of mechanized procedures and outsourcing. Employment in men's and boys' work clothing was 33,000 in 1987, of which

29,000 were classified as production workers. By 1992, total employment had fallen to 30,400, of which 26,400 were production workers. For the entire period total employment fell by 5.8 percent while production employment declined by 5.9 percent. Between 1992 and 1996, total employment dropped by 6.3 percent and employment in production declined even more sharply, with a decrease of 7.2 percent. In 1996, the industry's total work force numbered 23,400.

From 1987 to 1992 the industry's real wages fell without interruption, while value added per production worker rose, though not in a dramatic manner, suggesting that productivity improvements and real wages were moving in opposite directions. This trend slowed in the mid-1990s; in 1996, the average hourly wage was $7.17, a 4.3 percent increase over 1992's wages.

Compared to their employment rates in the overall manufacturing sector, the participation rates of women and African American and Hispanic workers within the industry exceed their national counterparts. In 1995 women comprised 70.0 percent of this industry's work force compared to a national average of 31.6 percent of women in manufacturing industries. Hispanic workers accounted for 24.0 percent of the industry's work force compared to a national average of 10.2 percent. The percentage of African American workers was 15 percent, slightly greater than the national average of 10 percent of African Americans in manufacturing industries. Taken collectively, over 1 million minority workers were active in the apparel industry's work force, while over 20 million worked in manufacturing industries in general.

FURTHER READING

Apparel Import Digest. Arlington, VA: American Apparel Manufacturers Association, 1997.

Apparel Industry Trends. Arlington, VA: American Apparel Manufacturers Association, March 1997.

Baker, Sandra. "Texas Rangers Player to Advertise Dickie's Work Clothing." *Knight-Ridder/Tribune Business News,* 11 April 1999.

Focus: An Economic Profile of the Apparel Industry. Arlington, VA: American Apparel Manufacturers Association, 1996.

Greco, Monica. "63 Years of Growth." *Apparel Industry,* December 1995.

Industry Surveys. New York, NY: Standard & Poor's, 1999.

"New Markets Discover Workwear." *Discount Store News,* 11 May 1998.

Shelton, Linda and Robert Wallace. "World Textile and Apparel Trade: A New Era." *Industry, Trade, and Technology Review,* October 1996.

U.S. Industry Profiles. Detroit, MI: Gale Research, 1995.

U.S. Industry & Trade Outlook '99. New York, NY: McGraw-Hill, 1999.

SIC 2329

MEN'S AND BOYS' CLOTHING, NOT ELSEWHERE CLASSIFIED

This category includes establishments primarily engaged in manufacturing men's and boys' clothing, not elsewhere classified, from purchased or woven fabrics. These items include, but are not limited to, athletic clothing, bathing suits, down-filled clothing, shorts, nontailored sports clothing, sweaters, athletic uniforms, and windbreakers. Establishments primarily engaged in manufacturing leather and sheep-lined garments are classified in **SIC 2386: Leather and Sheep-Lined Clothing.** Knitting mills primarily engaged in manufacturing outerwear are classified under **SIC 2253: Knit Outwear Mills.**

NAICS CODE(S)

315211 (Men's and Boys' Cut and Sew Apparel Contractors)

315228 (Men's and Boys' Cut and Sew Other Outerwear Manufacturing)

315299 (All Other Cut and Sew Apparel Manufacturing)

INDUSTRY SNAPSHOT

The U.S. Census Bureau estimated that 60 establishments manufactured clothing in this classification in 1997. They shipped $279 million worth of goods, spent $122 million on materials, and paid $5 million for buildings and other structures, machinery, and equipment.

ORGANIZATION AND STRUCTURE

While many manufacturers in this sector of the apparel industry were small, family-owned businesses, several large and growing establishments dominated the category, which was comprised of manufacturers, contractors, and jobbers. Contractors were independent manufacturers hired by various and often competing manufacturers. Contractors specialized in sewing the garment from pieces provided them. They were hired by producers that did not have their own sewing facilities or whose own capacity had been exceeded.

Jobbers were design and marketing businesses that were hired to perform specific functions, including purchasing materials, designing patterns, creating samples, cutting material, and hiring contractors to manufacture the product. After purchasing materials needed to produce the pieces, jobbers then sent the cut material to contractors for assembly.

In creating apparel from the purchased materials, manufacturers produced designs or bought them from freelancers, and they purchased the fabric and trimmings. Garments were usually cut and sewed in the manufacturer's factories, but outside contractors were hired when demand for an item exceeded the manufacturer's capacity or shipping deadlines could not be met. For the purposes of this entry, the term "manufacturers" will refer cumulatively to contractors, jobbers, and manufacturers.

BACKGROUND AND DEVELOPMENT

During the 1980s interest in men's fashions increased, augmented by the introduction of several new men's fashion magazines. Office wear became more comfortable and less formal, and sweaters and sports coats became acceptable in some work environments. As the men's apparel industry grew and diversified, manufacturers and retailers began to target specific markets according to income, age, and education—a strategy already common in the women's fashion industry. Many retailers expanded their men's wear departments, and the industry grew at a faster pace than women's wear throughout the 1980s and well into the 1990s.

As in other sectors of the apparel industry, consolidation and competition from imported clothing were the industry's primary concerns in the early 1990s. The economic recession of the early 1990s prompted manufacturers to produce more comfortable and moderately priced casual wear such as fleece sweat shirts, jackets, and pants. Shipments for all types of men's and boys' clothing were valued at about $2.3 billion in 1992, up from $1.6 billion in 1982. Employment in the industry expanded from approximately 44,600 people in 1982 to 53,300 in 1990.

The value of men's and boys' apparel production dropped 2.0 percent in 1996. However, retail sales of men's apparel climbed 7.3 percent, and retail sales of boys' apparel grew 4.4 percent. While the production of sweat pants, shorts, and sweaters declined in 1996, the production of team sport uniforms grew slightly.

CURRENT CONDITIONS

In 1998 the retail value of all apparel sold in the United States was $177 billion, up 4.7 percent from 1997, according to *Apparel Industry* magazine. Men's clothing increased by 6.8 percent, compared to 3.7 percent for women's clothing.

Casual wear accounted for the largest percentage of sales that year. This widespread trend toward dressing less formally helped the sportswear industry, since some companies began allowing employees to wear casual clothes to work instead of tailored suits. In the late 1990s, some clothing manufacturers were designing sportswear in modern, comfortable styles to appeal to younger men who wanted to look sophisticated yet casual. Some of these lines of sportswear were intended to be worn both at work and in leisure time.

Other companies offered innovative features to attract customers. For example, some swimwear designers were incorporating utilitarian cargo pockets and toggles into their products.

INDUSTRY LEADERS

Among firms that manufactured products in this classification as their primary business, Stone Manufacturing Co. (Greenville, South Carolina) was one of the largest with 2,000 employees and sales of $200 million in 1998. Founded in 1933, Stone specialized in men's and boys' active sportswear.

Another industry leader was Calvin Klein Sport Div. (a subsidiary of Calvin Klein Inc. based in New York, New York) with 1,100 employees and estimated sales of $190 million. This company had been known previously as Puritan Fashions Corp. It specialized in sportswear.

Russell Corp., based in Alabama, was one of the largest companies in this industry with sales of $1.18 billion in 1998. Other major companies in the category were Jos. A. Bank Clothiers Inc. of Hampstead, Maryland, with 1,150 employees and sales of $187 million; and Columbia Sportswear Co. of Portland, Oregon, with 450 employees and estimated sales of $140 million.

Among the large, diversified firms that also competed in this industry were Rennoc Corp. of Vineland, New Jersey, with estimated sales of $20.0 billion; Levi Strauss and Co. of San Francisco, California, with sales of $6.0 billion; Reebok International Ltd. of Stoughton, Massachusetts, with sales of $3.0 billion; and Eddie Bauer Inc. (a subsidiary of Spiegel Holdings Inc. based in Redmond, Washington) with sales of $1.6 billion.

WORKFORCE

Many of those employed in this category were sewing-machine operators, whose average wage in 1993 was $5.85 an hour. In 1995 the average wage for men's and boys' clothing production workers was $7.19. The average number of employees per establishment in the early 1990s was 66.

The Census Bureau estimated that in 1997 this segment of the apparel industry employed 4,300 people, including 3,464 production workers who earned an average hourly wage of $7.69. The 45 establishments that produced mainly athletic uniforms employed 4,169 people, including 3,368 production workers who earned an average hourly wage of $7.68.

A long-time center of the apparel business in the United States, New York was home to the majority of men's and boys' wear manufacturers in the early and mid-1990s. California, however, reported the greatest value of shipments at about $308.6 million. Tennessee reported having the highest number of employees in the industry at about 5,700. Alabama and Pennsylvania also had significant concentrations of workers in this category. In 1997 Tennessee led the men's and junior boys' athletic uniforms segment with shipments valued at $51 million. Shipments from Texas totaled $19 million, and shipments from California totaled $11 million.

AMERICA AND THE WORLD

In the 1960s the U.S. men's and boys' apparel industry began to lose significant market share to imports, which offered consumers lower prices and acceptable quality. By the 1990s imports had reached all-time highs. With U.S. manufacturers relying more heavily on off-shore assembly plants, the industry experienced further losses.

In the 1960s U.S. apparel makers began moving their manufacturing operations abroad, focusing on Hong Kong, Taiwan, and South Korea, where labor costs were low. By the 1980s, however, labor costs in these countries had increased and operations were moved to Bangladesh, Thailand, Pakistan, Indonesia, Malaysia, Sri Lanka, and India. By the early 1990s, China had replaced Hong Kong as the greatest supplier of imports to the United States. Hong Kong, Taiwan, and South Korea, as well as China, continued to lose market share to new players and represented only 28 percent of apparel imports in 1995. In the mid-1990s the largest gains in import market share belonged to the Caribbean countries and Mexico. These countries increased their market share from 20 percent in 1992 to approximately 54 percent in 1996.

The North American Free Trade Agreement (NAFTA) was ratified in 1993 to create a free-trade zone between the United States, Mexico, and Canada by gradually eliminating tariffs over 15 years. It was generally supported by executives in the men's apparel industry, but workers' unions tried unsuccessfully to stem the loss of jobs among Americans in the industry by limiting the imports allowed in the country.

During the early 1990s, more imports entered the United States under provision 9802 (formerly known as Section 807) of the Harmonized Tariffs Schedule of the United States. This provision allowed clothing assembled abroad—from pieces cut in the United States and then exported—to be reimported with duty paid only for the value added abroad. This meant that companies could pay foreign workers lower wages to complete the most labor-intensive part of the assembly process. Many U.S. manufacturers moved assembly operations to the Caribbean, where they expected to reduce costs and more successfully compete against imports from Asia. They encountered logistics problems, however, and it appeared that Mexico might ultimately become a more popular manufacturing location than the Caribbean.

The World Trade Organization (WTO) was established in 1995, and the Multifiber Arrangement (MFA), which allowed importing countries to limit the flow of imports from developing countries with lower labor costs, was replaced by the Agreement on Textiles and Clothing (ATC), which required the phasing out of MFA quotas over a ten-year period. According to Linda Shelton in an *Industry, Trade, and Technology Review* report, ''The elimination of MFA quotas likely will have a significant impact on the U.S. textile and apparel sector given the level of protection that such restrictions have provided domestic producers over the past two decades.'' Since the United States has until 2005 to implement the ATC, the legislation's effect on the men's and boys' apparel industry may not be realized for a few years.

RESEARCH AND TECHNOLOGY

In the battle against imports, U.S. apparel makers tried using more automation, delivering higher quality goods, and closely tracking consumer's needs and desires. Most of the larger manufacturers continually sought newer machinery to improve efficiency, but apparel manufacture remained a highly labor-intensive industry.

Another new strategy involved ''quick response,'' the idea that bringing apparel to the retailer more rapidly would shorten the production cycle, reduce inventories, improve productivity, and help manufacturers avoid overstocking. Using computers to track inventory, sales, and consumer response, domestic manufacturers hoped to compete more effectively with importers. Department stores and manufacturers worked together to speed deliveries and increase efficiency.

FURTHER READING

Apparel Import Digest. Arlington, VA: American Apparel Manufacturers Association, 1997.

Apparel Industry Trends. Arlington, VA: American Apparel Manufacturers Association, March 1997.

Dodd, Annmarie. ''Better Slates than Ever: Levi's Revamps Division with New Sportswear Line and Avedon Advertisements.'' *Daily News Record,* 30 August 1999.

Focus: An Economic Profile of the Apparel Industry. Arlington, VA: American Apparel Manufacturers Association, 1996.

''Import Growth Slowing, AAMA Says.'' *Apparel Industry,* June 1996.

Shelton, Linda, and Robert Wallace. ''World Textile and Apparel Trade: A New Era.'' *Industry, Trade, and Technology Review,* October 1996.

Spruill, Sandy. ''Staying Home.'' *Apparel Industry,* September 1996.

U.S. Department of Commerce. Census Bureau. *1997 Economic Census.* Washington, D.C.: GPO, 1999. Available from http://www.census.gov/prod/ec97/97m3152p.pdf.

SIC 2331

WOMEN'S, MISSES', AND JUNIORS' BLOUSES AND SHIRTS

This category includes establishments primarily engaged in manufacturing women's, misses', and juniors' blouses and shirts from purchased woven or knit fabrics. Knitting mills primarily engaged in manufacturing outerwear are classified in **SIC 2253: Knit Outerwear Mills.** Establishments primarily engaged in manufacturing girls', children's, and infants' blouses and shirts are classified in **SIC 2361: Girls', Children's, and Infants' Dresses, Blouses, and Shirts.**

NAICS CODE(S)

315212 (Women's and Girls' Cut and Sew Apparel Contractors)

315232 (Women's and Girls' Cut and Sew Blouse and Shirt Manufacturing)

INDUSTRY SNAPSHOT

U.S. Commerce Department figures for 1997 reported that more than 700 companies made women's and misses' blouses and shirts in 1997. This figure marks a considerable drop in the industry, for in the early 1990s there were more than 1,800 companies engaged in this area of manufacturing; much of the drop can be attributed to anemic product demand and the increased market share of international competitors. The value added by manufacture amounted to $1.6 million with material costs reaching $2.3 million. The 1997 value of shipments accounted for only $3.9 million compared to $4.1 billion in 1996.

In addition to the loss of market share to foreign companies, the domestic industry had also felt the sting of a declining trend in middle class discretionary incomes. The decline was particularly important since in former times the personal consumption expenditures of this income strata were a cornerstone of the industry target market, responsible for a major portion of apparel purchases of all types. The lingering overhang of takeover debt accumulated from the takeover frenzy of the late 1980s also imparted a growth-inhibiting effect on company profits. Other, less-significant factors contributing to the industry's decline included a stabilization in the number of women entering the workforce, as well as a change in consumer buying habits to discounters and off-price stores.

One positive trend for blouse and shirt manufacturers has been an increased ability to take advantage of overseas opportunities. The long-term decline in the value of the dollar spurred the export sales of women's and misses' blouses and shirts. In the early 1990s industry watchers remained enthusiastic about the prospects for export growth as a cure for the industry's economic woes. Their optimism was further buoyed with the 1993 passage of the North American Free Trade Agreement (NAFTA) and the elimination of significant world trade barriers as specified under the General Agreement on Tariffs and Trade (GATT).

On another front, while the industry itself was continuing to reel from the downsizing trend, the industry's larger firms had managed to increase their market shares and were investing in state-of-art apparel-related technologies and industry-related acquisitions.

In 1996 the women's and misses' blouses and shirts manufacturing industry was led by New York's Cygne Designs, the third largest women's wear maker in the United States with $516 million in sales and 5,000 employees. Other notable companies included Capucci Creations Internationale of California, Esprit de Corp. of California, and Bernaud Chaus Inc. of New York.

ORGANIZATION AND STRUCTURE

Because many establishments within the apparel industry group (including manufacturers of women's and misses' blouses and shirts) do not always make the entire garment within the establishment's premises or across the company's factories, the U.S. Census of Manufacturers separates the industry into three broad producer classifications. Just where a company or establishment falls within the classifications depends on the degree of comprehensiveness of its production activities. Producers are classified as manufacturers if they buy fabric and undertake the design, patternmaking, grading, cutting, sewing, and assembling of their garments from within their own establishment or firm. Because of their integrated structure, wholly owned manufacturers operate in a manner that allows them to exercise a considerable measure of control over the production quality of their garments. Since they require relatively large investment expenditures, such operations fall outside the financial reach of the majority of the establishments active in the industry.

A firm or establishment that carries out all garment making processes minus its sewing and (sometimes) its cutting operations, deciding instead to contract out these operations to independently owned outside firms, is defined as an apparel jobber. Many apparel firms, independent of their size, contract out their sewing and cutting needs, along with other highly skilled production functions such as embroidery, quilting, and pleating, which are performed using specialized machinery.

A firm or establishment that is independently owned and uses its own machinery and employees to sew and cut garments from the designs, materials, and specifications supplied by the apparel jobbers is classified as a contractor. The contracting system makes it possible to accommodate seasonal production peaks.

In 1987, when ranked according to their density within census regions, the largest number of establishments engaged in this industry were in the Pacific, Middle Atlantic, and South Atlantic regions. Alternatively, when ranked by the number of establishments per state, California was first with 485 and New York was second with 294, followed by Pennsylvania with 173 and Georgia with 76.

The major economic sectors responsible for the share of the industry's input supply flowed from imports (29.1 percent); broadwoven fabric mills (20.2 percent); apparel made from purchased materials (18.3 percent); and knit fabric mills (8.6 percent). The disaggregated share of the total output identified according to the category of its major product class indicated that women's and misses' knit shirts and blouses accounted for 30.1 percent of total sales, women's and misses' woven shirts and blouses represented 46.7 percent, contract work performed on women's and misses' blouses and shirts accounted for 16.5 percent, and about 6.7 percent went unspecified by kind.

BACKGROUND AND DEVELOPMENT

Up until the mid-nineteenth century, women's and misses' ready-made or ready-to-wear blouses and shirts were practically nonexistent. Dating back to early colonial times, U.S. women typically wore clothes that were made in the household. Popular women's magazines carried sewing instructions for making new patterns or styles. From the 1860s until the turn of the century, efforts to manufacture women's ready-wear garments met with little success. What was available was usually of inferior quality and questionable design, despite the invention and diffusion of sewing machine technology. For the most part, domestically produced garments continued to dominate the scene; mass produced ready-wear women's clothes were spoken about in derogatory terms.

Things changed slowly during the first two decades of the twentieth century, as women's ready-to-wear clothes encountered wider social acceptance. The combined influence of several concurrent social and economic forces explained this shift. For instance, ongoing improvements in European and U.S. textile technologies transformed the quality and availability of fabrics, enabling manufacturers to produce a more comfortable and style-conscious fit. Continuous upgrades in sewing machine technologies, cutting instruments, and pressing processes permitted the output of women's clothes to increase dramatically while their prices fell. Spurred on by the burgeoning women's movement, women were able to move beyond their traditional confines of home and family and participate more fully in social life. Women increasingly entered the workforce,

attended college, and became more active in sports and politics. World War I found many women taking over jobs once performed by men. Given their fuller participation in social affairs outside the home, women found the ready-to-wear clothes for themselves and their families a necessary convenience.

From the 1920s onwards, the women's apparel industry developed along the lines of small, privately-owned, single-product firms. By the late 1950s, things began to change as larger, publicly-held, multi-product firms started to move into the women's apparel industry. In most instances, their methods of gaining entry into the industry took the form of mergers with or acquisitions of existing firms. This growth in the industry continued unabated into the 1960s—there were only 22 publicly owned firms in women's apparel industry in 1959, but by the close of the 1960s their number exceeded 100. The forward march of large, publicly-owned firms continued more or less without interruption until the mid-1980s when the trend reversed itself and large manufacturing firms began to ''go private'' again during the era of leveraged buyouts.

The progressive growth of import penetration into the domestic market for women's and misses' blouses and shirts was a significant factor in the domestic industry's protracted tailspin. As part of industry-wide efforts to lower production costs, U.S. producers participated in this import deluge through the processes of ''outsourcing'' and relocation by foreign investment. Beginning around 1982 and still in force in the 1990s, price competition from foreign and domestic producers resulted in strong disinflationary pressures, which triggered a steep decline in the domestic industry's rate of capacity utilization. During the recession of 1981 to 1982, the percentage change in producer prices for women's apparel collapsed and then remained more or less flat for most of the period covering 1983 to 1990. Though not as dramatic as the previous recession, disinflationary forces hit once again during the 1990-91 recession, and then, most uncharacteristically, set out along the path of another steep decline despite being some two years into a recovery. During the past decade, capacity utilization fluctuated erratically, moving up and down between the 79 to 83 percent range during the 1981-82 recession. During the early years of the recovery it climbed, peaking at 89 percent in 1984. It then plummeted to settle at 76 percent in 1993, marking a drop of almost 15 percent in capacity utilization in the industry. As a direct consequence of the shakeout working through the industry's manufacturing sector, many traditional wholesale and retail links were sent into disarray or ruptured entirely, spawning a number of mergers and bankruptcy declarations.

During the 1980s another trend arose in the form of manufacturer-owned retail stores that were usually located in prime retail areas and carried a large and complete stock of the firm's product lines sold at regular prices. Such outlets provided manufacturers with a wealth of consumer information that was used to determine whether the prospect of future sales warranted future production runs.

According to the American Manufacturers Association, apparel imports grew only 10 percent in 1995. Imports of cotton apparel grew 1 percent; man-made fiber apparel imports increased 7 percent; and wool apparel imports rose 8 percent. Imports of fibers covered by the Multi Fiber Arrangement (MFA) fell 18 percent. In keeping with these overall industry trends, imports of women's knit shirts and blouses fell 12 percent in 1996, while import figures for women's shirts and blouses, not knit, remained similar to those of 1995. Although import growth was down and domestic production dropped in 1996, U.S. apparel consumption grew 5.8 percent. Retail sales of women's apparel grew 5.1 percent in 1996 compared to a 1.0 percent growth in 1995.

A new World Trade Organization (WTO) was established in 1995, and the Multifiber Arrangement (MFA), which allowed importing countries to limit the flow of imports from lower cost, developing countries, was replaced by the Agreement on Textiles and Clothing (ATC), which required the phasing out of MFA quotas over a 10-year period. According to Linda Shelton in an *Industry, Trade, and Technology Review* report, ''The elimination of MFA quotas likely will have a significant impact on the U.S. textile and apparel sector given the level of protection that such restrictions have provided domestic producers over the past two decades.'' Since the United States has until 2005 to implement the ATC, the legislation's impact on the women's apparel industry may not be realized for several years.

CURRENT CONDITIONS

Women's wear at the onset of the twenty-first century saw numerous examples of streamlining in an attempt to calm what had become a capricious area of commerce. A November 1999 issue of Apparel Industry Magazine reported that approaches such as portfolio expansion, information technology applications, and sourcing/distribution channel remodeling not only worked to shape the industry's future but also functioned as a driving force to establish the participant's position within it. In addition, the article noted that diversification was another new aim to regain lost market share. It further reported that executives and shareholders alike recognized that while fashion has always been notoriously fickle, consumer focus must remain at the forefront.

The apparel trade also employed various strategies to avoid further slumps yet still maintain a viable presence. Cost-cutting through the closing of duplicate or unprofit-

able subsidiaries and moving to offshore sourcing, especially in terms of labor and supply costs, proved to be one of the most economically advantageous tactics used by industry players. Growth through brand acquisitions in an effort to expand and diversify their presence was another measure adopted to remain competitive.

Along these lines, merchandisers and manufacturers worked to make industry processes faster and more efficient, mostly by incorporating smarter uses of computer technology and tools like the Internet and the World Wide Web. This resulted in just-in-time merchandise delivery, less stagnant inventory levels, lower costs, and instant information. It also led to an industry rejuvenation.

WORKFORCE

In 1997 the U.S. Census Bureau reported that 26,238 individuals were employed in the manufacture of women's and misses' shirts and blouses; of these, 19,263 were production workers. This was a precipitous drop from 1991, which showed 55,900 workers in this industry category. Such numbers proved the prevalence of increased U.S. plant closing and overseas assembly operations.

California employed the largest number of workers within this industry segment, followed by New York and Florida. Compared to the measures of employment by gender, race, and Hispanic origin for the U.S. manufacturing sector as a whole, women, black, and Hispanic workers active in the apparel workforce far exceeded their national counterparts. According to American Apparel Manufacturers Association estimates for 1995, women accounted for 70.1 percent of the apparel workforce, a figure considerably higher than the overall manufacturing average of 31.6 percent. Black apparel workers accounted for 15 percent of the workforce total—the total manufacturing average is 10.4 percent—and Hispanic workers accounted for 24.0 percent of the employee workforce, compared to the national average of 10.2 percent.

AMERICA AND THE WORLD

Ever since the end of World War II, the domestic producers of women's and misses' blouses and shirts have been vulnerable to import penetration. A particularly acute phase occurred from 1983 to 1992. Although they still account for the largest share of U.S. imports, the market share of the ''Big Four'' countries (the People's Republic of China, Taiwan, Hong Kong, and Korea) actually declined during this period, dropping from 63 percent in 1984 to 41 percent in 1992. Shipments from all of these countries declined with the exception of China, which recorded an increase of more than 100 percent. The ''Big Four'' continued to lose market share to new players such as Bangladesh, Indonesia, and Thailand and represented only 28 percent of apparel imports in 1995.

This was due in part to increased implementation of "quick response" and U.S. apparel manufacturers' ability to react more quickly to fluctuating consumer demands. By far the largest gains in import market share were enjoyed by the Caribbean countries and Mexico. These countries increased their market share from 20 percent in 1992 to approximately 54 percent in 1996.

To an increasing degree, many U.S. garment makers participated in this import binge and contributed to the erosion of domestic employment in the industry through their emphasis on foreign outsourcing. With respect to the Caribbean countries, this was true as a matter of policy ever since 1983 when Congress, fearful that the spread of poverty in the Caribbean would attract large portions of its citizens to communist politics, passed the Caribbean Basin Initiative (CBI) program. The CBI permitted almost all apparel items that had been cut within the United States to be shipped abroad for further processing and then to reenter the United States as manufactured or semi-manufactured goods. According to section 807 of the U.S. Tariff Code, the percentage of duty paid on the goods was equated to the value added abroad. And, as was often the case, this was set equal to the cost of foreign sewing labor, which was notoriously low when compared to the cost of U.S. workers. Among the countries participating in the program were Jamaica, the Dominican Republic, Haiti, Costa Rica, and, even though it was not a Caribbean country, Mexico. With the passage of NAFTA and GATT, trade relations between the United States and the rest of the world were supposed to be put on a more level playing field. Additional job losses in America, however, may well be one result. In discussing GATT's impact on the textiles and clothing industries, the *Christian Science Monitor* commented that "the accord puts the textiles sector back under multi-lateral trade rules, after a 20-year hiatus during which bilateral accords reigned under the Multifiber Agreement regime. Most tariffs and quotas in developed countries will be eliminated over the decade. Developing countries will take a growing share of textiles and clothing trade, worth $250 billion in 1992. Consumers should enjoy lower prices, while developed-world manufacturers, such as those in the United States, will continue to feel the heat."

Despite being caught up in an ongoing grip of establishment downsizing, major technological changes that began to affect the industry in the late 1980s led to a closer integration between retailers and manufacturers. New labor saving and lower cost technologies were introduced at larger companies, which widened the competitive cost differentials between themselves and the middle and lower tier firms in the industry. Unless rectified, this situation could also stoke the industry's downsizing trend.

A significant development in recent years between retailers and the industry's manufacturers has been the implementation of the quick response system, a computerized strategy that provides for the quick and precise replenishment of "hot-selling" garments. By means of electronic data interchange, participating apparel producers are privy to an instant and continuous flow of information concerning retail sales by styles, sizes, and colors, along with the level of retail inventory. With this information, manufacturers plan further production rounds on a more precise basis by discarding slow-moving styles and devoting their efforts toward fast selling items. As a result, they avoid costly markdowns and increase turnover.

New automated technologies were being installed to speed up the manufacturing process and reduce the labor time required per garment. Examples included automated marker and patternmakers, computer inspection of fabrics, scanning and measurement of fabric width variance, and shade recognition apparatus, which have all become automated parts of a fully integrated quality enhancing system. New programmable sewing units that use microprocessors were also instrumental in reducing sewing labor costs. Before the units' introduction, the sewing of a garment accounted for the largest portion of an article's labor cost, while anywhere from 70 to 80 percent of its in-process production time was spent handling and positioning a garment. To reduce in-process handling new automatic conveyor systems were being developed, along with robotics systems and automated warehouse facilities.

RESEARCH AND TECHNOLOGY

Positive in its intent but threatening to those unfamiliar with it, information technology, also called IT, revolutionized the apparel industry in the late 1990s. Combined with its many innovative computer-driven tools, this method of electronic commerce created a ripple effect that caused large and small industry players to evaluate their viability within the market. Those who could afford the necessary time and monetary investments usually saw worthwhile, if not significant, returns. Some who were cash-strapped or interested in sharing the risk opted for partnership. Others, like the smaller, family-owned businesses, chose to abandon their places within the industry.

While the logistics of each area's IT market entry and evolution, as well as the learning curve associated with it, saw various forms of upheaval and transition before the onset of success but the overall benefits stretched industry-wide. One apparel group executive noted that having access to IT-generated data not only made instant interpretation and understanding of fashion trends a reality but that it also encouraged cooperation among all the channels toward the seamless flow of goods to meet the demands, if not stay ahead, of those trends. Computer hardware and software, along with the Internet and World Wide Web, facilitated this new infrastructure and introduced systems that improved avenues of sales forecasting, product planning, warehouse management, manufacturing, distribution, order entry, and sales support.

FURTHER READING

Apparel Import Digest. Arlington, VA: American Apparel Manufacturers Association, 1997.

Apparel Industry Trends. Arlington, VA: American Apparel Manufacturers Association, March 1997.

Focus: An Economic Profile of the Apparel Industry. Arlington, VA: American Apparel Manufacturers Association, 1996.

Hill, Suzette. ''Women's Wear Makers Look Ahead to 2005.'' *Apparel Industry Magazine Online, 1999.* Available from http://aimagazine.com/nov99stor07.html.

''Import Growth Slowing, AAMA Says.'' *Apparel Industry,* June 1996.

Shelton, Linda, and Robert Wallace. ''World Textile and Apparel Trade: A New Era.'' *Industry, Trade, and Technology Review,* October 1996.

Statistical Abstract of the United States. Washington, D.C.: U.S. Department of Commerce, 1996.

U.S. Department of Commerce, Economics and Statictics Administration. *Annual Survey of Manufacturers: Statistics for Industry Groups and Industries.* Bureau of the Census, 1999. Available from http://www.census.gov.

SIC 2335

WOMEN'S, JUNIORS', AND MISSES' DRESSES

This entry describes establishments primarily engaged in manufacturing women's, misses', and juniors' dresses (including ensemble dresses), from purchased woven or knit fabrics, including woven or knit fabrics of paper, whether sold by the piece or by the dozen. Establishments primarily engaged in manufacturing girls', children's, and infants' dresses are classified in **SIC 2361: Girls', Children's, and Infants' Dresses, Blouses, and Shirts.** Knitting mills primarily engaged in manufacturing knit dresses are classified in **SIC 2258: Lace and Warp Knit Fabric Mills.**

NAICS CODE(S)

315212 (Women's and Girls' Cut and Sew Apparel Contractors)

315233 (Women's and Girls' Cut and Sew Dress Manufacturing)

INDUSTRY SNAPSHOT

At the onset of the twenty-first century, American manufacturers of women's, juniors', and misses' dresses had seen an immense drop in presence, production, and profits. In 1993, for example, 3,500 companies comprised this industry segment, but as of 1997, a mere 750 remained.

California and New York kept their places as the top two locations for dress manufacturing activity with 288 and 259 establishments, respectively. Next in line were Florida with 36, Texas with 30, and Pennsylvania with 22.

The clothing industry, particularly women's apparel, is sensitive to changes in economic conditions. In the 1980s, consumers were wearing designer labels and $100 jeans. The economic downturn in the early 1990s, however, caused consumers to look for value and savings. Consumer preferences shifted from fancy dressing to basic apparel at home as well as at work. As a result of this shift, manufacturers moved to the extremes of the industry: discounters and high fashion designers. Consequently, the number of women's apparel manufacturers declined. An increase in imports further increased the competition in this already volatile and difficult industry. Although imports increased by only 5 percent per year between 1988 and 1991, they jumped 15 percent in 1992, and again in 1993, slowing to 12 percent in 1994, 1995, and 1996. According to *Apparel Industry Magazine,* ''Weak consumer demand (prompted by factors that include consumers' anxiety about their jobs, the tendency of Baby Boomers to spend more on furniture and less on clothing, and casual Fridays)'' was to blame for sluggish apparel imports.

These events created increased competition and a reluctance on behalf of manufacturers and retailers to raise prices on apparel. Many small players were forced to close their doors, and the strength of the remaining manufacturers during the mid-1990s depended on an end to worldwide recessionary conditions. Between 1992 and 1997, average annual apparel employment decreased by 160,000 workers. In 1996, dress production fell 9 percent.

ORGANIZATION AND STRUCTURE

The American Apparel Manufacturers Association (AAMA) is the central trade association for the U.S. apparel industry. Throughout the 1990s, the AAMA represented three-fourths of the industry and provided its members with guidance and support through publications, statistical reports, and trade negotiations. In addition to the AAMA there are regional associations that focus on local issues and policies.

Business Centers. The industry's central business locations are New York City, Los Angeles, and Atlanta; each of these is supported by an apparel mart. These marts house showrooms in which manufacturers display their lines, and buyers and sellers converge at these marts to conduct the business of selling clothes. The selling periods for women's, misses', and juniors' dresses are typically condensed into monthly "market weeks." Retail buyers visit manufacturer showrooms to buy product for the coming season. In 1992, the women's apparel industry garnered retail sales of $64.5 billion. In 1995, domestic dress production reached $4.6 billion, and consumption of women's apparel grew by 1 percent; in 1996, consumption increased 5.1 percent.

The apparel industry operates under the principles of clustering. Clustering requires makers of similar products to congregate their operations in a small geographical location. This facilitates communication between buyers and sellers, increases the speed of innovation, and promotes a business culture that nourishes and supports an industry. Clustering is well-established in New York City and Los Angeles, thus ensuring their prominence as fashion centers for the United States.

Manufacturing Process. The manufacturing process requires an average of 6 to 8 months to move a particular line from design to sale. The process typically begins with a designer's sketch, which is turned into a pattern. Fabric is selected and a cost sheet is established to detail expenses. A wholesale price is determined by using the cost sheet as the base. The production department grades a pattern to accommodate the required size range and then cuts the fabric according to the patterns. The materials are then sewn and finished, and finally, the garments are pressed, then they are packed or hung on racks for shipment to the retail customer. Normally, design was the only process that manufacturers handled in-house. The ability of a manufacturer to maintain control of the remaining processes was a function of its size and capital equipment. The most frequently outsourced process was sewing and finishing. This process was given to small contractors, typically employing immigrant labor in sweatshop-like factories. The nature of the contracting business has made the tracking of operating businesses and gross sales nearly impossible.

Financial Structure. According to *Bobbin* magazine, two-thirds of apparel manufacturers factored their receivables in the early 1990s. This accounting method entails a contract between manufacturer and factor regarding credit approval for retailers. The factor, essentially a lender, buys the manufacturer's receivables for 80 percent to 85 percent of value, and in turn sells them to a retailer. This allows manufacturers to decrease risk and increase capital turnover.

BACKGROUND AND DEVELOPMENT

The 1830s marked the emergence of the women's ready-to-wear dress industry in America. Manufacturers were able to keep pattern making and fabric cutting on their premises, typically in the tailor shop, with the pieces contracted to workers who would sew and finish the product at home. By mid-century, several variables

emerged that pushed this nascent business towards an industry of mass production: (1) strengthening of domestic textile manufacturing techniques, (2) invention of a treadle-powered sewing machine by Isaac Singer, (3) influx of large numbers of immigrants, and (4) methods developed during the Civil War for the mass production of garments.

The easy availability of cheap immigrant labor encouraged the development of large sweat shops typically housed in lofts. Not until the turn of the century did the workers begin to mobilize and organize to promote better working conditions. Their actions resulted in the 1910 Protocol of Peace, which abolished home work, ended inside subcontracting, limited the workweek to 54 hours, and created an arbitration process for complaints. These benefits were granted at the expense of the workers' right to strike. The terrible images of 146 young women who died behind locked factory doors in the Triangle Shirt Waist fire of 1911 resulted in further reforms. By World War I, the International Ladies Garment Workers Union was one of the most powerful labor organizations in America.

New York City was the undisputed center of the women's ready-to-wear apparel industry. The city's dominance was secured during the 1920s when New York developers consolidated the industry around a group of buildings along Seventh Avenue that were designed to house workrooms and showrooms for apparel manufacturers.

The apparel industry was not immune to the effects of the Great Depression of the 1930s. Many manufacturers ceased operations as a result of bankruptcy; however, the manufacturing boom during World War II quickly reversed the fortunes of the industry. There were tremendous profits to be earned in servicing the needs of a fully employed population.

The labor intensive aspect of garment manufacturing requires an ongoing search for cheap sources of labor. It was this requirement, in addition to the increasing congestion and expense of doing business in New York City, that began the movement of manufacturers away from New York towards the South and West. The rise of large-scale manufacturing operations could benefit from economies of scale not possible in the small spaces typically found in New York. This led to the wholesale manufacture of staple garments such as jeans.

The unending search for cheap labor eventually led to an increase in imported goods. Under the terms of Tariff Item 807, now called 9802, a U.S. company can send semifinished garments overseas for incidental work, such as sewing and finishing. The company can then import the items back to the United States and pay duty only on the value-added portions of the garments. By the

1980s, the rise in imports was dramatic; 1985 imports were $15 billion, seven times that of 1972. By 1989, that number jumped to almost $24 billion. Manufacturers were pitted against retailers in their attempts to get protectionist legislation passed through Congress. The retailers argued that such legislation would result in an increase in domestic clothing prices. As a result, textile and apparel manufacturers established the Crafted with Pride in the U.S.A Council, designed to encourage consumers to buy American products.

Consolidation. Changing consumer buying patterns and the continuing increase in imported goods contributed to a decrease of 800,000 apparel and textile jobs during the 1980s. They also forced the industry to consider the increased usage of automated manufacturing processes. Although the industry was still labor intensive, computer integrated manufacturing principles and the use of electronic data interchanges for "quick response" in inventory and ordering had become increasingly popular among manufacturers. However, the capital outlays required for the transition to a more automated environment and increased economies of scale were often too costly for smaller manufacturers.

This led to an atmosphere of consolidation wherein heavily capitalized companies introduced automation, expanded their operations, and increased their access to a wider strata of retailers through the acquisition of other labels. Consequently, small, independent companies were squeezed by the ever-increasing import market and these large, domestic apparel corporations. For example, Liz Claiborne, Inc. diversified its holdings by purchasing several brands from Russ Togs Inc., and continued to sell its garments to department stores while these new brands allowed the company to do business with such high growth mass merchandisers as Sears Roebuck and Co. and J.C. Penney Company, Inc.

Licensing. Brand licensing was a strategy employed throughout the industry to increase market share or avoid the necessity of automating a manufacturing process. Through licensing, the brand owner can reap the benefits of its name without the attendant problems of manufacturing or contracting out the goods. Likewise, the licensee views a licensed brand as an opportunity to expand its line of offerings without the risk of financing a product launch. In a December 1992 *Bobbin* article, Craig Kalter, vice president of marketing and licensing for French Toast, noted that, "the advantage to the licensee is that it is able to benefit from a name that has a high degree of awareness and penetration in the marketplace."

NAFTA. The North American Free Trade Agreement (NAFTA) presented new challenges to the apparel industry. The agreement carried the possible threat of U.S. workers losing jobs to Mexico's cheaper labor source.

However, the advocates asserted that businesses only moved to Mexico production that was no longer viable in the United States. In its study of NAFTA, the Office of Technology Assessment commented that "Mexico has so far been a minor supplier of garments to the United States and will have difficulty dislodging established Asian producers. The threat to U.S. apparel jobs is global, not regional." Further, the American Apparel Manufacturers Association (AAMA), which supported NAFTA, argued that without NAFTA, such production would have moved to the Far East, thus completely eliminating U.S. involvement in the manufacturing process. A 1993 survey of AAMA membership indicated that despite NAFTA, only 3 percent of respondents expected an employment decline in the coming year. A full 50 percent expected no changes in their work force, while 46 percent of the manufacturers anticipated increasing their domestic employment.

The apparel industry in general, and women's and misses' dresses in particular, were very sensitive to economic and demographic changes. The economic conditions in the 1980s, boosted by the increase of women in the workplace, led to an average yearly business growth of 10 percent in terms of value of shipments for this category. During the recessionary climate of the early 1990s, however, the industry averaged only 2 percent growth. This sensitivity was further noted in the growth in sales for discount mass merchandisers at the expense of specialty boutiques and department stores. Manufacturers had to hold down costs and provide high quality garments to increasingly demanding and careful customers.

A report issued by the U.S. Department of Commerce projected moderate growth for the U.S. apparel industry through the mid-1990s. This forecast, based on a favorable long-term outlook for consumer spending, housing starts, and new car purchases, also noted the increasingly competitive nature of the industry as foreign producers work to increase their share of the U.S. market.

Overseas markets had become increasingly important to U.S. apparel manufacturers, particularly in the developing markets of the former Soviet Union and Eastern Europe. An economic newsletter published by the American Apparel Manufacturers Association paid particular attention to trends in Asia that suggested opportunities for domestic apparel manufacturers. Japan, for example, had huge stores of foreign exchange but the public's living standard is below that of U.S. citizens. The cultural climate in Japan was changing in the early 1990s and Japan's citizens were beginning to enjoy more leisure. It was anticipated that this would lead to an increase in the consumption of personal goods and services. Likewise, the opening of trade with China and the increasing interest in Western goods offered tremendous growth opportunities for U.S. apparel manufacturers.

A new World Trade Organization (WTO) was established in 1995, and the Multifiber Arrangement (MFA), which allowed importing countries to limit the flow of imports from lower cost developing countries was replaced by the Agreement on Textiles and Clothing (ATC), which required the phasing out of MFA quotas over a ten-year period. According to Linda Shelton in an *Industry, Trade, and Technology Review* report, ''The elimination of MFA quotas likely will have a significant impact on the U.S. textile and apparel sector given the level of protection that such restrictions have provided domestic producers over the past two decades.'' Since the United States has until 2005 to implement the ATC, the legislation's impact on the women's apparel industry may not be realized for several years.

CURRENT CONDITIONS

There were tremendous changes in the apparel industry during the final decade of the twentieth century, including women's, juniors', and misses' dresses. While most operations moved to locations outside the United States amid tumultuous reaction at home, overall outcomes for the dress segment were positive, far-reaching, and even forward-thinking.

Although overseas production dominated the industry, demand to fill American closets with smart, polished garments prevailed, and dress departments of the impending millennium revealed an inclination toward finery. Industry analysts reported Americans were looking for greater opportunities and occasions to literally dress up. While casual clothes remained a wardrobe staple, elegant attire found a rebirth among dress manufacturers. This trend influenced some brand expansions and corporate acquisitions despite rampant facility reductions. This industry segment additionally benefited from the latest computer tools and technologies like the Internet and World Wide Web, as well as improved processes like e-commerce and just-in-time merchandise delivery.

INDUSTRY LEADERS

Founded in 1976 and based in New York City, Liz Claiborne, Inc. grew into the leading manufacturer of dresses in the late 1990s. Industry analysts credit its success to the company's strategy of advertising its products as designer, but pricing them to attract a broader, more diverse market. Sold under size-segmented brands like Lizsport, Liz & Co., Elisabeth and Dana Buchman in outlet, retail, and department stores, the Liz Claiborne label is also licensed for cosmetics, shoes, sunglasses, watches, home furnishings as well as men's clothes. Employing 7,000, the company's 1998 sales topped $2.5 billion and boasted a net increase of $1.6 million for the year.

Leslie Fay Companies, Inc., which include the Leslie Fay Classic, Leslie Fay Collection, Albert Nipon, and Nipon Boutique lines, was founded in 1946 and had sales of over $800 million in 1992. A New York-based publicly traded company, Leslie Fay responded aggressively to consumer demands for moderately priced, value-oriented fashion by cutting prices in several of its dress lines. Due to their ''everyday value'' pricing strategy, the company gained the leading market share in the moderate-price dress category. Despite this market edge, the company's stock, which took a tumble in 1992, continued its downward trend, mirroring the sluggish women's apparel industry. In 1993, the company filed for Chapter 11 bankruptcy reorganization and continued its Chapter 11 operation through 1996.

Kellwood Co., the fifth largest apparel maker in the United States, grew rapidly during the mid-1990s. Despite a stagnant retail environment in 1995, the company's women's wear division grew at 11 percent.

WORKFORCE

The U.S. Census Bureau for 1997 reported that almost 30,000 employees worked in the manufacture of women's, juniors', and misses' dresses, a paltry showing compared to 100,000 employed in 1993.

AMERICA AND THE WORLD

Exports of apparel grew from 2 percent of total U.S. product shipments in 1987 to more than 7 percent in 1992. Total U.S. exports in that year were nearly $4 billion. Although much of this growth represented expansion of existing or new markets, a large portion of this gain was due to semifinished garments sent abroad for finishing and then returned to the United States under the provision of Harmonized Tariff Schedule of the United States (HTSUS) code 9802, formerly 807. Although section 807 existed since the Tariff Act of 1790, it only gained importance during the 1980s, as apparel imports dramatically increased. In the decade from 1980 to 1990, apparel imports increased 202 percent.

The 9802 program allows a manufacturer to pay duty only on the value added to the garment abroad, not the total value of the product. In 1992, HTSUS 9802 trade was slightly more than 14 percent of total imports, and nearly $900 million worth of HTSUS 9802 imports were produced in the Dominican Republic. Mexico produced approximately $700 million, followed by Costa Rica with $400 million.

Apparel trade is governed by the Arrangement Regarding International Trade in Textiles, also known as the Multifiber Arrangement (MFA). This agreement provides guidelines for member nations regarding international trade in textiles and apparel. Apparel is further controlled under the auspices of the General Agreement on Tariffs and Trade (GATT). The Uruguay Round of talks regarding GATT, begun in the late 1980s, were also expected to have an impact on the industry.

The largest suppliers of apparel to the United States were China, Taiwan, Korea, and Hong Kong, with almost $12 billion in sales for 1992. This represented nearly half of the $26 billion of all garments imported into the United States in 1992. Although labor costs in China, Pakistan, and India averaged only $0.23 per hour, wages in Singapore, Hong Kong, and Taiwan were $3.25 per hour, significantly higher than the $1.17 average hourly wage paid in Mexico. In the mid-1990s conventional Far East importers lost U.S. market share to new players such as Bangladesh, Indonesia, and Thailand. The ''Big 4'' (China, Hong Kong, Taiwan, and Korea) represented only 28 percent of apparel imports in 1995. This was due, in part, to increased implementation of ''quick response'' and U.S. apparel manufacturers' ability to react more quickly to fluctuating consumer demands.

FURTHER READING

Apparel Import Digest. Arlington, VA: American Apparel Manufacturers Association, 1997.

Apparel Industry Trends. Arlington, VA: American Apparel Manufacturers Association, March 1997.

Bonner, Staci. ''Kellwood's Vision Pays Off.'' *Apparel Industry,* November 1996.

''Dress YOUR Best in 1999.'' WWD Lifestyle Monitor—Cotton Incorporated, 1999. Available from http://www.cottoninc.com/wwd/homepage.cfm?PAGE+1061.

Focus: An Economic Profile of the Apparel Industry. Arlington, VA: American Apparel Manufacturers Association, 1996.

Hill, Suzette. ''Women's wear makers look ahead to 2005.'' Apparel Industry Online, 1999. Available from http://www.aimagazine.com/nov99stor07.html.

''Import Growth Slowing, AAMA Says.'' *Apparel Industry,* June 1996.

''Leslie Fay Seeks Post-Chapter 11 Lender Facility.'' *Women's Wear Daily,* 4 January 1996. Available from http://207.51.71.250/samples/archive/1996/000/069.htm.

Shelton, Linda and Robert Wallace, ''World Textile and Apparel Trade: A New Era.'' *Industry, Trade, and Technology Review,* October 1996.

U.S. Department of Commerce. *Statistical Abstract of the United States.* Washington: GPO, 1996.

U.S. Department of Commerce, Economics and Statistics Administration. *Annual Survey of manufacturers: Statistics for Groups and Industries.* Bureau of the Census, 1999. Available from http://www.census.gov/prod/ec97/97m3152k.pdf.

SIC 2337

WOMEN'S, MISSES', AND JUNIORS' SUITS, SKIRTS, AND COATS

This category covers establishments primarily engaged in manufacturing women's, misses', and junior's suits, pantsuits, skirts, coats (except fur coats and raincoats), and tailored jackets and vests, from purchased woven or knit fabrics. These garments are generally tailored and usually lined. Establishments primarily engaged in manufacturing fur clothing are classified in **SIC 2371: Fur Goods;** and those manufacturing raincoats are classified in **SIC 2385: Waterproof Outerwear.** Knitting mills primarily engaged in manufacturing knit outerwear are classified in **SIC 2253: Knit Outerwear Mills.**

NAICS CODE(S)

315212 (Women's and Girls' Cut and Sew Apparel Contractors)

315234 (Women's and Girls' Cut and Sew Suit Coat, Tailored Jacket, and Skirt Manufacturing)

INDUSTRY SNAPSHOT

The U.S. apparel industry, especially the women's apparel industry, underwent dramatic change beginning in the 1960s. The increased automation of the industry, the profound surge in imports, and fundamental shifts in the retail industry all affected the manufacture of women's clothing in the United States.

Industry statistics from 1997 reported 430 companies, employing slightly more than 20,000 workers, producing women's suits, coats, shirts, and jackets compared to 1993 figures of more than 1,000 companies and 49,000 workers. Previously, these industry establishments were small, family-owned operations but consolidation and foreign outsourcing created corporate conglomerates more readily adaptable to the fluctuating marketplace and better able to compete with imports. The value of shipments of women's suits, coats, skirts, and jackets in 1997 fell to $3.76 billion from $3.92 billion in 1995, and $3.93 billion in 1994, continuing almost a two-decade downward trend. Factors such as the increase of imports and a general shift toward more casual office wear had a negative impact on this segment of the U.S. market.

ORGANIZATION AND STRUCTURE

The apparel industry was composed of three types of producers: contractors, jobbers, and manufacturers. Contractors were independent firms performing specialized work, such as sewing a garment, for a number of competing firms. Contractors were hired by producers who either did not have their own sewing apparatus or whose own capacity had been exceeded. Contractors were not involved in the retail sale of merchandise. More than 50 percent of the plants making women's coats and suits were run by contractors.

Jobbers were design and marketing businesses that were hired to perform specific functions. For example, jobbers might purchase materials, design patterns, create samples, cut material, and hire contractors to manufacture the product. Most jobbers, however, did not sew garments, but instead hired contractors to sew and finish the products. These contracted sewing-machine operators completed specific parts of the garment, which were provided by the manufacturer. Through this system of piece work, operators could work more quickly and efficiently because they did not need to switch or adjust their machines.

Jobbers often had their own design staffs to create seasonal lines, or they might hire freelancers to do design work. A jobber bought the materials needed to produce the pieces and then created the patterns for different sizes. The cut material was then sent to contractors to be sewn and finished. Orders were taken for the garments, and the finished garments were then shipped to retailers.

Manufacturers were those establishments performing all functions involved in creating apparel from purchased materials. The manufacturer had a staff that produced designs, or it bought work from freelancers; it then purchased the needed materials (fabric and trimmings). Generally the cutting and sewing of the garment was done in the manufacturer's factory. However, when demand for an item exceeded the manufacturer's ability to supply it within shipping deadlines, outside contractors might be hired. The manufacturer's own sales and shipping staff took orders and sent them out.

When a manufacturer handled all stages of a garment's assembly, it clearly had greater control over the quality of the product. Nevertheless, the advantages to using contractors were numerous. For example, those companies without the capital to update machinery would find the system advantageous. Manufacturers who relied upon contractors also avoided the responsibility of hiring and training workers. And the contractor system was flexible—providing manufacturing capacity when needed at busy periods without needing to meet payroll obligations at off-peak periods.

BACKGROUND AND DEVELOPMENT

The growth of the U.S. women's apparel business began in the mid-nineteenth century when certain garments that did not need to be fitted, such as cloaks and mantles, started to be mass-produced. Small quantities of women's suits and skirts were turned out in a limited number of factories, but most women still made their own clothing at home.

Early in the twentieth century, the number of apparel manufacturers grew as more women chose to buy their clothing. New York City became the center of the women's apparel business for a variety of reasons. For example, manufacturers were able to take advantage of the inexpensive labor found in newly arrived immigrants—most of those working in the industry were young Jewish and Italian women. New York City also formed an ideal location for the industry due to its position as a port city and its proximity to the textile mills in New England and the South.

Soon, many manufacturers began to outgrow their quarters in an industry that was expanding rapidly. A consortium of apparel makers, investors, and a real estate developer came up with the idea of moving to an undeveloped area of New York City. Between 1918 and 1921, approximately 50 clothing makers moved to the area along Seventh Avenue, which came to be known as the garment district.

Since the garment industry was unregulated, the employees in these days often worked in crowded, unsafe, and poorly lit "sweat shops" for low pay. Early efforts to organize the workers into unions were met with industry-wide resistance—as one shop became organized, business would then simply shift to an unorganized one.

The Triangle Shirtwaist Factory fire in 1911, in which 146 employees were killed, was a tragedy that galvanized the industry. After much resistance from business owners, industry-wide minimum standards for worker safety were put into place. In the 1930s and 1940s, federal legislation made it easier for the unions to organize, and more labor standards were established. Two unions largely represented U.S. apparel workers, the International Ladies' Garment Workers' Union (ILGWU) and what eventually came to be known as the Amalgamated Clothing and Textile Workers Union (ACTWU). For many years they were able to negotiate contracts with yearly pay increases and benefits.

By the 1960s apparel manufacturers started to move their production facilities out of the United States to markets where the labor was plentiful and cheap. Apparel manufacturing became a global industry. Manufacturers from the United States first looked largely to Hong Kong and Taiwan but, as labor costs grew, manufacturers moved to other Asian nations and the Caribbean. Apparel imports into the United States increased from 9 percent in 1967 to 62 percent in 1992. The value of imports of women's suits, coats, skirts, and jackets reached $2.8 billion in 1995.

Another important development emerged in the 1960s—many textile companies, which produced the materials, and retailers, which bought the finished products, grew into huge companies. The apparel manufacturers responded in kind, as many merged to create large, publicly owned corporations. Historically, women's apparel companies were small businesses, often family-run. Although the new corporations were large, they sometimes lacked the flexibility needed in the ever-changing fashion industry. However, the larger companies were armed with the capital needed to upgrade machinery and modernize equipment to compete more effectively with imports.

Another trend that led to profound change in the industry was the dramatic increase in the number of women in the work force, which began in the 1970s. As a result, the demand for professional women's wear skyrocketed.

Personal-consumption expenditures on clothing nearly doubled during the 1980s, and women's apparel was an important part of that increase. As recession hit the industry in 1989, however, the spending splurge ended; manufacturers responded by cutting costs. While the women's apparel industry adjusted to the recession, the larger manufacturers grew stronger as the industry continued to consolidate. Some big manufacturers were able to take advantage of the weakened position of many smaller firms and strengthen their already dominant positions.

Other factors changed the women's apparel industry as well. For example, manufacturers began to sell their own products as the line between manufacturer and retailer blurred. Manufacturers were often unhappy with the way the retailers displayed their products or with the performance of sales staff. By opening their own retail spaces—either complete stores or free-standing ''shops'' within department stores—manufacturers could exert direct control of the sales, service, and environment. Another popular tactic was for manufacturers to sell through catalogs, again jumping over the middleman and appealing directly to the consumer. By marketing their own goods, manufacturers could avoid retailers who were looking to increase their profit margin at the manufacturers' expense.

Manufacturers responded to the surge in imports in a variety of ways. Some sold off their manufacturing facilities, hiring contractors to make products to their specifications; others contracted for their apparel to be produced almost exclusively offshore and then reimported. By contracting out, manufacturers could reduce their overhead and their inventories would be more flexible. Those who kept their facilities in the United States often stressed their reliability, on-time delivery, and quality.

The value of women's wear shipments declined gradually through the 1990s. One of the many reasons included a leveling-off of the number of women entering the work force. Historically, women's apparel accounted for half of all clothing sold, and it was sold primarily to working women, who by 1990 comprised 45 percent of the U.S. work force. In addition, office wear became more casual, and this particularly affected the sales of women's suits. And as the U.S. population aged, people often became less concerned with up-to-the-minute fashions than with saving for mortgage payments and children's educations. The market stabilized in 1996 and 1997 as manufacturers adjusted their lines to meet the demands of the more casual workplace. Nearly 63 million women were in the labor force in 1997, and they represented almost 50 percent of managerial and professional positions. As Anne D'Innocenzio reported in a *Women's Wear Daily* article, suits were expected to account for 10.8 percent of the tailored market in 1997, which meant the decline in women's suit sales had ceased. Blazers were expected to generate 27.7 percent of total tailored sales.

CURRENT CONDITIONS

Retailers themselves sought to cut costs and become more efficient as the market became more competitive. Retailers often looked to the larger apparel manufacturers that were providing merchandise that consumers recognized and respected. By limiting the number of manufacturers supplying them, retailers could reduce overhead expenses—thus favoring the larger manufacturers over the smaller ones.

Mass merchandising was the focus of the 1990s. The dawn of a new century improved upon this concept by incorporating the Internet into numerous stages within the industry process. This electronic commerce, sometimes called e-commerce or e-tailing, was a strategy that benefited both manufacturers and customers by moving goods to destinations almost instantly. A 1999 ApparelNews.net article reported that e-commerce represented only a sliver of annual sales, but the trend eventually found greater acceptance. These Internet-based transactions revolutionized the apparel trade in terms of turnaround and timelines. Access to this up-to-the-minute information, as well as the borderless venue, allowed for all parties to dramatically broaden their business reaches.

INDUSTRY LEADERS

Liz Claiborne, Inc. was the number one maker of clothes and accessories for career-oriented women, especially suits. One reason for its success was the company's strategy of advertising products as designer but pricing them to attract a broader market. Sold under size-segmented brands like Lizsport, Liz & Co., Elisabeth, and Dana Buchman in department, retail, and outlet stores, the Liz Claiborne label is also licensed for cosmetics, shoes, sunglasses, watches, and home furnishings, as well as men's clothes. Headquartered in New York City and employing 7,000 people, the company's 1998 sales topped $2.5 billion and boasted a net increase of $1.6 million for the year.

Specializing in the moderate to high-priced women's and career and casual sportswear, suits, dresses, and footwear was the Jones Apparel Group sold under such names as Jones New York, Jones & Co., Evan-Picone, Rena Rowan and others, including several labels licensed by Polo Ralph Lauren. Based in Bristol, Pennsylvania, with more than 8,000 people on its company payroll (and with products sold throughout department, retail, and outlet stores across the nation), Jones Apparel reported overall sales of $1.7 billion, as well as a net increase of almost $1.5 million in 1998.

Polo Ralph Lauren Corporation—one of the world's best known designer labels boasting such subsidiaries as Polo, Lauren, Chaps, and Club Monaco—designs and markets a variety of products such as men's and women's apparel and suits, accessories, fragrances and home furnishings. Its design strategy centers around overseeing the work of its many licensees (like its largest, Jones Apparel Group) and controls manufacturers in Asia and the United States. Its New York City-based operations, with 6,800 employees, reported 1999 sales of $1.7 billion and a net increase of $9.1 million.

WORKFORCE

As imports increasingly replaced American-made clothing, the number of employees in the industry predictably declined. The International Ladies' Garment Workers' Union (ILGWU) reported that from a peak in 1973, 34 percent of production worker jobs (nearly 25,000) were lost in 20 years in the women's and children's apparel industry, a process that accelerated in the 1980s.

U.S. Census Bureau figures for 1997 reported 20,378 workers involved in the manufacture of women's suits, coats, skirts, and jackets, down from 40,400 two years earlier. Hourly wages averaged $10.63, a $5.24 increase from 1995.

New York was the state with the largest number of employees in the women's apparel industry, while California, New Jersey, Texas, and Massachusetts also had significant concentrations of workers.

AMERICA AND THE WORLD

The U.S. women's apparel industry was dominated by imports by the early 1990s. Imports were attractive to consumers because they were often less expensive than domestically produced clothing and they had increased in quality over time. The industry began to lose market share to imports in the 1960s. The process began to accelerate in the 1970s and, by the early 1990s, imports reached all-time highs. From 1980 through the early 1990s, apparel imports tripled when measured in square meters. Also contributing to the industry's decline in the

United States was the reliance of manufacturers on offshore assembly of pieces cut domestically.

Manufacturers in the Far East represented a significant source of women's apparel. When apparel makers started to move their manufacturing bases out of the United States in the 1960s, they first went to Hong Kong, Taiwan, and South Korea to take advantage of the cheap labor there. By the 1980s, however, labor costs had increased, and capital and experience from those traditional low-wage markets moved to lower wage countries such as Bangladesh, Thailand, Pakistan, Indonesia, Malaysia, Sri Lanka, and India, which became the sources for more of the imports entering the U.S. market. By the early 1990s, China replaced Hong Kong as the greatest supplier of imported clothing to the United States. China, Hong Kong, Taiwan, and Korea represented only 28 percent of apparel imports in 1995.

The North American Free Trade Agreement (NAFTA), which created a free-trade zone between the United States, Mexico, and Canada by gradually eliminating tariffs over 15 years, took effect January 1, 1994. Since a similar agreement was already in effect between the United States and Canada, analysts expected NAFTA to increase trade with Mexico. Apparel-industry executives supported NAFTA. The ILGWU and the ACTWU, by contrast, sought to stem the loss of jobs in the apparel industry by limiting the imports allowed into the country. However, their arguments did not succeed in challenging the free-market philosophy that ultimately triumphed in the passage of NAFTA.

Any agreement to come from the negotiations of the General Agreement on Tariffs and Trade (GATT), started in 1986, would possibly have wide-ranging impact on the U.S. apparel industry. GATT was first established in the 1960s, and it created the Arrangement Regarding International Trade in Textiles, known as the Multifiber Arrangement (MFA). The MFA regulated apparel that was imported into the United States and other member nations, and it was renewed every three years. Proposals involved in the GATT negotiations would reduce the tariffs on imports into the United States by half over time, without guaranteeing U.S. products access to markets in other countries. Some countries that exported heavily into the United States—for example, China—did not allow corresponding access to their home markets. The MFA would be superseded by any agreement reached in the GATT talks, but if no agreement was reached, the MFA would be extended. The textile industry estimated that one million U.S. textile and apparel jobs would be lost under the provisions of GATT.

More and more imports entered the United States under provision 9802 (formerly known as Section 807) of the Harmonized Tariffs Schedule of the United States. This provision allowed clothing assembled abroad—

from pieces cut in the United States—to be reimported with duty paid for the value added abroad. Thus, the most labor-intensive part of the assembly process could be done at lower-wage rates. Many U.S. manufacturers took advantage of the provision and moved assembly operations to the Caribbean. They noted that they could reduce costs and more successfully compete against imports from Asia. More complex items could be assembled and turned around more quickly than if created in Asia. Disadvantages included sometimes cumbersome and time-consuming logistics considerations. By 1992, apparel assembled in the Caribbean comprised 14 percent of imports. The passage of NAFTA, however, led some observers to expect that the Caribbean would become less desirable than Mexico as a manufacturing destination.

U.S. women's apparel exports grew rapidly starting in the late 1980s. In 1995 exports of women's suits, coats, skirts, and jackets reached $259 million, more than double the value of these exports in 1989. U.S. clothing seemed to grow in popularity in Europe, perhaps due to the adoption by European women of a lifestyle more in line with the easy-care, comfortable clothing purchased by women in the United States. The weak U.S. dollar helped increase shipments to Japan and Canada, as well as Europe and the Middle East.

A new World Trade Organization (WTO) was established in 1995, and the Multifiber Arrangement (MFA)—which allowed importing countries to limit the flow of imports from lower cost, developing countries—was replaced by the ATC, which required the phasing out of MFA quotas over a ten-year period. According to Linda Shelton in an *Industry, Trade, and Technology Review* report, "The elimination of MFA quotas likely will have a significant impact on the U.S. textile and apparel sector given the level of protection that such restrictions have provided domestic producers over the past two decades." Since the United States has until 2005 to implement the ATC, the legislation's impact on the women's apparel industry may not be realized for several years.

The large firms in the women's apparel industry had the capital to invest in new technology, but many of the smaller firms, struggling against the tide of imports, were not in a position to do so. Nevertheless, the intrinsic "soft" quality of material made it difficult to use automated equipment widely, and apparel manufacture remained a highly labor-intensive industry.

One tool that was advocated to better meet the market's demands was "quick response"—the idea of bringing apparel to the retailer rapidly by shortening production cycles, reducing inventories, improving productivity, and relaying information regarding consumers' preferences quickly back to manufacturers. By using computers to track inventory and sales as well as consumers' responses to particular items, U.S. manufacturers could respond quickly to market demand—and thus get a jump on foreign producers. Department stores and manufacturers worked together to find ways to speed deliveries and increase efficiency. Mass merchandisers were among the first to implement the quick response concept.

RESEARCH AND TECHNOLOGY

E-commerce, the industry strategy employing computer-based tools like the Internet and the World Wide Web to streamline numerous facets within the trade, continued to evolve but was not without its occasional hiccups. The American Textile Manufacturers Institute noted that successful e-commerce required a solid infrastructure, especially in the areas of customer service and order fulfillment. Obstacles such as cost and lack of expertise prompted many vendors to created new processes or restructure old ones to help ensure operations with favorable outcomes. However, others chose to treat e-commerce as a separate channel partner by outsourcing their role to Web-savvy professionals who provided them a buffer as well as direction. Ultimately, their goal was seamless execution of sales and marketing efforts on all levels to all customers.

FURTHER READING

Apparel Import Digest. Arlington, VA: American Apparel Manufacturers Association, 1997.

Apparel Industry Trends. Arlington, VA: American Apparel Manufacturers Association, March 1997.

Brady, Jennifer L. "Analysts: Apparel on Slow Road to Recovery." *Women's Wear Daily,* 13 May 1996.

Conces, Elaine, and Margaret Brantley. "Textiles, Apparel Shoes and Accessories Industry." Austin, TX: Hoovers Online, 1999. Available from http://www.hoovers.com/industry/snapshot/0,2204,42,00.html.

D'Innocenzio, Anne. "McNaughton: New Directions." *Women's Wear Daily,* 20 March 1996.

"Dresses Excel in Tailored." *Women's Wear Daily,* 8 May 1996.

Focus: An Economic Profile of the Apparel Industry. Arlington, VA: American Apparel Manufacturers Association, 1996.

Hill, Suzette. "E-tailing: The Internet Meets SCM." Roswell, NM: Apparel Industry Online, 1999. Available from http://www.aimagazine.com/oct99stor09.html.

Nieder, Alison A. "Textile Presence on Web Grows as Sites Market E-Yardage." Los Angeles: ApparelNews.Net, 1999. Available from http://www.apparelnews.net/News/newsfast.html.

Shelton, Linda, and Robert Wallace. "World Textile and Apparel Trade: A New Era." *Industry, Trade, and Technology Review,* October 1996.

U.S. Department of Commerce. *Statistical Abstract of the United States.* Washington, D.C.: GPO, 1996.

SIC 2339

WOMEN'S, MISSES', AND JUNIORS' OUTERWEAR NOT ELSEWHERE CLASSIFIED

This industry includes establishments primarily engaged in manufacturing women's, misses', and juniors' outerwear, not elsewhere classified, from purchased woven or knit fabrics. Knitting mills primarily engaged in manufacturing outerwear are classified in **SIC 2253: Knit Outerwear Mills.**

NAICS CODE(S)

315999 (Other Apparel Accessories and Other Apparel Manufacturing)

315212 (Women's and Girls' Cut and Sew Apparel Contractors)

315299 (All Other Cut and Sew Apparel Manufacturing)

315238 (Women's and Girls' Cut and Sew Other Outerwear Manufacturing)

INDUSTRY SNAPSHOT

Globalization was a major influence on the women's, misses' and juniors' knit outerwear industry in the United States at the end of the twentieth century. While most design and sales operations were still primarily centered in California and New York, sourcing, sewing, and other labor moved overseas as a cost-cutting measure, sometimes at the expense of smaller family-based enterprises. The North American Free Trade Agreement (NAFTA) and the World Trade Organization (WTO) spurred the migration of operations overseas, forcing smaller U.S. businesses to close down and ushering in a new worldwide business approach. The industry also experienced technical innovations and advances that improved production and permitted enhanced international cooperation; new computer applications allowed operations spread over several countries to be seamlessly coordinated.

The global perspective that dominated the manufacturing side of the industry was evident in other aspects as well. Clothing designers were influenced by fashion developments and styles of other countries, indicated by the designs shown both on the high fashion runways and in retail clothing shops. American consumers had also become more diversified by the beginning of the 21st century: Asian and Hispanic American populations in particular were growing, especially female Hispanic American consumers, whose influence grew considerably during the 1990s. A 1999 survey by Cotton Inc. indicated that these women spent more on fashion and beauty items than any other market segment. Clothing merchants took notice of this trend and made special efforts to cater to these customers. Major retailer J.C. Penney, for example, created store signage in Spanish for its outlets in predominantly Hispanic areas like Los Angeles and Miami, further increasing sales to Hispanic American women.

Historically, the women's apparel industry has been particularly sensitive to changes in economic conditions. As the economic downturn of the early 1990s caused consumers to look for value and savings, consumer tastes shifted from a preference for designer labels during the economic boom of the 1980s to an increased interest in more casual, and inexpensive, apparel. This shift in consumer behavior resulted in a decrease in the number of women's apparel manufacturers and a growth in sales for discount mass merchandisers in the place of specialty boutiques and department stores. Manufacturers attempted to hold down costs and provide high quality garments for increasingly demanding and careful customers.

An increase in imports further increased competition in this already volatile and difficult industry. To help deal with these chaotic global circumstances, a new World Trade Organization (WTO) was established in 1995. Furthermore, the Multifiber Arrangement (MFA), which allowed importing countries to limit the flow of imports from lower cost, developing countries, was replaced by the Agreement on Textiles and Clothing (ATC) which required the phasing out of MFA quotas over a ten-year period. According to Linda Shelton in an *Industry, Trade, and Technology Review* report, "The elimination of MFA quotas likely will have a significant impact on the U.S. textile and apparel sector given the level of protection that such restrictions have provided domestic producers over the past two decades." Since the United States has until 2005 to implement the ATC, the legislation's impact on the women's, misses' and junior's outerwear industry was only beginning to be realized at the end of the 1990s. While imports increased by only 5 percent per year between 1988 and 1991, they jumped 15 percent in 1992. They rose another 15 percent in 1993 and increased 12 percent in 1994. Growth slowed to 10 percent in 1995, however.

Still, with the steady growth of the American economy and record highs in consumer confidence through the end of the 1990s, the women's apparel market experienced a rejuvenation. There were some growing pains as the industry scrambled to employ new technology and initiatives to streamline operations. Profound advancements in communication and availability of information, combined with smarter uses of computer technology and tools, introduced strategies and processes that benefited manufacturers and customers alike. Such pivotal improvements, including the broad application of the World Wide Web, inspired market time savers and positive outcomes like just-in-time merchandise delivery, fewer stagnant inventory levels, lower costs and instant order fulfillment and verification.

These improved business strategies facilitated cooperation among the various industry channels on all levels. While corporate acquisitions—in an effort to expand or diversify—were common in the late 1990s, a majority of industry participants collectively pooled their resources to better afford and understand these updated business methods. These industry innovations frequently required prohibitive investments of time and money, but many deemed the risk worthwhile and soon learned that doing so often resulted in significant savings and generous profits. Electronic commerce, a mode that had become a solid fixture in businesses large and small by the twenty-first century, proved to be one of the most important of the Web-based transactions. Although slow in its start and acceptance, it soon revolutionized the industry.

INDUSTRY LEADERS

Founded in 1976 and based in New York City, Liz Claiborne, Inc. was considered the top manufacturer of women's apparel. Many in the industry attributed its success to advertising its products as designer but pricing them to attract a broader market. The company sold a number of lines of segmented brands like Lizsport, Liz & Co., Elisabeth and Dana Buchman in an array of retail outlets. The label also licensed cosmetic items, shoes, sunglasses, watches, home furnishings, and men's clothes.

WORKFORCE

More than 22,000 people, or over 20 percent of this industry's workforce, were employed in California's 670 establishments engaged in women's, juniors', and misses' outerwear manufacturing in the mid-1990s. New York employed 12,800 people in this industry. The largest percentage of workers were employed as sewing machine operators, followed by pressing machine operators and inspectors. With the exception of sales and machine mechanics, all other employment categories in the industry were anticipating workforce reductions to continue through the turn of the century.

FURTHER READING

Apparel Import Digest. Arlington, VA: American Apparel Manufacturers Association, 1997.

Apparel Industry Trends. Arlington, VA: American Apparel Manufacturers Association, March 1997.

Conces, Elaine, and Margaret Brantley. "Textiles, Apparel, Shoes and Accessories Industry." Austin, TX: Hoovers Online, 1999. Available from http://www.hoovers.com/industry/snapshot/0,2204,42,00.html.

Focus: An Economic Profile of the Apparel Industry. Arlington, VA: American Apparel Manufacturers Association, 1996.

"A Global Perspective On Women and Women's Wear." *WWD Lifestyle Monitor, Cotton Incorporated,* 1999. Available from http://www.cottoninc.com/wwd/homepage.cfm?PAGE=2173.

Hill, Suzette. "Women's wear makers look ahead to 2005." *Apparel Industry Magazine Online,* 1999. Available from http://aimagazine.com/nov99stor07.html.

"Import Growth Slowing, AAMA Says." *Apparel Industry,* June 1996.

"Latina Fashionistas." *WWD Lifestyle Monitor, Cotton Incorporated,* 1999. Available from http://www.cottoninc.com/wwd/homepage.cfm?PAGE=2177.

Rotenier, Nancy. "Niki and Me." *Forbes,* 13 January 1997.

Shelton, Linda and Robert Wallace. "World Textile and Apparel Trade: A New Era," *Industry, Trade, and Technology Review,* October 1996.

SIC 2341

WOMEN'S, MISSES', CHILDREN'S, AND INFANTS' UNDERWEAR AND NIGHTWEAR

This category includes establishments primarily engaged in manufacturing women's, misses', children's and infants' underwear and nightwear from purchased woven or knit fabrics. Knitting mills primarily engaged in manufacturing underwear and nightwear are classified in **SIC 2254: Knit Underwear and Nightwear Mills.** Establishments primarily engaged in manufacturing women's and misses robes and dressing gowns are classified in **SIC 2384: Robes and Dressing Gowns,** and those manufacturing children's and infants' robes are classified in **SIC 2369: Girls', Children's, and Infants' Outerwear, Not Elsewhere Classified.** Establishments primarily engaged in manufacturing brassieres, girdles, and allied garments are classified in **SIC 2342: Brassieres, Girdles, and Allied Garments.**

NAICS CODE(S)

315212 (Women's and Girls' Cut and Sew Apparel Contractors)

315211 (Men's and Boys' Cut and Sew Apparel Contractors)

315231 (Women's and Girls' Cut and Sew Lingerie, Loungewear, and Nightwear Manufacturing)

315221 (Men's and Boys' Cut and Sew Underwear and Nightwear Manufacturing)

315291 (Infants' Cut and Sew Apparel Manufacturing)

INDUSTRY SNAPSHOT

The U.S. Commerce Department reported that 286 establishments were engaged in the manufacture of women's, misses', children's, and infants' underwear in 1997 compared to 340 in 1993. The value of total product shipments for 1997 was slightly more than $3.6 million;

the value added by manufacture reached $1.5 million while the cost of materials barely topped $2.0 million and the total capital expenditures crowned at $20,800.

Beginning in the early to mid-1980s, economic conditions in the women's apparel industry group turned from bad to worse. In 1982, for instance, there were approximately 604 establishments involved in manufacturing activities, and by 1989 that number had dropped to 383. During the same period, total employment declined from 67,800 to 49,400 people. This trend continued in the early to mid-1990s, and by 1995 total employment had dropped to 31,200 workers.

The ongoing concurrence of several major economic trends explained the industry's sagging fortunes. First, the decline in middle-class income levels, a trend that began in the mid- to late 1970s and picked up a full head of steam during the 1980s, led to the withdrawal of a considerable amount of consumer purchasing power formerly directed at the purchase of apparel products in general.

Second, and partly as a consequence of the above, established lines of distribution at both the retail and wholesale levels were in the throes of a bankruptcy-induced crisis. Around the same period, these sectors were also undergoing widespread structural change, owing to the introduction of advanced communication systems that greatly enhanced the flow of integrated information across retail, wholesale, and manufacturing levels.

Third, the change in women's apparel producer prices plunged during the recession of 1981 and 1982. Then, to the further detriment of the industry, as the recession ended, prices never climbed back to their previous levels but instead remained flat from 1983 into the first half of 1990s. With the onset of the 1990 through 1992 recession, women's apparel prices took another nosedive. Intense intra-industry competition from both domestic and foreign producers had played an important part in generating the unfavorable price climate and contributed to a significant 10-year decline in capacity utilization. After peaking in 1984 at 88 percent, capacity utilization began to plummet on an annual basis and stood at 78 percent in 1994. Finally, the lingering overhang of takeover debt, piled up from the late 1980s period of speculative merger mania, exerted a retarding effect on company profits and growth.

On the positive side, however, the steady decline in the value of the U.S. dollar proved advantageous to export sales of women's and children's underwear and nightwear, although it bears mention that export sales have traditionally figured as a rather insignificant component of the industry's overall U.S. sales. From 1989 to 1992, the annual change in nominal exports averaged 27.1 percent. In 1993, the value of exports grew to $186.0 million, and in

1995 exports in the industry were valued at $267.0 million. At the same time, the value of U.S. imports grew to $1.1 billion in 1993, $1.5 billion by 1995.

ORGANIZATION AND STRUCTURE

When tracking the density of establishments by their census region of concentration, the highest number of establishments were located in the Middle Atlantic, South Atlantic, and Pacific regions. When ranked by the number of establishments per state as well as total employment level per state, New York led the way, followed by California, New Jersey, North Carolina, and Pennsylvania.

An article appearing in *Sales and Marketing Management* estimated that, in 1987, large plants with 100 or more employees accounted for only 41 percent of the total number of establishments but were responsible for close to 87 percent of the industry's shipments. It noted that many of the smaller establishments survived by making specialized products to supply market niches.

Data available from the U.S. Bureau of the Census for 1982 and 1987 stated that primary materials consumed by the women's, misses', children's, and infants' underwear and nightwear industry ranked on a cost basis were materials, containers, and supplies; knit fabrics; miscellaneous materials and parts; and broadwoven fabrics. The Census also reported that the major economic sectors responsible for input supply came from imports, broadwoven fabric mills, apparel made from purchased materials, and knit fabric mills. When disaggregated, the total product share broken down by its major product classifications were women's and children's underwear with 38.3 percent; women's and children's nightwear with 46.4 percent; and contract and commission work on the two combined categories with 12.2 percent. The principal economic sectors responsible for the purchase of the industry's output were private personal expenditures with 82.7 percent; other manufacturers with 12 percent; exports with 1.5 percent; and the federal government with 1 percent.

BACKGROUND AND DEVELOPMENT

The modern history of women's underwear produced for mass consumption more or less began in the 1830s to 1840s with the manufacture of ready-made undergarments. Stay stitchers and gorers using hand techniques were employed in factories or worked from home as "outworkers." Around the early 1860s, the widespread use of sewing machines pushed underwear output to unprecedented levels. Other complementary technologies, like the band knife (which enabled garment workers to slice through several layers of material at once) proved instrumental in reorganizing the factory floor along the lines of the "batch" system.

During the 1870s, underwear was available in attractively packaged boxes with decorative and typically colored labels. Large-scale advertising campaigns trumpeting the virtues of underwear became commonplace by the end of the 1870s. Well into the 1880s, the marketing themes became more explicit in an attempt to match the luxury and erotic appeal of the undergarments. Underwear could be purchased from large department stores or by mail order from companies like Sears, Roebuck and Co. of Chicago or the Great Universal Stores located across the United States.

Fashion historians refer to the period of 1890 through 1913 as the "Belle Epoque." It was characterized as a period of extravagance and conspicuous consumption in women's dress in general and in women's underwear in particular. Underwear was much lighter in appearance, feel, and weight and, compared to its lackluster mid-Victorian antecedents, more luxurious and glamorous in conception. New luxury underwear first became available in sets that included nightwear and were christened with the group name "lingerie," a term derived from the French word "linge," meaning linen. Earlier material mainstays such as cotton longcloth and flannel were replaced by cambrics, merino, and silks. The extravagance in tastes and materials continued to lead the underwear fashion charge until the economic slump of the 1930s, which ushered in the era of mass-produced machine made rayon lingerie.

The nineteenth century introduction of elastene stretch fabrics exerted a tremendous influence on underwear production. Elastene was perfected in the 1930s, when the popularity of ready-made underwear began to seize the day. It supplanted the more upscale fabrics associated with the Belle Epoque.

During the 1940s, events surrounding World War II and its lingering after-effects put changes in the underwear industry on a 10-year hold as resources used throughout the apparel industry were diverted to wartime production. For instance, foundation wear finishing tape was used for cartridge belts; the production of hooks, eyes, and stocking supporters was supplanted by brass armaments manufacture; and ace machines were used for making camouflage nets. Nylon, invented in 1938, was used for glider tow ropes and parachutes; it wasn't used for the production of underwear until 1947.

During the 1950s, nylon and other manmade fibers entered into the production of underwear and dominated the scene. At the time, nylon's chief drawback was its nonabsorbent property, but later the fabric was somewhat modified and woven to obtain a more comfortable porous state. Another manmade material achieving popularity was rayon, which, when mixed with cotton, created a shiny and always new appearance. Other manmade 1950 notables were polyester and acrylic undergarments. In 1959 lycra, arguably one of the most important and versatile of manmade fibers, was introduced and was originally referred to as Spandex or elatomerics, only to be renamed elastene in 1976. Containing no natural fiber at all, lycra was lighter and proved far more durable than rubber elastic; it remained a foundation wear mainstay well into the 1990s.

The decade of the 1960s and early 1970s ushered in a tumultuous period of great social and political upheaval. Television exerted a powerful influence, and Maidenform Inc. became the first U.S. company to advertise underwear on a national level. *Vogue* and other glossy women's magazines were highly attuned to promoting a version of what the beautiful woman looked like in terms of both her outer-and innerwear garments. During this period, attitudes toward sex and the traditional woman's lifestyle, both outside and inside the house, were under assault, opening up new avenues for self-expression and lifestyle changes. More restrictive types of underwear previously equated with outdated notions of decency faded; in their place came bikini-style briefs. The popularity of the briefs, which were available for men and women alike, rested on their comfort and usability.

The teenage apparel market first became a distinct entity during the 1950s and became an institutional mainstay in the 1960s. The needs of younger girls (misses) for suitable and acceptable underwear reflecting their own stage of development and active involvement in various social activities was readily acknowledged. As a result, the U.S. company Lily of France introduced a special "Lilies" line of underwear for college-age girls, along with a preteen collection called "Teenform," which was later imported into Britain by Berlei.

By the 1990s, the 30-year transformation of children's and infants' underwear had achieved significant results. Unlike the underwear that was worn up to the late 1960s, undergarments in the 1990s washed easier; were more attractive, lightweight, and durable; and were less prone to induce irritation. The comfort provided from T-shirts made from cotton and simple crop tops left a favorable impression on the mother or child able to recall the discomfort related to wearing undergarments made from knitted wool; liberty bodices; and burdensome knickers lined with breakable elastic during the 1940s, 1950s, and early 1960s.

Downsizing due to the elimination of and mergers between establishments became a recognized trend by the late 1980s. By the mid-1990s things began to stabilize somewhat, yet it was not clear whether the trend had been entirely played out. The opening up of the countries of the former Soviet Union and Eastern Europe, where there resided a well-trained apparel workforce ripe for capitalist investment, also presented the industry with untapped opportunities that looked promising, even if they had not yet been fully explored. Further long term uncertainties were thrown into this mix with the 1993 passage of the North American Free Trade Agreement (NAFTA), and, later that year, the General Agreement on Tariffs and Trade (GATT).

Well into the 1980s, the entire U.S. apparel industry was negatively impacted by the erosion of middle-class income earners, who generally accounted for the over-whelming percentage of apparel purchases. At the same time, the growing trend toward the foreign relocation of apparel establishments—and the foreign outsourcing and re-entry into the United States of intermediate apparel-related work formerly performed in the U.S. under the auspices of provision 9802 of the Harmonized Tariff Schedule of the United States—did not bode well for U.S. job growth prospects. Apparel import competition leading to the progressive deterioration of domestic market share of U.S. apparel manufacturers also showed no sign of abating.

A new World Trade Organization was established in 1995, and the Multifiber Arrangement (MFA) that allowed importing countries to limit the flow of imports from lower-cost, developing countries was replaced by the Agreement on Textiles and Clothing (ATC), which required the phasing out of MFA quotas over a 10-year period. According to Linda Shelton in an *Industry, Trade, and Technology Review* report, "The elimination of MFA quotas likely will have a significant impact on the U.S. textile and apparel sector given the level of protection that such restrictions have provided domestic producers over the past two decades." Since the U.S. has until 2005 to implement the ATC, the legislation's impact on the women's, misses', children's, and infants' underwear and nightwear industry may not be realized for several years.

To date, the most far-reaching domestic response to the deteriorating conditions impacting the industry was to invest in state-of-the-art communication systems that facilitate the rapid flow of information used to immediately react to, and determine, consumer preferences formed in the marketplace. This consumer driven process, which the industry refers to as the "quick response" system, integrates several dimensions of the production cycle with the intent of shortening the cycle's duration. Via the immediate feedback of consumer sales information from the retail to manufacturing level, producers are able to implement productivity improvements and shrink inventory levels and their associated costs to a bare minimum. To determine the changing direction of consumer tastes, the quick response system compiles the results of consumer surveys, which express what consumers most likely will and will not purchase in the immediate future.

In addition to the quick response system, the industry also directed sizable investments at computer controlled automated machinery. With the primary intention of in-

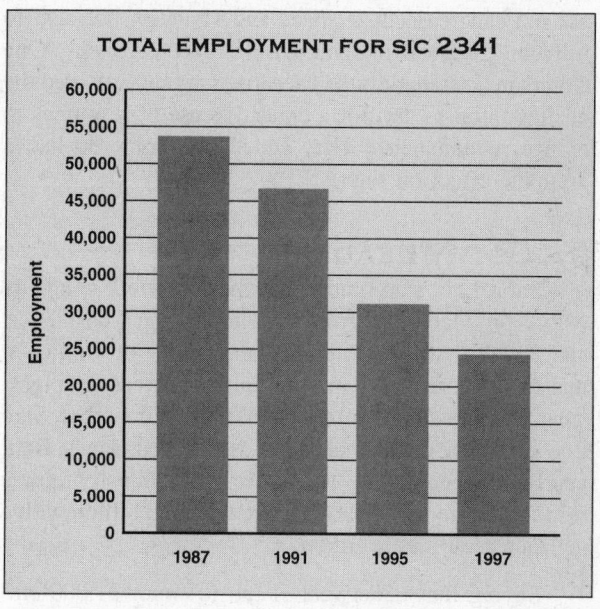

creasing productivity, these investments targeted the areas of design, cutting, embroidery, sewing, finishing, ticketing, and distribution operations. In order to compete within their own industry as well as against other nonapparel industries, the industry's leading firms were the first to implement these investments to any significant degree. Their ability to finance high-cost technological advances was related to their economies of scale and access to internally generated funds. With the passage of time, if the middle-and lower-tier firms failed to respond by adapting these new technologies, then an uneven pattern of technological change would result and most likely exacerbate the downsizing trend active throughout the industry.

CURRENT CONDITIONS

In the late 1990s, globalization best described the apparel industry as a whole, but especially the underwear and nightwear segment. Expected to continue into the next century, foreign sourcing, sewing, and manufacturing—compelling trends of the decade—prompted not only huge savings but also significant growth. A November 1999 issue of *Apparel Industry Magazine* reported "a seismic shift to overseas sewing;" industry player Fruit of the Loom saw these operations skyrocket from 12 percent to 95 percent, for example. Foreign sourcing of basic knit fabrics, the article also noted, grew 25 to 30 percent each year for the past two to three years.

Globalization owed part of its success to the industry's willingness to invest in the latest advancements in information and communication technologies, influencing another market trend industry leaders called speed-to-market, a streamlining process that put products on the shelves and racks more quickly. Many apparel companies implemented these systems enterprise-wide in an effort to not only increase their speed and visibility but also to fully integrate all of their business needs. Such "One Company" strategies, the executives argued, allowed the business unit to aim for a collective use of resources to reduce redundancies. They added that doing so had a dramatic effect on sales.

INDUSTRY LEADERS

Sara Lee Corporation, a multi-faceted company whose products span from food to polishes, cosmetics, and jewelry, was the number one maker of women's, misses', children's and infants' knit underwear and nightwear. Famous for its introduction of the Wonderbra, Sara Lee's intimate apparel subsidiaries included Hanes, Bali, and Bessin. Employing 138,000 in 1999, industry figures for the year boasted sales of more than $20 billion with a net increase of $1.2 billion.

Saying that underwear is fun to wear, 21,000-employee Warnaco Group closely followed Sara Lee's profit margins in this apparel group. With a 35 percent market stronghold, Warnaco focused its North American and European sales efforts on outlet, department, and specialty stores. Licensing its own brands as well as high-end ones like Calvin Klein and Warner, 1998 sales yielded almost $2 billion.

VF Corporation, most notable for its leadership in the denim market, was also a leader in intimate apparel via the Vanity Fair label. Industry analysts attributed the company's success to recent aggressive growth in select Latin American countries and their greater focus on improved quality of customer goods. With an employee roster of 70,000, VF saw 1998 sales reach almost $5.5 billion with a net increase of $388 million.

WORKFORCE

In 1997 the total number of individuals employed by women's and children's underwear and nightwear manufacturers fell to 24,402, compared to 31,200 in 1995. The majority of them (19,224) were classified as production workers who labored a total of 36,673 hours and earned $271,314 during the year.

In 1989 the average value added per production worker was $29,095—a figure considerably below the overall average of $105,881 for 459 U.S. manufacturing industries. Efforts to redress this productivity gap have been consistently, though not uniformly, percolating throughout the industry for some time. These have variously taken the form of labor-management cooperation schemes, technology diffusion, mergers, periods of protectionism meant to provide the time necessary to restructure the workplace, and the "outsourcing" to other domestic or foreign firms of work formerly performed within a company's premises.

The industry's employment picture had indicated a sharp decline going back as far as 1982. From 1987 to 1991, the industry's total employment fell from 53,700, of which 46,700 were classified as production workers, to 45,800, with 39,200 classified as production workers.

In 1990, the industry's major occupational categories were sewing machine operators; precision inspectors, testers, and graders; pressing machine operators; and blue collar supervisors. Close to 56 percent of the workforce was active in sewing machine operations. The remaining occupational categories each accounted for approximately 3.1 percent of the total workforce. The U.S. Bureau of Labor Statistics had forecast that many of these occupational categories were expected to decline by the year 2005. Assuming no great deviations from the industry's productivity trend, sewing machine operators were projected to experience the largest decline.

When compared to the measures of employment by gender and race for the U.S. manufacturing sector as a whole, women, Hispanic, and black workers were disproportionately represented in the industry's workforce to such a large degree that they dramatically exceeded their national average counterparts. In 1995, demographic data gathered from the American Apparel Manufacturers Association indicated that female workers comprised 70.0 percent of the industry's workforce, Hispanic workers 24.0 percent, and black workers 15.2 percent.

RESEARCH AND TECHNOLOGY

Computer technology and tools, including processes and products that resulted from them, helped the apparel industry make great strides in overall output with the approach of the twenty-first century. While such revolutionary accessories like information technology (also known as IT), the Internet, and the World Wide Web streamlined the business and introduced novel approaches like e-commerce, much of the focus remained on providing quality products in a timely manner. Cost proved to be a hurdle for most—if not all—industry participants, but many researched numerous methods and found various means to overcome it. Most of the initial challenges were met with improvements, some of which spawned industry innovations.

FURTHER READING

Apparel Import Digest. Arlington: American Apparel Manufacturers Association, 1997.

Apparel Industry Trends. Arlington: American Apparel Manufacturers Association, March 1997.

Darnay, Arsen J., ed. *Manufacturing USA.* 5th ed. Detroit: Gale Research, 1996.

Focus: An Economic Profile of the Apparel Industry. Arlington: American Apparel Manufacturers Association, 1996.

Guilford, Roxanna. "Understanding the Challenges of Underwear." *Apparel Industry Magazine,* 1999. Available from http://www.aimagazine.com/nov99stor11.html.

Shelton, Linda, and Robert Wallace. "World Textile and Apparel Trade: A New Era." *Industry, Trade, and Technology Review,* October 1996.

U.S. Department of Commerce, Economics and Statistics Administration. *Annual Survey of Manufacturers: Statistics for Industry Groups and Industries.* Bureau of the Census, 1999. Available from http://www.census.gov/prod/ec97/97m3152i.pdf.

SIC 2342

BRASSIERES, GIRDLES, AND ALLIED GARMENTS

Establishments primarily engaged in manufacturing brassieres, girdles, corsets, corset accessories, and allied garments are included in this industry.

NAICS CODE(S)

315212 (Women's and Girls' Cut and Sew Apparel Contractors)
315231 (Women's and Girls' Cut and Sew Lingerie, Loungewear, and Nightwear Manufacturing)

INDUSTRY SNAPSHOT

As the twentieth century came to a close, U.S. sales of brassieres, girdles, and allied garments far exceeded apparel sales. Bra sales rose by 50 percent in the last half of the 1990s, compared with 20 percent for the apparel industry as a whole. The introduction of new lines of sports bras contributed to this increase.

During its century of existence, the bra and allied garment industry had a number of ups and downs, influenced by a variety of factors—only some of them style-based. During World War II, for example, the cotton, rubber, silk, and steel used to make women's undergarments were needed instead for the war effort. The bra and girdle industry was forced to develop new products that made use of synthetic fabrics.

Although the braless look of the 1960s caused concern among manufacturers, who saw their profits literally going up in smoke during the burn the bra movement, bras and girdles did reappear—in different fabrics, shapes, and colors—and the industry remained strong. Fashion trends changed the shape of the bra and technology altered its fabric content, but the garment remained a big seller. In a 1989 tribute to the centennial of the bra, Life magazine estimated that more than half a million undergarments of this type were sold daily in the United States.

BACKGROUND AND DEVELOPMENT

The first bra was developed in France in 1889 by the corsetmaker Herminie Cadolle. Designed to replace the restrictive whalebone corsets that stylish women of the time were forced to wear, the bra supported a woman's breasts without constricting her diaphragm. Americans were introduced to the bra during the 1910s, the Flapper Era, when the ideal woman's silhouette was slim and boyish. An undergarment that would flatten a woman's breasts was an ideal accompaniment to the straight-cut, form-fitting flapper dress preferred by suffragettes and stylish debutantes in Europe.

The style was brought back to America, and in 1913 New York socialite Caresse Crosby designed a brassiere out of two handkerchiefs and silk ribbons. The patent for her design was registered in 1914. Shortly thereafter, it was purchased by the Connecticut-based Warner's Company for $1,500. Warner's, previously a corset company, became one of the first American manufacturers of the bra. Other companies followed, including the now-defunct Boyshform, whose name encompassed everything the new bra was supposed to do.

Until the 1930s, the bra was more or less a one size fits all product. Because of the manly styles of the 1920s, women did not want to emphasize the size or shape of their breasts; rather, they tried to conceal them. In the Depression era, however, fashion designers began to emphasize women's feminine form once again. Warner's introduced bras with fitted cups, ranging from A (small) to D (large) size, in 1935; other manufacturers quickly followed suit.

The rages of fashion shifted all the way from the World War I boyish look epitomized by the flappers, to the very womanly figure of such pinup girls as Betty Grable and Jane Russell during World War II. Even though the fabrics used to make bras and girdles—silk, cotton, and rubber—were reserved for the war effort, designers still found ways to manufacture bras and girdles that emphasized the curvaceous look favored by sweater girls and soldier boys.

Anecdotal evidence claimed that Howard Hughes's aeronautics firm once designed a bra for Jane Russell, star of the 1943 movie classic The Outlaw. Made of metal, the bra was heavy and uncomfortable, according to Russell, who claimed that she never wore it. But the use of metal did play an important role in the next phase of bra silhouettes. In 1946, undercup wiring was introduced. This engineering feat allowed bra designers to lift the bust even more, since the underwiring added extra support.

During the 1940s, bras were being manufactured by Maidenform Inc., founded in 1922; Playtex Apparel Inc., founded in 1932; Vanity Fair Mills Inc., founded in 1899; and other smaller companies including Bestform, founded in 1923; and Bali, founded in 1927.

Women's fashion took on a retro look in the postwar 1940s and 1950s, when returning soldiers reclaimed the workplace and many women returned to the role of homemaker. With sheath dresses that emphasized every curve of a woman's figure being shown in every fashion house in Europe and America, undergarment manufacturers introduced one-piece, constructed undergarments to hold in stomachs, nip in waists, and push-up busts. Another fashion favorite, the tight-bodiced, full-skirted dress, also required undergarments to pull in the waist and emphasize the bust.

During the 1950s, bra manufacturers experimented with a new look, the push-up bra, in which the cup section was cut in half, leaving the cleavage exposed. Usually strapless, to be worn under the strapless formal dresses so popular in the 1950s, the push-up bra gave every woman who wore it an ample-looking, high-bosomed silhouette. Cone-shaped bras, which emphasized a pointy-busted look, were also popular in the 1950s, and were returned to popularity briefly by singer Madonna in the late 1980s.

While bras changed in shape during the years they were manufactured by American companies, other undergarments also changed to keep up with the current styles. The Edwardian look of the last years of the nineteenth century and the first decade of the twentieth century involved the wearing of a firm foundation garment that pulled in the waist and supported the bust. Corsets of the 1920s flattened the figure, but they were often too long for the short dresses being worn by young women. In response, manufacturers developed corselettes—shorter corsets—as well as slide-on garter belts and other, even briefer, undergarments.

The technological innovations of the 1930s turned up in undergarments. Living Lastex, one of the earliest of the stretchy, shape-holding textiles, along with narrow, dependable zippers, allowed manufacturers to sell undergarments that not only helped a woman maintain a womanly shape, but also let her move and breathe with a bit more comfort. Panty girdles that were shaped like underpants were invented in the 1930s, to be worn under then more acceptable slacks and shorts.

Dior's New Look of the late 1940s and 1950s needed new-looking undergarments. To go with the cantilevered bras required by the new silhouette, women laced themselves into guepieres, or waist cinchers—a new back-laced corset. Also at this time the Merry Widow corset, an all-in-one bra and girdle combination that was popular at the end of the nineteenth century, was reintroduced. The industry giant Warner's was among the first manufacturers to make the new Merry Widow available to the masses by introducing them in retail stores in 1952.

The pulled-in, pushed-up look of the 1950s became the pulled-apart look of the 1960s, as women's liberation swept across America. Bras were suddenly seen as harnesses rather than supports, which held women back rather than up. Women's libbers burned bras in city streets. At the Miss America pageant of 1968—the height of the women's movement—protesters threw bras, girdles, and other symbols of enslavement, such as curlers and Cosmopolitan magazine, into a garbage can. Bras were out, and many women appeared in public without undergarments.

Bra and girdle manufacturers were undoubtedly concerned about their profits shrinking in the tide of the braless revolution. They worked hard at developing natural-looking undergarments, bras that held a woman's breasts without changing their natural shape, and minimal girdles. But it was not the revolutionary bra style that forced women back into underwear. Rather, it was the concern voiced by the medical community that women who went braless for a long period of time ran the risk of stretching their breast ligaments to a point where the breast would look elongated and feel uncomfortable.

Girdle manufacturers faced a revolution even more harmful than bra burning. It was the invention of pantyhose, all-in-one stockings and panties, which hurt manufacturers. Pantyhose did not require garters, garter belts, or girdles. Women's libbers, in fact almost every woman in the country, adopted pantyhose faster than anyone could possibly have foreseen.

As women became more confident about appearing in public without the entrapments of constricting undergarments, bra and girdle manufacturers had to scramble to keep up. Luckily, however, the exercise and fitness phenomenon of the 1970s and 1980s provided a new market for their wares.

Women and men throughout the United States became exercise fanatics, spurred on by such fitness gurus as Jane Fonda. Workout attire, such as sports bras, became popular. But for many women, especially those who suddenly found themselves part of the 24-hour-a-day corporate world, an exercise regimen was difficult to maintain on a regular basis. They needed help, and the bra and girdle manufacturers of America were prepared to support them with body suits, bras, body shapers (a synonym for girdle), and control-top underpants, all made of lycra, spandex, and other miracle synthetics.

By the late 1980s, the bra and girdle industry came almost full-circle as tastes and styles changed once again. Bras, girdles, and even corsets were popularized by performers such as Madonna, who almost single-handedly revived the bustiere industry; movies such as Dangerous Liaisons, in which the female characters were laced up in tight corsets; and couturiers who put their bras on the outside of dresses, rather than the inside.

Women's wear shipments, including bras and allied garments, were much lower than the industry average in the early 1990s. Among the factors affecting the growth of the industry were demographic trends; apparel expenses became a lower proportion of total personal expenditures for the baby-boom generation. These consumers reached the point in their lives when other expenses—mortgages and their children's college tuition, for example—began to take precedence over clothing purchases.

There was also a shift in consumer buying habits. Instead of patronizing retail stores, a majority of shoppers began making regular visits to discounters and off-price emporiums, where they could find bargains. Bra and girdle manufacturers began offering discount lines; although there might still be a small market for luxury underclothes, most women wanted to spend less on a bra than on an evening meal.

The fashion splurge of the 1980s, when expenditures on clothes practically doubled, was replaced with frugal shopping by recession-stressed consumers who frequented Kmart and Wal-Mart more often than designer boutiques and department stores. According to Standard and Poors Industry Survey's (1992), not only did the spending patterns of consumers change, but their buying patterns also took a new direction.

Basic apparel like T-shirts, sweatshirts, denims, and fleecewear were in, as were moderately priced name brands like Fruit-of-the-Loom and Van Heusen. The major manufacturers of bras and girdles began producing basic styles at popular prices, and in that way they were able to keep up with this latest trend.

Manufacturers of bras and girdles also realized that women and men would occasionally splurge on undergarments. Companies such as Victoria's Secret Stores and Gossard, manufacturer of the new super-uplift bra launched in 1994, continued to have success selling pure silk and lace undergarments for romantic occasions like Valentine's Day and honeymoons. They also served a number of women who desired a "little bit of femininity" under their business clothes.

Although the value of shipments of bras and allied garments increased 13 percent between 1987 and 1988, there was a 16 percent decline in the value of its shipments the following year. A modest 2 percent gain in 1989 to 1990 was offset by a 1 percent decline in 1990 to 1991.

As a result of the more frugal spending patterns of shoppers in the early and mid-1990s, discount stores held 30 percent of the bra market by 1997; bras were the most lucrative intimate apparel item of discounters. Chain stores accounted for 19.6 percent of the market, while department stores captured 18.7 percent. Between 1990 and 1997 bra sales at department stores increased 5 percent.

Mail order sales doubled from 1990 to 1999 due, in part, to the privacy afforded by mail order purchases. Catalog companies like Victoria's Secret depended on bras to generate 5.9 percent of catalog sales. By the end of the decade, mail order chains accounted for 13.4 percent of the bra market.

As manufacturers adjusted to meet consumer demands, the bra and allied garment industry grew slowly but steadily from shipment values of $1.2 billion in 1990 to shipment values of $1.8 billion in 1995.

CURRENT CONDITIONS

As the twenty-first century began, increasing bra sales made this segment one of the most dynamic in the apparel industry. Although traditional styles remained the strongest seller, the sales of sports bras was growing at a fast clip. Innovation in fabrics and the creation of styles and sizes to fit individual women was one of the reasons for the increase. Nike, for instance, introduced three styles of sports bras in 1999: external molded cups for full-busted women, internal structures for medium-busted women, and sculpted bras for small-to-medium-busted women. For the first time, these bra styles were available in varying cup and rib-cage sizes, and with adjustable straps.

Discount stores continued to account for the largest percentage of sales, generating 29 percent of dollars spent. Most of the major manufacturers also created Web sites in light of the popularity of online shopping. Intimate Brands' Victoria's Secret created a stir during the 1999 Super Bowl with its online fashion show. Over a million and a half people logged on to the site.

INDUSTRY LEADERS

One of the largest manufacturers of bras and related intimate apparel in the United States was New York City-based Warnaco, Inc., which markets under the Olga and Warner's label. Warnaco posted sales of $2 billion in 1998 and employed 21,000 workers. In 1996, the company acquired Lejaby, a $120 million European intimate apparel manufacturer. The acquisition allowed Warnaco to introduce its lucrative Calvin Klein underwear line in Europe. The company is headed by Linda Wachner, who purchased the company in a hostile takeover in 1986, thus becoming the first woman in the United States to buy and head a fortune 1000 company.

Playtex Apparel Inc. of Stamford, Connecticut, a subsidiary of the Sara Lee Corporation, posted sales of $400 million and employed 7,800 individuals in the latter half of the 1990s. Vanity Fair Mills Inc. of Monroeville, Alabama, a subsidiary of V.F. Corporation, had sales of $390 million and employed 8,500 people. Maidenform,

Inc. posted 1998 sales of $400 million and employed 8,900 workers. Bestform Foundations Inc., a privately held company based in Long Island, New York, had annual sales of $250 million and employed 2,220 in the late 1990s.

Intimate Brands, Inc, parent company of Victoria's Secret, reported sales of $4.2 billion in 1999. Victoria's Secret products are sold in about 800 stores in North America, through its catalog, and online.

RESEARCH AND TECHNOLOGY

Manufacturers of basic apparel, such as bras and girdles, were strong candidates for implementation of electronic data interchange (EDI) systems, which linked manufacturers with retailers via computer networks. Through these systems, retailers electronically scanned the bar codes on all merchandise as it was sold. Product data such as number, color, and size was transmitted automatically to manufacturers. EDI allowed manufacturers to plan production more efficiently and respond more quickly to consumer demand. Many such systems also provided for automatic replenishment, where manufacturers shipped replacement merchandise directly to retailers without the delay of processing paperwork. Manufacturers of basic apparel stood to gain most from EDI systems since their operations were more highly automated and less dependent upon fashion trends than other apparel manufacturers.

Environmental issues were another area of research that occupied bra and girdle manufacturers in the mid-1990s. The industry came under pressure to reduce the inks and dyes, fabric scrap, and packaging it used, which often ended up in landfills or water supplies. The industry responded by developing new production processes that reduced ink use and scrap, as well as reevaluating its packaging choices.

Consumer preferences also shifted toward natural, organically grown fabrics, so bra and girdle manufacturers increasingly tried to incorporate these materials into their garments. The increasing demand for well-fitting sports bras led to the use of high-tech fabrics such as LycraPower developed by DuPont and combinations of nylon, lycra, and polyester designed to absorb moisture.

FURTHER READING

Apparel Import Digest. Arlington, VA: American Apparel Manufacturers Association, 1997.

Apparel Industry Trends. Arlington, VA: American Apparel Manufacturers Association, March 1997.

Brady, Jennifer L. "Analysts: Apparel on Slow Road to Recovery." *Women's Wear Daily,* 13 May 1996.

Curan, Catherine. "Linda J. Wachner: Lingerie's first lady cut from strong cloth." *Crain's New York Business,* 27 September 1999.

DeMartini, Marilyn. "Basic training." *Sporting Goods Business,* 4 February 1998.

———. "Designs for Lifting: Innovations in brassiere technology improve on nature and boost sales." *Time International,* 31 May 1999.

———. "Victoria's Secret Seamless Bra Sews Up Sales." *Women's Wear Daily,* 8 May 1996.

Feitelberg, Rosemary. "Hyping Inner Actives." *Women's Wear Daily,* 19 April 1999.

Focus: An Economic Profile of the Apparel Industry. Arlington, VA: American Apparel Manufacturers Association, 1996.

Friedman, Arthur. "NPD: Price, Brands Drive Bra Sales." *Women's Wear Daily,* 5 October 1998.

Grish, Kristina. "Bra companies run with tech fabrics." *Sporting Goods Business,* 7 August 1997.

"Intimate Scores at Mass." *Women's Wear Daily,* 8 May 1996.

SIC 2353

HATS, CAPS, AND MILLINERY

This category includes establishments primarily engaged in the manufacture of hats, caps, millinery, and hat bodies. Establishments primarily engaged in manufacturing millinery trimmings are classified in **SIC 2396: Automotive Trimmings, Apparel Findings, and Related Products.** Establishments primarily engaged in manufacturing hats and caps of paper are classified in **SIC 2679: Converted Paper and Paperboard Products, Not Elsewhere Classified;** those manufacturing caps of rubber are classified in **SIC 3069: Fabricated Rubber Products, Not Elsewhere Classified;** those manufacturing caps of plastics are classified in **SIC 3089: Plastic Products, Not Elsewhere Classified;** and those manufacturing fur hats are classified in **SIC 2371: Fur Goods.**

NAICS CODE(S)

315991 (Hat, Cap, and Millinery Manufacturing)

INDUSTRY SNAPSHOT

Approximately 389 establishments were engaged in the manufacture of hats, caps, and millinery (the design, production, and sales of women's hats) in 1997. Altogether, these establishments were responsible for total product shipments estimated at $942.5 million. Total industry sales in 1987 were $663.0 million; in the past decade, the industry experienced a modest recovery, due in large part to the fad-driven popularity of team logo sports headwear. This was a welcome development for an industry whose fortunes had been steadily drifting downward since the early 1960s when there was a national trend toward hatlessness.

In addition to team logo sports headwear, the industry's output included straw harvest hats; jungle-cloth helmets; opera hats; panamas; and hat bodies made from fur-felt, straw, and wool-felt. To professional uniform services, the industry supplied chauffeur caps, police hats and caps (excluding protective headwear), and various other uniform hats and caps.

In the mid-1990s, hats began to be seen once again as fashionable accessories, and department-store hat sales increased. As fashion accessories, however, hats have always been subject to changing tastes. This was more of an issue for the industry in the late 1990s because even when a product achieved popularity, hats were not the fashion necessity they once were.

ORGANIZATION AND STRUCTURE

Of the 389 establishments engaged in the production of hats, caps, and millinery in 1997, 305 (78 percent) employed fewer than 50 employees. All together there were some 17,000 people employed in this industry (14,000 of whom were production workers). The average hourly wage was approximately $17 per hour.

According to the *1997 Census of Manufacturers,* the largest concentration of the industry's establishments was located in the mid-Atlantic region. In terms of the number of establishments per state, New York topped the others with 86, followed by California with 53, and Missouri with 37. Missouri, however, had the largest number of employees—3,245.

The industry leaders in 1998 give an idea of how the market shifted in just the past 10 to 15 years. Number one was Boston-based New Balance Athletic Shoe, Inc., with sales of $375 million and 1,100 employees. Second was Aris Isotoner of New York, with sales of $250 million and 200 employees. Hat Brands, Inc., which was ranked first in 1996, was ranked third in 1998, with sales (1999 estimate) of $180 million. Now known as Arena Brands, the company specialized in Western hats. These included Stetson and Resistol cowboy hats and Dobbs dress hats. "Name" hats obviously still carried a certain cachet, but sports and casual hats were still more popular.

In 1992 disaggregation of the industry's total output by its major product category indicated that cloth hats and caps, excluding millinery, accounted for a 56 percent share. Within this category, men's and boys' hats and caps dominated with 69 percent. It is important to note that the fad-driven growth in the sales of sports headwear bearing the team logos from the National Basketball Association, the National Football League, Major League Baseball, and the National College Athletic Association also fell within this major product category, but throughout the 1990s, their sales continued at a record pace.

The second major product category, accounting for 21 percent of the total output, was hats and hat bodies, except cloth and millinery. Next followed the classification of hats, caps, and millinery products, not specified by kind, accounting for 12 percent. The last major product category, responsible for 11 percent of the industry's total output, was millinery (women's, children's, and infants' trimmed hats made from hat bodies and other millinery materials). This included hats made from felt, straw, pile fabrics, and ribbon.

BACKGROUND AND DEVELOPMENT

Prior to the more recent era of hatlessness, which took root during the suburbanization wave of the 1950s and 1960s, no respectable man or woman would have thought of leaving the house without a hat. The question of whether the hat industry would survive or not was unheard of during this time. Instead, of vital concern to the successful firms competing in the industry was their ability to produce and market an unending procession of new styles or modified variations of current popular styles. Since the life of a hat as a fashion accessory was typically short, the faster a firm was able to get in and out of a hot-selling style proved the key to its success.

Although not totally isolated from historical forces of technological change sweeping through other apparel industries, up until the 1990s opportunities to mechanize and automate the industry had proven difficult. As a result, production methods frequently required a great deal of handwork; therefore, labor-intensive manufacture has long remained the industry's norm.

Men's Hats. As the twentieth century began, most men living in urban areas of the United States wore hats. During the first decade, men could choose from a large variety of hats with each style purported to reflect the wearer's personality. One of the most prominent was the "princely" brown or black derby hat, which was available in three basic styles. At the time, most successful or aspiring businessmen sported the derby look. One of the more notable was the financier J.P. Morgan, who popularized a flat-topped version of the derby.

The manufacture of the derby was a time-consuming and labor-intensive process. Made from felt treated with repeated applications of a shellac solution, the material was heated and then allowed to cool. As it cooled, it took on its stiffened state. Next came an oven process, which softened it to the touch, followed by an iron mold process. To press the hat into its distinctive derby shape, a rubber bag was inserted inside the hat into which cold water was forced. Finally, the hat's brim was curled through a highly skilled operation that required a set of specialized tools referred to as "shackles."

Almost as popular as the derby was the fedora, which was made from soft felt. Except for its shaping process, the fedora's manufacturing process mimicked many of the steps involved in producing a derby. The hat was available in black, brown, and gray and received its name from the popular drama *Fedora,* penned by Victorien Sardou.

Though derby and fedora hats were to remain popular U.S. favorites for decades to come, a challenge to their popularity arrived in the form of the homburg. Made popular by King Edward's recreational visits to the town of Homburg in southern Germany, the homburg was of Tyrolean origin and featured a small brightly colored feather in its side band's bow. By the time the hat achieved mass appeal, it was mostly available in black and was worn with an informal evening jacket.

During the 1920s the U.S. men's fashion scene was heavily influenced by the British, particularly items connected to the pastimes of the Prince of Wales or associated with displays of wealth. For instance, in 1925, the English international tennis team showed up to play in Newport, Rhode Island, wearing brown snap-brim soft felt hats that the prince, just a short time earlier, had been seen vacationing in. These hats became the rage with wealthy crowds frequenting tennis matches and then proceeded to gain mass U.S. appeal. As an emphasis on dressing in style for leisure events and travel to warmer climates of the United States became more popular, panamas, which were woven from such lightweight materials as oatmeal, coconut, and rice straws, increased in popularity. Bangkoks and Ballibuntals, made from bamboo grasses or bamboo saplings growing wild in the Philippines, also became popular. Another lightweight favorite were Milan hats, made from Tuscan straw grown in Italy. Woven loosely, these hats offered protection from the sun and allowed for good ventilation.

Except for the affluent few, the era of the Great Depression knocked the demand out of the market for hats. Just the same, British fashion influences continued, as was evidenced by the sensation created by the "porkpie" hat's arrival in 1934. A low-crowned hat of the telescope type and made from felt, the porkpie was first worn by well-to-do men who frequented polo games and horse races. Within a short time, the porkpie hat was accepted as appropriate attire for either business or casual settings. After its initial introduction in felt, the porkpie later became available in a variety of straws, including panamas, leghorns, and bangkoks.

Caps worn for purposes other than work also became popular during this decade. The checkered cap was deemed appropriate for golf and weekend motoring. For hunters, fishing enthusiasts, and country sports spectators, rough tweed caps were fashionable. Regardless of whether it was worn for work or leisure purposes, the production process for cloth-cap manufacture was practically the same. Cloth was cut by hand, usually with a manually operated knife, to ensure a precision pattern. The pieces were then sewn carefully to ensure that the cloth's design matched, with special attention paid to where the crown joined the visor. The cap was then steamed and ironed. Additional leather and linings were sewn in during the finishing stages. Should the cap be unlined, the crown seams were filled with tape so the threads did not appear on the outside of the cap.

With economic production geared toward military purposes, the war years of the 1940s witnessed little change in terms of style or material in men's hats. For the remainder of the decade, the war's aftershocks continued a dulling effect on the industry. By the early 1950s, the advent of manmade fabrics—many of which were washable and lightweight—dramatically transformed the material base from which most apparel garments were constructed. In turn, the reigning emphasis on lightweight materials translated into a boom for straw hats. Around the same time, the popularity of the low-crown porkpie hat increased, and the wearing of the small-shape strip tweed cap outside of its more narrowly defined traditional sporting events boundaries was common. By the decade's end, hats made from manmade material (such as nylon) displaced straw hats as they proved lighter in weight and came with more ventilation and durability.

The reversals in the industry's millinery branch appeared to be the most permanent. Although there were several short-lived, fad-driven waves, these were hardly sufficient to restore millinery back to the level of its formative years in the 1950s, when more than 400 companies supplied hats worn by the majority of U.S. women. By 1989 fewer than 80 companies produced millinery articles.

In the mid-1990s hats began to sell again as fashion accessories. To promote hats, 10 independent Chicago hatmakers formed the Millinery Arts Alliance in 1995. As department store sales increased in both 1994 and 1995, the industry seemed to be turning itself around, although to what level was still speculative. By 1997 graduates of New York's Fashion Institute of Technology, the only domestic school with a two-year millinery program, reached 500, 20 times the number of graduates in 1987.

Men's and boys' team logo sports headwear was the only other area breathing life into the struggling industry. Coupled with the increase in sales of hats as fashion accessories, this may have been sufficient enough to warrant a more optimistic outlook for the industry as a whole since data tracking the value of the industry's shipments for the period of 1987 to 1994 had risen significantly. In 1994 some of the top U.S. firms with leading market shares in the sports headwear market were: American Needle, Starter, Logo 7, A.J.D Cap, Drew Pearson, and Apex. In an effort to eliminate the high cost of sewing labor, some firms were experimenting with heat applied techniques to join sports headwear fabrics. The result of these undertakings were mixed as some products proved to be of inferior quality.

CURRENT CONDITIONS

As to what impact the market turnaround of the late 1980s and early and mid-1990s would have on the industry's domestic workforce was uncertain. For the most part, the leading firms in the sports headwear market became increasingly involved in foreign outsourcing, so while the industry's U.S. based firms might prosper, the same could not be said for its U.S. workforce. Add to the mix the passage of the North American Free Trade Agreement (NAFTA) and the trade-stimulating accord reached in the 1993 Uruguay Round of the General Agreement on Tariffs and Trade (GATT) and the near future domestic employment picture looked less than promising.

One pathbreaking technology figuring largely in all sports headwear firms' success came with the introduction of quick response (QR) systems. Seldom has a system been devised that was so in line with the apparel industry's business climate where rapid change, high-stakes risk, and oftentimes fickle consumer behavior play so important a role. By design, QR programs electronically linked textile manufacturers, apparel producers, and retailers into a computerized information network analyzing consumer sales information. Its ultimate purpose was intended to considerably shorten the turnaround time it took for hot-selling items to arrive in retail stores, minimize systemwide inventory levels, and reduce or eliminate slow-moving articles to prevent unwanted markdown. Other technological inroads were being forged through the application of computer aided design and manufacture and laser beams used to cut cloth.

After the World Trade Organization was established in 1995, the Multifiber Arrangement (MFA)—which allowed importing countries to limit the flow of imports from lower cost, developing countries—was replaced by the Agreement on Textiles and Clothing (ATC), which required the phasing out of MFA quotas over a 10-year period. According to Linda Shelton in an *Industry, Trade, and Technology Review* report, "The elimination of MFA quotas likely will have a significant impact on the U.S. textile and apparel sector given the level of protection that such restrictions have provided domestic producers over the past two decades." Since the United States had until 2005 to implement the ATC, the legislation's impact on the women's apparel industry might not be realized for several years.

WORKFORCE

In 1987 the industry's total employment was 17,200 people, of which 14,600 were classified as production workers. Employment levels dropped off in the early 1990s but picked up later in the decade. Interestingly, however, the number of production workers remained relatively steady through this period, which suggested that any job loss was confined to management personnel. During the same period, when compared to other apparel industries—most of which experienced higher levels of decline for the categories of total employment and production workers—the hats, caps, and millinery industry fared rather well. To a large extent, the reversal of the industry's fortunes after several decades of decline could be attributed to the growing influence of team logo sports headwear sales and the resurgence of hats as fashion accessories in the mid-1990s.

According to the Bureau of Labor Statistics (BLS), sewing-machine operators by far constituted the industry's largest occupational category in 1996, accounting for 55.5 percent of all occupations. Several other occupational categories that fell just slightly above or below the 3.0 percent level were precision inspectors, testers, and graders; blue-collar work supervisors; and pressing-machine operators. Traffic, shipping, and receiving clerks accounted for 2.1 percent of all occupational categories. Based on the expectation that the industry would continue along a moderate path of productivity growth, a BLS survey forecasting the growth of the industry's occupational categories until the year 2006 indicated negative growth for all categories, with sales-related occupations being the lone exception. Sewing-machine and pressing-machine operators were projected to be the hardest hit as improvements in sewing technologies and new stitch-free techniques would exercise a displacing effect.

The industry's workforce demographics, especially in terms of its race and gender components, bore little relationship to their national average counterparts for the manufacturing sector taken as a whole. According to research conducted by the American Apparel Manufacturers Association in 1995, women made up 70.0 percent of the industry's workforce against a national manufacturing average of 31.6 percent. Workers of Hispanic origin accounted for 25.7 percent of the industry's employment compared to a national manufacturing average of 10.2 percent. African Americans comprised only 14.4 percent of the industry's workforce. This figure was similar to the black participation rate for the apparel industry group as a whole and was also only slightly above the national manufacturing average of 10.4 percent.

FURTHER READING

Albrizio, Ann, with Osnat Lustig. *Classic Millinery Techniques.* New York: Random House, 1998.

Chandler, Susan. "Heady Days for Milliners." *Business Week,* 13 January 1997.

Focus: An Economic Profile of the Apparel Industry. Arlington, VA: American Apparel Manufacturers Association, 1996.

Shelton, Linda, and Robert Wallace. "World Textile and Apparel Trade: A New Era." *Industry, Trade, and Technology Review,* October 1996.

U.S. Census Bureau. *Manufacturing—Industry Series,* 1999.

SIC 2361

GIRLS', CHILDREN'S, AND INFANTS' DRESSES, BLOUSES, AND SHIRTS

This category covers establishments that are primarily engaged in manufacturing girls', children's, and infants' dresses, blouses, and shirts from purchased woven or knit materials. Knitting mills primarily engaged in manufacturing outerwear are classified in **SIC 2253: Knit Outerwear Mills.**

NAICS CODE(S)

315291 (Infants' Cut and Sew Apparel Manufacturing)

315223 (Men's and Boys' Cut and Sew Shirt (except Work Shirt) Manufacturing)

315211 (Men's and Boys' Cut and Sew Apparel Contractors)

315232 (Women's and Girls' Cut and Sew Blouse and Shirt Manufacturing)

315233 (Women's and Girls' Cut and Sew Dress Manufacturing)

315212 (Women's and Girls' Cut and Sew Apparel Contractors)

INDUSTRY SNAPSHOT

There were approximately 776 establishments that manufactured the items covered in this category in 1999. As was true for much of the U.S. apparel industry, these establishments tended to be small, family-run businesses, and they faced stiff competition from low-cost imports. Against this backdrop, the baby-boomer generation was having children leading to its own miniboom, and these parents were better educated and had more disposable income than their parents—factors influencing their purchasing decisions for their children's clothing. Also, children's clothing had become more fashionable and trendy than ever before.

ORGANIZATION AND STRUCTURE

Establishments that produce children's clothing are organized similarly to the rest of the apparel industry and are composed of contractors, jobbers, and manufacturers.

Contractors are independent manufacturers, hired by various, and often competing, manufacturers. Contractors specialize in sewing garments from pieces provided to them and are hired by producers who either do not have their own sewing facilities or producers whose own capacity has been surpassed.

Jobbers are design and marketing businesses hired to perform specific functions, for example, to purchase materials, design patterns, create samples, cut material, or hire contractors to manufacture the products. The cut materials are then sent to contractors to be assembled.

Manufacturers are those establishments that perform all functions, that is, creating apparel from purchased materials. Manufacturers have staffs that produce designs or buy them from freelancers and then purchase the materials (fabric and trimmings) needed. Generally the cutting and sewing of the garment is done on site. When demand for an item, however, exceeds the manufacturer's capacity or if shipping deadlines cannot be met, outside contractors would be hired. Most manufacturers have their own sales and shipping staff.

Children's clothing sizes are divided into separate categories for specific age groups. Clothing for infants includes newborns up to age one; clothing for toddlers covers ages two to three; clothing for children covers ages three to six; and clothing for girls covers ages seven to 14. Children's apparel manufacturers generally produce one line per season, typically creating four lines a year—winter, spring, summer, and fall.

BACKGROUND AND DEVELOPMENT

The children's wear industry developed early in the twentieth century around the same time as the women's apparel industry. As women joined the professional workforce, they turned away from making their own clothes, and they stopped sewing their children's clothing as well. Over time, children's clothing became more durable and the sizes became standardized.

A significant factor affecting the development of children's wear was the growing importance of television in children's lives after World War II. Children could emulate what other children wore on television, and they could be appealed to directly through advertising. Children began to demand a greater influence over the clothing their parents purchased for them and often asked for stylish and fashionable clothing. They became independent consumers themselves and were often very fashion conscious and brand-name aware.

The number of workers employed in this industry dropped throughout the 1980s even as the value of shipments rose. As in other sectors of the apparel industry, increased consolidation and the strength of imported clothing contributed to this trend. The value of shipments grew from $1.4 billion in 1982 to an estimated $5.2 billion in 1997.

The recession that began in the apparel industry in the late 1980s particularly affected children's apparel producers. Domestic manufacturers were hard hit while imports slowed only moderately. Nevertheless, it was expected that children's apparel sales would continue to increase as parents, grandparents, and children themselves purchased clothing manufactured in this industry.

CURRENT CONDITIONS

A solid U.S. economy, growing at a slow, steady pace throughout the 1990s, provided the apparel industry with low unemployment rates, along with low inflation and low interest rates. Consumer confidence and spending was high, and government forecasts called for continued solid growth. Between 1992 and 1997, however, personal consumption expenditures grew at an average annual rate of 5.4 percent, compared to a growth of only 4.2 percent for expenditures on clothing. There was a significant slowdown from the rate of growth experienced in the 1980s for apparel expenditures. Consumer buying habits shifted to shopping at discounters and off-price outlets. Lack of time, due to work schedules and preferences to spend more leisure time with family and friends, led many consumers to increasingly shop through the mail and over the Internet.

INDUSTRY LEADERS

OshKosh B'Gosh, Inc. was a dominant force in the children's apparel industry in the late 1990s. It operated more than 120 outlet and specialty stores as well as an online shopping site. In 1998 the company reported sales revenues of 423.2 million, an increase of 7.1 percent over 1997. The number of employees for 1998 was 3,800, an increase of 5 percent over 1997. The company made colorful clothing for children and still produced the overalls it had turned out since the late 1800s.

Another leading manufacturer in this category was The William Carter Company, a private company founded in 1864 and acquired in 1996 by Investcorp. The company's estimated revenues for 1998 were $408.2 million, an increase of 12.5 percent over 1997. Carter produced children's apparel under its own name as well as licensed apparel under several brands, including the Christian Dior and Campbell Kids labels. Carter manufactured newborn layette clothing, sleepwear, playwear, underwear, diaper bags, strollers, hair accessories, and shoes. The company operated approximately 145 outlet stores in the United States.

Gerber Childrenswear Inc. also produced clothing for children. Gerber reported revenues of $278.5 million in 1998, an increase of 37.8 percent over 1997. Gerber had 3,250 employees in 1998, an increase of 1.5 percent

over 1997. Gerber Childrenswear manufactured sleepers, cloth diapers, bedding, footwear, swimwear, layettes, playwear, underwear, knitwear, and vinyl baby pants.

WORKFORCE

The number of employees in this category declined throughout the 1980s. From 1982 to 1995, employment in this category fell from 38,000 people to an estimated 29,720 in 1997. California had the most establishments in this category with 288 establishments employing approximately 11,000 workers. New York had approximately 259 such establishments, employing about 10,000 workers, in 1997. Other states with noteworthy concentrations of workers in this category were Florida, Texas, and Pennsylvania.

AMERICA AND THE WORLD

The U.S. children's apparel industry began to lose significant market share to imports in the 1960s as did other sectors of the apparel industry; imports were attractive to consumers because of their lower prices and acceptable quality. The process began to accelerate in the 1970s and, by the 1990s, imports had reached all-time highs. Also contributing to the industry's decline in the United States was the reliance of manufacturers on offshore assembly of pieces cut in the United States.

More imports entered the United States under Provision 9802 of the U.S. Harmonized Tariffs Schedule (formerly known as Section 807). This provision allowed clothing assembled abroad (from pieces cut in the United States and then exported) to be reimported with duty paid for the value added abroad. Thus, the most labor-intensive part of the assembly process could be done at lower-wage rates but both import and export data were skewed. Many U.S. manufacturers were taking advantage of Provision 9802 and moving assembly operations to the Caribbean, noting that they could reduce costs and more successfully compete against imports from Asia. By 1992 garments manufactured in this manner comprised 14 percent of apparel imports. The passage of the North American Free Trade Agreement (NAFTA)—ratified in 1993 to create a free-trade zone between the United States, Mexico, and Canada by gradually eliminating tariffs over 15 years—however, led some to expect that the Caribbean would be a less desirable manufacturing destination than Mexico.

Asia-based manufacturers represented a significant source of children's apparel. When apparel makers started to move their manufacturing bases out of the United States in the 1960s, they first went to Hong Kong, Taiwan, and South Korea to take advantage of the cheap labor there. By the 1980s however, labor costs had increased, and capital and operations from those traditionally low-wage markets moved to lower wage countries such as Bangladesh, Thailand, Pakistan, Indonesia, Malaysia, Sri Lanka, and India, which became the sources for more of the imports entering the United States. By the early 1990s China replaced Hong Kong as the greatest supplier of imports to the United States. By 1997, Mexico, due to NAFTA, increased its imports to the point of surpassing Hong Kong as the second-greatest supplier of apparel imports to the United States.

The impact of the Asian financial crisis of the late 1990s created great uncertainty in the global apparel market. The five main countries affected by this crisis were Indonesia, Korea, Thailand, the Philippines, and Malaysia, and they were all important apparel producers. Because of the devaluation of the currencies, their products became less expensive, and it placed downward pressure on the pricing of products from competitor countries.

Employment in the apparel industry overall remained on a downward trend in 1997, even though exports had a modest expansion. Although technology improvements increased productivity in this industry, the manufacturing process is labor-intensive. As compared to other manufacturing industries, wages and profit margins were low. The earnings of employees in this industry were approximately 38 percent lower than employees of any other U.S. manufacturing industry. In the late 1990s, the Union of Needletrades, Industrial, and Textile Employees (UNITE) and the Clothing Manufacturers Association reached an agreement on a contract covering 25,000 tailored clothing workers that would provide a pay hike of 65 cents per hour over three years.

In 1997, as a result of concern about working conditions in the apparel industry, President Bill Clinton announced an agreement, the Apparel Industry Partnership, among industry, labor, and consumer and human rights officials that offered a voluntary code of conduct intended to uphold workers' rights in the United States and abroad. This code of conduct included a guaranteed minimum or prevailing industry wage, a maximum 60-hour workweek, and a prohibition against employing persons younger than 15 years of age.

RESEARCH AND TECHNOLOGY

In the battle against imports, U.S. apparel makers tried a variety of stratagems, including increased use of automation, delivering higher quality goods, and trying to more closely keep track of the consumers' needs and desires. Although the intrinsic "soft" quality of material made the extensive use of automated equipment difficult, most of the larger manufacturers tried to invest in newer machinery to improve efficiency. Nevertheless, apparel manufacture remained a highly labor-intensive industry.

One tool that was advocated to better meet the market's demands was "quick response": the idea of bringing apparel to the retailer rapidly by shortening the production cycle, reducing inventories, improving productivity, and sending information regarding consumers' preferences quickly back to the manufacturers, and thus avoiding overstocking. By using computers to track inventory and sales as well as consumers' responses to particular items, the ability to respond quickly to market demand—and thus get a jump on foreign producers often half a world away—domestic manufacturers could minimize their vulnerability to imports. Department stores and manufacturers worked together to find ways to speed deliveries and increase efficiency. Mass merchandisers were among the first to implement quick response systems.

The U.S. government was also assisting the industry with developing and applying new technologies. The American Textile Partnership was a joint venture between the industry and the U.S. Department of Energy to link textile mills, apparel manufacturers, wholesalers, and retailers in an electronic network that would allow all industry segments to respond more quickly to consumer spending patterns.

FURTHER READING

Baby and Junior: International Trade Magazine for Children's Fashions. Bamberg, Germany: Meisenbach GMBH, 1999.

Conditions in the Women's Garment Industry. International Ladies' Garment Workers' Union.

Earnshaw's Infants, Girls and Boys Wear Review. New York: Earnshaw Publications, Inc.

Fairchild Fact File: Children's Market, Infants', Toddlers', Girls', and Boys'—Apparel, Juvenile Products, Toys/Dolls. New York: Fairchild Publications, Inc.

SIC 2369

GIRLS', CHILDREN'S, AND INFANTS' OUTERWEAR, NOT ELSEWHERE CLASSIFIED

This category includes establishments primarily engaged in manufacturing girls', children's, and infants' outerwear, not elsewhere classified, from purchased woven or knit fabrics. This includes, but is not limited to, bathing suits, jeans, jogging suits, playsuits, shorts, skirts, slacks, and sweatsuits. Knitting mills primarily engaged in manufacturing outerwear are classified under **SIC 2253: Knit Outwear Mills.**

NAICS CODE(S)

315291 (Infants' Cut and Sew Apparel Manufacturing)

315222 (Men's and Boys' Cut and Sew Suit, Coat, and Overcoat Manufacturing)

315224 (Men's and Boys' Cut and Sew Trouser, Slack, and Jean Manufacturing)

315228 (Men's and Boys' Cut and Sew Other Outerwear Manufacturing)

315221 (Men's and Boys' Cut and Sew Underwear and Nightwear Manufacturing)

315211 (Men's and Boys' Cut and Sew Apparel Contractors)

315234 (Women's and Girls' Cut and Sew Suit, Coat, Tailored Jacket and Skirt Manufacturing)

315238 (Women's and Girls' Cut and Sew Other Outerwear Manufacturing)

315231 (Women's and Girls' Cut and Sew Lingerie, Loungewear, and Nightwear Manufacturing)

315212 (Women's and Girls' Cut and Sew Apparel Contractors)

INDUSTRY SNAPSHOT

In 1999 there were approximately 872 companies engaged in the production of clothing covered in this category. Of this, there were 121 establishments that either had more than 180 employees or more than $9 million in sales. The number of companies in this category steadily declined throughout the 1980s, because, as with much of the U.S. apparel industry, manufacturers faced stiff competition from low-cost imports. Nevertheless, during this time, a well-educated baby-boomer generation, with more disposable income than their parents had, were themselves having children and spending increasing amounts on children's clothing. Consequently, children's clothing became more fashion-oriented and expensive, as reflected in total industry shipments that totaled approximately $8 billion in 1997.

ORGANIZATION AND STRUCTURE

Clothing lines in this industry include "infant wear" for babies up to one year in age, "toddlers' wear" for children from ages two to three, "children's wear" for ages three to six, and "girls' wear" for girls between the ages of seven and fourteen. Children's apparel manufacturers generally produce one new line of clothing per season (spring, summer, winter, and fall) or four lines per year.

Establishments producing children's clothing are comprised of contractors, jobbers, and manufacturers. Contractors are independent manufacturers, hired by various—usually competing—manufacturers. Contractors specialize in sewing the garment from pieces provided to them and are hired by producers who either do not have their own sewing facilities or producers whose own capacity has been superseded.

Jobbers are design and marketing businesses hired to perform specific functions, including purchasing materials, designing patterns, creating samples, cutting material, and hiring contractors to manufacture product. After purchasing materials needed to produce the pieces, jobbers then send the cut material to contractors for assembly.

When creating apparel from the purchased materials, manufacturers retain staffs either to produce designs or buy them from freelancers, as well as to purchase the fabric and trimmings. While cutting and sewing the garment is generally performed in the manufacturer's factories, outside contractors are hired when demand for an item exceeds the manufacturer's capacity or shipping deadlines cannot be met. For the purposes of this entry, the term "manufacturers" will refer cumulatively to contractors, jobbers, and manufacturers.

BACKGROUND AND DEVELOPMENT

Children's apparel production developed early in the twentieth century, concurrent with the emergence of the women's apparel industry. During this time, as women joined the professional workforce in increasing numbers, they had less time for sewing their own or their children's clothing. Advances in the industry eventually led to the production of more durable children's clothing available in standardized sizes.

The growing popularity of television during the 1950s, particularly among children, provided a boost to the children's apparel industry. Not only did young people begin to emulate fashions worn by their peers on television, but they were especially responsive to advertising. During this time, children assumed a greater role in choosing the clothing purchased for them by their parents. Moreover, children came to represent an independent consumer market, purchasing clothing themselves with the money they received as gifts or for allowances. In the 1990s practically every major character on children's television shows or in the movies had a line of clothing available.

CURRENT CONDITIONS

The number of employees in the industry dropped throughout the 1980s as the value of shipments rose. As in other sectors of the apparel industry, increased consolidation and the popularity of imported clothing contributed to downsizing in the industry. In the late 1990s, however, employment in this industry appeared to be increasing.

The economic recession of the early 1990s particularly affected children's apparel producers; domestic manufacturers were hard hit while imports slowed only moderately. Nevertheless, analysts expected sales of children's apparel to continue to increase as parents, grandparents, and children themselves purchased more clothing for the offspring of the baby-boom generation.

INDUSTRY LEADERS

OshKosh B'Gosh, Inc. was a dominant force in the children's apparel industry in the late 1990s. It operated more than 120 outlet and specialty stores as well as an online shopping site. In 1998 the company reported sales revenues of 423.2 million, an increase of 7.1 percent over 1997. The number of employees for 1998 was 3,800, an increase of 5 percent over 1997. The company made colorful clothing for children, and still produced the overalls it had turned out since the late 1800s.

Another leading manufacturer in this category was The William Carter Company, a private company founded in 1864 and acquired in 1996 by Investcorp. The company's estimated revenues for 1998 were $408.2 million, an increase of 12.5 percent over 1997. Carter produced children's apparel under its own name as well as licensed apparel under several brands, including the Christian Dior and Campbell Kids labels. The William Carter Company manufactured newborn layette clothing, sleepwear, playwear, underwear, diaper bags, strollers, hair accessories, and shoes. The company operated approximately 145 outlet stores in the United States.

Another industry leader, Buster Brown Apparel, Inc., became a private company in 1993 when it was sold by Gerber Products Company. Originally founded in 1903, Buster Brown was once a highly profitable company, but leaner times necessitated Gerber's sale in an effort to cut costs. Its revenues in 1993 were estimated at $150 million, and it employed approximately 3,200 people.

WORKFORCE

Total employment for 1997 was 56,834 people and most of those employed in this category were production workers, approximately half of whom were union members. Production workers consisted largely of sewing-machine operators, whose average wage in 1997 was $8.10 an hour. While many manufacturers in this sector of the apparel industry, as with the industry as a whole, were small, family-owned businesses, there were a number of large and growing establishments dominating the industry.

Although New York was the long-time center of the apparel business in the United States, in 1997 California overtook that position. That year, approximately 313 establishments, employing about 14,000 workers, were headquartered in California. New York had approximately 139 establishments, with Florida, Pennsylvania, and Texas also having significant concentrations of workers in this category.

AMERICA AND THE WORLD

In the 1960s the U.S. children's apparel industry began to lose significant market share to imports, which offered consumers lower prices and acceptable quality. This trend accelerated in the 1970s, and, by the 1990s, imports had reached all-time highs. Moreover, with U.S. manufacturers relying more heavily on offshore assembly plants, the industry experienced further losses.

Manufacturers in the Far East represented a significant source of children's apparel. In the 1960s the U.S. children's apparel industry began moving manufacturing operations abroad, focusing on Hong Kong, Taiwan, and South Korea, where labor was cheap. By the 1980s, however, labor costs in these countries had increased and operations were moved to Bangladesh, Thailand, Pakistan, Indonesia, Malaysia, Sri Lanka, and India. By the early 1990s China replaced Hong Kong as the greatest supplier of imports to the United States. In the late 1990s, Asia remains the largest supplier of imports to the United States; Mexico's import growth, however, increased 278 percent between 1993 and 1997, and Caribbean imports increased 91 percent during that time.

The North American Free Trade Agreement (NAFTA)—ratified in 1993 to create a free-trade zone between the United States, Mexico, and Canada by gradually eliminating tariffs over 15 years—was generally supported by executives in the apparel industry. While the International Ladies' Garment Workers Union and other unions sought to stem the loss of jobs among Americans in the industry by limiting the imports allowed in the country, the free-market philosophy ultimately triumphed in the passage of NAFTA.

Throughout the 1990s, increasingly more imports entered the United States under provision 9802 (formerly known as Section 807) of the U.S. Harmonized Tariffs Schedule. This provision allowed clothing assembled abroad—from pieces cut in the United States and then exported—to be reimported with duty paid for the value added abroad. This meant that the most labor-intensive part of the assembly process could be accomplished for lower wages. Many U.S. manufacturers took advantage of provision 9802, moving assembly operations to the Caribbean, where they expected to reduce costs and more successfully compete against imports from Asia. While the process greatly decreased the turnaround time for assembling more complex clothing items, its logistics sometimes proved cumbersome and time-consuming as contractors in other countries managed the transportation, paperwork, and assembly required. Furthermore, the passage of NAFTA led some to expect that the Caribbean would largely be replaced by Mexico as a more desirable manufacturing destination.

In 1997, as a result of concern about working conditions in the apparel industry, President Bill Clinton announced an agreement—the Apparel Industry Partnership—among industry, labor, and consumer and human rights officials that offered a voluntary code of conduct intended to uphold workers' rights in the United States and abroad. This code of conduct included a guaranteed minimum or prevailing industry wage, a maximum 60-hour workweek, and a prohibition against employing persons younger than 15 years of age.

RESEARCH AND TECHNOLOGY

In the battle against imports, U.S. apparel makers tried several strategies, including increased use of automation, delivering higher quality goods, and trying to track consumers' needs and desires more closely. Although the intrinsic ''soft'' quality of material made the extensive use of automated equipment difficult, most of the larger manufacturers continually sought to invest in newer machinery to improve efficiency. Nevertheless, apparel manufacture remained a labor-intensive industry.

Another new strategy involved ''quick response,'' the idea that bringing apparel to the retailer more rapidly would shorten the production cycle, reduce inventories, improve productivity, and help manufacturers avoid overstocking by providing them with more timely information regarding consumers' preferences. Using computers to track inventory, sales, and consumer response, domestic manufacturers hoped to compete more effectively with importers. Department stores and manufacturers worked together to find ways to speed deliveries and increase efficiency.

FURTHER READING

Fairchild Fact File: Children's Market, Infants', Toddlers', Girls', and Boys' Apparel, Juvenile Products, Toys/Dolls. New York: Fairchild Publications, Inc., 1998.

OshKosh B'Gosh, Inc. Annual Report. Osh Kosh, WI: Osh Kosh B'Gosh, 1997.

U.S. International Trade Commission. *Industry & Trade Summary: Apparel.* Washington, DC: U.S. International Trade Commission, 1999.

SIC 2371

FUR GOODS

This category covers establishments primarily engaged in manufacturing fur coats, and other clothing, accessories, and trimmings made of fur. Those establishments that are primarily engaged in manufacturing sheep-lined clothing are classified in **SIC 2386: Leather and Sheep-Lined Clothing,** and those that are engaged in dyeing and dressing of furs are classified in **SIC 3999: Manufacturing Industries, Not Elsewhere Classified.**

NAICS CODE(S)

315292 (Fur and Leather Apparel Manufacturing)

Furs were once considered a luxury that only a few could afford. The huge influx of women entering the workforce in the 1970s, though, changed that perception forever. Their increased disposable income allowed many women to buy for themselves an item that historically had been purchased by men as gifts to their wives. After 1970 the U.S. fur market grew steadily and, by the 1980s, furs had surged in popularity.

Fur sales, however, dropped during most of the 1990s. Several factors contributed to this trend, including animal rights campaigns, warm winters, and a glut in the international fur market. The late 1990s saw a resurgence in interest in fur goods. Fur sales increased slightly, reaching their peak of $1.27 billion in 1997 and dropping slightly to $1.21 billion in 1998. The fur industry appeared to be in the midst of a renaissance, with interest in furs increasing worldwide. Fur goods caught the interest of several top clothing designers and many started to incorporate fur goods into their runway designs. In 1999 approximately 200 designers used fur goods in their lines, compared to 42 designers in 1985.

Internationally, the Chinese were emerging as a force to be reckoned with as both consumers and producers of fur goods. Hong Kong remained a force in fur exports and consumers in China started purchasing fur goods, focusing specifically on the darker pelts. Meanwhile Russia was struggling to maintain a presence in the international market. Farms in Russia produced only 4.5 tons of pelts in 1997 compared to the 12.0 tons produced six years previously. While Russians considered their pelts to be comparable to others on the market, they blamed the shift to a market economy for the poor processing of the pelts. In 1998 there were 96 farms in existence, compared to the 127 farms in production in 1992.

A surplus of pelts on the international market, a slow U.S. economy, warm winters, and price battles among retailers contributed to lower profits in the late 1980s. By 1991 U.S. fur sales had declined 44 percent from a high of $1.8 billion in 1987. Overproduction saw retail prices fall 40 percent below their peak of 1986. Animal rights groups—which had won much publicity in the 1980s with their advertising and public relations campaign against the fur industry, attempting to reduce the demand for fur—pointed to the declining numbers and claimed their campaign had been successful. Other analysts saw other factors (a series of mild winters, the slowdown of the economy, and a glut of pelts on the market) as much more important. By 1992 pelt prices began to turn around and the following year sales increased by 13 percent. In the early 1990s lower prices helped increase the unit sales of furs, but dollar sales remained constant. Some experts contended that in order for fur manufacturers to succeed in today's market, they needed to develop cross-promotional campaigns with other clothing manufacturers; in addition to the fur salons found in larger metropolitan areas, manufacturers needed to work closely with larger department stores such as Nordstrom's to raise awareness about fur goods among consumers.

By 1998 there were approximately 120 companies that manufactured fur goods in the United States, down from 503 in 1982. The number of workers employed by U.S. fur manufacturers plummeted from 2,600 in 1983 to 575 in 1997. More than half of those employed were sewing-machine operators. The industry was concentrated in the state of New York, with almost 90 percent of manufacturers based there in 1987. The four largest fur manufacturers and retailers were all located in New York: Mohl Fur Company, Inc.; Marc Kaufman; Associated Fur Manufacturers Co.; and J. Mendel Fourrure. According to the 1997 Economic Census, the majority of the industry continued to be family-operated companies with employees typically numbering fewer than 100.

Some industry analysts attributed the increase in fur sales in the late 1990s to a generally healthy economy and record snowfalls in the Northeast. In addition, the fur industry also saw a rise in worldwide fur prices, boding well for its future health. The threatened boycott by the European Union over U.S. use of leghold traps appeared to be on hold due to fear of challenge by the World Trade Organization.

FURTHER READING

"Commodities & Agriculture: Chinese Buyers Fill Fur Gap Left in Fur Market by Russians." *Financial Times,* 19 October 1999.

Emerson, Jim. "Fur Industry; Sidebar." *Direct,* September 1998.

Feitelberg, Rosemary. "Furriers Lament Spotty Season." *Women's Wear Daily,* 10 January 1995.

Munk, Nina. "Animal Magnetism." *Forbes,* 10 March 1997.

Riga, Andy. "Fur Industry Expects a Revival: Warm Winter Hurts Sales in 1997, Not the Anti-Fur Crusade: Group Says." *Gazette (Montreal),* 30 April 1998.

Rybak, Deborah Caufield. "Fur Flies Again Animal-Rights Activists Succeeded in Making Fur Unfashionable, but Designers Are Piling on the Pelts Again. Will Consumers Follow Suit?" *Star Tribune (Minneapolis),* 31 October 1999.

Sachs, Susan. "Russia's Riches-to-Rags Story/Fur Industry Takes Hit in Free Market." *Newsday,* 9 February 1998.

Schmitt, Jane. "Fur Coats, Accessories Gaining in Popularity." *Business First of Buffalo,* 15 November 1999.

Wilson, Eric. "Furriers Stress Fashion Over Function." *Women's Wear Daily,* 12 May 1998.

SIC 2381

DRESS AND WORK GLOVES, EXCEPT KNIT AND ALL-LEATHER

This industry includes establishments primarily engaged in manufacturing dress, semi-dress, and work gloves and mittens from purchased woven or knit fabrics, or from these materials combined with leather or plastics. Knitting mills primarily engaged in manufacturing gloves and mittens are classified in **SIC 2259: Knitting Mills, Not Elsewhere Classified;** establishments primarily engaged in manufacturing leather gloves are classified in **SIC 3151: Leather Gloves and Mittens;** those manufacturing sporting and athletic gloves are classified in **SIC 3949: Sporting and Athletic Goods, Not Elsewhere Classified;** and those manufacturing safety gloves are classified in **SIC 3842: Orthopedic, Prosthetic, and Surgical Appliances and Supplies.**

NAICS CODE(S)

315992 (Glove and Mitten Manufacturing)

Glove manufacturers produce gloves for a variety of purposes, ranging from the functional to the purely ornamental. Because of their utility in work, industry, fashion, and casual apparel, gloves have been a popular accessory for men, women, and children for centuries.

Gloves have been used since the fourteenth century B.C. Linen gloves were found in the tomb of King Tutankhamen. These accessories have served many purposes for both men and women throughout history and once were among the costliest items of clothing. In 1834 Xavier Jouvin, a French glove maker, invented a press that could cut six gloves simultaneously, bringing down the cost and increasing their popularity and availability. About 100 years later, the Singer Co. introduced the Pique sewing machine, designed with a thin post that held the glove for sewing the fingers.

During the first half of the twentieth century, Gloversville, New York, and the surrounding Fulton County region was considered the glove capital of the world, with around 300 manufacturing companies producing 90 percent of the world's leather gloves. Shortly thereafter, the glove industry had to move production offshore to become more competitive due to rising labor costs. This move began in the 1950s and continued into the 1990s, to places like the Philippines, India, and eventually China. During 1999 glove companies began targeting niche markets, such as specialty gloves for the government, using U.S. production in Gloversville.

The two major types of gloves include work or industrial gloves and casual or dress gloves. Casual and dress gloves are different from work gloves in many ways. Unlike their more durable counterparts, they are made from finer fabrics and weaves—including linen, silk, and fine weaves of cotton and wool. Their popularity as an accessory rises and falls according to the dictates of fashion.

Since industrial gloves are designed to provide protection, they are constructed of more durable materials, such as cotton, wool, or leather. In 1999, the American National Standards Institute and the Industrial Safety Equipment Association issued a hand protection standard ANSI/ISEA 105-1999. This standard provides glove selection criteria in 12 specific categories related to testing and performance properties, including puncture resistance, abrasion, protection from heat and cold, and chemical resistance.

Some of the leading work glove manufacturers in the late 1990s were Best Glove Manufacturing, Wells Lamont, Southern Glove Manufacturing, and Magid Glove and Safety Manufacturing. These companies shipped products directly to industries and retailers throughout the year. In 1998 Wells Lamont, an Illinois-based glove manufacturer, posted sales of $110 million and employed 2,000 workers.

In 1997, there were 80 establishments producing dress and work gloves valued at over $438 million, up from 73 in 1995. The value of shipments in 1998 was estimated at $400 million, which was expected to increase to roughly $428 million by 2000.

Employment by manufacturers of dress and work gloves has been on the decline since 1995, which was predicted to continue to decrease to a total of 2,200 workers by 2000. About 1,700 of these will be in production. North Carolina, Mississippi, and New York are the top producing states.

FURTHER READING

Fernberg, Patricia. "Standard Promotes Proper Selection." *Occupationa Hazards,* August 1998, 33.

"Glove Story." *Connoisseur,* February 1988, 65.

Rabon, Lisa. "Glovers Grip New Markets to Keep Their Hands in the Industry." *Bobbin,* January 1998, 24-29.

U.S. Department of Commerce. Census Bureau. *1995 Annual Survey of Manufactures.* Washington, D.C.: GPO, 1997.

SIC 2384

ROBES AND DRESSING GOWNS

Establishments in this industry are primarily engaged in manufacturing men's, boys', and women's robes and dressing gowns from purchased materials and

fabrics. This classification includes the manufacturing of bathrobes, caftans, housecoats, dusters, lounging robes, and men's smoking jackets. Companies primarily engaged in manufacturing girls', children's, and infants' robes from purchased fabrics are classified in **SIC 2369: Girls', Children's, and Infants' Outerwear, Not Elsewhere Classified.** Knitting mills which manufacture robes and dressing gowns are classified in **SIC 2253: Knit Outerwear Mills.**

NAICS CODE(S)

315231 (Women's and Girls' Cut and Sew Lingerie, Loungewear, and Nightwear Manufacturing)
315221 (Men's and Boys' Cut and Sew Underwear and Nightwear Manufacturing)
315211 (Men's and Boys' Cut and Sew Apparel Contractors)
315212 (Women's and Girls' Cut and Sew Apparel Contractors)

In 1997 there were more than 65 establishments in this industry, generating more than $300 million in sales and employing 6,000 workers.

The top three industry leaders for this category were Lillian Vernon of Rye, New York, with sales of $255 million for its fiscal year ended February 27, 1999; New York City-based NAP Inc., with sales of $100 million for 1997; and New York City-based Host Apparel Inc., with 1998 sales of $80 million. Other significant companies in the industry included New York City-based Movie Star Inc.; Russell-Newman Inc. of Denton, Texas; and Leading Lady Companies Inc. of Beachwood, Ohio.

In contrast with figures for 1993, this industry's sales decreased by $138 million and the number of workers decreased by 30 percent in 1996. Imported robes and loungewear competed for the domestic manufacturers' department-store market share, and some department stores had begun to contract with foreign mills to issue their own insignia bathrobes. In one instance in early 1997, this cost the Neiman Marcus Group almost $2 million in sales when 6,500 terry-cloth bathrobes were recalled at the request of the U.S. Consumer Products Safety Commission when the garments failed flammability tests, igniting upon exposure to flame.

In the mid-1990s, large leisure wear manufacturers also began expanding to include robes and loungewear for men and women, providing additional market competition for the dedicated robe and dressing gown manufacturers in the United States. Famous athletic name-brand robes matching their shoes became available in large department store chains as well as specialty shops for lingerie, sporting goods, and mail-order catalogs. Sports and leisure apparel outside of this primary category have enjoyed a significant increase in sales throughout the 1990s due to their diversification. Robe manufacturers experienced increased business from hotel-chain orders, particularly where terry-cloth towels are also provided.

While exact figures are not available, employment in this industry has been on the decline since the late 1970s. In 1995, more than 82 percent of this industry's workforce was comprised of production workers.

American companies manufacturing robes and dressing gowns have long been in competition with overseas manufacturing, mostly from China and Taiwan. In 1993, more than half of the robes and gowns sold in America were imported. American exports of these products have traditionally been small; however, their numbers increased to 9 percent of U.S. products in this apparel sector. American exports were expected to be one of the main factors in increased production in this industry by the end of the twentieth century.

Technological advances have helped manufacturers of robes and dressing gowns improve efficiency in production and distribution of their goods. Three areas in particular have been improved in this industry with technological developments: computer-aided design, production, and communications; modular manufacturing systems; and ergonomics (workplace equipment designed with respect to worker health and safety).

FURTHER READING

U.S. Census Bureau. ''1997 Economic Census, Manufacturing Industry Series.'' Washington D.C.: GPO, 1997.

U.S. Department of Commerce. *1995 Annual Survey of Manufactures.* Washington, D.C.: GPO, 1997.

SIC 2385

WATERPROOF OUTERWEAR

This category includes establishments primarily engaged in manufacturing raincoats and other waterproof outerwear from purchased rubberized fabrics, plastics, and similar materials. Included in this industry are establishments primarily engaged in manufacturing waterproof or water repellent outerwear from purchased woven or knit fabrics other than wool. Establishments primarily engaged in manufacturing men's and boys' oiled-fabric work clothing are classified in **SIC 2326: Men's and Boys' Work Clothing;** those manufacturing vulcanized rubber clothing and clothing made from rubberized fabrics produced in the same establishment are classified in **SIC 3069: Fabricated Rubber Products, Not Elsewhere Classified.**

NAICS CODE(S)

315222 (Men's and Boys' Cut and Sew Suit, Coat, and Overcoat Manufacturing)
315234 (Women's and Girls' Cut and Sew Suit, Coat, Tailored Jacket, and Skirt Manufacturing)
315228 (Men's and Boys' Cut and Sew Other Outerwear Manufacturing)
315238 (Women'S and Girls' Cut and Sew Other Outerwear Manufacturing)
315291 (Infants' Cut and Sew Apparel Manufacturing)
315999 (Other Apparel Accessories and Other Apparel Manufacturing)
315211 (Men's and Boys' Cut and Sew Apparel Contractors)
315212 (Women's and Girls' Cut and Sew Apparel Contractors)

Raincoats constitute the largest share of merchandise produced by establishments classified in this industry. In 1997 these companies shipped goods with a total value of about $95 million, a dramatic decrease from the $333-million value of shipped goods in 1987.

The 1990s brought a return of polyurethane-coated fabrics to the forefront of raincoat fashion. Polyurethane gives fabrics the shiny look associated with rain slickers of the 1960s. The newer versions of the shiny raincoat have benefited from improvements in the technology used to coat the fabrics. Softer fabrics such as rayon, cotton, and polyester can be used to back a very thin layer of polyurethane, creating a much more comfortable garment than was previously possible. Technological improvements have also expanded the number of softer styles available; some use new microfibers as well as sueded cotton and velvet treated with water-repellent chemicals. These improvements in waterproofing techniques have given linens an important role in outerwear for the first time.

Although the market for rainwear declined in the 1980s and 1990s, it appeared that rainwear was becoming more fashionable by the late 1990s. Some customers were buying raincoats as alternatives to other types of coats instead of focusing entirely on their functional aspects. The introduction of shorter raincoats (34 to 37 inches long instead of the traditional 48 to 50 inches) increased sales significantly. In addition, new ''high-tech'' fibers and finishes such as Tencel polynosics, suede and twill-weave polyester, and high-twist wools made raincoats wearable in all kinds of weather. These all-weather garments were known as hybrid coats or bridge coats.

The U.S. Census Bureau reported that, in 1997, the primary products of 16 establishments were men's and junior boys' overcoats, topcoats, and tailored car and suburban coats, including uniform and wool garments that were water repellant (except raincoats). These firms shipped $128.0 million worth of goods, spent $81.0 million on materials, and paid $1.4 million for capital expenditures.

The primary products of nine companies were raincoats and raincapes for men, junior boys, and toddler boys. These firms shipped $40 million worth of goods, spent $21 million on materials, and paid $818,000 for capital expenditures.

Among companies that made waterproof outer garments for women, misses, juniors, and girls (including smocks and dress shields, plastic or rubberized), three firms shipped at least $100,000 worth of goods. Shipments in this segment totaled $1.9 million.

A large percentage of production jobs in the waterproof apparel industry have left the United States in recent years. The industry employed only 1,400 U.S. workers in 1997, a 30 percent drop since 1992 and a 60 percent drop since 1987. Employment was concentrated on the East Coast, particularly Maryland, Massachusetts, and New Jersey, which together accounted for about 50 percent of the category's jobs. More than half of the establishments in the industry had fewer than 20 employees; in 1997 workers in this industry earned $39 million in wages.

The waterproof outerwear industry was dominated by Londontown Corp. (Eldersburg, Maryland), which produced the well-known London Fog line of outerwear. The company had 1,900 employees and sales of $350 million in 1998. Other companies whose primary business was waterproof outerwear included Galleon (a New York, New York, firm previously known as Chief Apparel Inc.), with 160 employees and sales of $145 million; Whaling Manufacturing Company Inc. (Fall River, Massachusetts), with 500 employees and sales of $55 million; Forecaster of Boston Inc. (Boston, Massachusetts), with 600 employees and sales of $34 million; and Blauer Manufacturing Co. (Boston, Massachusetts), with 500 employees and sales of $32 million.

FURTHER READING

Gellers, Stan. "Short Raincoats Long on High-Tech Fabrics." *Daily News Record,* 5 March 1997.

Maxwell, Alison. "Pairing the Right Partners." *WWD,* 20 October 1999.

Pagoda, Dianne M., and Arthur Friedman. "Finally, Some Sunshine for Rainwear." *WWD,* 16 April 1996.

Palmieri, Jean E. "Abboud Signs Rainwear Licensee." *Daily News Record,* 14 September 1998.

U.S. Department of Commerce. Census Bureau. *1997 Economic Census.* Washington, D.C.: GPO, 1999. Available from http://www.census.gov.

LEATHER AND SHEEP-LINED CLOTHING

This category consists of manufacturers of many types of leather and sheep-lined clothing, including coats, jackets, hats, pants, skirts, vests, and other garments. Companies that make leather gloves and mittens are included in **SIC 3151: Leather Gloves and Mittens.** Fur clothing is classified separately in **SIC 2371: Fur Goods.**

NAICS CODE(S)

315292 (Fur and Leather Apparel Manufacturing)

The top three industry leaders for this category were L.L. Bean Inc. of Freeport, Maine, with sales of almost $1.1 billion for its fiscal year ended February 28, 1998; DeLong Sportswear Inc. of Grinnell, Iowa, with 1998 sales of $25 million; and Avirex Ltd. of Long Island City, New York, with 1998 sales of $18 million. Other significant companies in the industry included New York City-based Swell-Wear Inc.; Gem Dandy Inc. of Madison, North Carolina; and Berlin Glove Company Ltd. of Berlin, Wisconsin.

In 1997 there were 105 establishments in the industry, down 22 percent since 1990. In 1995, the leather and sheep-lined clothing industry shipped about $129.3 million in products, a decrease of nearly 37 percent since 1990. Overall, retail sales of leather apparel almost quadrupled since 1985. These increases reflected the end of a rising trend in the price of leather. The cost of leather relative to other clothing materials has proved to be a reliable indicator of the leather apparel industry's performance from year to year. As is the case in the apparel industry in general, patterns of consumption can change rapidly as customer demand is influenced by fashion developments. Leather clothing, which is both high-fashion and high-cost in the world of apparel, is particularly susceptible to both of these kinds of fluctuations in demand.

Although demand for leather apparel is expected to rise slightly as the American economy continues to improves, the market share lost to imports is expected to increase as well. In addition, American companies are moving more of their manufacturing abroad to reduce labor costs. These are the most severe challenges facing the industry.

In the spring of 1997, the U.S. Air Force contracted Avirex to create a replica of the 1931 A-2 leather flight jacket with special artwork on it to commemorate the military branch's fiftieth anniversary. More than 400 high-ranking Air Force officials—including the Commander-in-Chief, President Bill Clinton—wore these special jackets at ceremonies celebrating the anniversary in Las Vegas. Subsequently, Avirex offered the jackets for sale to the public for about $320 at the Cockpit stores in New York City, Beverly Hills, and via a toll-free number.

FURTHER READING

Socha, Miles. "Avirex." *Daily News Record,* 5 May 1997.

U.S. Census Bureau. *1995 Annual Survey of Manufactures.* Washington, D.C.: GPO, 1996.

U.S. Department of Commerce. *County Business Patterns.* Washington, D.C.: GPO, 1996.

SIC 2387

APPAREL BELTS

This category includes establishments primarily engaged in manufacturing apparel belts. Companies that produce all types of belts for clothing are grouped in this industry, regardless of the material from which the belts are made.

NAICS CODE(S)

315999 (Apparel Accessories and Other Apparel Manufacturing)

The overall accessories business headed into the twenty-first Century with momentum. President of the accessories division at Liz Claiborne Helen Welsh called for continued momentum in belt sales through the year 2000, according to Wendy Hassen in *Women's Wear Daily* magazine. Customers' comfort with shopping on the Internet helped fuel this momentum, and the industry responded to the trend by investing in Internet infrastructures.

According to the U.S. Census Bureau's *1997 Economic Census—Manufacturing,* 161 establishments operated in this category for some or all of 1997. Industry-wide employment totaled 5,344 workers receiving a payroll of more than $131 million. Production workers accounted for 3,599 of these employees, and they received an average hourly wage of $8.53. Overall shipments for the industry were valued at a little more than $649 million, down from $678 million in 1995 shipments.

Leading the industry in overall sales was St. John Knits Inc. of Irvine, California, with $282 in sales for its fiscal year ended October 31, 1998. The family-run company, which had gone public in 1993 only to retreat back into private ownership in 1999, operated 17 retail boutique shops and counted Hillary Rodham Clinton and Diane Sawyer as two of its ultra-loyal customers. Lillian Vernon of Rye, New York, followed with $255 million in sales for its fiscal year ended February 27, 1999. Swank Inc. of Attleboro, Massachusetts, generated 1998 sales of just under $152 million. Tandy Brands Accessories Inc. of Arlington, Texas, rounded out the top 5 industry lead-

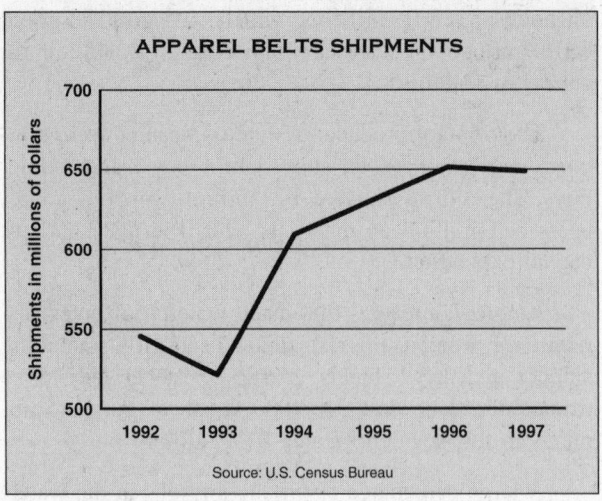

APPAREL BELTS SHIPMENTS

Source: U.S. Census Bureau

ers with $135 million in sales for its fiscal year ended June 30, 1998. In 1999, Chicago-based Florsheim Group Inc. contracted Tandy to design, manufacture, and market accessories, including a line of belts launched in fall 1999, under the Florsheim name.

Leather is by far the most important material for apparel belts, making up 67.5 percent of total shipments in 1995. Since the beginning of the 1990s, Nubuck suede has become an important material in the manufacture of apparel belts. Nubuck is a softened leather that is available in a variety of colors and textures. Nubuck first appeared as a footwear material and soon began to show up in women's accessories. Men's belts, which have traditionally been closely linked to footwear in terms of leather trends, followed soon thereafter.

An important factor in the belt industry's success throughout the 1990s has been an increasing emphasis on casual styles, as epitomized by the workday casual movement adopted by many American businesses by the mid-1990s. The glossy look of 1980s accessories had given way to a more down-to-earth and practical flavor in belts. With the comeback of jeans, belt manufacturers were producing "jean friendly" belts—belts with wider widths, braided belts, and belts with brushed textures—to work with the wider legs and roomier fit featured in many of the modern styles. Furthermore, the crossover market in men's belts continued to grow. What had until recently been mainly a replacement business had been spurred on by increasing attention paid to men by designers and manufacturers and ever-changing fashion trends such as textured belts and updated buckles. On the women's side, the reappearance of the fitted look and a renewed emphasis on the waistline contributed to the health of the belt industry in the 1990s.

A surge in the popularity of leggings and stretch pants for women that took place at the end of the 1980s, and new trends such as the grunge look and natural soft flowing fabrics in the early to mid-1990s, created a slump in sales for makers of belts. In general, however, industry sales were quite strong for much of the 1990s in spite of generally poor showings throughout much of the apparel industry.

Since the early 1980s, the number of U.S. jobs in this category has been on a steady decline. In 1982 the industry employed 11,700 U.S. workers; by 1997 that number was 5,344. Four states provided more than 70 percent of those jobs: New York, California, Texas, and Connecticut. Of the 245 companies operating in the industry, nearly two-thirds had fewer than 20 employees.

FURTHER READING

"Beltin' It Out." *Women's Wear Daily Accessories Supplement,* January 1995.

"Belting It Out; Florsheim has Signed a New Belt License." *Footwear News,* 12 July 1999.

Curan, Catherine. "Belts Won't Buckle Under." *Daily News Record,* 16 August 1996.

———. "Denim Demand Paves Path for Jeans Belts." *Daily News Record,* 3 May 1996.

Goldfield, Robert. "Hoity-toity Clothiers Coming to Broadway." *Business Journal—Portland,* 20 August 1999.

Hassen, Wendy. "Vendors See Boom Continuing." *Women's Wear Daily,* 6 December 1999.

"Total Women's Accessories." *Accessories,* January 1997.

U.S. Census Bureau. "Other Apparel Accessories and Other Apparel Manufacturing." *1997 Economic Census—Manufacturing,* 10 February 2000. Available from http://www.census.gov/prod/ec97/97m3159d.pdf.

SIC 2389

APPAREL AND ACCESSORIES, NOT ELSEWHERE CLASSIFIED

This industry consists of establishments primarily engaged in manufacturing suspenders, gaffers, handkerchiefs, and other apparel not elsewhere classified, such as academic caps and gowns, vestments, and theatrical costumes. Also included are establishments primarily engaged in manufacturing clothing by cutting and joining (for example by adhesives) materials such as paper and nonwoven textiles.

NAICS CODE(S)

315999 (Other Apparel Accessories and Other Apparel Manufacturing)

315299 (All Other Cut and Sew Apparel Manufacturing)

315231 (Women's and Girls' Cut and Sew Lingerie, Loungewear, and Nightwear Manufacturing)

315212 (Women's and Girls' Cut and Sew Apparel Contractors)

315211 (Men's and Boys' Cut and Sew Apparel Contractors)

During the early 1990s, the number of establishments in this industry gradually increased and reached 462 by 1994. The total value of shipments in 1995 was $893.9 million, up from $751.8 million in 1994.

The apparel and accessories industry comprises a wide variety of products. Ecclesiastical vestments and other clothing made up 12.5 percent of sales in this category in 1992 (a sharp drop from its 30 percent share in 1987). Academic caps and gowns, costumes, and theatrical clothing made up 41.5 percent. Garter belts made up 3.1 percent. Apparel and accessories, not elsewhere classified, made up 25.4 percent. Garters, hose supporters, arm bands, and suspenders accounted for 7.0 percent. Men's, boys', women's and children's handkerchiefs, combined with burial garments, accounted for 10.5 percent. Burial garments usually amount to about 2.0 percent of total sales in this category.

The U.S. Census Bureau reported that in 1997 there were 82 establishments manufacturing cut-and-sew apparel such as burial garments, academic caps and gowns, costumes, ecclesiastical vestments, and special garments for fraternal orders. The category includes theatrical costumes but does not include tailored clothing or military-type uniforms.

Companies in this industry shipped $358.0 million worth of goods, spent $154.0 million on materials, and paid $3.8 million for capital expenditures. They employed 4,072 people, including 3,223 production workers who earned an average hourly wage of $9.35. New York had the highest value of product shipments for this industry, followed by South Carolina, California, Florida, and Virginia.

In 1997 there were eight establishments that manufactured hose supporters, arm bands, suspenders, and handkerchiefs. They shipped $64.6 million worth of goods and spent $40 million on materials. They employed 827 people, including 634 production workers who earned an average hourly wage of $9.19.

Historically, about 80.0 percent of goods manufactured within this industry have been made for personal consumption, 12.0 percent have been used in apparel made from purchased materials, and 1.5 percent have been exported. The United States usually imports nearly twice as many products in this category as it exports. Others buying fractional amounts of the output of this industry include, in descending order the federal government; pleating and stitching operations; knit outerwear mills; hospitals; laundry, dry cleaning, and shoe repair operations; government agencies that buy items for hospitals and health organizations; portrait and photographic studios; and government agencies that buy items for public assistance and relief.

One of the largest firms whose primary business was in this classification was Cyrk Inc. (Gloucester, Massachusetts) with 1,300 employees and sales of $757.0 million in 1998. Cyrk's main focus was promotional screen and fabric screen printing. American Marketing Industries Inc. (Kansas City, Missouri) had sales of $218.0 million, mainly from manufacturing outerwear. Varsity Spirit Corp. (a subsidiary of Riddell Sports Inc. based in Memphis, Tennessee) had sales of $75.5 million, mainly from manufacturing uniforms for cheerleaders, dance teams, and booster clubs. Paris Accessories Inc. (New York, New York) had sales of $50.0 million, mainly from manufacturing women's belts and accessories. E.R. Moore Co. (Chicago, Illinois) had sales of $39.0 million, mainly from manufacturing choir robes, caps, gowns, and accessories.

Labor and occupations are specialized within this category. Historically, about 56.0 percent of the workers have been sewing machine operators; 3.2 percent have been garment inspectors, testers, and graders; and 3.0 percent have supervised precision blue-collar workers. Other occupations include pressing machine operators, shipping and receiving clerks, hand packers and packagers, helpers, laborers, and materials movers.

The number of employees in this industry rose from 10,400 people in 1992 to 12,900 in 1995. Production workers consistently accounted for about 80 percent of the labor force. In 1992 average hourly earnings for a production worker in this industry were $6.93. In 1995 that figure was down to $6.80, which was $0.74 per hour less than the average hourly earnings for all production workers in the broader apparel industry.

FURTHER READING

Darnay, Arsen J., ed. *Manufacturing USA*. Detroit: Gale Research, 1996.

U.S. Department of Commerce. Census Bureau. *1996 Annual Survey of Manufactures*. Washington, D.C.: GPO, 1998.

U.S. Department of Commerce. Census Bureau. *1997 Economic Census*. Washington, D.C.: GPO, 1999. Available from http://www.census.gov/prod/ec97/97m3159d.pdf.

———. *County Business Patterns*. Washington, D.C.: GPO, 1996.

SIC 2391

CURTAINS AND DRAPERIES

The establishments covered in this category are primarily engaged in manufacturing curtains and draperies from purchased materials. Those establishments primar-

ily engaged in manufacturing lace curtains on lace machines are classified in **SIC 2258: Lace and Warp Knit Fabric Mills,** and those manufacturing shower curtains are classified in **SIC 2392: Housefurnishings, Except Curtains and Draperies.**

NAICS CODE(S)

314121 (Curtain and Drapery Mills)

In 1997 there were 2,015 U.S. companies operating curtain and drapery mills, according to the U.S. Census Bureau. These companies shipped $1.8 billion worth of goods, up from $1.2 billion in 1995 and $1.0 billion in 1977. They spent $908 million on materials and paid $32 million for capital expenditures. Of the 2,087 plants operating in this segment, only 187 had at least 20 employees. States with high concentrations of establishments in this industry included California, Florida, Texas, and New York.

Most curtains were manufactured in standard, ready-made sizes. Draperies included ready-made items as well as custom-made versions. These made-to-measure draperies were ordered from a showroom or a catalog and then produced by the manufacturer.

Curtains and draperies were once considered the only options for dressing windows, especially in the home. Attitudes shifted over time, however, and by the 1980s, consumers wanted their homes to feel more comfortable and less formal. Spending on home furnishings grew throughout the 1980s. At that time imports did not have much effect on this segment of the market. The market for lined, pinched, and pleated draperies declined as one-inch mini-blinds became popular. By the early 1990s, many companies that manufactured traditional window treatments expanded into alternative products. Many analysts said that the manufacture of formal draperies was on a downward spiral but, by 1996, products such as sheer curtains and pinch-pleat draperies were regaining their popularity.

During the late 1990s, this industry began selling more merchandise via home improvement centers that offered items of interest to both men and women. Mass merchants sold about 50 percent of the category's goods in 1996, department stores sold nearly 33 percent, and the remainder was sold through specialty stores and catalogs. The market for soft window treatments was particularly robust in the late 1990s as consumers chose fashionable new designs that coordinated with their bedding and other home furnishings.

Most companies in this industry had fewer than 100 employees, but most of the business in this category went to the larger operations. Among the leading firms whose primary products were curtains and draperies was Decorative Home Accents Inc. of Abbeville, South Carolina, with sales of $176.7 million. Aberdeen Manufacturing Corp. (a division of Chicago-based CHF Industries Inc.) had sales of $160 million, and Arley Corp. of Taunton, Massachusetts, had sales of $160 million as well.

In 1997 the total number of employees working at establishments that manufacture curtains and draperies was 25,524. About 17,000 of those employees were production workers who earned an average hourly wage of $7.84.

FURTHER READING

American Textile Manufacturers Institute. "Press Release: U.S. Textile and Apparel Exports Increase in 1996. Mexico Surpasses Canada as Top U.S. Import and Export Market," 1997.

Conroy, David. "Arley Adds to Soft Windows." *HFN*, 22 April 1996.

Johnson, Sarah. "Window Fashion: Home Innovations' Upscale Launch." *HFN*, 30 September 1996.

Squire, Laurie. "When Window Dressing is More Than Mere Window Dressing." *Newsday*, 26 January 1997.

U.S. Department of Commerce. *1996 Annual Survey of Manufactures*. Washington, D.C.: GPO, 1998.

U.S. Department of Commerce. Census Bureau. *1997 Economic Census*. Washington, D.C.: GPO, 1999. Available from http://www.census.gov/prod/ec97/97m3141b.pdf.

SIC 2392

HOUSEFURNISHINGS, EXCEPT CURTAINS AND DRAPERIES

This category covers establishments primarily engaged in manufacturing housefurnishings from purchased materials, such as blankets, bedspreads, sheets, tablecloths, towels, and shower curtains. Those establishments producing housefurnishings primarily of fabric woven at the same establishment are classified, according to fiber, in **SIC 2211: Broadwoven Fabric Mills, Cotton; SIC 2221: Broadwoven Fabric Mills, Manmade Fiber and Silk; SIC 2231: Broadwoven Fabric Mills, Wool (Including Dyeing and Finishing); or SIC 2299: Textile Goods, Not Elsewhere Classified.**

NAICS CODE(S)

314911 (Textile Bag Mills)
339940 (Broom, Brush and Mop Manufacturing)
314129 (Other Household Textile Product Mills)

INDUSTRY SNAPSHOT

For many years, housefurnishings such as sheets, towels, and blankets functioned as basic household necessities. In the growing economy after World War II,

however, these products were manufactured with new technology in an expanding palette of colors, prints, and styles—thus becoming more of an expression of personal taste. By the 1990s, it was easy and affordable for consumers to redecorate their rooms with coordinated bedroom and bath products offered by companies in this industry. Record housing starts and home sales also helped to increase demand for bedding.

ORGANIZATION AND STRUCTURE

In 1997 there were 138 companies with 100 or more employees, totaling more than 36,000 employees whose primary products matched this industry's description. The manufacture of sheets and towels was dominated by a few large corporations. Some of the other products covered in this classification included tablecloths, pillows, boat cushions, laundry bags, shower curtains, slipcovers, and mattress pads. These were produced by a variety of small manufacturers, thus creating a very fragmented sector of the market.

Of the entire 1996 market for textiles, home furnishings shared 15 percent. In 1997, the fabricated textile products market (including home furnishings), accounted for 30 percent of the combined apparel and fabricated textile products market. Shipments of home furnishings and other textile products also grew much faster than other sectors.

BACKGROUND AND DEVELOPMENT

The housefurnishings market grew throughout the 1980s. Several factors contributed to the industry's relative strength. The home textile market was less penetrated by imports than other sectors of the textile industry. Also, home textiles were manufactured in a more automated process, with specialized machinery taking the place of the paid production worker. A large portion of the profits in this category were used to upgrade building and machinery. New capital expenditures—at $27 million in 1977—escalated to $81 million in 1995 as companies implemented new technologies at their manufacturing facilities. Companies continued to invest over the next several years; in 1997, capital expenditures reached $115 million.

CURRENT CONDITIONS

The top three companies with primary products in this category employed more than 1000 workers each, while about 70 percent of the remaining companies employed fewer than 100 workers. The value of shipments of all products in these establishments, including but not limited to the primary products of the industry, grew from $2.3 billion in 1977 to nearly $7.0 billion in 1997. Specifically, the value of shipments in the various market segments in 1997 were as follows: blankets, mattress protectors, table linens, and slip covers at $1.6 billion;

sheets and pillowcases at more than $1.4 billion; towels and washcloths at $849.3 million; bedspreads and bedsets at $272.0 million; and shower curtains at $147.7 million.

The U.S. Department of Commerce predicted that the value of shipments for all products would reach $7.10 billion in 1998, dropping slightly to $7.08 billion in 1999. Continued growth in the home remodeling business was expected to continue. Overall, 1998 sales of home textiles only grew a mere 0.6 percent, according to retail consultant Kurt Salmon Associates (KSA). Sales rebounded strongly in 1999 by 3.9 percent. Sales of home textiles in 2000 are expected to grow by approximately 5.0 percent.

However, some categories will not grow as quickly. Sales of towels in 1999 grew 7.2 percent, but they are only expected to grow 3 percent in 2000, KSA forecasts. Sales of sheets and pillowcases, after climbing 3.9 percent in 1999, are expected to rise 3.0 percent in 2000. Sales of other bedding items (including comforters, quilts, bedspreads, and throws) are expected to rise 5.0 percent in 2000, after an increase of 5.5 percent in 1999 and 8.7 percent in 1998.

INDUSTRY LEADERS

Companies in this industry earned more than $3.1 billion collectively in 1997. The top three manufacturers overall in 1998 (ranked by sales), according to *Home Textiles Today,* were Westpoint Stevens, Pillowtex (includes Fieldcrest Cannon), and Springs; all had 1998 sales of more than $1 billion. Pillowtex was number one in 1997, and its brand name Cannon was ranked the best household linen brand the same year by both discounters and discount shoppers. Of the top 15 manufacturers, the majority saw increases in 1998 sales compared to 1997, with acquisitions accounting for double-digit jumps.

Westpoint is the leader in sheets and pillowcases, whereas Pillowtex is the leader in several areas, including kitchen and bath towels, blankets, and pillows. Springs is the leader in comforters, bedspreads, and shower curtains. Pacific Coast Feather Co. is the largest manufacturer of down comforters and the second-largest bedding company behind Pillowtex. According to *Home Textiles Today* research, the company is the tenth largest supplier of home textiles in the United States. In 1998, it owned 21 percent of the bed, pillow, and down comforter market and had sales near $200 million. Sales were expected to top $225 million in 1999.

WORKFORCE

There were 42,100 production workers and 49,187 total employees in the housefurnishings industry in 1997. Production workers earned an average of $8.68 per hour and worked an average of 40 hours per week. Companies that manufactured sheets and pillowcases employed a total of 5,922 workers, with more than 90 percent in production. Employment has been decreasing in the home furnishings sector, but hourly earnings grew at the same rate as the industry average.

AMERICA AND THE WORLD

Imports have not had as much impact on the home furnishings market as with the apparel market. However, the value of imports grew from about $1.2 billion in 1992 to an estimated $2.1 billion in 1997. This was expected to reach more than $3.6 billion in 1999.

The World Trade Organization Agreement on Textiles and Clothing, which phases out quotas by 2005, is expected to cost the United States $4 billion in lost textile sales, according to the American Textile Manufacturers Institute. The largest threat will come from China, which imported almost 16 percent of all apparel and fabricated textile products in 1997.

Exports grew at a much slower rate, from $448 million in 1992 to an estimated $439 million in 1997, but they were expected to reach nearly $500 million in 1999. Overall, exports of both apparel and fabricated textile products accounted for 12 percent of shipments in 1997, up from 7 percent in 1992. Canada and Mexico were the fastest growing markets in the late 1990s.

FURTHER READING

American Textile Manufacturers Institute. "China's Entry into World Trade Organization Would Cost 154,5000 U.S. Jobs and Billions of Dollars in Lost U.S. Textile and Apparel Sales," 1999. Available from http://www.atmi.org/Newsroom/Releases/pr199932.html.

"Down Bedding Company Credits Growth to Research." *The Associated Press,* 10 November 1999.

Hogsett, Don. "KSA Predicts 4-5 Percent Home Sales Jump in '00," 21 December 1999. Available from http://www.hometextilestoday.com/.

"Home Textiles Today Top 15," 21 December 1999. Available from http://www.hometextilestoday.com/manufgiants1.htm.

U.S. Census Bureau. "NAICS 314129, Manufacturing—Industry Series." *1997 Economic Census.* Washington, D.C.: GPO, 5 November 1999.

"The Week in Business." *The Business Journal of Charlotte,* 25 November 1996.

SIC 2393

TEXTILE BAGS

This category includes establishments primarily engaged in manufacturing shipping and other industrial bags from purchased fabrics. Establishments primarily engaged in manufacturing plastic bags are classified under **SIC 2673: Plastics, Foil, and Coated Paper Bags;** those manufacturing laundry, wardrobe, shoe, and other textile housefurnishing bags are classified under **SIC 2392: Housefurnishings, Except Curtains and Draperies;** and those manufacturing luggage are classified under **SIC 3161: Luggage.**

NAICS CODE(S)

314911 (Textile Bag Mills)

In 1997 there were 432 textile bag mills in the United States, according to the U.S. Census Bureau. Of those, 42 made housefurnishings; the remaining 390 manufactured primarily textile bags (excluding bags for laundry, wardrobes, and shoes). About one-third of all textile bag mills had at least 20 employees. Only 29 had more than 100 employees. The greatest concentration of establishments in this category was in California, New York, Texas, and Washington. The highest concentration of the larger firms was in California.

The value of shipments for textile bags increased from $341 million in 1982 to $676 million in 1992. The value of shipments of all products these companies produced, including textile bags, increased from $422 million in 1982 to $779 million in 1992. The number of companies producing textile bags increased from 211 in 1977 to 298 in 1992. End-of-year inventories at these establishments increased substantially from $59 million in 1977 to $121 million in 1992. New capital expenditures went from $6 million in 1977 to $12 million in 1992 as manufacturers updated their machinery and buildings.

The value of shipments for all manufacturers who made textile bags reached $915 million in 1997, up from $871 million in 1995. Those establishments spent $458 million on materials, parts, containers, resales, fuels, electricity, and contract work. Their capital expenditures for new and used buildings, other structures, machinery, and equipment was $21 million.

Raytown, Missouri-based BHA Group Holdings Inc. led the category with sales of $142 million in 1998. Its subsidiary, BHA Company Inc. of Kansas City, Missouri, had sales of $121 million. Other firms that made textile bags as their primary business included MFRI Inc. of Niles, Illinois, with sales of $121.9 million; Super Sack Manufacturing Corp. of Savoy, Texas, with sales of $55 million; Cady Industries Inc. of Pearson, Georgia, with sales of $50 million; Menardi-Criswell of Trenton, South Carolina, with sales of $30 million; Bulk Lift International Inc. of Carpentersville, Illinois, with sales of $22 million; and Kenneth Fox Supply Co. of McAllen, Texas, with sales of $17 million.

This industry classification had an estimated 13,169 employees, including 11,098 production workers who earned an average hourly wage of $7.41. Total payroll in the segment was $238.6 million, up from $150.0 million in 1995.

In 1994 the United States, Mexico, and Canada implemented the North American Free Trade Agreement (NAFTA), a pact to gradually remove all tariffs and other trade restrictions from most goods made and sold in North America. In a press release issued by the American Textile Manufacturer's Institute (ATMI) in February 1997, President James M. Fitzgibbons said that the United States had been the biggest exporter to Mexico in the previous year. Fitzgibbons said, "This rapid increase in trade between the U.S. and Mexico is evidence that preferential trading agreements, when done correctly, can greatly benefit the U.S. textile industry."

FURTHER READING

"BHA Group Holdings Inc." *Hoover's Company Capsules.* Hoover's Inc., 1997. Available from http://www.hoovers.com.

"BHA Group, Inc. Changes Name to BHA Group Holdings, Inc." *Business Wire,* 19 February 1997.

U.S. Department of Commerce. Bureau of the Census. *1996 Annual Survey of Manufactures.* Washington, D.C.: GPO, 1998.

U.S. Department of Commerce. Bureau of the Census. *1997 Economic Census.* Washington, D.C.: GPO, 1999. Available from http://www.census.gov/prod/ec97/97m3149a.pdf.

"U.S. Textile and Apparel Exports Increase in 1996: Mexico Surpasses Canada as Top U.S. Import and Export Market." *American Textile Manufacturers Institute,* 21 February 1997. Available from http://www.atmi.org/.

SIC 2394

CANVAS AND RELATED PRODUCTS

This category covers establishments primarily engaged in manufacturing awnings, tents, and related products from purchased fabrics. Establishments primarily engaged in manufacturing canvas bags are classified under **SIC 2393: Textile Bags.**

NAICS CODE(S)

314912 (Canvas and Related Product Mills)

In the late 1990s, most companies primarily producing canvas and related products were small. Approximately 87 percent had fewer than 100 employees. California, Florida, and New York had the highest concentration of establishments in this industry.

Some of the top canvas products are awnings, non-camping tents, fitted tarpaulins, camping tents, flat tarpaulin, and sails. The industry also produces goods such as fabric roofs for sports arenas, canvas bags, and customized carry cases for electronic items. An important new product is flexible fabric sides, called curtainsiders, for truck trailers. Another innovation is synthetic textiles that resemble canvas but are cheaper and easier to clean. The more expensive, true canvas is still offered for consumers who desire a more durable product and are willing to pay the higher price for better quality.

The canvas and related products industry has become more of a custom industry since the 1950s, offering more colors than the well-known khaki or green, according to Tim O'Brien of *In Amusement Business*. The value of shipments of canvas and related products made from cotton, nylon, polyester, and other industrial materials was $991 million in 1992, up from $641 million in 1982.

In 1997 there were 1,665 companies operating in this category, according to the U.S. Census Bureau. Of the 1,680 establishments in the segment, only 225 had at least 20 employees and only 26 of those had at least 100 employees. The industry shipped $1.5 billion worth of merchandise in 1997, up from $1.3 billion in 1995, $1.0 billion in 1992, and $487.0 million in 1977. The cost of materials for the category was $723 million in 1997, and capital expenditures totaled $45 million.

Among companies whose primary business was the manufacturing of canvas and related products, Birdair Inc. (Buffalo, New York) had sales of $73 million in 1998; American Recreation Products Inc. (Creve Coeur, Missouri) had sales of $70 million; Hoover Industries Inc. (Miami, Florida) had estimated sales of $39 million; North Sails Group Inc. (Milford, Connecticut) had sales of $35 million; Service Manufacturing Corp. (Aurora, Illinois) had estimated sales of $28 million; and Anchor Industries Inc. (Evansville, Indiana) had sales of $25 million.

The canvas products industry employed 18,660 workers in 1997, up from 16,000 in 1995 and 14,000 in 1977. Payroll for all employees in 1997 totaled $413 million. The 14,024 production workers in these establishments earned an average hourly wage of $9.86.

FURTHER READING

American Textile Manufacturers Institute. "Press Release: U.S. Textile and Apparel Exports Increase in 1996. Mexico Surpasses Canada as Top U.S. Import and Export Market," 1997. Available from http://www.atmi.org/.

O'Brien, Tim. "Midways and Fairgrounds Are Seas of Multiple Colors Thanks to the Colorful Tents, Awnings, and Ballys." *In Amusement Business,* 14 March 1994.

U.S. Department of Commerce. *1996 Annual Survey of Manufactures.* Washington, D.C.: GPO, 1998.

U.S. Department of Commerce. Census Bureau. *1997 Economic Census.* Washington, D.C.: GPO, 1999. Available from http://www.census.com/prod/ec97/97m3149b.pdf.

U.S. Department of Labor. Bureau of Labor Statistics. *Career Guide to Industries, 1998-99 Edition. Bulletin 2503.* Washington, D.C.: GPO, 1998.

SIC 2395

PLEATING, DECORATIVE AND NOVELTY STITCHING, AND TUCKING FOR THE TRADE

The establishments covered in this category are engaged in pleating, decorative and novelty stitching, and tucking for the trade. Establishments primarily engaged in performing similar services for individuals are classified in service industries. Establishments primarily engaged in manufacturing trimmings are classified in **SIC 2396: Automotive Trimmings, Apparel Findings, and Related Products.** Establishments primarily engaged in manufacturing Schiffli machine embroideries are classified in **SIC 2397: Schiffli Machine Embroideries.**

NAICS CODE(S)

314999 (All Other Miscellaneous Textile Product Mills)
315211 (Men's and Boys' Cut and Sew Apparel Contractors)
315212 (Women's and Girl's Cut and Sew Apparel Contractors)

In the late 1990s, most of the companies in this category were private corporations with 100 or fewer workers. Workers at these establishments produced art needlework, quilted fabrics or cloth, Swiss loom embroideries, machine-made crochet ware, and sequined embroideries. Also made by companies in this industry are various products for the trade, including appliqueing, buttonhole making, eyelet making, hemstitching, looping, permanent pleating and pressing, pleating, ruffling, and scalloping.

During the 1980s, 200 companies dropped from this industry. However, the industry rebounded in the early 1990s when establishments grew to 756 in 1992, from a low of 685 in 1988. Companies continued to spend money to upgrade their buildings and machinery to meet the increased demand for their products. New capital expenditures totaled $12 million in 1987 and climbed to $27 million in 1995.

The U.S. Census Bureau estimated that, in 1997, 805 establishments with 15,001 employees were engaged in pleating and stitching. The value of product shipments of these establishments was $880 million. The 11,574 production workers in this segment earned an average hourly wage of $8.82. The cost of materials was $406 million, and capital expenditures were $45 million.

The primary product of 248 establishments was embroidery (excluding Schiffli machine embroidery). These companies employed 7,366 people, including 5,705 production workers who earned an average hourly wage of

$8.44. They shipped $456 million worth of goods, spent $211 million on materials, and paid out $16 million for capital expenditures.

Morning Sun Inc. of Tacoma, Washington, was one of the largest firms that did pleating and decorative and novelty stitching as its primary business. Like many companies that competed in this segment, Morning Sun was engaged in fabric screen printing and embroidering. Morning Sun had 375 employees and sales of $46 million in 1998.

Other leaders in the category included Caliendo-Savio Enterprises Inc. of New Berlin, Wisconsin, with 100 employees and sales of $38 million; Embroideries Inc. (a subsidiary of E.J.J. Inc. based in Monroe, Louisiana) with 150 employees and estimated sales of $36 million; Fabri Quilt Inc. of North Kansas City, Missouri, with 190 employees and sales of $35 million; and Wiener Laces Inc. of New York, New York, with 250 employees and sales of $35 million.

FURTHER READING

American Textile Manufacturers Institute. ''Press Release: U.S. Textile and Apparel Exports Increase in 1996. Mexico Surpasses Canada as Top U.S. Import and Export Market.'' American Textile Manufacturers Institute, 1997. Available from http://www.atmi.org/.

Nicolava, Rossitsa. ''Sew Fine: NKC Company Adopts Aggressive Strategy for Growth in Mature Quilting Industry.'' *The Kansas City Business Journal,* 19 March 1999.

U.S. Department of Commerce. *1996 Annual Survey of Manufactures.* Washington, D.C.: GPO, 1998.

U.S. Department of Commerce. Census Bureau. *1997 Economic Census.* Washington, D.C.: GPO, 1999. Available from http://www.census.gov/prod/ec97/97m3149e.pdf.

U.S. Department of Labor. Bureau of Labor Statistics. *Occupational Outlook Handbook 1998-1999.* Washington, D.C.: GPO, 1999. Available from http://stats/bls.gov/oco/ocos235.htm.

SIC 2396

AUTOMOTIVE TRIMMINGS, APPAREL FINDINGS, AND RELATED PRODUCTS

This category includes companies that manufactured automotive trimmings, apparel findings, and related products, and those that specialized in printing and stamping on garments and apparel accessories, including silk screen printing. Corporations classified in this industry made trimmings, bindings, and linings for items such as hats, suits, coats, neckties, purses, and luggage. They also made shoulder pads, shoulder straps, waistbands,

ribbons, bows, sweatbands and visors for caps, and other components to be used by the textile industry.

NAICS CODE(S)

336360 (Motor Vehicle Fabric Accessories and Seat Manufacturing)
315999 (Other Apparel Accessories and Other Apparel Manufacturing)
323113 (Commercial Screen Printing)
314999 (All Other Miscellaneous Textile Product Mills)

The value of shipments in the various product classes in 1995 were as follows: automotive trimmings, $3.4 billion; printing on garments and apparel accessories (including silk screen printing) and stamped art goods, $2.1 billion; automotive trimmings, apparel findings, and related products, not specified by kind, $533.0 million; other trimmings and findings, $502.0 million; and men's and boys' suit and coat findings, hatters' fur, and other hat and cap materials, $167.0 million. The value of shipments of all of the above products classes totaled $6.7 million in 1995.

According to the U.S. Census Bureau, 632 establishments manufactured automotive and apparel trimmings in 1997. They shipped $960 million worth of goods, spent $511 million on materials, and invested $46 million in capital expenditures.

In 1997 there were 63 companies that primarily manufactured apparel findings and trimmings, except men's and junior boys' coat, suit, and trouser findings. They spent $68 million on materials and invested $4 million in capital expenditures for new and used buildings and other structures, machinery, and equipment. The largest concentrations of firms in this segment were in New York, California, New Jersey, Massachusetts, Maryland, and Pennsylvania.

In 1998 QST Industries Inc. (Chicago, Illinois) sold $250 million worth of men's clothing component parts such as linings, shoulder pads, and waistbands. Among the leading companies in this classification that supplied the automotive industry were Prince Corp. (Holland, Michigan) with 5,000 employees and estimated sales of $875 million; Findlay Industries Inc. (Findlay, Ohio) with estimated sales of $529 million; Mexican Industries in Michigan Inc. (Detroit, Michigan) with sales of $171 million; TS Trim Industries Inc. (Canal Winchester, Ohio) with estimated sales of $131 million; and HFI Inc. (Columbus, Ohio) with estimated sales of $96 million.

The 632 establishments that manufactured automotive and apparel trimmings employed 12,301 people in 1997, including 9,800 production workers who earned an average hourly wage of $8.33. The 63 companies that primarily made apparel findings and trimmings employed

2,165 people, including 1,682 production workers who earned an average hourly wage of $8.28.

Companies in this industry operated plants outside the United States to better supply their customers. For example, Findlay Industries announced in 1997 that it would open a facility in Poland to supply nearby factories owned by General Motors Corp., one of its most important customers. Likewise, QST Industries had been operating a manufacturing plant in Hong Kong since the 1980s to supply pockets, interlinings, and other components to overseas textile plants. The company opened a new plant in Mexico in 1999 and planned to open a third plant in the Dominican Republic within another year. QST also had warehouses and sales facilities in dozens of countries.

FURTHER READING

Chirls, Stuart. ''Components: Better Service Boosts Market.'' *WWD*, 1 October 1996.

Maycumber, S. Gray. ''The Sun Never Sets on QST: Textile Component Supplier Goes Where the Apparel Business Goes.'' *Daily News Record*, 29 November 1999.

Sherefkin, Robert. ''3 Companies Are Going Global in Efforts to Increase Revenues.'' *Crain's Detroit Business*, 10 March 1997.

Smith, William C. ''Textiles in Automotives: the Market of Significance.'' *Textile World*, June 1996.

U.S. Department of Commerce. Census Bureau. *1996 Annual Survey of Manufactures: Value of Product Shipments*. Washington, D.C.: GPO, 1998.

U.S. Department of Commerce. Census Bureau. *1997 Economic Census*. Washington, D.C.: GPO, 1999. Available from http://www.census.gov/prod/ec97/97m3159d.pdf.

U.S. Department of Labor. *Employment, Hours, and Earnings, United States, 1988-1996*. Washington, D.C.: GPO, 1996.

SIC 2397

SCHIFFLI MACHINE EMBROIDERIES

This category includes establishments primarily engaged in manufacturing Schiffli machine embroideries.

NAICS CODE(S)

313222 (Schiffli Machine Embroidery)

Most companies whose primary business is Schiffli embroidery are relatively small and privately owned. Schiffli lace is produced by a machine with several hundred needles placed horizontally one above the other. With fabric held in a frame covering the full width of the machine, the needles move back and forth through the

material. The yarn used to embroider the fabric is supplied from individual spools.

Schiffli lace is a type of embroidery that once was made by hand with needles that were pointed at both ends. The lasting popularity of handmade lace led to the invention of lace-making equipment such as Schiffli machines. Many types of lace are machine made, frequently with geometrically shaped netting used as backgrounds. Although previously made only from cotton, Schiffli lace, like other laces, can be manufactured from man-made fibers.

During the mid-1990s manufacturers invested in high-technology machinery such as computerized embroidery machines. As the textile industry continues to become increasingly automated, operators and setters will need to understand complex machinery and have sufficient computer skills.

There were 235 companies with a total of 4,325 employees in 1997 compared to 357 Schiffli machine embroidery companies with a total of 6,000 employees in 1977. Capital expenditures were $5.8 million in 1997, with $930,000 going for buildings and other structures while $4.9 million went for machinery and equipment. The total cost of materials was $83.0 million. The value of shipments in this category was $262.0 million in 1997, compared to $320.0 million in 1995 and $254.0 million in 1992.

Of the 235 companies doing business in this industry, 38 had at least 20 employees. These larger firms produced $90 million of the $262 million total value of shipments in the category. New Jersey and California had the largest number of companies in this industry, 108 and 29 respectively.

One of the largest companies in this industry in 1999 was Emb-Tex Corp. of Travelers Rest, South Carolina. Founded in 1956, Emb-Tex had 550 employees and sales of $30.0 million in 1998. Other leading businesses in the industry included Garment Graphics Inc. (Mounds View, Minnesota), with 160 employees and $28.7 million in sales; Jubilee Embroidery Company Inc. (Lugoff, South Carolina), with 170 employees and $16.0 million in sales; Embroidered Corporate Image Inc. (Hayden, Idaho), with 60 employees and $15.0 million in sales; and Voyager Emblems Inc. (Sanborn, New York), with 450 employees and $13.0 million in sales.

Following an almost continuous decline since 1988, employment in all of the fabricated textile industries increased in the mid-1990s. However, the U.S. Department of Labor predicts a general decline in employment for all textile machinery operators through the year 2006. Such a decline would be caused primarily by the introduction of new machines and more efficient operating practices (which reduce the number of workers needed at textile factories), along with more relaxed international trade agreements (which could place U.S. companies and workers in greater competition with imported textiles).

Total earnings for all Schiffli workers were $63 million in 1995 and $84 million in 1997. The industry's 3,674 production workers earned $59 million in 1997. Their average hourly wage was $7.98.

In 1994 the United States, Mexico, and Canada implemented the North American Free Trade Agreement (NAFTA), which removed tariffs and other trade restrictions from most goods made and sold in North America. In a press release issued by the American Textile Manufacturer's Institute (ATMI) in February 1997, President James M. Fitzgibbons said that the United States was the biggest exporter to Mexico in 1996. Fitzgibbons said, "This rapid increase in trade between the U.S. and Mexico is evidence that preferential trading agreements, when done correctly, can greatly benefit the U.S. textile industry."

FURTHER READING

"Moritz Embroidery Works, Inc." Pocono, PA: Moritz Embroidery Works, Inc., 1997. Available from http://www.qdtmoritz.com/.

U.S. Department of Commerce. U.S. Census Bureau. *1996 Annual Survey of Manufactures.* Washington, D.C.: GPO, 1998.

U.S. Department of Commerce. U.S. Census Bureau. *1997 Economic Census.* Washington, D.C.: GPO, 1999. Available from http://www.census.gov/prod/ec97/97m3132c.pdf.

U.S. Department of Labor. Bureau of Labor Statistics. *Career Guide to Industries, 1998-99 Edition. Bulletin 2503.* Washington, D.C.: GPO, 1998.

U.S. Department of Labor. Bureau of Labor Statistics. *Occupational Outlook Handbook 1998-99.* Washington, D.C.: GPO, 1999. Available from http://stats/bls,gov/oco/ocos235.htm.

SIC 2399

FABRICATED TEXTILE PRODUCTS, NOT ELSEWHERE CLASSIFIED

This category covers establishments primarily engaged in manufacturing fabricated textile products, not elsewhere classified.

NAICS CODE(S)

336360 (Motor Vehicle Fabric Accessories and Seat Manufacturing)

315999 (Other Apparel Accessories and Other Apparel Manufacturing)

314999 (All Other Miscellaneous Textile Product Mills)

Companies in this category supplied textile products to the automotive industry. They also manufactured items such as cloth diapers, fishing nets, aprons, horse blankets, hammocks, pennants, and non-leather straps.

The number of companies that manufactured products in this category (not necessarily as their primary product) increased from 845 in 1977 to about 1,100 in 1992. The value of shipments from those corporations increased from $1.1 billion in 1977 to $3.2 billion in 1992.

The U.S. Census Bureau reported that in 1997 there were 865 establishments fabricating textile products in this category. They shipped $3.3 billion worth of goods, spent $1.8 billion on materials, and paid $85.6 million for capital expenditures on new and used buildings and other structures, machinery, and equipment.

The value of automobile seat covers and tire covers shipped in 1997 was estimated at $521 million, up from $383 million in 1992. Shipments of flags, banners, and similar emblems were valued at $272 million, down from $285 million in 1992. Shipments of sleeping bags were valued at $207 million, up from $192 million in 1992. Shipments of parachutes were valued at $59 million, down from $83 million in 1992. Shipments of industrial shop towels were valued at $37 million, down from $38 million in 1992. Shipments of miscellaneous fabricated products made primarily of fabric were valued at $440 million, up from $221 million in 1992.

Shipments from Georgia were valued at $667 million, placing that state far ahead of Kentucky ($330 million), South Carolina ($213 million), California ($204 million), Tennessee ($197 million), Texas ($173 million), and North Carolina ($119 million).

Takata Inc. Gateway Safety Systems Co. (a subsidiary of Takata Inc.), based in Olympia Fields, Illinois, was one of the largest companies whose primary business fell within this category. This manufacturer of automobile seat belts had 1,300 employees and sales of $90 million in 1998. Other industry leaders included TechnoTrim Inc. (a subsidiary of Johnson Controls Inc. based in Livonia, Michigan) with estimated sales of $72 million, and Dundee Mills Inc. Baby Products Div. (a subsidiary of Dundee Mills Inc. based in Gainesville, Georgia) with sales of $50 million.

In 1997 there were 32,409 people employed in this category, compared to 39,000 in 1995 and 31,000 in 1977. The industry's 26,407 production workers earned an average hourly wage of $8.99 in 1997. Total payroll was $658 million.

In 1994 the United States, Mexico, and Canada implemented the North American Free Trade Agreement (NAFTA), a pact that gradually removed all tariffs and other trade restrictions from most goods made and sold in North America. The American Textile Manufacturer's

Institute (ATMI) reported that the United States was the biggest exporter to Mexico in 1996.

FURTHER READING

U.S. Department of Commerce. U.S. Census Bureau. *1995 Annual Survey of Manufacturers: Industry Statistics.* Washington, D.C.: GPO, 1998.

————. *1995 Annual Survey of Manufactures: Value of Product Shipments.* Washington, D.C.: GPO, 1997.

————. *1997 Economic Census.* Washington, D.C.: GPO, 1999. Available from http://www.census.gov/prod/ec97/97m3149e.pdf.

LUMBER & WOOD PRODUCTS, EXCEPT FURNITURE

LOGGING

This category covers establishments primarily engaged in cutting timber and in producing rough, round, hewn, or riven primary forest or wood raw materials, or in producing wood chips in the field. Independent contractors engaged in estimating or trucking lumber, but who perform no cutting operations, are classified in non-manufacturing industries. Establishments primarily engaged in the collection of bark, sap, gum, and other forest products are classified in **SIC 0811: Timber Tracts; SIC 0831: Forest Nurseries and Gathering of Forest Products;** and **SIC 0851: Forestry Services.**

NAICS CODE(S)

113310 (Logging)

INDUSTRY SNAPSHOT

Logging, among the oldest of American industries, has become one of the most controversial. Environmentalists have severely attacked harvesting practices, and they have scored significant victories. The strife between the industry and its opponents ignited in August 1990 when the federal government listed the northern spotted owl as an endangered species and developed rules to ensure its survival by protecting government forests in the Pacific Northwest. The net result was strict restrictions: logging was prevented within a 2,000-acre radius around a known spotted owl nest, the largest trees in that zone had to be left uncut around a 500-acre area, and logging was prohibited within a 70-acre area around a nest. Ever since, the industry has been engaged in ongoing court cases, political wrangling, and regulatory proceedings to retain logging rights on government lands.

Conservationists have been winning the battle. In 1999 the U.S. Forest Service barred roads and logging on more than 40 million acres of undeveloped land in federal forests. It also increased restrictions on logging and the timber harvest in Alaska's Tongass National Forest, one of the world's largest temperate rain forests. In Washington state, nine timber sales in old-growth forests were blocked and others threatened because surveys had not been conducted of the 77 endangered animal and plant species in the areas. Also, the timber industry, Native American tribes, and the state government were developing a plan to protect salmon and wildlife habitats. This protection plan was expected to restrict logging on some 764,000 acres of private forest in Western Washington.

The conflicts have had a major impact on the geographic distribution of logging within the United States. The South and the Pacific Northwest have been the two traditional centers of U.S. logging. In the South, loggers have relied on private holdings, which account for some 90 percent of all timberland in the region. In the Pacific Northwest, however, much of the supply has come from federal forests. With harvesting of government-owned land down sharply, the Pacific Northwest has accounted for a shrinking portion of the nation's production. Western lumber production decreased 1.2 percent from 17.5 billion board feet in 1997 to 17.2 billion board feet in 1998. The decrease included a drop of 12.8 percent in hardwood production and of 0.9 percent in softwood production. During the same period, eastern lumber production grew 0.7 percent from 29.1 billion board feet in 1997 to 29.3 billion board feet in 1998. Southern yellow pine production decreased 0.1 percent, but hardwood production increased 1.5 percent.

The industry's health is tied to demand in the residential and light commercial construction sector, as well as to foreign markets. In the late 1990s, the U.S. demand for wood products was a mixed blessing—it sustained the industry, but did not result in higher prices, mainly because imports added to an oversupply worsened by the Asian economic crisis. Export markets, especially Japan, cut back on imports. In 1997, Canada overtook Japan as the top export country; it also continued to be the top import country. Only modest growth was projected for the next five years. Gains in sales of wood products to the repair and remodeling sector were forecast to be offset by a lower level of domestic building. Despite the easing of trade barriers through the North American Free Trade Agreement (NAFTA), and multilateral trade negotiations under the auspices of the World Trade Organization (WTO), exports were expected to decline 11 percent annually over 1998-2003. Imports were expected to increase 3 percent per year over the same period.

ORGANIZATION AND STRUCTURE

A diverse group of economic entities and individuals are involved in logging. Among the participants are the giant, integrated forest products firms, like Weyerhaeuser and Georgia-Pacific, which may own millions of acres of private timberlands; small sawmills that may harvest relatively few trees on federal lands for their own use; and independent cutters, who are compensated according to the number of trees they are able to distribute to mills. Logging activities are thus distributed among different types of firms and individuals, but they can also be integrated with other operations within a single, large company.

BACKGROUND AND DEVELOPMENT

In the United States logging is older than the country itself, and wood products have played a central role in the economy's development. The clearing and revival of the U.S. forest has been extraordinary. The land area of the coterminous United States is 1.9 billion acres. Between 822 and 850 million acres, or about 45 percent of the country's land area, was originally covered by commercial forest. By 1920, owing to agricultural clearing, lumbering, and other activities, the original cover had fallen to about 470 million acres, of which only 138 million acres were original forest (some 250 million acres were significantly disturbed through grazing, cutting, and burning and could not sustain second growth, while 81 million acres were nonrenewable and nonrestoring). By 1977, however, because of better management, the suppression of fire, replanting, and other factors, the trend had reversed—the commercial forest had grown to 483 million acres. The U.S. Forest Service estimates that there were 490 million acres of timberland in 1992.

Logging in the great forests of the Pacific Northwest was started by the Hudson Bay Company at its Fort Vancouver trading post on the Columbia River in 1820. In 1825, the Royal Horticultural Society of London sent

out a Scottish botanist, David Douglas, to the area; he returned to England with a sprig of what is now the most important commercial tree of these forests, the eponymous Douglas fir. Logging as an industry began in the region at the time of the Gold Rush, which produced a new market for timber in California. It was the timber barons from the East who saw the potential of the Pacific Northwest forests. Most famous among them was George Weyerhaeuser, who incorporated his company in 1900 in Tacoma, Washington. Often a pioneer in the industry, Weyerhaeuser began the practice of hand-planting new trees on clear-cut lands in 1938.

Most of the nation's timber supply has come from softwoods, which are used predominately in housing construction. In 1987, approximately 35 percent of the nation's softwood lumber came from sales of timber on federal lands in the Pacific Northwest. By 1992, that contribution had dropped to 25 percent. Sales of timber from federal forests in the region fell from 6 billion board feet in 1987 to 1.5 billion in 1992.

The curtailment of harvesting on federal lands had a disparate impact on firms in the wood products industry. In general, the major forest products companies performed poorly during 1991 and had mixed results in 1992, as the recession took its toll. In the first half of 1993, however, large firms that had extensive land holdings of their own recorded sharply higher earnings, as they benefited from the price increases that accompanied shrinking supply. Other companies, however, including many small sawmills without timber assets, faced increasing margin pressure as their raw material costs rose. In 1995 and 1996, wood product companies held their own in the face of continued flat prices. In 1995, wood chip demand from the paper industry and a strong level of Canadian imports created an oversupply of lumber and held back a return to stronger conditions. However, the paper industry demand for chips dropped, and an April 1996 Canadian lumber quota reduced the lumber supply.

The national recession during the early 1990s hurt the wood products sector badly, but as the recession waned, the industry began to recover. Due largely to the strength of higher housing starts and firmer timber prices, the wood products operations of the major forest products companies did better in 1992 and 1993 than in 1991. In the first half of 1993, profits at those companies that rely most heavily on wood products were up 179 percent from the same period in 1992. Nevertheless, the prospect of sustained cutbacks in the timber supply raised significant questions about the long-term health of the industry. In 1996, merger and acquisition activity was strong, with 5 million acres of timberland changing hands. Most of the land that changed hands was in the southern and western regions of the United States. About 7 percent of the estimated 68.6 million acres then owned by the industry were in those regions. Fifty percent of the 5 million acres that changed hands was in the South, 42 percent was in the West, and 8 percent was in the Northeast and Great Lake states.

Through the mid-1990s, smaller sawmill companies in the Pacific Northwest were hurt by contracting supply and continued to decline in number. Some observers blamed the companies since they tended to disregard forecasts, dating back to the 1970s, of a looming timber shortage during the 1990s. They also suggested that at the rate the loggers were cutting, the Pacific Northwest would have had severe supply problems by the year 2000, regardless of the spotted owl endangerment controversy.

Environmental constraints placed on logging in the 1990s reduced by 75 percent the amount of timber harvested from national forests in the United States. These logging restrictions did not have a major impact in most of the South, the Northeast, and North Central regions of the country. They did have a dramatic impact on the Pacific Northwest, which had supplied about half of the country's timber for wood products. The restrictions resulted in reduced production, and consequently the closing of some operations, and set off ongoing political and social problems for the industry. From their major victory in limiting logging in areas in which the spotted owl was found, environmentalists went on to secure habitat protection for other animal and plant species. Also, in the 1990s, the Forest Service began shifting use of national forests from logging to recreation, further limiting timber available to loggers.

Lumber markets improved in 1996 due to tightened lumber supplies and better pricing for lumber products. Housing starts increased 5 percent in 1996, aiding wood products sales. However, the industry also struggled against competing materials, namely steel for wood, in homebuilding. An increasing number of builders used steel-frame housing; an estimated 80,000 houses were built with the technology in 1996, compared to 800 houses in 1992. The availability of affordable wood products, however, dampened this building construction trend.

The Spotted Owl Controversy. On June 26, 1990, the government listed the northern spotted owl as a threatened species under the Endangered Species Act. Unlike most other species protected by the Act, the spotted owl's habitat covers a much larger area: it ranges from southern British Columbia, Canada, to Marin County, California. Under the terms of the Act, more than 5 million acres of forests were designated as conservation areas; these generally contained conifers of mixed varieties that were more than 200 years old—old-growth forests.

Technically, logging was still allowed within the conservation areas as long as it did not threaten the spotted owl, but as a practical matter, much of the owl's

habitat was off-limits to loggers. The U.S. Forest Service reported that in total it sold 4.45 billion board feet of timber in fiscal 1992—less than half of its sales in 1990. The agency managed to sell only 20 percent of the Congressionally approved volume in the Pacific Northwest and 40 percent in California. Most, if not all, of this shortfall stemmed from measures taken to protect the spotted owl and other species. Loggers cut 61 percent more national forest timber in 1992 than was sold during the year.

Some observers blamed the timber industry for its problems with the owl. They argued that the industry ignored the bird and tried to discredit research that showed the owl was truly endangered. They also said that the timber on the federal lands which the spotted owls inhabit represent public assets—assets that, in their view, have often been sold at below cost by the Forest Service and the Bureau of Land Management for the industry's benefit.

Many industry supporters, however, said there is much evidence that spotted owls of one subspecies or another are thriving on millions of acres of privately and publicly managed second-growth forests. They also noted that counts of the northern spotted owl have risen substantially over the past several years. They argued, additionally, that even if the spotted owl was indeed endangered, it did not provide sufficient reason to throw thousands of workers out of their jobs and destroy dozens of timber communities. The logging industry has fought for its livelihood through court cases.

Some observers within the industry and the environmental movement believe that efforts to save individual species are merely tactical devices in the battle to curtail logging. The environmental movement needed a weapon to shut down logging on federal lands, they say, and the Endangered Species Act happened to be conveniently at hand.

Environmentalists recognize that the total amount of woodland in the United States is not contracting—new plantings more than offset cuttings. Still, many are concerned that the way the nation's forests have been managed reduces biodiversity. When loggers cut down mixed forests with trees of different ages, they often replant with a single species (such as the Douglas fir, which reaches maturity in a relatively fast 50 years) of the same age. Some environmentalists argue that in a naturally regenerating forest, there are dead trees, clearings, old trees, and young trees, and each attracts its own group of plant and animal species. But when a forest consists solely of one tree type, all of the same age, only one set of species is attracted. Ecologists believe that this hurts the forest's ecosystem and leaves it prone to pest infestations.

In rebuttal, the industry's supporters pointed to the expansion in total timberland over the past 50 years and

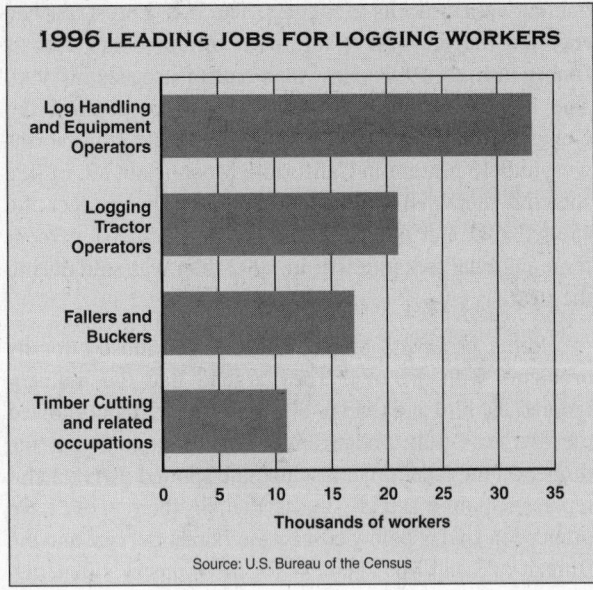

1996 LEADING JOBS FOR LOGGING WORKERS

Source: U.S. Bureau of the Census

the millions of acres, including much old-growth (trees over 200 years old), in national and state forests that are protected from logging. They also called attention to the significant advances in forestry management over several decades. For example, after the volcanic eruption of Mount St. Helens on May 18, 1980, Congress, in 1982, established a 110,000-acre National Volcanic Monument. In this area nature would be allowed to take its course, and the land would be left undisturbed. On the acreage adjacent to it, Weyerhaeuser and other companies salvaged the downed trees and planted new seedlings. According to some observers, the result of this effort is a forest not significantly different from the original (pre-1980) cover below the slopes of the volcano. By 1992, many of the trees Weyerhaeuser had planted were already 25 or 30 feet high. Next door, the National Volcanic Monument was recovering much more slowly—but, some would argue, more completely.

In February 1993, news reports indicated that the Clinton Administration was trying to modify the policies of the Department of Interior (DOI) so that "national train wrecks" (in the words of DOI Secretary Bruce Babbitt), like the one over the spotted owl in the Pacific Northwest, could be averted in the future. Instead of protecting single species, the DOI would seek preventive measures to insure long-term protection of whole ecosystems and all of their species. The theory behind such an approach is that conservation and business interests are better served by preplanning the fate of entire ecosystems before any single species is threatened.

Winners and Losers. Cutbacks of harvesting on federal lands has had a diverse impact on industry participants. Some believe that the largest companies—at least those with substantial timber holdings of their own—have been

less than vigorous in fighting curtailments of logging on federal land. These firms have huge plantations of genetically improved trees, which afford them ample supply. Their reliance on federal sales of old-growth trees is relatively small, and the spotted owl doesn't appear to thrive on their own second- and third-growth forests. It has been argued, therefore, that these companies have been willing, and even happy, to accept restrictions on logging of federal lands.

Small, independent sawmill owners, on the other hand, have relied since World War II on public lands to supply the old-growth logs that can be turned into specialty products. The trees they used were often as much as five centuries old; consequently, they were often inhabited by the spotted owl. The trees that have been engineered by big corporations are but a tenth the age and only half the height of the old-growth trees. Often they are too small for the saws and conveyor belts of the old-time sawmills.

The South. Level terrain, frost-free winters, and numerous highways made logging much easier in the South than it was in the Northwest. Trees in the region grew faster because of the relatively warm winters. Since most of the South's acreage was logged years ago, there is little of the old-growth forest that has aroused such strong environmental opposition in the Northwest. Most notably, some 90 percent of Southern timberland is privately owned.

The conflicts between the environmentalists and timber interests that halted logging in much of the Northwest has been comparatively rare in the South. The two sides have actually worked together to balance environmental and economic concerns. Georgia-Pacific (which moved its headquarters from Portland, Oregon, to Atlanta, Georgia, in 1982 and became an important presence in the region) believed in the mid-1990s that it was successfully dealing with the red-cockaded woodpecker, which some saw as a potential "spotted owl" of the South. Others, however, believed it was only a matter of time before the environmental movement began to become more aggressive in opposing logging in the South.

CURRENT CONDITIONS

A strong demand for wood products used in residential housing and light commercial construction provided single-digit growth in the late 1990s. However, housing starts were expected to decline 1 percent annually and adversely affect the industry. The decline was expected to be counteracted by an anticipated 2 percent annual increase in the repair and remodeling sector.

The Asian economic crisis hindered industry growth during the late 1990s. Reductions in Japanese demand for wood products, especially for housing applications, meant a reduction in exports to that country and contributed to oversupply in the United States. Imports and the growth in forest product capacity in emerging countries, which protected themselves with high tariffs, also contributed to oversupply. Imports of forest products, which topped exports by $2.9 billion in 1994, jumped to $9.4 billion in 1998 and were projected to continue their steady growth. The top five export countries in 1997 were Canada (22.0 percent share), Japan (17.5 percent), Germany (8.0 percent), the United Kingdom (6.7 percent), and Mexico (5.5 percent). The top five import countries were Canada (83.5 percent share), Indonesia (3.6 percent), Brazil (3.2 percent), Mexico (1.4 percent), and Chile (1.1 percent). The U.S. forest products industry saw the easing of trade barriers as critical. Government negotiators work to equalize international trade; however, a tariff agreement presented at the World Trade Organization meeting in December 1999 was not acted upon. The agreement would have eliminated tariffs on paper products between 2000 and 2002 and on wood products between 2002 and 2004.

While the clash between the timber industry and environmentalists (or preservationists, the term the industry prefers) has centered on the survival of the northern spotted owl, campaigns to protect other species may affect the industry in the future. Timber executives are also worried about the impact of logging on salmon. Because logging often damages the streams in which salmon spawn, the species could eventually become federally protected and thus further limit the industry in the Northwest.

INDUSTRY LEADERS

The leading companies in the logging industry in 1998 were MAXXAM Inc., RLC Industries Co., Plum Creek Timber Company, Pacific Lumber and Shipping Co., and Sealaska Corporation. MAXXAM is a holding company that had 1998 sales of $2.57 billion. RLC Industries had an estimated $740 million in sales in 1997. Plum Creek Timber Company had sales of $699 million in 1998. The company owned some 3.3 million acres of timberland in Arkansas, Idaho, Louisiana, Maine, Montana, and Washington and operated 11 wood-products conversion plants that produced lumber, plywood, and fiberboard. Pacific Lumber had 1997 sales of $320 million. Established in 1932, the company shipped softwoods and hardwoods to 40 countries on four continents. Pacific Lumber and its timber subsidiary owned an estimated 200,000 acres of old-growth redwood and Douglas fir timberlands in California, which conservationists worked to have preserved. Sealaska Corporation, owned by Alaska Native shareholders, is the largest private landowner in southeast Alaska. It had 1997 sales of $237 million.

Other companies with a stake in the logging industry included Crown Pacific Partners, Rayonier Inc., The Tim-

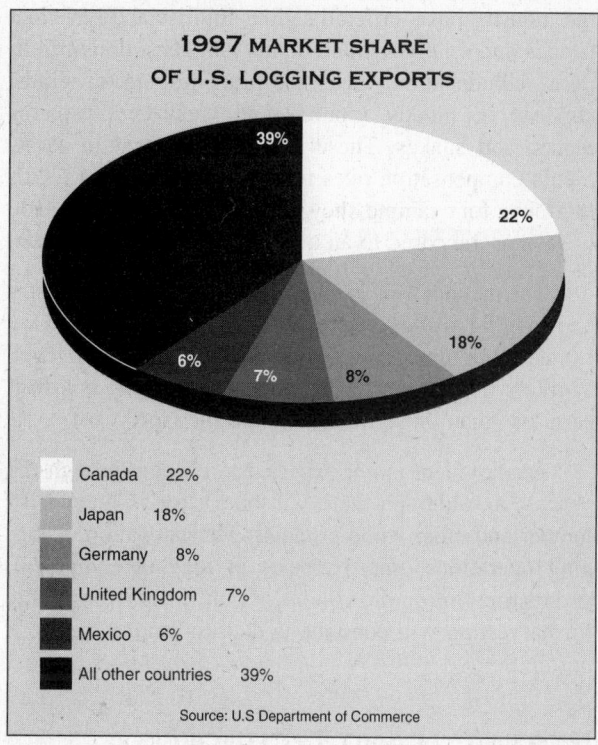

1997 MARKET SHARE OF U.S. LOGGING EXPORTS

Canada	22%
Japan	18%
Germany	8%
United Kingdom	7%
Mexico	6%
All other countries	39%

Source: U.S Department of Commerce

ber Company, and Weyerhaeuser Company. Crown Pacific Partners owned nearly 800,000 acres of timberland and had an annual log and lumber production capacity of 570 million board feet. It had 1998 sales of $667 million. Rayonier produced logs and other wood products for sale in 60 countries, and managed some 1.5 million acres of timberland in the United States and New Zealand. It had 1998 sales of $1 billion. The Timber Company is the subsidiary of Georgia-Pacific Corporation that owned or leased 5 million acres of timberland and is obligated to sell 80 percent of its timber to its parent. The company had 1998 sales of $514 million. Weyerhaeuser Company was the world's largest private owner of softwood timber, with holdings in the southern United States, the Pacific Northwest, and had cutting rights to 33.5 million acres in Canada. It had 1998 sales of $10.76 billion.

WORKFORCE

In 1996, logging workers held approximately 82,000 jobs, 200 more than in 1995. There were 33,000 log handling and equipment operators; 21,000 logging tractor operators; 17,000 fallers and buckers; and 11,000 workers in timber cutting and related logging occupations. In the late 1980s, some 88,000 people were employed in logging. Self-employed workers account for one of every three logging workers. About 40 percent of logging workers are employed in the Southeast and about 25 percent are in the Northwest.

Logging occupations are physically demanding, and the work can be very dangerous. Many workers within the industry have suffered serious injuries and have had friends and relatives killed on the job. Hazardous conditions include falling trees and branches, strong winds, slippery or muddy ground, foul weather, poisonous plants, and snakes. These risks are apparent in workmen's compensation rates for loggers. In the mid-1990s in Maine, for example, they ran about $37 for every $100 in salary, compared to an average of $12 for carpenters.

The median weekly earnings for all full-time forestry and logging workers were $445 in 1996. Earnings vary by size of employer, geographic area, and skill level. Workers in the South, where the cost of living is lower, earn less than those in Alaska and the Northwest.

Employment is not expected to change through the year 2006, although there will be a steady demand for lumber and other wood products. Mechanization of logging operations, improvements in logging equipment, and restrictions on the volume of public timber available for harvesting will continue to depress employment opportunities.

RESEARCH AND TECHNOLOGY

As a result of mechanization and automation, timber companies can log more efficiently while doing less harm to the environment. Huge "feller-bunches" have often replaced individual loggers in second-growth forests. These vehicles are built like tanks and have enormous "scissors" mounted on the front; they are able to snip mature trees and lay them down carefully to avoid smashing small, still-growing ones. Additionally, mechanized skidders that are used to haul logs out of the forest are being fitted with extra-wide tracks or oversized tires to spread their weight and reduce damage to the forest floor.

Timber companies are also experimenting with different forestry techniques. After harvesting, some loggers are leaving behind the odd mature tree, dead-sun-silvered trunks, and the usual litter of the woods. The hope is that, as new trees grow, their surroundings mimic what would follow a natural fire or windstorm, which a forest can survive.

Timber shortages and the possibility of higher lumber prices over the long-term are encouraging the creation of new offerings and the promotion of relatively inexpensive existing products. To fend off challenges, the industry is focusing on promoting such engineered wood products as oriented strand board and particle board.

FURTHER READING

Cory, M. James. "If a Tree Falls, etc., Market View, Editorial." *Home Improvement Market,* October 1996.

Darnay, Arsen J., ed. *Manufacturing USA.* Detroit: Gale Research, 1998.

Erb, George. "Timber or Salmon: Deal Would Reduce Logging." *Puget Sound Business Journal,* 22 January 1999.

"Forestry and Logging Occupations." *1998-99 Occupational Outlook Handbook.* Available from http://stats//bls.gov/oco/ocos178.htm.

Hoover's Online Company Capsules. Available from http://www.hoovers.com/co/.

"Lumber Production and Mill Stocks, 1998." U.S. Census Bureau, November 1999. Available from http://www.census.gov/ftp/pub/industry/1/ma24t98.pdf.

Seideman, David. "Out on a Limb." *Audubon,* November 1999.

"U.S. Wood Industry Reshaped By Timberland Acquisitions." *Wood Technology,* September 1996.

Whitman, David. "See Forests through Trees." *U.S. News & World Report,* 25 October 1999.

SIC 2421

SAWMILLS AND PLANING MILLS, GENERAL

This industry includes establishments primarily engaged in sawing rough lumber and timber from logs and bolts, or resawing cants and flitches into lumber, including box lumber and softwood cut stock; planing mills combined with sawmills; and separately operated planing mills that are engaged primarily in producing surfaced lumber and standard workings or patterns of lumber. The industry also includes establishments primarily engaged in sawing lath and railroad ties and in producing tobacco hogshead stock, wood chips, and snow fence lath. Establishments primarily engaged in manufacturing box shook or boxes are classified in wood container manufacturing industries; those manufacturing sash, doors, wood molding, window and door frames, and other fabricated millwork are classified in millwork, veneer, plywood, and structural wood industries; and those manufacturing hardwood dimension and flooring are classified in **SIC 2426: Hardwood Dimension and Flooring Mills.**

NAICS CODE(S)

321912 (Cut Stock, Resawing Lumber, and Planing)
321113 (Sawmills)
321918 (Other Millwork (including Flooring))
321999 (All Other Miscellaneous Wood Product Manufacturing)

INDUSTRY SNAPSHOT

Despite a strong U.S. economy in the mid- to late 1990s, which spurred demand for wood products in residential and light commercial construction, as well as for residential repair, remodeling, and home improvements, this industry experienced only modest growth. Nevertheless, sawmills and planing mills are the second largest sector in the forest products industry and the largest sector in the solid wood products industry. Their major product is sawn softwood (from coniferous trees) and hardwood (from deciduous trees) lumber. The industry's product shipments of $19.4 billion in 1996 increased 2 percent in 1997 to an estimated $22.0 billion. Between 1997 and 1998, however, production of lumber was unchanged at 46.6 billion board feet.

Several factors affected the industry. Although sawmills were closing, primarily due to curtailment of logging in Western federal lands, those still operating maintained active production, creating an oversupply that dampened market prices. Lumber prices peaked in 1996 at $480 per thousand board feet. In mid-1998 they were at a low of $260 per thousand board feet, but by March 1999 they had climbed to $340. Conditions in foreign markets also are contributing to oversupply. In 1998 imports accounted for 30.1 percent of consumption compared with 29.5 percent in 1997. Exports dropped from 6.4 percent in 1997 to 4.9 percent in 1998. The 1996 U.S.-Canada Softwood Lumber Agreement, intended to control imports from Canada, had little impact, as Canadian producers found it worthwhile to pay penalty fees for shipping large volumes of lumber. Canadian shipments to the U.S. decreased 2 percent in 1997, only to increase 3 percent in 1998. Imports from Latin American countries are also on the increase. Exports were negatively impacted by the Asian economic crisis. In addition, a 2 percent increase in 1997 in the national sales tax in Japan, the largest export market for U.S. softwood lumber, caused a major downturn in the housing market; export market share decreased from 54 percent in 1996 to 41 percent in 1997. Canada and Spain are the second and third largest export markets.

ORGANIZATION AND STRUCTURE

The largest companies operating sawmills and planing mills cut a large percentage of the total North American production. According to the *U.S. Industry & Trade Outlook,* "commodities manufactured by this sector are used in a wide range of applications, including residential construction and repairs as well as nonresidential construction, paper and allied products, millwork items, cabinetry and furniture, prefabricated housing units, and sporting goods and toys." The industry is affected by governmental environmental and land-use policies that regulate logging. In recent years those policies have contributed to consolidation of companies.

BACKGROUND AND DEVELOPMENT

The first sawmill in the United States is said to have been built in York, Maine, in 1623. Sawmills quickly became a common sight in frontier settlements. Most were small enterprises with one or two workers, and nearly all of these mills were on rivers, using running water as their power source. As railroads spread across the country in the nineteenth century, the best spot to put a sawmill became the bank of a log-driving stream where a railway crossed it. With the shift from water to steam power, mills became larger and more complex. One mill on the Saginaw River produced 14 million board feet during the first half of 1874 and employed 150 men. Circular saws replaced the old-fashioned up and down saws in the 1860s, and the contemporary invention of a method for repairing worn or broken teeth greatly extended their useful lives. Electric power began to replace steam power in the early twentieth century, and by 1929 it accounted for 45 percent of all energy sources.

The mid-1990s were the best and worst of times for sawmill owners. With the economy healthy and interest rates low, housing starts climbed, and lumber demand was buoyant. But while strong demand led to higher prices, lumber quotes continued to be highly volatile. Moreover, the supply side of the equation remained perilous. Conservationists remained committed to restricting timber harvesting, and the fight for control of the nation's forests was as polarized as ever. Thus mill owners had to scramble to find adequate supplies of raw material.

Relatively small mills without their own timber holdings came under increasing pressure as logging on federal lands declined—between 1987 and 1995, the Western lumber industry lost almost half its mills. The major, integrated forest products companies that had large timber holdings of their own, however, remained competitive. While the big firms were not insulated from losses related to environmental legislation, they were generally in a stronger position to benefit from the higher prices that followed restricted supplies.

There also was a notable shift in lumber production away from the Northwest and toward the South, where most timberlands are privately owned. During the 1980s the seven largest forest products companies cut their mill capacity in the Pacific Northwest by 35 percent, while they increased it in the South by 121 percent. In the 1990s, lumber production continued to shift to the South, where softwood output was approaching that in the West.

In 1994, the 20 largest lumber producers in the United States cut a total of 22.5 billion board feet, or some 38 percent of total North American production. These 20 firms operated 252 mills—down from 283 mills in 1991. The 100 largest companies in North America cut about 43 billion board feet, or about 71 percent of the industry's total production.

Even without any impact from curtailments of logging due to the spotted owl controversy, there was a general trend toward consolidation in this industry. One study completed on the lumber industry in Idaho noted that in 1956, the state had 311 sawmills, with 37 producing more than 10 million board feet. By 1990 the number of sawmills had fallen to 80, with 40 producing more than 10 million feet. In 1956, 73 percent of lumber production came from mills producing more than 10 million feet annually. In 1979, mills with yearly output of 10 million feet represented 93 percent of the state's lumber supply. In 1990, the forty mills in this category produced 98 percent of Idaho's 2.06 billion feet of lumber.

Lumber consumption increased about 6 percent in 1996 to 50.5 billion board feet, compared with 47.7 billion feet the year before. Annual housing starts increased by 9 percent to 1.48 million units from 1.35 million units in 1995, and were about level with 1.46 million starts in 1994. Repair and remodeling also did well, rising 6.5 percent.

Pricing. Because of the rise in new home construction and the increasing restrictions on the lumber supply, lumber prices rose dramatically in 1993 to about $500 per thousand board feet. For most of 1994, lumber prices were still quite high, fluctuating between $350 and $400. The high prices drove wood consumers to search for alternative materials, and the use of engineered wood and nonwood substitutes increased. In 1995, as prices eased further, the amount of lumber used per square foot of construction rose. In 1996, when prices again turned up, users once more considered lumber substitutes.

Wood Alternatives. Despite the frustration with lumber's price volatility, users were not rushing to buy other materials. As lumber prices climbed above $500 per thousand board feet in 1993 and future supplies became uncertain, steel producers envisaged a windfall from the construction sector. But it never materialized because lumber prices retreated in 1995. However, there were also significant, underlying impediments to switching over to steel. Building codes were written mostly for wood and masonry, and carpenters, accustomed to working in wood, had little desire to use steel. Thus steel's share of the market for home frames was just 2 percent in 1996. Still, users were not happy with the lumber situation. With harvesting of federal lands severely restricted and demand healthy, mill owners scrambled to find logs. High lumber prices did enable Western mills to pay the hefty quotes private owners demanded for their logs. But clear, blemish-free lumber comes from the mature trees of old forests, which environmentalists had mostly put under wraps; younger trees have a smaller percentage of clear wood. Thus the industry has become more sensitive to grade distinctions, with ''better'' (i.e., blemish-free) grades selling at a premium. Builders discovered that home buyers who watch their houses being built often demand this perfect lumber, even if other grades meet all structural requirements. But sometimes the difference in

grades isn't purely cosmetic. Some of the wood of the faster-growing, younger trees that private tree farmers harvest is less strong, and thus more wood must be used to cover the same span. While this is usually not a crucial matter in a typical single-family home, for light commercial builders it had become an important issue. Thus builders continued to search for reliable alternatives.

Move to the South. The wood products industry began to shift from the Pacific Northwest to the South in the late 1980s and 1990s, primarily because of environmental legislation and regulations that limited harvesting of federal timber lands. Even relatively small sales of federal timber lands became tangled up in lawsuits and court actions. In 1987, almost 10 billion board feet of timber was harvested from federal forests, compared with about 2.2 billion board feet in 1995—a drop of 78 percent in eight years. Overall, annual lumber production in the West fell by one-third over the period. Meanwhile, production of lumber from southern pine (mostly on private lands in the South) rose by about one-fifth.

Many sawmills in the Pacific Northwest, particularly those that had relied on old-growth trees from federal lands for their logs, experienced dramatically reduced profit margins and struggled to survive. The Western lumber industry had 702 mills operating in 1987; at the end of 1995, there were just 357 left. While the trend toward consolidation has been evident for decades, the difficulty of obtaining adequate supply certainly put increasing pressure on small mills.

Trade Conditions. The industry also was affected in the mid-1990s by international markets. Softwood lumber exports fell 3.2 percent in 1996 to 1.9 billion board feet. Exports to Europe and Japan were down 4 percent and 3 percent, respectively, while shipments to Australia and Mexico dropped 36 percent and 17 percent, respectively. In April 1996, Japan agreed to accept lumber grades that may have a few more imperfections but are still structurally sound. Lumber exporters hoped the agreement would shore up shipments to Japan, although some domestic users expressed concern that it would exacerbate lumber price inflation in the United States.

To meet expanding demand at home, the U.S. increased its lumber imports. In 1994, softwood lumber imports, mostly from Canada, rose 16 percent to $5.8 billion. To help even the flow of lumber between the two countries, on April 2, 1996, Canada agreed to restrict its softwood lumber exports to 14.7 billion board feet between April 1, 1996, and March 31, 1997. Lumber prices rose sharply after the agreement went into effect, and U.S. builders protested what they felt was the agreement's impact on lumber markets. However, the effect of the pact on prices was a subject of dispute—some in the lumber industry argued that strong demand and lower inventories importantly contributed to the short-term price changes.

CURRENT CONDITIONS

In the late 1990s, sawmills and planing mills were being affected by policies concerning logging in government forests. Curtailment of logging on federal lands began in the early 1990s when the spotted owl was placed on the endangered species list and its nesting areas were made off-limits to loggers. Further restrictions were imposed because of concerns about other species, including salmon. In 10 years, from a peak in 1987 of 12.7 billion board feet of timber, the timber harvest on federal lands fell to 3.3 billion board feet—a drop of 75 percent. In 1999, the Clinton Administration proposed to protect another 40 million acres of undeveloped forest from logging. These policies chiefly affected Western national forests, and consequently adversely affected Western sawmills, which relied on a supply of logs from federal lands. Many mills went out of business or consolidated. Eastern sawmills, which relied on logs generally cut from private lands, on the other hand, saw some improvement in production levels. Eastern lumber production increased from 29.1 billion board feet in 1997 to 29.3 billion board feet in 1998; Western lumber production decreased from 17.5 billion board feet in 1997 to 17.2 billion board feet in 1998.

The outlook for the industry appeared mixed. Moderate growth was expected through 2003. A healthy U.S. single-family housing market and home remodeling market was expected to sustain demand for lumber and other products produced by sawmills and planing mills; this demand was expected to offset declines in exports in ailing foreign markets.

INDUSTRY LEADERS

Large and small companies are engaged in sawmill and planing mill activities. They also are engaged in manufacturing products other than those classified under this category. The following sales figures cover all products produced by the companies. According to *Manufacturing USA,* in 1998 the top lumber producer in North America was Georgia-Pacific Group, with facilities in the United States and Canada. It had sales of $13.22 billion and was second in the forest and paper products category. Weyerhaeuser Company, in second place in 1998, had sales of $10.76 billion. *Hoover's Company Capsules* notes that "Weyerhaeuser is the world's largest private owner of softwood timber, with about 5.7 million acres in the southern U.S. and the Pacific Northwest and cutting rights to about 33.5 million acres in Canada."

Champion International Corporation ranked third in 1998 with sales of $5.65 billion. It controls about 5 million acres of timberland. Louisiana-Pacific, which controls some 950,000 acres of timberland, mainly in Texas and Louisiana, had $2.3 billion in sales in 1998. The company's "customers include large-volume building-products retailers and manufactured and traditional home builders," according to *Hoover's.* One of the oldest privately owned forest products companies in the Northwest, Simpson Investment Co., is the fifth leading company, with sales of $1.5 billion.

Other leading companies include: Rayonier Inc., which manages 1.5 million acres of timber, operates two lumber mills in the United States, and sells its products in 60 countries; Temple-Inland Inc., which produces lumber from the approximately 2.2 million acres of timber it controls; Crown Pacific Partners, L.P., which produces 570 million board feet annually from its six sawmills and some 800,000 acres of timber; Hampton Affiliates, which produces 825 million board feet of lumber annually from its five mills and some 182,000 acres of timber; Sierra Pacific Industries, which produces millwork products and lumber at its 12 planing mills and sawmills using timber from its 1.4 million acres; Plum Creek Timber Company, Inc., which owns 3.3 million acres of timber; and Pope & Talbot, Inc., whose chief wood products are specialty lumber and wood chips.

RESEARCH AND TECHNOLOGY

New technology and automation greatly improved productivity in the industry. In the 1990s, mills used computerized controls and laser scanners to maximize the amount of lumber obtained from a log. Automated graders were replacing humans. Waste materials were being used to fire boilers that provided mills with electricity, and some were being creatively marketed to consumers as dyed planer shavings and shrink-wrapped bundles of firewood. Because of improved machine and saw technologies, companies were able to increase profits by consuming the same or a lesser amount of wood. They also expanded their markets by offering cut-to-size parts, shaping beyond planing, panels, and other products and services to customers.

FURTHER READING
Blackman, Ted. "For a Look at High Tech, Head for Quebec Sawmills." *Wood Technology,* October 1996.

Darnay, Arsen J., ed. *Manufacturing USA.* Detroit: Gale Research, 1998.

"Forest Products." *Standard & Poor's Industry Surveys,* July 1999.

Holt, Shirleen. "No Knot, No Splinters, No Dice." *Oregon Business,* August 1996.

Kelly, Joseph. "Is More U.S. Lumber Bound for Japan?" *Home Improvement Market,* October 1996.

Shuster, Laurie. "Lumber Prices Continue to Climb." *Home Improvement Market,* October 1996.

Tooch, David. "Value-Added Dilemma: Is This Biz for You?" *Wood Technology,* July 1999.

U.S. Census Bureau. "Production and Mill Stocks," November 1999. Available from http://www.census.gov/ftp/pub/industry/1/ma24t98.pdf.

U.S. Industry and Trade Outlook '99. McGraw-Hill and U.S. Department of Commerce, 1999.

Whitman, David. "See Forests through Trees." *U.S. News & World Report,* 25 October 1999.

"Why Lumber Isn't What It Used to Be." *Home Improvement Market,* October 1996.

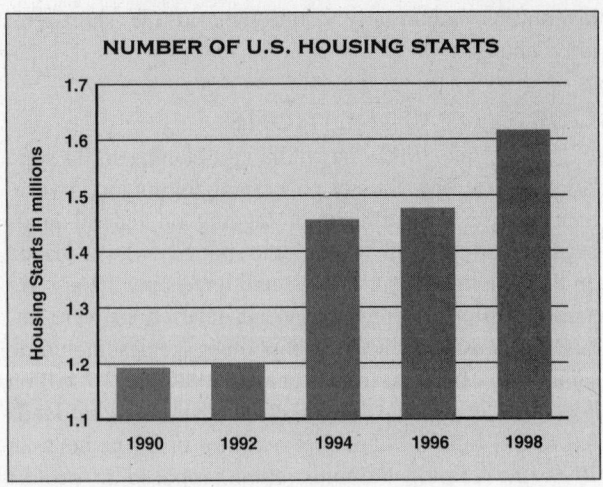

NUMBER OF U.S. HOUSING STARTS

SIC 2426

HARDWOOD DIMENSION AND FLOORING MILLS

This classification consists of companies that primarily make hardwood dimension lumber and workings therefrom; and other hardwood dimension, semifabricated or ready for assembly; hardwood flooring; and wood frames for household furniture. Companies that primarily make stairwork, molding, and trim are classified in **SIC 2431: Millwork;** and those making textile machinery bobbins, picker sticks, and shuttles are classified in **SIC 3552: Textile Machinery.**

NAICS CODE(S)
321918 (Other Millwork (including Flooring))
321999 (All Other Miscellaneous Wood Product Manufacturing)
337215 (Showcase, Partition, Shelving, and Locker Manufacturing)
321912 (Cut Stock, Resawing Lumber, and Planing)

Hardwood flooring and furniture components make up the largest shares of output in this industry segment. The remaining output includes many items, such as skis, golf clubs, and tool handles. Wood blocks for bowling pins and textile machinery accessories, rounds or rungs for ladders, and spool blocks and blanks are also produced by this industry.

The total value of all products and services sold by the hardwood dimension and flooring mills industry was $2.91 billion in 1995, up significantly from $1.74 billion in 1990. This figure represented a steady increase that continued throughout the 1990s. Since the health of this industry is tied closely to housing starts in the United States, the strong economy of the mid- to late 1990s brought rising revenues. There were 1.62 million housing starts in 1998, compared to 1.35 million in 1996 and 1.01 million in 1991. Housing starts in 1998 were up 9.7 percent over 1997 figures, and the industry's growth was expected to continue into the 2000s.

Among trends propelling the growth in this industry are the tendency for new houses to be bigger than those built in the early 1990s, the growth of interest in restoration and repair, and the increase in popularity of hardwood flooring. Wood flooring reached an industry low in 1982, but in the 1990s the installation of hardwood flooring increased nearly 10 percent. In 1996, the average new house used 244 board feet of lumber, compared to 172 board feet in 1990. The amount of hardwood flooring shipped in 1996 was more than 367 million board feet, compared to nearly 200 million board feet in 1991.

Oak, beech, birch, maple, and pecan are the species most often used in furniture and flooring manufacturing in the United States. Ash, cherry, poplar, and walnut are also frequently used. Moreover, four types of flooring are commonly made: strip, parquet, plank, and laminated.

Hardwood dimension and flooring generally account for 8 to 10 percent of hardwood lumber exports by value. Canada, Japan, and Taiwan are the most frequent destinations of dimension and flooring exported by the United States. In the mid-1990s, about 12 percent of the dimension and flooring consumed in the United States was imported, with the biggest suppliers being Canada and Japan. Throughout the late 1990s and early 2000s, wood product imports are expected to increase, especially from Canada. U.S. exports to Asian markets suffered during the Asian financial crisis of the late 1990s; exports were expected to increase as the difficulties the region wane.

Triangle Pacific Corporation of Dallas, Texas was an industry leader, with 1997 sales of $653 million and nearly 5,000 employees. Triangle Pacific made hardwood floors under the brand names Bruce, Hartco, and Robbins. The company's cabinet division made wood cabinets for kitchens and bathrooms with brand names such as Ultrawood, Baseline, and Gemini. Crown Pacific Partners, L.P. of Portland, Oregon was another industry leader with 1998 sales of $667 million and 1,200 employees. The company owns mature forests in Washington, Oregon, Idaho, and Montana that, combined, total over 700,000 acres and have a potential for billions of board feet of lumber.

In 1994 this industry employed 35,300 people, with approximately 31,400 working in production. This is a 30 percent increase from 1990, when the industry employed 24,600 production workers. Nationwide, there were approximately 730 companies in this industry in the early 1990s. Of those, only 3 companies had more than 500 employees; 79 employed between 100 and 500 workers; 162 companies had 20 to 49 employees; and 178 companies had fewer than 5 employees.

Several issues may affect the hardwood dimension and flooring industry in coming years. Changes in logging and land management regulations could have a major impact, as well as legislation affecting lumber imports or exports. Those changes, coupled with stricter air pollution laws, may drive up the cost of lumber. The industry will most likely remain vulnerable to any changes, good or bad, in the number of housing starts. As long as the booming economy and high consumer confidence of the late 1990s persist, new housing starts and a desire for furniture and flooring should remain strong. An interesting future trend, based primarily on environmental concerns, may be the refurbishing and marketing of "antique" floor and wall boards salvaged from condemned buildings.

FURTHER READING

Dwyer, D.K., et al. "Building Industry: The House Call." *Salomon Smith Barney,* March 16, 1999.

"Flooring Shipments and Housing Starts, 1996." The National Oak Flooring Manufacturers Association, Memphis, Tennessee.

Hoover's Company Capsules. Austin, TX: Hoover's, Inc., 1997. Available from http://www.hoovers.com.

Industry Surveys. New York, NY: *Standard & Poor's,* 1999.

National Wood Flooring Association. Available from http://www.nwfa.com.

Swenson, Steve E. "Hardwood Floor Firms Report Higher Sales."*Knight-Ridder/Tribune Business News,* November 23, 1997.

U.S. Department of Commerce. *1995 Annual Survey of Manufactures.* Washington: GPO, 1997.

U.S. Industry & Trade Outlook '99. New York, NY: McGraw-Hill, 1999.

"Wood and Ceramic Flooring Sweep Up Retail Sales." *HFN The Weekly Newspaper for the Home Furnishing Network,* January 25, 1999.

SPECIAL PRODUCT SAWMILLS, NOT ELSEWHERE CLASSIFIED

This industry classification includes mills, not elsewhere classified, that make excelsior (wood shavings used for packing or stuffing), wood shingles, and cooperage stock; or mills that make specially sawed products. This category also includes companies that make pads and wrappers made from wood excelsior, and makers of all types of wood shingles and shakes. Cooperage stock is comprised of the staves, headings, and hoops used for making barrels, although barrel construction is classified in **SIC 2449: Wood Containers, Not Elsewhere Classified.**

NAICS CODE(S)

321113 (Sawmills)
321912 (Cut Stock, Resawing Lumber, and Planing)
321999 (All Other Miscellaneous Wood Product Manufacturing)

Special product sawmills shipped $27.7 million worth of goods in 1997, down from $153.5 million in 1995 and $211.3 million in 1990. The U.S. Census Bureau reported that 71 establishments produced goods in this category in 1997. Those businesses spent $16 million on materials and paid $1 million for buildings and other structures, machinery, and equipment. They employed 342 people, including 297 production workers who earned an average hourly wage of $9.84. A large share of the operations in this category were located in Washington state.

As in previous years, wood shingles and shakes (hand-split, thicker shingles) made up nearly half of the industry's products in 1997. During the 1990s, the majority of shakes and shingles were made of red cedar, grown mainly in the Pacific Northwest. In 1987 red cedar shakes and shingles had accounted for more than 47 percent of the industry's production. Other woods used for shakes and shingles were northern white cedar, bald cypress, and redwood.

During the early 1990s, the use of wood shingles came under attack in areas prone to fires. In California, for example, several local governments banned new roofs made of wood products, due to the number of homes lost to fire during summer droughts. Wood shingle producers also faced competition from companies that made nonwood roofing materials, such as asphalt shingles.

In the early 1990s, cooperage stock made up about 16 percent of the industry's output. This included stock for both tight (used to hold liquids) and slack (for nonliquid use) cooperage, including buckets, hot tubs, storage vats, and barrels. Excelsior, also known as wood wool, accounted for another 7.5 percent of production.

Most special product sawmills were small operations with fewer than five employees. By 1998, one of the largest firms in the industry was Miller Shingle Company Inc. (Granite Falls, Washington), with 150 employees and estimated sales of $36 million. In addition to shingles, the firm made cedar logs, lumber, and shakes.

Shakertown 1992 Inc. (Winlock, Washington), previously known as Shakertown Corp., also made cedar shakes and shingles in addition to siding. It had 150 employees and sales of $24 million. Colonial Cedar Company Inc. (Kent, Washington), which made cedar lumber and siding products, had 40 employees and sales of $14 million.

Another industry leader was Blue Grass Cooperage Co. (Louisville, Kentucky) with 200 employees and sales of $26 million. This subsidiary of Brown-Forman Corp. made white oak whiskey and wine barrels. Independent Stave Company Inc. (Lebanon, Missouri) made white oak tight barrels, staves, and headings. It had 400 employees and sales of $23 million.

FURTHER READING

U.S. Department of Commerce. *1996 Annual Survey of Manufactures.* Washington, DC: GPO, 1998.

U.S. Department of Commerce. Census Bureau. *1997 Economic Survey.* Washington, DC: GPO, 1999. Available from http://www.census.gov.

SIC 2431

MILLWORK

This category covers establishments primarily engaged in manufacturing fabricated wood millwork, including wood millwork covered with materials such as metal and plastics. Planing mills primarily engaged in producing millwork are included in this industry, but planning mills primarily producing standard workings or patterns of lumber are classified in **SIC 2421: Sawmills and Planing Mills, General.** Establishments primarily engaged in manufacturing wood kitchen cabinets and bathroom vanities for permanent installation are classified in **SIC 2434: Wood Kitchen Cabinets.**

NAICS CODE(S)

321911 (Wood Window and Door Manufacturing)
321918 (Other Millwork (including Flooring))

INDUSTRY SNAPSHOT

According to the U.S. Labor Department and the U.S. Bureau of the Census, over 2,700 mills in America employ 64,000 workers to manufacture products almost entirely for the construction industry. The Bureau of the Census reported the value of output for the industry at over $7 billion in 1997. The composition of output shifted in the late 1980s as renovation and repair increased faster than new construction; however, new construction starts increased significantly throughout the 1990s, in accordance with the growth of the economy. According to the U.S. Department of Commerce, residential construction uses more than 60 percent of mill output, while nonresidential construction accounts for approximately 15 percent.

Continued environmental legislation has put the industry under tremendous supply pressures, although the effect on employment has been minimal compared to the logging, sawmill, and plywood industries. Nevertheless, the pressures are shifting the direction of technological change and marketing techniques in the industry. Most establishments specialize in one product class, such as wood door units, stairs, or railings. Although the industry was previously concentrated primarily in the Pacific Northwest, the Midwest, and Texas, new wood suppliers from South America and the second growth of forest in the southeastern United States have shifted some establishments to that area. Imports of both raw materials and milled products have increased dramatically over the last decade.

ORGANIZATION AND STRUCTURE

Mills in this industry cut down either raw logs or stock lumber to produce wood shapes for windows and door trims, baseboards, railings, window sashes, and other items. Wood pieces are also assembled with glass, vinyl, and aluminum cladding to make window sashes and frames. Often an inert gas such as argon fills the space between the glass panes to enhance insulation. Doors may be constructed out of solid pieces for high-end uses or, more commonly, consist of a frame, two-panels, and filling. Furthermore, exterior doors and interior apartment entrance doors often use steel to enhance security. In the 1990s, there was a shift away from expensive stain grade millwork to less expensive paint-grade, along with an increased use of medium density fiberboard (MDF).

Over time, the industry's dependence on new construction and repair decreased, and it turned its focus to remodeling, maintenance, and home improvements. During economic downturns, new construction subsides and repair work increases its share of construction activity. Repair work held steady during the recession in the early 1990s, while new construction grew more quickly during the mid- to late 1990s.

According to the reports of the U.S. Department of Commerce in 1996, the primary products manufactured by the millwork industry are doors (30 percent of total industry output), wooden windows and sashes (26 percent), and moldings (14 percent). Increasingly, doors and windows in particular are clad with vinyl, aluminum, or other metals; energy savings have led to the development of vinyl and aluminum windows. Wood windows are regaining popularity, however, because of their strength, beauty, and natural insulating properties. Recent industry developments have allowed aluminum and vinyl clad wood windows to be produced in unlimited shapes and sizes. Solid wood doors, on the contrary, have lost market share in recent years to nonsolid wood doors, steel, and steel-covered exterior doors.

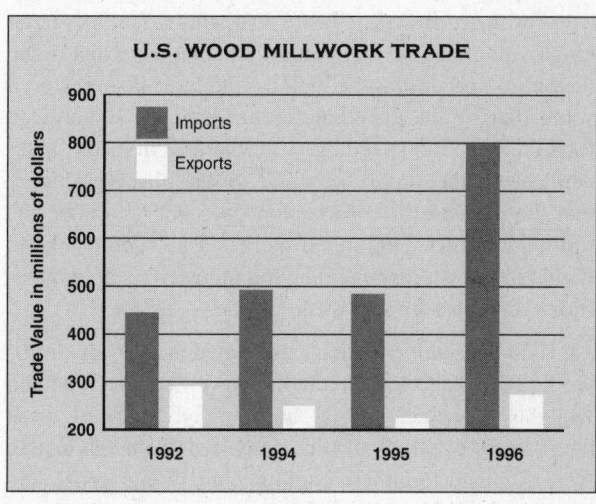

BACKGROUND AND DEVELOPMENT

The millwork industry has been impacted by a variety of environmental issues. Logging restrictions on federal lands, based on the concern for the future of the spotted owl and other species and a general desire to leave remaining forestlands untouched, is a major factor in the growth and direction of the wood products industries. Boycotts and export restrictions on tropical wood affect import and export markets. Concern over the effects of volatile chemicals on the health of workers and consumers has resulted in advances in wood treatment. Energy-loss concerns have led to major innovations in window and door production over the last 15 years.

Logging restrictions are a source of particular concern to the industry, as they directly influence the price and availability of millwork establishments' primary production materials. In 1989, environmental groups invoked the Endangered Species Act of 1973 to halt logging in many forests in order to protect the spotted owl. In 1993, the ban was extended to parts of California to protect the California spotted owl, which was listed only as a sensitive species, not endangered. The move sparked debate about trading jobs for the environment. Indeed, the effect of the logging restrictions on jobs was devastating in the northwestern logging and wood products industries. With timber harvests reduced by 75 percent from national forests, however, forest-products companies were seeing healthier markets and improved pricing in the late 1990s. Imports also dramatically increased, with the U.S. International Trade Commission estimating that imports of millwork products increased 80 percent during the period between 1992 and 1996.

On April 2, 1993, President Clinton held a timber conference in an attempt to find common ground and compromise between environmentalists and forest product workers. The compromise plan allowed 1.2 billion board feet a year to be cut from federal forests. This was approximately a quarter of the amount permitted at the height of the 1980s. The proposal also established spotted owl reserves and water system buffer zones to protect the owl from extinction and streams from erosion. The President also proposed the development of 10 intermediary zones. Loggers were allowed to experiment with new harvesting techniques in these zones, but forest management and environmental effects continued to be monitored. In 1999, in a continued effort to protect the forests, President Clinton proposed placing 40 million acres of federal forest off-limits to the timber and mining industries. While environmentalists applauded this proposal, industry spokesperson Chris Nance, the vice president of public affairs for the California Forestry Association, stated in an article in the San Francisco Chronicle that the U.S demand for wood nonetheless would increase 50 percent over the next 20 years, and that this proposal would only encourage increased imports from countries with little or no environmental laws. The debate over use of public lands and protection of environmentally threatened species is likely to remain a contentious issue in the industry.

CURRENT CONDITIONS

Forest product mills in the Pacific Northwest took a double beating in the 1990s. On the demand side, the early 1990's economic recession resulted in a downturn in housing starts. And, although housing starts have started to rise again in the mid-1990s, the industry was still affected by this slowdown.

On the supply side, environmental legislation, including the protection of the spotted-owl, has led to a reduction in timber harvests on federal lands. This legislation resulted in the closing of mills and loss of jobs in the Pacific Northwest. The impact on the profits for mill owners was mixed. Companies that had private sources of timber or were located away from spotted owl habitats, such as those in southern locales, benefited from the increased price of lumber. This also resulted in increased imports of raw material from foreign countries.

For the millwork industry as a whole, the impact on employment has been minimal. Jobs that were lost in the downturn and during the logging ban have been restored somewhat by the economic upturn, and the increase in total construction spending. Still, the mill industry is dependent on the supply of wood. Some observers argue that the increase in construction does not guarantee the millwork industry unlimited success. Environmental and regulatory concerns regarding the industry's staple materials—Douglas fir and western pine—remain.

Wood Technology magazine noted in 1999 that millwork plants have sought alternatives to western pine and Douglas fir, which are in short-supply. Some of these alternatives are radiata pine imported from Chile and New Zealand, southern yellow pine, white pine, and hardwoods. Both radiata pine and southern yellow pine are now used extensively in the industry. These alternatives require mills to be flexible in their handling of woods. Each species requires its own methods of treatment, drying, and handling of imperfections. This is necessary not only because of the unique characteristics of each kind of wood, but also because of the harvesting and storage practices of distant vendors, both in the United States and abroad. Good wood, or certified wood, is starting to make a name for itself in the industry. Forest owners are certified by an independent source as having sustained their forest—that is, no clear-cutting or other practices harmful to the long-term health of the forest.

INDUSTRY LEADERS

The privately owned Andersen Corp., based in Bayport, Minnesota, is the leading window and door manufacturer in the industry. It utilizes high-profile marketing to promote its product to the end user and keeps cost down by producing a large variety of standard sizes. The company's 1998 sales were estimated at $1.4 billion.

Pella Corporation, headquartered in Pella Iowa, is the second largest window and door manufacturer, with 1998 sales estimated at $600 million.

Morgan Products Ltd., of Williamsburg, Virginia, is a subsidiary of the Andersen Corporation and manufactures doors, windows, moldings, stairways, and mantels for new and renovated structures; their 1998 sales topped $383 million.

Trus Joist MacMillan is a joint venture of a Canadian forest products company, MacMillan Bloedel, and U.S based Trus Joist Corporation; the company has developed a long-term market strategy of focusing on engineered woods to improve strength and conserve old growth timber. TJM markets most of these products for structural uses such as beams and framing materials. Twenty-eight percent of its business, however, is in windows and doors, which it produces and markets through its subsidiaries, Dashwood Industries, Laffamme & Frere, and Norco Windows. It has begun marketing windows made with laminated strand lumber through these subsidiaries. Total sales for 1998 were $778 million.

Marvin Windows and Doors, with headquarters in Warroad, Minnesota, specializes in high-value custom production for replacement windows and doors and for unusual architectural arrangements on new construction.

Other leading companies in the millwork industry include Jeld-Wen Inc., of Klamath Falls, Oregon; Clopay Corp., based in Cincinnati, Ohio; and Huttig Sash and Door Co., of Chesterfield, Missouri.

WORKFORCE

Safety Issues. According to the U.S. Department of Commerce, the millwork industry has a high accident rate—49 percent higher than that of the general manufacturing industry. The accident rate for millwork was also higher compared to related industries of wood kitchen cabinets, hardwood veneer and plywood, softwood veneer, and plywood; it was lower, however, than industries categorized in **SIC 2439: Structural Wood Members, Not Elsewhere Classified.** The rate of injuries sustained per 100 full-time workers was greater in large mills (defined as 20 or more workers) than in small mills.

The Labor Department's Bureau of Labor Statistics lists back strain and hand and finger injuries as the two most common types of injuries in the millwork industry. Back strain injuries were primarily the result of lifting heavy objects; serious hand and finger injuries typically occurred while operating stationary saws and other machinery. Other safety issues that have received attention in recent years include the respiratory effects on workers involved in both sanding and the application of volatile materials such as polyurethane and formaldehyde. The U.S. Department of Labor believes that many accidents could be prevented through education, training, and minor machinery enhancements.

Employment. In 1999 the U.S. Bureau of the Census reported that 110,000 people were employed in the millwork industry in 1996, with an average yearly salary of $29,000 and a total payroll of over $2.2 billion in 1995. According to the U.S. Department of Labor, despite the large number and variety of machines employed in the industry, it is quite labor intensive. For each dollar of value that mills add to raw materials, it uses 72 percent more production-worker hours than in the manufacturing industry as a whole. According to Brad Knickerbocker, writing in the *Christian Science Monitor,* technical innovation has enabled the membership of the timber industry to record gains in productivity of as much as 40 percent; this has created a corresponding decline in timber industry employment. More recently, especially with the shortages of raw materials, technological innovation has taken a shift toward the maximization of materials savings, rather than labor savings.

The millwork industry is moving increasingly toward the use of computers in both the design and manufacturing processes. Although the employment outlook for woodworkers is expected to grow more slowly than average through 2006, according to the Occupational Outlook Handbook, skilled woodworkers with computer expertise will be in demand. It is also predicted that the increase in population and the strong economy at the turn of the century should provide steady employment in the millwork industry, as new homes are built and repair work is needed. Employment opportunities in the millwork industry are now available in all regions of the country, according to the U.S. Department of Commerce, with the vast majority of establishments employing under 100 people.

AMERICA AND THE WORLD

Trade patterns in millwork and other wood products have undergone considerable change recently due to environmental pressures, and the reduction of trade barriers. Total trade rose from $735.6 million to $1.1 billion between 1992 and 1996, according to the U.S. International Trade Commission. Throughout the mid-1990s the United States had a trade deficit in millwork. The only countries with which the United States had a surplus were Japan, South Korea, and the United Kingdom. This was a shift from the early 1990s, due in large part to a weak dollar.

Imports. Developing countries have the advantages of low-cost labor and cheap, abundant raw materials when competing in international trade. They have utilized these advantages to develop their woodworking industries and to consequently increase their exports of furniture and millwork products to America.

Imports of millwork increased an astounding 80 percent from 1992 to 1996. The total value of shipments rose from $445.3 million to $799.6 million during this time period. Imports came from Mexico (26 percent), Canada (21 percent), Chile (9 percent), Thailand (8 percent), Indonesia (8 percent), China (5 percent) and Malaysia (5 percent). Moldings were the largest category of imports, totaling 40 percent, followed by picture frames and doors. According to the U.S. International Trade Commission 80 percent of millwork imports were duty free, mainly due to the North American Free Trade Agreement and the Generalized System of Preferences (GSP). In 1995, Canada and the United States signed a timber pact that restricted U.S. duty-free timber imports to 14.7 billion board feet of Canadian lumber.

Environmental concerns have reduced the international supply of millwork's principal raw material, logs,

U.S. MILLWORK PRODUCT IMPORTS

although the U.S. Supreme Court's reversal of a federal law restricting log exports has somewhat eased international supply. Indonesia banned the export of logs in the early 1980s to slow the consumption of its own forests while expanding employment in wood products industries. By doing so, the Indonesian government stimulated the development of wood processing industries such as milling and plywood. According to a report in *The Nikkei Weekly*, however, plywood plants began shutdowns in 1996 due to a lack of logs. Only 70 percent of mill demands were met in 1995. Malaysia also recently restricted its exports of raw logs to preserve its forests and develop its woodworking industries.

Exports. Exports fell from $290.3 million in 1992 to $274.2 million in 1996. Lower exports to both Canada, which had lower housing starts, and Mexico, which suffered from an economic downturn, accounted for a large portion of the decline. The next largest market for U.S. millwork exports was Japan, which also suffered an economic downturn. In the late 1990s, the country began to recover and is expected to remain a strong market for U.S. millwork exports. The European Union is not considered a viable market for exports, as it is largely supplied by internal members. The majority of exported millwork products were doors, moldings, and windows, in that order.

RESEARCH AND TECHNOLOGY

Concerns about energy costs, maintenance requirements, and personal security have led to significant technological changes during the last two decades. Environmental restrictions on raw materials and worker safety are leading the current wave of changes.

For both doors and window frames, the newest technological advances are in the area of materials conservation. Sustained high costs for woods such as Douglas fir, Ponderosa, and other western pines have spurred innovation in window frame and door production, such as the increased use of radiata pine and regionalized species like southern yellow pine, an increase in painted products rather than stain-grade products, and an increased use of medium-density fiberboard rather than solid wood. Increasingly, composite materials are used as substitutes for solid wood parts, while window frames are produced from such engineered woods. As the industry continues to substitute engineered woods such as laminated strand lumber for sawed wood, it will have to focus its technological advances on worker safety issues such as exposure to dust, formaldehyde, and other volatile organic compounds. The increased use of technology will also play an important role in product design and manufacturing.

FURTHER READING

Andersen Corporation. *Company Web Page.* Available from http://www.andersenwindows.com.

"Clinton's Plan to Protect U.S. Forests." *The San Francisco Chronicle,* 14 October 1999, A1.

Hoover's Online. Available from http://www.hoovers.com.

Industry & Trade Summary: Millwork. USITC Publication 3096. U.S. International Trade Commission Office of Industries, April 1998.

JELD-WEN Inc. *Company Web Page.* Available from http://www.jeld-wen.com.

Marvin Windows and Doors. *Company Web Page.* Available from http://www.marvin.com/.

Morgan Products Ltd. *Company Web Page.* Available from http://www.morganproductsltd.com/.

Occupational Outlook Handbook. U.S. Bureau of Labor Statistics. Available from http://stats.bls.gov/ocohome.htm.

Pella Corporation. *Company Web Page.* Available from http://www.pella.com.

Sampson, William. "Modern Technology Makes Millwork Shop Competitive." *FDM,* November 1999, 58-65.

Stovall, Kevin. "Millwork industry faces opportunities, challenges." *Wood Technology,* March 1999, 48-54.

Trus Joist MacMillan. *Company Web Page.* Available from http://www.tjm.com/.

U.S. Bureau of the Census. 1997 Economic Census. Manufacturing. Industry Series. *Other Millwork (Including Flooring).* Available from http://www.census.gov.

U.S. Bureau of the Census. 1997 Economic Census. Manufacturing. Industry Series. *Wood Window and Door Manufacturing.* Available from http://www.census.gov.

U.S. Bureau of the Census. *Annual Survey of Manufacturers.* Available from http://www.census.gov.

U.S. Bureau of the Census. *Lumber Production and Mill Stocks,* November 1998.

U.S. Bureau of the Census. *Statistical Abstract of the United States,* 1999.

WOOD KITCHEN CABINETS

This industry includes establishments primarily engaged in manufacturing wood kitchen cabinets and wood bathroom vanities, generally for permanent installation. Establishments primarily engaged in manufacturing free-standing cabinets and vanities are classified in various furniture-manufacturing industries. Establishments primarily engaged in building custom cabinets for individuals are classified in **SIC 5712: Furniture Stores.**

NAICS CODE(S)

337110 (Wood Kitchen Cabinet and Counter Top Manufacturing)

According to a *Wood & Wood Products'* (*W&WP*) annual survey, 1997 sales for all those participating in the industry topped the $4.2 billion mark. The Kitchen Cabinet Manufacturers Association (KCMA) statistics showed that in 1998, more than two-thirds of manufactured cabinets were used in remodeling, with the remainder going towards new residential construction. W&WP's survey participants reported more of a 50/50 split. Remodeling a kitchen offers the highest return to the owner upon resale, recouping 102 percent of job cost.

From February 1996 through November 1999, kitchen and bath cabinet sales increased every month. Industry executives' biggest concern was attracting and retaining highly skilled employees, without which such growth could not be sustained. Other concerns included government regulations concerning wood finishing and wood dust, as well as the price and availability of wood.

According to the 1997 Bureau of the Census Manufacturing Industry Series, more than 99,000 people were employed in the industry, with most of the labor force in the states of Texas, Pennsylvania, Ohio, Florida, and Indiana.

Leading establishments in the wood kitchen cabinet manufacturing industry include Masco Corp. Cabinet Group, with 1997 sales of more than $1 billion; Master-Brand Cabinets Inc. and Mill's Pride, both with 1997 sales of $400 million; and American Woodmark Corp., with sales of $241 million in 1997. Other establishments include Omega Cabinets, Elkat Mfg. Co., and Triangle Pacific Corp. of Dallas, Texas, all posting near or over the $200 million mark in 1997 sales.

While the industry has seen few dramatic technological breakthroughs, several changes in the appearance of the industry have taken place in recent years. Raw material shortages are forcing some manufacturers to use more composite and engineered woods. Good wood, or certified wood, is starting to make a name for itself in the industry. Forest owners are certified by an independent source as having sustainably managed their forest, which means no clear-cutting or other practices harmful to the long-term health of the forest have been done. Companies view the use of good wood as good public relations. Frameless cabinetry design, in which shelf space can be utilized right up to the cabinet wall rather than sacrificing one inch around to the frame, is also increasing.

The demand for other room cabinetry has increased. Half of those surveyed by *W&WP* sell other-room products such as entertainment centers, bookcases, home-office furniture, and utility cabinets. Near the close of the century this subsection of the industry accounted for only 6 percent of sales, but it was projected to increase.

FURTHER READING

Adams, Larry. "Cabinet Companies Step Out of the Kitchen". *Wood & Wood Products,* March 1999.

Fried, Carla. "The Safe and Sane Way to Make Your House Everything You Want." *Money,* April 1997.

"KCMA Report." *Wood & Wood Products,* December 1999.

Kennedy, Kim. "Q1/97: Slower but Steady Gains Ahead." *Cahners Building & Construction Market Forecast,* March 1997. Available from http://members.aol.com/cahners/bcmf .html.

Schatz, Amy. "'Good Wood' Winning With the Green Crowd." *Wall Street Journal,* 17 May 1996.

U.S. Department of Commerce. "Wood Kitchen Cabinet and Counter Top Manufacturing." *1997 Economic Census Manufacturing Industry Series,* 1999.

SIC 2435

HARDWOOD VENEER AND PLYWOOD

This classification covers establishments primarily engaged in producing commercial hardwood veneer and those primarily engaged in manufacturing commercial plywood or prefinished hardwood plywood. This includes nonwood backed or faced veneer and nonwood faced plywood, constructed from veneer produced in the same establishment or from purchased veneer. Establishments primarily engaged in the production of veneer which is used in the same establishment for the manufacture of wood containers, such as fruit and vegetable baskets and wood boxes, are classified in various wood container manufacturing industries.

NAICS CODE(S)

321211 (Hardwood Veneer and Plywood Manufacturing)

INDUSTRY SNAPSHOT

The U.S. Census Bureau estimated that 332 establishments made hardwood veneer and plywood in 1997. They shipped $2.8 billion worth of goods, spent $1.7 billion on materials, and paid $72 million for buildings and other structures, machinery, and equipment. About 200 of these establishments had at least 20 employees; 68 of them employed at least 100 people. Those with fewer than 20 employees shipped only about 4 percent of the products in this category.

BACKGROUND AND DEVELOPMENT

According to U.S. Department of Commerce statistics, plywood sales constituted 45 percent of the industry's output for 1992, while hardwood veneer products constituted 25 percent. The U.S. Department of Commerce reported that nearly half of veneer and plywood output in the early 1990s went to construction, mainly residential. Roughly a quarter of the output was used in other lumber and wood products industries, and 11 percent was used in furniture and fixtures.

Veneer consists of layers of wood peeled from logs. Plywood can then be made by gluing these veneer sheets together, alternating the direction of the grain for each sheet. Typically, plywood sheets are four feet by eight feet. Veneer is also glued to lumber, fiberboard, and medium density fiberboard. It is also used in the production of oriented strand lumber and other engineered woods.

Plywood manufacturing and its related industries experienced hard times during the 1990s: a shortage of lumber increased operating costs, while the general economic recession of 1989-1991 resulted in numerous plant closings and lost jobs. Many small firms in the Pacific Northwest, dependent on timber from federal lands, were particularly affected. Industry critic Paul Ehinger claimed in a 1992 issue of *Forest Industries* that an estimated 133 sawmills, plywood, and veneer plants—20 percent of the mills in the Pacific Northwest—closed in this region between January 1990 and May 1992. This was an acceleration of a trend that saw 145 mills close in the 1980s. On the other hand, plywood firms with unlimited access to timber such as those in the South, or large firms with private sources of timber, profited from the soaring prices of plywood. According to a report of S.G. Warburg & Co. Inc., plywood prices rose 67 percent between 1991 and 1993.

To cope with supply pressures, firms developed new products like engineered woods. Some observers expected this trend to shift the composition of output in the industry. As predicted, the plywood and veneer hardwood industry lost market share to establishments involved in the manufacture of reconstituted panel products, which includes particleboard, medium density fiberboard, and oriented strand board (OSB), among other products. According to *Wood Technology,* the number of plywood plants decreased by 28 percent between 1987 and 1995, while OSB plants increased by 37 percent. David L. Fleiner, vice president of structural panels for Georgia-Pacific Corp, predicted that in the future plywood mills would have to produce less plywood and more specialties and veneer for laminated veneer lumber (LVL) in order to remain competitive.

Construction was hard hit by the 1990's recession and did not rebound as quickly as it had in past, despite low interest rates. Residential construction did not recoup its 1989 levels until late 1993, while the overall economy surpassed 1989 levels by mid-1992. Nonresidential construction continued its recession well into 1993. Both residential and nonresidential construction eventually recovered, with residential construction increasing by 8.9 percent in 1996 and nonresidential construction growing at 5.4 percent, according to *Cahners Building & Construction Market Forecast.*

Environmental Issues. During the 1990s, logging restrictions on federal lands, coupled with export restrictions of tropical hardwoods, affected the supply of raw materials for the industry. Legislation in the Pacific Northwest was designed to protect the spotted owl. Concerns regarding levels of dust, formaldehyde, and noise in plywood and hardwood veneer production also became an issue. The U.S. industry set voluntary formaldehyde emission standards.

According to David A. Pease, writing in *Wood Technology* in 1993, this concern was not limited to American manufacturers. The Dutch adopted strict dust level restrictions of 1.7 parts dust per million parts air (by weight). They set formaldehyde at 0.3 parts per million of air and noise exposure to 90 dBA with hearing protection. The Germans implemented similar limits. The Environmental Protection Agency (EPA) drafted a catalogue of indoor air pollutants, including formaldehyde and other volatile organic compounds, that result from the production of plywood, particleboard, medium density fiberboard, oriented strand board, and other engineered wood products.

In the early 1990s, the EPA launched a nationwide investigation of outdoor air pollutants generated by this industry as well. As a result, Weyerhaeuser Company paid more than $1.5 million in state fines and agreed to install millions of dollars worth of controls in its plants. Louisiana-Pacific pledged to install $70 million in control devices and paid $11 million in Federal fines. Georgia-Pacific, however, lobbied to curtail the EPA investigation to avoid fines and costly upgrades. Executives at Weyerhaeuser estimated that controls added an additional $1 million a year to plant operating costs.

The plywood industry experimented with several means of reducing these emissions. One was to use other chemicals to bond particleboard, plywood, and other products. Another possible solution was to treat the product with ammonia after it had been glued with traditional compounds. Further complicating efforts to address these environmental concerns, however, was the increasing emphasis on engineered wood production, which required the use of volatile organic compounds.

CURRENT CONDITIONS

In 1997, the U.S. Census Bureau reported that the 108 establishments that made hardwood veneer as a primary business shipped $1 billion worth of goods. Indiana, North Carolina, Wisconsin, and Michigan had the largest product shipments in this segment.

The 59 establishments principally manufacturing hardwood plywood shipped $1.3 billion worth of goods, mainly from Oregon, North Carolina, and Virginia. This category excluded prefinished hardwood plywood made from purchased hardwood plywood, which was the primary product at six establishments that shipped $155 million worth of goods, mainly from Indiana and North Carolina.

The 28 establishments that primarily made other hardwood plywood type products shipped $187 million worth of goods, with the largest shipments originating in Indiana and Oregon.

North Carolina had by far the largest concentration of establishments that manufactured hardwood veneer and plywood, followed by Indiana, Wisconsin, Virginia, South Carolina, Oregon, and Arkansas.

INDUSTRY LEADERS

One of the largest companies that made products in this category as its principal business was Ply Gem Industries Inc. (a subsidiary of Nortek Inc., based in Providence, Rhode Island) with 4,079 employees and estimated sales of $790 million in 1998. Roseburg Forest Products Co. (Roseburg, Oregon) had 3,975 employees and sales of $758 million. It made hard and soft plywood and particleboard. Columbia Forest Products Inc. (Portland, Oregon) had 3,500 employees and estimated sales of $500 million. It made hardwood plywood, hardwood veneer, and related products.

Numerous large, diversified companies also competed in this category. They included Georgia-Pacific Corp. (Atlanta, Georgia); Boise Cascade Corp. (Boise, Idaho); Champion International Corp. (Stamford, Connecticut); Stone Container Corp. (Chicago, Illinois); Temple-Inland Forest Products Corp. (Diboll, Texas); Louisiana-Pacific Corp. (Portland, Oregon); Herman Miller Inc. (Zeeland, Michigan); Carolina Builders Corp. (Raleigh, North Carolina); and Crown Pacific Partners L.P. (Portland, Oregon).

WORKFORCE

Workers in the plywood manufacturing industry often participate in management or own an interest in the company. For nearly three-quarters of a century, many plywood mills in the Pacific Northwest have been operated by worker cooperatives. The workers own and control these firms. Major decisions are made, policy is developed, and a board of directors is chosen democratically at the quarterly or semiannual meeting of the general membership.

A study of Pacific Northwest plywood cooperatives published in *Economic Analysis and Workers' Management* noted that proceeds from this type of enterprise are generally distributed according to work performed rather than on an equal basis or by capital stake. Members usually prefer to forgo earnings rather than suffer unemployment. These enterprises tend to use raw materials efficiently and are less capital intensive than conventional mills.

Some conventionally owned mills also encourage workers to participate in management. For example, workers sometimes influence a mill's production or the hiring of employees.

According to U.S. Department of Labor statistics, the hardwood veneer and plywood manufacturing industry has a high injury and illness rate—approximately 50 percent higher than for general manufacturing.

Employment varies considerably over time in hardwood plywood and veneer manufacturing establishments because of its dependence on the larger construction industry. U.S. Department of Commerce statistics indicate that employment in the industry plummeted 17 percent between 1989 and 1991. In 1992 approximately 20,000 people were employed in the industry, at an average hourly wage of almost $10. In 1997 the industry employed 22,025 people, including 19,186 production workers who earned an average hourly wage of $9.82.

AMERICA AND THE WORLD

According to the U.S. Department of Commerce, imports of plywood grew only 1.5 percent between 1989 and 1993, while exports shot up 62.0 percent. The United States, Indonesia, and Japan were the top three plywood producers, according to the FAO statistics. However, a 1996 *Nikkei Weekly* report indicated that plywood plants in Indonesia were shutting down due to a low supply of logs caused by overcutting.

In veneer production, China, Malaysia, and Canada were the leading producers during 1993. Chile experienced some growth in the veneer market with new startups by the Rio Itata group reported in 1995. The Chilean forestry industry was growing along with the nation's economy. The reduction of trade barriers between Canada, Mexico, and the United States as a result

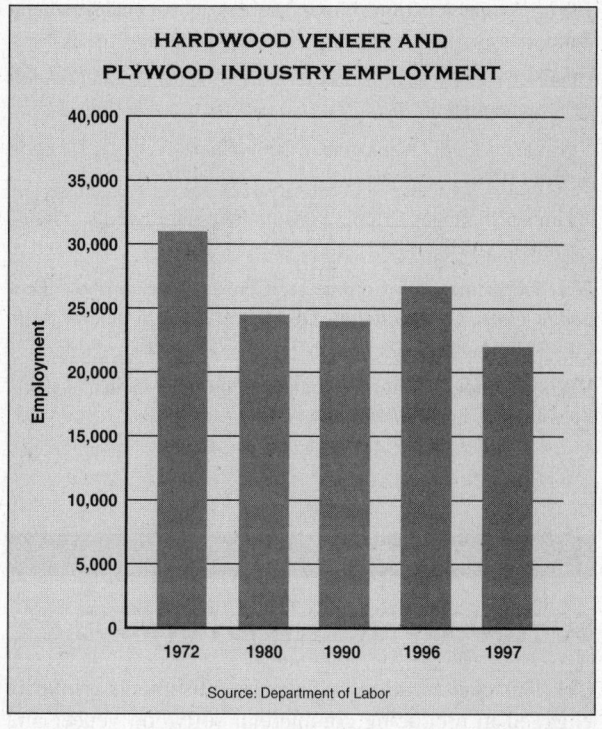

HARDWOOD VENEER AND PLYWOOD INDUSTRY EMPLOYMENT

Source: Department of Labor

of the North American Free Trade Agreement (NAFTA) continued to shift international trade patterns. Because of an outcry from the industry, a timber pact was made between Washington and Canada restricting imports by allowing only 14.7 billion board feet of lumber into the United States without a duty.

RESEARCH AND TECHNOLOGY

The emphasis in new technology has shifted from labor-saving innovation to material-saving innovation. To get more lumber from wood pulp, producers have been developing engineered wood products such as laminated veneer lumber, particleboard, medium density fiberboard, and oriented strand board. This trend represents a shift out of this industry and into reconstituted panel products (see **SIC 2493: Reconstituted Wood Products**).

FURTHER READING

Blackman, Ted. "Adding Value: Chilean Mills Get Full Value From Forests." *Wood Technology,* January/February 1996.

Einhorn, Cheryl Strauss. "Behind the Inflation Fears: Are Lumber and Energy Prices Really So Strong?" *Barron's,* 9 September 1996.

"Hardwood Plywood & Veneer Assn." *Wood & Wood Products,* December 1998.

Keil, Bill. "US Leads in Wood-Based Panel Output As Global Volume Rises To New Record." *Wood Technology,* January/February 1996.

Kennedy, Kim. "Q1/97: Slower But Steady Gains Ahead." *Cahners Building & Construction Market Forecast,* March

1997. Available from http://members.aol.com/cahners/bcmf
.html.

"Panel Capacity Race Starts to Slow down." *Wood Technology,* September 1996.

"Provinces Fight Over Lumber-Quota Shares." *Wood Technology,* 8 (1996).

"Timber Shortages Cripple Some Indonesian Plymills." *Wood Technology,* May 1996, 53.

U.S. Department of Commerce. Census Bureau. *1997 Economic Census.* Washington, DC: GPO, 1999. Available from http://www.census.gov/prod/ec97/97m3212a.pdf.

"Wood Products Mirror Modest Economic Gains." *Wood Technology,* January/February, 1996.

SIC 2436

SOFTWOOD VENEER AND PLYWOOD

This classification includes establishments primarily engaged in producing commercial softwood veneer and plywood from veneer produced in the same establishment or from purchased veneer. Establishments primarily engaged in producing commercial hardwood veneer and plywood are classified in **SIC 2435: Hardwood Veneer and Plywood.** Establishments primarily engaged in the production of veneer used in the same establishment for the manufacture of wood containers such as fruit and vegetable baskets and wood boxes are classified in various wood container manufacturing industries.

NAICS CODE(S)

321212 (Softwood Veneer and Plywood Manufacturing)

Plywood was first developed in 1905 in St. John, Oregon. Softwood veneer is made by cross-laminating veneers, such as pine, spruce, fir, and hemlock. The grains are placed at right angles to improve strength; panels are made in 4-by-8 foot sizes, with a thickness up to three-quarters of an inch. Veneers are bonded together using a waterproof or moisture-resistant adhesive. Plywood comes in different grades depending on the quality of surfaces and the type of adhesive.

The Bureau of the Census reported the value of output for the plywood and veneer (softwood) manufacturing industry as $5.4 billion for 1992. The demand for veneer and plywood depends on the construction industry. Nearly 48 percent of veneer and plywood output goes to construction, mainly residential. Roughly 25 percent of the output is used in other lumber and wood products industries, with an additional 11 percent in furniture and fixtures. Rough softwood plywood accounts for more than 50 percent of total product shipments, followed by

sanded softwood plywood and nonreinforced softwood veneer at 15 percent and 13 percent, respectively.

As with other construction material producing industries, this industry suffered during the economic recession of 1990-1991, but it benefited tremendously from the surge in housing construction at the end of 1993. Growth continued until 1996, when shipments dropped back to 1993 levels. In 1997, product shipments increased by 1 percent to about $5.8 billion compared to the previous year, which was again attributed to healthy housing starts. Increases of 1.5 to 2.0 percent were expected in 1998 and 1999. However, residential construction is expected to drop by 3.5 percent in 2000, according to The CIT Group/Equipment Financing.

Another challenge has been the cost of complying with growing environmental regulation of indoor pollutants. The industry set voluntary formaldehyde emission standards, and the U.S. Environmental Protection Agency (EPA) was collecting information on other forms of indoor pollutants. In the early 1990s, a national EPA investigation resulted in several companies paying millions of dollars in fines and equipment upgrades. On the other hand, timber companies and the products made from their wood were making efforts to become certified as being eco-friendly with regard to logging practices. The Forest Stewardship Council has certified 50 million acres of forest around the world.

Competition continues to increase from the Oriented Strand Board (OSB) industry since this product's average price is around 20 percent lower than plywood due to the simpler manufacturing process. In 1998, OSB owned more than 50 percent of the North American sheathing market. OSB production was expected to reach 19.45 billion square feet in 1999, up from 7.65 billion square feet in 1990, according to *Wood Technology.* U.S. and Canadian plywood production continued to decrease by an estimated 2 percent in 1999 to 19 billion square feet. By 2003, plywood production is forecast to go below 18 billion square feet, while OSB production could reach nearly 22 billion square feet.

Plywood manufacturers are trying to fight back by improving technology and looking for alternative markets. Better adhesives have made softwood plywood less expensive to produce. Specialty markets, including higher-valued products, are being pursued.

The United States had 92 mills producing plywood in 1997. Production shifted from the West to the South, which produced nearly 75 percent of all grades of softwood plywood. According to the U.S. Department of Commerce, the South should account for 77 percent of all plywood production by 2002. The West is expected to dominate in high-end construction applications.

Leading companies in the industry include Georgia-Pacific Corp., based in Atlanta, Georgia, with 1998 sales of $13.2 billion; Champion International Corp.'s Forest Products Group, headquartered in Stamford, Connecticut, with 1998 total sales of $5.7 billion; and Roseburg Forest Products Co., based in Roseburg, Oregon, with 1998 sales totaling $850 million.

According to the Commerce Department, total employment for the industry dropped 20 percent from 38,000 in 1987 to 31,000 in 1992. Average earnings for workers in the industry rose during that time span from just less than $10.00 an hour to approximately $10.50 an hour. Employment dropped to approximately 29,000 in 1997, with workers earning an average wage of $13.00 an hour. Most employees are found in the states of Oregon, Louisiana, Texas, and Arkansas.

International trade has been favorable but volatile for the U.S. softwood plywood and veneer industry in recent years. The economic recession led to sharp declines in imports by 32 percent between 1989 and 1991. The gradual economic recovery, coupled with timber-cutting restrictions that arose out of environmental concerns and the liberalization of trade, resulted in a sharp reversal of this decline in imports. Between 1991 and 1993, imports soared 55 percent, reaching $77 million. Between 1992 and 1996, imports slowed down, increasing only 10 percent overall. Imports jumped to $109 million in 1997, a 23 percent increase from the previous year, with more than three-fourths coming from Canada. Growth rates of less than 3 percent were expected for 1998 and 1999.

Exports surged as a result of trade liberalization, increasing 27 percent between 1989 and 1993, despite a 16 percent drop between 1990 and 1991. Between 1992 and 1996, exports saw a negative growth of 2 percent. However, exports increased 24 percent in 1997 (compared to the previous year) to $392 million, due to strengthening European markets. The United Kingdom, Canada, and Germany were the leading export markets. Growth rates in exports were expected to be only 1 to 2 percent until 2000. Competition from OSB also remained a threat for the export market.

FURTHER READING

Blackman, Ted. "World's Largest OSB Plant Churns Out Panels in Quebec." *Wood Technology,* May 1999. Available from www.woodwideweb.com/db_area/archives/1999/9905/OSB .html.

"Champion International Corporation Reports Earnings For Fourth Quarter and the Year." *Business Wire,* 16 January 1997. Available from http://biz.yahoo.com/news/cha.html.

Haddox, Katherine. "Strong Economy Supports Panel Growth, Stabilization." *Wood Technology,* October 1999. Available from http://www.woodwideweb.com/db_area/archives/1999/ 9910/panel.html.

Ince, Petter, and Henry Spelter. "Veneer Producers Can Cope with Cost-Price Squeeze." *Wood Technology,* October 1999. Available from www.woodwideweb.com/db_area/archives/ 1999/9910/spelterince.html.

Keil, Bill. "US Leads in Wood-Based Panel Output as Global Volume Rises To New Record." *Wood Technology,* January/ February 1996.

Kennedy, Kim. "Q1/97: Slower But Steady Gains Ahead." *Cahners Building & Construction Market Forecast,* March 1997. Available from http://members.aol.com/cahners/bcmf .html.

"Panel Capacity Race Starts to Slow Down." *Wood Technology,* September 1996.

"Plywood's Built Strong Following." *Los Angeles Times, Orange County Edition,* 30 May 1998.

U.S. Census Bureau. "NAICS 321212, Manufacturing-Industry Series." *1997 Economic Census.* Washington, D.C.: GPO, 13 August 1999.

"Wood Products Mirror Modest Economic Gains." *Wood Technology,* January/February 1996.

"Wood-Products Industry Turns Tables—Eco-Friendly Trend is Gathering Steam." *Seattle Times,* 15 November 1999.

SIC 2439

STRUCTURAL MEMBERS, NOT ELSEWHERE CLASSIFIED

This classification covers establishments primarily engaged in producing laminated or fabricated trusses, arches, and other structural members of lumber. Establishments primarily engaged in fabrication on the site of construction are classified in Division C, Construction. Establishments primarily engaged in producing prefabricated wood buildings, sections, and panels are classified in **SIC 2452: Prefabricated Wood Buildings and Components.**

NAICS CODE(S)

321912 (Cut Stock, Resawing Lumber, and Planing)
321214 (Truss Manufacturing)
321213 (Engineered Wood Member (except Truss) Manufacturing)

The U.S. Census Bureau estimated that this industry produced $2.5 billion worth of goods in 1992. In 1995 there were 170 structural panel plants, 35 glulam plants, and 47 I-joist and other engineered-wood plants, with combined sales of approximately $8 billion.

In the early 1990s, most of this industry's products were used in new construction, with a fairly even distribution between residential and nonresidential markets. While residential construction increased in 1992 and 1993, nonresidential construction grew at a sluggish rate

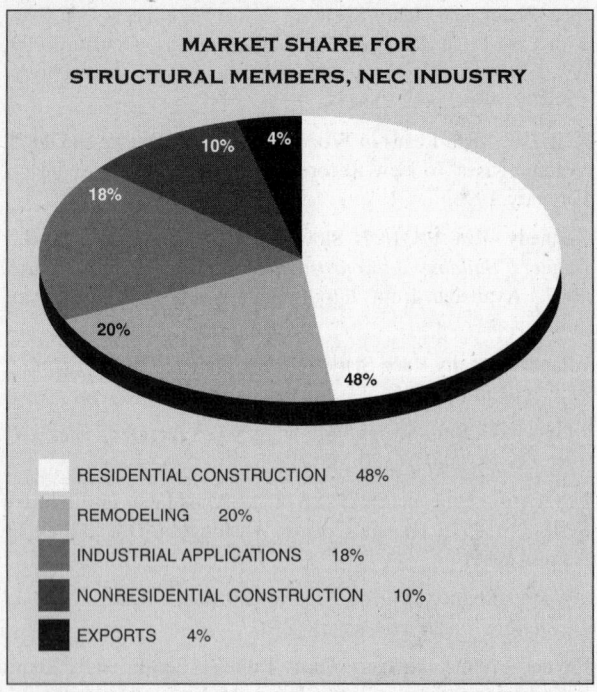

MARKET SHARE FOR STRUCTURAL MEMBERS, NEC INDUSTRY

RESIDENTIAL CONSTRUCTION   48%

REMODELING   20%

INDUSTRIAL APPLICATIONS   18%

NONRESIDENTIAL CONSTRUCTION   10%

EXPORTS   4%

during this period due to extensive building in the 1980s. In the mid-1990s *Wood Technology* stated that home building was the fastest growth area for structural composite lumber.

The industry faced the same supply constraints as did other wood-working industries. This was largely the result of environmental pressures, particularly the efforts to save the endangered spotted owl in the Pacific Northwest and to save tropical rain forests abroad.

Traditionally, mills in this industry had cut joists, beams, and other structural members from large logs, but, during the 1990s, engineered wood products became increasingly popular. These innovative building materials could be made from small young trees instead of the large old trees where endangered owls lived. Moreover, these new products were often stronger than a product sawed from a single piece of lumber.

One engineered product, laminated veneer lumber, was made by using adhesive, heat, and pressure to glue together numerous layers of high-grade veneer. It was used both for the flanges of I-joists and for the construction of beams. The production of laminated veneer lumber increased from 27.1 million feet in 1994 to 37.0 million feet in 1996. Production of a similar product, glulam timber, rose from 259 million feet in 1994 to 325 million feet two years later.

Engineered wood products such as parallel strand lumber and laminated strand lumber were made with strands of wood coated with adhesive and pressed into boards. When oriented strand board (OSB) was introduced during the 1980s, it was often mistaken for an inferior nonstructural panel, but, by the late 1990s, the production of OSB was one of the most rapidly expanding segments of the engineered wood products industry. OSB cost less than plywood but met the same structural performance standards.

Other engineered wood products included series joists, which were used to support floors or ceilings. Floors made with series joists were less apt to squeak, because they were less prone to warping. Similarly, wooden I-joists were so strong that they competed with steel I-beams in small buildings where building codes allowed the use of wood. The Engineered Wood Association reported that the production of wooden I-joists increased from 420 million lineal feet in 1994 to 580 million feet in 1996.

CURRENT CONDITIONS

In 1999 the Structural Board Association reported that OSB was the leading structural panel in North America used for residential sheathing. About 20 mills that made OSB had been started during the mid-1990s, and in 1999 at least nine firms were planning to either open new OSB mills or increase the capacity of existing operations. The increased production, however, created a temporary oversupply of the product. At the same time, demand decreased because of a financial crisis in Asia. Although prices dropped, the continuing strength of the U.S. housing market supported the industry until prices rose again. By 1998, OSB was selling at a higher price than plywood. At that time, OSB was expected to become increasingly popular for use in floors and in commercial and industrial applications. New resins and additives were being tested to increase the durability of OSB, and some types of OSB were being manufactured to resist moisture and intrusion by insects.

The Engineered Wood Association predicted that, in 1999, the engineered wood industry would produce 810 million linear feet of wood I-joists (up 15 percent from 1998), 50 million cubic feet of laminated veneer lumber (up 17 percent), and 312 million board feet of glulam lumber (up 4 percent). The association also expected residential construction to account for 48 percent of the market for engineered wood products that year, remodeling to account for 20 percent, industrial applications to account for 18 percent, nonresidential construction to account for 10 percent, and exports to account for 4 percent. In 1998, the average single-family house included 11,600 square feet of structural wood panels (plywood and oriented strand board), and the average multifamily unit contained 4,035 square feet of such products.

INDUSTRY LEADERS

The largest company with structural lumber as its primary product was TJ International Inc. (Boise, Idaho), with 3,735 employees and sales of $778 million in 1998. The company reported record sales in both 1997 and 1998, following a decade of steadily increasing revenues. Its subsidiaries, Norco Windows Inc. and Trus Joist Mac-Millan L.P., had combined sales of $706 million. Trus Joist MacMillan was the world's leading manufacturer and marketer of engineered lumber. It was jointly owned by TJ International and a Canadian company, MacMillan Bloedel Inc. In June 1999, MacMillan Bloedel was acquired by Weyerhaeuser Company, one of the world's largest forest products firms. In December of that year, Weyerhaeuser announced that it had also made an agreement to acquire TJ International within the next few months.

Another primary contender in the category was Boise Cascade Corp. (Boise, Idaho), with 23,039 employees and sales of $6.4 billion. Wickes Inc. (Vernon Hills, Illinois) had 3,766 employees and sales of $910 million. BMC West Corp. (a subsidiary of Building Materials Holding Corp. based in Boise, Idaho) had 3,500 employees and sales of $728 million. Lumbermen's of Washington Inc. (Olympia, Washington) had 1,400 employees and sales of $317 million in 1998.

Various large, diversified companies also made products in this classification. These included Georgia-Pacific Corporation's Building Products Division (a subsidiary of Georgia Pacific Corp., based in Atlanta, Georgia), with sales of $7.5 billion. Union Camp Corp. (Wayne, New Jersey) had sales of $4.5 billion. Masco Corp. (Taylor, Michigan) had sales of $4.3 billion. Carolina Builders Corp. (Raleigh, North Carolina) had sales of $1.2 billion. GAF Corp. (Wayne, New Jersey) had sales of $946 million.

According to the U.S. Census Bureau, 24,000 people were employed in the industry in 1992. Florida, California, Oregon, and North Carolina were the leading states for employment in this industry. Labor Department statistics indicated that during the mid-1990s the industry had one of the highest accident rates of any manufacturing industry, and that it had a higher accident and illness rate than the other woodworking industries.

In the mid-1990s, Canadian building authorities called for an objective-based National Building Code which, according to *Wood Leader*, would allow for greater use of wood-based structural members. According to the Structural Board Association, half of the goods produced at mills in Alberta, Canada in the late 1990s were products such as webs of I-beams made with oriented strand board. According to the Engineered Wood Association, about 70 percent of structural wood panels (oriented strand board and plywood) exported from North America went to Japan, Europe, and Mexico. Exports of structural wood panels reached 1.3 billion feet in 1998, and the association predicted that they would rise to 2.4 billion feet by the year 2003.

FURTHER READING

Adair, Craig. ''Regional Production and Market Outlook For Structural Panels and Engineered Wood Products 1996-2000.'' Tacoma, Washington: APA-The Engineered Wood Association, 1996.

Kennedy, Kim. ''Q1/97: Slower But Steady Gains Ahead.'' *Cahners Building & Construction Market Forecast,* March 1997. Available from http://members.aol.com/cahners/bcmf.html.

Lumbermen's of Washington Inc. website. Available from http://www.lumbermans-building.com.

''New Five Year Forecast Released by APA.'' Press release, APA (Engineered Wood Association) website, 2 April 1999. Available from http://www.apawood.org.

''OSB Developing Beyond a Commodity.'' Structural Board Association website, August 1999. Available from http://www.sba-osb.com/sba.industrynews.

''TJ International Reports Record Year-End Financial Results.'' *PR Newswire,* 3 February 1998.

''TJ International Reports Record Year-End Financial Results.'' *PR Newswire,* 2 February 1999.

U.S. Department of Commerce. Census Bureau. *1992 Census of Manufactures: Millwork, Plywood, and Structural Wood Members,* Washington, DC: GPO, 1995.

U.S. Department of Commerce. Census Bureau. *1997 Economic Census.* Washington, DC: GPO, 1999. Available from http://www.census.gov.

Walters, William R. ''Planning an Expansion Into Engineered Wood?'' *Wood Technology,* September 1996.

''Weyerhaeuser Purchse of TJ International Clears Hart-Scott-Rodino Waiting Period.'' *Business Wire,* 27 December 1999.

''Wood Products Mirror Modest Economic Gains.'' *Wood Technology,* January/February 1996.

''Year 2001 Code Strategy Will Benefit Wood.'' *Wood Leader,* February 1996. Available from http://www.cwc.metrics.com.

SIC 2441

NAILED AND LOCK CORNER WOOD BOXES AND SHOOK

This industry classification includes companies that are primarily engaged in the production of nailed and lock corner wood boxes (lumber or plywood) and shook for nailed and lock corner boxes.

NAICS CODE(S)

321920 (Wood Container and Pallet Manufacturing)

The nailed and lock corner boxes and shook classification covers the production of containers made wholly or partly of wood. Containers in this category include ammunition boxes, tool chests, wooden cigar boxes, and cases for

NAILED AND LOCK CORNER WOOD BOXES AND SHOOK

Shipments in millions of dollars

1992	420
1993	~423
1994	~414
1995	425
1996	
1997	405

Source: U.S. Census Bureau

packing produce. Shook refers to sets of box parts—sides, tops, bottoms, and ends—that are ready to assemble.

According to the U.S. Census Bureau's *1997 Economic Census—Manufacturing,* 318 establishments operated in this category for part or all of 1997. Industry-wide employment totaled 4,885 workers receiving a payroll of almost $109 million. Of these employees, 3,879 worked in production, putting in more than 7 million hours to earn wages of almost $69 million. Overall shipments for the industry were valued at approximately $406 million.

The top two industry leaders in this category were American Moulding and Millwork Co. of Stockton, California, with 1997 sales of $88.0 million and 800 employees; and Calpine Containers Inc. of Pleasant Hill, California, with 1997 sales of $63.5 million and 200 employees. Other industry leaders included North American Container Corp. of Mableton, Georgia; Michelsen Packaging Co. of Yakima, Washington; Gatewood Products L.L.C. of Parkersburg, West Virginia; and Woodland Container Corp. of Aitkin, Minnesota.

Woodland, which generated sales of $35 million with 350 employees in 1998, received its first ISO 9001 certification in December of that year. An ISO 9001 certification was the most stringent of the ISO 9000 certification series, an initiative toward international standardization of quality specifications. Woodland met the certification requirements for its industrial containers, which it manufactured to house snowmobiles, lawn and garden tractors, and watercraft, among other products. Because of the growth of business globalization, ISO 9000 certification was increasingly important across industries.

The nailed and lock corner wood box and shook industry consists mainly of smaller companies. In 1987 only 2 percent of these businesses employed 100 or more workers, while 50 percent of the companies had less than

10 employees. As of 1995, the top 21 companies in this category were all small and privately owned. The entire industry employed approximately 5,600 people in 1995 (with 4,600 in production), and had a total payroll of $108 million. Production workers averaged $8.30 per hour in 1995. This had increased to $9.86 by 1997.

Unlike pallets and skids, the largest segment of the wood container industry, sales of wooden boxes did not increase much during the 1990s. Fierce competition came from non-wood containers, such as boxes made of corrugated paperboard. Nailed and lock corner wood box makers also lagged behind the pallets and skids industry in the use of new, more efficient technology. Because of the diversity in the kinds of boxes made by this industry, most production runs are too small to benefit from automation. Improved conveyors and material handling equipment increased productivity for companies whose markets required large numbers of one kind of box. Elsewhere, however, nail guns were the most high-tech tools used to make boxes. Therefore, of the growth in output and productivity in the wood container industry between 1977 and 1995 (including **SIC 2448: Pallets and Skids** and **SIC 2449: Wood Containers Not Elsewhere Classified**), little came from sales of nailed and lock corner wood boxes.

In 1995, the industry shipped $483 million worth of goods. During the industry's peak in the 1970s, approximately 1 billion nailed wood boxes were made annually. The 1977 Census of Manufacturers estimated the value of nailed wooden boxes and box components shipped that year at $261 million. Adjusting for inflation, the industry lost some business to improved plastic and corrugated container technology (boxes from these materials cost far less to produce). Marketers hoped, however, that selling wood boxes as "specialty packaging items" would lend these products an air of quality. Both the durability and reusability of wooden boxes supposedly made them more attractive to consumers.

Like the wood containers industry as a whole, wood boxes have not historically faced much competition from foreign manufacturers. This industry's future primary concern will likely be the expense of making wooden boxes compared to cheaper, non-wooden containers.

FURTHER READING

Copeland, Julie. "Aitkin, Minn.-Based Industrial Containers Maker Gets Federal Certification." *Knight-Ridder/Tribune Business News,* 18 December 1998.

Infotrac Company Profiles. Available at http://web2.infotrac .galegroup.com (visited 1/25/00).

"The New Growth of Wooden Boxes." *Modern Packaging,* November, 1979.

Spencer, Albert G. and Jack A. Luy. *Wood and Wood Products.* Columbus, OH: Charles E. Merrill Publishing Company, 1975.

U.S. Census Bureau. ''Wood Container and Pallet Manufacturing.'' *1997 Economic Census—Manufacturingm,* 10 February 2000. Available from http://www.census.gov/prod/ec97/97m3219d.pdf.

U.S. Department of Commerce. *1995 Annual Survey of Manufactures: Statistics for Industry Groups and Industries.* Washington, D.C.: GPO, 1997.

SIC 2448

WOOD PALLETS AND SKIDS

This classification covers establishments primarily engaged in manufacturing wood or wood and metal combination pallets and skids.

NAICS CODE(S)

321920 (Wood Container and Pallet Manufacturing)

The manufacture of wood pallets and skids is the largest segment of the wood container industry. Pallets are made of platforms that are specially designed to allow heavy crates and boxes to be easily moved by forklift. Pallets play an important role in the shipping, handling, and storage of a huge variety of materials in an equally vast array of industries.

According to the U.S. Census Bureau's *1997 Economic Census-Manufacturing,* 2,349 establishments operated in this category for some or all of 1997. Industry-wide employment totaled 39,378 workers receiving a payroll of almost $729.0 million; 33,649 of these employees worked in production, putting in more than 61 million hours to earn wages of almost $531.0 million. Overall shipments for the industry were valued at almost $3.5 billion.

Industry leader PalEx Inc. of Houston, Texas, which generated 1998 sales of just under $320 million (up 43 percent from 1997), merged in 1999 with Munich, Germany-based International Food Container Organization (IFCO). PalEx manufactured, recycled, and rented wooden pallets from its 71 facilities in 23 states and 7 Canadian provinces, while IFCO supplied 50 million collapsible, reusable plastic produce containers to 15,000 supermarkets in 15 European countries. The combined company, named IFCO Systems, allowed PalEx to expand its pallet business into Europe and IFCO to expand its plastic container business into North America, setting the foundation for the combined firm to expand into Latin America and Asia.

Rounding out the top three industry leaders were Love Box Company Inc. of Wichita, Kansas, with $150 million in sales for its fiscal year ending September 30, 1997, followed by TRAK International Inc. of Port Washington, Wisconsin, with $96 million in sales for the

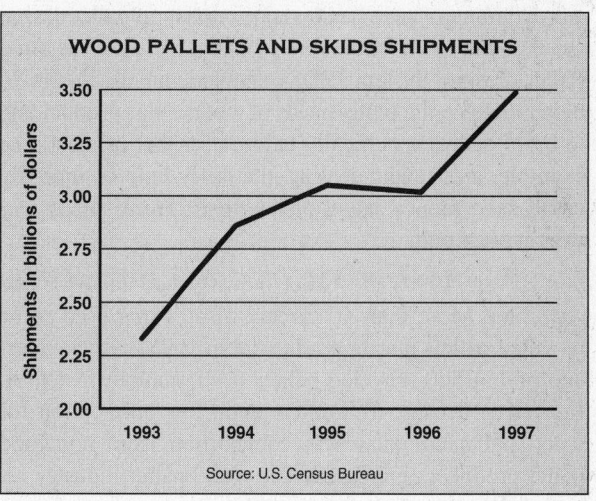

WOOD PALLETS AND SKIDS SHIPMENTS

Source: U.S. Census Bureau

same time period. Other industry leaders included Production Management Corp. of Harvey, Louisiana; AAR Cadillac Manufacturing of Cadillac, Michigan; and Piping Companies Inc. of Sand Springs, Oklahoma.

The vast majority of pallets and skids produced in the United States were made of wood. The remaining pallets were made of wood composite, cardboard/corrugated, metal, plastic, or other materials. In 1995, about 411 million new wood pallets and skids were manufactured in the United States. Used and/or repaired pallets added an additional 208 million to this total. The per firm annual production of pallets in the United States doubled between 1980 and 1995. The average firm produced 254,000 pallets annually in 1995, compared to an average of 112,000 pallets in 1980. The industry has grown at an annual rate of 5 to 7 percent since 1980.

Hardwood lumber, such as oak, was used for 62 percent of the wood in pallets in 1995. Other wood materials used in 1995 included stumpage, logs, and cants. Manufacturers used an average of 17.9 board feet of wood per pallet in 1995, up from 17.3 board feet in 1990. Waste materials were sometimes used by pallet manufacturers to make fuelwood, bedding, pulp, or charcoal, among other products.

The biggest pallet users are the food, paper and fiber, printing, steel and metal, and chemical industries. The most common pallet produced is the flushed stringer, double-face, nonreversible type measuring 48 by 40 inches, which is most often used by supermarkets. Since the 1980s, technology has played an increasingly important role in the pallet and skid industry, contributing to both production and design improvements. Most pallet manufacturers still used hand-held nailers and semi-automated equipment in 1980. By the 1990s, however, fully automated assembly systems allowed two laborers to put together 1,200 pallets in a day, at least four times the rate of production that hand nailers allowed.

Computers have had a major impact on pallet design since about 1980. In the mid-1990s, a computer-assisted Pallet Design System (PDS) enabled manufacturers to better analyze the pallet needs of a particular product and to build pallets specifically tailored for that product. For example, a company dealing in a fairly light commodity could save money using pallets made from softer, less expensive wood.

By the 1990s the pallet industry had incorporated recycling. More than 40 percent of all firms used some recycled pallets during production in 1995, with an average of 131,500 recycled pallets used annually per firm. Recycling became a more common low-cost option for wood pallet companies as competition from nonwood pallet producers increased. The wood pallet industry responded to this challenge with the development of "enhanced pallets," which are more resistant to fire and rot than conventional pallets. There was also a trend toward producing multiple-use pallets, which could be leased by customers and returned when worn out.

Several trends should continue to affect the pallet industry in coming years. In addition to growth in recycling and leasing pallets, and the use of nonwood materials, producers will continue automating the design and manufacturing process. Consolidation, like the PalEx-IFCO deal, should also continue. A shrinking labor force and future Occupational Safety and Health Administration (OSHA) and environmental legislation could also affect the industry, as well as the chance of reduced access to federal forest lands.

FURTHER READING

McCurdy, D.R., and John E. Phelps. *The Pallet Industry in the United States, 1980, 1985, 1990, and 1995.* Southern Illinois University, Carbondale, IL: Department of Forestry Publication, 1996.

"The Pallet Industry at a Glance." *Tech Talk.* Fact Sheet from The National Wooden Pallet and Container Association, February 1997.

Perin, Monica. "PalEx Agrees to Consolidate with German Container Concern." *Houston Business Journal,* 2 April 1999.

U.S. Census Bureau. "Wood Container and Pallet Manufacturing." *1997 Economic Census-Manufacturing.* Available from http://www.census.gov/prod/ec97/97m3219d.pdf.

SIC 2449

WOOD CONTAINERS, NOT ELSEWHERE CLASSIFIED

This industry classification includes companies that primarily make wood containers, not elsewhere classified, such as cooperage, wirebound boxes and crates, and other veneer and plywood containers. Companies that primarily make tobacco hogshead stock are in **SIC 2421: Sawmills and Planing Mills, General** and those making cooperage stock are in **SIC 2429: Special Product Sawmills, Not Elsewhere Classified.**

NAICS CODE(S)

321920 (Wood Container and Pallet Manufacturing)

This classification covers makers of nearly any wooden container that is not either a pallet or a nailed or lock corner box. Many containers in this classification are made from staves, heads, and hoops—a group of products called cooperage. Containers made in this way include barrels, storage vats, and buckets. Tight cooperage refers to containers used to store liquids, such as wine casks, beer barrels, or hot tubs. Containers built to hold solid materials are called slack cooperage. Cooperage is usually built in one facility from pieces constructed elsewhere.

The wood used for staves varies depending on the material to be shipped or stored. For instance, high quality white oak is used for aging bourbon, while seafood is often shipped in smaller kegs made of southern yellow pine. Hoops can be made from steel, wire, or wood.

Wirebound boxes are another part of this industry classification. About 60 percent of wirebound boxes are used for agricultural clients, such as fruit and vegetable growers. The military and private industries also use wirebound boxes. Unlike coopered container producers, wirebound box makers often process their own lumber or veneer. The technology for making wirebound boxes is relatively simple: box parts move down a conveyor belt, wire is stapled to the box, then a fastening machine binds the wire ends together.

According to the U.S. Census Bureau's *1997 Economic Census—Manufacturing,* 255 establishments operated in this category for part or all of 1997. Industry-wide employment totaled 5,679 workers receiving a payroll of almost $110 million. Of these employees, 4,676 put in almost 9 million hours to earn wages of just more than $75 million. Overall shipments for the industry were valued at more than $475 million.

The top two industry leaders in overall sales were large corporations that integrated wood container production into their own operations to create economies of scale. CNF Transportation Inc. of Palo Alto, California, which used wood containers in its trucking operations, led the industry with over $4.9 billion in 1998 sales. Brown-Forman Corp. of Louisville, Kentucky, which used wood containers to age and transport its distilled liquors, came in second in the industry with sales of over $2 billion for its fiscal year ended April 30, 1998. The third place company in the industry, Greif Bros. Corp. of

Delaware, Ohio, generated sales of $801 million for its fiscal year ended October 31, 1998, focusing primarily on container manufacturing.

The remainder of the industry leaders, which were smaller companies with lower revenues, included Sonoco Products Co. Baker Div. of Hartselle, Alabama; Calpine Containers Inc. of Pleasant Hill, California; Semac Industries Inc. of Millersburg, Ohio; and Marvil Package Co. of Wilmington, North Carolina. Market analysts at Salomon Smith Barney reported in December 1999 that Sonoco stood strong in its fourth quarter due to price increases in the United States and abroad, improving volume trends, and stable costs for raw materials.

Although the wood container industry as a whole grew throughout the 1990s, little growth came from miscellaneous wood containers. This is partly due to competition from containers made without wood, such as corrugated paperboard and plastic. Also, since the containers that clients want vary in size and shape, their production could not be automated as easily as a standard-sized product like wood pallets. Demand for quality wood containers probably will not fade, however, regardless of non-wood containers available. This, coupled with weak foreign competition, hints at a positive future for the U.S. wood container industry.

FURTHER READING

Infotrac Company Profiles, 25 January 2000. Available from http://web2.infotrac.galegroup.com.

Staphos, G.L. ''Equity Research.'' Salomon Smith Barney, 7 December 1999. Available from http://web2.infotrac.galegroup.com/itw/in...020224&dyn = 57!ar_fmt?sw_aep = umt_mansfield.

Spencer, Albert G., and Jack A. Luy. *Wood and Wood Products.* Columbus, OH: Charles E. Merrill Publishing Company, 1975.

U.S. Census Bureau. ''Wood Container and Pallet Manufacturing.'' *1997 Economic Census-Manufacturing,* 20 February 2000. Available from http://www.census.gov/prod/ec97/97m3219d.pdf.

U.S. Department of Commerce. *1997 Annual Survey of Manufactures: Statistics for Industry Groups and Industries.* Washington: GPO, 1999.

SIC 2451

MOBILE HOMES

This category covers establishments primarily engaged in manufacturing mobile homes and nonresidential mobile buildings. These units are generally more than 35 feet long, at least 8 feet wide, and often are equipped with wheels. Trailers that are generally 35 feet long or less, 8 feet wide or less, and with self-contained facilities are classified in **SIC 3792: Travel Trailers and Campers.** Portable wood buildings not equipped with wheels are classified in **SIC 2452: Prefabricated Wood Buildings and Components.**

NAICS CODE(S)

321991 (Manufactured Home (Mobile Home) Manufacturing)

INDUSTRY SNAPSHOT

This $32-billion industry declined since its peak in unit shipments was reached in the 1970s, but it made a resurgence in the last half of 1990s. In 1999, there were only 88 manufactured home corporations, compared to 261 companies in 1982. However, those manufacturers were approaching the 400,000 mark in shipments exceeded in the 1970s. Unit shipments increased 7 percent between 1995 and 1996 and 5 percent between 1997 and 1998. In 1998, manufacturers shipped a total of 372,843 homes—only 197,000 units were shipped in 1992. Large multi-section homes (some with three bedrooms) accounted for 15 percent of shipments in the early 1970s. January through August 1999, they accounted for 64.0 percent of industry shipments, compared with 60.2 percent through August 1998.

Yet, the industry showed signs of slowing. In 1998, the U.S. Census Bureau reported that 22.7 percent of single-family housing starts and 29.6 percent of new single-family homes sold was a manufactured home. These figures were down slightly from 23.8 percent and 30.5 percent, respectively, in 1997. Unit shipments January through August 1999 decreased 1.4 percent from the same period in 1998, mainly due to excess inventory.

The industry had been able to resurge in the mid- to late 1990s because it had virtually redefined its product. The old image of trailer parks, with metal-walled mobile homes and flat roofs, has been replaced, more or less, by an image of manufactured homes. Like the old mobile homes, a manufactured home is made in a factory and comes on its own chassis, with removable wheels that are taken off after it is trucked to its destination. But as Carlos Tejada reported in the *Wall Street Journal,* ''Today's multi-section manufactured home takes pains to hide those origins, with wood exteriors, wood-framed windows, porches, and shingled, peaked roofs.'' Many manufactured homes are indistinguishable from site-built homes. In pricing, too, the industry has gone farther upscale. Where mobile homes sold for less than $10,000 a couple of decades ago, in 1997 a single-section manufactured home sold for an average of $29,000 and a multi-section home sold for an average of $49,500. Indeed, even the name ''mobile home'' is something of a misnomer, because more than 90 percent of manufactured homes are never moved from their original site. In fact, the term "mobile home" only applies to manufactured housing units built before the U.S. Department of Housing and Urban Development (HUD) passed quality-assurance standards for this type of factory-built home in 1976.

Economics and demographics have played a part in the growth of manufactured housing. Manufactured homes typically cost just 20 to 50 percent of what traditional site-built homes do. This price advantage helped to attract first-time buyers, as well as retirees and "empty-nesters," who view the homes as an attractive option, either for a second vacation home or as a year-round residence. The availability of financing for manufactured homes, including longer loan terms, helped buyers. According to the Manufactured Housing Institute, other trends that contributed to industry growth included increased service-sector job creation in the Southeast and Southwest, improved construction quality and appearance, a population shift toward suburban and rural areas, and an increased ability to site homes in subdivisions. For all of these reasons, the surviving enjoyed solid financial performances in the late 1990s.

Due to the high costs associated with shipping mobile homes, manufacturing plants are generally located close to the market. Consequently, the industry's facilities dot the nation's landscape, with each manufacturing plant wedded, to a certain degree, to its surrounding market. The top five shipment states are Texas, North Carolina, Georgia, Florida, and South Carolina.

BACKGROUND AND DEVELOPMENT

During the mobile home industry's beginning, its products answered the need of a small percentage of the American populace: temporary shelter primarily used by migrant farm workers and equally nomadic construction workers. Although these were not the only buyers of mobile homes, they did account for the bulk of the industry's sales and, consequently, limited the potential of the industry's future expansion. Since both of these market niches composed a negligible portion of the nation's consumer base and any significant increase in their size—at least in proportion to the rate of population growth—appeared unlikely, the mobile home industry seemed destined to remain a relatively small industry.

This restrictive quality inherent in the industry's market would not inhibit mobile home manufacturers for long, however; once a product was made and marketed that could attract a more diverse clientele and fulfill a need overlooked by the traditional construction industry, sales would increase. But during the 1920s, when mobile homes were first emerging, and into the 1930s, as the industry began to take shape, sales figures remained unsubstantial.

The onset of World War II provided an unexpected boost for mobile home manufacturers, infusing the industry with production orders for military personnel shelters (essentially miniature barracks on wheels) and mobile housing for defense workers. By the conclusion of the war, mobile home manufacturers had several years of comparatively prodigious production levels, due primarily to defense contracts. Mobile homes had become, as a consequence of this war-related work, familiar fixtures in many encampments across the country. Moreover, once the war ended, America had, in effect, a standing army: a new social class of military personnel subject to the sometimes itinerant demands of military life. Mobile homes afforded members of the armed forces—especially those with families—the housing flexibility that their frequent relocation orders required, supplying mobile home manufacturers with a new market niche for their products. Two years after the war, in 1947, the mobile home retail market neared $150 million in sales, garnered from the sale of 60,000 units.

The following year sales eclipsed $200 million and unit sales leapt to 85,000 as the mobile home industry began to show signs of dramatic growth. In 1949, however, optimism regarding the industry's growth potential faded. Retail sales for the year were a disappointing $122 million and unit sales plunged to 46,200.

As the industry entered the 1950s, it effected a recovery from the dismal showings of 1949, posting successive gains in annual sales until 1956, a year that would mark the beginning of a new era in the mobile home industry. Originally, the size of mobile homes varied in length, but always measured 8 feet in width to conform to the maximum width permissible by law for vehicles on highways. These homes, after all, were intended to be mobile. But in 1956, manufacturers first introduced 10-foot-wide models, or "10 wides," which quickly became the industry standard. By 1958, 10 wides accounted for 65 percent of the industry's shipments and two years later, represented more than 85 percent.

It rapidly became apparent to manufacturers that mobility was not the primary asset mobile homes offered consumers. Instead, consumers were attracted by their affordability. To be sure, mobility was still an important feature, but mobile home owners moved their units on average only once every two and a half years, becoming for many a semi-permanent dwelling, and for some a house on wheels that never moved. Further, mobile homes came from the factory equipped with all the basic domestic appurtenances homeowners or renters of conventional houses ordinarily would have to buy separately, a total package for the mobile home customer that came with a significantly lower price tag than a bare conventional home.

The size of the mobile home industry had reached respectable proportions by relying solely on the production of 8-foot-wide models, reaching $462 million in sales from the sale of 111,900 units in 1955, the last year in which 8-foot-wide models represented 100 percent of the mobile home market. Although 10 wides quickly dominated the market, their introduction did not initially spark an exponential increase in unit production or in the industry's overall revenues. They did, however, provide the industry with a more stable and potentially rewarding foundation from which to build on. Newly married couples and those over 50 years of age became two of the industry's largest market segments, attracted by the affordability and flexibility mobile home housing offered at a time when both these components of the American populace were growing faster than the rate of population growth as a whole.

Along with these developments came the ills suffered by any industry whose target market has transformed into a more lucrative audience. For the mobile home industry these growing pains came in the form of increased competition during the late 1950s, as the low initial investment required to establish a mobile home manufacturing facility enabled hopeful entrepreneurs to enter the industry, causing the market to become saturated. This influx of small, single-plant manufacturers created considerable turmoil in the mobile home market in 1960 and 1961, when a number of small manufacturers failed and their inventories entered the market at panic prices. Units shipments for the industry fell from 120,500 in 1959 to 90,200 in 1961, while industry revenues dropped by roughly $100 million to $505 million.

The subsequent anxiety led to a period of industry consolidation during the early 1960s, as a handful of publicly owned conglomerates wrested control of the market from a scattered group of small, privately owned manufacturers through mergers and acquisitions. On the whole, however, the industry continued to be populated primarily by small, independent companies (the high cost of shipping mobile homes made large, centralized manufacturing consortiums impractical), but for the first time the industry's leaders were primarily comparatively larger, publicly held companies, such as Elkhart, Indiana's Skyline Homes; Dryden, Michigan's Champion Home Builders; New York's Divco-Wayne Corp.; and Redman Industries.

By 1963 the mobile home industry had recovered. Retail revenues stood at $862 million and unit sales topped 150,000, surpassing for the first time the figures recorded in 1959. By the following year, mobile homes accounted for one of every nine housing starts, with approximately 220 companies competing for the burgeoning business occasioned by the advent of 10 wides, which was finally coming to fruition six years later. Twelve-foot-wide mobile homes had been introduced two years earlier, in 1962, as the inevitable offshoot of 10 wides, garnering an encouraging 10 percent share of the

industry's 1964 sales. "Double wides," the joining of two 10 wides to form a single unit, were also widely popular as the industry entered the mid-1960s, giving owners up to 1,000 square feet of living space.

The consolidation of the previous years left the five largest companies controlling 30 percent of the market, the demographics of which had changed considerably in the previous 20 years. Families in which the head of the household was older than 51 years of age represented 35 percent of all mobile home residents, but only 8 percent of these owners were retired. Nomadic construction and factory workers, once the mainstays of the mobile home market, accounted for 19 percent of mobile home ownership, yet were surprisingly outnumbered by professional and business people, who represented 25 percent of all owners.

Added to these changes in the composition of the mobile home market was the emergence of an entirely new market segment in the early 1960s—commercial and industrial customers. Businesses such as banks used mobile "offices" as temporary branch outlets, manufacturing companies requiring temporary additional space to execute contract work used mobile home structures, and school systems used mobile homes as portable classrooms. These mobile "home" structures were custom built or converted from existing mobile home units, requiring the re-tooling of production machinery that many of the larger mobile home manufacturers found disruptive to their assembly lines. Consequently, the smaller manufacturers in the industry benefited from the majority of the commercial and industrial business, building each structure according to the specifications required for its particular application. Although industrial and commercial business accounted for only 5 percent of the industry's total sales during the early and mid-1960s, the market was just opening up and promised to develop into a lucrative component of the mobile home industry.

By 1965 mobile homes accounted for one out of every 6.5 housing starts, representing 324,050 unit sales for the year, while total revenues for the industry exceeded $1.2 billion. The industry also demonstrated encouraging independence from the traditional housing market in the mid-1960s as it matured and began to stand on its own, rather than exist as an adjunct to the construction industry. With the end of its dependence on the cyclical housing market, the mobile home industry was buoyed by the deleterious economic conditions. Mobile home manufacturers reaped business from prospective home buyers unwilling to spend the amount of money required to build homes.

Toward the close of the 1960s, the optimism pervading the industry grabbed the attention of those outside the industry, leading to some fantastic and, in retrospect, starry-eyed predictions for the industry's future. Some of these futuristic visions were extrapolations of the diverse applications for which mobile homes were used during the late 1960s. One such use was as an alternative to low-cost housing, a housing need particularly well-suited for mobile homes, considering their affordability and mobility. In 1968 alone, three cities (Atlanta, Chicago, and Washington, D. C.) began employing mobile homes as temporary housing for individuals forced from their homes as a result of rehabilitation or redevelopment projects. Mobile homes, with their wheels removed, were also stacked on top of each other to form low-rise apartment complexes in Baltimore; Amherst, Massachusetts; and Michigan City, Indiana. From these utilizations, plans for mobile home "skyscraper" structures were born. Architects were swept up by the enthusiasm surrounding the industry, envisioning the creation of mobile modular homes that could be removed and reinserted into high-rise structures, trailing the migratory travels of the owner. Although such structures never materialized, their creation, at least on paper, was indicative of the promising conditions characterizing the mobile home industry in the late 1960s.

Entering the 1970s, the industry had enjoyed a decade of prodigious growth, expanding at an annual rate of 20 percent throughout the 1960s and at 30 percent in the last two years of the decade. Unit shipments in 1970 topped 400,000, representing one mobile home for every 4.5 conventional housing starts, and revenues for the industry approached $3 billion.

At this point in the industry's history, several characteristics demonstrated by the industry augured increased growth for mobile home manufacturers, while some potentially hazardous market conditions loomed in the near future. On the favorable side, the average price for a mobile home had increased only negligibly, from $5,600 to $6,000, throughout the 1960s, while single-family housing construction costs had risen sharply. This disparity was primarily due to the cheaper labor costs incurred by mobile home manufacturers than the wages construction contractors were obliged to pay, increasing the industry's grip on the under-$20,000 housing market. In fact, considering that mobile home units had increased in size since the introduction of 10 wides in 1956, yet had increased only marginally in price during the intervening years, the price per square foot had actually declined. Additionally, financing a mobile home, a process resembling the financing of an automobile, was made easier through the enactment of the Housing and Urban Development Act of 1968, which permitted savings and loan associations to finance mobile home purchases.

The negative factors affecting the industry's future, however, were numerous. The most pressing was the decreasing space available for mobile homes. For the 400,000 units that entered the market in 1969, there were only an estimated 118,000 new mobile home park sites available, and the number of sites for future mobile home parks was scarce. Almost entirely relegated to rural areas, mobile home parks, in which roughly 80 percent of all mobile homes were parked, were generally not well respected by urban residential neighborhoods and were often banned from existing alongside conventional houses through zoning restrictions. This left mobile home manufacturers unable to respond to the urgent need for low-income housing—a large segment of the under-$20,000 housing market from which manufacturers derived almost all of their earnings—during the early 1970s. This additional business could have offset, in part, the mounting competition that continued to plague the industry, making market saturation an imminent reality. In 1969 alone, 110 new manufacturers joined the industry, attracted by the robust growth demonstrated by the industry and the low capital investment required to establish a mobile home manufacturing facility.

Despite the development of these conditions, the industry posted the most successful year in its history in 1972, recording remarkable production and sales volumes that would stand as benchmark figures for the rest of the decade. Unit shipments totaled 575,940 for the year and sales reached the $4-billion plateau, quelling observations that the industry was headed for less prosperous years. Two years later, the two decades of solid growth that had been marred only by several minor economic glitches came to a halt.

Unit shipments in 1974 plunged 42 percent and an additional 35 percent the next year to 212,690. Revenues in 1975 were $2.4 billion. The dramatic revenue spiral, however, did not reflect the actual extent of the losses incurred by the industry during these two years; artificially buoyed by soaring inflation, revenues in reality were lower than they appeared.

The losses suffered by the industry were severe and the reasons for the decline were manifold. Perhaps the single greatest contributing factor to the industry's demise was the economic downturn affecting the nation during this time. Unemployment rose and consumer income dropped, which threw a surfeit of repossessed mobile homes, more than 100,000, on the market. This, in turn, made financing a mobile home purchase more difficult, as the tight money conditions combined with the increasing size and price of mobile homes extended loan payback terms from 5 to 10 years, to 10 to 20 years. Since mobile homes depreciated in value, rather than appreciating like conventional houses, lenders were reluctant to provide loans, rejecting 60 percent of all mobile home loan applications during the two-year slump. Compounding these difficulties was the growing popularity of condominiums, which impinged on the mobile home market, eroding manufacturers' customer base further.

As a result of the losses sustained during this period, the proliferation of manufacturing facilities that preceded the recession (a net total of 295 plants had sprouted up between 1969 and 1973) was halted, then reversed, when more than 40 percent of the 550 firms involved in the market went bankrupt. Production capacity dropped by 43 percent from 1973 levels, nearly matching the increase in capacity during the four years leading up to the downturn.

To effect a recovery, several measures were taken—some which were initiated by the mobile home industry itself, while others came through federal intervention. Internally, mobile home manufacturers increased their output of larger mobile homes, concentrating on 14-foot-wide models and double-wides. Quality control was also a problem, engendered, in part, by unscrupulous manufacturers entering the field in the late 1960s and early 1970s. Many of these companies failed during the recession, solving part of the problem, but the more reputable companies also intensified their efforts toward producing higher-quality mobile units. To increase consumer confidence further, the federal government established uniform building codes and warranty standards, mandates that made entry into the industry by unethical manufacturers more difficult.

The federal government also eased mobile home financing by permitting federally chartered credit unions, which historically were short-term lenders, to provide longer-term credit to mobile home buyers. Also, the Veterans Administration increased the loan guarantee limits for mobile homes from 30 percent to 50 percent.

These ameliorations led to a slow recovery of the mobile home industry. Because of their expanded size and better workmanship, mobile homes began to appreciate in value after the mid-1970s, and began to increase their presence in conventional housing neighborhoods, as zoning restrictions eased. In 1976 unit shipments increased 16 percent to 246,120, still far below the level recorded in 1972, but, nevertheless, an improvement from the successive, precipitous drops suffered during the previous two years.

Also aiding the industry's recovery was the escalating price of conventional housing. Between 1974 and 1978, the average price of a new house rose 61 percent from $38,900 to $62,500, while the average price of a mobile home in 1978 was $15,900. Mobile homes had actually increased at a greater rate than conventional houses during this period, leaping 71 percent from 1974's average price of $9,300, but the price disparity between the two housing choices was great enough to invigorate sales for mobile home manufacturers. In fact, the soaring costs of conventional houses attracted a new breed of mobile home customers by the end of the decade— middle class consumers.

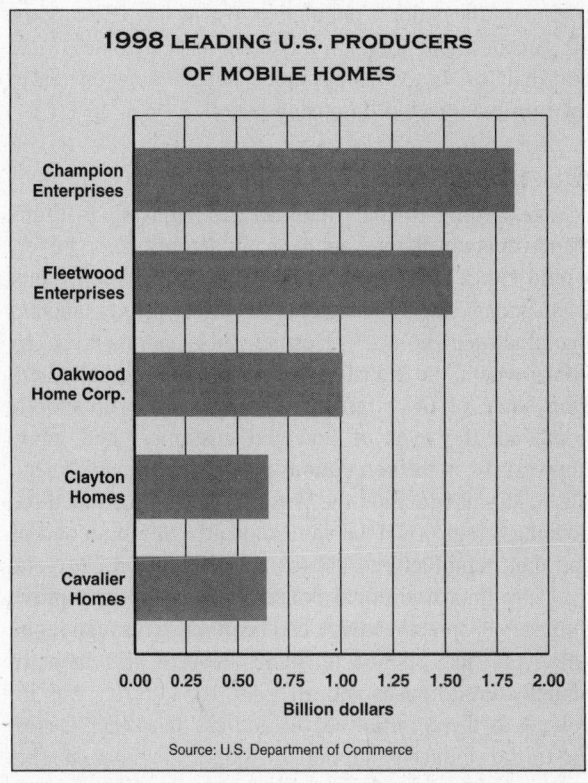

1998 LEADING U.S. PRODUCERS OF MOBILE HOMES

Source: U.S. Department of Commerce

Although these developments provided enough of an impetus to pull the industry out of its doldrums, a complete turnaround was not achieved, and growth of the industry remained stunted as it entered the 1980s. Unit shipments in 1980 were still well below half the total recorded in 1972 and even below the number of units shipped in 1976, the first year of the industry's recovery. After a 23 percent increase in 1983, unit shipments rose to 295,000, and topped 300,000 by the following year. Revenues during this period eclipsed the record year of 1972, peaking at $4.78 billion in 1983, and then dwindling down to slightly more than $4 billion a year for the rest of the decade.

According to the U.S. Census Bureau, mobile homes were the fastest-growing type of housing during the 1980s, a distinction earned primarily from robust sales in the fist half of the decade. The late 1980s brought recessive conditions to the fore once again, causing unit shipments to decline, but mobile home manufacturers avoided significant losses as mobile homes continued to be the only housing alternative for many consumers.

In the 1990s, the once-threatened industry was finding its new direction. Manufacturers were negatively affected, though, by zoning codes that restricted where owners could locate their mobile home for permanent residence. However, by 1992, 22 states had outlawed "anti-mobile home" zoning restrictions, declaring them discriminatory. In the mid-1990s, there were 7.3 million manufactured homes in America, housing 18 million people, or about 7 percent of the nation's population. By the late 1990s, some 10 percent of the population lived in mobile homes. More than half of the owner-occupied homes were on rented land (in manufactured housing parks).

CURRENT CONDITIONS

According to the Manufactured Housing Institute, "an average of 90 percent of manufactured home buyers would either recommend a manufactured home to their friends and family or would themselves buy another manufactured home." Despite this endorsement by homeowners, the industry's future growth requires shedding some of the stigmas still associated with mobile homes in the eyes of potential customers and, more importantly, in the perceptions held by American society. These stigmas include the perception that manufactured housing brings down the value of nearby site-built houses and that manufactured houses are of poorer quality and less safe than traditional houses. While this may prove impossible, some headway had been made through legislation that has opened up more areas to placement of manufactured houses and, in 1999, the industry was involved in three initiatives to address the other issues. First, the industry supported federal legislation that would update the Manufactured Housing Construction and Safety Standards Act of 1974 (HUD code) governing building technologies and safety features. Second, because "improper installation is thought to cause many of the problems and defects that are reported in manufactured homes," the industry was working with "states to pass laws that would require installation standards, training and licensing of installers and inspections." It also was developing installation systems. Third, the industry was working with several federal agencies "to improve manufactured home safety in natural disasters." Progress achieved in these initiatives should provide additional business to mobile home manufacturers in the twenty-first century.

INDUSTRY LEADERS

In 1998, the top 25 manufactured home producers accounted for 92 percent of total industry shipments, and the top 10 accounted for 78 percent. The industry leader in 1999 was Champion Enterprises, which produced 68,264 homes in 1998 with a dollar volume of $1.84 billion. Coming back from near-bankruptcy several years ago, the company overtook Fleetwood Enterprises through acquisitions and internal growth. Champion closed seven acquisitions of competing firms between 1994 and early 1997, including a merger with Redman Industries. The company manufactured homes at 60 plants in the United States and Canada. It sold homes, which ranged in cost from $15,000 to $150,000 and in size from 400 to 6,100 square feet, under the trade names A-1 Homes, Homes of America, and USA Homes.

Number two Fleetwood Enterprises had a dollar volume in 1998 of $1.54 billion, while number three Oakwood Homes Corporation had $1.01 billion. Fleetwood's housing featured vaulted ceilings, walk-in closets, and porches. Oakwood sold single- and multi-section homes, with the brand names of Freedom, Golden West, Villa West, and Peachtree. The least expensive model was $15,000. The company's financial services subsidiary provided financing for some 85 percent of company sales.

Rounding out the top five manufactured home builders were Clayton Homes, with a 1998 dollar volume of $652 million, and Cavalier Homes, with a 1998 dollar volume of $642 million. Clayton homes ranged in price from $10,000 to $75,000 and in size from 500 square feet to 2,400 square feet. The company sells more than 28,000 homes a year in 31 states and also provides financing and operates 75 manufactured home parks. Cavalier markets its low- to medium-priced homes mainly in the Southeast, Southwest, and Midwest, and it also provides financing services.

FURTHER READING

Byrne, Harlan S. "No Laughingstock: Once a Joke, Manufactured Housing Has Gained Respect and a Bright Future." *Barron's,* 6 January 1997.

Hood, John. "Factory-built Housing: The Path of Ownership?" *Consumers' Research Magazine,* August 1998.

Sherrid, Pamela. "An Oxymoron: Trailer Trash." *U.S. News & World Report,* 16 March 1998.

Tejada, Carlos. "Today's Mobile Home May Have a Hearth." *Wall Street Journal,* 14 June 1996.

SIC 2452

PREFABRICATED WOOD BUILDINGS AND COMPONENTS

Companies that primarily make prefabricated wood buildings, sections, and panels make up the prefabricated wood buildings and components industry. Manufactured and mobile homes delivered to a site are not part of this industry. Companies that assemble panels and components on-site are classified in various construction sectors.

NAICS CODE(S)

321992 (Prefabricated Wood Building Manufacturing)

INDUSTRY SNAPSHOT

The prefabricated wood components industry includes many products, including premade panels and sections for chicken coops, farm buildings, geodesic domes, marinas, sauna rooms, hotel rooms, and decks. The industry is fragmented and entrepreneurial and is represented by a wide range of companies.

By far the biggest segments of this industry are single-family homes, multifamily units, and institutional buildings, including hotels and motels, schools, hospitals, and prisons. With a strong economy pushing construction booms in both residential and nonresidential building, prefabricated wood buildings and components manufacturers experienced steady growth in many areas, most notably in larger, upscale homes and upscale log homes. Apart from the economy, factors influencing the growth of this industry during the 1990s included the availability of wood, advancements in design technology, and a move toward smaller class room sizes in education. A more accepting attitude towards prefabricated wood buildings and components—the result of improvements in quality and flexibility—was also a key factor in driving sales for this industry.

ORGANIZATION AND STRUCTURE

The advantage of prefabricated wood building products is that they save builders money. Because large pieces of the structure come from a factory and are designed for quick and easy assembly on-site, builders reduce on-site costs, such as labor, workers' compensation, and insurance. Assembly-line production also allows prefab manufacturers greater quality control.

The cost advantage of prefabricated buildings shows in the price gap between site-built and manufactured homes, which come to the site completely built. In 1997 the median price of a site-built, single-family home was $120,000, while the average price of a manufactured home was $40,000. Most prefabricated homes fell somewhere within this range.

The largest segment of the prefab wood products industry is single-family homes. Homes built using prefab units are called component, or prefabricated, housing. Typical prefab housing products include roof trusses, wall frames, and floors. Many builders also use pre-made wall units complete with insulation, plumbing, wiring, ventilation systems, and doors.

Builders of both detached and attached homes with prefab products use a systems approach to building, which is a hybrid of site-built and manufactured housing. The four types of systems-built housing include precut homes, for which all lumber and materials come to the site already cut; panelized homes, for which the main wall panels are shipped to the site, often with plumbing and wiring already installed; sectional, or modular, homes, which are 80 to 90 percent complete when they leave the factory and have cabinets and flooring already installed; and log homes, which are factory-made kit homes.

BACKGROUND AND DEVELOPMENT

Assembling wooden building components off-site has been practiced for centuries. The modern concept of prefabrication, which mass produces uniform panels and components, dates back to the early 1900s. Builders of that period, often the homeowners themselves, bought lightweight, premade frames and trusses to simplify construction. The use of gasoline-powered trucks in those early years boosted sales of prefab products and allowed manufacturers to build larger, heavier components.

The fledgling prefab industry grew during the post-World War II economic boom. As the economy and population grew, housing starts soared. Also, government housing programs, such as the Veteran's Administration Home Loan Guarantee Program of 1944, prodded demand for new construction. Single-family housing starts went from 139,000 per year in 1944 to 1.9 million in 1950.

Throughout the 1950s and 1960s, as the postwar economy thrived, families flocked to the housing market in a buying frenzy. Thousands of tract subdivisions were built on the edges of urban America, typically offering quality detached homes for less than $10,000 in the 1950s, with mortgage payments less than $100 per month. To keep up with demand, both residential and commercial builders sought more efficient production methods, including prefabrication.

New construction techniques and standard components made construction more viable during the 1950s, 1960s, and 1970s. New federal and state regulations were enacted, for example, mandating structural integrity and uniform building practices. Plywood, plastics, and aluminum, which all eventually went into wood prefab units, also increased sales.

Although demand for new construction remained high through the 1980s, several factors, including higher construction costs, slowed demand compared to past decades. As housing affordability and home ownership rates fell, many builders used component construction to cut costs. At the same time, higher quality components gave the industry a share of upscale markets. In addition, demand for heavy-duty commercial and industrial units rose.

Industry sales rose to nearly $2.5 billion by 1987, reflecting average annual growth of more than 12 percent between 1981 and 1987. Although commercial and residential construction markets stalled in the late 1980s and early 1990s, prefab industry revenues fell only marginally as the search for less-expensive production methods escalated. Sales slipped to about $2.3 billion in the early 1990s, but demand rose with better construction markets in the mid-1990s. The industry shipped goods worth $2.7 billion in 1995, down slightly from 1994.

CURRENT CONDITIONS

Total value of product shipments in this industry increased by nearly 33 percent between 1992 and 1997, according to the U.S. Census Bureau, reaching $2.88 billion dollars. Over half of that figure came from prefabricated stationary wood buildings shipped in three-dimensional assemblies, rather than in panel form, as packaged units, or as components. The value of shipments of three-dimensional assemblies, including both residential and nonresidential buildings, increased by 41 percent, marking the area of greatest growth in the industry. Other areas experiencing notable growth included prefabricated wood buildings shipped in panel form, particularly for structures other than single-family homes (although shipments in that area also increased). Multifamily residential units increased by 138 percent, and nonresidential units, including motels and hotels, increased by almost 110 percent. By contrast, shipments for components actually decreased slightly overall between 1992 and 1997, particularly those components used in nonresidential buildings.

Rapid growth in residential construction meant increased sales for several segments of this industry. In mid-1999, *ENR* reported a very tight market for premade wall panels as demand threatened to outrun supply. As a result, prices rose sharply in 1999, although industry experts also forecast an eventual drop in price as the market corrected itself. Traditional builders increasingly used panels for custom-built residential construction, as technological improvements in computer-aided design made the number of design options nearly limitless— once a drawback of using premade panels rather than building walls on-site. Other benefits of prefab wall panels include savings in cost and time.

The growth of the modular home industry was dramatic through the latter half of the 1990s. According to a report in *Automated Builder* magazine, 8 percent of all housing started in 1997 was modular, reflecting an 11 percent increase over 1996 and a 49 percent increase since 1993. The widespread acceptance of manufactured homes in the late 1990s—with one in three new single-family homes begun in 1998 being fully factory-built—suggested the potential for increasing growth of modulars as well.

As modular homes became more popular, bigger and pricier houses became more common in the industry. A sign of the growing acceptance of modular homes was the construction of one of the largest single-family homes ever built from prefabricated segments. Made by Westchester Modular Homes, the Greenwich, Connecticut, mansion encompassed 9,000 square feet. The house was 80 percent complete upon leaving the factory and was shipped to the site in 20 boxes. According to the builder, using prefabricated segments took off at least three months from the building schedule and saved between 10 to 12 percent of

the final cost of the home. In such larger—and more upscale—projects, the actual cost of materials may not be less than it is for conventional site-built homes, but the amount of time saved—sometimes a matter of years—still translates to a substantial cost savings.

Log Homes. Aside from more demand for prefabricated traditional homes, one large and growing segment of the industry was log homes. Log homes represented close to 7 percent of custom homes built in the United States in 1998 for a total of 23,000 log homes; exports of prefabricated log homes also increased. Like modular homes, log homes became more upscale. Because they use more wood than traditionally built housing—10 to 20 percent more—the wood favored for their construction continues to grow more scarce. Red cedar, which is especially popular in Southeast Asian markets, was expected to be difficult to come by within the first decade of the twenty-first century. Some makers have looked to other woods, including plentiful pine, to meet the demand.

Office and Schools. A shortage of office space was also a boon to manufacturers in this industry, as vacancy rates fell below 5 percent in some major cities. Modular office space allowed maximum flexibility for a business's growth and restructuring. In addition, the need to rewire or install additional wiring for rapid changes in technology made modular and panel-built offices an increasingly popular choice. Along with this trend, smaller panels came into favor in the United States for their increased flexibility.

Prefabricated building manufacturers aggressively pursued the school-building market in the late 1990s, but as of 1999, modular construction accounted for less than 1 percent of all new construction of educational facilities. Manufacturers battled against old stereotypical images of mobile trailers as temporary annexes to the brick-and-mortar school buildings. Some educational architects became proponents of using modular solutions, successfully lobbying school systems to adopt them. Advantages of using prefabricated buildings for school use included minimal disruption to classes and the ability to disassemble the structure and reassemble it at another site in the future. The nationwide push for smaller classroom sizes was also a positive factor for the industry.

One of the most notable educational projects undertaken in 1999 was the construction of Middlesex Community College in Bedford, Massachusetts, an entire college campus constructed from modular buildings encompassing over 126,000 square feet. According to a report in *School Planning and Management,* which is a major advocate for modular building, ''The new buildings, each two and three stories, are designed to model true New England neo-Georgian architecture with its classical brick exteriors and quoin work on the corners, and a running Flemish bond, as well as roof dormers, brick chimneys, and cupolas.''

Manufacturers participating in the education sector saw tremendous growth in the late 1990s. Modtech, the only major builder of modular classrooms in California—where smaller class sizes were a big political issue—watched its stock zoom up 260 percent in 1996. As of September of 1997, its work backlog alone was worth $40 million, compared to $4 million for year-end 1996. Industry analyst Steve Adams told *The Business Press* that, ''Over the next couple of years, they can probably achieve $100 million in total revenues with a pretax profit of about $10 million.'' The New York City schools present another big opportunity. A 1999 report in *Building Design and Construction* revealed that ''following a mandate to construct 100 new school buildings in four years, the New York City School Construction Authority recently completed a study to determine whether modular and pre-engineered construction could meet this goal.''

Other markets for growth included ground stands for concessions at amusement parks and fairs, which were endorsed by the International Association of Fairs and Expositions in 1997 as a more affordable and traditional alternative to trailers. Hospitals, prisons, and motels were other markets for this industry.

INDUSTRY LEADERS

About 709 companies participated in the prefabricated wood component industry in 1997. Because it is a localized industry by logistic necessity, most companies were small—only 249 had more than 20 employees. Pennsylvania was by far the leader in the production of three-dimensional assemblies; Wisconsin was the clear leader in production of buildings shipped in panel form. Top Pennsylvania producers in 1999 included Muncy Building Enterprises, Deluxe Homes of Pennsylvania, Simplex Industries Inc., and Haven Homes. Leaders in Wisconsin were Wausau Homes Inc. (which ranked sixth in the nation by sales), Wisconsin Homes Inc., and Stratford Homes Inc. Wisconsin is also a leader in log homes, home to leading companies Wilderness Log Homes, Greatwood Log Homes, and Pine Ridge Log Homes.

Firms leading the industry overall as of 1999 were Skyline Corp., with $612 million in sales and 3,500 employees; Horton Homes, with $250 million in sales and 1,500 employees, Liberty Homes, with $168 million in sales and 1,300 employees; and Cavco Industries, with $168 million in sales and 1,400 employees. Several industry leaders in this sector also had revenues from mobile and manufactured homes.

WORKFORCE

For production, the industry employed many assemblers, fabricators, and woodworkers. In 1997, 23,335 people worked in this industry, with 17,145 jobs in production, reflecting a slow but steady increase in employment for this industry. Total payroll for 1997 was $583 million, of which $352 million paid production wages.

Given the tight labor market in this industry and the overall economy, prefabricated buildings have been a blessing to contractors, as they require very little on-site labor.

RESEARCH AND TECHNOLOGY

Most technological advances throughout the mid-1990s centered around prefab housing's advantages of low cost, ease of construction, and uniform quality. Prefab makers also developed products to compete with traditional construction markets, such as high-rise buildings. For instance, component makers in Japan marketed sections and panels for medium-rise apartment buildings as high as five stories tall.

Japanese companies were leading technological advances in other areas of the industry, as well. Shimizu Corporation's Smart System, introduced in 1993, was designed to cut the number of man-hours required to complete a 20-story office building by 30 percent. The Smart System uses a network of nine computer-controlled cranes that scale the frame of the building and automatically attach components.

Technological developments that competed with the wood component industry in the 1990s included advances in wood substitutes. Producers in Saudi Arabia, for example, mass-produced prefab aluminum houses and buildings. Similarly, manufacturers in Poland shipped prefab metal and reinforced plastic components.

FURTHER READING

Bady, Susan. ''Factory-Built Housing Pushes the Envelope.'' *Professional Builder (1993),* October 1998.

Barnett, Robert Spencer. ''Better Building Blocks.'' *Building Design & Construction,* February 1999.

Byrne, Harlan S. ''No Laughingstock: Once a Joke, Manufactured Housing Has Gained Respect and a Bright Future.'' *Barron's,* 6 January 1997.

Evans, Rob. ''IAFE Panel: Ground Stands Can Be Affordable Alternative to Mobile Units.'' *Amusement Business,* 6 January 1997.

Feuerstein, Adam. ''Boom or Bust? The Area's Hot Office Market May Be Racing Toward Disaster.'' *San Francisco Business Times,* 8 May 1998.

Gribble, Jim. ''Log Home Mecca.'' *The Business Journal-Milwaukee,* 16 November 1996.

Grogan, Tim. ''Panels: Low Inventory, High Demand.'' *ENR,* 28 June 1999.

''The Modular Mansion.'' *Professional Builder (1993),* October 1998.

Savage, Chuck. "Dispelling the Myths of Modular Construction." *School Planning and Management,* July 1999.

Scott, Gray. "Smaller Classrooms Mean Bigger Profits for California Firms." *The Business Press,* 18 February 1997.

U.S. Census Bureau. *1997 Economic Census, Prefabricated Wood Building Manufacturing.* Washington, D.C.: GPO, 1999. Available from http://www.census.gov.

U.S. Department of Commerce. *1995 Annual Survey of Manufactures: Statistics for Industry Groups and Industries.* Washington, D.C.: GPO, 1997.

Watkins-Miller, Elaine. "Flexibility and Aesthetics, Head to Toe: Modular Floors and Ceilings Are New Standards in Today's Technology-Driven Workplace." *Buildings,* November 1998.

SIC 2491

WOOD PRESERVING

The wood preserving industry is comprised of establishments primarily engaged in treating wood—sawed or planed in other establishments—with creosote or other preservatives to prevent decay and protect against fire and insects. The industry also cuts, treats, and sells poles, posts, and pilings; however, establishments primarily engaged in manufacturing other wood products, which they may also treat with preservatives, are classified elsewhere.

NAICS CODE(S)

321114 (Wood Preservation)

People have been coating wood with crude preservatives, such as tar and pitch, for ages. Chemicals and processes developed during the nineteenth and twentieth centuries, however, have resulted in techniques for preserving wood for 35 years or more. Untreated wood exposed to the elements typically lasts about three years. Perhaps the greatest industry innovation during the 1900s was the high-pressure chemical treatment process, which accelerated wood's absorption of preservatives and increased the treatment's depth. During the 1990s, 95 percent of all preserved wood was treated using this process. Southern yellow pine accounts for 85 percent of all treated wood; the remaining 15 percent includes spruce-pine-fir, hemlock, Douglas fir, cedar, inland species of Ponderosa pine, and Brazilian pine. Demand for treated hardwoods is quite low.

Utility poles accounted for roughly 12.5 percent of sales, according to the 1997 Economic Census. Various residential, commercial, and institutional construction industries consume the bulk of industry output, with 77 percent being other wood products and the remaining 10.5 percent being contract wood preservation.

The majority of wood products are treated with water-borne preservatives, the most common being chromated copper arsenate (CCA), ammoniacal copper Quat (ACQ), and ammoniacal copper zinc arsenate (ACZA). Materials for decking, fences, gazebos, playgrounds, and the like are usually treated with this method. Pentachlorophenol, an oil-borne preservative, is used on utility poles and glued-laminated beams for vaulted ceilings.

Wood preservers have needed to adjust to new environmental restrictions. In 1990 the Environmental Protection Agency (EPA) identified the byproducts of wood preserving processes as hazardous waste and chose to begin regulating the industry in 1991. Naphthenate and other substitutes increasingly will offer viable alternatives to preservatives that spawn high-cost toxins. In 1996 Koppers Industries, an industry leader, reported ongoing problems with site and ground-water contamination from wood preservatives and had EPA violations at many of their facilities. The company reported the possibility of needing to install additional pollution control and monitoring devices at various facilities, and they participated in extensive cleanup operations.

The industry continues to deny that any pollution problems exist, despite research that shows that arsenic, in particular, leaches into the ground and water system, as well as rubs on those handling treated wood materials. The industry is also seeking alternative means of disposal of used treated materials since burying in a landfill, as well as burning the materials, releases chemicals into the ecosystem. Work is being done on reconstituting used treated woods into particle board.

The 1997 Economic Census lists the value of shipments in the wood preserving industry at $4.4 million from 449 companies employing 11,433 workers. Alabama and South Carolina were the top two states in value of product shipments, with Georgia and Virginia vying for third place.

During the 1990s, 15.4 percent of industry employees worked as assemblers, fabricators, and hand workers. Other occupations included sawyers; machine feeders; blue-collar supervisors and laborers; wood machinists; truck and tractor operators; freight and material movers; managers and executives; and coating, spraying, and painting workers. Despite the industry's growth in the 1980s and 1990s, employment is predicted to decline in the wake of productivity gains. Most occupations are expected to realize a work force reduction of 5 to 25 percent between 1990 and 2005, according to the Bureau of Labor Statistics.

Top companies in the industry in 1996 were Koppers Industries of Pittsburgh, Pennsylvania, which had sales of $465 million and 1,800 employees, and Fibreboard Corporation of Walnut Creek, California, which had sales of $364 million and 3,500 employees. Other leading companies included Tolleson Lumber Company, Walker-Williams Lumber Company, and Robbins Manufacturing Company.

FURTHER READING

American Wood Products Institute (AWPI). *Frequently Asked Questions About Treated Wood,* 1999. Available from http://primusweb.com/forest.

Koppers Industries 1996 Annual Report. Pittsburgh: Koppers Industries, 1997.

Long, Cheryl. "Just Say No to Wood Treated with Arsenic." *Organic Gardening,* July 1999.

Munson, Jacob M. "Reconstituted Particleboards from CCA-Treated Red Pine Utility Poles." *Forest Products Journal,* March 1998.

Southern Pine Council. *Pressure Treated Southern Pine,* November 1999. Available from http://www.southernpine.com/treated.htm.

SIC 2493

RECONSTITUTED WOOD PRODUCTS

The reconstituted wood products industry is comprised of establishments primarily engaged in manufacturing hardboard, particleboard, insulation board, medium-density fiberboard (MDF), waferboard, oriented strand board (OSB), and other panelized products made from wood chips and particles.

NAICS CODE(S)

321219 (Reconstituted Wood Product Manufacturing)

BACKGROUND AND DEVELOPMENT

Particleboard is created from wood flakes, shavings, or splinters that are discharged when wood products are processed. The particles are bonded together under pressurized heat using resin and adhesives to make an inexpensive, durable wooden panel. Approximately 80 percent of all particleboard is used to make furniture, cabinets, and doors. A hardboard, or fiberboard, panel is made from wood fibers that are steamed, rubbed apart, and then compacted under pressurized heat. Unlike particleboard, only a small amount of resin or adhesive is used to bond the fibers. Hardboard has a smooth finish and is used primarily for exterior house siding, indoor cabinets, and fixtures.

Commercially useful wood particle panels resulted from the chemical industry's development of high-tech synthetic resins and adhesives, particularly during the 1960s, 1970s, and 1980s. The value of reconstituted panel shipments increased steadily during the 1980s and 1990s to an estimated $5.1 billion by 1996. Shipments grew by about 3 percent to nearly $5.3 billion in 1997. For the

period 1998-2003, the U.S. Department of Commerce forecast an increase of 3.3 percent per year as demand for furniture and residential construction continues.

CURRENT CONDITIONS

Although the early-decade economic recession caused industry revenues to drop slightly, improved economic conditions in the 1990s saw a surge in shipments of particleboard and medium-density fiberboard (MDF) from U.S. mills. The Composite Panel Association estimated that U.S. particleboard and MDF shipments increased by 18 and 45 percent to almost 5 billion and 1.4 billion square feet, respectively, from 1993 to 1998. Particleboard shipments from Canadian mills increased by almost 14 percent in 1998 to 1.24 billion square feet.

However, Resource Information Systems, Inc. of Bedford, Massachusetts. Predicted slower growth rates in consumption in 1999 and 2000. Particleboard was projected to increase by approximately 4.2 percent in 1999 and 2000. MDF consumption increased by an estimated 16 percent in 1998, although Resource Information expects consumption to decrease to 10 percent in 1999 and 7 percent in 2000.

Rich Margosian, president of the Composite Panel Association, estimated that MDF shipments increased more than 50 percent between 1993 and 1998, which is an annual growth rate exceeding 10 percent. Applications like high-detail moldings and edge-detailed furniture continue to hold promise; MDF's share of the molding market grew from 20 percent in 1997 to 26 percent in 1998, according to Peter McKibbin, vice president of industrial products at Contact Lumber, Inc. Jeff Lundegard, vice president of sales and marketing for SierraPine Ltd., believes that in five years, MDF will have 85 percent of this market.

Wood panel manufacturers were starting to market their products with the Forest Stewardship Council's label, which certifies companies that are responsibly managing their timber lands. With the greening trend continuing, panels made of waste and alternative materials are also in demand. In 1999 CanFiber's Riverside, California, facility announced that it had produced the world's first MDF made from 100 percent post-consumer wastewood. Other companies are making boards made of rice straw, barley straw, or other agricultural fibers. Eight start-ups or expansions were planned for 1999 and 2000. Capacity of agricultural panel capacity quadrupled in 1998 to 169 million square feet with the startup of Isobord Enterprises' new plant. Iowa State University researchers have also developed a process to turn cow manure into MDF.

INDUSTRY LEADERS

The largest U.S. producers include Louisiana-Pacific Corporation (L-P), with 1998 total sales of $2.8 billion

(60 percent in wood products), and Masonite Corporation of Illinois, a subsidiary of International Paper. Masonite had 1998 estimated sales of more than $400 million. Twelve percent of International Paper's total sales includes forest products, which includes 945 million square feet of OSB and 300 million square feet of particleboard.

WORKFORCE

Despite overall growth, opportunities in most occupations in the industry are expected to decline significantly between 1990 and 2005, according to the U.S. Bureau of Labor Statistics. Jobs for assemblers and fabricators, which accounted for 14 percent of the work force in the early 1990s, are predicted to fall by more than 25 percent. Most positions, in fact, are expected to decline 5 to 20 percent by 2005. The industry employed approximately 25,000 workers in 1997, with more than 80 percent in production earning $13 per hour.

AMERICA AND THE WORLD

McKibbin estimated that the office furniture industry consumes 200 million square feet of particleboard and MDF every year. The Asian furniture market became a primary target for North American exports of particleboard; exports were expected to exceed 565 million square feet by 1997, primarily to Pacific Rim countries.

Worldwide production of MDF grew from less than 1 million cubic meters in 1996 to nearly 20 million cubic meters (11.3 billion square feet) in 1999 from more than 200 mills in 44 countries, according to market research consultant Leonard Guss. He predicts that global demand for MDF will increase 25 percent in the next 10 years. A worldwide survey by *Wood Technology* showed that 28 new MDF installations occurred in 1999, with 24 planned over the next several years; half of these 52 projects were in Europe.

Waferboard and oriented strand board (OSB) made up about 20 percent of industry sales in the early 1990s. Waferboard is similar to particleboard, but only three-inch, square wood flakes are used. OSB is a type of waferboard, but its flakes are layered and oriented in a way that makes it much stronger than waferboard, yet still less expensive than plywood. Global capacity of OSB is predicted to increase by 50 percent over the next decade, according to Guss.

OSB production capacity began to expand rapidly in the first half of the 1990s, and 27 new North American plants were built in 1995. Capacity expansion slowed by the end of the century. Globally, only 23 new plants were planned from 1999 through 2005, with 15 of these plants in North America.

North American OSB production grew from 7.65 billion square feet in 1990 to 19.45 billion square feet in 1999. OSB production was expected to reach nearly 22 billion square feet by 2003. The Engineered Wood Association also predicted that OSB will account for 44 percent of total production by 2000, up from 28 percent of the market in 1994 and 31 percent in 1995. Canada's panel production was predicted to be 82 percent OSB by the year 2000, up from 62 percent in 1994.

The hardboard market was relatively stable from 1986 to 1996, with shipments peaking in 1996 to 5.28 billion square feet. The next several years saw decreases of 4.5 and 4.3 billion square feet for 1997 and 1998, respectively.

The value of imports increased from 1992 to 1996 at a rate of 27.6 percent, reaching more than $1 billion. Growth was predicted to slow to 11 and 6 percent for 1998 and 1999, respectively. In 1997, more than 78 percent of the $1.1 billion in imports came from Canada, and this is expected to increase. The value of exports has slowed from about 15 percent in 1997 to an expected 6 percent in 1999. Exports reached $355 million in 1997—with Canada, the United Kingdom, Mexico, and Japan as the largest markets. Exports of particleboard in 1998 reached 291 million square feet, of which 110 million went to Canada. The U.S. exported 51 million square feet of MDF in 1998 and imported 277 million square feet, mostly from Canada.

FURTHER READING

"CanFibre Celebrates a World First by Producing Medium Density Fiberboard from 100 Percent Wastewood." *Canadian Corporate News, Inc.,* 15 June 1999.

"Consumption Could Affect MDF Prices." *Cabinetmaker,* July 1999.

Fitzgerald, Anne. "Manure Turned into Fiberboard." *Gannett News Service,* 8 August 1999.

"The Future of Composite Panels." *Furniture Design & Manufacturing,* June 1999.

Haddox, Katherine. "Strong Economy Supports Panel Growth, Stabilization." *Wood Technology,* October 1999. Available from http://www.woodwideweb.com/db_area/archives/1999/9910/panel.html.

Pease, Dave. "Market Will Determine Nature of Composites." *Wood Technology,* July 1999.

SIC 2499

WOOD PRODUCTS, NOT ELSEWHERE CLASSIFIED

This category includes establishments primarily engaged in manufacturing miscellaneous wood products, not elsewhere classified, and products made from rattan, reed, splint, straw, veneer, veneer strips, wicker, and willow.

NAICS CODE(S)

339999 (All Other Miscellaneous Manufacturing)
321920 (Wood Container and Pallet Manufacturing)
321999 (All Other Miscellaneous Wood Product Manufacturing)

This industry covers a plethora of wood products not categorized under other classifications, such as ship masts, dowels, rowboat oars, clipboards, rattan seat covers, shoe trees, tool handles, toothpicks, washboards, paint stirring sticks, and wooden ladders. Although the breadth of this industry is enormous, some categories account for a significant portion of overall sales. For example, wooden picture and mirror frames are by far the largest category, supplying 36 percent of industry revenues in the first half of the 1990s and garnering revenues of more than $1 billion by 1995.

Individuals, the largest consumers of miscellaneous wooden goods, accounted for about 22 percent of industry sales in the early 1990s. Office building owners and managers were the second-largest sector, representing about 4 percent of the market. Other major consumers of industry output were furniture manufacturers, makers of glass products, and paperboard mills. Exports accounted for 3.5 percent of production.

This industry is intangible and unstructured compared with most other industrial categories. The industry experienced wide swings in revenues during the 1980s, according to the U.S. Census of Manufactures. At that time 3,400 firms reported total sales of $3.4 billion. By 1992, the Census reported only 2,644 firms having $3.7 billion in total shipments of miscellaneous wooden items. By 1997, the number of firms had dropped to roughly 2,300 with a value of shipments of approximately $3.7 billion.

An estimated 52,705 workers served the industry in 1994; a slight increase since 1992, but an overall decline from the 61,000 workers reported in 1987. Production workers comprised 83 percent of employees. The number further declined in 1997 to about 42,000 workers, with a similar percent of production workers. These workers earned less than $10 per hour. Significant occupations in this industry include assemblers and fabricators, machine operators, sawers, blue-collar work supervisors, and truck drivers.

Long-term growth in industry sales and profits will depend on individual product segments. Overall employment is expected to decline significantly between 1990 and 2005, according to the Bureau of Labor Statistics. Assembler and fabricator jobs, for example, could plummet by more than 26 percent; positions for machine operators and bookkeepers also could decline. Most occupations, it is anticipated, will realize a 5 to 20 percent reduction in the workforce as companies seek to automate and increase productivity. Sales and marketing professionals, in contrast, will see positions in this industry grow by nearly 20 percent.

The largest producer of miscellaneous wood products throughout the first half of the 1990s was Masonite Corp. of Illinois, although the company's revenue and number of employees declined sharply during that period. Masonite generated revenue of $264 million from its diversified operations in 1996 and employed about 3,000 workers, down from revenue of $535 million and a workforce of 5,000 people in 1991. Masonite became second behind Longaberger Co. of Dresden, Ohio (with sales of $500 million), even though its sales grew to more than $400 million in 1997.

Other companies with sales of more than $200 million include ABT Building Products Corporation of Neehnah, Wisconsin; ABTCO of Troy, Michigan; Simpson Manufacturing Co. Inc. of Pleasanton, California; Intercraft Co. of Taylor, Texas; and Larson-Juhl, of Ashland, Wisconsin.

FURTHER READING

Darnay, Arsen J., ed. *Manufacturing USA*. 5th ed. Detroit: Gale Research, 1996.

"NAICS 321999." *Manufacturing-Industry Series*. U.S. Census Bureau, 8 September 1999.

U.S. Department of Commerce. *1995 Annual Survey of Manufactures: Value of Product Shipments*. Washington, D.C.: GPO, 1995.

FURNITURE AND FIXTURES

WOOD HOUSEHOLD FURNITURE

This classification consists of establishments engaged in manufacturing wood furniture commonly used in dwellings, with the exception of television, radio, phonograph, and sewing machine cabinets, which are classified in **SIC 2517: Wood Television, Radio, Phonograph, and Sewing Machine Cabinets;** also, millwork production is classified in **SIC 2431: Millwork;** wood kitchen cabinets are classified in **SIC 2434: Wood Kitchen Cabinets.** Cut stone and concrete furniture is classified in the major group for stone, clay, glass, and concrete products; laboratory and hospital furniture, except hospital beds, is in the major group for measuring, analyzing, and controlling instruments; photographic, medical, and optical goods; watches and clocks; and beauty and barber shop furniture is classified in the major group for miscellaneous manufacturing industries; and those engaged in woodworking to individual order or in the nature of reconditioning and repair are classified in non-manufacturing industries.

NAICS CODE(S)

337122 (Nonupholstered Wood Household Furniture Manufacturing)

The market for wood household furniture was estimated to be worth more than $11 billion in 1998, and the industry employed more than 127,000 people in the United States. Average salaries for furniture production workers were on average $10.89 per hour, nearly $2.00 less that the average in other production industries. Most furniture sold in this category (36 percent) was for the bedroom; with living rooms, dens, and libraries (25 percent), outdoor furniture (18 percent), kitchens and dining

rooms (17 percent), and infant's/children's (4 percent) accounting for the remainder of the market.

The industry's leading company in 1998 was Life Style Furnishings with sales of more than $2 billion. The company employed 30,000 people. Former first place leader Furniture Brands International fell to the second place spot with 1998 sales of $1.9 billion and 20,700 employees.

The Green Movement reached the furniture industry at the close of the 1990s. A few small companies started to recycle shipping pallets into fine furniture, such as coffee tables, desks, and dressers. These pieces are popular in businesses that like to "be green."

Ready-to-assemble (RTA) furniture was extremely popular in the 1990s, partly due to an improvement in quality—the products no longer smacked of dormitory living. Typical products offered wood veneer finishes and such details as rounded corners and beveled glass doors. A piece of RTA furniture can be assembled quickly, usually in less than an hour. O'Sullivan Industries has even utilized Velcro fasteners instead of screws to help hasten assembly. The low cost of RTA furniture and the ease of stocking it has made it popular among large mass merchandisers and warehouse-type stores, which have themselves become more popular among consumers. However, RTA furniture only accounted for 15 percent of 1997's total value of product shipments.

In 1999 the American Furniture Manufacturers Association (AFMA) started a five year public relations campaign to encourage people to buy more furniture. This was in reaction to a *Wall Street Journal* industry report that criticized the industry for excessive lead times, advertising low prices rather than value, and not keeping up with production-enhancing technology.

Most exports of American wood household furniture went to Canada (43 percent) and Mexico (7.4 percent).

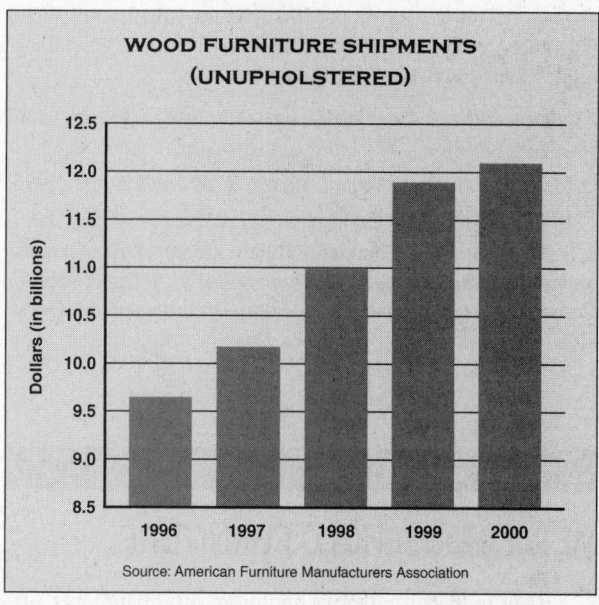

WOOD FURNITURE SHIPMENTS (UNUPHOLSTERED)

Source: American Furniture Manufacturers Association

Imports from the Pacific Rim countries (China, Indonesia, Japan, South Korea, Malaysia, Philippines, Taiwan, Thailand, and Vietnam) are on the rise, increasing by 19 percent during the first nine months of 1999 with imports of nearly $5 billion. Exports lagged behind, with only China and Vietnam showing increased purchases of U.S. wood furniture—17 and 53 percent, respectively. All other Pacific Rim countries cut back on U.S. purchases, ranging from a low of 19 percent less for Taiwan to a high of 84 percent less for South Korea. The 1998 trade deficit was more than $5.5 billion. Asian market share has decreased since the enactment of NAFTA—dropping from a 48.0 percent market share in 1994 to a 40.8 percent share in 1998. Canada and Mexico, however, have seen an increase from 24 percent in 1994 to 33 percent in 1998. U.S. wood exports to Canada and Mexico also increased during the first nine months of 1998, with a 10 percent rise (to $362 million) in Canadian purchases and an 18 percent rise (to $63.1 million) in Mexican purchases.

U.S. Environmental Protection Agency (EPA) regulations attempted to reduce volatile organic compound (VOC) emissions from chemicals used in furniture finishes. However, the industry was able to postpone some environmental legislation. Executives continue to be concerned about regulations governing finishing as well as wood dust.

FURTHER READING

Adams, Larry. "Soft Landing Means Economy to Grow, But Slow." *Wood and Wood Products,* January 1996.

"AFMA Report." *Wood & Wood Products,* December 1999.

Drill, Larry. "Stop the Ax." *Modern Paint and Coatings,* August 1996.

"Fine Furniture is Crafted from Used Pallets." *BioCycle,* May 1999.

"Furnituremakers' Pay Lags Behind national Averages." *Wood & Wood Products,* July 1999.

Iwanski, John. "The New Top 25 Benchmark: $100 Million." *Wood & Wood Products,* July 1999.

U.S. Department of Commerce "Nonupholstered Wood Household Furniture Manufacturing." *1997 Economic Census Manufacturing Industry Series.*

"Wood Furniture Trade Deficit on Record Pace." *Wood & Wood Products,* December 1999.

SIC 2512

WOOD HOUSEHOLD FURNITURE, UPHOLSTERED

This category covers those establishments primarily engaged in manufacturing upholstered furniture on wood frames. Shops primarily engaged in reupholstering furniture, or upholstering frames to individual order, are classified in Services, **SIC 7641: Re-upholstery and Furniture Repair,** or Retail Trade, **SIC 5712: Furniture Stores.** Establishments primarily engaged in manufacturing dual-purpose sleep furniture, such as convertible sofas and chair beds, are classified in **SIC 2515: Mattresses, Foundations, and Convertible Beds,** regardless of the material used in the frame. Establishments primarily engaged in manufacturing wood frames for upholstered furniture are classified in **SIC 2426: Hardware Dimension and Flooring Mills.**

NAICS CODE(S)

337121 (Upholstered Wood Household Furniture Manufacturing)

This industry is defined primarily by the materials with which the products are constructed, rather than the end product itself. All products feature wood frames and fabric or leather upholstery. Establishments within this industry produce a wide range of upholstered furniture for the home, including such upholstered living room furniture as chairs, rockers, couches, sofas, and recliners. Products manufactured in this industry include other household furniture as well as juvenile furniture.

Establishments in this industry produced goods that were sold to distributors or directly to retailers. Manufacturers produced goods for sale at a variety of price points and under a variety of brand names. *Standard and Poor's Industry Survey* estimated that approximately 44 percent of upholstered furniture was sold through furniture stores, 10 percent through department stores, and 44 percent through mass merchandisers. New retailing techniques were affecting the industry. Standard and Poor's noted a growing tendency among manufacturers to enter into agreement with a retailer to open a gallery devoted to the manufacturer's goods, a concept that was "very successful in attracting customers and generating sales." The arrangement was mutually advantageous because the retailer had proprietary rights on the goods while the manufacturer got a dedicated retail outlet for its merchandise.

Sales for the entire household furniture industry for 1998 were about $28.5 billion. In 1998 the United States imported $728.8 million worth of upholstered furniture, with the top importers being Italy, Mexico, Canada, China, and Taiwan. The United States exported almost $1.0 billion in upholstered furniture, with the top destinations being Canada, Norway, Saudi Arabia, the United Kingdom, and Japan.

Manufacturers of upholstered wood furniture benefited from an expanding market in the early 1990s, leading to approximately 5-6 percent growth between 1992 and 1993 alone. The industry was influenced by the rate of new home construction and the number of existing homes being remodeled. Standard and Poor's estimated that the upholstered wood household furniture industry would continue to expand through the end of 1990s due to changing demographics. Baby boomers were "getting older and richer and will soon want nicer things to suit their more upscale lifestyles."

In the late 1990s the economy was still going strong—umemployment was low, the stock market and consumer confidence levels were high. Housing starts were still strong and interest rates were low. Low interest rates spurred refinancing of homes, resulting in more money to spend on household furniture. People in the United States also had more disposable income than ever, resulting in strong furniture sales. Furniture sales are expected to slow by the end of 1999 and into 2000, due to export markets. The Asian financial crises continues to hurt the industry and the U.S. dollar is very strong. For domestic markets, the U.S. economy is nearing a record expansion, which may spur fears of a coming downturn and the holding off of major purchases.

The largest manufacturers in the industry in 1997 were Furniture Brands International (which included Broyhill, Lane, and Thomasville), with sales of $1.8 billion; LifeStyle Furnishings International, Ltd., with $1.7 billion in sales; and La-Z-Boy, Inc., with $1.1 billion in sales. The states with the highest percentage of people employed in this industry were North Carolina, Mississippi, Tennessee, and California. Between them, they accounted for 70 percent of the industry's employment.

FURTHER READING

International Trade Commission. "Top 25 U.S. Export Destinations for Upholstered Household Furniture." Available from http://www.ita.doc.gov/ocg/exp2512.htm. Accessed 24 November 1999.

———. "Top 25 U.S. Import Sources for Upholstered Wood Furniture." Available from http://www.ita.doc.gov/td/ocg/imp2512.htm. Accessed 24 November 1999.

Standard and Poor's Industry Surveys. New York: Standard and Poor's Corp., 1997.

U.S. Census Bureau. *Annual Survey of Manufacturers.* 1995. Washington, DC: GPO, 1997.

U.S. Department of Commerce. International Trade Administration. *U.S. Industry & Trade Outlook '99.* U.S. Department of Commerce/International Trade Administration and McGraw-Hill, 1999.

SIC 2514

METAL HOUSEHOLD FURNITURE

This industry category includes establishments primarily engaged in manufacturing metal furniture of a type commonly used in dwellings.

NAICS CODE(S)
337124 (Metal Household Furniture)

INDUSTRY SNAPSHOT
Although most people think of wrought-iron lawn chairs and tables when they think of metal household furniture, the offerings are considerably more varied. In addition to lawn items, metal furniture includes kitchen and dining room tables and chairs, cabinets, hostess carts, beds, folding cots, folding card tables, and children's furniture such as play yards and high chairs.

Total shipments of metal furniture in 1997, according to the U.S. Census Bureau, totaled $2.51 billion. There were approximately 420 companies that manufactured metal household furniture in the United States, employing some 24,000 people.

BACKGROUND AND DEVELOPMENT
Metal furniture dates back almost as far as the use of wrought iron. Society had witnessed an extraordinary increase in the use of metal furniture by the end of the eighteenth century. By the beginning of the nineteenth century, both English and American craftsmen began constructing Windsor-style chairs in wrought iron. In 1851 at the Great Exhibition in London, England, the American Chair Co. of New York exhibited a metal-framed, sprung, revolving chair, one of several styles with frames made largely of cast iron, steel, or a combination of the two. By the 1890s, metal beds had become one of the most popular-selling furniture items in America.

With the development of steel and other innovations in metal production by American manufacturing companies during the 1920s and early 1930s, major impacts on furniture design were felt. The abundance of ready steel made it a popular and reasonably cheap material for furniture. One of the most dramatic new processes, discovered in the early 1920s by an American inventor named Mannesman, produced seamless tubular steel. This new material had the combined advantages of being light, strong, and modern.

The role that bent metal furniture played in the design culture of the 1920s and 1930s has never been equaled by any other material or at any other time in design history. The designs seemed to encompass an era. The development of modern tubular steel furniture can be seen in terms of the technical accomplishments of modern industrialization with its improved methods of steel production, metal plating, and welding—all of which helped to disseminate the new furniture to a wider market. But above all of this is the fact that steel furniture came from the world of modern art and architecture and its preoccupation with the idea and image of the machine.

For that reason the major drawback to metal furniture was that its look appealed to a small, sophisticated market that enjoyed what was, at the time, called the Modern style of design. For that same reason, there remained for several years a great deal of resistance to its use in the home, with many feeling that it was too impersonal for domestic use, but perfectly suitable for hospitals and offices. The 1933 Chicago World's Fair exhibited a large number of pieces of tubular steel furniture. Seen as a symbol for modern life, the use of steel was advertised at the fair as, "natural, therefore that the modern spirit should express itself in striking, radically different kinds of furniture—and that furniture should be of steel, for this is the age of steel, and steel sounds the keynote of practicability, energy, and strength which dominates our modern life." By the mid-1930s tubular steel furnishing was being more easily accepted into domestic use, with steel items coming out of American factories in ever-increasing, large numbers.

Companies, such as the Chicago and Grand Rapids Co. of Michigan, immediately began producing large quantities of tubular steel furniture. American industrial designer Donald Deskey designed a line of metal furniture that was mass-produced around 1930 by the Ypsilanti Reed Furniture Co. A 1930 ad for the company pointed out that Ypsilanti Reed had pioneered steel furniture in America, "and in less than two years has assumed outstanding leadership in style and quality in this singular furniture."

By 1933 the Howell Co. of Geneva, Illinois, began mass-producing tubular steel furniture, including the best-selling "Beta," a chrome-plated, tubular steel and upholstered chair, as well as other innovative chair forms, such as the "S" chairs, with their bent metal frames, that were produced and sold in high volume throughout the 1930s.

Famous industrial designer Gilbert Rohde was among the first American innovators who worked with bent metal to create innovative furniture designs. His earliest tubular steel design was manufactured by the Troy Sunshade Co. of Troy, Ohio, in 1931. Because the company had additional offices in Amsterdam and Rotterdam in the Netherlands, Rohde's designs were sold in Europe as well.

The Kroehler Manufacturing Co. of Chicago, Illinois, also employed Rohde, who designed furniture not only from tubular steel, but from stainless steel, aluminum, and chrome. Rohde's pieces were advertised by the company as "functional and modern" with "a hygienic quality (no nooks and crannies to conceal dirt) that reduced dusting to a minimum while retaining their luster without the drudgery of polishing."

By 1930 Rohde moved on to take over design leadership for the Herman Miller Furniture company of Grand Rapids, Michigan. With Rohde at its helm, the company began an extensive program to produce modern furnishings, most of which incorporated the use of bent metal elements in many of their designs. In fact, throughout the decade leading up to World War II, the Herman Miller Co. continued to increasingly produce bent metal furnishings designed by Rohde.

Although metal furniture was seen as innovative by the American public, many American designers, such as Rohde, owed a great debt to their European counterparts during the decades between the two world wars. Many progressive European publications published designs for tubular steel furniture. In fact, some of the most copied modern tubular steel furniture designs belonged to Marcel Breuer, the avant-garde designer, and were originally created while he was at the Bauhaus, the German experimental design school, as early as 1925.

With the dissemination of European tubular steel designs to a wider world market and manufacturers producing their own interpretations of bent metal furniture, the originality and inventiveness of design had largely ended by the early years of the 1940s.

After World War II, profound changes in design and manufacturing moved the center of progressive development of metal furniture from Europe to the United States. Charles and Ray Eames, a husband and wife team of industrial designers, helped to develop new, and even more innovative, metal furniture designs for the Herman Miller Co. in the 1940s and 1950s.

Research into new materials such as molded plywood, and the use of light metal alloys (especially aluminum and magnesium, which were developed during the war) provided an entire new range of possibilities for postwar furniture.

The American furniture manufacturer, Knoll International, produced such innovative designs as the 1952 metal "Grid" chair by the artist/designer Harry Bertoia, as well as several other metal pieces. And, in the 1960s, Knoll produced the internationally acclaimed architect/designer Ludwig Mies van der Rohe's last body of furniture designs of tubular and flat steel.

But by the end of the 1950s, metal was being used less and less frequently for innovative furniture designs. The Herman Miller Co. and Knoll International continued to manufacture bent and tubular steel "design classics" from the 1930s, but with new and even more innovative materials, such as plastics, arriving on the scene, metal furniture was relegated to experimental, one-of-a-kind and limited edition pieces by artist/designers who did not look for mass production or wide audience acceptance.

Because metal was the symbol of the machine age, it was quite natural for metal furniture's high point to coincide with the era of the "machine age," that of the 1930s. The bent metal furniture designed and manufactured during that period was never equaled again. Throughout the 1990s metal furniture was still prevalent in schools and hospitals, but rather scarce for home furnishings. With the popularity of daybeds and futons in the mid-1990s, certain metals had a slight resurgence in the furniture industry.

Metal chairs and tables are still being produced in the United States today. Some of the newer 1990s forms of furniture were geared toward works of art rather than functional pieces of furniture. The trend toward home offices, which took off in the mid-1990s, was changing the scope and design of furniture across the board. A growing number of people were starting home-based businesses; many others were keeping their corporate jobs while "teleworking," spending part or all of their work time at home while hooked up to the company computer network. Particularly for those whose home offices consisted of a corner in their living rooms, durable and attractive household furniture, particularly pieces that could serve more than one function, would gain popularity.

This would likely mean that companies such as Steelcase Inc., Herman Miller, and Knoll, which had focused on office furniture, would gain more of a foothold in the household furniture business. Many pieces of furniture already blurred the lines between office and household. An attractive metal bookcase, for example, could be equally at home in a family room or an office. Steelcase, Herman Miller, and Knoll were all formidable companies. Steelcase had 1999 sales of $2.74 billion and Herman Miller had 1999 sales of $1.76 billion. Knoll's figures, for 1998, were $948.7 million.

Industry experts expected that the furniture industry overall would experience slow growth in the first two to three years of the twenty-first century. Economists speaking at the 1999 annual Economic Outlook Conference of the American Furniture Manufacturers Association noted that the anticipated slowdown in housing starts and existing home sales would mean fewer furniture purchases. The furniture industry should grow at a rate of between 2 and 4 percent annually as the new century began.

FURTHER READING

McIntosh, Jay. "Economists Predict Slower Sales Growth in 2000." *Furniture Today,* 2 January 2000.

U.S. Census Bureau. *Manufacturing—Industry Series,* 1999.

SIC 2515

MATTRESSES, FOUNDATIONS, AND CONVERTIBLE BEDS

This category covers establishments primarily engaged in manufacturing innerspring mattresses, box spring mattresses, and non-innerspring mattresses containing felt, foam rubber, urethane, hair, or any other filling material; and assembled wire springs (fabric, coil, or box) for use on beds, couches, and cots. This industry also includes establishments primarily engaged in manufacturing dual purpose sleep furniture, such as convertible sofas and chair beds, regardless of the material used in the frame. Establishments primarily engaged in manufacturing automobile seats and backs are classified under **SIC 2531: Public Building and Related Furniture;** those manufacturing individual wire springs are classified under **SIC 3495: Wire Springs;** and those manufacturing paddings and upholstery filling are classified under **SIC 2299: Textile Goods, Not Elsewhere Classified.**

NAICS CODE(S)

337910 (Mattress Manufacturing)
337121 (Upholstered Wood Household Furniture Manufacturing)

INDUSTRY SNAPSHOT

Producing more than 35 million units each year, U.S. mattress manufacturers make up a $4 billion enterprise, according to figures released by the U.S. Census Bureau. Mattress and durable bedding revenues amount to a 14 percent share of U.S. household furniture sales at the manufacturer level.

The U.S. mattress market is generally considered mature. Based on Census Bureau statistics for 1992-1997, annual sales growth at the industry level averaged around 6.9 percent, or about 4 percent after inflation is factored. Conventional wisdom holds that nearly everyone has a bed and that beds are replaced infrequently—on the order of once every 8-11 years, according to various industry estimates. Indeed, the International Sleep Products Association, an industry trade group, reports that replacements account for 70 percent of new mattress sales. Fifty percent of old mattresses, moreover, are reused by others, often transferred between family members or resold in the used furniture market.

As a result, mattress makers' growth prospects lie mainly in their ability to generate interest in new product launches and otherwise compel people to replace their existing bedding. Another growth generator is the expansion of the lodging industry (see **SIC 7011: Hotels and Motels**) and other industries that require bedding products. As in many industries, mattress manufacturers also seek out greater efficiencies and higher profit margins by buying out competitors in order to achieve economies of scale or access new markets.

CURRENT CONDITIONS

The U.S. bedding industry consists of some 624 mattress companies operating at 700 sites, but the top five companies account for the majority of sales. Most mattress manufacturers are privately held. Including convertible beds, which are sometimes counted as upholstered household furniture rather than bedding, industry sales in 1997 topped $4.3 billion and were expected to break the $5 billion mark in the early 2000s.

The Bureau of Labor Statistics reported that in 1998 the industry employed an average of 34,400 people, of whom 77.6 percent were production workers. Although the number of separate manufacturing establishments has been trending downward for some time, the industry's employee ranks have actually grown moderately from an early 1990s low of 27,700 people.

Product Marketing Profile. The growth economy of the mid- and late 1990s provided a hospitable market for mattresses and related products. Growth areas included premium bedding, especially mattresses touting special health-related benefits, and mattress sets featuring distinctive colors and fashion appeal.

By a slim margin, twin-size bedding is the most popular in the United States and is responsible for around 31 percent of unit sales. Queen size is the second most common, accounting for approximately 29 percent of mattress units sold. Larger mattresses—especially king and queen size—have been the fastest-growing categories, encouraged by industry marketing efforts to equate larger mattresses with getting a better night's sleep. The vast majority—some 90 percent—of mattress sales are of traditional innerspring mattresses, with products like waterbeds, air mattresses, and futons supplying the remaining 10 percent of sales. Not surprisingly, the most frequent buyers of mattresses are couples with children, and the median retail price for a mattress and box spring

set was $400 in 1997. On the retail side, the largest share of mattresses (42 percent) is sold through general furniture stores, followed by specialty mattress stores (24 percent) and department stores (11 percent), according to a 1997 study by two trade journals.

INDUSTRY LEADERS

A handful of manufacturers garner the bulk of industry sales; the top five are believed to account for as much as two-thirds of all U.S. bedding sales. The largest mattress producer in the United States, and by some reports, the world, is Sealy Corporation, headquartered in High Point, North Carolina. In 1998 this private company posted $891 million in sales, a 10 percent improvement from 1997, and was on track for a similar gain in the first three quarters of its fiscal 1999.

Serta, Inc. of Itasca, Illinois, is the second-largest U.S. mattress company, reporting $763 million in 1998 sales. Serta, which dominates the lodging market, is actually a licensing cooperative held by 12 regional manufacturers that license the Serta name and coordinate marketing and branding strategies.

Other major players in the industry include Simmons Company ($601 million in 1998), Spring Air Corporation ($386 million), and Select Comfort Corporation ($246 million).

FURTHER READING

Farrell, Nina. "Bring on the Mattress Boom." *HFN,* 1 February 1999.

International Sleep Products Association. "About the Industry." Alexandria, VA, 1999. Available from www.sleepproducts.org.

"Sleeping Your Back Pain Away." *Business Week,* 17 May 1999.

U.S. Bureau of the Census. *1996 Annual Survey of Manufactures.* Washington, D.C.: GPO, 1998. Available from www.census.gov.

———. "Manufacturing—Industry Series." *1997 Economic Census.* Washington, D.C.: GPO, 6 July 1999. Available from www.census.gov.

SIC 2517

WOOD TELEVISION, RADIO, PHONOGRAPH, AND SEWING MACHINE CABINETS

This category covers establishments primarily engaged in manufacturing wood cabinets for radios, television sets, phonographs, and sewing machines.

NAICS CODE(S)

337129 (Wood Television, Radio, and Sewing Machine Cabinet Manufacturing)

This industry makes such products as wooden speaker boxes, stereo cabinets, sewing machine cases, and television cabinets. It is part of the larger household furniture industry. About 60 percent of the industry's output in the early 1990s consisted of television cabinets or cases for television, stereo, or radio combinations. Stereo and radio cabinets constituted 20 percent of the market. Wooden sewing machine cases accounted for only 3 percent of sales, and miscellaneous items comprised the remainder. Nearly 85 percent of the industry's products were sold to radio and television manufacturers.

The U.S. Census Bureau reported that there were 98 establishments operating in this classification in 1997. They shipped goods worth $298 million, spent $150 million on materials, and paid $4.8 million for buildings and other structures, machinery, and equipment. About a third of these establishments had at least 20 employees. California and New York had the highest concentrations of businesses in this category.

A limited market existed for sewing machine cases and radio cabinets early in the twentieth century. Not until after World War II did the U.S. wooden cabinet business emerge as a small industry. A consumer spending boom, boosted by a surging demand for television cabinets beginning in the 1950s, resulted in healthy industry growth throughout the 1950s, 1960s, and much of the 1970s. By the early 1980s television and radio cabinet producers were shipping products worth more than $300 million per year and employing about 7,000 workers.

Although sales swelled to nearly $400 million in 1984, the market slumped soon afterward, primarily because of foreign competition and the increasing popularity of plastic. As imports of consumer electronics, particularly from Japan, ballooned throughout the 1980s, demand for domestically manufactured television and radio cabinets plummeted. Many U.S. factories switched from wood to cheaper, more versatile plastic cabinets. Wood cabinet sales tumbled at a rate of nearly 9 percent annually between 1984 and 1990, and the industry's yearly sales dropped below $250 million. Some companies left the industry during an economic recession in the early 1990s.

Thomson Crown Wood Products Inc. (Mocksville, North Carolina) was one of the largest firms that manufactured goods in this category as its primary business. Founded in 1980, the company was also known as General Electric Co. Crown Wood Products Inc. It had 650 employees and sales of $50 million in 1998. Its main product was wooden television cabinets.

Another industry leader, Sound-Craft Systems Inc., primarily made lecterns and portable sound systems.

Based in Morrilton, Arkansas, the firm had 28 employees and sales of $3 million in 1998.

Various diversified companies also competed in this category, including Kimball International Inc. (Jasper, Indiana); O'Sullivan Industries Inc. (Lamar, Missouri); and Child Craft Industries Inc. (Salem, Indiana).

To cut costs and increase productivity, the industry's workforce was slashed in the early 1990s to less than half its 1982 size. Total employment dropped from 5,900 in 1987 to 4,300 in 1994 and 3,764 in 1997. The category's 3,244 production workers earned an average hourly wage of $9.05 in 1997. Total payroll that year was $74.6 million, down from $89.8 million in 1994 and $96.7 million in 1995.

FURTHER READING

Darnay, Arsen J., ed. *Manufacturing USA.* 5th ed. Detroit: Gale Research, 1996.

Sound-Craft Systems Inc. Corporate WebSite, 2000. Available from http://www.sound-craft.com.

Thomson Crown Wood Products Inc. The Architect's Catalog, Inc. Corporate WebSite, 2000. Available from http://www.arcat.com.

U.S. Department of Commerce. Census Bureau. *1996 Census of Manufactures.* Washington, D.C.: GPO, 1998.

U.S. Department of Commerce. Census Bureau. *1997 Economic Census.* Washington, D.C.: GPO, 1999. Available from http://www.census.gov/prod/ec97/97m3371g.pdf.

SIC 2519

HOUSEHOLD FURNITURE, NOT ELSEWHERE CLASSIFIED

This industry category includes establishments primarily engaged in manufacturing reed, rattan, and other wicker furniture; plastics and fiberglass household furniture and cabinets; and household furniture not elsewhere classified.

NAICS CODE(S)

337125 (Household Furniture (except Wood and Metal) Manufacturing)

INDUSTRY SNAPSHOT

This industry, focusing largely, though not exclusively, on more specialized furniture production, was dominated in the late 1990s by small firms. Moreover, it was distinguished from most manufacturing sectors in that it was characterized by a trend toward more companies with fewer employees, against overall industrial trends. Of the 212 companies producing such furniture, only one-fifth maintained more than 20 employees; more than half had fewer than 5. In all, the industry employed 4,600 people in 1997, down from 5,400 in 1995; of that total, 3,600 were production workers, who earned an average of $10.63 per hour. Shipments for all products in this category totaled $529.5 million in 1997, up 5 percent since 1995.

BACKGROUND AND DEVELOPMENT

Wicker, Rattan, and Reed Furniture. Wicker furnishings have been used in American households since the seventeenth century. The first known craftsmen to advertise wicker furniture were early nineteenth-century basket weavers. During that period, straw and willow were replaced by rattan, which was imported by the East India Company.

In the mid-nineteenth century, wicker furniture, customarily styled with closely woven cane seats and looped reed backs and arms, became increasingly popular. Furniture frames were constructed from hickory and oak pieces that were steamed and bent into shape, then wrapped with split cane. At that time, construction of wicker furniture changed from craft to industry.

Between 1875 and 1910, wicker furniture reached the height of its popularity, in part because of its association with exotic, foreign countries. In 1917, Marshall B. Lloyd invented a wicker-weaving machine that used fiber material—the Lloyd Loom. Concurrently, many wicker manufacturers began to experiment with materials such as prairie grass and fiber. Wire grass, converted into a pliable twine and woven into furniture, was obtained from the prairie marshes of northwest America.

By the end of World War I, the skilled labor needed to weave wicker became scarce in the United States, and imports began replacing domestically manufactured goods. By the close of World War II, almost all wicker furniture sold in America was imported, a situation that continues to this day.

Plastics and Fiberglass Furniture. Although plastics had been developed in the late nineteenth century, it wasn't until 1909, when the American chemist Leo Baekeland developed Bakelite, that plastics gradually began to replace metal for body-shells in industrial applications. Baekeland, along with two Westinghouse Corporation engineers, Harold Faber and Daniel O'Connor, developed a laminate originally intended for electrical insulation. The development of this formula in 1913, however, eventually resulted in the establishment of the Formica Corporation. By the mid-1920s Formica's laminate was used to produce furniture.

With the demands for light-weight seat furniture brought on by the aircraft industry during World War II, the development of plastics for furniture construction increased. Two early pioneers of American furniture design,

Eero Saarinen and Charles Eames, began experimenting with molded polyester in 1941. Saarinen's "Womb" chair, the first fiberglass design to be mass-produced in America, was manufactured by Knoll Associates in 1946. The chair remained in continuous production for more than four decades. In 1950 New York's Museum of Modern Art held an exhibition entitled "Organic Design in Home Furnishings." The prize-winning fiberglass armchair, designed by Charles Eames, was manufactured by the Herman Miller Furniture Company. Eames' molded plastic chair series, which also included a stacking chair, became one of the most basic and popular lines of American seating furniture.

CURRENT CONDITIONS

Due to the wave of consolidation among retail furniture outlets, furniture makers across all categories have been forced to compete on the basis of access to distribution channels, with the larger firms typically gaining greater leverage in the process. While some of the major manufacturers in the miscellaneous household furniture category have been able to establish inroads in this domain, the bulk of the industry's players have been able to largely sidestep the whole process, focused as they are on niche products and smaller-scale production facilities. These companies have benefited greatly from the surge in e-commerce, allowing them to market their specialized products directly to customers. Wholesale outlets, home-shopping television, and mail-order distribution are the other primary marketing targets for these firms.

This miscellaneous household furniture industry is relatively strong in the outdoor furniture market, a sector that experienced 40 percent sales growth between 1992 and 1997, when sales of plastic and fiberglass seating and other outdoor furniture totaled $166 million. Reed and rattan furniture, mostly chairs and couches, generated sales of $98 million in 1997.

The surging number of home-office workers in the United States portends healthy sales in the early twenty-first century, as more and more individuals convert rooms in their homes into office space complete with all the features and amenities of their offices at work. Shipments of fiberglass and plastic shelves and cabinets were valued at $260 million in 1997, largely on the strength of this trend. Most of these products were shipped in pieces ready to assemble. The ready to assemble (RTA) market itself was particularly lucrative in 1999, valued at $13.1 billion, and industry analysts expect that figure will rise substantially in coming years, thus constituting an important market in which miscellaneous household furniture manufacturers will compete for position.

INDUSTRY LEADERS

The major players in this industry generally are diversified furniture manufacturers who generate the bulk of their revenue from furniture not classified under this category. Krause's Furniture, Inc. is a leading manufacturer of made-to-order furniture, with sales of $144.8 million in 1999 and 1,100 employees. O'Sullivan Industries, specializing in ready-to-assemble furniture, including plastic and fiberglass shelves, cabinets, and seating, employed 2,500 people in 1998, with $320.4 million in revenue. Another leader, Sealy Corporation, posted $800 million in revenue and maintained a payroll of 5,450 employees.

FURTHER READING

Griffin, Kate. "Higher-end Furniture Sales are the Ticket." *National Home Center News,* 3 May 1999.

"Home Office/Home Entertainment Producers Aim for Flexibility." *HFN,* 4 October 1999.

Lucie-Smith, Edward. *A History of Industrial Design.* Oxford, England: Phaidon Press Ltd., 1983.

"Making Space for Furniture." *National Home Center News,* 19 April 1999.

Menz, Katherine. *Nineteenth Century Furniture.* New York: Art & Antiques Books, 1982.

Sparke, Penny. *Design in Context.* London, England: Quarto Publishing, 1987.

U.S. Census Bureau. *1997 Census of Manufacturers.* Washington, D.C.: Department of Commerce, 1999.

SIC 2521

WOOD OFFICE FURNITURE

This classification covers establishments primarily engaged in manufacturing office furniture made chiefly of wood, including benches, bookcases, cabinets, chairs, desks, filing boxes and cabinets, panel furniture systems, stools, tables, partitions, and modular furniture systems.

NAICS CODE(S)

337211 (Wood Office Furniture Manufacturing)

INDUSTRY SNAPSHOT

Approximately 676 wood office furniture manufacturers operated in this industry during 1997, according to the U.S. Census Bureau. That year the industry employed nearly 31,000 people. Over the 1990s there was fierce competition in domestic and foreign markets as well as a flurry of mergers and acquisitions among some of the biggest names in the business.

According to the Business and Institutional Furniture Manufacturers Association (BIFMA) International, a leading trade group, shipments for the office furniture industry as a whole were worth $12.35 billion in 1998.

This was up from $11.46 billion in 1997. Wood products consistently made up about one-quarter of total office furniture sales.

The late 1970s and early 1980s were particularly profitable for the office furniture industry, with annual growth rates averaging 19 percent. The early 1990s saw an industry-wide recession. In 1990, for example, office furniture shipments increased by only .5 percent to $7.87 billion. The following year saw shipments drop by 8.1 percent to $7.2 billion. Growth since then remained in the vicinity of 6 to 8 percent, with the exception of 1997, when the value of office furniture shipments posted a gain of 14.1 percent.

ORGANIZATION AND STRUCTURE

West Michigan—most notably in and around the cities of Grand Rapids and Holland—was home to office furniture manufacturing giants Steelcase Inc. (whose product line focused on nonwood rather than wood furniture), Haworth Inc., and Herman Miller Inc., as well as a number of other firms. As a result, the area could boast that its facilities produced about 65 percent of all office furniture manufactured in North America. This dominance could be attributed to two factors—an abundant supply of good quality hardwood in Michigan forests during the industry's early years and the availability of highly skilled woodworkers.

When wood was still the material of choice for most manufacturers, stationery stores and office equipment dealers handled sales of office furniture. The concept of "office design" was unheard of; companies purchased desks and other pieces as needed, setting them up in rows in big, open spaces, creating an office environment that very much resembled a classroom.

Later, as the demand for office furniture increased and the market became more specialized and sophisticated, the major manufacturers developed their own sales staffs and dealer networks to handle large-scale orders. In addition, the introduction of new products such as computer desks and "systems furniture" (consisting of panels and other pieces that could be easily moved and reconfigured to accommodate changing needs) generated a need for office designers. So the bigger firms began to offer design assistance to customers eager to get the most out of their furniture purchases. Smaller companies that were unable to support their own sales and design staffs turned instead to manufacturers' representatives to provide the same services to customers.

In the 1990s, while a few manufacturers still sold directly to customers, most relied on other means of distribution. Distribution channels shifted over the past decade. According to a joint survey conducted by BIFMA and the Business Products Industry Association, nearly one-third of sales went through such channels as office products megadealers, superstores/warehouse clubs/other mass merchandisers, wholesalers, mail order, and the government. Superstores, warehouse clubs, and other mass merchandisers showed the strongest growth. In 1993 they represented 2.8 percent of total distribution; by 1996 they accounted for 6.3 percent of the total.

Office furniture manufacturers of all kinds showcased their newest products and services at a number of trade shows around the country, most notably the NeoCon World's Trade Fair. Held annually at the Merchandise Mart in Chicago, it was billed as North America's largest commercial interiors exposition.

BACKGROUND AND DEVELOPMENT

The wood office furniture industry first began to take shape in the late nineteenth century, a period of rapid industrial growth in the United States. This industrial growth—along with technical innovations such as the elevator, the typewriter, and the telephone—sparked a corresponding increase in the number of people working in offices. Manufacturers of residential furniture soon began to notice that more of their desks, tables, and bookcases were being put to use in a business setting. Some of them responded by designing and building pieces specifically suited to the needs of this new kind of employee, thus establishing office furniture as a separate segment of the overall furniture industry.

Wood dominated the market until the 1930s, when metal filing cabinets and desks became popular (and cheaper) substitutes for the old wooden models. The military's need for steel briefly interrupted this trend during World War II, but in the postwar years, metal office furniture once again reasserted itself as a serious threat to wood. Both sides responded by launching aggressive marketing campaigns emphasizing the advantages of their respective products.

The rivalry between the two camps gradually eased, however, as wood office furniture manufacturers began to incorporate steel parts in their designs, and metal office furniture manufacturers began to feature wooden tops. By the early 1960s the distinctions between the two industries had blurred to the point where the wood furniture manufacturers dissolved the trade association they had originally established to distinguish themselves from metal office furniture manufacturers. In 1973 office furniture manufacturers of all types officially recognized their common interests and concerns by joining forces in a single trade organization, BIFMA International. By 1997 BIFMA represented over 140 North American office furniture manufacturing companies located throughout the United States, Canada, and Mexico.

Growth was especially strong in the office furniture industry in the late 1970s and early 1980s, with average annual sales gains of 19 percent. Beginning in the late 1980s, however, significant white-collar downsizing in a number of Fortune 500 companies had a marked impact on office furniture manufacturers—fewer employees translated into less need for new desks, chairs, and other equipment. A recession in 1991-92 added to the industry's troubles, resulting in a drop of 8.5 percent in the value of shipments in 1991 over 1990 figures. The picture began to improve a bit in 1993, with shipments of wood office furniture showing a slight increase. Virtually no one, however, was forecasting a return any time soon to the strong growth of the early 1980s.

CURRENT CONDITIONS

Industry analysts continued to be cautiously optimistic in their predictions for the office furniture manufacturing industry as the 1990s drew to a close. Steady interest rates, a moderately growing economy, and low inflation all seemed conducive to a sustained period of modest sales gains in the range of 4 to 5 percent. Nevertheless, many wood office furniture manufacturers reassessed their markets in the middle of the decade, noting that the strongest demand for office furniture was coming from small companies with limited budgets and a desire to stretch their dollars as far as possible. The high-end products that large corporations typically purchased were simply out of reach for businesses with only a few dozen employees. A number of the major manufacturers responded to the situation by creating new lines of mid- and lower-priced furniture.

Wood office furniture manufacturers also began exploring new niche markets for their products during the 1990s. With an estimated 43 million people doing at least some work out of their homes as of 1996, companies looking for ways to expand their traditional customer base offered more and more pieces intended for home offices. Another growth market was ergonomically designed furniture, which client companies hoped would increase productivity, cut down on the number of repetitive strain injuries and backache (thus curbing health care costs), and reduce the threat of lawsuits from employees with work-related disabilities.

Industry observers also continued to express concern about the common practice of price discounting as much as 50 percent or more in a fiercely competitive market. Because it drained financial resources, discounting was blamed for the rise in the number of buyouts and mergers that occurred in the office furniture industry during the 1990s. The small company with a foothold in a niche market that a larger competitor wished to enter proved to be especially vulnerable to this kind of takeover. Major acquisitions were made by HON Industries Inc., Kimball International, and Haworth throughout the 1990s. Some companies did consolidate, though, such as Herman Miller in the late 1990s. Many companies called for an end to

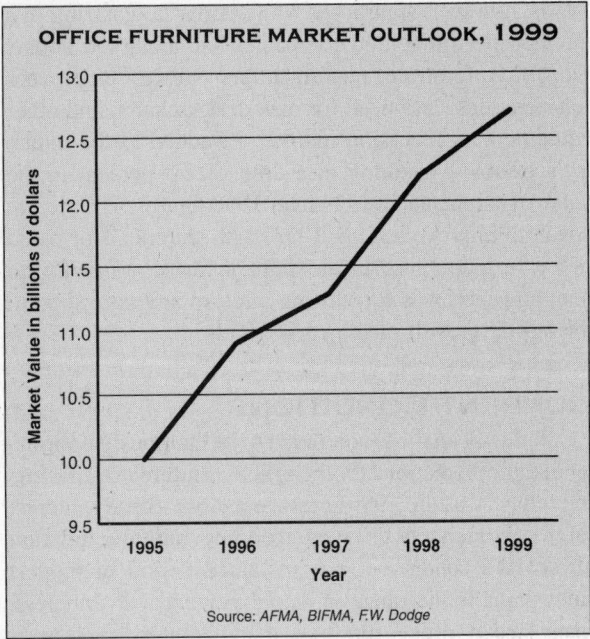

OFFICE FURNITURE MARKET OUTLOOK, 1999

Source: AFMA, BIFMA, F.W. Dodge

discounting and price wars, listing them among the greatest challenges the industry faced in the 1990s.

In a related action, office furniture manufacturers also joined together to fight for legislation to eliminate the competitive advantage enjoyed by the Federal Prison Industries (FPI) over private companies. By law, whenever the federal government was in the market for office furniture, it had to give preference to FPI and its prison-made products, regardless of cost. As a result, U.S. manufacturers lost tens of millions of dollars in sales every year.

In addition, wood office furniture manufacturers expressed apprehension about the effect of ongoing environmental legislation on their bottom lines. In their factories, they already incurred increased costs for disposing of hazardous wastes generated by the furniture-finishing process. They also had to abide by strict rules governing wood dust levels. In the marketplace, they faced mounting concerns about the effect of various pollutants on indoor air quality. Under the terms of the Clean Air Act Amendment of 1990, for example, various substances involved in the production of wood furniture were subject to regulation. Most commonly cited were the volatile organic compounds used in finishes and two types of adhesives, urea-formaldehyde resins and contact adhesives. To address these problems, some U.S. wood office furniture companies switched to water-based finishes and alternative glues, although some of these substitutes performed poorly.

Other challenges office furniture manufacturers faced as they headed into a new century included dealing with continued corporate downsizing, adjusting to the increasingly limited supply of wood and the subsequent rising price of wood and wood-based panels, and devel-

oping more products for home use in a market that was increasingly dominated by ready-to-assemble (RTA) furniture companies such as Sauder Woodworking Co., Bush Industries Inc., and O'Sullivan Industries Holdings, Inc. On the labor front, they were also concerned about the shortage of skilled workers (especially wood experts) and the need to work more efficiently to cut manufacturing costs.

INDUSTRY LEADERS

Publicly traded Herman Miller held the number-one spot among wood office furniture manufacturers. It ranked as the second-largest general office furniture manufacturer behind Steelcase (which specialized in nonwood products). For 1999 Herman Miller posted sales of $1.76 billion, up from $1.72 billion the previous year. Herman Miller began as a residential furniture manufacturer founded in 1923 by D. J. De Pree. He used money borrowed from his father-in-law, Herman Miller, to buy the Star Furniture Co., which had been in existence since 1905. De Pree then renamed the firm in honor of its major shareholder.

Herman Miller struggled to compete with larger local manufacturers during the Great Depression, most of whom were turning out reproduction pieces. To make his company's offerings stand apart from everyone else's, De Pree introduced a collection of furniture with a distinctively modern flair. Innovative design soon became a hallmark of the Herman Miller line of office furniture, some pieces of which were created by notables such as Charles and Ray Eames and Isamu Noguchi.

In the mid-1960s Herman Miller once again revolutionized the industry by introducing systems furniture. Its panels, storage units, and work surfaces made it simple to rearrange and customize open-plan office spaces. Since then, the company also devoted considerable research and design efforts toward developing ergonomic seating and other components that fulfilled the need for comfortable and multifunctional office furniture. Herman Miller also branched out into manufacturing furniture for hospitals and other health care facilities and entered the residential office furniture market as well with a line called Herman Miller for the Home.

For almost its entire history, Herman Miller was known as an unusually progressive firm in terms of its treatment of employees. In 1950, for example, it became one of the first companies in West Michigan to institute a participative management program that made it possible for all workers to be involved in setting goals for the firm, making suggestions for cost cutting and other improvements, and sharing in the profits. As a result, Herman Miller consistently ranked among the most admired companies in the United States.

The boom in office furniture sales in the 1980s led to record sales at Herman Miller in 1990. But a recession hit the following year, and by 1992, the company had posted the first loss in its history. It then began restructuring in an effort to combat the negative impact of the recession and decreased demands for its high-end products. With seven subsidiaries and operations in some 45 foreign countries that employed 8,500 people, Herman Miller continued efforts to compete more effectively in the marketplace by cutting jobs (including many in the executive ranks) and shutting down plants that failed to meet performance expectations.

The nation's second-largest wood office furniture manufacturer was Haworth Inc., a private company with estimated 1999 sales of $1.54 billion, up from $1.51 billion in 1998. Teacher Gerrard Haworth started the firm in 1948 in his garage, enjoying modest success with his wood and glass office partitions. But it wasn't until his son Richard patented a prewired, movable office panel in 1975 that sales really began to make it possible for customers to assemble and disassemble workstations to suit new office arrangements without having to call in an electrician. Before long, Haworth had vaulted into the top ranks of office furniture manufacturers. It aggressively defended itself against patent infringements by competitors, winning millions of dollars in damages from both Herman Miller and Steelcase over its prewired office panel.

Since 1988 Haworth pursued an ambitious policy of acquisition, buying up a number of smaller companies at home and overseas to broaden its product base and distribution channels. One of Haworth's acquisitions was the German company dyes, which specialized in desks and work tables. While making these acquisitions, Haworth paid very close attention to the bottom line. As a result, the company enjoyed a reputation for being one of the leanest and most profitable businesses in its category, with a solid manufacturing, marketing, and distribution presence throughout the world and a reputation for undercutting its rivals on price. The products manufactured and sold by its 10,000 employees included a full line of systems furniture, desk and guest seating, steel and wood casegoods (bookcases, cabinets, and other pieces that provide interior storage), files, tables, and desks. Haworth made these items available in nearly all price ranges but was increasingly emphasizing its less expensive lines.

Another notable wood office furniture manufacturer was HON Industries, with 1998 wood furniture sales of approximately $14.6 billion (out of total sales of nearly $1.7 billion). The company's sales grew 24.5 percent from 1997. HON, considered the leading manufacturer of value-priced office furniture, was a highly diversified company that designed and built mid-priced products for both office and home, including desks, chairs, file cabinets, credenzas, storage units, tables, bookcases, partitions, and panel systems. HON marketed its wood office furniture lines under the Gunlocke, Holga, and BPI brand names. It also manufactured metal office furniture. Nearly 9,800 people worked for HON.

A trend that had traditional office furniture manufacturers looking over their shoulders was the boom in ready-to-assemble (RTA) furniture. This inexpensive but serviceable alternative to traditional office furniture was fueled in part by the rise in home-based businesses. Some estimates put the number of Americans who worked at home at least part time at over 40 million. The number of strong players in this market was growing. Sauder Woodworking, with estimated 1998 sales of more than $500 million, was the largest RTA manufacturer, employing some 3,200 people. Second was Bush Industries, with 1998 sales at more than $413 million and 4,100 employees. O'Sullivan Industries, the number-three RTA manufacturer, employed some 2,350 people and posted 1999 sales of $379.6 million. Most RTA furniture (desks and tables, computer stands, credenzas, and cabinets) was sold through office superstores, mass merchants, catalogs, and furniture specialty stores.

WORKFORCE

Since 1988 employment steadily declined in all sectors of the office furniture manufacturing industry. The wood segment experienced the most significant losses but appeared to be making a comeback. After climbing steadily through the early and mid-1980s, the work force fell from 31,000 people in 1987 to 30,800 in 1988. It rose slightly in 1989 to 31,000 before falling to 28,200 in 1990. In 1991 it plunged to 22,500 as a result of the recession that began that year. Among production workers in particular, jobs fell from 24,600 in 1988 to 24,300 in 1989, 22,100 in 1990, and 17,000 in 1991. By the middle of the decade, total employment in the wood office furniture industry appeared to be stabilized at nearly 28,000. By 1997, however, the employment figure was around 30,600, with 24,600 production workers. Average hourly wages for production workers in the later 1990s hovered around the $11 mark.

Despite the leveling off of job losses, it appeared unlikely that all of the jobs lost in the office furniture industry since the late 1980s would be replaced. Instead, manufacturers were seeking to increase the productivity of existing employees. This disquieting loss of job security coupled with a new emphasis on bottom-line issues helped spark unionization drives during the 1990s at several West Michigan office furniture manufacturers, whose employees traditionally shunned unions. In 1993, for instance, the United Steelworkers tried to organize at both Steelcase and Haworth without much success. In 1997, however, the United Auto Workers mounted a campaign at Haworth that attracted far more attention and support.

AMERICA AND THE WORLD

With no rise in demand expected in the U.S. market any time soon, wood office furniture manufacturers looked overseas to increase their sales. Results were lackluster at best; as of the late 1990s, the major firms had yet to see much in the way of profits from their foreign divisions, often because of economic and political instability in certain markets.

The passage of the North American Free Trade Agreement in 1993 opened the doors to anticipated heavier volume of office furniture imports and exports. Overall, however, imports and exports of wood and nonwood office furniture continued to make up a fairly small percentage of total industry shipments. According to BIFMA, U.S. office furniture imports in 1998 totaled $1.53 billion, and exports totaled $410 million. Canada ranked as the country's main trading partner. In 1998 it received about 36 percent of all U.S. office furniture exports and provided more than 64 percent of all office furniture brought into the United States.

The growing popularity of Swedish furniture maker IKEA International, both in the United States and abroad, was still another factor in wood office furniture sales. IKEA, with estimated sales in 1998 of more than $7 billion, had more than 150 stores in nearly 30 countries. It offered stylish, affordable, (usually) RTA furniture, for both the home and the office.

RESEARCH AND TECHNOLOGY

In response to management trends stressing teamwork, ongoing corporate downsizing, concerns about occupational-related injuries, and the increasing number of people working out of their homes, office furniture manufacturers were devoting many of their research dollars to the development of multifunctional, ergonomically designed products. In larger offices, for example, cubicle clusters and movable panels were being replaced by a more open, less isolated environment that encouraged people to work together and made it physically easier for them to do so. Also growing in popularity were adjustable work surfaces and components that could serve more than one use, so as to accommodate workers whose jobs were no longer quite so narrowly defined. Designing all of these products to work better with rapidly changing computer technology was also a top priority.

Ergonomics was in the forefront, too, as employers and manufacturers both sought ways to comply with federal mandates (some resulting from the 1990 Americans with Disabilities Act) and ward off lawsuits filed by workers suffering from job-related aches and pains. The emphasis was on adjustability, such as motorized tables with multiple height settings to accommodate a person who was standing or sitting, and chairs that came in several sizes to fit a wide range of body types.

The need many people had for a comfortable and functional home office also led to creative new products from the design centers of U.S. manufacturers. Flexibility and good looks were especially important to this market, given that home office space might be very limited and any pieces had to blend well with home furnishings. So manufacturers were putting work centers and other components on wheels for portability, inventing desks that folded out or swung open for working and then closed up to hide office equipment, and creating adjustable tables that could do double-duty as coffee tables or typing tables.

FURTHER READING

Adams, Larry. "Blockbuster Deals Usher out 1995." *Wood and Wood Products,* February 1996.

"Are You Suited Comfortably?" *Management Today,* January 1995.

Blake, Laura. "Dealers Compete against New Distribution Options." *Grand Rapids Business Journal,* 12 June 1995.

———. "Industry Forecast Shows 4 Percent Growth." *Grand Rapids Business Journal,* 12 June 1995.

Brown, Christie. "You Say 65 Percent Off, They Say 71 Percent." *Forbes,* 20 May 1996.

Business and Institutional Furniture Manufacturers Association. "BIFMA Reflects on the Issues of the Day." *Wood and Wood Products,* February 1996. Available from http://www.bifma.com.

Christianson, Rich, and Larry Adams. "Back on Growth Track." *Wood and Wood Products,* February 1995.

Crook, David, and John Pierson. "New Products Bring Office Work Home." *Wall Street Journal,* 15 November 1996.

"Furniture Mart Reels from Layoffs." *Purchasing,* 20 April 1995.

Ghering, Mike. "Cubicle Clusters Out, 'Teaming' Panels Up." *Grand Rapids Business Journal,* 28 October 1996.

Jackson, Maggie. "Doing Right Can Be Financially Rewarding." *Grand Rapids Press,* 23 February 1997.

Kleeman, Walter B., Jr. "One Hundred Years of Wood Office Furniture Design." *Wood and Wood Products,* Special Annual Issue, 1995.

Palmer, Keasha. "No Place Like Home Office." *Grand Rapids Press,* 9 February 1997.

Tunison, John. "Furniture Firms Get Help from Lawmakers." *Grand Rapids Press,* 22 February 1997.

U.S. Census Bureau. *Manufacturing—Industry Series,* 1999.

Veverka, Amber. "Office Furniture Sales to Rise at Slower Pace." *Grand Rapids Press,* 26 January 1997.

Veverka, Amber, and Kyla King. "Union Drive Gets Serious at Haworth." *Grand Rapids Press,* 27 February 1997.

SIC 2522

OFFICE FURNITURE, EXCEPT WOOD

This category describes establishments primarily engaged in the manufacturing of office furniture, except furniture chiefly made of wood. Establishments primarily engaged in manufacturing safes and vaults are classified in **SIC 3499: Fabricated Metal Products, Not Elsewhere Classified.** The products manufactured by the industry include office benches, bookcases, chairs, cabinets, desks, filing cabinets, modular furniture systems, panel furniture systems, office partitions, stools, tables, and wall cases.

NAICS CODE(S)

337214 (Nonwood Office Furniture Manufacturing)

INDUSTRY SNAPSHOT

According to the Business and Institutional Furniture Manufacturers Association (BIFMA) International, a trade group that represented more than 140 North American office furniture manufacturing companies, shipments for the office furniture industry as a whole were worth $12.4 billion in 1998. Nonwood products consistently made up about 75 percent of this total. In 1998 that amounted to approximately $9.3 billion. This was up from an industry total of $11.5 billion in 1997 and $10 billion in 1996.

In the late 1970s and early 1980s the office furniture industry enjoyed an annual average growth rate of 19 percent, then the industry experienced a recession in the late 1980s and early 1990s. In 1990, for instance, office furniture shipments increased by only .5 percent to $7.9 billion. The following year saw shipments drop by 8.1 percent to $7.2 billion. In 1994 the value of office furniture shipments rebounded, posting a gain of 8.5 percent. Sales grew by a record 14 percent in 1997 and dropped to a respectable 8 percent in 1998. After seven years of steady growth, the industry once again experienced a slowdown in sales—predicted to be about 2 percent for 1999.

ORGANIZATION AND STRUCTURE

West Michigan—most notably in and around the cities of Grand Rapids and Holland—was home to office furniture manufacturing giants Steelcase Inc., Haworth Inc., and Herman Miller Inc., as well as a number of other firms. (Product lines at both Haworth and Herman Miller tended to focus more on wood office furniture, although the companies did produce nonwood pieces as well.) As a result, the area boasted facilities that produced about 65 percent of all office furniture manufactured in North America.

When wood was still the material of choice for most manufacturers, stationery stores and office equipment dealers handled sales of office furniture. The concept of "office design" was unheard of; companies purchased desks and other pieces as needed, setting them up in rows in big, open spaces, creating an office environment that very much resembled a classroom.

Later, as the demand for office furniture (including new nonwood products) increased and the market became more specialized and sophisticated, the major manufacturers developed their own sales staffs and dealer networks to handle large-scale orders. In addition, the introduction of new products such as computer desks and "systems furniture" (consisting of panels and other pieces that could be easily moved and reconfigured to accommodate changing needs) generated a need for office designers. So the bigger firms began to offer design assistance to customers eager to get the most out of their furniture purchases. Smaller companies that were unable to support their own sales and design staffs turned instead to manufacturers' representatives to provide the same services to customers.

In the 1990s, while a few manufacturers still sold directly to customers, most relied on other means of distribution. For example, contract office furniture dealers—those specializing in large-scale orders placed with industry giants such as Steelcase—handled nearly 65 percent of all office furniture sales in 1994, according to a joint survey conducted by BIFMA and the Business Products Industry Association (BPIA). The remaining 35 percent of sales were divided fairly evenly among six other categories: budget to mid-market furniture dealers; office product dealers; superstores, warehouse clubs, and other mass merchandisers; wholesalers; government; and mail order, direct sales, and other channels. Superstores, warehouse clubs, and other mass merchandisers showed the strongest growth from 1993 until 1994, increasing from 2.8 percent of the total to 4.1 percent.

Office furniture manufacturers of all kinds showcased their newest products and services at a number of trade shows around the country, most notably the NeoCon World's Trade Fair. Held annually at the Merchandise Mart in Chicago, it was billed as North America's largest commercial interiors exposition.

BACKGROUND AND DEVELOPMENT

Until the 1930s wood dominated the office furniture market. Then metal filing cabinets and desks emerged as popular, cheaper substitutes for the old wooden models. The military's need for steel briefly interrupted this trend during World War II, but in the postwar years, the metal office furniture industry launched an aggressive marketing campaign touting the advantages of its products, emphasizing durability and safety (offices filled with wood furniture posed a fire hazard). The rivalry between the two camps gradually eased, however, as wood office furniture manufacturers began to incorporate steel parts in their designs, and metal office furniture manufacturers began to feature wooden tops.

As recently as the 1950s, American offices and office furniture were generally drab, stark, and purely functional. Beginning in the late 1960s and early 1970s, however, office design, layout, and furniture began to be influenced by modern ideas of worker productivity and the realization that a link existed between employee performance and the quality of the office environment.

From the late 1970s through the early 1980s, office furniture sales grew by an average of 19 percent annually, according to BIFMA. The boom was fueled by the rapid growth of the white-collar workforce, especially in the computer industry and other information-related fields. These sales were largely driven by the demand for "systems furniture," or mix-and-match cabinets, desks, and wall panels or partitions. Changing work habits created a need for such products. For example, the rise of computers and related hardware helped spawn new types of workstations, printer tables, and movable walls and partitions that made it easy to reconfigure office space. Prewired partitions, which first appeared in the mid-1970s, facilitated wiring and networking of computers.

Beginning in the late 1980s, however, the entire office furniture industry felt the impact of white-collar downsizing at many firms. A recession in 1991-92 also hit furniture manufacturers extremely hard. From 1986 until 1992, average annual sales growth stood at just under 3 percent. Shipments for the metal office furniture manufacturing industry fell from $6.2 billion in 1989 to $5.6 billion in 1991. Exports, which had doubled between 1988 and 1989 from $86.7 million to $170.8 million, fell during this period as well.

The recession led to even more layoffs among office workers as one company after another downsized. Office space, which had mushroomed during the boom years of the 1980s when demand was high, sat vacant. As a result, few new offices were built during the late 1980s and early 1990s, which meant less demand for new office furniture. Corporations desperately searching for ways to save money began to regard new office furniture as a luxury item rather than a necessity. The weak economy eventually forced some office furniture manufacturing companies out of business, especially those that specialized in high-end products. To remain competitive, surviving manufacturers were forced to reduce their own staffs and increase productivity.

The economic picture began to brighten a bit in 1993, when office furniture sales hit $8.1 billion, a 5.1 percent increase over the previous year's sales figure of $7.7 billion. The improved fortunes of office furniture manufacturers in the mid-1990s reflected an overall upswing in the economy, including a surge in nonresidential building starts and falling unemployment rates. No one, however, envisioned a return to the boom years of the early 1980s.

CURRENT CONDITIONS

As the 1990s neared an end, analysts expressed guarded optimism about the future prospects and performance of the office furniture manufacturing industry. Steady interest rates, a moderately growing economy, and low inflation all seemed conducive to a sustained period of modest sales gains in the range of 2 to 5 percent. Yet the industry continued to suffer from too many suppliers competing for increasingly few customers. In fact, manufacturers were routinely forced to discount their prices by as much as 50 percent or more on high-volume purchases in order to win lucrative contracts.

Because most manufacturers realized that they could not necessarily compete on product alone, they began coming up with ways to provide more services to their customers. Terms such as "value-added partnering" became part of the industry lingo. This was just one way that the higher-end manufacturers tried to distinguish themselves from their lower-end rivals.

Another change since the early 1990s focused on distribution. Many of the industry leaders, including Steelcase, Haworth, and Herman Miller, switched to dedicated dealers. Others, including HON Industries, moved in the opposite direction and distributed their products through office supply superstores and other discount outlets.

Another strategy that high-end manufacturers in particular adopted as they reassessed their market involved acquiring smaller companies that already had a foothold in growing niche markets. For example, with an estimated 43 million people doing at least some work out of their homes as of 1996, companies eager to expand their traditional customer base offered more and more workstations, chairs, shelving units, file cabinets, and other components designed for the home office. This market, however, might not bring the expected sales boost, as start-up firms and those with home offices might not be willing to spend lavishly on office furniture.

Ready-to-assemble (RTA) furniture also captured the attention of some industry leaders. In late 1993, for example, Haworth purchased Globe Business Furniture, an RTA supplier specializing in partially assembled chairs. Globe's sales grew an average of 25 percent between 1981 and 1992, making it an attractive acquisition for a company such as Haworth that was intent on broadening its product line to include lower-priced furniture. Industry experts expected the trend to continue, but they warned producers against moving to RTA as a quick-fix method for regaining market share, in part because RTA required an entirely different cost structure than that used by traditional office furniture manufacturers.

Also lucrative was the market for ergonomically designed office furniture that offered maximum comfort and flexibility. As people became more aware of computer-related, white-collar occupational hazards such as repetitive strain injury, carpal tunnel syndrome, backache, and other ailments, they demanded furniture that would prevent or lessen the severity of these injuries. Office furniture manufacturers were at the forefront of the drive to design and produce ergonomic office furniture that their customers hoped would increase productivity, curb health care costs, and reduce the threat of lawsuits from employees with work-related disabilities.

Sales of high-end products—such as workstations that adjusted to let users sit or stand while they worked, and computer monitors and keyboards that could be positioned at various levels—helped to propel growth in the industry. Demand for less-expensive ergonomic furniture was also strong. Small companies concerned about liability for their employees' work-related injuries were often unable to afford traditional high-priced ergonomic furniture. Companies responded to this dilemma by coming out with new mid- and lower-priced lines that offered some adjustability.

The major players in the office furniture industry diversified their operations in other ways as well. In 1994 Steelcase announced plans to establish a consulting and service management subsidiary called Tangerine that would help companies identify their workplace needs, both on- and off-site, and then cater to those needs. This move by the industry leader underscored its recognition of the changing nature of the workplace.

Among the more pressing issues faced by the office furniture manufacturing industry in the 1990s was the growth of Federal Prison Industries (FPI), a program that employed prisoners to make various kinds of products, including office furniture. By law, whenever the federal government was in the market for office furniture, it had to give preference to FPI and its prison-made products, regardless of cost. As a result, U.S. manufacturers lost tens of millions of dollars in sales every year. With BIFMA, office furniture manufacturers joined together to fight for legislation to end the competitive advantage enjoyed by FPI over private companies.

In addition, office furniture manufacturers expressed apprehension about the effect of ongoing environmental legislation on their bottom lines. In their factories, they already incurred increased costs for disposing of hazardous wastes generated by the furniture-finishing process. In the marketplace, they faced mounting concerns about the effect of various pollutants on indoor air quality.

Among the most common offenders were formaldehyde (from pressed-wood products), adhesives, and paints and other finishes. To address these problems, some U.S. office furniture manufacturers switched to different kinds of finishes and alternative glues, although some of these substitutes performed poorly.

In the mid-1990s the U.S. Environmental Protection Agency (EPA) launched two major studies of indoor air quality in order to gain a better understanding of the problem in both public and private buildings. Results were not expected until the end of the 1990s. The EPA was to use those findings to develop a set of proposed national guidelines and standards for acceptable levels of indoor air pollutants.

Other challenges office furniture manufactures faced as they headed into a new century included dealing with continued corporate downsizing and developing more products for home use in a market that was increasingly dominated by ready-to-assemble furniture companies such as O'Sullivan Industries, Sauder Woodworking, and Bush Industries. On the labor front, they were also concerned about the shortage of skilled workers and the need to work more efficiently to cut manufacturing costs.

INDUSTRY LEADERS

The top company in the U.S. office furniture manufacturing industry was Steelcase Inc., which posted sales of $2.4 billion in the first nine months of 1999. This gave Steelcase a 25 percent share of the entire domestic office furniture manufacturing market that year. It had 49 production and service facilities worldwide and employed 21,500 people worldwide. Although it specialized in nonwood office furniture, Steelcase also manufactured wood office furniture, panels and partitions, lighting systems, and customized millwork. It even produced computer software that aided in designing office environments.

Steelcase's chief rivals in the high-end office furniture industry were Haworth and Herman Miller. In 1998, Haworth, a privately held company, posted nearly $1.6 billion in sales and employed 11,000 people; Herman Miller reported just under $1 billion in sales for the last six months of 1999. Other leaders in the metal office furniture market included HON Industries Inc., the Knoll Group, HMK Enterprises, and Krueger International.

WORKFORCE

Since 1988 employment in all sectors of the office furniture manufacturing industry has steadily declined, with the wood segment experiencing the most significant losses. When a recession struck in the early 1990s, it forced the industry's corporate customers to rethink their priorities and postpone furniture purchases that could be considered luxuries rather than necessities. Office furniture manufacturers responded by targeting their own payrolls for cutbacks. Since then, increased automation and efficiency also contributed to a reduction in the work force (especially in production), adding to the likelihood that those lost jobs would never be replaced.

At its peak in 1989, the office furniture industry as a whole employed 71,300 people. This fell to 68,000 in 1990, 62,600 in 1991, and 61,900 in 1992. Among production workers in particular, jobs dropped from 52,900 in 1989 to 50,600 in 1990, 46,100 in 1991, and 45,800 in 1992. By the middle of the 1990s, total employment in the metal office furniture segment of the industry appeared to have stabilized at about 33,500.

Since then, the decline in employment slowed somewhat, with job losses in the office furniture industry as a whole totaling about 2,200 from mid-1995 through mid-1996. The remaining workforce consisted of nearly 61,000 people, almost 45,000 of whom were production employees. Average hourly wages for production workers in mid-1996 stood at $10.81.

The disquieting loss of job security coupled with a new emphasis on bottom-line issues helped spark unionization drives during the 1990s at several West Michigan office furniture manufacturers, whose employees traditionally shunned unions. In 1993, for instance, the United Steelworkers tried to organize at both Steelcase and Haworth without much success. In 1997, however, the United Auto Workers mounted a campaign at Haworth that attracted far more attention and support.

AMERICA AND THE WORLD

With little hope of a rise in demand for their products in the United States any time soon, the country's biggest office furniture manufacturers bolstered their presence overseas. Results were lackluster at best; as of the late 1990s, the major firms had yet to see much in the way of profits from their foreign divisions, often because of economic and political instability in certain markets.

The passage of the North American Free Trade Agreement in 1993 opened the doors to anticipated heavier volumes of office furniture imports and exports. Overall, however, imports and exports of nonwood and wood office furniture continued to make up a fairly small percentage of total industry shipments. According to BIFMA, U.S. office furniture imports in 1998 totaled $1.5 billion and exports totaled $410 million. The top importing countries were Canada, China, Taiwan, Mexico, and Italy. The top countries that the United States exported to were Canada, Mexico, the United Kingdom, Japan, and Hong Kong.

RESEARCH AND TECHNOLOGY

In response to management trends stressing teamwork, ongoing corporate downsizing, concerns about occupational-related injuries, and the increasing number of people working out of their homes, office furniture manufacturers were devoting many of their research dollars to the development of multifunctional, ergonomically designed products. In larger offices, for example, cubicle clusters and movable panels were being replaced by a more open, less isolated environment that encouraged people to work together and made it physically easier for them to do so. Also growing in popularity were adjustable work surfaces and components that could serve more than one use, so as to accommodate workers whose jobs were no longer quite so narrowly defined. Designing all of these products to work better with rapidly changing computer technology was also a top priority.

Ergonomics was in the forefront, too, as employers and manufacturers both sought ways to comply with federal mandates (some resulting from the 1990 Americans with Disabilities Act) and ward off lawsuits filed by workers suffering from job-related aches and pains. It was felt that ergonomically designed furniture could increase worker productivity by 15 percent. The emphasis was on adjustability, such as motorized tables with multiple height settings to accommodate a person who was standing or sitting, and chairs that came in several sizes to fit a wide range of body types.

The need many people had for a comfortable and functional home office also led to creative new products from the design centers of U.S. manufacturers. Flexibility and good looks were especially important to this market, given that home office space might be very limited and any pieces had to blend well with home furnishings. So manufacturers were putting work centers and other components on wheels for portability, inventing desks that folded out or swung open for working and then closed up to hide office equipment, and creating adjustable tables that could do double-duty as coffee tables or typing tables.

FURTHER READING

Adams, Larry. "Blockbuster Deals Usher out 1995." *Wood and Wood Products,* February 1996.

Avery, Susan. "Technology Transforms New Designs." *Purchasing,* 22 April 1999.

Blake, Laura. "Dealers Compete against New Distribution Options." *Grand Rapids Business Journal,* 12 June 1995.

———. "Industry Forecast Shows 4 Percent Growth." *Grand Rapids Business Journal,* 12 June 1995.

Brown, Christie. "You Say 65 Percent Off, They Say 71 Percent." *Forbes,* 20 May 1996.

Business and Institutional Furniture Manufacturers Association. "BIFMA Reflects on the Issues of the Day." *Wood and Wood Products,* February 1996. Available from http://www.bifma.com.

———. "The U.S. Office Furniture Market." Available from http://www.bifma.com/statover.html. Accessed 16 December 1999.

Christianson, Rich, and Larry Adams. "Back on Growth Track." *Wood and Wood Products,* February 1995.

Crook, David, and John Pierson. "New Products Bring Office Work Home." *Wall Street Journal,* 15 November 1996.

"Furniture Mart Reels from Layoffs." *Purchasing,* 20 April 1995.

Ghering, Mike. "Cubicle Clusters Out, 'Teaming' Panels Up." *Grand Rapids Business Journal,* 28 October 1996.

Haworth Inc. "Haworth Inc. receives Federal Government Evergreen Award." Available from http://www.haworth.com/inout/news/business/evergreen.html. Accessed 23 December 1999.

Herman Miller Inc. "Herman Miller Inc. Reports Sales, Orders, and Profits for the Second Quarter of Fiscal 2000." Available from http://www.hermanmiller.com/news/12.21.99.html. Accessed 22 December 1999.

International Trade Commission. "Top 25 U.S. Destinations for Office Furniture, Except Wood." Available from http://www.ita.doc.gov/ocg/exp2522.htm. Accessed 24 November 1999.

―――. "Top 25 U.S. Sources for Office Furniture, Except Wood." Available from http://www.ita.doc.gov/td/ocg/imp2522.htm. Accessed 24 November 1999.

Palmer, Keasha. "No Place Like Home Office." *Grand Rapids Press,* 9 February 1997.

Steelcase Inc. "Steelcase Inc. Reports Record Net Sales for Third Quarter Fiscal 2000; Earnings in Line with Analyst Expectations." Available from http://www.corporate-ir.net/ireye/ir_site.zhtml?ticker=scs&script=410&script=410&layout=1&item_id=66036. Accessed 20 December 1999.

Stundza, Tom. "Demand for New Styles Is Lukewarm." *Purchasing,* 16 September 1999.

Tunison, John. "Furniture Firms Get Help from Lawmakers." *Grand Rapids Press,* 22 February 1997.

Veverka, Amber. "Office Furniture Sales to Rise at Slower Pace." *Grand Rapids Press,* 26 January 1997.

Veverka, Amber, and Kyla King. "Union Drive Gets Serious at Haworth." *Grand Rapids Press,* 27 February 1997.

SIC 2531

PUBLIC BUILDING AND RELATED FURNITURE

This category primarily encompasses establishments engaged in manufacturing furniture for public use in schools, theaters, assembly halls, churches, and libraries. Examples of such furniture include bleacher and stadium seating, church pews, library chairs and tables, and blackboards. The public building and related furniture category also includes seating for public conveyances such as automobiles, aircraft, and passenger trains. This category does not include manufacturers of stone furniture, which are classified under **SIC 3281: Cut Stone and Stone Products,** nor does it include those that manufacture concrete furniture, which can be found under **SIC 3272: Concrete Products, Except Block and Brick**

NAICS CODE(S)

322130 (Paperboard Mills)

INDUSTRY SNAPSHOT

An estimated 500 establishments were involved in the production of manufactured goods falling under the category of public building and related furniture in the United States. The total value of shipments generated by the industry amounted to an estimate of more than $6 billion by 1997. The companies that comprised this category differed greatly in structure, marketing strategy, and fiscal health, due to the variegated nature of the classification. Nearly half were smaller firms with fewer than 20 employees on the payroll, while roughly 10 percent were corporate subsidiaries. The majority of companies in the industry were "single establishment companies," which were not part of a larger parent corporation.

The variety of products manufactured by the public building and related furniture industry defies a general description of industry outlook. A smaller and less profitable segment of the industry involved the manufacture of church furniture, while providers of automobile seats to car manufacturers were more visible and fiscally sound. While early in the twentieth century much of the public seating furniture was made of wood, the incorporation of new technologies such as plastic radically altered manufacturing processes in this category. Throughout the 1990s, many companies were compelled to remarket their products to meet changing demands and a tougher economic situation. Increasingly stringent government regulations in regard to consumer safety and access for the disabled also forced periodic changes in the industry.

ORGANIZATION AND STRUCTURE

Most companies in the public building and related furniture industry were comprised of divisions responsible for different steps of the manufacturing process, including research and development, executive decision making, manufacturing, marketing strategy, and customer support. Many of the products manufactured in the industry were marketed to other companies or institutions, rather than the general public. Automobile seats, for example, were sold to firms specializing in seat frames and exteriors, which, in turn, sold the completed seating units to automobile manufacturers. Manufacturers commonly advertised in trade journals, such as *Automotive News, Library Journal,* and other publications aimed at executives, buyers, and other upper-level personnel.

During the economic recession of the early 1990s, many public building and related furniture manufacturers focused on customer satisfaction and product reliability as part of their plan to survive in the industry. This represented a particular challenge, as many public building and related furniture manufacturers marketed their products to other companies, rather than the ultimate consumer, making it difficult to gauge product satisfaction.

BACKGROUND AND DEVELOPMENT

Many of the firms engaged in manufacturing public building and related furniture date back to the late nineteenth century. During this period, the Industrial Revolution and the urbanization of America played a key role in the development and growth of the industry, as a variety of new demands for public-use furniture developed. For example, when educational reform in the United States led to the replacement of the one-room schoolhouse with large school buildings in consolidated districts, the subsequent demand for school desks and blackboards was filled by newly formed firms in the industry. Furthermore, newly prosperous industrial magnates founded and endowed hundreds of colleges and universities, necessitating the development of firms that could manufacture and ship seats and desks all over the country. U.S. Steel founder Andrew Carnegie funded the construction of over 2,800 public libraries across the country, and a new niche in the market arose to meet the demand for librarians' desks as well as patron tables and chairs.

The Industrial Revolution was also responsible for major shifts in population from rural regions to larger urban centers and, later, suburban communities. The shift in demographics was compounded by waves of immigrants from Europe, necessitating the construction of new and larger churches to serve the needs of evolving communities. A demand for more interior furniture, such as church pews, accompanied the exponential growth of churches.

The increased popularity of leisure and entertainment activities in the United States also played a key role in the genesis of the public building and related furniture industry. The development of organized community and collegiate sports, such as baseball and football, necessitated the construction of stadiums and arenas able to seat spectators. Moreover, as plays and motion pictures gained popularity, theaters were built in all but the most rural of American cities, and many competed to provide patrons with the most luxurious interiors, including plush seating.

Perhaps most importantly, the development of new technology in the transportation industry augmented the public building and related furniture industry. The growth of a network of railroads in America gave rise to the popularity of passenger rail travel. Companies evolved to provide comfortable seating for the new long-distance traveler. The invention of the automobile and its rapid rise as a major form of transportation necessitated the evolution of a parallel supplier industry for interior automotive equipment, including seats. During the 1950s and 1960s, the increasing affordability of passenger air travel fueled a great demand for new aircraft, with cabin accouterments and furnishings.

CURRENT CONDITIONS

The 1980s were a period of growth for the public building and related furniture industry. The value of shipments nearly doubled from $1.1 billion in 1982 to $2.0 billion in 1987; by 1991 this figure had reached $3.1 billion but showed a small decline from the previous year. In 1995 sales were $2.4 billion for seats for public conveyance (bus, train, etc.), $482.6 million for school furniture, $268.7 million for airplane seats, $223.2 million for chairs and seats, and $122.8 million for stadium and bleacher seats.

The number of employees in this field jumped from 18,800 in 1982 to 21,800 in 1987, and by 1996 this figure had reached an estimated 33,000. The largest and most competitive companies in this industry were automobile and airline seat manufacturers, which had to possess the working capital and financial solvency to meet the high costs of developing specialty seats built to withstand accidents. Such companies had to invest large sums in research and development, attract well-qualified engineers for product design, and have the promotional budgets to capture greater market share.

The automobile seating industry was innovating more towards comfort and technology. Johnson Controls, Inc., for example, had a Comfort Engineering Center that developed more comfortable seats and tested the durability of the comfort features. The future of automobile seating will be smart seats that adjust according to a passenger's height, weight, and preferred seating position. Active seats will incorporate technology that adjusts according to road conditions—maximizing passenger comfort.

INDUSTRY LEADERS

The companies that manufactured public building and related furniture were as diversified as their products. In the automotive industry, the main suppliers of car seats were Johnson Controls and Douglas and Lomason Co. Johnson Controls, founded in 1900 and headquartered in Milwaukee, Wisconsin, was a major manufacturer of automobile seats, but was best known as a provider of electronic control systems that regulated heating, cooling, and security for commercial buildings. Total sales for the auto segment were $12.1 billion in 1999 while total company sales were $16.1 billion. The international company employed 70,000. In 1991 Johnson Controls purchased Lahnwerk GmbH, a German company that supplied seat components and metal seat frames to the European auto industry. Two years later Johnson Controls acquired a similar Mexican firm, Grupo Summa. The company's 50 manufacturing plants involved in automotive seating were located in Michigan, Tennessee, and California, as well as in Portugal and Austria. More than 22.0 million vehicles carried Johnson interior equipment in 1999. Johnson Controls Automotive Division was the world's largest auto seating supplier for the major car companies. In October 1996 the company acquired Prince Automotive, which had been a smaller, yet still viable competitor.

The other large supplier of seats to the American automotive industry, Douglas and Lomason Co., a suburban Detroit, Michigan, firm, was founded in 1902. Douglas and Lomason primarily manufactured stamping and conveyer equipment for the industry.

Airline seats were an integral part of this industry as a whole. According to early 1990 statistics a row of seats in first class cost approximately $10,000 while a row of seating in coach cost $5,000. Aircraft cabin seating was the largest segment in this industry. The largest market share was held by BE Aerospace, Weber Aircraft Inc., and Burns Aerospace Corp. BE Aerospace, with over 5,600 employees, was the largest integrated supplier of aircraft cabin accessories, selling approximately 25 percent of the seat market according to early 1990 figures. Headquartered in Florida, the company was founded in 1987 and expanded in 1992 when it acquired the Connecticut-based aircraft cabin seat company PTC Aerospace. With other acquisitions of cabin supplier firms that produced such components as galley appliances and video monitors, BE Aerospace's sales went from nearly $233 million in 1996 to $701 million in 1999, providing the airline industry with all cabin products except for lighting fixtures and lavatories. Over 40 percent of the company's sales came from aircraft seats. Although demand for new aircraft declined in the early 1990s, BE Aerospace remained a strong leader in the field. Second in sales of aircraft cabin seats was the California-based firm of Weber Aircraft, controlling 19 percent of the market and employing 800. Burns Aerospace Corp., a subsidiary of Eagle Industries Inc., employed 700 and posted sales of $80 million, representing 16 percent of the market.

The largest supplier of library furniture in the 1990s was Gaylord Brothers, a Syracuse, New York, firm dating back to the end of the nineteenth century. Gaylord was started by two brothers, bank clerks, who developed a gummed parchment that they marketed to libraries for use in repairing books. When the business turned a profit in 1909, the Gaylord brothers quit the bank and developed their company into a full-service provider for American libraries. Their products included book shelving systems, magazine display units, storage facilities, librarians' desks, and patron chairs and tables. Gaylord Brothers, which became a subsidiary of the Croydon Co., marketed its products by catalog. By 1997 the company boasted over 11,000 different items in its product line.

WORKFORCE

In the public building and related furniture industry, the majority of jobs were concentrated in the actual manufacturing process. In 1995 the total number of jobs was 42,000 for the industry, with production workers accounting for 33,400 positions in that figure. The average hourly earnings for production workers in the industry was $10.15.

AMERICA AND THE WORLD

In the public building and related furniture industry, seating for public conveyances such as automobiles and airline cabins represented the most common export. The costs for importing other types of furniture, such as classroom or stadium seating, proved prohibitive for many foreign manufacturers who already had successful domestic furniture industries. American automotive seat suppliers such as Johnson Controls faced domestic competition from Japanese firms such as Atoma and Toyo Seat USA, and made acquisitions to expand into a lucrative foreign automobile market.

RESEARCH AND TECHNOLOGY

Government regulations prompted the development of new technologies in the public building and related furniture industry, particularly in automotive and airline seat manufacturing. Minimum criteria for car seats, set by the National Highway Traffic Safety Administration, stipulated that seats not have parts that might injure drivers or passengers on impact and that the seat withstand the force of a crash up to a specified gravitational force, requiring seat frames made of particularly resilient material attached firmly to the car floor.

Auto-seat manufacturers were also concerned with the seat's overall performance in terms of comfort, durability, and appearance. As changing demographic patterns engendered longer commuting times for many consumers, the average time spent sitting in a car seat increased. In response, researchers measured the amount of lumbar support various types of seat cushions provided, developing two methods used in the suspension of automotive seats. The most common type of seat consisted of foam block, a combination of a polyurethane cushion and springs, while another featured a light platform supported by a system of springs.

Governmental regulations, issued by the Federal Aviation Administration (FAA) and the National Transportation Safety Board, also affected the industry. Due to the potential for extremely high impact crashes in air travel, regulations on aircraft cabin seat construction were more stringent than for any other area of the public building and related furniture industry. Initially, the industry resisted modifications of cabin seating, complaining that heavier anchoring components used to bolt seats to the floor added too much weight to the aircraft. The development of new technology and materials in the 1980s, however, allowed for seats that could withstand up to 9 g in gravitational force. In 1988 the FAA ruled that all newly certified aircraft be outfitted with such seats, and proposed that all seats aboard U.S. aircraft meet a 16 g requirement by 1995. In accordance, most seat manufacturers, including Weber, switched production to the 16 g seats by 1990.

The fabric used in aircraft cabin seats was also regulated, ensuring cushions that were fire retardant and able to serve as floatation devices. Furthermore, regulatory officials continued to monitor the number and placement of seats on a given aircraft, a procedure that directly affected the profits of both the airline industry and the public building and related furniture industry. Some innovations in airline seating expected to be developed at the start of the twenty-first century included seats featuring attached shoulder harnesses, as well as seats that could rotate the passenger's legs upward and out of danger in the event of a crash.

FURTHER READING

Cole, David. "A New Way to Differentiate." *Inside Source,* winter 1999. Available from http://www.johnsoncontrols.com/asg-is/e/story8.html.

Johnson Controls Inc. "Johnson Controls Annual Report 1996." Available from http://www.jci.com/annual-report.

———. "Johnson Controls Reports Record 1999 Results." 19 October 1999. Available from http://www.jci.com/news_00yrend.htm.

———. "Seating and Interiors." 5 January 2000. Available from http://www.jci.com/asg-intro.

Lazich, Robert S. *Market Share Reporter.* Detroit: Gale Research, 1997.

Vasilash, Gary S. "Where Comfort Is an Engineering Discipline." *Automotive Manufacturing & Production,* January 1999.

SIC 2541

WOOD OFFICE AND STORE FIXTURES, PARTITIONS, SHELVING, AND LOCKERS

This category covers establishments primarily engaged in manufacturing shelving, lockers, and office and store fixtures, plastic-laminated fixture tops, and related fabricated products, chiefly of wood. It also includes prefabricated partitions made of wood if they are designed to be attached to floor; if they are designed to be freestanding or part of an office furniture panel system, they are classified under **SIC 2521: Wood Office Furniture.** This category excludes wooden refrigerated cabinets, showcases, or display cases, which are found under **SIC 3585: Refrigeration and Heating Equipment.**

NAICS CODE(S)

337110 (Wood Kitchen Cabinet and Counter Top Manufacturing)

337212 (Custom Architectural Woodwork, Millwork, and Fixtures)

337215 (Showcase, Partition, Shelving, and Locker Manufacturing)

INDUSTRY SNAPSHOT

In 1997 about 2,300 companies were engaged in the manufacture of wood shelving, partitions, and fixtures for commercial and residential use in the United States. The vast majority of them—nearly 80 percent—were firms of less than 20 employees. Industry sales were $8.5 billion in 1997, with about 60 percent of the manufacturers posting sales of less than $1 million. Sales in the industry are split fairly equally between wood and nonwood fixtures.

The industry is strictly commercial in nature, and its fortunes are tied to the retail industry. Most fixtures—about 85 percent—are sold to retail stores. The rest are sold to schools, banks, hotels, libraries, and other non-retail businesses.

At one time, the industry manufactured many types of products that are now either obsolete or only rarely made, including butcher shop display cases and telephone booths. Other products have become prohibitively expensive to both manufacture and purchase because of the high cost of materials and labor. Nevertheless, many of the firms that supply wood partitions and fixtures are still thriving due to the increased demand for retail shelving and wooden display units. The industry has also benefited from the development of laminated plastic coatings, which increase the durability of a much-used wood surface.

ORGANIZATION AND STRUCTURE

Most companies in the wood partitions and fixtures industry were originally organized into divisions reflecting their potential customers. In general, they focused on assembling and retaining a staff of highly skilled woodworkers. Research and development, marketing, and customer support typically did not receive a high priority, especially among smaller firms. Even today, only the largest companies can afford in-house staffs to handle those responsibilities.

Manufacturers of wood partitions, shelving, and fixtures usually reach out to their markets by advertising in trade journals such as *Restaurant Hospitality, Chain Store Age Executive,* and other publications aimed at business owners and managers. They sell to a wide range of customers, including major wholesalers, contract hardware jobbers, display and fixture jobbers, specialty wholesalers, independent hardware distributors, export outlets, government agencies, original equipment manufacturers, national mass merchants, large home centers, and building supply outlets.

BACKGROUND AND DEVELOPMENT

The wood partitions and fixtures industry emerged in the late nineteenth century during a period of tremendous expansion in the U.S. economy. Rapid industrialization attracted large numbers of people to cities, which in turn sparked the development of major urban commercial districts. The proliferation of small specialty shops and large department stores required a huge supply of fixtures for the display of merchandise.

Although they are no longer manufactured, wooden telephone booths once represented a small but important part of the industry. The first one was installed in 1889 outside a bank in Hartford, Connecticut. Western Electric continued to manufacture wooden telephone booths until the late 1940s, when the more durable glass and steel model was invented and went into production. By the 1990s, wooden phone booths were considered collectibles, and some sold for as much as $3,000.

The wood partitions and fixtures industry was hit hard by recession in the early 1990s, with the value of shipments declining from a 1990 peak of $3.1 billion to $2.8 billion in 1991. In addition to the economic downturn, this decline was attributed in part to the fact that many products became obsolete. The market demand for plastic imitations of wood, as well as the higher costs associated with fabricating real wood products, also had a significant impact on the overall health of the industry.

The mid-1990s, however, was a time of increased prosperity for the nation's wood shelving and fixtures manufacturers. By 1994, shipment values increased to $3.4 billion and were expected to reach $4 billion by 1998. Among their commercial customers, for example, the slow but steady growth of the economy and highly competitive retail atmosphere encouraged merchants to invest in new store fixtures to keep their product displays attractive. Manufacturers saw increased demand for both customization and flexibility. Retailers wanted a distinctive "look" that set them apart from their rivals. They were not interested in fixtures that could not be moved or changed to accommodate different kinds of displays, new inventory, or changing seasons.

Although metal fixtures gained popularity for their high-tech look and lower cost, wood was still the material of choice for those who preferred its warmer appeal. The market for combination wood and metal fixtures and shelving also grew during the 1990s, as did the demand for laminates. These gains, however, came at the expense of all wood products.

Wood shelving and fixture manufacturers in the 1990s were concerned about discounting and low bidding on projects, a practice they believed hurt the industry as a whole. Companies that operated in northern states were especially concerned about what they perceived to be unfair competition from Canada. The favorable exchange rate during the 1990s made it possible for Canadian firms to submit project bids that were substantially lower than those of their U.S. rivals.

CURRENT CONDITIONS

Sales of store fixtures reached nearly $8.5 billion in 1997, with about half—or $4.2 billion—coming from sales of wood fixtures. Of the 2,300 companies that manufacture fixtures, only about 25 percent of them concentrate on fixtures exclusively. Most companies in the industry are established businesses, with 70 percent of them in operation for 10 years or more. Fixtures companies tend to market their products both nationally and internationally, with only about 10 percent marketing their products regionally.

From 1995 through the end of the century, the fixture industry grew at a rate of 5 to 10 percent per year. This is mainly due to the continued economic expansion in the United States that, in turn, leads to more disposable income and more retail sales. Retailers continue to expand, remodel, and open new locations, driving the demand for store fixtures, which accounts for about 85 percent of the industry's sales.

Manufacturers in this category face a number of challenges. One of their top concerns is the shortage of highly skilled woodworkers. Without such workers, manufacturers find it impossible to keep up with production. To help alleviate the problem, some companies have started in-house training and apprentice programs.

Another barrier to growth was the increasingly limited supply of wood and wood panels. In particular, the industry did not have enough particleboard and fiberboard during the mid-1990s. This shortage kept wholesale prices fairly high, but, for the most part, manufacturers hesitated to pass along the rising costs to retailers.

Health concerns and environmental regulations also affect manufacturers of wood shelving and fixtures. Working in the wood industry brings with it a number of serious risks, including injuries caused by saws and drills and illnesses brought on by wood dust and paint vapors.

As a result, companies struggle with high healthcare costs and a growing number of workers' compensation claims. They also incur mounting costs for disposal of hazardous wastes generated by the wood finishing process; furthermore, they have to abide by strict rules governing wood dust levels in their factories. Manufacturers are also subject to regulations aimed at improving indoor air quality, which is adversely affected by fumes from finishes and adhesives. Yet some of the products that were developed as substitutes perform poorly, as evidenced by less durable finishes and glues that fail.

Fixture companies need to cultivate overseas markets as well as broadening their domestic market. They have to develop new fixtures and use new technologies to become even more efficient in their manufacturing processes, if they want to stay competitive in the future.

INDUSTRY LEADERS

Knape & Vogt Manufacturing of Grand Rapids, Michigan, was one of the largest suppliers of wood partitions, shelving, and fixtures during the 1990s. Founded in 1906, it employed 1,056 people in 1996 at facilities in four states and two Canadian provinces. It reported sales of $150.3 million in 1999, a figure that included not only sales of wooden store fixtures and shelving but also those made from materials other than wood as well as drawer slides, hardware items, and miscellaneous furniture components. This represented a 20 percent drop in sales from the previous year, however, when Knape & Vogt posted sales of $181.6 million.

Lozier Corp., based in Omaha, Nebraska, was another leading manufacturer of wood fixtures. It posted sales of $190 million during the mid-1990s and employed nearly 2,000 people. Smaller firms engaged in the manufacture of wood shelving, panels, and fixtures during the mid-1990s were Stevens Industries of Teutopolis, Illinois, with 400 employees and sales of about $42 million; Dorfile Storage and Shelving Systems of Memphis, Tennessee, with 550 employees and sales of about $35 million; and Bernhard Woodwork of Northbrook, Illinois, with 70 employees and sales of about $9 million.

WORKFORCE

In October 1999, the Labor Department reported that 544,600 people were employed in the furniture and fixtures industry; in October of 1998, the figure was at 532,700. The average hourly wage for production workers in the industry as a whole (both wood and nonwood segments) in 1999 was $11.37, up from $10.99 in October of 1998.

FURTHER READING

Adams, Larry. "Survey Says: 1995 Looking Good." *Wood and Wood Products,* March 1995.

Applefeld, Catherine. "Fixture Manufacturers Keep Up with Retailers to Stay Up-to-Date." *Billboard,* 16 September 1995.

"Customization Enhances Retailer Identity." *Chain Store Age Executive with Shopping Center Age,* July 1996.

"Fixture Flexibility Is Key: Trend Toward Modular, Customized Units." *Chain Store Age Executive with Shopping Center Age,* October 1995.

Hill, Dawn. "In Two Reports, Costs Put Drag on Net." *HFN: The Weekly Newspaper for the Home Furnishing Network,* 15 May 1995.

"Industry Overview." *National Association of Store Fixture Manufacturers,* 5 January 2000. Available from http://www.nasfm.com/tools/indoverview.html.

"Knape & Vogt's Quarterly Profits Inch Up." *HFN: The Weekly Newspaper for the Home Furnishing Network,* 20 February 1995.

"Knape & Vogt Reports 1999 Fiscal Year and Fourth-Quarter Results." *Knape & Vogt,* 5 August 1999. Available from http://www.corporate-ir.net/i.../ir_site.zhtml?ticker=knape&script=410&layout=7&item_id=4563.

"Looking At Business." *National Association of Store Fixture Manufacturers,* 26 November 1999. Available from http://www.nasfm.com/tools/lookbiznis/bizlooknov99.html.

Melaniphy, Margie. "Breaking into the RTA Storage Market." *Wood and Wood Products,* December 1995.

SIC 2542

OFFICE AND STORE FIXTURES, PARTITIONS, SHELVING, AND LOCKERS, EXCEPT WOOD

This category covers establishments primarily engaged in manufacturing office and store fixtures, shelving, storage racks, lockers, and related fabricated products, chiefly of materials other than wood. This industry also includes prefabricated partitions if they are designed to be attached to the floor; those designed to be freestanding or part of an office furniture panel system are instead classified in **SIC 2522: Office Furniture, Except Wood.** Establishments primarily engaged in manufacturing refrigerated cabinets, showcases, or display cases are classified in **SIC 3585: Air-Conditioning and Warm Air Heating Equipment and Commercial and Industrial Refrigeration Equipment.** Companies engaged in manufacturing safes and vaults are classified in **SIC 3499: Fabricated Metal Products, Not Elsewhere Classified.**

NAICS CODE(S)

337215 (Showcase, Partition, Shelving, and Locker Manufacturing)

INDUSTRY SNAPSHOT

The U.S. Census Bureau reported that in 1997 there were 31 establishments whose primary product was nonwood prefabricated partitions, 45 whose primary product was nonwood shelving and lockers, 91 whose primary product was nonwood storage racks and accessories, and 299 whose primary product was nonwood fixtures for stores, banks, offices, and other uses. These businesses shipped $4.8 billion worth of goods, spent $2.1 billion on materials, and paid $147.0 million for capital expenditures.

Overall, there were 926 establishments that made nonwood partitions and fixtures (not necessarily as their primary business). They shipped $5.2 billion worth of goods and spent $2.3 billion on materials. This was a thriving industry, due in part to an increased demand for unique store fixtures to showcase products for the burgeoning retail sector of the U.S. economy.

ORGANIZATION AND STRUCTURE

More than 1,800 companies in the United States were engaged in the manufacture of metal shelving, partitions, and fixtures for commercial and residential use during the mid-1990s. About 62 percent of these operations had fewer than 20 employees. Nearly 80 percent of the manufacturers in this category posted sales of less than $5 million in the mid-1990s.

BACKGROUND AND DEVELOPMENT

The growth of the metal partitions and fixtures industry in the United States was directly related to both the expansion of the retail segment of the economy and the development of new technology. After World War II, America's rapidly growing suburbs fueled the construction of large retail outlets such as supermarkets and shopping centers, which increased the demand for shelving and other fixtures. At the same time new manufacturing processes made it possible to craft fixtures and partitions from lightweight metal alloys to replace the standard wood fixtures. Metal shelves, cases, garment racks, and other products appealed to retailers because they were affordable and could be moved easily.

Demand for nonwood shelving and fixtures slumped in the early 1990s due to a recession but subsequently increased again. The highly competitive retail market and steady growth of the economy encouraged merchants to invest in new store fixtures to keep their product displays attractive and up to date.

Customization was a key word for retailers seeking a distinctive look to set them apart from their competitors. Flexibility was also important because few businesses were interested in buying fixtures that could not be moved or changed to accommodate different kinds of displays inventory. Metal wire emerged as a particular

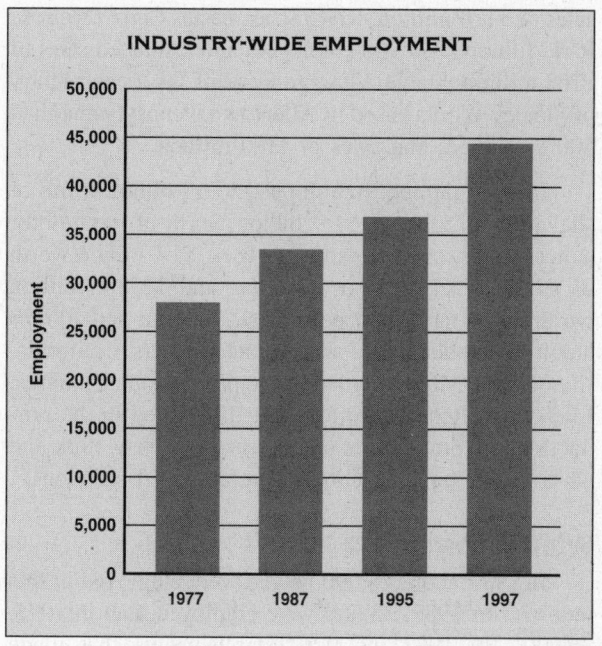

INDUSTRY-WIDE EMPLOYMENT

favorite because of its high-tech look. Combinations of wire and other materials (mostly wood and plexiglass) were also popular. This was due in part to the fact that metal products tended to cost less than wood because they could be manufactured quickly and efficiently, often on automated assembly lines.

Wire and wire combination products were also popular among residential customers for shelving, storage components, and fixtures. These products were often used in closets, kitchens, baths, laundries, and garages and were available at various retail outlets. They offered a less expensive alternative to similar wood and laminated wood products, which appealed to a more upscale market.

INDUSTRY LEADERS

One of the largest firms whose primary business fell into this category was Hoffman Engineering Co. (a subsidiary of Pentair Inc. based in Anoka, Minnesota) with 2,250 employees and sales of $310 million in 1998. Interlake Material Handling Div. (a subsidiary of Interlake Corp. based in Naperville, Illinois) had 1,100 employees and sales of $200 million. Madix Inc. (Terrell, Texas) had 1,600 employees and sales of $170 million. L.A. Darling Co. (a subsidiary of Marmon Group Inc. based in Paragould, Arkansas) had 2,700 employees and sales of $165 million. Its subsidiary, Darling Store Fixtures, had 2,000 employees and sales of $125 million. Falcon Products Inc. (Olivette, Missouri) had 4,440 employees and sales of approximately $143 million. Lozier Corp. (Omaha, Nebraska) had 1,400 employees and sales of $140 million. Lee/Rowan Co. (a subsidiary of Newell Co. based in Fenton, Missouri) had 1,500 employees and sales of $120 million. RHC/Spacemaster Corp. (Melrose Park, Illinois) had 900 employees and estimated sales of $105 million. Stanley Storage Systems Inc. (a subsidiary of Stanley Works based in Allentown, Pennsylvania) had 500 employees and sales of $100 million.

In 1997 the industry shipped $1.17 billion worth of shelving and lockers; $1.9 billion worth of fixtures for stores, banks, offices, and other uses; $1.1 billion worth of storage racks and accessories; and $277.0 million worth of prefabricated partitions. Alabama and Illinois led in the production of shelving and lockers. California, Illinois, and Minnesota led in the production of fixtures. Michigan, Ohio, California, and Illinois led in the production of storage racks and accessories. New York and Ohio led in the production of prefabricated partitions.

WORKFORCE

In 1977 about 28,000 people were employed in this industry. In 1987, 33,500 were employed, and in 1995, 36,900. By 1997 the 926 establishments that made nonwood partitions and fixtures employed 44,464 people, including 34,356 production workers who earned an average hourly wage of $11.84. The 466 establishments whose primary business was in this category employed 38,819 people, including 30,805 production workers who earned an average hourly wage of $11.81.

FURTHER READING

Applefeld, Catherine. "Fixture Manufacturers Keep Up with Retailers to Stay Up-to-Date." *Billboard,* 16 September 1995.

"Customization Enhances Retailer Identity." *Chain Store Age Executive with Shopping Center Age,* July 1996.

Darnay, Arsen J., ed. *Manufacturing USA.* 5th ed. Detroit: Gale Research, 1996.

"Fixture Flexibility Is Key: Trend Toward Modular, Customized Units." *Chain Store Age Executive with Shopping Center Age,* October 1995.

Gill, Penny. "Showers of Bath Storage Lines." *HFN: The Weekly Newspaper for the Home Furnishing Network,* 13 January 1997.

Hill, Dawn. "Lee/Rowan Targets Mass Retailers." *HFN: The Weekly Newspaper for the Home Furnishing Network,* 22 January 1996.

Hill, Dawn. "Schulte Adds Wood Laminate." *Discount Store News,* 7 August 1995.

Hill, Dawn. "Taming the Last Frontier: Garages," *HFN: The Weekly Newspaper for the Home Furnishing Network,* 13 January 1997.

Sellers, Pamela. "Kitchen Storage on the Rise." *HFN: The Weekly Newspaper for the Home Furnishing Network,* 13 January 1997.

U.S. Department of Commerce. Census Bureau. *1997 Economic Census.* Washington, DC: GPO, 1999. Available from http://www.census.gov/prod/ec97/97m3372d.pdf.

SIC 2591

DRAPERY HARDWARE AND WINDOW BLINDS AND SHADES

This category covers establishments primarily engaged in the manufacture of curtain and drapery rods, poles, and fixtures; venetian blinds; horizontal mini-blinds; and vertical blinds in all materials except canvas. Establishments primarily engaged in manufacturing canvas window shades and awnings are classified in **SIC 2394: Canvas and Related Products.**

NAICS CODE(S)

337920 (Blind and Shade Manufacturing)

INDUSTRY SNAPSHOT

Companies engaged in the manufacture of drapery hardware and window coverings have witnessed an astounding demand for their wares since the 1980s and have introduced many new types of products to satisfy consumer needs. However, U.S. manufacturers in this category face stiff competition from overseas companies that produce cheap imitations of higher-priced products for the consumer market. The trade gap for this industry is amongst the highest of all industries.

According to figures from the mid-1990s, venetian blinds (horizontal and vertical) made up nearly half the market for window coverings, with slightly more than half of the blinds sold being aluminum. Drapery hardware sales accounted for about 18 percent of the market. The value of shipments generated by this industry increased steadily in the last decade, from $1.7 billion in 1991 to an estimated $2.5 billion in 2000, a clear indication of the growth in this industry. Correspondingly, the drapery hardware and window blinds industry employed 13,600 workers in 1977, but by 2000 the number of workers employed in the industry had increased to an estimated 21,700.

ORGANIZATION AND STRUCTURE

Many of the U.S. firms that manufacture and sell drapery hardware and window blinds are private companies, but some are subsidiaries of much larger publicly-traded home furnishings conglomerates. Like other manufacturers, they are comprised of many specific divisions, but one of the largest concerns is in providing consumers with up-to-date and contemporary styles. For this reason, research and development departments play an important role in companies engaged in manufacturing drapery hardware and window blinds. This division keeps an eye on general trends in consumer lifestyle patterns, home furnishing expenditures, and overall color and pattern changes in the interior design industry. Design analysts in the research and development departments look for certain color groups and textures that they believe will appeal to the broadest range of consumers. For instance, in the 1980s, dramatic changes in the American lifestyle and consumer spending patterns caused by the burgeoning emphasis on high-tech products refashioned the home environment. A new edginess to interior design was manifested in sharp angles and artificial colors, such as mauve. Additionally, a downturn in the economy in the late 1980s, combined with a growing awareness of the concept of the global village, brought a new palette of colors to the window coverings industry and encouraged the introduction of the wood miniblind.

In the interior furnishings industry, window blinds fall under the category of home textiles, although they are not specifically textiles. Previously, curtains and drapes geared to match furniture and bedspreads were the dominant force in the category, but they were replaced by the popularity of miniblinds beginning in the 1980s and continuing through 1997. Consumers switched from buying pinch-pleated draperies and curtains to miniblinds accessorized with a "top treatment"—a swath of fabric that matched some other component of the interior. In the industry, miniblinds, vertical blinds, and pleated shades were first known as "alternative window treatments" to differentiate them from fabric-based draperies and curtains. Today, miniblinds are ubiquitous; they have become a standard in home furnishings. The lower-cost miniblinds, available at discount and chain retailers, have become a booming segment within the industry as a whole.

Manufacturers of miniblind products are divided between the two segments of the market, vinyl and aluminum. Vinyl blinds cost less to manufacture, do not rattle in the wind, and won't develop bend marks. Yet, vinyl blinds are susceptible to flapping on windy days, let a good deal of light through even when completely closed, can become discolored, and have a tendency to lose shape over time. They are popular with consumers, however, because of their low cost, range of standard sizes, relative ease of installation, and ultimate disposability. On the other hand, aluminum blinds are perceived as a much more durable investment. Heavier than vinyl, aluminum blinds do not flap in the breeze, keep out light more effectively, and their colors and finishes will last longer than plastic. Aluminum blinds may scratch a window, however, and can fall victim to surface dents and creases. Major manufacturers such as Hunter Douglas and Levolor concentrate primarily on the custom-made aluminum blind market and have left the vinyl blind market primarily to overseas manufacturers. However, some companies offer stock aluminum blinds in retail outlets and may also sell custom-made vinyl blinds.

In 1996, reports of unsafe miniblinds—particularly those manufactured overseas—led to a massive recall.

The miniblinds were found to contain lead and thus deemed unsafe for home usage, especially those homes with small children. Every retailer took part in the recall by pulling the affected miniblinds from the shelves and giving customers refunds.

Another large segment of the window coverings industry is newly geared to pleated shades to replace standard miniblinds and curtains. The pleated shades owe their development in part to new manufacturing processes that produce versatile fabrics in lightweight weaves to allow a great deal of light through, yet also possess insulating properties. The new processes have also introduced a variety of textures. A leading brand in this new segment of the industry is Duette, a brand manufactured by Hunter Douglas. The product was introduced in 1985 and proved popular with consumers, in part because the pull cord could be hidden. The company has also introduced another version of the pleated shade under the brand name Silhouette. Wood blinds, with their natural appearance, also occupy a growing segment of the window covering market.

In the field of drapery hardware and window coverings, department stores are the primary consumer retail outlets, led by the entrenched home-decorating departments of national chains such as J.C. Penney and Sears. However, the larger stores are being challenged in the home-furnishings market by such specialty retailers as Bed Bath and Beyond. These smaller national outlets provide consumers with either in-stock or custom-made window coverings in a large variety of styles, along with accompanying hardware.

BACKGROUND AND DEVELOPMENT

Prior to the miniblind-dominated era in interior window coverings, there was a relatively limited range of styles and options for consumers. Drapery hardware was relatively standardized and available in a narrow range of styles. Venetian blinds were originally made of wood, but later an aluminum version became ubiquitous. The companies that produced venetian blinds primarily sold them to institutions such as schools and offices. Most interior window treatments in kitchens, bathrooms, and bedrooms consisted of curtains made of a lightweight fabric with a pull-down vinyl shade spanning the window. Despite their popularity in office settings, venetian blinds were in fact found in the home with increasing frequency. It was not uncommon for people to hang blinds in their living rooms and bedrooms, and shades in the kitchen and bathrooms. In living rooms, heavy pinch-pleated draperies were the most popular window accessories, often paired with blinds or shades.

The popularity of the aluminum miniblind helped fuel the tremendous growth of this sector of the U.S. consumer home-furnishings industry. Later, vertical blinds and window shades developed from stronger, light-emitting materials were also introduced. However, in the late 1970s, Taiwan restructured its polyvinylchloride (PVC) manufacturing industry to mass-produce and import miniblinds. This resulted in the flooding of the U.S. market with cheaper plastic versions of the aluminum miniblinds. Manufacturers responded by diversifying their aluminum lines into a greater selection of colors and finishes, producing a competing line of more affordable vinyl blinds and keeping a strong foothold in the custom-made aluminum miniblind market. This has proven to be a popular segment of the window coverings industry. Consumers can take their window measurements to a retail outlet, sift through catalogs of styles, and in a few weeks have custom-crafted aluminum blinds installed throughout their home. These custom-made products accounted for 80 percent of the domestic miniblind market in the early 1990s. Many miniblind manufacturers (aluminum as well as vinyl) offer enough sizes that custom-made blinds are not the only option. Shades can generally be cut to fit any size window.

The drapery hardware segment of the industry has made a concerted effort to come out from behind the scenes. When long, heavy, pinch-pleated draperies were in vogue for so many years, the accompanying hardware was designed to stay hidden. The poles, rods, and tieback elements served a functional need and were correspondingly utilitarian in design. However, the emerging popularity of top treatments for windows—swaths of fabric that added a decorative element to the miniblind or pleat-shade covered window below—paved the way for a new emphasis on drapery hardware. These products are generally manufactured from a variety of metals, including steel, bronze, and brass, but some companies offer poles and rods in numerous wood finishes. Consumers may purchase drapery hardware in a variety of novelty styles. Drapery hardware products are available in both traditional and contemporary styles, and many now have removable decorative elements that give them a greater versatility.

CURRENT CONDITIONS

The economic restructuring and recession of the late 1980s and early 1990s had a negative impact on the drapery hardware and window coverings industry. Sales dropped during these years and, as with other manufacturing industries, some budgetary restructuring and across-the-board layoffs took place.

The industry was also witness to changes in its overall corporate structure through acquisitions and mergers that took place during this period. Companies struggled to hold on to their segment of the consumer-durables market while also introducing products to fill new niches. Consumers became increasingly price-con-

scious and firms competed to offer the best dollar value among a range of similar products. Industry leaders began to introduce more upscale products, such as aluminum blinds with elegant finishes, that appealed to consumers yet were inexpensively priced.

INDUSTRY LEADERS

Many of the top U.S. companies engaged in the manufacture of drapery hardware and window coverings are major corporations. One of the largest is Hunter Douglas, Incorporated of Upper Saddle River, New Jersey. It is a private company founded in 1963 that employs approximately 5,000 workers in the United States. Annual sales figures in the mid-1990s were $600.0 million. It is a subsidiary of the Hunter Douglas Group, which is headquartered in Rotterdam, the Netherlands; the company had worldwide sales of $1.5 billion and 13,500 employees in 1998.

Another corporate giant is Newell Rubbermaid, a major housewares conglomerate that sells window shades and drapery hardware under the brand name Window Furnishings. Based in Freeport, Illinois, the company traces its roots back to 1903 and reported annual sales of $6.4 billion in 1999 (a figure that represents the total for all of its corporate holdings, which include Rubbermaid products glassware, cookware, and hardware companies). In 1993, Newell acquired the Levolor Corporation of San Jose, California. Levolor was founded by the Lorentzen family in 1911, but in recent years, its brand name became nearly synonymous with the miniblind. At its peak, Levolor's annual sales neared $300.0 million, and it held onto a 40 percent share of the market. But during the 1980s, the company was beset by internal squabbling and suffered as a result. Instead of cultivating and maintaining valuable accounts with industry distributors, it instead concentrated on selling directly to the consumer and subsequently lost some major distributor accounts to more aggressive competitors. Sales declined, and in 1988 the company was sold to an investment firm for only $135.0 million. Newell also acquired drapery hardware and window coverings giant Kirsch, which in the mid-1990s had sales of $250.0 million.

Other leading companies in the window coverings manufacturing industry include Springs Windows Fashions, a division of Springs Industries, based in Fort Mill, South Carolina, whose brands include Bali, Nanik, and Graber; and Home Fashions, Incorporated of Westminster, California, which sells its products under the Del Mar brand name. The company employed 1,000 workers and reported 1998 sales figures of $110 million.

WORKFORCE

The workforce engaged in manufacturing drapery hardware and window coverings numbered 17,300 in

1991. More recent figures show that the industry's employment figures have continuously increased and should reach approximately 21,700 by 2000. Among these workers, roughly two-thirds are in the production sectors.

AMERICA AND THE WORLD

The relative ease with which window coverings can be manufactured by overseas companies, primarily in Taiwan, and exported into the U.S. market has negatively impacted the window coverings segment of this industry. The domestic drapery hardware business, meanwhile, has been invaded by a leading German manufacturer, Blome, which entered the U.S. market in 1991. The company has mainly distributed its products through intermediary outlets but also planned to market its wares in upscale department stores.

RESEARCH AND TECHNOLOGY

Industry critics of vinyl blinds, which are primarily imported from Taiwan, have decried their saturation in the U.S. market and charge that the imported products are not subject to the same lead content restrictions as U.S. manufacturers. Critics charge that the Taiwanese vinyl blinds are ecologically unsound, since they will eventually wind up in American landfills and take decades to disintegrate.

FURTHER READING

Burmingham, Geoffrey B. "An Old Favorite Is Back As a Window Dressing." *Orlando Sentinel,* 25 September 1999.

Moody's Industrial Manual 1999. New York: Moody's Investors Service.

SIC 2599

FURNITURE AND FIXTURES, NOT ELSEWHERE CLASSIFIED

This classification covers establishments primarily engaged in manufacturing furniture and fixtures, not elsewhere classified, including hospital beds and furniture specially designed for use in restaurants, bars, cafeterias, bowling centers, and ships.

NAICS CODE(S)

339113 (Surgical Appliance and Supplies Manufacturing)
337127 (Institutional Furniture Manufacturing)

According to the U.S. Census Bureau, 726 establishments made products in this classification in 1997. They shipped $2.3 billion worth of goods, spent $1.0 billion on materials, and paid $58.0 million for buildings and other structures, machinery, and equipment. The 162 establishments that manufactured merchandise in this category as their primary business shipped $1.3 billion worth of goods, spent $627.0 million on materials, and paid $32 million for capital expenditures.

The manufacturing of furniture and fixtures in this category primarily arose to fill specific needs within the service industry market. For instance, after World War II, the rise of bowling as a recreational sport necessitated the construction of a plethora of alleys across the United States to satisfy a growing demand. The factories and manufacturing plants that were built across the country needed specific interior furniture for a wide variety of purposes also, so this industry filled the needs of the growing industrial economy of the United States. Later, as orders for factory furniture declined due to the drop in overall manufacturing, the furniture and fixtures industry accommodated other segments of the economy. Hospital furniture manufacturing firms met the increased demand for new beds as medical facilities were built to serve more populous suburban communities. The growing consumer willingness to spend more entertainment dollars on dining out during the 1970s and 1980s fueled the construction of restaurants and the corresponding need for sturdy yet attractive furniture to fill them.

In 1996 nearly 47 percent, or $1.3 billion, of the industry's shipments were miscellaneous commercial products such as furniture for bowling alleys, factories, and ships, followed by commercial foodservice fixtures at 40 percent, or $1.1 billion, and hospital beds at 12.8 percent, or $366.0 million. The industry's 1995 performance reflected a 66 percent increase over 1985 dollar shipments.

The Census Bureau estimated that in 1997 this industry shipped about $1 billion worth of merchandise for restaurants, cafeterias, bars, and bowling centers. This included $149 million worth of wooden upholstered chairs and stools, up from $146 million in 1992; $37 million worth of wooden nonupholstered chairs and stools, up from $29 million in 1992; $89 million worth of metal chairs and stools, up from $78 million in 1992; and $106 million worth of booths, bars, and back bars, up from $101 million in 1992.

In 1997 the industry also shipped about $113 million worth of industrial work benches and stools, up from $63 million in 1992; $2 million worth of wooden drafting and drawing tables; and $607 million worth of items such as ship furniture and amusement game cabinets, up from $293 million in 1992.

California shipped about $147 million worth of products in this category in 1997. Shipments from Tennessee totaled $131 million, and shipments from Missouri totaled $81 million. Arkansas, Florida, Illinois,

Massachusetts, Michigan, Minnesota, and Wisconsin also shipped large amounts of merchandise in this classification.

Kinetic Concepts Inc. (San Antonio, Texas) was the largest company primarily engaged in the production of furniture and fixtures in this category. This hospital bed manufacturer had 2,100 employees and $330.5 million in revenues in 1998, up from $270 million in 1996 and $278 million in 1992.

Hill-Rom Inc., a subsidiary of Hillenbrand Industries Inc. (Batesville, Indiana), was another leading hospital bed firm. As of 1997 it claimed top sales in the electrically powered bed category. Hill-Rom employed approximately 3,700 people that year. Hillenbrand had 10,400 employees and sales of $2 billion in 1998. In the mid-1990s Kinetic Concepts and Hill-Rom had both filed antitrust charges with the U.S. Department of Justice. Kinetic Concepts accused Hill-Rom of attempting to monopolize the hospital bed market, and Hill-Rom countered by alleging that Kinetic Concepts was trying to monopolize the therapeutic bed market.

Other large companies competing in this industry included Restoration Hardware Inc. (Corte Madera, California); Invacare Corp. (Elyria, Ohio); Sunrise Medical Inc. (Carlsbad, California); Kimball International Inc. (Jasper, Indiana); Shelby Williams Industries Inc. (Chicago, Illinois); and Falcon Products Inc. (St. Louis, Missouri).

According to the Census Bureau, 22,347 people were employed in this industry in 1997, including 16,474 production workers who earned an average hourly wage of $11.51. Establishments that made goods in this category as their primary business employed 11,073 people, including 8,166 production workers who earned an average hourly wage of $11.62.

FURTHER READING

Darnay, Arsen J., ed. *Manufacturing USA.* 5th ed. Detroit: Gale Research, 1996.

Falcon Products, Inc. *Annual Report.* St. Louis, 1997.

Hillenbrand Industries, Inc. *Annual Report.* Batesville, IN, 1997.

Kimball International, Inc. *Annual Report.* Jasper, IN, 1996.

Kinetic Concepts, Inc. *Annual Report.* San Antonio, TX, 1997.

Shelby Williams Industries, Inc. *Annual Report.* Chicago, 1997.

U.S. Department of Commerce. Census Bureau. *1996 Annual Survey of Manufactures.* Washington, DC: GPO, 1998.

U.S. Department of Commerce. Census Bureau. *1997 Economic Census.* Washington, D.C.: GPO, 1999. Available from http://www.census.gov/prod/ec97/97m3371f.pdf.

PAPER & ALLIED PRODUCTS

SIC 2611

PULP MILLS

This category covers establishments primarily engaged in manufacturing pulp from wood or from other materials, such as rags, linters, wastepaper, and straw. Establishments engaged in integrating logging and pulp mill operations are classified according to the primary products shipped. Establishments engaged in integrated operations of producing pulp and manufacturing paper, paperboard, or products thereof are classified in **SIC 2621: Paper Mills** if primarily shipping paper or paper products; in **SIC 2631: Paperboard Mills** if primarily shipping paperboard or paperboard products; and in **SIC 2611: Pulp Mills** if primarily shipping pulp. Establishments primarily engaged in cutting pulpwood are classified in **SIC 2411: Logging.**

NAICS CODE(S)
322110 (Pulp Mills)
322121 (Paper (except Newsprint) Mills)
322130 (Paperboard Mills)

INDUSTRY SNAPSHOT
The U.S. pulp industry is by far the world's largest. In 1998 the United States produced 58.1 million metric tons of wood pulp, representing 33.1 percent of the 175.5 million metric tons produced worldwide. The next largest producer, Canada, produced 23.5 million metric tons. U.S. pulp mills make a wide variety of pulps for making paper and paperboard. Most of the pulp made in the United States is chemical pulp, which is produced by a chemical digesting process that converts wood chips into pulp by chemically liberating the cellulose fibers from the lignin that holds them together in the wood. Mechanical pulps are made with large "grinders" that physically shred the wood pulp into individual fibers. Some processes combine elements of mechanical and chemical pulping.

After the wood chips are digested or ground, they are called wood pulp. This wood pulp is cleaned, screened, and refined. If the pulp will be used for white paper, it is bleached (otherwise the pulp retains its natural brown color). At this point, the pulp is ready to be used in papermaking. Various grades of pulp can be made from softwood trees such as southern pine, hardwood trees such as oak, or from other sources that include recovered paper, rags, or agricultural products such as cotton linters, kenaf, bagasse, or straw.

In 1998 there were approximately 345 U.S. wood pulp mills producing a variety of pulps, down from 351 in 1997. Most of this pulp was used in integrated pulp and paper mills, which means that the pulp mill and the paper mill were owned by the same company and operated in many cases at the same location. There were numerous smaller paper mills, however, that were not connected with a pulp mill; they purchased "market pulp" on the open market from other pulp producers. Some companies produced only market pulp; other companies sold the excess pulp that could not be used by their paper machines.

ORGANIZATION AND STRUCTURE
U.S. pulp mills maintain a dominant share of the U.S. market for pulp—about 90 percent in 1998—and are also very strong competitors in global markets. One reason for this market strength is good economic fundamentals—U.S. pulp mills have access to low cost and abundant raw materials, a highly trained work force, and they operate world-class plants and equipment.

In most cases, pulp mills need to be located near their raw materials—trees or wastepaper—to minimize transportation costs. The United States has a very large growing stock of pulpwood in several areas: the Pacific Northwest, the upper Midwest, the Northeast, and the Southeast. This, combined with an efficient manufacturing base, makes the United States the low cost producer of many grades of pulp throughout the world. However, by the late 1990s, that position as low-cost producer was being challenged by a new generation of pulp mills, largely in South America and Southeast Asia. These mills have access to fast-growing hardwood and softwood fiber, which dramatically reduces operating costs. Many new, world-class pulp mills were built in South America and Southeast Asia in the 1990s, while virtually none were built in the United States and Canada. This new capacity made the global pulp market very competitive and, consequently, increased the volatility of pulp prices.

While the pulping and papermaking processes are very energy intensive, the industry has become an efficient user of energy by burning its own waste byproducts, such as tree bark and spent chemicals from the pulping process. In the late 1990s the pulp and paper industry generated well over half of the energy needed to run its mills. From the early 1970s to the mid-1990s, the industry reduced oil consumption by nearly 66 percent and natural gas consumption by 10 percent while increasing production capacity by 60 percent. Some mills even generate excess power and sell it back to local utilities.

Pulp mills and paper mills use a large amount of water from lakes, rivers and, in some cases, oceans. They must reuse and/or clean all of this water before it is returned to the body of water from which it came. In the early years of the industry, pulp mills would discharge untreated waste (effluent) back into the receiving body of water. Beginning in the late 1960s, however, the industry began operating under strict water use regulations that required primary, secondary and, in some cases, tertiary treatment of wastewater. These rules were tightened considerably during the following decades. Also, to cut down on treatment costs, mills reuse a large portion of the water they used elsewhere in the pulping and papermaking process. The process of cleaning and reusing water is commonly called ''closing the mill.''

In the mid-1990s, it took 65 percent less water to make a ton of paper than it did about two decades earlier. The water that cannot be reused goes to large outdoor water treatment plants. By 1999 the biochemical oxygen demand (BOD) of the treated water—a measure of environmental impact—had been reduced by more than 70 percent from 1974, even though total paper production increased more than 50 percent.

Captive Pulp. The vast majority of pulp produced in the United States—87.4 percent in 1998—is considered ''captive'' because it is used in an integrated pulp and

paper operation and is not sold on the open market. Market pulp sold on domestic and foreign markets accounted for the remaining 12.6 percent of total U.S. pulp production. While captive pulp accounts for the majority of pulp used in the United States, much more information and documentation is available for market pulp since it is bought and sold publicly.

The percentage of virgin wood fiber used in paper and board production in the United States and other countries has been steadily declining. Wood fiber, as a percentage of total global paper and board production, dropped from about 75 percent in 1970 to below 60 percent in 1998.

This decline is explained by several trends. While virgin wood fiber has long been the fiber of choice in most advanced papermaking operations, it is coming under sustained challenge from other fiber sources. For example, the use of recovered (recycled) paper is increasing dramatically and has displaced large amounts of virgin wood fiber in the pulping market. The increased use of recovered paper has been driven partly by society's desire to reduce the amount of paper going to landfills and partly by pulp producers realizing that virgin fiber will be increasingly hard to sustain in years to come.

North American paper producers have dramatically increased their use of recovered paper in recent years. The percentage of paper recycled in the United States rose from about 30 percent (of total paper produced) in 1990 to 47 percent in 1998. In the mid-1990s, growth in consumption of recovered paper was far out-pacing the underlying capacity growth at U.S. paper and paperboard mills. U.S. mill consumption of recovered paper rose 9.2 percent in 1996, or about two and a half times the rate of total paper and paperboard capacity growth. From 1997 to 1999, recovered paper consumption increased at an average rate of 2.9 percent, about twice the pace of paper and paperboard capacity growth during the same three-year period.

Virgin wood fiber also faces a challenge from the growing use of mineral coatings and inert fillers, mainly in printing and writing papers. Producers of these grades have completed a long-term shift from acid pulp to alkaline pulp. One reason for this shift is that paper produced from acid pulp becomes brittle and breaks up over time, while alkaline papers tend to last longer. The main reason, however, is that alkaline papermaking tends to be less expensive since it permits greater use of fillers, such as calcium carbonate, that replace a percentage of the wood fiber in the finished paper. In U.S. printing and writing papers, such as copy paper, the amount of filler can be 10 to 20 percent of the finished paper. The cost of fillers is about one third that of wood pulp, so paper mills have a financial incentive to increase their use of fillers. Papermakers use filler not only to reduce the amount of wood fiber used, but also to increase the smoothness and opacity of their finished products. As techniques to use more filler are developed, wood pulp will be displaced.

While the percentage of wood pulp in finished paper products will continue to decline, the use of wood pulp will still grow—at least slightly—as the entire market for paper expands. Global production of wood pulp should grow, on average, about 2 percent per year worldwide during the first two decades of the twenty-first century. In the United States, wood pulp will probably grow more slowly since growth in recycled fiber will be strong. For example, U.S. wood pulp capacity was projected to rise just 0.5 percent per year between 1999 and 2001. However, foreign markets will likely absorb an increasing amount of U.S. market wood pulp.

Chemical Pulp. Within the overall market for wood pulp, the use of chemical pulp—mostly kraft pulp, which is produced using the sulfate process—is increasing. In 1998 chemical pulp accounted for 69.7 percent of all pulp produced throughout the world, up from 66.0 percent in 1970. This figure was expected to reach 70.2 percent in 2001. In the United States, chemical pulp accounts for an even higher percentage of wood pulp capacity—82.2 percent in 1998. Semichemical pulp accounted for about 6.1 percent and mechanical pulp for 10.1 percent in 1995, with other grades accounting for the remaining 1.6 percent. The trend toward greater use of chemical pulp is driven by the need for greater strength as papermakers begin to blend less costly and weaker mechanical pulps and recycled paper fibers into the furnish they use to make paper.

As it has been for some time, chemical paper grade pulp was the primary product of the U.S. market wood pulp industry in the 1990s. In 1999 total U.S. market wood pulp capacity was 10.37 million tons. U.S. chemical paper grade market pulp mills held the vast majority of that total, at 9.27 million tons, while market dissolving pulp, at 1.10 million tons, accounted for the remainder. The two primary market chemical pulp grades in 1999 were bleached softwood kraft pulp, at 5.32 million tons, and bleached hardwood, at 3.32 million tons.

Overall, U.S. market wood pulp capacity was expected to essentially remain flat through the late 1990s and early 2000s. While some small fluctuations are expected, total market wood pulp capacity was expected to rise by a total of just 1.5 percent between 1997 and 2001, from 10.50 million tons to 10.66 million tons. The main reason for this stagnant market is that U.S. paper mills are using more recycled fiber than ever before.

The United States had 35.0 percent of the world's capacity to produce paper and paperboard in 1998 and 33.4 percent of the world's capacity to produce wood pulp. As mentioned earlier, the majority of U.S. paper

mills are integrated with captive pulp mills that do not sell pulp on the open market. Despite this fact, the United States is a major importer and exporter of market pulp. In 1998 the United States produced 8.57 million tons of market wood pulp, exported 5.94 million tons, and imported 4.15 million tons.

BACKGROUND AND DEVELOPMENT

Before the U.S. Civil War, paper was made exclusively from rags in the United States and around the world. Rag collection for papermaking was a major part of the U.S. economy. However, as the demand for paper continued to increase, the demand for rags began to outstrip supply.

This changed between 1851 and 1918 when wood pulp was invented, developed, and industrialized. The Civil War created a huge demand for both paper and rags; this helped spur research into using the fiber from trees for papermaking. This time period saw the development and commercialization of all the major wood pulping processes, including groundwood, soda, and sulphite and kraft (sulphate). Wood pulp quickly reduced the cost of papermaking, allowing the use of paper in new applications and new products.

Soda pulping was invented by Burgess and Watt in England and was patented in 1854 in the United States. Groundwood became established in the 1860s. The first chemical wood pulp was manufactured in 1864 in Manyunk, Pennsylvania, and the first kraft pulp mill came on line in 1909. Kraft pulping had been invented in 1884 by German chemist Carl Dahl using sodium sulfate as the pulping agent. The pulp produced a strong brown paper, which was then described with the German word for strong: kraft.

While other materials were used for pulping—including bagasse cactus, cudweed, straw, cornstalks and even cow dung—wood pulp quickly became the preferred source of pulp. By the 1870s, pulp mills were springing up in heavily forested areas such as New York, Massachusetts, Michigan, Ohio, and Wisconsin. These areas continued to develop as key pulp and paper regions throughout the early twentieth century and most remained so in the early 1990s.

The science of pulping continued to develop along with the growth of papermaking. Major pulping milestones included the invention of the recovery boiler, in which spent pulping chemicals are burned. This process recovers the energy in the chemicals and the chemicals themselves, which can then be reused. Another milestone was the development of the continuous digester, which replaced the slower batch digesting process.

More recently, in the 1980s, entire pulp mills were rebuilt to increase capacity and quality. Popular additions included new chip screening, handling and storage systems, new digester cooking controls, new washing systems, more screening and cleaning, new bleaching systems emphasizing oxygen, and better mixing. Pulp and paper mills also took advantage of process control to more closely control the process and produce better quality products.

The U.S. pulp industry in the 1990s saw much price fluctuation. In the early to mid-1990s low pulp prices and high levels of spending required to meet environmental demands depressed the U.S. pulp industry to such an extent that few if any pulp producers were profitable. By 1993 after factoring out inflation, the price of pulp was the lowest it had been in decades. However, in 1994, pulp prices began a meteoric rise that saw prices double in less than two years. The price for northern bleached softwood kraft market pulp (NBSK), a common benchmark for pulp producers, averaged $566 per metric ton in 1994 (during the year, prices increased from a low of $440 per metric ton at the beginning of the year to $700 per metric ton at year end). In 1995 the price for NBSK averaged $871 per metric ton, and many pulp producers reaped record profits (prices during the year increased from a low of $750 per metric ton at the beginning of 1995 to $910 per metric ton at year end). However, 1996 saw a steep fall in pulp prices. For the year, the average price for NBSK was $591 per metric ton, falling from a high of $860 per metric ton in the first quarter of 1996 to a low of $500 per metric ton in the second quarter. Prices recovered to $600 per metric ton at the end of 1996. Prices stayed in this range for the rest of the decade; in October 1999 the price per metric ton of NBSK was just $560. However, at the beginning of 2000, market pulp was in short supply and prices were expected to rise in one of the pulp market's cyclical recoveries.

CURRENT CONDITIONS

Water Regulations. Environmental pressure on pulp mills continues in three areas: water regulations, recycling, and timber harvesting. The most recent wave of water regulations has been spurred by the desire to eliminate or reduce to non-detectable levels the toxic chemical dioxin, which was discovered in small amounts in pulp mill water-borne effluent in the mid-1980s. Despite the lack of hard evidence that dioxin in minute quantities poses a human health risk, the paper industry voluntarily spent more than $1 billion to reduce dioxin discharges by more than 90 percent by the mid-1990s.

In 1993 the Environmental Protection Agency (EPA) proposed new regulations further restricting dioxin emissions by pulp mills, among other toxic chemicals. These regulations resulted from research the EPA had begun in the late 1980s when it formed a "pulp and paper cluster group" to coordinate regulatory actions involving the pulp and paper industry.

The EPA's pulp and paper cluster group focused on two major rule-making efforts. The first involved issuing revised effluent guidelines mandated by the Clean Water Act and required by a consent decree signed by the EPA after being sued by environmental groups over dioxin discharges from pulp mills. The second area involved defining maximum achievable control technology (MACT) emissions standards for pulp and paper mills, which was required under the Clean Air Act Amendments of 1990.

The Clean Air Act Amendments dramatically changed the allowable types and amounts of emissions. Based on emissions such as ozone, carbon monoxide, and particulates, regions of the United States can be classified as "nonattainment areas." These areas's pulp mills, like other industries, can be subject to severe restrictions.

While formulating new regulations, the EPA worked with the pulp industry through the "stakeholders" process. This allowed the pulp industry to develop new testing and process treatment methods; to introduce scientific data and research; and to offer advice on the environmental, economic, and industrial impact of EPA's findings. Through this cooperation, standards regulating chemical oxygen demand (COD), biochemical oxygen demand (BOD), color and absorbable organic halides (AOX) were revamped and made less costly to the industry. Final Cluster Rule regulations were issued on April 15, 1998, and the pulp and paper industry had up to three years from that date to comply with the new regulations.

The late 1990s resolved one controversy regarding pulp bleaching that arose in the early 1990s. Advocates of totally chlorine bleaching (TCF), in which no chlorine compounds are used to bleach pulp (including chlorine dioxide), argued that the process was environmentally superior to elemental chlorine free (ECF) bleaching, which uses chlorine dioxide. While the TCF process has some following in Europe, it has not caught on in the United States; no regulations have been passed requiring TCF bleaching. As a result, just two pulp mills in the United States were producing TCF pulp as of 1999.

Recycling. The second major environmental trend affecting the pulp industry is recycling. Public interest in paper recycling, driven by concerns about a potential landfill crisis, began to build in the late 1980s and peaked in the early 1990s. Consensus on landfills does not yet exist, as studies in the mid- to late 1990s suggested the landfill crisis to be less of a threat than previously reported.

Nonetheless, the push for recycling—primarily through federal and state legislation—continues, and paper companies now are marketing a wide variety of new recycled grades. Much of the new pulping capacity being built or planned uses wastepaper instead of virgin fiber as its raw material; this change has had a major impact on traditional pulping of wood fiber.

Much of the impetus for recycling came from government, and various local, state, and federal government rules still regulate the recycling process. Many of these laws specify precise levels of "postconsumer" content (paper that has been used and discarded by a consumer) and restrict the amount of "preconsumer" wastepaper that can be used. Examples of preconsumer wastepaper might include trimmings from the printing or papermaking process, unsalable newspapers, or overprints of magazines. There is, however, considerable disagreement over where the line should be drawn between postconsumer and preconsumer.

Paper companies also face other recycling regulations, including restrictions on products' use of "green labeling" claims; limits on permissible types of packaging; strict requirements on secondary fiber content; procurement preferences for certain kinds of recycled paper; and surcharges on paper products not meeting certain recycled standards. Consumers in some localities are required to collect and separate wastepaper for recycling.

Demand for recycled paper and recycling regulations are significant for pulp producers because they must manufacture the recycled pulp to be used in making the paper that meets the specifications. Throughout the 1990s, the pulp and paper industry responded by building large numbers of recycled paper processing plants. However, while paper recycling is an important part of waste minimization, it is only part of what is needed to reduce the generation of solid waste. It should also be noted that recycling itself generates a considerable waste stream. In recycled newsprint pulp mills, for example, only 85 percent of incoming newsprint is usable as fiber. The rest is unusable sludge that must be cleaned out of the process and then burned or placed in landfills. In some recycled grades, sludge can be up to 50 percent of the incoming waste paper.

Timber Harvesting. The third major environmental challenge facing pulp mills in the 1990s and early 2000s is timber harvesting, which is used to create lumber products as well as pulpwood. Access to pulpwood is vital for all virgin wood pulp mills, but that access has been severely restricted in some areas—most notably the Pacific Northwest. Court decisions in the early 1990s reduced harvesting drastically in many national forests and other federal areas in the Northwest. Through the Endangered Species Act, environmental groups filed successful lawsuits restricting harvesting in order to protect the northern spotted owl, among other species. While the Clinton Administration attempted to broker a compromise between timber interests and environmentalists in 1993, harvests throughout the remainder of the 1990s remained at about one-sixth the level of those in the 1980s.

This situation has led some pulp mills in the Northwest to close and others to seek raw materials from different sources, such as recycled paper and foreign wood chips. The long term effects are likely to permanently reduce tree harvesting and pulping in the Pacific Northwest, and pulp producers in foreign countries and the southern United States are likely to take up the lost volume. Indeed the U.S. Southeast saw a large increase in the number of chip mills operating in the late 1990s. Unlike the U.S. Northwest, where government agencies own the majority of timber-producing land, about 70 percent of forestland in the U.S. Southeast is privately owned, either by corporations or individuals. Private owners were selling more timber in the late 1990s, largely to make up for shortages in the Northwest. However, this increased volume of timber harvesting led to a backlash of protest by some environmental groups and other concerned parties.

Forest product companies and pulp and paper companies around the country still face pressure from environmental groups and government bodies to change their harvesting practices. Many groups want to eliminate clearcutting, which the industry argues is the most efficient harvesting method and is environmentally sustainable, provided that the clear cut is replanted. In the late 1990s, the U.S. forest products industries—which include the pulp industry—planted more trees than they cut down. In 1997 member companies of the American Forest & Paper Association reforested 1.3 million acres by planting, seeding, and natural regeneration. The effect of tree planting on government, corporate, and private land is that the net amount of forested land in the United States is actually increasing. From the early 1980s to the late 1990s, forest growth has exceeded the volume of trees cut or burned in forest fires. From the early 1970s to the late 1990s, the number of trees growing in the United States increased by 22 percent. Even in areas where the pulp and paper industry has access to virgin fiber, however, there is concern that the industry is effectively using all the pulpwood that is currently available and there may be shortages of virgin fiber. This potential shortage is one reason almost no new virgin pulp mills were being built in the United States during the late 1990s. Pulp producers hope that by improving the growth rate of trees through genetic research, they will be able to increase the amount of wood grown on the same amount of land.

The Business Cycle. Aside from environmental challenges, in the early to mid-1990s, U.S. pulp mills experienced volatile swings between profits and losses. When demand began to increase again in early 1994, there was little excess capacity to supply the new demand. Pulp prices surged dramatically and quickly, reaching $910 per metric ton by the third quarter of 1995. Market pulp producers again enjoyed record profits, and speculation centered on pulp prices remaining high into the next century. However, much of the run-up in pulp prices appeared to be caused by customers stocking up on inventory in anticipation of future price increases. When these customers stopped taking new shipments of pulp, prices dropped dramatically. Also, by the late 1990s, U.S. pulp producers were being directly affected by very large pulping capacity additions in Asia and South America. These trends appear to have made U.S. pulp producers very cautious about future capacity increases. Total U.S. wood pulp capacity—including market pulp and captive pulp—is slated to rise slightly from 70.66 million tons in 1998 to 71.64 million tons in 2001, an average annual growth rate of just 0.5 percent.

INDUSTRY LEADERS

Weyerhaeuser Company. Based in Tacoma, Washington, Weyerhaeuser has several core businesses, including growing and harvesting timber and manufacturing and distributing forest products (including logs, wood chips, building products, pulp, paper, and packaging products). In 1998, Weyerhaeuser had total sales of $10.77 billion and pulp, paper, and converted product sales of $4.38 billion. It was the largest producer of market pulp in the United States in 1998, with 2.22 million tons. In 1998, the company had 35,000 employees and owned 5.1 million acres of commercial forestland in the United States, with about half in the South and the other half in the Pacific Northwest. The company also had license arrangements on 18.9 million acres of Canadian forestland. In 1999, the company was poised to dramatically increase both its timber holdings and its market pulp production through its acquisition of MacMillan Bloedel, a large Canadian forest products company.

Georgia-Pacific Corporation. Atlanta-based Georgia-Pacific Group (G-P) has major interests in building products, pulp and paper, and paper chemicals. In 1998, G-P had total sales of $13.22 billion, including pulp, paper, and converted product sales of $5.65 billion. In addition to many other products, G-P is the world's second largest producer of market pulp, owning six mills with a combined annual capacity of 2.1 million tons in 1998, about 20 percent of U.S. market pulp capacity. G-P produces southern softwood, southern hardwood, and northern hardwood pulps for use in the manufacture of many paper grades. G-P is also a major supplier of fluff pulp (used in disposable diapers) and other specialty pulps. G-P exports about 60 percent of its market pulp.

International Paper Company. Founded in 1898 by the merger of 18 northeastern pulp and paper companies, International Paper Company (IP) was the world's largest pulp and paper company in 1998. In that year IP had total sales of $19.54 billion, which included $16.71 billion worth of pulp, paper, and converted product sales. World-

wide, IP produced 1.9 million tons of market pulp in 1998 for the paper, packaging, and specialty products industries. From the United States, IP exports market pulp to more than 40 countries. Some of IP's market pulp grades include Supersoft fluff pulp for hygiene products and dissolving pulp grades such as Estercell and Solvekraft, used for yarns, films, and plastics.

Parsons & Whittemore. While not among the largest pulp and paper companies in the United States, Parsons & Whittemore produces only market pulp and is the fourth largest U.S. producer of market pulp, making an estimated 1.2 million tons in 1998. The privately-held company, based in Rye Brook, New York, produced market pulp at three units in 1998: Alabama River and Alabama Pine in Perdue Hill, Alabama, and St. Anne-Nackawic Pulp Co. in New Brunswick, New Jersey.

Bowater. Bowater Incorporated, a pulp and paper company based in Greenville, South Carolina, became the fifth largest U.S. producer of market pulp when it purchased Avenor, a Canadian firm, in 1998. Bowater's total sales in 1998 (including Avenor) were $1.99 billion, and its pulp, paper, and converted product sales were $1.83 million. In 1998 Bowater produced 1.13 million tons of market pulp from four pulp mills. About 85 percent of its market pulp production was exported. Bowater says it is the only North American supplier with a mix of four grades of market pulp: southern hardwood and softwood pulps, and northern hardwood and softwood pulps.

WORKFORCE

Total employment in the pulp, paper, and converted product industries was 634,000 in 1997, with pulp mills accounting for about 10,300 of that total. The level of employment in pulp mills declined during the 1990s despite substantial capacity increases. Employee wage increases remained at or below the inflation rate in the 1990s, averaging about 2.2 percent. These increases were far below the average 7.5 percent annual increases recorded during the period from 1975 to 1985.

Like other manufacturing industries, the pulp and paper industry employs many unionized workers. However, the heaviest concentrations of union employees are in older mills that were organized years ago. Almost all new pulp and paper mills are nonunion operations, including mills constructed by companies with unionized mills in other locations. In general, the wages and benefits provided by nonunion mills are comparable to unionized mills.

There was relative labor peace in the pulp and paper industry during the 1980s and 1990s. In exchange for salary increases, management was able to obtain work rule changes that allowed workers to perform more jobs in the mill and eliminate pay differentials for Sunday and holiday pay. There were no major work stoppages in the pulp and paper industry during the 1990s.

AMERICA AND THE WORLD

Market pulp is a truly global commodity, with prices changing quickly in response to capacity changes, inventory levels, and purchase levels. While market pulp is produced in about 25 countries, more than two-thirds of world output comes from five northern countries: the United States, Canada, Sweden, Finland, and Norway. Global demand for wood pulp was 175.5 million metric tons in 1998. Non-wood pulp demand was more than 20 million metric tons in 1998.

Southern Hemisphere pulp producers expanded their operations extensively during the mid-1990s. New, technologically advanced market pulp mills were built in China, Indonesia, Brazil, Chile, and Argentina. Some of these mills include North American pulp and paper companies as investors. One major advantage of mills in South America and Southeast Asia is access to incredibly fast-growing pulpwood trees, such as eucalyptus and radiata pine species. These trees reach pulping maturity in about seven years or less, compared to 30 years in some northern countries. Other advantages of these new pulp mills include lower operating costs, lower labor costs, and less costly environmental regulation. Established pulp producers will need to carefully control costs and increase productivity in order to compete with these new market factors.

Increased Foreign Demand. In the mid- to late 1990s, production in the U.S. market wood pulp industry was relatively flat due to excess capacity in world markets, flat or declining domestic markets, and growing use of secondary fiber. That situation continued into the late 1990s, and U.S. market pulp capacity was expected to grow only 0.5 percent annually from 1999 to 2001.

U.S. wood pulp exports are a relatively small, but still significant, portion of total U.S. wood pulp production. In 1998 the United States produced 64.1 million tons of wood pulp and exported 8.05 million tons. Japan and South Korea have traditionally been the largest U.S. market pulp customers.

Despite producing and exporting large volumes of market pulp, the U.S. pulp and paper industry still imports a substantial amount. In 1998 the United States imported 4.2 million tons of market wood pulp. These imports accounted for less than 10 percent of total U.S. wood pulp consumption. Canada has traditionally been the leading U.S. supplier, accounting for around 83 percent of the total in 1998.

Reasons To Import. While the United States has the capacity to supply all the pulp it needs for domestic paper production, it still imports pulp in order to exploit the different properties of foreign market pulp. The domestic market pulp industry is largely based on southern pine and hardwood, and many U.S. mills prefer the special properties of other grades, such as NBSK produced in Canada, and eucalyptus pulp produced in countries such as Brazil. At the same time, a large number of foreign paper mills covet the southern pine and hardwood market pulp produced by U.S. market pulp mills.

Despite sluggish growth and new foreign competition, the United States was expected to remain a strong global market pulp competitor into the 2000s. The combination of relatively low cost fiber resources, energy and water supplies, and improvement in product technology and operating conditions will likely allow the U.S. pulp industry to remain the leader among world producers. However, competition for sales in the United States and overseas has intensified as foreign pulp and paper producers in developing regions such as Latin America, Asia, and Eastern Europe improve pulp quality and compete harder in major consuming markets in North America, Asia, and Europe. One major change in the global pulp market was the mid-1990s launch of pulp futures markets. While these markets were not an immediate success and trading volume remained under expectations into the late 1990s, there was enough trading volume to sustain at least one market, the Pulpex/Finnish Options Exchange. It was hoped that futures markets, widely used to trade futures in commodity products—such as copper, aluminum, sugar, and coffee—would bring more price stability to the pulp market and even out some of the extreme price fluctuations that have plagued the global market pulp industry.

RESEARCH AND TECHNOLOGY

Pulping processes, both chemical and mechanical, are likely to see continued improvement in research and technology. Pulp mills will focus on higher energy recovery, which can then be used in other mill processes. This will be essential to the future profitability of many mills facing competition from mills with lower cost structures. Energy is already a major cost for the pulp and paper industry, which is one of the largest industrial users of electricity. Other areas of improvement include the use of additives to speed up the chemical digesting process to increase fiber yields; new technical and environmental processes to reduce air and water pollution; and increased process control, monitoring, and automation. Similar measures to keep costs down and productivity high will be needed for the industry to remain competitive and expand its market share in world pulp consuming markets.

With more and more regulatory attention focused on pulp mill emissions, more research has been devoted to the "effluent free" mill, also called the "closed mill." In theory, the closed mill perfectly balances all the "inputs and outputs" to the pulping and papermaking process so that the mill reuses, recycles, or cleans all waste materials. This would mean that the mill produces no air or water pollution. There have been several totally closed pulp mills built, but these are groundwood pulp mills, not the kraft (chemical) pulp mills that are much more common.

Widely regarded as impossible just a decade ago, the closed kraft pulp mill appears to be feasible provided that current technology continues to develop and the cost of implementation decreases. For example, the Institute of Paper Science and Technology has been directed by its member companies to increase its research efforts on how heat and contaminants build up in closed pulping and papermaking systems; where the optimum "purge" points are in the process; and how to deal with the increased metal corrosion in closed systems. Many industry experts consider the truly closed kraft pulp mill to be a decade or two away. However, others argue that an effluent free mill, while feasible, may not be practical in that it will be too costly to implement. They argue that the industry should focus on the "minimum impact mill," which, while producing some effluent, does not harm the environment in any substantial way.

Another major research area affecting pulp mills is in high yield forestry. The industry needs to reduce the time it takes to produce a mature pulpwood tree from 28 years to about 7 or 8 years. There are two reasons for this. One is to compete with pulpwood from countries such as Brazil, which today can produce a mature pulpwood tree in seven years. The other is to reduce the amount of forestland used for harvesting trees. There is a great deal of pressure on the pulp industry to minimize its harvesting operations, and if it can produce the same amount of pulpwood from a smaller amount of land, it may mollify some of its critics. However, this will require major investment in plant biology and other high-tech genetic research. This area in particular will require more extensive networking between the pulp and paper companies, research institutions, and government agencies.

One of the major research initiatives involving the pulp industry is Agenda 2020, a cooperative research project involving the U.S. Department of Energy (DOE), pulp and paper research institutions, and leading paper companies. Agenda 2020 was prepared by the chief technology officers of major paper companies under the auspices of the American Forest & Paper Association. The development of the document was spurred by the DOE's "Industries of the Future" program, which seeks to fund research in specific manufacturing industries—including pulp and paper—that will reduce energy intensiveness and improve environmental performance. The DOE prepared a draft document on the "Pulp Mill of the Future," which the team of chief technology officers reviewed and modified to create Agenda 2020. It outlined six specific areas for research and development, including sustain-

able forest management, environmental performance, energy performance, capital effectiveness, recycling, and sensors and control. Many of the Agenda 2020 research projects involving pulping. For example, a research project underway at Auburn University and the Institute of Paper Science and Technology focuses on the bleachability of pulp. Decreasing residual lignin and modifying the chemical structure of the residual lignin to make it easier to remove by bleaching can reduce bleach plant effluent loadings. To make this process work, operators will need simple predictors of how easy the pulp will be to bleach. Once these predictors are in place, mills will be able to develop shorter bleaching sequences, which use less energy and fewer chemicals. This research may also make the use of pulping additives such as anthraquinone (AQ) more effective. Potential savings from this one research project in energy usage alone is estimated at $200 million per year, based on a projected 5.8 percent decrease in total energy usage for bleached and unbleached kraft pulping.

Another major industry project under development as of the late 1990s was "black liquor gasification." Traditionally, kraft pulp mills have burned the black liquor (spent chemicals) produced as a byproduct of the pulping process in large Tomlinson boilers, both to generate power and to recover the chemicals for re-use in the pulping process. Black liquor gasification changes this procedure by turning the black liquor into a gas before burning it. The process is said to have remarkable potential to reduce capital costs, improve energy efficiency, and reduce the emissions of greenhouse gases. As of 1999, the industry was in the process of setting up pilot plants at certain pulp mills and seeking grants from the Department of Energy to help fund the projects.

FURTHER READING

Biermann, Christopher J. *Essentials of Pulping and Papermaking.* San Diego: Academic Press, 1993.

"Market Pulp: Is There a Cure for Volatility?" *PIMA's International Papermaker,* February 1997.

"Market Pulp: Still Struggling." *PIMA's International Papermaker,* February 1999.

"Paper Markets Will Remain Weak as Demand Slows; Recovery Delayed." *Pulp & Paper,* January 1999.

Paper, Paperboard, Pulp Capacity and Fiber Consumption. Washington: American Forest & Paper Association, 1998.

"Papermaker's Top 50: Muddling Through." *PIMA's North American Papermaker,* June 1999.

"Pulp Markets are Almost Cleaned Out" *EUWID Pulp and Paper,* 20 October 1999.

U.S. Department of Commerce. Economics and Statistics Administration. *1997 Economic Census, Manufacturing Industry Series, Pulp Mills.* Washington, D.C.: GPO, November 1999.

SIC 2621

PAPER MILLS

This category covers establishments primarily engaged in manufacturing paper from wood pulp, wastepaper, and other fiber pulp, and they may also manufacture converted paper products. Establishments primarily engaged in integrated pulping and papermaking are included in this industry if they primarily ship paper or paper products.

NAICS CODE(S)

322121 (Paper (except Newsprint) Mills)
322122 (Newsprint Mills)

INDUSTRY SNAPSHOT

The United States produces more paper and paperboard than any country in the world. It has maintained this position by consistently producing about one-third of total world production, far more than any other country. While the paper industry remains prosperous and relatively unscathed by foreign competition, competition is rising across the globe as new regions—notably Asia and Latin America—develop strong paper industries.

Domestic U.S. paper and paperboard mills—of which there were 592 in 1998—produce about 90 percent of the paper consumed in the United States. In 1998, these mills used a total of 1,164 machines to produce all U.S. made paper and paperboard. The 1998 total included 775 machines producing paper and 389 machines producing paperboard. Taken as a whole, the U.S. pulp, paper, and converted paper products industry is the eighth largest U.S. manufacturing industry in dollar sales. While imports—mostly from Canada—account for about 10 to 12 percent of the paper consumed each year in the United States, domestic manufacturers dominate most segments of the industry.

While paper mills are separate from pulp mills in the Standard Industrial Classification System, the two are, in reality, directly connected. About 70 percent of all paper is produced at mills that are "integrated" with a pulp mill at the same site, both of which are typically owned by the same company. Most high volume "commodity" paper and paperboard grades—such as newsprint, uncoated free sheet, and linerboard—are produced in this fashion. Some smaller paper mills producing specialty grades may not be connected with a pulp mill. They procure pulp from other mills owned by the same company or buy "market pulp" produced by other companies.

Converters of paper products, which are often owned by paper companies, add value to paper and distribute their products to consumers and industrial users. This sector is more widely distributed and includes firms that are directly integrated with paper manufacturers as well as firms that purchase paper, paperboard, and plastic film from manufacturers. Converters transform these materials into thousands of different finished products. The largest number of converters are fully independent operations. However, the converters that are directly owned by or connected to paper and board manufacturers tend to be very large and account for a disproportionate percentage of total industry sales.

While growth in domestic markets has slowed in recent years, the U.S. paper industry still produces a vast amount of paper and paperboard. In 1998, total production was 94.5 million tons of paper and paperboard, with 44.8 million tons being paper and 49.7 million tons being paperboard. The 1998 total—94.5 million tons—was down from 95 million tons in 1997.

While papermaking is an energy intensive industry—being the third largest U.S. industrial consumer of energy—the pulp and paper industry itself produces more than 50 percent of the energy it uses through cogeneration and burning of waste fuels, such as bark and spent pulping chemicals.

ORGANIZATION AND STRUCTURE

Papermaking starts where the pulping process leaves off. The first step in papermaking is piping the pulp to the headbox of the paper machine. At this point the pulp—now called the furnish—is 99 percent water and 1 percent fiber. At the headbox, the pulp is laid onto a large mesh belt made of plastic, which is called a wire or a forming fabric. This wire can be as wide as 33 feet. As the water drains out, the fibers bond to each other and form a strong web. This web is taken off the wire by a series of rolls and put into a press section, where more water is squeezed or vacuumed out of the web. Then the web enters a long series of dryer rolls that are heated by steam. As the web comes in contact with these rolls, the water flashes off. By the time it leaves the dryers, the web is 3 to 4 percent water. After the paper is wound on a reel at the end of the paper machine, many things can happen, depending on the grade. It can be slit and shipped as a large roll or converted into paper products at the same location.

Paper mills are organized by the type of paper they produce. For example, some paper mills produce only printing and writing paper, while others produce newsprint. Many paper mills produce "white" paper, in which brown wood pulp is bleached to remove color and other impurities. Many paperboard mills, which are discussed in **SIC 2631: Paperboard Mills,** manufacture unbleached "brown grades" of paperboard, some of which are used for making corrugated shipping containers. However, some paperboard mills produce "white" products, such as the bleached paperboard used to make folding cartons for products such as breakfast cereal boxes.

Some paper mills produce unbleached brown paper for products such as grocery sacks.

Financial Structure. The paper industry is the most capital intensive of all basic U.S. manufacturing industries, requiring nearly continuous major investments for plant and equipment. According to one ranking, the pulp and paper industry is twice as capital intensive as any other major U.S. industry. This has led major paper companies to invest in enormous, high-speed machines that can use economies of scale to produce paper at the lowest possible cost.

The late 1980s and early to mid-1990s were a roller coaster for the U.S. paper industry. After paper companies enjoyed record profits in the late 1980s, the early 1990s saw a dramatic drop in paper prices and very difficult financial circumstances for many paper companies. Prices for most paper products started to drop in mid-1989 and remained low well into the 1990s. Despite low prices being paid for paper, many paper companies had embarked on major capital projects to build new paper machines and expand existing units. The twin conditions of new capacity coming on line and soft demand conspired to keep prices low even when demand began to recover in 1992 and 1993.

However, the spring of 1994 saw the beginning of one of the sharpest run-ups in paper prices ever. Supplies tightened, prices rose, and customers began stocking unusually large amounts of inventory in anticipation of future price increases. The result was that average prices for all paper and paperboard rose 8 percent in 1994 and a whopping 41 percent in 1995. However, the boom in paper prices was destined to be one of the shortest on record. Customers began to take stock out of inventory in the fall of 1995 and prices began falling again. By mid-1996 prices of some grades had fallen by a third. Prices for paper stabilized in late 1996 and stayed basically in the same low range until mid-1999, when prices began to creep upward. Prices were expected to slowly rise through late 1999 and into 2000.

This business cycle has plagued the paper industry for years. Plans for big greenfield (new) mills and machine additions are usually made in the middle of an economic recovery, when paper company profits are rising. These projects involve complicated engineering and take about three to four years to complete. This means new or expanded mills tend to come on line in the middle of a recession, which is what happened in the early 1990s. Also, since paper is a largely nonperishable product, both mills and customers can stock large amounts of paper in inventory. As a result, inventory adjustments can produce large swings in paper pricing.

After a burst of new mills and paper machines in the early 1990s, the mid-1990s saw relatively low growth in papermaking capacity. After increasing capacity at a 2.6 percent average annual rate from 1986 to 1995 and by 3.5 percent in 1996, paper and paperboard companies added just 2.8 percent capacity in 1997. From 1999 to 2001, capacity was expected to be added at a rate of just 0.9 percent annually. On a tonnage basis, U.S. paper industry capacity was expected to expand from 103.8 million tons in 1999 to 105.3 million tons in 2001—a three-year increase of 1.5 million tons.

In 1998, pulp and paper companies produced about 50 percent more tonnage with 5 percent fewer employees than in 1984. This was caused directly by paper companies' huge investment in higher capacity, heavily automated machines. For example, in 1998, the industry had the capacity to produce 102.5 million tons of paper and paperboard, up from 90.6 million tons in 1993, while operating 28 fewer machines than in 1993.

These large investments have created high fixed costs for paper companies. The expense of building and maintaining plants and equipment have become a much greater percentage of a paper company's total costs, while labor has become a lower percentage of costs. Because huge, automated mills need fewer people to run them, many in the industry assumed that paper companies could not adjust to lower demand by laying people off and taking capacity out for short periods. However, while that strategy appeared to be true during the paper industry's recession in the early 1990s, the industry used a completely different approach when prices began dropping in the mid-1990s. Beginning in 1996, many U.S. paper companies—particularly newsprint producers and linerboard producers—took extensive downtime to try to reduce both their own inventories and those of their customers. Paper companies continued to take extended periods of downtime throughout the mid- to late 1990s. Some companies took this a step further and announced permanent shutdowns of older, uncompetitive mills. For example, in 1998, Smurfit-Stone Container Corp. announced the shutdown of four mills that produced about 1.1 million tons of containerboard. The move followed the creation of Smurfit-Stone Container by the merger of Jefferson Smurfit Corporation and Stone Container Corporation in November 1998.

BACKGROUND AND DEVELOPMENT

American papermaking began just over 300 years ago in Philadelphia. In September of 1690, an entrepreneur named William Bradford—a recent English immigrant—built the first American paper mill on the shore of Wissahickon Creek in Philadelphia. At the time, paper manufacturing had not yet become an important part of the colonial economy. The small amount of paper consumed in the colonies was produced in Holland and France.

However, economic growth in the colonies soon created a booming market for paper. Bradford and other papermakers were soon ready to produce products for this market. Bradford built his mill with the assistance of William Rittenhouse, an immigrant from Holland, and other financial backers. The mill produced about 20 pounds of pulp, paper, and board a day. While at the time there was some mechanization of papermaking, it was largely a handmade process.

After 1690, the population of the American colonies grew quickly and so did the number of U.S. paper mills. By the time of the American Revolution—in which printed materials played a key role—there were more than 45 mills producing about 300 tons of paper per year. This production was used by more than 50 printers throughout the new nation.

At the beginning of the 1800s, an event occurred that would revolutionize the paper industry throughout the world. A Frenchman, Louis-Nicolas Robert, invented a machine to produce paper. Eventually, the machine patents were purchased by two English papermakers, the brothers Henry and Sealy Fourdrinier. After modification, the Fourdrinier machine began to catch on in England, and it later was produced in the United States as well. The name Fourdrinier is still used today to describe certain paper machines. The development of the paper machine changed what had been a lengthy and time consuming handmade art into a manufacturing process.

The other event that forever changed papermaking occurred in the middle of the nineteenth century. After 1851, the preferred fiber source for papermaking began to change from old rags to wood pulp. This event, along with the invention of the paper machine, in effect created the modern paper industry (see "Background and Development," **SIC 2611: Pulp Mills**). The size and speed of paper machines increased rapidly between 1850 and 1916. Paper use was booming by 1889, when the annual U.S. production of paper reached one million tons. This figure doubled in the next ten years.

At the end of World War I, the United States began a period of rapid economic growth, and the paper industry grew along with the general economy. Several new associations, including the Paper Industry Management Association and the Technical Association of the Pulp and Paper Industry were founded and developed during this time. Paper containers and packaging, a growing use of corrugated medium and linerboard to make shipping boxes, and a host of new products—such as tissues and sanitary napkins—all emerged as major trends in the postwar era. It was during this time that Canadian mills became dominant in newsprint manufacture, producing the majority of American newsprint. It is only recently that U.S. manufacturers have produced the majority of newsprint consumed in the United States.

Southern Growth. It was also during this period that the Pacific Northwest became a major pulp producer. The southern United States, however, saw the greatest growth. Prior to this time, it was difficult to use southern pine to make paper because of its high resin content. However, new processes were developed using southern pine to make bleached and unbleached kraft paper. Southern pine was ideal for this type of paper because its long fibers produced very strong paper and board. Kraft production in the South shot up from just 258 tons per day (tpd) in 1919 to 9,128 tpd in 1940. By the end of World War II, this total was up to about 13,000 tpd.

The growth of southern paperboard mills and other board mills around the country was greatly enhanced by a 1914 Federal Trade Commission (FTC) decision that legalized the use of corrugated medium packaging in shipping. Prior to that, wooden boxes were used for shipping goods around the country. Military development of paper packaging materials during World War I helped provide new technology and methods for producing superior paper packaging. Southern newsprint production also began during this time, due in large part to the talents of Charles H. Herty. Methods developed by Herty and his relentless promotion of southern papermaking helped create today's paper industry in the South.

While the Great Depression of the 1930s severely hurt other industries, it did not affect the pulp and paper industry as much since paper was being used in new ways throughout the economy. It was around 1930 that machine coated paper was first manufactured in the United States.

During World War II, the paper industry worked closely with the federal government to make sure that adequate supplies of paper were available both for domestic use and for the armed forces. Paper was one of the main materials used for shipping and storing military supplies. Recycling of paper reached a peak during the war years as well, with paper drives being common in many big cities.

Postwar Growth. After World War II, the paper industry continued growing. New pulping strategies and tree planting allowed the paper industry to develop the fiber sources it needed to meet the expanding demand. Prior to this time, paper companies tended to cut down trees and not replant. It was during this time that southern pine first began to be used to make white printing paper.

During the late 1940s, all areas of the paper industry were growing fast, but some new areas—such as milk cartons and drinking cups—saw exponential growth. Many of the growth trends were centered around the use of disposable paper products, a trend that had started in World War II.

In the 1950s and 1960s, paper machines grew wider and faster, which helped multiply the supply of paper and board. By 1970, however, the paper industry faced sustained challenges to its environmental practices. New clean air and water rules from federal and state governments in the early 1970s forced the industry to install expensive new treatment systems. Many other capital projects were put on hold and then frozen when the economy entered a recession in the early 1980s. However, in the mid- to late 1980s the paper industry initiated what has been called its greatest modernization ever. These capital intensive projects included mill-wide automation, technological innovations, mill modernization, environmental upgrades, and a push for total quality. The U.S. paper industry began competing more effectively in global markets during this time as well.

CURRENT CONDITIONS

The paper industry of the late 1990s was highly competitive, both in domestic and foreign markets. It had a modern, efficient manufacturing base, labor peace, and strong markets. However, the industry faced several major challenges, including financial performance, environmental compliance, recycling, and alternative media.

Financial Performance. The U.S. paper industry's financial performance throughout most of the 1990s was subpar, particularly compared to the rest of the U.S. economy, which enjoyed general prosperity. Some of the reasons for this poor financial performance were structural, such as the Asian financial crisis in 1997 and the volatile currency swings that accompanied it, a prolonged period of low inflation, and increasing environmental pressures. However, the paper industry is also said to have caused some of its own problems, notably by building more capacity to make paper than is justified by demand growth. Also, a tendency by most paper companies to focus more on production than on marketing their products is also said to have contributed to the industry's financial problems. The industry's inability to return acceptable profits to shareholders led to stagnant stock prices through much of the 1990s, at a time when other industry's stock valuations were soaring.

For example, from 1988 to 1997, operating profits for the U.S. paper industry grew at an annual rate of 3.9 percent, just half the rate of the Standard and Poor's (S&P) 500 Industrials, which grew at a 7.7 percent rate. Likewise, the industry's return on equity (ROE) averaged just 8.68 percent from 1988 to 1997, well below the 18.6 average posted by the S&P 500. As a result, stock prices for paper companies showed a compound increase of just 6.3 percent annually from 1988 to 1997, compared with 16.5 percent for the S&P 500.

Paper industry executives took note of this problem and pledged to remedy the situation by curbing capacity growth and pursuing consolidation. In the late 1990s, they made good on both pledges. Capacity growth in the late

1990s was less than half of historical averages, and several major mergers and acquisitions re-shaped the paper industry, notably Kimberly-Clark and Scott Paper; James River Corp. and Fort Howard; International Paper Co. and Union Camp; and Weyerhaeuser Co. and MacMillan Bloedel.

At the end of the 1990s, there was some evidence that this strategy was paying off. Stock prices for many paper companies rose sharply in 1999, as did company profits. Projections called for even further improvements in 2000.

Environment. Environmental compliance has been a daunting—and expensive—challenge for the paper industry in the 1990s. There is sustained opposition from environmental groups and increased government regulation in nearly all steps of production. For example, the lumber industry in the Pacific Northwest has been drastically reduced in scale. Due to successful court challenges by environmental groups under the Endangered Species Act of 1973, tree harvests in the early to mid-1990s dropped to one sixth of harvesting levels in the mid-1980s and stayed at those levels for the remainder of the 1990s.

Pulp and paper mills in the Northwest dependent on the residue of lumber operations for raw material have needed to look to new sources—even overseas—for sources of wood chips. Many northwestern U.S. mills have converted partially or completely to the use of recycled paper. Also, the pulping and bleaching of wood fiber was the focus of proposals for stringent and costly new federal regulation in the mid-1990s (see "Current Conditions," **SIC 2611: Pulp Mills**).

Recycling. While paper recycling was a major environmental challenge in the early 1990s, the industry's quick response to recycle more paper has convinced many of its critics—both in the public and government—that the industry is serious about recycling. The U.S. paper industry reached an overall recycling rate of 40 percent in 1993 and a 47 percent rate by 1998. It was expected that the industry would reach its goal of recycling 50 percent of all paper produced in the United States sometime in the early 2000s.

While highly touted as an environmental "silver bullet," recycling itself has some environmental liabilities. Most recycling mills generate a major waste stream and consume large amounts of purchased energy. With recycled newsprint, for example, only 85 percent of incoming newsprint is usable as fiber. The rest is unusable sludge that must be cleaned out of the process and then burned or placed in landfills. In some recycled grades, sludge can be up to 50 percent of the incoming waste paper. Considering that some mills make up to 2,500 tons per day of paper, sludge can become a major waste problem. Also, since recycling mills cannot burn bark or spent pulping chemicals to generate electricity on their own, they must purchase large amounts of power from local utilities.

In the mid-1990s, recycling began to change the geographic distribution of paper mills. So-called "mini mills" began to crop up near major U.S. cities. These mini mills remove ink and recycle old newsprint and other grades of wastepaper and make new newsprint and linerboard on relatively small paper machines. Since they are close to where much of the country's wastepaper is collected—major cities—they are able to greatly reduce shipping costs.

Alternative Media. A third major challenge to the paper industry comes from the electronic display and storage of information. In the 1970s and early 1980s, some people predicted that computers would soon replace paper in the so called "paperless office." In reality, computers encouraged users to print out even more paper than ever before, fueling a boom in printing and writing papers.

Today, however, computers are being used more often to replace paper for the storage and transfer of information previously accomplished only on paper, such as the filing of legal papers with the Securities and Exchange Commission (SEC), which as of 1996 began to require electronic submissions of some corporate documents. Some observers feel that this may curtail the growth of paper. However, other observers point out that computers have vastly expanded the amount of information that can be stored. Even if a smaller percentage of this information is printed out, it is predicted that the use of paper should still grow. Several studies concluded that alternative media is not likely to affect consumption of paper until 2005, and that even then, only select grades are likely to be negatively affected by alternative media. Still, some paper grades may feel the effects sooner than later. For example, newsprint usage in the United States was flat or declining in the late 1990s and was projected to fall further in the early 2000s. Some of the blame for this decline has been attributed to growing demand for Internet-based publications.

Financial Conditions. In the early 1990s, the paper industry produced more paper than ever before but was unable to maintain effective pricing. Paper prices fell in 1991 and 1992 before beginning a sharp recovery in 1994 that lasted through most of 1995. In fact, in 1994 and 1995 average paper prices were up more than 50 percent, with prices of some grades increasing at even higher rates. These high prices led to record U.S. paper company profits in 1995. However, 1996 saw prices—and profits—plummeting once again, though not falling as low as they had in the early 1990s. Prices remained at this same general level for the rest of the decade, though prices climbed slowly but steadily throughout 1999.

Operating rates are another key to profits in the paper industry. In general, operating rates—the percentage of

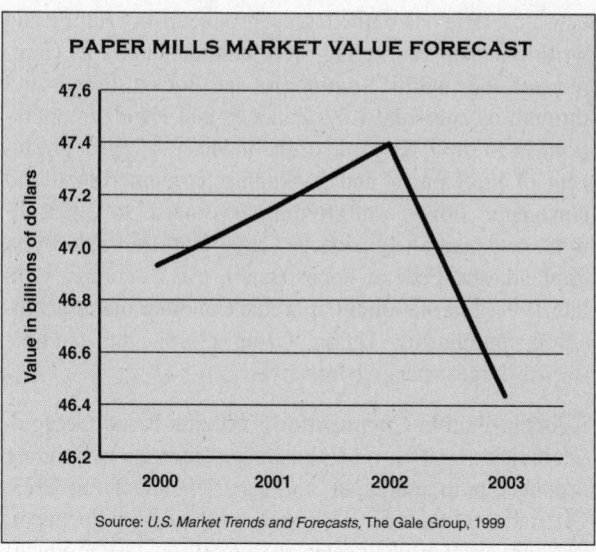

PAPER MILLS MARKET VALUE FORECAST

Value in billions of dollars

Source: *U.S. Market Trends and Forecasts*, The Gale Group, 1999

time that mills are in operation—need to be at or over 90 percent for the mill to be profitable. This means most large mills operate 24 hours a day, 7 days a week. Operating rates dropped in 1990 and 1991, but they rebounded to about 90 percent for paper producers and 95 percent for paperboard manufacturers in 1992. In 1993, the operating rate for all producers reached 93.7 percent and shot up to 96.0 percent in both 1994 and 1995. However, operating rates dropped dramatically in 1996 to about 89 percent as many producers took extensive downtime in an attempt to work off large inventories of pulp and paper products. In 1997, the average operating rate climbed to about 94.0 percent, but dropped back again to 92.2 percent in 1998.

Another measure of paper industry economic health is capital expenditures for new plants and equipment. When paper companies are profitable, they tend to reinvest a large share of their profits into capital expenditures. Capital expenditures for the U.S. pulp and paper industry peaked in 1990 at about $18 billion, and they stayed high in 1991 at about $17 billion. However, from 1992 to 1996, the rate of capital expenditures stayed within a range of $12 billion to $14 billion, and 1997 capital spending barely topped $10 billion. That decline continued in 1998, when capital expenditures dropped to $8.2 billion, and again in 1999, when they dropped to $7.2 billion, the lowest figure since 1984. Low capital expenditures were further evidence that domestic growth in paper capacity will remain low for some time.

INDUSTRY LEADERS

International Paper Company. Founded in 1898 by the merger of 18 northeastern pulp and paper companies, International Paper Company (IP) of Purchase, New York, was the world's largest paper company in 1998. In that year, IP had total sales of $19.5 billion, of which $16.7 billion were from pulp, paper, and converted product sales. IP is one of the largest producers of printing and writing papers, marketing these products under its Hammermill, Springhill, Strathmore, and Beckett brands and through its Aussedat Rey, Zanders, and Kwidzyn operations in Europe. IP is one of the industry's largest producers of kraft paper and packaging, containerboard and corrugated boxes, and folding boxboard. In 1995, IP made two major acquisitions: Carter Holt Harvey of New Zealand, and Federal Paper Board, a U.S. company. In late 1998, International Paper made another major acquisition, purchasing Union Camp Corp., the nation's twelfth largest paper company.

Georgia-Pacific Corporation. Atlanta-based Georgia-Pacific Corporation (G-P) has major interests in building products, pulp and paper, and paper chemicals. In 1998, G-P had total sales of $13.2 billion, including pulp, paper, and converted product sales of $5.6 billion. G-P produces containerboard and packaging, communications papers, market pulp, and packaging products at more than 80 facilities in the United States and Canada. In 1999, G-P purchased Unisource, the nation's largest distributor of printing and imaging products (paper), packaging systems, and maintenance supplies.

Weyerhaeuser Company. Based in Tacoma, Washington, Weyerhaeuser's main businesses are growing and harvesting timber; manufacturing and distributing forest products (including logs, wood chips, building products, pulp, paper, and packaging products); real estate development and construction; and financial services. In 1998, Weyerhaeuser had total sales of $10.7 billion ($4.4 billion of that in pulp, paper, and converted products) and employed 35,000 workers. Weyerhaeuser owned 5.2 million acres of commercial forestland in the United States, with about half in the South and the other half in the Pacific Northwest. The company also had license arrangements on 18.9 million acres of Canadian forestland. In 1999, Weyerhaeuser completed a major acquisition, purchasing MacMillan Bloedel, Canada's sixth largest forest products company.

Kimberly-Clark Corporation. Dallas-based Kimberly-Clark (K-C) is a leading global manufacturer of products for personal, business, and industrial uses. In 1998, K-C had total sales of $12.3 billion, all from pulp, paper, and converted product sales. K-C is best known for its consumer brands Kleenex, Huggies, Scott, and Kotex. In December 1995, Kimberly-Clark merged with Scott Paper Co., a global producer of sanitary tissue products. The $9.4-billion merger made K-C the largest tissue manufacturer in the world. As of 1999, K-C operated manufacturing operations in 38 countries, with products available in 150 countries.

The Procter & Gamble Company. This consumer products giant markets a wide range of household prod-

ucts, including paper products, worldwide. As of 1998, the company operated in 140 countries and had total 1998 sales of $37.2 billion. The company's paper segment had net sales of $10.9 billion in 1998. In 1998, the company spent $3.27 billion on acquisitions, most of them in the paper business. They included Tambrands Inc. and its brand Tampax; the Loreto y Pena Paper Company in Mexico; and the Ssanyong Paper Company in Korea.

Smurfit-Stone Container Corporation. Chicago-based Smurfit-Stone Container Corporation is one of the world's largest paper-based packaging companies and supplies about 11 percent of the world's containerboard. The company was formed on November 18, 1998, following the merger of Jefferson Smurfit Corp. and Stone Container Corp. Core products include corrugated containers, folding cartons, and specialty and bag packaging, supported by an integrated mill system and major fiber resources. The company operates more than 300 facilities worldwide and had 1998 sales of $7.7 billion, all of it in pulp, paper, and converted products.

Fort James Corporation. Created by a 1997 merger between James River Corporation and Fort Howard Corporation, this Deerfield, Illinois-based company manufactures tissue, toweling, and cups and plates for both home and away-from-home markets. Fort James also produces folding cartons and communications papers. Its 1998 sales were $7.3 billion, all of it in pulp, paper, and converted products. Fort James is North America's largest tissue provider and the second largest worldwide. The company has more than 65 manufacturing facilities and 28,000 employees around the world.

The Mead Corporation. Dayton, Ohio-based Mead Corp. is a forest products company with offices and operations in 30 countries. In 1998, Mead had total sales of $3.8 billion, all in pulp, paper, and converted products. In 1998, Mead had the capacity to produce 1.8 million tons of paper and 1.8 million tons of paperboard annually. It is a leading producer of coated paper, specialty paper, coated paperboard, containerboard, and multiple packaging. It is also a leading manufacturer and distributor of school supplies in the United States and Canada. In 1998, Mead divested several businesses, including its Zellerbach distribution unit.

WORKFORCE

Total employment in the pulp, paper, and converting industries was about 634,000 people in 1998, with pulp, paper, and board mills accounting for about 190,000 of that total. Throughout the 1990s, the industry exhibited a trend of stable or slightly declining employment despite large capacity increases. Employee wage increases remained at or below the inflation rate in the mid- to late 1990s, averaging about 2.1 percent. These increases were far below the average 7.5 percent annual increases recorded during the period from 1975 to 1985.

Like other manufacturing industries, the paper industry employs many unionized workers. However, the heaviest concentrations of union employees are in older mills that were organized years ago. Almost all new pulp and paper mills are non-union operations, including mills constructed by companies with unionized mills in other locations. In general, the wages and benefits provided by non-union mills are comparable to unionized mills.

There has been relative labor peace in the paper industry during the 1980s and 1990s. In exchange for salary increases, management was able to obtain work rules changes that allowed workers to perform more jobs in the mill and eliminate pay differentials for Sunday and holiday pay. One dramatic strike in the 1980s ended in failure when unionized workers at International Paper's mill in Maine were permanently replaced by new workers. Only a handful of the original workers regained their jobs. Since that strike, there have been no major work stoppages in the paper industry.

AMERICA AND THE WORLD

In 1998, the U.S. paper industry exported about 9.09 million tons of paper and paperboard, a decrease of 8.7 percent from the previous year. During this same year, the United States imported 14.5 million tons of paper and paperboard, an increase of 7.5 percent. Much of the imports came from Canada, and newsprint accounted for about half of the imports. (These figures do not include imports and exports of pulpwood chips and wood pulp, which are widely traded.)

Because of the large amount of newsprint imported from Canada, the U.S. paper industry usually runs a trade deficit. For example, in 1998 the value of all U.S. paper and paperboard exports was $6.4 billion, while imports in these categories totaled $10.1 billion. This figure does not include wastepaper exports, an area where the United States leads the world, with a large share of wastepaper exports going to the fiber-starved Asian countries. Japan and Korea are two of the leading Asian wastepaper importers.

Exports played a key role in stabilizing the paper industry during much of the 1990s. As domestic sales of paper and allied products (including pulp) experienced only slight growth from 1991 to 1996, at an average annual rate of 1.5 percent to 2 percent, exports increased 8.2 percent during the same period. However, in 1998 much of that growth was reversed as U.S. exports dropped and imports increased sharply. The worsening trade balance was the primary factor in the U.S. paper industry posting reduced production for 1999, the first decline in 13 years. The strong U.S. economy and the strong U.S. dollar, combined with weak economic conditions, made U.S. products less competitive. The U.S.

paper industry also argued that trade barriers in other countries hindered U.S. exports, and the industry pledged to try to remove the barriers through grade negotiations. One of those initiatives included an effort to have the World Trade Organization (WTO) approve a phase-out of tariffs worldwide on forest products.

In addition, China and the United States agreed, in 1999, to liberalize trade in forest and paper products. However, the deal was tied to China's application to join the WTO, a process that was expected to extend well into 2000 and beyond.

Newsprint Growth. Newsprint is one of the major areas where U.S. producers have become more competitive in the global economy. Canadian newsprint, which until the early 1980s held a dominant 60 percent share of total U.S. consumption, has fallen on hard times. In the late 1980s, Canadian newsprint became significantly less competitive with U.S. newsprint because of higher production costs, new state government requirements for recycled newsprint, and growing U.S. newsprint capacity. In 1998, Canadian newsprint accounted for less than 40 percent of U.S. newsprint consumption, compared with about 52 percent in 1991. Many Canadian newsprint mills are located in rural Quebec, far from recycled fiber sources, and are old and have high production costs. As a result, many market observers expect the Canadian market share to decrease. However, some Canadian producers have made aggressive moves to obtain recycled fiber and build mills closer to urban areas in order to compete in the market for recycled newsprint.

The Japanese market remains a major challenge for U.S. producers. Despite major cost advantages, U.S. producers have a very small market share of the $70-billion Japanese paper and paperboard market, which is second only to the United States in size. This low market share has been attributed to structural impediments in the Japanese market and a general reluctance by Japanese customers to use imported products.

In 1992 the U.S. industry achieved a major breakthrough, when, after lengthy negotiations, a formal five-year agreement was concluded between the governments of the United States and Japan on measures designed to open Japan's paper market to foreign suppliers. The agreement requires the Japanese government to encourage Japanese paper distributors, converters, printers, and other major consumers of paper products to use more imported paper and develop long-term buying relationships with foreign producers. Paper users in Japan are also expected to establish nondiscriminatory purchasing practices and develop purchasing guidelines that can be followed by both domestic and foreign suppliers of paper and paper products. Under the agreement, the two governments periodically review the implementation of the pact.

From 1992 to 1996, however, the U.S. share of the Japanese paper market increased by only 0.5 percent, from 3.6 percent to 4.1 percent. No further progress was achieved through the remainder of the 1990s. The United States contends that if all barriers were eliminated, Japanese imports of foreign paper products would increase fourfold. As a result of the lack of progress, in 1995 the U.S. Trade Representative placed the government of Japan on a Super 301 "Watch List," which allows the U.S. government to monitor trade activities of foreign country's markets in order to determine whether U.S. and other foreign suppliers are being discriminated against. As of 1999, that trade situation was still unresolved.

RESEARCH AND TECHNOLOGY

Traditionally, papermaking research has focused on making faster, wider machines that experience fewer paper breaks. To support these goals, research is continuing in every area of the paper machine: the forming section, the press section, the drying section, and the finishing and converting areas. Much of this research is being performed by supplier companies to the paper industry, which have traditionally assumed a much larger research role than the paper companies. However, paper companies—as well as suppliers—are expanding their support of cooperative research at the nation's pulp and paper schools, such as North Carolina State University, the University of Maine, and the University of Wisconsin-Stevens Point. They also support non-profit research groups such as the Institute of Paper Science and Technology, the Pulp and Paper Research Institute of Canada (PAPRICAN) and the Herty Foundation.

Recycled Research. Much of the research in the paper industry is focusing on how to effectively use more recycled fiber. This is particularly important as the paper industry works to meet its own challenge of recycling 50 percent of all paper produced early in the 2000s and government mandates such as presidential executives orders on recycled paper.

Much of this research will focus on improving the physical chemistry of the "flotation cells" of the deinking process. This technology uses air bubbles to literally "float" detached ink particles to the top of a mixture of ground up paper and water, where the inky froth is skimmed off. Improving the efficiency of this system would speed up production and lower costs.

Research will also focus on using new chemical processes to help produce recycled paper that matches virgin uncoated freesheet in quality. Uncoated freesheet, used in products such as copy paper, is one of the biggest grades of paper—and one of the most demanding in terms of quality.

One of the major initiatives involving the pulp and paper industry is Agenda 2020, a cooperative research project involving the U.S. Department of Energy (DOE), pulp and paper research institutions, and leading paper companies. Agenda 2020 was prepared by the chief technology officers of major paper companies under the auspices of the American Forest & Paper Association. The development of the document was spurred by the U.S. Department of Energy's "Industries of the Future" program, which seeks to fund research in specific industries—including pulp and paper—that will reduce energy intensiveness and improve environmental performance. The DOE prepared a draft document on the "Pulp Mill of the Future." That document was reviewed by the team of chief technology officers and modified to create Agenda 2020, which outlines six specific areas for research and development, including sustainable forest management; environmental; performance; energy performance; capital effectiveness; recycling and sensors; and control.

Information technology is another major area of development. Progress in paper machine process automation has been ongoing, but several major areas of development have emerged, including:

- Embedded process management, where automation, process and machinery know-how is totally integrated into new paper machines
- Open application platforms that allow the use of multiple systems
- Smart sensors and actuators that allow digital data transfer between field instruments and control equipment
- Fuzzy logic and neural networks that imitate human decision-making.

FURTHER READING

"Paper Markets Will Remain Weak as Demand Slows; Recovery Delayed." *Pulp & Paper,* January 1999.

Paper, Paperboard, Pulp Capacity and Fiber Consumption. Washington: American Forest & Paper Association, 1998.

"Papermaker's Top 50 North American Paper Companies." *PIMA's North American Papermaker,* June 1999.

Rowland, Jim. "Capacity Consolidation Continues to Cut Costs, Improve Performance." *Pulp & Paper,* March 1999.

Ryan, Rob. "Process Automation: Science Fiction Becomes Reality." *PIMA's North American Papermaker,* September 1999.

SIC 2631

PAPERBOARD MILLS

This industry consists of establishments primarily engaged in manufacturing paperboard from wood pulp and other fiber pulp. Paperboard mills may also manufacture converted paperboard products. Establishments primarily engaged in integrated pulp production and paperboard manufacturing are included in this industry if they ship mostly paperboard or paperboard products. Establishments primarily engaged in manufacturing converted paperboard products from purchased paperboard are classified in Industry Group 265 or 267. Establishments primarily engaged in manufacturing insulation board and other reconstituted wood fiberboard are classified in **SIC 2493: Reconstituted Wood Products.**

NAICS Code(s)

322130 (Paperboard Mills)

Industry Snapshot

U.S. paperboard mill production was 49.7 million tons in 1998—a 1.2 percent decrease from 1997 when production was 50.3 million tons. At this rate, paperboard outpaced production of paper in the United States in 1998, which checked in at 44.8 million tons.

The capacity of U.S. mills to produce paperboard was projected to grow from 53.9 million tons in 1998 to 55.5 million tons in 2001, a total increase of just 2.9 percent. (Paperboard production typically is about 88 percent to 98 percent of total capacity, depending on economic conditions.) Of this increase, about 40 percent will come from the construction of new machines and 60 percent from improvements to existing machines.

The most extensive use of paperboard is to make shipping containers, cartons, and packaging. U.S. paperboard producers manufacture the vast majority of paperboard consumed in the United States. In addition to dominating the domestic market, U.S. paperboard producers hold a strong position in the international market, with exports reaching 6.7 million tons in 1998, or 13.5 percent of total U.S. paperboard production, which was 49.7 million tons.

Two grades of paperboard—corrugating medium and linerboard—are used to make corrugated shipping containers. These two grades account for the majority of paperboard produced in the United States. A third grade—solid bleached sulfate (SBS), used for folding cartons such as those used in retail stores—accounts for a large share of the remaining production. Paperboard grades are also distinguished between folding and nonfolding grades. Folding grades have to be flexible enough so that when the board is folded to make a box—such as a cereal box—the surface will not split or crack.

Organization and Structure

Paperboard production in the United States is divided into four major categories:

- Unbleached kraft paperboard, which is made from pulp containing not less than 80 percent wood fibers

produced by the sulfate (kraft) process. Since it is unbleached, this type of paperboard retains a brown color. Unbleached kraft accounted for 23.2 million tons of all paperboard production in 1998, or 46.5 percent of all U.S. paperboard production.

- Recycled paperboard, which is manufactured from a combination of recycled fibers from various grades of paper stock, with the predominant portion of the pulp being recycled fibers and a minor amount being virgin fibers. Recycled paperboard that contains no virgin fibers is commonly called 100 percent recycled paperboard. Recycled paperboard accounted for 15.2 million tons of the total in 1998, or 30.5 percent of all U.S. paperboard production.

- Semichemical paperboard, which is made from pulp containing not less than 75 percent virgin wood fibers, the majority of which is produced by a semichemical process. Semichemical board accounted for 5.9 million tons in 1998, or 11.9 percent of all U.S. paperboard production.

- Solid bleached packaging paperboard, which is used in packaging and made from pulp containing not less than 80 percent bleached virgin wood fibers. This paperboard is white and is used for higher-end packaging applications, such as milk cartons and frozen food packaging. Solid bleached kraft accounted for 5.5 million tons of production, or 11.1 percent of all U.S. paperboard production in 1998.

More paper and paperboard is used to make packaging than in any other single application. While most paperboard is still made from virgin fibers (trees), paperboard mills have traditionally used a large percentage of recycled fiber because of favorable economics. The use of recycled fiber in paperboard production is growing quickly, especially in products in which the reclaimed pulp does not need to be cleaned. Combination boxboard, for example, is used in cereal cartons where two white outside layers mask a recycled, gray inner layer.

Paperboard produced on cylinder board machines has commonly been made from recycled fibers; this is because cylinder machines form the paperboard web in separate layers, which are then pressed together. This makes it possible to hide a layer of recycled board, which can have poor appearance and lower strength between two outside layers of virgin material.

Fourdrinier paperboard machines, which traditionally have made paperboard in a single web, are generally used to make virgin paperboard since it makes a superior web from one fiber source. Newer paperboard machines, however, include machinery that allows the formation of a single web from different fiber sources.

Kraft softwood has been the preferred pulp for making paperboard because of its superior strength characteristics. While most paperboard is unbleached, retaining the characteristic brown color of the pulp, bleached grades are often used where the consumer is likely to see the box—such as gift boxes and food and beverage packages. Besides food applications, cosmetics and other high-profit products use the more expensive bleached board because they can afford its higher cost.

Paperboard comes in a wide variety of styles and qualities, but can be divided into two categories based on its use: containerboard, which includes all the materials used for making corrugated boxes; and boxboard, which includes all the materials used for making non-corrugated packaging such as food containers and department store boxes. Containerboard is divided further into two subcategories: corrugating medium, the inner fluted part of the box; and linerboard, which makes up the outer faces, or layers, of the box. Corrugating medium—or just "medium," as it is often called in the trade—is made from both semichemical pulp and recycled fiber.

Boxboard is divided into three subcategories: folding boxboard, set-up boxboard, and milk carton/food service boxboard. Total U.S. production of boxboard in 1998 reached 15 million tons, virtually unchanged from the previous year. Most paperboard can be coated with a pigment such as clay to improve printing properties. Most grades of paperboard can also be made impermeable to air and liquids by using plastic coating and laminating; this is essential for products such as milk carton stock.

Corrugated Boxes. The universal use of corrugated containers for shipping manufactured goods by truck, train, or ship makes this grade one of the largest in the paper and board industry. There are a large number of converting plants located throughout the country that use corrugating medium and linerboard, which are glued together to make boxes. These converting plants are located close to users of the containers and are often owned by the same company that manufactures the linerboard and medium.

The main raw material used to make corrugating medium is semichemical hardwood pulp. Hardwood pulp, which is made from deciduous trees such as oak and maple, is used rather than softwood pulp made from conifers such as southern pine. Hardwoods are used because they are less costly and help make the corrugating medium stiff since they are less flexible than softwood fibers.

Unlike the pulp used in other types of paper and paperboard, the pulp used for making medium still contains some lignin, the chemical "glue" that holds fibers together in the tree. This is because medium pulp is not washed as intensively as pulps used in making other grades. As a result, the lignin and other wood by-products are left in the pulp and formed into the web of paperboard. When the paperboard web goes through the corrugator, the remaining wood by-products help form the rigid fluted shape.

Growth of Recycling. Like other predominantly virgin paper and paperboard grades, semichemical medium has seen its share of total capacity decline as a result of increased production of recycled products. Semichemical medium's share of total medium production declined to 60.4 percent in 1998 compared with 79.0 percent in 1980, while recycled medium's share grew to 39.6 percent. Much of that change occurred in the 1990s, when many paperboard mills expanded their capacity to produce recycled medium.

While there are many basis weights for both semichemical and recycled medium (including 22, 26, 33, 36, and 40 pound), the standard weight is 26 pound. It accounts for nearly 80 percent of all production.

Medium production is directly related to U.S. corrugated box shipments. In the late 1980s and early 1990s, box shipments grew faster than the general economy. Through the rest of the 1990s, growth in box shipments tracked more closely with growth in the general economy.

Linerboard. Total U.S. linerboard production reached 20.9 million tons in 1998, up 2 percent over 1997. Unlike medium, linerboard is made mostly from softwood fibers. However, linerboard may contain up to 20 percent hardwood pulp or recycled fiber. The recycled fiber may be made from cuttings from corrugating plants or other recovered corrugated material. Softwood is needed to give linerboard adequate strength. Most softwood pulp for linerboard is produced using the kraft pulping process. To suit the varied packaging needs of box consumers, bleached kraft linerboard is made in many different basis weights. The standard variety is 42 pound, but other major grades include 26 pound, 33 pound, and 69 pound. While production of recycled linerboard is significantly less than virgin linerboard, 100 percent recycled linerboard grew very fast in the United States from the late 1980s through the mid-1990s and was projected to grow even faster during the late 1990s.

SBS. Solid bleached sulfate (SBS) is a top-quality paperboard made from pulp that includes at least 80 percent bleached virgin fiber. Most U.S. produced SBS is coated with a clay solution to improve its surface for printing. SBS used as linerboard, folding boxboard, and for food packaging—such as milk carton stock—and is often coated with polyethylene. Basis weights for SBS range from 40 to 100 pounds. SBS is also used for products such as disposable cups and plates and as linerboard for corrugated boxes and displays that need an outside surface for high-quality, four-color printing. In 1998, the capacity of U.S. mills to produce SBS reached 5.81 million tons per year (tpy). By 2001, capacity was expected to grow to 5.96 million tpy. In 1998, actual SBS output was 5.50 million tons.

Another product made by some mills that produce SBS is bleached bristol. This product, usually a lightweight grade, is used for greeting cards, paperback book covers, and telephone directories, among other products. Bristol is usually classified under paper production, rather than paperboard.

BACKGROUND AND DEVELOPMENT

Since the majority of paperboard capacity is used to make materials for corrugated boxes, the background and development of paperboard mills tends to mirror growth in the use of these boxes.

Before corrugated containers became the accepted standard for domestic and international shipping, wooden crates and boxes were the preferred method. However, this began to change dramatically after the U.S. Federal Trade Commission (FTC), in the 1914 Pridham decision, legalized the use of corrugated packaging in shipping. Also, during World War I, the U.S. military spurred research and development of corrugated packaging to ship military supplies.

As new methods helped improve the strength and durability of corrugated containers, their use in the general economy increased dramatically. For example, between 1935 and 1942, 29 new paperboard machines came on line. Collectively, these machines produced 15,545 tons per day. During World War II, military needs fostered improvements in corrugated shipping containers, including water and temperature resistance. In the postwar years, the growth of corrugated containers more than kept pace with the general economy, which itself was growing rapidly. Also, the development of more disposable containers for products such as food and beverages fueled solid increases in the production of SBS board. Paperboard accounted for 52.6 percent overall production of paper and paperboard in the United States in 1998.

CURRENT CONDITIONS

Like other sectors of the U.S. pulp and paper industry, the 1990s were volatile for U.S. paperboard mills. The industry saw depressed conditions in the early 1990s; booming demand and huge price increases in 1994 and 1995; and falling prices in 1996. For example, year-end transaction prices for 42-pound kraft linerboard were $315 per ton in 1993 before shooting up to $430 per ton in 1994 and $480 per ton in 1995. However, this huge run-up was followed by a huge drop in 1996, to $360 per ton. Prices remained at those depressed levels for the remainder of the 1990s but began a cyclical recovery in 1999, a trend that was expected to continue into 2000. One of the reasons prices for linerboard and other paperboard grades plummeted in 1996 was that capacity increases far out-paced demand for the product, which was in some cases falling as customers worked off large

amounts of inventory they had purchased in anticipation of future price increases.

In the late 1990s, the U.S. paperboard industry made only modest increases in capacity. In addition, many mills took extensive downtime to reduce excess inventories of paperboard. Also, some paperboard companies went so far as to shut some aging mills that were contributing to excess capacity. For example, in 1998, Smurfit-Stone Container Corp. announced the shutdown of four mills that produced about 1.1 million tons of containerboard. The move followed the creation of Smurfit-Stone Container by the merger of Jefferson Smurfit Corporation and Stone Container Corporation in November 1998.

The total capacity of U.S. mills to make paperboard reached 53.9 million tons in 1998, just a 1.3 percent increase over the previous year. Within the overall paperboard category, containerboard grades were up 1.6 percent in capacity during 1998, an increase of 600,000 tons, and boxboard capacity was up 1.0 percent in 1998, by 100,000 tons. From 1998 to 2001, growth in U.S. paperboard production was expected to increase just 0.96 percent annually.

In 1998, the dollar value of U.S. production of paperboard commodities increased nearly 3 percent due to strong domestic and export performances by U.S. containerboard mills. U.S. producers of containerboard had noticeably higher sales to export markets, domestic corrugated and solid fiber box plants, and non-packaging containerboard end use markets. In the mid- to late 1990s, U.S. paperboard mills—particularly the containerboard segment—had record sales opportunities for many of their products in corrugated box, shipping container, and carton plants in southeast Asia, Europe, and Latin America, which led to a significant increase in paperboard exports.

While capacity, demand, and prices are the key elements determining the status of the U.S. paperboard industry, other factors have also come into play. U.S. linerboard is recognized worldwide as being the highest quality and best performing linerboard for most packaging applications. One of the major changes in linerboard occurred in the early 1990s when "Rule 41, Item 22" of the freight classifications was changed to emphasize "ring crush," which measures resistance to compression instead of bursting strength. This change allowed U.S. manufacturers to begin making more "high performance" linerboard, which is lighter in weight than traditional liner but still useful for shipping. As a result, U.S. producers have developed a number of high performance bleached and unbleached linerboard grades.

INDUSTRY LEADERS

Major paper companies produce large quantities of both paper and paperboard, thus the industry leaders are many of the same companies listed under **SIC 2621:**

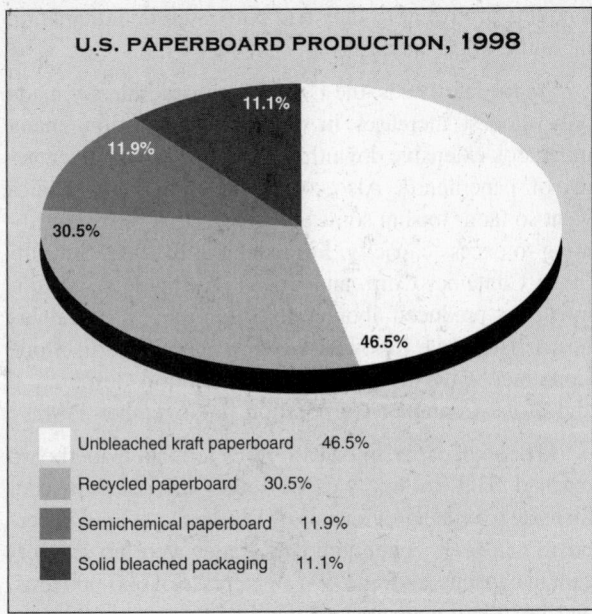

U.S. PAPERBOARD PRODUCTION, 1998

Unbleached kraft paperboard	46.5%
Recycled paperboard	30.5%
Semichemical paperboard	11.9%
Solid bleached packaging	11.1%

Paper Mills. However, some large companies, such as Smurfit-Stone Container Corp., Packaging Corporation of America, Inland Paperboard & Packaging, and International Paper, have much larger interests in paperboard than other companies in the industry.

Chicago-based Smurfit-Stone Container is the leading producer of paperboard in the United States, controlling the number one slot in three of four major paperboard grades. However, International Paper is the dominant leader in the fourth—bleached paperboard. In corrugating medium, total U.S. production capacity was 11.01 million tons in 1999, and the top five companies controlled about 54 percent. Smurfit-Stone Container was the clear industry leader, with 2.01 million tons of annual production capacity and about 18.2 percent of total U.S. capacity. Second place was held by Georgia-Pacific, with 1.16 million tons (10.5 percent) followed by Weyerhaeuser Co., with 1.07 million tons (9.7 percent); PCA, with 888 million tons (8.1 percent); and Mead, with 815 million tons (7.4 percent). Other significant companies in this grade included International Paper Co., Inland Paperboard & Packaging and Norampac.

In bleached paperboard, total U.S. production capacity in 1998 was 7.3 million tons, and the top five companies controlled 75 percent. International Paper Company (including acquired Union Camp operations) was three times larger than its nearest competitor, with 2.85 million tons of annual production capacity in 1998, good for 39 percent of all U.S. capacity in this grade. Second place was occupied by Westvaco, which had annual capacity of 965,000 tons (13.2 percent of capacity); followed by Inland Eastex, with 725,000 tons (9.9 percent); Potlatch, with 610,000 tons (8 percent); and Georgia-Pacific, with 340,000 tons (4.7 percent). Other leading companies included Blue Ridge Paper, Gulf States Paper, and Fort James Corp. As of late 1999, Westvaco had agreed to purchase the operations of Inland Eastex, a unit of Inland Paperboard & Packaging.

In linerboard, total U.S. production capacity in 1998 was 28.45 million tons, and the five top manufacturers together controlled 51.2 percent. Smurfit-Stone Container had 4.1 million tons of capacity in 1998 and held about 14.4 percent of the market. International Paper (including acquired Union Camp operations) had 4 million tons of capacity and 14.1 percent of the market, followed by Georgia-Pacific, with 2.53 million tons (8.9 percent); Inland Paperboard & Packaging, with 2.12 million tons (7.45 percent); and Weyerhaeuser, with 1.8 million tons (6.3 percent). Other significant producers included PCA, Gaylord Container, and Willamette Industries.

The production of recycled paperboard, a fast growing grade, was less concentrated than other paperboard grades. The top five producers controlled just 39.6 percent of the 17.75 million tons of total U.S. capacity in 1999. Smurfit-Stone Container Corp. had 2.0 million tons of capacity in 1999 and held about 11.4 percent of the market. It was followed by Caraustar Industries, with 1.4 million tons (8.0 percent); Newark Group, with 1.3 million tons (7.7 percent); Rock-Tenn, with 1.2 million tons (7.0 percent); and Inland Paperboard & Packaging, with 970.0 million tons (5.5 percent). Other significant producers included Sonoco Products Co., Weyerhaeuser, and Norampac.

AMERICA AND THE WORLD

Paperboard—particularly linerboard—is one of the strongest export products for the U.S. pulp and paper industry. U.S. linerboard mills, mostly in the southern United States, have traditionally been among the world's lowest-cost producers. In 1998, U.S. mills produced 6.68 million tons of paperboard for export with a value of $3.28 billion. Those exports represented 13.4 percent of total U.S. paperboard production.

Paperboard is a leading export product, accounting for about 60 percent of all paper, paperboard, and converted product exports in 1998. By contrast, the United States imported a relatively small volume of paperboard in 1995, just 167 million tons, with a value of $772 million.

Linerboard exports tended to increase and decrease sharply due to global economic trends, though the long-term trend has been upward. Prospects for paperboard exports remain strong but are subject to currency and price fluctuation.

RESEARCH AND TECHNOLOGY

Many of the research trends affecting paperboard mills are shared by paper mills (see **SIC 2621: Paper Mills**). However, there is some interest in using new concepts such as stratification in making paperboard. Stratification involves using a special headbox that can produce three or more layers simultaneously from different fiber sources. In this way, a layer of recycled fiber or some other lesser quality fiber source could be sandwiched between layers of better quality fiber. With newer model headboxes, these layers can be extremely thin.

Like other grades, much of the effort in research and technology in paperboard is to create machines that will produce a wider web of paperboard at higher speeds. In this way, paperboard mills can run their mills more productively. Also, as in other grades, mill processes are becoming more automated and less subject to product variation. This, and continual improvements in paperboard quality, are the main reasons that U.S. paperboard mills can continue to lead the world both in price and product quality.

FURTHER READING

Biermann, Christopher J. *Essentials of Pulping and Papermaking*. San Diego: Academic Press, 1993.

''Bleached Paperboard: Better Markets Ahead for Exports and Cartons.'' *Pulp & Paper*, October 1999.

''Downtime, Mill Shuts, Demand Turn Around Corrugating Medium Market in the U.S.'' *Pulp & Paper*, July 1999.

Kline, James E. *Paper and Paperboard: Manufacturing and Converting Fundamentals*. San Francisco: Miller Freeman Publications, 1982.

''Linerboard: Market Recovery Anticipated After Plummeting Prices, Exports in 1998.'' *Pulp & Paper*, January 1999.

Paper, Paperboard, Pulp Capacity and Fiber Consumption. Washington, D.C.: American Forest & Paper Association, 1998.

''Recycled Paperboard: Some Signs of Life, but Oversupply Problems Linger.'' *Pulp & Paper*, June 1999.

Thesaurus of Pulp and Paper Terminology. Atlanta: Institute of Paper Science and Technology, 1991.

''Global Outlook: More Misery or Muddling Through.'' *PIMA's North American Papermaker*, December 1998.

U.S. Trade and Industrial Outlook, 1999. New York: McGraw-Hill, 1999.

SIC 2652

SETUP PAPERBOARD BOXES

Establishments in this industry manufacture setup (rigid) paperboard boxes from purchased paperboard. This classification includes setup paperboard boxes, paperboard filing boxes, and metal-edged newsboard boxes. These products differ from other paperboard boxes in that they are not folded down, like corrugated boxes, and are shipped to customers in their final form.

NAICS CODE(S)

322213 (Setup Paperboard Box Manufacturing)

Setup paperboard box manufacturers comprise one of the smaller paper and board products industries. Sales have tended to increase and decrease sharply due to various market factors including economic conditions, inventory levels, and industry capacity. For example, the value of setup paperboard box product shipments grew a total of 18 percent over the ten years from 1984 to 1991, from $466.1 million to $554.9 million. While the average annual growth rate over this period was 1.8 percent, the setup paperboard box industry's sales performance was uneven. For example, after rising to $552 million in 1986, sales dropped dramatically the next year, to $436 million, before rising to a peak of $565.1 million in 1990. With the pulp and paper industry in recession in the early 1990s, the value of shipments of setup paperboard boxes dropped back to $430.3 million by 1993. By 1997 the value of shipments had recovered to $553 million, which was still below the 1990 peak of $565 million.

Since this is a small industry, some of the spikes in shipment values may be explained by changes in customers' inventory levels. If customers hold more product in inventory one year, they tend to purchase less the next year, even if their consumption rate is steady. However, an even more important factor is the price of the product, which tends to swing widely. The cost of materials rises and falls with the market price for paperboard, which during 1994 and 1995 rose as much as 50 percent before dropping back in 1996. Paperboard costs remained relatively stable throughout the rest of the 1990s, though prices were rising in 1999 and were expected to continue to rise in 2000. These wide price swings help explain the volatility of the value of shipments in the setup paperboard box industry.

The production of setup paperboard boxes is concentrated in the Eastern half of the country, with the three largest production states being New York, New Jersey, and Pennsylvania. The other production area combined Northeast and the North Central states, including Wisconsin, Illinois, Ohio, Michigan, and Indiana.

Customers of the setup paperboard box industry are divided among several different product groups. Setup boxes used by department stores and other retailers accounted for 16.7 percent of the market in 1997, while those used for textiles, wearing apparel, and hosiery accounted for 12.2 percent. Setup boxes used for cosmetics (including soap) accounted for 10.2 percent, while candy products manufacturers used 9.7 percent of the total. Setup paperboard boxes used for a wide variety of other products accounted for the remaining 51.2 percent of the market in 1997.

The value of shipments in the setup paperboard box industry is expected to remain flat in the early 2000s. While this is a "mature" industry with little chance for exponential growth, it appears to be a stable one. Since setup paperboard boxes are, by definition, rigid packaging, they face little competition from alternative materials—such as plastic—that cannot provide rigidity without undue cost. Also, the recyclability of setup paperboard boxes is seen as an environmental plus, and they can be made quite easily from recycled materials.

Most of the companies in this industry are smaller, "niche" manufacturers. Caraustar Industries, of Austell, Georgia, is the largest manufacturer in this industry, but it makes products in other industries as well. Other leaders in the setup paperboard box industry include Old Dominion Box Co., of Lynchburg, Virginia; Ward Paper Box Co.; Schiffenhaus Industries Inc., of Newark, New Jersey; and FN Burt Co., of Buffalo, New York.

In 1997 setup paperboard box plants employed 6,227 people nationwide with an annual payroll of about $146 million. Production workers accounted for 4,925 of that total and put in 9.5 million man-hours for an average hourly wage of $9.64. Total employment in this industry has been trending downward for years. Total employment in 1997 was a little more than one-half of what it was in 1983 when the industry employed 12,300 people.

FURTHER READING

Paper, Paperboard, Pulp Capacity and Fiber Consumption. Washington, D.C.: American Forest & Paper Association, 1998.

U.S. Census Bureau. *1997 Economic Census, Manufacturing Industry Series.* Washington, D.C.: GPO, August 1999.

Smook, Gary A. *Handbook of Pulp & Paper Terminology: A Guide to Industrial and Technological Usage.* Bellingham, WA: Angus Wilde Publications, 1990.

U.S. Industrial Outlook 1999. New York: McGraw Hill, 1998.

SIC 2653

CORRUGATED AND SOLID FIBER BOXES

This category covers establishments primarily engaged in manufacturing corrugated and solid fiber boxes and related products from paperboard or fiber stock. Important products of this industry include corrugated and solid fiberboard boxes, pads, partitions, display items, pallets, single face products, and corrugated sheets.

NAICS CODE(S)

322211 (Corrugated and Solid Fiber Box Manufacturing)

INDUSTRY SNAPSHOT

The United States is the world's largest producer of corrugated and solid fiber boxes, and as of the late 1990s, it accounted for more than a third of total world volume. Corrugated paperboard products are used to ship almost all of the non-durable goods manufactured in the United States—and a majority of the durable ones as well. They face relatively little competition from alternative shipping methods. The total value of corrugated paperboard and solid fiber box shipments in 1999 was expected to reach $32.6 billion.

The corrugated and solid fiber box industry employed 125,000 people in 1997, with an annual payroll of $4.27 billion. Of that total, 92,000 were production workers putting in 191 million hours for wages of $2.58 billion, which represents an average hourly wage of $13.47.

Corrugated paperboard products have long accounted for the majority of American paperboard container shipments, holding more than 60 percent of the total paperboard container market in the late 1990s. During that period, corrugated product shipments also held about 25 percent share of the overall domestic U.S. packaging market—which includes packaging made from wood, paper/paperboard, plastic, metal, glass, composites, and other materials.

The United States is a major consumer as well as a major producer of corrugated products. In the late 1990s, annual per capita U.S. consumption of corrugated products was the highest in the world—topping 80 kilograms (kg). Japan was the second leading consumer, at just under 70 kg. European nations make up the remaining per capita consumption leaders, with Germany at just under 50 kg, Italy at 45 kg, Spain at 40 kg and the United Kingdom at 30 kg.

Variations in End-Use Markets. The vast majority of corrugated products are used to package non-durable goods, such as food products. In 1998, for example, 77.7 percent of corrugated products were used to package non-durable goods. The percentage of corrugated products directed toward non-durable goods tends to rise during recessions since the number of high-ticket durable goods shipped—such as stoves and refrigerators—decreases.

Shippers and packagers of food products, the largest market for corrugated products, are likely to be the highest growth market for the corrugated industry. Also, shippers were using more corrugated pallets to replace wooden ones because of concerns about costs and recycling.

One of the key trends in corrugated boxes is recycling; this affects both the material used to make the boxes and how they are disposed of after use. Corrugated boxes are easily recycled and are biodegradable, which tends to help them compete well against plastic products among "green" consumers. Most corrugated products are unbleached, which exempts them from the controversies surrounding bleaching processes in the paper industry. In 1997, about 66 percent of corrugated products were recovered for recycling into new boxes or other paperboard products, which represents the second highest recovery level of any major consumable material (aluminum cans are first). Increased collection of corrugated boxes—including those coming from the homes of consumers—was expected to increase gradually each year through the 1990s until it nears 70 percent in the year 2000.

ORGANIZATION AND STRUCTURE

The corrugated box market is about 80 percent integrated. This means that 80 percent of all containerboard (the linerboard facing and corrugated fluting that together make a corrugated box) is not sold on the open market. Instead, it is delivered from containerboard mills to corrugated box plants owned by or affiliated with the same organization. The remaining 20 percent are sold by containerboard producers to independent box plants.

The value of corrugated and solid fiber box shipments reflect both the economic activity of the products shipped in them and the prices paid for boxes, which are typically pegged to the price of raw materials. These raw material prices tend to fluctuate widely. For example, the value of corrugated box shipments were up a strong 10.7 percent in 1994 to $22.7 billion, reflecting the recovery in the general economy, higher demand for corrugated boxes, and higher prices for boxes. That growth continued in 1995, as the value of shipments shot up to $27.9 billion, but in 1996 the value of shipments fell sharply, to $25.9 billion, as slackening demand, drawing down of inventories by customers, and sharp drops in raw material prices led to lower unit sales volumes and lower box prices. The market recovered, rising to $27.7 billion in 1997 and $30.1 billion in 1998. Projections called for 1999 to see a record $32.6 billion in value of shipments.

The U.S. corrugated product box industry produced all-time records in volume shipments during the 1990s as well. In 1996, shipments reached a record 376.2 billion square feet (bsf) of finished corrugated boxes, cartons, and shipping containers. By 1998 that total had reached another record, 402.6 bsf. Corrugated box and container product shipments accounted for 99 percent of the industry shipment total in 1998, while solid fiber boxes made up the small remainder.

Making Corrugated Board. Corrugated medium and linerboard are made into corrugated board at box plants. In 1998 the value of the corrugated board market in the

United States was more than $9.3 billion. Many weights, thicknesses, and combinations of liners and corrugated medium are used to make different types of corrugated board. In this process, flat corrugated medium board is softened with heat and moisture and passed between a set of corrugating rolls to form it into flutes. Adhesive is applied to the flute tip on one side of the medium. A separate, single face linerboard is then brought into contact with the fluted medium under heat and pressure to produce a single facer web.

This web is conveyed to the double backer station, where adhesive is applied to the exposed flute tips and the double back liner is applied. The combined corrugated board is then passed over a series of hot plates to set the adhesive. Modern corrugating machines run at a variety of speeds, ranging from as low as 100 feet per minute (fpm) to as high as 1,000 fpm, depending on the type of corrugated board under production.

After this, the corrugating board is cut into individual sheets, or blanks, on a trimmer-cutter. The blanks are then fed to a printer-scorer-slotter or some other device, which turns the blank into a flat box that can then be opened and glued by the end user.

Recycled Corrugated. Corrugated boxes have the image of being "environmentally correct" because they can be recycled into new boxes and other products. That image is to a large extent justified, since the recycled fiber content of corrugated is generally the highest of any paper product—as of 1997 it was 66 percent and still climbing. While corrugated products are often reused and the majority is recycled, some corrugated boxes do end up as waste in landfills.

To produce recycled linerboard and recycled corrugating medium, many paperboard mills use both preconsumer and postconsumer old corrugated containers (OCC). Preconsumer waste is corrugated materials such as off-rolls and trimmings from box plants. Postconsumer waste includes boxes that have been used for shipping and subsequently discarded. In 1997, pulp and paper producers used more than 16 million tons of OCC to make new containers, while another 3.7 million tons of OCC were exported.

Standard corrugated boxes are fairly easy to recycle since they are printed lightly and require little or no deinking. The pulp made from OCC needs little cleaning and does not need to be bleached. Unlike many grades of recycled paper, OCC suffers a minimal loss in fiber strength and other physical properties. However, there is a limit to how many times fibers can be recycled. For example, Asian corrugated boxes, which have been recycled many times due to chronic virgin fiber shortages in those countries, tend to be weaker and less resistant to water than U.S. corrugated boxes. The fiber quality of

Asian OCC is so low that many American recycling mills exclude it from their processes.

CURRENT CONDITIONS

At the end of 1997, the domestic corrugated box industry consisted of 1,740 establishments operated by a total of 996 companies. Of the 1,740 establishments, about 60 percent were independent operations (not associated with a paperboard mill that produces linerboard and corrugating medium) and 40 percent were fully integrated plants (where there is a paperboard mill, a corrugated plant, and a sheeting plant). These establishments include both corrugated plants, which take corrugating medium and linerboard and make it into containerboard, and sheeting plants, which take finished containerboard and make it into boxes. The total number of U.S. establishments continued to decrease in the late 1990s as downsizing and merger activity helped consolidate the industry and eliminate some smaller operations.

The southeast and west central regions of the United States have been among the fastest growing areas for the production of corrugated packaging. In the late 1990s, these regions accounted for more than 42 percent of total U.S. corrugated shipments. The Southwest has also been an area of significant growth.

The leading use of corrugated packaging is for food and other grocery products that are shipped to the nation's supermarkets and other retail outlets. In 1998, manufacturers of food, meat, dairy, and kindred products were expected to be the largest user of corrugated boxes, accounting for about 40 percent of all box deliveries used for nondurable goods. In this same nondurable category, the paper industry is its own second-best customer, with paper and allied products estimated to use about 21 percent of the nondurable total in 1998.

The durable goods market for corrugated products is considerably more fragmented, with toys and sporting goods leading the corrugated box users market in this category with just 5 percent of shipments.

One significant change for boxmakers in the early 1990s was the modification of Rule 41 and Item 22 of the freight classifications. These standards specify corrugated box design criteria and, after the modification, they now stress performance-based edge compression tests rather than the old mullen/burst strength-based test. This allows boxmakers to design lighter weight containment packaging. The revised classifications also create wider opportunities for the use of other types of corrugated boxes that use high performance linerboard (often with a predominantly virgin fiber furnish) and standard liners (usually having a fairly high recycled fiber furnish).

Industry Growth Predicated on Other Industries. The fortunes of the corrugated and solid fiber box manufac-

turing industry have historically risen and fallen with the shipping needs of other industries. In fact, some financial analysts use corrugated packaging as an indicator of overall economic activity. Corrugated container shipments were expected to continue to track with growth in the general economy throughout the late 1990s. The robust U.S. economy allowed the corrugated box industry to ship a record 402.6 billion square feet of finished product in 1998.

Pricing of U.S. box production generally reflects the pricing of its underlying materials—mostly linerboard and corrugating medium. In the early 1990s, domestic prices of corrugated boxes and their raw materials were quite low, shackled by the unusually long U.S. economic slowdown in the late 1980s and early 1990s, too much box making capacity, and lower demand for boxes. The average price for corrugated boxes ranged between about $44 per thousand square feet (msf) and $50 per msf through the 1990s, depending on the economy, available capacity, and inventories. Prices for box materials also varied significantly during the 1990s. After reaching a peak of $480 per short ton in 1995, linerboard prices plummeted, and by 1998 it was just $380 per ton. In 1998, the average price was $370 per ton. However, in 1999 linerboard prices began slowly increasing and that recovery was expected to continue into 2000. Corrugating medium followed much the same trend, reaching a peak of $470 per ton in 1995 before dropping dramatically to $265 per ton by 1998. In 1999, however, prices began to move up, reaching $325 per ton in March. Prices were expected to increase throughout 2000.

Preprinted Linerboard. One of the major recent changes in the corrugated box industry has been the growing use of preprinted linerboard. This product is used to make boxes with a white enamel surface that can be printed on with four-color graphics, while the rest of the box remains the same unbleached brown color. The main reason for the growth of preprint has been the growing belief by manufacturers that an attractive box can influence consumer buying decisions at the ''point of purchase'' in the store. Simply put, an attractively packaged product is more likely to be purchased than one in a brown box. Some studies have shown that up to 80 percent of buying decisions are made at the point of purchase, so the additional advertising from a colorful box can help influence that decision. Shipments of value-added, highly graphical boxes made from preprinted linerboard increased at a rate of about 7 percent a year throughout much of the 1990s, compared with growth of 2 percent for all corrugated packaging products.

Competitors. One of the market threats to corrugated packaging is flexible plastic films. These products—mostly stretch and shrink wraps—became more competitive with corrugated products throughout the 1990s, at least in domestic markets. Also, some companies began to employ re-usable plastic containers to ship products internally from one company location to another.

However, the corrugated container industry has responded to these kinds of market threats by producing lighter weight, higher strength products that reduce shipping costs for box users. In addition, features such as visual appeal (of boxes made from preprint linerboard) and improved resistance to moisture should help corrugated boxes compete in other areas.

INDUSTRY LEADERS

The industry leaders in this category tend to be the same as the leaders in the production of containerboard since so much of box production is fully integrated. Some of the leading corrugated and solid fiber box producers include Boise Cascade; Packaging Corporation of America; Smurfit-Stone Container Corp.; Weyerhaeuser Co.; and Temple-Inland, Inc. Other significant players include International Paper Co. and Willamette Corp.

AMERICA AND THE WORLD

The United States is a major player in the global market for corrugated products, both as a producer and as an exporter. Strong export demand for American corrugated products in the 1990s, in fact, helped keep the U.S. industry healthy. For example, in 1998 U.S. exports of corrugated paperboard products were up for the ninth consecutive year, with a 6 percent increase in value and a 4 percent increase in volume. In 1998, U.S. corrugators exported a record 2.33 million metric tons of finished corrugated boxes, containers, and related products. While U.S. sales have fluctuated in recent years, foreign sales have continued to be a growth area for domestic producers. Despite the Asian financial crisis, U.S. corrugators increased their sales noticeably to Japan and other Asian countries. In 1998, U.S. exports of corrugated containers and finished packaging commodities were shipped mainly to Mexico (55 percent) and Canada (21 percent). However, there were large increases in exports to several Latin American countries. Exports as a percentage of total corrugated box industry shipments grew from less than 1 percent in 1989 to nearly 3 percent in 1998.

The value of U.S. corrugated products imports was comparatively small in 1998, at $156 million. However, this was 132 percent higher than the 1993 total of $67.2 million. Imports increased every year from 1991 to 1998. Principal suppliers of corrugated products to the United States in 1998 were Canada (65 percent) and Mexico (10 percent).

International Competitiveness. Since U.S. containerboard producers are often the low-cost producers in world markets, U.S. corrugated products tend to be very competitive in global markets. When the U.S. dollar is low against foreign currencies, U.S. corrugated products are even more competitive. This was the case in the early to mid-1990s, when U.S. corrugated exports boomed. However, by 1996 the combined effect of Mexico's fiscal crisis and the rising value of the dollar threatened to erode some of these export gains—since Mexico's ability to purchase corrugated products was damaged and the rising dollar raised the effective cost of U.S. products in foreign markets. The U.S. dollar remained relatively strong through the rest of the decade, though it weakened somewhat in 1999. Despite these currency difficulties, the U.S. foreign shipment level in 1998 was roughly 30 percent higher than foreign sales of European Union corrugators and almost four times the amount shipped by Japan.

Worldwide shipments of corrugated packaging reached $54 billion in 1995 and were expected to reach $64 billion by 2000. As the global low-cost producer, the United States was expected to maintain its 35 percent share of the total number of boxes produced into the early 2000s; that share amounted to more than 28 million metric tons in 1998. Growing economies in Asia, Eastern Europe, and South America may become more important to the U.S. industry if they are unable to satisfy domestic needs for packaging and shipping containers. However, pulp and paper facilities are being constructed at a rapid pace in many of these markets—particularly in Asia—and many nations may be able to satisfy their domestic demand for corrugated packaging more quickly than was once thought.

Although the U.S. corrugating industry is the world's largest, it needs to continue to increase the productivity of its corrugator and sheet plants by staying competitive on labor and operating costs. The industry will also need to do a better job of responding to customers by developing or implementing new graphics, coatings, inks, and dyes. Through computer technology, the industry will also have to streamline the process of ordering, producing, and transporting corrugated products, both domestically and worldwide.

RESEARCH AND TECHNOLOGY

Much of the research and technology in corrugated box production throughout the 1990s focused on improved process control and computerized order entry and production scheduling.

One area of concern to researchers is twist warp—the loss of flatness—in linerboard when it is converted into corrugated board. This problem was relatively unknown until the past few years, when corrugating machines began to run at faster speeds—around 1,000 feet per minute. At these speeds, linerboard with twist warp can cause malfunctions on the corrugator. While paperboard producers are currently focusing on making operating changes to minimize the problem, more research is needed into the fundamental reason for twist warp in order to help solve the problem.

Another promising research area for corrugated products manufacturers involves recycling. Traditionally, manufacturers of boxes for applications where the box becomes wet (such as for shipping produce) used corrugated materials treated with chemical wet strength agents. Although these agents make the box resistant to moisture, they also make it almost impossible to recycle since it will not break down during the recycling process. However, a paper chemical manufacturer, Georgia-Pacific Resins Inc., has researched and developed a wet strength agent that will break down during recycling. It is expected that this will expand the recyclability of many old corrugated containers.

Other research efforts will focus on how to maximize quality and minimize cost as the U.S. corrugated box industry attempts to preserve its strong market advantages throughout the next century.

FURTHER READING

"Can Industry Reverse the Profit Crisis?" *Pulp & Paper,* January 1999.

"Global Outlook: More Misery or Muddling Through?" *PIMA's North American Papermaker,* December 1998.

Paper, Paperboard, Pulp Capacity and Fiber Consumption. Washington, D.C.: American Forest & Paper Association, 1998.

U.S. Trade and Industrial Outlook, 1999. New York: McGraw Hill, 1999.

SIC 2655

FIBER CANS, TUBES, DRUMS AND SIMILAR PRODUCTS

Establishments in this industry are primarily engaged in manufacturing fiber cans, tubes, drums, cones, and similar products from purchased paperboard. These products can be made with or without metal ends. This industry segment produces a wide variety of products, including paper fiber bottles, fiber bobbins, composite cans, all-fiber cans, fiber drums (metal-end or all fiber), fiber cores, mailing cases and tubes, and tubes for chemical and electrical use.

NAICS CODE(S)

322214 (Fiber Can, Tube, Drum, and Similar Products Manufacturing)

Fiber can and drum manufacturing is a mature industry, with growth at or below the rate of increase in the U.S. gross domestic product (GDP). From 1984 to 1997, the value of this industry's product shipments increased 36 percent, from $1.69 billion to $2.30 billion. With an annualized growth rate of 2.7 percent, this industry ranks among the slower growing paper products industries, but is still close to matching the country's average growth in GDP. In the late 1980s and early to mid-1990s, the fiber can and drum industry plateaued, with the value of shipments inching up each year from $1.83 billion in 1989 to $1.92 billion in 1992 and $2.00 billion from 1993 to 1995. In the late 1990s, the industry exceeded growth projections, producing shipments worth $2.30 billion in 1997.

The number of establishments in the industry in 1997 was 285, down from 301 in 1992. In 1997, this industry employed 11,549 people with a total payroll of $356.6 million (compared with 13,000 people in 1992). Of that 1997 total, 9,524 were production workers who put in 19.3 million hours for wages of $262.4 million, an hourly average of $13.57.

The manufacture of fiber cans, tubes, and drums is concentrated east of the Mississippi River. The top three producing regions, in terms of total shipments, are the north central, the southeast/mid-Atlantic, and the northeastern regions of the United States. In 1997, Georgia was the leading producer of fiber cans and drums, with $154 million in product shipments, followed by Ohio with $152 million, Wisconsin with $120 million, and North Carolina with $103 million.

Fiber cans, tubes, and similar products are, by far, the largest category of products produced by this industry, accounting for $1.66 billion of the industry value of shipments in 1997. Paperboard fiber drums, a larger-sized product, accounted for $374 million of total fiber cans, drums, and similar product shipments in 1997. Products not specified by kind accounted for $122 million. All other products accounted for the remaining $144 million.

Paper and paperboard (not including boxes and containers) represented the single largest category of materials used by the fiber can, tube, and drum industry in 1997, accounting for $683.0 million worth of materials consumed. Metal closures and crowns for containers claimed another $81.8 million, while sheet steel and strip claimed $60.7 million. Glues and adhesives cost $48.7 million and all other materials combined claimed about $340.0 million.

Like other paper product producers, the makers of fiber cans, tubes, and drums have been using more recycled paperboard and less virgin paperboard in order to satisfy end user demands. In the 1990s, this industry appeared to benefit from the desire by consumers and the government to use more products made from recycled materials or materials that were more recyclable than competing products. This environmental factor was a distinct advantage for industry manufacturers as many competing products are made from plastic, which is perceived to be a less recyclable product.

The paper industry is a good customer as well as a supplier for the fiber can, tube, and drum industry. Many mills use heavy-duty fiber cores to wind their paper and paperboard rolls. These cores are either shipped in long lengths and cut at the mill or pre-cut by the core manufacturer. This market shows little sign of moving toward alternative products, such as steel cores.

The fiber drum has seen its market share decline as many industrial users are trying to eliminate the use of disposable containers. For example, for regulatory reasons, the chemical industry is moving away from using drums of any kind, including fiber or metal. Instead, they are using more portable chemical feed containers that are dropped off by the chemical manufacturer and then picked up to be reused when empty.

Some of the industry leaders in this category are integrated manufacturers, in that they produce fiber cans, drums, and tubes, as well as the paperboard from which they are made. Other fiber can, tube, and drum manufacturers are independent converters of purchased paperboard. One of the leading companies in this industry, Sonoco Products Co. of Hartsville, South Carolina, is an integrated producer. Other leaders in this industry include Greif Bros. Corporation of Delaware, Ohio; Star Paper Tube Inc. of Rock Hill, South Carolina; Anvil Cases Inc. of Hacienda Heights, California; and Niemand South Inc. of Marion, Alabama.

FURTHER READING

Darnay, Arsen J., ed. *Manufacturing USA*. 6th ed. Farmington Hills, MI: Gale Group, 1998.

Lazich, Robert S., ed. *Market Share Reporter*. Farmington Hills, MI: Gale Group, 1997.

Paper, Paperboard, Pulp Capacity and Fiber Consumption. Washington, D.C.: American Forest & Paper Association, 1998.

Smook, Gary A. *Handbook of Pulp & Paper Terminology: A Guide to Industrial and Technological Usage.* Bellingham, WA: Angus Wilde Publications, 1990.

U.S. Department of Commerce. Census Bureau. "Fiber Can, Tube, Drum, and Similar Products Manufacturing," *1997 Economic Census.* Washington, D.C.: GPO, November 1999.

U.S. Trade and Industrial Outlook 1999. New York: McGraw-Hill, 1998.

SIC 2656

SANITARY FOOD CONTAINERS, EXCEPT FOLDING

This category includes establishments primarily engaged in manufacturing non-folding food containers from special foodboard. Industry products include paperboard beverage cartons, round and nested food containers, paper cups for hot or cold drinks, and stamped plates, dishes, spoons, and similar products. Establishments primarily engaged in manufacturing similar items from plastic materials are classified in Industry Group 308; those making folding sanitary cartons are classified in **SIC 2657: Folding Paperboard Boxes, Including Sanitary.**

NAICS CODE(S)

322215 (Non-Folding Sanitary Food Container Manufacturing)

Sanitary food containers have been a strong growth market for the paper industry. Despite increasing consumer interest in reducing usage of disposable products, the convenience of disposable paper products has continued to appeal to growing numbers of consumers. Also, the use of paperboard milk cartons in alternative, nonfood markets has given that part of the industry a healthy boost.

In the 1990s, the value of U.S. sanitary food container product shipments rose and fell, largely in concert with the fortunes of the paper industry, which produces the raw materials from which these products are made. When paper prices dropped, as they did in the early 1990s, so did the value of sanitary food container product shipments. When paper prices recovered in 1995, sanitary food containers did likewise. For example, in 1991 the value of shipments reached a record $2.72 billion, but dropped back sharply in 1992 to $2.49 billion, and dropped again in 1993 to $2.46 billion. However, the value of shipments of sanitary food containers recovered in 1994, and by 1997 had increased to a record $2.74 billion.

This industry consists of three major segments. Cups and liquid-tight paper and paperboard containers were a bit less than half ($1.35 billion) of the value of all industry shipments in 1997. Milk and milk-type paperboard cartons were the next largest category, at $684.0 million; other sanitary paper and paperboard food containers, boards, and trays, except folding accounted for $641.9 million; and all other products took up the remaining $65.0 million.

Sanitary-food-container manufacturers employed 14,925 people in 1997, down from 15,700 in 1990. There were 83 establishments in the industry in 1997, slightly lower than the total of 86 in 1990. Annual payroll for all employees was $441.4 million in 1997, up from $392.0 million in 1990.

The market for paper cups, plates, and other disposable paper products was healthy in 1990s. Despite the fact that these products are relatively difficult to recycle—most are contaminated with food or beverages after use—the category continued to grow throughout the decade. In the mid-1990s, manufacturers of sanitary food containers were able to answer some of their environmental critics by including recycled fiber in their products. This was made possible when the Food and Drug Administration (FDA) issued guidelines for the use of recycled paper in products that come in contact with food. Also, the increased strength and grease resistance of paper products, particularly plates, allowed for their use in an increasing number of applications. Household use of paper cups showed no signs of abating.

Paperboard milk cartons have a formidable competitor in milk jugs made from high density polyethylene (HDPE). These plastic milk jugs captured a growing share of the milk market in the 1970s and 1980s, most particularly in the gallon size, but also in the half-gallon size. However, an extended decline in sales of paperboard milk cartons began to slow and even stop in the 1990s when it became widely known that paperboard milk cartons retain vitamins better than their plastic counterparts (fluorescent lights in dairy cases leach vitamins from milk in translucent plastic jugs). This knowledge led some dairies and consumers to once again favor paperboard. Also, major efforts to promote the recycling of milk cartons by milk carton manufacturers, notably International Paper Co., helped improve the appeal of this type of packaging. Product innovations, such as adding spouts with resealable caps to paperboard orange juice cartons, have also helped increase the use of carton packaging.

Because of paperboard milk-style carton's ease of storage and ability to withstand repeated access, additional domestic uses for it were developed. These included packaging for nondairy flavored drinks, fruit juices, dry pet foods, laundry detergents, candy, and hardware. Such alternative uses helped increase the sale of milk cartons: in 1980, nondairy carton tonnage accounted for only 13 percent of all milk-carton sales. By 1997, that percentage had topped 32 percent.

Leaders in this industry include a mixture of major paper companies and independent converting companies. The leading company is Fort James Corp., manufacturer of Dixie Cups and other sanitary paper products. Other key market players include International Paper Company and Blue Ridge Paper Co.—both of which manufacture milk carton stock—Solo Cup Company; Sealright Company, Inc.; Keyes Fibre Company; and Imperial Bondware Inc. While many of these leading companies produce branded products, sales of private label products are very strong in key categories, such as disposable dishes. For example, private label products accounted for close to 50 percent of the disposable dish market (including paper and plastic) in 1997. The leading paper disposable dish brand was Fort James' Dixie Livingware, followed by Keyes Fibre's Chinet brand. As of 1998, Fort James operated 11 tabletop/foodservice converting plants employing 3,300 people.

FURTHER READING

Lazich, Robert S., ed. *Market Share Reporter*. Detroit: Gale Research, 1997.

Paper, Paperboard, Pulp Capacity and Fiber Consumption. Washington, D.C.: American Forest & Paper Association, 1998.

Smook, Gary A. *Handbook of Pulp & Paper Terminology: A Guide to Industrial and Technological Usage*. Bellingham, WA: Angus Wilde Publications, 1990.

U.S. Department of Commerce. Census Bureau. "Nonfolding Sanitary Food Container Manufacturing," *1997 Economic Census*. Washington, D.C.: GPO, November 1999.

U.S. Trade and Industrial Outlook 1999. New York: McGraw-Hill, 1998.

SIC 2657

FOLDING PAPERBOARD BOXES, INCLUDING SANITARY

Establishments in this industry are primarily engaged in manufacturing folding paperboard boxes from purchased paperboard, including folding sanitary food boxes or cartons (except milk cartons). Products include folding paperboard boxes such as cereal boxes; folding cartons; frozen food containers; ice cream containers; folding sanitary food pails, such as those used for takeout food from restaurants; and paperboard backs for blister packages.

NAICS CODE(S)

322212 (Folding Paperboard Box Manufacturing)

INDUSTRY SNAPSHOT

While the folding paperboard box industry demonstrated sales growth for most of the 1990s, it encountered some difficulties in the middle part of the decade before recovering in the late 1990s. The value of folding paperboard box shipments grew from $7.93 billion in 1992 to $8.63 billion in 1995. While the value of shipments slipped slightly in 1996, to $8.49 billion, it continued growing again in 1997, reaching $8.94 billion. Projections called for continued, if moderate, growth throughout the 2000s.

The tonnage of folding paperboard boxes and cartons advanced steadily throughout the 1990s, rising from 2.60 million tons in 1992 to 3.22 million tons in 1997, a gain of 24.0 percent, or about 4.8 percent per year. That figure was more impressive considering that folding paperboard boxes were "lightweighted" throughout the 1990s, meaning that less packaging materials were needed to create boxes with the same performance characteristics.

Food and beverage products represented some of the best markets for the folding paperboard box industry, with strong growth reported in packaging materials for both the bottled and canned beverages and dry food and produce industries. Together, those two categories accounted for 46 percent of the tonnage of folding paperboard boxes produced in 1997. Some of the biggest beverage markets are for 6-, 12-, and 24-packs of canned soft drinks and beer.

Other important categories included frozen foods (10.3 percent); soaps and detergents (8.7 percent) carry-out boxes and trays (8.7 percent); paper goods (7.5 percent); and tobacco products (6.0 percent).

Overall, about 62 percent of the volume of folding carton shipments went to food-related applications and 38 percent to non-food applications in 1997.

ORGANIZATION AND STRUCTURE

In 1997, the U.S. folding paperboard box industry was made up of about 575 establishments. Shipments by the U.S. folding carton industry were concentrated in four main regions: North Central, Eastern, Southern, and Pacific. In the early 2000s, leading states in the industry included California, with 54 establishments; Illinois, with 51; Ohio, with 44; and Pennsylvania, with 42.

The growth of food-related packaging and other retail applications helped expand the retail market for folding paperboard boxes. The growing use of folding boxes as beverage carriers also helped fuel growth in folding paperboard box sales. Both beer and soda bottlers used 24-can ''cases'' as promotional vehicles in the mid-1990s. As a result, more of those products were sold in folding paperboard boxes and fewer in the traditional six-packs held together by plastic carriers.

In the late 1990s, folding box manufacturers expanded production of high-quality, high-whiteness boxes suitable for four-color-process printing. Better visual appeal of such packaging often translated into higher impulse purchases by consumers, and folding boxboard customers often would pay a premium price for goods so boxed.

However, unlike its corrugated container cousins, the folding paperboard box has faced direct competition from alternative materials, principally the bewildering array of plastics. The growth of flexible bags, pouches, and wraps, as well as rigid carriers and containers made from plastics, has created a serious challenge to the dominance of the folding paperboard box in the packaging marketplace.

Folding paperboard boxes have also faced competition from some other paperboard products. In some retail applications, corrugated products and carded ''blister packs'' (paperboard backings that hold a molded plastic insert) have been used as a substitute for paperboard boxes.

Sales in the folding carton industry traditionally have been seasonal. The industry typically starts the year strongly after a slump in sales during December. Sales usually slow down slightly from April to July, and then they rebound from August to November before slowing down again in December.

CURRENT CONDITIONS

The U.S. folding paperboard box industry set records in 1998 in both the volume and value of product shipments. The strong U.S. economy led to increased domestic sales, and export sales were higher than expected. This allowed the folding paperboard box industry to have record sales in nearly all of its end use markets. This was the second straight year of renewed growth for the industry after a drop in sales during 1996.

While still facing formidable competition from alternative packaging, the folding paperboard box industry was expected to grow into the 2000s. Improved strength and lighter weight folding boxboard helped to improve the competitive position of folding paperboard boxes in the packaging marketplace. Folding paperboard boxes also benefited from the fact that they were recyclable and contain recycled fiber. Both of these attributes were actively promoted on retail packages.

Paperboard's recyclability is significant since packaging in general has garnered a reputation for increasing the amount of solid waste produced in the United States each year. In the early 1990s, recycling was a important issue and there was much public discussion of the landfill crisis, which presumed that the United States was running out of landfill space. The use of paperboard packaging (and other forms of packaging) was criticized as being inherently wasteful. Manufacturers were encouraged to reduce or eliminate packaging for their products.

The folding boxboard industry and other sectors of the paper and paperboard industry responded by increasing the amount of recycled fiber used in their products. This successful campaign led to the paper industry recovering 47 percent of the paper and paperboard produced in the United States in 1998, up from just 28 percent in 1986. Also, the landfill crisis turned out to be more imaginary than real, with major amounts of new landfill capacity coming on stream in the mid-1990s. The combination of these two developments helped curtail pressure to reduce the use of paperboard packaging, and shipments of folding paperboard boxes were expected to increase—not decrease—through the end of the 1990s and into the 2000s.

Production of the raw material for folding paperboard boxes—folding boxboard—was growing steadily in the mid-1990s. The United States produced 6.66 million tons of folding boxboard in 1998, up 2.6 percent over 1997, when production was 6.49 million tons.

There are three grades of U.S. folding boxboard: solid bleached sulfate (SBS), which is bleached white for high brightness; unbleached kraft, which retains the natural brown color of paperboard; and recycled. Of the 6.66 million tons of folding boxboard produced in 1998, 2.86 million tons were recycled folding boxboard (43 percent); 2.14 million tons were SBS (32 percent) and 1.66 million tons were unbleached kraft (25 percent).

SBS is favored by manufacturers of folding paperboard boxes for the packaging of cigarettes, frozen and wet foods, meats, non-prescription drugs, bakery foods, and cosmetics. These manufacturers appreciate its superior visual and performance characteristics. Throughout the 1980s and early 1990s, SBS accounted for about 35 percent of the folding boxboard used by the domestic folding paperboard box industry.

In the early 1990s, SBS was challenged by two market forces—competition from lower cost alternatives and the growth of recycling. As the quality of lower-cost kraft and recycled-board grades increased, some boxmakers opted for the cost savings those grades could provide. Also, many companies purchasing folding paperboard boxes wanted to demonstrate environmental awareness to their retail customers by providing the ultimate end-user with products encased in recycled packaging.

However, in the mid- to late 1990s, SBS staged something of a comeback, and in 1995 production of SBS increased—to 2.07 million tons from 2.02 million tons the previous year—while production of recycled folding boxboard declined slightly, to 2.86 million tons from 2.87 million tons. By 1998, production of SBS was up to 2.14 million tons, while recycled boxboard was steady at about 2.85 million tons. Growing demand for SBS can be attributed to demands by domestic packagers for better graphics on their packages and growing export demand for SBS.

Recycled folding boxboard—the leading folding boxboard grade—was an environmental success story for the industry. The success of this grade was due to several factors, including the tremendous interest in recycling. But most industrial users would be unwilling to accept an inferior product simply because it was more environmentally friendly. Better recycling procedures and improvements in strength, formation, and surface coating have allowed quality recycled clay-coated board to compete in several markets from which it was previously excluded.

The capacity to produce all three grades of folding boxboard was expected to increase throughout the late 1990s. Unbleached kraft folding capacity increased from 2.07 million tons in 1997 to 2.25 million tons in 1999. By 2001, capacity was expected to reach 2.33 million tons. SBS folding boxboard capacity increased from 3.03 million tons in 1997 to 3.07 million tons in 1999. Capacity was expected to increase to 3.20 million tons in 2001.

Capacity to produce recycled folding boxboard reached 3.00 million tons in 1997 and grew slightly to 3.05 million tons in 1999. Capacity was expected to remain virtually unchanged through 2001.

In the 1990s, folding paperboard box volume shipments tended to mirror the general economy, growing only as fast or slightly slower than gross domestic product (GDP). However, since these figures are based on tonnage, it must be taken into account that today's folding paperboard box manufacturers are producing lighter weight boxes that still meet existing strength tests and other industry standards. As a result, lighter boxes—which reduce industry tonnage—are replacing heavier products.

Product shipments of folding paperboard containers and boxes are expected to increase about 1.6 percent annually from 1999 to 2004 as the U.S. economy grows at a rate of 2.2 percent per year. On a volume basis, exports of folding cartons should increase about 6.0 percent and imports 7.0 percent annually during this period. Mexico and Canada should remain the main export markets, but the industry was expected to develop new markets as well, primarily in Latin America, Asia, and Eastern Europe.

Folding paperboard box plants employed 50,197 people in 1997. About 39,900 of those were production workers who earned on average $13.79 an hour.

INDUSTRY LEADERS

The folding paperboard box industry is highly integrated. This means that the leading producers of folding paperboard boxes also produce the folding boxboard used to make the product. Leading producers of folding paperboard boxes include Georgia-Pacific Corporation, Fort James, Smurfit-Stone Container Corp., Westvaco Corp., Packaging Corporation of America, and Rock-Tenn Co. Other leading companies include Green Bay Packaging Inc., Waldorf Corp., and Gulf States Paper Corp.

AMERICA AND THE WORLD

The folding paperboard box industry has traditionally imported more than it has exported—a trend that continued into the late 1990s. In 1998, U.S. exports of all folding cartons and related products amounted to 151,250 metric tons, an increase of 2 percent over 1997. In 1998, folding cartons represented about two-thirds of the total volume exported, while sanitary food and beverage containers made up one-third. The leading U.S. export markets by volume for finished folding cartons in 1998 were Canada, with 40 percent; Mexico, 30 percent; and China, 11 percent. In spite of the Asian financial crisis in 1997, export growth in this category was expected to continue growing throughout the late 1990s and into the 2000s.

In 1999, U.S. exports in this category were expected to be valued at $315 million, compared to $292 million in

1998 and $278 million in 1997. By comparison, imports of folding paperboard boxes were valued at $402 million in 1999, compared to $362 million in 1998 and $315 million in 1997.

While exports of folding paperboard boxes have continued to grow, they are still a relatively small portion of total production. In 1998, for example, exports accounted for just 3 percent of total folding paperboard box production. It usually makes the most economic sense to export folding boxboard in sheets or rolls and then convert them into boxes locally. Many U.S. folding paperboard box manufacturers possess sites for foreign conversion for this reason. As a result, exports of unconverted folding boxboard were roughly three-and-a-half times the size of finished folding paperboard box exports in the late 1990s.

Foreign trade was expected to continue to play a minor but growing role in total industry shipments through the end of the 1990s. With exports to Mexico, other Latin American countries, and Pacific Rim countries expected to increase, folding carton product shipments were anticipated to increase 11 percent in value in 1997 and 8 percent in 1998. The domestic market will likely remain the central focus of folding paperboard box manufacturers. The historically high U.S. per capita consumption of folding paperboard boxes—approaching 40 pounds per year—will help maintain that focus. By comparison, western European per capita consumption has been documented as only about half that of the United States.

FURTHER READING

Folding Paperboard Box Manufacturing, 1997 Economic Census, Manufacturing Industry Series Washington, D.C.: U.S. Census Bureau, August 1999.

Lazich, Robert S., ed. *Market Share Reporter 2000.* Detroit: Gale Research, 1999.

Paper, Paperboard, Pulp Capacity and Fiber Consumption. Washington, D.C.: American Forest & Paper Association, 1998.

U.S. Trade and Industrial Outlook 1999. New York: McGraw-Hill, 1998.

SIC 2671

COATED AND LAMINATED PACKAGING PAPER AND PLASTICS FILM

This classification covers establishments primarily engaged in manufacturing coated or laminated flexible materials made of combinations of paper, plastics film, metal foil, and similar materials (excluding textiles) for packaging purposes. These are made from purchased sheet materials or plastics resins and may be printed in the same establishment. Establishments primarily engaged in manufacturing coated or laminated paper for other purposes are classified in **SIC 2672: Coated and Laminated Paper, Not Elsewhere Classified,** including establishments manufacturing all gummed or pressure sensitive tape. Those establishments that manufacture unsupported plastics film are classified in **SIC 3081: Unsupported Plastics Film and Sheet.** Establishments manufacturing aluminum foil are classified in **SIC 3497: Metal Foil and Leaf,** while those manufacturing paper from pulp are classified in **SIC 2621: Paper Mills.**

NAICS CODE(S)

322221 (Coated and Laminated Packaging Paper and Plastics Film Manufacturing)
326112 (Unsupported Plastics Packaging Film and Sheet Manufacturing)

Note: The U.S. Economic Census now reports industrial information under the North American Industry Classification System (NAICS) instead of the Standard Industrial Classification (SIC) system. As a result, the data reported below is for **NAICS 322221** (the replacement for **SIC 2671**), and includes only a small portion of what used to be reported for **SIC 2671.** For example, the 1995 value of shipments for **SIC 2671** was estimated at $4.14 billion; in 1997, the value of shipments for **NAICS 322221** was reported at $1.58 billion.

The coated and laminated packaging paper and plastics film industry is one of the smallest segments within the paper industry group, totaling just $1.58 billion in 1997. It makes the raw materials used to make specialized packages, such as those used for razor blades and other ''carded'' products, as well as other packaging products. The industry is more fragmented than most other paper industries, with a number of small players competing either in highly specialized product niches or regions. A company might, for example, have a leading position in one segment but have no products in any of the other segments. A distinguishing feature of the industry is the fact that an inordinately high percentage (approximately 20 percent) of potential clients such as manufacturers package their own goods, which means that firms within the industry often compete with potential clients.

This industry was made up of 91 establishments operated by 78 companies in 1997. The industry employed a total of 5,753 people in 1997, including 4,445 production workers. Those production workers had total wages of $132 million and logged 9.7 million hours, for an average hourly wage of $13.63.

Three product categories make up most of this industry's shipments. Single-web paper, coated rolls and sheets, including waxed, for flexible packaging uses, accounted for $965 million of the value of product shipments in 1997. Multiweb laminated rolls and sheets, except foil and film, for flexible packaging uses accounted for another $456 million. Coated and laminated packaging paper and plastics film, not specified by kind, represented $119 million.

Companies in this industry were located primarily east of the Mississippi River, and five states dominated the industry. Massachusetts was the leading producer, accounting for $183 million of the industry's value of shipments in 1997. Tennessee followed at $156 million; Wisconsin at $135 million; Missouri at $114 million; and Michigan at $104 million. Other leading states included Illinois, New York, Ohio, and Texas.

The paper, coated, and laminated packaging industry, while small, has been resilient for much of the 1980s and 1990s, producing a gain in the value of shipments even during recessions. Since 1987, the value of shipments for this industry increased every year; this growth continued through the late 1990s. A stronger national economy in the late 1990s, more emphasis on research and development, and the expansion of niche markets appeared to be driving this industry toward increased sales and new markets. Demand for all types of plastic film—one of the key raw materials used by this industry—was expected to increase 17 percent (in volume) between 1993 and 1998, moving from 10.66 million pounds in 1993 to 12.44 million pounds in 1998.

Some of the more notable changes the industry has experienced include: new materials, environmentally conscious products, specialization, and technological innovation. The industry experimented with new materials as customers demanded lighter weight, stronger materials for packaging. Some of the new materials include lighter, high-tech plastics and reinforced paper. The increased popularity of the microwave, for example, has produced a growing need for a wider range of uses for existing and new materials.

Biodegradable, recyclable, and recycled materials have become essential in the packaging industry. Packaging accounted for more than 30 percent of U.S. solid waste in the late 1990s. In response to environmental pressures as well as to higher prices for landfill usage, producers have incorporated "green" products and recycled raw materials into their packaging. However, there was some doubt about whether or not "green" products were commercially viable. While in surveys consumers often say that they want to buy more environmentally friendly products, when asked to pay more for them, they usually decline.

With manufacturers demanding more from packaging, producers have needed to incorporate new skills and materials into producing packages. This has led to specialization and technological innovation. An example of such innovation is razor packaging, which has been made to simulate the look of a mirror.

Bemis Corporation of Minneapolis, primarily active in flexible film packaging, was one of the leading companies in this industry. Consolidated Papers Incorporated, a major paper manufacturer of paper and converted paper products, sold its coated and laminated packaging operations to St. Laurent Paperboard, a Canadian company, in 1999. Printpack Incorporated of Atlanta; Instrument Systems Corporation of Jericho, New York; and Minnesota Mining & Manufacturing (3M) of St. Paul, Minnesota, were other leading companies in the industry.

FURTHER READING

Darnay, Arsen J., ed. *Manufacturing USA*. 6th ed. Detroit: Gale Research, 1998.

Coated and Laminated Packaging Paper and Plastics Film Manufacturing, 1997 Economic Census, Manufacturing Industry Series. Washington, D.C.: U.S. Census Bureau, August 1999.

Lazich, Robert S., ed. *Market Share Reporter*. Detroit: Gale Research, 1997.

Paper, Paperboard, Pulp Capacity and Fiber Consumption. Washington, D.C.: American Forest & Paper Association, 1998.

Smook, Gary A. *Handbook of Pulp & Paper Terminology: A Guide to Industrial and Technological Usage.* Bellingham, WA: Angus Wilde Publications, 1990.

U.S. Department of Commerce. Census Bureau. "Coated and Laminated Packaging Paper and Plastics Film Manufacturing," *1997 Economic Census.* Washington, D.C.: GPO, 1999.

U.S. Trade and Industrial Outlook 1999. New York: McGraw-Hill, 1998.

SIC 2672

COATED AND LAMINATED PAPER, NOT ELSEWHERE CLASSIFIED

This industry covers establishments primarily engaged in manufacturing coated, laminated, or processed paper and film from purchased paper, except for packaging. Also included are establishments primarily manufacturing gummed paper products and pressure sensitive tape with backing of any material other than rubber, for any application. Establishments primarily engaged in manufacturing coated and laminated paper for packaging are classified in **SIC 2671: Packaging Paper and Plastics Film, Coated and Laminated;** those manufacturing carbon paper are classified in **SIC 3955: Carbon Paper and Inked Ribbons;** and those manufacturing photographic and blueprint paper are classified in **SIC 3861: Photographic Equipment and Supplies.**

NAICS CODE(S)

322222 (Coated and Laminated Paper Manufacturing)

INDUSTRY SNAPSHOT

This classification incorporates a wide variety of products and companies. In 1997, the value of shipments for the laminated and coated paper industry reached nearly $12 billion, up sharply from $8.87 billion in 1994. Industry establishments employed approximately 41,541 workers in 1997, including 28,504 production workers. This industry has grown rapidly over the past 20 years as more specialty applications for its products have been developed. For example, in the late 1990s, the U.S. Postal Service rapidly expanded its use of self-stick postage stamps, representing an enormous market for this industry.

ORGANIZATION AND STRUCTURE

Most companies in this industry limited their activities to the coating of paper or other materials, but produced diverse products from this process. Of the many products in the industry, the vast majority of shipments came from one of two sectors: pressure-sensitive products and "other" coated and laminated paper not produced at paper mills. The pressure-sensitive products group included cellophane tape, almost all labels, and a variety of other pressure-sensitive adhesives (PSAs), but did not include gummed tape. Other coated and laminated paper products included paper that was treated or coated to enhance the paper's utility. PSAs were by far the largest product class produced by this industry, accounting for $7.1 billion, or about 60.0 percent, of all shipments in 1997, according to the U.S. Economic Census. The next largest category was wallcoverings, which held 3.8 percent of all shipments, followed by gift wrap (3.6 percent); coated and processed papers (3.4 percent); and gummed paper products (1.7 percent). All other products accounted for 27.5 percent of the total.

Pressure-Sensitive Products. Even within this subsegment of the industry, there was a great deal of diversity. Pressure-sensitive products ranged from cellophane tape to shrinkable labels to sealing tapes. Advances in adhesive technology and continuing development work by manufacturers of PSAs led to increases in applicability and quality. Lighter weight products offering greater flexibility and lower cost than traditional materials allowed some types of adhesives to be used in place of rivets, bolts, and chemical compounds in assembly processes. Even heavy industrial processes such as engine manufacturing and truck frame assembly found applications for PSAs.

To produce PSAs, manufacturers used paper, plastic films, nonwoven cloth, or polyethylene as a base. A chemi-cal solvent or waterborne acrylic, which provides the adhesive necessary for the PSA to stick, is applied to the base, usually to one side. PSAs can be measured using three different criteria: tack, PSA's bonding quality with a given surface; peel, difficulty of removing the tape from the surface; and shear resistance, PSA's response to "creep" over time. The type of adhesive that coats the film depends on the PSA's desired application. Labels can be made of paper, polystyrene, film, or other materials, but the defining feature of a label is its mode of application.

The value of shipments for label base stock reached $2.18 billion in 1997, according to the 1997 U.S. Economic Census. Total U.S. sales of finished pressure-sensitive labels was $3.93 billion in 1998, according to the 1998 North American Label Study, commissioned by the Tag & Label Manufacturers Institute. According to the study, the market is projected to reach $5.35 billion by 2003, representing a 6.4 percent compound annual growth rate. That means the industry's growth rate slowed from 8 to 10 percent annually in the early 1990s to between 5 and 7 percent at the end of the decade.

Competing Technologies. Pressure-sensitive labels faced competition from several other technologies, the two most common being wet glue and shrink sleeve. Wet glue applications affix a paper or plastic label using a preapplied adhesive. Beverages and foods in glass containers often use wet glue labels. Glue-applied labels were the leading labeling method, holding an estimated 50 percent share of the total label market in the late 1990s, compared to about 40 percent for PSAs. All other technologies had about 10 percent of the market.

Shrink sleeve applications, in which the label is wrapped around the product and then shrunk directly on to it to form a bond, were most common on batteries and film products. Other competing technologies included heat transfer, heat seal, and in-mold labels. Gummed labels, with about 25 percent of the label market in the 1960s, have dropped to below 2 percent and are not a significant competitor. Most of the erosion in the gummed label market has been linked to increased use of pressure-sensitive labels.

Other Coated and Laminated Papers. The products produced through the coating and laminating process ranged from specialty papers to wax paper, carbonless, and thermographic business papers. For this category, the U.S. Economic Census includes only paper produced at establishments other than base paper producers. As a result, this category does not include the vast majority of coated paper produced in the United States, which is produced on site at paper mills (see **SIC 2621**). Most coated paper manufacturers have off- or on-paper machine coaters that can be set to coat the paper (or be left off to produce uncoated paper) as it leaves the production line. Paper produced in this fashion (coated on site) is classified under **SIC 2621.** The coated and laminated paper that is included in **SIC 2672** is produced by companies that purchase "base stock" paper from paper mills and then coat or laminate it. In fact, three-fourths of the "other coated and laminated papers" category in **SIC 2672** is accounted for by carbonless paper coated at establishments other than where the paper was produced.

The value of coated printing paper included in **SIC 2672** (paper coated at establishments other than where the paper was produced) is extremely small, compared with the value of the entire coated printing paper market, which is included in **SIC 2611.** For example, U.S. shipments of paper coated at establishments other than where the paper was produced had a 1997 value of $270.5 million, compared to the value of coated printing paper produced at U.S. paper mills, which amounted to more than $5.0 billion.

Some of the factors involved in coating papers include the printing process (offset, rotogravure, nonimpact, etc.), the type of ink used (colored, black and white, thickness), and environmental considerations. Coating must take into account the uniformity of the coating application, the evenness of the coat weight, and the smoothness and uniformity of the coat. There are five grades of coated paper, the first one being the heaviest and generally the highest quality.

Paper is coated with pigments, which can consist of either chemical solutions or clay compounds. Titanium dioxide has long been a favorite coating material because of its opacity, though substitutions are usually sought since titanium dioxide is fairly costly. Other popular coatings include calcium carbonate and kaolin (clay), a naturally occurring mineral.

Within the coated and laminated paper sector, converters may apply any number of coatings to change the function or quality of paper—gummed resins to make flypaper or gummed adhesive tape; cloth or fluids to produce cloth-lined or porous impregnated papers. The carbonless paper segment of this industry had continuing growth in the 1990s. This type of paper is manufactured by weaving small beads of ink into the paper fiber itself. When pressure is applied, the beads are broken and ink darkens the paper to emulate the pen strokes of the writer.

BACKGROUND AND DEVELOPMENT

Technological advances in coatings, paper manufacturing processes, and adhesives have long been the driving force behind developments in the coated and laminated paper industry. One clear event that prodded the growth of the label industry was the development of the self-adhesive label by Stanton Avery in 1935. From this initial product line came a whole range of self-adhesive (now called pressure-sensitive) products, including ther-

mal films, airline bag tags, computer imprintable films, and thermal transfer self-adhesives. A wide range of industries now make extensive use of pressure-sensitive labels, including airlines, automotive, consumer durables, food and beverages, health and beauty aids, chemicals, pharmaceuticals, retailing, and transportation.

CURRENT CONDITIONS

The coated and laminated paper industry is generally characterized by small firms that have sought to stake out dominant shares in niche markets. However, there is one industry giant (3M Corporation) and several other relatively large companies (Appleton Papers, Nashua Corporation, and Wausau-Mosinee Paper Corporation) that hold commanding positions in this industry segment.

Coated Paper Markets. Along with much of the rest of the paper industry, the coated market experienced slow growth through the downward business cycle of the early 1990s. However, coated paper prices shot up dramatically in 1994 and 1995 as demand surged and supplies remained tight. While prices retreated in 1996, they remained relatively stable for the rest of the decade. One trend, however, may have changed the long-term market for coated papers. Publishers faced with enormous price hikes during the 1994-1995 period (as much as 75 percent in a 12-month period) cut back on the number of magazine or catalog pages they printed or dramatically trimmed circulation in order to conserve paper.

One problem facing producers of coated papers in the early 1990s—demands for more recycling—has eased for two reasons: manufacturers are now producing more coated papers made at least partially from recycled paper, and magazines and catalogs printed on coated paper are being recycled in greater volumes. While paper recyclers once shunned coated paper because of the coating materials used, recycling operations have learned how to process this type of paper. Still, coatings and fillers typically account for a large part of the paper. When the paper is recycled, these materials have to be separated, removed from the process, and landfilled. Some coated papers can consist of as much as 50 percent coating and filler, which greatly reduces the amount of recoverable paper fiber. As a result, most recycling operations tend to mix small amounts of coated paper with much larger volumes of uncoated paper.

Growth in Pressure-Sensitive Products. Applications for pressure-sensitive products have been driven by the bewildering array of technology options available to manufacturers and new products targeted toward the consumer sector. Removable adhesives—such as those found in Post-It notes—have driven growth, as have new applications of traditional products. For example, the U.S. Postal Service has converted most of its stamp products to PSAs.

Label markets grew faster than the U.S. gross domestic product (GDP) in the late 1990s. Some of the factors contributing to the growth of this sector include increased use of bar codes at end point-of-sale processors (such as supermarket deli counters); legislation requiring food manufacturers to disclose an increased amount of information on food labels; and advances in application and material technologies, which have allowed manufacturers to increase the use of labels.

In terms of the "face stock" used to produce pressure-sensitive labels, the fastest growing segment is sheeted laser paper, reflecting the increase of in-house printing of information by label users. Laser paper usage was growing at a rate of 20 percent annually in the mid- to late 1990s, and in 1998, it accounted for more than 15 percent of the face stock used by pressure-sensitive label manufacturers. General paper is the largest single face material used and accounted for about 50 percent of the market in 1998. General paper is said to be growing more slowly than the market as a whole, reflecting displacement by film face stock in some applications. Film prices were declining and approached high-end paper grade prices. Film accounted for more than 25 percent of the market in 1998.

While the use of pressure-sensitive labels is growing, they face more competition from other technologies. For example, the use of shrink sleeve and in-mold labels greatly increased in the mid-1990s. Shrink sleeve labels, which dominated much of the plastic beverage bottle market, grew 7 percent annually in the late 1990s. In-mold labels, used on blow-molded plastic containers, had a high penetration rate in the health and beauty products and household chemicals markets and had an annual growth rate of 10 percent in the late 1990s.

INDUSTRY LEADERS

The fragmented and specialized nature of the coated and laminated paper industry makes true dominance across all sectors a virtual impossibility. Certain firms, however, have managed to carve out strongly defensible niches and have consistently maintained innovation and expertise to keep a strong position in their particular sector. Appleton Papers, Incorporated, a division of the UK firm Arjo Wiggins Appleton (AWA), is a market leader in carbonless and thermographic papers. Among the notables in the pressure-sensitive products area is the Minnesota Mining & Manufacturing Company (3M). 3M pioneered cellophane tape and manufactures some of the best-known brand names in the industry with its Scotch tape and Post-It notes. 3M manufactures only part of its products within this industry but still has a sizeable representation within the industry leaders.

One challenge to companies in this industry continued to be in-house label manufacturing units at large companies. For example, Anheuser-Busch, the nation's largest beer brewer, was manufacturing its own labels in 1999. Advances in graphics technology made it possible for smaller companies to do the same.

According to the 1998 North American Label Study, leaders in this industry also need to develop and incorporate prepress/digital technology for pressure sensitive applications. The study showed that most companies in the label industry have avoided digital technology because it is costly and not fully developed. However, the study also noted that this technology offers the capacity to handle shorter and faster runs and that the label companies should consider implementing these innovations.

WORKFORCE

Because of the extremely specialized nature of the industry, those who work with coated and laminated papers tended to be more specialized than workers within the rest of the paper industry group. At the same time, the wide array of activities within the classification tended to minimize variance of wages; wages for production workers in the industry averaged $14.78 per hour in 1997, roughly on par with the rest of the paper industry. Because of the dispersion and fragmentation of the industry, organized labor tended to be less represented.

AMERICA AND THE WORLD

A high value-to-weight ratio along with the unique nature of many of the products within the industry have contributed to a globalization of the industry. Since technologies are often proprietary, few barriers existed to stop products from migrating from one market to another. A list of the world's leading thermal coaters, for example, would list few U.S. firms. Another factor hindering U.S. growth in this sector is the fact that many of the advances in coating equipment technology have come from overseas. This has meant a delay in the diffusion of technology to the United States and a subsequent lag in U.S. competitiveness in certain sectors.

It has also been noted that large PSA converters need to develop successful market entry strategies for Latin America. According to the 1998 North American Label Study, Mexico was showing strong growth in the label sector, with the rest of Latin America not far behind. The study advised U.S. converters to identify strategies for success in these markets.

FURTHER READING

Bottiglieri, Janice. "The Future Is Clear for Coating Technology." *PIMA Magazine*, May 1996.

Coated and Laminated Paper Manufacturing, 1997 Economic Census, Manufacturing Industry Series. Washington, D.C.: U.S. Census Bureau, August 1999.

1998 North American Pressure Label Study. Naperville, IL: Tag & Label Manufacturers Institute, Inc., 1999.

1999 North American Pulp & Paper Factbook. San Francisco: Miller-Freeman, Inc., 1998.

SIC 2673

PLASTICS, FOIL AND COATED PAPER BAGS

This category covers establishments primarily engaged in manufacturing bags of unsupported plastic film, coated paper, metal foil, or laminated combinations of these materials. These bags can be printed or unprinted. Establishments primarily engaged in manufacturing uncoated paper bags and multiwall bags and sacks are classified in **SIC 2674: Uncoated Paper and Multiwall Bags;** those manufacturing textile bags are classified in **SIC 2393: Textile Bags;** and those manufacturing garment storage bags, except of plastics film and paper, are classified in **SIC 2392: Housefurnishings, Except Curtains and Draperies.**

NAICS CODE(S)

322223 (Plastics, Foil, and Coated Paper Bag Manufacturing)
326111 (Unsupported Plastics Bag Manufacturing)

Note: The U.S. Economic Census now reports industrial information under the North American Industry Classification System (NAICS) instead of the Standard Industrial Classification (SIC) system. As a result, the value of shipments data reported below is for **NAICS 322223** (the replacement for **SIC 2673**), and includes only a small portion of what used to be reported for **SIC 2673**. For example, the 1994 value of shipments for **SIC 2673** was reported at $6.02 billion; in 1997, the value of shipments for **NAICS 322223** was reported at just $512 million.

The performance of the plastic, foil, and coated paper bag industry produced a value of shipments of $512 million in 1997 (NAICS data). However, the NAICS definition does not include the primary product in **SIC 2673**—plastic merchandise bags. Under the SIC definition, the industry grew at an above average annual rate of 4.4 percent in the 1990s. The outlook for the industry is generally thought to be quite positive as more retail outlets convert to plastic merchandise bags and as other applications are developed.

While this category is classified under paper and allied products, the industry actually uses very little paper in its products, and even that small percentage is declin-ing. The vast majority of products in this industry are made exclusively from plastic.

Products found in this classification include merchandise bags, trash bags, waste bags, frozen food bags, garment storage bags, and wardrobe bags. The vast majority of products manufactured in this sector are specialty bags and liners made from polyethylene single-web film. This segment accounted for 80 percent of total shipments in the late 1990s, up from 58 percent in 1987.

Other significant industry products include multi-web bags and liners. Another category, specialty bags and liners made from coated single-web paper, appeared to be on the decline. These are the products that comprise the new **NAICS 322223** category.

The biggest purchaser of plastic, laminated, and coated paper bags continues to be retail trade outlets (not including eating and drinking establishments). These retail outlets purchased about 60 percent of all bags produced in this category in the mid-1990s. Personal consumption and wholesale trade each accounted for less than 10 percent of the output. The remainder of product shipments were purchased by a wide variety of other sectors of the economy, mostly in manufacturing.

The vast majority of products produced by companies in this industry are made from plastic resins or sheets. Plastic resins used in granule, pellet, powder, or liquid form accounted for about 40 percent of the materials consumed by this sector in the mid-1990s. Plastic products used in the form of sheets, rods, tubes, and other shapes accounted for about 15 percent. By contrast, paper accounted for just 5 percent of industry purchases. Other significant raw materials for this category include printing ink, paperboard containers, boxes and corrugated paperboard used to ship finished products, and glues and adhesives.

A large portion of this industry's output is in branded products, with trash bags being one of the leading products. Of the total U.S. trash bag market in 1995, private label products held a 20.5 percent share of the market—equal to the leading national brand, Glad, which also held a 20.5 percent share. Other leading brands include Hefty Cinch Sak (8.2 percent); Hefty (4.6 percent); and Glad Stress Flex (2.1 percent).

The plastic, foil, and coated paper bag industry has made extensive use of new plastic materials to make products that are both lighter and stronger. For example, the use of high-density polyethylene by all manufacturers was expanding at a healthy 6 percent annual rate in the late 1990s and reached 1.7 billion pounds in 1998. High-molecular weight resins offer major performance improvements over linear-low density polyethylene. While the primary application for this product is retail plastic bags, trash bag manufacturers are using this material as well to take advantage of its strength, toughness, and printability.

FURTHER READING

Darnay, Arsen J., ed. *Manufacturing USA,* 6th ed. Detroit: Gale Research, 1998.

Lazich, Robert S. *Market Share Reporter.* Detroit: Gale Research, 1997.

Plastics, Foil and Coated Paper Bag Manufacturing, 1997 Economic Census, Manufacturing Industry Series. Washington, D.C.: U.S. Census Bureau, July 1999.

U.S. Trade and Industrial Outlook, 2000. New York: McGraw-Hill, 1999.

SIC 2674

UNCOATED PAPER AND MULTIWALL BAGS

This classification includes establishments primarily engaged in manufacturing uncoated paper bags or multiwall bags and sacks, whether or not coated or containing plastics film or metal foil. Establishments primarily engaged in manufacturing bags from plastics, unsupported film, foil, coated paper, or laminated or coated combinations of these materials, are classified in **SIC 2673: Plastics, Foil, and Coated Paper Bags.** Those establishments manufacturing textile bags are classified in **SIC 2393: Textile Bags.**

NAICS CODE(S)

322224 (Uncoated Paper and Multiwall Bag Manufacturing)

INDUSTRY SNAPSHOT

The uncoated paper and multiwall bag industry faced steady declines in shipment volumes of its products in the 1990s. While some of these declines can be explained by the "lightweighting" of products (newer bags that are lighter yet as strong as older bags), the industry has steadily lost market share due to sustained and intense competition from rival products made from plastic. Between 1992 and 1997, industry volume declined in both of its major categories, grocery/variety/shopping bags and shipping sacks/multiwall bags. Since they were able to sell higher valued added products, sales in this industry remained stable between 1992 and 1997, increasing by a fraction from $2.83 billion in 1992 to $2.85 billion in 1997. However, when inflation is factored in, the value of shipments actually declined.

In all uncoated paper and multiwall (three-ply or more) bag applications, the package must contain and protect the product or contents. Paper is used because of its ability to contribute strength and stiffness or rigidity to the container. Plastics may also offer strength, but paper is more resilient than plastics over a wider temperature range. Paper is better for printing than other materials. However, in many applications paper bags must be coated with waxes or plastics (or laminated to plastic films or foil) to develop effective barriers to water, vapor, gases, or odors.

Market Shares. The uncoated paper and multiwall bag industry is split between two categories. Shipping sacks and multiwall bags accounted for 60 percent of the industry's sales in 1997, up from 56 percent in 1992 and 51 percent in 1987. Grocers' bags, sacks, variety, and shopping bags held 38 percent of the market in 1997, down from 43 percent in 1992 and 48 percent in 1987. A small "not specified by kind" category accounted for the remaining 2 percent of shipments in 1997. The gap between the two categories will likely grow as the grocers' bag market continues to decline.

In the shipping sack and multiwall bag subcategory, the dominant product is multiwall shipping sacks and bags, holding about 84 percent of production in the subcategory, with single- and double-wall sacks and bags a distant second at 16 percent. In 1997, U.S. manufacturers produced 891,000 tons of multiwall bags and 174,000 tons of single or double-wall bags, compared with 1.04 million tons and 193,000 tons, respectively, in 1992. Of this total, the largest customer category was agriculture and food, followed by building materials, chemicals, and minerals.

In the uncoated paper grocers' bags, sacks, variety, and shopping bags subcategory, the leading product is still uncoated paper grocer's sacks, with 55 percent of shipments in 1997. However, that figure is down sharply from 1992 when grocer's sacks accounted for 68 percent of shipments. In 1997, uncoated shopping bags accounted for 10 percent and uncoated paper merchandise bags 9 percent of this subcategory. All other uncoated paper bags and pouches, including specialty bags, comprised the remaining 26 percent.

ORGANIZATION AND STRUCTURE

In the industry's terminology, paper sacks refer to the large bags used to hold customers' supermarket purchases. The 1/6th barrel sack is the standard paper sack used in supermarkets. It is called that because in the early 1900s, when paper bags were gaining in popularity, they were used to hold 1/6th of a barrel of flour. Another popular size is the 1/8th barrel sack.

Paper sacks come in a variety of basis weights. Single-ply bags range in basis weight from 60 pound to 80 pound. Some stores prefer a double-ply bag, made of two 40-pound basis weight bags, since it can hold heavier items. Stores using this double-ply bag can avoid the "double bagging" common at checkouts of supermarkets using single-ply bags.

The bag industry refers to smaller, lighter weight bags as "grocery bags." These bags are used in outlets such as convenience stores and fast food restaurants. They come in a variety of sizes, from 1/2-pound bags to 25-pound bags. These weights are also based on early 1900s terminology, when paper bags were graded by how much sugar they could hold. Retail trade establishments remain this manufacturing industry's primary customer.

The uncoated paper and multiwall bag market was a steadily growing and relatively stable industry into the 1970s. Paper accounted for the vast majority of bags produced for retail outlets, such as supermarkets. However, in the 1970s, plastics manufacturers began to perfect the single-ply polyethylene shopping bag, which could compete effectively with the traditional paper sack. While lacking some of the characteristics of the paper sack, such as stiffness, the plastic sack had one big advantage—lower cost. Today, individual plastic bags cost about one-third as much as the average paper sack. This price advantage increased when kraft paper prices skyrocketed along with other grades of paper in 1994 and 1995. For example, the price of 70-pound grocery sack paper rose from $320 per ton in 1993 to $490 in 1994 and $530 in 1995, before falling back to about $410 per ton in 1996. In 1997 and 1998, the price rose slightly, to $450 per ton. With supermarket net profits averaging about one cent for every dollar of sales, these retailers have been quick to convert to plastic bags. While most supermarket chains still stock paper bags for customers that ask for them, many have stopped asking the question "paper or plastic" at the checkout, leading to increased use of plastic bags.

Prices prevalent in the late 1990s clearly demonstrate the cost differential. For example, the average paper grocery sack cost $34-$36 per 1,000, or 3.4-3.6 cents each, while the typical high density, 1/2 mil polyethylene sack cost $12-$14 per 1,000, or 1.2 cents-1.4 cents each. While plastic bags do not hold as much as comparable paper bags, supermarket chains still see substantial cost savings in using plastic bags. While a few supermarket chains use paper sacks extensively and others still stock paper bags, that has not stopped the steady erosion of paper's market share. Also, other retail outlets, such as mass merchandisers, use plastic bags exclusively. Kmart Corporation converted from paper in the 1980s. This led Union Camp Corporation (purchased by International Paper Company in 1999), formerly a major supplier of paper sacks to Kmart, to invest in plastic bag manufacturing in order to continue supplying Kmart. In the early 1990s, Wal-Mart Stores, Inc., the nation's largest retailer, converted to using plastic bags exclusively. In the mid-1990s, Union Camp scaled back its production of paper bags and sacks and closed its flagship Savannah, Georgia, bag-making unit.

Multiwall Market. Multiwall paper bags, which use three or more plies of paper, are used heavily in industrial applications for the transport and sale of products such as seed and fertilizer. They have fared better than the grocery bag market. Multiwall bags have continued to expand their share of this market at the expense of single- and double-wall bags. Multiwall bags are used for many business-to-business transactions, such as the sale of fertilizer to farmers, and also for consumer transactions, such as pet food. As a result, multiwall bags are sold in a variety of shapes, sizes, and constructions, from the plain brown bags used for cement mix to the high quality, four-color, plastic-lined packages used for pet food or lawn fertilizer.

Multiwall bag producers divide their market into two categories: paper multiwall packaging, designed for products weighing 20 pounds and more; and consumer packaging, designed for products weighing five to ten pounds, such as pet food and charcoal.

The number of packaging layers depends on the application. For example, multiwall bags for products being shipped overseas may have as many as five or six layers to withstand severe handling and extreme temperature conditions. Pet food bags, on the other hand, may have just three layers, with one being a grease-resistant paper. Cement bags usually include a polyethylene liner to keep the product's moisture away from the outer paper layers. However, some bag manufacturers, in order to make their bags more "environmentally friendly" and recyclable, are looking for ways to eliminate the plastic film inner layer by using specially-treated paper instead.

BACKGROUND AND DEVELOPMENT

Paper bags have been a major product for the paper industry for more than 100 years. One of the earliest bag makers, Union Paper Bag Machine Co. (now part of International Paper Company), was founded in 1861 in Bethlehem, Pennsylvania, to make and sell machines for manufacturing paper bags. In the late 1800s and early 1900s, the use of paper bags continued to grow along with the economy. The bag market received a major boost from the invention and development of self-serve grocery stores in the early 1900s. As self-serve stores continued to expand in other retail environments, the use of paper bags boomed.

CURRENT CONDITIONS

The big issue for the uncoated paper and multiwall bag industry continued to be the penetration of plastic bags into markets previously dominated by paper. The severity of this problem is illustrated by the long-term decline in production of the kraft paper from which bags and sacks are made. The long-term decline in demand for unbleached kraft packaging papers, particularly for grocery bags and sacks, caused paper producers to reduce production capacity by 40 percent from 1985 to 1995, from about 3.9 million tons in 1985 to 2.5 million tons in 1995. Production capacity continued to decline through the rest of the decade, but appeared to stabilize in 1999 at about 2.2 million tons. Capacity for bleached kraft paper, used to make white paper bags, was about 440,000 tons in 1999.

The damage that plastics have done to the paper bag market varied greatly by category. In the paper sack market, plastics had taken over 80 to 85 percent of the market in the late 1990s. That was a dramatic reversal from the early 1980s, when paper sacks accounted for the majority of the market. Paper was expected to "bottom out" and hold onto about 15 to 20 percent of the market, since many customers still prefer the paper sack in supermarkets. However, much of those sales depend on supermarkets' willingness to continue stocking two types of sacks. In the late 1990s, grocery bag manufacturers introduced a version of the grocery sack with handles in order to better compete with plastic.

In the grocery bag market, plastics penetration has been far less pervasive. In the late 1990s, paper still accounted for 65 to 70 percent of the market. Much of the strength in this market is accounted for by the growth of the fast food marketplace. Fast food chains such as McDonald's Corporation and Burger King use a very high volume of small bags to package customers' orders. Plastics have almost no penetration in this particular market segment. The main reason is that plastics have no rigidity, a real problem when food, drinks, and other items are placed in one bag. Also, these chains use the high-quality printing surfaces of the bags for promotions and advertising.

The product mix in the fast food bag segment changed radically in the 1990s as demand for recycled products grew. For example, the McDonald's chain converted from a bright white bleached bag made from virgin fiber to a 100 percent recycled, unbleached brown bag. Other chains, such as Burger King, soon followed with other types of bags made from recycled paper. Changes demanded by large customers such as McDonald's are highly significant. For example, in 1985, McDonald's used 285,000 tons of packaging materials (much of that in bags), with 86 percent being paper and 14 percent plastic. The average recycled content in McDonald's packaging increased from 17 percent in 1990 to 42 percent in 1995 and was expected to continue increasing.

Also, some "high-quality" retailers use paper bags to promote store image, since plastic bags tend to be associated with discount outlets. For example, in the late 1990s Starbucks Coffee was using a highly printed, intricately patterned brown paper bag at its retail outlets.

The "notions and millinery" sector includes the flat bags (without folded bottoms) used to hold customer purchases in variety stores and department stores. Plastic made heavy inroads into paper's market share in this category, accounting for about 75 to 80 percent of the market in the late 1990s. However, paper held on to its 20 to 25 percent of the market in 1998.

The only paper bag product line seeing any real growth in the mid-1990s was heavy duty, cord-handled shopping bags used by many department store chains. Many retail outlets used these bags for marketing purposes, since they can be made from high-quality, bleached, clay-coated paper for four-color printing. Many stores used these bags as a customer service—often charging for them—so that customers could consolidate their purchases from different areas of the store.

The multiwall bag market grew at an annual rate of 1.5 to 2 percent per year in the mid-1990s and was even slower in the late 1990s. Some of this slow growth was attributed to inroads made by low-density plastic bags and wraps. One of the fastest growing bag applications, for example, was multilayer industrial plastic film bags, which were replacing multiwall paper bags for products such as herbicides, pesticides, and fertilizers.

By the late 1990s, plastics had claimed close to 30 percent of the market previously held exclusively by multiwall paper bags. For example, plastic bags were often used for high-moisture products, such as bark chips.

Manufacturers were also producing combination bags, which included several outer layers of paper and inner liners made of plastic. This hybrid bag combines the barrier properties of plastic with the rigidity and strength of paper. Also, manufacturers found that layers of different materials, such as paper and plastic, provide a better odor barrier in some instances than either material alone.

However, some multiwall bag applications have been converted to 100 percent plastic; they may use three or more layers of different plastics to accommodate specialized packaging processes. For example, some products are packaged with a "hot fill" process, where the product is put into the package while still hot. The inner plastic layer can handle the hot product while the outer layers are designed to protect the product in transit.

INDUSTRY LEADERS

While there are many companies operating in this industry, the major manufacturers of uncoated paper and multiwall bags include Duro Bag Manufacturing Company, Gaylord Container Corporation, International Paper Company, Longview Fibre Company, and Southern Bag Company. Duro Bag and Gaylord were among the largest players in the late 1990s.

Gaylord and Stone Container Corporation, the two largest U.S. retail grocery sack and bag manufacturers, merged their sack and bag operations in 1996, forming S&G Packaging. The joint venture was 35 percent owned by Gaylord and 65 percent by Stone Container. In 1998, Stone Container merged with Jefferson Smurfit Corporation, forming Smurfit-Stone Container. In late 1999, Smurfit-Stone sold its share of S&G Packaging to Gaylord, which now owns 100 percent of the unit. S&G Packaging is the world's leading producer of paper handle sacks and is the largest U.S. producer of retail grocery sacks and bags, with annual sales of $250 million in North America and the Caribbean.

Duro Bag and Gaylord are also leaders in the production of multiwall bags. Gaylord produces multiwall bags through its Mid-America Packaging unit. Other leaders in multiwall bag production include International Paper and Longview Fibre. Duro Bag is "fully integrated," in that it also has extensive Interests in plastic bags.

WORK FORCE

The uncoated paper and multiwall bag industry employed 16,858 people in 1997 with a payroll of $464.3 million. In 1994, the industry had employed 14,249 production workers who put in 30.6 million total hours at an average pay rate of $11.38.

FURTHER READING

"Kraft Paper: Industry Shipments, Pricing and Mill Operating Rates Are Improving." *Pulp & Paper,* November 1999.

Paper, Paperboard, Pulp Capacity and Fiber Consumption. Washington, D.C.: American Forest & Paper Association, 1998.

Uncoated Paper and Multiwall Bag Manufacturing, 1997 Economic Census, Manufacturing Industry Series. Washington, D.C.: U.S. Census Bureau, August 1999.

U.S. Trade and Industrial Outlook 2000 New York: McGraw-Hill, 1999.

SIC 2675

DIE-CUT PAPER AND PAPERBOARD AND CARDBOARD

Establishments in this industry are primarily engaged in die-cutting purchased paper and paperboard and in manufacturing cardboard by laminating, lining, or surface coating paperboard. Establishments primarily engaged in laminating building paper from purchased paper are classified in **SIC 2679: Converted Paper and Paperboard Products, Not Elsewhere Classified.**

NAICS CODE(S)

322231 (Die-Cut Paper and Paperboard Office Supplies Manufacturing)
322292 (Surface-Coated Paperboard Manufacturing)
322298 (All Other Converted Paper Product Manufacturing)

Products in this industry classification include pasted chip board; bottle caps and tops; cardboard foundations and cutouts; pasted, laminated line and surface coated paperboard; plain paper cards; tabulating cards; die-cut paper and paperboard; egg cartons and egg case fillers and flats; and filing folders, index cards, and paperboard library cards.

As of 1997, the die-cut paper and paperboard industry consisted of 356 establishments operated by 335 companies across the United States. The performance of the die-cut paper and board industry was erratic in the 1990s. The value of shipments reached an all-time high of $2.29 billion in 1991, but it fell sharply the following year to $2.01 billion—before recovering to $2.02 billion in 1993 and $2.24 billion in 1994. By 1997, the value of shipments had fallen back again, to $2.19 billion. Projections called for small declines in subsequent years. The slow or negative growth experienced by this industry reflects the fact that the market for many of its traditional products is a mature one. Also, many products produced by the industry are traditional office supplies, such as file folders, index cards, and paper rolls for business machines. Usage of these products is said to be declining, in part due to the growing importance of electronic data transfer and electronic document management systems.

In 1997, die-cut paper and board office supplies accounted for 53 percent of industry shipments (by value). Within this category, file folders represented the biggest seller, followed by hanging and expandable file folders, index cards, and report covers.

The next largest category was paper supplies for business machines, which accounted for 34 percent of industry shipments. Leading products in this category were paper rolls for adding and other business machines and other unprinted paper supplies. All other products accounted for the remaining 11 percent of industry shipments.

Die-cut paper and board manufacturers tend to be located in areas where business activity is highest. As a result, industry activity is greater in such states as Illinois, which accounted for 12.7 percent of industry shipments in 1997; California, 10.8 percent; Massachusetts, 8.6 percent; and Ohio, 8.3 percent.

This industry manufactures a wide variety of products, yet it is closely linked to the production of corrugated boxes since many of its products are used as box inserts. Also, many products are made from recycled fiber—often 100 percent recycled fiber. The desire by consumers and businesses to buy products made from recycled materials appears to have increased demand for some products from the die-cut paper and board industry.

Die-cut paper and board industry leaders tend to be independent converters; there are few major paper companies with holdings in die-cut paper and paperboard. Some of the leading companies include Esselte Pendaflex Corp. of Garden City, New York; Fleer Corp. of Mount Laurel, New Jersey; Book Covers Inc. of Newark, New Jersey; and Advertising Display Co. of Englewood Cliffs, New Jersey. Chesapeake Corp. is one of the few paper companies with a large market share in this industry through its Chesapeake Display Co. in Winston-Salem, North Carolina.

The die-cut paper and board industry employed a total of 12,208 employees in 1997, including 9,683 production workers. These totals were down sharply from 1992. The average hourly wage for production workers was $11.14 in 1997, up from $10.40 in 1992.

FURTHER READING

Darnay, Arsen J., ed. *Manufacturing USA,* 6th ed. Detroit: Gale Research, 1998.

Die-Cut Paper and Paperboard Office Supplies Manufacturing, 1997 Economic Census, Manufacturing Industry Series. Washington, D.C.: U.S. Census Bureau, July 1999.

Paper, Paperboard, Pulp Capacity and Fiber Consumption. Washington, D.C.: American Forest & Paper Association, 1998.

Smook, Gary A. *Handbook of Pulp & Paper Terminology: A Guide to Industrial and Technological Usage.* Bellingham, WA: Angus Wilde Publications, 1990.

U.S. Trade and Industrial Outlook 1999. New York: McGraw-Hill, 1999.

SIC 2676

SANITARY PAPER PRODUCTS

This classification covers establishments primarily engaged in manufacturing sanitary paper products from purchased paper, such as facial tissues and handkerchiefs, table napkins, toilet paper, paper towels, disposable diapers, and sanitary napkins and tampons.

NAICS CODE(S)

322291 (Sanitary Paper Product Manufacturing)

INDUSTRY SNAPSHOT

The sanitary paper products industry manufactures paper into finished products with sanitary applications. The value of shipments in the sanitary paper industry was approximately $9.77 billion in 1997 (about 5.8 percent of the paper and allied products industry group as a whole). Projections indicate a steady increase throughout the next decade at about the rate of increase in the gross domestic product (GDP). A large majority of the products contained in this classification are branded consumer products sold in many different retail outlets, so the sanitary paper industry spends more on advertising than any other part of the paper industry.

There are three broad subcategories within the sanitary paper products industry: disposable diapers, which accounted for $3.93 billion (40.2 percent) of the value of shipments in 1997; sanitary tissue paper products, for $3.46 billion (35.4 percent); and sanitary napkins and tampons, for $2.16 billion (22.1 percent). A small "not specified by kind" segment accounted for the remaining 2.3 percent.

Many of the products within this classification are considered nondiscretionary and, as a result, sales within this classification have followed different business cycles than those of more commodity-oriented paper lines. While new sanitary products, such as adult incontinence products, have helped to expand the market, this industry tends to grow only as fast as overall GDP. As in many mature markets, competition for customers is fierce. For example, tissue manufacturers continually seek to lower production costs since small gains can lead to major gains in either profit margins or market share. In order to maintain growth, firms have begun to focus on expansion abroad while at the same time continuing to segment the market and introduce new products domestically. Production of sanitary paper products is one of the few areas of the paper industry where major global corporations—notably Kimberly-Clark Corporation, The Procter & Gamble Company, and Fort James Corporation—operate manufacturing facilities in many locations around the world.

Most of the major companies in the sanitary paper products industry are integrated, in that they produce the raw materials for finished products, such as parent rolls of tissue at large paper mills, as well as the converted sanitary paper products, such as packages of bathroom tissue.

ORGANIZATION AND STRUCTURE

The majority of sanitary paper products are made from pulp or paper, though a significant percentage are made using the "nonwoven" process in which natural or synthetic fibers are bonded together by cohesion, friction, and/or adhesion. Sanitary paper products are usually divided into two sectors: consumer or commercial and industrial (C&I). Customers in the C&I category of sanitary paper might be schools, hospitals, or offices. C&I shipments comprise about 40 percent of sanitary tissue sales and a much smaller percentage of nonwoven sales.

Sanitary Tissue. Sanitary tissue products, the second largest segment of this industry, is divided into several subcategories. The largest of these is retail toilet tissue, which accounted for about a third of all sanitary tissue product shipments (by value) in the late 1990s. Commercial and industrial toilet tissue accounted for about 12 percent of shipments. Retail paper towels is another large subcategory, accounting for more than 22 percent of sanitary tissue product shipments, while industrial paper towels were another 10 percent of the market. Facial tissues were 9 percent while industrial paper napkins (hand towels) accounted for 7 percent. Retail paper napkins held 4 percent of the market. All other sanitary tissue products accounted for nearly 6 percent of the market.

The processes used to make sanitary tissue products are very similar to those used to create other types of paper. In the standard papermaking process, wood fibers are stripped from wood chips in either a chemical or mechanical process to produce wood pulp. This pulp, a combination of wood fibers and water, is then spread on a continuous fine screen. The resulting mat is then passed over vacuum boxes (to remove some water) and run through successive drying and pressing processes until the finished paper product is achieved.

The major differences between general paper manufacture and tissue manufacture lie in the type of raw material used and the converting processes. Because of the relationship between the softness of the raw material and the softness of the final product, lightly refined softwood fibers are generally preferred for consumer-oriented products. These fibers come both from virgin fiber (wood) and from recycled fiber. In fact, the sanitary tissue products industry is one of the largest recycling industries in the United States. As of 1998, about 47 percent of all U.S. tissue was produced with fiber from purchased wastepaper (recycled paper), and 20 percent was produced from purchased virgin pulp. The remaining fiber was produced on site at integrated pulp and paper mills. Products for the C&I market typically place a higher premium on strength as opposed to softness, and are made from recycled paper or coarser grades of wood.

Once the tissue paper is formed, large, integrated producers typically convert it into consumer products on-site. (Smaller, nonintegrated converting operations purchase "jumbo rolls" of tissue paper on the open market.) Depending on the type of product, dyes and perfumes may be added and the paper may be embossed. The tissue is then prepared for market—facial tissues are folded and boxed, and bathroom tissue is rolled and prepared for shipment.

Nonwoven Sanitary Products. The nonwoven sanitary paper market consists of products that incorporate nonwoven fabrics in their manufacture. Nonwoven products include disposable diapers and training pants, feminine hygiene products, adult incontinence products (including consumer and institutional adult pads and bed pads), and premoistened tissues (including baby wipes). Advances in nonwoven technology have increased the number of nonwoven applications and enhanced the use of nonwovens in existing applications.

Nonwovens are so named because the fibers (synthetic or wood pulp) used in their fabrication are bonded together instead of woven, as they would be in textile-type products. This bonding can take the form of an adhesive applied to the fiber mat before or after forming, or it can be the result of a chemical reaction. The typical nonwoven product incorporates many steps into its fabrication. A diaper, for example, will begin with a polyethylene outer shell. Dry formed wood pulp (fluff pulp) within layers of impervious nonwoven fabric is bonded to the shell. Glues, resins, and adhesives are used to bind the various components to one another. The typical adult incontinence pad, sanitary napkin, and tampon incorporate many of the same steps into their manufacture.

In the manufacturing process, nonwovens are often treated with super-absorbent polymers (SAPs) which can absorb as much as 70 to 80 times their weight in liquid. A further distinguishing feature of SAPs is that, unlike a sponge or other woven absorbent products, SAPs retain water even when squeezed. A sponge, for example, retains water in channels or pores. SAPs chemically bind with the fluid to form a gel. Under extremely heavy pressure, SAPs might release a type of gel, but most liquids remain in their chemical compound.

Aside from sanitary applications, nonwovens can also be found in other applications either as a substitute for cloth or in applications requiring a high degree of absorbency (filters, car covers, durable shop towels). Since most producers of nonwoven sanitary products are also producers of nonwoven fabrics, the strength of these related industries can also have an impact on these companies' results.

Marketing. After the final product is ready, the process moves from manufacturing to marketing. The need to market effectively drives two additional defining features of the industry. First, there is the need for extensive promotion: companies within the sanitary paper industry spend the highest percentage on advertising of any paper-producing industry. Second, companies have also recognized the need for sophisticated marketing techniques. Increased segmentation and "database marketing," using elaborate information banks to determine lifestyle predictors for a target segment, have become important success factors in the industry.

Establishment Size and Distribution. Unlike other grades of paper, many sanitary paper products—notably tissue products—are bulky, and it is not cost effective to ship them long distances. As a result, sanitary product converters have traditionally been located close to their end use markets. This is especially true for more commodity-oriented product lines such as bathroom tissue and household towels. This is one of the reasons sanitary paper product manufacturers have developed a global network of manufacturing plants. For higher value added products such as tampons and ultrathin pads, or niche products such as premoistened tissues and baby wipes, producers typically supply markets from only one or two manufacturing facilities.

The twin requirements of converting massive amounts of raw materials and a highly-competitive consumer marketplace have led to a high degree of concentration in the U.S. sanitary paper products industry. For example, at the end of 1999, four firms—Fort James Corporation, Kimberly-Clark, Procter & Gamble, and Georgia-Pacific Corporation—controlled 76 percent of U.S. tissue paper manufacturing capacity, with the top two firms controlling half of the total. Fort James (created by the 1997 merger of James River Corporation and Fort Howard Corporation) held about 29 percent of U.S. tissue paper manufacturing capacity, while Kimberly-Clark, following its 1995 merger with Scott Paper Company, held 21 percent of capacity. Procter & Gamble controlled an additional 14 percent, followed by Georgia-Pacific Corporation with about 12 percent. Georgia-Pacific's share increased substantially in 1999 when it agreed to form a joint venture with Chesapeake's Wisconsin Tissue unit, which combined the companies' tissue making operations. The new unit, called Georgia-Pacific Tissue, was 90 percent owned and effectively controlled by Georgia-Pacific Corporation.

In the disposable diaper segment, market concentration is even more pronounced. The two leading firms, Kimberly-Clark and Procter & Gamble, shared about 80 percent of the market in 1998, with roughly equal shares. Private label products accounted for 18 percent, while other brands held 3 percent of the market.

BACKGROUND AND DEVELOPMENT

The development of the sanitary paper market in the United States has paralleled the development of two broader categories the market represents, the paper and consumer products industry groups. The advances made in paper production technology from the latter half of the nineteenth century to the early part of the twentieth century that had an impact on the paper industry as a whole also impacted the sanitary paper industry.

Sanitary Tissue Products. As with most of the paper industry, the sanitary tissue sector owes much of its growth to advances in automation and wood processing made in the last century. The development of the fourdrinier paper machine in the first half of the nineteenth century allowed greater volumes of paper to be produced at a lower price.

This process is particularly relevant for sanitary tissue since it is still the ideal process for lighter weight grades in general and tissue manufacture in particular.

Since 1850, ongoing developments in wood processing have provided paper manufacturers with a cheap, reliable source of raw materials. Prior to these discoveries, the main raw materials for paper production were rags, cloth, and straw. By the 1850s, mechanization had already substantially reduced the costs of producing paper, but constraints on the supplies of raw materials limited paper production to specific applications. Once a process was developed for wood fiber to be converted into pulp, greater applications for paper became possible and the sanitary paper industry was born. Paper began to find its way into more and more households and assumed the roles previously held by towels, leaves, and rags.

The marketing of sanitary paper products did not assume its current importance until the early part of the twentieth century. Prior to that, competition in the industry seemed to be oriented toward consolidation and acquisition. The United Paper Company made a series of acquisitions in the 1890s in an attempt to form a "tissue trust," but the trust was broken and the company forced into bankruptcy when other paper producers switched to tissue production and undercut the trust's position.

From the early part of the twentieth century, developments in the sanitary sector were not so much technology- as consumer-driven, and the role of the sanitary paper producer switched from being a provider of specific products to responding to consumer needs. The development of one company, Scott Paper Company, reflects many of these changes. In 1902, the company introduced Waldorf, one of the first branded bathroom tissues, and moved quickly into a position of dominance in this product line. Scott's invention of paper towels in 1907 further consolidated the company's position. By the 1950s, Scott held more than 50 percent of the sanitary tissue market. Over time, however, new product introductions and sustained marketing efforts by competitors reduced Scott's market dominance.

Perhaps it was Kimberly-Clark's long experience with marketing that allowed it to gain some of Scott's market share. In 1915, Kimberly-Clark developed Cellucotton, an absorbent wadding that was later used in feminine hygiene products. In 1924, Kimberly-Clark introduced one of the most ubiquitous brand names in America—Kleenex. Originally developed as a tissue for removing cold cream, the company found that it sold better as a disposable handkerchief; due to technological innovations in folding and packaging, Kimberly-Clark was able to market it as such.

Since these developments, the sanitary tissue sector has been marked more by evolutionary realignments than revolutionary innovations. The basic product offerings of the major producers in the sector have remained essentially the same, but improvements in quality, strength, and packaging, have been the driving forces in the market. Since the 1960s, the sanitary paper market has witnessed intensified competition among a number of strong competitors. Low-cost producers have captured large segments of the low-end market, while marketing and consumer product giants have gained substantial market share in the premium branded segments. James River Corporation of Virginia, founded in 1969, used acquisitions and joint ventures to expand its activities rapidly. James River evolved from a start-up operation in the early 1970s to the third largest tissue producer in the United States in the mid-1990s. In 1997, it merged with Fort Howard Corporation, the nation's leading producer of tissue for the C&I market, to form Fort James Corporation.

Nonwoven Sanitary Products. The nonwoven sector, with its emphasis on consumer goods, reflects the development of the power of marketing on American lifestyles. At the same time, the technological innovations in superabsorbent polymers and nonwoven fabrics have marked advances in the sector.

Disposable diapers comprise the largest subsegment in the sanitary products industry, with the value of product shipments reaching $4.13 billion in 1997. Procter & Gamble invented the category when it introduced disposable diapers with the Pampers brand in 1961. Since that time, the market has exhibited steady growth based mainly on increasing penetration rates. Continuous product enhancements and forceful marketing by the two main players in the disposable diapers field, Procter & Gamble and Kimberly-Clark, led to high usage rates. Annual new product introductions have kept competition high and have continuously improved the image of disposable diapers. Advances in nonwoven technology have led to improvements in absorbency and size reductions, enabling producers to achieve savings in transportation and packaging. The next generation of diapers is expected to allow for even greater absorbency, so as to stay dry even through multiple wettings. Another major development was the introduction by Kimberly-Clark of the Pull-Ups brand of disposable training pants for older children, which expanded the market.

Sanitary napkins and tampons generated about $1.56 billion in value of shipments in 1997. Kimberly-Clark first entered the consumer products segment in the 1920s with a sanitary napkin called Kotex. At first, societal norms prevented feminine care products from being publicized and displayed. Many magazines refused to carry advertising for feminine care products, and stores were reluctant to stock them. However, despite these barriers and the relatively high prices, consumer acceptance of the products was high.

CURRENT CONDITIONS

The sanitary paper market experienced steady growth in the mid-1990s. The nondiscretionary nature of many of its product lines seems to ensure a strong demand base. At the same time, many producers see limited growth opportunities in the domestic market. The aging of the American population, the relatively stable birth rate, and increasing competition all pose significant challenges for this industry.

The 1990s were marked by a series of massive mergers in the sanitary products market. The trend was started by the 1995 merger of Kimberly-Clark Corporation and Scott Paper Company. The merger of these two industry giants was valued at $9.4 billion, with Kimberly-Clark (K-C) being the surviving corporation. The new K-C is a massive presence in the sanitary paper products industry, controlling nearly 30 percent of the sanitary tissue market and about 40 percent of the disposable diaper market. The U.S. Justice Department, concerned about excessive market concentration, reached a consent decree with K-C before it approved the merger. Under the decree, K-C agreed to sell the Scotties facial tissue brand and its Fort Edward, New York tissue mill to Irving Tissue Inc., It also sold the former Scott wipes plant to its leading competitor, Procter & Gamble (P&G). The latter sale gave P&G a one-third share of the baby wipes market.

The K-C/Scott merger was followed by the 1997 linkup of James River and Fort Howard to create Fort James Corporation and the 1999 combination of the tissue units of Georgia-Pacific and Chesapeake Corporation. Fort James became the number one tissue producer in the U.S. and the number two producer worldwide.

Two of the major U.S. sanitary paper products producers moved away from vertical integration in the 1990s. Both Procter & Gamble and Kimberly-Clark sold much of their pulp making capacity, in order to establish long-term agreements with independent pulp producers. Both companies cited the need to put more money into their core marketing, operations, and research and development units as reasons for the divestitures.

Since production of tissue and tissue products is highly integrated, one of the major factors affecting the financial performance of the industry is the capacity to produce tissue. If there is excess capacity, prices of tissue tend to drop, as do retail prices for tissue products. When demand exceeds growth in capacity, tissue prices can rise sharply, as they did in 1994 and 1995. U.S. tissue manufacturing capacity grew 3.4 percent in 1999 to 7.1 million tons, thanks to the startup of several new machines and the "ramping up" of machines that came on line in 1998. Capacity was expected to grow an additional 2.8 percent in 2000, as more machines were brought on line. However, growth was expected to slow to 1.7 percent in 2001 and 0.2 percent in 2002. For the period from 1999 to 2002, tissue paper capacity was projected to grow at a rate of 1.6 percent per year, compared with 2.1 percent per year from 1990 through 1999.

Sanitary Tissue Markets. While unit volume of sanitary tissue products grew steadily at about 2 percent in the mid- to late 1990s, the value of shipments was somewhat erratic, largely due to low underlying prices of tissue. However, the value of shipments began increasing again in 1994 and 1995 as major producers raised prices in response to dramatically higher prices for tissue paper and the wood pulp and wastepaper from which it is made.

In 1996, however, sharp drops in wood pulp and wastepaper prices helped increase profitability for major sanitary tissue product producers. These lower raw material prices allowed manufacturers to reduce prices modestly while still maintaining profitability. For example, Procter & Gamble instituted a 5 to 8 percent price cut in early 1996 for various consumer tissue products.

Despite a sharp drop in pulp prices in late 1995 and early 1996, the overall decline in tissue pricing was only 3 percent in 1996. Steady demand, rising operating rates, and an increase in pulp prices during 1997 drove prices up modestly. The prices of tissue product stabilized in the late 1990s due to relatively low prices for tissue paper and low inflation in the general economy.

Producers have seen slow but steady growth in the disposable diaper market since the product's introduction. The value of shipments in this category was $4.13 billion in 1997, according to the 1997 Economic Census. Growth in the domestic diaper industry reached a plateau in the late 1980s and early 1990s with a decline in net births and stabilization of market penetration. Much of the sector's growth can be accounted for by increased market penetration and higher usage rates as the product has improved, yet marketers foresee limited opportunities for domestic growth.

As diaper penetration rates have stabilized, makers of disposable diapers have used their capabilities to introduce products for market segments exhibiting increasing growth. Some of these products include training pants (for children making the transition from diapers) and adult incontinence products. The adult incontinence segment is considered one of the fastest-growing in the country, albeit from a small base.

In the feminine care sector, sanitary napkin usage continued to decline in the mid- to late 1990s in favor of tampon usage. The value of shipments in the total sanitary napkin and tampon market was $1.56 billion in 1997, with feminine pads accounting for $866 million of the total (55.5 percent) and tampons accounting for $694 million (44.5 percent). The share of tampons peaked at around 50 percent in the late 1970s, but declined in the

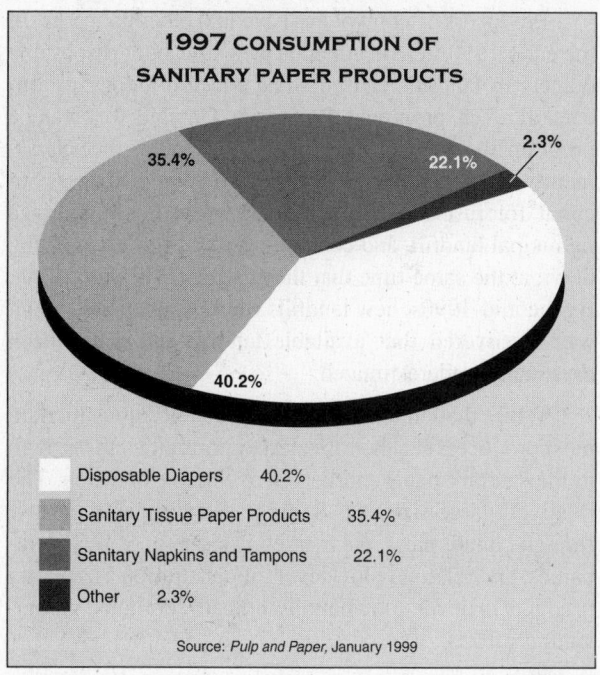

1997 CONSUMPTION OF SANITARY PAPER PRODUCTS

- Disposable Diapers — 40.2%
- Sanitary Tissue Paper Products — 35.4%
- Sanitary Napkins and Tampons — 22.1%
- Other — 2.3%

Source: *Pulp and Paper*, January 1999

1980s, due to adverse publicity associated with toxic shock syndrome (TSS). Since then, medical improvements in tampon manufacture have led to increased acceptance of these products, and the tampon market rebounded.

Environmental Concerns. In the early to mid-1990s, environmental concerns and long-term access to fiber were two of the top issues facing the paper industry group. Restrictions on timber-cutting, new environmental regulations, and potential long-term fiber shortages are all concerns for many sectors of the industry. However, timber-cutting restrictions in the Northwest, continued throughout the late 1990s, have had less of an impact on sanitary paper products industry, mainly because a large proportion of the industry's fiber base is in recycled paper.

Manufacturers of tissue, like other producers of bleached paper products, faced stricter air and water regulations under the Environmental Protection Agency's "Cluster Rule," which was issued in its final form in April 1998. This rule further limited air and water discharges from bleached kraft pulp mills and other paper industry facilities, focusing on limiting discharges—particularly of dioxin, chloroforms, and other chlorinated organics arising from the pulp manufacturing process. Mills also faced new regulations promulgated by the EPA under revisions to the Clean Air Act of 1970 and Clean Water Act of 1972. However, mills that use recovered paper were expected to be less affected by these new rules than mills using wood pulp. This is significant for the sanitary paper products industry since nearly 50 percent of all tissue produced in the United States is made from recycled paper.

Producers of nonwovens have had other concerns. In the early 1990s, environmental pressure about disposable diapers in landfills caused some concern among producers. It even prompted Procter & Gamble to create a program to compost used diapers, although the experiment was eventually discontinued. However, diapers account for just 2 percent of solid waste in the average municipal landfill, and concern over this issue was dying down at the same time that the landfill crisis was easing. By the mid-1990s, new landfills were being opened and it was discovered that available landfill space had been drastically underestimated.

While the United States is still an enormous market, most producers see their greatest opportunities for growth in the sanitary paper markets in overseas expansion. The relatively large size of U.S. producers compared to their foreign counterparts, the marketing strength of U.S. companies, and relatively low levels of penetration of sanitary products in developing nations indicate continued globalization efforts.

INDUSTRY LEADERS

The largest companies within the sanitary paper product industry are Fort James Corporation, Kimberly-Clark Corporation, The Procter & Gamble Company, and Georgia-Pacific Corporation.

Fort James Corporation is the combination of two large paper companies: James River and Fort Howard. James River expanded rapidly in the 1970s and 1980s by acquiring mills considered obsolete and retooling them for efficient use. Its purchase of Dixie-Northern in 1982 made the company a serious competitor in the bathroom tissue market. Fort Howard Corporation was the acknowledged leader in the commercial & industrial market for paper towels, bath tissue and napkins, with the vast majority of its products made from recovered wastepaper.

Today, the company is a leading international consumer products company, manufacturing tissue, toweling, cups, and plates. It had 1998 sales of $7.6 billion. Fort James also produces folding cartons and communications papers. Fort James is North America's largest tissue provider and the second largest worldwide. The company has more than 65 manufacturing facilities and 28,000 employees in North America, Western Europe, Russia, and China.

Since its merger with Scott Paper Company, Dallas-based Kimberly-Clark Corporation has grown into an even more dominant presence in the sanitary products market. In 1998, K-C's sales were $12.3 billion. This made K-C the second largest U.S. paper company according to PIMA's North American Papermaker Magazine's annual ranking survey. K-C is a global manufacturer and marketer of products for personal, business, and industrial uses. Nearly all of its products are made from natural and synthetic fibers. K-C now operates manufacturing facilities in 38 countries with products available in 150 countries.

Kimberly-Clark holds commanding market shares in many segments of the sanitary paper products industry. Its diaper brands accounted for about 40 percent of the North American market in 1998, and its facial tissue brands held over 50 percent of the North American market. K-C also dominates the adult incontinence products market, with over 50 percent market share in 1998.

Procter & Gamble of Cincinnati, Ohio, is one of the world's largest consumer products companies with revenues of $37.2 billion in 1998. P&G had pulp, paper, or converted product sales of $10.9 billion, which ranked it third on PIMA's North American Papermaker Magazine's listing of top paper companies. P&G operates in 140 countries and in 1998 spent $3.27 billion on acquisitions, most of them in the paper business. They included Tambrands Inc. and its global leading brand, Tampax; the Loreto y Pena Paper Company in Mexico; and the Ssanyong Paper Company in Korea. In North America, the company's paper sector generated 10 percent unit volume growth compared with 1997.

P&G's Charmin brand dominates the U.S. consumer toilet paper segment, holding 30 percent of the market in 1997. In second place is Northern, made by Fort James, which held 14 percent. Scott was third at 12 percent. With about 37 percent of the disposable diaper business in 1998, P&G continues to battle with K-C, which held about 40 percent of the market.

The U.S. feminine hygiene market has a number of players: Tambrands Inc. (acquired by Procter & Gamble in 1997) holds a dominant share of the tampon market, with about 43 percent in 1998, followed by Playtex Products Inc. with 26 percent, and Kimberly-Clark, with about 21 percent.

WORKFORCE

The sanitary paper products industry employed 21,791 people in 1997, including 16,981 production workers. Wages in this industry for production workers are much higher than other industries in the paper and allied products group, averaging $16.95 per hour in 1997.

AMERICA AND THE WORLD

The capital-intensive nature of paper manufacturing means that cheaper overseas labor has less of an impact on manufacturing costs than in other, more labor-intensive industries. U.S. manufacturers face little threat from abroad; only one foreign paper manufacturer, Finland-based Molnlycke, has established a significant presence in U.S. sanitary markets. The internationalization of the sanitary paper industry has meant U.S. firms going abroad. Superior product quality and marketing ability has given the United States a competitive advantage in a number of foreign markets.

For most sanitary paper producers, Europe is viewed as particularly promising—the European Community contains 5 percent of the world's population but consumes only 25 percent of the world's sanitary tissue. This compares with 3 percent and 40 percent, respectively, in the United States. This is one of the factors behind Procter & Gamble's acquisition of VPS AG, a major European tissue manufacturer, in 1995. Through the 1990s, nearly all of the large U.S. producers had secured market positions in the European Union. Fort James even ventured into Russia, setting up a production and distribution venture there.

The prospects of greater access to global markets was one of the key elements behind the merger of Kimberly-Clark and Scott Paper in 1995. Scott Paper had more extensive European operations than K-C, and the combination of the two made K-C a powerful competitor in Europe. In fact, before the deal was allowed to go through, governing bodies of the European Union required significant divestitures, including selling the Kleenex tissue and towel lines in Europe, Scotties boxed facial tissue, and Handy Andies facial tissue in the United Kingdom and Ireland. K-C was also forced to sell its Prudhoe, England, tissue mill. In 1998, K-C was the leading European producer of consumer tissue products, though its operations there were challenged by aggressive competition from local manufacturers.

In Asia, U.S. sanitary paper producers have had limited success penetrating the Japanese market but much more success in the rest of Asia. While the Japanese market is highly fragmented and thus viewed as vulnerable to the sophisticated marketers of U.S. products, intricate supplier-retailer relationships have thus far prevented any U.S. producer from establishing a significant presence.

However, U.S. companies' penetration of the fast-growing "rest of Asia" market is much greater. For example, Kimberly-Clark holds a strong position in Taiwan, Korea, and the Philippines. K-C joint ventures in Indonesia, Malaysia, and China are also generating strong sales growth.

RESEARCH AND TECHNOLOGY

Changes in the manufacture of paper have historically been evolutionary rather than revolutionary. The processes used to manufacture paper from rags in the middle of the nineteenth century are in many forms still used today. Much of the research and technology in this industry is focused on lowering incremental manufacturing costs, since the ability to be the low-cost producer can translate into a strong market advantage. Also, the ability to produce softer and stronger paper is a significant focus of sanitary

paper products research and development. For example, Procter & Gamble's development of "through-air-drying" helped it develop the Charmin brand, which had superior bulk and softness compared with other products.

Because companies in this industry are highly competitive, their research and development programs are tightly guarded secrets. Many companies will not allow tours of their tissue-making operations for fear of industrial espionage.

FURTHER READING

"Outlook 1999: Paper Markets Will Remain Weak As Demand Slows; Recovery Delayed" *Pulp & Paper,* January 1999.

Paper, Paperboard, Pulp Capacity and Fiber Consumption. Washington, D.C.: American Forest & Paper Association, 1999.

"Papermaker's Top 50 Paper Companies." *PIMA's North American Papermaker Magazine,* June 1999.

"The Changing Face of U.S. Tissue Manufacturing" *PIMA's North American Papermaker Magazine,* August 1999.

"Tissue, Towel Producers Conquer Market with Form and Function." *Pulp & Paper,* April 1998.

United States Trade and Industrial Outlook 1999. New York: McGraw-Hill, 1998.

SIC 2677

ENVELOPES

This category includes establishments primarily engaged in manufacturing envelopes of any description from purchased paper and paperboard. Establishments primarily engaged in manufacturing stationery are classified in **SIC 2678: Stationery, Tablets, and Related Products.**

NAICS CODE(S)

322232 (Envelope Manufacturing)

INDUSTRY SNAPSHOT

The envelope category is classified as a converting operation, since it transforms a finished product (rolls and sheets of paper and paperboard or synthetic materials) into envelopes. In 1998 U.S. manufacturers shipped 178 billion envelopes and had sales of $3.04 billion, according to figures from the Envelope Manufacturers Association. That compares with 175 billion envelopes and sales of $3.08 billion in sales in 1997.

The latest U.S. Economic Census places the value of shipments for the envelope industry in 1997 at a higher level, $3.58 billion. Commercial white or colored mailing envelopes accounted for about 60 percent of that total.

Kraft mailing envelopes represented 7 percent of the total, followed by clasp and string/button envelopes, at 2 percent. All other envelopes, including padded shipping envelopes, accounted for the remaining 31 percent.

The envelope industry is obviously a major consumer of paper. In 1997 envelope converters consumed $1 billion worth of paper and paperboard in their manufacturing processes, mostly uncoated freesheet and kraft paper, according to the U.S. Economic Census. Mailing and in-house envelopes, which use adhesive seals, metal clasps, or string-and-button closures, are another important segment of the industry, as are heavy-duty padded shipping envelopes and mailers. Converters also used $109 million worth of paperboard containers, boxes, and corrugated paperboard—primarily to ship their products. Additionally, converters used $40 million worth of glues and adhesives and $94 million of plastic film and sheet. The industry also used $359 million worth of other materials.

The envelope industry is not a growing industry; it can be considered static since it is neither growing nor declining rapidly. Envelope shipments ranged between 166 billion units and 178 billion units from 1988 to 1998, with small increases or declines each year. The value of shipments is also relatively static.

U.S. envelope sales were $2.75 billion in 1994, $2.82 billion in 1995, $3.01 billion in 1996, and $3.08 billion in 1997. In 1998 however, sales declined to $3.04 billion according to the Envelope Manufacturers Association.

The chief threat to the envelope industry is alternative means of transmitting information, from mediums such as the Internet, fax machines, voice mail message systems, electronic mail, and other electronic communications systems. However, despite these threats some industry observers point out that new technologies rarely eliminate "old" technologies; they simply move them into new applications. Just as television did not eliminate radio broadcasts, electronic communications are not likely to completely eliminate the use of "old-fashioned" mail.

ORGANIZATION AND STRUCTURE

Envelope manufacturing is widely distributed throughout the United States and basically involves folding, gluing, and printing on high-speed converting equipment. There are many companies involved in envelope manufacturing, including numerous small producers. As in other industries though, the envelope industry is consolidating as larger, more efficient producers buy up smaller entities or force them out of business.

The domestic envelope sector continued to suffer from over capacity, low capacity utilization rates, and flat or declining prices in the late 1990s. In simple terms, there was too much envelope-folding machine capacity

compared to total envelope demand. Many converters reacted by scrapping older, less-efficient equipment or even closing some plants. Little new plant construction was anticipated in the late 1990s, as converters instead pursued a strategy of rebuilding or refurbishing older machines so that they could compete more effectively with new equipment.

While paper envelopes have traditionally been made from 100 percent virgin fiber, many converters have reacted to public demand for more environmentally friendly products by introducing standard business and specialty envelope products that contain varying amounts of recycled materials. Since the products themselves can be recycled, they hold an advantage over newer plastic and olefin envelopes. In fact, some municipal collection programs collect "junk mail," giving paper-based envelopes an environmental plus.

Most paper envelopes are made from uncoated freesheet, one of the largest grades produced by U.S. paper mills. In 1998, envelope grades accounted for about 10 percent of the 13.7 million tons of uncoated freesheet produced by U.S. mills.

Specialty Envelopes. While standard business and commercial stationery envelopes still account for the majority of envelopes produced in the United States, in the mid-1990s specialty envelopes emerged as the fastest-growing segment of the envelope industry. This growth has been spurred by several factors, including the proliferation of specialty "quick print" shops and home-based envelope printing. Many quick print shops use personal computers and laser printers to create custom-printed business forms, stationery, and envelopes.

Envelopes for the specialty market must be able to accept the output of laser printers, which use dry plastic toner ink that is fused to the paper in a heating process similar to that of copier machines. Specialty envelopes also require special adhesives and cannot use windows, snaps, buttons, or clasps. They must also be made of paper, since nylon, plastics, and olefin cannot accept the dry ink process.

Shipping Envelopes. Another growing market for envelope converters is the parcel delivery industry. Providers of overnight services, such as Express Mail, Federal Express, and United Parcel Service, offer shipping envelopes free to their customers. These envelopes are made from several materials, including paper, paperboard, nylon, spunbonded olefin, plastic, and plastic resin. The overnight package delivery industry, begun in the 1970s, was delivering more than 4 million packages daily in the late 1990s.

Catalog services, which proliferated in the 1980s and 1990s, are a major market for shipping envelopes as well. Aided by the vast expansion of credit cards and toll-free telephone numbers, catalogs exist for every imaginable consumer need. Each catalog order must be shipped in envelopes or paperboard boxes. More recently, e-businesses operating on the Internet have expanded the market for home shopping, adding to demand for shipping envelopes.

In addition to catalogs and e-business, telemarketing and television shopping networks are major users of shipping envelopes and mailers. Envelopes and mailers for catalog and direct mail orders must meet strict shipping requirements and thus are heavier and more expensive than other envelopes. They come in a wide range of shapes, sizes, and combinations of base construction materials.

Direct Mail. Third-class, direct mail advertisers are another major market for envelope converters. Consumers responding to direct mail solicitations often trigger an avalanche of paper use, including the paper and envelope for the solicitation, the paper and return envelope containing the order, and the envelope or box in which the product is shipped to the consumer. Direct mail experienced an enormous boom in the 1980s and 1990s, despite perceived negative consumer perceptions about the practice. While costly, direct mail allows manufacturers to target their marketing efforts directly to consumers most likely to purchase their products, avoiding the "waste" of traditional mass media, where many consumers reached by an ad are unlikely to buy the product or service it promotes. The expansion of consumer databases and the ability by marketers to more closely define certain market "niches" has allowed marketers to fine tune their direct mail solicitations, leading to long-term growth in this advertising and marketing vehicle.

One of the major costs of direct mail advertising is postage. Postal rates have been rising far faster than inflation as the U.S. Postal Service (USPS) attempts to come closer to recouping its actual costs for each class of mail. Direct mail advertisers were aware that the major postal rate hike in 1994 and a smaller one in 1997 would likely be followed by others, so they look for ways to reduce the cost of each mailing. One way of reducing costs is by "lightweighting" envelopes, using envelopes made with either lighter paper or with lightweight plastics or composites. Envelopes made from nontraditional materials are more resistant to tearing and puncturing and are more resistant to water. However, traditional paper envelopes still dominate both the standard and specialty envelope sectors because of their low cost and other properties, such as high strength, rigidity, and resistance to curl and fold.

CURRENT CONDITIONS

The USPS remains the dominant carrier of envelopes and plays an integral part in sustaining this industry. In

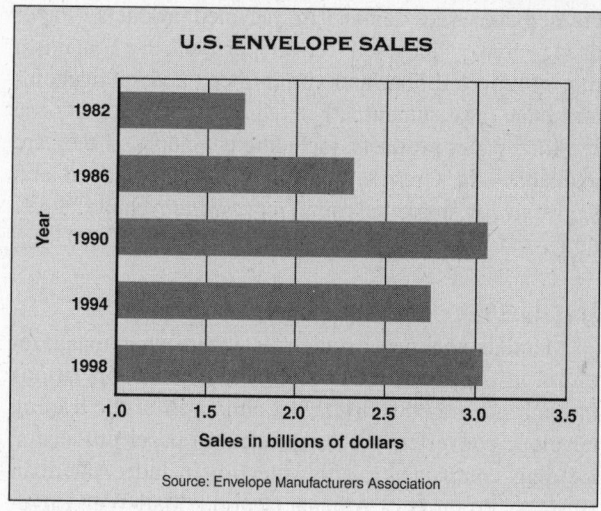

U.S. ENVELOPE SALES

Source: Envelope Manufacturers Association

1995, the USPS handled about 95.3 billion pieces of first-class mail and 71.1 billion pieces of third-class mail, which translates into an enormous demand for a wide variety of envelopes, particularly plain, unprinted envelopes. The volume of both first-class mail and third-class mail was up from 1992, when volumes were 90.1 billion and 62.0 billion units respectively. However, mail volume was expected to begin to decrease in the 2000s. According to the U.S. General Accounting Office (GAO), first-class mail volume will decline at an average annual rate of 0.8 percent in U.S. government fiscal years 1999 to 2008. While first-class mail is projected to grow at an average annual rate of 1.8 percent in fiscal years 1999 to 2002, it is also projected that growth will then decline at an average annual rate of 2.5 percent in fiscal years 2003 to 2008. If realized, this would be the first decline in the history of the USPS and would have a major negative effect on envelope production.

For the early 2000s, the envelope industry is expected to sustain very modest growth. However, the rest of the decade is more uncertain, particularly if projections of a first class mail decline come true. Other factors, such as higher mailing costs, may also negatively impact the industry as the decade continues.

In the late 1990s, the U.S. envelope industry improved operating efficiency and reduced heavy over capacity in converting equipment. This strategy boosted the relatively low operating rate (the percentage of time equipment is operating) that plagued the industry in the early 1990s. As less efficient converters with aging plants become uncompetitive, more plant closures and layoffs are expected in the envelope industry. In fact, employment of production workers in envelope converting slipped from a high of 21,100 in 1989 to 19,200 in 1997.

By the late 1990s, many envelope manufacturers had dramatically increased their purchases of envelope stock containing recycled fiber in order to accommodate increased consumer demand for recycled products. (Paper used to make "recycled" envelopes typically contains a mix of recycled fiber and virgin fiber.) Federal agencies and state government are required by law to choose recycled paper products, including envelopes, if they are available. As a result, converters have developed and aggressively marketed new recycled/recyclable envelopes and mailers.

INDUSTRY LEADERS

Unlike other paper categories, where paper manufacturers also control most of the converting operations through integrated subsidiaries, almost all of the leading envelope converters are independent of paper producers. Leading companies in this category include American Business Products of Atlanta, Georgia; Mail-Well Envelope of Englewood, Colorado; New York Envelope of Long Island City, New York; and Tension Envelope of Kansas City, Missouri.

WORKFORCE

The envelope segment employed 25,500 people in 1997 with a total payroll of $782 million. Production workers accounted for 19,200 of that total and earned hourly wages averaging $13.11. The number of people employed by envelope converters has been dropping as the industry decreases the total number of plants producing envelopes and invests in more heavily automated operations.

AMERICA AND THE WORLD

International trade in envelopes is relatively small, since envelopes tend to be manufactured close to where they are ultimately used. Nonetheless, U.S. converters have expanded their exports, mostly to nearby trading partners such as Canada and Mexico. The North American Free Trade Agreement (NAFTA) with Mexico and Canada, ratified by the United States in 1993, was expected to help expand the exports of efficient U.S. converters.

RESEARCH AND TECHNOLOGY

Much of the research and technology in envelope manufacturing has focused on improving converting equipment, which allows envelopes to be produced faster and with better quality. Indeed, slower pre-1970 equipment is slowly going out of production, since capacity utilization on this equipment has dropped from 57 percent in 1994 to 48.9 percent in 1996. Capacity utilization of higher-speed, post-1970 equipment remained high at 84.9 percent in 1994 and 85.1 percent in 1996, according to the Envelope Manufacturers Association.

As the speed of the envelope converting equipment increases, however, new problems emerge. Previously, for example, most paper was produced using an acid process. However, due to the desire to reduce costs and improve the life of paper products, nearly all mills producing fine paper, which is used in many envelopes, have converted to the alkaline process.

Alkaline paper is usually produced with a synthetic "sizing" product, such as alkylketene dimer (AKD), to improve the surface of the paper. AKD is used to produce many fine paper grades, including envelope paper. On newer, high-speed precision converting equipment, AKD paper has been known to "slip," causing runnability problems. Recent research though, has prompted the development of new sizing products that allow envelope manufacturers to use alkaline paper without concerns about runnability. Such innovations have helped improve efficiency and keep the industry competitive.

Envelope converters clearly face competition from electronic personal communications and electronic data interchange. For example, while electronic bill payment was still in its infancy at the beginning of the 2000s, it was expected that this method of bill payment would grow dramatically, reducing demand for envelopes. Still, while envelopes may be a smaller percentage of the total communication market, their use will continue as the entire market grows even faster. In addition, the fact that envelopes are still a very low cost, attractive way to send information means that the envelope market will remain stable, or at least not experience massive declines, for the foreseeable future.

FURTHER READING

Darnay, Arsen J., ed. *Manufacturing USA*. 6th. Ed. Detroit: Gale Research, 1998.

Envelope Manufacturers Association Fact Sheet. Alexandria, VA: Envelope Manufacturers Association, 1999.

Outlook for Envelopes, 2000. Alexandria, VA: Envelope Manufacturers Association, 1999.

Paper, Paperboard, Pulp Capacity and Fiber Consumption. Washington, D.C.: American Forest & Paper Association, 1998.

U.S. Trade and Industrial Outlook 2000. New York: McGraw-Hill, 1999.

SIC 2678

STATIONERY, TABLETS, AND RELATED PRODUCTS

Establishments in this industry are primarily engaged in manufacturing stationery, tablets, loose-leaf fillers, and related items from purchased paper. Products include correspondence-type tablets, paper desk pads, loose-leaf filler paper, memo books, newsprint tablets and pads, notebooks, stationery, and various other padded paper products.

NAICS Code(s)

322233 (Stationery, Tablet, and Related Product Manufacturing)

The stationery products industry turned in an erratic performance in the mid- to late 1990s, although sales did increase in the latter part of the decade. After reaching a high of $1.48 billion in 1993, sales fell to $1.47 billion in 1994, before climbing to $1.53 billion in 1995 and $1.85 billion in 1997. On average, the industry was growing at about the rate of the gross domestic product (GDP).

The stationery products industry consists of three categories: stationery; tablets, pads, and related products; and stationery, tablets, and related products not specified by kind (NSK). Tablets and pads accounted for a great majority of industry products in 1997, with 79 percent of industry shipments (by value), followed by stationery with 16 percent. The NSK category accounted for the remaining 5 percent.

Within the tablet and pad category, the leading product is bound notebooks, followed by tablets and pads and loose-leaf paper fillers. The two leading products in the stationery category are boxed stationery and portfolios, and wedding and social announcements.

Stationery products are produced by a wide range of companies. Some of the larger paper manufacturing companies have divisions that convert and distribute their own brands of stationery products. Smaller independent stationery converters have also managed to survive and thrive in this market.

Consumers account for the majority of stationery products purchased, at slightly more than 50 percent. The remaining customers for stationery products comprise a wide range of businesses and government agencies, including retail trade, wholesale trade, and doctors and dentists.

School supplies are a vital part of the market for this industry. For example, sales of stationery at discount stores, including products not classified in **SIC 2678,** amounted to $5.32 billion in 1996. Of these sales, 31.0 percent were accounted for by back-to-school products; 30.5 percent by greeting cards; 19.0 percent by office supplies; 6.2 percent by party goods; and 13.3 percent by other products.

As one might expect, paper mills are the largest supplier to the stationery products industry, providing almost 60 percent of all product inputs. Other suppliers of products and services include the wholesale trade;

paperboard mills; motor freight transport firms; and railroads.

The stationery products industry is considered a mature industry, meaning that sales increases are likely to track closely with general growth in the economy. The industry has been negatively impacted by the increased use of personal computers for home and office use, which has reduced the demand for a wide variety of stationery products. While computer printers have increased the use of paper in general, such increases have come in the use of continuous-form computer paper and laser printer paper, which are not included in this classification. Also, extensive downsizing at many U.S. companies in the mid- 1990s negatively affected the use of all office paper products, including stationery. The trend toward home-based offices, however, has been a bright spot for stationery product manufacturers.

One major change in the stationery products industry has been the manner in which its products have been marketed to consumers. While stationery products were once sold primarily by small, independent stationery stores, much of that sales volume has been captured by office product ''superstores'' such as OfficeMax, Inc. and Office Depot, Inc., which have been able to force smaller retailers out of the marketplace and drive wholesale prices down.

Several large paper companies are leaders in the stationery products industry, including International Paper Company of Purchase, New York; Georgia-Pacific Corporation of Atlanta, Georgia; and Mead Corporation of Dayton, Ohio. However, there has remained room for some mid-sized independent converters such as Smead Manufacturing Co. of Hastings, Minnesota.; Ampad Corp. of Dallas, Texas; Demco Inc. of Madison, Wisconsin; and Roaring Spring Blank Book Co. of Roaring Spring, Pennsylvania.

The stationery products industry employed a total of 9,094 people in 1997, about the same amount as in 1991. The 1997 total included 6,590 production workers who earned average hourly wages of $11.57 per hour, which was comparable to other industries in the paper and allied products group.

Further Reading

Lazich, Robert S., ed. *Market Share Reporter 2000.* Detroit: Gale Research, 1999.

Paper, Paperboard, Pulp Capacity and Fiber Consumption. Washington, D.C.: American Forest & Paper Association, 1999.

Stationery, Tablet and Related Product Manufacturing, 1997 Economic Census, Manufacturing Industry Series. Washington, D.C.: U.S. Census Bureau, August 1999.

U.S. Trade and Industrial Outlook 2000. New York: McGraw-Hill, 1999.

SIC 2679

CONVERTED PAPER AND PAPERBOARD PRODUCTS, NOT ELSEWHERE CLASSIFIED

Establishments in this category are primarily engaged in manufacturing miscellaneous converted paper or paperboard products, not elsewhere classified, from purchased paper or paperboard. Products in this classification include gift wrap, pressed and molded pulp goods, laminated building papers, fiber conduits, crepe paper, pressed and molded pulp cups, pressed and molded dishes, molded pulp egg cartons, and converted filter paper.

NAICS CODE(S)

322215 (Non-Folding Sanitary Food Container Manufacturing)
322222 (Coated and Laminated Paper Manufacturing)
322231 (Die-Cut Paper and Paperboard Office Supplies Manufacturing)
322298 (All Other Converted Paper Product Manufacturing)

Note: The U.S. Economic Census now reports industrial information under the North American Industry Classification System (NAICS) instead of the Standard Industrial Classification (SIC) system. As a result, the value of shipments data reported below is for **NAICS 322299** (the replacement for **SIC 2679**), and it includes only a portion of what used to be reported for **SIC 2679**. For example, the 1995 value of shipments for **SIC 2679** was reported at $5.16 billion; in 1997, the value of shipments for **NAICS 322299** was reported at $4 billion. **NAICS 322299** also includes portions of the following SIC industries: **SIC 2675: Die-Cut Paper and Paperboard and Cardboard** and **SIC 3999: Manufacturing Industries, NEC.**

The paper products in this classification are best described as specialty products because of their diversity. In 1997, this industry had a value of shipments of $4.0 billion (NAICS data). The largest product category in this industry is "other converted paper and paperboard products," accounting for $2.7 billion (68 percent) of the value of industry shipments in 1997. This category includes such diverse products as paper party and holiday goods ($195 million of the total); cellulose insulation/paper doilies/placemats ($184 million); paper filters and "other" paper wrapping products ($228 million); and "other" die-cut paper and paperboard products ($209 million).

The next largest category is molded pulp goods, including egg cartons, florist pots, and food trays. This segment accounted for $466 million of the value of shipments in 1997. All other products accounted for the remainder of the total.

The total value of raw materials used in converted paper and paperboard products not elsewhere classified in 1997 amounted to $1.9 billion. Of this total, paper and paperboard was the largest raw material category at $634.8 million. Other leading raw material categories include recovered paper at $41 million; paperboard containers, boxes, and corrugated paperboard at $42 million; plastics at $23 million; and glues and printing inks at $23 million. The "all other materials" and raw materials not specified by kind (nsk) categories accounted for a rather large portion of the total, at $1.14 billion.

Paper mills have traditionally been the largest supplier to this industry, providing almost 30 percent of its raw materials. Imports accounted for the next-largest volume, at 21.0 percent; followed by wholesale trade with 9.2 percent; paperboard mills with 6.6 percent; and plastics materials and resins with 2.5 percent.

Personal consumption expenditures accounted for the largest share of purchases from the industry, at close to 30 percent of the total. The wholesale trades were the next-largest customer, with 11 percent of total purchases.

Trends for this industry are highly product-specific. Gift wrap continued to grow with the general economy, despite admonitions by environmental groups for consumers to reduce or eliminate the use of gift wrap. Sales of gift paper are directly related to the level of gift purchasing in the United States. After several mediocre years during the recession in the early 1990s, gift paper enjoyed an upward sales trend through the remainder of the 1990s as gift buying—particularly during the key Christmas period—accelerated along with the general economy.

Molded pulp products—primarily egg cartons—enjoyed a resurgence in the 1990s due to public interest in recycling. These gray cartons, often made of recycled newsprint, lost share in the 1980s to molded plastic products. But as consumers began to express some displeasure with hard-to-recycle plastic cartons, some egg producers responded by moving back to molded pulp products. Schools and fast food outlets also stepped up their use of molded food trays in the 1990s.

The converted paper products not elsewhere classified industry employed 24,188 people in 1997. Of that total, 18,775 were production workers, earning an average hourly wage of $11.96 and working 37.2 million hours.

FURTHER READING

All Other Converted Paper Product Manufacturing, 1997 Economic Census, Manufacturing Industry Series. Washington, D.C.: U.S. Census Bureau, November 1999.

Darnay, Arsen J., ed. *Manufacturing USA.* 6th ed. Detroit: Gale Research, 1998.

Smook, Gary A. *Handbook of Pulp & Paper Terminology: A Guide to Industrial and Technological Usage.* Bellingham, WA: Angus Wilde Publications, 1990.

U.S. Trade and Industrial Outlook 2000. New York: McGraw-Hill, 1999.

PRINTING, PUBLISHING & ALLIED INDUSTRIES

SIC 2711

NEWSPAPERS: PUBLISHING, OR PUBLISHING AND PRINTING

This category includes establishments primarily engaged in publishing newspapers, or in publishing and printing newspapers. These establishments carry on the various operations necessary for issuing newspapers, including the gathering of news and the preparation of editorials and advertisements, but may or may not perform their own printing. Commercial printing is frequently carried on by establishments engaged in publishing and printing newspapers, but even though the commercial printing may be of major importance, such establishments are included in this industry. Establishments not engaged in publishing newspapers, but which print newspapers for publishers, are classified in **SIC 2759: Commercial Printing, Not Elsewhere Classified.** News syndicates are classified in **SIC 7383: News Syndicates.**

NAICS CODE(S)

511110 (Newspaper Publishers)

INDUSTRY SNAPSHOT

Since the 1960s, newspaper management has undergone a transformation from essentially family-run companies to the concerns of multimedia corporations. According to Ellis Cose, author of *The Press,* 1963 brought the first sign that the newspaper industry was in for a change. That year, the Chandler family, owner of The Times Mirror Company, whose chief holding was the *Los Angeles Times*, listed the company on the New York Stock Exchange. Soon other newspapers went public,

making their actions accountable to shareholders and not just the families that ran them. This trend led to the growth of newspaper chains and the proliferation of a corporate culture, which stressed profits and growth over conventions of journalism. By 1989 five companies—Washington Post Company, Times Mirror Company, The New York Times Company, Gannett Co., Inc., and Knight-Ridder Inc.—were responsible for one-fourth of the newspapers read each day in the United States. In 1998, the top ten newspaper companies owned more than 270 newspapers, accounting for 45 percent of total daily circulation. In keeping with the transformations of the industry, corporations that controlled newspapers began to branch out into other related ventures such as book publishing and marketing, and as a result their newspapers became part of entire communications systems, rather than self-contained enterprises.

The newspaper industry has been feeling pressure since the late 1980s. Many papers with long histories have been forced to shut down, and many others have reported financial losses. To counteract this crisis, publishers reduced editorial and production staffs through layoffs and hiring freezes, raised newspaper prices and advertising rates, experimented with new layouts, and increased automated processes. The industry's advertising revenues rose from $41.3 billion in 1997 to $43.9 billion in 1998, a 6.3 percent increase. Circulation contributed another $10.3 billion, making newspapers a $54 billion industry.

Even so, circulation figures have declined steadily since 1987 at a rate averaging 1 percent a year. In 1998, total daily circulation was 56.2 million, the lowest level since the mid-1950s. Newspaper readership—the percentage of adults who read newspapers—has also been declining, from 77.6 percent of adults in 1970 to 58.6 percent in 1998, according to the Newspaper Association of America. To stimulate readership and circulation, the NAA hired an advertising agency in 1997 to promote newspaper reading with a three-year, multimedia campaign.

ORGANIZATION AND STRUCTURE

A variety of publications could be called newspapers. The most common format is the gatefold, which is divided into individual sections. Pagination in a gatefold restarts in every section. The other major format, the tabloid, is read like a book or a magazine. Tabloids usually have fewer articles than gatefolds, and are paginated without interruption from beginning to end. Traditionally, the content of tabloids has been considered less serious and less comprehensive than that of gatefolds.

Frequency of publication is another variable among newspapers. The papers with the greatest circulation are dailies; most of these issue a denser, more expensive Sunday edition. There are far more weeklies in operation, though their circulation is smaller. The two most common types of weeklies are the community newspaper and the alternative newspaper. The community newspaper highlights local current events such as education, sports, and politics. The alternative newspaper provides coverage of news items and arts-related activities that are often overlooked by the mainstream press. Since advertising provides the bulk of revenue for weeklies, these newspapers are often free.

Advertising. Most newspapers rely on circulation and advertising to finance their operations. Measured in linage, advertising amounts to about 80 percent of an average newspaper's income. Placement of advertisements is a significant factor; the section and page of an ad, as well as its size, will determine its price. Department stores traditionally have been a major source of advertising dollars, filling pages with pictures of their merchandise. Classified advertising is also a reliable and profitable endeavor for newspapers, adding up to 37 percent of total advertising income. This type of advertising is sold by the word.

One recent and controversial development in newspapers is the "advertorial," or paid announcement on the opinion page or in another section where the advertiser expects to gain from its context. Other advertisements of this type consist of multi-page inserts or theme magazines distributed with papers. Paid announcements are labeled as such to avoid confusion, however, many editors feel the ads jeopardize the integrity of the newspaper.

Circulation. Newspapers are sold in vending machines and privately owned newsstands, or by subscription, which allows customers to pay a reduced rate per issue and have the paper delivered to their home or business. Newspapers profit from subscribers because they mean guaranteed, consistent sales. In determining a price for newspapers, publishers have to weigh the potential earnings from sales against what readers are willing to pay. If the price is too low, circulation might be healthy, but profits could decline. If the price is too high, circulation could drop.

Averaging 50-60 percent of total costs, personnel represented the largest expenditure for newspapers. Departments include management, editorial, advertising, circulation, and production. Within the editorial department, the staff is divided according to paper sections, which may include: local and national news, sports, entertainment and the arts, business, opinion, and others, depending on the paper's size and focus.

Newsprint was the second-highest expenditure, averaging one-quarter of total costs. The United States consumes more than one-third of the world's newsprint, most of that going for the nation's newspapers. A dip in newsprint costs can save a newspaper during hard times, and since a failed newspaper means loss of business for the newsprint manufacturer, most offer substantial discounts from list prices. However, publishers such as the New York Times Company and the Tribune Company also own paper mills, and consequently suffer when newsprint sells at a low cost. Equipment such as printing presses and cameras represents the third-largest expense for newspapers.

BACKGROUND AND DEVELOPMENT

Newspapers served to inform the public of events and circumstances pertaining to society, government, and commerce. The providers of information were expected to be reliable and current, without neglecting their other function of entertaining the literate population. The Acta Diurna of the Roman empire and the Chinese gazettes of the first century A.D. are the distant ancestors of today's newspapers. The first modern newspapers appeared in Europe in the sixteenth century.

Newspaper reporters had a responsibility to act as watchdogs against injustice, corruption, and impropriety; the right to expose these qualities in public figures is protected in the First Amendment to the Constitution of the United States. The first great moment in American journalism came in 1735 with a court case deciding the issue of freedom of the press. Editor John Peter Zenger was brought to trial on charges of seditious libel for printing articles that were critical of colonial governor Sir William Cosby. In his successful defense of Zenger, Alexander Hamilton invoked the Magna Carta and stressed that opposition to the establishment was a basic civil liberty, thus creating the foundation on which the American press was built.

An overriding objective for American newspapers was to reach as many readers as possible. One early manifestation of this aim could be seen in the *New York Tribune,* founded by Horace Greeley in 1841. Priced at one penny, the paper was written by Greeley and other advocates of social change in a style that was described as simple but not condescending. It boasted a tremendous readership throughout the country, which led to enthusiastic support from its advertisers. The populist instincts that Greeley embodied eventually evolved into "Yellow Journalism," a term originally referring to the practices of many of the New York daily newspapers during the late 1800s. Joseph Pulitzer, editor of the *New York World,* and William Randolph Hearst, editor of the *New York Journal* strove to increase circulation through a variety of aggressive tactics, such as reporting sensational stories, setting headlines in extremely large type, making extensive use of pictures, and issuing Sunday supplements with color comics.

Telegraph lines, which by the turn of the century reached points all over the United States and crossed the Atlantic Ocean, were essential to the dissemination of news, and they facilitated the rise of cooperative news gathering. The Associated Press, originally formed by the morning newspapers of New York City, allowed member newspapers to run each other's stories. England's Reuters news service and other similar European agencies established reciprocal agreements with the Associated Press, fostering the potential for newspapers to run stories from around the world. The United Press and the International News Service were established to compete with Associated Press during the 1920s. In 1958, these two services merged to form United Press International.

In the early twentieth century, newspapers began to contend with the rise of new media that was capable of quickly bringing more information into American homes. The formation of the Radio Corporation of America (RCA) in 1919 represented the first of these challenges. In 1929, advertising revenues at newspapers were still far ahead of those of radio, but the newer medium was quickly growing. The Depression, which left the newspaper industry with barely more than half of its advertising income, had little effect on radio advertising, which doubled in the years from 1929 to 1933. A second news forum arose in the 1930s—the newsreel, which was shown between features at movie theaters.

The 1950s brought another challenge for print journalism. Television captured the imagination and leisure time of many Americans. As it quickly became the medium of choice, television siphoned advertising dollars away from newspapers. Network television news became more readily identified with major events, such as the assassination of President John F. Kennedy. The 24-hour Cable News Network (CNN) debuted in 1980, and its phenomenal growth contributed to the sense that newspapers were becoming an outmoded form of transmitting breaking stories. The late 1980s and 1990s saw an even greater expansion of cable television, and American

viewing habits changed accordingly. By 1995, the average adult spent approximately 1,580 hours watching television—30 hours per week. During the same time period, newspapers across the country were battling circulation losses, and the number of daily newspapers dropped from 1,745 in 1980 to 1,489 in 1998.

The economic recession at the end of the 1980s brought heavy losses in advertising and circulation revenues. The effects were even felt by new publications. The *St. Louis Sun,* a tabloid created by Ralph Ingersoll II with money from junk bonds, debuted in September 1989 and closed the following August. Another new publication, *The National,* a nationwide sports daily, ran only eighteen months before folding in June 1991. By 1991, papers with long histories, many of which had survived the Depression, were beginning to shut down as well. These included *The State-Times* of Baton Rouge, Louisiana, and the *Dallas Times Herald.* The latter closing left 900 people unemployed and made that city the largest in the country with only one daily paper. In 1991, United Press International filed for bankruptcy for the second time in six years.

One solution to these dire conditions was the Joint Operating Agreement (JOA). Under the Newspaper Preservation Act of 1970, newspapers were largely exempt from antitrust suits. In a JOA, two or more newspapers are allowed to share the costs associated with operations, while maintaining separate editorial departments. However, the papers must prove that one would not survive if not for a JOA. One of the most substantial and controversial agreements, between Knight-Ridder's *Detroit Free Press* and Gannett's *Detroit News,* was finalized in November 1989 after a lengthy court battle. While similar agreements have saved newspapers in other cities, both of these papers continued to lose money and circulation.

CURRENT CONDITIONS

Newspapers have enjoyed increasing advertising revenues since 1992, following 1990 and 1991, the two worst years ever for the newspaper industry. For the first time since the Depression, there were back-to-back losses in annual advertising revenues as national, retail, and classified linage all shrunk. Ad revenues began to rise again in 1992, with a 3.9 percent gain, followed by 5.2 percent gain in 1993. Advertising revenues reached $39 billion in 1996, a 7.7 percent gain from 1995, and a $5 billion increase from 1994. The industry's advertising revenues rose from $41.3 billion in 1997 to $43.9 billion in 1998, a 6.3 percent increase.

The trend toward consolidation has continued in the newspaper industry, with numerous mergers and acquisitions taking place every year. In 1998, more than 160 daily newspapers changed hands, compared to 73 dailies in 1994. Mergers and acquisitions are fueled not only by considerations of economies of scale, but also by the desire for strategic clustering in specific geographic areas.

One major concern of the newspaper industry has been readership. Through academic studies and marketing surveys, publishers attempted to discover who was reading the newspaper with regards to such factors as age, sex, and financial status; frequency and duration of an average read; the instances where one newspaper was shared by two or more readers; and the sections of the newspaper that were read or ignored. In most cases these inquiries yielded discouraging results. A study by journalism professor Gerald Stone determined that between 1967 and 1989, the number of people aged 18 to 29 who read a daily paper declined 35 percent. According to Stone, this was due to parents passing on to their children their disinclination for newspaper reading, resulting in an ever-deepening alienation from the publications. The trend was linked to a pervasive apathy towards current events. A study by the Times Mirror Center for the People and Press found that merely 42 percent of those under age 30 showed an interest in the fall of the Berlin Wall, an event given a great deal of attention by newspapers.

USA Today was the industry's most revolutionary gesture towards appealing to a mass readership. Pioneered by Gannett's Allen Neuharth in 1982, *USA Today* modified the approach of other newspapers aiming at the entire nation—the *New York Times, The Wall Street Journal,* and the *Christian Science Monitor.* The paper was printed in regional plants via satellite transmissions from its editorial centers. Aware that advertisers and readers tended to regard the average daily newspaper as visually bland and difficult to navigate, designers of *USA Today* incorporated such features as an easily read index on the front page, bold graphics featuring statistical information related to the day's events, and a large color weather map. The newspaper was even sold in vending machines designed to resemble television sets. Neuharth limited the number of sections in his paper to four: a news section emphasizing the positive side of current events; a "Money" section devoted to business coverage with a strong consumer orientation; an extensive sports section providing many pictures and ample statistical data; and a "Life" section encompassing health, education, and entertainment. In 1999, its U.S. circulation of 1.8 million put it slightly ahead of *The Wall Street Journal* as the leading national newspaper. Gannett claimed that *USA Today* had worldwide circulation of 2.2 million and was available in 60 countries in 1999.

Readership continues to be the primary problem facing the industry. According to a 1996 American Opinion Research poll, only half of those in the industry said that it would be "healthy" in ten years. As noted earlier, newspaper readership has declined from a high in the early 1970s, when approximately three of every four

NEWSPAPERS MARKET VALUE FORECAST

Source: *U.S. Market Trends and Forecasts,* The Gale Group, 1999

adults read a newspaper, to less than six of every ten adults in 1998. Daily circulation, likewise, continues to decline. For the six-month period ending March 31, 1999, daily circulation at seven of the nation's top ten metropolitan newspapers declined. Only the *New York Times, Los Angeles Times,* and *New York Daily News* reported circulation gains for the period.

INDUSTRY LEADERS

A diversified news and information company headquartered in Arlington, Virginia, Gannett Co., Inc., ranked first in daily circulation in 1999 with 74 daily newspapers with a combined circulation of more than 6.7 million. Founded by Frank Gannett in 1906, the company began acquiring newspapers throughout New York State. It owned 22 dailies by 1947, the year he died. Allen Neuharth joined the company in 1963, and he is credited for making it a major force in the industry. After going public in 1967, Gannett absorbed small newspapers all over the country, bringing to them exacting management requirements and transforming them into profitable enterprises. Additionally, Gannett augmented its holdings with radio and television stations, and entered the field of billboard advertising. The birth of *USA Today* in 1982 was facilitated by the fact that Gannett's reporters, editors, and technology were established in every region of the nation. In 1999, Gannett had revenues of $5.3 billion, up 2.7 percent from 1998, and net income of $1 billion, a 4.2 percent increase. It also employed a total of 45,800 people. In 1998 the company divested its remaining radio stations and acquired three television stations.

Knight-Ridder, Inc., which is involved in news and information services and graphics and photo services in addition to newspaper publishing, is the second-largest newspaper company in terms of circulation with an average daily circulation in 1998 of 4.0 million. The company resulted from the 1974 merger of the Knight and Ridder newspaper chains. In addition to owning such respected newspapers as the *Philadelphia Inquirer, Miami Herald,* and *Detroit Free Press,* Knight-Ridder became a leader in the related field of information services, acquiring Dialog Information Services in 1988. In late 1996, Knight-Ridder announced a joint venture with Financial Times Information and Dow Jones & Company, Inc. for the co-development of a global electronic news resource for corporate, research, government and academic customers. Knight-Ridder/Tribune Business News was slated to be distributed independently through the companies' respective electronic information services beginning in mid-1997. The company has been very forward-looking in its use of information technology, and in 1999 *Information Week* ranked it second among 500 companies for its use of information technology. Knight-Ridder's revenues for 1999 were $3.2 billion, up 4.4 percent from 1998. The company employed 22,000.

The Times Mirror Company of Los Angeles, California, publishes five metropolitan and two suburban daily newspapers. It also provides professional information services and publishes a variety of special-interest magazines. Unlike Gannett and Knight-Ridder, which own a great number of small newspapers, Times Mirror's holdings are concentrated on large city dailies, including the *Los Angeles Times, The Baltimore Sun,* and Long Island's *Newsday.* In 1999 the company had net income of $259 million on revenues of $3.03 billion.

The New York Times Company, owner of the *New York Times,* the *Boston Globe,* and 21 regional newspapers, is a diversified media company that is also involved in magazines, television and radio stations, and electronic information and publishing. The *New York Times,* ranks third in circulation behind *USA Today* and the *Wall Street Journal.* The *Times* has been a longtime stronghold of journalistic standards, beginning when Adolph Ochs and his son-in-law Arthur Hays Sulzberger emphasized comprehensive coverage and news writing of the highest order. In 1999 the New York Times Company reported net income of $310 million, up 6.6 percent from 1998, on sales of $3.1 billion.

WORKFORCE

The newspaper industry employed 4.4 million people in 1996, including more than 2 million women. Production workers accounted for 34 percent of total employees, earning an average hourly wage of $12.39. In light of the changes in newspaper management and production during the late 1980s and early 1990s, those working in the industry were obligated to learn new skills and take on new duties. Foremost among these were related to the computer revolution, as word processing programs and developments in page design proliferated

in newsrooms. Some of the tasks that previously belonged to production departments, such as typesetting, either were made obsolete or were dramatically altered with technological developments. In addition, some departmental differences began to disappear, meaning that former specialized positions now required proficiency in many areas, as well a general knowledge of all newspaper operations.

RESEARCH AND TECHNOLOGY

In the early 1990s, some newspapers began migrating to supplying electronic information. They made their databases available to subscribers, creating special editions, and enhancing their classified ads. The five newspapers with the highest circulation—*Wall Street Journal, USA Today, New York Times, Los Angeles Times,* and the *Washington Post*— were among the first to have online versions. By the end of 1998, more than 900 U.S. newspapers had Web sites, and internationally more than 3,000 newspapers were available online. Competing with newspapers were a variety of Web-based news and information services offered free or on a subscription basis.

Despite being touted as the most important development in the industry since the invention of the printing press, online publications pose some challenges. Creating an online newspaper is both expensive and labor intensive. Since reading an on-screen publication is different than reading a newspaper, design and graphics are even more important—content must be adjusted accordingly. If an online newspaper has no subscription fee, advertising revenue must absorb the costs. Advertisers supporting the online version may pull their dollars from the print. Finally, it is not clear if there are enough potential readers, although the number of U.S. households that have computers with modems is growing rapidly. How much this market will grow is unknown.

A 1998 survey by industry magazine *Editor & Publisher* found that among the more than 700 media Web sites surveyed, nearly 20 percent were profitable in 1998. Among newspaper sites, a reported 25 percent were profitable. Other media operating profitable Web sites included magazines and television and radio stations.

FURTHER READING

Cose, Ellis. *The Press.* New York: Morrow, 1989.

"Editor & Publisher Interactive." New York: The Editor & Publisher Co., 1997. Available from http://mediainfo.elpress .com.

Foroohar, Kambiz. "Chip off the Old Block." *Forbes,* 17 June 1996.

"Knight-Ridder, Inc., 1998 Annual Report: Financial Highlights." Available from http://www.kri.com.

"Gannett Company Profile," available at http://www.gannett .com/map/gan007.htm, 8 December 1999.

"Knight Ridder," *Editor & Publisher,* 9 October 1999.

Lazich, Robert S., ed. *Market Share Reporter.* Detroit: Gale Research, 1997.

"More Strong Postings," *Editor & Publisher,* 1 May 1999.

Moses, Lucia. "Profits Strong Despite Ad Slowdown," *Editor & Publisher,* 6 February 1999.

"New York Times Company: Regional Newspaper Group." Available from http://www.nytco.com/company/busi.reg.html, 8 December 1999.

"The Paperless Paper," *Institutional Investor,* November 1998.

Seabury, Jane. "Circulation Down at Most Big Papers, Audit Bureau Says," *Knight-Ridder/Tribune Business News,* 4 May 1999.

Standard & Poor's Industry Surveys: Publishing. New York: Standard & Poor's Corporation, 14 October 1999.

"Times Mirror Lifts Earnings," *Editor & Publisher,* 13 February 1999.

"Times Mirror: About Us." Available from http://www.tm .com/about/, 8 December 1999.

"Times Mirror Reports 1998 Results," company news release, 8 February 1999. Available from http://www.tm.com/financial/ 1998earningstext.html

"Welcome to the Newspaper Association of America." Vienna, VA: Newspaper Association of America, 1997. Available from http://www.naa.org.

Ziegler, Bart. "Stop the Presses: Publishers Scramble into On-line Services, but Payoff is Unclear." *Wall Street Journal,* 26 April 1995, 1.

SIC 2721

PERIODICALS: PUBLISHING, OR PUBLISHING AND PRINTING

This category covers establishments primarily engaged in publishing periodicals, or in publishing and printing periodicals. These establishments carry on the various operations necessary for issuing periodicals, but may or may not perform their own printing. Establishments not engaged in publishing periodicals, but which print periodicals for publishers, are classified in commercial printing industries.

NAICS CODE(S)

511120 (Periodical Publishers)

INDUSTRY SNAPSHOT

The first American magazines appeared in 1741, but like many of their successors, were doomed to swift failure. This inauspicious start notwithstanding, the periodicals industry burgeoned steadily over the following 250 years, employing an estimated 131,000 Americans by 1996, distributing upward of 11,000 publications and generating annual revenues of more than $24.786 billion. By 1998 the number of business and consumer magazines had grown to 18,608, according to the consumer magazine industry association, Magazine Publishers of America. In 1998, the top 500 magazines had an estimated $26.1 billion in revenues, representing an estimated 75 percent of the industry's total revenue. Indispensable to Americans as a source of entertainment and information, magazine publishing also provides an essential advertising medium for other industries.

In the first half of the twentieth century the magazine publishing industry progressed steadily, without meteoric rises until the early 1980s, when new production technology, positive demographic trends, and an accelerated need for information all came together to spur a doubling in revenues over the span of the decade. Unfortunately this growth spurt did not last. A widespread recession started in the late 1980s, just when periodical markets were starting on a tendency towards maturity and saturation. In response, major advertisers hastened to slash their budgets, bringing diminished revenues and dwindling profits to the publishing industry generally.

The beginning of the 1990s found magazine publishers scrambling both to reduce costs and retain their share of U.S. advertising expenditures. To keep advertisers interested, many companies introduced niche periodicals that catered to smaller audiences, but offered their advertisers useful, tightly focused audiences. This eased the advertising situation somewhat, but also split the magazine market into highly-fragmented target areas. Between 1988 and 1998, the following ten categories added the most new titles: business and industry, health, education, computers and automation, travel, regional interest, automotive, entertainment, lifestyle, and women's interest.

ORGANIZATION AND STRUCTURE

Periodical publishers earn money either by selling advertising space in their pages to companies wanting display areas for their products or by charging readers for subscriptions or individual issues. Thus the periodical's content is essentially a tool which can be fine-tuned in order to boost sales and ad revenues. Many publishers also generate income through database marketing techniques, such as selling subscriber lists or marketing "back-end" products and services to their customers.

Periodicals sales and ad revenues each account for about 50 percent of the average publisher's receipts. Although more than 80 percent of all periodicals are purchased through mail-order subscriptions, 30 percent of sales dollar volume is garnered through newsstand sales. As is the case with most items, the prices of magazines rose during the 1990s. In 1992 the average annual subscription price of a U.S. periodical was about $27, while the typical newsstand price per individual issue was about $2.85. By the end of 1998, however, newsstand prices averaged $3.45, and subscription rates had risen to an average $33.00.

Markets. In 1988, according to McCann-Erickson, magazines received a 5.1 percent share of the print-media advertising market. By the end of 1996, their share had risen to 5.3 percent. This prompted publishers to find innovative ways to attract more advertising dollars. Some, like top-ranked *TV Guide,* cut their ratebases to advertisers, making up the difference in revenues by boosting the newsstand price of the magazine. Others started custom publishing magazines tailored to the needs of specific clients. In November 1996 *Business Week* noted two interesting examples. One, a richly illustrated Conde Nast publication, advertised only the expensive watches specified in its title, *Patek Phillipe;* the other, from Hachette Filipacci Magazines, was *Mercedes Momentum,* launched in 1995 specifically to attract more female purchasers to the Mercedes Benz automobile.

A second way to multiply advertising dollars is by paying close attention to previously skirted markets and introducing new magazines targeted to them. For example, Essence Communications, publisher of the highly successful *Essence,* a magazine for African-American women, introduced *Latina,* a bilingual Spanish-English magazine in May 1996. From 1994 through 1997 an average of 800 new magazines were launched each year to reach new audiences.

The leading magazine advertisers include automobile manufacturers, consumer goods companies, entertainment conglomerates, and tobacco firms. The top ten magazine advertisers in 1998 included four automotive firms (General Motors, DaimlerChrysler, Ford Motor, and Toyota), two consumer goods firms (Procter & Gamble and Unilever), two tobacco companies (Philip Morris and RJR Nabisco Holdings), and two entertainment and media companies (Time Warner and Sony). General Motors led all magazine advertisers with $460 million in expenditures, followed by Procter & Gamble with $407 million, Philip Morris with $384 million, and DaimlerChrysler with $355 million. Altogether, the top 50 magazine advertisers spent $5.6 billion on magazine advertising in 1998. During the 1990s the magazine industry enjoyed a trend of increased advertising revenues from year to year.

Competition. More than 18,000 American magazines are published each year, yet the industry is dominated by large companies that tend to be diversified media conglomerates with interests in other media as well as magazine publishing. In 1998, the ten largest consumer magazines had a combined advertising and circulation revenue of $5.6 billion, or 21 percent of the $26.1 billion in revenues for the top 500 magazines. While figures representing total industry revenues are not available, industry magazine *Folio* estimated that the top 500 magazines accounted for three-fourths of the industry's total revenues. The top-grossing magazine for several years has been *TV Guide,* with revenues of $1.1 billion in 1998. Notably, *TV Guide* was acquired in 1999 by Gemstar for $9.2 billion.

Because competition for ad and circulation dollars is intense, the turnover rate of publications is enormous—particularly for start-up periodicals. From 1994 through 1997 an average of 800 magazines debuted each year, but statistically speaking, 50 percent are doomed to failure. Low barriers to entry in comparison to most other industries contribute to the high failure rate, because anyone with several thousand dollars and an idea can start a new periodical. Poor business planning and inadequate market research, however, usually accompany such endeavors.

BACKGROUND AND DEVELOPMENT

Periodicals evolved from book notices that were inserted in European newsbooks published during the early 1600s. By the 1640s publishers were beginning to include critical commentary, and by the 1650s, the notices began appearing as regular features of newsbooks and papers. About the same time that book notices were developing, digests and abstract journals began appearing. These periodicals provided summaries of published books, biographies, and reports on important philosophical, literary, and scientific matters of the time. The *Journal des scavans,* first issued in Paris on January 5, 1665, is recognized as the parent of the modern periodical industry.

Throughout the remainder of the seventeenth century, several publishers, mostly in Great Britain, began to produce periodicals offering opinion, news, and entertainment. Next, early in the 1700s, journals of political opinion became particularly popular. Great Britain's *Spectator,* for example, achieved a circulation of 4,000. Other well-received British journals during the eighteenth century included *Farmer's Magazine, Gentlemen's Magazine,* and *London Review.* During the nineteenth century as the European industry evolved, journals appealing to a broad range of interests emerged. Great Britain's *Westminster Review,* Italy's *Scena Illustrata,* and Russia's *Russky Vestnik* were popular, as were new magazines targeting special interest groups such as children, physicians, and women.

The first American periodicals were Andrew Bradford's *American Magazine* and Benjamin Franklin's *General Magazine,* both of which started and failed in 1741. Other early efforts included *The Columbian* and Thomas Paine's *Pennsylvania Magazine.* In all, about 100 magazines were eventually started in the colonies;

most of them failed within a few years. After numerous duds and over 500 new periodical start-ups during the early 1800s, by 1825 about 100 magazines and journals were circulating on U.S. soil. Spurred by a demand for weekly literary journals, as well as children's, women's, religious, and political periodicals, the total number of magazines in circulation rose to 600 by 1850. Two famous titles of that time were *North American Review* and *Southern Literary Messenger.*

With the 1850s came a new era for the periodicals industry. It began with *Harper's New Monthly Magazine,* a richly illustrated periodical that spurred a horde of highly successful imitators. *The Nation, Outlook, Scribner's Magazine,* and *Christian Union* were a few of the titles that rocketed the number of U.S. periodicals to 1,200 in 1870, 2,400 in 1880, and nearly 3,000 by 1890. In the 1890s, moreover, low-priced illustrated monthlies were introduced that cost only 15 cents per copy, compared to the 35 cents charged by their predecessors. Many of these magazines were "muckrakers" that exposed government corruption.

The number and circulation of periodicals continued to proliferate rapidly during the early twentieth century. Among the most popular publications were *Good Housekeeping* and *Ladies' Home Journal,* which were joined by *Life* in 1923, and *Newsweek* ten years later. *Reader's Digest,* founded in 1922, became a classic American success story, its circulation soaring to a stunning 21 million during the 1950s. *Life* and a similar publication called *Look,* achieved success in the 1960s, reaching combined sales of 7 million dollars.

The periodical publishing industry found itself facing new challenges during the 1950s and 1960s. Most visible was the immediate popularity of television. In company with radio, television altered American reading habits and allowed periodical publishers an increasingly smaller proportion of overall advertising expenditures. Augmenting this trend were diminished profit margins caused by growing production expenses and higher postal rates, though media competition and rising costs could not suppress strong circulation growth throughout the middle years of the century. Publications like *Playboy* and *Seventeen* opened up entirely new, and massive, market segments. Likewise, a plethora of trade and business journals boosted industry breadth and earnings. In addition, entire sub-industries sprang up during the 1970s to serve automotive enthusiasts, fashion fans and other niche readers. New marketing channels, such as the Publisher's Clearinghouse Sweepstakes, also spurred growth. By the end of the 1970s, the periodicals industry was grossing more than $10 billion in sales and employing a work force of over 90,000.

The periodicals industry continued to expand steadily during the 1980s. A general increase in the demand for all types of current information and escalating advertising expenditures helped to boost circulation. Other stimulants came from burgeoning electronics technology, spurring a $275 million market niche for computer and office equipment magazines which had not existed at the beginning of the decade. Other industries which significantly increased their magazine ad expenditures included apparel and travel.

As periodical demand rose and ad revenues climbed, the number of periodical titles increased from 10,700 in 1982 to about 11,000 by 1990. During the same period, total industry sales jumped from $11.5 billion to $23.1 billion, representing an average annual growth rate of more than 7 percent. Some of the readership niches that offered the best opportunities were newsweeklies, women's, men's sports, and travel.

Periodical prosperity waned in 1989 and the early 1990s. A U.S. and global economic recession blasted ad revenues, stalled subscription growth, and slashed newsstand sales. In addition, some analysts believed that the market was becoming saturated and mature, thus offering fewer profit opportunities. Finally, periodical producers were slowly losing their share of U.S. ad dollars to other media, such as direct mail and catalogs.

Cost control became an important factor in maintaining magazine profitability. Besides subtly reducing the number of issues per year, publishers were also trying to reduce costs through other strategies. For instance, by presorting mail and including four-digit zip code suffixes to address labels, some producers were able to cut second-class postage costs by as much as 5 percent. Other publishers were switching to lightweight paper and trucking magazines to regional distribution centers. Many producers were also increasing their database marketing efforts and striving to garner follow-up retail sales from their subscribers. The largest gains, though, were being accomplished through layoffs, salary freezes, and benefit cutbacks.

Winners and Losers. As the economic recovery took hold in the early and mid-1900s, the magazine publishing industry enjoyed steady increases in advertising revenues. Circulation figures, which had declined from 1990 to 1992, began to rise again in 1993. The industry's optimism was reflected in the number of new magazine launches, with an average of 800 new magazines being introduced annually from 1994 through 1997.

The most popular magazine category in terms of new titles introduced between 1988 and 1998 was business and industry, which grew from 358 titles in 1988 to 694 in 1998. The number of health magazines nearly tripled during the period, increasing from 169 in 1988 to 494 in 1998. Education magazines more than doubled, from 227 titles in 1988 to 519 titles in 1998. Other categories

PERIODICALS MARKET VALUE FORECAST

Source: *U.S. Market Trends and Forecasts,* The Gale Group, 1999

rounding out the top ten in growth were computers and automation, travel, regional interest, automotive, entertainment, lifestyle, and women's interest.

CURRENT CONDITIONS

Magazine publishers enjoyed strong growth in advertising revenues in 1999. The more than 200 magazines audited by the Publishers Information Bureau (PIB), an affiliate of the trade association Magazine Publishers of America, showed an 11 percent increase in year-to-year advertising revenues through August 1999. The growth was attributed both to increases in advertising rates and in the number of advertising pages. For the 227 consumer magazines tracked by PIB in 1998, there were 242.4 million ad pages, compared to 231.4 million pages for 216 magazines tracked in 1997.

Through October 1999, automotive advertisers increased their magazine advertising expenditures by 10.4 percent for the year, from $1.35 billion to $1.49 billion. Even higher growth was reported for technology advertisers (up 15.2 percent to $1.06 billion); home furnishings and supplies (up 15.9 percent to $922.6 million); drugs and remedies (up 18.7 percent to $828.1 million); financial, insurance, and real estate (up 23.5 percent to $784.0 million); media and advertising (up 19.5 percent to $589.5 million), transportation, hotels, and resorts (up 17.4 percent to $589.0 million); and retail (up 10.8 percent to $539.5 million).

The number of new magazine launches declined in 1998 to 476 new magazines. The top categories, each with more than 30 new launches in 1998, were media personalities, sex, crafts/games/hobbies, sports, computers, and metro/regional/state. There were 27 new business and finance magazines launched in 1998.

The magazine industry experienced heightened merger and acquisition activity in 1998, and the trend was

likely to continue in 1999 and 2000. According to *Folio,* some 100 mergers and acquisitions took place in 1998 with an estimated value of more than $6.8 billion, comparable to the number of mergers and acquisitions in 1997. Major deals included the $1.2 billion acquisition of Petersen Cos. By EMAP; the sale of ten magazines including *Country* by Reiman Publications Inc. to the private equity firm Madison Dearborn Capital Partners for $640 million; and the acquisition of Mecklermedia by business-to-business publisher Penton Media.

Major transactions in 1999 included the sale of *TV Guide* by co-owners Liberty Media and News Corp. for $9.2 billion to Gemstar, a company traditionally involved in technologies related to electronic program guides. Advance Publications, a privately held company run by the Newhouse family with $1.4 billion in magazine revenues in 1998, purchased Fairchild Publications from Walt Disney Co. Fairchild published *Women's Wear Daily (WWD), Footwear News, Supermarket News,* and other retail trade magazine. Also in 1999, technology publisher Ziff-Davis was put up for sale by its Tokyo-based parent company, Softbank Corporation. Analysts estimated Ziff-Davis could fetch $3 billion, despite its 1998 losses of $78 million.

In the late 1990s, magazines increasingly turned to online services, which offer benefits such as decreased dependence on advertisers. Many well-known magazines have offered electronic versions on consumer online services such as America Online and Compuserve. With the popularity of the World Wide Web, publishers have also begun hosting their own sites that often include back issues and other special features. There have also been numerous Internet-only publications, sometimes called e-zines, that offer similar content and format as their print-based competitors. This does not mean that publications in print form are on their way out. There are many situations, such as when traveling, when consumers may not have access to their computers, and therefore turn to printed magazines. Also, there are still millions of households across the country which do not have computers. In an effort to pursue ever-greater advertising revenues, magazines have begun offering different ads and editorial sections for the same publication, so that different customer segments will receive issues tailored to their demographic profile.

INDUSTRY LEADERS

The industry leaders in magazine publishing tend to be diversified media companies with interests in other media as well as in magazines. In terms of 1998 magazine advertising revenue, as reported by *Advertising Age,* the industry leaders were Time Warner Inc. with $3.3 billion in magazine advertising revenues, The Hearst Corporation ($1.6 billion), and Advance Publications Inc.($1.4 billion).

Time Warner is a diversified media and entertainment conglomerate with interests in movies, television, music, and book publishing, among other areas. In addition to its flagship weekly news magazine *Time,* it also publishes *People Weekly, Sports Illustrated, Life, Entertainment Weekly,* and *Vibe.*

The Hearst Corporation is a diversified communications company with interests in newspaper, book, magazine, and business publishing. It is a partner in cable network A & E Network and owns radio and television stations. Its subsidiary, Hearst Magazines, claims to be the world's largest publisher of monthly magazines, with sixteen U.S. titles and 98 international editions distributed in more than 100 countries. Among the well-known titles it publishes are *Cosmopolitan, Esquire, Country Living, Good Housekeeping, Harper's Bazaar, House Beautiful, Popular Mechanics, Redbook, Smart Money,* and *Town & Country.*

Advance Publications Inc. is a private company controlled by the Newhouse family. It is the parent of Conde Nast Publications Inc., which publishes fashion titles including *Vogue, Glamour, GQ, Mademoiselle, Allure,* and *Brides.* In 1999, Advance acquired Fairchild Publications, which published *Women's Wear Daily* (*WWD*) and *Footwear News* as well as other retail trade periodicals.

Reed Elsevier, with $969 million in 1998 magazine advertising revenue, is an international publisher and information provider for the North American and European markets. Its periodicals cover three business segments: scientific, professional, and business-to-business. It is a publicly traded company that is owned by two international parent companies, Reed International P.L.C. and Elsevier NV.

Primemedia, with an estimated $928 million in 1998 magazine advertising revenue, is a media company that publishes 250 magazine titles, 232 business and consumer information products, and a variety of education titles. It owns nearly 50 trade shows and offers more than 200 Web sites. Founded in 1989 as K-III Communications Corporation, it publishes consumer, special interest, and technical and trade magazines. Its best-known consumer titles include *American Baby, Modern Bride, New York, Seventeen, Soap Opera Digest,* and *Soap Opera Weekly.* It also publishes consumer magazines for teenagers, including *16 Magazine, Teen Beat,* and *Tiger Beat,* among others.

WORKFORCE

The periodical industry's 6,298 establishments employed roughly 137,550 workers in 1997, according to the U.S. Census Bureau. Workers in the industry are relatively well paid and work fewer hours than the average manufacturing industry employee. The average production worker earned $16.34 per hour in 1997. Further-

more, the average work week in this industry was only 37.1 hours in 1995, compared with 41.6 hours for all other manufacturing sectors.

The industry is a major employer of writers, editors, and technical writers, which together constitute 13 percent of its workforce. Many employees begin as copywriters, copyeditors, or production editors, and work their way up to various editorial management positions. Senior editors, for example, traditionally write copy and may also manage other editorial employees or freelancers. But a salary survey presented in August 1996 by *Folio* pointed to an increased workload for senior editors, as a result of the corporate downsizing that has taken place during the 1990s. The average senior editor's salary, $43,400 in 1993, rising through the top third averaged $62,600, according to a survey with 404 respondents in the August 1, 1993 issue of *Folio.* By 1996, salaries had risen considerably. The average senior editor on a business publication could now expect to earn $49,900 per year, while consumer magazines offered an average annual salary of $63,300, with the top third yielding $81,200 on average.

Managing editors coordinate the editorial, art, and production departments of a publication and oversee proofreading and copywriting functions. Salaries for this job averaged $41,000 in 1993 and $48,500 by 1996, with business magazines paying an average $48,100 and consumer publications slightly more, at $48,900 per year. Editors, who are responsible for directing the content of a publication, averaged $47,000 in 1993, though the top one-third of survey respondents earned over $70,000. By 1996, however, the average was $65,100, with the top third earning $102,700. Editorial managers, who may be called publishers, are responsible for setting editorial policy and managing operations. The average salary for this function was $66,400 in 1993, with the top third of the group earning more than $100,000. By 1996, the average for this position was $73,400, while top wages averaged $112,700. Base salaries as well as bonuses for all positions vary primarily according to the circulation volume of each periodical, by the frequency of its appearance, and by the number of pages in each issue.

Periodical producers also employ a large number of ad salespeople, who make up 12 percent of industry employment. According to a *Folio* survey, the average director of ad sales earned $90,208 in 1993. When the same survey was repeated in 1996, the top one-third of the directors, averaged $137,310. Branch and regional ad sales managers averaged $72,000, with the top salary reaching $122,000. Also included in this group were ad salespeople, whose average salary in 1996 was $46,000 for business publications, and $41,000 for consumer magazines; the highest salary was $110,000. *Folio's* 1999 survey indicated that salaries for ad sales positions were either flat or declining between 1998 and 1999, in spite of an overall increase in advertising revenue.

Although overall compensation slumped in the early 1990s, the long-term employment outlook for the periodicals industry was very positive going into the mid-1990s. Jobs for writers and editors were expected to increase by over 50 percent between 1990 and 2005, according to the Bureau of Labor Statistics. Sales and related positions, moreover, were expected to grow by over 65 percent. Indeed, almost every occupation in the industry was forecast to jump by over 30 percent. Jobs for executives, for example, should rise 28 percent, and administration and support staff will likely grow by over 30 percent. Opportunities for computer programmers are expected to increase nearly 80 percent by 2005.

AMERICA AND THE WORLD

In an effort to boost earnings in slow domestic markets, many periodical publishers in the early 1990s were seeking growth overseas. Although total industry exports amounted to only 3.5 percent of receipts in 1993, cross-border shipments had grown almost 100 percent since 1989 and were expected to increase at a rate of 5 to 10 percent annually through the turn of the century. Furthermore, U.S. publishers had a stranglehold on domestic markets, as imports amounted to less than $170 million in 1993 and the industry's trade surplus topped $600 million.

Canada consumed about 78 percent of all periodical exports in the early 1990s, but other countries were exhibiting solid market growth. The United Kingdom, for example, purchased 6 percent of periodical exports, and Mexico and the Netherlands each purchased 3 to 4 percent. Consumer and farm magazines were the greatest sellers. Helping to increase foreign sales in the early 1990s were U.S. joint ventures with overseas publishers that were directing local marketing and publishing efforts. For example, IDG, a global computer-related publisher, entered a joint venture in China to publish *Electronics International,* while 1996 brought a joint venture between *Newsweek* and a Russian banking, real estate, and communications conglomerate called Most, to produce *Itogi,* a newsmagazine aimed at the emerging highly educated new middle class in Russia. Top magazine circulations in Russia may run as high as 2 million, *FIPP Magazine World* claimed in January 1997.

While the majority of magazine exports have traditionally gone to English speaking foreigners, U.S. publishers began significant efforts during the 1980s and early 1990s to establish foreign editions of their publications. Some of these efforts were quashed by the global recession of the early 1990s.

Other companies that had successfully invaded foreign periodical markets in the early 1990s included Miller Freeman, Inc., of California, PennWell Publishing of Texas, Advanstar Communications of Ohio, and several others. Cahners Publishing, of Illinois, for example, was selling 38 percent of its 58,000 monthly circulation of *Hotels* to overseas readers in 1993. Likewise, Paisana Publications was shipping over 68,000 issues of the semimonthly *Easyriders,* a Harley Davidson motorcycle enthusiasts magazine, to foreign customers. *Surfing,* published monthly by California's Western Empire Publishing had about 13,744 overseas subscribers in 1993, and by the end of the same year *Scientific American* was selling 113,000 copies of a total 663,000 overseas, and *Fortune* magazine introduced a new Chinese-language edition at the end of 1996.

Despite some overseas success, the export potential for U.S. periodicals remained limited by multiple factors going into the mid-1990s. Most important, postal rates in most European and Asian countries are much higher than U.S. rates. This severely restricts subscription sales. U.S. publishers also often incur great difficulty obtaining effective mailing lists that they can use to market their publications. The U.S. list industry is highly advanced by comparison. Furthermore, some important markets like Germany have strict environmental and privacy regulations that limit periodical sales through the mail.

U.S. exporters will likely experience little relief from foreign regulations in the near future, depending on revisions to the European Union's law on privacy and data protection, which threatened to make it very costly for U.S. publishers to acquire customer lists. Nevertheless, Europe, as well as Asia and Latin America, will remain the focus of joint ventures and licensing arrangements aimed at boosting overseas sales. The North American Free Trade Agreement (NAFTA), signed in 1994, was expected to have a negligible impact on industry participants.

RESEARCH AND TECHNOLOGY

In 1993 a data-gathering service called Periodical Retail Information Management (PRIM) was introduced. The system was designed to provide timely and accurate data to retailers, wholesalers, and publishers. The system was expected to eventually assist with the distribution of more than 3,000 titles to more than 189,000 retailers each month, and would keep close track of title data related to each retailer's sales, including promotion and discount information.

In the long term, periodical publishers will start to view their role as providers of information services, rather than just product publishers. This will occur as electronic and digital publishing proliferates, and as publishers seek to enhance revenue streams through advanced media options. Many publishers were already experimenting with multimedia markets in the early 1990s, and several had been offering their periodicals on CD-ROM or online since the 1980s. Some analysts believed that electronic publishing, in some form, would dominate the industry by the 2010s, with paper publishing used only as a side or specialty media.

Indeed, as the number of American households with a modem-equipped personal computer rose from 13 percent in 1993 to more than one-third in 1998, publishers were increasingly striving to take advantage of this media by launching Web sites on the World Wide Web. Whether or not such electronic publishing ventures were profitable was another question. According to a 1998 survey of more than 700 media Web sites, only 20 percent were profitable. Of all magazine Web sites surveyed, 24 percent were profitable in 1998, and 40 percent expected to be profitable in 1999.

Evidencing the trend toward electronic media was a partnership formed in 1993 by Jeffrey Dearth, president of the *New Republic,* and Rob Raisch, president and founder of The Internet Co. Their online partnership, The Electronic Newsstand Inc., was designed to give print publishers a "point of presence" on the Internet. More than 50 magazines were represented on The Electronic Newsstand by 1994, including such titles as *Arthritis Today* and *New Yorker.* By the end of 1996, this number had soared dramatically, with *Publisher's Weekly* counting some 800 magazines on line. In November of 1996, *Folio* reported that on-line publishers had joined with members of other businesses to form a trade association called the Internet Advertising Bureau. Adweek Magazines, Hearst, and Time Warner Inc.'s New Media were among 70 others who paid their first annual $70,000 fee, in order to join discussions of such topics as advertising to children and agency and marketer relations.

By 1999, periodical Web sites were common and took several different forms. Some offered editorial content from their print publications, supplemented by unique content and other interactive features. Others were strictly marketing sites, providing such services as e-mail newsletters and links to advertisers and other sites listed in the print product's editorial matter. Still other magazines were only available electronically. These e-zines or Webzines, as they were called, provided original content and competed with the existing Web sites of print periodicals. Some periodical publishers established separate operating units to handle electronic publishing. Fashion magazine publisher Conde Nast established CondeNet in 1994, offering four sites with original material as well as content from its magazines. It launched Vogue.com late in 1999, but CondeNet had yet to turn a profit. The proliferation of online databases of periodical articles also offered periodical publishers another source of revenue.

The advent of electronic publishing for magazines, newspapers, and databases raised certain copyright issues and concerns among freelance writers regarding electronic rights. In September 1999, the U.S. Circuit Court of Appeals ruled in favor of freelancers, represented by the National Writers Union, and against the *New York Times* and other publishers, saying that publishers must provide additional compensation to freelancers for use of their articles on their Web sites and in electronic databases.

FURTHER READING

Callahan, Sean. "Ziff-Davis Faces Uncertain Future," *Business Marketing,* 1 August 1999.

Chang, Suna. "Out of Print: Webzines with Names Like Word, Nerve, and Salon Have Pulled in Mainstream Respect and Devoted Followers," *Entertainment Weekly,* 5 February 1999.

"Circ City: Here We Come!" *Folio,* 1 July 1996.

"CondeNet," *Adweek Eastern Edition,* 20 September 1999.

"Folio: M&A Scorecard," *Folio,* August 1999.

"Gemstar Buys TV Guide," *Television Digest,* 11 October 1999.

Hearst Corporation. "About Hearst Magazines," available at http://www.hearstcorp.com/mag29.html

"The Latina Link in Two Languages." *Folio,* 1 September 1996.

Levine, Joshua. "Go Break a Leg." *Forbes,* 3 June 1996.

Lockwood, Lisa. "Advance's Fashion Crown Adds Another Jewel," *Footwear News,* 30 August 1999.

Lockwood, Lisa. "Mags Online: Different Strokes," *WWD,* 9 April 1999.

Magazine Publishers of America. "About MPA," available at http://www.magazine.org/aboutMPA/mission.html

Magazine Publishers of America. "Circulation Revenue for Top 100 ABC Magazines," available at http://www.magazine.org/resources/fact_sheets/cs11_8_99.html

Magazine Publishers of America. "Growth of Magazines by Category," available at http://www.magazine.org/resources/fact_sheets/ed4_8_99.html

Magazine Publishers of America. "Magazine Advertising Pages," available at http://www.magazine.org/resources/fact_sheets/adv7_8_99.html

Magazine Publishers of America. "Magazine Advertising Revenue by Classification, 1998," available at http://www.magazine.org/resources/fact_sheets/adv6_8_99.html

Magazine Publishers of America. "Magazines' Role in the Media Mix," available at http://www.magazine.org/resources/fact_sheets/adv3_8_99.html

Magazine Publishers of America. "New Magazine Launches," available at http://www.magazine.org/resources/fact_sheets/adv6_8_99.html

Magazine Publishers of America. "October Posts Highest Growth in Advertising Pages This Year," available at http://www.magazine.org/news/press_releases/991109_oct_pib.html

Magazine Publishers of America. "Single Copy and Subscription Circulations Per Issue for All A.B.C. Magazines, 1960-1998," available at http://www.magazine.org/resources/fact_sheets/cs5_8_99.html

Magazine Publishers of America. "Sold and Merged Magazines, 1998," available at http://www.magazine.org/resources/fact_sheets/ind1_8_99.html

Magazine Publishers of America. "Top 50 Magazine Advertisers," available at http://www.magazine.org/resources/fact_sheets/adv13_8_99.html

Maurer, Rolf. "Tepid Raises," *Folio,* 1 September 1999.

"Newsmagazines Take Hold in Russia." *Folio,* 1 November 1996.

Oder, Norman. "Freelancers Win Copyright Suit," *Library Journal,* 15 October 1999.

Owens, Jennifer, and Heather Holliday. "Analysts: Ziff-Davis Could Go for $3B in Sale," *Folio,* August 1999.

Pogrebin, Robin. "Magazines Multiplying As Their Focuses Narrow." *New York Times,* 2 January 1997.

Primedia, Inc. "Company Overview," available at http://www.primediainc.com/html2/company.html, 8 December 1999.

Primedia, Inc. "Specialty Consumer Magazine Group," available at http://www.primediainc.com/html2/media.html, 8 December 1999.

"Read All About It." *Business Week,* 18 November 1996.

Reed Elsevier. "Annual Review 1998: Business Description," available at http://www.r-e.com/redescrp.htm, 9 December 1999.

Rogers, Michael. "National Online Meeting Tackles E-Journals and More," *Library Journal,* 15 June 1999.

Sarbin, Hershel. "The Multimedia Imperative," *Folio,* 15 April 1999.

Silber, Tony. "Outpacing Inflation . . . And Then Some." *Folio,* 1 August 1996.

Standard & Poor's Industry Surveys: Publishing, New York: Standard & Poor's Corporation, 14 October 1999.

"Trade Group Forms for Online Publishers." *Folio,* 1 November 1996.

U.S. Census Bureau. *1997 Economic Census.* Washington: GPO 1999.

SIC 2731

BOOK PUBLISHING

This category includes establishments primarily engaged in publishing, or in publishing and printing, books and pamphlets. Establishments primarily engaged in printing or in printing and binding (but not publishing) books and pamphlets are classified in **SIC 2732: Book Printing.**

NAICS CODE(S)

511130 (Book Publishing)
512230 (Music Publishing)

INDUSTRY SNAPSHOT

The book publishing industry experienced extraordinary growth from 1963 to 1993, with annual book sales of $1.68 billion in 1963 rising to $17.17 billion by 1993. In 1998 American consumers spent $28.7 billion on books, while the Association of American Publishers estimated total net sales of books for 1998 at $23 billion. The most significant categories accounting for book sales in 1998 were trade (including adult and juvenile titles) with $6.15 billion in sales, up 6.5 percent from 1997; professional, scientific, technical, and medical with $4.4 billion (up 6.3 percent); elementary-high school (el-hi) texts and materials with $3.3 billion (up 10.3 percent); college texts and materials with $2.9 billion (up 8.2 percent); and mass market paperbacks with $1.5 billion (up 5.6 percent).

Books sales are driven by a number of factors. Favorable demographics have contributed to sales growth in such categories as adult trade, children's books, college texts, and el-hi sales. Publishers have found support in a growing literate population with high disposable personal incomes. Other factors affecting sales of different categories include school enrollments and state funding for school-related books. With a growing number of high school graduates and more targeted marketing programs, college sales have been strong. Children's book sales have benefited from merchandising tie-ins with movies and television shows. Demand for adult trade books reflects strong best-seller lists and other factors.

Changes in the way consumers purchase books have had a positive impact on book sales in the 1990s. In the early 1990s it was the proliferation of large retail bookstore chains. By offering conveniences such as comfortable browsing areas, coffee bars, and special events such as book-signings, author readings, and children's story hours, these chains created "superstores" that provided an enjoyable atmosphere for consumers while expanding the overall market for books. The two biggest players that emerged in this arena were Borders Group Inc. and Barnes & Noble Inc. In the late 1990s it was the growth of online bookselling, pioneered by Amazon.com. It wasn't long before both Barnes & Noble and Borders Books & Music had established Web sites to offer books over the Internet. In 1999 Barnes & Noble raised $25 million by spinning off barnesandnoble.com as a separate, publicly-traded company while maintaining a 37 percent interest in it.

ORGANIZATION AND STRUCTURE

In some respects, book publishing appeared to be a fragmented industry, with over 25,000 companies participating in the United States in the late 1990s. In reality, however, the industry was dominated by several giant publishing houses. According to *Trade Book Publishers,*

1996: Analysis by Category, as quoted in *Media Daily,* the top dozen trade book publishers accounted for nearly 85 percent of the overall U.S. book publishing market. These large publishers consolidated many of their smaller imprints in the 1990s in order to cut costs and reposition themselves for the onset of electronic publishing. According to Malcolm Jones of *Publishers Weekly,* most of these companies considered themselves to operate within ''the publishing aspect of the communications industry.'' However, this concentration of power among relatively few publishers led to criticism regarding the quality and diversity of materials published. Industry observers saw an increasing role for small presses to publish works of literary quality that did not necessarily have enormous sales potential. Because of the proliferation of smaller publishers, the book publishing industry is not highly concentrated compared to other industries. In many categories there are relatively few barriers to entry.

Products within the book publishing industry could be divided into six major categories: adult trade; juvenile trade; mass market; professional, technical, and reference; university press; and religious books. Trade books, representing the largest share of the book market, encompassed all general-interest publications, such as adult and juvenile fiction, nonfiction, advice, and how-to books. In 1998, the trade category had net dollar sales of over $6.1 billion according to the Association of American Publishers. In the mass market paperback category, publishers' net dollar sales were $1.5 billion in 1998, compared to $1.35 billion for 1995; net dollar sales for professional titles reached $4.4 billion in 1998, up from almost $3.87 billion in 1995 The expansion of large chain bookstores and the population growth among school-age children and high-income adults were among the factors that contributed to the growth of these sales.

The book publishing process was fairly similar across these product categories. Most books originated as a concept or idea, which was either submitted by an outside author or generated internally by the publisher. The concept was usually refined using market analysis, and the final decision to proceed resulted from a comparison of the product's expected costs and potential revenues. Such decisions were increasingly made by committee consensus versus the decree of one individual editor. Next came the actual compilation of the book's content, followed by editorial work to ensure its quality and tailor it specifically to a target market. Meanwhile, the marketing and art departments designed the finished product, including type style, page size and layout, presentation of graphics, and appearance of the cover. Then the book was typeset (set in final, camera-ready form for printing), either by an outside vendor or with an in-house desktop publishing system. Finally, the book was transformed into plates, printed, and bound, usually by an outside

vendor or affiliated company rather than the publishing house.

Volume, or the size of a book's print run, is an important factor in achieving profitability. Non-educational publishers normally held first hardcover runs to 5,000-50,000 copies while new books by bestselling authors may have merited first runs of over 300,000 copies. Per unit fixed costs were a function directly related to the size of the print run. The American Association of Publishers indicated that the typical manufacturing costs for a mass-market paperback were less than 10 percent of gross sales, while the average for all books was approximately 25 percent.

Returned books represented a substantial cost to publishers, and one that rose ominously throughout the mid-1990s. The cost of returns included ''handling, processing, and disposal,'' and, according to *Standard & Poor's,* such costs cut heavily into publishers' pretax profit margins. The *New York Times* noted the following in August 1996, ''Returns are the most significant barometer of the financial success of a book, a measurement more critical than a ranking on a best-seller list because rejects cut directly into profits. Historically, publishers have agreed to take back returns and absorb the loss to entice bookstores to stock their titles.'' According to the American Association of Publishers, from 1990 to 1995, industry losses on returned hardcover books rose by 60 percent to over $530 million; as a point of contrast, gross sales grew during the same period by 47 percent.

Book publishers sold their products to the following primary markets: chain and independent retail bookstores; college bookstores; elementary and high schools; and libraries, universities, and other institutions. Among these markets, large chain bookstores proliferated and gained importance in the early 1990s—making book-buying into a form of entertainment and siphoning sales away from mail order and book clubs. In addition, the library market, though small, was considered crucial in that it guaranteed publishers a minimum number of sales and, traditionally, required comparatively little in terms of marketing attention. On-line bookselling, the newest and fastest growing retail format, provided consumers with relatively quick access to over 1 million titles purchasable via the Internet.

BACKGROUND AND DEVELOPMENT

The U.S. book publishing industry grew after the Civil War, as the country moved from an agrarian to an industrial society and people increasingly sought information about emerging technology. World War I increased demand for engineering manuals, especially with regard to radio communication, aviation, construction, and aerial photography. During World War II, training manuals gained importance as factories had to hire untrained people to replace soldiers. Publishers who could provide this information quickly received special allocations of paper, which was scarce during wartime.

Beginning in the mid-1800s, publishing houses provided gathering places for literary talent of the time, especially in London and New York City. Most writers formed relationships with particular editors—who often became well-known public figures in their own right—and followed them from one publishing house to another. Several publishing houses became prominent in the fight against censorship in the early twentieth century. One celebrated case occurred in the 1930s when Bennett Cerf, one of the founders of Random House, intentionally notified U.S. Customs about the arrival of James Joyce's allegedly obscene novel *Ulysses* from Paris. Cerf wanted Customs to confiscate the book so that he could fight the censorship in court. Publishing houses that supported freedom of speech often attracted the top literary and editorial talent.

Paperback books first appeared in the United States in the 1770s, but they did not gain a wide audience until Simon & Schuster introduced its line of Pocket Books in 1939. These early softcover editions sold for 25 cents each and met with great success—over 25 million copies were shipped overseas during World War II. Public acceptance of paperbacks increased the overall market for books and made it necessary for publishers to adopt high-volume, low-cost production methods.

In *Publishers Weekly,* John F. Baker called the 1940s and the 1950s "the golden age of publishing," when the industry was a "comparatively small business producing a comparatively limited number of books for a dozily elite readership whose access to bookstores was limited by geography." As the U.S. population grew and became more educated, however, book publishing boomed. This rapid growth culminated in what Baker described as "the decade of the Great Communications Conglomerate Takeover" in the 1960s. Publishing houses either acquired one another or joined forces with communications conglomerates that held interests in newspapers, magazines, television, and motion pictures. By the early 1970s, the industry was dominated by about 15 giant companies. The consolidation of power continued into the early 1990s, when about seven publishers controlled the industry.

Many of the challenges facing the book publishing industry were reflected in the children's literature boom of the late 1980s. Children's books traditionally represented a quiet, consistent segment of the market, and were virtually ignored by most large houses except for the revenue generated by the classics year after year. However, sales of children's books exploded during the "baby boomlet"—a result of the financially secure baby-boom generation reaching child-bearing age—from $336 million in 1985 to $1.1 billion in 1992. As more

publishers jumped on the bandwagon and expanded their children's divisions, annual output grew from 3,800 titles in 1985 to over 5,000 in 1991 and the number of children's-only bookstores doubled. However, such rapid expansion led to an oversaturation of the market with books of mediocre quality, which was compounded by the recession and decreases in library budgets. As a result, sales growth suddenly dropped by half, retailers returned unprecedented numbers of unsold books, and many publishers were forced to reevaluate their approaches in the face of fierce competition. According to M. P. Dunleavy in *Publishers Weekly,* "the publishing of children's books has not only grown up but completed an odyssey," and the industry learned in the process that it must adopt a longer-term outlook in order to survive.

The book publishing industry faced a transformation entering the mid-1990s. Many observers noted that the industry, which once could be characterized as gentlemanly and literary, had quickly become more cutthroat and businesslike. *National Review* cited as evidence the trend for large publishing houses to replace long-time chief executives, best known for their "literary sensibilities," with industry outsiders steeped in "modern management techniques." As a result, many employees within the publishing industry shifted their focus from building relationships with authors and carefully tailoring manuscripts to cutting costs and analyzing profit and loss statements. Former Pantheon managing director Andre Schiffrin noted in *The Nation* an increasing trend among modern day publishing houses to set higher and higher profit targets, which often ranged from 12 to 15 percent in 1996; this figure contrasted starkly with the typical 1920s publishing company's average profit of 4 percent. Rising overheads also contributed to the financial strain placed on publishers in the mid-1990s, making many companies even more vulnerable.

Some analysts felt that this shift toward modernization was overdue, since book publishing faced challenges on a number of fronts yet lagged behind other industries in seeking efficiencies in production, distribution, and marketing. One problem addressed by many large houses was their overproduction of titles, which resulted in an average of 30 percent of trade books (and up to 48 percent of paperbacks) being returned unsold for credit. Retailers tended to over-order some titles to attain volume discounts and hopefully predict the next best-seller. In response, some publishing houses utilized new technology to make shorter production runs more profitable, and their average first-runs dropped significantly in the late 1980s. In addition, several publishers began experimenting with "no-return" policies with the goal of encouraging booksellers to make more realistic orders.

Another factor affecting the book publishing industry was the proliferation of large, influential retail bookstore chains. While these chains expanded the overall market for books, they also had the power to limit pricing and affect the selection of books that publishers could offer profitably. Some critics argued that by catering to a mass market, chains caused publishers to create books of broad appeal, but low quality. For example, the early 1990s saw many publishers adopt genre publishing—focusing on books with similar themes in order to limit their risk. One highly criticized result of this trend was the battle to attain publishing rights for headline-grabbing, "true-life" stories of questionable literary value, such as celebrity scandals and lurid crimes. Some analysts also worried that chains would disrupt the business of independent booksellers, who were often closely linked to tastes within their communities and provided a market for more eclectic books. *The Nation* noted in 1996 that, "In a series of lawsuits brought by the American Booksellers Association, the independents have charged that the large publishers favor the chains through unfair practices." The argument was that the big publishers allegedly paid generously to have their bestsellers prominently displayed and advertised within the stores while the smaller publishers did not have the means to compete in such a system.

The two biggest retail bookselling chains, Borders Books and Music and Barnes & Noble Inc., expanded aggressively throughout the United States, opening outlets reaching from New York's World Trade Center to the West Coast. In 1995, Borders boasted sales of $1.75 billion while Barnes & Noble posted a total revenue figure of $1.97 billion. By 1998, Barnes & Noble had $2.5 billion in store sales revenue, and Borders had $1.56 billion, not counting online sales. However, with only 203 stores compared to Barnes & Noble's 493 stores, Borders had higher average sales per store, $7.7 million per unit. In 1999, Barnes & Noble more than doubled its store count to 1,009 units, while Borders added another 47 stores through August. Newcomer chain, Books-A-Million, based in Birmingham, Alabama, had 165 stores in 1998 and sales of $348 million.

Book publishers also faced a challenge to their continued profitability due to the 1980s legacy of offering huge cash advances to prominent authors. Examples of this included HarperCollins' highly publicized 1994 offer to pay Congressional House Speaker Newt Gingrich an advance of $4.5 million for future writings, and—in 1996—an offer by Random House of $2.5 million to former Clinton administration political strategist Dick Morris. Some industry executives likened the impact of this trend to mass suicide by publishers, since it meant that only one in five products were successful enough to turn a profit. In addition, large advances were criticized within the industry for preventing publishers from nurturing talented, yet less well-known authors. However,

other industry observers argued that the proceeds from one best-seller could often support a number of "more literary" releases. Overall, many publishers expressed their intention to limit future advances.

Book publishers competed for the leisure time of their traditional customers with cable television, VCRs, video games, multimedia products, and the Internet. On a positive note *Publishers Weekly* cited a study in 1996 that indicated "spending on reading material by households with computers is at least as high as spending on such material by those without." In addition, the recession of the early 1990s led to cutbacks in education and library funding, with subsequent reductions in book purchases by these markets. These trends reinforced industry concerns about declining literacy rates in the United States, and led several publishing houses to participate in programs to encourage a more book-oriented culture. Many publishers also faced shrinking profit margins in key areas. For example, author royalties generally accounted for 10 to 15 percent of the cover price of trade books, which left publishers with an average margin of 9.5 percent. For textbooks and professional books, however—which were less expensive to produce and usually sold in larger quantities—houses obtained an average margin of 20 percent. Many book publishers responded to these challenges by cutting costs, streamlining operations, adopting new technologies, and investigating the marketing potential of electronic products such as CD-ROMs and on-line information delivery.

As John F. Baker explained in *Publishers Weekly,* "Publishing is changing quite markedly, to the extent that there's more caution, a much greater sense of the potentials, up and down, of the market, and a determination to focus more sharply, among the big houses; new skills, better distribution, and a real sense of a significant role to play, among the smaller ones." As the U.S. economy began to recover in the mid-1990s, the outlook for the book publishing industry also began to improve. Shifting demographics pointed toward higher enrollment levels in schools and colleges, while the Clinton administration appeared likely to increase funding for libraries and the arts. Many publishers expected growth among medical and health care-related titles to correspond with concerns of the aging U.S. population, as well as growth in professional and technical titles to support rapid changes in office technology. In 1995, the latter expectation was born out and evidenced in part by an 82 percent increase in revenues from the sale of computer books for that year alone.

CURRENT CONDITIONS

Book sales in all categories remained strong in 1998, showing increases over 1997, according to the Association of American Publishers. Two developments most

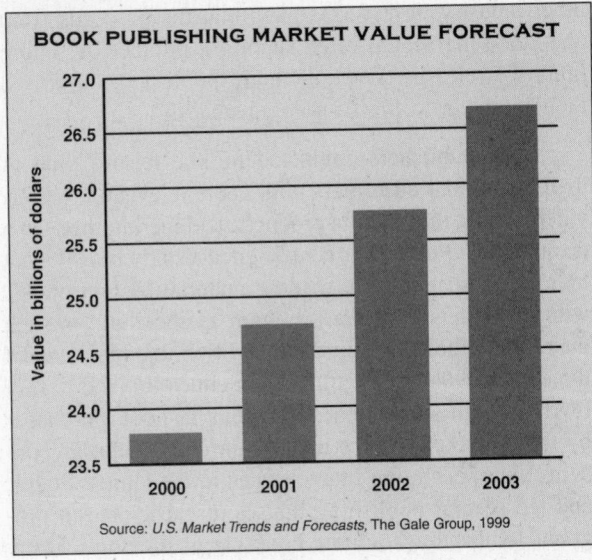

BOOK PUBLISHING MARKET VALUE FORECAST

Source: *U.S. Market Trends and Forecasts*, The Gale Group, 1999

likely to have the greatest effect on the book publishing industry are industry consolidation and changing patterns of book distribution. Mergers and acquisitions seemed to reach a peak of activity in 1998 as consumers were making book purchases from a variety of sources.

Adult trade publishing became more concentrated in 1998 with the acquisition of the largest U.S. trade publisher, Random House, Inc., by German conglomerate Bertelsmann AG and subsequent merger with Bantam Doubleday Dell (BDD), which Bertelsmann already owned. The two publishers together accounted for 66 new bestsellers in 1998 and held 43 percent of *Publishers Weekly's* available weekly bestseller positions. Counting Random House and Bantam Doubleday Dell as separate entities, the top seven adult trade publishers accounted for more than 88 percent of *Publishers Weekly's* bestseller lists in 1998. The other top five adult trade publishers were Simon & Schuster, Penguin Putnam Inc., HarperCollins, Time Warner, and Hearst.

Another major deal involved Simon & Schuster and the United Kingdom-based Pearson P.L.C. Simon & Schuster sold off its Education, Reference, and International Group as well as its Business and Professional Group to Pearson for $4.6 billion. Following the acquisition Pearson divested several of its newly acquired reference, business, and professional operations that did not fit with its core educational publishing program. Pearson was also required by the U.S. Department of Justice to sell off some 55 college textbooks before it would approve the acquisition. Also in 1998 The Times Mirror Co., deciding to focus on its newspaper publishing operations, sold several book publishing operations to Reed Elsevier P.L.C., including legal publisher Matthew Bender.

Further consolidation of adult trade book publishing occurred in mid-1999, when News Corp. acquired Wil-

liam Morrow and Avon Books from Hearst Corporation. The acquisition of the Hearst Book Group was estimated at $180 million. News Corp. already owned HarperCollins and religious publisher Zondervan Publishing, among other properties.

In 1998, consumers were buying books through a variety of distribution channels. According to the NPD Group, large chain bookstores accounted for 25.3 percent of adult book purchases, followed by book clubs (18.0 percent), and independent and small chain bookstores (16.6 percent). Other channels each accounting for less than 10 percent of adult book purchases included warehouse clubs, mass merchandisers, mail order, food and drug stores, discount stores, used books, the Internet, and multi-media.

INDUSTRY LEADERS

Following mergers and acquisitions through mid-1999, the top four trade publishers ranked by worldwide sales were Random House, HarperCollins, Penguin Putnam USA Inc., and Simon & Schuster.

Random House was already the largest general trade book publisher in the English-speaking world when it was acquired by German entertainment and publishing conglomerate Bertelsmann AG in 1998 and merged with Bantam Doubleday Dell (BDD), which Bertelsmann already owned. The new publishing entity continued with the name of its senior partner, Random House Inc., and had estimated worldwide sales of $1.6 billion in fiscal 1999 ending June 30, with 80 percent of its sales in North America. Random House's publishing operations included The Ballantine Publishing Group, Bantam Books, Broadway Books, The Crown Publishing Group, Dell, Doubleday, The Knopf Publishing Group, Random House Audio Publishing Group, and Fodor's Travel Publications, among others.

HarperCollins, a subsidiary of Rupert Murdoch's News Corporation Ltd., became the second-largest trade publisher in 1999 when it acquired Hearst Corp.'s trade book publishing imprints William Morrow & Co. and Avon Books. The new entity would have an estimated $900 million in worldwide revenues. News Corp. also owned Basic Books, Regan Books, Westview Press, and Zondervan Publishing.

Penguin Putnam USA is a subsidiary of London-based holding company Pearson P.L.C., which also owns controlling interests in numerous publishers in England and the United States. The Pearson conglomerate originated with holdings in construction and oil, began acquiring banks and newspapers in the 1920s, and expanded into book publishing throughout the 1980s. Falling under the Pearson umbrella are such notable publishing imprints as Addison Wesley Longman, Berkley, Dutton, HP

Books, Jossey-Bass, Macmillan, Perigree, Prentice Hall, Signet, and Viking.

Simon & Schuster Inc. was founded in New York City in 1924 by Richard L. Simon and M. Lincoln Schuster. The company went public in 1966 and was acquired by Gulf + Western in 1975. Simon & Schuster expanded aggressively during the 1980s by launching a dozen new imprints and acquiring interests in textbooks and software. In 1993, Simon & Schuster acquired the 150 year old Macmillan, Inc. from the estate of British media mogul Robert Maxwell. In 1998, Simon & Schuster sold off its Education, Reference, and International Group as well as its Business and Professional Group to Pearson P.L.C. of the United Kingdom for $4.6 billion. The sale reduced Simon & Schuster's worldwide trade sales to $550 million.

Time Warner's book publishing companies in 1998 included Warner Books; Little, Brown, and Co.; Time-Life Books; Oxmoor House; and Book-of-the-Month-Club.

Outside of general trade publishing, The McGraw-Hill Companies encompasses educational, financial, business, governmental, and professional publishing and information services. It is the world's largest educational publisher with overall revenues of more than $3 billion annually.

Other large media companies with interests in book publishing include Walt Disney Co. and Viacom Inc.

WORKFORCE

In an assessment for *Black Enterprise,* Lolis Eric Elie called book publishing ''an industry that rewards creativity, treasures personal taste, and provides opportunities to combine work with a socially responsible endeavor.'' In addition to editorial work, publishing offered career potential for individuals with backgrounds in business, marketing, sales, graphic design, and computer applications. Traditionally, however, ''low entry-level salaries, long hours, and slow advancement have deterred those who tried their hand in the field,'' Elie continued.

Publishers Weekly conducts an annual survey of salaries in the book publishing industry. The 1999 survey, based on more than 600 respondents, indicated that publishing company presidents and CEOs earned the highest average annual salaries in the industry, ranging from an average of $99,159 at smaller publishing firms with revenues between $1 million and $9.9 million, to an average of $542,500 at the largest houses (with revenues greater than $100 million). Those at mid-sized firms with sales between $10 million and $99.9 million earned an average of $238,250 according to the survey. Executive and senior vice presidents earned an average of $77,229

at smaller houses, $125,222 at mid-sized firms, and $193,000 at the largest publishing companies.

Editorial positions covered in the survey included editorial assistants (earning between $20,500 and $25,000 depending on the employer's size), copy editors and proofreaders ($38,000 average), product development and acquisitions editors ($42,400 to $52,667), associate editors ($28,613 to $32,000), editors ($32,750 to $83,333), senior, executive, and managing editors ($44,330 to $91,494), and editorial directors and editors-in-chief ($69,850 to $177,397). The magazine cautioned that the results of the survey should not be interpreted as definitive because of the small number of respondents for some job categories.

In 1998, the book publishing industry's work force was affected by several mergers and acquisitions. Respondents to the *Publishers Weekly* salary survey indicated that at firms with more than $100 million in sales, more than half of employee turnover was due to mergers and acquisitions. The turnover rate for small publishers was 16 percent, 19 percent for mid-sized publishers, and 21 percent at large publishers.

Some industry observers predicted that technology would redefine the roles of everyone in the publishing industry in the late 1990s. As Susan Trowbridge, vice president of publishing technology at Addison-Wesley, explained in *Publishers Weekly,* ''the new technological capabilities are causing us to re-examine the roles and procedures of all the publishing participants, from author to editor to designer to manufacturer.'' Trowbridge foresaw desktop publishing technology moving upstream into editorial functions as well as downstream to manufacturers; a more coordinated focus on the development of multimedia products, involving teamwork between editorial, marketing, and technical experts; and increased automation of administrative processes, such as scheduling and cost-tracking. Employees in all sectors of the publishing industry increasingly required knowledge of computers in order to be successful in their careers.

AMERICA AND THE WORLD

The U.S. publishing industry was by far the world's leading exporter of books. Exports accounted for nearly 10 percent of U.S. publishers' shipments in 1993, or about $1.7 billion. According to the U.S. Department of Commerce, book exports reached $1.76 billion in 1995 (displaying a 4 percent increase over 1994) while unit sales increased to over 885 million. Half of U.S. exports were textbooks or professional and technical products. The major markets for U.S. book exports were Canada, the United Kingdom, Japan, Australia, Germany, and Mexico. In 1995, the biggest increase was in exports to South Korea. The predominance of U.S. exports was explained in part by the increasing numbers of people worldwide who used the English language to conduct business. Total U.S. imports of books reached $1 billion in 1992, an increase of 13 percent over the previous year. By 1995, 530 million books worth $1.2 billion entered the United States with the largest increases coming from Canada, Mexico, China, and Italy according to *Publishers Weekly*. The United Kingdom, Hong Kong, Japan, Thailand, South Korea, and Canada were the sources for most imported books, although the figures also included shipments of books manufactured abroad for U.S. publishers.

Industry analysts in the early 1990s expected international sales of U.S. books to continue to improve, particularly in emerging markets such as the former Soviet Union, Mexico and Latin America, and the Asia. U.S. publishers faced some challenges in international sales, however, due to inconsistent application of copyright, or intellectual property right, laws overseas. Publishers of audio books and electronic products, in particular, were displeased with the lack of specific protection afforded by the General Agreement on Tariffs and Trade (GATT) when it concluded in late 1993.

RESEARCH AND TECHNOLOGY

The traditional printed book might never disappear completely, but new technology has revolutionized production, distribution, and nearly every other aspect of operations in the publishing industry in the 1990s. As *Publishers Weekly* predicted, "The definition of 'publisher' will change. It won't just refer to a person who makes books, but a person who holds information or intellectual property, and disseminates that information in any way he or she can benefit from it." Most publishers began to store information in digital form on computer systems so that it could be readily translated into a variety of electronic product formats. While the conversion to the new technology was often difficult and costly for publishers, most electronic products essentially repackaged information the publishers already owned and thus offered higher margins than print products.

The advent of new technology raised a number of interesting issues within the publishing industry. Publishers faced unprecedented competition from software and communications companies entering the electronic publishing market. These industries began to converge—through partnerships and acquisitions—into something analysts called "the new media." Authors and publishers disagreed about who owned electronic publication rights, and significantly more complex contract negotiations became the norm. Additionally, some confusion arose about which channels of distribution would be most appropriate for electronic products, since bookstores, software stores, on-line subscriptions, and direct mail all formed possible outlets. Many publishers were concerned about what would emerge as the dominant technological platform for

electronic publishing. Libraries initiated the movement toward electronic publishing by purchasing reference products in on-line and CD-ROM formats. However, since millions of American homes were equipped with personal computers in the mid-1990s, this presented a formidable market for entertainment and educational products on CD-ROM or diskette. In addition, small, hand-held electronic books such as the Sony Data Discman and the Philips CD-Interactive, which sold for $400-600 each, gained acceptance as their prices fell. Some observers predicted that CD-ROM drives might become standard accessories on television sets in the near future, while others claimed that telecommunications would provide the next mass-distribution medium for electronic publishing. Finally, all of these issues had strong implications for the current organization and future staffing of book publishers. They had to become more flexible and technologically adept in order to compete.

By 1996, many publishing companies had to make the decision of whether or not to abandon their fledgling efforts in the CD-ROM market. According to *Multimedia Business Report,* "One of the biggest problems for many book publishers is that the CD ROM publishing model is moving away from the book model. Three or four years ago, a CD ROM title could be published for not much more than it cost to publish a book, and marketing costs were minimal. Today, CD ROM budgets are headed in the direction of movie budgets. Text is the forgotten media, compared to video, audio, and animation."

Accessing information electronically offered a number of advantages for consumers. For example, CD-ROM products allowed easy sorting of information from a wide variety of databases, as well as made it possible to combine text, graphics, sound, and animation. Some examples of innovative CD-ROM products included a dictionary that could pronounce words, an encyclopedia that could show video clips about entries, and a book that could help a child learn to read. Another common format for electronic information was on-line through computer subscription services and via the Internet. On-line materials were less expensive for publishers to distribute than paper, easier—in some cases—for users to search, and also provided quick publication for time-sensitive information such as medical advances.

With the growth of the Internet, textbook publishers were establishing Web sites that provided online learning resources tied in to their print products. Scott Foresman, a subsidiary of Pearson P.L.C., created the Know Zone, an interactive, online environment that linked classroom work for elementary and middle school students with home study. After the National Science Teachers Association developed sciLINKS, which links textbook topics to relevant Web sites, science textbook publishers Holt,

Rinehart & Winston and Harcourt Brace incorporated sciLINKS into their textbooks.

Computers also had a significant impact on book production technology. Desktop publishing systems—which featured sophisticated yet simple graphic design software to manipulate digitized text and images into publishable form—made many operations quicker and less expensive for publishers. For example, desktop publishing made it possible for houses to reprint fewer copies of books more often, and thus avoid inventory costs. In addition, the technology allowed publishers to save up to 70 percent in typesetting and other production costs. However, since publishers performed more operations themselves, desktop publishing led to significant changes in the roles of suppliers. In response, many typesetters and printers offered creative services—such as 24-hour turnaround, consulting and training in the use of electronic systems, and management of huge amounts of data—in order to continue to add value.

On-demand printing is a technology that has been available for most of the 1990s, but publishers have been slow to embrace its possibilities. Book distributor Ingram initiated its "Lightning Print" program, which enables publishers as well as authors to bring an out-of-print title back into print with a minimal investment. Once such an "on-demand" book is back in stock at Ingram, it also becomes immediately available through every Internet retailer, including Amazon.com, Borders, and Barnes & Noble. On-demand printing has the capability to make it economical to bring back into print many out-of-print titles that would otherwise remain unavailable.

Technology also began to impact distribution and marketing within the book publishing industry. In the early 1990s, one such system was PUBNET, an electronic book-ordering system that linked 65 publishers with 2,400 bookstores. PUBNET had the capacity to provide publishers with timely, in-depth sales information, which they hoped to better incorporate into upstream decisions.

By the mid-1990s, the Internet was being used by hundreds of publishing companies and distributors alike not only as a vehicle to advertise their goods and display product catalogs online, but also as a means to sidestep the middleman in sales transactions. By 1996, the leading on-line book provider was Amazon.com, a company founded only two years earlier in a garage. Owned by Jeff Bezos, the firm employed 85 people, had estimated sales of $5 million, boasted a stock list of over 1 million titles, and was experiencing extraordinary sales growth. As of 1998, the company employed 2,100 people. In 1999 it posted sales of $1.64 billion and had an income of $720 million. According to Steve Potash, as quoted in *Publishers Weekly,* "After software, books are the most popular type of product sold on the Internet." Sales of books over the Internet have been projected to account for as much as 25 percent of all book sales by 2005. One effect of Internet book sales has been to give new life to backlist titles, as consumers spread their book-buying dollars over a broader range of titles through online purchases.

Several industry analysts predicted that environmental issues would gain importance within the publishing industry. For example, some consumer groups demanded that books, especially paperbacks, be made recyclable. Publishers cooperated with printing and binding companies to make book-binding processes and cover materials more environmentally sound, and some products were developed that could be unbound easily. In 1995, the Environmental Protection Agency announced, as part of its 1994 Common Sense Initiative, an air toxins rule for the printing and publishing industry that would cut dangerous air emissions resulting from printing and package production processes. The proposal was expected to impact 127 existing printing and publishing facilities in the United States and any future facilities to be built.

FURTHER READING

"AAP Sales Report," *Publishers Weekly,* 23 August 1999.

"Barnes & Noble," *Billboard,* 4 September 1999.

Book Industry Trends 1999. New York: Book Industry Study Group, Inc., 1999.

"Books@ Random: About Random House." Available from http://www.randomhouse.com/backyard/, 11 December 1999.

"Books@ Random: Divisional Information." Available from http://www.randomhouse.com/backyard/div.html, 11 December 1999.

Carvajal, Doreen, "Returns are Swamping the Publishing Industry," *The New York Times,* 1 August 1996.

"Computer Books Fastest Growing Sector—Study." *Media Daily,* 18 July 1996.

"Harper Sells its CD-ROM Rights." *Publishers Weekly,* 21 October 1996.

Stand & Poor's Industry Surveys: Publishing. New York: Standard and Poor's Corporation, 14 October 1999.

Jones, Margaret. "Mergers-and-Acquisitions Aftershocks," *Publishers Weekly,* 20 September 1999.

Manes, Stephen. "Gutenberg Need Not Worry—Yet," *Forbes,* 8 February 1999.

"The Market for Children's Books Is Still Large, But It Is Changing Significantly," *YouthMarkets Alert,* 1 June 1996.

Maryles, Daisy. "They're the Tops!," *Publishers Weekly,* 4 January 1999.

Milliot, Jim. "Good Times Returning for Children's Publishing?," *Publishers Weekly,* 22 February 1999.

Milliot, Jim. "News Corp. to Acquire Morrow, Avon from Hearst," *Publishers Weekly,* 21 June 1999.

Milliot, Jim. "Salary Survey," *Publishers Weekly,* 5 July 1999.

Milliot, Jim. "Veronis, Suhler Study Sees Positive Outlook for Books." *Publishers Weekly,* 7 August 1995.

Milliot, Jim, and John F. Baker. "IDG Books Buys Macmillan General Reference," *Publishers Weekly,* 5 July 1999.

Milliot, Jim, and Sally Taylor. "Book Exports Slightly Up in '95." *Publishers Weekly,* 25 March 1996.

Moran, Susan. "Amazon.com Forges New Sales Channel." *Webweek,* 19 August 1996.

"Multimedia Future Uncertain for Many Book Publishers." *Multimedia Business Report,* 7 June 1996.

Muffer, John. "Unit Sales Fell in '98," *Publishers Weekly,* 10 May 1999.

Mutter, John. "The Inevitable Future," *Publishers Weekly,* 15 November 1999.

Mutter, John. "The Bookstore of the 21st Century." *Publishers Weekly,* 22 July 1996.

Roback, Diane. "Licensed Tie-ins Make Registers Ring," *Publishers Weekly,* 29 March 1999.

Schiffrin, Andre. "The Corporatization of Publishing." *The Nation,* 3 June 1996.

Shatzkin, Mike. "Fasten Your High-Tech Seatbelts," *Publishers Weekly,* 24 May 1999.

"The 60-Second Book: A New High-Tech Publishing Technique is Creating a Literary Big Bang for America's Would-Be Authors," *Time,* 2 August 1999.

"63 Percent of Heaviest Book Buyers are Women." *About Women and Marketing,* 1 July 1996.

"Slow Growth in Consumer Book Purchases Last Year, New Study Shows." *American Association of Publishers Monthly Report,* September 1996. Available from http://www.publishers.org/news/releases/9610.html.

"Store Count, E-Commerce Top Priorities," *Discount Store News,* 9 August 1999.

"U.S. Book Exports Edge Up 1.5 Percent." *Publishers Weekly,* 9 September 1996.

"What's New with . . . Textbooks and Technology," *Technology & Learning,* May 1999.

"Wiley Buys Pearson College Titles," *Publishers Weekly,* 24 May 1999.

SIC 2732

BOOK PRINTING

This category includes establishments primarily engaged in printing, or in printing and binding, books and pamphlets, but not engaged in publishing. Establishments primarily engaged in publishing, or in both publishing and printing, books and pamphlets are classified in **SIC 2731: Books: Publishing, or Publishing and Printing.** Establishments engaged in both printing and binding books, but primarily binding books printed elsewhere, are classified in **SIC 2789: Bookbinding and Related Work.**

NAICS CODE(S)

323117 (Book Printing)

INDUSTRY SNAPSHOT

The earliest printing techniques were developed in China in the second century A.D. The printing industry was inaugurated in the Western world when Johannes Gutenberg, Johann Fust, and Peter Schoffer invented movable type and the printing press around the middle of the fifteenth century, producing the first printed books in the Western world with this newly developed equipment. Printing came to the United States with some of the earliest English immigrants; the first book printed in the new world was the *Bay Psalm Book,* printed by Stephen Day in 1640. Since that time, design improvements and new inventions have made the process quicker and less costly. Almost from the beginning, printing and publishing were separate enterprises, and not much has changed since then: today, publishers decide what to print and how it will look, and printers put the words on the page to the publishers' specifications.

The continued movement toward automation, computerization, and new technologies caused radical changes in the industry. Desktop typesetting and formatting at point of origin (the author), digitized color scanning and imaging, electronic publishing over the World Wide Web, and new media formats available for the conveyance of information were all some of the driving forces of the industry.

Book printers are generally divided into two categories: long-run printers and short-run printers. For the largest book printers, such as industry leader R.R. Donnelley and Sons and Quebecor Printing, Inc., book printing was just one of several types of printing services they offered. Donnelley, for example, served five end-markets including book publishers, magazine publishers, directories, financial services, and merchandise media. Short-run printers, on the other hand, tended to specialize in book printing. They typically offer publishers both hard and softcover printing on editions of 500 to 15,000 copies.

ORGANIZATION AND STRUCTURE

An overview of the major segments of the printing industry, including commercial printing, is provided through the various affiliates and sections of the Printing Industries of America: Electronic Prepress, Graphic Arts Marketing and Information Service, Graphic Communications Association, International Thermographers, Label Printing Industries of America Printing Industry Financial Executives, Sales & Marketing Executives, the

Web Offset Association, and the Non-Heatset Web Section. In addition, the Printing History Association and Research and Engineering Council of the Graphic Arts Industry help preserve the heritage of printing and coordinate production techniques and new technologies.

Historically, books are separated into many different categories, such as trade, mass market paperback, textbooks, scientific, technical, reference, and professional books. These have been marketed through traditional bookstores, super- or mega-bookstores, book clubs, and via direct-mail order. Several companies are now also adding web site marketing.

The book printing industry is influenced by several factors: the publishing industry in general with its mass and specialized book marketing, the economy at large, and technological innovations, particularly those relating to increased quality or production.

The publication of books in the United States is characterized by a clear division of labor between book printer and book publisher. The publisher selects the books to be printed, makes all of the decisions regarding the appearance of the final product, from page layout and illustrations to type font and paper quality, and finances the production. The printer takes either a camera-ready copy or a film negative and reproduces them in the quantities required by the publisher, on the paper specified and often already purchased by the publisher. The printer's role in the publishing process is one of reproduction rather than production.

Depending on whether the publisher supplies the camera-ready copy, a phototypeset film negative, or a computer text file, the printer's job begins either with making film negatives of each page or printing plates. In some cases, graphic artists working for the publisher take the corrected typeset hard copy of the text and lay out each page with any necessary graphics. These camera-ready pages, called mechanicals, are then sent on to the printer. The printer then photographs these mechanicals to produce the film copy necessary in the plate-making process. With recent advances in computer graphics capabilities, many computer systems can bypass both the lay-out process and the photographing process. Computer programs can combine text and graphics, so page layout can be done on a computer rather than the drafting table. Hardware peripherals can generate output in the form of a film, ready for platemaking.

Metal, paper, or plastic plates are what actually put the images of the text onto the paper. Using photochemical processes, the image to be printed is transferred from the film negative onto the plate. The prepared plate has image areas that chemically accept ink and can therefore pass the ink onto a piece of paper, and nonimage areas that chemi-cally repel ink and therefore pass nothing onto the paper, leaving spaces between the letters, images, and lines.

Having made the plates, the printer can begin the reproduction process. Most printing is offset. The inked plates pass a reverse image onto a rubber sheet, which then passes a positive image onto the paper; offset tends to produce a clearer image than direct printing. Black and white graphics, and text-only pages, need pass through the machine only once to produce the complete image. Color pictures complicate the process, however, and are usually sent through several times for different colored inks. After the actual printing, some print shops also bind the books; others ship the product back to the publisher or to the bindery unbound.

BACKGROUND AND DEVELOPMENT

It is generally thought that the Chinese invented the earliest printing. During the second century A.D., they carved religious texts and images into marble columns around their temples; devotees and pilgrims would ink the columns and press paper to it to make their own copies of the text. Small seals were carved for similar purposes, and, by the sixth century, artisans carved wood blocks with which to make prints as well. The oldest known printed works were made with wood blocks in Japan in the eighth century. A million Buddhist charms were printed on paper and distributed to followers around 770 A.D. One of the oldest printed books now extant, the *Diamond Sutra* (a Chinese version of the Buddhist scriptures), was printed in 868 A.D. using wooden blocks on seven sheets of paper attached at the top and bottom ends to form a single 16-foot roll. Although movable clay block type had been invented nearly 400 years earlier, it took the rebirth of knowledge, an abundant paper supply, ink that could be applied to metal and transferred to paper, a wooden press, and the availability of an alphabet to allow printing to become a major force in communication.

The geographical containment of Europe and sociological needs of the Renaissance, along with four essential elements (paper, ink from painters, a press from the olive and grape vine yards and metal casting from the goldsmiths) and the synthetic genius and tenacity of Gutenberg set the stage for typography. Nonetheless, it took yet another 500 years for the age of automated typesetting and computer generated camera-ready copy to arrive.

Paper-making, a necessary predecessor to printing, came to Europe via the Arabian presence in Spain between the twelfth and the thirteenth centuries. Wood-carving prints survive from the fourteenth century, but the printing industry really started in Germany in 1455 with the invention of metal movable type and a printing press by Johannes Gutenberg. Gutenberg made molds of individual letters that then could produce many type pieces of the same letter, all identical. The printer then arranged the pieces in a composing stick in the proper order, and fastened each stick onto the press, which could print many copies of each page. Type pieces could then be removed from the composing stick and revised for the next page.

In the first century of printing, printers were publishers and publishers were printers: that is, the printer decided what to print and provided the initial financial investment, and the publisher did the rest. In the sixteenth century, for example, as the church and different governments gained control over the trade and determined what would and would not be printed, they granted licensing rights to only a small number of men to produce a small number of politically acceptable books. In England, booksellers were granted these rights rather than the printers; because of this, the printers lost the power to decide what to print, and the publishing industry was born. The English booksellers' guild, called the Stationers' Co., had the authority to inspect any printing office and destroy unauthorized publications; the members of the company became the sole (legal) publishers in the country, and law-abiding printers worked on commissioned jobs.

Printing and publishing have always been separate ventures in the United States. The Reverend Jose Glover, who might rightfully be called the father of printing in the United States, brought the first printing press from England to America in 1638, and hired Stephen Day, a locksmith, to do the printing. Glover died during the voyage; the press was passed on to his wife, who brought the press to the newly established Harvard College. The first president of Harvard, Henry Dunster, oversaw the printing in 1640 of the first book in this country, *The Whole Booke of Psalmes Faithfully Translated into English Meter,* (also known as the *Bay Psalm Book,*) by Stephen Day and his son, Matthew.

The history of the U.S. printing industry is essentially the history of the technology. Minor changes in design and processes eventually became continuous improvements in the speed and efficiency of the presses, and major new inventions periodically altered production. In the process of stereotype, for instance, molds were made for each page before printing in order to free the type pieces before the printing process, which in turn allowed more than one press to be used simultaneously. By the end of the next century, photography was applied to the process, and photoengraving was invented. This process used film, light, and chemical reactions to engrave the text on a thin plate that was then used for printing. New desktop publishing capabilities have demystified the process of printing. Now authors, familiar with various type styles, point sizes, and page formats, can adapt their computer-generated text at the point of origin to the styles required by publishers.

Composition, the process of setting the type, also underwent several changes. By the late nineteenth century, the invention of the Linotype and monotype machines improved typesetting speeds over hand composition. The first quarter of the twentieth century was characterized by innovative and creative breakthroughs in typography, such as sans serif type, which were driven by consumer needs rather than artistic design. In the middle of the twentieth century, the invention of computers revolutionized typesetting once again. Today, the computer is used to set the type, and can either produce a hard copy on paper that is then photographed to make the plates, or can generate the image on film to be used immediately to produce a plate; some of the newest machines can even make plates directly from the computer file, sidestepping the film stage completely.

The medium for printed matter is rapidly changing. CD-ROMs and the World Wide Web (with its ability to transmit text, color images, and even full-motion color video) are providing new media for the printed word. Once data or text are entered into a computer for book production, it is an easy step to transmit this data over the wire to a publisher or a consumer.

CURRENT CONDITIONS

Predictably, the printing industry has been affected by general economic trends. During the economic growth years of the early 1980s, the industry grew tremendously. The recession of the early 1990s, brought this growth to a somewhat screeching halt. The modest recovery that began in the mid-1990s, however, helped the printing industry regain its strength over the latter years of the decade. Book sales in all categories remained strong in 1998, showing increases over 1997, according to the Association of American Publishers (AAP). In 1998 American consumers spent $28.7 billion on books, while the AAP estimated total net sales of books for 1998 at $23 billion.

Acquisitions and mergers in the printing industry continued to occur as the industry leaders become even larger. In September 1999 Quebecor Printing, the second-largest book printer in North America, announced it would acquire World Color Inc. for $2.7 billion. The new company, called Quebecor World Inc., would be the largest magazine printer in the United States.

New media formats are redefining the word "printing" to at least include CD-ROMs, electronic publishing, among other modern products. Many reference books and technical manuals are now sold with a CD-ROM in their pocket. Furthermore, the perception of the industry is changing as the diversification of media for transmitting information increases. Increased attention is being paid to the marketing end of the printed or produced product, to digital technology, and to establishing a place on the information highway via whatever process is necessary.

INDUSTRY LEADERS

A few large corporations dominated the book printing industry in the late 1990s. Some were part of large conglomerates that also owned publishing houses. Bertelsmann USA, for example—the American branch of a German media conglomerate—included not only Bertelsmann Printing and Manufacturing Corp., but also the Random House publishing group.

The largest printing companies had subsidiaries all over the country and the world. R.R. Donnelley and Sons, headquartered in Chicago and considered by *Graphic Arts Monthly* to be the largest printer in the United States, had operations in nearly 200 worldwide locations, including manufacturing operations in North America, South America, the United Kingdom, Central Europe, and Asia. It had 40 sales offices and manufacturing locations in North America. It was the number-one book printer in North America as well as the world's leading printer of telephone and business-to-business directories. It also was the leading North American printer of consumer and trade magazines and offered a wide range of other printing services. For 1998 Donnelley reported $488 million in earnings (excluding one-time items) on sales of $5 billion.

Montreal-based Quebecor Printing was the second-largest book manufacturer in North America. It printed more than 500 million books in 1997, with a client list that included the major U.S. book publishers Random House, Simon & Schuster, Thomas Nelson, Time Warner, McGraw-Hill, Penguin USA, Houghton-Mifflin, and Harlequin. Its U.S. subsidiary, Quebecor Printing (USA) Corp. was formed in 1990 to consolidate the company's U.S. operations. Both the parent company and its U.S. subsidiary grew through a series of acquisitions, including the additions of book printers Arcata Corp. and William C. Brown. Quebecor's other print products, in addition to books and directories, included magazines, Sunday magazines and comic books, inserts and circulars, catalogs, and specialty printing products. Quebecor Printing's (USA) annual sales reached $2.1 billion in 1998.

BookCrafters, based in southeastern Michigan, was a vertically integrated company that emerged to fulfill a special niche by printing, storing, and shipping books for publishers in specialized markets as well as self-publishers. It used 21 presses, web, belt roll-fed and color sheet-feed presses, in addition to its own in-house bindery. It was a leading short-run printer.

Another short-run printer was the Thomson-Shore company of Dexter, Michigan. It was a small company, but a leader among short-run printers. It was founded by Ned Thomson and Harry Shore, both of whom worked for another Ann Arbor, Michigan, small press, left their jobs and started their own company with their own business philosophy. Decisions were made by committees of employees, who owned one-third of the company. They em-

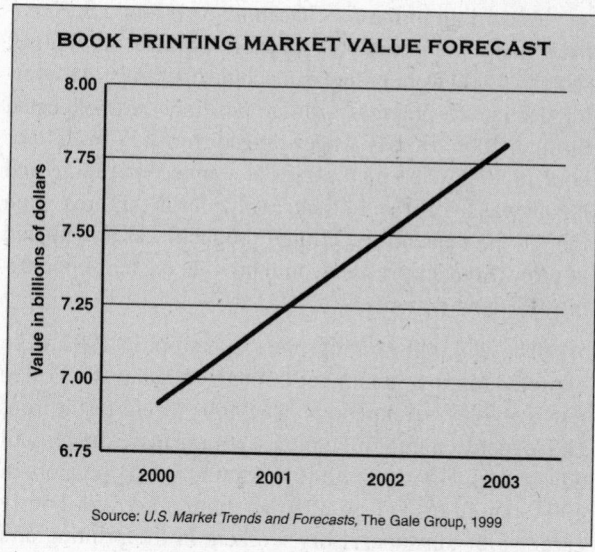

BOOK PRINTING MARKET VALUE FORECAST

Source: *U.S. Market Trends and Forecasts*, The Gale Group, 1999

ployed no sales force, "Customers come to us, and we've made our entire effort based on the idea that quality would sell for us if we did better than our competition."

After almost 20 years of just printing books, Thomson-Shore began to branch out into pre-and postpress activities. They added a bindery operation and a page-making program for their computers with an eye towards eventual composition work. They specialized in short runs, because reprint costs were considered cheaper than carrying long-term inventories. Thomson-Shore's average runs were between 300 and 5,000 copies.

WORKFORCE

Printing companies employed skilled technicians, mid-level management, and high-level management. The actual production was carried out by skilled workers using highly complex machines. Vocational and technical colleges offered training, as did some high schools and two-year colleges. Workers could often rise to mid-level management jobs, such as foreperson or production control. A college education was frequently required for the higher-level management positions. A few schools offered degrees in printing technology, but science, art, or business degrees could also be helpful.

Printing occupations were divided into three main stages: prepress, press and binding, or postpress. The industry was rapidly moving to "digital imaging" or direct conversion of customer-submitted computerized text to printing plates. Typesetting and layout was frequently done prior to coming to press and increasingly at the source. Authors now produced their product on a preformatted computerized layout that was transmitted directly to the publisher via e-mail or disk. Hot-type composition was replaced with electronic type or computer-to-plate technology.

According to the *U.S. Occupational Outlook Handbook,* there were 169,000 prepress workers in 1994, of which 25,000 were prepress machine operators. An overall decline in prepress worker positions was expected through 2005. Hourly wages ranged from $17 to $21 per hour in 1995. The increase of at-source typesetting and layout was likely to eliminate many jobs in this area, even though the demand for printed products was anticipated to grow. Smaller presses would provide the best opportunity for new entrants.

The 244,000 printing press operators in 1994 were expected to grow in number through 2005 but at a slower rate than other occupations. New jobs would result from U.S. expansion into foreign markets and more direct-mail advertising. Hourly wages for printing press operators in 1994 ran from $11 to $19 per hour. Average hourly earnings of nonsupervisory workers in the printing and publishing at large remained relatively stable over several years and was between $12 and $13 per hour in 1996.

Book printing was largely dependent on the publishing industry. The printing and publishing industry combined experienced a growth in employment from 1.2 million workers in 1983 to 1.5 million in 1994, or an annual growth rate of 1.6 percent, with a projected yearly growth rate of 0.5 percent to reach 1.6 million workers from 1994 to 2005. The total number of employees in the book printing industry alone rose from 121,000 to 123,000 from 1990 to 1995, while production workers dropped slightly from 66,000 to 65,000. The average hourly earnings of production workers rose from $10.10 to $11.57 per hour during the same period.

AMERICA AND THE WORLD

Historically, printing has been a national business. American copyright laws have kept foreign printers from American publishers, and American printers have been kept busy within the domestic market. In the early 1990s, however, American printers began to take on more international business. Long-standing disadvantages to overseas work included language barriers, shipping costs, cultural differences, and periodically fluctuating exchange rates. As the Eastern bloc countries began to open up, however, American technology and supplies, far superior to those available in many other countries, became increasingly in demand. Some companies, such as R.R. Donnelley, had subsidiaries overseas as well. Exports in the printing and publishing industries grew steadily in the 1990s.

A favorable balance of trade existed in the book industry in spite of a surge in U.S. imports due to the strength of the dollar in 1995, with a ratio of exports to imports of 1 to 1.41 in 1995, though that was down slightly from previous years. The value of all U.S. book exports totaled $1.7 billion in 1995, with 885.5 millions of copies shipped. This represented a 4 percent increase in exports from 1994 to 1995. Japan and Colombia, who had the largest number of printing contracts, experienced a 10 percent decline in contracts, but China and Mexico absorbed some of these contracts. In 1994 the North American Free Trade Agreement (NAFTA) had an impact on the book printing industry by heating up the Mexican market where U.S. printers were competing for Mexican work. Pesano Printing of San Francisco opened offices in Mexico. Book imports totaled $1.2 billion.

After experiencing a rapid growth rate, Japan's printing related industries experienced a downward trend in 1996. This was documented in the reduction in the production of printing machines, plate-making machines, and bookbinding machines, in part reflecting export reactions to changes in the yen. Book printers in Hong Kong were migrating to mainland China.

RESEARCH AND TECHNOLOGY

Book printers were becoming increasingly responsive to the needs of their different customers. Publishing firms that needed large quantities of best sellers were only one segment of their market. Demands for shorter runs and quicker turnaround in a computer environment increased. The printing industry sought new technology to meet these needs.

To help printers keep up with rapidly changing printing technologies, some of the manufacturers of book manufacturing machinery and systems set up the Book Technology Group in 1995. This international group held meetings and helped printers utilize the latest in book production technology. Heidelberg, a well-known manufacturer, was in the process of establishing a Print Media Academy in a 12-story building, with completion due in 2000.

Small publishers, and publishers producing books with limited appeal, such as university presses and the scholarship they support, frequently did not want large runs of books. Usually, the fewer the books printed at one time, the more each book cost to make, primarily because of the time needed for composition. Because more and more publishers were gravitating toward shorter runs, to cut down on storage costs and to realistically reflect the market, book printers were beginning to specialize in smaller runs, with new computer composition techniques. Computer graphics produced illustrations more efficiently than draftsmen. New machinery introduced new methods of plate production directly from a computer file without the middle step of a film. Each reduction in the time and cost of composing reduced the cost and increased the efficiency of shorter book runs. Some companies could produce any number of books—from 25 to 5,000—cost-effectively.

Newer formats, such as CD-ROMS and Web publishing, could demand new skills but increase profitability. Printing on demand was also becoming popular and necessary. Computer storage and laser technology meant that books need never be out of print. On demand and short-run color printing bypassed film intermediaries, created printed images directly from data, and was growing twice as fast as conventional printing. Digital printing systems were having an impact on printing. The definition of a digital color press varied although most used electrophotographic imaging. E-Print 1000, Xeikon, or Agfa Chromapress represented some of this new equipment. CTP (computer-to-plate), such as Linotype Hell's Gutenberg, was suggested in 1995 as a major trend for the next five years. Over 1,600 shops planned to buy this technology as early as 1995. This digital electronic printing was expected to grow to a $2 billion industry by 1998 according to James Vanderslice of Pennant, the IBM Printing Systems, in *Marketing News*.

Many large industrial or technological firms needed to produce manuals for their employees and consumers, but did not want to get into the printing business. Companies, such as Corporate Publishing Services of Fremont, California, were established to fill their needs. Its goal was to take data from their clients, usually in the form of computer files, and with their high-quality computer printers, xerographic copying machines, and in-house bindery presses, provide custom quantities of publications within hours. Recent advances in computer laser printing and computer composition made this realistic and economically feasible.

Digital printing was a new technology that gradually was replacing traditional print processes in several segments of the printing industry. In book printing, digital printing made on-demand book production systems possible. Ingram, the largest book distributor in the world, introduced its Lightning Print digital on-demand library, which allowed single copies of books to be printed on demand. At the 1999 Book Expo America trade show, Lightning Print produced hundreds of perfectbound books during the show. Another system shown at Book Expo was the InstaBookMaker, which joined a single-color desktop laser printer with binding equipment to produce finished books. In 1999 Borders Books and Music announced it would test printing books on demand in its stores, with a possible rollout in 2000 if the system worked. In the book printing industry, digital printing was in its early adoption stage in 1999 and was expected to grow over the next five years.

In a development related to digital printing, Microsoft Corp. and R.R. Donnelley and Sons announced they would cooperate in producing and distributing electronic books in 2000. Under the agreement, Microsoft would offer book publishers software to store tens of thousands of titles and convert them to e-book formats. Donnelley would then work with retailers to print and distribute the books and deliver them in whatever format customers asked for.

An overall increase in the book-buying population; NAFTA, which should favor increased exports; the General Agreement on Tariffs and Trade, which should increase royalties through better protection of copyrights; and improved technology—all of these things drive the industry to new heights. The biggest challenges facing the industry would be to increase productivity while keeping up with new technological developments and new media formats.

FURTHER READING

"AAP Sales Report." *Publishers Weekly,* 23 August 1999.

"B&N Will Launch Online Bookstore on AOL." *Publishers Weekly,* 3 February 1997.

The Bowker Annual Library and Book Trade Almanac. 41st ed. New Providence, NJ: R.R. Bowker, 1996.

Delano, Daryl. "Economic Outlook: Rollin' but Slowin'." *Graphic Arts Monthly,* December 1996.

Dilger, Karen Abramic. "Pressing On." *American Printer,* October 1996.

Dzilna, Dzintars. "Printer Dynamics Change with Birth of Quebecor World." *Folio,* 1 September 1999, 62.

Hilts, Paul. "Donnelley, Microsoft Team to Expand eBook Business." *Publishers Weekly,* 8 November 1999, 11.

Lamparter, William C. "Something for (Almost) Everybody." *American Printer,* October 1999, 69.

Quebecor Printing, Inc. "Products." Available from http://www.quebecorprinting.com/htmen/html/4_0.htm. 22 December 1999.

"Quebecor Printing, Inc.: Pressing All the Right Buttons." *Canadian Shareowner,* March/April 1996.

Rebsamen, Werner. "Bound to Deliver." *American Printer,* April 1999, 66.

R.R. Donnelley and Sons. "About R.R. Donnelley & Sons Co." Available from http://www.rrdonnelley.com/about. 22 December 1999.

———. "Book Publishing Services." Available from http://www.rrdonnelley.com/products/books. 22 December 1999.

———. "What We Do." Available from http://www.rrdonnelley.com/about/businesses. 22 December 1999.

Sharples, Hadley. "New Technologies Divide Short-Run, On-Demand." *Graphic Arts Monthly,* September 1995.

Shirai, Hiroshi. "Developments in Japan's Printing-Related Industry." *Japan 21st,* April 1996.

"Tracking the Trends." *American Printer,* July 1996.

U.S. Department of Commerce. Economics and Statistics Administration. Bureau of Economic Analysis. *Survey of Current Business.* Washington, DC: GPO, 1997.

U.S. Department of Commerce. Economics and Statistics Administration. Census Bureau. *Statistical Abstract of the United States, 1996.* 116th ed. Washington, DC: GPO, 1996.

U.S. Department of Labor. Bureau of Labor Statistics. *Occupational Outlook Handbook,* 1998-99 ed. Washington, DC: GPO, 1998. Available from http://stats.bls.gov/ocohome.htm.

Vincour, Richard M. "What's behind the Urge to Merge?" *American Printer,* November 1996.

"Whatever Happened to the Book Market?" *Publishers Weekly,* 6 January 1997.

Zwang, David L. "Real World PDF." *American Printer,* June 1999, 70.

SIC 2741

MISCELLANEOUS PUBLISHING

This classification includes establishments primarily engaged in miscellaneous publishing activities, not elsewhere classified, whether or not engaged in printing. This includes the publishing of atlases, business service newsletters, calendars, catalogs, directories, guides, maps and map globe covers, paper patterns, race track programs, racing forms, sheet music, shopping news, technical manuals and papers, telephone directories, and yearbooks, as well as the activity of micropublishing.

NAICS CODE(S)

511140 (Database and Directory Publishers)
512230 (Music Publishers)
511199 (All Other Publishers)

INDUSTRY SNAPSHOT

The various sectors encompassed in the classification of miscellaneous publishing maintained strong sales figures through the mid- and late 1990s. Miscellaneous publishers typically are rather small; less than one-fifth of all establishments employ more than 20 people. Overall, about 3,260 companies made up the industry, employing slightly less than 70,000 workers. The shipment value for all miscellaneous publishing products totaled $14.6 billion in 1999. The industry, almost entirely domestic, depends heavily on the U.S. economy's advertising expenditure, and thus in turn correlates rather closely with the state of the overall U.S. economy, which meant good news for miscellaneous publishers in the late 1990s. Overall growth projections were set at one percent annually through 2003.

The opening of the Internet toward electronic commerce may also prove beneficial to certain industry players, such as directory or newsletter publishers, because such publications are often fairly time sensitive and require frequent printings to keep information to date. An online publication can therefore allow publishers to quickly update information without necessitating costly reprintings,

while revenue can still be garnered from advertisers. Other sectors, such as trading cards or calendars, were not likely to be directly affected by the Internet.

Miscellaneous publishers tend to be specialized within their respective categories. However, in addition to independent publishing companies, some book and periodical publishers also have divisions or departments engaged in miscellaneous publishing. The industry spans a range of some of the largest companies in publishing down to sole-proprietorship enterprises. The activities of some miscellaneous publishers more closely resemble book publishers, while others more closely resemble periodical publishers.

ORGANIZATION AND STRUCTURE

The largest category within miscellaneous publishing, comprising about a third of the industry's revenues, is telephone directory publishing. More than 6,000 telephone directories are published in the United States annually by approximately 200 publishers; this includes both telephone companies or their subsidiaries and independent publishing companies. There are several kinds of telephone directories. The utility, or core directory, is the standard directory provided by telephone companies for their service areas, with an edition distributed free to the owner of each phone line. Directories for smaller regional areas, such as a specific town, neighborhood, or larger regions than the core directories cover, may be published by either a telephone company or an independent publisher. Telephone company publishers also publish business-to-business directories whose listings include establishments that would be of interest to other businesses. Finally, there are independent companies that publish special interest directories, such as those targeted to specific ethnic groups.

The telephone directory publishing industry is often synonymous with the term yellow pages publishing because the same companies publish both comprehensive alphabetical telephone listings and categorized paid advertising listings known generically as yellow pages. Even if certain directory editions do not contain classified business listings, their publishers earn their revenues from the yellow pages that they publish, whether as part of a directory or in a separate volume. Telephone directory publishing is thus an unusual industry because the bulk of its revenues are earned through advertising services and not the selling of the publications. The yellow pages account for 85 percent of the directory printing market.

Directories. Directories that do not base their revenues on selling advertising space usually provide more comprehensive information on their entries than merely the telephone number and street address—and list individuals or organizations based on a common specialization.

These directories are published by a different category of publishers than the telephone directory publishers. These publishers typically create and own their own databases of information to be published. Directory publishers may be primarily publishers of periodicals, such as trade journals, and publish directories focused on their journals' specialization. Other comprehensive directories, which provide substantive additional information, are published by reference book publishers. Directories are also published by nonprofit organizations, such as professional or trade associations.

Two new revenue streams are emerging for directory publishers: as reference works and as sources of names and addresses for new business purposes. Beardsley Ruml began producing medical directories in 1995, recognizing a market for publishing directories of physician practices. This Medical Support Systems group, which started in the early 1990s was predicted to gross more than $5 million in before-tax revenues in 1996. Demand for these directories was attributed to the growing retirement population and the emergence of managed care operators.

Catalogs. The catalog industry is primarily a printing industry because catalogs are usually produced on contract for manufacturing, wholesale, or retail companies for the marketing of their products. In some cases, however, publisher-printers create catalogs on their own as a business initiative.

Business Service Newsletters. Newsletters geared toward businesses and industries have proliferated rapidly in the mid- and late 1990s, surpassing the billion-dollar sales mark in 1995 and reaching nearly $1.5 billion by the close of the decade. The field is crowded with more than 5,000 publications. Nearly half of their income is from related products and services, as these publications depend heavily on revenues from advertising. Profitability is also tied to the cost of postage. While there were some concerns about postal rates, many publishers cut costs by reducing paper weight and more accurately targeting their audiences. Relatively new is fax publishing, which is usually done on demand.

The distinction between business service newsletters and regular periodical publishing is often blurred. In general, business service newsletters contain no advertisements, charge high subscription rates, are narrowly focused, and contain articles, tables, or graphs oriented toward data rather than commentary. Such newsletters are often available in electronic form in addition to or instead of print. Companies in this industry may be independent firms, but the largest publishers are often divisions or subsidiaries of market research or financial information services firms. Other business service publications besides newsletters are sometimes grouped with

this category; these would include such publications as bibliographic databases.

Sheet Music. Like trade book publishers, publishers of sheet music publish, market, and hold existing copyrights to creative works of independent composers and lyric authors. Many music publishers, however, derive the majority of their revenues from sources other than sheet music, namely from performance royalties or recorded music royalties for the music to which they own the copyrights. Thus, these publishers are categorized instead under the financial industry for patent and trademark owners and lessors. Publishers that gain most of their business from printed sheet music publishing, and thus are part of the miscellaneous publishing industry, tend to be publishers of classical music, in which most of the written music is in the public domain and no royalties are paid. Vocal music is another major category in printed music publishing. Sheet music publishers may also publish collections of their music as books.

Maps and Atlases. Map and atlas publishers create maps with their own copyright, using data from public domain geographic surveys. The publishers' cartographers draw up their own maps according to these surveys, altering the map sizes and adding or deleting data to the maps. Major publishers publish their maps both in book form as atlases and as free-standing, poster-style maps. Smaller map publishers create local and regional maps for their local market. Smaller cartographic companies draw up maps on request for clients, which are typically book publishers and advertising agencies. Other book or periodical publishers may also publish atlases as a secondary activity.

Trading Cards. The trading card industry is dominated by baseball cards but also includes the publishing of other sports cards and entertainment cards, depicting personalities or scenes from films, television shows, and music. Companies may publish a full range of cards or they may specialize. Sport trading card publishers have licenses from the professional sports leagues and pay royalties to the players or teams pictured. There are about 80 companies in the sports and entertainment trading card business. Sport cards were originally sold with bubble gum but are increasingly sold separately and marketed toward adult collectors. Trading card publishers are often categorized under the printing industry instead of publishing. The value of individual cards after time has been proven by such instances as a single 1910 Honus Wagner baseball card, which was sold for $640,500 in 1996—and was immediately advertised for sale for $1 million.

Calendars. More than 200 companies published calendars in the United States in the late 1990s. These comprise both specialized calendar publishers and those with other publishing or non-publishing activities. The industry does not include the multitude of companies that have calendars produced in their name as marketing devices. Calendars are among the most effective conventional ways to boost business.

Micropublishing. Micropublishing comprises microfilm and microfiche publishing, known collectively as microform. Publishing on microform typically involves the reproduction of printed material, especially periodicals, for distribution primarily to libraries. Microform publishers usually are not the original copyright holders of documents but must obtain licenses from the original print publishers to publish microform editions. Newspapers and magazines are usually reproduced on reels of microfilm, whereas government documents and telephone directories are the texts most commonly published on microfiche. Some print publishers, such as The New York Times Company, publish their own microform versions.

UMI, a Bell & Howell company, has been aggressively acquiring business information service providers such as Data Times, establishing cooperative relationships with index producers, and making the Worldwide Web central to its strategy. Both text and images from more than 3,000 journals, magazines, and other titles were available from Telnet, CD-ROMs, or the Web using its ProQuest Direct services and Z39.50 compliant servers. Selected articles indexed in ABI/Inform and Periodicals Abstracts are provided directly to library users in seconds upon their request from any terminal they are using. OCLC, the largest provider of library services, has agreed to make such access available via its Web site. Increasingly, such full-text databases are being offered online for membership-access fees. Electronic, on demand publishing and delivery of archived articles will continue to make UMI a viable force. The foremost publisher of microfilm for other newspapers, magazines, and academic dissertations is University Microfilms International. Microforms have not yet been completely replaced with electronic, digitized formats, however.

Globes. Globe publishing began with Johann Schiner, a German mathematician, who was the first to produce globes in quantity in 1515, shortly after the appearance of the printing press. Antique globes constitute a lucrative sub-market in this sector, attracting the attention of collectors, and auction prices for eighteenth century versions have brought up to $20,000.

BACKGROUND AND DEVELOPMENT

Telephone Directories. The first telephone directory, which listed 50 names, was published in New Haven, Connecticut, in 1878, just two years after Alexander Graham Bell invented the telephone. The first directory with classified business headings was published in 1883. It is said that the first yellow pages were printed in 1883 when a printer in Cheyenne, Wyoming, ran out of white paper and had to use yellow sheets instead. Telephone directories were originally produced as a service for telephone users, and the business of taking in revenues from advertising developed later.

The telephone company American Telephone and Telegraph (AT&T), a major phone company in the United States, became the largest directory publisher, earning more than $1.5 million from its yellow pages business in the late 1970s. AT&T had introduced the name "Yellow Pages" and the famous walking fingers logo but chose not to trademark either name or logo, which have since been adopted by numerous publishers. When AT&T divested its Bell companies in 1984, the directory publishing business was also divided among the seven new regional holding companies, resulting in a publishing subsidiary or division for each company. This led to greater competition for advertisers, as the regional Bell companies introduced directories for regions beyond their own service areas. Meanwhile, independent yellow pages publishers had existed for decades.

The yellow pages industry grew rapidly in the 1980s from revenues of $2.9 billion in 1980 to $8.9 billion in 1990, including non-publishing marketing and advertising service sales. The number of directory editions published increased steadily to a peak of 6,500 in 1986, when the number began to decline somewhat. The regional Bell companies withdrew to publishing for only their own territories in response to consumer confusion and advertiser complaints over multiple yellow pages for the same region. Also, some niche publications, such as one by Southwestern Bell that targeted the elderly, were unsuccessful. Although traditionally considered a recession-proof industry, yellow pages advertising sales slowed, but did not decline during the recession of 1990-92.

Several trends affected yellow pages publishing in the early 1990s. Publishers are increasingly relying on third-party marketing agencies. The industry was working toward a standardized advertising menu in 1993. Targeted niche marketing is being further developed. The growth of 800 numbers has led to an increase in national advertising whereby a company chooses to advertise in various yellow pages throughout the country. Recently, audiotex services were being introduced in some areas. Sometimes referred to as "talking yellow pages," voice information services permit callers to enter in codes for information on the advertised product or service. Yellow pages publishers, both independent and utility, are teaming up with newspaper publishers to offer these information services. Another trend among telephone directory publishers is a greater dedication to community service with the publishing of community-oriented information pages. Recently efforts were made to overcome the old dusty image and to consider the yellow pages as the first place to shop. Directories rating World Wide Web sites for beginners and listings or evaluations of CD-ROMs are also being published.

CURRENT CONDITIONS

The total value of shipments for miscellaneous publishing as a whole rose from $12.3 billion in 1994 to $14.6 billion in 1999 on steady growth. While analysts expected the early 2000s to continue to offer growth opportunities to miscellaneous publishers, the rapid emergence of new technologies and shifting consumer trends made it impossible to provide fixed predictions for the industry as a whole, as the various sectors were likely to go in their own directions.

More than 17 billion catalogs were mailed in 1998, the equivalent of 64 for every person in the United States. By 1999 that number was estimated to hit 17.6 billion, consuming about 3.35 million tons of paper. Such news has not gone unnoticed by environmentalists, for whom the Internet is a welcome development in this case. By the end of the 1990s, many catalog publishers had not fully integrated the World Wide Web into their operations, a fact that some industry proponents were trying to mitigate. There is a rapid movement toward electronic cataloging and consolidating design and prepress operations to bring them in-house. Catalog growth expanded by 8 percent annually between 1993 and 1998 but is expected to fall to 6.4 percent from 1999 to 2003, as consumers shift to buying directly from the Internet. In 1997 106.7 million Americans shopped from catalogs.

Telephone directories constituted a nearly $12-billion sector in the late 1990s, by far the largest category in the miscellaneous publishing industry, though these revenues include advertising-related services as well. The growth-hungry U.S. business environment played no small part in the sector's strong sales; yellow pages advertising revenues were up 8 percent in 1999 to reach $2.16 billion. Despite these strong figures, however, the industry's voracious competition kept advertising prices fairly low. The 1996 Telecommunications Act opened the door for independent directory publishers to gain footing in this industry by forcing phone companies to release their listings databases. By 1998, independent publishers had achieved an 8 percent share of the directory market. Observers expected the early 2000s to be marked by consolidation among directory publishers. Meanwhile, American Business Information took advantage of opened directory listings to develop a white-page database with more than 100 million residential listings for use in Internet directories and telemarketing.

The Yellow Pages Publishers Association embarked on its first national marketing campaign in years, shedding its famous "walking fingers" logo in favor of a yellow light bulb, in an effort to promote the yellow pages as an idea source. Meanwhile, in urban markets such as New York, yellow pages geared toward specific ethnic groups experienced great success in the late 1990s. Such directories focus on people and businesses of specific ethnic groups in their own languages, catering to customers with an affinity for doing business within a sub-community and promoting strong identity ties within ethnic populations. This niche market, with its more specialized advertising, is becoming a popular and profitable supplement income for yellow pages publishers.

The global market for sheet-music publishing continued its slow but steady growth through the mid-1990s. The 1999 International Survey of Music Publishers, conducted by the National Music Publishers Association, listed total publishing revenues of $6.29 billion worldwide in 1997. This included both mechanical royalties and performance revenue. The gap between these segments is widening in favor of the former. Mechanical royalties are based on the reproduction of published music, and they generated an income of $2.74 billion, or 44 percent of total publishing revenues. However, growth in sheet music publishing revenues is limited by the tendency toward copyright violations. Since sheet music is usually only a few pages long, it is easily photocopied illegally. In 1998 U.S. music publishers signed a 10-year royalty contract with record labels, securing publishing revenues into the 2000s. However, of growing concern to publishers and labels alike was the emergence in the late 1990s of online music distribution, of which the industries have yet to iron out the legalities.

The 1990s were an exasperating decade for the trading-card industry. Companies were forced to adapt quickly to survive a shaken market as sales across all categories declined, greatly exacerbated by a series of sports strikes. In 1998 manufacturers and licensers formed the Sports Card Association, Inc. in order to pool efforts following a 60 percent decline in total industry sales, dropping from $1 billion in the early 1990s to $450 million in 1998. The association launched huge promotional campaigns, including offers of trips to sports All-Star games as well as large sports- and entertainment-card displays in retail stores. In early 1999 baseball cards comprised 37 percent of sales; footballs cards, 34 percent; and all others, 24 percent.

And then came Pokemon. Through 1999 the children's sensation almost single-handedly resuscitated the trading-card market. The release of Pokemon movies portends sustained sales through 2000 and is anticipated to generate the first increase in trading card sales since 1991. Meanwhile, the secondary market of dealers and collectors has been growing recently due to increases in sales to adults, sophistication in marketing, and the use of nonexclusive licensing contracts by professional sport leagues as a means of improving their images and marketing their players and teams.

Yearbook sales are likely to continue their strong growth patterns well into the 2000s due to demographic trends; the growing number of elementary school students through the 1990s will lead to increasing numbers of high school graduates as those children come of age. The yearbook market was estimated at about $500 million. Yearbook publishers greatly enjoy the benefits received from the unpaid creative efforts of students. However, the sector's intense competition was characterized by the victory of Taylor Publishing Co. in an antitrust lawsuit against market leader Jostens, Inc. in 1997, which held that Jostens had interfered with Taylor's sales representatives.

The super graphics segment of the industry (oversized posters, murals, banners, signs, and maps) has been expanding into new markets such as "tied" formats in large collages and historical exhibits. Using new technology, they then print on transfer paper to vinyl, textiles, canvases, and even wood. Large-format output is one of the largest areas of anticipated growth.

Other solid miscellaneous publishing sectors in the late 1990s included micropublishing, with revenues of $146.2 million in 1997; pattern publishing for clothing and other purposes, with $197 million; and calendars, with revenues of $220.4 million enjoyed by companies specializing in calendar production.

INDUSTRY LEADERS

The major telephone directory publishers in 1998 were the leading regional Bell companies—Bell Atlantic Corporation ($2.26 billion in revenues), Bell South Corporation ($1.89 billion), U.S. West Incorporated ($1.27 billion), and Ameritech Corporation ($1.77 billion)—as well as GTE Corporation ($1.53 billion), Reuben H. Donnelley Corporation ($590 million), Sprint ($384 million), Yellow Book U.S.A. ($250 million), and Alltel ($120.3 million).

Reuben H. Donnelley Corporation derives most of its revenue from advertisement services. Its publishing business was given over to Ameritech in 1998 in a joint venture between the two firms and DonTech. The bulk of the firm's yellow pages operations, meanwhile, were sold to Yellow Book U.S.A. Yellow Book, the largest independent phone-directory publisher in North America, was acquired in 1999 by British Telecommunications, an alliance that merged the two companies' Internet databases.

The leading business service publishers include Dow Jones and Company Incorporated; Dun & Bradstreet Corporation and its Moody's Investors Service subsidiary; Thomson Information Publishing Group; Value Line Incorporated; and Disclosure Incorporated.

The January 2000 merger between EMI Group PLC and Time Warner, Inc. created the largest music-publishing firm in the world, as EMI Music Publishing Worldwide and Warner Brothers Publications expected to control about one-third of the world market for combined mechanical and performance royalties.

The nation's largest catalog publisher-printer is R.R. Donnelley and Sons Company. The firm engages in a variety of printing and publishing activities as well as online and electronic-commerce services, generating revenues of $5.1 billion in 1998 for all its activities.

Sagging industry sales resulted in the re-shuffling of the leading sports-card publishers in the late 1990s. Long-time market leader Topps Company, Inc. maintained its position with sales of $326 million in 1999, largely owing to its copyright over the stellar Pokemon series but also deriving from candy products and comic books. However, many of Topps' traditional competitors were swallowed in the late 1990s by Playoff Corp., which acquired the trading-card rights of Donruss, Score, and Leaf on its way to sales of $25 million in 1999. Donruss maintained its hockey- and baseball-card lines.

Rand McNally Company remained the world's largest commercial map publisher through the late 1990s, which sells more than 10 million road atlases annually in addition to its hardcover world atlases. The firm's diverse business lines employed 31,000 people and brought $5.13 billion in revenues in 1998. Also that year, Rand McNally purchased another of the leading map publishers, Thomas Brothers, whose specialty in digital mapped street guides produced annual sales of $30 million and will be incorporated into Rand McNally's burgeoning CD-ROM mapping products. Successful products in this line included the Business Traveler's Suite CD-ROM package. National Geographic Society, meanwhile, dropped its non-profit status in 1997 amidst declining contributions, and expanded its map and atlas businesses, which had previously been made available only to members, to the public. Other leading map and atlas publishers included Simon & Schuster, which owns Mobil Road Atlas and H.M. Gousha, and Hammond Incorporated.

Jostens Incorporated prints about half of all high school yearbooks in the United States, with sales of $769 million in 1999, though that figure also includes its line of class rings. Jostens' chief competitor in the yearbook market was Taylor Publishing Company, which derived 91 percent of its $100 million in revenues from yearbooks in 1999. Other yearbook publishers included Herff Jones, Inc. and Walsworth Publishing Company.

WORKFORCE

The miscellaneous publishing industry was one of the top 20 industries at the three-digit SIC level for rate of employee growth during the 1980s. Its workforce increased 79.6 percent between 1979 and 1989. This growth cooled considerably in the mid- and late 1990s, reaching 70,400 in 1998. Of this total, about 25,000 workers were engaged in production, earning an average of $14.28 per hour. The U.S. market for published information is expected to continue its breakneck pace into the 2000s, portending a voracious labor market for employees in this category.

AMERICA AND THE WORLD

Most companies engaged in miscellaneous publishing have little or no international presence. Only about one percent of all products in this category are set for exports; thus, firms focus little on international marketing campaigns.

One area that has experienced increasing international activity is directory publishing. After British Telecommunications purchased Yellow Book U.S.A., many analysts expected to see an increase in international merger activity, particularly in the market for online directory publishing. As the global business climate integrates, firms will likely desire access to detailed information on overseas businesses, thus heightening the need for internationally based directories.

As the U.S. directory market splinters following the 1996 Telecommunications Act, which put an end to the monopoly power wielded by telephone companies, foreign operations increasingly maintain the largest yellow pages publishing operations. While local and national telephone utilities continue to publish the alphabetical directories, the commercial market has been left wide open for experienced North American publishers. However, U.S. publishers have taken considerable strides to compete with these larger firms in untapped markets where no large-scale yellow pages had existed. U.S. publishers have won contracts to publish directories in Eastern Europe and Russia as those countries move toward a free-market economy.

Sheet music publishing is a lucrative international business, along with music publishing as a whole. Publishers contract with licensed distribution agents in each country or region in which they distribute their music. In printed music, the United States is the world leader. The revenues of U.S. music publishers have been growing faster internationally than domestically. After the United States, the countries with the largest music-publishing industries were Germany, the United Kingdom, Japan, and France. Taken together, these top five countries enjoyed 69.6 percent of the world music-publishing market.

Affected by a logic of globalization similar to that of directory publishers, business-service newsletter publishers are increasingly marketing their publications internationally to serve business people interested in market conditions in different countries. Newsletters are much lighter than business magazines and therefore ship well by airmail. Whether companies are sending articles, bibliographic or directory databases, or numeric tables, business service publications in electronic formats are by far the easiest to "export."

RESEARCH AND TECHNOLOGY

For much of the miscellaneous publishing industry, the potential consequences of the World Wide Web and other online technologies remains clouded. Catalog publishers are likely to realize enhanced revenues from electronic commerce, while sheet-music publishers fear that the Internet will allow wide proliferation of published music on the Web and through e-mail programs from which companies will be unable to collect royalties. Maps and atlases are often published online, though the large graphic files are often slow to download. Map publishers, therefore, have focused much more on digitizing their information for use in CD-ROM programs.

Throughout the miscellaneous publishing industry, in fact, many publishers of printed material have begun publishing versions of their books or periodicals on CD-ROM, while others license their data to specialized CD-ROM publishers and online vendors. A wide range of miscellaneous publishing exists on CD-ROM: telephone directories, other directories, maps, business service publications, business newsletters, guides, and even forms of catalogs and yearbooks. Some business service publishers now publish more information in electronic form than either print or microform. Fax and online information services are being utilized—especially by business newsletter publishers who need to provide speedy delivery of information.

CD-ROMs have the physical attributes, low production costs, and standardization necessary to make it an almost ideal medium for publishing, data distribution, and archival material for the business consumer. Computerized maps of the entire United States with adjustable scales now fit on one CD-ROM. Rand McNally, along with several other map producers, have expanded into the CD-ROM market. One CD-ROM can contain maps of the entire United States. Rand McNally has enjoyed strong sales from its TripMaker, StreetFinder, and Quick Reference Atlas CD-ROMs. New products and markets include outsized posters, banners, and maps for exhibits or murals and a variety of surfaces. Many reference books, technical manuals, and even children's books are packaged with a CD-ROM version accompanying them. CD-ROMS are increasingly used for technical manuals because of their ease of indexing and compactness. The manufacturing industry at large still relies heavily on paper technical manuals, however.

FURTHER READING
"ABI Offers White Pages Database of Residential Listings." *Information Today,* June 1998.

"B-to-B Catalog Industry at a Glance." *Business Marketing*, December 1997.

"Does a Category Have to Hit Bottom Before Licensees and Licensors Start to Pull Together?" *The Licensing Newsletter*, 16 March 1998.

"Grand Prairie, Texas, Company Acquires Sports-Card Brands From Rival." *Fort Worth Star-Telegram*, 21 July 1999.

"Look Out (Thud!)—It's an All-Out Phone-Book War." *Wall Street Journal*, 10 June 1999.

"Mechanical Pact Set." *Billboard*, 2 August 1997.

International Survey of Music Publishers. New York: National Music Publishers' Association, 1999. Available from http://www.nmpa.org/nmpa/nv-s99/iis.html.

"New York Merchant Bank to Buy Dallas Yearbook-Publishing Company." *Dallas Morning News*, 21 December 1999.

"Newsletters Find Haven Online." *New York Times*, 7 July 1997.

Osterman, Jim. "Fingerectomy at Yellow Pages." *AdWeek Southeast*, 21 December 1998.

"Outlook for Print Shows Slower Growth." *Pulp & Paper*, March 1998.

"Those Free Catalogs Cost Us All, Critics Say." *USA Today*, 29 November 1999.

"Top Yellow Pages Publishers." *Advertising Age*. 16 August 1999.

"Trading Up." *Sporting Goods Business*, 22 June 1998.

Trager, Cara. "Fingers Go On Walking Tour of Ethin Neighborhoods: Polyglot Directories Win Diverse Ad Dollars." *Crain's New York Business*, 29 June 1999.

U.S. Department of Commerce. Bureau of the Census. *1997 Census of Manufacturers*. Washington, D.C.: GPO, 2 November 1999.

U.S. Department of Commerce. International Trade Administration. *U.S. Industry and Trade Outlook 1999*. New York: The McGraw Hill Companies, 1999.

SIC 2752

COMMERCIAL PRINTING, LITHOGRAPHIC

This category includes establishments involved primarily in printing by various processes involving lithography. It includes printers using web and flat sheet technologies. Terms describing the processes include offset printing, photo-offset printing, photolithography, and planography.

Most of this industry's work is done on a custom-job basis. Typical products include advertising posters, circulars, coupons, and labels. In addition, some products such as calendars, maps, posters, and decalcomanias are bulk manufactured and offered for sale. Greeting card printers, however, are classified in **SIC 2771.**

Lithographed newspapers and periodicals made by printing companies that are not publishers are also included in this industry. Establishments primarily involved in printing books are classified in **SIC 2732.** Newspaper, periodical, and book publishers are classified in SICs **2711, 2721,** and **2731,** respectively.

Establishments primarily involved in preparing plates and related prepress services are classified in **SIC 2796.** Establishments offering photocopying services are classified in **SIC 7334.**

NAICS CODE(S)

323114 (Quick Printing)
323110 (Commercial Lithographic Printing)

INDUSTRY SNAPSHOT

"Lithography" describes the printing process in which ink is transferred from a plate with a level surface that has been chemically treated to make some areas ink-receptive and others ink-repellent. The term "offset lithography" was coined to describe the process by which an image is transferred from a lithographic plate onto a rubber blanket cylinder and then pressed from the cylinder onto paper or other substrates. About 50 percent of all the printing done in the United States is lithographic.

In 1998, the commercial printing industry pulled approximately $73 billion in shipments, which was expected to rise in 1999 to $76 billion, and employed 374,000 workers. Offset lithography was expected to retain the lion's share of the commercial printing market into 2000. Advertising printing was offset lithography's largest single category in 1996, counting for 31 percent of all production. It was projected that direct advertising materials would continue rapid growth to combat the electronic media. Examples of advertising products were direct mail circulars, letters, pamphlets, mailing inserts, and brochures. Other large categories included periodical printing and general business paperwork printing.

Offset lithographers as a whole reported an average of 6 percent growth in sales in 1996, but of that category, commercial offset "quick printers" reported 19 percent growth in sales, with their biggest category being multi-color jobs. Quick printers are geared to turn work around in less than a week.

Industry watchers expected stable growth for the entire industry at 2 to 3 percent annually through 2000. Commercial printing continued to be challenged by the rapid growth of electronic media and the relative scarcity of electronically savvy employees, greater expenditures for pollution management and Occupational Safety and Health Administration (OSHA) compliance, and fluctuating paper cost and supply—but the impact of these factors would be lessened by U.S. population growth increases, rising new business starts, and the increasing demand for English-language publications internationally.

BACKGROUND AND DEVELOPMENT

The term "lithography" comes from two Greek words: *lithos,* meaning "stone," and *graphien,* meaning "to write." The process was developed by the German inventor Aloys Senefelder, who discovered that by treating limestone with gum arabic, nitric acid, and a mixture of soap and tallow, he could make parts of the stone repel printing ink and parts of it repel water. In 1798, he perfected his process for use in printing.

Early lithographic plates were made from limestone, and presses were made of wood. During the first two decades of the 1800s, technical advances were made. Cast iron plates helped improve impression quality, and steam-driven cylinder presses increased operating efficiency. The ability to print in color was developed in 1837. A typical nineteenth century press could print approximately 600 impressions per hour.

The twentieth century brought innovations to increase press speeds and improve image resolution. Ira W. Rubel and Caspar Hermann, both of New Jersey, developed thin metal plates in 1904. Their success enabled the development of rotary lithography, a procedure in which the plate was mounted on a cylinder. By the late 1980s, advances in offset rotary press technology had produced presses capable of making 30,000 impressions per hour, printing on both sides of the paper, and receiving paper in sheets or from large rolls called "webs."

Despite its widespread use, many people find lithography more difficult to understand than other printing processes. Unlike methods in which printing plates contain raised or etched images, lithographic plates are flat. To create a lithographic plate, a plate maker begins with a thin piece of metal coated with an oil-based emulsion. A photographic negative of the image to be printed is placed over the plate, which is then exposed to a bright light. The light reacts with the uncovered emulsion so that when the plate is chemically washed the emulsion remains only in the image area. During the printing process, water is used to wet the bare metal, non-image areas of the plate. Printing ink, an oil-based product, is able to adhere only to the emulsion in the image area.

According to the U.S. Department of Commerce, commercial printing by lithography earnings totaled $32.7 billion in 1987. Of this amount, $30 billion represented products considered primary to the industry. The combined value of commercial printing by all methods in 1987 was estimated at $44.7 billion.

By 1991, the commercial printing industry had grown to $55.7 billion. However, profit margins for many establishments were down as a result of intensified price competition during the national recession.

According to figures published by the National Association of Printers and Lithographers, commercial printing represented the fifth largest manufacturing industry in the United States. During the early 1990s, government statistics indicated that commercial printing was growing faster than general manufacturing in all 50 states. The industry continued striving toward faster presses, quicker set-up, improved color reproduction, and better material handling procedures. One noted trend was toward shorter but more numerous press runs. Industry analysts attributed this to "just in time" inventory systems and to advertisers' ability to target markets with greater precision. Six-color systems became the new industry standard.

Compliance with national, regional, and local environmental regulations posed a challenge to the industry. Commercial lithography depended on the use of solvents, volatile organic compounds (VOC), and other substances classified as toxic. The printing process also generated waste materials that were considered hazardous. In addition, some environmental groups criticized the industry for its mass production of newspapers, periodicals, catalogs, and direct mail items that used paper resources and congested the nation's landfills.

Another observed trend was the increased use of color. Previously, four-color presses were considered the industry standard for reproducing photographic images. Four-color process printing created shades and tones of color by employing a technique called color separation, which involved filtering an image through a screen to produce a series of single-color plates, each containing an image comprised of tiny dots. Six- and eight-color presses enabled printers to exactly match distinctive colors, take advantage of special effects such as the application of metallic inks, and apply coatings or other finishes.

According to a July 1996 article in *American Printer,* a survey of the top fifth of domestic printing firms indicated that more than half were involved in mergers or acquisitions. The larger the company, the more likely the chance of merger. In February 1997, *Publishing & Production Executive* suggested that the consolidation trend was fueled by the printing customer's demand for a one-stop shop. The huge capital investments required to stay competitive in the industry were also a factor.

The National Association of Printers & Lithographers identified seven key industry trends in a November 1996 report published in *GATF World,* the magazine of the Graphic Arts Technical Foundation. The trends, in order of importance, were: more color, graphics, and complex designs; shorter run-lengths; paper and material cost inflation; severe price competition among printers; much quicker turn-around times; black and white printing now going to copying machine technology; and, clients insisting on higher quality.

An increasingly pressing challenge for the industry was training and retaining qualified employees. The industry was revamped during the 1980s and 1990s, and traditional mechanical printers' skills were not sufficient in leading shops. From electronic prepress to digital presses, the new standard of commercial printing equipment was redefining the craft in terms of the electronic era. New technology was a two-edged sword. According to a 1996 study by the National Association of Printers and Lithographers, the cost of staying "state-of-the-art" with regard to new software and hardware was the leading threat to overall profitability for the industry. Interestingly, the same survey identified the key strength of the industry as having state-of-the-art equipment that could handle a broad range of work. The second most serious "threat to profitability" was closer kin to it—the learning curve of keeping current with new technology and converting to new systems.

The mid-1990s was a trying time for many in the industry. Rising postage costs, rising paper costs, and threats of recession kept many companies lean. Aggressive competition among printers cut profit margins.

CURRENT CONDITIONS

The "hot" markets beyond 2000, said Ron Davis of the Printing Industries of America (PIA), would be "general marketing and promotional." The PIA predicted that the industry would do well into the late 1990s, seeing a growth in sales of approximately 6 percent. The driving trends were toward more color, faster color, digital proofing, and a preference among customers for shops that could combine all-in-one digital proofing, printing, fulfillment, and delivery service.

In the late 1990s, the dominance of six-color presses was being challenged by eight-color sheet-fed "perfectors" that could print both sides of a sheet of paper during one pass through the press. At prices ranging from $2.7 to $4.0 million dollars, these behemoth machines were considered expensive, but incredibly productive—and a sure contender for the wave of the future. By 1997, they were already widely adopted by printers in Europe.

Another important development within commercial lithography was the growing impact of environmental regulations. Systems used to produce proofs (samples made before printing to exactly depict the finished product) were criticized because of their reliance on solvents associated with air and water pollution. Many local ordinances controlled waste water discharges from printing establish-

ments by defining acceptable pH levels, restricting the discharge of ignitable substances, and banning the presence of heavy metals. Worker safety regulations mandated chemical exposure limits, and the storage and handling of hazardous substances were controlled by legislation. The Clean Air Act Amendments of 1990 required companies to obtain permits for press equipment, and some states also ordered permits for vented prepress equipment. In some places, local governing authorities restricted the number of hours a day certain types of presses were allowed to run and limited the acquisition of additional printing capacity.

The race for new technology and the challenge of finding technologically savvy workers are two factors that were expected to hold back industry expansion. But by far the largest obstacle was the rising cost of paper, expected to continue to increase into 2003.

INDUSTRY LEADERS

One of the largest commercial printers operating in the United States during the 1998 was Quebecor Printing Inc., of Boston, Massachusetts. The company's parent organization, Quebecor Inc., was founded in 1965, and its corporate headquarters is in Montreal, Canada. In 1997, Quebecor operated 48 printing and related service plants in the United States, mostly concentrated in the Northeast, and in 1998, it had 170 locations worldwide. The company reported 1998 sales of $3.8 billion and employed more than 27,500 workers.

Quebecor's principal products included advertising inserts, circulars, flyers, magazines, catalogs, and books. Other divisions included specialty printing, directory printing, securities printing, newspaper printing, and other printing services such as prepress support, circulation fulfillment, and list management.

Another industry leader is Quad/Graphics, Inc., founded in 1971 by entrepreneur Henry Quadracci in Pewaukee, Wisconsin. In 1998, Quad/Graphics was the largest privately held printing company in North America, with annual sales in excess of $1.4 billion dollars and 11,000 employees. Quad/Graphics also operates extensive digital design, gravure, book publishing, mailing, and fulfillment centers.

Other industry leaders in 1998 included R. R. Donnelly & Sons Company, a Chicago printing giant founded in 1866, with annual sales of $5 billion; and Big Flower Holdings, Inc., with 1998 sales of more than $1 billion.

WORKFORCE

In 1998, the U.S. Bureau of Labor Statistics noted that there were 76,000 offset lithography press operators out of a total of 224,300 press operators nationwide. The jobs were well distributed through the country, with only slightly heavier concentrations in New York, Los Angeles, Chicago, Philadelphia, Washington, D.C., and Dallas.

Workers within the commercial printing industry were facing rapid changes as new production methods and materials were adopted. Changes resulted in the elimination of some job classifications but created shortages of experienced labor in others. The prepress and postpress areas were expected to yield the greatest gains in employment opportunity, while traditional jobs such as those of ''strippers'' were being eliminated by computerized prepress.

The National Association of Printers and Lithographers stated that ''though commercial printing is a huge industry, it is an industry of numerous small businesses, embodying the U.S. entrepreneurial spirit.'' Forty-three percent of commercial printing establishments employed fewer than four employees; 66.2 percent employed fewer than 10; 85.0 percent fewer than 20; and 93.4 percent of the nation's commercial printers employed fewer than 50 employees.

In the mid-1990s, the median weekly wage for a press operator was $432, according to the U.S. Bureau of Labor Statistics. Employment in this sector was expected to grow slowly through 2005 because, although demand for the printed product was expected to increase, technology would enable one professional offset press operator to print more quickly and more efficiently than several were able to do in the past. Most employment growth in 2000 and beyond will result from direct mail efforts and expansion into industry globalization.

RESEARCH AND TECHNOLOGY

Evolving technology played a vital role in the development of the commercial printing industry. Analysts estimated that printers invested more than $2 billion in new technology during 1991 to maintain their competitiveness. The development of high-quality copying machines drove printers to adopt presses capable of offering more benefits. Innovations brought improvements in color capacity, press speeds, and automation.

As press speeds approached 2,500 feet per minute, automated equipment became increasingly important because of human physical limitations. New methods of feeding paper into the press and taking printed matter away from the press were developed. Researchers designed computers to help achieve optimal results by automatically monitoring press temperatures, plate register (how images fit together), and web tension. One device that facilitated the development of higher speed presses was a densitometer. A densitometer was a device used to insure color integrity throughout an entire press run by automatically making adjustments to the ink fountains. Prior to the development of densitometers, ink fountain adjustments were made by an experienced pressman based on visual perception.

In the industry's quest for decreased production time and increased efficiency, commercial printers were turning to the International Cooperation for Integration of Prepress, Press, and Postpress (CIP3). This digital technology was being embraced in 1999 as an answer to the quick electronic media. Half-size webs were also becoming more popular as a quick alternative to the larger webs.

Other technological changes were aimed at improving the ability to quickly set up a press and to reduce paper waste. One area under study was the automatic setting of press variables from prepress operations. For example, if computerized color separations could be used to directly set press ink keys, exact color reproductions could be made without wasting time and paper in experimental attempts to duplicate the required visual results. Other evolving technologies included faster plate changes, reductions in the amount of blank space required to lock plates onto press cylinders, additional in-line finishing capabilities, optimized material handling at the end of the press run, and better photographic reproductions.

One system that gained acceptance was called dry lithography. Dry lithography used waterless ink systems. In traditional lithography, water was necessary to dampen the plate. A precise ink/water balance was essential for superior quality. Systems printing without water achieved higher-quality results and operated more efficiently. Waterless printing also enabled printers to work with higher resolutions. For example, commercial printers traditionally reproduced photographs using screens of 150 lines per inch. Using waterless technology, printers could employ screens of 300 to 500 lines per inch. The investment required to ''retro-fit'' presses for dry lithography, however, delayed the penetration of this technology into the market. The technology required special inks and special plate materials able to repel the inks from non-image areas. In addition, press temperatures were more difficult to control. Using traditional water systems, the water served not only to keep ink away from non-image areas but also to cool the press. Waterless systems required chilling rolls to carry off excess heat or ink adjustments to compensate for higher temperatures.

At the close of 1999, technological advancements in digital prepress and printing was expected to define the market for the next century. Digital technology offers better quality products, decreased production time, and allows the industry to remain competitive with fast-growing electronic media.

FURTHER READING

Dun's Business Rankings. Bethlehem, PA: Dun & Bradstreet, 1996.

''Eight Is Enough: Printers Look to Eight-Color Perfectors.'' *American Printer,* February 1997.

Esler, Bill. "The Quick Print Giants." *Graphic Arts Monthly,* December 1996.

"Hoover's Company Capsules." *Hoover' Online,* 1999. Available from http://www.hoovers.com.

Ferris, Fred. "A Step Ahead of the Crowd: Short-Run Digital Color Requires a Fresh, Aggressive Marketing Approach." *American Printer,* April 1996.

Lamparter, William C. "Web Press Wonders." *American Printer,* May 1999.

Milburn, David L. "Connects Pixels to Paper—1996 Technology Forecast." *GATF World,* March/April 1996.

"Printer's Perspective: 1996 in Review." *Publishing & Production Executive,* February 1997.

"Printers' Profits Remain Healthy Despite Drop." *GATF World,* July/August 1996.

"Quebecor Printing (USA) Company Overview." Boston: Quebecor, 1997. Available from http://www.quebecorusa.com/facilityglb.htm.

"The More Complete Sheet." *Printing Impressions,* February 1997.

Toth, Deborah. "CIP3 Compatibility Buffs Rosy Sheetfed Outlook." *Graphic Arts Monthly,* June 1999.

"Tracking the Trends: Merger Activity in Top Printing Firms." *American Printer,* July 1996.

U.S. Bureau of Labor Statistics. International Trade Administration. *Occupational Outlook Handbook.* Washington, D.C.: GPO, 1998. Available from http://stats.bls.gov/oco/ocos231.htm.

SIC 2754

COMMERCIAL PRINTING, GRAVURE

This category includes establishments primarily engaged in commercial printing using the gravure process. Other terms often used to describe current methods of gravure production are "photogravure," "rotogravure," and "intaglio." Examples of products in this industry include magazines, postage stamps, dollar bills, calendars, fine art prints, wallpaper, catalogs, coupons, directories, newspaper advertising inserts, playing cards, postcards, gift wrap, and product packaging and wrappers.

NAICS CODE(S)

323110 (Commercial Gravure Printing)

INDUSTRY SNAPSHOT

Gravure is a form of intaglio printing. "Intaglio" comes from an Italian word meaning "to engrave;" the word "gravure" is taken from the French and has the same meaning. Intaglio printing methods were developed by carving or engraving an image in stone or metal. In contemporary commercial gravure printing, a reversed image is cut into a thick metal plate wrapped around a cylinder. Ink, applied to the plate and wiped off the surface with a blade, remains in the incised image cells so that when paper is placed against the plate it absorbs the ink and produces a crisp copy of the image.

The contemporary gravure printing process has generally been used for very long press runs on projects requiring superior color accuracy and clarity on thin papers. Gravure is preferred in runs of more than 300,000 copies, like printing weekly or monthly magazines or mass-distributed catalogs. Gravure's primary advantage over other forms of printing is its ability to produce millions of impressions without suffering image deterioration. Gravure can also print a superior image on lighter papers than other printing methods can, since gravure lays down wet ink over dry. Other commercial printing methods lay wet ink over wet ink, which causes the image to degrade more quickly. Gravure's disadvantages include generally higher costs and increased press set-up time.

Catalog and directory printers represented a substantial segment of the gravure market. Twenty percent of the catalogs and 15 percent of the newspaper inserts published domestically were gravure, according to the Gravure Association of America (GAA). Roughly 26 percent of the gravure industry was devoted to the category of catalog and directory printing, which also included direct mail catalogs and telephone and business directories.

Approximately 16 percent of the gravure printing industry was devoted to magazine printing in the late 1990s. Roughly one-third of all consumer magazine circulation was gravure, as were more than 90 percent of Sunday magazines. In the late 1990s, according to the GAA, 30 magazines were printed gravure, including *Family Circle, McCalls, Better Home & Garden, Reader's Digest, Parade,* and *TV Guide.* Another 27 percent of the gravure industry profited from producing advertising flyers, leaflets, and direct mail ad campaigns.

Gravure is also used for packaging designs, such as the printed plastic wrapping around many perishable foods or around beverage containers. Fifteen percent of the gravure's printing market in the mid- to late 1990s was devoted to printing labels and wrappers.

BACKGROUND AND DEVELOPMENT

The gravure printing process developed from copperplate engraving techniques employed during the fifteenth century. Early plates were flat and needed to be hand engraved. The development of engraved cylinders to replace flat plates led to rotary gravure, called "rotogravure." Rotary gravure presses operate by squeezing paper between the image cylinder and a second cylinder called an impression cylinder. Rotary technology enabled the development of presses with increased printing speeds. A process by which rotary gravure presses were able to print on both sides of the paper was patented in 1860 by Auguste Godchaux, a Paris publisher. A photographic etching technique developed in 1878 by a Czech painter helped simplify platemaking procedures.

Gravure printing was further refined in 1908 when two German textile printers, Ernst Rolffs and Eduard Mertens, developed the "doctor blade." Gravure printing techniques relied on creating height differences between the image and non-image areas of the plate. An image was formed by making small recessed ink cells. The doctor blade assured the removal of excess ink from the surface level and enhanced the quality of reproductions.

One of the most popular items reliant on gravure technology was the Sunday newspaper magazine section. Many magazine sections even used the term "rotogravure" as part of their name. Although gravure newspaper supplements were not suited for up-to-the-minute reporting because of their lengthy preparation requirements, they made color advertising possible.

Despite advances made in gravure technology during the early twentieth century, plate engraving expenses and the length of time required to set up press runs remained problematic. The industry responded with efforts aimed at increasing gravure's efficiency. By the mid-1980s computerized preparation and computer-to-plate (CTP) techniques had cut the pre-press time drastically. Lithography printing and gravure printing were practically equal in the late 1990s in terms of pre-press time. However, the costs associated with gravure were still higher, including costs to engrave and handle the heavy gravure press cylinders.

In comparison with offset lithographic presses, gravure presses tended to be larger, faster, and more expensive. In the mid-1990s, the cost of an average no-frills American-made gravure press hovered around $10 million, not including additional thousands of dollars spent in buying impression rollers, safety cages, and on-site installation. Other costs associated with buying a new gravure press included "extras" that most shops find to be necessities, such as cylinder-loading, viscosity, plumbing, and duct systems. Gravure presses were, at the time, often more than nine feet wide and more than 13 1/2 feet long.

During the early 1990s, analysts noted uncertain conditions within the commercial gravure industry. Among catalog and directory printers, gravure held approximately one fourth of the market share, and growth in gravure print orders for catalogs was growing at a faster rate than the overall growth rate for catalog printing.

In other areas, however, gravure printers were experiencing decreasing demand as publishers and advertisers turned to other print processes. According to figures re-

leased in 1989 by the Gravure Association of America (GAA), annual increases in gravure advertising totaled only 6.0 percent during the 1980s while offset advertising print orders had increased at an annual rate of 13.6 percent. In addition, gravure's market share for inserts had dropped to 8.5 percent from 19 percent in 1982. Among magazine printers, annual increases in page production fell short of increases in print capacity and productivity. This led to increased competition and reduced profit margins.

According to the GAA, gravure Sunday magazine production was 12 percent higher in 1988 than in 1987, but the total number of individual magazines produced had dropped. By the end of the decade, they numbered less than 50, and the 1990s reduced their numbers further. Discontinued magazines included publications offered by the Des Moines *Register, Denver Post, Oakland Press, Sacramento Union,* New York *Daily News,* and *Newsday.*

The fact that total production had not also fallen was attributed to two growing national Sunday supplements, *Parade* and *USA Weekend,* both gravure products.

In addition to competition among gravure printers, the commercial gravure industry as a whole faced competition for advertising dollars from television and other printing processes. Trends toward shorter press runs to produce demographic editions of large-circulation magazines and similar trends among catalog publishers toward smaller specialty catalogs lessened the economic advantages offered by gravure's long run capability. At the same time, improvements in the ability of competing print processes to achieve high-quality photographic reproductions further eroded gravure's traditional advantages.

CURRENT CONDITIONS

In the 1990s, the commercial printing industry experienced a period of discomfort caused by a series of large acquisitions and mergers, an increase in the cost of paper supplies, and postage rate increases. Gravure, as a subset of the industry, felt these changes keenly since its profit margin relied on an affordable paper supply. In the July 1996 issue of *American Printer,* 50 percent of the country's top 20 printing firms were involved in a merger. Gravure printers and heatset web plants (another kind of printing used primarily for magazines) were the most aggressive in seeking mergers.

According to GAA's executive director, Cheryl Kasunich, in 1997 gravure comprised 20 percent of the commercial printing market. From 1989 to 1997, the industry employed between 80,000 and 90,000 people. Gravure printing shipments in 1996 were estimated at just under $4 billion—a relatively static figure since 1990. Gravure was expected to continue its growth, albeit slowly, into 2000. The surge of digital technology was responsible for a slowed employment rate at the turn of the century, since it required less time and fewer workers.

Trends within the industry toward shorter print runs aimed at more focused markets lessened gravure's advantages and brought increased competition from other print technologies, especially offset. During the mid-1990s, computer magazines, weekly magazines, and direct mail prospered, all contributing to a steady overall profitability for the gravure—albeit with little significant growth. In early 1997, the industry hoped to take advantage of strong magazine starts. Lawrence Rasie's 1995 Directory of Business Information had indicated a magazine industry sales increases of 1 to 2 percent per year until 2000— a fortuitous sign for gravure.

Industry forecasters expect that the highest rate of growth in 2000 will be in the catalog and magazine sectors, as direct mail to targeted audiences and school enrollment increase. Globalization of the industry and stiff competition from electronic media were expected to drive the industry toward faster and better quality products than ever before. Technological advances such as CPT and CIP3 were expected to become an industry standard. From 1997 to 2002, media sales were expected to grow by $34.7 billion, a growth rate that included the gravure industry. While the outlook was encouraging, this growth rate is smaller than that predicted for electronic media.

Some industry prognosticators foresaw more consolidation and merger activity among printers, as well as a continuing challenge for gravure to remain viable in the face of competition from the more flexible and often more cost-effective offset printers. But industry forecasters expect that catalog and magazine production will continue to rise more markedly than other industry products on into the year 2000 and beyond, due to increasing U.S. demand, especially in the business sector.

By the late 1990s, gravure had made tremendous strides to overcome its high cost of set-up, lengthy cylinder engraving process, and environmentally unsound ink solvents; however, offset presses—the competition— improved quality, turn-around time, and ability to print longer runs with better quality. Pre-press costs were about equal for offset and gravure process by the late 1990s, but gravure cylinders were still substantially more expensive. Plates for an offset press can cost as little as $200, while a typical gravure cylinder cost $1,000 to $1,200. The future of gravure technology within the publication industry is unsure. Gravure technology may move away from traditional commercial printing and become reserved for operations in which it is undisputed master—like decorating vinyl wall and floor covers. As of 1999, the biggest challenges to the industry were cost-effectiveness and timeliness, in addition to the strong need for niche marketing.

INDUSTRY LEADERS

One of the largest gravure printers operating in the United States was Quebecor Printing, Inc., a multi-billion dollar Canadian firm whose U.S. headquarters were in Boston, Massachusetts. In 1998, Quebecor had annual sales (including non-gravure commercial printing) of $3.8 billion, 170 locations, and nearly 28,000 employees. Quebecor produced Sunday newspaper magazines— including Parade and USA Weekend—and retail inserts. The company's major advertising clients included Sears, Dayton-Hudson, Montgomery Ward, Radio Shack, and Woolco-Woolworth. Quebecor also printed catalogs for L.L. Bean, and magazines including Time, Reader's Digest, and People.

In late 1994, Quebecor signed an additional agreement with USA Weekend magazine to print 17 million copies a week of its regional editions until July 2004. Despite its heavy involvement in gravure printing, however, Quebecor's primary classification was under **SIC 2752: Commercial Printing, Lithographic.**

Founded in 1971 in Pewaukee, Wisconsin, by entrepreneur Harry Quadracci, Quad/Graphics was the largest privately held printing company in North America—with 18 plants, 11,000 employees, and $1.4 billion in annual sales. Quad/Graphics, in the late 1990s, operated 12 Cerutti-built gravure presses in two all-gravure printing plants—one in Lomira, Wisconsin, and the other in Martinsburg, West Virginia. Both shops were 100 percent direct-digital engraving. Quad/Graphics prints Lillian Vernon and Hanover Direct catalogs, as well as mass-market magazines such as Newsweek, Time, and Wired.

R.R. Donnelly & Sons Company, of Chicago, posted 1998 sales of more than $5 billion and had more than 36,000 employees in its 50 facilities. The third largest commercial printer worldwide, Donnelly was the largest catalog printer in 1998 and the largest magazine printer in 1999. Its sales are mostly comprised of catalogs and magazines, in addition to other products such as inserts and books. Donnelly's products were produced in a 100 percent digital production process.

AMERICA AND THE WORLD

The printing industry was only behind Germany in product exports as of the late 1990s. Gravure's popularity increased faster in Europe during the late 1980s than in the United States. Large gravure presses capable of all-at-once production were used to print magazines in a single print pass. Popular weekly news magazines featuring topical issues, televisions listings, and celebrity news required regular press runs of several million copies. In Europe, gravure was successfully used to print much shorter press runs of only 150,000 copies, as opposed to the 300,000 to 500,000 copy minimum practiced in the United States. Analysts noted that the European gravure market did not need to weather the same bottom-line, cost-conscious mentality as many American companies.

Some industry watchers noted that U.S. printers and publishers were poised to succeed as agreements such as the North American Free Trade Agreement (NAFTA) and the Uruguay Round of the General Agreement on Tariffs and Trade (GATT) increased the viability of exporting U.S. printing abroad and increased U.S. copyright protection. Also, U.S. printers looked forward to reaping the advantage of having American English as the world's standard language of trade, science, and commerce.

RESEARCH AND TECHNOLOGY

Lawson Mardon Packaging's Marcel J. Pilon, in a presentation at the GAA's 1996 Annual Convention, pointed out that gravure is the process of choice—and had better results than other methods of printing—when the job required a lot of florescent ink, extremely tight registration, printing on foil, or extremely long runs. In these areas, gravure still had an edge on litho, but industry reports at the end of the 1990s indicated that competing processes were closing the gap.

Digital Process. By the late 1990s, digital engraving technology was helping to overcome one of gravure's traditional problems—lengthy cylinder engraving time. Direct digital engraving methods used laser technology to etch cylinders without making an intermediate film copy of an image. Reportedly, by the mid-1990s all gravure shops used digital engraving for some portion of their work, and by 2000, digital technology was expected to dominate the industry. Getting rid of the film step in the printing process removed a large cost component, saved time, and also reduced waste and the environmental impact of the manufacturing process. Max Daetwyler Corp., of Huntersville, North Carolina, developed one of the first complete digital systems, using a laser to engrave on a non-reflective metal alloy. Lasers could cut 25,000 to 30,000 image cells per second.

Coming into focus at the close of the century was the use of coatings in packaging web presses, due to the quality and protection of the finished product. Press manufacturers were designing coating-equipped machines, in addition to manufacturing retrofits. Industry forecasters suggested that coatings offered a company a bigger competitive edge than digital technology, primarily because there was less competition—most companies had coating capabilities inferior to the available technology.

Environment. The 1990s saw a great deal of research into improving the environmental impact of gravure because of U.S. Occupational Safety and Health Administration (OSHA) compliance issues, the Pollution Prevention Act of 1990, and the Clean Air Act Amendment. Traditional toluene-based inks, which were strictly regulated and rated by the U.S. Environmental Protection Agency as Volatile Organic Compounds (VOC) and Hazardous Air Pollutants (HAP), were slated to be phased out by water-based inks. However, the technology was still in a developmental stage. Promising developments included mixing acetone, a non-hazardous but flammable substance, with water to increase ink drying time and multicolor press runs that used a water-based ink as only one of the colors. One study noted that in a typical four-color (cyan, yellow, magenta, and black) printing run, if a water-based ink were used just for the yellow component, toluene emissions would be reduced 35 percent. Full color water-based printing was not a reality in the late 1990s.

Competition Online. Many short-run publications were complemented by material on CD-ROM or on a Web site. Referenced in the February 1997 *Publishing & Production Executive,* a study of 1,000 U.S. consumers commissioned by the Printing Industries of America (PIA) found that only 21 percent of those surveyed thought that electronic media would replace print. Many felt that electronic and print media would remain independent methods of information. The advance of electronic media into the short-run market, however, could be a driver to encourage printers to expand into electronic publishing or to take over increasingly large segments of what has been traditionally gravure's domain—long, multicolor press runs.

Going into the late 1990s, industry leaders appeared in agreement that long-run magazine and catalog publishing was unthreatened by electronic publishing—at least for the next decade. Many industry giants, like Quebecor and Quad/Graphics, welcomed digital publishing by advertising their services online and using Web pages as marketing tools.

FURTHER READING

"A Commitment to Gravure Excellence." *Gravure,* fall 1996.

"Austrian Machine Corporation." Cranston, RI: Austrian Machine, Inc., 1997.

Chorvat, Bill, et al. "Waterbased Inks: What Are the Real Issues?" *Gravure,* fall 1996.

"Electronic Media Not Likely to Replace Print." *American Printer,* July 1996.

Hobson, Garnett. "Package Printing Technology Change with the Times." *Gravure,* winter 1996.

"Hoover's Company Capsules" *Hoover' Online,* 1999. Available from http://www.hoovers.com.

Kirby, Gretchen A. "1996: Looking Back—The Year in Review." *Publishing & Production Executive,* February 1997.

Lamparter, William C. "A Coat of Many Colors." *American Printer,* March 1999.

———. "Web Press Wonders." *American Printer,* May 1999.

"Printing Press Operators." *1998 Occupational Outlook Handbook*, 1999. Available from http://stats.bls.gov/oco/ocos231.htm.

"Quad/Graphics Breaks Ground in Martinsburg, WV for First All-Digital Gravure Printing Plant." *Gravure*, winter 1995.

Quad/Graphics. "Quad/Graphics: Who Are We?" Company brochure. Pewaukee, WI, 1997. Available from http://www.qg.com/who.html.

Quebecor Printing USA Corp. "Quebecor Printing USA Corp. Company Overview". Boston: Quebecor Printing USA Corp., 1997. Available from http://www.qubecorusa.com/facilglb.htm.

Robbins, Scott. "Gravure and the Environment." *Gravure*, fall 1996.

"R. R. Donnelly & Sons Company." *Folio: the Magazine for Magazine Management*, October 1999.

"Tracking the Trends." *American Printer*, July 1996.

SIC 2759

COMMERCIAL PRINTING, NOT ELSEWHERE CLASSIFIED

This industry classification is comprised of diverse establishments involved in commercial or custom-job printing not categorized elsewhere. Example products include newspapers and periodicals printed on behalf of publishers, engraved announcements, circulars, maps, tags and labels, directories, stock certificates, and currency. Procedures include screen printing, flexography, letterpress, digital printing, embossing, engraving, debossing, and thermography on substrates such as paper or plastic, but not textile. For information on commercial lithographic printing, see **SIC 2752.** For commercial gravure printing, see **SIC 2754.**

NAICS CODE(S)

323112 (Commercial Flexograph Printing)
323113 (Commercial Screen Printing)
323114 (Quick Printing)
323115 (Digital Printing)
323119 (Other Commercial Printing)

INDUSTRY SNAPSHOT

In 1997, shipments for this industry totaled $12.2. Nearly 111,000 people were employed in the industry in 1997. The industry included 6,931 establishments in 1997; this was projected to decrease to 6,656 establishments by the year 2000.

Commercial flexographic printing of items such as labels and wrappers held 38 percent of the market in 1997, the largest single share. Screen printing of items such as signs, posters, and bumper stickers shared the second spot (20 percent of the market) with other commercial printing of items like scientific chart paper, letterpress newspapers, and tags. A great deal of excitement was generated in the late 1990s by an emerging technology that relied solely on an electrochemical reaction to produce an image. This dynamic plateless and filmless process still had no firm nomenclature in early 1997, but one of the developing companies, Elcorsy Technology of Montreal, registered the name "elcography." Images could be changed or manipulated in real-time, while the press was still running. A memory buffer in the system allowed another job to be "moved into line" while the press was still printing a previous piece. The transition from job to job was accomplished seamlessly, with no need to recalibrate the press.

ORGANIZATION AND STRUCTURE

Letterpress and flexography are two common relief printing methods. In relief printing, plates are cast or engraved to produce a raised image. The image is transferred by applying ink to the plate's surface and pressing it against paper or other substrates. Letterpress and flexographic technologies are similar, except that letterpress plates are made from metal and flexographic plates are made from rubber or photopolymer materials. As a result of its different plate composition, flexographic processes require special inks to avoid plate damage.

Screen printing (sometimes called porous printing or silk screening) employs a screen stencil. The image area is left open and nonimage areas are sealed using a substance called "resist." Ink is applied to the screen and forced through its mesh onto paper or other substrates such as glass, plastics, and metal (including highway signs). Screen printing is commonly used for limited quantity outdoor posters such as billboards and point-of-purchase advertising displays. Screen printing is unique in that it allows printing onto uneven, oddly shaped, or extremely large substrates.

Thermography, also called raised printing, is used primarily for business cards, social invitations, and stationery. The raised effect is achieved by applying a colorless resin powder to the wet ink. The powder then assumes the color of the underlying ink and, when heated, it bubbles and bonds to the paper. Some printers use pearlescent and glitter powders to create special effects.

BACKGROUND AND DEVELOPMENT

Human interest in making multiple copies of art and documents dates back many centuries. The Chinese, credited with the invention of paper, designed a kind of wooden movable type based on Chinese characters. Modern print methods, however, trace their beginnings back to the early 1400s when Johannes Gutenberg, a German publisher, developed movable metal type based on alphabetic characters. Gutenberg created molds for individual letters and cast them using a metal alloy made of lead, antimony, and tin. He hand-assembled text, letter by letter, from pieces of type which were kept in a special "type case," with compartments for each letter, accent mark, and punctuation mark. To print, Gutenberg locked the type in a frame and placed the frame in a fixed position on a hand-operated wooden press. He spread ink made of soot and linseed oil on the surface of the type and pressed paper against it with a movable flat platen.

Wilhelm Haas, a Swiss typemaker, developed a metal hand press in 1787. Haas's press produced higher quality impressions than previously existing wooden presses. Further print improvements came during the early 1800s, when flat platens were replaced with steam-driven "impression cylinders." Because an impression cylinder rolled over a plate, it created even pressure across the entire surface and required less energy to operate. The first press to replace its flat platen with a metal cylinder was constructed in the United States by Richard Hoe in 1844.

A major innovation in typesetting technology occurred in 1884 when Ottmar Mergenthaler, a German immigrant to the United States, invented the Linotype machine. It operated by casting lines of type rather than individual letters. A Linotype machine stocked engraved letter dies in a storage area. The letters were released by typing on a keyboard. The machine ordered them, along with punctuation marks and spaces, into entire lines that could then be cast into metal bars. After lines were cast, the individual letters were routed back into storage for future use. The metal bars of type were used to make printing plates. Prior to the invention of the Linotype machine, typesetters could set approximately 1,400 characters per hour. A Linotype machine could set 6,000 characters per hour.

Other typesetting refinements included the Monotype machine, which was invented in 1897. The Monotype machine produced a perforated paper tape to control type-casting equipment. René Higonnet and Louis Moyroud developed photographic typesetting techniques during the 1940s. During the 1950s, computer technology was first employed. Further progress over the next several decades brought additional improvements in typesetting capabilities through the advancement of Optical Character Recognition and digital scanning. Prior to the development of offset lithography during the early twentieth century, letterpress was the most common form of printing in the United States and other developed nations. Even during the latter twentieth century, it remained the most popular printing method in economically developing nations.

Because of advances in offset lithography, some predicted that letterpress and flexography would fall into disuse. Enhanced technologies emerged, however, and

brought increased interest in flexo. A 1992 article in *Graphic Arts Monthly* claimed that nearly all telephone directories and full-color newspaper comics were being printed by flexography and that the volume of regular newspaper sections printed by flexography had doubled within the previous few years. The report anticipated that the future availability of better paper grades and improved inks would also bring increased use among magazine printers.

The flexo trend among newspapers continued into the mid-1990s because flexo continued to offer several advantages over other printing methods; those advantages included water-based, environmentally friendly inks that didn't rub off, brighter colors, an enhanced ability to print on light paper stocks, and competitive make-ready time. According to Dr. Gregory D'Amico, the publisher of *Flexo Today* who was quoted in a 1997 issue of *GATF World,* nearly 47 daily North American newspapers are printed at least partially with flexography, and another 75 are poised to begin flexographic production. The *Pittsburgh Post-Gazette,* for example, began flexo printing in 1996. Quoted in *Flexo Today,* Robert Higdon, general manager of the newspaper, said they made the switch because of environmental impact issues, ease of production, and quality.

Screen printers also benefited from four-color-process work refinements, computerized design, increased press speeds, and environmentally responsive improvements. In anticipation of governmental regulations mandating cuts in solvent use, screen printers began turning to water-based inks cured with ultraviolet (UV) light. Traditional inks contained solvents to aid in drying; UV inks were dried with UV light.

According to *American Printer,* the screen printing industry was previously a secretive and "unwieldy group of individualistic entrepreneurs." Screen printers put images on everything from highway signs to pens and computer components. The market's four leading categories were decals and labels, electronic components, point-of-purchase displays, and signage.

To meet future challenges, the Screen Printing Association International, headquartered in Fairfax, Virginia, established the Screen Printing Technical Foundation in 1985. The nonprofit foundation was charged with the responsibility of developing guidelines, testing methods, and uniform practices. Specific areas under study included ink opacity, weather exposure, process colors, ink-drying techniques, and ways to eliminate *moiré,* a problem pattern caused by improper screen alignment. Screen printers hoped that standardization would help the process become more conventional and result in increased sales.

In the mid-1990s, a new kind of printing technology emerged that allowed digital files to be uploaded into the memory of an elcographic press. No film and no plates were used; rather, the image in the memory was translated into a series of electrical pulses. A special ink—a waterbase with pigment polymers and salts to enhance conductivity—coagulated in response to the pulses, and was cold-offset onto the paper. This new process was first utilized in short-run, high-speed markets, and industry prognosticators expected it to grow quickly into the high-speed publishing arena.

CURRENT CONDITIONS

Reflecting a healthy U.S. economy, the printing industry was expected to do well in the late 1990s. Growth rates for the commercial printing industry were predicted at 2.6 percent for 1998 and 2.3 percent for 1999. Business spending in the industry was projected at a 0.6 percent growth rate for 1998. For broader industry grouping **SIC 27,** production in 1997 increased 3.3 percent over levels in 1996. **SIC 27** was projected to grow 1.1 percent in 1998 and 1.9 percent in 1999. According to data cited in *Graphic Arts Monthly,* this industry enjoyed growth in 1997 second only to the industry's surprising growth spurt of 5.9 percent in 1993.

An emerging global economic crisis slowed industry expectations during 1999, even with a booming domestic economy. Global economic conditions were expected to particularly impact the industry's exports to Asian markets, but local markets were expected to remain strong. Tighter economic conditions also caused industry establishments to consider consolidation in order to serve increasingly diverse markets. Industry leaders were well aware of global effects; only 33.1 percent of a National Association of Printers and Lithographers Business Panel expected increased business during the first six months of 1999 (down from 44.2 percent in March of 1998).

Diversification in the late 1990s in the industry was driven by customer demand as well as the economic climate. Commercial printers found themselves offering additional services including database management, facilities management, Web site design, and production of CD-ROMs. Industry establishments planned to diversify using a number of strategies, including offering all services in-house, partnering, or merging/acquiring other companies.

WORKFORCE

In 1997, this industry's 6,931 establishments employed 110,927 people. Of this total, 69.7 percent worked in production and earned an average hourly wage of $12.57.

INDUSTRY LEADERS

One of the largest organizations in the industry was the Deluxe Corporation. Deluxe was the largest check printer in the United States at the end of the 1990s, with more than half the marketshare and 15,000 employees. Through its divisions, Deluxe provides short-run computer forms, business forms, electronic tax filing services, and screen printed promotional items like pens and coffee mugs. Deluxe's subsidiary, Current, Inc., is the nation's largest direct-mail marketer of specialty products. In 1999, Deluxe's sales reached $1.7 billion, an increase of 14.6 percent. Deluxe divested of its specialty paper business in order to build its financial services. The company planned expansion overseas.

The American Banknote Corporation, formerly the United States Banknote Corporation, was one of the largest security printers in the world. In 1995, the company reported sales of $206 million. In 1993, the company expanded into Brazil, and in subsequent years the ABN-Brazil division accounted for 38 percent of the company's sales. ABN produced a wide variety of security items for corporate and commercial customers. These included products such as stock and bond certificates, travelers' checks, gift certificates, promotional coupons, dividend checks, union benefit stamps, certificates of deposit, and motor vehicle certificates of origin. ABN also supplied certificates for the emerging stock and bond exchanges in Eastern Europe and some of the former Soviet republics. In 1994, the company lost the annual U.S. postage stamp contract. During the 1990s, Mastercard, VISA, Discover, and EuroPay all carried a holograph made by ABN. At the beginning of the twenty-first century, ABN remained under investigation by the Securities Exchange Commission for alleged misrepresentation of finances by its former American Bank Note Holographics unit. About 75 percent of its sales come from overseas markets.

One of ABN's fastest growing products was currency printed for foreign governments. The company's customers include Lithuania, Estonia, Malaysia, Haiti, and Venezuela. Under normal usage, paper currency is generally replaced after approximately 15 months in circulation. However, the political turmoil experienced around the globe during the early 1990s resulted in more frequent changes. Changing political regimes caused some nations to redesign their money, newly independent countries sought to establish their own national currency, and countries experiencing rapid inflation required increased amounts of currency and changes in its denominational units. According to a report published in the *New York Times,* an ABN spokesperson estimated the cost of money was between $26 and $45 per thousand bills regardless of the denomination. Price variables depended on features employed against potential counterfeiting and other options.

RESEARCH AND TECHNOLOGY

The entire commercial printing industry has relied on continuously improving technology to remain competitive. One area under study during the late 1980s and early 1990s, was the development of better flexographic inks containing higher levels of pigment solids to improve drying and color density. Letterpress operators investigated keyless inking systems. One such system, the Civilox system, employed an ink-carrying drum to provide a continuous, evenly distributed and automatically monitored ink supply. Advocates of Civilox technology noted that converting letterpress equipment would cost an estimated $100,000, much less than the $1 million to switch to an offset press.

Another innovation developed during the early 1990s was a hybrid of web-fed technology and plateless printing, in which a special light-sensitive drum was used to print variable information for each impression made during a press run. This computer-enhanced system enabled its operators to offer personalized, mass-printed output. One industry analyst predicted that as computer and printing technologies advanced, future recipients of documents would be unable to tell the difference between an item printed on a printing press and one individually generated with a computer.

The most significant technological strides in flexography surrounded direct-to-plate (DTP) flexo technology, which was fully realized for the first time in 1996. The Illinois *Decatur Herald & Review* was the first of several newspapers to commercially use DTP in every section of the full-color newspaper. Other flexographers were moving toward DTP technology, which is advantageous because of time, resource, and environmental savings.

One recently discovered and unexpected environmental bonus for flexo is that a mixture of baking soda effectively cleans press rollers. Previous roller cleansers were hazardous to the environment, whereas the Environmental Protection Agency considers baking soda nontoxic. Printers also found that the baking soda mixture is gentle on the rubber composition rollers, and thus preserves the life of expensive equipment better than harsh cleaning agents.

By the mid-1990s, researchers at institutes like the Graphic Arts Technical Foundation were still looking for ways to address optimum ink control on flexographic presses. Of special concern was the fact that barcodes were difficult to reproduce well—the consequences of a finished job with defective bar-coding were, of course, disastrous. A new procedure called "echotopography,"—a computerized schematic of press capabilities in a given situation—was in development and would allow printers to determine exact ink density for specific kinds of paper.

In mid-1999, Fuji Film announced a new product line for the industry, including the Multi-Laser Imagesetter and the FinalProof digital halftone proofing system. According to Fuji, film-based production remained a viable and very workable part of the commercial printing process. The Multi-Laser Imagesetter complemented the Celix imagesetters and the Plate Jet 4 and 8 devices; the FinalProof digital halftone proofing system had the capability to be retrofitted to Hewlett Packard imagers to create two-sided digital bluelines. One graphic arts industry expert quoted in *Graphics Arts Monthly* expected film use to continue in the industry until at least 2010. Combs predicted the demand for film in the industry to be contributed to by the flexology sector, a new market being pursued by Fuji at the end of the 1990s.

FURTHER READING

"American Banknote Corporation," 20 March 2000. Available from http://www.hoovers.com.

"American Banknote 1995 Annual Report." American Banknote Corporation: New York, 1996.

Castegnier, Pierre. "Elcography: a New Digital Printing Alternative." *GATF World,* January/February 1997.

Darnay, Arsen J., ed. *Manufacturing USA.* 5th ed. Detroit: Gale Research, 1996.

"Deluxe Corporation," 20 March 2000. Available from http://www.hoovers.com.

Annual Report. Deluxe Corporation: Shoreview, MN, 1997. Available from http://www.hoovers.com.

Falkman, Mary Ann. "Bio-Lab Makes a Splash with In-house Bottle Decorating." *Packaging Digest,* September 1996.

"High-Speed Hot Stamp Is for In-Line Decorating." *Plastics World,* September 1996.

Kendra, Erika. "1997 Technology Forecast—Flexography." *GATF World,* January/February 1997.

———. "1997 Technology Forecast—Screen Printing." *GATF World,* January/February 1997.

———. "Single Width, CTP for Flexo, Too." *Editor & Publisher,* 4 May 1996.

Massa, Michelle. "Great Balls of Fire: The U.S. Economy Continues to Shine Despite Looming Clouds Overhead." *Graphic Arts Monthly,* June 1998.

Paparozzi, Andrew D. "Slow: Curves Ahead." *American Printer,* December 1998.

U.S. Bureau of Labor Statistics. "2759—Occupations Employed by SIC 275." *Industry-Occupation Matrix.*

U.S. Census Bureau. *1997 Economic Census—Manufacturing.* Washington: GPO 1999.

Ynostroza, Roger. "In Plain Sight: Serving Film's Legacy Base." *Graphic Arts Monthly,* May 1999.

SIC 2761

MANIFOLD BUSINESS FORMS

This category covers establishments primarily engaged in designing and printing, by any process, special forms for use in the operation of a business, in single and multiple sets, including carbonized or interleaved with carbon or otherwise processed for multiple reproduction.

NAICS CODE(S)

323116 (Manifold Business Form Printing)

The status of the manifold business form industry is directly tied to the overall health of the U.S. business sector. A bustling economy, with established businesses reporting growth and new enterprises entering the field and surviving during their first years of operation, breeds a demand for business products. The establishments engaged in printing and manufacturing manifold business forms generally limit their product lines to such forms. The number of these establishments has grown steadily throughout the 1970s, 1980s, and 1990s. Dun & Bradstreet reported 941 establishments as of 1996, an increase of approximately 100 establishments over the course of a decade. The value of shipments for 1999 was expected to be $6.8 billion, down from $7.0 billion in 1998 and $7.4 billion in 1992. Industry leaders in the late 1990s were Standard Register Co., of Dayton, Ohio; New England Business Service, Inc., of Groton, Massachusetts; and Shade/Allied, Inc., of Green Bay, Wisconsin.

In 1999 U.S. manifold business forms were exported to (dollar amounts are from January through September 1999): Canada, with $10.0 million; Mexico, with $298,000; Venezuela, with $106,000; United Kingdom, with $101,000; and Hong Kong with $89,000. The countries that imported to the United States were (dollar amounts are from January through September 1999): Canada, with $5.3 million; Mexico, with $92,000; Singapore, with $43,000; Japan, with $26,000; and Austria, with $18,000.

The number of people employed by the industry began to decrease in the early 1990s. In 1987 the industry employed 53,000 people, of which production workers accounted for 37,100. As of the mid-1990s, however, the industry employed only 45,000 people, with production workers accounting for only 32,000. This decline was partly due to the growing use of computers in businesses of all sizes. Affordable laser printers can easily produce mass-volume custom business forms of all types, rendering the need to purchase standard manifold forms unnecessary. The proliferation of electronic financial transactions has also hurt the industry, resulting in a reduced demand for standard commercial checkbooks. In addition, many companies and government facilities have started to make their forms available for download over the Internet. While widespread use of laser printers for on-demand forms, along with other industry-related factors such as increasing paper prices, suggests a challenged industry, the continued increase in revenues shows every indication of stability, albeit with a smaller workforce.

Manifold business forms are printed by commercial printing establishments and then sold to other businesses for use in all manner of transactions. Many of the establishments in this industry are regional in scope, gearing their sales and distribution efforts to a limited area. Such companies may market their products through an in-house sales team that targets area businesses, or they may sell their wares through retail office supply outlets or local printing shops. The products can be classified into two subcategories: custom and stock. Custom forms are printed to a specific enterprise's particular needs, while stock forms can be sold to and used by a wide range of establishments. Stock manifold business forms include sequentially numbered tickets, cash receipt journals, message memo pads, invoice books, and spreadsheet books. Blank standard legal documents, such as lease agreements for landlords and incorporation forms, are also a vital component of the manifold business form industry. Most Americans encounter manifold business forms in a variety of daily public transactions, but their use is often vital to behind-the-scenes business operations as well.

FURTHER READING

"Bowater to Sell Star Forms Business Unit." *Pulp & Paper,* November 1996.

"Illinois Offers Forms On-line." *St. Louis Post-Dispatch,* 11 May 1996.

"Printing and Publishing." *U.S. Industry & Trade Outlook '99.* New York: McGraw-Hill, 1999.

"Top 25 U.S. Destinations for Manifold Business Forms." *International Trade Administration,* 30 November 1999. Available from http://www.ita.doc.gov/td/ocg/exp2661.htm.

"Top 25 U.S. Sources for Manifold Business Forms." *International Trade Administration,* 30 November 1999. Available from http://www.ita.doc.gov/td/ocg/imp2661.htm.

United States Department of Labor, Bureau of Labor Statistics. *Employment, Hours, and Earnings, United States, 1990-95.* Washington, D.C.: GPO, September 1995.

SIC 2771

GREETING CARDS

This category includes establishments which publish and/or print greeting cards for all occasions. Producers of hand-painted greeting cards are classified in **SIC 8999: Services, Not Elsewhere Classified.**

NAICS CODE(S)

323110 (Commercial Lithographic Printing)
323111 (Commercial Gravure Printing)
323112 (Commercial Flexographic Printing)
323113 (Commercial Screen Printing)

323119 (Other Commercial Printing)
511191 (Greeting Card Publishers)

INDUSTRY SNAPSHOT

According to the Greeting Card Association, over 6.8 billion cards were sold in 1998. Two manufacturers dominate this business in the world: American Greetings Corporation, the largest publicly owned greeting card manufacturer in the world, and Hallmark Cards, Inc., the largest privately owned manufacturer. Together, these two companies closed out the 1990s controlling 80 percent of the $7.5 billion annual U.S. greeting card market. Gibson Greetings, Inc. was a distant third with 10 percent of industry sales. By 1998, according to the *Wall Street Journal,* American Greetings commanded a 33 percent share of the market, and Hallmark claimed 47 percent.

Throughout the latter part of the twentieth century, this industry has grown annually by roughly 1 percent, based on sales revenues. However, the Greeting Card Association has predicted an annual growth rate of 5 percent by the start of the twenty-first century due to developments in marketing and technology. *Progressive Grocer* reported that 1995 greeting card sales in supermarkets alone reached $1.9 billion. Representing a 4 percent rise in this category over 1994, this one year growth pattern shows hefty progress in what is a $3.6 billion industry.

ORGANIZATION AND STRUCTURE

Greeting card companies run their establishments on two structural models. Larger establishments have in-house creative staff, including graphic artists, designers, creative consultants/directors, and writers. Smaller companies typically use freelancers to provide these services. Generally, printing is done in-house by both large and small establishments; the notable exception to this, however, is Hallmark Cards, Inc., which has used an outside printer since the late 1940s. Common to both types of establishments is the emphasis on marketing. Leaders in this industry have highly developed distribution and marketing research and promotion systems.

Distribution. Since greeting cards formerly appeared in drug and grocery stores in relatively small quantities, manufacturers relied heavily on small-package delivery services. Hallmark Cards, Inc. used long-haul trucks and trains to ship cards from their distribution centers in Liberty, Missouri and Enfield, Connecticut to regional offices throughout the country. From there, smaller courier services handled regional distribution. But since 1995, reports *Material Handling Engineering,* Hallmark has handled all phases of its own distribution from its Research Distribution Operations division in Kansas City, a 226,000 square foot facility that uses ergonomic operator workstations, high-tech carousels, and a state-of-the-art tracking system to triple its throughput.

Other manufacturers, however, rely heavily on their relationship with couriers, notes *Distribution.* Because of the seasonal nature of most greeting cards, companies require timeliness of shipments and a courier that is able to handle the returned unsold cards at the end of a season. Moreover, throughout the year unsold cards need to be returned and replaced speedily as part of this industry's marketing strategy.

Marketing Research and Promotion. Manufacturers have structured their marketing divisions to engage in marketing research and promotion at two levels. One level addresses retailers and works with each store or regional chain to create a product mix and display specific to each retailer's sales record. The other level addresses customers directly by using consumer-specific research. The industry uses demographic studies and surveys of consumer tastes and purchasing behaviors extensively.

BACKGROUND AND DEVELOPMENT

Louis Prang, a German-born immigrant who founded a lithography business in Boston, made the first commercially printed greeting cards in America during the Christmas season of 1874. His folded cards contained messages inside, copying the newly formed tradition of Victorian English Christmas cards. Since Americans were not accustomed to purchasing greeting cards, Prang's first year of business went exclusively to England. He put his cards on the American market the following year and soon added birthday and Easter cards to his product line. But sales were slow, and by 1890 he had stopped producing cards. In *The Romance of Greeting Cards,* Ernest Dudley Chase suggests that Prang's lack of success with the American market was due in large part to the popularity of less expensive German-made greeting cards, which resembled postcards rather than greeting cards. Prang's cards costs more to produce due to their use of colors.

Joyce C. Hall, founder of Hallmark Cards, entered the greeting card industry in the early 1900s by producing postcards similar to the German-made cards. Hall had predicted that the postcard craze would not last because he felt that postcards were an inadequate means of personal communications. Hall's prediction was realized at the onset of World War I. At this time greeting cards, as known from the Victorian era, were reintroduced to the American consumer market because the war curtailed postcard shipments from European manufacturers. Greeting cards also filled a niche by providing sentiments and morale boosters sent to soldiers.

World War II saw another increase in card sales, as greetings were again sent to soldiers overseas. But this time, card sales continued to grow in post-war America as more people moved across the country and corresponded more by mail. Also, the industry grew with increased competition; at the end of the war, American Greeting Publishers (later named American Greetings Corp.) entered the market and by the mid-1950s proved to be a major competitor for Hallmark. The competition between these two industry leaders and the increase in television advertising evolved into the marketing-oriented greeting card industry of the late twentieth century.

Sales Trends. From the 1970s to the early 1990s marketing underwent major changes within this industry. At the retail level, sales to chain variety stores and drug and grocery stores increased while sales to card shops decreased. This shift from card shops to departments of other retail stores resulted in large part from changes in consumer habits, for people wished to purchase cards at the same store where they made their other purchases. In the mid-1980s, this shift was fueled by a price war among industry leaders, which dramatically reduced prices for retailers while retaining the same pre-printed prices for consumers.

Marketing directed at consumers has been historically difficult for this industry. According to *Drug Topics,* studies have revealed that card shoppers (90 percent of whom are female) do not tend to purchase cards on the basis of brand names. One approach to this marketing problem has been to attract customers through messages available in greeting cards, which reflect trends in consumer interests and lifestyles. In *Discount Merchandiser,* Ela Schwartz observed that "when it comes to responding to shifts in consumer behavior or picking up on the latest trends, greeting-card vendors are in the forefront."

The 1980s marked a departure from tradition for card manufacturers as they responded to changes in consumer behavior with "alternative" or "non-occasion" cards. The demand for such cards emerged from changes in letter-writing habits and in personal relationships. As Karen Durand, product manager at Gibson Greetings, explained to *Discount Merchandiser,* "The customer doesn't want to spend 20 minutes writing a letter, but they will spend 10 to 20 minutes finding the right card." The alternative cards assist personal communications by dealing with such topics as drug and alcohol addiction. These cards have also responded to changes in personal relationships with messages addressing topics such as coping with a divorce or living with a step-parent. Alternative cards grew in sales by nearly 10 percent per year in their first few years of production.

Another notable shift in the types of messages in greeting cards has been movement away from the more traditional poetry to conversational verse and prose. Marketing research for alternative cards showed consumers wanted straightforward messages written in a straightforward style. An exception to this trend for prose messages has been in religious cards. All of the industry leaders produce a religious or inspirational line of cards, which experienced an increase in sales during the 1990s.

By the mid-1990s the concept of market segmentation had evolved further. *Progressive Grocer* noted in August 1996 that Hallmark had developed an ethnic line with Mahogany, a highly successful selection of cards for the African American market, and that specially-designed Tree of Life cards enjoyed a growing popularity with Jewish customers.

During the mid-1990s, drugstores and supermarkets continued to be among the most important outlets for greeting cards. Since card suppliers maintained card displays, a store rarely carried more than one brand, and often worked in tandem with the manufacturer to maximize its profits. The Copps supermarket chain based in Stevens Point, Wisconsin, advertised its American Greetings cards about 15 times per year, centering efforts round seasonal events. Each store also cross-marketed by displaying birthday cards in the bakery department, Thanksgiving cards alongside turkeys, and get-well cards in the in-house drugstore. According to *Progressive Grocer* of January 1996, these efforts paid handsome dividends for Copps. The 17 corporate stores selling greetings cards enjoyed a 20 percent rise in revenues since their promotions beginning.

Innovations and Developments. Throughout the mid-1980s and early 1990s significant developments in production and distribution of greeting cards took place. In the mid-1980s an innovation in printing added to the many printing processes used by greeting card manufacturers. A process called Prismatic Imaging stamps a card with a silver dye and then prints on top of the stamping. By 1991, the House of Gold, New Jersey, which has exclusive license on the process, stamped 40 million cards annually for the greeting card industry.

In 1991, Gibson Greetings introduced a line of recyclable cards. At that time, Hallmark Cards and American Greetings had started using recyclable paper to a lesser extent in some of their products. Gibson Greetings also began using other environmentally sensitive materials in production, such as organic dyes, inks, and cleaning solutions.

A significant development in the distribution of greeting cards emerged with the use of electronic ordering and inventory control systems, known as electronic data interchange (EDI). Replacing the use of the postal service, EDI systems allow retailers to order cards through a computer linked directly to the manufacturers and independent distributors. This has facilitated speedier ordering and more accurate inventory controls.

In 1992, Hallmark and American Greetings introduced self-access personalized greeting cards, which enabled customers to create their own greeting cards at an in-store computer kiosk. A variety of designs, colors and typefaces made it possible to buy cards, which were far more original than mass-produced ones and a personal message helped to express a senders' personality.

While the idea was potentially profitable, the path of the computer kiosks was not a smooth one. Since several companies chose to introduce them almost simultaneously, there was a controversy over patent rights. In 1992, Hallmark filed a claim against American Greetings, claiming that Hallmark had marketed the concept first with its Touch-Screen Greetings, patented in July 1991 while American Greetings patented CreataCard in October 1991. Also heavily involved in the dispute was Custom Expressions, Inc., the company which had invented the technology behind these kiosks.

Nevertheless, Morry Weiss of American Greetings predicted that his company's CreataCard kiosks would generate nearly $500 million in annual sales by the end of the century, according to *Industry Week*. His reasoning, given the fact that customers were now able to express their own personal taste, was that the kiosks would not only encourage more card-buying by younger shoppers and by men, but would also make it easier for market researchers to gauge the tastes of the buying public. However, as the *Kansas City Star* noted, these kiosks did not fulfill their early promise. By June 1995, Hallmark was expected to close 1,500 of its 2,700 centers, based on a two-year survey of sales.

Other innovations of the mid-1990s came from Hallmark and American Greetings, both of whom provide card and gift shopping services through their own Web sites and online services such as America Online (AOL). Another trend ties cards to the movies. In July 1995 *Chain Drug Review* reported that Hallmark had made licensing arrangements with Disney and Warner Brothers to produce theme cards based on popular movies.

INDUSTRY LEADERS

Founded in 1910 as Hall Brothers, Hallmark Cards, Inc. has become the leading producer of greeting cards sold in the United States, with 1998 sales of $3.6 billion. Along with the other industry leaders, American Greetings Corporation ($2.2 billion in 1998 sales) and Gibson Greetings, Inc. ($398 million in 1998 sales), Hallmark also manufactures wrapping paper and other gift and novelty items.

In 1998, the privately held Hallmark employed 20,100 workers, with roughly 5,000 working in production (printing, lettering, die-cutting, and related jobs) and 700 in writing and designing. Up until the early 1990s, staff developing new cards worked independently within their own department. Hallmark reengineered this pro-

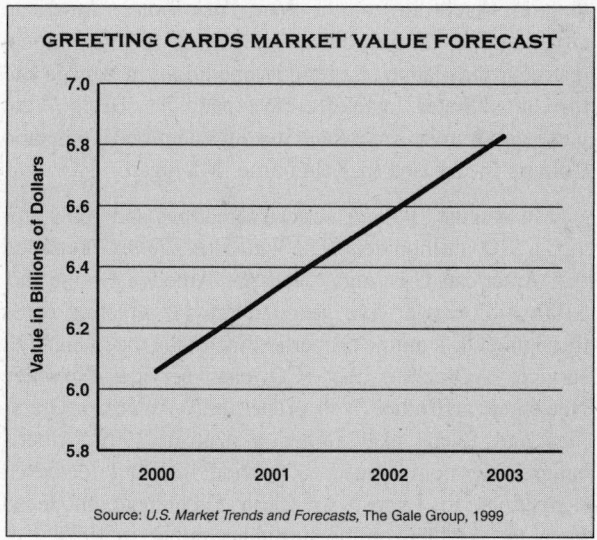

GREETING CARDS MARKET VALUE FORECAST

Value in Billions of Dollars

Source: *U.S. Market Trends and Forecasts*, The Gale Group, 1999

cess so that a team of mixed-occupation personnel (artists, writers, lithographers, merchandisers, and administrators) worked on a single holiday. This system is not expected to completely replace departments, but "should cut cycle time in half, which will not only save money, but will also make the company more responsive to changing tastes," according to *Fortune*.

Due to the growth of this industry, Hallmark and other industry leaders have diversified into new markets. In July 1999, Hallmark announced that it had bought Dayspring Cards Inc. from Cook Communications Ministries. According to the *New York Times,* Hallmark bought Dayspring with the hopes of "broadening Hallmark's appeal in the fast-growing Christian card market." Dayspring published more than 150 million cards and had sales of $52 million in the fiscal year that ended in May 1999. In addition to producing 3.5 billion Hallmark cards, Hallmark also owned Hallmark Entertainment, which produced prime time television movies. Hallmark also owns Binney and Smith, the makers of Crayola crayons and the portrait studios Picture People.

The company Web site, Hallmark.com, sought to integrate these brands and offered e-cards, gifts, and e-tools such as an online calendar and address book that would remind registered users when to send gifts and cards. Hallmark.com originally offered 1,600 e-cards, 1,200 of which were free. In October 1999, the *Wall Street Journal* reported that Hallmark would stop charging for any of the e-cards and users would be able to send any card for free. John Sullivan, a Hallmark senior vice president in charge of on-line business, said that "Hallmark views its online mission as a way to drive sales in its stores."

During 1999 American Greetings was busy with international restructuring, acquisitions, and Web site development. In June, the greeting card company cut 650 jobs in Canada, closing manufacturing and distribution plants in

Ontario. According to the *New York Times,* American Greeting said the job cuts were part of an international restructuring plan to integrate its operations in Canada and the United States. In an effort to expand their DesignWare party-goods unit, American Greetings acquired Contempo Colours Inc., based in Kalamazoo, Michigan.

In August 1999, American Greetings and AOL created a $100 million deal. The *Wall Street Journal* reported that American Greetings ''will pay America Online Inc. $100 million over five years to provide greeting cards through AOL's online properties, including the main AOL service; AOL.com; the ICQ chat service; Netscape Netcenter; and other Web properties.'' American Greetings and Lycos also signed a deal in 1999. Americangreetings.com agreed to provide free and fee-based e-greetings to Lycos. American Greetings announced plans to take their online subsidiary public in 1999.

The Internet brought significant changes to the face of retailing during the late 1990s. As both Hallmark and American Greetings developed e-commerce sites of their own, smaller greeting card publishers were also on the Web attracting Internet users. In 1994, Stephen Schutz and Susan Polis Schutz, owners of the Blue Mountain Arts Publishing Company, created Bluemountain.com to be a ''spirtual and emotional center for the Web,'' giving away e-greeting cards. The *New York Times* reported that Bluemountain.com only used ''word-of-mouth advertising, and swiftly grew to be one of the most consistently popular sites on the Web.'' According to MediaMetrix, a company that measures the Internet audience, Bluemountain.com ranked 14th among sites on the Internet. In October 1999, Excite@Home, an Internet gateway which is majority owned by the AT&T Corporation, paid up to $1 billion to acquire Bluemountain.com. According to the *New York Times,* ''Excite@Home predicted that the acquisition would increase its audience by 40 percent, to encompass approximately 34 percent of Internet traffic.'' Both Excite@Home and Bluemountain.com benefited from being able to raise their advertising rates.

WORKFORCE

In the United States, greeting card manufacturers employ an estimated 60,000 workers. Administrative and marketing staffs make up 50 percent of the workers; additional marketing and public relations agencies frequently provide temporary personnel. Printers and production specialists make up nearly 40 percent of this work force. Graphic artists and writers account for only ten percent, but their numbers are expected to increase with increased production of alternative cards.

AMERICA AND THE WORLD

According to the Greeting Card Association, this industry has virtually no competition from foreign manu-facturers selling in the United States. As exporters of greeting cards, the American industry has limited its business due to the high cost of small shipments. American exporters primarily license foreign printers to print their cards. Canada and the United Kingdom are the largest importers of American-made greeting cards.

FURTHER READING

''American Greetings Acquisition.'' *Wall Street Journal,* 31 August 1999.

''American Greetings and AOL Set $100 Million Alliance.'' *Wall Street Journal,* 5 August 1999.

''American Greetings to Cut 650 Jobs and Take a Charge.'' *New York Times,* 24 June 1999.

''American Greetings, Lycos Deal.'' *Wall Street Journal,* 10 October 1999.

Brooklyn Public Library. *Business Rankings Annual 1999.* Farmington Hills, Michigan: Gale Group, 1998.

Brown, Jeannette. ''Flowers, Candy and an e-Valentine.'' *Business Week,* 22 February 1998.

———. ''Carousels Drive Hallmark's New Selection System.'' *Material Handling Engineering,* November 1995.

Cheng, Kipp. '' Hallmark.com Revamps Consumer-Targeted Site.'' *Mediaweek,* 24 May 1999.

Cohen, Jeffrey. ''It's in the Cards.'' *Progressive Grocer,* January 1996.

''Company to Stop Charging for Electronic Greetings.'' *Wall Street Journal,* 26 October 1999.

''Greeting Cards.'' *Progressive Grocer,* August 1996.

''Greeting Cards: Party On.'' *Progressive Grocer,* June 1996.

''Hallmark Buys a Rival.'' *New York Times,* 22 July 1999.

''Hallmark Keeps Close Eye on Emerging Market Trends.''*Chain Drug Review,* 3 July 1995.

''Hallmark Shifts Card Strategy.'' *Kansas City Star,* 21 June 1995.

''Hallmark Takes to the Net and Sentiments Go E-Mail.'' *Kansas City Business Journal,* 15 November 1996.

Kaufman, Leslie. ''Excite@Home to Acquire Bluemountain.''*New York Times,* 26 October 1999.

Market Share Reporter 2000, Farmington Hills, Michigan: Gale Group, 1999.

McCormack, Kevin. ''Greetings from Hallmark.'' *Adweek,* 11 November 1996.

Stern, William M., ''Loyal to a Fault,'' *Forbes,* 14 March 1994.

Symons, Allene ''Alternative Card Lines Attract Younger Market.'' *Drug Store News,* 7 June 1999.

Symons, Allene ''Card Manufacturers Face Productivity Changes.'' *Drug Store News,* 7 June 1999.

Symons, Allene ''Greeting Cards Go for the Heart of the Market.'' *Drug Store News,* 14 December 1998.

Ward's Business Directory of U.S. Private and Public Companies 2000, Volume 4 Farmington Hills, Michigan: Gale Group, 1999.

SIC 2782

BLANKBOOKS, LOOSELEAF BINDERS AND DEVICES

This industry consists of establishments primarily engaged in manufacturing blankbooks, including checkbooks and books with ruling paper, and looseleaf binders. Other items included in this industry are albums, ruled chart and graph paper, and record albums.

NAICS CODE(S)

323110 (Commercial Lithographic Printing)
323111 (Commercial Gravure Printing)
323112 (Commercial Flexographic Printing)
323113 (Commercial Screen Printing)
323119 (Other Commercial Printing)
323118 (Blankbook, Loose-leaf Binder and Device Manufacturing)

While blankbooks have been produced since the advent of the first printing presses, the modern-day concept of the looseleaf binder is less than 50 years old in the United States. The production of blankbooks, which includes checkbooks, ledgersheets, accounting books, and diaries, has changed little in its U.S. history, until recently. Modernization has replaced letterpress with offset printing for the small amount of actual printing involved in blankbook manufacturing.

The largest checkbook producers looked to product diversification for increased profits in the early 1990s, but mid-size checkbook companies in the late 1990s were reportedly focusing on improving existing check printing systems to meet the ever-growing volume of checks written in the United States each year. One report stated that 61 billion checks were written in 1995, a figure that was increasing in the late 1990s by about 2 percent per year.

The looseleaf binder manufacturers have seen growth through innovation and diversification within their product lines. According to Fred Ferris of *American Printer,* the ''most exciting development'' in this sector of the industry in recent years has been the use of 4-color lithograph on vinyl. This has greatly eased the majority of the industry's manufacturing, which entails the production of custom-designed binders with company logos and other artwork.

Another major development for looseleaf binder manufacturers was the introduction of new flexible vinyls for binder covers; these vinyls are more durable and tighter fitting than their predecessors. However, these new vinyls have posed problems for the industry because they are harmful to the environment; the vinyl does not decompose in landfills and releases a hazardous chemical when incinerated.

Competition among manufacturers is generally concentrated in the area of accessories, such as supplementary pockets and slots designed to carry additional awkward items. From the mid-1980s, binders with accessories have remained in strong demand with the advent of organizers—looseleaf datebooks with inserts, such as foldout maps and charts. For looseleaf binder manufacturers involved in the production of organizers, diversification has also been realized with profits derived from the sale of a large variety of insert refills.

Despite recurring predictions that blankbooks and looseleaf binder manufacturers would suffer as a result of the emergence of the computer industry, the industry has experienced considerable growth during the 1980s and 1990s. In fact, with the increase of computer use, this industry has increased its production for computer-related products.

In 1999 the largest company, nationally and internationally, in sales for blankbooks and looseleaf binders was ACCO World Corp., with $1.3 billion in sales and 9,200 employees. Its U.S. subsidiary, ACCO USA, Inc., generated $1 billion in sales and had 4,000 employees. Safeguard Business Systems, Inc., ACCO USA, Inc., and Holson Burnes Group, Inc., totaled approximately $480 million in sales for that year. According to a Dun & Bradstreet study, there were 851 establishments within this category in 1996, with the value of shipments estimated at $4.3 billion.

In 1999, more then 60,000 people worked in this industry. Production workers earned an average of $11.05 hourly for an average work week of 39.2 hours with 2.9 overtime hours.

FURTHER READING

Average Hours and Earnings of Production and Nonsupervisory Workers on Private Nonfarm Payrolls, Bureau of Labor Statistics, 1999. Available from http://www.bls.gov.

Dun's Census of American Business 1996, Bethlehem, PA: Dun & Bradstreet, 1996.

Employment—National, Not Seasonally Adjusted Data, Bureau of Labor Statistics, 1999. Available from http://www.bls.gov.

SIC 2789

BOOKBINDING AND RELATED WORK

This industry covers establishments providing edition, trade, job, and library bookbinding and related services, such as paper bronzing, gilding and edging, and mounting of maps and samples. The classification covers only establishments primarily binding books printed elsewhere; establishments binding books printed at the same establishment are classified in **SIC 2731: Books: Publishing, or Publishing and Printing** and **SIC 2732: Book Printing.**

NAICS CODE(S)

323121 (Tradebinding and Related Work)

INDUSTRY SNAPSHOT

While some feared that the Internet Age would signal a decline in bookbinders' business, no such losses had been realized by the late 1990s. The total value of bookbinding shipments jumped to nearly $2 billion in 1999, up from $1.38 billion in 1994. In 1997 1,250 bookbinderies were in operation in the United States, employing more than 31,350 individuals. Only 400 establishments had more than 20 employees, while an equal number had fewer than five. More than two-thirds of the industry's labor force worked in the 150 largest binderies. The majority of small to medium binderies were subsidiaries of the commercial printing industry.

ORGANIZATION AND STRUCTURE

Bookbinding falls into several categories: edition (large runs), job binding (short runs), library, pamphlet, manifold (business forms or ledgers), and blankbook binding. Highly specialized preservation bookbinders usually attempt to restore original bindings of old books. Bookbinders are generally also involved in postpress work, including collating, perforating, folding, glueing, die-cutting, stamping, and other operations. These peripheral activities generated about $550.1 million in revenues for bookbinders in 1997.

There were three major associations concerned with bookbinding: Book Manufacturers Institute, Bookbinders' Guild, and the Society of Bookbinders.

BACKGROUND AND DEVELOPMENT

Until the 1980s, few developments were made in the binding process, although more establishments emerged in response to the demand for more magazines and books. In 1988 Otava Publishing in Finland introduced America to a binding process called Otabind, which enables books to stay open and lie flat without damaging the spine of the book. The process was developed in 1980 and has since been used increasingly throughout Europe. Otabind has proven highly valuable to trade printers who produce computer manuals, previously made with costly spinal binders. The predecessors to Otabind were the centuries-old casebinding, wherein cases (folded sheets of paper) were stitched together, and perfect-binding, a modern innovation that applied durable adhesives directly to the edge of unfolded paper, replacing the time-consuming folding and stitching process.

Given the expense of new machines and adhesives needed to implement the Otabind process, it was slow to gain popularity with binders. In order to justify costs, binders needed to take on large runs using Otabind. This problem was reduced with the introduction of RepKover—meaning reinforced paperback cover—which uses cloth strips for pre-assembly of covers, allowing printers to send partially bound books to a binder for Otabinding. This has enabled binders to accept numerous small orders, adding up to a large run. By the end of the 1990s, a number of versions in of the Otabind process were in use throughout the United States.

New equipment to improve binding included Xerox's ChannelBind System that provided 2.5 tons of clamping force; the Muller Martini Trendbinder; the BQ-440 perfect binder; and the Profinish CT-1000 casing machine that doubled the amount of hand production from 50 to 100 per hour. Bindery equipment manufacturers all emphasized equipment that utilized digital technology to integrate components, simplify set-up steps, and boost productivity. In the mid-1990s new saddle-stitching systems were introduced, among them the Stahl USA ST-90 with the capability of converting untrimmed signatures into completed books.

Other significant innovations in this industry have come from the use of new adhesives and less labor-intensive machines. Polyurethane resin (PUR) added durability to bindings, and Polyvinyl acetate (PVA) added flexibility. PVA proved valuable in manufacturing because it can be applied cold. Less labor-intensive machines have also appeared in binderies in response to employee health problems, such as carpal tunnel syndrome—a result of hand gathering and feeding.

CURRENT CONDITIONS

Hardbound edition printing, which includes textbooks for all levels of schooling as well as hardcover technical, business, consumer, trade, and professional books, accounted for $83.6 million in shipments in 1997. Library binding, involving the hardcover binding of libraries' periodicals collections, generated sales of $181.6 million. Binding of pamphlets and similar softcover products totaled $157.3 million. Total shipments for other book and pamphlet binding and related work were valued at $1.23 billion.

The traditional customer base for bookbinderies was centered in the library market, binding periodicals and books for libraries shelving systems. In the late 1990s, however, bookbinderies were shifting an increasing proportion of their business to commercial printers. In many cases this lead to the wholesale integration of binding activities into the printers' operations.

Bookbinders themselves were also expanding their capacity during this period, as well as integrating more technologically sophisticated operations into their facilities. Market leader Bindagraphics, for instance, upgraded its plant to incorporate a more diverse product line in-house, thus enabling the firm to handle complex orders efficiently and quickly at one facility.

Changes were occurring both in the processing and the promotion of bindery products and services, among them targeted advertising and increased distribution. General binding and finishing were among the top services provided in-house at many small commercial and quick printers. Guillotine cutters found a home as an accessory for on-demand color printers and direct-imaging presses.

Throughout the 1990s, new concerns arose over the education and safety of employees. The rapid technological changes in the industry required employee training and specialized education. Employee safety became increasingly important with discoveries that the new adhesives were hazardous to air quality. This factor also gained the attention of customers, who were concerned about the contents of the chemicals used in the binding process and the environmental consequences of getting rid of bound materials. There was some concern regarding recycling ethylene-vinyl acetate (EVA)—a hot-melt adhesive preferred for its excellent adhesion to a variety of paper and cardboard stocks. Water dispersible hot melt adhesives were the only type that could be repulped. In the late 1990s, chemical manufacturers successfully negotiated with the Environmental Protection Agency (EPA) to avoid a rewrite of the Toxic Substances Control Act, which most likely would translate into significantly increased operating costs for bookbinders. In place of a rewrite, chemical manufacturers were testing high-production volume (HPV) chemicals to ensure their safe exposure levels. Furthermore, greater consumer awareness of environmental hazards posed by chemical levels spurred the bookbinding industry to turn away from traditional solvents toward "green" materials such as thermoplastic polyurethanes (TPUs).

INDUSTRY LEADERS

Leading firms in the bookbinding industry at the end of the 1990s included Bindagraphics of Baltimore, Maryland, with more than 200 employees and 1998 revenues of $15 million; Reindl Bindery Company of Glendale, Wisconsin; Universal Printing Co., Inc. of St. Louis, Missouri; Houchen Bindery Ltd. of Utica, Nebraska; and CPI Graphics, Inc. of Lansing, Michigan.

WORKFORCE

More than 31,350 workers were employed in the bookbinding industry in 1997 with media weekly earnings of $460. About 80 percent of these were production workers, earning an average of $10.67 per hour. The

majority of jobs were in commercial printing plants. The demand for bindery workers was expected to grow more slowly than for most other occupations through the year 2005. Demand for printed material is expected to increase, but heightened productivity will be accomplished increasingly on more efficient processes and automation.

FURTHER READING
Adams, Cheryl. "Build It And They Will Come." *Printing Impressions,* March 1999.

"Bound For Change." *Graphic Arts Monthly,* May 1990.

Fairley, Peter. "HPV Rule: Legal Hammer or Litigation Bait." *Chemical Week,* March 1999.

Larkin, Jim. "Simplify, Don't Digitize." *Printing Impressions,* January 2000.

Marks, P.J.M. *The British Library Guide to Bookbinding : History and Techniques.* Toronto: University of Toronto Press, 1998.

U.S. Bureau of the Census. *Census of Manufacturers 1997,* Washington, D.C.: GPO, 3 November 1999.

U.S. Department of Commerce. International Trade Association. *U.S. Industry and Trade Outlook 1999,* New York: The McGraw Hill Companies, 1999.

SIC 2791

TYPESETTING

This classification includes establishments primarily engaged in typesetting for the trade, including advertising typesetting, hand or machine composition, photocomposition, phototypesetting, computer-controlled typesetting, and typographic composition.

NAICS CODE(S)
323122 (Prepress Services)

INDUSTRY SNAPSHOT

In 1997, the industry shipped $2.35 billion worth of goods, up from $1.81 billion in 1992. The industry employed 27,754 people, 74 percent of whom were production workers earning an average hourly wage of $16.05. California shipped $585.8 million worth of goods and employed 6,054 people, both high marks for the nation.

By the 1990s, the typesetting industry had been revolutionized by electronic technology, resulting in frequently upgraded equipment, redefined job functions, retraining of workers, and expansion of services provided to clients. New technology allowed faster turnaround on jobs, and typesetting companies were under pressure to continue to improve their equipment for even faster results.

The growing popularity of desktop publishing allowed many of typesetting's traditional clients to produce their own newsletters, advertising, and other print materials instead of contracting with typesetters for the work. Many organizations and businesses, however, elected not to become their own publishers and continued to contract with typesetters and other preprint services. With the burst of personal computers at home and in businesses, many producers of printed materials used a combination of their own computer-based technology and outside typesetting services. Typesetting remained in the 1990s an essential service industry for book publishers, magazine publishers, advertising agencies, catalog companies, and other large and small businesses.

ORGANIZATION AND STRUCTURE

The typesetting industry includes large, multimillion dollar shops with several hundred employees as well as small shops with only a few employees. Many of the larger companies offer related services, including printing, bookbinding, development, and sales of custom computer systems for desktop publishing or typesetting to client companies. Many large typesetting companies have areas of specialization as well, producing catalogs for car parts companies, textbooks, trade paperbacks, financial reports, and so on.

Jobs that come into typesetting establishments must be compatible with the typesetting system. Creating this compatibility can be complex. Typesetting companies accept word processing disks from clients and convert them for use on their own systems. With the new flexibility—but potential incompatibility—of increasingly sophisticated systems, software, and hardware, the typesetting shop may enter the publishing process sooner than it has in the past. With electronic capabilities, the client and typesetting shop may test various formats and styles before actually doing the typesetting job to make sure that the two systems will work together without glitches and to be sure that the client's word processing control codes can automatically be converted to phototypesetting control codes. Most of the code conversion can be done automatically, with the typesetting operator making few decisions other than those concerning hyphenation, justification, and final output.

Desktop systems offer "what you see is what you get" technology. That is, the screen displays the text and layout exactly as it will appear on the finished page. Commercial digitized typesetting equipment also offers this electronic pagination. Once material is input, the page can be automatically arranged according to batch page processing, or an operator can manipulate the elements on the page. Because the material can be altered on screen before any hard version has been produced, changes are less expensive and time-consuming.

Large companies, such as Black Dot Graphics in Crystal Lake, Illinois, have expanded their services to a point where they are considered "electronic prepress service bureaus." They provide technical assistance as well as typesetting to their clients. According to *Publishers Weekly,* these companies "are at the forefront of technical innovation in a field where technology is advancing at a breathless rate." When Black Dot began in the 1960s, it provided photocomposition services to book publishers. By the 1990s, Black Dot and other typesetters were providing a broad range of services for both color and black-and-white jobs, from initial input of data to output of printing plates or final page proofs, or any services in between, including illustration, pagination, and integration of words and graphics.

BACKGROUND AND DEVELOPMENT

Typesetting changed drastically during the last 40 years of the twentieth century. For hundreds of years, type was set with metal printing elements; this was called "hot type" because molten lead was used to manufacture individual letters, which were then set into complete words, sentences, and paragraphs. At first, the molten lead letters were set by hand, one letter or space at a time. The letters were mirror images of actual letters so that, when printed, they would read correctly. The set type was locked into a frame and ink applied to it, and the paper was printed directly from the type.

In 1886, Ottmar Mergenthaler invented a typesetting machine, which became known as a Linotype machine. This was also a hot type method, but it sped up typesetting considerably. Typesetting machines became faster and more sophisticated for the next 80 to 90 years, but operated on the same principle as the one Johann Gutenberg used in the 1400s when he invented movable type.

Unlike hot type, which is three-dimensional, "cold type" is two-dimensional. Cold type is generally regarded as any of a variety of methods in which photographic principles are used to create an image on specially treated paper. It came into widespread use in the 1970s. As a typesetter keyed in the letters, the machine made photographic images of them and reproduced those images on photosensitive paper or film. The images were arranged on a layout sheet and the printer photographed it to make a film negative from which a printing plate was then made.

Cold type has undergone several generations of change in both data storage and output. They all begin with keying in the text on a keyboard like that of a typewriter. That data input may be done by a typesetter, but generally that is now done by authors as they compose with word processors.

The first phototypesetting equipment stored the text on paper tape. The tape was punched using a special keyboard, and this specially-punched encoded tape drove the typesetting equipment, sending instructions about typeface, size, and appearance of the set type.

The next development in phototypesetting brought equipment with powerful software, photo fonts, and magnetic data storage. This was actually the first true phototypesetting machinery, and in the 1990s, was still in use in many typesetting operations.

The next generation of cold type created characters from digital information instead of a photo negative. Output is produced on photosensitive paper or film. This equipment became the standard in the 1980s. Subsequent generations of equipment employed various laser technologies for output. This is not phototypesetting since it does not employ photographic technology and output is on regular paper rather than photosensitive paper.

CURRENT CONDITIONS

The application of electronics and computers moved the industry to digitized imaging in which material is printed directly from the computer to paper or a printing plate. More typesetting companies are offering extensive preprinting services, including digital color scanning with electronic dot generation, electronic color page composition, electronic page layout, and off-press color proofing. Although many typesetting shops were still using traditional phototypesetting equipment in the early 1990s, digital typesetting is likely to make such methodologies obsolete in years to come.

Digitized typesetting opened up a world of possibilities for interface technology, the ability of two computers to communicate with one another. Some experts in the typesetting industry were predicting that by the year 2000, 50 to 75 percent of typesetting would be accomplished via interface technology.

Data may be transferred through direct or remote interfacing. Direct interface includes a cable connection with other computers such as word processors or personal computers; optical character recognition by means of scanners; media conversion (conversion of word processing program on disk to typesetting software; or reading magnetic or paper tape). Remote interfacing refers to telecommunication through a modem.

Interfacing, regardless of the method, however, requires appropriate software for conversion from word processing to typesetting equipment. Not all word processing programs and typesetting equipment, however, are compatible, requiring client and typesetter to coordinate their work in advance of transmission. Typesetters do not ordinarily have the capability to convert all of the hundreds of word processing programs to their typesetting programs; however, a third-party service bureau can handle most conversions.

Such varied technological advances, however, allowed publishers to transmit manuscripts to keyboarders or typesetters in other countries with lower wages, thereby cutting publishing costs. Use of satellite and other technology is expected to further expand publishers' options.

The role of typesetting is expected to expand to include some layout or "paste-up" work as well. Desktop publishing systems offer this capability, and its use in commercial typesetting is growing. While in the past, typeset copy was passed on to an artist who arranged the various graphic and textual components on the page and then pasted them onto a layout sheet, components can now be arranged on the computer screen and corrections made before anything is printed out on paper or film. Even photographs or illustrations can be inserted on screen by use of digital scanners. Once the layout is complete, it is transmitted for reproduction onto paper, film, or even directly onto a plate for printing.

INDUSTRY LEADERS

The typesetting industry was led throughout the 1990s by Merrill Corporation, a public company based in St. Paul, Minnesota, that boasted 1999 sales of $509.5 million. The company had 34 U.S. offices and employed 3,933 people.

Other typesetters of note include the Black Dot Group, headquartered in Crystal Lake, Illinois; York Graphic Services Incorporated, based in York, Pennsylvania; and Composing Room Incorporated, based in Pennsauken, New Jersey.

WORKFORCE

There were 2,069 U.S. typesetting establishments as of 1997, more than half of which had fewer than five employees. The U.S. Census Bureau reported a 26 percent decrease in the number of employees in this industry between 1987 and 1997—from 37,600 to 27,754. However, while it may be true that technology tends to reduce the labor needed to attain the same results over time, the typesetting industry may see improvements in their employment statistics as typesetting needs arise for electronic publications such as Web sites. Adobe Systems, for instance, a leader in providing software to the typesetting industry, began in the mid-1990s to offer software for creating Internet documents. Indeed, several of the typesetting software leaders, such as Corel Corporation and Microsoft Corporation, began to incorporate Internet publishing tools within their already popular typesetting packages.

Electronic technology changed the nature of work that typesetters do, requiring knowledge and familiarity with computers and a multitude of software programs. In typesetting, as in other prepress functions, technology required constant upgrading of skills and retraining of the workforce as more and more functions become computerized.

FURTHER READING

"Computers:Software." *Standard & Poor's Industry Surveys.* New York: Standard & Poor, 10 October 1996.

Dun's Census of American Business 1996. Bethlehem, PA: Dun & Bradstreet, 1996.

Hilts, Len. "Avoiding Potholes in the Desktop Publishing Road." *Publishers Weekly,* 18 October 1991, 34-36.

Hoover's Company Capsules, 20 March 2000. Available from http://www.hoovers.com.

McCollum, Tim. "In-House Publishing, Professional Results." *Nation's Business,* November 1996.

Perenson, Melissa. "Do-It-Yourself Publishing." *PC Magazine,* 21 January 1997.

Rosenberg, Jim. "Technology Progress '95." *Editor & Publisher,* January 1996.

Sucov, Jennifer. "Invested Interest." *Folio,* 15 October 1996.

U.S. Bureau of the Census. *1992 Census of Manufactures.* Washington: GPO, 1996. Available from http://www.census.gov/epcd/www/mc92ht27.html.

U.S. Census Bureau. *1997 Economic Census—Manufacturing.* Washington: GPO, 1999.

U.S. Department of Labor. *Employment, Hours, and Earnings, United States, 1990-95.* Washington: GPO, 1995.

Ward's Business Directory of U.S. Private and Public Companies. Detroit: Gale Research, 1997.

SIC 2796

PLATEMAKING AND RELATED SERVICES

This category covers establishments primarily engaged in making plates for printing purposes and in related services. Also included are establishments primarily engaged in making positives or negatives from which offset lithographic plates are made. These establishments do not print from the plates they make, but prepare them for use by others. Engraving for purposes other than printing is classified in **SIC 3479: Coating, Engraving, and Allied Services, Not Elsewhere Classified.**

NAICS CODE(S)

323122 (Prepress Services)

INDUSTRY SNAPSHOT

The platemaking and related services industry was comprised primarily of companies that made printing plates used in offset lithographic printing processes. It also encompassed platemaking for numerous miscellaneous printing processes, such as gravure and letterpress. Lithography was introduced in 1796 and became popular during the 1900s. Offset printing, first applied in 1902, came to represent about 40 percent of all U.S. printing.

Steady demand growth for lithographic and related printing boosted platemaking service industry revenues to about $2.4 billion in 1987, the first year in which this industry was separately classified. Steady growth in printing markets pushed platemaking industry sales steadily upward to nearly $3.5 billion by the mid-1990s. Likewise, sales and employment are forecast to continue growing through the early 2000s, bolstered by new printing technologies and greater demand.

ORGANIZATION AND STRUCTURE

Most companies in the platemaking industry served lithographic printers. Lithography was a printing process whereby ink was applied to a flat printing surface (plate) that was treated with grease. Blank, or nonimage, areas of the surface repelled the ink, while the greased areas held it. The inked surface could then be transferred directly to paper by means of a press. In the popular offset (planographic or litho-offset) process, the inked image was first printed on a rubber cylinder and then transferred to other materials.

Platemaking companies created the templates that printers used to transfer images to the rubber cylinder or other printing media. The plate cylinder was usually zinc, aluminum, or a special alloy. Its porous surface was coated with a photosensitive material. When exposed to an image, the coated area hardened and the coating on the nonimage areas was washed away. Ink, which was continually deposited on the plate cylinder by inking rollers, was accepted by the greasy image on the plate. Modern offset printing plates were usually cylindrical, allowing them to provide a continuous transfer of ink to a rubber-covered, or blanket, cylinder.

A variety of plates were used for different offset printing processes and print jobs. Basic monometal plates were made of zinc or aluminum and functioned as described above. The plate was usually exposed to an image by covering it with a negative of text or illustrations and exposing it to intense light, after which the coating on the unexposed areas was washed away. A slight variation was the presensitized plate, which had a coating with a longer life span and could be made of paper or plastic for short print jobs.

Deep-etch plates, in contrast to monometal, exposed the plate to a positive of the text or illustration. The nonprinting areas were hardened and the printing areas were washed away. A mild acid bath etched the metal of the printing areas. The plate was then treated with an ink-receptive lacquer. Deep-etch plates were used for longer print runs of 250,000 or more copies. Bi-metal and tri-metal plates were more durable and could dependably endure runs of 500,000 copies or more. They were created using two or three metal plates, one or two of which covered the primary plate as a microscopic film. A photoengraving process partly removed the thin metal layers.

In addition to conventional offset plates were several other platemaking processes. Electrostatic (xerographic) plates, for example, were electrically charged plates that absorbed images. A negatively charged powder (stuck to the positively charged image) was heated and hardened and acted as the ink-receptive printing surface. Similarly, immediate offset plates incorporated a polymer layer that responded to heat, as opposed to light.

In addition to lithography, other types of printing processes used plates. Rotogravure, for example, transferred fluid ink contained in the cells of the printing cylinder, or plate. Nonprint areas of the plate were kept ink-free through constant wiping. Rotogravure plates were made in a process that utilized carbon tissue paper soaked in an emulsion and exposed to an image. The carbon-imprint was then transferred to a (usually copper) cylindrical plate. Rotogravure was often used to produce high-quality color illustrations. In addition to plates for rotogravure printing were plates for collotype printing, which generated high-quality color photo reproductions; flexographic printing, used for large-scale commercial printing (for newspapers and magazines); and other miscellaneous processes.

BACKGROUND AND DEVELOPMENT

During the second century A.D., the Chinese were capable of printing on paper using ink on stone surfaces with carved impressions, precursors to modern day printing plates. In about 1040, Chinese alchemist Pi Sheng designed a crude printing plate consisting of an iron plate coated with a mixture of resin, wax, and paper ash. Other rough printing plate forms were used in subsequent print processes, such as xylography (fourteenth century), metallographic printing (1430), typography (fifteenth century), and stereotypy (eighteenth century).

Czechoslovakian Alloys Senefelder envisioned the lithographic printing process in 1796. The first mechanized lithographic printer, complete with a plate cylinder, was built in 1850. Importantly, technological advancements during the early 1800s related to etching and photosensitivity made Senefelder's design possible. Gravure and rotogravure platemaking processes were first used in the 1890s.

It was not until the early 1900s that lithographic platemaking became widespread. The popularity of lithography, and even of modern day printing techniques, was largely a result of American Ira W. Rubel's discovery of offset printing in 1902. Rubel accidentally trans-

ferred an image from a plate cylinder to a rubber blanket, discovering that the rubber offset produced a superior image to that of the metal plate. The popularity of offset lithography spawned a flurry of advancements during the mid-1900s in the area of chemical etching, electroplating, and other technologies that were integrated into the printing and platemaking process.

Besides general economic expansion during the 1960s, 1970s, and 1980s, new inks and printing processes bolstered platemaking industry revenues. By 1987, the first year in which this industry was separately classified, platemaking companies garnered about $2.4 billion annually and employed a workforce of more than 30,000 people. Industry sales expanded to more than $3 billion annually in the 1990s.

CURRENT CONDITIONS

The continual increase in revenues is stimulated by a general increase in demand for printed materials as well as technological advancements that increased the use of plate printing processes. For example, markets for several types of printed packaging ballooned, as did demand for direct mail and catalog printing. And higher quality, faster, and less expensive printing processes, such as waterless sheetfed printing, boosted demand. Likewise, new computer technologies improved the platemaking process. Advanced desktop publishing software, for example, was integrated into digital platemaking processes to quickly produce relatively inexpensive, high-quality plates.

In the 1990s, lithographic platemaking services accounted for about 57 percent of industry sales. Color film platemaking represented the large majority of the lithographic segment, followed by various noncolor plate services. Deep-etch metal plates accounted for less than 0.5 percent of industry receipts, as did multi-metal plate processes. Aside from lithography, gravure cylinders made up almost 6 percent of industry revenues, and flexographic plates represented about 3 percent. Miscellaneous services, such as letterpress and electrostatic platemaking, comprised the remainder of sales.

Commercial printers of consumer packaging, marketing materials, and a plethora of other media accounted for roughly 75 percent of the demand for platemaking services in the early 1990s. The balance of the market was comprised of newspaper publishers, book printers, and publishers, magazines, and numerous smaller markets.

The mid-1990s saw an exciting development in the platemaking industry. Computer-to-plate systems, (CTP), had taken over the industry spotlight. CTP promised a quantum leap in productivity for printers. It required fewer materials and less labor while offering enhanced quality and faster turnarounds. At the turn of the century, commercial printers moved toward exclusive use of the digital technology, which included digital copy and proofing. The completely digital technology offered a better quality product because of the precision and decreased production time that CTP offers. Film-based work was rapidly becoming obsolete.

However, the change from conventional methods will be slow. DuPont Printing & Publishing projects that, by 2003, the percentage of pages printed via conventional means will fall only 30 percent from its 1996 level of 95 percent. As of late 1996, *Graphic Arts Monthly* reported plate manufacturer expectations that CTP will account for 15 percent of all printing plates by 2001 and that conventional plates won't disappear for "some time. In addition, in 1999, plates made from polyester rather than from metal were coming into use. The polyester material is more flexible and less expensive than its metal counterparts."

INDUSTRY LEADERS

More than 1,700 U.S. companies provided platemaking services in 1996. The industry was highly fragmented, consisting mostly of small, localized manufacturers with just a few employees. Polychrome Corp., of Fort Lee, New Jersey, was the largest industry participant, with $500 million in sales and about 1,700 workers in 1996. Eastman Kodak followed with 1996 sales of $260 million from platemaking services. The companies were combined by 1999 into Kodak Polychrome Graphics. Another industry leader was Matthews International Corp. of Pennsylvania, which had sales of around $50 million in 1998.

WORKFORCE

Contrary to employment prospects for most U.S. manufacturing industries, job growth in printing trade services was expected to be robust between 1990 and 2005, according to the Bureau of Labor Statistics. Overall employment for platemaking laborers was forecast to rise 30 percent by 2005, despite anticipated productivity gains resulting from automation. Even positions for general managers and executives should rise an estimated 20 percent.

FURTHER READING

Dun's Census of American Business 1996, Bethlehem, PA: Dun & Bradstreet, 1996.

Duschene, Stephanie. "A Running Start Into Computer-to-Plate." *American Printer,* 22 February 1999.

Esler, Bill. "Conventional Plates Hold Their Ground." *Graphic Arts Monthly,* July 1996.

Employment, Hours, and Earnings, United States, 1990-95. Washington, D.C.: United States Department of Labor, Bureau of Labor Statistics, September 1995.

Hilts, Paul. "CTP for the Rest of Us." *Publishers Weekly,* 15 April 1996.

"Hoover's Company Capsules." *Hoover's Online: The Business Network,* 1999. Available from http://www.hoovers.com.

Johnston, Peter. "CTP: Poised on the Brink of Success." *Graphic Arts Monthly,* April 1996.

O'Brien, Katherine. "Polyester Becomes Fashionable." *American Printer,* 9 March 1999.

"Prepress Workers." *1998-99 Occupational Outlook Handbook,* 1999. Available from http://www.bls.gov.

Shepherd, Gary. "Pre-Press House Skips a Generation, Goes Digital." *Tampa Bay Business Journal,* 22 July 1996. Available from http://www.amcity.com/tampabay/stories/072296.

CHEMICALS & ALLIED PRODUCTS

ALKALIES AND CHLORINE

This industry classification includes establishments engaged in manufacturing alkalies and chlorine. Examples of products include compressed or liquefied chlorine, sodium or potassium hydroxide, sodium bicarbonate, and soda ash (not produced at mines). Alkalies produced by mining are classified in **SIC 1474: Potash, Soda, and Borate Minerals.**

NAICS CODE(S)

325181 (Alkalies and Chlorine Manufacturing)

INDUSTRY SNAPSHOT

The two primary commodities offered by the alkalies and chlorine industry are chlorine and sodium hydroxide (caustic soda), together representing about 82 percent of all shipments. Soda ash, an alkali product used in glassmaking, water treatment, pulp bleaching, and detergent manufacturing, accounts for only 14 percent of shipments. Other products account for the remaining 4 percent.

Chlorine and caustic soda have consistently appeared on lists of the top ten U.S. chemicals according to production weight. They are co-products of the same chemical process. This means that they are created at the same time and that the production of one results in the production of the other. Although there are several modern procedures used to produce chlorine and caustic soda, most rely on a technique called electrolysis. As electricity is passed through brine (a salt water solution), the brine's components, salt (sodium chloride) and water (made up of hydrogen and oxygen), recombine to form chlorine and sodium hydroxide (caustic soda) in approximately equal amounts. Some hydrogen gas also results from the process.

Organic chemical manufacturers are the primary chlorine users in the United States. Some examples of chemicals produced with chlorine are ethylene dichloride, carbon tetrachloride, and methylene chloride. These and other chlorinated organic chemicals are used to make many products, including flame retardants, herbicides, solvents, refrigerants, polyvinylchloride (PVC) pipe, and pigments. The second-largest chlorine user is the pulp and paper industry, which uses chlorine as a bleaching agent. Chlorine products are also used as raw ingredients in household and commercial bleaches, scouring powders, and automatic dishwashing compounds. Other chlorine uses include water treatment, sewage treatment, sanitizing, and metal extracting.

Caustic soda has a wide range of industrial applications. It is used in petroleum exploration and by water treatment facilities, tanneries, and the textile industry. It also plays a role in food processing, metal fabrication, and chemical manufacturing. Caustic soda is also used in industrial complexes to remove boiler scale.

According to U.S. Department of Commerce statistics, shipments within the alkalies and chlorine industry totaled $2.5 billion in 1997. In current dollars, the industry more than doubled since 1987 when it shipped $1.5 billion worth of products. Growth patterns of the various industry segments varied. Although overall growth within the chlorine and alkalies industry was expected to increase at a rate of 2 percent to 3 percent through the mid-1990s, some industry forecasters predicted the slowest growth would occur within the chlorine segment.

During the late 1980s, chlorine production increased, but, by the early 1990s, demand and production declined. The shift was attributed to economic and environmental conditions. As the national economy suffered during the recession of the late 1980s and early 1990s, construction slowed and demand for PVC products fell sharply. At the same time, pulp and paper manufacturers were turning away from chlorine-based processes because of concerns about the toxicity of dioxins, which are formed from the combination of chlorine and residue organic compounds. Other major chlorine products such as chlorofluorocarbons (CFCs) and chlorinated solvents were also under increasing criticism because of their damaging effects on the environment.

Conditions within the chlorine segment of the industry affected other products. Dropping demand for chlorine led to an oversupply, which consequently reduced chlorine prices from $145 per ton in 1986 to about $50 per ton in 1991. But because caustic soda is a co-product of chlorine, cuts in chlorine production led to shortages and higher prices within the caustic soda market. The price of caustic soda rose from approximately $120 per ton in 1986 to $300 per ton in 1991. High caustic soda prices in turn led to increased demand for alternative products such as hydrogen peroxide and soda ash.

Although soda ash has been manufactured synthetically from the evaporation of brines, it is primarily produced from trona, a mined product. The last synthetic soda ash facility in the United States closed in 1986, idling 700,000 tons of capacity. Operators closed the plant because it could not produce soda ash at prices low enough to compete with the trona-reliant process. Almost half of the domestic production of soda ash is used by glassmakers.

ORGANIZATION AND STRUCTURE

Approximately 99 percent of the chlorine and alkali chemical manufacturers in the United States and Canada belong to the Chlorine Institute, a group founded by ten industry leaders in 1924. Although its original purpose was to further the demand for chlorine, its focus shifted to providing the industry with supervision and direction following a destructive hurricane in 1926 that wrought havoc on Florida's water treatment facilities. Thousands of chlorine cylinders were shipped to the state to aid in restoring safe water supplies, but many could not be used because the industry had no previously adopted standardized fittings. The emergency chlorine supply sat idle until adapters and valves could be obtained.

As a result of this experience, the group initiated a study of valve and fitting designs and recommended a standard that was voluntarily adopted by producers. Federal officials later relied on information from the Chlorine Institute in establishing standards for all compressed gases.

The Chlorine Institute also began working on programs to improve the safety record of the industry. In the 1930s an informal policy was established for responding to emergencies. Later the institute developed a formal program called CHLOREP (Chlorine Emergency Plan).

CHLOREP consisted of volunteer teams available to respond to chlorine emergencies 24 hours a day, seven days a week. By 1991 the Chlorine Institute had trained 250 CHLOREP teams composed of members from more than 40 companies, and they were placed at more than 100 locations throughout the United States and Canada.

In addition to establishing standards and emergency response programs, the Chlorine Institute has published a wide range of manuals, pamphlets, and audiovisual materials to provide technical and safety information. The group has also worked on behalf of its members with the government agencies responsible for regulating various aspects of chemical production and shipment such as the Department of Transportation (DOT), the Interstate Commerce Commission (ICC), the Coast Guard, and the Occupational Safety and Health Administration (OSHA).

BACKGROUND AND DEVELOPMENT

The use of chlorine compounds in chemical processes dates back to at least 77 A.D., but the isolated element itself was not produced until 1774. Although chlorine is a common element, in nature it exists only in compounds because it reacts readily with other substances, both organic and inorganic. For example, ordinary table salt, or sodium chloride, consists of chlorine and sodium.

A Swedish chemist, Carl Wilhelm Scheele (1742-1786), is acknowledged as the first person to create and identify chlorine. Scheele (who also co-discovered oxygen) generated a greenish-yellow gas during experiments with sea water. He called it "dephlogisticated marine acid air." The word "dephlogisticated" referred to the fact that it was not susceptible to combustion. The phrase "marine acid air" identified the new gaseous material produced from the acid obtained from marine brine. In 1810, when Sir Humphry Davy (1778-1829) used electricity to prove that the gas was an element, he coined the word "chlorine" from *chloros,* the Greek word for greenish yellow

The bleaching effects of chlorine were first put to commercial use by textile makers in France near the end of the eighteenth century. Natural cottons and linens were light brown and required bleaching before they could be dyed with light or bright colors. Traditionally this had been accomplished by spreading the fabrics out and exposing them to the sun. Bleaching fabrics in this manner took as long as three months for cotton and as long as six months for linen. Chlorine bleaching compounds enabled textile manufacturers to keep up with the increasing speed of production that followed improvements in spinning and weaving methods.

Chlorine products were greatly improved by technology during the late eighteenth and early nineteenth centuries. In 1792 a process for bleaching rags used in paper

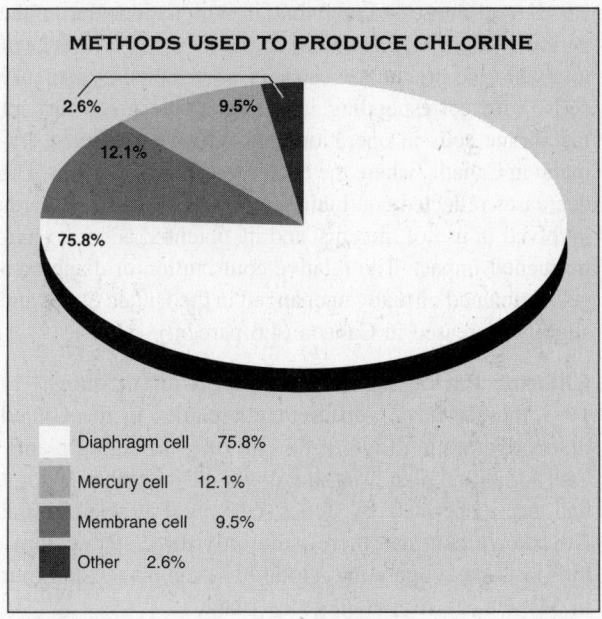

METHODS USED TO PRODUCE CHLORINE

2.6%   9.5%

12.1%

75.8%

Diaphragm cell   75.8%

Mercury cell   12.1%

Membrane cell   9.5%

Other   2.6%

making was developed. Bleaching powder, or calcium hypochlorite, was first introduced in 1799. The ability to transport chlorine to markets distant from manufacturing plants was achieved through the formation of potassium hypochlorite, a liquid product created with chlorine and caustic potash.

The development of chlorine production based on electrolysis lowered chlorine prices and increased the chemical's popularity. Electrolysis methods evolved through the mid-nineteenth century and, by the century's close, had become commercially viable in areas with low-cost electricity. The first commercial plant in the United States opened in Rumford, Maine in 1893.

As the twentieth century began, chlorine was being used for an increasing number of purposes. Jersey City, New Jersey was the first city to use chlorine to disinfect drinking water supplies. It began chlorination in 1908 and was soon followed by other major cities, including New York. Sewage treatment methods based on liquid chlorine were first adopted in Altoona, Pennsylvania, in 1913. The use of chlorine by water and sewage treatment facilities helped virtually eliminate diseases such as cholera, typhoid, and dysentery.

Not all chlorine's uses, however, were benevolent. During World War I, chlorine gas, an extremely poisonous substance, was used as a weapon against the Allies. Despite the horrors associated with chlorine gas, the U.S. chlorine production industry benefited from the war. Imports of chemicals from Europe were sharply curtailed because of submarine warfare. As a result, domestic production tripled and continued to grow after the war. Chlorine has also played a role in the development of insecticides, anesthetics, dry cleaning fluids, and firefighting compounds. The fledgling plastics industry re-

lied on chlorine to make its vital vinyl chloride products. Between 1955 and 1970, chlorine usage grew approximately 5.8 percent per year.

The 1970s ushered in an era of changes. Although the decade closed with chlorine production at a historic high, growth stagnated. Environmental questions hampered producers, and economic woes diminished demand by users. By the early 1990s, chlorine production and demand were still less than they had been in 1979.

Despite improvements lessening the environmental impact of chlorine and caustic soda production, the industry continued to suffer from adverse publicity concerning chlorine use. Chlorine compounds react with organic substances to form dioxins, which are suspected carcinogens and pose potential health hazards including birth defects and damage to the human skin, liver, neuroendocrine system, and immune system.

Controversy about dioxins affected usage by pulp and paper producers, one of the largest chlorine-consuming industries. Chlorine was traditionally used to bleach pulp and create white paper products. Increasingly, manufacturers were turning to innovative oxygen and hydrogen peroxide bleaching technologies. Analysts estimated that the pulp and paper industry used only about 9 percent of the domestic chlorine production in 1994, a drop from 15 percent in 1990.

Environmental groups increasingly protested the use of chlorine in other areas as well. Chlorofluorocarbons (CFCs) are suspected of damaging the ozone layer of the earth's upper atmosphere. Chlorinated solvents were considered a source of air pollution because of their emissions. In addition, some water treatment facilities began turning away from chlorine to other methods of water purification. According to the Chlorine Institute, however, calls to eliminate chlorine are unreasonable because of the heavy financial burden of meeting such restrictions.

Despite the problems associated with chlorine and its declines in traditional markets, industry analysts anticipate overall demand to grow and prices to increase as much as 15 percent by 2002. Vinyl exports and PVC use in new construction and in remodeling are expected to make up for the declines in other areas.

Soda Ash. In the 1990s, the global soda ash industry saw many non-U.S. companies acquire U.S. producers. For example, Solvay, the world's largest soda ash producer (headquartered in Brussels), purchased Tenneco's soda ash division in 1992. As a result of the acquisition, Solvay controlled almost half of U.S. soda ash production and was positioned to expand in the Asian Pacific and Latin American markets. By 1997 a Korean company, OCI, also entered U.S. soda ash production, operating the Big Island Mine and Refinery in Green River, Wyoming.

Humanitarian Aid. In early 1997, PPG Industries donated 11 million metric tons of calcium chlorite, and Olin Corporation donated an additional 1 million, for a total of 12 million metric tons to help residents of Cuba still recovering from the effects of Hurricane Lili, which struck the island in October 1996. The calcium chlorite was for use in disinfecting drinking water.

CURRENT CONDITIONS

Modern methods of chlorine production were developed around electrolysis. The three most-used technologies—diaphragm cells, mercury cells, and membrane cells—produce chlorine and caustic soda by decomposing brine (salt water). Combined, they accounted for 97 percent of U.S. chlorine production in 1997. Other methods in operation in 1997 included electrolysis of either molten magnesium chloride or molten sodium chloride; electrolysis of hydrochloric acid; and non-electrolytic processes. The brine used as a raw material is obtained from natural deposits under the earth's surface or is made from salt and water.

Diaphragm cells, the oldest and most widely used of the modern methods, produces more than three-quarters of the nation's chlorine. Direct current is used to separate salt and water into chlorine, hydrogen, and sodium hydroxide (caustic soda). An internal asbestos fiber-coated device called a "diaphragm" keeps the chlorine and caustic soda separate. Manufacturers rely on additional evaporation and drying procedures to create products in marketable concentrations.

Mercury cells accounted for 12.1 percent of U.S. chlorine production in 1997. They employ a different technique for keeping manufactured chlorine and caustic soda separate. Because of the presence of mercury during the application of the cell's electric current, the sodium is isolated and dissolved into the mercury. A secondary process recaptures the mercury and releases the sodium to form sodium hydroxide (caustic soda). During the early 1990s producers were moving away from mercury cells because of environmental concerns surrounding the mercury content of plant waste water.

The membrane cell accounted for only 9.5 percent of U.S. chlorine production in 1997 but is the most rapidly growing production technology, using an ion exchange membrane to separate the chlorine and caustic soda. Membrane technology requires less electricity and produces grades of chlorine and caustic soda with higher purity than other methods.

The remaining 2.6 percent of U.S. chlorine capacity was contributed by alternate methods. By comparison, in Canada, diaphragm cells retained their role in 85.3 percent of the production capacity, with membrane cells at 11.9 percent and mercury cells at 2.8 percent of the total.

It is of interest to note that, in both nations during the period 1988-1997, there was a decrease in the percentage of total chlorine production capacity contributed by mercury cells, with corresponding increases in the percentage of membrane cells in operation. This change was most dramatic in Canada, where the decrease was 12.5 percent. The decreases reflected continuing concerns about the hazards involved in use of mercury and its potential adverse environmental impact. The relative contribution of diaphragm cells remained virtually unchanged in the United States and slightly increased in Canada (4.6 percent).

Chlorine Packaging Plants in the United States. In 1997 there were 27 different companies in the United States operating a total of 86 chlorine packaging plants. One additional plant was shut down in November 1996; it had been operated by Jones Chemical in Henderson, Nevada. In contrast, there were only three such companies in Canada operating a total of seven plants, and four in Mexico, each operating one plant.

Chlorine and Caustic Soda Producers. In 1997 there were 24 companies in the United States operating 45 chlorine production plants with a total production capacity of 39,558 tons per day. By comparison, the seven Canadian plants had a daily production capacity of only 11 percent of the U.S. figure (3,561 tons per day), while the five operating Mexican plants were at 1.3 percent of U.S. capacity (529 tons per day).

Five companies either completed or were engaged in plant expansions and modernization in the United States as of late 1996—Dow Chemical, Occidental Chemical, Formosa Plastics, and a joint venture between Olin Corporation and Geon.

Figures released by Dow Chemical for 1996 showed their global chlorine production capacity at 11.5 billion pounds per year and global caustic soda production capacity at 12.5 billion pounds per year. About 50 percent of the caustic soda produced was sold, generating global sales of $500 million in 1996. A plant expansion in Freeport, Texas, in late 1996 increased Dow chlorine production capacity by 440 million pounds (200,000 metric tons) per year. The company heralded its first ever commercial use of membrane cell technology in its plant expansion in Stade, Germany, which added additional capacity of 260 million pounds (118,000 metric tons) per year. These increases were earmarked for the company's internal chlorine demand, which consumed over 95 percent of the chlorine generated.

Of Dow Chemical's total chlorine production in 1996, approximately one-third was directed towards production of 10 billion pounds of ethylene dichloride (EDC), which in turn was used for synthesis of vinyl chloride monomers (VCM). The latter were sold to other companies principally for production of polyvinyl chloride (PVC). An additional one-third of the chlorine production was directed towards synthesis of propylene oxide, with production of 3 billion pounds per year reported in 1996. Roughly 25 percent of this was destined for synthesis of propylene glycol, important in products such as aircraft de-icing fluids. The remaining one-third of Dow's chlorine production was used for production of other chlorinated compounds.

Occidental Chemical (Oxychem), the second-largest producer, but largest merchant marketer of chlorine and caustic soda, reported that it had completed expansions and improvements at several of its chlor-alkali facilities. Since 1993, Oxychem's U.S. chlorine production capacity was increased by 400 tons per day, with plans to add 600 tons per day additional capacity at three Gulf Coast plants, where the bulk of its production was concentrated by the end of 1998. This was slated to bring the total domestic capacity to roughly 9,000 tons per day. About 60 percent of the company's chlorine production in 1996 was directed towards its vinyls product chain, including EDC and VCM, ultimately used to manufacture PVC. The vinyls chain was the largest and most rapidly growing market for Oxychem's chlorine.

According to the U.S. Department of Commerce, chlorine capacity remained fairly stable from 1991 through 1996, with a general upward trend beginning in 1995. By 1996 the U.S. capacity (38,416 short tons per day) had slightly surpassed the 1985 value (38,298 tons per day) but not yet returned to the 1980 level (39,391 short tons per day).

Statistics released by the Chlorine Institute revealed an overall trend towards increased domestic U.S. production of chlorine gas (and its alkali co-product) as well as the amount liquefied from 1991 through the start of 1997. Chlorine production for 1991 and 1996 was, respectively, 11,489,896 and 13,168,384 short tons. Equivalent values for liquefied chlorine were, respectively, 9,340,125 and 10,179,100 short tons. For the same period, liquid sodium hydroxide production was 12,151,285 and 13,856,531 short tons per year, respectively. The amount of dry sodium hydroxide produced during these years, although only a small percentage of the total, actually decreased from 266,137 short tons per year in 1991 to a value of 183,062 in 1996, a low of 173,925 short tons having been reached in 1995. By comparison, dry sodium hydroxide production was considerably greater in 1980 at 418,178 short tons. For the first two months of 1997, there were slight increases over the same two months of 1996 in production of chlorine and both liquid and dry sodium hydroxide.

Figures released by the U.S. Bureau of Census for the chlor-alkali industry in 1995 showed domestic total production at $3.3 billion in shipments, with contributions to this total from chlorine (compressed or liquefied)

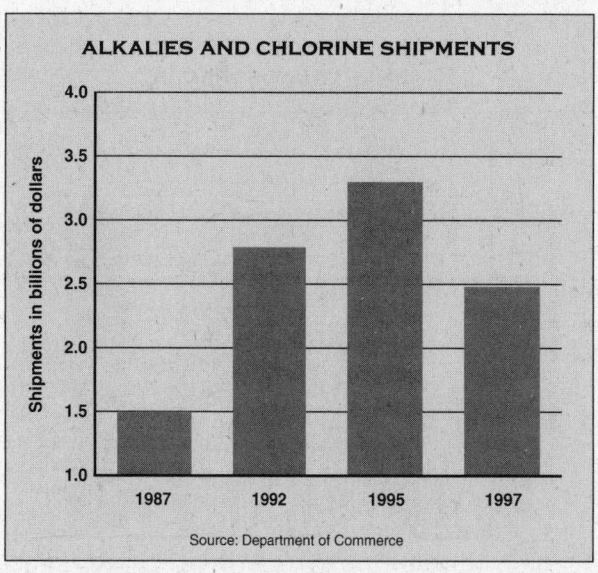

ALKALIES AND CHLORINE SHIPMENTS

Shipments in billions of dollars

Source: Department of Commerce

at $849.7 million, sodium hydroxide or caustic soda at $2.06 billion, and other alkalies at $382.3 million.

Prices for chlorine increased by $25 to $40 per ton at the end of 1996 and again in early 1997, by Dow, Occidental, and Vulcan. Increases were caused by (1) previous expansions in downstream production of chlorine derivatives not having been matched by corresponding expansions in chlor-alkali plants, with demand thus exceeding supply; (2) failures at two Dow chlor-alkali rectifiers (Freeport, Texas), with resultant production delays due to repairs; (3) a 30-day loss of production at the LaRoche Industries Gramercy, Louisiana plant, caused by a fire that caused a daily 50 percent reduction in the normal 300 tons per day output; and (4) the seasonal spring increase in homebuilding, with its attendant increase in demand for PVC products.

Caustic Soda. During the first quarter of 1997, caustic soda prices continued to decrease with prices reported in February at about $95 per ton on the Gulf. Although caustic soda prices dropped $100 per ton in the year from early 1996 to early 1997, it was believed by April 1997 that prices had bottomed out. Severe flooding in the Midwest, limited transport on the Mississippi River due to elevated levels, the Dow and LaRoche production problems, and other unforeseen difficulties during the first quarter helped to stabilize prices in part by their effects on caustic soda inventories. By 1998 the Dow plant at Freeport, Texas, was producing 4.5 million short tons per year of caustic soda with an increase of 325,000 short tons in capacity added in late 1999. In 1998 Bayer began building a plant at Baytown, Texas, to produce 1,065 tons per day of caustic soda. OxyChem generated almost 3.2 million short tons of caustic soda in 1998 at its facilities in Texas, Louisiana, Alabama, New York, and Delaware, and PPG followed with 1.9 million short tons at two plants in Louisiana and

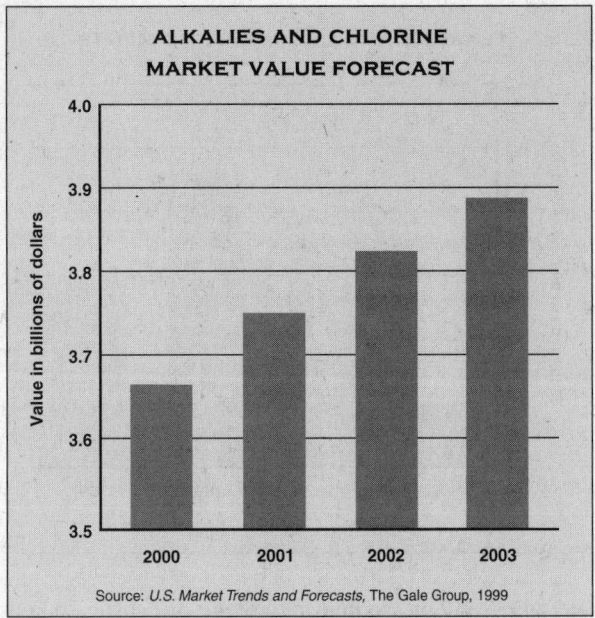

ALKALIES AND CHLORINE MARKET VALUE FORECAST

Source: *U.S. Market Trends and Forecasts,* The Gale Group, 1999

West Virginia. Demand for caustic soda increased from 13.9 million tons in 1997 to 14.2 million tons in 1997 and is expected to climb to 15.7 million tons by 2001. Two percent growth per year is predicted through 2001, and the 1998 price per ton is $300.

EPA Limits On Toxic Pollution. In 1994 the Environmental Protection Agency announced that chemical companies in the United States would have to cut their manufacturing plants' toxic air pollution by almost 90 percent from 1990 levels. The rule, noted the *Detroit Free Press,* ''requires the companies . . . to install equipment to better prevent evaporation and leaks of 112 toxic chemicals. . . . About 370 chemical plants in 38 states will be forced to cut toxic air pollution by a total of 506,000 tons, an EPA statement said.'' While the new rules, instituted as a part of the 1990 Clean Air Act, would involve significant expenditures on capital improvements for the affected companies, regulators noted that chemical companies have already taken significant steps to address the new requirements in anticipation of the announcement.

Hydrogen Peroxide. Environmental issues continued to affect the worldwide chlorine industry in 1997, matters that were clearly reflected in the peroxide market, which is linked to the pulp and paper market. Due to excessive pulp inventories in 1996, pulp prices declined. Prior to the crash, peroxide growth was forecast at 10 to12 percent annually through 2000, but afterward, at only 5 to 8 percent.

EPA regulations provided the initial impetus for increased hydrogen peroxide demand in the pulp and paper industry. These regulations prompted conversion of pulp mills from elemental chlorine use to either chlorine diox-

ide (which may be generated, in turn, from sodium chlorate) or hydrogen peroxide.

By the beginning of 1997, most U.S. pulp plants had stopped using elemental chlorine for bleaching and substituted chlorine dioxide to eliminate dioxin production. During the same period, a bill was introduced in Congress to force U.S. pulp plants to use totally chlorine-free (TCF) bleaching processes, a move favored by many environmentalists as a means of reducing dioxin pollution. The EPA was therefore debating between two possible rules—to either allow chlorine-based plants to substitute chlorine dioxide or to require partial substitution of chlorine dioxide with oxygen. The Chlorine Chemistry Council and paper workers' unions supported the shift to chlorine dioxide, arguing that partial substitution of oxygen would be very costly (perhaps $1 billion), and the expense would potentially eliminate thousands of jobs.

As of early 1997, the Canadian pulp industry was believed to have substituted other materials for elemental chlorine in 89 to 90 percent of its operations, with the United States lagging behind at perhaps only 45 percent. Worldwide, Scandinavian pulp producers adopted total chlorine-free (TCF) substitution due to pressure from the Green Movement in Europe. Of related interest in 1997 were proposals to the European Commission by EURO-CHLOR (an industry group of European chlorine producers) for new air and water emissions standards for mercury-based chlor-alkali production processes. Proposed limits for air and water were 1.9 grams of mercury per metric ton of chlorine produced. Final legislation will take effect in 2005.

The trend away from chlorine use was highly beneficial for the peroxide market, and, by 1996, the six producers in North America (DuPont, Solvay, Degussa, Chemprox, FMC, and Eka Nobel) were gearing up for plant expansions to increase North American capacity to roughly 2 billion pounds by 1998, an increase of more than 800 million pounds over previous levels.

Despite the efforts to reduce or eliminate elemental chlorine use, strong growth was predicted in 1997 for both chlorine and non-chlorine bleaching agents in foreign markets, principally Latin America and Asia. Growth was also predicted for the U.S. domestic market for both oxygen- and chlorine-based bleaches, up from the 1996 estimate of 10.4 billion pounds valued at about $2.9 billion. Forecasts were for annual market growth of 5.1 percent, reaching a value of $3.5 billion by 2000, with pulp bleaching accounting for about 66 percent of the total value, followed by water treatment, and finally by cleaning compounds.

WORKFORCE

The U.S. Census Bureau reported that the chlorine and alkalies industry employed 4,900 workers in 1997.

This figure was down by 2,700 employees from 1994 but up 25 percent from the mid-1980s. In 1997, 19 of the 39 American manufacturers had 50 to 250 employees, and only five firms had more than 250. Louisiana, New York, and Washington led all states in producing chlorine, and Louisiana and Washington also produced 44 percent of American-made caustic soda. The average hourly wage for production workers in 1997 was $24.85.

AMERICA AND THE WORLD

Chlorine production in the United States accounts for almost 30 percent of the world's capacity, but there is little international movement of chlorine because of difficulties related to its transportation and storage. Producers generally prefer to erect production facilities in regions where demand exists.

In 1998 analysts predicted that worldwide chlorine demand would decline as the effects of the Asian economic crisis spread and slowed construction and use of PVC resins amounting to nearly 40 percent of demand. By contrast, demand for caustic was strong in 1998, and producers struggled to put new facilities on line, increase production (at the Stade, Germany, plant operated by Dow Chemical, for example, where 120,000 metric tons of capacity were added in late 1998), and acquire the chlor-alkali facilities of other firms.

In 1996 soda ash had been predicted to grow in Asian exports from 130,000 metric tons to 140,000 tons in 1998; the economic catastrophe forced the industry to consider cutting back soda ash exports by as much as 100,000 metric tons in 1998 instead. Pulp and paper manufacturers and water treatment facilities were among those using soda ash as a caustic soda substitute; as the price of caustic soda rose in 1997 to $160 per ton, these industries switched back to soda ash, which helped balance Asian losses.

FURTHER READING

Brand, Tony. "Bleaches Brighten Abroad." Special Report, *Chemical Market Reporter,* 27 January 1997.

"Caustic Soda." *Chemical Market Reporter,* 1 June 1998.

"Chlorine Surge to Taper Off, but Long-Term Growth Is Seen." *Chemical Marketing Reporter,* 11 January 1993.

"CI Industry Aids Victims." *Chemical Market Reporter,* 27 January 1997.

Fairley, Peter. "Zero Discharge Bill Introduced." *Chemical Week,* 2 April 1997.

Johnson, Dexter. "Chloralkali products face uncertain year." *Chemical Market Reporter,* 5 January 1998.

———. "Chlorine Makers Hike Prices Again As Plant Outages Tighten Up Market." *Chemical Market Reporter,* 24 February 1997.

———. "Hydrogen Peroxide Outlook Strong, Despite the Effect of Cluster Rules," *Chemical Market Reporter,* 3 February 1997.

———. "Sodium Chlorate Market Doing Well Despite Still Flagging Pulp Business." *Chemical Market Reporter,* 13 January 1997.

Kirschner, Elisabeth. "Total Chlorine Phaseout Would Cost $102 Billion/Year, Says CI." *Chemical Week,* 28 April 1993.

Mullin, Rick and Emily Pilsher. "Bit Ticket Changes in Store for North American Pulp and Paper." *Chemical Week,* 21 April 1993.

North American Chlor-Alkali Industry Plants and Production Data Report—1996. Washington: The Chlorine Institute, 1997.

Scott, Alex. "Chlor-Alkali Standards Proposed." *Chemical Week,* 12 March 1997.

Westervelt, Robert. "Caustic Market Starts to Settle." *Chemical Week,* 2 April 1997.

Williams, Mike. "EPA Sets New Limits on Toxic Pollution." *Detroit Free Press,* 2 March 1994.

U.S. Bureau of the Census "Alkalies and Chlorine Manufacturing." *1997 Economic Census: Manufacturing Industry Series.* August 1999.

SIC 2813

INDUSTRIAL GASES

This industry classification contains establishments primarily involved in manufacturing industrial gases (organic as well as inorganic) that may be sold in compressed, liquid, or solid form. Industrial gases include acetylene, argon, carbon dioxide, helium, hydrogen, neon, nitrogen, nitrous oxide, and oxygen. Fluorocarbon gases are covered under **SIC 2869: Industrial Organic Chemicals, Not Elsewhere Classified.** Industrial gas distributors, including liquid oxygen shippers, are classified in **SIC 5169: Chemicals and Allied Products, Not Elsewhere Classified.**

NAICS CODE(S)

325120 (Industrial Gas Manufacturing)

INDUSTRY SNAPSHOT

In the United States, industrial gases touch virtually every facet of life. The three major atmospheric gases—oxygen, nitrogen, and argon—are used in steel production. Oxygen enhances kiln firing to reduce brick-making costs. Liquid oxygen and liquid hydrogen fuel rockets. Nitrogen is used in brewing beer, recycling tires, and applying metallic finishes on toys. Ammonia is synthesized from nitrogen for use in fertilizers, nitric acid, hydrazine, amines, and urea. It is also important in the production of nitrous oxide (also known as laughing gas) that is used as an anesthetic in some types of surgery. Liquid nitrogen and liquid carbon dioxide are used to make plastic fittings for moldings, enhance oil recovery from wells, and enable solvent recycling. Argon contributes to stainless steel manufacturing and serves as a component in fluorescent lighting.

The industrial gas industry differs from many other types of manufacturing because its raw materials are primarily extracted from the atmosphere. The two principal gases produced by the industry are nitrogen and oxygen. Dry air is composed of 78.1 percent nitrogen, 20.9 percent oxygen, and just under 1 percent argon. All other atmospheric gases, often called rare gases, make up the remaining one-tenth of 1 percent. Additional industrial gases such as hydrogen, acetylene, and carbon dioxide are obtained as co-products or by-products of other operations. Production costs within the industry are divided among labor, energy, and distribution.

The industry uses three different techniques to separate gases from the atmosphere. Cryogenic methods are the oldest and most widely used. Cryogenic separation relies on cooling and pressurizing the air until it becomes liquid. Oxygen, when held at a pressure of 80 pounds per square inch, liquefies at minus 274 degrees Fahrenheit; nitrogen liquefies at a colder temperature. As the atmospheric gases liquefy, they are extracted by means of a distillation process. Additional distillation steps are necessary to produce argon and other rare gases such as krypton and xenon. Helium liquefies only at temperatures approaching absolute zero. As a result, cryogenic production is not economically feasible for helium. Most commercially available helium is derived from natural gas rather than from the atmosphere.

Two non-cryogenic gas production methods are membrane separation and pressure swing absorption (PSA). Membrane separation uses hollow fibers, most frequently made of organic polymers, to recover gases such as hydrogen from oil refineries or carbon dioxide from natural gas supplies. Pressure swing absorption (PSA) relies on a molecular sieve material that selectively absorbs atmospheric components at specific temperatures and pressures.

According to the U.S. Census Bureau, the industrial gases industry shipped products valued at $3.9 billion in 1997. Although industry sales declined in the late 1980s, growth was achieved during the 1990s, with shipments increasing over 25 percent from 1992's $3.1 billion. In 1996 U.S. oxygen production was estimated at 668 billion cubic feet; nitrogen production at 1.03 trillion cubic feet; hydrogen production at 271 billion cubic feet; and argon production was approximately 18 billion cubic feet. The United States likewise produced more than 5 million short tons of liquid carbon dioxide and 235,000 short tons of solid carbon dioxide.

In addition to its major products, the industry produced almost 100 different specialty gases such as krypton, xenon, and neon. Many specialty gases were used for medical, communications, electronics, aerospace, laser, and special lighting applications. Although specialty gases accounted for only about 8 percent of the industry's total production in 1992, they accounted for 29 percent of its revenues.

ORGANIZATION AND STRUCTURE

The industrial gas industry is divided into two major segments. The first, called the "tonnage" or "supply scheme" market, is composed of large-volume users who usually receive gas via a direct pipeline from an on-site production facility. Under typical on-site contracts, a gas supplier constructs a production plant at or adjacent to a gas user's facility. The gas supplier owns and operates the plant for the benefit of the gas customer. Long-term contracts dictate that the customer take a specified volume of gas, often the entire amount produced. Many contracts contain adjustment clauses to account for increasing energy prices, variances in productivity, or changes in labor costs. Within this market segment, gas sold is measured in terms of tons per day. Examples of customers who routinely purchase industrial gases on the tonnage market include chemical, petroleum, electronics, and steel manufacturers.

The other major market segment is known as the "merchant" or "bulk liquid" market. Customers within this market generally have fluctuating demand rates or operate multiple facilities in scattered locations. They often purchase gas products under short-term contracts of less than five years in duration. Suppliers deliver liquid gas in cryogenic tanker trucks or by rail. Gases are shipped and stored in liquid form because of volume constraints. For example, liquid oxygen takes up less than 1 percent of the space required to contain the same amount in a gaseous state. Examples of customers in this category include the metal, food processing, electronics, chemical, aerospace, plastics, medical, glass, and paper industries.

A third, but much smaller market segment, consists of cylinder gas deliveries. Cylinder gas shipments are generally limited to expensive specialty gases and mixtures. A typical tanker truck carries the equivalent of 1,600 large cylinders. A train of ten cars carries the equivalent of 57,000 cylinders.

BACKGROUND AND DEVELOPMENT

The gases that make up the multi-billion-dollar industrial gas industry were discovered by various researchers living in several different countries beginning in the later half of the eighteenth century. Nitrogen was isolated in 1772 by Daniel Rutherford (1749-1819), a British physician; in 1776, it was identified as an elemental gas by the great French chemist Antoine-Laurent Lavoisier (1743-1794). Also about 1776, oxygen was discovered by two chemists working independently in Europe; the English scientist Joseph Priestley (1733-1804) and Swedish chemist Carl Wilhelm Scheele (1742-1786) share credit for the discovery. During the late 1800s, it was used for medical purposes and put to commercial use in welding. Oxygen was also used to generate limelight for theaters and music halls.

Acetylene was discovered in 1863 and first produced commercially in 1892. In 1897, Georges Claude (1870-1960), a French researcher, developed a method of dissolving acetylene in acetone at low pressures. Claude's process enabled the development of methods that allowed the movement of the gas via transportation cylinders. The first acetylene-burning torches were developed around 1900.

In 1877, two researchers, Louis-Paul Cailletet (1832-1913) in France and Raoul Pierre-Pictet (1846-1929) in Switzerland, developed similar processes for the fractional distillation of liquid air. This procedure made it possible to produce large volumes of oxygen economically. In 1903 the Linde Air Products Company constructed the first commercial oxygen plant in the United States.

Events of the early twentieth century demanded increasing amounts of industrial gases. World War I required large amounts of oxygen and acetylene for welding; during World War II pilots of high-altitude aircraft needed oxygen for their flights. Following the wars, researchers used inert gases such as argon and helium in electric arc welding.

Growing industrialization in the Western world brought rapid expansion to the gas industry. Oxygen demand continued growing through the 1950s as steel manufacturers turned to the gas to improve production methods. Maturing uses for nitrogen, previously considered a waste material, developed during the 1960s, along with advances in the uses of helium and argon. The 1970s brought large-scale expansions in the nation's capacity to produce industrial gases. The decade also saw growth in the use of specialty gases by the electronics industry. By the mid-1980s, the electronics industry used an estimated 15 percent of the nation's nitrogen output.

CURRENT CONDITIONS

Although demand for nitrogen in 1960 had been practically nonexistent, by the early 1990s nitrogen sales surpassed the sales of all other industrial gases. Nitrogen and oxygen sales combined accounted for approximately 41 percent of the industry's sales in 1997. Carbon dioxide and acetylene ranked third and fourth.

Because nitrogen does not readily react with other materials, several industries use it as a "blanketing agent," which is a compound able to prevent unwanted reactions. For example, when nitrogen is used as a blanketing agent with embers, it prevents them from igniting. Nitrogen is therefore used to ensure product quality and improve plant safety. Oil producers use nitrogen to stimulate and pressurize wells. The gas is also valuable in steel processing, food production, cooling, refrigeration and freezing systems, solvent recovery, chemical and glass production, and in the electronics and aerospace industries. Nitrogen production rebounded in 1996 after a decline in 1995.

Measured in terms of sales volume, the second most significant industrial gas in the 1990s was oxygen, which is used to intensify or control combustion in a variety of industries. Its other uses include speeding fermentation, providing life support, and controlling odors. Chemical manufacturers, brick makers, and metal fabricators all rely on oxygen. Innovative uses include processes aimed at restoring or maintaining environmental integrity. Oxygen is used in hazardous-waste cleanup, waste-water treatment facilities, and coal gasification systems (a process designed to reduce the hazardous emissions associated with burning coal). One of the fastest growing areas of oxygen use in the 1990s, however, was as a replacement for chlorine in bleaching, especially by pulp and paper manufacturers because the oxygen process pollutes less.

Another gas with a rapidly growing demand in the early 1990s was helium. Traditionally used in welding, balloons, and leak detection, helium is finding new applications in cryogenic cooling. Liquid helium is the only gas known to become cold enough for use in the superconducting magnets used in body scanners. By 1991 the cooling requirements of superconductive magnets such as those used by magnetic resonance imaging (MRI) diagnostic equipment accounted for more than one-fourth of the world's demand for helium. The United States produced 3.4 billion cubic feet of helium in 1995.

Demand for specialty gases such as krypton, xenon, and neon is also growing. Low-power lamps rely on krypton, high-intensity filament lamps and CAT scanners depend on xenon, and neon is necessary for lasers, display lighting, and bar-code scanners. All three rare gases were used to develop radial keratotomy, a form of laser surgery for eyes.

INDUSTRY LEADERS

In the mid-1980s Union Carbide was the largest industrial gas supplier in the United States. It provided approximately one-third of the nation's merchant gas. In 1985 the company opened six new nitrogen plants, with most of its production capacity aimed at the fast-growing high-tech market. In 1992 Union Carbide's industrial gas unit was spun off to become an independent entity, Praxair, Inc., which had revenues of $4.4 billion in 1996. In 1997, Praxair's president, Paul Bilek, cited economics, environmental regulations and issues, and globalization as the three forces affecting future growth of industrial gas manufacture.

Another major producer was Air Products and Chemicals, Inc. Founded in 1940, Air Products pioneered on-site industrial gas manufacturing. In 1991 the company introduced small volume, low cost, non-cryogenic nitrogen for use by metal heat-treating firms. In 1998 Air Products employed more than 16,700 workers, and its global sales exceeded $4.9 billion, of which almost half was derived from industrial gas sales. The firm's industrial gas segment was growing less rapidly than its chemical and related businesses.

Liquid Air Corporation, a subsidiary of the French company L'Air Liquide, entered the U.S. market in 1968. By the mid-1980s L'Air Liquide operated in 66 countries. Liquid Air is the company's headquarters for its operations in North and South America. It supplies products including oxygen, nitrous oxide, hydrogen, nitrogen, specialty gases, chemical gases, and rare gases to a wide variety of industrial users. Big Three Industries, another L'Air Liquide unit, sells most of its production to chemical and petroleum producers via a pipeline system located in the Gulf Coast region.

Another international gas producer with a strong presence in the U.S. market is the BOC Group., which derived more than half of its worldwide sales in 1996 from industrial gases. The BOC Group originated in England with the incorporation of the Brins Oxygen Company Limited in 1886. BOC acquired the American company Airco in 1978. By the mid-1980s Airco provided 20 percent of the U.S. domestic merchant gas. BOC's expansion continued; by the late 1990s, the company operated units on all continents except Antarctica.

WORKFORCE

In the United States, the Census Bureau reported that the industrial gases industry employed a total of 8,787 workers with a payroll of more than $354 million in 1997. The statistics show a continued increase in industry employment since the early 1990s. The three leading states by employment were New Jersey, Texas, and California. Production workers received an hourly wage of $17.31 on average in 1997.

AMERICA AND THE WORLD

The global market for industrial gases experienced $29 billion in sales 1996 and is expected to reach $41 billion by 2003. Because of problems related to the transportation and storage of gas products, most production occurred close to its point of use. There was, therefore, very little international trade in industrial gases. Instead of transporting products, large international corporations functioned by operating production facilities in many countries.

The types and volumes of gases provided in an area depended on the development of the region's economy. Regions with emerging economies typically required high volumes of oxygen, whereas countries with economies based on high technology and service needed greater amounts of nitrogen. According to the BOC Group, the ratio of nitrogen sales to oxygen sales could be used as a measurement of a nation's industrial development.

RESEARCH AND TECHNOLOGY

During the 1990s, pollution abatement was one of the most rapidly developing areas of study within the industrial gases industry. Waste water treatment has successfully been improved by oxygen injection, and oxygen is also used in hazardous waste incineration. Large quantities of oxygen and hydrogen are consumed in the production of directly reduced iron, which replaces scrap metal resources (expected to be exhausted by 2001) in producing steel for electric-arc furnaces. Recovery systems using nitrogen to condense and recapture solvents and chemical vapors helped manufacturers come into compliance with the Clean Air Act Amendments of 1990. An innovative technology based on carbon dioxide offered promise for reducing the environmental impact of solvent use within the paint and coatings industry. Additionally, carbon dioxide-based refrigeration systems were introduced to replace systems that relied on chlorofluorocarbons (CFCs).

Research into new or refined uses for industrial gases also continued. Liquid nitrogen was being considered as a possible aid in reducing problems associated with cracking in structural concrete. Xenon provided sun-like brightness to meet the special lighting needs of airports, stadiums, the motion picture industry, and copying machine manufacturers. Other rare gases were also being developed for use in diagnostic technologies and pharmaceutical applications.

FURTHER READING

Air Products and Chemicals, Inc. *1996 Annual Report.* Allentown, PA, 1996.

Johnson, Dexter. "Industrial gas industry is driven by economic, environmental forces." *Chemical Market Reporter.* 22 September 1997.

U.S. Census Bureau. "Industrial Gas Manufacturing." *1997 Economic Census: Manufacturing Industry Series.* October 1999.

———. *1995 Annual Survey of Manufactures.* Washington: GPO, 1997.

———. "Industrial Gases." *Current Industrial Reports.* Washington: GPO, 1997.

———. *1992 Census of Manufactures.* Washington: GPO, 1995.

SIC 2816

INORGANIC PIGMENTS

This industry classification is comprised of establishments engaged in manufacturing inorganic color pigments, white pigments, and black pigments, including animal black and bone black. Carbon black is classified in **SIC 2895: Carbon Black.** Organic color pigments are classified in **SIC 2865: Cyclic Organic Crudes and Intermediates, and Organic Dyes and Pigments.**

NAICS CODE(S)

325131 (Inorganic Dye and Pigment Manufacturing)
325182 (Carbon Black Manufacturing)

INDUSTRY SNAPSHOT

Inorganic pigments serve the purpose of imparting color to various compounds. They also add properties such as rust inhibition, rigidity, and abrasion resistance. Pigments are insoluble substances that can be incorporated into a material to selectively absorb or scatter light. Depending on the specific pigment used, different visual effects are produced. Inorganic pigments may be obtained from a variety of naturally occurring or synthetically produced mineral sources. The counterpart, organic pigments, are carbon compounds derived from petroleum sources.

In comparison with organic pigments, inorganic pigments are generally better able to withstand the affects of sunlight and chemical exposure. They provide superior opacity, which means they can render a substance or object opaque by prohibiting light from passing through it. Inorganic colors, however, tend to be less bright, pure, and rich than their organic counterparts. Because inorganic pigments possess less tinting strength, more pigment is needed to produce the desired effect. This generally makes them more durable. Almost all inorganic pigments are completely insoluble. Consequently they do not bleed or leach out of coatings, inks, or plastics. In addition, inorganic pigments are usually less expensive than similar organic colors.

Pigments differ from dyes as a result of their distinctive chemical natures. Dyes are soluble, and to impart color they are dissolved in a carrier and applied by a process that involves chemical changes. Pigments however, remain unchanged physically and chemically. They function without altering their crystalline, particulate, or metabolic structures.

Inorganic pigments are classified as single-metal oxides, mixed-metal oxides, and earth colors. Single-metal oxides include pigments made from titanium, zinc, cobalt, and chromium. Mixed-metal oxides include pigments such as cobalt aluminate blue, which is used in ceramic glazes, and nickel antimony titanate, manganese antimony titanate, and chromium antimony titanate, which are used for outdoor coatings and plastic siding. Earth colors, including siennas, ochers, and umbers, are generally made from iron oxides and lead chromates. A method of high-temperature firing called calcination is used to produce pigments with improved heat resistance.

Pigment manufacturers supply inorganic colors in a variety of forms such as powders, pastes, granules, slurries, and suspensions. Pigment users include manufacturers of paints and stains, printing inks, plastics, synthetic textiles, paper, cosmetics, contact lenses, soaps and detergents, wax, modeling clay, chalks, crayons, artists' colors, concrete and masonry products, and ceramics.

Within the inorganic pigments classification, the largest selling individual pigment is titanium dioxide (TiO_2), a white pigment with opacifying characteristics. Titanium dioxide is by far the most widely used white pigment in the world. It is a solid that melts at over 1800 degrees Celsius. It has a higher refractive index than everything except diamonds. It is polymorphous and exists in three crystal structures: rutile, anatase, and brookite. To utilize titanium dioxide's special properties, it must be developed to an ideal particle size. Most often, the particle size is one half the wavelength of visible light or about 0.3 microns.

BACKGROUND AND DEVELOPMENT

The use and exploitation of color dates back to the prehistoric era. Pigments were made by grinding naturally colored materials into minute particles and then mixing them into a binder material. Some of the substances used to produce paintings on cave walls were still used during the twentieth century. For example, the reds used to produce the drawings in the Lascaux caves of southern France were made from red iron oxide.

During the early part of the twentieth century, the pigments industry relied heavily on lead-based ingredients. One ingredient, lead carbonate (white lead) was known to be toxic as early as the late nineteenth century, and although some countries began imposing restrictions on its use in the 1920s, the United States was not among them. The toxicity of lead carbonate, especially to children who ate paint chips, received increasing publicity. By the mid-1960s paint manufacturers were required to begin phasing out its use.

According to industry researchers, lead carbonate caused lead poisoning because of its solubility. The solubility enabled it to interfere with the human body's biochemical system. Investigators claimed that other lead pigments suffered from non-specific adverse publicity resulting in regulations that failed to differentiate between soluble and insoluble lead compounds. A reduction in the use of lead chromate pigments during the 1970s resulted in increased costs of more than $1 billion because available replacements were inferior. Into the late 1990s, this problem still existed and lead carbonate was still in use to some degree; advancements in the industry continued to make substitutes that were economically feasible and comparable in color strength.

To address issues such as environmental matters, tariffs, toxicity, and worker health, the Dry Color Manufacturers Association (DCMA) was formed. Originally organized in 1925 and headquartered in New York City, the trade association moved to New Jersey and then to Washington, D.C. In 1993, the organization changed its name to the Color Pigments Manufacturers Association, Inc. (CPMA) and as of 1997, it was located in Alexandria, Virginia.

Growth in production and demand for titanium dioxide increased rapidly through the 1980s. By 1989, production was 67 percent above the 1982 level. Although demand declined in 1990, industry analysts predicted annual domestic growth within the titanium dioxide market of about 2 percent through the decade. Globally, demand was expected to increase about 3 percent per year. Paint and coatings manufacturers used almost half of the titanium dioxide produced in the United States. Other users included the plastics, rubber, printing inks, floor coverings, ceramics, textiles, cosmetics, and paper industries.

Manufacturers used two basic processes to make titanium dioxide. The sulfate process, which produced slightly less than half of the world's supply of titanium dioxide, was the older method. It used sulfuric acid to dissolve the titanium dioxide. Further refinement was required to produce different grades of the finished product.

The newer method, called the chloride process, centered around the use of chlorine and accounted for 51 percent of the world's titanium dioxide capacity. By this method, chlorine was reacted with titanium-containing minerals to produce titanium tetrachloride. The titanium tetrachloride was reacted with oxygen to form titanium dioxide and recyclable chlorine. Advantages of the chloride process included its ability to create higher grades of titanium dioxide without additional handling, its use of less labor and equipment, and its ability to produce in a continuous, as opposed to a batch, process.

The chloride process also produced a smaller volume of waste by-products. Up to 12 tons of waste material were generated when the sulfate process was used in making one ton of titanium dioxide from ilmenite. The

chloride process generated four to five tons of waste in producing the same amount of titanium dioxide. A large part of the wastes generated by the chloride process, however, consisted of iron chloride. Disposal of iron chloride created controversy because of its acidic properties and hazardous nature. To reduce the amount of iron chloride waste, manufacturers were forced to rely on higher priced rutile or other purified forms of titanium-containing raw materials. High grade rutile generated only about 70 pounds of iron chloride to yield one ton of titanium dioxide.

New and existing grades of titanium dioxide were made more similar to each other as paint formulas became more standardized around the world. Slight regional differences, such as particle size or degree of opacity, were being phased out by the industry. Leaders in this trend as of 1996 were DuPont's R-706 multi purpose pigment for coating applications and SCM's RCL535. Kronos and Kerr-McGee were also working on similar products.

Titanium dioxide was also being used to create synthetic pearlescent pigments. Pearlescent pigments, a twentieth century innovation, were developed in an attempt to create the visual sense of depth associated with natural pearls. Initial pearlescent pigments were made from crystals obtained from fish scales. Rosary bead manufacturers were among the first users of these products.

Researchers identified two chemical compounds with similar light reflective properties. One of these, carbonate white lead, was withdrawn because of its toxicity. The other bismuth oxychloride found wide use in applications such as cast polyester buttons, automotive paints, fingernail enamels, cosmetics, wall papers, and plastics.

Synthetic pearlescent pigments, however, failed to exactly duplicate those of fish scales. The search for other synthetic pearlescent pigment compounds led to the use of such minerals as mica. Mica, when coated with titanium dioxide, was judged to reflect light in a manner suitable for use in pearlescent pigments.

The second largest family of pigments was iron oxides. Although iron oxides produced pigments in a wide range of colors, reds accounted for almost half the consumption. By the early 1990s, synthetic iron oxides had captured two-thirds of the market. Industry forecasters expected increased interest in synthetic iron oxide pigments because they offered improved color strength over naturally occurring ores. The primary users of iron oxide pigments were paint and coatings manufacturers.

Lead chromates represented the third largest family of pigments. In the early 1990s, approximately 42 million pounds of these pigments were still being sold annually. Traffic paint manufacturers used nearly 18 million pounds of these pigments. Despite their popularity, lead chromates were being subjected to increasing congressional scrutiny because of concerns about lead toxicity and environmental integrity.

Silica encapsulation involved encasing pigment particles or crystals within a shell of silica (a glass like substance). Researchers claimed that encapsulated lead chromate pigments were protected from chemical, photochemical, and thermal degradation. The encapsulation process also reduced their toxicity by making them less soluble in the body. Researchers also claimed that silica encapsulation improved the brightness and intensity of the pigments, making them better suited for use in high-temperature applications such as plastic manufacturing.

CURRENT CONDITIONS

According to figures released by the U.S. Department of Commerce, shipments of inorganic pigments were valued at an estimated $4.1 billion in 1999. The largest end user was the paint and coatings industry. This was a marked increase from the $3.73 billion shipped in 1997.

The industry's 74 establishments employed 8,608 people, 5,666 of whom were production workers. These production workers earned an average hourly wage of $21.27, far above the manufacturing industry's average.

As the inorganic pigments industry entered the 1990s, the largest single product produced was titanium dioxide. Titanium dioxide production relied on two different raw materials containing titanium: ilmenite and natural rutile. Both minerals were primarily mined in Australia and South Africa. Ilmenite contained less titanium than rutile, but it was more plentiful and less expensive.

The industry implemented several price increases in 1995, and 1996 saw a downturn in the market for titanium dioxide. The worldwide price index dropped several cents per pound. Pigments in general showed a moderate growth, indicating a mature market. Demand for titanium dioxide grew moderately through the 1990s and toward the end of the decade began to pick up—as did prices.

Environmental Impacts. Questions about environmental degradation and the toxicity of heavy metals challenged the inorganic pigment industry throughout the 1980s and early 1990s. Heavy metals such as lead, cadmium, chromium, and mercury were associated with ailments including cancer and liver disease. Both the Congress and the Environmental Protection Agency (EPA) considered legislative and regulatory initiatives to control, limit, and in some cases ban, the use of several of the industry's essential raw materials. Some manufacturers responded by backing away from heavy-metal pigments. Others defended their formulations and offered evidence

that if raw materials were banned, certain colors would become unavailable.

In addition to struggling with direct toxicity problems, pigment manufacturers faced charges claiming that their disposal of heavy-metals used in pigments were threatening the nation's water supplies. Products undergoing incineration or degradation in landfill sites created a potential hazard as heavy metals were released into the environment. As a result of this growing environmental concern, the Conference of North East Governors (representing nine northern states) and the legislatures in several other states, began working toward bans on heavy metals in packaging materials. During the early 1990s, industry watchers expected the number of environmental regulations regarding the use of heavy metals in pigments to increase.

Many inorganic pigment formulas relied on heavy metals. Some colors were not even achievable without their traditional raw materials. In other cases, colors could be matched using organic ingredients but the resulting pigment suffered from decreased light stability, poor opacity, and an inability to withstand high-temperature processing. Acceptable organic pigment substitutes were often more expensive than the inorganic pigments. Analysts suggested that switching to organic pigments could increase the price of a color concentrate by as much as 300 percent.

An often cited example of the difficulties faced by industries forced to switch away from heavy metal inorganic pigments was the problem of the Pennzoil oil bottle. The Pennzoil oil bottle, fabricated from an identifying bright yellow plastic, depended on yellow lead chromate. During the early 1990s yellow lead chromate cost between $1.00 and $1.50 per pound, but as legislation was likely to continue to limit the use of lead chromate, the company was forced to look for substitutes for the ingredient. One commonly used substitute cost between $6.00 and $7.00 per pound and other organic yellows cost up to $30.00 per pound. Facing a similar situation, Caterpillar (a manufacturer of heavy equipment) switched from its traditional color to a less bright yellow.

INDUSTRY LEADERS

The largest U.S. corporation producing inorganic pigments in 1999 was Millennium Chemicals, Inc. of Iselin, New Jersey. With sales of $1.6 billion, Millenium has approximately 5,300 employees and is the second largest producer of titanium dioxide. Ferro Corp. of Cleveland, Ohio had 1999 sales of $1.3 billion and 6,900 employees. Ferro began operating in 1919 as a frit manufacturer. Frit is a special glass material used to produce porcelain enamel and ceramic glaze. Color pigments for the ceramics and coatings industries were added to the company's product line in 1939. The company began supplying pigments to the plastics industry in 1947. By 1993, Ferro operated 12 color production facilities and sold its products in more than 100 countries.

Ferro's line of inorganic mixed metal oxide pigments are used primarily to color vinyl siding, window profiles, appliance housings, garden tools, and automotive components. The company's ultramarine blue and violet pigments are manufactured in Spain from sodium aluminum sulfosilicate complexes. They find use in thermoplastic resins, rubber compounds, paints, printing inks, artists' colors, and roofing granules. A third line of colors, called complex inorganic color pigments, are man-made minerals that are heat-stable, light-stable, and weather resistant. According to the manufacturer, they are the most chemically resistant pigments known to exist. They are recommended for use in exterior building applications and engineering plastics.

Other large inorganic pigment companies in the United States in 1999 were NL Industries Inc. of Houston, Texas; Kronos Div. of Houston, Texas; and Engelhard, Inc. of Iselin, New Jersey.

AMERICA AND THE WORLD

In 1990, estimates suggested that titanium dioxide accounted for about 30 percent of global pigment sales, and demand for the white pigment was expected to grow at approximately 3 percent per year. Industry forecasters expected new global production capacity that would add 850,000 tons between 1990 and 1995, resulting in a slight over-supply that would stabilize prices.

Western Europe however, was expected to see reduced production. Approximately 73 percent of the region's existing capacity was based on the sulfate process, which was subject to increasing criticism from environmental groups. A European Union directive to stop ocean dumping of wastes, slated to take effect at the end of 1993, was expected to increase operating expenses by about 15 percent and force older plants out of the global market.

Heavy metal pigment manufacturers were also facing difficulty in some parts of the world. In Japan, cadmium was replaced in 1980. European manufacturers began phasing it out several years later. An estimated 50 to 60 percent of European cadmium production had been eliminated by 1990. Some industry observers suggested that the banning of heavy metal pigments resulted in an increased reliance on duller colors.

Rare-earth-based red and orange pigments were scheduled for production in the 3rd quarter of 1997 when Rhone-Poulenc SA planned to start its 500 metric ton per year operation at La Rochelle, Les Roches-Roussillon and Clamecy. This inorganic pigment, trade-named Neolor, would be an environmentally friendly alternative to cadmium and lead-based paint types.

An advance in the making of complex inorganic color pigments by Englehard Corp. brought about the reddest pigment of it kind for use in PVC, nylon and other engineering plastics in 1996. Meteor Plus 9384 had 70-80 percent greater color strength than the next closest complex inorganic color pigment with a red value.

FURTHER READING

Alperowicz, Natasha, and Ian Young. ''DuPont to Raise Prises; SCM Plans to follow Suit.'' *Chemical Week* 11 December 1996.

Darnay, Arsen J., ed. *Manufacturing USA.* 6th ed. Detroit: The Gale Group, 1999.

Dry Color Manufacturers' Association. ''Pigments—A Primer.'' *American Ink Maker,* June 1989. Reprinted by Color Pigments Manufacturers Association, Inc. (formerly DCMA).

———. ''Inorganic Mixed Metal Oxide Pigments.'' Cleveland, OH: Ferro, nd.

''Inorganic Pigments.'' *Standard & Poor's Industry Surveys.* New York: Standard & Poor's Corporation, 1997.

MacDonald, Cindy. ''New Technologies Boost Performance.'' *Canadian Plastics,* February 1996.

Parkingson, Gerald. ''Rhone-Poulenc Will Commercialize 'Friendly' Pigments.'' *Chemical Engineering,* October 1996.

''Production By the U.S. Chemical Industry: Production Growth Sputtered in Most Sectors.'' *Chemical and Engineering News,* 24 June 1996.

SCM Chemicals. *Titanium Dioxide in Today's Environment: A Responsive and Responsible Industry.* Baltimore, MD: SCM, nd.

''SCM to Reduce TiO2 Capacity, Hike Prices.'' *Modern Paint and Coatings,* September 1996.

Shearer, Brent. ''Pigments Fade.'' *Chemical Marketing Reporter,* 21 October 1996.

———. ''Ultramarine Pigments.'' Cleveland, OH: Ferro, nd.

SIC 2819

INDUSTRIAL INORGANIC CHEMICALS, NOT ELSEWHERE CLASSIFIED

This category includes establishments primarily involved in manufacturing industrial inorganic chemicals not elsewhere classified. A few examples are alum, ammonium compounds (except for fertilizer), industrial bleaches (sodium or calcium hypochlorite), chemical catalysts, hydrazine, hydrochloric acid, hydrogen peroxide, inorganic sodium compounds, and sulfuric acid.

Establishments primarily engaged in mining, milling or otherwise preparing natural potassium, sodium, or boron compounds (other than common salt) are classified in **SIC 1474: Potash, Soda, and Borate Minerals;** establishments primarily engaged in manufacturing household bleaches are classified in **SIC 2842: Specialty Cleaning, Polishing, and Sanitation Preparations;** those manufacturing phosphoric acid are classified in **SIC 2874: Phosphatic Fertilizers;** and those manufacturing nitric acid, anhydrous ammonia, and other nitrogenous fertilizer materials are classified in **SIC 2873: Nitrogenous Fertilizers.**

NAICS Code(s)

325998 (All Other Miscellaneous Chemical Product Manufacturing)

331311 (Alumina Refining)

325131 (Inorganic Dye and Pigment Manufacturing)

325188 (All Other Inorganic Chemical Manufacturing)

Industry Snapshot

The inorganic chemicals industry makes up the bulk of basic chemical production. Inorganic chemicals are those derived from inanimate earth materials such as minerals and the atmosphere. They are differentiated from organic chemicals, which are derived from plant and animal sources. Organic chemicals are based on carbon; inorganic chemicals are based on all other naturally occurring and synthetically produced elements.

The major chemicals within this classification are known as "basic" chemicals. They are also sometimes referred to as "heavy," "bulk," or "commodity" chemicals. Manufacturers typically produce them from ores or brines, or as co-products or by-products of other processes. They serve industrial users who put them to work in the creation of other products. Some common applications include processing aids and chemical catalysts. Inorganic chemicals are also used as ingredients in nonchemical products. The primary markets for chemical products are paper, housing, automobiles, water treatment, fertilizer, petroleum refining, steel production, manufacturing, and soap and detergent production.

Sulfuric acid is by far the largest volume inorganic chemical. It is used primarily as a chemical reagent in a variety of industrial processes with the largest end use in fertilizer production. About three-fourths of domestic sulfuric acid is used for phosphate fertilizer.

Hydrogen peroxide is a rapidly growing sector of the inorganic chemicals industry. Pulp and paper manufacturing account for more than half the demand for hydrogen peroxide as it becomes a more viable option than chlorine for the chemical bleaching of paper. It is also used to remove ink from paper before the recycling process. Other uses for hydrogen peroxide are in water and waste treatment and for bleaching textiles.

Organization and Structure

Chemical producing companies range in size from small establishments providing a single chemical to multinational corporations offering thousands of different chemical products. The Chemical Manufacturers Association (CMA) was established to represent the industry's interests in local, state, and national affairs. According to the CMA, the industry's challenge was to balance self-interests with those of its many publics—legislators, regulators, the courts and especially, employees and neighbors.

Historically, regulators proved a large and demanding public. Several governmental agencies existed to regulate specific facets of the industry. For example, regulations covering railroad shipments of hazardous materials were instituted following the Civil War; and during the closing years of the 1800s, the Bureau of Chemistry (within the U.S. Department of Agriculture) was responsible for overseeing the safety of chemicals used in foods and drugs.

Governmental efforts to ensure product safety, establish worker safety laws, and protect the environment intensified during the 1970s, beginning with the establishment of the Environmental Protection Agency (EPA) in 1970. The decade brought the following host of new regulations: revisions of the Clean Air Act (1970 and subsequent amendments), the Occupational Safety and Health Act (1970), the Resource Recovery Act (1970), the Federal Water Pollution Control Act (1972), the Safe Drinking Water Act (1974), amendments to the Federal Insecticide, Fungicide, and Rodenticide Act (1972), the Resource Conservation and Recovery Act (1976), and the Toxic Substances Control Act (1976). The 1980s opened with the passage of the Comprehensive Environmental Response, Compensation, and Liability Act (also known as the "Superfund" Act).

Federal regulations mandated that new chemicals be evaluated for safety before use, that new uses of existing chemicals be evaluated, and that all chemicals meet specific safety and health standards. In addition, governmental bodies regulated by-products and co-products, controlled transportation, and monitored waste disposal. In her 1984 work *Toxic Substances Controls Primer* Mary Devine Worobec noted that "Virtually every chemical and substance used in the United States is subject to some type of control. During manufacture, workers who are exposed must be monitored. During use, by-products are created that must be treated in specified ways and when use of a substance is completed, the wastes that remain must be disposed of in approved ways. And at each juncture, the chemical must be transported to the site of the next stage in a proper manner."

Background and Development

The first attempt to identify the "elements," basic indivisible materials, resulted in a list of four substances:

earth, air, water, and fire. The ancient Greeks identified nine modernly recognizable elements: gold, silver, mercury, copper, lead, tin, iron, sulfur, and carbon. As elements and compounds were identified and understood, they were put to work. Early uses for chemicals included dyeing, bleaching, tanning, brewing, embalming, baking, mining, and cleaning. Chemicals were also important to the development of art and medicine.

One of the first products of the chemical industry was borax. A naturally occurring compound containing sodium, boron, and oxygen, borax was known to the Babylonians and Egyptians. Marco Polo inaugurated trade in borax between the Far East and Europe. Another early product (still traded in modern times) was alum. Alum was used during the fifteenth century to stop bleeding, and served as an additive to dyes to improve their ability to adhere to fabrics.

The modern inorganic chemicals industry has its roots in the discovery of the elements. The first element discovered since the time of the ancient Greeks was phosphorous. A German alchemist, Henning Brand, discovered it in 1669 during his attempts to make gold. Modern applications of phosphorous include matches (invented in 1831) and tracer bullets.

During the 1700s, a Dutch chemist decomposed borax to make boric acid. French chemists further decomposed the boric acid and discovered the element boron. Uses of boron compounds in the twentieth century have included water softeners, cleansers, fiberglass, gasoline additives, rocket fuel, fire proofing and fire fighting compounds, cosmetics, pharmaceuticals, and soldering flux. One of the most well known products is Pyrex glass. Pyrex glass is made with boron oxide to reduce the amount of expansion that occurred upon heating. As a result, unlike regular glass, Pyrex is not susceptible to cracking during heat changes. Boron has also been used as a neutron-absorbent material to help control nuclear energy during power production.

In 1730, innovative procedures led to the production of sulfuric acid on a commercial scale. The corrosive substance had been used since the eighth century for a variety of purposes including tanning, tin-plating, brass founding, and hat and button making, but the time-consuming methods employed created only weak acid. Changes introduced by Joshua Ward and improved upon by John Roebuck during the eighteenth century led to the industry's ability to produce stronger acid in greater volumes. By the end of the twentieth century, sulfuric acid topped the list of the most widely sold inorganic chemicals.

Other eighteenth-century discoveries included Georg Brandt's identification of cobalt, Axel Cronstedt's discovery of nickel, and Nicolas Vauquelin's identifica-

tion of chromium. Cobalt chloride achieved popularity as an invisible ink, and in 1948 cobalt-60, a radioactive isotope, was found to be helpful in treating cancer, preserving foods, and sterilizing medical supplies. Nickel, previously thought to be a form of copper, was used to strengthen gold, silver, and copper. Twentieth-century applications have included use in high-strength magnets and household appliances. A chromium compound developed in 1913 by Harold Brearely, an English metallurgist, became widely known as "stainless steel." By the late eighteenth century, 30 elements were known.

During the early nineteenth century, researchers learned more about separating the components of naturally occurring compounds. It was a time of rapid discovery, and many more ingredients used by the modern inorganic chemicals industry were identified. For example, Sir Humphry Davy, an English scientist, discovered sodium, potassium, magnesium, calcium, barium, and strontium. A French chemist, Bernard Courtois, accidentally discovered iodine during experiments with seaweed in which he was trying to produce sodium nitrate to make gunpowder for Napoleon's army. Antoine Balard, another French chemist, discovered elemental bromine. Although pure bromine was poisonous, compounds have been used as sedatives and in synthetic dyes. Silver bromide, a light-sensitive compound, is a critical component used to produce photographic film. In gasoline, bromine serves as an anti-knock additive. Johann Afrwedson, a Swedish chemist, discovered lithium. Lithium, a light alkali metal, weighed only one fifth as much as aluminum and burned when exposed to air. Copper and steel manufacturers exploited this tendency and used lithium to eliminate gas pockets that occurred during metal fabrication. Lithium compounds were also used during World War II to lift emergency radio antennas. They have also served as solid rocket fuels.

In 1860, German chemists Robert Bunsen and Gustav Kirchhoff discovered cesium. Cesium was the first element to be found with a light spectroscope, a device used to measure the light given off from a heated material. According to spectroscopic theory, no two materials emitted the same light pattern. Each element had its own "fingerprint." Cesium, an element that easily releases its electrons when exposed to light, was later used in the development of television and space technologies.

Another discovery made during the 1860s was the creation of elemental fluorine by the English chemist George Gore. Gore succeeded in creating only a small amount of fluorine however, which spontaneously exploded. In 1886 Henri Moissan, a French chemist, developed a way to produce fluorine in platinum vessels without explosive results. In the twentieth century, fluorine has been used in the separation of uranium for atomic weapons, as a component in liquid rocket fuel, and in combination with carbon to make fluorocarbons. Fluorocarbons have been used to replace ammonia in refrigeration systems and as propellants in aerosol cans (before they were banned due to their damaging environmental impact). Fluorine has also been used as a water additive to prevent tooth decay.

The 1860s also brought the development of synthetic dye manufacturing in Germany. The German synthetic dye producers evolved into world chemical production leaders. BASF (Badische Anilin und Soda Fabrik), for example, was established in 1861 originally as a manufacturer of alkali and related products. A BASF chemist enabled the company to expand by developing a method to produce alizarin (a yellowish-red compound) on a commercial scale. Other large German dye companies were Hoechst and Bayer. By the early twentieth century, the German companies held almost 90 percent of the world's dye production ability.

The Dow Chemical Company, founded in 1897, originally sold bromine and chlorine. The first additions to its product line included chloroform, sodium, magnesium, and calcium. Soon after, other corporations joined the roster of chemical manufacturers. They included the Hooker Electrochemical Company (1905), American Cyanamid (1907), Shell Chemical (1912), and Occidental Chemical (1920).

One of the biggest influences on the early twentieth century chemical industry was World War I. During this period, governments sponsored research and guaranteed purchase contracts for finished products. As a result, chemical companies developed new products more quickly than would have been economically possible during times of peace. Following World War I, the German chemical companies regrouped and formed IG Farben, the largest chemical group outside the United States. According to one estimate, IG Farben employed one out of three chemical workers in Germany by 1928. After World War II, IG Farben was divided back into the three largest companies that had merged for its creation: BASF, Bayer, and Hoescht.

In the United States, DuPont invested its war profits by expanding into production of rayon, plastics, ammonia, heavy chemicals, insecticides, electrochemicals, paints, pigments, and varnishes. American Cyanamid, originally a producer of fertilizers, also expanded. New areas included chemicals and chemical catalysts.

During the 1920s, mergers and acquisitions expanded the political influence held by U.S. chemical companies. Allied Chemicals was formed in 1920 through the merger of five previously existing chemical companies. Allied specialized in heavy inorganic chemicals and dyes. Union Carbide was founded in 1920 from three previously existing firms. Domestic chemical producers benefited from

reduced foreign competition in the years between World War I and World War II. The Fordney-McCumber Act of 1922, for example, required that imported chemical products be sold at the same price as domestically produced chemicals. As a result, the chemical industry was one of the fastest growing industries in the country. By 1935, the combined value of the 26 U.S. chemical companies was estimated at $1.7 billion.

World War II brought increased demand for chemical products. These included chemical weapons, bombs, and incendiary devices, as well as a host of new products designed to meet the demands of developing technologies such as aviation. Other products developed by the industry included flameproofing and waterproofing materials. From 1947 to 1978, U.S. chemical production increased 900 percent. During the 1970s however, environmental issues came to the forefront of the nation's conscience and challenged the safety of many products produced by the inorganic chemicals industry. The Environmental Protection Policy Act of 1970 established the Environmental Protection Agency (EPA), and subsequent legislative and regulatory efforts had far reaching effects on the industry. For example, the Toxic Substances Control Act of 1976 gave the EPA authority to regulate chemicals posing a risk to the environment or to human health.

Nevertheless, expansion continued. By the mid-1980s, approximately 60,000 chemicals were being used in the United States, and new industrial chemicals were being developed at a rate of about 1,000 per year. Concerns about safety also escalated, and waste disposal methods were criticized. In 1984, Lee Niedringhaus Davis, a writer specializing in the social impact of high technologies, wrote, ''Each person now contains within his or her body a mixture of poisonous chemicals that no generation throughout humankind's entire history ever accumulated. Their long-term consequences we can only guess at.''

Chemical-producing companies employed numerous methods to reduce the amounts of waste generated. Among them was recapturing and reusing materials previously discharged, using wastes as raw materials for other products, increasing the efficiency of chemical reactions, using waste materials as energy sources, and processing wastes into products by finding innovative uses for them. As companies began to change their views about waste materials, terminology changed. According to Davis, the increasing popularity of the term ''coproduct'' reflected a changing attitude where substances previously discharged as polluting wastes were instead viewed as potential products.

In 1987, the U.S. Department of Commerce reported that the value of shipments within the inorganic chemicals industry totaled $13.2 billion. Products were provided by approximately 700 establishments. About half of these firms were small companies that produced small volumes of specialty chemicals. These types of establishments accounted for only 4 percent of the industry's total shipments, but according to government projections, demand for specialty chemicals was expected to grow faster than demand for commodity chemicals.

The 1990s brought more questions about pollution and environmental health concerns. One chemical under increasing criticism was hydrofluoric acid (HF). Overall demand for HF, an ingredient in the manufacture of chlorinated fluorocarbons (CFCs), was falling during the early 1990s as a result of CFC phaseouts. Some industry analysts expected demand for the chemical to continue declining, but others anticipated a rebound as CFCs were replaced with chemicals containing greater percentages of HF.

Hydrofluoric acid, however, has many other uses. It has been commonly used for the manufacture of other chemicals, aluminum production, stainless steel pickling, and as an octane booster in the petroleum industry. Some well-known end products created with HF technology included computer screens, fluorescent light bulbs, semiconductors, and fluoride toothpaste. Despite its widespread use, *Audubon* magazine called HF "the most dangerous chemical in town." Hydrofluoric acid, a hazardous material, boils at 68 degrees Fahrenheit. As a result, spills of the chemical form dense, low-lying toxic clouds. One accident in 1987 sent more than 1,000 people to the hospital.

A legal action against Mobil Oil Company in California led to the issuance of a consent decree in 1990 requiring all refineries in the state to stop using HF by the end of 1997. Industry watchers estimated that nationwide consumption of HF by gasoline refineries totaled 40 million pounds per year. Nevertheless, only half the gasoline refineries in the country depended on HF; the rest relied on sulfuric acid. According to Mobil, expenses related to switching from HF to sulfuric acid were expected to approach $100 million. Sulfuric acid, although still considered a hazardous chemical, posed less danger than HF. Sulfuric acid has a much higher boiling point, 625 degrees Fahrenheit, and as a result, remains in a liquid state if spilled. Because sulfuric acid does not boil at naturally occurring ambient temperatures, the threat of toxic cloud formation is eliminated.

Since the early 1990s, the largest single chemical produced within the industry has been sulfuric acid. In 1991, producers generated 43 million tons of the chemical. Although some sulfuric acid was manufactured as a by-product of smelting operations and some was regenerated from previously used acid, most was created through the oxidation of sulfur.

Annual demand for sulfuric acid was expected to top 45 million tons by the mid-1990s. As the petroleum refining industry turned away from HF, some industry watchers predicted increased domestic demand for sulfuric acid. Others, however, expected no overall demand increase because of its reduced use in historically important markets, such as rayon production. Sulfuric acid has been used in phosphate and nitrogen fertilizers, ore processing, inorganic pigments, inorganic and organic chemicals, pulp and paper manufacturing, synthetic rubber production, plastics, water treatment, and soaps and detergents.

In the 1990s, hydrazine faced environmental and safety challenges. Approximately 40 percent of the hydrazine produced in the United States is used as an anticorrosion agent in boilers. Users began turning to alternative products however, after hydrazine was identified as a carcinogen. Some hydrazine producers began promoting closed handling systems to permit customers to continue using hydrazine without exposing their workers to dangerous concentrations of the chemical.

One chemical product benefiting from the increased emphasis on environmental safety has been hydrogen peroxide. Although production volumes fell short of other products in the early 1990s, its growth rate and potential were notable. A report published in 1993 suggested that the North American hydrogen peroxide market was expanding at a rate of about 10 to 12 percent annually. One of its primary uses has been as a substitute for chlorine in the pulp and paper industry. Other areas of anticipated growth include the detoxification of cyanide used in gold mining, laundry and cleaning products, chemical manufacturers, water treatment facilities, and pollution control. More potential users of hydrogen peroxide are the textiles industry, suppliers of laundry products, electronics manufacturers, and food processors.

EPA Limits on Toxic Pollution. In March 1994 the Environmental Protection Agency announced long-expected regulations regarding toxic air pollution as part of the 1990 Clean Air Act. Under the rule, "The nation's chemical companies will have to cut their plants' toxic air pollution by almost 90 percent from 1990 levels," according to the *Detroit Free Press*. "The rule requires the companies . . . to install equipment to better prevent evaporation and leaks of 112 toxic chemicals." Environmental Protection Agency Administrator Carol Browner called it the most far-reaching effort ever taken to reduce air toxins. Prior to the new regulations, only 13 air toxins were federally regulated, with others regulated in varying fashions at the state level. To meet requirements, the EPA estimated that approximately 370 chemical plants across the nation would be forced to cut toxic air pollution by a total of 506,000 tons. *The Detroit Free Press* pointed out that "the chemical industry will have to spend $450 million on capital improvements and another $230 million a year in ongoing costs to satisfy the requirements, which will go into effect in most cases within three years.'' The *Free Press* noted that chemical companies have, in many cases, already initiated efforts to improve their pollution emissions in anticipation of the EPA ruling. Company spokespersons for Dow Chemical and Upjohn, for instance, say that both companies have reduced air pollution levels at their plants by more than 50 percent in recent years.

The chemical industry as a whole was experiencing a slow recovery after a national economic slowdown during the early 1990s. Forecasters expected the overall industrial inorganic chemicals industry to grow at a rate comparable to the nation's economic growth rate.

The outlook for inorganic chemicals by 1996 was mixed. The hydrogen peroxide commodity was sold out and prices were expected to remain the same until more product became available. Chlorine and sodium chlorate were expected to drop slightly from their strong 1995 levels, and sodium bicarbonate sales would reflect growth in gross domestic product.

The demand for hydrogen peroxide was 1 billion pounds in 1994, 1.1 billion pounds in 1995, and was expected to grow at a rate of 8 to 10 percent. In 1996 however, the pulp market crashed. As the pulp market used 60 percent of all hydrogen peroxide in North America, the pulp and paper industries dictated to a large degree the livelihood of hydrogen peroxide. The market had been going so well up until then, that hydrogen peroxide makers were not incredibly hurt by the sudden decrease in activity, and some manufacturers welcomed the opportunity for maintenance.

Gains in the fertilizer market caused the demand for sulfur to increase 5 percent from 1993 to 1994. Another healthy gain occurred in 1995 due to increased fertilizer consumption. Sulfur sales were expected to remain closely tied to U.S. and world fertilizer demand.

Sulfuric acid recovered well in 1995 from reduced levels in 1993 and 1994. In March of 1994, the industry hit bottom with prices falling to $8 and $9 per ton. By 1995 sulfuric acid was up to $35 per ton. This was beginning to approach the $50-per-ton record high of the late 1980s.

The healthy market in the mid-1990s was due to an increase in demand for phosphate fertilizers and more use by the copper industry. As copper prices doubled in the first two months of 1995, more sulfuric acid was suddenly needed as copper miners tried to extract as much copper as quickly as possible. Another contributing factor was that imports of sulfuric acid from non-Canadian sources were almost nonexistent in 1995. The import rate had dropped from 684,000 metric tons in 1993 to 333,000 metric tons in 1994. Shipping prices from Germany, for example, were more expensive per ton than the sulfuric acid was worth.

CURRENT CONDITIONS

The chemical industry as a whole grew in the last years of the 1990s, boosted in part by the strong economy and in part by a growing export market. Collectively, the industry's 665 establishments shipped $18 billion worth of products in 1997. Alumina was responsible for $1.2 billion of this total. The Chemical Manufacturers Association reported in February 2000 that 1999 exports for the industry as a whole had reached a record $70 billion. The industry had expected exports to be flat, but a number of factors including a strong global demand for chemicals bolstered the performance. Inorganic chemicals are expected to do fairly well in 2000 and beyond, although consolidations and streamlining would likely continue to reduce the number of workers.

INDUSTRY LEADERS

The leaders of the inorganic chemical industry include E.I. DuPont de Nemours and Co. of Wilmington, Delaware; Dow Chemical Co. of Midland, Michigan; and FMC Corp. of Chicago, Illinois.

In 1999, Du Pont was the largest company in the entire chemicals industry. It showed revenues of $27.9 billion and employed 101,000 people. Du Pont has facilities in some 65 countries around the world.

The Dow Chemical Company was founded in 1897 by Herbert Henry Dow, and its first two products were bromine and chlorine. Other products added during the company's early years included sodium, magnesium, calcium, synthetic dyes, chemical fertilizers, food preservatives, solvents, and caustic soda. Throughout the twentieth century, Dow acquired other companies and diversified into many areas including chemicals, plastics, hydrocarbons, energy, pharmaceuticals, and consumer products.

Dow was an early pioneer in toxicology work. The company established its first toxicology laboratory in 1933 following the deaths of workers from chemical exposure. Dow was also working to reduce the environmental impact of its products and manage solid wastes in a more responsible manner. In 1991, Dow created a Corporate Environmental Advisory Council, the first of its kind in the industry. The Council was composed of professionals from the government, education, environmental protection, and scientific communities who met together to discuss issues concerning environment, health, and safety. In 1999, Dow's sales totaled $18.9 billion, and the company employed 39,000 people.

The FMC Corporation reported sales of $4.1 billion in 1999. FMC divisions held top positions in several segments of the inorganic chemicals market. FMC is the world's leading producer of soda ash, and its Peroxygen Chemicals Division was one of the world's largest producers of hydrogen peroxide and served such customers as the pulp and paper, textile, detergent, electronics, and environmental industries. FMC Foret, S.A., the company's European division, supplied products to a variety of users including other chemical manufacturers and the detergent industry.

Like many of its competitors, FMC has been heavily affected by environmental legislation. The company reported that its waste releases were decreased by 30 percent between 1987 and 1992. In addition, FMC voluntarily participated in an Environmental Protection Agency (EPA) program to reduce its emissions of specific hazardous chemicals.

One newcomer to the industry isn't actually a newcomer in the strictest sense of the word. Solutia, Inc., which posted 1999 sales of $2.8 billion and had 8,700 employees, was spun off by the Monsanto Corporation as part of its effort to focus on the life sciences industry.

WORKFORCE

According to government estimates, the inorganic chemicals industry employed 59,700 workers in 1999. Overall employment figures declined somewhat since the early 1990s, although there was a slight rise in the mid-1990s. (In 1981, U.S. Department of Labor statistics indicated a total work force in the industry of more than 107,000 employees.) Most of those employees are located in three states: South Carolina, Washington, and Tennessee. Of the more than 700 companies classified in the industry, more than 55 percent employed fewer than 20 people. The average hourly wage for production workers in this industry was $22.19 in 1997.

One of the major issues confronting the industry's labor force was worker health and safety. The chemical industry has had a long history of exposing its workers to hazardous situations. For example, in the latter half of the 1800s, the Leblanc method of reacting sulfuric acid on salt to produce alkali created hydrochloric acid gas as a by-product. The hydrochloric acid gas rotted workers' teeth, led to chronic bronchitis, and caused skin ailments. Moreover, industrial accidents involving chemicals often resulted in greater harm to workers and the environment than accidents in other industries.

To address the needs of workers, Congress passed the Occupational Safety and Health Act of 1970. The Act created the Occupational Safety and Health Administration (OSHA) within the U.S. Department of Labor. OSHA's responsibilities include establishing safe standards for chemical exposure and keeping workers informed of potential risks. Chemical companies also began to address safety needs with greater vigor and introduced increasing numbers of voluntary measures to help ensure employee and public safety.

RESEARCH AND TECHNOLOGY

As the chemicals industry evolved during the twentieth century, the cost of investigating and developing new products was very high. Many new compounds studied by researchers were rejected because they failed to meet expectations, were too expensive to produce, or posed safety problems. Another related problem was rapid obsolescence of products and related manufacturing methods. Because technologies changed so quickly, new products were sometimes outdated before their developing companies could recapture costs associated with research and development. Additionally, as technologies changed, many manufacturing methods also became obsolete.

By the 1990s, many products within this industrial classification were considered basic commodities. As a result, research activities to develop new products were conducted with less vigor than in other segments of the chemical industry. Instead of focusing on new product development, most research focused on ways to reduce production costs by reducing labor costs, cutting energy needs, improving process efficiencies, and finding new applications for existing products. Researchers also investigated ways to meet environmental mandates by curtailing emissions, putting waste products to work, recapturing materials, and rendering hazardous substances inert.

The Santa Cruz In Situ Mining Research Project was conducted in 1996 to explore new uses for sulfuric acid. This project demonstrated the environmental, technical, and economic feasibility of in situ, or "in place" mining. The goal was to reach copper that was buried too deeply and was of too low a grade to be mined by conventional methods. A dilute solution of sulfuric acid was injected nearly 1,600 feet below the earth's surface into undisturbed granite bedrock containing soluble copper oxide minerals. The solution was then recovered through wells and pumped to the surface where it was processed and re-injected into the mining zone in a closed loop.

FURTHER READING

Chapman, Peter. "Chemical Outlook '96: Inorganic Chemicals." *Chemical Marketing Reporter* 15 January 1996.

———. "Peroxide Producers Jolted by Pulp Crash." *Chemical Marketing Reporter* 19 February 1996.

———. "Sulfuric Acid Market Regains its Strength." *Chemical Marketing Reporter* 11 September 1995.

Darnay, Arsen J., ed. *Manufacturing USA.* 6th ed. Detroit: The Gale Group, 1999.

Dow At a Glance, Midland, MI: nd

The Dow Chemical Company. Available from http://www.dow .com/index2.html.

"DuPont At a Glance . . ." Available from http://www.dupont .com/corp/gbl-company/overview.html.

Gallagher, Matthew. "Sulfuric Acid Aided By 'Diverse Factors'." *Chemical Marketing Reporter* 27 March 1995.

"Hydrogen Peroxide." *Chemical Marketing Reporter* November 1995.

"New Use For Sulfuric Acid?" *Chemical Marketing Reporter* 4 March 1996.

U.S. Census Bureau. *1997 Economic Census—Manufacturing.* Washington, DC: GPO, 1999.

SIC 2821

PLASTIC MATERIALS AND RESINS

The plastic materials and resins industry is comprised of companies primarily engaged in manufacturing various resins and plastics for sale to other industries that create plastic sheets, rods, films, and other products. Information on related products can be found under **SIC 2822: Synthetic Rubber, SIC 2823: Cellulose Manmade Fibers,** and **SIC 2824: Organic Fibers—Noncellulosic.**

NAICS CODE(S)

325211 (Plastic Material and Resin Manufacturing)

INDUSTRY SNAPSHOT

Synthetic plastic was invented late in the eighteenth century and did not reach widespread use in the United States until the 1900s. Swift advances in chemical and manufacturing technologies during the twentieth century, however, made plastic one of America's most important manufacturing materials. Massive demand for plastic had propelled the industry to $274 billion in shipments in 1996, a 55 percent increase since 1991, according to the Society of the Plastics Industry (SPI) with the industry employing 1.3 million. If upstream employees are counted, this figure grows to 2.3 million. Upstream includes those workers who supply the plastics industry with products and services. In 1996 the plastics industry ranked fourth in shipments among the top manufacturing industry groups behind motor vehicles, petroleum refining, and electronic components and accessories, up from fifth in 1994.

Adjusting for inflation the plastics industry grew at an annual rate of 4.1 percent over the last 25 years as plastics increasingly invaded markets formerly dominated by wood, metal, glass, and paper products. Moreover, growth was spurred by the development of new and better plastics that spawned new uses for industry output. Although an economic recession in the early 1990s caused growth to lag, the long-term outlook for plastics is optimistic, with the industry registering a 4.9 percent

increase in the production of resins for the first four months of 1999 compared to the same period in 1998. Sales and internal use increased by 7 percent.

Much of the initial growth of the industry came from plastic replacements of wood, metal, and glass products. Nevertheless, 95.6 million metric tons of thermoplastic resins were consumed worldwide in 1996. This represents a 12.5 percent increase in consumption over 1994. (In 1998 the production of plastic materials and resins by weight was 81.7 million pounds). The same figure for 1994 was 68.9. It is forecast that worldwide demand for plastic materials and resins will reach 160 million metric tons by 2003, mostly for thermoplastics. This increased demand, coupled with developing technologies is expected to boost production and profits into the twenty-first century.

ORGANIZATION AND STRUCTURE

Plastics provide an important alternative to natural materials for a plethora of applications. One of the most important distinguishing factors between plastic and other materials is plastic's ability to "creep" under load, or gradually stretch or flow when subjected to stress. While metals and ceramics exhibit this property as well, they do so only at much higher temperatures. Plastics also resist erosion and do not require a coating to protect them against inorganic acids, bases, and water or salt solutions. Perhaps the greatest advantage that plastics offer, however, is their ability to be molded into any shape and to be processed to exhibit any of a massive number of physical characteristics.

Competition and Market Structure. The synthetic materials industry is considered a segment of the overall chemical industry; synthetic materials manufacturers represent about 20 percent. The plastics industry comprises about 70 percent of the entire synthetic materials industry, which also encompasses rubber and manmade fibers. Manufacturers produce about 500 different types of resins and compounds. Each of these products is available from various suppliers in multiple grades, each grade offering varying physical properties and prices.

Production. Plastics are giant polymers, or long-chain molecules that contain thousands of repeating molecular units. When combined with other ingredients called additives, the polymers can be shaped and molded under heat and pressure into a resin. Resins are produced through chemical processes that combine carbon with other elements such as oxygen, nitrogen, and hydrogen. Resin usually takes the form of pellets, flakes, granules, powder, or a syrupy liquid. Most resins are not used in their natural state, but are instead combined with other materials by mixing or melt-state blending. The end result is a plastic compound, still in the form of pellets, granules, or powder, that is ready to be delivered to a processor. There are two basic kinds of plastics: thermoplastics, which can be re-softened to their original condition by the application of heat; and thermosets, which cannot be resoftened. The production of thermoplastic resins surpasses the production of thermosetting resins by a ratio of about 8 or 9 to 1. Thermosetting resins include epoxy and polyester. Thermoplastic resins include polyethylene and polyvinyl chloride, more commonly known as PVC.

The physical properties of the final plastic product can be altered at various stages of the polymerization and production process. The most versatile method of varying properties is by compounding. With this method, additives—such as colorants, flame retardants, heat or light stabilizers, or lubricants—may be added to the resin to achieve a desired result. Fillers or reinforcement—such as glass fibers, particulate materials, or hollow glass spheres—may instead be added to the resin, as may other polymers, which form a polymer blend or alloy.

Plasticizers are the most common additives used to alter plastic resins. Plasticizers increase a resin's flexibility and are often used to make polyvinyl chloride resins used in construction products. Impact modifiers are an additive used to boost a plastic's resistance to stress. Similarly, antidixodiants retard the oxidation and breakdown of plastics, and heat stabilizing additives help resins to maintain their physical structure during processing. Light stabilizers filter out radiation that can cause a plastic to deteriorate as a result of exposure to sunlight, and flame retardants enable resins to resist combustion. Colorants are another major additive used in the compounding process.

Four major commercial divisions of plastic resins are manufactured. Commodity resins, which represent the bulk of industry production, are low-tech plastics available in standardized formulas from many companies throughout the world. Intermediate resins are generally considered more advanced and somewhat specialized in comparison to commodity resins. Similarly, engineering resins generally exhibit more advanced performance characteristics and are produced on a smaller scale than other types of resin. Finally, advanced resins are generally those most capable of withstanding impact and high heat, carrying loads, and resisting attacks by chemicals and solvents.

Thermoplastics. Thermoplastics accounted for about 88 percent of industry output in 1998. They solidify by cooling and may be remelted repeatedly to form new shapes. Examples of thermoplastic resins are polyethylene, polypropylene, and polystyrene. Polyethylene is the highest volume plastic, accounting for about 40 percent of thermoplastic production, and is used primarily to create packaging, though many consumer and institutional products are made from it as well. About 27 billion

pounds of polyethylene were produced in 1998. Major manufacturers of this resin include Quantum Chemical, Union Carbide, and Dow Chemical Co.

Polyvinyl chloride (PVC) makes up the second largest share of the thermoplastics segment. It is used primarily to make gutters, pipes, siding, windows, and other products used by construction and building industries. About 14.5 billion pounds of PVC were shipped in 1998. Major producers include Occidental Petroleum, Shintech, and Formosa Plastics. Polypropylene, another thermoplastic, accounted for about 13.8 billion pounds of production in 1998. This resin is used mainly in the creation of fiber and filaments, as well as in the production of packaging and molded consumer products.

About 6.2 billion pounds of polystyrene, a fourth major thermoplastic product, were produced in 1998. This resin is used to make disposable packaging, furniture finishings, and miscellaneous consumer products. Other thermoplastics segments include polyamide resins, styrene-butadiene, and some polyesters.

Thermosets. Thermosets, the other division of the plastics industry, account for about 12 percent of output. Unlike thermoplastics, thermosets harden by chemical reaction, and cannot be melted and shaped after they are created. Thermosets are also considered the more mature and less dynamic segment of the industry.

Typical thermosets include phenolics, urea-formaldehyde resins, epoxies, and polyester. Phenolics, which account for over 50 percent of all thermoset production, are used principally for construction products. Such materials include plywood adhesives, insulation, laminates, moldings, and abrasives. Urea, the second largest segment of the thermoset division, is also used as an adhesive for plywood and particle board. Other uses of this resin include protective coatings and textile and paper treating and coating.

Thermoset polyesters are used to create plastics that are reinforced with glass fiber and other materials. They are also used to make various construction supplies such as boat and marine equipment, transportation products, and electronics. Epoxy is primarily used as a protective coating for metal goods, but is also used in multiple construction applications. In 1998, 639 million pounds of epoxy were produced.

BACKGROUND AND DEVELOPMENT

The first plastic used in the United States was a natural material known as Keratin, which was made from animal hooves, horns, feathers, and hair. Keratin was used as a fabricating material to make lantern windows and other items as early as 1740. In the late 1800s, Americans copied a technique observed among Malayan natives, who molded a plastic made from gutta percha, or gum elastic, into knife handles and other articles. This technique had a variety of applications in the United States, from ocean cable insulation to billiard balls. Samuel Speck, regarded as the first American to mold plastics, helped to introduced shellac plastics in the 1850s. By then, different types of natural plastics were being used to produce such items as checkers, buttons, picture frames, and insulators.

"Parkesine," the first synthetic plastic, was invented in 1862 by Alexander Parkes, an Englishman. Recognizing the important plasticizing effect in the Parkesine production process, American John Wyatt renamed the substance celluloid in 1870 and was credited with originating the production of synthetic plastics in the United States. Celluloid, despite its inflammability, was used to make carriage and automobile windshields and motion picture film.

Dr. Baekland, also an American, invented the world's first moldable plastic material in 1909. Baekland's thermosetting phenolformaldehyde resin provided a tremendous impetus for other inventors, who began developing molding techniques and adding resins to paints and varnishes. Baekland's resin, later called "bakelite," was also used in the electrical industry to make some of the first molded synthetic plastic components. The first colorless resin, urea-formaldehyde, was invented in 1918 and sold commercially in 1928.

Plastics research and development began to proliferate in the 1920s and 1930s. The Germans pioneered the creation of many new thermosetting resins, while Americans and several Europeans made significant contributions in the area of plastic molding and extrusion machines, and later in the advancement of thermoplastics. During World War II, the plastics industry realized significant advances, as warring nations hurried to develop new and better materials for their war machines.

Postwar economic expansion augmented the development of the plastics industry. As demand for all types of consumer, commercial, and institutional products soared, plastics producers scrambled to keep pace with expanding markets. Successive breakthroughs in chemical technology and production techniques opened up vast new markets for manufacturers. Most importantly, however, producers in other industries began to realize the advantages of substituting plastics for more expensive, less flexible, natural materials. By the 1970s the plastics industry was shipping more than $10 billion worth of resins per year. U.S. producers also controlled a major share of aggregate world exports.

Sales of all types of plastic resins continued to multiply throughout much of the 1980s. A variety of factors, such as excess capacity and high petroleum costs, contributed to brief periods of slow production or decreased profits. In general, however, industry participants benefited from several factors. Growth in exports, for example, contributed to the industry's success; although U.S. chemical firms lost world market share, exports grew from $7 billion in 1992 to nearly $14 billion in 1999, imports also grew during these years from $2 billion in 1992 to $5.6 billion in 1999.

New additives and plastic alloys also increased in demand, opening entirely new markets for resins and prompting other industries to substitute plastic for more expensive, less flexible organic products. Furthermore, as many segments of the industry matured and became more competitive, falling prices allowed plastics to penetrate a number of metal, glass, and wood markets. Reinforcing downward pricing pressures were massive industry investments in research, development, and more efficient production facilities, allowing producers to remain extremely competitive domestically.

Between 1992 and 1999, plastic industry shipments grew at a slow but steady pace from $31.6 billion to $47.7 billion, with predictions of $47.6 billion in shipments in 2000. In percentages, the growth rate for the plastic industry was 6.1 percent between 1992 and 1996; 9.5 percent between 1996 and 1997; 4.5 percent between 1997 and 1998; and 4 percent between 1998 and 1999. Industry employment also grew at a slow but steady pace from 54,000 in 1982 to almost 70,000 in 1995. In 1996, however, employment had sunk to 58,600, a decade low. Nevertheless this figure is predicted to climb back to 69,500 by 2000.

CURRENT CONDITIONS

Much of the demand for plastics comes from the packaging and consumer markets, two sectors that, according to Standard & Poor's, are fairly resistant to recessionary pressures. In fact in 1997 the largest single market for plastics was packaging products such as bags, bottles, and food containers. These products alone consumed 26 percent of all plastics according to the SPI. Building and construction was the second largest market with structural materials, pipes, conduits, and fittings accounting for 21 percent of 1997 plastics production. Consumer and institutional goods such as kitchen wares, toys, sporting goods, and medical products accounted for 13 percent; transportation for 5 percent; furniture and furnishings and electronic appliances and components each accounted for 4 percent; exports for 12 percent; adhesives, inks, and coatings for 2 percent; and all other uses for 13 percent.

Thermosets, however, are not quite as recession resistant as thermoplastics. In 1997, 66 percent of thermoset production was consumed by the building and construction industry, an industry that is highly cyclical.

Many industry analysts predicted 1999 and 2000 to be a good years for the plastics materials and resins

VALUE OF SHIPMENTS FOR PLASTICS MATERIALS AND RESINS

Source: U.S. Industry & Trade Outlook '99

industry following a worldwide slump in resin prices in 1998. The 1998 slump in resin prices was a direct result of the Asian economic crisis. Asian plastics producers, in an effort to raise cash, flooded the market with exports. These actions, however, resulted in a slump in prices due to oversupply. Brazil, which also faced its own economic crisis in 1998, saw a 13 to 17 percent drop in the price of its resins. Depressed prices carried over into early 1999, with *Modern Plastics'* Robert Colvin predicting that a buyer's market would continue well into the year, especially for polyethylene.

Standard & Poor's, however, noted that production rose in the first four month's of 1999 with most resins reporting gains with the exception of PCV prices, which remained close to 1998 levels. Howard R. Blum, vice-president of The Catalyst Group was quoted by *Chemical Market Reporter* as foreseeing 1998's 106 million metric ton global thermoplastic market growing at an annual rate of 3.2 percent and thus reaching 156 million metric tons by 2010. Blum predicted that the 2010 thermoplastic market would consume: 91 million tons of polyolefins; 34 million tons of PVC and styrenics; 26 million tons of PET and nylon fibers; and 15 million tons of ETPs. *European Chemical News* was also optimistic in its forecast of a 9 percent growth between 1998 and 1999 with polymer demand in Romania, the Czech Republic, Slovakia, Hungary, and Poland reaching 2.5 million tons in 1999.

Purchasing predicted price rises in the year 2000 for many basic products including plastics. Quoting a study by Thinking Cap Solutions, *Purchasing* predicted a price jump of 5.5 percent in 2000 following price drops of 8.8 percent in 1998 and 3.2 percent in 1999.

The 1990s also witnessed compression and consolidation in the U.S. plastics industry. Standard & Poor's

quoted Impact Marketing Consultants as estimating that there were only 17 large U.S. producers of polyethylene and 14 large U.S. producers of polypropylene in 1995. They also noted that in 1996, the number of U.S. polystyrene producers dropped from eight to six when two producers sold out to competitors. Other important mergers and buyouts included: the formation of the Equistar Chemical partnership formed by the partial merger of Lyondell Chemical and Millennium Chemicals, Inc., which made Equistar the largest producer of ethylene and polyethylene in North America, with 1998 revenues of $4.4 billion; the acquisition of Rexene Corp. by Huntsman for $60 million in 1997; the partial merger of Geon Co. and Occidental Petroleum in 1999, which formed Oxy Vinyls L.P., a move expected to provide cost savings of $80 million by 2000; and the merger of Amoco Corp. with British Petroleum and the pending merger of Exxon Corp. and Mobil. BP Amoco reported chemical sales of $9.7 billion in 1998.

INDUSTRY LEADERS

The largest U.S. company actively producing chemicals, plastics, hydrocarbons, and agricultural and specialty products in 1998 was Dow Chemical Company of Midland, Michigan. This diversified company employed over 42,800 in 1997 and generated over $20 billion in sales. Allied Signal of Morristown, New Jersey was second with sales of nearly $14 billion. Allied, however, employed nearly 77,000.

Ashland Inc. was the third largest with 1998 sales revenue of $12 billion. The Chemical Group of the Monsanto Company of St.Louis was fourth with sales of just over $12 billion. Dow Chemical U.S.A., with 1998 revenues of $9.5 billion, and Exxon Chemical Co. of Houston, Texas, with 1998 sales revenue of $8.6 billion, ranked fifth and sixth in the United States respectively.

The Ciba-Geigy Corp. of Terrytown, New York was the seventh largest competitor in the industry in 1998 with revenues of $6.7 billion and 20,000 employees. Other large competitors included Polymer Products of Wilmington, Delaware, $6.6 billion in 1998 sales; Union Carbide Corp. of Danbury, Connecticut, with $6.1 billion in sales; and Occidental Chemical Corp. of Dallas, with sales revenue of $5.4 billion.

WORKFORCE

In 1995, about 70,000 were employed in the U.S. plastics industry, including 41,500 production workers. Total compensation was $3.3 billion and the average hourly wage was $19.97. Total employment had been expected to drop to 58,500 in 1996 and then begin climbing again to 69,500 by 2000.

Despite these relatively flat employment figures, the plastics industry is expected to offer steady opportunities for highly trained individuals, especially in technical fields. Average wages per hour in the plastics industry in 1996 were $20.50 as compared to $12.68 for the average of all manufacturing establishments. The first production step in making plastic products is the preparing and mixing of resins with other ingredients to form powders. These tasks are usually performed by drier operators, blenders, and oven tenders. Molding machine operators are then responsible for setting and monitoring heat and pressure gauges on the molding machinery and pouring the powder into the machines. The operators then remove the molded plastic products from the machines and send them to finishing rooms where drill press operators, grinders, and buffers finish the products. Plastics regrinders are responsible for grinding scrap plastic for recycling.

The plastics industry remains a major supplier of high-paying jobs for those specializing in technical fields, particularly chemists, chemical engineers, and plastics engineers. A chemical engineer with a bachelor's degree could be expected to earn a starting salary of $42,800 in 1997. With post-bachelor degrees, the starting salary could be boosted to just under $60,000. Starting salaries for chemists are generally higher. In 1997 the average starting salary for a chemist with a bachelor's degrees was $49,400, $56,200 with a master's degree, and $71,000 with a doctorate. For chemical engineers, the prediction is for above average employment opportunities in the plastics industry. In 1996 chemical engineers represented 2.9 percent of industry employment and chemists represented 1.3 percent. The highest job classification in the industry was chemical equipment controller, which represented 11.3 percent of industry employment followed by extruding and forming machine operators at 8.2 percent.

AMERICA AND THE WORLD

The U.S. plastics industry, by far the largest and most advanced in the world, was heavily dependent on exports throughout the 1990s. In 1995 the U.S. plastics industry exported $10.3 billion worth of products. This figure was expected to climb to $13.9 billion in 1999. Import figures are $4 billion and $5.6 billion, respectively. The SPI estimates that exports were responsible for 118,000 industry jobs in 1996, up 22 percent from 1992. The society also notes that the U.S. plastics industry had a $5.5 billion trade surplus in 1996, a 34 percent increase over 1992. The strongest export sector of the plastics industry is plastics raw materials, which had a $6.3 billion trade surplus in 1996. Plastics products had a positive trade balance of $659 million. Molds and machinery, however, showed a deficit. The U.S. Department of Commerce predicted that the United States, Japan, and western Europe will continue to dominate in the production and the consumption of plastics materials and products, although the markets in both Latin America and

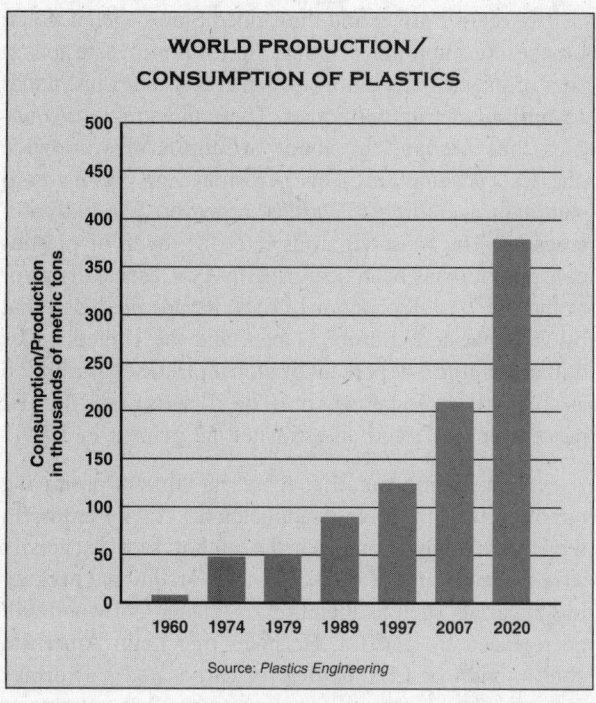

WORLD PRODUCTION/ CONSUMPTION OF PLASTICS

Source: *Plastics Engineering*

Asia will grow at a faster rate. This will be especially true in Brazil, China, and Mexico. Growth in Thailand, South Korea, and other fast-developing areas of southeast Asia is expected to be slow as a result of the 1998 Asian economic crisis-but then rebound by 2003.

There are, however, both short-and long-term export challenges for the U.S. plastics industry. Still prevalent currency problems in Asia are expected to dampen the demand for U.S. exports, and export growth was expected to be slow throughout 1999. Many Asian countries, especially South Korea and China, are expanding their plastics manufacturing capacity, which will lessen their demands for imports while creating global competition for U.S. firms.

Writing in *Plastics Engineering* Francoise Pardos of Pardos Marketing in Orgeval, France predicts that by 2007, the global market for solid polymers will reach 210 million metric tons and climb to 400 million metric tons by 2020. These figures reflect a 7.8 percent annual growth rate between 1960 and 1997 (8 million metric tons to 125 million metric tons respectively) and a 5 percent annual growth rate between 1997 and 2020. Pardos draws a correlation between per capita average income and per capita consumption of plastics by major countries and regions of the world. In this analysis, consumption refers to raw plastics consumed by converting industries. Pardos believes that as a general rule of thumb, an average GNP of US$15,000 per capita or higher converts to a per capita consumption of 60 kilograms of plastics (about 132 pounds), while an average GNP of US$2500 or less would mean an average plastics consumption of less than 15 kilograms (about 33 pounds) per capita.

Western Europe and the United States each account for the consumption of about 30 million metric tons a year of plastics in solid form. Japan consumes just under 15 million metric tons a year. These three regions/countries thus account for about two-thirds of worldwide plastics consumption. This percentage of plastics consumption according to Pardos, however, is rapidly decreasing. The most vigorous rate of growth of plastics consumption has been occurring in Asia, especially prior to the 1997-1998 economic crisis. Pardos predicted that by 2020 western Europe, Japan, and the United States will account for 40 percent of global plastic consumption as compared to 75 percent in 1974, 70 percent in 1985, 62 percent in 1997, and an estimated 52 percent in 2007.

"Developing countries represent areas of promising opportunities for plastics application," says Pardos. In these developing countries the author sees especially strong growth in four market sectors. Traditional packaging materials such as metal, glass, paper, and wood will be replaced by plastics. He notes that Latin American consumption of PET bottles for carbonated soft drinks and water has a staggering annual average growth rate of 20 percent, which translated in 1997 to 500,000 metric tons, or nearly 50 percent of the similar European market. Pardos also sees strong growth in applications such as building and construction, automotive parts, and agricultural films. "The future demand for plastics is expected to be fueled by the continuing requirement in developed countries—where growth is slower, but production is based upon very large tonnage—and buildup of demand from developing countries." "Imaginative and creative applications of new polymers, blends, and combinations can play a part in solving some of the most urgent problems of developing countries," Pardos concludes.

RESEARCH AND TECHNOLOGY

Technology and performance are keywords in the plastics industry's search for new markets and the maintenance of existing ones. "It's an exciting time in the business right now," claims Daniel DeLegge, Technical Director of Resins for Lawter International. Lawter, which was recently acquired by Eastman Chemical, is driven by environmental concerns, cost containment, and performance, especially the performance of inks under the new demands of high-speed, high-pressure, and high-temperature printing machine technologies. "We are looking for resins that will handle the demands of high-speed presses," says DeLegge. To meet these demands Lawter has come up with a new series of OMNI-REZ resins that are based on a hybrid technology of phenolics and hydrocarbons.

Plastics technology also continues to play an increasingly important role in heavy industry. DaimlerChrysler engineers, for example, have developed a lightweight, fully recyclable thermoplastic that will make its debut as a hardtop on the 2001 Jeep Wrangler. The new plastic weighs 30 percent less than comparable use plastics, costs 10 percent less, and doesn't require painting, thus saving $75 million in paint shop emissions-control equipment alone. Paint is injected directly into the plastic before taking on its final shape as a door or hardtop. As a result, the new auto part won't chip, scratch, or rust. The result, however, is a matte finish, not a glossy one. "We are on the cusp of revolutionizing the vehicle manufacturing process," says Al Power, president and chief executive officer of Decoma International, a bumper fascia supplier and project collaborator. The new hardtops will be made of injection-molded thermoplastic at Husky Injection Molding Systems of Novi, Michigan.

FURTHER READING

Campbell, Paul D.Q. "Environmental, Cost and Performance Factors Drive Resin Developments in 1999." *American Ink Maker,* October 1999, 131+.

Career Information Center. 7th ed. New York: Macmillan Reference USA, 1999.

"DaimlerChrysler AG's (Germany) Engineers and Its North American Suppliers Jointly Develop High-Tech Thermoplastic." *Detroit Free Press,* 2 November 1999.

Darnay, Arsen J. *Manufacturing U.S.A.* 6th ed. Detroit: Gale Research, 1998.

"Global Engineering Thermoplastics Consumption Will Total 2.2 bil lb/yr by 2000." *Appliance,* September 1999.

"Goodbye Deflation! Prices Forecast to Rise in 2000." *Purchasing,* 21 October 1999, 28-30.

Hoover's Masterlist of Major U.S. Companies 1998-1999. Austin, Texas: Hoover's Business Press, 1998.

Pardos, Francoise. "Forecast for the World Plastics Industry to 2020." *Plastics Engineering,* November 1999, 53-57.

Plastics Material and Resin Manufacturing: 1997 Economic Census-Manufacturing-Industry Series. Washington: GPO, 1999. Available from http://www.census.gov/prod/ec97/97m3252a.pdf.

"Polymers Set to Grow By 9 Percent." *European Chemical News,* 8 November 1999, 11.

"Report From Dusseldorf: K'98 Show News (Pastics Technology Fair)." *Plastics Technology,* January 1999, 44-60.

"Resin Supply At the Crossroads." *Modern Plastics.* January 1999, 49-72.

Richards, Don. "World Thermoplastics Market Appears Set for Lasting Growth." *Chemical Market Reporter,* 11 August 1999.

Society of the Plastics Industry. *SPI: The Society of the Plastics Industry Trade Association.* Washington: Society of the Plastics Industry, 1999. Available from www.plasticsindustry.org.

Standard & Poor's Corp. *Chemicals: Basic.* New York: Industry Surveys, 1999.

U.S. Industry & Trade Outlook '99. New York: McGraw-Hill, 1999.

U.S. Superintendent of Documents. *1998-1999 Occupational Outlook Handbook.* Washington: Superintendent of Documents, 1998.

SIC 2822

SYNTHETIC RUBBER (VULCANIZABLE ELASTOMERS)

This category covers establishments primarily engaged in manufacturing synthetic rubber by polymerization or copolymerization. An elastomer, for the purpose of this classification, is a rubber-like material capable of vulcanization, such as copolymers of butadiene and styrene, or butadiene and acrylonitrile, polybutadienes, chloroprene rubbers, and isobutylene-isoprene copolymers. Butadiene copolymers containing less than 50 percent butadiene are classified in **SIC 2821: Plastics Materials, Synthetic Resins, and Nonvulcanizable Elastomers.** Natural chlorinated rubbers and cyclized rubbers are considered as semifinished products and are classified in **SIC 3069: Fabricated Rubber Products, Not Elsewhere Classified.**

NAICS CODE(S)

325212 (Synthetic Rubber Manufacturing)

INDUSTRY SNAPSHOT

Production of synthetic rubber on a commercial scale began in the United States during the 1930s, though natural rubber has been used since the early 1800s for multiple applications. The United States assumed an early lead in the development and production of vulcanizable elastomers—a position that it maintained throughout the twentieth century. Indeed, by 1997 the more than 100,000 people employed in the industry were churning out approximately 2.7 million metric tons of synthetic rubber. The value of shipments increased from $4.74 billion in 1994 to $4.98 billion in 1995 and $6.06 billion in 1997.

Rubber manufacturers were holding their own in the late 1990s, following a gradual industry decline during the 1980s. Product maturity, stagnant demand growth, and increasing foreign competition were the dominant factors suppressing industry profitability. Although producers tried to counter this downward momentum with increased productivity and the development of new rubbers, falling prices and a sluggish world economy in the early 1990s offered little reason for optimism. Ironically, past industry successes contributed to the industry's malaise. Long-lasting rubbers, for instance, reduced demand in large market segments such as the tire industry. Competitors were looking to new rubbers for growth in the 2000s.

Holding out some hope for increased synthetic rubber demand in the new millennium was a continuing shortage of natural rubber. In the fall of 1999, the London-based International Rubber Study Group predicted that global production of natural rubber in 2000 would fall short of demand for the second year in a row. According to the IRSG's projections, international natural rubber output would rise in 2000 to 6.79 million metric tons, up from 6.68 million in 1999. World consumption of natural rubber was expected to hit 7.03 million metric tons, up from 6.78 million metric tons in 1999.

ORGANIZATION AND STRUCTURE

The synthetic rubber industry represents about 8 percent of the entire U.S. synthetic materials manufacturing sector. Plastics (**SIC 2821: Plastics Materials, Synthetic Resins, and Nonvulcanizable Elastomers**) and manmade fibers (**SIC 2824: Manmade Organic Fibers, Except Cellulosic**) are the other synthetics.

The synthetic materials industry is considered part of the overall U.S. chemical industry, of which synthetics account for about 25 percent. Natural rubber, which represents about 20 percent of all rubber consumed in the United States, is derived from rubber trees and other organic sources. Production and processing of natural rubber is not included in this industrial classification.

Synthetic rubber offers important advantages over natural materials. Among its most beneficial characteristics are its great resistance to corrosion caused by fluids and gases, its very poor electrical conductivity, and its ability to flex and then regain its original shape. Because of the endless variety of compounds that can be created, synthetic rubber has increasingly been used as a substitute for more expensive, lower performance natural materials. Besides displacing woods, metals, and ceramics in many traditional applications, rubber has allowed the creation of completely new products.

The synthetic rubber industry shipped $6.06 billion worth of material in 1997, which was equivalent to about one-quarter of the value of sales by U.S. tire and inner tube manufacturers. By 2000, this number was expected to increase to $6.68 billion. Despite its relative economic insignificance, however, the industry supplied billions of pounds of material and has been an integral part of the U.S. and global industrial machine. Rubber serves a vital role in transportation industries but is also an important production material for medical supplies, packaging and sealing devices, construction equipment, and other goods. Furthermore, U.S. producers supply about one-quarter of total world rubber consumption.

Competition and Markets. The industry is highly consolidated, with only about 120 firms competing in the late 1990s. Of the 143 U.S. rubber production establishments operating in 1997, only 57 employed a workforce of 20 or more. Geographically, nearly 33 percent of the U.S. industry's 143 establishments—or 47 establishments in all—were located in the five states of Texas, Louisiana, Ohio, Florida, and Indiana. Even more telling, the 47 establishments in those five states employed 6,617 workers in 1997 which was more than half of the total U.S. synthetic rubber workforce of 12,009.

Tire and inner tube manufacturers consumed about 35 percent of industry output in the late 1990s. The remainder of the rubber market, though, is highly fragmented and is represented by a vast array of fabricated rubber products. Paper mills and floor covering producers each use about 5 percent of all rubber absorbed domestically, while about 2 percent of output is required to make hoses and belts. Adhesives, gaskets, sealants, and packing devices also consume about 5 percent of production. Other popular uses of rubber include the manufacture of sporting goods, medical supplies, footwear, paint, printing ink, chemical preparations, communication equipment, batteries, and cord. Outside of North America, tires and inner tubes represent about 60 percent of rubber demand.

Rubber Production. Synthetic rubber is produced by first chemically rearranging molecules in a process called polymerization, during which the molecules are made to link up in very long chains. The polymer exists as a soft, tacky thermoplastic, which can be remelted and manipulated. The thermoplastic resin is then treated with heat and chemicals to create a thermoset, a compound that cannot be remelted and formed. This process, called vulcanization, is what contributes to the resilience and elasticity of rubber compounds—physical properties that have earned rubbers the name elastomers. Most elastomers are made using petroleum, although potatoes and grains, coke (made from coal), limestone, salt, or sulfur may also be used.

Endless varieties of rubbers are produced, each of which offers different physical properties and comes in a variety of grades. Different rubbers are created during the production process, for instance, by integrating additives, adding processing chemicals, or creating alloys with natural rubber or other thermoplastics. Numerous chemical processing agents include accelerators, activators, vulcanizing agents, antidegradants, antioxidants, flame retardants, and stabilizers. Additives include reinforcement fibers, fillers, colorants, and catalysts, such as carbon black and sulfur.

The two major elastomer divisions are commodity and specialty. Commodity elastomers, which account for the bulk of industry sales, are available at relatively low prices from several manufacturers. The most popular commodity rubber is styrene butadiene rubber (SBR), which represented about 25 percent of total output (by value) in the late 1990s. SBR is used primarily in tires and inner tubes, though it is also found in industrial applications such as carpet backing, nonwoven materials, and paper coatings. Major manufacturers of this compound include Uniroyal, Goodrich Tire Company, and Goodyear.

Polybutadiene, the third largest industry segment at about 7.6 percent of sales (by value), is also used mostly to create tires and treads. In addition, it is an important production material for hoses and belts. Ethylene-propylene elastomers (EP) accounted for approximately 10.9 percent of shipments in the late 1990s. This compound is used in the construction supply industry for such products as roof membranes and foundation sealants. It is also used as an impact modifier for plastic resins. Other uses include oil viscosity additives and various auto parts, such as gaskets and seals, hoses, belts, and tubing. Other commodity thermoset elastomers include nitrile, butyl, polyisoprene, polychloroprene, and silicone.

Specialty elastomers, the second division of the synthetic rubber industry, represented about 8 percent of sales in the mid-1990s. Specialty elastomers offer enhanced performance characteristics, are typically more expensive, and are sold by fewer competitors than commodity elastomers. The two main categories of specialty rubbers are silicones and fluorocarbons. Silicones are used to make vehicle mechanical parts and sealants, adhesives for construction, and electronic products. Fluorocarbons are used for O-rings, seals, and gaskets, as well as and for high-tech aerospace, automotive, electrical, and petrochemical applications.

In addition to thermosets, the specialty category also encompasses a relatively new category of rubbers called thermoplastic elastomers (TPEs). TPEs are often more economical to produce and easier to process than are thermosets. TPEs can be categorized as styrenics, polyolefins, elastomeric alloys, polyurethanes, copolyesters, and polyamides. They are often used to create high-performance adhesives, to modify plastics during the production process, and in various consumer goods applications. TPEs provide benefits associated with recycling, and typically offer greater durability, hardness, and chemical resistance.

BACKGROUND AND DEVELOPMENT

Natural rubber has been in use since at least the fifteenth century. Christopher Columbus, for one, witnessed Haitian natives playing games with balls "made of the gum of a tree." The first record of rubber used for purposes other than recreation was made by explorer

F. Juan D. Torquemada in 1615. He saw Indians brush rubber on their cloaks as waterproofing and also witnessed them compressing rubber in earthen molds to create footwear and bottles. Rubber was brought to Europe in the eighteenth century from the East Indies and used to rub out lead pencil marks—hence the term "rubber." Rubber was later transported to Europe to make raincoats and rubber thread.

A recognizable natural rubber industry evolved in the United States by the 1830s, as numerous factories sprouted along the eastern seaboard. U.S. producers pioneered many important processing machines that furthered industry growth. For example, Edward M. Chaffe invented a rubber milling and rolling machine in 1836. Chaffe's machine, which was nicknamed "The Monster," was completed in 1837 at a cost of $30,000 and a weight of 30 tons. In another important industry breakthrough of the late 1830s, rubber's tendency to soften with heat and harden with cold was mitigated. Indeed, Charles Goodyear's discovery of vulcanization in 1839 lead to the use of rubber in many demanding mechanical applications.

Realizing the potential benefits of creating a synthetic replacement for natural rubber, scientists had been searching for a formula since the early 1800s. In 1826, Michael Faraday, an English scientist, was one of the first to successfully chemically analyze rubber. It was not until 1910, however, that S.V. Lebedev, a Russian, polymerized butadiene to produce the first synthetic rubber. This breakthrough, combined with processing and vulcanizing technologies developed during the 1800s, initiated a new era for the rubber industry.

By the 1930s, synthetic rubbers were being produced on a commercial scale only in Russia and Germany. World War I and World War II both pushed synthetic advances, as countries on all continents sought to sever their dependency on foreign natural rubber supplies. The United States, traditionally dependent on South American suppliers for natural rubber, shifted into overdrive during World War II in its quest for an inexhaustible synthetic supply. Between 1939 and 1945, in fact, U.S. production of synthetic rubber rose from a negligible experimental yield to about 820,000 tons per year.

World War II Era. World output of synthetic rubber was estimated at 10,000 tons in 1935, and 72,000 tons by 1939. Germany and Russia produced all but a small fraction. By the end of World War II, though, global production had skyrocketed to well over million tons per year, of which the United States supplied the lion's share. Correspondingly, the share of U.S. rubber consumption served by natural rubber declined during the 1940s. In 1939, about 0.3 percent of all rubber used in the United States was synthetic. By 1950 that share had grown to 43.0 percent, and the United States was devouring a whopping 55.0 percent of total global elastomer output.

Although large quantities of synthetic rubber continued to be produced after World War II, natural rubbers still dominated the market because of their superior physical characteristics. Advances in the use of recycled natural rubber boosted its popularity. In 1953, however, German chemists Karl Ziegler and Giulio Natta discovered a polymerization process that resulted in a synthetic rubber virtually identical in molecular structure to that of natural rubber. Commercial production of cis-1, 4-polyisoprene was immediately undertaken in the United States, which became the dominant supplier for many war-ravaged European countries.

Augmenting the proliferation of synthetic rubber in the 1950s and 1960s was the development of new additives. New reinforcing materials allowed manufacturers to strengthen synthetics and reduce production costs, while at the same time achieving advanced performance. Asbestos, hard clay, limestone, and carbon black were among these fillers. Similarly, plasticizers and softeners allowed producers to develop synthetics with physical properties superior to many natural rubbers. Curing and vulcanizing agents, accelerators, and age-resistors all lead to the substitution of synthetics for natural rubbers and other organic materials.

Besides advances in quality and variety, synthetic rubber also benefited from simultaneous breakthroughs in processing and molding technology used in other industries. Furthermore, the postwar U.S. economic expansion generated huge demand growth. Most importantly, the staggering growth of the automobile and truck industries during the 1950s and 1960s resulted in a vast market for tires, inner tubes, belts, and hoses. Construction and consumer markets ballooned as well. By 1960, global production of synthetic rubber stood at more than 2 million tons per year. The United States alone produced about 1.5 million tons and devoured more than 40 percent of global output. Although natural rubber still held more than 50 percent of the world rubber market by 1960, synthetics supplied about 70 percent of U.S. rubber demand.

While it continued to realize growth during the 1960s and 1970s, the rubber industry had clearly surpassed its stage of rapid expansion by the 1970s. Even the 1960s showed evidence of industry maturation, such as consolidation. The number of competitors manufacturing tires, for instance, plummeted from about 60 in the late 1940s to just a handful of big producers by the 1970s. Spiraling petroleum prices during the late 1970s, moreover, dampened industry profitability. Furthermore, popular synthetics that were once cutting edge materials, such as styrene-butadiene, became low-margin commodities. Foreign competition, too, began eating away at U.S. global dominance.

The 1980s and 1990s. By 1980, U.S. synthetic rubber output was about 1.8 million metric tons per year. This represented a relatively slight increase over production levels of the late 1960s and early 1970s. Falling energy prices and an uptick in demand during the early 1980s, however, boosted industry output and profitability. Although the value of shipments jumped less than 1 percent between 1982 and 1983, the cost of production materials fell by about 3 percent as output jumped nearly 8 percent. In 1984, moreover, output value leapt over 8 percent as demand climbed steadily, causing revenues to surpass $3.4 billion.

After 1985, overall U.S. rubber output stagnated. Despite a healthy economy, U.S. synthetic rubber manufacturers were hurt by several factors, including increased imports of automobile, tire, and rubber products; the trend toward smaller cars that used smaller tires; and the increased use of long-lasting radial tires. Exports from southeast Asia, as well as other regions of the world, were also cutting into demand from other market segments. Between 1982 and 1990 total industry output grew just 22 percent, from about 1.8 million to 2.2 million tons.

Despite sluggish demand in traditional commodity synthetic rubbers, such as SBR, the industry managed to maintain a fairly strong revenue growth rate of about 5 percent during the 1980s. This was accomplished through the development and sales of improved compounds and specialty rubbers. Production volumes of polybutadiene and ethylene-propylene, for instance, advanced 44 percent and 89 percent, respectively, between 1982 and 1991. Specialty TPEs, moreover, grew from a negligible share of the market in the early 1980s to account for about 8 percent of domestic industry consumption by 1991.

Although their share of the world rubber market declined in the 1980s and early 1990s, industry participants enjoyed solid export growth as foreign consumption of rubber slowly, but steadily escalated. Despite sluggish domestic markets, exports grew between 3 percent and 5 percent per year in the late 1980s and early 1990s. The demand for proprietary high-tech rubbers by overseas consumers was particularly strong.

Synthetic rubber manufacturers were able to buoy earnings throughout the early 1990s. Unfortunately, though, a domestic and global economic recession that began in 1989 and lingered through 1993 put the squeeze on industry profitability. Shipment volume declined .03 percent in 1989, .07 percent in 1990, and more than 4 percent in 1991, while plant utilization dipped to a depressing 68 percent. Industry revenues grew about 1 percent per year in 1987 dollars during that period. Although output jumped a surprising 9 percent in 1992, revenues gained only 4 percent, rising to about $4.4 billion, and an industry profit slump persisted.

A tepid economic recovery helped to boost industry expectations in 1992 and 1993. Analysts were discouraged, however, by fundamental weaknesses in rubber markets. Importantly, demand by the auto industry, which consumes 70 percent of SBR, was recessed. Overall production of SBR, in fact, had slipped from 876,000 tons to about 850,000 by 1992. Although shipments to tire producers rose about 8 percent in 1992, long-term growth in that segment was expected to remain weak.

Although commodity polybutadiene and ethylene-propylene elastomers generally outperformed SBR during the 1980s and early 1990s, continued expansion of these segments was in question. As it entered a phase of maturity, polybutadiene was expected to offer a tepid growth rate of only 2 percent through the mid-1990s. Commodity ethylene-propylene markets were already recessing in the early 1990s, following a rapid rise during the early and mid-1980s. Although sales surged slightly in 1992, weak auto and construction markets were expected to restrain demand for this thermoset.

High-Tech and Thermoplastic Opportunities. To sustain profits going into the mid-1990s, producers were looking to smaller industry segments for expansion. The greatest opportunities for profits in the mid-1990s were expected to be in TPEs. Besides their recyclability and often lower production costs, thermoplastics combined the rubber-like flexibility characteristic of thermoset rubbers with the heightened processing versatility of plastic. As a result, TPEs were expected to grow by 7 percent or more per year throughout the 1990s. Furthermore, worldwide consumption of TPEs should rise from 680,000 tons in 1992 to more than 1.1 million tons by the year 2000.

Besides cannibalizing market share held by thermoset rubbers, TPEs were creating entirely new markets for the industry. Styrenic TPEs, for example, offered significant potential for use as an asphalt modifier to keep roofing and roadways from cracking. High-tech niche TPEs were making inroads into industries such as medical, construction, and food packaging. New TPEs, for example, were being used in the plumbing industry to deliver drinking water that could meet strict new federal standards. Other TPEs were being developed to make everything from ski boots and swimwear to auto body panels that could be painted without a primer coat.

Like TPEs, high-performance thermosets also promised to buoy the earnings of the most savvy producers. Growth rates for some specialty ethylene-propylene elastomers, for instance, were expected to exceed 15 percent in the mid-1990s. High-performance nitrile rubbers were finding use in applications that required heat, chemical, and abrasion resistance. Some nitrile rubbers were forecast to realize 15 percent to 35 percent growth during the mid-1990s.

After growing 3.1 percent to 3.3 million metric tons in 1998, North American consumption of synthetic rubber was expected to slow to a growth rate of 1.5 percent per year through 2003, according to the International Institute of Synthetic Rubber Producers (IISRP). This would bring North American consumption to about 3.6 million metric tons by 2003. Fueled by 3.9 percent growth in the U.S. economy, North American synthetic rubber consumption enjoyed its seventh consecutive annual increase. That growth, however, was expected to moderate somewhat into the early years of the new millennium.

Environment. One of the greatest obstacles to success for synthetic rubber producers in the mid-1990s was environmental controls. The overall chemical industry was by far the largest polluting industry in the United States, and rubber producers contributed significantly to that reputation. Besides emitting large doses of hazardous chlorofluorocarbons (CFCs) into the air during the production process, rubber producers were also charged with creating end-user products that would not degrade. Furthermore, rubber manufacturers suffered from environmental controls that affected their consumers, such as fuel efficiency and emissions standards that were encouraging the production of smaller cars (and tires).

Environmental mandates (see **SIC 2821: Plastics Materials, Synthetic Resins, and Nonvulcanizable Elastomers**) were forcing manufacturers to bring their production facilities into compliance with federal and state rules. Such retrofitting was costing many companies millions of dollars.

Partially in an effort to allay criticism of non-degradable rubber waste, the Rubber Manufacturer's Association (RMA) took a lead role in reclamation and recycling efforts during the 1980s and 1990s. Although thermoset elastomers cannot be truly recycled, efforts were underway to convert rubber waste to other uses in the mid-1990s, such as highway asphalt production and fuel for energy plants. Tires, which consume about 60 percent of all elastomer output, were a focal point of such endeavors. In 1990, about 8 percent of the 240 million tires discarded annually were reused. By 1992, this percentage had jumped to 24 percent. By the mid-1990s, the RMA's Scrap Tire Management Council estimated that figure would double to nearly 50 percent.

CURRENT CONDITIONS

Several years of sluggish demand resulted in consolidation of the synthetic rubber industry and its suppliers. One of the biggest resulting mergers was that of Monsanto Company and Akzo Nobel's rubber chemicals business into a new company Flexsys. The synthetic rubber business was expected to grow no more than 1.5 percent per year in industrialized nations and 2.0 to 3.0 percent per year worldwide. The world demand for TPE's on the

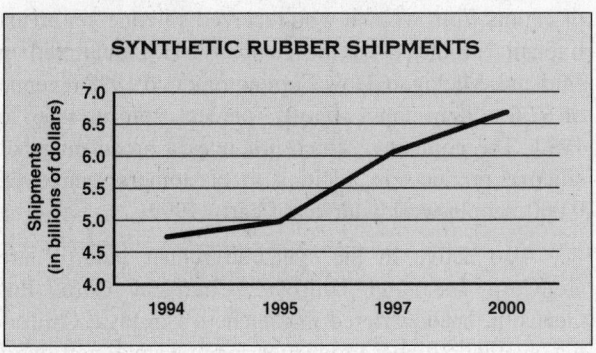

SYNTHETIC RUBBER SHIPMENTS

other hand was expected to increase from 1.3 million metric tons in 1998 to about 1.7 million metric tons in 2003, an increase of more than 6 percent per year.

In 1997, there were 121 operating U.S. companies in the synthetic rubber industry. Consumption of synthetic rubber increased marginally faster than natural rubber consumption in global marketplaces during the 1990s, due in part to a shortage of natural rubber in the latter years of the decade. The major increases in synthetic rubber consumption were in Asia, central Europe, and eastern Europe.

There were two contradictory trends prevalent in the synthetic rubber industry. While consumption was increasing, producers were unable to increase prices to make up for the increasing raw materials prices. The economic recovery of industrialized nations, upsurge in automobile production and the related demand for tires, belts and hoses were the causes for the increased demand and consumption for synthetic rubber. Even though a 2.7 percent annual global increase in synthetic rubber consumption was predicted from 1998 to 2003, the declining price of natural rubber was expected to have a dampening effect on synthetic rubber prices.

Stocks in the tire and rubber industry, which showed average performance in the mid-1990s, were expected to appreciate significantly from 1998 to 2000 because of aging auto fleets and the promising market for replacement tire sales worldwide.

INDUSTRY LEADERS

Most of the major players in the U.S. synthetic rubber industry are large, diversified chemical companies, producing a wide variety of products not limited to elastomers. Within the industry, Shell Chemical Co., headquartered in Houston, Texas, was a leader, reporting international sales of about $1 billion in 1998. An operating unit of Shell Oil Co., based in the Netherlands, the company employed a workforce of about 5,000 people as of late 1999.

Also a major force in the industry historically has been Dow Corning Corp., which in 1999 was operating under protection from its creditors because of thousands of claims from women who received silicone gel breast implants produced by the company. Headquartered in Midland, Michigan, Dow Corning reported 1998 revenue of $2.6 billion, down almost 3 percent from its sales in 1997. The company, which produces a broad range of silicone products in addition to elastomers, employed 9,000 people worldwide as of early 1999.

Also active in the synthetic rubber industry are GenCorp Inc. and Uniroyal Chemical Corp. For GenCorp, headquartered in Ranchero Cordova, California, synthetic rubber production is but a small portion of its overall business, which includes its Aerojet aerospace-defense systems subsidiary. Uniroyal, headquartered in Middlebury, Connecticut, reported 1998 sales of $1.2 billion, up 2.2 percent from the previous year.

WORKFORCE

The economic stability of some of the larger players in the industry was largely the result of actions taken during the 1980s and early 1990s. To combat downward profit pressures, manufacturers attempted to cut costs and boost productivity. A large portion of the massive capital investments made by the industry during the 1980s, in fact, was used to automate production facilities and improve information systems. Many companies also realigned their management structure and moved production facilities to foreign countries. The end result of such efforts was stagnant employment growth. Despite production increases, the number of U.S. workers employed in the industry actually declined between 1982 and 1992, from 11,800 to 11,100. However, by 1997, the industry's workforce had rebounded to a total of 12,000 people.

Regardless of workforce cutbacks, the synthetic rubber industry, like most chemical businesses, remained a high-paying haven for most of those fortunate enough to find jobs. The average rubber production worker, for instance, earned about $46,900 per year (overtime included) in 1997. The average annual salary for all members of the industry's workforce in 1997 was $51,735, including overtime.

Slight productivity gains combined with stagnant output growth forecasts for the 1990s and early twenty-first century bode poorly for future employment in the synthetic rubber industry. Jobs for most machine operators, which accounted for about 10 percent of the workforce, should decline by more than 25 percent between 1990 and 2005, according to the U.S. Bureau of Labor Statistics. Positions for chemical equipment controllers, which made up 7 percent of the workforce, will fall by more than 15 percent. Indeed, most blue collar jobs will dwindle by at least 5 to 10 percent. On the bright side, occupations related to sales and marketing will leap by more than 15 percent, and work for systems analysts and computer scientists will increase by a hearty 37 percent.

The synthetic material industries are major employers of chemists and engineers. Jobs for these professionals in the rubber industry will likely grow by 10 to 15 percent by 2005. For more information about chemical and engineering employment in this industry, see **SIC 2821: Plastics Materials, Synthetic Resins, and Non-vulcanizable Elastomers.**

AMERICA AND THE WORLD

In the second half of the 1990s, the United States remained a strong net exporter of synthetic rubber, outpacing imports by nearly two to one. The largest export market for U.S. synthetic rubber was Canada, which accounted for nearly 25 percent of all U.S. exports. Canada also was a major supplier of the synthetic rubber being imported into the United States, accounting for about one-third of total U.S. imports. The economic slowdown in Asia in the late 1990s was responsible for some significant changes in the pattern of U.S. exports. Sales to Japan dropped off sharply, while sales to some non-Asian markets increased dramatically. U.S. synthetic rubber sales to Brazil, for example, increased almost 900 percent.

The United States has gradually lost the dominance of world rubber markets that it enjoyed in the 1950s, when U.S. synthetic rubber producers supplied more than 50 percent of global demand. Nevertheless, the U.S. elastomer industry remains the largest, most advanced, and most productive in the world. The United States produced about 23 percent of total global output in the early 1990s—far more than any other nation. It also exported more than $1 billion worth of rubber and maintained a hefty trade surplus of about $450 million.

U.S. exports rose approximately 17 percent in 1995. The export uptrend slowed somewhat in 1996, increasing only 6.3 percent. In 1997, exports fell nearly 3.0 percent. Although exports resumed their upward climb in 1998, the rate of increase was only about 0.5 percent. Capital investments made during the 1980s that helped domestic producers become more competitive globally were partially responsible for export growth. Canada, the largest buyer of U.S. elastomers, accounted for 24.2 percent of total U.S. exports in 1997. Belgium took 13.7 percent of overseas shipments, while Mexico and Brazil purchased 8.7 and 7.6 percent, respectively.

U.S. consumers purchased between $680 million and $740 million worth of overseas elastomers per year in the late 1990s. In 1997, Canada supplied 33.4 percent of these imports, while Japan and France delivered 12.2 and 8.6 percent, respectively.

In the late 1990s, global demand for both natural and synthetic rubber was being held down by weakness in Far East markets, including Japan, which were burdened with a major economic slowdown. The best prospects for increased consumption into the early years of the new millennium are likely to come in central and eastern Europe, China, and the countries of the former Soviet Union.

Through the year 1999, the International Institute of Synthetic Rubber Producers (IISRP) projected growth of about 2.4 percent per year worldwide, with just 1.0 percent per year growth for North America, 2.2 percent per year for western Europe, 3.9 percent per year for Asia-Oceania, and 4.7 percent per year for Latin America.

While Asia accounted for the majority of rubber producing nations, Japan, North America, and Europe accounted for more than half of the world's total consumption of rubber.

RESEARCH AND TECHNOLOGY

Companies in the synthetic rubber industry are heavily dependent upon research and development to maintain competitiveness. The average rubber manufacturer in the late 1980s, for instance, invested more than four times more money per employee in research and development than did the average U.S. manufacturer. This amounted to 5 to 7 percent of total industry sales. In 1990, moreover, the industry funneled a full 9 percent, or $380 billion, of total revenues into capital investments.

Technological advances in regulatory compliance were essentially a reaction to the 1990 Pollution Prevention Act, the Clean Air Act, and a multiplicity of other state and federal controls. Although producers were making large investments in new equipment and compounds that would allow them to produce rubber with fewer hazardous emissions, they were also focusing on the development of new recyclable rubbers that would result in less after-market waste. The most important of these was recyclable TPEs. Besides offering many advantageous physical characteristics, TPEs were increasingly being used as a substitute for many nondegradable thermoset rubbers.

Progress in the recovery of thermoset rubber waste was advancing, though at a relatively slow pace. Industry participants were still searching for economically viable uses for the nondegradable compounds. Besides asphalt modification and waste-to-energy applications, elastomer refuse was being used in several civil engineering functions. It was being utilized, for example, to create road embankments, artificial reefs, and as a replacement for gravel in water cleansing systems. Some recycled rubber was also being used as a filler for tires, and to make low-tech items like mud guards for trucks.

In addition to demands for more environmentally friendly rubber products, elastomer manufacturers were constantly under pressure to create new high-performance, cost-efficient products. While huge breakthroughs in tire longevity had been achieved throughout the 1960s, 1970s, and 1980s, producers in the early 1990s were

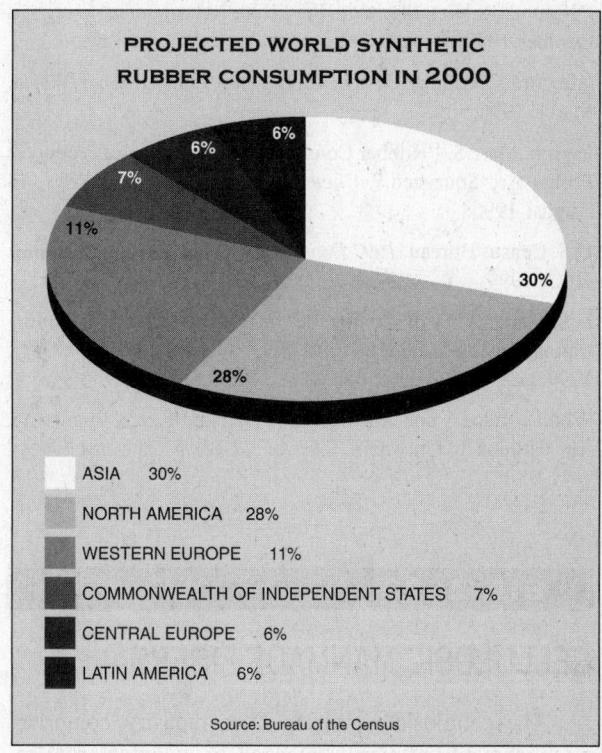

PROJECTED WORLD SYNTHETIC RUBBER CONSUMPTION IN 2000

- ASIA 30%
- NORTH AMERICA 28%
- WESTERN EUROPE 11%
- COMMONWEALTH OF INDEPENDENT STATES 7%
- CENTRAL EUROPE 6%
- LATIN AMERICA 6%

Source: Bureau of the Census

introducing much better products. In 1991, for example, Michelin, the French tire company, introduced a cutting edge tire called the XH4. The company guarantees the tire to last 80,000 miles, which is longer than most people own their car. Michelin also introduced a tire in Europe in 1993 called the MXN. It delivers 4 to 5 percent better gas mileage than competing tires.

Many breakthroughs occurred in the area of specialty elastomers in the early 1990s. One such example was hydrogenated nitrile, a product for which demand was expected to grow by 15 to 35 percent per year in the mid-1990s. Besides allowing manufacturers to more easily meet environmental emissions requirements, the substance offered superior thermo and mechanical properties. Hydrogenated nitrile can withstand temperatures of more than 300 degrees Fahrenheit, for example, compared to normal nitrile, which remains stable only to 212 degrees Fahrenheit.

FURTHER READING

Azman, Syed. "No Successor to World Rubber Pact on Horizon." *Reuters,* 2 October 1999.

Darnay, Arsen J. *Manufacturing USA.* 5th ed. Detroit: Gale Research, 1998.

"India, China to Lead Asian Rubber Markets." *Financial Express,* 9 March 1998.

International Rubber Study Group. "Rubber Statistics." Available from http://www.rubberstudy.com/STATS.htm.

Ita, Paul A., and Gross Andrew C. "Industry Corner: World Rubber and Tire." *Business Economics,* January 1995.

"Natural Rubber Shortage Predicted." *Associated Press,* 18 October 1999.

"Record Consumption for Rubber in 1995." *Rubber World,* March 1996.

Reisch, Marc S. "Rubber Consumption Is Rising But Producers Profits Are Squeezed." *Chemical and Engineering News,* 14 August 1995.

U.S. Census Bureau. *1997 Economic Census.* Washington, D.C: GPO, 1999.

U.S. Department of Commerce. International Trade Administration. *U.S. Industrial Outlook 1999.* Washington, D.C.: GPO, 1999.

Wood, Andrew, and Ira Breskin. "Demand Keeps Improving, But Outlook Is Uncertain." *Chemical Week,* 26 April 1995.

SIC 2823

CELLULOSIC MANMADE FIBERS

The cellulosic manmade fiber industry comprises establishments primarily engaged in manufacturing rayon and acetate fibers in the form of monofilament, yarn, staple, or tow. These fibers are suitable for further manufacturing in other industries on spindles, looms, knitting machines, or other textile processing equipment. Synthetic fibers, which represent more than 90 percent of all U.S. manmade fiber output, are classified in **SIC 2824: Manmade Organic Fibers, Except Cellulosic.**

NAICS CODE(S)

325221 (Cellulosic Manmade Fiber Manufacturing)

Cellulose fibers are made from modified wood pulp that has been dissolved in a liquid and treated with chemicals. The solution is forced through small holes called spinnerets; the extrusion dries into a hard filament. The shape and physical properties of the fiber can be modified during extrusion and processing to yield numerous fiber types and grades.

Cellulosic manmade fiber, of which rayon accounts for by far the largest portion, continued to lose ground in the late 1990s to synthetic fiber, falling to less than 10 percent of total U.S. and worldwide man-made fiber output. According to data from the Fiber Economics Bureau's World Surveys of Manufactured Fiber Production, cellulosics had fallen to about 7 percent of worldwide manmade fibers production by 1998. Global production of all manmade fiber in 1998 was 29.9 million metrics tons, more than double the 14.3 million metric tons produced 20 years earlier in 1978. However, while the output of synthetic fibers, such as polyester, has seen strong long-term growth, averaging 5 percent annually, the production of cellulos-

ics, including rayon and acetate, has declined an average of 2 percent per year between 1978 and 1998.

In the early 1990s, more than 90 percent of industry output was rayon; this fiber is used to make apparel, home furnishings, nonwoven products, tires, and industrial goods. Less than 10 percent of production in the early 1990s was acetate, which is primarily used to create apparel, home furnishings, and cigarette filters. In the mid-1990s, health concerns and "sin" taxes were expected to reduce the demand for cellulose cigarette filter tow. According to *Market Share Reporter 1997,* a shift in production did occur in 1995, and rayon accounted for only 55.8 percent of the market.

The largest consumer of rayon and acetate was the broadwoven fabric industry, which consumed more than 40 percent of total production. Apparel linings accounted for a large portion of the market, along with special occasion apparel and acetate/spandex blended fabrics. Knit fabric manufacturers accounted for 20 percent of the U.S. market, and 3.5 percent of industry revenues were garnered from exports.

The fibers, when made into fabrics, are identified by generic classifications that were established by the Textile Fiber Products Identification Act of 1960, and generic names were assigned by the Federal Trade Commission (FTC). The Identification Act also states that products must be labeled with the manufacturer's name and country and list the percentage of fiber content.

The first patent related to the manufacture of cellulose fibers was granted in 1855. In 1883 Sir Joseph Wilson Swan, a British scientist, created the first nonflammable cellulose fiber. Commercially viable rayon fibers were invented during the 1890s. Acetate filaments were developed in the late 1800s as well, but did not receive commercial acceptance until the 1920s. During both world wars, particularly World War II, fiber development and production ballooned as warring nations sought inexhaustible supplies of apparel and textile fibers.

Rayon increased in popularity during the post-World War II U.S. economic expansion. In fact, by 1980 U.S. companies were generating more than 580 million pounds of fiber each year. Despite past growth, however, cellulose fibers were quickly losing favor to newer and better synthetic fibers, such as polyester and nylon. Between 1970 and 1990 the percentage of U.S. fibers (including organic filaments) made from cellulose declined from 28 percent to 6 percent. The industry was coping with environmental concerns and standards while trying to improve quality.

Worldwide, cellulosic fiber production reached its peak in the early 1980s and has been trending steadily downward since then. Besides the increasing popularity of synthetic fibers, foreign competition, particularly from

Asia, battered industry participants. Between the early 1980s and 1998, Asian countries increased their production of cellulosic fibers by some 425,000 metric tons, while all other regions of the world reported declines in production. The sharpest decline came in eastern Europe, where total output plummeted from a high of 1.1 million metric tons in the early 1980s to only 174,000 metric tons in 1998. Cellulosic fiber production in western Europe and North America saw moderate declines during this period. U.S. producers of cellulosic manmade fibers shipped close to $1.1 billion worth of product in 1997, down sharply from 1992 shipments of nearly $1.7 billion.

Revenues lagged behind inflation with an average growth rate of less than 1 percent per year, and industry employment fell from more than 14,000 people in the early 1980s to about 11,000 by 1992. The employment rate was continuously falling from approximately 7,500 people in 1995 to 4,800 in 1997. Further declines in the cellulosic fiber workforce were predicted into the new millennium. The number of establishments was also declining from 18 in the mid-1980s to 9 in 1995, and then only 6 in 1998. In the shrinking world of U.S. cellulosic fiber production, Buckeye Technologies Inc., formerly known as Buckeye Cellulose, is a major player. Headquartered in Memphis, Tennessee, Buckeye employed a workforce of 1,800 people and reported sales of $618 million for fiscal 1999 (the 12 months ending June 30, 1999.)

In the mid-1990s, the surviving U.S. cellulose fiber producers were hoping that lyocell, a new fiber, might spare the struggling industry. Two of the largest competitors, Courtaulds Textiles PLC and Lenzing Fibers Corp., were vying for domination of this new market segment. Lyocell offered superior performance compared to rayon and could be manufactured with fewer hazardous waste emissions. However, by and large, lyocell failed to live up to its early promise. Fiber makers were also hoping to benefit from massive capital investments made during the 1980s to improve productivity and develop better fibers.

Despite manufacturer's efforts, the long-term industry outlook remained bleak. Producers in emerging industrial nations, such as China and Malaysia, would likely devour greater global market share. More stringent environmental regulations would also take their toll on U.S. competitors (see **SIC 2824: Man-Made Organic Fibers, Except Cellulosic**). Employment of cellulosic fiber production workers was forecast to continue falling by 15 to 25 percent between 1990 and 2005, according to the Bureau of Labor Statistics. Even high-paying research and engineering jobs were expected to increase only slightly during that period.

FURTHER READING
American Fiber Manufacturers Association. "FiberFacts," 2000. Available from http://www.fibersource.com.

Darnay, Arsen J., ed. *Manufacturing USA,* 6th ed. Detroit: Gale Research, 1998.

Duncan, Beth. "Fiber Facts." Mississippi State University, 10 April 1996. Available from http://www.ces.msstate.edu/pubs/is1250.htm.

Lazich, Robert S., ed. *Market Share Reporter.* Detroit: Gale Research, 1997.

U.S. Bureau of the Census. *1997 Economic Census.* Washington, D.C.: GPO, 1999.

U.S. Department of Commerce. International Trade Administration. *U.S. Industrial Outlook 1999.* Washington, D.C.: GPO, 1999.

SIC 2824

ORGANIC FIBERS—NONCELLULOSIC

Establishments primarily engaged in manufacturing noncellulosic, or synthetic, fibers comprise the manmade organic fibers industry. The fibers are created in the form of monofilament, yarn, staple, or tow suitable for further manufacturing on spindles, looms, knitting machines, or other textile processing equipment. Textile glass fibers and cellulosic manmade fibers, such as rayon and acetate, are classified elsewhere.

NAICS CODE(S)
325222 (Noncellulosic Organic Fiber Manufacturing)

INDUSTRY SNAPSHOT
Although experimental organic fibers existed as early as 1913, the first commercially viable synthetics were invented during the 1930s and 1940s. Explosive industry growth occurred mid-century as new fibers, such as polyester, made synthetic materials a strong part of American life. In the late 1970s and early 1980s, U.S. industry participants were generating more than 3.5 million tons of fibers annually, worth more than $8 billion.

Rapid industry expansion subsided in the 1980s, as important sectors of the fiber business matured. Although production tonnage and revenues increased slightly throughout the decade, profit margins were confined by stagnant export growth and a rising tide of imports in the form of apparel and textiles. Environmental regulations and economic recession in the late 1980s and early 1990s suppressed profits further as manufacturers scrambled to consolidate and reduce costs.

The industry seemed to be entering a stage of modest recovery in 1992. Production increased for the first time in four years, and prices surged. Nevertheless, producers still faced stiff foreign competition and sluggish market growth, which they sought to combat by taking advantage of new technologies that allowed productivity gains and the development of new types of fibers.

By 1998, the worldwide production of synthetic fibers was 27.8 million tons. However, a major geographic shift in production had occurred in the 20 years from 1978 to 1998. Asian production had surged to a total of about 15.8 million metric tons, while North American production had increased very modestly to a total of 5.4 million metric tons. Production for all of Europe totaled 5.1 million metric tons in 1998, but output in eastern Europe had plummeted from a peak of 1.9 million metric tons in the late 1980s to only 800,000 metric tons in 1998.

ORGANIZATION AND STRUCTURE

Manmade fibers offer a less expensive substitute for many natural fibers, such as cotton, wool, and silk. In addition, many synthetic fibers have greater durability, hold their shape better, and are more uniform than natural fibers. Products created with manmade fibers typically afford greater resistance to aging and breakdown as a result of exposure to the elements. Because they can be modified to create a great variety of filaments with different physical properties and grades, synthetics provide great flexibility for manufacturers of apparel and textiles.

The two categories of manmade fibers are cellulosic and synthetic. Cellulosic fibers include such products as rayon, acetate, and triacetate, which are derived from modified wood pulp that has been dissolved in a liquid. Synthetic fibers are derived from molecules containing various combinations of carbon, hydrogen, nitrogen, and oxygen. Examples of products in this group are nylon, olefin, polyester, and spandex.

Synthetic fibers accounted for about 93 percent of U.S. manmade fiber output in 1998. Manmade fibers constituted approximately 25 percent of the larger U.S. synthetic materials industry, which also encompassed plastics and rubbers. Synthetic materials, in turn, represented about 25 percent of the overall $300-billion per year U.S. chemical industry.

Nearly 70 U.S. firms competed in this highly consolidated industry during the late 1990s. Even among the handful of competitors, earnings were top-heavy; the combined revenues of the top five firms in the business were nearly four times greater than the aggregate sales of the next five largest companies. Moreover, the majority of the largest 20 establishments employed fewer than 200 workers, compared with between 10,000 and 20,000 employees at each of the top few companies. Extremely high start-up capital requirements, entrenched market leaders, and proprietary technology necessary to produce high-margin fibers discouraged potential market entrants from joining this exceptionally competitive business.

The largest U.S. market for synthetic fibers during the 1990s was floor covering manufacturers. This sector consumed almost 35 percent of fiber output to create carpeting for commercial, institutional, and consumer applications. Apparel producers commanded about 25 percent of industry production during this time, and makers of various home textile products controlled 8 percent of output. Industrial products and miscellaneous consumer goods, representing 25 percent of consumption, included such items as tire reinforcements, rope, surgical and sanitary supplies, fiberfill, electrical insulation, and plastic reinforcements. Nearly 8 percent of total output was shipped to other countries.

Production Process.   Synthetic fibers are extremely long, threadlike molecules composed of hundreds of thousands of atoms strung together in chains. They typically originate from petroleum-based chemicals, which must first be converted into a liquid state by either being dissolved into a solution or by melting. The free-moving molecules that form the liquid are then extruded through small holes called spinnerets. The fine strands of liquid that emerge from the spinnerets are hardened to form long, silk-like filaments.

The three most popular spinning processes are known as dry, wet, and melt. In dry spinning, the fiber-forming substance is dissolved in a solvent, extruded through a spinneret, and then exposed to hot air. The heat causes the solvent to evaporate from the fiber, leaving a solid filament. Wet spinning works in a similar manner, except that the extrusion is jettisoned into a coagulating bath, which causes the fiber to harden as a result of chemical or physical change. Melt spinning is accomplished by simply melting and extruding a substance that dries upon contact with the air.

During the spinning process, the filament can be manipulated to result in various physical properties and forms. This manipulation determines such attributes as drapability, softness, elasticity, perceived coolness or warmth, stiffness, roughness, and resilience. Fibers that are formed to have a dog-bone or lobed cross-section, for instance, result in fabrics with greater density, while flat fibers give fabrics a rough feel.

After spinning, fibers go through a stretching and orientation process. During this procedure, the long molecules that constitute the fiber are pulled into alignment along the longitudinal axis of the filament. Through various techniques, the molecules can be aligned, packed, and manipulated to result in a variety of different physical characteristics. Tensile strength, dyeing properties, stretching ability, water penetrability, and resistance to breakdown are a few of the attributes that are influenced through stretching and orientation of the molecules.

Finished fibers are usually formed into monofilament, yarn, staple, or tow that can be used by other manufacturing sectors. Monofilaments are single, long strands of fiber used to create items such as nylon stockings and toothbrush bristles. Staple consists of fibers that have been cut into short lengths, usually between one and six inches. Staple can be mixed with other natural or manmade fibers to create yarns and fabrics. Tow is a fiber that is spun with hundreds of thousands of filaments bundled together into a loose rope and wound onto a spool. Tow is used like staple, but the cutting is done at a later stage to ensure that the filaments remain parallel to one another.

Products. Polyester fibers, the largest industry segment by production tonnage, constitutes about 40 percent of inorganic fibers shipments. Among other qualities, polyester sports low moisture retention, good electrical insulation characteristics, and high resistance to solvents. Nearly 80 percent of polyester fibers were used to produce textiles, apparel, and home furnishings. Eight percent of this segment was purchased by the tire industry to be used as rubber reinforcements, 7 percent was used for other industrial applications, and 5 percent went towards the production of carpeting. The majority of polyester was sold in the form of either yarn or staple. Tow represented a relatively small share of segment sales.

The second most popular synthetic fiber is nylon. This fiber, which comes in a multitude of characteristics and grades, accounts for nearly 30 percent of industry output. Nylon's advantages include a high strength-to-weight ratio, excellent recovery from deformation, and high abrasion and flex resistance. Seventy percent of nylon output was used to make carpeting, while about 20 percent was integrated into apparel and noncarpet home furnishings. Manufacturers of industrial products, such as tires and rope, represented the remaining 10 percent of this market. Most nylon was sold as yarn, though a substantial share of output took the form of tow.

Much of the remaining 30 percent of synthetic fiber revenues were derived from the sale of olefin and acrylic fibers. Olefins, which were the fastest growing segment of the industry in the early 1990s, are used to create durable carpeting and other textiles. Acrylic, the smallest volume synthetic fiber at about 5 percent of the market, is used to make clothing and home furnishings, such as blankets.

BACKGROUND AND DEVELOPMENT

Evidence suggests that hemp, presumably the oldest cultivated fiber plant, was grown in China as early as 4500 B.C. Furthermore, Egyptians were already weaving and spinning linen by 3400 B.C. The spinning of silk, which provided a major impetus for the creation of artificial fibers, dates back to 2640 B.C. Flax and wool fabrics dating back to the sixth and seventh centuries B.C. have been excavated in Switzerland.

English physicist Robert Hooke was one of the first scientists to explore the possibility of extruding artificial silk, proposing a mechanical device that mimicked the silkworm. Louise Schwabe, an English weaver during the nineteenth century, was the first to successfully produce filaments from molten glass. He forced the liquid through nozzles, which caused a strand of glass to protrude and harden into a fiber. These early experiments initiated the discovery and development of manmade cellulose filaments (see **SIC 2823: Cellulosic Manmade Fibers**).

Chemists carried out the first extensive research into possible methods of creating synthetic fibers after World War I. Finding that many polymers (long chains of molecules) could be dissolved in solvents, they began extruding different polymers in spinnerets. Their initial goal was to imitate rayon, a cellulosic fiber. Breakthrough synthetic fibers were produced by German chemists in 1913 and through the 1920s. Important advances occurred in 1928, for example, when vinyl chloride and vinyl acetate were used to produce fibers. This breakthrough lead to the development of the first commercially viable synthetic textile fibers in 1936.

The synthetic industry got its practical start in 1935, when American Wallace H. Carothers, working at E. I. DuPont de Nemours & Company, developed the first nylon fiber. This important discovery prompted intense research during and after World War II that resulted in many new classes of commercially useful synthetic textile filaments. The first polyester fiber, for example, was invented in 1941 by British researchers. Eastman Chemical Products Inc. of the United States introduced a vastly improved and more marketable version of that fiber in 1958. Acrylics and other polyvinyl-based fibers were developed during the 1950s.

Rapid technological advances during and after World War II paved the way for a massive synthetic fiber industry expansion during the 1960s and 1970s. Although polyester and vinyl fibers had existed for several years, public acceptance of textiles and apparel created with artificial filaments lagged behind technology. During the 1960s, however, fiber producers began making a wide variety of different products. Furthermore, they opened new markets and persuaded every feasible manufacturing sector to consider their products.

Nevertheless, the fiber industry was still dominated by cotton and other natural materials. Increased public acceptance of synthetics, combined with other influences, began to change this situation during the 1970s. For instance, pivotal synthetic fiber technology was developed for the space program, as well as for the military during the Vietnam era and the Cold War. These advances inspired new products that found favor in civilian markets. Most importantly, new production and processing techniques evolved, such as texturizing and chemical crimping, that allowed competitors to vastly improve the quality, look, and feel of their fibers.

In the early 1950s, manmade fibers accounted for about 13 percent of worldwide fiber production— synthetic fibers represented a negligible share of this total. By the late 1960s, however, manmade fibers met over 30 percent of global fiber demand, and synthetics were quickly displacing their cellulosic cousins. Boosted by postwar economic expansion, worldwide manmade fiber production rocketed from just 4.6 billion pounds in the early 1950s to over 16.2 billion pounds by 1970. Furthermore, the United States supplied a major share of global exports in this new, high-tech industry.

Continued technological advances prompted expansion of the synthetic fiber industry throughout the 1970s. While no completely new apparel and textile fibers were invented during that decade, modifications and processing advancements were numerous. Du Pont developed Antron nylon, as well as extremely lightweight, thin polypropylene fibers. Similarly, BASF introduced conductive nylon carpet fibers that reduced static. Popular anticling nylons were developed as well. ''Pluscious'' brushed nylon, created by Dow Chemical Co., became the preferred fiber for women's and children's sleepwear. Moreover, new polypropylene fibers with improved pigments and ultraviolet light inhibitors became popular in automotive and outdoor markets.

As industry revenues and output skyrocketed, the synthetic fiber industry adopted a more consolidated structure. The industry consisted of a multitude of innovators attempting to establish themselves as leaders in this new high-tech industry. However, commercial development of synthetic fibers proved to be an extremely capital-intensive endeavor, and research and development costs, plant construction, and ongoing fiber improvement expenditures became more than many companies could bear. As a result, many fiber making companies merged.

Polyester and nylon fabrics became more and more popular throughout the 1970s, and the industry surged ahead. By 1979, polyester accounted for 50 percent of all shipments by weight, while nylon held a 30 percent share of the market, and olefin and acrylic fibers each comprised 10 percent. Overall synthetic fiber output peaked at about 6.5 billion pounds in 1979.

Despite this impressive expansion, industry growth stalled in the 1980s. High petroleum prices helped to depress profits during the early part of the decade, and the industry faced more fundamental and long term obstacles as well. Specifically, the major innovations that had propelled growth during the previous 20 years were no longer new, and the synthetic fiber industry was entering a stage of maturity.

The declining market for polyester, the industry's mainstay, was of primary concern for struggling manufacturers in the 1980s. U.S. production jumped an encouraging 11 percent in 1983, but slipped for four consecutive years to only 3.3 billion pounds by 1986. Total production in this important segment climbed only 1 percent annually between 1982 and 1991. The other major class of fibers, nylon, reflected a similar growth pattern. From 1.9 billion pounds of output in 1982, demand rose an average of just 2 percent per year through 1991, to 2.5 billion pounds.

Olefin fibers continued to realize strong demand. That segment grew an average of 11 percent per year during the 1980s, topping 1.8 billion pounds per year by 1990, when olefin fibers accounted for over 20 percent of industry shipments. Acrylic fibers, by contrast, plummeted from 624 million pounds sold in 1982 to just 454 million by 1991, exhibiting an average annual decline of 4 percent. Consumer preference for cottons and polyester served to reverse expansion in this sector.

During this time, stiff foreign competition in commodity fiber markets emerged. The U.S. fiber makers faced a serious challenge from Europe, Japan, and emerging industrial nations. Taiwan and Korea became particularly aggressive competitors during the decade, and significant additions to the market also came from low-cost producers in Indonesia, Bangladesh, and Malaysia.

U.S. synthetic fiber imports reached more than $900 million per year by 1992, approaching 10 percent of domestic sales. Besides cutting into domestic profits, foreign filament producers were quickly capturing global market share. As U.S. apparel and textile manufacturers moved their production facilities overseas, they often turned to cheaper foreign fiber suppliers. By 1990, the total U.S. share of global industry output fell to 18 percent, down significantly from the more than 50 percent the country held in 1950.

In an effort to combat downward price and profit pressures exerted by foreign competitors, U.S. companies scrambled to cut costs and improve their products. Massive capital investments made during the early 1990s were used to update manufacturing facilities, increase automation, and integrate new information management systems. Investments also were used to create thinner, lighter, stronger, and more versatile fibers. Despite these efforts, however, industry sales climbed an average of only 4 percent per year between 1982 and 1990, to about $11.5 billion. Total output during that period remained stagnant at about 3.2 billion pounds. Only gains in productivity helped to buoy profits for many struggling competitors.

As if heightened competition and stagnant demand were not enough of a challenge for U.S. synthetic fiber manufacturers, the country experienced economic recession from 1989 through 1991. Output slipped about 1 percent in 1989 before plunging 4 percent in 1990. Revenues fell 4 percent as well. Sales slipped again in 1991 by less than 1 percent, disappointing many who had anticipated a significant recovery. Besides increased imports of apparel and textiles, fiber makers were hit particularly hard by a depression in the construction industry, a major consumer of carpet fibers.

Supported by overall improvement in the U.S. economy, American synthetic fiber markets began to show definite signs of recovery in 1992 and 1993. The value of shipments rose 4.0 percent (2.0 percent in inflation adjusted dollars), and output climbed 3.6 percent.

CURRENT CONDITIONS

The synthetic fibers industry had a mixed year in 1998, experiencing only 1 percent real growth in shipments. However, despite the economic slowdown in Asia, U.S. exports of synthetic fibers rose more than 8 percent to almost $2.4 billion. Imports trailed exports, totaling $1.7 billion. Worldwide production totaled 27.8 million metric tons, an increase of only about 2 percent, well below the annual average growth of 5 percent observed between 1978 and 1998.

Into the 1990s, manufacturers of polyester were benefiting from management and production restructuring, as well as from a slowdown in the growth of apparel imports that occurred in the late 1980s. Demand for polyester was also increasing from producers of high-performance tires and nonwoven products, such as disposable medical garments. Market demand for new polyester microfibers, which give polyester the feel of silk, encouraged manufacturers as well.

Nylon producers expected to benefit from an increase in carpet demand in the mid-1990s. Despite generally weak markets, nylon fiber makers were scrambling to fill surging demand in the automotive air bag market, a lucrative niche expected to grow 12-fold between 1995 and 2005. Overall nylon production grew less than 1 percent in 1992, to 2.5 billion pounds. U.S. producers maintained a 28 percent share of global nylon fiber production in the mid-1990s.

The long term health of the U.S. synthetic fiber industry was questionable as the new millennium dawned. Opportunities for impressive productivity gains seemed limited. Most competitors were already operating at low costs compared to foreign producers—particularly those in Europe and Japan—and gains allowed by automation and information technology had been largely exhausted.

Industry analysts expected the United States to experience a continued decline in its share of the global market. Fiber producers in such newly industrialized countries as South America and Asia were likely to dominate those regions, exerting downward pressure on global fiber prices as they competed in markets around the world. Also, increasingly stringent environmental rules and regulations reduced U.S. profit margins. To reduce toxic emissions, federal and state governments began requiring producers to meet strict manufacturing regulations (see **SIC 2821: Plastics Materials and Resins.**) In order to comply, U.S. companies were spending millions of dollars retrofitting their factories and searching for cleaner production technologies.

INDUSTRY LEADERS

The largest company competing in the synthetic fibers industry in the 1990s was E.I. Du Pont de Nemours of Delaware. This mammoth chemical company reported 1998 revenue of $24.8 billion, off nearly 38 percent from its performance in 1997. Its net income, however, jumped 86.3 percent to $4.48 billion. Du Pont, the inventor of nylon, remained the world's largest producer of that fiber, as well as the largest chemical company in the United States.

Throughout the 1990s, Du Pont made substantial investments to reduce emissions and to modernize its polyester production facilities and expand filament capacity. As of late 1998, the company employed a workforce of 101,000 people worldwide.

Though Du Pont did not rank as one of the top five producers of organic fibers in 1997, it was still the largest producer of nylon in North America. Also, Du Pont was the largest company in the entire chemicals industry. Its nylon, polyester, and specialty fiber businesses accounted for slightly more than 43 percent of the company's 1998 revenue. Operating in almost every corner of the globe, Du Pont earned nearly half of its 1998 revenue, or $11.67 billion, outside the United States.

Other major players in the U.S. synthetic fibers industry in the late 1990s were BASF Corp., Honeywell International Inc., and Wellman Inc., all of which were based in New Jersey. Headquartered in Mount Olive, New Jersey, BASF Corp. is the North American subsidiary of Germany's BASF AG. With more than 15,000 employees, BASF reported 1998 sales of $7.5 billion, up 13.5 percent from 1997. Formerly known as Allied Signal, Honeywell International in late 1999 acquired Honeywell and changed its name. Headquartered in Morristown, New Jersey, Honeywell employs a workforce of more than 70,000 and posted 1998 sales of $15.1 billion, up 4.5 percent from the previous year. Wellman, based in Shrewsbury, New Jersey, employed about 3,000 as of late 1998 and reported 1998 revenue of $968 million, down 10.6 percent from the previous year.

WORKFORCE

About 37,000 workers were employed in the U.S. synthetic fiber industry in the late 1990s. This reflected an employment decline of more than 35 percent since 1982, when more than 60,000 workers served the industry. Although many jobs had moved overseas to factories in low-cost regions, workforce reductions were largely a result of huge productivity gains. Heavy investments in labor saving automation, for instance, resulted in the elimination of many production workers. Similarly, new information systems reduced the demand for managers and support staff.

Employment prospects for the long-term remained discouraging. Most chemical equipment controllers and machine operators, which accounted for approximately 20 percent of the industry's labor force, were likely to see their positions decline in number by 15 to 25 percent between 1990 and 2005. Nevertheless, high-paying jobs for chemists, engineers, and scientists were expected to increase by 5 to 15 percent by 2005. Moreover, experts projected that positions related to sales and marketing would surge about 17 percent. The greatest opportunities would likely arise in the fields of systems analysis and computer science, with a potential increase of more than 35 percent by 2005.

Despite unenthusiastic expectations for workforce growth, those established in the industry were relatively well-paid. In 1996, for example, the average production worker earned $15.66 per hour, significantly higher than the average for all other U.S. manufacturing sectors.

The highest paid workers in the business were generally scientists and engineers, particularly highly educated chemists involved with management or research and development. Salaries for these professionals averaged between $70,000 and $105,000 in 1998, depending on education level. For more information on chemical engineering jobs in the synthetic materials industries, see **SIC 2821: Plastics Materials and Resins.**

AMERICA AND THE WORLD

After experiencing record production growth of 12 percent in 1997, the world synthetic fibers industry stagnated during 1998, in large part due to the widespread financial distress being experienced in Asia, Russia, and Latin America. According to Folkert Blaisse, president of Cirfs, the Brussels-based European fibers industry association, the near-term outlook is for U.S. and European producers to increase their production of industrial and specialty fibers while decreasing their commodities output. "I expect growth to be in the 3 to 5 percent range in industrial fibers and specialties," Blaisse said, adding that carbon fibers and nylon for air bag applications are the fastest growing fibers in this market segment.

Worldwide, the market for manmade fibers was estimated at $40 billion annually, of which Asia, excluding Japan, accounts for about $13 billion. The United States and Europe account for about $8 billion and $7.5 billion,

respectively. In 1998, textile fibers accounted for slightly more than 80 percent of global fibers output. In this category, polyester filament grew by 6 percent in 1998, while nylon carpet yarn production climbed 2 percent, trailed by polyester staple fiber, which grew 1 percent.

In 1998, the synthetic fibers industry increased production capacity by 8 percent, but weak demand caused a drop in capacity utilization in much of the world, increasing competition and weakening prices. The synthetic fiber industry's share of world fiber consumption—including cotton and wool—climbed 1 percent in 1998 to 58 percent.

Japan's economic downturn led to a 5 percent decline in Japanese production of synthetic fibers in 1998. U.S. production declined 3 percent. The market share of both Japan and the United States declined by 1 percent. Although western Europe's fiber production dropped 2 percent, it managed to hold onto its market share. China's production of manmade fibers rose sharply in 1998, climbing 7 percent.

RESEARCH AND TECHNOLOGY

Significant capital investments were made during the 1980s and 1990s to increase productivity and reduce hazardous manufacturing emissions. In 1990, synthetic fiber makers invested over $800 million, or about 10 percent of total revenues, back into their businesses, a figure roughly equal to three times the investment per employee of the average U.S. manufacturer and double the amount spent by the industry less than 10 years earlier.

U.S. producers sought to develop cutting-edge fibers that could deliver high profit margins and displace commodity fibers increasingly supplied by emerging industrial nations. One significant product introduction during the early 1990s was Hoechst Celanese's Polarguard high void continuous filament (HV), which provided greater warmth from lightweight, outdoor polyester fiberfill products. Similarly, the company introduced a 100 percent recyclable, all-polyester carpet system in 1993.

Also in 1993, Du Pont was improving its Micromattique MX, intended as a substitute for cotton in sportswear. Furthermore, Du Pont revealed plans to develop nylon recycling technology. Planning to market recyclable fibers by 1997, the company hoped to eventually command 85 percent of the used nylon market. Seeking to revive the struggling acrylic sector, American Cyanimid Corp. introduced MicroSupreme, a microfiber product that offered superior softness and strength as well as greater wicking and heat barrier characteristics.

Promising technological breakthroughs were also occurring outside of the private sector. Researchers at the University of Minnesota developed a method of growing poly fibers in a vertical glass tube. The system, which allowed the shape and diameter of the fiber to be altered, offered an alternative to the traditional extrusion process.

FURTHER READING

Alperowicz, Natasha. ''Specialties Improve, But Commodities Unravel.'' *Chemical Week,* 19 May 1999.

American Fiber Manufacturers Association. ''FiberFacts,'' 2000. Available from http://www.fibersource.com/f-info.

Chapman, Peter. ''Nylon Producers Completing Year of Record Output.'' *Chemical Market Reporter,* 6 January 1997.

''Chinese Purchasing Buoys Fibres Markets.'' *ECN-European Chemical News,* 4 November 1996.

Darnay, Arsen J., ed. *Manufacturing USA,* 6th ed. Detroit: Gale, 1998.

Garcia, Carmen. ''Mixed Bag for Man-made Fibres.'' *ECN-European Chemical News,* 20 May 1996.

Sudershan, O.P. Kharbanda. ''Fibers and Intermediates Makers Lose Their Shirts; Overcapacity Drowns Strong Demand.'' *Chemical Week,* 11 September 1996.

''Synthetics Climb to Summit of Success.'' *Daily News Record,* 30 October 1995.

U.S. Bureau of the Census. *1997 Economic Census.* Washington, D.C.: GPO, 1999.

U.S. Department of Commerce. *U.S. Industry and Trade Outlook '99.* Washington, D.C.: GPO, 1999.

SIC 2833

MEDICINAL CHEMICALS AND BOTANICAL PRODUCTS

This classification covers establishments primarily engaged in manufacturing bulk organic and inorganic medicinal chemicals and their derivatives, as well as processing—grading, grinding, milling—bulk botanical drugs and herbs. Included in this industry are establishments primarily engaged in manufacturing agar and similar products of natural origin, endocrine products, manufacturing or isolating basic vitamins, and isolating active medicinal principals from botanical drugs and herbs.

NAICS CODE(S)

325411 (Medicinal and Botanical Manufacturing)

INDUSTRY SNAPSHOT

Companies in this industry segment furnish the active ingredients used by pharmaceutical firms to manufacture finished products, called pharmaceutical preparations (see **SIC 2834: Pharmaceutical Preparations**). Active ingredients are the portion of a finished drug that create the desired effect—therapeutic or preventive—for humans and animals. Extracts of crude drugs (not yet processed) derived from plant or animal sources are important examples of the components produced by this industry sector. By the 1960s synthesized chemicals—either a manufactured copy of an organic or inorganic substance or a new chemical entity (NCE)—had become common active ingredients in pharmaceuticals from vitamin pills to hormones. Meanwhile, the biotechnology revolution, beginning in earnest in the 1980s, resulted in ways of inserting genetic material into small microorganisms. This made them miniature factories for the production of active drug ingredients like insulin and, in the process, created new molecular entities (NMEs) that could be patented.

By the late 1990s, the primary market for this industry—the pharmaceutical industry—risked high research and development costs for the prized billions of dollars it could generate with new products. While many drug companies have vertically integrated production lines, a trend grew to favor outsourcing chemical intermediates and active ingredients to smaller fine chemicals companies.

ORGANIZATION AND STRUCTURE

A large number of the medicinal and botanical establishments are divisions or subsidiaries of other firms, including pharmaceutical industry giants such as Merck and Hoffman-La Roche. Parent firms that have developed in-house active ingredient suppliers are said to be ''back-integrated,'' and their chemical products are referred to as ''captive,'' dedicated to the parent firm. Chemicals produced by firms independent of the final purchaser are called ''merchant.''

Many ''fine'' chemical companies producing for the merchant market are contracted to large pharmaceutical companies to supply custom, or specialty chemicals, while others produce and sell them on the open market. The latter often manufacture well-known bulk pharmaceutical compounds, like those used in the production of aspirin. Custom and specialty chemicals are produced in smaller quantities than bulk chemicals and frequently combine several different chemical compounds called intermediates, which are more expensive. Traditionally, fine chemicals were those with fewer impurities than the industrial chemicals not intended for human consumption.

Both the back-integrated firms and the independent fine chemical companies are involved in the complex processes of producing extracts of natural substances, synthetic inorganic and organic chemicals, or combinations of any or all of these, that go into most modern medicines. The specific formulas for these substances can be found in academic monographs or in the official U.S. Pharmacopeia (USP) and the National Formulary (NF). If they have not yet been manufactured on an industrial scale or are entirely new compounds (NCEs or NMEs), the pharmaceutical firm creates a document as a reference for its own in-house producers or as a guide to firms contracted to supply active ingredients. These references provide manufacturers with the acceptable legal standards of purity and potency for products. A new manufacturing process, as well as an NCE or NME, can be patented in the United States.

Active ingredients from natural sources start as crude drugs. According to the standard text on drug extraction from natural sources, *Pharmacognosy,* crude drugs from vegetative or animal—even insect—origins are "natural substances that have undergone only the processes of collection and drying." Natural substances are those "found in nature . . . that have not had changes made in their molecular structure." The sources of these substances, medicinal plants or the animals from which glands and organs are needed, can either be raised commercially or collected in the wild. But environmental concerns tended to support the former in the 1980s and 1990s. Especially with plants, it is of vital importance that the correct species be identified before collection. Once a crude drug has been collected and the needed portions separated and cleaned, it must be safely stored or immediately processed according to how quickly the active ingredient might spoil on lose its potency. Plants are often stored over long periods to help decompose unwanted plant components while leaving the desired portions intact. Animal glands and organs, however, are generally processed quickly to avoid deterioration.

If the crude drug is a plant, the active constituent—the ingredient desired for the final drug product—must be extracted. The first step in this procedure is grinding and mincing the appropriate plant parts, such as the leaves or the seeds. Production facilities in this industry house hammer mills, knife mills, and teeth mills designed to reduce leaves, stems, seeds, or roots to a manageable powder composed of evenly sized granules. Some plant products, such as herbal remedies, can be packaged at this point for sale or combined into other preparations. For most plant-derived drugs, the powdered plant must be submitted to a series of solvent baths (a process called maceration) in alcohol or ether, or the plant goes through a series of distillation procedures (in the case of volatile oils) that separate the desired ingredient from the crude material. Animal glands or organs are also minced, then mixed with a solvent that aids extraction and often preserves the substance. After centrifugation, the animal extract is filtered to separate remaining impurities. Antibiotic molds, on the other hand, are actually grown in large fermentation tanks. The molds release their medicinal yield into a fermenting medium or solution. These fluid mixtures of either mold, plant, or animal materials are submitted to "precipitation," which involves the application of either heat or freezing cold or the addition of

salts or some other compound that separates or isolates the target active ingredient from the fluid. Isolates are then sent to the customer in either powdered or fluid form to be assembled into a marketable drug.

Manufacturers of active ingredients ship finished products in "batches" to the preparation firm awaiting them. The chemical composition of these shipments must match a parent batch to ensure purity and strength and must meet with the approval of the U.S. Food and Drug Administration (FDA) as well as the client company. Firms that desire a regular supply of high-quality materials will often inspect manufacturing plants before assigning a production contract for active ingredients. Besides comparing active ingredients to the standard, the FDA is responsible for ensuring that every step in the process of pharmaceutical raw material production meets specific production standards.

BACKGROUND AND DEVELOPMENT

Raw material suppliers for pharmaceutical companies, in the form of fine chemical producers, actually predated the pharmaceutical industry. Until well into the nineteenth century, doctors and apothecaries—pharmacists—collected and processed their own botanical remedies and compounded their own medicinal chemicals. Drugs in the limited and non-standardized pharmacopeia were herbal remedies whose provenance dated back centuries and could be prepared simply. Pharmacists could produce what chemical treatments there were in drugstores using comparatively unsophisticated equipment. Because of the similarity of pharmaceutical chemicals to the processes for making industrial chemicals, small-scale producers often engaged in the manufacture of both. In fact, many modern medicinal chemical suppliers, like Dow and Hoechst, produce industrial chemicals as well.

An increase in the scientific study of chemistry and botanical extracts in the nineteenth century yielded a whole range of new chemicals and isolates with pharmaceutical potential. Included among these were the anesthetics ether and morphine. These new drugs required a greater degree of standardization and production expertise than earlier treatments. Their efficacy also increased public demand. Pharmacists, like H.E. Merck in Germany, as well as doctors and fine chemical producers, started developing and building the manufacturing capacity to meet these needs. The new pharmaceutical firms called themselves "ethical" manufacturers in order to differentiate themselves from the "patent" medicine producers, who bottled popular concoctions with broad therapeutic claims but dubious medicinal value. The makers of ethicals clearly labeled the contents of products and promoted the therapeutic strength and purity of their medicines.

Many early active ingredient suppliers for both the American ethical and patent producers were European fine chemical companies. But such events as the War of 1812, the Civil War, and World War I tended to disrupt European supplies and spur American companies to increase capacity for domestic chemical manufacture. American companies like Squibb—which became Bristol Myers-Squibb Company—established themselves by supplying medicines for the Union armies.

By the first decades of the twentieth century, breakthroughs in understanding the bacteriological basis of many diseases by Louis Pasteur and the effect of chemicals on certain parts of the body by Paul Ehrlich led to a new era in pharmaceutical science in which specific compounds could be screened for effectiveness against known disease organisms. The discovery of such "wonder drugs," like the anti-infective sulfanilimides and various vaccines, increased the demand for reliable new drug treatments. Most drugs, however, with the exception of injectables, still did not reach the physician or pharmacist in finished form. Pharmaceutical firms still purchased fine chemicals from companies like Pfizer Inc. or Merck and Co., Inc. and compounded them into pharmaceutical mixtures for distribution to hospitals and pharmacists. Pharmacists mixed these bulk ingredients into finished form in the drugstore. However, it is important to note that these treatments did not displace botanical products as the dominant form of drug treatment until after World War II.

With its emergency demand for the new antiinfectives like the antibiotic penicillin (as well as sulfa drugs), World War II changed the structure of the pharmaceutical industry. Bulk suppliers like Pfizer Inc. and Merck and Co., Inc. found themselves producing drugs on a massive scale in both finished and bulk form. After the war, these companies stayed in the profitable ethicals business, making prescription-only pharmaceutical preparations. With a high public demand for new life saving or extending medications, companies began to finance enlarged research and development departments to discover and develop important—and profitable—new therapies. A vast array of new drugs resulted in the 1940s, 1950s, and 1960s, including tranquilizers, steroids, vaccines, and more antibiotics. Many of these drugs were derived from the laboratory screening of botanicals and animal products, like steroids from yams used to make a cortisonal treatment for arthritis and insulin from animal pancreas extracts used to control diabetes. The limits of natural supply, however, prompted many pharmaceutical companies to synthesize the active ingredients in these medicines.

Meanwhile, new federal regulatory requirements slapped tight new restrictions on the production of drugs after 1962, when a popular European sleeping pill, Thalidomide, was found to cause severe birth defects in some newborns. In response, Congress passed the 1962 Kefauver-Harris Amendments to the 1938 Food, Drug, and Cosmetic Act. The legislation required FDA licensing and oversight of all pharmaceutical manufacturing facilities and processes, including those of bulk pharmaceutical suppliers. Similar production controls had already been instituted after 1949 for "batches" of bulk penicillin.

Kefauver-Harris reinforced trends in the industry toward in-house production of active ingredient supplies for pharmaceuticals. Because the pharmaceutical company was ultimately responsible for the purity of its product, even if an outside supplier provided ineffective or dangerous compounds, companies thought it safer to have internal oversight and production control. Perhaps as important to major firms was a desire to maintain command of active ingredient supply even after patents had run out on new medications. In his history of the pharmaceutical industry titled *The Structure of American Industry,* Walter S. Measday cited a situation in which "upwards of 150 companies" offered Vitamin C in dosage form while "the entire output of the vitamin itself is produced by Merck, Pfizer, and Hoffman-La Roche, Inc." If ethical pharmaceutical companies could control bulk supplies for more advanced medications than Vitamin C even after product patents ran out, they would effectively extend their patent period—and associated high profits—indefinitely.

In the late 1980s and early 1990s, pharmaceutical firms began to reverse the trend toward the in-house production of active ingredients in favor of a more complex combination of captive production and long-term contracts with outside custom suppliers. Among the factors fueling this trend were the 1992 economic recession and excess world chemical capacity, the increasing costs in both time and money to negotiate regulatory hazards, the complexity of new drug compounds, and the desire to avoid tying up too much capital in supply factories.

Meanwhile, the highly politicized drive for healthcare reform in the late 1980s and early 1990s created downward pressure on the prices the big pharmaceutical firms could charge for their prescription drugs, even for new "breakthrough" treatment therapies costing considerable amounts of money to develop. The immediate winners in this contest over drug prices seemed to be the smaller independent generics companies. Generics, markedly cheaper therapeutic and chemical equivalents of prescription patented medicines, went into production once the patent protection on a prescription drug expired. Generics companies could manage cheap prices because they only had to copy—not research and develop—the drugs they produced.

Because of this, however, the active ingredients in generics accounted for almost one-half of the sale price—a ratio three to four times greater than prescription versions of the same drug. This made the generic companies susceptible to changes in the supply of active ingredients worldwide. When, as *Drug Topics* reported in 1994, the European Economic Community temporarily "outlawed the exportation of bulk/fine chemicals," generics companies were faced with a 85 percent cutoff of supply. At the same time, the prescription pharmaceutical firms controlled the current capacity on the active ingredients in their drugs coming off-patent. Combined with a wave of takeovers or start-ups of generics firms by large pharmaceutical producers, the cutoff in supplies threatened to squeeze independent generic producers out and effectively extend prescription patents and higher drug prices much longer than healthcare reform advocates desired.

CURRENT CONDITIONS

The fine chemicals sector of the industry was very fragmented, with the top 25 companies accounting for less than 25 percent of the $60-billion market in 1999, according to Jan Zuidam of DSM Fine Chemicals. Of the $21-billion U.S. market, 44 percent of sales were generated by the pharmaceuticals industry and 54 percent were Agro chemicals, according to reports by Frost and Sullivan and Kline and Co. Inc.'s president Andrew A. Boccone.

As life sciences industries underwent a growth boom, companies in this industry likewise looked forward to strong growth as pharmaceutical companies focused more on research and development and increasingly outsourced active-ingredient production. Outsourcing reduced the burden of drug development while accelerating the process for pharmaceutical companies. Additionally, pharmaceutical companies were no longer responsible for costs associated with maintaining manufacturing facilities.

The botanicals segment of this industry also offered tremendous growth potential as consumer awareness and demand grew in the global nutritional industry. According to International Research Institute, U.S. sales of botanical medicines in 1998 totaled $4 billion. Companies were able to add value to natural ingredients by developing and patenting methods of standardized extraction of active plant constituents. One such company, Inter-Cal, a subsidiary of Zila, Inc., patented Ester-C brand products and a standardized extract of Saw Palmetto for treatment of benign prostate hyperplasia, affecting 50 percent of the male population by age 60. Additionally, Congress called for funding for university research grants to increase scientific information available for botanical dietary supplements. In 1999 the National Institute of Health granted $7.5 million to UCLA's new Center for Dietary Supplements Research: Botanicals.

While the botanicals segment was taking steps to gain public trust, seven leading vitamin manufacturers

pled guilty in the largest criminal settlement in U.S. history and agreed to pay combined fines of $1.8 million in 1999. Five of the companies pleaded guilty to charges of conspiracy to fix and inflate vitamin prices. Fined most heavily were Swiss pharmaceutical giant Hoffman-LaRoche, Inc., which agreed to pay $500 million, and German BASF AG, which agreed to pay $225 million. The scheme lasted nearly a decade, according to Assistant Attorney General Joel I. Klein, affecting more than $5 billion in U.S. commerce in common household products. Dr. Kuno Sommer, former director of worldwide marketing for Hoffman-LaRoche Vitamins and Fine Chemicals Division agreed to plead guilty and serve a four-month prison term and pay a $100,000 fine.

INDUSTRY LEADERS

In the 1990s, Merck & Co. Inc. continued to dominate the market by delivering, developing, manufacturing, and marketing a broad range of human and animal health products. Overall sales in 1998 totaled nearly $27 billion, with a 13.8 percent sales growth from the previous year. The company employed 57,300 people worldwide in 1998. Although the company continued to form partnerships with biotech companies and academic scientists for research, the company was not among the "aggressive outsourcers," for botanicals and fine chemicals. In contrast, in 1998 as global demand for Merck products grew, the company sought to expand its bulk chemicals capacity and broke ground for a new chemical manufacturing facility in Singapore.

Roche Holding AG, of Switzerland, generated 1998 sales of approximately $17.9 billion—a 39.7 percent increase over the previous year. The company's pharmaceutical products comprise 60 percent of its sales. Roche manufactures pharmaceutical products, diagnostics, fragrances, and flavors. In 1998 Roche employed approximately 66,707 people worldwide (28 percent in North America). The company's Vitamins Division manufactured thirteen vitamins, several carotenoids, medicinal feed additives, amino acids, citric acid, polyunsaturated fatty acids, UV filters, emulsifiers, and antitussives (cough-reflex inhibitors). In 1999 the division employed approximately 7000 people. In 1998 the division's sales reached 3.63 billion Swiss Francs (some 2.4 billion U.S. dollars), undergoing a slight decline due to heavy price pressures. That year the company invested in four new vitamin production facilities in Scotland, Poland, Germany, and China. In 1999 the company expected a favorable net profit despite the $500 million penalty in the vitamin price-fixing suit agreed to by the company's subsidiary Hoffman-LaRoche, Inc.

AMERICA AND THE WORLD

Despite the twentieth century revolution in chemical pharmaceuticals, it was reported in *The Medicinal Plant*

Industry that "50 percent to 80 percent of the developing world depends on traditional therapies for their health care," namely plant-derived remedies. In China and Southeast Asia, indigenous industries process and package plant-based remedies based on ancient recipes. Some processors utilize the same machinery and manufacturing expertise as American companies, while others are extremely small and use traditional methods. This system of traditional active ingredient production for drugs, except to the extent that Western-style medicines were adopted or locally produced for export to the West, remained relatively untouched by American corporate influences.

Suppliers of fine chemicals for American pharmaceuticals, however, have never been limited to the country's borders. European chemical companies, except for temporary alterations during various wars, have always had—and continued to have in the late twentieth century—a large presence in the American market. The *Chemical Processing on the Web* reported in 1999 that of the top 25 fine chemicals firms in the world, 15 were European, 7 were from the United States, and 3 were Japanese. Of the $60-billion world market, U.S. companies had sales of only $25 billion. American producers, however, more than held their own in domestic markets. In the 1990s industry leadership remained in European and American hands, which, with the addition of Japan, were estimated to control almost 90 percent of the market. A growing threat to this Western fine chemical hegemony were Asian and Indian producers, who do not have the strict Western environmental codes applied to U.S. producers. Asian producers showed themselves particularly competitive in the bulk pharmaceutical and intermediates classes.

FURTHER READING

"About Roche." F. Hoffmann-LaRoche Ltd., 1999. Available from http://www.roche.com.

"Chairman of Pharmanex, Inc. Medical Advisory Board Awarded Unprecedented $7.5 Million Grant By National institutes of Health (NIH) to Research Botanical Dietary Supplements Dr. David Heber to Head New 'UCLA Center for Dietary Supplements Research: Botanicals (CSRB)' to Investigate Red Yeast, Green Tea Extract, Soy, St. John's Wort and Others." *PR Newswire,* 12 October 1999.

"Hoover's Company Capsules." Hoover's, Inc., 1999. Available from http://www.hoovers.com.

Howlett, Elizabeth. "Outsourcing by the Pharmaceutical Industry Provides Opportunities for Fine Chemical Producers Worldwide." *Industry, Trade, and Technology Review,* October 1999.

"Leading Chemical Industry Management Consulting Firm Shares Views of Industry Outlook." *PR Newswire,* 27 September 1999.

Lichtblau, Eric. "Seven Vitamin Makers Settle Antitrust Suit for $1.8 Billion." *Los Angeles Times,* 4 November 1999.

Merck 1998 Annual Report. Whitehouse Station, NJ: Merck and Co., Inc., 1999. Available from http://www.merck.com.

McKinley, Ed. "Growth and Consolidation for Fine Chemicals." *Chemical Processing on the Web,* July 1999. Available from http://www.chemicalprocessing.com.

"Roche Sees 'Good' FY Despite Special Charges in Vitamin Case." *AFX Europe,* 14 October 1999.

Storck, William. "Industry's Bright Outlook." *Chemical and Engineering News,* 12 January 1998.

Sniffen, Michael. "Vitamin Giants Sued Millions." *San Francisco Examiner,* 6 November 1999.

Tyler, Varro, et al. *Pharmacognosy.* 8th ed. Philadelphia, PA: Lea and Febiger, 1981.

Wijesekera, R.O.B. *The Medicinal Plant Industry.* Boca Raton: CRC Press, 1991.

"Zila's Inter-Cal Launches Palmexx Saw Palmetto Extract, Based on New Purextrax Technology." *PR Newswire,* 11 November 1999.

SIC 2834

PHARMACEUTICAL PREPARATIONS

This industry includes establishments primarily engaged in manufacturing, fabricating, or processing drugs in pharmaceutical preparations for human or veterinary use. The greater part of the products of these establishments are finished in the form intended for final consumption, such as ampoules, tablets, capsules, vials, ointments, medicinal powders, solutions, and suspensions. Products of this industry consist of two important lines, namely pharmaceutical preparations, promoted primarily to the dental, medical, or veterinary profession; and pharmaceutical preparations promoted primarily to the public.

NAICS CODE(S)

325412 (Pharmaceutical Preparation Manufacturing)

INDUSTRY SNAPSHOT

Since World War II, which established the American drug industry on a permanent footing, pharmaceutical firms have enjoyed a high level of profitability. The discovery and development of dozens of life-saving medications in company research labs created enormous demand for pharmaceuticals, while patent protection and sophisticated marketing structures maintained sales and profits. The high cost of drug development and marketing, though, tended to concentrate industry earnings in several large firms. In fact, the top ten companies accounted for 40 percent of the market up until 1999. Even with strict regulatory oversight and periodic crises, like the Thalidomide scare of 1962, the American pharmaceutical industry, or at least its major players, managed to remain both profitable and beneficial to world health, while avoiding the price controls commonplace in other industrialized nations.

The trend toward corporate mergers gained momentum at the end of the century, allowing companies to shift from depending heavily on one or two drugs for the bulk of their sales. The major pharmaceutical companies also had the capital to fuel corporate alliances with biotechnology companies offering platform technologies with potential to produce new drugs. By the year 2000, 20 percent of research and development dollars was spent on such research collaborations, according to reports by Advancetech Monitor.

ORGANIZATION AND STRUCTURE

Pharmaceutical production and employment was concentrated in the northeast states of New Jersey, Pennsylvania, and New York. About 20 percent of the nation's drugs were shipped from New Jersey, home to industry leaders American Home Products Corp., Johnson & Johnson, and Merck and Co., Inc. Other states with high concentrations of drug companies were California, Illinois, Texas, Indiana, and Florida.

Companies marketing pharmaceutical preparations, or finished-form drugs, maintained their traditional leadership of the industry into the late 1990s. Companies in this sector share similar manufacturing techniques—they combine active medicinal ingredients, chemicals, or natural products with excipients (i.e., buffered powders) or sterile water to produce the finished, or dosage, drug form. The most common dosage forms are oral (tablets and liquid suspensions), parenteral (by injection), or solid (suppositories and ointments). More novel drug delivery systems appeared in the 1980s and 1990s, including polymer implants, transdermal patches, and controlled-release sponges inside tablets.

Preparations firms also concentrated on the development, production, and marketing of therapeutic agents—drugs designed to treat, cure, or prevent specific diseases (antibiotics); suppress symptoms (analgesics); or supplement deficiencies (vitamins). Meanwhile, other industry segments concentrated on making drugs to create immunities (vaccines) or aid in diagnosis (radioactive iodine for X-rays). Within the general area of therapeutics, pharmaceutical companies developed expertise in one or more of the eight therapeutic classes of drugs, such as cardiovasculars, or even a specific disease, such as hypertension. Industry leaders generally manufactured and marketed drugs in several therapeutic categories, while some small companies produced only one drug.

All companies in the pharmaceutical industry operate within a strict regulatory environment. Because these companies manufacture potentially harmful, yet socially necessary products, but must also make a profit, the pharmaceutical industry has had a complex relationship with government regulators. These regulators are charged with protecting the public and encouraging business growth at the same time. Major incidents of adverse or fatal reactions from drugs, evidence of collusion or corruption within the industry, and the government's desire to move the industry in a particular direction have historically prompted new regulation. From the Food and Drug Administration (FDA) to the Federal Trade Commission (FTC), pharmaceutical companies and the federal government are linked at all stages, including development, production, and marketing.

Division and segmentation also characterized the industry. Some of this was the result of federal regulation, while the pressures of a highly competitive marketplace were responsible for the rest. One point of division for regulatory agencies was that between "ethical" and over-the-counter (OTC) drugs. Ethical drugs require a prescription from a physician before being dispensed to the patient, while consumers can purchase OTC medications (such as aspirin and antacid) without a doctor's prescription.

The ethical drug segment of the industry is further subdivided into "patented" and "generic" prescription drugs. Patented drugs are therapies developed by pharmaceutical companies whose formulas, production processes, and trade names (often called branded prescription drugs) enjoy 17-year protection under U.S. patent laws. Patented prescription drugs were the driving force behind pharmaceutical industry sales after World War II and continued market domination into the mid-1990s. Branded prescriptions included almost all of the major breakthrough therapies developed in drug research labs since the 1940s, continuing the drug industry's unusual combination of health- and profit-driven research. Meanwhile, an alternative to some of the most popular remedies were generics, markedly cheaper chemical and therapeutic equivalents of patented prescription drugs that go into production once brand name therapies have come "off-patent." Generics' share of the prescription drug market was expected to increase from 22 percent in 1985 to more than 66 percent by the turn of the century.

In addition to drugs for human consumption, pharmaceutical companies produce drugs for the veterinary market. Accounting for a relatively small percentage of overall industry sales—nearly $1.6 billion in 1995, according to the U.S. Census Bureau's *Current Industrial Reports*—many drug industry leaders either maintained specific animal health divisions or were involved in the animal health care industry.

Beginning in the early 1980s, a new force entered the pharmaceutical arena—biotechnology. From the discovery of DNA structure in 1953 and new knowledge of "genetic blueprints" that direct protein growth by messenger RNA, scientists were able to clone proteins in the laboratory. Knowledge of a specific protein's function in the body—to stimulate infection-fighting cells or block a destructive internal process, for example—allowed physicians to induce desired reactions in patients by injecting biotechnology-produced cloned proteins, or "Magic bullets," into the body. Though biotech companies managed to create and patent many exciting new treatments in the 1980s, they were generally inconsequential, lacked marketing structure, consumed vast amounts of research capital, and created little profit compared to those offered by the industry leaders. Nevertheless, because of the potential to continue providing "breakthrough" treatments and vaccines for some of our most stubborn diseases, biotechnology companies were the target of buyouts, mergers, and joint ventures in the 1980s and 1990s. In one such move, industry giant Roche purchased controlling interest in biotechnology pioneer Genentech in 1990.

BACKGROUND AND DEVELOPMENT

Prior to the late nineteenth century, the American pharmaceutical industry barely resembled its current structure. Simple chemical compounds such as iodine chlorate, along with plant extracts such as quinine, constituted the prime ingredients of available remedies. However, these drugs lacked specific scientific formulas. Thus a doctor's order for a medication might not yield the product intended. To offset this problem, doctors often dispensed medicines in addition to prescribing them. But they did not have a monopoly on medical advice or drug selection for patients. Given the uneven quality of medical care before the twentieth century, patients often chose to dose themselves with "patent" medicines or to describe symptoms to the druggist who would obligingly offer his own remedy for purchase. Some traditional treatments, like digitalis, remain part of the pharmacological arsenal.

The War of 1812 and the Civil War stimulated an increase in domestic pharmaceutical manufacturing capacity. Both events temporarily disrupted the supply of "fine" chemicals (those with a purity level high enough for human consumption) from Europe with which pharmacists and doctors produced what few chemical medicaments they knew. Advances in the isolation and creation of new chemical substances, such as the 1840 discovery of the medicinal applications for nitrous oxide (laughing gas) by an American dentist, Horace Wells, stimulated demand for more fine chemical capacity. During the Civil War, American firms like Squibb were able to establish themselves profitably by providing advanced machinery and quality products to the Union Army.

As the century progressed, other companies turned to the production of "ethical" drugs for physicians and hospitals. These drugs had clearly labeled and pharmacologically reliable contents (and were thus termed "ethical"). They were intended to supply drugs of standardized quality. Brand name ethicals were also promoted as alternatives to the wide variety of other proprietaries, mainly bottled "patent" medicines. These extremely popular elixirs claimed great therapeutic value while the contents—often only colored water, alcohol, and opiates—were generally ineffectual and occasionally dangerous. The reliability of the new ethical suppliers, on the other hand, induced doctors to begin requesting branded pharmaceuticals in prescriptions by the end of the century.

Following scientific breakthroughs in understanding the causes and potential treatments for many of the diseases that had long been the scourge of mankind, demand for these reliable drugs and vaccines soon increased. The germ theory of disease, based upon the research of bacteriologists like Pasteur, revolutionized medicine and drug therapy in the 20 years immediately before and after World War I. Laboratory isolation of disease organisms meant that physicians could diagnose patients by tracing illnesses to specific infectious organisms, while drug researchers finally had a clear therapeutic target. New knowledge of the manner in which chemical treatments operated in the body, based upon the research of the German scientist Paul Ehrlich, opened up pathways of attack against these disease organisms. By World War I, "medical science," as this marriage of disease and therapeutic research came to be called, had created significant breakthroughs, especially in the development of vaccines and what Ehrlich called "chemotherapy."

Larger pharmaceutical companies like SmithKline expanded clinical departments in response to the popularity and promise of medical science. They increased research into new drug therapies and quality control activities. On the eve of World War I, however, these companies lagged far behind German manufacturers like Bayer in the development and patenting of new therapies. German companies had a long history of combining basic bacteriological research with the applied science of drug development. And, unlike American firms, they had no compunction about creating exclusive markets for therapeutic inventions by patenting drugs in the United States and Germany. Novel treatments, such as the popular antisyphilitic arsenical drug, Salvarsan, discovered by Ehrlich and produced by chemical giant Hoechst, illustrated the potentially large new markets for "scientific" pharmaceuticals. When, during the war, most German companies had American patent rights suspended, American pharmaceutical firms began manufacturing patented drugs invented in Germany (like Salvarsan and Bayer aspirin) and reaping the profits.

In the time between World War I and II, American firms copied the research orientation and patenting habits

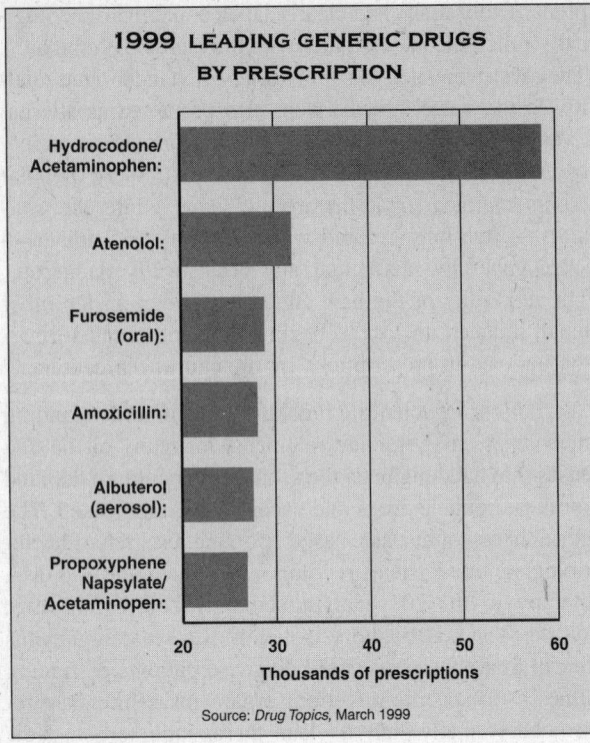

1999 LEADING GENERIC DRUGS BY PRESCRIPTION

Hydrocodone/Acetaminophen:

Atenolol:

Furosemide (oral):

Amoxicillin:

Albuterol (aerosol):

Propoxyphene Napsylate/Acetaminopen:

20   30   40   50   60

Thousands of prescriptions

Source: *Drug Topics*, March 1999

to produce marketable quantities of the "wonder drug" for use by armies and general populations. By 1945, the American manufacturing capacity for drugs had expanded so quickly that penicillin prices fell from $20 to $1 per dose, less than the labeled bottle containing it. This vastly expanded the productive capacity on the part of pharmaceutical companies and the awareness of the potential market for antibiotics, and it led to American domination of world markets after the war. Those factors resulted in the establishment of American pharmaceutical firms as research, manufacturing, and marketing powerhouses.

The first important federal law governing drug production came in 1902 with a law requiring the inspection and licensing of biologicals (vaccines and antitoxins) by a new federal agency, the Hygienic Laboratory, precursor of the National Institutes of Health (NIH). Soon thereafter, public outcry over the dangers of adulterated foods after the publication of Upton Sinclair's *The Jungle* secured passage of the second major piece of legislation covering therapeutic drugs, the Pure Food and Drug Act of 1906. This act prohibited adulterated or misbranded food or drugs from interstate commerce and granted authority to ban dangerous drugs.

In 1937, an American sulfanilimide producer, the Massengill Company of Tennessee, marketed a sore throat remedy that dissolved the sulfa drug in diethylene glycol, now the main ingredient in radiator antifreeze. Apparently, the manufacturer chose this particular solvent because of its pretty red color and sweet taste. No clinical trials for toxicity were performed. More than 100 reported deaths from kidney failure resulted from its ingestion before investigators determined the source of the fatalities. Public clamor over this incident led to the passage of the Food, Drug, and Cosmetic Act of 1938. This legislation required that all drugs must submit to tests for proof of safety by the newly created Food and Drug Administration (FDA). Packaging was required to carry labels clearly describing the contents of the drug, how it should be administered, and possible side effects. Attendant legislation gave the Federal Trade Commission (FTC) responsibility for ensuring valid drug advertising. Experience showed, however, that most consumers did not bother to read the extensive labels on medication. As a result, the Durham-Humphrey Amendment of 1951 exempted prescription drugs from full labeling requirements. These drugs, to be dispensed only by a licensed pharmacist under written direction of a physician, carried a "legend" label that read, "Caution: Federal law prohibits dispensing without a prescription." Legend drugs thereafter became another name for prescription or ethical drugs.

Despite regulatory hurdles, World War II and America's sustained postwar economic dominance secured the foundation for phenomenal growth in the pharmaceutical

of German counterparts. Merck and Squibb opened direct ties with academic research institutions, financing research fellowships, laboratories, and institutes in the natural sciences. Drug companies hired academic research leaders to head or staff in-house labs. Firms developed some interest in basic research, but the major concern was using expanded research and development area capabilities to create new drug products for the expanding market. Major companies like Squibb, Merck, Abbott, and Upjohn all had research staffs of about 20 with budgets of at least $100,000 by World War II. Nevertheless, the discovery of the two major drug treatments of the war years, the sulfanilimides and the antibiotics, both resulted from European research. The sulfa drugs, chemotherapeutic anti-infectives derived from coal tars, were first developed at Bayer in 1935. One of the most important drug therapies of the twentieth century, mold-derived anti-infective penicillin, was first isolated and described by Alexander Fleming in England in 1928. Both the sulfa drugs and antibiotics became cornerstones of the American pharmaceutical industry from the 1930s to the 1950s.

Patent protection for the sulfas expired in the 1930s, and American companies, including Merck and American Cyanimid, began domestic manufacture of the anti-infectives. Meanwhile a grant by the Rockefeller family brought penicillin to America, where, in a Peoria, Illinois, lab in 1941 scientists discovered how to mass-produce penicillin mold by deep fermentation (as opposed to the slower surface culture). Several drug companies— including Pfizer, Squibb, and Merck—quickly geared up industry. The desire to find new drugs, especially antibiotics, led companies to sometimes absurd extremes. Pfizer requested that people send them samples of dirt from all corners of the world on the chance that some might contain new molds from which to extract antibiotics. In fact, a Pfizer employee did find a profitable new treatment, terramycin, in a sample of dirt outside a company plant in Indiana. This and other ''broad-spectrum'' antibiotics, effective for a wide range of illnesses, provided revolutionary therapeutic regimens for physicians after the 1940s. Other breakthrough medications in the 1950s included Jonas Salk's polio vaccine, and tranquilizers and amphetamines, like Librium and Dexedrine, which promised to significantly aid patients suffering from mental illness. According to the Pharmaceutical Manufacturers Association (PMA) in its 1980 *Factbook,* new drug introductions increased from an annual average of 10 to 30 in the 1940s to an average of 30 to 50 in the 1950s.

The array of new products available meant that individual physicians and pharmacists could not know all the available treatments at any one time. Pharmaceutical companies began to send out sales representatives, or ''detail'' men, as both educators in new therapies and promoters of company brands. Spending large sums on free physician samples and advertising in professional journals led to increased brand loyalty on the part of doctors. This marketing structure was expensive but also supported high profits. Trained to think only of treatment regimens, doctors, often unaware of drug prices, prescribed medication where cheaper and equally efficacious therapeutic alternatives existed. Even if pharmacists wanted to substitute a cheaper generic for a doctor's prescription, doing so made little sense for a drugstore's profitability, might anger the physician, and was illegal in some states. The relationship established in the 1940s and 1950s between drug companies, pharmacists, and doctors, therefore, tended to perpetuate itself.

Fallout from another scandal, the Thalidomide crisis of 1962, however, placed more pressure on the industry. A popular European sleeping pill, Thalidomide was under investigation in 1962 by an American firm, the William S. Merrell Company, which wanted to start U.S. sales of the drug. The company's tests revealed that the drug could cause severe birth defects in babies if taken by a pregnant mother. Despite the fact the drug was never sold in the United States, its inadequate premarket testing in Europe and near-entry into the American market revealed that a thin line of regulation was all that stood between dangerous drugs and the general public. As James Nielson wrote in *The Handbook of Federal Drug Law* in 1992, the Thalidomide disaster made it clear ''that people were taking drugs'' for which ''neither the prescriber nor the manufacturer had a clear knowledge of their effects.'' The Thalidomide crisis, along with public dissatisfaction with exorbitant drug-company profits, meant ''drugs never again received the universal public acceptance they had previously enjoyed.''

The federal government responded to the uproar over the Thalidomide crisis by passing the Kefauver-Harris Amendments of 1962. These amendments to the Food, Drug and Cosmetic Act of 1938 required pharmaceutical companies to prove both safety and efficacy before a drug entered the marketplace. Formal procedures for new drug applications (NDAs) to the FDA and for the clinical investigation of potential therapies were established. All adverse drug reactions in clinical studies would have to be fully reported, and human clinical subjects had to be informed of the dangers of involvement in trials before giving consent. Additionally, the act required that drugs must follow specific production guidelines, called Good Manufacturing Practices (GMP). Manufacturing plants became subject to both registration and inspection procedures. Finally, advertising for prescription drugs was placed under FDA supervision, while OTC drug advertising continued under FTC oversight. The price controls for pharmaceuticals included in Senator Kefauver's original legislative proposal were dropped along the way.

The immediate effect of the Kefauver-Harris amendments was to drastically lower the rate at which pharmaceutical manufacturers introduced new drugs to the market. According to the Pharmaceutical Manufacturers Association (PMA), drug introductions fell from 45 to 24 annually between 1961 and 1962 alone. In the 1970s they stayed below 20 in most years. Despite this slump, by the 1980s reinvigorated research efforts using advanced techniques in ''molecular biology and biochemistry were promising a new generation of highly effective drugs for specific ailments, or magic bullets.'' One of the magic bullets was SmithKline Beecham's Tagamet, an anti-ulcer medication that quickly became ''one of the most widely prescribed pharmaceuticals in the world'' and prompted an increase in the research investments of pharmaceutical companies from ''$1 billion in 1976 to $4 billion in 1985.''

These larger research budgets yielded a whole crop of profitable new drug therapies in the 1980s, including drugs for hypertension (Merck's Vasotec), cholesterol treatment (Lopid from Warner-Lambert and Mevacor from Merck), and blood clot dissolvers for heart attack victims (Genentech's TPA). Meanwhile, Ortho Pharmaceutical's (owned by Johnson & Johnson) anti-acne Retin-A and Upjohn's baldness treatment Rogaine created new markets for cosmetic drugs. Even standbys like aspirin enjoyed increased sales as a result of studies that showed its potential to avert some heart attacks.

Despite some victories, by the end of the 1980s the prospects for the preparations industry did not look bright. Decades of expensive applied research, a wide patent umbrella, strong overseas sales, and aggressive marketing had sustained high profit and growth in the American prescription pharmaceutical industry since World War II. The system produced important new therapies that prolonged lives, banished ancient diseases, and made the aches and pains of modern existence easier to bear for those who could afford to purchase these new medications. But the highly structured corporate research, manufacturing, and marketing systems of industry leaders also required that wonderful new medications carry, what seemed to many, improperly inflated price tags. Some analysts felt that price was determining costs rather than the other way around. This trend continued into the 1980s. Thus, some industry critics claimed that the big brand pharmaceutical companies were charging unjustifiably high prices for drugs while spending more money on advertising, brand support, and lobbying efforts than they did for research and development. The prices of drugs were less related to cost inputs, therefore, than to companies' needs to maintain corporate structures. Meanwhile, the soaring costs of health care in general in the 1980s and early 1990s added fuel to demands for drug price control policies similar to those in Europe. Medications sold in Europe and America were reported to have price differentials exceeding 50 percent. Meanwhile, continued reports of industry profits added fuel to reform fires. According to industry analyst Robert Helms, quoted in a 1992 *Drug Topics,* "profits for the top ten drug companies averaged 15 percent of sales, compared to 4 percent for all other industries."

In 1991 legislation allowed state-funded Medicaid insurance programs to demand rebates from drug manufacturers for medications purchased by program recipients that resulted in downward price pressures. Standard and Poor's reported in its 1994 *Industry Surveys* that Medicaid accounted for about 15 percent of all U.S. pharmaceutical sales. Similar programs for the federal government's Medicare program were included in President Clinton's 1993 health care reform proposals. Downward pressures on drug prices also resulted from the advent of private managed care organizations such as health maintenance organizations (HMOs) in the 1980s and 1990s. Standard and Poor's estimated that HMO enrollment alone may top 50 percent of the population by the year 2000. These organizations increasingly adopted restrictive drug formularies (lists of drugs that could or could not be purchased by an organization) that stressed economical medication in therapeutic groups, often demanding discounts from manufacturers and the use of cheaper brands or generics to treat illness. Both of these movements created what one industry analyst, Paul Hanson, in an April 1994 *Chemical Week* article called a "strategic shift in power in pharmaceuticals from suppliers to consumers."

The price- and consumer-oriented generics and over-the-counter (OTC) segments, in fact, were poised to benefit from the health care reform movement. At least since the passage of the Drug Price Competition and Patent Term Restoration Act of 1984 (commonly called the Waxman-Hatch Act), the federal government attempted to increase industry competition and help supply cheaper drugs for the public by aiding the generally smaller and independent generics manufacturers. The act allowed generics companies to present a shorter version of the standard New Drug Application (NDA) to the FDA's anti-ulcer Zantac, which reached the open shelves of drugstores and groceries in the 1990s. Like generics, OTCs represented a significant price advantage over branded prescriptions. In addition, patients were more likely to diagnose and treat themselves with the drugs than to visit a doctor and receive a prescription. Fueled by these factors, sales of OTC drugs increased at a compound annual rate of 6 percent from 1985 to 1995. The OTC segment was expected to grow by more than 45 percent from $9.6 billion in 1995 to $14.0 billion by the year 2000.

U.S. drugmakers also faced the threat of increased regulation—including price controls—in the early 1990s. While it was defeated in 1994, the Clinton administration's health care proposal did have an indirect effect on the industry, inspiring wholesale belt-tightening and a rash of mergers and acquisitions. Furthermore, the industry's earnings growth slowed from an annual average of 18 percent from 1987 to 1992 to 9 percent from 1991 to 1993. Downsizing helped boost the earnings growth rate to 12 percent by 1995.

The pharmaceutical preparations industry continued to be dominated by existing large branded firms in the mid-1990s. Through buyouts and in-house start-ups, as well as a continuation of the merger movement begun in the late 1980s, large companies adjusted to both market changes and reform movements. Many of the bigger companies, including industry leaders Marion Merrell Dow and Hoescht, moved swiftly to buy or create generics divisions in the early 1990s. Industry sources estimated that approximately 40 percent of the generics market was already controlled by the leading branded pharmaceutical companies in 1992. Meanwhile, most major OTC companies were also prescription producers, and the majority of prescriptions to OTC switches could easily be carried out within these companies. As Roche did with Genentech, the majors also moved to purchase smaller competitors or start their own innovative biotechnology companies. Along with a number of new and important breakthrough drugs coming out of the majors' drug research pipelines, an aging population with greater drug demand, and what Standard and Poor's *Industry Surveys* called the "recession-resistant nature of the business'' boded well for at least some of the industry's large companies.

CURRENT CONDITIONS

By the late 1990s, this $265-billion industry of high stakes and potentially huge profits was marked with frenzied buy-outs and turf wars. *Hoover's Industry Snapshots* reports that in 1996 alone, the 27 U.S. mergers valued $9.4 billion and mergers between U.S. and international companies valued $1.9 billion. The tremendous time and money investment required to bring a drug to market created a constant pressure on drug companies to have new products nearly approval-ready at about the time patents for current money-makers expired.

The 1999 battle over Warner-Lambert illustrated the extent of this pressure. The company had a five-year marketing agreement with Pfizer Inc. to market its top-selling cholesterol-reducing drug Lipitor, with sales expected to total more than $6 billion in 2002. After Warner-Lambert made a $67-billion merger agreement with American Home Products, Pfizer initiated an $82-billion hostile takeover bid for Warner-Lambert in an attempt to derail the merger. A provision of the Warner-Lambert/American Home Products agreement required a $2-billion payment if either walked away from the deal. Pfizer sued Warner-Lambert, contending it violated a standstill provision when it failed to inform Pfizer of merger talks with American Home Products. The following week Warner-Lambert initiated a lawsuit, claiming the takeover offer was illegal and the information Pfizer used to make the offer was confidential to the Lipitor agreement.

On another battleground, AstroZeneca, maker of the only proven breast-cancer prevention drug tamoxifen, sued the Eli Lilly and Co. for ''off-label'' promotion of the same claim for its osteoporosis drug Evista. In 1997 the FDA denied approval of Evista for cancer prevention but granted its approval for use against osteoporosis. The FDA issued warning letters to the Eli Lilly Co. for implying the drug's cancer-prevention properties in a 1998 $40-million ad campaign. Sales representatives for Evista strongly implied it was proven to prevent cancer and even misrepresented its labeling to doctors. In July 1999 a federal judge granted a preliminary injunction to stop the advancement of unapproved claims.

INDUSTRY LEADERS

Hundreds of companies are involved in the pharmaceutical preparations industry, but the top five companies generally account for more than 30 percent of American sales. Buyouts and competition among the major pharmaceutical companies continued to shift the rankings from year to year, but a handful of giants provided consistent leadership in both the ethical pharmaceutical and OTC segments of the field.

Merck and Co., Inc., a traditional industry leader in prescription drug research, had sales of $26.9 billion in 1999, more than triple its $8.6 billion in 1991. Merck was the number-one drug maker in the United States and was one of the world's largest prescription drug companies. The company introduced five new drugs in 1998. That year the company also retained three joint-venture partnerships, sold its interest back to the Dupont Pharmaceutical Co. in another venture, and re-structured a venture with Astra AB of Sweden.

Merck originated as a German apothecary shop, and the family name was associated with pharmaceutical manufacturing for more than 300 years in that country. In 1891, George Merck began American operations. In World War I, Merck avoided confiscation by giving the majority of its stock to the U.S. government, which sold it after the war to start American Merck. In the 1930s and 1940s, Merck created a name for itself by making breakthroughs in the discovery and synthesis of vitamins, including B12 in 1948. Outside the drug area, Merck's *Manual of Diagnosis and Therapy* became a medical standard. Merck scientists also led in the synthesis of steroids and funded research that resulted in the discovery of streptomycin in 1943. Five Merck scientists received Nobel Prizes in the 1940s and 1950s for these and other pharmaceutical breakthroughs.

Merck's drug pipeline fell to a trickle and company fortunes slumped in the 1960s. But renewed commitment to research and development, started by new Chairman John Horan (1976) and continued by his biochemist successor Roy Vagelos (1985), yielded important new therapies. Two of these, Vasotec, an anti-hypertensive, and Mevacor, which lowered cholesterol levels, reached annual sales of $1 billion each. One of the few large companies to take advantage of biotechnology breakthroughs, Merck began marketing the first genetically engineered human vaccine for hepatitis B late in the decade.

Rather than join the merger and buyout trend of the late 1980s and early 1990s, Merck sought to complement its industrial leadership in ethical pharmaceuticals by moving into joint ventures with companies like chemical industry leader DuPont and OTC leader Johnson & Johnson. However, Merck did buy mail-order drug distributor Medco Containment Services for $6.6 billion in 1993. This, and new supplier agreements with Managed Care Organizations (MCOs), showed that even giants like Merck were girding themselves for the changes wrought by health care reform. In 1992 Merck established what would become known as ''the Rahway pledge,'' vowing not to increase prescription drug prices faster than the general inflation rate. The company had several reasons

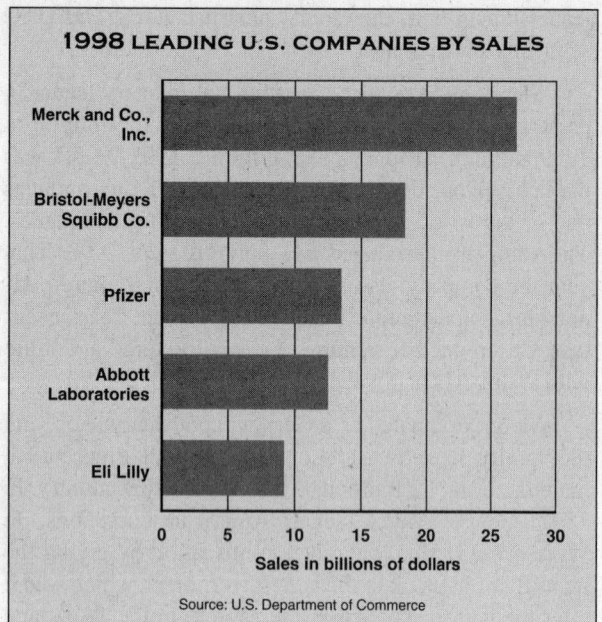

1998 LEADING U.S. COMPANIES BY SALES

Sales in billions of dollars

Source: U.S. Department of Commerce

and type II diabetes treatment Glucophage, with sales of $861 million.

One of the largest pharmaceutical firms in the world, Johnson & Johnson, also was an industry leader in OTC sales in the late 1990s. The company had 1998 sales of $23.7 million. Prescription to OTC switches for its popular yeast infection treatment Monistat 7 and its antidiarrheal Immodium promised to improve its OTC position even further. Johnson & Johnson also managed to bring Tylenol back to its position as the best-selling nonprescription drug in the country in the 1990s. Other familiar OTC products from Johnson & Johnson include the athlete's foot medication Micatin and the sinus medication Sine-Aid. The company expanded its product line through the more than 30 company acquisitions it made in the span of the 1990s.

Headquartered in New Brunswick, New Jersey, Johnson & Johnson got its start when founder Robert Wood Johnson decided to begin the production and distribution of plaster wound dressings he observed during the Civil War. High-quality sterile dressings, including the world famous Band-Aid, made the familiar Johnson & Johnson red cross logo ubiquitous in hospitals and bathroom medicine cabinets. The company also successfully promoted the placement of first-aid kits in homes, railroad cars, and businesses. Beyond Band-Aids, Johnson & Johnson became best known for its familiar line of baby-care products. The purchase of McNeil labs in 1959 expanded Johnson & Johnson's product line into prescription drugs like sedatives, muscle relaxants, and eventually the analgesic Tylenol, which went to OTC status in the 1960s. Other successful prescription introductions for the company have included the acne treatment Retin-A and the Ortho-Novum group of oral contraceptives.

Pfizer had $13.5 billion in 1998 sales and more than 46,000 employees. Pharmaceuticals accounted for more than 85 percent of the sales for the company, which was best known for its impotence treatment Viagra. Other major sellers were the blood pressure-control drug Norvasec, antidepressant Zoloft, and the antibiotic Zithromax. Pfizer co-marketed cholesterol-reducing Lipitor—the drug central to the Warner-Lambert takeover bid spurred by a merger agreement between Warner-Lambert and American Home Products.

Abbott Laboratories was another leader in the pharmaceutical industry in 1998, with sales revenues of $12.5 billion. Abbott produced Similac infant formula, antibiotics, synthetic hormones, and Norvir, a treatment for children with HIV and AIDS. Abbott marketed products in more than 130 countries and employed more than 56,000 people in 1998. The company spent more than $1 billion in 1999 on research and development in areas such as: immunoscience, anti-infectives, neuroscience, and aging and degenerative diseases. Dr. Wallace C. Abbott

for optimism as it entered the new century. With older patented drugs maintaining profitability, 14 new drugs introduced in the four years prior, and a continuing commitment to research and development expenditures, Merck continued to enjoy a position of strength.

With 1998 revenues of $18.3 billion, Bristol-Myers Squibb Company is a diversified firm with interests in medical devices and household products as well as pharmaceutical preparations, which comprised some 70 percent of company sales. The company's top ethical drugs in the early 1990s were Capoten, a hypertension treatment, and Pravachol, a cholesterol-lowering drug. Bristol-Myers Squibb also sells health and beauty aids under the Clairol and Matrix essentials brands.

Bristol-Myers Squibb was formed via the 1989 acquisition of Squibb by Bristol-Myers for $12.7 billion. Named for founder Edward Squibb, the older of the two companies traced its roots to a New York City firm that specialized in such anesthetics as pure ether and chloroform. William Bristol and John Myers launched the firm in 1887 and initially named it for its hometown, Clinton, New Jersey. After the merger, the company shed many of its consumer products to concentrate on pharmaceuticals, especially anti-cancer and high blood pressure drugs. In the late 1980s, the company's Oncogen subsidiary began testing DDI, an AIDS treatment. When the drug won FDA approval in 1991, it was released under the brand name VIDEX. In 1996, the company formed an alliance with drug delivery company Sano Corp. to offer Bristol-Myers Squibb's anti-anxiety drug BuSpar in a transdermal patch. The company's top products in 1998 were the cholesterol-reducer Pravacol, with $1.6 billion in sales; the chemotherapy drug Taxol, with sales of $1.2 billion;

founded Abbott in 1888. His "dosimetric granules," which enabled precise measurement of drug dosages, revolutionized the industry.

Eli Lilly, headquartered in Indianapolis, Indiana, was another leader with $9.23 billion in 1998 sales. It made the world's best-selling antidepressant Prozac, which had been prescribed to than 24 million patients as a remedy for depression in its ten years on the market as of 1997.

More than 20 companies were merged throughout its history to form industry leader Pharmacia & Upjohn, the largest of which were those between KaviVitrum and Pharmacia in 1990, between Kabi Pharmacia and Farmitalia Carlo Erba in 1993, and between Pharmacia and Upjohn in 1995. Net sales for Pharmacia & Upjohn in 1998 were $6.9 billion, a 2.7 percent increase over 1997 sales. The company is a global leader in areas such as infectious diseases, metabolic diseases, women's health, and ophthalmology. Between 1995 and 1998, Pharmacia & Upjohn expected to launch at least 25 new products, including rescriptor, an antiviral drug to fight AIDS. OTC medications manufactured included Cortaid, Kaopectate, and Motrin IB. The company also manufactured Nicorette/Nicotrol and Rogaine.

WORKFORCE

Work in the preparations segment of the pharmaceutical industry is concentrated in the largest companies. Merck and Squibb have been described as fulfilling places to work because of their aggressive research departments. Merck did, however, endure a 15-week strike by its unionized workers in 1985. Johnson & Johnson has also enjoyed a solid reputation as an employer, offering progressive child care and maternity leave policies. Industry observers noted that ongoing rationalization of overcapacity would put "thousands more" out of work before the end of the decade.

AMERICA AND THE WORLD

Industry analysts estimated in 1999 that American pharmaceutical firms accounted for more than 30 percent of the $265-billion pharmaceuticals market, while the domestic market consumed approximately 65 percent of this output.

The formal economic integration of European Union countries did not immediately fulfill industry expectations. Before unification, American companies selling or producing in Europe navigated a minefield of conflicting national price controls (most European countries have national health care systems that control costs), quality standards, and approval requirements for each new drug introduction, while also worrying about adequate patent protection.

Nevertheless, progress toward the creation of a free market in Japan, the country with the highest per capita consumption of pharmaceuticals in the world with more than 20 percent of the global market. In 1998 the Pharmaceutical Research and Manufacturers of America collaborated with Members of Congress and U.S. government officials to promote a market-based health-care system, helping to produce the Summit Report on the Enhanced Initiative on Deregulation. In the report, the Japanese Government recognized the free-market system as a valuable tool for bringing new medicines to the Japanese market.

The importance of international relationships illustrated the traditionally global character of the pharmaceutical industry. Like European and Japanese counterparts, American companies historically produced, manufactured, and marketed in each other's backyard. Rather than directly investing in full-scale overseas operations, many formed joint licensing agreements or joint ventures with home companies overseas to manufacture and market products in other countries. In the 1990s American OTC leader Warner-Lambert started a joint venture with British Glaxo to develop and market an OTC version of Glaxo's blockbuster anti-ulcer drug Zantac. Many American pharmaceutical firms, including Warner-Lambert, however, continued to have overseas production and marketing networks under their own control. Giants such as Merck, American Home Products, and Eli Lilly operated worldwide, while many European firms maintained extensive U.S operations.

RESEARCH AND TECHNOLOGY

Though the federal government and academic institutions pursue both basic and applied research that often directly affects drug development, approximately 90 percent of new drugs come from the drug industry. However, analysts emphasize that the importance of researchers financed by the National Institutes of Health (NIH) in initiating path-breaking drug developments and the role of academic researchers (often with both NIH and drug company financing) in revolutionary cell-receptor research as well as initial chemical trials cannot be denied.

The Pharmaceutical Research Manufacturers Association estimated in 1999 that its member companies invested $24 billion annually—20 percent of domestic sales—in the research and development of new drugs. The drug industry's ratio of research-to-sales ranks as the highest of all major domestic industrial groups.

For patented prescription producers, the actual research and development of new drugs, especially after the adoption of the 1962 FDA regulatory guidelines, had always been an intricate process, sometimes referred to as "playing chess with nature." Company researchers began by screening or developing any number of New Chemical Entities (NCEs) that showed promise in a therapeutic class, on a specific disease, or with a specific cell receptor. Once one of these showed therapeutic potential, the company proceeded to move the new compound through a series of preclinical trials with animals to determine its toxicity at various doses. After initial testing, the research company generally patented its new chemical and announced to the FDA its intention to begin human trials. The potential drug then moved through three distinct phases of human clinical trials, often taking seven years. The process was designed to expose possible adverse reactions, determine safe and effective dosages for humans, and test treatment. Once an NCE successfully survived these trials, and 19 of 20 did not because of ineffectiveness or toxicity, the company submitted a completed New Drug Application (NDA) to the FDA seeking final market approval for the new therapy. Even after market approval, a fourth phase could result in a recall or new label warnings if the drug showed adverse reactions in the larger population.

By its own regulations, the FDA was supposed to complete an NDA review within six months. By the 1990s though, review time in the understaffed agency had risen to over two years. Thus, by the time a company's new drug reached market, almost ten of its 17 years of patent exclusivity had disappeared, a point drug companies used to justify high prices. To address this problem, and to raise more revenue in order to add review staff to the FDA, Congress passed the Prescription Drug User Fee Act in 1992. This legislation generated more than $325 million in five years and helped speed average NDAs by ten months. The user fee program was refined under the Food and Drug Modernization Act of 1997, allowing the FDA to hire more reviewers to speed up approvals. In 1998 30 drugs received approval in an average of 11.7 months, compared with a 30-month average per drug before user fees. The law also required the FDA to aim to review "priority" drugs within 6 months and to facilitate patent access to experimental drugs.

Drug delivery systems and biotechnology were two particularly active areas of research and development in the late 1990s. Seeking ways to improve the therapeutic and economic performance of products, pharmaceutical companies began to expand beyond traditional delivery systems to inhalation, transmucosal, transdermal, and implantation methods. Examples include: timed-release capsules, implantable pumps, computerized inhalers, and "lollipop" sedatives.

FURTHER READING

"About Abbott." *Abbott Laboratories Company Web Site*, 1999. Available from http://www.abbott.com/about/index.htm.

"About Pharmacia & Upjohn." *Pharmacia and Upjohn Company Web Site*, 1999. Available from http://www.pharmacia.se/about/history.html.

Alger, Alexandra. "Giding the Lilly." *Forbes*, 1 November 1999.

Bristol-Meyers Squibb Company Web Site, 1999. Available from http://www.bms.com.

Galewitz, Phil. "Warner-Lambert Sues to Cut Pfizer Out of Deal." *The Ann Arbor News*, 30 November 1999.

Goldman, Jonathan. "Pharmaceuticals Are Looking Good." *Institutional Investor*, December 1996.

Knox, Noelle. "Warner Asks Pfizer to Drop Bid." *The Ann Arbor News*, 10 November 1999.

McKinley, Ed. "Growth and Consolidation for Fine Chemicals." *Chemical Processing On the Web*, July 1999. Available from http://www.chemicalprocessing.com/protected/cp799/indtrend.html.

"Pfizer Initiates $82.4 Billion Offer with Warner-Lambert." *PR Newswire*, 4 November 1999.

PhRMA Annual Report 1999. Washington: Pharmaceutical Research and Manufacturers Association, 1999.

"Pharmaceutical Results Improve Helped By New Product Launches." *Chemical Market Reporter*, 27 January 1997.

"Recently Published Reports Reveal Industry Insights into Successful Strategies for Pharmaceutical and Biotechnology Research Alliances." *Business Wire*, 19 October 1999.

Spilker, Bert. *Multinational Drug Companies: Issues in Drug Discovery and Development*. New York: Raven Press, 1989.

SIC 2835

IN VITRO AND IN VIVO DIAGNOSTIC SUBSTANCES

This category covers establishments primarily engaged in manufacturing in vitro ("in glass," such as a test tube) and in vivo ("in the body") diagnostic substances, whether or not packaged for retail sale. These materials are chemical, biological, or radioactive substances used in diagnosing or monitoring the state of human or veterinary health by identifying and measuring normal or abnormal constituents of body fluids or tissues.

NAICS CODE(S)

325412 (Pharmaceutical Preparation Manufacturing)
325413 (In Vitro Diagnostic Substance Manufacturing)

Often viewed as an extension of the pharmaceutical industry, the diagnostics industry is closely intertwined with cutting-edge developments in the treatment of human and animal disorders. This includes a multitude of genetic research and studies centered around high-profile diseases like cancer and AIDS. Simultaneously, much of the industry's output involves comparatively low-tech, routine diagnostics like allergy assays and home pregnancy tests.

In vitro diagnostics, those used outside the body, constitute by far the largest share of industry sales. In 1997, according to Census Bureau statistics, in vitro test product shipments from U.S. firms were valued at more than $5.8 billion. In vivo substances, by contrast, garnered $1.2 billion in sales. (Under the North American Industry Classification System (NAICS), in-vivo diagnostics are considered part of the general pharmaceutical preparation industry.)

The primary market for these diagnostic substances is in hospitals and laboratories, but sales to physicians and individual consumers have seen considerable growth. In the commercial markets, in particular, users have emphasized the need for more automated test systems that free up staff time and reduce the likelihood of error. Diagnostic applications attracting the greatest market interest include those for sexually transmitted diseases, diabetes, and cellular disorders.

Most, if not all, of the industry's products are regulated by the U.S. Food and Drug Administration (FDA). The agency sets standards for safety and quality in manufacturing, and depending on the diagnostic, usually requires products to be formally reviewed and approved before they are used. For diagnostics an average review lasts two years.

The current trend in the industry is to miniaturize the machinery and make them more portable. This point-of-care (POC) testing is expected to present the greatest growth area in the near future for in vitro diagnostics. Already, the technology has found its way into hospitals and medical centers and will soon be available in the home health care field. FDA approval of other products, such as an imaging agent for use with ultrasound technology, is expected to help bolster the industry. Yet, as the industry has grown, FDA approval time has often been slow and more stringent regulations have been enacted.

The industry's ties to the pharmaceutical business mean that, like pharmaceuticals, diagnostics are a global business dominated by a handful of wealthy companies. The largest diagnostics makers are some of the world's top drug companies. These deep-pocketed drug makers increasingly see the diagnostics business as a complement to their pharmaceutical operations—a test can indicate whether a patient needs a drug or how well an administered drug is working.

Integrated Pharmaceutical Leaders. Heading the list is Switzerland's Roche Group, which was believed to hold 17 percent of the $18 billion global diagnostics market in the late 1990s. Roche attained its standing mostly through acquisitions.

Close behind was Abbott Laboratories, with an estimated 15 percent share. In 1999 Abbott's diagnostics business was slapped with an unprecedented $100-million penalty for failing to meet FDA manufacturing quality standards. None of Abbott's products were found to be defective or harmful, but the drug maker was accused of repeatedly flouting FDA rules.

Johnson & Johnson was another sizable competitor, estimated at an 11 percent share of the world market. Well-known for its consumer products, Johnson & Johnson maintains a large and growing presence in the medical instrument and pharmaceutical markets.

Germany's Bayer AG, a major pharmaceutical and chemical conglomerate, likewise has made inroads into the diagnostics market. In 1999 it acquired the diagnostics wing of the biotechnology firm Chiron Corp.

Independent Diagnostics Leaders. One of the leading independent suppliers of diagnostic kits is Bio-Rad Laboratories, Inc. Based in Hercules, California, Bio-Rad supplied more than 4,500 different products for laboratory and medical research including chemicals and instruments to diagnose and monitor diseases such as anemia, diabetes, and AIDS. The company developed clinical diagnostics test kits and analytical instruments, including a blood glucose analyzer. Established in 1957 with four employees, by 1999 Bio-Rad employed 2,675 workers in the United States and abroad. Its 1999 sales for the 12 months ending September 30 reached $474 million.

Los Angeles-based Diagnostic Products Corporation (DPC) is an independent diagnostic manufacturer focusing on tests for immune-system disorders. The $200 million company employed 1,600 people in 1999. Its products are used to identify allergies, thyroid disorders, fertility problems, and some forms of cancer, among other things. DPC also markets a line of automated instruments for use with its diagnostic tests.

Another large independent firm focusing on diagnostics is IDEXX Laboratories, Inc. of Westbrook, Maine. With 1999 sales in excess of $350 million, IDEXX is a leader in the veterinary diagnostics market. Included in its more than 400 products are common diagnostics for pet illnesses and diseases, as well as a line of tests for measuring environmental pollution.

FURTHER READING

Banks, Howard. "How Roche Got an Edge on Its Competitors." *Forbes,* 2 November 1998.

Health Industry Manufacturers Association. "In Vitro Diagnostics: Medical Tests That Save Lives and Reduce Health Care Costs." Washington, 1999. Available from http://www.himanet.com.

Hensley, Scott. "A 'Clear Message' for Abbott." *Modern Healthcare,* 8 November 1999.

Marquez, Rachelle C. "Home Self-Testing Market Grows as Medical Costs Rise." *Business Journal,* 3 November 1997.

U.S. Census Bureau. *1997 Census of Manufactures.* Washington: Department of Commerce, 1999. Available from www .census.gov.

SIC 2836

BIOLOGICAL PRODUCTS, EXCEPT DIAGNOSTIC SUBSTANCES

This category covers establishments primarily engaged in the production of bacterial and virus vaccines, toxoids, and analogous products (such as allergenic extracts), serums, plasmas, and other blood derivatives for human or veterinary use, other than *in vitro* and *in vivo* diagnostic substances. Included in this industry are establishments primarily engaged in the production of microbiological products for other uses. Establishments primarily engaged in manufacturing *in vitro* and *in vivo* diagnostic substances are classified in **SIC 2835: In Vitro and In Vivo Diagnostic Substances.**

NAICS CODE(S)

325414 (Biological Product (except Diagnostic) Manufacturing)

INDUSTRY SNAPSHOT

According to statistics compiled by the U.S. Department of Commerce, establishments classified in **SIC 2836: Biological Products, Except Diagnostic Substances** shipped products valued at $2.16 billion in 1990. By 1996, shipments had reached an estimated $6.15 billion, an increase of almost 10 percent over 1995. Exports stood at $1.56 billion in 1995, while imports totaled $613 million, up 10 percent over 1994. The largest class of products within the industry were blood and blood derivatives. By 1998 the international sales for blood and its derivatives were approximately $18.5 billion per year. Other major product classifications were vaccines, toxoids and antigens; biological products for veterinary, industrial and other uses; and antitoxins, antivenoms, immune globulins, therapeutic immune serums, and allergic extracts.

In the late 1990's the biotech industries reflected a strong focus on financial investment in research and development and numerous alliances between biotechnology companies and between government and the private sector. Often small biotechnology companies relied on pharmaceutical companies to supply approximately half of the capital necessary for company development, according to Ligand's. As the century came to a close,

biotech companies were expected to reap the profits as new products entered the market, with net profits of $2 billion in 1999, up from $1.5 billion in 1998.

BACKGROUND AND DEVELOPMENT

Biological products were created with biotechnology, the scientific and engineering procedures involved in manipulating organisms or biological components at the cellular, subcellular, or molecular level. These manipulations were carried out to make or modify plants and animals or other biological substances with desired traits. Although examples of primitive biotech processes dated back to ancient times (such as the use of fermentation in brewing and leavening agents in baking), their use in medical and pharmaceutical applications was an innovation of the latter decades of the twentieth century. Some analysts compared the biotech industry's impact on global medical care with the computer industry's impact on communication.

Biotech researchers produced products in essentially three ways: by developing ways to achieve commercial production of naturally occurring substances; by genetically altering naturally occurring substances; and by creating entirely new substances. Some of the tools used by biotech researchers included recombinant DNA and monoclonal antibodies. Recombinant DNA involved the ability to take the deoxyribonucleic acid (DNA) from one organism and combine it with the DNA from another organism thereby creating new products and processes. By using recombinant DNA techniques researchers were able to select specific genes and introduce them into other cells or living organisms to create products with specific attributes. Monoclonal antibodies were developed from cultures of single cells using cloning techniques. They were designed for use in attacking toxins, viruses, and cancer cells.

The U.S. Food and Drug Administration (FDA) required extensive scrutiny of products developed by biotech researchers before they could be offered for sale. Because the biological products presented for approval often involved new technologies or innovative therapies for diseases that had not been previously treated successfully, the approval process frequently proved to be long and costly. Many companies struggled financially through the 1980s waiting for an FDA determination.

One of the earliest biological products introduced to the U.S. marketplace was a blood protein first sold in 1966. The blood protein, called Factor VIII, was used by patients with hemophilia A to control bleeding episodes. Factor VIII, the blood factor responsible for normal clotting action, was manufactured from human blood received from donors. It was followed by the development of Factor IX for patients with hemophilia B.

During the early 1980s, problems arose as a result of AIDS contamination in the blood supply used to produce blood clotting factors. In 1984 manufacturers began using a heat treatment process to guard against future contamination, but, according to a report in the *Wall Street Journal*, approximately half of the nation's 20,000 hemophiliacs contracted AIDS, primarily through the use of Factors VIII and IX.

The earliest FDA approval for a modern biotech product designed for human therapeutic use was given to human insulin in 1982. Human insulin was used for treating patients with diabetes. Other product approvals followed in subsequent years. In 1984 the FDA approved an agricultural vaccine against colibacillosis (a disease commonly called scours, which causes diarrhea or dysentery in newborn animals). Approval was given in 1985 to a human growth hormone (HGH) for the treatment of dwarfism.

The first genetically engineered vaccine approved for use in the United States was a vaccine against hepatitis-B. It received approval in 1986. The vaccine had been created by inserting part of a hepatitis-B virus into yeast cells. Although the portion of the hepatitis-B virus used was not infectious, it caused an immune reaction against infection from the entire hepatitis-B virus.

Other firsts occurring in 1986 included the approval of therapeutic monoclonal antibodies (MABs) and alpha interferon. MABs were approved for use along with immunosuppressive drugs to help prevent kidney rejection in transplant patients. Alpha interferon's first approved use was in the treatment of hairy cell leukemia. Other approved uses for alpha interferon followed: for Kaposi's sarcoma in 1988, venereal warts in 1988, non-A/non-B hepatitis in 1991, and hepatitis-B in 1992. A product to dissolve blood clots in patients with acute myocardial infarction (heart attack) was approved in 1987. An agricultural vaccine to protect against pseudorabies won FDA approval the same year.

Erythropoietin (EPO), which was to become the largest single biotech product, received its first FDA approval in 1989. EPO, a protein that stimulates production of red blood cells, won initial approval for use with anemia associated with kidney disease. In the same year, the Health Care Financing Administration agreed to pay for EPO given to dialysis patients under the Medicare program. Within a few years, EPO was being used by approximately 82,000 dialysis patients in the United States. In 1991 the FDA gave additional approval for its use in treating AIDS-related anemia.

Advances continued during the 1990s. As the industry matured, cooperation between product developers and government regulators improved. The steps in the approval process became more predictable, and a shift in

technology was also noted. The primary products of the 1980s had involved the use of recombinant DNA proteins without further alterations. During the early 1990s, researchers turned their attention to products requiring more extensive genetic modification and to more obscure applications.

During the first few years of the 1990s, the FDA granted approval for several products with uses targeting human conditions. These included a treatment for chronic granulomatous disease (a genetic abnormality affecting the immune system and resulting in severe or life-threatening infections), for acute pulmonary embolism, to aid in chemotherapy and bone marrow transplants, and for kidney cancer. Products wining FDA approval for veterinary use included a vaccine against feline leukemia and a treatment for canine lymphoma.

By the end of the 1980s, sales of products developed around recombinant DNA technology exceeded $1 billion according to a study done by Consulting Resources and reported in *Chemicalweek*. Consulting Resources expected such sales to reach $4.29 billion by 1995 and to more than double again by the end of the century. The industry surpassed those estimates in 1994 by having $4.39 billion in sales—and in 1996 the value of shipments were estimated to have reached $6.15 billion.

In the 1990s FDA granted approvals for vaccines against rabies, tetanum toxoids, and pertussis. According to government statements, vaccines were one of the most effective and cheapest ways to eradicate some diseases. Accordingly, the National Institute of Health's Office of Financial Management reported that funding for vaccine research and development rose 65 percent from 1993 to 1999. Concern about health care costs during the early 1990s focused the national spotlight on the pharmaceutical industry and questions were raised about the high cost of biological products.

CURRENT CONDITIONS

In the late 1990s advances in research methods, a faster FDA approval process, and strategic alliances formed a strong network for growth in the biotechnology industry in the United States and internationally. While approval of a therapeutic product by the U.S. Food and Drug Administration (FDA) could last as long as 15 years; the FDA sought to reduce the length of time for the final approval process. A user fee program, which was refined under the Food and Drug Modernization Act of 1997, allowed the FDA to hire more reviewers to speed up approvals. In 1998 30 drugs received approval in an average of 11.7 months, compared with a 30-month average per drug before user fees. The FDA Fiscal Year 2000 budget increased to $216 million in 2000, and funding for the Center for Biologics Evaluation rose to $317 million and the Center for Biologics Evaluation and Research.

Global initiatives aimed toward eradicating deadly childhood diseases as well as steps toward the prevention of common illnesses such as ear infections promised thriving growth for the industry through the year 2005. Patient compliance was expected to increase as new technologies allowed the development of combination vaccines and new "needleless" vaccines. Manufacturers tapped into a new source of income from the more "user-friendly" vaccines by charging a premium for them. According to Frost and Sullivan, revenues from worldwide pediatric vaccine markets grew 4.5 percent in 1998 to $1.8 billion.

INDUSTRY LEADERS

One of the leading establishments classified in this category was Genentech, Inc. Headquartered in San Francisco, Genentech pioneered the development of first-generation biotech products including recombinant human insulin. In 1988 the therapeutic Activase won FDA approval for dissolving blood clots in heart attack patients. Approval, however, came only after a lengthy regulatory review and initial sales failed to meet projections. These difficulties left the company financially unstable. Roche Holdings Ltd., a Swiss pharmaceutical maker, acquired majority ownership of Genentech in 1990. Under Roche's umbrella, Genentech continued to make significant contributions to the industry.

In late 1999 the company manufactured and marketed seven products in the United States: three growth hormone products; a treatment to dissolve blood clots occurring during a heart attack, in the lungs, or in the brain during a stroke; an inhalant for cystic fibrosis; and two cancer treatments for a specific lymphoma and breast cancer. The company received royalties on sales of its products worldwide under a 1995 merger agreement with Roche Holdings Ltd. and other licenses.

Genentech operated from the world's largest research facility devoted solely to biotechnology. With 3,389 employees its 1998 revenues totaled $1.15 billion, up 21.5 percent from the previous year; while net income rose 41.0 percent to $181.9 million. That year Genentech reinvested more than a third of its revenues into research and development. Several new products were in development; a cardiovascular agent was to be marketed with partner Boehringer International GmbH pending BLA approval and Genentech filed for FDA approval of sustained-release growth hormone with partner Alkermes.

Genzyme Corporation, another major producer of biological products, produced products in niche markets, especially those targeted at genetic diseases. Headquartered in Cambridge, Massachusetts, the company produced biopharmaceuticals in a $75-million facility. Genzyme's 1998 sales reached $688.5 million, and they employed 3,500 workers.

One of the best known Genzyme products was Ceredase, which was used to treat Type 1 Gaucher's disease. Gaucher's disease, an incurable metabolic disorder most common among people of Eastern European Jewish ancestry, affecting between 2,000 and 3,000 people in the United States. By 1996 the company began transitioning U.S. patients from tissue-derived Ceredase to Cerezyme, which was produced by recombinant DNA technology. By mid-1999 the transition was completed globally.

In 1998 Genzyme's therapeutics line was broadened with the FDA approval of two new products: Renagel, for the control of blood phosphorous levels in late-stage kidney patients and Thyrogen, a product for follow-up screening of patients who had been treated for thyroid cancer.

In October 1999 Genzyme entered an agreement to acquire Cell Genesys for approximately $350 million, according to a company press release. The acquisition offered Genzyme access to Cell Genesys's extensive intellectual property portfolio in gene therapy and to the human monoclonal antibody technology developed by Abgenix.

Alpha Therapeutic Corporation is a leading provider of human blood and plasma products is with between $250 and $500 million in sales in the late 1990's and over 2,900 employees. The company, headquartered in Los Angeles, was founded in 1948 and was incorporated in 1978 by its parent company, Yoshitomi Pharmaceutical Industries, Ltd., Japan's tenth largest pharmaceutical company. In 1999 Alpha Therapeutic was undergoing a major facilities expansion.

Alpha Therapeutic's products included a plasma expander for maintaining blood volume in critical situations, three coagulation factor products for the treatment of hemophilia, and an immune globulin product to replace missing antibodies in people with compromised immune systems.

AMERICA AND THE WORLD

Exports by U.S. biotech companies exceeded imports. According to government statistics, exports totaled $973 million in 1990, $1.19 billion in 1992, and $1.56 billion in 1995. Imports totaled $271 million in 1990, $420 million in 1992, and $613 million in 1995.

Although U.S. biotech companies pioneered the development of the industry, other countries were making significant progress. For example, research for an AIDS vaccine led to increased understanding of therapeutic vaccines in Switzerland. Industry watchers also noted that Japanese scientists were making gains. Some feared that future market domination by the Japanese could parallel the earlier experience of the electronics industry.

RESEARCH AND TECHNOLOGY

In 1987 the U.S. Patent and Trademark Office announced that it would issue patents on non-naturally occurring nonhuman animals, thus opening the door for patenting biotech-engineered animals. Although some hailed the decision as a boon to biotechnical research, others objected on ethical and religious grounds. The decision also drew protests from animal rights activists and environmental groups.

By 1998, 54 therapeutics were approved to treat human diseases such as heart attack, hemophilia, growth deficiency, diabetes, hepatitis, genital warts, several cancers, and genetic disorders. The Pharmaceutical Research and manufacturers of America reported 350 new medicines in development based on biotechnology, with 140 companies performing the research and development. Of these, 151 were for treating cancer, 77 were vaccines, 29 were for the treatment of HIV infection and AIDS, 19 were for autoimmune disorders, and eight were for blood disorders.

AIDS research also received considerable attention throughout the 1990s. By 1998 60 medicines were available to treat AIDS and related infections. Recombinant DNA techniques had been used to demonstrate the life cycle of the human immunodeficiency virus (HIV) and show how the virus caused AIDS. Recombinant DNA techniques were also being used in the search for vaccines and therapeutic agents for AIDS treatment. Other areas of ongoing research in ways to use DNA focused on heart disease, cancer, Parkinson's disease, and bone marrow recovery in patients following transplantation.

FURTHER READING

"1999 Washington Biotechnology and Medical Technology Annual Report: Carl Feldbaum CEO Interview." *Washington Biotechnology and Medical Technology Online,* April 1999. Available from: http://www.wabio.com/ind/annrpt/ceo_feldbaum.htm.

Alpha Therapeutic Company Web Site, 1999. Available from http://www.alphather.com.

Burton, Thomas M. "Hemophiliacs Sue Firms, Foundation Over AIDS in '80s." *Wall Street Journal,* 1 October 1993.

Darnay, Arsen, ed. *Manufacturing USA.* 5th ed. Detroit: Gale Research, 1996.

"Drugs and Biotech Prognosis 1999." *Businessweek,* 11 January 1999. Available from http://www.businessweek.com.

Edwards, Mark and Joan O'C. Hamilton. "10 Deals That changed Biotechnology." *Signals,* 17 November 1998. Available from http://www.signalsmag.com.

Folkers, Gregory, and Anthony S. Fauci. "The Role of U.S. Government Agencies in Vaccine Research and Development." *Nature Medicine Vaccine Supplement,* May 1999.

"Frost and Sullivan- New Combination Pediatric Vaccines Provide Lucrative Market Opportunities." *PRNewswire,* 28 September 1999.

Genentech. "The Biopharmaceuticals: FDA-Approved Biopharmaceutical Drugs and Vaccines." Access Excellence, 1997. Available from http://www.gene.com.ae.

Genentech. "Genentech, Inc. Scientific Achievements." Access Excellence. 1999. Available from http://www.gene.com.ae

"Genzyme to Acquire Cell Genesys." Cambridge: Genzyme Corporation, 18 October 1999. Available from http://www.genzyme.com.

Genentech, Inc. Corporate Web Site, 1999. Available from http://www.gene.com.

Genzyme Corporate Web Site, 1999. Available from http://www.genzyme.com.

Heller, Karen. "For Investors, It's More Than Just Hope Now." *Chemicalweek,* 17 January 1990.

"Hoover's Company Capsules." Hoover's, Inc., 1998. Available from http://www.hoovers.com.

Matveld, H. Edward, and Karen L. White. "Alpha Therapeutic Corporation." 1997. Available from http://www.biospace.com.

"1998 Survey: Biotechnology." Washington: Pharmaceutical Research and Manufacturers of America, 1998. Available from http://www.phrma.org.

Starr, Douglas. "Book Excerpt: Blood An Epic History of Medicine and Commerce." *Businessweek Online,* 1999. Available from http://www.businessweek.com.

SIC 2841

SOAP AND OTHER DETERGENTS, EXCEPT SPECIALTY CLEANERS

This category includes establishments primarily engaged in the manufacture of soap and detergents. It includes companies who make crude and refined glycerin products from fats, or synthetic detergents such as laundry detergents, dishwashing compounds, and personal cleansing bars. Establishments primarily involved in the manufacture of specialty cleaning products are classified in **SIC 2842: Specialty Cleaning, Polishing, and Sanitation Preparations.** Establishments primarily involved in the manufacture of shampoos and shaving products are classified in **SIC 2844: Perfumes, Cosmetics, and Other Toilet Preparations.**

NAICS CODE(S)

325611 (Soap and Other Detergent Manufacturing)

INDUSTRY SNAPSHOT

The soap and detergents industry's $4.4 billion marketplace in the United States faced increasing competition during the late 1990s. Having to contend with increasing globalization, the U.S. market expanded 2.4 percent in 1998. High performance formulations that omitted bleach were among the largest growing segments of this industry. Another breakthrough came in 1998 when liquid detergent sales outpaced powders for the first time ever. The liquid detergents, priced higher than the powders, captured 52 percent of the overall market. In addition to environmental and health questions, societal transformation propelled changes in the soap and detergent industry during the late 1990s. Among the numerous factors presenting challenges to detergent formulators were: the need for improved sanitation; the increasing numbers of women working outside the home; the development of time-saving appliances; the trend towards using less energy by lowering wash temperatures; the need to conserve water; and changes in textiles and other cleanable surfaces.

Detergent modifications were also spurred by technical innovation, such as bleach additives, better optical brighteners, and improved technologies to release soils. Marketers packaged products differently to meet the needs of specialized users such as households with infants or with men performing tasks traditionally associated with women's roles. To meet the needs of various market segments, the industry saw a proliferation of brands and varieties. For example, a typical large supermarket might contain more than forty varieties of laundry detergents including both liquids and powders.

Industry trends for the late 1990s included the environmentally friendly "Ultra" or concentrated detergents and liquid soaps. However, analysts claimed that the increasing popularity of liquid soaps would not affect the sales of bar soaps in any way. Another popular trend was the consumers' growing interest in small soaps and detergents shops, such as Crabtree and Evelyn and The Body Shop, which used herbal and natural materials in their products.

BACKGROUND AND DEVELOPMENT

The soap and detergent industry's origins are obscured in antiquity. Michael C. Crossin, writing for *Soap, Cosmetics, Chemical Specialties,* stated "the caveman who fell into the river with his fur still on quickly learned that water is an excellent aid in the removal of soils and odors from garments." Crossin calls this find "the single most important discovery in laundry history."

Water alone, however, was not sufficient for all cleaning needs. The next important breakthrough was the development of soap. Different accounts place its invention between 2500 B.C. and 300 B.C. The word "soap" may have been derived from Mt. Sapo, near Rome, a place where burnt offerings were made to the gods. People discovered that the fat and ash residue from the offerings had cleaning properties.

By definition, soap is a cleansing product created through the chemical process of combining a fat or natural oil with an alkali (such as wood ashes or lye) under controlled conditions. Soap-producing factories developed in France and Italy, where olive oil was plentiful and used as the main ingredient, throughout the sixteenth, seventeenth, and eighteenth centuries. In the nineteenth century, palm oil began to replace olive oil in formulations. By the turn of the twentieth century, many people still made soap by boiling fats and lye to produce solid cakes.

In the United States, the soapmaking industry marks 1837 as an important year. In that year, William Procter and James Gamble established a candle and soapmaking business. Their company, Procter and Gamble, went on to become one of the foremost soap and detergent makers in the country. Procter and Gamble's famous "Ivory" soap bar was first introduced in 1882. Lever Brothers, another major soap and detergent company, offered "Lifebouy" and "Sunlight" soap bars in 1895.

Procter and Gamble introduced Oxydol, a flaked laundry soap, in 1924. Oxydol was followed in 1933 by Dreft, the nation's first synthetic household detergent. Instead of soap, Dreft's formula was based on alcohol sulfates. Alcohol sulfates were the first type of surfactants to make a significant impact in the formulation of cleaning products.

The term "surfactant" comes from shortening the phrase "surface active agent." A surfactant is a type of chemical capable of changing the surface properties of a liquid. As a result of their chemical nature, surfactants help wash-water wet the surface to be cleaned quickly and thoroughly. When water and mechanical action combine to remove soils from a surface, surfactants also help keep the soil suspended in the liquid so that it does not redeposit on the item being cleaned. Surfactants are basic ingredients in most products intended for use in washing clothes and dishes.

The first synthetic detergents based on sodium dodecylbenzene sulfonate were developed in 1939. They were followed by detergents based on alkylbenzene sulfonate (ABS), which provided better cleaning and more suds than traditional soaps at lower prices. ABS grew in popularity and its use expanded with the introduction of front-loading drum washing machines.

In addition to surfactant technology, the 1930s brought the introduction of "built" soap powders and detergents. "Builders" were materials used to enhance the efficiency of a cleaner. Although they had several purposes, such as providing alkalinity to aid cleaning, keeping removed soil from redepositing, and helping to emulsify oil and grease, one of their primary functions was to overcome problems associated with water hardness. Water hardness is a measurement of the soluble metal salts (primarily formed from calcium, magnesium, iron, or manganese) in the water supply. According to the U.S. Geological Survey, water is termed ''soft'' when it is relatively free of soluble metal salts. It is termed ''moderately hard,'' ''hard,'' or ''very hard'' based on the amount of hardness chemicals present.

When soap products were used in hard water, a substance called ''soap curds'' or ''lime soap'' formed. The lime soap precipitate, which would not dissolve, formed in the water and stuck to surfaces causing films and deposits. Builders were used to help counteract these problems. Several types of builders were developed and they worked in different ways. Sodium carbonate, a precipitating builder, caused the water hardness materials to precipitate from the wash solution. Sodium aluminosilicate, another type of builder, inactivated water hardness materials by a chemical process called ion exchange. The most commonly used builders, complex phosphates, worked by holding water hardness materials in the wash solution through a process called sequestration.

By the late 1930s, built soaps and soap in granular form had virtually replaced laundry bar soaps. A decade later, built detergents were becoming popular. The shift from soap to detergent formulations was driven primarily by efforts to overcome problems associated with water hardness.

Detergents, although similar in function to soaps, differed from them chemically. Detergents were made from other raw materials including petroleum products and fatty acids. They often contained additional ingredients such as fluorescent whitening agents, antiredeposition agents, corrosion inhibitors, suds control agents, nonchlorine bleaches, colorants, fragrances, enzymes, blueing, and processing aids.

Built detergents, like built soaps, also contained builders to help improve cleaning efficiency. The first and most widely used builder was sodium tripolyphosphate (STPP). Formulators found STPP effective and relatively easy to process in granulated detergent. Although most built detergents were designed for laundry use, some were adapted for nonlaundry household chores. Typically these adapted formulas were high sudsing detergents and could be used for tasks such as hand dishwashing or floor care.

In 1946, Procter and Gamble test marketed their new phosphate-built Tide. Tide was launched nationally in 1947 and gained widespread acceptance. Built detergents based on surfactants continued to increase in popularity and by 1953 the poundage of surfactant products sold exceeded that of soaps. The rapid expansion of synthetic

detergents, however, led to problems. Reports of foaming in streams and wastewater treatment plants were first heard in the late 1940s, and by the early 1950s scientific evidence identified synthetic detergents as the cause. ABS, the most widely used surfactant, was not biodegradable and led to water contamination.

In 1951, the Association of American Soap and Glycerine Producers, predecessor to the Soap and Detergent Association, began to study the industry's environmental concerns and search for biodegradable surfactants. The federal government also investigated the environmental impact of detergents and began to address national concerns with the Federal Water Pollution Control Act of 1956.

During the early 1960s, chemists developed a new form of ABS with a different molecular structure. The new surfactant, called linear alkylbenzene sulfonate (LAS), possessed the appropriate characteristics necessary for biodegradability. In 1965, U.S. detergent manufacturers switched from ABS to LAS in household laundry detergents. Within a few years the number of foaming incidents had dropped and the amount of surfactants in the nation's waterways had been reduced.

Foaming in waterways and treatment facilities, however, was only one problem with early synthetic detergents. Another was ''eutrophication.'' Eutrophication refers to the process of adding nutrients to bodies of water. Excess nutrients caused excessive algae growth, and when the algae decayed, oxygen levels in the water decreased. With diminished levels of oxygen, water bodies were unable to support their fish populations.

Although eutrophication occurs in nature, it takes place over thousands of years. Accelerated eutrophication of water bodies, sometimes referred to as cultural eutrophication, occurred when wastewater carrying nutrients such as phosphorous and nitrogen was dumped into lakes and streams. The phosphate builders used in synthetic laundry detergents were one source of phosphorous in the nation's wastewater.

How much laundry detergents contributed to cultural eutrophication was a controversial question. Proponents of phosphate bans cited studies indicating that 25 to 30 percent of wastewater phosphorus came from laundry detergents. Those opposing phosphate bans claimed that detergents contributed only three percent of the phosphorus entering the nation's surface water, and that most eutrophication could be attributed to agricultural practices.

In the early 1970s, the United States faced rising concern about environmental issues and the problems associated with phosphates. Initial phosphate bans were enacted during the early 1970s. By 1992, statewide phosphate bans for household laundry products were in effect in Georgia, Indiana, Maryland, Michigan, Minnesota,

New York, North Carolina, Pennsylvania, Vermont, Virginia, and Wisconsin. Additionally, the city of Washington, DC and parts of Idaho, Illinois (including Chicago), Montana, New Hampshire, Ohio, Oregon, and Washington had instituted similar bans. The states of Connecticut, Florida, and Maine, while not banning phosphates outright, limited their use.

Industry analysts differed in their predictions over future demand for phosphate-built products. Some predicted steady or expanded use. They noted that by the early 1990s the rate at which bans overseas were being enacted had dropped, and that in 1991 the United Kingdom refused to institute a ban. They expected domestic demand to remain stable and demand for exports, particularly to Mexico and South America, to increase. Others, however, predicted that phosphates would be completely replaced in laundry products as alternatives were developed. Citing distribution problems associated with meeting varied local regulatory requirements and prevalent consumer perceptions connecting phosphates with environmental jeopardy, they anticipated phosphates would be phased out by the end of the century.

In the United States, phosphate bans helped encourage the development of liquid laundry detergents which were formulated without phosphates. Liquids began to achieve popularity by the mid-1970s and by the close of the 1980s had captured about half the market.

The Early 1990s. The early 1990s also saw a move away from premium pricing for name brands as customers became more value conscious. Although exceptions existed, many soaps and detergents were seen as undifferentiated commodity items. In 1992, reduced value pricing was being used by approximately 40 percent of detergent manufacturers. Typically, a value-priced product cost $1 or more less than a premium-priced product.

A similar trend brought the increased popularity of "value added," multipurpose products. These included items such as detergent with bleach or fabric softener and three-in-one personal cleansing bars. Moisturizing, deodorant, and antibacterial multibenefit synthetic detergent (also called syndet) bars and soap/syndet combination bars became popular following the introduction of Lever 2000 in 1990. Analysts expected multibenefit bars to capture 10 to 20 percent of the soap market by the mid-1990s.

The automatic dishwashing detergent (ADD) market was also undergoing transformations. Although customers had rejected first-generation ADD liquids because they separated and were difficult to get out of their bottles, gels were gaining acceptance. ADD gels, first introduced in 1991, were easier to dispense than their liquid predecessors and maintained product consistency.

By the beginning of 1992, gels accounted for 35 percent of the ADD market.

While the ADD market was not as directly impacted by the growing concern over environmental issues as was the laundry detergent market, it was influenced. ADD formulas contained four basic types of ingredients: builders, bleaching agents, surfactants, and fragrances. The builder most often used was sodium tripolyphosphate (STPP). During the early 1990s, an estimated 250 million pounds of STPP were used annually in ADD products.

By 1992, phosphate use in ADD products had not been banned as it had been for laundry detergents, and no acceptable alternative for widespread use in household, institutional, and industrial applications had been discovered. In some jurisdictions, however, phosphate use had been limited, typically to 8.7 percent of the product by weight. Even in areas unaffected by such restrictions, manufacturers often reduced the phosphate content of their products from previous levels of 14 to 16 percent to 8.7 percent for the purpose of simplifying the national distribution of their merchandise.

By the end of 1992, Shaklee Corporation was the only U.S. company having a no-phosphate ADD product on the market. Industry analysts expected consumer demand for environmentally safe products to stimulate other manufacturers in their efforts to develop additional no-phosphate ADD alternatives. Environmental concerns were also expected to move the ADD market toward concentrated formulations. The ability to produce concentrated automatic dishwashing detergents was expected to be more difficult than reformulating laundry detergents had been because ADDs do not have as many inert fillers.

Within the laundry detergent segment of the industry, environmental concerns remained primary. Along with environmental issues came an emphasis on "natural" products because they were perceived by consumers to be better for the environment. Formulations were developed for detergents without added fragrances or colors to reduce the number of chemicals used. Manufacturers also promoted "mildness" because it was seen as less harsh for the environment.

The environmental movement led to the promotion of "green" products, products said to be "earth friendly." In contrast to general trends toward value pricing, U.S. consumers demonstrated a willingness to pay slightly higher prices for environmentally friendly products. U.S. consumers, however, were not willing to accept "green" products that were inconvenient to use or those with diminished performance capabilities.

Concern for the increasing amounts of solid waste in U.S. landfills also factored into the development of concentrated detergents. The nation produced 90 million tons of garbage annually in 1960; by the 1990s that amount had risen to 160 million tons, and some forecasters expected it to reach more than 190 million tons by the year 2000. Manufacturers discussed the nation's growing problems with solid waste management experts and developed responses. Concentrates used smaller volumes of some chemicals, required less packaging, and reduced transportation expenses. The percentage of plastic in the nation's garbage had been less than 3 percent in 1970, but was expected to reach 9 percent by 2000. To emphasize their proactive environmental policies, manufacturers promoted the waste-reduction benefits of cartons made from recycled paper, measuring scoops made from recycled plastics, and containers that were recyclable.

The use of phosphates continued to be controversial. By 1990, phosphate usage in laundry products for household use had been banned in all the Great Lakes states and in many states draining into the Chesapeake Bay. The issue was still politically alive in the Pacific Northwest, and the industry continued its search for cost-effective, high-performance alternatives. Industry watchers expected major manufacturers to turn more heavily to non-phosphate detergents even in areas unaffected by bans because of distribution problems associated with supplying different formulas to different regions.

In addition to environmental questions, another area of concern for manufacturers involved the use of animal testing. During the 1970s and 1980s, animal testing had been widely used as a tool in investigating the safety of detergent ingredients. Animals were used to determine the likelihood of human reactions, the severity of possible injuries, and the time necessary for healing. Rabbits and monkeys were frequently used to discover if certain chemicals or combinations of chemicals would cause eye irritation. Animal rights organizations promoted bans on certain kinds of tests and favored regulations which would require labels to state if animal testing had been used in developing a product. The soap and detergent industry responded with claims that it was working on developing alternatives but some animal tests were still required. One promising alternative was the development of "in vitro" (meaning "in glass") tests.

According to Keith A. Booman, Technical Director for the Soap and Detergent Association, the use of animal testing was reduced by 64 percent between 1980 and 1988. In 1989, Booman wrote in *Soap, Cosmetics, Chemical Specialties,* "Further reductions in animal testing by the detergent industry at this time would impair its ability to evaluate the safety of new products for consumers." He predicted, however, that with further research the causes of chemical-induced injuries would be better understood. The results would thus assist researchers in their efforts to develop batteries of nonanimal tests to help further reduce reliance on animal testing.

In 1997, the soap and detergent industry's shipments were valued at $17.8 billion, up 23.6 percent from 1991 shipments of $14.4 billion. The 1997 shipments total represented an increase of 12.7 percent over figures from 1996 but was only 10.6 percent ahead of shipments in 1995. In 1992, U.S. exports of soap and detergent products took just more than 5 percent of total shipments.

The household detergent segment of the market in 1998 totaled $4.4 billion, which was split between liquids ($2.3 billion) and powders ($2.1 billion). The U.S. household market also consumed approximately $522 million worth of automatic dishwasher detergent (ADD) in 1998. Nearly 50 percent of that market was captured by Procter and Gamble's Cascade brand, of which $254.8 million was sold. The second best seller in the ADD market was Electrasol, a product of the United Kingdom's Reckitt Benckiser PLC, which sold $92.5 million. Coming in third was Unilever's Sunlight brand, which sold $83.1 million worth of ADD in 1998.

The bar soap market, which had grown at an average rate of about 4.1 percent annually in the early 1980s, entered the 1990s with a growth rate of about 4.9 percent. Industry analysts attributed the increase to the introduction of body soaps and multipurpose bar soaps. Beauty bars comprised the fastest growing segment of the bar soap market, with sales increasing at a rate of about 7 percent per year. Later in the decade, however, bar soap began to lose some ground to shower gels. In 1998, bar soap sales grew only 1.5 percent in value and slipped 4.5 percent in unit terms, while shower gel sales increased dramatically. However, even with their 18.1 sales gain in 1998, the shower gel market, with total sales of $450 million, remained slightly less than a third the size of the bar soap market, which totaled $1.4 billion in value in 1998.

One of the most significant challenges facing the soap and detergent industry during the early 1990s was a growing concern over environmental issues. Consumer demand and government regulations combined to push producers toward reformulating products with an emphasis toward "earth friendly" materials. As a result, manufacturers intensified their efforts to develop detergent formulas capable of meeting environmental concerns without sacrificing product performance or convenience.

The development of concentrated and super-concentrated formulas was an important step in these efforts. Concentrates and super-concentrates required fewer filler materials and chemicals than standard formulations. Their smaller size reduced transportation costs and decreased the volume of packaging materials required. Producers highlighted their environmental emphasis by offering many of the new formulations in recyclable packages made of recycled materials containing postconsumer waste. Despite the heavy emphasis on advertising environmental benefits, some industry watchers reported that consumers placed safety, cost, and performance ahead of environmental issues. Melinda Sweet, director of environmental affairs at Lever Brothers, told *Soap, Cosmetics, Chemical Specialties* that confusion about recycling caused some people to think that recycled products were used products. As a result, some customers thought that products in recycled packages ought to be cheaper.

CURRENT CONDITIONS

American consumers in the late 1990s were very demanding and value minded. They weighed many factors before buying any products. According to *Soap, Cosmetics, Chemical Specialties,* aging baby-boomers were looking for milder, less irritating products. Soaps using vegetable-based fats, with no animal fats or animal testing, were also in demand. Other popular items included loofahs, oatmeal products, and chamomile leaves. In general, customers demanded performance and value in all their soap, shampoo, and detergent products, which were the driving factors behind the soap and detergents industry at the turn of the century. Sales of shower gels made dramatic gains in the latter half of the 1990s, rising more than 18 percent in 1998. Although the market for bar soap remained large at about $1.4 billion, sales in this area showed an increase in value of only 1.5 percent and were off nearly 5 percent in unit terms.

For the first time ever, liquid laundry detergent sales outpaced powder sales in 1998. Liquids, typically priced higher than powders, took 52 percent of the total market. Sales of liquids totaled $2.35 billion, up 9.5 percent over 1997 levels, while powder sales dropped 4.5 percent to about $2.1 billion. Overall, the laundry detergent market grew 2.4 percent in 1998, compared with growth of 4.1 percent in 1997.

The U.S. automatic dishwashing detergent market totaled $522 million in 1998 and was dominated by Procter and Gamble's Cascade brand, which took more than 48 percent of total sales. Runners-up were Reckitt Benckiser's Electrasol, which took 17.7 percent of the market, and Unilever's Sunlight brand, which captured 15.9 percent of the ADD market.

INDUSTRY LEADERS

One of the oldest and largest companies in this industry is Procter and Gamble (P&G). Headquartered in Cincinnati, Ohio, P&G reported fiscal 1999 (ended June 30,1999) sales of more than $38 billion and employed a workforce of 110,000. Founded in 1837 by two brothers-in-law, the company originally made soap and candles. As of the late 1990s, P&G provided some 300 brands to more than 140 countries. Its product list included laundry and cleaning products (Tide, Mr. Clean, Downy, Spic and Span), health and beauty aids (Noxzema, Clearasil, Head

& Shoulders, Secret, Ivory), paper products (Charmin), and even foods and beverages. In the worldwide market, P&G's laundry detergents held the largest share and overseas trade represented P&G's fastest growing market. Slightly more than half its revenue was generated outside the United States in fiscal 1999.

One of P&G's biggest competitors in the United States and abroad, and the second largest player in this industry, was the London-based Unilever conglomerate. Widely diversified, Unilever reported 1998 sales of $47.5 billion, up 1.8 percent from 1997. Worldwide, the company employed a workforce of 265,000 as of late 1998. The rivalry between Unilever and Procter and Gamble goes back nearly 50 years. Although P&G had entered the European continental market in 1954, Unilever had already begun marketing a synthetic detergent, OMO, in Italy in 1951. In the United States, Lever Brothers (a Unilever unit) and P&G faced off in several areas. One market in which they both competed was automatic dishwashing detergents. Between them for several years, they held the top two leading automatic dishwashing detergents. P&G's Cascade was the nation's best seller; Lever's Sunlight was number two. However, by the end of the decade, Unilever's Sunlight had fallen into third place in the ADD market, being succeeded in second place by Electrasol, which is marketed by another U.K.-based company, Reckitt Benckiser PLC. P&G's Cascade held on to the number one spot in the ADD market, capturing nearly 50 percent of the market.

Another area in which the two companies competed was the bar soap market. In 1990, Lever Brothers introduced a new three-in-one moisturizing, deodorant, and antibacterial cleansing bar called Lever 2000. Lever 2000 competed with several P&G products such as Safeguard, Coast, and Zest. As of 1998, another Lever product, Dove, climbed to the top selling position among bar soaps, supplanting Dial, which had been the historic market leader in this market. Dove accounted for 19.2 percent of bar soap sales in 1998, compared with 13.6 percent for Dial. Lever 2000 took third place among bar soaps with 9.7 percent of the market. Dial continued to hold its top position, however, in the liquid soap category.

Following Unilever, holding third place among soap manufacturers, was Colgate-Palmolive with 1998 sales of $8.97 billion and 38,300 employees. In an attempt to be more competitive, Colgate-Palmolive replaced its original Palmolive soap with Palmolive Gentle Skin Bar. In liquid soaps, the company's SoftSoap made gains but still lagged behind Dial Liquid in market share. Colgate-Palmolive's total assets and net sales, however, exceeded those of Dial.

In addition to providing products in the soap and detergent industry, Colgate-Palmolive manufactured oral and personal care products such as toothpastes, toothbrushes, oral rinses, and shampoos. The company also operated divisions in specialty fabric care products and in pet dietary care products. Colgate-Palmolive's domestic sales accounted for only about 30 percent of its total revenues in 1998. European sales accounted for 23 percent; sales in Latin America generated 27 percent; and the Asian and African markets combined to total 16 percent.

Other major players in the industry included Amway Coporation ($6 billion), S. C. Johnson and Son Inc. ($4.2 billion), and Clorox Co. ($4 billion). Dial Corporation, another example of a diverse, global company, reported 1998 revenues of $1.5 billion. Its products included bar soaps (Dial, Tone, Pure & Natural, Mountain Fresh, Spirit, Fels Naptha), Liquid Dial, Purex laundry products, and Brillo scouring pads. The company also produced specialty cleaners, personal care products, and food items, and operated divisions in transportation manufacturing and service companies. Another foreign-based player in the U.S. soap and detergents market was Reckitt Beckiser PLC, which markets such well-known cleaning products as Electrasol, Calgonite, Lysol, Resolve, Easy-Off, and Lime-A-Way. Based in Windsor, England, Reckitt Benckiser reported 1998 revenue of $3.7 billion, up 1.2 percent from 1997. Worldwide, the company employs 15,900.

WORKFORCE

In 1987, soap and detergent establishments employed 31,700 workers, 2 percent less than in 1986 and 10 percent less than in 1982. Ten years later in 1997, the size of the industry's workforce had slipped still further to a total of 31,158, of whom just over 18,000 were production workers. As the industry has increased its level of automation during the 1980s and 1990s, worker productivity has increased. Government officials attributed the ability to keep U.S. products competitive on the overseas market to the industry's high level of automation. States with the highest employment in the industry were California, Texas, Illinois, and Ohio.

AMERICA AND THE WORLD

The soap and detergent industry is an international industry, and during the early 1990s world demand for its products increased 1 to 3 percent per year. Many of its participants competed on a global basis. Analysts, noting a firm correlation between a nation's standard of living and its usage of soap and detergent products, expected the market to continue growing in both industrialized and developing nations.

U.S. companies involved in foreign trade found the markets in western Europe, Japan, and East Asia to be about the same size as the U.S. market. In Japan and Europe, demographic shifts toward older populations and smaller households were similar to the U.S. situation.

SOAP DETERGENT INDUSTRY EMPLOYMENT

Source: Department of Labor

Forecasters expected the greatest future export opportunities to occur in the developing economies of eastern Europe. Eastern Europe was also considered a good location for new manufacturing plants.

One of the world's largest non-U.S. soap and detergent manufacturers was the Kao Corporation. Kao, an industry leader in Japan, supplied a broad range of products including laundry detergents, dishwashing detergents, cleaners, toilet soaps, and personal care products. In 1988, Kao entered the U.S. market through its acquisition of the Andrew Jergens Company. By the early 1990s, its global network included several Asian and Pacific nations and the company planned to expand into Australia.

Japanese and other foreign marketers, like their U.S. counterparts, struggled with environmental issues. For example, by 1990 superconcentrates had captured 80 percent of Japan's powdered detergent market, and Kao was switching its formulations to natural-based surfactants. In Europe, environmental efforts resulted in regulations stricter than many enacted in the United States. Refillable containers, which were considered innovations in the United States in 1992, were already popular in Holland and Germany. In addition, German consumers were required to return all outside packaging. Issues of water consumption and energy use were also prompting changes in overseas markets faster than in domestic markets. Some industry analysts expected that trends toward washing with room temperature water and with less water would eventually spread to the United States.

The controversy over phosphates affected soap and detergent marketers on virtually every continent. Sodium tripolyphosphate (STPP) use increased in some areas but fell in others. In Canada during the fall of 1990, a brand war emphasizing the environmental benefits of phosphate-free detergents caused phosphate detergents to drop from 90 percent of the market to 40 percent in only six months. In 1991, however, forecasters expected phosphate sales to increase in eastern Europe and Asia. Industry analysts also predicted continued growth in phosphate usage within the industrial and institutional segment of the market and in automatic dishwashing detergents.

RESEARCH AND TECHNOLOGY

The need to meet environmental regulations both in the United States and abroad drove many of the research efforts undertaken by the soap and detergent industry during the early 1990s. Zeolite, sodium citrate, sodium carbonate, and sodium nitrilotriacetate were under investigation as possible builders to replace phosphates. Other questions being addressed included product safety, water quality, chemical disposal, the ability to wash in unheated water, and indoor air quality.

Although technological developments and an expanding understanding of chemical processes had improved the industry's ability to restore soiled garments and other objects to their presoiled condition, available soaps and detergents still failed to achieve perfect results. Chemical scientists, therefore, continued to work on developing innovative laundry additives such as new enzymes and oxygen bleaches.

FURTHER READING

D'Amico, Esther. "Soaps and Detergents the Push to Perform." *Chemical Week,* 24 January 1996.

Darnay, Arsen J., ed. *Manufacturing USA,* 6th ed. Detroit: Gale Research, 1998.

"Dishwasher Detergent Market, 1998." *Advertising Age,* 30 November 1998.

Fitzgerald, Patrick. "Ultra's in the Drivers Seat: Liquids Are the Growth in the Detergent Market." *Chemical Market Reporter,* 22 January 1996.

Gerry, Roberta. "Cleaning Up the Body and Spirit: Soap Market is Bubbling with New Body Washes Gaining Significant Market Share." *Chemical Marketing Reporter,* 22 January 1996.

———. "Stain, Stain Go Away." *Chemical Marketing Reporter,* 27 January 1997.

Hoover's Company Profiles. Hoover's Online, 2000. Available from http://www.hoovers.com.

Moore, Samuel K. "Bath Wash Gets Bigger: Market Opportunities Start to Gel." *Chemical Week,* 27 January 1999.

"Top Bar Soap Brands, 1999." *Household and Personal Products Industry,* December 1998.

U.S. Department of Commerce. *U.S. Industry and Trade Outlook '99.* Washington, D.C.: GPO, 1999.

U.S. Department of Commerce. U.S. Census Bureau. *1997 Economic Census.* Washington, D.C.: GPO, 1999.

Walsh, Kerri, and Claudia Hume. "Soaps and Detergents: Sharing the Risks and Rewards." *Chemical Week,* 27 January 1999.

SIC 2842

SPECIALTY CLEANING, POLISHING, AND SANITATION PREPARATIONS

This category includes companies that primarily make specialty cleaning products (those designed for specific surfaces such as bathrooms, ovens, drains, carpets, and upholstery), polishes and waxes (such as for furniture, metal, flooring, and glass), and other sanitation preparations including disinfectants and deodorizers. This category also includes companies making products such as household bleaches and ammonia, laundry starches, and fabric softeners. Companies that primarily make industrial bleaches are in **SIC 2819: Industrial Inorganic Chemicals, Not Elsewhere Classified.** Companies that primarily make household pesticides are in **SIC 2879: Pesticides and Agricultural Chemicals, Not Elsewhere Classified.**

NAICS CODE(S)

325612 (Polish and Other Sanitation Goods Manufacturing)

INDUSTRY SNAPSHOT

The U.S. Census Bureau estimated that in 1997 there were 728 establishments manufacturing products in this category. They shipped $8.4 billion worth of merchandise, spent $3.2 billion on materials, and invested $154.0 million in new and used buildings and other structures, machinery, and equipment. About 29 percent of these establishments had at least 20 employees. The largest number of operations was in California, followed by Texas, New York, Florida, and Illinois.

Goods in this category were often classified as commodity cleaners or specialty cleaners. Commodity cleaners were usually sold in bulk at lower prices. Specialty cleaners were sold in smaller quantities at higher prices. About 65 percent of products were sold to the industrial and institutional market, which included contract cleaning firms, office buildings, restaurants, hospitals, schools, hotels, and nursing homes.

BACKGROUND AND DEVELOPMENT

The specialty cleaning, polishing, and sanitation preparations industry made hundreds of products, each serving specific cleaning needs of consumers in different markets. Products were developed as a response to changes in technology, consumer need, government regulation, and other factors. This makes it hard to generalize about the industry's development, but the history of fabric softeners serves as an example of how certain factors have affected this category.

Fabric softeners were introduced during the early 1950s after synthetic laundry detergents became popular. Because detergents stripped natural oils out of fabrics as they cleaned, clothes came out scratchy and often developed negative ionic charges (static cling) in the dryer. The first fabric softeners were liquids that were added to the laundry during the rinse cycle. In the 1970s fabric softeners for use in the dryer were developed. Some were porous foam sheets doused with softener, while others were sprays and dispensing bars. The 1980s brought all-in-one detergents with fabric softeners for use during the wash cycle.

Because the coating action of softeners caused fabric to appear dingy, manufacturers invented optical brighteners, also called fluorescent whitening agents (FWAs). FWAs were chemical compounds that made fabrics appear brighter by converting ultraviolet light into visible blue light.

Fabric softeners made fabrics fluffy by coating fibers with fatty compounds. They eliminated static cling using "cationic surfactants," chemicals added to liquids to allow the wetting, foaming, dispersing, emulsifying, or penetrating actions of the solution on a fabric while adding positive charges to offset the negative ionic charges from static electricity. In addition to cationic surfactants, which did not clean effectively when used alone, the industry developed other surfactants. Anionic surfactants carried negative charges and were typically high sudsing. Nonionic surfactants carried no functional ionic charges but worked against oily soils. Amphoteric surfactants might be either positively or negatively charged depending on water conditions.

A national trend toward mild, natural, and environmentally safe products affected fabric softener development through the mid-1990s. Historically, customers wanted softeners to add fragrance, but an emphasis on using fewer chemicals led to new formulas. Procter & Gamble, for example, introduced Bounce Free, which had no perfumes, inks, or extra additives. The environmental movement's campaign to reduce packaging waste led to the development of concentrates and refills. In 1990 Procter & Gamble introduced Downy Refill, which customers mixed with water to make full strength. It required 75 percent less packaging than the original 64-ounce bottle. By mid-1991 refills made up 40 percent of Downy's sales.

Fabric softener sales rose 2 to 3 percent in the early 1990s. Sales of fabric softeners for use in dryers rose faster than sales of traditional liquid softeners made to be added during the washing machine's rinse cycle. Sales of detergents with added softeners declined.

Environmental concerns also affected polishes and waxes. Few ingredients and industry by-products were biodegradable. The Clean Water Act challenged floor wax makers to meet product disposal requirements. Regulations concerning volatile organic compounds led some makers to phase out solvent-based products in favor of water-based systems. Zinc was also regulated, since it harmed sewage treatment facilities.

During the early 1990s, the market for household polishes and waxes declined. The popularity of no-wax floors and a desire for more convenient products lowered demand for floor wax. Within the industrial and institutional market, improvements in maintenance technology, such as high-speed floor buffers, reduced the need for floor wax. New acrylic floor materials also required less maintenance.

Demand for other floor care products increased, however. The growing popularity of mineral surfaces, such as marble, terrazzo, quarry tile, and ceramics, brought a need for new types of cleaners. In addition, old asbestos flooring required constant care to keep it sealed and polished.

Carpet cleaner sales grew as manufacturers introduced products with deodorizers. The carpet care industry also reacted to environmental concerns about indoor air quality. Formulas that were less harsh, nontoxic, and pleasant smelling were emphasized, while some companies promoted all-natural formulas. Many aerosol cans were replaced by plastic spray-pump bottles. More communities were able to recycle plastic than steel, so plastic was seen as a better choice for the environment. In addition, aerosols were perceived to be environmentally dangerous, even though CFCs (chlorofluorocarbons) had been banned since 1978.

Within the household bleach market, environmental concerns had less effect. Although perborate bleaches (the most widely used type of non-chlorine bleach) seemed safer for the environment and gentler on clothes than chlorine-based bleaches, consumer acceptance of perborates was not as strong as analysts anticipated, because these bleaches performed poorly at the low wash temperatures preferred by many Americans. In Europe, where higher wash temperatures were popular, perborates captured 80 percent of the bleach market. One product expected to bring increased acceptance of perborates was Tide with Bleach, which contained a patented low-temperature activator called sodium nonanoyloxbenzene sulfonate (SNOBS).

Another trend during the early 1990s was an interest in disinfectants to control the spread of infectious diseases, especially HIV, the virus connected to Acquired Immuno-Defiency Syndrome (AIDS). Disinfectants were widely used by hospitals, clinics, schools, building service contractors, and hotels. Developing countries also began buying more disinfectants. For example, disinfectants were used in South America to fight cholera.

One problem involved products for stopping the spread of HIV and hepatitis. Occupational Safety and Health Association (OSHA) regulations required health care employees to work assuming all body fluids were infected with HIV or hepatitis. Disinfectant makers complained the EPA measured disinfectant strength according to its ability to kill bacteria responsible for tuberculosis. According to the industry, the efficacy tests were not comparable because tuberculoides were airborne and most disinfectants used against HIV and hepatitis were designed for surface use.

The disinfectant industry came under scrutiny in 1990 because of a report by the U.S. General Accounting Office. The report stated that up to 20 percent of disinfectants were ineffective, and the Environmental Protection Agency (EPA) could not ensure that registered disinfectants worked according to their claims. The Chemical Specialties Manufacturers Association (CSMA) responded by evaluating the quality of the data used in the tests. It also conducted its own random product reviews and reported that U.S. disinfectants worked and had passed the most stringent testing in the world.

Disinfectant registration brought contention, with industry leaders complaining that registration took too long and made it too costly to create new products. They claimed the process was further complicated by individual state requirements, which were often different from EPA requirements. The CSMA favored standardized, nationwide regulations.

Because of pressure from the environmental movement, manufacturers looked for ways to reduce volatile organic compounds and make products more biodegradable. In addition, marketers turned to packaging made of recycled postconsumer waste.

Environmentalists also criticized dry cleaning chemicals, which were often improperly discarded or leaked from faulty equipment and seeped into the ground, contaminating wells and aquifers. One of the biggest offenders was perchlorethylene (PCE, also called perc). More than 80 percent of U.S. dry cleaners used perc, and approximately 500 million pounds of perc were produced in the United States annually. The Clean Air Act of 1990 listed perc as a hazardous pollutant that could cause dizziness and headaches. Some studies also linked perc to miscarriage and cancer. The EPA proposed that dry cleaners reduce perc emissions 13 to 26 percent by 1996.

In 1987 the specialty cleaning, polishing, and sanitation preparation industry shipped goods worth $5.6 billion. Of this total, $3.9 billion were considered primary to the industry and $1.5 billion were secondary products. Miscellaneous transactions made up the remaining $227.9 million. By 1991 shipments totaled $6.0 billion, exports totaled $455.0 million, and imports totaled $175.0 million. By 1995 sales reached $8.7 billion.

CURRENT CONDITIONS

The Census Bureau reported that in 1997 the industry shipped more than $1 billion worth of household chlorine and other inorganic bleaching compounds, $5 billion worth of specialty cleaning and sanitation products, and $1 billion worth of polishing preparations and related products. This included $194 million worth of nonagricultural disinfectants for industries and institutions; slightly more than $1 billion worth of laundry aids; $713 million worth of air and room fresheners; $264 million worth of household glass window cleaners; $24 million worth of industrial and institutional glass window cleaners; $39 million worth of automotive windshield washer fluid; $104 million worth of oven cleaners; $250 million worth of household toilet bowl cleaners; $39 million worth of industrial and institutional toilet bowl cleaners; $180 million worth of drain pipe solvents; $437 million worth of bathroom, tub, and tile cleaners; $131 million worth of household rug and upholstery cleaners; $50 million worth of industrial and institutional rug and upholstery cleaners; $11 million worth of household ammonia; and $525 million worth of other specialty detergents such as waterless hand cleaners.

In terms of the value of products shipped, California led the household chlorine and other inorganic bleaching compounds segment. Ohio led the specialty cleaning and sanitation products segment, followed by Wisconsin, New Jersey, and Missouri. Wisconsin led the polishing preparations and related products segment, followed by Illinois and Ohio.

INDUSTRY LEADERS

Among firms that made products in this category as their primary business, Du Pont Performance Coatings (a subsidiary of E.I. du Pont de Nemours and Co. based in Troy, Michigan) was one of the largest with 6,000 employees and sales of $3.0 billion. S.C. Johnson and Son Inc. (Sturtevant, Wisconsin) had 12,500 employees and estimated sales of $2.8 billion. Its products included Glade air freshener, Shout laundry stain remover, Pledge furniture polish, and Windex glass cleaner. Clorox Co. (Oakland, California) had 6,600 employees and sales of $2.7 billion. Clorox, a former division of Procter & Gamble, had become independent in 1969 due to antitrust regulations. In addition to Clorox brand bleaches, the firm's products included Formula 409, Soft Scrub, Liquid Plumr, and Pine-Sol.

Other industry leaders included Madison BiOnics (a subsidiary of Systems General Inc. based in Tempe, Arizona) with 10,380 employees and estimated sales of $2.2 billion; and Reckitt and Colman Inc. (a subsidiary of the British company Reckitt and Colman PLC based in Wayne, New Jersey) with 2,500 employees and estimated sales of $1.3 billion.

Several large, diversified companies also competed in this category. They included Unilever Group (London, England) with sales of $47.5 billion; Dow Chemical Co. (Midland, Michigan) with sales of $18.4 billion; Colgate-Palmolive Co. (New York, New York) with sales of $8.9 billion; and MotorVac Technologies Inc. (Santa Ana, California) with sales of $4.2 billion.

WORKFORCE

According to the U.S. Department of Commerce, 21,989 people were employed in this industry in 1997, compared to 23,000 in 1995 and 21,700 in 1991. Total payroll was $724.6 million, compared to $702.3 million in 1995. The industry's 14,132 production workers earned an average hourly wage of $12.54 in 1997.

RESEARCH AND TECHNOLOGY

During the 1990s, changing regulations and environmental concerns brought more ''earth friendly'' technologies and products. One new development was packages made of resin from recycled products. Clorox, for example, increased its use of postconsumer waste in containers. Clorox claimed its efforts saved eight million pounds of virgin plastic, glass, and corrugated paperboard in 1992. Other efforts to reduce packaging materials included making caps and labels smaller and eliminating exterior packaging.

To make safer cleaning products without losing performance or convenience, manufacturers explored ways to reduce volatile organic compounds use in solvent-based formulas, make products more biodegradable, and lessen products' effect on sewage treatment plants. Some efforts toward making products that would be less harmful to the environment were the industry's response to federal and state regulations. Other efforts were market driven. Some industry analysts predicted innovations in ''environmentally friendly'' formulas would come from small suppliers.

FURTHER READING

Poppe, Carolyn J. ''Scour Town.'' *Soap-Cosmetics,* 1 March 1997.

Stapinski, Helene. ''Let's Talk DIRTY.'' *American Demographics,* November 1998.

U.S. Department of Commerce. U.S. Census Bureau. *1996 Annual Survey of Manufactures.* Washington, D.C.: GPO, 1998.

U.S. Department of Commerce. U.S. Census Bureau. *1997 Economic Census.* Washington, D.C.: GPO, 1999. Available from http://www.census.gov/prod/ec97/97m3256b.pdf.

SIC 2843

SURFACE ACTIVE AGENTS, FINISHING AGENTS, SULFONATED OILS, AND ASSISTANTS

This industry classification includes establishments primarily involved in making compounds that, when dissolved in water, reduce the water's surface tension. Products include preparations such as wetting agents, emulsifiers, and penetrants. These ingredients are raw materials for soap and detergent manufacturers. This industry classification also includes establishments primarily involved in producing sulfonated oils and fats and related products.

NAICS CODE(S)

325613 (Surface Active Agent Manufacturing)

In 1997 shipments of surfactants (surface active agents) were valued at $7 billion, up from $4.68 billion in 1995, according to the U.S. Census Bureau. The 211 establishments that manufactured products in this category employed 9,471 people, including 4,998 production workers who earned an average hourly wage of $18.39. The industry spent $3 billion on materials and $289 million on capital expenditures. About 50 percent of the establishments in this industry had at least 20 employees. The largest concentrations of businesses in the category were located in North Carolina, South Carolina, New Jersey, California, and Illinois.

Customer demand and legislative requirements changed the industry during the early 1990s. Manufacturers worldwide developed milder products, used more natural ingredients, and emphasized environmental safety. One of the most profound changes was the shift to concentrated and superconcentrated products for use in homes, industries, and institutions. Some industry analysts feared that the increasing demand for superconcentrated surfactants produced by large manufacturers would impede the development of small companies because the formulas were difficult for smaller manufacturers to reproduce.

Formulas were also changed to comply with environmental regulations. Personal care product manufacturers required solutions with less alcohol, makers of specialty cleaners were shifting from solvents and volatile organic compounds to water-based systems, and some communities upgraded biodegradability standards.

During the 1990s the industry experienced significant consolidation as large global corporations bought smaller companies, leaving fewer independent manufacturers.

Stepan Company, of Northfield, Illinois, led the industry with 1,372 employees and sales of $610.5 million in 1998. Other companies whose primary business was in this category included Harcros Chemicals Inc. (a subsidiary of Harrisons and Crosfield Inc. based in Kansas City, Kansas) with estimated sales of $98 million; Rite Industries Inc. (High Point, North Carolina) with sales of $90 million; and High Point Chemical Corp. (a subsidiary of Kao Corporation of America based in High Point, North Carolina) with sales of $70 million.

Although the market for surfactants grew slowly in North America, parts of Europe, and Japan during the late 1990s, demand increased significantly in developing nations where standards of hygiene and household cleanliness were rising. The detergent industry used more than 50 percent of all surfactants manufactured worldwide. In North America a large percentage of surfactants were used by the petroleum industry and other industrial ventures.

FURTHER READING

Feng, Pang, and Gui Hua. "China's Surfactants Market: Opportunities and Risks." *Chemistry and Industry,* 19 April 1999.

Karsa, David K. "Coming Clean: The World Market for Surfactants." *Chemistry and Industry,* 7 September 1998.

McCoy, Michael. "Stepan Eyes Specialty Surfactants and Overseas Markets for Growth." *Chemical Market Reporter,* 9 March 1998.

Stepan Company. *Stepan 1996 Annual Report.* Northfield, IL, 1996.

U.S. Department of Commerce. Census Bureau. *1996 Annual Survey of Manufactures.* Washington, D.C.: GPO, 1998.

U.S. Department of Commerce. Census Bureau. *1997 Economic Census.* Washington, D.C.: GPO, 1999. Available from http://www.census.gov/prod/ec97/97m3256c.pdf.

SIC 2844

PERFUMES, COSMETICS, AND OTHER TOILET PREPARATIONS

This category includes establishments primarily engaged in manufacturing perfumes, cosmetics, and other toilet preparations. Manufacturers of shampoos, shaving products, personal deodorants, hair preparations, suntan lotions and oils, talcum powders, toothpastes and powders, mouthwashes, and premoistened towelettes are included.

NAICS CODE(S)

325620 (Toilet Preparation Manufacturing)
325611 (Soap and Other Detergent Manufacturing)

INDUSTRY SNAPSHOT

There were approximately 770 establishments in the toilet preparations industry in 1996, employing an estimated 60,000 workers. The total value of industry shipments was $19.7 billion in 1994; by 1997 this number had increased to an estimated $22.8 billion. California and New Jersey had the largest number of establishments in the 1990s, with approximately 140 and 105, respectively.

The nation's economic condition during the 1980s and early 1990s brought about changes in the industry's distribution patterns. Traditionally, retail products had been classified as upscale, mid-level, or low-scale, depending on where they were sold and their pricing structure. Upscale product lines were typically sold in major department stores or specialty boutiques; mid-level product lines were sold in department stores at lower prices; and low-scale product lines were sold in drug stores or through catalogs. Industry analysts reported that customers were turning away from upscale products and switching to lower priced brands that were increasingly being sold in mass market outlets. Department stores had sold almost 20 percent of upscale cosmetics in 1985, but by 1991 the figure had dropped to 12 percent, according to a study conducted by Business Trend Analysts reported in *Drug and Cosmetic Industry.*

Due to a mature and stagnant market in the United States, manufacturers met with global success in the mid-1990s in Europe and emerging markets such as Asia and Latin America. A leader in this market, Gillette has the largest international market base with nearly 70 percent of its sales from foreign customer accounts. Procter & Gamble expects to boost its international sales, which in 1996 accounted for about 50 percent of the total.

ORGANIZATION AND STRUCTURE

Many participants in the cosmetics, fragrances, and personal care products industry were members of the Cosmetic, Toiletry and Fragrance Association (CTFA). The CTFA, which was founded in 1894, represented manufacturers and distributors as well as industry suppliers. It provided scientific, legal, regulatory, and legislative services.

The federal agency most often involved in regulatory encounters with the industry was the Food and Drug Administration (FDA). The FDA required that color additives be tested and approved before use. It banned or restricted the use of some specific ingredients including mercury compounds, chloroform, and methylene chloride. Other regulations dictated that cosmetics contain no poisonous or harmful substances and no filthy, putrid, or decomposed substances; they must also be made and held under sanitary conditions. The FDA also instituted labeling requirements that compelled manufacturers to list cosmetic ingredients in descending order according to the quantity used, with some flexibility allowed for the protection of trade secrets. The FDA also had the authority to take legal action against cosmetic companies if problems developed with the safety of products already on the market. To do so, the agency was required to prove in court that the product was harmful or misbranded.

The FDA, however, did not require the same type of pre-market approval for cosmetics as was required for drugs. According to a report published in *FDA Consumer,* cosmetics were legally defined as "articles other than soap that are applied to the human body for cleansing, beautifying, promoting attractiveness, or altering the appearance." The FDA recognized 13 categories of cosmetics: skin care products, fragrances, manicure products, eye makeup, makeup other than eye makeup, hair coloring preparations, shampoos and other hair products, deodorants, shaving products, baby products, bath oils and bubble baths, mouthwashes, and sunscreens.

The distinction between cosmetics and drugs was sometimes vague. According to FDA guidelines, products claiming to offer medical benefits or physiological effects were over-the-counter (OTC) drugs. Examples of items with controversial classifications included antiperspirants, which were classified as OTC drugs in the late 1970s, sunscreen products that listed a Sun Protection Factor (SPF) number, hair care products claiming to protect or restore hair, and shampoos professing to cure or remove dandruff. If the FDA deemed a cosmetic product to be an OTC drug, it was regulated as a new drug. The manufacturer was then required to demonstrate product safety and efficacy to gain FDA approval.

The cosmetic industry, under the sponsorship of CTFA, developed the Cosmetic Ingredient Review (CIR) in the mid-1970s to gather information about ingredient safety and make the information available to manufacturers. Reviews were conducted by a panel of scientific and medical experts. One report claimed that by 1988, 85 percent of the most frequently used 700 cosmetic ingredients had been reviewed, were under review, or were being regulated or studied by other procedures such as the FDA's process of reviewing OTC drugs. Another report claimed that a review performed by the National Institute of Occupational Safety and Health found that 884 of the 2,983 chemicals used as ingredients in cosmetics were toxic substances. The CTFA refuted the claim and maintained that scientific and medical studies demonstrated the safety of ingredients used within the industry.

The fragrance segment of the industry organized the Research Institute for Fragrance Materials (RIFM) in the mid-1960s to independently test and certify the safety of natural and chemical aromatics. During its first 25 years of operation, the RIFM tested approximately 1,400 different materials. The studies resulted in recommendations to restrict or prohibit about 100 of the ingredients reviewed. In an effort to further cooperation between cosmetic and fragrance manufacturers and the FDA, the regulatory agency instituted a voluntary registration program in which manufacturers participated in monitoring adverse reactions to products.

BACKGROUND AND DEVELOPMENT

The use of cosmetics, fragrances, and personal care products can be traced back to human's earliest days. Neanderthal man painted his face with reds, browns, and yellows derived from clay, mud, and arsenic. Bones were used to curl hair. Makeup, tattoos, and adornments conveyed necessary social information.

During the reign of the Pharaohs, Egyptian aristocrats wore cones of solidified perfume that would melt under warm temperatures to provide cooling and mask odors. A mineral called hematite was applied as rouge and faces were painted with white lead. Black kohl encircled eyes. Aloe vera was known as an anti-irritant.

Greek women also painted their faces white and put red circles on their cheeks. Galen, an ancient Greek physician, invented cold cream. The Romans used oil-based perfumes on their bodies, in their baths and fountains, and applied them to their weapons. In the ninth century, Arabs developed alcohol-based perfumes. Crusaders of the thirteenth century brought fragrances back to Europe from the Far East.

The perfumes developed during the sixteenth century were powders or gelatinous pastes. They could be applied to scented fans or carried in jewelry with fragrance compartments. The ability to create new fragrances by blending ingredients was developed during the seventeenth century in France. Some of the compounding establishments developed in France during the eighteenth and nineteenth centuries were still operating at the close of the twentieth century. America's first cologne water, Caswell-Massey's Number Six, was a blend of 27 ingredients and was said to have been a favorite of George Washington.

Natural perfumes were made from a variety of ingredients containing aroma. These included: essential oils, which were found in flowers, roots, fruits, rinds, or barks depending on the type of plant; resinoids, which were gums or resins that were purified with a solvent; and absolutes, which were aromas extracted with solvents existing in viscous liquid form. Natural perfumes were expensive, primarily because of the labor involved in gathering ingredients.

Chemical formulations developed during the nineteenth century began to replace expensive natural ingredients and make perfumes more widely available. Early synthetic fragrances included vanilla and violet. In the United States, Francis Despard Dodge developed citronella with various floral scents.

The nineteenth century also brought changes in facial makeup. Ceruse, a cosmetic that had been widely used in Europe since the time of the second century, was replaced by a powder made from zinc oxide. Ceruse, made from white lead, was discovered to be toxic and was blamed for causing physical problems such as facial tremors, muscle paralysis, and even death.

Antiperspirants and deodorants were developed during the 1890s. Aluminum chloride, the original active ingredient, frequently caused skin irritation and damage to clothes. These difficulties were overcome during the 1940s when aluminum chlorohydrate was developed. Although additives were subsequently produced to improve antiperspirant activity, aluminum chlorohydrate remained the primary ingredient in antiperspirants for the remainder of the twentieth century.

Cosmetics played a role during World War II. Leg makeup was developed in response to shortages of stockings. In Germany, women sacrificed lipstick, but U.S. officials judged it vital and necessary. Following the war, biological ingredients began to receive attention. Human placental products were first used in cosmetics during the 1940s. Cosmetic makers claimed that they stimulated tissue growth and removed wrinkles. The FDA ruled that such claims were medical in nature, and as a result classified these products as drugs and declared them ineffective. Placental products later reappeared in cosmetics but were listed only as a source of protein. Other biological ingredients (derived primarily from cows) included amniotic liquid, collagen (a protein substance), and cerebrosides (fatty substances with carbohydrates produced at the deepest layer of skin).

Fashion trends continued to bring new innovations. Artificial skin tanning aids were developed during the late 1950s. False eyelashes became popular during the 1960s. The 1960s also saw the introduction of "natural" products based on botanical ingredients such as carrot juice and watermelon extract.

During the 1970s, the growing environmental movement brought challenges to the cosmetic and fragrance industry. The use of some popular ingredients was banned following the enactment of endangered species protection legislation. Some examples included musk (from Himalayan deer, Ethiopian civet, and certain types of beaver) and ambergris (taken from sperm whales).

Concerns about contaminated makeup emerged during the late 1980s. An FDA report in 1989 found that more than 5 percent of samples collected from counters in department stores were contaminated with molds, fungi, and pathogenic organisms. Such contamination was supposed to be controlled by preservatives in the cosmetics. Preservatives, however, proved ineffective against the microorganisms responsible for causing product contamination when they lacked stability or when a particular product was kept longer than the shelf life of its preservative system.

Although cosmetic products seldom caused serious injury, some problems did occur. Most common among them were eye infections (caused by scratching the eyeball with a contaminated mascara wand) and allergic reactions. Fragrance additives were often blamed as a source of allergic responses. Two fragrances, acetylethly tetramethyltetralin (AETT) and 6-methyl coumarin (6-ME), caused sufficient numbers of adverse reactions for the FDA to take action against them. AETT, a neurotoxic, caused flushing, dizziness, nausea, and other reactions. 6-ME, which was frequently used in sunscreens, was photo-toxic and interacted with UV radiation occasionally leading to irreversible skin depigmentation and/or hyperpigmentation.

Manufacturers began to offer products labeled "hypoallergenic" or "natural." The term "hypoallergenic" meant a product was considered by its manufacturer to offer less potential for allergic reaction. Some makers conducted clinical tests to determine the likelihood of allergic responses. Others merely reformulated products without adding fragrances. An effort by the FDA to regulate a precise meaning for the term "hypoallergenic" was overturned in the courts. The industry used the word "natural" to refer to any ingredient that was not synthetically produced. It had no regulated meaning implying "pure" or "clean."

Controversy continued into the 1990s over cosmetic ingredients and claims. Some popular materials were Nayad, liposomes, and vitamins. Nayad (a trade name) was a yeast extract said to make the skin look and feel smoother by reducing lines and wrinkles. Liposomes were round, microscopic sacs made of fatty substances that cosmetic makers claimed could penetrate the skin's surface to deliver other ingredients into deeper skin layers. Vitamins were listed on display labels to imply that their usage would nourish the skin. The FDA, however, prohibited manufacturers from making therapeutic claims based on the vitamin content of skin care products.

CURRENT CONDITIONS

As the perfume, cosmetic, and toiletry preparations industry entered the 1990s, it faced many challenges including regulatory changes, product safety concerns, calls for scientific data to document product claims, increasing environmentalism, and pressure from the growing animal rights movement. Congress began investigating possible revisions to the traditional "drug" and "cosmetic" definitions established under the Food, Drug and Cosmetic Act. A report titled *Classification and Regulation of Cosmetics and Drugs: A Legal Overview and Alternatives for Legislative Change* included provisions for a third category of "cosmeceuticals" to include products like sunscreens that fell in the gap between "drugs" and "cosmetics." Some industry analysts welcomed legislative changes to clarify product distinctions but doubted whether manufacturers would accept proposals that would require safety and efficacy testing to substantiate label claims.

The FDA continued compiling complaints from customers about neurological reactions to perfumes including symptoms such as burning of the eyes, nose, and throat; flushing; dizziness; nausea; difficulty in breathing; memory loss; and drowsiness. Some hospitals banned the use of perfumes by operating room nurses. A group calling itself the National Foundation of the Chemically Hypersensitive wanted to ban the use of fragrances in public meeting places.

Some spokesmen within the fragrance and cosmetic industry claimed that, because no one had ever been killed or seriously injured as a result of fragrance use, the FDA's resources would be better spent on bigger health problems. They advocated individual avoidance of offending ingredients as a solution to skin irritations and allergic responses. Although the industry's safety record before the 1990s had been good, some seasoned industry watchers expressed concern about continued safety as many small, new companies emerged.

Growing concern about environmental issues also affected the industry. Several surveys demonstrated increased awareness of pollution and related issues. In 1990, Find/SVP (a New York survey group) estimated that 18.8 million U.S. households were environmentally interested shoppers. These consumers, called "Green consumers," accounted for about 20 percent of the U.S. population and their number was expected to increase. In a report on Green consumers, Find/SVP cited three main concerns: animal rights and species preservation, availability of clean air and water, and waste management.

One of the most controversial environmental matters facing the fragrance industry was pressure to reduce its use of volatile organic chemicals (VOCs). The most popularly used VOC was ethyl alcohol, which functioned as a solvent. The industry claimed that water was not a good substitute for ethyl alcohol because many fragrance ingredients were not water soluble. Ingredients designed to help materials dissolve in water affected product tex-

ture and also presented possible safety concerns. Propellants and many other ingredients used within the industry were also VOCs.

VOCs were blamed for contributing to ground-level ozone. In California, VOC emissions from colognes, perfumes, toilet water, aftershaves, and body splashes were estimated at almost 1,700 pounds per day. Consequently, in the early 1990s, California proposed limits on VOC usage in fragrances. New York and other states were expected to follow. In California, regulations took effect January 1, 1995, that limited VOCs to 70 percent of perfumes, colognes, and toilet waters; 60 percent of aftershaves; and 50 percent of other fragrances. Colognes, perfumes, and toilet waters that were on the market before the regulations took effect were exempt.

In addition to planned compliance with VOC regulations, many fragrance and cosmetic companies brought "green" products to the market place. Estee Lauder introduced its Origins Natural Resources line of skin care, body products, aromatherapy, and makeup. The line was promoted as natural and non-animal tested. Items were sold in recyclable containers. Revlon brought out New Age Naturals, skin care products made of all degradable ingredients, and Pure Skin Care, a line of products developed without animal testing. Mary Kay Cosmetics' Countryside Colors line emphasized its use of recyclable packaging made from recycled materials. Mary Kay also eliminated most external packaging on men's skin care products. As some companies eliminated, reduced, or refabricated outer packaging to emphasize their concern about waste disposal problems, others, particularly fragrance manufacturers, expressed concern about the trend because packaging contributed to their image.

Critics claimed that many of the environmental efforts advertised by cosmetic and fragrance manufacturers were exaggerated, false, or meaningless. For example, "biodegradable" packages were incapable of degrading under conditions present in most landfills. Some products were labeled "ozone friendly" because they did not contain chlorofluorocarbons (CFCs), but CFCs had been banned since the late 1970s. "Recyclable" notations on plastic containers were meaningless when recycling plants for particular plastics (like polystyrene) were not available.

Along with increased environmental awareness came concern for healthy products. Items seen as safe for the environment were perceived as healthy for users. This philosophy drove a trend toward increased use of natural products containing ingredients such as proteins and vitamins. It also brought expanded use of botanical ingredients such as aloe, cucumber, and berry extracts. In perfumes, the trend led to the increasing popularity of discreet scents, floral freshness, and sea smells. In makeup, consumers began turning to functional products.

Cosmetics were expected to do more than add color and cover skin imperfections. Buyers wanted products to contain ingredients such as sunscreens and emollients to nourish and protect their skin. The focus on natural products also led to more realistic product claims.

The emphasis on natural ingredients, however, extended only to plant sources. Animal products were shunned and animal testing fell into disfavor. Many companies promoted cosmetic lines that were developed without animal testing. One example was SafeBrands Inc, which prohibited the use of animal testing in the development of its products and by its raw ingredient suppliers.

The Cosmetic, Toiletries, and Fragrance Association (CTFA) remained firm in its support of some animal testing, however. According to the CTFA, even products that claimed to use non-animal test methods relied on models that were acquired as a result of animal testing. The organization believed that human health and safety were more important than animal rights. The CTFA reported that 74 percent of Californians polled opposed legislation that would prohibit animal testing to insure product safety.

In addition to the social and political concerns surrounding animal testing, environmentalism, and product safety, the industry was also affected by the nation's economic situation. The perfume, cosmetic, and personal care products industry had established a "recession proof" image when sales of inexpensive cosmetics had outsold mid-priced food items and clothing during the Depression of the 1930s. Cosmetics also did well during the recessions of the 1960s and 1980s. The recession of the early 1990s, however, brought new challenges. Counterfeit products were offered at low prices. Customers resisted high prices and demanded value. The numbers of distribution channels for upscale lines decreased as traditional department stores closed. Costs associated with product promotion increased and marketers turned more often to expensive strategies such as giving free products.

In an effort to move away from traditional department store cosmetic counters, upscale manufacturers turned to self-serve packaging and sold greater volumes to discounters. This enabled retailers to place items on sale. Depressed pricing, however, sometimes diminished a product's image. Bridge brands were increasingly aimed at a niche between the upscale and mass markets. Mass marketers focused on increasing volumes to generate more profit. In 1999, it was reported that one of the major movements in the industry was a trend toward providing consumers with premium versions of health and beauty products.

Due to the growing trend toward industry globalization, industry leaders have focused product lines and

marketing at the ethnic niche market, primarily targeting the specific makeup and skincare needs of Asian, African American, and Latino consumers. This segment reported sales of $210 million in 1997, and this market is expected to continue its rapid growth.

INDUSTRY LEADERS

One of the largest companies involved in the perfume, cosmetic, and toilet preparations industry was Procter & Gamble (P&G), which posted total sales in 1999 of $38.1 billion (including some noncosmetic items) and employed 110,000 workers. In the early 1990's, P&G's Cover Girl held 59 percent of the makeup market; Oil of Olay was the leader in mass-market skin care with a 29.7 percent share; and in men's products, Old Spice was a best seller. To expand Old Spice's appeal to younger men, P&G developed a new marketing campaign, which focused on sports and action.

P&G increased its involvement in the global cosmetics market through the purchases of Beatrix and Max Factor. Beatrix, a German cosmetic manufacturer, had annual sales estimated at $200 million. Max Factor's sales were estimated at $600 million per year. Domestic sales accounted for only 25 percent of the total. Japan and the United Kingdom were the largest overseas customers.

Max Factor, the company, took its name from the Hollywood makeup artist Max Factor. In 1914, Factor began making cosmetic products according to the demands of the technologically evolving film industry. One Factor creation, Pancake makeup, first appeared on the screen in 1937. Max Factor continued to develop new formulas to meet the needs of Technicolor movies and color television. In 1990, the company introduced a new makeup designed to meet the demands of high density television in Japan. New Definition Perfecting Makeup used four times more pigment dots than other products. Max Factor was also a leader in cosmetic development outside the film industry. In 1988, the company introduced the "no makeup look" with a no-color mascara and "Invisible Makeup," made of light-diffusing ingredients to blur skin imperfections. The "Transparencies" line, introduced in 1991, used a new combination of color pigments to avoid heaviness or opacity.

Johnson & Johnson, a diversified healthcare product manufacturer, was involved in producing consumer toiletries as well as pharmaceuticals and professional medical products. In 1998, the company brought in sales of more than $23.6 billion and employed 93,100 workers.

Within the fragrance segment of the industry, The Estee Lauder Companies Inc. was one of the nation's largest companies. Estee Lauder first began marketing skin products in 1946. Lauder's earliest perfume, called Youth Dew, was introduced in 1953. Since then, other perfumes were developed including Estee, Cinnabar, and

Beautiful. Lauder's marketing efforts presented American women with the idea of wearing perfume all day long, not just on special occasions. During 1999, Lauder's estimated world sales totaled $3.9 billion, most of which was in prestige markets. Industry analysts expected the company to be heavily affected by a trend away from traditional department store cosmetic and fragrance counter sales. But as of 1999, sales and employee growth continued to rise.

Within the men's toiletries market, many companies were experiencing declining profits in the early 1990s. An exception was Gillette. Gillette, founded in 1901, was the world's leader in sales of razors and blades. The company's 1998 sales were $10 billion. The company's line of toiletries was one of the top sellers in the United States yet pulled in about 60 percent of its revenues from outside the United States. The innovative Gillette Sensor razor was introduced in 1990 and sold at premium prices that helped bolster the company's bottom line. As a result of the Gillette Sensor's success, the company expanded efforts to upscale some of its lines and aim them at a market niche between mass market items and upscale products. Gillette was also working toward encouraging retailers to group men's grooming products together in a single section containing shaving supplies as well as men's fragrances.

WORKFORCE

Although industry shipment figures demonstrated overall growth during the 1980s and the early 1990s, employment figures fell. In 1988, the toilet preparation industry employed 72,200. In 1991, several manufacturers including Colgate-Palmolive, Gillette, Revlon, Procter & Gamble, and American Cyanamid closed plants or announced future plant closings. With the trend toward untapped ethnic markets and globalization of the industry, employment is rising quickly. In 1999, the industry employed approximately 742,000 workers.

AMERICA AND THE WORLD

At the turn of the century, globalization of the industry was exploding. Eastern Europe, Latin America, Russia, and the Asia Pacific region are driving up sales. The global industry reported 1998 sales of $125.7 billion, with fragrance leading the pack in growth, with sales of $24.2 billion. Skincare was reported at $30 billion, haircare at $24.6 billion, makeup at $23.7 billion, and personal care products at $23.2 billion.

In the early 1990s, the United States was a net exporter of perfumes, cosmetics, and toilet preparations. Canada, the United Kingdom, Japan, and Mexico were major purchasers of U.S. goods. About 55 percent of the nation's imports were received from France. Other countries supplying products to the U.S. market included the United Kingdom, Japan, and Mexico. Within the fragrance segment, U.S. demand represented the largest national market in the world, only slightly smaller than the entire European market. Demand in Japan was estimated to be about one third the size of the U.S. market.

As the industry moved increasingly toward globalization, new markets were developing in Latin America, Eastern Europe, and the Pacific Rim. While American companies like Procter & Gamble increased their penetration in overseas markets, foreign companies increased their involvement in American markets. Globalization brought efforts to adopt common terminology, particularly in describing ingredients. The Cosmetic, Toiletries and Fragrance Association (CTFA) expected wider use of the CTFA Ingredient Dictionary.

RESEARCH AND TECHNOLOGY

During the 1990s, research and technological improvements within the industry focused on reformulating products to move away from synthetic chemicals and to rely on natural products. Consumers were becoming more knowledgeable about products that were good for them, demanding effective and appealing products. Within the class of natural products, the primary emphasis was on vegetable and plant materials. Chemists also sought to meet customer demands for mildness and reduced toxicity. Within the growing sun-care segment of the industry, scientists researched products with improved protection, especially against year-round ultraviolet rays. Color market formulators worked to develop new silicon-based products that promised better color retention and improved waterproofing capabilities.

According to a report published in *Seventeen* magazine, Tony Barone, vice president of Barone Cosmetics, predicted further changes within the cosmetic industry. He guessed that as Americans shunned the sun because of health concerns, paler faces would become more fashionable. He speculated that modern habits of living in controlled environments would lead to a loss of body hair including diminished eyebrows and less head hair. Barone considered the advancement of medical cosmetics, where beauty doctors would tattoo permanent makeup in place and perform routine cosmetic surgery, a possible future development.

FURTHER READING
Benham, Michelle, and Ben Blinder. "Functional Materials in Skin Care." *Drug & Cosmetic Industry,* November 1998.

Bittar, Christine. "Moving Upscale with Day to Day Items." *Brandweek,* 21 June 1999.

"Datamonitor's Futures and Perspectives." *Drug and Cosmetic Industry,* 1 October 1998.

Darnay, Arsen, ed. *Manufacturing USA,* 5th ed. Detroit; Gale Research, 1996.

''Employment—National, Not Seasonally Adjusted Data.'' *Bureau of Labor Statistics,* 1999. Available from http://www.bls .gov.

''Hoover's Company Capsules.'' *Hoover's Online: The Business Network,* 1999. Available from http://www.hoovers.com.

''Overseas Consumers Flock to U.S. Household and Personal Care Brands.'' *STREETnet,* 26 July 1996. Available from http:// www.streetnet.com.

''State of the Industry.'' *Global Cosmetic Industry,* June 1999.

SIC 2851

PAINTS, VARNISHES, LACQUERS, ENAMELS, AND ALLIED PRODUCTS

This industry category includes establishments primarily engaged in manufacturing paints (in paste and ready-mixed form); varnishes; lacquers; enamels; shellac; dry powder coatings; putties, wood fillers, and sealers; paint and varnish removers; paintbrush cleaners; and allied paint products.

Establishments primarily engaged in manufacturing carbon black are classified in **SIC 2895: Carbon Black;** those manufacturing bone black, lamp black, and inorganic color pigments are classified in **SIC 2816: Inorganic Pigments;** those manufacturing organic color pigments are classified in **SIC 2865: Cyclic Organic Crudes and Intermediates, and Organic Dyes and Pigments;** those manufacturing plastics materials are classified in **SIC 2821: Plastics Materials and Resins;** those manufacturing printing ink are classified in **SIC 2893: Printing Ink;** those manufacturing caulking compounds and sealants are classified in **SIC 2891: Adhesives and Sealants;** those manufacturing artists' paints are classified in **SIC 3952: Lead Pencils, Crayons, and Artists' Materials;** and those manufacturing turpentine are classified in **SIC 2861: Gum and Wood Chemicals.**

NAICS CODE(S)

325510 (Paint and Coating Manufacturing)

INDUSTRY SNAPSHOT

According to the U.S. Census Bureau, U.S. manufacturers shipped about 1.3 billion gallons of paint, valued at $15.4 billion in 1998. About 700 firms produced paint in the United States in the mid-1990s, down from more than 900 early in the decade. The paint and coatings business was considered a mature industry, with growth projected at about 1 to 2 percent annually.

Historically, paint remained a comparatively small, yet influential industry into the mid-1990s. Despite its relatively minor revenues, the industry's products affected virtually every aspect of modern life. From cars and homes, to containers for food and beverages, to appliances and furniture, paints and coatings protected, personalized, and beautified our surroundings. Some economists consider it a leading economic indicator.

The paint industry has become essential to nine major manufacturing industries, including: automobiles, trucks and buses, metal cans, farm machinery and equipment, construction machinery and equipment, metal furniture and fixtures, wood furniture and fixtures, major appliances, and coil coating (high-speed application of industrial coatings to continuous sheets, strips, and coils of aluminum or steel). Additionally, paint manufacturers influence the wider chemicals industry via their purchase of billions of dollars worth of raw materials. Paint and coatings were also an integral contributor to the new and resale housing industry.

The paint industry underwent significant changes in the early 1990s, including a gradual expansion of specialized end-user markets, progressively stricter environmental regulations, an increase in foreign corporate ownership, and an accelerating pace of consolidation. But in the mid-1990s, as raw material prices eased and demand in two key markets (automotive and housing) surged, paint manufacturers experienced an increase in sales.

ORGANIZATION AND STRUCTURE

The paint industry's first national professional organization, the National Paint, Oil, and Varnish Association, was founded in 1888 in Saratoga, New York. Industry associations proliferated in the early twentieth century until the Great Depression, when government officials and top paint company executives urged the creation of a single national organization. The National Paint, Varnish, and Lacquer Association was formed in 1933, and was later renamed the National Paint and Coatings Association (NPCA).

The NPCA's membership constituted over 75 percent of the entire paint industry in the 1990s. The organization existed to represent the industry to government regulators and the general public. Its public relations and educational programs focused primarily on the technical and aesthetic qualities of architectural paint. The group's annual ''Clean-Up, Paint-Up, Fix-Up'' campaign, which encouraged neighborhood pride through house painting, was first undertaken in 1912 and lasted through the early 1970s. In the 1990s campaigns countered paint's persistently bad image as a noxious, but necessary, maintenance product. Following the lead of such successful ''category marketers'' as the cotton and milk industries, the NPCA promoted paint as a versatile decorating tool.

Competitive Structure. Numerous mergers, the high cost of regulation, and increasingly expensive, complex manufacturing processes began to have a cumulative effect on industry composition in the mid-1990s. Mergers and acquisitions reduced the number of companies in the industry from more than 900 to about 700 over the course of the early 1990s. By that time, the top three producers accounted for about 45 percent of U.S. shipments, up from less than 30 percent in 1990. The 10 largest manufacturers comprised nearly two-thirds of the market. Industry observers expected consolidation to eliminate another 300 companies by the year 2000.

The geographic dispersal of paint manufacturers was historically dictated by the high transportation costs associated with paint distribution. The weight of prepared paint encouraged the development of a regionalized structure of small manufacturers by the end of the nineteenth century. Paint companies gravitated toward major population and industrial centers such as Cleveland, New York, St. Louis, and Chicago. This arrangement dominated the industry until the 1940s and 1950s, when the leading paint manufacturers began to consolidate paint plants and develop wider distribution networks.

By the early 1960s, however, that trend reversed, and smaller branch plants were built to lower freight costs, avoid some state taxes, and facilitate more personalized service. In 1967 about 66 percent of paint was consumed within 500 miles of its manufacture. Decentralization persisted through the 1990s, represented by the industry segment of tenacious small-to- medium-sized paint manufacturers who served limited regional markets.

Market Segments. Three basic segments existed within the industry: architectural coatings, original equipment manufacturer (OEM) product coatings, and special purpose coatings. Architectural coatings, known in the industry as trade sales paint and commonly referred to as house paint, comprised the largest segment, contributing 44 percent of annual gallonage and 38 percent of revenues in 1995. About 60 percent of the 617.5 million gallons of architectural coatings sold in 1995 were interior paints. Exterior paints contributed 36 percent (225.1 million gallons), and lacquers and all others accounted for the remainder of architectural paint shipped. Water-based, or latex, paints constituted 76 percent of trade sales in 1996, up slightly from 73 percent in 1990.

The bulk of architectural coatings were distributed through wholesale and retail outlets. Marketing these paints encompassed both formulation and aesthetic factors. Safety, durability, consistency, washability, and convenience were some common consumer concerns with regard to formulation. But color and appearance were also important, so paint manufacturers were often obliged to keep up with decorating trends.

Sales in this industry segment were keyed to weather (which could limit the application of exterior paints), new

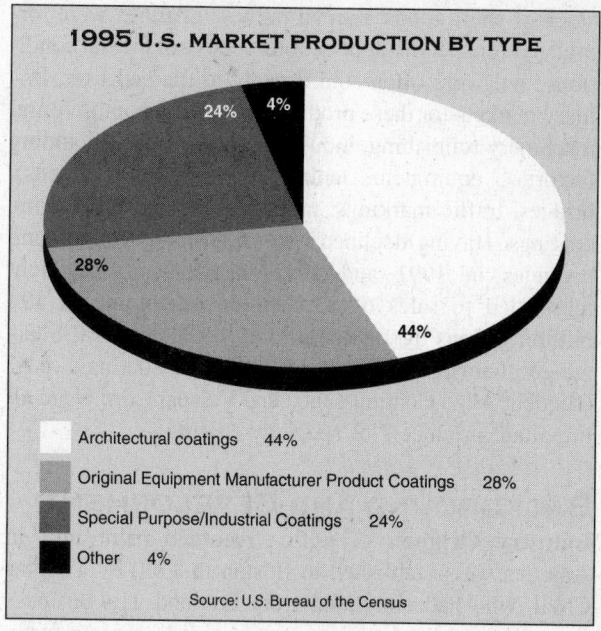

1995 U.S. MARKET PRODUCTION BY TYPE

24% | 4% | 28% | 44%

☐ Architectural coatings   44%

▨ Original Equipment Manufacturer Product Coatings   28%

▨ Special Purpose/Industrial Coatings   24%

■ Other   4%

Source: U.S. Bureau of the Census

housing starts, sales of existing homes, and to a lesser degree, commercial and industrial construction. Architectural coatings were subject to competition from vinyl siding, wallpaper, wood paneling, and glass. Major producers for this segment included Sherwin-Williams Co.; PPG Industries, Inc.; Grow Group; Valspar Corp.; Glidden Co. (a subsidiary of Great Britain's ICI Paints); and Benjamin Moore and Co.

OEM paints constituted about 28 percent of industry gallonage in 1995. These products were often custom formulated in consultation with the end-user and applied during manufacturing. These coatings were used in such durable goods markets as automobiles, aircraft, appliances, furniture, metal containers, sheet and coil metals, and industrial equipment. Dollar shipments for this industry segment in 1995 were a record $5.3 billion, up more than 25 percent from 1990. Strong automobile and consumer durables markets helped fuel volume growth as well, which rose from 339 million gallons in 1990 to 389.6 million gallons in 1995.

One major challenge facing OEMs in the early 1990s was the increased use of plastics in automobiles and appliances, which created the need to match the paint finish of metal panels with plastic panels that were painted separately. Development of new applications technologies was another primary concern. Major companies with interests in OEM markets included E. I. DuPont de Nemours, PPG Industries, Grow Group, and Glidden.

Special purpose or industrial coatings, which developed largely after World War II, accounted for less than one-fourth of industry volume in 1994. While similar to architectural coatings in that they could be classified as stock or shelf goods, special purpose coatings were formulated for specific applications or environmental conditions, and were often sold directly to the end user. Primary markets for these products included automotive and machinery refinishing, industrial maintenance (including factories, equipment, tanks, utilities, and railroads), bridges, traffic markings, metallic coatings, and marine coatings. Having declined both in terms of volume and revenues in 1991 and 1992, this industry segment rebounded to sales of $3.1 billion in volume of 194 million gallons by 1994. DuPont; PPG Industries; Sherwin-Williams; RPM Inc.; Courtaulds Coatings, Inc.; Glidden; Akzo Coatings, Inc.; and Valspar Corp. were all important producers of specialty coatings.

BACKGROUND AND DEVELOPMENT

Industry Origins. The first recorded paint mill in America was established in Boston in 1700 by Thomas Child, who had emigrated from England. His business manufactured the components of paint in a paste form. During most of the nineteenth century, professional painters mixed their own paints from linseed oil, white lead, turpentine, and pigments. Their formulas were inconsistent, and the paint they produced had virtually no shelf life.

In 1867, D. R. Averill, an Ohioan, patented ready-to-use paint. But early factory-made paints were notorious for their poor quality and unreliable performance. It was not until the 1880s that quality ready-mixed paints were produced. By 1888 the paint industry generated about $45 million in annual revenues.

During World War I, paint and varnish were vital to the U.S. military effort for protection and camouflage of equipment and personnel. The war exposed the industry's dependence on imported raw materials, and frequent shortages encouraged the development of domestic and synthetic replacements. By 1922 annual industry volume neared $300 million.

Paint and coatings were vital to the Allied effort during World War II, as the products once again preserved and camouflaged virtually everything. The unique needs of the military spurred the development of specialized paints and coatings. There were acid-proof, corrosion-proof, and waterproof coatings; fire-retardant, ice-repellent, fungus-resistant, weather-resistant, and water-resistant compounds that enhanced fabrics; and phosphorescent and fluorescent paints that proved strategically vital. The NPCA's "Paint Protects America" slogan summed up the industry's wartime contributions.

A Maturing Industry. After more than quadrupling from 1933 to 1947, it took the paint industry 17 years to increase from $1.25 billion to $2 billion. The American market was nearing saturation, and the same high trans-

portation costs that prevented the consolidation of paint plants impeded expansion into overseas markets.

Overcapacity, increased competition, and rising expenses also plagued the paint industry. The U.S. Department of Defense reported on overcapacity in the paint industry during World War II, noting that "only 100 of the then 1,400 paint manufacturers, working only one shift, could meet any emergency needs of the entire country." By the 1960s, such alternatives as aluminum siding, concrete, and stucco for exterior application, and vinyl, wood, and paper wallcoverings for the interior, entered the already crowded market. Paint producers began to sacrifice their profit margins in an attempt to maintain market share.

At the same time, labor, packaging, and distribution costs rose dramatically. From 1965 to 1970, wage costs rose 33 percent, but the dollar value of industry-wide shipments rose only 26 percent and productivity increased only 2 percent—not enough to account for the difference. By 1970 the industry's average return fell to 6.2 percent, compared to a 10.1 percent average for all industries.

As the growth and profits of the paint industry trailed the rest of the economy, top paint manufacturers diversified into everything from fertilizer to foods to garner profits. But promotional sales exacerbated the profit squeeze during the 1970s. Many in the industry blamed mass merchandising of paint. Discounters could afford to slash margins and even take a loss to capture market share. Paint manufacturers were forced to follow suit to hang onto their share. Another factor that emerged during the 1970s was the oil crisis, which caused the price of many of the industry's raw materials to rise rapidly.

As the paint industry matured and profit margins decreased, many firms merged to consolidate their resources and achieve economies of scale. In 1960 there were about 2,000 companies in the industry. Between 1963 and 1968 alone, 71 paint companies changed hands, often merging several smaller businesses into one substantial company. The larger, more powerful companies sought increased market share and the higher sales.

Rebound. The paint industry endured a recession in the early 1980s along with the rest of America, but from 1983 to 1990 growth was buoyed by strong construction and durable goods markets. Volume increased dramatically, from less than 420 million gallons shipped in 1982 to over 1 billion gallons in 1990. The physical increase was accompanied by a leap in dollar sales, from about $3.1 billion in 1982 to about $9.3 billion in 1985 and over $11.7 billion in 1990. Consolidation of the paint companies continued during the 1980s. By the end of 1992, fewer than 900 companies remained, down from 1,100 in 1984. Manufacturers also sought to increase their profit margins through applied research and development directed at refining existing technologies.

After decades of practice, paint and coatings companies anticipated environmental regulation and tried to prepare for it in advance. So when the Environmental Protection Agency estimated that coatings solvents were responsible for 8 to 10 percent of all volatile organic compounds (VOCs) released in the United States, coatings formulators stepped up their efforts to produce high-performance, low-VOC paints before solvents were banned.

Sales volumes in the paint and coatings industry fell 4.9 percent to about $11.39 billion in 1991, largely due to the recession's impact on the architectural and special purpose segments. From 1988 to 1991 raw materials prices increased 24 percent, but paint prices increased only 12 percent.

The financial picture brightened in 1992 and 1993, as sales of existing homes increased due to low interest rates. Some analysts noted that owners of offices and light manufacturing buildings purchased more paint to maintain their properties as well. These factors kept the paint industry growing slowly at an annual rate of about 2.9 percent from 1987 to 1992.

In the 1990s the primary concerns of paint manufacturers centered on progressively stricter environmental regulations, increasing foreign ownership, greater likelihood of mergers and acquisitions, and accelerating technological advances.

Growth in manufacturing, especially automobiles and construction in the mid-1990s, fueled healthy expansion of the paint industry. Paced by double-digit volume gains in the water-based exterior coatings segment, dollar volume advanced 9 percent from 1993 to $15.9 billion in 1995. This trend accelerated into the first half of 1996, when volume increased 12.5 percent to 685 million gallons over the first half of 1995 and value jumped 16.4 percent to $8.3 billion in the period. The Freedonia Group forecast that domestic sales of paint and coatings would expand at an average annual rate of almost 2 percent, reaching $18 billion on volume of 1.3 billion gallons by the year 2000. Industrial coatings, especially powder and radiation-cured types, were expected to account for a significant portion of the growth.

CURRENT CONDITIONS

In 1999 the expected growth for the industry was 2 to 3 percent, driven mostly by new housing starts. Other factors contributing to growth were better economic conditions in South America and Asia, and strong demand in Europe, as well as in the United States. Through June 1999, the industry produced 667,776,000 gallons of paints and coatings, up from 671,808,000 through June

1998. The value of the production in 1999 was $8.3 billion, up from $7.7 billion the year before.

While the architectural paint industry remained fragmented, with few national brands, the industry leaders were busy buying local retailers and regional distributors. PPG bought Wattyl Paint, an Atlanta-based retailer with 21 stores, in June 1999, to expand in the South. Benjamin Moore added $45 million a year in sales when it bought New York metro-area retailer Janovic in June 1998. The key to sales growth was to have outlets for the products in three areas: company-owned stores, independent stores, and home centers. Sherwin-Williams focused mainly on its company-owned stores, which provided over half of the company's sales. The division responsible for sales to the other channels declined in the late 1990s. Some analysts felt that Sherwin-Williams needed to have more of its sales coming from home centers—in the late 1990s the company sold only low-volume, high-end products through home centers.

Another trend in the architectural market was negotiating contracts with the large home centers to take advantage to the do-it-yourself market. The largest home centers, Lowe's and Home Depot, grew rapidly in the 1990s and showed no sign of slowing—Home Depot had plans to quickly double the number of stores it operated. Sales growth was slowing for the paint companies, however; as the home centers reduced their inventories from a six-week supply to two weeks worth of product. The bankruptcy of another home center chain, Hechinger's, particularly hurt Sherwin-Williams and to a lesser extend, PPG.

Due to higher raw materials costs, many companies raised prices in 1999. Most companies were keeping the increases as low as possible—5 percent or less—as competition kept them from raising prices any higher. In the paint industry, raw materials normally accounted for 65 to 70 percent of cost of goods sold. Most of the companies in the industry were trying to cut costs to raise profits and attached a higher price to new and high performance products. Since there was little difference in architectural paint products, companies had to differentiate themselves by advertising and price.

Trying to hold costs down, many industry leaders were shutting plants or had plans to reduce staff and plants in 1999. Once its acquisition of Herbet's was complete at the end of 1999, DuPont planned on closing six plants—in Italy, Germany, Mexico, and the United Kingdom—in addition to the plants already closed in Portugal and Brazil. With a targeted completion of March 2000, the closings were expected to eliminate 13,000 DuPont jobs and save the company $100 million per year.

The automotive OEM industry was much more specialized and not as fragmented—PPG, DuPont, and BASF had 29 percent of the market—yet prices for those products were also flat, in fact falling 2 percent. The trends for the automotive OEM market were for better inventory management. The companies had more of a say in the automakers' inventories, their orders, and warehouses. PPG went further, offering a "pay as you paint" plan. This way the automakers paid only for the number of cars painted. The OEMs were becoming more involved with their customers, extending their knowledge and research results. All of these policies made for lower administrative costs and reduced disputes between the paint companies and auto manufacturers.

Fresh from their success against the tobacco industry, the late 1990s saw lawyers and state attorneys general filing lawsuits against the paint and coatings industry. In late 1999 the state of Rhode Island filed suits against the Lead Industry Association (LIA) and eight paint industry leaders, including DuPont, Glidden, and Sherwin-Williams. Rhode Island claimed that the industry knew of the dangers of lead-based paints as early as the 1930s and that the LIA conspired with the industry to hide evidence that lead paint was a health hazard. The industry said they would vigorously defend themselves, noting that they had won similar cases in the past.

INDUSTRY LEADERS

Mergers and acquisitions modified the upper ranks of the U.S. paint industry in the mid-1990s, bringing an end to longtime leader Sherwin-Williams' dominance and adding new names to the list. Ongoing industry consolidation guaranteed that the standings would continue to change in this close-run horse race.

PPG Industries, Inc. Formerly known as Pittsburgh Plate Glass, this company was founded in 1883. As its name implied, paint was historically not its primary product: in the late 1960s, coatings constituted less than 20 percent of PPG's annual sales. By the mid-1990s, however, PPG had expanded its paint interests to become its primary division with over $3.5 billion in annual revenues in 1999, with automotive OEM leading the way with $1.4 billion. A spate of acquisitions in the mid-1990s vaulted the company over Sherwin-Williams to make it the top manufacturer in the industry. PPG acquired business from 1997 to 1999 that added $2 billion in sales and 9 of the 10 purchases from 1998 to 1999 were of coating companies. About half of PPG's operating profit in 1999 came from the automotive industry. Its key brands of architectural coatings included Lucite house paint and Olympic wood stain, both acquired from Clorox in 1989.

Sherwin-Williams Co. One of the founding firms of the American paint industry, Sherwin-Williams celebrated its 130th anniversary with estimated paint sales of $1.4 billion in 1995. The Cleveland-based company was America's largest paint manufacturer from 1905 until the early 1990s, when it relinquished its standing to PPG

Industries. Its vertical integration, which extended from raw materials and packaging to retail stores, helped the company become a low-cost manufacturer and the broadest distributor of architectural coatings in the United States.

Sherwin-Williams always emphasized architectural coatings, offered under the company's namesake brand and its acquired Dutch-Boy label, but by the early 1990s also produced industrial finishes for the automotive aftermarket and painting accessories. In 1990 Sherwin-Williams acquired Krylon brand aerosol paint and DeSoto, a major producer of architectural paints. In 1995 it merged with Pratt & Lambert United Inc., formerly two mid-sized companies that merged in 1994.

By 1999 Sherwin-Williams was the third-largest paint company in the world, with a strong position in the North American markets and, with the acquisition of Herbet's, a leader in the European market. Its worldwide sales were predicted to be $4 billion in 1999. In the third quarter of 1999 Sherwin-Williams paint group saw sales increase 4.9 percent, but not enough sales at home centers continued to plague the company; the consumer coatings group saw sales drop 6.3 percent.

Other key players included Masco, Rohm and Haas, Glidden Co., RPM, Valspar Corp., and Benjamin Moore and Co.

WORKFORCE

The paint and coatings industry employed an estimated 51,600 Americans in 1997, up from about 50,500 in 1996. Production workers comprised just over half of that total. Almost 25 percent of the industry's employees were managers and administrators, and 20 percent were professional chemists and sales representatives.

Production workers operated and fixed machinery, moved raw materials, and monitored the production process. High school graduates qualified for entry-level production jobs, and advancement into better-paying jobs requiring higher skills or more responsibility was possible through on-the-job experience or additional vocational training at a two-year technical college. Production workers in the industry earned about $605 a week.

Most administrative and management positions required a bachelor's degree and experience in the industry. Support workers often held two-year technical degrees or had some college, but these were not required.

Research and development specialists in the paint industry included chemists and chemical engineers. They typically conducted research and experimented with new products and processes. Advanced degrees were often essential for these positions. Some senior chemists were promoted to management positions.

Marketing and sales representatives promoted sales of their companies' products by developing new products, creating plans to market them, and advertising them to retail and industrial customers. These positions often required a degree in marketing, chemistry, or chemical engineering.

Employment in the paint and coatings industry was projected to continue its steady decline through the year 2005, with machine operators bearing the brunt of the cuts. Those positions were expected to decline by 29 percent. In line with the industry's strong emphasis on research and development, the number of chemists employed was expected to increase by over one-fourth by 2005. More efficient production processes, increased plant automation, growth of environmental awareness, health and safety concerns, and rising foreign competition were all expected to influence paint and coatings employment significantly and negatively.

AMERICA AND THE WORLD

Due to prohibitive shipping expenses, overseas trade historically did not contribute significantly to the U.S. paint market. Nevertheless, the United States dominated what global paint trade did exist after World War I, when Germany relinquished its top position in chemicals. But after World War II, foreign countries grew increasingly self-sufficient.

In 1960 the industry's total export business constituted less than 2 percent of total production. During this decade tariffs, quotas, licensing and exchange restrictions, and special import fees hamstrung U.S. coatings manufacturers' world trade. Trade barriers encouraged some paint producers to enter into joint ventures with their foreign competitors so that they could market their products overseas.

Trade liberalization and reductions in transportation costs in the 1990s encouraged international trade. By mid-decade, foreign sales represented a small, but growing percentage of total domestic revenue, with exports doubling from 1989 to 1993. More than half of the goods went to Canada and Mexico. While the U.S. paint industry maintained a positive balance of trade in the early 1990s, Canada, Germany, Japan, and Belgium had become the most significant importers.

In the first and second quarters of 1999 the industry exported $531.5 million of paints and coatings, while the United States imported $60.5 million. Architectural and OEM industrial segments accounted for about 40 percent each of that total, with 20 percent coming from special purpose coatings. Paintings and coatings are predicted to grow about 2 percent worldwide through 2003, with Europe growing about 1.5 and the Asia-Pacific Rim area about 2.5 percent.

Globalization. Globalization of the paint industry occurred as U.S. companies followed their primary OEM customers from America to the Far East and other lower-cost areas. Economic liberalization drew many of the world's leading paint manufacturers to China, where joint ventures promised a piece of double-digit sales growth. At the same time, foreign producers sought growth through acquisition of U.S. paint companies. These international movements enabled some large corporations to capitalize on their technological advantages in new markets.

Imperial Chemicals Industries (ICI) was an aggressive acquirer of U.S. paint companies, purchasing the Glidden paint operations of SCM Corp. in 1986 and both Grow Group and Fuller-O'Brien Paints in 1995. The Glidden acquisition marked ICI's entry into the U.S. paint industry and made the British conglomerate the world's largest paint company.

By 1995, 10 multinational companies held an estimated 60 percent of total world production, compared with one-fifth in 1980. By that time, the top five companies worldwide were ICI, Akzo-Nobel, PPG Industries, Sherwin-Williams, and Kansai. The Europeans and Japanese, historically the stiffest competitors of the United States, emerged in a particularly strong position internationally.

RESEARCH AND TECHNOLOGY

At the end of the 1990s, paints and coatings incorporated a myriad of chemical compounds uniquely formulated to fulfill the varied requirements of hundreds of thousands of applications. The need for regulatory compliance helped make research and development a paramount concern—and a major budget item. But the industry was not always so technically inclined.

From its inception in 1700 until the mid-1900s, paint formulation remained relatively unchanged. The switch from paste to ready-mixed paint in the 1860s and the mechanization of the manufacturing process in the mid-1880s were two significant innovations. But for the first half of the twentieth century, the manufacture of paint was a relatively simple process of mixing and grinding oils and pigments using "secret" recipes usually concocted by trial and error.

As previously mentioned, World War II inspired many innovations in paint formulation. One observer noted that there was more technological progress in the paint industry from 1947 to 1967 than in the previous 1,000 years. Product developments occurred so quickly that an estimated 90 percent of 1960's trade sales consisted of items that did not exist a decade before.

Most of the raw materials used in the contemporary paint industry were developed during the postwar era.

They were derived from petroleum, then mixed in varying proportions with specific chemical agents to produce such distinct characteristics as durability, elasticity, and chemical and thermal resistance. By the mid-1960s, the major industrial paint manufacturers offered as many as 20,000 different products.

The 1980s and 1990s brought the industry's most significant and rapid changes. As one industry executive told *Industrial Paint & Powder* in 1994, "Technology has changed more in the last eight years than in the previous 80 years of our coatings business." At the start of the twenty-first century, paint manufacturers were developing paints with fewer chemical compounds, moving from solvent-based to water-based products. The industry was also moving more toward powder coatings, as they were less harmful to the environment.

Color. During the late 1950s some manufacturers of architectural paint offered an increased selection of colors to consumers by shipping a white base paint to retailers with separate oil or powdered pigments. The desired paint color would be mixed at the point of sale upon the customer's request. This system gave the customer a wider choice of colors (more than 1,000 in some cases) and reduced the retailer's risk of overstocking an unpopular color. By 1960 these "custom" systems constituted about 5 percent of retail paint sales.

Latex Revolution. The architectural paint market, and eventually the entire industry, was revolutionized by the introduction of waterborne, or latex, paint. Unlike its oil-based predecessors, latex paint required no ventilation, was nonflammable and scrubbable, gave a good finish, was easy to remove from brushes, and dried in about 20 minutes.

Latex ascent began in the industry in the 1950s. Before that time, solvent- or oil-based products dominated gallonage consumption, while waterborne, high-solids, and powdered coatings constituted only 10 percent of industry volume. By the early 1990s water-based paints alone constituted over 75 percent of gallonage. Convenience was clearly a factor in the widespread commercial acceptance of water-based paints, but in the 1970s, another strong influence drove their industrial acceptance: government regulation.

Government Regulation Drives Innovation. Regulation of the industry accelerated dramatically during the environmentally conscious 1970s, when federal clean air regulations were adopted to encourage the production of less-polluting, less-toxic paints. By the beginning of the 1980s nearly every aspect of the paint business was regulated. The Occupational Safety and Health Administration monitored the workplace. The Environmental Protection Agency regulated the introduction, generation, transportation, treatment, and disposal of hazardous materials used in or produced by the coatings industry. The Consumer Product Safety Commission protected paint customers by controlling what could be bought and sold.

Although many in the paint industry resisted government efforts to monitor the business, state and federal regulation actually encouraged several technological advances. An early example of this phenomenon occurred just after the turn of the century, when legislation was enacted in North Dakota requiring formula labels on house paints. The idea gained popularity among consumers and members of Congress throughout the country. But paint manufacturers feared revealing their "secret formulas," and warned that the new law would inhibit research on new formulations. In hindsight, the rules encouraged the use of quality ingredients and fostered more scientific formulations.

Lead. Once a primary component of paint, lead ranked as the top environmental threat to children's health in the 1990s. Lead poisoning affected the nervous system, the gastrointestinal tract, and the blood-forming tissues, and was especially harmful to children. The deleterious effects of lead (which was also used in gasoline, ceramic finishes, plumbing, and many other products) were discovered in the 1930s. White lead pigments were essentially eliminated from architectural paints in the 1940s, but it was not until 1977 that the use of lead-based paints was outlawed in the United States.

Government and medical reports published in the late 1980s and early 1990s revealed evidence that lead poisoning could occur with much lower doses than was previously thought, so the lead problem was more pervasive than earlier believed. Some public health officials estimated that there could be accessible lead paint in up to 42 million homes and apartments housing 12 million children.

In the increasingly litigious American society, paint manufacturers rightly feared a wave of lawsuits. Some analysts predicted that lawsuits involving lead-paint poisoning could eventually eclipse asbestos suits. And in 1993, all paint manufacturers in California were assessed special fees under that state's Childhood Lead Poisoning Act of 1991. Paint industry spokespersons contended that the fees unfairly punished manufacturers and sellers who may not have been in business when the lead paint was sold, and that parents, contractors, and property managers should share the blame and the cost.

Superfund. In addition to the environmental concerns of producing and applying paints and coatings, manufacturers increasingly bore responsibility for disposal. Proposed in 1979, the Comprehensive Environmental Response, Compensation and Liability Act of 1980 (also known as Superfund) mandated the accumulation of a multimillion-dollar fund to pay for the cleanup of oil and hazardous waste spills and disposal sites. The fund would be amassed through fees assessed to businesses, municipalities, and individuals who were designated as ''potentially responsible parties'' in the pollution of the sites. Since the Resource Conservation and Recovery Act of 1976 had already classified paint wastes as hazardous materials, virtually all paint manufacturers found themselves subject to fee collection under Superfund. Representing the paint industry, the National Paint and Coatings Association (NPCA) argued that it was unfair to single out certain industries for problems created by the entire society.

Volatile Organic Compounds. Organic solvents, the oils that liquefied many paints, were blamed for some air pollution. As paint dried, the liquid portion evaporated. When the liquid was an organic solvent, volatile organic compounds (VOCs) were released in the drying process. VOCs reacted with sunlight to contribute to smog. State VOC regulations started to proliferate in the wake of 1977's Clean Air Act and subsequent amendments, which required states to regulate geographic areas that failed to meet ambient air quality standards. Control of VOCs was a significant aspect of compliance. California was one of the first, and most stringent, state-level regulators.

Rather than resisting these state laws, the NPCA called for uniform federal guidelines, as opposed to the confusing array of state and local initiatives that cropped up. The NPCA supported the ''bubble concept'' of plant compliance, which allowed individual factories to develop plant-wide emission reduction plans using an average emission level of VOCs. Some companies went further, aiming for ''zero-waste generation:'' the elimination of plant emissions and reuse and recycling of materials.

Four basic coatings designed to save energy and pollute less were developed. For the most part, they exemplified different strategies to achieve the same purpose: to reduce the proportion of toxic solvents in paint. One industry executive predicted the eventual eradication of solvents from coatings. The development of water-soluble paint, for example, reduced the use of petroleum-based solvent in paints by about 90 percent. High-solids paints contained more resins and pigments than solvents. Accelerated cure coatings were dried by ultraviolet light or an electron beam. Powdered coatings, which contained virtually no organic solvents, also sidestepped the VOC problem. New application processes also helped reduce the volume of paint required to perform a particular function. Most of these products were intended for industrial use.

The Glidden Co. became the first paint manufacturer to introduce major architectural paint lines containing no VOCs, in 1992. Although consumers in the 1990s were clearly interested in environmentally sound products, zero-VOC paints had several drawbacks, including a reduced range of colors and lower performance.

Polyurethane automotive coatings for OEM and refinishing application offered durability and enhanced beauty at the same time. These included water-based coatings for cans, prefinished wood, and flat board.

Powder and radiation-curable coatings were considered two of the more exciting new developments, with a growth rate of 12.5 percent from 1990 to 1992. Industry analysts pegged growth at 15 percent through 1999. Powder coatings were sprayed on dry and electrically adhered to the surface. Major markets for powder coatings in the mid-1990s were metal finishing, appliances, automobile applications, and architectural products. Radiation-curable coatings, intended for use on vinyl flooring, wood furniture and paneling, paper, and metals, were hardened by ultraviolet light or electronic-beam energy. Although the conversion to these new techniques was costly, such factors as increased material utilization, reduced energy and lab costs, and the elimination of solvent emissions promised to more than offset the initial cost disadvantages. Growth in the powder and radiation-curable coatings segments outstripped that of more traditional paints and coatings. These products were expected to eventually replace many conventional solvent-based coatings.

FURTHER READING

Bourguignon, Edward W. ''Paint Industry Enjoys Strong First Half 1996.'' *American Paint & Coatings Journal,* 11 November 1996, 19.

Darnay, Arsen J., ed. *Manufacturing USA.* Detroit: Gale Research, 1996.

Fattah, Hassan. ''Paints and Coatings: Mergers Create an Altered Image.'' *Chemical Week,* 23 October 1996, 33-34.

Minnis, Glenn. ''LIA, Paint Makers Face R.I. Suit.'' *American Metal Market,* 2 November 1999.

National Paint & Coatings Association. ''Paint & Coatings Industry Facts.'' 15 December 1999. Available from http://www.paint.org/ind_info/facts.htm.

Padow, Mark. ''Not a Bad Year, Most Say, All Things Considered.'' *American Paint & Coatings Journal,* 16 December 1996, 17-18.

———. ''Sherwin-Williams, ICI, Others Were 'Serious' about Acquisitions in '95.'' *American Paint & Coatings Journal,* 29 April 1996, 14-15.

''Paints, Coatings Manufacturers Sales Highest in Decade.'' *American Paint & Coatings Journal,* 15 January 1996, 11.

''PPG Industries: Deemed to Be One of the Biggest Makers of Automotive & Industrial Coatings in the World.'' *Paint and Coatings Industry,* July 1996, 49.

Reilly, Christopher. ''Moderate Growth, Rising Prices Forecast in Mature Market.'' *Purchasing,* 7 October 1999.

Sissell, Kara. ''Ethyl, DuPont Named in Lead Poisoning Lawsuit.'' *Chemical Week,* 13 October 1999.

Standard & Poor's Industry Surveys. 8 February 1996, C51-C54.

U.S. Census Bureau. "Current Industrial Reports, Paint, Varnish and Lacquer - Second Quarter 1999." Available from http://www.census.gov/cir/www/ma28f.html.

Van Arnum, Patricia. "High-Value Deals Mark Coatings Industry." *Chemical Market Reporter,* 11 October 1999.

Walsh, Kerri. "Sherwin-Williams Names Connor CEO; Earnings Beats Estimates." *Chemical Week,* 3 November 1999.

Walsh, Kerri, and Rick Mullin. "Paints and Coatings: A Whole Lot of Shakin' Going On." *Chemical Week,* 20 October 1999.

SIC 2861

GUM AND WOOD CHEMICALS

The gum and wood chemicals industry comprises of establishments primarily engaged in manufacturing hardwood and softwood distillation products, natural dyes, tanning materials, and related products. Companies that make synthetic organic tanning materials and synthetic organic dyes are classified in **SIC 2869: Industrial Organic Chemicals, Not Elsewhere Classified** and **SIC 2865: Cyclic Organic Crudes and Intermediates, and Organic Dyes and Pigments,** respectively. Gum and wood chemical producers are part of the larger, industrial organic chemical industry.

NAICS CODE(S)

325191 (Gum and Wood Chemical Manufacturing)

INDUSTRY SNAPSHOT

According to the U.S. Census Bureau, 63 establishments manufactured gum and wood chemicals in 1997. They shipped $815 million worth of goods (up from about $776 million in 1993), spent $349 million on materials, and paid $34 million for buildings and other structures, machinery, and equipment. About 27 percent of those businesses had at least 20 employees. These larger operations accounted for about 93 percent of the industry's shipments. Missouri had the largest concentration of businesses in this classification.

BACKGROUND AND DEVELOPMENT

This industry grew substantially after World War II when construction companies, for example, needed wood treatment chemicals, adhesives, and sealants. The increasing popularity of outdoor barbecue grills during the 1950s and 1960s boosted sales of charcoal briquettes. Revenues and profits declined during the 1980s, however. Synthetic chemicals displaced many natural wood and gum chemicals in everything from dyes to sealants. In addition, environmental laws restricted the burning of charcoal.

Like organic chemicals derived from petroleum and natural gas, thousands of natural chemical products can be distilled from wood. Turpentine, for example, is extracted from pine gum and pine wood. Numerous oils and finishes can also be obtained from pine or other woods, as can many dyes, fuels, and resins.

By the mid-1990s the outlook seemed brighter as environmental concerns about synthetics brought renewed interest in natural chemicals, such as dyes and fuel additives. At that time about 40 percent of the industry's revenues came from sales of hardwood charcoal briquettes, 30 percent came from hardwood distillates such as oak extract, and 17 percent came from softwood distillates such as resin and turpentine.

Most merchandise in this category is sold to individual consumers who primarily purchase charcoal, turpentine, and other products for home use. Manufacturers of plastics used 11 percent of production in the early 1990s to create base resins and additives. Other industries used distillates and extracts to manufacture soaps, detergents, paperboard, drugs, paints, printing ink, leather tanning chemicals, rubber, adhesives, sealants, and many other goods. About 12 percent of production in the early 1990s was exported.

In 1995 weak demand, low prices, stiff competition (especially from cheaper Asian products), and new styles of clothing brought the U.S. dyes industry to a ten-year low, according to *Chemical Week* magazine. Prices throughout the gum and wood chemicals industry dropped substantially in 1996, according to *Chemical Market Reporter.*

CURRENT CONDITIONS

The Census Bureau estimated that in 1997 the industry shipped about $357 million worth of hardwood charcoal and charcoal briquettes, $263 million worth of crude tall oil, $51 million worth of refined tall oil, $20 million worth of rosin and other tall oil derivatives, and $239 million worth of other gum and wood chemicals.

INDUSTRY LEADERS

Among companies that made gum and wood chemicals as their primary business, Royal Oak Enterprises Inc. (Roswell, Georgia) was one of the leaders with 400 employees and sales of $61 million in 1998. Royal Oak was the largest privately owned charcoal manufacturer in the world, and it made more private label (store brand) charcoal than any other company.

Hickory Specialties Inc. (a subsidiary of Bob Evans Farms Inc. based in Brentwood, Tennessee) also specialized in charcoal. It had 150 employees and estimated sales of $29 million. Campfire Charcoal Company Inc. (Jacksonville, Texas) had 65 employees and estimated sales of

$20 million. It was a subsidiary of Arrow Industries Inc., which was part of the ConAgra Inc. conglomerate.

WORKFORCE

This industry employed 2,267 people in 1997, including 1,708 production workers who earned an average hourly wage of $14.94. The total workforce had been about 3,500 people in the early 1980s and had dropped below 2,500 in the early 1990s.

FURTHER READING

Darnay, Arsen J., ed. *Manufacturing USA.* 5th ed. Detroit: Gale Research, 1996.

Foroohar, Kambiz. ''A Tough Market Forces Dyes Suppliers to Realign.'' *Chemical Weeks,* 2 August 1995.

Lerner, Mathew. ''Gum Arabic Price Decrease Makes Suppliers Optimistic.'' *Chemical Marketing Reporter,* 17 June 1996.

Meltzer, Mark. ''Royal Oak to Build its Headquarters in Roswell: Charcoal Maker Plans Corporate Campus with Lake.'' *Atlanta Business Chronicle,* 6 March 1998.

U.S. Department of Commerce. Census Bureau. *1996 Annual Survey of Manufactures.* Washington, D.C.: GPO, 1998.

U.S. Department of Commerce. Census Bureau. *1997 Economic Census.* Washington, D.C.: GPO, 1999. Available from http://www.census.gov/prod/ec97/97m3251h.pdf.

SIC 2865

CYCLIC ORGANIC CRUDES AND INTERMEDIATES AND ORGANIC DYES AND PIGMENTS

This industry covers establishments primarily engaged in manufacturing cyclic organic crudes and intermediates and organic dyes and pigments. Important products of this industry include (1) aromatic chemicals such as benzene, toluene, mixed xylenes, and naphthalene; (2) synthetic organic dyes; and (3) synthetic organic pigments.

NAICS CODE(S)

325110 (Petrochemical Manufacturing)
325132 (Organic Dye and Pigment Manufacturing)
325192 (Cyclic Crude and Intermediate Manufacturing)

INDUSTRY SNAPSHOT

Organic chemicals contain carbon, are usually combustible, are mostly insoluble in water, have liquid or solid forms, and have relatively low melting points. Aromatics are included in a group called *basic organics,* which also includes aliphatics and methanol. These substances are obtained directly from raw materials, primarily crude oil and natural gas. Intermediates are often grouped with solvents and are made from basic chemicals for the purpose of making other chemicals and chemical products.

The 50 U.S. companies in the cyclic crudes and intermediates industry employed 8,000 workers and shipped almost $6 billion worth of products in 1997, according to the U.S. Census Bureau. Almost 93 percent of these shipments consisted of cyclic intermediates, while the remaining 7 percent included tar, tar crudes, and tar pitches. In the dye and pigment manufacturing portion of this product class, 112 firms employed over 8,000 employees in 1997 and shipped $2.5 billion worth of products. Organic dyes made up 40 percent of these shipments, and pigments and toners accounted for 60 percent. Industry output provided an important supply of base manufacturing material for pharmaceutical, dye, fuel, and agricultural sectors.

Crude industry sales surged by about 10 percent from 1992 to 1997. Prices declined in the early 1990s because of large capacity additions that came into effect. During the early 1990s, temporary price upswings caused by the war in the Persian Gulf were the only relief periods for the industry. Sales improved again by 1994 and into 1995 as prices and margins began to rise. This period was the industry's best financial performance since the late 1980s. In 1997 varying levels of growth were observed in all major segments of the industry.

One reason for the instability of the industry was the inability to predict the supply and demand for organic materials. For example, benzene, styrene, and mixed xylenes saturated the market from July through December 1996, while cyclohexane and phenol were not being produced rapidly enough to meet demand. Demand for some organic products, such as toluene, fluctuated from year to year, making it difficult to gage production.

The synthetic organic dye industry also experienced growth from 1992 to 1997, with an increase in shipments of about 25 percent; the pigment portion declined about 20 percent during the same period.

ORGANIZATION AND STRUCTURE

Industrial organic chemicals are created from substances that contain carbon, such as petroleum, coal, and natural gas. Though inorganic chemicals may also contain carbon, they are found within the earth's crust and derive from materials without animal or plant origins. The aromatics classified in this industry are distinguished from other organics by their closed-ring molecular structure. This structure allows them to be combined with other chemicals, including inorganics, to make a vast array of intermediate compounds. Intermediates are consumed by other industries for the production of plastics, pharmaceuticals, and fertilizers.

In 1992 chemicals classified in this industry constituted 20 percent of the $53 billion U.S. industrial organic chemical industry, which also includes gum and wood chemicals and industrial organics not elsewhere classified. Industrial organic chemicals, in turn, represented 66 percent of the overall chemical industry, which includes inorganic and agricultural chemicals. The encompassing chemical and related products industry represents a $230 billion business, of which organics account for about one-third. Many products and compounds generated in the fine chemicals industry, however, are used to produce other chemicals and related goods.

In the early 1990s, 20 percent, or about $2.2 billion, of the $11.0 billion worth of aromatic, intermediate, and synthetic dye output was consumed by manufacturers within the industry to produce other fine chemicals. For example, an aromatics producer might sell benzene to a company that makes the intermediate chlorobenzene. Plastics materials and resin manufacturers consumed 13 percent of U.S. production, as did the organic synthetic fiber industry. Though they each accounted for less than 3 percent of the fragmented market, other major customers included petroleum refiners, pharmaceutical companies, paint and coating manufacturers, and semiconductor producers. Exports made up 13 percent of industry shipments during the early 1990s.

The three primary aromatic chemicals used to create intermediates are benzene, xylene, and toluene. These three chemicals represent about 10 percent of U.S. industry output. Intermediates created using these base organics, however, account for an additional 70 percent of total production. Benzene, the simplest and most widely used aromatic, is combined with sulfuric acid and other chemicals to create many intermediates. U.S. manufacturers generated over 1.6 billion gallons of benzene in 1993. Benzene intermediates are used to produce plastic resins, epoxy, nylon, polyurethanes, synthetic rubber, and detergents.

The most common derivative of benzene is ethyl benzene/styrene, which accounts for 50 percent of demand for this aromatic. Nearly 21 billion pounds of ethyl benzene and styrene were produced in 1992. Styrene is a major ingredient in plastics and synthetic rubber. Cumene/phenol and cyclohexane represented 21 and 14 percent, respectively, of benzene-derivative sales. Phenol is used to produce adhesives and high-grade plastics and epoxies. Other major intermediates in this category include: nitrobenzene/aniline (6 percent), alkybenzene (2 percent), and chlorobenzene (2 percent).

Xylene is primarily utilized as a gasoline additive and a solvent. It is separated into three commercial substances: paraxylene, orthoxylene, and metaxylene. Paraxylene derivatives are used to make polyester fiber and films, beverage bottles, and specialty engineering resins. Consumption of this chemical topped 5.6 billion

pounds in 1992. Also in 1992, 918 million pounds of orthoxylene were generated. Orthoxylene is required to make intermediates that can be utilized in the production of plasticizers (plastic additives) and polyester resins. Metaxylene has limited uses in the manufacture of coatings and plastics.

The last primary aromatic chemical is toluene. In 1992, the industry produced 833 million pounds of toluene. This aromatic is used to create benzene. End markets for toluene also include manufacturers of adhesives, solvents, photographic film, textiles, pharmaceuticals, inks, and coatings.

Besides aromatics and their intermediate offspring, organic dyes and pigments each make up about 8 percent of industry sales. Tar and pitch compounds round out industry offerings, capturing 4 percent of sales revenue. Approximately 245 million pounds of synthetic organic dyes and pigments, valued at $761 million, were shipped by U.S. manufacturers in 1991. Two-thirds of dye and pigment production was consumed by textile industries. Dyes are typically obtained from petroleum through lengthy chemical processes and must conform to rigid safety standards before they can be used to color food, clothing, and other goods.

BACKGROUND AND DEVELOPMENT

William Henry Perkin (1838-1907), an Englishman and the father of the organic chemical industry, was the first chemist to synthesize an organic chemical for commercial use. In 1856 he accidentally created mauve, a synthetic dye, from a piece of coal tar. Friedrich Kekule von Stradonitz (1829-1896) was the first to explain Perkin's invention when he proposed his breakthrough theory of the benzene ring in 1865. During the remainder of the nineteenth century, German chemists developed most of the dye classes, and many of the individual dyes, that were still being used in the early 1990s.

The advancement of aromatics, intermediates, and dyes, in the wake of Kekule's discovery, were considered relatively unimportant outside of Germany. It wasn't until World War I that Great Britain, France, and the United States frantically developed an organic chemical industry. World War II also brought massive industry expansion, especially as producers learned to derive aromatics from petroleum rather than coal tar. By the end of World War II, the United States was the major global supplier of aromatics and intermediates. Industry growth was rampant during the postwar U.S. economic expansion.

The aromatic, intermediate, and synthetic dye industry grew at a healthy rate of 5 percent per year between 1982 and 1990. Though this reflected a decline in growth rates compared to the 1960s and 1970s, it exceeded gains achieved by most other U.S. manufacturing sectors. Sales rose from $7.1 billion in 1982 to $10.9 billion by 1990.

The demand for new high-performance intermediates, particularly by pharmaceutical and agricultural sectors, drove this sales growth.

In addition to revenue gains, producers also benefited from increases in productivity and the development of new processing techniques during the decade. Productivity gains of approximately 4 percent per year during the 1980s were the result of massive capital investments in automation and information systems. These investments allowed manufacturers to eliminate both production workers and managers. Indeed, as production volume steadily rose throughout the 1980s, industry employment gradually shrank. The work force declined from more than 27,000 in the early 1980s to about 23,000 by the early 1990s. In addition to cutting labor costs, many manufacturers were able to reduce productions costs through advanced processing techniques.

Despite massive capital investments surpassing $43 billion during the 1980s, productivity and manufacturing gains were substantially offset by changing dynamics in the global organic chemical industry. Two primary factors stunting profit growth in the 1980s and demand into the 1990s were increased foreign competition and environmental regulations. In addition, regulatory intervention in important end markets, such as pharmaceuticals, was hindering competitors. Also hurting industry participants in the early 1990s was a U.S. and global economic recession. Overcapacity, a result of slower-than-expected growth in the early 1990s, was causing severe price suppression and reduced profits for most companies. Even as the United States experienced a modest recovery in 1992 and 1993, overseas markets remained flat.

During the mid-1990s, aromatic, intermediate, and dye producers continued to suffer from downward price pressures due to oversupply. For example, while the demand for styrene grew about 13 percent between 1990 and 1993, excess production capacity in the United States crushed price growth in that segment. Many producers of benzene derivatives were experiencing a similar scenario, as were producers of xylenes. Only phenol suppliers dodged the burden of oversupply. In 1993 U.S. prices and demand recovered slightly, but primary global markets remained recessed.

Besides slack markets, increasingly stringent environment regulations were also taking their toll in the mid-1990s. A string of new rules implemented during the 1980s to cap hazardous waste emissions were heavily impacting manufacturers. The Clinton administration supported efforts to reduce waste from this high-polluting industry. The Clean Air Act Amendment of 1990, the Environmental Protection Agency's (EPA) Toxic Inventory Release (TIR) program, the federal Emergency Planning and Community Right-to-Know Act, and voluntary Chemical Manufacturers Association (CMA) programs

were just a few of the initiatives expected to cost the industry millions of dollars during the mid-1990s.

Perhaps the greatest challenge for most intermediate and dye producers in the mid-1990s was growing foreign competition. Although the European Community, Japan, and the United States remained the primary global suppliers for this industry, emerging industrial nations posed a real threat to their dominance. East Asian nations, excluding Japan, were capturing market share, as were producers in South America, Eastern Europe, India, and other developing regions.

Access to cheap labor and freedom from strict environmental regulations were expected to help manufacturers in these nations advance rapidly in the mid-1990s. For example, the average Chinese worker cost a company $1,000 per year in 1992. By contrast, the average U.S. aromatic production worker received over $35,000 in salary alone. As a result, dye imports to the United States almost doubled between 1981 and 1991 as the total value of U.S. dye production fell. Although intermediates had fared much better than dyes, U.S. global organic market share diminished from 30 to 25 percent between 1988 and 1992.

CURRENT CONDITIONS

Benzene. From 1982 to 1997 global demand for benzene doubled, and steady growth was predicted to continue at about 5 percent through the year 2000. Demand in 1996 was more than 27.0 million metric tons and was expected to increase to about 28.5 metric tons in 1997. The top U.S. benzene producers, including Amoco, Dow, Exxon, and Shell, controlled roughly half, or one billion gallons, of the total 2.4 billion gallons of U.S. benzene production.

Cyclohexane. Demand for cyclohexane was expected to grow from the 1.0 million metric tons of 1996 to approximately 1.1 million tons in 1997. No new cyclohexane plants were expected to come into operation until 1999, when Chevron planned to open a 75-million-gallon facility in Saudi Arabia. The market will have little impetus to change until this facility is built.

Toluene. The end of 1996 saw toluene at its highest price levels since early 1995. This was because toluene was the aromatic of choice for blenders who were adding octane to their gasolines.

Xylenes. In 1996 an increase in crude prices and a drop in chemical prices occurred. Many producers had to operate refineries at minimum levels, which significantly cut the production of mixed xylenes. After reducing inventories and production levels, supplies of mixed xylenes were decreased, allowing prices to rise again.

Styrene. Worldwide demand of styrene was approximately 17 million metric tons in 1996. With annual growth at 4.5 percent, demand should approach 18 million metric tons in 1997.

Phenol. In 1996 the U.S. demand for phenol was more than 4.1 billion pounds. By the year 2000, if growth remained at 3 percent, it was expected to be over 4.7 billion pounds.

Dyes and Pigments. Demand for synthetic organic pigments and dyes will increase, but U.S. production will likely remain stagnant or will decline as exports flood the market. Pharmaceutical intermediates and fuel additives will offer some of the greatest profit potential, as will environmentally safe compounds. To remain competitive in the global markets of the 1990s, U.S. producers have been forced to focus their efforts on the development of high-tech, high-margin specialty intermediates and dyes. Consumers of large-volume, low-tech, commodity-like aromatics, intermediates, and dyes will continue to seek low-cost producers in emerging nations.

INDUSTRY LEADERS

The fine chemicals industry is consolidated in comparison to most other U.S. manufacturing industries. There were only 180 U.S. companies competing in the early 1990s. The top five companies generated a combined revenue of approximately $1.7 billion. The majority of the top 25 firms, moreover, had sales of over $50 million and employed more than 300 workers. By contrast, the bottom 140 competitors each generated revenues of less than $1 million and employed fewer than 100 people.

In 1997 the largest company in the industry was First Mississippi Corp. of Jackson, Mississippi. It had total sales of $645 million and employed 1,600 people. Crompton and Knowles Corp. of Stamford, Connecticut, was the second largest with sales of $590 million and employing 2,700. Clariant Corp. of Charlotte, North Carolina, had sales of $400 million and employed 1,200 people. Systems Bio-Industries Inc. of Trevose, Pennsylvania, had sales of $300 million and employed 600. Warner-Jenkinson Co. of St. Louis, Missouri, had sales of about $140 million and employed 300 people. Major aromatics and intermediates producers primarily active in other industries included Exxon, Dow Chemical, Shell, Occidental Petroleum, Amoco, and Lyondell Petrochemical.

In terms of production by state, Texas led Louisiana, Pennsylvania, and Ohio in the production of cyclic intermediates with over half of the total U.S. production in 1997. South Carolina led the synthetic organic dye industry, while Ohio dominated the production of synthetic organic pigments, lakes, and toners in 1997.

WORKFORCE

Into the mid-1990s there were limited job prospects in the industry. Opportunities were being depleted as a result of productivity gains at the expense of the labor force, movement of production facilities overseas, and increased competition. Positions for chemical equipment controllers, which account for about 9 percent of the work force, are predicted to plunge by 25 percent between 1990 and 2005. Similarly, opportunities for machine operators and laborers will decrease. Among the last job positions expected to decrease are for general managers, top executives, and support staff, which will plummet by about 20 percent. On the other hand, jobs in sales and marketing should rise by about 5 percent, and engineering positions should increase by 1 to 4 percent.

AMERICA AND THE WORLD

In the early 1990, with sales of about $11 billion per year, U.S. producers accounted for roughly 25 percent of global fine chemicals output. The European Community met 40 percent of worldwide demand, and Japan represented 20 percent of production. Like the United States, which shipped $1.4 billion of its output overseas in 1992, Japan and the European Community were major chemical exporters within the global marketplace. These three regions also represented most of the world's chemical consumption.

In the mid-1990s market share held by all major producers was steadily eroding. For example, in 1993, Eastern European and South American manufacturers generated approximately $2 billion and $1 billion worth of product respectively. At the same time, they were striving to boost exports. Also, East Asia, which sold $2 billion to $3 billion of aromatics and intermediates in 1992, was growing its output by 8 to 10 percent per year.

Two of the fastest growing export nations were China and India. China exported $800 million worth of intermediates in 1992, while India shipped approximately $500 million. Both countries were expected to surpass U.S. exports by the turn of the century. "China is in a major, major buildup," said Joshua Pratter, manager of technical marketing and planning at ICG, a California-based intermediates producer, in the August 30, 1993 issue of *Chemical Marketing Reporter.* "They're buying a lot of technology." China designated the petrochemical industry (including cyclic intermediates and all related manufactures) as one of four 'pillar' industries for its Ninth Five-Year Plan ending in 2000; however, the Asian economic crisis slowed China's ambitions in fine chemicals, as did severe flooding, high unemployment, a weakening of domestic demand for these products, and extensive smuggling into China. South Korea experienced heavy losses in this industry into 1998 and is seeking foreign investment. The Asian crisis is also expected to have a spill-over effect into Latin America because of the extent of trade among the nations of these two continents.

Another trend taking place in the early 1990s was the movement of U.S. production facilities overseas. Dow Chemical, for example, received a license in 1992 to build a polystyrene plant at Map Ta Phut, Thailand. This plant would be its fifth in that country. Many other producers were moving production to Mexico, Singapore, and other developing regions. By the late 1990s major restructuring, downsizing, and merging were occurring in Asia (to absorb financially stressed joint ventures) and in countries like Canada, where industrial giants are consolidating to fund new plants to produce fuels additives, among others.

In the pigment industry, prices remain depressed (as of 1998 figures) because of oversupplies and environmental regulations. Demand is expected to grow most significantly in China, India, and Southeast Asia. Eastern Europe is experiencing serious shortages of pigments, so demand is increasing there, although the beginning base for growth is much smaller than in Asia. Organic pigments are expected to grow faster than inorganic pigments, and inorganics based on heavy metals such as cadmium and chromium are expected to be withdrawn almost entirely from the marketplace because of their high environmental risk. Iron oxide (used extensively in pigments for the construction industry) is also experiencing growth in the late 1990s, and producers in Western Europe are the world's top suppliers. According to the Stanford Research Institute, the pigments industry worldwide should grow 2-3 percent per year through 2001.

RESEARCH AND TECHNOLOGY

U.S. manufacturers were making capital investments during the early 1990s of more than $5.5 billion per year. This represented an investment, per employee, about five times greater than the average U.S. manufacturer. Indeed, the United States maintained the most productive and technologically advanced intermediates industry in the world. In the 1980s and early 1990s, the industry spent billions of dollars attempting to raise productivity through automation and information systems, to increase capacity, and to comply with environmental laws. By the mid-1990s, new product research and development were the primary investment focus.

Intermediate and dye manufacturers were scrambling to develop high-tech molecules and compounds to open new markets and battle foreign commodity producers. For example, advances in intermediates used to make pharmaceuticals allowed the most savvy producers to reap significant rewards. Also in demand were high-performance intermediates that could be used to make cleaner fuel additives, new resins and fibers, better rubber, and environmentally friendly chemicals.

In the early to mid-1990s, numerous breakthroughs were occurring throughout the industry. In 1993, Mon-

santo Corp. was perfecting a method for producing aromatics using an environmentally safe process. The development offered potentially major commercial consequences.

An important growth area predicted for the late 1990s is peptide intermediates. Drugs using peptides were already being developed in the early 1990s. These drugs can be used to cause chemical changes in the human body that fight off diseases. Peptide-based drugs offered potential therapy for cancer, AIDS, and other major afflictions.

FURTHER READING

Anderson, Earl V.. "Foreign Trade: U.S. Chemical Trade Surplus Declines." *Chemical & Engineering News,* 13 December 1993.

"The Battles of the Alliances Begins." *Chemical Week,* 22 July 1998.

———. "Japan: Once Booming Economy Struggles Through Times." *Chemical & Engineering News,* 13 December 1993.

———. "Developing Nation's Chemical Exports Surge." *Chemical & Engineering News,* 2 August 1993.

Bahner, Benedict. "Intermediates '93: Hanging in There." *Chemical Marketing Reporter,* 30 August 1993.

Brand, Tony. "Aromatics: A Mixed Review." *Chemical Market Reporter* 251 no.2, 13 January 1997.

"Chemical Industry R&D Rose 7 percent in 1992." *Chemical & Engineering News,* 23 August 1993.

"Facts & Figures for the Chemical Industry." *Chemical & Engineering News,* 28 June, 1993.

"Industrial Organic Chemicals: Growth Projected for Organics." *Standard and Poor's Industry Surveys.* New York: Standard and Poor's Corporation, 1997.

Jiang, David and Warburton, Richard. "China's petrochemical industry: a waking giant." *Chemistry and Industry.* 19 April 1999.

Layman, Patricia. "Europe: Definite Though Modest Recovery Forecast for 1994." *Chemical & Engineering News,* 13 December 1993.

Loesel, Andrew. "Intermediates '93: Getting Smarter." *Chemical Marketing Reporter,* 30 August 1993.

Naude, Alice. "Intermediates '93: Waiting for Harvest." *Chemical Marketing Reporter,* 30 August 1993.

Reisch, Marc S. "New Woes May Trigger Another Shakeout for U.S. Dye Producers." *Chemical & Engineering News,* 5 July 1993.

———. "Top 50 Chemicals Production Recovered Last Year." *Chemical & Engineering News,* 12 April 1993.

Rzadzki, John. "Intermediates '93: Region on the Rise." *Chemical Marketing Reporter,* 30 August 1993.

Shon, Melissa. "Intermediates '93: Shakeout Time." *Chemical Marketing Reporter,* 30 August 1993.

Sissell, Kara. "Latin America: Evaluating Strengths." *Chemical Week,* 15 July 1998.

Springer, Neil. "Intermediates '93: Looking Outward." *Chemical Marketing Reporter,* 30 August 1993.

Standard & Poor's Industry Surveys. New York: Standard & Poor's Corporation, 20 January 1994.

Storck, William J. "United States: Chemical Industry Lackluster This Year." *Chemical & Engineering News,* 13 December 1993.

Tilton, Helga. "Asian Economic Crisis Worsens And May Spread to Latin America." *Chemical Market Reporter,* 21 September 1998.

Tomasula, Dean. "Cumene Yet to Benefit From Economic Recovery." *Chemical Marketing Reporter,* 3 January 1994.

U.S. Census Bureau. "Cyclic Crude and Intermediate Manufacturing." *1997 Economic Census: Manufacturing Industry Series.* August 1999.

U.S. Census Bureau. "Synthetic Organic Dye and Pigment Manufacturing." *1997 Economic Census: Manufacturing Industry Series.* August 1999.

U.S. Department of Commerce. International Trade Administration. *U.S. Industrial Outlook 1993.* Washington: GPO, 1993.

Wood, Andrew. "No Relief in Sight for Pigment Makers." *Chemical Week,* 12 August 1998.

SIC 2869

INDUSTRIAL ORGANIC CHEMICALS, NOT ELSEWHERE CLASSIFIED

This industry includes companies primarily engaged in the production of organic chemicals used by other manufacturing industries. It encompasses the majority of U.S. organic chemical output and represents the single largest segment of the overall chemical industry. Materials created using these chemicals, such as plastic and fiber, are classified in their respective industries.

NAICS CODE(S)

325110 (Petrochemical Manufacturing)
325188 (All Other Inorganic Chemical Manufacturing)
325193 (Ethyl Alcohol Manufacturing)
325120 (Industrial Gas Manufacturing)
325199 (All Other Basic Organic Chemical Manufacturing)

INDUSTRY SNAPSHOT

Scientists began producing synthetic organic chemicals in the 1850s. Not until the 1900s, however, did production grow to surpass inorganic output. Rapid expansion during the twentieth century made the overall chemical industry one of the largest businesses in the

United States and the biggest exporting sector of the American economy. In 1999, U.S. organic chemical manufacturers sold an estimated $68 billion worth of materials and employed 93,200 workers. They shipped almost $11 billion worth of exports and accounted for about 25 percent of global organic chemical output.

The industry realized healthy revenue and profit growth during the late 1980s. Production volume and sales continued to climb in the early 1990s. However, overcapacity and a weak global economy diminished manufacturers' earnings. As they entered the mid-1990s, producers faced other roadblocks as well. To combat these negative influences, manufacturers were increasing their productivity, focusing on high-margin specialty chemicals, and restructuring their organizations. One result of this increased productivity and company restructuring has been a steady overall decrease in the number of workers.

The 1990s also saw massive efforts to reduce waste to the environment. Between 1988 and 1994, toxic chemical emissions were reduced 60 percent, according to materials submitted to the Environmental Protection Agency (EPA) in 1996. A number of companies have agreed to voluntary compliance programs, such as the Responsible Care Initiative, whose member companies work in partnership with the public to ensure chemical safety standards within the community.

ORGANIZATION AND STRUCTURE

The chemical industry is divided into organic and inorganic substances. Inorganic chemicals, which are derived from the inanimate material of the earth's crust, include compounds such as sulfuric acid, sulfur, phosphoric acid, and hydrogen peroxide. Organic chemicals are so named because in the industry's early days they were obtained from living organisms. Today they are derived from substances that contain carbon—such as petroleum, coal, and natural gas. Petroleum-based chemicals, or petrochemicals, account for about 80 percent of industry output by weight and 50 percent of production by value.

Organic chemicals, particularly petrochemicals, play an indispensable role in modern society. They are essential ingredients in plastics, synthetic fibers, rubber, fertilizers, and chemical intermediates, which are converted into a plethora of consumer and industrial products. They are the primary building blocks of important materials supporting the health, food, transportation, and communication industries. Organic substances also have made possible many important specialty items, such as protective clothing and materials used for space exploration.

Because organic chemicals are used to make so many products within the overall chemical and related products divisions, the industry eludes clear definition. In fact, most industrial organic chemicals are consumed by chemical-related businesses. For instance, companies that produce cyclic crudes and intermediates, such as aromatics and dyes (see **SIC 2865: Cyclic Organic Crudes and Intermediates, and Organic Dyes and Pigments**), purchased about 20 percent of industry output in the 1990s. Plastic resin manufacturers (see **SIC 2821: Plastics Materials, Synthetic Resins, and Nonvulcanizable Elastomers**) consumed 13 percent of production. Synthetic fiber producers (see **SIC 2824: Manmade Organic Fibers, Except Cellulosic**) accounted for about 6 percent of industry revenues, and elastomer companies (see **SIC 2822: Synthetic Rubber—Vulcanized Elastomers**) absorbed 3 percent of production. Another 13 percent of organic chemical sales were garnered from exports.

The remaining 45 percent of organic output was used by numerous manufacturing sectors. Steel and aluminum mills, paper mills, semiconductor manufacturers, drug companies, carpet mills, and battery producers were relatively large customers. Other chemical uses included the production of items such as pipe, photographic equipment, electrical insulation, and food containers.

Production. The organic chemical industry serves one primary purpose: to take a relatively few fundamental raw chemicals that contain carbon and combine and transform them into new substances with desirable physical properties. Using carbon as a basic building block, chemists are able to unite other elements—such as nitrogen, hydrogen, oxygen, sulfur, and chlorine—to generate a multitude of different compounds. Furthermore, each resultant compound can be manipulated with heat or additives to produce an infinite variety of characteristics and grades.

The most common category of organic chemicals are aliphatics, or olefins, which are straight-chain hydrocarbons. Olefins can be made using petroleum or natural gas, though most U.S. manufacturers use the latter. To produce Olefins, natural gas is separated into ethane, propane, and butane. From these gases, smaller percentages of marketable ethylene, propylene, and butadiene are extracted. These three substances are the basic building blocks for most organic chemicals and synthetic materials. Major producers of aliphatics include Dow Chemical, Union Carbide, Occidental Petroleum, and Quantum Chemical.

Ethylene is the largest volume organic chemical produced in the United States. Approximately 75 percent of all ethylene is utilized to produce plastics such as polyethylene, polyvinyl chloride, and polystyrene. It also is widely used to make antifreeze, synthetic fibers, rubber, solvents, and detergents. Derivatives of ethylene also represent a significant share of total industry output. The second largest olefin by production volume is propylene.

Forty percent of propylene is used to make polypropylene, which in turn is utilized to manufacture film, packaging, foams and coatings, solvents, gasoline, and fibers. In addition, propylene is used to make other popular chemicals, such as acrylonitrile, propylene oxide, isopropanol, and cumene. Butadiene, the third most popular olefin, is employed primarily in the manufacture of synthetic rubber. The remaining one-third of butadiene production is consumed by makers of latex, resins, and nylon fibers.

Aside from olefins and their offspring, synthetic methanol accounts for a large share of industry output. Important derivatives of methanol include formaldehyde, acetic acid, methyl methacrylate, and various solvents. About 50 percent of all methanol is utilized in the production of adhesives, fibers, and plastics. In addition, it is an important ingredient in antifreeze and gasoline additives. Methyl tert-butyl ether (MTBE), a methanol derivative, is used as an oxygenate in automobile gasoline.

Environmental Impact. Laws and initiatives regarding hazardous emissions generated during organic chemical production and use are important dynamics that shape the industry. The chemical business is by far the largest polluting U.S. industry—generating at least three times more pollution than the second greatest offending industry.

As late as 1991, chemical producers released more than 1.5 billion pounds of toxins—as defined by the Environmental Protection Agency's (EPA's) Toxics Release Inventory (TRI). This figure represented a full 46 percent of all U.S. industrial toxic emissions. Forty percent of this waste was dumped into the air, 40 percent into underground wells, and the remainder was released into water and land.

To minimize the detrimental effects of chemical industry pollutants, multiple local, state, and federal laws govern producers. For example, the federal Emergency Planning and Community Right-to-Know Act requires many manufacturers to submit detailed emissions data to the EPA. Similarly, the Pollution Prevention Act (1990) requires those same companies to report their waste management and pollution reduction activities.

Other federal regulations impacting producers include the Safe Drinking Water Act, the Clean Air Act Amendments of 1990, and other laws that restrict hazardous wastes. In addition to legal restrictions, both the EPA and the Chemical Manufacturers Association (CMA) sponsor successful voluntary pollution reduction programs that encourage environmental sensitivity. The EPA has continued to monitor the industry, and in today's current political climate, which places strong emphasis on chemical safety and pollution controls, it is likely that regulations will continue to be added and modified.

The Responsible Care Initiative, launched by CMA in 1988 and joined by the Society of Organic Chemical

Manufacturers Association in 1990, is a voluntary program whose member companies work with the public to address such issues as chemical safety. This is done through a combination of soliciting information from the public about its concerns and reporting progress back to the public.

BACKGROUND AND DEVELOPMENT

Ancient Egyptians and Chinese were the first to experiment with chemical processes in carrying out dyeing, leather tanning, and glassmaking activities. It was not until 1790, however, that Nicolas Leblanc, a Frenchman, gave birth to the chemical industry. He is credited with being the first person to successfully carry out a deliberate plan to convert one or more chemical products into one wholly different substance, keeping in mind not only the end product but also the economics of the process. Leblanc was inspired by a reward of 12,000 francs offered by the French Academy of Sciences to anyone who could devise a method for making inexpensive alkali.

While Leblanc's discovery was neglected in France, it became extremely important in England in the soap and textile industries. As British alkali producers advanced the inorganic chemical industry during the 1800s, they laid the foundation for organic chemistry. Although organic compounds had been known to man for centuries, it was not discovered until early in the nineteenth century that they all contain carbon. Once scientists realized that they could unite carbon with other common elements, they quickly began to create their own substances. At first chemists sought to create elements that imitated natural, known substances. Later on, they learned how to create a vast variety of unknown compounds.

The first chemist to synthesize an organic chemical for commercial use was Englishman William Henry Perkin, the father of the organic chemical industry. At 18 years old, Perkin, working in his father's house in 1856, accidentally created a synthetic dye using a piece of coal tar. Although he received knighthood for his efforts, it wasn't until 1865 that the chemical structure of Perkin's dye was understood. In that year, Friedreich von Kekule announced his breakthrough theory of the benzene ring. Using Kekule's theory, chemists were able to build millions of new organic chemicals during the nineteenth and early twentieth centuries, many of which displaced natural materials and dyes.

Chemists did not begin synthesizing petroleum and natural gas to create petrochemicals on a commercial scale until the 1920s. A huge demand for gasoline, rubber products, textiles, detergents, and plastics that could be created with petrochemicals in the 1920s and early 1930s boosted industry growth. However, it was World War II that launched the organic chemical industry to national prominence. During this period, a shortage of natural and manmade materials that had previously been supplied by other sources resulted in rapid industry expansion. For example, production of synthetic rubber bolted from just 72,000 tons in 1939 to more than 800,000 tons in 1945.

Organic chemical sales continued to balloon after WWII as the post-war U.S. economy expanded. The explosion in automobile production during the 1950s, 1960s, and 1970s, for example, created a massive demand for chemicals utilized in the production of rubber, paint, and gasoline. Importantly, commercial and residential construction booms generated a huge need for paneling, roofing, insulation, carpet, draperies, upholstery, varnishes, and other chemical-based building materials. Likewise, the call for clothing created from organic chemicals ballooned as a rising population sought viable alternatives to costly natural fibers. Defense and consumer products markets grew as well. Moreover, besides meeting demand in domestic markets, the United States became a major chemical supplier to European countries that had been devastated by war.

As organic chemical revenues blossomed throughout most of the period between the 1950s and 1970s, overall chemical industry sales, including inorganics, reached approximately $50 billion. Production volume of ethylene and propylene, combined, topped 30 billion pounds, while total organic output climbed past 120 billion pounds. Heading into the 1980s, industrial organic chemical producers were employing more than 120,000 workers and shipping more than $5 billion in exports.

In the early 1980s, organic producers were battered by high petroleum prices and a deep U.S. economic recession. As sales stalled throughout the early years of the decade, inventories swelled and profit margins collapsed. However, demand started recovering in 1983, pushed by a revival in housing starts and automobile markets. The demand for organics used to create plastics and textiles was especially strong, and consumption by paperboard and furniture markets recuperated. Sales climbed 9 percent in 1983—from $30.4 billion to $33.3 billion—and about 8 percent in 1984—to $35.8 billion.

Despite a temporary downturn in 1985 and 1986, industry expansion accelerated during the late 1980s. Sales rose to $42.0 billion in 1987 before jumping 16 percent to $49.1 billion in 1988. Prices and profits also improved following stagnation throughout most of the decade. For example, overall chemical industry profits rose to $4.0 billion in 1987, from just more than $2.0 billion per year between 1982 and 1985. Profit margins climbed from 4 percent in 1985 to a peak of almost 10 percent in 1988, boosting overall earnings past an annual rate of $7.0 billion in early 1989.

Production volume of many organics mushroomed during the 1980s. For example, propylene output rocketed from 12.5 billion pounds in 1982 to 21.8 billion by 1990, representing annual growth of more than 6 percent. Consumption of butadiene rose similarly, to about 3 billion pounds by 1990. Ethylene production climbed at an annual rate of more than 5 percent, from 24.5 billion pounds in 1982 to 36.5 by 1990. More importantly, however, many derivatives of the three major olefins realized average annual growth rates in excess of 10 percent throughout the decade. In anticipation of continued growth, producers responded in the late 1980s by making heavy capital investments to increase their production capacity.

Notwithstanding a surge in the latter years of the decade, chemical market growth during the 1980s was modest in comparison to the expansion enjoyed during the previous three decades. Indeed, many organic chemical producers realized that the industry was entering a new stage of maturity. The massive growth opportunities of the mid-twentieth century, propelled by economic expansion and uncontested global dominance, had diminished significantly even by the late 1970s.

Particularly disconcerting to producers of commodity-like organics was the steep rise of foreign competition that occurred in the early 1980s. Besides expanded output by Japan and the European Community, U.S. producers also were being challenged by low-cost producers in Korea and Singapore. Despite overall export growth by domestic chemical manufacturers in the mid-1980s, the U.S. share of the world chemical export market plummeted from about 17 percent in 1984 to less than 14 percent in 1987. Although inorganic commodity chemicals represented much of this decline, the share of U.S. exports represented by organic chemicals slipped from more than 30 percent in the mid-1980s to about 25 percent by the early 1990s. The U.S. global chemical export market share recovered slightly in 1989, to about 15 percent.

To combat long-term downward profit pressures exerted by relatively flat market growth and increased competition, many producers in the early 1980s began cutting costs, consolidating operations, increasing research and development spending, and implementing cost-saving automation and information systems. Most producers who were slow to implement such initiatives had climbed aboard the bandwagon by the late 1980s, and these efforts were evidenced by a decline in employment. Even as organic manufacturers scrambled to boost their productivity during the 1980s, employment fell from 111,000 in 1982 to about 100,000 by 1990. This occurred despite steady growth in production volume.

After steady growth through 1989, industrial organic chemical manufacturers suffered serious setbacks in the early 1990s. A U.S. and global economic recession stumped profit growth, as the value of petrochemical and related products sales dropped 1.5 percent in 1990 to $54.1 billion. Sales rose just 1 percent in both 1991 and 1992 (using inflation adjusted dollars), and overall organic chemical output rose only slightly between 1990 and 1992. Moreover, this tepid growth was offset by stagnant prices and declining profits. From its peak of nearly 10 percent in 1988, chemical industry profit margins sank to about 5 percent in 1992.

Compounding industry woes in the early 1990s was excess production capacity, the result of expansion in the previous half decade. Oversupply was still depressing organic prices into the mid-1990s, thus eliminating profit growth. Despite ongoing successful efforts to increase productivity and improve products, U.S. competitors were unable to overcome the effects of the latest downturn. Even a slow but steady increase in organic exports did little to alleviate the impact of sluggish domestic markets. After all, U.S. imports rose at a rate about 15 times greater than U.S. exports in 1992, augmenting downward price pressures.

In an effort to buoy earnings, domestic competitors continued restructuring in the 1990s. Companies were cutting costs out of every phase of the production process, often leading to massive layoffs. For example, DuPont announced a workforce reduction of as many as 4,500 people in late 1993, adding to about 5,500 layoffs made by that company since 1991. Likewise, Dow Chemical eliminated 4,700 jobs in 1993, and Air Products reduced its workforce by 1,300. Many companies also were restructuring by selling unprofitable operations and focusing on their core competencies.

CURRENT CONDITIONS

While revenues improved and prices gained slightly in 1993, overcapacity and weak markets persisted into 1994. Industry shipments grew between 1 and 2 percent in 1993 and were expected to increase similarly in the near term. However, this growth eventually was expected to reduce overcapacity, allowing manufacturers to raise prices slightly. The effects of a reduction in oversupply may be offset by the diminished stature of U.S. producers in the global marketplace. U.S. firms will increasingly be forced to shift production from high-volume, commodity-like organics to low-volume specialty and high-tech compounds that demand higher prices.

Shipment growth rates of ethylene were expected to be at 3 to 4 percent through the year 2000. As ethylene demand continues to grow, the industry will be forced to add new facilities at the estimated rate of one per year. Production of propylene rose 7.3 percent in 1995, and at year's end, inventories of propylene were twice those of 1994 and above average historical levels; this caused prices to drop by nearly 30 percent. Demand for propylene has grown moderately since then—estimates place the growth rate at 3.5 percent per year between 1995 and 2000.

Though the United States produces more than 3 billion pounds of butadiene per year, it historically has imported most of its butadiene from Europe. As with propylene, higher inventory in the mid-1990s caused prices to drop. As for methanol, the price almost tripled in 1994 reaching $1.55 per gallon, but by the end of 1994 it was back down to 42 cents. Since then prices have decreased even more. Still, there is ongoing interest in the use of methanol as an alternative to gasoline, and new methanol plants are being constructed in such countries as Chile, Saudi Arabia, Trinidad, Equatorial Guinea, and Iran.

Methyl tert-butyl ether production topped 10.5 billion pounds in the early 1990s as prices were driven up by the Clean Air Act Amendments of 1990, which required the use of gasolines containing oxygenates such as MTBE. Beginning in 1992, the sale of oxygenated fuels was required during the winter months in 37 U.S. metropolitan areas that did not meet the federal air standards for carbon monoxide. In January 1995, year-round use began in 9 regions as dictated by the Clean Air Act. However, the demand for MTBE was not as high as expected in 1995, as some states were able to get out of the program. In 1999, the National Research Council of the National Academy of Sciences released a report claiming that gasoline enhanced with MTBE could create ozone violations. Early in 2000, organizations such as Northeast States for Coordinated Air Use Management, the American Lung Association, and the American Petroleum Institute announced their support for a pending law eliminating the 1995 Clean Air Act regulations. These actions have been vigorously fought by the Oxygenated Fuels Association, which claims that oxygenated fuel has actually led to a 22 percent reduction in air toxins.

Regulatory Impacts. While increasing federal and state regulations posed an ongoing challenge to chemical industry participants, positive signs indicated that the industry was successfully clearing these hurdles and was even benefiting from some laws. The overall chemical industry has managed to reduce its emissions of TRI wastes, even as industry production has increased. Nonetheless, regulatory issues are an ongoing major concern to the industry.

Despite industry gains, chemical pollutants remained a major concern for regulators, and President Clinton's administration planned to increase efforts to reduce toxic emissions. However, some regulations were expected to boost industry profits. For example, the Clean Air Act Amendments of 1990 required automobile carbon-monoxide emissions to fall below certain levels by 1995. As a result, the demand for organic gasoline additives that allow such reductions grew rapidly.

Besides environmental restrictions, manufacturers also were burdened with increased costs related to new safety initiatives initiated by both the EPA and the Occupational Health and Safety Administration (OSHA) law, passed by Congress in 1992, which was aimed at preventing accidents in the work place. Costs associated with the EPA and OSHA rules were not small, but they were expected to more than make up for this in cost savings from reduced environmental damage and response costs. Moreover, corporate commitment to environmental and safety concerns is invaluable to companies from a public relations standpoint; good consumer and community relations are critically important for companies that wish to remain competitive.

Information submitted to the EPA has shown that emissions of toxic chemicals had decreased considerably in the past decade. The most recent edition of the Toxic Release Inventory (1997 figures) showed that chemical manufacturing accounted for 48.9 percent of TRI total production-related waste management. The total amount of production-related waste that was managed by the industry was 11.3 billion pounds.

The EPA considered underground injection wells "safer than virtually all other waste disposal practices." To dispose of highly diluted wastes, they were injected into EPA-permitted wells, drilled deep into special geologic formations that contained, and in some cases neutralized, the waste.

In 1994, the EPA added 286 chemicals to its inventory list, nearly doubling its size to 643 reportable chemicals. The CMA contended that some of these were innocuous, and the EPA stood the risk of confusing the public with what truly was hazardous and what was not.

INDUSTRY LEADERS

About 700 companies participated in the industrial organic chemical industry in the late 1990s. More than 30 had sales of more than $1 billion from various businesses, and many of them employed several thousand workers. However, most of the top 75 firms in the industry had fewer than 500 workers and generated revenues of less than $200 million per year. The industry is highly consolidated in relation to most other U.S. manufacturing sectors. High startup costs, technical expertise, and entrenched segment leaders discourage new competition.

Large-scale consolidation has impacted the industry. The 1999 merger of Exxon and Mobil created a monolith with sales of $187 billion. However, its organic chemical production was handled by two subsidiaries—Exxon Chemical Co., with 1998 sales of $11.9 billion and 12,000 employees; and Mobil Chemical Co., with 1998 sales of $3.3 billion and 4,100 employees.

The merger of Amoco and British Petroleum formed London-based BP Amoco, with 1998 sales of $68.3 billion and 96,650 employees. A move on BP Amoco's part to acquire Atlantic Richfield Corp. was thwarted by the U.S. Federal Trade Commission (FTC) early in 2000.

Other companies that held prominence in the industry included Ashland Inc., with 1999 sales of $6.8 billion and 23,000 employees; Solutia Inc., a spinoff of Monsanto with 1999 sales of $2.8 billion and 8,700 employees; and Dow Corning, with 1998 sales of $2.6 billion and 9,000 employees.

WORKFORCE

An estimated 93,200 workers served the industrial organic chemical industry in 1999. In 1982 the industry employed 111,800 people; except for a few spikes, the number has gone steadily down. Production workers accounted for about 55,200 workers in 1999. Productivity increases achieved by manufacturers were largely to blame for cutbacks in both white and blue collar jobs.

Employment growth in the organic chemical industry is expected to remain weak, and future employment prospects are bleak. Blue collar workers will suffer the most from long-term trends. Positions for chemical equipment controllers, which account for a full 9 percent of the organic chemical industry workforce, will fall steadily over the next several years, according to the Bureau of Labor Statistics. In fact, jobs for most production workers—such as technicians, supervisors, and machine operators—are expected to plummet by 5 to 35 percent by 2005.

The number of jobs for white collar workers and support staff also will fall. By 2005, the demand for administrators and managers will have declined 14 percent from 1990; clerical jobs will plunge almost 25 percent. General management and top executive positions will drop, and even chemists will see opportunities erode somewhat. On the bright side, some engineering jobs will rise, as will sales and marketing positions. The need for systems analysts and computer scientists in this industry is expected to increase steadily.

A primary factor driving workforce cutbacks in the 1980s and early 1990s was high wages. Indeed, workers in the organic chemical industry are among the highest paid manufacturing employees in the United States. The average organic chemical production worker earned $17.23 per hour in 1992, compared with the average of just $10.49 for all U.S. manufacturing laborers. By 1999 that figure was an estimated $23.79. For the entire organic chemical industry, payroll per employee topped $40,000 per year in 1992; by 1999 that figure had risen to an estimated $61,000.

The best paying jobs in the industry go to highly educated chemists involved in research or management; chemists with doctorate degrees can earn much more than chemists who hold only master's degrees. However, the job market is very competitive.

When it comes to employment, chemical engineering is a notoriously cyclical field. For example, graduates entering the chemical industry in 1993 could expect to earn $25,000 per year at the undergraduate level, $33,000 with a graduate degree, and about $50,000 with a doctorate. However, 25 percent of graduating chemical engineers in 1992 were still seeking employment 8 months after graduation. Even among chemists employed by the industry in 1993, surveys showed that one out of 25 had experienced joblessness during the past year. The steady decrease in the number of jobs might make the industry less cyclical into the twenty-first century, but it is not unreasonable to assume that for the top jobs there will continue to be upward and downward spikes.

AMERICA AND THE WORLD

The U.S. organic chemical industry remains the largest and most technologically advanced in the world. However, its supremacy has waned considerably since the 1950s when U.S. organic producers supplied more than 50 percent of global output.

Despite the strength of the industry, foreign competition continued to erode its comparative might. Economic stagnation in key export markets—such as Japan and the European Community—and recovering U.S. demand helped importers to increase their share of the U.S. market in the early 1990s. However, long-term structural changes in global chemical markets also were at work. Importantly, producers in emerging economies were increasingly challenging U.S. suppliers for both domestic and export sales.

In the long term, growing foreign organic chemical production will result in fierce competition and reduced opportunities for U.S. manufacturers. The United States, Europe, and Japan will remain the key producers, but much of the market for high-volume, commodity-like organics will be surrendered to emerging powers. To sustain profitability, U.S. competitors will be forced to boost their production of high-tech compounds that will outperform existing chemicals and open new markets.

RESEARCH AND TECHNOLOGY

The organic chemical industry continues to invest a major share of its revenues in research and development. Most expenditures are used to increase productivity and to meet stringent environmental regulations. Estimates indicate that the average organic manufacturer made capital investments equivalent to $55,418 per employee in 1999.

As the industry continues to consolidate, and as environmental issues continue to command center stage, research and development will occupy an increasingly prominent place in the industry.

FURTHER READING

Darnay, Arsen J., ed. *Manufacturing USA.* 6th ed. Detroit: Gale Group, 1999.

Hess, Glenn. "Toxic Emissions Decline." *Chemical Marketing Reporter,* 7 October 1996.

"Organic Chemicals," 2000. Available from http://www.bayer .de/bayer/english.

SIC 2873

NITROGENOUS FERTILIZERS

This category includes establishments primarily engaged in manufacturing nitrogenous fertilizer materials or mixed fertilizers from nitrogenous materials produced in the same establishment.

NAICS CODE(S)

325311 (Nitrogenous Fertilizer Manufacturing)

The number of establishments producing nitrogenous fertilizers was 166 in 1993, 168 in 1995, and 143 in 1997. The industry shipped $4.2 billion worth of goods in 1994, $3.5 billion in 1996, and $3.8 billion in 1997. The cost of materials was $2.0 billion in 1997, and capital expenditures totaled $574.0 million.

Employment fell from 8,000 in 1994 to about 6,300 in 1996 and 5,483 in 1997. The industry's 3,490 production workers earned an average hourly wage of $20.84 in 1997. Nearly 40 percent of the establishments in this category had at least 20 employees. The largest concentration of establishments was in California, followed by Florida, Missouri, Arkansas, and Iowa.

The main source of nitrogen for fertilizer production is atmospheric nitrogen, of which there is abundant supply; it has been estimated that there are about 35,000 tons of nitrogen over every acre of land. For plants to utilize this element, however, it must first be combined with either oxygen or hydrogen in a process called "fixation."

The primary ingredient of most nitrogenous fertilizers is anhydrous ammonia, which the fertilizer industry typically forms by fixing atmospheric nitrogen with the hydrogen found in the natural gas methane. The resultant compound is a gas that is 82.25 percent nitrogen. This gas is stored in containers that are pressurized and usually refrigerated. It may be injected beneath the soil surface as a fertilizer. In 1992 natural gas prices shot upwards and accounted for 70 percent to 85 percent of ammonia production costs. This put the United States at a cost disadvantage compared to countries such as Russia, Canada, and Mexico, which have abundant and lower-priced sources of natural gas.

Anhydrous ammonia may be combined with nitric acid to produce ammonium nitrate, an excellent fertilizer that is highly combustible. A third type of fertilizer, urea, can be made by combining anhydrous ammonia with carbon dioxide. Urea has a higher nitrogen content and is easier and safer to store and handle than ammonium nitrate. Some nitrogenous fertilizer materials are made from organic substances such as sewage sludge.

The U.S. Census Bureau estimated that in 1997, the industry shipped $4.4 billion worth of synthetic ammonia, nitric acid, and ammonium compounds, up from $3.6 billion in 1992. Shipments of urea totaled $785 million, up from $709 million in 1992. Shipments of nitrogenous fertilizer materials of organic origin totaled $70 million, down from $155 million in 1992.

Demand for urea and other nitrogen-based fertilizers was strong during the mid-1990s, but in 1997 the industry floundered when China withdrew from the market. In an attempt to curtail imports and support its own domestic production, China imposed an import tax on urea, which substantially increased the product's price there. The resulting oversupply caused the price of urea to slump in other countries. Along the Gulf of Mexico, the domestic delivery point for the raw commodity, the price dropped from $191 per ton to $110 per ton in just 10 months. As manufacturers reduced their production of urea and began making more ammonia instead, the price of ammonia also dropped. Conditions were not expected to improve until China began buying nitrogenous fertilizers again.

Meanwhile, one of the largest U.S. producers of nitrogen fertilizer was acquired by a Canadian company that made potash fertilizer. Arcadian Corp. (Memphis, Tennessee) merged with Potash Corporation of Saskatchewan Inc. in the spring of 1997 to form PCS Nitrogen Inc. In 1998 Potash Corporation had sales of $2.3 billion, and Arcadia had sales of $1.1 billion.

Other leaders in this category included Terra Industries Inc. (Sioux City, Iowa) with sales of $2.5 billion; CF Industries Inc. (Long Grove, Illinois) with sales of $1.2 billion; Pursell (Los Angeles, California) with estimated sales of $1.2 billion; and Scotts Co. (Marysville, Ohio) with sales of $1.1 billion.

FURTHER READING

Conner, Charles. "International Market Fluctuations Affect Fertilizer Producers." *Knight-Ridder/Tribune Business News,* 3 April 1998.

———. "Tennessee-Based Fertilizer Maker's Shareholders Approve Sale." *Knight-Ridder/Tribune Business News,* 5 March 1997.

Darnay, Arsen J., ed. *Manufacturing USA.* 5th ed. Detroit: Gale Research, 1996.

"Fertilizer Materials—1995." *Current Industrial Report,* September 1996. Available from http://www.census.gov/industry/ma28b95.txt.

Johnson, Dexter. "Nitrogen Fertilizers Slump, Potash Rebounds." *Chemical Market Reporter,* 20 October 1997.

Lazich, Robert S., ed. *Market Share Reporter.* Detroit: Gale Research, 1997.

Muirhead, Sarah. "PCS Completes Arcadian Purchase, Internally Restructures." *Feedstuffs,* 17 March 1997.

Nielsen, Karol. "Terra Sells Distribution Arm to Survive Fertilizer Slump." *Chemical Week,* 12 May 1999.

U.S. Department of Commerce. U.S. Census Bureau. *1997 Economic Census.* Washington, D.C.: GPO, 1999. Available from http://www.census.gov/prod/ec97/97m3253a.pdf.

SIC 2874

PHOSPHATIC FERTILIZERS

This category includes establishments primarily engaged in manufacturing phosphatic fertilizer materials, or mixed fertilizers from phosphatic materials produced in the same establishment.

NAICS CODE(S)

325312 (Phosphatic Fertilizer Manufacturing)

The U.S. Census Bureau estimated that 61 establishments manufactured phosphatic fertilizers in 1997. They shipped $5.7 billion worth of goods, spent $3.6 billion on materials, and paid $248.0 million for capital expenditures. About 62 percent of these establishments had at least 20 employees. The greatest number of phosphatic fertilizer operations were located in Florida and Louisiana.

During the 1990s Florida had a multibillion-dollar phosphate industry. In 1995 Jacksonville exported 293,000 tons of phosphate rock, while Tampa exported 3.44 million tons and shipped 6.6 million tons within the United States. Tampa also shipped 9.6 million tons of fertilizer in 1995.

Although the original sources of phosphorus for plant fertilization were guano (bird and bat excrement) and ground bone, a more plentiful source was found in phosphate rock, which was the only commercially important source of fertilizer phosphorus in the 1990s. The United States is the world's leading producer of phosphatic fertilizers. The Kola Peninsula in Russia is another primary source, and so is Morocco, which has phosphate rock deposits four times larger than those in the United States.

After mining, the phosphate rock must be refined and concentrated for use as fertilizer. Sometimes, finely ground phosphate rock is applied directly to soil, but usually sulfuric acid is used to convert it into a more water-soluble form.

About 45 percent of the phosphatic fertilizer produced in the United States is used on the domestic corn crop, so corn acreage is one determinant of domestic demand. Other determinants are grain prices, the ability of U.S. farmers to compete globally, and the weather. Short-term fluctuations in the domestic market are thus difficult to predict.

In the early 1990s the most widely used of the phosphatic fertilizers was diammonium phosphate (DAP). During 1991, about a fifth of the 10.7 million tons of DAP exported by the United States went to India, and nearly half went to China. Expecting a boom year for the industry in 1992, manufacturers increased their DAP inventories, but this contributed to an oversupply of the product as demand slumped in domestic and foreign markets. Prices fell to the lowest point in nearly 15 years.

From 1994 to 1995 phosphate fertilizer production increased 3.2 percent, exports increased 10.9 percent, and consumption increased 2.2 percent. Phosphatic fertilizer shipments were valued at $5.165 billion in 1995.

Demand for phosphates was so strong in the spring of 1998 that much of the inventory warehoused throughout North America was depleted. The price of two primary raw materials for DAP (ammonia and sulfur) was low, while the price of DAP was up until demand for the product dropped because of bad weather and the usual seasonal slowdown. Government financial aid to farmers and a growing demand for phosphates in China and India were two of the main reasons for the strong showing that year.

Nevertheless, some fertilizer manufacturers initiated significant cost-cutting measures. For example, in 1998 one of the world's largest producers of phosphate fertilizers, IMC Global Inc., began consolidating its phosphate and potash operations, a move that included the elimination of hundreds of jobs and the closure of several mines and processing plants. The next year IMC Global formed a joint venture with two of its primary rivals, CF Industries Inc. (Long Grove, Illinois) and Cargill Fertilizer Inc. (Riverview, Florida), to open a sulfur remelting facility called Big Bend Transfer Co., LLC, in Tampa, Florida.

IMC Global subsidiary Freeport-McMoRan Resource Partners L.P. (New Orleans, Louisiana) was one of the leading companies in this industry with 1,000 employees and sales of $957 million in 1998. Another subsidiary, IMC Kalium (Bannockburn, Illinois) had 2,500 employees and estimated sales of $600 million. A third subsidiary, IMC-Agrico Co. (Uncle Sam, Louisiana) had 650 employees and estimated sales of $184 million. It had previously been known as Agrico Chemical Co.

Among other industry leaders, Cargill had 1,354 employees and sales of $600 million. LESCO Inc. (Rocky River, Ohio) had 1,244 employees and sales of $417 million. Mobil Mining and Minerals Co. (a subsidiary of Mobile Corp. based in Pasadena, Texas) had sales of $161 million. Koch Agriculture Company Inc. Agri Service Div. (a subsidiary of Koch Industries Inc. based in Arapahoe, Nebraska) had sales of $150 million.

The Census Bureau reported that this industry employed 8,878 people in 1997, including 6,188 production workers who earned an average hourly wage of $17.31.

FURTHER READING

Brown, Robert. "Phosphate Fertilizers Await Spring as Demand Faces a Seasonal Slowdown." *Chemical Market Reporter,* 9 November 1998, p. 5.

Cargill Fertilizer Inc. corporate Web site. Available from http://www.cargill.com.

Cristy, Matt. "Phosphate Treasure Draws Little Interest." *Jacksonville Business Journal,* 31 March 1997. Available from http://www.amcity.com/jacksonville/stories/033197/story3.html.

Darnay, Arsen J., ed. *Manufacturing USA.* 5th ed. Detroit: Gale Research, 1996.

IMC-Agrico Co. corporate Web site. Available from http://www.imc-agrico.com.

Johnson, Dexter. "Nitrogen Fertilizers Slump, Potash Rebounds." *Chemical Market Reporter,* 20 October 1997, p. 5.

Lazich, Robert S., ed. *Market Share Reporter.* Detroit: Gale Research, 1997.

LESCO Inc. corporate Web site. Available from http://www.lesco.com.

Sunil, Saraf. "Potash and Gas Lead to Middle East." *MEED Middle East Economic Digest,* 10 January 1997, p. 16.

U.S. Department of Commerce. *Statistical Abstract of the United States.* Washington, DC: GPO, 1996.

U.S. Department of Commerce. Census Bureau. *1996 Annual Survey of Manufactures.* Washington, DC: GPO, 1998.

U.S. Department of Commerce. Census Bureau. *1997 Economic Census.* Washington, DC: GPO, 1999. Available from http://www.census.gov.prod/ec97/97m3253b.pdf.

U.S. Department of Labor. *Employment, Hours, and Earnings, United States, 1988-96.* Washington, DC: GPO, August 1996.

SIC 2875

FERTILIZERS, MIXING ONLY

This category covers establishments primarily engaged in mixing fertilizers from already-processed fertil-izer materials. In the industry, "fertilizer materials" refers specifically to fertilizers that have no more than one of the three primary plant nutrients (nitrogen, phosphorus, and potassium). This category also includes manufacturers of compost and potting soil, which condition the soil to promote plant growth but contain relatively small amounts of plant nutrients.

NAICS CODE(S)

325314 (Fertilizer (Mixing Only) Manufacturing)

The production of mixed fertilizers is an industry that has seen periodic declines during the past 30 years. The value of mixed fertilizer shipments in 1997 was $2.9 billion, up from $2.2 billion in 1995 and $1.9 billion in 1992. Though single nutrient fertilizers have dominated the fertilizer market since the 1970s, mixed fertilizers remain a necessity for American farmers. A total of more than 19 million short tons of mixed fertilizers was consumed in the United States in 1998.

According to the United States Department of Agriculture (USDA), mixed fertilizers, which are also termed multiple-nutrient fertilizers, are typically of four varieties: nitrogen, phosphorous, and potassium mixtures (N-P-K); nitrogen and phosphorous mixtures (N-P); nitrogen and potassium mixtures (N-K); and phosphorous and potassium mixtures (P-K). In 1998, N-P-K multiple-nutrient fertilizers were used most frequently in the United States, with more than 10 million short tons consumed. More than 7 million short tons of N-P mixtures were purchased in 1998, followed by 796,000 short tons of N-K and 618,000 short tons of P-K.

Mixed fertilizers can also be classified according to the method manufacturers use to combine the component fertilizers—homogeneous mixtures, bulk blends, and fluids. A key process performed by producers of homogeneous mixtures (and one that is performed by producers of fertilizer materials as well) is granulation. Nongranulated dry fertilizer powders have a tendency to form hardened cakes, which make the product difficult to handle. The hardened cakes are not always broken up easily, and explosives are sometimes used to break these cakes up into heaps of stored fertilizer. Another problem with nongranulated fertilizer mixes is the propensity for the component fertilizer materials to segregate by particle sizes during transport and handling. Granulation addresses the problem of caking and segregation by shaping the constituent parts of the fertilizer mix into larger granules which are relatively equal in size and which each have the same nutrient composition. The manufacture of this type of mixed fertilizer is a complex process requiring sophisticated equipment.

Bulk blending plants, by contrast, do not perform granulation or any chemical processes and their basic equipment needs are rudimentary (such as bins, front-end loaders, mixers, and scales). They keep an assortment of fertilizer materials on site, from which they select desired proportions for mixing together, often to suit the specific nutrient needs of the customer. The mix may be bagged or it may be taken directly to the customer's field and applied. In 1998, $2.15 billion worth of dry mixed fertilizers—including potting soil—were shipped.

Fluid mixed fertilizers have the smallest share of the mixed fertilizer market, accounting for only about $300.0 million of the total $2.9 billion of mixed fertilizer product shipments in 1998. Fluid mixed fertilizers are generally made by either the hot-mix or cold-mix process. Hot-mix plants combine ammonia with phosphoric acid, a reaction which releases considerable heat. The cold-mix process usually does not involve heat-producing chemical reactions, and the equipment needs of cold-mix plants are simpler than those of hot-mix plants.

The commercial usage of multiple-nutrient fertilizers is somewhat controversial. Some governments have argued against the practice on the grounds that optimal results are obtained when farmers tailor their fertilizer usage to their specific crop/soil combination, and that this is best done with the use of single-nutrient fertilizers applied in the proper proportions. Research results have supported that argument, and advances in soil nutrient analysis technique have made it easier to determine which specific nutrient a particular plot of land may need. The result of this debate has been a trend away from the use of mixed fertilizers. Data for fertilizer consumption in the United States, covering the period between 1955 and 1980, indicates that beginning in 1955, the use of mixtures was roughly twice that of direct application fertilizer materials. Over the subsequent years, the use of single-nutrient fertilizers grew, both in absolute terms and relative to mixtures and, in the early 1970s, it surpassed the use of mixtures. According to the USDA, the 19.3 million short tons of multiple-nutrient fertilizer consumed in 1998 was down from the 19.6 million short tons used in 1997. Moreover, single-nutrient fertilizers were used almost twice as often. In 1998, more than 31 million short tons of single-nutrient fertilizers were consumed in America. But the convenience of applying commercially-mixed fertilizer as opposed to determining the precise chemical balance appropriate for each plot of land ensures that the manufacture of mixed fertilizers will remain a major agricultural industry.

In 1997, 445 establishments were engaged in this industry, up from 413 in 1993. With its 39 fertilizer mixing facilities, Florida had the highest number of such businesses in the United States. Texas and New York followed with 38 and 17 businesses, respectively. More than 8,700 American workers were employed in the manufacture of mixed fertilizers in 1997 and, on average, earned $7.50 per hour.

The leader of the mixed fertilizer industry in 1998 was the agronomy company Cenex/Land O'Lakes Ag Services. This joint venture between Cenex Harvest States Cooperative and Land O'Lakes reported 1998 sales of about $1.5 billion, according to the *Kansas City Star*. Other key companies in this sector include the Tennessee Farmers Cooperative and Royster-Clark Incorporated of North Carolina, whose 1998 sales topped $1.0 billion.

FURTHER READING

Darnay, Arsen J., ed. *Manufacturing USA*. 5th ed. Detroit: Gale Research Inc., 1996.

Long, Victoria Sizemore. "Farmland Plans Joint Venture to Reduce Costs." *Kansas City Star,* 2 September 1999.

SIC 2879

PESTICIDES AND AGRICULTURAL CHEMICALS, NOT ELSEWHERE CLASSIFIED

This category includes establishments primarily engaged in the formulation and preparation of ready-to-use agricultural and household pesticides from technical chemicals or concentrates, and the production of concentrates that require further processing before use as agricultural pesticides. This industry also includes establishments primarily engaged in manufacturing or formulating agricultural chemicals, not elsewhere classified, such as minor or trace elements and soil conditioners. Establishments primarily engaged in manufacturing basic or technical agricultural pest control chemicals are classified in industries that manufacture industrial organic or inorganic chemicals.

NAICS CODE(S)

325320 (Pesticide and Other Agricultural Chemical Manufacturing)

INDUSTRY SNAPSHOT

Dominant forces affecting the agricultural chemicals industry during the late 1990s were increased government regulation, public concern over pesticides and a growing organic movement, and general economic trends including globalization and large mergers. Nonetheless, the industry overall saw gains in revenues for the period.

In 1997, domestic sales of both U.S. and imported pesticides were $8.8 billion, an increase of 5.5 percent; exports of domestically produced pesticides also grew, totaling $2.8 billion in sales for the same period. Most pesticide sold in the United States is used for crops including corn (24 percent), soybeans (19 percent), and cotton (10 percent). Seventeen percent of pesticides sold in 1997 were used for lawn, garden, and other noncrop purposes.

Pesticide sales can be subdivided into three main categories: herbicides, insecticides, and fungicides. Herbicides, which are used to kill weeds and brush, made up 68 percent of U.S. pesticide sales in 1997, primarily for crop use. Insecticides made up 21 percent of the market; with $1.9 billion in sales, that market dropped more than 20 percent due to advances in biotechnology including insect-resistant plants and seeds. Fungicides represented 7 percent of sales.

BACKGROUND AND DEVELOPMENT

Prior to World War I, pesticide use in the United States was limited. The Insecticide Act of 1910 imposed some regulations on pesticide manufacturers, but was mainly concerned with product effectiveness rather than public safety. After World War II, pesticides became more sophisticated, and their use more widespread. In 1947, Congress updated the Insecticide Act with the more comprehensive Federal Insecticide, Fungicide, and Rodenticide Act (FIFRA). The new legislation required pesticides, which were distributed across state lines, to be registered with the U.S. Department of Agriculture (USDA). However, the emphasis was on proper labeling and product efficacy.

It was not until 1954 that public health concerns were addressed by legislators. In that year, Congress amended the Federal Food, Drug, and Cosmetic Act (FDC Act) with a section (408) that directed the Food and Drug Administration (FDA) to set residue tolerance levels (i.e., maximum allowable pesticide residue) for pesticides used on raw produce. These tolerance levels were set using a risk/benefit analysis, whereby public health risks were weighed against benefits to the food supply. Four years later, in 1958, Congress added the controversial Delaney Clause, requiring pesticides that remain in processed foods in amounts that exceed their tolerance for raw produce, and that have been found to cause cancer in laboratory animals, not be approved for any use on food crops, regardless of any countervailing benefit of those pesticides. The Delaney clause applied only to processed foods, not to fresh produce, or to crops the EPA did not consider processed, such as frozen vegetables. In fact, the Delaney Clause had minimal impact on pesticides precisely because the overwhelming majority of pesticide residues decrease or remain at the same levels when fresh food is processed.

In 1970, the newly created Environmental Protection Agency (EPA) was given responsibility for setting residue tolerances. Enforcement of the EPA pesticide tolerances remained the responsibility of the FDA. In 1972, Congress amended FIFRA with the Federal Environmental Pesti-

cides Control Act. The new act required all pesticides manufactured in the United States to be registered with the EPA. It also provided for civil penalties of up to $5,000 for each violation and criminal penalties of up to $25,000, plus one year in prison. In 1976, Congress enacted the Toxic Substances Control Act, which required the EPA to monitor the production of chemical substances, including pesticides, and to impose testing requirements on the manufacturers of those chemicals to determine any threat to the environment or to public health that those substances may present. In 1988, Congress amended the FIFRA to require the re-registration of all pesticides previously registered before November 1, 1984.

In general, the political climate in the 1990s did not favor the domestic pesticide industry. The EPA struggled to find the best interpretation for administering the Delaney Clause. In 1988, it announced it would grant exceptions to the Delaney Clause when the pesticide in question posed only a minimal risk of cancer in processed food, but in July 1992 a decision by the U.S. Ninth Circuit Court of Appeals ruled such exemptions were contrary to the legislation. The decision, however, was controversial. This "zero risk" criterion was considered to be unreasonable by many in the agrochemical industry, and in the spring of 1993, two members of the U.S. House of Representatives introduced the Food Quality Protection Act in an attempt to loosen the EPA's pesticide tolerance-setting criteria. Both the National Association of State Departments of Agriculture and the National Food Processors Association supported the proposed act. But any lessening of pesticide regulations would receive opposition from environmental groups, especially in light of a National Academy of Science study released in June 1993, which charged that federal regulators were not adequately protecting children from pesticide poisoning.

The argument over pesticide regulation extended further than the Delaney Clause. In 1992, the U.S. Supreme Court ruled that state and local governments have the right to enact pesticide regulations that are more stringent than those required by the federal government, as about 12 states had done. In response, Congress began considering passage of the Federal-State Pesticide Regulation Partnership Act, which would prohibit local regulation of pesticides.

The Clinton administration announced a program to reduce the use of agricultural pesticides in the United States, and appeared to support the proposed Circle of Poison Prevention Act, which would prohibit U.S. manufacturers from exporting those pesticides that are banned in this country. The "circle of poison" refers to the U.S. export of pesticides that are banned domestically, and the subsequent use of those pesticides on crops in foreign countries, which are then imported back into the United States. The pesticide industry argued that the proposed bill would inappropriately apply U.S. risk/benefit criteria to countries where the benefits may outweigh the risks, thereby depriving those countries of needed improvements to their food supply; would fail to distinguish pesticides that have been refused registration by the EPA for public health reasons from those pesticides that the manufacturers have decided not to register in the United States due to a poor domestic demand; and would simply allow competitors from other countries to gain global market share by selling identical pesticides to the same countries. The combination of industry-adverse regulation in the United States and the proposed export restraint on pesticides was the impetus for the trend among pesticide manufacturers to send research and development and production operations overseas.

Lawsuits stemming from product liability issues also hurt leaders in the industry throughout the 1990s. A case in point was E.I. Du Pont de Nemours, the parent company of Du Pont Agricultural Products. The company reported sales of $3.29 billion in 1995, versus $2.73 billion in 1994, but almost $114 million was recorded as a loss, principally from costs associated with product liability litigation. In June of 1993, the company paid out $500 million in out-of-court settlements to 2,000 farmers who used the product and then claimed that it adversely affected their flowers and shrubs. These payments caused a 7.5 percent reduction in Du Pont's 1991 net income, and an 8.3 percent reduction for 1992. After Du Pont scientists purportedly found evidence that the Benlate DF was not at fault, the company discontinued its policy of settling the claims. Other costly measures have been taken to control the damage done by the industry. For example, in 1996, FMC Corp. faced spending an estimated $8.4 million to clean up a 30-acre hazardous waste landfill, following a plan crafted by the EPA and the New York State Department of Environmental Conservation.

CURRENT CONDITIONS

On August 3, 1996, President Clinton signed the Food Quality Protection Act. Under that law, all exposures to pesticides must be shown to be safe for infants and children, with a clear consideration of the sensitivity of the young to these chemicals. In addition, when determining a safe level for a pesticide in food, the EPA must explicitly account for all infant and child exposures to other pesticides and toxic chemicals that share a common toxic mechanism. Based on those standards, in 1998 the Environmental Working Group completed a study finding that 77,000 infants each day consume unsafe levels of pesticides. The group proposed a ban on the use of organophosphate pesticides in commercial baby food.

In August 1999, the EPA announced plans to restrict the use of azinphos-methyl and to ban the use of methyl parathion, two commonly used insecticides that fall un-

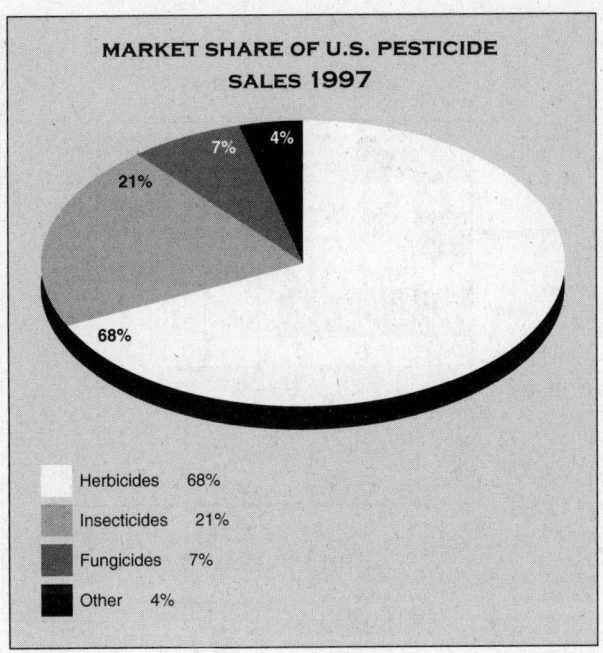

MARKET SHARE OF U.S. PESTICIDE SALES 1997

Herbicides   68%
Insecticides   21%
Fungicides   7%
Other   4%

der the category of organophosphates. U.S. makers of those products included Bayer Corp., Cheminova Inc., and Elf Atochem. Jay Vroom, president of the American Crop Protection Association, said in *The Chemical Market Reporter* that the pesticide industry was "disappointed and deeply concerned" by EPA's decision because of the precedent it set for the implementation of the Food Quality Protection Act.

The EPA further frustrated pesticide makers in 1999 with a 3.68 percent increase in the fees charged for processing petitions for determining legal residue levels. In addition, according to *The Chemical Market Reporter*, a proposed rule would allow the EPA to charge for all costs associated with processing tolerance actions, a move that could result in 10-fold increases in current fees.

INDUSTRY LEADERS

Leading U.S. establishments in this category include DuPont Agricultural Products, Griffin Corp., and Monsanto Company. Some of the larger foreign manufacturers have U.S. subsidiaries. In 1996, Novartis AG, created when Ciba-Geigy and Sandoz Ltd. merged, became the largest pesticide manufacturer in the world in one of the largest mergers in corporate history. In July 1997, Novartis purchased Merck and Company for $910 million. Another foreign leader, Rhne-Poulenc, was purchased by U.S.-based Scotts Co. in 1998.

In late 1997, Griffin Corp, once a small, family owned business, announced plans to form a joint venture with DuPont. That move increased their sales from $285 million to more than $450 million per year, making Griffin a new leader in the pesticide industry. According to *Chemical Week*, the venture "combines all of Griffin

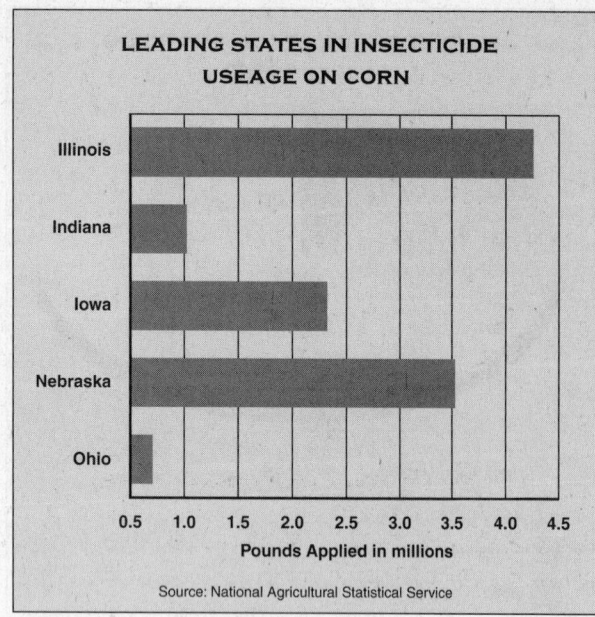

LEADING STATES IN INSECTICIDE USEAGE ON CORN

Pounds Applied in millions

Source: National Agricultural Statistical Service

with four of DuPont's postpatent pesticides lines—diuron, linuron, mancozeb, and fenbutatin oxide—along with DuPont's plants in Colombia and Brazil.''

The Agriculture and Nutrition division of E.I. DuPont de Nemours, constituted by its Crop Protection Productions and its Nutrition and Health business, reported sales of $3.2 billion in 1998, an increase over sales of just over $2 billion in both 1996 and 1997. In 1998, DuPont reached an agreement with FMC Corp. for exclusive use of its sulfentrazone herbicides, Authority and Canopy XL, used on soybean crops. Overall sales for DuPont in 1998 were $24.7 billion. In late 1999, AM-VAC Chemical Corp. announced plans to buy DuPont's Fortress insecticide business.

Monsanto company, which includes Ortho Consumer Products division, is the maker of Roundup, the world's top-selling pesticide. The product is a glyphosate salt under patent protection in the United States until 2000. With the success of that product, the firm funded a $200 million upgrade of its production facilities. In order to protect its leading product following the expiration of its patent, Monsanto developed ''Roundup Ready'' crops, including soybeans, corn, and cotton, which are the only crops that tolerate the product. In 1998, the maker of Roundup's main competitor, Zeneca's Touchdown, sued Monsanto for monopolistic practices. Monsanto had already filed suit against Zeneca for illegally acquiring Roundup Ready seeds for testing Touchdown.

In 1998, Monsanto reported total revenues of $7.36 billion, $4.26 billion of which came from its agricultural division. That figure marked a decline from sales earnings of $9.26 billion in 1996. Monsanto looked to make a recovery in 1999; the revenues just for the first three quarters totaled $6.84 billion, with $4.02 billion from

agricultural products. Earnings for each quarter were higher than those of individual quarters in 1999. Monsanto held reports on its fourth quarter in order to release them along with the sales figures from Pharmacia & Upjohn, with which Monsanto announced a planned merger in late 1999, expected to be complete the second quarter of 2000. The combined company was estimated to have total sales in 1999 of $17 billion. The firm also announced plans to make the agricultural business a separate entity and to offer up to 19.9 percent of the company in an Initial Public Offering.

WORKFORCE

Between 1982 and 1993, employment levels in the pesticide industry, as well as the agricultural chemical industry in general, stayed close to 16,000, peaking at 17,000 in 1990. Sharper declines began in 1994, with the number of workers decreasing to 13,800 in 1996. Projected employment levels through the year 2000 were higher, at about 15,500. Occupations utilized by the industry include chemical equipment controllers, chemical plant and system operators, maintenance repairers, truck drivers, secretaries, mechanics, chemists, electricians, warehouse workers, shipping clerks, and office workers. Declines in the industry have generally been in clerical positions; increases through the year 2006 were projected to occur in engineering fields—including chemical, computer, and mechanical—and in marketing and advertising. Wages for production workers in this industry tended to be higher than average for the manufacturing industry as a whole: in 1996, the average agricultural chemicals worker earned $19.45 per hour, compared to an average of $12.68 per hour across all manufacturers.

AMERICA AND THE WORLD

The United States is the world's largest manufacturer of pesticides, followed by Germany and Japan. The largest market for U.S. exports of pesticides is Japan, which accounted for about 10 percent in 1996. The world market for pesticides was $30.2 billion in 1997, an increase of 2.6 percent from the previous year; the U.S. Department of Commerce projected slow but continued growth in 1998. Factors influencing the worldwide market included poor weather conditions caused by El Nino and unstable economies in Asia.

RESEARCH AND TECHNOLOGY

Research and development costs have risen to high levels and are expected to continue to rise as regulatory requirements for more environmentally safe pesticides increase. The 1990s ushered in a trend among agrochemical manufacturers to develop low-dosage pesticides as a means of reducing the amount of chemical residue left on crops. Monsanto, for example, has a policy that any new pesticides that it develops must be designed for low-dosage application, must have low toxicity, and must be low impact on the environment.

Another area which holds promise for the industry is biotechnology. Biotechnology involves the genetic engineering of plants to make them resistant to diseases, insects, drought, pollution, and herbicides, in addition to the use of bacteria and viruses to create biological insecticides. One especially promising group of viruses for use as "bioinsecticides" is the baculoviruses. These viruses are naturally occurring and only attack specific insects; they pose no threat to humans, wildlife, or non-targeted insects. In 1992, American Cyanamid Co.'s Agricultural Research Division signed an agreement with the University of Georgia Research Foundation Inc. to develop ways to make these viruses more effective. The development of herbicide-tolerant plants has allowed companies who participate in both pesticide manufacturing and biotechnology to monopolize a market on particular crops, such as Monsanto's pairing of Roundup and Roundup-tolerant soybeans. In November 1999, American Cyanamid announced an agreement with Northwest Plant Breeding Company for research and development on herbicide-tolerant varieties of wheat, the largest agricultural crop in the world.

FURTHER READING

"American Cyanamid and Northwest Plant Breeding Company Sign Research and Commercialization Agreement to Produce Herbicide Tolerant Wheat." *PR Newswire,* 30 November 1999.

"American Cyanamid Signs Research Agreement with the University of Georgia Research Foundation." *Business Wire,* 24 February 1992.

"Amvac to Buy DuPont Biz." *Chemical Market Reporter,* 13 December 1999.

Chapman, Peter. "Roundup's Growth is a Boon for Monsanto and Its Suppliers." *Chemical Market Reporter,* 10 March 1997.

Darnay, Arsen J., ed. *Manufacturing USA.* 6th ed. Detroit: Gale Research, 1998.

DuPont 1998 Annual Report. Available from http://www.dupont.com.

"Du Pont Pesticide Shown to Contaminate Ground Water, According to Study." *PR Newswire,* 30 June 1993.

"EPA Raises Its Fees For Reviewing Pesticides." *Chemical Market Reporter,* 7 June 1999.

Hess, Glenn. "EPA Restricts Two Major Pesticides Drawing Sharp Criticism From Industry." *Chemical Market Reporter,* 9 August 1999.

Monsanto and Pharmacia & Upjohn To Merge, Creating Global Leader in Pharmaceuticals with Top-Tier Growth Prospects. Available from http://www.monsanto.com/monsanto/mediacenter/99/99dec20_pnu.html.

Monsanto Company 1998 Annual Report. Available from http://www.monsanto.com.

Owens, Jennifer. "Study: Baby Food has Unsafe Pesticide Levels." *Supermarket News,* 9 February 1998.

Steyer, Robert. "Monsanto Sued Over Herbicide, Genetically Altered Crops." *Knight-Ridder/Tribune Business News,* 28 July 1998.

U.S. Department of Commerce. *U.S. Industry and Trade Outlook, 1999.* McGraw-Hill, 1999.

Walsh, Kerri. "Monsanto Completes Pesticides Sale; More Divestments to Come." *Chemical Week,* 25 November 1998.

Wood, Andrew. "Griffin Gets Big in Generic Pesticides." *Chemical Week,* 17 December 1997.

SIC 2891

ADHESIVES AND SEALANTS

The adhesives and sealants industry consists primarily of manufacturers of industrial and household adhesives, glues, caulking compounds, sealants, and linoleum, tile, and rubber cements from vegetable, animal, or synthetic plastics materials, purchased or produced in the same establishment. Establishments primarily engaged in manufacturing gelatin and sizes are classified in **SIC 2899: Chemicals and Chemical Preparations, Not Elsewhere Classified,** and those manufacturing vegetable gelatin or agar-agar are classified in **SIC 2833: Medicinal Chemicals and Botanical Products.**

NAICS CODE(S)

325520 (Adhesive and Sealant Manufacturing)

INDUSTRY SNAPSHOT

The adhesives and sealants industry includes two chemically similar but functionally different groups of formulated products, adhesive and sealants. Adhesive products are used to create a bond between two different or similar materials. Sealants are used to create an impenetrable barrier to gas or moisture. Adhesives and sealants are made from precise blends of petroleum-derived plastic resins, synthetic rubber elastomers, and agents or additives used to enhance certain characteristics. The final formulation ultimately depends on the end use. Industries that typically use adhesives and sealants include construction, consumer products, assembly, packaging, labeling, and transportation.

The industry grew at a rate of about 4 percent through most of the 1990s, but analysts expected growth to slow heading into the next century. Individual companies seeking to increase their revenues looked to mergers and acquisitions, particularly in foreign markets, where industry growth was expected to surpass that in the United States. At the same time, foreign companies increasingly invested in U.S. firms, such that the industry became both more globalized and more consolidated.

Major factors influencing the growth of this industry include the stability of other industries using its products, the availability of raw materials, and environmental concerns. Measured by the value of product shipments, the market for natural-base glues—with the exception of most animal-based glues—increased tremendously between 1992 and 1997; however, synthetics should continue to dominate the industry, particularly water-based products and hot melt adhesives.

BACKGROUND AND DEVELOPMENT

The adhesives and sealants industry's development can best be explained by the economy-wide transition from conventional materials (glass, stone, wood, and metal) to lighter and more economical resources, mainly petroleum-based plastics. These new materials mandated new methods of assembly, and suitable bonding components. A generation of new products emerged to service this rapid growth area.

The market for reactive adhesives grew as the automotive industry moved away from mechanical fasteners. At the same time, packaging applications for reactives were on the rise, adding buoyancy to the adhesives industry. In the early 1990s, the reactives sector of the industry was dominated by epoxy and polyurethane systems, with urethanes taking a significantly larger portion of the market. About 100 million pounds of urethane resin went to adhesive and sealant applications in the early 1990s, compared to 28 million pounds of epoxy resin. Urethanes are most often used with flexible materials in high-impact applications, while epoxies are known for their hardness and are used with more rigid substances.

The development of epoxy/urethane hybrids attracted particular interest because of the broad range of demands placed on adhesives used in the automotive industry. Both manufacturers and users of these products were looking for the best of both worlds: combining high-tensile strength and compatibility with flexible materials. The problem was that a sacrifice was usually made in shelf life, toughness, or curing flexibility; the development of these hybrids minimized the number of sacrifices required. Developments in reactive adhesives for the auto industry also brought benefits to other industrial sectors, including appliance manufacturing.

In the latter half of the 1990s, the sealants industry continued to suffer from the vagaries of the construction market, especially in maintenance and repair. Growth was expected to continue at 3 percent per year, especially if the construction market continued to pick up as predicted.

CURRENT CONDITIONS

The adhesives and sealant industry grew throughout the 1990s—at a rate of 4 percent annually from 1991 to 1996—but growth began to slow somewhat in 1998, and the slowdown was expected to continue through 2001. ChemQuest, a Cincinnati consulting firm, predicted a 3 percent growth rate for adhesives and a 2.5 percent rate for sealants.

In 1998, the adhesives and sealant market was valued at $9.2 billion, with sales split among these primary groups: industry assembly (24 percent), packaging (23 percent), construction (16 percent), wood bonding (16 percent), transportation (11 percent), and consumer products (6 percent). For adhesives alone, the largest markets were construction and packaging, each with a nearly 40 percent share of demand, as measured by volume (rather than by sales). Revenues in this industry climbed steadily since 1987, and were expected to continue into the twenty-first century. Measured by the value of shipments, the industry grew 36 percent between 1992 and 1997, with growth rates between 3 and 5 percent projected through 2003. The value per pound of industry products was expected to grow about 12 percent from 1997 to 2002, from 89 cents per pound to $1 per pound.

Products showing the greatest growth between 1992 and 1997 included natural-base glues and adhesives—specifically, those made from natural gums, shellac, lacquers, and varnishes—with a 300 percent increase; hot melt adhesives, with an 87 percent increase; epoxy adhesives, with 74 percent; rubber cements, with nearly 95 percent; and sealants, with 44 percent. Pressure-sensitive adhesives also increased, by almost 60 percent. Products that fell included several kinds of synthetic resin and rubber adhesives, rubber and synthetic resin combinations, and protein and dextrine vegetable natural adhesives. Nonetheless, when measured by value of product shipments, synthetic resin and rubber adhesives held 58 percent of the market share (this group includes epoxies, hot melt adhesives, rubber cements, and pressure-sensitive adhesives).

Into the twenty-first century, products expected to see the most growth included electronics adhesives for printed wiring boards, hot melt systems, and automotive adhesives. In 1998, the U.S. hot melt adhesives market was valued at $1 billion, and was expected to grow 3 percent per year. The most common end-uses for hot melt adhesives were packaging, with 38 percent of the market, and disposable and pressure-sensitive products, each with 15 percent of the market.

Growth, however, is controlled by the availability of raw materials. Hot melt adhesives—favored among most industry watchers as the most likely product to outstrip the market with its growth—require hydrocarbon resins; demand for those resins was expected to increase by 2.6 percent annually through 2001. Some producers of the resins, including Eastman Chemical and Hercules, said in 1998 that they expected supply to keep up with demand, but Exxon Chemical reported the possibility of running short. Many manufacturers were attempting to expand their production capabilities to keep up with the growth of the raw materials market; demand was expected to increase at a rate of 4 percent annually. Even if supply remains adequate, prices were already rising, meaning that the largest companies would be best positioned to compete for available raw materials.

While revenues and product volume increased from 1987 to the year 2000 overall, the number of establishments declined slowly, bottoming out in 1995; it is expected to rise slightly through 2000. This change likely reflects trends toward consolidation—mergers and acquisitions—prevelant in all sectors of the economy. In 1997, Stephen Einhorn, president of Einhorn Associates, said in *Chemical Week* that there were nearly 40 mergers in the industry in 1996. According to Einhorn, the agreements were ''driven by the strategic push for specialized knowledge, market entry, and the ability to take this knowledge around the world.''

Industry watchers did not expect the larger companies to push out smaller competitors. As specialized applications for adhesives increase in demand, smaller firms should be able to carve out their own unique niches. Nonetheless, larger companies began to take a larger portion of market share. As of 1997, over 55 percent of the market was controlled by the top 20 companies, compared to 50 percent in 1982. According to Bill Broxterman, president of ChemQuest, ''All a small entrepreneurial company needs to do is to maintain a relationship with one or two customers to stay in business. Small companies will always be there; it is the medium-sized ones that are more likely to disappear.''

Because the adhesive and sealant markets depends greatly upon secondary industries, trends in other sectors of the economy can have a big impact on this industry. One sector showing increasing interest in adhesives and sealants was the automotive industry. Several U.S. automakers joined with adhesive and sealant makers to develop industry-specific applications that will cut costs, reduce weight, and even increase recyclability of cars made with these products. David Freeman, president and CEO of Loctite, said in *Chemical Week* that for automakers, ''using chemical methods is cheaper than mechanical methods, so the component suppliers are using more adhesives.'' Freeman reported a 20 percent increase in volume for 1997, the result of such outsourcing, and predicted 25 percent growth in automotive sales through the year 2001. More conservative estimates for growth in sales to the automotive industry averaged around 6 percent.

Other factors contributing to the growth of the industry include the use of adhesives as a substitute for metallic fasteners such as nails and staples, and as a substitute for paint. Broxterman reported in 1997 that ''much of the artwork that you see on the skins of airplanes and the

sides of large trucking fleets, such as rent-a-trailers, is actually decals and is no longer painted.''

Concerns over the environmental impact of adhesives and sealants increased following the passage of the Clean Air Act Amendments of 1990. Under that legislation, the Environmental Protection Agency (EPA) was required to set standards for volatile organic compounds (VOC) content and emissions reduction. In 1999, the agency was expected to propose a regulation that required adhesives products purchased by consumers to have a VOC content of 10 percent or less (although the EPA reported delays due to government shutdowns). Because the regulation was based on California guidelines already in place, most companies with a nationwide market were not expected to be greatly affected. Such regulations increased the production and demand for water-based and hot melt products, although water-based adhesives may still contain toxic residues.

INDUSTRY LEADERS

In 1997, the adhesives and sealants industry was comprised of more than 692 U.S. establishments employing approximately 21,737 people, just 12,000 of whom were production personnel. Many of these establishments were small business—of the 692, just 39 percent had more than 20 employees. Ranked by the number of production workers, the top five states in 1997 were Ohio, Missouri, Michigan, California, and Illinois.

According to a survey by Impact Marketing Consultants in 1998, these were the largest corporations in the industry, as ranked by market share: National Starch and Chemical Company and H.B. Fuller, each with a 5.0 percent share; Henkel, with a market share of 3.5 percent; 3M, at 3.0 percent; and Reichhold, Morton International, and General Electric tied for fifth place, each with 2.5 percent. Other top companies included Sonoco Products, Hercules Incorporated, and Borden Inc. Cytec Industries was the leading aerospace adhesives producer in 1998. Industry analysts mentioned Fieldco Industries and Devcon as two smaller companies with the potential for growth in the specialized adhesives market.

AMERICA AND THE WORLD

Because most products in this industry are based on commonly held formulas and because of the high cost of overseas shipping, exports are not a large part of this industry, with the exception of some high-performance, application-specific products.

U.S. firms instead worked to increase global market share via international acquisitions. For example, Reichhold purchased two firms in Italy (one in 1996, and one in 1996), while H.B. Fuller purchased three European firms in the United Kingdom and Germany. Foreign firms also provided growth opportunities for midsize U.S. companies; among the firms that took advantage of that opportunity in the late 1990s were Sovereign Chemical Company and TACC International. Sovereign also purchased a portion of former industry leader B.F. Goodrich's adhesives and sealants business. At the same time, European companies increased investments in American firms; major foreign firms included Imperial Chemical Industries, Henkel, and Elf Atochem. As of 1998, Henkel was considered the top-selling company in the industry worldwide.

Gaining a foothold in the global marketplace was crucial for companies seeking larger scale growth. In 1998, the United States represented just under half of the worldwide consumption of adhesives and sealants, and growth in foreign markets was expect to outstrip domestic growth for the industry. Some analysts suggested that Latin America was a region ripe for market development. A study by the Freedonia Group predicted demand in that area would increase from 885,000 metric tons in 1997 to 1.1 billion metric tons by 2002. According to Freedonia, leading markets for the industry include Brazil, Argentina, Chile, Colombia, and Venezuela.

RESEARCH AND TECHNOLOGY

Adhesives and sealants manufacturers are counting on proactive research and development to keep them one step ahead of environmental regulators and market demands. Among the challenges faced are regulations aimed at reducing volatile organic compound emissions and bolstering pollution prevention measures.

Newer areas of technological challenge in terms of bonding are glass-reinforced polyesters. One emerging plastic technology is resin transfer molding (RTM). This is a polyester material, based on resin, that is being used in lower volume auto and truck applications such as sporty or upscale car models.

A growing number of players in the adhesives and sealants industry have expressed a desire to move away from the use of primers in adhesive systems because of their flammability and volatility. Such a change, however, presents difficulties in getting the right adhesion to certain materials. Physical and chemical changes can be made to the surface of these materials, but the focus of new development is to make adhesives and sealants that will incorporate the function of a primer. Environmental mandates on chlorofluorocarbons, volatile organic compound emission standards, and other ecological considerations are thus forcing adhesive formulators to nudge solvents out of their products and find alternatives. Research continues on meeting high-performance parameters such as water resistance, durability, and humidity resistance without using such solvents.

In addition, a number of large users of solvent-borne adhesives have already installed equipment to recapture and recycle, or properly incinerate, solvent and are less likely to change to solventless products. Already, adhesive manufacturers have moved production of industrial adhesives away from solvents to 100 percent solids, epoxies, and urethanes. With respect to pressure sensitive adhesives such as duct tape and heavy-duty industrial tapes, manufacturers have raised solid content to 65 percent, from as low as 35 percent.

A growing area of research in the late 1990s was soy-based adhesives, particularly for wood-bonding applications. Trials in 1996 and 1997—some sponsored by Borden Chemicals—found that adhesives made from soy hydrolyzate created a waterproof bond that exceeded industry standards for strength. The United Soybeans Board hoped to develop adhesives to replace both urea-formaldehyde and phenol-formaldehyde. Such products would also have a reduced volatile organic compounds (VOC) content.

Developments in cloning technology may also hold potential for the creation of new adhesives. Seeking an improved waterproof adhesive, scientists at the University of California, Santa Barbara, studied mussels. According to the Department of Energy's Idaho National Engineering and Environment Laboratory, "the 'feet' of mussels secrete a viscous substance—a protein with adhesive-like properties—that hardens into attachment threads in about one minute. Unfortunately, it takes about 10,000 mussels to produce just one gram of adhesive." Scientists hope to clone the proteins to make their production economically feasible.

FURTHER READING

"Adhesives Demand Rises." *Chemical Market Reporter*, 15 February, 1999.

Chapman, Peter. "Adhesives Stick it Out." *Chemical Market Reporter*, 28 April 1997.

Cozier, Muriel, and Doris Leblond. "Sealing a Place in the World market." *ECN-European Chemical News*, 8 June 1998.

D'Amico, Esther. "Squeezing Out Profits: Adhesives Makers Get Set for Growth." *Chemical Week*, 27 March 1996.

Dun & Bradstreet/Gale Industry Reporter. Detroit: Gale Group, 1999.

"Eureka!" *R & D*, October 1999.

Gain, Bruce. "Adhesives & Sealants." *Chemical Week*, 18 March 1998.

———. "Adhesives and Sealants: Customizing the Formula." *Chemical Week*, 26 March 1997.

"Hot Melts Heat Up." *Chemical Week*, 20 May 1998.

Market Share Reporter, 2000. Detroit: Gale Group, 2000.

Pease, David A. "Research Moves Forward on Soy-based Adhesives." *Wood Technology*, September 1997.

Pospisil, Ray. "Automakers Develop Chemical Dependence." *Chemical Week*, 18 March 1998.

Scheraga, Dan. "Sticking Around for Niche Applications." *Chemical Market Reporter,* 24 August 1998.

Stringer, Judy. "EPA Consumer Product Proposal on the Way: VOC Reduction Effort Continues." *Chemical Week,* 27 March 1996.

U.S. Department of Commerce. *U.S. Industry & Trade Outlook.* McGrawHill, 1999.

U.S. Department of Commerce/U.S. Census Bureau. *Adhesive Manufacturing: 1997 Economic Census.* Washington: GPO, 1999. Available from http://www.census.gov.

Walsh, Kerri. "Optimism in the Raw." *Chemical Week,* 18 March 1998.

SIC 2892

EXPLOSIVES

This industry covers establishments primarily engaged in manufacturing explosives. Establishments primarily engaged in manufacturing ammunition for small arms are classified in **SIC 3482: Small Arms Ammunition,** and those manufacturing fireworks are classified in **SIC 2899: Chemicals and Chemical Preparations, Not Elsewhere Classified.**

NAICS CODE(S)

325920 (Explosives Manufacturing)

Historically, the explosives industry has been closely aligned with the coal mining industry. According to *The Institute of Makers of Explosives* (IME) the coal industry consumed 67 percent of explosives manufactured in the United States in 1998 and remained the largest application for explosives use in the United States. Historically, explosives such as black powder have been used in the United States to mine for minerals, break rock, clear fields, and build roads. After Alfred Nobel invented dynamite and the blasting cap required to make it explode, he licensed his discoveries in the United States. Mines could now be dug deeper and more quickly with dynamite, thereby making mining more profitable.

By 1905, E.I. DuPont de Nemours and Company, one of the largest U.S. explosives companies, supplied 56 percent of the production of explosives in the United States. DuPont continued to strengthen its hold on the market; by 1907 the U.S. government had begun antitrust proceedings against the company. In 1912 DuPont was forced to divest segments of its business, which resulted in Atlas Chemical Industries and the Hercules Powder Company. Later, Atlas was purchased by Imperial Chemical Industries PLC, DuPont's explosives division was sold to Explosives Technologies International, and Hercules' explosives division was sold to Dyno Nobel, Inc.

In the early years of the industry, the volatile nature of explosives played a significant role in the organization of explosives manufacturers. Companies operated numerous small plants to ensure that their entire business would not be wiped out in the event of an explosion. In addition, plants were located near the consumer rather than the raw materials sources because of the danger in transporting the product.

Products of the explosives industry have changed dramatically over the years. ANFO, or ammonium nitrate mixed with fuel oil, was invented in 1953. Since 1959, it has become the most widely utilized explosive in surface coal mining. By the early 1990s, ANFO held 75 percent of the market. Thus, dynamite declined in importance from about one billion pounds in the mid-1950s to approximately 100 million pounds in 1993. Because of the drastic decline in the use of dynamite, manufacturing plants for that product decreased from 30 in the 1950s to just one, which was owned by Dyno Nobel, in 1993. In place of dynamite, emulsions gained popularity in the 1990s because of their water resistance and low density.

In 1997, 101 establishments, employing 7,770 people, were in operation in the explosives manufacturing industry. In 1998, 2.89 million metric tons of explosives were produced in the United States. This was a 9 percent increase over 1997, and sales of explosives were recorded in all states. The coal industry continued to be the largest domestic user, accounting for 67 percent of total explosives consumption. The rest of the explosives production was distributed among quarrying and nonmetal mining industries (14 percent), the metal mining industry (9 percent), construction industries (7 percent), and miscellaneous uses (3 percent). Ammonium nitrate-based explosives accounted for 99 percent of production, or 2.86 metric tons—a 9 percent increase from 1997.

While 1998 was a good year for the explosives industry, explosives consumption declined slightly in 1999 but was expected to increase slightly again in 2000. Coal mining, the largest domestic user of explosives, showed its greatest growth in the West. Western surface mines contained less overburden rock and thus required fewer explosives to reach the coal. That trend could be offset by changes in weather patterns, which would result in a greater demand for coal, which could also have a substantial impact on coal demand and, thus, impact the consumption of explosives in the new century.

As a result of the 1993 World Trade Center bombing in New York City and the 1995 bombing of the Federal Building in Oklahoma City, there was a push at the federal level to require that all explosives and potential explosive components such as fertilizer be manufactured with taggants—color-coded, multilayered particles. These particles bear a unique signature and can be seen under a microscope, enabling identification of the manufacturer's batch lot by an explosives expert. In 1996, Congress enacted anti-terrorism legislation, which mandated the study of the feasibility of placing identification taggants in explosives. This study was the responsibility of the Department of the Treasury's Bureau of Alcohol, Tobacco and Firearms (ATF) and was contracted out to the National Academy of Sciences (NAS) to conduct a third-party examination. The NAS report was completed and issued in March 1998 and concluded that it was not appropriate to require commercial explosives to contain identification taggants considering the level of threat in the late 1990s. The ATF also issued an interim report in March 1998 that stated that any effort intended to have a measurable impact on the prevention and investigation of bombing incidents had to be an integrated one. In October 1999 the IME's recommendation was that it was not in the best interests of the industry, the public, the environment, or law enforcement to mandate taggants in commercial explosives. It also seemed likely that the explosives manufacturers would not welcome any further action on the part of Congress.

In response to the 1995 Oklahoma City bombing, a joint voluntary campaign called "Be Aware for America" was formed by The Fertilizer Institute (TFI) and the ATF. The goal of this program was to provide fertilizer retailers with information to identify suspicious ammonium nitrate purchasers and thus help avoid intentional criminal use of that product. To further strengthen the program, the ATF requested that ammonium nitrate dealers identify the local law enforcement agencies that would most likely be contacted in the event of theft or vandalism at the dealer's property. The law enforcement agencies were then contacted to discuss their responses to such incidents.

FURTHER READING

"Be Aware for America." *The Fertilizer Institute,* 1999. Available from http://www.tfi.org/beware.htm.

"The Debate About Invisible Detectives." *U.S. News & World Report,* 16 September 1996.

"Explosives Manufacturing." *U.S. Census Bureau, 1997 Economic Census, Manufacturing, Industry Series,* August 1999.

Kramer, Deborah. "Explosives." *Minerals Yearbook, Volume 1—Metals and Minerals, U.S. Department of the Interior, U.S. Geological Survey,* 1998. Available from http://minerals .usgsgov/minerals/pubs/commodity/explosives/index.html.

"Product Liability Could Be the Real Issue With Taggants." *Chemical & Engineering News,* 26 August 1996.

Robinson, Kevin. "Devices Detect Explosive Residue." *Phonics Spectra,* July 1998.

"Taggants Become an Issue." *Coal Age,* December 1996.

"Taggants in Explosives." *Institute of Makers of Explosives,* October 1999.

"Tagged Out." *Science News,* 14 September 1996.

SIC 2893

PRINTING INK

This classification includes establishments primarily engaged in manufacturing printing ink, including gravure ink, screen process ink, and lithographic ink. Establishments primarily engaged in manufacturing writing ink and fluids are classified in **SIC 2899: Chemicals and Chemical Preparations, Not Elsewhere Classified.** Those establishments manufacturing drawing ink are classified in **SIC 3952: Lead Pencils, Crayons, and Artists' Materials.**

NAICS CODE(S)

325910 (Printing Ink Manufacturing)

The printing ink industry is one of America's oldest, dating back to the pre-Revolutionary War days. After more than 200 years of similar operating procedures, there was little change in the structure of the industry entering the 1990s. However, the 1990s brought massive consolidation to the sector. Because the market for printing inks was mature and profits were low, the largest ink companies acquired smaller firms as a way to boost market share. By September 1999, four companies controlled more than half of the global printing ink market, according to *Chemical Market Reporter.*

The National Association of Printing Ink Manufacturers (NAPIM)—the trade organization representing ink producers in the United States—reported that industry shipments were valued at $4.3 billion in 1998, up from $3.7 billion in 1996. Printing ink imports increases 11.6 percent from 1997 and 1998, and exports rose 9.7 percent.

The printing ink industry is classified by ink type. In 1997, lithographic and offset printing ink shipments comprised the largest category, with shipments valued at $1.97 billion—45.8 percent of the total shipments. With 15.9 percent of the total market, lexographic printing inks were the second-largest sector, with 1997 shipments topping $683 million. Gravure printing inks shipments totaled $541 million, representing 12.6 percent of the total, while letterpress printing ink shipments were more than $153 million, or 3.6 percent of the total. Nonimpact digital inks were the smallest individual ink category, with approximately $115 million in shipments (accounting for 2.7 percent of the total). The remaining 19.4 percent of the market was comprised of nonclassified printing inks.

In 1997, 565 establishments were involved in the production of printing ink, and 200 of these were larger companies with more than 20 employees. California was home to the largest number of printing ink manufacturers with 54 companies, followed by Texas with 36, and New Jersey with 33. With shipments valued at more than $333 million, California accounted for 7.7 percent of the industry's total, far ahead of the next largest-shipping state—New Jersey—which shipped more than $219 million worth of printing ink in 1997 (5.1 percent of the total).

A total of 13,026 people worked in the printing ink production industry in 1997, with 6,895 of those directly involved in production. Production employees worked an average of 40 hours per week and earned an average wage of $16.56 per hour.

The 1994 Vegetable Ink Printing Act of Congress exerted a powerful influence on the industry. The bill mandated that printers with government contracts use vegetable oil-based inks instead of volatile petroleum-based inks whenever possible. The main concerns were due to the hazardous effects of using crude oil as the ink base, as was done for most of the history of printing inks. Emissions from volatile organic compounds (VOCs) and emissions of hazardous air pollutants (HAPs) had to be controlled. Printing inks also had to be developed to make the de-inking and recycling of paper easier. Printers wanted inks that stuck to paper, and recyclers wanted inks that could be easily removed.

During the recession at the beginning of the 1990s, raw material prices stabilized considerably. Purchasing experts in the ink industry found that there were only a few areas where upward price pressure could continue throughout 1990. The major factor affecting prices was the stable price of crude oil, from which more than 75 percent of the raw materials for ink was derived. The industry's membership sought to take full advantage of the relatively low raw material costs, resisting any price increases from raw materials suppliers unless they were fully justified. In some product areas, the companies were able to negotiate price reductions, which helped the industry hold the line on its own prices.

The printing ink industry has made efforts to reduce the environmental burden of its products. Before passage of the Clean Air Act, printing ink manufacturers were developing water-based ink systems to replace inks containing volatile organic compounds. Many years before the first "CONNEG Law" was passed to reduce heavy metals in packaging, the printing ink industry had been reducing the use of lead-bearing pigments in packaging inks.

Growth in vegetable-based inks leveled off in 1996 as most of the users with environmental concerns switched to newer inks. Another increase in vegetable- and water-based inks will only be likely if environmental pressure increases again.

Further change in the industry occurred in the late 1990s as the pace of consolidation accelerated. In 1998, Flint Ink of Ann Arbor, Michigan, acquired Mander plc

for $167 million. Flint continued its buying spree in November of 1999, with its acquisition of Sacramento, California-based The Ink Co. Flint—the second-largest ink producer in the world—made the purchases to remain competitive with the industry's global leader, Dainippon Ink & Chemical of Japan. Dainippon's U.S. subsidiary, Sun Chemical Corp., was the second-largest American ink producer behind Flint.

FURTHER READING

"Flint Ink Absorbs Rival, Adds Market Share." *Crain's Detroit Business,* 1 November 1999.

"FlintINK Research Center." Detroit: Flint Ink Corporation, 1997. Available from http://www.flintink.com/research.html.

Gentile, Deanna M. "Ink Outlook: Steady Growth and Evolving Technologies." *Modern Paint & Coatings,* July 1996.

Lustig, Ted. "Outlook for Printing Inks, '95." *Graphic Arts Monthly,* March 1995.

———. "Ink Suppliers Seek Rebound in 1996." *Graphic Arts Monthly,* March 1996.

McConville, Daniel J. "Getting Bigger by Staying Small." *Chemical Week,* 1 May 1996.

Miceli, Donna L. "Alternate Inks Mark the Spot." *Chemical Marketing Reporter,* 26 August 1996.

Poirier, Mark. "Expect Another Ink Price Hike." *Catalog Age,* July 1995.

"Printing Inks Market Consolidates." *Chemical Market Reporter,* 20 September 1999.

Savastano, David. "Building a Successful Legacy." *Ink World,* August 1999.

U.S. Census Bureau. "Printing Ink Manufacturing," October 1999. Available from http://www.census.gov/prod/ec97/97m3314c.pdf.

SIC 2895

CARBON BLACK

This category covers establishments primarily engaged in manufacturing carbon black (channel and furnace black). Establishments primarily engaged in manufacturing bone and lamp black are classified in **SIC 2816: Inorganic Pigments.**

NAICS CODE(S)

325182 (Carbon Black Manufacturing)

INDUSTRY SNAPSHOT

Carbon black is essentially an oil by-product used to strengthen rubber. It is made by shooting a hot mist of oil particles into a flame, a very expensive process that has limited the number of competitors in the industry. Carbon black is a general name for a variety of trade name products such as acetylene black, attrited black, channel black, flame black, furnace black, lamp black, and thermal black. Carbon black production requires large amounts of heat. In addition to its main use in tires, the powdery reinforcing agent is used to make inks and other everyday products.

In 1997, U.S. carbon black shipments were worth more than $990 million, and carbon black sold at prices between 28 and 46 cents per pound, depending on the grade. The vast majority of carbon black produced in the United States in the late 1990s was consumed by rubber and tire manufacturing companies.

ORGANIZATION AND STRUCTURE

Carbon black is largely a homogenous product with many trade names. It is essentially an oil by-product used to make tires, inks, and other products. The principal economic industries responsible for the purchase of carbon black were domestic manufacturing industries, which purchased nearly 95 percent of the industry's shipments. A 1998 ranking of purchased carbon black output found these industries responsible for carbon black usage: tires and inner tubes, which purchased approximately 50 percent of the industry's shipments; industrial applications, which used 15 percent of the carbon black manufactured in the United States; and specialty applications, such as wiring, plastics, and coatings, which used 10 percent.

In 1997, 22 establishments were engaged in the production of carbon black. These establishments employed 1,769 workers. In the late 1990s, the U.S. carbon black industry was centered primarily in southern states. Eight companies operated out of Texas, while five were based in Louisiana.

BACKGROUND AND DEVELOPMENT

The Cabot family was involved in carbon black production from the industry's outset. In 1882, Godfrey Cabot built a carbon black plant in Buffalo Mills, Pennsylvania. At the time, carbon black was made by impinging a gas flame against steel. After World War I, it was discovered that carbon black had properties for reinforcing rubber products. It was this innovation that fueled the industry's growth.

As early as 1864, carbon black was used as a printing ink and it is still employed in this sector in the late 1990s. The most revolutionary application was developed for the rubber industry, which discovered that carbon black made tires tougher. In 1920, the rubber industry consumed only 40 percent of the carbon black produced. Today, the rubber industry is the largest market for carbon black.

By 1972 carbon black prices were deteriorating because production capacity was greater than production. Production was three billion pounds per year, while production capacity was about four billion pounds per year. In addition, the cutback in gasoline usage that followed the oil embargo of 1973 took a heavy toll on carbon black demand. At that time, 95 percent of carbon black use was associated with automobile applications; 70 percent went into tire production alone. Higher costs were also having a detrimental effect on the industry. As carbon black prices increased, demand for the industry's products was reduced. Carbon black production capacity fell from an estimated 4.21 billion pounds in 1979 to 3.38 billion pounds in 1981. The decline in 1978 and 1979 mirrored the downturn in the U.S. automotive industry, but export business buoyed the industry.

By the 1980s, with four or five years of increasing prices behind it, relative stability had returned to the carbon black market. Prices for carbon black generally followed oil prices. As oil prices stabilized, so did prices for carbon black.

The total value of industry shipments increased 21 percent from $570 million in 1987 to $692 million in 1990. This number declined to a decade low of $604 million in 1991, but continually rose to $800 million by the mid-1990s. Despite the increase in carbon black shipments, leading producers in the fiercely competitive and sagging U.S. auto industry compelled producers to enter overseas markets. In the early 1990s, U.S. producers established operations in Europe and in Japan. The leading U.S. producer was Cabot Corporation, with total mid-1990s sales of $1.69 billion. It recorded negligible profits in the United States, but generated huge profits abroad.

Leading companies, including Cabot Corporation, continued to expand into international markets in the early 1990s. In 1992, Cabot opened a new carbon black plant, Cabot Kashima, in Kashima, Japan, which produced special grades of carbon black. Many in the industry were also expanding into the budding capitalist societies of eastern Europe. Also during this time of exploration into international markets, new low cost production processes were developed, and recycling efforts in the rubber and tire industries were encouraged. All these improvements within the carbon black industry were implemented to enable U.S. producers to compete against international export companies.

As the carbon black industry entered the mid-1990s, U.S. producers were facing stiff competition from traditionally import-oriented countries. U.S. producers were seeking new markets in developing economies such as China. The demand for carbon black in China was expected to grow 6.6 percent per year during the 1990s. U.S. consumption of carbon black was also projected to increase an average of 2.7 percent annually to $640 million in 1997. This projection was predicated on the gradual recovery of the auto industry.

By March 1995, U.S. demand for carbon black caused a 10 percent increase in price. This dramatic increase was not to be repeated the following year, however. Instead, 1996 operating rates were high and pricing was weak as carbon black sold for 28 to 50 cents per pound. Industry leaders attempted to raise prices 5 percent but were unsuccessful. Tire manufacturers, who purchased 50 percent of U.S. produced carbon black, resisted the price increase.

CURRENT CONDITIONS

Despite tire manufacturers protestations, carbon black prices rose in 1997 and 1998, as demand for the commodity outstripped supply. The automotive sector, which consumed carbon black for tires, boomed in the bull market of the late 1990s. Moreover, the growing popularity of sport utility vehicles—which used bigger tires that wore out faster than on cars—fueled demand for carbon black. Carbon black manufacturers also enjoyed low crude oil prices, which kept production costs to a minimum.

However, in 1999, rising crude oil prices impacted the carbon black market. While demand for tires remained strong in North America, a surge of cheaper import tires undercut carbon black prices. Tires originating in Korea and Brazil claimed an increasing share of the market, which grew at a rate of about 2 percent in 1998.

INDUSTRY LEADERS

The Boston, Massachusetts-based Cabot Corporation was the world's largest producer of carbon black in 1998, producing some 995 million pounds. The Cabot Corporation was a conglomeration of specialty metals, chemical, and energy businesses. When the carbon black market staggered in the early 1980s, Cabot expanded into fields such as high-technology ceramics. Cabot also kept effective control over the slow-growth carbon black market segment of through restructuring efforts, including drastic reductions in unit costs to counter the heavy fixed capital investment required for carbon black production.

In 1996, Cabot bought a plant in Merak, Indonesia. The plant was expected to double its capacity to 60,000 metric tons per year. Also in 1996, Cabot instituted a system that measured the performance of its 71 carbon black plants and conveyed the information to all plant managers. Cabot was able to stay ahead of competitors and quadruple earnings per share through cutting costs, modernization, and restructuring. In 1997 the company introduced a new line of carbon black pigments, which helped it remain at the forefront of the industry. Cabot's efforts were rewarded. Sales in 1998 were approximately $1.7 billion, and the company employed 4,800 workers.

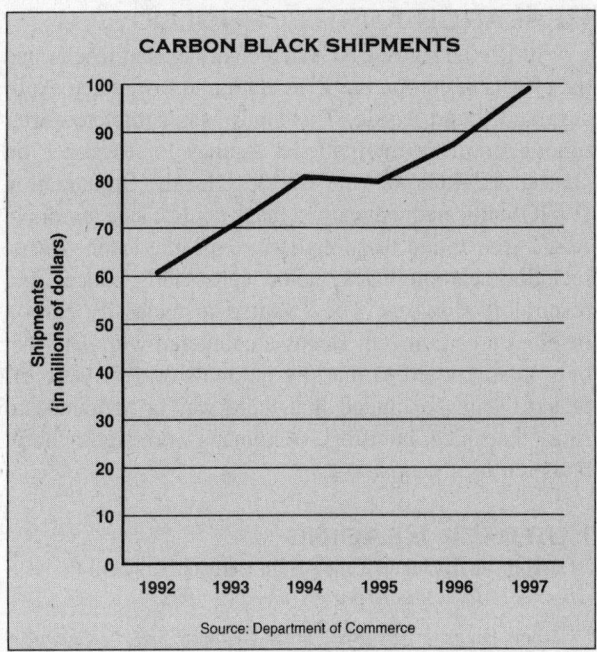

CARBON BLACK SHIPMENTS

Source: Department of Commerce

The second-largest producer of carbon black was Columbian Chemicals Co. of Atlanta, Georgia. In 1996, Columbian underwent a 25 percent expansion that increased its global capacity by 180,000 pounds. This restructuring cost approximately $60 million. The company operated 11 plants in 8 countries. Columbian's total sales were $260 million in 1998, and they employed 1,400 people.

Another major industry player was Degussa's Carbon Black Division of Ridgefield Park, New Jersey, with $150 million in sales and 300 employees. In 1998, Degussa moved aggressively to capture a greater share of the Asian market for carbon black by acquiring the carbon black division of LG Chemical in South Korea. Other leading carbon black producers included JM Huber Corporation's Engineered Carbons Division (bought by Gantrade Corporation in 1995) of Borger, Texas, and Norit Americas Inc. of Atlanta, Georgia.

WORKFORCE

In 1997 approximately 1,769 workers were employed in the carbon black industry. Of this total number, 1,123 were production workers who earned an average wage of $19.71 per hour. On average, these production employees worked a total of 46 hours each week.

The U.S. Bureau of Labor Statistics forecast that most of the industry's occupational categories were expected to increase until 2005, reflecting the projected growth in demand for the industry's products. However, many of the occupations expected to grow most rapidly were nonproduction jobs, such as sales workers and highly skilled professional positions.

RESEARCH AND TECHNOLOGY

In 1996, Degussa AG, an industry leader, researched the effects of carbon black in relation to workplace exposure and found it safe. This study was completed after reports from the International Agency for Research on Cancer (IARC) of the World Health Organization (WHO) indicated that carbon black could cause tumors in rats. IARC found that long-term exposure to fine dusts, including carbon black, could cause lung cancer and respiratory diseases. They wanted to reclassify carbon black as a carcinogen. Degussa countered with data that only rats exposed to massive amounts of dust were effected. They concluded that there was no evidence to show that mice, hamsters, or humans were significantly bothered by the dust.

FURTHER READING

"Carbon Black Makers Enjoy High Demand, Low Oil Prices." *Chemical Marketing Reporter,* 27 April 1998.

"Carbon Black Poses No Threat Degussa Says." *Chemical Marketing Reporter,* 5 August 1996.

Cho, Aileen. "Waste Toner May Beef Up Asphalt." *ENR,* 30 September 1996.

"Columbian Has Details on Hike in Carbon Black." *Chemical Marketing Reporter,* 22 April 1996.

Henry, Brian. "Cabot Using Technology to Transform Carbon Black." *Chemical Marketing Reporter,* 21 October 1996.

Landau, Peter. "Rising Feedstock Costs Crimp Profit Margins for Carbon Black." *Chemical Marketing Reporter,* 8 November 1999.

Morris, Gregory DL. "Columbian Details Expansions." *Chemical Week,* 24 April 1996.

Shearer, Brent. "Carbon Black Makers Adding New Capacity." *Chemical Marketing Reporter,* 23 September 1996.

U.S. Census Bureau. "Carbon Black Manufacturing," October 1999. Available from http://www.census.gov/prod/ec97/97m3314c.pdf.

Warren, J. Robert. "Cabot Sees Strong Asian Markets for Carbon Black." *Chemical Marketing Reporter,* 25 March 1996.

SIC 2899

CHEMICALS AND CHEMICAL PREPARATIONS, NOT ELSEWHERE CLASSIFIED

This industry consists primarily of establishments engaged in manufacturing miscellaneous chemical preparations, not elsewhere classified, such as fatty acids, essential oils, gelatin (except vegetable), sizes, bluing, laundry sours, writing and stamp pad ink, industrial compounds, such as boiler and heat insulating compounds, metal, oil, and water treating compounds, waterproofing compounds, and chemical supplies for foundries. Establishments primarily engaged in manufacturing vegetable gelatin are classified in **SIC 2833: Medicinal Chemicals and Botanical Products;** those manufacturing dessert preparations based on gelatin are classified in **SIC 2099: Food Preparations, Not Elsewhere Classified;** those manufacturing printing ink are classified in **SIC 2893: Printing Ink;** and those manufacturing drawing ink are classified in **SIC 3952: Lead Pencils, Crayons, and Artists' Materials.**

NAICS CODE(S)

325510 (Paint and Coating Manufacturing)

311942 (Spice and Extract Manufacturing)

325199 (All Other Basic Organic Chemical Manufacturing)

325998 (All Other Miscellaneous Chemical Product Manufacturing)

As the specialty chemical industry entered the 1990s, many corporations implemented organizational restructuring coupled with cost reduction measures. Based on these management decisions, the industry appeared to be in the beginning of a business recovery from the cyclical downturn experienced during the last portion of the 1980s. However, the pickup was more difficult and slower than expected, in part because of the continued sluggishness of foreign economies. This factor reduced the export demand for chemicals and, consequently, the industry's trade surplus.

Total industry shipments were valued $12.7 billion in 1997, up from $9.9 billion in 1992. Chemical preparations, including essential oils, were the most important category in this industry in 1997. Shipments in this sector were about $6.5 billion, which accounted for 51.2 percent of total shipments. Water treating compounds were the second-largest category with shipments reaching more than $2.7 billion, or 21.3 percent. Shipments of automotive chemicals, such as antifreeze and engine cleaning chemicals, were $744 million in 1997, representing 5.9 percent of the total. Gelatin shipments were more than $558 million, while evaporated salt shipments topped $451 million, comprising 4.4 percent and 3.6 percent respectively. Matches were the weakest category in the industry, accounting for only $79 million, or less than 0.7 percent of total shipments.

The growth of miscellaneous chemicals, such as sodium chlorate, posted double-digit growth since the late 1980s. Sodium chlorate is used in the form of chlorine dioxide as a substitute for traditional chlorine in pulp and paper bleaching. While the substitution of this chemical has been greater in Canada than the United States due to greater environmental concerns over chlorine, the use of

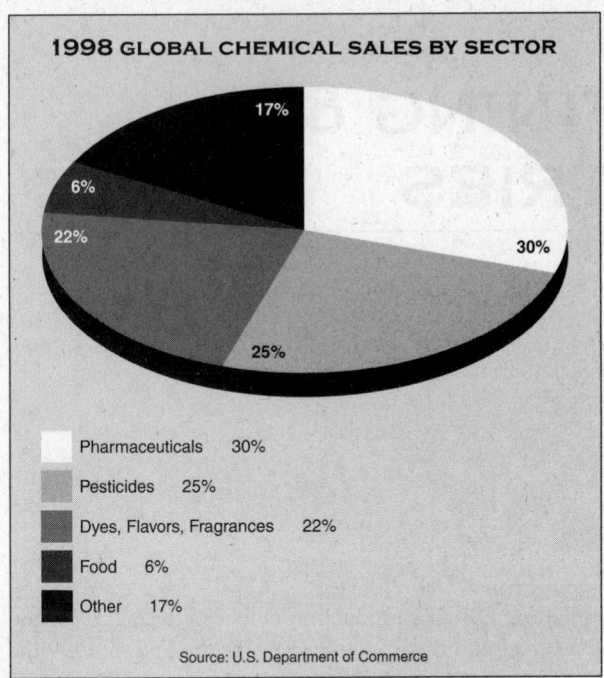

1998 GLOBAL CHEMICAL SALES BY SECTOR

17%

6%

22%

30%

25%

Pharmaceuticals   30%

Pesticides   25%

Dyes, Flavors, Fragrances   22%

Food   6%

Other   17%

Source: U.S. Department of Commerce

the chemical in the United States is expected to continue increasing. About two-thirds of the North American production capacity of sodium chlorate was located in Canada. Considering the dramatic growth prospects for sodium chlorate, major producers have made sizeable capacity expansions in recent years.

Demand for basic chemicals strengthened in response to the prolonged economic expansion of the 1980s. Output in the early 1990s, as measured by the Federal Reserve Board (FRB) Basic Chemicals Production Index, was at its highest level since the prior peak reached in the late 1970s. Over the long run, the demand for basic chemicals was expected to pace the rise in real (inflation-adjusted) gross domestic product (GDP), with the automobile, housing,

export, agricultural, and paper markets, in particular, holding sway. The prolonged economic upswing of the mid-and late-1990s brought further growth to the industry.

The number of establishments involved in this industry in 1997 was 1,149—down from 1,409 in 1996. According to *Chemical Week,* considerable consolidation in the chemical industry has reduced the number of key players. The vast majority of companies in this sector employed less than 20 workers. Only 424 of the total number had 20 or more employees in 1997. With 127 companies, Texas led other states with the greatest number of chemical preparation establishments, followed by California with 114 and Illinois with 67.

Employment in this industry has dropped recently due to consolidation. The number of employees decreased from 36,500 people in 1994 to 35,897 in 1997, of which 21,536 were production employees. Production workers earned on average $14.76 per hour. Texas was home to the greatest number of employees in this industry, with 3,722, followed by Illinois with 3,000.

Major United States corporations that produce specialty chemicals include Mobil Corp., Kich Industries Inc., Texaco Inc., and Merck and Company Inc. Other leading companies are Nalco Chemical, a subsidiary of Suez Lyonnaise des Faux; as well as Akzo Nobel Inc. and Henkel of America, a subsidiary of German chemical giant Henkel.

FURTHER READING

"Akzo, Dow, and BASF Rise to the Top". *Chemical Week,* 24 March 1999.

Darnay, Arsen J., ed. *Manufacturing USA.* 5th ed. Detroit: Gale Research, 1996.

U.S. Department of Commerce. "Value of Product Shipments." *Annual Survey of Manufactures,* Washington, D.C.: GPO, 1995.

PETROLEUM REFINING & RELATED INDUSTRIES

PETROLEUM REFINING

This category covers establishments engaged primarily in producing gasoline, kerosene, distillate fuel oils, residual fuel oils, and lubricants through fractionation or straight distillation of crude oil, redistillation of unfinished petroleum derivatives, cracking, or other processes. Establishments primarily engaged in producing natural gasoline from natural gas are classified in mining industries. Those manufacturing lubricating oils and greases by blending and compounding purchased materials are classified in **SIC 2992: Lubricating Oils and Greases.** Establishments primarily engaged in manufacturing cyclic and acyclic organic chemicals are classified in various chemicals and allied product manufacturing industries.

NAICS CODE(S)

324110 (Petroleum Refineries)

INDUSTRY SNAPSHOT

The $150 billion U.S. refinery industry continues its path toward consolidation and cost efficiency in the face of price instability and tightening environmental regulations. From 1990 to 1999 the number of operable refineries in the United States declined 22 percent, while capacity held steady with late 1980s levels. In 1999 the 159 operable refineries had a total operating capacity of 16.26 million barrels per day, a quarter of the world's capacity. Meanwhile, U.S. demand has grown at 1 to 2 percent a year, a trend expected to continue in the early 2000s.

Price instability plagued the overall oil business in the late 1990s. From historic low prices in 1998 and early 1999, when oversupply dragged crude oil prices below $10 a barrel, a Depression-era low when adjusted for inflation, OPEC's production cutbacks during 1999 and 2000 caused oil prices to surge. By the end of 1999 the average monthly price had soared nearly 150 percent since the beginning of the year.

Although refiners weren't hit as hard by price swings as other segments of the oil industry were, consolidation due to price pressures transformed the refining side greatly. Within a two-year span, the U.S. industry saw corporate mergers between such giants as Exxon and Mobil, and British Petroleum and Amoco, along with a refining joint venture between Marathon and Ashland. In addition, a complex refining and marketing combination between Shell, Texaco, and Saudi Refining produced two large regional refiners named Motiva and Equilon. Similar transactions took place in foreign operations. Refiners, as well as integrated oil companies generally, sought cost savings and other economies of scale that these mergers were expected to provide. The companies hoped to better insulate themselves against the oil business' notorious price cycles.

Refiners must contend with a host of environmental issues at both the state and national levels. Recent federal regulatory proposals have included a drastic reduction of sulfur in gasoline and diesel fuel, against strenuous objections from refiners. Another area of growing regulatory attention has been the elimination of methyl tertiary butyl ether (MTBE), an oxygen-adding compound used in reformulated gasoline to reduce motor vehicle emissions. MTBE has been found to contaminate water supplies, and as a result, was banned in California starting in 2002. Other states and federal authorities were considering restrictions on MTBE as well.

ORGANIZATION AND STRUCTURE

Downstream. The process of turning crude oil into refined products, the "downstream" side of the oil business, involves several key participants and cannot be fully understood without a rudimentary knowledge of the "upstream" side of the oil business, the process of obtaining crude oil. Upstream operations consist of exploration, geological evaluation, and the testing and drilling of potential oilfield sites; that is, all of the procedures necessary to get oil out of the ground (see **SIC 1311: Crude Petroleum and Natural Gas**). Downstream operations include pipelining crude oil to refining sites, refining crude into various products, and pipelining or otherwise transporting products to wholesalers, distributors, or retailers.

Because many downstream companies are subsidiaries of conglomerates that also maintain upstream subsidiaries, the sale of raw materials to refiners is often essentially a transfer of products between different operating units of the same corporation. Petroleum refiners, therefore, often depend on the upstream arms of their parent corporations for supplies of crude, and, in turn, supply wholesalers (who then sell to independent retailers) and retailers (company-owned gasoline stations, for example) that are also part of the same corporation. All major oil operating in this system are known as "integrated oil companies" and non-integrated companies are often referred to as "independents".

This tendency toward massive, integrated supply systems affects the oil industry and refiners in that any shift in condition at any point in the crude-to-product chain is felt equally at all levels; economic trickle-down, as it exists in other industries, offers no stabilization.

Processes and Terms. Petroleum refineries turn crude oil into a variety of intermediate forms that are then used in a wide range of products from asphalt to plastics. All products begin in much the same way: with the distillation, or vaporization, of crude. Distillation begins when crude oil boils; components within crude condense at different rates and so are extracted at progressive points along a time/temperature continuum. Lighter, high-value products—propanes, butanes, gasoline, jet fuel—condense at lower temperatures while heavier compounds require high temperatures or a special extraction method to be transformed into such products as diesel fuels, heavy fuel oil, and asphalts. The components of distillated crude vary according to the make-up of the raw crude, with some batches containing large amounts of sulfur, for example, while others may be bituminous and full of heavier compounds.

Before distillation, crude is stored in groups or "farms" of steel tanks. Distillation then occurs in a fractionating tower, in which the various fractions, or portions, of the crude are separated. The "straight runs" obtained in the fractionating tower are treated in secondary stages to create final products.

Some secondary processing involves simple heat and pressure manipulations, while others include complex chemical reactions. Thus not all refineries are capable of all processing techniques. Some of the most common processes include coking, which creates gasoline and gas oils from the heaviest molecules of the crude. Catalytic cracking uses heat, pressure, and a chemical catalyst to double the gasoline yield in a barrel of crude by converting heavy cuts to lighter products. Hydrocracking uses hydrogen to make 100 percent gasoline from the light gas oils that catalytic cracking and coking produce. Hydrofining removes sulfur from the crude, making a cleaner-burning base fuel and allowing the sulfur to be sold as a byproduct. Reforming rearranges molecules in a low-octane gasoline to produce a higher octane. Alkylation enlarges propane and butane molecules, allowing them to be mixed with gasoline.

From these processes emerge products that can be sorted into three main headings. Gas and gasoline, or "white" products, which comprise the lighter end of the barrel, usually about 20 percent of the total yield, are used for automobile gas, aviation fuel, and feedstocks for petrochemicals. Middle distillates, the middle quarter of the barrel, yield kerosene and light gas-oil, heating oil, diesel oils and waxes. Fuel oil and residuals, comprising the heaviest, bottom 55 percent, make up heavy fuel oils—for use in power stations and ship furnaces—asphalt and bitumen.

Petroleum products have a wide variety of uses. Solvents, for example, go into ink, oil-base paints, dry cleaning solutions, rubber cement, and metal cleaners. Sodium hydrosulfide improves paper pulp and tans leather, while organic chemicals serve an entirely, separate spectrum of uses as petrochemicals.

Ethylene, the largest-volume organic produced in the United States, goes mostly into fabricated plastics but is also used in antifreeze, synthetic fibers and rubbers, and detergents. Propylene has several chemical offshoots that are used mainly in film, packaging, and fibers. Butadiene goes primarily into synthetic rubber, but it is also used in ABS resins, latexes, and nylon fibers.

Aromatics, including benzene, toluene, and the xylenes, are primarily useful as blending agents in gasoline, as well as in increasing the octane rating of unleaded gas. Methanol is traditionally used in formaldehyde, acetic acid, solvents, and polymers for adhesives, fibers, and plastics. But in years to come, methanol is likely to be in greater demand to make the oxygenate MTBE (methyl tertiary butyl ether). MTBE, used since 1979 when lead additives began to be phased out, is a component of reformulated gasolines in cities designated by the Clean Air Act of 1990. Its use grew rapidly during the 1990s in the effort to comply with air-quality standards; however, by the late 1990s it was found to contaminate groundwater and was being phased out in states like California.

Product yields per barrel have shifted with demand. In 1981, 10.4 percent of a barrel went toward residual fuel oils, only 6.7 percent was used in such fuel oils in 1991. Moreover, while 7.6 percent of a 1981 barrel went for jet fuel, 10.3 percent of a 1991 barrel was used in jet fuel. This trend should continue, and may become more pronounced, as various emissions regulations are adopted. Federal requirements for low sulfur diesel fuel and reformulated gasoline should change the yield of a barrel of crude; at the same time, wastewater and toxic solids limitations will change the methods of obtaining yields.

Financial Structure. Once crude oil has been refined, its products may be sold as raw materials to other manufacturers, such as plastics or pharmaceutical companies. Other products may be in a final, packaged form and destined for retail sale in service stations or chemical companies.

Within an integrated oil company, a refinery's profits then are part of the total profits made on the front-end. Its ability to compete depends entirely on efficient production without excessive expenditures so that retail prices can remain low. Like the supply side interdependency of integrated oil companies, integrated profit margins are cumulative. They must absorb the costs of every aspect of the oil business, including geological research, refining procedures, and trucking the finished product, to show real net gain.

For refiners operating independently, turning a profit traditionally rested in purchasing crude at low enough rates to allow final product levels to match those of the integrated oils. Free from the overhead of exploration and test drilling, independents were able to compete effectively for years simply by taking advantage of plentiful, cheap supplies of crude. However, the increasingly stringent environmental requirements of the 1980s and 1990s put independents at a distinct disadvantage. Even with low crude prices, facility upgrading cut deeply into revenues and forced profit margins to fall.

Competitive Structure. The U.S. industry is made up of integrated international oil companies, integrated domestic oil companies, and independent domestic refining/marketing companies. Like the oil business in general, refining is dominated by integrated internationals, specifically a few large companies such as BP Amoco, Exxon Mobil Corporation, and Chevron Corporation.

Of the nonintegrated refining companies—independents that focus exclusively on refined goods production and marketing—Marathon Ashland and Tosco stood out as major players. However, no independent companies competed on the same level as any integrated international in terms of net profits or refined goods sold.

Capacity also distinguishes leading refiners as arms of integrated oils. Exxon Mobil, BP Amoco, and Chevron have more than one million barrels per day capacity, with Marathon Ashland and Tosco trailing them closely. In 1999 the top ten refiners controlled an estimated 58 percent of U.S. capacity; this proportion was expected to rise when announced mergers and joint ventures were factored in. At that time around 30 U.S. companies had capacities of 100,000 barrels per calendar day (b/cd) or greater.

As the costs of upgrading refineries escalates, the difficulties of small refining operations will probably intensify. Only with mass infusion of capital can existing refineries remain viable, and only large integrated oils have cashflow to divert. Even the majors struggled: Shell, once the largest U.S. refiner in terms of capacity, has allied nearly all of its U.S. refineries in joint ventures with Texaco and others. Many believe that upgrading and compliance costs will continue to shift the competitive structure of the American refined petroleum products market toward an oligopoly by integrated internationals.

BACKGROUND AND DEVELOPMENT

The use of semi-refined fossil fuels dates back several millennia. Six thousand year-old inscriptions in Mesopotamia include descriptions of oil and asphalt used as waterproofing materials. Egyptians embalmed their dead in asphalt, and Romans wrote by the light of oil lamps and drove chariots with wheels lubricated by crudely refined greases.

Early Development. The invention of the kerosene lamp by Dr. Abraham Gesner of Pittsburgh prompted the formation of the Pennsylvania Rock Oil Company in 1854. During this time Americans sought alternative lamp fuels in response to a shortage of whale oil. Dr. Gesner extracted his "improved illuminating oil" from coal, but his methodology proved invaluable to petroleum refining's founding father, Benjamin Silliman, Jr., who wrote a treatise on the chemistry of petroleum in 1855 and then promptly figured out how to distill it. Steam was introduced into the distillation process in 1858. In 1860, the first semi-continuous refining system, operating in a battery of stills, was patented by D.S. Stombs and Julius Brace of Virginia. Luther Atwood cracked petroleum later that year, and Jean Lenoir then produced a three horsepower motor, which ran on benzene. The first full-fledged refinery began production in 1861 near Titusville, Pennsylvania, adjacent to the site where Edwin Drake and W.A. Smith had discovered the first producing oil field in the country at Oil Creek. The refinery churned out little except kerosene; contemporaneous demand for lubricating oils and greases wasn't high enough to keep anyone in business, and petroleum as a transport fuel was still several decades away.

Julius Hock's invention of the noncompression petroleum engine in Vienna in 1869 perhaps marked the beginning of the modern refining process, as engine fuel would become the primary vehicle for petroleum markets worldwide. ''Horseless carriages''—powered by burning hay, steam, or electricity until Frank and Charles Duryea built the first gasoline-powered automobile in 1892—eventually became the channel through which refined petroleum captured public attention. The internal combustion engine suddenly brought petroleum to a pinnacle of economic significance.

Industrial Age. In the early part of the twentieth century, new technology was developed in petroleum-driven locomotion; automobiles, airplanes, and military vehicles proliferated as petroleum exploration and refining outpaced itself annually. Intense demand for petroleum products during World War I led to production facilities that would continue to produce innovations even after the war; solutions to agricultural, industrial, and transportation problems came with each new piece of understanding about the capabilities of a barrel of crude. Even food supply was drastically affected, as gasoline powered tractors enabled farmers to increase their productivity, and asphalt surfaces on highways allowed diesel-powered trucks to speed goods to market.

World War II also prompted an upsurge in refining capacity, yielding subsequent massive peacetime productivity. American consumers during the 1950s demanded large, stylish automobiles, warm houses, and air travel. For nearly three decades, Americans found uses for more refined petroleum. The ''more is more'' credo became refining's byline; a constant, steadily increasing demand for new products was met by the constant, steadily increasing supply of new crude oil supplies. Unfettered by environmental controls or financial limits, refiners expanded and enjoyed a long, golden age of prosperity.

Oil Crisis. Then, in 1973, a political crisis in the Middle East spurred a severe recession and highlighted the extent to which America had become dependent of foreign oil supplies. Furthering the crisis, the overthrow of the Shah of Iran in 1979 precipitated a series of supply interruptions and price increases. Overcompensating for the shortages brought on by Iran's domestic turbulence, refiners misjudged the oil demand for the early 1980s. While worldwide refining capacity increased tenfold between 1938 and 1981, ''more is more'' no longer held true, and in the 1980s refiners faced a loose market with substantial excesses in place.

Trends in the 1990s. Refiners entered the 1990s burdened by unpredictable supply and demand factors and the potential business consequences of the burgeoning environmental movement. Such issues as recycling, air quality, global warming, and water pollution were high on America's legislative agenda. Consequently, the business strategy of refiners shifted toward finding cleaner-burning, more efficient fuels for smaller cars, as well as finding more environmentally friendly ways in which those fuels could be created.

A mild recovery in demand for refined goods could not alleviate the strain refiners experienced in the early 1990s due to unimproved profit margins. Reduced operations, refinery closures, and low sales characterized a gloomy market. The 1991 recession had taken its toll, and the industry was braced in anticipation of new federal manufacturing standards. These new standards, prompted by a growing concern for the environment, meant that depressed market conditions were compounded by rigorous, expensive mandatory upgrading.

Petroleum refining, like the rest of the oil industry, saw profits dwindle to a five-year low in 1992, while spending on refining simultaneously rose 8.3 percent in an effort to meet costs of upgrading and research into alternative processing. Moreover, the recession had prompted shutdowns totaling 114,850 b/cd capacity and had dampened domestic refined product consumption.

Profit margins remained subdued for most of the decade but improved overall toward the late 1990s. Among large refiners tracked by the U.S. Energy Information Administration, refined product margins rose from a meager $0.77 a barrel in 1994 to a modest $1.58 a barrel in 1998. During that period marketing costs were cut substantially, while energy and other operating costs fluctuated.

Environmental Regulation. Environmental legislation and regulations have had a significant impact on the industry. The Clean Air Act of 1990 required that America's 39 smoggiest cities substitute oxygenated gasoline for winter use beginning in November 1992. By 1995, the country's nine smoggiest cities—Baltimore, Chicago, Hartford, Houston, Los Angeles, Milwaukee, New York, Philadelphia, and San Diego—were to have implemented its Phase I specifications. Phase I stipulated that oxygenates (MTBE) be substituted for aromatics (which do not burn completely) in octane enhancers, essentially prescribing a complete reformulation of automotive gasoline.

The new gasoline must have a minimum oxygen content of 2 percent by weight, a maximum of 1 percent benzene by volume, a maximum aromatics content of 25 percent, and no heavy metals. It must not cause an increase in nitrogen oxide emissions and must create lower tailpipe emissions of volatile organic compounds and toxic air pollutants (relative to a baseline of 1990 summertime gasoline). The cost to refiners of implementing substitutions and reformulations prescribed in Phase I was estimated to run $3 billion to $5 billion.

Furthermore, the California Air Resources Board (CARB) instituted standards exceeding those of the Clean Air Act, requiring them to be met by 1996. Some analysts predicted the CARB standards would eventually replace Clean Air standards nationwide.

Estimates for upcoming compliance costs for U.S. refiners fall within the $20 billion range, as four more major amendments of the Clean Air Act come into play. In October 1993 ultra low-sulfur diesel fuel (.05 percent by weight) was to be required nationally. January 1995 marked the deadline for nationwide Stage I gasoline reformulation, and Stage II should have been met by January 1997, requiring adherence to a "complex" model as opposed to Stage I's "simple" model. January 2000 was to see an additional 10 percent reduction in organic compounds and air toxins from the 1990 baseline fuel, with no increase in nitrogen oxides.

CURRENT CONDITIONS

In 1999 the 159 operating U.S. petroleum refineries produced an average of 8.0 million barrels of gasoline per calendar day (b/cd), 1.6 million b/cd of jet fuel, 3.4 million b/cd of distillate fuel oil, and 700,000 b/cd of residual fuel oil, according to figures published by the Energy Information Administration. Gasoline typically supplies around half of the industry's revenue. Excluding closing stocks, total U.S. demand for refined petroleum products was estimated at 19.44 million b/cd that year, or 9.7 percent above 1995 levels and 14 percent above 1990 levels. Demand was forecast to reach 19.95 million b/cd by 2001, a 2.6 percent volume increase over 1999.

Price Volatility. Oil prices remain a thorny issue for refiners. The late 1990s price volatility was brought on primarily by OPEC policies and softness in world oil markets. Prices tumbled in 1998 when OPEC producers failed to curb their crude oil output despite recession in Russia and parts of Asia and South America. With heavy supply and light demand, prices sank to levels not seen in decades. According to one analyst, the 1998-1999 low reached Depression-era levels when adjusted for inflation.

In early 1999, however, OPEC ministers agreed to limit production in order to cut crude oil supply and resuscitate prices. Within months, prices more than doubled, surpassing the Gulf War nadir of 1990. They remained high into 2000. This, in turn, provoked diplomatic efforts to get OPEC to raise output and stabilize prices. U.S. crude imports were expected average more than $21 a barrel through at least 2001.

Oil companies, including refiners, can be hurt by both low and high prices. In general, low prices benefit downstream business (refining and marketing), whereas high prices benefit upstream operations (exploration and production). Thus, low prices tend to hurt integrated companies most, as their exploration and production operations yield less revenue—and usually profit—on the oil they extract. Meanwhile, high prices tend to squeeze refiners because they must pay more for crude, and especially amid price volatility, they have trouble passing higher costs on to customers. The process is complex,

though, since inventories and other factors can alter individual companies' results.

New Environmental Measures. New environmental laws and regulations continue to challenge the industry. January 2000 marked the introduction of the EPA's Phase 2 regulations for reformulated gasoline (RFG) under the Clean Air Act Amendments of 1990. The second phase continued the EPA's requirement that gasoline contain at minimum 2.1 percent oxygen by weight and no more than 0.95 percent benzene by volume. Going further, it mandated that gasoline provide greater reductions in vehicle emissions of toxic air pollutants, volatile organic compounds, and nitrogen oxides.

Refiners achieve these specifications by formulating their products in different ways, and the changeover can involve considerable cost. In 2000 the U.S. market for Phase 2 reformulated gasoline (RFG) was estimated at 34 percent of total gasoline demand, although the penetration rate varied widely by region. Because not all areas are legally required to use RFG, getting the proper formulation to the correct market can also create logistics costs and challenges for oil marketers.

Meanwhile, even as refiners ramped up operations to produce RFG that complied with the regulations, an unintended side effect of boosting oxygen in gasoline was creating separate environmental worries. Research found that a leading oxygenate, methyl tertiary butyl ether (MTBE), was contaminating groundwater. The pollution was apparently nonlethal but nonetheless troublesome. In 1999 California's governor reacted by banning MTBE effective 2002; other states and the federal government were considering restricting it as well. Abraded by the turnaround on MTBE, which would likely mean another round of expensive refinery upgrades, industry officials pressed for more time and research before MTBE is banned outright.

One of the most controversial new regulations, also issued by the EPA as part of its implementation of the Clean Air Act, is about sulfur content in gasoline. Under so-called Tier 2 requirements, in 1999 the EPA followed another California initiative that reduces sulfur in gasoline by almost 90 percent. The new regulation, to take effect in 2004, was expected to cost the industry $3 billion to $5 billion to implement. Industry representatives had advocated a more gradual, targeted switch to low-sulfur blends, citing the costs and "unproven technology" involved in the conversion. One industry executive estimated that meeting the new RFG and sulfur regulations would cost the industry upwards of $10 billion.

INDUSTRY LEADERS

Exxon Mobil. By refining volume, the biggest U.S. petroleum refiner in 1999 was Exxon Mobil Corporation, which output an average of 1.93 million barrels of refined products per day from its U.S. plants. And its U.S. production amounted to just one-third of Exxon Mobil's global refinery throughput. The company was formed by a merger that took effect that year between two of the world's largest integrated oil companies. Revenue from all operations in 1999 totaled $187 billion; only a fraction of that came from U.S. refining, however.

Exxon was created in 1934 by the merger of Standard Oil Company of New Jersey and Anglo-American Oil Company Ltd.; it took Exxon as its name in 1972. Exxon spent much of the 1990s reeling from bad publicity and large payouts surrounding a massive 1989 Alaskan oil spill by its *Valdez* tanker. Mobil evolved from two other spin-offs of Standard Oil, Standard Oil of New York and Vacuum Oil, adopting the Mobil name in 1976.

BP Amoco. Formed by another weighty merger of the late 1990s, BP Amoco p.l.c. was second in 1999 U.S. refinery capacity and throughput. The oil giant was formed in 1998 when British Petroleum and U.S.-based Amoco merged. U.S. refineries of the London-based company reported in 1999 average daily throughput of 1.34 million barrels, down 10 percent from a year earlier. Worldwide throughput that year fell 6.5 percent, to 2.52 million b/cd, although the U.S. pullback accounted for most of that decline. The company attracted headlines in 1999 when it proposed to buy Atlantic Richfield Company (ARCO), a move opposed on anticompetitive grounds by a sharply divided Federal Trade Commission (FTC).

Chevron. San Francisco-based Chevron was the third-largest U.S. refiner in 1999. That year it sold 1.30 million b/cd of products from its U.S. refineries, with volume up 4.7 percent from 1998. Chevron's 7 U.S. refineries supplied 59 percent of its refined product volume worldwide.

WORKFORCE

Employment in the refinery business has declined with technological advances, corporate consolidation, and movement of operations overseas. In 1999 refiners employed 92,000 workers in U.S. operations, a decline of 12 percent since 1995 and 22 percent since 1990. In 1999 nearly two-thirds of the industry's employees were production workers, and they earned an average of $24.41 an hour.

Within refineries, operators and craftsworkers monitor products via computers. They analyze data and make adjustments to machinery to ensure optimum yields, repair faulty equipment, and make statistical reports on output. Mechanical engineers work closely with operators, developing new machinery and making improvements whenever possible. These highly skilled technicians and scientists are the core of all refineries' staffs.

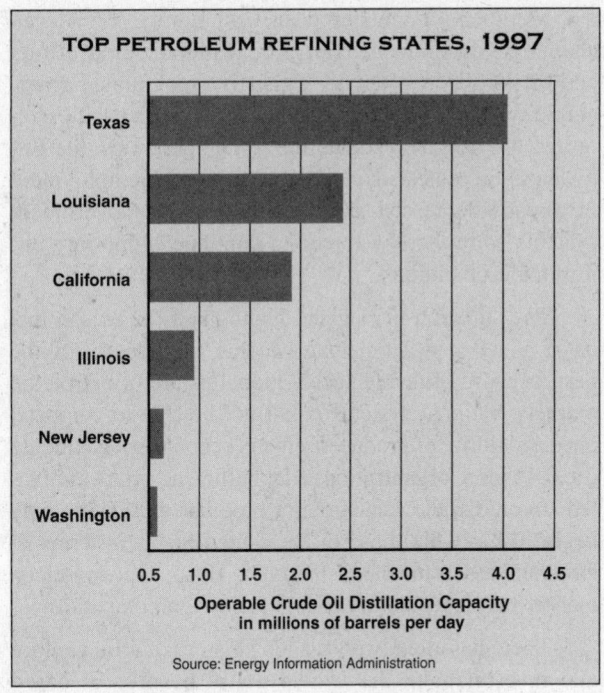

TOP PETROLEUM REFINING STATES, 1997

Operable Crude Oil Distillation Capacity in millions of barrels per day

Source: Energy Information Administration

AMERICA AND THE WORLD

Refining, as with the broader oil industry, is highly internationalized in many respects. Most large oil companies have considerable holdings in multiple regions of the world, and some, like Exxon Mobil and BP Amoco, derive greater revenues from international operations than they do in their home markets.

Because of its strategic importance and other factors, the oil business in some nations has close ties to government agencies; in some places petroleum upstream and downstream activities are performed by government-owned corporations or regulated monopolies. As international trade liberalization and related political and economic forces have gained sway, a trend toward privatizing government monopolies has impacted the oil business in a number of countries. Many major national systems being privatized in the early 1990s were inspired by Mexico, whose president, Carlos Salinas de Gortari, used privatization as one method to turn around his country's flagging economy. Although it shortly suffered a serious economic setback for other reasons, Mexico has been viewed by some as a lesson in the ills of planned economies and the virtues of market controls.

In 1993, the Italian state petroleum holding company Ente Nazionale Idrocarburi began to unfold one of the largest privatization programs ever. Most key oil producing nations in Latin America, growing economies in the Asia-Pacific region, and much of western Europe, were all in various stages of privatization in the early 1990s, depending on freer markets to sustain their national economies.

Members of the European Community (EC) faced challenges in both their individual privatization efforts and their collective energy legislative programs. For example, when EC efforts to reduce excess capacities required that England streamline some operations, the English public protested, claiming that mass unemployment in already-depressed areas would follow. Government systems were thereby forced to continue supporting unprofitable operations.

The situation in England highlighted the reason that nationalized petroleum may become an industry of the past; because of the decidedly global nature of petroleum markets, national systems might not be able to compete, once a majority of producer/refiners become private industries. As more organizations adopt efficient, profit-motivated structures, the standards for products worldwide may begin to resemble those in the United States in terms of stringent environmental standards. If so, the American market may become accessible to foreign competition.

There has already been a long history of joint venture and investment in the United States by refiners based overseas, and some of the integrated internationals that dominate in the United States are based in foreign countries, such as the Royal Dutch/Shell Group and British Petroleum.

The state energy companies of several OPEC countries, particularly Kuwait, Saudi Arabia, and Venezuela, invested heavily in U.S. downstream capacities in the early 1990s. Petreolos de Venezuela S.A. (PDVSA, the state petroleum company of Venezuela and Saudi Arabia) acquired the remaining 50 percent interest in Citgo Petroleum in 1991, becoming the full owner of this subsidiary. Star Enterprise, a 50/50 petroleum refining and marketing joint venture between Saudi Arabia's Aramco and Texaco, began operating in 1989. And Delta International, another state-owned Saudi company, began negotiating a joint venture with Fina Oil and Chemical, the U.S. subsidiary of Petrofina, a Belgian firm, for its U.S. refining and marketing operations. Furthermore, the as yet unprivatized Pemex Corporation of Mexico acquired a 50 percent interest in Shell Oil's Deer Park, Texas, refinery and began negotiations with other Gulf Coast refiners.

The increasingly complex subsidiary networks of integrated internationals should link many refineries in the United States in the next decade. As the global economy shrinks and ties between nations become stronger, the already cosmopolitan arena of petroleum refining will know increasingly fewer political borders. Consequently, American refiners may compete more directly with foreign firms for markets both at home and abroad.

RESEARCH AND TECHNOLOGY

Although new advances in reformulating gasoline, substituting cleaner fuel bases, and eliminating production waste represent significant innovations in the industry, perhaps the most important revolution in petroleum refining technology involved the implementation of computers. In the early 1990s, distilling and manufacturing industries relied on mainframes that could record, compile, and recall data on all elements, from viscosity to sulfur levels, in any given barrel of crude. Everything from measuring proportions of ingredients to monitoring chemical reactions could be performed with computers, and engineers relied as much on three-dimensional graphic and diagramming software as on actual valves and gages to determine improvements in processes.

With upstream technology breakthroughs such as 3-D seismography, horizontal and directional drilling, and enhanced oil recovery (EOR) helping to ensure that every drop of oil was pumped from the ground, the impetus to utilize every drop of oil at maximum efficiency had never been stronger. Computers allowed such efficiency not only by storing and retrieving data in a central, accessible medium, but also by cutting the time required for compilation and computation. Moreover, by implementing self-cleaning machines monitored by more sophisticated computers, petroleum refiners should be able to produce the low-toxicity fuels in demand and eventually find new areas for growth.

Nevertheless, patience, thrift, and ingenuity will be paramount to survival in the refining industry. Demand for petroleum products is forecast to grow at only half the rate of the U.S. economy. New regulations will limit the use of products that once had diverse applications, restricting them by season, geographical area, applications, and production costs. Federal standards requirements are likely to continue to proliferate, absorbing time and capital and human resources for research and experimentation.

FURTHER READING

Anderson, Robert O. *Fundamentals of the Petroleum Industry.* Norman: University of Oklahoma Press, 1984.

Beck, Robert J. "Resurgent Oil Demand, OPEN Cohesion Set Stage for Optimistic Outlook for the Oil Industry at the Turn of the Century." *Oil and Gas Journal,* 18 October 1999.

"Expansions, Mergers Boost U.S. Refining Capacity 6 Percent Over Two Years." *Oil Daily,* 29 June 1999.

Frank, J. Louis. "New Mandates Present Fuel Challenges for U.S. Refiners." *Oil and Gas Journal,* 13 December 1999.

Kronenwetter, Eric. "Industries Bemoan EPA Stand on New Diesel." *Oil Daily,* 4 November 1999.

Leffler, William L. *Petroleum Refining in Nontechnical Language.* 3rd ed. Tulsa, OK: Pennwell, 2000.

U.S. Census Bureau. *1997 Economic Census.* Washington, 1999. Available from www.census.gov.

U.S. Energy Information Administration. *Annual Energy Outlook.* Washington, 2000. Available from www.eia.doe.gov.

———. *Petroleum Supply Annual 1998,* vol. 1. Washington, 2000. Available from www.eia.doe.gov.

———. *Short-Term Energy Outlook.* Washington, February 2000. Available from www.eia.doe.gov.

SIC 2951

ASPHALT PAVING MIXTURES AND BLOCKS

This category describes companies principally employed in manufacturing asphalt and tar paving mixtures and paving blocks made of asphalt mixed with other materials.

NAICS CODE(S)

324121 (Asphalt Paving Mixture and Block Manufacturing)

INDUSTRY SNAPSHOT

The asphalt paving mixtures and blocks industry was poised for good times in 2000, with increases in road construction imminent after passage of federal legislation. Highway construction in the private sector, a fairly good indicator of general economic health, was increasing about 11 percent annually in the late 1990s and was expected to reach $55.2 billion in 2000. The demand for mixtures should parallel this growth. In 1997, there were 1,168 establishments involved in the production of asphalt paving mixtures and blocks. The vast majority of these (1,005) employed fewer than 20 workers, while only 16 employed more than 100. The industry's total reached $6 billion in 1998, up 20 percent since 1996 and 35 percent since 1994.

Asphalt is a blackish-brown material with a consistency ranging from a viscous liquid to a glassy solid. Most asphalt is obtained as a byproduct of the distillation of petroleum or other materials. Natural asphalt, rarely used by the 1990s, is formed during the early stages of the breakdown of organic marine deposits into petroleum.

Asphalt is used most often in the construction of roads, parking lots, walkways, and other paved surfaces. Of the 2.27 million miles of paved road in the United States, 94 percent of them are surfaced with asphalt, including 65 percent of the interstate system. With the passage of the Transportation Efficiency Act, those figures are expected to increase substantially by 2010.

Asphalt is also commonly utilized in reservoir linings, dam facings, and other harbor and sea applications. Highway and street constructors purchased about 50 per-

cent of industry output in the early 1990s, and an additional 25 percent or more was used in the construction of parking lots and walkways for commercial buildings. The remainder of the asphalt market was fragmented.

The primary advantages of asphalt—over concrete—are cost, flexibility, and durability. Because it softens when heated and is comparatively elastic, asphalt offers a high degree of adaptability in construction applications. Its physical properties also make it less susceptible to cracking and weathering; it is also more resistant to salts and chemicals used to clear and maintain roads in inclement weather. Furthermore, asphalt is easier to remove and costs much less than either concrete or natural paving materials. Finally, asphalt is 100 percent recyclable. An entire road surface, for instance, can be excavated and remixed for use in new surfaces.

The main asphalt paving product is hot mix asphalt, in which asphalt cement is used to bind a mixture of stone, sand, and gravel. The hot mix asphalt (HMA) industry employed about 300,000 people in 1998. Another 600,000 jobs revolved around the HMA industry. This included workers and administrators involved in paving activities and was not limited to companies primarily engaged in production of paving mixtures. Organizations involved in this industry are the National Asphalt Pavement Association (NAPA) of Lanham, Maryland, and the Asphalt Institute's National Asphalt Training Center II in Lexington, Kentucky.

BACKGROUND AND DEVELOPMENT

Historic uses of asphalt date back to 3000 B.C., when natural asphalt was used to seal a reservoir at Mohenjo-Daro, Pakistan; it was later used throughout the Middle East to pave roads and seal waterworks. Pitch Lake on the Island of Trinidad was the first large commercial source of the material. The development of petroleum-based materials such as asphalt during the eighteenth, nineteenth, and twentieth centuries gradually replaced natural supplies.

The demand for asphalt that accompanied the post-World War II economic expansion in the United States drew primarily on petroleum-based supplies. By the early 1990s, asphalt paving mixture producers used more than 50 million barrels of asphalt per year, selling more than $4 billion worth of mixtures and blocks annually.

Asphalt sales in the final decades of the twentieth century generally mirrored the health of the overall economy, expanding throughout the 1980s from about $3.0 billion in 1982 to more than $4.5 billion by 1988. The glut in construction in the late 1980s and early 1990s, in part a result of the rapid building of the 1980s, paced the economic recession, before rebounding throughout the mid- and late 1990s.

CURRENT CONDITIONS

Perhaps the most significant, and certainly the most welcome, development in the asphalt industry in the late 1990s was the passage, in 1998, of the Transportation Efficiency Act for the 21st Century (TEA-21). This legislation, authorizing a host of construction projects and funding, promises to be a boon to highway construction and, thus, to asphalt companies. The Act paves the way for the repair of more than 20,000 lane miles of highways in the United States, along with the construction of 3,000 miles of new road construction. The Act also provides more hands-on aid to the industry as well, in the form of the Institute of Safe, Quiet, and Durable Highways at Purdue University. The Institute, funded in part by TEA-21, was created to study the interaction of tire design and highway surfaces with an eye toward increasing the comfort and durability of the nation's highways. Of concern to manufacturers of asphalt paving mixtures and blocks are the efforts to isolate the proper mixture of asphalt conducive to limiting sound radiation caused by the interaction of road surfaces with tires. Examinations have been underway on porous asphalt and rubber-modified asphalt.

The federal Superpave program, a performance-based specification system developed by the Strategic Highway Research Program (SHRP) to improve national road durability, has gained a dramatic foothold nationwide. Superpave involves a volumetric mix design aimed at resisting wear and cracking due to low temperatures and a liquid-binder specification. In 1998, one-third of all hot-mix asphalt projects were Superpave. The number of Superpave projects awarded skyrocketed from 93 in 1996, when Superpave was introduced, to 1,339 in 1998. The most common usage was for large highway projects. Almost all states had implemented Superpave binder specifications by 2000, and 39 states had adopted its volumetric mix-design procedures.

An increasing number of states are beginning to lean toward rubberized asphalt, a surface that incorporates crumb rubber into its aggregate mix, for new highway projects. Rubberized asphalt was first developed in the late 1960s and began to be used widely in the early 1990s. By 2000, rubberized asphalt was used in 40 states.

Relatedly, the asphalt industry was increasingly attracted to the use of recycled materials in mix designs. Rubberized asphalt, in particular, was especially noteworthy for its incorporation of scrap tires in its mix design—a practice that analysts held could reduce the nation's tire stockpiles significantly with only minimal application. The processing of recycled aggregate was becoming a major business in its own right in 2000, and companies were increasingly incorporating this practice into their production. About 67 million tons of construction aggregate were recycled in 1998, up from 54.6 mil-

lion tons in 1993. The increase in waste-disposal costs and, relatedly, heightened environmental concerns relating to aggregate production and general waste has furthered the trend toward the use of recycled materials, even including old computers and electronic equipment, in asphalt paving mixtures. Asphalt companies trying to trim costs are finding the recycled aggregate sector an attractive niche.

Despite these positive developments, the industry was still facing challenges from environmentalists, many of whom have filed suit against companies, alleging violations of standards enacted by the Clean Air Act of 1990. More generally, the increase in highway construction has pushed the issue of urban sprawl into the political arena, which could make the prospects for asphalt paving mixtures and blocks in some urban and suburban markets more murky than the broader industry's trends would suggest.

INDUSTRY LEADERS

The asphalt industry is highly fragmented, with companies ranging from small firms engaged only in mixtures to large construction firms involved in highway paving and other construction.

Vulcan Materials Company, with 6,970 employees, was the largest U.S. producer of construction aggregates in 1999, having manufactured 10 million tons of asphalt products. Vulcan was able to generate 10 percent annual sales growth throughout the mid- and late 1990s. In 1998, the firm acquired industry leader CalMat Company, leading to 1999 sales of $2.19 billion, of which Construction Materials accounted for 70 percent.

Martin Marietta Materials, another major industry player, went on a spending spree in 1999, acquiring nine companies and boosting sales to $1.2 billion, a 20 percent increase over 1998. The firm maintained a payroll of 5,700 employees.

WORKFORCE

The asphalt paving mixture industry employed just under 14,000 workers in 2000, of which production workers, earning an average of $17.47 per hour, significantly above the average for manufacturing sectors, numbered 10,000.

A concern to the asphalt industry, revealed in 1992 by the U.S. Department of Labor's Occupational Safety and Health Administration (OSHA), was that 500,000 workers were potentially exposed to asphalt fumes that could cause headache, skin rash, fatigue, reduced appetite, throat and eye irritation, and cough. OSHA was developing an action plan to reduce exposures to this hazard but had not initiated any further action.

RESEARCH AND TECHNOLOGY

Among the most prominent technological breakthroughs in the industry in the 1990s was stone mastic asphalt (SMA). Developed in Europe, SMA incorporates cellulose fibers that make it stronger than conventional asphalt. Efforts to use recycled rubber tires as an asphalt ingredient were encouraged by 1991's Intermodal Surface Transportation Efficiency Act (ISTEA), which mandated the use of scrap tires in federally funded state roads.

FURTHER READING

Defendis, Megan. "Deal to Turn Tires Into Asphalt Blend." *Waste News,* 2 March 1998.

Halal, Anne Marie. "Hot Mix." *Waste News,* 11 August 1997.

Kett, Irving. *Asphalt Materials and Mix Design Manual,* New Jersey: Noyes Publications, 1998.

Moore, Miles. "Institute to Research Tire, Highway Noise." *Rubber & Plastics News,* 20 September 1999.

Nichol, Kyle. "Is Recycling the Waste To Go?" *Pit & Quarry,* May 1997.

"Superpave Projects Increase Fourfold." *Pit & Quarry,* August 1998.

Usmani, Arthur M. *Asphalt Science and Technology.* Monticello, NY: Marcel Dekker, 1997.

U.S. Census Bureau. *1997 Census of Manufacturers.* Washington, D.C.: Department of Commerce, 1999.

SIC 2952

ASPHALT FELTS AND COATINGS

This category is comprised of establishments that manufacture asphalt in roll or shingle form—either smooth or faced with grit—and roof cements or coatings. Examples of products include asphalt brick siding, tar coating compounds, roofing fabrics, pitch, shingles, and tar paper. Manufacturers of asphalt paving mixtures and blocks are described in **SIC 2951: Asphalt Paving Mixtures.**

NAICS CODE(S)

324122 (Asphalt Shingle and Coating Materials Manufacturing)

Asphalt is a compound made of hydrogen and carbon, with minor proportions of nitrogen, sulfur, and oxygen. It exists in forms ranging from a black liquid to a glassy solid. Most asphalt is obtained as a byproduct of the distillation of petroleum or other natural materials. Some natural asphalt, however, is extracted from organic mineral deposits in the early stages of their breakdown into petroleum.

When formed into felts and coatings, asphalt provides a reliable protectant and sealant. It is extremely water-repellent, tolerates temperature fluctuations, and resists the breakdown and decay caused by exposure to the elements. These characteristics make asphalt ideal for roofs, coatings, floor tilings, and waterproofing. Asphalt coatings and sheets are also popular soundproofing materials. Roofing shingles represented 40 percent of the total industry output in the early 1990s, and all roofing and siding fabrics combined made up 75 percent of production. Roofing cements and coatings accounted for an additional 15 percent of sales. In the late 1990s, asphalt shingles accounted for over 60 percent of the residential roofing market.

Although asphalt was used to line reservoirs as early as 3000 B.C., it did not achieve widespread commercial application until the twentieth century. Aided by technological advancements in petroleum-based materials during World War II, the U.S. asphalt felt and coating industry mushroomed during the post-war economic expansion. Specifically, residential and commercial construction booms launched the industry to nearly $3 billion in sales by the late 1970s.

Industry growth stalled during the 1980s, as a reduction in the number of housing starts and competition from new synthetic materials cut into producer's profits. Sales rose from $3.3 billion to $3.6 billion between 1983 and 1990, lagging behind the rate of inflation. By 1996, sales were at $3.8 billion. A year later, however, the value of total shipments rose more sharply, to around $4.9 billion.

Likewise, industry employment declined from about 14,000 to 13,316 by 1997, as manufacturers utilized automation instead of an increased workforce to boost productivity. Depressed construction markets in the late 1980s and early 1990s further reduced earnings. The average hourly wage in 1987 was $11.75, which increased 30 percent to $15.24 by 1996 and reached $15.36 a year later.

As profitability declined during the 1980s and early 1990s, the already consolidated industry became even more concentrated. The number of industry participants declined from 273 in 1982 to 245 in 1992, dropping again in 1997 to just 149 total establishments. The combined revenues of the top ten companies in 1996 comprised over half of total industry sales.

Many large corporations, such as Toledo, Ohio-based Owens Corning, participated in this industry without focusing on it exclusively. Of those companies that focused primarily on asphalt felts and coatings, however, the industry leaders were Carmel, Indiana-based Firestone Building Products Co., with $420 million in 1997 sales; Indianapolis, Indiana-based Reilly Industries Inc., with $350 million in 1997 sales; and Carlisle, Pennsylva-

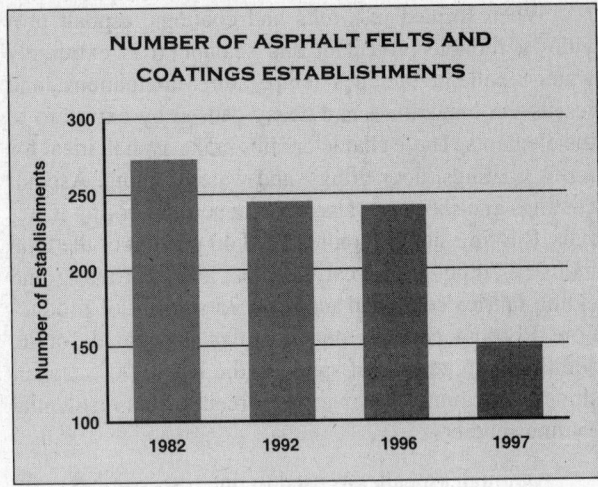

NUMBER OF ASPHALT FELTS AND COATINGS ESTABLISHMENTS

nia-based Carlisle SynTec Inc., with 1997 sales of $320 million. Other industry leaders included GS Roofing Products Co. of Irving, Texas, with 1997 sales of $275 million; Elcor Corp. of Dallas, Texas, with fiscal 1998 sales of $268 million; and Tamko Roofing Products Inc. of Joplin, Missouri, with 1997 sales of $240 million.

Firestone also led the industry in technological innovation by equipping its Contrator Services group with wearable personal computers manufactured by Xybernaut Corporation, allowing for on-site inspectors of roofing installations to electronically interface digital information with the corporate offices. On the other hand, some innovations, like the photovoltaic modules used combination roofing and solar energy-collecting units, worked against the industry. Another challenge to the industry was recycling: reroofing generated an estimated 6.8 million tons of waste yearly in the late 1990s, accounting for almost 3 percent of all municipal solid waste. Although recycling technologies existed, they were not fully utilized due to their complexity and cost.

FURTHER READING

Darnay, Arsen J., ed. *Manufacturing USA*. Detroit: Gale Research, 1996.

"Firestone Places Initial Order With Xybernaut." *PR Newswire,* 28 December 1999.

Infotrac Company Profiles, 7 January 2000. Available from http://web4.infotrac.galegroup.com.

National Association of Home Builders. "Photovoltaic (PV) Roofing," 7 January 2000. Available from http://www.nahbrc.org/homebase/pandt/tech/abstracts/roofsab1.html.

National Association of Home Builders. "Waste Management Update #2: Asphalt Roofing Shingles," 7 January 2000. Available from http://www.nahbrc.org/homebase/rrr/techres/wstroof.htm.

U.S. Census Bureau. *1997 Economic Census,* 15 February 2000. Available from http://www.census.gov.

SIC 2992

LUBRICATING OILS AND GREASES

This category includes establishments primarily engaged in blending, compounding, and re-refining lubricating oils and greases from purchased mineral, animal, and vegetable materials. Petroleum refineries engaged in the production of lubricating oils and greases are classified in **SIC 2911: Petroleum Refining.**

NAICS CODE(S)

324191 (Petroleum Lubricating Oil and Grease Manufacturing)

INDUSTRY SNAPSHOT

Slow growth has bedeviled the mature U.S. lubricants industry since the 1990s. The industry's estimated 414 establishments shipped $6 billion worth of product in 1997. In real terms, from 1992 to 1997 industry sales grew just 6.4 percent. Manufacturers of lubricating oils and greases employed 11,300 people in the late 1990s and produced more than 50 million barrels of finished compounds annually.

The fastest-growing segment continued to be synthetic and synthetic blend lubricants. Although they represented only 11 percent of the market, synthetic product sales were expected to rise at an 11 percent clip annually through 2003. Synthetics have gained popularity because they're longer lasting and less toxic than conventional lubricants.

In a similar vein, an area under development was eco-friendly vegetable-oil lubricants. These new compounds, which blend a variety of familiar oils such as canola and soybean, were touted as being nontoxic and renewable, thereby greatly reducing the environmental impact of producing and disposing of lubricants. What's more, some research indicates vegetable-based lubricants can perform better in motor vehicle engines and other applications than their petroleum-based counterparts.

ORGANIZATION AND STRUCTURE

Manufacturers in this industry compete directly with petroleum refiners in many instances. However, some argue that the increasing degree of specialization required within the lubricants market gives lubricant manufacturers an edge over general refiners in that specialized equipment and multiple blending agents are more difficult to maintain in an integrated refining plant than in a lubricants plant.

Product Overview. The several thousand different lubricant products manufactured in the United States fall into three categories: automotive lubricants, industrial lubricants, and greases.

Within the automotive category, the three main types are crankcase oils, transmission and axle lubricants, and fluids for hydraulic torque converters and fluid couplings used in automatic transmissions. Each category had subdivisions based on viscosity, or resistance to molecular rearrangement or flow. Automotive lubricants kept various parts of auto bodies and engines running smoothly by cushioning adjacent metal pieces, oiling moving parts, and keeping dirt out of combustion chambers.

Industrial lubricants range from machine oils to steam-turbine oils. These products serve similar purposes as automotive lubricants, with added endurance capacity, which allows them, for example, to prevent rust from high-temperature steams. Viscosity represents the main difference between lubricant uses. In 1997, the U.S. market for industrial lubricants was worth about $3 billion. Growth of industrial lubricants was expected to remain lower—less than 1 percent annually—than other segments of the industry through the late 1990s.

A lubricating grease is a solid or semisolid lubricant composed of a fluid lubricant with an added thickening agent. Generally the fluid base is petroleum derived, while the thickening agent usually consists of soap made from aluminum, barium, calcium, lithium, sodium, or strontium. Sometimes, if wide temperature variations will be encountered in use, the fluid base is a synthetic, such as silicone or polyalkylene glycol. In some instances, non-soap thickeners such as modified clay or fine silica may be used. The trend in grease manufacturing in the late 1990s was toward longer lasting products.

Lubricating oils accounted for more than 75 percent of the industry's dollar sales, while greases amounted to less than 7 percent and miscellaneous lubricants brought in the remainder. The single largest market for lubricating oils was the consumer market, which accounted for about 25 percent of the industry's shipments.

INDUSTRY LEADERS

Pennzoil-Quaker State Company, based in Houston, Texas, led the U.S. lubricants industry in the early 2000s with an estimated 37 percent market share. Formed by the 1998 merger of the lubricants businesses of Pennzoil Company and Quaker Chemical Corp., Pennzoil-Quaker State took in $960.5 million from its lubricants and consumer products segment. The firm also runs the Jiffy Lube quick-oil-change chain and other oil-related businesses. Lubricants and consumer product sales accounted for about half of the company's total sales.

Valvoline Company of Lexington, Kentucky, was another leading producer. A division of oil-refining giant Ashland Inc., Valvoline produced automotive and indus-

trial lubricants and maintained a sizable presence in the consumer market. In 1999 Valvoline posted sales of $1.26 billion. These results included revenue from the company's oil-change outlets as well as from sales of non-lubricant car care products.

Large, integrated oil companies, often dubbed the "majors," also supplied a substantial portion of lubricant output. These included Chevron, ExxonMobil, and BP Amoco. The majors participated in the lubricant industry as a side enterprise to their oil exploration, production, refining, wholesaling, and retailing operations.

AMERICA AND THE WORLD

Although the United States was the largest national market for lubricants, on a regional basis, Asia consumed the most. Based on 1996 estimates, Asia purchased 29 percent of the 8.25 billion gallons of lubricants made worldwide. Asia has also been the fastest-growing regional market. North America was second largest in consumption, at 26 percent of global demand, followed by Central and Eastern Europe (18 percent), Western Europe (14 percent), and Latin America (8 percent).

FURTHER READING

Ashland, Inc. *Annual Report.* Russell, KY, 1997.

"Chemicals, Fluids Demand Expected to Top $6 Billion by 2003." *Aftermarket Business,* December 1999.

Messina, Philip. "Lubricant and Lube Additives Face Tough Times." *Chemical Market Reporter,* 24 August 1998.

Papanikolaw, Jim. "Veg Oil-Based Engine Lubricants Impact Market and Environment." *Chemical Market Reporter,* 7 June 1999.

Pennzoil-Quaker State Company. *Annual Report.* Houston, TX, 1999.

U.S. Census Bureau. *1997 Economic Census.* Washington, D.C.: GPO, 1999.

SIC 2999

PRODUCTS OF PETROLEUM AND COAL, NOT ELSEWHERE CLASSIFIED

This category includes establishments primarily engaged in manufacturing packaged fuel, powdered fuel, and other products of petroleum and coal not elsewhere classified. Products in this industry include calcined petroleum coke, regular petroleum coke, fireplace logs, fuel briquettes, or petroleum waxes, independently of petroleum refineries.

NAICS CODE(S)

324199 (All Other Petroleum and Coal Products Manufacturing)

Plummeting crude oil prices in the late 1990s adversely affected this industry, which relies on oil as the source for petroleum production. On September 29, 1998, crude oil futures closed on the New York Mercantile Exchange at $15.98 per barrel, as compared to one year earlier, when it closed at $21.18 per barrel. The price had bottomed out in late 1997, falling to $11.58 per barrel. Whereas these low oil prices translated into cheap gasoline for consumers, it spelled trouble for this industry.

This small composite industry shipped $1.035 billion worth of products in 1996, a 28.9 percent increase over 1992, according to the U.S. Census Bureau. Exports made up 32.9 percent of the industry's output for 1995. In 1997, approximately 80 establishments employing a total of 2,100 workers comprised the miscellaneous petroleum and coal products industry. More than 50 percent of production was concentrated in the states of Louisiana, Texas, California, and Pennsylvania.

Raw materials for companies grouped in this area are procured from petroleum refineries or coal processors, and the goods produced are shipped either to distributors for the retail market or to other manufacturers. Solid packaged fuels, including fireplace logs and fuel briquettes produced by companies, are sold for general consumer use.

Petroleum waxes and coke are often lucrative side businesses generated by such leading U.S. oil refineries as Pennzoil Company, Mobil Corporation, Shell Oil Company, and Exxon Corporation, which are classified under **SIC 2911: Petroleum Refining.** Smaller firms that are primarily classified in this industry hold a relatively small market compared to the oil giants. Niche markets that demand specialty wax applications, however, require blending capacities that are regarded as too costly for major refiners to install and maintain.

Industry leaders include New York City-based Schlumberger Ltd., with $11.8 billion in 1998 sales; Salt Lake City-based Questar Corp., with $2.2 billion in 1998 sales; and Houston, Texas-based Apache Corp., with $876.4 million in 1998 sales.

Petroleum Coke. A by-product generated from the thermal cracking of reduced crudes and residuums, coke serves as a domestic and industrial fuel. In its refined form, petroleum coke is used primarily for heating in the eastern United States, where most of its manufacturers are based. This fuel is also used in aluminum anodes, furnace electrodes and liners, carbonaceous pastes and cements, as well as various carbon and graphite products. Highly purified graphite derived from petroleum coke can be used for construction materials in nuclear plants. In the 1990s, petroleum coke accounted for 54.8 percent of this industry's shipments.

Petroleum Waxes. In general, waxes made up 19.3 percent of industry production during the 1990s. Driven by high demand, U.S. manufacturers produced roughly 2.4 billion pounds of petroleum waxes in 1996, up 8.2 percent from 1995. These waxes, which include paraffin wax and petrolatum, are used primarily in paper manufacturing; both the manufacture of paper and the coating and impregnating of paper and paperboard for protective wrapping of foods require petroleum wax. In the manufacture of rubber tires, petroleum waxes serve as an antiozonant, while in PVC manufacturing, the waxes serve as internal lubricant. Paraffin wax is used in making candles, cosmetics, and pharmaceuticals.

FURTHER READING

Aven, Paula. "Oil, Gas Firms Over a Barrel." *Denver Business Journal,* 2 October 1998.

Darnay, Arsen J., ed. *Manufacturing USA.* 5th ed. Detroit: Gale Research, 1996.

Infotrac Company Profiles, 7 January 2000 Available from http://web4.infotrac.galegroup.com.

U.S. Census Bureau. *1992 Census of Manufactures.* Washington, 1995.

U.S. Census Bureau. *1996 Annual Survey of Manufactures.* Washington: GPO, 1998.

RUBBER & MISCELLANEOUS PLASTICS PRODUCTS

SIC 3011

TIRES AND INNER TUBES

This category covers establishments primarily engaged in manufacturing pneumatic casings, inner tubes, and solid and cushion tires for all types of vehicles, airplanes, farm equipment, and children's vehicles; tiring; camelback; and tire repair and retreading materials. Establishments primarily engaged in retreading tires are classified in **SIC 7534: Tire Retreading and Repair Shops.**

NAICS CODE(S)

326211 (Tire Manufacturing (except Retreading))

INDUSTRY SNAPSHOT

After years of intense price wars, consolidation, and layoffs, the tire and inner tube industry was highly concentrated in 2000. The top three firms controlled two-thirds of the global market; the capital-intensive nature of the industry lends itself to such patterns. While raw materials prices are relatively stable and assured, since most manufacturers maintain their own rubber plantations (most of them in southeast Asia), the cost of manufacturing operations is particularly high, making it difficult for smaller firms to generate economies of scale. The 1980s and 1990s were spent bearing out the consequences of these industry dynamics, with non-stop restructuring, acquisitions, and consolidation.

There were 110 companies in the U.S. tire and inner tube industry in 1997, employing 64,000 workers. The total shipment value for all products under this category was $14.66 billion, up from $14.05 billion since 1995. The largest portion was derived from passenger car pneumatic tires, valued at $6.6 billion. Truck and bus pneumatic tires placed second with $5.6 billion in sales. Other products included tractor and industrial pneumatics, at $969.0 million; and inner tubes, at $149.6 million.

The tire industry developed in the twentieth century as a major supplier to the manufacturers of automobiles and other vehicles and to consumers seeking replacement tires. The tire and rubber industries have traditionally been based in Akron, Ohio, where most tire and rubber companies' headquarters were located.

The tire business is reasonably assured of stable sales. While the demand for vehicles can fluctuate with changing economic conditions, the purchase of replacement tires cannot be long deferred, giving a relative evenness to the rate of tire purchases. Unfortunately for industry players, however, the increased durability of tires (because of technical improvements) has decreased the rate of replacement purchases, forcing manufacturers to compete along lines of durability, innovation, and, increasingly in the late 1990s, style.

ORGANIZATION AND STRUCTURE

Most tires are manufactured by relatively large companies that produce a wide range of types and sizes; smaller tire producers tend to limit output to specialized product groups. While a major portion of sales in the industry are to vehicle manufacturers for installation as original equipment, a much larger share are sold as replacements through various distribution channels; while manufacturers have made substantial inroads into the retail distribution market, this area is still dominated by independent dealerships.

The tire and inner tube industry depends chiefly on rubber suppliers for raw materials and automobile manufacturers for sales. More than 50 percent of the world's production of rubber goes into the manufacture of auto-

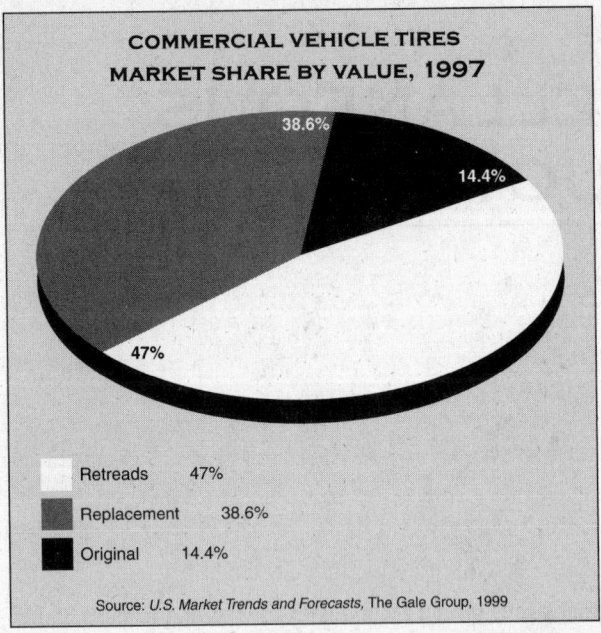

**COMMERCIAL VEHICLE TIRES
MARKET SHARE BY VALUE, 1997**

38.6%

14.4%

47%

Retreads   47%

Replacement   38.6%

Original   14.4%

Source: *U.S. Market Trends and Forecasts,* The Gale Group, 1999

mobile tires. The tire and inner tube industry is the largest element of the rubber industry group as a whole, constituting more than 40 percent of that group's product sales. The rubber industry group is represented by the Rubber Manufacturers Association (RMA). RMA members make up more than three-fourths of the dollar sales of the rubber industry group as a whole.

The industry's strength and stability belies an undercurrent of competition and economic issues that have changed the industry's structure and led to abandonment of plants, reductions of employees, and limited profitability.

In the late 1980s, the U.S. tire and inner tube industry's ownership concentration was shifted overseas. Whereas U.S. tire manufacturers once dominated the world industry, by the 1990s the four largest companies were owned by French, Japanese, and Italian nationals. British interests have attempted, unsuccessfully, to acquire control of remaining leading U.S. tire producers. Competition has become more severe and more international in scope. These ownership changes have been a part of a trend toward mergers of many of the major companies, resulting in larger but fewer independent companies in the top structure of the industry. Within the United States, production is concentrated in southern states; North Carolina, Oklahoma, and Alabama accounted for half of all U.S. tire output.

Tire Types and Characteristics. Though a small number of tires sold consist of solid rubber, practically all are pneumatic, or inflated with air. The pneumatic tire was developed in the late 1800s for use in bicycles, just prior to the onset of the automobile industry. Later, thousands of sizes and types of pneumatic tires were made available

for passenger cars and other vehicles, including trucks, buses, tractors, motorcycles, airplanes, and construction vehicles. Tire sizes range from less than two pounds to more than three tons for earth-moving equipment.

Tire casings are made from layers of rubber compounds and synthetic fibers or steel wire. The design and arrangement of these layers, or plies, affect qualities like cornering ability, vibration absorption, and durability.

Relationship with the Auto Industry. The tire and inner tube industry has always been heavily dependent upon the automobile industry. Competition among the tire manufacturers has been fierce, particularly competition for status as original equipment for automakers. Since car buyers tend to purchase replacement tires of the same brand originally sold on the car, it behooves a tire producer to cut prices and induce auto producers to select its brand. For each tire included as original equipment, an average of three replacement tires will be bought.

BACKGROUND AND DEVELOPMENT
The History of Rubber. Christopher Columbus noted the existence of rubber on his second voyage to the New World when he observed indigenous groups playing with balls they had made from a liquid obtained from a tree. Practical uses of rubber products began in earnest in the early 1800s, particularly with the use of rubber in clothing as a means for waterproofing. However, widespread applications were limited because the rubber material was somewhat sticky, odorous, and easily affected by shifts in temperature.

An American inventor, Charles Goodyear, developed the vulcanization process of rubber in 1839. By incorporating lead and sulfur with rubber and applying heat, Goodyear created qualities of durability and stability, which facilitated the use of rubber in many practical and beneficial products, particularly tires.

In 1876, Sir Henry Wickham planted some rubber trees in Kew Gardens from rubber tree seeds he brought from Brazil. These trees were transferred to Ceylon (Sri Lanka) and the Malay Peninsula where a rubber plantation industry developed that produced almost 3 million tons a year. Some of the larger tire producers later acquired and managed their own rubber plantations.

Tire Design Developments. The pneumatic principle was first developed in 1845 by a British engineer, Robert William Thomson, who applied it with modest success to carriage tires. However, solid rubber tires remained more popular until John Boyd Dunlop patented a more practical pneumatic tire in 1888. Dunlop's tire consisted of a vulcanized rubber and canvas tube with a valve attached to a solid wood wheel.

In 1890 further tire design refinements were developed by Charles Kingston Welsh and William Erskine

Bartlett. A design featuring a detachable pneumatic tire, created and patented by Welsh, continued to be used in the twentieth century. Bartlett developed the beaded edge for the tires so that the tire's edge could be hooked securely to the wheel's rim and remain firmly attached by compressed air in the tire.

Synthetic Rubber. The early 1900s saw the growth of the automobile and tire industries. The business increased when the steel wheels of agricultural tractors were replaced with rubber tires. All tires were made from natural rubber until the 1940s when the supply of natural rubber was cut off from Asian plantations as a result of World War II hostilities. Out of necessity, a synthetic rubber was quickly developed and remained an important raw material in the industry. In the 1960s, synthetic rubber sales equaled that of natural rubber as a raw material for tires, and synthetic rubber eventually became the preferred material.

Tire Structure and Features. Tires are manufactured by assembling plies of rubberized fabric on a cylindrical drum. Various materials may be used in the plies, including cotton, rayon, nylon, and polyester. Steel wire or glass fiber is incorporated in radial tires, perpendicular to the direction of the tire's motion, providing more stability.

Radial tires were first sold in the United States after World War II by France's Michelin. They were not produced extensively by U.S. tire manufacturers until the Lincoln Continental adopted Michelin radials as standard for its 1968 model. Radials eventually became the most popular tire, comprising more than 90 percent of the passenger car tires and 65 percent of truck tires purchased in 1990.

The performance of tires has improved greatly over the years. Manufacturers have improved durability, traction, cornering, shock absorption, and ease of mounting. Designs for tires with greater width and lower height have given vehicles greater contact with the road, lowering the center of gravity.

Changing Company Ownership. Except for French-owned Michelin, technically and commercially successful since the late 1800s, the tire market was dominated by well-known U.S. company brand names such as Goodyear, Goodrich, Uniroyal, Firestone, Dunlop, General, and Armstrong. However, producers of most of these brands were purchased by foreign companies between 1985 and 1993.

A major reason for the purchase of U.S. tire companies by foreign firms over this period was the decreasing value of the dollar. Furthermore, due to the weak economy, U.S. tire companies and foreign-owned companies operating in the United States were unable to overcome the fact that more tires have been imported to than were exported from the United States between 1971 and 1999.

CURRENT CONDITIONS

Entering the 2000s, tire sales were expected to cool along with the overall economy; from 5 percent sales growth in 1999, growth was expected to decline to only 1 percent in 2000. This largely reflects an expected slowing of automobile sales. The replacement tire market, booming in the late 1990s, still offered attractive growth potential though.

The growth of niche markets has offered the industry a much-needed break from vigorous price-war-based competition. The growing demand for everything from tires for specific weather conditions to tires in demand for their style or even color has necessitated an increased flexibility in production facilities, so as to avoid tallying excessive manufacturing costs in the attempt to bring diverse product lines to market. However, such streamlining calls for significant investment, further squeezing many smaller companies. The drive toward technological innovation and product diversification characterized the tire industry in the late 1990s.

Original-equipment light truck tires were the fastest-growing market category in 1998, with shipments of 8.5 million units, up 21 percent from the previous year. Replacement passenger car tires clearly led the overall market in production, at 191 million units, while 81 million original automobile tires were manufactured. Total production of all tire categories reached a record 295 million units, of which 215 million were replacements.

Tire manufacturers faced growing competition from tire-retreading firms in the late 1990s. In 1998, these companies sold 30.9 million retreaded tires in North America, worth more than $2 billion. In pricing, long the focus of tire competition, retreads cost 30 to 50 percent less than new tires. Moreover, retread firms can highlight their products' environment-friendly characteristics, as they reduce waste and save tires from landfills, a concern to many environmentalists as the nation's scrap-tire production reached 270 million units in 1998, nearly 100 million of which were added to stockpiles. However, in 1999 retreads suffered a wave of negative publicity, including skepticism and concern relating to their safety on highways. Nonetheless, major manufacturers have taken note; Michelin North America, Inc. moved into the retread market in 1999, and Bridgestone/Firestone was expected to follow suit.

INDUSTRY LEADERS

Goodyear Tire & Rubber Co. Traditionally the global center of the tire and rubber industries, Goodyear has for years made more tires than any other tire producer. Since most of Goodyear's domestic tiremaking competitors were acquired by foreign firms by the mid-1980s, Goodyear, based in Akron, Ohio, became the only leading tire producer headquartered in the United States. In 1998,

Goodyear controlled 29 percent of the global tire market, posting revenues of $12.63 billion and employing 97,100 people.

Goodyear was founded in 1898 by Frank A. Sieberling, who named the company after Charles Goodyear, inventor of the vulcanization process. By World War I, after making a variety of technical and practical design improvements, Goodyear had the largest tire sales volume of any company. Between the two world wars, the company survived some financial difficulties, developed production operations in four other countries, owned and managed rubber plantations, and created the famous Goodyear blimp as a promotional tool. After World War II, Goodyear set up production facilities in six more countries and promoted the development of synthetic rubber. Goodyear addressed tough competition from Michelin's radial tire by developing its own design innovations, creating a new all-weather tire, and expanding its interests into the field of gas and oil pipelines.

In 1986, a British financier attempted to buy Goodyear. To fend off this move, Goodyear sold its cotton growing and aerospace businesses, including its blimp manufacturing activity. Using those resources and heavy borrowing, Goodyear bought back $2.6 billion of its stock. After slumping in the early 1990s, the firm bounced back strongly throughout the remainder of the decade with innovative new products like the Aquatred premium-priced tire, renewed emphasis on the replacement market, distribution through mass retailers, and expansion into the emerging markets of Latin America and Asia.

Compagnie Generale de Establissements Michelin. Headquartered in Clermont-Ferrand, France, Michelin was one of the earliest producers of tires for bicycles and carriages and has become one of the world's manufacturers of tires and inner tubes, with 127,000 employees and revenues of $12.17 billion in 1998. Michelin North America, Inc. boasted a 22 percent share of the U.S. tire market.

In 1863, two brothers who had operated a rubber products business for some 30 years formed a new company, developing a detachable pneumatic bicycle tire in 1891 and producing similar products for carriages and then automobiles. In the early 1900s, Michelin pioneered tire design improvements including the first tubeless tire and a low profile shape. The company soon added plants in Italy and the United States to its French production facilities. Michelin marketed the first radial tire, which significantly helped tire traction and wear, in the 1930s. U.S. tire producers did not follow Michelin's lead in radials until decades later.

Always a leader in Europe, Michelin broke into the United States market by selling its innovative radials to Ford and other automakers in the 1960s. By 1980, Michelin had four tire facilities in the United States. In 1989 Michelin bought the Uniroyal-Goodrich Tire Company, a firm formed when two struggling tire companies merged in the mid-1980s. Absorbing these troubled organizations, along with a highly competitive tire market, resulted in heavy losses for Michelin in 1991. With its development of the ecological tire in 1992, Michelin anticipated the later trend toward more efficient niche models. The company maintained its own rubber plantations in Nigeria and Brazil and was poised for continued expansion into North America.

Bridgestone/Firestone, Inc. Bridgestone was a leading Japanese tire manufacturer, as well as a producer of bicycles, sporting goods, and various rubber industrial products, when it decided to merge its Bridgestone U.S.A. operations third-ranking tire producer in the United States, Firestone Tire and Rubber Company, in 1990. Bridgestone bid for Firestone against Italy's Pirelli in 1988 and ended up paying $2.6 billion for the U.S. firm.

"Bridgestone" is an English translation of its founder's name. The company evolved from a family clothing business that added a rubber sole to its line of footwear. A line of tires was initiated in 1923. After the Korean War, Bridgestone established tire plants in Singapore, Thailand, and Indonesia, and it also formed a collaborative effort with Spaulding in the United States for making golf balls. In the 1980s, Bridgestone began tire production at a Firestone plant it acquired in Tennessee and, a few years later, it purchased the entire Firestone company.

Firestone was formed in Akron, Ohio, by Harvey S. Firestone in 1900, and Ford was one of its early and regular customers. Later Firestone encountered several problems, including defects in its steel-belted radial tires and alleged tax violations and illegal campaign contributions. These problems led to a period of retrenchment during which plants closed, employment dropped, and several businesses were sold.

Based in Nashville, Tennessee, Bridgestone/Firestone was the third-largest tire manufacturer in the United States, controlling a 21 percent market share in 1999. That year, it had 45,000 employees and generated sales of $3.7 billion.

Cooper Tire & Rubber Co. Cooper's Tire Operations division accounted for 70 percent of the company's 1999 revenue of $1.99 billion. With 10,750 employees, Cooper produced automobile, truck, and motorcycle tires, as well as inner tubes. Cooper held 6.5 percent of the U.S. tire market, distinguishing itself from many of its competitors by targeting the replacement tire market and a more ample gross margin rather than competing with the larger industry players for position with the major automobile manufacturers. Based in Findlay, Ohio, Cooper marketed its products throughout the Americas, Western Europe, the Middle East, Africa, and Asia distributing about half its tires via independent distributors and the other half as private brand labels through oil company retail systems. However, despite its success in the robust replacement tire market, the company's business focus was slowly shifting away from its concentration on tires, as a series of acquisitions in the late 1990s positioned it firmly in the automobile equipment parts market.

WORKFORCE

Throughout the mid- and late 1990s, employment in the tire and inner tube industry hovered around 65,000 people. By 1998, it was just below that figure, at 64,000. Of that total, 54,000 were production workers, who earned an average of $20.11 per hour, up from $19.74 in 1996 and very strong relative to other manufacturing sectors. The flat employment trends were expected to continue into the 2000s. The most plentiful jobs in the industry were in the production and maintenance areas. More technical activities were in the research and development, production planning and control, accounting and finance, and information systems functions. Career paths can proceed from production operator to supervisor, department head, and plant manager. Such lateral moves can be made as from production supervisor to production control technician.

Opportunities for careers in the industry have generally been fewer than in other industries, largely because of severe competition resulting from mergers and acquisitions and excess capacity. Meanwhile, the relatively high wages were offset by the drive by most companies to keep prices low in order to gain or maintain market share, thus limiting employment figures. Nevertheless, some companies planned to increase prices and production capacity. Furthermore, at the top levels, opportunities have been created for business leaders to help organizations overcome losses or unsatisfactory profit margins.

Unions. The United Rubber Workers (URW) have represented employees at American tire companies since the 1930s and 1940s. Firestone's union workers endured long strikes in 1936 and 1976; in 1981 its URW members agreed to wage reductions. The URW instituted "pattern bargaining" to negotiate contracts in 1946. Having won modest concessions from the URW in the 1980s to help meet its competitive challenges, Goodyear came to a relatively generous agreement with the group in 1994. The URW expected Goodyear's largely foreign-owned competitors with U.S. operations and subsidiaries to follow suit, but many, including Michelin (whose anti-union stance is well-known) and Bridgestone, balked at the demands. In 1995, Bridgestone hired 2,000 replacements for striking workers, prompting the URW to seek strength in numbers via a merger with the United Steel Workers,

resulting in one of the largest, most significant strikes in recent U.S. history and a victory for the workers. In 1999, the United Steelworkers lead a year-long strike against Continental General Tire's North Carolina passenger-tire plant, rejecting the company's proposed increase in shift hours from 8 to 12, claiming the production of large bias-ply tires with the plant's aging equipment required too much physical strain to withstand a 12-hour shift.

AMERICA AND THE WORLD

The United States is a net importer of tires, though that has been somewhat mitigated by the North American Free Trade Agreement (NAFTA), the region that received 60 percent of U.S. tire exports. NAFTA likewise accounted for 36 percent of imports, followed by Japan, at 25 percent. U.S. exports in 1997 totaled $2.40 billion, while imports amounted to $3.36 billion. Most of the leading companies had tire plants in several countries and sold their products in international markets. Since the latter part of the 1980s, the tire industry has also become much more multinational in ownership as many of the top U.S. tire companies were bought by foreign concerns. In fact, the multinational mergers and acquisitions have left few tire companies in the United States unaffiliated with foreign firms.

RESEARCH AND TECHNOLOGY

Recent research has emphasized creating and improving the design and specifications of tire products to meet customers' needs and wishes, especially in the realm of durability. Though technical skills have always been applied to production methodology and cost controls, operating efficiency has been a dominant objective in the 1980s and 1990s because of the intense competition in that period.

Tire Design and Specifications. Historically, research and technology have been used to design better tire products for the purpose of developing strong competitive positions in the marketplace. Major breakthroughs included pneumatic tires for cushioning, removable tires for convenience, synthetic rubber to overcome material shortage, and radials to enhance durability and performance. Tire companies were increasingly keeping an eye on technological developments in the automobile industry. A future prospect centered on the development of tires with low rolling resistance for use with automobiles running on efficiency-based alternative fuels.

Goodyear and Bridgestone have developed a tire that can run safely for 200 miles after a flat, eliminating the inconvenience and dangers of changing a tire on the roadside. While "run-flats" were in high demand entering the 2000s, the challenge faced by manufacturers centered on how to offer the prolonged post-damage durability without sacrificing a smooth ride during the tire's regular performance. Goodyear also has been working on microprocessors to monitor the tire's air pressure, temperature, and wear, which might extend a tire's life by 15 percent. Meanwhile, Bridgestone has developed a tire capable of healing itself upon being punctured. The tire design incorporates a polymer material, called Sealix, which can liquify and harden around a tire puncture. Other research involves extending tire life, enhancing traction in adverse conditions, and increasing fuel efficiency and lowering auto emissions by reducing rolling resistance.

Environmental Concerns. The tire industry's environmental efforts have focused primarily on the reuse, recycling, and safe disposal of scrap tires. Reuse programs include retreading, a well-established niche of the tire industry, as well as newer anti-erosion programs. Recycled tires have been used in asphalt-based road coverings, shoes, household items, and even new tires. But in spite of all these programs, nearly 100 million tire discards went to landfills in the mid-1990s.

Some processes attempt to avoid the problem of scrap tires before it begins. Goodyear patented a process by which around 80 percent of a tire's rubber can be recovered and reused in rubber products, including recycled tires. The specialized devulcanization process, whereby the tire's essential ingredients are broken apart from the sulfur and other tire components so that they may be reused, could generate dramatic waste reduction.

Manufacturing and Cost Controls. Since the mid-1980s, when merger and acquisition activities dominated the industry, the intensified competition has encouraged or required the tire producers to reduce costs so they could trim prices and survive with slimmer profit margins. To cut costs, producers have engaged in "downsizing," eliminating inefficient plants, and streamlining operations. These cost improvement activities have required the companies' technical staffs to design better production methods and apply computer techniques to save workers' time, speed processes, and improve quality. Most tire-manufacturing facilities still involve hand-made assembly by a series of workers, though many firms, like Bridgestone, have set upon a course to allow machines piece together the various components, leaving workers to monitor the process and perform quality checks.

FURTHER READING

"1999 A Vintage Year for Tire Sales." *Rubber & Plastics News,* 6 December 1999.

Craig, Rochelle. "Firm Develops New Recycling Method." *Tire Business,* 25 October 1999.

Dawson, Brad. "Tire Industry Growth to Slow." *Rubber & Plastics News.* 8 November 1999.

French, Michael J. *The U.S. Tire Industry: A History.* Boston: Twayne, 1991.

Moore, Miles. "Goodyear Finds Way to Recover Used Tire Rubber." *Crain's Cleveland Business,* 20 September 1999.

Slaybaugh, Chuck. "Best or Worst?" *Tire Business,* 3 January 2000.

U.S. Census Bureau. *1997 Census of Manufacturers.* Washington, D.C.: Department of Commerce, 1999.

Yip, Jeff. "Better, Smarter, More Colorful: Makers Staking Future on Run-Flats, 'Smart' Tires. Energy-Saving Tires." *Tire Business,* 27 September 1999.

SIC 3021

RUBBER AND PLASTICS FOOTWEAR

This category covers establishments primarily engaged in manufacturing fabric-upper footwear having rubber or plastic soles vulcanized, injection molded, or cemented to the uppers, as well as rubber and plastics protective footwear. Establishments primarily engaged in manufacturing rubber, composition, and fiber heels, soles, soling strips, and related shoe making and repairing materials are classified in **SIC 3069: Fabricated Rubber Products, Not Elsewhere Classified;** those manufacturing plastic soles and soling strips are classified in **SIC 3089: Plastics Products, Not Elsewhere Classified;** and those manufacturing other footwear of rubber or plastics are classified in **SIC 3140: Footwear, Except Rubber.**

NAICS CODE(S)

316211 (Rubber and Plastics Footwear Manufacturing)

INDUSTRY SNAPSHOT

The rubber and plastics footwear industry in the United States was worth $1 billion in 1997. The market reeled from a decline in consumer spending on athletic footwear but tried to capitalize on the shift in demand toward outdoor footwear, including rugged shoes for hiking and winter-sports footwear. The other shift in consumer tastes—toward casual street fashion—was not of particular help to this industry as leather products tend to dominate that category of footwear.

The United States is the world's largest importer of footwear, accounting for one-quarter of the world's imports. Asian and Middle Eastern manufacturers are responsible for about 70 percent of worldwide production. The major manufacturing countries include China, India, and Indonesia, where many U.S. companies also produce a large portion of their own shoes to take advantage of lower labor and materials costs. This fact has, in recent years, generated controversy for the footwear industry as a whole, as news of harsh labor practices in U.S. manufacturing facilities unleashed a backlash against the use of sweatshop labor in particular, and exploitative labor practices in general, and spurred calls for regulations establishing worldwide labor standards, including minimum wage and safety provisions.

This industry consists primarily of two product categories. One area includes the waterproof footwear worn over shoes to protect them from inclement weather. Such products are often referred to as overshoes, rubbers, galoshes, and arctics. Also included in this area are rubber boots that are not worn over shoes but protect the feet from mud and water. In addition to the retail market, protective footwear is more or less guaranteed a strong institutional customer base with restaurants, large construction crews, municipal snow-removal workers, and a host of other industries in relatively stable need of protective footwear. Within these limits, there is a great deal of specialization, with products often tailored specifically for different occupations.

The second area consists of rubber soled canvas shoes, generally known as sneakers. While nearly all sports shoes have a rubber or plastic sole, and athletic shoes other than the canvas sneakers featuring rubber soles and a fabric upper are considered in this category, those with leather uppers belong to other SIC classifications.

The rubber footwear industry is largely based on the ability of rubber to protect against water and rain. An early breakthrough was made around 1920 by a Scottish chemist, Charles Macintosh, who developed rubberized waterproof cloaks that became known as "mackintoshes." Later, Macintosh's associate, Thomas Hancock, devised ways to process rubber so that it could be used as a material for footwear. By the 1990s, the manufacture of footwear required more rubber than that of any other product except tires. The sewing of uppers to rubber soles had been superseded by the use of adhesives or vulcanizing directly.

CURRENT CONDITIONS

There were 50 manufacturers of rubber and plastics footwear in 1997, employing 8,300 workers, down from 9,600 in 1995. Of these, production workers, earning an average of $8.23 per hour, totaled 6,890. In all of 1997, U.S. manufacturers produced 49.2 million pairs of rubber or plastic-soled, fabric-upper shoes, worth $532 million. Just under half of these were athletic shoes, including sports shoes made with cleats and spikes. Athletic shoes, however, accounted for about 70 percent of the shipment value for this area. While quantity sales for this category were significantly from 1995's total of 63.5 million, the dollar value was slightly higher.

Rubber and plastic protective footwear generated sales of $224.1 million in 1997, with 15.5 million pairs sold; both figures were down from 1995, when 16.87 million pairs, worth $253 million, were shipped.

U.S. employment in the industry decreased by 65 percent between 1972 and 1987, caused in part by moves to lower cost suppliers overseas. Total employment had risen from 10,900 people in 1987 to 11,700 in 1991, but continuously declined throughout the decade to only 8,300 in 1997, a pattern predicted to continue into the twenty-first century.

Sportshoe manufacturer Nike received worldwide criticism because of substandard conditions and harsh treatment of workers, including corporal punishment and child labor abuses, at its factories in both Indonesia and Vietnam. The firm hired the Goodworks International Group in early 1997, headed by former United Nations ambassador and mayor of Atlanta, Andrew Young, to review a new code of conduct for its overseas factories. Nike also expanded its U.S. advertising team, adding Goodby, Silverstein & Partners to help counteract the bad publicity. Criticism of Nike, however, has hardly abated, despite its return its continued profit margins; in fact, it has generalized into a more widespread outcry affecting the entire apparel industry. Labor activists, human rights groups, and religious organizations have forced politicians to take action against such practices, and President Clinton created a task force to mitigate the abusive child labor practices employed by U.S. manufacturers in Third World countries. As the issue becomes more integrated into social consciousness, manufacturers in this industry will be further obliged to take note, while some analysts expect that refraining from such practices can be turned into a selling point.

INDUSTRY LEADERS

Leaders in this industry included large, diversified shoe and apparel manufacturers and smaller firms focusing on more specific products. Decker's Outdoor Corporation, employing 200 workers, generated revenues of $112.9 million in 1999 from its outdoor rugged footwear and sports shoes and sandals. Vans, Inc. of Orange, California, produced a range of footwear for casual and rugged wear, including snow boots and biking shoes, employing 1,040 people and posting sales of $234.0 million. Converse, Inc., a global manufacturer based in North Reading, Massachusetts, with sales of $244.7 million and 2,650 employees, was a leader in this category thanks largely to its popular All-Star brand of canvas, rubber-soled sneakers. LaCrosse Footwear, Inc., based in LaCrosse, Wisconsin, with 1,250 employees, specialized in protective, sporting, and occupational footwear, generating sales of $128.3 million.

A number of established names also participated in the rubber and plastics footwear industry, but derived most of their revenue from the $14.7 billion sneaker industry, of which products in this category are only a part. The leading manufacturers of this larger industry were Nike, controlling 34 percent of the market; Reebok, a distant second at 13 percent; and Adidas, with 6 percent.

RESEARCH AND TECHNOLOGY

Supporting the industry's technological development front was the Shoe and Allied Trades Research Association (SATRA), which maintains a Footwear Technology Centre in England. This group of 180 scientists, technicians, and support staff assists its 1,200 members in 70 countries by helping to control manufacturing costs and improve quality by evaluating materials and production. It aids the business side of the industry through its consulting activities and by developing management information systems tailored to the industry. Its members are footwear manufacturers, material and machinery suppliers, repairers, and retailers.

SATRA has done a great deal of pioneering research, providing industry members with technology too costly for the smaller companies in the footwear business to develop on their own. For example, SATRA has developed beneficial concepts in the areas of ergonomics, color durability, the environment, materials standards, quality control, and computer applications like CAD/CAM, robotics, and bar coding.

FURTHER READING

"A Floor Under Foreign Factories?" *Business Week,* 2 November 1998.

"Athletic Footwear Marketscope." *Sportstyle,*17 May 1999.

"Footwear, Rugged and Casual." *Sportstyle,* 24 May 1998.

"To Protect and to Serve." *Footwear News,* 3 May 1999.

U.S. Census Bureau. *1997 Census of Manufacturers.* Washington, D.C.: Department of Commerce, 1999.

U.S. Census Bureau. *Current Industrial Reports.* Washington, D.C.: Department of Commerce, 1999.

SIC 3052

RUBBER AND PLASTICS HOSE AND BELTING

This category covers establishments primarily engaged in manufacturing rubber and plastics hose and belting, including garden hoses. Establishments primarily engaged in manufacturing rubber tubing are classified in **SIC 3061: Molded, Extruded, and Lathe-Cut Mechanical Rubber Goods** and **SIC : 3069: Fabricated Rubber Products, Not Elsewhere Classified.** Those companies manufacturing plastics tubing are classified in

SIC 3082: Unsupported Plastics Profile Shapes. Those establishments manufacturing flexible metallic hoses are classified in **SIC 3599: Industrial and Commercial Machinery and Equipment, Not Elsewhere Classified.**

NAICS CODE(S)

326220 (Rubber and Plastics Hoses and Belting Manufacturing)

INDUSTRY SNAPSHOT

More than 200 companies make hoses and belting in the United States in a market worth approximately $2.6 billion in sales in the mid-1990s. Manufacturing companies range from a myriad of small shops filling niche markets all the way up to several firms producing broad product lines with sales approaching or exceeding $1.0 billion a year. In 1996 industry-wide shipments totaled $3.3 billion.

The number of companies in the industry, however, actually dropped off from the late 1980s to the early 1990s because of the effects of restructuring and a move toward automation. These actions, though, helped the remaining players be more productive.

Hose and belting products find usage in a wide variety of industries. Hoses are used in such varied markets as automobiles, construction, and oil and gas. Transmission belting is used to help power cars, industrial machinery, agricultural equipment, household appliances, and construction equipment. Flat belting, commonly known as conveyor belting, finds usage from traditional markets such as mining and material handling as well as in lighter weight applications such as food handling and airline luggage conveyor systems.

Economies of scale are difficult to achieve except for some of the larger firms because a large number of products need short runs, and many of the lines have differences in chemical compounds and machinery needs. States with the greatest volume of hose and belt production include Colorado, Nebraska, North Carolina, and Ohio.

Rubber remains the predominant material in the market, accounting for between 70 and 80 percent of the products. For example, rubber is the main material for hoses, except in garden hoses, where plastic takes the majority of the share. Other materials, though, are expected to make some inroads as higher performing products are needed.

ORGANIZATION AND STRUCTURE

Much of the structure of the hose and belting industry is organized around how the product gets to its end user—either in the original equipment (OE) or replacement market. Looking at the automotive market, the OE market is much more straightforward, as most of the products are sold directly to the auto makers.

Sales to the aftermarket, though, are a bit more complicated, going through either a three-step or two-step distribution process. In the three-step process, the manufacturer sells his hose or belting to a wholesale distributor that handles automotive parts lines. The distributor in turn sells the product to what is known as a jobber, an example of which would include the NAPA store chain. The final step is for the jobber to sell the hose and belting to the installer—the repair shop that does work on automobiles, for example. Some manufacturers have increasingly tried to shorten the process by skipping the initial step and selling directly to the jobber.

Historically, this has been the most efficient way to get to market, ensuring that there is plenty of inventory in the aftermarket so that people can get the necessary parts for their car at almost any time. Hose and belt manufacturers, however, have had to shift with the times as the places where people get their automobiles serviced have evolved. While the total number of outlets for repair service has remained virtually unchanged, the make-up has changed considerably.

Prior to the growth in popularity of self-serve gasoline stations, about 150,000 gas stations in the United States also offered automotive service. By 1990, however, that number had declined to approximately 100,000. Conversely, the number of repair-only shops had grown from 110,000 to 140,000. Moreover, import car owners used to be much more likely to get their automobiles fixed at the dealer; but that has changed as repair shops have become more attuned to repairing imports. The number of retail auto stores also increased, from about 27,000 in 1980 to 40,000 a decade later, taking additional volume away from the jobbers.

Through all these changes, the hose and belt makers have had to ensure that their distribution system is getting the parts to the proper outlet in a timely fashion. Distribution also plays an important role in the industrial hose and belt markets. Many of these distributors also serve as fabricators, placing needed attachments and accessories onto the basic hose and belts for their final usage. The distributors in this sector also are more likely to play a role in OE accounts, especially for an account that needs to have local inventory. As for the aftermarket, a major portion of the business is sold through distribution sectors, although some hose and belt makers do sell some product directly to the end user.

Distributors also play a major role in times of over-capacity. While only four to five firms make broad lines across many industries, there are enough niche manufacturers to ensure stiff competition in all product areas. This situation gives the distributor an advantage in getting a lower price on products.

Types of Products. A hose is a flexible pipe or conduit that is intended to serve as a means to move material from one place to another. The three basic elements of a hose are the tube, carcass, and cover. The tube is the part of the hose that comes in contact with the fluid and therefore must be resistant to the material. The carcass gives the hose strength to withstand any forces, external or internal, that might be encountered, while the cover protects the product from environmental forces.

Although hoses can be referred to by their usage—such as gasoline, air, or garden hoses, manufacturers and users generally classify the products by the method of reinforcement. The common hose types include:

Knitted Hose. A flexible product knitted in an open-loop manner. The garden hose is a typical example of this kind of product. This type generally is subjected only to low pressure.

Braided Hose. One of the more common hose types, it is produced when a single or multiple ends of yarn cord or wire are woven over the tube. The size and type of reinforcement material, as well as the angle, help establish the strength of the hose. These hose types find a variety of usage, from air, water, garden, spray, or low-pressure liquid transfer, to more demanding applications like hydraulic, steam, and high-pressure transfer of liquid and gases.

Wrapped Fabric Hose. This type of hose is reinforced with an impregnated woven fabric that can be applied by hand or machine. This makes for a stiff, bulky hose that is commonly used in suction or vacuum applications.

Wire Spiraled Hose. Used for hose facing high-impulse pressures, wires are placed in opposite directions to counter the twisting effect of applying the spiral wire.

Woven Jacket Hose. Looms are used for circular weaving of jackets for the hose; often used for fire hoses. The design allows the hose to lie flat when not transporting water, for more efficient storage.

Hand-Built Hose. Used to make the large hose that needs great strength and excellent crush resistance. Uses include rotary drill hoses and oil suction and discharge hoses.

Belting. Power transmission belts are more commonly known as V-belts. Given their name because they transmit power and motion between V-shaped sheaves, the belts are made in numerous sizes and lengths. V-belts are preferred where there is limited space. Major applications are in automotive, industrial, agriculture, fractional horsepower, and recreational uses. In automotive use, though, a poly-V, or serpentine belt, has become much more popular in newer car models.

Flat belting also is used in some limited power transmission applications, but the overwhelming use for these products is in conveying uses. Basic components of conveyor belts include the carcass, which bears the load and is usually made of several piles of rubber-coated textile fabric or a single layer of steel cable; the rubber cover, which must resist wear, cracking, and element pressures; the breaker, which improves adhesion between the carcass and cover; and the skim coating, used to hold the load-bearing plies together.

Conveyor belts are used for a variety of purposes, from the grocery market check-out stand, to coal mines where coal is conveyed from deep within the mine, to growing applications in recycling and waste management programs.

BACKGROUND AND DEVELOPMENT

This industry has undergone significant change over the past several decades. In the automotive market—the top market for hose and transmission belting—a catalog of about 50 V-belts and 100 hoses covered most of the cars on the road shortly after World War II. Cars became more complicated, however, and smaller cars that required smaller engine compartments assumed increased market share ever since the 1970s and 1980s. Hose and belt manufacturers responded with products that conformed to the new size and weight demands of the automotive market.

The serpentine belt also made great inroads over the years. While designs at one time had several V-belts in the engine compartment, producers discovered that one serpentine belt could drive a number of accessories simultaneously, resulting in weight and space savings. In 1982, there were approximately 50 sizes of serpentine belts; a decade later that number had increased to up to 250.

Belts and hoses also last much longer in the modern era of manufacturing. Such products used to last 10,000 miles. In the modern era, however, hoses and belts commonly last for 40,000 miles or more of use.

CURRENT CONDITIONS

According to a study conducted in 1999 by the Freedonia Group, Inc., a leading provider of industry studies, demand for rubber hoses and belting was expected to rise 5 percent per year through 2002. This was a slightly smaller increase than the 5.3 percent growth expected for the rubber industry as a whole. Most of the growth would come from repair and replacement applications as opposed to original equipment manufacturers (OEMs), according to the study.

The Fredonia Group predicted that one factor contributing to the growth in the rubber hoses and belting industry would be the pricing of raw materials needed to manufacture hoses and belts. Prices of raw materials were expected to slow compared with the highs experienced in the mid-1990s. This in turn would allow hose and belt manufacturers to keep their prices down. Of course,

prices for belts and hoses are also affected by business conditions within the industries that use the products, especially the automotive industry. As the automotive industry strives to provide more dependable, long-lasting products in response to customer demand, this leads to the need for more durable belts and hoses, which often must be priced higher to cover the manufacturing costs.

The rubber hose and belting industry is directly related to the general economy. As the economy grows or declines, so does the rubber hose and belting industry. This industry is also related to the seasons of the year. Demand, especially for hoses, tends to increase in the third quarter as consumers prepare their vehicles for autumn. Demand then tends to slack off in November and December.

The Fredonia study also predicted a strong growth in the demand for plastic and metal belting and hoses. In fact, growth in the plastic and metal hose and belting market was expected to take away from the demand for the rubber products.

Although the automotive industry has traditionally represented the largest market for hoses and belting, aerospace was also becoming a significant area for growth in this industry in the late 1990s and was expected to continue to be an important market. As the aerospace industry grows in response to increasing demand for commercial aircraft, the need for hoses and belts to be used in those aircraft also increases.

INDUSTRY LEADERS

Gates Corporation, Dayco Products Incorporated, and Plastic Specialties and Technologies Incorporated were the top three companies in this industry in sales in 1999.

Founded in 1911, Denver-based Gates had 10 hose and belt plants in the United States, two in Canada, and three in Mexico, as well as another 15 facilities around the world in the mid-1990s. The firm has a major presence in automotive, industrial, and hydraulic markets, and posted worldwide 1999 rubber product sales—mainly from belts and hoses—of $1.6 billion.

Dayco, headquartered near Dayton, Ohio, is the largest operating unit of publicly held Mark IV Industries Inc. Dayco had 27 production facilities worldwide, including 14 in the United States, and had annual sales $850.0 million in 1999.

WORKFORCE

Total employment in the industry was estimated at 19,900 in 1996 and was expected to remain steady through 1998. Of these, about 15,200 were production workers earning about $11 to $12 an hour, according to government figures. Other occupations include chemists, product designers, engineers, and sales people.

The average number of workers per factory has decreased over the years because of increased productivity traceable to improved processes and automation. In 1972, 19 hose and belt plants in the United States—about 21 percent of facilities—accounted for 76 percent of employment and 75 percent of shipments. A decade later, just 9 plants employed 500 workers or more, accounting for 44 percent of employment and 39 percent of shipments. The average number of workers per plant dropped from 354 in 1972 to 124 in 1987 to just 100 in 1995, and just below 100 in 1996.

AMERICA AND THE WORLD

Importers generally compete more easily in commodity lines than specialty ones, putting pricing pressure on U.S. firms. One trend that increased competition in the United States in this industry was the emergence of transplant auto makers, especially from Japan. As these Japanese firms began production in the United States, it was not uncommon for their traditional domestic suppliers to follow them to America. Examples include power transmission belters MBL (USA) Incorporated, located in Illinois, and Bando Manufacturing of America, which built its plant in Kentucky. There also was an increase in the number of joint ventures between Japanese and U.S. firms to supply the transplant car firms.

Global expansion is also an important force driving leading companies in the industry. "Much of the logic behind the current activity is to supply the global automotive industry," according to the *European Rubber Journal*.

In July 1995, Britain's Tomkins PLC purchased Gates Rubber Company for $1.2 billion in preferred stock. In return, Gates received a 15.7 percent stake in Tomkins, giving Gates an ever-increasing presence in Europe. Gates is also expanding eastward with two new plants in China and one in India. According to Lo Estenfelder, president of Gates Europe NV, "1996 sales for Gates Europe increased about 4 percent over 1995, which in turn was about 40 percent higher than 1994."

Mark IV, the parent company of Dayco, also plans to expand globally. Mark IV plans to double turnover by 2001 from about $1.0 billion, split 65/35 OE/aftermarket, to about $2.0 billion, splitting sales 50/50, between the U. S. and the rest of the world, according to Kurt Johansson, the president of Mark IV's automotive business. Pointing out Mark IV's joint venture in India and its manufacturing plant in Australia, Johansson commented that most hose and belt suppliers are interested in Asia.

RESEARCH AND TECHNOLOGY

Rubber hoses, while still used in the overwhelming majority of industrial hose products, will face increased competition from other materials. Driving the need for new materials are a number of factors, such as the evolution of some of the traditional applications of the product. For example, alternate fuels and higher operating temperatures bring different requirements for hose products. When states begin to require higher alcohol content in fuel in order to reduce emissions, the hose materials must change as well. Specialty rubbers, plastic, Teflon, and nylon are among materials expected to challenge commodity rubber.

Like hoses, belts will be impacted by the shrinking of auto engine compartments. Because of hotter temperatures, belt makers will be forced to turn to new materials that will withstand the environment in which they are used. Some of the commodity types of rubber also will face competition from specialty rubbers and plastics.

FURTHER READING
"Activity Intensifies in Hose Y Belt." *European Rubber Journal,* December 1996.

Darnay, Arsen, ed. *Manufacturing USA.* 5th ed. Detroit: Gale Research, 1996.

Fredonia Group, Inc. Study #1033 Abstract *Industrial Rubber Products to 2002.* 1999. Available from: http://ecnext.imrmall .com/free-scripts/ip_catalog_all.pl?0001&9&1033

"Heavy Duty Belting Digs Up Growth: Mining Stirs Steady Rise For Firms." *Rubber Plastics News,* June 1996.

Genna, Albert "Growth Is In Repair and Replacement Market." *Rubber Plastics News,* August 1999.

Plehwe, Dieter. *Change and Concentration in the World Rubber Industry.* Brussels, Belgium: International Federation of Chemical, Energy and General Workers' Unions.

"Study: Gaskets, H&B Markets to Grow: Replacement Engine Seals to Cool Down." *Rubber & Plastics News,* February 1995.

U.S. Bureau of the Census. *1992 Annual Survey of Manufactures.* Washington: GPO, Updated 1996. Available from www .census.gov/epcd/ec92/mc92ht30.html

SIC 3053

GASKETS, PACKING, AND SEALING DEVICES

This category covers establishments primarily engaged in manufacturing gaskets, gasketing materials, compression packings, mold packings, oil seals, and mechanical seals. It includes gaskets, packing, and sealing devices made of rubber leather, metal, asbestos, and plastics.

NAICS CODE(S)
339991 (Gaskets, Packing, and Sealing Devices)

INDUSTRY SNAPSHOT

By definition, a seal is a "device for eliminating or controlling the leakage of liquids and/or gases while preventing the entrance of external contaminants such as dust and dirt," according to John J. Carr in the *Vanderbilt Rubber Handbook.*

Seals are divided into two classifications: static or dynamic. Static seals are used on surfaces where there is no relative motion between the surfaces. An example of a static seal would be an engine cylinder-head gasket. Dynamic seals are used wherever relative motion exists between two surfaces, either intermittently or continuously. Examples are engine crank-shaft seals and hydraulic cylinder-rod seals.

There are several basic types of seals. Cup-packings are mainly used as piston-head seals. Previously made from leather, elastomers are now used for low-pressure, smaller cups, while an elastomer/fabric blend is used for high-pressure applications. Cup-packings are particularly effective where clearance between surfaces to be sealed is excessive—for example, when sealing rough metal surfaces.

Gaskets typify the compression-sealing method. They are made from a wide variety of materials, often times used in combination with one another. For example, cork and elastomers are a popular combination in automotive usage because cork's compressibility and rubber's resiliency combine to give excellent results in such uses as engine gaskets. Gaskets can be molded or cut from a sheet. They are installed between two surfaces, and pressure from bolting or clamping provides the sealing force.

Elastomeric gaskets are the most common type of nonmetallic gasket. They can be made of synthetic rubber or thermoplastic elastomers (TPEs)—materials that have properties similar to rubber but are processed like plastics. Elastomeric gaskets are produced in a variety of sizes, colors, and finishes. They also can be produced to be especially resistant to such things as temperature, oil, chemicals, weathering, aging, and abrasion. With all these variations, as well as the variety of elastomers available, the applications vary tremendously. Simple applications would include such things as plumbing gaskets, while other, more sophisticated gaskets find advanced applications in aerospace products.

The simplest and most common sealing device, O-rings are used in numerous systems. They can be used in static and dynamic applications, depending on the proper design. Among their primary uses are as components in automotive steering and brake systems, off-road heavy equipment, aircraft, and other industrial and household items.

Mechanical face seals are a multicomponent sealing device used to create a leakage-free seal between a rotating shaft and a member through which the shaft passes. They are used in automotive water pumps and in the chemical process industries.

Molded packings and seals are mainly used in such things as fluid handling pumps, valves, cylinders, piston-type accumulators, and other equipment. They can be used as seals on the rod, ram, piston, plunger stem, or spool to develop and maintain hydraulic working power. They find their main applications in static sealing uses. Molded seals include squeeze-type ring seals and lip types. Squeeze seals are used in low-pressure applications, with lip seals finding more usage in high-pressure needs.

Radial lip seals are used in dynamic, low-pressure applications. Many are available in standard sizes but the trend is to customized production.

U-packings are pressure-activated sealing devices commonly used in low to moderate dynamic sealing applications. They can be found in such things as pneumatically or hydraulically activated door openers.

Three or more seals are often used together in the low-speed, high-pressure dynamic applications common to V-packings. In one of this type of seal's many end-product uses, V-packings are found in heavy-duty hydraulic cylinders of off-road earth-moving equipment.

Gaskets and seals are vital to the operation of many types of equipment. Three markets—transportation equipment, industrial equipment and machinery, and electrical equipment—account for more than 90 percent of total demand. Of this, sales to original equipment manufacturers (OEMs) account for about 40 percent of revenue, and aftermarket sales an additional 60 percent.

Transportation equipment, including automobiles, is the largest OEM customer, accounting for 40 percent of total sales. The cyclical nature of the market resulting from such dependency on automobile sales has been offset by the relative stability of aftermarket demand for industry products.

By 1996, U.S. shipments in the seal and gasket industry totaled $4.4 billion according to government figures. This figure is approximately double that of a decade earlier. Compressed, nonmetallic gaskets and gasketing held the greatest share at $1.3 billion, followed by molded gaskets and gasketing at $920.7 million, metallic gaskets and machined seals at $588.0 million, and other nonmetallic gaskets and gasketing at $277.0 million.

ORGANIZATION AND STRUCTURE

This industry supports varied manufacturing and other industries, gaining its existence from the end use of its products rather than from the products themselves. Because of the industry's dependency on the health of the economy in general, the demand for gaskets, seals, and packings mirrors the cycles experienced by the makers of the durable goods that utilize such supplies.

Makers of gaskets and seals are also influenced by their customers in areas such as product development, production processes, marketing, and pricing. With the large number of suppliers available, end users can bargain not only for better pricing, but for better service as well.

Other variables outside the control of U.S. gasket and seal manufacturers combine to affect the market. For example, since the early 1980s the industry saw a rise not only in the amount of gaskets and seals imported into the United States, but also in the variety of types of machinery in which such products were used. Varying levels of industrial production have also impacted the market.

Transportation equipment has traditionally been the leading market for gaskets and seals. Other markets include industrial equipment and machinery, electrical equipment, and photographic equipment, among others.

There are two professional organizations associated with the gasket and seal market: the Gasket Fabricators Association and the Fluid Sealing Association. Founded in 1979, the Gasket Fabricators Association had approximately 100 members in 2000. The association consists of gasket cutters and industry suppliers who come together to discuss problems within the industry and to develop possible solutions to those problems. The organization also develops industry standards. The Gasket Fabricators Association meets twice per year and publishes a technical handbook as well as a quarterly newsletter. The Fluid Sealing Association is an international trade association founded in 1933. Its membership is heavily concentrated in North America but includes companies from other continents as well. According to its web site, the objective of the Fluid Sealing Association is to "serve as the point for worldwide efforts to improve the manufacturer's understanding and application of fluid sealing devices and to promote a safe, clean environment."

BACKGROUND AND DEVELOPMENT

Historically, a number of different types of seals have been used in general applications. They are: gaskets, U-packings, V-packings, cup-packings, and O-rings. In time, the uses for seals have multiplied and improvements in materials and technology have allowed seal manufacturers to offer a product with extended life and better performance.

The sealing industry encountered many challenges during the 1980s and 1990s as applications for sealing products became more complex. Aeronautical and oil-field consumers were among the first to push for more demanding requirements. Elastomeric seal chemists and engineers were forced to advance technology from a "so-called art," to an "engineering science," according to Kerry C. Smith in *Rubber & Plastics News*.

Traditional materials such as cork, rubber, paper, and felt soon began to give way to specialty materials. For example rubber gaskets used to be found in low-pressure and temperature uses. However, rubber is not always the material of choice for gaskets, because contact with oil and grease negatively impacts its performance in such uses as the automobile aftermarket. The success of rubber in such usage is dependent on proper installation. Higher engine temperatures also negatively impact the selection of rubber for automobile gaskets. Specialty rubbers and TPEs more easily met the newer, more demanding standards and allowed the number of possible gasket applications to grow.

The synthetic rubber category can be broken into three subcategories: commodity rubbers, medium performance rubbers, and specialty rubbers. The commodity types generally cost the least, but offer less in the area of performance. In the past, these types generally took the largest percentage of elastomeric gasket usage. More recently the trend has been toward the medium-performance and advanced rubbers. Among medium performance types, ethylene-propylene rubber, commonly known as EPDM, has found greater acceptance because it offers better weatherability and abrasion resistance.

Specialty rubbers are usually available in low volume and give the best performance, but at a markedly higher cost. These advanced materials have seen wider applications in head gaskets, manifold gaskets, and oven-door and other appliance gaskets. A number of these elastomers offer higher heat resistance, along with high fuel and oil resistance. Silicone rubber, especially, is being used more and more in aerospace applications.

Various TPEs find gasketing applications because they are resistant to oil and other engine fluids, are lightweight and offer superior durability. But TPEs haven't achieved greater market share because their heat resistance has not been comparable to some of the specialty rubbers. TPEs are expected to continue to gain in noncritical uses and will grow into more critical areas after their heat resistance is improved.

About 80 percent of the elastomeric gaskets manufactured have been made of various synthetic rubbers, with TPEs accounting for the remainder. Since the early 1980s, however, TPEs have increased their share. By the early 2000s, seals and gaskets made from carbon and aramid fibers were projected to show the most growth in demand.

Examples of increasingly demanding design requirements and life requirements in automotive applications have included the ability to seal the nonchlorinated refrigerants that began replacing the chlorofluorinated refrigerants (CFCs) that were historically used. Automakers looked for near-zero permeation but also expected seals to last up to 150,000 miles in engines operating at increasingly higher temperatures.

CURRENT CONDITIONS

While the early 1990s saw a substantial increase in the demand for gaskets and seals, that demand was projected to rise more slowly through the year 2006 according to a 1998 study conducted by the Freedonia Group, a leading provider of industry studies. The group predicted that this decrease in growth would be sharpest among original equipment manufacturer products. The group attributed this decrease to a slow-down in motor vehicle production and capital spending. Another factor that was expected to contribute to the deceleration in the demand for seals and gaskets was that the technology and materials used to manufacture gaskets and seals is constantly improving, so consumers do not have to replace them as often. The Freedonia Group also predicted that growth in the demand for seals and gaskets made from carbon and aramid fibers would continue to surpass growth in demand for more traditional products such as compression packings and gaskets made from less reliable materials like cork, paper, or commodity rubber.

Although the use of more reliable and more expensive materials would cause some increase in the value of shipments, the U.S government nonetheless predicted that the value of shipments would not grow as rapidly as it had in the early 1990s. According to government figures, the value of shipments increased an average of 7.6 percent per year between 1990 and 1996, topping out at $4.4 billion in 1996. By contrast, the government predicted the value of shipments to increase by an average of only 3.4 percent per year through the year 2000.

INDUSTRY LEADERS

In 1999, the three leading companies in this industry in sales were the Parker Seal Group of Irvine, California, with $210 million in sales; Garlock Sealing Technologies of Palmyra, New York, with $208 million in sales; and John Crane Inc. of Morton Grove, Illinois, with $200 million in sales. Since these firms derive revenue from sales of other products besides seals, packing, and gaskets, it is difficult to pinpoint how much of their sales figures can be attributed directly to these products. Other firms with a significant presence in this industry include Freundenberg-NOK of Plymouth, Michigan, and Niantic Seal Inc. of Lincoln, Rhode Island.

As with many other industries in the late 1990s, mergers were common among gasket and seal industry leaders. Both Freundenberg-NOK and Niantic Seal closed big deals. Niantic and Sealing Devices Inc. of Lancaster, New York created a joint venture for sealing

distribution and elastomeric parts fabrication. Mergers of this kind were expected to continue in the next decade.

WORKFORCE

Total industry employment in 1996 was about 38,500 according to the latest figures available from the U.S. government. This was a 2.5 percent increase over the employment rate in 1995. The range of employment varied extensively, from factory workers producing the products, to chemists and engineers who develop the compounds and designs, to the sales force that deals with OEM and aftermarket accounts. The average number of workers per establishment was approximately 65.

Projected employment for 2000 was 41,200 workers. This would mean an average increase of 1.7 percent per year since 1996. Of the 41,200 workers employed in 2000, 29,700 of them were expected to be production workers earning an average of $13.14 per hour.

RESEARCH AND TECHNOLOGY

In response to increasing imports, many makers of gaskets and seals took a proactive stance: cutting manufacturing costs, going to advanced production concepts such as computer-aided design, and after-uses that had the opportunity to provide greater than average growth. Examples of such applications are nonasbestos gasketing, or seals designed to reduce emissions in process industries. Industry participants also spent to improve product design. These actions helped the industry maintain steady growth since the early 1980s.

Despite their uses in highly complex applications, gasket and seal technology itself is more defined. Developments have come in the form of the new materials being used and demands from customers for longer lasting materials. Capital costs aren't immense, but investment has been needed to keep up with these continuing shifts.

One new type of material is an oil-resistant liquid-silicone-rubber (LSR) introduced by Dow Corning STI in Plymouth, Michigan. Typical applications of this product are gaskets, O-rings, grommets, rollers and electrical components. These new silicones should extend "hot-oil performance and high speed processing to manufacturers of automotive, off-highway, and industrial equipment"; according to *Mechanical Engineering*. The automobile industry demanded a new type of silicone due to rising temperatures in engine compartments, and the need for longer service-life in the automobile industry.

Technology is also sometimes governed by regulation. For health and safety reasons, the Department of Environment, Transport and the Regions banned the use and supply of white chrysotile asbestos as of November 24, 1999. Use of the material as a sealing material was allowed until January 2001 for saturated steam, superheated steam, and particularly hazardous substances. Seal manufacturers that once used this material will have to develop alternatives.

FURTHER READING

Carr, John J. *The Vanderbilt Rubber Handbook.* Norwalk, CT: R. T. Vanderbilt Co. Inc, 1990.

"Chlorine Producers Refuse to Adopt Non-Asbestos Seals." *Engineer.* 24 September 1999.

D&B Million Dollar Directory. Dun and Bradstreet, 1999.

Darnay, Arsen J., ed. *Manufacturing USA.* 5th ed. Detroit: Gale Research, 1996.

Fluid Sealing Association Home Page. Available from: http://www.fluidsealing.com

Fredonia Group, Inc. Study #959 Abstract *Gaskets and Seals to 2001.* 1998. Available from: http://ecnext.imrmall.com/free-scripts/ip_catalog_all.pl?0001&9&959

Gasket Fabricators Association Home Page. Available from http://www.gasketfab.com

GBR Document. *5053, General Statistics.* Detroit: Gale Group, 1999.

GBR Document. *5053, Product Share Details.* Detroit: Gale Group, 1999.

"Sealing Devices and Niantic Seal from Sealing Devices for Elastomer Parts Fabrication and Seal Distribution." *Rubber and Plastics News,* 8 November 1999.

Smith, Kerry C. "Seal Industry Rediscovers Stress Relaxation." *Rubber and Plastics News,* 31 January 1994.

"Technology Focus: Oil Resistant Silicone." *Mechanical Engineering,* September 1996.

U.S. Bureau of the Census. *1992 Annual Survey of Manufactures.* Washington: GPO, Updated 1996. Available from http://www.census.gov/epcd/ec92/mc92ht30.html.

SIC 3061

MOLDED, EXTRUDED, AND LATHE-CUT MECHANICAL RUBBER GOODS

This category covers establishments primarily engaged in manufacturing molded, extruded, and lathe-cut mechanical rubber goods. The products are generally parts for machinery and equipment. Establishments primarily engaged in manufacturing other industrial rubber goods, rubberized fabric, and miscellaneous rubber specialties and sundries are classified in **SIC 3069: Fabricated Rubber Products, Not Elsewhere Classified.**

NAICS CODE(S)

326291 (Rubber Product Manufacturing for Mechanical Use)

INDUSTRY SNAPSHOT

Molded, extruded, and lathe-cut goods are used in various types of machinery and equipment. End uses for these products exist in automobiles, oil and gas equipment, appliances, farm equipment, and construction machinery. About 600 firms in the United States make molded, extruded, and lathe-cut goods. Due to the diversity of end uses, the market is fragmented and no single company has dominated the industry. The sector also faces strong foreign competition.

According to estimated figures for 1999, value of shipments for this industry was $6.5 billion, and the number of employees totaled 63,100 (of whom 52,200 were production workers).

Many of the products in this segment are custom-made to various end-user specifications. As such, manufacturers often sell them with a higher profit margin. Such customer orders have helped this sector show a higher rate of growth in shipment value compared to other industries.

Entering the late 1990s, the recovery of the U.S. automobile industry was projected to fuel growth in industrial rubber products, which find more than half their end uses in cars. Other areas of growth were expected to be manufacturing, mining, construction, oil and natural gas, appliances, and agriculture.

Competition from imports and other materials such as plastics, which cut processing time by eliminating the curing step necessary to rubber production, were expected to hold back overall growth. As automakers continue to ask for just-in-time delivery to decrease inventories, the advantage of plastics provides a competitive edge in some uses.

BACKGROUND AND DEVELOPMENT

The term "molded goods" encompasses a wide-ranging group of products whose shape is determined by the mold in which they are produced. Markets using molded goods include automotive and other types of transportation, appliances, oil and gas fields, off-highway machinery, and equipment used in such industries as construction, farm, lawn and garden, and mining. Benefits of molded goods include resiliency, insulation, cushioning, flexibility, and vibration or noise dampening.

Among the myriad of products produced in this segment are automotive and off-highway air springs; chassis bumpers; engine and truck mounts; automotive vibration dampers; weather-stripping; wiper blades; pedals and pedal pads; rubber marine bearings; bellows, grommets, and mounts used in appliances; drill pipe protectors; shock absorber mounts; conveyor wheels; pool table bumpers; and railroad-crossing pads.

The rubber mold, normally made from steel, is the most important component in the molding process, giving the part its shape and ensuring that it has the proper dimensions, look, and functions. The choice of molding process—compression, transfer, or injection—takes into account many variables because none of the three main methods can handle all applications. Some hybrid processes, combining two of the three molding techniques, have become popular in some uses.

Due to its relative simplicity, compression molding is the most widely used technique. The material is placed in the mold and compressed using hydraulic clamp pressure. When the cycle is completed, the clamp is released and the product removed from the mold. The mold can be virtually any size as long as sufficient clamping pressure exists. This process generally has the least-expensive mold and yields minimal amounts of waste rubber. Drawbacks include having the longest cure time (the cycle it takes for the product to be formed), the number of finishing operations necessary to render the product usable, and the lack of control over meeting exact customer specifications.

Transfer molding is a more precise process. The material is transferred from a pot, normally located above the mold cavities, down to the mold at the desired time. The technique gives better tolerance control, ensures the mold is closed before rubber is introduced to eliminate exposure to the environment, can be used when other items are to be inserted into the rubber product, and sometimes offers a substantially shorter curing time. Transfer molding, however, leaves more waste, requires moderate secondary operations, and requires a more expensive mold.

Injection molding requires the most expensive press and molds, but often yields the lowest overall cost to produce the part, as it gives more options for automation. Material is injected into a closed mold from an injection barrel. One injection system can be used to feed material into several molds, either by having the injector automatically moved to different molds, or by having several molds rotate to a fixed injection unit. The part removal operation is also a good candidate for automation. Other benefits include high-precision parts, lowest rubber prepping cost, shortest cycle times, and minimal exposure to the environment during the molding process. Drawbacks to injection molding include expensive tooling and the potential for large amounts of waste if proper precaution is not taken.

An extruder is a power-driven screw enclosed in a cylinder. In the extruded molding process, material goes in one end and is sent through the cylinder by a rotating screw. At the other end, the material is fed through a die, which is a steel mold designed to produce the desired shape of the product being made. Among the products made using extrusion are cables, wire insulation, door and deck automotive lid seals, window and glass chan-nels in cars, wiper blades, and rubber tubing used in medical, automotive, and appliance applications.

Extruders have been in use for more than 150 years in industry. Originally, the rubber going into the extruder had to be prewarmed so it could be conveyed through the extruder. This hot-feed extrusion method was time consuming and required great amounts of labor to complete the warming process.

Earlier in the twentieth century, however, cold-feed extruders were developed. These machines accept material at room temperature and include components designed to warm and soften the material for final forming. These machines are sometimes three times longer than hot-feed extruders, but they result in faster cycles, lower labor costs, and more uniform products. Extruded goods are flexible and good for sealing. They offer the advantage of low-cost permanent tooling and high production rates. Extrusion dies to make prototypes can be produced swiftly and for little cost. Recent studies have emphasized new designs for more effective self-feeding of the material and higher output rates.

While non-automotive, lathe-cut goods are the smallest segment of the industry, automotive lathe-cut goods represent a larger segment. Lathe-cut products in the automotive industry include oil filter washers, fuel system components, disc brake washers, and electric and electronic parts. Other areas using these goods are agriculture, communications, filtration, material handling, printing, and pumps and valves used in water systems.

CURRENT CONDITIONS

As automakers remain the single largest customer of molded, extruded, and lathe-cut products, their demands have a large impact on the industry. During the 1990s, for example, it was common for manufacturers to reduce their supplier base. While in the past an automaker may have bought a single part from many firms, the same company is now more selective in vendor selection, buying parts from fewer and fewer vendors. Auto companies became more stringent in their requests for high quality, on-time delivery, quick response to requests, and, as always, competitive pricing.

Automakers also began to ask suppliers of these products to provide the technical capability to develop a component from conception to finished product. This enabled vehicle manufacturers to cut their own development overhead and leave certain design work to companies with expertise in that particular discipline. Full-service molders and extruders, therefore, were expected to make the most gains.

While there have been an increasing number of companies in this industry gaining size, industry executives agree that there will always be a place for the so-called "job shops," which do custom work on products that often are short-run. These firms offer quick turnaround on prototypes and fill niche markets that larger molders cannot service cost-effectively. Job shops are often run by entrepreneurial types, carry lower overheads, and are highly flexible. One government study found those single-establishment companies with up to 20 employees accounted for 7 percent of the total value of shipments in this category.

Growth prospects for U.S. consumption of molded goods has been reasonably healthy. Areas expected to remain strong are transportation, off-highway machinery, appliances, and other miscellaneous applications—all above 6 percent a year. Capital spending in these areas increased when the economy began its steady rise after the recession of the early 1990s.

Growth in molded products for oil and gas machinery is expected to lag behind, at just 2 percent a year—in part because of a drop in U.S. oil production, and only a slight increase in natural gas production.

Other areas in which strong growth is anticipated include certain niche markets such as wiper blades and vibration control products, extruded rubber products, automotive extrusions, weather stripping, and lathe-cut goods.

Technology is evolving, however, to a future in which cars will have adaptive or active vibration control systems. Computer-controlled actuators and sensors will be used in conjunction with the rubber mounts, allowing the product to adapt to numerous frequencies.

INDUSTRY LEADERS

Because of the fragmented nature of the industry, no one firm or small group of firms dominate. Several companies do, however, have a substantial presence.

The Cooper Tire & Rubber Company, based in Findlay, Ohio, is a major supplier of molded goods for automotive vibration controls. The company had sales in 1999 of $2.2 billion and employed more than 10,000 workers. Aeroquip Corporation/Automotive Group, located in Maumee, Ohio, manufactures hoses and fittings for the automotive industry. Estimated sales in 1999 were over $500 million. GenCorp, Corporate Technology Center, located in Akron, Ohio, is the automotive products subsidiary of GenCorp Inc., based in Rancho Cordova, California. The company overall had sales of $1.7 billion in 1999 and employed more than 10,000 workers.

WORKFORCE

The mechanical rubber goods industry employed an estimated 63,100 workers in 1999. The number has been growing slowly but steadily since 1990. Average hourly wage in 1999 was estimated at $10.40, somewhat below the average for the manufacturing sector as a whole.

AMERICA AND THE WORLD

Imports from Europe and the Far East have played a significant role in the market. Some U.S. firms, in turn, explored service niches or specialty markets that have traditionally been harder for imports to penetrate than markets for commodity products.

Joint ventures, especially with Japanese-owned companies, also became prevalent. These helped U.S. firms gain business with both foreign automakers as well as transplant companies that make cars and other products in America.

RESEARCH AND TECHNOLOGY

Plastic products are expected to continue to challenge rubber for end-product applications that require more stringent characteristics. As automakers design smaller engine compartments in an effort to improve fuel efficiency and work in conjunction with front-wheel drive systems, they will demand better-performing products. As smaller compartments lead to hotter engine temperatures, automotive components will need to be made of materials with higher heat tolerances.

While traditional rubbers have continued to be used, other materials have been tested. Specialty elastomers, a synthetic rubber made for such specific uses, and thermoplastic elastomers, a material that is processed like a plastic but has the properties of rubber, are among the materials vying for increased usage. New fuels, mandated to reduce harmful emissions into the air, will also factor into material selections in the future.

New techniques will continue to evolve. One such predicted growth area is liquid injection molding (LIM) using silicone rubber. This process was unveiled in the late 1970s amid much hype as to how it would simplify life for molders. According to early literature, the liquid material went directly into the machine and the finished product came out—supposedly eliminating the need for several secondary operations necessary with traditional rubber molding.

While the reality of LIM did not quite meet its promise when it was first introduced, improvements in its technology in the early 1990s increased its popularity. Molders of components for medical devices, especially, adopted the process, with many adding or expanding LIM capability. The draw for medical molders has been the ability to make a clean product—the finished component emerges virtually untouched—that meets tight tolerances.

Cellular manufacturing has also gained in prominence. In this process, molding and secondary finishing operations all take place in one "cell," eliminating the necessity for the product to be moved to different areas of the plant. This improves quality, product flow, and efficiency, and helps reduce staffing requirements as well.

A new fully integrated system for high-yield molding of trimless/flashless parts is the industry's newest technology, developed by Hull/Finmac Inc. in Warminster, Pennsylvania, and Trimless/Flashless Design Inc. (TFD) in Chantilly, Virginia. The system is a combination of a 35-ton compression press and a unique modular mold, a first for the rubber industry. The system's purpose is to reduce scrap rates and eliminate most deflashing operations, improving speed and quality in molding natural or synthetic rubber.

Industry products themselves are expected to continue to evolve. One such area is in the field of vibration control products for automobiles, which have traditionally been passive systems. With use of a rubber mount, engineers can control a single frequency that causes noise or motion of the vehicle. More advanced mounts have been designed to control two frequency-related problems.

Technology is evolving, though, to a future where cars will have adaptive or active vibration control systems. Computer-controlled actuators and sensors will be used in conjunction with the rubber mounts, allowing the product to adapt to numerous frequencies.

FURTHER READING

"Advanced Elastomer Introduces New TPE." *Rubber and Plastics News.* 13 November 1995.

Darnay, Arsen J., ed. *Manufacturing USA.* 6th ed. Farmington Hills, MI: Gale Group, 1999.

Long, Harry, ed. *Basic Compounding and Processing of Rubber.* Akron, OH: American Chemical Society Inc. Rubber Division, 1995.

Smith, Maurice, and James F. Walder, contributors. *The Vanderbilt Rubber Handbook.* Norwalk, CT: R.T. Vanderbilt Co. Inc., 1990.

"Technology Focus: Integrated System for Rubber Molding." *Mechanical Engineering,* September 1996.

SIC 3069

FABRICATED RUBBER PRODUCTS, NOT ELSEWHERE CLASSIFIED

This category covers establishments primarily engaged in manufacturing industrial rubber goods, rubberized fabrics and vulcanized rubber clothing, and miscellaneous rubber specialties and sundries, not elsewhere classified. Included in this industry are establishments primarily engaged in reclaiming rubber and rubber articles. Establishments primarily engaged in the wholesale distribution of scrap rubber are classified in **SIC 5093: Scrap and Waste Materials.** Establishments primarily engaged in rebuilding and retreading tires are classified in

SIC 7534: Tire Retreading and Repair Shops; those manufacturing rubberized clothing from purchased materials are classified in **SIC 2385: Waterproof Outerwear;** and those manufacturing gaskets and packing are classified in **SIC 3053: Gaskets, Packing, and Sealing Devices.**

NAICS CODE(S)

313320 (Fabric Coating Mills)
326192 (Resilient Floor Covering Manufacturing)
326299 (All Other Rubber Product Manufacturing)

INDUSTRY SNAPSHOT

This industry includes more than 100 rubber products not classified in other rubber products industries such as toy balloons, rubber brake linings, rubber rafts and pontoons, and many others. The total value of U.S. shipments for these products was an estimated $9.5 billion in 1999. There were approximately 1,226 establishments in the industry in 1999, employing some 58,900 workers. Sales and shipments rose steadily since the beginning of the 1990s.

ORGANIZATION AND STRUCTURE

Growing demand among manufacturers for rubber products fueled shipment increases, although higher consumer spending was also a major factor. Demand for items used in automobiles and those related to health protection forecast larger-than-average percentage increases. With a large number of players in these market segments, firms would continue to focus on improved customer service, product design, and delivery. U.S. firms exported a good deal of products to industrialized countries, but also imported a considerable amount of low-cost products from developing nations. Manufacturers were expected to continue focusing on flexible, customer-oriented production. Development of new materials also forecast improved product quality and durability.

CURRENT CONDITIONS

Gloves and Condoms. With the AIDS crisis escalating throughout the 1980s and continuing into the 1990s, more attention has been focused on latex gloves and condoms than on any other fabricated rubber product. Both products are made by a dipping process in which a form in the shape of the product desired (such as a hand) is dipped into latex. Condom sales fell between 1991 and 1994 according to the American Psychological Association and based on scanner data from retail outlets. The top U.S. condom firms are Carter-Wallace Inc.; SSL International PLC (the largest condom maker outside the U.S.) and Ansell Healthcare Inc.

Ansell International, the world's largest exam glove firm, closed a plant in Arizona and shifted much of its production to its Asian facilities. Ansell still maintained two U.S. medical glove facilities, as well as two factories in Malaysia and one in Thailand. Another multi-national, Smith & Nephew PLC., closed an exam glove plant in Ohio and concentrated on the more regulated surgical glove market.

Latex gloves, long used routinely during examinations and surgery, are used by virtually all health care personnel whenever they perform a task that requires contact with a patient. Besides physician's exams, the gloves also are widely used in dental procedures. Despite high expectations however, neither the glove or condom market reached the enormous proportions projected in the 1980s. One official at a glove firm said that from 1986 to 1990 the demand for latex examination gloves may have doubled, but the capacity quadrupled. Medical institutions helped to unrealistically raise apparent demand by placing duplicate orders with multiple distributors in an effort to ensure delivery. This situation led to a consolidation in the glove industry, with many start-up firms going out of business and larger, multi-national firms scaling back production.

Firms that produced examination gloves in the United States faced stiff competition from overseas companies, much of it economically driven. Many companies locate plants in Malaysia because of the country's readily available supply of latex. Also, the Malaysian government placed duties between five to ten percent on exported liquid latex, but none on exported finished gloves. Malaysia also offered economic incentives and cheaper labor than that found in the West. But even glove firms in Malaysia were hurt when demand did not meet expectations. From 1987 to 1990, the government issued 300 permits for glove factories. By late 1988 only 90 had begun operating and by the end of 1990 only 30 plants remained.

Entering the mid-1990s, glove and condom makers began studying a new problem: the use of alternate materials for those allergic to latex. Reactions to latex range from relatively minor problems such as localized contact dermatitis, to much more severe symptoms such as systemic dermatitis and anaphylactic shock, which can be life-threatening. From October 1988 to April 1992, there were 1,036 severe reactions and 15 deaths related to latex allergies that were reported to the U.S. Food and Drug Administration. Studies showed that employee groups most exposed to latex, such as operating room nurses, were more susceptible to latex allergies.

To counter these problems, glove and condom makers produced and tested more hypoallergenic latex products. By the mid-1990s, a few companies in North America began making gloves of thermoplastic elastomers, a material with the characteristics of rubber but processed like a plastic. In 1993 the FDA approved a polyurethane condom made by London International, and approved a polyurethane condom for women produced by Pharmacal of Wisconsin. None of the nonlatex products though, made a major impact on the glove and condom market by the mid-1990s.

Single-Ply Rubber Roofing. This is another market expected to grow tremendously that never fulfilled predictions. The most common type of rubber roofing used in commercial building was developed in 1963 by DuPont. Two reasons this type of roofing evolved are the poor weather durability of other roofing materials and the energy crisis of the 1970s, which resulted in higher material costs for asphalt-based roofs. Roofers were looking for flexiblity and superior weather and water resistance over long periods of time. Rubber roofing increased in popularity because it could accommodate movement, was functional at high and low temperatures, resisted environmental elements, and was not subject to the effects of ponded water.

From a small 1980 base of $70 million, rubber roofing demand in the United States quadrupled by 1985 to $287 million, and then doubled by 1991 to an estimated $608 million. Annual growth of 11.1 percent was expected, but the rubber roofing market staggered early in the 1990s, according to the Rubber Manufacturers Association (RMA), which represents rubber product firms. Single-ply roofing hit a peak in 1990 and stagnated for the next several years.

The RMA reported 1990 usage at one billion square feet, but said the market fell to 850 million square feet in 1991 because of a drop in the U.S. economy. Shipments recovered to 910 million square feet in 1992 and 968 million square feet in 1993.

The rubber roofing market has seen much consolidation, with many firms entering the fray but later dropping out, especially after a 1983 price war that virtually wiped out profits for many companies. The two leading firms in the United States are Carlisle SynTec Systems, which pioneered the product's usage, and Firestone Building Products Company, which is owned by tire maker Bridgestone/Firestone Inc. Both of the leaders made major acquisitions in 1993. Carlisle bought the roofing business of Goodyear Tire & Rubber Company after making the product for Goodyear for two years under a private-label arrangement. Firestone purchased the roofing operations of Colonial Rubber Works Inc.

Rubber-Covered Rollers. Rubber covered rolls consist of three parts: a metal core, a rubber bonding adhesive applied to the core, and a rubber cover. The largest market for these products is the graphic arts industry, which uses rolls in printing presses to convey the ink onto the printing plate. Other applications are in paper making, plastic film production, printing, steel fabricating, textile manufacturing, metal coating and leather processing. In the paper industry, the rolls are used to squeeze water out of newly formed paper web so it compresses to the correct thickness. Steel mills use rolls in many strip processing lines as the rubber coverings reduce noise, provide traction, give a wringing action between processes, and protect the metal from corrosion.

Growth of rubber covered rolls has been gradual since 1980. U.S. usage was at $189 million in 1980, growing to $232 million in 1985. Growth slowed a bit in the early 1990s but picked up as the economy began to boom.

Sheet Rubber. This rubber product is made using a machine called a calender. A strip of material fed into one side of the machine is flattened and emerges as a rubber sheet, which is used in various industrial applications like packing and lining. The process makes sheet goods in various widths and thicknesses. U.S. consumption of sheet rubber goods has varied since 1980. At that time, shipments were valued at $119 million, a figure that rose to $153 million in 1985. By 1991 though, demand dropped to $142 million, although it picked up later in the decade.

Sponge Rubber Products. Sponge rubber goods are classified as either open-cell or closed-cell. Open-cell sponge rubber derives its name from natural occurring sponge. G.R. Sprague of Colonial Rubber Works defined open-cell sponge rubber in the *Vanderbilt Rubber Handbook* as "an elastic mass made porous by interconnecting cells." Typical open-cell products include carpet underlay, mattress and upholstery filling. Closed-cell sponge is different because the cells do not connect. Applications of this type of sponge rubber include insulation, automotive weatherstripping, architectural gaskets, swimsuit material, pipe insulation, and mattress and upholstery filling.

Hard Rubber Products. Rubber products usually can stretch to at least twice their dimensions when stress is applied, and then return to their original form once the stress is removed. Hard rubber products do not follow this guideline, although the goods retain many of the qualities of rubber. Typical hard rubber products include steering wheels, caster wheels, electrical insulation, battery boxes and bowling balls.

Rubberized Fabrics. The making of rubberized fabric is one of the oldest forms of rubber manufacturing. When latex was discovered, it was spread on a fabric and placed in the sun. When the water evaporated, the resulting product was a type of coated material. Historically, makers of rubberized fabrics considered their processes an art and kept such production methods secret. This created an environment in which only a few manufacturers made highly specialized products. The technology for making coated fabrics evolved from an art into a science, and the information spread through the industry so that applica-

tion has grown tremendously. Polyurethane coatings simulate leather, especially in the apparel, shoe, and upholstery industries. Rubber fabric products include inflatable safety equipment such as life vests, life boats, and escape slides carried on aircraft.

INDUSTRY LEADERS

Leading companies in the industry include Plumley Companies, Inc., Gates Corporation, and Foamex International, Inc. Plumley, a division of the Dana Corporation, is a manufacturer of molded products, including hoses, tubing, and extrusions for home and industry. (Dana had overall sales of $13.1 billion in 1999.) The Gates Corporation (a subsidiary of UK-based Tomkins PLC) produces belts and hoses for automotive and other industrial uses, batteries, formed fiber products, and other automobile accessories. Gates had 1998 sales of $2.5 billion. Foamex manufactures flexible polyurethane foam and foam products. Its 1998 sales totalled $1.3 billion.

WORKFORCE

In 1997 the industry employed almost 54,000 people. Production workers earned an average hourly wage of $12.05 and comprised 76 percent of the workforce. Over 1,000 establishments were doing business in this industry in 1997.

FURTHER READING

Darnay, Arsen J., ed. *Manufacturing USA.* 6th ed. Farmington Hills, MI: The Gale Group, 1999.

U.S. Census Bureau. *1997 Economic Census—Manufacturing.* Washington, DC: GPO, 1999.

The Vanderbilt Rubber Handbook. Norwalk, CT: R.T. Vanderbilt Co. Inc., 1990.

SIC 3081

UNSUPPORTED PLASTICS FILM AND SHEET

Establishments primarily engaged in manufacturing unsupported plastics film and sheet from purchased resins or from resins produced in the same plant are classified in this industry. Establishments primarily engaged in manufacturing plastics film and sheet for blister and bubble formed packaging are classified in **SIC 3089: Plastics Products, Not Elsewhere Classified.**

NAICS CODE(S)

326113 (Unsupported Plastics Film and Sheet (except Packaging) Manufacturing)

INDUSTRY SNAPSHOT

The estimated value of shipments in the plastics film and sheet industry in 1999 was $16.0 billion. About 870 establishments operated in the industry, and 62 percent of these establishments had 20 or more employees. The average firm size as measured by the number of production workers per establishment was 34 percent larger than that for the manufacturing sector as a whole.

The plastics film and sheet industry employed approximately 63,200 workers in 1999, 46,500 of whom were production workers. This was roughly double the number employed in 1987. The industry was highly capital-intensive, and its annual hours and hourly wages for production workers were slightly higher than those in the manufacturing sector at large.

ORGANIZATION AND STRUCTURE

The states ranking in the top 10 by value of shipments were, in order of descending value: Massachusetts, Texas, South Carolina, Ohio, Virginia, New Jersey, California, Illinois, Indiana, North Carolina, and Pennsylvania. Together, these states accounted for 60 percent of total shipments and 61 percent of total employment for the industry. The average number of employees per establishment varied widely across these states. South Carolina had 10 times as many employees per plant (413) as California (40).

BACKGROUND AND DEVELOPMENT

Although the terms are sometimes used interchangeably, plastics films are generally defined as being less than 0.010 inches in thickness, whereas plastics sheet is thicker. The plastics film and sheet industry had its origins in the rapid growth of the organic chemical industry in the late nineteenth century. The first commercially successful plastics film was cellulose nitrate. Although this film had many desirable properties, its flammability limited the scope of its use. In his book *Plastic Films*, John Briston called regenerated cellulose, or cellophane, "the most important development in films." The commercialization of this film followed the development of continuous-process film production machinery for which the Swiss chemist J.E. Brandenburger received his first patents in 1911. Cellophane was initially used for the packaging of luxury and semi-luxury goods, but its use expanded rapidly thereafter.

Plastic Films: Technology and Packaging Applications, by Kenton Osborn and Wilmer Jenkins, summarized the growth of the industry as follows: "The commercialization of cellophane in the 1920s revolutionized the flexible packaging of consumer goods. For the first time, the buyer could see the contents of the package through a film that protected the packaged items from dirt, moisture, and atmospheric gases. Countless items previously packaged in heavy metal or fragile glass containers began to appear in this safe, convenient, light-weight film. As a result, the flexible packaging industry grew from a small, paper-based operation into the . . . giant it is today."

Cellophane remained the dominant film in the industry until the commercialization of polyethylene film in the 1950s. One of the key advantages of polyethylene film was its lower cost, which made it practical for large tonnage packaging applications. As of 1987, cellulose films made up only 7 percent of the industry's product share, compared to 29 percent for polyethylene films. The rapid growth of the pre-packaged food industry in the post-World War II period provided an ever-growing demand for polyethylene films. The use of polyethylene films expanded to the packaging of textiles and toys, as well as heavy sacks for industrial and agricultural uses.

The industry introduced polypropylene films in 1959. This film was stiffer than polyethylene film, and thus, readily lent itself to packaging with high-speed machinery. Polypropylene film made up 7 percent of the industry's product share in 1987, and was expected to grow more rapidly in use than polyethylene films.

The rapid market growth of plastics films was enabled in part by ever-lowering costs. This changed to some extent after the Oil Crisis of 1972, which slowed the growth of the industry. Nonetheless, plastics film continued to grow at the expense of cellophane and other traditional, flexible packaging materials. Considering that the production of aluminum foil was up to four times as energy-intensive as the production of plastics film, Osborn and Jenkins noted that "Rising energy costs will continue to favor flexible over rigid packaging, plastics films and paper over foil, and may cause a minor shift in the paper/plastics balance in the favor of paper. The latter effect can not be large, since paper has only a few of the many packaging-friendly attributes of plastics." The authors conclude that the diminishing supply of oil and gas will not significantly affect the production of plastics films for two reasons. First, of products produced with oil and gas, plastics have the highest value added in the production process. Second, plastics packaging used only one-half percent of all oil and gas consumed in the United States.

One of the relatively new important markets for plastics films was agricultural production. The agricultural industry used plastics films for greenhouses, row covers, irrigation channels, and mulches. Plastics mulches reduced weeds, fungi, and insects, and held in ground moisture. The use of plastics mulches resulted in yield increases of up to 250 percent in certain field tests.

CURRENT CONDITIONS

The value of shipments in the plastics film and sheet industry has nearly doubled since the late 1980s. Capital investments increased by 17 percent over this same period, with 1992 a strong year. Capital investments rose to $592.3 million in 1992, then declined until 1995, then peaked at $767.6 million in 1996. After another decline, the investments have been rising steadily with estimated figures of $702.7 million in 1999. Except for a slight drop-off in the early 1990s, employment of production workers has moved steadily upward over the last dozen years; by the end of 2000, the industry expected to employ some 64,500 workers, of whom 47,600 would be production workers. The industry employed 39,867 production workers in 1997, paying an average hourly wage of $14.35.

One of the important challenges facing the plastics film and sheet industry was the need to develop more environmentally friendly products and processes. Two researchers at Cornell University published a study that addressed the biodegradability of plastics films. The researchers tested 12 films claimed by their manufacturers to be biodegradable and judged that only one of these films, produced by E.I. DuPont de Nemours & Company (DuPont), was truly biodegradable. This film was relatively expensive and may not be economically feasible for such applications as trash bags. Among other films claimed to be biodegradable, the best of them simply broke into small pieces.

Demand for biodegradable and recycled plastics was expected to have a lasting impact on the industry. In an early 1990s conference titled "Greener and Better: Packaging Challenges for the 1990s," the subject was addressed by Richard Mayer, CEO of Kraft General Foods. The *Journal of Plastic Film and Sheeting* summarized his keynote speech as follows: "Mayer emphasized that unity and partnership are needed by material producers, converters, packagers, wholesalers, and retailers if the industry is to meet the consumer's challenge for better and lighter packages, which use much recycled material. Since consumers are demanding legislative action to obtain source reduction, reuse of packages, and minimum recycling requirements, it is becoming increasingly important that the packaging industry respond with both action and education."

INDUSTRY LEADERS

Among the key players in the plastics film and sheet industry as of 1998 were Reynolds Metals Company in Richmond, Virginia; the Hunstman Corporation in Salt Lake City, Utah; and W R Grace and Company of Boca Raton, Florida. These companies are quite diversified and plastics film and sheeting make up only part of their overall sales and production. Other noteworthy players in the industry include Borden Chemicals and Plastics Limited in Geismar, Louisiana; and Viskase Companies, Inc. of Bedford Park, Illinois.

Borden Chemicals and Plastics Limited is a limited partnership that was formed in 1987 to acquire and operate chemical plants in Louisiana and Illinois that were previously owned by Borden, Inc. In addition to plastics film and sheet, the company produces other PVC polymer products; methanol and derivatives; and nitrogen products. Total company revenues in 1999 totaled $554.2 million, showing 3.5 percent growth from the previous year. The company employed approximately 800 workers in early 1999.

Viskase, formerly known as Envirodyne Industries, was founded in 1970, and had $409.2 million in sales and 3,050 employees in 1998. Producing shrink wrap and plastics film for food packaging, the firm was a subsidiary of the privately held Emerald Acquisition Corporation, also of Oak Brook. Viskase acquired its plastics production facilities in its 1986 purchases of Union Carbide Corporation's film packaging business and of Filmco International Limited.

RESEARCH AND TECHNOLOGY

Plastics film and sheet was produced by feeding molten plastics through either a flat or tubular die. After being shaped, the film was cooled or "quenched," either by coming into contact with a cooled roller or by being immersed in water. Water quenching more uniformly cools films and was preferred, especially when film clarity was a consideration.

One of the most important outputs of the industry was laminated plastics films. Lamination enabled a film that combined the optimal characteristics of each of the component materials, whether that characteristic be imperviousness, stiffness, clarity, strength, or wrinkle-resistance. Laminates were produced either by adhesive bonding of separately produced films or by the newer process of coextrusion. In coextrusion, two or more films were simultaneously formed and heat-bonded either by a set of adjacent dies or by a manifold die. By creating laminated plastics films in one continuous process, coextrusion greatly reduced their cost. One of the disadvantages of coextruded films is that it was not possible to print on the protected inside surface since component layers are formed and bonded almost simultaneously. The quality of print was of great importance for the marketing of packaged food products. New developments in surface printing were underway to address this problem.

The industry developed a number of new products and processes in the 1990s to address the issue of environmental safety. A project undertaken by Dow Plastics and Advanced Environmental Recycling Technologies of Rogers, Arkansas, created a new process to remove dirt and other wastes from recycled polyethylene grocery sacks and stretch film. Grocery and merchandise bags constituted the bulk of recycled plastics film products. DuPont developed a new polyester film, Mylar OL, that enabled dependable seals for packaging with the use of adhesives, making the film more readily recyclable.

The Exxon Chemical Company started up a new film production line in 1993 that was capable of producing seven million pounds of plastics film a year, using up to 50 percent post-consumer plastics. Mobil Chemical developed a new low-density polyethylene called 'Super Strength' that enabled films to be produced that were 30 percent thinner, yet just as strong as conventional plastics films. Highly impervious silica-coated plastics films began to be commercialized in the United States in the 1990s after having been developed in Japan and in Europe. Aside from their desirable packaging properties, silica-coated films more readily lent themselves to recycling than laminates containing vinyl-based resins.

Airco Gases of Murray Hill, New Jersey, developed a new cooling technology known as cryogenic bubble cooling. This process eliminated a long-standing bottleneck in the production of plastics films and enabled output increases of up to 60 percent.

FURTHER READING

Briston, John H. *Plastic Films.* 2nd ed. Harlow, England: Longman Scientific and Technical, 1983.

Darnay, Arsen J., ed. *Manufacturing USA.* 6th ed. Detroit: The Gale Group, 1999.

Osborn, Kenton and Wilmer Jenkins. *Plastic Films: Technology and Packaging Application.* Lancaster, PA: Technomic Publishing Company, Inc., 1992.

U.S. Census Bureau. *Manufacturing Industry Series: Unsupported Plastics Film and Sheet,* 1999. Available from www.census.gov.

SIC 3082

UNSUPPORTED PLASTICS PROFILE SHAPES

This industry covers establishments primarily engaged in manufacturing unsupported plastics profiles, rods, tubes, and other shapes. Establishments primarily engaged in manufacturing plastics hose are classified in **SIC 3052: Rubber and Plastics Hose and Belting.**

NAICS CODE(S)

326121 (Unsupported Plastics Profile Shape Manufacturing)

ICON Health and Fitness Inc.—the industry leader and manufacturer of indoor fitness equipment such as Nordic Track—experienced turbulence in the late 1990s. After Sales skyrocketed from $403.0 million in May 1994 to $836.2 million in 1997, sales in 1998 plummeted 10.4 percent, by $86.9 million, down to $749.3 million. Ironically, the company had just taken on more debt,

attempting to leverage higher profits. Eventually the bottom fell out of the indoor fitness equipment business, forcing ICON to restructure yet again with the assistance of Wall Street investment bank Credit Suisse First Boston. Company sales rebounded in summer 1999, indicating a positive shift for the company.

Other industry leaders included Fraser, Michigan-based Venture Industries Inc., with $568.0 million in 1997 sales; Troy, Michigan-based Cadillac Plastic Group Inc., with $270 million in fiscal 1997 sales; Sheboygan, Wisconsin-based Vinyl Plastics Inc., with $250 million in fiscal 1997 sales; and Columbus, Ohio-based Crane Plastics Company L.P., with $150 million in 1997 sales.

The value of shipments in the plastics profile shapes industry in 1996 was $4.465 billion, up from $3.344 billion in 1992, according to the *1997 Census of Manufactures.* The industry employed 27,600 production workers in 1995, up from the 27,000 employed in 1994 and above the previous peak of 21,300 in 1989. The states that dominated the industry in numbers of residents employed for 1992 were Ohio, Illinois, California, and Pennsylvania. Together these states account for about 33 percent of total value of shipments.

The top products by share in the industry are those made from vinyl (16 percent), polyethylene (16 percent), polypropylene (12 percent), polystyrene (10 percent), nylon (4 percent), acrylates (4 percent), and styrene copolymer (1 percent).

FURTHER READING

Boulton, Guy. "Logan, Utah-Based Fitness-Equipment Maker Restructures to Cut Debt." *Knight-Ridder/Tribune Business News,* 10 October 1999.

Darnay, Arsen J., ed. *Manufacturing USA.* 5th ed. Detroit: Gale Research, 1996.

Infotrac Company Profiles, 7 January 2000. Available from http://web4.infotrac.galegroup.com.

U.S. Bureau of the Census. *1997 Census of Manufactures.* Washington: GPO,1999.

SIC 3083

LAMINATED PLASTICS PLATE, SHEET, AND PROFILE SHAPES

This category covers establishments primarily engaged in manufacturing laminated plastics plate, sheet, profiles, rods, and tubes. Establishments primarily engaged in manufacturing laminated flexible packaging are classified in **industry group 267 (Converted Paper and Paperboard Products, Except Containers and Boxes).**

NAICS Code(s)

326130 (Laminated Plastics Plate, Sheet, and Shape Manufacturing)

Industry Snapshot

This industry confronted the prospect of its own maturation in the late 1990s, forcing companies to devise inventive means of driving continued growth. Many companies hit upon the solution of increasing service as a way to promote growth. Specifically, companies such as GE Plastics of Pittsfield, Massachusetts, turned to product customization as a way of luring small-lot customers, especially those that utilized GE's just-in-time inventory system. Analysts predicted that the maturation of the industry would inevitably lead to consolidation, as with other industries.

Organization and Structure

In 1996 approximately 328 establishments were engaged in the production of laminated plastic plate and sheet. Those establishments employed 14,600 workers, 10,800 of whom were production workers. During 1994, the average value added per production worker was $105,925—a figure which compared less than favorably with an overall average of $134,084 for all U.S. manufacturing industries.

In terms of geographic concentration, the largest number of establishments was located in the East North Central region of the United States, followed by the Middle Atlantic region, and then the Pacific region, including Alaska and Hawaii. Alternatively, when ranked by the number of establishments per state, California was first with 44, followed by Ohio with 28, Illinois with 20, and Pennsylvania with 17. Ohio's establishments generated the most money from shipments, with $307.0 million.

Market concentration was relatively high in the laminated plastics plate and sheet industry. In 1992 it was estimated that the largest eight companies accounted for approximately two-thirds of the industry's $2.8 billion in sales. While three of the largest companies in the industry at that time were divisions of larger companies, most of the leading companies were subsidiaries. Only one company in the top 10, Spartech Corporation, was publicly traded.

The primary materials consumed by the laminated plastic plate and sheet industry, when ranked by delivered costs (not adjusted for inflation) were: materials, ingredients, containers, and supplies of various kinds, valued at $993.6 million in 1992; paper and paperboard products, except paperboard boxes, containers, and corrugated paperboard ($233.4 million); and other materials and components, parts, containers and supplies ($168.5 million).

The major sources of input for the plastics industry were overwhelmingly from the manufacturing sector, which accounted for nearly 63 percent of sector input. The single major input was plastic materials and resins, which comprised 36.2 percent. Wholesale trade accounted for 8.5 percent of inputs, while imports—undifferentiated by industry sector—contributed 5.8 percent.

If disaggregated by total product share, the industry's output was divided among the following product classes: thermosetting products were approximately 38 percent of total output in the early 1990s; thermoplastics were 29 percent; and other laminates were 28 percent. Plastic laminates (excluding flexible packaging), laminated plastics plate, and sheet and profile shapes accounted for the remaining 5 percent.

In the mid-1990s, the principal sectors responsible for the purchase of miscellaneous plastics products were hospitals, which bought 5.6 percent of sector output, followed by electronic components with 5.2 percent, and personal consumption with 4.3 percent. Exports made up 4.0 percent of total product sales.

Background and Development

Laminated plastic plate and sheet products are defined, in rather technical terms, as plastic materials consisting of superimposed layers of synthetic resin-impregnated or coated filler that have been bonded together by means of heat and pressure to form a single piece. Plastic sheet is distinguished from plastic film by its thickness—sheet is more than 0.010 of an inch in thickness. Sheet is known for its resistance to corrosion and is used in applications from building construction to production of appliances and other consumer durables. When discrete separate layers of plastics are joined together by an adhesive, heat, or other method, the finished product is called a laminate. The term ''composite'' is used to describe sheets that result when two or more plastics are combined.

The history of laminated plastics can perhaps be best understood in the context of the development of the plastics industry in general. Some have referred to the twentieth century as the ''plastic century,'' when plastics technology applications were thought to be virtually limitless. In some respects this optimism was justified, as plastic in general began to make vast inroads as a lighter replacement for steel and other natural materials. With the boom in consumer spending following World War II, the idea of what some referred to as a ''plastics utopia'' was not all that farfetched. After the mid-1950s, laminated plastic was everywhere, with applications proliferating at an unprecedented rate.

One of the earliest and most famous names in laminated plastics history is Formica, the trade name developed by the Formica Corporation (Formica Laminate) over 80 years ago, spawning a vast array of products. It was during the 1950s that Formica took on its most characteristic use as kitchen countertops. Formica was sold as a durable nonporous material that required only the wipe of a damp cloth to clean the surface. Eventually, Formica surfaces would be able to imitate any type of surface.

Formica laminate was perfected by two former Westinghouse employees—Daniel J. O'Conor and Herbert A. Faber. They developed a process for making rigid laminated sheets that could be cut into various shapes. The Formica Insulation Company started in Cincinnati in 1913 as a venture of these two enterprising former Westinghouse employees. The new product was called "Formica" to distinguish it from other products such as Westinghouse's "Bakelite-Micarta," which had distinguished itself from the previous "Micarta." While early laminates were dark in color and homogeneous, it wasn't long before Formica's surface could hold any color, pattern, or texture including stone, wood, and textile. Other companies, such as Redmanol Company and Bakelite (founded by plastics pioneer Leo Baekeland), as well as smaller companies such as Continental Fibre and Diamond State Fibre, were all selling virtually the same product in the 1920s and 1930s. Sales of laminates boomed as laminate panels covered the interiors of railroad cars, decorative laminates covered the lobbies of many buildings, and Formica laminate even lined the Queen Mary ocean liner.

By the 1950s, technological change, lower resin prices, and new thermoplastic materials derived from petroleum led to a massive proliferation of laminates. Technological applications in the consumer appliance industry—including washing machines, vacuum cleaners, and refrigerators—all benefited from Formica parts. During this time, Formica took on its most characteristic use as kitchen countertops. Shortly afterward, the company was making dinette tops and chairs. Industry competition became fierce. By 1950 weekly production of Formica dinette sheets was 55,000 units, compared with just 28,000 units two years earlier.

In the 1950s the plastics industry expanded at an astounding rate that was far more rapid than most other American industries. Plastic laminate applications boomed as well, especially in consumer industries. In 1969 Formica ceased production of industrial grade laminate, one of its first applications. And in 1971 they received a patent for the development of a heavy-ink process used as another surface texturing technique. One year later a metallic laminate line was produced. In 1982, Formica laminate went three-dimensional by way of ColorCore, a surfacing material that made it possible to achieve volumetric as well as intaglio or cameo effects.

Establishments engaged in the manufacture of plastic plates, sheets, and related products shipped goods valued at $2.3 billion in 1993 (not adjusted for inflation). This figure remained in line with a generally flat trend in the industry in recent years. The total value of shipments increased by 5 percent from 1987 to 1990. The industry lagged behind the growth of plastics products in general, which experienced growth in shipments of over 17 percent during the same period. By 1996 the value of shipments increased to $2.6 billion.

The relatively flat trend in laminated plastic plate and sheet production has been attributed to several economic forces. Continuing weakness in the manufacturing sector due to the prolonged economic recession undoubtedly contributed to the stagnation in the demand for the industry's products during the late 1980s and early 1990s. On the positive side, however, laminated plastic makers have been able to maintain an advantage over competitors in nonplastic plate and sheet. In addition, research and development has resulted in better products and cheaper methods of production. Continuing advancements in processing technology are opening new markets throughout the world, most notably the recycling market.

CURRENT CONDITIONS

October 1999 saw price increases for acrylonitrile butadiene (ABS) resins, bolstering profits for companies in this industry. GE Plastics raised its price for Cycolac ABS by 7 cents per pound on October 11, followed by Dow Plastics on October 15. These companies and others that also raised prices explained the inflation as a result of the rising costs of raw materials as well as the tightening global market. The industry shipped $3.1 billion in products in 1997.

INDUSTRY LEADERS

Of the companies that focused primarily on this industry (as opposed to Dow Chemical Co. of Midland, Michigan, which focused on multiple other industries besides just this one), the industry leader was GE Plastics of Pittsfield, Massachusetts, with 1998 sales of $6.7 billion. In early 1999, GE expanded capacity at its Ottawa, Illinois, facility by 80 to 100 million pounds, and added compounding capacity to its St. Louis plant. GE also expanded overseas, adding 300 million pounds of capacity to its polycarbonate facility in Cartegena, Spain.

Premark International Inc. of Deerfield, Illinois, generated 1998 sales of $2.7 billion. Spartech Corp. of Clayton, Missouri, garnered $653.9 million in sales for its 1998 fiscal year. Fiscal 1999 sales of $767.9 million represented the company's eighth consecutive year of record sales; late that year, the company acquired High Performance Plastics, Inc., formerly a subsidiary of Uniroyal Technology Corporation. Other industry leaders included Klochner Capital Corp. of Gordonsville, Virginia, with $546.0 million in fiscal 1998 sales, and Wilsonart International Inc., with $370.0 million in 1997 sales.

LAMINATED PLASTICS PLATE, SHEET, AND PROFILE SHAPES INDUSTRY EMPLOYMENT

WORKFORCE

In 1994, employment dropped slightly from the previous year to 16,000 workers, including 12,000 production workers. The industry showed little growth between 1994 and 1997, when the most current figures were available. Employment increased in 1997 by just over 300 workers above 1994 levels—to a total of 16,356 people—including more than 12,000 production workers

Employment figures from earlier in the decade show that the industry tends to follow a cyclical pattern. Total employment remained relatively flat between 1987 and 1990. It was 17,300 in 1987, rose 8 percent to around 18,600 in 1988, then dropped to 17,600 in 1990, for an overall increase of only 2 percent for the entire period. Production worker employment followed roughly the same trend, rising from 12,900 in 1987 to 14,000 in 1988, and falling to only 13,400 for an overall increase of 4 percent over the entire period.

Average hourly earnings of production workers in laminated plastics was $13.86 in 1997—which is high relative to other plastics industries. This was a 14 percent increase from 1994. Regional differentials in average wages per hour for production workers ranged from a high of $13.39 in Ohio to a low of $7.40 in Indiana.

RESEARCH AND TECHNOLOGY

U.S. producers were continually developing new products and processes. This effort was reflected during the early and mid-1990s through the computerization of nearly all aspects of the laminated plastics production cycle, including design, manufacture, and distribution. Specifically, this has meant increased applications of computer-aided design and computer-aided manufacturing. At the sales level, these innovations include individualized customer design, which will lead to shorter delivery times and better quality control. By allowing

manufacturers to determine precise product demand, these new methods of production and delivery will allow users of these techniques to achieve quick delivery and short turnover times.

Of course, all of these innovations, while increasing productivity and reducing unit costs, involve major investments in computer-automated machinery. As a result, firms have tried to reduce relative labor costs, which remain high when compared to other plastics industry groups. With their economies of scale and access to internally generated funds, the larger companies will be better positioned to implement these expensive, large capital commitment operations. This will undoubtedly lead to a pattern of technological change that is anything but uniform across firms in the industry.

Finally, most firms in the industry recognized the trend toward recycling and are devoting considerable research efforts to developing recyclable materials and technologies that hold potentially profitable applications.

FURTHER READING

Darnay, Arsen J., ed. *Manufacturing USA.* 5th ed. Detroit: Gale Research, 1996.

Infotrac Company Profiles. Available at http://web4.infotrac .galegroup.com.

Ouellette, Jennifer. "ABS Producers Mulling Price Increases." *Chemical Market Reporter,* 22 November 1999.

"Spartech Corporation Announces Agreement to Purchase Uniroyal Technology's High Performance Plastics Group." *PR Newswire,* 27 December 1999.

Tullo, Alex. "Engineering Plastics Market Grows in Wake of Innovative Strategies." *Chemical Market Reporter,* 20 September 1999.

U.S. Bureau of the Census. *1995 Annual Survey of Manufactures.* Washington: GPO, 1997.

———. *1994 County Business Patterns* Washington: GPO, 1996.

SIC 3084

PLASTICS PIPE

This category covers establishments primarily engaged in manufacturing plastics pipe. Establishments primarily engaged in manufacturing plastics pipe fittings are classified in **SIC 3089: Plastics Products, Not Elsewhere Classified.**

NAICS CODE

326122 (Plastic Pipe and Pipe Fitting Manufacturing)

INDUSTRY SNAPSHOT

Establishments manufacturing plastics pipe produced an estimated $4.2 billion dollars worth of product in 1999. Although the industry has grown fairly steadily over the past decade, it has lagged behind the growth of plastics products in general.

In the late 1990s however, plastics pipe as a commodity maintained a large advantage over competitors in nonplastics piping. Although markets stagnated in the 1980s and early 1990s, plastics piping markets grew at a rate four times faster than that of nonplastics markets. In addition, research and development spurred new products and cheaper methods of production. The continuing advancements in processing technology are opening new markets and applications throughout the world.

ORGANIZATION AND STRUCTURE

In 1999 an estimated 298 establishments were engaged in the production of plastics pipe. In 1996, each establishment employed an average of approximately 49 employees, 34 of which were production workers. The estimated number of employees overall in 1999 was 16,300.

In terms of major geographic concentration, the largest number of establishments were located in the Pacific region of the United States—including Alaska and Hawaii—followed by the west South Central region. California had the largest number of establishments, followed by Texas, North Carolina, Indiana, and Florida.

Market concentration was relatively high in the plastics pipe industry. In 1999, it was estimated that the five largest companies accounted for approximately 38 percent of the entire industry's sales. Dominant players in the plastics pipe industry were Phillips Chemical Company, with 1998 revenues of $1.0 billion; Central Sprinkler Corporation, (a division of Tyco International), with 1998 revenues totaling $187.0 million; and Advanced Drainage Systems, with 1998 revenues of $160.0 million. Most of the leading companies were private companies. In fact, 31 of the top 50 companies were private companies.

Consolidation was evident in this industry. One noteworthy partnership announced in 1999 was a joint venture between Phillips Chemical and Chevron Chemicals. The two companies have a combined value of $6.1 billion, and finalization of the venture was expected in mid-2000.

BACKGROUND AND DEVELOPMENT

Plastics pipe was first manufactured commercially in the United States in 1940, when the Southern California Gas Company used a type of plastics pipe, butyrate pipe, to distribute natural gas. Prior to that time, polyvinyl chloride (pvc) pipe had been used in Germany as early as 1930. Then, plastics pipe was being produced as well by several U.S. companies for use in chemical services. Plastics pipe production in the U.S. commenced in 1948 with the development of polyethylene pipe for water services. Initial applications of the new pipe included use on farms for drainage and various applications in the petroleum industry.

Plastics pipe and tubing is the final stage of value-added production into consumer or industrial products. In general, plastics manufacturing is as follows: plastics materials (monomers) are chemically altered to produce polymers, which are then mixed with certain materials to impart certain characteristics such as durability, flexibility, and chemical resistance. Then, other manufacturing processes are used to produce final products such as plastics pipe. The production processes specific to plastics pipe manufacturing—processes including a variety of methods such as coating, extrusion, molding, and laminating—allow for continuous production of piping. Plastics pipes have various functions for long and short distance transportation of fluids. Also, plastics pipes have various intermediary purposes for final use in building construction.

Plastics soften but do not melt when heated, thereby allowing them to change shape without losing cohesion. Before the 1930s, industrial products were largely based on coal as the basic chemical feed stock. The surge and rapid expansion of the production and consumption of plastics was directly related to the advent of petroleum as the main chemical feedstock. Thus, the petroleum and plastics industry are intrinsically related, and petrochemicals provide the basis for mass production of plastics, and conversely, plastics provided petroleum with their main downstream market.

The boom in plastics piping in the post-World War II period is intertwined with the boom in plastics manufacturing, which has a close relation to the advancement of consumer society in the United States, most notably the substitution of plastics material for other materials such as copper, aluminum, and steel. This enabled the use of plastics products to seriously challenge metal or alloy applications in such fields as aerospace, transportation, electricity, and engineering industry. In general, the plastics industry is the single, most-important "downstream" industry in the petrochemicals value-added chain. Plastics products are produced by various chemical processes that allow the formation of usable products by heating, milling, or extrusion.

Retail sales of plastics pipe for various applications were up to $500,000 by 1948 and annual sales volume grew to $10 million by 1952. The new major classes of rigid thermoplastics pipe, namely acrylonitrile-butadiene-styrene (ABS) and polyvinyl chloride (PVC) were introduced in 1949 and 1950, respectively, and became widely used in new markets, competing effectively with other

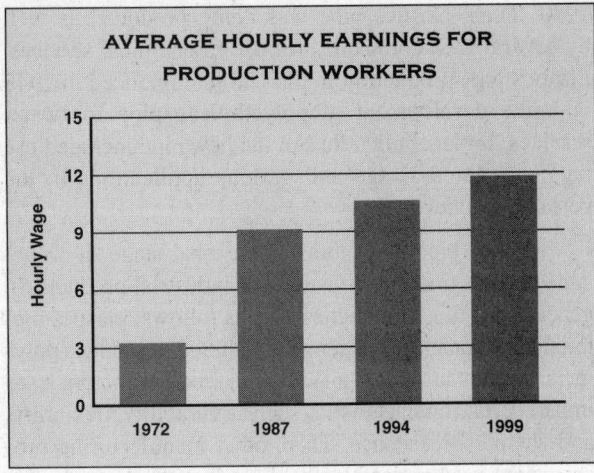

AVERAGE HOURLY EARNINGS FOR
PRODUCTION WORKERS

materials such as steel and copper piping. Plastics piping became widely used in drain, waste, and vent applications; natural gas distribution; and in the chemical industry. Styrene rubber pipe for sewer and drainage services became common material by around 1956. This was followed by other successful materials—thermoplastics piping, acetal, polypropylene, and polyvinyl dichloride. Sales grew to $25 million in 1957, $75 million in 1963, $100 million in 1964, and $120 million in 1965.

Applications became very wide-spread in construction and building, as piping of all sizes pervaded the economic development of the post-World War II period in the United States. New standards for municipal building codes were being written, and new standards were adopted to provide for the now dominant use of plastics pipe. In addition, the competitive effect on other materials products, such as steel and copper pipe producers, was such that manufacturers sought to protect their markets by acquiring manufacturers and distributors. This was especially important in oil piping where hundreds of miles of tubular goods are involved.

Plastics pipe's competitive advantage over various metals was the result of many factors, not the least of which was low cost. In addition, plastics pipe offers other advantages to users in that it is lightweight and resistant to varying environmental conditions. It is also relatively easy to install, minimizes solid deposits, has low frictional losses, and has self-insulating characteristics. However, metal pipes exhibit superior performance in some applications where temperature and pressure are significant factors.

Specific among plastics pipe's many applications are water supply and distribution, including water utilities, municipal water treatment plants, chemical feed lines, sludge lines, and water distribution; natural gas distribution; drain, waste, and vent services, where plastic is resistant to chemicals; industrial uses, including food and beverage piping, acid and corrosive drain lines, chemical, electric and communication conduits, water and gas ser-

vice, and general drainage; and irrigation of farm and ranch systems, including movement of water and gas, fertilizer and insecticide.

In any case, the 1960s and 1970s were boom times for plastics in general and plastics piping in particular. Approximately 55 companies were engaged in the manufacture of plastics pipe by the mid-1970s. From 1964 to 1970 total sales more than doubled from 150 million pounds to 345 million pounds. In 1967, sales were 320 million pounds valued at $240 million dollars. By 1969, plastics pipe accounted for 1 to 2 percent of the $5 billion per year total pipe market, and was growing at a rate of about 15 percent per year, about two times as fast as the growth of the chemical industry. Sales topped the $500 million mark by the mid-1970s. Steel would lose 5 percent of its market to plastic pipe—over $100 million in sales—while copper lost 50 percent, and aluminum lost 20 percent.

CURRENT CONDITIONS

The underground piping market is the largest use segment of plastics pipe—water, drain, waste, vent, sewer and drain, gas, irrigation, conduit and pressure— and remains the largest market for plastics piping not only in the United States but in the world. The industry shipped $4.2 billion worth of goods in 1997.

Significant recycling advances have been made in the industry but the portion of total plastics recycled remains low compared with total production or consumption. The industry responded to public pressure to develop environmentally safer products and to advance recycling into all of its product areas. Efforts were made between the industry and federal, state, and local governments to evaluate the merits of various policies.

While new technologies will further the trend toward the replacement of non-plastics materials with plastics, there is some concern over the feasibility of plastics recycling which may lead some to shift back to older materials such as aluminum, copper, and other metals. From the production side, industry efforts to implement computer-aided design and manufacture (CAD/CAM) is expected to lead to drastic reductions in costs, reductions in turnover time, and decrease some of the environmental concerns by minimizing material waste. These continuing advancements in process technology remain the key factors behind the plastics piping products' success and future growth.

WORKFORCE

Except for a blip in the mid-1990s, total employment in the plastics pipe rose steadily in the last decade of the century.

In 1990, the major occupational categories for the entire plastics products industry were: plastics molding machine operators, assemblers and fabricators, and packers and packagers. The Bureau of Labor Statistics forecasted that all of these occupational categories would grow by the year 2005, reflecting the projected growth in demand for the industry's products. However, the occupation that made up the bulk of the industry's employment in 1987, plastic molding machine operators, was projected to grow 29.5 percent by 2005, trailing 12 other categories in projected job growth. The percentage of production workers within total employment has drifted downward slowly since 1972 to about 77 percent in the late 1990s from 80 percent in 1972.

The job categories with the largest projected growth (ranked by projected percentage growth) into 2005 were largely nonproduction jobs: sales and related workers were projected to grow by 69 percent by 2005; industrial production managers have a projected growth of 64.2 percent; industrial machinery mechanics are expected to increase by 50.9 percent; tool & die makers have a projected growth of 44.9 percent. Blue collar worker supervisors; hand packers and packagers; inspectors, testers, and graders; freight, stock, and material movers; and extruding and forming machine operators occupations were forecast to grow by 35.8 percent.

While average hourly earnings of production workers in plastic pipe production rose from $3.30 in 1972 to an estimated $11.80 in 1999, the purchasing power of these money wages actually declined over the same period. General payroll per employee, adjusted for inflation, actually fell over this same period. In terms of value added per production worker, money wages per hour rose about two-and-one-half times while the value added per hour by these production workers increased over three times, indicating a shift in income distribution away from wages and toward profits. (When comparing industry figures for plastic piping over time, plastic piping was included as part of **SIC 3079: Miscellaneous Plastics Products** in 1972, and the workforce figures were calculated on the 1972 SIC basis.)

FURTHER READING

Chasis, David A. *Plastic Piping Systems.* Industrial Press, Inc., 1988.

Darnay, Arsen J., ed. *Manufacturing USA.* 6th ed. Detroit: The Gale Group, 1999.

U.S. Bureau of the Census. *1995 Annual Survey of Manufactures.* Washington, DC: GPO, 1997.

SIC 3085

PLASTICS BOTTLES

Included in this category are establishments primarily engaged in manufacturing plastics bottles.

NAICS CODE(S)

326160 (Plastic Bottle Manufacturing)

INDUSTRY SNAPSHOT

In 1997 467 U.S. establishments shipped $6.3 billion worth of plastic bottles. Imports into the United States reached $162.0 million in 1995, while exports totaled $220.0 million. As of 1998, both import and export prices were dropping.

ORGANIZATION AND STRUCTURE

This industry is dependent on nine separate plastic bottle markets: soft drink, milk, medicinal, household chemical, toiletry and cosmetic, automobile and marine, juice and water, food (excluding milk), and industrial. All of these markets had moderate and steady growth over the last 10 years. The use of plastic in bottles has been steadily replacing the use of aluminum and glass because of its convenience and cost effectiveness.

BACKGROUND AND DEVELOPMENT

In 1990, plastic bottles comprised 22.7 percent of the container market by material shipments, metal cans were 59.1 percent, and glass containers were 18.2 percent. A report by the Freedonia Group entitled ''Beverages & Containers: Markets & Materials'' claimed that metal would remain the dominant packaging material for beverages, but plastic would continue to gain market share at the expense of glass throughout the 1990s.

At the heart of this growing industry are the suppliers of plastic resins, which, for the majority of plastic bottles, are one of three types—polyethylene terephthalate (PET), high density polyethylene (HDPE), and vinyl.

Bottle demand for PET in the United States was 1.3 billion pounds in 1992, about 70 percent of the total PET market. The largest market for PET is carbonated soft drink containers at 910 million pounds. Single serving carbonated soft drink containers in 12, 16, and 20 ounce sizes are now a 225 million pound market that is growing 25 percent annually.

PET resin producers supply the bulk ingredient to make plastic bottles, and their production in 1991 capacity rose to only 68,000 tons, while demand shot up to 206,000 tons. By 1992 demand had increased to 219,000 tons, while new capacity more than doubled, reaching 140,000 tons. Plants worldwide should be reaching capacities of upwards of 93 percent. Eastman Company expanded domestic resin production by 300 million pounds in 1993 and 1994, and 250 million pounds in 1995. In early 1992, PET resin stood at 65 to 67 cents per pound and fell at the end of 1992 to 62 to 64 cents per pound. Prices should rise with increased demand for PET resin. Technology Forecasts of Westport, Connecticut, projected an 8 percent annual growth rate in PET resin use through 1997.

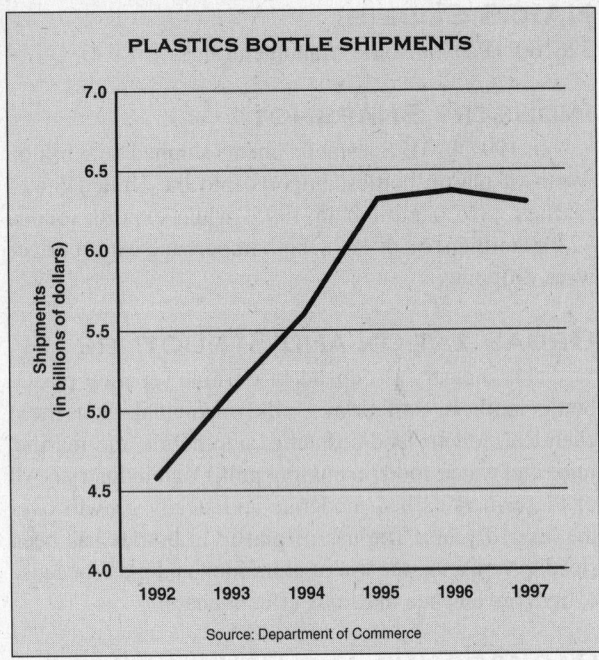

PLASTICS BOTTLE SHIPMENTS

Shipments (in billions of dollars)

7.0
6.5
6.0
5.5
5.0
4.5
4.0

1992 1993 1994 1995 1996 1997

Source: Department of Commerce

In 1992, PET resin demand from the soft drink industry topped 900 million pounds, and by 1997 it approached to 1.4 billion pounds. With PET resin bringing higher prices and worldwide demand exceeding supply, lightweighting of plastic bottles is PET manufacturer's highest priority. Environmental and pricing pressures are prompting PET producers to investigate methods for reducing the weight of the two-liter bottle below its current weight of 55 grams. A one-gram reduction of PET from the current container would be a 22 million pound savings to the beverage industry and a cost savings of about $15.0 million per year. One way to achieve this goal is to make all PET bottles with plastic closure finishes instead of aluminum closures. The removal of basecups is also another potential solution. One-piece PET bottles in the United States could then fall to 50.5 grams. In Europe, PET producers are marketing a one-way PET bottle that weighs between 48 and 49 grams.

The recycled version of HDPE, the second type of plastic resin, had previously cost more than its virgin plastic, and many packagers have been using recycled HDPE to satisfy environmental concerns. But in 1994, there were indications that the gap between these plastics has significantly narrowed or, in some cases, disappeared. Important variables between these markets are the availability of high quality, well-sorted HDPE and the degree to which collection is subsidized by municipalities. As state lawmakers and major retailers insist on recycled content packaging, demand will rise for this resin.

Vinyl, the third type of plastic resin, is used mostly for packaging household chemicals, liquid soap, shampoo, edible oils, and bottled water. In Europe, vinyl is the leading packaging material for bottled water, and 36 percent of U.S. and Canadian water bottlers reported that they used one or more sizes. For clean, one-gallon water bottles, vinyl is the leading material.

The market research firm SRI International of Menlo Park, California, projects U.S. consumption of recycled PET will increase 12 percent annually through the late 1990s, due mostly to the success of curbside collection efforts. There are now 3,100 community programs in the United States that accept PET in their recycling bins, up from 575 in 1990. Approximately 3.7 billion PET bottles were recycled in 1992. The major soft drink manufacturers now use PET bottles that contain a percentage of recycled resin. Some 19 percent of all plastic bottles were recycled in 1992, led by the 41.5 percent recycling rate of soft drink bottles. In 1991, 14 percent of all plastic bottles were recycled, also led by the 36 percent recycling rate of soft drink bottles.

CURRENT CONDITIONS

In 1999, the majority of PET was used for soft drink bottles, but other drinks, such as juice, water, and beer, as well as nonfood items, had increased consumption to a weighty 40 percent of the market. Production of PET bottles was taking off. Manufacture of PET beer bottles has not been as successful as others. For one reason, the darker-colored bottle makes it difficult for local recyclers to easily identify and separate it from other recyclables. Early bottles did not protect against the introduction of oxygen, which dramatically shortens beer's shelf life. Also, increased cost made consumers less likely to purchase beer in plastic bottles. But new bottles designed with numerous layers were making progress toward lengthening shelf life, and beer in plastic bottles was expected to sell well at outdoor sporting events and other outdoor entertainment, where cost is not the same kind of issue as it is in a retail store.

Also less successful than soft drinks was water in plastic bottles. Until late 1999, a harmless PET byproduct called acetaldehyde could be detected in bottled water by its slight but fruity flavor. A researcher at Aston University was developing additives that would act as barriers to the chemical's taste.

According to the Freedonia Group report, blow-molded bottles will likely present the greatest opportunities for growth, particularly in small contoured carbonated soft drink bottles and hot-fill bottles, where the material has cost and performance advantages over metal and glass. While the strongest growth in volume terms will occur in the United States, the polyethylene terephthalate market will grow at a faster pace in Canada and Mexico. An expected growth rate of 18 percent in Mexico is attributed to the country's status as the second largest per capita consumer of soft drinks, poor tap water quality, hot climate, and PET advantages over glass.

INDUSTRY LEADERS

In 1999, CONSTAR Plastics Inc. of Philadelphia was the industry leader with $540.0 million in sales. Second was Johnson Controls Inc., of Manchester, Michigan with $400.0 million in sales. Another major player was Crown Cork and Seal Company, Inc, of Philadelphia.

WORKFORCE

In 1997, 34,142 employees worked for an estimated 467 establishments in the plastic bottle industry, up from 25,100 employees in 1987. In 1997 28,967 were production workers. Payroll in 1997 reached $744.8 million.

California is the largest plastic bottle manufacturing state in the United States, with 36 companies shipping more than $340.0 million worth of bottles. It accounts for 12 percent of industry shipments and employs approximately 3,000 workers. Other states in the top five are Ohio, with 26 companies shipping $319.0 million and employing 3,200; New Jersey, with 23 companies shipping $282.0 million and employing 2,700; Texas, with 22 companies shipping $216.0 million and employing 1,500; and Illinois, with 22 companies shipping $200 million and employing 2,100. The bulk of the nation's plastic bottles comes from the Great Lakes region, which represents about 40 percent of total industry shipments.

AMERICA AND THE WORLD

Outside the United States, PET containers are battling glass for market share in the refillable-container soft drink market, especially in Europe where refillable PET is being driven by regulations, and in Latin America where it is cost effective to use. Beverage containers account for 80 percent of the PET used in Europe, and just 4 percent was recycled in 1992. A Pan-European association called Petcore, which was formed by PET resin producers and bottle converters, is aiming to reach a recycling target of at least 15 percent, which would be in line with the European Packaging and Packaging Waste Directives. Petcore will work with public sector groups and industry to increase the recycling of blow-molded PET containers up to five liters in size. Petcore wants to achieve a recycling target of 30 percent. Petcore's U.S. counterpart, NAPCORE, reached a 27 percent recycling level in 1992. "Reaching 15 percent in five years will be tough. The problem is not recycling capacity, but getting the PET back from the customer," states Dr. Vince Matthews, coordinator of Petcore. But recycling increased in 1997 to 649 million pounds, most of which were PET soft drink bottles. Prices for recycled PET, mostly for fiber uses, were also increasing. But late 1990s modifications in bottle manufacturing was expected to cause further problems for local recyclers.

Since 1991, German law has required manufacturers, distributors, and retailers to take back product packaging.

Though 64 percent of all plastics were to be recycled by the mid-1990s, only 4 percent is recycled now in Germany, but an industry consortium called Duales System Deutschland (DSD) wants to improve that level. All costs of DSD systems are internalized and passed along to the consumer, and the estimated yearly per capita cost is $33. By weight, nearly 80 percent of the food and beverage container market in Germany is glass, approximately 18 percent is metal, and 2 percent is plastic. The program cost $6.0 billion to start and $2.6 billion annually, and it has come under criticism from German citizens. A comparable program in the United States could cost $18.0 billion annually.

RESEARCH AND TECHNOLOGY

Two University of Pittsburgh scientists are designing plastic that can be made without toxic by-products and recycled with help from an enzyme. If the technology can be developed in an economically feasible manner, it could aid in efforts to recycle plastic bottles. Drs. Alan Russell and Eric Beckman are working on developing "bioplastic"—instead of being made with organic solvents it is made with carbon dioxide. Carbon dioxide fluid can chemically sort out mixed batches of melted plastic, enabling recyclers to shred plastic and dump the pieces into a high pressure tank of supercritical carbon dioxide. The same type of plastic, usually the lightest, floats to the top of the tank. Several companies are considering licensing the technology.

To aid in the recycling of plastic bottles, plastic labels are being widely produced in the same polymer type as the plastic bottle, and closures are also being made increasingly compatible. The packaging market for stretch blow-molded plastic bottles may also expand. Favorable market potential is attributed to a new thermoplastic polyester resin and a number of new process technologies.

Other advances include single piece PET bottles, stretch blow molding by cyrogenics, and thin-walled molded PET. Because wall thickness is more important to bottle performance than other variables such as weight, new techniques for measuring thickness have been developed in the late 1990s. Late 1999 research also focused on the presence of Bisphenol A, a primary ingredient in plastic bottles, and its possible link to obesity in children.

FURTHER READING

Demetrakakes, Pam. "Brewers Look at Plastic Again." *Food Processing,* September 1999.

U.S. Census Bureau. *Economic Census 1997.* Available from http://www.census.gov.

"Hormone Mimic Linked to Obesity in Mice." *Chemistry and Industry,* 1 November 1999.

"Improving and Increasing PET Container Recycling." *Beverage Industry,* January 1999.

"Landmark PET Bottle Patents." *Beverage Industry,* July 1998.

Lazich, Robert S., ed. *Market Share Reporter.* Detroit: Gale Research, 1997.

"Recycling Plastic Beer Bottles" *Beverage Industry,* June, 1999.

Rice, Judy. "PET Container QC." *Beverage Industry,* July 1998.

Stack, E. Gifford. "Use of PET Bottles is Exploding." *Beverage Industry,* May 1999.

Thomas, William D., et al. "Producer Price Highlights 1998." *Monthly Labor Review,* July 1999.

"Water Bottles All in Good Taste." *Chemistry and Industry,* 15 November 1999.

SIC 3086

PLASTICS FOAM PRODUCTS

This industry covers establishments primarily engaged in manufacturing plastics foam products.

NAICS CODE(S)

326150 (Urethane and Other Foam Product (except Polystyrene) Manufacturing)
326140 (Polystyrene Foam Product Manufacturing)

INDUSTRY SNAPSHOT

Despite the industry-wide implementation of cost-saving initiatives, plus volume gains and the recovery of Asian markets, prices for plastics foam products still decreased in early 1999. These lower selling prices, as well as negative currency impacts and weak economies in Europe and Latin America, adversely affected sales results.

ORGANIZATION AND STRUCTURE

In 1996, approximately 1,300 establishments were engaged in the production of plastic foam products. These businesses employed approximately 49 employees per establishment, of which 34 were production workers. The average value added per production worker was $72,991, a small figure compared to an average of $93,930 calculated for the average of all U.S. manufacturing industries.

The largest number of plastic foam products establishments were located in the East North Central region, followed by the middle Atlantic region and the Pacific region. However, when ranked by the number of establishments per state, California was first with 171, followed by Texas with 83, North Carolina with 70, Ohio with 62, Pennsylvania with 60, and Michigan with 59. It was estimated that the largest five companies producing plastic

foam products accounted for approximately $2.6 billion, or more than 59 percent of the entire industry's sales.

BACKGROUND AND DEVELOPMENT

Plastics foam, sometimes called expandable plastics, are versatile materials that were first used in the post-World War II plastics boom. Plastic foam products are used both as original and replacement materials in industries. Foam products emerge out of a unique chemical process. Foamed plastic is an expanded material with a distinct cellular structure that can be either rigid or flexible. Rigid foam consists of hollow spheres attached together, while flexible foam has its cells connected, thus giving it a spongy structure. Polystyrene and polyurethane are used for rigid foams and vinyls and cellulose acetate. Linear polyurethanes have been traditionally used in flexible foams. By 1969, flexible urethane dominated the market with polystyrene running second, rigid urethane third, and polyvinyl chloride fourth.

Following World War II, plastics foam consumption in the United States grew tremendously, increasing more than ten-fold from 1955 to 1970. By 1967, total consumption of plastics foam products rose to 700.0 million pounds, or $60.0 million; by 1970, output weight was 1.0 billion pounds. It took only five years for this figure to double. More than 700 companies in the 1970s were in some way involved in the production of plastics foam, including most major chemical companies, rubber and tire companies, textile mills, and drug companies.

By the end of the 1960s, the threat of oversupply prompted the industry to step up research and development to improve materials and develop new market outlets, notably tires, sporting goods, advanced military equipment, and highway safety barriers. Rigid urethane and polystyrene were used for industrial purposes, such as industrial walls and cold storage insulation. The foams came in many forms—slabs, logs, sheets, rods, tubes, and particles.

In general, plastics are manufactured as follows: plastic materials (monomers) are chemically altered to produce more complex materials called polymers, which are then mixed with certain materials to impart characteristics such as durability, flexibility, and chemical resistance. Subsequent manufacturing processes produce final products, such as the rigid and flexible foam used in consumer durable goods, buildings, and refrigerated transport. Foam production processes involve a variety of methods, and the output takes the form of slabs, blocks, boards, sheets, molded shapes, and extruded insulation. Foam can also be produced onsite for building insulation and cushioning applications. Extrusion and injection molding are used to produce most grades of foam. More than half of foamed plastic is polyurethane, and the rest consists of expandable polystyrene and vinyl, phenolic, epoxy, urea, and silicone.

The post-World War II boom in plastics foam products was intertwined with the growth in general plastics manufacturing, growth stemming from a burgeoning U.S. consumer base and from the substitution of plastics for materials such as copper, aluminum, and steel. Plastic products seriously challenged metals and alloys in the aerospace, transportation, electricity, and engineering industries. In general, the plastics industry is the single most important "downstream" industry in the petrochemicals value-added chain. Plastics are produced by various chemical processes that allow end-products to be formed through heating, milling, or extrusion. Plastics soften but do not melt when heated, thereby allowing them to change shape without losing cohesion. Before the 1930s, industrial products were largely based on coal as the basic chemical feed stock. The surge in production and consumption of plastic was directly related to the availability of petroleum, which is plastic's main chemical feedstock. The petroleum and plastics industries are closely linked; petrochemicals provide the basis for the mass production of plastics and, conversely, plastics provide petroleum with their main downstream market.

Total plastics foam production tripled from 1970 to 1980. Increased production was fueled during this period by skyrocketing demand for consumer goods such as furniture cushioning, mattresses, bedding, and other items that use mostly urethane foams. Rigid foam found growing use in buildings, refrigerated transports, household refrigerators and freezers, dehumidifiers, dishwashers, packaging, and marine salvage.

The main concern of industry leaders is, of course, market growth and expansion. Of particular interest are consumer durable goods, construction, and health care, which make up a large portion of demand for the industry's products. The early 1990s upturn in consumer spending, especially for durable goods such as appliances (which use large quantities of rigid foam and adhesives), buoyed the market for plastic foams; construction, another rigid foam user, underwent similar growth.

In the mid-1990s, the industry manufactured products estimated to valued at $10.1 million dollars. This figure remained in line with a generally upward production trend in the industry since 1987. Total value of shipments increased by over 31 percent from 1987 to 1993, higher than the increase in general plastic production, which grew at a 17 percent rate over the same period. By 1996, the value reached $12.1 billion.

CURRENT CONDITIONS

According to a study conducted by Philip Townshend Associates, the largest interior use for plastics is in automotive paneling, which used over 1.1 billion pounds of plastics material in the 55 million vehicles produced worldwide in 1997. Polyurethane accounted for 90 percent of this market, with polypropylene and polyethylene accounting for 6 percent of consumption and polyvinyl chloride accounting for 4 percent of the market. As the exteriors of cars became more similar, manufacturers sought to express a car's individuality through their instrument panels, which challenged the plastics foam industry to provide ever-stronger, ever-lighter materials that could be molded to their specifications. One solution the industry developed was single-material panels, which recycled easier than the traditional blended-composition panels.

INDUSTRY LEADERS

Dow Chemical Co. of Midland, Michigan, led the industry in overall sales with $18.4 billion in 1998 sales, while Tennaco Inc. of Greenwich, Connecticut, generated $7.6 billion that year. It should be noted, however, that these revenue totals also reflect other industries in which Dow and Tennaco are active besides the plastics foam industry. Of the companies that focused primarily on this industry, Sealed Air Corp. of Saddle Brook, New Jersey, led the way with 1998 sales of $2.5 billion. Boca Raton-based W. R. Grace and Co. garnered $1.5 billion in 1998 sales. Courtaulds United States Inc. of Purchase, New York, ended its fiscal year on March 31, 1999 with $1.1 billion in sales.

WORKFORCE

In 1995, the major occupational categories for the plastics products industry (these data relate to the three-digit **Industry Group 308** for miscellaneous plastics products rather than the specific four-digit SIC for plastics foam products) were: plastic molding machine operators, who made up 17.8 percent of total employment; assemblers and fabricators, who made up 8.6 percent; and packers and packagers, who comprised 4.8 percent. Approximately 20 percent of industry employees were engaged in some type of managerial or supervisory function or clerical, transportation, and accounting/financial tasks. The remaining employees were engaged in production activity.

The U.S. Bureau of Labor Statistics has forecast that all these occupational categories will grow by the year 2005, reflecting the growth in demand for this industry's products. The occupation making up the bulk of the industry's employment, plastic molding machine operators, should grow 29.5 percent to the year 2005, trailing 12 other industry categories in projected growth.

The industry job categories with the largest projected growth through 2005 were largely nonproduction jobs: sales and related workers, which are projected to grow by 69 percent; industrial production managers, 64.2 percent; industrial machinery mechanics, 50.9 percent; and tool and die makers, 44.9 percent. Categories uniformly forecast to grow by 35.8 percent were: blue-collar worker supervisors; hand packers and packagers; inspectors, testers and graders; freight, stock, and material movers; and extruding and forming machine operators.

Over the period covering 1991 to 1994, total employment in the plastics products industry overall rose by 13 percent. Production worker employment followed roughly the same trend, rising from 47,800 to 55,800 in 1996.

Concerning the industry's income distribution, while average hourly earnings of production workers in plastic products production rose from $3.27 in 1972 to $8.43 in 1987, the purchasing power of these wages actually declined by 10 percent. General payroll per employee, adjusted for inflation, fell from an average of $18,215 to $17,903 during that time. From 1987 to 1996, average hourly earnings rose by about 28 percent to $11.62. From 1972 to 1987, in terms of value added per production worker, wages per hour rose about two and one half times, while the value added per hour by these production workers rose by over three times, a shift in income distribution away from wages and toward profits.

RESEARCH AND TECHNOLOGY

The plastics industry faces challenges due to environmental damage caused by its use of certain processes and chemicals. The industry must comply with federal and worldwide environmental rules aimed at banning use of chlorofluorocarbons (CFCs), which are said to deplete the ozone layer. The rules have led to a competitive race to develop replacements for CFCs. In addition, political pressure is forcing companies to develop recycling processes; as of the early 1990s, only a small portion of plastics in general were recyclable.

The industry has devoted significant resources to developing alternatives to CFCs. It has been very successful in the flexible foam sector, but rigid foam makers have made less progress. For rigid foams, some firms are developing new formulations that use hydrochlorofluorocarbons (HCFCs), which have a lower ozone depletion potential than CFCs while retaining some of CFCs' desirable properties. Flexible foams are also being reformulated. New machinery has been developed that is tailored to the low boiling point agents that are gradually replacing CFCs.

Recycling efforts are also underway. For example, construction board has been made from rigid foam scrap and carpet pad has been produced from auto seating scrap. Though most of the focus in the recycling movement has been on bottles and foamed polystyrene containers, the push is on for polyurethane recycling. The plastics foam products industry and federal, state, and local governments are evaluating the merits of various recycling policies.

Finally, in addition to their recycling efforts, firms in the industry hope to improve the aesthetic of urethane foams, particularly in automobiles. For example, technology is being developed that would reduce foam scorching at high temperatures. And, in another effort, some are attempting to eliminate fogging that occurs on the insides of car windows when sunlight heats up plastics in passenger compartments.

FURTHER READING

Chang, Joseph. "Specialty Makers Report Mixed Results." *Chemical Market Reporter,* 2 August 1999.

Darnay, Arsen J. *Manufacturing USA.* 5th ed. Detroit: Gale Research, 1996.

Infotrac Company Profiles. Available at http://web4.infotrac.galegroup.com.

"Instrument Panels Challenge Materials Suppliers, Molders." *Molding Systems,* March 1998.

SIC 3087

CUSTOM COMPOUNDING OF PURCHASED PLASTICS RESINS

This category covers establishments primarily engaged in custom compounding of purchased plastics resins. For more information related to this industry, see the **SIC 2821: Plastic Materials, Synthetic Resins, and Nonvulcanizable Elastomers.**

Custom compounding companies purchase plastic resins from plastic manufacturers. They alter and manipulate the resins to form new compounds, which they usually sell to companies making plastic products. They contribute to the plastic manufacturing process by upgrading the quality and performance of resins, improving the efficiency of the compounding process, and developing entirely new plastic substances. Custom compounding emerged as a separate industry during the 1980s and is credited with increasing the breadth of the U.S. plastics business during that decade. About one-third of all U.S. polymer production undergoes some sort of compounding.

NAICS CODE(S)

325991 (Custom Compounding of Purchase Resin)

INDUSTRY SNAPSHOT

There were 832 establishments in the industry in 1997, up from 644 in 1995. Industry shipments totaled $7.8 billion in 1997, an increase of 76 percent over 1995, when shipments totaled $6.0 billion. There were 27,573 employees in 1997—a gain of 7.4 percent since 1995, when 25,531 found work in the industry. In 1997, 18,224 employees were directly involved in production. On average they earned $13.92 per hour.

ORGANIZATION AND STRUCTURE

Plastics are extremely long polymers, or long-chain molecules, which are shaped and molded under heat and pressure to form a resin. Resins typically take the form of pellets, flakes, powder, granules, or liquid. Although many resin manufacturers process their own resins and even make plastic products, they often sell resins to companies that make custom compounds. Custom compounders alter the physical properties of the resins they purchase by: mixing or melt-state blending several resins together, introducing additives, or adding fillers and reinforcements. An almost infinite number of compounds, each with varying grades and performance characteristics, can be created.

Several categories of additives are used to make compounds. Plasticizers, the most common additives, are chemicals that increase a resin's flexibility. Similarly, impact modifiers increase stress resistance. Plasticizers and impact modifiers are used, for example, to increase the resilience of plastic automobile body panels or to make polyvinyl chloride (PVC) resins used in construction materials. Various stabilizers and antioxidants are used to retard the oxidation and breakdown of resins that results from exposure to heat, light, air, and moisture. Heat stabilizers, for instance, help resins to retain their physical structure during processing. Flame retardants are added to reduce flammability, and colorants are used to change a resin's hue.

Fillers and reinforcements are used to add texture, strength, and other characteristics to resins without changing their polymer structure. Examples of fillers are cotton and asbestos flocks, glass fibers, chopped monofilaments, carbon fibers, hollow glass spheres, metal powder, and carbon. Glass fiber, which is integrated as whole or chopped mat, and carbon fiber have traditionally accounted for the majority of filler and reinforcement material used in the plastics industry.

Plastic compounding companies work with and create four general grades of resins and compounds. Commodity resins, which receive little attention in this industry, are low-tech plastics made with standardized formulas. Intermediate resins are slightly more advanced. Engineering resins exhibit higher performance characteristics. Advanced resin compounds, the most expensive class, are those most able to withstand exposure to heat, weight, impact, acids, and other forces. They are typically used for applications in aerospace, microelectronics, and other high-tech industries.

BACKGROUND AND DEVELOPMENT

The first plastic, a natural material called Keratin, was developed in the early 1700s. Parkesine, the first synthetic plastic, was invented in 1862 by Englishmen Alexander Parkes; but, it was American John Wyatt who recognized the important plasticizing effect of the Parkesine production process. Wyatt renamed the substance Celluloid in 1870 and is recognized as the founder of modern plastic making in the United States.

The use of plastics increased rapidly during the early 1900s as new processing techniques, such as molding, evolved. Compounding occurred, but in relatively simple ways. Resins were combined with paints and varnishes, for example, to increase their durability. Not until World War II were more advanced compounding processes used on a broad scale—to make items such as airplane gun turret covers and lightweight field equipment. Huge advances in the chemical additives industry during the 1950s, 1960s, and 1970s created a strong demand for new compounds with specific characteristics. As compounders learned to make resins more flexible, durable, attractive, and flame retardant, the need for plastics compounds grew. By the early 1980s, the plastics industry was shipping $15 billion worth of resins, about 30 percent of which were compounded by resin manufacturers or plastic goods producers.

During the 1980s, the U.S. plastics industry began to shift its focus from commodity-like resins and compounds to higher grade products that could be used to replace steel, glass, and other natural, more expensive materials. The development of high-tech additives and alloys allowed U.S. producers to retain their global industry lead in spite of fierce foreign competition from low-cost manufacturers. As the need for advanced, efficient compounding processes expanded, custom compounding firms proliferated.

By 1987, custom compounders were processing about 8.5 billion pounds of resins annually and grossing $2.5 billion. Despite a late 1980s recession, production volume jumped to 12.5 billion pounds by 1990, and industry revenues climbed to $5,080.1 billion by 1993, reflecting average annual sales growth of 8 percent between 1987 and 1993. As plastics consumers increasingly sought the expertise and efficiency of custom compounding companies, revenues swelled at a rate of approximately 7 to 10 percent annually during the early 1990s.

CURRENT CONDITIONS

The plastics custom compounding market was strong in the late 1990s because the key consumers of plastic—the automotive, electronics, appliance, and construction industries—flourished in the booming U.S. economy. The strength of the automotive industry played a particularly key role in custom compounders' success. By 1998, 25 percent of all plastic compounds were used in that industry, and in 1999, car sales reached an all-time high of over 18 million vehicles. The auto industry increasingly turned to custom compounders to produce inexpensive plastic parts that could be engineered for a set purpose. Underhood and seating applications were the most common new uses for plastic compounds.

The electronics and appliance industries were equally healthy, and further drove demand for custom compounded plastics. While appliances accounted for about 13 percent of the total market for custom compounds, plastics' role in the sector was expected to increase. As plastic increasingly came to supplant metal in small appliances such as toasters, blenders, and mixers, custom compounders looked forward to burgeoning sales to appliance makers. Moreover, consumers' growing use of personal computers and portable electronics (such as pagers and cellular phones) assured plastic compounders a stable future market.

But the industry was not free from challenges. Compounders were plagued by rapidly escalating resin prices in 1999, which significantly drove up their operating costs. Moreover, they could not simply pass the increased costs along to their customers—end users of plastic compounds were reluctant to pay a higher price, since cheaper import compounds were gaining a foothold in the market.

INDUSTRY LEADERS

The leading custom compounder in 1999 was The Geon Company of Avon Lake, Ohio. Controlling a 10 percent share of the custom compounding plastics market, Geon reported 1998 sales of $1.3 billion and employed 2,400 workers. Like other companies in the industry, Geon had expanded its operations through acquisition in the late 1990s. In 1998 alone, Geon purchased three companies—Adchem Inc., Plast-O-Meric Inc., and the Wilflex Ink Division of Flexible Products Co. Another key player in the industry was the Cleveland, Ohio-based M. A. Hanna Company, with 1998 sales of $2.3 billion and 7,130 employees. Hanna's share of the market had been on an upswing as the company engaged in a protracted series of acquisitions, purchasing 25 companies in 12 years. A. Schulman Inc. also was a leading company, with its 1999 sales topping $986 employees. Schulman operated 13 manufacturing facilities in North America, Europe, Mexico, and Asia and maintained a workforce of 2,400. In 1998, Schulman teamed up with Du Pont to produce the brightly colored plastic compounds that were used in the bumpers of Dodge and Plymouth's model year 2000 Neon.

RESEARCH AND TECHNOLOGY

A technological focal point in the mid-1990s was the development of techniques that allowed resin processors to create compounds and alloys while extruding plastic into molds. By melting and mixing compounds during the molding process, processors were able to eliminate problems caused by heating resins twice. Such compound/molding techniques were already resulting in higher performance and less expensive plastic products by the early 1990s. Specifically, new grades of materials created using these new compounding techniques were capable of making products with thinner walls, greater product uniformity, and more even molecular distribution—improvements that allowed for increased use of plastics in automobiles and packaging industries, for example.

Significant expenditures were also being directed toward the development of new environmentally safe compounds. Companies were striving to meet new chlorofluorocarbon (CFC) emission regulations by developing compounds that would not require hazardous manufacturing processes. Similarly, new additives and compounds were under development that would accelerate the natural breakdown of plastics products and reduce landfill waste. Although technologies like weak-link and bacterial polymers showed promise, extremely high production costs made them commercially impractical for most purposes in the late 1990s.

FURTHER READING

Darnay, Arsen J., ed. *Manufacturing USA*. 5th ed. Detroit: Gale Research, 1996.

Esposito, Frank. "Compounders Add Dash of Optimism." *Plastics News*, 19 July 1999.

———. "Schulman Expanding Products for Cars, Film." *Plastics News*, 13 December 1999.

U.S. Census Bureau. *1994 County Business Patterns*. Washington: GPO, 1996.

U.S. Census Bureau. "Custom Compounding of Purchased Resins." Available from http://www.census.gov/prod/ec97/97m3314c.pdf. October 1999.

———. *1995 Annual Survey of Manufactures*. Washington: GPO, 1997.

SIC 3088

PLASTICS PLUMBING FIXTURES

This category includes establishments primarily engaged in manufacturing plastics plumbing fixtures. Establishments primarily engaged in assembling plastics plumbing fixture fittings are classified in **SIC 3432: Plumbing Fixture Fittings and Trim.** Establishments primarily engaged in manufacturing plastics plumbing fixture components are classified in **SIC 3089: Plastics Products, Not Elsewhere Classified.** As a result of the 1987 Standard Industrial Classification (SIC) reclassification, information is unavailable for the industry prior to 1987 at this level of aggregation.

NAICS CODE(S)

326191 (Plastics Plumbing Fixtures Manufacturing)

INDUSTRY SNAPSHOT

Plastics plumbing fixtures manufacturers produced items such as bathtubs, sinks, lavatories, shower stalls, and whirlpool baths. The market for plastic plumbing supplies is linked to the overall construction and building industry. The construction of new buildings, as well as the remodeling of existing structures, helps drive sales of plumbing products. The U.S. plastic plumbing fixture market benefited from the expanding American economy in the late 1980s, although the Asian economic crisis of 1997 caused a decrease in exports in 1998 and 1999. Industry shipments were valued at $2.18 billion in 1997, up considerably from $709 million in 1987. U.S. plastics plumbing products manufacturers face competition from imports, as well as from producers of ceramic and metal plumbing fixtures.

In 1997, 572 establishments were involved in the production of plastics plumbing fixtures, and 205 of these—more than one-third—were larger companies with 20 or more employees. The industry employed an estimated 19,359 workers in 1997, 15,006 of whom were production workers. The industry was relatively capital intensive. On average, production employees worked about 38 hours per week and earned $10.10 per hour.

ORGANIZATION AND STRUCTURE

Production was concentrated in the relatively recently industrialized states of the South and Southwest portions of the United States. The top-ranking states by number of establishments were, Florida (with 38) and Georgia (with 27), followed by North Carolina and Pennsylvania (each with 18). Together these 4 states accounted for 19 percent of all establishments and 17 percent of total employment for the industry.

The industry is served by the Plumbing Manufacturers Institute, headquartered in Glen Ellyn, Illinois. Founded in 1956, the association has more than 50 members. The Institute, which organizes semiannual conventions, has committees on codes, government affairs, standards, intra-industry, and statistics.

BACKGROUND AND DEVELOPMENT

The development and use of plumbing fixtures increased rapidly after the introduction of pressurized water supply and sanitary drainage systems in the 1840s. Kitchen sinks and toilets were the first fixtures installed, followed by washtubs and bathtubs. The earliest sinks and tubs were made of wood lined with sheets of metal. Thereafter, cast iron and glazed pottery sinks came into broad use. One significant early improvement in sinks was the built-in overflow.

The 1870s saw the increased popularity of bathing and new techniques of bathtub production. These new tubs were made of enameled cast iron and were mass-produced by a New York manufacturer.

The first modern toilet was designed by the Englishman Joseph Bramah in about 1790. Known as a valve closet, this design saw long use in the toilet compartment of railroad cars. The valve closet was followed by the less expensive pan closet, which was in common use from the 1830s to the 1870s. Also developed in England, the pan closet had a lead bowl with a hole in the bottom sealed by a hinged copper pan. In the 1850s glazed pottery toilets came into use, and in the 1880s the first all-earthenware toilets were developed in England.

The early plumbing fixtures were primarily of English design. This changed after the 1880s, when the United States became a center of fixture design. Louis Nielsen describes this change and possible causes for it in his book *Standard Plumbing Engineering Design*. After the 1880s, he writes, ''developments in plumbing fixture design proceeded independently and at an accelerated pace in the United States. Much of this may be attributed to . . . U.S. industrial expansion and the continuous increase in population due to waves of immigration, and the tremendous demand for new homes and buildings to house the swelling numbers in industrial centers all over the country.''

Many of the designs and materials developed in the United States around the turn of the century dominated the industry until very recently. Key among these was the development of the washdown toilet, similar in principle to today's toilet. One of the key advantages of this toilet was that it remained sanitary after extended use, thereby rendering earlier toilet designs obsolete. A number of improvements were made to this basic design in the twentieth century. These involved combining the components of the washdown toilet into a single integrated unit, using siphon jets to strengthen the flush, and reducing noise of operation.

With regard to materials, one of the key developments around the turn of the century was glazed vitreous chinaware. With its smooth impervious surface, vitreous chinaware was the dominant material for many plumbing fixtures, until the rapid growth in the use of plastic fixtures in recent years. Introduced by plumbing fixture manufacturers in 1952, plastics came to be widely used for toilets, bathtubs, whirlpool baths, shower stalls, utility and laundry sinks, and sink-washtray combinations in bathrooms.

The creation of industry-wide standards was important to the development of the industry. Nationwide standards first appeared just after World War I. Contemporary standards were established by the American National Standards Institute's Committee A112. These standards address both design and materials suitability. Regarding

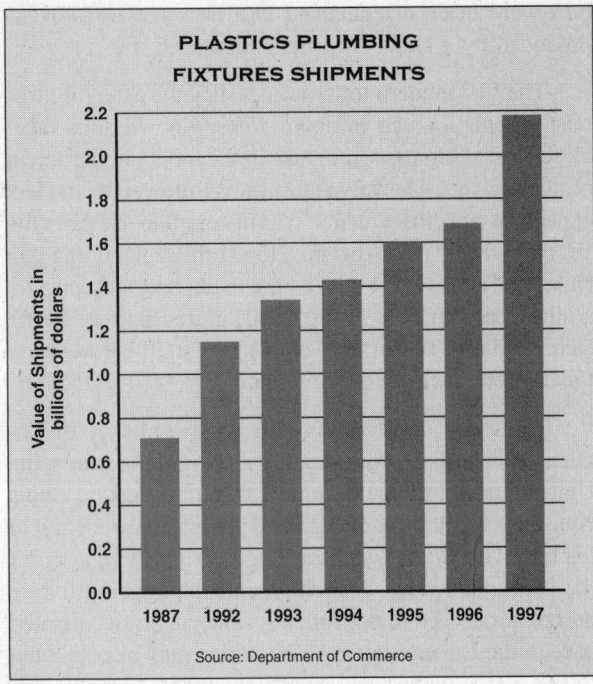

PLASTICS PLUMBING FIXTURES SHIPMENTS

Value of Shipments in billions of dollars

Source: Department of Commerce

the general quality of fixtures, standards require that fixtures ''shall have smooth impervious surfaces, shall be durable for the uses intended, and shall be free from defects and concealed fouling surfaces.'' The regulations also detailed standard dimensions and other specifications for fixtures.

The overall trend in shipments was strongly upward from 1987 to 1996, increasing by 49 percent in real terms over the period, with 1996 a peak year. Capital investments increased even more rapidly, with $15 million invested in 1987, $19 million in 1988, $69 million in 1989, $110 million in 1990, and $91 million in 1991. There was a sharp drop-off in 1992 to $31 million, after which investments started rising again to $31.2 million in 1993 and $57 million in 1994. The value of imports of plastics plumbing fixtures increased from $24 million in 1989 to an estimated $59 million in 1996, while the value of exports increased from $19 million to $40 million for these same years.

CURRENT CONDITIONS

The market for plastics plumbing fixtures in the late 1990s was strong. Since demand for plumbing products is linked to new housing and building construction, the industry was buoyed by the expanding economy at the close of the decade, in which low interest rates fueled new home purchases. Of particular importance to the plumbing industry was the trend toward an increasing number of bathrooms in new housing. From the early 1980s to the early 1990s, the number of newly built single occupancy homes with two and one-half or more baths doubled to 44 percent.

Plastics plumbing fixtures compete against vitreous china fixtures, as well as metal ones, for a greater share of the plumbing fixture market, and have had success in doing so. According to *Ceramic Industry,* ''in recent years, plastic has displaced vitreous and metal materials.'' In 1998 more than 30 percent of all lavatories were comprised of plastic, as well as 90 percent of shower stalls, and almost all whirlpool tubs. Plumbing products made of plastics accounted for approximately 48 percent of total shipments in 1997.

Plumbing fixtures are primarily made of three materials and are classified into three different industries accordingly. In addition to the plastics plumbing fixtures industry are **SIC 3261: Vitreous Plumbing Fixtures** and **SIC 3431: Metal Plumbing Fixtures.** The primary demand for plumbing fixtures results from new construction. New construction slumped after the late 1980s and picked up again after 1992, and the fortunes of the plumbing fixtures industries followed accordingly.

The use of plastic plumbing fixtures grew at the expense of the vitreous and metal plumbing fixtures industries. While from 1987 to 1994 the real value of shipments suffered overall declines of 8 percent for the metal plumbing fixtures industry and 15 percent for the vitreous plumbing fixtures industry, the real value of shipments of plastic plumbing fixtures increased by 52 percent over these same years.

Exports have played a key role for plastics plumbing products manufacturers in the 1990s. The rapidly expanding economies of Asia in the early 1990s helped increase exports, as American companies supplied plumbing products for the construction boom. Between 1990 and 1997 plumbing fixture exports to Asian nations grew at an average annual rate of 13 percent. However, the financial crisis of 1997—which resulted in currency devaluation—slowed exports.

Imports have challenged U.S. manufacturers's primacy at home. According to *Ceramic Industry,* the United States ''ran a deficit of more than $300 million . . . across all four product categories (sinks, lavatories, toilets, and bathtubs).'' Imports were expected to grow at an annual rate of 4 percent between 1997 and 2002.

INDUSTRY LEADERS

Leading firms in the industry in the late 1990s included the Wisconsin-based Kohler Co., with 1998 sales of more than $2.2 billion and 18,000 employees, and Eagle Industries Inc., of Chicago with 1998 sales of $993 million and 7,000 employees. Eljer Industries Inc. was another key player. Headquartered in Dallas, Texas, Eljer achieved sales in excess of $397 million in 1998 and was home to some 3,700 workers. Founded in 1902, The Hancor Company was also an industry leader. The private firm was originally a producer of clay drainage tiles, but by 1995 had 14 plants dedicated to plumbing fixtures and announced plans to substantially expand its manufacturing facilities throughout the decade. In 1998 Hancor employed 1,200 and had sales of $220 million.

Other leading companies included the Aqua Glass Corporation—a wholly owned subsidiary of the Masco Corporation since 1984. With $135 million in sales and 155 employees, Aqua Glass manufactured acrylic bathtubs, showers, and whirlpools. The firm began marketing its products on the West Coast in the early 1990s, and in 1993 announced the opening of its first West Coast office in Klamath Falls, Oregon. Pomona, California-based California Acrylic Industries reported sales in 1998 of $140 million and 1,250 employees.

RESEARCH AND TECHNOLOGY

The key areas of industry development concerned water conservation and accommodation of the disabled and elderly. Conventional fixtures were wasteful of water, with waste rates of 70 percent for conventional toilets and 50 percent for conventional showers. The *U.S. Industrial Outlook* for 1994 described the development of water-conserving fixtures as an emerging trend in the market because of the increasing popularity of products that use substantially less water. Industry standards mandating their use in new installations were scheduled throughout the 1990s. Among these regulations was the National Plumbing Products Efficiency Act of 1991.

Although water conservation fixtures typically cost up to 30 to 50 percent more than conventional fixtures, they sold well nationwide, but particularly in drought-afflicted California. In 1992 Toto Niki USA introduced a tankless computerized toilet that not only conserved water but flushed quietly. The industry standard for faucets was for flows of 2.5 to 2.7 gallons per minute in the early 1990s. New York State had the nation's strictest regulations regarding faucet flow in the 1990s, and 90 percent of bath faucets produced met these standards.

Industry manufacturers, prompted by the Americans with Disabilities Act (ADA) of 1990, also accelerated the design and production of fixtures to accommodate the disabled. The ADA defines disability sufficiently broadly that some 43 million Americans are covered by it, and the ADA requires owners and landlords of buildings defined as "public accommodations" to provide sinks, toilets, and drinking fountains that are accessible to those with disabilities.

FURTHER READING

"Plastics Continue to Make Inroads Into U.S. Sanitaryware Market." *Ceramic Industry,* 1 August 1998.

U.S. Census Bureau. "Plastics Plumbing Fixture Manufacturing," October 1999. Available from http://www.census.gov/prod.

PLASTICS PRODUCTS, NOT ELSEWHERE CLASSIFIED

This category covers establishments primarily engaged in manufacturing plastics products not classified elsewhere. Establishments primarily engaged in manufacturing artificial leather are classified in **SIC 2295: Coated Fabrics, Not Rubberized.**

Companies in this industry manufacture a multitude of items, ranging from clothespins and air mattresses to shoe soles and septic tanks. This industry accounted for approximately 60 percent of all plastics products sales in the early 1990s. For more information about manufacturing processes and the history of plastics products, see other entries in industry group **3080.** For information regarding resin manufacturing, see **SIC 2821: Plastics Materials, Synthetic Resins, and Nonvulcanizable Elastomers.**

NAICS CODE(S)

326122 (Plastic Pipe and Pipe Fitting Manufacturing)
326121 (Unsupported Plastics Profile Shape Manufacturing)
326199 (All Other Plastics Product Manufacturing)

INDUSTRY SNAPSHOT

There are at least 12 major processing techniques used to form plastics goods. A traditional and popular technique is extrusion, which entails melting and compressing plastic granules in a tube. A screw conveyor inside the tube forces the plastic through a nozzle at the end of the tube. The physical characteristics of the plastic can be altered by applying heat or cold to the barrel, adjusting the screw pressure, or by using different types and sizes of screws. Extrusion processes are used to make pipe, sheeting, films, and various forms.

Another popular processing technique is blow-molding, whereby extruded plastic is forced into a bottle-shaped mold. Compressed air inflates the hot plastic and pushes it against the cold sides of the mold, resulting in thin-walled plastic containers. Injection molding, one of the most popular processing operations, entails extruding plastic directly into a mold, where it hardens into a solid form. Sheets of plastic are created through calendaring or film and sheet extrusion. Foam is made in a process called foaming. Other popular plastic processing techniques include film casting, rotational molding, laminating, and casting.

The two main classes of plastics are thermosets and thermoplastics. Thermosets, which account for only 10 percent of the material used in this industry, harden by chemical reaction and cannot be melted and reshaped once they are created. Primary products created with thermoset plastics are epoxies and phenol formaldehyde (Bakelite). Epoxies are used to manufacture flooring, protective coatings, adhesives and cements, electrical hardware, and particleboard. Bakelite is formed into electrical parts, pot handles, and various knobs.

Thermoplastics include acrylics, cellulose proportionate (Forticel), ABS (acrylonitrile-butadiene-styrene), polyphenylene oxide (Noryl), and polysulfone. Acrylics are utilized in the production of windows, signs, vehicle light covers, and textiles. Forticel is applied in the manufacture of items such as pens, typewriter keys, telephone housing, and other applications that require impact strength. ABS, which has very high impact resistance, is used to make drain pipes, automobile parts, and small appliances and tools. Noryl, which combines high impact strength with temperature stability, is used for products like machine parts and equipment housing. Lastly, polysulfone, which is heat resistant, is used in battery casings, smoke alarms, electronic connectors, and shower heads.

Although the markets for miscellaneous plastics products are extremely fragmented, a few major categories stand out. For instance, miscellaneous plastic packaging, such as caps, food trays, and bubble wrap, constituted a leading 12 percent of shipments in the 1990s. Fabricated plastics used for vehicles, such as turn indicator housings, also made up 12 percent of the market. Plastics used to make electrical devices accounted for about 8 percent of industry sales, and plastic siding contributed 2 percent of revenues. Other major product groups included doors and window frames, dinnerware and kitchenware, and plastic furniture parts.

BACKGROUND AND DEVELOPMENT

Keratin, a natural plastic, was used in the United States to make lantern windows and other simple items as early as 1740. Gutta percha, or gum elastic, was first used during the middle 1850s to make billiard balls and ocean cable insulation. Manufacturers borrowed forming and processing techniques from Malayan natives. Shellac plastics, developed by Samuel Speck, also emerged during the mid-1800s, and were used to create goods such as checkers, buttons, and insulators.

Following the invention of the first synthetic plastics in the late 1870s (see **SIC 2821: Plastics Materials, Synthetic Resins, and Nonvulcanizable Elastomers**), plastics products sales began to accelerate. American Dr. Baekland introduced the first moldable plastic, Bakelite, in 1909. Bakelite prompted a flurry of new molding techniques and resins during the early 1900s. Advances during World War II also bolstered the industry. The rampant proliferation of new synthetic chemicals and production processes during the 1950s, 1960s, and 1970s resulted in massive industry expansion. By the late 1970s, plastics products had become a staple of American life and were rapidly displacing conventional materials in a range of applications.

U.S. sales of miscellaneous plastics products expanded rapidly during the 1980s, but increased competition, both at home and abroad, contributed to lagging price growth. Total U.S. plastics products shipments were $105.0 billion by 1995. About 53 percent—or $55.3 billion—of that total was comprised of miscellaneous goods from this industry. Despite a late 1980s and early 1990s U.S. recession, shipment growth persisted as new additives and processing techniques were introduced.

Stiff competition and weak prices continued to plague manufacturers in the early 1990s, but increased sales of plastic goods for automobiles, packaged goods, and construction materials boosted margins for many competitors. Output of all plastics products grew throughout the 1990s and prices in some important market segments rose an estimated 3 percent to 5 percent per year. Sales in some depressed sectors, such as high-tech engineering plastics, were rebounding. Industry receipts were expected to climb at a rate of 3 percent to 6 percent annually through the mid-1990s.

In the long term, the use of plastics products will proliferate. But successful manufacturers will be forced to develop and implement improved processing techniques that reduce costs and improve quality. As foreign competition mounts—particularly for commodity-like products—U.S. technological superiority in plastics will become paramount.

As in the early 1990s, many companies will respond to increased competition by acquiring or merging with competitors to reduce research and development costs, establish a global presence, and pool capital investment dollars for expensive new equipment. Some smaller firms with niche expertise will also find growth.

Despite industry consolidation during the late 1980s and early 1990s, the miscellaneous plastics products industry remained relatively fragmented. About 8,330 companies competed going into the mid-1990s, up from only 8,045 in 1990. The number of companies was projected to drop slightly to about 8,200 by 1998. The average industry participant shipped about $6.6 million worth of goods, slightly less than 70 percent as much as the average U.S. manufacturer. The majority of producers are small and specialized.

CURRENT CONDITIONS

Sustained growth in plastic packaging sales fueled this industry in the late 1990s, as demand for durable, cost-effective packaging increased. Annual consumption of resins used to manufacture rigid and flexible packaging increased in 1997 to 19 billion pounds. However, the industry also relied on plastic recycling, which was on the decline in late 1997 as both a revenue stream and a source for raw materials. Analysts attributed this shortfall of recycling to the cyclical nature of the market.

INDUSTRY LEADERS

A mere 576 workers at the Columbus, Ohio-based Core Materials Corp. generated an astonishing $65.4 billion in 1998 sales, translating into $114.0 million in sales per employee. Moosup, Connecticuts Griswold Rubber Company employed 125 workers who garnered $13.4 billion in 1998 sales, creating per-employee earnings of $107.0 million. In contrast, Crown Cork and Seal Company Inc. of Philadelphia employed 39,459 workers who created $8.3 billion in 1998 sales for sales per employee of $210,345. Similarly, Greenwich, Connecticut-based Tenneco Inc. employed 48,000 workers who produced $7.6 billion in 1998 sales, or $158,271 per employee.

WORKFORCE

The industry's 470,000-member work force will benefit in the future from strong growth in demand for plastics products. However, productivity gains achieved through automation and the integration of more efficient processing techniques will contribute to a lag between shipment growth and new jobs. Opportunities for laborers will likely expand 30 to 40 percent between 1990 and 2005, according to the U.S. Bureau of Labor Statistics. For example, jobs for molding machine operators—which account for about 17 percent of the work force—will likely grow by 30 percent, as will positions for managers and executives. Better yet, jobs for sales professionals, industrial machine operators, and machinery mechanics will skyrocket 50 to 70 percent by 2005. Unfortunately, workers in this industry receive, on average, only 80 percent of the wages paid in other U.S. manufacturing industries.

AMERICA AND THE WORLD

Although exports and imports have traditionally played a minor role in the plastics products industry, imports (excluding bottles and plumbing) into the United States swelled six-fold during the 1980s to about $3.8 billion by 1991. By the early 1990s, the U.S. plastics products industry trade surplus had been whittled to only $200.0 million. While a weak dollar and increased industry productivity helped to buoy the trade surplus in 1992 and 1993, foreign competition was expected to increase in the long term.

One of the regions of greatest growth was China. Its plastics products shipments soared more than 200 percent during the 1980s, reaching approximately 4.1 billion tons by the early 1990s and reflecting average annual growth of about 12.5 percent. Chinese manufacturers suffered, however, from a lack of production equipment and access to processed raw materials. Although China's economic growth will stimulate increased imports, a low per capita plastic consumption will keep overall growth to 7 percent annually between 1997 and 2001. As capacity accelerates to meet demand during the 1990s, China will likely become a formidable competitor in export markets, particularly in fast growing east Asian countries. Asia, in general, is a strong growth area, with predicted annual growth rates of 10 percent, especially in ethylene propylene, vinyl chloride, and acrylonitrile. Within the Asian market, the largest increases could occur among ASEAN (Association of Southeastern Asian Nations) members, as new complexes come online. The rapid increase of plastics consumption within the Asian market has stimulated U.S. producers to look at investing in local production plants.

Imports also rose in the wake of the North American Free Trade Agreement, as U.S. manufacturers move production facilities south of the border to Mexico to take advantage of inexpensive labor and reduced environmental restrictions. After Canada, Mexico was the second biggest importer of plastics goods into the United States during the mid-1990s. Mexican imports should rise rapidly over the next 5 to 10 years as Asian producers infiltrate the Mexican market to meet NAFTA requirements that 6 percent of a duty-free product's components be made in North America. The General Agreement on Tariffs and Trade (GATT) treaty has limited international import duties on resins to 6.5 percent by the year 2000, down from an average of 12.5 percent. The impact of the new tariffs on the market structure is still uncertain, although most predictions lean toward further increases in international trade.

RESEARCH AND TECHNOLOGY

Going into the mid-1990s, major technological trends in the plastics products industry included recyclability and faster concept-to-production cycles. Indeed, many companies were ardently seeking flexible processing, extrusion, and molding techniques that would allow them to design and quickly manufacture new products. One of the most important recycling tactics was "design-for-recycling," whereby plastics products and devices are created in such a way that they can be efficiently ground, melted, and reused. For example, glue and adhesives that can contaminate reground materials were being eliminated from manufactured plastic goods.

FURTHER READING

Aronhalt, Frank and Ron Perkins. "The Wave of Recycling Bumps into the Seawall of Economic Reality." *Modern Plastics,* 15 November 1999.

Darnay, Arsen J., ed. *Manufacturing USA.* 5th ed. Detroit: Gale Research, 1996.

Infotrac Company Profiles. Available at http://web4.infotrac .galegroup.com.

Mastio, Richard C. "Annual Use of Resins for Rigid and Flexible Packaging Tops 19 billion lbs." *Modern Plastics,* 15 November 1999.

LEATHER & LEATHER PRODUCTS

LEATHER TANNING AND FINISHING

This category includes establishments primarily engaged in tanning, currying, and finishing raw or cured hides and skins into leather. Converters and dealers who buy hides, skins, or leather for processing under contracts with tanners and/or finishers are also included in this category.

NAICS CODE(S)

316110 (Leather and Hide Tanning and Finishing)

INDUSTRY SNAPSHOT

Leather tanning and finishing in the United States is a multibillion dollar industry. According to the United States Census Bureau, the dollar value of U.S. leather industry shipments in 1997 was $3.4 billion, up from $3.1 billion in 1995. Production shipments in 1997 were approximately $3.2 billion. In the United States, automotive upholstery and casual footwear make up most of the leather market. The number of companies engaged in leather tanning and finishing has declined since the 1980s, as larger firms acquired smaller ones. The number of U.S. tanning and finishing establishments decreased from 342 in 1982 to 328 in 1997. Competition from overseas leather tanners—especially in developing nations—has adversely affected the industry in the United States.

Leather tanning in the United States is primarily the work of privately held companies. The vast majority of the leather processed in the United States is cattle hide. So-called specialty leathers—including deer, calf, pig, goat, sheep, lamb, kangaroo, and various reptiles—represent only about 5 percent. With 72 establishments, New York has the most companies engaged in leather tanning and finishing. Massachusetts, California, Texas, Wisconsin, Pennsylvania, North Carolina, and New Jersey are each home to more than ten tanneries.

ORGANIZATION AND STRUCTURE

Leather tanning is a process in which chemical agents and extracts are applied to various types of hides and skins in order to prevent rotting. Not all tanneries follow the same method of processing hides into leather. However, the process described here is used by the majority. First, the hides must be prepared for tanning at the packing house. This includes unhairing (a lime solution loosens the hair, making removal easier), fleshing (cleaning off the inner side of the hides), and bating (removing the lime from the hides). Next, the skins and hides are cured—salted or soaked in brine to preserve them until they reach the tannery. Once at the tannery, the hides are soaked to remove the salt. Two primary methods are used to then convert the raw material into leather: chrome tanning and vegetable tanning. The method used depends on the intended use of the leather. Chrome tanning, which involves the use of soluble chromium salts such as chromium sulfate, is used primarily to tan leather for the upper parts of shoes. Vegetable tanning, which uses tannic acid, is used to tan heavy leather for shoe soles, bags, straps, harnesses, and other products used in industrial equipment. Chrome tanning is the most widely used method in the United States.

Several basic stages are involved in the tanning process. First, the underlying layer of the hide is "split" off and shaved to uniform thickness. Tanning drums are then used to saturate the hides in the tanning solution, which preserves the hide and adds strength. The hides are tanned again, where dyes and oils are added to provide, color, softness, and durability. Then the hide must be stretched and dried to remove all excess moisture. At this point, the leather is firm, flat, and ready to be trimmed. Finally, the hide is conditioned and finished. The finishing process involves softening the hide mechanically, spraying final colors onto the leather to meet customer requirements, and embossing to the required texture.

BACKGROUND AND DEVELOPMENT

Tanning—the process that turns raw animal hides into the soft, pliable, and enduring material called leather—is one of the world's oldest industries. Recovered specimens of leather tents and shoes date as far back as 6,000 B.C., and ancient Egyptian carvings show tanners at work. Early Romans used leather not only for shoes, shields, and harnesses, but also as currency. As the centuries passed, tanning grew into a highly developed art. Twelfth-century England gave rise to tanners' guilds, and in America, early settlers learned that tanning was not new to the Native Americans. Advances in the chemical and mechanical processes of tanning and the invention of the thermometer and hydrometer—for measuring density—opened up the industry worldwide and brought tanning from the realm of the arts to the sciences.

The Leather Industry in America. The first English leather worker to come to the New World was a shoemaker named Experience Miller. Miller arrived in Plymouth Colony in 1624 and soon found that the Native Americans used bark tanning to preserve cattle and other hides. The abundance of deer hides and water resources in the colonies led to the development of a flourishing tanning industry. By 1650 there were more than 50 tanneries in Massachusetts alone. Early colonial tanneries were small and often moved when the vegetable tanning materials or the source of hides in one area were exhausted. The first tanning machine used in the United States was a stone mill used to grind tree bark. It was invented by Peter Minuit, Governor of New Amsterdam. By 1800 there were 2,000 tanneries in the United States.

Technological innovations in the nineteenth century increased production. In 1805 Sir Humphry Davey, an Englishman, discovered that many trees other than oak could be used in the tanning process. The hemlock, mimosa, chestnut, and ash were also used, since all were abundant in the United States. An American, Samuel Parker, further advanced the tanning industry in 1809 by inventing a machine to split hides. Prior to this, it took one man a whole day to split four hides. With the aid of Parker's invention, one man could split 100 hides in one day. These developments made leather cheaper, opening the leather market to all classes. In 1884 August Schultz discovered that chromium salts could be used in the tanning process instead of vegetable material. This method, perfected ten years later by Martin Dennis, allowed more attractive and flexible leathers to be produced at a faster rate.

Other procedural changes and inventions, including a machine to remove hair and flesh from the skins, gave the U.S. leather industry an added boost by increasing the supply of leather. By the end of the nineteenth century, tanneries had begun to consolidate. The larger tanneries produced more goods than had the many smaller operations, since they could better maintain heavy, expensive machinery and a large work force. In 1899, 1,306 tanneries produced leather valued at $204 million, versus 6,664 tanneries producing only $40 million worth of leather in 1850. Integration and growth continued into the twentieth century. In 1919, 680 tanneries produced $900 million worth of leather. The number of tanneries continued to shrink with the slowdown of the Depression and the competition from synthetics after World War II. In the 1970s the decline in meat consumption further decreased the availability of hides for tanning, which in turn began increasing the cost of leather worldwide.

Beginning in the 1970s, the United States's role as a leather tanner and processor began to lessen. Although the United States was the leading producer of bovine hides, the manufacturing costs of converting these hides into leather rose. As a result, developing nations—with their lower labor costs and weaker environmental regulations—gained a greater share of leather tanning business. According to *Leather*, "to an increasing extent, developing countries import raw hides and skins from developed countries for processing, manufacturing, and re-exporting as value-added products to developed countries." In 1992 imported leather goods were valued at $631 million.

CURRENT CONDITIONS

The role of imports continued to grow in the late 1990s. By 1999 U.S. leather imports totaled over $1.2 billion, up from $1 billion in 1996. Moreover, as Charles Myers, president of Leather Industries of America, Inc., (an association of leather tanners and related industries) noted, the tanning industry—which once produced primarily for U.S. markets—had by 1997 become an aggressive exporter. "We now export more raw material than finished product to countries that can finish more cheaply than we can, and we have a very small domestic customer base."

In the tanning and finishing leather industry in the United States, automotive upholstery was a growth sector in the late 1990s. As leather seats and leather interiors became more commonplace in American automobiles, the market for upholstery leather boomed. In 1997 upholstery product shipments topped $1 billion, up from about $682 million in 1992. Although footwear manufacturers remained an important market for American leather tanners, the industry was hurt by the Asian financial collapse of 1997, which dampened demand for leather shoes.

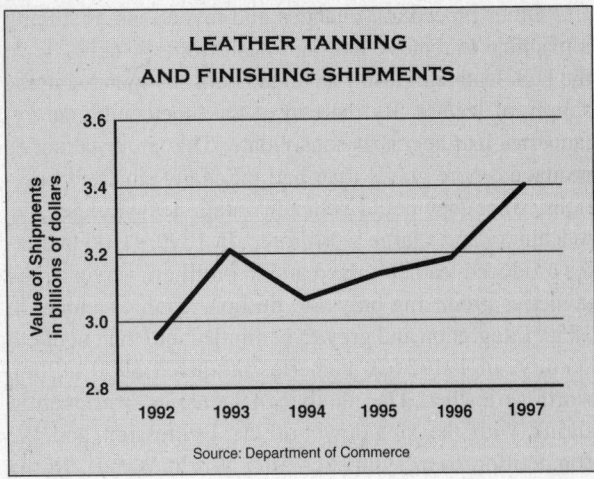

LEATHER TANNING AND FINISHING SHIPMENTS

Value of Shipments in billions of dollars

Source: Department of Commerce

York, and Wisconsin each supported over 1,000 employees in the industry.

Associated work for the tanning industry lay in the fields of chemistry and environmental management. The outlook for leather workers depends upon the continued demand for leather products and the availability of hides.

AMERICA AND THE WORLD

Although U.S. leather exports grew consistently through the mid-1990s—from $705 million in 1992 to $950 million in 1997—this trend did not last through the close of the decade. U.S. exports fell nearly 11 percent from 1997 to 1998. Industry experts in the early 1990s had been optimistic about the role of the United States in the export of treated leather products. But cheap labor in developing nations meant that leather tanning was increasingly moved abroad. As *Leather* explained, "tanning and leather manufacturing industries have been shifting to developing nations, where manufacturing costs are lower." U.S. exports to Japan fell 48.7 percent from 1997 to 1998, and during the same period, exports to Austria, Germany, and Taiwan dropped 82.5 percent, 41 percent, and 28 percent, respectively.

According to Charles Myers: "U.S. automobile upholstery leather tanners are expanding offshore and constructing cutting operations in Mexico, South Africa and Europe following the movement of their auto manufacturing customers into these areas. In addition, there is considerable potential for the U.S. in Asia, where a number of U.S. tanneries have located factories and warehouses. This strategy positions major American footwear leather tanners closer to where their U.S. and European customers are sourcing shoes."

Finished leather imports continued to rise in the United States, accounting for $1.18 billion in 1998, up from $1.16 billion in 1997. Mexico was the leading importer in 1998, with $614 million of goods (up 17.9 percent from 1997). While Argentina and Italy remained the second and third largest importers in 1998, products from Columbia, Thailand, and Brazil increased substantially—34.3 percent, 22.7 percent, and 10 percent, respectively.

Furthermore, leather tanners in developing nations gained a greater share of the footwear market.

INDUSTRY LEADERS

One of the leading leather tanners in the late 1990s was the Milwaukee, Wisconsin-based United States Leather, Inc. The company, which produced finished leather for shoes, furniture, and car makers, sold its goods under several brand names—including Lackawanna Leather, Pfister & Vogel, A.L. Gebhardt, and A.R. Clarke. Although United States Leather had 1998 sales of over $250 million, the company had been hit hard by a slump in the footwear and specialty leather business. In 1996 United States Leather closed its Trading Division, which dealt with unfinished hides and their by-products. In 1998 United States Leather survived a short period in Chapter 11 Bankruptcy proceedings.

Albert Trostel and Sons Co. was another major player in the U.S. leather industry. Also a Milwaukee-based company, Albert Trostel was owned by Evertt Smith Group. Albert Trostel's estimated 1998 sales of $500 million were due in part to the flourishing market for automotive leather. The company primarily produced leather seats and interiors for car makers, as well as custom leather seals and precision-molded leather components for car companies. With more than 3,500 employees, Albert Trostel rounded out its operations with the production of leather for use in furniture.

WORKFORCE

The industry is unionized, but also highly mechanized. In 1997, 15,317 employees worked in domestic leather tanning and finishing. 12,425 of these were production laborers, who worked an average of approximately 38 hours per week. Production employees earned an average wage of $12.10 per hour, up from the $11.62 reported in 1996. The leading state for employment in 1997 was Pennsylvania, which was home to 2,332 workers in the leather tanning business. Massachusetts, New

RESEARCH AND TECHNOLOGY

Innovations. The leather tanning industry began a series of technological innovations in the late 1970s and 1980s in response to the need to assess the effect of tanning chemicals used on the environment. The Leather Industries of America Research Laboratory, based in Cincinnati, Ohio, worked on changes relating to the chemical aspects of hide processing.

Research support continues to make the industry more cost-effective and helps it respond to demands made by environmental protection laws passed in the 1980s and 1990s. The U.S. tanning industry spends millions of dollars each year in research and development, and fierce competition from abroad will fuel the need for U.S. companies to develop state-of-the-art equipment, new technologies, and leathers. In addition to studies performed by individual firms, the Leather Industries of America Research Laboratory conducts ongoing industry research.

Environmental Issues. The leather tanning and finishing industry must meet Environmental Protection Agency (EPA) waste standards on three fronts: liquid, solid, and air. In 1985 the EPA established new standards to control pretreatment of the liquid wastes that tanners discharge indirectly to publicly owned waste treatment facilities. These standards applied to waste acidity and to wastes containing sulfides and chromium. All tanners discharging directly into waterways were required to operate with the EPA-approved National Discharge Elimination System (NDES) permits. The EPA standards for this group required control of conventional pollutants such as solids and biological oxygen as well as sulfides, chromium, and acidity. Further, the 1990 Clean Air Act and other strict federal standards curbing the emission of volatile organic compounds into the air have encouraged the industry to develop low-solvent or solvent-free finishing technologies.

In 1992 waste scrap leather and tannery sludge that contained chromium was exempt from hazardous waste regulation. Tanning systems that recycled chromium had been developed and were widely used throughout the industry to reduce the amount of chromium that appeared in the final waste. There had been talk of removing the exemption on waste from leather products, which would force the leather industry to come up with new techniques for the disposal of those products. However, in 1995, the EPA did a retrospective study on the industry's effluent guidelines and pollution prevention progress. The study found that the industry had taken major steps in modifying the chrome tanning process in order to get more of the chromium into the leather and less in the waste. Through these measures, chromium fixation was increased from 50 percent in 1982 to 90 percent in 1995. In addition, the industry's water use was reduced by 50 percent.

FURTHER READING

Darnay, Arsen J., ed. *Manufacturing USA.* 5th ed. Detroit: Gale Research, 1996.

Gallum, Alby. "US Leather Hopes to Rise Above the Herd." *Milwaukee Business Journal,* 4 September 1998.

International Trade Administration. "Top 25 U.S. Export Sources for Leather Tanning," 30 November 1999. Available from http://www.ita.doc.gov.

International Trade Administration. "Top 25 U.S. Import Sources for Leather Tanning," 30 November 1999. Available from http://www.ita.doc.gov.

"Projections to the Year 2005." *Leather,* 1 April 1999.

Rieger, Nancy. "Irving Tanning Expands Plant, Product Lines." *Footwear News,* 23 January 1995.

U.S. Census Bureau. "Leather Tanning and Finishing," October 1999. Available from http://www.census.gov/prod.

U.S. Department of Labor. Bureau of Labor Statistics. *Employment and Earnings,* December 1996.

U.S. Environmental Protection Agency. *Effluent Guidelines, Leather Tanning, and Pollution Prevention: A Retrospective Study,* June 1995.

SIC 3131

BOOT AND SHOE CUT STOCK AND FINDINGS

Establishments that fall under this category are primarily engaged in manufacturing leather soles, inner soles, and other boot and shoe cut stock and findings. The industry also includes finished wood heels. Establishments primarily engaged in manufacturing heels, soiling strips, and soles made of rubber, composition, plastics, and fiber are classified in the major group for rubber and miscellaneous plastics products.

NAICS CODE(S)

321999 (All Other Miscellaneous Wood Product Manufacturing)
339993 (Fasteners, Button, Needle, and Pin Manufacturing)
316999 (All Other Leather Good Manufacturing)

In 1996, the boot and shoe cut stock findings segment continued to suffer from the growing penetration of relatively low-cost imported footwear into the United States. According to footwear industry statistics, in 1966 the United States market for nonrubber footwear totaled 735 million pairs, and 641 million pairs were made in America. By 1996, the market had grown to 1,218 million pairs, but the U.S. produced only 143 million pairs. The import/export imbalance was even more telling—1,098 million pairs were imported in 1996, while only 24 million were exported.

In this environment, many footwear plants have been forced to close. Between 1966 and 1996, there was a net loss of 783 nonrubber footwear plants in the United States, and plant openings had slowed to a trickle. Pricing was also under intense pressure: the average factory price for nonrubber footwear increased about 2 percent to an estimated $21.16 a pair in 1993—the smallest advance in three years because of competition from imported shoes. In the labor intensive footwear industry, U.S. makers simply could not compete with manufacturers overseas whose wage rates were far below U.S. levels.

The drop in domestically produced footwear, of course, depressed the business of companies that supply shoe manufacturers. According to government statistics, shipments for the boot and shoe cut stock and findings segment in 1995 totaled $282 million, down from $319 million in 1994 and $425 million in 1981. Moreover, the number of workers totaled 3,100 in 1995—down from 3,400 in 1994 and 7,000 in 1981. Besides the dramatic increase in shoe imports, leather sole makers also had to contend with a shift by consumers to more casual footwear and the rising cost of leather. While there remained a market for the fine leather shoe, many Americans were no longer dressing up for work and did not require several pairs of dress shoes.

During the recession of the early 1990s, the repair trade picked up somewhat, as consumers have traditionally mended old shoes when they did not have the money to buy new ones. Some manufacturers thought sales were less robust than in previous recessions, however, because of the loss of white collar jobs. There was also concern about longer term trends in the repair market. During the Second World War, the number of repair shops totaled nearly 70,000; by 1996, there were fewer than 12,000. One estimate showed that only 8 to 10 percent of consumers made use of shoe repair shops, and the average customer was 45 years old. The availability of inexpensive imported footwear may also encourage people to simply buy new shoes rather than repair old ones.

The late 1990s did not show any encouraging signs for the industry's success. The number of employees plunged from mid-1990s levels to 1,358 in 1997. Also, the value of shipments dropped to only $176 million.

FURTHER READING

"Statistics." *Footwear Industry Association,* 14 April 1997. Available from http://fia.org.

Kukolla, Steve. "Shoe Repair Suppliers See Business Slipping." *Knight Ridder/Tribune Business News,* 9 January 1996.

U.S. Census Bureau. "Manufacturing-Industry Series." *1997 Economic Census.* Washington, D.C.: GPO, 19 October 1999.

SIC 3142

HOUSE SLIPPERS

This classification includes establishments primarily engaged in manufacturing house slippers of leather or other materials.

NAICS CODE(S)

316212 (House Slipper Manufacturing)

The house slippers industry falls under the auspices of the nonrubber footwear industry, which produces all types of footwear except rubber protective and rubber-soled "sneakers." House slippers may be constructed with leather, vinyl, plastic, cloth, or textile uppers for both genders of all ages.

The modern structure of house slipper manufacturing is characterized by several major brand names with primary distribution through department store venues. The leading brand names differentiate themselves by comfort and fashion levels. In the late 1990s, the leading brand names included Dearfoams by R.G. Barry Corporation and Isotoners by Aris. However, consumers' footwear buying habits had shifted to form, function, and comfort—away from brand names. Many consumers were seeking lower-priced house slippers in strip shopping centers and outlet stores instead of in traditional shopping mall department stores.

A portion of the house slipper consumer market is represented by house-bound invalids and hospitalized patients. This sector of the market seeks products that are light-weight, comfortable, easy to put on and take off, and unlikely to fall off the feet. *American Salesman* magazine also listed house slippers among the items one should never fail to pack when traveling. Sales people and other frequent travelers opt for house slippers that are fashionable, light-weight, and easy to pack.

The house slippers industry is the smallest division within the nonrubber footwear industry. There were an estimated 19 establishments in 1996, the lowest in 15 years, down from 31 in 1992. In 1995 shipments of house slippers declined almost 50 percent from 1994 to a product value of $113 million. Of nonrubber footwear product shipments, house slippers accounted for about a quarter of the quantity but only 3 percent of the value, primarily because most slippers are produced from lower-cost vinyls and other textiles. In 1995 2,000 employees worked for the industry, 1,800 of which were production workers who earned substantially less than the average manufacturing worker. House slipper manufacturers earned an average of $7.67 per hour compared to $12.37 per hour for all of manufacturing.

Showing increases from the mid-1990s, 25 establishments in 1997 named house slipper manufacturing as their primary function; the number of employees was 2,753. The shipment value also showed an improvement—at $263 million.

In order to maintain profitability in the face of declining demand, the house slipper industry considers new technology essential to increasing productivity and lowering costs of manufacturing. The increased use of computers has already integrated design, management, manufacturing, and marketing functions. Overall, the industry emphasizes such nonprice factors as quality and quick delivery in competition with imports. The industry has turned to computer-aided design (CAD) and computer-aided manufacturing (CAM). Through these methods, companies can link computer system data to auto-stitchers, milling, and turning machines. The industry has also increased its use of three-dimensional CAD, which produces more accurate slipper patterns and reduces the number of prototypes needed.

FURTHER READING

U.S. Census Bureau. "Manufacturing-Industry Series." *1997 Economic Census.* Washington, D.C.: GPO, 1 December 1999.

U.S. Department of Labor. Bureau of Labor Statistics. *Employment, Hours, and Earnings: United States, 1988-96.* Washington, D.C.: GPO, August 1996.

SIC 3143

MEN'S FOOTWEAR, EXCEPT ATHLETIC

This category includes establishments primarily engaged in the production of men's footwear designed for dress, street, and work. Establishments primarily engaged in the production of such protective footwear as rubbers, rubber boots, storm shoes, galoshes, and other footwear with rubber soles vulcanized to the uppers are classified in **SIC 3021: Rubber and Plastics Footwear.** Establishments primarily engaged in the production of athletic shoes and youths' and boys' shoes are classified in **SIC 3149: Footwear Except Rubber, Not Elsewhere Classified,** and those manufacturing orthopedic extension shoes are classified in **SIC 3842: Orthopedic, Prosthetic, and Surgical Appliances and Supplies.**

NAICS CODE(S)

316213 (Men's Footwear (except Athletic) Manufacturing)

INDUSTRY SNAPSHOT

In the late 1990s, the men's footwear market was being shaped by two powerful forces. First, the American footwear industry had continued to be affected by the increasing dominance of imported shoes. Although 178 U.S. factories were engaged in the manufacture of men's dress, casual, and work footwear in 1998, shoes produced in nations such as China, Brazil, and Indonesia accounted for over 80 percent of the men's footwear purchased by American consumers—continuing a trend that began more than three decades ago. Second, the men's footwear market has also changed as more casual work attire has become more acceptable in American offices. As a result,

men's dress shoe sales have fallen, while those of casual, dress/casual, and outdoors shoes have soared.

BACKGROUND AND DEVELOPMENT

New England had become the center of a thriving footwear industry as early as 1800, and by 1850, the United States was exporting large quantities of high quality, inexpensive shoes to England and other European countries. Micajah Pratt, who began making and selling shoes in Lynn, Massachusetts in 1812, was considered an innovator in the industry. He was among the first to use standard patterns and sole cutting machines. Pratt eventually employed about 500 workers; many of whom lived in other towns and worked at home; with this arrangement he was able to produce almost 250,000 pairs of shoes annually.

Shoemaking became industrialized in the early 1860s, prompted by the development of machinery for attaching the leather part of a shoe, known as the upper, to the sole. In 1858, Lyman R. Blake of Abington, Massachusetts, invented a machine that attached the leather uppers with nails and wooden pegs. Soon after, Gordon McKay, also of Abington, improved on Blake's invention by substituting thread for the cumbersome nails and pegs. Recognizing the threat that McKay's sewing machine posed to their livelihood, shoemakers staged the first general strike in the footwear industry in 1859. Nevertheless, by 1864, the Blake sewer was used by most U.S. shoemakers.

The most important technological advance, however, was probably the shoe-lasting machine, invented in 1882 by Jan Ernst Matzeliger, who also worked in a Lynn shoe factory. "Lasting" was the process of shaping the leather upper over a wooden form before attaching it to the sole. Matzeliger's shoe-lasting machine, patented in 1883, allowed shoes to be mass produced for the first time.

Technology has remained relatively unchanged in recent years, but the U.S. industry has been dramatically altered nonetheless by the growing penetration of imports versus domestically produced shoes. According to Footwear Industries of America (FIA), import penetration in the American shoe market increased from 21.5 percent in 1968 to 89.5 percent in 1995. As import shoes claim the market, domestic production of footwear has dropped. Between 1978 and 1995, the pairs of shoes manufactured by companies in the United States sunk from over 418 million to about 145 million. And while the export of American-made men's footwear to other countries is still a significant factor at around 22 percent of the total, according to FIA statistics, primary destinations have shifted from England and other European countries a century ago to Japan, Canada, and Mexico.

CURRENT CONDITIONS

Men's footwear accounts for a substantial portion of the total pairs of non-rubber footwear produced by companies in the United States. In 1998, nearly 34 million of the 159 million total pairs of these shoes made in America were men's, according to FIA. These shoes were being released into a receptive environment. While the overall shoe market increased at an annual rate of less than 2 percent from 1996 to 1998, three men's footwear categories experienced annual double-digit growth—hiking boots, work boots, and sandals. According to FIA, men's retail footwear sales in the United States even outperformed women's in 1998, as men' shoes generated $17.4 billion in sales, compared to women's $16.8 billion.

Nevertheless, U.S. made men's footwear comprised only a small percentage of these booming retail sales. In 1998, 190.8 million pairs of men's shoes were imported into the United States (accounting for better than 15 percent of the 1.23 billion pairs of shoes imported that year). American production has decreased every year since 1968, and this trend held true in 1998, as U.S. footwear production declined 1.2 percent from 1997. While import shoes represented only 21.5 percent of those purchased in the United States in 1968, more than 92 percent of shoes bought in the United States in 1998 were manufactured abroad. In the men's footwear segment of the market, more than 80 percent of the shoes consumed by Americans in 1998 were not produced domestically. China was the most voracious exporter to the United States, producing more than 72 percent of footwear imports to the United States. Brazil was the second most popular country of origin for foreign shoes purchased in the United States, but it lagged far behind China, accounting for only 6.7 percent of the import market. Indonesia stood in third place at 4.8 percent, Italy in fourth at 3.9 percent, and Spain in fifth at 1.8 percent. This decline in U.S. based shoe manufacturing has taken its toll on American factories. As production continues to shift overseas to take advantage of lower labor costs, American facilities have closed at a rapid rate. Forty-one factories closed between 1995 and 1998 alone.

But U.S. companies have striven to find other markets for their goods. Approximately 27 million pairs of non-rubber footwear were exported by U.S. companies in 1998, of which 6 million were men's shoes. Canada imported the most, with 37.3 percent of the total, followed by Japan with 10.8 percent. Mexico, the leading importer of American-made shoes in 1992 with 13.6 percent of the market, dropped to third place with 7.1 percent by 1998.

INDUSTRY LEADERS

Timberland Company. A manufacturer of rugged, upscale hiking boots, walking shoes, and casual shoes,

The Timberland Co. has become a leader in the men's footwear market as the so-called "brown shoes" it produces have become fashionable. The company rang up $862 million in sales in 1998, and it employed more than 5,200 workers. Although Timberland was a staunch supporter of domestic manufacture, in 1994 burgeoning competition in the casual shoe market led the company to close some of its American plants and outsource production to the Dominican Republic and Puerto Rico. Timberland sells its products at its 75 independently-owned retail and outlet stores, as well as in department stores and athletic footwear shops.

Russian immigrant Nathan Swartz founded Timberland when he purchased half interest in the Abington Shoe Company in 1951. His partner died four years later and he purchased the rest. His sons, Herman and Sidney, joined him in the business, and for the next 15 years they produced inexpensive, private-label men's shoes and work boots in a converted Boston warehouse. Their dress shoes were most often sold through discount stores, while their work boots became a staple in Army/Navy surplus stores.

Sales of Abington's leather work boots increased unexpectedly around 1970, as the company was one of the first to stumble upon a new fashion trend that combined styles and gear previously favored by outdoors enthusiasts. "When we visited the stores, we saw that a lot of young people, college students, were buying them. You don't have to be a genius to know that something's going on," Herman Swartz later told *INC.* magazine.

Abington had by then relocated to Newmarket, New Hampshire, and in 1973 selected the "Timberland" name from a list suggested by an advertising agency. The company created a subsidiary to manufacture its new line of insulated and waterproof leather boots, which were distinguished by their thick rubber soles. It produced just 2,500 pairs that first year, compared to 490,000 shoes and boots in the Abington line.

The company initially marketed Timberland and Abington boots by appealing to hunters and fishermen who shopped the Army/Navy surplus stores, and sales of the new line were unimpressive. However, in 1975 a marketing consultant suggested the company position Timberland as a fashion item sold through upscale department stores and retail outlets. A new advertising campaign was funded through a hefty price increase and launched with the slogan, "A whole line of fine leather boots that cost plenty, and should." In 1979, Abington officially changed its name to the Timberland Co. That year, it sold 500,000 pairs of Timberland boots as revenues topped $16 million. The company opened its first retail store in 1986, and made its first public stock offering in 1987. After fierce competition in the "brown shoe" sector eroded Timberland's sales, in 1997 the company began updating its retail stores. In 1998, Timberland introduced its "beige shoe"—a hybrid between a boot and a sneaker—and in 1999 debuted its line of Mountain Athletics products, which targeted younger men.

Florsheim Shoe Group Inc. Chicago-based Florsheim Shoe Group Inc., was perhaps the best known maker of men's dress shoes in the United States in the early 1990s when it accounted for about 20 percent of the market. By 1998, though, its share had dipped and its sales reached only $244 million.

The company was founded in 1892 by Milton S. Florsheim. He created one of the earliest brand names in the shoe industry by stamping the company name into the sole of every shoe it produced. In the early 1900s, Florsheim began advertising nationally in magazines such as *The Saturday Evening Post*. It was one of the first manufacturers to open its own retail stores, and was credited with introducing low-cut dress shoes for men.

A consumer survey in the early 1990s found the Florsheim brand name was associated with high prices, so the company reduced prices on four of its most popular men's dress styles. In an effort to capture a greater share of the profitable casual shoe market, Florsheim launched a rash of new models aimed at appealing to younger consumers. The company's line of @ease shoes, as well as its Frogs golf shoes were introduced in the mid-1990s. Florsheim also embarked on a major redesign of its retail stores—including the bold step of offering its competitors' shoes in an attempt to increase traffic into the stores.

Other Leaders. The outdoor look pioneered by Timberland spread throughout the industry, and several other companies were also achieving success with it. Wolverine Worldwide tallied $669.3 million in sales in 1998, at least partially because of its appeal. Wolverine also manufactures Hush Puppies, which are extremely popular with baby boomers. Hush Puppies sales have soared as more relaxed office dress codes have empowered men to wear casual shoes to work. The Rockport subsidiary of Reebok International Ltd. is another key player in the men's footwear industry. With recorded sales of $447.6 million in 1996 Rockport was one of the few bright spots for the parent company.

WORKFORCE

The U.S. non-rubber footwear industry employed 33,533 people in 1998 and 28,867 of them were production workers, the FIA reported. The total represented a 15 percent decline from the prior year and an 86 percent decrease since 1968, when employment stood at 233,400. Production employees earned an average of $8.92 per hour in 1998—up 5 percent from the $8.49 per hour they averaged in 1997. A rough comparison of this figure with China's basic monthly wage for its shoe-making workers of about $50 graphically illustrates why production has

largely shifted to those countries in recent years. Even the average salary in Taiwan, reportedly the highest among major foreign competitors, was less than half the U.S. amount.

AMERICA AND THE WORLD

Considered one of the most open footwear markets in the world because it was one of the few industrialized nations that did not impose high import tariffs, FIA reported that imports to the United States grew 229 percent—at an average annual rate of 11 percent—from 1978 until 1998.

After 1968 (when President Lyndon Johnson cut tariffs in half) several attempts were made to impose higher import tariffs, most notable of which was the Textile, Apparel, and Footwear Act of 1990 vetoed by President George Bush. Similar bills had been rejected by Congress in 1985 and 1988. Also during this time, the industry filed complaints about unfair trade practices with the International Trade Commission (ITC), but in 1984 the ITC ruled that the U.S. footwear industry was not being harmed by imports. A Senate recommendation for five years of global quotas was tabled in the early 1990s.

After the Textile, Apparel, and Footwear Act was vetoed in 1990, the FIA, which had lobbied for import protection, effectively gave up the fight. Fawn Evenson, then executive director of the FIA, told *The Journal of Commerce and Commercial* in 1992, "We literally spent millions of dollars on trade cases. We almost went broke trying to protect jobs."

In 1990, FIA voted to expand its membership to include importers and tacitly supported the North American Free Trade Agreement (NAFTA) by focusing its efforts on ensuring that Mexico would not become a transit point for duty free shoes from other countries, most of which imposed tariffs of 25 percent or more on U.S. exports or locked out U.S. companies entirely. Evenson explained, "We are importers. We've stopped quota battles. We're going to spend a lot more time on market access and on exports. We're now going to devote our efforts to companies that are surviving."

FURTHER READING

Baber, Bonnie. "Casual Shoe Demand on Upswing with Consumers Across the Board." *Footwear News,* 23 October 1995.

Bentz, Kristen. "True West." *Footwear+,* March 1997.

Chandler, Susan. "Florshem Sizes Up Its Alternatives After Loss in Fourth Quarter." *Chicago Tribune,* 3 March 1999.

Clifford, Mark. "Pangs of Conscience." *Business Week,* 29 July 1996.

"Current Highlights of the Nonrubber Footwear Industry." Washington, D.C.: Footwear Industries of America, April 1999. Available from http://www.fia.org/.

Lagnado, Ike. "Men's Sales on Solid Footing." *Footwear News,* 29 April 1996.

Saporito, Bill. "Can Nike Get Unstuck?" *Time,* 30 March 1998.

Schneiderman, Ira. "Battle of the Sexes." *Footwear News,* 26 July 1999.

Waxler, Caroline. "Walking Wounded." *Forbes,* 20 May 1996.

SIC 3144

WOMEN'S FOOTWEAR, EXCEPT ATHLETIC

This category covers establishments engaged in the production of women's footwear designed primarily for dress, street, and work. Establishments engaged in the production of athletic shoes and misses', children's, infants', and babies' footwear are classified in **SIC 3149: Footwear, Except Rubber, Not Elsewhere Classified.** Establishments primarily engaged in the production of rubber or plastic footwear are classified in **SIC 3021: Rubber and Plastics Footwear,** and those manufacturing orthopedic extension shoes are classified in **SIC 3842: Orthopedic, Prosthetic, and Surgical Appliances and Supplies.**

NAICS CODE(S)

316214 (Women's Footwear (except Athletic) Manufacturing)

INDUSTRY SNAPSHOT

The U.S. women's footwear industry is dominated by large companies that design and manufacture a wide variety of shoes each year. Since the early 1990s it has been heavily influenced by the continuing popularity of rubber soled athletic shoes and other outdoor oriented casual models that do not fall directly into this category. A steady market of consumers eager for new styles, along with the short life span of a pair of shoes, have produced lucrative profits for the nation's well-established footwear manufacturers. According to Footwear Industries of America (FIA), U.S. companies produced and shipped approximately 37.0 million pairs of women's shoes in 1998. In relation to the overall footwear industry, women's models accounted for about 30 percent of all shoes produced by manufacturers in the United States. The import of foreign-made footwear has been the biggest problem for domestic shoe manufacturers as comparably stylish but lower priced models made outside the United States continue to dominate the market. Approximately 92 percent of shoes sold in the United States in 1998 were made abroad, arriving primarily from China, Brazil, and Indonesia. These imports were able to undercut their American counterparts in large part due to the lower labor and production costs incurred by foreign shoe companies.

ORGANIZATION AND STRUCTURE

Unveiling a wide assortment of new shoe styles each season is how industry leaders regularly improve their product lines and increase their market shares. A key aspect of this process consists in the work of a shoe company's in-house design staff, which develops appropriate new versions of their firm's basic products by monitoring European and American fashion trends. As this is one of the most expensive parts of the entire manufacturing process, more and more American companies have attempted to reduce overall costs by relocating many preliminary manufacturing tasks to foreign factories where labor expenses are lower. Nevertheless, shoes are frequently returned to the United States for a number of final production steps, at which point the finished footwear is distributed to stores across the nation. Marketing teams from each manufacturer then negotiate with retail outlets and department stores in an effort to place as much of their company's products on display shelves as possible. Competition is fierce, and dramatic shifts within the industry based on the smallest stylistic or structural innovation are commonplace. To keep up with these changes, much of the industry's design, marketing, and management personnel meet at annual trade gatherings like the Fashion Footwear Association of New York show, the National Shoe Fair, and Shoes in New York.

CURRENT CONDITIONS

The U.S. market for women's footwear has undergone a significant transformation in recent years. This shift has been driven by two distinct yet interrelated trends. First, women have come to prefer comfort over style when selecting their footwear. A study cited by the September 29, 1997, *Footwear News* revealed that 82 percent of women ranked comfort ahead of fashion on their list of shoe-buying criteria. Second, with the proliferation of "casual Fridays" and other corporate dress-down occasions, a greater number of women wear less formal shoes to work. As a result, women's dress shoe sales have fallen by more than 30 percent since 1991 (and those of pumps by nearly 37 percent in the same period), while casual shoe sales have soared—becoming the second most popular market in the U.S. behind athletic shoes. As the massive baby boom generation ages, the market for women's casual footwear is expected to continue to expand, as these consumers seek more comfortable shoes.

Despite the growth of the casual footwear segment of the women's shoe market, American footwear manufacturers have continued to lose ground to their foreign rivals. Although the total number of pairs of women's nonathletic shoes produced in the United States remained relatively constant between 1996 and 1998, domestic shoe companies controlled a dwindling percentage of that market. 92.8 percent of all shoes purchased in the United States in 1998 were manufactured abroad, an increase of 1.5 percent from 1996 and 4.1 percent from 1994. Imported women's footwear, which reached nearly 533.0 million pairs in 1998, dwarfed the 37.0 million pairs manufactured domestically that year. 6.8 million pairs of these shoes were exported from the United States.

INDUSTRY LEADERS

Nine West Group Inc. manufactures and markets such venerable brands as Easy Spirit, Bandolino, Enzo Angiolini, and Pappagallo. With over 15,000 employees and 1999 sales topping $1.9 billion, Nine West dominates the market for casual, career, and dress footwear. The company's wares are sold at 1,500 of its own retail stores, as well as at over 7,000 locations in department stores and specialty shoe outlets. Nearly 92 percent of Nine West's shoes are manufactured in Brazil, China, and other foreign countries. Despite a series of profitable acquisitions in the early 1990s, Nine West faced flagging sales and excess inventory in 1998. As a result, the company was purchased in 1999 by Jones Apparel Group, whose brands include Jones New York and Todd Oldham.

Nine West was founded in 1977. The publicly- held firm quickly attained a place of distinction by sourcing out many of its manufacturing tasks to factories in foreign countries, which enabled Nine West to offer fashionable products at extremely competitive prices. Its shoes developed high brand recognition and were found in department stores as well as the company's own retail outlets. This strategy proved successful, and by the early 1990s, its original Nine West stores—which accounted for 30 percent of all company sales at the time—tallied one of the industry's highest sales-per-square-foot ratios. With its popular brands Nine West, Calico, and Enzo Angiolini moderately priced between $25 and $55, Nine West appealed to younger working women who wanted chic shoes at a reasonable price. In particular, its Enzo Angiolini division made great strides in the early 1990s against several major competitors who also offered affordable, European-style dress and career shoes.

Nine West's inroads proved disastrous for the United States Shoe Corp. As Nine West's fiercest rival, U.S. Shoe Corp. produced footwear brands such as Bandolino, Selby, Easy Spirit, Vittorio Ricci, Capezio, Amalfi, Evan Picone, Pappagallo, Texas Boot, and Wrangler Boot. Founded in 1931, U.S. Shoe Corp. had by 1995 emerged as not only one of the largest American manufactures of women's shoes, but also as a franchiser of retail shoe,

apparel, and eyeglass stores. With over 40,00 employees and annual sales of nearly $2.6 billion, U.S. Shoe Corp. operated the August Max Woman, Caren Charles, Pappagallo, and Casual Corner nationwide retail apparel outlets, as well as LensCrafters optical-goods outlets.

U.S. Shoe began suffering major losses to Nine West in the early 1990s, especially as its once dominant Bandolino division—offering dress and career shoes priced from $55 to $70 and targeted at fashion-conscious working women—fell victim to unfavorable exchange rates stemming from its manufacture in Italy, and the fresher styles in the same price range introduced by competitors such as Nine West. Retailers began discounting Bandolino and the brand's all-important image suffered among consumers; as demand decreased department stores ceded more shelf space to Nine West, and U.S. Shoe and Bandolino lost even more ground.

U.S. Shoe had made some strides during the early 1990s by emphasizing its Easy Spirit line of dress shoes, which it had introduced in 1988. This label was a direct response to the growing needs of women in the workforce who were pairing business attire with athletic footwear for street travel, carrying their uncomfortable dress pumps in a bag, and then changing shoes after arriving at work. Pump sales had peaked in the mid-1980s but dropped off as they became less of a fashion staple and more of a basic wardrobe necessity. Trying to capitalize on women's continuing need for a dressy shoe but increasing unwillingness to torture their feet in high heels, U.S. Shoe combined low- to medium-heeled pumps with flexible soles and padded linings. Advertising campaigns depicted women playing basketball in the shoes and trumpeted the slogan, "Looks like a pump, feels like a sneaker." Priced at around $100 a pair, the shoes cost more than average pumps, but nonetheless proved popular.

Ultimately, however, such efforts—as well as the company's decision to move the production of its more casual shoe models to lower-cost Brazilian and Far Eastern factories—proved insufficient to stem the negative tide. In 1995, U.S. Shoe was acquired by Luxottica. Although Luxottica kept LensCrafters within its corporate fold, it sold U.S. Shoe's women's apparel division to an Italian concern. Nine West purchased U.S. Shoe's footwear business in 1995 for $600.0 million.

Nine West immediately began incorporating various U.S. shoe lines into its own operation, placing a number of shoe stores (such as Easy Spirit and Easy Spirit Outlet) under its management arm, and announcing in early 1997 that it would close three of its former rival's domestic manufacturing facilities and transfer the additional production overseas. This maneuver reduced Nine West's U.S.-produced footwear from 8.5 million pairs in 1995 to about five million pairs—then representing less than 10 percent of its total production and continuing the strategy that helped it overtake U.S. Shoe in the first place. The move also eliminated about 1,000 of the company's 1,900 American manufacturing jobs.

In 1998, Nine West was forced to cut production by 40 percent. Plagued by a surplus of inventory and stagnate sales, the company laid off 6 percent of its workforce. After announcing in 1999 that it was under investigation by the Federal Trade Commission for its pricing policies, Nine West's travails continued. Later that year, Nine West was acquired by Jones Apparel. More job cuts were forecast.

Kenneth Cole Productions Inc., also a relative newcomer to the women's footwear industry, is another market leader. Founded in 1982, this publicly-owned company has over 1,000 employees and 1998 sales of over $219 million. The company's strength is in marketing its relatively-expensive trendy shoes. With its reputation for cutting-edge fashion, Kenneth Cole is increasingly known for its controversial advertising campaigns that combine corporate imagery with politically oriented messages. (Several of its ads in the mid-1990s, for example, centered on AIDS.) The company, which also sells eyewear, practices what it preaches by making corporate financial donations to a variety of social causes and encouraging its employees to become involved in charitable projects. In addition to selling its products at 3,500 department and specialty stores, Kenneth Cole also operates 50 of its own retail stores, a mail order catalogue, and a web site. Most Kenneth Cole goods are manufactured by contractors in Brazil, China, and India.

The Stride Rite Corp. is another a key player in the industry, although its women's division is only one part of its overall footwear operation. With its major brands including Grasshoppers, Keds, Sperry Top-Sider, and Stride Rite, the company reported 1998 sales of $539.4 million. The Massachusetts-based Stride Rite boomed in the 1980s by remarketing its lightweight canvas Keds sneaker, a standard product which it had made for more than 70 years. The renewed success of this casual shoe led to the reemergence of a similar product line, carrying the Grasshoppers label, which was aimed at older women. Models in this line included Keds-style canvas casuals, leather casuals, espadrilles, and leather sandals. Despite its success, the company was slow to adopt the bigger shoes and thicker soles that became fashionable in the early-1990s. In 1993, the company quickly strove to update its product lines. After closing 80 of its underperforming retail stores in 1995 and 1996, Stride Rite returned to profitability. In 1997, Stride Rite entered a licensing agreement with clothing designer Tommy Hilfiger to produce women's and men's shoes.

While many key players in the women's footwear business emphasize more dress-oriented models, the continuing popularity of casual footwear based on athletic-shoe styling and comfort has revolutionized the women's shoe industry. Footwear manufacturers, including many athletic shoe companies themselves, jumped into this niche in the early 1990s and began offering comfortable quasi-athletic shoes made with leather uppers and an emphasis on unique styling. This trend coincided with a general relaxation of office dress codes and created a new half-casual, half-workplace type of shoe.

Skechers U.S.A., Inc. has reaped the rewards of catering to this rapidly-growing market. Founded in 1992 by Robert Greenberg, who had previously co-launched the popular L.A. Gear athletic footwear company in the early 1980s, Skechers experienced phenomenal growth. Recognizing that younger consumers had tired of the athletic shoes sported by their baby boomer parents, Skechers debuted an array of rugged leather casual shoes. Although they utilized popular athletic-shoe materials and compressed air-cushioning pockets that were placed in the heel and the front of each sole, Skechers were intended primarily to complement casual apparel. Targeting 12 to 25 year old consumers, Skechers designed advertising that featured teenage skateboarders sporting Skechers shoes and plenty of attitude. The strategy was successful. According to *Business Week*, 17 percent of teenagers had purchased a pair of Skechers in 1998. Even more impressive was the company's burgeoning sales, which tripled between 1995 and 1998. 1998 sales grew 102 percent to reach $372.7 million, while 1998 net income was $24.4 million, an increase of over 121 percent from 1997. Skechers sells its trendy shoes at U.S. department and specialty stores, as well as at 40 of its independently owned retail stores.

Other companies also sought to claim a stake of this market. Airwalk, Vans, and Simple, which all traced their roots to the skateboarding and beach cultures of Southern California, gained a following of loyal consumers. Although these companies initially aimed their sneaker-like products at young men, in 1995 they began broadening their marketing approaches and design plans to include young women as well. "We've had a ton of people asking for cool but comfortable women's shoes," Simple president Eric Meyer told *Action Sports Retailer* magazine as one reason for the new emphasis.

WORKFORCE

Footwear manufacturers based in the United States have increasingly moved their production operations overseas to boost their profits. As a result, imports have gained a substantial foothold in the American footwear market. By 1998, 92.8 percent of all nonrubber footwear designed for American consumption was produced outside the U.S. This shift away from domestic footwear manufacture has had obvious consequences on the American workers once employed in the industry. 1,200 U.S.

shoe factories closed between 1968 and 1995, resulting in the loss of nearly 180,000 manufacturing jobs. An additional 41 U.S. shoe-making facilities were shuttered between 1995 and 1998. By 1998, only 33,533 Americans were employed in the footwear industry—down from 53,800 in 1995 and 233,400 in 1968. According to FIA, these workers earned an average hourly pay of $8.92 in 1998 (a 5 percent increase from 1997). American shoe-making facilities are located primarily in Maine, Texas, California, New York, Puerto Rico, Pennsylvania, Wisconsin, Missouri, Mississippi, and Massachusetts.

The surge of footwear production away from the United States has also impacted foreign workers. Factories are often re-located to countries noted for their dearth of government regulations on working conditions, health and safety matters, and the right to unionize.

AMERICA AND THE WORLD

Manufacturers of women's footwear in the United States continue to face strong competition from cheaper imports. The amount of imported shoes on the American market has increased exponentially in recent years, from 175 million pairs in 1968 to 374 million in 1978, and from 941 million pairs in 1986 to 1.3 billion in 1998. Over 533 million pairs of women's shoes alone were imported in 1998. The majority of these shoes now come from the Far East, with imports from China growing by 39 percent each year since 1981 to top 895 million pairs in 1998. Chinese factories produced 72.8 percent of the import shoes sold in the United States in 1998. Brazil and Indonesia accounted for an additional 10.5 share of the import market. Several aggressive newcomers also have sought entrance into the U.S. marketplace. Chief among these is Vietnam, according to *Footwear News*.

U.S. companies learned to reduce costs further by shipping cut footwear patterns to plants in Third World countries, where they were then either partially or completely assembled. The firms did this because it was cheaper for the footwear to be only partially assembled abroad, since American companies pay a lower duty (typically 5 percent) on unfinished goods being re-exported to the United States. The final, less labor-intensive manufacturing details such as bottoming, finishing, and packing are then completed at home.

On the other side of the international trade front, American companies shipped more than 27 million pairs of footwear abroad for sale in 1998, of which about 6 million were women's models. Canada was the chief destination for American-made shoes, receiving 37.3 percent of exports in 1998. Japan followed with 10.8 percent; Mexico, the biggest foreign market for American footwear only five years earlier, fell to just 7.1 percent. The United Kingdom, Venezuela, the Netherlands, Panama, and Honduras accounted for nearly the rest of the exports.

RESEARCH AND TECHNOLOGY

Like other industries, the production and sale of U.S. women's footwear has been greatly changed by computer technology. Companies have invested large sums of money to integrate the latest electronic equipment into all facets of their operations. In the research and development segment, the use of computer-aided design (CAD) is now common, and many firms have integrated it with computer-aided manufacturing (CAM) processes. The combination allows shoes to be produced in America more quickly and accurately, which dramatically lowered production costs but also eliminated jobs. The women's footwear industry has additionally brought robotics technology into the manufacturing process, utilizing robots to move shoes from one production module to the next. Computers are also used extensively in the industry's management sector, usually tracking production figures and coordinating them with distribution results and sales totals.

FURTHER READING

Agins, Teri. "Kenneth Cole Firms Up Position As Top Fashion Brand." *Wall Street Journal,* 1 February 1999.

Bailey, Steve and Syre, Steven. "Shoes and Support CEO Thinks Stride-Rite Is headed Toward Comeback Trail." *Boston Globe,* 2 February, 1996.

"Current Highlights of the Nonrubber Footwear Industry." Washington: Footwear Industries of America, April 1999. Available from http://www.fia.org/.

Hajewski, Doris. "Rare Size Fits Some Shops." *Milwaukee Journal Sentinel,* 1 April 1998.

Lagnado, Ike. "The Highs and Lows of Women's Shoe Sales." *Footwear News,* 29 April 1996.

Lucas, Allison. "Heart and Sole." *Sales & Marketing Management,* May 1996, 30.

MacDonald, Laurie. "Kenneth Cole: Seriously." *Footwear News,* 5 February 1996.

MacDonald, Laurie. "NSRA Parley Brings Key Issues To Table." *Footwear News,* 15 January 1996.

"Market Pros Say Comfort, Casual Are Industry's Future." *Footwear News,* 29 September 1997.

Morris, Kathleen. "Sketchers Has To Watch Its Step." *Business Week,* 27 September 1999.

"NSRA Conference in Las Vegas." *Footwear News,* 27 February 1995.

Patterson, Philana. "Athletic Shoe Market Looks Worn Out." *The Raleigh News and Observer,* 25 December 1997.

Peale, Cliff. "Luxottica Settles Terms of U.S. Shoe Sale." *Cincinnati Post,* 30 May 1996.

Rossi, William. "Going Nowhere: Is Footwear Retailing Stuck In A No-Growth Rut?" *Footwear News,* 18 December 1995.

Rothman, Howard. "Rising to the Occasion." *Action Sports Retailer,* February 1995, 45.

Strassel, Kimberly. "Nine West Plans U.S. Plant Closings, Paring 1,000 Jobs." *The Wall Street Journal,* 13 February 1997, C16.

Tedeschi, Mark. "Colombia Out To Lure Shoe Business." *Footwear News,* 4 March 1996, 2.

Underwood, Elaine. "The Nike of Women's Shoes (Nine West Group Inc.)." *Brandweek,* 25 March 1996.

SIC 3149

FOOTWEAR, EXCEPT RUBBER, NOT ELSEWHERE CLASSIFIED

This classification includes establishments primarily engaged in the production of shoes, not elsewhere classified, such as misses', youths', boys', children's, and infants' footwear and athletic footwear. Establishments primarily engaged in the manufacture of rubber or plastics footwear are classified in **SIC 3021: Rubber and Plastics Footwear,** and those manufacturing orthopedic extension shoes are classified in **SIC 3842: Orthopedic, Prosthetic, and Surgical Appliances and Supplies.**

NAICS CODE(S)

316219 (Other Footwear Manufacturing)

INDUSTRY SNAPSHOT

The nonrubber footwear industry manufactures all types of footwear except rubber protective and rubber-soled fabric upper (the traditional "sneaker"). Nonrubber footwear may be constructed with leather, vinyl, plastic, or textile uppers or combinations of these materials for all ages and both genders. Men's footwear producers, classified in **SIC 3143: Men's Footwear, Except Athletic,** and women's footwear producers, classified in **SIC 3144: Women's Footwear, Except Athletic,** compose their own independent industries.

The main categories of nonrubber footwear include athletic shoes, outdoor shoes (such as boots), and safety footwear. The safety footwear segment includes heavy leather work boots with steel toes for extra protection. U.S. consumers purchase more than 1 billion pairs of shoes a year, spending more than $41 billion. Sales in the footwear industry are influenced by economic conditions, demographic trends, and pricing. Fashion trends generally play a limited role in overall market demand. Since 1993 consumers shifted away from designer brands and became more price conscious. With more companies allowing casual dress, the demand for dress shoes declined. In addition, consumers increasingly choose "brown shoes," which are rugged, yet comfortable, instead of athletic shoes for casual wear.

Because of lower manufacturing costs and modified trade rules, most footwear (or the parts requiring the most labor) was produced in Mexico, Central America, and Asia during the late 1990s and, consequently, employment in U.S. footwear factories plunged. Automation also contributed to the decline.

During the same period, unit sales of shoes declined, although dollar sales increased slightly. Price increases for men's, women's, and infants' shoes contributed to the sales increases. Lower-priced shoes and athletic footwear dominated the market. To improve market share, manufacturers consolidated, increased marketing, and opened their own retail stores. Some also increased sales operations abroad; demand in some countries, however, was lessened by the Asian economic crisis.

BACKGROUND AND DEVELOPMENT

According to *Footwear News,* shoe style cycles have historically "averaged two years in ascendancy, two years at peak, two years in descendency." Those averages held for various popular styles—such as loafers, platforms, and dress boots—and their design characteristics until athletic-footwear manufacturers captured nearly one-third of the total footwear market in the early 1970s. Over a span of more than 25 years, American consumers spent $300 billion on 7.5 billion pairs of athletic shoes. Athletic-shoe companies built empires by spending huge sums on innovative marketing strategies that included sports-celebrity endorsements and advertising and promotion with tie-ins to college and other sports. Reebok International Ltd. and Adidas became $3.5 billion companies, while Nike Inc. became the first-ever $9.5 billion company. In 1998, however, athletic footwear for casual wear began to lose out to leather boots and more rugged casual footwear, and companies started to downsize, reduce inventories and production, and trim their advertising and celebrity endorsement budgets.

In 1987 there were 120 companies operating 129 establishments in this industry. In 1992 that number had gone down to just 84 companies operating 94 establishments. By 1996 the number of establishments had dropped to about 52, with 12 factories closing since 1995. Many of the plants that closed in the early 1990s were owned by the largest manufacturing and retailing companies, which opted to source more footwear from less expensive producers overseas. In 1996 total employment declined about 11 percent to 46,100; production employment also declined by about the same amount.

As a group, the nonrubber footwear industry reported a 2.6 percent decline in shoe production in 1996 from 1995 figures, and recorded a 19.5 percent decline in profits. The two largest athletic-footwear producers, however, were responsible for 94 percent of the group's total profits. Four companies, including the third-largest athletic-footwear producer, recorded losses in 1992.

In 1994 shipments of footwear began to steadily decline, dropping approximately 24 percent to 19 million pairs in 1995. The value of these shipments decreased 68 percent from 1994 to an estimated $139 million in 1996. Shipments of footwear in this group accounted for 15 percent by quantity and 7 percent by value of all categories of footwear sold. Production of all types of footwear within this industry fell in 1996, dropping by an annual rate of 3 percent over the previous five years.

More than half (56 percent) of the nonrubber footwear produced in the United States had leather uppers in 1996. This was up from 51 percent in 1991. Only 31 percent of juvenile types of shoes had leather uppers, while almost all athletic footwear had leather uppers.

Ups and Downs of Personal Consumption. Historically, consumers have primarily purchased their footwear at footwear specialty stores and department stores. In the past, customers were strongly brand-loyal and most often selected footwear purchases on the basis of brand recognition and style. During the 1980s, consumers took great interest in their appearance and became slightly extravagant at the sales counter. Personal consumption of footwear and other apparel nearly doubled, with an average annual growth rate of 7.3 percent. Hurt by a recession, weak growth in disposable income, and high unemployment, however, consumers in the early 1990s became much more frugal.

Along with these economic changes came changes in consumer psychology. Designer names, high-priced shoes and apparel, and frequent shopping sprees became things of the past in 1993, as consumer tastes in general shifted away from designer brands. Consumers became more value-conscious and began purchasing less expensive products at lower-end retail establishments, such as mass merchandisers, stores in strip shopping centers, and outlet stores. Department stores' share of all apparel expenditures fell to 24.3 percent in 1993, down from 33.6 percent in 1985, as women were buying more of their families' shoes and other apparel at mass merchandisers, such as Kmart and Wal-Mart, and shopping less frequently at department and specialty stores.

In addition to opting for different types of retail establishments, shoppers also were selecting different types of merchandise by the early 1990s. Basic footwear and moderately priced brand-name shoes were often the best-selling items. This pattern reflected a more value-oriented consumer, as well as an aging population seeking comfort and less formality in footwear. In the late 1980s and early 1990s, many mass merchandisers added more recognizable national brand names to their in-store inventory. Previously, most brand names were distributed only through department stores.

During the 1990s, formal attire lost some of the popularity it had enjoyed in the 1980s, and footwear sales reflected this trend. A decrease in the size of the white-collar work force and a trend toward more relaxed office attire contributed to a slide in the sale of formal footwear.

Acquisitions and Consolidations. Throughout the late 1980s, the ten largest publicly traded apparel companies saw their market share increase by nearly 5 percent. Part of this growth was attributed to increased demand for these companies' products, but a series of acquisitions and consolidations was also beneficial. This consolidation of the footwear manufacturing industry paralleled developments in the retail industry as a whole. As large department store retailers merged in the late 1980s, they consolidated their buying functions. Larger apparel and footwear manufacturers benefited from this because it became more efficient for the fewer number of buyers to use one vendor rather than several. In response, growth-oriented apparel and footwear manufacturers increased their acquisition activity in search of new brands and broader product offerings.

In addition, the enormous growth of large mass merchandisers drove the industry to consolidate. From 1981 through 1991, Sears, Roebuck and Co.—then the nation's largest retailer—saw its sales increase rapidly, as did Wal-Mart and Kmart. Savvy footwear manufacturers understood they could increase their sales and market share by offering these retail giants a broad array of brand-name merchandise. Historically, many brand-name manufacturers sold their goods only to department stores; as time went on, however, they sold nearly identical merchandise to mass merchandisers in order to participate in that sector's phenomenal growth. Not surprisingly, this affected manufacturers' relationships with department stores, which sought exclusivity in their products. To remedy the situation, many manufacturers began to produce several different categories of brand names, each of which was distributed through a different type of retailer.

Throughout history, retailers and footwear manufacturers have had an adversarial relationship because of issues centered around pricing. In the mid-1990s, pricing was still an important factor, but retailers also wanted special services from manufacturers. Storage of inventory was one of the highest expenses a retailer faced. To reduce this expense, more and more retailers demanded that manufacturers carry the inventory instead and make deliveries when the retailers' stock was low. In order for this type of relationship to work, especially when dealing with large quantities of merchandise required by stores such as Wal-Mart or Kmart, retailers and vendors found it necessary to form partnerships. Quick response was the most important aspect of this relationship. Orders had to be replenished automatically via computer links called electronic data interchange.

Retailers also demanded a continual flow of new merchandise. Some footwear manufacturers responded to this need by creating "flow replenishment" programs, in which new products were introduced in a continual flow rather than in seasonal batches. In addition, retailers were demanding more marketing support and other services. Many manufacturers, as a result, created their own point-of-sale fixtures and advertised their products nationally.

Experts traced the growing appeal of outlet stores back to the value-conscious shopper. The primary attraction of outlet stores was the price of their products. Customers generally purchased footwear and other apparel items at up to half the cost charged by conventional department and specialty stores. In many cases, the merchandise offered was no longer just the irregulars, overruns, or odd lots; often, the merchandise was first quality, coming from current inventory. Many footwear manufacturers, however, used their own outlet stores to dispense extra or second-quality merchandise. Manufacturers preferred this form of distribution to off-price retailers because they could avoid tarnishing their brand names. Risk to brand names often occurred when too much merchandise was sold through discounters. In addition, outlet stores also tended to be located far from the selling areas of conventional department and specialty stores. This decreased the chance that the manufacturer's regular retail store would lose sales to the outlet store.

Athletic Footwear. Athletic footwear was the largest-selling category in the footwear industry, and the only division within nonrubber footwear to post any gains in the mid-1990s. Production of athletic footwear reached a peak of about 6.5 million pairs in 1993, but declined to 5.5 million pairs in 1995. Consumption of athletic footwear, which included imports, rose from a 1993 total of 382 million pairs to 408 million pairs in 1995. Representing 99 percent of consumption, imports continued to dominate the market, while U.S. production continued to decline. Imports have risen by an average of 3.5 percent per year since 1990. Even though the number of shoes purchased declined, the sales of athletic shoes actually increased, to $11.4 billion. Athletic footwear represented about 26 percent of combined nonrubber and rubber-fabric footwear consumption of approximately 1.6 billion pairs in 1995. Imports of juvenile footwear in 1996 were down from 1995 but were still higher than any previous year; similarly, imports of athletic nonrubber footwear increased from 1995 but were still lower than any other year in the early 1990s.

The largest selling and most consistently popular brand of athletic footwear was from Nike—men bought Nike 70 percent of the time, while women purchased this brand 61 percent of the time. Reebok was not far behind, and was in fact the only brand that gave stiff competition to Nike. Reebok International Ltd.'s shoes represented 46 percent of purchases for men and 57 percent of purchases for women. Adidas, Converse, and Fila rounded out the top five brands, but none had more than 23 percent of purchases.

The Summer Olympics of 1996 gave the top athletic brands a chance to compete with each other for sponsorship and advertising rights. The general target audience was 18 to 34 year-olds, and marketers reached them with a mix of sports, lifestyle television programming, and magazine titles. While Nike, Converse, and Avia built strong followings in the performance shoe business, Reebok and L.A. Gear had more of a fashion than a performance-based image. Nike, though not an official sponsor of the Olympic games, led the way by spending more on advertising, and in fact, many people believed they were a sponsor. Reebok teamed with The Athlete's Foot in downtown Atlanta to show off "Planet Reebok," hoping to cash in on its proximity to the athletes and spectators. Most athletic-shoe companies relied on high-priced, prime-time television advertisements and major sporting event television advertisements for most of their media advertisements.

The nation's largest-selling footwear company, Kinney Shoe Corp., launched its own private label of athletic footwear in August 1993 through its Foot Locker sneaker and sports apparel retail chain. The new shoe brand, In the Zone or ITZ, had its own independent marketing budget and was set to compete with the volatile second tier of athletic-shoe brands, such as L.A. Gear, Adidas, Converse, and Asics.

Outdoor Footwear. One of the fastest-growing categories in the footwear industry during the mid- to late 1990s was outdoor footwear. Outdoor footwear includes rugged hiking boots and casual outdoor sandals. In 1995, hiking boot sales exploded, selling 27 million pairs over the course of that year, compared with just 22 million in 1994 and 11 million in 1992. Sales grew 14 percent to top $1 billion for the first time. Sales grew in spite of an average price drop in hiking boots, going from around $42 a pair to just $38 a pair. Many traditional athletic-footwear companies recognized the potential profit in this category and were scrambling to participate.

In the athletic outdoor shoe category, Teva sandals, manufactured by Deckers Outdoor Corp., were one of the most popular styles of outdoor sports sandals in the 1990s. Sales for 1996 dropped by less than 1 percent to $102 million as the market was flooded with imitation Tevas and a wide array of sports sandals from all the major athletic-shoe companies. After the initial excitement waned, however, consumers went back to the original, and Deckers' first quarter sales for 1997 increased 20 percent over first quarter 1996, with sales of Tevas increasing by 30 percent.

One of the fastest-growing companies in the outdoor shoe category was Timberland Co. In addition to streamlining its operations, Timberland cultivated the casual outdoor fashion that began to increase in popularity in the early 1990s. Sales increased by 125 percent since 1992, reaching $655 million in 1995. Many companies were attempting to imitate Timberland's style, but consumers still considered Timberland to be the ''original.''

Safety Footwear. Safety footwear constituted yet another segment of the footwear industry. This type of footwear was worn mainly by workers with hazardous, physically demanding jobs. In the mid-1990s, safety footwear started to look much more like mainstream retail footwear. Workers who cared as much about style and comfort as they did about protection, and were more inclined to wear shoes that were aesthetically pleasing, drove the trend. The most successful safety footwear manufacturers were designing shoes that combined a safe environment for the foot with an overall stylish appeal.

Juvenile Footwear. After many years of rapid growth due to the heavy sales demands of the postwar baby-boom era, juvenile footwear sales slowed in the early 1990s. Despite reaching the peak of the baby boom, competition among this category's competitors was still tight. Production of juvenile footwear steadily declined through the 1990s, dropping below 10 million pairs for the first time ever, in 1996.

The undisputed leader in juvenile footwear was Stride-Rite Corp. In 1993, after 27 consecutive quarters of increased earnings, company sales started dropping from $585 million in 1992 to $448 million in 1996. Stride-Rite's primary competition in the juvenile footwear industry included Keds (a brand also owned by Stride-Rite), Weebok (owned by Reebok), Sebago, Sam & Libby, and Toddler University. As in the case of adult footwear, the industry witnessed a trend away from shopping at higher-priced department stores and specialty-shop retailers, toward lower-priced mass merchandisers and outlet stores. Also, with more two-career families, parents were finding less time to take children shopping. As a result, the industry witnessed a trend toward direct-mail purchasing through catalogs.

New Markets. With limited prospects for domestic growth, many footwear companies in the early 1990s were looking for growth opportunities abroad. For footwear merchandise, market penetration was limited since tastes in fashion apparel differed from one country to the next; every country in the world, however, looked to sell in America, the world's leader in footwear consumption.

China's exports to the United States grew 2,600 percent since 1986, at an average rate of 40 percent annually. In 1996 China exported 750 million pairs of shoes; Brazil was the second-biggest exporter to the United States, shipping over 91 million pairs. The import penetration rate ballooned, going from around 40 percent in 1976 to more than 90 percent for the first time in 1996.

Overall exports in nonrubber footwear improved, shipping just under 25 million pairs in 1996. Athletic shoes improved slightly, while exports in slippers (which included the sports sandal) tripled from 1995, going from 607 million pairs to 1.8 billion pairs in just one year. Juvenile footwear also showed strong international sales in 1996, almost doubling its 1995 showing, increasing to 5 million pairs. Japan enjoyed its second year as the main importer of U.S. footwear, taking the mantle from Canada in 1995. Exports to Japan totaled 3.6 million pairs in 1996, while Canada took 2.4 million pairs. The U.K. market continued to grow, importing 1.6 million pairs, and Mexico imported 1.1 million pairs of U.S. footwear.

Many manufacturers believed that basic footwear, such as tennis shoes and children's shoes, had the potential for a large international market. Many brand-name products, such as NIKE, became major international franchises in the mid-1990s. In 1996 international sales accounted for 36 percent of NIKE's total sales of $6.4 billion. Total worldwide orders for athletic footwear were $3.9 billion in 1996 compared to only $2.5 billion in 1995. Such rapidly rising worldwide sales were especially important to NIKE as it struggled to overcome slow growth in the United States. In China, NIKE found that its challenge was to get its shoes into stores and ensure that those stores knew how to display products that were extremely expensive by Chinese standards. In the Philippines, 20 percent of NIKE's shoe sales were made by door-to-door salespeople who sold the shoes on credit. Keeping control of its distribution operation and remaining flexible in the face of cultural differences were keys to boosting NIKE's sales in the region. NIKE gained control of its distribution in Taiwan, Hong Kong, Malaysia, China, Singapore, Australia, and New Zealand within a three-year period. NIKE executives spoke of creating an emotional tie with the consumer in these countries, and as a result, NIKE was one of the world's most recognized brand images in the 1990s and was the world's largest supplier of athletic footwear.

Timberland Co. also was successful in exporting its footwear. In 1983, the company had no interest in foreign markets; 13 years later, nearly 30 percent of its business came from overseas markets, and Timberland owned franchises and retail stores for its products in 50 countries. Timberland's executives developed an interest in the export business when they joined forces with an Italian consumer-goods distributor to establish European operations.

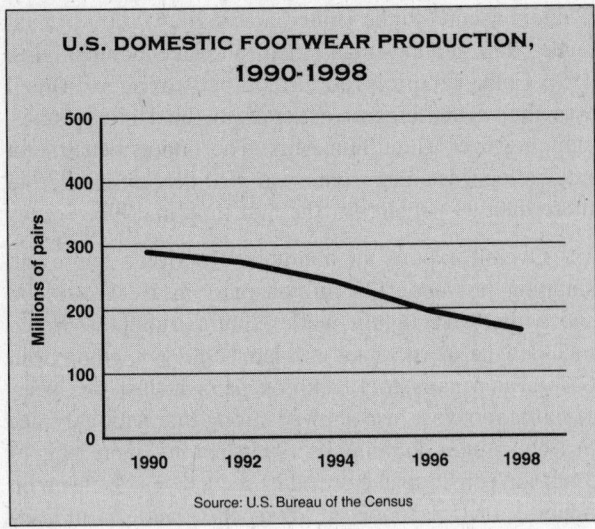

U.S. DOMESTIC FOOTWEAR PRODUCTION, 1990-1998

Source: U.S. Bureau of the Census

unchanged since 1995. In 1998 imports of nonrubber foot-wear from China, the leading supplier to the United States, increased by 6 percent to 881 million pairs ($6.6 billion), while imports from all other sources combined decreased 10 percent to 322 million pairs ($4.8 billion). China's share of the U.S. market was 67 percent in 1998. Brazil, the second-leading supplier, saw its imports drop 9 percent from the 1997 level, to 81 million pairs valued at $1 billion, due to price competition from Italy, Spain, and China in women's leather footwear. The third-leading supplier was Indonesia, followed by Italy, Spain, and Thailand. Economic conditions in Asia affected production. Shipments from the once-dominant suppliers of Korea and Taiwan declined by 18 percent in 1998 as production moved to China and Vietnam. Vietnam became the 14th-leading supplier as U.S. imports rose 18 percent to 3.4 million pairs. In the Western Hemisphere, Mexico and Caribbean countries also had drops in imports to the United States.

According to *U.S. Industry & Trade Outlook,* Japan was the top export market of U.S. nonrubber footwear in 1997, receiving 15 percent of products. Canada, the Netherlands, Mexico, and the United Kingdom rounded out the top five export markets. Besides constructed shoes, the United States exports cut footwear parts and components to countries such as Mexico and the Dominican Republic, which finish or partly finish the footwear, then reexport it to the United States. Often final manufacturing operations requiring less labor are completed in the United States.

Consumers spent almost 5 percent more on footwear in 1998 than in 1997. According to Standard & Poor's *Apparel & Footwear Industry Survey,* 46 percent of shoes sold were lower priced, 19 percent were moderately priced, and 19 percent were higher priced. Athletic footwear accounted for approximately 40 percent of all footwear purchases, although the trend toward brown shoes was beginning to affect that category's share of the casual-shoe segment and sales. Between 1997 and 1998, sales dropped from $14.7 billion (346.6 million pairs) to $13.87 billion (325.4 million pairs). Between 1998 and 1999, sales of pairs were expected to fall 5 percent and revenues 1 percent, as the shift to casual footwear continued.

Manufacturers sought to enhance sales by opening their own retail outlets to sell excess inventory, instead of letting discounters sell their products, a practice that often eroded brand image. Many manufacturers also were establishing relationships with other well-known brands to increase sales.

In the future, per capita consumption of nonrubber footwear was expected to remain steady; the U.S. market would continue to be dominated by imports from countries with low-cost labor. These foreign producers would also provide stiff competition for U.S. footwear manufacturers.

Once there, they learned that international marketing campaigns needed to be country-specific to succeed. Timberland became very sensitive to cultural differences and won many European customers by developing new flexible marketing techniques, which included "concept shops," "specialty shops," and filling retailers orders quickly.

CURRENT CONDITIONS

U.S. production of nonrubber footwear declined steadily in the late 1990s. From 1997 to 1998, production dropped 1 percent in quantity of pairs (to 122.2 million pairs) and 2 percent in value. The 1998 decline, however, was not quite as severe as in previous years. In 1995 there was a 10 percent drop in quantity of pairs and a 16 percent drop in value; in 1996, the drops were 13 and 7 percent, respectively; and in 1997, they were 3 and 8 percent. Shipments fell from 642 million pairs in 1968 to approximately 99 million pairs in 1998. The largest declines were in the slippers and women's footwear categories. Athletic-footwear manufacturers also were experiencing declines as teens and young adults began purchasing boots and other brown shoes for casual wear.

Industry employment fell along with production. In 1998 total employment dropped 13 percent (5,400 employees) to 35,100 employees—a drop that followed declines of 9 percent in 1997, 15 percent in 1996, and 9 percent in 1995. The number of operating plants plummeted from more than 1,000 establishments in 1968 to around 390 in 1992. Three plants closed in 1998 and 11 closed in 1997. Three plants opened in 1997.

Although U.S. production declined, U.S. consumption increased from 1.282 billion pairs in 1997 to 1.327 billion pairs in 1998. The per capita consumption was about 4.9 pairs, up from 1997, but still below the levels of the 1980s when athletic footwear boosted demand above five pairs. Imports accounted for 92 percent of consumption and 83 percent of value in 1998, figures that remained relatively

INDUSTRY LEADERS

According to Standard & Poor's, the top footwear companies in the late 1990s were Brown Group, Justin Industries, K-Swiss Inc., NIKE, Nine West Group Inc., Reebok International, Stride-Rite Corp., Timberland Co., and Wolverine World Wide. K-Swiss sold tennis shoes, children's shoes, and sports sandals, which were manufactured by independent suppliers and sold in specialty retail stores in more than 50 countries. Nine West Group sold women's casual, career, and dress footwear under the Nine West, Easy Spirit, Bandolino, Enzo Angiloini, and Pappagallo brands, and the licensed Calvin Klein label.

Hoover's Online noted that "NIKE is the world's #1 shoe company and controls more than 45 percent of the U.S. athletic-shoe market." The company made shoes for numerous sports and operates Niketown shoe and sportswear stores. Selling its products in 110 countries and online, it posted an 8.1 percent increase in sales in 1999 despite the trend of teens and young adults toward brown shoes for casual wear. Reebok, the second largest maker of athletic shoes, also made Rockport walking and casual shoes.

Stride-Rite Corp. was a designer and marketer of casual and athletic footwear for adults and children. Brands included Grasshoppers, Keds, Munchkin, Pro-Keds, Sperry Top-Sider, Street Hot, and Stride-Rite.

The Timberland Co. made waterproof hiking boots, boat shoes, dress and outdoor casual shoes, and sandals. Wolverine World Wide was the producer of Hush Puppies casual shoes, slippers, and boots, and of Merrell outdoor boots, Bates military boots, and Hy-Test and Wolverine industrial boots. It also produced Caterpillar, Coleman, and Harley-Davidson branded footwear.

Other footwear companies included Red Wing Shoe Co., Inc.; New Balance Athletic Shoe, Inc.; Skechers U.S.A., Inc.; and Deckers Outdoor Corp. Red Wing first made its Red Wing brand work shoes designed for specific occupations in the United States in 1905. The company outsourced its Vasque, Irish Setter, and WORX brands. New Balance made its athletic shoes for men and women in the widest selection of shoe widths. It also made children's shoes. Skechers was a leader in casual footwear aimed at 12 to 25 year olds. Its 900 styles of oxfords, boots, sneakers, sandals, and semi-dressy shoes resulted in a nearly 103 percent rise in sales in 1998. Deckers Outdoor was the marketer of the Teva sports sandal, Simple casual and athletic footwear, and Ugg sheepskin boots.

RESEARCH AND TECHNOLOGY

Like most industries, manufacturers in the nonrubber footwear industry were under extreme pressure to limit the size of their work force, while boosting productivity and efficiency at the same time. For that reason, the industry considered new technology essential to increase growth and profitability. In the 1970s and 1980s, the use of computers integrated design, manufacturing, management, and marketing tasks. Computerized production allowed manufacturers to emphasize nonprice factors such as quality and quick delivery to compete with imports.

Many footwear producers turned to computer-aided design (CAD) and computer-aided manufacturing systems and software. As a result, these manufacturers produced tooling from CAD-generated data and linked it to auto-stitchers, milling, and turning machines. In the early 1990s, the industry witnessed a resurgence of interest in three-dimensional CAD, which produced more accurate shoe patterns and reduced the number of prototypes required to take a new shoe design to the retail level. By the late 1990s, CAD systems enabled athletic-footwear manufacturers to put a new design into production within a few months.

In the footwear industry, computers also enabled manufacturers to combine several operations or machines under fewer operators, thereby reducing handling time and the number of employees, while improving quality. The industry also developed computerized robots to handle and transfer operations within and between production modules.

In order to meet the demands of retailers' quick response requirements, more and more manufacturers were utilizing electronic data interchange (EDI). The goal of quick response was to maintain lean inventories and avoid overstocking, while ensuring that retailers had the merchandise customers wanted to buy. EDI allowed retailers and manufacturers to link themselves together.

In the EDI system, interlinked computer systems were placed at every point of the manufacturing and sales process. Through use of an electronic scanner and bar code tagged to the merchandise, retailers recorded which type of footwear was sold at the point of sale. All sales data on the individual products, including details of color and size, were transmitted immediately to the manufacturer. Through this method, the manufacturer kept track of every store's retail sales trends. This first-hand view of consumer purchasing trends allowed manufacturers to produce apparel based directly on customer demand. The information contained in the bar code set automatic reordering into motion. The industry also referred to this type of inventory replenishment as "flow" or "just in time." In addition to allowing automatic replenishment, EDI also ameliorated distribution and shipping processes. For example, once a shipment was ready to go, the manufacturer created a labeling document, and EDI sent an invoice automatically.

A great deal of this new technology was developed and used in Europe before coming to the United States.

Most of it was easily transferred to Far Eastern footwear producers, depending on the availability of capital. For these Far Eastern manufacturers, however, the labor-saving benefits of this new technology were not as great as for producers with higher production costs. Industry experts predicted that the net effect of such technology would reduce the costs of U.S. production relative to Far Eastern production, although the latter would continue to maintain a competitive advantage for most categories of footwear.

FURTHER READING

"Apparel & Footwear." *Standard & Poor's Industry Surveys,* July 1999.

Footwear Industries of America. "Statistics." Washington, DC: Footwear Industries of America, 1997.

Rossi, William A. "Athletic Footwear: Facing Hard Realities." *Footwear News,* 25 May 1998.

Sporting Goods Manufacturers Association. "Athletic Footwear Sales Slip 2 Percent in 3rd Quarter; Back-to-School Market Soft Again." 8 December 1999. Available from http://www.sportlink.com/press_room/1999_releases/m99-030.html.

"Switch Consumers Bought Fewer Athletic Shoes in 1995, but Spent More." *AFA News,* 26 March 1996. Available from http://www.sportsite.com.

"Teens Give Boot to NIKE." *U.S. News & World Report,* 9 March 1998.

U.S. Census Bureau. "Current Industrial Reports: Footwear Production - 1997." 13 August 1998. Available from http://www.census.gov/pub/industry/1/ma31a97.pdf.

———. *1995 Annual Survey of Manufacturers,* Washington, DC: GPO, 1997.

U.S. Department of Commerce. International Trade Administration. *U.S. Industry & Trade Outlook '99.* U.S. Department of Commerce/International Trade Administration and McGraw-Hill, 1999.

U.S. International Trade Commission. "Nonrubber Footwear Statistical Report, 1998." Washington, DC: U.S. International Trade Commission, 1999. Available from ftp://ftp.usitc.gov/pub/reports/studies/PUB3174.PDF.

SIC 3151

LEATHER GLOVES AND MITTENS

This category includes establishments primarily engaged in the manufacture of dress, semi-dress, and work gloves that are made exclusively of leather or leather with lining of other materials. Excluded are establishments primarily engaged in the manufacture of athletic gloves, classified in **SIC 3949: Sporting and Athletic Goods, Not Elsewhere Classified;** semi-dress and work gloves made primarily of cloth, classified in **SIC 2381: Dress and Work Gloves, Except Knit and All-Leather;** and safety gloves, classified in **SIC 3842: Orthopedic, Prosthetic, and Surgical Appliances and Supplies.**

NAICS CODE(S)

315992 (Glove and Mitten Manufacturing)

Historical data shows that the industry has been shrinking in both output and the number of manufacturers over the latter part of the twentieth century due to competition from lower-priced imports. The U.S. glove industry began about 1760 when Sir William Johnson, founder of Johnstown and Gloversville, New York, brought in a group of glove makers from Perthsire, England, to make deerskin mittens and heavy gloves for nearby farmers. Native Americans had shown Johnson how to use the local barks for dying and tanning. The abundant supply of deer hides and the availability of streams and lakes for tanning the hides and transporting the finished gloves to nearby farm communities helped the industry flourish.

Nineteenth-century inventions that mechanized glove cutting and sewing increased productivity in the industry, but the industry still needed skilled workers. In the 1890s, many glove workers came from Italy. Fulton County, where Johnstown and Gloversville are located, remained the U.S. glove-making center and was home to the now-defunct industry association and union headquarters. Through the 1930s, the U.S. Department of Labor noted, men cut most of the materials for gloves in the area's many small factories, and most of the sewing was performed by women. Sewing of the heavier work gloves was done in the factories on heavy duty machines, while work on the dress and semi-dress gloves was often done on a piece-work basis in homes.

After World War II, competition from cheaper labor abroad began to cut into the American market. In 1997, the largest single segment of the U.S. glovemaking industry remained in the Johnstown-Gloversville area of upper New York State. Some industry leaders included Elmer Little and Sons, Inc. and Aris Isotoner, Inc.

This segment of the entire glove and mitten manufacturing industry is relatively small. Of the 132 establishments, only 52 primarily deal with leather. The leather segment employs 2,059 people, while the fabric segment employs 4,467. The value of all glove shipments was also relatively small—of the 1997 total of nearly $678 million, only $239 million was from leather gloves.

FURTHER READING

U.S. Census Bureau. "Manufacturing-Industry Series." *1997 Economic Census.* Washington, D.C.: GPO, 29 November 1999.

SIC 3161

LUGGAGE

This category covers establishments primarily engaged in manufacturing luggage of leather or other materials. The luggage industry produces a wide variety of products, including suitcases, briefcases, attache cases, hand luggage, tote bags, trunks, and occupational cases. Materials used in addition to leather include plastics, nylon, cotton, linen, and metals. Many products use a combination of these materials. Construction methods include sewing, molding, and laminating.

NAICS CODE(S)

316991 (Luggage Manufacturing)

INDUSTRY SNAPSHOT

Luggage shipments increased about 17.1 percent between 1988-1989 reaching to almost $1.13 billion in 1996. Total industry employment declined 3.7 percent, to 13,000 employees, but employment in the area of production increased about 4 percent, to 10,200. This indicated that the industry was lowering overhead labor, while increasing production. In 1997 the number of employees again declined (to 9,655 people); of those 7,038 were production workers. There are more than two dozen types of occupations in the luggage/leather products industry, including sewing machine operators, plastic molding machine operators, leather workers, assemblers, inspectors, and packagers.

In 1996, the moderate economic recovery continued and resulted in slightly more travel and, hence, more demand for luggage. Luggage purchases amounted to $2.2 billion in the mid-1990s, up about 12 percent from earlier in the decade. Similarly, imports increased about 15 percent from 1.8 billion in 1994 to $2.1 billion in the mid-1990s. The value of shipments was $1.4 billion in 1997.

BACKGROUND AND DEVELOPMENT

Luggage—defined as a product designed to carry items by hand from place to place—has been around in some form or another since the beginning of time. Cave men and women likely carried sticks, stones, bones, and furs in small leather sacks or large skins as they moved from cave to cave. Egyptians packed precious objects into casket-shaped trunks and buried them in tombs with their kings and queens. In those early days, separate trunks or chests were used to transport different types of items; for example, there were jewelry, linen, and wardrobe cases. This practice endured for centuries and is still popular with those who have no need to travel lightly.

How one traveled dictated what type of luggage one used. When traveling by foot, for example, a simple sack was often sufficient. If beasts of burden were available, items were boxed or bagged and secured atop the animal. Travel by ship or barge made it possible to use large trunks and chests. Of course, the more money one had, the grander the style of travel and the type of luggage. "Heaven only knows how many people it took to get Cleopatra's barge up the Nile, Marco Polo to China, or Mrs. Vanderbilt across the Atlantic," wrote Diane Sustendal in *Showcase*. "It's only in recent years that hopping the Concorde with a single bag has become a status way to travel. Prior to that, three or more matched pieces of luggage lined up at a dock, train station, or airport said something about the status of the traveler."

Whole groups of people, she noted, have been identified by the types of luggage they carried. The "Casket Girls of Louisiana," young women sent from France to the colonies (now the United States) to marry, carried their belongings in caskets. Carpetbaggers got their name from the bags in which they carried cash and clothing to the South following the Civil War. "Old Saddlebags" referred to the early Pony Express riders who carried mail in such pouches on the back of horses. Some types of luggage have gotten their names from modes of transportation, including the coach bag, train case, flight kit, pullman case, and steamer trunk. The luggage lexicon has also been affected by war. British soldiers during World War I had their "kit bag." American G.I.s packed their belongings in a "duffle bag" or "furlough bag."

The luggage industry bubbled with new ideas after World War II. Many materials developed for the wartime effort were put to use in the industry, including rip-stop nylon, fiberglass, plastics, simulated fabric, leather, and aluminum. Manufacturers learned to design products that were durable, yet light enough to meet plane travel requirements. Luggage became available in three categories: constructed, or molded luggage; semi-constructed, with such features as side zipper entry and compartments for easy packing; and soft luggage, which is lightweight and collapsible.

Color added a fashion statement previously missing from luggage. Fashionable women travelers could choose from such colors as bright red, pale blue, pink, and cream; men had gray, navy, forest green, and burgundy as alternatives to the more conservative black or brown. In the late 1960s, the colors of luggage mimicked the colors of fashion—hot pink, neon yellow and orange, and bright blue.

By the 1970s, with the idea of space travel no longer a distant reality, luggage resembling space suit fabrics first appeared. During that same time period, "designer luggage" became the vogue, and luggage sported designer logos. As plane travel became faster and more efficient, travelers began placing a higher priority on speed. Manufacturers recognized this and devoted more of their attention on carry-on luggage, which permitted passengers to save time by avoiding check-in lines and baggage claim areas. The Mac Pac by Casecraft Incorporated illustrated this trend. This European-styled set consisted of a three-suit garment bag, a four-zipper expandable boarding case, and a 10-inch grooming kit.

In the 1980s, an era known for conspicuous consumption, customers demanded that their luggage demonstrate their wealth, status, and personal taste. They looked for classic styling, quality, and high-fashion touches. Leather, tweeds, and stripes were big sellers. For example, Henry Rosenfeld Travelware introduced several new tweeds and leather designs in 1988. One line of luggage featured interchangeable sets. Popular colors included earth tones, blue-black, burgundy, melon, pumpkin, olive green, and deep gold.

Responding to the consumers' increasing interest in quality, name-brand luggage, vendors introduced luggage with better fabrics and more features, such as zippers, pockets, and compartments to hold such items as shirts, hair dryers, running shoes, and tennis racquets. Peters Bag Corporation introduced a Sasson Executive Style Luggage set in 1989, which included a garment bag with full front zippered pocket, adjustable shoulder strap, boarding bag with dual zipper opening, front and side zipper pockets, and a utility kit with a fully-lined interior and two-way zipper.

Business Cases. Attache cases or briefcases have been around as long as people have called on clients. Scribes and physicians may have been the first to use some form of business case. Blacksmiths, cobblers, carpenters, seamstresses, musicians, and artists used bags, boxes, and small cases to transport the tools of their trade. The attache, with its hard sides and box-like construction, is a direct descendant of an artist's paint box and the scribe's writing box. Early coverings designed to protect books, letters, sketches, and legal briefs were forerunners of today's portfolios or briefcases.

Throughout the twentieth century, the functions and appearance of the business case have changed frequently and sometimes dramatically. While leather business cases are still popular, there are now more choices than ever before—molded cases of plastic or metal, fashion cases, canvas cases, and cases made of exotic skins. In the late 1980s, R.F. Kilpatric and Associates even introduced a wooden briefcase from Sweden, available in natural wood and a mahogany color. Briefcases that doubled as luggage also made their appearance.

Like luggage, business cases eventually became available in a variety of colors. Gray, burgundy, tan, forest green, even red, white, and blue became acceptable options for business executives. Such features as contrasting trim, gleaming or burnished hardware, detachable shoulder straps, and retractable handles also became available. Compartments for holding pens, business cards, calculators, checkbooks, cellular phones, computers, and mini-televisions were added to many of the new designs, as were sleeves to accommodate portfolios, notepaper, computer readouts, legal pads, agendas, and reports.

Business cases and attache's were expected to retain their traditional flavor throughout the 1990s. Sales for business cases rose 4 percent in 1996.

CURRENT CONDITIONS

In the United States, 279 establishments claimed luggage manufacturing as their primary occupation; the highest number of establishments (41) was in California. New York had 32 and Illinois had 18. Although Washington only had 8 establishments, its shipment value was higher than that of Illinois.

In terms of shipment value, the largest industry segment in 1997 was luggage with a leather or mostly leather outer surface ($90 million). Business cases of leather or mostly leather had a shipment value of $35 million that same year.

INDUSTRY LEADERS

Samsonite Corp., headquartered in Denver, Colorado, is the world's leading manufacturer of luggage. In 1996, the company had an estimated $800 million in sales. In 1999 the company reported sales of $697 million. Samsonite was founded in 1910 as the Shwayder Trunk Manufacturing Company. It was not until 1966 that the company operated under the name Samsonite. From a one-room business near downtown Denver with 10 employees, Samsonite has grown into a network of 30 manufacturing and distribution centers employing 10,000 individuals throughout the world. Samsonite products are sold in more than 100 countries.

Samsonite established its reputation by producing a product that was extremely durable. The company's original slogan (''Strong enough to stand on'') was first illustrated by a picture of founder Jess Shwayder, his father, and three of his brothers standing on a plank that rested on a Shwayder hardcase. Samosonite became famous in the 1980s with it's television commercial featuring a gorilla throwing around Samsonite luggage; the commercial emphasized the durability of the product. Today Samsonite makes both hardside and softside luggage. Hardside luggage is made by the molding and assembly of plastic components, utilizing either vacuum forming or injection molding techniques. Samsonite's softside luggage involves the manufacturing of hand-assembled luggage made of synthetic fiber materials and steel or plastic frames. The company's hardside luggage sales continued to grow dramatically in the early 1990s, particularly in the European market. Samsonite is the leading manufacturer of hardside luggage in the world. Samsonite holds 900 patents worldwide for it's luggage designs and is the parent company of the number two brand of luggage, American Tourister.

A major foreign player in the luggage industry was LVMH Moet Hennessy Louis Vuitton SA, a manufacturer of high quality luggage based in Paris, France. This company also handles champagnes, wines, and cognacs; perfumes; and fashions.

AMERICA AND THE WORLD

The resurgence of pride in America and American-made products in the 1980s prompted many luggage manufacturers to focus on American-made goods and push the "Made in the U.S.A." logo. Promoting U.S. made luggage was often challenging, however, since few luggage products are actually made in the United States. "Almost all nylon goods, whether it's Samsonite, American Tourister, Verdi, it's all imported," said Gallup. "It has the good old American name but basically it's an import." According to American Tourister manager Karl Czerny, however, approximately 25 percent of their merchandise is made in the United States. That percentage is made up primarily of hardside luggage, which is bulky and expensive to import.

FURTHER READING

Hoover' Company Profiles. Hoover's Online, 2000. Available from http://www.hoovers.com.

LeTellier, George. "Higher Fashion Key in Luggage." *Upscale Discounting,* March 1987.

Sustendal, Diane. "Where We've Been: A History of Luggage, Business Cases, Personal Leather Goods and Components." *Showcase,* November-December 1988.

U.S. Census Bureau. "Manufacturing-Industry Series." *1997 Economic Census.* Washington, D.C.: GPO, 24 January 2000.

SIC 3171

WOMEN'S HANDBAGS AND PURSES

This classification includes establishments primarily engaged in manufacturing women's handbags and purses of leather or other materials, except precious metals. Establishments primarily engaged in manufacturing precious metal handbags and purses are classified in **SIC 3911: Jewelry, Precious Metal.**

NAICS CODE(S)

316992 (Women's Handbag and Purse Manufacturing)

INDUSTRY SNAPSHOT

The women's handbag and purse industry produces all women's handbags and purses of leather and other materials, except precious metals. Approximately 64 percent of the domestic handbags shipped in the United States in the 1990s were made of leather. Handbag production shipments declined about 29 percent in 1997 to an estimated $214 million. Total industry employment plunged from the 1992 figure of 5,200 workers to just 3,530 in 1997, but increased to 7,000 in 1999.

BACKGROUND AND DEVELOPMENT

Historically, women have made most of their handbag purchases at boutique specialty stores and department stores. Consumers in the purse and handbag industry most often made handbag purchases on the basis of designer recognition and style. During the 1980s, consumers took great interest in their appearance and became slightly extravagant. Sales of high-priced and mid-range brands, such as Coach and Dooney & Bourke, proliferated. Personal consumption of handbags and other apparel accessories nearly doubled in the 1980s, with an average annual growth rate of 7.3 percent. Then, hurt by the recession, weak growth in disposable income, and high unemployment, consumers became much more cost-conscious.

Along with these economic changes came changes in consumer psychology. Designer names, high-priced accessories, and frequent shopping sprees were not as popular as they once were. Consumers became more value conscious and began purchasing less expensive products at lower-end retail establishments and mass merchandisers. A writer for *Footwear News* indicated that leather buying habits started shifting to form, function, and comfort, away from designer names.

Despite the recessionary economy, however, Coach and Dooney & Bourke products, which ranged from just above $100 to more than $400 in 1996, remained consistently strong performers. But other high-priced segments of the handbag business have not fared as well. High-priced lines like Liz Claiborne stumbled badly at the retail counters. Many experts attribute the success of Coach and Dooney & Bourke to the lines' classic/casual styling versus Liz Claiborne's dressier appearance.

Shoppers changed their handbag buying habits throughout the early 1990s. Consumer purchasing shifted toward the most basic, functional accessories. Rather than purchasing a handbag to match each outfit—the pattern during the first three-quarters of the twentieth century—shoppers began purchasing a single handbag versatile enough to match many outfits. This pattern reflected a more value-oriented consumer, as well as an aging population seeking comfort and casualness. In the past several years, many mass merchandisers have added more recognizable national brand names to their in-store inventory. In the past, most brand names were distributed only through department stores.

In 1992 specialty and department store retailers were optimistic about the growth of the handbag category, according to *Stores Magazine*. At the time, retailers were predicting increases in handbag sales ranging from a low of 8 percent to a high of 20 percent. Through 1996, however, sales were continuing to drop by an average of 4 percent a year. The key for sales success was to have the right assortment of handbags, from the moderate-priced to the higher-priced brands. By 1992, the moderate-priced handbag business doubled its 1990 sales level. Brand names such as Perry Ellis America, Capezio, and Esprit led the pack in producing fashionable handbags at moderate prices and giving retailers new inventory options.

CURRENT CONDITIONS

Shoppers began spending again in the late 1990s as the economy recovered and financial security returned. In turn, the department store shares of sales began creeping up again, and shoppers who were seeking more basic handbags and lower-priced goods in strip malls and outlet stores were going back to the department stores. According to the National Retail Federation, department store share of all apparel expenditures began rising again to 48 percent in 1996, up from 39 percent in 1995, and 30 percent on 1994. Discount stores still held the largest share at 60 percent, down from 64 percent the year before, but had loosened their grip on retailing somewhat as the economy recovered and consumers were willing to shop at the specialty and department stores. For mass retail stores such as K-mart and Wal-Mart, brand name recognition was still important, and such brands as Chic and Gitano were particularly successful. Abe Chehebar, president of Gitano handbags, told *Discount Merchandiser* that functional, organizer-style bags have been solid performers for his company. As a result, shoulder bags and totes continue to be strong performers. Chehebar also considers designer signatures on handbags to be important features because they elevate the accessories as status items.

The biggest challenge at the end of the 1990s continued to be increased competition from overseas markets. Shipments were estimated to have declined almost 14 percent from 1997 to 1998, and another 11 percent from 1998 to 1999. The next few years were expected to show a decline of another 11 percent. With a decline in production and consumption, the future is uncertain.

Storage of inventory is one of the highest expenses a retailer faces. To reduce this expense, retailers were increasingly demanding that a manufacturer carry the inventory instead and make deliveries when the retailers' stock was low. In order for this type of relationship to work, especially when dealing with the large quantities of merchandise required by stores such as Wal-Mart or K-mart,

retailers and vendors found it necessary to form partnerships. Quick response is the most important aspect of this relationship; orders must be replenished automatically via computer links called electronic data interchange (EDI).

Experts attribute the growing appeal of outlet stores to the value-conscious shopper. Outlet stores' primary draw is price. The merchandise is often top quality and comes from current inventory, although many manufacturers use their own outlet stores to move surplus and low-quality merchandise. Manufacturers prefer this form of distribution to off-price retailers because they avoid tarnishing their brand names, which can occur when too much merchandise is sold through discounters. In addition, outlet stores tend to be located away from the selling areas of conventional department and specialty stores. This decreases the chance that the manufacturer's regular retail customers will lose sales to the outlet stores.

INDUSTRY LEADERS

Throughout the late 1980s, the 10 largest publicly traded apparel and accessory companies saw their market share increase by nearly 5 percent. Part of this growth can be attributed to increased demand for these companies' products. But the remaining growth was a result of acquisitions and consolidations. As large department store retailers merged in the late 1980s, they consolidated their buying functions. Larger manufacturers benefited from this because it became more efficient for a fewer number of buyers to use one vendor rather than several. In response, growth-oriented handbag and purse manufacturers increased their acquisition activity in search of new brands and broader product offerings.

In addition, the enormous growth of large mass merchandisers was driving the industry to consolidate in the mid-1990s. From 1981 through 1991, Sears—the nation's largest retailer—saw its sales increase rapidly, as did Wal-Mart and K-mart. Historically, many brand-name manufacturers sold their goods only to department stores, but they soon began selling nearly identical merchandise to mass merchandisers and catalogues in order to participate in the phenomenal growth experienced by those sales channels. Not surprisingly, this affected the manufacturers' relationships with the department stores, who seek exclusivity in their products. To remedy the situation, many manufacturers began to produce several different categories of brand names, each of which was distributed through a different type of retailer. Each retailer had brand exclusivity within its own category.

As of 1999, the industry leaders were Pyramid Handbags Inc., Jaclyn Inc., AD Sutton and Sons, Koret Inc., JLN Inc., Ima Fashions Inc., Coach Leatherware Company Inc., Chaus Accessories, LANA MARKS Boutique, Nine West Accessories Inc., Ponte Vecchio International, and Michael Stevens Limited.

In the leather industry, 20 percent of the total work force is employed in the handbags and purses industry. However, employment was expected to continue its decline through the year 2006 due to increased competition from overseas markets and their cheaper goods and lower wages.

AMERICA AND THE WORLD

Because labor costs represent such a high proportion of total production costs, handbags and other personal leather goods industries encountered significant import competition in the 1980s and early 1990s. This competition came primarily from developing nations where wage rates are far below those in the United States. China, for example, has rapidly become the dominant supplier to the United States of all these products. Some of the world's leading brands of these goods are now produced in developing countries—a trend that is expected to continue because of the drastic differences in labor costs. Furthermore, because international demand for handbags and other leather goods rose in the early 1990s, many more developing countries with appropriate supplies of leather and suitable production skills could possibly enter the trade. Most of these developing nations enter the trade by producing travel goods or small leather articles, which tend to stay in fashion longer than women's handbags. This way, the producers have opportunities to establish steady export businesses before turning to the production of the seasonal women's handbags.

U.S. exports of handbags, luggage, and personal leather goods were $46.5 million in 1997. Mexico, Japan, and Canada were the leading exporters. Mexico was the largest market by quantity, accounting for 51 percent of all U.S. exports. However, most of these exports were cut parts for handbags that were assembled in Mexico and re-exported to the United States as finished goods. Japan was the leading market for finished U.S. handbags.

The total value of U.S. imports of women's handbags or purses was $1 billion. China and Italy commanded this market in 1997.

RESEARCH AND TECHNOLOGY

More than many other industries, production of handbags and purses is labor intensive. Therefore, like most companies, large producers of women's handbags are under extreme pressure to limit their number of employees by boosting productivity and efficiency. The industry considers new technology to be the key to increasing growth and profitability and keeping more production jobs in the United States. In recent decades, the increased use of computers has integrated design, manufacturing, management, and marketing functions. Computerized production allows manufacturers to emphasize such nonprice factors as quality and quick delivery to compete with imports.

Many handbag producers have turned to computer-aided design (CAD) and computer-aided manufacturing

(CAM) systems and software. As a result, these manufacturers can produce tooling from CAD data and link it to auto-stitchers, milling, and turning machines. Computers also enable manufacturers to combine several operations or machines under fewer operators—thereby reducing handling time and number of employees—and improve quality. The industry has also developed computerized robots to handle and transfer operations within and between production modules.

In order to meet the demands of retailers' quick response requirements, more manufacturers are utilizing electronic data interchange (EDI), which allows retailers and manufacturers to instantly communicate. The goal of quick response is to maintain lean inventories and avoid overstocking, while ensuring that retailers have the merchandise customers want to buy. In the EDI system, interlinked computer systems are placed at every point of the manufacturing and sales process. Through use of an electronic scanner and bar code that has been tagged to the merchandise, retailers record at the point of sale which merchandise has been sold. All sales data on the individual products, including details of color and size, are transmitted immediately to the manufacturer. Through this method, the manufacturer keeps track of every store's retail sales trends. This first-hand view of consumer purchasing trends allows manufacturers to produce handbags based directly on customer demand. The information contained in the bar code sets automatic reordering into motion. The industry also refers to this type of inventory replenishment as "flow" or "just-in-time." The manufacturer can quickly restock a retailer's shelves, using no more than a computer for communication. In addition to allowing automatic replenishment, EDI also enhances distribution and shipping. For example, once a shipment is ready to go, the manufacturer creates a labeling document and EDI sends an invoice automatically. In the future, EDI is likely to include electronic funds transfer as well.

Much of this new technology was developed and used in Europe before coming to the United States. Most of it can be readily transferred to Far Eastern producers, depending on the availability of capital. For these manufacturers, however, the labor-saving benefits of this new technology will not be as great as for producers with higher costs of production. Industry experts predict that the net effect of such technology will reduce the costs of U.S. production relative to Far Eastern production, although the latter will continue to maintain a competitive advantage for most categories of handbags.

Handbag producers are also making environmental breakthroughs. In late 1993, a company by the name of Holiday Fair began producing handbags made of EEKO, a mainly water-based combination of natural and synthetic rubbers with the look, feel, and colorability of leather. Holiday Fair's management team hopes this new material will eventually replace leather and leather substitutes. To promote its product, the company is placing heavy emphasis on retail and consumer educational programs that include detailed point-of-purchase literature and a store video. The company also intends to assume responsibility for the safe disposal, recycling, and reuse of all its products by using tags that offer consumers a value coupon toward their next Holiday Fair purchase if they return used handbags to the company. In January 1994, Holiday Fair also began shipping a new line of handbags made of polypropylene EEKO2, a material that emulates cotton, for products ranging from tote bags to belts.

FURTHER READING

Darnay, Arsen, J., Ed. *Manufacturing USA.* 5th ed. Detroit: Gale Research, 1996.

Hensell, Lesley. "Tandy Brands Adds Fashion Names." *Dallas Business Journal,* 24 March 1997.

Hoover's Company Capsules. *Hoover's Online.* 2000. Available from http://www.hoovers.com.

U.S. Bureau of the Census. *Economic Census 1997.* 2000. Available from http://www.census.gov.

U.S. Bureau of the Census. *1995 Annual Survey of Manufactures.* Washington: GPO, 1997.

U.S. Bureau of Labor Statistics. *Employment Statistics.* 2000. Available from http://www.bls.gov.

U.S. Bureau of Labor Statistics. *1998-99 Occupational Outlook.* 2000. Available from http://stats.bls.gov.

*U.S. Industry and Trade Outlook.*The McGraw-Hill Companies, 1999.

SIC 3172

PERSONAL LEATHER GOODS, EXCEPT WOMEN'S HANDBAGS AND PURSES

This category covers establishments primarily engaged in manufacturing small articles normally carried on the person or in a handbag, such as billfolds, key cases, and coin purses of leather or other materials, except precious metal. Establishments primarily engaged in manufacturing similar personal goods or precious metals are classified in **SIC 3911: Jewelry, Precious Metal.**

NAICS CODE(S)

316993 (Personal Leather Good (except Women's Handbag and Purse) Manufacturing)

The overall economic health of the personal leather goods industry is tied to the status of the domestic leather production industry as a whole. Both this small segment and its parent category are affected by many of the same

problems in manufacturing, labor costs, and competition with foreign-made products. The products manufactured by this industry are sometimes referred to as flatgoods due to their small dimensions; they are generally designed to fit into pockets or handbags. Such items include wallets and billfolds, coin purses, and key and cigarette cases; these goods may be manufactured wholly or partially of leather, plastic, or fabric, or from a combination of these materials.

Wallets and billfolds have historically represented the largest production segment of this industry, accounting for almost a third of all goods produced in 1989 and more than 75 percent of the total monetary value of shipments. Travel kits are the next largest portion of the flatgoods market, followed by jewelry boxes and small items such as key and eyeglass cases. This was still the case in 1997, according to the U.S. Census Bureau. Typically, manufacturers offer several product lines each season in a variety of colors and prices. Many of the products are interrelated, meaning consumers of both sexes can purchase a wallet and accompanying accouterments in a single style at the department store counter, traditionally the largest retailer of such products. This industry category also includes such items as watchbands, compacts, and business-card cases, if made from leather.

According to U.S. Department of Commerce estimates, the value of shipments for this segment of the leather manufacturing industry totaled $437.3 million in 1995. This figure represented a nearly 20 percent increase since 1990. The value of shipments fell in 1997, however, to $332.7 million. Total number of employees in this segment of the industry fell to 5,300 in 1995 from 6,400 in 1990; this number fell even further in 1997 when only 4,784 people were employed. The number of production workers in the industry, a figure that has generally accounted for nearly 80 percent of all workers engaged in the industry, stood at 3,800 in the mid-1990s, down from 5,200 in 1990; the number was 3,604 in 1997.

The number of firms engaged in the production of flatgoods has been in decline since the early 1970s. Approximately 244 firms were classified as manufacturers in this industry in 1972, but by 1987 that number declined 15 percent to 208. By 1995, there were approximately 166 establishments in the industry. The number increased slightly—to 174—in 1997. The largest number of establishments was located in California and New York.

Since the early 1970s, the personal leather goods industry in the United States has been dramatically affected by foreign-made products. Due to the skilled nature of the work, labor costs for domestic manufacturers are relatively high. The estimated average hourly wage in the industry was $7.75 for a production worker in 1995. Foreign manufacturers, most notably in China, Korea, India, and Italy, can produce flatgoods at a much reduced cost due to significantly lower wages. Because of this, the American consumer market for these products has become saturated with imported wallets, key cases, and eyeglass cases that have lower retail prices than their domestically produced counterparts.

In 1995, the United States imported $475 million in flatgoods. However, while imports continue to increase, so do exports of domestically produced flatgoods. A strong dollar and increased trade with Japan and Canada have helped to double the amount of exports since 1989. Industry leaders in the late 1990s include Tandycrafts, Inc. of Fort Worth, Texas, and Aristocraft Leather Products of Northvale, New Jersey.

FURTHER READING

U.S. Census Bureau. *County Business Patterns.* Washington, D.C.: GPO, 1996

———. "Manufacturing-Industry Series." *1997 Economic Census.* Washington, D.C.: GPO, 27 July 1999.

SIC 3199

LEATHER GOODS, NOT ELSEWHERE CLASSIFIED

This category covers establishments primarily engaged in manufacturing leather goods, not elsewhere classified, such as saddlery, harnesses, whips, embossed leather goods, leather desk sets, razor strops, and leather belting. Establishments primarily engaged in manufacturing gaskets and packing are classified in **SIC 3053: Gaskets, Packing, and Sealing Devices.** Establishments primarily engaged in manufacturing leather and sheeplined clothing are classified in **SIC 2386: Leather and Sheep-Lined Clothing.**

NAICS CODE(S)

316999 (All Other Leather Good Manufacturing)

The industry category of manufacturers of miscellaneous leather goods encompasses a broad array of unusual products with somewhat archaic uses. For example, a significant number of items classified relate to antiquated equestrian pursuits and the reliance on the horse as a primary form of transportation, as it was during the eighteenth and nineteenth centuries in the United States. For this reason, the miscellaneous leather goods industry can trace its roots back to the first skilled leather craftspeople who arrived on the North American continent with early European settlers, and even before that, back to near prehistoric times when militia units roamed much of Eurasia on horseback. The demand for such items as

saddles, feed bags, halters and harnesses, riding crops, helmets, and stirrups made from leather later declined with the advent of the industrial era.

More recently, the miscellaneous leather goods industry shifted to manufacturing products for use in factories and other mechanical establishments. Such items included textile machinery aprons, machinery belting, and sleeves and leggings for welders. Declines in the manufacturing segment of the economy led to another shift toward consumer products. This area, which dominated the industry in the 1990s, is involved in manufacturing small leather novelty items, such as leather collars and harnesses for household dogs and cats. A large portion of earnings in this industry is derived from the manufacture and sale of leather desk accessories.

Leather desk sets and holsters had the highest shipment value in 1997 at nearly $157 million. Industrial leather products and pet accessories followed with shipment values of $123 million and nearly $114 million, respectively. Equestrian accouterments accounted for $108 million, while leather novelties accounted for almost $102 million.

In the mid-1990s, there were 403 establishments in the industry, an increase of over 15 percent since 1987, when there were 349 establishments. The majority of establishments employed less than 20 people. Total value of shipments in 1995 was $507.9 million, an increase from $390.6 million in shipments in 1987. The number of workers in the industry was 7,900 in 1992, up 11 percent from 1987. By 1994, that figure was down to 6,600 and then rose slightly to 6,700 in 1995.

In 1997 the total number of establishments engaged in the industry's pursuits was 434. The number of employees also saw an increase—to 8,805. The value of shipments reached $700 million. The leading states, in terms of number of establishments, were Texas and California. The leaders, in terms of shipment value, were California and Ohio.

While finished leather accounts for the majority of material utilized by the miscellaneous leather goods industry, broadwoven fabrics, coated plastics and fabrics, and other forms of plastics are also used in industry production. In 1977, the cost of materials used by the industry in manufacturing was $154 million; five years later, the figure had risen to just $165.3 million. In 1987, the cost of materials totaled $181.4 million, a somewhat dramatic jump from the previous year's figure of $134.5 million. In 1995, the cost of materials was $149.4 million; this rose drastically in 1997 to $370.0 million.

FURTHER READING

U.S. Census Bureau. "Manufacturing-Industry Series." *1997 Economic Census.* Washington, D.C.: GPO, 19 October 1999.

STONE, CLAY, GLASS & CONCRETE PRODUCTS

FLAT GLASS

This group includes establishments primarily engaged in manufacturing flat glass. This industry also produces laminated glass, but establishments primarily engaged in manufacturing laminated glass from purchased flat glass are classified in **SIC 3231: Glass Products, Made of Purchased Glass.** Manufactured flat glass covered under this industry includes such types as building glass, cathedral glass, float glass, colored glass (including both cathedral and antique), insulating glass, laminated glass, optical glass, picture glass, sheet glass, structural glass, and window glass.

NAICS CODE(S)

327211 (Flat Glass Manufacturing)

INDUSTRY SNAPSHOT

The flat glass manufacturing market is dominated by products intended for use by the office and housing construction industry. In 1999, the construction market accounted for more than 50 percent of flat glass demand in the United States, the automotive industry accounted for a quarter of total demand, and the specialty glass market (mirrors, solar panels, and signs) accounted for 17 percent.

The fate of the flat glass industry, like that of most manufacturing industries, is inextricably linked to the status of the nation's general economy. Thus the industry suffered during the recession of the late 1980s and early 1990s, which was accompanied by a decrease in housing and nonresidential construction starts. The value of U.S. flat glass product shipments had fallen from $3.5 billion in 1987 to an estimated $2.8 billion in 1998.

As the new millennium dawned, the flat glass industry faced many challenges, including more stringent expectations for environmental responsibility and the need, shared by many industries in an age characterized by sophisticated consumers and impatient stockholders, to produce better, more technologically advanced products more cheaply. But it is also reaping benefits from a number of new technologies and new uses of glass.

One of the avenues for the industry's growth comes through an expansion of shipments abroad. U.S. flat glass producers have been somewhat frustrated in this arena by the tariff and nontariff barriers many countries have erected to keep out U.S. flat glass. In November 1999, Japanese government officials indicated that they saw no need to negotiate a new flat glass trade agreement with the United States. Under the 1995 flat glass accord, which expired at the end of 1999, U.S. and Japanese officials agreed to facilitate Japan's purchases of foreign-made glass. In rejecting U.S. pleas for a new glass trade agreement, Hideo Hato, director of the Ministry of International Trade and Industry's press division, told United Press International: "The market for flat glass is sufficiently deregulated and the object of the agreement has already been attained. It's not necessary to extend the '95 measures."

Senator Mike DeWine (R-Ohio), in assessing the barriers to U.S. flat glass exports, observed in early May 1999 that "American businesses face tough and often unfair competition in foreign markets that often do not have the same commitment to free and open markets that we have. I am pleased many of the issues and concerns raised during our last international antitrust hearing have been successfully resolved, but I remain disappointed Japanese flat glass manufacturers continue to engage in anti-competitive practices to limit competition. Those of us on Capitol Hill grow weary of Japan's tactics of delay and denial, and its failure to take meaningful steps to put an end to the anti-competitive scheme between manufacturers and distributors in its flat glass market.''

ORGANIZATION AND STRUCTURE

Flat glass producers can be divided into two major classes: makers of raw float glass and fabricators, or companies that treat raw glass with special coatings for finished products. Two popularly used types of treated glasses are tempered and laminated flat glass. Tempered glass is discussed in more detail below; information on laminated glass and other glass products can be found in **SIC 3231: Glass Products, Made of Purchased Glass.**

The U.S. flat glass industry is clearly dominated by one company, PPG Industries Inc. of Pittsburgh, Pennsylvania, whose total net sales topped $7.5 billion in 1998. Other major players in the U.S. flat glass market include Minneapolis-based Apogee Enterprises and Libbey-Owens-Ford Co., an operating unit of British-based Pilkington PLC.

The distribution of flat glass once it has been manufactured and, when applicable, processed with special coatings, occurs along a multi leveled chain, with sales possible at all levels. According to *Glass Magazine,* the normal distribution routes for domestic and imported flat glass are directly from domestic or foreign producers to fabricators, glazing contractors, and retailers or through independent glass distributors who, in turn, serve manufacturers, fabricators, glazing contractors, and retailers. However, many companies, which may have originated as either manufacturers or distributors, have found it profitable to expand from one segment of the market into another and have integrated manufacturing, fabrication, and sales into their operations.

The flat glass industry is subject to regulation by many government agencies and branches, including but not limited to the Consumer Product Safety Commission, the Environmental Protection Agency (EPA), the Occupational Safety and Health Administration (OSHA), the National Bureau of Standards, and the Department of Commerce. Standards and recommendations for the glass industry are also set by such groups as the American National Standards Institute and the Building Officials and Code Administrators International, and more specialized groups such as the National Glass Association, the Chemical Manufacturers Association, the Glazing Industry Code Committee, and the American Architectural Manufacturers Association.

BACKGROUND AND DEVELOPMENT

Archeological remains indicate that glass was first made in the form of beads or small rods in the near East (possibly Mesopotamia), beginning about 2500 B.C. Ancient glass was made from the same basic raw materials as

modern glass: sand, soda, and lime, with other materials like dolomite and salt cake added. Early glass was used to make beads, vases, and other largely aesthetic objects; its fragility and limited transparency and the difficulties inherent in its production precluded other uses.

From ancient times until the beginning of the nineteenth century, glass was made by laborious hand methods. But mechanization followed on the heels of the great advances made in science and technology in that century, and this led to decreased production costs. Flat glass also became more functional, and by 1925, 42 plants in the United States were producing 600 million square feet of sheet glass.

In 1959, the English firm of Pilkington Brothers perfected the revolutionary float glass manufacturing process, which enabled flawless clear or tinted glass to be produced without the cumbersome grinding and polishing steps that had previously been necessary. The transparency of the new float glass allowed 75 to 92 percent of visible light to be transmitted to the interior of a room. The float glass manufacturing process also brought about savings: capital investment costs decreased by 25 to 50 percent per ton of glass, and manufacturing outlays decreased by 15 to 30 percent.

The energy crisis of the 1970s forced glass manufacturers to develop energy efficient glasses, like tinted and coated glasses. However, since such glasses absorb and reflect heat, they reach higher temperatures than ordinary windows. Thus, manufacturers developed tempered glass, which is heat-treated to increase its strength and ability to resist thermal stress. Tempered glass is considered safer than ordinary glass because when broken, it shatters into cube-shaped particles without jagged edges. Tempered glass is thus ideal for high- and rough-usage areas and those that come into contact with high heat, for example, storefronts, shower doors, and fireplace screens. In addition, tempered glass cannot be cut, drilled, or edged, so it is used as a security glass in the construction and motor vehicle industries. However, use of tempered glass is limited in situations where building codes require fire-resistant glazing. In 1972, demand for tempered glass was at 317 million square feet; that number rose to 1 billion square feet in 1996.

In 1983, the glass industry took energy efficiency a step further by introducing ''low-emissivity'' glass. ''Emissivity'' refers to an object's power to radiate heat, light, etc.; in the flat glass industry, the term is used to measure the ability of window glass to control energy and minimize heat loss in cold weather. The lower a product's emissivity, the more energy efficient it is. The development of low-emissivity (low-E) glass is considered the industry's greatest advance in energy efficiency since the 1970s. Low-E glass is similar to aluminum foil in that it has an invisible, colorless, thin metallic coating that reflects radiant heat and maintains cool temperatures. It is believed that the use of low-E glass in commercial buildings decreased heating, cooling, and lighting needs by as much as 40 percent.

A trend that became apparent in the 1980s was an increased use of glass walls in new construction. Designers and building owners choose to incorporate them into building design for many reasons, including their dramatic aesthetic effect and the fact that glass is cheaper per square foot than most other, comparable, building materials.

The financial success of the flat glass industry waxed and waned over the years, usually in company with the health of the U.S. economy. The industry entered a healthy growth period in 1983, which peaked in 1987, when the value of product shipments reached $3.5 billion, the highest in 15 years. The value of flat glass shipments diminished in each subsequent year until 1992, however, when only $2 billion in flat glass products were shipped.

Concurrently, the industry experienced growing prices for raw materials. In 1992, *Glass Magazine* reported that "the cost of materials as a percentage of the value of industry shipments rose from 31.8 percent in 1970 to 38.9 percent in 1989."

The industry's labor force also suffered during this time. In 1990, the flat glass industry employed 17,000 people; in 1992, at the height of the U.S. recession, it employed only 14,700. In fact, the trend toward a smaller work force started much earlier than the recession. As early as the 1970s, manufacturers began actively seeking ways to further automate production processes, largely in an effort to reduce payroll costs. Their efforts resulted in a smaller glass work force.

The recession and its effects on demand and sales levels were not the only challenges the industry faced in the 1980s and 1990s. For example, the flat glass industry's pricing methods came under scrutiny. Since the eighteenth century, it had been standard practice for glass manufacturers, distributors, and fabricators to calculate the price of total square footage by rounding up fractional amounts. However, after a glass retailer complained of unfair pricing due to this method, officials began to reexamine the flat glass industry's overall pricing methodology. Suggested alternatives included the adoption of either a unit price method or a fractional-inch computational method. Both methods require manufacturers, wholesalers, and the entire distribution chain to reprogram or recalculate glass costs to the actual fractional-inch square footage.

The industry was also rocked by a new standard proposed by the American Society of Heating, Refrigeration, and Air Conditioning Engineers (ASHRAE). ASHRAE 90.2, which was adopted in 1993, imposes limits on fenestration (the arrangement and design of windows and doors in a building) in the design of energy-efficient, low-rise residential buildings. Fenestration area is normally 20 percent of conditioned floor area in a newly constructed single family detached home, but ASHRAE 90.2 limits that amount to 15 percent. It has been estimated that the new limitation could lead to a projected 2.75 million fewer windows sold for single-family detached homes and 750,000 fewer patio doors.

The industry also faced challenges in the 1980s and 1990s on environmental, energy, and safety fronts. Several landmark legislative actions were handed down by the Environmental Protection Agency (EPA), the Department of Energy, and various local regulatory agencies. The EPA's Clean Air Act Amendments of 1990 specifically address the hazardous rate of air pollutants emitted by specific facilities and processes. The flat glass industry has been forced to find ways to manufacture high-quality glass more cleanly; some of the technological developments in this area are discussed in the "Research and Technology" section below. The costs connected with the new law and standards, which are associated with the requirements of the law itself, the steps that a manufacturer must take to obtain an EPA permit, and the penalties that can be and are levied against the law's violators, represent one of the most serious and long-lasting legacies of this period. Other environmental concerns include water pollution and waste recycling.

CURRENT CONDITIONS

Laid low by the U.S. economic recession of the early 1990s, the flat glass industry struggled to recover, managing to increase shipments from slightly less than $2.1 billion in 1992 to nearly $2.7 billion in 1996. Shipments in 1997 and 1998 were projected to reach $2.7 billion and $2.8 billion, respectively.

Much promising research and product development took place during the 1990s, much of it focused on making glass windows more energy efficient. It has been found that adding gas between the sections of an insulating glass unit improves both thermal and sound control values. Heat loss by conduction occurs because of the tendency of heat to flow toward cooler temperatures. Argon gas filling in insulating glass slows the flow of building heat to the outside in winter and reduces the amount of outdoor heat entering the building.

Fire-resistant glass is another important and exciting segment of the glass market in the late 1990's. So-called "fire-rated glazing" is expected and required to both contain fire and allow visibility for building occupants and fire fighters during a fire. Various building codes and construction standards dictate the types of buildings, as well as which areas within buildings, must be fitted with fire-rated glass. Glass fire ratings are given in terms of time (e.g., 45 minutes). In the United States, a fire rating is achieved by first subjecting a particular glass to high-temperature flames. If a rating of more than 30 minutes is sought, the glass must then be blasted with water from a fire hose. Thus, most fire-rated glass is expected to not only withstand heat but to remain intact (and thus continue to contain fire) even after being sprayed with water from a fire hose. A related concern is the ability of glass to resist heavy impact; glass that has been tested for impact resistance is called "safety-rated" glass. In many cases, builders are required to install glass that is both fire rated and safety rated.

Wired glass was the original fire-rated glass, and in 1996, wired glass continued to be the most popular type of fire-rated glass both because of its relatively low cost (at $7 to $12 per square foot, it is by far the cheapest fire-rated glass) and because it is the oldest and best-known fire-rated glass on the market. Most wired glass carries a fire rating of 45 minutes.

But wired glass has some limitations, such as its less than artful appearance and the fact that standards prohibit its use in sizes larger than 1,296 square feet. These have increasingly made wired glass an unattractive choice for building designers and owners seeking to use larger, clear glass windows and even walls in new construction. Two of the more promising alternatives that have gained acceptance in the 1990s are glass ceramic and transparent wall panels. Glass ceramic looks like ordinary window glass and can be manipulated like glass, but its ceramic properties enable it to easily pass both portions of the fire test with ratings up to three hours. Safety-rated versions of glass ceramic are also manufactured. A transparent wall panel is, like wired glass, fire rated and safety rated, but since it has no wire mesh reinforcement, it looks better. Because it is able to act as a barrier to heat, it can be classified as a wall, not a window, and thus it is not restricted to a limited size. Transparent wall panels are made of several laminated sheets of float glass; the lamination enables them to carry the highest levels of glass safety ratings.

The issue of window labeling exploded in the 1990s. In 1995, the Canadian Window and Door Manufacturers Association (CWDMA) began a voluntary labeling program, which sets and uses a uniform "Energy Rating" (ER) standard for windows. This standard makes it easier for consumers to compare products and for building inspectors to confirm code compliance. The Canadian market is extremely important to U.S. glass manufacturers, so the Canadian initiative helped push the National Fenestration Rating Council (NFRC) of the United States to begin developing similar window and door energy performance standards. Those efforts were still underway in early 1997, but other, distinctly nonvoluntary, labeling programs have already begun in the United States. The

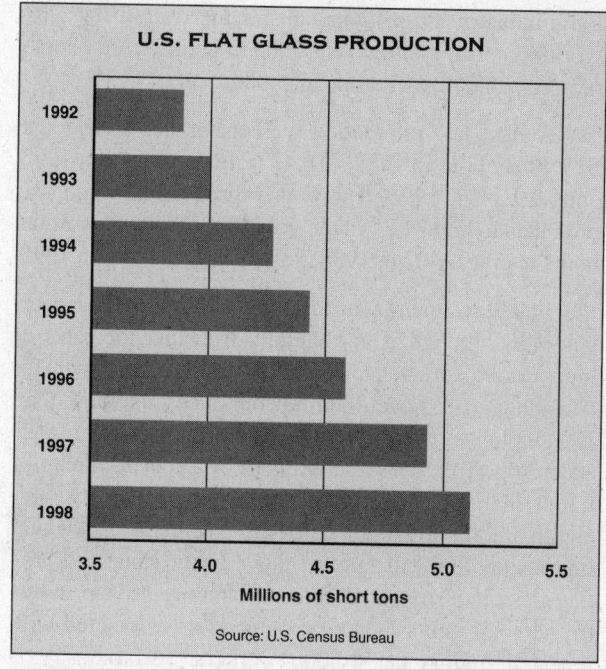

Source: U.S. Census Bureau

1996 Building Codes include detailed and fairly complex rules on the labeling of wired and laminated glass. In some cases, the labels must be permanent; the code specifies that labels for tempered glass be either etched or ceramic fired. A February 1996 *Glass Magazine* article, "Building Codes Update," quoted an industry analyst saying that the new regulations were "one of the most onerous things that have happened to the glass industry."

INDUSTRY LEADERS

The three leading U.S. flat glass manufacturers were PPG Industries Inc.; Apogee Enterprises Inc. of Minneapolis, Minnesota; and Libbey-Owens-Ford Co., an operating division of the United Kingdom's Pilkington PLC.

PPG, a flat glass and fiberglass manufacturer, is by far the overall U.S. glass industry leader. PPG sales were reported at $7.5 billion dollars in 1998, up 1.8 percent from the previous year. A distant second in terms of U.S. flat glass sales, Apogee Enterprises reported 1998 sales of $792 million, down more than 13 percent from the previous year. Pilkington PLC, the British parent of Libbey-Owens-Ford, reported total worldwide earnings of nearly $4 billion in fiscal 1999, the twelve months ended March 31, 1999.

WORKFORCE

In 1979 the flat glass industry employed about 19,500 workers; by 1996 that number had fallen to 11,500. The number of production workers experienced a parallel decline, from 15,200 in 1979 to 9,300 in 1996. Analysts attribute the work force reduction to manufacturing automation and production trimming, as well as to the oft-mentioned recession and its effects on the flat glass industry. Projections call for the overall flat glass workforce to fall in the year 2000 to about 9,700 people, of whom 8,000 will work in production.

A flat glass production worker earned, on average, $15.90 per hour in 1987, $16.49 in 1992, $17.95 in 1995, and $19.39 in 1996. The hourly production wage was projected to hit $21.34 in the year 2000. Weekly overtime hours averaged 7.7 in 1988, 5.9 in 1992, and 7.1 in 1995.

Flat glass manufacturing can be difficult and dangerous work, though it is generally true that the rates of injury and work-related illness tend to be lower for companies with fewer than 50 employees and more than 100 employees than for mid-size establishments. In 1995, according to the U.S. Department of Labor's Bureau of Labor Statistics, the flat glass industry ranked twenty-eighth among private industries for incidents of nonfatal injuries per 100 full-time workers. In the same year, the flat glass industry rated sixteenth among private industries for incidents of nonfatal disorders associated with repeated trauma per 10,000 workers. (An industry is considered "high rate" in either category if it ranks among the top 25).

AMERICA AND THE WORLD

Most U.S. flat glass manufacturers are engaged in some type of international commercial activity, either through joint ventures with foreign firms, licensing of technology to foreign producers, or acquisition of all or part of foreign flat glass manufacturers. The industry experienced a trend toward globalization in the 1980s. For example, in 1986, one of the major U.S. flat glass manufacturers, the Libbey-Owens-Ford Co., was bought by the British glass making giant, Pilkington, while U.S. firms like Guardian and PPG expanded by setting up factories overseas.

The value of flat glass exports from the United States rose each year from 1989 through 1996. In 1989, the United States exported $333 million worth of flat glass products, while in 1997, it exported shipments worth $810 million. The value of imports did not change as drastically during this period: in 1989, the United States imported $302 million worth of flat glass, while in 1996, it imported flat glass worth $492 million.

According to the January-February 1996 issue of *Chemical Industries Newsletter*, North America is the largest consumer of flat glass in the world, with 32 percent of total demand, followed by Asia/Oceania (29 percent), western Europe (26 percent), eastern Europe (6 percent), Africa and the Middle East (4 percent), and Central and South America (3 percent). It is expected that the majority of growth in flat glass demand through the year 2000 will come from the industrializing regions of South America and Asia.

Major foreign players in the international flat glass industry are Asahi Glass of Japan, Pilkington of England, and Saint-Gobain of France.

RESEARCH AND TECHNOLOGY

Computers and the Internet are causing major changes in the way that glass manufacturers, distributors, and retailers do business. Most obviously, information about glass products and manufacturing standards and specifications is increasingly available via the World Wide Web, so consumers can compare products and prices at many "stores" from home and manufacturers can access important information instantly. Plant management has also been revolutionized by new, increasingly advanced and user-friendly business computing tools.

Research continues in the area of energy efficiency. While great progress has already been made in improving the ability of window glass to keep heat and sound in or out of a room, some researchers have turned their attention to the window edge, where spacer design and construction can lead to significant heat loss, decreasing overall window energy efficiency by as much as 25 percent. "Warm edge technology" is helping manufacturers to better seal window perimeters by replacing the traditional frost-prone metal window spacers with high strength, thin stainless steel, molded-in thermal breaks, and split spacers or silicone foam. This not only helps to keep the temperature of the entire window higher, but reduces the incidence of condensation and frost. Though products using warm edge technology were available in 1997, it is fair to say that the technology is still developing. It is not yet known, e.g., how long existing products can be expected to last. And manufacturers are looking for a way around the facts that warm edge materials are often more expensive than standard ones and that many require an entirely new production system.

Improving low-E glass technology was considered a cutting-edge research problem in the late 1980s and early 1990s, and great strides were made in reducing emissivity. In the late 1990s, a better and more energy efficient window is still on many researchers' to-do lists, but now more demands have been added. In the May 1996 issue of *Glass Digest*, Day Chahroudi noted in "Smart Windows," that "it is becoming apparent that the glass industry expects its next major market expansion to come from . . . optical shutters, or smart windows." The technologies referred to here as "optical shutters" allow windows to perform some of the same functions as shutters or curtains—keeping sunlight out of a room, allowing it into a room, and even allowing daytime one-way viewing.

Another promising product under consideration is switchable glass, a liquid crystal glass that can be wired to any structure's electrical system and operated by flipping a switch. Liquid crystals make the glass cloudy but permit sufficient light without obstructing visibility. The electrical current changes the glass from opaque to clear. Its current use is in interior applications such as partitions and conference rooms, where privacy and optional visibility are desirable.

Tighter environmental regulations, specifically emissions standards, have brought about a significant manufacturing innovation—oxygen-fuel (oxy-fuel) combustion. According to Rich Deal, in *Glass Industry,* oxy-fuel offers many significant advantages over conventional combustion systems. Most crucial among these to the U.S. industry is significantly lower NOx and particulate emissions, but others include higher melt rates, reduced fuel consumption, improved workability of the resulting glass product, and the declining cost of producing on-site oxygen. Manufacturers in the late 1990s are still making the switch to oxy-fuel, and there are some real, if predictable, technological and efficiency issues still to solve.

FURTHER READING

Button, David A. "Glass for the Year 2000." *Glass Digest,* 15 January 1990.

"CEH Abstract: Glass Industry Overview." *Chemical Industries Newsletter,* January-February 1996.

Chahroudi, Day. "Smart Windows." *Glass Digest,* 15 May 1996.

Cunningham, R.C. "Industry Survey Finds Optimism in all Segments." *Glass Digest,* 15 June 1996.

Deal, Rich. "1997 Forecast Sees More Industry Change." *Glass Industry,* January 1997.

"The Evolution of the Industry over the Past Seven Decades." *Glass Digest,* 15 August 1996.

Francke, Hans-Christian. "Recommendations for Low-Emissivity Glasses." *Glass Digest,* 15 May 1996.

"How the Industry Fared in 1996." *Glass Industry,* July 1996.

Joelson, Daniel. "It's Blue Skies in 1996, But There are Some Clouds, Too." *Glass Digest,* 15 January 1996.

Johns, Nicole. "Building Codes Update." *Glass Magazine,* February 1996.

"Looking at Economic Factors, Things Appear Bad." *Glass Digest,* 15 August 1996.

Penrod, Bret E. "Trends in Flat Glass Raw Materials." *Glass Digest,* 15 August 1996.

Pilkington PLC. "Interim Results for the Six Months to 30 September 1999." Available from http://www.pilkington.com/mediafoc/index.htm.

PPG Industries Inc. "PPG Reports on 3rd Quarter; Posts $57 Million in Charges," 1999. Available from http://www.ppg.com/frames/finnews.htm.

"A Preview of Fenestration in the Year 2000." *Fenestration.* New York: Ashlee Publishing Company, 1989.

Razwick, Jerry. "Fire-Rated Glazing Comes of Age." *Glass Magazine,* February 1996.

U.S. Bureau of the Census. *1995 Annual Survey of Manufactures.* Washington, D.C.: GPO, 1997.

U.S. Bureau of the Census. *Current Industrial Reports.* Washington, D.C.: GPO, 1998.

U.S. Bureau of Labor Statistics. *Employment, Hours, and Earnings. United States, 1988-96.* Washington, D.C.: GPO, 1996.

SIC 3221

GLASS CONTAINERS

This category includes establishments primarily engaged in manufacturing glass containers for commercial packing and bottling, and for home canning. Products include ampoules; bottles, containers, jars, and jugs for packing, bottling, and canning; carboys; cosmetic jars; fruit jars; medicine bottles; packers' ware; vials; and water bottles.

NAICS CODE(S)

327213 (Glass Container Manufacturing)

INDUSTRY SNAPSHOT

In 1998, the industry shipped 253.7 million gross of glass containers, a decline of less than half a percent from 1997 shipments of 254.5 million gross. Imports of glass containers in 1998 totaled 24.8 million gross, compared with 23.9 million gross in 1997. Glass container exports totaled 9.4 million gross, compared with 8.2 million gross in 1997. There were approximately 61 establishments in the industry in 1998, a decrease of 38 percent from 1990. The industry's workforce in 1998 totaled about 19,000 workers, a decline of more than 48 percent from payroll levels in 1990.

Production of glass containers in 1998 totaled 256.4 million gross, an increase of 3.6 percent from the 247.4 million gross produced in 1997. More than three-quarters of the glass containers produced in 1998 were of the narrow-neck variety, with the remainder falling into the wide-mouth category. Nearly 80 percent of the glass containers shipped in 1998 were of the narrow-neck variety, with the remainder consisting of wide-mouth containers.

A *Packaging* magazine survey in 1986 proved that promotion of glass containers had been successful. For several years, advertisers within the glass manufacturing industry have focused on the positive aspects of glass container use. At one point, glass container manufacturers sponsored advertising campaigns touting their product as a naturally pure, recyclable taste protector. Particularly innovative was the industry's Nickel Solution Trust, formed in 1983 by a coalition of labor organizations and glass container manufacturers. Employees of glass container companies pledged a nickel of each hourly pay, and the employers contributed matching funds to pay for glass promotions. Since its inception, the trust has expended more than $21 million for recycling program development and management. Despite aggressive promotions such as these, the glass container market remained sluggish. Consequently, the glass container industry has become smaller but also much smarter. Promotion, however, continues to target those areas where glass retains a winning edge as a premium product.

ORGANIZATION AND STRUCTURE

The glass container industry manufactures two basic types of containers: narrow neck and wide mouth containers. The industry further classifies containers by their end use, creating categories of glass designated for food, beverages, beer, liquor, wine; chemical, household, and industrial uses; toiletries and cosmetics; and other uses including medicinal and health supplies. Wide mouth and narrow neck bottles are used interchangeably, depending on the product, but tradition or utility occasionally dictates specific bottle types. For example, milk is normally packaged in wide mouth containers, both wide mouth and narrow neck bottles are used for cosmetics, while narrow neck bottles are more practical for perfumes.

Consumer preferences and marketing strategy often combine to determine whether a product is packaged in a wide mouth or narrow neck container. One company used feedback from consumer focus groups to determine the best container for mustard. Participants expressed preference for a wide-mouth jar that would allow the use of a large serving spoon or spatula. The company's selection of a wide mouth container originated from an entirely different perspective. A smaller jar, in the company's estimation, connoted saving the product for special occasions rather than using it as a special item for everyday meals. Thus, the selection of wide-mouth jars satisfied consumer preferences and complemented the company's marketing strategy.

Shape is the most important feature of a bottle. To be practical, a bottle must be able to stand up, have a filling mouth, and withstand a variety of mechanical handling devices such as washing machines, filling tubes, labelers, and conveyors. According to experts, spherical-shaped containers present the most efficient use of glass container weight. After the sphere, the most efficient use of glass is a cylinder with similar dimensions of diameter and height. The container industry generally favors glass shapes characterized by broad, rounded shoulders, edges, and corners. To ensure maximum strength, the industry avoids the use of square or rectangular shapes, flats or panels, or offsets. Glass containers are also designed to convey a brand image. Clear beveled-edge bottles offer

high profile products an advantageous shelf presence and easy handling benefits for consumers.

Even more marketable are glass containers combining eye-catching designs with a functional after-life as decanters or collector items. A few decades ago, small, odd-sized and shaped bottles were replaced by standardized bottles, in part because manufacturers discovered that standardized bottles could be produced faster using the old machinery. While most odd-shaped bottles have disappeared, they are now prized and traded as antique collectibles. In the 1990s, Dr Pepper issued a commemorative bottle saluting the involvement of U.S. troops in Operation Desert Storm. In contrast, plastic or aluminum containers rarely offer any collectible value. For the industry, bottle collecting could increase industry share of the beverage market by 3 percent and account for 25 percent of all glass beverage bottles.

Manufacturers capitalize on designer appeal of glass containers by constantly adding innovative styles. Each year, the Glass Packaging Institute recognizes creative glass containers by granting awards in several categories, including food, beverage, package design, label, environmental awareness, and mature product repositioning. In 1989, Fireworks Popcorn captured first place as winner in the overall food category. The award winning package highlighted the product's vivid popcorn colors by using a clear, reusable 15-ounce jar shaped like a home canning jar. In the beverage category, first place honor went to Ocean Spray's choice of a large, collector-type glass carafe packaging its premium fruit juice.

Changing the design of a glass container entails more than adding a new face. Most design changes create a ripple effect on the overall product manufacturing process, affecting cost and product positioning. Even the slightest modifications—such as availing a round food jar or adding a modest blown-in decorative effect—can increase the container's weight by 20 percent. Maintaining lighter weight without reducing container strength highlights one persistent industry concern. One solution to the weight problems is the use of the narrow neck press and blow technology capable of manufacturing more efficient containers at 15 to 20 percent lighter weights. Another possible solution to weight reduction of glass containers is the development of a process that uniformly maintains glass wall thickness and enhances the container strength through some type of coating. The results would be a 12-ounce capacity container made in the 3 to 4 ounce weight range. According to an industry spokesperson, once manufacturers improve control over the container production process, weight problems will be alleviated.

Many gloriously designed containers generate both consumer delights and production havoc. For example, Welch's redesign of a popular jelly jar featuring a new tear drop-shaped container proved popular with consumers but caused countless cost and handling problems. Because the tapered glass jar was smallest at the bottom, with jar-to-jar contact only at the shoulder, containers frequently toppled over on the conveyors. Case packing of the tear-drop jars necessitated manual rather than the usual mechanical handling, thereby adding three packers per shift. Because of the additional costs accompanying the new design, the company redesigned the container by making the container base the same diameter as the shoulders. The slightly heavier jar caused a modest increase in freight costs, but by eliminating the jar's tip-over tendency, case packing increased by 2,000 per shift, thereby eliminating the need for additional production shifts.

For many other products, the image qualities of glass containers combine with other features to convey a unique premium appeal. Glass packaged wine coolers, for example, were tremendously popular in the mid-1980s, with sales as high as three million bottles daily. Analysts attributed the boom in part to the popularity of the single-serving bottle, a concept that was virtually unknown a few years earlier. Successful demonstration of the concept with wine coolers led to single-serve juice beverages and later bottled water. Gatorade, for one, reported a 30 percent sales increase in one year following introduction of a 16-ounce, single-serve, wide mouth bottle, conveniently suitable for carrying "at the point of sweat." More than 100 companies later joined the promotion of the single-serve bottles' health advantages. The single-serve concept also motivated distilled spirits producers to carve their niche by introducing spirit coolers in single-serve glass bottles.

BACKGROUND AND DEVELOPMENT

For centuries, glass objects were made by artisans using hand blowing methods. Many products created by these highly trained craftsmen now adorn art museum collections. Mechanization came to the glass-making industry with the industrial revolution and subsequent introduction of pressing machines. This and other refinements promoted a range of new designs and uses of glass containers. Wide mouth Mason jars became popular in the United States in the early 1900s, while the popularity of narrow neck jars developed more slowly.

M.J. Owens and E.D. Libbey initiated a new process of bottle making by filling and dipping the first or blank mold into hot glass and evacuating the air from the mold. Several years of experimentation finally led to the development of an automated bottle machine. By 1920, 200 of these automatic machines accounted for approximately 45 percent of the total U.S. bottle production.

In 1975, the Environmental Protection Agency (EPA) issued standards and guidelines covering wastewater discharges from glass container manufacturing plants. The regulations targeted oil and grease pollution

that originated from soluble oils used in glass shearing, machine lubrication, and condensation from compressed air systems. Oil and grease pollution stems from the biodegradable nature of emulsified oil that subjects cullet quench systems (broken or refuse glass added to new material to facilitate the glass-making procedure) to severe biological growth problems. According to *Glass Magazine,* biological growth within cullet quench systems degrades oil and grease removal efficiency, often resulting in discharge values exceeding regulatory standards. Additionally, the biologically fouled cullet quench system precipitates a potential health hazard in the form of Legionnaire's Disease, as well as contributes to unpleasant working conditions.

CURRENT CONDITIONS

In 1998, production of glass containers amounted to 256.4 million gross, while shipments totaled only 253.7 million gross. The previous year, glass container output totaled 247.4 million gross, outpaced by shipments of 254.5 million gross. Shipments of narrow neck containers in 1998 totaled 200.9 million gross, while wide mouth container shipments numbered 52.8 million gross. This compared with 1997 shipments of 200.5 million gross of narrow neck containers and nearly 54.0 million gross of wide mouth containers. Production and shipment of narrow neck containers consistently outrank those of wide mouth containers. Wide mouth containers are most popular for food, including dairy products, and have held steady sales and production over the last few years. The lowest shipment and production levels are for narrow neck and wide mouth chemical, household, and industrial containers. At best, the glass container industry can be described as flat. Bottle shipments, according to analysts, will likely remain flat. Continued overcapacity and the threat of conversion to alternative packaging stands to keep price increases in the 3.0 to 3.5 percent range.

Several factors contribute to the flat conditions of the glass container industry. Since the 1980s, the glass container market has suffered a steady loss of market share to alternate plastic and can packaging. Analysts point to the beer industry as a major factor causing the decline of the glass container industry. More than 85 percent of the decline was due to brewers switching to aluminum cans, and the lingering residual of this change still poses an imminently significant threat, in the industry's opinion. Statistics may well support this threat. Although shipment and production of beer bottles remain high, at about 88 million, analysts feared a decline as higher price tags forced consumers to switch to lower-priced canned beer.

One drawback to recycling cited by the Glass Packaging Institute relates to forced deposit laws requiring a consumer to pay a deposit and then return the containers to the store for a refund. The industry perceives such legislation as devastating to the market share of environmentally friendly glass containers and argues that it sways consumers to use plastic. GPI believes the most effective way to reduce solid waste is not forced deposit laws, but comprehensive curbside recycling. The practice of bottle refilling as an alternative to recycling may experience a comeback.

The Glass Packaging Institute noted that the 1990s began with five major bottling companies switching from plastic to glass containers, because of consumer preference, environmental climate, and packaging costs. According to investment analysts, however, falling resin prices could be an omen signaling a return to plastic. In 1989, a price differential of 20 percent between plastic and glass caused plastic to lose its market share to glass, primarily in the area of 16-ounce containers. When the differential was closer to 5 percent or less, plastic regained some of its share. Until the glass container industry develops a more cost-competitive, lighter weight, or break-resistant package, analysts foresee fewer gains derived from the anticipated growth of the soft drink market.

Another challenge facing the glass container industry involves raw materials leftover from the manufacturing process. According to an industry spokesperson, only 85 to 90 percent of the melted raw materials are converted to a marketable product. The remaining 10 to 15 percent of raw material becomes cullet or discarded waste, mostly broken glass. Industry leaders are attempting to devise satisfactory uses for this cullet.

Hurt during the first nine months of 1999 by "severe economic conditions in emerging markets in South America and Eastern Europe," industry leader Owens-Illinois reported in October 1999 that increased domestic shipments of beer, juice, and tea containers had largely offset declines in the demand for certain food, liquor, drug, and chemical containers. Joseph H. Lemieux, the company's CEO, said that "despite current problems in some international markets, most of our businesses are continuing to perform well. We believe that our businesses have excellent potential for long-term earnings growth, including the operations in countries where we have experienced recent difficulties due to adverse economic conditions."

INDUSTRY LEADERS

The undisputed leader in the glass container industry is Owens-Illinois, which posted 1998 revenue of $5.3 billion. Other major players in the North American market include Anchor Glass Corp., a subsidiary of Canada's Consumers Packaging; Ball Corp.; and Mexico's Vitro. Toronto-based Consumers, which employs 2,400 worldwide, reported 1998 sales of about $891.0 million, while Ball Corp., based in Broomfield, Colorado, posted revenue of $2.9 billion. Vitro's sales in 1998 hit $2.5 billion.

WORKFORCE

In 1998, the industry employed about 19,000 people, down more than 48 percent from 1990. Production workers' average weekly hours were 44.8 in 1998, up from 42.1 in 1990. Production workers' average hourly earnings were $17.81 in 1998, up from $14.38 in 1990.

Noting significant improvements in labor productivity per unit, an Owens-Illinois spokesperson commented that producing a quality product still requires an excessive amount of work. Labor constitutes 35 percent of the cost of glass, but only 9 percent and 13 percent for cans and plastic, respectively. Although use of sophisticated control systems in the future will require more operator interpretation rather than intervention, production workers must be better trained and more knowledgeable than most manufacturing employees.

RESEARCH AND TECHNOLOGY

Flexibility may determine the glass container's response to its environmental challenges. Glass is 100 percent recyclable. A used glass container can be melted and repeatedly made into a new glass container. Furthermore, glass recycling creates no additional waste or byproducts. Yet glass recycling ranks lower than that of plastic. The Glass Packaging Institute (GPI), the glass container industry's trade group, questions the Environmental Protection Agency's (EPA) statistics quoting the recycling rate for glass at 10 to 12 percent, plastic at 20 percent, and aluminum cans at 55 percent. Still, glass retains a positive recyclability perception. In contrast, recyclability of plastic beverage containers is accepted by only 20.7 percent of consumers.

Recent testimony before a Congressional subcommittee by the Glass Packaging Institute cited three major problems for the glass industry's recycling program: Plants are located primarily on the East and West coasts and the Southeast, transporting recycled glass from community collection facilities to these plants proves expensive; recycling of increasing amounts of imported green containers exceeds the domestic demand for these containers; and loose quality control at local collection sites, mixing recyclable and nonrecyclable glass, damages the manufacturing process. The most viable recycling solution, according to some experts, comes from less packaging. In the last 10 years, 16-ounce glass bottles have been reduced by 30 percent, thus lowering the amounts of materials and waste.

To date, a few technologies have demonstrated capacity for breaking up oil and grease found in glass container plant wastewater. One technology consists of carbon absorption, a process in which wastewater passes through a bed of activated carbon that absorbs the oil and grease. This process is more applicable to small flows with relatively low oil and grease loadings. The process of chemical coagulation followed by dissolved air flotation (DAF) is another process where chemical emulsion breakers and other processes are added to wastewater to break emulsion. DAF has been successfully used and research studies continue to study various emulsion breaking chemistries.

Since 1975, compliance with national standards has enabled glass container manufacturers to make significant improvements in control of oil and grease in wastewater. In the 1990s, companies placed greater emphasis on research and development to upgrade wastewater treatment technologies to comply with stringent state and local effluent standards.

In the future, the recyclable features of glass products could play a major role in safe disposal of hazardous waste, according to the editor of *Glass Industry*. The Department of Energy opened a new $1.3-billion Defense Waste Processing Facility in South Carolina designed to test the feasibility of encasing radioactive materials in glass. This process, known as vitrification, entails encasing hazardous waste in ''logs'' of strong glass, wrapped in steel. Steel cylinders measuring 10 feet high and 2 feet around each hold 165 gallons of waste.

Parallelling this project was an experiment during the 1990s at the California-based Lawrence Livermore National Laboratory on radioactivity released from glass. A computer model was designed to predict the release of radioactivity, if any, from a nuclear waste repository incorporating glass. To ensure adequate leakage prevention of harmful radioactive material from glass, scientists performed a variety of laboratory experiments and computer simulations of potential environmental scenarios that might be affected by radioactive leaks.

Large and small glass container manufacturers have spent millions for high-tech equipment and computerized operations. Part of the $40 million Anchor Glass expended in the 1990s was for the installation of sophisticated quality control equipment on all the company's production lines. Wheaton Glass completed a $10 million investment in manufacturing operations of containers for the parenteral drug and the cosmetics industries. Over a period of three years, Kerr invested in excess of $22 million for improvements such as computerized furnace control systems, high-productivity forming machines, and quality control equipment.

Considerable industry attention now focuses on eliminating weak spots of containers by uniform redistribution of glass. The benefits would be strong, lightweight containers with less glass produced faster and less expensively than at present. Several companies have achieved outstanding results by improving traditional machinery such as the latest press-and-blow molding. Owens-Illinois's ''ten-quad machine'' claims to be the fastest forming machine for glass containers in the United States. It operates at speeds of more than 450 containers per minute.

Glass coatings remain a significant aspect of research and development. Through a program identified as the Advanced Glass Treatment Systems, various coatings for strength enhancement of glass containers are being studied. Manufacturers are also experimenting with sophisticated hot- and cold-end coatings to reduce breakage and scuffing. These coatings also increase container filling speeds. A New York-based company developed a coating procedure identified as the Brandt Color Coat process. The water-based acrylic coating expands colors and textures of glass beverage bottles. Glass can be tinted in a range of desired colors combined with transparent opaque, matte, or frost finishes. The process offers more cost-effectiveness and more scratch-resistance than conventional bottle-tinting methods, plus a resistance to ultraviolet light, normally harmful to beverages such as beer. It also allows bottle labels to be printed with UV-cured inks without fear of harm to the contents. Anchor Glass Container is the only U.S. manufacturer to offer this new product.

In August 1999, industry leader Owens-Illinois announced that it had developed a new bottle making process that substantially reduces the amount of glass consumed. The end result is a lighter bottle, more easily handled by the consumer, and a production process that is quicker and more cost effective. The company said its new Duraglas XLT bottles retain all the functionality of current bottles but add increased strength while lowering the consumption of energy and raw materials in the production process. In announcing the new technology, Joseph H. Lemieux, Owens-Illinois chairman and CEO, said that, ''The process for producing Duraglas XLT bottles is a major advance in glass container manufacturing, which will enable our customers to offer consumers the premium image of glass on an even more efficient and competitive basis with other rigid packaging materials. By dramatically reducing the amount of raw material and energy required in the manufacturing process and increasing the rate of production, Duraglas XLT containers help make glass one of the most cost effective and environmentally friendly, 100 percent recyclable choices in packaging.''

FURTHER READING

''Owens-Illinois Builds a Better Glass Bottle.'' *PR Newswire,* 16 August 1999.

''Owens-Illinois Reports Third Quarter Results.'' *PR Newswire,* 21 October 1999.

Tooley, Fay V., ed. *The Handbook of Glass Manufacture.* Vol. 2. Ashlee Publishing Co., 1985.

U.S. Bureau of the Census. *1995 Annual Survey of Manufactures.* Washington, D.C.: GPO, 1997.

U.S. Bureau of the Census. *Current Industrial Reports.* Washington, D.C.: GPO, 1998.

U.S. Department of Commerce. ''Glass Containers: Summary for 1996.'' *Current Industrial Reports.* Washington, D.C.: GPO, 1996.

SIC 3229

PRESSED AND BLOWN GLASS AND GLASSWARE, NOT ELSEWHERE CLASSIFIED

This category includes establishments primarily engaged in manufacturing glass and glassware, not elsewhere classified, pressed, blown, or shaped from glass produced in the same establishment. Establishments primarily engaged in manufacturing textile glass fibers are also included in this industry, but establishments primarily engaged in manufacturing glass wool insulation products are classified in **SIC 3296: Mineral Wool.** Establishments primarily engaged in manufacturing fiber optic cables are classified in **SIC 3357: Drawing and Insulating of Nonferrous Wire;** and those manufacturing fiber optic medical devices are classified in the surgical, medical, and dental instruments and supplies industries. Establishments primarily engaged in the production of pressed lenses for vehicular lighting, beacons, and lanterns are also included in this industry, but establishments primarily engaged in the production of optical lenses are classified in **SIC 3827: Optical Instruments and Lenses.** Establishments primarily engaged in manufacturing glass containers are classified in **SIC 3221: Glass Containers,** and those manufacturing complete electric light bulbs are classified in **SIC 3641: Electric Lamp Bulbs and Tubes.**

NAICS CODE(S)

327212 (Other Pressed and Blown Glass and Glassware Manufacturing)

INDUSTRY SNAPSHOT

The pressed and blown glassware industry manufactures products ranging from television tubes, ashtrays, candlesticks, stemware, tobacco jars, and optical lenses to Christmas tree ornaments. Throughout the 1980s and 1990s, the industry maintained a steady level of employment at about 37,000 workers, while the value of shipments rose steadily to reach $6.1 billion by 1997. The total number of establishments engaged in the industry also grew during the 1980s and 1990s, from 331 in 1982 to 515 in 1997.

ORGANIZATION AND STRUCTURE

The companies involved in the pressed and blown glass industry displayed much diversity in earnings and employment levels. Of the 515 industry establishments in 1997, only 111, or 21.5 percent, employed 20 or more people. However, the industry was dominated by large companies related in some way to Corning Incorporated, such as Owens-Corning, Owens-Illinois, and Owens-Corning Fiberglass. Anchor Hocking Glass, a division of Newell Rubbermaid Inc., was another giant in the industry, although dwarfed by the Corning units. Steuben Glass (a Corning company) and Lenox Crystal were among those companies making handmade stemware, both of which shared the international market with Waterford Crystal of Ireland.

Due to the resurgence of interest in glass blowing in the United States, small craft shops could be found across the country where artisans sold their wares, displayed their techniques, and often taught classes. However, these shops were generally neither involved nor interested in producing the mass quantities of machine-made glassware supplied by such large corporations as the Corning conglomerate.

The product share within the industry was split between five types of goods. Textile glass fiber accounted for 33 percent of the overall market; machine-made table, kitchen, art, and novelty glassware claimed roughly 17 percent; machine-made lighting and electronic glassware took another 30 percent; all other machine-made glassware accounted for about 16 percent; and handmade pressed and blown glassware claimed approximately 4 percent. The materials consumed in the greatest amounts by the industry included all types of glass sand; sodium carbonate (soda ash); industrial organic chemicals other than sodium carbonate; other chemicals and allied products; and wood boxes, pallets, skids, and containers.

BACKGROUND AND DEVELOPMENT

The Mesopotamians were credited by archaeologists with making the world's first glass, circa 2500 B.C. However, it was not until the Roman Empire that glass making evolved as a standard craft, much like baking and jewelry making. Venice eventually became known as the glass making capital of the world and remained so through the 1600s. Glass making in the United States was very much a crude art form until the eighteenth century, but it nearly died out several times. Glass items of any quality, such as windows or glassware, needed to be bought from England. However, several small shops where glass was blown provided wares for limited customer bases, and eventually larger manufacturers, such as Bakewell and Company of Pittsburgh, entered the marketplace. For the cosmetic enhancement of glass, etching was practiced during the seventeenth and eighteenth centuries. However, the ability to press glass in very large quantities did not develop until the nineteenth century.

The glass industry in the United States started to boom after the War of 1812. Between 1800 and 1825, America experienced strong demographic, economic, and political growth. Luxury items were in ever-increasing demand, creating a need for machine-made glass products. Glass pressing was already common in Europe by the late 1700s, although the pieces were small and made with waffle-iron-type presses. American inventors developed the first large, hand-operated pressing machine.

The introduction of glass pressing created a new challenge for glass makers. Only specific glass mixtures were adequate for pressing, which required experimentation. Also, experience was required to know how much molten glass could be placed in a press without scrapping the piece and how much time was required to produce the glass before it started to cool and crack. By the time these processes were perfected, glass makers started to produce molds exhibiting ornate designs, referred to as ''lacy glass.'' Glass pressing continued to evolve during the colonial era, expanding to candlesticks and lamps. The Victorian era heavily influenced glass making, and by the 1880s, colored glass was the order of the day. Glass collecting became a pastime for many and an obsession for some, evidenced by collectors willing to pay heavily for early American, lacy, carnival, and depression glassware.

CURRENT CONDITIONS

The pressed and blown glass industry in the late 1990s experienced low margins, high competition, and high technology. While glass tableware and cooking dishes did not share the high-tech image of fiber optic cables and devices, research and development continued for better materials for these purposes. Likewise, new marketing approaches, such as creative packaging and merchandising, were constantly investigated.

INDUSTRY LEADERS

In the 1990s, many of the top-ranking companies in the entire glass industry were related in some fashion to Corning Inc., of Corning, New York—Owens Corning and Owens-Illinois Inc., both of Toledo, Ohio, and Corning Consumer Products Co. of Elmira, New York.

Corning Inc. posted 1998 revenue of about $3.5 billion, nearly 15 percent less than 1997. The company, with more than 15,000 employees worldwide, changed its name in 1989 from Corning Glass Works to better reflect its increasingly diverse product line. The founder, Amory Houghton, moved his glass operation from Brooklyn to Corning, New York, in 1868. By 1875, Corning Glass Works was incorporated, and Houghton became president of the company—a position he retained until 1911.

The technical expertise of the company was recognized early, as Thomas Edison asked for its help in making electric light bulbs in 1880. In 1912, Corning invented borosilicate, which was used to produce Pyrex in 1915. Pyrex immediately became standard in the scientific community for laboratory equipment, although the consumer markets were not tapped until years later. Another significant milestone for Corning was the 1934 manufacture of a 200-inch diameter mirror for the Mount Palomar telescope. The company surpassed this accomplishment by creating the world's largest single-piece telescope mirror for the Japanese government in 1992. In the 1960s, Corning created the ceramic heat-resisting reentry shields and glass windshields for the Apollo moon program. The most significant research for Corning in past years was in the development of fiber optics. Corning realized the potential of the material in the 1960s and continued research and development even though market demand was low and, by 1984, the company invested $87 million in new fiber optic plant facilities.

Owens-Illinois Inc., with nearly 39,000 employees worldwide, is a leader in the manufacture of glass containers and other glass products, as well as a major producer of plastic packaging materials. Headquartered in Toledo, Ohio, the company posted 1998 sales of $5.3 billion, up 13.9 percent from the previous year. Owens Corning, a major producer of glass fiber, employs 21,000 people worldwide and reported 1998 sales of $5 billion, up 14.5 percent from the previous year. Corning Consumer Products Co., in which Corning Inc. retains an interest of less than 10 percent, reported 1998 revenue of $533.1 million, nearly 7 percent less than 1997.

Other leaders in the industry include Anchor Hocking Glass, of Lancaster, Ohio, and Libbey Inc., of Toledo, Ohio. Anchor Hocking traces its roots back to 1905, when founder Ike Collins convinced a group of seven investors to contribute to the Hocking Glass Company's original capitalization of $25,000. By the end of its first year of manufacturing and marketing lamp chimneys and other glass items, the company had generated sales of $20,000. By 1919, Hocking boasted 300 employees (many of them highly skilled glass blowers) and $900,000 in annual sales, and it had diversified from lamp chimneys (which were made obsolete by the invention of the incandescent light bulb) into glass tableware.

Acquisitions and mergers expanded the company's interests into glass containers, plastics, and hardware, increasing annual sales to a peak of more than $900 million in the early 1980s, but intense competition forced Anchor Hocking to sell out to the Newell Company (renamed Newell Rubbermaid Inc. in 1999 after its acquisition of Rubbermaid) in 1987. Sales of Anchor Hocking's parent company in 1998 totaled $3.7 billion, up 15 percent form the previous year.

With more than 3,800 employees worldwide, Libbey Inc. is a leading producer of glassware, flatware, and ceramic dinnerware, all of which are distributed throughout North America and to more than 100 other countries. In 1998, the company posted revenue of $436.5 million, up 5.9 percent from the previous year.

WORKFORCE

In 1997, the pressed and blown glass industry employed a total of 35,156 workers—with 29,255 working in production. In 1982, 37,600 people worked in the industry—78 percent as production workers. The average hourly wage had increased to $15.42 by 1997 from $9.41 in 1982. By 2000, the industry's workforce was expected to shrink to 33,200, but hourly wages were expected to increase to $16.64.

Projections for occupations in the glass industry were not bright going into the twenty-first century. All industry employees—with the exception of extruding and forming machine workers, who were expected to increase about 22 percent—were expected to decrease in numbers by 33 to 51 percent by the year 2005.

FURTHER READING

Hoover's Online. "Hoover's Company Capsules," 1999. Available from http://www.hoovers.com.

U.S. Census Bureau. "1997 Economic Census: Other Pressed and Blown Glass and Glassware Manufacturing." Washington, D.C.: GPO, 1999. Available from http://www.census.gov/prod/www/abs/97ecmani.html.

SIC 3231

GLASS PRODUCTS, MADE OF PURCHASED GLASS

This category covers establishments primarily engaged in manufacturing glass products from purchased glass. Establishments primarily engaged in manufacturing optical lenses, except ophthalmic, are classified in **SIC 3827: Optical Instruments and Lenses,** and those manufacturing ophthalmic lenses are classified in **SIC 3851: Ophthalmic Goods.**

NAICS CODE(S)

327215 (Glass Product Manufacturing Made of Purchased Glass)

INDUSTRY SNAPSHOT

In 1997, the industry was made up of 1,528 companies operating more than 1,650 establishments. These companies generated shipments valued at $9.67 billion,

up more than 40 percent from 1992 shipments of $6.89 billion and up 22 percent from shipments of $7.90 billion only two years earlier in 1995. Employment in the industry, which hovered around 50,000 in the mid-1980s, has increased more modestly, reaching a total of 60,881 in 1997, an increase of 21.8 percent from the mid-1980s. Of the more than 60,000 workers employed by the industry in 1997, nearly 48,000 of them were involved in production operations. The annual payroll for all employees in the industry totaled $1.83 billion in 1997.

ORGANIZATION AND STRUCTURE

Firms in the purchased glass products industry are distinguished from other glass manufacturing firms—known as primary glass manufacturers—in that their products are not made directly from raw glass materials but from secondary glass bought from other companies.

Companies within the industry make everyday home glass products, such as mirrors, beverage glasses, shower doors, bathtub enclosures, picture glass, ash trays, lighting fixture glass, glass top tables, display shelving, window glass, automobile glass, clock glass, patio doors, oven door panels, novelty and souvenir glass items, appliance glass, and cosmetic and perfume containers. Industry products are also used in an extensive number of industrial, technical, and other non-household applications such as safety and bullet-proof glass, instrument dials, precision glass tubing, stained glass, industrial safety glasses and welding lenses, greenhouse glass, glass fiber used in optical components and for data and nondata transmission (faceplates, sensors, and glass-based optical coatings), chemical glassware, instrument panels, cathode ray tube screens, and high-tolerance specialty glass products such as elapsed-time indicators and gravity-sensing electrolytic transducers.

Important subgroups of industry products include beverage glasses such as tumblers and stemware, beer glasses, crystal and casual glassware, and glass fiber used in optical components and for data and non-data transmission.

Product Manufacture. Because industry firms do not make glass from raw materials as do primary glass manufacturers, the methods for making glass products from purchased glass vary with the specific product. Firms within the industry buy glass in the following forms: float glass (a type of flat glass manufactured by floating the glass in a bath of molten tin), sheet glass, plate glass, glass sand, and "cullet" or glass scrap.

Other materials and supplies used in the manufacture of purchased glass products include industrial inorganic chemicals, plastic film and sheets, ground or otherwise treated nonmetallic minerals, and sodium carbonate (soda ash), as well as paperboard containers, wood boxes and pallets, and lumber.

Some of the more common glass products, which illustrate different glass manufacturing methods, include laboratory glass, laminated glass, mirror glass, ornamental glass, safety glass, and stained glass.

Laboratory Glassware. Laboratory glass products such as test tubes, beakers, vials, and glass for distilling liquids are often made of borosilicate glass (a combination of boric oxide, silica sand, and other chemicals) because it has a high natural resistance to temperature change and corrosion, making it ideal for scientific, pharmaceutical, and some household uses. A common manufacturing method for laboratory glassware is machine blowing, in which molten glass is fed into a blowing element where jets of air are blown into the liquefied glass, causing it, with the aid of molds, to expand and conform to predetermined dimensions. Another common glass making method is machine pressing, where molten glass, cut at regular intervals into individual dollops, is dropped into molds where it is then shifted beneath a plunging or pressing element that gives the glass, when cooled, its final shape.

Laminated Glass. Laminated or compound glass is comprised of two or more sheets of glass and a layer of plastic fused together by heating in a pressurized tank or autoclave. When laminated glass products such as automobile windshields are broken, they crack rather than shatter because the fragments adhere to the plastic layer, maintaining the glass' transparency and preventing the scattering of shards.

Mirror Glass. Mirrors are made by treating washed float glass with a tin-based mixture, then spraying the surface with a ''silvering'' solution made of silver nitrate and water, followed by a ''reducing'' agent. The combination of the tin solution and the reducing agent creates a reflective silver film on the glass surface, which is then treated with a layer of copper and a protective lacquer and allowed to dry.

Ornamental Glass. Ornamental glass products are made by running sheets of glass through rollers that shape or emboss the glass surface according to the specific (and often trademarked) design of the individual firm. Some types of ornamental glass, each made using different techniques, include light scattering glass, ''wave'' glass, lined glass, curved or semicircular ''roundel'' glass, and glass with flower or other decorative impressions.

Safety Glass. Safety or tempered glass is designed to break into small, rounded pieces of a predetermined size when shattered, thus reducing the creation of dangerous sharp fragments. Such glass is manufactured by heating sheets of flat glass, then subjecting them to bursts of cold air, which causes the interior of the glass to cool more slowly than the surface. The physical bond between the interior and external glass layers is such that when the pane is broken, the fragments are small, uniformly sized, and noninjurious.

Stained Glass. Stained glass consists of segments of individually colored panes joined together to create an image or pattern. The three methods for staining glass are painting, fusion with metallic oxides, and enameling. Glass painting involves applying pigments to hardened glass, then permanently burning or baking the pigment onto the surface of the glass in an oven. Alternatively, metallic oxides of varying colors can be added to glass while it is still molten, changing the tint of the glass itself when it cools. Metallic oxides are also used in enameling methods but are applied to hardened rather than molten glass. The enamel coating is then bonded with the glass by firing or baking.

Industry Specialization. Many industry firms manufacture more than one type of glass product. For example, Apogee Enterprises Inc. of Minnesota produces insulating, heat-tempered, laminated, non-glare, picture, automotive, and bullet-resistant glass. A few firms, however, such as American Mirror Company, Inc., of Virginia; Fisher Skylights, Inc., of New York; and Riordan Stained Glass Studio, of Ohio, specialize in a single line of glass products. Industry specialization in glass product manufacturing is also reflected in the names of some industry firms, such as Artistic Shower Door & Mirror Company Inc., Pilkington Aerospace Inc., National Bullet Proof Inc., and Christmas by Krebs Corporation, among others.

End-Users. The major users of glass products, including some non-industry products but excluding containers such as bottles and jars, consist of individual consumers; manufacturers, such as motor vehicle and car body; exporters; restaurants, bars, and other eating and drinking establishments; automotive repair shops and service businesses; lighting fixture and equipment manufacturers; miscellaneous plastics products manufacturers; hotels and other hospitality businesses; and electric lamp manufacturers.

BACKGROUND AND DEVELOPMENT

Between 1972 and 1987, the purchased glass products industry experienced continuous solid growth, with the only declines in the value of shipments occurring in the mid-1970s. In that 16-year period, the value of industry shipments more than quadrupled from $1.3 billion to $5.4 billion, the number of industry firms increased 38 percent from 817 to 1,325, and employment grew 52 percent from 33,700 to 51,100. At the same time, the cost of materials and payroll as a percentage of total shipment value declined from 73 to 67 percent industry wide.

In the 10-year period between 1987 and 1997, the industry's shipments again showed dramatic growth, climbing 79 percent from $5.40 billion in 1987 to $9.67 in 1997. By contrast, the number of companies in the industry grew a much more modest 15.3 percent from 1,325 in 1987 to 1,528 in 1997. The cost of materials and payroll as a percentage of total shipment value inched downward from 67 percent in 1987 to 64.7 percent in 1997.

Faced with decreased demand for glass products, industry firms entered into joint ventures, introduced new products, and improved facilities in the early 1990s to stimulate sales. Between 1992 and 1994, glass container shipments averaged about 70,000 per quarter, with seasonal fluctuations.

INDUSTRY LEADERS

Major players in the industry in the late 1990s included Guardian Industries Corp., Donnelly Corp., and Safelite AutoGlass Corp., all of which made automotive glass products. Guardian, headquartered in Auburn Hills, Michigan, near the North American home of DaimlerChrysler, also makes glass products for use in construction applications. Guardian's 1998 sales hit $2.2 billion, an increase of 10 percent over the previous year. Donnelly of Holland, Michigan, is the world's leading manufacturer of rearview mirrors. For fiscal 1999, the 12 months ended June 30, 1999, the company posted revenue of $905 million, an increase of 18.6 percent over the previous year. Based in Columbus, Ohio, Safelite is best known for the manufacture of automobile windshields. Safelite posted sales of $876.8 million in fiscal 1999, the 12 months ended March 31, 1999. This represented a whopping 310 percent increase over its showing the previous year.

WORKFORCE

In 1997, the industry employed 60,881 people, an increase of 19.1 percent over the 1987 workforce of 51,100, but a decrease of 2.3 percent from 1995 when 62,300 worked in the industry. Production workers made up 78.6 of the workforce in 1997, reflecting little change from 1995 when 76 percent of the workforce was involved in production. The industry's payroll in 1997 was $1.83 billion, of which $1.25 billion went to production workers.

The glass-making occupations with the greatest number of workers were glass product assemblers and fabricators (12 percent of glass industry employment); general helpers, laborers, and material movers (8 percent); hand packers and packagers of manufactured products (6 percent); glass manufacturing machine feeders and offbearers—workers who deliver raw materials and carry them away from glass manufacturing machines (5 percent); and blue collar worker supervisors (5 percent). The remaining two-thirds of industry employees consisted of other production workers—such as glass product cutting and slicing machine setters, operators, and tenders; precision glass product inspectors, testers, and graders; glass hand cutters and trimmers; glass furnace, kiln, or kettle operators and tenders; and glass product coating, painting, and spraying machine operators—and nonproduction administrative positions such as sales staff, general managers and executives, support and clerical staff, and industrial production managers.

FURTHER READING

Darnay, Arsen J. *Manufacturing USA.* 5th ed. Detroit: Gale Research, 1998.

U.S. Bureau of the Census. "1997 Economic Survey: Glass Product Manufacturing Made of Purchased Glass." Washington, D.C.: GPO, 1999. Available from http://www.census.gov/prod/www/abs/97ecmani.html.

——. *1994 County Business Patterns.* Washington, D.C.: GPO, 1996.

SIC 3241

CEMENT, HYDRAULIC

Establishments primarily engaged in manufacturing hydraulic cement, including portland, natural, masonry, and pozzolana cements.

NAICS CODE(S)

327310 (Cement Manufacturing)

Cement is manufactured by grinding minerals, typically a controlled mix of limestone and clay, in either a wet or a dry environment. The ground material is then heated in a kiln, chemically changing it into a substance called "clinker" that is cooled and reground with additional minerals such as gypsum. This leaves a finished powder—the cement itself—that reacts with water and can be mixed with gravel or sand to create concrete.

In the mid-1990s the United States produced 75 million metric tons of portland cement, which accounted for 90 percent of this industry's output, and consumed 86 million metric tons. U.S. cement makers shipped more than $6 billion worth of hydraulic cement in 1998. The U.S. cement industry ranked third largest in the world, following China and Japan. Growth in the industry was fueled by general strength in the economy, particularly the robust construction industry of the mid-1990s.

Cement is used in a variety of construction-related industries, particularly in building and roadway construction. In the mid-1990s buildings commanded roughly 55 percent of U.S. cement consumption, followed by streets and highways at 29 percent, water systems at 9 percent, and miscellaneous construction and nonconstruction uses at 7 percent.

The industry, which runs an annual trade deficit, has significantly reduced its reliance on imports as a proportion of consumption since the mid-1980s, when import volume was as much as 20 times greater than export volume. In the mid-1990s imports declined and exports increased, bringing the deficit down to less than a factor of 10. In 1998, prices were continuing to increase.

Industry employment dropped steadily since the 1970s due to automation and a decline of small producers. Approaching the twenty-first century, the industry was expected to increase employment levels by more than 10 percent, however, in three occupations: industrial machinery mechanics, sales workers, and industrial production managers. Most other occupations were expected to face reductions; those most significantly affected were hand packers, furnace operators, secretaries, and crushing and mixing machine operators. Positions for general managers and top executives will possibly decline by more than 5 percent as the hydraulic cement industry reaches the year 2000.

In 1997 there were approximately 279 establishments manufacturing cement throughout the United States. Plants were typically located near the regional market they served to minimize transportation costs. During the mid-1990s construction boom, cement plants operated at just over 90 percent capacity. The Portland Cement Association (PCA) estimated that 65 percent of U.S. cement capacity was held by foreign companies.

With $2.4 billion in 1999 revenues, Lafarge Corporation of Reston, Virginia, was the industry leader. Second was CBR-HCI Construction Materials Inc. of Allentown, Pennsylvania, with $1.4 billion. Third was Holnam Inc. of Dundee, Michigan, with $1.1 billion. In late 1999 approximately 17,400 workers were employed by the industry, of which 12,700 were in production. The average work week was 43.7 hours with 5.6 hours of overtime, and the average salary was $19.30 per hour.

FURTHER READING

Bureau of the Census. *Economic Census 1997*. Washington, D.C.: GPO, 1999. Available from http://www.census.gov.

Employment Statistics. Bureau of Labor Statistics, 2000. Available from http://www.bls.gov.

Portland Cement Association Homepage. Skokie, IL: 1997. Available from http://www.portcement.org.

Thomas, William D., et al. "Producer Price Highlights 1998." *Monthly Labor Review*, July 1999.

U.S. Industry and Trade Outlook '99. New York: The McGraw-Hill Companies, 1999.

SIC 3251

BRICK AND STRUCTURAL CLAY TILE

This category covers establishments primarily engaged in manufacturing brick and structural clay tile. Establishments primarily engaged in manufacturing clay firebrick fall under **SIC 3255: Clay Refractories;** those manufacturing nonclay firebrick are grouped under **SIC 3297: Nonclay Refractories;** those manufacturing sand lime brick are classified in **SIC 3299: Nonmetallic Mineral Products, Not Elsewhere Classified;** those manufacturing architectural terra cotta and other miscellaneous structural clay products are classified in **SIC 3259: Structural Clay Products, Not Elsewhere Classified;** and those manufacturing glass brick are classified in **SIC 3229: Pressed and Blown Glass and Glassware, Not Elsewhere Classified.**

NAICS CODE(S)
327121 (Brick and Structural Clay Tile Manufacturing)

ORGANIZATION AND STRUCTURE
In 1997, the leading product types for this industry were building or common brick and face brick, accounting for 91.6 percent of the value of total shipments, and glazed brick and paving, floor, and sewer brick, making up about 5.3 percent of total shipments. Among the specific products produced by the industry in the late 1990s were clay book tile, clay ceramic glazed brick, corncrib tile, clay radial (rounded) chimney blocks, hollow and vitrified (heat-fused into glass or a glassy material) brick, clay building tile, clay floor arch tile, clay furring tile, clay fireproofing tile, clay flooring brick, clay paving brick, clay partition tile, silo tile, and slumped brick (brick with an expanded or "slumped" base).

The characteristics of brick and structural clay tile products vary depending on the type of clay or raw mineral material used, the manner in which they are manufactured, the temperature at which they are burned or baked, the relative absorptive and strength qualities, and the severity of the climates they will be used in. The standard dimensions of U.S. bricks range between 4 and 6 inches thick, 2 3/4 to 4 inches high, and 8 to 12 inches wide. Bricks come in roughly 10,000 different colors besides the traditional red, weigh about six pounds, and cost between 25 and 50 cents each. Typical uses for brick and clay structural tile have historically been in the construction of homes—66 to 76 percent of all industry brick sales—as well as office buildings and industrial and other structures.

In its most common form, brick is made from clay that has been mixed with water, formed or "tempered" into a rectangular block, dried, and burned in a kiln. "Common brick'' refers to brick in its undifferentiated state as it comes from the kiln, and it is used as ''backup'' masonry for wall thickness and structural support behind face brick. Face brick is chosen based on its uniformity of appearance for use in the exterior or visible portions of walls and is divided into various grades of color, texture, and perfection. Glazed brick is brick that has been treated with a coating of melted ground glass to repel moisture, engender easy cleaning, and/or create a desired appearance.

Unlike the most common ceramic home floor tile, which is typically thin and flat, structural tile more resembles concrete construction blocks in that it is hollow or cored and is primarily used for structural support rather than for aesthetic, decorative purposes. Structural clay tile is derived from clay, ceramic, and refractory minerals including kaolin and ball clay, mixed with industrial chemicals, molded into specific dimensions by forcing the raw material through dies, and burned or baked in kilns or ovens. The basic types of structural clay tile are load-bearing wall tile to bear the weight of floors, roofs, and facings; nonload-bearing tile used in the construction of partitions in building interiors and for backing up walls made of two or more materials; furring tile used to line the inside of walls and to provide an air space between the plaster and the wall; and fireproofing tile used to protect steel girders, beams, columns, and other structural elements from fire. Flooring tile—not to be confused with everyday decorative floor tile—is used in floor and roof construction, and structural clay facing tile is used in exposed or visible interior and exterior walls and partitions.

BACKGROUND AND DEVELOPMENT

The first bricks in North America appeared in the form of the ballast of English ships, but a native brickmaking industry soon emerged in which clay was pressed into wooden molds and baked in beehive-shaped kilns. This handmade method endured until the 1870s when early brick production machines began to transform the industry. Besides the handmade method, two basic brickmaking methods soon emerged. Machine-molded brick resembled the traditional method except that the moist clay was forced into the molds by machine. Extruded brick—the most common method today—uses a machine to press a continuous tube of moist clay through an aperture, after which a wire cuts the individual bricks at preset intervals.

The use of uniform or modular standards for brick and structural clay tile by the construction industry and the brick and structural clay tile manufacturing industry has a long history, and industry products are governed by precise specifications with respect to tile length, width, and thickness—as well as strength, endurance, and appearance. For example, in the early 1960s there were 12 distinct modular sizes or specifications for structural load-bearing wall tile. Sizes that become unpopular may be dropped, however, and new ones can be added as construction industry demand dictates. Traditionally, few manufacturers have produced all the tile sizes accepted as standard by the industry. Between 1985 and 1994, the U.S. brick industry languished with an annual growth rate well below 2.5 percent.

CURRENT CONDITIONS

In 1997, the brick and structural clay tile manufacturing industry consisted of 129 companies operating 225 establishments. The industry's shipments in 1997 reached a value of $1.45 billion, compared with 1992 shipments of $1.12 billion, generated by 117 companies operating 186 establishments. In 1997, the top brick producing states were North Carolina, which accounted for 17 percent of total shipments; Texas (10.2 percent); and Ohio (7.6 percent). Government economists were predicting that the industry would see a healthy growth rate of close to 3 percent into the early years of the new millennium.

Issues confronting the industry in the 1990s included conforming to environmental protection regulations, managing labor costs, coping with fluctuating construction demand, financing new facilities and expansion, and competing with imported products. Industry firms have increasingly benefited from improved brick making technologies, including better kiln designs, improved knowledge of brick and tile raw materials and their characteristics, greater use of modern manufacturing technology, and better control over the firing or baking process.

The explosive spread of computers in American industry has led to computer control of the brick manufacturing process and the adoption by some industry firms of the World Wide Web as a marketing tool. In the mid-1990s, brick makers continued to address the growing demand for the ''human'' feel (handmade bricks) by returning to historical handmade brick-by-brick manufacturing methods and by altering the look of machine-made bricks to give them a less uniform appearance. The use of recycled brick from demolished structures also continued to grow in the 1990s, as producers looked to cheaper raw material alternatives to clay.

The building boom of the late 1990s created occasional shortages of brick, prompting manufacturers to place limits on their shipments to retailers. Brick manufacturers in 1999 turned out about 8 percent more bricks than they produced in 1998, but demand still outstripped supply, according to Tom Perry, a spokesman for the Brick Industry Association, a trade group representing manufacturers. ''We are behind demand because it is an extremely robust home buying market.'' Perry pointed out that building booms do not usually last as long as the one seen in the latter half of the 1990s. In the fall of 1999, there were some signs that the building frenzy was beginning to slow down, hopefully enough to allow brick producers to catch up with demand.

INDUSTRY LEADERS

In the late 1990s, leading manufacturers included GTE Precision Materials of Danvers, Massachusetts; Justin Industries Inc. of Fort Worth, Texas; Coors Ceramics Co. of Golden, Colorado; Boral Bricks Inc. of Atlanta, Georgia; and Cherokee Sanford Group Inc. of Sanford, North Carolina.

WORKFORCE

In 1997, the brick and structural clay tile manufacturing industry employed 14,428 workers, of whom 11,438 were involved in production. That's nearly identical to the 14,200 workers employed in 1992.

FURTHER READING

"The Brick Industry: Markets and Trends." *Ceramic Industry,* 1 October 1996.

Brozda, Mike. "Building with Brick." *Home,* November 1995.

Ceramic Industry. Troy, MI: Business News Publishing Co.

Darnay, Arsen J., ed. *Manufacturing USA,* 6th ed. Detroit: Gale Research, 1998.

Masonry. Oak Brook, IL.: Mason Contractors Association of America.

U.S. Bureau of the Census. *1997 Economic Census: Brick and Structural Tile Manufacturing.* Washington, D.C.: GPO, 1999. Available from http://www.census.gov/prod/www/abs/97ecmani.html.

SIC 3253

CERAMIC WALL AND FLOOR TILE

This industry covers establishments primarily engaged in manufacturing ceramic wall and floor tile. Establishments primarily engaged in manufacturing structural clay tile are classified in **SIC 3251: Brick and Structural Clay Tile,** and those manufacturing drain tile are classified in **SIC 3259: Structural Clay Products, Not Elsewhere Classified.**

NAICS CODE(S)

327122 (Ceramic Wall and Floor Tile Manufacturing)

INDUSTRY SNAPSHOT

Nearly 99 percent of this industry's product share is composed of glazed and unglazed floor tile and wall tile, including quarry tile and ceramic mosaic tile. Because this industry is so focused on decorative tiles, it is com-

pletely dependent on the economic health of the construction and remodeling industries.

Clay, ceramic, and refractory materials such as kaolin and ball clay are the raw materials consumed in the manufacture of ceramic tiles. Other industrial chemicals, some lead based, are also used to produce ceramic tiles. Because of the industry's use and disposal of these lead-based chemicals, ceramic manufacturers are forced to comply with a wide array of Environmental Protection Agency (EPA) regulations.

This industry has been experiencing steady growth through the 1990s in terms of establishments, shipments, and employment levels. In 1988, 112 establishments were present, with 53 employing 20 or more people. By 1997, 142 establishments were engaged in the industry, with 58 employing 20 or more people. Leading states involved in ceramic wall and floor tile manufacturing included California, Texas, and Ohio. By the end of 1997, the total workforce was estimated at 9,065 people, with 85 percent of the employees working in a production capacity.

BACKGROUND AND DEVELOPMENT

The evolution of clay tiles began with the introduction of roofing tiles, followed by flooring and wall tiles. The Roman historian Pliny wrote that tiles were invented in Greece on the isle of Cyprus by Cinyra, son of Agrippa. The earliest baked clay roof tiles, which date to around 1800 B.C., were excavated near Argos, Greece. The technique for production of this architectural medium was transported to southern Italy and Sicily and slowly spread throughout the rest of continental Europe. Until the Industrial Revolution when tile making was mechanized somewhat, only the very rich could afford tiled roofs and floors. This is evident in the 89 B.C. Charter of Tarentum, which stated that Senate membership and voting privileges were restricted to those men who owned housing within Tarentum, roofed with at least 1,500 tiles.

As with all industries, the Industrial Revolution forever changed the manufacture of clay tiles. By the 1850s the British led the industry in machinery innovation and heavily influenced production methods in Germany, France, Belgium, Holland, Spain, and Portugal. The introduction of machines to aid in the manufacturing process resulted in dramatically higher production levels and far greater availability of tiles.

The ceramic tile industry in the United States entered its own period of enlightenment in the 1870s. The art form in ceramic tiles developed its own uniquely American twist during the Philadelphia International Centennial Exhibition of 1876; glazed tiles were produced in the United States approximately 30 years previously, though. This progress is documented by Charles Thomas Davis, writer of *Manufacture of Bricks, Tiles and Terra-Cotta,* published in 1884. He wrote, "Nothing in the history of pottery is so remarkable as the progress which has been made in the manufacture of encaustic and decorative tiles, but especially in the latter, in this country since the Centennial Exposition of 1876." However, during 1870 and 1900, many American-produced tiles imitated the lifestyle in Victorian Britain, mainly because many of the artisans were trained either in Britain or directly by the British.

A new, distinctly different generation began to infuse the American ceramic tile industry in the early 1900s. These artisans were trained in American potteries and art schools and prided themselves on original, handmade tiles. The leaders in innovation were the small companies that created a broad diversity in style and technique. This period was struck a deadly blow by the Great Depression of 1929 when the construction industry shuddered to a halt, and many small tile firms were forced to close their doors.

The United States then entered World War II, and the Art Deco movement again changed the design of ceramic tiles. Screen printing became an important method of coloring tiles, and production methods were improved to lend great consistency to final tile products. The tile industry in the United States today is dominated by international conglomerates like Armstrong World Industries, which owns American Olean Tile. However, much of the artistry in the industry is still spurred by smaller tile companies.

CURRENT CONDITIONS

The ceramic tile industry is closely tied to the construction industry, both residential and nonresidential. In the first quarter of 1996, construction began an overall decline. Due to depressed sales, inventory accumulation stalled production of various ceramic products. Likewise, poor weather conditions throughout the United States slowed construction, directly affecting the sales and shipments of ceramic products. During the remainder of 1996, however, clay floor and wall tiles experienced strong growth in shipments because of economic recovery in other industries. Due to lower interest rates and general economic improvement, housing starts and residential remodeling were projected to grow into the late 1990s. In the latter part of the decade, ceramic tile was being used for upscale remodeling and building of bathrooms and kitchens. This growth would serve as a tremendous boon to establishments involved in ceramic wall and floor tile manufacturing.

Since the late 1990s, shipments increased each year, following the trend toward greater consumption. It was estimated that into the year 2003 consumption would rise up to three percent annually. Imported products would also continue to grow in volume due to reduced tariffs under the North American Free Trade Agreement (NAFTA). Most ceramic tile was imported from Italy.

INDUSTRY LEADERS

American Olean Tile Company of Lansdale, Pennsylvania, is owned by Armstrong World Industries of Lancaster, Pennsylvania. This acquisition, completed in 1988 in an effort to boost profitability, was the first of several restructuring moves for Armstrong, the largest outfit in this industry in terms of sales. Armstrong, a public company employing almost 20,000 workers in 1999, posted annual sales of almost $3.0 billion. Other key companies in this industry included Dal-Tile International of Dallas, Texas, with 1999 sales of $720.0 million, and American Biltrite Inc., of Wellesley Hills, Massachusetts, with 1998 sales of $423.9 million.

WORKFORCE

In the late 1990s, the workforce engaged in tile manufacturing works in a highly mechanized, if not totally automated, setting or works in a small, specialty studio setting, creating highly artistic and functional tiles.

The industries producing stone, clay, and mineral products are expected to engage in downsizing efforts across a variety of occupations by the year 2000. The number of hand packers and packagers is expected by some industry observers to be reduced by nearly 25 percent, largely as a result of increasing automation. Other occupations expected to experience workforce reductions of about 15 percent include assemblers and fabricators; furnace, kiln, oven, and kettle operators; crushing and mixing machine operators; precision inspectors, graders, and testers; packaging and filling machine operators; machine feeders and offbearers; hand freight, stock, and material movers; secretaries; cutting and slicing machine operators; grinders and polishers; and metal and plastic machine forming operators. Occupations expecting growth in the industry include sales workers, industrial machinery mechanics, and industrial production managers.

RESEARCH AND TECHNOLOGY

Production methods for manufacturing ceramic tiles have greatly improved since the end of World War II. Machine decoration has increased overall output, while improved drying machines move tiles to shipping quicker. Additionally, new advances in airless and microwave drying techniques hold the promise of revolutionizing the drying process while cutting production time dramatically.

Increasing customer demand for greater variety in styles and uses of tiles has broadened the base of techniques used to produce final artistic effects. The most revolutionary of these procedures enables customers to choose designs from a computer's memory and see the finished product on a computer simulation of the customer's own bathroom. In the future computers—

combined with machine tile decoration—will allow customers to design their own tiles for the manufacturer to then produce. While clay tile making continues to resemble many of the practices used 1,000 years ago, better production methods and materials lend new levels of quality and consistency to the final product.

FURTHER READING

"An Overview of the Economy." *Ceramic Industry,* August 1996.

"Blending Pottery Art With Computer Technology." *Ceramic Industry,* January 1996.

Earl, David. "The Feasibility of Microwave Drying Ceramic Tile." *Ceramic Industry,* October 1996.

Hoover's Company Capsules. Hoover's Online, 2000. Available from http://www.hoovers.com.

Jones, John. "Advances in Tile Manufacturing Technology." *Ceramic Industry,* April 1996.

Sheppard, Laurel. "New and Better Additives Ensure Fabrication of Quality Ceramics." *Ceramic Industry,* March 1997.

Stubbing, Thomas. "Airless Drying Improves Productivity and Reduces Energy." *Ceramic Industry,* March 1996.

U.S. Bureau of the Census. *Economic Census 1997.* Washington, D.C.: GPO, 1999. Available from http://www.census.gov.

U.S. Industry and Trade Outlook. New York: The McGraw-Hill Companies, 1999.

SIC 3255

CLAY REFRACTORIES

This category covers establishments primarily engaged in manufacturing clay firebrick and other heat-resisting clay products. Establishments primarily engaged in manufacturing nonclay refractories and all graphite refractories, whether of carbon bond or ceramic bond, are classified under **SIC 3297: Nonclay Refractories.**

NAICS CODE(S)

327124 (Clay Refractory Manufacturing)

INDUSTRY SNAPSHOT

Refractories are mineral- and chemical-based materials with very high heat-resisting properties, which make them ideal for use in the construction of walls, ceilings, and associated elements of iron and steel industry blast furnaces, glass manufacturing tanks, cement kilns, hot stoves, ceramic kilns, open hearth furnaces, nonferrous metallurgical furnaces, and steam boilers. Most clay refractory products are manufactured in the form of bricks, but refractory clay may also be formed into special shapes, such as the T-sections of refractory pipes or the small

stands that support ceramic products during firing in a kiln. Refractories have been an essential element in heat engineering plants since the 1960s, where they were successfully used to improve performance and energy efficiency.

ORGANIZATION AND STRUCTURE

In 1995, the clay refractory industry consisted of four general product groups: refractory bricks and shapes, with 61 percent of the value of industry shipments; unshaped clay refractories, with 34 percent; other lump or ground refractory materials, with 2 percent; and unspecified refractories, with 2 percent. Included in the refractory bricks and shapes category were fireclay bricks and shapes, pouring pit refractories, clay kiln furniture, and radiant heater elements. As many as 38 U.S. firms made unshaped clay refractories in 1995, which included everything from refractory bonding mortars and plastic refractories to ramming mixes, castable refractories, and fire clay gunning mixes. Fifteen industry firms made lump or ground refractory materials in 1995. These were generally sold directly to customers in raw form or as an export.

The refractory brick and shapes industry was a highly specialized supplier to such heat manufacturing industries as the iron and steel industry, the ceramics industry, and the glass-making industry. Its terminology and the specific products it sold to end-user industries were as specialized as the products they helped to make. For example, one industry product, known as refractory tank blocks, consisted of blocks of refractory clay used in the lower portions of glass-tank furnaces; and refractory feeder parts were devices for supplying refractory raw materials to a preparation machine prior to firing in a ceramic or glass oven. Many industry products were specific to the iron and steel making industries. Refractory "nozzles," for example, were used in ladles for extracting molten steel; "runners" were refractory-lined channels in which molten iron flowed from a blast furnace when tapped; and ladle gate parts included refractory pouring spouts for molten iron or steel. Other specialized products manufactured by industry firms included clay refractory cement, refractory tile made out of fire clay, and various refractory elements used in glass manufacturing, such as glasshouse floaters, melting pots, rings, saggers, and stoppers.

One of the most common methods for manufacturing clay refractories was extrusion, in which moist refractory clay was forced by pressure through a die of specific dimensions, creating a rectangular shaft of clay that could then be cut at regular intervals to form bricks. The extruded bricks could then be sent through tunnel driers or dried on hot floors. Another common manufacturing process for noncomplex refractory shapes was power pressing, in which brick presses weighing as much 3,600 tons produced bricks of up to 28 inches in length. Unlike brick extruding machines, brick presses did not require large amounts of water, and thus simplified the drying and handling of the bricks.

Other methods of refractory manufacture included slip casting, hydrostatic pressing, fusion casting, and hand molding. After initial forming, clay refractory bricks and shapes were often fired in tunnel-shaped kilns to strengthen the brick or shape and stabilize it at a temperature equal to or higher than it would experience in actual use—often 1800 degrees Fahrenheit or more.

Because of its low cost in comparison to other refractories, fire clay—a mixture of kaolinite clay and silica sand—was the preferred material for clay refractory brick, which was classified as "low," "intermediate," "high," and "superduty," according to the temperature at which softened when fired or baked. Typical specific uses of fire clay refractory bricks were boiler furnace linings, blast furnace linings, molten iron casting pit refractories, and other applications that did not entail extremely high temperatures.

Plastic fire clays were refractories that were moldable when mixed with water and were often used for furnace linings or as a binding agent in fire clay brick manufacture. Fire clay could be combined with other raw materials to increase its refractoriness and to reduce its shrinkage during firing. Because of improvements in the combustion properties of fuels used in industrial furnaces, performance requirements for refractory materials continued to be upgraded to extend operational life and conform to harsher furnace environments. This led to the development of "superrefractories" that consist of 50 to 80 percent alumina, a form of aluminum oxide found in minerals such as corundum and bauxite, used in the manufacture of aluminum.

In 1997, by value, more than 57 of the materials consumed in the manufacture of clay refractories consisted of clay, ceramic, and refractory minerals, such as kaolin and ball clay, extracted and processed by mining firms (see **SIC 1455: Kaolin and Ball Clay,** and **SIC 1459: Clay, Ceramic, and Refractory Minerals, Not Elsewhere Classified**). More than 18 percent consisted of clay or nonclay refractories, while less than 2 percent came from industrial chemicals.

Between 1972 and 1987, the value of clay refractories shipments more than doubled from $336 million to more than $788 million. Shipments in 1997 reached $1.1 billion.

CURRENT CONDITIONS

Since about 1990, the industrialized world has experienced a significant drop-off in the amount of refractories produced and consumed. A number of factors contributed to this downward trend: a decrease in the production of steel around the world during this period; the use of higher-grade refractory materials; the use of new non-refractory technologies in heat engineering industries; improvements in the durability of refractories already produced and sold; and the discontinuation of thermal pretreatment in the use of some raw materials.

Industry trends in the clay refractory industry in the 1990s included the emergence of new seamless refractory furnace linings that reduced air leakage into and out of industrial furnaces. Improvements in furnace operation and refractory materials resulted in increases in the number of tons of steel (up to 1 million) that could be produced before refractory linings needed replacing. Partnerships were also formed between refractory suppliers and steelmakers to develop new refractory materials and techniques. The industry continued to seek ways to find purer grades of refractory minerals that would increase the temperature-resisting limits of refractory products.

The long-term trend toward increased automation of refractory manufacturing processes, such as automatic brick batching, also continued in the 1990s. The development of robotic and remote control gunning machines enabled furnaces to be relined and refractory coatings applied without the expense of temporarily shutting down the furnace. The major issues facing refractories producers in the 1990s were environmental antipollution standards, increases in cost for materials, and changing markets.

INDUSTRY LEADERS

Major players in the clay refractory manufacturing industry included Indresco Inc. of Dallas, Texas; North American Refractories Co. of Cleveland, Ohio; Adience Inc. of Pittsburgh, Pennsylvania; A.P. Green Industries Inc. of Mexico, Missouri; and Harbison-Walker Refractories of Pittsburgh. Ohio, Missouri, Illinois, and Pennsylvania accounted for 66 percent of the industry's total shipments in 1997.

WORKFORCE

The industry grew from 86 firms to 111 firms between 1972 and 1987, while industry employment fell from 11,200 to 6,400 workers (production and nonproduction). By 1997, the number of companies in the industry had inched back up to 115 firms employing 6,131 people, three-quarters of whom worked in production.

FURTHER READING

Ceramic Industry. Troy, MI: Business News Publishing Co.

Darnay, Arsen J., ed. *Manufacturing USA,* 6th ed. Detroit: Gale Research, 1998.

Refractory News, Pittsburgh, PA: Refractories Institute.

"Refractories - Trends and New Developments." *Industrial Ceramics,* 1 September 1996.

U.S. Bureau of the Census. *1997 Economic Census: Clay Refractory Manufacturing.* Available from http://www.census.gov/prod/www/abs/97ecmani.html.

SIC 3259

STRUCTURAL CLAY PRODUCTS, NOT ELSEWHERE CLASSIFIED

This industry classification includes establishments engaged in the manufacture of clay sewer pipe and structural clay products, not elsewhere classified. Other products include adobe brick, clay chimney pipe, clay drain tile, and clay roofing.

NAICS CODE(S)

327123 (Other Structural Clay Product Manufacturing)

Although this small industry's shipments increased regularly in current dollar value during the 1980s, by the mid-1990s both its shipments and employment were declining. The industry shipped $150.4 million worth of goods and employed 1,800 workers in 1995, which marked a 14 percent decline, not including inflation, since the industry's 1989 peak of $175.0 million in shipments. After inflation this reduction amounted to almost 30 percent. In 1997 the industry shipped $118.3 million worth of goods and employed 1,332 workers.

Production in the largest segment of this industry, vitrified clay sewage pipe and fittings, declined by nearly 40 percent between 1990 and 1995, from 255.6 million short tons of product in 1990 to only 152.3 million tons in 1995. Estimated 1996 production of clay sewage pipe was down to 112.9 million metric tons, representing about $40 million worth of product. Only seven companies manufactured clay sewer pipes in 1996, and an estimated total of 51 establishments comprised the whole industry in 1997.

Total employment was down by 18 percent since 1988, falling from 2,200 workers in 1988 to 1,800 workers in 1995 to 1,300 workers in 1997; production workers totaled more than 1,000 for 1997. Production workers' average wages in the industry, about $11 per hour in 1997, were lower than the U.S. average for manufacturing wages but were nearly equal to the average for all structural clay production combined. The industry was regionally concentrated in the 1990s, with California and Ohio accounting for roughly two-thirds of the industry's employment.

Some industry observers expect significant downsizing to continue in this industry during the next decade. The only occupations expected to increase employment

levels include extruding and forming machine operators, industrial machinery mechanics, sales workers, maintenance repairers, truck drivers, industrial production managers, and coating machine operators. Those occupations expected to face reductions are primarily in the realm of assembly/production and include assemblers, furnace operators, crushing and mixing machine operators, inspectors, hand packers, packaging machine operators, machine feeders, material movers, secretaries, cutting machine operators, general machine operators, grinders, and machine forming and machine tool cutting operators.

The top firm in this industry in 1999 was A & M Products Inc., of Danbury, Connecticut, with sales of $149 million. Next was KMG Minerals of Kings Mountain, North Carolina, and U.S. Tile Company of Corona, California, both with sales of $15 million.

FURTHER READING

U.S. Census Bureau. *1995 Annual Survey of Manufactures.* Washington, D.C.: GPO, 1997.

U.S. Census Bureau. *Current Industrial Reports.* Washington, D.C.: GPO, 1997.

U.S. Census Bureau. *Economic Census 1997.* Washington, D.C.: GPO, 1999. Available from http://www.census.gov.

SIC 3261

VITREOUS CHINA PLUMBING FIXTURES AND CHINA AND EARTHENWARE FITTINGS AND BATHROOM ACCESSORIES

This industry classification consists of establishments primarily engaged in manufacturing vitreous china plumbing fixtures and china and earthenware fittings and bathroom accessories. Items manufactured in this industry include flush tanks, lavatories, bidets, urinals, toilet fixtures, closet bowls, drinking fountains, and sinks. Other items include vitreous china and earthenware bolt caps, bathroom accessories, faucet handles, soap dishes, and towel bar holders.

NAICS CODE(S)

327111 (Vitreous China Plumbing Fixture and China and Earthenware Fitting and Bathroom Accessories Manufacturing)

INDUSTRY SNAPSHOT

Manufacturers of vitreous china plumbing products function in the larger plumbing industry. The industry imposes strict standards that regulate everything from the width of pipe holes to the number of gallons used in each toilet flush. The manufacture of U.S. plumbing products suffered during the recession of the late 1980s. Of 156 manufacturing industries rated by the U.S. Department of Commerce's International Trade Administration, this industry was ranked 142 in its compound annual growth rate of −3.9 percent from 1988 to 1993.

Vitreous china is a ceramic product made primarily with specially treated clays and other chemicals including feldspar and silica, then glazed and fired at high temperatures in a kiln. The vitreous product lasts forever and does not absorb water or other materials; it has changed plumbing throughout the world.

ORGANIZATION AND STRUCTURE

The vitreous china plumbing industry is driven by trends in construction spending. Therefore, when the housing starts and remodeling trends plummeted in the 1980s, the industry suffered tremendously. Since vitreous china plumbing products are needed in residential and commercial settings, both construction industries affect the industry. Foreign-trade conditions also affect the manufacturers since imports still provide much of the plumbing ware in the United States.

Many manufacturers sell their wares only to distributors, who in turn sell the products to contractors and plumbers. Home centers, which have begun to change the way many Americans furnish or remodel their homes and businesses, have had an effect on the vitreous plumbing industry as well. For example, one large manufacturer, American Standard Inc., sells to independent wholesalers who sell to the trade. The company allows their wholesalers to sell American Standard products to home centers and other retailers. Their new line is actually being manufactured in Thailand to be sold in the United States.

Conversely, another major U.S. manufacturer, Kohler Company, still insists on selling its products only through distributors. Many manufacturers have begun to sell their wares directly to the home centers to prevent competitors from gaining too much market share.

BACKGROUND AND DEVELOPMENT

From the time civilization reached the point when populations were centralized, plumbing has been an important concern. Typhoid fever and dysentery spread during the Industrial Revolution when sewage systems were still combined with systems for drinking water. Once separate systems were designed, different plumbing fixtures were used to deliver drinking water and to remove waste materials from buildings.

Thomas Crapper invented the flush toilet, or water closet as it was known in England, in 1884. The mechanism he designed—with its float, valves, and arms that regulate the water in the flush tank—has remained virtu-

ally unchanged to the present. The early toilets as well as the earliest bathtubs, washbasins, and drinking fountains, were made from enameled cast iron. Vitreous china plumbing products were not introduced for several more decades.

By 1927, Walter Kohler was making vitreous china lavatories and toilets in his Wisconsin pottery operation, which emerged at that time as the third largest plumbing products company in the United States. As consumers began to customize their bathrooms, Kohler created vitreous china plumbing products in colors that matched the enameled cast iron bathtubs and accessories. In 1964, Kohler began manufacturing a self-rimming lavatory that eliminated the need for a metal frame or rim on the counter.

In the second half of the twentieth century, the American attitude toward the bathroom changed. People were spending more time there and were using the bathroom not just for hygiene purposes, but also as a bastion of relaxation. Manufacturers also thrived as a result of the increasing numbers of bathrooms being placed in each residential setting.

CURRENT CONDITIONS

From 1994 through 1998, the value of U.S. shipments of vitreous china plumbing fixtures has ranged from a high of $941 million in 1994 to a low of about $860 million in 1996. With shipments in 1997 and 1998 of $876 million and $884 million, respectively, the trend has been slightly upward, although much of these modest increases may be accounted for by inflation. In volume terms, shipments of vitreous china and other nonmetallic lavatories, for example, declined in 1998 to 5.69 million units from 5.79 million units the previous year.

Competition from Abroad and from Other Materials. Imports of foreign vitreous plumbing fixtures have had a harmful impact on U.S.-made products. The value of U.S. imports of vitreous china fixtures jumped nearly 35 percent in 1998 to $68.0 million from $50.5 million in 1997. U.S. exports, however, declined, falling from $68.4 million in 1997 to $65.7 million in 1998. The U.S. Bureau of the Census measures apparent U.S. consumption of vitreous plumbing fixtures by subtracting exports of U.S.-produced fixtures from the total of imports plus U.S. manufacturers' shipments. This apparent consumption rose from $859 million in 1997 to $886 million in 1998. The percentage of imports to apparent consumption rose from 5.9 percent in 1997 to 7.7 percent in 1998.

In the late 1990s, the vitreous china plumbing fixtures industry experienced stiff competition from plastics and fiberglass. The value of shipments of plastic and fiberglass plumbing fixtures in 1996 was $1.4 billion, compared with $859.7 million for vitreous china fixtures.

The following year, the value of vitreous china fixtures, at $876.8 million, was roughly 57 percent that of plastic and fiberglass fixtures, which totaled $1.5 billion. In 1998 the value of vitreous china fixtures, totaling $883.7 million, had slipped to just over 51 percent that of plastic fixtures, which came in at about $1.7 billion. Although vitreous china has retained much of the toilet bowl market, it has lost ground to plastics in the manufacture of lavatory sinks and toilet water tanks. Included within the plastics category are cultured marble and fiberglass-reinforced plastics (FRP).

Environmental Consciousness. Water conservation became an important issue in the industry beginning in the 1970s. Most flush toilets used an average of 3.5 gallons per flush (gpf). A federal bill known as the National Plumbing Products Efficiency Act (NPPEA) was signed into law at the end of 1992 as part of the Comprehensive National Energy Policy Act. The bill regulated the amount of water required per flush of a toilet or urinal. It also regulated the flow rate of showerheads and faucets. The American Society of Plumbing Engineers Research Foundation conducted field studies in the early 1990s to explore the possibility of replacing 3.5 gpf toilets with 1.6 gpf fixtures. Despite the fact that they found more clogging in the low-flow fixtures, environmental concerns overrode their criticisms, and the new U.S. code was enacted.

Manufacturers of vitreous plumbing fixtures worked with other plumbing industry advisors to coordinate low-flow products, as well as other new products that were developed in response to consumer concerns. One group of these products featured so-called universal design. These plumbing fixtures were equally accessible by wheelchair-bound and elderly consumers. Another recent trend was the development of lead-free plumbing. New requirements for plumbing systems came as a response to several lawsuits involving faucets. California's 1986 law, known as Proposition 65, specified toxic substances that were prohibited from being discharged into drinking water. These changes, which required implementation of lead-free plumbing, meant that entire plumbing systems had to be reworked.

Because of intense competition, from within the United States and abroad, manufacturers have had to expand their product lines, innovate with new technology, cut production costs, and improve their relationships with distributors. Advertising costs had risen, and consumers exhibited a greater interest in the plumbing fixtures they bought.

INDUSTRY LEADERS

The two biggest players in the vitreous china plumbing fixtures market are Kohler and American Standards. Kohler, headquartered in Kohler, Wisconsin, is family-owned and sells its vitreous fixtures under the Kohler and Sterling brand names. Because it is privately owned, Kohler is not required to publicly disclose its financial results. However, industry estimates indicate that the company generated total revenue of $2.4 billion in 1998, an increase of 8.6 percent over the previous year. Founded by John Kohler and partner Charles Silberzahn in 1873, the company was originally known as Kohler & Silberzahn. Charles Silberzahn left the company seven years after its founding. It was not until the mid-1920s that Kohler added vitreous china lavatory sinks and toilets to its product line. Operating more than 44 manufacturing facilities worldwide, Kohler employs a total of 18,000 people.

The 1990s were not particularly kind to American Standards, which lost money for most of the decade. In 1998, the company reported a net loss of $16 million on revenue of $6.7 billion. Despite its financial difficulties during the 1990s, the company remains a major manufacturer of vitreous china plumbing fixtures in the United States. The company was created in 1929 when American Radiator and Standard Sanitary merged to form American Radiator & Standard Sanitary, a name shortened to American Sanitary in 1967. For a time during the 1960s, American Standard was the world's leading manufacturer of plumbing fixtures. Headquartered in Piscataway, New Jersey, the company operates 116 manufacturing facilities in 33 countries and employs more than 57,000 people worldwide.

Other key manufacturers of vitreous china plumbing products in the United States include Eljer Industries of Dallas, Texas; Briggs Industries Inc. of Tampa, Florida; Gerber Plumbing Fixtures Corp. of Chicago; and Universal-Rundle Corp. of New Castle, Pennsylvania. During the economic downturn of the 1980s, several manufacturers in the industry were forced out; the industry saw many mergers and acquisitions.

WORKFORCE

Average hourly earnings for workers in the vitreous plumbing fixtures industry, most of whom are involved in actual production, rose from $11.96 in 1990 to an estimated $14.56 in 1999. Wages in 2000 are projected to average $14.89. Many of the plants where vitreous china plumbing products are manufactured are unionized. Some belong to the Glass Molders, Pottery, Plastics and Allied Workers International Union (GPPAW), while some factories are part of the local United Auto Workers (UAW). The GPPAW publishes a health and safety manual that identifies potential workplace hazards for manufacturers of vitreous china products. Unions also negotiate wages, certain workplace standards, vacation time, and other benefits for their members.

Many workers in this industry spend their entire careers perfecting one job. Each job in production is unique, from the creation of the special clay mixture (called slip) to the packaging of the final products.

Some plants have a sliphouse where there are machine operators and mixers who bring the raw materials to exactly the right consistency before it is cast. Casters pour the slip into plaster of Paris molds, where it dries. Finishers remove coarse edges and seams. Glazing is done manually or with glazing machines before fixtures are taken to be fired in kilns. Kiln operators must deal with the intense heat needed to meld glazes and ceramics. Kilns reach temperatures of up to 2,300 degrees Fahrenheit. Inspectors and selectors check the finished products, sending some to packaging, others to be reground, reglazed, or refired.

AMERICA AND THE WORLD

The manufacture of vitreous plumbing fixtures is a labor-intensive business. Costs for U.S. manufacturers have risen dramatically over the past decades, and foreign competition has increased, in part because of the low labor costs that foreign companies incur.

The value of U.S. imports of vitreous plumbing fixtures in 1991 was $64.4 million, in which range it generally remained through 1994. By 1995, it had gone up to $71.2 million, just shy of the high of $72.6 million in 1989. Imports slipped to $64.8 million in 1996 and then fell sharply in 1997 to $50.5 million. However, imports jumped dramatically in 1998, rising to $68.0 million. The value of exports in 1991 was $46.1 million, rising to $61.1 million in 1995 and $65.7 million in 1998.

RESEARCH AND TECHNOLOGY

Vitreous china materials and basic toilet designs have not changed significantly in the past half century. Much of the industry's research efforts have concentrated on perfecting current manufacturing methodologies. Quick-dry glazes, for instance, enable manufacturers to upgrade their rate of production. Many experiments in plumbing fixtures have gone by the wayside, while others are constantly being introduced. For example, Kohler recently introduced the Rosario Lite toilet, which flushes automatically when the user closes the lid.

Several foreign companies have proven adept in their aggressive efforts to improve their product line. Toto, one of Japan's largest plumbing products manufacturers, has introduced several new features, not yet available in the United States, for plumbing fixtures. The company's Washlet toilet features hot-water cleaning and hot-air drying. Toto's Sound Princess, developed in response to the practice of many Japanese women of flushing repeatedly during one sitting, plays a recording of flushing water so that the user does not feel compelled to flush to mask obtrusive noises. Japanese manufacturers also have produced toilets that send urine for medical tests. Another new product features an armrest that can simultaneously measure one's blood pressure, temperature, and pulse. As the population ages in the United States, these features might be requested more often, and local manufacturers may begin producing them.

FURTHER READING

Darnay, Arsen J., ed. *Manufacturing USA*. 5th ed. Detroit: Gale Research, 1998.

U.S. Bureau of the Census. *Current Industrial Reports*. Washington, D.C.: GPO, 1998.

U.S. Department of Commerce. U.S. Bureau of the Census. *1995 Annual Survey of Manufactures*. Washington, D.C.: GPO, 1997.

SIC 3262

VITREOUS CHINA TABLE AND KITCHEN ARTICLES

This industry consists of companies that manufacture vitreous china table and kitchen articles, such as bone china, vitreous china tableware, vitreous china dishes, and china cooking ware. Manufacturers of fine earthenware table and kitchen articles are In **SIC 3263: Fine Earthenware (Whiteware) Table and Kitchen Articles.**

NAICS CODE(S)

327112 (Vitreous China, Fine Earthenware and Other Pottery Product Manufacturing)

Manufacture of vitreous china table and kitchen articles is an anomaly in twentieth- and early twenty-first-century America. It is a very labor-intensive industry, with skilled craftsmen perfecting work that has extremely high standards of quality. In this industry, much of the technology is the same as it was ages ago. Many glaze recipes, clays, molds, casting, and firing processes have remained unchanged, but potters' wheels are electric, and jiggerblades quickly shape the pieces.

Porcelain was being made in China as early as the ninth century. Many centuries later, the Ohio River valley became the first china manufacturing center in the United States. Here manufacturers had easy access to kaolin, the soft, white clay that is essential to the manufacture of china and porcelain.

Vitreous china is made of clays that are glazed and fired at extremely high temperatures. The temperatures cause the glaze to fuse with the clay and become nonporous. This china is both delicate and extremely durable. For this reason, it is used in hotels and restaurants more often than the semivitreous earthenware manufactured in **SIC 3263.**

The industry is closely tied to economic conditions because many people consider china to be a luxury. Also, since the manufacturers sell to the hotel and restaurant trade, they suffer when there is a slump in new hotel and restaurant openings. The bridal market accounts for a large percentage of sales of bone china and other vitreous china table articles, and when this market suffers, so does the industry. Competition from abroad is intense. Imports account for about half of the U.S. market of housewares, kitchenware, and tableware. Some U.S. manufacturers have part of the work done overseas and finish their pieces in this country.

As consumer confidence recovered following the economic downturn in the 1980s, the industry improved. Manufacturers began to respond to consumer concerns about lead content in chinaware. California's Proposition 65 required labeling on chinaware, warning consumers if a product exposed them to more than 0.5 micrograms of lead per day.

According to the 1995 *Annual Survey of Manufactures,* 5,200 people were employed in this industry with 4,200 working in production. The cost of materials used by the industry was $80.2 million dollars in 1995, a $1.0 million decline from 1994, but the value of industry shipments rose almost $7.0 million to $368.0 million. In 1997 it was estimated that there were 1,000 establishments producing vitreous china, as well as fine earthenware, discussed in **SIC 3263: Fine Earthenware (Whiteware) Table and Kitchen Articles,** employing a total of 20,548 workers.

Most industry leaders have been in the business for many years. Pfaltzgraff, founded in 1811 and headquartered in York, Pennsylvania, is said to be the oldest continuously operating pottery in the country. It is owned by the privately held company Susquehanna Broadcasting. Pfaltzgraff purchased another well-known chinaware manufacturer, Syracuse, in 1983. Lenox China, founded in 1889 in Trenton, New Jersey, was bought by Brown-Forman in 1983. Oneida, which bought Buffalo China in 1983, was founded in 1848 and was originally known for its quality flatware. Homer Laughlin was founded in 1871 in West Virginia.

The three top companies in 1999 were Corning Inc., of Corning, New York, with nearly $3.5 billion in sales; Lenox Inc., of Lawrenceville, New Jersey, with sales of $370 million; and Mikasa, Inc., of Carson, California, with sales of $363 million.

Industry jobs include machine operators in the sliphouse; mold runners, casters, and jiggermen who shape and form the clay; cutters and finishers who dry and secondary shape; glaze grinders and decorators; kiln firemen and loaders; inspectors, selectors, and stampers; and packers. Average hourly wages for production workers in this industry were $10.58 in the late 1990s. Kiln operators earned hourly wages of $6.06 to $9.26, while molders and casters earned $4.61 to $9.86 per hour.

The U.S. industry endures heavy worldwide competition, especially with Japan, Taiwan, China, and England. However, a weaker dollar has meant that exports from the United States have increased, especially to Taiwan, Canada, and Mexico, while foreign products have become more expensive, making domestic products more attractive at home.

Some manufacturers were looking in new technological directions to beat foreign competitors, such as Pfaltzgraff, the first in the industry to have a dry press system, which formed, finished, decorated, glazed, and fired china in one continuous process. It vastly increased productivity. The company also invested in a CAD/CAM system that provided 3-D images of finished china products.

FURTHER READING

Bureau of the Census. *Economic Census 1997.* Washington, D.C.: GPO, 1999. Available from http://www.census.gov.

Darnay, Arsen J., ed. *Manufacturing USA.* 5th ed. Detroit: Gale Research, 1996.

U.S. Department of Commerce. Bureau of the Census. *1995 Annual Survey of Manufactures.* Washington, D.C.: GPO, 1997.

SIC 3263

FINE EARTHENWARE (WHITEWARE) TABLE AND KITCHEN ARTICLES

This industry consists of companies manufacturing semivitreous earthenware table and kitchen articles. These include fine semivitreous whiteware, semivitreous earthenware used for cooking and serving food, and both commercial and household earthenware. Manufacturers of vitreous china table and kitchen articles are included in **SIC 3262: Vitreous China Table and Kitchen Articles.**

NAICS CODE(S)

327112 (Vitreous China, Fine Earthenware and Other Pottery Product Manufacturing)

Fine earthenware table and kitchen articles have been made for centuries. Earthenware is porous, coarse, and opaque—unlike vitrified porcelain and bone china, which are nonporous and translucent. All are considered pottery and begin with clay and other raw materials, but earthenware is fired at lower temperatures and is more breakable.

Many styles and types of earthenware have become popular as everyday dinnerware. Since earthenware was less expensive than bone china or other vitreous tableware, sales of it were less affected by the economic downturn of the 1980s. China and porcelain products have begun to draw more consumers, however, especially from high-income households headed by 45- to 54-year-olds. The bridal market also accounted for a large percentage of retail sales of semivitreous earthenware.

The oldest form of pottery, earthenware, was made in China as early as the ninth century, where it was dried in the sun. Kilns have become the source of heat to fire pottery that becomes modern dinnerware, but in the industry as a whole, much of the technology is the same as it was centuries ago. Not much has changed—including the labor-intensive nature of the work and the skilled craftsmen who are employed to manufacture products with high standards of quality—but pottery wheels are electric, and a jiggerblade can speedily shape a plate.

In the early 1990s, manufacturers were beginning to respond to consumer concerns about lead content in chinaware. Some manufacturers changed the recipes of their glazes to reduce the lead content. Ceramic goods imported from other countries were more often to blame since many countries did not have strict lead content rules. California's Proposition 65, the Safe Drinking water and Toxic Enforcement Act of 1986, required labeling on chinaware, warning consumers if a product exposed them to more than 0.5 micrograms of lead per day.

Although most of the same companies that manufactured earthenware also manufactured vitreous china, far fewer people worked directly on these products. In 1997, approximately 20,548 people were employed in both industries, of which only a few hundred worked in the earthenware industry, and this number was expected to continue its decrease. Of the 600 workers in 1996, an estimated 500 worked in production. The value of industry shipments in 1994 was $57.0 million, but this was expected to decrease to $36.8 million by 1998. Combined industry shipments in 1997 were estimated at more than $1.0 billion.

Industry jobs included machine operators in the sliphouse; mold runners, casters, and jiggermen who work to shape and form the clay; cutters and finishers who dry and again shape the product; glaze grinders and decorators; kiln firemen and loaders; inspectors, selectors, and stampers; and packers. The only occupation expecting growth through the year 2005 was painting, coating, and decorating workers. Extruding and forming machine workers were expecting the most dramatic decrease—80.6 percent.

Average hourly wages for production workers in this industry were $11.27 in 1990. Kiln operators earned hourly wages of $6.06 to $9.26, while molders and casters earned hourly wages of $4.61 to $9.86. By 1997 the hourly wage remained at $10.58 and was expected to decline further to $8.62 by 1998.

The industry leaders in 1999 were Zrike Company of Pompton Plains, New Jersey, with sales of $14 million, and Bonny Products Inc., of Washington, North Carolina, with sales of $6 million.

Imports accounted for about 50 percent of the sales in earthenware and kitchenware in the mid-1990s. Most foreign competition came especially from Japan, Taiwan, China, and England. However, exports to Taiwan, Canada, and Mexico increased as the dollar weakened.

FURTHER READING

Bureau of the Census. *Economic Census 1997*. Washington, D.C.: GPO, 1999. Available from http://www.census.gov.

Margulies, Jeffrey B. "The Prop 65 Page," 1996-1999. Available from http://members.aol.com/calprop65/about.html.

U.S. Department of Commerce. Bureau of the Census. *1995 Annual Survey of Manufactures*. Washington, D.C.: GPO, 1997.

SIC 3264

PORCELAIN ELECTRICAL SUPPLIES

This category consists of manufacturers of porcelain electronic insulators, molded porcelain parts for electrical devices, other electrical insulators, ceramic electronic and electrical supplies, and spark plug and steatitic porcelain.

NAICS CODE(S)

327113 (Porcelain Electrical Supply Manufacturing)

Unlike other pottery product industries, the porcelain electrical supplies industry relies on high technology. Only the base material, clay, makes it similar to other pottery products. The products manufactured in this industry are ideal insulators for electrical currents because of the way they dissipate heat. The United States has the technological edge in most electronic ceramic components used in these high-performance markets.

The value of product shipments in this industry rose steadily in the late 1980s, from $759 million in 1987 to $936 million in 1990. Due in part to the decrease in U.S. military spending, the value of product shipments dropped in the early 1990s, to $927 million in 1991. The industry experienced rapid growth in the mid-1990s however, as the value of product shipments reached $1.4 billion in 1995, dropping somewhat to nearly $1.2 billion in 1997. The worldwide advanced ceramics market was estimated to be worth between $2 and $3 billion in 1996, with U.S. companies dominating the industry overall. The structural and electronic ceramics segment of the market was estimated at nearly $1 billion. The U.S. Advanced Ceramics Association projected 9 percent annual growth in the advanced ceramics market through the end of the twentieth century.

In 1997 there were 10,082 people working in the porcelain electrical supplies industry, 78 percent of whom were production workers. The annual salary for production workers fell 2 percent in 1995, to $25,700, in line with the national average for production workers in manufacturing. Salaries in 1997 were an average of $27,760. Professional staff in the industry include inspectors, metrology and process workers, and application engineers.

The Adolph Coors Company, whose primary business is malt beverages, was also making technical ceramics at a separate facility until late 1992, when the brewery became a separate company. Coors Ceramics Company, which was one of the largest U.S.-owned manufacturer of technical ceramics, became a part of the holding company called ACX Technologies. Although company outputs were primarily absorbed by Adolph Coors Company, sales for ACX fell more than 20 percent, from $910 million in 1995 to $712 million in 1996. Coors Ceramics represented about 30 percent of ACX net sales in 1995, with $271 million. In 1999, ACX Technologies posted $988 million in sales, and Coors Ceramics Company posted $300 million.

Many of the companies working in this industry also make engineering supplies that are not porcelain based. Some of the companies are small job shops making small quantities of a specific product and others are large international corporations. Brush Wellman Inc., for example, makes beryllia ceramics and beryllium alloys used as insulators for microelectronics. These products represent only about 10 percent of their business.

Some of the latest technology employed by manufacturers in this industry includes dry press production equipment, automation such as computerized tool control systems and computer-aided design, high volume tunnel kilns, and statistical process control that is integrated on a network. Precision operations include grinding, lapping, and polishing.

FURTHER READING

ACX Technologies, Inc. "The ACX Businesses." Golden, CO: Lighthouse Communications Group, Ltd., 1996. Available from http://www.acxt.com:80/ccc.html.

Bureau of the Census. *Economic Census 1997.* Washington, D.C.: GPO, 1999. Available from http://www.census.gov.

Darnay, Arsen J., ed. *Manufacturing USA.* 5th ed. Detroit: Gale Research, 1996.

U.S. Bureau of the Census. *1995 Annual Survey of Manufactures.* Washington, D.C.: GPO, 1997. Available from http://www.census.gov/prod/www/titles.html#mm.

SIC 3269

POTTERY PRODUCTS, NOT ELSEWHERE CLASSIFIED

This industry consists of manufacturers of art and ornamental pottery, industrial and laboratory pottery, unglazed earthenware florists' articles, and earthenware table and kitchen articles, as well as those establishments primarily engaged in firing and decorating white china and earthenware for the trade.

NAICS CODE(S)

327112 (Vitreous China, Fine Earthenware, and Other Pottery Product Manufacturing)

INDUSTRY SNAPSHOT

The manufacture of pottery products, like the manufacture of vitreous china table and kitchen articles (see **SIC 3262: Vitreous China Table and Kitchen Articles**) is an anomaly in twentieth-century American industry. It is labor-intensive and to a large extent involves machinery and techniques that have changed little in the last half century.

Pottery is made of clays that are mixed with other chemicals. Some pottery products are made on modern versions of potters' wheels, and some are glazed and fired at extremely high temperatures to become vitreous china. Pottery that is glazed and fired in a kiln becomes vitrified, or nonporous and glass-like, when the high temperatures cause the glaze to fuse with the clay; this china is both delicate and extremely durable. For this reason, it is used for fine giftware such as bone china figurines and lamp bases.

Competition from abroad is intense. Pottery products are sold in the United States from Japanese, English, Chinese, and Spanish manufacturers, among others. Imports account for almost three-quarters of the U.S. gift market. During the first half of the 1990s, weakness in the U.S. dollar helped to even the playing field somewhat, allowing U.S. manufacturers to sell more of their wares in Canada, Taiwan, and Mexico. However, as the decade progressed and the dollar again strengthened, foreign manufacturers regained the upper hand.

The industry is also closely tied to economic conditions, as many consumers consider art and ornamental pottery to be a luxury. Although the U.S. economy was recovering in the early 1990s, the upturn in the giftware market was slower than in other industries. Even fine china, once considered a staple of the bridal market, was being rejected in the late 1990s by some young couples who preferred to put more money into electronic equipment or more expensive housing.

ORGANIZATION AND STRUCTURE

The pottery products industry is led by several manufacturers who also create tableware and kitchenware made of vitreous china and semivitreous earthenware. Much of the equipment used by these manufacturers is the same for all of these products. Glazes and kiln temperatures vary widely, however, and the manufacturers often keep their different lines separate. Some manufacturers, for example, create their unglazed red earthenware lines in a separate plant from their semivitreous tableware lines.

The giftware market is critical for these manufacturers. Some of the promotional or commemorative pottery items slid through the recession without suffering, as corporate buyers continued to purchase promotional ceramics at much the same rate.

BACKGROUND AND DEVELOPMENT

Porcelain was being made in China as early as the ninth century. By the seventeenth and eighteenth centuries, fine porcelain art objects were being created in Europe as well. When immigrants came to the United States, they brought their crafting techniques with them. The Ohio River Valley, where manufacturers had easy access to kaolin (the soft, white clay that is essential to the manufacture of china and porcelain), became the first pottery manufacturing center. By the late 1990s, more of the companies working with pottery products were in California, but companies in Ohio and Pennsylvania still accounted for nearly 15 percent of the industry's total shipments.

The Industrial Revolution changed the manufacture of porcelain products just as it had changed other industries. Around the world, potters, who had created hand-thrown ware and then painstakingly decorated their work one piece at a time, began to change the procedures they used. Mass copies of pottery objects became available at lower prices as the processes became more efficient. Some manufacturers objected to the new ways, however, and insisted on maintaining individuality and high quality in their wares.

Potters in the United States also had to adapt to the changing tastes and needs of their communities late in the nineteenth century. They had to compete with increasingly available glass and tin containers, and many of them expanded their product lines to include red earthenware pots, which became the only luxury many consumers allowed themselves through World War I and the Depression. For many U.S. potteries, these flowerpots were the company staple for decades.

CURRENT CONDITIONS

During the recession of the late 1980s the giftware market suffered. Even affluent consumers who purchased artware, stoneware, and earthenware items were becoming more price conscious. Manufacturers had to lower prices or develop newer lines to compensate for losses. However, while the retail market was sluggish, many manufacturers covered their losses by responding to increased demand for promotional giftware and tableware. In the dinnerware market (also covered in **SIC 3262: Vitreous China Table and Kitchen Articles** and **SIC 3263: Fine Earthenware (Whiteware) Table and Kitchen Articles**) more than half of sales were through mass merchants and department stores.

Giftware in the 1990s became increasingly diverse. New designs of ceramic and pottery items reflected interest in the environment and in multicultural themes. Both wholesalers and retailers displayed collections of pottery and stoneware that were reminiscent of specific cultures, or that were politically correct, environmentally friendly, or both. One popular cookie jar was designed to resemble the earth, complete with raised continents. Certain traditional items, such as elegant china and earthenware figures still sold well.

The increasing concern about lead content in earthenware, pottery, and other ceramics led to the establishment of the Coalition of Safe Ceramicware (CSC). In early 1992, the CSC pledged that its members complied with all of the Food and Drug Administration (FDA) standards regarding safe levels of lead, with Proposition 65, which required labeling on chinaware warning consumers if a product exposed them to more than 0.5 micrograms of lead per day, and with the California Tableware Safety Program.

The U.S. economic boom during the latter half of the 1990s was another indication that the giftware business would be improving steadily. As consumer confidence increased, small shops were again optimistic that their sales would increase accordingly.

According to the U.S. Census Bureau's *1997 Economic Census,* the value of shipments in the industry was $996.4 million, up from $591.7 million in 1990; $519.7 million in 1987; and only $146.9 million in 1972. These figures included the shipments of products that were primary and secondary to the industry. Most of the value of product shipments for this industry came from art and decorative ware made either of china and porcelain, or of earthenware and stoneware. Projections toward the year 2000 anticipated continued growth in the industry.

INDUSTRY LEADERS

In the late 1990s, most of the recognized leaders in the manufacture of pottery products also manufactured fine earthenware and/or vitreous china table and kitchen products. Most industry leaders had been in the business for many years. Pfaltzgraff, founded in 1811 and headquartered in York, Pennsylvania, was recognized as the oldest continuously operating pottery in the country. Operated by the Pfaltzgraff family for generations, the company expanded throughout the 1980s, purchasing another well-known manufacturer of pottery products, Syracuse, in 1983. In 1988, Pfaltzgraff bought Treasure Craft, a California company that was known for its giftware and household ceramic products. Privately held, Pfaltzgraff is not required to disclose details of its financial performance.

Lenox China, founded in 1889 in Trenton, New Jersey, was purchased by Brown-Forman Corp. of Louisville, Kentucky, in 1983. The china company's founder, Walter Scott Lenox, formed the Ceramic Art Company, which made table items as well as gift and art pieces including parasol handles, vases, inkstands, and thimbles. Lenox opened a new facility in 1985 in Oxford, North Carolina, expressly for the manufacture of Lenox China giftware. Other Lenox China plants were in Pomona, New Jersey, and Kinston, North Carolina.

WORKFORCE

Many workers in this industry spend their entire careers perfecting one job. Each job in production is unique, from the creation of the special clay mixture, called slip, to the packaging of the final products. Training a potter takes many years, and most manufacturers in this industry hire production workers with the intention of investing the time required so that the workers learn the craft from top to bottom.

Some plants have a sliphouse, where there are machine operators, mixers, and others who must bring the raw materials to exactly the right consistency before it can be cast. Casters pour the slip into plaster-of-Paris molds where it dries for a specified length of time. The porous molds draw moisture out of the slip until enough of a shell forms the outlines of the product. If it sits too long, when the rest of the slip is poured out, the shell will be too thick to be glazed and fired. Each manufacturer has its own recipe for the slip and its own methods for casting, but each step is carefully monitored.

After pouring out excess slip, casters and finishers sponge the products, removing coarse edges and seams left over from the mold. In some plants, jigger men work in shaping and forming the clay, and cutters and finishers work in drying and secondary shaping. The pottery where the products are cast can be very dusty during the drying operations. During certain hours each day all workers are required to wear respirators. The pottery, then known as greenware, must dry, usually overnight, before it is ready to be glazed and fired.

Most glazing is done by a glazer; glazes are sprayed onto one piece at a time. Some glazes are applied by glazing machines. In most factories, loaders place greenware onto tiered carts that can be moved from the casting room through the glazing department and directly through the kilns. Kiln operators and loaders get used to the intense heat needed to vitrify the greenware. Glazes and ceramics become melded together, forming the impermeable vitreous china. Kilns reach temperatures of up to 2,300 degrees Fahrenheit; therefore, they are almost never shut down, since it would take close to two weeks to get them back up to firing temperature.

Once they emerge from the kiln, the products are checked by inspectors and chosen by selectors. Pieces that are slightly defective are sent back for regrinding, reglazing, and refiring. Many items, especially in giftware, are then specially adorned by decorators. These must also be seen by inspectors before being sent to the packing department.

The manufacturers also have support departments, including machine shops, where machinery can be repaired or cleaned; mold departments, where plaster molds are made and repaired; and warehouses that handle shipping and receiving. They also have administrative departments covering human resources, public relations, corporate development, and other general business needs.

In the 1990s, many of the plants where pottery products were manufactured were unionized. Some of the organized workers belonged to the Glass Molders, Pottery, Plastics and Allied Workers International Union (GPPAW). The GPPAW published a health and safety manual that identified potential workplace hazards for manufacturers of dinnerware, chinaware, and other pottery products. The unions were also active in negotiating wages, certain workplace standards, vacation time, and other benefits for their members.

According to the *1997 Economic Census* published by the U.S. Bureau of the Census, 14,363 people worked in the pottery products industry that year. Of these, 11,307 worked in production. In 1985 there were only 7,100 people working in the industry. The average hourly wage for production workers in 1997 was $10.02, up from $7.06 in 1987, $5.96 in 1982, and $3.87 in 1977.

AMERICA AND THE WORLD

Nearing the year 2000, the U.S. pottery industry faced heavy world competition, especially with Japan, Taiwan, China, and England. For much of the 1990s, the weaker U.S. dollar meant that exports from the United States increased, especially to Taiwan, Canada, and Mexico, while foreign products became more expensive and made domestic products more attractive at home. However, as the dollar strengthened later in the decade, competition from imports gathered strength once again.

U.S. potteries tried to capitalize on the desire of local consumers to buy products made in their country. They tried to keep close tabs on marketplace trends and to respond with items the American consumers would want.

RESEARCH AND TECHNOLOGY

Much of the technology employed by the pottery industry in 1997 was the same as it was centuries ago. The factories in the early twentieth century used more machinery to produce more pottery, but the essential ingredients remained. For example, hand-throwing techniques were supplemented with hand-jigger machines. Today's potter's wheel is electric, and a jigger blade is usually used to quickly shape a plate. Salt glazing was gradually replaced by dip-glazing, in which the ware was dipped before firing. In some plants, pottery is glazed automatically, while in others, glazers spray glaze onto only one item at a time. Only slight changes have been made in the recipes for clays, the shape and type of molds, casting methods, and firing techniques.

However, some manufacturers were looking in new technological directions to keep foreign competitors at bay. Pfaltzgraff was the first in the industry to have a dry press system, which formed, finished, decorated, glazed, and fired pottery products in one continuous process. It vastly increased productivity, especially for plates and small bowls. The company also invested in a CAD/CAM system that provided 3-D images of finished products so that problems could be anticipated and corrected before production began. In 1997, the company estimated that it saved 9 to 18 months in production and discarded one-quarter fewer pieces of china because of the CAD/CAM improvements.

The larger changes for the pottery products industry were in the general way business was conducted. In order to survive, these small, family-owned potteries had to become businesses that competed not only in the national but also the international market. It was no longer enough to make a quality product. Manufacturers also had to market and sell their wares, create new innovations, and pass on to a new generation of potters the desire to keep this age-old craft thriving.

FURTHER READING

Deutsch, Claudia H. "Not Making Them Like They Used To," *New York Times,* 31 March 1997.

The Fine China and Crystal Story. Lawrenceville, NJ: Lenox China, September 1990.

Glossary of Fine China and Crystal Terms. Lawrenceville, NJ: Lenox China, July 1991.

Pfaltzgraff: America's Potter. York, PA: Historical Society of York County, 1989.

Rotenier, Nancy. "The Gifty Business," *Forbes,* 22 April 1996.

U.S. Bureau of the Census. "1997 Economic Census: Vitreous China, Fine Earthenware and Other Pottery Product Manufacturing." Washington, D.C.: GPO, 1999. Available from http://www.census.gov/prod/www/abs/97ecmani.html.

SIC 3271

CONCRETE BLOCK AND BRICK

This category covers establishments engaged in manufacturing concrete building block and brick from a combination of cement and aggregate. Contractors engaged in concrete construction work are classified in the construction segment (see Vol. 2, Chapter 3: Construction Industries) while establishments primarily engaged in mixing and delivering ready-mixed concrete are classified in **SIC 3273: Ready-Mixed Concrete.**

NAICS CODE(S)

327331 (Concrete Block and Brick Manufacturing)

In 1999 the concrete block and brick industry had approximately 20,300 employees, of which 13,400 were in production. Establishments in the industry shipped products with a total value of $2.8 billion in 1997, and net output increased 2 percent by the following year. The employees in the industry in 1999 earned a total of $717.9 million.

Although the industry has had slow and fluctuating growth in the 1980s and early 1990s, the part of the market that is expected to be strong in the latter 1990s is the public works segment, which should be helpful to the concrete block and brick industry. Dominant states in the industry include Pennsylvania, California, Texas, and Michigan.

The first solid concrete block patent was granted in 1832, and the first hollow concrete building block patent was in 1850, both in England. Harmon S. Palmer patented a concrete block machine in 1900 in the United States. Since then, the concrete block has continued to increase in popularity because of the product's durability and economy. The industry also advanced in terms of product quality, production and distribution methods, and installation procedures. Concrete's fire safety compared to that of wood has been a major factor in its appeal. In the early days, small concrete manufacturing facilities sprouted up rapidly in most urban areas in the United States because they needed to be located near their users' destinations. A block machine could be bought for $100 in 1906, and the business opportunities appealed to entrepreneurial instincts.

The National Concrete Masonry Association (NCMA) was an affiliate of the Portland Cement Association in the 1930s. The NCMA became independent in

1942 and has since supported concrete block producers, machinery manufacturers, and related interests. Since its founding, the NCMA has conducted research and testing on concrete block products and structures.

Establishments in this industry tend to be relatively small, local operations, since it is generally not economical to ship concrete block and brick more than 50 miles because of its weight. For this reason, companies in the industry have grown by organizing or purchasing added concrete block and brick production operations in new areas.

Another factor in the structure of the industry is that most of the companies that produce concrete block and brick also produce other concrete-related products, including ready-mixed concrete, concrete pipe, or various precast or prestressed products, such as building structural parts, which can be fabricated centrally and shipped to locations where they will be installed. Sales of these secondary products in 1992 were an estimated $127.0 million with an additional $451.6 million in earnings attributable to miscellany.

Most concrete block and brick establishments have one or more competitors in their areas of operation and compete in matters such as price, location, service, quality, and reliability. They also compete with other building products such as lumber, clay brick, and steel.

Companies within this industry segment spent $1.4 billion on materials services and fuels in 1999, with the products shipped valued at nearly $2.9 billion. In 1997 there were 940 establishments operating within this industry sector.

None of the larger companies in the concrete industries has concrete block and brick as the primary product line. These larger companies produce concrete block as one part of a group of products in the concrete and other construction-related fields. Leading corporations within this industry segment ranked by revenue as of 1999 included Glen-Gery Corporation of Wyomissing, Pennsylvania, with $150 million in sales; Featherlite Building Products Corporation of Austin, Texas, with $45 million in sales; and Clayton Block Company of Lakewood, New Jersey, with $21 million in sales.

Research has continued in the 1990s to improve the characteristics of concrete block as well as to make possible different features to fit varying users' needs and desires. New exterior appearance attributes have been developed such as ribbed, fluted, and split-faced surfaces, which have met the needs of innovative architects for the walls of buildings. Blocks of lighter weight have been created by mixing different raw material aggregates with the cement and water. New uses have been found for concrete blocks, such as in drainage systems. Research

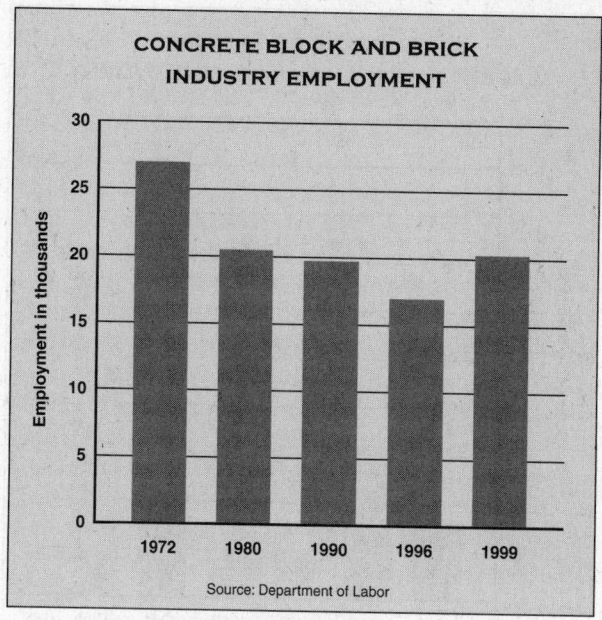

has also been conducted on ways in which concrete block might be constructed automatically into building walls.

FURTHER READING

Bureau of the Census. *Economic Census 1997*. Washington, D.C.: GPO, 1999. Available from http://www.census.gov.

Bureau of Labor Statistics. *Employment Statistics*. Washington, D.C.: GPO, 1999. Available from http://www.bls.gov.

Thomas, William D., et al. "Producer Price Highlights." *Monthly Labor Review*, July 1999.

SIC 3272

CONCRETE PRODUCTS, EXCEPT BLOCK AND BRICK

This category covers establishments primarily engaged in manufacturing concrete products, except block and brick, from a combination of cement and aggregate. Contractors engaged in concrete construction work are classified in the construction industries, and establishments primarily engaged in mixing and delivering ready-mixed concrete are classified in **SIC 3273: Ready-Mixed Concrete.**

NAICS CODE(S)

327999 (All Other Miscellaneous Nonmetallic Mineral Product Manufacturing)
327332 (Concrete Pipe Manufacturing)
327390 (Other Concrete Product Manufacturing)

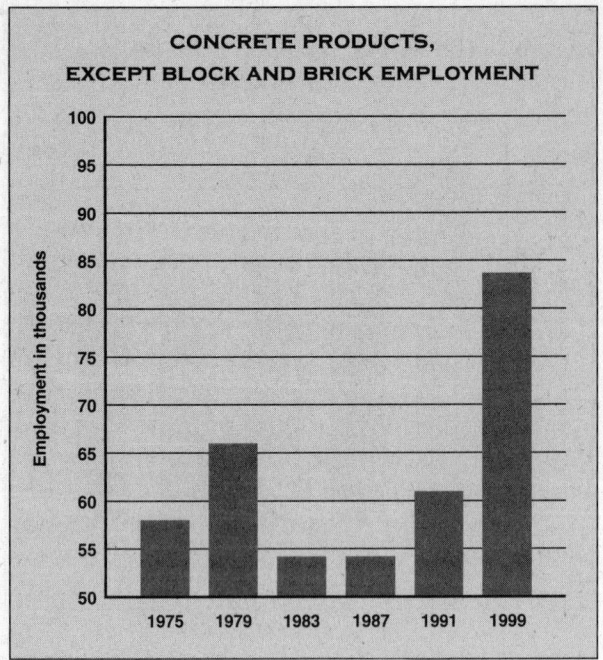

CONCRETE PRODUCTS,
EXCEPT BLOCK AND BRICK EMPLOYMENT

INDUSTRY SNAPSHOT

The products included in this industry are made of concrete, formed and hardened at the cement facility, and shipped in finished form to customers or users. Many of the items were prefabricated parts to be assembled into buildings, bridges, or parking structures. Pipe was another major segment of the industry. Other products included a variety of utilitarian and decorative items, such as burial vaults, septic tanks, monuments, and bird baths.

In contrast to products that were poured on-site, the products of this industry were made in a controlled environment, away from a construction job site. Such controlled production conditions enabled concrete products to be made more structurally sound and in accordance with construction specifications.

In 1999 the concrete products industry employed 83,700 people, of which 65,400 were in production. In 1987 the states with the greatest employment in the industry were California, Florida, Pennsylvania, and Texas, which accounted for 35 percent of the total industry employment.

ORGANIZATION AND STRUCTURE

The great majority of customers for concrete products were building contractors and construction firms. This required industry firms to deal with architects and engineers as well as management. Many of the industry's sales comprised standard or off-the-shelf items that were produced, warehoused, and sold to multiple customers. Other items were tailor-made to the specific design of particular buildings, bridges, parking structures, or other

facilities. Where products made of plastic or lumber were possible alternatives, precast concrete products were sometimes preferred and selected for environmental reasons.

Companies in the industry tended to grow by acquisitions and mergers. The greater size enabled the companies to spread their marketing, research, and engineering costs over a larger number of activities. Industry firms also joined to form several trade groups, which generally conducted research into materials and methods to improve the products, performed promotion of the product specialty, and represented the industry in governmental matters. These associations included the American Concrete Institute, the American Concrete Pressure Pipe Association, the Concrete Reinforcing Steel Institute, the Post-Tensioning Institute, the Portland Cement Association, the American Segmental Bridge Institute, and the Precast/Prestressed Concrete Institute.

Industry firms continually conducted research to improve the qualities of concrete products. Areas of focus included workability, strength, durability, weight, and insulating ability. Minimum quality standards for products were established by the American Society for Testing and Materials (ASTM) and were continuously modified as technology developed and changed.

BACKGROUND AND DEVELOPMENT

Concrete was made by mixing together cement, sand, gravel, possibly other aggregates, and water. The concrete then was molded and might be reinforced in a variety of ways to meet its different purposes. Molds were made of wood, fiberglass, concrete, or other materials. Precast concrete was poured into molds of the desired product shapes, in which it was hardened and cured. Reinforced concrete was strengthened by inserting steel rods or mixing in fibers. Prestressed concrete had steel wires or rods inserted and stretched so as to compress the concrete and make it resist tensile stresses. Other qualities of concrete were modified by use of different types of sand, gravel, crushed stone, and cement in differing proportions. All of these factors affected the properties relating to its strength, durability, workability, curing time, resistance to temperature and humidity changes, and appearance.

CURRENT CONDITIONS

In 1967 there were 2,687 companies in the concrete products industry, employing 70,000 workers and shipping products valued at $5.8 billion. By 1982 there were 2,749 companies, employing 20 percent fewer employees and shipping 39 percent less product value. In 1997 there were approximately 2,743 establishments and fewer than 70,000 employees. Total shipments for that year were estimated at $8.0 billion.

The concrete products industry often experienced cyclical changes along with the construction industries on which it largely depended. The industry's business fluctuations were most apparent in the total number of employees. For example, the industry stood at 58,000 workers in 1975; 66,000 in 1979; 54,200 in 1983; 70,000 in 1987; 61,000 in 1991; and 83,700 in 1999.

U.S. total cement consumption grew by 19.2 percent between 1991 and 1994; March 1995 cement prices were 5.3 percent higher than the previous year. Also, production in 1995 was reported to be reaching capacity, save in New England and California, where the industry was feeling the impact of slower economic recovery.

Construction in public works projects in the United States—infrastructure construction ranging from construction of public buildings, highways, and conduits for utilities—was predicted to increase, then level off at about $120 billion through 1998. For example, a 1992 review found many of the 600,000 bridges in the Federal Highway Administration's jurisdiction as requiring either replacement or significant repairs. The water distribution system in New York City also broke and caused frequent flood conditions in the 1980s and early 1990s. In response to increased demand, the concrete products industry was expected to continue to enhance concrete's qualities and usefulness through engineering improvements.

INDUSTRY LEADERS

By far the 1999 leader in this industry sector was Oldcastle Inc. of Atlanta, Georgia. Oldcastle posted sales of nearly $2.5 billion and employed 15,000 workers. A distant second was Tarmac America Inc. of Norfolk, Virginia, with sales of $400.0 million and 2,300 workers. Third was Hydro Conduit Corporation of Houston, Texas, with $250.0 million in sales and 2,000 employees.

WORKFORCE

The concrete products industry employed 83,700 people in 1999. More than 78 percent of the industry's employees were production workers who earned an average of $12.25 per hour. The average work week was 44.5 hours with 7.5 hours of overtime. The industry's white collar jobs encompassed accounting, engineering, estimating, marketing, and management.

RESEARCH AND TECHNOLOGY

Industry firms conducted continuous research throughout the twentieth century to enhance the qualities of concrete products and construction operations and to improve the methods for producing and delivering concrete. Additional advancements were made by business-

men and managers, as with the adaptation of trucks for deliveries and mixing in the early part of the century.

Continual and sometimes dramatic changes in science and engineering produced positive changes in the industry. Industrialization of the precast concrete products industry began in earnest in the 1960s and 1970s as an increasing number of improvements in the strength and other qualities of concrete were made by scientific, engineering, and chemical research and analyses. Technicians in these specialties combined steel with concrete to enable its use in large bridge and skyscraper structural elements, as well as applied computers and automation to control and mix raw material ingredients accurately. Many studies and tests were conducted to determine the effects of different material ingredients, and varying proportions of those ingredients, in producing desired new concrete qualities. These scientific activities were performed by both individual companies—each hoping to improve its own competitive position—and industry-supported trade associations and institutes.

"Basically, most 'new' products in the precast concrete industry are an evolution of existing elements," according to one industry overview. "Nevertheless, the industry has developed (and is successfully marketing) valuable solutions in fields relative to, for instance, environmental problems such as sound barrier walls to protect residents living near highways or railways from noise hindrance."

In the mid-1990s there was some controversy in the United States regarding the manufacture of concrete-related products using cement made in hazardous waste burning kilns. It was thought that perhaps the toxic chemicals not destroyed in the process could leach through the pipe or other products and into the environment; however, there has been little research that would either support or refute these claims. The concern spawned legislation at the local government level banning the use of or sale of "toxic cement," including the use of concrete pipe manufactured with cement made from hazardous waste fueled kilns in public water supplies.

The use of used tires as a kiln fuel was also challenged by environmental regulations. Proponents, however, as is the case with the use of hazardous waste as a kiln fuel, argued that using spent tires was an effective form of recycling. Both practices have met with numerous legal challenges.

FURTHER READING
Bureau of Labor Statistics. *Employment Statistics.* Washington, D.C.: GPO, 1999. Available from http://www.bls.gov.

"Set in Concrete: Trade." *The Economist,* 3 June 1995.

U.S. Census Bureau. *Economic Census 1997.* Washington, D.C.: GPO, 1999. Available from http://www.census.gov.

SIC 3273

READY-MIXED CONCRETE

This category covers establishments primarily engaged in manufacturing portland cement concrete manufactured and delivered to a purchaser in a plastic and unhardened state. This industry includes production and sale of central-mixed concrete, shrink-mixed concrete, and truck-mixed concrete.

NAICS CODE(S)

327320 (Ready-Mix Concrete Manufacturing)

INDUSTRY SNAPSHOT

A material similar to stone, concrete is made by mixing selected proportions and qualities of cement, sand, gravel, and sometimes other aggregates. Water is added and the soft mixture is formed into desired shapes. Water and cement interact chemically to form a solid mass, binding the ingredient particles together, but the mixture remains soft so that it can be shaped before the concrete hardens.

Concrete was a leading material resource for building construction and for various products because of its strength, its ability to be molded into any shape, its resistance to fire and weather, and the availability of materials from which it is made. Concrete's limited strength under tensile stress was substantially overcome by reinforcement with steel and other materials in various ways.

According to the National Ready Mixed Concrete Association (NRMCA), the U.S. industry's leading trade association, the key to achieving a long-lasting concrete product lies in the proportioning and mixing of the ingredients. A mixture that lacks sufficient paste, made up of cement of water, to fill all the voids between the aggregates will be difficult to handle and will produce rough surfaces and porous concrete. However, a mixture with too much paste, though easy to place, will be more susceptible to cracking and in the long run will be uneconomical. NRMCA suggests that the ideal mixture will have the necessary workability for the fresh concrete and the desired strength once the mixture has hardened. A typical mixture contains by volume about 10 to 15 percent cement, 60 to 75 percent aggregates (usually sand, gravel, and rock), and 15 to 20 percent water.

Concrete businesses throughout the 1990s furnished much of the basic raw material for the construction industries, as well as for utilitarian and artistic products like railroad ties and birdbaths. A few of the larger construction contractors made their own concrete materials and products, while others relied on concrete producers for their products.

The ready-mixed concrete industry included businesses that made concrete and delivered it to contractors or other customers for constructing buildings, bridges, roads, sidewalks, or other facilities. The concrete production process involved the use of large-scale equipment and machinery located reasonably close to where the concrete was to be used so that the concrete could be delivered while it was still soft enough to be shaped.

The concrete ready-mixed industry was heavily dependent on its primary customers, which were constructors of homes, industrial and office buildings, highways, and bridges. Consequently, the industry's market generally shadows the cyclical markets served by construction industries. For example, in the early 1990s the market for public works construction was strong while the other building markets were weak. At the midpoint of the decade, as residential and industrial construction began to strengthen, the level of public works construction continued strong. These public works projects included the construction of government buildings, highways, and public utility facilities. Concrete industries developed technologies in the 1980s and 1990s to make concrete building parts stronger and more attractive, which helped the industry to reinforce its market in the construction industries.

ORGANIZATION AND STRUCTURE

Many ready-mixed concrete companies were relatively small, having customers in one community or a limited region, primarily because soft concrete cannot be delivered beyond about 20 miles from where it is made. Yet to produce the concrete economically requires considerable expenditures for plant and trucking facilities. Most concrete plants were fixed, but some were portable and could be moved close to major construction sites. Many larger companies have grown by expanding their territories as well as by buying smaller local firms. In 1992 there were more than 5,250 establishments producing ready-mixed concrete. Of those, less than 1,400 employed 20 or more employees. With increasing consolidation within the industry, the total number of establishments was projected to fall to about 5,000 by the year 2000, of which about 1,400 would employ 20 or more people. The number of establishments is greater than the number of companies in this sector, as several of the larger players in the concrete business maintain multiple production establishments.

Most of the ready-mixed concrete producers also were involved in related concrete businesses, such as the mining of sand and gravel, the production of crushed stone, cement manufacturing, or the manufacturing of concrete blocks, pipe, building structural elements, and other concrete products.

Most industry establishments competed against several concrete businesses in a small market area. In addition, several non-concrete products substituted for concrete provided another arena of competition. These alternative resources included lumber, asphalt, brick, and steel.

The NRMCA was the primary trade group supporting the industry. Headquartered near Washington, D.C., the NRMCA helped its more than 1,000 members by fostering research, training and product promotion programs, and by representing the industry before federal and professional groups. The NRMCA worked with many other trade associations in the ready-mixed concrete industry including the Portland Cement Association (PCA), the American Concrete Pavement Association (ACPA), the Concrete Reinforcing Steel Institute (CRSI), the Post-Tensioning Institute (PTI), and the American Concrete Institute (ACI).

The American Society for Testing and Materials (ASTM) began providing guidelines for the manufacture and testing of concrete products in 1933. Throughout its existence, the organization continued to revise its specifications as the ready-mixed concrete industry, and the technology it utilized, evolved. Additional organizations, including ACI and NRMCA, published other specifications.

BACKGROUND AND DEVELOPMENT

Though the first use of concrete dates back many centuries, widespread usage did not occur until the nineteenth century, when improvements in the materials combined to form the cement ingredient were made. In the twentieth century, reinforcement techniques were developed that made cement structural components for skyscrapers and large bridges over highways and rivers practical. The development of trucks equipped to mix concrete in transit in the 1920s made it possible for the ready-mixed approach to become the dominant process for concrete use by the 1990s.

Portland cement was invented in 1824 by Joseph Aspdin, a British engineer, and had strength and water resistance qualities superior to those of previous cements. Limestone and clay were portland cement's principal ingredients. These raw materials were ground finely, combined, and heated in a kiln to form clinker, which was then pulverized. The name ''portland'' came from the Isle of Portland, where limestone was quarried. Portland cement was the primary type of cement used from its origination.

In 1909 concrete was first mixed in transit in a horse drawn wagon with gears from the wheels activating paddles in the mixing process. In 1913 concrete was taken to the work site in a dump truck. The first company to market a revolving horizontal drum mixer was the Paris Mixer Company in 1926. Between 1925 and 1930, the number of ready-mixed concrete plants in the United States increased from 25 to 100. The NRMCA was formed in 1930 and helped foster industry growth.

Concrete, like stone, has very good compressive strength; it withstands considerable pressure from above without crumbling. However, concrete does not have great tensile strength. A concrete beam between two posts will crack if too much pressure is placed in the middle of the beam. To overcome tensile limitations, steel rods were placed in the concrete before it hardened, reinforcing its tensile strength. Reinforcing concrete techniques were begun in the first decade of the twentieth century. Prestressed concrete can withstand even greater tensile stresses. Rods or wires are stretched before the concrete hardens around them. The released wires or rods then compress the concrete, providing additional tensile strength. Prestressed technology enabled cement to be used in much greater spans as required in the construction of large-scale buildings and bridges.

Between 1982 and 1996, the number of employees in the industry increased from 81,600 to 94,500, while the number of establishments producing concrete decreased from 5,379 to less than 5,100, reflecting a number of acquisitions and mergers.

CURRENT CONDITIONS

The latter half of the 1990s saw a boom in construction throughout the United States, fueled by a healthy economy and low interest rates. However, as the millennium neared its end, there were signs that the boom was beginning to slow. Dun & Bradstreet's November 1999 survey of 200 U.S. construction executives indicated that the industry was entering a period of slower growth, giving it time to work off some of its back orders. The outlook through early 2000 pointed toward fewer orders, lower employment levels, and softer prices. ''Our November survey suggests that the sector is entering a slow-down period, a trend that industry experts, and our survey respondents, have been predicting for some time,'' said David T. Kresge, Dun & Bradstreet's chief economist.

Many of the larger ready-mixed concrete companies benefited from centralized purchasing, marketing, and engineering operations. Many were involved in manufacturing fields related to concrete production, such as making concrete pipe, railroad ties, and construction structural elements. Because of the benefits of size, it was expected that the trend toward larger companies in the industry would continue.

There was steady improvement in the durability, appearance, and other qualities of ready-mixed concrete. Lower production costs and greater quality control also were achieved. These advancements were spurred by competition and aided by the many trade groups conducting research and providing training.

INDUSTRY LEADERS

Major players in the U.S. ready mixed concrete industry in the late 1990s included Holnam Inc., Lafarge

Corp., Lone Star Industries Inc., U.S. Concrete Inc., Florida Rock Industries Inc., Centex Construction Products, Vulcan Materials Co., Texas Industries Inc., Giant Cement Holding Inc., and CSR America. One indication of the strong hold foreign cement producers have on the industry is the fact that at least 50 percent of the industry's leaders are owned wholly or in part by foreign companies.

Holnam Inc., headquartered in Dundee, Michigan, is a subsidiary of Switzerland's Holderbank Fianciere Glaris. The largest cement producer in the United States, Holnam employs close to 2,500 in its U.S. offices and plants. As a subsidiary of Holderbank, Holnam is not required to report on its financial results, but its 1997 revenue is estimated at close to $1.1 billion.

Based in Reston, Virginia, Lafarge Corp. is 52 percent owned by Lafarge SA, a French building products giant. Although the U.S. company is also involved in the production of gypsum wallboard and asphalt, its cement business accounts for nearly 45 percent of its annual revenue, which hit $2.45 billion in 1998, up more than 35 percent from the previous year.

A subsidiary of Germany's Dyckerhoff, Lone Star Industries is headquartered in Stamford, Connecticut. Producing Portland cement and ready-mixed concrete, Lone Star operates five cement plants in the Southwest and Midwest and also holds a quarter interest in Kosmos Cement, the owner of two additional cement plants. With more than 1,000 employees, Lone Star posted 1998 revenue of $347.1 million, down slightly from the previous year.

Two other major players in the U.S. ready-mixed concrete market with foreign ties were Giant Cement Holding Inc., which in late 1999 was being acquired by Cementos Portland of Spain, and CSR America, the North American subsidiary of Australia's CSR. Giant Cement, of Summerville, South Carolina, reported sales of $154.1 million in 1998.

In addition to its operations in cement and concrete, Texas Industries is involved in the production of steel, manufacturing a variety of steel products from recycled material. Headquartered in Dallas, Texas, the company posted revenue of $1.13 billion for fiscal 1999, the twelve months ended May 31, 1999. Its principal customers are involved in construction in Colorado, Louisiana, Oklahoma, and Texas.

Based in Birmingham, Alabama, Vulcan Materials Co. produces concrete along with a wide variety of other construction materials, particularly aggregates. Vulcan also manufactures a number of industrial and specialty chemicals. The company posted 1998 revenue of $1.78 billion, up 5.8 percent from the previous year.

Florida Rock Industries Inc., based in Jacksonville, Florida, sells its products throughout much of the eastern United States. In addition to ready-mixed concrete, the company produces concrete block and a wide variety of construction aggregates. For fiscal 1999, the 12 months ended September 30, 1999, the company posted revenue of $579.3 million, an increase of nearly 18 percent over the previous year.

Centex Construction Products Inc., headquartered in Dallas, is 60 percent owned by homebuilder Center Corp., of which it once was a division. Although the company produces a variety of building materials, its cement business accounts for nearly 50 percent of its total revenue, which was $336 million in fiscal 1999, the 12 months ended March 31, 1999.

U.S. Concrete Inc., based in Houston, employed about 600 people as of the late 1990s. The company posted 1998 sales of $194.1 million.

WORKFORCE

Most of the employees in the ready-mixed concrete industry were production workers. Larger companies and many smaller companies used computers not only for accounting but for controlling the processes of concrete mixing and other production operations. The larger companies in particular employed engineers to help refine mixing and production processes.

The 94,500 employees in the industry in 1996 earned a total of $2.93 billion in wages. Production workers made up the biggest segment of the industry's total payroll in 1996, totaling 73,900 workers, each of whom earned an average of $13.07 per hour.

Employment in the ready-mixed concrete industry in the year 2000 was projected to total just under 93,000, up modestly from 1991 employment of 86,100, but below 1996 figures. Industry shipments, valued at about $11.7 billion in 1991, were projected to hit nearly $20 billion in 2000.

AMERICA AND THE WORLD

The principal international relationships of the ready-mixed concrete industry have been that some of the raw materials have been received from overseas, growing operations in the United States have been foreign owned, and some American companies have had facilities that produced concrete in other countries.

Concrete transactions between countries were somewhat limited by the fact that ready-mixed concrete production and sales were local operations. Also, hardened concrete products, like pipe and concrete block, were prohibitively expensive to ship overseas because of their weight. However, there have been significant cases of international ownership of ready-mixed and other concrete operations.

In the 1980s, cement from foreign sources filled 15 percent of U.S. needs, but not without conflict. A battle between cement producers in the United States and Mexico started in the late 1980s and escalated through the next decade. Mexico's Cemex—the largest producer in that country as well as the globe's fourth largest firm in the industry—was accused of dumping product in the United States. The Department of Commerce started tacking on anti-dumping duties in 1990, which were raised again in May 1995 from 43 to 62 percent. *The Economist* reported that 19 U.S. manufacturers grumbled because the duty was considered too low.

Reports were that U.S. cement companies prepared several proposals in order for the U.S. trade officials to address the issue, including the chairman of Lone Star Industries, Inc. Failing in his efforts to reduce import levels, Lone Star then became the largest importer of cement. By 1992, imported cement had dropped to 8 percent of consumption in the United States, but it quickly increased because manufacturers were reaching plant capacity and sales had increased. The United States imported 11.3 million tons of concrete in 1994, 60 percent more than was imported in 1993 and the most since 1990, according to *The Economist*. However, the latter half of the 1990s saw relatively modest growth in U.S. imports of cement.

The ironic aspect of this dispute was that approximately two-thirds of all U.S. cement companies were foreign-owned. Subsidiaries of companies such as Lafarge, Mitsubishi Materials Corporation, and Blue Circle Industries PLC either fully owned or controlled significant financial interests in many cement and cement products plants throughout the United States.

Many U.S. cement companies had been acquired by foreign interests in the early 1990s because reduced profits had made them vulnerable to takeovers. More than 65 percent of U.S. cement production facilities were acquired by foreign interests. The two largest cement producing companies in the United States were foreign owned.

For example, Lafarge, the largest cement producer in North America and a major manufacturer of ready-mixed concrete, was a subsidiary of a French construction company, Lafarge Coppee. Lafarge Coppee was a major building materials company operating in 35 countries.

RESEARCH AND TECHNOLOGY

With keen competition forcing ready-mixed concrete companies to improve service and cut costs, many of the larger companies looked toward research and technology to improve the quality of concrete products and reduce their production costs. Lafarge, for example, used scrap tires as a fuel and industrial by-products, such as spent refractory bricks and iron mill scale, as low-cost raw materials for concrete. This practice was not without controversy, and soon the manufacture of concrete-related products using cement made in hazardous waste burning kilns in the United States was questioned. It is thought that perhaps the toxic chemicals not destroyed in the process leach through the pipe or other products and into the environment; however, there has been little research that would either support or refute these claims. The concern spawned legislation at the local government level in the mid-1990s that would ban the use of or sale of "toxic cement," including the use of concrete pipe manufactured with cement made from hazardous waste-fueled kilns in public water supplies.

Using used tires as a kiln fuel was also challenged by environmental regulations. Proponents, however, as is the case with the use of hazardous waste as a kiln fuel, argued that using spent tires was an effective form of recycling. Both practices have met with numerous legal challenges.

For years concrete producers and industry groups endeavored to improve concrete's strength, durability, uniformity, appearance, drying time, and weight. By the early 1990s, concrete's compression strength had been increased to withstand 20,000 pounds per square inch (psi), while in laboratory experiments strengths of 100,000 psi were reached. In the 1960s, 5,800 psi was considered high-strength concrete.

The American Society of Civil Engineers established the Civil Engineering Research Council (CERC) to spearhead a program of construction product improvements the society considered to be essential to meet infrastructure needs for the twenty-first century. The CERC developed plans to work with government, industry, and trade groups in designing and perfecting higher strength concrete.

Other research was conducted to create new types of concrete that would enable their use in products previously made from ceramics, plastic, or aluminum. Lone Star developed a new product named Pyrament that dried quickly enough to allow traffic on a road four hours after the concrete was laid. Greater strength-to-weight ratios and improved ability to absorb energy were achieved by incorporating reinforcing materials such as wood, glass, carbon, or steel into concrete.

Computer hardware and software were used by ready-mixed concrete manufacturers in the late 1980s to prepare job estimates, control production processes, and schedule deliveries. For example, Raia Industries Inc., of Hackensack, New Jersey, reported a 200 to 300 percent increase in productivity once it computerized its operations.

Ready-mixed concrete companies as well as trade groups were continuously seeking more efficient manufacturing and processing approaches. Examples included enabling longer delivery span, reducing truck and equipment maintenance costs, facilitating filling of bags, and automating the setting of concrete curbs.

In the late 1980s, Master Builders Inc. developed a technology that slowed the hardening process in the formation of concrete, thus enabling it to be transported over longer periods of time and distances. This technique was called the DELVO system and was said not to be detrimental to strength or other concrete characteristics.

However, as Lionel W. Vincent of National Cement Company of California Inc. wrote in *Concrete Products,* "The zeal for putting all that information into the end product is for naught without implementing the basics of concrete production. Over the years, our reliance on obtaining concrete durability has been unrealistically tied to a dependence on the increasing use of chemical admixtures, mineral additives, specialty cements, etc. . . . The cost of a cubic yard of basic concrete containing the three basic ingredients—cement, aggregates and water—can now be doubled by adding anywhere from three to five (or more) special additives. What is evident here is that after 40 years of innovative technology and 'allege' improved knowledge, the 'back to basics' theory is still very valid. . . . If you rely on additives or special cements and you disregard the basics of good concrete, you will most likely not attain durable concrete."

FURTHER READING

CSR. "About CSR," 1999. Available from http://www.csr.com.au/about/index.html.

Darnay, Arsen J., ed. *Manufacturing USA,* 6th ed. Detroit: Gale Research, 1998.

"Expected Slowdown in Construction Finally Shows Up; Order Books, Employment, and Prices All Weaken." *Business Wire,* 7 December 1999.

National Ready Mixed Concrete Association. "Concrete Basics," 1999. Available from http://www.nrmca.org/concrete_basics.

"Set in Concrete: Trade." *The Economist,* 3 June 1995.

Vincent, Lionel W. "Concrete: from A-Z and Back to A." *Concrete Products,* June 1993.

SIC 3274

LIME

The lime industry is comprised of establishments primarily engaged in manufacturing quick-lime, hydrated lime, and miscellaneous lime-related products. It is considered part of the larger concrete, gypsum, and plaster products industry.

NAICS CODE(S)

327410 (Lime Manufacturing)

Lime, or quick-lime, is calcium oxide derived from naturally occurring calcium carbonate. Its total production in the United States ranked fifth among all chemicals. Lime is produced at 85 establishments. The total value of the product shipments in 1997 was more than $1 billion.

One of the oldest products of chemical reaction known to man, lime is a white or grayish-white solid with numerous applications. Its history dates to ancient Egypt, where it was used in mortar and plaster. Lime was traditionally used as a construction product until the Industrial Revolution when its usage began expanding. The growth of the chemical industry at the start of the twentieth century gave lime production another boost and, of that produced, an estimated 90 percent is used in some sort of chemical process. Solid lime, for example, is used extensively as a fertilizer and building material. It is also commonly utilized as a chemical neutralizer to treat solid and gaseous wastes. Quick-lime accounted for approximately 72 percent of industry revenues in the early 1990s.

When mixed with water, lime turns into calcium hydroxide, or slaked lime, which is used to make mortars, plasters, and cement. Slaked lime represented about 19 percent of industry output in 1991. Lime is also used to make calcium carbide, which decomposes in water to form the flammable acetylene gas used in welding torches.

Blast furnace operators and steel manufacturers consume the largest amounts of lime products to melt and process steel. Steel production usage, the traditional driving force in this industry, consumed about 31 percent of industry output in 1994. Total use in chemical and industrial applications represented 64 percent of the lime market. Chemical firms, for example, use lime-related products in the production of plastic resins. Environmental uses, such as water, sewage, and smokestack emissions treatment, accounted for 26 percent of lime usage in 1994, and construction industries consumed about 8 percent, with refractory, or heat-resistant, dolomite usage consuming 2 percent of total U.S. lime production.

Lime is considered a commodity, and industry profit margins are typically low. However, new applications for lime allowed the industry to realize steady demand growth throughout the mid-1900s and even through the 1980s. Between 1982 and 1988, for instance, sales of lime expanded 35 percent, from $543 million to about $830 million. Growth faltered in the late 1980s and early 1990s, and lime production dipped to about 17.5 million tons and $720 million in 1991. World production has been tapering off each year since 1990. U.S. lime producers were poised for recovery in 1993 and 1994; production in those years was 16.8 million metric tons at a value of $965 million, according to the Bureau of Mines, and 17.4 million metric tons worth more than $1 billion, respectively. The total value of the product shipments in 1997 was $1.2 billion.

While some core lime markets remained stagnant in the mid-1990s, other segments were expected to buoy production volume and industry earnings throughout the next decades. Flue gas desulfurization in 1996 accounted for 15 percent of all lime sales and, as the market segment with the fastest growth, was poised to continue with utility deregulation. As environmental restrictions increase, so too will lime uses related to treating wastes. In 1995 alone, two midwestern utilities that invested in new lime scrubbers increased the market by a single-year record amount. By mid-1996 Dravo, one of the nation's leading producers of lime, announced production increases and expected operations at full capacity, particularly with the introduction of a new product for the lime-based environmental technologies market.

The largest U.S. lime producer in 1999 was Dravo Corporation of Pittsburgh, Pennsylvania, with sales of $321 million. Second was Martin Limestone Inc., of Blue Ball, Pennsylvania, with sales of $36 million.

WORKFORCE

A recovering economy and new lime applications will help boost industry employment between 1990 and 2005, according to the Bureau of Labor statistics. Lime manufacturers employed about 5,524 workers in early 1997. Despite continued productivity gains, however, jobs in most occupations should rise by 5 to 20 percent by 2005. Truck drivers, who make up about 30 percent of the entire workforce, will see their opportunities jump by 13 percent. Industrial production management jobs will grow approximately 23 percent. Sales and marketing positions will likely increase 27 percent.

FURTHER READING

Bureau of the Census. *Economic Census 1997*. Washington, D.C.: GPO, 1999. Available from http://www.census.gov.

Chapman, Peter. "Lime Growth Doesn't Meet Expectations." *Chemical Marketing Reporter*, 1 January 1996.

"Lime Demand Eases, But Market Remains Strong." *Industrial Specialties News*, 6 May 1996.

Minerals Yearbook: Metals and Minerals, Volume I. Washington, D.C.: U.S. Department of the Interior, Bureau of Mines, n.d.

SIC 3275

GYPSUM PRODUCTS

Companies predominately employed in manufacturing plaster, plasterboard, and other gypsum products con-

stitute the gypsum products industry. The manufacturers in this industry make products such as acoustical plaster, wallboard, cement, insulating plaster, orthopedic plaster (for casts), plaster of paris, and gypsum rock, lath, and tile.

NAICS CODE(S)

327420 (Gypsum and Gypsum Product Manufacturing)

INDUSTRY SNAPSHOT

Gypsum product manufacturing is nearly synonymous with wallboard production, which represents more than 90 percent of industry sales. As such, the gypsum industry's fortunes are closely tied to those of the construction business.

The late 1990s construction boom carried the otherwise mundane gypsum industry to record production levels, topping 29 billion square feet of board in 1999. That figure amounted to a 7.4 percent increase over 1998's record level. During the period, demand was so furious that manufacturers couldn't keep pace, leading to minor shortages and driving prices up sharply in places. However, a slowdown in new construction in the early 2000s promised to decelerate growth down to more sustainable rates. Ironically, because wallboard makers raced to add new capacity—a potential 30 percent boost between 1999 and 2002—supply may outpace demand in the early 2000s.

ORGANIZATION AND STRUCTURE

Gypsum, or hydrated calcium sulfate, has been an important construction material for centuries. It is mined from hardened ocean and saline-lake brine deposits. Natural supplies of the material are abundant, particularly in the United States, Canada, France, Italy, and Britain. The largest U.S. gypsum-producing states are Oklahoma, Iowa, Texas, Michigan, Nevada, California, and Indiana. In 1998 these states contributed 73 percent of domestic gypsum production. Companies that only mine gypsum without producing finished or semi-finished goods aren't considered part of this industry, however.

In 1998 just 10 U.S. companies calcined, or dehydrated, gypsum for use in wallboard manufacturing. Calcining is an intermediate process that occurs after grinding gypsum into a powder. The process is necessary in order to reconstitute a mineral paste for use in wallboard. The activity was spread among 65 plants in 28 states, often close to sites where the material was mined or quarried. The top four companies (USG Corp., National Gypsum Co., Georgia-Pacific Corporation, and Celotex Corp.) supplied almost 80 percent of U.S. calcined gypsum.

Gypsum is used as a fertilizer, a filler in paper and textiles, and a retarding agent in cement. About 80 percent of total gypsum output, however, is used to make plaster that is formed into building products. When combined with water and additives, plaster becomes a white cementing material that sets and hardens by chemical reaction. It is an excellent construction material for interior walls because it is inexpensive, easy to install, fire retardant, and acts as a noise insulator.

The United States remains the world's largest producer and consumer of wallboard. About 75 percent of the gypsum consumed in the United States is used in wallboard. Forty percent of wallboard products are used in new residential construction. Another 35 percent of industry output is used for remodeling and repair, while 10 percent goes into new commercial construction. The remaining 15 percent of the market consists of numerous miscellaneous applications, such as mobile home walls.

BACKGROUND AND DEVELOPMENT

Gypsum-based wallboard was first developed around 1900 in the United States. Strong housing markets during the post-World War II U.S. economic expansion pushed industry sales close to $2 billion in the late 1970s. But a housing slump in the early 1980s kept revenues to $2.3 billion in 1982.

A recovery in housing starts boosted gypsum industry sales to a peak of nearly $2.7 billion in 1987. A U.S. economic recession and depressed housing markets in the late 1980s and early 1990s, however, pummeled industry participants. Receipts plunged below $2 billion a year in the early 1990s, and wallboard prices crashed from $127 per thousand square feet in 1985 to $67 in 1992. Prices recovered in the mid- to late 1990s as construction picked up and as wallboard manufacturers held the line on adding new capacity. From a plateau of $110 in 1995 and 1996, prices edged upward from 1997 to 1998, nearing $130 by 1998. In 1999 prices peaked around $160, lifting wallboard makers' profits handsomely. Over the period of 1994 to 1999, output had climbed 30 percent, crossing 29 billion square feet in 1999. The value of gypsum product shipments in 1999 was estimated at $4.5 billion.

INDUSTRY LEADERS

USG Corp., formerly United States Gypsum Co., of Illinois, is the largest U.S. wallboard maker. Aftershocks from financial hurdles that beset the firm in the 1970s and 1980s, which ranged from antitrust matters to a hostile takeover bid to lawsuits over asbestos-contaminated products, forced the company to retrench under Chapter 11 bankruptcy protection. By the late 1990s, USG emerged triumphant. As of 1999, USG commanded a third of the U.S. wallboard market. Approximately 80 percent of its $3.6 billion in sales that year came from its North American Gypsum unit, its wallboard arm. USG also markets ceiling tiles and commercial ceiling systems.

National Gypsum Co., the second-largest U.S. producer, also had a brush with bankruptcy in the early

1990s. The erstwhile public company was recapitalized with private financing in 1995. Delcor Inc., an investment concern owned by C.D. Spangler, then National Gypsum's chairman, became the parent company. Since being taken private, National Gypsum hasn't released detailed financial and production figures, but it is widely regarded as the industry's number-two player, and its 1999 revenues were estimated at upwards of $1.2 billion. In 1994, its last full year as a public company, the firm recorded annual sales of $630 million.

Other participants in the gypsum industry include forest-products giant Georgia-Pacific Corp., Celotex Corp., Temple-Inland Inc., Republic Gypsum Co., James Hardie Gypsum, and Lafarge Corporation.

WORKFORCE

According to 1997 estimates by the Census Bureau, the industry employed more than 11,000 people. That figure was essentially flat since the early 1990s. The average hourly wage for production workers was $14.47 in 1997, compared to the manufacturing average of $13.91. Production laborers averaged a 44-hour work week that year.

FURTHER READING

Balazik, Ronald F. ''Gypsum.'' *Mineral Industry Yearbook.* Washington, D.C.: U.S. Geological Survey, 1999. Available from http://www.minerals.usgs.gov.

Gypsum Association. ''Another Record Setting Year for Wallboard Production.'' Washington, January 2000. Available from http://www.gypsum.org.

Tejada, Carlos, James R. Hagerty, and Carl Quintanilla. ''World-Trade Wallflower, Drywall Is Rare Example of Scarce Commodity.'' *Wall Street Journal,* 15 March 1999.

Tejada, Carlos, and Patrick Barta. ''Drywall Demand Eases, But Prices Remain High.'' *Wall Street Journal,* 17 January 2000.

SIC 3281

CUT STONE AND STONE PRODUCTS

This category covers establishments primarily engaged in cutting, shaping, and finishing granite, marble, limestone, slate, and other stone for building and miscellaneous uses. Establishments primarily engaged in buying or selling partly finished monuments and tombstones, but performing no work on the stones other than lettering, finishing, or shaping to custom order, are classified in either the wholesale or retail trade divisions. The cutting of grindstones, pulpstones, and whetstones at the quarry is classified in the mining division.

NAICS Code(s)

327991 (Cut Stone and Stone Product Manufacturing)

Industry Snapshot

Dimension stone sales expanded steadily during the 1990s as construction markets grew. Shipments were valued at $1.3 billion in 1997. Despite a severe construction industry recession beginning in the late 1980s, a trend toward the use of stone in new buildings buoyed industry earnings, as did new technology that delivered productivity gains.

Organization and Structure

The three main materials utilized in this industry are granite, marble, and limestone. Granite products accounted for more than 50 percent of industry output in the 1990s. Granite is a light-colored rock—usually found in mountainous regions—that is comprised primarily of varying amounts of quartz and feldspar. About half of all cut granite is used in buildings, the remainder being consumed to create monuments and miscellaneous products.

Marble, which represented approximately 20 percent of production during the 1990s, is also used mostly in buildings. It is metamorphosed limestone and is usually quarried from the core of young mountains in the Rockies or from the exposed roots of ancient mountains in the Appalachians. The presence of impurities and other minerals during metamorphosis is responsible for the many colors and streaks found in different types of marble. Its strength and appearance make it a popular stone for statuary and decorative applications.

Limestone, a sedimentary rock, is comprised primarily of calcite that resulted from the sedimentation of coral and dead organisms. Limestone varies greatly in texture and color. Although most limestone is crushed for use as agricultural lime or cement, cut limestone is often used as building stone. Limestone products, almost all of which are building stone, accounted for about 10 percent of industry shipments during the 1990s. Aside from the three major stone products groups, miscellaneous cut stone comprised the remaining almost 20 percent of sales. Slate, for example, is commonly used in construction and to make items such as billiard tables and chalkboards.

Dimension stone is usually removed from open pits in rectangular blocks, although some rock is mined from tunnel-type quarries. A channeling machine is used to cut softer rocks, such as limestone, marble, and sandstone, into blocks that are removed by cranes and hauled away. The rock may also be cut by wire sawing, which involves pulling a wire surrounded by an abrasive slurry back-and-forth along the stone.

From the quarry, the stone is hauled to a processing plant where it is cut, shaped, polished, and/or coated. Most dimension stone is finished into masonry veneer for use as fascia on buildings. The stone veneer is anchored to a structural frame or backing, often giving the impression that the structure is built with stone blocks. A significant portion of cut stone is shaped and finished into surfaces for floors, walls, tables, and counters.

Background and Development

Dimension stone was quarried as early as Egyptian times. The Egyptian pyramids were built from quarried stone in about 2800 B.C.; the largest pyramid contains 2.3 million blocks with an average weight of 2.5 tons. The Babylonians used cut stone in 600 B.C. to build the renowned Hanging Gardens. The Greeks and the Romans also used cut and finished stone widely as construction, decorative, and statuary material. In fact, the Greeks quarried marble as early as 447 B.C.

Stone was quarried in America as a building and paving material before the Revolutionary War. But the U.S. cut stone industry lagged behind European production until the development of a railway system during the mid-1800s. Mechanized cutting and finishing tools and methods during the late 1800s and early 1900s significantly boosted industry activity, as did the building boom of the 1920s. Early U.S. stone structures include St. Patrick's Cathedral (1879) and the Cathedral of St. John the Divine (started in 1892 and completed in 1996), both in New York City.

Although stone remains an important building material, new construction materials and methods developed during the twentieth century have limited its use almost entirely to a finishing element of mostly decorative value. Steel frames and concrete have particularly infringed on conventional uses of stone. Furthermore, new synthetic materials have replaced stone in many decorative and functional applications, such as counter tops, wall coverings, and architectural ornamentation. Many synthetic substitutes with the look and feel of marble or granite are less expensive, more durable, and easier to manufacture, ship, and install than real stone. Nevertheless, stone is still a popular and cost-effective building material for many indoor and outdoor construction projects and consumer products.

Current Conditions

Although synthetics and glass became popular building materials during the 1980s, an escalation in commercial construction spurred cut stone industry expansion. Sales climbed from about $900.0 million in 1988 to almost $1.3 billion in 1996. Despite slow building activity during the 1990s, revenues continued to ascend to nearly $1.5 billion by 1996. Shipments were valued at $1.3 billion in 1997. Furthermore, increased interest in stone building materials, as opposed to concrete and glass, continued to buoy sales into the middle of the decade.

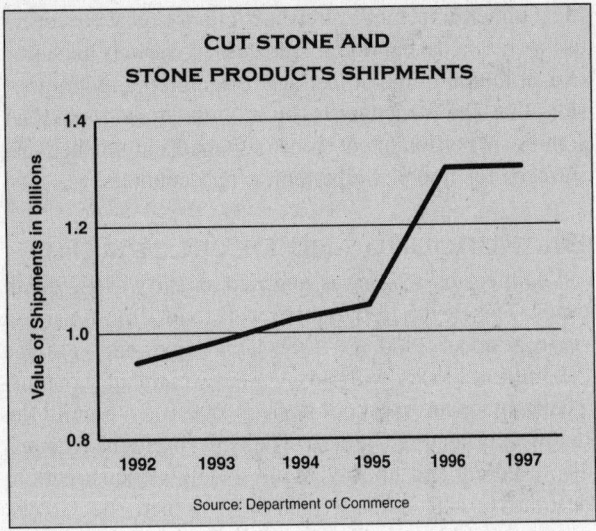

CUT STONE AND STONE PRODUCTS SHIPMENTS

Value of Shipments in billions

Source: Department of Commerce

spot on the horizon for the industry is the expected continued surge in historical restoration projects that require considerable amounts of stone to replace damaged pieces from the original construction.

INDUSTRY LEADERS

Because of its logistical characteristics (transportation costs), the cut stone industry is highly fragmented into relatively small, local manufacturers. In 1997 slightly more than 1,000 establishments competed. The largest producer was Pluess-Staufer Industries Inc., of Proctor, Vermont, with sales of $130 million. Second was Alabama Limestone Company Limited, of Russellville, Alabama, with $60 million in sales.

WORKFORCE

The employment outlook for the cut stone and stone products industry was dismal. In fact, most labor positions were expected to decline by about 20 percent by 2005, according to the U.S. Bureau of Labor Statistics. Jobs for helpers and material handlers, which account for 8 percent of the workforce, will likely diminish 22 percent by 2005; work for cutting machine operators, truck drivers, and finishers will fall 10 percent. Even management positions will decline 12 percent or more. Only opportunities for production managers are forecast to increase, though only slightly.

RESEARCH AND TECHNOLOGY

New cutting, finishing, and construction technologies in the mid-1990s were helping the cut stone and stone products industry remain competitive against new synthetics and low-cost imports. For example, advanced construction techniques were used in Washington, D.C., in 1992 to create and erect massive 50-foot-tall limestone columns for the Market Square Arena—800,000 cubic feet of limestone were quarried to produce the 80,000 cubic feet of material actually contained in the columns. An advanced horizontal lathe rounded and fluted the huge structures, which were put into place as the concrete frame of the building was poured. The project was indicative of a trend toward greater use of natural stone in restorative building projects.

Cut stone producers were also benefiting from improved quarrying techniques, such as laser rock-face profiling and robotic drilling and cutting machines. While much of this technology was being developed for extraction of crushed stone and other minerals, cut stone producers were finding applications for these and related innovations.

FURTHER READING

Cook, Hugh. "The Keys To Historic Masonry Restoration." *Building Design and Construction,* February 1997.

Many cut stone and stone product companies were crunched by the construction slowdown of the 1980s and early 1990s. As demand slowed, prices dropped and profit margins slipped as a result of overcapacity and increased competition. Most industry segments were stable, however. Granite producers, for example, were achieving greater demand at the expense of marble. Marble had been losing market share since the 1980s when it was determined that most varieties are affected by acid rain. Although granite producers were fighting stiff foreign competition, the use of granite for headstones and monuments remained strong, and a construction industry uptick in the mid-1990s bolstered the bottom line for many competitors.

Some companies were also benefiting from productivity gains implemented during the slowdown. The industry had succeeded at increasing its workforce only 25 percent during the 1980s as its shipment value surged almost 80 percent. New automated cutting and finishing equipment, as well as advanced transportation and information systems, were credited with increasing efficiency. But while some producers had been able to boost profitability through automation, stone cutting remained a labor intensive industry susceptible to imports from low-cost emerging nations. India, for example, has made steady inroads into the U.S. granite industry throughout the 1990s.

The long-term industry outlook was generally lackluster going into the 2000s. Limited opportunities for further productivity gains, coupled with greater foreign competition, were expected to hurt many industry sectors. Most traditional domestic markets, such as construction, will realize tepid growth at best. In addition, superior synthetic substitutes will continue to make gains. Because of stone's weight-to-value ratio, moreover, opportunities for U.S. export growth are slim with the exception of niche specialty stones. U.S. producers exported about 2 percent of production in 1996. A bright

"Construction Growth Tied to Population." *Pit and Quarry,* October 1996.

Gregerson, John. "Old Reliable." *Building Design and Construction,* March 1997.

Hernan, Patrick. "Southeast Report." *Pit and Quarry,* January 1997.

Paslawskyj, Michael. "The Outlook is High." *Pit and Quarry,* July 1996.

U.S. Census Bureau. *Economic Census 1997.* Washington, D.C.: GPO, 1999. Available from http://www.census.gov.

SIC 3291

ABRASIVE PRODUCTS

This classification covers companies that primarily make abrasive grinding wheels of natural or synthetic materials, abrasive-coated products, and other abrasive products. Companies cutting grindstones, pulpstones, and whetstones at the quarry are classified under mining industries.

NAICS CODE(S)

332999 (All Other Miscellaneous Fabricated Metal Product Manufacturing)
327910 (Abrasive Product Manufacturing)

INDUSTRY SNAPSHOT

The value of industry shipments in 1999 was estimated at $4.62 billion, up nearly 18.5 percent from shipments of $3.9 billion in 1990. Capital investment in the sector during 1999 was estimated at $146.8 million, up from $135.4 million in 1990. By the late 1990s, there were more than 400 U.S. companies in the abrasives industry, roughly half of which employed 20 or more employees.

Among the natural abrasives used in the manufacture of abrasive products are diamonds, corundum, garnet, pumice, talc, quartz, sandstone, and certain vegetable fibers. Synthetic abrasives, first invented by Edward G. Acheson in 1891, include silicon carbide (also known as Carborundum), aluminum oxide, and boron carbide. Aluminum oxide, produced from bauxite, is used to cut hard metals, while boron carbide is one of the hardest abrasives.

This industry employed about 15,100 production workers in 1999, down from 16,400 in 1990. The industry invested about the same money per production worker as other manufacturing sectors. Annual hours worked by production workers in the industry were about the same as those worked in the manufacturing sector at large.

ORGANIZATION AND STRUCTURE

Ranked by sales, two-thirds of the top 30 firms in the industry were subsidiaries and divisions of larger firms, while the others were private companies. Of the industry's 75 leading companies, 84 percent were private corporations. Each of the industry's top 30 companies generated more than $10 million and employed 100 or more workers.

The top four types of abrasive products by product share, as of the early 1990s, were nonmetallic coated abrasive products and buffing and polishing wheels (45 percent); nonmetallic abrasive products, including diamond abrasives (23.7 percent); nonmetallic sized grains, powders, and flour abrasives (17.2 percent); and other nonmetallic shapes, coated or impregnated with any natural or artificial abrasive material, cloth-resin, and waterproof bond (12 percent).

The largest organization serving the industry is the Abrasive Engineering Society (AES), headquartered in Butler, Pennsylvania. The Society was founded in 1957 and has 400 members (its name changed from the American Society for Abrasive Methods in 1975). In addition to an annual technical conference and semiannual educational seminars, AES publishes the quarterly *AES Magazine,* circulation 3,000, and otherwise promotes the exchange of technical information about abrasive materials and their uses. The industry is also served by a number of smaller organizations, including the Grinding Wheel Institute, the Abrasive Grain Association of Cleveland, the Coated Abrasives Fabricators Association, the Diamond Wheel Manufacturers Association, and the Association of Electroplaters and Surface Finishers.

BACKGROUND AND DEVELOPMENT

Abrasives have been vital to making metal products since the earliest days of metallurgy in ancient times, but the modern abrasive products industry arose from the technical developments of the late nineteenth century. These developments involved not only abrasives, but also the binders used to create bonded abrasive products.

A key development for the industry was synthetic abrasives. In 1891, Edward G. Acheson synthesized silicon carbide, the first synthetic abrasive grain to attain broad, commercial success. Fused aluminum oxide abrasives, pioneered by C. B. Jacobs in the 1890s, became a commercial product by 1904. Along with the naturally occurring corundum, garnet, and diamond, silicon carbide and fused aluminum oxide dominated the abrasive products market into the 1930s. In 1938, a new technique for producing aluminum oxide was developed, resulting in the most successful abrasive grain for precision grinding that existed to date. In the 1950s, aluminum oxides were produced by nonfusion methods. Fused mixtures of aluminum and zirconium oxides also became commercially viable.

Diamonds gained widespread use as abrasives in the 1930s. This resulted from the creation of the first bonded wheels, using industrial diamonds, and was accelerated by the need for a very hard abrasive to grind tungsten carbide, which became important in the 1930s. Synthetic diamonds were produced in 1960 by General Electric. Along with cubic boron nitride, diamonds made up the hardest class of abrasives, known as "superabrasives."

In 1987, aluminum oxide and silicon carbide, the oldest synthetic abrasives, led industry output, with $104 million and $51 million in value consumed, respectively. Ranking next in order of value of materials used were natural abrasive materials ($30 million), diamond ($27 million), aluminum-zirconium oxide ($23 million), and cubic boron nitride ($7 million).

The development of binders for bonded abrasive products, including grinding and buffing wheels and flexible abrasives such as sandpaper, were as important as the development of synthetic fibers. Rubber was used to bond abrasives for grinding wheels in the 1850s. Sand, corundum, and diamond bonded by shellac were used to make grinding wheels in India in the early nineteenth century. The shellac process was utilized by the Waltham Emery Wheel Co. Rubber and shellac remained the only organic binders until synthetic resins came about in the 1920s.

Inorganic binders were developed in the late nineteenth century to simulate the properties of sandstone. Key among these were vitrified products commercialized by the Norton Co. of Massachusetts in the late 1800s. In addition to these binders, so-called "active" fillers were used to make grinding wheels. Active fillers enabled cooler grinding, increased wheel porosity, and increased the uses for grinding wheels.

CURRENT CONDITIONS

During the early 1990s, abrasive product shipments showed some weakness, reflecting the recessionary economic climate. Shipments in 1991, 1992, and 1993 failed to reach the $3.9 billion level recorded in 1990. However, a turnaround began in 1994, when shipments hit $4.1 billion. Shipments in 1995 and 1996 totaled $4.4 billion and $4.7 billion, respectively. Shipments for 2000 were projected at $4.7 billion.

Among the abrasive materials that showed weakness during the 1990s were fused aluminum oxides and metallic abrasives. The use of silicon carbides, aluminum-zirconium oxides, and superabrasives showed strength, with the most dramatic growth seen in the sale of superabrasives. The market share of superabrasives was expected to show sharp growth during the mid- and late 1990s. U.S. firms lagged behind competitors in Europe and the Far East in using high-technology superabrasives.

Theodore L. Giese, business manager of the Abrasive Engineering Society, argued in *AES Magazine* that the industry depended on developing formal education in abrasives technologies. Noting that only two U.S. universities had recognized programs in these technologies, the University of Connecticut and the University of Massachusetts, Giese wrote, "We have learned that trial-and-error methods for solving problems are inefficient tools for product development and troubleshooting grinding operations. Measurement-oriented strategies such as statistical process control (SPC) are necessary. Control of a grinding operation now requires an understanding of the grinding system and the concepts behind the grinding process. That means . . . a better comprehension of ideas behind the technology we use. All this translates into the need for more education."

INDUSTRY LEADERS

The leader in the U.S. abrasives industry at the end of the 1990s was the Norton Co. of Worcester, Massachusetts, an indirect wholly owned subsidiary of France's Compagnie de Saint-Gobain, which posted 1998 revenue of $20.8 billion. In addition to being the world's leading manufacturer of abrasives, Norton produces ceramics, plastics, and chemical process products. In late October 1999, Norton acquired Furon Co., a leading designer and manufacturer of engineered products made primarily from high-performance polymers. Worldwide, Norton employs 16,000 people and operates 88 production facilities in the United States and 19 other countries.

Founded in 1885, the Norton Co. was acquired in July 1990 by Saint-Gobain, which bought a majority share of the American company's common shares. The French firm also owned Norton-affiliated makers of abrasives and ceramics in Australia, Bermuda, Japan, Germany, Belgium, Luxembourg, the Netherlands, Italy, Spain, Norway, the United Kingdom, Canada, and Brazil. Norton Co. restructured after the buyout by Saint-Gobain, including $50 million in modernization investments over three years.

WORKFORCE

From a high of 17,500 production workers in 1984, employment levels in the abrasives industry generally have trended downward, except for three or four years in the late 1980s and early 1990s when the workforce plateaued at about 16,400 workers. Employment in 1999 was estimated at about 15,100 people, with a workforce of only 14,900 projected for the year 2000.

RESEARCH AND TECHNOLOGY

Much of the research and new technical developments in the industry were related to the increased importance of superabrasives. In *Superabrasive Grinding,* J.L. Metzger summarized future areas of superabrasives development, ''Our experience indicates major developments are likely to continue—possibly even to accelerate—in the following areas: (1) New, custom-designed, 'hard-to-grind' materials for an ever widening spectrum of industrial applications; (2) Creep feed grinding, also known as plunge or deep feed grinding; (3) High performance, high-speed grinding of hardened steels with CBN-wheels; (4) Form or profile grinding, in part with electroplated, in part with crushable wheels, in high removal, high precision, high surface quality applications; (5) CNC-control of production grinding machines, with, possibly, partial adaptive control optimization.'' Other developments regarding superabrasives included the use of chemical vapor deposition for optimal bonding of diamond coatings. Flexible belt superabrasive products were advocated over bonded wheel superabrasives for grinding ceramics because flexible products were less likely to chip and crack ceramics.

Additional areas of technical development for the industry included improvements in coated (sandpaper-like) abrasives, such as new backings, adhesives, grains and joint designs (for belt abrasives), and the use of cushioned belts. These improvements made coated abrasives faster and more economical than traditional grinding and cutting techniques for many applications. Substantial research was also undertaken to improve liquid coolants and lubricants used in many grinding operations.

An exciting development was announced in July 1999 when Norton Co. introduced a line of ''engineered'' abrasives. Norton claims the line, trade-named NORaX, lasts up to 10 times longer than conventional abrasives and provides higher cut rates at lower pressures. The NORaX line consists of fine-grit products in which the abrasive and bond are formed in a distinct three-dimensional structure rather than in a single layer.

FURTHER READING

Darnay, Arsen J., ed. *Manufacturing USA,* 6th ed. Detroit: Gale Research, 1998.

Metzger, J.L. *Superabrasive Grinding.* London: Butterworth & Co., 1986.

''New Line of 'Engineered Abrasives' Offers Higher Cut Rates, Longer Life for Final Finishing; Products Can be Custom-Designed for Each Application.'' *Business Wire,* 14 July 1999.

''Norton Company Completes Tender Offer for Furon Company.'' *PR Newswire,* 26 October 1999.

U.S. Department of Commerce. *1995 Annual Survey of Manufactures: Statistics for Industry Groups and Industries.* Washington, D.C.: GPO, 1997.

SIC 3292

ASBESTOS PRODUCTS

This category includes companies that primarily make asbestos textiles, asbestos building materials (except asbestos paper), insulating materials for covering boilers and pipes, and other products composed wholly or chiefly of asbestos. Companies that primarily make asbestos paper are in **SIC 2621: Paper Mills.** Those making gaskets and packing materials are in **SIC 3053: Gaskets, Packing, and Sealing Devices.**

NAICS CODE(S)

336340 (Motor Vehicle Brake System Manufacturing)
327999 (All Other Miscellaneous Nonmetallic Mineral Product Manufacturing)

INDUSTRY SNAPSHOT

Serious health concerns have all but dismantled the asbestos industry in the United States. Use of asbestos plummeted after medical studies in the early 1970s linked airborne asbestos fibers to a couple of serious illnesses: asbestosis and mesothelioma. Asbestosis scars the lungs and interferes with respiratory function, while mesothelioma is a rare and deadly form of cancer. Acting on these health concerns, the Environmental Protection Agency (EPA), in 1973, banned the use of spray-on asbestos insulation, and the U.S. tile and floor-covering industry, once a major consumer, voluntarily stopped asbestos use by 1986. According to the Census Bureau, the value of asbestos products made in the United States in 1990 was about $352 million. By 1995, sales fell so low that there were no figures available.

In 1989, the EPA issued a ruling that would have eliminated asbestos use in the United States by 1996. However, the ban was declared unreasonable by the federal courts, which permitted asbestos use in products imported or made in the United States as of July 1989. The courts upheld an EPA ban on any new products with asbestos.

By the late 1990s, only a handful of U.S. companies manufactured products containing asbestos. Most of those still involved in asbestos production produced friction products for automobile brakes. The rest made roofing materials, heat-resistant gaskets, and safety clothing. Most of the asbestos used by U.S. manufacturers was chrysotile asbestos imported from Canada.

Once enormously popular in construction applications because it is nonflammable and a poor conductor of heat, asbestos use in construction is virtually nonexistent with the exception of limited use in roofing materials. No satisfactory substitute for asbestos has been developed, although there was a glimmer of hope in the late 1990s that new products with a safe form of asbestos might soon reach the market.

BACKGROUND AND DEVELOPMENT

Asbestos is a group of soft minerals composed of tiny fibers that is nearly impervious to acid, fire, and biological decay, and is a poor conductor of heat and electricity. During the late 1800s, when it was first widely used to insulate boilers, steam pipes, and other high-temperature industrial equipment, asbestos became known as "white gold," especially in Canada, which was the world's leading supplier.

Since 1900, asbestos was used in more than 3,000 products made in the United States, from safety clothing and automobile brake linings to textured paints and electrical insulation. The most extensive use of asbestos was as construction insulation. The United States used thousands of tons of asbestos insulation in ships built during World War II. Another surge in asbestos insulation use was in the 1960s when it was routinely sprayed on structural beams and roof decks. In the mid-1970s, the United States used an estimated 700,000 tons of asbestos per year, most of it in insulation products.

Health Concerns. The ancient Greeks first noticed a link between asbestos and respiratory illness. However, the first medical studies were not done until the early 1900s when asbestos use became widespread. When asbestos' hook-shaped fibers are inhaled, they attach to the insides of the lungs. The body reacts by covering the fibers with proteins. As this scar tissue increases, the lungs clog and lose elasticity. The scarring and resulting respiratory problems are called asbestosis. Evidence also suggested prolonged exposure to asbestos increased the risk of cancer, including mesothelioma, which affects the visceral membranes. Asbestos exposure also greatly increased the risk of lung cancer for cigarette smokers.

In 1931, Great Britain became the first country to pass laws regulating exposure to asbestos; the United States did not pass similar laws until the early 1970s. In the 1960s, Dr. Irving Selikoff, an epidemiologist at Mount Sinai Hospital in New York, studied the incidence of respiratory diseases in men who had worked in the asbestos industry or in the shipyards during World War II. Selikoff also noted more respiratory problems in wives who shook asbestos dust out of their husbands' work clothes. Selikoff's controversial conclusion was that no level of exposure to asbestos was safe. However, later studies disputed Selikoff's conclusions. In the late 1980s, the United Kingdom Health and Safety Commission concluded the long-term risk to office workers in a building with asbestos insulation was so low it was comparable to inhaling one puff of cigarette smoke every day for a lifetime.

Federal Regulation. The United States began regulating industrial exposure to asbestos dust in the early 1970s. In 1986 the EPA declared, "no level of exposure to asbestos is without risk," and tried to ban asbestos use in consumer products. The EPA order would have phased out almost all use of asbestos by 1996. However, The Asbestos Institute, supported by the Canadian asbestos-mining industry, filed a petition for review of the ban with the U.S. Court of Appeals. In 1991 the court ruled the ban was unreasonable.

In its ruling, the court said the EPA overstepped its authority by trying to ban all asbestos use and failed to consider the financial costs and health risks posed by asbestos substitutes. The court said many proposed substitutes "actually may increase the risk of injury Americans face." The court found, based on the EPA's own studies, "a complete ban would save less than one statistical life over 13 years."

Under the court ruling, affirmed in 1993, U.S. companies could keep making asbestos products that were either imported or manufactured in the United States at the time the EPA announced the ban in 1989. The court let stand an EPA ban on new uses of asbestos or asbestos products.

In 1993, the EPA issued a report on what products were permitted under the court ruling. These included asbestos clothing; roofing materials; gaskets; and friction products for automotive use including brakes, brake linings, and clutch facings. Friction products accounted for about 70 percent of asbestos used by U.S. manufacturers. These products concerned the appeals court because automobile makers testified that non-asbestos-lined brakes were less reliable, especially for trucks and heavier cars. The appeals court found there was "credible evidence that non-asbestos brakes could increase significantly the number of highway fatalities." After the court ruling, the EPA asked car makers to switch to non-asbestos brakes voluntarily by 1994, but no major manufacturers agreed to do so in 1993.

Asbestos in products allowed by the court order was considered "locked-in" or "encapsulated," and not considered a health risk. Asbestos fibers in friction products were mixed with various binders and only a small amount were released into the air during normal use. Auto repair shops used special equipment to sweep asbestos fibers from the air. The asbestos fibers in roofing materials and gaskets were surrounded by asphalt, latex, rubber, or other resilient material.

Johns-Manville Corporation. The Johns-Manville Corporation was created in 1901 from the merger of two asbestos products companies. In 1969, Clarence Borel, a laborer who had spent more than 30 years installing asbestos insulation, sued Johns-Manville and other asbestos products makers alleging they knowingly manufactured a hazardous product *(Borel v. Fibreboard Paper Products Company, et al).* Borel, who suffered from asbestosis, testified that in all his years as an installer, no one had ever told him asbestos could make him ill.

In addition to Johns-Manville, the suit named the Pittsburgh Corning Corp., Owens-Corning Fiberglass Corp., Union Asbestos & Rubber Co., Combustion Engineering Inc., Eagle-Picher Industries Inc., the Philip Carey Corp., Armstrong Contracting & Supply Corp., Rubberoid Co., and the Standard Asbestos Manufacturing & Insulation Co. Those companies testified that most laborers knew the dangers but refused to wear breathing masks provided by insulation contractors. As the industry leader, Johns-Manville argued that it put warning labels on its products starting in 1964, as soon as it had sufficient evidence that installation workers were at risk.

The jury found Borel and the asbestos-products companies guilty of negligence. More importantly, Borel died in 1970 before the verdict was rendered, and the jury found the asbestos-products companies liable for his death. The jury awarded Borel's widow nearly $80,000. The U.S. Court of Appeals upheld the decision in 1973 and found that Johns-Manville and the other defendants could have foreseen the dangers to Borel "at the time the products causing Borel's injuries were sold." That ruling opened the floodgates to litigation. By 1981, more than 16,000 lawsuits were filed against Johns-Manville. Most of the suits were filed by insulation workers and people who worked in shipyards during World War II. Johns-Manville put the projected costs of the lawsuits at $2 billion—twice the company's assets at the time—and, in 1982, the company filed for protection under Chapter 11 of the U.S. Bankruptcy Code. It was the largest U.S. corporation to ever file for bankruptcy.

Johns-Manville filed a plan for reorganization in 1983. As part of the plan, the company, which changed its name to the Manville Corporation, established a trust fund to pay for asbestos-related claims. The Manville Personal Injury Settlement Fund owned 80 percent of the reorganized company, which also stopped using asbestos. Initially, the trust fund held $1 billion. However, as the number of claims increased—to more than 200,000 by 1993—the fund was increased to almost $3 billion. Because asbestosis and other asbestos-related diseases develop over time, the Rand Corp. estimated claims against Manville and other asbestos companies could reach more than $50 billion.

After a decade of court battles, in 1993, two insurance companies, Chubb Corp. and CNA Financial Corp., agreed to pay up to $3 billion for asbestos-related claims against the Fibreboard Corp., which spun off from Louisiana-Pacific in 1988. More than 145,000 people claimed to have been harmed by Fibreboard products. The decision was expected to keep Fibreboard from declaring bankruptcy. However, at least a dozen other asbestos-products companies declared bankruptcy due to asbestos litigation along with Johns-Manville, including National Gypsum Co., Celotex Corp., and Eagle-Picher.

CURRENT CONDITIONS

Canada, the world's largest producer of the chrysotile form of asbestos, received a major blow in early 1997 when France banned the production and importation of all asbestos products. Angered by the sweeping French ban, Canadian government trade officials petitioned the World Trade Organization to mediate the dispute. The European Commission, executive body of the multination European Union, preempted any decision in July 1999 by banning almost all remaining asbestos applications throughout the trade bloc. The only product exempted from the ban is electrolysis diaphragms used in chlorine plants. The ban will be implemented in all member countries of the European Union no later than January 1, 2005.

FURTHER READING

"Asbestos: Manufacture, Importation, Processing, and Distribution in Commerce Prohibitions; Final Rule." *Federal Register,* 12 July 1989.

Darnay, Arsen J., ed. *Manufacturing USA,* 6th ed. Detroit: Gale Research, 1998.

"EC ban." *Mining Journal,* 1 October 1999.

SIC 3295

MINERALS AND EARTHS, GROUND OR OTHERWISE TREATED

This category includes establishments operating without a mine or quarry and primarily engaged in crushing, grinding, pulverizing, or otherwise preparing clay, ceramic, and refractory minerals; barite; and miscellaneous nonmetallic minerals, excluding fuels. These minerals are the crude products mined by establishments of Industry Groups 145 (clay, ceramic, and refractory minerals) and 149 (miscellaneous nonmetallic minerals, except fuels), and by those mining barite in **SIC 1479: Chemical and Fertilizer Mineral Mining, Not Elsewhere Classified.** Also included in this category are establishments primarily crushing slag and preparing roofing granules. The improvement or preparation of the minerals and metallic ores and the cleaning and grading of coal are classified in Mining, whether or not the operation is associated with a mine.

NAICS CODE(S)

327992 (Ground or Treated Mineral and Earth Manufacturing)

Products in this classification include barium, blast furnace slag, clay for petroleum refining, ground clay, activated clay desiccants, diatomaceous earth, filtering clays, Fuller's earth, kaolin, black lead, mica, pulverized earth, pumice roofing granules, talc, and vermiculite. The value of shipments in this industry tended to spike up and down throughout the 1980s and early 1990s, dropping as low as $1.17 billion in 1985 and rising as high as $1.85 billion in 1993. In 1997 the value of shipments was $2.30 billion.

No single product dominated this industry, with no product taking more than 13 percent of the market. In 1996 lightweight aggregate held the largest share of the market, at 13.2 percent, followed closely by crushed slag at 8.8 percent, dead-burned magnesia at 5.8 percent, and natural graphite at 4.5 percent. A wide range of other materials and earths held the remaining 58.5 percent of the market. Kaolin was one of the biggest products within the industry in both intake and output, being an ingredient in several products. Once the kaolin was processed, it was sent to many different industries with a wide range of products. The biggest consumer in 1995 was the fiberglass industry, taking 29.3 percent of the kaolin. Rubber and elastomeric industries took the next highest share at 25.6 percent. Sanitaryware and filler or extender each took about 13 percent, and refractories took 6 percent. Dinnerware accounted for 3 percent, ceramic tile took 2 percent, and electrical porcelain took 1 percent. The remaining 7 percent went to miscellaneous products.

The products produced by this industry tended to have a relatively low value compared to their weight. As a result of weight, truck transportation, warehousing, and rail transportation accounted for the highest percentage of the inputs used by the minerals and earths industry in the 1990s. The raw materials accounted for the next highest percentage of all inputs. The power required to process ground mineral and earth products were also important inputs, with gas and electric utilities accounting for another high percentage of all inputs.

The production of ground minerals and earths was concentrated in five states, with Pennsylvania, Ohio, Illinois, Louisiana, and California accounting for 30.2 percent of all product shipments. Pennsylvania was the largest single producing state, with 7.6 percent of the total and $134.5 million in shipments.

In 1999 the leading companies in the ground minerals and earths industry included Eagle-Picher Industries Inc., of Cincinnati, Ohio, with $849 million in sales; Engelhard Corp. Pigments and Additives of Iselin, New Jersey, with $500 million in sales; and Edward C. Levy Co. of Detroit, Michigan, and ECC International of Roswell, Georgia, both with sales of $200 million. Many companies operated out of the southeastern and midwestern United States, where abundant supplies of clay (kaolin) were located.

This industry employed an estimated 9,888 people in 1997. The total industry payroll was $455.9 million. Employment for production workers was expected to decline into the year 2006.

FURTHER READING

Bureau of the Census. *Economic Census 1997.* Washington, D.C.: GPO, 2000. Available from http://www.census.gov.

Darnay, Arsen J., ed. *Manufacturing USA.* 5th ed. Detroit: Gale Research, 1996.

"Production Occupations Not Studied in Detail." *1998-99 Occupational Outlook Handbook,* 2000. Available from http://stats.bls.gov.

U.S. Department of Commerce. Bureau of the Census. *1995 Survey of Manufactures.* Washington, D.C.: GPO, 1997.

SIC 3296

MINERAL WOOL

This category includes companies that make mineral wool and mineral wool insulation products made of such siliceous materials as rock, slag, glass, or combinations of these. Companies that primarily make asbestos insulation products are classified in **SIC 3292: Asbestos Products,** and those making textile glass fibers are classified in **SIC 3229: Pressed and Blown Glass and Glassware, Not Elsewhere Classified.**

NAICS CODE(S)

327993 (Mineral Wool Manufacturing)

This industry's products include mineral wool acoustical board and tile; fiberglass insulation; glass wool; mineral wool roofing mats; and insulation made of rock wool, slag, and silica minerals. The value of industry shipments grew relatively steadily throughout the 1980s, from $2.3 billion in 1982 to a peak of $3.4 billion in 1988. However, the mineral wool industry—like others in the United States—was hit hard by a major recession in 1989; by 1991, the industry's value of shipments had fallen back to $3.1 billion. By 1997, the industry rebounded with total shipments of $4.4 billion. Prices for mineral wool continued to rise the following year.

This industry produced two major product categories: mineral wool for thermal and acoustical envelope insulation, which held about 70 percent of the market in 1987; and mineral wool for industrial, equipment, and appliance insulation, which accounted for roughly 25 percent.

Within the first category, batt, blanket, and roll insulation products had the largest market share; this area includes the familiar fiberglass insulation found in residential attics. Fiberglass insulation used in the upper stories and ceilings of homes varies by type. Acoustical mineral wool holds the next highest market share in the mineral wool industry.

Within the second major category—industrial, equipment, and appliance insulation—sales are spread among four categories: special purpose insulation pieces (9 percent), other (4.9 percent), flexible blankets (4.5 percent), and pipe insulation (3.73 percent).

Owens-Corning of Toledo, Ohio, was the leading manufacturer of mineral wool, with 1999 sales of $5 billion and approximately 20,000 employees. The company was also the leading U.S. maker of industrial asphalt and residential roof shingles. Owens-Corning had 83 manufacturing plants worldwide as of 1997, including 4 in China, and seemed well-positioned for expanding in a global economy.

The next leading company was Knauf Fiberglass of Shelbyville, Indiana, with $140 million in sales and 1,000 employees. Third was CTA Acoustics Inc. of Corbin, Kentucky, with $74 million in sales and 500 employees.

Employment for the industry remained stable throughout the 1980s, dropping from 19,700 in 1982 to 19,000 in 1990. In 1997, the mineral wool industry had a payroll of more than $1 billion. In 1999, approximately 25,000 people worked in the industry.

FURTHER READING

Bureau of the Census. *Economic Census 1997.* Washington, D.C.: GPO, 2000. Available from http://www.census.gov.

Bureau of Labor Statistics. *Employment Statistics.* Washington, D.C.: GPO, 2000. Available from http://www.bls.gov.

Thomas, William D., et al. ''Producer Price Highlights 1998,'' *Monthly Labor Review,* July 1999.

U.S. Department of Commerce. *1995 Annual Survey of Manufactures: Statistics for Industry Groups and Industries.* Washington, D.C.: GPO, 1997.

SIC 3297

NONCLAY REFRACTORIES

This category includes establishments primarily engaged in manufacturing refractories and crucibles made of materials other than clay. This industry also includes establishments primarily engaged in manufacturing all graphite refractories, whether of carbon bond or ceramic bond. Establishments primarily engaged in manufacturing clay refractories are classified in **SIC 3255: Clay Refractories.**

NAICS CODE(S)

327125 (Nonclay Refractory Manufacturing)

A refractory is a product such as brick that is resistant to intense heat. Some of the main uses of refractories are to create fire-resistant construction materials for industrial buildings and to create crucibles. Crucibles are vessels made of a substance that will withstand extreme heat and are used for melting metals or minerals. Another use of refractories is to create furnaces and other devices. While those are the biggest divisions within the industry, refractories are used for a wide variety of industries, from boiler combustion chambers and incinerators to rotary kilns and mine ore dryers. Generally, refractory products are needed where commercial production processes exceed temperatures of 700 degrees Fahrenheit.

This industry includes establishments primarily engaged in manufacturing all graphite refractories, whether of carbon or ceramic bond. Products produced by the nonclay refractories industry include alumina-fused refractories; bauxite, carbon, and refractory brick; nonclay castable refractories; high temperature cement; magnesia cement; crucibles made of graphite, chrome, silica, or other nonclay materials; dolomite brick; nonclay gunning mixes; nonclay plastics refractories; nonclay refractory cement; and pyrolytic graphite.

The value of shipments in this industry grew dramatically through most of the 1980s from $691.0 million in 1982 to $954.5 million in 1987 and $1.1 billion 1989. By 1997, the value of the industry's shipments continued to grow to an estimated $1.4 billion, recovering from a U.S. recession in the early 1990s that hurt overall sales. The iron and steel industry accounted for about one-half of the U.S. refractory market, and steel and refractory production actually paralleled each other.

Materials, ingredients, containers, and supplies were by far the largest category of materials consumed by the nonclay refractories industry in 1995, with an estimated delivered cost of $455.6 million. The next highest category, clay, ceramic, and refractory minerals, cost the industry $143.9 million, while dead-burned magnesia or magnesite had a delivered cost of $54.4 million. Clay or nonclay refractories accounted for another $60.4 million worth of materials. Miscellaneous products, components, ingredients, parts, containers, and supplies cost the industry a total of $177.5 million.

Monolithic refractories—those that do not have to be fired—account for about 50 percent of the market. Castables, plastics, and gunning mixes are the most popular of the nonfiring refractories, with new mixes, such as alumina-carbon and alumina-silica, creating stronger and longer lasting refractories. All refractories have to be replaced eventually, but because of industry improvements, the rate at which they are replaced is diminishing. Also, as the steel industry continues to change, refractory manufacturers need to constantly adapt.

The nonclay refractories industry is concentrated in two states—Ohio and Pennsylvania—which accounted for an estimated 41.6 percent of all U.S. production in 1996. In 1999, leading companies included J.E. Baker Co. of York, Pennsylvania, with $185 million in revenues; MINTEQ International, Inc. of New York, with revenues of $110 million; and C-E Minerals, Inc., of King of Prussia, Pennsylvania, with revenues of $70 million.

Unlike many other American industries, the nonclay refractories industry increased employment during the 1980s, moving from 6,800 people in 1982 to 8,500 in 1989. In 1997, the workforce dropped to only 7,621 workers. All occupations, from laborer to top executives, were expected to decline through 2005 by about 20 percent, with extruding and forming machine positions estimated to plunge by 80 percent. Only hand painting, coating, and decorating positions were expected to grow by about 50 percent. On average, workers in this industry made $15.80 an hour in 1997.

FURTHER READING

Anderson, George. "An Introduction to Industrial Refractories." *George Anderson's Home Page,* 1 February 1997. Available from http://vanbc.wimsey.com/~gandersn/refrac.html.

Darnay, Arsen J., ed. *Manufacturing USA.* 5th ed. Detroit: Gale Research, 1996.

U.S. Census Bureau. *Economic Census 1997.* Washington, D.C.: GPO, 1999. Available from http://www.census.gov.

Heine, Hans J. "Refractories Revisited: A Review and Outlook." *Foundry,* March 1996.

SIC 3299

NONMETALLIC MINERAL PRODUCTS, NOT ELSEWHERE CLASSIFIED

This category is comprised of firms that manufacture goods made from plaster of paris, papier-mâché, sand lime, and other miscellaneous nonmetallic mineral products. Examples of industry output include synthetic stones, clay and plaster plaques, architectural plaster work, plaster of paris sculptures, miniature gypsum images, plaster of paris flower boxes, and gypsum urns.

NAICS CODE(S)

327420 (Gypsum and Gypsum Product Manufacturing)
327999 (All Other Miscellaneous Nonmetallic Mineral Product Manufacturing)

Markets for miscellaneous nonmetallic mineral products are extremely fragmented. The largest single industry product category is statuary and art goods, which accounted for about 17 percent of industry output during the mid-1990s. The largest consumer of this industry's offerings is the nonferrous wire-drawing industry, which uses tubing made from quartz to produce electrical wire. Other major consumers include fabricated rubber product manufacturers and motor and generator makers, who also use quartz tubing. About 9 percent of production was exported in the mid-1990s.

The industry is relatively low-tech and manufactures many commodity-like products. The average amount of value contributed per production worker was about 65 percent lower than the U.S. manufacturing average in the mid-1990s. Likewise, capital investment per employee represented 72 percent of the national manufacturing average. As a result, many producers of nonmetallic mineral products were highly susceptible to competition from low-cost foreign producers.

U.S. sales of miscellaneous nonmetallic mineral products topped $400 million in the early 1980s. During the mid-1980s, however, shipment growth slowed compared to the 1960s and 1970s. Although domestic demand for products such as electrical wiring and art supplies increased, foreign competition reduced profit opportunities in many sectors. Revenues increased at a tepid 5 percent annually between 1982 and 1990, slightly lagging behind inflation. Furthermore, a U.S. recession in the late 1980s and early 1990s stalled expansion—annual sales hovered around $650 to $700 million. General economic improvement in the mid-1990s, as well as a boost in new commercial and residential construction, led to increased demand for electrical wire, which helped the industry resume average growth to more than $1.7 billion in shipments in 1997. Prices rose again the following year.

About 498 establishments competed in the industry in 1997. The majority of the top 25 firms generated revenues of less than $25 million per year. The industry leader was Carborundum Company of Niagara Falls, New York, with around $340 million in 1999 sales and about 3,200 employees. Ranking second was CeramTec North America Electronic Applications Inc. of Mansfield, Massachusetts, which had sales of about $210 million and 1,800 employees.

In the mid-1990s, there was significant development in the area of advanced materials such as ceramic fibers. Ceramic fibers are used primarily in composite materials, which are lighter, stronger, and more heat-resistant than pure ceramics or metals. In 1997, the market introduced "core-sheath" ceramic fibers, which are the result of a new process called biocomponent extrusion that increases strength, heat resistance, and efficiency in production. The new fibers provide advantages to end users such as auto and aircraft industries, which use composite materials in high-tech applications such as jet engines.

Miscellaneous nonmetallic mineral product manufacturers employed a workforce of about 11,026 people in 1997. The average annual salary for production workers was $27,700. Future prospects for employment in this industry were generally dismal, as positions for most laborers will likely decline by 15 to 20 percent between 1996 and 2005, according to the Bureau of Labor Statistics.

FURTHER READING

Farrar, Gary. "Changes in the Indexes for Nonmetallic Building Materials." *The Oil and Gas Journal,* 4 October 1999.

"Spinning a Tough Yarn." *Financial Times,* 17 January 1997.

Thomas, William D., et al. "Producer Price Highlights 1998." *Monthly Labor Review,* July 1999.

U.S. Department of Commerce. Economics and Statistics Administration. Bureau of the Census. *1995 Annual Survey of Manufactures.* Washington, D.C.: GPO, 1997. Available from http://www.census.gov/prod/www/titles.html#mm.

U.S. Census Bureau. *Economic Census 1997.* Washington, D.C.: GPO, 1999. Available from http://www.census.gov.

PRIMARY METALS INDUSTRIES

STEEL WORKS, BLAST FURNACES (INCLUDING COKE OVENS), AND ROLLING MILLS

This classification includes establishments primarily engaged in manufacturing hot metal, pig iron, and silvery pig iron from iron ore and iron and steel scrap; converting pig iron, scrap iron, and scrap steel into steel; and in hot-rolling iron and steel into basic shapes, such as plates, sheets, strips, rods, bars, and tubing. Merchant blast furnaces and by-product or beehive coke ovens are also included in this industry. Establishments primarily engaged in manufacturing ferrous and nonferrous additive alloys by electrometallurgical processes are classified in **SIC 3313: Electrometallurgical Products, Except Steel.**

NAICS CODE(S)
324199 (All Other Petroleum and Coal Products Manufacturing)
331111 (Iron and Steel Mills)

INDUSTRY SNAPSHOT
The first steel mill in North America was built in the 1600s, making the industry one of the oldest in the country. During much of the twentieth century the steel industry served as the measure of the U.S. economy. In 1998, 79 U.S. steel companies employed about 159,000 people and shipped more than 102 million tons of steel. Despite its impressive size, the steel industry began declining in the mid-1970s and suffered a devastating depression between 1982 and 1986. After peaking in 1978 at over 137 million tons, U.S. steel production slipped to less than 90 million tons in 1991. Anemic market growth, expensive labor, increased production costs, and stagnant prices pummeled many manufacturers in the industry. In addition, the proliferation of foreign competition and the popularity of substitute materials, such as plastics and aluminum, gouged industry profits.

In response to a more competitive environment, the U.S. steel industry continued to restructure itself in the late 1980s and early 1990s. By 1993, new production techniques and facilities, as well as increased automation, had made U.S. steelmakers among the most productive in the world. From the low point in 1991, U.S. steelmakers steadily increased production during the 1990s, reaching peak levels in 1997 of 108.6 million tons produced and 105.9 million tons shipped. As productivity in the steel industry increased, the labor force declined to about 159,000 jobs in 1998, down from 171,000 in 1996.

Domestic steel production accounted for more than 12 percent of total world production annually from 1993 to 1998, reversing a downward trend from 26 percent in 1960 to less than 11 percent in 1991. Although U.S. steelmakers enjoyed strong domestic demand for steel in 1997 and 1998, especially from the automotive, construction, and industrial machinery and equipment production markets, they faced increasing competition from foreign steelmakers. There were record levels of imported steel in 1998, with U.S. steelmakers uniting to charge foreign producers with dumping steel into the U.S. market at below-market cost.

ORGANIZATION AND STRUCTURE
Steel companies are involved in the manufacture of hot metal, pig iron, and silvery pig iron from iron ore, iron, and steel scrap. They are also involved in converting pig iron, scrap iron, and scrap steel into steel as well as hot-rolling iron and steel into plates, sheets, strips, and bars. These end products are purchased by companies in

other industries, which usually shape and manipulate the steel to create finished products.

Products offered by steelmakers are classified into five categories according to the manner in which they were processed and their chemical compositions. Carbon steels are used mostly for flat rolled products because of their high malleability. Machines, auto bodies, ships, and building structures are made with this type of steel. In fact, carbon steels accounted for about 54 percent of all U.S. steel production in the 1990s. Alloy steels, which made up about 10 percent of the market, integrate elements into steel to enhance its physical properties. Corrosion resistance, greater strength, and increased conductivity are a few of the advantages offered by some alloys.

In comparison to carbon and alloy steels, stainless steels are highly resistant to rust and may be stronger or offer resistance to temperature changes. Accounting for 4.7 percent of the steel market volume, stainless steel is often used in pipes, tanks, and in the medical field. Tool steels and high-strength low alloy (HSLA) steels accounted for less than 1 percent of industry production, combined. They are used in applications in which strength and weight are critical.

Integrated Manufacturers vs. Minimills. Steel manufacturers can be divided into two camps—traditional integrated mills and non-integrated "minimills." Integrated steel mills undertake every step of the steel making process. These facilities typically begin by converting mixtures of iron ore, limestone, and coke (made from coal) into molten iron using a blast furnace. Basic oxygen furnaces (BOFs) are next used to convert the molten iron into steel, which is then cast into ingots. Ingots are then shaped into slabs, billets, or blooms of steel.

Increasing numbers of integrated mills in the 1990s were using a process called continuous casting to bypass the production of ingots and cast billets, slabs, and blooms directly from molten iron. Compared to the old ingot teeming process, continuous casting is less complicated and yields a superior product. In this process, molten steel from a furnace is quickly carried in a ladle directly to a refractory lined container, or tundish, at the top of the caster. The molten metal is then poured into the tundish, which feeds it continuously into the caster, the core of which is water-cooled mold open at both ends. When molten steel enters one end of the mold and cools, a "skin" of metal forms around a liquid core. The material leaves the other end of the machine and is further cooled by water sprays, solidifying the metal. Continuous casting cuts time, consume less energy, and increases yield. It has been estimated that it cuts operating costs by about $30 a ton. Steelmakers next convert the finished, or semi-finished, steel into rolls, plates, bars, tubes, rails, or other more marketable products, especially for the auto

industry, at a rolling mill. By 1995, every major U.S. manufacturer relied on continuous casting.

In the 1990s, minimills, or non-integrated facilities, were using the same process as integrated mills with a few exceptions. Rather than process base materials—iron ore, coke, and limestone—minimills typically start with scrap iron or steel. The scrap, melted in an electric arc furnace (EAF), rather than a blast or basic oxygen furnace, is continuously cast into blooms and billets. Minimills typically produced fewer finished products than integrated mills. Although many manufacturers were broadening their offerings to include steel pipes, plates, and sheets, most minimills emphasized rods and bars used in light construction.

Minimills are capable of producing from 150,000 to 2 million tons of steel per year. In contrast, most integrated mills can generate 2 to 4 million tons per year. Minimills are also typically able to produce steel at a much lower cost than their larger cousins. Because minimills do not have to be located near supplies of raw ingredients, for instance, they are able to operate closer to their customers, thus reducing product transport costs. In addition, more minimills are located in the southern United States and benefit from less expensive, non-union labor. Integrated mills, on the other hand, employ union labor. Union contracts prevent integrated companies from reducing compensation costs when production declines due to downturns in demand. Furthermore, minimills are more likely to employ more advanced technology, such as continuous casting and EAFs, that reduce production costs and improve quality.

Competitive Structure. Integrated steel producers have been steadily losing market share to minimills. In 1992, integrated steelmakers accounted for approximately 75 percent of U.S. steel industry production. In 1998, integrated steelmakers accounted for only 55.4 percent of U.S. steel production, compared to more than 90 percent in 1960. Minimills, on the other hand, increased their share of production from 8.4 percent in 1960 to 44.6 percent in 1998.

Compared to minimills, integrated steelmakers are more capital and labor intensive. On average, minimills realized about $500 in capital costs per ton of steel produced, while integrated mills incurred about $2,000 per ton. Likewise, during the mid-1980s and early 1990s, minimills generated about $32 in operating profit per ton of steel, compared to just $3 per ton for integrated mills. The availability of cheap scrap steel was also a factor in keeping costs down at minimills.

Minimills have been able to achieve greater labor productivity than integrated mills, in part because they employ nonunion labor. Nucor, the leading minimill manufacturer and the third largest steel producer in the

United States, produced 1,333 tons per employee in 1998. By comparison, Bethlehem Steel, the second-largest integrated steel manufacturer in the United States, produced only 573 tons per worker in 1998.

The domestic steel industry remains fairly concentrated, but is a far cry from the oligopoly characteristic of the early twentieth century. Of the 79 companies in the U.S. steel industry, the top three—USX-U.S. Steel Group, Bethlehem Steel, and Nucor—accounted for 27 percent of total shipments in 1998. The top nine firms accounted for nearly 52 percent of industry shipments in 1998.

The main consumers of steel are the automotive industry, construction, and industrial machinery and equipment manufacturers. Service and distribution centers consumed 21 to 23 percent of U.S. steel production in 1995. The largest steel customer that built consumer products was the automobile industry, which used 13.5 million tons in 1995, or about 16 percent of total steel production. The construction industry purchased about 11.7 million tons of steel in 1995, and machinery manufacturers used about 2 million tons. Other large steel consumers included oil and gas companies with 2.7 million tons, container manufacturers with 3.8 million tons, and various commercial equipment producers with 700 thousand tons.

BACKGROUND AND DEVELOPMENT

Steel is an alloy of carbon and iron that is harder and stronger than iron. The first ironworks were established in British North America in Jamestown, Virginia, in 1621, and the Saugus ironworks was established in Massachusetts in 1645. By the beginning of the eighteenth century iron making was underway in almost every other colony. Despite English parliamentary acts that tried to restrict the burgeoning industry, manufacturers in North America continued to build new iron mills, and eventually finished steel mills, throughout the 1700s. Iron production in this early period entailed the use of charcoal fuel or water power, along with a small labor force, to melt iron ore in a blast furnace. Entrepreneurs could start a mill with several hundred dollars. By 1800, approximately 84,000 tons of iron were being produced in North America.

The coming of the steam age in the early part of the nineteenth century created a huge demand for iron. Up to this time most iron mines, forges, and blacksmiths were small operations. Steam created a demand for rolled iron to be used in making boilers. In addition, more than 30,000 miles of railroad track with iron rails were laid in the United States between 1830 and the outbreak of the American Civil War in 1861. As a result, iron mills became major enterprises.

The production process changed very little throughout the 1800s, although advances in transportation freed the industry from many geographical constraints. The U.S. steel industry did not develop on its own until after the American Civil War. Up until that time steel was too expensive to manufacture by the methods then available. Its use prior to the American Civil War was confined primarily to high-value products, and the United States imported nearly all of its steel until after the American Civil War.

Two inventions in the 1850s resulted in the rapid rise of the steel industry, which supplanted the iron industry by the end of the nineteenth century. One was the Bessemer process for making steel, developed by British engineer Henry Bessemer in 1856. The second was the Siemens-Martin open-hearth method, introduced in 1858. These processes, once perfected, greatly reduced the cost of producing steel. The first Bessemer converter in the United States was built in 1864, and the first open-hearth furnace, which was better suited to American iron ore, was built in 1868. These spurred steel production in the United States. By 1873 the United States was producing nearly 115,000 tons of steel rail, approximately one-eighth of all U.S. rail production. As the price of steel continued to drop, steel rails replaced iron rails, which became brittle and required frequent repairs. The iron age was over.

Toward the end of the nineteenth century the structure of the industry changed as it became more concentrated and the number of firms dwindled. Between 1880 and 1900, U.S. steel production increased from 1.25 million tons to more than 10 million tons. The industry underwent consolidation as mill owners sought economies of scale. Led by Andrew Carnegie, Henry Clay Frick, Charles Schwab, and others, the modern steel industry took shape. Companies such as Bethlehem Steel and Illinois Steel Company were born. It was also during this time that the first steel import tariffs and trade associations were instigated. Many bitter and deadly labor disputes rocked the industry during the late 1800s and early 1900s, notably the Homestead strike of 1892, and the steel industry would not be fully unionized until the 1930s. In 1901 financiers J. Pierpont Morgan and Elbert H. Gary formed the United States Steel Corporation. With a capitalization of $1.4 billion, it was the largest industrial enterprise in the world. By 1910 the United States was producing more than 24 million tons of steel, by far more than any other country.

In the early 1900s, the development of the open hearth furnace (OHF) made it possible for companies to produce higher quality steel and to use scrap metal in the production process. Improved steel quality was an important advantage for firms that were striving to serve the needs of the new automobile industry. Indeed, the massive growth in demand for new steel during the early 1900s, particularly in the 1920s, was a boon to the industry. After suffering setbacks during the Great Depression, when over 50 percent of U.S. steel production capacity stood idle, steel markets expanded significantly throughout World War II.

In the 30 years following World War II, U.S. steelmakers dominated the global steel industry. In addition to the fact that many European and Japanese producers had been stifled by damage during the war, U.S. plants were technologically superior. Additionally, U.S. facilities were also an average of more than three times larger than those in other industrialized nations. In 1950, over 45 percent of the world's raw steel was produced in the United States. American firms produced about 90 million tons of steel, compared to about 30 million tons and less than 5 million tons produced by Europe and Japan, respectively.

Because U.S. firms enjoyed great economies of scale and technological supremacy, their steelworkers were by far the highest paid in the world. U.S. manufacturers enjoyed immediate access to the fastest growing economy in the industrialized world. These and other factors helped to push U.S. steel production from around 90 million tons in 1950 to nearly 140 million tons by the 1970s. Although the U.S. steel industry maintained a significant lead over the European Community (EC) and Japan from the 1950s through the 1970s, companies in those two regions gained quickly on their U.S. counterparts. By 1970, the EC and Japan were producing about 120 million and 90 million tons of steel per year, respectively.

Despite its size and its rapid growth, the U.S. steel industry began experiencing problems in the 1960s and 1970s. In addition to high labor costs, slowing growth in domestic markets, and a declining world market share, the industry was also beginning to pay the price for failing to invest the resources necessary to maintain its technological lead. Most companies, for example, had been slow to convert their operations to more productive basic oxygen furnaces (BOFs), which were replacing the old OHFs. Indeed, by the mid-1970s it was clear that U.S. companies had lost their leadership role in world steel markets—despite a flurry of capital investment by steelmakers in the late 1960s.

Since the Mid-1970s. The U.S. steel industry experienced its first significant reversal in the mid-1970s. A rise in energy prices was one of most significant factors that contributed to the industry's decline. In 1975, after oil prices had jumped from $3 to $12 per barrel in less than two years, U.S. steel production dropped by 20 percent. To make matters worse, U.S. companies had substantially increased their production capacity in anticipation of strong market growth—a dreadful miscalculation. High labor costs continued to plague U.S. competitors as well, adding to their comparative inefficiency in the global market.

Other miscellaneous factors battered down industry profits. Environmental regulations, for example, forced the industry to spend a peak of nearly $400 million in 1981 to reduce pollutants. Also, government-subsidized imported steel was cutting into domestic market revenues. The dumping problem became so bad that the U.S. government enacted Voluntary Restraint Agreements (VRAs) in the early 1980s—which essentially amounted to anti-dumping legislation for 29 importing countries. Finally, steel substitutes were further reducing steel's market share. For instance, the average amount of steel and iron contained in an automobile fell from 2,535 pounds in 1977 to 1,757 pounds in 1992, but the average amount of plastic in an automobile rose from about 180 pounds to 245 pounds.

The proliferation of minimills also added to the woes of large steel producers. Although minimills had originated in the 1960s, by the late 1970s these facilities were beginning to compete directly with large producers in specific market niches. The more efficient and technologically superior minimills particularly benefited from EAFs, which proved much more productive than even the BOFs in which large manufacturers continued to invest. As a result, the market share of the top six producers declined from 64 percent in 1980 to about 50 percent by 1990.

The end result of the problems affecting the industry was decreased production and profits beginning in the late 1970s and continuing throughout most of the 1980s. Total U.S. steel production declined from a peak of 136 million tons in 1979 to a low of about 81.5 million tons in 1986. U.S. manufacturers' share of world steel production also plummeted from over 17 percent in 1976 to about 11 percent in 1990. Furthermore, industry employment plummeted from about 300,000 in 1982 to less than 190,000 by 1990. Industry profits fell through the floor, declining to a loss of over $1.8 billion in 1985, and a staggering loss of nearly $4.2 billion in 1986. Although industry net income jumped to over $1 billion in 1987, profits remained relatively stagnant throughout the decade.

Industry Restructuring. In response to the metamorphosis of steel markets, U.S. producers launched a major industry restructuring in the 1980s. Companies greatly increased investments in new production technologies. Integrated mills alone invested $23 billion in the 1980s to modernize their plants. The percentage of steel produced in older OHFs, for instance, fell from nearly 20 percent in 1977 to less than 5 percent by 1990. During the same period, steel produced using efficient EAFs increased from just over 20 percent to nearly 40 percent. Most importantly, manufacturers increased the amount of steel that was produced using continuous casting from just 15 percent in 1980 to over 75 percent by 1991—nearing the levels found in the EC and Japanese industries.

U.S. steelmakers made important gains in other areas, too. Investment in pollution controls declined to just over $100 million in 1990, although those costs began to rise again in the early 1990s. Manufacturers also succeeded in stabilizing their labor costs, although it was estimated that labor still represented 28 percent of the cost of production in as of 1994. Large investments in automation, however, had helped to bring labor expenses in line with overseas competitors. Also bolstering industry competitiveness was the success of highly efficient minimills that could produce steel nearly twice as fast as integrated facilities. By 1995, minimills represented 40.4 percent of industry production.

Domestic producers had also succeeded in reducing steel dumping by importers with such legislation as the VRAs. Furthermore, American companies had increased the quality of their products by investing in new production technology. They had developed new products, for instance, that allowed them to compete with many plastic substitutes. New steel products were being offered that had the corrosion resistance and weight advantages of many plastics, yet cost less to create.

CURRENT CONDITIONS

As a result of restructuring during the 1980s and 1990s, U.S. steel companies in 1996 were the third most productive in the world. Manufacturers had dramatically reduced the average amount of labor required to produce one ton of steel from 11 man-hours in 1982 to 3 man-hours in 1994—less than both Japanese and European producers. At least one study estimated that pretax production costs in the United States were lower than costs in any other major steel producing nation, except Britain. Furthermore, exports, which have since slowed to 7 percent in 1995, had reached a peak of 8 percent of production in 1992, despite a more than 5 percent decline in foreign demand since the late 1980s. At the same time, an upturn in the U.S. economy in 1995 and early 1996 buoyed domestic demand.

By the mid-1990s the U.S. steel industry was in good economic shape. Restructuring continued during the 1990s, and from 1992 to 1998 the steel industry spent an aggregate of $50 billion to modernize its plants. Steel companies improved their financial position by reducing debt, underfunded pension plans, and other liabilities. After two strong years industry performance slackened slightly in 1996 as some plants suffered breakdowns after running at full capacity. Raw steel production during 1996 was 99.4 million tons, up from 97.1 million tons in 1995. Steel shipments rose in 1997 to 105.9 million net tons, then fell 3.5 percent in 1998 to 102.1 million tons.

Strong demand in the United States for steel in 1997 and 1998 resulted in a significant increase in imported steel of various kinds. Cheap imports from Russia, Japan,

Brazil, and other countries forced the price of commodity grade steel down more than 10 percent. To prevent other countries from dumping steel into the United States market, the U.S. steel industry filed antidumping petitions with the U.S. International Trade Commission, under the U.S. Department of Commerce, and the International Trade Administration. ''Dumping'' refers to the practice of one country selling commodities or finished products in another country at below cost or fair market value. Since 1980 the steel industry has used antidumping complaints as a tool to curb imports, and in 1998 it filed complaints against Japan, Russia, and Brazil.

The major markets for flat-rolled steel are automotive, accounting for 50 percent; construction, 20 percent; and production of industrial machinery and equipment, 30 percent. All of these markets enjoyed increased production during the 1990s, resulting in growing demand for steel. High levels of vehicle production and increasing truck share, which are more steel-intensive than automobiles, have explained much of the strength in steel volume in recent years.

Steel prices have dropped due to a combination of softer demand, a drop in domestic steel operating rates, a steep decline in scrap prices, competitive pressures from imports, and expanded domestic capacity. However, steel prices started to turn upward in mid-1999 as the major producers announced price hikes.

The steel industry's profitability continued to be affected by a wave of low-priced steel imports in 1999. *American Metal Market* reported that only five of the 14 integrated producers that it tracked were profitable for the first half of 1999. The 14 integrated steelmakers posted a combined operating loss of $519 million for the first six months of 1999, compared to a combined operating profit of just over $1 billion for the same period of 1998.

The Future of Steel. The steel industry remains highly competitive. Domestic producers face competition not only from foreign steelmakers, but also from substitute materials, such as glass, ceramics, aluminum, and plastics. World steel consumption was expected to decline by nearly 3 percent in 1999, followed by a modest recovery in 2000. Excess world capacity was expected to put pressure on U.S. steelmakers despite the many antidumping complaints being filed. Any increase in steel prices would act as a stimulant to encourage even more expansion of low-cost capacity.

Integrated steelmakers, which were under severe profit pressure during the 1980s, were expected to reap the most benefits from increased prices. Nevertheless, analysts expected that minimills would continue to gain market share and to significantly outperform integrated facilities. Minimills promised to pose a growing threat as they expanded their offerings to include flat-rolled sheet steel and large structural products—formerly the domain of integrated producers. Furthermore, rapid advancements in minimill production technology were allowing this sector to compete with integrated manufacturers in a growing number of markets.

Direct steelmaking is the most likely long-term solution to problems caused by the capital-intensive nature of the integrated steelmaking process. Widespread implementation of the direct steelmaking process would also eliminate the need for coke ovens, many of which are badly in need of being rebuilt and have been the source for harmful emissions. One direct-process plant has been in operation since 1989. Located in Pittsburgh, this experimental facility is capable of producing five tons of steel an hour. It uses a coal-based, continuous in-bath melting process that substitutes a single vessel for coke ovens, blast furnaces, and basic oxygen furnaces. This technique's energy requirements are about 20 percent lower than those of conventional steelmaking, which uses three separate processes. A second, larger experimental facility was completed in 1995, and several foreign competitors have built similar plants.

INDUSTRY LEADERS

In 1998, the top nine steel producers accounted for 51 percent of all U.S. steel shipments. Ranked by steel shipments, they were U.S. Steel Group (a subsidiary of USX Corp.), Bethlehem Steel, Nucor, LTV, National Steel, AK Steel Holding, WHX Steel, Weirton Steel, and Rouge Steel.

The largest domestic steelmaker, USX's U.S. Steel Group, had annual sales of $6.3 billion in 1998, down from $6.9 billion in 1997. The company's net income declined from $452 million in 1997 to $364 million in 1998. In 1973, this company produced a record 35 million net tons of raw steel. By 1990, however, its total steelmaking capacity had shrunk from 37 million to 19 million tons. The capacity reduction was the result of a restructuring effort in the 1980s that eliminated or modernized its facilities.

Another large U.S. steel producer, by revenues, was LTV Corporation, of Dallas. In the mid-1990s, this industry giant had annual sales exceeding $4 billion and employed 15,300 people, down by 20,000 since 1991. LTV Steel, LTV Corporation's steelmaking subsidiary, was formed as a result of the merger of Jones & Laughlin and Republic Steel in 1984. Shortly thereafter, following a price collapse in 1985, LTV Steel filed for bankruptcy. Massive capital investments, joint ventures, and automation efforts helped revive the company in the late 1980s. However, after rebounding with a profit in 1991, it again showed a loss in 1994 of $127 million. In 1997 the company turned a profit of $30 million on sales of $4.4 billion. In 1998, a $55 million pretax charge related to

restructuring, combined with an increase in steel imports, resulted in a net loss of $27 million on sales of $4.3 billion. For the first nine months of 1999, the company reported a net loss of $145 million.

Other large integrated steel producers included ARMCO, with sales of $1.7 billion and a profit of $347 million in 1998 (ARMCO merged with AK Steel Holding in 1999); Bethlehem Steel Corp., with sales of $4.5 billion and a profit of $78.4 million in 1998; and National Steel Corp., with sales of $2.8 billion and a profit of $83.8 million in 1998. Another major producer, Inland Steel, was acquired in 1998 by London-based Ispat International for $1.4 billion.

One of the most progressive and successful steel producers was Nucor Corporation, of Charlotte, North Carolina. In contrast to the larger producers already mentioned, Nucor produces steel in minimills. With a net income of $263.7 million and sales of $4.2 billion in 1998, this company was one of the most profitable of the large producers and was continuing to build new facilities. Established in 1967 with a single mill in South Carolina, Nucor had added five plants by 1991 with a production capacity of about 4 million tons per year. Using state-of-the-art technology, such as EAFs and continuous casting, Nucor was able to produce steel from scrap at a fraction of the cost incurred by its larger competitors.

Nucor has also been a leader in expanding the markets served by the minimill sector. In the early 1990s, the company broke into the flat-rolled steel market, which previously was controlled entirely by integrated producers and accounted for about 45 percent of their production. To produce this sheet steel, Nucor was utilizing a new technique called thin-slab casting. In this process, a machine employs a funnel-shaped mold to squeeze molten steel down to a thickness of 1.5 inches to 2.0 inches. This eliminates the need for primary stands that reduce the larger slabs, typically eight to ten inches thick, that conventional casters produce. This method has proved much less costly than conventional casting methods. Nucor's thin-slab casting operation became profitable in June 1990, only ten months after it started production, and was operating at its maximum capacity of 800,000 tons per year by 1992.

In July of 1992, Nucor opened a new $330-million, one-million-ton-per-year, thin-slab casting sheet plant in Arkansas. By 1996, both it and Nucor's Indiana plant were operating at full capacity. The company also announced plans to control 20 percent of the sheet steel market in 2000 by progressing to 8 million tons of capacity. In addition to its attack on the sheet steel market, Nucor also constructed a mill in partnership with Yamato of Japan to roll wide-flange beams—a product produced primarily by integrated mills in the early 1990s. As of mid-1996, five other steel companies had announced plans to build thin-slab plants.

WORKFORCE

Labor productivity in the U.S. steel industry tripled between 1980 and 1998, from an industry-average of 10.1 man-hours per ton in 1980 to 3.2 man-hours per ton in 1998. Many North American facilities were able to produce a ton of finished steel in less than two man-hours per ton and some in less than one man-hour. These factors, combined with a reduction in demand since the late 1980s, dealt a lethal blow to many jobs in the industry. The trend toward automation was expected to maintain a trend toward fewer workers. Jobs in the steel industry declined from 171,000 in 1996 to 159,000 in 1998.

While overall steel employment declined through the 1990s, new positions were expected in the emerging minimill sector where a wide gap existed in labor productivity between minimills and integrated producers. Between 1986 and 1991 employment growth at minimills rose by an average of 19 percent, while employment at integrated companies fell by 30 percent. Minimills typically employed nonunion labor. Steel workers at integrated producers were represented by the United Steelworkers of America.

AMERICA AND THE WORLD

U.S. exports of steel typically accounted for less than 10 percent of total shipments during the 1990s, due in part to the fact that the U.S. domestic market is the largest in the world. Imported steel, on the other hand, reached a staggering 42 million tons in 1998 compared to an average of 23 million tons per year from 1990 to 1997. Among the countries showing the biggest increase in exports to the U.S. market in 1998 were Japan (5.5 million tons, up 157 percent from 1997), Russia (4.4 million tons, up 46 percent), and South Korea (2.9 million tons, up 105 percent). The largest exporters by volume to the United States were the European Union, Canada, Brazil, and Mexico.

Total global steel production fluctuates from year to year due to a variety of circumstances. In 1998, global production fell 3 percent to 775.3 million tons, due in part to the financial crisis in Russia, an economic crisis in Southeast Asia, and a lengthy strike at U.S. automaker General Motors. China was the largest producing country with 114.3 million tons, 14.7 percent of the world's output.

RESEARCH AND TECHNOLOGY

Rather than expanding production capacity, producers in the late 1980s and 1990s were relying on new technology to help achieve greater efficiency and quality. Because the overall global steel market has matured, companies in the mid-1990s could grow only by increasing market share, raising profit margins, or by developing new steel products.

In addition to continuous casting, thin-slab casting, and EAFs, companies were experimenting with a variety of new production techniques. For example, an array of devices were being employed in the early 1990s to help companies spot, map, describe, and classify defects in sheet steel that were as small as .02 inches in diameter. Strobe lights, laser beams, and artificial intelligence systems were all at work ensuring higher quality output. Furthermore, continuing advancements in alloys and steel coatings were allowing manufacturers to create new steel products that could compete with advanced plastics and ceramics.

Nucor has also been experimenting with an electromagnetic braking system, designed to improve surface quality of the sheet by reducing turbulence in the mold. Less turbulence should result in fewer surface defects and allow for greater casting speed. In addition, AK Steel has pioneered an oxygen-blowing technique that shows some promise in the fight to become more competitive. AK uses a form of oxygen injection in its blast furnaces to increase output and to improve its ability to cope with the world steel market. It is believed that oxygen injection will allow a decrease in the break-even volume for making steel in a blast furnace.

Besides new production techniques, U.S. steelmakers were also realizing productivity gains in the mid-1990s through information technology. Bethlehem Steel, for instance, entered a 10-year contract with Electronic Data Systems, Inc. (EDS) to coordinate its operations. EDS will eventually provide Bethlehem with all necessary resources for data center management, applications development support, and process control activities. The goal of the effort was to fully integrate all aspects of Bethlehem's operations and to allow the company to concentrate on steelmaking, rather than information management.

With the growth of the Internet in the late 1990s, the steel industry also embraced electronic commerce. By late 1999 the industry had two major electronic commerce ventures, MetalSite and e-Steel. MetalSite, based in Pittsburgh, was founded in 1998 by Weirton Steel, LTV Steel, and Steel Dynamics. It held its first steel auction in December 1998. New York-based e-Steel began conducting trial sales in 1999 and enjoyed financial backing from the same venture capital firms that had invested in other successful Internet businesses, such as Amazon.com and America Online.

FURTHER READING

"Armco Earnings up Despite Lower Sales," *American Metal Market,* 22 January 1999.

Baker, Stephen. "Metals: Prognosis 1997." *Business Week*, 13 January 1997.

"Bethlehem's Profit Drops 67 Percent," *American Metal Market*, 1 February 1999.

Boselovic, Len. "Basic Steel Prices Head Upward," *Knight-Ridder/Tribune Business News*, 28 April 1999.

Boselovic, Len. "Import Prices Lead U.S. Steel to Reduce its Work Force," *Knight-Ridder/Tribune Business News*, 4 November 1998.

Boselovic, Len. "Pittsburgh-Based Online Steel Venture Gains Two New Partners," *Knight-Ridder/Tribune Business News*, 2 September 1999.

Boselovic, Len. "Tidal Wave of Cheap Steel Imports Sends Industry into Tailspin," *Knight-Ridder/Tribune Business News*, 14 October 1998.

Boselovic, Len. "U.S. Businesses Face Costly, Unsure Battle to Fight 'Dumping,'" *Knight-Ridder/Tribune Business News*, 14 June 1999.

Boselovic, Len. "U.S. Steel Industry is Quick to Embrace Electronic Commerce," *Knight-Ridder/Tribune Business News*, 22 June 1999.

Boselovic, Len. "U.S. Steel Makers Complain about Cheap Steel Imports," *Knight-Ridder/Tribune Business News*, 13 October 1998.

Boselovic, Len. "U.S. Steel Makers Enter Gray Area as Import Prices Drop," *Knight-Ridder/Tribune Business News*, 3 November 1998.

Burgert, Philip. "World Steel Production Falls 3 Percent in 1998," *American Metal Market*, 21 January 1999.

Carter, Walter F. "Modest Recovery in World Steel, U.S. Slowdown Foreseen," *American Metal Market*, 14 September 1999.

Darnay, Arsen J., ed. *Manufacturing USA: Industry Analyses, Statistics, and Leading Companies*. Sixth edition. Farmington Hills, MI: The Gale Group, 1998.

Dolan, Kerry A. "Carnegie Would Be Jealous," *Forbes*, 23 August 1999.

"Foreign Steel Slams Bethlehem into Red," *American Metal Market*, 28 April 1999.

Gale Encyclopedia of United States Economic History. Farmington Hills, MI: The Gale Group, 1999.

Hall, Christopher. *Steel Phoenix: The Fall and Rise of the U.S. Steel Industry*. New York: St. Martin's Press, 1997.

"Low Prices, Shipments Put LTV in Red," *American Metal Market*, 18 October 1999.

"LTV Slides $27M in the Red in '98," *American Metal Market*, 29 January 1999.

Misa, Thomas J. *A Nation of Steel: The Making of Modern America, 1865-1925*. Baltimore: Johns Hopkins University Press, 1995.

"National Steel Posts Lower Sales, Profits," *American Metal Market*, 4 February 1999.

"Nucor Earnings Slip 10.4 Percent for Year," *American Metal Market*, 4 February 1999.

"The Power of the New Steel Industry," American Iron and Steel Institute, 26 November 1999. Available from http://www.steel.org/facts/power/.

Prizinsky, David. "Stage Set for Steel Talks: U.S. Steel Group, Bethlehem Lead off in Negotiating Effort," *Crain's Cleveland Business*, 17 May 1999.

Robertson, Scott. "Import Flood Sinks Steel Profits," *American Metal Market*, 4 October 1999.

Roth, Daniel. "Annual Report on American Industry: Metals." *Forbes*, 12 January 1998.

Sacco, John E. "'98 U.S. Steel Mill Shipments Off 3.5 Percent," *American Metal Market*, 10 February 1999.

Sacco, John E. "AK Stockholders OK Armco Merger," *American Metal Market*, 1 October 1999.

Sacco, John E. "Four Steelmakers Seek OCTG Hikes," *American Metal Market*, 20 August 1999.

Sacco, John E. "Steel Mill Products Roll to Import Record in '98," *American Metal Market*, 23 February 1999.

Sacco, John E. "Strong U.S. Market Drawing Steel Imports," *American Metal Market*, 8 September 1997.

Sheridan, John H. "A Global Future," *Industry Week*, 18 January 1999.

Standard & Poor's Industry Surveys: Metals: Industrial. New York: Standard & Poor's Corporation, 15 July 1999.

"Steel Imports for 9 Months of 1999 Remain High Due to Country and Product Switching; Average Import Prices Remain Depressed - Down 25 Percent," American Iron and Steel Institute press release, 21 October 1999. Available from http://www.steel.org/news/.

"USX Corporation, Financial Highlights: U.S. Steel Group," U.S. Steel Group, 24 November 1999. Available from http://www.usx.com/ussfin.htm.

Woker, Craig. "The M&A Question: Buy or Build?" *New Steel*, 1 January 1999.

SIC 3313

ELECTROMETALLURGICAL PRODUCTS, EXCEPT STEEL

This category includes establishments that manufacture metal additive alloys for both ferrous and nonferrous metals using electrometallurgical or metallothermic processes. Establishments primarily engaged in manufacturing electrometallurgical steel are classified in **SIC 3312: Steel Works, Blast Furnaces (Including Coke Ovens), and Rolling Mills.**

NAICS CODE(S)

331112 (Electrometallurgical Ferroalloy Product Manufacturing)

331492 (Secondary Smelting, Refining, and Alloying of Nonferrous Metals (except Copper and Aluminum))

The following alloying metals are those most commonly used to enhance iron and steel: nickel, molybdenum, manganese, silicon, aluminum, phosphorus, calcium, sulfur, lead, and selenium. Tungsten carbide powder and spiegeleisen also are produced in this industry. Alloys have three main purposes: to eliminate undesired elements in a base metal; to add special characteristics, such as strength, heat resistance, and corrosion resistance; and to neutralize unwanted properties of a metal.

Electrometallurgical products firms were shipping about $1.3 billion worth of products per year in the late 1990s. Nickel and molybdenum are the most common alloys produced in the industry. Nickel is used primarily to create stainless steel; molybdenum is used to strengthen steel for aerospace and other specialty steel applications. Specialty metals production accounts for about 65 percent of primary nickel consumption. About 75 percent of all molybdenum consumed in 1998 went into iron and steel, with major end-use applications as follows: machinery, 35 percent; electrical, 15 percent; and transportation, 15 percent.

North American metal workers have been strengthening and enhancing iron and steel with alloys since the 1600s. Only since World War II, however, has the mining and production of the alloying metals emerged as a significant industry. Since that time, the federal government has promoted the extraction and processing of various ferrous and nonferrous alloys as a means of insuring reserves for national defense and security.

Demand for alloy metals surged from the 1950s through the 1970s, as the U.S. economy expanded and new alloying technologies broadened the industry's market. The auto and capital equipment industries, particularly, became major consumers of ferroalloys during that period. By the end of the 1970s, the electrometallurgical industry employed about 6,000 workers and was shipping about $700 million worth of products each year.

As maturing markets, high production costs, and metal substitutes reduced U.S. steel production in the 1980s, growth of alloy demand slowed—despite the fact that the percentage of metals that used alloys continued to rise. The value of shipments ranged from $707 million in 1982 and $661 million in 1983 to $667 million in 1986. Employment in 1986 plummeted to 3,600 people.

As steel and other metal orders rose in the late 1980s, the alloy market rebounded, sending the value of shipments past $1.2 billion by 1988. Despite a huge increase in production tonnage, however, industry profitability sagged as the competitive and glutted market steadily eroded prices. The price of nickel, for instance, fell from $6.49 per pound in 1988 to about $3.55 by 1996. Similarly, molybdenum prices dropped to about $3.20 per pound in the late 1990s; it had traded at $7.00 to $8.00 per pound as recently as 1994. Therefore, the value of all electrometallurgical shipments remained at around $1.30 billion in 1996 and 1997.

Entering the 1990s, producers of ferrous and nonferrous alloys expected a mild reprieve from glutted markets and faltering prices. However, nickel prices were expected to rebound only slightly, perhaps to $4.00 per pound. As the 1990s ended, there was an oversupply of nickel, leading to a sharp drop in prices. In 1998, prices averaged only around $2.20 per pound, with a 1999 price averaging $2.33 per pound.

Molybdenum was forecast to rise in price slightly by the end of the century, to $4.00 or $4.25. In 1997, prices held steady at $4.50 per pound until the last quarter, when they fell below $4.00 per pound. A more volatile year was 1998, with prices first rising to $4.30 per pound then dropping to $3.75 by mid-year and finally dropping to a low of $2.15 per pound in the fall. In summer 1999 the price was $2.60 per pound.

U.S. consumption of molybdenum in steel applications dropped about 10 percent from 1997 to 1998. Several North American producers reduced production in 1999. World demand for molybdenum in alloys, including stainless steel, was expected to be about the same in 1999 and 2000 as in 1998. Increased usage in duplex steels was expected to compensate for reductions in other areas.

Producers expected little revenue growth going into the new century, as world steel production remained static. Through 2003 U.S. steel shipments were forecast to grow by only 1 to 2 percent. Weak demand globally, coupled with large inventories, were also expected to keep prices low and even to lead them to decline over a ten-year period. U.S. steel mill exports were expected to remain around the 1997 level of 5.4 million tons for the following two years.

Increased production of nickel-based superalloys in the late 1990s was expected to do little to bolster nickel's price due to the alloy's growing stockpile, up 6 percent from 1995 to 1996. This overcapacity continued; in 1998, Special Metals, the world's largest producer of nickel-based alloys, announced a 10 percent reduction in its workforce as a result of a net loss in the first half of 1988.

In 1997, an increase in stainless steel production increased nickel consumption by 9.3 percent to 930,000 metric tons. However, the resulting oversupply of stainless steel in 1998 was expected to lead to a nickel demand of just 1.0 percent. The nickel market was expected to be in surplus for 1999, leading to a similar growth rate. The outlook for 2000 looked better, at 4.0 percent.

Stagnant prices at the end of the century were viewed against a backdrop of price-fixing accusations levied against some of the largest electrometallurgical products companies. One federal civil antitrust complaint was filed in 1997 against five silicon firms, alleging a price-fixing conspiracy to boost sales prices. Defendants in the suit were American Alloys Incorporated of New Haven, West Virginia; Applied Industrial Materials Corporation of Pittsburgh; Elkem Metals Company of Pittsburgh; Globe Metallurgical Incorporated of Cleveland, Ohio; and SKW Metals & Alloys of Niagara Falls, New York.

Also in 1997, Elkem Metals Co. and American Alloys Inc. pleaded guilty to price-fixing violations of the Sherman Act in a U.S. Justice Department criminal suit. Criminal charges against SKW Metals & Alloys also were filed. Other civil suits were filed in the late 1990s, as well. Allegheny Teledyne, for example, filed lawsuits alleging price-fixing, fraud, and violations of the Racketeer Influenced and Corrupt Organizations (RICO) Act against American Alloys Inc. and Globe Metallurgical Inc.

The largest producer in the industry in the late 1990s was Elkem Metals Company of Pittsburgh, Pennsylvania, with annual sales of $190 million. Founded in 1962, the company employed 2,000 workers in the mid-1990s, but that roster dropped to roughly 1,300 in the late 1990s as the steel industry increasingly looked to buy its ferroalloys overseas. Second-largest was Globe Metallurgical Inc. of Cleveland, Ohio, with other operations in Alabama and Oregon and a subsidiary in Ardingly, England. Globe's annual sales in 1998 were $160 million.

Other large electrometallurgical corporations in the late 1990s included Steel of West Virginia of Huntington, West Virginia, with estimated sales around $113 million; Thompson Creek Metals Company of Englewood, Colorado, with annual sales around $100 million; and American Alloys Inc. of New Haven, West Virginia, with annual sales around $50 million.

In 1997, the electrometallurgical products industry employed approximately 3,300 workers, with 2,400 in production. Ohio employs the majority of all U.S. workers at roughly 40 percent. Production workers earned an average of about $17 per hour the same year, up from $15.60 in 1992.

However, because income growth in the industry comes largely from increased productivity, employment was expected to decrease or hold steady toward the turn of the century. The number of workers employed in most sectors of the industry was expected to decline by 10 to 50 percent by 2005. Similarly, every occupation in the steel industry was forecast by the Bureau of Labor Statistics to decline between 1994 and 2005. New manufacturing and information technologies that increase automation will yield most of the productivity gains.

FURTHER READING

Adams, William. "New Stainless Startups to Boost Nickel Demand." *American Metal Market,* 7 January 1997.

Anthony, Michael. "1999 Annual Commodities: Molybdenum." *Engineering & Mining Journal.* PRIMEDIA Intertec, 1999.

"Armco Sues Silicon Firms." *Purchasing,* 16 January 1997.

Blossom, John W. "Molybdenum-1998." *Annual Mineral Survey.* U.S. Geological Survey, 1998.

"Ferro-alloys: Let the Bears Take Stock." *Metal Bulletin,* 30 September 1996.

Fitzpatrick, Dan. "Elkem Puts Its Technology Center on the Block." *Pittsburgh Business Times and Journal,* 25 March 1996.

Phillips, E.H. "Memory Alloys Key to 'Smart' Wing." *Aviation Week & Space Technology,* 22 July 1996.

Rotondo, Michael. "Moly Market Continues to Fuel Wishful Thinking." *American Metal Market,* 7 January 1997.

"Special Metals Narrows Losses, Remains Cautious." *Reuters Business Report.* Reuters Ltd., 1999.

Standard & Poor's Industry Surveys. New York: Standard & Poor's Corporation, 12 November 1992.

"Steel Mill Products." *U.S. Industry & Trade Outlook '99.* U.S. Bureau of the Census/McGraw-Hill, 1999.

Stundza, Tom. "Alloying and Plating Metals: There's Plenty—And It's Cheap." *Purchasing,* 12 December 1996.

"Transaction Prices." *Purchasing,* 17 October 1996.

"Molybdenum." *Mineral Commodity Summaries.* U.S. Geological Survey, January 1999.

SIC 3315

STEEL WIREDRAWING AND STEEL NAILS AND SPIKES

This category covers establishments primarily engaged in drawing wire from purchased iron or steel rods, bars, or wire, as well as those which may be engaged in the further manufacture of products made from wire. Establishments primarily engaged in manufacturing steel nails and spikes from purchased materials are also included in this industry. Rolling mills engaged in the production of ferrous wire from wire rods or hot-rolled bars produced in the same establishment are classified under **SIC 3312: Blast Furnaces and Steel Mills.** Establishments primarily engaged in drawing nonferrous wire are classified in other industry categories.

NAICS CODE(S)

331222 (Steel Wire Drawing)

332618 (Other Fabricated Wire Product Manufacturing)

INDUSTRY SNAPSHOT

Steel wiredrawing plants manufacture a wide variety of products including barbed and twisted wire, steel baskets, brads, cable, chain link fencing, fence gates, posts and fittings, form ties, horseshoe nails, steel nails, paper clips, spikes, staples, wire cages, tacks, tie wires, wire fabric, wire carts, wire cloth, and wire garment hangers.

The steadily growing U.S. economy helped steel wiredrawing manufacturers continue the industry's expansion through 1998. Demand for steel wire was fueled by a significant increase in highway construction, residential housing construction, and the continued strength of the automotive industry. In spite of these positive factors, U.S. steel wire drawing industries faced growing competition from imports in the late 1990s. While total shipments were valued at $4.89 billion in 1997, U.S. producers lobbied fiercely for relief from imports that kept prices near record lows.

ORGANIZATION AND STRUCTURE

In 1997, 273 companies produced steel wire and related products, down from 350 in 1995. The vast majority of establishments in this industry were larger companies employing 20 or more employees. Of all steel wire manufacturers, only 76 employed 20 or less in 1997. The largest concentration of firms by shipment value were in the Great Lakes region of the United States, with the southeast and New England regions ranking second and third, respectively. The largest producing states in descending order of shipments were Pennsylvania, Missouri, Illinois, Ohio, Tennessee, Texas, and Oklahoma.

Six major classes of steel wire and related products comprised the steel wire industry. Noninsulated ferrous wire rope, cable, and strand manufactured in wiredrawing plants represented approximately 19 percent of the dollar value of the steel wire and related products industry shipments in 1997, down from 22.1 in 1995. Steel nails, staples, tacks, spikes, and brads made up 9.2 percent of this industry's total product shipments, a 37 percent decrease from 14.6 percent in 1995. Steel wire produced in mills not producing steel rods or hot-rolled bars accounted for 44.4 percent of total product shipments, up from 37.2 percent in 1995, while other fabricated ferrous wire products, except springs, represented 18.1 percent of steel wire product shipments, up from 13.3 percent in 1995. Shipments for the other two industry categories (steel fencing and fence gates made in plants that draw wire, and ferrous wire cloth and other ferrous woven wire products made in plants that draw wire), together accounted for the remaining 28.3 percent of the industry's shipments.

BACKGROUND AND DEVELOPMENT

The demand for steel wire evolved from the housing, construction, and automotive industries. To service these markets, steel wire makers bought steel rod from both domestic and foreign mills and drew it into wire and other related products. While steel wiredrawing companies shopped globally for the least expensive sources of steel bar, their ability to buy from foreign sources depended on the trade climate between the United States and its competitors. The rapid expansion of the Chinese, Russian, and South African steel industries saw steel supplies increase substantially in the 1990s. Steel consumption increased at the same time as the demand for wiredrawing products, particularly in housing and highway construction, aided growth.

During the 1980s, increases in imports of finished products during the recession coupled with high dollar valuations led many domestic steel wire producers to call for extended voluntary restraint arrangements and duties on imported steel wire and products. The high inflation rates, interest rates, and high value of the dollar made offshore sources of steel wire attractive and affordable for domestic users. Industry shipments dropped 21.4 percent between 1981 to 1982.

From the mid-1980s to the early 1990s, American steel wire producers charged many countries with unfair trading practices, most notably with dumping product at prices less than the cost of production. In February 1989, 30 Japanese producers were subject to duties as high as 29.8 percent. The Specialty Steel Industry of the United States, which represented virtually all U.S. producers of stainless and alloy tool steels and other high technology metals, found that import penetration grew to 20.2 percent of the U.S. market, up from 18.6 percent in 1990.

Imports remain a problem for the industry. In the mid-1990s, the Specialty Steel Industry asked the Clinton administration to work quickly in establishing a Mutual Specialty Steel Agreement with the European Union and the rest of the world on stainless steel imports. Stainless steel buyers purchased 24 percent of their product from foreign mills, depressing domestic prices. More than 500,000 tons of stainless steel were imported in 1996, spurred by a 5 percent increase in consumption.

CURRENT CONDITIONS

Demand for steel wire in the late 1990s remained high, as a booming American economy drove the automotive and construction industries—the primary consumers of wire. Especially promising for wire mills was the continued rise in housing construction, fueled by low and moderate interest rates. Steel-framed housing construction became more prevalent, further increasing demand for wiredrawing products. Nevertheless, a U.S. International Trade Commission Report filed in September of 1999 revealed that domestic producers struggled to remain profitable in the first half of 1999. American firms were forced by a flood of cheaper imports to slash prices. Because of the 1997 Asian economic crisis and the currency devaluations that followed, wire mills based in Asia found it more profitable to sell their goods in the United States, especially as the construction industry stalled in Asia as a result of the economic downturn. Those countries cited for "dumping" inexpensive wire in the United States included India, Japan, South Korea, Spain, Canada, and Taiwan. Moreover, while these imports drove down U.S. steel wire prices, U.S. producers lost markets abroad, as Asian economies remained sluggish. To further compound the problem, the Russian economy collapsed in the late 1990s, eliminating another potential market for U.S. steel wire drawing products.

In December of 1999, workers from various steel wire sectors rallied at the White House to convince President Clinton to take action on the matter. "Our losses are mounting, and imports are surging into the United States at record levels," an industry spokesperson proclaimed in a press release.

INDUSTRY LEADERS

While the majority of steel wire producers were privately held firms, a relatively sizeable number were subsidiaries or divisions of larger companies. Some of the largest producers by sales and number of employees in 1998 included BICC Cables Corp., a division of BICC General ($3 billion in sales and 13,000 employees); Ohio-based Bekaert Corp. ($500 million in sales and 1,400 employees); Northwestern Steel and Wire Co. Of Sterling, Illinois ($596.4 million in sales and 2,000 employees) Keystone Steel and Wire Co. of Peoria, Illinois ($300 million in sales and 500 employees); and Mount Airy, North Carolina-based Insteel Wire Products ($266 million in sales and 1,056 employees).

WORKFORCE

Employment in the industry peaked in 1979 at 33,800 and then reached an industry low in 1985, with a work force of 20,900. While sharp increases in hiring led to employment figures of 27,100 in 1989, employment fell through 1992. In 1997, the industry employed 23,293. Of this total number of employees, 18,644 were production workers, most of whom were represented by the United Steel Workers of America. On average, these workers earned $13.29 per hour. The average work week was about 41 hours. In 1997, Pennsylvania was home to the greatest number of steel wiredrawing employees, with 2,353, followed by Illinois with 1,677 and Missouri with 1,557.

Steel wire makers faced several employment issues in the 1990s, including spiraling health care costs and the need for fully funded company pension plans. During this time, many smaller companies had health care costs that exceeded company earnings.

RESEARCH AND TECHNOLOGY

Competition from companies offering specialty metals and new processes posed a continual challenge to the

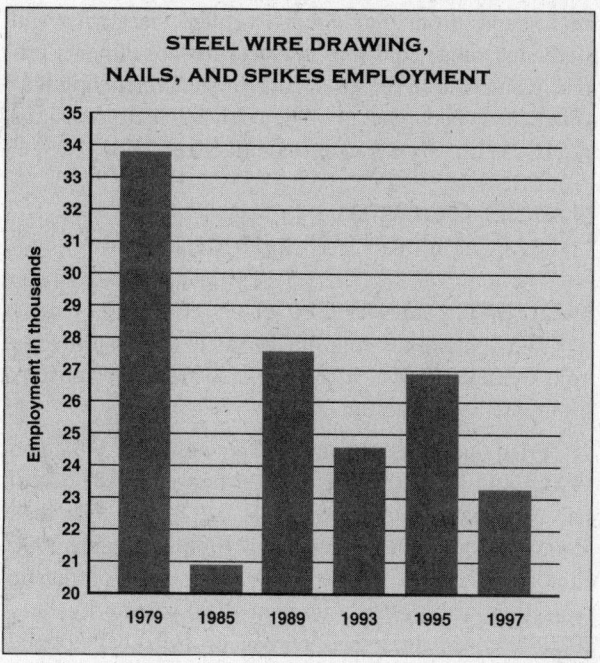

industry, as their traditional markets, such as the automotive and construction industries, looked to use lighter, stronger, and cheaper materials. Seeking to expand its market as well as its sources for raw materials, the industry regarded recycling as a potentially important area.

FURTHER READING

Adams, Chris. "U.S. Producers Accuse Six Countries of Unfair Trade Trade in Stainless-Steel Wire." *Wall Street Journal,* 30 March 1998.

Kelly, Nancy. "With All Chips on ITC Table, Producers Playing for US Market Pot." *American Metal Market,* 15 April 1999.

Marcus, Peter F. "Metal Tags Encounter Fork in the Road." *Purchasing,* 16 January 1997. Available from http://www .manufacturing.net/magazine/purchasing/archives/1997/ pur0101.97/011mnnews.htm#ME.

"Steelworkers Rally at White House." *PR NewsWire,* 8 December 1999.

Stundza, Tom. "Supply Overwhelms a Weakening Market." *Purchasing,* 13 February 1997. Available from http://www .manufacturing.net/magazine/purchasing/archives/1997/ pur0213.97/021bars.htm.

SIC 3316

COLD FINISHING OF STEEL SHAPES

This industry covers establishments primarily engaged in cold-rolling steel sheets and strip from purchased hot-rolled sheets; cold-drawing steel bars and steel shapes from purchased hot-rolled steel bars; and producing other cold finished steel. Establishments primarily engaged in the production of steel, including hot-rolled steel sheets that are then cold-rolled are classified in **SIC 3312: Blast Furnaces and Steel Mills.**

NAICS Code(s)

331221 (Cold-Rolled Steel Shape Manufacturing)

Industry Snapshot

The demand for cold finished steel comes primarily from the automotive, aerospace, construction, housing, and home appliance industries.

Price increases dominated the news in 1998 and 1999 for this industry. The price of the source, sheet steel slabs, peaked in early 1998 at $265 per ton, then plummeted to $150 by the end of 1998, and spent 1999 climbing back up to the $200 mark, with optimistic projections calling for a price of $250 per ton by early 2000. Accordingly, industry producers steadily increased the prices they charged for the end products, hot- and cold-rolled sheets and coated sheets. Industry producers attributed the hikes to the tight market. And industry analysts further elaborated by pointing out that strong demand, continued low inventories, and increasing backlogs led to reduced imports, as European shortfalls started eating up excess stocks of Asian steel.

Organization and Structure

Cold-rolling is the process of rolling steel without first reheating it. This method produces a smooth steel surface that reduces thickness and enhances machinability. Cold-rolling gives steel the ability to be stretched and shaped without cracking and provides it with a bright finish. The three main product classes within the industry are steel sheet, steel strip, and steel bars.

Steel sheet and strip are both flat products that are generally less than 1/4 inch thick. Sheet is the wider of the two by 12 inches or more and is produced to less exact thickness than the strip. Steelmakers produce most sheet and strip in the form of large coils that the user can cut into pieces of any desired length. Much of the sheet and strip manufactured is used in automobile bodies, but thousands of other products also contain these forms of steel.

Steel companies make bars in many sizes and various shapes, including squares, circles, ovals, hexagons, and rectangles. Products made from steel bars include many precision-engineered components that power automobiles, trucks, tractors, hand tools, washing machines, and lawn mowers.

There were 187 establishments producing cold steel products in 1997, down from 219 in 1993. The largest concentration of firms by shipment value could be found in the Great Lakes region of the United States. The

northeast and West Coast were second and third, respectively. The largest producing states in descending order of shipments were Ohio, Pennsylvania, Illinois, Michigan, Indiana, Connecticut, and New York.

Background and Development

The production of cold finished steel became industrialized early in the twentieth century, prompted by the mass marketing of automobiles, household appliances, and industrial machinery. New and more efficient steel production methods ensued at a rapid pace.

During World War II, the American steel industry boomed, while other countries' steel manufacturing facilities sustained considerable damage. American firms dominated global steel markets during the post-war years, and, by 1960, American shipments of cold finished steel shapes totaled 17 million tons, rising to 20 million tons by the middle of the decade. During this time, however, Japan and several European countries focused on rebuilding their steel industries, using the most modern facilities and equipment available, while American steelmakers continued to use older, less efficient equipment. Consequently, American shipments fell below 17 million tons in 1970.

Worldwide inflation and high interest rates in the early 1970s curtailed foreign steel production, particularly in developing nations, allowing U.S. shipments to realize significant gains. In 1973, U.S. shipments stood at 24.09 million tons, the highest level experienced by the industry in over two decades. Economic recession in the United States, however, eventually pushed shipments back down to 20.76 million tons in 1979.

The cold finished steel industry faced intense foreign competition during the 1980s. Due to the high value of the dollar, foreign steel became significantly less expensive than American steel. Furthermore, having rebuilt and improved their facilities, foreign producers were marketing a superior product, and this quality gap widened significantly during the decade. Consequently, American companies operating with outdated equipment and production methods were often priced out of the market. From 1979 to 1980, U.S. shipments of cold finished steel dropped 24 percent. The industry recovered slightly in 1981, with shipments rising 8 percent; the following year, however, shipments fell 25 percent to a 30-year low.

Hoping to become more competitive by realizing productivity gains, some American companies began installing completely automated, high-speed production equipment with computer controlled systems. In 1988, industry shipments were valued at $6.3 billion, representing a small increase over previous years. The Gulf War and the early 1990s economic recession, however, depressed the value of shipments to a low of $5.4 billion in 1991. By 1995, the industry increased production as world steel demand surged to levels higher than those before the Gulf War. In 1995, shipments of cold finished products stood at more than $7 billion.

Many analysts doubted that cold finished steel makers would again reach the shipment levels enjoyed during the 1960s and 1970s. Steel sheet and bar shipments had apparently peaked in 1973 at 20.38 and 2.25 million tons each, while steel strip shipments peaked earlier, at 1.58 million tons in 1966.

Nevertheless, the industry regarded the 1990s with optimism. As the industry gradually shed its excess capacity, its ability to raise prices in the face of increasing demand was expected to help buoy profits. Steelmakers also relied on investments in new technologies and commitments to reducing costs to increase their chances for survival and long-term profitability.

While prices did rise somewhat throughout 1996, worldwide steel capacity surged as foreign production, particularly from China and Russia, began to swell market reserves. The influx of foreign steel on the market diminished domestic producers' ability to pass on increasing cost to consumers. Some industry leaders, like Worthington Industries and LTV Corporation, sought to expand their operations to produce economies of scale and to diversify into more value-added steel products. The growth of nonunion steel mill competitors forced older members of the industry to seek additional cost-containment strategies to sustain profit margins.

The value of cold-finished steel shipments rose substantially in 1995 and was projected to make similar rises throughout the rest of the decade. As consumers pushed for cost reductions from all parts suppliers, however, some steel bar manufacturers were expected to have difficulty passing along their rising costs. Steel sheet price was 5 percent higher in 1996 than 1995, but remained well below 1994 levels. Imports were the major factor in keeping prices down.

As the industry entered the mid-1990s, its success hinged on its ability to meet the needs of domestic durable goods customers in a climate of rising competition, business costs, labor difficulties, and alternative uses of new metals and plastics. The industry was therefore called upon to improve quality, technology, and productivity while working in partnership with their customers to enhance their prospects for long-term survival.

CURRENT CONDITIONS

On January 30, 1998, several companies simultaneously announced their price increases for finished sheet steel. Middletown, Ohio-based AK Steel Corp., Bethlehem, Pennsylvania-based Bethlehem Steel Corp., and Mishawaka, Indiana-based National Steel Corp. raised their prices for hot-rolled sheet by $10 per ton from $310, for cold-rolled sheet by $15 per ton from $460, and for coated

sheet by $20 per ton from $520. Price hiking continued throughout 1999, starting with increases in February 1999 by Allegheny Ludlum, Armco, and J&L Specialty, raising the price 4 percent above 1998 lows. Allegheny initiated another price increase of 7 percent on stainless hot- and cold-rolled strip, sheet, and continuous mill plate as of July 19, 1999. Armco followed on Allegheny's heels with the same hike, effective August 1, 1999.

Then, on August 5, 1999, Cleveland, Ohio-based LTV Steel Company Inc. effectively raised its prices by lowering its competitive discounts by $30 per ton of flat-rolled steel (hot- and cold-rolled as well as coated) as of October 3, 1999; other companies, such as Chicago-based Ispat-Inland Steel Co., Pittsburgh-based US Steel Group of USX Corp., Wheeling, West Virginia-based Wheeling-Pittsburgh Steel Corp., Weirton, West Virginia-based Weirton Steel Corp., National Steel, and Bethlehem Steel, followed suit. National then raised its hot-rolled sheet prices by $25 per ton, its prices for cold-rolled sheet, as well as hot-dip galvanized and electrogalvanized by $20 per ton on January 2, 2000.

INDUSTRY LEADERS

LTV Steel Company of Cleveland, Ohio led the industry with 1997 sales of $4.4 billion, according to the most recent available data from Infotrac. National Steel Corp. followed with $2.8 billion in 1998 sales. Ispat International took over Inland Steel Co. on July 16, 1998, to form the Ispat-Inland Steel Co. For the first six months of 1998 before the takeover, Inland generated sales of $1.23 billion, slipping slightly from sales of $1.25 billion for the same six months of 1997. AK Steel Corp. posted sales of $2.4 billion in 1998, and Armco Inc. garnered $1.7 billion in 1998 sales. For its fiscal year ended May 31, 1998, Columbus, Ohio-based Worthington Industries Inc. reported sales of $1.6 billion.

WORKFORCE

In the early 1990s, attrition and early retirement incentives were used more often than layoffs to cut back on labor costs. Flexible assignment of employees helped reduce the number of classes of skilled steel trades. Approximately 14,348 employees served the industry in 1997, a slight decrease from the 15,100 in 1994.

Average production wages per hour reached $20.29 in 1997. Payroll costs were $440 million. Nearly all non-management employees belong to the United Steelworkers of America (USWA), one of the largest labor unions in the United States. WHX Corp., the third largest company in the sector, experienced substantial labor problems in 1996. The USWA walked out of talks with the company over the issue of pensions. Work ceased at eight of the companies' facilities, even though both sides engaged a federal mediator to resolve the dispute.

AMERICA AND THE WORLD

In the early 1990s, the U.S. steel industry filed charges of unfair competition against several foreign firms. Upon review, the U.S. International Trade Commission (ITC) found that 25 of the claims were justified and assessed duties accordingly. Due to the increased potential for duties imposed by the ITC on their steel, many foreign steelmakers reduced their exports to the United States in 1993.

Some domestic manufacturers filed complaints with the International Trade Commission protesting the imports of plate steel from China, Russia, South Africa, and Ukraine. Domestic imports from those countries increased four-fold between 1993 and 1995 and were expected to surpass 1 million tons in 1996.

The 1993 passage of the North American Free Trade Agreement (NAFTA) was implemented to help eliminate tariffs placed on foreign steel entering America. Mexico, Canada, and the United States were scheduled to drop all tariffs on cold finished steel traded among the three countries before the year 2004. As of 1993, the tariff on steel sheet, strip, and bar exported by Mexico was 10 percent. Canada's tariffs on sheet and strip were between 6.8 and 10.2 percent, and on bar between zero and 12.5 percent. The U.S. tariffs on sheet and strip were between 2.4 and 6 percent, and on bar between 3.3 and 10.6 percent.

RESEARCH AND TECHNOLOGY

In the early 1990s, the industry was concerned with improving the quality and reputation of steel in the face of aggressive marketing techniques by makers of alternative metals. Manufacturers that purchased steel bar typically looked to obtain straight components, tight tolerances, fast machining rates, and quality surfaces—characteristics that could be furnished by alternative materials such as plastics, aluminum, and brass. The low density of aluminum, for example, was found to lengthen tool life and productivity in machining operations as well as to produce a lighter weight, and thereby more fuel efficient, automobiles. Moreover, steep declines in brass and aluminum prices made those materials more attractive to manufacturers.

In order to compete for market share, the steel industry sought a better understanding of the product's end use and to communicate to customers the advantages of steel. By becoming a part of their customers' product problem-solving and supplier development teams, steel firms hoped to win back lost markets and combat the substitution of alternative metals for their cold-finished steel.

FURTHER READING

"Allegheny Ludlum, Armco, and J&L Specialty Steel are raising selling prices." *Purchasing,* 11 February 1999.

"Armco tries for stainless hike." *American Metal Market,* 29 July 1999.

Haflich, Frank. "Steel slabs reviving from slump." *American Metal Market,* 24 August 1999.

Infotrac Company Profiles. Available from http://web6.infotrac.galegroup.com (visited 1/7/00).

"Inland Steel sales, earnings slide." *American Metal Market,* 23 July 1998.

"LTV hiking flat-rolled steel." *American Metal Market,* 5 August 1999.

Marcus, Peter F. "Metal Tags Encounter Fork in the Road." *Purchasing,* 16 January 1997. Available from http://www.manufacturing.net/magazine/purchasing/archives/1997/pur0101.97/011mnnews.htm#ME.

"National to increase sheet." *American Metal Market,* 18 October 1999.

Robertson, Scott. "Sheet steel price hikes planned." *American Metal Market,* 30 January 1998.

Stundza, Tom, "Supply Overwhelms a Weakening Market." *Purchasing,* 13 February 1997. Available from http://www.manufacturing.net/magazine/purchasing/archives/1997/pur0213.97/021bars.htm.

———. "On-Time Means a Lot to Steel Buyers." *Purchasing,* 3 April 1997. Available from http://www.manufacturing.net/magazine/purchasing/archives/1997/pur0403.97/041steel.htm.

SIC 3317

STEEL PIPE AND TUBES

Included in this category are establishments primarily engaged in the production of welded or seamless steel pipe and tubes and heavy riveted steel pipe from purchased materials. Establishments primarily engaged in the production of steel, including steel skelp or steel blanks, tube rounds, or pierced billets, are classified under **SIC 3312: Blast Furnaces & Steel Mills.**

NAICS CODE(S)

331210 (Iron and Steel Pipes and Tubes Manufacturing from Purchased Steel)

According to the U.S. Census Bureau's *1997 Economic Census—Manufacturing,* 325 establishments operated in this category for part or all of 1997. Industry-wide employment totaled 27,723 workers receiving a payroll of more than $1 billion. Within this workforce, 21,707 of these employees worked in production, putting in almost 46 million hours to earn wages of more than $679 million. Overall shipments for the industry were valued at almost $7.6 billion.

After some years of declining sales, the American steel pipe and tubes industry entered a period of stronger economic growth in the mid-1990s. During the first seven months of 1993, shipments were running 22.1 percent ahead of 1992's first seven months. Total shipments were $6.374 billion in 1996, up almost 6 percent from the 1994 level of $6.038 billion. Rising demand, the increasing price of raw material, and energy costs drove the prices of seamless carbon tubing up to $973 per ton, welded tubing up to $739 per ton, seamless carbon casing up to $701 per ton, and welded casing up to $560 per ton.

In the United States, the automotive, display fixture, juvenile furniture, and exercise and recreation equipment industries showed healthy increases in demand for steel pipes and tubes. Regionally, the midwest, mountain, and southern states exhibited high demand, while sales in the Northeast and on the West Coast remained stagnant.

In the steel pipe and tube industry, 243 establishments employed 25,300 workers; of these, 19,800 were involved in production during 1995. That year total compensation reached an estimated $798.2 million. The largest producing states in descending order were Pennsylvania, Ohio, Illinois, and California, which together shipped 55 percent of total U.S. shipments. New capital expenditures on plant and equipment totaled $181.5 million, an increase of over 50 percent from 1990 levels.

The American steel mill products industry, which includes steel tubes and pipes, exported $13.4 billion in 1995, a 44 percent increase over the 1994 level. Imports of foreign steel pipe and tubes totaled $3.2 billion, an increase of 7.3 percent from 1994.

In 1992, the U.S. International Trade Commission and U.S. Commerce Department ruled in favor of many American pipe and tube manufacturers, concluding that foreign countries were dumping their shipments into the U.S. market at less than the cost of production or values sold at home. The countries guilty of dumping in 1992 (with corresponding duties assessed) were Brazil (103.38 percent); South Korea (4.9 to 11.6 percent); Mexico (32.6 percent); Taiwan (19.5 to 27.7 percent); and Venezuela (52.5 percent).

Cleveland-based LTV Steel Company Inc. led the industry with sales of more than $4.4 billion in 1997. LTV's Steel Tubular Products Co. division, located in Youngstown, Ohio, contributed $300 million to the company's 1998 sales. Following LTV was Babcock and Wilcox Co. of Barberton, Ohio, which generated $1.2 billion in sales for its fiscal year ended March 31, 1999. Bringing up third place in the industry was Houston-based Quanex Corp., with $797.5 million in sales for its fiscal year ended October 31, 1998. Other industry leaders included Sandvik Inc. of Fair Lawn, New Jersey, Marmon/Keystone Corp. of Butler, Pennsylvania, and Ameron International Corp. of Pasadena, California.

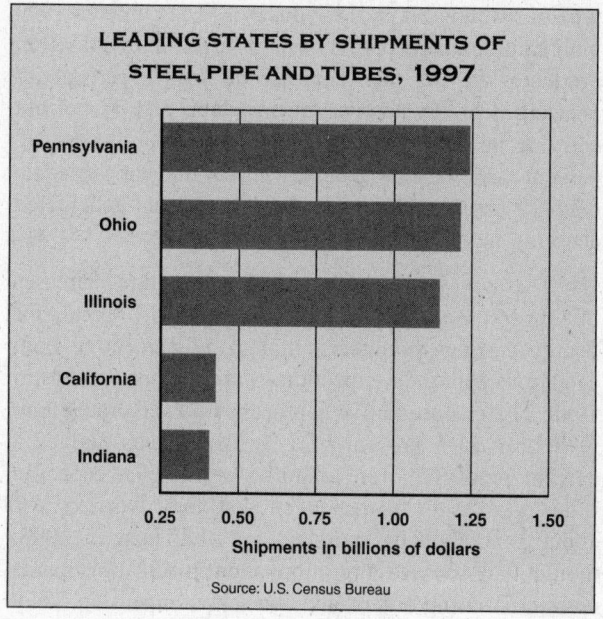

LEADING STATES BY SHIPMENTS OF STEEL PIPE AND TUBES, 1997

Shipments in billions of dollars

Source: U.S. Census Bureau

FURTHER READING

Darnay, Arsen J., ed. *Manufacturing USA*. 5th ed. Detroit: Gale Research, 1996.

Infotrac Company Profiles. Available at http://web6.infotrac.galegroup.com (visited 1/25/00).

U.S. Census Bureau. *1995 Annual Survey of Manufactures*. Washington, D.C.: U.S. Government Printing Office, 1997.

———. *1997 Economic Census-Manufacturing*. Available at http://www.census.gov/prod/ec97/97m3312a.pdf.

U.S. Department of Commerce. International Trade Administration. *U.S. Industrial Outlook 1995*. Washington, D.C.: U.S. Government Printing Office, 1996.

SIC 3321

GRAY AND DUCTILE IRON FOUNDRIES

This classification covers establishments primarily engaged in manufacturing gray and ductile iron castings, including cast iron pressure and soil pipes and fittings.

NAICS CODE(S)

331511 (Iron Foundries)

INDUSTRY SNAPSHOT

According to a 1998 *Foundry Management and Technology* magazine survey of 110 industry executives, gray iron castings shipments rose 2.1 percent from 1996 to 1997 and ductile castings shipments increased by 3.7 percent. However, many of those queried responded that they experienced a slowdown in late 1998, or, "some type of leveling off in the industry.'' They entered 1999 with cautious anticipation, with 37 percent of gray iron producers staying their increase of debt, 8 percent increasing debt, 18 percent retiring debt, and 37 percent carrying no debt. Of the ductile castings producers, 42 percent carried the same debt, while 27 percent carried no debt, 19 percent retired debt, and 12 percent anticipated accruing more debt.

The survey called for capital expenditure increases of 8.6 percent for gray iron producers and 5.1 percent for ductile castings producers, though 53 percent of both categories kept their expenditures at the same level as in 1998. These conservative approaches slowed production, with only 81.4 percent of gray iron plants and 82.7 percent of ductile iron foundries working at capacity. Industry executives responded that they worried less about general labor shortages in 1999 than in 1998, though they worried a bit more about medical insurance costs, decreasing orders, and overseas competition. They worried much less about on-time deliveries.

ORGANIZATION AND STRUCTURE

This industry is heavily engaged in manufacturing pipes and pipe fittings; however, other segments of the industry are growing in response to changing market demands. For example, the automotive industry has switched most engine components to aluminum in response to consumer demands for lighter, more fuel efficient cars. While this move has hurt some gray and ductile iron foundries, it has forced them to find alternative markets. This is readily apparent, since 52.6 percent of product share is claimed by other gray iron castings and 19.9 percent is claimed by other ductile iron castings. Only 3.9 percent of product share is due to cast iron pressure, soil pipe, and fittings, whereas 14.0 percent is attributed to ductile iron pressure pipe and fittings.

Historically, the automotive and aerospace industries were the largest customers for gray and ductile iron foundries. When demand was at its highest, each of the Big Three automakers owned several foundries. In mid-1980s, the poor financial performance of both the domestic automotive and aerospace industries forced closings of many self-contained foundries. Companies in these industries found that outsourcing the casting business was a cheaper alternative than under-utilizing plant and labor capacities.

In the 1980s and 1990s, the corporate average fuel economy (CAFE) standards mandated that automobile manufacturers produce lighter, more fuel efficient cars. As a result, the 650 pounds of iron casting found in a 1981 automobile was reduced to 350 pounds of gray iron per vehicle by 1995 and is expected to fall another 40 percent by 2005. Ductile iron, on the other hand, has experienced some growth in the automotive industry as

the mechanical properties of the metal make it an attractive alternative to heavier cast components.

BACKGROUND AND DEVELOPMENT

Humans have been casting metals for at least 5,000 years. This is evidenced by the progression of early societies from the Stone Age to the Bronze Age, when people started extracting ores and shaping them by melting or hammering methods. The Iron Age began in Europe circa 1100 B.C. Cast iron came into commercial use in the early 1700s when a mechanic named Abraham Darby and some Dutch workmen established a brass foundry in Bristol, England. It was there that Darby and his men started experimenting with iron as a replacement for brass. Because brass and iron are completely different pouring mediums in terms of their reaction with sand and solidification patterns, Darby faced many technical difficulties in his early experiments. With the help of John Thomas, a boy working in his shop, Darby succeeded in casting a complete iron pot. For proprietary reasons, Darby and Thomas entered into an agreement in which the boy was to remain his servant to keep the secret.

Ductile iron was not discovered until after World War II. Laboratory metallurgists at International Nickel Company noticed that the addition of a higher content of magnesium than is normally required for gray iron produced a structurally different material. When observing the material at a microscopic level, researchers noticed that the graphite particles had taken on a spheroidal shape, thus coining the name ''nodular iron'' in the United States and ''spheroidal graphite cast iron'' in Great Britain. The recognition of nodular iron's mechanical strength—and its ability to provide more ductility than other metals in its class—provided it with its more commonly accepted name, ductile iron. Since its release to the marketplace in 1949, ductile iron has gained acceptance as an important engineering material and has replaced many of the previous applications formerly reserved for steels and other irons. The discovery of ductile iron was one of the greatest achievements in the engineering materials community in the twentieth century.

The metal casting industry was wounded severely in the 1980s. During the 1970s, the industry was filled with back orders that exceeded annual capacity, providing a seller's market. The pricing strategies reflected this, as did profit margins. However, shipment volume—not quality—was the key issue during the 1970s. During the 1980s, foreign competitors who offered timely delivery of better quality castings at lower prices emerged. During the recession of the late 1980s and early 1990s, consumers turned to overseas suppliers, leaving the domestic producers behind. Consequently, U.S. foundries were operating at no more than 50 percent capacity by the mid-1980s.

By 1995, the foundry industry had been cut in half from 1955 levels, when the number of establishments involved in ferrous and nonferrous casting across the country was 6,000. Only 3,100 establishments remained in 1995, with approximately 700 engaged in casting gray and ductile iron. However, due to technological advancements and capacity gains through consolidations, output per remaining producer rose.

Gray and ductile iron foundries rely on the health of the U.S. economy to spur growth within their industries. With the increase in new housing during the late 1990s, there will also be a corresponding increase in the demand for gray iron needed for boiler and radiator castings, valves and fittings, and pumps and compressors. This industry is also being aided by an increased volume in exports of heavy equipment, such as diesel engines and farm and construction equipment. At the same time, plastics are replacing gray iron; this substitution is also being seen in the refrigerant and air conditioning markets.

The automobile market is expected to sustain ductile iron growth into the twenty-first century as the preferred replacement for forged gears and shafts in power transmissions. Specialty industrial machinery—such as those used for paper, printing, and plastic manufacturing and for farm and construction equipment—will maintain the demand for ductile iron. The recent development of austempered ductile iron (ADI) allowed this metal to challenge forgings and cast steels in operations requiring strength and durability.

The foundry industry has also increased its worldwide marketability by certification through the International Organization for Standardization. This series of certifications, referred to as ISO 9000, offered distinct competitive advantages for those who qualified and passed the certification audit. Although the audit was intensive, the result was the receipt of an internationally recognized benchmark standard, which signified the recipient was paying attention to details and distinguishing itself as a manufacturer of quality castings, engineered with integrity.

In 1995, total industry shipments were at only 33 percent of the tonnage shipped in 1978. Gray iron suffered a huge decline between 1978 and 1982, dropping from approximately 18.5 million tons to 9.5 million tons. Throughout the remainder of the 1980's, gray iron shipments continued to decrease. In the mid-1990s, they finally leveled off at approximately 6 million tons per year. Ductile iron, however, has shown growth in shipments since 1982, continuing a trend that started in 1966. In 1994, shipments of ductile iron surpassed 4 million tons for the first time since the metal was invented; ductile tonnage is expected to surpass gray metal by the turn of the century. The growth of ductile iron was largely due to its increasing recognition as being more economical and

structurally sound than gray and malleable irons; in some cases, it can replace steel forgings and weldments.

CURRENT CONDITIONS

In 1997, the industry consisted of 668 gray iron foundries, which shipped $11.9 billion dollars worth of goods. The industry also saw total capital expenditures exceed $4.5 billion.

For all its rhetoric of improving industry standards, in practice the industry shrugged off the ISO 9000 accreditation initiative as unnecessary unless customers required it—which they didn't, making the issue moot. Only 13 percent of companies in the gray iron industry and 33 percent in the ductile iron industry bothered to get ISO 9000 accreditation by October 1998. Only 20 percent of gray iron producers anticipated seeking accreditation in 1999, while half of the ductile iron industry felt compelled to seek certification.

INDUSTRY LEADERS

Industry leader AMSTED Industries Inc., which acquired Varlen Corp. for $790 million in a late-1999 merger, generated $1.4 billion in 1999 sales. Memphis-based Mueller Industries Inc., which owned its own railroad in the west and its own gold mine in Alaska, garnered $1.2 billion in 1999 sales. Birmingham, Alabama-based Citation Corp. posted $724 million in fiscal 1998 sales. Additionally, revenues increased 8.6 percent in the first quarter of fiscal 1999 to $184.9 million, as compared to $170.2 million for the first quarter of 1998. Grede Foundries Inc. generated $633 million in 1998 sales.

WORKFORCE

In general, most labor-intensive occupations in the gray and ductile iron foundries experienced continued work force reductions through the 1990s. The occupations facing the most substantial reductions—30 percent and more—included worker supervisors, plastic and metal machine workers, plastic and metal grinding machine operators, maintenance, electricians, and machine tool cutting operators. Other occupations facing reductions—20 to 30 percent—included fabricators, assemblers, hand workers, general laborers, precision workers, molding machine operators, inspectors, welders, truck and tractor operators, and mechanists. The only occupations expecting to gain employment levels were hand grinders and polishers.

Hourly compensation in this industry was, on the average, substantially higher in comparison to other forms of manufacturing. In 1994, the industry's average hourly wage was $15.22, while the average hourly wage of all other manufacturing concerns was $12.09. In 1994 Ohio and Illinois offered the highest hourly compensation in the industry, paying hourly wages of $19.19 and

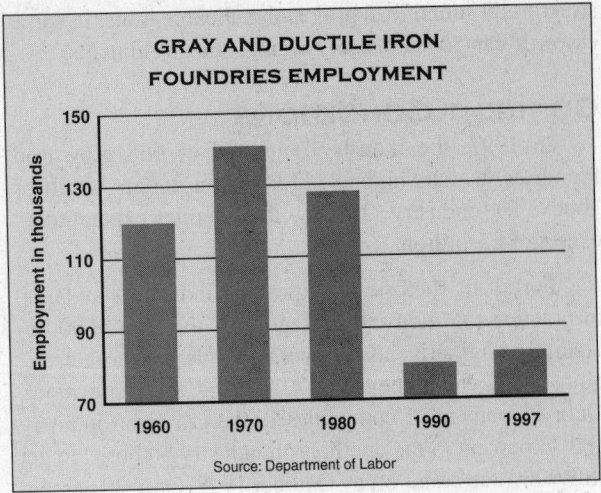

GRAY AND DUCTILE IRON FOUNDRIES EMPLOYMENT

Employment in thousands

Source: Department of Labor

$18.20, respectively. Ohio and Pennsylvania have the highest concentration of gray and ductile iron foundries. In 1997, more than 30 percent of the entire shipment activity in the United States was due to the combined efforts of the states of Ohio and Wisconsin. In 1997, the industry employed 83,678 people, over 80 percent of which were production workers. The average hourly wage for production workers was $16.00.

AMERICA AND THE WORLD

The foundry industry faced tremendous challenges in the global marketplace in the 1990s. During the five-year period from 1991 to 1995, there was a shift in metal cast production from the Pacific Rim to North America. The United States and Canada increased 63 and 56 percent respectively, while Japan dropped 12 percent. The five largest gray and ductile iron producers in 1995 were: the United States, 20 percent; China, 16 percent; the Commonwealth of Independent States (CIS), 15 percent; Japan, 10 percent; and Germany, 6 percent. With the demise of communism in the former Soviet Union, much of that region's production capacity remained underutilized. For example, Ukraine produced 6 million tons of casting in 1985 and reported a little less than 1 million tons in 1995.

The financial impact of environmental and safety regulations continued to beleaguer foundries throughout the 1990s. For example, Mexico was being pressured by the United States to install air pollution control devices in the early 1990s. However, Mexican laws included a loophole that did not require the devices for companies to operate. In Korea, foundry workers were not provided with safety equipment, such as eye protection, hard hats, respiratory devices, or earplugs. Additionally, workman's compensation and minimum wage levels were much higher in the United States. The benefits enjoyed by American workers added significantly to U.S. companies' costs. In financial terms, foreign competitors legally had an edge when it came to earning profits during the 1990s.

RESEARCH AND TECHNOLOGY

Conditions in the iron foundry industry—in particular ductile iron operations—have improved during the 1990s. The U.S. government was interested in replacing many forged steel components with cast ductile iron. Specifically, the U.S. Navy was researching the increased lethality of ductile iron projectiles over those made from steel. Other contractors were looking for less expensive alternatives to forged steel components—in lower stress applications, the mechanical properties of ductile iron suffice. However, more research and development was needed for this material because other, lighter weight materials were replacing ductile iron in lower stress applications. Ductile iron's low production price tag was enticing to both manufacturers and consumers and served as one of the primary incentives for its use.

Cast thermal analysis—also called numerical modeling/simulation—was used to improve quality and productivity in the foundry through pattern design optimization. The benefits of using numerical modeling were substantial, especially in relation to cost savings associated with time and material waste. Computer technology displaced the standard "pour and pray" method of metal casting and helped engineers optimize casting designs.

For the foundry industry as a whole, the advent of rapid prototyping technology was perhaps one of the most exciting advancements of the 1990s. Rapid prototyping is a computer-integrated method of accelerating the step between design and manufacture of the part. Under normal circumstances, a foundry would take weeks to construct a pattern (and core boxes if necessary) from an original design. With rapid prototyping, this process took only days, in some cases only hours, to create a limited production pattern. The competitive edge this technology offered was substantial, especially considering the accuracy it lent to the price quoting process.

FURTHER READING

Cahill, Virginia D. "Outlook '99: Holding Steady." *Foundry Management & Technology,* December 1998.

"Citation's First Quarter Fiscal 1999 Exceeds Estimates." *Foundry Management & Technology,* February 1999.

Darnay, Arsen J., ed. *Manufacturing USA.* 5th ed. Detroit: Gale Research, 1996.

"Dividends and Earnings." *Crain's Detroit Business,* 19 July 1999.

Hoovers Company Capsules, 20 March 2000. Available from http://www.hoovers.com.

Infotrac Company Profiles, 7 January 2000. Available from http://web6.infotrac.galegroup.com.

U.S. Census Bureau. "Iron Foundries," 11 February 2000. Available from http://www.census.gov/prod/www/abs/97ecmani.html.

MALLEABLE IRON FOUNDRIES

This industry is made up of establishments primarily engaged in the manufacturing of malleable iron castings.

NAICS CODE(S)

331511 (Iron Foundries)

INDUSTRY SNAPSHOT

Casting molten metal is one of the most efficient and economical ways of shaping metal products. Malleable iron foundries are typically large plants in which workers make metal products called castings by pouring molten metal into molds that then are left to harden. Malleable iron is made from white cast iron by annealing it at temperatures from 1500 to 1850 degrees Fahrenheit over several days. When annealed, the iron carbide breaks up, producing rosettes of graphite. The iron is known for its shock resistance, strength, machinability, and ductility. Products such as engine blocks, iron ornaments, and valves can be made from malleable iron castings. The automotive, railroad, construction, agricultural implement, and hardware industries have wide uses for malleable iron castings.

According to the U.S. Census Bureau's *1997 Economic Census—Manufacturing,* 26 establishments operated in this category for some or all of 1997. Industry-wide employment totaled 2,628 workers receiving a payroll of almost $114 million. Within this workforce, 2,227 of these employees worked in production, putting in almost 5 million hours to earn wages of almost $94 million. Overall shipments for the industry were valued at almost $353 million.

ORGANIZATION AND STRUCTURE

Castings are used in 90 percent of all durable goods. In 1999, there were 2,950 metal foundries in the United States with a capacity to ship 17.7 million tons of castings annually. Actual shipments amounted to an estimated 14.7 million tons in 1998, up from 1997 shipments of 14.2 million tons valued at $25.7 billion. Iron castings (including gray iron, ductile iron, and compacted iron graphite, in addition to malleable iron) accounted for 73 percent of the overall metal tonnage shipped and sold, but only 35 percent of the overall value.

In 1995, there were more than 3,100 U.S. metal foundries making over 100,000 distinct products. Malleable iron casting production represented approximately 1.7 percent of the total U.S. casting output. Capacity utilization in 1990 for malleable iron foundries was 78 percent, just slightly better than the 75 percent average for the entire foundry industry. This reflected the high rate of disinvestment in plants and equipment that occurred during the 1980s.

As an indication of the decline of this industry, government statisticians classify malleable iron foundries as job shops. These foundries generally operate on a job or order basis by manufacturing castings for sale to others, or for interplant transfer. In the 1970s, half of all malleable iron foundry castings came from in-house or captive plants. But in the 1980s, a major shift occurred when large independent manufacturers of railroad cars, oil-drilling equipment, heavy machinery, automobile, trucks, and major appliances sold off, shut down, or consolidated their captive operations. Near the end of the century, upwards of 75 percent of all malleable iron castings came from independent or custom casters.

These foundries produce two types of malleable iron: standard malleable iron and pearlitic malleable iron. In the early 1990s, the value of shipments for each of these two product classes of malleable iron castings were 145,800 metric tons (mt) for standard malleable iron (62.1 percent of total) and 89,100 mt for pearlitic malleable iron (37.9 percent of total).

Most of the malleable iron foundries are found in the nation's midwestern and northeastern states. The largest malleable iron-producing states, in descending order of shipments, are Wisconsin, Pennsylvania, Michigan, Connecticut, New York, Ohio, and Illinois.

BACKGROUND AND DEVELOPMENT

Cast iron was first made by the Chinese around the eighth century B.C. It was not until the invention of the blast furnace by the Europeans in the fourteenth century, however, that large quantities of cast iron were produced. North America's first operational foundry was built in 1642 along the Saugus River, near Boston. About eight tons per week of gray iron castings were produced at the site.

Malleable iron, also called American blackheart iron, replaced grey iron as the standard cast-metal around 1820, when the commercialization of secondary heat treating of the metal was first used. In 1966 malleable iron castings production in the United States accounted for 50 percent of the total malleable iron cast in the world. The year 1967, however, saw ductile iron castings production surpass malleable iron castings production in the United States. U.S. malleable iron castings production accounted for roughly 12 percent of the world's total production in 1995.

During the 1960s, average yearly production of malleable iron castings reached its peak at around 983,300 mt. Production during the decade of the 1970s remained at respectable average yearly production levels of 854,900 mt. The 1980s, however, reflected the difficult

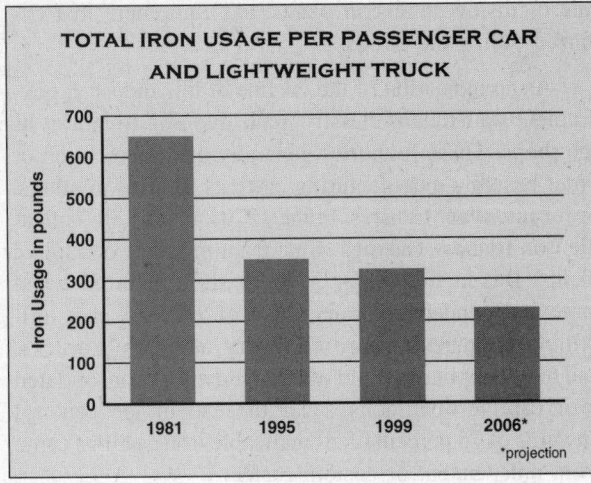

TOTAL IRON USAGE PER PASSENGER CAR AND LIGHTWEIGHT TRUCK

economic times for the industry, with average yearly production levels shrinking to 346,100 mt.

The foundry industry still ranks within the top ten manufacturing segments in the United States. Still, it has been battered by technological and competitive forces throughout the last two decades. The high inflation rates, high interest rates, high value of the dollar, and deep recession during the early 1980s hurt this industry tremendously. The largest customers of malleable iron castings, the domestic heavy equipment manufacturers, realized that these economic conditions favored offshore sources of malleable iron castings. Foreign competitors not only had lower prices when compared to American malleable iron sources, but they also had high quality manufacturing capabilities. Consequently, the value of castings shipments in the United States dropped 55 percent from the 1977 level of $721.9 million to $323.2 million in 1982.

The high interest rates also raised the industry's cost of capital, which is the price to finance and replace existing operations. This in effect halted any new capital expenditures on plant and equipment in the United States. Capital reinvestment dropped 85 percent between the years 1978 and 1983. Again, the high dollar, high interest rates, and high cost of capital made it very expensive to reinvest in the business of producing malleable iron castings. The lower rates of reinvestment by American malleable iron casters at a time when foreign competitors were raising their levels of casting quality put U.S. foundries at a technological disadvantage. In 1986, the Reagan Administration's decision to not sanction import restrictions further hurt the industry.

To illustrate the damaging effects of adverse economic conditions and increased foreign competition, total shipments of 1.17 million mt of malleable iron castings in 1969 fell to production levels of 284,000 mt in 1982. A small recovery in the industry occurred in 1984 when production increased to 380,000 mt., but production soon

slid back to 299,000 mt in 1989 and hit the all-time low of 207,000 mt in 1991. Production then increased to 260,000 mt in 1994 before slipping yet again to 249,000 mt in 1995 and even further down to an estimated 226,000 mt in 1996. The number of establishments producing malleable iron castings also decreased during this period, from 73 in 1972 to 26 in the late 1990s.

The industry was in severe decline, with no expectations of returning to its glory days of the 1960s. More than a third of the malleable foundries in the United States have been closed since the early 1980s, with further consolidation likely to continue. The factors that have contributed to this decline are strong foreign competition, the substitution of other metals and materials for malleable iron, rapid changes in technology, and unfavorable domestic economic conditions.

CURRENT CONDITIONS

Malleable iron foundries faced an ironic dilemma in late 1999, as demand from the booming auto industry surpassed expectations, pushing foundry capacity to the limit. Auto sales of 17 million units far exceeded predictions of 15 million, leaving foundries flat-footed in the race to keep up with auto-part needs. A production line operation running 24 hours a day took its toll: machinery had no down-time for maintenance; workers burnt out on overtime; and companies had to payroll this overtime, as well as paying premium rates for just-in-time shipments. Instead of profiting from this increased demand, foundries lost money.

Other current challenges facing the malleable iron foundry industry include:

Demand for Cheaper, Lighter, and Stronger Components. Many U.S. end use manufacturers are substituting plastics, ceramics, composites, lighter alloys, and nonferrous castings for malleable iron in appliances, aerospace equipment, builder's hardware, and automotive components to help them compete in a global economy and to meet government regulations. Cast iron usage per passenger car and lightweight truck was approximately 600 pounds in 1980. By 1999, the usage had dropped to 325 pounds and industrial analysts estimated that usage could drop to 230 pounds per vehicle by the year 2006. Similarly, only 25 percent of the intake manifolds produced for domestic vehicles in 1995 were made of iron. Many components that were once castings may now be weldments, forgings, or mechanical assemblies.

Changing Markets. The forecast for a continued expansion of the economy to the end of the century leads to an optimistic outlook for the casting industry. Steady demand for American-made cars, trucks, farm equipment, machine tools, freight cars, and oil field machinery should maintain the need for malleable iron castings. On the down side, however, proposed changes in plumbing fittings and electrical standards could further erode an already dwindling demand.

Replacement by Ductile Iron Castings. Related to the need for lightweight and high-strength components and parts is the growth in the replacement rate of ductile iron castings for malleable iron castings. Malleable iron competes with ductile and grey iron in the traditional light and heavy industrial manufacturing markets, but ductile iron is lighter than malleable iron. Ductile iron actually doubled its share of the market in the last decade because of its unique compatibility with new casting techniques called "near-net-shapes." This new method of casting allows for thinner-walled castings with intricate and complex shapes and sizes. Secondary finishing like blasting and sanding are virtually eliminated through the use of this process. In the automotive industry, ductile iron engine blocks are increasingly replacing malleable iron engine blocks. In the housing industry, ductile iron valve castings are expected to continue to replace malleable iron valve castings because of their superior resistance to shock and impact. Ductile castings are also replacing malleable castings in the farm equipment, electrical fittings, and plumbing fittings markets.

Foreign Competition. In the 1980s, overseas competitors adapted more quickly to changes in the industry than did domestic producers. They also used the strong dollar of the early 1980s to gain a foothold in the U.S. market that they have yet to relinquish. Approximately 28 percent of all malleable plumbing fittings used in the United States in 1995 were imported. Thailand has been particularly responsible for the decline in American foundry's market shares in plumbing and electrical fitting castings. In an effort to increase their sales price in the United States, tariffs have been levied on these imported products.

INDUSTRY LEADERS

Industry leader Intermet Corp. of Troy, Michigan, with $841 million in 1998 sales, was hard-hit by increased demands from the car industry in late 1999, when third-quarter profits fell 20 percent to $7.4 million in spite of revenues rising by 16 percent to $225 million. Milwaukee-based Grede Foundries Inc. generated 1998 sales of $633 million. McWane Corp. of Birmingham, Alabama garnered 1998 sales of $587 million. CMI International Inc. of Southfield, Michigan followed with almost $574 million in sales for its fiscal year ended June 30, 1998. Rounding out the top five were American Cast Iron Pipe Co. of Birmingham, Alabama, with $500 million in 1998 sales. Other industry leaders included Lufkin Industries Inc. of Lufkin, Texas; Waupaca Foundry Inc. of Waupaca, Wisconsin; and Burnham Corp. of Lancaster, Pennsylvania.

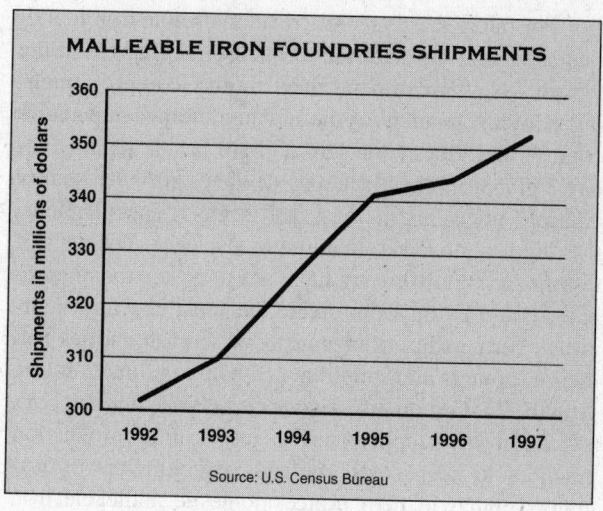

MALLEABLE IRON FOUNDRIES SHIPMENTS

Source: U.S. Census Bureau

WORKFORCE

Total employment in malleable iron foundries in the mid-1990s had fallen to 2,800, as compared with the 16,000 employed workers in 1980. Production workers numbered 2,400, accumulating 5 million production hours. Employment in the malleable foundry industry reached its peak in 1951 at 32,289, of which 28,388 workers were in production. Total payroll compensation in the mid-1990s was $112.3 million, with hourly wages at $18.90 as compared to $11.27 a decade earlier.

AMERICA AND THE WORLD

According to *Modern Castings'* "30th Census of World Casting Production," the world's production of malleable iron castings was approximately 2.1 million mt in 1995. This was roughly a drop of 38 percent from the record production levels of 3.4 million mt reached in 1973.

In 1995, the United States' share of total world production was roughly 12 percent (down from 50 percent in 1966). The largest producer of malleable iron castings was the Commonwealth of Independent States (CIS) with 40 percent of total world production. China's share of world production totaled 20 percent, Japan tallied 7 percent, and India and Germany contributed 4 percent each to global production of malleable iron castings.

RESEARCH AND TECHNOLOGY

Many industry observers regard exotic materials and thin-walled castings as the wave of the future. Some of the rapid technological changes occurring around malleable iron casters are new mold designs; new metal casting techniques; new computerized casting, finishing, and monitoring; and new purchasing procedures by domestic consumer and industrial product manufacturers. The industry is under attack by new technology parts-making processes, and it has been slow to change to compete with these more efficient casting processes.

For future survival, American malleable iron foundries must keep up with the technological changes in the industry. New investments in operations to improve melting, alloying, metal flow, die and mold filling temperature control, and lubrication will all help in this regard. Today's global marketplace also demands stronger quality control, price restrictions, and tighter specifications. Casting has moved from an art to a science. The days of testing sand moisture by hand are over, for today computer controls are what create the most exacting tolerances. Partnership arrangements between foundries and their customers and suppliers will help to promote future growth. Pricing, quality assurance, service, and the consolidation of suppliers using just-in-time production practices to keep costs low and response time to customers high will help protect domestic malleable iron casting operations from further market declines.

FURTHER READING

American Foundrymen's Society. ''Facts and Figures about the U.S Foundry Industry.'' Available at http://www.afsinc.org/Trends/FactsandFigures.htm.

Infotrac Company Profiles. Available at http://web6.infotrac.galegroup.com (1/25/00).

Malleable Iron Castings. Ann Arbor, MI: Ann Arbor Press, Inc., Malleable Founders Society, 1960.

''Modern Casting Census of World Casting Production.'' *Modern Casting,* December 1992.

Sanders, Clyde A. *History Cast in Metal.* Cast Metals Institute, American Foundrymen's Society, 1960.

U.S. Census Bureau. *1995 Annual Survey of Manufactures.* Washington, D.C.: U.S. Government Printing Office, 1997.

———. *1997 Economic Census-Manufacturing.* Available at http://www.census.gov/prod/ec97/97m3315a.pdf.

SIC 3324

STEEL INVESTMENT FOUNDRIES

This classification covers establishments primarily engaged in manufacturing steel investment foundries.

NAICS CODE(S)

331512 (Steel Investment Foundries)

INDUSTRY SNAPSHOT

Shipments from steel investment foundries were valued at $2.34 billion in 1997, a decrease of 66 percent from the previous year, when shipments reached $3.5 billion.

The industry is subdivided into four product classes. In 1997, the largest of these sectors—high temperature metal investment castings—accounted for 42 percent of total industry shipments, with over $987 million in shipments. Carbon and alloy steel investment castings were the second-largest category in 1997, with shipments valued at over $801 million, or 34 percent of total shipments. Stainless steel investment castings claimed 18 percent of total shipments in 1997, garnering $423 million. Nonspecific steel investment foundries represented the remaining 6 percent of total industry shipments.

The materials consumed by this industry were primarily those used to make steel. The delivered cost of pig iron was $1.2 million in 1997, while the delivered cost of iron and purchased steel scrap accounted for a collective delivered cost of $49.0 million. Other metals included: cobalt-based alloys ($36.8 million); nickel-based alloys ($100.1 million); and all other ferrous shapes and forms ($29.4 million). Sand had a delivered cost of $12.3 million, and clay refractories had delivered costs of $3.2 million. Industrial dies, molds, jigs, and fixtures that were used to produce the wax patterns reported delivered costs of $18.0 million. Grinding wheels and other abrasives had delivered costs of $19.7 million. Industrial patterns carried a cost of $3.45 million and all other materials, components, parts, containers, and supplies reported delivered costs of $175.2 million.

ORGANIZATION AND STRUCTURE

In 1997, 159 establishments were involved in this industry. Of this total, 116 companies, or about 72 percent, were larger companies with more than 20 employees. California, with 19, was home to the greatest number of steel investment foundries, followed by Michigan with 18 and Ohio with 16. California also led the nation in shipments of steel investment castings in 1997, with shipments valued at over $260 million, or about 11.0 percent of the U.S. total. Ohio's shipments accounted for 10.1 percent of the total, while Michigan produced steel investment castings worth over $224 million, which represented 9.6 percent of the nation's total.

Steel investment foundries are not necessarily in a class of their own. Many foundries practice investment casting regardless of the metal type, and many steel foundries may practice several casting processes beside investment. For example, the art industry used investment casting to create bronze sculptures, while the jewelry industry used investment casting to produce intricate designs. Relatively few steel foundries, with respect to the entire steel foundry industry, used the investment casting process exclusively.

The Environmental Protection Agency and the Occupational Safety and Health Administration keep watchful eyes on the industry and continually impose regulations. One particular advantage of the investment casting process is that, compared to other casting processes, it is not harmful to the environment. The sand used can be further recycled; and, since the process involves no chemical binders, there is no danger of producing hazardous fumes. With less waste and fewer pollutants produced, this process was not severely affected by increasing environmental legislation.

BACKGROUND AND DEVELOPMENT

According to Paul DeGarmo in *Materials and Processes in Manufacturing*, "investment casting actually is a very old process. It existed in China for centuries, and Cellini employed a form of it in Italy in the sixteenth century. Dentists have utilized the process since 1897, but it was not until World War II that it attained industrial importance for making jet turbine blades from metals that were not readily machinable. Millions of castings are produced by the process each year, its unique characteristics permitting the designer almost unlimited freedom in the complexity and close tolerances he can utilize."

Investment casting is also known as precision casting or the lost wax process. A pattern of wax or other expendable material is created and is attached, sometimes in clusters, to expendable down sprues. This conglomeration is then invested, or surrounded, by a refractory slurry, which then dries and hardens at room temperature. The mold is then heated to melt or burn out the wax or other expendable material. In the hollow cavity, molten metal is cast. This casting process is particularly adapted to the production of small, intricate parts using metals of higher melting points than are feasible for use in die-casting. Steel is one of the primary metals used in the industry.

Investment casting is a high precision process and is therefore expensive. The process allows highly complex shapes to be produced while maintaining good dimensional accuracy and surface finishes. The ability to produce thin wall sections are another advantage of using the investment casting process. Sections as thin as 0.015 inches, for example, have been cast.

CURRENT CONDITIONS

Steel investment casting survived the recession of the early 1990s, which eroded the industry's key markets: the aerospace, automotive, and energy industries. The middle of the decade, however, brought another set of challenges. Foremost among these was the continuing decline of the aerospace industry. The end of the Cold War resulted in the Department of Defense slashing its arms expenditures, which fell from $81 billion in 1990 to $45 billion in 1998; in 1994 and 1995, the commercial sector of the aerospace industry dropped as well. Although commercial plane building has surged again in the late 1990s, investment casters are effected by the rampant consolidation that has swept through the industry. As

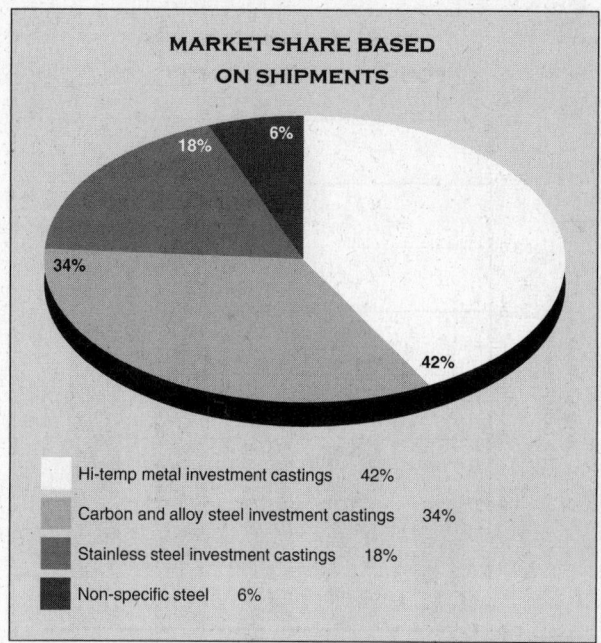

MARKET SHARE BASED ON SHIPMENTS

- Hi-temp metal investment castings — 42%
- Carbon and alloy steel investment castings — 34%
- Stainless steel investment castings — 18%
- Non-specific steel — 6%

aerospace companies merge, they turn to fewer and fewer suppliers for their precision cast parts. A similar consolidation has occurred in steel investment casting.

Steel investment foundries have also been impacted by the increasing use of aluminum cast parts in the automotive industry. According to Ducker Research Company, the average aluminum content per passenger vehicle has risen at annual rate of 4.3 percent since 1977, and overall aluminum content in automobiles doubled during the 1990s. Car manufacturers are turning to aluminum because it is easily recyclable, as well as being lighter than steel. With federal regulations mandating specific levels of fuel efficiency, automotive companies turn to aluminum cast parts rather than steel to reduce the weight of vehicles.

Another issue facing steel investment foundries concerns the quality of the steel required to cast intricate parts. Because extreme precision is needed to produce these castings, any inclusions in the metal will ruin a part. The primary quality issue facing the steel industry in the 1990s was the cleanliness of steel. Clean steel is essential to the industry because steel that is free of tramp elements, slag, and dross creates better quality parts. According to John Svoboda, "[i]n the early 1980s a high level management task force representing the steel industry identified oxide macroinclusions as the major factor responsible for the lack of acceptance of steel castings by the design engineering community. This study augmented the already well-known requirements for cast steel to be free from tramp elements, gases, and microinclusions. In short, the mandate for 'clean steel' has been issued." By the 1990s, significant progress had been made in clean steel production. Moreover, future

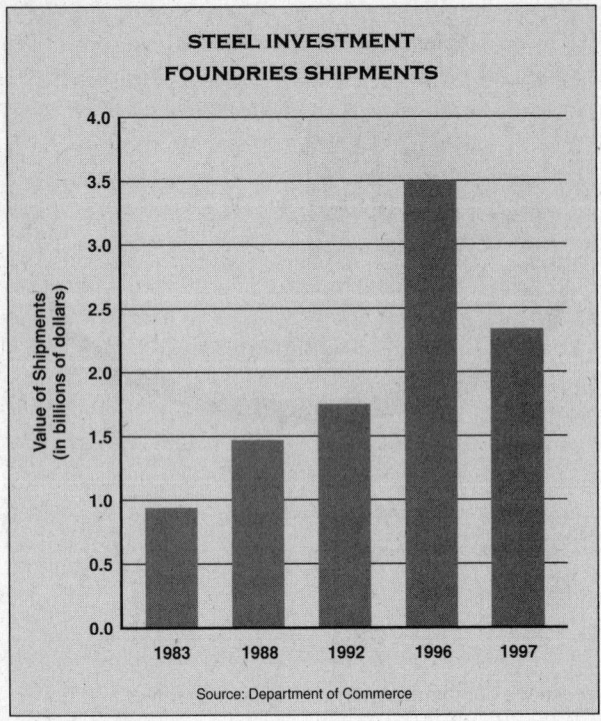

STEEL INVESTMENT
FOUNDRIES SHIPMENTS

Value of Shipments
(in billions of dollars)

Source: Department of Commerce

studies were expected to establish a method of quantifying the cleanliness of steel and find the relationship between cleanliness, mechanical properties, and design performance.

A major technological advancement in the foundry industry was developed in the early 1990s. This advancement was known as both Rapid Prototyping and Functional Prototyping. Rapid prototyping is a computerized system that uses stereolithography and selective laser sintering to create a three-dimensional shape that has been drawn on a computer aided drafting station. A computer takes the three-dimensional model and mathematically slices it into layers of specific thickness. Each layer is transmitted digitally from the design unit to the production unit where the material of choice is used to build the shape layer by layer. Using this new technology, a designer could take a customer's idea, design it, and in several hours or days, depending on the size of the part, have a prototype available for the customer to evaluate. The new technology dramatically reduced both the time and expense of producing intricate designs.

The largest producer of rapid prototyping equipment in 1996 was 3D Systems of Valencia, California. They sell a system that uses ultraviolet light driven by a CAD program to slice through a photopolymer pool. The company is developing a process called QuickCast to improve the accuracy of the stereolithographic models used to produce the patterns for investment casting. The CAD program divides a part to be cast into a core and cavity then generates a negative of the part. Next, the product is molded with QuickCast and built in steel to produce a

mold insert. In the December 1996 issue of *Modern Casting,* Matthew Duke of Precision Technology Inc. remarked that stereolithography allows a great reduction in lead time when used in the right applications, but for many parts the cost is still prohibitive.

INDUSTRY LEADERS

Pechiney Corp. was the leading steel investment foundry in 1998, reporting sales of $2.78 billion and 28,000 employees. The company was also involved in various forms of aluminum production. Portland, Oregon-based Precision Castparts Corp. was the industry's second-largest company in 1998. Precision produced investment castings that were used in the aerospace industry, as well as other industrial sectors. Although aerospace industry casting accounted for over half of Precision's 1998 sales, the company was striving to limit its dependence on that cyclical sector. Through a series of acquisitions in the late 1990s, Precision had entered into new markets, primarily fluid management technology. Between 1996 and 1999, the company had reduced the portion of its sales linked to aerospace 10 percent. Precision's most notable clients included General Electric, Pratt & Whitney, and Rolls Royce. Its 1999 sales were $1.47 billion, and the company employed 12,355 workers.

Atchison Casting Corporation of Birmingham, Alabama, was another key player in the industry. The company, which produced castings ranging in size from several ounces to over 200 tons, provided castings to the automotive, railroad, military, mining, and utility industries. Its significant customers included Caterpillar, General Electric, Deere & Co., and General Motors. The company's 1999 sales were $475 million. With 4,500 employees, Atchison had been one of the driving forces in the industry's consolidation during the 1990s. Additional industry leaders included the Whitehall Casting Division of the Howmet Corp. of Greenwich, Connecticut (1998 sales of $1.3 billion, 11,500 employees); Portland, Oregon-based PCC Structurals Inc. (1998 sales of $285 million, 2,600 employees); and Citation Corporation of Birmingham, Alabama. Citation, which reported 1998 sales of $724 million, operated 23 facilities in 10 states and employed over 6,330 workers. Citation derived the bulk of its sales from the automotive sector.

WORKFORCE

The iron and steel foundry industry faced substantial employment reductions during the mid- to late 1990s. The number of workers employed in steel investment foundries dropped from 37,100 in 1995 to 22,673 in 1997. Eighty-one percent of steel investment foundry employees were production workers. On average, these 18,418 employees earned $13.41 per hour and worked 38.5 hours each week. With 2,586 employees, Ohio contained the greatest number of steel investment casting workers, followed by California with 2,388 and Texas with 1,863.

FURTHER READING

Darnay, Arsen J., ed. *Manufacturing USA.* 5th ed. Detroit: Gale Research, 1996.

Delch, D. K. "Free Trade: Patient Needs Resuscitation." *American Metal Market,* 25 November 1996, 14.

Ducker Research Company. "Report on Aluminum Content in 1999: North American Passenger Cars and Light Trucks." Available from http://www.aec.org/ducker_report.htm. 1999.

Horton, Robert. "Risk Demand Fuels Investment Casting Technology Innovations." *Modern Casting,* December 1996, 45.

Schmitt, B. "Group Seeks Harmony in the Discord of Free Trade." *Am. Met. Mark,* 18 May 1995, 6A.

"30th Census of World Casting Production - 1995." *Modern Casting,* December 1996.

U.S. Census Bureau. "Steel Investment Foundries." Available from http://www.census.gov/prod/ec97/97m3314c.pdf. October 1999.

SIC 3325

STEEL FOUNDRIES, NOT ELSEWHERE CLASSIFIED

This classification covers establishments primarily engaged in manufacturing steel castings, not elsewhere classified.

NAICS CODE(S)

331513 (Steel Foundries (except Investment))

According to the U.S. Census Bureau's *1997 Economic Census—Manufacturing,* 288 establishments operated in this category for part or all of 1997. Industry-wide employment totaled 23,982 workers receiving a payroll of almost $762 million. Within this workforce, 19,789 of these employees worked in production, putting in almost 41 million hours to earn wages of more than $563 million. Overall shipments for the industry were valued at almost $3 billion.

The Great Lakes area has the heaviest concentration of steel foundries, and Ohio's 24 establishments ranked first in terms of shipments, which amounted to $285.1 million in the early 1990s. At the same time, Pennsylvania had more foundries than any other state; however, its 32 establishments were ranked third, with shipments of $190.8 million. Wisconsin ranked second with $233.4 million worth of shipments generated by 18 establishments. Hourly wages between these three states did not vary significantly during this period. Workers in Ohio

were paid the highest hourly wage, compared to Pennsylvania and Wisconsin, at $13.86. Wisconsin and Pennsylvania paid workers an average of $11.42 and $10.41 per hour, respectively.

The Bureau of Labor Statistics projected a bleak future for this industry's occupations. Except for industrial machinery mechanics, sales workers, millwrights, and industrial production managers, all other occupations are expected to face reductions in employment levels. The many steel foundry occupations expected to face over a 10 percent reduction going into the year 2000 include general laborers, grinders, precision workers, blue collar worker supervisors, mold assembly and shakeout operators, inspectors, metal pourers, truck operators, grinding machine operators, furnace machine operators, welders, assemblers, hand workers, electricians, material handlers, and janitors.

Leading the U.S. industry in overall sales was Dallas-based Commercial Metals Co., with 7,350 employees and sales of just under $2.4 billion for its fiscal year ended August 31, 1998. Worthington Industries Inc. of Columbus, Ohio, followed Commercial Metals, with 6,500 employees and just over $1.6 billion in sales for its fiscal year ended May 31, 1998. Rounding out the top three industry leaders was Pittsburgh-based Allegheny Ludlum Corp., with just under $1.5 billion in 1997 sales. Other industry leaders included Inco United States Inc. of Saddle Brook, New Jersey; New York City-based Renco Corp.; and Nucor-Yamato Steel Co. of Blytheville, Arkansas.

Allegheny, which employed 6,000 workers, sought to capture market share by setting up a production line at its Massillon, Ohio plant (acquired in 1998 from Bethlehem Steel Corp.) capable of producing 72-inch wide stainless steel coiled plate. Allegheny was the only producer of such a product at this width.

Carbon steel castings held 44 percent of the market share in 1987, while high alloy and other alloy steel castings each held just over 22 percent of the market. Approximately 11 percent of the market was non-specific in 1987. On the whole, this industry steadily downsized its employment levels between 1982 and 1986, with the highest level being 36,900 and the lowest level being 19,700. By the mid-1990s, however, the industry had begun a slow recovery. According to the *1995 Annual Survey of Manufactures,* employment levels in 1995 had risen to 25,700, an increase of 7.5 percent over 23,900 in 1994.

FURTHER READING
"Allegheny Ludlum Offers Wide Plate." *American Metal Market,* 29 November 1999.

Darnay, Arsen J., ed. *Manufacturing USA.* 5th ed. Detroit: Gale Research, 1996.

Infotrac Company Profiles. Available at http://web4.infotrac .galegroup.com (visited 1/28/00).

U.S. Census Bureau. *1995 Annual Survey of Manufactures.* Washington, D.C.: U.S. Government Printing Office, 1997.

U.S. Census Bureau. *1997 Economic Census—Manufacturing.* Available at http://www.census.gov/prod/ec97/97m3315c.pdf.

SIC 3331

PRIMARY SMELTING AND REFINING OF COPPER

This industry consists of companies that smelt copper from ore and refine copper by electrolytic or other processes. Those establishments engaged in rolling, drawing, or extruding copper are classified in **SIC 3351: Rolling, Drawing, and Extruding of Copper.**

NAICS Code(s)

331411 (Primary Smelting and Refining of Copper)

Industry Snapshot

Copper has excellent properties that make it useful to many industries. As a base metal, copper is used both alone and in alloyed combinations with other metals. The electrical, communications, and construction industries use copper in many of their products. Approximately 70 percent of U.S. copper consumption is for electrical and electronic uses, according to the U.S. Geological Survey. Copper faces increasing competition, however, from other materials such as plastics and other highly engineered materials in electronics and electrical applications.

Organization and Structure

Companies engaged in smelting and refining copper create products for a variety of national and international industries. End-use markets for copper and copper alloy can be categorized into five different functional uses. In 1994, 55 percent of copper products were used for electrical purposes and 25 percent of the products were used because they were corrosion resistant. Another 11 percent of copper products were used in heat transfer functions, while 8 percent went toward structural purposes. The final functional use is the aesthetic use of copper products, which accounted for only 2 percent of the total number.

The end-use markets for copper were primarily building related or industrial machinery and equipment related. For 1994, the 10 largest copper markets in the United States were: heating and plumbing, with 16 percent of the market share; building wire, 14 percent; commercial refrigeration and air conditioning and power utilities; each 8 percent; automotive electrical, telecom-munications, and in-plant equipment, each 7 percent; electronics, 5 percent; and industrial valves and fittings and automotive nonelectrical, each 4 percent. The remaining 21 percent of the United States copper market was unspecified.

Copper in the United States went from the mines to the smelters. In some cases, the same company owned both, and in some cases, the mining and smelting were performed at nearby facilities. The mining and smelting companies are the producers of copper materials, while the wire rod mills, brass mills, and foundries work with copper and prepare the metal for delivery to manufacturers in various industries.

Mining companies process copper ores, most of which are retrieved from open-pit mines. These ores are refined and sometimes alloyed with other elements, such as zinc or beryllium. A primary smelting reactor such as a reverberatory furnace produces copper sulfide from concentrated ore. Some reverberatory furnaces were replaced by oxygen/flash smelting, which created less air pollution. The final step in smelting and refining work involves an electrolytic or other refining process. The resulting copper is often close to 100 percent pure.

Background and Development

Copper mining had origins in the Middle East, but reached its zenith in America. In the mid-eighteenth century, miners in the colonies discovered copper ores in what is now the northeastern United States. They mined these ores, but English law prohibited the establishment of smelting works in the colonies, so the ore was sent to England for smelting and refining.

After the American Revolution, miners and smelters moved to the newly created United States and began working in American mines and refineries. Copper sheathing began to be used on wooden ships as early as the 1790s. The copper protected the ships from the pressure and corrosive effects of the ocean. Great demand from the shipping industry helped the budding copper industry, but the United States still depended on copper imports from England and South America. In 1806, U.S. importers of copper asked Congress to exempt copper from customs duty. The protests lodged by copper industry pioneers succeeded in lowering tariffs applied to copper imports.

In the early 1800s U.S. companies began to use blast furnaces for smelting and refining copper. Later, with the rise of American industry, growing copper works created stripping, boiler plates, rivets, and other copper-based items that were used in an increasingly diverse number of industries and products. Copper nails replaced cast iron nails in building, a windfall for the copper industry since towns and cities were being built as fast as possible all across the new nation.

The reserves of copper in the United States have not suffered appreciably during the twentieth century. Although copper has been in use for more than 10,000 years, about three-quarters of all copper consumed has been produced since World War II. In recent years, new deposits have been found and better mining and extracting methods developed by copper companies.

U.S. smelter production of copper reached its peak in the early 1970s at 1.8 million metric tons annually. At that time, the trend in the copper smelting industry was for oil companies to purchase smelters, refining companies, and mines. In the following decade, almost all of these oil companies sold off their copper companies, leaving them independent again, but this time with a renewed sense of the marketplace. Workers in some of these companies learned new technologies that enabled them to compete in the international copper arena. Instead of the pyrometallurgy of the reverberatory furnaces, many smelters introduced hydrometallurgical processing that produced copper whose purity and quality matched that of electrolytically refined copper.

The 1980s were not boom years for many players in the various copper-related industries. The three largest U.S. producers of copper—Asarco, Phelps Dodge Corporation, and AMAX, Inc.—lost almost $2.5 billion from 1982 through 1985. These companies, however, remained leaders in the field despite their difficulties. Many other companies in the copper industry went out of business, though. Those that remained made drastic changes to cut operating costs and improve efficiency. These cost-cutting measures at times exacerbated difficulties with labor.

The copper smelting business has been growing since the early 1980s. In 1987, shipments were valued at $2.55 billion and the size of the total work force was 3,300. Five years later, shipments had grown to $5.58 billion with total employment at 5,600. By 1994, shipments had grown to $6.18 billion and total employment was at 6,400. The average hourly wage in the industry had grown from $14.34 in 1984 to $18.14 in 1994. The number of establishments dedicated to copper smelting reached a low during the 1980s; approximately 12 establishments existed in 1986. By the mid-1990s, there were approximately 20 establishments.

In 1994, the largest share of the market was refined primary copper, representing 60.4 percent. Noncommercial grade copper smelter products, which are produced for further refining, comprised 39.5 percent of the market. Nonspecific primary copper products filled the remaining tenth of a percent of the industry. Nearing the end of the twentieth century, all of the players in the copper industry were involved in the recyclability of copper. Recycled copper is highly valued, as "high-grade" scrap often retains more than 90 percent of the value of newly mined copper.

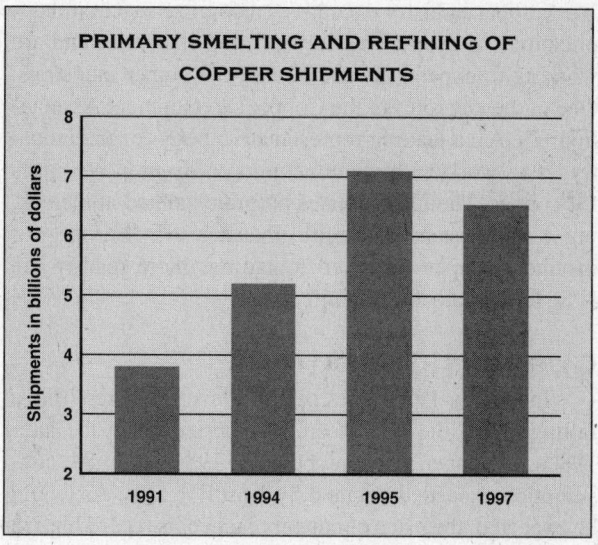

PRIMARY SMELTING AND REFINING OF COPPER SHIPMENTS

In dollars, copper consumption had fallen during the late-1980s and early-1990s. The compound growth rate for copper consumption from 1972 through 1991 was 1.3 percent. In 1991, the value of all shipments of primary copper hit a low of $3.8 billion.

After the declines of the early 1990s, the industry posted modest growth during the mid-1990s. Its 1994 shipments were valued at $5.2 billion; by 1995 shipments had climbed to $7.1 billion in current dollars, although production was actually lower than in 1994. Despite the growth of plastics as a substitute for copper pipe and fittings, industry analysts expect copper markets to grow at approximately 1 percent per year through the year 2000.

The United States maintained its world leadership in copper production during the 1990s. U.S. companies produced 1.8 million metric tons of copper ores and almost 2.7 million tons of refined copper products in 1995. Consumption of copper throughout the world was expected to increase into the twenty-first century. One important factor has been the stabilization of supply levels of copper from mines in Peru, which had begun to solidify by the late-1990s due to the combined efforts of the World Bank, the International Monetary Fund, and various financial organizations. Those groups took important measures to restructure debt in Peru thereby improving mining in that country and thus ensuring a smoother supply of copper to the world.

Total worldwide smelter production of copper in 1993 was 9.5 million short tons, a decrease from the high of 9.7 million in 1989, according to the U.S. Geological Survey. International competition was a factor in the 1990s, as was an increased environmental consciousness in the United States. One copper company declined to build a new smelting facility in Texas after environmental groups protested.

Copper industry executives recognize successful applications of copper in many existing industries and are working to expand the use of copper in other industries. One of the key roles of the Copper Development Association (CDA), a leading representative body for the industry, is to work with manufacturers to develop new uses for copper. The CDA creates programs aimed at increasing copper usage in specific industries. In Europe, for instance, copper was used four times more than in the U.S. for architectural applications.

CURRENT CONDITIONS

In the late-1990s, the copper industry suffered from a falling-off of the golden era it experienced in the late-1980s. In copper's heyday between 1986 and 1988, consumption exceeded demand by 1 million tons. As would be expected, the price of copper reached its record high in 1988, averaging $1.15 per pound and closing in December at $1.64. In contrast, the industry experienced a reversal of those boom times a decade later when production outstripped demand between 1996 and 1998. Copper supplies increased 9 percent in 1997, leading to an oversupply in 1998. Copper prices plummeted accordingly, closing in December 1998 at 66.8 cents per pound, a few cents shy of a full one-dollar drop in price compared to the closing price a decade earlier. Copper averaged 75 cents per pound in 1998, a 27 percent decrease from the 1997 average of $1.03. The industry's 16 establishments shipped $6.54 billion worth of goods in 1997.

INDUSTRY LEADERS

Phoenix, Arizona-based Phelps Dodge Corp. led the industry with $3.1 billion in 1999 sales, a 1.7 percent increase from the previous year. Lower copper prices contributed to the sluggish sales growth. New York City-based Arasco Inc. chalked up 1998 sales of $2.2 billion. New Orleans-based Freeport-McMoRan Copper and Gold Inc. generated 1999 sales of $1.9 billion. Southwire Co. of Carrolton, Georgia, garnered an estimated $1.4 billion in sales for 1998.

WORKFORCE

In 1997, the industry employed 7,360 people; 78 percent of them worked in production. The average hourly wage for production workers was $17.29, down from $18.14 in 1994.

AMERICA AND THE WORLD

According to *Standard and Poor's Industry Surveys,* the United States was the world leader in smelter production of copper entering the 1990s. In 1994, 1.7 million short tons of copper were smelted in the U.S. In comparison, 1.4 million short tons were smelted in Chile, which is the second-ranked country in copper smelter production. During that same year, 560,000 short tons were

smelted in Canada, 296,000 in Germany, 1.1 million in Japan, and 585,000 in African nations. The Commonwealth of Independent States (CIS) smelted 900,000 short tons of copper in 1993.

That same year, the United States ranked second in mine production of copper at 1.8 million metric tons. In comparison, top-ranked Chile mined 2.2 million metric tons.

The copper industry was becoming increasingly global in its outlook in the 1990s. Smelters and refiners of copper were looking toward developing countries as markets for copper-based products. Those countries that were improving their infrastructures with telecommunications cables, power cables, and other basic building tools needed more copper. The Asian markets of China, Taiwan, and South Korea were expected to provide large new markets.

In 1993, a politically charged topic in the industry was the General Agreement on Tariffs and Trade (GATT). Copper industry leaders met with U.S. trade officials to request a reduction of Japanese and European tariffs under GATT. Their aim was to eliminate global tariffs on copper to gain better access to foreign markets; they argued that the Japanese market was too heavily protected. The U.S. International Trade Commission (ITC) rejected high tariffs on imported metals.

The U.S. formed an International Copper Study Group in the 1990s in conjunction with 17 other countries involved in the copper industry. Their aim was to allow information exchanges between producing and consuming countries and to increase copper production and consumption. The members of the group included Germany, China, Chile, Peru, and France.

RESEARCH AND TECHNOLOGY

A low-cost method of production being used in the 1990s in U.S. copper companies was known as SX-EW, or solvent extraction-electrowinning. Solutions of sulfuric acid were applied to dumps of copper-bearing ores, then the dissolved copper was recovered by depositing copper onto electrically charged cathodes. This process was known as electrowinning. SX-EW had fewer steps and caused less pollution at a lower cost than earlier production methods. But only some of the world's ore could be processed by this method. Primary sulfide ore, which is located deeper in mines and is usually found combined with other elements, was not eligible for SX-EW. The process was effective for oxide ore and secondary sulfide ore, which are found closer to the mine's surface, where the ore has been oxidized. Unfortunately, the contents of U.S. mines often mainly contain primary sulfide ores rather than oxide ores or secondary sulfide ores. Another process for copper production is known as the Escondida ammonia leach process. This process employs air combined with a solution of ammonia-ammonium sulfate, which leaches cuprous salts from chalcocite solutions. Approximately half the copper is leached and the remainder can be recovered by a flotation recycle. This process was developed by and named for the Escondida mine in Chile and has been used successfully to produce cathode copper. An innovative leaching process, piloted at Chatwoods Australia, is known as the Intec process. This method of leaching has the added advantage that gold can be recovered on activated carbon at the same time that copper is being separated as its halogen complex. The metal from the Intec process is used for copper briquettes and wire or strips.

The technical research and market development area of the copper industry has promoted new technologies that use copper materials in a wide array of applications. These new applications include the use of copper radiators in the automobile industry. The copper industry emphasizes copper's positive features, such as its corrosion resistance and strength, and notes that the new radiators are also lighter and more durable than current copper radiators, which they would replace.

Other proposed uses of copper include solar energy systems, nuclear waste disposal canisters, and superconductivity applications. Industrial applications, such as valves, fittings, and power utilities, remain steady users of copper. Until 1982, another copper user was the U.S. mint, which coined pennies using a copper alloy. In 1982, the copper alloy was replaced by zinc. Another loss to the industry was the increasing use of fiber optics products, which began to replace some copper telecommunications equipment.

Recyclability became increasingly important as copper companies faced the next century. Because copper was more easily recycled than many other metals, more copper was recovered from recycled material than was obtained from newly mined ores. This combination of recycled copper materials and healthy U.S. deposits of copper made the country highly self-sufficient in copper. Aluminum, which competed with copper in many areas, was a more difficult metal for the United States to obtain.

FURTHER READING

"Excess Supply Tarnishes Copper Pricing." *Purchasing,* 1 September 1998.

Gross, John E. "Copper Market Adjusting to New World Order." *American Metal Market,* 18 February 1999.

Hoover's Company Profiles, 20 March 2000. Available from http://www.hoovers.com.

McNamara, Thomas. "Copper's Prognosis Expected to Remain Bleak." *American Metal Market,* 18 February 1999.

Silva, Enrique R. "Copper: Impact of Expectations and Speculative Factors." *Engineering & Mining Journal,* March 1999.

U.S. Census Bureau. *1997 Economic Census—Manufacturing.* Washington: GPO 1999.

Yafie, Roberta C. "PD Results Reflect Restructuring." *American Metal Market,* 14 July 1999.

SIC 3334

PRIMARY PRODUCTION OF ALUMINUM

This classification includes establishments primarily engaged in producing aluminum from alumina and in refining aluminum by any process. Excluded from this classification are establishments primarily engaged in rolling, drawing, or extruding aluminum, which are classified in the following product groups: **SIC 3351: Rolling, Drawing, and Extruding of Copper; SIC 3353: Aluminum Sheet, Plate, and Foil; SIC 3354: Aluminum Extruded Products; SIC 3355: Aluminum Rolling and Drawing, Not Elsewhere Classified;SIC 3356: Rolling, Drawing, and Extruding of Nonferrous Metals, Except Copper and Aluminum;** and **SIC 3357: Drawing and Insulating of Nonferrous Wire.**

NAICS CODE(S)
331312 (Primary Aluminum Production)

INDUSTRY SNAPSHOT
Divided into product groups, the aluminum industry comprises three distinct segments: primary aluminum manufacturers, semi-fabricated aluminum manufacturers, and secondary, or scrap aluminum manufacturers. Of these segments, the primary aluminum industry is the smallest, based on its number of manufacturers.

To produce aluminum, primary aluminum manufacturers first process bauxite (an ore that is the basic raw material of aluminum) to create alumina. A powerful electric current is then passed through a solution containing alumina to produce aluminum in its most basic form. This type of aluminum, shaped into either a mass of metal in a bar or a block shape (referred to as an ingot) or a smaller rectangular bar (referred to as a billet), serves as the raw material for manufacturers engaged in producing aluminum products. Primary aluminum manufacturers supply aluminum to semi-fabricated aluminum manufacturers and to a diverse array of manufacturers outside the aluminum industry who utilize aluminum to make their products.

Throughout much of its existence, the primary aluminum industry comprised fewer than 10 manufacturers, but as of 1998 approximately 21 manufacturers were involved in producing primary aluminum. In 1997 these companies generated $5.03 billion in sales, an aggregate value of shipments substantially derived from the production of aluminum ingot, which accounted for over 80 percent of the industry's total shipments. Billet primary aluminum, the only other type of aluminum produced by the industry that accounted for any appreciable revenue, represented 19.7 percent of the industry's shipments.

These shipments were purchased primarily by participants in a few discrete industries. In 1998 the bulk of the industry's aluminum was utilized by manufacturers involved in the building and construction, container and packaging, and transportation industries, which when combined accounted for 65.7 percent of the industry's total shipments. Exports accounted for approximately 12 percent of aluminum shipments in 1998.

Throughout the 1990s, the growth of aluminum was driven by the automotive industry. Car makers continue to produce lighter passenger vehicles and trucks in order to conform to the Corporate Average Fuel Economy (CAFE) regulations. By substituting one pound of aluminum for steel parts, the auto designers are able to remove 2.0 to 2.5 pounds of cast iron, making the use of aluminum very attractive. This growth trend is expected to continue into the twenty-first century.

ORGANIZATION AND STRUCTURE

Although the industry consists of relatively few manufacturers, the size of a primary aluminum manufacturing facility, when defined in terms of the number of people employed per establishment, was comparatively large when measured against other manufacturing industries. All of the 21 establishments involved in producing primary aluminum in 1997 employed 20 or more employees, and 19 of these establishments employed over 1,000 workers. Geographically, a majority of the establishments involved in the primary aluminum industry in 1998 were located in the Pacific Northwest. These firms accounted for 38.4 percent of total U.S. shipments. The Ohio Valley was the country's second most productive region, generating 31.9 percent of shipments.

Primary aluminum producers faced high overhead costs. In fact, the average cost per facility for the raw materials necessary to operate is higher in the primary aluminum production industry than in any other manufacturing industry. This disparity is mainly due to two key factors. First, aluminum production requires a tremendous amount of electrical energy, meaning that producers face staggering utility bills. Second, very little bauxite is found in this country, and, as a result, aluminum producers incur high costs for importing this essential ore. Consequently, running a primary aluminum manufacturing facility is very expensive: operating expenses are sometimes 14 times higher than an average manufacturing establishment. According to 1997 figures, the average cost for materials per establishment in the primary aluminum industry was $71

million. The average investment per establishment (that is, the average expense earmarked for purchasing and maintaining manufacturing facilities and machinery, as well as paying for production retooling) was also significantly higher in the primary aluminum industry. In 1997 primary aluminum manufacturers paid an average of $16.9 million for such expenditures.

BACKGROUND AND DEVELOPMENT

In 1886, the concurrent development in the United States and France of an economical electrolytic process for refining aluminum immediately spawned widespread optimism. Many manufacturers regarded the discovery as the new metal of the future. Aluminum would continue to be regarded as the metal of the future throughout its first century of existence, indeed well past the time its future should have arrived. All of this optimism led aluminum manufacturers and government officials to overestimate demand for the metal on occasion. But the creation of a process to economically produce aluminum did, however, warrant its fair share of hyperbole, even if the expectations associated with its production sometimes ran too high. The metal possessed desirable conductive and thermal properties, was lightweight, and could be used to form many hard, light, corrosion-resistant alloys. As American manufacturing industries slowly moved toward creating products that were lighter in weight, aluminum would prove to be an integral component in a wealth of manufacturing processes, eventually establishing a pervasive, global presence that would validate the hopeful projections held by aluminum's early proponents.

But in 1886, there was really no clear plan regarding how aluminum could become, in practical terms, the metal of the future. Discovery of the myriad applications for the new wonder metal fell entirely to the only aluminum manufacturing company of any consequence at the time, the Pittsburgh Reduction Company, later renamed the Aluminum Company of America, and more commonly known as Alcoa. Indeed, Alcoa would remain the only manufacturer of any consequence for the aluminum industry's first 60 years, establishing a monopoly over the U.S. aluminum market during the interim and, consequently, solely guiding the industry's direction for the first half of the twentieth century.

Under the partial stewardship of Charles Martin Hall, a young chemist who discovered the more economically feasible process of aluminum production while working in his woodshed, Alcoa faced the daunting chore of first creating both a need and a demand for aluminum. Initially, the company utilized aluminum to manufacture a line of cooking utensils, which later, in 1901, were successful enough to merit the organization of a cookware subsidiary named American Cooking Utensil. The biggest market for aluminum, however, proved to be the automobile industry, a market that would fuel the industry's growth for its first five decades of operation. By 1915, 65 percent of all primary aluminum was utilized in automotive parts.

At this time, Alcoa still stood alone in the U.S. aluminum market, with the only competition coming from foreign manufacturers, whose penetration of the U.S. market was limited by high tariffs and comparatively higher energy costs. America's entrance into World War I quelled the negligible affect foreign manufacturers had on Alcoa and provided the opportunity for America's uncontested primary aluminum giant to begin exporting aluminum to Great Britain, France, and Italy. On the home front, Alcoa enjoyed commensurate success, supplying the federal government with aluminum for military applications.

By the end of the war in 1918, Alcoa was producing 152 million pounds of aluminum annually and stood poised to further develop export markets it first explored during the war. The manufacturing of aluminum had become a lucrative business, due largely to escalating demand during the war and to the fervor with which the automobile industry embraced the still new metal. Alcoa, almost entirely responsible for creating this burgeoning demand, sought to capitalize on the boom wherever it could and, as such, spent the 1920s acquiring factories, bauxite mines, and power-generating facilities in Scandinavia, western Europe, and Canada. Toward the end of the decade, however, Alcoa's ubiquitous presence overseas made efficient management and production too difficult. In 1928, the company divested all of its foreign operations, excluding the bauxite mines it owned in Dutch Guiana, which were spun off as Aluminum Limited and later renamed Alcan Aluminum Limited.

Reorganized and focused on domestic production, Alcoa struggled through the Great Depression, during which the company's sales plummeted from $34.4 million to $11.1 million and half of its work force was laid off. Once demand for aluminum returned in 1936, Alcoa quickly recovered from the earlier losses, still maintaining an omnipotent grip on the U.S. aluminum market. This enviable position, however, would not be enjoyed by the company for long, as the end of the 1930s signaled the beginning of a new era of competition in the U.S. primary aluminum industry, although it would be over a decade before competition in the industry would begin in earnest.

Anti-trust suits had been filed against Alcoa by the U.S. Justice Department dating back to 1911 without much success, but in 1937 a suit filed by U.S. Attorney General Homer Cummings, charging Alcoa with monopolization and restraint of trade, initiated proceedings that finally wrested control of the U.S. aluminum market away from Alcoa. The trial lasted from 1938 to 1940 and several appeals were made. Although a district court ruled in Alcoa's favor in 1942, the final decision, in 1945, sustained the government's appeal.

While lawyers for both parties submitted a series of appeals that made the Alcoa anti-trust suit the largest proceeding in the history of U.S. law at that time, America entered another war, spurring demand for aluminum. The military applications for aluminum significantly increased during the 23-year span between World War I and World War II, creating a military appetite for aluminum that Alcoa, still the lone manufacturer in the United States of any consequence, found unable to satiate. Frustrated by Alcoa's inability to supply all the aluminum that was needed, the war department stepped in and financed new plants to provide additional production capacity.

These plants, built and operated by Alcoa, swelled the nation's output of aluminum and enabled the heightened demand to be met. As the war drew to a close and victory appeared assured, government officials were left with the responsibility of what to do with the additional capacity created during the war, which would be superfluous during peacetime. The answer to the problem was the solution of another exigency: namely, how to effectuate an equitable conclusion to the anti-trust suit levied against Alcoa? The decision was made to offer the government-financed aluminum production plants at reduced prices to two fledgling aluminum manufacturers, Reynolds Metals Company and Permanente Metals Corporation, both of which were owned by industrialist Henry Kaiser. In 1950, a district court decree parceled out the U.S. aluminum market among the three manufacturers, giving Alcoa 50.9 percent of the nation's production capacity, Reynolds Metals 30.9 percent, and Permanente Metals, by this time renamed Kaiser Aluminum & Chemical Corporation, 18.2 percent of production capacity.

Although the seven-year debate concerning the redistribution of the U.S. aluminum market did not necessarily spawn an industry comprised of numerous participants but instead left control of the market to a tightly knit cadre of manufacturers, competition was nevertheless quick in coming, particularly from Reynolds Metals. The company's aluminum production capacity doubled as a result of acquiring six of the government-financed plants, which enhanced its ability to capitalize further on the introduction of its aluminum foil products several years earlier in 1947. Although much smaller in terms of sales volume and production capacity than Alcoa, Reynolds Metals established itself as the more aggressive marketer, expanding overseas at a rapid rate, while still focusing on developing innovative applications for aluminum that would later help elevate the company's magnitude in relation to Alcoa's.

A postwar housing boom infused the industry with an increased demand for aluminum, but the problem of smelting over-capacity, unresolved by the government's actions following the war, remained as a potential impediment to the industry's continued success. Although the hazards posed by excess supply did not threaten primary aluminum manufacturers to any great extent during the 1950s, the danger still remained. To exacerbate matters, production capacity tripled during the decade, partly due to justifiable increases engendered by the rising demand for aluminum from the housing, construction, and transportation industries. But demand was also fueled by federal orders to augment aluminum production to meet the demand created by the nation's involvement in the Korean War. The industry was protected from the negative affects of oversupply during the early 1950s due to an agreement with the federal authorities that guaranteed the purchase of excess aluminum at market prices by the government, referred to as a "put." But federal intervention merely masked the problem of over capacity, a problem that would plague manufacturers in the years to come.

Despite their inherently precarious position, primary aluminum manufacturers entered the 1960s rightfully optimistic. The decade would bring with it the development of several new applications for aluminum that would enrich the industry considerably and fuel its growth for the next several decades. The utilization of aluminum to manufacture automobile engines, used in only one model in 1960, became more widespread during the early 1960s, and 1961 commenced with eight automobile models boasting aluminum engines. Further, aluminum bumpers and other new applications for automobiles were being developed, contributing to a rise in the amount of aluminum utilized per automobile to 62.1 pounds by 1961. A year earlier, Reynolds Metals introduced the first aluminum drill pipe, which was met with encouraging enthusiasm by other manufacturing industries. Reynolds Metals' greatest gift to the future success of the primary aluminum industry came in 1963, however, with its fabrication of an aluminum beverage can. The utilization of aluminum in beverage cans would increase dramatically for the next 30 years, supporting the industry's growth throughout the 1960s and 1970s, and become a linchpin to primary aluminum manufacturers' survival in the 1990s.

These developments, combined with a housing construction boom and the growing popularity of mobile homes, which contained a large amount of aluminum, drove demand from domestic customers upward, while the industry's export activity accelerated at a rapid rate. Foreign demand for U.S. aluminum tripled between 1959 and 1960, totaling over 500 million pounds in the first year of the decade, and enabling U.S. manufacturers to sidestep the pernicious affects of oversupply.

To foster the further development of overseas markets, U.S. manufacturers of primary aluminum also began striking affiliation agreements with foreign aluminum producers in the early 1960s. In addition to joint ventures already existing at that time in Guinea and elsewhere, primary production facilities were opened in Greece and Australia in 1960, concurrent with the development of a hydroelectric and aluminum project in Ghana.

By aggressively developing new markets for their product, instead of patiently waiting for demand to catch up to supply, which was the general practice in former years, primary aluminum manufacturers had ameliorated their position in the aluminum marketplace. As sales climbed for each manufacturer and production increased, however, industry participants found they were actually recording smaller profits, causing one manufacturer to describe the industry's performance as characterized by "profitless prosperity." Indeed, profitless prosperity was an apt description, and one that would be equally applicable in the ensuing years. The deterioration of aluminum prices, shrinking profit margins, and an excessive amount of unused production capacity saddled manufacturers with a growing percentage of operating costs that did not generate revenue. To exacerbate matters, the importation of primary aluminum into the U.S. market saturated a market already sufficiently supplied with aluminum. Consequently, U.S. producers of aluminum were shipping more aluminum but reaping reduced earnings. The three largest manufacturers watched with dismay as their combined net profit margins slipped from 10.7 percent in 1956, to 5.2 percent by 1960. Alcoa, for example, which produced 36 percent of all the aluminum manufactured in the United States at this time, posted a sales total within 1 percent of its record high in 1960, yet lost $40 million, the company's worst profit performance in a decade. Thus, the paradoxical nature of the primary aluminum industry became readily apparent in the early 1960s—innovative applications for primary aluminum promised increased demand and production levels grew, but manufacturers garnered comparatively prosaic earnings.

By the mid-1960s, the primary aluminum industry was comprised of seven companies operating 23 separate plants. Conditions had improved considerably in the five years since earnings slipped from more lucrative levels, as the industry recorded its fourth consecutive record year in shipments in 1965. Significant gains were realized in several markets that relied on primary aluminum for manufacturing purposes, most notably the burgeoning demand for aluminum to fabricate truck trailers, mobile homes, and related equipment. Aluminum usage in this segment of the transportation market jumped 32 percent in 1964, complementing an increase in the usage of aluminum per automobile to nearly 70 pounds. The electrical market also provided additional business for aluminum manufacturers, as aluminum usage for underground residential distribution cable, building wire for industrial, commercial, and residential uses, and extra high voltage transmission lines increased 19 percent.

These surges in demand experienced by the primary aluminum industry's key end-use markets were related to the concerted search by aluminum manufacturers for new ways in which aluminum could be used. This, however, was nothing new; manufacturers had been exploring aluminum's potential applications for years, beginning with Alcoa's initial research and development efforts back in the 1890s. What was new, and what sparked a resurgence in optimism regarding the primary aluminum industry's future by manufacturers and industry observers alike, was a stabilization of aluminum prices, which previously had fluctuated wildly, glutting production capacity and squeezing profit margins. Also, the affiliations with foreign aluminum manufacturers that were initiated earlier in the decade began to buoy the industry's performance, as manufacturers benefited from high-volume, global operations.

Providing further impetus to the industry's growth was a trend toward incorporating aluminum into many new large-scale construction projects during the mid-1960s, such as in skyscrapers and large ships. These emboldening developments led industry observers to note that perhaps the primary aluminum industry was emerging from its extended adolescence and had indeed become the metal of the future after nearly 80 years of commercial availability.

By the end of the decade, 9 manufacturers representing 13 companies were involved in the production of primary aluminum. The building and construction market continued to be the largest consuming segment of primary aluminum, accounting for 23 percent of the industry's shipments. The transportation industry ranked second, purchasing 20 percent, followed by the electrical market, which accounted for 13 percent, and the rapidly growing packaging and containing market—enlarged by the increasing popularity of aluminum beverage cans—accounted for 10 percent. During the 1960s, aluminum shipments increased by an annual average rate of roughly 9 percent and the price of aluminum continued to remain stable. The estimated average price index for primary aluminum in 1969 reflected only a 4 percent increase from the 1960 level.

In the early and mid-1970s, an energy crisis touched off recessive economic conditions that sent many manufacturing industries' earnings spiraling downward. For primary aluminum manufacturers, the deleterious effects of the energy crises were particularly harsh, since their production facilities were the most energy-intensive of all manufacturing activities. Aluminum manufacturers consumed four percent of all the electric power generated in the United States, the purchase of which represented greater than a third of the total manufacturing cost of

aluminum. Consequently, when the price of electricity soared, primary aluminum manufacturers suffered the brunt of the damage engendered by escalating energy costs. In 1975, the nadir of the recession, primary aluminum operating capacity dropped to 75 percent and the industry's total shipments plummeted 28 percent from the previous year's total.

Despite the decline in shipments, primary aluminum inventories swelled during the recession. It took two years to work off the aluminum ferreted away during the general economic decline once the economic scene improved, prolonging the industry's recovery. Not surprisingly, primary aluminum manufacturers intensified their efforts toward developing primary aluminum processes that reduced their dependence on electricity. Laudable achievements already had been achieved toward this objective; the energy consumption required to produce aluminum dropped from 12 kilowatt hours per pound following World War II, to roughly eight kilowatt hours by this time. But, after the recessive mid-1970s, manufacturers invested more time and money into developing alternative methods to produce aluminum. Additionally, a majority of primary aluminum manufacturers began concentrating more on the secondary smelting of aluminum, which required far less electric power.

Once the industry recovered from the negative affects of the energy crises in the late 1970s, manufacturers were unable to meet the rising demand for aluminum, as conditions within the industry quickly reversed. The transformation was only temporary however, for demand just as quickly disappeared in the early 1980s, due in part to a significant decline in housing and construction activity. Compounding the situation, aluminum prices plummeted, causing the closure of a substantial percentage of production capacity. Despite the diminished production capacity, total operating smelter capacity in the United States fell to 72 percent, 3 percentage points below the low recorded in 1975. By the mid-1980s key aluminum markets had become saturated, with foreign aluminum manufacturers carving out a 21 percent share of the U.S. primary and fabricated aluminum market, up from the 9 percent market share they secured in 1980.

Sales in the U.S. aluminum market grew at twice the rate of the gross national product during the 1960s and 1970s, but in the 1980s the expansion into new, untapped markets was no longer possible. Buffeted by a rapidly growing scrap aluminum industry that benefited from the trend toward recycling and an increasing use of plastic instead of aluminum for beverage containers, primary aluminum manufacturers faced unfavorable prospects as the industry faltered in its tenth decade. The fabrication end of the aluminum industry, which generated 80 percent of the overall aluminum industry's revenues by the mid-1980s, began to attract more primary aluminum manufacturers as the decade drew to a close. Between 1982 and 1987 the number of manufacturers climbed from 15 to 34. At the same time, primary production facilities sprouted up overseas, signaling for some the beginning of a new era in U.S. aluminum production.

CURRENT CONDITIONS

The primary aluminum production industry in the late 1990s was undergoing a number of consolidations. In 1999 aluminum prices fell to a five year low because of global over-capacity and a flood of cheaper imports into the United States. Seeking a way to insulate themselves from the industry's cyclical downturns, a number of primary aluminum producers merged in 1998. After acquiring Alumax and Inespal, Alcoa made a bid to purchase Reynolds in 1999. Alcoa's chief executive, Alain Belda, explained the impetus behind his company's acquisition binge to the August 25, 1999, *Wall Street Journal* as an effort to obtain ''greater efficiencies and cost reductions'' in the face of the ''industry's lowest prices in years.''

Primary aluminum production is not a high growth industry. Although buffeted by periodic price fluctuations, primary aluminum producers can rely upon steady demand from the various industries that consume aluminum. Since 1994 the automobile industry has been the largest consumer of aluminum—accounting for 30.9 percent of net shipments (over 7 billion pounds) in 1998 alone. Aluminum sales to automobile manufacturers have increased 110 percent since 1990. Although steel is the most commonly used metal in car production, aluminum is playing a greater role as pressure for more fuel-efficient—and lighter—cars grows. Aluminum can save up to 50 percent in weight over some steel parts and can match steel's safety as well. According to the August 12, 1999, *Wall Street Journal*, car manufacturers used 4 percent more aluminum in their model year 2000 vehicles than they had in the prior year. Future growth in this market is anticipated since car and light truck sales continue to rise.

The second-largest end use for aluminum is packaging. Soft drink and beer cans, food containers, and household and institutional foils accounted for 21.6 percent of all aluminum shipments (over 5 billion pounds) in 1998. The building and construction industry—fueled by projects in the residential, industrial, commercial, farm, and highway sectors—purchased 13.2 percent (3 billion pounds) of total shipments. Aluminum is also becoming important in the building of infrastructure, such as bridges and oil rigs. Because it is lightweight as well as strong and durable, increasing numbers of construction contractors incorporate aluminum in their projects. Other traditional markets requiring aluminum components, such as computers, office machines, and small engines, continue to be seen as markets for long-term growth into the twenty-first century.

In addition to being subject to price fluctuations and market demands, the primary aluminum production industry continues to be affected by the price of electricity. Aluminum smelters require massive amounts of electricity, and a manufacturer's profitability is in large part determined by energy costs. According to the August 25, 1999, edition of the *Wall Street Journal*, electricity accounts for about one-third of the total cost of aluminum production. The industry as a whole consumed over $2 billion worth of electricity in 1998. Not surprisingly, aluminum-producing companies have strenuously advocated the deregulation of the American electric utility industry, which would theoretically introduce competitiveness into electric pricing. By mid-1999, California, Connecticut, Illinois, Maine, Massachusetts, Montana, Pennsylvania, and Rhode Island were implementing deregulation, while Idaho, Nevada, New Hampshire, New Jersey, New York, and Washington had instituted experimental pilot programs. Aluminum producers, though, had taken successful steps to reduce energy consumption long before deregulation. Since 1970 the industry as a whole improved its energy efficiency by about 20 percent. Even more impressive is the fact that since 1930 the average amount of electricity needed to make a pound of aluminum has dropped from 12 kilowatt hours to about 7 kilowatt hours.

Primary aluminum producers' profits are also influenced by environmental regulations. The domestic construction of new smelting capacity was limited by the amended Clean Air Act of 1990, which in part required electric utilities to reduce sulfur dioxide emissions. The costs incurred by electric utilities in making these emission reductions were in turn passed on to primary aluminum manufacturers. Aluminum producers have also had to invest large sums of capital into advanced scrubber systems in order to satisfy the Clean Air requirements. As a result, U.S. aluminum companies have begun to look for alternate suppliers of electricity and have made efforts to start a futures market for electric power.

INDUSTRY LEADERS

In the mid-1990s, a number of mid-sized and large establishments were engaged in the primary production of aluminum. Prompted by low aluminum prices, however, the industry began to consolidate rapidly in the final years of the decade. After a spate of acquisitions, Alcoa Inc. regained its historic place as the most powerful aluminum producer in the world. With over 103,000 employees worldwide, Alcoa's 1998 sales topped $15 billion. The company had played a pivotal role in primary aluminum production since the industry's beginning. Indeed, for the first 60 years of the industry, primary aluminum production meant Alcoa. Its patent for the electrolytic process that first made the production of aluminum commercially feasible gave Alcoa a jump-start on its competitors. Negatively affected by the overall slide of the primary aluminum industry during the 1980s, Alcoa diversified its operations to mitigate its losses from the decline and placed a lesser emphasis on the production of primary aluminum. Instead, Alcoa concentrated more on the fabrication end of the aluminum industry, as well as smelting secondary aluminum harvested from recycled aluminum. In 1998 Alcoa acquired Alumax, Inc.—with sales of over $3 billion and some 15,000 employees—and Norada Aluminum Inc. After its archrival the Canadian company Alcan Aluminums merged with Pechiney of France and Alsuisse Lonza (of Switzerland), Alcoa turned its eyes towards its largest American competitor, Reynolds Metals. Reynolds accepted Alcoa's take-over bid of $4.4 billion, though at the close of 1999, Alcoa was still waiting for federal approval for the merger. If successful, the deal would create an aluminum super-power with annual sales of over $22 billion.

WORKFORCE

Total employment in the primary aluminum industry declined throughout much of the 1980s, then stabilized toward the latter end of the decade. By 1988 the industry's employment base was nearly 26,000, and during the period from 1990 to 1992 decreased to approximately 25,000 workers. Further reductions in the industry's production capacity and the trend toward relocating smelting facilities abroad eroded the industry's total employment level to 15,763 in 1997.

Of the 15,763 people employed in the primary aluminum industry in 1997, an overwhelming majority—more than 12,500—were employed as production workers. Salaried employees, or those performing managerial, administrative, or technical duties, composed the balance of the industry's workforce.

Generally, production workers were employed by the industry on a full-time basis. Average hourly wages in the primary aluminum industry were considerably higher than the average amount earned by production workers employed by all other manufacturing industries. In 1997 production workers in the industry were paid an average of $19.67 per hour.

As a consequence of the comparatively high hourly wage paid to production workers in the industry, the personnel costs per manufacturing facility, including both production workers' wages and salaries paid to managerial, administrative, and technical staff, were appreciably higher than the personnel costs incurred by the average of all other manufacturing industries. In 1997 the average payroll per establishment in the primary aluminum industry was over $33 million.

Prognostications for the industry's work force in the year 2005 suggested a general decline for nearly every occupation employed by the primary metals industry, of which the primary aluminum industry is a subdivision.

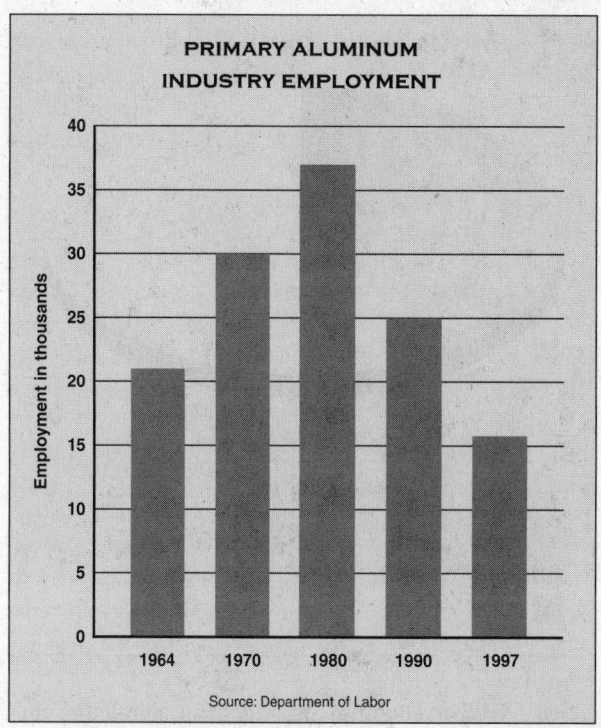

PRIMARY ALUMINUM INDUSTRY EMPLOYMENT

Source: Department of Labor

According to U.S. Bureau of Labor estimates, furnace operators, materials and ceramic engineers, and metallurgists are expected to proportionately increase their representation in the industry by the end of the twentieth century. Occupations expected to be affected most severely were machine operators, material and stock movers, and bookkeeping and accounting clerks, each of which were expected to decline by 22 to 31 percent by the year 2005.

AMERICA AND THE WORLD

Domestic aluminum producers have often accused their foreign competitors of "dumping" aluminum, or selling their products at artificially low prices in the United States to increase their market share. This situation was especially tense in the early 1990s, as the amount of aluminum originating in the former Soviet Union ballooned from 250,000 metric tons to 1.6 million metric tons between 1989 and 1993. As a result of this flood of aluminum unleashed on the domestic market, U.S. producers cut production by 796,000 metric tons, or 20 percent of capacity, and laid off 1,300 employees. In 1995, the 14 aluminum smelters in the Commonwealth of Independent States (the countries that had previously comprised the Soviet Union) were privatized. Without subsidies from the Russian government, the CIS manufacturers were liable for their own operating costs. They could no longer afford to sell aluminum below open market cost and remain operational.

Because U.S. tariffs imposed on products imported from foreign aluminum mills are much lower than those

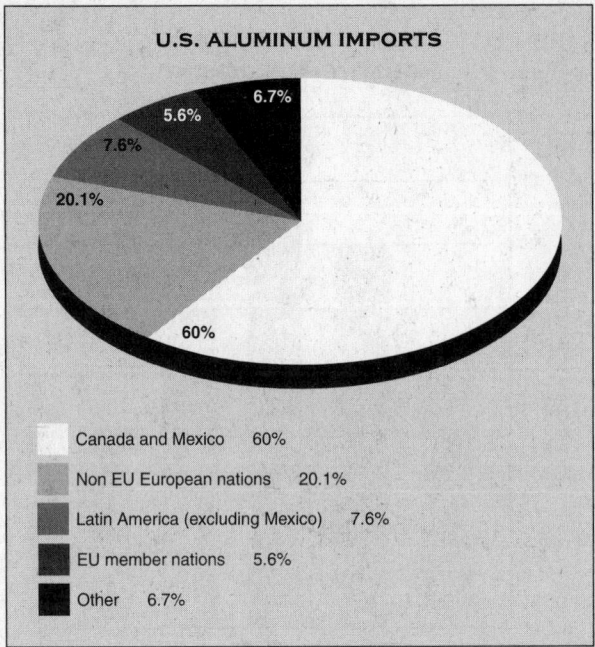

U.S. ALUMINUM IMPORTS

6.7%
5.6%
7.6%
20.1%
60%

Canada and Mexico   60%

Non EU European nations   20.1%

Latin America (excluding Mexico)   7.6%

EU member nations   5.6%

Other   6.7%

Misner, Scott. "User Benefits Foreseen as a Result of Energy Deregulation." *American Metal Market,* 30 April 1999.

Osterland, Andrew. "Russian Overture." *Financial World* 164, no. 7, 14 March 1995, 24.

Regan, B. "Aluminum Can Shipments Inch Up." *American Metal Market,* 27 January 1997.

"Smelter Electric Rate a Success, BPA Says." *American Metal Market,* 31 October 1996.

"US Aluminum Companies Fight for Competitive Power." *Platt's Metals Week,* 23 September 1996.

SIC 3339

PRIMARY SMELTING AND REFINING OF NONFERROUS METALS, EXCEPT COPPER AND ALUMINUM

This classification covers establishments primarily engaged in smelting and refining nonferrous metals, except copper and aluminum. Establishments primarily engaged in rolling, drawing, and extruding these nonferrous primary metals are classified in **SIC 3356: Rolling, Drawing, and Extruding of Nonferrous Metals, Except Copper and Aluminum,** and the production of bullion at the site of the mine is classified in various mining classifications.

NAICS CODE(S)

331419 (Primary Smelting and Refining of Nonferrous Metals (except Copper and Aluminum))

INDUSTRY SNAPSHOT

This industry supplies nonferrous metals for further consumption to secondary smelting and refining establishments. The metals refined include antimony, babbitt, beryllium, bismuth, cadmium, chromium, cobalt, columbium, germanium, gold, iridium, lead, magnesium, nickel, platinum, rhenium, selenium, silicon, silver, tantalum, tellurium, tin, titanium, zinc, and zirconium. These metals are extracted from their ores and poured into basic shapes, such as slabs, pig molds, or ingots.

According to the U.S. Census Bureau's *1997 Economic Census—Manufacturing,* 141 establishments operated in this category for part or all of 1997. Industry-wide employment totaled 10,018 workers receiving a payroll of more than $405 million. Within this workforce, 7,135 of these employees worked in production, putting in more than 16 million hours to earn wages of almost $254 million. Overall shipments for the industry were valued at more than $3.5 billion.

levied by other countries on American aluminum, imports still account for a substantial portion of the total U.S. aluminum supply. Aluminum imports rose 16.4 percent in 1998. In fact, nearly one-third of all aluminum consumed in the United States in 1998 came from abroad. Aluminum from Canada and Mexico together represented over 60 percent of all imports in 1998. European nations not within the European Union (EU) accounted for 20.1 percent of all imported aluminum, followed by Latin American countries with 7.6 percent, and by EU member nations with 5.6 percent.

On the opposite side of the trade equation, the United States did export aluminum to other countries. In 1998 exports accounted for 12 percent of the total market for U.S. aluminum. Sixty-two percent of U.S. aluminum exports were destined for Canada and Mexico, while 22 percent were sent to East Asia. Latin America was the end market for 8.6 percent of U.S. aluminum exports, followed by EU members at 3.8 percent.

FURTHER READING

Amos, J. "Reynolds Looks for the Low Power Rates." *American Metal Market,* 105, 1997, 14.

Deogun, Nikhil and Matthews, Robert Guy. "Reynolds Metal Yields to Alcoa's Bid." *Wall Street Journal,* 20 August 1999.

Holman, W. Jenkins, Jr. "Oh Horrors! A Beverage Can Oligopoly." *Wall Street Journal,* 25 August 1999.

Klebnikov, Paul. "Does Size Matter?" *Forbes,* 6 September 1999.

Matthews, Robert Guy. "Suddenly Consolidation Rolls All Over Aluminum Industry." *Wall Street Journal,* 12 August 1999.

CURRENT CONDITIONS

In its March 1999 issue, *E-MJ—Engineering and Mining Journal* reported on the market status of many of the metals in this industry, including cobalt, lead, nickel and zinc. Lead experienced increased consumption due to steady demand for lead acid batteries. The lead market had been depressed in the early 1990s, recovering in the mid-1990s. Lead prices on the London Metal Exchange (LME) averaged 28 cents per pound in 1995 and 1997, peaking in 1996 to 35 cents per pound; the price continued to fall to 24 cents per pound in 1998. Seventy percent of domestic lead production, however, occurred at secondary smelters, which primarily recycled lead acid batteries; this left only 30 percent of production for primary smelters.

Cobalt prices plummeted in 1998 due to weak end-markets and inventory stockpiling. Producers had been hoping for price reductions to spur consumption, but the price fell further than expected while consumption failed to increase, creating an imbalance. The future of the cobalt market promised continued consolidation to weather its fluctuations. Similarly, nickel prices plunged 33 percent in 1998, averaging $2.13 per pound across the year. Western world consumption grew slightly, while Western production grew 2.3 percent to 713,000 metric tons. These conditions combined to create a volatile market for nickel, with recovery at the mercy of global economic growth. Zinc experienced similar market conditions, with prices on the LME falling from 48.7 cents per pound at the opening of 1998 to 41.6 cents per pound at the year's close, averaging 46.5 cents per pound—a significant decrease from 1997's average of 59.8 cents per pound. Western world consumption similarly declined.

INDUSTRY LEADERS.

Dominating the industry in overall sales were New York City-based Asarco Inc., with more than $2.30 billion in 1998 sales, and Degussa Huls of Ridgefield Park, New Jersey, with about $2.15 billion in sales for its fiscal year ended September 30, 1998. Other industry leaders included New York City-based Renco Group Inc., St. Louis-based Doe Run Co., and New York City-based Horsehead Industries Inc.

RESEARCH AND TECHNOLOGY

Late in October 1993, researchers at the National Institute of Standards and Technology in Boulder, Colorado announced they had developed a new alloy. The alloy is a combination of nickel, chromium, manganese, molybdenum, copper, nitrogen, and iron. It can withstand temperatures below −269 degrees Celsius (−516 degrees Fahrenheit), and is expected to find use in fusion energy studies, superconducting magnets, and physics experiments funded by the U.S. government. The importance of the alloy will lie in welding seams in superconducting magnets, which must resist fracture in such low temperatures.

FURTHER READING

Deelo, Michael L. "Lead: Millenium to Bring Happiness?" *E-MJ—Engineering and Mining Journal,* March 1999.

Kertes, Noella. "Silver's Use Seen Growing; Industrial, Decorative Applications Most Promising." *American Metal Market,* 8 January 1997.

Kielty, Edward R. "Cobalt: A Market Still Not Satisfied," *E-MJ—Engineering and Mining Journal,* March 1999.

LaRue, Gloria T. "LME Proves its Status as the Biggest Gold Forum." *American Metal Market,* 3 February 1997.

Ozols, Victor, and Tsukasa Furukawa. "Gold Loses Luster; a Deflated Image?" *American Metal Market,* 5 February 1997.

Rudnitsky, Howard. "Metals: After a Tough Year Prices Are Climbing Back." *Forbes,* 13 January 1997.

"Russia Tungsten Exports Fall." *American Metal Market,* 4 December 1996.

Seddon, Mark. "Recovering CIS States Exporting." *American Metal Market,* 22 August 1996.

"Short Silver Supply Seen in 8th Consecutive Year." *American Metal Market,* 3 March 1997.

Upton, Doug. "Nickel." *E-MJ—Engineering and Mining Journal,* March 1999.

U.S. Census Bureau. "Primary Smelting and Refining of Non-ferrous Metal (Except Copper and Aluminum)" *1997 Economic Census-Manufacturing.* Washington, D.C.: U.S. Department of Commerce, 1999. Available from http://www.census.gov/prod/ec97/97m3314b.pdf.

"U.S. Tungsten Market Expected to Rebound." *American Metal Market,* 3 October 1996.

Yates, E. M. "Zinc: Asian Problems Predominate." *E-MJ—Engineering and Mining Journal,* March 1999.

SIC 3341

SECONDARY SMELTING AND REFINING OF NONFERROUS METALS

This classification comprises establishments primarily engaged in recovering nonferrous metals and alloys from new and used scrap and dross, or in producing alloys from purchased refined metals. This industry includes establishments engaged in both the recovery and alloying of precious metals. Also included in this industry are plants involved in the recovery of tin through secondary smelting and refining, as well as by chemical processes. Excluded from this classification are establishments primarily engaged in assembling, sorting, and breaking up scrap metal without smelting and refining the metal. These establishments are classified in **SIC 5093: Scrap and Waste Materials.**

NAICS CODE(S)

331314 (Secondary Smelting and Alloying of Aluminum)

331423 (Secondary Smelting, Refining, and Alloying of Copper)

331492 (Secondary Smelting, Refining, and Alloying of Nonferrous Metals (except Copper and Aluminum)

INDUSTRY SNAPSHOT

Metal, utilized by nearly every manufacturing industry in the United States and abroad, is produced through two basic production methods: primary and secondary. Primary manufacturers produce metal by subjecting particular extracted ores to various metallurgical processes, creating metal in large block or bar form. Secondary manufacturers smelt, refine, and sometimes blend metal recovered from either the shaping and trimming of primary metal during production and fabrication, or from recycled metal. The secondary smelting and refining of nonferrous metals, as defined by **SIC 3341,** comprises the secondary production of metals that do not contain iron, such as aluminum, copper, gold, lead, nickel, silver, tin, and zinc. These metals are used in a wide variety of manufactured products, including ammunition, beverage cans, coins, automobiles, household appliances, and a wealth of other products that encompass the breadth of U.S. manufacturing activity.

Copper, possessing superior electrical conductivity, is a strong, durable metal used in a variety of structural applications as well as for power, lighting, and communications transmissions. Domestically, the major markets for copper are construction, electrical and electronics, and industrial machinery and equipment.

Aluminum, the most widely used nonferrous metal, possesses several positive attributes, such as light weight, corrosion resistance, and high electrical and thermal conductivity that make the metal suitable for a variety of applications. Container and packaging manufacturers purchase a majority of the domestically produced aluminum, while other major end-use markets include the transportation sector, the buildings and construction sector, and the electrical sector.

Lead is primarily used for the manufacture of storage batteries, which in turn are incorporated into automobile ignition starters, uninterruptible power supplies for computer systems, and standby power supplies for emergency lighting systems and telephones. Other market sectors that purchase lead include paint and glass manufacturers and building products manufacturers.

Zinc is primarily used to galvanize products found in the automobile, steel, and construction industries, but a greater percentage of secondary zinc is used to produce brass and bronze, as well as assorted chemicals and dusts. Additional applications include the blending of zinc-based, die-cast alloys and brass alloys.

Approximately 350 companies in the United States were involved in the secondary smelting and refining industry in 1997. These manufacturers recorded $8.65 billion in sales for products included in this classification, an aggregate value of shipments primarily derived from the production of the industry's five key products: secondary aluminum, secondary precious metals (gold, silver, platinum), secondary copper, secondary lead, and secondary zinc. Although the secondary smelting and refining industry produces other metals, such as nickel and tin, these five metals accounted for the bulk of the industry's total shipments. Of all the metals produced by the industry, secondary aluminum represented the largest product category, accounting for nearly 42 percent of the industry's aggregate shipments. Secondary copper was the industry's second largest product category, representing 14.7 percent of total shipments, followed by precious metals, which accounted for 13.1 percent. Secondary lead represented 8.2 percent and zinc was 3.5 percent.

ORGANIZATION AND STRUCTURE

In terms of the number of people employed per establishment, the secondary smelting and refining industry has been historically populated by relatively small manufacturing facilities. Of the 395 secondary smelting and refining establishments in operation in 1997, 173, or nearly 44 percent, employed less than 20 people, while the remaining 222 employed 20 people or more. These 395 establishments represented all of the individual production facilities operated by the approximately 354 companies engaged in smelting and refining secondary nonferrous metals in 1997. The average number of employees per establishment in the secondary smelting and refining industry in 1997 was 52.

Geographically, a majority of the secondary smelting and refining production facilities in the 1990s were located in a four-state area comprising Michigan, Illinois, Indiana, and Ohio. Together, these states contained 99 production facilities. The mid-Atlantic states of Pennsylvania, New York, and New Jersey formed the second largest regional concentration of facilities, with 65 establishments. The Pacific region was the third largest area of production solely by virtue of the 37 establishments located in California—the greatest number located in any one state and the only state within the region that contained any secondary smelting and refining facilities. When ranked according to the number of establishments per state, California was followed by Pennsylvania, with

34 production facilities, and Ohio, with 33 establishments. The 17 manufacturing facilities in Alabama and Georgia together accounted for a whopping $719.4 million in shipments in 1992, 77.5 percent more than the $405.4 million generated by the 37 establishments in California.

The expenses incurred from operating a secondary smelting and refining facility were substantially higher than the amount of money required to operate the average manufacturing facility in the United States. This disparity was most evident in the average cost per establishment, that is, the average amount of money paid for raw manufacturing materials. According to 1994 figures, the average cost per establishment in this industry was $12.8 million, more than three times greater than the $4.2 million averaged by all other manufacturing industries. At $399,225, the average investment per establishment in the secondary smelting and refining industry for production machinery and other equipment necessary in the recovery of primary metal, however, was 43 percent higher than the average investment per establishment in all other manufacturing industries, which required only $278,244.

BACKGROUND AND DEVELOPMENT

In the historiography of secondary smelting and refining, one chronicler traces the origins of recovering scrap metal to the seventh descendent of Adam, back to the founder of the iron and steel industry, and by implication, the founder of the scrap metal industry—Tubal-Cain. The writer then proceeds to chart the utilization of scrap metal throughout the span of civilization, making references along the way to documented accounts of scrap metal usage by such notable personages as Moses, Chaucer, Shakespeare, Paul Revere, Captain Kidd, and Thoreau. While this exploration into the depths of scrap metal's history may strike some as overindulgent, it does indicate the pervasiveness and integrality of secondary metal in the history of human existence. It also suggests that scrap metal has been used as long as metal has been used by mankind.

But, obviously, the processing of scrap in the days of Tubal-Cain bore no resemblance to the modern secondary metal industry. The smelting and refining of scrap metal as an organized and structured industry—the type of industry that operated in the 1990s—was a modern creation of the United States. It formed in the early 1900s as secondary smelting and refining manufacturers began to shed their image as junk peddlers, and gradually became regarded as legitimate operators of an enterprise essential to the existence of modern manufacturing industries. This transition was hastened by the formation of the National Association of Waste Material Dealers in 1913, which gave manufacturers, for the first time, formalized

rules of operation, a code of ethics, and uniform specifications for scrap metal production. The creation of this governing body, renamed the National Association of Secondary Material Industries (NASMI) in 1960, lent cohesion to a loosely structured group of manufacturers struggling to attain order in a rapidly changing manufacturing environment.

Although the advent of NASMI helped define and shape the industry, the smelting and refining of secondary nonferrous metals had been occurring in an industrial setting for quite some time before NASMI came into existence. No statistical record of scrap consumption in the United States exists prior to 1900, but, in the first year figures were recorded, U.S. manufacturers consumed 5.1 million gross tons of ferrous and nonferrous secondary metal. Indeed, the first American scrap metal company, Cline & Bernheim, based in Nashville, Tennessee, had begun operating nearly 40 years before industry-wide consumption figures were recorded in 1862. According to these records, the first market coverage of the scrap industry was published in 1865, when the *Commercial Bulletin of Boston* began providing scrap metal prices. And, even further back in time, the first commercial use of scrap metal in the United States occurred at an iron works in Lynn, Massachusetts, in 1642.

Although some of these early uses of scrap metal were of the ferrous variety, the tradition of scrap metal usage had its roots stretching back to the founding of the United States. Accordingly, the scrap metal industry gathered more than a modicum of momentum by the time NASMI emerged. Once it did emerge, however, the modern version of the secondary nonferrous metal industry began and the recovery, smelting, and refining of such metals became distinguished from the production of primary metals, rather than lumped together under the more general and generic metal industry umbrella.

Following the founding of NASMI, secondary nonferrous production occurred at a predictable, steady rate, without any significant influence from external market forces that would have otherwise proportionally boosted the industry's production volume. Military build-up during World War I, which had a positive effect on many manufacturing industries, provided less than its expected impact on secondary metal producers, largely due to the conspicuous absence of wartime scrap metal drives. A tremendous increase in secondary nonferrous metal production did occur however, as a result of America's entrance into World War II. By early summer in 1942, the first summer after the Japanese bombed Pearl Harbor, the nation embarked on a virtually uninterrupted campaign to recover scrap metal, elevating the importance of secondary producers in the metal manufacturing industry.

During the immediate post-war years, a majority of American manufacturing industries flourished, and the secondary nonferrous metal industry, as a supplier of the raw material for much of the accelerated production, shared in the explosive growth of the American economy. By 1950, primary manufacturers of nonferrous metals held a commanding lead in the global market, producing nearly half of the world's supply of refined copper, aluminum, and zinc, and more than 25 percent of the world's supply of lead. Secondary producers of these metals, who literally benefited from the crumbs of the prodigious production volume, were well positioned to profit from the increased demand for nonferrous metals, converting ''old'' scrap, or metal recovered from recycled products, and converting ''new'' scrap gleaned from the trimming and shaping of primary nonferrous ingot (referred to as ''home'' scrap).

This closely knit, interdependent relationship secondary producers maintained within the nonferrous metal industry, which had matured and strengthened in the nearly four decades since the establishment of NASMI, invigorated production during robust economic conditions, but also made industry participants vulnerable to the vagaries of the overall metal industry. Although conditions were favorable in the 1950s, several portentous developments arose during this time that would create a somewhat bleaker future for all manufacturers of nonferrous metal.

The consumption of nonferrous metals increased exponentially since the turn of the century, fueled by a rapidly growing population and its need for products manufactured with this type of metal. By the time the United States entered World War II, this increased demand had depleted the country's metal ore reserves to the extent that the self-sufficient production of several key nonferrous metals, such as zinc and lead, was no longer possible. To compound this problem, the manufacturing of another key nonferrous metal, aluminum, required an ore more commonly found in countries other than the United States.

During the 1950s, this development persuaded many primary manufacturers of nonferrous metals to either affiliate with foreign metal manufacturers to meet existing U.S. demand or to establish wholly owned operations overseas, where ore deposits were plentiful. While this expansion into foreign metal markets narrowed the gap between supply and demand and sparked the overall metal industry's growth, it also fostered the growth of the global nonferrous metal market, establishing the first manufacturing facilities in less-developed countries and encouraging output in more sophisticated, foreign markets. Repercussions from this shift overseas were not immediate, but, in the years ahead, the evolution of a genuine global metal industry would create a highly competitive nonferrous metal market.

Another development affecting industry participants was a technological innovation developed by primary manufacturers in the 1950s that promised to impinge directly on the demand for secondary nonferrous metal. The underlying principle behind this innovation was relatively simple: introduce oxygen into the furnaces in which pig iron is converted to steel.

The addition of oxygen quickened the conversion process, reducing the energy requirements of metal production. Most harmful to secondary producers, however, was that the process required far less scrap metal with which to manufacture ingot. Without oxygen, primary manufacturers needed a high percentage of scrap metal to efficiently produce metal, but with oxygen the proportion of scrap metal dropped to as low as 40 percent. Initially, steel manufacturers employed this new process, but, by the mid- and late 1960s, the utilization of oxygen in the production of nonferrous metals had begun, as aluminum manufacturers also adopted the process. Of course, the use of oxygen also reduced the conversion time in the production of secondary metals, but the losses suffered as a result of the diminished role scrap metal played in the manufacturing of primary metal were significant.

Fortunately for secondary metal producers, the popularity of this new production method was roughly concurrent with the increased interest in consumer product recycling efforts, which bolstered the industry's production output and marked the beginning of a movement that would serve as a linchpin to the industry's existence and success into the 1990s. To varying degrees, the recycling of used products and materials had been occurring for many decades prior to the late 1960s and early 1970s— the existence of the secondary metal industry itself, comprised of former junk peddlers, was a testament to the long tradition of recycling. But these efforts were intensified due to the growing outcry against pollution and waste, as landfills dotting the nation's landscape brimmed with refuse. Also, recycling had been generally limited to the recovery of industrial, or commercial byproducts, not the recycling of consumer products such as storage batteries, aluminum, and tin cans.

Once recycling began in earnest, secondary producers of nonferrous metals began to play a more dominant role in the overall nonferrous metals industry, outpacing primary manufacturers in terms of production volume and capitalizing on governmental efforts aimed at reducing the amount of national waste. Federally led and financed attempts to reduce waste received an initial push from the creation of the Office of Solid Waste Management in 1965, which was strengthened in 1970 by the promulgation of the Resource Recovery Act. The Resource Recovery Act of 1970 authorized a three-year budget of $461 million, but, most important to secondary nonferrous metal producers, the Act changed the Office of Solid Waste Management's primary objective from the sanitary dumping of solid wastes to the recycling of those wastes. In a short time, the effect of this concerted push toward recovering solid wastes improved the secondary nonferrous industry's position, driving scrap manufacturer's production output upwards. By 1971, roughly 50 percent of the total lead consumption in the United States was supplied by secondary metal producers and the proportional representation of other secondary nonferrous metals were no less impressive: 45 percent of secondary copper, 35 percent of secondary aluminum, and 23 percent of secondary zinc.

By the mid-1970s, however, a recession and a worldwide energy crisis nearly crippled all sectors of the ferrous and nonferrous metal industry, as successive oil shocks shook the foundations of an industry that relied on relatively large amounts of energy to exist. Indeed, the deleterious effects of the energy crises plagued metal manufacturers for the rest of the decade and stood as a turning point for the health of metal manufacturers worldwide. The annual growth rates in the consumption of nonferrous metals from 1979 to 1988 stood well below the pace recorded from 1950 to 1974. Indeed the annual consumption rate of aluminum, worldwide, from 1950 to 1974 was 9 percent, while from 1979 to 1988 the rate dropped to 2.3 percent; copper fell from 3.9 percent to 1.1 percent; lead from 2.7 percent to 0.5 percent; and zinc from 3.9 percent to 1.2 percent.

Entering the 1980s, a period of corporate restructuring began, as companies purchased, sold, and merged operations to enhance their competitiveness. Still, the key metals within the industry were each affected, either negatively or positively, by conditions peculiar to their markets. The production of secondary copper suffered a decline in total shipments in the early 1980s after effecting a rebound from the pernicious 1970s. By 1989, however, shipments eclipsed the one-year surge experienced at the start of the decade, as manufacturers combated difficulties associated with aging production facilities and environmental regulations. Over the entire decade, secondary production accounted for 26 percent of the total U.S. copper production, a more encouraging representation than the 20 percent share recorded from 1975 to 1979.

Secondary aluminum production fared comparatively better during the 1980s, increasing 40 percent over the decade. Hampered by decreasing primary production of aluminum in the United States and a nearly glutted beverage can market, secondary aluminum manufacturers also experienced capricious fluctuations in demand during much of the decade. Nevertheless, secondary aluminum producers concluded the 1980s with three solid years of production output, during which they recorded much of the production growth of the decade.

Primary lead manufacturers, struggling with the sharply decreased demand for tetraethyl lead (TEL), which is used to produce leaded gasoline, witnessed secondary manufacturers of lead increase their representation of total lead consumption during the 1980s. The reclamation of lead acid storage batteries, the largest market for lead and typically recyclable, elevated the importance of the secondary lead industry. In 1980, primary and secondary lead production was about equally split, with secondary producers supplying half of the nation's total lead. By the end of the decade, however, secondary lead manufacturers supplied approximately 65 percent of the total lead consumed in the United States.

Secondary zinc manufacturers also figured more prominently within their nonferrous metal niche during the 1980s. The demand for zinc, both from primary and secondary suppliers, increased throughout much of the decade, excluding a temporary decline in 1982. Overall consumption rose 21 percent over the course of the decade, while secondary zinc producers increased their share of the total zinc production to 23 percent.

CURRENT CONDITIONS

As the secondary smelting and refining industry entered the late 1990s, an intensified interest in recycling by both the consumer and industrial sectors buoyed the production output of industry participants. From 1990 to 1997, shipments of nonferrous castings rose 9 percent, indicating a revitalization in this sector of the market. Each of the metals within the industry were expected to demonstrate a positive but slow growth forecast by the expected increase in the reclamation of industrial and consumer solid waste. Additional success in this direction will continue to elevate the industry's importance within the overall nonferrous metal industry and fuel its future growth.

While secondary aluminum production accounted for only about 25 percent of total supply in 1989, by 1997 secondary production—at 3.76 million metric tons—had for the first time exceeded primary production, which totaled only 3.6 million metric tons. One of the most important factors spurring increased secondary aluminum production was the 95 percent savings realized in energy costs. Above-average growth is expected for secondary aluminum production in the early years of the new millennium. At the same time, copper is expected to remain steady or increase only modestly into 2000 and beyond. Zinc, on the other hand, is being constantly replaced by plastics and may experience either no growth or limited growth into the new millennium. Lead consumption is expected to experience a continual decline as this metal is removed from various metal formulations for toxicity reasons.

INDUSTRY LEADERS

Ranked according to sales volume, the largest manufacturer in the secondary smelting and refining industry in 1998 was Commercial Metals Company, located in Dallas, Texas, with 7,500 workers and $2.3 billion in sales.

Second is Connell L.P., located in Boston, Massachusetts. Connell, a holding company with operations involved in fabricating special dies, plate work, and metal forming machine tools, as well as sheet metal production, is engaged in the secondary smelting and refining industry through its Wabash Alloys division, the leading producer of aluminum casting alloys in the United States. Deriving a majority of its business from the automobile industry, Wabash converts aluminum scrap into aluminum casting alloys, which are then sold to major automobile manufacturers or to die-casting companies that cater to the automobile industry. With 2,800 employees, Connell posted roughly $1.1 billion in sales in 1998.

The U.S. Reduction Company, a more diversified producer of secondary nonferrous metals than Wabash, reported 1998 sales of $76 million and employed 400 people. RSR Corp., headquartered in Dallas, Texas, recycles scrapped batteries into refined lead.

WORKFORCE

Total employment in the secondary smelting and refining industry dropped throughout much of the 1980s, with a slight rise occurring during the late 1980s and into the 1990s. In 1982, the industry's total employment stood at 19,200, then slipped to 12,500 by 1987. The largest precipitous drops occurred during 1982 and 1983, and during 1986 and 1987. After 1987, the nadir of the industry's employment decline, total employment increased by an average of 800 per year. In 1994, the industry's employment base continued to rise, although at a less robust pace than during the late 1980s, reaching 14,400 by the end of the year. Perhaps fueled to some degree by the increasing popularity of recycling, the late 1990s saw a sharp uptrend in the size of the industry's workforce, which swelled to about 20,600 by 1997.

Of the 20,600 people employed in the secondary smelting and refining industry in 1997, 5,570 were salaried employees, or those performing managerial, administrative, or technical duties, while the balance of the industry's work force comprised just over 15,000 production workers. A typical secondary smelting and refining facility in 1997 employed 38 production workers and 14 salaried employees.

Generally, production workers are employed on a full-time basis, averaging 12 percent more hours per year than the average number of hours worked by production workers in all other manufacturing industries. On average, the production workers employed by the secondary smelting and refining industry earned slightly less than the typical production worker. In 1994, a typical production worker employed by a manufacturing industry earned $11.55 per hour, while production workers involved in the secondary smelting and refining industry earned $11.20 per hour.

Prognostications for the industry's work force in the year 2005 suggest a general decline for nearly every occupation employed by the primary metals industry, of which the secondary smelting and refining industry is a subdivision. According to the U.S. Bureau of Labor, only furnace operators, metallurgists, and ceramic and materials engineers are expected to proportionately increase their representation in the industry between the years 1994 and 2005. Occupations expected to be affected most severely are machine operators, material movers, bookkeepers, and accounting clerks, each of which are expected to decline by 22 to 31 percent by the year 2005.

AMERICA AND THE WORLD

The U.S. nonferrous metal industry, once the prominent, global leader in production volume, entered the 1990s harried by escalating production costs and mounting foreign competition. Consequently, foreign manufacturers of nonferrous metals, some of whom were located in countries rich in metal ore deposits, were able to gain ground on domestic manufacturers during the 1980s, and, with certain metals, supplant the United States as the leading metal manufacturer. This situation was further exacerbated for U.S. manufacturers because some of the state-owned foreign manufacturing companies pursued political rather than economic objectives. This affected domestic manufacturers of primary nonferrous metals more severely than secondary producers, although any significant cutbacks in primary production eventually and inevitably affect secondary producers.

Despite the increasing competition and the flight of primary manufacturing facilities, secondary producers in the United States maintained a leading position in the international nonferrous market well into the 1990s. With five secondary smelters, two electrolytic refineries, and six fire refineries operating in 1992, the U.S. secondary copper industry ranked as the largest producer in the world, accounting for 35.3 percent of the 1.2 million metric tons of secondary copper produced by all countries with market economies. The Federal Republic of Germany ranked as the second largest producer, supplying an estimated 23 percent of the copper, followed by Japan, which accounted for 6 percent. Other prominent secondary copper-producing nations are the United Kingdom with 2.6 percent and Italy with 6.2 percent. The region responsible for producing most of the secondary copper is Europe with 47.5 percent, followed by North America with 37.8 percent.

The United States' secondary aluminum producers held a larger lead in the global secondary aluminum market than their copper counterparts, manufacturing 44.6 percent of the 6.1 million metric tons produced in 1992. America's closest rival, Japan, produced 17.4 percent of the total, and an estimated 13.7 percent was produced by the Commonwealth of Independent States (CIS). Other important producers of secondary aluminum in 1992 were Italy with 5.7 percent and France with 3.6 percent. The production of this metal was divided regionally between North America with 47.3 percent, Asia with 32.4 percent, and Europe with 18.7 percent.

The production of secondary lead was regionally divided between Europe with 41.2 percent of the 1.7 metric tons produced worldwide in 1992. Asia was responsible for 22.0 percent and North America for 32.8 percent. The United States was the leading producer of secondary lead with 26.7 percent, and the Federal Republic of Germany produced approximately 15.9 percent. The United Kingdom was responsible for an estimated 11.0 percent of the world production of secondary lead, and Italy produced 5.0 percent.

The international secondary zinc market was sharply contested in the late 1980s, as the former U.S.S.R. maintained a precarious lead over its two strongest competitors, the United States and the Federal Republic of Germany. Of the 349,602 metric tons of zinc produced globally in 1992, the United States controlled 36.5 percent of the market, followed closely by the Commonwealth of Independent States (CIS), which accounted for 35.4 percent of total production. The Federal Republic of Germany supplied an estimated 10.0 percent of the international market. Japan accounted for 9.3 percent, and France produced 4.0 percent. The production of secondary zinc was divided regionally between Asia with 44.7 percent, North America with 36.5 percent, and Europe with 17.3 percent.

FURTHER READING
Darnay, Arsen J., ed. *Manufacturing Worldwide*. Detroit: Gale Research, 1995.

U.S. Bureau of Census. *1997 Economic Census*. Washington: GPO, 1999.

U.S. Department of Commerce. International Trade Administration. *U.S. Industry and Trade Outlook '99*. Washington: GPO, 1999.

SIC 3351

ROLLING, DRAWING, AND EXTRUDING OF COPPER

This industry consists of establishments that roll, draw, or extrude copper, brass, bronze, and other copper-

based alloys. These establishments create basic shapes such as plate, sheet, strip, bar, and tubing.

NAICS CODE(S)
331421 (Copper (except Wire) Rolling, Drawing, and Extruding)

INDUSTRY SNAPSHOT
The 128 companies in the rolling, drawing, and extruding of copper industry are commonly known as copper fabricators. Wire rod mills, brass mills, ingot makers, and powder plants are all classified as copper fabricators. Wire rod mills and brass mills account for about 85 percent of all copper fabricators in the United States. Copper foundries are discussed in **SIC 3366: Copper Foundries.** After receiving smelted and refined copper ore and copper scrap, fabricators convert the raw copper into wire, strip, sheet, plate, rod, bar, and other copper products used by various industries.

Key end-use markets for copper and copper alloy are the building/construction, electrical and electronic products industries, and the transportation, industrial machinery and equipment, and consumer products industries. More than 41 percent—or 3.5 billion pounds—of all refined copper in 1998 was consumed by the building/construction sector. Valued for its conductivity, copper wire is essential to heating and cooling systems and is the primary type of building wire used.

After a decade of overcapacity and falling prices in the 1980s, the copper industry stabilized in the late 1990s. However, like other commodities markets, the copper industry is prone to cyclical price fluctuations. Shipments for 1997 topped $7.6 billion. Fueled by a strong domestic building and transportation market and an increasing need for copper in developing nations, demand remained high in the late 1990s.

ORGANIZATION AND STRUCTURE
Copper in the United States passes from the mines to the smelters. In some cases these facilities are owned by the same company, and in some cases the mining and smelting are done nearby. The mining and smelting companies produce copper, and the wire rod mills, brass mills, and foundries are the consumers of copper who prepare the metal for delivery to manufacturers in various industries.

Mining companies process copper ores, most of which comes from open-pit mines. The ores are refined and sometimes alloyed with other elements, such as zinc or beryllium. The percentage of copper and copper alloys that went to wire rod mills in 1997 was 56 percent, while 36 percent went to brass mills, 4 percent went to ingot makers, and 2 percent to foundries. All of these fabricators created copper-based products used throughout U.S.

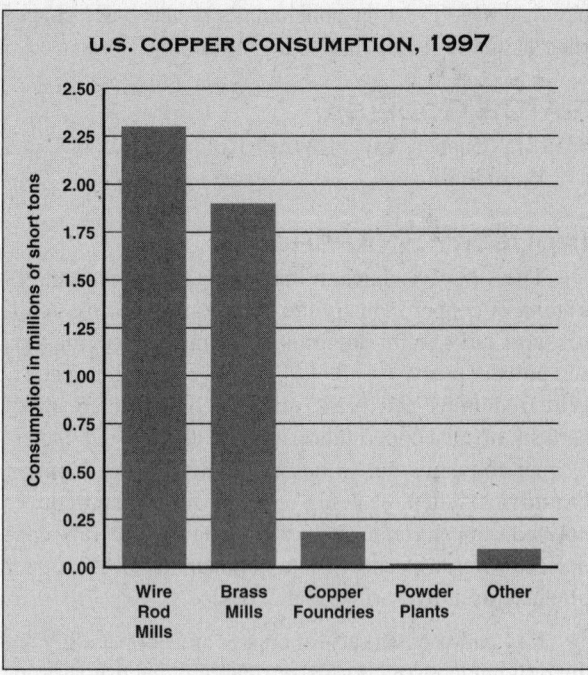

U.S. COPPER CONSUMPTION, 1997

industries. The total refined production of primary copper was 2.69 million short tons in 1997, and net imports of refined copper were 646,000 short tons.

Most brass mills in the United States operate in three areas. While one division produces rod, bar, and shapes, another division manufactures strip, sheet, and plate, and the third division produces commercial and plumbing tube. Brass rod and brass strip, two of the most popular copper alloys produced in the industry, possess the kind of corrosion resistance, machinability, and electrical properties that enable them to be used under adverse climatic conditions. Air-conditioning tube and plumbing tube are two examples of the unalloyed copper and high-copper alloys that comprise another major segment of the mill's output.

There are several associations for copper production. Foremost is the Copper Development Association, which tracks market statistics and releases public relations reports. The American Copper Council—also a trade organization central to the copper industry—tried to increase its audience by expanding its Internet presence during the 1990s.

BACKGROUND AND DEVELOPMENT

Copper mining began in the Middle East and reached its zenith in the American West. Small mining operations spawned prosperous towns in Michigan and Arizona. In the mid-eighteenth century, miners in the colonies discovered copper ores in what is now the northeastern United States. They mined the ores, but English law forbade construction of smelting works, so the ore was sent to England for smelting and refining.

After the American Revolution, many copper workers moved to the new United States. Copper sheathing began being used on wooden ships as early as the 1790s. The copper protected the ships from the pressure and corrosive effects of the ocean. Great demand from the shipping industry helped the budding copper industry, but the United States still depended on copper imports from England and South America. In 1806 U.S. importers of copper asked Congress to exempt copper from customs duty. Protests by copper industry pioneers resulted in lower tariffs on copper imports.

Steamships had copper parts by this time, because copper was better than pinewood at containing steam in boilers. Later, with the rise of American industry, growing copper fabricators created stripping, boiler plates, rivets, and other copper-based items that were used in an increasingly diverse number of industries and products. Copper nails replaced cast iron nails in building, and the boom in building towns and cities across the new nation resulted in a windfall for the copper industry.

Development of efficient flotation processes around the turn of the century and advances in open-pit mining techniques quickly turned the United States into the world's largest producer of copper.

The brass mill industry began in Connecticut during the early days of colonial America. There were copper mills from Waterbury south to Ansonia, where melting and rolling techniques were developed and tested. Though largely forgotten in Connecticut, the industry remains centered in the eastern United States.

Like many other mineral and mining industries, the copper market was plagued by overcapacity and falling prices in the 1980s. As a result, companies began merging to try to improve efficiency and gain some protection from the fluctuations of the market. This continued in the early 1990s, as buyouts and consolidation led to a leaner field. Mining companies were previously tied to large, multiproduct wire and cable mills, but in the mid-1990s, they spun off their fabricators to try to become more efficient. Some refining companies, however, added continuous cast wire rod mills to the end of their production process, thereby effectively opening their own millworks.

According to an article in the trade magazine *Copper Talk,* shipments of strip, sheet, and plate declined in the 1980s, but demand for copper products increased slightly. Shipments to the electrical and electronic products markets grew to represent 36 percent of shipments; this was an increase of 12 percent from two years earlier, according to Copper and Brass Development Association statistics. The percentage of copper mill products that were consumed by the building construction industry was more than 40 percent in 1991. Electrical and electronic products industries received 24 percent, and the industrial machinery industry accounted for 13 percent.

In 1996 the copper industry was shaken again—this time by a trading scandal at Sumitomo Corp. Yasuo Hamanaka, Sumitomo's chief copper trader, was exposed as a heavy speculator in copper futures. His unauthorized dealings cost the company more than $1.8 billion and sent the price of copper plummeting. By mid-June 1996, copper prices had fallen 64 percent to 79 cents per pound; they rebounded in the fall to 91 cents per pound. The price for raw copper remained unsettled as traders feared that Sumitomo had such huge quantities of the metal that, if it were sold, prices would be depressed even more. By 1997, copper prices stabilized, and demand became steady. A 1997 strike at Chile's Escondida copper mine, the world's largest, made copper prices rise as inventories fell. Stockpiles at the London Metal Exchange were low, falling in a year by more than 50 percent to 149,100 metric tons.

CURRENT CONDITIONS

In 1997, the value of refined copper shipments was more than $7.6 billion. That year, wire rod mills, brass mills, ingot makers, powder plants, and other industries in the copper fabrication sector consumed more that four million short tons of copper. Wire rod mills—the largest segment of the industry—consumed approximately 2.3 million short tons of refined copper and 28,000 short tons of scrap copper. As *Trends in the Use of Copper Wire & Cable in the USA* noted, "Nearly all newly mined copper . . . goes into the production of wire rod, and thence to wire and cable products." Brass mills consumed a total of 1.9 million short tons of copper, alloy, and ingot, while powder plants used more than 19,000 short tons and other industries a total in excess of 95,000 short tons. (Copper foundries consumed 185,000 short tons.)

The building/construction industry—including building wiring, plumbing and heating, and air-conditioning and commercial refrigeration—was the most sizable end-market for fabricated copper products, accounting for 41.4 percent of the 1998 market. Electrical and electronics products, such as power utilities, telecommunications systems, business electronics, and lighting and wiring devices, absorbed 26.0 percent of fabricated copper in 1998. The third largest consumer of fabricated copper was the transportation industry, which accounted for 12.4 percent, incorporating copper parts into cars, trucks, buses, railroads, ships, and aircraft. Industrial machinery and equipment—such as in-plant equipment, industrial valves and fittings, non-electrical instruments, off-highway vehicles, and heat exchangers—represented 11.2 percent of the 1998 market. Consumer and general products, mainly appliances and electronics, used 9.0 percent of fabricated copper produced in the United States in 1998.

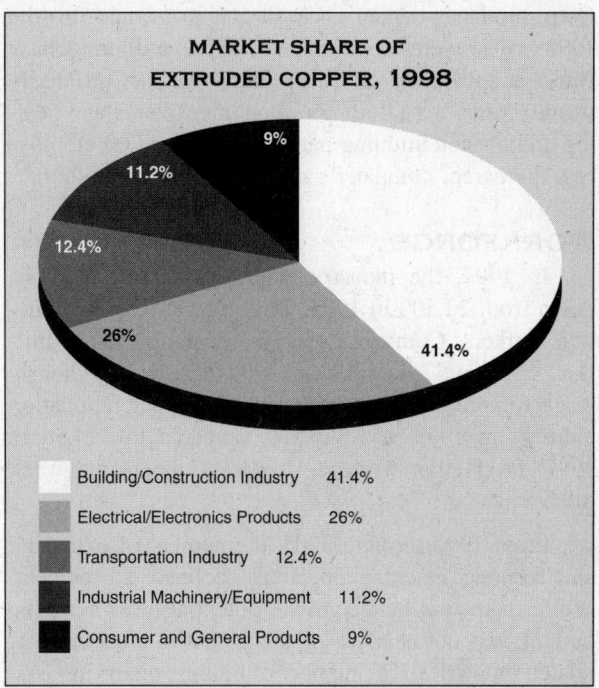

MARKET SHARE OF EXTRUDED COPPER, 1998

- Building/Construction Industry 41.4%
- Electrical/Electronics Products 26%
- Transportation Industry 12.4%
- Industrial Machinery/Equipment 11.2%
- Consumer and General Products 9%

Copper demand in the United States during the late 1990s was driven in large part by the booming economy, which fueled the industrial, commercial, and residential housing markets. As the most popular metal for building wire, copper benefited from the upturn in construction. Moreover, the demand for electrical services (which use copper wire as their primary conduits) continued to soar in the late 1990s as more appliances—especially computers—became commonplace in American homes. The auto industry also profited from the nation's good economy. As cars became increasingly reliant on electronic systems, copper played a more central role in this industry, as well. While no slowing in these sectors was predicted, copper was losing ground in telecommunications, where fiber-optic cables began supplanting copper wire.

INDUSTRY LEADERS

Major companies engaged in copper rolling, drawing, and extrusion processes include Marmon Group, Inc., a conglomerate of more than 100 autonomous manufacturing and service companies, that racked up more than $6 billion in sales in 1998 and employed 35,000 people. Marmon's primary copper subsidiary is Hendrix Wire and Cable Inc. Mueller Industries Inc., a manufacturer and distributor of copper tubing and related fittings, reported 1998 sales exceeding $929 million. As one of the leading U.S. manufacturers of copper and copper alloy tube for commercial products, Wolverine Tube Inc. manufactured fabricated copper for residential air-conditioning units, heat exchangers, and utilities. With 3,316 employees, Wolverine Tube's 1998 sales were $617.5 million. Through its Olin Brass subsidiary, Olin

Corp. produces copper alloy sheets, strips, and foil. Its 1998 sales were approximately $1.4 million. Chase Brass, a subsidiary of Chase Industries Inc., primarily manufactures brass rods for plumbing fixtures and heating and air-conditioning parts. With about 700 employees, the parent company's sales topped $433 million.

WORKFORCE

In 1997, the industry employed 21,110 workers, down from 22,500 in 1995. There were 16,580 production workers. Compensation was reported at $785 million, up from $711 million in 1995. The average hourly wage for production workers in the copper fabrication industry in 1998 was $15.53, compared to $14.56 in 1995. Production workers worked 42 hours per week on average.

From 1990 through 2005, the number of extruding and forming machine operators declined 1.1 percent. While there was better growth potential elsewhere, the outlook was not nearly as bleak as that in other copper-related industries. The number of mining, quarrying, and tunneling occupations, for instance, was expected by some observers to fall by almost 20 percent, while the number of foundry mold assembly and shakeout workers was expected to fall more than 20 percent.

AMERICA AND THE WORLD

According to the *Asian Wall Street Journal,* the U.S. copper industry was "pinning its hopes for future growth on an expected strong demand for the metal from the emerging economies of China and Central Europe". Copper demand rose as developing nations built infrastructures with telecommunications cables, power cables, and other basic building tools. Besides China, Taiwan, and South Korea offered potentially large markets. Total wire mill product exports in 1997 were 446 million pounds, a substantial gain since 1993 when 274.5 million pounds were exported. Bare copper wire, insulated wire and cable, cooper strip, sheet, plate, and foil products also were being exported. Total fabricated copper exports in 1997 exceeded 766 million pounds, compared to 471 million pounds of exports reported in 1993.

U.S. fabricating industries closely watched their international competitors so they would not dump products below market costs into the country; overcapacity quickly leads to price declines. Imports occupied a sizable role in the U.S. market. In 1997, 320.5 million pounds of wire mill products were imported, up from 147.5 million pounds in 1993. Brass mill imports accounted for an additional 587 million pounds of imports, and total fabricated copper imports in 1997 exceeded 912 million pounds.

The United States formed an International Copper Study Group in the early 1990s along with 17 other countries in the copper industry, including Germany, China, Chile, Peru, and France. They aimed to allow informational exchanges between producing and consuming countries, and to increase copper production and consumption.

RESEARCH AND TECHNOLOGY

Patricia Foley, a copper executive writing in the trade magazine *Copper Talk,* said, "In the late 1980s, most strip and sheet producers invested to serve the growing electronic markets. They installed automatic gauge control and statistical process control capabilities to enable them to produce strip with consistent and close tolerances." The emphasis on these new precise technologies was apparent in most of the companies involved in the rolling, drawing, and extruding of copper. For them to remain competitive in the market, their products had to meet a higher standard of excellence and precision. Companies improved their productivity and efficiency, which enabled the U.S. industry to increase production.

FURTHER READING

Black, William. "Trends in the Use of Copper Wire and Cable in the USA." New York: Copper Development Association, 1995. Available from http://www.marketdata.copper.org/trends-cable.html/.

"Copper Prices Rise a 5th Day As Chile Strike Slows Output." *New York Times,* 24 April 1997.

Einhorn, Cheryl Strauss. "Red Metal Rising." *Barron's,* 6 January 1997.

Hyde, Charles. *Copper for America: The United States Copper Industry from Colonial Times to the 1990s.* Tempe: University of Arizona Press, 1998.

Levinson, Marc. "The Mighty Copper King." *Newsweek,* 24 June 1996.

Penson, Stuart. "West Pins Copper Sector Growth on Emerging Nations' Demand." *Asian Wall Street Journal,* 21 May 1997.

"Short Term Copper Price Looks Sour." *Metals Week,* 18 October 1998.

U.S. Census Bureau. "Copper Rolling, Drawing, and Extruding," October 1999. Available from http://www.census.gov.

"U.S. Copper Industry Continues Record Growth." *PR Newswire,* 15 October 1999.

SIC 3353

ALUMINUM SHEET, PLATE, AND FOIL

This classification covers establishments primarily engaged in flat rolling aluminum and aluminum-alloy basic shapes, such as sheet, plate, and foil, including establishments producing welded tube. Also included are establishments primarily producing similar products by continuous casting.

NAICS CODE(S)

331315 (Aluminum Sheet, Plate, and Foil Manufacturing)

INDUSTRY SNAPSHOT

"The aluminum sheet market is like a box of chocolates: you never know what you're gonna get." With due credit to Forrest Gump, David Hamill of *American Metal Market* aptly described the volatility of this sector in the mid-1990s. In the 1993-96 period alone, the market bottomed out, peaked, and drew back once more. While the gyrations made life interesting for speculators, they were anathema to users who sought stable, predictable pricing. By the late 1990s, the industry had begun to consolidate considerably—most notably with the merger of giants Alcoa and Reynolds. Industry shipments totaled $13.8 billion in 1997.

Over the past several decades, aluminum makers have been successful in developing new products and taking market share from competitors like steel. Much of the industry's gains could be traced to the intrinsic qualities of the metal—aluminum is strong, lightweight, and eminently recyclable, all qualities that were still highly prized in the 1990s. Skilled management and smart marketing, however, had also been significant factors in the industry's advance. Thus it had come to dominate the beverage can market and had established an increasing presence in automobile manufacturing.

While the industry had done an excellent job in spurring demand, the volatility in aluminum markets was causing more than a few users to have second thoughts about the metal. In the important automotive market—and even in cans—some executives were taking another look at steel. Nevertheless, producers remained optimistic that aluminum's physical traits would make it the metal of choice in a growing variety of applications.

Aluminum sheet, plate, and foil represent the aluminum industry's major product group and accounts for the majority of shipments from aluminum producers. Aluminum is first produced in the form of sheet ingot. These ingots, which may weigh as much as 20 tons, are flat-rolled and rerolled until the desired thickness, or gauge, is achieved. The gauge determines what product has been produced: plate is a quarter-inch thick or more; sheet is .006 inch to .249 inch; and foil is less than .006 inch. Sheet is by far the most widely used form of aluminum and is found in all of the industry's major markets, including containers and packaging (most notably beverage cans) and transportation (i.e. panels for automobile bodies). Plate is used for the skins of jetliners and to make

storage tanks, among other heavy-duty applications. Foil is used, of course, to wrap the Thanksgiving turkey, but is also utilized in building insulation and electrical capacitors, as well as a wide variety of packaging applications.

ORGANIZATION AND STRUCTURE

Vertical integration in the aluminum industry is extensive—it goes well beyond the mining, refining, and smelting of primary aluminum (including sheet ingot, casting ingot, and extrusion billet) to the production of semifabricated and fabricated products downstream, including sheet, plate, and foil offerings. Alcoa, formerly the Aluminum Company of America, has dominated the industry; its scheduled May 2000 merger with other industry leader Reynolds Metals, coupled with the restructuring of the former Tenneco, Inc., will give it a huge presence in the industry. Canadian manufacturer Alcan, however, has launched something of a challenge with planned mergers of its own.

BACKGROUND AND DEVELOPMENT

The aluminum industry is relatively young. The first major application, cast cooking utensils, did not appear until the 1890s. Following the turn of the century, however, prices fell, production rose, and applications grew. World War I greatly expanded use of the metal, as armies searched for lightweight, durable materials for military equipment. In the 1920s, high-strength alloys were developed that were used in the development of the commercial airline industry in the 1930s. During World War II aluminum output increased, primarily due to demand from warplane production and soldiers' rations packaging. While consumption dropped briefly right after the war, consumer demand soon picked up the slack. In the early 1950s The Korean War produced another surge in aluminum shipments. As consumer demand grew during the postwar prosperity, the range of applications increased accordingly. Use of aluminum building products in commercial and residential construction expanded, and aluminum foil became a staple of the American kitchen.

The advent of a strong environmental movement gave new prominence to the industry, since aluminum was particularly suited to recycling. To produce aluminum from recycled scrap requires only 5 percent of the energy that it takes to make it from scratch. Since the economics of recycling make so much sense, industry participants have supported the efforts of environmentalists in this area. Moreover, as governments pressure automakers to increase gas mileage of their vehicles and thus save energy, lightweight aluminum is gaining favor among manufacturers in a variety of applications.

Aluminum is a notoriously cyclical business, and after a very strong performance at the end of the 1980s, a few lean years might have been expected. The extent of the downturn, however, was an alarming one for industry participants and well beyond expectations. In the early 1990s the aluminum industry became one of the un-intended victims of the Cold War's aftermath. Russia no longer needed much aluminum for its defense sector, but it did hunger for export earnings. Before the fall of the Berlin Wall in 1989, Russia sent about 250,000 metric tons of aluminum overseas each year; by 1993 they were shipping aluminum at an annual rate of 1.2 million metric tons. As Clifford Gaddy, a Brookings Institution economist, told the *Wall Street Journal,* "We were used to a world in which one of the biggest commodity producers was the most stable and predictable—everything was planned five years ahead with the absolute minimum of surprise. Now it's switched to the exact opposite, where even their own government doesn't know what's happening."

In 1994, however, the industry staged a strong recovery on the back of an improved economy and tighter supply. Overall demand for aluminum sheet increased 11 percent; the transportation sector was particularly strong, with usage in passenger cars up 23 percent. Moreover, under the so-called Memorandum of Understanding, the aluminum-producing nations agreed to shut down 1.5 million to 2-million tons of overall capacity. Russia alone cut its production by 500,000 tons a year. As demand grew and supply was restricted, inventories fell, prices strengthened, and profits rose.

In late 1995 and 1996, however, market conditions again took a turn for the worse. Some industry observers traced the weakness to protracted "destocking" by aluminum consumers. Pricing for aluminum ingot on the London Metal Exchange—which has a strong effect on sheet and can stock prices—averaged 68 cents per pound in 1996 versus 82 cents per pound in 1995. According to statistics of the Aluminum Association, sheet, plate, and foil volume fell 4 percent in 1996 to 10.7 billion pounds. At that level, the three products accounted for 59 percent of the industry's total shipments. Demand for sheet fell 5 percent to 9.2 billion pounds; plate was down 16 percent to 0.3 billion pounds; and foil production rose 2 percent to 1.2 billion pounds. The lower level of shipments and weak pricing were reflected in the 1996 pretax profits of the six largest aluminum producers, which fell 36 percent. The industry began to turn around in the late 1990s, although employment figures continued to drop. Consolidation within the industry will probably lead to further restructuring.

CURRENT CONDITIONS

The three major markets for aluminum in North America are packaging, building and construction, and transportation. Building and construction in the United States, despite a building boom in the late 1990s, is a mature industry. And while shipments to the beverage industry had been the major factor driving new demand through the early 1990s, in mid-decade they had begun to stagnate. Thus the industry looked to the transportation sector for new markets and continued growth.

Transportation. In the 1990s the aluminum industry invested substantial resources in both research and development and marketing to displace steel as the metal of choice in automobiles, and by mid-decade it had made significant progress toward that goal. According to the Aluminum Association, in 1998 aluminum shipments to North American carmakers was 7.16 billion pounds, accounting for 31 percent of the total market. To provide some perspective, automakers used 2.9 billion pounds of aluminum in 1994, up 386 million pounds from the level of a year earlier. Sheet aluminum accounted for the greatest volume.

The potential for increased aluminum content is substantial. According to one estimate, only 5.8 percent of the typical family vehicle in 1995 consisted of aluminum, versus 67.5 percent for steel and 7.7 percent for plastic. In 1996 the average car had about 247 pounds of aluminum. Estimates of the proportion of aluminum content in passenger vehicles by the end of 2000 vary, but some observers put the figure at 350 to 400 pounds. The large producers are optimistic that aluminum usage in cars will increase steadily.

In the automotive market, as in others, aluminum's advantages are its recyclability (at a time when governments and environmentalists are aiming for a totally recyclable car) and, especially, its light weight (which improves fuel economy). While aluminum is only 35 percent as dense as steel (its specific gravity is 2.7 versus 7.8 for steel), it can be nearly as strong, depending on car assembly methods. The development of higher-strength alloys has increased the attractiveness of aluminum in recent years. Some observers believe that the Japanese auto industry has a particular interest in incorporating aluminum into vehicles because of the high price of gasoline in Japan and the high proportion of imported raw materials. Others believe that the electric car is the most promising market for aluminum, because such automobiles must be light to compensate for the presence of heavy batteries.

One drawback of aluminum, however, is the relatively high cost, which has led some observers to believe that "all-aluminum" cars will continue to be restricted to luxury models. In 1996 there were only two such BIW (body-in-white) aluminum cars: the Honda Acura NSX and the Audi A8, and both were high-priced, low-volume sports cars. The Acura's aluminum BIW weighed 309 pounds, or 40 percent less than what a hypothetical steel model would have cost. But many observers believed that there would not be an affordable, all-aluminum, high-volume car for many years, owing to the more problematic assembly methods and the higher metalmaking cost. Aluminum requires more energy in spot welding and is less formable in stamping than steel.

Can Sheet Production. In 1963 almost none of the beverage cans were made from aluminum; 35 years later, all beverage cans were aluminum. Shipments of can sheet rose steadily throughout the 1980s and early 1990s, increasing from 2.9 billion bounds in 1982 to 4.3 billion pounds in 1992—24 percent of the aluminum industry's total shipments. Aluminum displaced both glass and bimetal cans partly because of its light weight and stackability. Moreover, in a period that saw rising ecological concern, aluminum's recyclability meant it was environmentally friendly. In 1998, 64 billion aluminum cans were recycled, according to the Aluminum Association.

But perhaps the main selling point for aluminum was its lower overall cost. In 1994, however, as supply contracted and prices rose, beverage makers had sticker shock. In December 1994, Coca-Cola announced that it would replace aluminum with steel in some of its European and Asian markets, and many beverage makers talked of switching to cheaper materials. By 1997, though, there were still no major changeovers. As Norm Nieder, group director of packaging at Anheuser-Busch told *Beverage World* in 1995, "Outside the United States, steel cans may offer a nice alternative, but they produce higher coating emissions than aluminum cans do. There's no way you could run a steel can plant in California today, for instance, that's for sure."

Anticipating still-higher can sheet prices in 1995, beverage makers stockpiled inventories—soft drink can shipments rose 10.4 percent in 1994—which hurt the market during the mid-1990s. A longer-term trend in the beverage industry has potential repercussions for aluminum producers. So-called New Age drinks have been increasing in popularity, and these have traditionally been sold in glass bottles. While the industry has tried to convert New Age bottlers to aluminum, in 1994 bottlers shied away from marketing their products in 24-ounce aluminum cans because of the high price. Meanwhile, in the beer segment, aluminum makers must contend with the growing popularity of products from microbreweries, which package their beer in bottles.

Moreover, for a variety of reasons, can makers are adopting smaller lid designs and are using thinner aluminum. As a consequence, manufacture of each can requires smaller amounts of aluminum than in past years. Thus, greater unit demand for cans does not necessarily translate into an equal rise in aluminum requirements. Additionally, there appears to be a trend toward the more economical large, plastic bottle as well. Producers had been hopeful that overseas beverage can markets, where aluminum's penetration has on average been much lower than in the United States, would pick up the slack. But with Coca-Cola and other producers shifting at least some of their packaging to steel, these expectations may be dashed.

Aerospace. The aluminum industry has aggressively penetrated the aerospace market; nearly all defense planes have an aluminum content of 70 to 90 percent. Demand for aluminum from the aerospace segment was strong during the 1980s, as both defense spending and commercial aircraft orders were buoyant. By the early 1990s, however, the aerospace segment was in decline. The airlines cancelled or delayed orders as their profits disappeared, and with the Cold War over the government cut outlays for the military. According to Aluminum Association statistics, annual shipments of both heat-treatable sheet and heat-treatable plate, which are primarily used in defense and aerospace applications, fell 23 percent and 19 percent, respectively, between 1989 and 1992.

In early 1994 some industry participants thought a bottoming out had been reached and that this industry niche would recover a bit. By 1996 the commercial jet aircraft market proved to be one of the few bright spots in an otherwise lackluster aluminum picture. Price hikes of 10 to 15 percent in some heat-treated and heat-plated products were announced at the end of the year by Alcoa, Reynolds, and Ravenswood Aluminum.

The aluminum producers continued to maintain a dominant role in the aircraft market despite the attempts of other materials makers to steal share. In the 1980s proponents of nonmetallic advanced composites claimed that by the second half of the 1990s they would account for up to 80 percent of commercial airframe weight. In 1994, those predictions appeared overblown. Aluminum in the newest commercial transport, the Boeing 777, accounted for about 65 percent of total weight, down from previous generations of airliners but nowhere near the 20-25 percent level that some pessimistic observers had forecast. The composites have made the most headway in the plane's tail, which in the 777 represents a loss of about 25,000 pounds of aluminum products.

Meanwhile, the industry continues to work on new alloys and new processes. Despite cutbacks in its budget, the Pentagon remains committed to maintaining its technological edge, which encourages aluminum companies to make new investments in research and development to service the military's needs.

INDUSTRY LEADERS

The largest aluminum producer in the world is Alcoa (Aluminum Co. of America). Indeed, in the early part of the century it was the only aluminum producer of conse-

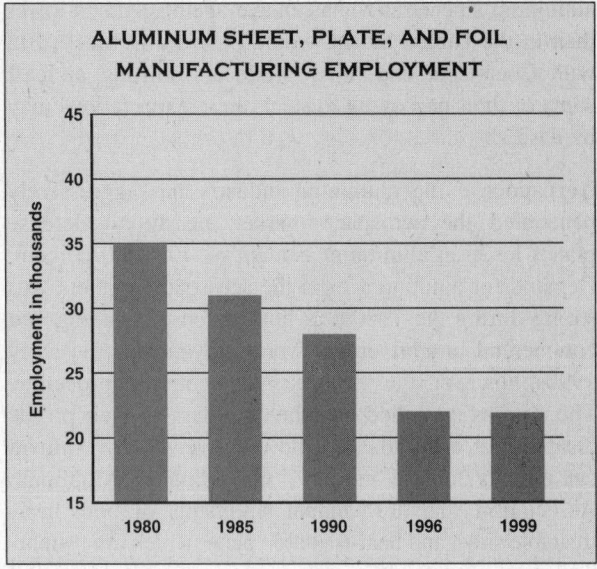

ALUMINUM SHEET, PLATE, AND FOIL MANUFACTURING EMPLOYMENT

quence in North America. In 1928 it spun off its foreign operations into Alcan, the large Canadian producer, as it continued to dominate the U.S. market. In 1950 Alcoa's domestic monopoly—which had already been somewhat diluted by the federal government's efforts to create competitors during and following World War II—came to an end as the courts dismantled the company.

In the early 1960s the reconfigured company began to produce more semifabricated and fabricated products as it expanded output of can stock and products for the aerospace industry. In the late 1980s, after the acceptance of diversification earlier in the decade, the company refocused on its aluminum business. Alcoa stresses the importance of safety in its operations, and in the early 1990s had the best safety record of the major producers. In 1996, Alcoa's sales rose 5 percent to $13.1 billion; net profit fell 35 percent to $514 million, primarily due to lower prices for aluminum products. By 1999 sales were at $16.3 billion and income at $1.05 billion.

Consolidation seems to be the name of the game in the aluminum industry, and Alcoa is leading the way. In the summer of 1998 Alcoa merged with Alumax, another key player in the industry, purchasing some 27.5 million Alumax shares at $50/share. Alumax, which derived about 30 percent of its income from the construction market, had itself acquired extruded aluminum manufacturer Cressona in 1996. A year after the Alumax deal, Alcoa announced plans to acquire the venerable Reynolds Metals Company. This deal, set for completion in May 1999, came in the form of an all-stock bid valued at $4.3 billion dollars. Reynolds Metals Co. has been a leader in developing new aluminum products, from baseball bats to grain bins. It introduced the aluminum beverage can in 1963, when steelmakers had a lock on that market. Reynolds' two-piece can took about one-fifth the

time to make and used 40 percent less metal than the three-piece can of its steel rivals, which it quickly displaced. In 1968, the company pioneered the huge can recycling program that gave makers a cheap source of aluminum and was cheered by environmentalists.

Reynolds had the wisdom to stick with its famous aluminum foil when it was a money-loser. It has built on the popularity of its foil by expanding into plastic and paper household packaging products. On the other hand, in the mid-1990s the company was criticized for investing in too many businesses and losing its strategic focus; it was also accused of having a high cost structure. Sales of $3.5 billion in 1996 yielded net income of $89 million, sharply below earnings of $389 million in 1995. In 1999, sales were $7.8 billion and revenues were $124 million.

Meanwhile, Montreal-based Alcan, with 1999 sales of $7.5 billion, is planning to acquire two companies, the French manufacturer Pechiney and the Swiss manufacturer Alusuisse Lonza. Alcan will still be smaller than Alcoa, but it will be a formidable presence nonetheless.

WORKFORCE

The manufacturing work force of the major aluminum companies is heavily unionized. The industry's two major unions are the United Steelworkers and the Aluminum, Brick, and Glass Workers. New long-term labor agreements covering unionized workers were ratified in mid-1996. The agreements set broad, new goals for employee safety, job security, influence, control, and accountability for the work environment. Some observers, however, thought labor peace had come at a considerable price. Analyst John C. Tumazos, aluminum analyst at Donaldson, Lufkin & Jenrette, told *American Metal Market* that they were "more expensive than the national inflation rates and our own expectations." Not surprisingly, given the labor agreements and the consolidation, the number of workers in the aluminum industry has been slowly decreasing, except for a small blip in the mid-1990s. In 1983 there were 28,100 workers; by 1999 the figure was down to 21,900. The industry's 70 establishments in 1997 employed 19,400 production workers, who were paid an average hourly wage of $20.09.

AMERICA AND THE WORLD

Historically, the U.S. aluminum industry has been adept at expanding overseas and capitalizing on its foreign assets. Indeed, the aluminum industry has a greater presence abroad than many other U.S. industries. Some 50 percent of Alcoa's sales is derived from overseas sources; for Reynolds, the figure is 23 percent.

Russia. In the early 1990s international developments were the source of the industry's major problems. While shipments in the U.S. in 1992 were healthy as the economy pulled out of recession, conditions in Europe and

Japan remained depressed; meanwhile, Russia was rapidly increasing its aluminum exports. Since 1978 the price of aluminum ingot (which is eventually reflected in sheet, plate, and foil quotes) has been set on the London Metal Exchange (LME): it fell from above a peak of $1.65 in 1988 to $.50 in late 1993. With the international supply/demand equation unbalanced, producers worldwide were suffering. As Lloyd T. O'Connell, Reynolds Metals' chief economist, told the *Wall Street Journal:* "If the demand is weak abroad, it's almost as bad as if demand is weak domestically. The LME doesn't care where the metal is."

Thus, in 1994, the industry signed a two-year Memorandum of Understanding to limit worldwide supply; it reduced overall capacity by 1.5 million to 2 million tons, and Russian capacity alone by 500,000 tons. With the expiration of the agreement in 1996, some analysts predicted that Russian product would eventually be needed for rising demand from both industrialized and developing countries. Initially, however, Russian aluminum exports to the United States fell sharply, declining to 8,800 tons for the first ten months of 1996 compared with 112,500 tons for the same period in 1995. The sharp drop reflected the quality problems some users had encountered in even the most basic sheet alloys.

Japan. In recent years, U.S. producers have strengthened ties with Japanese aluminum and steel companies. In September 1990, Alcoa and Kobe Steel announced a strategic alliance to exploit worldwide opportunities in aluminum that resulted in four joint ventures in the United States and Japan. The agreement was particularly noteworthy because the steelmaker has strong relationships with the automobile industry.

Mexico. With the passage of the North American Free Trade Agreement (NAFTA), trade between the United States and Mexico in aluminum has received increased attention. The role of Mexican aluminum manufacturers in the U.S. auto industry was expected to grow significantly between 1997 and the year 2000. Such companies as Nemak SA of the Alfa Industrial Group should be a major source for aluminum castings, particularly in power train applications. The increase in trade wasn't expected to be in just one direction: Mexico's imports of secondary aluminum rose to 20,000 tons in 1996, owing to increased auto production following the passage of NAFTA.

RESEARCH AND TECHNOLOGY

The enormous strides that aluminum has made in displacing steel and other materials in the container/packaging, automotive, aerospace, and construction markets demonstrates the substantial investment it has made in research and development. This effort has been instrumental in developing a wide range of new aluminum products including beverage cans, baseball bats, grain bins, roofing, windows, appliance parts, and truck trailers; it has also yielded stronger, lighter, cheaper alloys, and improved production processes. A comment of David Moison, a consultant at Resource Strategies, to the *Wall Street Journal* is telling: "People in aluminum don't have the belief somebody's going to use it just because they make it. They've had to fight like hell to convert people to aluminum."

Producers have also made remarkable strides in improving productivity, which has advanced from 15 manhours per ton in the 1960s to 6 man-hours per ton in the early 1990s. Since aluminum by weight costs six times as much as steel and is so energy-intensive, the industry has had to strive constantly to reduce its costs to remain competitive. In 1994 Alcoa received grants totaling $33 million from the Department of Energy to develop more efficient methods for producing both alumina and aluminum sheet.

FURTHER READING

Alcoa, Inc. Available from http://www.alcoa.com.

Aluminum Association, Washington, DC. Available from http://www.aluminum.org.

Ambrosia, John. "Aluminum Tries to Recycle its Past Success." *Iron Age,* June 1992.

Boselovic, Len. "Alcoa accepts month delay in Reynolds merger," 21 March 2000. Available from http://www.hoovers.com.

Hamill, David. "U.S. Aluminum Sheet Market Is Like a Box of Chocolates." *American Metal Market,* 12 July 1995.

Petry, Corinna. "Aluminum Producers Optimistic About Future Markets." *American Metal Market,* 15 November 1996.

Pieters, Nancy. "Increasing Production and Mixed Signals." *New Steel,* May 1996.

Red, Brendan. "Steel vs. Aluminum in Detroit." *New Steel,* October 1995.

Regan, Bob. "Alcoa Lands Energy Research Pact." *American Metal Market,* 12 May 1994.

———. "Aluminum Softness Takes Financial Toll." *American Metal Market,* 17 February 1997.

———. "Aluminum Wage Pacts May Prove Expensive." *American Metal Market,* 5 June 1996.

———. "Russia's Aluminum Products Seen Losing Popularity in US." *American Metal Market,* 9 May 1996.

———. "Subdued Aluminum Market Creeps Ahead Cautiously." *American Metal Market,* 25 February 1997.

Sfiligoj, Eric. "At What Price?" *Beverage World,* June 1995.

Smosarski, Greg. "Steel Cans Rank as Tops in Europe Metals Race." *American Metal Market,* 25 March 1996.

Stuckey, John A. *Vertical Integration and Joint Ventures in the Aluminum Industry,* Cambridge, MA: Harvard University Press, 1983.

"Transportation Market Becomes Large Market for Aluminum Industry." *American Metal Market,* 20 October 1995.

U.S. Census Bureau. *Survey of Manufacturers,* 10 February 2000. Available from http://www.census.gov/prod/www/abs/97ecmani.html.

Wrigley, Al. "Mexico's Aluminum Market Casting Bigger Net." *American Metal Market,* 25 February 1997.

ALUMINUM EXTRUDED PRODUCTS

This classification covers establishments primarily engaged in extruding aluminum and aluminum-based alloy basic shapes, such as rod and bar, pipe and tube, and tube blooms, including establishments producing tube by drawing.

NAICS CODE(S)

331316 (Aluminum Extruded Product Manufacturing)

INDUSTRY SNAPSHOT

The process of extruding aluminum has been compared to squeezing toothpaste from a tube, with the metal (initially in the form of extrusion billet) taking the shape of the die through which it has been pressed. While commercially pure aluminum is used in some extrusion applications, more often the aluminum is mixed with other metals—particularly magnesium and silicon—to form alloys. Aluminum extrusions are used to make windows, doors, and gates; as components in cars, trucks, and jet aircraft; in the manufacture of major appliances, furniture, and electrical equipment; and in a host of other applications, ranging from cranes to athletic goods.

The aluminum extrusion industry exhibited strong growth during the late-1990s. In 1998, U.S. aluminum industry shipments of extruded aluminum shapes and tubes increased 15.2 million pounds to reach nearly 4.06 billion pounds. The construction industry is the largest consumer of extruded aluminum products. However, in 1998 and 1999, the aluminum extrusion industry made substantial gains in the automotive sector—which offers the greatest potential for the industry's expansion. Extruded aluminum is classified in one of three key markets by the Aluminum Association—the shapes market, pipe and tube, and extruded rod and bar.

ORGANIZATION AND STRUCTURE

To some extent, the extrusion segment may be divided between the commodity-like output of large producers, which may be said to be sold by the pound, and specialty production of smaller makers, sold by the part.

As in other industries, extruders have their areas of specialization. Some work primarily in certain alloy series, while others specialize in close tolerances, miniature shapes, or extremely large shapes.

The aluminum extrusion industry consolidated substantially during the 1980s and 1990s. Between the mid-1980s and mid-1990s, about 40 aluminum extruders went out of business, and a number of independent aluminum extruders were swallowed up by the biggest players. According to the U.S. Census Bureau, 160 companies were involved in the aluminum extruding business in 1997. Of this total number, 151 had 20 or more employees. California, Ohio, and Indiana were home to the greatest number of aluminum extruders.

The trend toward consolidation was furthered in 1996, when Alumax Inc. bought the largest privately owned extruder, Cressona Aluminum. Two years later, Alcoa Inc. acquired Alumax for $3.8 billion. In early 1997, Reynolds Metals announced that it would sell its aluminum extrusion plant in El Campo, Texas, to Tredegar Industries, which had highly profitable extruding operations. In 1999, Alcoa made a $4.4 billion hostile bid for Reynolds. Finally, in July of 1999, Easco Inc. (the largest American independent aluminum extruder after Cressona was subsumed) was purchased by Caradon Inc., the U.S. division of Great Britain's Caradon PLC.

BACKGROUND AND DEVELOPMENT

The first aluminum extrusion press in North America was opened by Alcoa in New Kensington, Pennsylvania, in 1904. During the 1930s large strides were made in the extrusion process, permitting the formation of virtually any type of aluminum cross section for a wide variety of applications. During World War II, the use of aluminum in aerospace applications grew rapidly, as the strength of Allied air forces was key to the war effort. In the postwar period, extruders continued to expand, benefitting from the growth in the residential housing sector.

The extrusion segment has been subject to the same price volatility shown by other sectors of the aluminum industry. Moreover, the extruded aluminum products industry rides on the fortunes of its primary consumers—the construction and transportation sectors. The recession of the early 1990s, which affected the automobile and housing market, also damaged the extrusion industry. Total extruded products dropped from 3.07 billion pounds in 1988 to 2.5 billion pounds in 1991 and 2.86 billion pounds in 1992. Shipments rose steadily from 3.09 billion pounds in 1993 to 3.93 billion pounds in 1997.

CURRENT CONDITIONS

The extruded aluminum products industry was strong in the late-1990s. Buoyed by the American economic boom that drove car sales, new home and building construction, as well as infrastructure construction, extruded aluminum's future prospects looked bright.

Automotive. The automobile sector presents the greatest opportunity for the aluminum extrusion industry. Aluminum products of all types (both castings and extrusions) have become increasingly essential to automotive manufacturers. Since aluminum is lighter than steel, iron, and copper and is easily recyclable, the metal fits well with a strategy of reducing energy consumption. In 1991, the average American car had 182 pounds of aluminum; by 1999, aluminum content had risen to 248 pounds.

Although aluminum castings are typically used much more frequently in the automotive industry than extruded products, extruded products have begun to play an essential role in the sector. In 1999, 7.5 percent of all automotive aluminum was in the form of extrusions. Shipments of extrusions for use in passenger cars, trucks, and buses rose from 865 million pounds in 1994 to 1.17 billion pounds in 1998. In February of 1999, General Motors announced that it would use extruded aluminum in its bumper beams for all its Buick, Oldsmobile, and Pontiac cars. With each bumper weighing about 26 pounds, GM estimated that it would incorporate an additional 8.3 billion pounds of extruded aluminum each year, according to *American Metal Market.* Moreover, GM also utilized aluminum extrusion alloys to make engine cradles in two Chevrolet car lines, as well as radiator enclosures in Chevrolet, GMC, and Cadillac light trucks.

One application that particularly excites producers is the spaceframe, where aluminum extrusions are used to make the skeletal system of the car's structure. Rather than spot welding as many as 300 stamped steel components, less than 100 aluminum extrusions and interconnecting die-cast nodes are robotically welded to form the spaceframe. The spaceframe offers a weight saving of about 35 percent over steel bodies. In 1993, Alcoa began operating a plant in Soest, Germany, to supply aluminum spaceframes to Audi AG. In 1994, Audi began selling its A8 luxury sedan in Europe—the first car to utilize a complete aluminum spaceframe body structure.

Building and Construction. The use of aluminum extruded products in the building and construction sector has remained relatively flat since 1988. The market sagged in the recession of the early 1990s, but recovered to earlier levels in 1998. That year, 1.41 billion pounds of extruded aluminum products were used in building and construction. The shapes market and the pipe and tube market were particularly important to the building and construction industry. In 1998, 1.4 billion pounds of shapes were employed in building and construction, as well as an additional 400 million pounds of pipe and tube.

In an effort to boost demand, some extruders began providing customers with an increasing number of value-

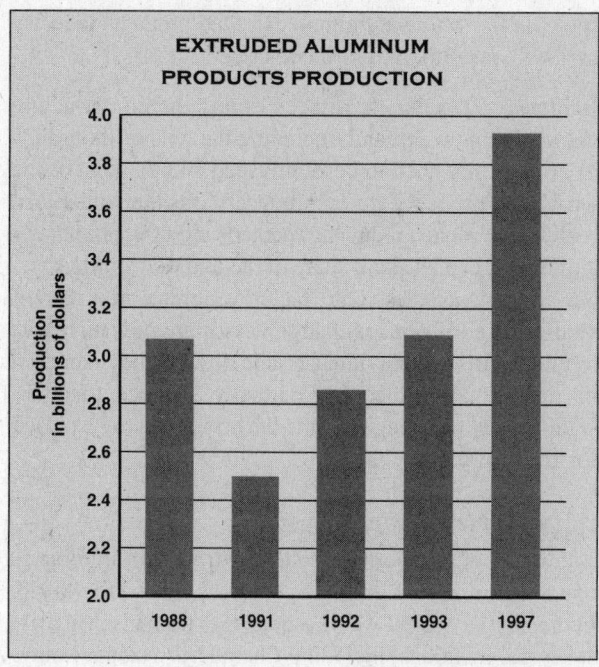

added services downstream. By offering a variety of machines for extra processing, extruders helped their customers get new products to market more quickly and saved them the costs of investing in the equipment themselves. This also reduced questions of accountability for poor quality, since the customer didn't have to send the parts on to a fabricator or finisher before using them. While some observers note that providing additional services hasn't always resulted in increased profitability, they add that it has helped in developing customer loyalty.

Aircraft. The market for aircraft aluminum extrusions was depressed during the early 1990s because of the decline in U.S. military spending and a drop in orders for commercial airplanes. The segment underwent a shakeup in 1992 as one of the largest makers of small press aerospace alloy shapes, International Light Metals, went out of business; the company had at one time accounted for as much as 35 percent of aircraft extrusions of less than 5-inch circle size. The two major surviving producers were Alcoa, the largest maker, and Universal Alloy, owned by Swiss parent, AG Menziken. In a bid to find a niche between industry giant Alcoa and the distributors (who have traditionally accounted for most shipments to end users), Universal Alloy decided to sell the bulk of its shapes directly to end-users or their contractors. In early 1996, however, the aviation market appeared to have recovered. In 1995, Universal Alloy sold 10 million to 15 million pounds of light shapes, its largest market, compared with about half that in 1993.

Despite the positive outlook, however, the use of extruded aluminum products in aircraft slumped in 1998. According to *American Metal Market,* "the only weak spot'' in the whole aluminum extruded products industry in 1998 was ''the aircraft/aerospace sector.''

Bridges. Extruders have been eyeing the infrastructure market for new demand, including the tens of thousands of bridges that need to be refurbished. While most of the work will probably go to producers of other materials, with each repair requiring perhaps 50,000 pounds of aluminum, even a small share of the market would generate significant sales. One factor weighing in favor of aluminum extrusions is that processes are now available to tailor parts to individual bridge design; they can then be quickly assembled and virtually snapped together, significantly reducing the time the bridge has to be closed for reconstruction.

INDUSTRY LEADERS

Alcoa is the world's leading extruder of aluminum, operating numerous extrusion facilities around the world. In the United States, Alcoa produces extrusions primarily at several locations, including Chandler, Arizona; Lafayette, Indiana; Baltimore, Maryland; Tifton, Georgia; and Delhi, Louisiana. With the 1998 sales of over $15 billion, Alcoa employed over 103,000 workers. It has been a primary force in the massive consolidation of the aluminum extrusion sector. In 1998, Alcoa acquired Alumax, and handily increased its extrusion capacity with the transaction. A mere two years earlier Alumax had acquired Cressona Aluminum, which was as the time the largest independent extruder in the United States. Alcoa's growth spurt continued. In 1999, Alcoa made a bid to take over Reynolds Metals, its largest competitor in the United States.

WORKFORCE

The manufacturing facilities of the major producers are heavily unionized; the two major unions are the Aluminum, Brick, and Glass Workers and the United Steelworkers. Contract talks between these unions and the major producer have a significant influence on pay rates throughout the industry.

Workers in the extruded aluminum products industry numbered 30,357 in 1997, of which 24,556 were directly involved in production. These production employees worked an average of 41 hours per week, and earned an average wage of $12.53 per hour. With the greatest number of aluminum extrusion employees, Indiana was home to some 2,720 workers in 1997, followed by California with 2,351, and Florida with 1,820.

FURTHER READING

Courter, Eileen. ''Despite Gains, Extrusion Market's Still a Dogfight.'' *American Metal Market,* 4 September 1996.

Ducker Research Company. ''Report on Aluminum Content in 1999 North American Passenger Cars and Light Trucks: Executive Summary,'' 28 December 1999. Available from http://www.aec.org/ducker_report.htm.

————. ''Extrusions on the Rise.'' *American Metal Market,* 27 September 1995.

Haflich, Frederick. ''Aluminum Extruder Sees Light; Firming Aircraft Market Prompts Expansion.'' *American Metal Market,* 8 February 1996.

Owen, Jim. ''Flat '96 Not Necessarily Bad News for Extruders.'' *American Metal Market,* 12 January 1996.

Pinkham, Myra. ''New Auto Applications Drive Extrusion Demand.'' *American Metal Market,* 25 February 1997.

Regan, Bob. ''Aluminum Extrusions Register 'Good Year'.'' *American Metal Market,* 2 July 1999.

''Reynolds's Metals to Sell Aluminum Extrusion Plant to Tredegar Industries.'' *PR Newswire,* 7 March 1997.

Schroeder, Manfred. ''Extruders Press for Further Shipment Gains.'' *American Metal Market,* 12 July 1995.

U.S. Census Bureau. ''Aluminum Extruded Products Manufacturing,'' 23 October 1999. Available from http://www.census.gov/prod/ec97/97m3314c.pdf.

Wrigley, Al. ''GM in Big Aluminum Switch.'' *American Metal Market,* 5 February 1999.

SIC 3355

ALUMINUM ROLLING AND DRAWING, NOT ELSEWHERE CLASSIFIED

This classification refers to establishments primarily engaged in rolling, drawing, and other operations resulting in the production of aluminum ingot including extrusion ingot, and aluminum and aluminum-base alloy basic shapes, not elsewhere classified, such as rolled and continuous cast rod and bar. Establishments primarily engaged in producing aluminum powder, flake, and paste are classified in **SIC 3399: Primary Metal Products, Not Elsewhere Classified,** and those producing aluminum wire and cable from purchased wire bars, rods, or wire are classified in **SIC 3357: Drawing and Insulating of Nonferrous Wire.**

NAICS CODE(S)

331319 (Other Aluminum Rolling and Drawing)

Overall, the domestic aluminum industry struggled in 1998 with shipments increasing only 1.1 percent. According to the Aluminum Association, industry sales volume decreased by almost 4 percent through September 1998 as compared to the same period in 1997, with most of this loss resulting from a weak flat-rolled sector. Aluminum extrusion sales volume increased 5 percent by mid-1998, however, prompting a three cents per pound price hike in mid-August. Shipments of extruded shapes and tube also rose 3.1 percent over the first 7 months of 1998, amounting to 934,228 tons.

According to the U.S. Census Bureau's *1997 Economic Census—Manufacturing,* 19 establishments operated in this category for part or all of 1997. Industry-wide employment totaled 2,580 workers receiving a combined payroll of more than $96 million. Of these employees, 2,024 worked in production, putting in more than 4 million hours to earn wages of more than $69 million. Overall shipments for the industry were valued at almost $1.3 billion.

Aluminum rod, bar, and wire products are often grouped together in a single product category. Wire is made from rod or bar, and by definition is less than three-eighths of an inch in diameter, while rod and bar are generally thicker. Electrical transmission lines represent the major end-use of rod/bar/wire products, but they are also used to make rivets, nails, screws, and bolts, and parts of machinery and equipment.

Houston-based MAXXAM Inc. led the industry in overall sales, with 1998 revenues reaching almost $2.6 billion. The Essex Group Inc. of Fort Wayne, Indiana, followed with 1998 sales of over $1.8 billion. Houston-based Quanex Corp. rounded out the top three industry leaders with sales of almost $798 million for the fiscal year ending October 31, 1998. Other industry leaders included Reynolds Metals Co. Metals Div. of Richmond, Virginia; Alcoa Building Products of Sidney, Ohio; and AFC Cable Systems Inc. of Providence, Rhode Island.

Rod, bar, and wire production slumped during the late 1980s and early 1990s. According to the Aluminum Association, rod, bar, and wire shipments fell 0.7 percent during 1996 to 551 million pounds, representing 3 percent of all aluminum industry shipments. In general, aluminum wire dominates the electrical transmission and distribution market, with copper a distant second. During the 1980s, however, demand for electrical transmission lines fell, as new construction was lackluster and electricity usage remained flat. Furthermore, use of aluminum wire in buildings fell sharply in the 1980s. In the mid-1970s, aluminum had a 31 percent share of this market, but following the publicity of the hazards of aluminum wire, its share dwindled to 8 percent in 1994. Several of the major aluminum companies thus elected to retreat from the electrical conductor market. In 1994 and 1995, however, there was a recovery in demand for rod, bar, and wire products. Larger shipments to the transmission and distribution sector were a result of increased housing starts and the need to upgrade existing systems. Some producers have moved to expand their plants.

FURTHER READING

Infotrac Company Profiles, 28 January 2000. Available from http://web4.infotrac.galegroup.com.

Petry, Corinna. ''Aluminum Producers Optimistic About Future Markets.'' *American Metal Market,* 15 November 1996.

Regan, Bob. ''Weak flat-roll sector drags down overall aluminum bookings.'' *American Metal Market,* 2 October 1998.

The Story and Uses of Aluminum. Washington: Aluminum Association, 1993.

U.S. Census Bureau. *1997 Economic Census—Manufacturing,* 10 February 2000. Available from http://www.census.gov/prod/ec97/97m3313f.pdf.

SIC 3356

ROLLING, DRAWING, AND EXTRUDING OF NONFERROUS METALS, EXCEPT COPPER AND ALUMINUM

This classification covers establishments primarily engaged in rolling, drawing, and extruding nonferrous metals other than copper and aluminum. The products of this industry are in the form of basic shapes, such as plate, sheet, strip, bar, and tubing. Excluded from this classification are establishments primarily engaged in recovering nonferrous metals and alloys from scrap or dross. Such establishments are classified in **SIC 3341: Secondary Smelting and Refining of Nonferrous Metals.** Those establishments primarily engaged in manufacturing gold, silver, tin, and other foils, except aluminum, are classified in **SIC 3497: Metal Foil and Leaf;** and those establishments manufacturing aluminum foil are classified in **SIC 3353: Aluminum Sheet, Plate, and Foil.**

NAICS CODE(S)

331491 (Nonferrous Metal (except Copper and Aluminum) Rolling, Drawing, and Extruding)

INDUSTRY SNAPSHOT

The industry shipped $4.8 billion worth of product in 1997, up significantly from the $2.9 billion shipped in 1996 and the $3.6 billion shipped in 1989.

In 1997 approximately 184 establishments derived the bulk of their revenue from the rolling, drawing, or extrusion of nonferrous metals other than aluminum and copper.

More than half of the manufacturing establishments in operation in 1996 in this industrial sector employed 20 people or more, while the typical establishment employed 90 workers, slightly more than twice the size of the average manufacturing establishment involved in all other manufacturing industries.

Geographically, semi-fabricated metal manufacturing establishments were concentrated primarily in Pennsylvania, New Jersey, New York, and Michigan. The mid-Atlantic states, the Great Lakes region, and New England contained the greatest number of establishments, though production was also distributed throughout the South and West.

As with the other branches of the metal industry, the operating costs in the semi-fabricated metal industry are significantly higher than the costs incurred by the average manufacturing establishment. In 1994 the average cost per establishment in the semi-fabricated metal industry, that is, the average amount earmarked for raw materials, was $16.9 million, nearly double the average expense incurred by other manufacturing industries. However, the cost of materials for production continued to decline from highs established in the early 1980s. In 1997 material costs reached $2.5 billion, nearly $1.0 billion more than the previous year.

ORGANIZATION AND STRUCTURE

Nonferrous metals are utilized by nearly every manufacturing industry in the United States and abroad, their existence critical to the production of a wide variety of products from tin cans to semiconductors. The metals used by manufacturers to produce their products are purchased from three types of metal manufacturers, depending on the particular needs of the buyer: primary metal manufacturers, secondary metal manufacturers, and semi-fabricated metal manufacturers, each of which share an interdependent relationship with the other. Primary manufacturers produce metal by subjecting particular extracted ores to various metallurgical processes, thereby creating metal in its most basic form. Secondary manufacturers smelt, refine, and sometimes blend metal recovered from the shaping and trimming of primary metal during production and fabrication, or from recycled metal. The metal produced by these two types of manufacturers leaves the production site in either large bar or block form known as ingot. As ingot, the metal exists in a convenient and efficient state for storage or shipping, ready for delivery to manufacturers requiring metal cast in this form, or ready to be shipped to a facility equipped to further shape or extrude the metal.

These latter facilities, the semi-fabricated metal manufacturing establishments classified in this industry, take metal in its basic form, then roll, draw, or extrude the massive bar or block ingot into various shapes to make the metal suitable for a wide variety of applications. As semi-finished products, the metal is formed into plate, sheet, strip, bar, or tubing, then delivered to manufacturers involved in a multitude of industries.

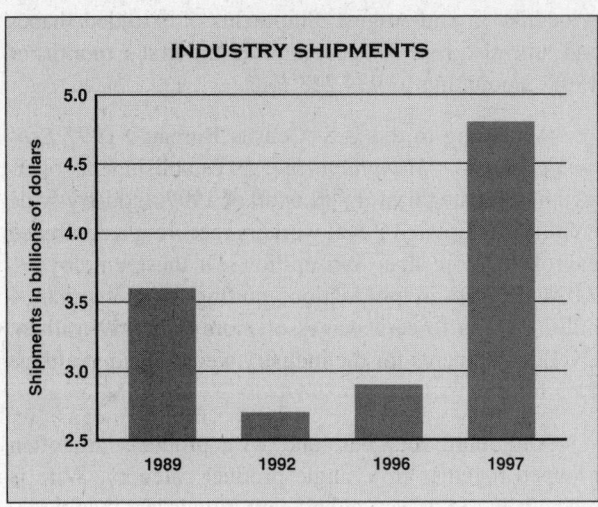

Establishments in this sector are involved in shaping and forming precious metals, nickel, titanium, magnesium, lead, zinc, and other nonferrous metals (copper and aluminum are not included). The production of magnesium, lead, tungsten, molybdenum, and other nonferrous metal shapes account for 28.3 percent of production. Nickel and nickel-based alloys comprise 26.3 percent, while precious metals, titanium, and unclassified nonferrous rolling and drawing account for 20.5, 19.35, and 5.4 percent of production, respectively.

BACKGROUND AND DEVELOPMENT

Historically, growth in the semi-fabricated metal industry depended on the metal market as a whole; if demand for particular metals experiences an increase, then semi-fabricators generally enjoy a commensurate upswing in business. As a result, the industry's history mirrored the growth and decline of primary and secondary nonferrous metal producers, functioning as a dependent arm of the metal manufacturing industry and realizing earnings from the sundry markets that spur activity in the primary and secondary metal manufacturing industries.

Following World War II however, a number of technological developments directly benefited semi-fabricated, nonferrous metal manufacturers. These stand as noteworthy achievements peculiar to the industry, and enabled manufacturers to play a more prominent role in the metal industry.

One of these technological advances made two of the less widely used metals more popular in the semi-fabricated metal industry. In 1964, after the conclusion of a seven-year research and development program financed by the U.S. Air Force and conducted by Republic Aviation Corp., a method was found by which titanium could be extruded more thinly than previously possible and at significantly lower costs, a capability that greatly enhanced titanium's applicability to the then burgeoning jet airplane and aerospace industries. In 1963, one year before the extrusion process was fully developed, 5,000 tons of titanium were consumed in the United States. Five years later, U.S. consumption had climbed to 25,000 tons and showed no signs of slowing. During this five-year period, enormous technological strides in extracting the metal from its ores were achieved under a joint venture between Reactive Metals Inc. and Titanium Metals Corporation of America.

As the production of a supersonic transport aircraft neared completion in the late 1960s, domestic titanium consumption approached 80,000 tons annually, largely because supersonic transports and other high-speed aircraft required an appreciably greater percentage of titanium than slower aircraft because of temperature resistance qualities. Consequently, supersonic transports were 80 percent titanium, while slower aircraft such as Boeing Company's 727, were manufactured with less than 2 percent titanium. As the nation's space program intensified, the applications for titanium broadened, leading to widespread use of titanium in the aviation and aerospace industries in the 1990s.

Shortly after the titanium extrusion process was developed, another nonferrous metal began a similar rise in popularity, once again as the result of an extensive research and development program. This time the work was conducted outside U.S. borders by Canada's Cominco, Ltd., the world's largest producer of refined lead and zinc during the late 1960s. In 1964, concurrent with the conclusion of the U.S. Air Force's titanium research program, Cominco began exploring possible methods to improve the extrusion technology of zinc. Five years later, a suitable method was discovered that enabled zinc to be extruded without tearing, cracking, or sticking to the dies, problems that had restricted the use of zinc in the past. Prior to Cominco's discovery, zinc occasionally had been rolled or drawn, but it was more commonly known in the metal industry for its galvanizing and die casting properties. The capability to extrude the metal however, greatly improved the metal's suitability for a host of component parts used in the production of automobiles and appliances. By using zinc, manufacturers could match colors more accurately, giving zinc an aesthetic advantage over aluminum and other metals. Consequently, the use of zinc by semi-fabricated metal manufacturers began in earnest during the 1970s, eventually becoming one of the key metals utilized by the industry in the early 1990s.

Essentially affected by the same market factors that dictate the economic health of primary and secondary metal manufacturers, semi-fabricated metal manufacturers entered the mid-1990s bolstered by the strong performance of some metals and negatively affected by the static performance of others. Rarely is the industry's future easy to ascertain since its overall performance is dependent on the separate markets for individual metals, which frequently experience divergent bouts of growth and decline.

Emerging from the recessive early 1990s, however, the semi-fabricated metal industry's future was shaped by the encouraging strength of the lead market and the discovery of several new consumer markets for titanium. The zinc markets remained weak due to high levels of supply. Nickel prices remained unsettled due to strong supply and weak global demand for stainless steel, the principle end-use for nickel. Overall, the industry shipped $2.9 billion worth of product in 1996, up marginally from its 1992 low of $2.7 billion in shipments and well below its high of $3.6 billion in 1989.

The worldwide demand for lead continued to expand through 1996 and record consumption and production continued through 1997. This increase was largely attributable to an increase in storage battery production and battery replacement, the primary end-uses of lead. Prices rose in 1996, but were tempered by fallout from the Sumitomo commodities trading scandal, which depressed the market price for many nonferrous metals. Demand for lead was especially strong in the United States, but was weak in Europe and Japan due to sluggish economic growth.

Titanium producers entered the 1990s facing substantial cutbacks in defense spending and fluctuating demand for aircraft parts. However the development of high-content titanium golf equipment brought a change in fortune for the industry. Titanium golf club heads increasingly replaced traditional wood heads in the mid-1990s. The light metal offered golfers a larger and more favorable hitting surface. Titanium shipments increased from 34.4 million pounds in 1992 to 43.6 million in 1995. Moreover, titanium found its way into such diverse consumer products as eyeglass frames, cameras, bicycles, inline skates, cookware, and watches. Titanium product producers looked to increase this new segment of the industry not only as a substitute for falling defense needs, but to cushion the cyclical changes traditionally experienced in the commercial aviation industry, a large titanium consumer.

CURRENT CONDITIONS

As of April 1997, strong demand from the thriving aerospace industry led to increased titanium consumption and earnings. By 1999 aerospace demand accounted for 41 percent of titanium consumption. Then, in May 1999, prices for titanium ingot plummeted 25 percent to between $5.75 and $5.90 per pound, a drop of more than $1 since the third quarter of 1998. Boeing Commercial Airplane Group, the largest end-market customer for titanium, fixed the price it paid for titanium at $7.62 per pound when supplies were tight, thus buoying the industry some. However, Boeing's orders rose from 563 aircraft in 1998 to 620 in 1999, but fell 22 percent to 480 in 2000, thus exerting less of a compensatory effect on the industry that year. In fact, titanium orders industry-wide were down 15 percent in 1999 and projections called for the depressed market to continue until 2003.

INDUSTRY LEADERS

The Essex Group Inc. of Fort Wayne, Indiana, which went public in a February 1997 stock offering, led the industry with 1998 sales of $1.8 billion. In 1999 Essex merged with Superior Telecommunications Inc. to form Superior Essex Communications Group and Superior Essex Industrial Group. New York City-based TGB Industries Inc. posted sales of $770 million in its fiscal year ended November 30, 1997, according to Infotrac databases. Titanium Metals Corp., a subsidiary of Tremont Corp. of Denver, Colorado, generated revenues of $708 million in 1998. Boeing contracted Titanium Metals to supply as much as 70 percent of its titanium.

WORKFORCE

In October 1997, 240 employees at the Essex Group's Columbia City, Indiana building-wire plant (belonging to Lodge 113, Local 2520 of the International Association of Machinists and Aerospace Workers) went on strike to reduce their hours to a regular 40-hour week. Two years later the industry was laying off workers in order to salvage what profit they could from lean times.

Total employment in the semi-fabricated metal industry fluctuated throughout the 1980s, effecting slight, sporadic gains, then suffering proportionate declines. In 1982 the industry employed 20,000, and by the mid-1990s, employment fell to 15,500, reflecting general consolidation and cost-cutting in the industry. Employment made a slight recovery and by 1997 totaled 17,237.

Production workers are generally employed on a full-time basis and earn more per hour than their counterparts in other manufacturing industries. The industry had nearly three times the average payroll per establishment in 1994 as did the rest of the manufacturing sector. Average payroll per employee in 1994 was $35,419 versus $30,620 for the wider manufacturing category. In 1997, 69 percent of the labor force worked in production, earning an average hourly wage of $17.15.

FURTHER READING

Allegheny Teledyne Incorporated Report 10-K for the Year Ended 12-31-96. *Securities and Exchange Commission*. 27 March 1997.

"An Overlooked Metal Broadens Its Appeal." *Business Week*, 17 May 1969, 124.

Bierck, Richard. "How Golf Saved a Defense Supplier Hole in One." *U.S. News & World Report*, 2 December 1996, 56.

Chase, Martyn. "Aerospace woes have rapid effect on titanium field." *American Metal Market*, 20 October 1999.

Haflich, Frank. "Hard times hurt leading US titanium producers." *American Metal Market*, 6 October 1999.

Haflich, Frank. "Strong aero demand boost titanium earnings." *American Metal Market*, 25 April 1997.

Haflich, Frank. "Titanium ingot slides lower." *American Metal Market*, 5 May 1999.

Infotrac Company Profiles. 2000. Available from http://web4 .infotrac.galegroup.com.

"Striking Workers at Essex Group Plant in Indiana to Vote on Contract." *Knight-Ridder/Tribune Business News*, 9 October 1997.

Stundza, Tom. "What the Trading Scandal Did!" *Purchasing*, 6 October 1996.

"Superior, Essex renamed." *American Metal Market*, 31 May 1999.

Tremont Corporation Report 10-K for the Year Ended 12-31-96. *Securities and Exchange Commission*. 31 March 1997.

U.S. Department of Commerce. *Annual Survey of Manufactures*. Washington: GPO, 1996.

U.S. Census Bureau. *1997 Economic Census—Manufacturing*. Washington, DC: GPO, 1999.

SIC 3357

DRAWING AND INSULATING OF NONFERROUS WIRE

This classification covers establishments primarily engaged in drawing, drawing and insulating, and insulating wire and cable of nonferrous metals from purchased wire bars, rods, or wire. Also included are establishments primarily engaged in manufacturing insulated fiber optic cable. Establishments primarily engaged in manufacturing glass fiber optic materials are included in **SIC 3229: Pressed and Blown Glass and Glassware, Not Elsewhere Classified,** while those manufacturing fabricated wire products from purchased wire are classified in **SIC 3496: Miscellaneous Fabricated Wire Products.**

NAICS CODE(S)

331319 (Other Aluminum Rolling and Drawing)
331422 (Copper Wire Drawing)
331491 (Nonferrous Metal (except Copper and Aluminum) Rolling, Drawing, and Extruding)
331522 (Fiber Optic Cable Manufacturing)
335929 (Other Communication and Energy Wire Manufacturing)

INDUSTRY SNAPSHOT

Nonferrous wire manufacturers shipped $19.1 billion worth of products in 1997, up from $15.2 billion in 1995. While shipment values increased, so too did the cost of raw materials and capital investment.

Manufacturers involved in drawing and extruding nonferrous wire and cable supply five primary markets with various types of products manufactured from aluminum and copper—the two most widely utilized nonferrous metals—and other nonferrous metals. These products, ranging from fiber optic cable to insect wire screening, are drawn or extruded from wire bars or rods, a process that essentially winnows the larger bar and rod shapes into wire or cable. The wire and cable is then insulated with assorted materials such as paper, rubber, or other materials, including polyethylene and polyvinyl chloride. Once insulated, the wire and cable is used in an assortment of applications, including wiring for residential and commercial buildings, communication networks, power distribution, automobiles, and appliances.

Historically, the five primary markets for the industry's products have been communication industries; electric utilities; automobile, truck, and boat manufacturers; the construction industry; and manufacturers of home appliances and industrial machinery. Since the conclusion of World War II, the composition of the industry's primary markets has remained unchanged, although the order of importance of each market to the industry has fluctuated.

ORGANIZATION AND STRUCTURE

In the nonferrous wire drawing and insulating industry, approximately 380 companies in the United States were deriving the bulk of their revenue from the fabrication and insulation of wire and cable at the close of the twentieth century. These companies, many of which owned more than one manufacturing establishment, operated roughly 545 separate manufacturing facilities. Of these facilities, 357—or nearly 65 percent—employed 20 or more workers. The average size of a wire drawing and insulating establishment, in terms of the number of employees per establishment, was more than twice the size of the average manufacturing establishment.

Geographically, a majority of the industry's manufacturing establishments were located in the northeastern United States. By value of shipments, Indiana, Georgia, North Carolina, Illinois, and Texas lead the list. In terms of the greatest number of establishments located in one state, California led the nation with 60 manufacturing establishments.

Manufacturing establishments in this industry have historically been relatively expensive to operate, with operating costs at more than three times the national average. This has been attributed primarily to the high price of raw materials needed to operate a wire drawing and insulation manufacturing establishment. The required production machinery was also appreciably more expensive than the national standard posted by other manufacturing establishments.

BACKGROUND AND DEVELOPMENT

The wire and cable manufacturing industry has changed enormously over the years because of technological progress, both in its own operations and in the systems and needs of its customers. The modern wire and cable manufacturing industry emerged in the late nineteenth and early twentieth century, a time during which the industrialization of the United States created a need for wire and cable products and provided a means for their production.

Once America became an industrialized nation, wire became a fundamental product underpinning the nation's growth, both industrially and commercially. For years, copper had been the preferred metal for a majority of the wire and cable manufacturing industry's products; its high conductivity elevated the metal above all others. Aluminum, which would eventually gain widespread acceptance in the industry, was first introduced as a cable conductor during the 1930s, but did not represent an appreciable portion of the market until the 1950s, when a tightened supply of copper forced manufacturers to search for an alternative.

Manufacturers' selection of aluminum to augment their copper supply came at an opportune time in the country's development: the population was rapidly expanding, creating a housing boom; televisions and radios were being manufactured at unprecedented levels; a community antennae television (CATV) market was burgeoning; more automobiles were being manufactured; and electric power generation in the country was about to begin two decades of exponential growth. Wire and cable manufacturers served each of these markets, experiencing enviable growth as the nation enjoyed an age of prosperity. By the beginning of the 1970s, the industry had evolved into a $3 billion entity, primarily due to the growth of the national economy over the previous two decades.

The use of aluminum by the industry's products, however, particularly in the wiring of residential homes, caused considerable anxiety for some manufacturers when the U.S. Consumer Product Safety Commission (CPSC) filed a lawsuit against 26 manufacturers in 1977. Charging that 1.5 million homes wired with aluminum between 1965 and 1973 were in danger of catching fire, the CPSC sought to force manufacturers responsible for producing the wire to pay for rewiring at an estimated cost of $300 per home.

The potential for fire stemmed from the poorer conductivity of aluminum when compared to copper. Since aluminum was less conductive than copper, more aluminum was required to form a wire, which created a thicker stock that wire installers were unable to fit tightly into wall outlets. This led to loose connections that, in turn, caused the wiring to overheat. The problem was corrected for all homes wired after 1973, but the scare sent aluminum's share of the wiring market cascading downward from 17.0 percent to 1.4 percent during the 1970s.

CPSC's revelation, however, did not dissuade manufacturers from using aluminum as a key raw material in the production of wire and cable. By the late 1980s, manufacturers purchased more primary aluminum than any other nonferrous metal to produce wire and cable products.

As the wire drawing and insulating industry entered the mid-1990s, manufacturing activity resumed its pre-recession levels, thanks largely to continuing strengths in the construction industry and increasing use of fiber optic cable by the telecommunications industry. Strong private residential housing starts augured well for manufacturers involved in producing building wire. Other wire and cable markets effected recoveries as well, enabling the industry to stanch its shrinking revenue volume. The brightest prospect for the industry's future lay in the growth of the fiber optics industry, for which the wire drawing and insulating industry supplies fiber optic cable.

From 1989 to 1993, U.S. shipments of fiber optic equipment—including optical fiber and cable as well as other products excluded from the wire drawing and insulating manufacturing industry—increased 13 percent annually, with industry observers calling for still greater growth through the end of the decade. In the mid-1990s, the world market for fiber optic equipment was estimated to be $5 billion, a market in which U.S. manufacturers maintained a lead over European and Japanese producers, although the gap separating the United States from other manufacturers was closing. Some observers expected this market to double in value by the end of the decade, promising lucrative profit potential for manufacturers of fiber optic cable. As the conventional markets supporting cable and wire manufacturers' core business once again fueled the industry's growth, those manufacturers able to afford the costly nature of exploring ''next-generation'' technology began turning to the production of fiber optic cable in increasing numbers.

CURRENT CONDITIONS

Even as the strong economy of the late 1990s kept the construction industry busy, and the booming technology industries demanded communication and fiber optic cable, this industry experienced some fluctuation. The volatility of this market was demonstrated in September 1997, when

the *Leader* of Corning, New York, ran a story reporting potential weaknesses in Corning Inc.'s fiber optics division due to stiffer international competition, decreased demand, and reduced growth rates. That day, Corning's stock price plummeted on the New York Stock Exchange, resulting in a $1 billion loss. The company criticized the newspaper story as inaccurate, and dumped sales racks from their premises onto the parking lot at the newspaper. The *Leader* defended its story by pointing out that Corning officials failed to respond to repeated requests to confirm or refute the reported facts, and furthermore the company revised its financial projections for the division two days later, substantiating the validity of the article.

But the industry did experience some good news at the end of the 1990s. In December 1999, Hewlett-Packard subsidiary Agilent Technologies of Palo Alto, California, agreed to lease $400,000 worth of equipment to VisionGlobal Corporation for use in the completion of the company's broadband wireless data radio network. Such agreements bode well for the industry, as the boom in wireless communications would require hardware infrastructures using nonferrous wire. This rising demand could offset the effects of falling prices for communications cables and building wire in 1999.

Superconducting markets also blossomed at the turn of the century. In December 1999, industry leader Intermagnetics General Corp. (IGC) of Latham, New York, entered a $1 million contract to supply superconducting wire to Samsung Advanced Institute of Technology. The superconducting wire was used in nuclear fusion magnets in Samsung's Korean National Fusion Project and the Korean Superconducting Tokamak Advanced Research (KSTAR) project. This deal represented the second such supply agreement between IGC and Samsung, with projections calling for orders of 20 additional metric tons of niobium-tin wire through the year 2001.

INDUSTRY LEADERS

IGC generated sales of $102.9 million, for 1999. Of companies that focused primarily on this industry (as opposed to second-place AT & T Network Systems, which garnered little of its $9.2 billion in sales from this industry), Agilent led the pack with $8.3 billion in 1999 sales. Corning created $4.3 billion in overall sales for 1999, with its focus concentrating more and more on its technologies instead of its traditional market of housewares. BICC General of Highland Heights, Kentucky, formerly known as General Cable Corp., generated $2.1 billion in 1999 sales.

WORKFORCE

Total employment in the wire drawing and insulation industry declined throughout the 1980s and 1990s. A large percentage of this decline was attributable to the diminishing number of production jobs; in 1982 there were 50,000 production workers employed by the industry, but by 1996 their numbers had fallen to 44,100. In 1997, however, the industry's 446 establishments employed 51,371 production workers, a marked increase from the previous year, possibly due to the increased demand for high-tech products. These production workers earned an average hourly wage of $17.76.

FURTHER READING

"BICC General's 2d-Qtr. Net Slides 28 Percent." *American Metal Market,* 23 July 1999.

Infotrac Company Profiles, 14 January 2000. Available from http://web4.infotrac.galegroup.com.

"Intermagnetics to Supply Additional $1 Million in Superconducting Material for Major South Korean Reactor." *PR Newswire,* 8 December 1999.

Jones, Stacy. "Booster Turned Goat." *Editor & Publisher,* 11 October 1997.

Miller, Andy. "A Special Report: Georgia's Private Companies: No. 3: Southwire Cable Manufacturer Wired to International Market." *Atlanta Journal and Constitution,* 22 September 1996. Available from http://www.elibrary.com/s/cox/.

Securities and Exchange Commission. *Raychem Corp Report 10-Q Quarterly Report for the Period Ended September 30, 1996,* 8 November 1996. Available from http://www.sec.gov/cgi-bin/srch-edgar.

Torpy, Bill. "Southwire's Split Personality: Irony and Conflict: The West Georgia Company Is a Study in Contradiction: On Issues Ranging from Environmental Conscience to Politics." *Atlanta Journal and Constitution,* 12 February 1995. Available from http://www.elibrary.com/s/cox/.

U.S. Census Bureau. *1997 Economic Census—Manufacturing.* Washington: GPO 2000.

U.S. Department of Commerce. *Annual Survey of Manufactures,* Washington: GPO, 1995.

"VisionGlobal Corporation Announces Signing of Equipment Lease Documents With Hewlett-Packard Subsidiary, Agilent Technologies." *PR Newswire,* 1 December 1999.

SIC 3363

ALUMINUM DIE-CASTINGS

This classification is comprised of establishments primarily engaged in manufacturing die-castings of aluminum (including alloys).

NAICS CODE(S)
331521 (Aluminum Die-Castings)

INDUSTRY SNAPSHOT

Aluminum die-castings differ from other types of aluminum castings because of the difference in the type of mold used and the process by which the molten metal is delivered to the die. Whereas casting molds may be made of many different materials—including sand, plaster, iron, steel, and polystyrene—dies are made only of metal, most frequently steel. In die-casting, the die is filled with molten metal that is forced into it under pressure, unlike other casting processes where liquid metal is poured by gravity. Die-casting techniques are used to produce greater volumes of cast products than other types of casting.

According to the U.S. Census Bureau's *1997 Economic Census—Manufacturing,* 317 establishments operated in this category for part or all of 1997. Industry-wide employment totaled 27,487 workers receiving a payroll of more than $897 million. Within this workforce, 22,702 of these employees worked in production, putting in more than 47 million hours to earn wages of more than $672 million. Overall shipments for the industry were valued at almost $3.8 billion.

BACKGROUND AND DEVELOPMENT

Herman Doehler, founder of Doehler-Jarvis, developed the first die-casting machine around the turn of the century. The first commercially produced aluminum die-castings in the United States were manufactured in 1915. In 1946, the U.S. Department of Commerce reported that aluminum die-casting production totaled 73 million pounds, representing about 16 percent of the total die-casting production for all metals that year. Prior to the late 1960s, zinc was used in a majority of die-cast products, but, in 1967, aluminum production surpassed that of zinc. Throughout the 1970s, aluminum production continued to expand dramatically, and, by 1988, aluminum die-casting production reached the 1.5 billion-pound mark.

As the die-casting industry entered the 1990s, aluminum remained in the top position. Its chemical and physical properties offered many advantages to industrial users. For example, aluminum die-castings weighed about 60 percent less than identical iron products, resisted corrosion, and were stronger than permanent mold or sand castings. Automated production methods produced high quantities at low per-unit costs. By the late 1990s, the automotive industry had discovered the benefits of aluminum and consequently became the largest market for aluminum castings, buying 25 percent of all aluminum produced and nearly one-half of all aluminum die-castings produced.

In 1995, the value of U.S. shipments of aluminum die-castings totaled $4.2 billion. In that year, the industry employed 28,000 people in 292 establishments, most of which were centered in the Great Lakes area because of its

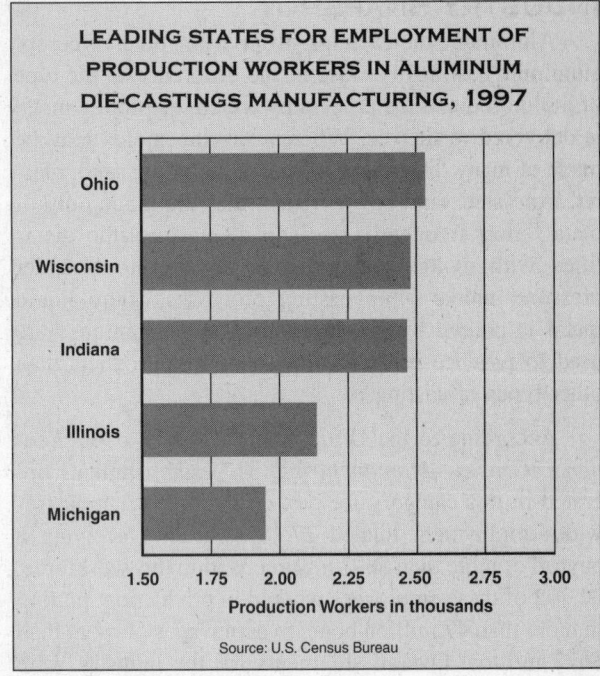

LEADING STATES FOR EMPLOYMENT OF PRODUCTION WORKERS IN ALUMINUM DIE-CASTINGS MANUFACTURING, 1997

Production Workers in thousands

Source: U.S. Census Bureau

proximity to the automotive industry. Wisconsin, Michigan, Ohio, and Illinois accounted for almost 50 percent of die-cast production. Establishments generally employed twice as many workers compared to all of manufacturing, yet paid them a smaller average wage at $11.79 an hour (compared to $12.09 per hour for all manufacturing). As automation became the standard, however, the workforce diminished throughout the rest of the decade.

INDUSTRY LEADERS

Leading this industry in overall sales was ACX Technologies Inc. of Golden, Colorado with 1998 sales of over $988 million on the strength of 5,600 workers. ACX developed innovative new technologies for its die-cast aluminum products, such as vibration damping for its baseball bats and mountain bike suspension systems. Second-place Varlen Corp. generated sales of just under $647 million for its fiscal year ended January 31, 1999, with 3,758 employees. Pace Industries of Fayetteville, Arkansas garnered sales of $397 million for 1997. Other industry leaders included Gibbs Die Casting Corp. of Henderson, Kentucky; Ohio Decorative Products Inc. of Spencerville, Ohio; and Contech Div. of Portage, Michigan.

Another industry leader in terms of innovation is Doehler-Jarvis, inventors of the first die-casting machine. During its long history, the company boasted many "firsts" in die-casting technology, including the first transmission case casing, the first die-cast oil pan, and the first automotive cylinder block. In 1979, the company made another breakthrough when it introduced computer-assisted design, or CAD, a technology that permitted dies to be made with electronic information and

eliminated the need to make blueprints. In 1980, Doehler-Jarvis introduced the "doehlercore system," a patented and proprietary process using expendable cores in high-pressure castings. This process enabled the company to cast parts with complex internal shapes.

Doehler-Jarvis decided to automate its production in 1997, with a full line of robots on the production line. With CAD and robotic production, Doehler-Jarvis remained on the leading edge of technological methods and product precision. Several robots, implemented in the summer of 1997, were to handle and produce all complex die-castings, including products for Doehler-Jarvis' largest market, the automotive industry. By the early 1990s, Doehler-Jarvis operated three casting centers with combined manufacturing space totaling 2 million square feet. The company reported annual shipments of 75,000 tons valued at $300 million. In the mid-1990s, Doehler-Jarvis employed 1,500 workers and reported revenues of $200 million.

FURTHER READING

Darnay, Arsen J, ed. *Manufacturing USA.* 5th ed. Detroit: Gale Research, 1996.

Doehler-Jarvis. *Aluminum Casting Alloys Fact Book.* Toledo, OH: Doehler, 1991.

Diecaster to the World. Toledo, OH: Doehler, 1992.

"Doehler-Jarvis Selects FANUC Robotics to Automate its Die Casting Operations." *PR Newswire,* 4 April 1997. Available from http://www.companylink.com/item.cfm/1718804.

Houlder, Vanessa. "Absorbing the Shock of Impact." *The Financial Times,* 13 November 1997.

"Striking Bat Improvement." *The Financial Times,* 9 July 1998.

U.S. Census Bureau. "Aluminum Die-Casting Foundries" *1997 Economic Census-Manufacturing.* Washington, D.C.: U.S. Department of Commerce, 1999. Available from http://www.census.gov.

SIC 3364

NONFERROUS DIE-CASTINGS EXCEPT ALUMINUM

This classification is comprised of establishments primarily involved in manufacturing die-castings from nonferrous metals and alloys other than aluminum. Establishments primarily engaged in manufacturing die-castings from aluminum and aluminum alloys are classified in **SIC 3363: Aluminum Die-Castings.**

NAICS CODE(S)

331522 (Nonferrous (except Aluminum) Die-Castings)

INDUSTRY SNAPSHOT

According to the U.S. Census Bureau's *1997 Economic Census—Manufacturing,* 278 establishments operated in this category for part or all of 1997. Industry-wide employment totaled 17,143 workers receiving a payroll of more than $500 million. Within this workforce, 13,678 of these employees worked in production, putting in more than 27 million hours to earn wages of more than $353 million. Overall shipments for the industry were valued at over $2 billion.

According to figures released by the U.S. Census Bureau, zinc die-castings represented the largest category of die-castings other than aluminum. In 1996, domestic production totaled 140,000 tons. Industry analysts, however, expected that number to drop in 1997 as the automotive industry continued to move increasingly towards the use of lighter metals and plastics. Casting shipments of magnesium, another important non-aluminum die-casting metal, totaled 29,000 tons in 1996 and were expected to grow to about 31,000 tons in 1997, with sales of $171 million.

BACKGROUND AND DEVELOPMENT

Die-casting techniques, which rely on injecting molten metal into steel molds under pressure, were developed around the turn of the twentieth century. Industrial development and needs spawned by both world wars brought increased use of die-castings.

In 1946, shipments of die-castings reached nearly 460 million pounds. Of this total, 376 million pounds represented die-castings fabricated with zinc. Zinc remained the top metal for die-casters until it was surpassed by aluminum in 1967. The 1970s and 1980s brought additional challenges to zinc die-casters when automakers began replacing zinc components with plastic products, and domestic manufacturers faced increased challenges from imported products. Improvements in the ability to cast zinc parts using thin-wall technology were expected to help zinc recapture some of its lost market share.

Innovations in the 1980s permitted fabricators to purify magnesium of contaminants associated with poor corrosion resistance. Refined magnesium possesses qualities making it competitive with aluminum, steel, plastics, and other traditional materials. These improvements resulted in dramatic increases in magnesium die-casting shipments. In 1983, for example, magnesium shipments totaled 4,700 tons. By 1990, the figure had increased to 15,500 tons. Although magnesium shipments dropped slightly in 1991 to 15,000 tons, industry analysts expected sales to rebound.

Another die-casting metal receiving increased interest during the early 1990s was titanium. Titanium possesses low weight, high strength, and good corrosion resistance. Although it had been used since the early 1950s in aerospace applications, widespread acceptance failed to develop because of the high costs associated with titanium production. Innovations developed during the 1980s, however, opened the door to expanded use.

As the die-casting industry prepared for the 1990s, the North American Die Casting Association (NADCA) predicted that technological improvements would increase demand for die-cast products. In addition to refinements in zinc production, the ability to work with magnesium held promise.

CURRENT CONDITIONS

Magnesium shipments fulfilled the industry expectations by doubling its shipments by 1996, and were expected to continue growing substantially throughout the rest of the decade. The largest user of magnesium die-castings is the automotive industry. According to industry predictions, magnesium casting use in automobiles increased to an estimated 12,000 tons in 1997. Magnesium parts for cars include various housings, brackets, and steering column components. Other significant users of magnesium castings include manufacturers of chain saws, fishing rods, and power tools.

INDUSTRY LEADERS

Leading the nonferrous die-castings industry was Labinal Inc. of Lombard, Illinois, with $290 in 1998 sales on the strength of 2,800 workers. Gibbs Die Casting Company, which generated 1997 sales of $272 million, built a new magnesium and aluminum casting plant in Harlingen, Texas called Rio Grande Die Casting that year. The 40,000-square-foot plant, which went online in June 1998, made magnesium steering wheel armatures among other products. Henderson, Kentucky, where the company makes its headquarters, was becoming the home of casting, as Gibbs built the third castings plant in the city, a 70,000-square-foot facility housing 10 casting machines.

Rounding out the top three industry leaders was Contech Division of Portage, Michigan, with 750 workers creating 1997 sales of $150 million. Other industry leaders included New York City-based Lexington Precision Corp.; Lindberg Corp. of Rosemont, Illinois; and Dynacast Inc. of Yorktown Heights, New York.

FURTHER READING

Kirgin, Kenneth H. "1997 Metalcasting Forecast and Trends: Solid Casting Markets Fuel 1997 Expansion." *Modern Casting,* January 1997. Available from http://www.moderncasting.com.

U.S. Census Bureau. "Nonferrous (Except Aluminum) Die-Casting Foundries" *1997 Economic Census-Manufacturing.* Washington, D.C.: U.S. Department of Commerce, 1999. Available from http://www.census.gov/prod/ec97/97m3315e.pdf.

"U.S. Zinc Diecasting Industry Hit by Indirect Imports." *Foundry Management and Technology,* January 1991.

Wrigley, Al. "Gibbs Plant to Open New Casting Facility." *American Metal Market,* 23 January 1997.

SIC 3365

ALUMINUM FOUNDRIES

This category includes establishments primarily engaged in manufacturing aluminum (including alloys) castings, except die-castings, which are classified in **SIC 3363: Aluminum Die-Castings.**

NAICS Code(s)

331524 (Aluminum Foundries)

Industry Snapshot

Aluminum foundries create castings by pouring heated, liquefied metal into hollowed-out molds. As the molten metal cools, it hardens and assumes the shape created by the mold's cavity. Aluminum foundries typically work with metal purchased in the form of ingots from primary producers or from secondary aluminum recyclers. Some foundries located in close proximity to primary smelters obtain aluminum in molten form.

There were 4.9 billion pounds of aluminum castings shipped during 1998, up 7.8 percent from 1997. The industry has grown steadily since the 1960s when 1.3 billion pounds were shipped.

The largest user of aluminum castings is the automotive industry. Overall automotive content doubled in the 1990s, as car companies incorporated more aluminum to help reduce vehicle weight and meet federally mandated fuel efficiency standards. In 1998, 92.5 percent of all aluminum used in the automotive industry was in the form of castings. The second largest market for aluminum was in containers and packaging such as food containers, beverage cans, and institutional and household foil. Building and construction were the third largest market for cast aluminum products.

In 1997, 625 establishments were involved in aluminum casting. Only 276 of these companies employed 20 or more workers. With 81 companies, California had the greatest number of aluminum foundries in the United States, followed by Ohio with 80, and Pennsylvania with 45.

Background and Development

Aluminum is the most abundant metal in the earth's crust, but it never occurs naturally in isolation. It is a component of many gem stones such as rubies, turquoise, and jade, and it exists in the mineral bauxite. Clays with high aluminum content were used to make pottery in prehistoric times, and aluminum compounds were used by several ancient civilizations as well. The ability to break the chemical bonds between aluminum and other elements to produce the isolated metal was first discovered during the 1800s.

Bauxite, the source for virtually all modern aluminum, was first discovered in Lex Baux, France in 1821. Advances made during the nineteenth century in chemistry and electrolysis made practical the commercial production of aluminum metal from bauxite. In 1855, aluminum cost $115 per pound, but improvements in chemical production led to price reductions. By 1859, the price had dropped to $17 per pound.

Although falling prices permitted the introduction of some aluminum products such as surgical instruments and novelty items, aluminum was still too expensive to gain widespread industrial use. The most important breakthrough came later in the century when Charles Martin Hall of the United States and Paul L. T. Héroult of France independently developed commercial aluminum production methods based on electrolysis. As a result, by the turn of the twentieth century, aluminum prices had dropped to $0.33 per pound.

One of the most famous aluminum castings in the United States was placed on the tip of the Washington Monument in 1884. The first aluminum household utensils were created during the 1890s and gained popularity during the early 1900s. By the mid-1960s, more than half of the cookware on the U.S. market was aluminum.

In 1903, aluminum reached new heights when Wilbur and Orville Wright launched the Kitty Hawk Flyer. Its converted engine contained 30 pounds of aluminum parts.

During World War I, items such as canteens, mess kits, ammunition cases, and tent pins were made from cast aluminum. The emerging automotive industry required engines, manifolds, crankcases, oil pans, and valve covers. World War II increased aluminum casting demands by the military, and brought growing needs within the aeronautic industry.

Modern Casting Techniques. During the mid-twentieth century, aluminum foundries relied on several different casting technologies to meet the diverse demands of their customers. The casting techniques are differentiated by the type of mold used and the process by which the molds are filled. One of the most common types of casting is called "sand casting." Sand castings are created using molds formed from precise blends of sands, clays, and moisture. After a mold is formed, molten aluminum is poured into it. When the aluminum hardens, the sand is removed. The advantages of sand casting are its versatility and low cost for producing small quantities. Its principle disadvantage is its slowness compared to other casting methods.

Shell mold casting is a type of sand casting that relies on a thin mold made of preformed, baked sand. Plaster mold casting is similar to sand casting but molds are fabricated from plaster instead of sand. Plaster mold casting produces products with an improved surface finish.

Permanent mold castings employ molds made of iron or steel into which aluminum is poured. Although aluminum die-casting also uses permanent steel molds, it differs from permanent mold casting by using pressure to force the molten aluminum into the dies, instead of relying on gravity. Permanent mold casting technology produces the strongest castings.

Investment casting is a complex type of casting in which two or more permanent molds are assembled with an intervening wax lining or in which a wax shape is formed and dipped into a special liquid ceramic. When dried, the ceramic creates a shell around the shape. In both cases, the wax is heated and drained to create a hollow for the liquid aluminum. Because the melted wax is drained out of the mold, investment casting is sometimes referred to as the "lost wax" method. After cooling, the mold is broken and an exact aluminum replica of the former wax image remains. One advantage of investment casting is its ability to duplicate intricate patterns.

One of the most recently developed casting processes is called expendable pattern casting, sometimes referred to as "lost foam casting" or "evaporative foam pattern casting." Expendable pattern casting employs a polystyrene pattern made from fused polystyrene beads surrounded by a special sand pack. When liquid aluminum is poured into the mold the polystyrene vaporizes. This procedure yields a casting of the same dimensions as the pattern. Thus, the process holds many advantages such as a reduction in finishing costs and an improved ability to make more complicated designs. According to one estimate, production cost savings associated with expendable pattern casting are as much as 50 percent over traditional casting techniques.

Why Aluminum? Many industrial users favor aluminum because of its physical and chemical properties. Aluminum reflects light, conducts heat and electricity, and weighs only one-third as much as an equal volume of steel. It is also nonmagnetic, nontoxic, and naturally resistant to corrosion. Cast aluminum products are made of pure aluminum or aluminum alloys. Pure industrial aluminum is defined as aluminum containing less than 1 percent impurities. Many of the alloys incorporated into aluminum are added to improve the mixture's hardness, tensile strength, or corrosion resistance. Binary aluminum alloys are made of aluminum and one other element, while complex alloys contain two or more other elements. The most frequently used metals in aluminum alloys include copper, magnesium, manganese, and zinc. Another element often alloyed with aluminum is silicon. Alloys of aluminum with silicon have a lower melting point which results in improved castability.

CURRENT CONDITIONS

The driving force for aluminum castings in the United States is the automobile industry's efforts to conform with the Corporate Average Fuel Economy (CAFE) governmental regulations. According to a study commissioned by the Aluminum Association, the average North American passenger car or light truck contained 183 pounds of aluminum parts in 1991. By 1996, the aluminum content per vehicle had increased more than 80 percent to 248 pounds. Indeed between 1977 and 1999, the average aluminum content per vehicle rose by 150 pounds per vehicle—4.3 percent per year. Approximately 63 percent of the total amount of aluminum in 1999 model cars was recycled metal.

The substitution of aluminum for steel in automobiles has provided a weight savings of approximately 55 percent. Typically, 1 pound of aluminum can replace 2.25 to 2.5 pounds of cast iron. In 1996, the Aluminum Association indicated that the lifetime fuel savings of the lighter 1996 model passenger cars and light trucks could amount to more than 600 gallons of gasoline in the United States. In addition to fuel savings, the Association cited other benefits of increasing reliance on aluminum, including better acceleration, improved stopping, enhanced handling, and less vibration.

Another trend in the automotive industry fueling the use of aluminum castings was the growing popularity of light trucks (including pick-up trucks, sport utility vehicles, and minivans) in the late-1990s. On average, light trucks in 1999 contained 256 pounds of aluminum, compared to 241 pounds for passenger cars. While the average passenger car had gained 8 pounds of aluminum between 1996 and 1999, the average light truck gained 34 pounds of aluminum. Analysts for the Aluminum Association predict that the demand for aluminum in the automotive sector should slow somewhat in the early twenty-first century. Nevertheless, aluminum should continue to play a still greater role in the automotive industry, especially in closure panels, body structures, chassis and suspension components, and engine blocks.

Other traditional markets such as computers, office machines, and small engines, will also continue to provide aluminum with opportunities for long-term growth. Recent advances in the refrigeration and air conditioning market sectors should spur increased aluminum sales as well.

In an effort to save energy, natural resources, and landfills, more Americans are recycling. In 1998, 33 percent of the total supply of aluminum was recycled. In 1998, all beverage cans produced were made from aluminum and of the 103 billion cans produced that year, approximately two-thirds of those were recycled. The change from 2.3 billion recycled cans in 1974 to 64 billion recycled cans in 1998 was made possible by the increase in recycling centers—there are now more than 10,000 throughout the nation. Moreover, almost 90 percent of automotive aluminum in 1998 was reclaimed and recycled. The aluminum industry continues to support and promote recycling.

The aluminum foundries are still experiencing difficulties in complying with the U.S. Environmental Protection Agency (EPA) policies on the treatment and disposal of used aluminum potliners. The agency classified the potliner contaminants (arsenic, cyanide, and fluoride) as hazardous waste in 1989 and revised the levels in 1996.

In response, the casting industry began investigating ways to reduce the amount of waste generated through programs such as sand reclamation and reuse. Some governmental jurisdictions instituted studies to evaluate potential applications for foundry waste. Proposed uses included: fill for highway embankments, sub-base materials for concrete slabs, and raw material for making construction products such as bricks.

INDUSTRY LEADERS

One of the largest aluminum foundries in the United States is CMI International, Inc. of Southfield, Michigan. CMI is a major producer of machine-cast and molded parts primarily for the automotive industry. Its products include intake manifolds, cylinder heads, engine blocks, suspension and chassis systems, and drive train components. The foundry also produces castings for trucking, mining, and construction equipment. Other industry leaders were Wabash Alloys of Wabash, Indiana; Columbia Aluminum Corporation of Vancouver, Washington; and General Housewares Corporation, headquartered in Terre Haute, Indiana, with 500 workers and $119 million in sales.

WORKFORCE

Aluminum foundries employ a wide variety of skilled and unskilled workers. Typical employees with specialized skills include technicians, engineers, and chemists. Other specialists include patternmakers (who produce the patterns necessary to create castings), molders (who make the sand molds), and coremakers (who make sand cores). Aluminum foundries also employ many workers with skills not specific to metal-casting. These include industrial hygienists, electricians, and millwrights.

A total of 34,094 people were employed at aluminum foundries in 1997. Of this total, 27,829 were production workers, who were employed an average of 40 hours

a week and earned an average wage of $12.39 per hour. With 4,818 workers involved in the aluminum casting industry, Ohio employed the largest number of foundry workers in the United States, followed by Wisconsin with 3,627, and California with 2,676.

According to the American Foundrymen's Society (AFS), approximately 25 universities in the United States offered Cast Metals Studies programs. In addition, the Cast Metals Institute, established by the AFS in 1957, provided ongoing training to individuals within the industry.

Among employees in aluminum foundries, burns have been one of the leading causes of work-related injuries. To help protect workers from the inherent dangers involved in handling hot, liquid metal, the Aluminum Association's recommended safety precautions include the use of shields and the establishment of areas in which personnel must wear protective equipment. Special protective clothing for workers directly exposed to molten aluminum is deemed essential because some types of fabrics are subject to igniting or melting upon contact with the liquid metal. As a result, industry standards require wrist to ankle coverage and mandate the use of special footwear, gloves, headgear, and safety glasses.

RESEARCH AND TECHNOLOGY

Ongoing research efforts within the cast aluminum industry have been aimed at alleviating specific casting problems and producing castings of a better quality. Because aluminum shrinks as it cools, casting were sometimes prone to "hot tears," a type of fracture caused by the stresses created during solidification. Breaks in the finished product caused by insufficient metal flow during the casting process can lead to another problem. These types of deficiencies are known as "shrinkage cracks."

One of the biggest challenges, however, has been the elimination of hydrogen-induced porosity in cast products. Under certain conditions, hydrogen, which was soluble in aluminum, can cause tiny pores within a casting's metal structure. According to Hans J. Heine, International Editor of *Foundry Management & Technology*, these tiny holes represent "a primary cause for rejection of an aluminum casting."

To help reduce hydrogen-induced porosity, a method was developed to pass nitrogen gas through the molten aluminum solution. The nitrogen was not soluble in aluminum and the action of its presence helped the mixture release trapped hydrogen prior to casting. Some researchers experimented with refinements using argon, freon, and chlorine. Although these methods were deemed effective, industry analysts judged them to be too expensive. Another promising method of reducing hydrogen-induced porosity involved degassing the molten aluminum under a partial vacuum. Pressurized conditions caused the gas to float to the surface of the molten mixture.

To produce castings with specific qualities, sometimes heat treatments are used. When a cast product is heated and cooled under precise conditions, it develops a uniform internal structure, removes stresses, and improves its strength, stability, and hardness. One type of heat treatment, called annealing, involves heating a casting to a temperature above the point where its metal crystals would melt and then cooling it to recrystallize the metal.

FURTHER READING

"Compliance Date Extended." *American Metal Market,* 14 January 1997, 6.

Ducker Research Company. "Report on Aluminum Content in 1999 North American Passenger Cars and Light Trucks: Executive Summary," 28 December 1999. Available from http://www.aec.org/ducker_report.htm.

Kirgin, Kenneth H. "Nonferrous Foundries Vie for Continued Growth." *Modern Casting,* September 1996, 40.

U.S. Census Bureau. "Aluminum Foundries," 29 October 1999. Available from http://www.census.gov.

SIC 3366

COPPER FOUNDRIES

This industry consists of companies primarily engaged in manufacturing copper and copper-alloy castings, except die-castings. Establishments that produce copper castings and also are engaged in fabricating operations for a specific product are classified in the industry of the specific product. Therefore, some of the companies considered to be a part of the copper foundry industry are not included in this classification, although some of the statistics covering the copper foundry industry do include these "captive" foundry departments of manufacturers.

NAICS CODE(S)

331525 (Copper Foundries)

INDUSTRY SNAPSHOT

Copper processing actually has many divisions, including such diverse activities as mining, smelting, refining, and fabricating. Copper is mined and refined before alloys are added to it. Copper and copper alloys are sold to fabricators who create such products as forgings, rods, bars, and tubes that are used in the construction industry, telecommunications industry, and in various manufacturing industries.

Copper is renowned for its corrosion resistance, electrical and thermal conductivity, machinability, color, and ease of finishing. Foundries combined copper with several other elements to create alloys with a wide range of qualities. Copper-based castings are strong and corrosion-resistant, making them essential as a basic tool in the building, plumbing, and automobile industries.

Foundries cast copper in many different ways. The most common of these are sand casting, centrifugal casting, continuous casting, investment casting, permanent mold casting, and shell mold casting. Sand casting, in which molten metal is poured into a sand mold, is the most widely used method of producing large quantities of copper and copper alloy castings. Because the cost of the sand mold patterns is usually reasonably low and sand is an incredibly reusable and then recyclable resource, this method of casting is ideal.

Centrifugal casting consists of pouring molten metal into a revolving or rotating mold, which in turn holds the molten metal against the wall by centrifugal force. This method is often utilized for casting bearings, gears, or machinery pieces. In a continuous casting system, molten copper alloy is fed through an open-ended mold to yield bar, tube, or other shaped cables.

Investment casting—also called precision casting—has an extensive history that predates the Egyptian pyramids. In the late twentieth century, it was still used to produce decorative copper applications and aircraft parts.

According to the U.S. Census Bureau's *1997 Economic Census—Manufacturing,* 312 establishments operated in this category for part or all of 1997. Industry-wide employment totaled 8,909 workers receiving a payroll of more than $260 million. Within this workforce, 7,423 of these employees worked in production, putting in more than 15 million hours to earn wages of more than $192 million. Overall shipments for the industry were valued at almost $855 million.

ORGANIZATION AND STRUCTURE

Most U.S. foundries are small by the relative standards of U.S. industry. Forty percent of the copper foundries employed less than 100 people, and in 1994 there were 195 copper companies employing fewer than 20 people. The number of workers in the copper foundry industries remained relatively steady, dropping only slightly from 8,200 in 1987 to 8,100 in 1994. The number of hours worked per year per production worker in these foundries was 2,138 in 1994, as compared to the industry standard of 2,056. That same year, hourly pay, at $9.67 per hour, was considerably less than the hourly wage for all other manufacturing industries, at $12.09.

According to the "30th Census of World Casting Production" compiled by the trade magazine *Modern Casting,* there were approximately 2,100 foundries of nonferrous metal in the United States operating in 1995. These foundries produced 311,000 metric tons of copper and copper-alloys. Foundries in the United States pro-

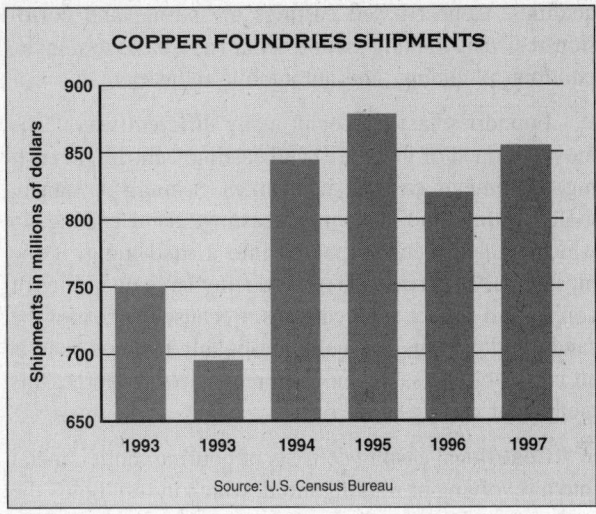

COPPER FOUNDRIES SHIPMENTS

Source: U.S. Census Bureau

BACKGROUND AND DEVELOPMENT

Copper-based castings have a long history. Copper artifacts have been dated back to 8700 B.C., and smelting was being performed as early as 5000 B.C. Casting, especially sand casting, is one of the oldest known methods of producing metal components. As agricultural equipment, shipping equipment, and plumbing developed, so did the need for advanced castings. Nonferrous castings, including copper-based castings, also became essential to the modern world with the proliferation of automobiles, televisions, airplanes, and telecommunications equipment.

In the 1950s and 1960s, induction furnaces were used in most foundries to melt brass and other copper alloys. Core, or channel, furnaces and coreless, or crucible, furnaces were both induction furnaces in which current was induced into the metal before it was melted. The temperature of the metal to be poured was carefully monitored by a pyrometer. Pyrometers became increasingly accurate and easier to read as the technology improved during the 1960s.

There were tremendous advances in technology and environmental science from the 1960s through the 1980s. As foundry practices began to adapt to these advances, the improvements saved money, increased efficiency, and assisted U.S. foundries in maintaining world leadership in the field, which was becoming an increasingly difficult task with the emergence of casting producers in foreign countries. Many of these foreign foundries boasted state-of-the-art facilities, low labor costs, and subsidized work. Having difficulty competing with these imports, U.S. foundries accused their foreign counterparts of dumping products below costs.

The metalcasting industry is a basic component of all industrial societies, but the economic upheavals in the 1970s and 1980s brought tremendous change to the industry. Many foundries had to close their doors, while many merged into larger companies.

CURRENT CONDITIONS

Copper foundries rely on the health of the U.S. economy and the success of their customers in the manufacturing industries in order to prosper. The business environment for copper-related industries has remained somewhat flat during the last decade of the twentieth century. The copper foundries have experienced a continual fight between the eroding plumbing fitting market by plastic substitution and increased commercial growth in industrial valves and fittings. The latter market has been aided by reduced imports as U.S producers become more competitive. Some foundries have survived by investing in new plants and equipment to accommodate changes in technology. Many have cut their labor forces to become more cost

duced more copper-based castings than anywhere else in the world.

U.S. foundries consumed 17,200 short tons of refined copper in 1995, which was less than the high of 19,000 short tons in 1994. The foundries consumed far less refined copper than both wire rod mills and brass mills. They consumed more, however, than ingot makers and powder plants. According to the U.S. Department of Commerce, the supply of copper content in wire mill products was 3.83 million short tons in 1995—a new high—while the supply of foundry products fell from 425,000 short tons in 1994 to 395,000 short tons in 1995. Approximately 25 to 30 percent of the castings output in the United States came from captive foundry producers—those within a vertically integrated operation—in the 1990s.

One of the mainstays of the U.S. copper industry is the Copper Development Association (CDA). Its members include the primary copper producers, miners, and smelters described in **SIC 3331: Primary Smelting and Refining of Copper;** manufacturers of mill products such as sheet, strip, rod, bar, tube, and pipe described in **SIC 3351: Rolling, Drawing, and Extruding of Copper;** as well as the copper foundries of this industry. CDA tracks market statistics and publishes handbooks, reports, and bulletins as part of its efforts to broaden copper markets in this country and abroad.

The American Foundrymen's Society (AFS) comprises the foundries of the United States, Canada, and Mexico. It is a professional, technical, and management association that works with government leadership to influence Congress on legislative issues, prepare educational programs, and perform research for its members and interested lay people. With almost 13,000 members in more than 47 countries, it is the leading metalcasting association in North America.

effective. The surviving foundries have also worked with users of their end products to customize castings.

Twice during the summer of 1999, copper prices jumped at the news of decreasing mining or production capacity. First, in early July, when Phelps Dodge Corp. announced its intention to cut output while the Highland Valley Copper Co. closed one of its copper mines, copper prices reacted by jumping 4.1 cents to reach 75.7 cents per pound before closing the day at the London Metal Exchange (LME) at 75.15 cents. Later, in early August, Phelps Dodge, Cyprus Amex Minerals Co. and Asarco Inc. hiked their premiums by 0.25 cents in reaction to limited rod manufacturing capacity and rising prices. At the same time, Broken Hill Proprietary (BHP) Co. Ltd. closed its 365,000 ton-a-year San Manuel, Arizona smelter, tightening supply throughout the industry.

INDUSTRY LEADERS

Federal-Mogul Corp. of Southfield, Michigan led the industry with 1998 sales of just under $44.7 billion created by 54,350 workers. Phoenix-based Phelps Dodge followed with 1998 sales of almost $3.1 billion. Olin Corporation's Brass Division of East Alton, Illinois rounded out the top three industry leaders with sales of $829 million for 1997, according to the most recent results available on Infotrac databases. Other industry leaders included Tucson-based BHP Copper North American Operations; JSJ Corp. of Grand Haven, Michigan; and Revere Copper Products Inc. of Rome, New York.

FURTHER READING

Copper Development Association Inc. "Annual Data: 1996: Copper Supply and Consumption, 1972-1995," New York, 1996.

————. "Copper in the USA: Bright Future—Colorful Past." New York, 1996.

Infotrac Company Profiles. Available at http://web4.infotrac .galegroup.com (visited 1/28/00).

U.S. Census Bureau. *1997 Economic Census—Manufacturing.* Available at http://www.census.gov/prod/ec97/97m3315g.pdf.

Yafie, Robert C. "Copper Prices Surge on Supply News." *American Metal Market,* 1 July 1999.

————. "Copper Rod Premiums Up." *American Metal Market,* 4 August 1999.

SIC 3369

NONFERROUS FOUNDRIES, EXCEPT ALUMINUM AND COPPER

This industry includes establishments primarily engaged in manufacturing nonferrous metal castings, including alloys, except aluminum and copper castings and all die-castings.

NAICS CODE(S)

331528 (Other Nonferrous Foundries)

Metalcasters in this industry pour molten metals such as nickel, zinc, magnesium, beryllium, and titanium into molds made from sand, plaster, or other materials. When the metal cools, it forms a casting that can be used either as a part of a tool or machine to manufacture other products or as a component of a product being manufactured. Major casting products include parts for motor vehicles and other machine parts. Generally less costly than die-casting, these castings are also used to produce prototypes of machine parts for testing and evaluation prior to mass production.

According to the U.S. Census Bureau's *1997 Economic Census—Manufacturing,* 141 establishments operated in this category for part or all of 1997. Industry-wide employment totaled 6,529 workers receiving a payroll of almost $215 million. Of these employees, 5,163 worked in production, putting in more than 10 million hours to earn wages of more than $141 million. Overall shipments for the industry were valued at more than $959 million.

Industry leader Budd Co. of Troy, Michigan, with 1998 sales of $3.7 billion, won three major contracts in 1998: manufacturing BMW's exterior sheet steel body panels and subassemblies for its sports utility vehicles (SUV); building steel frames for General Motors's SUVs; and assembling Ford's exterior sheet panels and welded body subassemblies for compact Ford Explorers and Mercury Mountaineers.

The Wyman-Gordon Group of Grafton, Massachusetts, which held second place in the industry in 1999 with $849 million in sales, experienced downed forging presses in both 1998 and 1999. In March 1998, the malfunction of Wyman-Gordon's 29,000-ton press demonstrated the commercial aircraft industry's overwhelming reliance on this company's supply of titanium. On December 1, 1999 the aircraft industry again suffered delays in delivery of titanium when Wyman-Gordon's 50,000-ton forging press—the largest press in the industry, along with Alcoa's twin press—shutdown for 3 weeks. Even though it was replaced during its downtime by a 35,000-ton press that handled 95 percent of the workload, considerable delays were inevitable. And, finally, when the larger press returned to the production line, it operated at less than full capacity. Other industry leaders included American Cast Iron Pipe Co. of Birmingham, Alabama (with 1998 sales of $500 million); Copper and Brass Sales Inc. of Eastpointe, Michigan; Cleveland-based Brush Wellman Inc.; and Dallas-based TIC United Corp.

The category is relatively new to the SIC system, as a reclassification took place in 1987 to narrow the scope of this industry. From a total of $339.9 million in 1987 shipments, the industry increased steadily to $617.1 million before inflation by 1995. Industry product share in the 1990s was distributed between nickel castings with 21.8 percent of the total share; zinc castings accounted for 7.9 percent; magnesium and magnesium-base alloy cast in sand molds claimed 7.1 percent; and the remaining 63.2 percent share of the industry was made up of titanium and miscellaneous nonferrous castings.

In 1995 the industry employed 4,600 laborers, 3,200 of whom were production workers. Production workers earned an average wage of $12.81 per hour, which was 3.6 percent higher than the average for all U.S. manufacturing.

Approaching the twenty-first century, the occupational outlook for this industry was favorable compared to other manufacturing industries. Employment levels were expected to drop by less than 2 percent for grinders and polishers, inspectors, mold assembly and shakeout workers, metal pourers, assemblers, metal machine operators, machine forming operators, and secretaries. Those occupations expected to grow more than 20 percent include machinists, combination machine tool operators, tool and die makers, industrial machinery mechanics, maintenance repairers, sales workers, and industrial production managers.

In the late 1990s, manufacturing trends for the industry were similar to those for other metalcasting industries—that is, producing castings with lower-cost materials and with greater efficiency. Research and development has focused on several technologies: developing new materials, particularly alloys, with similar or better physical characteristics and lower costs to produce than conventional metals; finding more energy-efficient processes, since the energy needed to melt metals amounts to as little as 25 percent of production costs; and implementing process improvements to make production less labor intensive and to reduce waste materials.

FURTHER READING

Darnay, Arsen J., ed. *Manufacturing USA*. 5th ed. Detroit: Gale Research, 1996.

"Downed forging press points up supply chain's delicate balance." *Aviation Week & Space Technology*, 2 March 1998.

Haflich, Frank. "Wyman-Gordon's big press hit with 3-week shutdown." *American Metal Market*, 17 November 1999.

Infotrac Company Profiles, 28 January 2000. Available from http://web4.infotrac.galegroup.com.

U.S. Census Bureau. *1995 Annual Survey of Manufactures*. Washington: GPO, 1997.

———. *1997 Economic Census—Manufacturing*, 10 February 2000. Available from http://www.census.gov/prod/ec97/97m3315h.pdf.

U.S. Department of Energy. Office of Industrial Technologies. *Industries of the Future: The Metalcasting Industry*. Washington, 1996. Available from http://oit.eh.doe.gov/pudesc/metal.htm.

Wrigley, Al. "Budd Gets Big Ford SUV Contract." *American Metal Market*, 7 September 1998.

———. "Budd to Supply Frames for GM's Compact SUVs." *American Metal Market*, 1 June 1998.

SIC 3398

METAL HEAT TREATING

This category covers establishments primarily engaged in heat treating of metal for the trade.

NAICS CODE(S)

332811 (Metal Heat Treating)

The various forms of heat treating are used to make metals more durable and to improve their mechanical performance for manufacturing. Heat treating processes include brazing, annealing, hardening and tempering, normalizing, nitriding, and carburizing. In each of these processes, controlled heat is generated from an electrical or gas-based source and applied to metals, making heat treatment an energy-intensive industry. Heat treated metals are required in components produced for aerospace, industrial machinery, heavy equipment for construction and agriculture, motor vehicles, and general manufacturing.

According to the U.S. Census Bureau's *1997 Economic Census—Manufacturing*, 805 establishments operated in this category for some or all of 1997. Industry employment totaled 22,318 workers receiving a payroll of almost $791 million. Of these employees, 17,263 worked in production, putting in almost 36 million hours to earn wages of more than $523 million. Overall shipments for the industry were valued at almost $3.5 billion.

In 1998, Cleveland-based industry leader LTV Corp., which generated sales of almost $4.3 billion, joined together with Steel Dynamics Inc. (Butler, Indiana) and Weirton Steel Corp. (Weirton, West Virginia) to create a World Wide Web-based dynamic portal trading system called MetalExchange, through which to sell steel. Weirton's existing online sales site generated about $50 million per year during the two years prior. Then, in late 1999, General Motors announced it would conduct all $87 billion worth of its steel purchasing online within two years. Online commerce promised increased efficiencies, reducing purchase order processing from $100 to $10 by 2001. GM chose to conduct its business through MetalSite, an outgrowth of MetalExchange with added equity partners Bethlehem Steel Corp. of Bethlehem, Pennsylvania, and

Chicago-based Ryerson Tull Inc. GM's proposed processing fee of 1 to 2 percent fell to between 0.25 and 0.5 percent before even getting online, with steel industry hopes that it would disappear altogether.

Other industry leaders included Southington Savings Bank of Plantsville, Connecticut, with $521 million in 1998 sales; Wheeling-Nisshin Inc. of Follansbee, West Virginia; Curtiss-Wright Corp. of Lyndhurst, New Jersey; and Bodine Aluminum Inc. of Overland, Missouri.

An estimated 670 U.S. establishments performed metal heat treating in 1996. The total number of establishments declined slightly between the 1980s and 1990s. Industry shipments of heat-treated metals totaled $3.19 billion in 1995, which was roughly a 23 percent pre-inflation increase over the previous year. In the 1990s the value of this industry's output grew by more than 50 percent before inflation.

Of the 19,500 workers in the industry in 1995, some 14,600 were engaged in production labor and earned an average of $12.77 per hour—about 3 percent higher than average for manufacturing employees in the United States.

As the twenty-first century approached, the employment levels of many occupations in the primary metal products industry, which includes heat treatment facilities, were expected to decrease. Those occupations expected to face reductions of more than 25 percent included miscellaneous hand workers, electricians, metal pourers, metal/plastic machine workers, furnace operators, and welders. Those occupations expected to face reductions between 10 and 25 percent included production worker supervisors, general laborers, heat treating machine operators, furnace operators, truck and tractor operators, crushing and mixing machine operators, inspectors, crane operators, material movers, machine tool workers, secretaries, machine feeders, science and mathematics technicians, material moving equipment operators, and metal molding machine operators. Sales workers were expected to be in demand, as the employment level in this occupation was expected to increase by 12.5 percent by the year 2000.

FURTHER READING

Darnay, Arsen J., ed. *Manufacturing USA: Industry Analysis, Statistics, and Leading Companies,* 5th ed. Detroit: Gale Research, 1996.

Infotrac Company Profiles, 1 January 2000. Available from http://web2.infotrac.galegroup.com.

Machlis, Sharon. "Steelmakers set up portal to Web." *Computerworld,* 24 August 1998.

Robertson, Scott. "GM Moves to Internet to link with suppliers." *American Metal Market,* 10 November 1999.

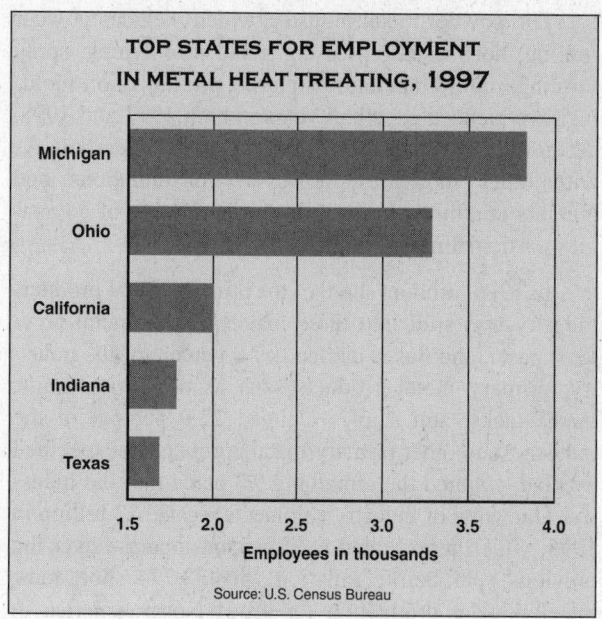

TOP STATES FOR EMPLOYMENT IN METAL HEAT TREATING, 1997

Employees in thousands

Source: U.S. Census Bureau

U.S. Census Bureau. *1997 Economic Census—Manufacturing,* 2 February 2000. Available from http://www.census.gov/prod/ec97/97m3328a.pdf.

———. *1995 Annual Survey of Manufactures.* Washington: GPO, 1997.

U.S. Department of Labor. Bureau of Labor Statistics. *Occupational Outlook Handbook, 1996-97.* Washington: GPO, 1996. Available from http://stats.bls.gov:80/ocohome.htm.

SIC 3399

PRIMARY METAL PRODUCTS, NOT ELSEWHERE CLASSIFIED

This category covers establishments primarily engaged in manufacturing primary metal products, not elsewhere classified, such as nonferrous nails, brads, and spikes, and metal powder, flakes, and paste. Steel nails, brads, spikes, and stables are classified under **SIC 3315: Steel Wiredrawing and Steel Nails and Spikes.**

NAICS CODE(S)

331111 (Iron and Steel Mills)
331314 (Secondary Smelting and Alloying of Aluminum)
331423 (Secondary Smelting, Refining and Alloying of Copper)
331492 (Secondary Smelting, Refining, and Alloying of Nonferrous Metals (except Copper and Aluminum))
332618 (Other Fabricated Wire Product Manufacturing)
332813 (Electroplating, Plating, Polishing, Anodizing, and Coloring)

The powder metal industry, which includes powder forging, hot isostatic pressing, rapid prototyping, spray forming, high-temperature sintering and injection molding, experienced excellent years in both 1997 and 1998, according to the Metal Powder Industries Federation. As with other industries, however, consolidations and mergers continued to push down the number of companies participating in the industry.

In 1996, product share of the primary metal products industry was split into three major groups: metal powders, paste, and flakes claimed 67.8 percent of the industry; primary metal products such as nonferrous nails, brads, tacks, and staples claimed 22.9 percent of the industry; and other primary metal products, not specified by kind, claimed the remaining 9.3 percent of the industry. The value of industry shipments was $3.13 billion in 1995, which represented a 32 percent increase over the previous year before inflation. At 433,774 short tons, metal powder production for all of North America in 1995 was up only 1.8 percent from the previous year, according to the Metal Powder Industries Federation. New capital expenditures for plant and equipment investment amounted to $137.8 million in 1995, up roughly 60 percent from 1994.

The vast majority of metal powders, more than 66 percent according to the Metal Powder Industries Federation, are used in the automotive industry. Other applications include office equipment, sporting goods, medical devices, industrial machinery and household appliances.

Leading the industry was Praxair Inc. of Danbury, Connecticut with more than $4.8 billion in 1998 sales on the strength of 24,834 employees. Ferro Corp. of Brecksville, Ohio, which generated 1998 sales of almost $1.4 billion, introduced a new line of stock-powder coatings in 1999 called ''Vista,'' with 62 colors in a choice of 13 textures. Rounding out the top three industry leaders was United States Surgical Corp. of Norwalk, Connecticut, with almost $1.2 billion in 1998 sales. Other industry leaders included St. Louis-based Doe Run Co.; Norandal

USA Inc. of Brentwood, Tennessee; and West Company Inc. of Lionville, Pennsylvania.

At $13.89 per hour, the average wage for production workers in this industry in 1995 was approximately 12 percent higher than the average for the manufacturing industry as a whole. Growing in the 1980s, the total number of establishments in the industry leveled during the mid-1990s to about 260.

As the twenty-first century approached, the employment levels of many occupations in the primary metal products industry, including nonferrous foundries and heat treatment facilities, were expected to decrease. The occupations expected to face reductions of more than 25 percent include miscellaneous hand workers, electricians, metal pourers, metal/plastic machine workers, furnace operators, and welders. The occupations expected to face reductions between 10 and 25 percent include blue collar worker supervisors, general laborers, heat treating machine operators, furnace operators, truck and tractor operators, crushing and mixing machine operators, inspectors, crane operators, material movers, machine tool workers, secretaries, machine feeders, science and mathematics technicians, material moving equipment operators, and metal molding machine operators. Sales positions were expected to increase, however, by as much as 12.5 percent during the 1990s.

FURTHER READING

Darnay, Arsen J., ed. *Manufacturing USA*. 5th ed. Detroit: Gale Research, 1996.

Infotrac Company Profiles. Available from http://web2.infotrac.galegroup.com. 1/29/00.

Metal Powder Industries Federation. *Metal Powder Industries Federation*. Princeton, NJ, 1996. Available from http://www.mpif.org.

U.S. Census Bureau. *1995 Annual Survey of Manufactures*. Washington: GPO, 1997.

Wrigley, Al. ''P/m consolidation continuing.'' *American Metal Market*, 8 June 1998.

FABRICATED METAL PRODUCTS, EXCEPT MACHINERY/ TRANSPORTATION EQUIPMENT

METAL CANS

The metal can and shipping container industry includes companies engaged in the manufacture of metal cans from purchased materials, primarily steel and aluminum. The majority of the cans and containers produced in this industry are used to package various foods and beverages. Foil containers are excluded from this classification.

NAICS CODE(S)

332431 (Metal Can Manufacturing)

INDUSTRY SNAPSHOT

In the late 1990s, several segments of the can manufacturing industry experienced steady growth. Aluminum soft drink can producers, for example, recovered from a slip in 1995, and reported that 1998 shipments were up 2.2 percent. However, the market for aluminum beer cans decreased. Moreover, aluminum cans faced fierce competition from polyethylene terephthalate (PET) plastic bottles that came to claim a greater share of the beverage container market each year. The steel can market also dwindled in the late 1990s, and the entire metal can industry consolidated, as companies sought to remain profitable. The long term outlook for the maturing metal can industry depends on the industry's ability to exploit burgeoning foreign markets, new production technologies, and recycling opportunities.

ORGANIZATION AND STRUCTURE

The metal can industry was divided along the lines of the raw material used in manufacturing: steel and aluminum. Of the two types of cans, steel proved less expensive to produce, easier to heat, and stronger, while alumi-

num offered a greater strength-to-weight ratio, making it less expensive to transport. Moreover, consumers generally preferred aluminum cans over steel for some products, particularly beverages. Technological advances in the recycling industry generally applied to aluminum rather than steel cans.

The manufacture of steel cans typically involved three pieces—a top, bottom, and body. The body of the can was rolled and then soldered, welded, or cemented at the seam, and the can's top and bottom were later mounted to the ends of the body. Tin-plated steel cans, on the other hand, were generally constructed from two pieces, including a body and bottom, which were stamped and drawn from one piece of metal, and a top that was later attached. Aluminum cans were also produced from two pieces of metal, but usually featured a slight "neck" at the top of the body, which reduced the amount of material needed.

Because of its packaging properties, steel was used to produce the vast majority of all food cans and containers made from metal in the late 1990s. Steel also comprised about half of all non-food metal containers. Vegetables, pet food, aerosol cans, fruit and fruit juices, seafoods, and baby food were all commonly packaged in steel cans.

Aluminum cans were used primarily as beverage containers, largely because they were recyclable and held a greater appeal for consumers. Aluminum can manufacturers used more aluminum than any other U.S. industry. Of containers used by soft drink manufacturers in 1998, 48 percent were made of aluminum, while about 53 percent of the beer industry's containers were aluminum.

Recycled cans provided an important source of production material for manufacturers. Of the 102 billion aluminum cans produced in 1998, 63 percent (or 64 billion) were recycled, according to The Aluminum Association. While both steel and aluminum cans were nearly 100 percent recyclable, aluminum can manufacturers favored the process due to the high price of new aluminum, which was nearly double that of steel. Recycling saved 95 percent of the energy necessary to produce finished aluminum, and eliminated altogether the mining, shipping, refining, and reduction processes. While new steel production was a less expensive process, many steel can producers were also using recycled materials, given its cost-effectiveness and the country's increasing concern for environmental conservation.

BACKGROUND AND DEVELOPMENT

The canning industry traces its origins to 1809, when French confectioner Nicolas Appert developed a method for preserving food, using glass jars that had been boiled in water. The ability to keep raw food from spoiling over long periods of time proved an important discovery, of particular benefit to French troops at war during this time. The basic canning principles developed by Appert closely resembled canning processes still used in many applications in the 1990s; carefully prepared raw food was sealed in a container, heated to a predetermined temperature to destroy spoilage organisms, and then cooled.

The glass bottle was eventually replaced by the tin can in a procedure patented in England by Peter Durand. While canning technology reached the United States in 1820, the tin-coated steel container did not gain widespread use in America until 1939. In 1861, Isaac Solomon discovered that adding sodium chloride to the preserving and canning process allowed for a longer shelf life. Subsequent advancements in canning during the Civil War hastened industry growth.

The canning industry experienced rapid proliferation beginning in the early 1900s, when advancements in can and glass jar technology lowered costs and improved canning reliability. For instance, soldered seams, which sometimes contaminated the food, were replaced by more reliable welding techniques during this time. Furthermore, the development of new machinery allowed producers to manufacture and fill mass quantities of cans.

Progress in can coatings and preservatives during the 1950s, among other technological breakthroughs, helped establish the United States as a world leader in the canning industry. By 1965, in fact, the United States was producing about 1.7 billion cans per year. The canning industry continued to enjoy high growth rates over the next two decades, as potential uses for the traditional steel can increased dramatically, most notably perhaps as a container for carbonated beverages. Although carbonated beverages constituted a negligible market for cans in the 1960s, by 1975 manufacturers were producing over 26 billion beverage cans per year, eclipsing the use of cans for food.

However, while the market for cans expanded, alternative packaging methods began offering stiff competition. Plastic and aluminum containers, which were developed into viable canning techniques during the early 1960s, began to enjoy widespread use in the 1970s. Because they offered price, weight, and convenience advantages important to beverage producers, aluminum cans quickly began to overtake that market segment. Furthermore, in 1974, Reynolds Metals Co. developed a pull-tab for the aluminum can that remained attached to the can after opening. This innovation proved safer than the traditional steel pull-tab and also produced less litter, making the aluminum can especially attractive to the beverage market.

The market for metal beverage cans continued to escalate in the 1980s—from about 50 billion cans produced in 1980 to over 97 billion by 1995—and aluminum cans captured an increasing share of the market. Having entered the industry in 1961, aluminum's market share reached 79 percent by 1975, 82 percent by 1980, and accounted for 95 percent in the 1990s. Furthermore, the beverage can market had grown to dominate the entire can industry. By the early 1990s, nearly three times more aluminum cans than steel cans were being produced. Plastic containers, which accounted for more than 25 percent of all food container production, were also competing for can consumers.

During this time, the introduction of the aluminum can recycling industry bolstered the popularity of the aluminum can. The amount of aluminum cans recycled annually leapt from about 300 million pounds in 1979 to nearly two billion pounds by 1991. In 1995, 62 percent of the 100 billion cans produced were recycled.

Although they had effectively been nudged out of the beverage can industry, steel can manufacturers continued to control the food and consumer products can market. Throughout the 1980s and early 1990s, steel cans represented approximately 95 percent of that market. By the mid-1990s, however, steel container revenues were in decline, due largely to increased competition from microwave and frozen food products that utilized plastic packaging. During this time, shipments of steel cans and containers remained between 4.1 and 4.5 billion tons.

U.S. aluminum can manufacturers faced a slow economy and a mature domestic market in the mid-1990s. Growth in this segment of the industry slowed to 3.9 percent in 1990 and just over 3 percent in 1992. Beer sales showed a decline as new products and microbrewers turned to glass bottles. As a consequence, can shipments to the beer industry fell from 36.8 billion units in 1994 to 35.1 billion units in 1995. Furthermore, sales to the soft drink industry, normally an increasing segment, dropped from 66.3 billion units in 1994 to 62.6 billion units in 1995.

A rise in aluminum prices at the beginning of 1996 had can fillers pre-buying sizable shipments in late 1995 and early 1996 to beat the increase. This price-sensitive purchasing caused gains for those periods but overall aluminum can manufacturers were cutting back on production. In 1996, Reynolds Metals Co. closed a 1-billion-can-a-year plant in Fulton, New York, and in 1997, discontinued operations of a 14-million-can-a-year plant in Houston. Crown Cork & Seal Company, Inc. closed two can plants and shut operations on another plant that produced beverage can ends. While both companies were shrinking their U.S. can capacity, however, they began expanding their operations in other parts of the world.

In addition to the industry-wide maturation of markets, steel can manufacturers in particular were challenged by slight gains experienced by producers of aluminum and plastic containers. Shipments of steel containers posted disappointing declines of 4.4 percent in 1991 and 5.7 percent in 1992, following nearly a decade of stagnation. The most notable blow to the industry was delivered in 1993, when Bev-Pak Inc., one of the nation's largest remaining producers of steel beverage cans, announced plans to switch to aluminum cans. Weirton Steel Corporation also announced its decision to end marketing efforts of steel cans.

CURRENT CONDITIONS

The aluminum can industry recovered from its slump of 1995 and 1996. Overall aluminum can shipments in the United States grew 2.2. percent in 1998 to reach 102.9 billion cans. Of this total number, soft drink cans accounted for over 67 percent with 69.5 billion cans. Beer cans represented about 32 percent (33.4 billion cans) of total aluminum beverage can shipments in 1998. According to *Beverage World*, the aluminum beverage can market is expected to continue to grow at about 2 percent per year through 2002.

Despite the positive aspects of the aluminum beverage can sector, several daunting challenges threaten the industry. Foremost among these is the rise of PET plastic bottles in the soft drink industry. Just as aluminum cans once overtook steel as the packaging material of choice for soda companies, PET bottles have made substantial inroads into the market, beginning in the late-1970s. In 1990, plastic bottles claimed only about 34 percent of the soft drink packaging market, while aluminum cans had a 54 percent share. However, by 1998 PET had acquired a 51 percent of soft drink packaging, compared to aluminum's 48 percent share. PET bottles have proved particularly successful in the "on-the-go" market of gas stations and convenience stores, where consumers appreciate the convenience of 20 ounce PET bottles.

Aluminum can manufacturers have fought back. Producers have stressed to beverage companies and bot-

tlers the benefits of aluminum cans—they are easier to stack and store on shelves than PET bottles and can be emblazoned like miniature billboards. Aluminum can manufacturers also began to tinker with can design to offer beverage companies aluminum packaging that could differentiate products. For instance, the development of thinner aluminum in the early 1990s was the enabled can manufacturers to adjust can shapes and production methods. The fluted can body resulted from experiments in this arena, as did the "202" beverage can, which sported a top that was one quarter of an inch smaller than most beverage cans used. Furthermore, Ball Corp. developed a spin-flow necking process that slimmed down both ends of its aluminum cans and thereby reduced the amount of aluminum required for manufacture as well as the amount of energy required in the production process. Even more promising, though, was can manufacturer's development of embossing techniques and high definition graphics. By 1999, worldwide sales of embossed cans neared 1 billion.

Steel cans did not fare as well as their aluminum counterparts in the late 1990s. In 1997, steel can shipments were valued at about $4.7 billion, which represented 39 percent of total shipments that year. Steel food can production fell from over 32 billion cans in 1997 to 31.7 billion in 1998.

The overall can industry of the late 1990s has been marked by consolidation, as manufactures seek to maximize profits. Between 1982 and 1992 the number of metal can manufacturing companies declined from 397 to 301. By 1997, only 272 companies were involved in can production, and 198 of these were larger companies with over 20 employees. The most significant event in the late 1990s occurred in August of 1998 when Ball Corp. acquired can-making division of Reynolds Metal Co. to vault ahead of its competitors.

INDUSTRY LEADERS

Based in Muncie, Indiana, Ball Co. is the largest can producer in the United States and the world. 1998 sales topped $2.89 billion, and the company employed 12,100 workers. About 25 percent of Ball's annual worldwide sales was derived from its can business with Coca-Cola and PepsiCo bottlers. American National Can Group, was the second-largest can manufacturer in the United States. Operating over 22 plants in the U.S., American National provided cans to the Adolph Coors Company, as well as to the Coca-Cola Company and its bottlers (which accounted for nearly half of American National's sales). The biggest can manufacturer in Europe, American National's 1998 sales were $2.45 billion and it employed 4,735. A third key player in the can industry was Crown Cork & Seal Company, Inc. based in Philadelphia, with 38,459 employees and sales of $8 billion in 1998.

Although these three companies were much larger than any of their competitors, their revenues were augmented significantly by a wide variety of operations outside of metal can manufacturing. The metal can industry as a whole remained relatively diversified, supporting several firms that generated revenues of less than $50 million and employed fewer than 500 employees.

WORKFORCE

Increased productivity in the industry prompted a reduced workforce, and between 1982 and 1990, as industry employment declined from about 50,000 to around 35,000. This trend continued in the 1990s with total employment in the industry falling from 30,900 to 27,241 between 1994 and 1997. This reduction was fueled by increased automation and the movement of production facilities to less-regulated, low-wage paying countries, such as Mexico. Jobs for machinery mechanics, which accounted for 10 percent of the workforce in 1993, were expected to decline by about 20 percent between 1990 and 2005. Positions for machine forming operators and tenders (7.4 percent of the work force) were expected to see declines in workforce of over 45 percent during the same period. In fact, every occupation in the industry would likely plunge by 10 to 50 percent, with most job opportunities—including those for top executives and managers—decreasing by at least 30 percent.

Nevertheless, production workers were essential to can manufacturing in the late 1990s. 23,000 of the 27,241 industry employees were directly involved in production in 1997. These workers earned an average wage of $19.84. California had the most employees in the industry in 1997, with 4,082, followed by Ohio with 3,348 and Illinois with 2,151.

AMERICA AND THE WORLD

Foreign food and beverage markets offered huge growth potential for U.S. canners, particularly aluminum can producers, who stood to benefit from the global shift away from steel cans. While 50 percent of all beverage cans produced outside the U.S. were steel in 1992, U.S. aluminum canners, operating the most technologically advanced and productive plants in the world, were poised to gain market share as other countries sought the environmental benefits associated with aluminum.

RESEARCH AND TECHNOLOGY

In addition to the strides made in improving aluminum cans, several steel beverage can developments also occurred in the early 1990s, as some producers tried to revive that market, including several Japanese firms. Despite these developments, most countries, including Japan, switched to aluminum in the 1990s. But steel cans had a slight resurgence in 1995, as six European can makers changed from aluminum to steel. Additionally, Northern Can System, of Canton, Ohio, introduced a steel can made with a steel end (instead of the industry norm of aluminum) to be used with a variety of non-carbonated beverages. And in Germany, Coca-Cola debuted a contoured can that could only be made from steel because of the distortion limitations of aluminum.

FURTHER READING

Darnay, Arsen J., ed. *Manufacturing USA.* 5th ed. Detroit: Gale Research, 1996.

Kidwell, Karen. "Beverage Can Shipments Overall Continue to Climb." *Beverage World,* 15 June 1999.

Lenderman, Maxim. "On the Up and Up." *Beverage World,* June 1996.

"Light Metals Processing." *JOM,* March 1996.

Pinkham, Myra. "Can Growth Expected Despite Inroads by PET." *American Metal Market,* October 27, 1999.

Regan, Bob. "Can Plant Shutdowns Announced by Crown." *American Metal Market,* 3 October 1995.

U.S. Census Bureau. "Metal Can Manufacturing," October 1999. Available from http://www.census.gov/prod/ec97/97m3314c.pdf.

"Can Shipment Rate Declines." *American Metal Market,* 26 December 1996.

"Can Shipments Slowed in 1995 Aluminum Tally." *American Metal Market,* 24 January 1996.

"Cans Staying Under 1994's Record Pace." *American Metal Market,* 29 November 1995.

———. "The Shape of Cans to Come." *Beverage World,* June 1996.

SIC 3412

METAL SHIPPING BARRELS, DRUMS, KEGS, AND PAILS

This category includes establishments primarily engaged in manufacturing metal shipping barrels, drums, kegs, and pails.

NAICS CODE(S)

332439 (Other Metal Container Manufacturing)

According to the U.S. Census Bureau's *1997 Economic Census—Manufacturing,* 151 establishments operated in this category for some or all of 1997. Industry wide employment totaled 6,098 workers receiving a payroll of more than $185 million; 4,814 of these employees worked in production, putting in more than 10 million hours to earn wages of almost $126 million. Overall shipments for the industry were valued at almost $1.3 billion.

Dallas-based Trinity Industries Inc. led the industry with sales of over $2.9 billion for its fiscal year ended March 31, 1999. Menasha Corp. of Neenah, Wisconsin, a fifth-generation privately owned firm, followed with $933 million in 1998 sales. Greif Bros. Corp. of Delaware, Ohio, rounded out the top three industry leaders with sales of $801 million for its fiscal year ended October 31, 1998. Other industry leaders included Longview Fibre Co. of Longview, Washington; Park-Ohio Holdings Corp. of Euclid, Ohio; and Russel-Stanley Corp. of Bridgewater, New Jersey, which in late 1999 introduced a new 55-gallon tight head steel drum with a ''W'' style hoop enclosure for maximum freight usability and vacuum seal.

The metal shipping barrels, drums, kegs, and pails industry has changed little since 1982. The value of shipments has remained fairly flat, only rising from $1.21 billion in 1990 to an estimated $1.30 billion in 1996, while employment levels have dropped slightly. There were 146 establishments in the industry in 1996, employing 6,600 people, of which 4,600 were production workers. When compared to other forms of manufacturing, this industry paid lower-than-average hourly wages of $11.86 in 1994; the average was $12.09. Steel shipping barrels and drums accounted for more than 67 percent of the industry's market share, with steel pails claiming 23.1 percent of the market. The remainder of the market was split between non-specific barrels, drums, and pails.

Five states held well over one-half of the industry's establishments and accounted for 60 percent of U.S. sales. Illinois' 19 establishments shipped $180.5 million worth of metal barrels, drums, kegs, and pails in 1996 and accounted for 18 percent of U.S. sales. Ohio's 20 establishments shipped $148.9 million and cornered a 13.1 percent share. Texas's 11 establishments shipped $145.2 million, with a 12.8 percent share of sales. California's 17 establishments shipped $106.4 million, accounting for 9.4 percent, and Pennsylvania's 11 establishments shipped $101.4 million, with an 8.9 percent share. Illinois' workers averaged the highest wages in 1994, at $13.05 per hour. Hourly workers in Texas were paid the lowest wages, at $8.82 per hour.

Employment levels of most occupations in this industry were expected to decline approaching the year 2005. Those facing reductions of more than 40 percent were machine feeders (expected to decline 40.4 percent), metal/plastic workers (a 41.3 percent decline), maintenance and repairers (40.5 percent), hand packers (43.3 percent), punching machine operators (47.0 percent), material handlers (47.1 percent), miscellaneous machine operators (41.6 percent), and welding machine setters (40.4 percent). All other types of employment were expected to decline by about 35 percent by 2005.

Modifications in the design of steel drums and higher quality steel have improved drum and pail performance considerably. The U.S. Department of Transportation (DOT) has also helped in improving the quality of the industry when their Performance-Oriented Packaging Standards went into effect in October of 1996. The new standards called for better formed individual drum parts, improved gasket and closing rings, and more secure joining of individual parts.

Both the improvement of technology and superior steel products have made incredible improvements to the drum and barrel industry. Computer controlled operations within the steel processing industry have improved thickness tolerances, resulting in stronger, yet thinner steel, and also eliminated pinholes. This meant that steel container manufacturers in the late 1990s had far better raw materials than they had just a few years before.

FURTHER READING

Darnay, Arsen J., ed. *Manufacturing USA: Industry Analysis, Statistics, and Leading Companies,* 5th ed. Detroit: Gale Research, 1996.

Infotrac Company Profiles. 29 January 2000. Available from http://web2.infotrac.galegroup.com.

''New container review.'' *Purchasing,* 7 October 1999.

Steel Shipping Container Institute. ''Steel Container Performance Improved Under POP Standars.'' *Packaging Vision,* October 1996. Available from http://www.steel.org/markets/containers/oct96.htm.

U.S. Census Bureau. *1997 Economic Census—Manufacturing.* Available from http://www.census.gov/prod/ec97/97m3324d.pdf (visited 2/10/00).

SIC 3421

CUTLERY

This category includes establishments primarily engaged in the manufacture of items such as pocket knives, safety razors, razor blades, straight razors, table cutlery, scissors, shears, manicure tools, kitchen and butcher knives, and artisan's knives. Establishments primarily engaged in manufacturing precious metal cutlery and table cutlery with handles of metal are classified **SIC 3914: Silverware, Plated Ware, and Stainless Steel Ware;** those manufacturing electric razors, knives, or scissors are classified in **SIC 3634: Electric Housewares and Fans;** those manufacturing hair clippers for human use are classified in **SIC 3999: Manufacturing Industries, Not Elsewhere Classified;** those manufacturing them for animal use in **SIC 3523: Farm Machinery and Equipment;** and those manufacturing power hedge shears and trimmers are classified in **SIC 3524: Lawn**

and Garden Tractors and Home Lawn and Garden Equipment.

NAICS Code(s)

332211 (Cutlery and Flatware (except Precious) Manufacturing)

Industry Snapshot

Rated in 1872 by J.B. Hyde as one of America's "great industries," cutlery manufacturing has witnessed significant change during the twentieth century. Instead of small craft shops producing innovative but simple utensils, modern cutlery firms are more likely to be mass producers of one or two extremely simple products that can be sold anywhere in the world. However, sales of the various cutlery products showed steady growth throughout the century, increasing from $37,002 in 1921 to $1.1 billion in 1987. The value of shipments in the industry for 1997 was $2.16 billion, up from $1.89 billion in 1995 and $1.80 billion in 1994.

Organization and Structure

The industry can be divided into two main components: kitchen and table cutlery, and nonelectric razors and razor blades. Shears and scissors comprise a third—but proportionately tiny—segment of the industry. Of the $2.16 billion in industry shipments, kitchen and table cutlery and shears and scissors accounted for $870 million; nonelectric razors and razor blades accounted for $1.18 billion.

There were 162 establishments manufacturing cutlery in 1997, according to the U.S. Census Bureau's *Economic Census.*, an increase from 104 in 1995. In 1997, 55 of these companies were larger establishments—with 20 or more employees. New York had the largest number of cutlery companies, with 20, followed by California with 16, and Ohio and Pennsylvania with 12 each.

Most cutlery products are sold by retail chain stores, warehouse clubs, specialty stores, or catalogue operations. Manufacturers supported retail sales with national advertising campaigns, promotional offers, and sales training programs.

In 1998, mass merchandisers like Wal-Mart, Kmart, Target and Bradlees accounted for 34 percent of all kitchen and table cutlery sales, according to a 1999 *Weekly Home Furnishings Newspaper* article. Department stores accounted for 33 percent of sales in this category, especially in higher-end products.

Background and Development

The production of quality cutting tools required skilled artisans, most of whom worked in the communities of Sheffield, England and Solingen, Germany. Because the cost to transport the finished product was small, early American efforts could not compete with the quality or price of imported products. The American industry was helped by a 20 percent ad valorem tax imposed in 1792 and an innovative machine-forged knife introduced in 1844. The U.S. industry continued to push for even higher tariffs in the 1890s with some success, but its greatest victory came during World War I.

Between 1914 and 1919, all German products disappeared from the Americas along with most British manufactures. Tariff increases in 1922 solidified the industry gain, ensuring both prosperity for the industry and high consumer prices, although the 1930s saw a shift in demand to lower-priced products.

One of the biggest problems for the industry was the quality of steel available. Sheffield set the standard with its invention of crucible steel in 1740. That process took imported Swedish "blister" steel, known for its consistent quality, and melted it in clay crucibles along with precise amounts of manganese, carbon, and other materials. The result was a steel well-suited for knives and other blades. American firms imported this steel, thereby increasing production costs, until late in the nineteenth century. At the time, American crucible steel proved unreliable and experiments with cold and hot rolled carbon steel produced an inferior product. In 1910 stainless steel in the form of an alloy of cobalt, chromium, and steel made its debut as the "rustless steel," but the lack of accurate measuring instruments, like pyrometers and thermometers, along with the scarcity of skilled annealers to judge the preparation of the metal, often resulted in brittle knives or soft edges.

However, technology and demand continued to evolve, and by 1930 a consistent material became available and competition prompted its almost universal use in many product lines. Half of all cutlery produced during the early 1930s used the new stainless steel mixtures of steel, chromium, and cobalt, molybdenum, silicon, vanadium, or magnesium. Electric smelting furnaces provided the control necessary to produce high-quality steel consistently.

Meanwhile, the American mass production system made inroads into the cutlery plant, displacing expensive, hard-to-find craftsmen like grinders with automated machinery that required no special skills to operate. Generally, firms specialized in a narrow range of products like butchers' knives or ax heads, but with excess manufacturing capacity available, especially just after World War I, many new firms entered the industry and produced cheaper knock-offs of the original products. The competition forced established firms to expand product lines and reduce inventory stock. At the same time, new product designs came and went as technology helped the product evolve.

The industry fought competition and falling prices with manufacturers' associations like the American Cutlers Association, which was founded in 1870 in Greenfield, Connecticut. It established uniform pricing, discount rates, and a method of absorbing freight costs into the price structure. The result was the continued dominance of East Coast firms as the market expanded westward. After fading for a few years, the association reappeared during World War II as a government lobbying group.

Trade unionism began to flourish in the early 1880s as a depression in the industry prompted manufacturers to attempt to reduce wages. In 1884, workers began to strike, although no official union backed the labor action at that time. Unofficially, the Knights of Labor Assembly was commonly accused of inflaming the workers. Despite intense labor organization and decades of strikes, the cutlery manufacturers associations managed to resist unionization and its demands by standardizing wages and hiring policies throughout the industry. The final blow to skilled labor came with industry-wide use of the grinding machine, which made the specialized artisans' skills obsolete.

The post-World War II period saw an influx of inexpensive Japanese and Chinese cutlery, along with a gradual reduction of import tariffs in the 1950s. The traditional centers of skilled trade for the industry gradually eroded as mass production techniques flooded the world markets. In the United States before tariff reductions, 50 domestic manufacturers supplied almost the entire country's demand for shears and scissors. By 1993, only six firms operated in the United States. Traditionally, cutlery manufacturers operated small plants in established rural communities, drawing on a base of family artisans.

In 1933, more than half of all cutlery produced in the United States came from cities of less than 500,000 people; most of those communities had fewer than 2,500 people. However, new industrial strategies gave the advantage to large cities with sizable pools of unskilled labor. Even so, some older firms like those in the Connecticut Valley retained a large portion of the market for certain specialty knives and other quality cutlery.

During the latter part of the twentieth century, small firms continued to join or be absorbed by large, diversified corporations. By 1987, only 61 establishments in the cutlery industry listed any form of cutlery as their primary product, according to the *Census of Manufactures*. The other 80 produced cutlery as a secondary or even tertiary product line.

The industry saw signs of an upturn during the 1980s, however, as a newly favored domestic lifestyle promised increased demand for products like cutlery, particularly high-tech innovative products that emphasized increased convenience. ''Never-sharpen'' knife sets with a $50 to $100 price range set the pace, but consumers quickly showed a predilection for mid-range products. For instance, good-quality stainless steel flat-

ware became the preferred alternative to silverware. At the same time, consumers insisted on brand-name products, but refused to pay high-end prices.

The industry reacted by consolidating production with universal products and reducing product lines to specialty, high-value, high-tech merchandise. In 1994, Gillette Company, the largest American razor manufacturer, announced it would reorganize its production arrangements by laying off 2,000 workers, or 6 percent of its work force, while hiring an equivalent number to increase production at other plants around the world. This strategy eliminated multi-product facilities, dedicating each plant to a specific product. Gillette's chairman and chief executive, Alfred Zeien, claimed the move was a continuation of his efforts to position the company as a global enterprise by producing universally accepted products that could be produced in large numbers and sold worldwide.

Other American cutlery firms became aware of the need to consider their global position with the introduction of ISO 9000 standards. Developed by the International Organization for Standardization, which was formed in Switzerland in 1946, the guidelines sought to reach across political boundaries and homogenize such industrial procedures as design, manufacturing, inspection, packaging, marketing, quality control, and measurement. European industry quickly moved to adopt ISO 9000 as the new international standard, but acceptance was slower in the United States.

CURRENT CONDITIONS

Cutlery sales across categories were strong in the late-1990s. Kitchen and table cutlery performed especially well in 1998, despite the fact that the sector was considered mature by many industry analysts. Sales rose 6.7 percent in 1998 to reach $678.9 million. The market for kitchen and table cutlery burgeoned as manufacturers released new designs and styles. Consumers were influenced by an emphasis on gourmet cooking. The number of cooking television shows rose dramatically during the decade, and buoyed by the booming economy of the late 1990s, consumers bought the brands they saw their favorite television chefs use. Kitchen and cutlery sales also increased as entertaining at home gained popularity in the final years of the decade. As a cutlery executive explained to *HFN*, ''The cocooning trend still comes into play.'' Mid-priced cutlery in this category proved especially successful in 1998. Consumers sought out well-known brands in favor of private label ones. A sales representative from Ekco Houseware explained to *HFN* that ''as you move into better-quality goods, brand is important.''

The U.S. razor market advanced in 1998 as well, with product innovation driving sales. Gillette's introduc-

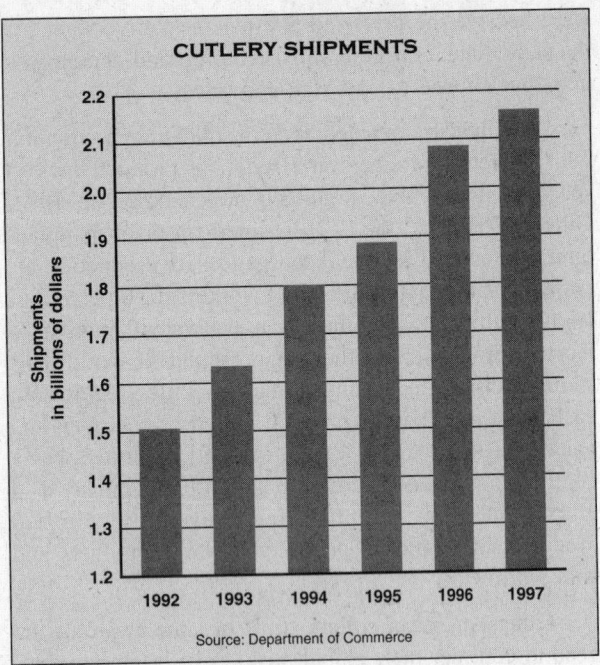

CUTLERY SHIPMENTS

Shipments in billions of dollars

Source: Department of Commerce

tion of the Mach 3 men's razor was the most important development in this sector in 1998, as the triple-bladed razor—comprised of a nondisposable handle and disposable blades—quickly became the best-selling brand in the category. Another key growth area consisted of razors specifically designed for—and marketed to—women. In 1998, the third best-selling razor was the Gillette Sensor Excel for Women.

Strong performance in the Swiss army knife, multi-tool, and lock back categories further contributed to a very favorable outlook for this industry. Multi-tools in particular had been steadily gaining in popularity since their introduction in 1983, cutting in on traditional knife sales.

INDUSTRY LEADERS

Most companies in this category were relatively small operations, with larger firms usually producing items in addition to cutlery. Some of the larger firms in the industry group include Gillette Company, BIC and American Safety Razor for the razor segment, Fiskars' Gerber Legendary Blades and Buck Knives for knife manufacturing, and Fiskars Inc. for scissors.

Gillette Company, the largest in the cutlery industry, commanded about 65 percent share of the razor market. Based in Boston, the firm began operations in 1901. Gillette employed 43,100 workers for total sales of $10 billion in 1998. The second largest company in the industry was Scott Fetzer Co. of Westlake, Ohio, with sales revenues of $935 million and 14,500 employees. Alcas Corp. ranked third with sales revenues of $551 million and 600 employees, while Oneida Ltd. was fourth with 1998 sales of $465.9 million and 5,010 employees.

Ranking fifth, BIC Corp of Milford, Connecticut, employed 2,500 workers and rang up sales of $439.3 million in 1998, compared to the $409.2 million in sales its next-biggest competitor, Viskase Companies Inc., reported that year. Nashua, New Hampshire-based Ekco was the seventh-largest company in this industry, with sales of $330 million and 1,070 employees, followed by Mirro Co. with 2,000 employees and sales of $300 million.

WORKFORCE

Employment in the cutlery industry declined from 13,400 in 1972, to 11,200 in 1995, and 11,102 in 1997. Of this total, 8,682 people were production workers in 1997, earning an average wage of $13.91 per hour. The workweek of production workers averaged approximately 37 hours. With 1,965 employees, New York was home to the greatest number in the industry, followed by California with 718 and Pennsylvania with 553.

AMERICA AND THE WORLD

The nature of the typical cutlery firm changed dramatically by the 1990s. The small shop still existed, but was rare. Despite complaints of unfair competition and "dumping" from the traditional centers of the industry, accompanied by demands for ever-higher tariff protection, mass marketing firms in countries like China, Japan, Brazil, and Korea made steady inroads and forced the old firms to reassess their operations.

Many failed, but some, like Westall Richardson of Britain, succeeded. Westall Richardson became Europe's largest producer of kitchen knives by 1987 and captured 33 percent of the British market. Most of its 400 employees were unskilled laborers; the company concentrated its expertise in engineering and marketing.

By the late 1980s, Sheffield, the mecca of the industry, could only support a small number of specialized firms as well as an equally small collection of master cutlers, known as "little Masters." In the late 1980s, one of the few remaining cutlery factories in Sheffield, the Globe Works, received a $1.5 million historic restoration grant. Because the center was built as an integrated factory in 1825, it included facilities for every part of the cutlery manufacturing process, from charcoal-burning furnaces to grinding and finishing workshops.

The grant was used to restore the workshops and manager's residence destroyed in a fire in 1970. The restored works provided a site where the vanishing skills of the little masters could be passed on to later generations of crafters. Plans call for the complex to become a showplace for the industry and a training facility for the British Cutlery and Silverware Association.

Certainly the concept of specialization was a boon for the Swiss firm, Victorinox. The makers of the internationally renowned Swiss Army knife produced at least

4 million of their distinctive pocketknives annually as of 1984. Actual sales figures are a closely guarded secret. In addition to pocketknives, Victorinox makes kitchen and butcher's knives. Even Victorinox, however, felt threatened by foreign competition from mass-production factories.

Cheap knock-offs of the original Swiss pocket knife appeared routinely in Taiwan and Japan; the Far East, West Germany, Austria, and the United States were just as likely to have firms copying and marketing look-alike products. Even the Swiss Helvetia Cross appeared on the copies. Such copyright infringement invariably brought diplomatic protests, but the company found its only effective protection was to clearly brand "Victorinox, Switzerland, Stainless, and Rostfrie" on every knife it made.

Such careful branding, which also included date and place of manufacture, helped create the hobby of pocket knife collecting, which became one of the hottest new crazes in American antique collecting in the 1990s. With each knife clearly identified, value and collectability could be determined and agreed upon easily.

RESEARCH AND TECHNOLOGY

The twentieth century began with the introduction of stainless steel as the preferred metal in cutlery manufacturing. That led to mass production machinery and plant specialization as the old skills of the trade, geared to old metals, became increasingly obsolete. By the end of the century, stainless steel also faced the possibility of obsolescence as the industry sought high-tech replacement materials for increasingly rare and expensive natural resources like iron and aluminum. The new, computer-designed substances offered the advantages of being stronger, lighter, more durable, and easier to work with, which reduced the skill-level needed to form the finished product.

As Robert Newnham, professor of solid-state science at Pennsylvania State University, told *Time* magazine, "At one time, we had to settle for whatever Mother Nature gave us. Now if we're not satisfied we can go out and create our own materials." These materials were beginning to appear in 1990 in such products as ceramic scissors that never rusted and never got dull. The United States led the world in materials research for much of the century, but by the last decade the Japanese were forging ahead. While the American preoccupation with military and aerospace applications restricted research for industrial and consumer applications, the Japanese targeted those areas specifically.

FURTHER READING

Darnay, Arsen J., ed. *Manufacturing USA.* 5th ed. Detroit: Gale Research, 1996.

Lloyd, Simon. "Gillette's Mach 3 is Brought Back to Earth." *Business Review Weekly,* 27 August 1999.

Thau, Barbara. "Cutting Edge: Cutlery Gets a Makeover." *HFN The Weekly Newspaper for the Home Furnishing Network,*5 July 1999.

U.S. Census Bureau. "Cutlery and Flatware Manufacturing," October 1999. Available from http://www.census.gov/prod.

Werner, Holly M. "Cutlery Brands vs. Private Label." *HFN The Weekly Newspaper for the Home Furnishing Network,* 4 November 1996.

————. "Regent Sheffield Cutting Loose; Hones Campaign to Add Share, Widen Markets." *HFN The Weekly Newspaper for the Home Furnishing Network,* 22 July 1996.

SIC 3423

HAND AND EDGE TOOLS, EXCEPT MACHINE TOOLS AND HANDSAWS

Firms in this industry manufacture simple, edged hand-tools such as files, axes, chisels, prying bars, rulers, soldering irons, tongs, rakes, and cutters for metalworking, woodworking, and general maintenance. Saws and saw blades are discussed in **SIC 3425: Saw Blades and Handsaws,** while metal-cutting dies and power-driven hand tools, attachments, and accessories appear under the major group for industrial and commercial machinery and computer equipment.

NAICS CODE(S)

332212 (Hand and Edge Tool Manufacturing)

According to the U.S. Census Bureau's *1997 Economic Census—Manufacturing,* 1,066 establishments operated in this category for part or all of 1997. Industry-wide employment totaled 42,906 workers receiving a payroll of more than $1.3 billion; 32,743 of these employees worked in production, putting in almost 66 million hours to earn wages of more than $838 million. Overall shipments for the industry were valued at almost $5.7 billion.

Houston-based Cooper Industries Inc. led the industry with 1998 sales of almost $3.7 billion behind the strength of 28,100 workers. Danaher Corp., based in Washington D.C., followed with 1998 sales of more than $2.9 billion created by 18,000 employees. Rounding out the top three industry leaders was Stanley Works of New Britain, Connecticut, with more than $2.7 billion in 1998 sales generated by 18,000 employees. Using stereolithographic models from CAD drawings and infrared photography, Stanley introduced a new line of tools with ergonomically redesigned handles in mid-1999. Other industry leaders included SPX Corp. of Muskegon, Michigan; Snap-On Inc. of Kenosha, Wisconsin; and Toro Co. of Minneapolis, Minnesota.

The industry provides basic hand tools for both domestic and professional use. According to the 1995 *Annual Survey of Manufactures,* industry shipments reached $4.6 billion that year. In the mid-1990s, there were about 900 establishments employing around 40,700 people. While the number of establishments was projected to decline to 890 by 1997, the number of employees was expected to rise to 41,200. Firms in this industry averaged 50 employees per establishment in the mid-1990s, according to *Manufacturing USA.*

Traditionally, production in this industry was centered in the New England area, paralleling the development of **SIC 3421: Cutlery.** In the early 1900s, Massachusetts and Connecticut commanded 47 percent of the hand and edge tool and cutlery industries. The shift toward mass-production techniques and away from a reliance on skilled craftsmen, however, resulted in the increasing movement of the hand and edge tool industry to the heartland states. The industry tended to follow the source of cheap materials and markets, differentiating it from cutlery by its marked westward migration. In the early 1990s, the four main states producing hand and edge tools were Ohio, Minnesota, Connecticut, and South Carolina.

Employment figures for 1995 show that the industry was experiencing slow growth by the mid-1990s. According to the *1995 Annual Survey of Manufactures,* 42,000 workers were employed in the industry in 1995, an increase of 2.6 percent over the 40,900 employed in 1994. Payrolls also increased from $1.14 billion to $1.19 billion during that year, representing an increase of 4.3 percent. The value of industry shipments increased 5.8 percent from $4.80 billion in 1994 to $5.08 billion in 1995.

FURTHER READING

Darnay, Arsen J., ed. *Manufacturing USA: Industry Analysis, Statistics, and Leading Companies,* 5th ed. Detroit: Gale Research, 1996.

Taber, Martha Van Hoesen. *A History of the Cutlery Industry in the Connecticut Valley.* Northhampton, MA: Smith College, 1955.

U.S. Census Bureau. *1997 Economic Census—Manufacturing.* Available from http://www.census.gov/prod/ec97/97m3322b.pdf (10 February 2000).

1995 Annual Survey of Manufactures. Washington: GPO, 1997.

SIC 3425

SAW BLADES AND HANDSAWS

This category covers establishments primarily engaged in manufacturing handsaws and saw blades for hand- and power-driven saws. Establishments primarily engaged in manufacturing power driven sawing machines are classified in the major group for industrial and commercial machinery and computer equipment.

NAICS CODE(S)

332213 (Saw Blade and Handsaw Manufacturing)

According to the U.S. Census Bureau's *1997 Economic Census—Manufacturing,* 176 establishments operated in this category for some or all of 1997. Industry-wide employment totaled 9,149 workers receiving a payroll of almost $301 million; 6,614 of these employees worked in production, putting in almost 14 million hours to earn wages of more than $180 million. Overall shipments for the industry were valued at almost $1.5 billion.

Blount International Inc. of Montgomery, Alabama, the industry leader with 1998 sales of almost $832 million and 5,300 employees, merged with Lehman Brothers Merchant Banking Partners II L.P. in an April 1999 consolidation worth $1.35 billion. Vermont American Corp. of Louisville, Kentucky held second place in the industry with sales of over $525 million for 1997 and 4,300 employees. In 1998 Vermont American implemented training and teamwork programs for its nonunionized manufacturing workers and its unionized distribution center workers, resulting in improved customer service, improved turnover of inventory, and profits surpassing corporate projections. Other industry leaders included Black & Decker Corp.'s Power Tools and Accessories division of Towson, Maryland; L.S. Starrett Co. of Athol, Massachusetts; and W.C.I. Outdoor Products Inc. of Nashville, Arkansas.

Shipments for the saw blades and handsaws industry in 1994 totaled $1.35 billion. By 1995 that figure had risen to $1.38 billion, an increase of a little more than 2 percent. During the same period, employment had risen from 7,800 workers to 11,000, a 41 percent increase, and payrolls advanced from $237.2 million to $334.8 million, also an increase of 41 percent.

Traditionally, production in the saw blades and handsaws industry was centered in the New England area of the United States, paralleling the development of **SIC 3421: Cutlery.** The shift towards mass-production techniques and away from a reliance on skilled craftsman resulted in the establishment of the industry in heartland states. The industry tended to follow the source of cheap materials and markets, differentiating it from cutlery by its marked westward migration.

The challenge to the industry towards the end of the twentieth century was to maintain a high level of precision for the cutting edges and to produce new metals and composites to cut the increasingly diverse range of hard-to-cut man-made materials. Modern blades must be able to last long periods of time, operating in unmanned, automatic feed industrial applications.

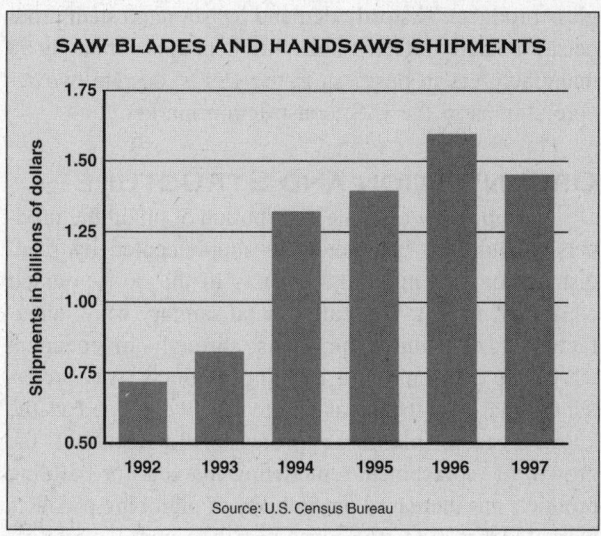

SAW BLADES AND HANDSAWS SHIPMENTS

Source: U.S. Census Bureau

Sales in the saw industry were tied closely to the health of such industries as steel, housing, and lumbering, which used large quantities of saw blades and handsaws. Generally, in both America and Japan, the production of saws and blades increased steadily after World War II. Japanese exports went mainly to Asia, but North America took 27 percent of its production in 1990.

FURTHER READING

"Blount International Inc." *Outdoor Power Equipment,* May 1999.

Darnay, Arsen J., ed. *Manufacturing USA: Industry Analysis, Statistics, and Leading Companies,* 5th ed. Detroit: Gale Research, 1996.

Infotrac Company Profiles. 1 January 2000. Available from http://web4.infotrac.galegroup.com.

U.S. Census Bureau. *1997 Economic Census—Manufacturing,* 10 February 2000. Available from http://www.census.gov/prod/ec97/97m3322c.pdf.

———. *1995 Annual Survey of Manufactures.* Washington: GPO, 1997.

Williams, Mark K. "Teaming up with training for world-class performance." *National Productivity Review,* winter 1998.

SIC 3429

HARDWARE, NOT ELSEWHERE CLASSIFIED

This category covers establishments primarily engaged in manufacturing miscellaneous metal products usually termed hardware, not elsewhere classified. Establishments primarily engaged in manufacturing nuts and bolts are classified in **SIC 3452: Bolts, Nuts, Screws,** **Rivets, and Washers;** those manufacturing nails and spikes are classified in the major group for primary metal industries; those manufacturing cutlery are classified in **SIC 3421: Cutlery;** those manufacturing hand tools are classified in **SIC 3423: Hand and Edge Tools, Except Machine Tools and Handsaws;** and those manufacturing pole line and transmission hardware are classified in industry group **SIC 3640: Electric Lighting and Wiring Equipment.**

NAICS CODE(S)

332439 (Other Metal Container Manufacturing)

332919 (Other Metal Valve and Pipe Fitting Manufacturing)

332510 (Hardware Manufacturing)

This industry manufactures a diverse range of products, including brackets, clamps, couplings, door locks, fireplace equipment, handcuffs, nut crackers, and piano hardware.

Industry leader Ingersoll-Rand Co. of Woodcliff Lake, New Jersey, (1998 sales of almost $8.3 billion) bought the door hardware assets of Master Lock in 1998 from Fortune Brands Inc. of Old Greenwich, Connecticut. Sandwiched between Ingersoll-Rand and third-place Fortune Brands (which generated 1998 sales of over $5.2 billion) was Delphi Interior and Lighting Systems of Warren, Michigan, with sales of almost $5.6 billion for 1997.

In 1995, industry shipments reached $10.6 billion, according to the *1995 Annual Survey of Manufactures*—an increase of 26 percent over the 1987 figures, but an increase of only about 1 percent over the 1994 figures. During 1994 and 1995, employment in the industry decreased from 79,000 to 77,800 employees. Payrolls, however, increased during the same period, rising from $2.26 billion to $2.28 billion, an increase of 0.8 percent.

Traditionally, production in this industry was centered in the New England area. Many small blacksmith shops produced simple but useful household items made of low grade iron and steel, known as "Yankee notions." The availability of rail and ship transport allowed for rapid distribution along the eastern seaboard and the central United States. The shift toward mass production techniques and away from a reliance on skilled craftsman, however, resulted in the migration of the industry to the Midwest. The industry tended to follow the source of cheap materials and markets, differentiating it from cutlery by its marked westward migration. The industry adapted its production methods to the use of numerical control production (NC) with great success in both productivity and precision.

Both employment and sales in the industry increased steadily throughout the 1980s, but declined substantially in accordance with the general economic downturn near the end of the decade. The industry was particularly hurt by the soft housing market, since businesses in that sector use a substantial amount of hardware. By the early 1990s, the hardware industry showed signs of recovery, and once dismal unemployment figures showed signs of improvement.

FURTHER READING

Darnay, Arsen J. ed. *Manufacturing USA*. 5th. Detroit: Gale Research, 1996.

Infotrac Company Profiles. Available at http://web4.infotrac .galegroup.com (visited 1/29/00).

Taber, Martha Van Hoesen. *A History of the Cutlery Industry in the Connecticut Valley*. Northhampton, MA: Smith College Department of History, 1955.

U.S. Bureau of the Census. *1995 Annual Survey of Manufactures*. Washington: GPO, 1997.

Washburn, Dan. "Master Lock sells door hardware assets." *Home Improvement Market,* February 1998.

SIC 3431

ENAMELED IRON AND METAL SANITARY WARE

This category includes establishments primarily engaged in manufacturing enameled iron, cast iron, or pressed metal sanitary wares, such as bathtubs, sinks, toilets, and other bathroom and household plumbing fixtures. Nonmetallic plumbing products are listed in **SIC 3088: Plastic Plumbing Fixtures, SIC 3261: Vitreous Sanitary Ware,** and **SIC 3469: Porcelain Enameled Kitchen, Household, and Hospital Ware.**

NAICS CODE(S)

332998 (Enameled Iron and Metal Sanitary Ware Manufacturing)

INDUSTRY SNAPSHOT

Metal sanitary ware manufacturers compete in the household, commercial, and industrial plumbing product markets, producing products made of cast iron, enameled iron and steel, and stainless steel. Traditionally, these markets are directly influenced by the nation's construction markets and, therefore, are extremely cyclical.

During the 1990s, the increased use of plastic and fiberglass plumbing products reduced the demand for iron and steel plumbing products. In response to this change, manufacturers have developed composite materials that combine the strength and durability of metal with the lightweight and rustproof features of plastic and fiber-

glass products. A steady demand for stainless steel products, especially kitchen sinks, has kept approximately 90 manufacturers in business in the 1990s, despite two severe slumps in the U.S. construction market.

ORGANIZATION AND STRUCTURE

Traditional wholesale distribution of plumbing products to building contractors is supplemented by retail distribution of plumbing products to the do-it-yourself consumer market. Typically, metal sanitary ware manufacturers distributed products through independent wholesale distributors of building products. Any advertising was of a technical nature and was aimed at the knowledgeable plumbing professional. Recently, the growth of replacement/remodeling markets for building products has increased profitability of plumbing products marketed directly to the consumer. In response, manufacturers have expanded marketing efforts, focusing on a consumer more concerned with function and style than with the technical specifications of the product.

BACKGROUND AND DEVELOPMENT

The fate of the plumbing producer has always been tied to the health of the nation's new construction markets. Economists label the demand for new construction a leading indicator of this industry's growth because it provides insight into the future conditions of the overall economy. Hence, a decline in the demand for new construction usually precedes a slowdown in the nation's gross national product (GNP) growth. This held true in the recessions of 1982 and 1991, as construction activity began to decline a year before the rest of the economy slid into recession. Metal sanitary ware manufacturers felt the recessions early as well, as demand for their products fell with slowed construction activity.

During the 1980s, several trends in the construction industry impacted metal sanitary ware producers. Severe declines in construction activity in 1980 and 1982 caused many manufacturers to shut down. The number of metal sanitary ware manufacturing establishments dropped to 77 in 1982. After these severe declines, however, construction demand boomed in 1983 and 1984, as consumer optimism fueled demand for new houses. In addition, an unprecedented cut in the tax on capital gains implemented by the Reagan administration suddenly made business investment in commercial offices, stores, residential condominiums, and apartments extremely attractive. As a result, demand for both residential and commercial plumbing products boomed in the mid-1980s.

By the end of 1990, however, the construction industry suffered a serious decline, as housing starts fell to near record lows. The industry employed approximately 6,000 workers in 1995, 5,000 of whom were involved in production. The decrease in profit margins has caused production workers' wages to remain stagnant. Despite yearly productivity gains, workers' wages have barely kept up with inflation. Production workers' hourly wages have hovered around $11.00 during the mid-1980s and early 1990s.

The cause of the decline was primarily attributed to an oversupply of commercial office space and residential housing caused by the building spree of the mid-1980s. Analysts suggested that this glut in the supply of newly constructed properties would take many years to clear, holding down construction growth well into the 1990s. While metal sanitary ware manufacturers suffered through this latest downturn in construction, the decline was not as deep as was expected. This was attributed to plumbing ware manufacturers' success in the less cyclical home remodeling market.

In the late 1980s, remodeling projects and do-it-yourself repairs became popular hobbies for many homeowners. Disgust over the high cost of plumbing repairs and the urge to modernize bathrooms and kitchens led many people to undertake plumbing projects they would have avoided only a few years earlier. As a result, manufacturers often marketed installation guides to consumers in the form of books or videos.

On the other hand, the move toward larger bathrooms with jacuzzis and whirlpools threatened metal sanitary ware manufacturers' bathtub market. Shower stall and wall-surround bathtubs with whirlpool technology can not feasibly be made using cast iron and enameled steel. In response, several metal sanitary ware manufacturers developed composite materials that combined the features of steel and cast iron with the lighter weight and ease of transportation and installation of plastics and fiberglass products. Acceptance of these composite materials would allow metal sanitary ware manufacturers to take advantage of demand for more luxurious bathtub products. The industry was successful in shifting its focus from bathtubs to the kitchen and sink markets. In fact, sales for the industry doubled in the 1980s, despite a fall in bathtub market share from 62 percent to 38 percent during the decade.

The demand for stainless steel kitchen sink offset the decline in cast iron and enameled steel bathtub demand. While sales nearly doubled during 1980s, profit margins for the industry declined steadily. As a percentage of total costs, material costs grew from 42 percent to 52 percent during the decade. The decline in profit margins was the direct result of a skyrocketing increase in the cost of materials for stainless steel production.

Entering the 1990s, metal sanitary ware manufacturers faced a construction market in which slow growth was predicted for several years. This forced the industry to seek growth through other markets—mainly, the replace-

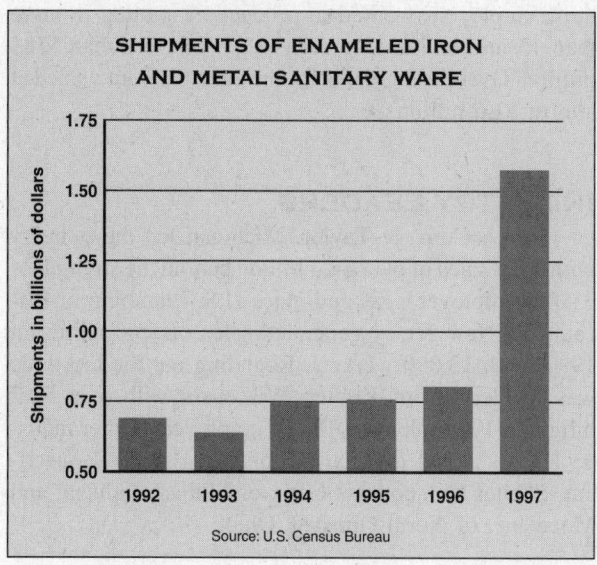

SHIPMENTS OF ENAMELED IRON AND METAL SANITARY WARE

Source: U.S. Census Bureau

ment and remodeling plumbing fixtures market. In addition, plumbing manufacturers faced a more environmentally aware consumer who demanded efficient, water conserving plumbing products. Concern for the environment caused metal sanitary ware manufacturers to use recycled metals and to provide more efficient products. Many states, for example, passed legislation requiring that all new toilets use only 1.6 gallons of water per flush as opposed to the traditional 3.5 gallons per flush.

The growth in remodeling and replacement markets for plumbing products was attributed to the increasing desire for homeowners to entertain within the home. This phenomenon was expected to affect plumbing ware manufacturers for many years to come. Especially fruitful for metal sanitary ware manufacturers was the increased emphasis on the kitchen and the basement in the scheme of the house. Stainless steel was the most popular material for kitchen and bar sinks, primarily because of its low-price and ease of installation for the do-it-yourself homeowner.

In the mid- to late 1990s, however, new construction was again on the rise. The Turner Corp., the nation's leading builder, announced that first quarter results for 1997 were up 14 percent from 1996 to $1.2 million in net income. This, in combination with continued growth in the remodeling and replacement markets, could in turn spur favorable growth in the sanitary ware market as well. U.S. manufacturers' shipments of metal plumbing fixtures totaled approximately $757 million in 1995.

CURRENT CONDITIONS

According to the U.S. Census Bureau's *1997 Economic Census—Manufacturing,* 88 establishments operated in this category for part or all of 1997. Industry-wide employment totaled 9,994 workers receiving a payroll of more than $280 million. Within this workforce, 7,860 of these employees worked in production, putting in more than 15 million hours to earn wages of more than $183 million. Overall shipments for the industry were valued at almost $1.6 billion.

INDUSTRY LEADERS

Masco Corp. of Taylor, Michigan led the industry with 1998 sales of over $4.3 billion behind the strength of 31,700 employees. Second-place U.S. Plumbing of Piscataway, New Jersey generated sales of $3.6 billion in 1997, with 13,000 workers. Rounding out the top three was Kohler Co. of Kohler, Wisconsin with over $2.2 billion in 1998 sales and 18,000 employees. Other industry leaders included Esstar Inc. of New Haven, Connecticut; Shelter Components Corp. of Elkhart, Indiana; and Moen Inc. of North Olmsted, Ohio.

AMERICA AND THE WORLD

The U.S. market for plumbing ware fixtures does not include a large percentage of imported products. The added cost of shipping large cast iron and enameled steel products overseas usually makes imports too expensive for the U.S. market. This lack of import competition has given U.S. producers of plumbing ware products a luxury that many other industries do not enjoy. On the other hand, the export of metal sanitary ware manufacturers is limited for the same reasons. This makes U.S. producers highly vulnerable to the fluctuations of the domestic market for plumbing products.

The majority of U.S. trade in metal sanitary ware products occurs with Canada and Mexico. Transportation costs to these markets are minimal. Companies in the United States also compete in many overseas markets through foreign production in proximity to the particular market. Either through direct ownership of a plant on foreign soil, or through licensing agreements with foreign manufacturers, U.S. companies participate in foreign markets while eliminating expensive shipping costs.

The protection from foreign competition for U.S. metal sanitary ware producers has saved many domestic manufacturing jobs. Primarily, production job declines have been caused by productivity improvements; however, two significant occurrences threatened to change this in the 1990s. First, the stainless steel sink market was more open to foreign competition because these products are lightweight and, therefore, do not incur the high shipping costs of cast iron and enameled steel products. Secondly, the North American Free Trade Agreement (NAFTA) gave metal sanitary ware manufacturers access to low wage production workers without the large addition in shipping costs usually associated with foreign production.

FURTHER READING

Darnay, Arsen J., ed. *Manufacturing USA*. 5th ed. Detroit: Gale Research, 1996.

"Male Plumbing." *Advertising Age,* 4 October 1999.

U.S. Census Bureau. *1995 Annual Survey of Manufactures.* Washington, D.C.: GPO, 1997.

U.S. Census Bureau. "Enameled Iron and Metal Sanitary Ware Manufacturing" *1997 Economic Census-Manufacturing.* Washington, D.C.: U.S. Department of Commerce, 1999. Available from http://www.census.gov/prod/ec97/97m3329l.pdf.

SIC 3432

PLUMBING FIXTURES AND FITTINGS

Companies that produce metal plumbing fixtures and parts make up the plumbing fixture and fittings industry. This classification also encompasses establishments engaged in the assembly of plastic components into fixtures and fittings. Companies that manufacture plastic, ceramic, earthenware, and other types of plumbing fixtures are classified in separate industries, as are firms that make steam or water line valves.

NAICS CODE(S)

332913 (Plumbing Fixture Fitting and Trim Manufacturing)

332999 (All Other Miscellaneous Fabricated Metal Product Manufacturing)

INDUSTRY SNAPSHOT

Although advanced plumbing systems have existed since 2000 B.C., metal pipes and fittings were not commonplace in the United States until the early 1900s, when they began playing an important role in the development of industrialized society. By 1997, the plumbing fixtures and fittings (PFF) industry had shipments valued at $3.58 billion and the industry had just over 16,000 employees. The PFF industry is largely dependent on the new housing market. Other important market sectors are commercial and institutional construction, and replacement and renovation.

As fixture manufacturers approached the close of the twentieth century, they looked forward to sustained market growth and increased profits. The industry had experienced steady expansion since the 1970s, despite economic recessions. Through the mid-1990s the industry enjoyed an average annual growth rate of between 5 and 5.5 percent. This rate of growth, however, was predicted to slow through 1999 and 2000. To maintain profitability and growth in the mid-1990s, competitors by the mid-1990s had begun introducing new products, increasing productivity, and taking advantage of propitious demographic trends.

ORGANIZATION AND STRUCTURE

Plumbing refers to the system of pipes, fixtures, and other apparatus in a structure that supplies water and removes liquid and waterborne wastes. The foremost role of an integrated plumbing system is to safely deliver and remove water; therefore, fixtures and fittings must conform to strict codes, regulations, and trade standards. Manufacturers of fixtures are also concerned with producing styles that appeal to consumers by reflecting current trends in home decoration.

Most plumbing fixtures and fittings are built for residential use. Primary residential applications include kitchens, bathrooms, utility rooms and gardens. Fixtures also complement various commercial, industrial, and institutional plumbing systems. Most fixtures and fittings may be divided into one of four groups: traps, tubes, and drains; pipe fittings; faucets and toilets; and shower fixtures. Manufacturing metals used by the industry include copper, brass, bronze, and iron.

In 1997 the largest single product share of the PFF market was for miscellaneous plumbing fixtures and fittings and trims (brass goods) valued at more than $1.5 billion. The second largest product share was for single lever plumbing fixture controls, two or three handle bath or shower fittings, and anti-scald bath or shower valves valued at nearly $1.3 billion. The last was for nearly $800 million worth of lavatory and sink fittings (except single control) including drains and overflows.

Basin drains usually incorporate traps or tubes. Traps are essentially drainage pipes with a bend, or trap, beneath the drain for holding water and preventing odors and gases from backing up out of the drain. P, J, and S shaped traps are commonly used for sinks, while drum and bottle-type traps, which are typically used for bathtub and kitchen drains, consist of a cylindrical metal box or settling basin attached to the waste pipe. Other types of traps include grease, laundry tray, and slop sink. Most traps incorporate a clean-out plug or screw to remove debris caught in the trap. Tubes are used to connect traps, garbage disposals, dishwasher drains, and other drains and devices. They come in a variety of shapes and materials to suit all applications and configurations.

Pipe fittings are used to connect pipes and tubes and come in a multitude of shapes and sizes; several categories of fittings exist. Nipples are used to extend a pipe and to provide proper threading for connection to other pipes. Couplings are used to join standard sizes of pipe. Similarly, floor flanges connect pipes to a wall, floor, or other flat surface. Elbow fittings make it possible to change the direction of a straight pipe. Reducers, when incorporated with couplings, provide a means of connecting different sized pipes. Three- and four-way tees allow a pipe to branch out into two or three other pipes, often of smaller size. Other common fitting types include return bends, flair and compression fittings, wye (Y) bends, slip joints, and ground joint unions.

Faucets are available in several different forms. Compression faucets, common in residential plumbing, use a washer to control water flow and are operated by turning a lever, moving a ball, or shifting a handle. Fuller ball faucets work similarly, but use a ball stopper instead of a washer mechanism. Ground-key faucets use a copper plunger to regulate water flow. Sill cocks, which are designed to resist freezing, are heavy duty exterior faucets.

Toilet fixtures and fittings include levers and other parts that control the flush and water inlet valves. The ballcock assembly is the primary mechanism that controls water supply in the tank and toilet.

Standard shower heads are typically made of chrome-plated brass or plastic, and they offer adjustable spray, swivel-ball joints, and self-cleaning rims. Massaging showerheads incorporate a diverting valve that allows for a pulsating action. Continental showers allow the shower head to be removed and used as a hand shower. Popular shower head enhancements include water-saving flow control mechanisms and anti-scald valves. Some regional building codes mandate inclusion of anti-scald valves in public facilities, as well as for showers in multi-family structures.

Sundry devices include water fountain heads, lawn hose nozzles and sprinklers, shower rods, various plumber's tools and supplies, water-saving devices, and anti-scald bath and shower valves. Special equipment of more durable material and incorporating a higher degree of technology is produced for hospitals, industrial plants, laboratories, and other niche markets.

BACKGROUND AND DEVELOPMENT

Latrine-like receptacles with crude drains are known to have existed as early as 8000 B.C., and advanced plumbing systems built of terra cotta and burned brick were used as early as 2500 B.C. The first latrine with a water flushing reservoir dates back to 2000 B.C. in the royal palace of the Minoans. Clay plumbing pipes were introduced by the Greeks in about 200 B.C., and, later, the Romans began developing complex plumbing infrastructure that incorporated the use of lead pipes. By 300 A.D., the Roman system was carrying over 50 million gallons of water per day to residents.

Advancements in plumbing technology languished after the fall of the Roman Empire until the seventeenth and eighteenth centuries. While cast iron pipes were introduced into plumbing in London in 1619, metal plumbing systems were not used on a significant scale in the

United States until the nineteenth century. Between 1850 and 1900, the industry expanded rapidly, and by 1900, almost all U.S. towns with more than 2,000 residents had relatively advanced plumbing systems.

During the economic expansion that occurred in the United States after World War II, demand for metal fixtures and fittings escalated. Over the next three decades, massive increases in new single family homes, as well as growth in commercial and institutional structures, prompted a huge demand for all types of faucets, drains, fittings, and other fixtures. As the U.S. population skyrocketed, the percentage of families owning their own homes also increased from about 45 percent in 1940 to nearly 65 percent by the late 1970s. By 1980, metal plumbing fixture manufacturers were shipping about $1 billion worth of products each year.

Growth in the industry slowed in the late 1970s and 1980s, due to higher interest rates, demographic shifts, and other economic factors. Nevertheless, plumbing fitting and fixture manufacturers continued to report gains during the 1980s. Furthermore, the amount of plumbing fixtures used to build the average house during this time rose steadily. For instance, while most homes built prior to 1960 had only one bathroom, most homes built in the 1980s featured at least two baths. Moreover, kitchens became larger and utilized more elaborate fixtures than earlier homes, and new amenities, such as hot tubs and dual sink decks also helped the industry to sustain growth during this time. Importantly, the replacement market for existing home fixtures and fittings augmented the new home market.

From $1.3 billion in shipments in 1982, industry sales steadily rose to $2.6 billion in 1991, representing an average annual growth rate of around seven percent. In the early 1990s manufacturers were looking forward to continued industry growth. 1992 showed a 20 percent rise in new home construction and the trend was towards larger and more luxurious bath and kitchen amenities. The average new home in the early 1990s included 2.5 bathrooms, while the master bathroom was generally 30 percent larger than those of 25 years ago. By 1996 16 percent of all new homes had three or more bathrooms, 33 percent had two and a half baths, 41 percent had two baths, and only ten percent had one and a half baths or less. Between 1995 and 1998. however, the market continued to grow although much more slowly. In 1995 shipments were valued at $2.96 billion up only 1.5 percent over 1994. 1996 was a little better with shipments of $3.07 billion representing an increase of 3.7 percent. 1997 shipments increased only .2 percent to $3.07 billion.

1998 shipments were predicted to be worth $3.03 billion representing a decline of 1.4 percent. In early 1998 industry insiders blamed this expected decline on the construction industry. "We see a slowdown in residential construction and in commercial as well," said Charlie Whipple, vice president/sales and marketing at Chicago Faucets in a *Contractor* interview. Fortunately for the industry PFF shipments turned around and increased 5.5 percent to $3.45 billion. Predictions for 1999, however, were less optimistic. "Growth is expected to be modest in 1999, more in line with the 1995 pause that refreshed, as the housing market cools a bit while nonresidential construction accelerates moderately," said economic analyst Daryl Delano in an early 1999 *Contractor* interview. The year 2000 is predicted to show renewed growth in the residential and commercial construction markets prompting a hoped for 4.4 percent increase in PFF shipments valued at about $3.6 billion.

Prices for plumbing fixtures showed a 3.4 percent increase in 1995. In 1996 and 1997 prices increased 2.9 percent and 1.7 percent respectively. 1998, however, showed a price increase of only .1 percent.

The National Energy Policy Act, passed by Congress in 1992, set maximum water-flow rates allowed for residential and commercial fixtures. Manufacturers hoped that this legislation would boost replacement market sales, as well as sales of new water-flow devices. Residential and commercial regulations, which were scheduled to take effect in the mid-1990s, allowed only 1.6 gallons-per-flush (gpf) for water closets, 1 gpf for urinals, and 2.5 gallons per minute for faucets and showerheads.

There has been, however, growing consumer and grass roots opposition to the 1.6 gpf legislation and calls for its repeal because of less than satisfactory flushing with many of the new devices. The PFF industry, however, is against any change in the 1992 law. A repeal of the law would cost the industry tens of millions of dollars that would ultimately be passed along to the consumer according to Gerber Plumbing Fixture's Bill Ficken. Industry insiders feel that the chances of any changes in the law are "slim to none."

Fixture and fitting producers also benefited throughout the 1990s from new distribution channels. Discount hardware and home center warehouse stores were quickly becoming a primary outlet for consumer sales, as increasing numbers of consumers sought to install and repair plumbing themselves in order to avoid large mark-ups charged by plumbers and traditional hardware stores. HQ, Home Depot, and Builder's Square were a few of the massive warehouse chains that were bringing new buyers into the market.

Some manufacturers, however, are cautious about changes in the way their products are distributed. "In spite of the big box/home center situation, companies are investing in traditional plumber wholesaler organizations because they believe it is the correct way to service the market-place and eventually the consumer," says Ficken.

"From the figures I see, two-thirds of all plumbing products are sold through traditional distribution."

CURRENT CONDITIONS

The PFF market was expected to show moderate growth through 2000. The value of shipments in 1997 was nearly $3.6 billion. The figure was predicted to grow to $3.9 billion, $4.1 billion, and nearly $4.3 billion in 1998, 1999, and 2000. Value of shipments through 2003 is expected to grow at between three and four percent.

Demand for plastic fixtures and fittings is expected to show greater growth than the more traditional metal and vitreous ones. Plastics are showing especially strong growth in conjunction with residential bathtub, shower stall, lavatory sink, and whirlpool applications. Overall shipments of plastic fixtures (plastic and fiberglass) were worth $1.43 billion in 1996 representing 46 percent of the market. Vitreous china shipments in 1996 accounted for $860 million (27 percent) and metal fixtures accounted for $644 million (20 percent.)

The domestic PFF industry is facing growing competition from foreign manufacturers. By 1997 imports were nearly double their 1992 figure with the value of shipments rising from $375 million to $717 million. This figure was projected to reach $815 million in 1999. Exports actually dropped from $254 million in 1992 to $245 million in 1996 with slight rises in 1993, 1994, and 1995. Exports were expected to be worth $320 million in 1999, less than half the import figures for the same year.

INDUSTRY LEADERS

Masco Corp. of Taylor, Michigan, is one of the PFF industry's most aggressive companies, especially in terms of acquisitions. Over the last 30 years Masco has acquired more than 100 home improvement companies with annual sales of $1 million to $100 million. In a September 1999 in a $3.8 billion dollar deal Masco acquired five companies which make such products as glue guns, radiators, kitchen and bathroom cabinetry, and stains and varnishes. Masco had also acquired five other companies earlier in the year. "Our goal is to grow our business 16 percent in sales annually, and we've done that for 40 years and will continue to do so," said Masco's Richard Manoogian in a *Detroit Free Press* interview. The five acquired firms also had exclusive contracts with retailing home improvement giant The Home Depot. Masco had 1997 sales of $3.76 billion and employed just over 28,000. The company is best known for its Delta Faucet line, which was established in 1955. Other plumbing fixtures marketed by the company include Alson hand held shower systems, Peerless kitchen, bathroom, and tub and shower faucets, and its premium line of Rubinetterie Mariani S.p.A. kitchen and bath

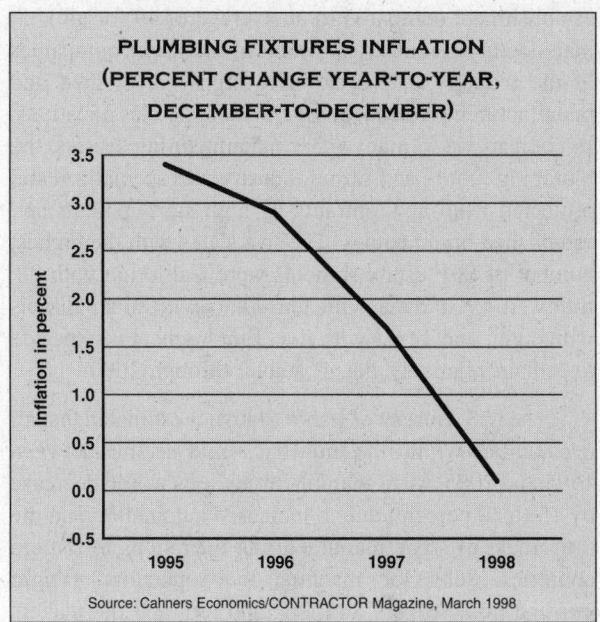

PLUMBING FIXTURES INFLATION (PERCENT CHANGE YEAR-TO-YEAR, DECEMBER-TO-DECEMBER)

Source: Cahners Economics/CONTRACTOR Magazine, March 1998

faucets. Masco has manufacturing facilities in Europe, Mexico, and Taiwan as well as North America.

The Kohler Company of Kohler, Wisconsin, controls about 25 percent of the U.S. plumbing fixtures market. Kohler has 43 manufacturing plants and has various PFF products including PRO sinks, faucets, and cook centers as well as Fairfax Faucets, Camber and Timpani lavatory sinks, and its MasterShower Thermostatic Valve system. Kohler had 1997 sales of $2.2 billion and employed 18,000. Kohler also manufactures small engines, generators, electrical switchgear, and high-end furniture, and has hotel and real estate interests. The Kohler family owns 98 percent of the company.

American Standard of Piscataway, New Jersey, makes air conditioning systems, automotive parts, and plumbing products at 108 facilities in 35 countries. American Standard had 1997 sales of $6 billion and employed 51,000. Sales of plumbing fixtures accounted for 25 percent of 1997 sales revenue with 1998 figures rising 5 percent to a record $1.5 billion. Plumbing products are marketed under the brand names American Standard, Ideal Standard, and Porcher. In a $417 million 1999 deal American Standard bought the bathroom unit of Blue Circle Industries PLC. The acquisition added annual sales of $283 million to the company's plumbing products division.

WORKFORCE

In 1997, 110 PFF establishments had 16,159 employees of which 11,692 were production workers. Total industry payroll was $496.2 million of which $314.7 million represented wages. The average hourly wage in 1997 was expected to be $11.74 and rising to $12.57 by 2000. In 1996 the industry averaged 108 employees per establishment compared to an average of 49 for all U.S. manufacturing industries. Many of the larger companies in the industry, however, were highly diversified and manufactured products in several industry classifications. In comparison to many other manufacturing sectors, the plumbing fixture and fitting industry was specialized and protected from new entrants by high start-up costs and established brand names. The five states with the highest number of PFF establishments were California with 28, followed by Indiana with ten, Ohio with nine, Illinois with eight, and Texas with five. Employment is expected to remain relatively flat, if stable, through 2000.

The U.S. Bureau of Labor Statistics estimated that all occupations within the industry would decline between 1994 and 2005. Most manufacturing jobs would decrease by 15 to 30 percent, due to increased automation and the movement of some manufacturing operations to foreign countries. Jobs for machine tool operators, freight movers, bookkeepers, drafters, and tool and die makers were expected to realize the greatest decreases (more than 30 percent).

RESEARCH AND TECHNOLOGY

The late 1990s saw the PFF industry dealing with innovative products, new methods of distribution, and following the lead of European manufacturers, more emphasis on design and aesthetics. In 1998 the Waterless Co. introduced a waterless urinal marketed under the name No-Flush Urinal. The urinal uses no water and thus has no flush valves and no mechanical parts. The urinal instead has an Eco-Trap that is filled with BlueSeal fluid. BlueSeal is lighter than urine thus the waste flows down through it and the fluid forms a surface seal that odors can't pass through. No-Flush urinals have been installed in more than 40 government buildings, resulting in savings on water and maintenance costs. "People can't flush these with their feet, there will be no overflow problems and kids can't stick things down the drain," according to Klaus Reichardt, president of Waterless. "That way owners don't have to pay to have them fixed and maintained all the time."

1999 saw the introduction of Internet sales of plumbing fixtures when Amazon.com, the Internet's largest retailer of books, videos and music, announced it would begin selling plumbing products in November of that year. Although the site will be aimed at professional contractors, sales to homeowners are also welcome. Faucets, fittings, valves, and various other plumbing parts and fixtures will be available. In an interview with *Contractor* Amazon.com's Joe Galli elaborated on the new service. "We offer a full, exhaustive line of equipment they [contractors] use every day," Galli said. Any product purchased through Amazon.com/homeimprovement will be shipped anywhere in the country, regardless of

weight, for $4.95. Overnight delivery will be an extra-cost option. "The No. 1 advantage we have is our selection," according to Galli. "We have upwards of 400 brand-name products available that professionals have come to respect and trust." While some contractors are enthusiastic about the new online service others are more reserved. "I don't do any purchasing over the Internet yet," said Patrick Wallner of Redding, California's Wallner Plumbing. "I'll always go to my wholesaler over anyone else, even if it means not saving a buck. The years I've put into the relationship with my wholesaler are not worth saving a few bucks."

By 1999 industry analysts were becoming increasingly aware of European trend setting in PFF design and innovation. "Since Europe has had such a strong influence on plumbing design trends during the past 20 years, the show [Frankfurt, Germany ISH trade show] is increasingly watched by U.S. manufacturers for early warning signs of new directions," according to Don Arnold in a special report for *Contractor*. Arnold feels that under the influence of European designers the lines between products designed for commercial use and those designed for residential use are becoming increasingly blurred. Commercial products are becoming more aesthetic and products for the home are showing more innovation with such things as electronic proximity faucets, pre-rinse faucets, and the increasing use of stainless steel in home plumbing fixtures and accessories. Newer plumbing fixtures for commercial applications no longer have what Arnold terms "early penal-colony" design but rather have more enhanced styling and a far greater breadth of material options including glass, wood, and solid surface. On the electronic frontier are whirlpool tubs that respond to voice commands and proximity faucets with portable touch pad controls. Another tub comes with a monitor that allows its user to watch television, check e-mail, and surf the Internet. Toilets with concealed in-the-wall tanks were also featured at the show as well as toilets with a water saving two-stage flush system which delivers different volumes of water for flushing solid or liquid waste.

Other European innovations are aggressive ad campaigns for premium designer faucets and fixtures. Germany's Grohe reported a sales rise of 49 percent following a $5 to $10 million ad campaign for its sleek new line of faucets designed in Italy. Its premium priced sub-brand Groheart reportedly boosted company sales to $39.5 million in 1998 as compared to $33.3 million in 1997 and $26.4 million in 1996. A sales increase of 49 percent is astonishing when compared to an average growth rate of 3.7 percent for other European companies.

In 1998 Underwriters Laboratories announced that it would begin testing and certifying a variety of plumbing components and assemblies including fixtures, fittings, piping, appliances, and water treatment units. Previously these items were tested and certified by various multiple organizations.

FURTHER READING

"American Standard and Blue Circle in $417 Million Deal." *New York Times,* 3 September 1999.

Arnold, Don. "A Walk on the Wet Side of ISH '99." *Contractor,* May 1999.

Darnay, Arsen J. *Manufacturing U.S.A.: Industry Analyses, Statistics, and Leading Companies.* 6th ed. Detroit: Gale, 1998.

D & B Million Dollar Directory: America's Leading Public & Private Companies. Bethlehem, Pennsylvania: Dun & Bradstreet Corp., 1999.

Delano, Daryl. "Housing Market May See Cooling Trend." *Contractor,* December 1999.

———. "Nonresidential Spurt Mostly Commercial." *Contractor,* November 1999.

"Euro Effie Awards: Profits Flow From Famous Faucets." *Advertising Age International Supplement,* December 1999.

Hezelbart, Rob. "Amazon.com To Sell Plumbing Products." *Contractor.* December 1999.

"Manufacturer Updates: UL Expands Plumbing Services." *National Home Center News,* 9 November 1998.

"Masco Makes Five Acquisitions for $3.8 Billion." *New York Times,* 2 September 1999.

"Masco Main Supplier for The Home Depot." *Contractor,* November 1999.

"Plumbing Market's Growth Will Stabilize in 1999." *Contractor,* January 1999.

"Taylor, Mich. Based Construction Material Firm Swallows Five Companies." *Detroit Free Press,* 2 September 1999.

U.S. Census Bureau. *Plumbing Fixture Fitting and Trim Manufacturing: 1997 Economic Census, Manufacturing Industry Series.* Washington: GPO, 1999. Available from: http://www .census.gov/prod.

SIC 3433

HEATING EQUIPMENT, EXCEPT ELECTRIC AND WARM AIR FURNACES

This category covers establishments primarily engaged in manufacturing heating equipment, except electric and warm air furnaces, including gas, oil, and stoker coal-fired equipment for the automatic utilization of gaseous, liquid, and solid fuels. Establishments primarily engaged in manufacturing warm air furnaces are classified in **SIC 3585: Air-Conditioning and Warm Air Heating Equipment and Commercial and Industrial Refrigeration Equipment;** cooking stoves and ranges

are classified in **SIC 3631: Household Cooking Equipment;** boiler shops primarily engaged in the production of industrial, power, and marine boilers are classified in **SIC 3443: Fabricated Plate Work (Boiler Shops);** and those manufacturing industrial process furnaces and ovens are classified in **SIC 3567: Industrial Process Furnaces and Ovens.**

NAICS CODE(S)

333414 (Heating Equipment(except Electric and Warm Air Furnaces) Manufacturing)

INDUSTRY SNAPSHOT

The heating equipment industry is comprised of firms primarily engaged in manufacturing heating devices other than electric equipment and warm air furnaces. Residential and low-pressure boilers are included in this classification, as are steam and hot water furnaces, fireplaces, room heaters, heating stoves, and other mechanisms. Making fire and building devices to utilize the resultant heat were among the earliest and most noteworthy human achievements. Some stove, furnace, and other equipment designs implemented as early as 600 B.C. were still in use throughout the world in the twentieth century.

In 1997, the U.S. heating equipment industry was shipping about $3.7 billion worth of products each year. The industry was characterized by maturity, consolidation, and increasing foreign competition. In order to remain competitive, industry participants in the 1980s and 1990s reduced employment, increased productivity, and moved manufacturing facilities abroad.

ORGANIZATION AND STRUCTURE

The heating equipment industry generally encompasses all non-electric devices used to heat spaces in homes, buildings, and industrial structures. Such heaters are powered by coal, oil, gas, wood, or solar power. In addition to their different energy sources, industry offerings can be categorized as fireplaces and wood-burning stoves; supplemental heaters; or low-pressure steam and hot water boilers and furnaces. Warm-air furnaces and high-pressure steam and hot water systems, which are often used as central heating systems for larger structures, are included in **SIC 3585: Air-Conditioning and Warm Air Heating Equipment and Commercial and Industrial Refrigeration Equipment** and **SIC 3443: Fabricated Plate Work (Boiler Shops),** respectively.

Low-Pressure Boilers. Low-pressure steam and hot-water boilers differ from other industry offerings in that they are often used as central heating devices to warm several spaces within a structure. A hot-water system usually consists of a centrally located cast-iron boiler and a network of steel or copper pipes that are connected to satellite radiators. Water is heated in the boiler and transferred up through the pipes to the radiators. As the water travels through the metal radiator, it releases heat, becomes more dense, and falls back down to the boiler where it is reheated. Motor driven pumps are used to increase pressure and to allow rooms below the boiler to receive heat.

Steam heating systems work similarly to hot water systems. Because steam is a gas, however, it cannot hold heat as well as water and it is more susceptible to sharp temperature fluctuations. As a result, steam systems generally require more apparatus and are less efficient for many residential, as well as some commercial, applications.

Supplemental Heaters. Non-electric supplemental heaters are used to heat spaces that are not connected to centralized heating systems, such as garages and warehouses. In addition, they are often used for "zone" heating, a complement to a central heating system that can reduce overall energy costs. Space heaters typically run on natural gas and oil.

Kerosene space heaters have traditionally been a popular residential device. Although they are cost-efficient and relatively easy to operate, safety concerns have reduced the desirability of these heaters in relation to competing products. Open flame kerosene heaters deplete oxygen and emit carbon monoxide. In addition, they can become a fire hazard if misused or poorly maintained. As a result, some local ordinances have banned kerosene heaters.

Gas and liquid propane (LP) supplemental heaters are of three types: infrared-radiant, which transfer most of their heat through direct infrared radiation from the heater to the objects in a room; convection, which heat and recirculate air, and; catalytic, which produce heat when gas is distributed and ignited over a platinum-plated grid. Gas and LP heaters are comparatively clean-burning and inexpensive to operate. They also require little or no ventilation.

Portable forced-air heaters are commonly used to heat work areas, such as outdoor construction sites. Although they are fueled by oil, kerosene, or gas, they may also use electric fans to disperse the heat. Industrial forced-air systems can supply as much as 600,000 British thermal units (BTUs) of heat. Other supplemental heating devices include baseboard units, duct fans, solar heaters, and various oil-filled heaters—many of which incorporate electrical devices.

Fireplaces and Woodburning Stoves. Because they use a relatively inexpensive and renewable energy source, fireplaces and woodburning stoves are a popular alternative to boiler and supplemental heating systems. Wood-fueled heat, however, is relatively inefficient and emits more pollution than oil, gas, or LP. A standard fireplace, for instance, is only 5 to 15 percent energy efficient when a fire is burning, and -5 to -10 percent inefficient when the fire is dying. Although many woodburning stoves are 40 to 65 percent energy efficient, most other heaters are much more efficient and pollution-free. Many furnaces, for example, offer greater than 70 percent efficiency.

The three principal types of woodburning stoves are: traditional box (radiant), airtight (circulating), and pellet-fed. Airtight stoves have a sealed firebox, a tight-fitting door, and a manually or thermostatically controlled air intake damper that controls burning. Pellet-fed stoves burn processed wood pellets that are fed into the stove's combustion chamber electronically, allowing greater heat control and efficiency.

Fireplace heating products offered by manufacturers in the industry include artificial gas fireplaces and various heat-saving accessories. Heat recovery systems, for instance, generate heat through convection and radiation using energy from an open fire. Tube grates pull cool air out of the room and blow hot air back out. Similarly, heat extractors, which are often installed in a chimney, heat and circulate air in a room using energy from the fireplace.

Market Structure. In the early 1990s, cast-iron boilers, radiators, and convectors used in steam and hot water systems accounted for about 25 percent of industry sales—this represented the largest single industry segment. Floor and wall systems, unit heaters, infrared heaters, and stokers accounted for about 16 percent of production. Of that 16 percent, supplemental unit heaters made up about half. Domestic heating stoves of all fuel types represented about 13 percent of industry output. Various miscellaneous heating equipment accounted for about 45 percent of production. Such devices included fireplace accessories, parts and attachments for boiler systems, and domestic stoves, forced-air devices, and specialty oil-burning heaters.

Residential and personal uses accounted for about 32 percent of heating equipment expenditures in the mid-1990s. Office buildings consumed about 10 percent of production, and miscellaneous farm, industrial, and commercial uses accounted for about 51 percent of the market. Exports consumed the remaining 7 percent of production.

BACKGROUND AND DEVELOPMENT

Woodburning stoves, believed to be the earliest heating devices, were first used by the Chinese in 600 B.C. Central heat was first used in 350 B.C., when the Greeks began building flues beneath building floors to heat rooms. The Romans developed more complex central heating systems called hypocausts in the early Christian era. These systems transferred heat from a furnace using conduction, convection, and radiation. Although the chimney was not developed until the fourteenth century, heating systems designed for European castles in the eleventh and twelfth centuries were important precursors to the flue and other space heating contraptions.

Woodburning and coalburning stove technology continued to advance before and during the Middle Ages. In fact, stoves similar in design to the earliest Chinese units were still in use throughout Russia and parts of Europe in the 1990s. The first manufactured cast-iron stove, which was essentially an iron box, was produced in Lynn, Massachusetts, in 1642. Benjamin Franklin improved this design in 1744 by joining the stove to a fireplace. The first round cast-iron stoves, which became popular in the nineteenth century, were built in Pennsylvania in 1800 by Isaac Orr.

Central heating system technology, in contrast to advances in stove systems, languished after the fall of the Roman Empire. The first central hot-water system that used pipes to heat a building, for instance, was created in 1792 to heat the Bank of England. Not until 1840, did similar technology reach the United States. Central steam heaters were also developed in the late 1700s and were implemented in the United States in the late 1800s. Not until the early twentieth century were hot air systems, similar to those used in the Roman hypocausts, revived for practical use.

In addition to new heat delivery methods, such as steam and hot water, central furnaces, and iron stoves, the burgeoning U.S. heating equipment industry also benefitted from the commercial application of new fuels in the nineteenth and twentieth centuries. In the early 1900s, particularly in the 1920s, heating devices that could efficiently utilize gas and oil increased the scope of the market served by traditional woodburning and coalburning device manufacturers. Likewise, the availability of liquified propane in the 1940s significantly boosted demand for gas-powered heaters.

Gas- and oil-powered heating equipment, as well as electrical equipment classified in other industries, proliferated during the 1940s through the 1970s. As a result, the share of the heating equipment market represented by coalburning and woodburning devices declined. Nevertheless, shipments of nearly all types of heating equipment ballooned in the postwar economic boom. As housing starts swelled in the 1950, 1960s, and 1970s, the demand for space heaters, stoves, and fireplace accessories blossomed. Booming commercial, industrial, and institutional markets hiked the production of boiler and radiator systems. The even faster proliferation of warm-air furnaces and electric heating equipment, however, cannibalized growth in some industry segments.

Despite solid market growth throughout much of the 1970s, manufacturers realized by the end of that decade that the heating equipment industry had entered maturity. Although fluctuations in energy prices caused temporary spurts in demand in various industry segments, the overall demand for heating equipment had stabilized. Throughout the 1980s the value of industry shipments stagnated at about $2.1 billion. Although energy-availability shortages in the late 1970s and early 1980s aroused interest in some alternative heating equipment, such as solar-powered systems, sales from these segments collapsed in the mid-1980s as energy costs stabilized and alternative-energy tax incentives faded.

Although some manufacturers were able to take advantage of budding foreign markets during the 1980s, domestic producers generally found themselves under increasing pressure from foreign rivals in their core U.S. market. Stagnant revenue growth and declining profit margins plagued many producers throughout the decade.

In response to idle markets and downward pressure on margins, heating equipment manufacturers in the early 1990s were continuing two trends which they started in the early 1980s—consolidation and increased productivity. Like companies in other mature businesses, heating equipment producers were consolidating the industry through merger and acquisition, or by exiting the market and abandoning market share. The primary benefits for competitors of mergers and acquisitions were related to multiple economies of scale and increased financial strength.

Increasing productivity, the second trend, was being achieved primarily through automation and work force reduction. Between 1980 and 1990, the total number of workers employed in the industry declined nearly 30 percent, from over 26,000 to about 18,500. Some producers also realized gains by exporting some production activities and by increasing use of foreign parts. By 1991, for instance, imported parts accounted for a full 35 percent of materials used by heating equipment producers.

Going into the mid-1990s, manufacturers were facing a slight reprieve from the tepid growth that plagued them for more than a decade. This growth represented marked improvements over sales in the early 1990s. For instance, total unit sales of all types of heating equipment fell from $2.4 million in 1989 to $2.2 million in 1990. In 1992, conversely, sales of residential boilers jumped 8.7 percent to 321,942 units; this jump followed five successive years of decline.

In 1993, the residential heating business boomed. The result was a record shipment of 2.5 million gas furnaces. Thirteen of the 14 types of home heating equipment indexed by the Gas Appliance Manufacturers Association (GAMA) showed gains in 1993. Gas warm air

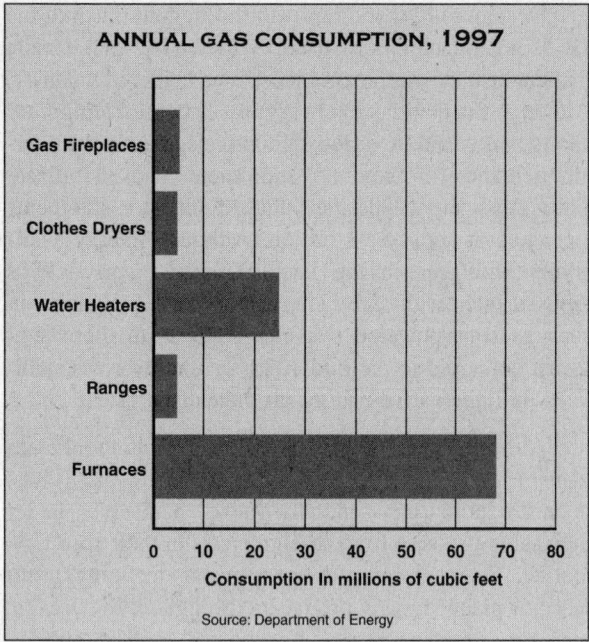

ANNUAL GAS CONSUMPTION, 1997

Consumption In millions of cubic feet

Source: Department of Energy

furnaces had the warmest year in 1993, with shipments of 2.5 million units, up 21 percent from 1992. These furnaces accounted for more than half of all heating equipment shipments. Oil warm air furnaces showed a gain of 5.5 percent, with shipments of 148,803 units. Hydronic residential heating systems were also up. Gas boilers totaled 187,378 shipments, a growth of 4.7 percent. Oil-fired boilers totaled 118,119 units, a gain of 11.2 percent. The only negative statistic in the business was for gas floor furnaces, which were down 11 percent at 13,583 shipments.

Sales of residential baseboard and convector devices jumped in 1993, by an estimated 13.7 percent. Miscellaneous room heater sales were expected to rise by a less dramatic 9 percent in 1993. Increases in residential markets, caused by a surge in homebuilding activity, were partially offset by commercial and industrial sectors. Demand for nonresidential boilers, for instance, was projected to continue its steady 2 percent per year decline.

CURRENT CONDITIONS

By the year 2000, potentially 2 million furnaces and 3,000 boilers will need to be replaced; this will provide the majority of sales of heating equipment through the end of the 1990s. Replacement of central heating systems continues to lead the field, accounting for almost 70 percent of all central heating systems shipped, and virtually all homes that are built are built with central heating systems. This new construction accounts more than 1.3 million units a year, with about two-thirds of single family homes using a gas-heat furnace.

Despite the remarkable performance of 1993, on average, productivity gains declined in the 1990s. Produ-

cers were only able to increase margins by moving production to other countries, such as Mexico. Passage of the North American Free Trade Agreement in 1993 made this move easier.

In the future, increased automation and movement of some production activities overseas will likely exert downward pressure on wage growth for traditional heating equipment manufacturing jobs. But job prospects for highly technically skilled workers were expected to grow through 2006 to keep up with increasing demand for products.

The value of shipments increased slowly, from $2.1 billion in 1987 to $2.3 billion in 1996, a mere 7 percent in 10 years. But in 1997, shipment value made a sizable jump to over $3.7 billion. Sales continued to be bolstered by demand for energy efficient systems by the turn of the century.

Low energy prices will dilute opportunities for sales growth of high-tech, energy-efficient products. The energy intensive, comparatively low-tech nature of heating equipment minimized opportunities for technological breakthroughs that might otherwise spur large numbers of replacement sales. However, producers in 1993 continued to make technological strides in several areas. The "zero-clearance" fireplace, which inserts into a traditional fireplace, promised up to 90 percent efficiency and reduced emissions of pollutants. Similarly, developers of "thermoformers," which use catalytic gas-fired infrared heaters, claimed their innovation could save up to 80 percent on electrical costs.

INDUSTRY LEADERS

The top company in this industry sector for 1999 was Falcon Building Products Inc., of Chicago, Illinois. Falcon posted $686 million in sales and 4,200 employees. Second was Schutte and Koerting Division of Bensalem, Pennsylvania, which posted $127 million in sales and employed around 100 workers. Third was Sterling Radiator Division of Westfield, Massachusetts, which employed 1,400 workers and posted $112 million in sales.

There were a total of 469 establishments in this industry in 1997, which collectively employed 20,300 workers in 1999, 13,900 of whom were in production. This marked a decline of nearly 18 percent from 1997. Wages averaged $12.76 an hour in 1999, and a typical workweek was 43.3 hours with an average 4.6 hours of overtime.

WORKFORCE

Employment prospects in the heating equipment industry were bleak going into the mid-1990s. The U.S. Bureau of Labor Statistics estimates that employment in most heating equipment manufacturing positions will decline by 15 percent to 25 percent between 1990 and 2005.

Positions for assemblers and fabricators, which account for a leading 15 percent of total jobs in the industry, were expected to decline by 23 percent. Jobs for grinders and polishers, machine tool workers, and lathe operators will also decline by over 20 percent. Manufacturing opportunities will arise, however, for some machinists, sheet metal workers, and tool and die makers. Furthermore, sales positions are expected to increase by over 22 percent.

FURTHER READING

Darnay. Arsen J., ed. *Manufacturing USA.* 5th ed. Detroit: Gale Research, 1996.

Heating, Air Conditioning, and Refrigeration Technicians. *1998-99 Occupational Outlook Handbook. Bureau of Labor Statistics.* 2000. Available from http://stats.bls.gov.

Ward's Business Directory of U.S. Private and Public Companies. Detroit: Gale Research, 1999.

SIC 3441

FABRICATED STRUCTURAL METAL

This classification includes establishments primarily engaged in fabricating iron and steel or other metal for structural purposes, such as bridges, buildings, and sections for ships, boats, and barges. Establishments primarily engaged in manufacturing metal doors, sash, frames, molding, and trim are classified in **SIC 3442: Metal Doors, Sash, Frames, Molding, and Trim;** and establishments doing fabrication work at the site of construction are classified in the Construction industries.

NAICS CODE(S)

332312 (Fabricated Structural Metal Manufacturing)

INDUSTRY SNAPSHOT

The fabricated structural metal industry was strong in the late 1990s. In 1997, total fabricated structural metal shipments were valued at $16.1 billion. Since a primary market for fabricated structural metals was the building and construction industry, metal fabricators benefitted from the American construction boom of 1997 and 1998. Nevertheless, competition from cheaper imported products was a concern for fabricated structural metal producers. Moreover, the economic collapse in Asia eroded export markets for U.S. fabricated structural metal manufacturers.

The industry's products were divided into five categories by the U.S. Census Bureau. The largest sector—fabricated structural metal bar joist and concrete reinforcing bars—accounted for over 65 percent industry shipments in 1997. The second category—structural

metal for bridges—represented 3.2 percent of total shipments, while fabricated structural iron for ships, boats, and barges (category three) made up 1.9 percent. Other fabricated structural metal products (category four) comprised 20.5 percent, and the final category—fabricated structural metal, not specified by kind—accounted for the remaining 9 percent.

ORGANIZATION AND STRUCTURE

A total of 3,040 establishments were involved in the production of fabricated structural metal in 1997. 1,176 of these facilities (about 40 percent) were larger companies with more than 20 employees. With 260 fabricated structural metal establishments, California led the nation in this regard. The state's 1997 shipments were valued at $1.1 billion, or approximately 6.6 percent, of total shipments. Although Texas had fewer establishments in this industry—with 237—its shipments were the highest in the country. In 1997, Texas' shipments of fabricated structural metal products were $1.6 billion, or about 9.6 percent of the total. Ohio was home to the third-highest number of companies in this industry in 1997. Its 177 establishments produced shipments worth over $762.0 million, or 4.7 percent of the total.

BACKGROUND AND DEVELOPMENT

At first, metals were hammered into shape, then when it was found that fire could alter the structure of the ores, furnaces were built to cast metals into useful shapes. The use of ferrous metals, however, did not begin until 7,000 years after copper and bronze were first smelted. Once technology advanced and iron smelting began, iron rapidly replaced copper for tools and weapons. By 100 B.C. the use of iron as a semi-structural material was recognized.

By the 1990s the kiln, hammer, and anvil had been replaced with blast furnaces and multi-ton presses. Structural shapes were continuously cast and forged, later to be cut to standard lengths. Although greater understanding of the metallurgical properties of metals occurred over the course of the industry's development, and manufacturing processes evolved, which served to lend uniformity and structural integrity to the final product, working conditions in the industry changed little. While steel and iron mills were much safer places to work in the early 1990s, thanks largely to the Occupational Safety and Health Act and the Environmental Protection Agency, hazards remained, making mill work a fairly dangerous occupation in comparison to other manufacturing jobs.

Industry shipment levels remained fairly constant between 1982 and 1994. In 1982 the value of shipments was $8.8 billion. By 1995 this value reached a high point of $10.8 billion. The lowest level during this period was in 1983 when the value of shipments was $8.0 billion.

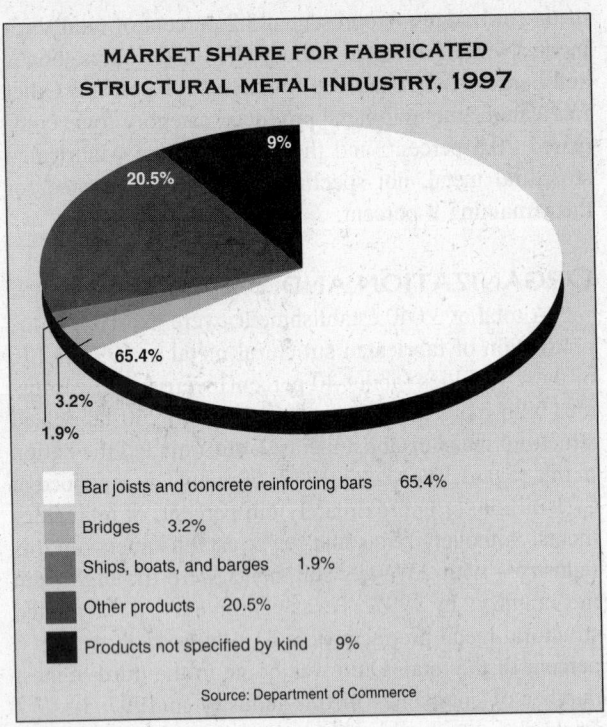

MARKET SHARE FOR FABRICATED STRUCTURAL METAL INDUSTRY, 1997

9%
20.5%
65.4%
3.2%
1.9%

☐ Bar joists and concrete reinforcing bars   65.4%

▨ Bridges   3.2%

▨ Ships, boats, and barges   1.9%

▨ Other products   20.5%

■ Products not specified by kind   9%

Source: Department of Commerce

CURRENT CONDITIONS

The fabricated structural metal industry was bolstered by the overall strong American economy. Most important to the industry was the construction boom of the late 1990s. As a result of increased demand from the construction sector, shipments of fabricated structural iron or steel products for commercial, residential, institutional, or public buildings generated shipments rose to more than $5.6 billion in 1997, or about 34 percent of all fabricated structural metal product shipments. The market for fabricated structural metal for bridges was promising, as well. A report issued by the U.S. Department of Commerce revealed that over one third of American bridges were in need or replacement or repair.

Imports remained a threat, however. With the devaluation of Asian currencies in the wake of the financial crisis of 1997, steel imports flooded into America. As a result of this oversupply, profits remained low. At the same time that import levels rose, U.S. saw key fabricated structural metal markets in Asia and Russia dwindle. The construction industry stalled in Asia, thereby reducing demand for the offerings of U.S. firms.

INDUSTRY LEADERS

Valmont Industries Inc. was a leading company in this industry. The Valley, Nebraska-based firm's 1998 sales were $606.3 million, up from $522.0 million in 1995. The company, which employed 3,859 workers, derived about 49 percent of its 1998 sales from engineered metal structures, which it sold primarily to lighting, util-

ity, and communications companies. Another key player in the industry was Acme Metals Incorporated. With over 2,000 employees and 1998 sales of $459.9 million, Acme's fabrication division—Acme Packaging—earned about half of the company's profits. Acme Packaging obtained the steel for its fabricating operations from Acme Steel.

Nucor Corporation of Charlotte, North Carolina, realized significant growth in the late 1990s because of the considerable capital investments it had made during the decade. Its Jewett, Texas, mill received a continuous caster, which went online in June 1994. The company's Hickman, Arkansas, hot-rolled sheet mill received a $35.0 million thin-slab caster. These investments toward expansion helped Nucor record a 59 percent rise in profits in 1993 and gave the company the second-highest operating profit, $432.3 million, in 1995.

In December 1996, Nucor Corporation announced plans to spend an additional $250.0 million for modernization and capital improvement projects. These expenditures included $80.0 million for increased capacity and functioning of the Norfolk, Nebraska, mill; a galvanizing line at Berkeley, South Carolina, capable of producing 10 million tons of steel a year at an estimated cost of $40.0 million; $30.0 million of improvements at the Crawfordsville, Indiana, facility; and a new steel-deck facility in Fort Payne, Alabama, at a cost of $10.0 million. These capital improvements reduced costs and increased Nucor's tonnage so that it could meet competition from other mini-mills such as Gallatin Steel Co., North Star BHP Steel Ltd., and Steel Dynamics Inc. The result of Nucor's efforts was 1998 sales of $4.2 billion. With 7,200 employees, the company was the fourth-largest steel maker in the United States.

WORKFORCE

Employment levels steadily decreased in the 1980s, falling from 103,500 total employees in the industry in 1982 to 70,700 in 1993. With the economic expansion of the mid and late 1990s, however, more people found work in this industry. By 1995, total employment had risen to 73,700, and by 1997 the work force had grown to 83,783. Of this total number, 60,969 employees were production workers, who on average earned $12.78 per hour during a 39 hour work week.

Texas contained the greatest number of workers in this industry, with 9,194, followed by California with 6,972. Fabricated structural metal employees in California earned an average of $14.35 per hour—a higher wage than the industry-wide norm—while their counterparts in Texas received $11.71 per hour. With 5,486 workers, Pennsylvania had the third highest number of employees in this industry. Production workers were paid $14.59 per hour.

RESEARCH AND TECHNOLOGY

Innovations in casting technology boosted the productivity of structural metal manufacturers. One manufacturer of casting equipment and systems, Rokop Corporation, was experiencing growth as a result of two companies' capital investments. Nucor Corporation requested another continuous caster, making it the fourth piece of such equipment installed in its facilities. The other company making a capital investment with Rokop was Tennessee Valley Steel Corporation. This project added a dual-stream ladle sequencing system, the fourth ladle system project for Rokop, two of which were sold to casters in China and Hungary. A fifth system of this sort was sold to Keystone Steel & Wire Company.

Rokop Corporation's projects were indicative of a trend in the structural metal industry to modernize facilities. Steel mills and iron casters have been around for centuries, while the principal technology has changed little. However, controlling processes to improve quality and reduce costs enabled great technological innovations. Bethlehem Steel participated in this strategy by investing $100 million in modernization of its new subsidiary, Bethlehem Structural Products, which was a leading supplier of structural steel and sheet-piling to the construction industry. The aim of this three-year project was to increase productivity, cut costs, and improve quality. However, in 1995, Bethlehem Structural Products Corp. underwent major overhauls that resulted in the discontinuation of its steel making operations.

FURTHER READING

Petry, Corinna. "Nucor's Cash Headed Into Modernization." *American Metal Market,* 30 December 1996.

Robertson, Scott. "Import Flood Sink Steel Profit." *American Metal Market,* 4 October 1999.

Teaff, Rick. "Steel Chiefs Dash for Cash." *American Metal Market,* 30 May 1996.

U.S. Census Bureau. "Printing Ink Manufacturing." Available from http://www.census.gov/prod/ec97/97m3314c.pdf. October 1999.

SIC 3442

METAL DOORS, SASH, FRAMES, MOLDING, AND TRIM

Companies in this industry are engaged primarily in manufacturing ferrous and nonferrous metal doors, sash, window and door frames and screens, molding, and trim. Establishments primarily engaged in manufacturing metal covered wood doors, windows, sash, door frames, molding, and trim are classified in **SIC 2431: Millwork.**

NAICS CODE(S)

332321 (Metal Window and Door Manufacturing)

INDUSTRY SNAPSHOT

The metal doors, sash, frames, molding, and trim industry is an extremely competitive industry with a low profit margin. It has experienced moderate but steady growth in shipments since 1982, except for a slight dip in 1990 and 1991. Shipments were valued at $4.69 billion that year. Shipments grew to $8.20 billion in 1996, and an estimated $8.62 billion for 1998. Employment levels grew slightly in the early 1980s but flattened between 1986 and 1988. In 1982 approximately 66,300 people were employed by this industry, 47,600 of those being production workers. These figures grew to 67,800 total employees and 49,300 production workers by 1996. Total employment numbers were expected to decline to 67,400 in 1998, with the number of production workers remaining the same.

Workers are paid poorly in this industry compared to average pay in all manufacturing industries combined. In 1982 the average hourly wage was $6.61; the figure grew to $9.73 by the end of 1996. That same year the average hourly wage for all manufacturing workers was $12.40. By 1997 the average hourly wage had reached $10.43, still well below the national manufacturing average. Other comparative ratios indicate this industry rates below the manufacturing average in terms of value added, cost, shipments, and investment per establishment, employee, and production worker. In fact, in terms of investment this industry ranks more than two-thirds below the average manufacturing industry.

ORGANIZATION AND STRUCTURE

This industry is dominated by small independent companies with fewer than 20 employees. In 1982, of the 1,738 establishments engaged in this industry, only 673 employed more than 20 people. By 1996 the total number of establishments fell to an estimated 1,268, while those employing more than 20 people fell to 553.

The product share is divided into six areas. Metal doors and frames, except storm doors, held 47.54 percent of the total market share in the early 1990s. Metal window sash and frames, except storm sash, held 24.16 percent; metal molding and trim and store fronts held 4.86 percent; metal combination screen, storm sash, and storm doors held 6.09 percent; metal window and door screens and metal weather strip held 3.97 percent; and metal doors, sash, and trim, not specified by kind, held 13.39 percent of the market share in the early 1990s.

In the early 1990s the leading states in employment were California, Texas, Pennsylvania, Ohio, and Florida. California led the industry in shipments with 192 establishments engaged in the manufacture of metal doors, sash, frames, molding, and trim. These establishments shipped 10.6 percent of the U.S. total in this industry, amounting to $756.8 million for that year. The total number of people employed in this industry in California was 7,700, averaging 40 people per establishment, who earned an average of $9.21 per hour. Ohio's 62 establishments shipped $601.2 million worth of product and employed 4,200. Ohio's employees earned an average $10.67 per hour. Texas's 105 firms engaged in this industry shipped $545.5 million worth of products and employed 5,600 workers who earned an average $7.51 per hour. Pennsylvania's 67 establishments had gross revenues of $460.5 million and employed 4,600 who earned an average $10.08 per hour. Tennessee's 42 companies had sales of $403.4 million and employed 3,600 earning $9.56 per hour. Florida's 116 companies had sales of $386.2 million and employed 4,200 who earned an average $7.80 per hour.

CURRENT CONDITIONS

According to *U.S. Glass Metal & Glazing* projections, the U.S. demand for windows and doors reached $26 billion by the year 2000. Older house maintenance helped increase sales of windows and doors within the U.S. by 4.7 percent per year in the late 1990s. More energy-efficient products and regulations coupled with a lack of timber resulted in the highest demand increase for vinyl/plastic products, although wood windows and doors still made up more than 56 percent of sales through 2000. Increase in metal doors and windows was slow because of the lack of insulation of metal products.

Anything involved in the building industry, both commercial and residential, had an effect on this industry. A strong real estate market coupled with a strong economy was creating more growth and expansion, and causing small companies, like Hollow Metal Door of Wichita, Kansas, to expand and grow. When housing was up, sales were up. But even when housing was not up, people were remodeling, adding skylights, columns, and stairs; this created even more sales than housing.

INDUSTRY LEADERS

Lowe's Companies Inc. of North Wilkesboro, North Carolina, led this industry with overall sales of $12.2 billion for its fiscal year ended January 30, 1999, representing an increase of 21 percent over the previous year's sales. In April 1999 Eagle Garden & Hardware, which experienced sales of $1.1 billion for its 1998 fiscal year, a 12 percent increase over its previous year's sales, merged with Lowe's. Toledo, Ohio-based Owens Corning generated $5 billion in 1998 sales. Atlanta-based Alumax Inc. posted sales of $2.9 billion in 1997 and $1.6 billion for the first six months of 1998, before it was taken over by the Aluminum Co. of America (Alcoa). Lancaster, Pennsylvania-based Armstrong World Industries Inc. garnered 1998 sales of $2.7 billion.

None of the above companies listed this industry as their primary focus, however. Jeld-Wen Inc. of Klamath Falls, Oregon, on the other hand, was considered the biggest door and window maker in the world. In 1998 Jeld-Wen created sales of $1.5 billion, employed 11,000 workers worldwide, owned more than 150 companies in 40 states as well as overseas, and was listed 119th on the *Forbes* private 500. The company followed an unorthodox diversification strategy that did not create apparent synergies; its list of subsidiaries included resorts, a dairy farm, a wood pellets manufacturer, and, as of January 1999, a multimedia marketing house. Nonetheless, Jeld-Wen continued to thrive.

WORKFORCE

Jeld-Wen was renowned for its tactic of buying out a company, dismissing all its employees, and then rehiring them at lower wages in the name of creating efficiencies. While this strategy might make sense from a corporate perspective, the workers viewed the action as unfair and cut-throat, prioritizing profits over providing a living wage. In 1998, when Jeld-Wen acquired an Oshkosh, Wisconsin, door and window manufacturing plant run by Morgan Products Ltd. for the previous 128 years, it cut all jobs and then rehired workers at wage rates as much as $2.70 per hour lower, with no signed labor agreement, and without healthcare benefits. The United Brotherhood of Carpenters Local 1363 picketed the plant in response.

As the industry looks toward the year 2005, a decrease in demand for workers overall is anticipated. Sheet metal workers and duct installers were expected to be reduced by 58.8 percent, followed by structural metal and precision fitters with a 50.6 percent decline; those were the sharpest declines estimated for this industry. Coating, painting, and spraying machine operators were expected to be reduced by more than 50 percent. Other occupations expected to be reduced between 30 and 50 percent included metal and plastic machine forming operators; drafters; hand freight, stock and material movers; and bookkeeping, accounting, and auditing clerks. In 1997 the industry's 1,375 establishments employed 71,308 people, 72 percent of whom worked in production.

RESEARCH AND TECHNOLOGY

A process called UNI-SAN 6500 that fuses glass and metal was made available in viewing windows from Jacoby-Tarbox. The process is reported to eliminate common causes of window breakage through its improved strength. Increased safety and durability are key to these single-unit windows.

In 1996 Wayne-Dalton Corporation of Mt. Hope, Ohio, premiered the Ironmax Classic Entry Door. The product was made of durable, 26-gauge steel panels; its core was filled with forced-in-place high-density polyurethane. The doors featured electrostatically applied prime coating and a warranty against warping or peeling was included.

FURTHER READING

"Alcoa buy pulls down Alumax net." *American Metal Market,* 10 July 1998.

Bump, Greg. "Workers at Oshkosh, Wis., Door Manufacturer Protest Lack of Labor Agreement." *Knight-Ridder/Tribune Business News,* 16 July 1998.

Darnay, Arsen J., ed. *Manufacturing USA: Industry Analysis, Statistics, and Leading Companies,* 5th ed. Detroit: Gale Research, 1996.

Infotrac Company Profiles. 14 January 200. Available from http://web4.infotrac.galegroup.com.

"Local Door Company to Expand." *Witchita Business Journal,* 23 August 1996.

"Lowe's and Eagle post record years." *Do-It-Yourself Retailing,* April 1999.

Lubove, Seth. "Construction." *Forbes,* 13 January 1997.

U.S. Census Bureau. *Survey of Manufacturers,* 10 February 2000. Available from http://www.census.gov/prod/www/abs/97ecmani.html.

"U.S. Demand for Windows and Doors to Reach $26 Billion by 2000." *U.S. Glass Metal & Glazing,* 1 December 1995.

Ward's Business Directory of U.S. Private and Public Companies. Vol. 5. Detroit: Gale Research, 1997.

"Wayne-Dalton Releases Ironmax Door." *National Home Center News,* 5 August 1996, 230.

Wojahn, Ellen. "The 1 billion-pound elephant." *Oregon Business,* June 1998.

SIC 3443

FABRICATED PLATE WORK—BOILER SHOPS

This classification includes establishments primarily engaged in manufacturing power and marine boilers, pressure and nonpressure tanks, processing and storage vessels, heat exchangers, and weldments and similar products; these are made by cutting, forming, and joining metal plates, shapes, bars, sheets, pipe mill products, and tubing to custom or standard design for factory or field assembly. Excluded from this category are establishments primarily involved in manufacturing warm air heating furnaces, which are classified in **SIC 3585: Air-Conditioning and Warm Air Heating Equipment and Commercial and Industrial Refrigeration Equipment.** Those establishments primarily engaged in manufacturing nonelectric heating apparatus other than power boilers are classified in **SIC 3433: Heating Equipment, Except Electric and Warm Air Furnaces.** Also excluded from the fabricated plate work classification are manufacturers of household cooking apparatus and those manufacturing industrial process furnaces and ovens. The former are covered in **SIC 3631: Household Cooking Equipment,** and the latter are listed under **SIC 3567: Industrial Process Furnaces and Ovens.**

NAICS CODE(S)

332313 (Plate Work Manufacturing)
332410 (Power Boiler and Heat Exchanger Manufacturing)
332420 (Metal Tank (Heavy and Gauge) Manufacturing)
333415 (Air-Conditioning and Warm Air Heating Equipment and Commercial and Industrial Refrigeration Equipment Manufacturing)

INDUSTRY SNAPSHOT

Plating—the application of a thin metal layer on a surface to enhance wearing quality, to prevent leakage, and to protect against corrosion—is used in the fabrication of many products. The manufacturing process generally is consigned to manufacturers involved in the fabricated plate work industry. Although the bulk of the industry's shipments comprises a multitude of products manufactured through plating processes, the core of the fabricated plate work industry essentially includes the manufacturing of power and marine boilers and various types of plate tanks and storage vessels.

Power boilers, as classified by the American Society of Mechanical Engineers, operate at greater than 15-psig steam pressure and are intended for stationary service, which excludes locomotive boilers from the scope of the fabricated plate work industry. Boilers operating at 15-psig steam pressure or lower, known as low-pressure heating boilers, are classified in **SIC 3433: Heating Equipment, Except Electric and Warm Air.** Power boilers, designed to operate at high pressures and temperatures, generate steam to provide power for utility companies and for various industrial processes. The boiler itself consists of two principal parts: the furnace, which provides heat, usually by burning fuel, and the boiler proper, in which water is converted to steam by the heat piped in from the furnace. A steam engine derives its power from steam generated under pressure in a boiler. Marine boilers are designed and fabricated for use aboard a wide range of vessels, including tugboats, oceanliners, oil drilling barges, freighters, and aircraft carriers.

ORGANIZATION AND STRUCTURE

The fabricated plate work industry is comprised of large and small manufacturing facilities. In 1997, a total of 25,074 workers were employed by 1,034 fabricated plate work establishments.

Geographically, fabricated plate work manufacturing occurs throughout much of the United States, with 43 states containing 5 or more manufacturing facilities. The bulk of manufacturing activity in the mid-1990s took place in Texas, Pennsylvania, California, Ohio, and Oklahoma. Together, these states contained 712 manufacturing establishments, which generated $3.6 billion in sales and accounted for 38.9 percent of the total domestic shipments delivered by the industry. These states employed 37.2 percent of the industry's workforce.

Texas, with 210 establishments, contained the greatest number of fabricated plate work manufacturing facilities in any one state and had the highest total revenue collected and shipment volume, posting $987.5 million in sales and accounting for 11 percent of the industry's total shipments. While California's 181 establishments topped Pennsylvania's 127, Pennsylvania came in second in terms of revenue and shipments with $864.3 million in sales and 9.5 percent of total U.S. shipments. California garnered third place with $576.7 million in total sales, which was 6.3 percent of total U.S. shipments.

Operating a manufacturing establishment in the fabricated plate work industry generally is a less expensive venture than operating other typical manufacturing establishments, particularly in the area of average costs incurred. In 1989, the average cost incurred from purchasing the necessary raw materials for manufacturing fabricated plate work per establishment was $2.7 million, 41 percent lower than the average recorded by all other manufacturing industries. A greater difference is found in the area of average investment per establishment. In 1989, the average investment expenditure per establishment was $162,996 (approximately 50 percent below the $321,011 incurred by a typical manufacturing facility).

BACKGROUND AND DEVELOPMENT

The origins of the fabricated plate work industry may be traced to the early development of boilers, which began in the Middle Ages when inventors experimented with the idea of harnessing the power of steam. For centuries, improvements were made in both the theory of deriving power from steam and in steam generators themselves. Seventeenth-century inventor Giovanni Battista della Porta was the first to discover that when steam condensed in a closed vessel it created a vacuum that could draw up water. Thomas Savery, an English engineer working in the late seventeenth century, created the first machine to provide mechanical power by utilizing steam. By 1800, vast improvements had been made in designing steam engines and boilers, but the expense involved in developing prototypes was prohibitive.

In 1800, a landmark development in the history of boiler development occurred when Richard Trevithick put together a steam engine and boiler, which eventually, through the addition of tubes carrying gases from a fire, increased the heating surface and efficiency of the boiler. Several decades after Trevithick's achievements, John Stevens, an American engineer, developed one of the first boilers in which tubes carried water to be converted to steam, instead of gases from a fire. This "water-tube" boiler represented the culmination of roughly 50 years of work by Stevens in his efforts toward constructing an efficient steam system to power ships along the Hudson River. By the mid-nineteenth century, further improvements had been made in the water-tube design, which allowed the water to circulate more easily, provided more heating surface, and lowered the risk of boiler explosions.

During this time, boiler design was fostered by the industrialization of Great Britain. The shift from an agrarian and commercial society to an industrial society was prompting a similar transition in the United States, shaping that country into a modern manufacturing nation. Steam powered both of these industrialization movements; the power it provided proved intrinsic to the movement toward large and distinct manufacturing industries. In the United States, residences and local industries were the primary users of these steam generators until the latter half of the nineteenth century. At that time, the applications for steam power broadened and spurred the emergence of a market segment for the fabricated plate work industry that would fuel its growth throughout the twentieth century.

The unveiling of this new use for steam took place at the 1876 U.S. Centennial Exhibition in Philadelphia, during which the practicality of generating electricity by steam power was demonstrated to the attending public. Five years later, four boilers were powering the Brush Electric Light and Power Co. in Philadelphia, the nation's first commercial electric generating station, marking the beginning of a new era for both the United States in general and boiler manufacturers in particular. From this time forward, power boilers in mills and factories appeared with increasing frequency, particularly in sugar refining companies, as the industrialization of the United States neared its greatest intensity.

Similar advances had been made with marine boilers, another integral product that bolstered the U.S. fabricated plate work manufacturers, helping them to form a genuine, organized industry after the turn of the century. Beginning with the *Great Britain* in the early nineteenth century, marine engineers began exploring the possibilities of providing power to becalmed ships through steam. Eventually sails and masts were discarded and boilers became the sole source of power for ships of all classes and sizes, from the 1,154-ton *Britannica,* which "sailed" from Liverpool to Boston in 1840, to the *Monitor* and the *Virginia,* two iron-hulled steamboats pitted against each other during the American Civil War.

By the time boilers had become common in American industry, marine boilers also were fueling a majority of the U.S. vessels on water. Accordingly, by the end of the nineteenth century, fabricated plate work manufacturing, essentially comprising the fabrication of power and marine boilers, was being conducted in earnest. In 1889, the American Boiler Manufacturers' Association (ABMA) was chartered with elevating the standards of boiler design and manufacture and preventing the production and sale of boilers deemed unfit for safe operation. Moreover, the establishment of a national association for boiler manufacturers cohered a loosely organized group of manufacturers, marking the formal beginnings of the boiler shop, or fabricated plate work industry in the United States.

Before the fledgling industry could emerge as an integrated and uniform group of manufacturers, national boiler manufacturing standards needed to be created and the alarming frequency of boiler explosions needed to be quelled, something the formation of the ABMA had failed to do. Another association with a vested interest in the production of boilers, the American Society of Mechanical Engineers (ASME), also had failed to curb the number of accidents related to boiler explosions, despite formulating a code entitled "Standard Method for Steam Boiler Trials" in 1884. In 1914, a committee under the purview of ASME published the "Boiler and Pressure Vessel Code," which provided manufacturers with standard specifications for the design, fabrication, installation, and inspection of boilers and pressure vessels. The adoption of nationwide standards helped to curtail the number of boiler explosions while providing manufacturers with a universal manufacturing language in which to communicate and enabling them to produce higher-quality boilers that conformed to the diverse needs of their customers.

Once ASME's Boiler Code gained widespread acceptance, many of the fabricated plate work industry's internal, organizational problems were resolved, or at least made more manageable, facilitating—and in some cases invigorating—the industry's growth. Technological improvements in the design of boilers followed at a rapid pace, as the onus of spearheading future design and production innovations fell to the companies involved in the industry, rather than to the independent engineers.

Several historic achievements followed the publication of the Boiler Code, the first of which involved the opening of the Edgar Steam Electric Station in Weymouth, Massachusetts. The electric station, operated under the aegis of the Boston Edison Co., opened in 1925 with a high-efficiency turbine and boiler system able to produce electricity at the rate of one kilowatt hour per one pound of coal. For its time, this ratio represented a considerable leap in efficiency—conventional power plants competing on the vanguard of technology were consuming 5 to 10 pounds per kilowatt hour—and the station remained a model of efficiency until it was dismantled and sold to a South American power company in the 1970s.

Thirty-three years after the Edgar Steam Electric Station demonstrated to the world the efficiency of steam generated electrical stations, President Dwight D. Eisenhower tripped a switch that activated the first North American commercial central electric-generating station to utilize nuclear energy. Located in Shippingport, a town northwest of Pittsburgh, the Shippingport Atomic Power Station was designed by the Westinghouse Electric Corp., the Division of Naval Reactors of the Atomic Energy Commission for the Department of Energy, and the Duquesne Light Co. Generating 60,000 kilowatts of electricity, the Shippingport Station was small compared to the generating capacity of similar electric stations to follow, but it heralded the advent of a new method for generating electricity, a process that incorporated the use of boilers.

In 1960, the first commercial geothermal, electric generating station in North America began operating in Sonoma County, California, north of San Francisco. This geothermal field, from which generators received naturally produced steam, was first discovered in 1847 and then tapped in the early 1920s, but the steam and hot water billowing from the earth proved too corrosive for pipes and other equipment of the 1920s. By the late 1950s, however, significant advances in anticorrosion technology enabled the Pacific Gas and Electric Co. to successfully generate steam from the Sonoma field, which further broadened the applications for boilers in the production of energy.

These benchmark events in the development of additional uses for boilers, coupled with the increasing utilization of boilers by the industrial sector, accelerated the growth of the fabricated plate work industry. By the early 1960s, boiler shop manufacturers—producing power and marine boilers, pressure and non-pressure tanks, processing and storage vessels, heat exchangers, weldments, and various other plate products—represented a $1.5 billion a year industry. Consistent improvements in design and the increased requirements of U.S. industry led to the fabrication of massive boilers, some of which were able to generate 6.5 million pounds of steam per hour, heated by furnaces approximating the size of 40 medium-sized houses. In the electrical power field, the use of boilers in thermal power plants, which accounted for roughly 80 percent of all electrical power generated in the nation, was pervasive, as boiler manufacturers benefited from their position as suppliers of equipment essential to a diverse customer base.

As the industry entered the 1970s, the demand for power boilers remained strong, stronger than manufacturers were able to satisfy. However, growing concern for the potentially harmful effects of additional electrical generating facilities on the environment began to make the selection of future power plant sites difficult. Consequently, an electrical production deficit existed during the late 1960s, which sparked a wave of concern by utility operators regarding the availability of the equipment necessary to construct additional facilities, as demand outpaced supply. During the 1960s, this gap between production and consumption created a commensurate gap between new orders for power boilers and the production of power boilers. This gap narrowed by the beginning of the 1970s, when electric utility operators began ordering steam-generating equipment in advance as a hedge against an anticipated shortage of power boilers. For manufacturers in the fabricated plate work industry, particularly those focusing on the fabrication of power boilers, this panic boosted sales volume. The value of power boiler shipments increased 18 percent from 1969 to 1970, the culmination of a decade that saw industry-wide power boiler revenue climb from $341 million in 1963 to $631 million in 1970.

The 1970s, however, marked a turning point for the fabricated plate work industry. During the mid-1970s, utility companies became increasingly concerned about the availability of fuel, environmental exigencies, and future demand for energy, resulting in an energy crisis. Energy conservation efforts and soaring energy costs sharply reduced new orders for utility boilers. The fabricated plate industry also experienced slackening, reflecting the losses incurred by nearly every manufacturing industry in the United States during the energy crunch.

Revenue garnered from the production of power boilers fell from more than $1 billion in 1974 to $860 million in 1978, while total boiler production fell from 90 million pounds of capacity to 36.5 million pounds, prompting manufacturers to plead for federal intervention. In response, the National Energy Act and the Industrial Fuel Use Act were passed in 1978. While the government hoped such measures would reduce the number of industrial boilers dependent on gas and oil for fuel, the fabricated plate work industry hoped they would invigorate the stagnant boiler market. Neither occurred, as both manufacturers and their customers became confused about which fuel was to be used.

As a result of the somewhat bleak prospects facing manufacturers in the industry, expected profit margins were reduced in the early 1980s, and competition intensified for the dwindling number of new orders. To mitigate their losses, some manufacturers exited the business entirely, while others began concentrating more on retrofitting and converting existing boilers. Although the latter were able to stave off the negative effects of the six-year downturn, their strategy did not preclude serious losses.

Nationwide energy conservation by both of the industry's primary markets—industrial and utility—imposed, in effect, a limit on the extent to which boiler manufacturers could recover. In 1980, the Department of Energy estimated that the concerted movement toward conservation had reduced the growth in energy demand to half the growth rate of the gross national product, an unsettling discovery considering that the two growth rates, historically, had been roughly equal.

Consequently, manufacturers entered the mid-1980s struggling to maintain their precarious presence in the boiler and fabricated plate work market. Electric utilities at this time were operating old electric generating equipment approaching the end of its economic life, but boiler manufacturers did not expect to realize any significant wave of new orders until the early 1990s, as electric utility operators forestalled the purchase of new equipment as long as possible. An increasing percentage of the industry's work continued to be the rebuilding and refurbishing of older units but, for a considerable number of manufacturers, this type of work did not generate enough money to sustain operations, and the roster of fabricated plate work manufacturers shrank.

By the late 1980s, conditions had not improved greatly. Manufacturing operations were consolidated and some facilities were shut down due to decreased demand. As manufacturers looked toward the future, a reversal of the depressed state of the industry was largely predicated on the equipment purchasing decisions by electric utility companies and a return to more aggressive capital expansion programs by the industrial sector, both of which were stunted by the recessive economic conditions of the early 1990s.

Approximately 1,034 U.S. companies were involved in producing fabricated plate work in 1997. This figure reflected the latest of a decade-long decline in the number of manufacturers engaged in the industry. The sharpest decline occurred from 1982 to 1987, when the number of participants dropped from 1,743 to 1,584. Total revenue garnered by the industry during the 1980s declined as well, dropping from $8.23 billion in 1982 to a low of $6.15 billion in 1986. In the late 1980s, however, the industry's performance improved, as revenue increased for three consecutive years to conclude what otherwise had been a decade of consistent decline. In 1987, the industry's revenue total increased to $6.79 billion, then leapt to $7.81 billion the following year.

CURRENT CONDITIONS

Since 1990, there has been a steady growth in the number of fabricated plate work manufacturers with the largest increase from 1991 to 1992, when the number jumped from 1,694 to 1,942, leveling off in 1993 to 1,922. As the industry entered the 1990s, its sales volume eclipsed the total recorded in 1982, climbing to $8.65 billion in 1990. In 1993 revenue reached $9.11 billion, fell slightly to $8.94 billion in 1994, but rebounded to $10.08 billion in 1995. Shipments climbed to $11.30 billion in 1997. Growth in this industry was expected to be slow due to trends away from replacement and large units.

Sales shipments are predominately derived from the industry's five primary product groups: heat exchangers and steam condensers; fabricated steel plate; steel power boilers, parts, and attachments; metal tanks and vessels (custom fabricated at the factory); and fabricated plate work not conforming to the parameters of standard fabricated plate work. This last product category, attesting to the wide range of products manufactured by the industry, was the most abundantly produced product by fabricated plate work manufacturers, accounting for 20.1 percent of the industry's total shipments. Standard fabricated plate work represented the industry's second largest product category, accounting for 16.7 percent of total shipments, followed by heat exchangers and steam condensers, which accounted for 14.4 percent. Steel power boilers and their parts and attachments represented 10.3 percent of the industry's shipments and were closely trailed by metal tanks and vessels manufactured in a factory setting and according to customer specifications, which represented 10.2 percent. The remainder of the industry's products comprised storage tanks (5.3 percent), nuclear reactor steam supply systems (5.5 percent), and gas cylinders (3.7 percent).

INDUSTRY LEADERS

Ranked according to sales volume, the three largest companies involved in the fabricated plate work industry in 1999 were McDermott Inc., based in New Orleans, Louisiana, with sales of $1.7 billion and 15,000 employees; Columbus, Ohio-based Worthington Cylinder Corp., with $1.5 billion in sales and 1,500 workers; and Babcock & Wilcox Co. of Barberton, Ohio, with sales of $1 billion and 12,000 employees.

McDermott Inc., controlled by McDermott International Inc., earned its position in the industry largely through a merger in 1978 with The Babcock & Wilcox Co., resulting in Babcock & Wilcox as a subsidiary in McDermott's Power Generation Systems and Equipment Division. Formed in 1867 as Babcock, Wilcox and Co., the company's roots actually stretch back to 1856, when a 26-year-old engineer from Rhode Island, Stephen Wilcox, applied his knowledge of water circulation theory to perfect a new boiler concept utilizing inclined water tubes. Later referred to by Thomas Edison as "the best boiler God has permitted man yet to make," the success of Wilcox's system persuaded him and his friend George Herman Babcock to form Babcock, Wilcox and Co.

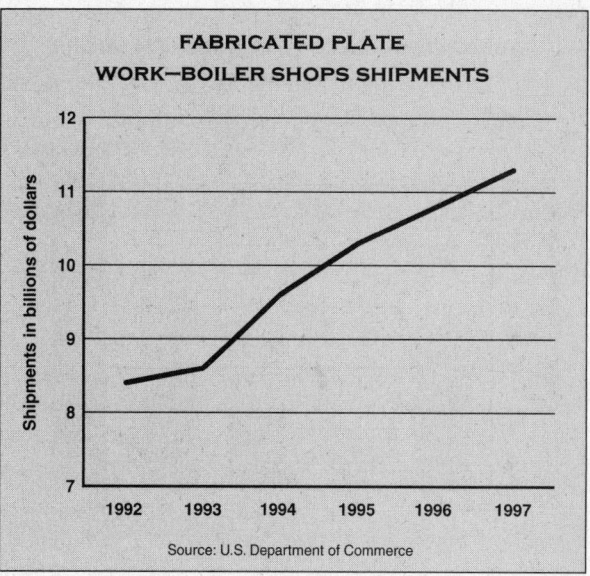

FABRICATED PLATE WORK—BOILER SHOPS SHIPMENTS

Shipments in billions of dollars

Source: U.S. Department of Commerce

Initially, the two partners sold a majority of their boilers to sugar refineries. Then, in 1881 the company began supplying the boilers for the country's first central electric power station at the Brush Electric Light and Power Co. in Philadelphia. In subsequent years, Babcock & Wilcox boilers would continue to represent the vanguard of power generation technology, pioneering significant advances in utility steam generation design and marine boiler development. Moreover, the company helped to shape the industry by playing an instrumental role in the development of the American Society of Mechanical Engineers' Boiler and Pressure Vessel Code in 1914.

Into the early 1990s, Babcock & Wilcox continued to set the pace for other companies involved in the industry, thriving as a major supplier of nuclear steam generating equipment, critical heat exchanges, and replacement recirculating steam generators. Employing approximately 20,000 workers, McDermott Inc. garnered $2.3 billion in sales for 1995. In April 1997, Babcock & Wilcox was awarded a $35-million contract to design and manufacture steam generator components for a nuclear plant in China that was expected to be completed in 1999.

WORKFORCE

Total employment in the fabricated plate work industry declined sharply during the 1980s, falling most precipitously from 103,200 people to 71,200 between 1982 and 1986, a period during which the industry's aggregate revenue experienced a commensurate decline. Toward the latter half of the decade, as sales recovered slightly, the industry's employment base grew. As the industry entered the 1990s, employment increased but was still far below the employment total of the early 1980s.

Total employment in the industry fell from 81,500 people in 1990 to 73,500 in 1991. By 1993, the number

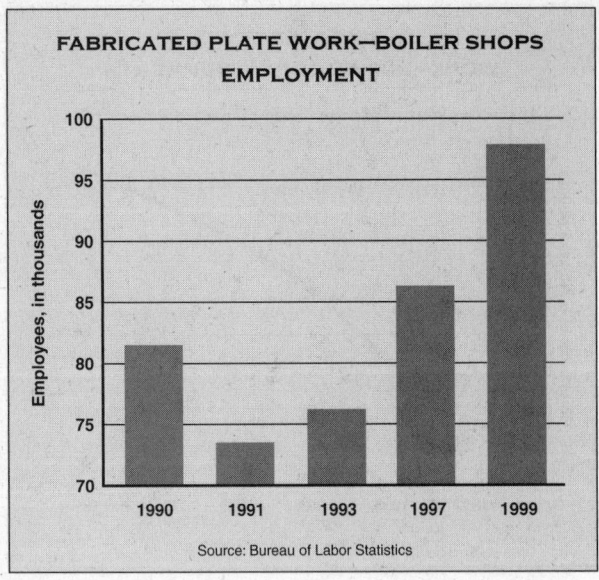

FABRICATED PLATE WORK—BOILER SHOPS
EMPLOYMENT

Source: Bureau of Labor Statistics

had begun to climb back with 76,200 total employees, and levels reached more than 80,000 in 1994 and 97,900 in 1999.

Of the people employed in the industry, an overwhelming majority were employed as production workers, while salaried employees—those performing managerial, administrative, or technical duties—composed the balance of the industry's workforce. In 1994, the typical fabricated plate work manufacturing establishment employed 33 production workers and 13 salaried employees.

In general, production workers in the fabricated plate work industry are employed on a full-time basis. In 1999, a production worker's hourly wage was $14.40. They worked an average of 42.2 hours per week with 5.1 hours of overtime.

In terms of the total payroll per establishment, the fabricated plate work industry's workforce expenditures were slightly less than the average payroll expenditures for all other manufacturing industries, largely because the fabricated plate work industry employed fewer workers per establishment than the average for manufacturing industries.

RESEARCH AND TECHNOLOGY

During the 1980s, two technological developments in particular enabled manufacturers in the industry to increase production efficiency and improve the quality of their products. One of these advances, acoustic emissions technology (AET), had been available to manufacturers of metal-related products for centuries but was not utilized in the production of fabricated plate work in a widespread fashion until much later. The other, computer-aided design, or CAD technology, was developed in the 1980s as an inevitable extension of the rapid technologi-

cal advancements achieved by the computer industry as a whole during the decade.

The use of AET emerged during the 1980s as a viable and effective means to gauge the quality of plate work, and its adoption by manufacturers quickly spread. Acoustic emission, the sound produced by various types of materials during production processes, was first used commercially by those involved in the production of pottery. Potters relied on the audible cracking sounds clay pots produced while cooling in a kiln. These sounds enabled the practiced listener to determine which pots would eventually crack. An application more closely related to the type employed by fabricated plate work manufacturers, however, was used by tin manufacturers, who listened to the sounds of smelted tin, known as "tin cry," to detect structural flaws in the manufactured metal. For manufacturers involved in the fabricated plate work industry, acoustic emissions provided similar information in identifying the inherent structural weaknesses of their products.

Perhaps the most valuable contribution that monitoring acoustic emissions provided was the ability of manufacturers to determine the rate of deterioration of their products, rather than merely the condition of the metal at the time of inspection. Moreover, the structural integrity of metal could be determined without cutting into it, which conventional methods required. By the late 1980s, AET was embraced by manufacturers throughout the United States and regarded in the industry as the most reliable method of monitoring the structural defects of fabricated plate work during production.

Complementing the emergence of AET, the fabricated plate work industry also benefited from the increasing advancements in computer design and software applications during the 1980s, helping manufacturers to reduce the operating and production costs of their products and to improve their designs. The advent of CAD, in particular, provided manufacturers with an invaluable tool to determine the most economical and efficient design of power boilers and other products manufactured by the industry. Additional software applications—designed for use in industrial settings and able to perform tasks that previously had consumed a considerable portion of research and development expenditures—reinforced the industry's dependence on computers to effectively compete in a market that demanded the most sophisticated resources available.

FURTHER READING

"Boilermakers." *1998-99 Occupational Outlook Handbook,* 2000. Available from http://stats.bls.gov.

"Employment Statistics." *Bureau of Labor Statistics,* 2000. Available from http://www.bls.gov.

"Foster Wheeler Sues Over Repeal of Retail State Law." *Waste Age,* May 1996.

"McDermott Gets Job in China." *Wall Street Journal Interactive Company Briefing Book,* 24 April 1997.

Young, David. "Chicago Bridge & Iron Set for Spinoff." *Chicago Tribune,* 6 March 1997.

SIC 3444

SHEET METAL WORK

This industry encompasses companies primarily engaged in manufacturing sheet metal work for buildings (not including fabrication work done by construction contractors at the place of construction) as well as stovepipes, light tanks, and other products of sheet metal.

NAICS CODE(S)

332322 (Sheet Metal Work Manufacturing)

INDUSTRY SNAPSHOT

In 1997, the 4,201 companies involved in the U.S. sheet metal work industry employed 128,534 workers and generated $15.8 billion in shipments. California, Ohio, Illinois, and Texas accounted for more than 33 percent of the industry's total shipments. The most common end uses for sheet metal that same year were electronic enclosures (such as personal computer housings or casings, accounting for 21.8 percent of end uses); roofing and roof drainage equipment (8.7 percent); air conditioning ducts and stove pipes (10.3 percent); sheet metal flooring and siding (7.6 percent); awnings, canopies, cornices, and soffits (4.2 percent); culverts, flumes, irrigation pipes (2.9 percent); and other or unspecified uses (44.5 percent). These categories cover a myriad of products used by every industry from aircraft manufacture (air cowls), building construction (siding, stove hoods, and gutters), heating, ventilation, and air conditioning (HVAC) applications (ducts, furnace flues), mineral processing (coal chutes), and highway construction (guardrails) to agriculture (irrigation pipes), business machines (computer casings, shipbuilding (ship ventilators), postal delivery (mail boxes), and food preparation (vats and bins).

ORGANIZATION AND STRUCTURE

Sheet metal forming is one of the most basic and pervasive manufacturing processes in U.S. industry. In general, sheet metal products manufactured by industry firms have thin walls, simple as well as complex designs, and a large quantity of surface area in relation to thickness. They are generally lighter in weight and more versatile than metal products formed and shaped through casting and forging processes. The manufacture of sheet metal products is generally characterized by low to moderate costs for labor, equipment, and dies.

Industry sheet metal products are manufactured with a wide range of metal-forming machine tools. Several different techniques can be used to produce the same sheet metal part. The factors determining which method to use include the cost of the die, the amount of labor available, the number of sheet metal parts to be made, and the speed of production. Deep-drawing methods, for example, involve more complicated machinery and cost more than other methods, but they are also faster and more cost effective for jobs involving the manufacture of many parts.

In 1997, the sheet metal industry consumed 45 percent the value of its total shipments on materials and supplies, primarily from blast furnaces and steel mills and aluminum rolling and drawing companies. Low-carbon steel was the most widely used metal for sheet metal processes because of its low cost and high strength and formability.

CURRENT CONDITIONS

From 1972 to 1993, the sheet metal industry experienced steady, uninterrupted growth. The number of firms grew from 2,960 to 4,600, and the value of shipments more than quadrupled, from $2.7 billion to $11.1 billion. In the same period, employment rose from 74,000 to 106,400.

In the late 1990s, sheet metal work remained a strong market, fueled by the booming American economy. HVAC systems and business/computer machines were the two largest buyers of the sheet metal work industry's products, and demand for HVAC systems and computer goods remained high at the end of the century. Moreover, low interest rates bolstered new home and building construction, which in turn fostered demand for many sheet metal work products for roofing and siding. Demand for steel sheet metal work was especially robust, and a slew of companies strove to fill consumers' needs. The supply of steel sheet metal rose in 1998 and 1999 as cheaper imported steel flooded the U.S. market. At the same time, U.S. production capacity expanded as a result of a new generation of new steel "mini-mills." Both these factors kept steel prices low, according to *The Value Line Investment Survey.* Although domestic steel producers suffered, sheet metal work industry firms benefitted from the low prices of steel sheet metal needed for their work. Because of the importance of HVAC systems and business/computer machines to the U.S. economy, these two largest buyers of the sheet metal work industry's products seemed to offer the greatest opportunity for future industry growth.

INDUSTRY LEADERS

The leading U.S. sheet metal work firms in 1995 were Consolidated Systems Inc. of South Carolina ($160 million in sales, with 400 workers), Alcan Building Products of Ohio ($120 million, 1,200 employees), Bouras

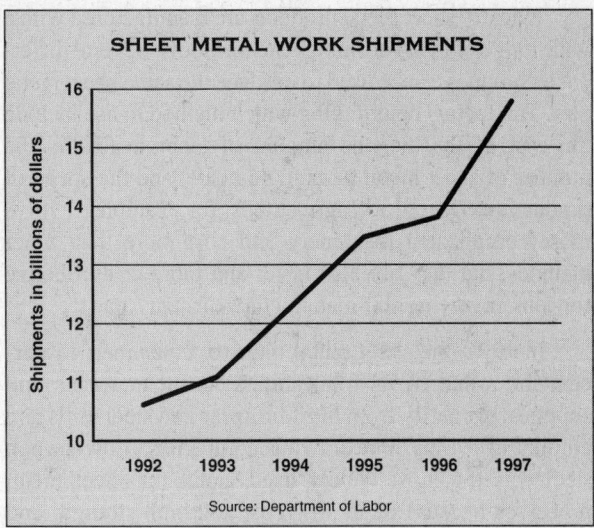

SHEET METAL WORK SHIPMENTS

Source: Department of Labor

Industries Inc. of New Jersey ($110 million, 500), Harrow Corporation of Michigan ($110 million, 1,200), and Hart and Cooley Inc. of Michigan ($100 million, 1,200). Other leading firms included Syro Steel, Symons Corporation, ASC Pacific Inc., and Coastline Distribution Inc.

In 1995, Consolidated Systems announced it was constructing a manufacturing plant and warehouse in Jackson, Mississippi, and the same year Alcan Building Products—a major manufacturer of canopies, awnings, and other exterior building products—was bought out by its management and renamed Alument Building Products. In 1996, Harsco Corporation announced that it had acquired Symons Corporation, a maker of prefabricated concrete forming equipment, and Watsco Inc. purchased Coastline Distribution, a maker of HVAC-related products.

WORKFORCE

In the late 1990s, the vast majority of the nation's sheet metal workers toiled for firms outside the sheet metal industry, such as on-site construction contractors, for example, or in the plumbing and HVAC business. The sheet metal industry's 95,419 production workers, however, represented an important segment of the American sheet metal work force, and were represented in part by the Sheet Metal Workers' International Association (SMWIA). That union, formed in Toledo, Ohio, in 1888, claimed 134,000 members and 205 local unions in the mid-1990s. In 1996 in Milwaukee, the SMWIA Local 18 experimented with a novel way to ensure job security by offering consumers rebates if they bought furnaces or central air conditioning systems from union contractors. Sheet metal workers often learned the trade through apprenticeships involving four to five years of combined classroom and on-the-job training. The average production worker in the sheet metal work industry in 1997 earned $13.05 an hour and $26,223 per year.

RESEARCH AND TECHNOLOGY

Technological advances in the sheet metal work industry in 1990s were revolutionizing the efficiency and precision with which sheet metal products were fabricated. These advances centered in large part on improving tools, dies, and other equipment; relying more extensively on automated machinery; and embracing the benefits of the computer, new software, and—for marketing purposes—the World Wide Web.

A new turret punch press introduced in the 1990s allowed machine tool operators in the sheet metal industry to punch, cut, separate, and sort finished metal blanks in a single operation rather than the three-part operation previously required. The machine's 21 hole-punching tools could be adjusted to perform simple unsupervised operations or more complicated processes involving automatic retrieval and storage of parts. Even more impressive was the Trumatic 2000 Rotation compact punching and forming machine, which was introduced in 1998 by the German tool manufacturer, Trumpf GmbH & Co. The Trumatic 2000 could punch up 900 hits per minute, and could make prototypes as well as medium production runs. Similarly, electromechanically operated industrial robots were used extensively to accurately and tirelessly perform the continuous machining motions once performed by humans.

Although Japanese and European firms led U.S. manufacturers in the use of laser-cutting technology for cutting sheet metal to product specifications in the early 1990s, the United States gained ground on its foreign competitors in this crucial manufacturing technology as the decade progressed. In the mid-1990s, an Ohio State engineering professor began experimenting with the use of lasers and light-emitting diodes (LEDs) to detect the wrinkles that develop when the pressure exerted by a die is inappropriately calibrated to the strength of the sheet metal being pushed into it. By detecting wrinkles instantaneously, just as they begin to occur, the sensors enabled a computer to automatically re-adjust the pressure on the metal before the wrinkles marred the sheet. A laser application, developed in the mid-1990s for sheet metal work in the aerospace industry, combined the precision and automation of laser technology for finishing and trimming metal parts with the design and efficiency benefits of CAD/CAM (computer-aided design/computer-aided manufacture) software to reduce project lead time by two-thirds and costs by up to a quarter. In 1998, Rofin-Sinar and the Frauenhofer Institute of Germany debuted a multi-kilowatt diode-pumped Nd:YAG laser for industrial processing.

In response to the need to cut costs and increase equipment durability, some industry firms turned to plastics, epoxy, and polyurethane in the 1990s to replace more traditional metallic tools and dies. Software programs using finite element analysis (FEA) also enabled product designers to predict the effectiveness of sheet metal stamping dies for the manufacture of products with intricate surfaces, and identified potential strains and stresses in the metal. FEA also enabled manufacturers to accurately predict potential problems in sheet metal bending operations before any metal was actually machined. Software packages such as "PE/Sheet Advisor" used a combination of "expert system" logic and three-dimensional modeling to enable sheet metal product manufacturers to incorporate data gathered from manufacturing operations into the design of new products.

Large sheet metal operations used central computers to direct all sheet metal-forming operations. This "systems approach" managed entire sheet metal processes using vast unified databases containing information on materials, tool and die parameters, and the mechanical properties of the variables of the sheet metal manufacturing process. The efficiency of such CAD/CAM programs as AutoCAD (the industry standard) was estimated to be four to five times greater than traditional methods. Small- to medium-sized firms—which were generally unable to afford the costs of a truly integrated and centralized sheet metal CAM system—could purchase simulation or modeling CAD software to eliminate the costly trial-and-error methods for developing and manufacturing new products. "MetalMan," a Windows-based software program designing sheet metal parts, used a graphic user interface that simulated a machine shop, enabling designers to form three-dimensional solid models of the parts they wished to fabricate, exchange data with other CAD programs, and add to and evaluate new operations in the fabrication process. Such programs could also produce cost quotes and estimates, maintain manufacturing schedules, keep inventories, and generate specification reports for each part.

FURTHER READING

"Combination Machining." *Mechanical Engineering,* October 1996, 34.

Cummings, Chris. "Gaining the Competitive Edge." *Canadian Machinery and Metalworking,* 1 January 1999.

"Getting the Wrinkles Out of New Cars." *USA Today Magazine,* June 1996, 8.

"Harsco Corp. Pursues Privately-held Symons." *Pit & Quarry,* February 1996, 35.

Holley, Paul. "Union Hopes Rebates Spur Business." *Business Journal Serving Greater Milwaukee,* 15 June 1996, 5.

"Inter-City Products Sells Coastline Distribution to Watsco." *Air Conditioning Heating & Refrigeration News,* 2 December 1996, 1.

Katz, Harvey. "Steel (General) Industry." *The Value Line Investment Survey,* 1 January 1999.

Russell, Kelly. "South Carolina's Consolidated Systems to Build Jackson Facility." *Mississippi Business Journal,* 16 October 1995, 7.

Strope, Leigh. "Alcan Execs Join Forces for Buyout." *Dallas Business Journal,* 21 April 1995, 9.

Stundza, Tom. "Suddenly, the Outlook Is Cloudy." *Purchasing,* 9 May 1996, 32B1.

U.S. Census Bureau. "Sheet Metal Work." Available from http://www.census.gov/prod/ec97/97m3314c.pdf. October 1999.

SIC 3446

ARCHITECTURAL AND ORNAMENTAL METAL WORK

This category includes establishments primarily engaged in manufacturing architectural and ornamental metal work, such as stairs and staircases, open steel flooring (grating), fire escapes, grilles, railings, and fences and gates, except those made from wire. Establishments primarily engaged in manufacturing fences and gates from purchased wire are classified in **SIC 3496: Miscellaneous Fabricated Wire Products;** those manufacturing prefabricated metal buildings and parts are classified in **SIC 3448: Prefabricated Metal Buildings and Components;** and those manufacturing miscellaneous metal work are classified in **SIC 3449: Miscellaneous Structural Metal Work.**

NAICS CODE(S)

332323 (Ornamental and Architectural Metal Work Manufacturing)

Manufacturers in the architectural and ornamental metal work industry provide construction contractors with building and finishing materials for all divisions of the development market. Product offerings include bank fixtures, guide rails for stairways and ramps, permanent ladders and stairways, lamp posts, flag poles, metal grates, fire escapes, decorative fences and posts, brass fixtures, and various metal adornments. Classified in other industries are firms that specialize in producing wire fences, prefabricated metal buildings and parts, and miscellaneous metal work.

According to the U.S. Census Bureau's *1997 Economic Census—Manufacturing,* 1,742 establishments operated in this category for part or all of 1997. Industry-wide employment totaled 30,907 workers receiving a payroll of almost $874.0 million. Of these employees, 22,107 worked in production, putting in more than 44 million hours to earn wages of almost $519.0 million.

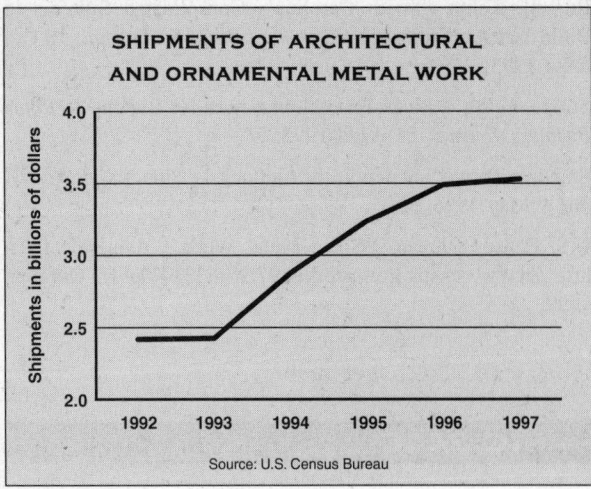

SHIPMENTS OF ARCHITECTURAL AND ORNAMENTAL METAL WORK

Source: U.S. Census Bureau

Overall shipments for the industry were valued at more than $3.5 billion.

Architectural and ornamental metal work industry leaders included Baltimore-based Northrop Grumman Corporation's Electronic Sensors and Systems Division, with almost $9.9 billion in 1997 sales (the most recent results available on Infotrac databases) and the Harsco Corporation of Camp Hill, Pennsylvania, with 1998 sales of over $1.7 billion. Subsidiary Patent Construction Systems of Paramus, New Jersey, handled Harsco's architectural metal work business, contributing $272.0 million to its parent company's sales. Patent manufactured metal works for specialized applications: for example, the sidewalk grating that Marilyn Monroe stood on when her dress was billowed by a passing subway in the 1954 movie "The Seven-Year Itch" was made by Patent. Patent's business grew by 168 percent between 1994 and 1999 on the strength of the construction industry's rebound from its early-1990's bust. Other industry leaders included Houston-based Aluma Systems USA Inc.; Drew Industries Inc. of White Plains, New York; and Bissell Inc. of Grand Rapids, Michigan.

Metal working is one of the world's oldest trades. It originated in about 2500 B.C. when bronze was discovered, although smiths prior to that time produced architectural ornaments using gold. It was not until the discovery of iron in 1200 B.C., however, that the craft of structural metal work truly developed. The industry in the United States flourished when architectural styles progressed from the applied ornament period of the nineteenth century to the organic, or functional, ornament period of the 1900s. U.S. economic boom periods in the 1920s, 1950s, and 1960s all served to increase the size and scope of the industry.

Architectural and ornamental metal work firms realized market growth during most of the 1980s and early 1990s as a result of a fairly active construction market.

Industry shipments climbed from less than $1.5 billion in 1982 to $2.9 billion by 1995. Industry employment rose from about 23,000 in 1982 to 30,000 in 1992, but declined to 27,000 by 1995.

A construction lull during the late 1980s and early 1990s stymied growth in the industry, but, by 1991, shipments were again on the rise. And, even though building markets still sagged in 1993, architecture and ornamental metal work firms were benefiting from a combination of increased public construction spending, renovation work mandated by the Americans with Disabilities Act, and an increase in the popularity of metal ornament in some building sectors. Products most highly in demand in 1995 were stairways, fences, railings, and gates, which accounted for a combined total of more than 24 percent of the market. Open flooring, grating, and studs made up about 16 percent of the market; and grilles, registers, and air diffusers represented another 12 percent of demand.

Historically, small private firms have dominated the industry. In fact, in 1996 most of the top 80 firms employed 100 or fewer people; 79 percent of companies had 19 or fewer employees, and only 3 percent of companies employed more than 100. Furthermore, three-fourths of those companies generated revenues of less than $10 million. Predominant locations for the greatest number of firms in the industry were California, New York, Florida, Pennsylvania, and Texas.

The architectural and ornamental metal work industry is served by several trade and/or professional associations. The National Ornamental and Miscellaneous Metals Association, headquartered in Forest Park, Georgia, has 675 member companies and publishes the bimonthly *NOMMA Newsletter*. The National Association of Architectural Metal Manufacturers, based in Chicago, Illinois, has 124 member companies. The largest organization, the International Association of Bridge, Structural, and Ornamental Iron Workers, headquartered in Washington, D.C., has 135,000 individual members and publishes *The Iron Worker*. Affiliated with this organization are Architectural and Ornamental Iron Workers local unions.

FURTHER READING

Baehr, Guy T. "Paramus, N.J.-Based Scaffolding Maker's Work Stands Up over Time." *Knight-Ridder/Tribune Business News,* 26 November 1999.

Braun-Feldweg. *Metal Design and Technique.* London: B.T. Batsford Ltd., 1975.

Darnay, Arson J., ed. *Manufacturing USA.* 5th ed. Detroit: Gale Research, 1996.

Directory of Corporate Affiliations: Who Owns Whom. New Providence, NJ: National Register Publishing, 1996.

Geerlings, Gerald K. *Metal Crafts in Architecture.* New York: Charles Scribner's Sons, 1929.

Infotrac Company Profiles. Available at http://web4.infotrac .galegroup.com (1/29/00).

U.S. Bureau of the Census. *1995 Annual Survey of Manufactures.* Washington, GPO 1997. Available from http://www .census.gov/prod/www/abs/asm95as1.html and http://www .census.gov/prod/www/abs/msmfgo7c.html.

U.S. Census Bureau. *1997 Economic Census-Manufacturing.* Available at http://www.census.gov/prod/ec97/97m3323f.pdf (2/10/00).

U.S. Department of Commerce. International Trade Administration. *Occupational Outlook Handbook.* Washington GPO, 1997. Available from http://stats.bls.gov:80/ocohome.html.

SIC 3448

PREFABRICATED METAL BUILDINGS AND COMPONENTS

This category covers establishments primarily engaged in manufacturing portable and other prefabricated metal buildings and parts and prefabricated exterior metal panels.

NAICS CODE(S)

332311 (Prefabricated Metal Building and Component Manufacturing)

According to the U.S. Census Bureau's *1997 Economic Census-Manufacturing,* 603 establishments operated in this category for part or all of 1997. Industry-wide employment totaled 25,967 workers receiving a payroll of more than $775 million. Of these employees, 17,782 worked in production, putting in almost 36 million hours to earn wages of almost $442 million. Overall shipments for the industry were valued at almost $4.21 billion.

Epic Systems Inc. of Darby, Montana led the industry with 1998 sales of almost $6.5 billion, behind the strength of a mere 30 employees. United Dominion Industries Inc. of Charlotte, North Carolina followed with more than $2 billion in 1998 sales created by 11,000 employees. Rounding out the top three industry leaders was Butler Manufacturing Co. of Kansas City, Missouri, with 1998 sales of $962 million and 5,205 employees. Other industry leaders included Houston-based NCI Building Systems Inc.; Skyline Corp. of Elkhart, Indiana; and American Buildings Co. of Eufaula, Alabama.

In 1996, the prefabricated metal buildings industry manufacturer's shipped $4.22 billion worth of such products as portable buildings and houses, silos, greenhouses, carports and garages, and other prefabricated metal buildings. The largest division within this industry was nonresidential or farm prefabricated building systems, which included industrial and commercial, institutional, medi-

cal, and religious buildings. That section of the industry accounted for 60 percent of 1996 sales, for a total of $2.54 billion in total shipments. Residential, farm, and portable dwellings and greenhouses made up 27 percent and $1.48 billion. The remaining 13 percent was accounted for by miscellaneous metal structures, which brought in $278 million in shipments.

Employment levels climbed steadily over the 1980s, growing from 23,500 people in 1982 to 30,000 in 1990. Throughout the early 1990s, however, the employment rate fluctuated from a high in 1990 to a low of only 21,000 in 1992. By 1996 the number evened off at 24,000, but was expected to decline by about 22 percent through 2005. The total number of establishments declined from an all-time high of 569 in 1982 to 517 in 1996. Establishments had been dwindling throughout the 1990s except for 1993, when 555 establishments—the most during the 1990s—were in operation. Wages for this industry climbed steadily from the early 1980s but, in 1994, were still far below the average for the manufacturing sector as a whole. While the number of employees and production workers per establishment were the same, metal building workers made only $10.51 per hour compared to average manufacturers' earnings of $12.09.

Due to a decrease in the construction of both office buildings and commercial and industrial sites in the early 1990s, the prefabricated metal building industry suffered a slight decline in sales. Nevertheless, the industry continued to grow steadily, with new technologies and environmental concerns giving the industry a small boost. Steel was the most heavily recycled product in the world—more than plastic, paper, aluminum, and glass combined—and, as such, construction firms often turned to steel as a way to satisfy new environmental regulations. The steel industry also revolutionized new techniques in manufacturing to give those who process steel products the best raw materials the industry had ever seen. Furthermore, as the residential construction industry continued to grow, an increase in demand for products relevant to that division of the industry was predicted to make up for the slack in commercial demand.

The Universal Prefab Metal Framing and Seismic Component System was seeking to revolutionize the industry with its computer automated system, introduced in 1997. The Universal system, though still fairly new and not widely used, claimed it could substantially cut costs by reducing production time, lowering insurance rates, and cutting workers' compensation funds. The system was an automated cutting and design system that could be programmed to clients' demands, allowing the operator to cut and shape by the push of a button or by hydraulic controls. The worker was no longer required to cut the steel by hand—an admittedly dangerous, laborious, and time-consuming task. The end product was a stronger and more precise structure. Though the product was too new to be widely used, preliminary testing indicated it was superior to older methods, according to a study by Sandia National Laboratories, a division of the U.S. Department of Energy, and the University of California State, Hayward.

FURTHER READING

Darnay, Arsen J., ed. *Manufacturing USA*. 5th ed. Detroit: Gale Research: 1996.

Infotrac Company Profiles. Available from http://web4.infotrac .galegroup.com (visited 1/30/00).

"OECA Prefabricated Metal Sector Notebook." *Envirosense*, 14 December 1995. Available from http://es.inel/gov/comply/ sector/fab/fabintro.html.

U.S. Census Bureau. U.S. Department of Commerce. *1995 Annual Survey of Manufactures*. Washington: GPO, 1997.

U.S. Census Bureau. *1997 Economic Census-Manufacturing*. Available from http://www.census.gov/prod/ec97/97m3323a .pdf (visited 2/10/00).

SIC 3449

MISCELLANEOUS STRUCTURAL METAL WORK

This category includes establishments primarily engaged in manufacturing miscellaneous structural metal work, such as metal plaster bases, fabricated bar joists, and concrete reinforcing bars. Also included in this industry are establishments primarily engaged in custom roll-forming of metal.

NAICS CODE(S)

332114 (Custom Roll Forming)
332312 (Fabricated Structural Metal Manufacturing)
332321 (Metal Window and Door Manufacturing)
332323 (Ornamental and Architectural Metal Work Manufacturing)

In the first three quarters of 1998, Japan "dumped" almost 5.5 million tons of steel, selling it below manufacturing costs into the United States; this represented a 157 percent increase over 1997 U.S. imports. Domestic prices fell in response, as did domestic production. Officials blamed imports for the loss of 10,000 steel industry jobs. The fabricating segment of the industry, however, did not suffer as much as production did, since fabrication took advantage of the low prices of its raw materials.

In 1997, Cleveland-based Alcan Aluminum Corp. led the industry with sales of almost $3 billion on the work of 3,500 employees, according to the most recent results available on Infotrac databases. Minneapolis-

based Apogee Enterprises Inc. followed with sales of almost $793 million for its fiscal year ended February 28, 1999, behind the strength of 6,367 workers. Rocky Mountain Steel Mills Div. of Pueblo, Colorado rounded out the top three industry leaders with 1998 sales of $356 million.

In October 1997, about 1,000 union workers walked off the job at Rocky Mountain and few had returned by the beginning of 2000. The parent company Oregon Steel hired replacements and kept them on even when the strikers called off the walkout after a year. The AFL-CIO called a national union boycott of both Oregon Steel products and its financiers, including Wells Fargo Bank of San Francisco, which lost an estimated $1.2 billion in deposits as a result. San Francisco's Board of Supervisors officially asked the Bay Area Rapid Transit District (BART) "to refrain from purchasing rail for track replacement and repair from Rocky Mountain Steel Mills" to honor the union boycott until Oregon Steel reinstated its workers.

Roughly 50 percent of U.S. structural metal work sales were derived from manufacturing custom roll-formed metals, which brought in $2.4 billion of the industry's $4.5 billion total revenues in 1996. Another 32 percent of industry sales came from fabricated bar joists and concrete reinforcing bars. The remaining 18 percent was split between manufacturing metal plaster bases, curtain walls, and other miscellaneous metal work.

Closely related to the construction and automobile industries, structural metal work manufacturers were heavily affected by the recession of the late 1980s and early 1990s, following a $1 billion boom in shipments between 1986 and 1988. Shipment values, after dropping sharply in the early 1990s, recovered and leveled out in 1993.

One reason for this stagnation was the industry trade deficit between the United States and its foreign competitors. Customers of steel firms were adversely affected by complaints filed by U.S. firms against foreign steel manufacturers concerning this trade deficit. The deficit continued into the mid-1990s, as imports of steel drastically increased in 1996 to the second-highest tonnage ever: 29 billion net tons of steel were imported, up an enormous 19.5 percent from 1995. The deficit, combined with U.S. steel producers' protests, diminished business at U.S. ports, increased prices for steel products, and left a shortage of specialty plate and sheet products previously supplied by foreign suppliers. As a result, some U.S. steel-using firms were contemplating relocation to Canada, Mexico, and other Pacific Rim countries.

Concentrated in the Great Lakes region, this industry employed an estimated 22,000 people in 694 establishments by 1996, paying average earnings of more than

$12.74 per hour. Compared to other forms of manufacturing in the 1990s, this industry typically employed fewer people per establishment and paid average wages.

With increased automation, the face of the industry was expected to change into the year 2000. Heavy reductions in employment of production workers were expected, while job prospects for sales personnel, industrial production managers, and cost estimators were expected to increase.

In the mid-1990s, the industry focused on cost reduction through process improvement and materials research. In 1993 CF&I Corporation invented a new process that produced rails continuously for a quarter of a mile, reducing the need for welding and reducing construction costs. Ford Motor Company, in partnership with Alcan Rolled Products Company, experimented with the effects of hybrid aluminum-steel sheet metal on an automobile's fuel economy, durability, service, and performance. A new rigid rod-polymer, developed in 1995, has the capability to replace structural metals, such as stainless steel and aluminum. The new polymer, which is four times stiffer than conventional plastics and can be injection molded, extruded, or compressed, posed a threat to the structural metal industry.

FURTHER READING

''1996 Steel Imports up 19.5 Percent.'' *American Iron and Steel Institute,* 19 February 1997. Available from http://www.steel.org/industry.impdec96.htm.

Chamberlain, Gary. ''Technology Bulletin: Late Developments That Shape Engineering.'' *Design News,* 8 May 1995.

Darnay, Arsen J., ed. *Manufacturing USA: Industry Analyses, Statistics, and Leading Companies,* 5th ed. Detroit: Gale Research, Inc., 1996.

Haflich, Frank. ''USW presses Oregon boycott.'' *American Metal Market,* 5 August 1999.

Infotrac Company Profiles. Available from http://web4.infotrac.galegroup.com (30 January 2000).

Perez, Gayle. ''Pueblo, Colo., Steelworkers Rally on Strike Anniversary.'' *Knight-Ridder/Tribune Business News,*5 October 1998.

Scott, Jonathan. ''Mixed market: steel producers sweat imports while fabricators continue to flourish.'' *Memphis Business Journal,* 5 February 1999.

SIC 3451

SCREW MACHINE PRODUCTS

This category includes establishments primarily engaged in manufacturing automatic or hand screw machine products from rod, bar, or tube stock of metal, fiber, plastics, or other material. The products of this industry consist of a wide variety of unassembled parts and are usually manufactured on a job or order basis. Establishments included in this industry may perform assembly of some parts manufactured in the same establishment, but establishments primarily engaged in producing assembled components are classified according to the nature of the components. Establishments primarily engaged in manufacturing standard bolts, nuts, rivets, screws, and other industrial fasteners on headers, threaders, and nut-forming machines are classified in **SIC 3452: Bolts, Nuts, Screws, Rivets, and Washers.**

NAICS CODE(S)

332721 (Precision Tuned Product Manufacturing)

INDUSTRY SNAPSHOT

According to the Precision Machine Products Association (formerly the National Screw Machine Products Association), more than 1,600 companies employed more than 56,000 highly skilled workers throughout North America in the late 1990s. These companies utilized traditional methods combined with cutting-edge technologies, such as automatic screw machines, computer-controlled (CNC) single- and multiple-spindle lathes and CNC turning and machining centers, to manufacture billions of component parts to precise specifications. This industry machined components used in a multitude of end products, including anti-lock brakes, transmissions, fuel injection systems, car airbags, computer hard drives, video recording equipment, medical diagnostic equipment, and power tools, to name just a few.

The screw machine products industry is defined more by the process of manufacture than by any specific product. Although screw machine products manufacturers produce a wide variety of products for many types of industries, they all use a variation on the screw machine—a large, usually cam-driven piece of machinery that allows roughly cylindrical material to be subjected to a variety of tooling and machining operations as the material is turned about its axis. Screw machines may have as many as eight spindles that act upon the part being machined, and are able to produce highly precise parts quickly. The screw machine, by ensuring the interchangeability of manufactured parts, was a major contributor to the development of modern manufacturing and assembly processes.

Screw machine products manufacturers are located primarily in the industrialized sectors of the Northeast and Midwest and near aerospace manufacturers in the West. The industry is dominated by smaller companies employing fewer than 50 workers, most of whom are highly skilled machinists. Many of the shops are privately owned, and most are located close to the industries to which they supply parts. In addition, many larger companies that use screw machine products manufacture those products in-house. The automotive industry is the major purchaser of screw machine products and accounts for 30 percent of the industry's shipments.

ORGANIZATION AND STRUCTURE

The vast majority of screw machine products are manufactured on a job or order basis. The purchaser of a product provides the manufacturer with a precise description of the part desired, and the manufacturer then sets up its machines to produce that part. Part runs may call for the manufacture of as few as a hundred or as many as a million parts, requiring a single screw machine or a shop full of machines to produce the part on time. Because of the nature of their business, screw machine products manufacturers rely on the flexibility of their equipment and employees to accommodate the different needs of the various screw machine products purchasers.

Three types of screw machines are used by manufacturers: swiss, single-spindle, and multiple-spindle machines. Using these machines, a machinist may perform up to 32 different types of cutting and forming operations. Fred W. Lewis, discussing the screw machine products industry in the *Handbook of Product Design for Manufacturing,* stated, "The amount of work done is limited only by the number of tool positions available and the tool layout engineer's ingenuity." The tool layout engineer designs the cams that control the various machining operations and sets up the machine, which is then capable of producing millions of identical pieces. Many manufacturers are turning to computer-controlled rather than cam-controlled operations, because of the longer set-up time required for cam-driven machines and the level of expertise required to operate them. Computer-controlled screw machines, however, are not necessarily more productive than cam-driven machines.

The flexibility inherent in both machine and machinist allows screw machine products manufacturers to produce parts for many types of industries. While larger manufacturers have diversified their production, smaller companies have tended toward specialization and may produce as much as 80 percent of their total output for one company. This degree of commitment means small manufacturers experience whatever economic downturns or upturns their customer experiences. The actual screw machines account for the major capital expenditures of manufacturers in this industry. The screw machine is a remarkably durable piece of machinery, however; it can be rebuilt and overhauled, and computer controls can be added to enhance the machine's flexibility, thus spreading capital outlay out over a long period of time.

The screw machine products industry is characterized by a high degree of structural stability: the machinery it uses, the processes involved in manufacture, and the kinds of products it produces have remained essentially the same for nearly 100 years. Many manufacturers use screw machines that are decades old. Most employees learn their trade through hands-on training or a form of apprenticeship, though workers are increasingly receiving training in vocational education programs. Thus, the screw machine operator of two generations ago would recognize many of the operations being conducted in today's shop, though the veteran workers might be surprised to see young operators who had not gone through an apprenticeship programming computer-controlled screw machines to work on plastics and fibers as well as metals.

BACKGROUND AND DEVELOPMENT

Although the first machine-cut screws were produced in 1800, at the dawn of the first industrial age, the concept of a screw dates back as far the third century B.C., when the Greek mathematician Archimedes designed a water-powered, screw-driven system to lift water. Much later, in the mid-1400s, Leonardo da Vinci drew plans for a screw-cutting lathe. But it was Henry Maudslay, an English mechanic, who in 1800 first cut a piece of lead on a lathe into the helical pattern we know as a screw. Early screw manufacturers were hampered by the lack of any standards for measuring their products or ensuring their uniformity. Thus, each producer made a different size and pitch of screw, making it very difficult to replace parts when needed.

The early manufacture of machined metal parts in the United States occurred primarily in the increasingly industrialized Northeast states, where small shops produced parts for the machines that would drive American economic growth. Such shops used belt-driven lathes that were powered by water or, occasionally, an ox tied to a treadmill outside the factory. It was not until the middle of the nineteenth century, however, that a small group of machinists centered around Windsor, Vermont, created the machine tools that preceded today's screw machines. Out of this innovative environment of skilled inventors and machinists, which included pioneers Francis A. Pratt, Richard Lawrence, and James Hartness came Christopher Spencer, who in 1873 created the Hartford Automatic Screw Machine.

According to Donald E. Wood, editor of *Automatic Machining* and author of *From Archimedes to Automation: The History of the Screw Machine,* Spencer's automatic screw machine was "the prototype for all single-spindle machines in use today." This machine was manufactured by the Hartford Machine Screw Co., which is the oldest continuing screw product manufacturer in the country. Soon Pratt & Whitney Co. of Hartford, Connecticut, and Brown & Sharpe Manufacturing Co. of

Providence, Rhode Island, began manufacturing screw machines that were famed for their precision and accuracy. The creation of precision screw machines contributed greatly to the development of modern manufacturing, as screw machines made products for the growing automotive industry and other developing industries. According to Wood, ''The mass production of consumer goods, and its parallel problem, precise interchange ability of goods components, came only after machine tools had been devised which could make products alike in a rapid manner, and standardization of measurement had been established.''

Although the screw machine was initially designed to produce threaded fasteners, users of the machine soon recognized that it was capable of producing a vast number of products. In fact, standardized screw thread manufacturers soon turned to a different process, called cold-heading, and this industry is now classified as **SIC 3452: Bolts, Nuts, Screws, Rivets, and Washers.** Because the screw machine could create any roughly cylindrical, symmetrical piece of stock, it soon was used to manufacture gears, pulleys, push rods, rollers, and other products. By 1960 more than 1,500 screw machine product manufacturers employed more than 30,000 workers and operated over 40,000 screw machines to produce nearly $1 billion in annual sales of special component parts.

CURRENT CONDITIONS

Although the screw machine product industry generally feels the effects of national economic downturns, it nevertheless fared relatively well in the overall economic downturn of the early 1990s. Between 1982 and 1996 there was growth in shipment levels. In 1982 the value of shipments was $2.17 billion, and by 1996 it reached $4.41 billion. The value of shipments for the industry was relatively stagnant in the late 1980s through 1991. However, shipment values grew from $2.97 billion in 1991 to $3.83 billion in 1992. This increase was tied to the strong recovery of the domestic automobile industry, which sought to cut costs even if this meant purchasing screw machine products from independent manufacturers rather than captive screw machine departments. Industry shipments reached $8.33 billion in 1997.

As American manufacturing concentrated in the midwestern states of Michigan, Illinois, and Ohio, so did the screw machine products industry. Michigan's 213 establishments led the nation in value of shipments in 1992, which reached 728.7 million. This accounted for 19 percent of total U.S. shipments. Ohio followed closely behind with 181 establishments and $534.2 million in shipments and accounted for 13.9 percent of total U.S. shipments. Michigan's 7,000 employees earned an average of $11.97 per hour, ranking well below Massachusetts's $12.94 per hour average wage.

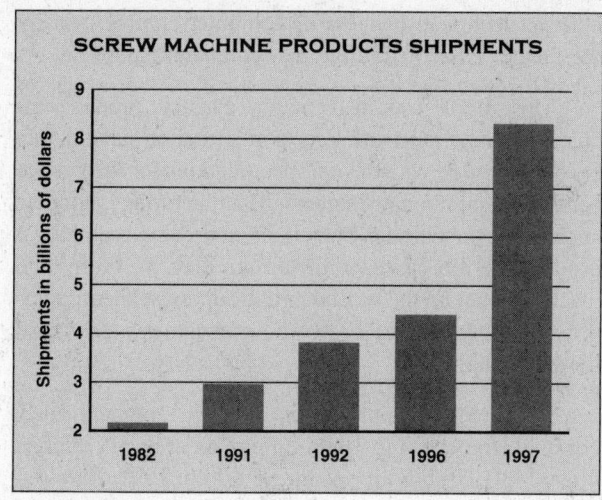

SCREW MACHINE PRODUCTS SHIPMENTS

Industrywide sales totaled approximately $5.4 billion in 1997, according to the most recent statistics available from the Precision Machine Products Association. Companies averaged sales of $3.3 million, and the average growth rate of the industry, adjusted for inflation, was projected to be 3 to 5 percent into the new millennium.

INDUSTRY LEADERS

Detroit-based United Technologies Automotive Inc. Engineered Systems Div. led the industry with $975 million in 1997 sales, according to the most recent information available on Infotrac. Cerro Metal Products Co. of Bellefonte, Pennsylvania, generated $250 million in 1997 sales, and the Kurt Manufacturing Co. garnered $108 million in 1997 sales. The U.S. Environmental Protection Agency's Region 5 office slapped a $20,000 fine on Kurt in 1997 for not disposing of polychlorinated biphenyls (PCBs) on time.

WORKFORCE

Manufacturers of screw machine products have traditionally employed a highly skilled workforce, although the aging of highly trained employees and the availability of more accessible computer-controlled machines suggests that the work force of the future will be younger and somewhat less skilled. Because learning to set up a cam-controlled screw machine takes years of training, finding qualified employees has been one of the industry's biggest problems. Operators traditionally learned the intricacies of setting up a machine through an apprenticeship; but vocational training programs and on-the-job training have now supplanted formal apprenticeships. In addition, the Precision Machine Products Association, located near Cleveland, Ohio, provides training manuals, videos, and seminars for its members. The industry's move to greater computerization is driven less by the inherent technical benefits of computer control than by the greater ease of training that computers allow.

Most employees in the screw machine products industry are machinists of some sort. Because manufacturers are provided with design specifications for their products, they employ no designers. Manufacturing engineers specify the machining operations and cams required to produce the job based on the design they are given, and machinists set up the machines and supervise their operation. In many smaller firms, the principal owner is also the head engineer.

Total employment for the industry remained fairly constant from 1984 to 1988. Employment levels reached 45,900 in 1989 but dropped to 40,600 in 1991. Employment later rebounded, and in 1996 the industry employed 47,700 people. Production workers' employment levels followed a nearly identical pattern to total employment levels, with a low of 32,300 in 1991 and a high of 41,900 workers in 1994. This number leveled off to 38,400 in 1996.

In 1997, there were approximately 2,745 establishments in the United States that manufactured screw machine products. Only 40 percent of these establishments employed more than 20 employees. Average wages for this industry have steadily increased from $7.72 per hour in 1982. However, the average pay of $11.25 per hour in 1994 was slightly lower than the national standard of $12.09 for all manufacturing industries. By 1997 the average hourly wage for the 63,715 production workers in the industry was $13.28.

FURTHER READING

Darnay, Arsen J., ed. *Manufacturing USA: Industry Analysis, Statistics, and Leading Companies,* 5th ed. Detroit: Gale Research, 1996.

Infotrac Company Profiles. 1 January 2000. Available from http://web5.infotrac.galegroup.com.

"Kurt Manufacturing to pay $20,000 fine." *American Metal Market,* 4 March 1997.

Lewis, Fred W. "Screw Machine Products." *Handbook of Product Design for Manufacturing: A Practical Guide to Low-Cost Production.* New York: McGraw-Hill, 1986.

Precision Machine Products Association. 18 January 2000. Available from http://www.pmpa.org.

U.S. Census Bureau. *Survey of Manufacturers,* 10 February 2000. Available from http://www.census.gov/prod/www/abs/97ecmani.html.

Ward's Business Directory of U.S. Private and Public Companies. Detroit: Gale Research, 1997.

Wood, Donald E. *From Archimedes to Automation: The History of the Screw Machine.* Brecksville, OH: National Screw Machine Products Association.

BOLTS, NUTS, SCREWS, RIVETS, AND WASHERS

This category includes establishments primarily engaged in manufacturing metal bolts, nuts, screws, rivets, washers, formed and threaded wire goods, and special industrial fasteners. Rolling mills engaged in manufacturing similar products are classified in the major group for primary metal industries (33); establishments primarily engaged in manufacturing screw machine products are classified in **SIC 3451: Screw Machine Products;** and those manufacturing plastic fasteners are classified in **SIC 3089: Plastics Products, Not Elsewhere Classified.**

NAICS CODE(S)

332722 (Bolt, Nut, Screw, Rivet, and Washer Manufacturing)

INDUSTRY SNAPSHOT

Manufacturers in this industry produce the materials that hold American industry together: bolts, nuts, screws, rivets, and washers. Producing these items in lots as small as 1,000 and as large as 20 million, manufacturers make both custom-ordered and standard fasteners using processes quite different from that of the screw machine product industry, **SIC 3451: Screw Machine Products,** with which it otherwise shares many similarities. While screw machine product manufacturers produce goods using some form of screw machine that cuts into a metal product to produce the needed tooling, fastener manufacturers use a variety of cold-forming and rolling processes to produce simpler parts with greater strength. Both industries trace their beginnings to the early stages of industrialization, which made innovations in the field of fastener engineering possible.

The fastener industry is remarkably decentralized, with hundreds of small shops producing the majority of fasteners. Manufacturers in the fastener industry tended to cluster around the industries that purchased its products—traditionally the automotive, defense, and aerospace industries. The industry is therefore concentrated in the auto-producing states of the upper Midwest and the defense and aerospace-oriented regions of California. But such dependence has had its costs. Slumps in the auto industry during the 1980s posed severe challenges to fastener manufacturers, and defense downsizing in the 1990s posed an equally significant threat. Domestic fastener manufacturers were also seriously threatened by an influx of cheap, foreign-made fasteners in the 1970s and 1980s. The Fastener Quality Act of 1990, passed in response to complaints about poor quality and fraud on the part of foreign fastener manufacturers, promised some protection for the domestic industry.

ORGANIZATION AND STRUCTURE

Manufacturers in this industry produce a wide and ever-changing variety of products that fall under the general name "industrial fasteners." According to the Industrial Fastener Institute, the trade association for the industry, a fastener is "a mechanical device for holding two or more bodies in definite position with respect to each other. A high percentage of fasteners have threads as part of their design, but unthreaded items such as rivets, clevis pins, machine pins, etc., are considered fasteners as well." The industry produces fasteners using the primary manufacturing operations of heading, upsetting, forming, forging, and extruding. Fasteners primarily use ferrous metals for products, usually carbon and alloy steels. Most fasteners begin as wire, rod, or bar, which is cut to length, headed, and then threaded.

A typical hex-head bolt begins as a shaft of metal whose length is a number of times longer than its diameter. This shaft is placed in a die, a metal holder that maintains the shaft's position when it is struck by a punch, which is designed to impart the hexagonal shape of a bolt head to the shaft. Multiple punches are sometimes used to impart more intricate head shapes or to form harder metals. The headed shaft is then given an external thread in another cold-forming process called thread rolling. In thread rolling, the headed shaft is pressed between stationary and moving hardened-steel dies, which squeeze the material into the desired thread form. The nut that accompanies this bolt may also be cold-formed using a thread-forming tap that displaces rather than removes metal to form the interior thread. These and other processes like them constitute the major means by which industrial manufacturers produce goods.

According to the *Manufacturers' Capability Guide,* published by the Industrial Fastener Institute, "Cold forming is a high-speed, high-volume production process, with economical production rates determined by part size, design complexity, and degree of forming required—all factors that determine the number of blows required to form the part and thus the complexity of the tooling and equipment required." Cold-forming has the advantage of allowing the manufacturer to produce many thousands of products an hour. According to John E. Neely and Richard R. Kibbe, authors of *Modern Materials and Manufacturing Processes,* "Production rates on upsetting machines can be as high as 36,000/hr. for small unpierced rivets, and No. 8 size screw blanks can be made at 27,000/hr." Such economies of scale allow manufacturers to offset the very high costs of cold-forming equipment. Cold-forming also has the advantage of wasting no material, since the metal is pressed into shape rather than trimmed away by machin-

ing, and of allowing the metal grain to form in continuous unbroken lines, improving tensile and shear strengths and resistance to fatigue.

BACKGROUND AND DEVELOPMENT

According to *The Heritage of Mechanical Fasteners,* a publication produced by the Industrial Fastener Institute, "Man's conquest of nature has depended upon his ability to fasten useful things together." Ever since an axle was bound to a wheel to provide the means of moving a cart, humans have been using fasteners to make lives easier. People were fashioning nails as early as 2800 B.C., and the first screw appeared around 250 B.C., but it was not until the fifteenth century that what we now know as threaded fasteners began to appear in common usage. In this century, the first printing press was held together and run by a screw, tiny screws held Swiss-made watches together, and French mathematician Jacques Besson designed the first practical machine for cutting screws.

The Industrial Revolution, which swept the Western world in the late eighteenth century, brought about many of the technological innovations that gave birth to the modern fastener industry. In 1760, Job and William Wyatt became the first known manufacturers of threaded fasteners. The English brothers employed 59 people in their water-powered factory, producing 1,200 gross of wood screws a week. Screw makers started up throughout England and America, but purchasers of their products were faced with a serious problem. Because fastener makers shared no common rules for size and thread pitch, a nut from one shop had little chance of fitting a bolt from another. Nuts and bolts had to be carefully paired, for once separated they were practically useless.

"The one man most responsible for starting threaded fasteners on the way to becoming the high-precision, freely interchangeable, taken-for-granted components we know today was the English inventor Henry Maudslay," according to *The Heritage of Mechanical Fasteners.* Maudslay invented a bar lathe capable of making highly accurate and duplicable threads, and his ideas led others, including American inventor David Wilkinson, to design machines that would form the basis for the new machine tool industry. Most early threads were cut on a screw machine, but in 1836 William Keane of New York invented a process known as thread-rolling that formed threads without cutting away material. That process, which later became prevalent, differentiates the fastener industry (**SIC 3452: Bolts, Nuts, Screws, Rivets, and Washers**) from the screw machine products industry (**SIC 3451: Screw Machine Products**).

In 1834, the C. Read & Company of Providence, Rhode Island, became the first significant manufacturer of screws in the United States. In 1840, Rugg & Barnes of Marion, Connecticut, became the first American firm that solely manufactured and sold nuts and bolts. In 1842 the A.P. Plant Company of Plantsville, Connecticut, became the first company to issue a price list and discount large orders. The 1840s also saw other advances in the industry: in 1844 Julius B. Savage introduced machine-made nuts, and in 1847 William E. Ward patented the first automatic cold-heading machine.

Fastener manufacturers benefited from the Civil War—when all of American industry was mobilized in the production of firearms, machinery, and railroad equipment to feed a war that devoured machinery as fast as it did men. Shortly after the war, the center of the American fastener industry shifted from the Northeast to the Midwest (then referred to as the West) in order to stay close to the expanding railroads and growing iron and steel production facilities. By the end of the nineteenth century, Cleveland, Ohio, was the capital of the American fastener industry, and most of the processes for creating its products had been established.

Beginning in 1864, U.S. fastener manufacturers adopted the Sellers Thread System over the Whitworth Screw-Thread used by the British, and in 1884 the American standard for screw threads, bolt heads, and nuts was established. Having different thread systems posed no problem for the two countries, until it came time for them to cooperate during World War I. American manufacturers were not equipped to manufacture the British threads, and field repairs of machinery were disastrous. The fiasco was nearly repeated in World War II, but temporary adjustments helped avert disaster. In 1931 a dozen fastener manufacturers met in Cleveland and formed the American Institute of Bolt, Nut, and Rivet Manufacturers, which in 1949 became the Industrial Fasteners Institute.

In 1964 the International Organization for Standardization (ISO) announced two universal thread systems: ISO Inch and ISO Metric. Despite occasional efforts to convert manufacturers to the metric system, the United States remains the only country in the world still tied to the inch system. This practice leads to dual manufacturing facilities and inventories, but American manufacturers and the American public have resisted conversion to the metric system.

By 1969, the U.S. fastener industry had reached its peak of production. In that year, 450 companies operating 600 plants and employing more than 50,000 people manufactured more than 2 billion fasteners each year. By 1984, however, the industry decreased in size to 250 manufacturers operating 350 plants and employing 35,000 people because of severe challenges from foreign competition and dramatic changes in the requirements of original equipment manufacturers (OEMs). The biggest challenge came from foreign fastener producers, who took advantage of inexpensive Third-World labor and material costs to produce cheap "standards," or fasteners

that met nationally recognized product standards. The Industrial Fastener Institute reported that domestic manufacturers went from supplying 80 percent of American bolts, nuts, and large screws in 1969 to just 44 percent in 1984. During the same period, OEMs, especially automobile manufacturers, were pressing fastener manufacturers to develop specialized products at lower costs. The production of these items sustained many companies, but it drove the smaller, less technologically advanced companies out of the industry.

Beginning in the mid-1980s, the American fastener industry began to rebound. Many manufacturers allied themselves with companies in need of technically sophisticated products rather than simple standardized commodities, and the falling value of the U.S. dollar drove the prices of foreign products up. Then, in 1985, reports began surfacing in newspapers across the country of "bogus bolts," bolts that were graded to withstand high loads but were failing in service, leading to the destruction of property and, in one case, the loss of life. The Industrial Fastener Institute began an investigation and, in 1986, urged an investigation by the U.S. Customs Service.

In 1988, after an 18-month investigation, a U.S. House subcommittee published a report entitled *The Threat from Substandard Fasteners: Is America Losing Its Grip?* The report stated that "the failure of substandard and often counterfeit fasteners has killed people, reduced our defense readiness, and cost both the American taxpayer and the American industry untold millions in breakdowns, downtime, reconstruction, and other unnecessary inefficiencies." The subcommittee concluded that the substandard and counterfeit fasteners at fault were largely foreign made. The "bogus bolts" controversy ended in the passage of Public Law 101c-92, the Fastener Quality Act (FQA), in 1990. This act provided for the "testing, certification, and distribution of certain fasteners used in commerce within the United States." Perhaps more important than the law, the investigation challenged the quality of the fasteners imported from abroad while affirming the quality of fasteners made in the United States. Passage, but not the actual implementation, of the FQA resulted in a soaring demand for fasteners made in the United States because they had quality control records that were both traceable and well documented.

Surprisingly, the FQA was never fully implemented because the U.S. government was reluctant to interfere with the $6-billion American fastener industry, and the government wanted to give the industry time to establish or contract for approved testing facilities. By early 1999, more than 400 such facilities were operational. Since its passage, however, many fastener manufacturers and end users of their products have sought to water down the

FQA. "Powerful forces, including the American Automobile Manufacturers Association-the nation's largest user of industrial fasteners-and the General Aviation Manufacturers Association want to defang the Fastener Quality Act," writes David Sharp in *Engineering News Record.* The American fastener industry had long felt that its own internal policies, policing and record keeping would assure a safe, high quality product and that full implementation of the FQA would only hamper the industry.

In June 1999 the American fastener industry got its wish when President Clinton signed into law a series of amendments to the FQA, which according to *Industrial Distribution,* "makes the legislation more focused and less burdensome." Clinton signed the legislation less than a month from the deadline for full implementation of the FQA. Supporters of the amending legislation claim it shifted the policing focus from government mandated regulations to more "preventative measures." The new legislation also recognized decade long industry improvements in quality control and for the most part eliminated tests performed at government approved facilities. Clinton's signing also limited coverage of the FQA to high-strength fasteners and allowed companies to transmit and store records and reports electronically. "The amendments contained in the law respond to all the problems the industry had with the original law," David Edgerly, former director of the National Institute for Standards and Technology and industry consultant, told *Industrial Distribution* after the signing. The Fastener Industry Coalition, the National Fasteners Distribution Association, and the Industrial Fasteners Institute all lobbied for the amended legislation.

CURRENT CONDITIONS

The industrial fastener industry experienced little or no growth through the late 1980s and into the early 1990s. By 1994 employment within the industry had dropped to 31,900 production workers, down from 38,700 in 1987. In the mid-1990s, however, the industry began to rebound and, by 1995, the last year for which government figures are available, employment of production workers had climbed to 34,000. Total employment in the industry had also climbed to 46,000 in 1995, up from 43,000 a year earlier, but this figure is expected to again drop to around 43,000 by the year 2000. Average hourly earnings for 1995 were $13.58 and this was expected to rise to $14.79 by 2000. The forecast value of shipments of industrial fasteners in 1999 was $6.9 billion compared to $6.5 billion in 1996. Much of this rise is due to exports, which increased in value by 29 percent in 1996. Much of this increase in exports went to automobile production in Canada and Mexico, which increased its importation of industrial fasteners by more than 80 percent in 1996. These exports to Mexico were valued at $529 million.

Canada imported $520 million worth of industrial fasteners in the same year.

Although the U.S. industrial fastener industry is continuing to export more products, it also faces challenges from foreign countries, especially Taiwan. In 1997 Taiwan was the world's largest exporter of fasteners—1 billion kilograms worth $1.31 billion U.S. dollars. Despite the Asian financial crisis, these figures were expected to grow by 11 percent in 1998. In January through May 1999, more than 56 percent of Taiwan's exported fasteners went to the United States. Joe Costello of J. Cost, Inc. told *Industrial Distribution* in 1998 that roughly 60 percent of all fasteners used in the United States are imports. There are, of course, trade-offs for low foreign prices. "It may take an extra two-four weeks to get a product from Taiwan, but you'll save 20 percent to 30 percent on cost," according to Costello. "It's pretty hard for a U.S. manufacturer paying $30 per hour for labor to meet the price of a manufacturer in Taiwan who pays his help $2 per hour."

Despite foreign competition the U.S. industrial fastener industry is expected to grow 3 to 4 percent annually according to *Purchasing's* Agatha Ciancarelli. This figure, however, represents a decrease from the 9 percent growth spurt the industry enjoyed in 1998. Fastener sales are expected to climb to $9.33 billion in 2001. Ciancarelli also expected prices to remain relatively stable throughout 1999. Ciancarelli, however, foresaw the fastener manufacturers facing growing competition from the adhesives industry as more and more products are being made with plastic, a product oftentimes best joined together by adhesives.

An expanding market for fasteners into the twenty-first century is the aerospace industry. The Freedonia Group told *Purchasing* that a 9 percent annual growth in fasteners for the aerospace industry can be expected. U.S. manufacturers are best equipped to meet this demand since specifications usually call for high-end products that are used in critical applications. The Freedonia Group predicts that U.S. shipments of industrial fasteners will grow to $8.9 billion by 2001.

INDUSTRY LEADERS

Fastener manufacturers have long congregated near the industries that buy their products, and according to Industrial Fastener Institute sources, the major purchasers are automobile manufacturers, the federal government, and electronics, machinery, aerospace, and appliance manufacturers. For this reason, Illinois, Ohio, Michigan, and Pennsylvania lead all states in fastener production. California, home to major players in the defense and aerospace industries, is also a major producer of fasteners. Illinois Tool Works (ITW), with headquarters in Glenview, Illinois, is by far the largest producer of industrial fasteners in the United States, with total company sales of $5.6 billion in 1998 sales and more than 24,000 employees. ITW has prospered by following a policy of decentralization. In an interview, Vice Chairman Frank Ptak told *Industry Week* that when an ITW division hits $50 million it's time to split it into three $15-million to $18-million divisions. As an example Ptak offered the company's experience with their Deltar Division, which focused on plastic fasteners for the automotive market. It took that division seven years to reach $2 million as part of the company's Fastex industrial fastener group. When Deltar was separated as part of a decentralization program, it grew sevenfold in four years and has since been split four times into even smaller units.

SPS Technologies Inc. of Jenkintown, Pennsylvania, came in second with $410 million in sales and 4,100 employees. In 1995, Textron Inc. purchased Elco Industries Inc. and formed Elco Textron Inc. (based in Rockford, Illinois) and garnered the third spot with $238 million in sales revenue and 2,200 employees. Other major manufacturers include Camcar Textron Incorporated of Rockford, Illinois, and Huck International Incorporated based in Irvine, California.

RESEARCH AND TECHNOLOGY

In the early 1990s, the fastener industry improved technology due to demands for stronger, lighter, and easier-to-use products. This trend for light, small fasteners continued throughout the decade—especially with the growth in popularity of laptop computers. Buyers were also demanding a variety of innovative and diverse fasteners such as self-locking, self-cinching, or self-sealing screws, bolts, nuts, and threaded inserts according to a *Purchasing* article on fasteners and the aerospace industry. Fastener manufacturers were also working to develop more environmentally friendly products, such as fasteners that maintain lubricity without the use of such plating materials as cadmium, a suspected carcinogen.

Throughout the decade there was much industry effort aimed at improving quality control so as to make total implementation of the FAQ unnecessary. "Improved industry standards, enforcement of those standards, and quality control personnel at both the distributor and manufacturer levels have made the FAQ redundant," according to Barbara Somerville in a 1998 article for *Industrial Distribution*. Towards this end, the industry instituted end-of-line quality control assessments and state-of-the-art manufacturing techniques such as quality assessment on the assembly line. The result has been greatly improved quality control and fewer rejects. "Under the old system, it wasn't uncommon to have a defect ratio of 50K/1 million," says Robert Harris, Managing Director of the Industrial Fastener Institute. "To-

day's in-line quality assurance techniques have reduced defects to below 100 ppm."

FURTHER READING

"Aerospace's Appetite for Fasteners Continues to Grow." *Purchasing,* 7 May 1998.

Aircraft Locknut Manufacturers Association. "Aircraft Locknut Manufacturers Association." Wayne, PA: 1999. Available from http://www.almanet.org.

Ciancarelli, Agatha. "Adhesives & Fasteners: Mixed Reviews on Pricing." *Purchasing,* 11 March 1999.

Cicione, Maryellen. "Fastening the Maker's Needs." *Industrial Distribution,* July 1998.

"Clinton Signs Toned Down FQA." *Industrial Distribution.* July 1999.

Handbook of Bolts and Bolted Joints. New York, NY: Marcel Dekker, 1998.

The Heritage of Mechanical Fasteners. Cleveland, OH: Industrial Fastener Institute, 1991.

Industrial Fasteners Institute. "Industrial Fasteners Institute: IFI." Cleveland, OH: 1998. Available from http://www.ifi-fasteners.org.

Modern Materials and Manufacturing Processes. Upper Saddle River, NJ: 1998.

National Fastener Distribution Association. "National Fastener Distribution Association." Cleveland, OH: 1998. Available from http://www.nfda-fastener.org.

Sharp, David F. "Tell Congress: Ban Bogus Bolts." *Engineering News Record (ENR),* 17 May 1999.

Somervill, Barbara A. "Global Fasteners: It's in the Specs." *Industrial Distribution,* November 1998.

Stevens, Tim. "Breaking Up Is Profitable To Do: A Paragon of Decentralization, Illinois Tool Works." *Industry Week,* 21 June 1999.

SIC 3462

IRON AND STEEL FORGINGS

This industry includes establishments primarily engaged in manufacturing iron and steel forgings, with or without the use of dies. These establishments generally operate on a job or order basis, manufacturing forgings for sale to others or for interplant transfer. Establishments that produce metal forgings for incorporation in end products produced in the same establishment are classified on the basis of the end product. Establishments further processing forgings are classified according to the particular product or process.

NAICS CODE(S)

332111 (Iron and Steel Forging)

INDUSTRY SNAPSHOT

The forging processes of the iron and steel forging industry—not the industry's end products—characterize the industry. Forging reconfigures a substance by pressing, hammering, or constricting it with a great deal of pressure. Most substances are forged after they have been heated, but not melted. Liquefying metals to make parts is called casting.

There are three main processes for forging metal: closed die or impression die forging, which compresses a metal between two dies that contain an impression of the end product; open die forging, which hammers metal between two flat dies but moves the piece between blows to shape the end product; and seamless rolled ring forging, which punches a hole in the work piece and then rolls and squeezes it into a thin, seamless ring.

All forging processes make very resilient parts known as forgings. Forgings are strong because forging processes create a grain flow in the parts of the finished product that require maximum strength. Forging processes also impart beneficial metallurgical properties, such as ductility, resistance properties, dimensional stability, and absence of porosity. Although companies may forge many types of metal, the most commonly forged metals are carbon steel and alloy steel.

Establishments in the iron and steel forging industry are concentrated in the Midwest and Northeast, with the highest number of establishments in Ohio, Michigan, and Illinois. Texas, California, and Pennsylvania also have a large number of forging establishments.

Industry shipments were valued at $4.9 billion in 1997. The industry's primary consumers tended to be companies engaged in industries that were concentrated in the same general regions as the forging companies themselves, even though forging companies do market their products nationally and internationally. The largest purchasers of forged products are the aerospace, national defense, and automotive industries, as well as agricultural, construction, mining, material handling, and general industrial equipment manufacturers.

BACKGROUND AND DEVELOPMENT

Humans first forged metals by hand-hammering them. The steam hammer automated the forging industry in 1843—the steam raised the hammer, but the weight of the hammer was the only pressure used to shape the metal. By 1888, a double-acting hammer used steam to supplement the pressure exerted by the falling hammer. Technology continued to advance the industry.

A census taken by *Forging* reported that two forging methods dominated the industry in 1992: closed die and open die methods. The closed die method was used by 248 companies, while the open die method was used by 109 companies, a margin of more than two-to-one. The ring rolling method was used as a primary method by 16 plants; 13 plants in the census cited other unnamed primary methods of forging. The *Forging* census included 32 Canadian companies and companies classified in **SIC 3463: Nonferrous Forgings.**

Forging developed as more of an art than a science, and even in the 1990s, when most forging was almost completely mechanized, forging processes could not be completely predicted with scientific methods. The unique problems posed by forging are the result of the many factors manufacturers must take into account. The most common factors to consider are the properties of the metal to be transformed, the strain or amount of pressure required to shape the metal, the rate at which the pressure can be applied to the metal for deformation, and the appropriate temperature for the deformation to occur without scaling or breaking the material. All the factors must be balanced to achieve consistently desired results from any of the forging processes.

Even with advances in technology, the complexity of some forging problems have not been solved. Determining the kind of die lubricant to use for forging operations is an example. Before the industrial revolution, animal oils, coal, soapstone, and crude oils were used because the products were "simple" and the processes requiring lubricants were "minimal," according to *Forging*. The advent of the steam-hammer demanded new lubricants, which were developed by the end of the nineteenth century. The new lubricants were steam-refined mineral oils, sawdust, salt water, fatty soap solutions, and oil and graphite flake combinations.

The oil and graphite mixtures proved to be effective as forging speeds increased with automation, but because those mixtures were explosive, other lubricants needed to be developed. Mixtures of water and graphite replaced the oil-based mixtures by 1970. In response to health related problems caused by graphite lubricants, research on synthetic lubricants began in the 1970s. In 1993, *Forging* reported that "water-based graphites make up about 60 percent of the forging industry sales, synthetics 15 percent, and oil-based graphites 15 percent."

The success of the forging process relies on the effectiveness of the lubricant, but no simple method for selecting a lubricant exists. Each lubricant has advantages as well as disadvantages. Oil and graphite applies easily and works well at many temperatures, but is explosive and expensive. Water and graphite costs less and helps cool dies, but requires careful application to work; in addition, graphite dust can collect in the work area and cause problems for workers. Synthetic lubricants are cost effective and less hazardous but must be applied through spraying, may impede metal flow, and are ineffective to use for forging complex shapes.

The industry has seen many changes in the cost of production. From a low of $1.2 billion in 1983, material costs rose dramatically to just over $2.0 billion in 1989, to $2.5 billion in 1997.

CURRENT CONDITIONS

There are three types of forging orders: custom forgings, which are made at the request of a customer; captive forgings, which are made for the company's own internal use; and catalog forgings, which consist of standardized parts that are resold through various sources. Forged products range from precision aircraft parts to everyday hammer heads and wrenches.

Forgers faced significant competition from other industries in the mid 1990s, as end-users looked for lighter, cheaper materials. Powdered metal, cast metal, plastics, and ceramics posed the greatest threat to the iron and steel forge industry. Industry analyst Joshua Billings told *Metals Watch* that "the competitive pressure from plastics and new metal alloys will force forgers to reduce the weight of their components." Billings added, however, that "[f]orgings may lose some market share for smaller parts to castings and powder metal parts, but will retain their preeminence for very large items or parts that are neither complex nor intricate."

In addition to the challenges presented by rival materials, iron and steel forgers experienced a drop in demand in the late 1990s. Although the U.S. economy boomed for the closing years of the decade, forgers were affected by the collapse of Asian economies in 1997. According to the *Milwaukee Business Journal,* the slowing of the aerospace industry had the greatest potential to harm iron and steel forging business. Since air travel decreased in the wake of the financial crisis, major airlines canceled or delayed orders for new planes. Iron and steel forgers—who produced highly engineered parts for airplane engines—were expected to experience a corollary drop in demand.

INDUSTRY LEADERS

The majority of the most successful forging companies are privately held. Among the leading establishments in 1997 was Ladish Co., Inc. Based in Cudahy, Wisconsin, Ladish derives 90 percent of its sales from the aerospace industry. The company's 1998 sales increased 8.1 percent from 1997 levels to reach $226.0 million. Ladish employed 1,130 workers. Another key player in the iron and steel forging industry was the publicly-held Defiance, Inc., which manufactured the bulk of its products for the U.S. automotive sector. A subsidiary of GenTek, Defiance reported 1998 sales of $89.3 million and employed 691. SIFCO Industries, Inc. enjoyed major commercial airlines as its primary clients. Based in Cleveland, Ohio, SIFCO's 1999 sales were $115.0 mil-

lion, and employment levels remained stable at 848 workers.

WORKFORCE

Forging requires large amounts of capital investments to maintain the expensive equipment, but the industry sustains companies of a wide variety of sizes. While companies have between 50 and 250 employees, there are thriving businesses with as few as 10 and as many as 1000. In 1997, 47 percent of establishments in the iron and steel forgings sector employed 20 or more. The industry as a whole employed 26,243 workers in 1997, of which 19,950—76 percent—were directly involved in production. These production employees earned an average wage of $16.42 per hour. The greatest number of iron and steel forging employees resided in Ohio. In addition to these 3,810 workers, 3,381 called Texas home. Pennsylvania contained the third highest number of iron and steel forging employees, with 2,912.

RESEARCH AND TECHNOLOGY

The industry expects to make significant investments in research and development in the coming decades. $80 billion in federal funding was made available to American manufacturers by a mandate from the Clinton Administration. Roger W. Werne, the associate director for engineering and technology transfer for Lawrence Livermore National Laboratory, noted in *Forging* that under the Clinton Administration's increased funding for national laboratories, the labs can act as an "'insurance policy' that can enhance the probability of success of a U.S. company or consortium of companies that decides to push the limit of their technology beyond existing boundaries." About the development of new technologies, the executive editor of *Forging,* John R. Wright, stated that "America is on the verge of wholesale new areas of technology development. We are close to breakthroughs—a technology blast that will carry this country for the next 30 years."

FURTHER READING

Stundza, Tom. "Forging News," *Metals Watch: The Newsletter.* Vol. 2, April/May 1996. Available from http://www.steelforge.com/metals/issues.html.

Stundza, Tom. "Forging News." *Metals Watch: The Newsletter.* Vol. 2, December 1996. Available from http://www.steelforge.com/metals/issues.html.

U.S. Census Bureau. "Iron and Steel Forgings," October 1999. Available from http://www.census.gov/prod.

Velocci, Anthony. "Aerospace Suppliers Preoccupied with Possible Cyclical Downturn." *Aviation Week and Space Technology,* 31 May 1999.

NONFERROUS FORGINGS

This category includes establishments primarily engaged in manufacturing nonferrous forgings, with or without the use of dies. These establishments generally operate on a job or order basis, manufacturing forgings for sale to others or for interplant transfer. Establishments that produce metal forgings for incorporation in end products produced in the same establishment are classified on the basis of the end product. Establishments that further process forgings are classified according to the particular product or process.

The forging industry as a whole, which includes **SIC 3462: Iron and Steel Forgings,** is characterized by its forging processes rather than its end products. Because many companies forge many types of metals, including both ferrous and nonferrous, industry information for this industry classification and **SIC 3462: Iron and Steel Forgings** are often reported together. The Forging Industry Association, for example, does not distinguish between the two SICs, presenting information on sales for the entire industry. Therefore, this entry will focus on the unique characteristics of the nonferrous forgings industry, and general information on forging can be found in the essay on **SIC 3462: Iron and Steel Forgings.**

NAICS CODE(S)

332112 (Nonferrous Forging)

According to the U.S. Census Bureau's *1997 Economic Census—Manufacturing,* 84 establishments operated in this category for some or all of 1997. Industrywide employment totaled 9,129 workers receiving a payroll of almost $367 million; 6,952 of these employees worked in production, putting in more than 15 million hours to earn wages of almost $259 million. Overall shipments for the industry were valued at almost $1.86 billion.

In the late 1990s Los Angeles-based Teledyne Inc. led the industry with sales of over $2.5 billion generated by 18,000 employees. Second in the industry, Wyman-Gordon Co. of Grafton, Massachusetts, with almost $753 million in sales for its fiscal year ended May 31, 1998 on the work of 4,285 employees, entered into a titanium supply agreement with Titanium Metals Corp. (Timet). In one of several "strategic transactions," Wyman transferred its Millbury, Massachusetts vacuum arc remelting (VAR) plant to Timet for the supplier to process Wyman's titanium.

Amcast Industrial Corp. rounded out the top three industry leaders, with more than 4,500 workers and $574 million in sales for its fiscal year ended August 31, 1998. Other industry leaders included Textron Inc. Turbine

Engine Components Div. of Euclid, Ohio; RMI Titanium Co. of Niles, Ohio; and Cerro Metal Products Co. of Bellefonte, Pennsylvania.

Aluminum is the metal most often forged in this industry classification. It is "the most forgeable of all metals," according to *Forging.* Aluminum and its alloys can be forged into many different shapes and sizes. The metal is unique because it can be heated to the same temperature as the dies that will form it. The hardness of the dies is also lower than dies used for forging steel. The most common lubricant for forging aluminum is a graphite-water solution, with soap, to help the flow of the metal. Aluminum can also be forged into precision parts that need no further machining for use. Gravity or drop hammers are used for open die forgings, mechanical presses for closed die forgings, and hydraulic presses for complex pieces.

Other nonferrous forgings are made from magnesium and its alloys, whose coarse grains require that the metal be forged slowly in hydraulic presses; copper and its alloys, including brass and bronze; and titanium and its alloys, which are very sensitive to temperature changes but are extremely strong and resistant to corrosion.

The number of companies engaged in primarily manufacturing nonferrous forgings was only one-fifth the number of companies engaged in forging iron and steel. In 1986, 60 companies primarily used nonferrous metals to manufacture their forgings, a decrease of four companies since 1982. Capital investment within the industry slid in 1986 to 44 percent ($43.8 million) of that which was invested in 1982. Production in value of shipments also declined during that period by 1 percent, to $1.09 billion. As the value of shipments fell, however, the cost of materials and the value added by manufacture increased, by 3 and 8 percent to $586.1 million and $497.8 million, respectively.

In the 1990s the nonferrous forging industry continued to be a small part of the total forging industry. In a 1993 census taken by *Forging,* 40 of 386 plants across the United States and Canada concentrated their efforts on forging aluminum, while 13 facilities concentrated on titanium and 12 on copper-base alloys. The forging of nonferrous metals is not limited to these companies, however; the total number of plants that engage in nonferrous metal forging to some degree is significantly higher. When asked to provide all the types of metals a company forged, the number of plants that indicated at least a modicum of aluminum forging was 57 percent, while those engaged in titanium forging reached about 20 percent, and about 9 percent reported forging copper-base alloys.

In 1994 the entire metal forgings and stampings industry employed 247,000, and the value of shipments

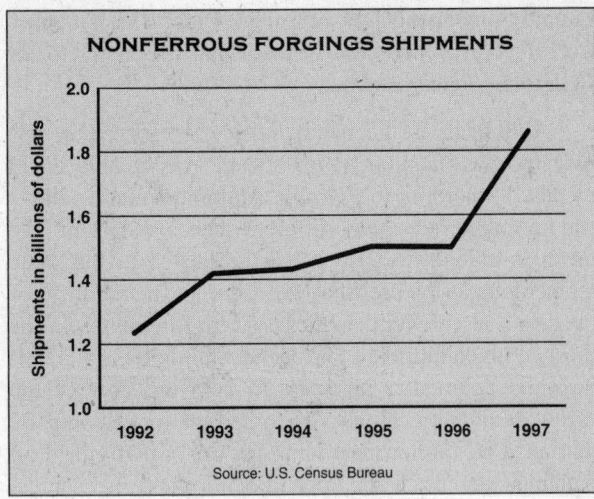

NONFERROUS FORGINGS SHIPMENTS

Shipments in billions of dollars

Source: U.S. Census Bureau

was $36.750 billion. The nonferrous forgings segment had about 90 establishments in 1996. Capital investment was around $29 million, and the cost of materials was $664 million. The value of shipments was approximately $1.213 billion. In 1998 the industry had an estimate 94 establishments and shipment values of approximately $1.200 billion. Capital investment fell to an estimated $24 million, but the cost of materials rose to an estimated $674 million.

Compared with other manufacturing establishments, the nonferrous forging industry is labor-intensive. The industry employs almost twice as many workers per company than other manufacturers, with 80 workers per establishment on average as opposed to 49. The 1987 *Census of Manufactures* reported that the nonferrous forgings industry employed 7,300 employees, a drop of 8 percent since 1982. In 1994 the industry employed 6,900, and this number was expected to fall to 6,700 by 1998.

By 2005 employment is expected to decrease in a majority of the occupations in this industry. Metal and plastic machine forming operators are expected to fall by almost 70 percent. Freight, stock, and material movers are expected to fall by 31 percent, along with janitors and cleaners. Combination machine tool operators are expected to rise about 28 percent, however, and punching machine operators are expected to increase by 15 percent. In the late 1990s California's 20 establishments generated 19.4 percent of U.S. shipments. Illinois' and Connecticut's 9 establishments were producing about 12.0 percent of the U.S. total.

FURTHER READING

Darnay, Arsen J., ed. *Manufacturing USA: Industry Analysis, Statistics, and Leading Companies,* 5th ed. Detroit: Gale Research, 1996.

Infotrac Company Profiles, 1 January 2000. Available from http://web4.infotrac.galegroup.com.

"Metals and Alloys." *Forging,* spring 1993.

"Taking a Tally of the U.S. Forging Industry." *Forging,* summer 1993.

U.S. Census Bureau. *1997 Economic Census—Manufacturing,* 2 February 2000. Available from http://www.census.gov/prod/ec97/97m3321b.pdf.

U.S. Department of Commerce. *1987 Census of Manufactures.* Washington: GPO, 1987.

———. *Statistical Abstract of the United States.* Washington: GPO, October 1996.

SIC 3465

AUTOMOTIVE STAMPINGS

This category includes establishments that primarily manufacture metal auto parts, such as body panels, hubs, and trim pieces, usually for sale to other manufacturers or for use in assembly facilities located off-site. Those firms that utilize the stamped products in the manufacture of end products in the same establishment are categorized by that end-product.

NAICS CODE(S)

336370 (Motor Vehicle Metal Stamping)

INDUSTRY SNAPSHOT

The automotive stamping industry remains closely dependent on the health of the domestic U.S. automobile market. With the decline of domestic car and truck production after 1988, the demand for stampings also decreased. The value of product shipments has decreased since the late 1980s. The industry was worth $16.0 billion in 1987. That figure changed to $20.6 billion in 1995, a net decrease in value after inflation over the nine-year period. In 1996, the industry's value decreased again to $15.8 billion. In 1996 the industry employed 105,100 workers at roughly 699 facilities in the United States. This represented an approximate 12 percent decrease in employment for the industry since 1987. The technical expertise of industry production workers is increasing rapidly as the industry adapts to new production techniques and strategies, the challenges of new metal alloys, and the competition of plastic alternatives.

ORGANIZATION AND STRUCTURE

As with all manufacturers of automotive parts, stamping firms produce for two major market components: the original equipment manufacturer (OEM) and the after-market or replacement parts sector. Typical components include fenders, roofs, floor pans, exhaust systems, brake shoes, and trim pieces. Such large pieces require a considerable investment in tooling and scale of operation. Consequently, businesses engaged in their manufacture are usually operated by the major automotive manufacturers or contracted by them. Small components, such as brackets, valves, and hangers, do not require the same level of sophisticated engineering investment, which allows small, independent firms to specialize in such items. As a rule of thumb, automotive manufacturers contract out any stamped part needed in volumes below 200,000 pieces annually.

Between 1987 and 1996 the number of production workers employed dropped from 99,900 to 87,000. At the same time, the number of establishments also dropped from 713 to 699. Although the number of production workers and establishments has been decreasing, the stamping plants that still exist tend to be large operations employing many production workers. In 1996 the average number of production workers per establishment was 129. Because the automotive stamping industry is a major supplier to automotive manufacturers, firms in the industry are concentrated in Michigan, Ohio, Indiana, and Illinois, near the major U.S. automakers. These states accounted for 80 percent of the employment in the automotive stamping industry in 1996.

BACKGROUND AND DEVELOPMENT

The process or art of stamping metal to form hundreds or even thousands of identical parts evolved with the automotive industry. In 1912, Philadelphian Edward Budd convinced the Hupp Motor Co., the Oakland Motor Co., and Garford Motors to begin incorporating metal into the design of their car bodies instead of the traditional wood. For the next few years, cars were made using a combination of both materials. In 1914, however, the Dodge brothers moved the automotive and the stamping industries into the modern era of industrial manufacturing with an order for 5,000 all-steel touring sedan bodies.

Stamping, or cold-forming, involves the use of power-operated clamping devices. A moving die, or forming-tool, presses into a sheet of metal and against a fixed die. The metal undergoes what is known as plastic deformation to take on the desired shape and thickness. Until the 1930s, the method was more art than science. Skilled artisans would produce relatively simple dies and use their collective experience to effectively produce parts mainly by trial and error. They often used an array of special tools and rituals to trick the sheet metal into shape.

As the industry needed to produce more sophisticated components, the unitized body, which eventually replaced the frame entirely on domestic automobiles, was developed. With the unitized body, once the die design, the metal material, and the blank sheet dimensions were chosen and found to be correct, the tool-system could create thousands of duplications under the supervision of relatively unskilled labor. That cost-saving attribute appealed to the needs of mass production manufacturers

and overcame the disadvantage of the time-consuming process of die development. The new stamping process would require each individual component of the process to have a unique set of custom-designed dies.

A major advancement in press design came in the 1950s with the use of numerical controls. They made the new presses more accurate, faster, and easier to set up, allowing the industry to begin manufacturing a new range of products including mufflers, oil filler caps, some gears, engine mounts, and brackets. By the 1970s, this technology gave way to computer numerical controls. The computer allowed the presses to run faster and operate more precisely, creating a need for automatic systems and robot loaders and unloaders.

The growing popularity of fuel-efficient Japanese-built cars challenged the mass-production philosophy of the American automotive manufacturers, particularly in the 1980s. The stamping industry felt the pressure directly. Its manufacturing philosophy prescribed large, regional facilities supplying several assembly plants in various geographic locations. However, the number of car models being produced, including foreign models, was steadily climbing. In 1986, there were 51 models sold in the United States; by 1990 there were 90. The capacity of press lines in operation had increased as older lines were replaced with more modern, efficient systems, which meant competition increased along with the number of required die changes.

Increased foreign competition also meant the domestic manufacturers had to improve the quality of their product. They needed new metals with better corrosion resistance. Instead of the standard 0.040-inch-thick carbon steel the industry had been using, manufacturers began specifying Zincrometal, one-sided and two-sided galvanized and coated alloy-steels. In addition, customers became far less tolerant of part variations that showed up as poor fit and finish. In 1981, many firms introduced Statistical Process Control and begin to implement just-in-time manufacturing systems in order to tighten the production belt. The resulting retrenching turned into downsizing and a massive reduction in production employment. Between 1972 and 1982, the number of production workers in the industry dropped from 103,000 to 74,500.

A major impediment to improved efficiencies in American stamping plants was the age of the equipment inventory. According to the thirteenth *American Machinist* inventory of metalworking machinery, almost one-half of all American metalforming equipment was at least 20 years old in 1983. Much of this equipment was cumbersome, designed for long production runs with long periods of shut down for maintenance and die replacement. During the 1980s, rebuilt and upgraded parts for these presses rose to 29 percent of all machine tool manufacturer's shipments. Even with the efforts to modernize, however, some machines could not be made competitive with the newer, more flexible Japanese technologies.

One of the most important battles for the American industry to win was the challenge of the rapid die change. Traditionally, American stampers took hours and sometimes days to change the dies in their machines. With the lines shut down for maintenance, one shift out of three working, and a warehouse full of finished product inventory in case of an unexpected breakdown, such long change-out times had not been a problem. However, with just-in-time production methods, inventories shrank to only hours of reserve parts and the number of die-changes increased to several per day. In contrast, in Japan during the early 1980s, die-changes took 10 minutes, using small armies of workers. By 1991, Hirotec Corporation of Hiroshima could consistently change a die set in 80-to-90 seconds using just three men.

The difference between the United States and Japanese stamping processes was equipment design and planning. Older American machines required the complete removal of the old die before a new one could be installed. To do that, workers had to unfasten bolts and brackets. Having placed the new die, they would then set the piston stroke height and adjust the die position. Japanese presses use hydraulic clamps to hold standardized dies, and have openings on either side to allow the new die to be inserted as the old is withdrawn.

To remain competitive, in the early 1990s the big three U.S. automakers (Ford Motor Company, General Motors Corporation, and Chrysler Corporation) spent billions of dollars for new presses and new stamping plants tied to particular assembly facilities. The on-site stamping plant produces all the major parts required for the assembly of a specific car, cutting down on transportation costs and increasing the efficiency of shorter production runs. However, in 1991 the Big Three still had 22 major regional facilities that would be expensive to abandon and replace.

To increase the efficiency of those older plants, the industry began to standardize the die heights and improve the die designs and body panel designs so as to reduce the number of strokes needed to complete the forming process and reduce the amount of scrap steel produced. Formed parts almost always require multiple hits by the die or a series of dies to take the desired finished shape. Reducing the number of strokes required increases the rate of production and the life of the die. American molds typically average five and one-half hits per panel compared to less than three and one-half for Japanese systems.

During the early 1990s, the competitive need for higher efficiency through better quality control and increased flexibility drove the auto-makers to rethink their stamping arrangements and manufacturing philosophies.

The traditional method of sourcing parts from several suppliers working from a manufacturer-supplied design gave way to a more cooperative and interactive approach. Copying the Japanese method, the manufacturers began to involve specific suppliers early on in the design stage and to require them to provide much of the engineering expertise, which reduced costs to the manufacturer and allowed the supplier to maintain an economy of scale in its actual production. It also meant fewer but larger suppliers. At the same time, manufacturers moved to on-site stamping plants equipped with sophisticated technology that effectively automated the process from start to finish. The increased efficiencies allowed the industry to compete effectively with foreign firms and to resist pressure from other materials like aluminum and plastics.

INDUSTRY LEADERS

The largest stamping firms in the OEM portion of the industry remain the automotive manufacturers themselves, but those firms outsource about 25 percent of their new car stamping requirements to independent firms. In 1999, the largest of the independent stamping firms was Minneapolis-based Tower Automotive, Inc. Founded in 1955 and lead by CEO Dugald K. Campbell, Tower took the lead in the stamping industry for the first time in 1999. Tower employed almost 9,000 people in 1999 and generated approximately $1.2 billion in sales. Although Tower's headquarters are in Minneapolis, the company has a number of subsidiaries throughout the United States and is involved in various aspects of the automotive industry in addition to stamping.

The second largest independent metal stamper in 1999 was The Budd Company of Troy, Michigan, a subsidiary of Thyssen AG of Germany. Budd employed 10,000 workers to produce more than $1 billion in sales in 1999. Founded in 1912, the company pioneered the development of metal stampings throughout the early part of the century, racking up such firsts as the first four-door, all steel sedan body (Dodge), the first all-steel unitized body (Nash), stainless steel "streamliner" trains of the 1930s, the Navy's Conestoga RB-1 stainless steel cargo plane built during World War II, the prototype for the French Citroen, and the all-plastic-bodied 1954 Studebaker Coupe.

Metal stampings make up more than 50 percent of the company's sales, but it also manufactures fiberglass and plastic composite body panels, truck brake and wheel components, iron castings, and cold weather products like engine block heaters and interior car warmers. The German steel manufacturer and stamping firm, Thyssen AG, bought Budd Co. in 1978. The American firm had extended itself into many nonautomotive areas like aerospace and nuclear energy, reaching an employment high of 21,500, but it was loosing money. Thyssen propped up the company with influxes of capital, trimmed company operations, and limited operations to the automotive business to help it through the recession of the 1980s.

WORKFORCE

Traditionally, the large stamping plants, using large quantities of relatively unskilled workers, have operated with union labor. The main unions are the United Auto Workers (UAW) in the United States and the Canadian Automobile Aerospace and Agricultural Implement Workers (CAW) in Canada. However, many transplant operations have tried to use non-union labor throughout their operations including the on-site stamping plants.

With the shift to advanced automation at the newer plants, the traditional union stance of clearly defined job descriptions and classifications is giving way to more flexible arrangements like Ford's Modern Operating Agreement at its Wayne, Michigan, on-site stamping facility. Under that agreement, only one category of production worker exists. Each worker receives training on the entire manufacturing process to produce a teamwork approach. Displaced by sophisticated automation, the number of unskilled operators continues to decline. In their place, skilled tradesmen and craft-workers design and maintain the complicated production machinery and its robot servers.

Manufacturers and a growing number of labor leaders see automation as the key to preventing manufacturing facilities from relocating in Mexico with the advent of the North American Free Trade Agreement (NAFTA). Without the competitive edge of tireless automation, the lower wages accepted by Mexican workers would force manufacturers to relocate to stay competitive.

AMERICA AND THE WORLD

The American stamping industry in the 1990s played catch-up with their European and Japanese counterparts. American plants typically wasted twice as much material, used more press operations, and ran presses at half the speed of foreign plants with production runs five times as long. Body panel sets costing $300 in a Japanese plant could cost $700 in its American counterpart. By building newer, more flexible plants and up-grading old presses where possible, American manufacturers began to slowly overcome their impediments.

RESEARCH AND TECHNOLOGY

Modern stamping plants are using advanced technology to redefine themselves. Once the labor-intensive blacksmith shop of the auto industry, stamping now taps the skills and ingenuity of its workers to produce machines and computer monitoring systems to do repetitive work. At a fully automated plant like Ford's $600-million Wayne, Michigan, stamping plant, for example, human operators are used only to load raw steel into the plant and to remove the finished product at the end of the production line. Automatic guided vehicles follow roadways of wires embedded in the factory floor carrying bar-coded metal to the correct storage area or the next press that needs that particular type of material. Transfer presses pass the metal down lines of six or eight similar machines to form complicated components. The completed parts exit the production area, and enter the transfer area where operators manually check them and rack them on a conveyor. Their next stop is the assembly facility.

Transfer presses need less production floor room, but often achieve only 25 to 30 percent operating efficiency because of their complexity. Simpler, easier to repair robot systems may become the technology of choice where the need for flexibility dominates. Robot systems appeal to small-batch producers like Budd Company. A ''hard-tooled'' automation system like a transfer press line may need expensive retooling every few years, but a ''soft-tooled'' robotic system can be upgraded by reprogramming and minor physical relocations.

The computer has also improved new die design and raw material usage, reducing both the production costs due to wastage and the design time needed for the evolution of a new car. Such programs can reduce the skilled man-hours needed for die face design by 50 percent, die face manufacture by 30 percent, and die tryout and corrective modification by 30 percent. Such improvements went a long way in reducing the traditional domestic car manufacturers' five-year new car design period, putting it in line with Japanese design periods of two or three years.

FURTHER READING

D&B Million Dollar Directory. Dun and Bradstreet, 1999.

U.S. Bureau of the Census. *1997 Annual Survey of Manufactures.* Washington, D.C.: GPO, 1999. Available from www .census.gov.

SIC 3466

CROWNS AND CLOSURES

This category covers establishments primarily engaged in manufacturing metal crowns and closures, including both bottle caps and jar crowns and tops.

NAICS CODE(S)

332115 (Crown and Closure Manufacturing)

INDUSTRY SNAPSHOT

The crowns and closures industrial classification is a portion of the larger stamped metals industry that is

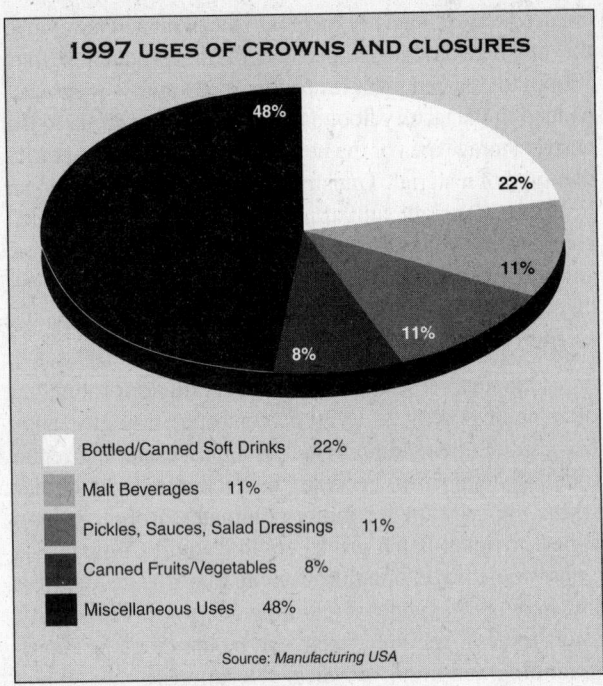

1997 USES OF CROWNS AND CLOSURES

48%
22%
11%
11%
8%

Bottled/Canned Soft Drinks   22%

Malt Beverages   11%

Pickles, Sauces, Salad Dressings   11%

Canned Fruits/Vegetables   8%

Miscellaneous Uses   48%

Source: *Manufacturing USA*

try's products are also used in the packaging of roasted coffee, wines, brandy, brandy spirits, toilet preparations, and confectionery products.

BACKGROUND AND DEVELOPMENT

Shipments in the metal crowns and closures industry increased in the early and mid-1990s, moving from $720.2 million in 1990 to $770.9 million in 1995. Shipments reached a peak in 1993 at $837.1 million. Much of the increase was attributed to a shortage in plastic closures, forcing some bottlers to turn to metal. Employment in this industry, however, has steadily fallen. In 1983, this industry employed 7,100 people, 5,700 of who were production workers. By 1995, this total was 4,300, with 3,500 production workers.

Industry sales have fluctuated in reaction to conditions in the plastics market. For example, metal closure sales picked up somewhat in the mid-1990s when a high worldwide demand for polypropylene—a type of resin used to manufacture plastic closures—slowed the shift from metal to plastic closures. At the same time, some bottlers' market research has showed that in certain cases, consumers actually prefer metal closures to plastic. Alcoa, for example, found that consumers favor the popping sound aluminum closures make when a vacuum-packed glass bottle is opened. That technology does not yet exist in plastic closures, so some select segments of the beverage market are moving back to aluminum.

INDUSTRY LEADERS

Philadelphia-based Crown Cork and Seal Company, which led the industry with 1998 sales of $8.3 billion, announced late that year that lower earnings prompted them to cut 7 percent of its workforce—about 2,700 workers—in order to return profits of $0.80 instead of $1.05 to its shareholders. On the other hand, AptarGroup subsidiary Valois, a French-based manufacturer of perfume and pharmaceutical pumps, considered doubling its workforce over a two-year period. AptarGroup Inc. of Crystal Lake, Illinois generated 1999 sales of almost $714 million. Rounding out the top four industry leaders were Indianapolis-based Alcoa Closure Systems International and Alltrista Corp. of Muncie, Indiana.

Alltrista is best known for its Ball home canning jars and closures (the Ball brand dates back to 1884). In addition to producing metal closures, the company's metal fabrication operations manufacture a wide range of zinc-based products, from battery cans to coin blanks to industrial components. In 1996, Alltrista acquired the Kerr Group Inc., another maker of home canning products, and consolidated Kerr's manufacturing facility into Alltrista's existing operations. To complement its line of home canning products, Alltrista also makes a variety of food preservation products used in canning.

fading into a highly fragmented industry. As bottlers seek lower production costs, more tamper-evident packaging, and better printability for product differentiation, many continue to move away from metal closures, preferring plastic ones instead.

According to the U.S. Census Bureau's *1997 Economic Census—Manufacturing,* 66 establishments operated in this category for part or all of 1997. Industry-wide employment totaled 4,627 workers receiving a payroll of more than $164 million. Within this workforce, 3,842 of these employees worked in production, putting in more than 8 million hours to earn wages of more than $121 million. Overall shipments for the industry were valued at almost $949 million.

ORGANIZATION AND STRUCTURE

The product share of this industry is split into three sections. Metal commercial closures and metal home canning closures comprise 84.39 percent of the total market, and metal crowns for glass and metal containers represent 14.08 percent. Non-specific crowns and closures represent the remaining 1.53 percent. Aluminum, in the form of sheet, plate, and foil, is proportionately the industry's largest input. Tin plate, tin-free steel, terneplate, and blackplate represent the second most highly consumed materials. Carbon steel sheet and strips are also used.

Bottled and canned soft drink manufacturers use up 22.3 percent of the industry's outputs. Malt beverage makers use 10.6 percent; pickles, sauces, and salad dressings consume 10.5 percent; and canned fruits and vegetables take 7.7 percent of the industry's outputs. The indus-

WORKFORCE

Machine operators in the fabricated metal products industry earned about $510 a week in 1994. This is somewhat less than many other metalworking and plastics-working machine operators; those in primary metals industries earned $640 weekly and those in industrial machinery and equipment earned $570 a week.

Employment is expected to decline through the year 2005 for both metalworking and plastics-working machine operators. Those employed in metalworking are likely to be affected more than those employed in plastics because, in recent years, plastic products have increasingly been used in place of metal in consumer and manufacturing products. Another reason for the employment decline is the widespread use of computer-controlled production equipment.

AMERICA AND THE WORLD

According to Alltrista's 1996 Annual Report, the home canning products segment of this industry was hampered by a poor U.S. growing season in both 1995 and 1996, resulting in lower earnings for establishments producing these products. The cyclical nature of seasonal weather patterns, however, almost guarantees an improvement in this part of the industry.

RESEARCH AND TECHNOLOGY

A new development in aluminum can closures surfaced in 1996, building on the existing concept of the "eco-lid." The eco-lid is a tab that allows the consumer to open a beverage can by pushing the lid inside the body of the container. The lid stays attached to the can, reducing solid waste. Some hygienic concerns still exist over the eco-lid, since the beverage unfailingly comes in contact with the exposed part of the package that gets pushed inside the can. An innovation called S.H.E.S (which stands for "Safe, Hygienic, Easy, Simple") addresses this concern with a fully recyclable dispenser inside the can. The dispenser is pulled out when the can is opened. S.H.E.S. represents about a 5 percent production cost increase over current can closure technologies. As of early 1997, this development had not been widely adopted by closure manufacturers.

FURTHER READING

Alltrista Corporation. *1996 Annual Report.* Muncie, IN: Alltrista Corporation, 1997.

"Alltrista Corporation Profile." Alltrista Corporation, 1997. Available from http://www.alltrista.com.

"AptarGroup Inc. Acquires Somova." *Global Cosmetic Industry,* August 1999.

Bureau of Labor Statistics. *Metalworking and Plastics-Working Machine Operators.* Washington, D.C.: GPO, 1996. Available from http://www.stats.bls.gov.

"Crown Cuts Jobs, Costs." *Soap-Cosmetics-Chemical Specialities,* December 1998.

Darnay, Arsen J., ed. *Manufacturing USA.* 5th ed. Detroit: Gale Research, 1996.

Sfiligoj, Eric. "Cap Squeeze." *Beverage World,* June 1995.

———. "'S.H.E.S.' the One." *Beverage World,* September 1996.

U.S. Census Bureau. "Crown and Closure Manufacturing" *1997 Economic Census-Manufacturing.* Washington, D.C.: U.S. Department of Commerce, 1999. Available from http://www.census.gov.

U.S. Department of Commerce. *1995 Annual Survey of Manufactures.* Washington, D.C.: GPO, 1996.

SIC 3469

METAL STAMPINGS, NOT ELSEWHERE CLASSIFIED

This category includes establishments primarily engaged in manufacturing metal stampings and spun products, not elsewhere classified, including porcelain enameled products. Products of this industry include household appliance housings and parts, cooking and kitchen utensils, and other non-automotive job stampings.

NAICS CODE(S)

339911 (Jewelry (including Precious Metal) Manufacturing)
332116 (Metal Stamping)
332214 (Kitchen Utensils, Pot and Pan Manufacturing)

According to the U.S. Census Bureau's *1997 Economic Census—Manufacturing,* 2,161 establishments operated in this category for part or all of 1997. Industrywide employment totaled 92,694 workers receiving a payroll of more than $3 billion. Of these employees, 71,523 worked in production, putting in more than 148 million hours to earn wages of more than $1.9 billion. Overall shipments for the industry were valued at almost $12 billion.

Corning Inc. of Corning, New York led the industry with 1998 sales of almost $3.5 billion behind the strength of 15,400 workers. U.S. Industries Inc. of Iselin, New Jersey generated more than $3.3 billion in sales for its fiscal year ended September 30, 1998, and employed 24,000. Ball Corp. of Broomfield, Colorado employed 12,100 workers, who helped to create almost $2.9 billion in sales. Snap-On Inc. of Kenosha, Wisconsin rounded out the top four industry leaders with 1998 sales of almost $1.8 billion.

The largest portion of the industry stamps metal for motor homes, aviation, agricultural equipment, computers, electrical appliances, radios, televisions, kitchen appliances, and laundry equipment. Cooking and kitchen utensils, such as tea kettles, metal spoons, baking pans, and stainless steel mixing bowls, claim a distinct majority of the industry's product base. In 1995, aluminum made up 39.4 percent of cookware shipments, while bakeware accounted for 22.7 percent.

The stamping industry is currently entering into a new age of technology. Although computer-aided drafting and manufacturing tools have been used to great advantage in the metal-cutting industry, the related metal-forming industries have not used available software tools. Specialized software is now being developed to add precision to the stamping process. Not only does computer software design improved stamping dies, but it can also be interfaced with the machinery to tell the operator when the die is beginning to dull, or when the machine itself is beginning to malfunction.

The implementation of computer technology helps manufacturers reduce costs throughout the spectrum of machining operations. For larger production lines, the area of specialty tooling is gaining importance as more companies cut costs and competition grows. With specialty tooling, several operations can be combined by using unique punch dies. Louver, countersink, embossing, lettering, and lance-and-form tools are gaining popularity as more industry leaders seek to improve product quality and cost through process redesign.

Over 2,700 companies were engaged in the metal stamping industry in 1988. That year, the industry employed 97,000 people at an average hourly wage of $9.65. The value of shipments increased $2 billion between 1982 and 1988, while employment levels remained stable. A major reason for the increase in shipment values was the rising cost of materials. In 1995, the value of product shipments was $11.9 billion.

Significant reductions in the labor pool are expected in several production line occupations by the year 2005. The largest segment of employment in the industry is occupied by metal and plastic forming machine operators. This segment, however, is expected to be one of the hardest hit with layoffs, with over 65 percent of the positions being eliminated. Other occupations facing reductions include welding machine setters and machine feeders (23 percent), assemblers and fabricators (18 percent), precision inspectors, truck and tractor operators, and sheet metal workers (15 percent), and cutting tool operators (13 percent). The only occupations expected to grow more than 10 percent include punching machine operators, combination machine tool operators, and machine tool cutting and forming.

FURTHER READING

Darnay, Arsen J., ed. *Manufacturing USA*. Detroit: Gale Research, 1996.

Infotrac Company Profiles, 2 December 1999. Available at http://web6.infotrac.galegroup.com.

Lazich, Robert S., ed. *Market Share Reporter*. Detroit: Gale Research, 1997.

U.S. Bureau of the Census. *1995 Annual Survey of Manufactures*. Washington: GPO, January, 1997.

U.S. Census Bureau. *1997 Economic Census-Manufacturing*. Available at http://www.census.gov/prod/ec97/97m3321e.pdf (visited 2/12/00).

SIC 3471

ELECTROPLATING, PLATING, POLISHING, ANODIZING AND COLORING

This category includes establishments primarily engaged in all types of electroplating, plating, anodizing, coloring, and finishing of metals and formed products for the trade. Also included in this industry are establishments that perform these types of activities on their own account, on purchased metals or formed products. Establishments that both manufacture and finish products are classified according to their products.

NAICS CODE(S)

332813   (Electroplating, Plating, Polishing, Anodizing, and Coloring)

INDUSTRY SNAPSHOT

The value of the industry's shipments in 1997 was $5.94 billion, up from $2.7 billion in 1982. There were 3,399 establishments in 1997.

In the 1990s there were two types of firms in the industry: small, private corporations and large, publicly held companies that were either subsidiaries or divisions of larger parent corporations. While larger firms were often more diversified in the number of electroplating and finishing processes they utilized, smaller firms tended to specialize in one or two types of finishing processes. During the 1950s and 1960s, many companies established their own finishing operations, but with the onset of increased environmental regulation of the industry in the 1970s many manufacturing firms opted to subcontract for finishing services, thus avoiding the added costs of waste treatment. In the 1990s the trend once again was for manufacturing firms to own and operate their own finishing operations, often integrating production and finishing processes.

BACKGROUND AND DEVELOPMENT

Historically, the most important activity in this industry was electroplating. Electroplating entailed adhering a thin metal coating to an object by immersing it into an electrically charged solvent containing the dissolved plating metal. Metals commonly used in plating included copper, nickel, chromium, zinc, lead, cadmium, tin, brass, and bronze, as well as precious metals such as gold, silver, and platinum. Electroplating served a number of functions, such as protecting from corrosion and wear, decoration, and electrical shielding.

Alessandro Volta's creation of the battery in 1800 first made electroplating possible. Commercial electroplating began around 1840. Before the development of commercial nickel plating in the 1910s, the metals most commonly used for plating were silver, gold, and brass. Nickel plating tarnished and developed green corrosion, but that problem was eradicated in the late 1920s with the development of commercially practical chromium plating. This was a key development in the history of the industry, especially in regard to plating applications for the automobile and appliance industries. Though nonmetallic materials had been electroplated since the mid-nineteenth century, they became increasingly important for the industry after the 1963 development of ABS plastic, which lent itself to electroplating.

Of increasing importance for the industry in the 1980s and early 1990s was plating utilized as electrical shielding, particularly for the plastic housings of computers. The Crown City Plating Company, based in El Monte, California, developed the electroless process used for such shielding around 1970.

The solvents used to dissolve plating metals often were highly toxic. Cyanide, for example, was a commonly used solvent. In addition to being one of the most toxic of commonly found pollutants, its toxicity was heightened when mixed with certain plating metals. Cyanide also interfered with water treatment processes and formed a toxic gas when converted to an acid. Of the plating metals, cadmium, chromium, and lead were the most problematic. The increasing regulation of the use of such solvents had a great impact on the industry's development.

Key statutes affecting the industry included the Federal Water Pollution Control Act Amendments of 1972, the Resource Conservation and Recovery Act of 1976, the Clean Water Act of 1977, and the Comprehensive Environmental Response, Compensation, and Liability Act of 1980, better known as Superfund.

The number of enforcement actions by the Environmental Protection Agency (EPA) increased steadily from the late 1980s into the 1990s. In 1996 a record number of criminal enforcement actions were taken by the EPA. In that year criminal fines amounted to more than double the previous record. A record 262 criminal cases were referred by the EPA to the Department of Justice in 1996, and $76.7 million in criminal fines were assessed. Total criminal, civil, and administrative fines and penalties in 1996 were the highest in EPA history, totaling $173 million, indicating that pollution abatement would continue to be a key issue for the industry.

The significant effect of environmental and safety regulations on the industry was suggested by the aims of one of the industry's trade organizations. Founded in 1955 and located in Chicago, the National Association of Metal Finishers (NAMF) had 850 members in the late 1990s who were managing executives of firms in the industry. Often committees of the NAMF were devoted to issues of regulation.

Difficulties facing the industry from the 1970s through the 1990s included increasing production costs, excessive competition, and a shortage of experienced employees. Excessive competition had a number of implications, one of which was the relatively slow rate of productivity growth in the industry. From 1958 to 1974 the value added per production worker hour more than quadrupled for computers and related machines and doubled for motor vehicles and parts and household laundry equipment. During the same period, the metal finishing industry experienced only a 17 percent increase. As of 1994, the value added per production worker in the plating industry was only half that of the average of the manufacturing sector as a whole.

A 1992 study of the industry's future concluded that development of the industry lay in the nature of environmental regulations as well as future demand for more sophisticated finishes. As parts to be finished became larger and more complex, finishing processes also became more complex.

Demand for the industry's products was dependent on the demand for durable goods and thus dependent on growth in the manufacturing sector at large. Growth and profitability also were dependent on the creation of environmentally safe manufacturing techniques. The pace of technical change was brisk entering the 1990s, which suggested that the industry could meet environmental and safety regulations in a cost-effective manner.

The automotive industry represented a significant end-consumer of this industry's products. From the 1970s through approximately 1985, the plating industry enjoyed brisk sales of zincrometal (zinc priming applied to the unexposed side of cold-rolled steel) to the auto industry. In the mid- to late-1980s 1.2 million tons zincrometal were sold annually. However, in the mid-1980s the auto industry began to use electrogalvanized steel, which was treated right at the steel mill instead of being processed by a separate company. In 1998 all transportation industries (including automotive) bought only 470,000 tons of coated steel coil (including zincrometal.)

In the 1990s capital investment in the industry was very low compared to the average capital expenditure in all other manufacturing industries. In 1994 the average investment per establishment in the metal finishing industry was 83 percent below the national average for manufacturing industries. This enabled relatively easy entry into the industry and accounted for the large number of small, often family-owned, private firms.

The ease of entry into the industry made for highly competitive conditions in which small, independent companies were positioned between large suppliers of finishing machinery and materials and the large corporations for which they provided services. This meant relatively low profits for small manufacturers.

Smaller firms' dilemma of keeping abreast of innovative techniques was exacerbated by their need to adhere to a host of environmental regulations. This problem was deepened by the less sophisticated control procedures many smaller companies were forced to utilize due to lower cost. For example, quality finishes could only be obtained through highly sophisticated processes often unavailable to smaller firms.

One bright spot for smaller companies arose from the EPA's own broad mandate to regulate industry with an overstretched budget. In 1995 the EPA proposed deferring Clean Air Act operating permit requirements for non-major sources in three industries, one being the decorative chromium electroplating and chromium anodizing segment. The EPA recognized the difficulty small businesses had in meeting the requirements and the massive assistance they would require from regulators. The deferral would last for five years; certain electroplating operations would be exempted permanently.

The value of the industry's shipments in 1996 was an estimated $5.7 billion, up from $2.7 billion in 1982. There were just under 3,200 firms in the industry in 1996, 34 percent of which had 20 or more employees, up from 26 percent in 1982. In 1994 average firm size in the industry as measured by production workers per establishment was 50 percent lower than that of the typical manufacturing industry.

CURRENT CONDITIONS

The industry capitalized on studies suggesting trends that its products could address. For example, a late-1990s study revealed that corrosion (or expenses incurred repairing corrosion) amounted to approximately 4 percent of the gross national product. Statistics such as this worked in the industry's favor, as plating represented one of the main means of combating corrosion. Similarly, the

nickel used in the industry was thought to be carcinogenic until studies showed this to be false (one non-industry study concluded that potential carcinogenicity was "not able to be determined," according to J. Kelly Mowry in the industry magazine *Finishing Line*.)

INDUSTRY LEADERS

Iselin, New Jersey-based Engelhard Corp. maintained a commanding lead in the industry with 1999 sales of $40.5 billion. Following far behind was Sequa Corp. of New York City, with 1998 sales of $1.8 billion, up from sales of $1.6 billion in 1997 and of $1.5 billion in 1996. Minneapolis-based Vincent Metal Goods generated $560 million in 1997 sales, the most recent report available from Infotrac. Siegel-Roberts Inc. of St. Louis garnered $487 million in its fiscal year ended July 31, 1998. Rounding out the top five was Material Sciences Corp. of Elk Grove Village, Illinois, with $469 million in sales for its fiscal year ended February 28, 1999.

WORKFORCE

The industry employed 79,700 workers in 1995, up from 62,000 in 1982. The industry was relatively labor-intensive, having an average of only 33 percent of the investment per production worker as that of the manufacturing sector as a whole. Annual hours worked by production workers in the industry were about the same as those averaged by production workers in a typical manufacturing industry, while hourly wages were 21 percent lower. For workers in the industry, continued competition brought uncertainty, but increases in employment for most job positions were predicted through the year 2005 for the overall metal services industry. In 1997 the industry employed nearly 75,000 people, 78 percent of whom were production workers whose average hourly wage was $11.42.

RESEARCH AND TECHNOLOGY

Throughout the 1990s many significant technical developments in the industry arose in response to environmental regulation. The Torrington Company of Connecticut demonstrated a method to recover cadmium and chromium from electroplating rinsewaters. In one study using the ion exchange method, both cadmium and cyanide were removed, sometimes to below detection levels, while the pH of the rinsewater remained constant. Following the exchange, cadmium was recovered and regenerated, while less cyanide was necessary for wastewater treatment.

In the 1990s pollution prevention methods often took the path of reducing the need to coat or plate at all, sometimes by using coating-free materials such as titanium, reinforced plastics, weathering steel, and aluminum alloys. In addition, alternatives to traditional coating systems were found in emerging technologies. Studies found promise in nonelectroplating methods, including electron beam-cured coatings, super-critical carbon dioxide coating systems, and radiation-induced thermally cured coatings.

Some of the most promising technologies, such as the dry application of metal powders, were classified in **SIC 3479: Metal Coating & Allied Services.** The success of such techniques was expected to lead to a shift in production away from the plating industry.

Sandia National Laboratories in Albuquerque developed methods for gold-plating onto microelectronic devices that did not use cyanide. Metal-ceramic coatings were substituted for cadmium coatings for certain high-priced parts. Handy and Harman Electronic Metals Corporation, the seventh-largest firm in the industry, developed a formable silver-tin oxide as a replacement for silver-cadmium oxide for coating electrical contacts. Previously used silver-tin oxides were not formable, so the process of applying them was more labor-intensive and costly. In addition to their reduced environmental hazard, silver-tin oxides were also more highly conductive.

GE Research and Development devised a method for nickel-plating plastics to shield computer housings. This process did not use chromium, unlike Crown City Plating's process, and was applied with a water-based solution.

FURTHER READING

American Electroplaters and Surface Finishers Society. "Corrosion Principles & Control via Metal Finishing," 22 January 2000. Available from http://www.aesf.org/newsflash.htm.

Arnett, Harold E., and Donald N. Smith. *The Metal Finishing Industry: A Framework for Success.* Ann Arbor, MI: University of Michigan, 1977.

Bassett, Susan M. "Title V Permitting Delayed for Some Non-Major Sources." *Pollution Engineering,* 1 March 1996.

Darnay, Arsen J., ed. *Manufacturing USA: Industry Analysis, Statistics, and Leading Companies,* 5th ed. Detroit: Gale Research, 1996.

Haflich, Frank. "Coaters target auto market." *American Metal Market,* 21 April 1999.

———. "USS-Posco Expansion Spurs Further Growth on West Coast." *American Metal Market,* 6 August 1996.

———. "USS-Posco Weighs $100M Tin Upgrade." *American Metal Market,* 6 December 1996.

Jaszczak, Sandra, ed. *Encyclopedia of Associations.* 32nd ed. Detroit: Gale Research, 1997.

Mowry, J. Kelly. "NAMF Update—Nickel Controls." *Finishing Line,* April/May 1999.

Park, Kyung Hee. "Analysts Warn Depressed Prices of Steel Will Keep Posco Down." *Asian Wall Street Journal Weekly,* 28 October 1996.

"Plunge in Profits for Pohang Iron." *New York Times,* 5 March 1997.

Quinn, Barbara. "EPA Does Pollution Prevention Research." *Pollution Engineering,* 1 September 1995.

———. "Looking at Technology We Already Own." *Pollution Engineering,* 1 January 1996.

———. "The Surface Coating Industries Try on New Coats." *Pollution Engineering,* 1 February 1995.

"Sequa Corp. of Chester, S.C., Reports Higher Profits." *Knight-Ridder/Tribune Business News,* 26 February 1998.

U.S. Census Bureau. *Survey of Manufacturers,* 10 February 2000. Available from http://www.census.gov/prod/www/abs/97ecmani.html.

U.S. Environmental Protection Agency. *Enforcement Records Set for 1996,* 25 February 1997. Available from http://www.epa.gov/docs/PressReleases/1997/February/Day-26/pr-1009.html.

SIC 3479

COATING, ENGRAVING, AND ALLIED SERVICES, NOT ELSEWHERE CLASSIFIED

This industry includes establishments primarily engaged in performing the following types of services on metals, for the trade: (1) enameling, lacquering, and varnishing metal products; (2) hot dip galvanizing of mill sheets, plates and bars, castings, and formed products fabricated of iron and steel; hot dip coating such items with aluminum, lead, or zinc; retinning cans and utensils; (3) engraving, chasing, and etching jewelry, silverware, notarial, and other seals, and other metal products for purposes other than printing; and (4) other metal services, not elsewhere classified. Also included in this industry are establishments that perform these types of activities on their own account on purchased metals or formed products. Establishments that both manufacture and finish products were classified according to the products.

NAICS CODE(S)

339914 (Costume Jewelry and Novelty Manufacturing)
339911 (Jewelry (including Precious Metal) Manufacturing)
339912 (Silverware and Plated Ware Manufacturing)
332812 (Metal Coating, Engraving, and Allied Services (except Jewelry and Silverware) to Manufacturing)

INDUSTRY SNAPSHOT

The larger firms that participated in this industry were often more diversified in their finishing activities, while independents tended to specialize in one or two types of finishing. During the 1950s and 1960s, there was a tendency for manufacturing firms to set up their own finishing operations. With the increased environmental regulation of the industry beginning in the 1970s, many manufacturing firms opted to subcontract for finishing services, thus getting around the added costs of waste treatment. Parts to be finished were typically shipped to finishing firms by their customers, after which they were shipped back. Since the mid-1970s, about three-fourths of a finishing firm's business came from within a 50-to-75-mile radius of the firm. Since finishers needed to be near their customers, their operations were located in the same areas as producers of durable goods.

In the 1990s, the tendency was once again for manufacturing firms to undertake finishing operations, often integrating production and finishing processes. In 1997, the industry consisted of 2,207 establishments. The value of product shipments in 1997 was $8.5 billion, up from the $7.0 billion of 1995 and the $4.9 billion shipped in 1990.

ORGANIZATION AND STRUCTURE

Just over one-half of the output of this industry consisted of the application of organic coatings such as paints, varnishes, and lacquers. Next to the application of organic coatings, galvanizing was the largest activity in the industry, making up 22 percent of output. Metal coating and allied services, not specified by kind, made up 21 percent of output; and the remaining 6 percent consisted of engraved and etched products.

The industry is served by the National Association of Metal Finishers, located in Chicago, Illinois. Founded in 1955, the Association had 850 members in the mid-1990s, who typically are managing executives of firms in the industry. The American Galvanizers Association (AGA) also serves the industry. Founded in 1935, it has 150 members, who are galvanizers, material and equipment suppliers, and service companies in the industry.

BACKGROUND AND DEVELOPMENT

The value of product shipments in 1995 was approximately $7.0 billion, up from $4.9 billion in 1990. Growth of output and employment stagnated entering the 1990s, but profit rates remained close to the average for the period 1982 to 1992. The industry benefited from growth in the use of galvanized steel and in the use of alternatives to electroplating that it offered.

The industry's primary focus is the application of coatings including paint, lacquer, and varnish. Although metals had been coated by like means since ancient times, their modern application was dependent on the development of phosphating as a surface preparation. Phosphating involved treating a metal, usually steel, with phosphoric acid. This greatly improved the adhesion and durability of coatings. Phosphating alone was also used as an anti-corrosive coating on steel in conditions where the potential for corrosion was not high. Although phosphating was developed in the 1860s, treatment times were exceedingly

long until iron filings were added to the phosphoric acid bath after 1906 (following Thomas Watts Coslett's patent), shortening treatment time to about two-and-one-half hours. The treatment time was shortened to ten minutes by the addition of copper salts in 1929, after which the process became generally used as a surface preparation for organic coatings. More recent developments lowered treatment times to just five seconds.

Galvanizing is the process of dipping steel or iron into a bath of molten zinc. The zinc coating served as a corrosion prohibitor, and was applied to structural parts, sheeting, pipe, various containers, and hardware. During this process, the metal to be coated was immersed until it reached the same temperature as the bath (typically 1,562 degrees Fahrenheit). Thus, the process could not be used on springs or other objects in which desirable properties would be lost by such exposure to heat. Since uniformity of thickness was not readily controllable in hot dip processes, galvanizing was limited to applications in which such uniformity was not required. Electroplating with zinc was sometimes also referred to as galvanizing or electrogalvanizing. This process was done cold, and could assure high uniformity of thickness, getting around the above-mentioned problems.

As with all metal-coating processes, it was vital that parts were thoroughly cleaned before being galvanized. This typically involved treating the parts to be galvanized in an acid bath, after which they were fluxed, a process that generally used hydrochloric acid. The wastes produced by such pre-treatment were toxic, as were the solvents used in the organic coatings processes. The minimization of such wastes continued to be central issues for the industry, as did the development of alternative solvents.

The industry received a boost in the early 1990s with the Intermodal Surface Transportation Efficiency Act of 1991, which required that all highways, bridges, and tunnels built with federal funds take into account the costs of materials over their life-cycles. This strongly favored the use of galvanized metals. The American Galvanizers Association estimated early in the decade that use of galvanized steel would double through the 1990s, largely as a result of increased use for highways, bridges, and wastewater treatment systems.

The industry was also strongly effected at the end of the 20th century by increased concerns about the environment. The most promising of the environmentally friendlier alternatives to electroplating were the application of metal powders and vacuum deposition, processes that were projected to become increasingly important. Thus, the effects of environmental regulation provided substantial benefits to the industry, and growth prospects appeared promising. From the perspective of the firms, the question remained whether plating or coating firms could more readily diversify into these technologies.

The relative ease of entry into the industry made for highly competitive conditions in which small independents were sandwiched between the large suppliers of finishing machinery and materials and the large firms for which they provided services. This meant relatively low profits for independents. Profit rates varied greatly among firms in the industry. Taking rates of return on equity, a firm ranking at the median had less than half the profitability of a firm ranking at the upper quartile.

Theoretical knowledge, as opposed to empirical knowledge, rapidly increased in importance in the 1990s. Equipment and material suppliers developed many new techniques. Thus, smaller firms were able to obtain some of the same innovations as larger firms. Nonetheless, given the greater purchasing power of the captive and large independent firms, suppliers allocated a disproportionate amount of their research and technical support to such firms.

Another issue inhibiting investment by smaller firms in more capital-intensive techniques was that, unlike large captive firms, they were less able to absorb the losses resulting from excess capacity in the face of an economic downturn. Because the greater profitability of the more successful firms could be used to finance techniques that were more productive and sophisticated, the gap between large captive firms and smaller independents was likely to remain, if not widen.

CURRENT CONDITIONS

The industry continues to be strongly influenced by environmental factors, and innovative techniques continue to effect finishing processes. With shipments valued at $8.5 billion in 1997, the industry showed steady growth from the beginning through the end of the 1990s.

Starting in early 1997 and continuing into the 2000s, the National Metal Finishing Strategic Goals Program allied the industry with the Environmental Protection Agency and other environmentalists to cooperate in creating blueprints of how best to solve the environmental challenges facing the industry. Instead of working as adversaries, the groups worked together to devise and implement realistic guidelines for issues such as the storage, recycling and disposal of wastewater treatment sludges. Often, the industry had better solutions to the problems than the EPA or environmentalists could suggest, since the industry understood its own processes best. In this sense, the Goals Program sought to move "beyond compliance" in ways that benefited the industry and the EPA and satisfied environmentalists.

INDUSTRY LEADERS

Leading the industry in overall sales was H.B. Fuller Co. of St. Paul, Minnesota, with revenues of $13.5 billion for its fiscal year ending November 30, 1998. However, in 1999 Fuller divested itself of its powder coatings business, thus exiting this industry. Paint giant Sherwin-Williams Co. of Cleveland placed next in this industry with 1998 sales of $4.9 billion. LTV Steel Company Inc., also of Cleveland, followed close on its heels with sales of $4.4 billion in 1997.

Chicago-based Morton International Inc. generated sales of $2.3 billion for its fiscal year ended June 30, 1997. At that time, Morton was poised for growth, with $750 million in capital from the spin-off of its air-bag division to Autoliv AB of Sweden. However, Morton went on an acquisition binge, depleting its coffers to $156 million within one year. This strategy did not succeed as planned, and in 1999 Morton was acquired by Philadelphia-based chemical company Rohm & Haas for $4.9 billion in cash and stock.

WORKFORCE

The number of industry employees increased from 44,100 in 1990 to an estimated 49,700 in 1996, 38,500 of which were production workers earning approximately $11.58 per hour. In 1997, the number of production workers increased again, to 44,821; these workers earned an average $12.21 per hour. The total workforce in 1997 swelled to 56,484.

RESEARCH AND TECHNOLOGY

As with the metal-plating industry, a number of innovations in the metal-coating industry were motivated by increasingly pressing environmental regulations. For the process of stripping coatings from rejected parts, blasting with plastic particles was seen as a viable alternative to the more toxic methods of chemical stripping and incineration. In the early 1990s, Whirlpool Corp. installed a pre-treating line in its Evanston, Illinois, plant that made use of a safer alternative to traditional phosphating. The line used a chrome-free rinse and cleaners that lessened the production of heavy metal wastes. The new line also improved the quality of coatings and consumed less energy.

New developments in the deposition of metal coatings were expected to cause a shift away from electroplating to alternative methods, such as new forms of vacuum deposition. This process involved reducing pressure in a closed container to produce a vacuum in which pure metals could be vaporized at low temperatures and then allowed to condense on a surface. Laboratory tests of new vacuum methods produced high-quality coatings with fast coating times. Vacuum coating also had the significant advantage that it did not generate the toxic sludges of electroplating processes. Another technology of increasing importance was the application of metal powders by spraying or through the use of centrifugal force. As with vacuum deposition, such applications of metal powders had the significant advantage that they did not produce toxic sludges.

While the initial costs of pollution abatement technologies may have been prohibitive to some firms, a number of these technologies could lower production costs. The BASE Corp. reported that pollution abatement measures at two of its coating plants saved it $1.3 million in the early 1990s, and that the payback period after initial investments ranged from 15 to 20 months. New technologies in the application of powder coatings made them not only an environmentally friendlier, but also a cost-effective alternative to electroplating.

FURTHER READING

Darnay, Arsen J., ed. *Manufacturing USA.* 5th ed. Detroit: Gale Research, 1996.

Infotrac Company Profiles, 1 January 2000. Available from http://web7.infotrac.galegroup.com.

Izenberg, Jerry. "Paint, Coating Demand to Hit $18 Billion in U.S." *Rubber World,* December 1996.

National Association of Metal Finishers. "Strategic Goals Effort Works for Industry." *Legislative Line,* April/May 1999. Available at http://www.namf.org/nwsltr/99AprMay/99aprmaylegline.htm.

Snyder, David. "Salt in Chicago's Wounds: Why'd Morton Have to Go?" *Crain's Chicago Business,* 15 February 1999.

U.S. Census Bureau. *1997 Economic Census—Manufacturing.* Washington: GPO, 2000.

Walsh, Kerri. "Fuller Beats Analysts' Estimates." *Chemical Week,* 29 September 1999.

SIC 3482

SMALL ARMS AMMUNITION

This industry includes establishments primarily engaged in manufacturing ammunition for small arms having a bore of 30 millimeters (1.18 inches) or less. Establishments primarily engaged in manufacturing ammunition, except for small arms, are classified in **SIC 3483: Ammunition, Except for Small Arms;** those manufacturing blasting and detonating caps and safety fuses are classified in **SIC 2892: Explosives;** and those manufacturing fireworks are classified in **SIC 2899: Chemicals and Chemical Preparations, Not Elsewhere Classified.**

NAICS CODE(S)

332992 (Small Arms Ammunition Manufacturing)

INDUSTRY SNAPSHOT

The late 1990s were marked by increased sales for small arms and small arms ammunition manufacturers, following a sluggish period in the mid-decade. Ongoing controversy over gun laws helped boost sales and interest in shooting sports, as did concerns about self-defense. The possibility of power outages, food shortages, and communication failures as a result of computers turning over to the year 2000 (the "Y2K bug") spurred large numbers of first-time gun buyers, closing the century with a sharp spike in arms and ammunition sales.

Specialized, niche products helped lead the industry out of its short-term slump, including top-end high-performance ammunition, "cowboy-action" loads, and light recoiling ammunition targeted for the growing market segment of women gun consumers. A strong overall economy gave gun owners both money and leisure time for pursuing shooting sports.

ORGANIZATION AND STRUCTURE

Ammunition producers manufacture both cartridges and shells. The two types of cartridges used in rifles and pistols are rimfire and centerfire. Rimfire cartridges are comprised of a soft lead bullet, a case most often made of brass, and the smokeless propellant (powder). The priming compound is spun into the rim of the case, and, when the firearm's firing pin strikes and indents the rim of the cartridge, the priming mixture ignites and in turn ignites the propellant—hence the name "rimfire." Centerfire cartridges differ from rimfire cartridges in that a separate primer is seated in the base or head of the cartridge. When struck by the firing pin, the primer ignites the propellant via the flash hole in the base of the cartridge—hence the name "centerfire."

Prior to the Civil War, both large- and small-bore rifle and pistol cartridges were rimfire. In the post-Civil War period, however, more powerful cartridges began to be developed. These cartridges reached subsequently higher pressures and thus required case heads too thick to be indented by a firing pin. The centerfire ignition system solved this problem, and was still being used in the same configuration in the 1990s for high-pressure cartridges. Shotgun shells are also centerfire but are made up of a paper or plastic cylinder with a brass base or head. The shell is filled with powder followed by a cupped plastic wad filled with birdshot or much larger buckshot. While birdshot may be made of either lead or steel, buckshot is always made of lead. Federal law mandates that all duck and goose hunting be done with steel shot. It has been found that wildfowl accidentally ingesting spent lead shot while feeding are subject to lead poisoning. Shotgun shells may also be loaded with a single heavy slug, which in various configurations is made of lead or a lead alloy. Slugs are used both in law enforcement and for hunting big game such as deer. In addition to cartridges and shells, the small arms ammunition industry also includes the manufacture of BBs and pellets, which are most commonly fired from spring- or pneumatic-powered pistols and rifles.

Rimfire cartridges were typically .22 caliber and used in rifles and pistols designated "small-bore". Their share of small arms ammunition shipments increased by just over 85 percent from 1992 to 1997, accounting for 13 percent of total shipments. In 1997, centerfire rifle cartridges showed the largest decline in that period, falling from the top to the fifth position among the seven categories of ammunition; after accounting for 21 percent of market share in 1992, these cartridges garnered only 12 percent just five years later. Centerfire pistol cartridges, including those cartridges such as the .44 Magnum that could be interchanged between pistols and rifles, increased market share by 26 percent by 1997, second in sales only to shotgun shells, which accounted for about 22 percent of total industry shipments. Shipments of industrial shells and cartridges, airgun ammunition, and percussion caps, as a group, fell markedly—from 18 percent of the total in 1992 to just over 10 percent in 1997. Other major sectors of the industry in 1997 included components (wads, shot cases, bullets, and bullet jackets), with 19 percent of shipments, and primers, with 3 percent of shipments.

Consumers and Trade Representatives. Most of the ammunition made by manufacturers in this industry is sold to private consumers: 44 percent in 1992, up from 40 percent of industry sales in the 1980s. Sales to the federal government for military and other uses accounted for about 19 percent of sales in 1992, a slight decline from 20 percent in the 1980s. Exports, the third largest category for sales in the 1980s, jumped to second place in the early 1990s, increasing from 10 percent of sales to 28 percent. State and local government, including police and corrections officers, accounted for nearly 9 percent of sales in 1992, a slight increase from the previous decade.

There are three industry and consumer groups that represent ammunition interests in the United States. Most ammunition industry executives are affiliated with the National Shooting Sports Federation (NSSF), which promotes hunting and target shooting. The NSSF's sister organization, the Sporting Arms and Ammunition Manufacturers Institute (SAAMI), sets voluntary national standards for ammunition and firearm design. These groups rarely participate in political lobbying efforts, although ammo producers have traditionally donated money to support game populations and preserve hunting areas. The third and best-known organization, the National Rifle Association (NRA), is heavily involved in lobbying efforts, most of which are of interest to ammo manufacturers and users. As of 1996, only 12 percent of all hunters, however, belonged to this organization.

An Obscure Industry. In 1996, the ammunition industry was about 70 percent as large as the entire firearms industry that it complements. The comparably high-profile firearm industry receives large amounts of press and is often the target of state and federal regulatory initiatives. Ammunition makers, however, operate in relative obscurity, with little publicity, regulation, or outside analysis of the industry.

One reason that the industry has such a low profile is that most of its products are homogenous, resulting in a commodity-like business environment that is not dynamic. In addition, the largest producers in the industry are owned by massive conglomerates that view ammo operations as relatively small sideline businesses.

BACKGROUND AND DEVELOPMENT

The use of gunpowder to propel projectiles dates back to fourteenth century Europe. Iron darts with brass fittings were mounted on shafts, much like crossbow arrows of the time. The shaft held the gunpowder and was wrapped with leather to keep gases from the burning powder from leaking out of the sides of the shaft. During the fourteenth, fifteenth, and sixteenth centuries, armies experimented with a variety of projectiles. Gunpowder was used to fire rocks in the 1300s, though metal balls became the ammunition of choice by the 1400s. Hot shot, or heated metal balls, added a deadly twist to this technique.

The advent of rifled barrels following the American Revolution created a demand for new types of bullets. Although barrels were being rifled as early as the 1500s in Germany, it was not until the late 1700s that this manufacturing technique became popular. Long spiral grooves or rifling cut into a barrel's inner surface causes a fired projectile to spin on its axis, imparting ballistic stability and greatly increasing the firearm's accuracy and range. Because elongated projectiles benefited most from the rifling technique, elongated bullets grew in popularity throughout the nineteenth century, gradually replacing the solid lead ball. All pistols and rifles manufactured in the 1990s have rifled barrels; shotgun barrels, however, are not rifled.

Muskets, which fire rounded lead balls and similar projectiles, were dominant in North American until the end of the Civil War. Westward expansion following the Civil War, however, created a market for heavier and more powerful firearms. Buffalo hunters needed long range rifles, and settlers on lonely farms needed repeating firearms such as the Winchester lever action rifles. The cartridge technology used in the 1990s originated in this era and consisted of an elongated bullet enclosing powder and primer in a brass cartridge. The cartridge was powerful, virtually oblivious to weather, and could be used in repeating firearms. This technological breakthrough quickly spelled the end of the muzzle-loading Kentucky rifle of Daniel Boone fame.

Winchester rifles, Colt revolvers, and other famous weaponry created markets for a variety of new ammunition during the westward U.S. expansion. Widespread use of smokeless gunpowder, which was perfected in the late 1880s, hastened ammunition industry growth. Most importantly, advances in ammunition and firearms during both World Wars broadened the scope of the industry to include specialized ammunition for automatic weapons and other new firearms.

In addition to a huge demand for ammunition by the military, ammunition producers in the United States enjoyed a large market for hunting products throughout the twentieth century. Not counting times of war, hunters remained the largest consumers of all types of small arms ammunition throughout the nineteenth and twentieth centuries.

Industry Conditions from 1970 to 1996. Following steady growth in commercial sales during the first half of the twentieth century and throughout the 1960s, the general public's demand for ammo began to slip in the 1970s. Although military consumption provided sporadic boosts in sales, the industry's core market, hunters, stagnated.

Stalled growth in hunting impeded the expansion of profits for some manufacturers throughout the 1970s and early 1980s. After Ronald Reagan was elected to office in 1980, however, an increase in ammo sales to the military boosted revenues. Profits were further buoyed by an increase in target shooting. By the mid-1980s, the military consumed nearly 30 percent of industry production, and handgun and target shooters had become the primary growth market for manufacturers.

To boost profits, small ammo producers began raising productivity, selling through new marketing channels, and offering new niche products. In the 1980s, manufacturers invested an average of $25 million per year in production facilities, a very low investment compared to most other industries. Despite that low figure, industry employment fell from about 7.4 million to 6.3 million workers during the decade, even though overall production increased.

Winchester, for instance, installed computer-controlled cartridge loading machines that allowed the company to produce 9 mm cartridges and other popular ammo at a rate of up to 450 units per minute. Despite industry efforts at low-cost, high-volume production in some areas, most manufacturers still used some very old production techniques. Even at Winchester factories, many low-volume products in 1993 were still loaded at rates of 40 to 60 per minute using machines the company acquired in 1931.

Along with moderate productivity gains, producers were benefited from new marketing channels in the early 1990s. Discount stores, such as Wal-Mart and Kmart, accounted for 30 to 50 percent of commercial sales by 1992. In addition, mail order catalog sales were becoming an increasingly important channel of distribution. One of the largest ammunition catalogers, AcuSport Corp. of Ohio, increased mail order sales from $30 million in 1988 to over $75 million by 1992.

As the mid-1990s approached, an area of potential growth for industry competitors was the export market. Productivity gains realized in the 1980s allowed U.S. producers to stem an influx of cheap import ammunition from Brazil and the Far East during that decade. Exports already accounted for more than 10 percent of total U.S. production in the early 1990s. Foreign producers had captured less than 20 percent of the U.S. ammo market by 1992, and import growth seemed to have stabilized.

Increasing Regulation. Despite measures aimed at controlling the manufacture and sales of guns during the 1990s, the small arms ammunition industry remained loosely regulated. Congress, with the support of the NRA, had succeeded in banning certain types of "cop-killer" bullets, designed to penetrate bulletproof vests. That ban represented the only piece of legislation ever passed to directly limit the sale of small arms ammunition.

Senator Daniel Patrick Moynihan (New York) proposed legislation in the early 1990s to ban the sale of 9 mm, .25 caliber, and .32 caliber ammunition, which together accounted for 50 percent of the bullets fired at police officers. He also tried to pass legislation making many pistol cartridges prohibitively expensive. Moynihan was unsuccessful in both attempts. Critics argued that such laws could not be enforced and would have a negligible effect on crime. Nevertheless, the Clinton administration had indicated support for similar types of legislation.

In 1994, President Clinton signed the Brady Bill, which called for a waiting period for handgun purchases and required local police authorities to conduct an investigation before issuing a permit to purchase a handgun. Because of a general fear of crime and social and civil unrest, however, the sale of handguns and those military style assault rifles that were still legal skyrocketed along with ammunition for these arms. Many such firearms and ammunition were in short supply, causing a booming business among gun stores, distributors, importers, and manufacturers.

Spurred by 1994 Republican majorities in the U.S. House and Senate, pro-gun grass roots organizations began active campaigns to promote gun safety and shooting activities. In an attempt to increase its membership of young males, the 4-H Clubs of America formed a Shooting Sport Committee, which developed a shooting sports program in cooperation with various manufacturing interests. By mid-1996, the program had spread to chapters in 38 states. The Boy Scouts of America revived many of their shooting sports programs and began laying the groundwork for a nationwide Young Hunter Education Challenge. The National Rifle Association continued its "Eddie Eagle" firearms safety program and played a major role in "right to carry" legislation at the state and local level. In 1996, South Carolina became the 31st state to pass such legislation.

CURRENT CONDITIONS

Driven by fears of the Y2K bug and the threat of increased regulation by the federal government, sales of small arms and small arms ammunition boomed in the late 1990s, after a mid-decade slump following a sales boom in 1994. *The Wall Street Journal* offered anecdotal evidence of huge sales increases in 1999: The small Los Angeles manufacturer U.S.A. Magazine—widely known to gun control proponents for its controversial products and marketing tactics—predicted a 50 percent increase in sales over its $10 million in 1998. Retailers reported increases in 1999 sales of up to 112 percent, reflecting a "stampede" of first-time gun buyers.

Moderate growth began in 1997, as wholesalers, retailers, and buyers began to deplete excess inventory following the 1994 boom. In 1998 sellers and consumers finally needed new supplies, continuing the upswing. Targeted marketing and consumer demand for more and more specialized and technologically advanced products also enhanced sales.

Despite slow growth in the area of hunting, the strong economy of the 1990s, changing demographics, and increased leisure time all combined to spur sales of top-end hunting ammunition. Richard Carreon, vice president of sales for Federal Cartridge Corp., was quoted in *Shooting Industry:* "About 46 percent of the hunters today are 35 to 54 years old and have relatively high disposable incomes coupled with a high degree of free time. . . . They don't necessarily want the best deal on .30-'06 hunting ammunition, for instance. They are often technology-oriented and are looking for anything that will give them an edge in the field. Hence the very strong sales of virtually every company's high-end, or premium hunting ammo lines."

So-called "cowboy-action" ammo also contributed to sales, marking one success in the gun industry's effort to project a more family friendly image. Cowboy-shooting competitions took place at Wild West festivals and often involved elaborate costumes; the sport appealed especially to women. Black Hills, Winchester, and Hornady were among leading manufacturers of dedicated cowboy-action ammunition.

Despite a ban on the controversial Black Talon expanding bullet made by Winchester, production of high-performance specialty ammo continued to be strong even during the sluggish mid-1990s, supported by a solid market in personal protection. Winchester replaced the Black Talon with another expanding bullet, the less controversial SXT; bullets popular with law enforcement, such as Federal's Hydra-Shok, were also popular with consumers. Personal protection also drove the market for gender-specific products. In 1998, Federal and Winchester were among small ammo producers who developed light recoiling ammunition, designed for women concerned with losing control of their handguns due to heavy recoil.

Throughout the 1990s, the industry continued to battle increased government restrictions, the threat of which contributed to the increase in sales for the industry. The Clinton Administration continued the work begun with the Brady Bill and the Assault Weapons Ban by pressing for further regulations and increased enforcement for current laws. On Nov. 30, 1998, the federal government approved the National Instant Criminal Background Check System, a national database containing names of individuals banned from buying weapons, a system required by the Brady Bill. Although frustrated retailers complained about delays and downed computer systems, the effect on sales was minimal.

An even more serious threat to the industry than legislative regulation was from judicial decisions. In early 1999, a federal jury in Brooklyn, New York, found that 15 of the nation's largest gun manufactures were engaged in negligent distribution and marketing of guns. "In the past, gun companies have defeated lawsuits charging that they made defective guns or objects that were inherently dangerous, but the Brooklyn suit was the first to take a broader perspective and charge them with negligent marketing," said a CNN report.

According to CNN, gun industry attorney James Dorr said that it was unfair to "hold the manufacturers of a lawful, legitimately sold product responsible for acts of outlaws who are totally outside their control. . . . The case is simply wrong." According to Adam Cohen, writing for *Time,* the Brooklyn case won because it was built on an innovative theory: "It argued that gunmakers should pay for injuries from illegally obtained guns because their distribution practices let guns fall into the hands of criminals. The suit exposed a netherworld of gun trafficking, including the 'straw buyers,' who resell guns to minors and convicted felons, and the 'iron pipeline' of illegal guns that flows from states with lax gun laws, like Georgia, to states with tough ones, like New York." Following the success of the Brooklyn suit, and a wave of large settlements in the big tobacco lawsuits of the late 1990s, several other cites initiated their own lawsuits or expressed the intent to consider doing so.

The gun industry also went to the courthouse to combat regulations proposed by Massachusetts Attorney General Scott Harshbarger. In early 1998, the American Shooting Sports Council filed suit in Boston to protest restrictions that it claimed were a "back-door approach to gun prohibition," according to Richard Feldman, ASSC's executive director.

The industry also found support from a Republican Congress generally hostile to further gun control. In 1999, the Senate ignored a request from the Clinton White House to close a gun show "loophole" allowing certain sales of guns without background checks, instead expanding the loophole to include pawnshops. Pro-gun activists also declared victory when, in early 2000, President Clinton announced a national gun enforcement initiative, seeking a record $280 million to step up enforcement of current gun laws. According the NRA, this approach to crime prevention follows the path pro-gun activists have recommended all along.

Industry watchers have long noted that gun control debates have generally had a positive impact on sales. *The Wall Street Journal* reported in 1999 that "the gun market historically booms whenever consumers perceive a threat that regulations will make it harder to obtain firearms or their accoutrements." Moreover, most attempts at regulating firearms leave ammunition untouched, while most attempts to regulate ammunition have failed. Ironically, the 1994 Assault Weapons Ban was a boon to makers of clips. According the *The Wall Street Journal*, "A customer who in years past might have bought an extra 18-round clip with his Glock, for a total of 36 rounds, today has to buy three extra clips to match that firepower."

The Internet proved to be a new and controversial venue for guns and ammunition sales. Online sales in general went through the roof in the late 1990s, but concerns about controlling sales caused some sellers to change course. eBay, the Internet's leading auction site, reversed its policy in 1999 and halted the sale of weapons and ammunition after sharp criticism. Because each state had its own laws regulating the sale of firearms, online sellers found it difficult to comply with regulations. Others have found the Internet to be a way to flout gun laws: U.S.A. Magazine used its website to advertise high-capacity clips that were illegal to manufacture, but not illegal to sell. Mass market retailers like Kmart and Wal-Mart, which accounted for up to half of sales in 1992, began to decrease their stock in guns and ammunition. In 1998, *Shooting Industry* pronounced, "The industry must find an outlet to replace sales lost in the mass market."

INDUSTRY LEADERS

In November 1997, Blount International Inc. acquired Federal Cartridge Company, the industry leader in sales, from Pentair Inc. According to a Blount press release, "The transaction was structured as an all-cash acquisition for approximately $112 million." In 1998, Federal's estimated sales were $90 million, double that of its nearest competitor, and the company employed nearly 1,000 workers. Other industry leaders included Crosman Corp., with $45 million in total sales; Day and Zimmerman, also with $45 million in sales; and Hornady, with $19 million in sales.

The other approximately 100 companies that made up the industry were comparatively small. Most of them employed fewer than 100 workers and had sales of less than $1 million per year. Several companies focused on producing specialty cartridges, construction industry products, and reused rounds.

WORKFORCE

Employment in the small arms ammunition industry dropped steadily throughout the 1990s, according to the U.S. Bureau of Labor Statistics. In 1997 there were 6,863 workers employed in the small arms ammunition industry, down from just over 10,000 15 years earlier. That figure was expected to decline to around 6,000 by 2000. Productivity gains, movement of production facilities to countries with cheaper labor, and stagnant domestic market growth were expected to contribute to this trend. Jobs for assemblers and fabricators, which represented 12 percent of industry positions, were forecast to fall by more than 10 percent. Other manufacturing positions, which accounted for the bulk of industry employment, were also expected to decline by 10 percent. General management and executive positions were likewise expected to drop by more than 10 percent. Workers already employed in the industry, however, continued to enjoy higher wages than workers in most other U.S. manufacturing industries in the 1990s.

FURTHER READING

Ayoob, Massad. "High-performance Ammo Still Sells." *Shooting Industry,* January 1997.

"Blount International, Inc. Completes Acquisition of Federal Cartridge Company from Pentair, Inc." Available from www.blount.com/FedAcq.html.

Buel, Stephen. "eBay Will End Online Auctions of Guns, Ammunition." *Knight-Ridder/Tribune Business News,* 22 February 1999.

Calandra, Bob. "State of Shooting Sports." *Sporting Goods Business,* 15 December 1997.

Carpenter, Kristin. "Checking Guns at the Door." *Sporting Goods Business,* 15 December 1998.

Cohen, Adam. "Where There's Smoke . . . The Siege of Big Tobacco and a Brooklyn Verdict Provide a Strategy to Take Aim at Gun Manufacturers." *Time,* 22 February 1999.

Darnay, Arsen J., ed. *Manufacturing USA.* 6th ed. Detroit: Gale Research, 1998.

"Gun Industry Finds Itself at Wrong End of the Barrel." Available from www.cnn.com/SPECIALS/1988/guns/overview.

Knox, Neal. "Knox's Notebook." *American Rifleman,* August 1996.

Parsons, Lisa. "Light Recoiling Ammo Ideal for Women." *Shooting Industry,* June 1998.

Parsons, Lisa. "Step Back in Time and Step Forward on your Bottom Line." *Shooting Industry,* July 1997.

"President Clinton and Vice President Gore: Working to Close the Gun Show Loophole." Available from www2.whitehouse .gove/WH/Work/042799.html.

Robinson, Jerome B. "The Next Generation of Shooters." *Field & Stream,* May 1996.

"Sarah Brady and Handgun Control Applaud President Clinton's National Gun Enforcement Initiative; Call on Gun Lobby to Support President's Plan." Available from www .handguncontrol.org/press.

Sundra, Jon R. "Ammo Makers Offer More Choices." *Shooting Industry,* May 1996.

Sundra, Jon R. "Blount Continues to Expand." *Shooting Industry,* August 1997.

U.S. Department of Commerce. *1997 Economic Census,* Washington: GPO, 1999.

"Targeting 1998 ammo sales." *Shooting Industry,* January 1998.

Thurman, Russ. "Industry Sues to Halt Gun Regulations." *Shooting Industry,* February 1998.

SIC 3483

AMMUNITION, EXCEPT FOR SMALL ARMS

This category covers establishments primarily engaged in manufacturing ammunition, not elsewhere classified, or in loading and assembling ammunition of more than 30 millimeters (or more than 1.18 inches), including component parts. This industry also includes establishments primarily engaged in manufacturing bombs, mines, torpedoes, grenades, depth charges, chemical warfare projectiles, and their component parts. Establishments primarily engaged in manufacturing small arms are classified in **SIC 3482: Small Arms Ammunition;** those manufacturing explosives are classified in **SIC 2892: Explosives;** and those manufacturing military pyrotechnics are classified in **SIC 2899: Chemicals and Chemical Preparations, Not Elsewhere Classified.**

NAICS CODE(S)

332993 (Ammunition (except Small Arms) Manufacturing)

According to the U.S. Census Bureau's *1997 Economic Census—Manufacturing,* 53 establishments operated in this category for part or all of 1997. Industrywide employment totaled 9,427 workers receiving a payroll of more than $379 million. Of these employees, 4,953 worked in production, putting in almost 9 million hours to

earn wages of almost $141 million. Overall shipments for the industry were valued at almost $1.5 billion.

St. Louis-based McDonell Aircraft Co. led the ammunitions industry with almost $8.2 billion in 1996 sales, according to the most recent records available on Infotrac databases. Olin Corp. of Norwalk, Connecticut was a distant second, with 1998 sales of more than $1.4 billion; closely following Olin, however, was Duchossois Industries Inc. of Elmhurst, Illinois, with 1998 sales of almost $1.3 billion. Alliant Techsystems Inc. of Hopkins, Minnesota, which generated almost $1.1 billion in sales for its fiscal year ended March 31, 1999, made news in late 1997 when it returned 1,200 acres of Native American property in the Black Hills of South Dakota to the Great Sioux Nation. Blount Industries rounded out the top five industry leaders with 1999 sales of $832 million.

About 45 percent of U.S. large ammunition industry output in the early 1990s was bombs. An additional 40 percent of production included miscellaneous bullets and other projectiles, casings, and components. Rockets made up the remaining 30 percent of shipments. Nearly 80 percent of all sales in 1991 were sold under U.S. government contract, mostly to the armed services. Another 15 percent of industry output was exported, and about 5 percent was consumed by various manufacturing sectors. Examples of manufacturing uses include demolition and mining.

The industry declined precipitously in the mid-1990s, in part because of the end of the Cold War and anticipation of military spending cuts. While the industry had employed 415,000 people in 1987, that number had dropped to 234,000 by 1992, and to only 12,000 in 1995—a decrease of almost 75 percent, according to the *1995 Census of Manufactures.* Those goods shipped in 1995 were valued at $2.034 billion, which was a slight increase over the 1994 figure of $2.008 billion, but still well below the $3.100 billion reported in the *1992 Census of Manufactures.*

Gunpowder was first employed to project missiles early in the fourteenth century, when large dart-like objects were propelled through the air during medieval battles. Darts were soon replaced by more reliable, rounded projectiles that were fired from cannon-type devices. Napoleon III released one of the first written works about artillery that included large ammunition in 1338, entitled *Etudes Sur . . . l'artillerie.* Stone shot was replaced by iron shot in the mid-1300s, because iron allowed greater penetration of stone walls. Soon thereafter, shells were invented that could be filled with gunpowder, fired from cannons, and made to explode. Rounded metal balls and shells remained the principal types of large ammunition from the fifteenth through the nineteenth century.

The large ammunition industry in the United States arose as a result of both internal and external military conflicts, particularly the Civil War and both World

Wars. Development of the rifled artillery barrel and smokeless gunpowder in the nineteenth century lead to the proliferation of elongated bullets and shells. This ammunition type dominated production throughout most of the twentieth century.

Although production of some large ammunition types peaked during World War II, the manufacture of other types of projectiles and explosives proliferated between 1950 and the late 1980s. Nuclear bombs and guided missiles, particularly, contributed to industry growth throughout the Cold War. By 1988, the industry employed about 26,000 workers and was producing a record $4.3 billion in shipments per year. During the Reagan presidency alone, the ammunition industry had grown from just $1.8 billion in shipments and about 16,000 workers.

The end of the Cold War in the late 1980s, punctuated by the demise of the Soviet Union, pummeled the large ammunition industry. As defense purchases plunged, sales dropped to $3.1 billion in 1990 and continued to plummet in 1991 and 1992. Likewise, industry employment crashed to about 14,500. Adding to employee woes were moderate increases in manufacturing productivity—the result of more than $600 million in capital investments by producers in the early and mid-1980s.

Entering the late 1990s, large ammunition manufacturers expected continued cuts in U.S. defense expenditures by the Clinton administration. Employment in every position in the industry was forecast to fall by 25 to 50 percent. For example, jobs for assemblers and fabricators, which accounted for a leading 14 percent of all workers, were expected to fall by 51 percent between 1990 and 2005. Even white-collar jobs were forecast to decline by more than 40 percent during that period. Companies were counting on export growth to partially offset domestic declines.

FURTHER READING

"Alliant Techsystems Returns Black Hills Tract to Sioux Tribe." *Knight-Ridder/Tribune Business News*, 25 December 1997.

1995 Census of Manufactures. Washington: Office of the Census, 1997.

U.S. Census Bureau. *1997 Economic Census—Manufacturing*. Available at http://www.census.gov/prod/ec97/97m3329g.pdf (2/12/00).

SIC 3484

SMALL ARMS

This category includes establishments primarily engaged in manufacturing small firearms or parts for small

firearms. Small firearms, defined as having a bore of 30 millimeters (mm) or less, include pistols, revolvers, rifles, shotguns, and submachine guns. This category also includes establishments that manufacture weapons with bores greater than 30 mm but that nevertheless are carried and employed by individuals, including grenade launchers and heavy field machine guns. Establishments primarily engaged in manufacturing artillery and mortars having bores greater than 30 mm are classified in **SIC 3489: Ordnance and Accessories, Not Elsewhere Classified.**

NAICS CODE(S)

332994 (Small Arms Manufacturing)

INDUSTRY SNAPSHOT

In 1999 there were nearly 400 gun makers in the United States, which together generated annual sales of $1.5 billion. Nearly all of the major gun manufacturers in the United States were privately owned companies; the only public company was Sturm, Ruger & Co. *Business Week* named Smith & Wesson Corp. as the leading handgun producer in 1997, commanding 19 percent of the handgun business. The other large domestic producers controlled 36 percent of the market, while foreign imports and a few small producers split up the remaining 45 percent.

Historically, the small-arms industry has been cyclical and subject to many external pressures, including the general state of the economy, worldwide military conflicts, and public and political vagaries concerning private ownership of firearms. A rash of school shootings—from Jonesboro, Arkansas to Littleton, Colorado, and from Fort Gibson, Oklahoma to Conyers, Georgia—put the handgun industry itself on the firing line. In the 1999, 28 U.S. cities, as well as the National Association for the Advancement of Colored People, filed suits against U.S. gun manufacturers based on the much-debated theory that gun makers bear responsibility for gun violence. Moreover, the push to install new federal legislation, including limits on gun sales, mandatory background checks for all gun-show purchases, and the so-called "smart gun" technology, a safety device that allows only the owner to fire the weapon, gained momentum.

ORGANIZATION AND STRUCTURE

Many small-arms companies began operation in the late nineteenth century in the Connecticut River Valley between Hartford and Springfield, Massachusetts, which soon became known as Gun Valley because of its concentration of armories. Because of this long tradition, several small-arms companies that no longer had manufacturing facilities in Gun Valley maintained headquarters there at the start of the twenty-first century.

Following the Great Depression, many surviving small-arms companies diversified or were purchased by

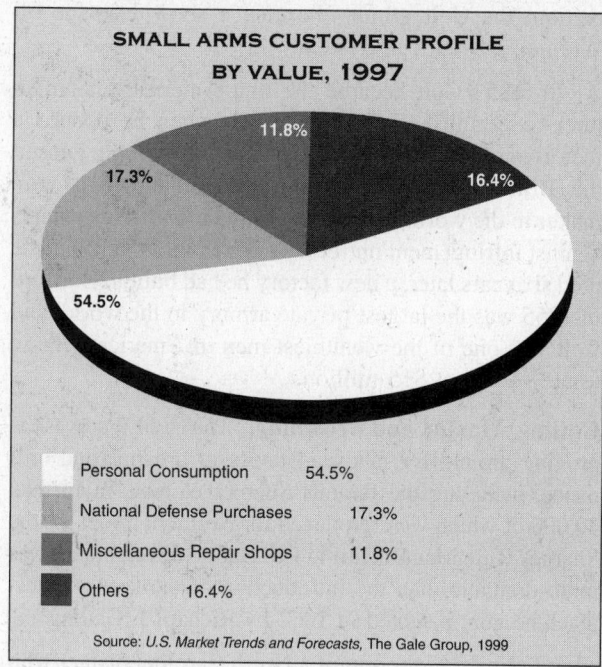

SMALL ARMS CUSTOMER PROFILE BY VALUE, 1997

11.8%
17.3%
16.4%
54.5%

Personal Consumption	54.5%
National Defense Purchases	17.3%
Miscellaneous Repair Shops	11.8%
Others	16.4%

Source: *U.S. Market Trends and Forecasts*, The Gale Group, 1999

large corporations. The trend towards amalgamation reversed itself in the 1980s when two of the largest corporations in the industry, Colt Industries and the Olin Corp., divested themselves of poorly performing firearms divisions to form stand-alone companies. One of those new companies, the U.S. Repeating Arms Co., maker of Winchester rifles, was then sold to Belgian firearms conglomerate Fabrique Nationale Herstal, and then acquired by the French government-owned GIAT Industries. Fabrique Nationale and Italian firearms maker Pietro Beretta Fabbrica Amri also had large manufacturing facilities in the United States.

BACKGROUND AND DEVELOPMENT

The small-arms industry played an important part in both the historical development of the United States and in the myths and ideals that accompanied that development. Early to mid-nineteenth-century guns pioneered the use of interchangeable standardized parts, the technology that gave rise to modern manufacturing. Moreover, guns bearing the names Remington, Winchester, and Colt were associated with the settlement of the Old West, Manifest Destiny, and the development of the United States as a world power.

Although many prominent craftsmen produced firearms in colonial America, gun making as an industry did not truly begin until 1775, when the Continental Congress established the Committee of Safety, whose responsibilities included ensuring that the Continental Army had sufficient firearms. The Committee of Safety established specifications for manufacturing flintlock muskets and awarded contracts to various American gun makers. In 1794 Congress established a national armory at Springfield, Massachusetts that stored and manufactured muskets for military use. A second armory was established at Harper's Ferry, Virginia in 1796. The armory at Harper's Ferry would eventually be burned in 1861 to keep it out of the hands of Confederate forces. The Springfield armory was in operation until 1975.

In 1808, as tensions mounted between the United States and England (which would eventually erupt into the War of 1812), the federal armories tooled up to manufacture 40,000 muskets a year. Private gun makers were also awarded contracts to manufacture between 2,500 and 10,000 muskets each, with the goal of supplying nearly 100,000 militiamen. The federal armories provided "pattern" muskets for the private manufacturers to copy.

Early Innovators. One of the earliest gun makers to receive a government contract was Eli Whitney, best known as the inventor of the cotton gin, who had established an armory in New Haven, Connecticut in 1798. Whitney was a Yale-educated engineer who realized that the most efficient and cost-effective way to make guns was to manufacture interchangeable parts that could then be assembled by unskilled workers. Although Whitney was far from being the most successful gun maker of the day, he amazed government officials who were inspecting his plant by assembling muskets from parts chosen at random. Whitney was the first U.S. industrialist to manufacture interchangeable parts and was considered the father of mass production long before Henry Ford began building cars. By the 1850s, Whitney's "American System" of manufacturing was known throughout Europe. The Whitney Armory continued to manufacture guns until 1888.

Although rifles were invented in the early 1500s and the famous Pennsylvania-made Kentucky rifles were used by some militiamen during the American Revolution, smoothbore muskets remained common into the early nineteenth century. Despite their inaccuracy, they were easier to load and fire than a firearm with a rifled barrel. Then, in 1810, an American gunsmith, John H. Hall, invented a breech-loading flintlock rifle that could be loaded quickly using a paper cartridge containing ball and powder. The U.S. Army ordered 200 rifles in 1818 for experimentation, and Hall supervised their construction at the federal armory at Harper's Ferry. The rifles performed well, but the military continued to rely on muskets up until the Civil War. Although the Springfield Armory did not begin manufacturing rifles until 1858, it produced more than 840,000 by the end of 1865. On the other hand, hunters and frontiersmen who favored accuracy switched to breech-loading rifles much sooner. The 200 Hall rifles built in 1818 were also the first firearms manufactured in a government armory using interchangeable parts.

Samuel Colt. Samuel Colt was the first great American gun maker. He was born in Hartford, Connecticut in 1814 and left school at the age of 10 to work in his father's silk mill in Ware, Massachusetts. At the age of 16, he joined the crew of a ship bound for London and Calcutta. In London, Colt apparently saw a display of early attempts at designing repeating firearms. During the voyage home, and possibly inspired by the ship's clutch-controlled rotating capstan, he whittled a crude wooden model of a pistol with a revolving cylinder.

Between 1832 and 1835, Colt financed development of his revolving pistol as a lecturer and "practical chemist," billing himself as "the celebrated Dr. S. Colt of London and Calcutta" and giving demonstrations of laughing gas in the United States and Canada. He sent money and ideas for improvements in his design to John Pearson, a Baltimore gunsmith, who created a working model. Colt received patents on his design from England and France in 1835, and from the United States in 1836. The most unique feature of Colt's design was a ratchet that rotated and locked the cylinder in place when the gun was cocked.

Colt established the Patent Arms Manufacturing Co. in Paterson, New Jersey in 1836 to produce revolving pistols and rifles. The head of U.S. Army Ordnance, however, was not impressed with a demonstration, and the company failed to receive a military contract. Although the army eventually did order about 100 rifles and a few five-shot revolvers for fighting the Seminole Indians in Florida, Colt was forced to close down his company in 1842.

At the start of the Mexican War in 1846, General Zachary Taylor, who had used an early Paterson-model Colt revolver, asked Colt for 1,000 revolvers to be delivered within three months. Captain Samuel Walker of the Texas Rangers, who had used Colt revolvers to fight the Comanches, also asked for guns, but he wanted a larger caliber revolver that would fire six shots. Colt designed a gun to Walker's specifications, but without a factory of his own, Colt subcontracted the manufacturing to Eli Whitney Jr., who was then running the armory his father had founded and was the army's primary contractor for muskets. Colt, however, personally supervised the manufacturing. The .44 caliber six-shooter became known as the Walker gun. Tragically, Walker was killed in action four days after he received a set of Walker-model revolvers from Colt.

In 1847 the army ordered another 1,000 revolvers and Colt set up the renamed Colt's Patent Arms Manufacturing Co. in a leased space in his hometown of Hartford. He also hired a talented machinist, Elisha K. Root, to manage the operation. Root, who received twice the salary he had made at a farm-implements company, was given a free hand in setting up the factory. He designed belt-driven machinery for turning gun stocks, boring rifling barrels, and making cartridges. Under Root's di-

rection, the Colt armory became a showplace for Eli Whitney's American System.

In 1853 Colt became the first American manufacturer to establish a foreign branch when he opened a factory on the Thames River in London to supply guns to the British government. Colt became known as gun maker to the world and successfully defended his patents against infringement until they expired in 1856. When he died six years later, a new factory he had built in Hartford in 1855 was the largest private armory in the world, and Colt was one of the wealthiest men in America with an estate valued at $15 million.

Gatling, Maxim, and Browning. The Civil War was the proving ground for many advances in firearms and ordnance, including the famous Sharpes carbine, more than 80,000 of which were produced for Northern troops by the Sharpes Rifle Manufacturing Co. But no development was more dramatic than the introduction of the first practical machine gun, patented in 1862 by Richard J. Gatling.

Gatling was the son of a North Carolina planter who spent most of his career improving agricultural methods and inventing farm machinery. Gatling's hand-cranked machine gun actually performed erratically during the Civil War, but with some mechanical improvements the design was officially adopted by the U.S. Army in 1866. He later sold his patent to the Colt's Patent Arms Manufacturing Co.

In 1884, another American-born inventor, Sir Hiram Stevens Maxim, developed the first semiautomatic rifle, when he modified a Winchester rifle so the power of the recoil would eject the spent cartridge and load the next round. In 1889 Maxim also developed the first fully automatic machine gun. Maxim's designs were adopted by every major power in the world between 1900 and World War I. English models of the Maxim machine gun, known as the Vickers, were used by both sides in World War II, and the North Koreans employed outdated Maxim machine guns in the Korean War.

Maxim also experimented with internal combustion engines, steam-powered flight, and electric lights, losing a critical patent lawsuit to Thomas Edison. A native of Maine, Maxim moved to England and became a British citizen in 1900. He was knighted in 1901. His son, Hiram Percy Maxim, invented the silencer, which mutes the report of a gunshot.

John M. Browning, the son of a Utah gunsmith, was the most prolific and successful American gun designer in history. He developed one of the earliest semiautomatic pistols and the first gas-operated machine gun. Browning sold or licensed most of his designs to the Colt Patent Arms Manufacturing Co., including several machine-gun designs. He also licensed designs to the Winchester Repeating Arms Co., including the first lever-action rifle strong enough to use the high-power cen-terfire cartridges of the day. This rifle, named Model 1886, made Winchester the best-known name among American rifle makers.

In 1888, when no American companies expressed interest in his semiautomatic pistol, Browning licensed the design to the Belgian gun-making firm of Fabrique Nationale Herstal. He also licensed the Browning name for use outside of North America. Browning and Na-tionale Fabrique later collaborated on some of the most famous firearms in history, including the Browning Auto-matic Rifle, or BAR, used during World War I and World War II. Fabrique Nationale purchased controlling interest in Browning Arms in 1977.

Browning also designed the first successful gas-operated machine gun. In 1890 he sold the design to Colt, which produced the Colt Machine Gun Model 1895, the first fully automatic machine gun used by U.S. mili-tary forces. In 1990 Colt also became the first U.S. com-pany to produce an automatic pistol, also based on a Browning design.

CURRENT CONDITIONS

The late 1990s brought bad news for gun manufac-turers. "Not since George Washington established the Springfield (Mass.) Armory to defend the young repub-lic," wrote William C. Symonds in *Business Week,* "has the American gun industry faced a more serious crisis." The influence that gun lobbies once wielded with national and state lawmakers eroded amid rising public concern about gun violence. Gun-control advocates worked to channel public outrage at increased school and workplace shootings, combined with gun accidents by children, into a Congressional mandate.

The new gun-control efforts were much stronger than previous ones. In the *Business Press,* Adam Eventov reported that, in May 1999, the Senate passed a bill "that would close loopholes in the 1993 Brady Handgun Vio-lence Prevention Act, tighten background checks at gun shows, outlaw the importation of large-capacity clips, require safety locks on new handguns and prohibit juve-niles convicted of felonies from owning firearms as adults." State legislatures were also enacting tougher laws. In California, a formerly firearm-friendly state, ini-tiatives to require manufacturers to install new safety devices and meet stricter performance standards, such as a handgun being able to survive a three-foot drop, were proposed.

Ironically, however, the likelihood of stricter regula-tions actually spurred gun sales in 1999, as consumers tried to stock up before the new laws took effect. A similar spike occurred during 1993 and 1994, when Presi-dent Bill Clinton made gun control a national priority. The 1993 Brady Bill called for a five-day waiting period

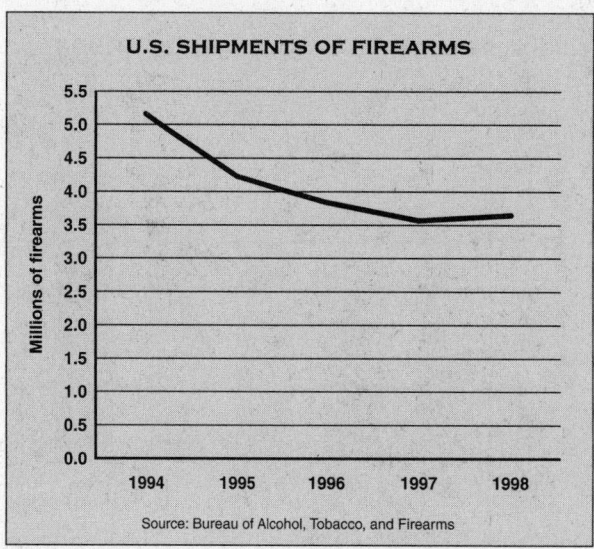

U.S. SHIPMENTS OF FIREARMS

Source: Bureau of Alcohol, Tobacco, and Firearms

(and background check) before a customer could pur-chase a handgun. In 1994 Congress passed a law banning 19 types of assault weapons. But due in part to the effective lobbying efforts of the National Rifle Associa-tion (NRA), these laws contained numerous loopholes that allowed gun manufacturers to sidestep the regula-tions. By making minor design changes on their weapons, gun manufacturers were able to continue manufacturing and selling assault weapons. A three-year sales slump followed in which production fell more than 30 percent.

The legislative action told only part of the story. Gun makers were also facing an onslaught of litigation. The success of class-action lawsuits against tobacco giants inspired similar product liability claims against gun man-ufacturers. By December 1999, 28 cities filed suit against the handgun industry, seeking compensation for the costs associated with gun violence and pushing for reforms in the industry's marketing practices. But gun makers said they were not responsible for criminal misuse of their products. In the *New York Times,* Barry Meier cited New York University Law School professor Stephen Gillers as saying that the cause-and-effect legal claim that un-derpinned the gun cases appeared far weaker than in the tobacco lawsuits. Nevertheless, the plaintiffs were likely to win by default, as the cost of the litigation would drive gun companies out of business and gun costs out of the reach of most consumers.

Gun companies responded to the hostile environ-ment in a variety of ways. Some companies, such as Colt Manufacturing, Smith & Wesson, and Mossberg, entered into settlement talks; others, backed by the 2.9 million-member NRA, refused to compromise. In 1999 four small companies filed for bankruptcy protection. Several large manufacturers were working to develop codes of conduct for gun distributors and dealers. In addition, gun companies were developing new marketing strategies,

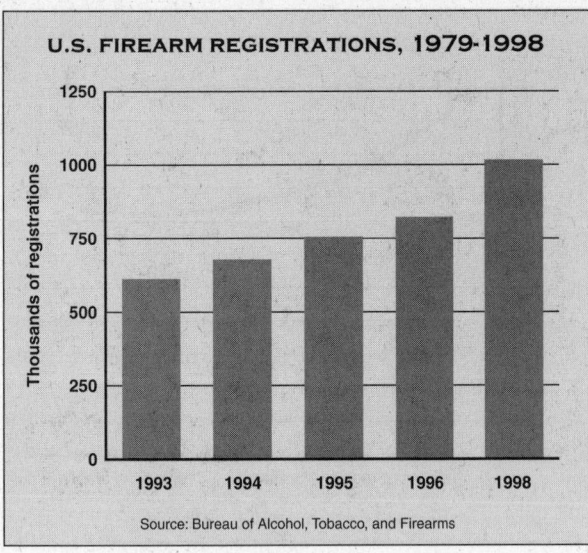

U.S. FIREARM REGISTRATIONS, 1979-1998

Source: Bureau of Alcohol, Tobacco, and Firearms

such as targeting women, and diversifying their product lines by adding items such as titanium golf club heads and specialty clothing.

INDUSTRY LEADERS

Remington Arms Co., Inc. In 1999 Remington was owned by a Delaware holding company, DuPont Chemical and Energy Operations, Inc. The company transferred its headquarters from Wilmington, Delaware to Rockingham County, North Carolina in 1995. In the mid-1990s, it built new facilities in Kentucky and North Carolina, organized a shooting school in New York, and launched a web site where customers could buy guns with the click of a mouse. In 1992 and 1996, Remington introduced a number of new handguns and rifles but discontinued its hunting apparel line in 1995.

Remington traced its heritage to Eliphalet Remington, an early American gunsmith who produced his first flintlock rifle in 1816. Raised in Central New York, Remington purchased land along the Erie Canal in 1828 and established an armory. The town that developed around the armory became known as Remington's Corners until Eliphalet Remington insisted the town change the name to Ilion. Remington's manufacturing facilities were still in Ilion in 1993. The company was known as E. Remington & Sons during the Civil War. The Depression of 1884 forced the company into bankruptcy, but it was reorganized in 1888 as the Remington Arms Co. Du Pont purchased Remington in 1933.

Remington was considered a leader in introducing new technology and production techniques. After World War II, Remington began manufacturing parts that were interchangeable between models. The company also simplified the shape and design of many gun parts, which initially caused gun enthusiasts who were used to the elaborate showpieces of the past to treat newer Remington models with scorn. Some parts designed in the early 1950s were still being used on models introduced in the 1980s.

In the late 1980s, Remington became one of the first gun makers to install computer-aided design and computer-aided manufacturing equipment to reduce costs and increase its ability to respond to consumer trends. Paradoxically, the new manufacturing process produced parts by traditional machine tooling rather than stamping or casting, which most companies had turned to in the middle of the twentieth century to save money. The Remington plant in Ilion was considered one of the most advanced metalwork facilities in the United States.

O.F. Mossberg & Sons, Inc. Based in New Haven, Connecticut, O.F. Mossberg had revenues of $20 million in 1996. Oliver F. Mossberg was a Swedish immigrant who worked for several U.S. gun makers before he began making .22 caliber ''novelty guns'' in his spare time to put his sons, Iver and Harold, through college. In 1919 the Mossbergs formed O.F. Mossberg & Sons. Between 1919 and 1932, they produced about 37,000 .22 caliber ''Brownie'' pistols. They began manufacturing .22 caliber rifles in 1922. Oliver Mossberg died in 1937.

The company continued to produce .22 caliber pistols and rifles after World War II, but also expanded into bolt-action shotguns. The first pump-action Mossberg shotguns were introduced in 1957. In 1986 Mossberg ended production of all rifles and pistols to concentrate solely on shotguns. Mossberg shotguns were widely used in law enforcement and the military. Mossberg claimed to be the oldest family-owned and operated firearms manufacturer in the United States. In 1993 Alan I. Mossberg, grandson of the founder, was president and CEO.

U.S. Repeating Arms Co., Inc. The U.S. Repeating Arms Co. (USRAC) was a major manufacturer of shotguns and rifles under the legendary Winchester brand name. In 1991 USRAC produced more than 126,000 shotguns and 113,000 rifles, generating revenues of $74 million. The company was owned by GIAT Industries, a private company wholly owned by the French government.

Oliver F. Winchester founded the Winchester Repeating Arms Co. in New Haven, Connecticut in 1866. Winchester was a shirtmaker by trade, but became involved in gun making when he purchased the assets of the defunct Volcanic Repeating Arms Co. Volcanic had been founded in 1855 by Horace Smith and Daniel B. Wesson, later of Smith & Wesson fame. Winchester was an early investor in the company, which went bankrupt in 1857. The Winchester Model 1866 was the first successful lever-action-repeating rifle. Later models made the Winchester name synonymous with American-made rifles.

When the market for guns collapsed during the Great Depression, the Olin Corp. purchased Winchester. In 1981 a group of Olin employees purchased Olin's Winchester gun division in a leveraged buyout, calling the new company the U.S. Repeating Arms Co., and licensing the Winchester name from Olin. Unfortunately, gun sales in the United States plummeted in the early 1980s, and USRAC filed for bankruptcy. USRAC was then purchased in 1987 by a group of investors led by Fabrique Nationale, a Belgium gun maker and at one time the largest private arms company in the world. Fabrique Nationale became the sole owner in 1990 and was purchased by GIAT Industries in 1992.

Sturm, Ruger & Co., Inc. Sturm, Ruger & Co. was the only U.S. gun maker active in all four small-arms categories: rifles, shotguns, revolvers, and pistols. It produced over 50 models of guns, which had more than 300 variations. In addition to guns, it also produced a line of specialized castings for industrial clients representing aerospace, automotive, medicine, and golf. Based in Southport, Connecticut, Sturm, Ruger employed a work force of more than 2,000 in 1999.

Sturm, Ruger was founded in 1948 by William Batterman Ruger with a $50,000 stake from Alexander Sturm, a family friend and gun collector. Ruger had been a firearm designer for the U.S. government's Springfield Armory and the Auto Ordnance Corp. Sturm and Ruger started by manufacturing a .22 caliber semiautomatic target pistol designed by Ruger, but gained special favor with gun enthusiasts in the early 1950s when it began producing Old West-style six-shooters that capitalized on the popularity of adult TV Westerns. Sturm, Ruger also utilized a manufacturing process known as investment casting. Rather than machine-tooling parts for its guns, Sturm, Ruger cast parts from molten steel using the "lost wax" process. The parts were not only cheaper to produce, they were stronger. Since perfecting this process, Ruger cast parts for other manufacturers to the tune of $16 to $18 million annually or about 8 to 9 percent of sales. This figure jumped by nearly 70 percent in the first quarter of 1995, however, due to a large contract for titanium Big Bertha golf-club heads for Callaway Golf Co.

Between 1982 and 1992, when sales of small arms in the United States fell by almost 50 percent, Sturm, Ruger increased sales by nearly 75 percent. In 1986, Sturm, Ruger forced its distributors to choose between its guns and those made by Smith & Wesson. About half chose to stay with Sturm, Ruger.

Between 1953 and 1972, Sturm, Ruger produced more than 1.5 million of the single-action revolvers patterned after the legendary 1873 Colt Peacemaker. Like the original Peacemaker, unfortunately, Sturm, Ruger six-shooters often discharged accidentally if the gun was dropped or if the hammer was struck. In 1994 for instance, 24 liability cases were tried, dismissed, or settled out of court. The average settlement was approximately $55,000.

Sturm, Ruger redesigned its single-action revolvers in 1972 to make them safer. In 1982 Sturm, Ruger offered to retrofit older models with a safety device at no cost to their owners; fewer than 10 percent of the 1.2 million old model revolvers were modified, however. The company also ran a series of advertisements from 1981 to 1983 urging gun owners to load revolvers with only five bullets and leave the hammer resting on an empty chamber.

By 1995 Barron's reported that Sturm, Ruger could boast of a "squeaky-clean" balance sheet, superb profitability and 45 years in business without a negative balance sheet. Sturm, Ruger continued to be profitable despite the antigun mood of much of America because most of its customers were hunters, law enforcement personnel, gun collectors, and sportsmen. Ruger also survived the "assault weapons" legislation as all of its products were exempted and named "legitimate sporting firearms."

In 1999 the company boasted that it not only led the industry in new technology, but it also stressed safety and responsibility in its catalogs and advertising more so than other gun makers.

Marlin Firearms Co. The privately owned Marlin Firearms, a leading maker of .22 caliber rifles, had revenues of $50 million in 1996. Marlin was founded in New Haven, Connecticut in 1870 by John Mahlon Marlin, who had worked for the Colt Patent Firearms Co. during the Civil War. After 100 years at the same site, the company opened up a new plant a few miles away in North Haven, Connecticut. Trick-shooter Annie Oakley used a specially made Marlin Model 1889 in Buffalo Bill Cody's Wild West show in the 1890s. Marlin was also known for its Colt-Browning machine guns and military rifles made during World War I, when it was known as the Marlin Rockwell Corp. After the war, Rockwell had no interest in sporting guns and auctioned off the firearms division. Frank Kenna, whose family owned and operated Marlin Firearms into the 1990s, purchased the business for $100. In addition to firearms, Marlin produced razor blades from 1936 until the 1960s.

Smith & Wesson Corp. Smith & Wesson was the leading manufacturer of small arms in the United States in 1999. Smith & Wesson's most popular revolver was the .38 Special, widely used by police officers, both in the United States and abroad. The Royal Canadian Mounted Police carried 9 mm Smith & Wesson pistols. The company also manufactured the .44 Magnum revolver used by Clint Eastwood in the "Dirty Harry" movies. In the late 1980s Smith & Wesson became a leader in the emerging market for handguns designed especially for women, with the Lady Smith. The Lady Smith was a .357 Magnum with a grip and trigger mechanism designed for smaller hands. Many women's magazines refused to run ads for Lady Smith when it was introduced in 1988.

Horace Smith and Daniel B. Wesson formed their first partnership in 1851, creating the Volcanic Repeating Arms Co., which they later sold to Oliver F. Winchester. In 1856, when the Colt patents expired, Wesson developed a revolver that used a metallic rim-fire cartridge. He and Smith then formed Smith & Wesson in Springfield, Massachusetts, in 1856. Smith retired from the business in 1873, but Wesson and his descendants continued to run the company until 1967, when it was purchased by the Bangor Punta Corp. In 1984 the company became part of the Lear Siegler Holdings Corp. Lear Siegler eventually sold the company to F.H. Tompkins PLC, a British manufacturer of plumbing supplies and lawn mowers, in 1987. In 1996 the company had revenues of $140 million and a work force of 1,500.

Colt Manufacturing Co.   At one time the largest and most important gun maker in the United States, the Colt Manufacturing Co. was a relatively small maker of rifles and pistols in the early 1990s, producing 70,000 pistols and 38,000 rifles in 1991. Colt was owned by an investment group that included the United Auto Workers union and the state of Connecticut. It had revenues of about $73 million in 1996.

Colt's Patent Arms Manufacturing Co., founded by inventor Samuel Colt in 1847, provided the Union Army with more than 107,000 revolvers during the Civil War. The famed Peacemaker, a six-shooter used in the Old West, was introduced in 1873 and manufactured continuously until 1941, and Colt produced commemorative Peacemakers after World War II.

The Colt family owned the company until 1901, when it was sold to a group of investors. The company suffered several setbacks in the 1920s and 1930s, beginning with its decision to stop manufacturing the Thompson submachine gun because it had become popular with gangsters. Nearly 2 million of the popular tommy guns, as they were called, were produced during World War II by another contractor. Ironically, 60 years later Colt ended production of the AR-15, a popular semiautomatic civilian model of the military's M-16, in part because it was being used by drug dealers.

Like most other small-arms manufacturers, Colt was hard hit by the Great Depression. Its difficulties were compounded by a violent strike in 1935, during which the home of its then-president Sam Stone was firebombed, and a hurricane in 1936, which destroyed most of what was left of the Colt Manufacturing Co. The company seemingly rebounded during World War II, but mismanagement later led to a financial crisis and manufacturing stopped altogether between 1945 and 1947.

In 1955 Colt was purchased by the Penn-Texas Corp., a corporate raider that was expected to dismantle the company. In 1962, a stockholders' revolt forced out Penn-Texas and the company was reorganized as Colt Industries. In 1963 Colt became the sole contractor for the army's new M-16 automatic assault rifle.

After nearly two decades of growth, during which Colt Industries became a diversified billion-dollar corporation, the Firearms Division suffered another series of market defeats in the 1980s. In 1985 the U.S. government dropped the Colt .45, standard military issue since 1911, and adopted a 9 mm semiautomatic pistol, produced by the Beretta USA Corp., in its place. Then, in 1986, the United Auto Workers (UAW) struck the Colt plant in Hartford. Replacement workers were hired, but the lingering strike and concerns about quality might have caused Colt to lose the M-16 contract in 1988. (An order for 500,000 rifles went to FN Manufacturing, the American manufacturing subsidiary of Fabrique Nationale.)

In 1990, a group of investors that included the state of Connecticut purchased the Firearms Division from Colt Industries. The UAW agreed to end the strike in exchange for rehiring striking workers and an 11 percent share of the company. The division was renamed the Colt Manufacturing Co. The new owners almost immediately found themselves embroiled in an old controversy when Colt announced plans in 1991 to market a rifle similar to the discontinued AR-15. At the time, Connecticut, with a 47 percent stake in the company and $25 million of its employee pension funds at risk, was considering a ban on all assault-style rifles.

FURTHER READING

Eventov, Adam. ''Ontario, Calif.-Area Gun Makers Face Litigation, Legislation.'' *Business Press,* 28 June 1999.

''Fishing Flounders, but Firearms Is Still a Sure Shot: Women Shooters Give Manufacturers New Target.'' *Discount Store News,* 6 February 1995.

''Guns in America.'' *Economist.* 3 July 1999, 17-19.

Hausman, Robert M. ''U.S. Repeating Arms Co.'' *Shooting Industry,* March 1996.

The History of Marlin Firearms. North Haven, CT: Marlin Firearms Co.

Levin, Myron. ''Gun Makers, Plaintiffs Discuss Settlement.'' *Los Angeles Times,* 28 September 1999.

———. ''NAACP Files Lawsuit against Handgun Makers.'' *Los Angeles Times,* 17 July 1999.

Marlin Firearms Co. ''Marlin Shotguns.'' Available from http://www.marlinfirearms.com/history_8.html#today. Accessed 21 December 1999.

Meier, Barry. ''It Just Looks Like a Smoking Gun.'' *New York Times,* 12 December 1999.

Nicholas, Peter. ''Philadelphia Mayor Schedules Meeting to Seek Compromise on Guns.'' *Philadelphia Inquirer,* 11 June 1999.

Remington Arms Co. "History of the Firearms Business, 1816-1998." Available from http://www.remington.com/AboutUs/corphistory.htm.(21 December 1999).

Sturm, Ruger & Co. "Fifty Years of Fine Firearms." Available from http://www.ruger-firearms.com/misc/fftyhstr.html. (21 December 1999).

Symonds, William C., Lorraine Woellert, and Susan Garland. "Under Fire." *Business Week,* 16 August 1999.

Thurman, Russ. "Firearms Business Analysis." *Shooting Industry,* June 1996.

———. "Local Gun Sales Healthy." *Shooting Industry,* May 1996.

Tomkins, Richard. "The Four-Gun Family in Their Sights." *Financial Times,* 2 March 1996.

Winchester and U.S. Repeating Arms Co. Available from http://www.winchester-guns.com/faqs/faqs.htm. Accessed 21 December 1999.

Wolffe, Richard. "Mayors May Drop Action against Gun Group." *Financial Times (London),* 8 June 1999.

SIC 3489

ORDNANCE AND ACCESSORIES, NOT ELSEWHERE CLASSIFIED

This category covers establishments primarily engaged in manufacturing ordnance and accessories, not elsewhere classified, such as naval, aircraft, anti-aircraft, tank, coast, and field artillery having a bore more than 30 mm. (or more than 1.18 inch), and components. Establishments primarily engaged in manufacturing small arms and parts 30 millimeters or less are classified in **SIC 3484: Small Arms;** those manufacturing tanks are classified in **SIC 3795: Tanks and Tank Components;** and those manufacturing guided missiles are classified in Industry Group 376 (Guided Missiles and Space Vehicles and Parts).

NAICS CODE(S)

332995 (Other Ordnance and Accessories Manufacturing)

According to the U.S. Census Bureau's *1997 Economic Census—Manufacturing,* 70 establishments operated in this category for part or all of 1997. Industry-wide employment totaled 12,285 workers receiving a payroll of more than $547 million. Of these employees, 4,825 worked in production, putting in almost 9 million hours to earn wages of almost $215 million. Overall shipments for the industry were valued at almost $1.8 billion.

Los Angeles-based Northrop Grumman Corp., which led the industry with 1998 sales of $8.9 billion,

sent its new electronic warfare equipment through 6 weeks of successful live-testing in late 1998: the AAQ-24 DIRCM replicated the ultraviolet signature of missiles's rocket engines. Salt Lake City-based Cordant Technologies Inc. generated almost $1.8 billion in sales for its fiscal year ended June 30, 1998. GenCorp. Inc. of Fairlawn, Ohio, reported more than $1.7 billion in sales for its fiscal year ended November 30, 1998. ITT Defense and Electronics Inc. of McLean, Virginia placed fourth in the list of industry leaders with 1997 sales of $1.6 billion. Alliant Techsystems Inc. of Hopkins, Minnesota, rounded out the top five industry leaders with sales of almost $1.1 billion for its fiscal year ended March 31, 1999.

The Ordnance and Accessories industry declined in the post-Cold War era, along with other high-tech industries (aerospace, search and navigation equipment manufacturing). The decline in defense spending, along with the private sector recession of 1990 and 1991, were the main causes of the employment losses and downturns experienced in this industry since 1987.

The value of shipments in the ordnance and accessories industry was $1.31 billion in 1991. Shipments declined every year since 1989, and reached a five-year low in 1996. The industry peaked in 1984, with $1.93 billion in shipments and 14,700 workers involved in production. Still, in accordance with the steady descent of shipment values, the number of workers in this field has dropped slightly every year since 1984.

The industry is highly labor intensive, having only 19 percent as much investment per production worker as that for the manufacturing sector as a whole. Annual hours worked by production workers in the industry are slightly lower on average than those worked in the manufacturing sector at large, although hourly wages are 49 percent higher. The average hourly wage in 1996 was about $20. This was expected to increase to $21.54 by 1998.

In 1996, there were approximately 60 establishments in the ordnance industry, just over half of which had 20 or more employees. The heaviest concentration of establishments was in California, with eight. Other states with a large number of establishments in the industry were Ohio (6), Florida, Texas, and Michigan (5 each). Together, these five states account for about 64 percent of all industry establishments in the United States.

The top five industries and sectors buying the outputs of the ordnance and accessories industry are listed as follows: federal government purchase, national defense, with a 72.0 percent share; exports, with a 24.4 percent share; ordnance and accessories, not elsewhere classified, with a 2.4 percent share; change in business inventories, with a 1.0 percent share; and small arms ammunition, with a 0.2 percent share.

FURTHER READING

Hetrick, Ron L. "Employment in High-Tech Defense Industries in a Post Cold War Era." *Monthly Labor Review,* August 1996, 57-63.

Infotrac Company Profiles. Available from http://web6.infotrac .galegroup.com (visited 2/12/99).

Klass, Philip J. "Live-fire tests demonstrate AAQ-24 DIRCM capabilities." *Aviation Week & Space Technology,* 26 October 1998.

U.S. Census Bureau. *1997 Economic Census-Manufacturing.* Available from http://www.census.gov/prod/ec97/97m3329i .pdf (visited 2/12/00).

SIC 3491

INDUSTRIAL VALVES

This category covers establishments primarily engaged in manufacturing industrial valves. Establishments primarily engaged in manufacturing fluid power valves are classified in **SIC 3492: Fluid Power Valves and Hose Fittings;** those manufacturing plumbing fixture fittings and trim are classified in **SIC 3432: Plumbing Fixture Fittings and Trim;** and those manufacturing plumbing and heating valves are classified in **SIC 3494: Valves and Pipe Fittings, Not Elsewhere Classified.**

NAICS CODE(S)

332911 (Industrial Valve Manufacturing)

INDUSTRY SNAPSHOT

A valve is a device designed to regulate the flow of a gas, liquid, slurry, or dry material through a pipeline or a chute. Valves not only regulate the flow of material but also the rate, volume, pressure, and direction of the flow. The Valve Manufacturers Association observes that valves are basic yet indispensable items in our society; they are required in "virtually all manufacturing processes and every energy production and supply system." Today's valves are made from a variety of materials and range in complexity from simple to highly sophisticated. They range in size from a fraction of an inch to more than 30 feet in diameter, and they can handle pressures ranging from a vacuum to more than 20,000 pounds per square inch, as well as temperatures ranging from cryogenic extremes to more than 1,500 degrees Fahrenheit.

In 1997, according to the U.S. Bureau of the Census, 427 companies with 53,264 employees were engaged in the manufacture and distribution of industrial valves in the United States. Of these employees, 34,815 were production workers. Total payroll for the industry was $1.897 billion and total payroll for production workers was $1.025 billion. In 1996 the average wage for the industrial valve industry was $13.78. This figure was expected to reach $15.16 by the year 2000.

The Valve Manufacturers Association of America totaled the 1997 value of industrial valve shipments at $3.08 billion. This was down from a total value of $3.11 billion in 1996.

Compared to other manufacturing industries, the industrial valves segment was both labor and capital intensive. High-tech equipment was used in researching, designing, manufacturing, and testing products. Comparative ratios of employees, production workers, wages, and hours worked per establishment were much higher than in other manufacturing industries. Cost, shipments, and investment per establishment were also higher than the manufacturing average.

The U.S. valve industry was segmented, with several large companies making a wide variety of valve products but with the majority of industry players being small and medium-sized companies focusing on a particular market niche. Throughout the 1990s acquisitions and mergers in the industry focused on expanding product lines, increasing sales, and providing long term viability for companies. The industry was also experiencing shrinking demand for traditional cast iron valves and fittings but growing demand for high technology products, especially automated valves. According to Wendy E. Jovan, a research analyst for the Freedonia Group, and Stanton G. Cort, a Case Western Reserve University marketing professor, the investment in technology necessary to produce these advanced valves exacerbated the capital intensive nature of the industry.

ORGANIZATION AND STRUCTURE

Valves are made from metals, including brass, bronze, iron, steel, and alloys, as well as from plastics. In the late 1990s some valve companies operated their own foundries to make the castings from which the valves were fashioned. Sourcing parts offshore was another practice that some valve companies engaged in.

According to the Valve Manufacturers Association of America (VMAA), shipments of industrial valves are divided among six product groups. These groups and the value of their 1997 shipments were: gate, globe, and check valves ($481.7 million); ball valves ($548.7 million); industrial butterfly valves ($282.9 million); plug valves ($195.1 million); automated valves ($936.0 million); and pressure relief valves ($176.9 million). This totaled to $3.08 billion in 1997 shipments, with 1998 shipments forecast to reach $3.2 billion.

According to Jovan and Cort, valves typically accounted for 5 to 10 percent of an end-user's capital budget in the 1990s. The VMAA lists 15 categories of end-users for industrial valves. These end-users and their forecast percentage of 1998 industrial valve shipments were: chemical industry (17.6 percent); water and sewage industry (17.0 percent); petroleum production (12.7 percent); power generation (10.7 percent); pulp and paper industry (7.0 percent); oil and gas transmission (5.6 percent); commercial construction (5.0 percent); gas distribution (2.4 percent); food and beverage industry (2.3 percent); iron and steel industry (1.9 percent); co-generation (1.7 percent); marine industry (1.5 percent); mining (0.6 percent); textiles (0.5 percent); and other (2.6 percent).

In the late 1990s, there was a trend toward integrated supply programs in the industry. These allowed for closer relationships between valve producers, distributors, and customers, resulting in more accurate usage forecasts for the valve industry.

BACKGROUND AND DEVELOPMENT

The invention of the valve, like the invention of the wheel, is obscured by antiquity. It is known that the ancient Greek and Egyptian cultures used primitive valves to divert the flow of water for agricultural use and public consumption. The ancient Romans refined the concept and developed plug valves and check valves for their plumbing systems. Further developments in valve technology did not occur until the Renaissance, when Leonardo da Vinci designed canals, irrigation projects, and hydraulic systems that incorporated valves.

Valves first began taking a modern bent in design with the introduction of Thomas Newcomen's industrial steam engine in 1705. The development of steam engines and valves paralleled and complemented one another, as steam engines required more sophisticated valves that could withstand high pressures and high temperatures. However, large scale production of valves did not occur until the proliferation of municipal water systems began with New York City's Croton Waterworks project in 1842.

As the Industrial Revolution continued and the scope of industry expanded, so did the development of the modern industrial valve. The quarter-turn plug valve was developed in the 1920s, and the diaphragm valve was developed during the 1940s. Since then, the use of synthetic materials as valve linings has greatly increased the performance of valves. The ability to automatically control valves is another development of the last half of the twentieth century.

CURRENT CONDITIONS

According to the Freedonia Group, a Cleveland market research firm, demand for industrial valves was expected to grow 5.8 percent per year in the United States through the year 2003. This growth would be fueled by new construction in the utility industry and increased activity in chemical process industries. Demand for automated valves and some ball and high-performance butterfly valves was expected to be strong.

Data from Thinking Cap Solutions, Inc., showed that valve prices increased in the late 1990s despite adequate supplies of valves on the market, reduced demand due to the Asian financial crisis, strong competition among valve producers, and low costs for raw materials. Valve prices in February 1999 were up 3.2 percent over 1998 prices, 5.5 percent over 1997 prices, and 7.6 percent over 1996 prices. Meanwhile, direct manufacturing costs in February 1999 were 3.2 percent lower than in 1998 and 6.5 percent lower than in 1997 due to low metals and plastics prices.

INDUSTRY LEADERS

In 1997, according to Jovan and Cort, the top seven industrial valve manufacturers in the United States were Watts Industries, Emerson Electric, Crane Valves, Neles-Jamesbury, Tyco International, Duriron, and Keystone International. These seven companies accounted for 20 percent of the U.S. industrial valve market, with Watts Industries and Emerson Electric accounting for 9 percent of valve sales.

Watts Industries Inc. is located in North Andover, Massachusetts. The company began in the late 1800s as Watts Regulator and produced valves for water heaters and boilers. By the 1970s Watts had become one of the world's most diversified valve makers, supplying the market with state-of-the-art quarter-turn valves and actuators. In 1984 Watts surpassed $100 million in sales and embarked on a selective acquisition strategy. By 1995 Watts' sales were totaling $750 million annually.

Emerson Electric, located in St. Louis, Missouri, is a diversified company with 60 divisions, a number of which produce a variety of valves.

Crane Valves of Stamford, Connecticut, was founded in 1855 by Richard Teller Crane and manufactured its first valve in 1858. Crane produces cast steel, bronze, iron, ball, and butterfly valves. The company also has a subsidiary, Crane Nuclear, Inc., that is a valve vendor for the nuclear power industry. In 1997 Crane acquired the nuclear valve products and services of ITI Movats, Inc. from Westinghouse.

AMERICA AND THE WORLD

The United States is the largest market for and largest producer of industrial valves. According to Jovan and Cort, the United States produces 23 percent of the world's valves. Other major producers of valves are Germany, Japan, Italy, France, and the United Kingdom, as well as Russia, China, and Taiwan. Other major markets for valves, in order of market size, are Germany, Japan, China, the United Kingdom, Italy, and South Korea.

RESEARCH AND TECHNOLOGY

There is an ongoing trend in the valve industry to produce technologically advanced automated valves that can be activated by pneumatic, solenoid, electric, hydraulic, or digital mechanisms. These valves can be used in remote or hazardous environments, such as in oil pipelines in the Arctic or within nuclear power plants. Such specialty products provide a growing market segment for valve producers, but they also require costs to be incurred in the form of materials research, product design and testing, and more sophisticated production methods.

FURTHER READING

Baumann, Hans. "Noise Regulated; Aerodynamic Noise Prediction Using Control Valves." *Process Engineering,* October 1996.

"Crane Co. Announces China Joint Venture." *PR Newswire,* 14 June 1995.

Farrar, Gary. "Indexes for Selected Equipment Show Moderate Increase." *Oil & Gas Journal,* 5 April 1999.

Genna, Albert. "Prices Inch Up, but Supplies Are Good." *Purchasing,* 6 May 1999.

Jovan, Wendy E., and Stanton G. Cort. "A World View of Industrial Valves." *Business Economics,* April 1997.

Kirgin, Kenneth H. "Solid Casting Markets Fuel 1997 Expansion: Industry Overview." *Modern Casting,* January 1997.

Murphy, Elena Epatko. "Prices Rise Slightly in Healthy Market." *Purchasing,* 13 August 1998.

Rhodes, Anne K. "Integrated Process Plant Management Systems Proliferating." *Oil & Gas Journal,* 7 October 1996.

Rudnitsky, Howard. "Metals." *Forbes,* 13 January 1997.

Sherwood, Robert J. "Who's Where in the Industry Groups." *Forbes,* 13 January 1997.

Skousen, Philip L. *Valve Handbook.* New York: McGraw-Hill, 1998.

"Taking Control of Industrial Processes." *Manufacturing Chemist,* February 1997.

"Transtech Industries Announces that it has Completed the Sale of its Hunt Valve Subsidiary." *Business Wire,* 4 March 1996.

"Uniroyal Chemical and Fisher-Rosemount Systems Win Microsoft Technical Innovations in Manufacturing Awards." *PR Newswire,* 11 March 1997.

U.S. Bureau of the Census. *Industrial Valve Manufacturing 1997: Economic Census, Manufacturing, Industry Series, November 1999.* Washington, D.C.: GPO, 1999. Available from http://www.census.gov.

Zappe, R.W. *Valve Selection Handbook.* Houston: Gulf Publishing, 1999.

SIC 3492

FLUID POWER VALVES AND HOSE FITTINGS

This classification covers establishments primarily engaged in manufacturing hydraulic and pneumatic valves, hose and tube fittings, and hose assemblies for fluid power systems. Establishments primarily engaged in manufacturing fluid power cylinders are classified in **SIC 3593: Fluid Power Cylinders and Actuators;** those manufacturing fluid power pumps are classified in **SIC 3594: Fluid Power Pumps and Motors;** and those manufacturing hydraulic intake and exhaust motor vehicle valves are classified in **SIC 3592: Carburetors, Pistons, Piston Rings, and Valves.**

NAICS CODE(S)

332912 (Fluid Power Valve and Hose Fitting Manufacturing)

INDUSTRY SNAPSHOT

The National Fluid Power Association (NFPA) calculates the total 1998 U.S. fluid power market at $13.5 billion. The U.S. government's 1998 estimate for the value of shipments for fluid power valves and hose fittings was nearly $5.3 billion. The value of direct exports of U.S.-manufactured fluid power products in 1997, according to the NFPA, was just shy of $1.3 billion, excluding compressors. The estimate for indirect trade fluid power products (fluid power products exported as parts of end user machinery) in 1997 was $2.6 billion.

In 1996, the last year for which shipment figures are available, the value of shipments within the fluid power industry totaled $4.9 billion. This figure is predicted to grow to $5.7 billion by 2000. Employment in the industry is expected to remain relatively flat despite the increase in the value of shipments. In 1996 the industry employed 31,500 people with nearly 22,000 being production workers, and in 2000 these figures are expected to be 31,800 and 22,400 respectively. Average hourly wages in 1996 were $13.09 and are predicted to be $14.26 in 2000. The leading states for the production of fluid power valves and hose fittings are all east of the Mississippi and include Connecticut, Minnesota, Texas, New Jersey, Michigan, and Ohio.

According to the NFPA, the fluid power industry underwent two periods of sustained growth in the 1980s and 1990s. The average annual growth rate of the industry between 1987 and 1990 was 9.5 percent, and this figure climbed to 11.7 percent for the years 1993 through 1995. This remarkable growth was due to the expansion of existing markets and new markets, especially robotics and active suspension systems on automobiles—due to the introduction of electrohydraulic and electropneumatic technologies.

ORGANIZATION AND STRUCTURE

According to the NFPA, fluid power is energy that is transmitted and controlled through a pressurized fluid—liquid or gas. Fluid power valves regulate the liquid or gas as it moves through valves, hoses, and fittings. The term fluid power thus applies to both hydraulics and pneumatics. Hydraulics utilizes liquid, oil, or water under pressure, while pneumatics refers to the use of compressed air. Fluid power is often used in conjunction with other technologies such as sensors, transducers, and microprocessors. Included in the total fluid power market are fluid power valves and fittings as well as hydraulic and pneumatic pumps, cylinders, rotary actuators, motors, filters, hose accumulators, air preparation accessories, stationary compressors, and other products.

The fluid power industry is generally divided into three large segments: mobile hydraulic, industrial hydraulic, and pneumatic. Historically, mobile hydraulic applications have accounted for about 50 percent of fluid power sales while the other two segments each share about 25 percent of the market. The mobile hydraulic segment (heavy truck, construction equipment, and agricultural machinery), although the largest, is also the most volatile.

The aerospace industry, construction equipment, heavy truck, agricultural equipment, and the machine tool and materials handling industries account for about 75 percent of the total fluid power consumption in the United States. The other 25 percent is divided amongst more than 500 other industries. In 1992, the last year for which figures have been published, the top five product share by type in order of dollar value were: nonaerospace-type hydraulic and pneumatic fittings and couplings for hose; aerospace-type hydraulic and pneumatic fluid power hose or tube end fittings and assemblies; aerospace-type hydraulic fluid power valves; nonaerospace-type flareless fittings and couplings (including nonmetal fittings) used in fluid power transfer systems; and nonaerospace-type pneumatic directional control valves. The rest of the market was divided by eight other categories by type.

Most of the establishments engaged in this industry employ more than 20 people. Therefore, this industry is characterized by larger businesses and labor-intensive processes. Throughout the 1990s the amount of employees per establishment was higher than the average of all manufacturing—as were payroll, hours worked, and wage statistics and shipments per establishment. Shifting from earlier trends, shipments per establishment also were higher than average, but investment per establishment was average.

Fluid power valves rely heavily on a number of economic sectors and industries for business inputs. The highest percentage of input is provided by blast furnaces and steel mills at 12.9 percent, followed by wholesale trade materials at 12.7 percent. Manufactured pipe, valves, and pipefittings represent 8.8 percent; manufactured goods from iron and steel foundries, 7.4 percent; and screw machine products, 4.8 percent. The remaining input categories are all less then 4.0 percent.

CURRENT CONDITIONS

The National Fluid Power Association (NFPA) is optimistic about industry growth even though fluid power consumption growth in 1998 was less than in 1997. Reasons for optimism include a strong and continued global demand for consumer goods and growth in demand for capital equipment in Eastern Europe and South America. Exports have played an increasingly important role in the U.S. fluid power industry. In 1989 U.S. fluid power exports were valued at $500 million, but by 1996 this figure had more than doubled to $1.1 billion. This represented an average annual export growth rate of about 17 percent. In 1997 exports stood at $1.3 billion.

Fluid power imports, however, are also rising. In 1989, U.S. imports of fluid power products stood at $350 million, but by 1996 this figure had increased to $1.1 billion. In 1997 imports stood at $1.2 billion. The five top importing countries of U.S. fluid power goods were: Canada with $370 million, Mexico with $115 million, the United Kingdom with $125 million, Germany with $96 million, and Japan with $88 million. These countries purchased 61 percent of all U.S. fluid power exports in 1997. Surprisingly four of these countries were also the largest exporters of fluid power products to the United States— Germany with $324 million, Japan with $233 million, Canada with $142 million, the United Kingdom with $141 million, and Italy with $66 million. In 1997, 74 percent of U.S. fluid power imports came from these five countries.

INDUSTRY LEADERS

The top companies engaged in the fluid power industry include: ITT Industries; Vickers, Inc.; SPX Corporation; and the Cooper Cameron Corporation.

ITT Industries of White Plains, New York, makes a wide variety of products and services in many fields through its ITT Fluid Technology division including pumps, valves, mixers, and other fluid technology products including Koni shock absorbers and struts for the automotive market. ITT Aerospace Controls manufactures fuel, hydraulic, pneumatic, and solenoid valves. ITT generated $2.1 billion in sales in the fluid power market in 1998 and has 13,000 employees.

Vickers, Inc. has been part of the Eaton Corp. since 1999 and is headquartered in Maumee, Ohio. Vickers was once part of Aeroquip-Vickers, which had sales of $2.1 billion in 1998. Vickers was founded in 1921 in Los

Angeles to design and build hydraulic machinery. Aeroquip-Vickers produces a wide range of products for the fluid power industry, including all pressure ranges of hoses, fittings, adapters, couplings, and other fluid connectors along with motor pumps, valves, and electrohydraulic, hydraulic, and pneumatic cylinders. Its Fluid Power Division produces and services 400 products and 34,000 components, including hydraulic and electrohydraulic equipment for global aerospace, marine, and defense markets. Vickers, Inc. employs nearly 4,900 people. In 1999 Aeroquip-Vickers opened an $11-million automotive hose and fittings factory in Queretaro, Mexico, for automotive air conditioning and power steering systems.

The SPX Corporation of Muskegon, Michigan, nearly doubled its size with the acquisition of General Signal Corporation in 1998. SPX's Hytec division produces high-pressure hydraulic pumps, rams, valves, pullers, and other equipment. Its Power Team produces hydraulic equipment for automotive and industrial markets as well as high-pressure hydraulic pumps, cylinders, and valves. In 1997, prior to its acquisition of General Signal, SPX had sales of $922 million and employed nearly 4,600 people.

Cooper Cameron Corporation of Houston, Texas, produces land and offshore hydraulic control and drilling systems for the oil industry as well as hydraulic industrial equipment including compressor systems. Products include oil and gas pressure control equipment including valves, wellheads, chokes, and blowout preventors. It also produces assembled systems for oil and gas drilling, production, and transmission. In 1997 Cooper Cameron had sales of $1.81 million and employed 9,600 people.

RESEARCH AND TECHNOLOGY

Research in the fluid power industry is aimed at three key issues, according to the NFPA: higher operating pressures, lower noise levels, and less environmental contamination due to leakage. The industry has always been driven towards higher operating pressures, and this demand is not expected to subside. The noise issue is relatively new and has come because of more stringent government noise regulations. The leakage issue applies more to hydraulics than it does to pneumatics, especially hydraulic oil leakage; this is being addressed with increased use of straight thread connectors, a renewed interest in water in hydraulic systems, and more environmentally friendly fluids.

Under continuing pressure from the Environmental Protection Agency (EPA), the fluid power industry is turning towards more environmentally friendly fluids for use in hydraulic systems and products. To be considered environmentally safe, fluids must be readily biodegradable and virtually non-toxic; however, many such products, especially vegetable oils, have a deteriorating effect on commonly used urethane seals through *hydrolysis.* Parker Seals Packing has, however, developed a high grade urethane (known as P4301A90) that resists hydrolysis. Thus, environmentally friendly oils such as rapeseed oil can be used in some hydraulic applications. Another problem with the use of vegetable oils in these applications was the propensity for rapid oxidation at high temperatures—oils are not fire resistant. To deal with this problem, Houghton International of Valley Forge, Pennsylvania, has begun marketing a Canola Oil based hydraulic fluid called Cosmolubric B-230 that is described as a ". . . vegetable oil derived fire-resistant hydraulic fluid with additives to enhance corrosion protection, metal passivation, and oxidative inhibition."

Other trends include the use of exotic materials, miniaturized pneumatic valves, and solid-state pressure switches. In 1999 Parker Hannifin, for instance, introduced corrosion free compression tube fittings made from a titanium alloy. The company also produces compression tube fittings made of Hastelloy, a nickel-molybdenum alloy as well as Alloy 400, a nickel-copper alloy.

Kenneth Korane, managing editor of *Machine Design,* sees a growing demand for miniaturized pneumatic valves. "The world of pneumatics is getting smaller. A growing need for economical systems that are durable, flexible, and fast is feeding demand for downsized components," writes Korane. Smaller valves are easier to install, take up less space, and answer the growing need for valves that can be mounted on moving actuators and end effectors according to Frank Latino, senior product engineer for the Festo Company. Weight is also a growing issue. "More and more, pneumatic valves are used in portable equipment where weight and size become critical," according to Jim Crain, vice president of the Cincinnati based Clippard Instrument Laboratory. "Small valves are put into everything from clinical chemistry instruments to medical equipment itself," concurs Les Greenberg, business unit manager for Vector Engineering.

Solid state pressure switches used in fluid power circuits provide fast and precise operations and a longer cycle life than conventional electromechanical switches, according to Richard Schneider, an editor at *Hydraulics & Pneumatics.* "In addition, microprocessor circuitry makes possible performance features which extend the basic capabilities of pressure switches and allow solid state models to handle difficult applications." Schneider feels that the integration of solid-state technology into these applications represents significant technological advance for the industry.

FURTHER READING

Adams, R. , J.P. Kromdyk, and T. Noblit. "Canola Oil-Based Fluid is Gentle on Environment." *Hydraulics & Pneumatics,* April 1999.

Cooper Cameron Corp. *Connected @ Cooper Cameron.* Houston, TX: Cooper Cameron Corp., 1999. Available from http://www.coopercameron.com.

D & B Million Dollar Directory: America's Leading Public and Private Companies. Bethlehem, PA: Dun & Bradstreet, 1999.

Hitchcox, A.L. "Fluid Formulations Continue Evolutionary Improvements." *Hydraulics & Pneumatics,* September 1999.

Hoover's Masterlist of Major U.S. Companies 1998-1999. Austin, TX: Hoover's Business Press, 1998.

ITT Industries, Inc. *ITT Industries: Engineered for Life.* White Plains, NY: ITT Industries, Inc., 1999. Available from http://www.ittind.com.

Korane, Kenneth J. "Mini Pneumatics Joins the Big Leagues." *Machine Design,* 9 October 1997.

National Fluid Power Association. *NFPA: Solutions Through Motion Technology.* Milwaukee, WI: National Fluid Power Association, 1998. Available from http://www.nfpa.com.

"Parker Hannifin has Exotic Alloy Fittings." *Manufacturing Chemist,* April 1999.

Pentair, Inc. *Pentair.* St. Paul, MN: Pentair, Inc., 1999. Available from http://www. pentair.com.

SPX Corp. *SPX Corporation.* Owatonna, MN: SPX Corp., 1999. Available from http://www.spx.com.

Schneider, Richard T. "Solid-State Pressure Switches are Coming On Strong." *Hydraulics & Pneumatics,* May 1999.

Vickers Inc. *Vickers.* Maumee, OH: Aeroquip-Vickers, 1999. Available from http://www.vickerssystems.com.

Wangsaard, M.F. "Keeping Environmentally Safe Hydraulic Fluids in Their Place." *Hydraulics & Pneumatics,* February 1999.

SIC 3493

STEEL SPRINGS, EXCEPT WIRE

This category includes establishments primarily engaged in manufacturing leaf springs, hot wound springs, and coiled flat springs. Establishments primarily engaged in manufacturing wire springs are classified in **SIC 3495: Wire Springs.**

NAICS CODE(S)

332611 (Steel Spring (except Wire) Manufacturing)

According to the U.S. Census Bureau's *1997 Economic Census—Manufacturing,* 128 establishments operated in this category for part or all of 1997. Industry-wide employment totaled 5,375 workers receiving a payroll of more than $174.0 million. Of these employees, 4,108 worked in production, putting in almost 9 million hours to earn wages of more than $120 million. Overall shipments for the industry were valued at more than $761 million. According to the *1995 Census of Manufactures,*

the specific segment of the industry covered by **SIC 3493: Steel Springs, Except Wire** employed 4,000 people and had a payroll of $126.3 million. Industry shipments were valued at $570.9 million, a decline of about 4 percent from the 1994 level of $593.5 million. For more information on the spring manufacturing industry as a whole, consult the essay on **SIC 3495: Wire Springs.**

Barnes Group Inc. of Bristol, Connecticut led the industry with 1998 sales of more than $651 million. Kuhlman Corp. of Savannah, Georgia followed with sales of more than $643 million in 1997, according to the most recent information available on Infotrac databases. Third place in the industry was occupied by Chicago-based American Steel Foundries, with $300 million in sales for its fiscal year ended September 30, 1997. Firestone Industrial Products Co. of Carmel, Indiana placed next with 1998 sales of $109 million, while Reyco Industries Inc. of Springfield, Missouri generated sales of $52 million for its fiscal year ended March 31, 1998. Rounding out the top six industry leaders was Spirol International Corp. of Danielson, Connecticut, with sales of $50 million for its fiscal year ended September 25, 1998.

The automotive industry is the largest consumer of steel springs. The Spring Manufacturers Institute Inc. (SMI) reported that sales to automotive customers accounted for the largest portion—41.3 percent of industry sales in 1992—followed by industrial equipment customers, which accounted for 8.8 percent of sales. Alloy, carbon, and stainless steels were the most commonly used spring materials because of their strength. Titanium, however, was gaining popularity in the early 1990s because of its superior strength, light weight, and resistance to corrosion. Titanium's high cost was once prohibitive, but new, less expensive titanium alloys expanded its use.

Advances in technology have boosted the production capabilities of some spring manufacturers, but this is not a requirement for survival in the industry. In *Springs,* George Keremedjiev, president of Tecknow Education Services Inc., noted that spring manufacturing companies were using anything from "state-of-the-art electronics in tooling to machinery and tooling that seemingly is frozen in time back in the 1950s." In other words, the technology employed in spring factories can run the gamut from old machines fitted with electronic sensors that check spring positioning to the Spring Manufacturers Institute Inc.'s (SMI) Spring Design software program, which enables the most novice engineer to successfully design springs. The lack of nationwide standards for spring making has hindered the greater implementation of technology.

Because the capital investments required for advances in technology are high, companies must consider both the competitive advantages and cost-effectiveness of modernization. If a company is able to maintain or increase sales volume with old assets, it may not be beneficial to modernize its machinery because of the cost involved. SMI's *1992 Annual Market Summary* noted that modernization would be an inefficient use of assets unless it helped "to produce a higher profit percentage on net sales." Nevertheless, Keremedjiev predicted in *Springs* that modern methods of production are needed for a spring manufacturer "to achieve world class quality in the production process." Furthermore, according to Scott Rankin of Vulcan Spring in *Springs,* there is universal recognition that technology will change the industry. Spring making, once known as the "black art" because of its difficulty, can now be mastered by a "spring maker with a month's knowledge and the ability to type numbers on a keyboard," noted Rankin.

As trade barriers are removed throughout the world, the American spring industry has had to compete for foreign manufacturing customers. Supplying American springs to foreign customers will keep the industry competitive because, according to SMI president Pete Peterson, "We don't worry too much about Japanese springs landing in America. But we must worry about the finished products coming here." To compete globally, some American spring makers have counteracted manufacturers' preferences for national suppliers by forming joint ventures with prominent foreign spring makers. One such joint venture allowed America's largest spring maker, Associated Spring of the Barnes Group, to establish relationships with Japanese automakers through its association with NHK Spring Co. Ltd. of Japan, Japan's largest spring maker.

FURTHER READING

1995 Census of Manufactures, Washington: U.S. Department of Commerce, 1997.

Infotrac Company Profiles. Available at http://web6.infotrac .galegroup.com (2/12/99).

Keremedjiev, George. "Sensors and Electronics in Spring Manufacture . . . the Key to Savings and Quality." *Springs,* May 1993.

"Looking Ahead—Not Back—as SMI Celebrates its 60th Anniversary." *Springs,* October 1993.

Peterson, Bud. "The Family Tree of Springmakers Withstands the Winds of Change." *Springs,* May 1993, 77-85.

"Petersons Stamp Success on Spring Industry." *Springs,* October 1993.

"Removing the Veil of the 'Black Art,° Newcomers Share Their Enthusiasm for the Springs Industry." *Springs,* October 1992.

"Spring Design Enters New Era." *Springs,* October 1992.

U.S. Census Bureau. *Annual Survey of Manufactures,* Washington: U.S. Census Bureau, 1991.

U.S. Census Bureau. *1997 Economic Census—Manufacturing.* Available at http://www.census.gov/prod/ec97/97m3326a.pdf (visited 2/12/00).

Additional information provided by the Spring Manufacturers Institute Inc.

SIC 3494

VALVES AND PIPE FITTINGS, NOT ELSEWHERE CLASSIFIED

This category includes establishments primarily engaged in manufacturing metal valves and pipe fittings, not elsewhere classified, such as plumbing and heating valves, and pipe fittings, flanges, and unions, except from purchased pipes. Establishments primarily engaged in manufacturing plastics pipe fittings are classified in **SIC 3089: Plastics Products, Not Elsewhere Classified;** those manufacturing plumbing fixture fittings and trim are classified in **SIC 3432: Plumbing Fixture Fittings and Trim;** and those manufacturing fittings and couplings for garden hoses are classified in **SIC 3429: Hardware, Not Elsewhere Classified.**

NAICS CODE(S)

332919 (Other Metal Valve and Pipe Fitting Manufacturing)
332999 (All Other Miscellaneous Fabricated Metal Product Manufacturing)

According to the U.S. Census Bureau's *1997 Economic Census—Manufacturing,* 222 establishments operated in this category for part or all of 1997. Industry-wide employment totaled 17,652 workers receiving a payroll of almost $559 million. Of these employees, 12,964 worked in production, putting in almost 27 million hours to earn wages of almost $363 million. Overall shipments for the industry were valued at almost $2.8 billion.

Parker Hannafin Corp. Refrigerating Specialties of Broadview, Illinois led the industry with $5 billion in sales for its fiscal year ended June 30, 1998. ITT Industries Inc. of West Harrison, New York generated 1998 sales of almost $4.5 billion. Third place in the industry was occupied by Delphi Energy and Engine Management Systems of Flint, Michigan, with 1998 sales of more than $3.8 billion. Despite its financial success, controversy surrounded Delphi in November 1999 when the Madison County chapter of the NAACP raised allegations of discriminatory hiring practices. The NAACP logged an estimated 150 complaints that Delphi conducted interviews with questions that did not pertain to job demands, that its interviewers refused to explain unclear wording of questions, and that the company refused to specify the reasons behind applicants' rejections. NAACP board member and attorney Donald Hurst characterized Delphi's applicant tests as ''not racially neutral,'' and suggested that the NAACP might consider filing a class-action lawsuit.

Other industry leaders included Grinnell Corp. of Exeter, New Hampshire, which garnered sales of almost $3.1 billion for its fiscal year ended June 30, 1997. Rounding out the top five industry leaders was the Crane Co. of Stamford, Connecticut, with 1998 sales of almost $2.3 billion.

The valves and pipe fittings industry relies heavily on both the oil and construction industries. The domestic oil industry has been depressed since the mid-1980s, but the retrofitting of pipes in the housing market has served to maintain a level of stability in this industry.

Growth in the industry was assured because of changes in fire sprinkler laws. A fire in a Puerto Rico hotel in the early 1990s caused the federal government to review and change laws regarding automatic fire sprinkler systems in buildings exceeding six stories. Additionally, a low-rise hotel fire in Chicago, which killed 15 people in 1993, caused the federal automatic fire sprinkler laws to change regarding buildings lower than seven stories. As a result, many buildings started retrofitting to comply with new safety regulations; as a secondary consequence, demand increased for many of the products manufactured in this sector.

In the late 1990s, approximately 69 percent of the metal valve and pipe fitting industry was engaged in producing metal fittings, flanges, and unions for piping systems. Another 23 percent of the industry was engaged in producing plumbing and heating valves.

FURTHER READING

Darnay, Arsen J., ed. *Manufacturing USA*. 5th ed. Detroit: Gale Research, 1996.

Heikens, Norm. ''Anderson, Ind., Auto Parts Maker Faces Discrimination Complaints.'' *Knight-Ridder/Tribune Business News,* 19 November 1999.

Infotrac Company Profiles, 2 December 1999. Available at http://web6.infotrac.galegroup.com.

U.S. Bureau of the Census. *1995 Annual Survey of Manufactures.* Washington: GPO, January 1997.

U.S. Census Bureau. *1997 Economic Census-Manufacturing,* 2 December 2000. Available at http://www.census.gov/prod/ec97/97m3329d.pdf.

SIC 3495

WIRE SPRINGS

This industry consists of establishments primarily engaged in manufacturing wire springs from purchased wire. Establishments primarily engaged in assembling wire bedsprings or seats are classified in the Furniture and Fixtures industries.

NAICS CODE(S)

332612 (Wire Spring Manufacturing)
334518 (Watch, Clock, and Part Manufacturing)

INDUSTRY SNAPSHOT

In 1997 the value of shipments in the wire springs industry was approximately $2.22 billion, which was extremely close to the 1996 figure of $2.23 billion. This figure is expected to increase to approximately $2.6 billion through 2000. The value of precision mechanical wire springs produced by the industry in 1997 was slightly over $900 million, and the value of other wire springs was about $1.3 billion. The largest bloc of material consumed by the wire springs industry in 1997 was steel wire and wire products valued at nearly $535 million. There were 394 establishments in the industry in 1997, which is close to 1996's figure of 383 but down sharply from the 432 establishments reported in 1982. Of these 394 establishments, 199 had 1 to 19 employees; 147 had 20 to 99 employees; and 48 had 100 or more employees.

ORGANIZATION AND STRUCTURE

The capital requirements for the wire springs industry are generally low, with average investment per establishment around 40 percent of that for the manufacturing sector as a whole. ''Someone who gets to be a proficient springmaker may decide he doesn't have to be working for someone else anymore. He will go out on his own and get the financing to get started with a few pieces of equipment. This is going to be as constant a thing in the future as it has been in the past,'' predicted Rich Chud, president of Wesco Spring Co., during a 1998 *Springs* round table on the future of the spring industry.

Prior to the 1980s, it was rare for firms to cooperate in the production of springs, but this has changed in the last two decades. Firms learned to cooperate on a number of bases. For example, some firms developed expertise in grinding springs at high tolerances, while others developed high levels of efficiency in looping the wire on the ends of springs. Other spring-producing firms found it advantageous to hire these specialty firms for such operations. ''We as a small spring company probably couldn't survive if it weren't for other spring companies that we've met through the SMI (Spring Manufacturers Institute) and do work for,'' Dave Habicht, president of the Kirk-Habicht Co., told the *Springs* round table. ''We make parts for about 12 other spring companies. That's our sales force.''

The smallest firms have fewer than 25 employees and generally do not design the springs they produce, relying instead on specifications provided by their customers. They typically produce small batches of springs made from larger wires (up to about 3/8 inches in diameter), as well as both large and small batches from smaller diameter wires (up to about 0.08 inches in diameter). These versatile firms typically have one or two hand-operated spring coilers and several automatic spring coilers, in addition to a lathe or two for coiling heavier wires. Furthermore, these small firms typically have a number of machines devoted to the other processes necessary for spring production, including grinders, spring testers, baking ovens, and various machine tools. "If you look at the SMI membership, I would say 80 percent of them are ma and pa spring companies," Chud told his fellow spring makers. "As far as the future is concerned, I'd say there will always be ma and pa spring companies serving particular markets. There will always be a local market or niche where they can find a place for themselves in the industry." In 1997, companies with 19 or fewer employees made up the largest segment of the industry. But Dan Sebastian, president of MW Industries sees the spring industry of the future being dominated by fewer and larger companies. "If you look at the spring industry 25 or even 50 years from now, I think you'll see four or five players controlling the vast majority of the spring marketplace," he told the round table. "I also see a lot of small companies still existing for individual niche areas for a particular reason. But I think we're going to see more Associated Spring, Peterson Spring-sized companies over the next few years because it's the nature of the beast," he concludes.

Medium-size companies have 20 to 99 employees, and these made up the second largest share of companies in the industry. These firms typically employ engineers to design and test springs. Medium-size firms usually specialize in producing coil springs in large batches or are diversified in the production of a large number of spring types. These firms employ processes similar to those used in smaller firms, and the main distinctions regarding capital goods were the number and size of machines. These firms also typically have a greater variety of machines to supplement core production processes, such as electroplating equipment. Using computers in the design and production of springs throughout the 1990s has led to greater qualitative distinctions in the production processes of smaller and larger firms.

Large firms have more than 100 employees and typically have a larger technical and scientific staff. There were about 48 such establishments in the United States in 1997. In addition to engineers, such firms often employ metallurgists and highly trained inspectors. These firms also devote substantial resources to specialized research equipment, such as fatigue testers and wire-twisting machines. These large establishments are typically diversi-

fied in the production of all major spring types and are often diversified across industry lines. The Peterson Spring Company of Southfield, Michigan, for example, has about 900 employees. The company has a home office engineering staff that complements the production engineers working in Peterson's various plants as well as engineers and metallurgists involved in product design, performance analysis, and research and development.

In the years just after World War II, production of springs was tightly concentrated in the northeastern states of Connecticut, New York, Pennsylvania, Illinois, and Ohio. By 1997, however, the top five states with spring manufacturing establishments were Illinois with 51, California with 45, Ohio with 37, Michigan with 34, and Connecticut with 29. Many plants in the industrial Midwest produce springs for the automobile industry while many California firms produce springs for the aircraft industry.

The output of the wire spring industry is widely dispersed across industry and sector lines reflecting the great extent to which the industry is dependent not only on the production of manufactures, but on the production of the economy at large. The top ten industries and sectors buying the outputs of the wire springs industry in 1998 were new construction (6.9 percent); repair and maintenance (6.4 percent); personal consumption (5.1 percent); mattresses and bedsprings (5.1 percent); miscellaneous fabricated wire products (5.1 percent); non-farm residential structures (4.9 percent); exports (4.6 percent); motor vehicles and passenger car bodies (4.5 percent); maintenance and repair of residential structures (4.2 percent); and retail trade (3.5 percent.)

BACKGROUND AND DEVELOPMENT

The wire spring manufacturing industry grew rapidly in the post-World War II period. The number of plants producing precision springs increased by about six-fold from 1940 to 1980. Membership in the Spring Manufacturers Institute (SMI) increased from 40 establishments in 1940 to about 350 in the late 1990s.

The SMI was founded in 1933 and is headquartered in Oak Brook, Illinois. The SMI publishes the quarterly *Springs: The Magazine of Spring Technology*, books such as the *Handbook of Spring Design* and various publications on topical subjects such as computer software, federal regulations relating to health and safety issues, etc. In 1998 SMI undertook a partnership with Wright State University in Dayton, Ohio that introduced engineering students to the spring industry, spring design, and performance analysis. A number of programs are involved ranging from industry internships to courses of study including a full college level course in spring design. The industry is also served by the American Society of Mechanical Engineers, the American Society for Testing and Material, and the American Society for Metals.

There are three primary types of wire springs: compression springs absorb energy as they are compressed, extension springs as they are extended, and torsion springs as they are twisted. The design and production of wire springs has been referred to as a "Black Art" because of the complexity of interactive variables that must be taken into account. The industry used about 100 types of metals in the production of springs. The choice of the optimal metal depends on such conditions as the potential for corrosion, conductivity, the loads to be borne by the spring, the temperature ranges to which the spring will be exposed, the desired working-life of the spring, and size constraints. The basic types of metals used in spring production include high-carbon steels, steel alloys, stainless steels, and copper and nickel-based alloys. Since the cost of materials can vary from one to hundreds of dollars per pound and safety was often a factor (in production of vehicles, for instance), the optimal choice of materials was vital.

Production begins with the process of coiling metal wire. For smaller batches (several hundred or less), the manufacturer uses a hand-operated coiler or a lathe. Larger batches require automatic coilers. Whereas in the mid-1970s, many coilers produced at the rate of 3,000 to 5,000 springs per hour, by the 1980s machines were sold that coiled up to 18,000 springs per hour. After being coiled, springs were baked to stabilize their shape. Thereafter, they were compressed to remove any set that would accumulate during usage. Lastly, the ends of the springs were shaped (in the case of extension and torsion springs) and ground. Precision grinding was among the most time-consuming and expensive operations in the production of springs. After they were thus formed, springs were typically finished by oiling, painting, electroplating, or oxidizing.

In addition to the more common wire spring types are hairsprings. These are spiral springs made from very fine flattened wire (as thin as 0.0002 inches). These springs were used in clocks and watches, as well as specialized precision instruments. Only only a few firms produced hairsprings.

CURRENT CONDITIONS

In the early 1990s, the value of shipments rose slightly and then decreased to $1.743 billion in 1992. Since 1992, the value of shipments rose steadily, and by 1995 it reached $2.223 billion. It was expected to reach $2.587 billion in 2000. In total, the industry employed 18,798 in 1997, with 15,128 involved in production. These figures are expected to increase slightly by 2000 to approximately 19,500 total employees of which 15,300 will be production workers. The average wage in 1996 was $12.29 per hour; this figure is expected to increase to

$13.69 per hour in 2000. Total industry wages reached $3.89 billion.

In 1998 *Springs* gathered together eight industry leaders for a round table discussion on the current state and future of the wire spring industry. John Petry, vice president/general manager of Sandvik Steel-Spring Products almost immediately noted that the industry was growing between 6 and 8 percent a year or almost double the GDP growth rate. In spite of this growth rate, the spring industry is nevertheless threatened by growing demand for non-wire or non-mechanical springs such as gas springs and plastic products. Other participants were heartened by the growth of new markets for the industry. "The amount of parts we put into electronic components today versus 20 years ago is mind boggling. Innovation may change the size and nature of springs, but they're still there," said Dan Sebastian, president of MW Industries.

INDUSTRY LEADERS

In 1998 the top four American manufacturers of wire springs, excluding manufacturers of wire springs for furniture and bedding, were Associated Spring, the aforementioned Peterson Spring, Newcomb Spring, and Mid-West Spring. Associated Spring of Farmington, Connecticut is part of the Barnes Group. Founded in 1857, it has since become the largest manufacturer of springs and precision metalforms in North America. The company has 2,000 employees and was a $280 million business in 1998. Associated has 10 manufacturing divisions in five countries, and it produces 13,000 different parts including compression, extension, torsion, die, stock, and power springs and wireforms for its over 3,000 customers worldwide.

Peterson Spring of Southfield, Michigan was founded in Detroit in 1914 and is part of the international group of Peterson-American companies—the largest privately owned spring group in North America. Peterson has 14 manufacturing plants in the United States, Canada, Mexico, and England and produces compression, torsion, and extension springs, as well as multiform clips and wireforms. In 1998 Peterson had sales of $95 million and 900 employees.

The Newcomb Spring Corporation is located in Southington, Connecticut and manufactures compression, extension, and torsion springs as well as wire and strip forms and metal stampings. Newcomb also specializes in the production of battery contact springs for a variety of battery powered devices. In 1998 Newcomb had 300 employees and sales of $40 million. Mid-West Springs is located in Romeoville, Illinois and employed 500 and had sales of $38 million in 1998.

RESEARCH AND TECHNOLOGY

In the mid- to late 1990s there were no major breakthroughs in spring design or spring technology. Instead, the industry concentrated on and expanded the use of computer software in spring production and design and the use and development of new materials. This included software developed by the SMI for the design of compression, extension, and torsion springs. The program is based on parameters drawn from the *SMI Handbook of Spring Design*, and enables the design of optimal springs working under various sets of constraints.

Computer Numerically Controlled (CNC) springmaking equipment is also being employed by spring manufacturers after years of lagging behind the machine tool industry because of the cost of the machines, the relatively small size of the spring industry, and because of the complex set of operations required for the production of springs. CNC technology, however, has made possible increased speed of production, lesser setup and training times, greater precision, and lower costs.

New materials also played an increasing role in spring production throughout 1990s, including memory alloy springs, beryllium copper, which is especially well suited for springs needing increased production speeds and decreased product size and springs made from titanium alloys. Springs made from titanium alloys weigh one-half of those made from steel and are also highly resistant to corrosion. The high cost of titanium makes it prohibitively expensive for many applications, but new and less costly titanium alloys are responsible for expanded use of the metal in the spring industry.

FURTHER READING

Associated Spring. *Associated Spring*. Farmington, Connecticut: Associated Spring, 1999. Available from http://www.asbg .com.

Capaldi, F. "Beryllium Copper Flat Springs." *Springs: The Magazine of Spring Technology*. Spring 1999, 32.

D & B Million Dollar Directory: America's Leading Public & Private Companies. Series 1999, Bethlehem, PA: Dun & Bradstreet, 1999.

Darney, Arsan J., ed. *Manufacturing USA.*, 6th ed. Detroit: Gale Research, 1999.

Domsch, David and David Bywaters. "Looking Ahead to the 21st Century." *Springs: The Magazine of Spring Technology*. Winter 1999, 9-12.

"Educating Tomorrow's Spring Engineers." *Springs: The Magazine of Spring Technology*. Winter 1999, 14-16.

Halleran, L. Michael. "Beryllium Copper." *Springs: The Magazine of Spring Technology*. Summer 1998, 75.

"Making History: A Chronicle of Companies That Shaped the Spring Industry." *Springs: The Magazine of Spring Technology* Spring 1999, 8-31.

Mitteer, John. "Bend or Slide: Sometimes It Makes More Sense To Use CNC Wire Forming Equipment . . ." *Springs: The Magazine of Spring Technology*. Winter 1999.

Newcomb Spring. *Newcomb Spring*. Southington, Connecticut: Newcomb Spring, 1998. Available from http://www .newcombspring.com.

Peterson Spring. *Peterson Spring*. Southfield, Michigan: Peterson Spring, 1999. Available from http://www.pspring.com.

Schauer, Rita. "On the Table: A Mixed Outlook for Future Spring makers." *Springs: The Magazine of Springs Technology*. Summer 1999.

Spring Manufacturers Institute. *Spring Manufacturers Institute*. Oak Brook, Illinois: Spring Manufacturers Institute, 1999. Available from:http://www.smihq.org.

U.S. Bureau of the Census. *Spring (Light Gauge) Manufacturing. 1997 Economic Census: Manufacturing—Industry Series*. Washington: G.P.O., 1999. Available from http://www.census .gov/prod/ec97/97m3326b.pdf.

Ward's Business Directory of U.S. Private and Public Companies 1998. Detroit: Gale Group, 1999.

SIC 3496

MISCELLANEOUS FABRICATED WIRE PRODUCTS

This category includes establishments primarily engaged in manufacturing miscellaneous fabricated wire products from purchased wire, such as noninsulated wire rope and cable, fencing, screening, netting, paper machine wire cloth, hangers, paper clips, kitchenware, and wire carts. Rolling mills engaged in manufacturing wire products are classified in the Primary Metal Industries. Establishments primarily engaged in manufacturing steel nails and spikes from purchased wire or rod are classified in **SIC 3315: Steel Wiredrawing and Steel Nails and Spikes;** those manufacturing nonferrous wire nails and spikes from purchased wire or rod are classified in **SIC 3399: Primary Metal Products, Not Elsewhere Classified;** those drawing and insulating nonferrous wire are classified in **SIC 3357: Drawing and Insulating of Nonferrous Wire;** and those manufacturing wire springs are classified in **SIC 3495: Wire Springs.**

NAICS CODE(S)

332618 (Other Fabricated Wire Product Manufacturing)

According to the U.S. Census Bureau's *1997 Economic Census—Manufacturing,* 1,253 establishments operated in this category for part or all of 1997. Industrywide employment totaled 41,821 workers receiving a payroll of more than $1.0 billion. Of these employees, 32,234 worked in production, putting in more than 62 million hours to earn wages of more than $641 million. Overall shipments for the industry were valued at almost $4.6 billion.

Engelhard Corp. of Iselin, New Jersey, a diversified firm involved in a variety of other businesses, led this industry in 1999 with overall sales of more than $40.5 billion. New York City-based Alpine Group Inc., which focused primarily on this industry, generated more than $919 million for its fiscal year ended April 30, 1998. UOP of Des Plaines, Illinois, placed third in the industry with sales of $770 million for 1997, according to the most recent results available on Infotrac databases. Columbus McKinnon Corp. of Amherst, New York garnered sales of more than $735 million for its fiscal year ended March 31, 1999. Belden Inc. of Clayton, Missouri rounded out the top five industry leaders with 1998 sales of almost $724 million.

The miscellaneous fabricated wire products industry produces a wide variety of wire-based goods, including barbed wire, bird cages, conveyor belts, hog rings, and paper clips. The largest single product produced by the industry is noninsulated ferrous wire rope and cable, representing 12.9 percent of the total product share in the 1990s. While ferrous and nonferrous wire cloth, ferrous woven wire products, fencing, and fence gates all claim significant shares of the market, the production of the majority of products produced by this industry is too limited to be represented statistically. The materials consumed by the industry include steel castings, plastics and bolts, stainless steel, and copper and aluminum wires. Steel wire is the most heavily consumed category of wire, with a delivered cost to the industry of $689.1 million in 1992.

The number of establishments involved in this industry fluctuated wildly during the 1980s and 1990s. The value of shipments rose from $2.4 billion in 1982 to almost $4.1 billion in 1994. The industry workforce grew moderately, rising from 36,800 employees in 1982 to 41,100 by 1994. In 1994, the 31,600 production workers in this industry averaged wages of $8.92 per hour. End users of these products vary widely, ranging from mattress and bedspring makers to tire makers, logging camps, and highway and building construction.

Barbed wire, the most famous of miscellaneous fabricated wire products, changed the course of American history. According to Henry D. and Frances T. McCallum, authors of *The Wire that Fenced the West,* ''The introduction of barbed wire in the 1870s had remarkable social and economic consequences. Before the wire's invention, fences were intended to keep animals and trespassers out. Because barbed wire effectively kept animals in, the landholding concepts of cattlemen and small settlers changed radically with the new power that barbed wire gave them.''

Before barbed wire, ranchers used plain wire, wooden fences, and natural hedges to mark their territory. These boundaries, however, were generally impractical, labor intensive, and highly penetrable. When a rancher

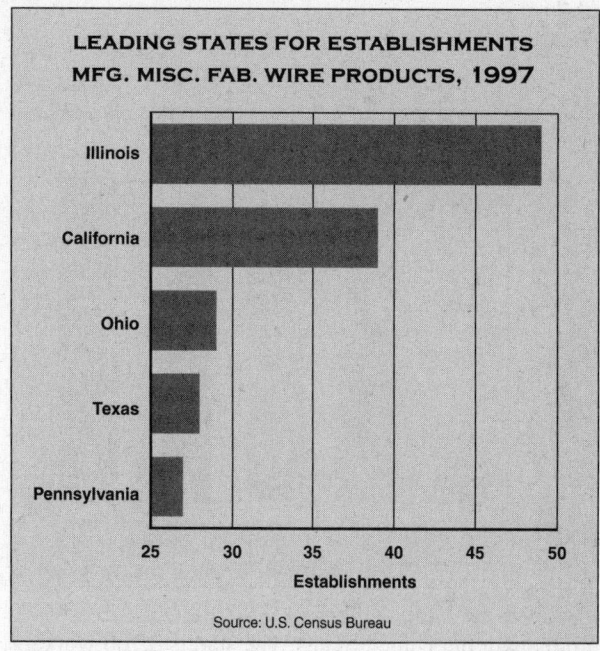

LEADING STATES FOR ESTABLISHMENTS
MFG. MISC. FAB. WIRE PRODUCTS, 1997

Source: U.S. Census Bureau

had only his family to tend the animals, maintaining a fence around the perimeter of hundreds or thousands of acres was out of the question. Because containment was so difficult, the rancher kept his stock to a low, manageable number. Getting rich in the West off of cattle and horses required a considerable investment in cowhands and a steady cash flow to keep them. The invention of barbed wire paved the way for large herds of cattle that needed little supervision. Credit for the invention is generally given to Isaac Ellwood and Joseph Glidden, who saw a sample of a wooden fence with sharp wire projections on display at the 1873 DeKalb County Fair in Illinois, and quickly set about patenting and manufacturing barbed wire.

Barbed wire also influenced how wars were fought. Barbed wire was first used as a war defense system during the Russo-Japanese War of 1904-1905. In 1914, the American Steel & Wire Division of United States Steel Corporation and many other U.S. manufacturers sent mile after mile of barbed wire to Europe, where it was tangled into barriers that were impenetrable by ground forces. In World War II, a new military occupation was created as a result of barbed wire's use. ''Frogmen'' were trained to cut clearings for submarines and ship propellers through the carloads of barbed wire dumped by the Japanese into the sea.

The Great Lakes region traditionally led the nation in shipments of miscellaneous fabricated wire products, due to the area's access to raw materials. By 1992, however, the regional breakdown had shifted. In the mid-1990s, Pennsylvania's 71 establishments ranked first in shipments for an individual state. Its shipments of $331.2 million represented 9.3 percent of the value of all wire

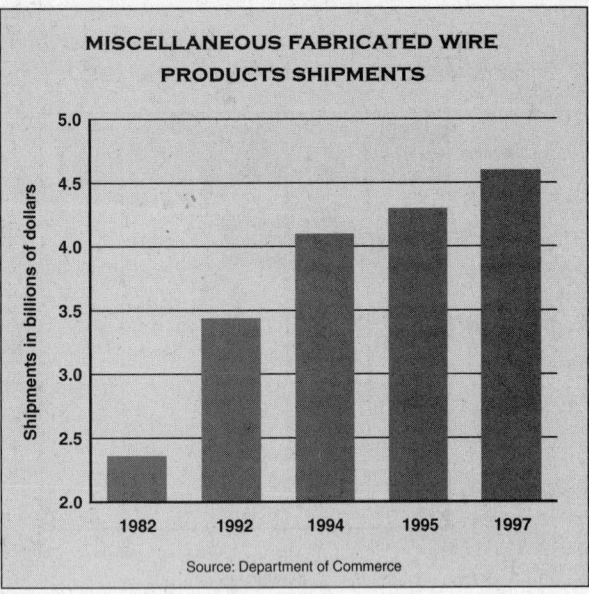

MISCELLANEOUS FABRICATED WIRE PRODUCTS SHIPMENTS

Source: Department of Commerce

products in the United States. The state's 2,700 workers averaged $10.61 per hour. Illinois ranked second, generating $321.0 million in shipments. Its 108 establishments employed 3,500 people at an average wage of $9.21 per hour. California's 125 establishments shipped $242.2 million and employed 2,500 people at an average hourly wage of $9.08. Missouri's 25 establishments shipped $229.9 million in goods. The 3,100 wire workers in Missouri averaged $7.41 per hour. Texas' 70 establishments shipped $198.0 million and employed a total of 2,500 people at an average hourly wage of $8.49.

FURTHER READING

Darnay, Arsen J., ed. *Manufacturing USA: Industry Analysis, Statistics, and Leading Companies.* 5th ed. Detroit: Gale Research Inc., 1996.

Infotrac Company Profiles. Available at http://web6.infotrac.galegroup.com (2/12/99).

McCallum, Henry D., and Frances T. McCallum. *The Wire that Fenced the West.* Norman: University of Oklahoma Press, 1985.

U.S. Census Bureau. *1997 Economic Census—Manufacturing.* Available at http://www.census.gov/prod/ec97/97m3326c.pdf (2/12/00).

SIC 3497

METAL FOIL AND LEAF

This category covers establishments primarily engaged in manufacturing gold, silver, tin, and other metal foil (including converted metal foil) and leaf. Also included are establishments primarily engaged in converting metal foil (including aluminum) into wrappers, cook-

ware, dinnerware, and containers, except bags and liners. Establishments primarily engaged in manufacturing plain aluminum foil are classified in **SIC 3353: Aluminum Sheet, Plate, and Foil.**

NAICS CODE(S)

322225 (Laminated Aluminum Foil Manufacturing for Flexible Packaging Uses)

332999 (All Other Miscellaneous Fabricated Metal Product Manufacturing)

INDUSTRY SNAPSHOT

The value of product shipments in the metal foil and leaf industry in 1996 was $3.6 billion. This figure was expected to rise to $4.1 billion by the year 2000. In 1995 there were 116 establishments involved in the industry. Of these, 78 establishments had 20 or more employees. In 1996 the industry employed approximately 8,500 people. Average hourly wages in 1996 were $15.95 and were expected to rise to $17.36 by 2000. In 1998 New Jersey and California led the country with the number of establishments involved in the metal foil and leaf industry, with 16 and 13 respectively. However, Kentucky and North Carolina were the leaders in terms of the value of shipments, totaling nearly 30 percent of U.S. output in the industry.

ORGANIZATION AND STRUCTURE

Aluminum foil, the bulk of which is converted into food containers and packaging for food and other products, is a major component of this industry. In 1995 a full 43 percent of the industry's output consisted of laminated aluminum foil rolls and sheets for flexible packaging uses, especially foil-paper laminate. Another 30 percent of the industry's output consisted of converted, unmounted aluminum foil packaging products. As a consequence, the fortunes of the industry were closely tied to the prosperity of the food packaging industry.

The remaining 27 percent of the industry's output consisted of unconverted metal foil and leaf and converted foil for non-packaging applications, many of which were on the cutting edge of technology, especially in the field of electronics. The industry was thus divided between those facets producing everyday household products—such as aluminum foil popcorn containers—and high technology foils—such as ultra-thin (3 microns) copper foil—to answer industry demands for the miniaturization of electronic components.

The largest segment of the metal foil and leaf industry was served by the Aluminum Foil Container Manufacturers Association, headquartered in Savannah, Georgia. This association, founded in 1955, was comprised of 14 member companies. Its journal, *Paper, Film and Foil Converter,* provided information to producers in the industry.

Firms involved in the production of metal foil and leaf were not generally involved in the production of metals. As Hamilton Bowman wrote in his *Handbook of Precision Sheet, Strip and Foil,* a foil producer's "operations are generally confined to the cold rolling, heat treating, flattening, slitting, and edge conditioning of coils of flat-rolled metal produced for him by a basic mill." However, the scope of operations in the industry had widened considerably in the latter years of the twentieth century as the use of foil for containers, packaging, electronics, and holograms became increasingly important.

BACKGROUND AND DEVELOPMENT

Metalsmiths have produced flat metal sheets for centuries. In its earliest form, metal foil was produced by hammering malleable metal against a flat surface. As early as the seventeenth century, metal foils were produced by hand-operated rolling mills. These early mills made use of two parallel iron cylinders through which metals were passed in a number of successive stages, depending on the thickness of foil desired. Thinner products were referred to as sheet and thicker products as plate. By the mid-nineteenth century, a great many powered rolling mills were in use in Europe and the United States. The use of parallel cylinders remains the dominant method of foil production today, and hammering techniques are still used in the production of gold leaf and foil.

By the end of the nineteenth century, continuous-process roller mills came into use. These mills differ substantially from their predecessors. Instead of reducing the metal to the desired thickness by making a series of passes, continuous-process mills operate on a longer piece of metal that is flattened to the desired thickness by being passed once through a series of roller pairs set at ever-closer distances to each other. These mills substantially reduce the cost of production by optimizing the flow of materials and reducing set-up times.

Until the mid-1920s continuous-process mills (also referred to as tandem or strip mills) were not able to produce widths greater than 24 inches. Then, more powerful mills were developed that could accommodate greater widths and, subsequently, narrower widths were produced by slitting broader widths of material.

A wide variety of metals are converted to foils, among them copper, gold, lead, magnesium, nickel, platinum, silver, tin, and zinc. Foil is generally defined as being 0.005 inches or less in thickness. Some foil producers also produce precision sheet and strip, which are materials between 0.015 and 0.005 inches in thickness.

The cold rolling of foil and precision sheet and strip requires much greater precision than the cold rolling of thicker sheets. Variations in thickness, temper, and finish need to be more controlled. Consequently, foil is produced at much slower speeds than thicker sheets, and

complex systems are required to monitor variation. Key developments in the post-World War II period include the use of smaller diameter rollers, the more rigid mounting of rollers, and more sophisticated drive mechanisms and systems of control.

Larger diameter rollers have the disadvantage of greater surface contact with the rolled metal. Greater force is required to overcome the greater frictional resistance of large rollers. Thus, for any given amount of energy used, large rollers reduce sheet thickness by lesser amounts than smaller rollers. The greater flexibility of smaller rollers requires that they be backed up by large adjacent rollers, called backup or support rolls. In four-high mills, each contact roller is backed up by a single support roll. In cluster mills, each contact roller is typically backed by nine support rolls. Steckel mills are four-high mills in which the rolls are not driven. Metal sheet is instead pulled through the rolls, permitting a great deal of thickness control, though somewhat less reduction per pass than a standard four-high mill. Large-diameter, two-high mills permit reductions of only 10 percent per pass, whereas four-high mills permit reductions of 50 to 60 percent and cluster mills reductions of 75 percent per pass. Smaller contact rollers enable not only greater reductions but also lesser variation in foil thickness.

Cold rolling makes metal harder and more brittle. Depending on the thickness of foil desired, cold rolled metals need to be heat treated, or annealed, in order to soften them for further reduction. Reductions obtained through cycles of annealing and cold rolling are constrained only by the mechanical limitations of the rolling machinery and by handling considerations.

Development of the metal foil and leaf industry was based on these basic technologies. In *Handbook of Precision Sheet, Strip and Foil,* Hamilton Bowman wrote that the growth of the industry since the 1960s resulted "as designers have come to appreciate the unique advantages of economy, weight saving, and dimensional precision inherent in these metals."

CURRENT CONDITIONS

The overall value of shipments for the metal foil and leaf industry increased steadily, but slowly, throughout the 1990s. In 1992 the value of shipments was $3.1 billion. By 1995 this figure had reached $3.7 billion, and by 2000 it was expected to be $4.2 billion. In 1997 the total value of shipments of laminated aluminum foil for flexible packaging usage totaled $1.4 billion. Employment in the industry grew slowly throughout the early 1990s, reaching a peak of 107,000 production workers in 1995. This figure, however, was expected to decline to 104,000 by the year 2000. The price of aluminum sheet, plate, and foil was expected to decrease 4 percent in 1999, with the year 2000 showing a 5.2 percent increase.

The future of the industry is dependent in large part on technical developments within and outside of the industry. A number of viable substitutes for metal foil laminates were developed in the 1990s, cutting into the market of the most important product of the industry. Among these new materials were metallized polypropylene, metallized paper, polyethylene, and ethylene vinyl alcohol. However, such new products as extremely thin steel foils and improved foil products for baking suggested the possibility of growth for the core products of the industry.

INDUSTRY LEADERS

In 1998 the top four U.S. companies in the metal foil and leaf industry were Gould Electronics, Hampden Papers, Alumax Foils, and Circuit Foil USA.

Gould's Foil Division, located in Eastlake, Ohio, was the leading supplier of copper foil in Europe and North America and the number two supplier in Pacific Rim countries. Gould produces specialty metal foils, such as nickel- and tin-plated copper foil and copper-aluminum-copper laminates. In 1998 Gould's foil division had 800 employees and did $67 million in business.

Hampden Papers of Holyoke, Massachusetts, produces packaging laminates. In 1998 it employed 200 people and generated $32 million in business.

Circuit Foil USA of Bordentown, New Jersey, produces electro-deposited copper foil for electronic applications. In 1998 the company employed 170 workers and had sales of $25 million.

Alumax Inc., located in Atlanta, became part of Alcoa in 1998. It is the third-largest U.S. producer of aluminum products, behind Alcoa and Reynolds. Alumax Foils, Inc., produces light and heavy aluminum foil. In 1998 the foil division had 200 employees and had sales of $31 million.

RESEARCH AND TECHNOLOGY

At the turn of the century, much of the ongoing research and development within the industry was aimed at producing ever-thinner foils for a variety of applications. Japan's Mitsui Mining & Smelting developed ultra-thin copper foil for electronic applications and Germany's Thyssen Krupp AG was producing a thin foil—Aluchrom 7A1 YHF—to be used in meeting new emissions standards for catalytic converters. The new product employed aluminum, yttrium and hafnium.

In the United States, the API Group introduced Atalfa in 1999. This was a new "optimum moisture barrier substrate" that employed 200 times less metal than aluminum foil. Atalfa has been approved for food contact.

Ultra-thin foils were also being developed for emergency equipment repairs, in which a flame from a match or a spark from a battery could trigger a "molecular marriage." This foil was being developed at Johns Hopkins University and consisted of a microscopic layering of two elements in alternating rows, each 50 to 100 atoms deep.

FURTHER READING

"API Group is Introducing Atalfa." *Packaging Week,* 26 August 1999.

Bowman, Hamilton B. *Handbook of Precision Sheet, Strip and Foil.* Metals Park, OH: American Society for Metals, 1980.

CF: Circuit Foil USA Web Site, 1999. Available from http://www.circuitfoilusa.com.

D & B Million Dollar Directory: America's Leading Public and Private Companies. Bethlehem, PA: Dun & Bradstreet, 1999.

"Fiery Foils Produce New Sealing Process." *USA Today,* June 1997.

"Goodbye Deflation! Prices Forecast to Rise in 2000." *Purchasing,* 21 October 1999.

"Mitsui Mining & Smelting Has Developed an Ultra-Thin Copper Foil for Microelectronic Printed Circuit Boards." *American Metal Market,* 18 May 1999.

Russell, John J., ed. *National Trade and Professional Associations of the United States, 32nd ed.* Washington, D.C.: Columbia Books, 1997.

"Thyssen Krupp's Krupp VDM Unit Developed a New Thin Foil for Catalytic Converters." *American Metal Market,* 11 May 1999.

U.S. Bureau of the Census. *1995 Annual Survey of Manufactures.* Available from http://www.census.gov.

———. *Occupational Outlook Handbook, 1996-97.* Available from http://stats.bls.gov.

SIC 3498

FABRICATED PIPE AND PIPE FITTINGS

This industry covers establishments primarily engaged in fabricating pipes and pipe fittings from purchased metal pipe by processes such as cutting, threading, and bending. Establishments primarily engaged in manufacturing cast iron pipe and fittings, including cast and forged pipe fittings that have been machined and threaded, are classified in **SIC 3321: Gray and Ductile Iron Foundries;** those manufacturing welded and heavy riveted pipe and seamless steel pipe are classified in **SIC 3317: Steel Pipe and Tubes;** and those manufacturing products such as banisters, railings, and guards from pipe are classified in **SIC 3446: Architecture and Ornamental Metal Work.**

NAICS Code(s)

332996 (Fabricated Pipe and Pipe Fitting Manufacturing)

According to the U.S. Census Bureau's *1997 Economic Census-Manufacturing,* 857 establishments operated in this category for part or all of 1997. Industry-wide employment totaled 29,491 workers receiving a payroll of more than $874 million. Of these employees, 22,328 worked in production, putting in almost 46 million hours to earn wages of more than $566 million. Overall shipments for the industry were valued at more than $4 billion.

Van Dusen and Meyer Inc. of Shelton, Connecticut led this industry with sales of $7.0 billion for its fiscal year ended March 31, 1999. Cleveland-based LTV Corp. followed with 1998 sales of almost $4.3 billion. Grinnell Corp. of Exeter, New Hampshire placed third in the industry with sales of almost $3.1 billion for its fiscal year ended June 30, 1997, according to the most recent results available on Infotrac databases. Harsco Corp. of Camp Hill, Pennsylvania generated over $1.7 billion in sales during 1998. Milwaukee-based A.O. Smith Corp. rounded out the top five industry leaders with 1998 sales of $917.5 million.

The U.S. fabricated pipe and pipe-fitting industry is strongly dependent on the health of the domestic construction industry, which, after enduring rough economic conditions in the late 1980s and early 1990s, rebounded in the mid-1990s. Improvements in the domestic as well as international economic climate, along with the replacement of old manufacturing processes, helped the industry rebound during the latter part of the 1980s and weather the downturn of the early 1990s. In the late 1990s, pipe, valve, and fitting manufacturers experienced marked gains in the industry's ability to meet the steady demand for fire protection flow control products. The industry's recent positive fortunes have also been due in part to increased global competitiveness. Overseas producers have been chased away from the U.S. market by increased domestic quality, lower dollar valuations, and strong antidumping legislation.

Texas's 96 establishments produced 15.1 percent of the U.S. shipment total in the mid-1990s. California had the second highest number of establishments with 90, producing 6.6 percent of U.S. shipments; and, although Michigan had just 69 establishments, it produced 8.6 percent of U.S. shipments. Employment highs in the industry were recorded in 1979, when 32,900 employees worked in the industry's manufacturing facilities. Projections called for employment decreases in this industry, however. Some industry occupations expected to decrease by 2005 were metal and plastic machine workers (29 percent); bookkeeping, accounting, and auditing clerks (25 percent); and tool and die makers (19 percent). The occupations with the

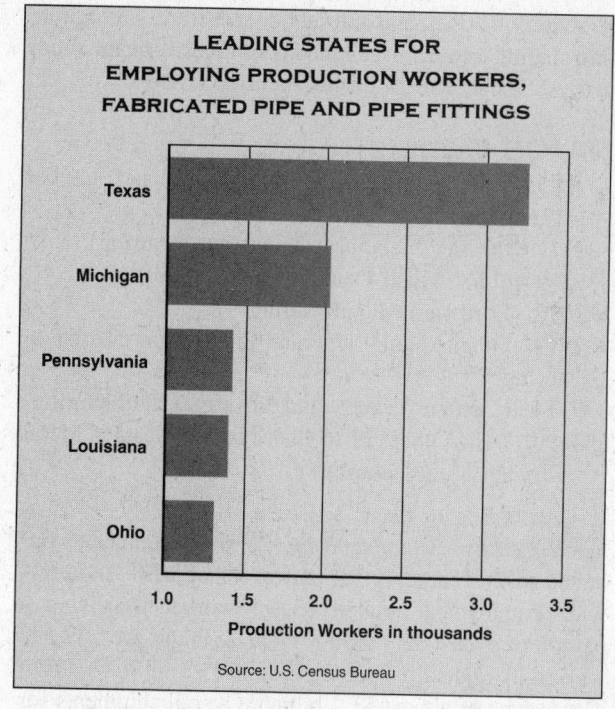

LEADING STATES FOR EMPLOYING PRODUCTION WORKERS, FABRICATED PIPE AND PIPE FITTINGS

Production Workers in thousands

Source: U.S. Census Bureau

largest expected increases were combination machine tool operators (51 percent) and metal and plastic machine tool cutting operators (42 percent).

Further Reading

Darnay, Arsen J., ed. *Manufacturing USA.* 5th ed. Detroit: Gale Research, 1996.

Infotrac Company Profiles. Available at http://web6.infotrac .galegroup.com (visited 2/12/99).

U.S. Bureau of the Census. *1992 Census of Manufactures.* Washington: GPO, 1995.

U.S. Census Bureau. *1997 Economic Census-Manufacturing.* Available at http://www.census.gov/prod/ec97/97m3329j.pdf (visited 2/12/00).

U.S. Department of Commerce. "Value of Product Shipments." *Annual Survey of Manufactures.* Washington: GPO, January 1997.

SIC 3499

FABRICATED METAL PRODUCTS, NOT ELSEWHERE CLASSIFIED

The fabricated metal products not elsewhere classified industry encompasses establishments that manufacture miscellaneous metal goods for both commercial and residential applications. Examples of industry output include metal ladders, ironing boards, steel safes, toilet fixtures, trophies, lawnmower wheels, chairs, barricades, ammunition boxes, and automobile seat frames. For more information about miscellaneous fabricated metal products, see other entries in this industry group.

NAICS CODE(S)

337215 (Showcase, Partition, Shelving, and Locker Manufacturing)

332117 (Powder Metallurgy Part Manufacturing)

332439 (Other Metal Container Manufacturing)

332510 (Hardware Manufacturing)

332919 (Other Metal Valve and Pipe Fitting Manufacturing)

339914 (Costume Jewelry and Novelty Manufacturing)

332999 (All Other Miscellaneous Fabricated Metal Product Manufacturing)

According to the U.S. Census Bureau's *1997 Economic Census—Manufacturing,* 2,590 establishments operated in this category for part or all of 1997. Industrywide employment totaled 63,372 workers receiving a payroll of almost $1.9 billion. Of these employees, 47,299 worked in production, putting in almost 92 million hours to earn wages of almost $1.2 billion. Overall shipments for the industry were valued at almost $7.5 billion.

Intermagnetics General Corp. of Latham, New York led this industry with sales of almost $96.0 billion for its fiscal year ended May 31, 1998. New York City-based Tomen America Inc. was a distant second, with 1997 sales of more than $2.6 billion, according to the most recent information available on Infotrac databases. Pittsburgh-based Armco Inc. placed third in the industry with 1998 sales of more than $1.7 billion. HON Industries of Muscatine, Iowa generated sales of approximately $1.7 billion for its fiscal year ended January 3, 1999. St. Louis-based Aigma-Aldrich Corp. rounded out the top five industry leaders with 1998 sales of almost $1.2 billion.

The background and development of the industry varies by product category. During the post-World War II U.S. economic expansion, the industry was characterized by a general surge in demand, and, approaching the 1980s, industry participants were churning out about $4.4 billion worth of goods per year and employing a work force of 65,000 people. Moreover, healthy economic growth during most of the 1980s boosted sales and profits. A surge in housing starts, for example, boosted shipments of metal furniture parts and ladders. Likewise, bank and vault manufacturers benefited from growth in the savings and loan industry.

By 1989, industry sales had reached more than $6.9 billion, representing average annual revenue growth of 7 percent since 1983. In contrast to many other manufacturing sectors, both the number of employees and companies in the industry grew during the decade, to 80,000 and 900, respectively. Unfortunately, an economic recession in the early 1990s stalled this expansion. Revenues actually declined about 1 percent in 1990 and remained flat throughout 1991 and 1992. For example, shipments of metal containers dropped about 6 percent in 1992, and purchases by the ailing savings and loan industry remained depressed. An upturn in housing and automobile markets in the mid-1990s, however, renewed optimism in some segments.

In the late 1990s, California had the highest number of establishments with 380, but they only produced 8 percent of the total U.S. shipments. Pennsylvania's 211 establishments generated 11 percent of U.S. shipments. Overall, shipment values in the industry were expected to increase from about $8.4 billion in 1996 to $9.0 billion in 1998.

Because of its specialized nature, the industry is highly fragmented. The average industry participant grossed about 28 percent as much as the average U.S. manufacturer in the mid-1990s and employed about half as many workers.

Although the industry is fragmented, a few product segments stood out in the late 1990s. Fabricated metal safes and vaults accounted for about 3 percent of production, and metal ladders accounted for about 4 percent. Flat metal strapping accounted for about 5 percent; powder metallurgy parts represented approximately 14 percent of production. The largest segment of production, at 50 percent, was for all other fabricated metal products, not elsewhere classified, which illustrates the industry's fragmentation. In 1995, fabricated metal products', not elsewhere classified, shipment value was $5.3 billion, while powder metallurgy parts' value was $994 million.

Despite steady sales and employment growth throughout the 1980s, job prospects for the overall industry are dim. Automation and the movement of manufacturing facilities to locations outside the United States will curtail job growth. At 77,400 industry workers, employment levels were fairly high for the industry in 1996. Openings for many positions will decline by between 3 and 29 percent between 1994 and 2005. Jobs for assemblers and fabricators, which make up a leading 11 percent of the work force, will increase by about 1 percent. The occupations with the highest projected growth are combination machine tool operators (51 percent) and metal and plastic machine tool cutting operators (42 percent).

FURTHER READING

Darnay, Arsen J., ed. *Manufacturing USA*. Detroit: Gale Research, 1996.

Infotrac Company Profiles. Available at http://web6.infotrac.galegroup.com (2/12/99).

U.S. Census Bureau. *1997 Economic Census—Manufacturing*. Available at http://www.census.gov/prod/ec97/97m3329m.pdf (visited 2/12/00).

INDUSTRIAL & COMMERCIAL MACHINERY & COMPUTER EQUIPMENT

STEAM, GAS, AND HYDRAULIC TURBINES, AND TURBINE GENERATOR SET UNITS

This industry covers establishments primarily engaged in manufacturing steam turbines; hydraulic turbines; gas turbines, except aircraft; and complete steam, gas, and hydraulic turbine generator set units. Also included in this industry are manufacturers of wind and solar powered turbine generators and windmills for generating electric power. Establishments engaged in manufacturing nonautomotive type generators are classified in **SIC 3621: Motors and Generators;** those manufacturing aircraft turbines are classified in **SIC 3724: Aircraft Engines and Engine Parts;** and those manufacturing windmill heads and towers for pumping water for agricultural use are classified in **SIC 3523: Farm Machinery and Equipment.**

NAICS CODE(S)

333611 (Turbine and Turbine Generator Set Unit Manufacturing)

INDUSTRY SNAPSHOT

This industry's 85 establishments employed almost 20,000 people in 1997. Of this total, 11,000 were production workers who earned an average hourly wage of $20.54.

Turbine manufacturers faced challenging business conditions in the 1990s. Early in the decade, a new generation of gas turbines helped the industry recover from its prolonged slump in the 1980s. But by 1994 U.S. electric utilities were under renewed pressure to cut

spending, and outlays for power plants was lackluster. At mid-decade turbine capacity outstripped demand by as much as 30 percent. On the bright side, demand in Asia (particularly from China) was growing much faster than in the United States or Europe. With all companies focusing on the same customers, however, price competition was severe.

Nearly all of the companies that entered the wind turbine business in the early 1980s—when the industry was in its heyday—have simply disappeared. By 1987 only three manufacturers of the larger-scale turbines used by utilities were still in business, and only one was producing turbines in significant numbers. The number of companies making small wind turbines for stand-alone power has also contracted substantially. In March 1995 the U.S. wind power industry received a fatal blow: the Federal Energy Regulatory Commission (FERC) overturned a decision that had forced utilities in California— the key U.S. market—to buy wind-generated power. Overseas demand presented a much brighter picture, however. The European wind power industry was doing well because of the European Union's encouragement of renewable energy resources. China also was looking to wind power as a way of reducing the pollution generated by its utilities.

BACKGROUND AND DEVELOPMENT

While early steam engines were reliable generators of electricity, they were big, heavy, inefficient devices. The modern steam turbine was developed in the late nineteenth century to replace them. Westinghouse shipped its first steam turbine in 1897, a few years before rival General Electric. By 1910 the largest steam turbine-generator unit could produce 30,000 kilowatts, compared with just 1,200 kilowatts ten years earlier. By 1940 single turbine units with a capacity of 100,000 kilowatts were in general use. During the 1950s and 1960s, steam turbines continued to dominate an expanding power-generation market, as fossil fuel prices remained low and ever-larger steam turbines were brought on line. In the 1980s, however, additions to the power capacity of utilities slowed because of erratic growth in consumption and the difficult political climate for utilities in many states.

In 1986 General Electric introduced a new series of advanced gas-fired turbines that turned around its faltering power systems segment. GE's relatively small and inexpensive gas turbines were ideal for utilities seeking to adjust to fluctuating demand by adding capacity selectively. In 1994 operating profits of its power division business reached a record $1.2 billion on $5.9 billion in sales.

Just one year later, however, profits had fallen about one-third, to $770.0 million, owing to several factors. Because of design flaws that could lead to cracks, GE had to make one of the biggest and most expensive recalls in the electric power business. In total, 22 GE turbines in the United States and overseas had to be shut down to be fixed; an additional 28 being shipped or installed required retrofitting with new components. GE has also lost some orders to competitors in Asia, including a key contract in China.

In the industry downturn of the 1980s, Westinghouse nearly exited the business, but by the mid-1990s it was doing better. In 1996 Westinghouse won a coveted partnership with Shanghai Electric Corp. of China, which is expected to be the largest market for power equipment over the next decade. Westinghouse Vice President Randy Zwirn told the *Wall Street Journal* in 1996 that, with an equity interest in Shanghai, ''we've got the crown jewel.'' Westinghouse also won contracts in April 1996 valued at nearly $300.0 million to build power plants in South Korea and Pakistan.

Wind Power. Small wind turbines were set up in rural areas of the Midwest during the early twentieth century, but power from utilities largely displaced them during the 1930s. As oil prices surged in the 1970s, however, renewable energy resources became popular, and the wind industry was resuscitated. Tax relief was offered for wind farms, and research was greatly expanded. About 14,000 wind turbines were installed between 1980 and 1985, the vast majority of them in California. When oil prices dropped below $20 a barrel and tax incentives were eliminated, however, much of the domestic wind industry collapsed.

In the wind power segment, the biggest U.S. company has been Kenetech of Livermore, California, founded in 1979 as U.S. Windpower. In early 1995 the company seemed to be poised for a turnaround. It made major sales to India and South Wales as well as to Palm

Springs and Minnesota. However, a March 1995 decision by the FERC that freed California utilities from the requirement that they buy wind power cost the company contracts worth $945.0 million. Wind power needed this regulatory support because it remained uneconomical, in part because of the short fatigue life (five years) of a wind turbine's major components and their expensive replacement costs. At best, Kenetech, the world's leading producer of wind-generated electricity, could produce power at five cents per hour, compared with three cents per hour for conventional natural gas plants. In the wake of this regulatory change, Kenetech first laid off 115 employees, or about 12 percent of its work force. By June 1996 the company had filed under Chapter 11 of the U.S. Bankruptcy Code.

Overseas markets, however, were healthier. The European Union (EU) set a target for renewable resources to account for 8 percent of Europe's primary energy by 2005. More specifically, the EU plan forecast that wind power would meet 2 percent of Europe's electricity demand by the same year. China, too, was encouraging the growth of wind power to satisfy its domestic energy needs.

INDUSTRY LEADERS

The list of industry leaders in the late 1990s represented a shift from earlier configurations of market share domination. Gone were General Electric and Westinghouse Electric from direct control of the market, and in their place was Foster Wheeler Corp., with Cooper Cameron Corp., Sequa Corp., and McDermott Inc. vying for control of the industry.

Clinton, New Jersey-based Foster Wheeler outpaced its rivals with 1998 sales of $4.6 billion. In 1998 Foster Wheeler won a design/build/operate/transfer contract with the University of Minnesota to renovate its historic Southeast Steam Plant, built in 1903, by installing a pollution-reducing boiler capable of burning 30 different fuels. *ENR* magazine named this one of the ''Best Projects'' of 1998.

Houston-based Cooper Cameron generated 1998 sales of almost $1.9 billion, up from $1.8 billion in 1997 sales. Sequa, based in New York City, followed closely, with more than $1.8 billion in 1998 sales, and McDermott's sales amounted to just under $1.8 billion for its fiscal year ended March 31, 1997 (the most recent results available on Infotrac). Rounding out the top five was Teleflex Inc. of Plymouth Meeting, Pennsylvania, with 1998 sales of over $1.4 billion, up from 1997 sales of $1.1 billion.

AMERICA AND THE WORLD

During the 1990s the turbine market increasingly became international in scope. Major American and European manufacturers strengthened their presence in each other's backyard. For example, the German industrial conglomerate Siemens AG took over a spin-off of Allis-Chalmers Co., known as A-C Equipment of Wisconsin and invested $30.0 million in its Milwaukee plant.

More than 60 percent of Westinghouse's new orders in 1996 were coming from customers outside the United States. "Asia is the biggest power market in the world," Westinghouse's Mike Asquino told the *Orlando Business Journal* in 1996. "That's where we're seeing significant growth." Indeed, China was expected to be the world's fastest-growing market. In 1996 it had a total installed generating capacity of 200,000 megawatts, which was being expanded by 10,000 megawatts per year.

Wind Power. In overseas markets, Denmark, Germany, and Britain have been in the forefront of developing wind energy. Wind energy accounted for less than 0.1 percent of Europe's total power generation in 1992. However, under a European Community directive, that figure is slated to rise to 2 percent by 2005. In 1996 the European wind power market was the world's largest, with installed capacity of 2,420 megawatts. The wind industry in Europe enjoys government subsidies and is growing quickly; it has also been a pioneer in developing wind farms offshore.

China also offered excellent opportunities for the wind industry. It has a set a target of 1,000 megawatts of installed wind power by the year 2000, more than 20 times the 1996 level of 44 megawatts. While 1,000 megawatts would still only represent 0.3 percent of China's anticipated capacity at the next millennium, it would still require 2,000 to 3,000 large wind turbines. Chinese authorities were eager for a more environmentally friendly source of power, since three-quarters of its generating units were powered by coal.

RESEARCH AND TECHNOLOGY

Many of the advances in gas turbines over the past decade have their roots in jet engine technology, as manufacturers have adopted techniques perfected for the airlines and the Pentagon for power generation. Older gas turbines have a thermal efficiency of 25 percent—they capture and convert to electricity about one-quarter of the energy value of their fuel—versus a 33 percent thermal efficiency posted by steam turbines. Using the technologies developed for aircraft, however, some newer gas turbines have reached thermal efficiencies of 40 percent. Other recently developed gas turbines have achieved even higher efficiency levels through combined cycle generation, in which the turbines use the exhaust gases from the turbine to boil water into steam, which is then used in a steam turbine to generate additional electricity. A variation of this method is to boil water with the exhaust gases and inject some of the steam back into the

gas turbine, so it is running on a combination of gases and steam. Some industry participants believe that gas-fired and combined-cycle power systems will be the leading technologies of the 1990s, representing about half of all new capacity additions worldwide. Fossil-fueled steam turbines, hydroelectric power, and nuclear plants will account for the balance.

The wind industry has made progress on several fronts that have historically hampered its growth. One major problem for the industry has been the variability and intermittent nature of wind. Traditional, fixed-speed wind turbines have had a relatively low capacity factor compared with other energy sources because they have not been able to take advantage of the full range of wind velocities. Improvements in wind turbine design and technologies, however, have allowed finer control of power output at both low and high wind speeds. Other advances, including more accurate weather forecasting, improved methods of picking the best sites for wind farms, and blades that can better cope with the destructive effects of dead insects have contributed to more efficient wind energy production.

FURTHER READING

"California's Kenetech Windpower Inc. to Serve Customers During Chapter 11." *Knight-Ridder/Tribune Business News*, 5 June 1996.

Cole, Benjamin Mark. "Generating Power Without Much Fuss (Capstone Turbine Corp.'s Small Turbine Power Plants)." *Los Angeles Business Journal*, 28 October 1996.

"Cooper Cameron Profits Fall." *Oil Daily*, 29 January 1999.

Demoss, Timothy. "Modern Technology Breathes New Life Into Old Turbines." *Power Engineering*, August 1996.

Dillon, Paul. "Westinghouse Becomes Bigger in Asia." *Orlando Business Journal*, 26 April 1996.

Foroohar, Kambiz. "Blowing in the Wind." *Forbes*, 4 December 1995.

General Electric 10-K, 1996. Fairfield, CT: General Electric, 1997.

Hindley, Angus. "Thinking Long-Term in the Gulf." *Middle East Economic Digest*, 31 January 1997.

"Historic steam plant goes hi-tech with option to burn 30 fuels." *ENR*, 21 December 1998.

"Teleflex Incorporated." *Barron's*, 15 February 1999.

U.S. Census Bureau. *Survey of Manufacturers*, 10 February 2000. Available from http://www.census.gov/prod/www/abs/97ecmani.html

Zhang, Don. "China Sets 1000 MW Wind Power Goal." *Modern Power Systems*, June 1996.

Zink, John. "Steam Turbines Power an Industry: A Condensed History of Steam Turbines." *Power Engineering*, August 1996.

SIC 3519

INTERNAL COMBUSTION ENGINES, NOT ELSEWHERE CLASSIFIED

This industry includes establishments primarily engaged in manufacturing diesel, semidiesel, or other internal combustion engines, not elsewhere classified, for stationary, marine, traction, and other uses. Establishments primarily engaged in manufacturing aircraft engines are classified in **SIC 3724: Aircraft Engines and Engine Parts,** and those manufacturing automotive engines, except diesel, are classified in **SIC 3714: Motor Vehicle Parts and Accessories.**

NAICS CODE(S)

336399 (All Other Motor Vehicle Parts Manufacturing)
333618 (Other Engine Equipment Manufacturing)

According to the U.S. Census Bureau's *1997 Economic Census—Manufacturing,* about 300 establishments operated in this category for part or all of 1997. Industry-wide employment totaled nearly 56,000 workers receiving a payroll of more than $2.3 billion. Almost 41,000 of these employees worked in production, putting in more than 81 million hours to earn wages of almost $1.5 billion. Overall shipments for the industry were valued at almost $19 billion.

The Environmental Protection Agency (EPA) and the U.S. Justice Department rocked the industry in 1998 when they cracked down on diesel engine manufacturers' installation of "defeat devices," or software that changed engine performance and emissions under highway driving conditions. The industry defended itself by pointing out that the use of the defeat devices was filed on public record, and that the EPA never expressed opposition to this use until the sudden crackdown. Regardless, the EPA slapped the industry with what it called the largest civil penalty in the history of environmental law: an $83.4 million fine, on top of an estimated $850 million in costs for meeting tighter emissions standards on a quicker schedule than before the settlement. Additionally, six companies, including the "Big Three" industry leaders, would have to rebuild existing engines in order to meet cleaner emissions specifications and recall pickup trucks to remove defeat devices from them.

Industry leader Caterpillar Inc. of Mossville, Illinois, which generated almost $21.0 billion in 1998 sales, shared the brunt of the civil settlement with third place Cummins Engine Company Inc. of Columbus, Indiana, which had 1998 sales of almost $6.3 billion. Each company paid $25.0 million of the $83.4 million fine. Second place industry leader Navistar International Corp. of Chicago, which garnered more than $7.8 billion in sales for its fiscal

year ended October 31, 1998, boasted that it paid the least share of the fine at $2.9 million. Additionally, Navistar was not required to conduct the environmental projects that cost Caterpillar and Cummins $35.0 million each.

The other companies that shared the blame (as well as the fines) were Mack Trucks Inc., which paid $13.0 million of the civic penalty and $18.0 million in environmental projects; Detroit Diesel Co., which paid $12.5 million on the civic fine as well as $12.0 million in environmental projects; and Volvo Truck Corp., which spent $5.0 million on the civic penalty and $9.0 million on environmental projects. The settlement did not indict the fourth place industry leader, Brunswick Corp. of Lake Forest, Illinois, which generated 1998 sales of more than $3.9 billion.

Despite this setback, or perhaps even spurred by it, the industry continued to introduce innovative new engine designs that increased both efficiency and power. For example, Caterpillar replaced its 3406E model with the C-15 and the C-16. Not only did this extend the company's model numeration past C-10 and C-12, it also incorporated design specifications from these other models into their designs, such as the ADEM (Advanced Diesel Engine Management) 2000 electronic control system to monitor the engine's function. The new models were 200 pounds lighter, quieter, more reliable, and more fuel-efficient than was their predecessor, the 3406E. Cummins also introduced new designs: the ISX series with optional additional torque and the Signature 600 engine, delivering 600 horsepower at 2,000 revolutions per minute.

Sixth-place industry leader Detroit Diesel Corp., a relative newcomer to the industry spotlight, was founded in 1988 when former auto racer Roger Penske bought control of the company from General Motors and proceeded to raise its share of the U.S. heavy-duty diesel truck engine market from 3 percent in 1987 to more than 26 percent in 1995. That year, sales totaled more than $2 billion, more than double what they were when Penske took over the company. Detroit Diesel's turnaround can be traced to its Series 60 engine, which provided far better fuel efficiency than previous models, as well as computerized features that could diagnose mechanical problems and monitor driver productivity.

As Detroit Diesel advanced, Cummins receded: it lost 10 points of market share in 2 years and posted substantial losses in both 1990 and 1991. The company already had suffered through tough times in the mid-1980s, when the firm cut both its prices and profitability to defend its markets against Japanese manufacturers. By the mid-1990s, however, Cummins had made a strong recovery: it reported earnings of $160 million on sales of $5.2 billion in 1996. That same year, it took about 35 percent of the heavy-duty diesel truck engine market, about the same

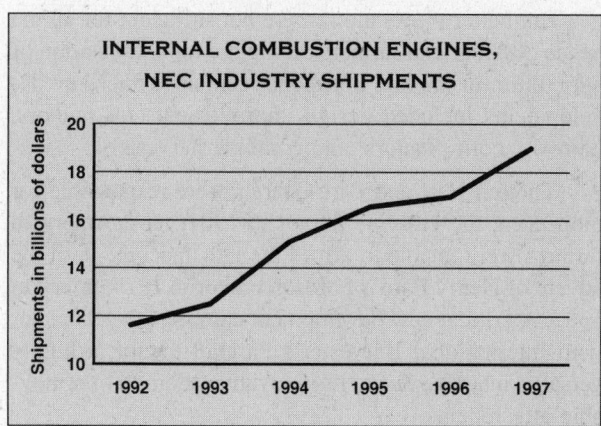

INTERNAL COMBUSTION ENGINES, NEC INDUSTRY SHIPMENTS

(Graph: Shipments in billions of dollars, 1992–1997)

level as it had taken in 1994 and 1995. This return to profitability reflected a strong upturn in demand for heavy-duty trucks, a more competitive product line, corporate downsizing, and an increased emphasis on establishing a presence in non-truck diesel engine markets, including a renewed focus on recreational vehicles.

Diesel engines are used primarily in large trucks and buses, in high-powered farm tractors, and in heavy construction machinery. Other markets include marine vessels and lawn-and-garden equipment. The industry dates from 1893, when Rudolph Diesel, a young German engineer, filed a patent application entitled "Theory for the construction of a rational thermal engine to replace the steam engine and other internal combustion engines currently in use." Four years later, Diesel built the first diesel engine.

The fortunes of U.S. diesel engine makers depend heavily on the market for heavy-duty trucks. The end-user has the option of choosing his own engine, so companies must impress both truck operators and truck makers, which may decide to make an engine standard on a specific line. Although the heavy-duty truck market fell about 23 percent in 1996 from the record level of 245,000 units in 1995, it was still healthy by historical standards. Some industry observers thought the traditional boom-and-bust cycle of the industry had softened somewhat, due to modest inflation and a more stable economy.

FURTHER READING

"A Brief History of the Diesel Engine." *PSA Website,* 14 March 1997. Available from http://www.psa.fr/en_psaBB0026 .html.

Infotrac Company Profiles. Available from http://web6.infotrac .galegroup.com (2/12/99).

Koenig, Bill. "Cummins Engine Hope More Products, International Sales Will Boost Earnings." *Knight-Ridder/Tribune Business News,* 10 April 1996.

McElroy, John. "Miracles in the Heartland: How to Buy Part of GM and Make It Immediately Profitable." *Automotive Industries,* June 1995.

Osenga, Mike. "Cat Introduces Dual Truck Engines." *Diesel Progress Engines & Drives,* August 1996.

"Diesel industry confronts the emission settlement." *Diesel Progress North American Edition,* December 1998.

U.S. Census Bureau. *1997 Economic Census—Manufacturing.* Available from http://www.census.gov/prod/ec97/97m3336d .pdf (2/12/00).

Wilson, Rob. "C-15 and C-16 Thoroughbreds Replace 3406 Diesel Warhorse." *Diesel Progress North American Edition,* October 1999.

"New Trucks, New Engines Make Their Way in Markets Where Y2K Hedge Shipping Exacerbates Frenzied Boom." *Diesel Progress North American Edition,* November 1999.

Zirnhelt, George. "Soft Landing, Soft Rebound Likely for Engine Markets in the Year Ahead." *Diesel Progress Engines & Drives,* December 1996.

SIC 3523

FARM MACHINERY AND EQUIPMENT

This category covers establishments primarily manufacturing farm machinery and equipment, including wheel tractors, for use in the preparation and maintenance of the soil; planting and harvesting of the crop; preparing crops for market on the farm; or for use in performing other farm operations and processes. Included in this industry are establishments primarily engaged in manufacturing commercial mowing and other turf and grounds care equipment. Establishments primarily engaged in manufacturing farm handtools are classified as the Cutlery, Handtools, and General Hardware industries; and those manufacturing garden tractors, lawnmowers, and other lawn and garden equipment are classified in **SIC 3524: Lawn and Garden Tractors and Home Lawn and Garden Equipment.**

NAICS CODE(S)

333111 (Farm Machinery and Equipment Manufacturing)

332323 (Ornamental and Architectural Metal Work Manufacturing)

332212 (Hand and Edge Tool Manufacturing)

333922 (Conveyor and Conveying Equipment Manufacturing)

INDUSTRY SNAPSHOT

The 1990s took the farm machinery and equipment industry on a roller coaster ride, with sales and revenues rocketing up then crashing down, seemingly without warning. An upswing in the farm sector of the U.S. economy initially seemed to bode well for manufacturers, but in late 1998, the market turned, with sales in some areas falling as much as 36 percent. Nonetheless, most indicators predicted that the farm sector will continue slow but steady growth, suggesting that the farm machinery and equipment industry will have another opportunity to rebound.

Factors affecting the U.S. economy generally also play a significant role in the organization of this industry. Globalization and consolidation have allowed industry leaders to maintain growth or minimize losses in a poor domestic market. Nonetheless, the collapse of many Asian economies in the mid- to late-1990s resulted in decreasing exports of equipment and decreasing Asian imports of U.S.-grown agricultural products. Other factors important to the stability of this industry include government subsidies of U.S. farms, relationships with equipment dealers, and the availability of raw materials.

BACKGROUND AND DEVELOPMENT

The major expansion period for U.S. agriculture came during the late nineteenth century. A total of 408 million acres had been farmed prior to 1870, and in the next 30 years an additional 431 million acres were newly cultivated. As the scale of U.S. agriculture dramatically increased, so did its complexity, with locally oriented farmers later engaged in an international system of storing, shipping, and selling, engendered by increased mechanization, cash crops, and stock trading in commodities.

At the onset of these developments, the most significant role was played by the largest farming enterprises. Heralding increased mechanization, greater crop specialization, and a trend towards farming on a large scale, the 40,000-acre or more farms were run with military efficiency. The pace of mechanization was so rapid and extended into so many areas of farming technology that in 1860 alone, the U.S. Patent Office issued new patents for corn shellers, corn huskers, corn cultivators, corn-shock binders, cornstalk shocking machines, cornstalk cutters, corn cleaners, corn and cob crushers, seed drills, corn harvesters, rotary harrows, corn and cob mills, smut machines, and hundreds of corn planters.

The types of plows used since the earliest development of agriculture proved to be unsuitable in dense, heavy prairie, so new designs were essential. A first step came in the form of an adaptation of Jethro Wood's 1814 iron plow, a "prairie breaker" that was very heavy, clogged easily, and moved slowly, even when pulled by a team of oxen. In 1837, a blacksmith in Grand Detour, Illinois, developed the first "singing plow" by combining a wrought iron moldboard with a steel share scavenged from a broken band saw, enabling a far more thorough and clog-free scouring of the prairie. By the 1850s, this blacksmith was manufacturing approximately 10,000 examples of his invention annually at his mass-production plant in Moline, Illinois.

But better plows alone were not sufficient for all the needs of American farmers during the rapid escalation of agriculture in the late nineteenth century. Other key developments included design improvements for tractors, harrows, corn planters, and combine harvesters.

Though Hart and Parr Charles were responsible for pioneering the gasoline tractor in 1901, most American farmers were unable to afford the new machine until the advent of Henry Ford's Fordson tractor in 1917, priced at $397. A critical new development came seven years later with International Harvester's Farmall tractor, a highly versatile machine due to its innovative addition of removable attachments.

During the nineteenth century, harrows rapidly became stronger and more complex. Before the introduction of the tractor, these had to be dragged by animals. The first designs of hoes and brush harrows were outmoded in the 1840s by the Geddes, a hinged triangular construction of wood with teeth made of iron, which, in turn, was outmoded several decades later by an all iron and steel model. This design was later outmoded by a harrow called the Nishwitz rotary disk harrow, which through rollers or clod-crushers, sifted and tamped down the soil.

The planting of corn was both time-consuming and inaccurate until technological advances permitted the mechanization of the planting and the measuring involved as well. In Galsburg, Illinois in the 1850s, George W. Brown pioneered a semi-mechanized method of corn planting with a horse-drawn vehicle that dropped seed by hand. Next, shoes or "furrow openers" were added to the front of the vehicle for better preparation of the soil, and the seed-dropping mechanism was refined, permitting vehicle operators to divide the tasks of driving and navigating. The latter improvement enabled operators to pay closer attention to where the corn was being dropped.

Developments in combine harvesting technology took a slower and more interrupted course than did those of the other forms of farming equipment. The steam-driven reaping and threshing machines introduced in the 1880s were replaced by the versatility of the Farmall tractor. The Second World War delayed the full implementation of the technological advances marked by Allis Chalmers' All-Crop Harvester of 1936, a gleaner equipped with a special corn-head attachment. With the resumption of peace, the versatile and efficient but expensive combines initially took a back seat to the much cheaper picker-sheller machinery. Only with the proliferation of silos and their efficient storage of vast quantities did the diesel-driven combines' capacity for mass harvesting give them an unbeatable advantage.

CURRENT CONDITIONS

Based on the improving health of the farm sector of the U.S. economy, the farm equipment industry also experienced a turnaround in the 1990s. Value of shipments in 1992 bottomed out at $7.2 billion before climbing to $14 billion in 1997, with continued increases expected. Between 1996 and 1997, value of shipments increased by 7.5 percent. Tractor sales for the first three quarters of 1998 were 13 percent higher than the same period in 1997; increases in combine sales were particularly dramatic—41 percent between the first five months of 1998 and the same period in 1997.

The industry turned another corner in 1999, as sales of farm equipment appeared to have reached a maximum. According to a 1999 survey by the Equipment Manufacturers Institute (EMI), sales of most farm implements were down in early 1999 after the 1998 highs, and were expected to remain depressed in the year 2000. A striking example of the saturated market was reflected in the sales of self-propelled combines, which were expected to fall by at least 36 percent in 1999 and an additional 1.8 percent in 2000. Sales of tractors were expected to be down 5 percent compared to 1998, and sales of rectangular balers, forage harvesters, grinder mixers, manure spreaders, windrowers/swathers, field cultivators, chisel plows, and disk harrows were also expected to be soft in 1999 and 2000. EMI predicted positive numbers for farm loaders, with a 0.7 percent increase in 1999 and 5.4 percent increase in 2000, and for dairy mechanization equipment and milking machines, with an increase of 10 percent for 1999. Reports from major manufacturers Deere and Co. and Case Corporation forecasted a 35 percent drop in North American demand for large-scale agricultural equipment for 1999, and an 8 to 10 percent drop globally. According to *Implement and Tractor*, "Initial forecasts for [2000] indicate that retail demand for farm machinery could be 5 to 10 percent lower than in 1999."

A study released in 1999 by the Food and Agricultural Policy Research Institute and reported in *Implement and Tractor* suggested that while the next three years would reflect decreasing demand and increased supply for farm products, the overall outlook for the first decade of the twenty-first century was positive.

At the same time, while the number of farms has been decreasing for several years, the size of those farms has been increasing, further pushing the market for farm machinery. In 1999, 80 percent of farms had fewer than 500 acres, but those farms produced only 20 percent of total U.S. output, making larger corporate farm businesses the most important market for makers of farm equipment. The Farm Bureau predicted that without federal aid, as many as 30 percent of small farmers in some states would be forced to shut down. In order to save family farms, the Farm Bureau in 1999 lobbied Congress to pass its AgRecovery Action Plan, which called for $9 billion in aid. The aid package included $4 billion for direct assistance, $2 billion for export initiatives, and $2 billion for reform and expansion of the federally supported risk management safety net. The Bureau also requested $5 billion to help farmers with the cost of complying with federal regulations. The plan would help reverse the effects of the 1996 Freedom to Farm Act, which cut federal farm subsidies through the year 2002.

Forecasting to 2005, the U.S. Department of Labor saw positive signs for the agricultural equipment industry, noting that farmers had generally recovered from the losses and excessive debts incurred during the 1980s. Farmers were expected to replace machinery that they had been unable to replace when times were hardest, and to invest in new machinery, taking advantage of improvements brought about by advanced technology. Indicative of this trend was 1997's 4 percent first quarter increase in non-real estate loans. In addition, farm inputs, equipment, and machinery accounted for 50 percent of the increase in farm loan value in 1996, which rose to $2.3 billion, up 3.2 percent from 1995.

During the late 1990s, federal legislation continued to play a key role in the farm and farm equipment industry. A major development occurred with the passage of the Federal Agriculture Improvement and Reform Act of 1996. The Act ended the federal requirement that farmers leave idle a portion of their land in order to receive government income support, meaning that farmers became free to plant on additional land without losing an important source of income—both positive indicators for farm equipment manufacturers.

In 1999, farm equipment manufacturers filed suit to protest a law regulating producers' relationships with dealers. *The Business Journal-Milwaukee* reported that "the law makes it harder for manufacturers to terminate a dealership contract if the dealer changes ownership or management. In addition, it prevents manufacturers from canceling a contract if the dealer refuses pay for national advertising initiatives or refuses to accept delivery of certain equipment." Emmett Barker, president of the Equipment Manufacturers Institute, said that such laws likely resulted from the efforts of farm-equipment makers to reduce the number of dealers representing them, another cost-cutting measure in a soft market.

Other government restrictions on the farm equipment industry came from the Environmental Protection Agency (EPA). The EPA standards concerning exhaust emissions were designed to take effect for engines of over 750 horsepower in the year 2000, for those of 50 to 100 horsepower in 1998, for those of 100 to 175 horsepower in 1997, and for those of 175 to 750 horsepower in 1996. According to *Implement and Tractor*, clean air legislation creating new diesel fuel standards was seen as making viable an otherwise too expensive diesel blend containing soy oil, and leading to a decline in carbon monoxide and hydrocarbon emissions. From the point of view of farmers, this cleaner fuel was not believed to have consequences for torque output, even if it did lead to small reductions in horsepower.

INDUSTRY LEADERS

This industry is highly consolidated, with four to five companies manufacturing most of the products. In 1998, Deere and Co. of Moline, Illinois had sales of over $13.8 billion, with 37,000 employees. Not only did Deere lead the farm machinery industry in the United States, but it also led worldwide. With factories in nine countries, Deere distributed its products to about 120 countries around the world.

Deere has been the industry leader for years, but the company has faced some perilous challenges in the last decade. Deere posted net losses of $902 million in 1993, but turned the business around within a year to record its most profitable fiscal year ever. Acquisitions were a part of Deere's growth strategy. In late 1999, for example, Deere bought up 49 percent of Cameco Industries, a farm equipment manufacturer with $100 million in the year before. The year before, Deere rolled out a program aimed at maintaining a steady supply of steel, whatever the market conditions. The company hoped to convince its parts suppliers to rely on only two distributors for their steel needs: Earle M. Jorgensen Co. and Olympic Steel Inc. Although company spokesmen projected the program would take several years to be implemented, its benefits would include cost reductions for both parts suppliers and for Deere, as well as consistent quality and availability of the industry's most important raw material.

Deere was hard hit by the downturn of the market in 1999, posting an operating loss of $8 million for the third quarter of its fiscal year, compared with a $282 million operating profit for the same period in 1998. Reacting to declines in demand, Deere's agricultural equipment division began production shutdowns and a voluntary early-retirement program.

AGCO Corp. ranked second in the industry in 1998 with $2.9 billion in sales. AGCO marketed its diversified agricultural products worldwide and employed 11,000 people. Under the guidance and leadership of CEO Robert J. Ratliff, AGCO became the Cinderella of the farm machinery industry. *Implement and Tractor* noted that Ratliff transformed a relatively small and unprofitable $200 million company into a $2 billion industry leader. Ratliff launched the changeover by expanding the company's narrow product line, thereby increasing its worldwide tractor market share to 20 percent. In fact, by 1994 AGCO dominated the tractor market outside the United States. To help build and reinforce the AGCO empire, Ratliff purchased the domestic and international operations of Massey-Ferguson in 1993 and 1994, respectively.

To cope with the disappointment of the market's late '98 downturn, AGCO implemented extensive cost-cutting measures. The firm cut 1,400 jobs in the United States and laid off hundreds more workers, closing plants in Missouri, Ohio, Texas, and Minnesota. Only the Hesston, Kansas, production facility was slated to remain open and functioning. The company released a statement saying it expected 1999 earnings to reflect a 75 percent decrease from 1998 earnings, and a buy-out of the company was rumored in the stock market. As of late 1999, AGCO's stock was climbing rapidly, doubling from $6 per share to $12 per share between March and August.

The third major company in the industry was New Holland North America, of New Holland, Pennsylvania. New Holland's prominence resulted in part from their purchase of former industry leader Case Corp. In 1998, Case Corp. of Racine, Wisconsin, ranked as the North America's second largest farm machinery operation and as the world's largest small and medium size construction equipment manufacturer. The company posted 1998 sales of $6.1 billion, with 17,700 employees. In second-quarter 1999, however, Case announced a 71 percent drop in net income, the result of "weak demand for big agricultural equipment and unfavorable foreign currency exchange rates," according to *Implement and Tractor.* The negative numbers also reflected Case's planned merger with New Holland Grand Island. New Holland did not suffer as much from the downturn in the market, posting second quarter net revenues of $1.6 billion, compared to $1.7 billion for the same period in 1998. Although New Holland shut down its Nebraska plant and cut production of some equipment by up to 17 percent, it also spent aggressively toward future growth, with a $13 million plant renovation project, and acquisitions of Case and Orenstein & Koppel. As of October 1999, stock prices for both companies remained strong and growing. The merger was complete November 12, 1999, although a press release issued by Case confirmed that "the multiple brands and corresponding distribution networks of both the Case and New Holland organizations will be maintained in the marketplace."

AMERICA AND THE WORLD

Throughout the 1990s, exports of farm machinery and equipment have out-valued imports every year except 1994. The value of exports increased over 21 percent between 1996 and 1997, and although it decreased 5 percent the next year, between 1998 and 1999 that value was expected to rebound, making the 1999 value of exports almost 20 percent higher than in 1996. Growth of exports between 1992 and 1996 was 15 percent, while imports increased by just over 10 percent in that period.

According to the *WEFA Industry Monitor,* the following countries were the top export markets for this industry: Canada, with a 25 to 30 percent share; Mexico, with 8 to 10 percent; Australia, with 6 to 7 percent;

Germany, with 5 percent; France, with 3 to 5 percent; and the United Kingdom, with 3 to 5 percent. Countries leading imports into the United States included Canada, Germany, Japan, and the United Kingdom.

Seeking new markets was a crucial strategy in increasing exports. According to the U.S. Department of Agriculture, members of the Commonwealth of Independent States, such as Ukraine, could provide U.S. manufacturers with a new market for their farm machinery. The country's slow transition to a market economy and the privatization of agriculture has forced Ukrainians to seek farm equipment and other agricultural products elsewhere. In 1996, Ukraine purchased Deere combines for $187 million, the company's largest sale ever. Furthermore, Pakistan reported that it would increase its importation of U.S. tractors from 22,000 to 25,000 from 1995 to 1998. The Pakistani government drove this increase by urging the cultivation of more of the country's 79 million acres of arable land to meet agricultural consumption requirements. As of 1996, Pakistan cultivated only 50 million acres of its arable land.

Industry leaders sought to increase their footprint abroad through acquisitions, joint ventures, and contract manufacturing. AGCO purchased Xaver Fendt GmbH & Co., the German manufacturer of the Fendt tractor, making AGCO number one in Germany and number two in France, when ranked by market share. Deere held contracts with companies in Italy, Spain, France, and the Czech Republic, enabling them to reach markets in Latin America, Australia, the Pacific Rim, South Africa, and South America. In late 1999, Deere announced a joint venture with the Hattat Group of Turkey for the production of tractors. Case bought its way into a majority stake in Austrian equipment manufacturer Steyr, providing the company entry into Eastern European markets.

As in many sectors of the U.S. manufacturing industry, the Asian economic crisis of the late 1990s hit the export market hard. Half of the United States' agricultural exports went to Pacific Rim countries before the impact of the crisis, including 40 percent of U.S. crops. The depreciation of foreign currency was another factor in the fall of Asian economies. For example, the depreciation of the Japanese yen had the effect of increasing the price of U.S.-made products by 20 percent. Results of a 1999 survey reported in *Implement and Tractor* showed almost 75 percent of farm equipment dealers reporting a downturn in business, and among those the amount of the decrease averaged close to 20 percent. The slump in Asia was expected to last until the year 2000 or even 2003.

RESEARCH AND TECHNOLOGY

The industry has made some technological breakthroughs that can substantially reduce producers' dependence on manual laborers. In 1995, Automated Harvest-ing Systems developed a pepper picker for harvesting delicate pepper varieties without damaging the vegetables. This diesel-powered harvester includes a liquid-cooled diesel engine and rated 86.9 horsepower at 2200 rpm, according to *Diesel Progress Engines and Drives*. The pepper picker has the potential of harvesting as much as 150 manual pickers, which would save farmers considerable labor costs. In addition, The Robotics Consortium is developing a robotic harvester that uses imaging sensors and intelligent motion control, according to *Design News*. The machine has been tested on alfalfa fields with success, marking a new frontier in farm machine design.

FURTHER READING

"Asian Crisis Has Hurt Dealers." *Implement and Tractor,* March 1999.

Banham, Russ. "Export Opportunities Sprout for U.S. Producers." *Journal of Commerce and Commercial,* 8 November 1996.

"Case Corporation and New Holland Complete Merger." 12 November, 1999. Available from http://www.casecorp.com/corporate/press/index.html.

Darnay, Arsen J., ed. *Manufacturing USA.* 6th ed. Detroit: Gale Research, 1998.

"Deere and AGCO Report Record '94 Sales." *Implement and Tractor,* January/February 1995.

"Deere and Co. (Tractor Company Buys 49 Percent of Farm Machinery Firm Cameco Industries Inc.)" *Implement and Tractor,* January/February 1998.

"Deere Enters Tractor Joint Venture in Turkey." *Diesel Progress North American Edition,* October 1999.

"FAPRI: Despite Bleak Spots Ahead, 10 Year Outlook is Bright." *Implement and Tractor,* May 1999.

"Farm Bureau Seeks Emergency Farm Relief." *Implement and Tractor,* July 1999.

"Financial." *Implement and Tractor,* March/April 1995.

Freiberg, Bill. "AGCO Corporation: A Living Example of the American Dream." *Implement and Tractor,* May/June 1995.

Gallun, Alby. "Case, Farm Equipment Makers Sue Over South Dakota Law." *The Business Journal-Milwaukee,* 27 August 1999.

Hays, JoAnn. "From the Dealer's Seat." *Successful Farming,* November 1996.

Hill, Peter. "Tractor Makers Eye European Market." *Implement and Tractor,* May/June 1997.

"Machinery." *Institutional Investor,* October 1999.

McNeely, Mark. "Holy Peno, Now That's a Pepper Picker." *Diesel Progress Engines and Design,* December 1995.

"More 'Adjustments' to Poor Farm Economy." *Implement and Tractor,* July 1999.

"North American Mid-Year Sales Review and Outlook." *Implement and Tractor,* July 1999.

Shepherd, Mary. "Reflections of Ag in a Falling Global Economy." *Implement and Tractor,* September 1998.

U.S. Census Bureau. *1997 Economic Census.* Washington, D.C.: U.S. Government Printing Office, 1999. Available from http://www.census.gov.

Waxler, Caroline and Carleen Hawn. "Out to Pasture." *Forbes,* 15 December 1997.

Wrigley, Al. "Deere Shifts its Focus from the Many to Just Two." *American Metal Market,* 11 November 1998.

SIC 3524

LAWN AND GARDEN TRACTORS AND HOME LAWN AND GARDEN EQUIPMENT

This entry discusses establishments primarily engaged in manufacturing lawn mowers, lawn and garden tractors, and other lawn and garden equipment used for home lawn and garden care. It also includes establishments primarily engaged in manufacturing snowblowers and throwers for residential use. Other equipment classified here includes: wagons and carts for lawn and garden use, lawn mover grass catchers, power hedge trimmers, power lawn edgers, loaders for garden tractors, mulchers, plow attachments for garden tractors, rototillers, seeders, and residential lawn vacuums.

Establishments primarily engaged in manufacturing farm equipment and machinery are classified in **SIC 3523: Farm Machinery and Equipment.** Those manufacturing hand lawn and garden shears and pruners are classified in **SIC 3421: Cutlery,** and those manufacturing other garden handtools are classified in **SIC 3424: Hand and Edge Tools, Except Machine Tools and Handsaws.**

NAICS CODE(S)

333112 (Lawn and Garden Tractor and Home Lawn and Garden Equipment Manufacturing)
332212 (Hand and Edge Tool Manufacturing)

INDUSTRY SNAPSHOT

Lawn and garden equipment companies manufacture a variety of tools, including walk-behind power mowers, lawn tractors, tillers, string trimmers, leaf blowers, snow blowers, and other gas- and electric-powered equipment. In 1997, the value of industry shipments was $7.46 billion. Lawn and garden equipment manufacturers are influenced by a number of factors, such as weather conditions, the housing market, demographics, and the overall economy. The industry has been strong in the late-1990s, as aging and affluent baby boomers—those consumers

born between 1947 and 1964—take up gardening and buy high-end equipment.

In 1997, the industry was comprised of 145 establishments. Wisconsin supported the greatest number of lawn and garden equipment manufacturers with 12 companies, followed by Pennsylvania with 10 and California with 7. With shipments valued at $3.57 billion, consumer non-riding lawn, garden and snow equipment outperformed the riding varieties in 1997. Nevertheless, the future of riding lawn and garden equipment looks promising, as baby boomers seek out less strenuous tools.

BACKGROUND AND DEVELOPMENT

The nation's enthusiastic interest in lawn maintenance is relatively new, though the lawn mower itself (developed in England) has been around since the 1830s. During the same time John Deere was promoting his sodbreaking plow as the most important piece of equipment frontier farmers of the prairie could own, the push lawn mower was familiar to children of antebellum America.

In the 1930s, U.S. lawn mower sales held at about 50,000 units annually. Following World War II and the American migration to suburbs, homeowners began to take a growing pride in tending their lawns, hedges, and gardens. During this same time, new grass seed varieties were also being developed, and the quest for the "perfect" lawn became a popular hobby and a point of pride.

Reel mowers were the standard home lawn grooming device until the 1950s, when gas-powered rotary motors developed into more than a rough cutting tool. By the end of that decade, power mowers outsold reel mowers by a margin of 9 to 1. The rise in the popularity of power garden equipment was accompanied by a corresponding surge in lawn mower accidents—wounds from flying debris and toe and finger amputations. In the mid-1990s, design changes combined with news stories about equipment safety that appear in the spring (as well as when the first mower-related accident is reported) have raised public awareness.

Some of the first safety measures included attaching decks to handles with bolt-on brackets instead of cotter pins and the positioning of the starter cord away from the discharge chute. Through the development of safety standards, injuries from walk-behind power mowers have decreased 40 percent since 1983.

An era of consumer activism began in 1969, with the publishing of *Unsafe at Any Speed* by Ralph Nader, a book focused on the automobile industry's "indifference" to safety concerns. In 1972, the federal Consumer Product Safety Act created a Consumer Product Safety Commission (CPSC); one of the initial concerns of that agency was power lawn mower accidents. At the time an estimated 77,000 people each year were injured by the whirling blades of this equipment. Following 10 years of CPSC data gathering and testimony from experts and consumers, the first safety requirements for power lawnmowers—the deadman control and blade housing and shield designs to prevent foot injuries—were adopted.

The deadman control prevents hand injuries that can occur when operators attempt to clear the chute of wet grass without shutting down the engine. It is now standard for lawn mower (as well as snowblower) blades to stop rotating once the operator releases a spring-loaded control on the handle. Less expensive mowers may feature a simple control that shuts down the entire engine when the operator releases the handle; more expensive models stop the blade action but allow the engine to keep running.

Blade housings and shields prevent an operator's foot from accidentally slipping under the deck of the mower and into the blade. Manufacturers are required to perform a standard "foot-probe test" to ensure their product designs meet this safety requirement.

Another design change initiated by the industry requires debris (nails, rocks, small branches) be deflected onto the ground rather than flying out the chute. All of these standards have added more than $25 to the cost of mowers—which generally range in price from $100 for lower-end mowers to $700-plus for riding tractors for home consumer use. These design changes, combined with an increase in liability insurance for power mower manufacturers, accounted for a near doubling in the price of garden equipment

CURRENT CONDITIONS

After surviving a period of recession in the early 1990s—in which increasing numbers of consumers opted not to hire professional landscaping companies—the lawn and garden equipment industry has recovered. According to a press release issued by the Outdoor Power Equipment Institute (the trade organization representing 95 percent of lawn and garden equipment manufacturers), 1999 sales for consumer and commercial lawn care products were "solid" for most product categories. In 1997, manufacturers' shipments of lawn mowers rose 3.5 percent, while front engine lawn tractors increased about 5 percent, according to Do-It-Yourself Retailing.

The resurgence of lawn and garden equipment in the late-1990s was due to a number of factors. In addition to an overall booming American economy, new housing starts were up in 1998 and 1999—meaning that more consumers were now responsible for lawn care. More important to the fate of the industry, though, are the demographics. The largest generation in American history—the baby boomers—have reached their prime years for gardening and lawn care (between the ages of 45 and 64 years old). These consumers are more affluent than most generations that preceded them, and are thus more likely to purchase more expensive equipment. In 1998, the National Gardening Association reported to National Home Center News that boomers accounted for about 42 percent of all purchases in the lawn and garden segment.

Another trend influencing the industry is the rise of giant home center stores, such as Home Depot. While consumers previously purchased their lawn and gardening tools from hardware stores, these new superstores have claimed a greater stake of the market. According to Do-It-Yourself Retailing, hardware stores' share of the outdoor power equipment market fell from 16 percent in 1978 to 6.3 percent in 1992. During this same period, home centers' saw their share of this market rise from 1 percent to 8.7 percent.

INDUSTRY LEADERS

The Bloomington, Minnesota-based Toro Company is a leading producer of consumer and commercial care lawn mowers, as well as snow blowers. With 1998 sales above $1.2 billion, the company offers its products under a variety of brand names, including Toro, Exmark, and Dingo. Commercial sales now account for two-thirds of total revenue. Faced with declining sales for snowblowers in the winter of 1997 (because of unseasonably mild weather) and declining export revenue (because of the Asian economic crisis), Toro stopped selling its equipment exclusively through its independent dealers. By 1999, the company offered its goods at about 1,500 home centers.

The Black & Decker Corporation is another key player in the lawn and garden equipment industry. Its 1998 sales topped $4.6 billion (of which lawn equipment was only a portion). Headquartered in Towson, Maryland, Black & Decker sells such products as Grass Hog, Groom 'N' Edge, Leafbuster, and Hedge Hog. Deere and Company expanded its operations into lawn care equipment in 1991, and by 1998 sold $2.1 billion of products such as leaf blowers, mowers, small tractors, snow blowers, string trimmers, and utility vehicles. Lawn care equipment accounted for 20 percent of Deere's sales in 1998. In 1999, Deere teamed up with the Home Depot in promotions to boost sales.

WORKFORCE

In 1997, 28,617 workers were involved in the lawn and garden equipment industry, and 22,936 were production workers. Tennessee was home to the largest number of employees in this industry, with 5,739 workers, followed by Wisconsin with 3,355 and Indiana with 982. On average production employees in this sector worked 38.2 hours per week and earned $11.16 per hour.

RESEARCH AND TECHNOLOGY

Environmental concerns are driving a number of technological changes in the industry. A growing number of states and municipalities across the country are banning grass clippings and other organic wastes from local landfills; this has been seen as an incentive to produce a growing number of mulching mowers and composting equipment. With increasing government concern directed at the amount of particulate pollution generated by the smaller motors that power home lawn equipment, a resurgence in the sale of the classic push mower is also showing itself.

The Environmental Protection Agency continues to be a strong motivator when it comes to improving lawn and garden equipment. It has been the EPA's position for some time that lawn mowers are significant polluters. A recent EPA-funded study compared gasoline mowers typically used across the country with cordless electric mowers. Gasoline-powered equipment emitted eight times more nitrogen oxides, 3,300 times more hydrocarbons, 5,000 times more carbon monoxide, and more than twice the carbon dioxide per hour of operation compared to the electric models.

The EPA study concluded that if just 20 percent of U.S. homeowners with gasoline mowers switched to cordless electric mowers, there would be annual emissions reductions of 10,800 tons of hydrocarbons, 340 tons of nitrogen oxides, 84,000 tons of carbon monoxide, and 70,000 tons of carbon dioxide. Gay MacGregor, a division director at the National Vehicle and Fuel Emissions Laboratory in Ann Arbor, Michigan, believes that "[p]eople think that because these engines are so small, they must not pollute so much." Whereas automobiles have been regulated for 20 years, lawn mowers and other lawn and garden equipment have remained unregulated and now represent a significant source of pollution. The industry responded to many of these problems with cleaner mowers. Those mowers manufactured after September, 1997, used small four-cycle engines that exceeded EPA emission standards for small spark-ignition engines.

FURTHER READING

"Baby Boomers Are Digging into a New Hobby." *National Home Center News,* 20 July 1998.

Baker, Stephen. "Operation Push Mower." *Business Week,* 10 June 1996.

Doyle Driedger, Sharon. "Ever Greener: Gardening is Big Business in Canada." *MacLean's,* 22 April 1996.

Elstrom, Peter. "This Cat Keeps on Purring." *Business Week,* 20 January 1997.

"Lawn and Garden." *Do-It-Yourself Retailing,* 1 July 1997.

"Lawn and Garden Equipment to Near $9 Million in 2002." *Appliance Manufacturer,* 1 February 1999.

U.S. Census Bureau. "Lawn and Garden Tractor and Home Lawn and Garden Equipment Manufacturing," October 1999. Available from http://www.census.gov/prod.

SIC 3531

CONSTRUCTION MACHINERY AND EQUIPMENT

This industry includes establishments primarily engaged in manufacturing heavy machinery and equipment used primarily by the construction industries, such as bulldozers, cranes (except industrial plant overhead and truck-type cranes), dredging machinery, pavers, self-propelled backfillers, backhoes, aggregate spreaders, construction plows, and power shovels. This industry also includes establishments primarily engaged in manufacturing forestry equipment and certain specialized equipment, not elsewhere classified, similar to that used by the construction industries, such as elevating platforms, ship cranes and capstans, aerial work platforms, and automobile wrecker hoists. Establishments primarily engaged in manufacturing mining equipment are included in **SIC 3532: Mining Machinery and Equipment, Except Oil and Gas Field Machinery and Equipment**; those manufacturing industrial plant overhead traveling cranes are classified under **SIC 3536: Overhead Traveling Cranes, Hoists, and Monorail Systems**; and those establishments manufacturing industrial truck-type cranes are classified under **SIC 3537: Industrial Trucks, Tractors, Trailers, and Stackers.**

NAICS CODE(S)

336510 (Railroad Rolling Stock Manufacturing)
333923 (Overhead Traveling Crane, Hoist, and Monorail System Manufacturing)
333120 (Construction Machinery Manufacturing)

INDUSTRY SNAPSHOT

The construction machinery and equipment industry is dynamic. After experiencing a growth of 12 percent in 1997, the industry went on to enjoy its eighth year of consecutive growth in 1998. Construction equipment shipments were valued at $21.7 billion worth in 1997, representing a 16 percent increase since 1995. Low interest rates and a booming American economy fueled residential, public, and commercial construction in the United States, which in turn boosted demand for construction machinery and equipment. In 1997, 721 establishments were involved in the production of construction equipment, compared to 919 in 1995. With 58 facilities, Wisconsin was home to the greatest number of construction equipment manufacturers. California and Illinois followed, with 56 and 51 establishments, respectively. Exports of U.S.-made construction machinery in 1998 were $6.88 billion, down 2.5 percent from 1997.

ORGANIZATION AND STRUCTURE

This industry provides several major categories of equipment for use by the larger construction industry. Earthmoving machinery is utilized by companies involved in residential and commercial construction, as well as those involved in highway construction and dam-building. Caterpillar Inc. is the industry leader in the production of earthmoving machinery, which has historically been the cornerstone of its product line.

Excavators and cranes are used in a variety of construction areas. Excavators are used in most construction jobs and come in a wide variety of sizes and configurations, ranging from small tractor-mounted backhoes to large power shovels. Cranes are used for bridge, highway, large commercial or industrial construction jobs, and in offshore oil drilling. Other construction equipment includes underground mining machinery, asphalt and concrete pavers, air compressors and tools, pumps, hoists, and rock-crushing and screening equipment.

CURRENT CONDITIONS

Construction machinery manufacturers emerged from the recession of the early-1990s leaner and more productive. For instance, Caterpillar embarked on a six year, $1.8 billion modernization program in 1993 that automated many facets of factory production. The industry was also aided in its recovery by the burgeoning American economy of the mid-1990s. With low interest rates fueling a housing boom (new homes sales in 1997 alone topped 800,000), the construction business needed equipment and machinery to keep up with demand. Commercial building also fared well. The lowest vacancy rates in office buildings in a decade spurred the construction of office parks and urban commercial buildings. The strong economy also led to the construction of new football stadiums and other sports arenas—again driving sales of earthmovers, scrapers, pavers, and other heavy equipment to complete the projects.

Manufacturers of construction equipment also received a boon from infrastructure projects. In June of 1998, the *Transportation and Efficiency Act for the 21st Century* passed the U.S. Congress. This bill—the biggest public works bill in U.S. history—set aside $219 billion for transportation needs; $175 billion was earmarked for road and bridge repair and construction alone. The bill's impact on the construction equipment market was extremely positive. As *Construction Equipment* noted on December 1, 1998, "the Highway Act is one reason the U.S. construction market will feel little pain from global financial cooling." Moreover, bridge-building reached

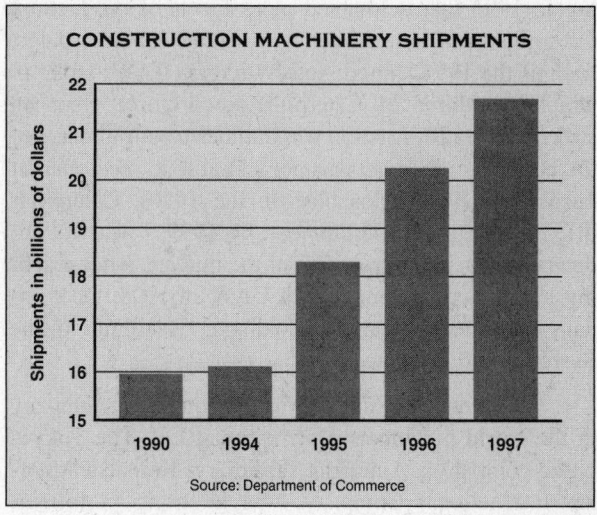

CONSTRUCTION MACHINERY SHIPMENTS

Source: Department of Commerce

new levels in the late 1990s after the U.S. Department of Commerce reported that over one-third of the country's bridges were in need of repair. Such work requires highly automated bituminous and concrete paving equipment, milling machinery, and high-powered pavement breakers. Other public sector projects—which in 1998 accounted for $295 billion—included the construction of urban pollution control facilities, such as solid waste disposal and wastewater treatment facilities.

The outlook for the construction equipment industry was not entirely rosy, however. The Asian economic crisis of 1997 cut into American firms' exports. In the wake of the collapse, construction projects for new housing, roads, and offices slowed dramatically, dragging down demand for construction machinery. Exports of U.S.-made construction equipment to Asia dropped 33 percent in 1998 to $808.5 million. Russia's economic collapse of the late-1990s also hurt the American industry.

INDUSTRY LEADERS

The world's leading manufacturer of construction equipment, with total sales and revenues in 1998 of nearly $21 billion, is Caterpillar Inc., of Peoria, Illinois. Construction machinery and equipment accounted for $13 billion of its sales that year. Ranked 58th among the *Fortune 500* companies, 1998 marked Caterpillar's seventh consecutive year of growing revenue and profits. Originally incorporated in 1925 as the Caterpillar Tractor Company, the company boasts more than two dozen major production facilities in 22 countries, as well as 195 dealerships. After suffering significant losses during the 1980s, the company embarked on a series of changes to regain its previous form, cutting its workforce from 90,000 to 60,000, closing 30 percent of its plants, introducing new machinery, and moving aggressively into foreign markets. After completing the massive restructuring in 1993 that automated more facets of production, Caterpillar was able to better withstand labor disputes, such as the 1994 United Auto Workers (UAW) strike in which two-thirds of Caterpillar's workforce went on strike. The transformation was at times a painful one, but the company emerged stronger and able to meet market needs quickly. For instance, in the 1980s, Caterpillar offered little paving equipment; by 1999, it was the industry leader in this segment of the market. After reaching a contract agreement with UAW in 1998, the company acquired Veratech Holdings, Handling Crane Systems, and Wrightech.

The second-largest construction equipment company in the world is Komatsu International Ltd. The Tokyo-based company's American subsidiary, Komatsu America International Company, was a strong performer. Based in Vernon Hills, Illinois, Komatsu America conceives, manufactures, sells, and maintains earth-moving machinery for North American construction and mining firms. The company's forte is in dump trucks and crawler bulldozers. Sales 1n 1998 were above $8 billion.

Incorporated in 1868, Deere and Company is one of the largest agricultural and industrial equipment manufacturers in the United States. An industry innovator since founder John Deere introduced the first successful self-cleaning steel plow in 1837, the company has factories throughout the world and distributes its products through independent retail dealers. In 1998, Deere and Company employed 37,000 people and achieved sales of over $11.0 billion. Construction equipment accounted for 19 percent—about $2.6 billion—of total sales. John Deere produced backhoe loaders, crawler bulldozers, and drive train components, in addition to engines, excavators, motor graders, and scrapers. The company was hit hard by the economic collapse in Asia and Russia. In 1998, John Deere announced that 2,400 workers would be laid-off because of dwindling exports.

WORKFORCE

The industry employed 74,868 in 1997, down from 78,200 in 1995. The number of production workers also dropped substantially from 53,300 in 1995 to 50,565 in 1997. Increasing automation in the construction equipment industry led to the declining number of workers. Production workers toiled an average of 39 hours per week. Average earnings in 1997 were $17.36 per hour. Illinois was home to the greatest number of workers in this industry in 1997—with 12,740. Iowa followed with 9,290 and Wisconsin with 7,539.

Labor is a huge part of operating expenses for leading domestic construction equipment manufacturers such as Deere & Co. and Caterpillar. Labor at both companies is represented by the United Auto Workers, and both companies had their share of labor disputes in the 1990s.

RESEARCH AND TECHNOLOGY

Construction equipment itself has often been considered relatively "low-tech," but "intelligent" machinery is increasingly being developed for field work. Kraft TeleRobotics of Kansas, for instance, is testing Haz-Trak, an excavator and materials handler that can be operated by remote control from hundreds of yards away, allowing operators to handle dangerous materials such as radioactive waste from a safe distance. The excavator, it was hoped, can eventually be operated from even greater distances.

Another trend in the industry is the quest for automated construction equipment, which, as *Construction Equipment* explained, would "reduce operating costs and increase productivity on the construction site and in the mine." The magazine predicted that, within 15 years, a fleet of machines could be operated by a single human operator. Armed with the latest in technology these machines of the future should be able to "detect problems and then proactively inform the human overseer."

FURTHER READING

Bares, John. "Coming Next Decade: More Machine Automation." *Construction Equipment,* 1 August 1999.

"Caterpillar Inc." *The Wall Sreet Journal,* 4 April 1997, C30.

Merwin, Donald. "Construction Headed for 8th Year of Growth." *Construction Equipment,* 1 December 1998.

U.S. Bureau of the Census. *1994 County Business Patterns.* Washington: GPO, 1996.

———. "Construction Machinery Manufacturing." Available from http://www.census.gov/prod/ec97/97m3314c.pdf. October 1999.

"U.S. Machinery Exports Decline." *Gulf Construction,* 1 May 1999.

1995 Annual Survey of Manufactures. Washington: GPO, 1997.

SIC 3532

MINING MACHINERY

This category includes establishments primarily engaged in manufacturing heavy machinery and equipment used by the mining industries, such as coal breakers, mine cars, mineral cleaning machinery, concentration machinery, core drills, coal cutters, portable rock drills, and rock crushing machinery. Establishments primarily engaged in manufacturing construction machinery are classified in **SIC 3531: Construction Machinery and Equipment;** those manufacturing well-drilling machinery are classified in **SIC 3533: Oil and Gas Field Machinery and Equipment;** and those manufacturing coal and ore conveyors are classified in **SIC 3535: Conveyors and Conveying Equipment.**

NAICS Code(s)

333131 (Mining Machinery and Equipment Manufacturing)

Industry Snapshot

Mining machinery and equipment manufacturers experienced a downturn in the late 1990s. Diminishing demand for domestically produced minerals fueled the initial decline, decreasing mining activity substantially. To combat weakened demand, mining equipment companies relied on the export market for business opportunities, but this market has been far from stable. The Asian economic crisis of 1997 decimated exports of mining equipment, as did the collapse of the Russian economy. While mining equipment shipments in 1997 were valued at over $2.6 billion, the leading mining equipment company, Harnischfeger Industries, Inc., reported that mining machinery sales dropped 28 percent between 1997 and 1999.

Organization and Structure

The mining equipment industry is highly dependent on mining activity in the United States and the world. When demand for mined materials is high, mine operators order new machinery; when demand is low, orders fall off. Mining machinery manufacturers are cushioned somewhat from demand cycles because different kinds of mines use similar machinery. Thus a decline in coal mining, for example, may be offset by a boom in salt mining.

The market share divisions within this industry were split among several categories. Underground mining machinery claimed 30.9 percent of the industry in 1997, up from 15.4 percent in 1995. In 1997, crushing, pulverizing, and screening machinery held 21.6 percent of the market, a jump of over 10 percent from 1995. Drills and other mining machinery, not elsewhere classified, controlled 5.3 percent of the market, down from 9.4 percent two years earlier. The remaining categories accounted for the other 42.2 percent.

The mining machinery industry draws its supplies from a variety of sources. Mill shapes and forms made from carbon alloy, stainless steel, copper, and aluminum are the most highly consumed materials. Castings from gray and malleable iron, steel, aluminum, and copper, and forgings from iron and steel are also heavily consumed. Fabricated structural metal products, speed changers, gears, industrial high-speed drives, and roller bearings constitute other significant materials consumed by the industry.

In 1997, 297 establishments manufactured mining machinery and equipment. Of this total number, 129 were larger companies that employed 20 or more workers. West Virginia led all other states in the number of businesses engaged in this industry, with 38 factories; Pennsylvania was home to 27 mining machinery manufacturers, followed by Illinois with 18. In terms of shipment volume, Pennsylvania generated the highest dollar-amount with $703.4 million, 26.6 percent of total industry-wide shipment value. West Virginia placed second, with shipments worth $223.4 million, 8.5 percent of the total.

Background and Development

Mining came late to the United States, for early surveyors assumed that there were no significant mineral resources to be found in the country. Politicians and statesmen arguing over currency shortly after the Revolutionary War ruled out gold and silver because the United States supposedly did not have the resources to produce this type of exchange. Benjamin Franklin said, "Gold and silver are not the produce of North America, which has no mines." Another eighteenth-century observer, Cornelius de Pauw of the Netherlands, remarked that "In all the extent of America there are found but few mines of iron, and these so inferior in quality to those of the old continent that it cannot even be used for nails." As history has shown, these remarks proved wildly presumptuous. Explorers moving westward across the country in the nineteenth century discovered rich reserves of gold, silver, lead, copper, iron, nickel, coal, and many other ores and minerals. The country proved far richer than any of the original settlers imagined.

The first mechanisms to dig and extract mineral resources from the earth were hammers, chisels, shovels, and buckets. More advanced operations used single cars on rail ways to convey materials to the surface of underground mines. The hammer and chisel were the first instruments to be replaced by pneumatically-powered cutting devices. British inventors were nearly one decade ahead of the Americans in the development of mechanical power to cut into the ground. In 1850, a Glasgow mine owner proved compressed air could be used to power underground machinery. By 1853, a cutting chain machine was developed, which matured into a machine called the Gartsherrie, patented in 1864. The Gartsherrie is considered the precursor of modern coal cutters.

A rock drill was invented and patented by Simon Ingersoll in 1870. After Ingersoll's patent changed hands several times and improvements to his invention had been made, Addison Rand was able to persuade mining companies to use his new technology instead of hammers and chisels. The two inventors came together in 1905 and advertised themselves as "the largest builder of air power machinery in the world." Ingersoll's side of the operation specialized in construction work, while Rand's specialized in underground mining. Today, Ingersoll-Rand is a highly diversified company with many interests, most of which are related to its origins in mining.

Though the industrial revolution was dependent on abundant supplies of coal to generate power, the coal mining industry lagged far behind others in using machinery to ease the work of men. Men manually shoveled coal into coal cars well into the twentieth century. Keith Dix, author of *What's a Coal Miner to Do?*, wrote: "It is ironic that the advance in technology and management, which gave modern industry its momentum, bypassed the one industry on which most others depended." By 1948, roughly 33 percent of the country's underground coal continued to be loaded by hand.

Joseph Joy, who was responsible for the mechanization of coal loading, is considered the single most significant inventor in this industry; he was awarded 106 patents between 1904 and 1944. Joy developed the Joy Loader in response to two insistent demands: American industry's demand for an increasing supply of coal and newly-organized mineworkers' demand for improvements in working conditions that were frequently subhuman. Following the development of the Joy Loader, men would no longer need to shovel coal by hand, though many would lose their jobs as a result. The Joy Manufacturing Company, known today as Joy Technologies Incorporated, claimed that Joy Loaders accounted for 72 percent of all coal loaded mechanically by 1954.

During the 1970s, the U.S. Government pushed the development of new mining technologies through legislation on health and safety, air and water pollution, and environmental protection of the land mined. Such efforts changed the face of the mining industry, requiring skilled staff to operate and maintain mechanized production. Productivity in underground coal mines was hampered due to additional resources required to prevent accidents, black lung disease, and acid-runoff. In surface mining, additional resources were necessary to meet land restoration standards and to negotiate with those who claimed the land for agricultural purposes. Mining machinery manufacturers sought to capitalize on the changing industry by providing machines to do the required jobs.

The mining equipment industry suffered a substantial drop in shipments during 1982, when shipments were valued at $2.1 billion. By 1983 they fell to $1.5 billion and only recovered to $1.6 billion by 1991. The industry continued a slow growth trend with total sales at approximately only $1.7 billion in 1996.

By the 1980s, U.S. Government interest in mining was concerned with addressing import-export imbalances. A 1986 report suggested that foreign penetration of the U.S. machinery market was primarily due to the strength of the dollar, high domestic material and capital costs, and generous financing and credit terms offered by some foreign governments to support export sales. The report projected that U.S. mining equipment manufacturers would face a steadily growing export market, shifting to Latin America, Asia, and Africa. Current world events, such as the North American Free Trade Agreement, the emergence of Korean and Taiwanese manufacturers, and the plea from South Africa, a major mining country, to lift trade sanctions, underscore the significance of these projections and the importance for U.S. manufacturers of developing the export market.

Due to the high price of new mining machinery, the used-machinery market was very healthy, especially outside the United States. This demand created an incentive for thieves to steal equipment, which is a relatively easy task. Machinery is usually left in unsecured areas, and is easy to start, difficult to trace, and easy to sell. The increase in equipment thefts in the early 1980s spurred Deere & Company to issue a Manufacturer's Certificate of Origin (MCO),which was adopted by the Construction Industry Manufacturers Association in 1983. Since then more than 20 manufacturers have used the MCO, which has reduced the thefts of certain machinery. As used-equipment buyers become more aware of the frequency of machinery theft, more MCOs have been requested upon the purchase of used-equipment.

U.S. manufacturers maintained a significant, though not a leading, share of the world mining machinery industry in the early 1990s. The strongest competitors in the world market were Japan, Germany, France, Canada, South Korea, Taiwan, and South Africa. While mining in the United States dropped sharply due to a worldwide surplus of metal and mineral supplies, mining abroad expanded quickly, opening new markets for U.S. manufacturers. The largest potential market was the former Soviet Union, which had vast amounts of natural resources. Although much of this marketplace was speculative in the early 1990s, analysts suggested that the way to jump-start the economy of Russia and the other nations was to enter the world marketplace through the sale of these resources. Many of the former Soviet Union's mines were in dire need of modernization and capital investment, providing a ready market for U.S. mining machinery equipment.

CURRENT CONDITIONS

The mining equipment industry's reliance on exports was the source of many of its challenges in the late 1990s. Asia—once a key market for mining equipment—suffered from a severe economic downturn in 1997. Once-busy mining operations in China and Australia slowed or halted production, thereby limiting the amount of equipment they needed. At the same time, other Asian industries also cut back production in the wake of downturn. As factories limited production, they needed less coal, which adversely impacted the mining equipment industry as well. According to the *Wall Street Journal*, "coal consumption . . . slowed world-wide" in 1998. Russia's mining operations encountered hard times, as well, and U.S. equipment manufacturers watched as this important market for their goods dried up.

The situation in the United States was not much better. 1998 copper prices were near record lows, which stalled copper mining operations. Nevertheless, in July of 1999, P&H MinePro, the above-ground mining business of Harnischfeger Industries received a substantial order. Southern Peru Copper Corp. purchased over $20 million of equipment for its expanding Cuajone copper mine in southwestern Peru. P&H sold two electric mining shovels, three rotary blasthole drills, and a large wheel loader in this transaction.

INDUSTRY LEADERS

The leading mining equipment manufacturing company in 1998 was the Milwaukee-based Harnischfeger Industries. Harnischfeger's operations included P&H MinePro Services, which produced above-ground mining equipment and Joy Mining Machinery, which focused on below-ground equipment, as well as a pulp and paper-making machinery division. With its mining equipment sales for 1998 topping $1.2 billion, Harnischfeger controlled about 70 percent of the total market. Despite its considerable size, though, Harnischfeger had fallen on hard times. Like others in the industry, it struggled to overcome disappearing markets in Asia and Russia. Moreover, the company sought to diversify in the late 1990s, which left it dangerously overextended. Harnischfeger cut 20 percent of its work force in August of 1998. In 1999, the company was forced to enter Chapter 11 restructuring proceedings. Other key players in the industry included Texas-based Letourneau, Inc., Bucyrus International, and Svedala Industries, Inc., which manufactured mineral processing equipment, grinding mills and crushers.

WORKFORCE

The employment level in this industry dropped sharply between 1984 and 1987, to 13,600 people. From 1989 to 1991, employment rose about 10 percent from the 1987 level, but then began to decline again in 1992. In 1997, mining machinery and equipment manufacturers employed 13,224 people, of which only 8,905 were production workers. The employees directly involved in production earned an average wage of $14.38 per hour, and worked an average of about 40 hours each week. Pennsylvania was home to the greatest number of workers in this industry, with 2,821 in 1997, and West Virginia followed with 1,235.

U.S. Department of Labor projections for the year 2005 indicate that the workforce of the mining machinery industry will change significantly. Welders and cutters, who account for the largest segment in this industry, are expected to reduce their numbers by 11.1 percent. Others facing drops of 10 percent or more include assemblers, welding machine setters, machine builders, secretaries, inspectors, truck and tractor operators, and material handlers. Machinists are expected to increase employment levels by 6.8 percent, sales workers by 18.2 percent, mechanical engineers by 9.5 percent, numerically controlled machine tool operators by 9.5 percent, industrial machinery mechanics by 18.3 percent, industrial production managers by 15.7 percent, engineering technicians by 6.0 percent, combination machine tool operators by 8.3 percent, and coating/painting/spraying machine operators by 7.5 percent.

RESEARCH AND TECHNOLOGY

Mining equipment is considered mature in terms of design and innovation. Therefore, any improvements rely on research and development of new materials and advanced sensing, control, and computer techniques. Innovations in technology have typically sought to achieve gains in productivity or worker safety. The dangers of underground mining prompted underground machinery designers to develop remote controlled and automated mining systems. These systems reduce production costs, increase productivity, and increase worker safety.

Other technological devices are found in surface mining, where sensing and control systems are frequently installed. Blast hole drills employ automated systems that regulate the speed and feet rate of the drill bit. Mining shovels have on-board microprocessors, which relay information and record data. Because they can be added to existing equipment, these technologies have been developed by many manufacturers.

Another new machine is Caterpillar's autonomous truck control system, which was introduced to the commercial market in 1998 in limited numbers. The benefits of the driverless robot mine truck include: it's less expensive than hiring human truck drivers; it works continuously with no breaks; and it will operate in remote locations, such as northern Canada, where it is difficult to hire and get truck drivers to the machines at all. The Caterpillar truck was one of several robot mine trucks that was expected to be in general operation worldwide by the year 2000.

FURTHER READING

Darnay, Arsen J., ed. *Manufacturing U.S.A.* 5th ed. Detroit: Gale Research, 1996.

Laing, Jonathon. "Grave Digger: How Harnischfeger's Flashy Chieftan Drove the Firm to Ruin" *Barron's* 12 July 1999.

Leach, Mark, et. al. "Machinery (Construction and Mining)." *The Value Line Investment Survey (Part 3 - Ratings and Reports).* 8 November 1996.

National Mining Association. ''Mining Equipment Statistics'' Available at http://www.nma.org/eqipstats.html

Quintanilla, Carl. ''Harnischfeger Has Loss, To Cut Work Force 20 Percent'' *Wall Street Journal* 27 August 1998.

Woof, Mike. ''Look - No Hands!'' *World Mining Equipment,* December 1996

SIC 3533

OIL FIELD MACHINERY

This category covers establishments primarily engaged in manufacturing machinery and equipment for use in oil and gas fields or for drilling water wells, including portable drilling rigs. Establishments primarily engaged in manufacturing offshore oil and gas well drilling and production platforms are classified in **SIC 3731: Ship Building and Repairing.**

NAICS CODE(S)

333132 (Oil and Gas Field Machinery and Equipment Manufacturing)

INDUSTRY SNAPSHOT

The health of the oil and gas field machinery industry is inextricably tied to capital expenditures in the oil and gas extraction industries whose health in turn is dependent on the price of oil. Fortunes of the oil industry are also very cyclical.

In the 1970s the Organization of Petroleum Exporting Countries (OPEC) produced more than half of the world's oil. For a variety of reasons, most of which had little to do with supply and demand, OPEC began aggressively pricing oil and consumers were willing to meet their price. But OPEC could not maintain production quotas amongst its member and the market was soon glutted with oil and the price subsequently fell. Demand for OPEC oil fell from 31 million barrels a day in 1979 to 17 million barrels a day in 1985. In 1997 and 1998 OPEC again boosted production as demand growth stagnated due to global economic problems.

The fortunes of the oil and gas field machinery industry likewise rose and fell in relation to the going price for a barrel of crude oil. Because of depressed oil prices throughout the 1990s the cost of drilling for oil often did not produce satisfactory returns. Therefore, with little drilling activity, there was little need for oil and gas field machinery. Investment reports by industry analysts such as Merrill Lynch and Standard and Poor's shared the same opinion: oil and gas prices would remain relatively flat especially when compared to the early 1980s.

However, 1999 produced cautious optimism in the industry due to late decade improvements in the price of gas and oil. The industry showed a growth rate of 23 percent in 1996 and nine percent in 1997. This represented the first back-to-back 2 years of growth in the industry since 1991. In early 1999 the Organization of Petroleum Exporting Countries (OPEC) and some non-OPEC countries announced plans to cut daily oil production by 2.1 million barrels a day in an attempt to raise prices by reducing supply. In early 1999 the price of a barrel of the benchmark West Texas Intermediate Crude was $12.00. By May it was $18.50.

The later years of the 1990s also saw a plethora of oil and gas field industry acquisitions and mergers. Companies were attempting to diversify products, capitalize on new technologies and innovations, improve efficiency, and reduce costs.

In 1995, there were 513 establishments in the oil and gas field industry, with predictions that this figure would drop to only 258 by 2000. The decade high for this figure was 1991, which hosted 582 such establishments. The value of shipments in 1996 was nearly $4.7 billion, a far cry from the more than $11.0 billion worth of shipments in 1982. The figure was projected to drop to less than $1.7 billion by 2000. Industry establishments are located primarily in Texas with a scattering of others in Oklahoma and other states.

By 1997 there were 497 companies involved with oil and gas field machinery industry with 29,452 employees. Of this figure 19,512 were production workers. The industry's payroll for 1997 was nearly $1.17 billion with wages representing almost $641 million. The delivered cost of materials consumed by kind was: hydraulic and pneumatic fluid power valves—$26 million, other valves—$107 million, fluid power pumps, motors and hydrostatic transmissions—$18 million, other pumps—$33 million, and fluid power cylinders and rotary actuators—$9 million.

ORGANIZATION AND STRUCTURE

The oil and gas field machinery industry includes field tools, oil derricks, drilling rigs and tools, well logging and surveying equipment, and general gas well and oil field machinery and equipment. Many companies exist in the United States that make specialty drilling equipment and other related machinery. Other companies, such as machine tool makers, produce smaller parts either for assembly at the more specialized companies or to meet replacement needs while the rig is in service. The companies producing drilling rigs usually maintain a field service department. Private consulting firms, however, may also specialize in field repair of all oil field related equipment. Oil and gas field machinery companies thus provide equipment and services to the oil industry that are used in drilling, testing, and finishing oil and gas wells as well as enhancing existing wells. Equipment may be premanufactured or it may be built and assembled in the field. These companies may also provide on-site service once a well begins operating. Customers of the industry are oil and gas producers and drilling companies. In the United States, approximately 97 percent of the drilling rigs are owned by drilling contractors, not the oil and gas producers.

The oil industry finds itself variously controlled, compromised, regulated, influenced and lobbied for or against by organizations like the Organization of Petroleum Exporting Countries (OPEC) the American Petroleum Institute, the ever volatile geopolitics of the Middle East, and the vagaries of the American consumer. Domestically, the industry is also controlled, to a great extent, by regulations imposed by the U.S. government and the governments of international competitors. The Environmental Protection Agency has begun to place stringent restrictions on companies selling crude oil, which ultimately affects the cost of producing oil. This can drive profits downward, especially if coupled with low oil prices. Given these conditions, oil drilling is being performed more and more by major oil-selling companies, like Exxon, Texaco, and Citgo. This is in sharp contrast to the early 1980s, when drilling rigs were common sights in the front yards of southern and midwestern private homes.

Any decrease in drilling activity world-wide adversely effects the oil and gas field machinery industry. Smaller support machinery businesses that thrived in the early 1980s amidst high oil prices either went out of business or were bought out. This trend continued throughout the 1990s and by the end of the decade the industry consisted mostly of very large, well-diversified companies. For example, IRI National of Houston and Norways's HitecASA merged to form IRI Hitec which focused on the design, engineering, and manufacturing of technically advanced offshore and land-based drilling equipment. In 1997 the Halliburton Company acquired the Numar Corporation and in 1998 acquired Dresser, making Halliburton the largest provider of oil field services. Halliburton purchased Dresser so as to bring together oil field, engineering, and construction services. Numar was purchased because of its patented Magnetic Resonance Imaging Logging tool that evaluates subsurface rock formations in new wells. Another important industry event was the 1998 acquisition of Western Atlas by Baker Hughes. By the late 1990s the three dominant companies in the industry according to Standard & Poor's were Halliburton with 1998 revenues of $17.4 billion, Schlumberger Ltd. with revenues of $11.9 billion, and Baker Hughes at $1.7 billion.

BACKGROUND AND DEVELOPMENT

In the United States, oil drilling evolved as a result of seeking salt brine. Without refrigeration, one of the few

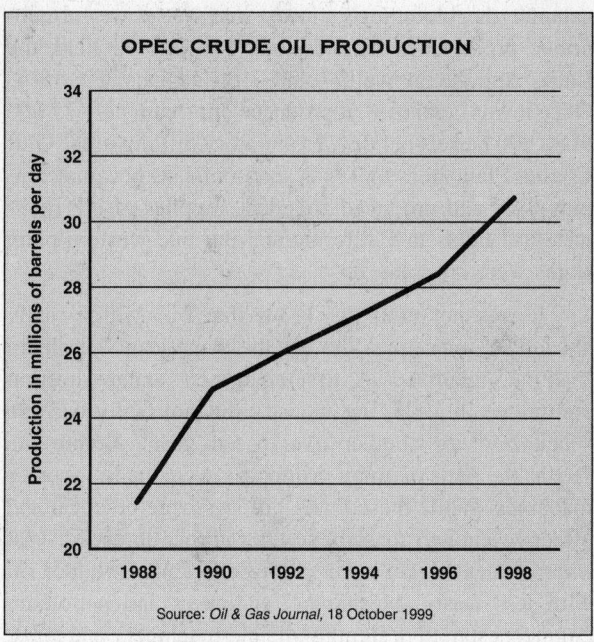

OPEC CRUDE OIL PRODUCTION

Source: *Oil & Gas Journal*, 18 October 1999

means of preserving meat was through packing it with salt. Therefore, salt brine was a commodity in heavy demand. In 1806 two brothers, David and Joseph Ruffner, established a business supplying settlers near Charleston, West Virginia, with salt brine. Quickly, the demand for the salt became so great that the brothers devised a way to drill a hole to intercept the flow of the brine seepage. This well, responsible for developing the spring pole and drilling line, was the first well drilled in America with tools. From this point, other types of wells were drilled in the Ruffner fashion. In 1814, near Burkesville, Kentucky, the ''American Well'' was drilled, which was 475 feet deep and supposedly produced 1,000 barrels of oil per day.

The invention of the steam engine in tandem with cable tools changed the nature of oil and gas drilling from 1860 to 1930. During this time, crude oil was gaining favor as an illuminant, replacing whale oil used for lamps. Also, the use of machinery to aid man's endeavors was more widespread, and crude oil was known to be an excellent lubricant. Its use as a fuel was also gaining popularity. These three developments created a demand for oil drilling; thus the industry gained momentum. The first well drilled in America strictly for oil production to supply the machinery industry was the Drake well. Following the Drake well, patent applications were filed in abundance for a wide assortment of tools, rigs, and machines to support oil drilling activities. Among these patents were predecessors to common modern oil industry machinery, including rolling cutter rock bits, an offshore drilling rig, and rotary and percussion motion devices.

From this point, the oil boom was upon the world. An oil field in Corsicana, Texas, was the first well to catapult the blooming industry into the powerful economic prominence it holds today. In this oil field, the Lucas Spindletop well "blew" on January 10, 1901. Once it was contained, it produced approximately 75,000 to 80,000 barrels per day. Exploratory drilling in the Gulf Coastal Plain areas of Texas and Louisiana became commonplace and produced abundant supplies of oil. Likewise, oil fields in California and the mid-western plain states were cropping up.

It was not until the 1930s that oil drilling really became a science. Although the American Petroleum Institute organized its first equipment standardization committee in 1925, the industry did not really become specialized for another five to ten years. Before the 1930s, the parts of an oil drilling rig were made for other machines. While these makeshift rigs were practical and effective enough to achieve the purpose intended, vast improvements were necessary to efficiently produce oil with less waste. Mechanical engineers and petroleum engineers started designing oil field machinery and tools. From these efforts the following were created: better tooth and ball bearing designs of rock bits, roller bearing enclosed engines, automatic controls for steam generating plants, and gas engine electric generator sets with motors. Also, drilling rig personnel were becoming more educated about professional and safety practices.

Basically, the same principles are employed today as in the past. Aside from the demise of oil derricks, which have given way to pumping units, and the off-shore drilling methods used along the coast lines, the industry has not radically changed since its inception. The oil drilling industry can be summarized as an evolution of improved techniques, which will continue as long as oil lies beneath the earth's surface.

Standard & Poor's June 1999 *Industry Survey* was anticipating a re-bound in oil prices as 2000 approached. Foremost among factors influencing their optimism was OPEC's determination to cut production. As stated previously the price of a barrel of West Texas Intermediate crude oil jumped from $12.00 a barrel in early 1999 to $18.50 a barrel by May of that year. In spite of this rise in the price of a barrel of oil, oilfield activity remained low in 1999. For instance, the Baker Hughes rig count (the number of oil drilling rigs exploring for oil and gas) was at 507 in June, 1999, down 42 percent from May of 1998 but a bit higher than the April 1999 count of 488 rigs. This in fact is the lowest number since Baker Hughes began counting rigs in 1944.

However, *U.S. Industry & Trade Outlook '99* quotes an Offshore Data Services report showing a worldwide offshore rig fleet utilization rate of 95.6 percent, which reflects a steady rise since a 1986 low. High rig utilization rates are usually a precursor to rising day rates, which is the price paid to a drilling contractor for a day's work,

which in turn reflects higher profits. Also quoted is a forecast from the Energy Information Administration predicting an increase in the energy market share of petroleum from 38 percent (1996) to 40 percent in 2020, which would increase exploratory drilling and perhaps contribute to rig shortages, especially in the Gulf of Mexico and the North Sea.

On the other hand, the 1998 domestic rig count by the Reed Tool Co. showed U.S. rig utilization at 77 percent in mid-1998, down from 87 percent a year earlier. The report also showed that while day rates for offshore rigs increased 62 percent in 1997 and 17 percent in 1998 the rate for land rigs fell 5 percent in 1998 after a 1997 increase of 19 percent. Between mid-1998 and early 1999, however, it was likely that onshore and offshore utilization rates slipped and day rates declined significantly due to a decline in drilling activity. Making predictions even murkier is uncertainty over the amount of oil Iraq will be allowed to sell because of United Nations (UN) sanctions resulting from the Persian Gulf War, recent oil discoveries in Algeria and Nigeria, and current Venezuelan plans to increase production.

CURRENT CONDITIONS

World oil production was expected to decline 1.7 percent in 1999 but show a small 0.5 percent increase in 2000. Much depends on OPEC's production discipline and the subsequent price of oil. If OPEC's policies hold fast, oil prices will rise. As they rise, however, non-OPEC countries, and perhaps some OPEC countries, will be encouraged to raise production. Natural gas production is expected to rise slightly worldwide but decline in the U.S. although natural gas exploration is rising faster than oil exploration. Standard & Poor's predicted world oil demand would increase by 1.0 percent in 1999 or about 700,000 barrels a day. Nearly 50 percent of this growth, however, is expected to be in the United States. U.S. consumption would thus have grown about 2.2 percent in 1999. Demand growth in various Asian nations would show 1.6 percent for the same period.

Because of forecasts showing firm prices and solid demand growth, oil and gas companies are increasingly spending more money on exploration and production. Capital expenditures, however, declined 5 percent in 1998 and were expected to be even lower in 1999. Capital expenditures by oil and gas companies represent, of course, the total revenue of the oil and gas field machinery industry. Although capital expenditures for exploration and production in the oil and gas industry rose 26 percent in 1997 compared to 1996 Standard & Poor's estimated these same expenditures to fall 25 percent in 1999. A capital expenditure survey by the *Oil & Gas Journal* showed that U.S. companies were expected to spend $32.6 billion on U.S. projects in 1999, down over

20 percent from the 1998 figure of $41.0 billion. For the period 1988-1998 industry capital spending outlays have averaged about $34.5 billion a year. If oil price gains continue, however, Standard & Poor's predicts that capital spending could experience ". . . a double digit increase in 2000."

INDUSTRY LEADERS

Standard & Poor's reported in 1999 that the three dominant industry participants were the Halliburton Co., Schlumberger Ltd., and Baker Hughes Inc. The Halliburton Company, of Dallas, Texas had sales of nearly $8.9 billion in 1997 and a net income of just over $454 million. Halliburton has an assortment of divisions that provide a wide range of oil field services. Bariod Drilling Fluids, as its name implies develops and sells oil drilling fluids for various applications. NUMAR with its Magnetic Resonance Imaging Logging measures the potential of new wells to produce oil or gas in commercial quantities. Security DBS supplies roller cone rock bits, fixed cutter bits, coring equipment and services, and downhole tools. Halliburton's purchase of Dresser Industries made Halliburton the world's largest supplier of oil field services. Prior to its acquisition by Halliburton, Dresser had sales totaling just under $7.5 billion in 1997 and a net income of $318.0 million. In 1997 Dresser had 31,300 employees. Baker Hughes had 21,500 employees the same year. Dresser Wheatley provides safety valves, flow control equipment, surface safety systems, and well screens as well as plunger pumps, liquid meters, and gas measurement equipment. Sperry-Sun provides drilling engineering services, tools, sensors, software for integrated systems, and rig site information services. 1999 revenues for Halliburton were expected to be in the neighborhood of $20.0 billion.

Schlumberger Ltd. of New York likewise provides a variety of oilfield services and electronic measurement products. The company had sales of over $10.5 billion in 1997 and a net income of nearly $1.3 billion. In 1998 Schlumberger had revenues of $11.8 billion. The company has seven divisions that provide a wide variety of oil field services: Anadrill, Dowell, Geco-Prakla, GeoQuest, Integrated Project Management, Sedco Forex, and Wireline & Testing. By late 1999 Schlumberger was expected to spin off its offshore drilling unit, Sedco Forex Offshore and merge it with Transocean Offshore. This merger would result in the creation of the world's largest offshore drilling company. The merger comes as a result of the high cost and high technological demands of offshore drilling.

Baker Hughes was formed in 1987 when amidst a global oil slump Baker Oil Tools and the Hughes Tool Company merged. In 1998 Baker Hughes merged with Western Atlas to form the third largest oil field services

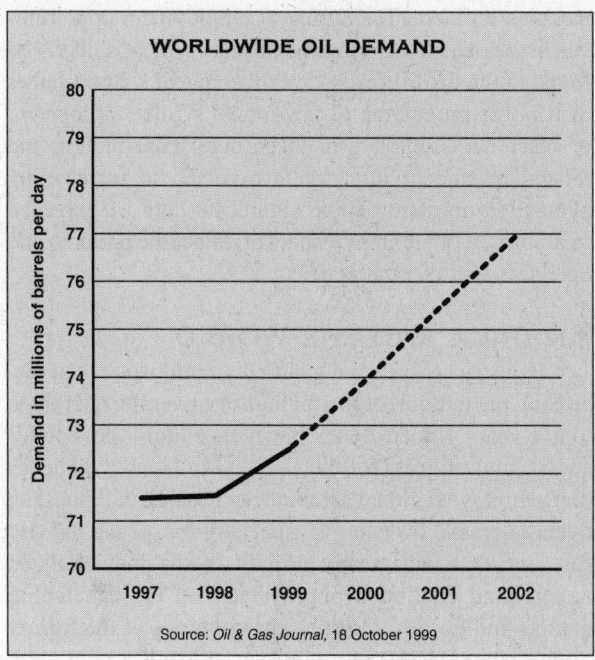

WORLDWIDE OIL DEMAND

Demand in millions of barrels per day

Source: *Oil & Gas Journal,* 18 October 1999

firm which retained the name Baker Hughes. The bid was reported to be between $5.1 and $5.5 billion. The company makes oil field equipment and provides oil field services for drilling, completing and operating oil and gas wells. Baker Hughes has nine divisions providing a wide variety of oil field services: Baker Atlas, Baker Oil Tools, Baker Petrolite, Baker Process, Centrilift, E & P Solutions, Hughes Christensen, and INTEQ. Baker Hughes has 30,000 employees worldwide and had 1998 revenues of $6.3 billion.

WORKFORCE

Between 1982 and 1994, over half of the establishments in this industry either went out of business or were consumed by larger companies. This trend continued throughout the remaining years of the decade. In 1995 there were 513 establishments in the industry, a figure expected to drop to 258 by 2000. In 1995 total employment in the industry was approximately 24,000 with about 15,000 being classified as production workers. Although the total number of establishments decreased employment was on the upswing. In 1997 the industry employed 29,452 with 19,512 of them being production workers. Payroll in 1997 was $1.20 billion with wages being nearly $647.00 million. In 1997 the value of shipments for the industry was estimated to be just over $5.00 billion and this figure is forecast to remain steady through 1999. Average wages are also expected to remain relatively flat through the end of the century. In 1995 the average hourly wage was $15.05 and is predicted to be $16.73 in 2000.

The industry is primarily composed of blue collar workers, such as welders, assemblers, machinists, and machine builders. The strongest employment opportunities in the industry in subsequent years will most likely be found in the fields of service and technical support rather than in the production of new units. While employment of machine assemblers in the general construction and related machinery industry is expected to increase by almost two-thirds by 2005, significant cuts are expected in almost all other areas, especially machine builders and operators and clerical staff.

AMERICA AND THE WORLD

Industry analysts are guardedly optimistic when discussing the outlook of the oil industry over the next three to five years. Robert Beck, managing editor—economics and special projects for the *Oil & Gas Journal,* believes that a three-year global economic expansion will boost an overall demand for energy, especially for oil and gas. He foresees slow but steady growth in the industrialized nations and continued improvement in the developing nations and Eastern Europe. The countries of the former Soviet Union (FSU) are, however, a bit of a wild card. "The economic situation in the FSU is chaotic and its outlook uncertain," Beck writes. It is hoped that the global economic downturn of 1997 and 1998, which was due in great part to the Asian economic crisis, has run its course. The International Monetary Fund is projecting an average annual growth rate of 4.9 percent for developing countries in 2000. Economic growth in the developing nations of Asia is expected to be 5.7 percent with the countries of Latin America registering 3.5 percent. *Oil & Gas Journal* also predicts a 0.6 percent growth in energy consumption for every 1 percent gain in economic activity. Total energy consumption of member countries of the Organization for Economic Cooperation and Development (OECD) is expected to rise 3.9 percent between 1999 and 2000. Total worldwide energy demand by 2002 is expected to increase 6.7 percent over 1999. The demand for natural gas is expected to increase 4.6 percent by 2002 and petroleum consumption is expected to increase 6.1 percent by the same year.

There is also guarded optimism concerning the ability of OPEC to maintain discipline amongst its members. OPEC did succeed in 1999 in limiting production which subsequently boosted oil prices. OPEC must be careful, however, not to raise prices too high, which would most likely result in a drop in demand and capital investment in other forms of energy. Iraq, however, is not part of the quota agreement and its vast reserves, coupled with rising prices, may cause that country to boost output rapidly should UN sanctions be lifted.

RESEARCH AND TECHNOLOGY

By mid-1999 there was cautious optimism in the industry about research and development and new oil field services technology. This optimism was based on an apparent rebound of oil prices and the belief that new technologies are needed to meet growing demands on the industry, both gas and oil. "Technologies are critical to drilling economics, and advances in drilling technology are allowing drillers to work much smarter," says John Cochener, principal analyst of resource evaluation for the Gas Research Institute.

A study by the Gas Research Institute that was cited in an *Oil & Gas Journal* article on oilfield technology predicts that ultra deepwater drilling will grow from 3 percent of total offshore activity in 2000 to 24 percent by 2015. Drilling trends in the industry favor looking at deeper and deeper wells, especially in offshore drilling. This trend is based on new technologies and favorable regulatory rulings. In 1984 Shell Oil drilled a well in 6,952 feet of water. This record was broken in 1987 when Shell Oil drilled a well in 7,520 feet of water. Ships are presently being constructed with capabilities of drilling in 10,000 feet of water. A joint-industry project (JIP) that began in 1996 has spent over $14.0 million on the development of a dual-gradient mud lift drill system that is expected to push operational limits beyond 10,000 feet of water. "Our goal . . . is to deliver a 12.5 inch well bore to virtually any geologic depth in water depths of 10,000 feet and beyond in the Gulf of Mexico," according to Ken Smith, JIP project manager.

The oil and gas field machinery industry is also looking at exotic materials to enhance efficiency. A JIP between RTI Energy and Grant Prideco has produced and put into use a titanium drill pipe. The pipe is designed with high stress, short radius drilling applications in mind and is being used in Greeley County, Kansas. The titanium drill pipe which is fitted with fatigue resistant steel tool joints is resistant to chemicals and weighs half as much as steel with twice the flexibility.

"In the oilfield services sector, the companies that succeed will be those that develop new technologies for increasing the efficiency and reducing the cost of producing oil and gas," according to a 1999 Standard & Poor's survey. The high cost of research and development is, however, expected to exacerbate the industry trend of continued mergers and acquisitions.

FURTHER READING

Baker Hughes Inc. "Welcome to Baker Hughes." Houston: Baker Hughes, 1999. Available from: http://www.bakerhughes.com.

"Baker Hughes Records Revenues of $6.3 bil in 1998 . . ." *Forbes.* 9 August 1999, 82.

"Baker Hughes, Western Atlas Agree to Merge." *Oil & Gas Journal.* 18 May 1998, 30.

Beck, Robert J. "Low Oil Prices Cause U.S. and Canadian Firms to Curtail Capital Outlays in 1999." *Oil & Gas Journal.* 5 April 1999, 44-51.

Beck, Robert J. "Resurgent Oil Demand, OPEC Cohesion Set Stage For Optimistic Outlook For Oil Industry At The Turn of the Century." *Oil & Gas Journal.* 18 October 1999, 49-62.

Brantly, J.E. *History of Oil Well Drilling.* Houston: Gulf Publishing Company, 1971.

Darnay, Arsen J. *Manufacturing USA: Industry Analyses, Statistics, and Leading Companies.* 6th ed. Detroit: Gale, 1998.

Fisher, Daniel. "Mr. Outside Saves the Day." (Halliburton's R. Cheney) *Forbes.* 11 January 1999, 162 +.

Gaddy, Dean E. "Industry Group Studies Dual-Gradient Drilling." *Oil & Gas Journal.* 16 August 1999, 32-33.

Haflich, Frank. "RTI Energy Systems and Grant Prideco Design Titanium Drill Pipe." *American Metal Market.* 19 October 1999, 9.

"OTC: Technology Outlook, Oil Price Rebound Support Returning Industry Confidence." *Oil & Gas Journal.* 10 May 1999, 21-29.

Salpukas, Agis. "Merger is Planned to Create Biggest Offshore driller: Schlumberger Unit and Transocean to Join." *New York Times* 13 July 1999, C7.

U.S. Bureau of the Census. *Oil and Gas Field Machinery and Equipment Manufacturing. 1997 Economic Census: Manufacturing-Industry Series.* Washington: GPO, 1999. Available from http://www.census.gov/prod.

SIC 3534

ELEVATORS AND MOVING STAIRWAYS

This classification comprises establishments primarily engaged in manufacturing passenger or freight elevators, automobile lifts, dumbwaiters, and moving stairways. Establishments primarily involved in manufacturing commercial conveyor systems and equipment are classified in **SIC 3535: Conveyors and Conveying Equipment,** and those manufacturing farm elevators are classified in **SIC 3523: Farm Machinery and Equipment.**

NAICS CODE(S)

333921 (Elevator and Moving Stairway Manufacturing)

INDUSTRY SNAPSHOT

The elevator and moving stairway industry manufactures a series of products designed for the vertical transportation of both materials and passengers. Machines manufactured for the exclusive purpose of moving materials, such as freight elevators and automobile lifts, comprise a small niche of the wide-ranging materials handling market. The majority of company revenues are generated by manufacturing passenger elevators and escalators, producing parts required for elevator renovation and modernization, and servicing elevators.

The livelihood of this industry is based mostly on the well-being of the construction industry, since new buildings need new elevators. The demand for elevators in the United States in the late 1990s was fairly high, as the strong economy fueled the construction of new commercial and public buildings. However, the 1997 collapse of Asian economies—and the subsequent stalling of the construction industry in countries such as China and Korea—eroded an important market for American elevator manufacturers. In 1997, industry shipments were valued at $1.6 billion, up 71 percent from 1996 shipments of $1.1 billion.

ORGANIZATION AND STRUCTURE

One hundred ninety-five establishments were engaged in manufacturing elevators and moving stairways in 1997. Elevators and moving stairways accounted for 79 percent of total shipments, while parts and attachments produced for separate sale represented 21 percent. Electric and hydraulic passenger elevators—40 percent of the industry's total 1997 shipments—were the largest product groups within the industry. Automobile lifts—16 percent of the total figure—were the next largest group, followed by freight elevators, other types of non-farm elevators, and moving stairways and escalators—which each comprised less than 6 percent of total shipments.

Establishments in the elevator and moving stairway industry employed an average of 48 people each. Of the 195 companies operating in 1997, 58 percent (112 firms) employed fewer than 20 workers. However, 38 percent of all employees in the industry were concentrated in establishments employing more than 50 people. The greatest concentration of industry employees was in the Midwest and the East. Indiana was home to some 1,590 employees, followed by New York with 783 and Illinois with 761. Combined, these three states employed over one third of the industry's total work force, and housed over 17 percent of all companies.

In 1997, this industry as a whole spent more than $849.0 million on raw materials, which translated to about $4.4 million per establishment. New capital expenditures totaled $38.8 million for the industry as a whole, approximately $199,000 per establishment.

The application of modern technology to the elevator industry has also fostered greater competition among major contractors (who engaged in manufacturing new elevators as only a part of their operations) and smaller independent firms (who derived their business exclusively from the service market). In an effort to guarantee future service and renovation contracts on elevators they manufactured, many of the larger companies in the industry attempted to guard the technical data governing their elevators so that outside contractors lacking proper access codes would be unable to service their product. Although this form of proprietorship was frowned upon by governing organizations such as the National Association of Elevator Contractors (NAEC), the profit margin on new elevators—about 5 percent—encouraged companies to protect their large capital investments in this manner.

BACKGROUND AND DEVELOPMENT

The genesis and evolution of the elevator industry closely paralleled the historical development of the Otis Elevator Company. The company was founded by Elisha Otis, the inventor of the first "safe" hoist—a technological development that generated public confidence in the elevator for the first time and laid the foundation for the elaborate vertical transportation systems of the twentieth century. An innovative advertiser as well as a skillful engineer, Otis brought his new invention to the Crystal Palace Exposition in New York City in 1854. During the middle of his demonstration, Otis stunned the crowd by cutting the rope that held up the hoist platform on which he stood, only to be kept securely in place by the release of the wagon spring safety mechanism he had invented. While Otis himself died before he was able to realize the financial rewards of his inventions, the company he founded reached the $1.0 million mark in sales in 1870 through the leadership of his sons, Charles and Norton.

As technology made the construction of taller buildings possible, the Otis-dominated elevator industry kept pace with developments of its own, introducing the hydraulic elevator in 1878, the electric elevator in 1889, and the gearless traction electric elevator in 1903. These innovations would later become the backbone of the industry, enabling passengers to be transported safely at greater speeds and to greater heights in buildings such as the 102-floor Empire State Building and the 110-floor World Trade Center.

With increases in the volume of passengers and the construction of taller buildings, the need arose for federal safety codes regulating the industry. In 1922, the American standard safety requirements for elevators were established, codifying the informal laws that had previously governed the industry. By keeping such concerns at the forefront, the industry was able to maintain an excellent safety record, strengthening consumer confidence and paving the way for the public acceptance of new technologies in future years.

As elevator speeds reached 700 feet per minute, the need for an automated control system became more evident. Consequently, in 1924 Otis developed the Signal Control System, which took the guesswork away from the operator by automatically slowing down the elevator as passengers on various floors pushed call buttons. The system was further refined with the invention of Peak Period Control, a control device which automated the job of the elevator starter, further increasing efficiency.

The widespread use of electronics in World War II ushered in a new era of technological advances in the elevator industry. In addition to providing improvements in safety devices, such as the development of a sensor that automatically returned the elevator doors to the open position when a person occupied the doorway, electronics technology finally eliminated the need for elevator operators and starters. With Otis's development and refinement of Autotronics, a system that electronically controlled when elevator doors should be opened and closed, most commercial elevators were fully automated by the mid-1950s.

The next two decades were marked by continued refinement of the automatic control systems developed in the 1950s. By 1970, for instance, solid state circuitry, which contained hundreds of printed circuit boards per system, was applied to the elevator industry. This innovation significantly reduced the size and weight of the control system, while improving its reliability and ease of maintenance in comparison to earlier models. New methods of production were introduced as well, such as the concept of the pre-engineered elevator, which brought forth the mass production of uniformly designed elevators. This manufacturing philosophy not only lowered production costs, but, by providing the architect with the exact hoistway dimensions and other elevator specifications, eliminated much of the arduous work required in designing elevators to fit individual construction projects. Such innovations enabled the industry to surpass the $1.0 billion mark in shipments by 1982, more than twice the total of a decade earlier.

As the 1980s progressed, however, the pattern of growth characteristic of earlier years was not sustained. An increased demand for escalators in shopping malls and other public buildings throughout the country was not enough to overcome the slowdown in the elevator market, a direct result of the severe decline in multi-story buildings. At the close of 1991, total shipments of $1.2 billion were recorded, reflecting only a 5 percent increase over the previous 10 years. In a similar fashion, new capital expenditures fell from $31.2 million to $16.3 million, nearly a 48 percent decline.

While the future of the industry largely depended on the condition of the real estate and construction markets, it would also be influenced by firms' abilities to sell clients on new technological developments, particularly those implementing the use of computerized control systems, which promised to revolutionize the industry in the 1990s. With the advent of various types of new computer technology, the future of the industry would largely be determined by the ability of elevator manufacturers to convince consumers that extensive modernization projects were indeed necessary. Without the support of a strong U.S. economy in the future, it appeared doubtful that such expenses would be justified by companies attempting to cut costs.

The value of U.S. shipments rose each year from 1991 to 1996. In an attempt to combat the unfavorable economic conditions of the early 1990s, the elevator industry attempted to fill the void in new elevator contracts by shifting its attention to the renovation and modernization of models installed 20 or more years ago. By replacing old control panels with new machinery and computer technology, the elevator industry hoped to survive the effects of the glutted real estate market. Elevator manufacturers also looked to take advantage of the new opportunities for renovation made available by legislation passed during the early 1990s requiring that elevators be updated to provide greater handicapped accessibility in public and private buildings.

From 1990 to 1995, the demand for elevators and escalators fell from 90,000 units annually to 70,000 units. Large international firms and small local companies all suffered. They responded to the crunch by cutting costs, decreasing the number of employees, simplifying designs, and consolidating. In 1991, there were 175 companies operating in this industry; by 1997, there were only 34—with the industry leaders consisting of subsidiaries of larger, diversified corporations.

In 1996, the elevator industry faced increased competition, and a slow construction industry made business difficult. Large European companies were in financial straits, such as the Swiss engineering firm Schindler. Their 1995 profits were one-half the preceding year's. Kone, a Finnish company, closed several of its factories. The American firm Otis, which controlled about one-fifth of the market, saw a 20 percent rise in operating profits in 1995; with $5.3 billion in sales, the company made $511.0 million in profits.

Historically, the servicing of elevators has been the privilege of the manufacturer, but the servicing of elevators has become a fiercely competitive market of its own. Servicing contracts are of great importance because generally, in the first twenty years of its life, an elevator will cost its owner as much in repairs as the initial cost. To offset this, Otis started installing elevators equipped with electronics that allowed engineers to remotely monitor elevators for faults and upcoming problems. The remote monitoring enabled engineers to spot problems, and elevators can be serviced before breakdowns occur.

CURRENT CONDITIONS

The U.S. market recovered in the late 1990s. Commercial building construction boomed, as vacancy rates in office buildings were at their lowest in a decade. Demand for elevators in office buildings was high. An overall strong economy boosted construction of public

buildings—many of which also needed elevators—as well as new football stadiums and other sports arenas.

However, the rising need for elevators and moving stairways in the United States was undercut by the precipitous drop in demand in Asian markets. Damaged by currency devaluation and widespread financial panic, construction projects in Asia slowed dramatically. American elevator companies were not immune to the crisis. For example the industry's worldwide leader, Otis Elevator Company, had depended on Asian nations for over 19 percent of its sales in 1997. In 1998, the company was forced to restructure its Far Eastern operations.

INDUSTRY LEADERS

Farmington, Connecticut-based Otis Elevator Company has historically been the leader of elevator companies. This status quo continued through 1998, as Otis achieved total sales of over $5.6 billion. A wholly-owned subsidiary of United Technologies Corp. since 1976, Otis employed 63,000 people in more than 1,700 locations worldwide. The company claimed that over 1.2 million of its elevators were in service, and dispatched an army of 22,000 mechanics to service them. Otis also produced escalators and moving walkways. In 1998, over 80 percent of its revenue was derived from exports.

Other key players in the elevator industry included Dover Corp., a multi-national conglomerate, which owned a successful elevator division. This subsidiary—Dover Elevator International Inc.— was headquartered in Memphis, Tennessee, and reported $4.0 billion in sales in 1998. Dover Elevator employed 23,350 workers. Schindler Elevator Corp. of Morristown, New Jersey, achieved $700.0 million of sales in 1998, and had a work force of 6,200 employees. With 1,100 workers, the El Cajon, California-based United States Elevator Corp. had sales of $170.0 million in 1998, while rival Amtech Elevator Services of Whittier, California reported sales of $74 million.

WORKFORCE

Total employment in the elevator and escalator industry encountered a period of gradual decline in the early and mid-1980s. After reaching a decade high of 13,000 total employees in 1982, employment figures declined to 10,200 in 1987 and to 8,400 in 1996. However, in 1997, employment increased to 9,389.

Of the total 9,389 people in the elevator and escalator industry, 6210—66 percent—were production workers, while the remaining 3,179 held technical, managerial, or administrative positions. Those in managerial and laboring positions all suffered from the general decline of the industry during the mid- and late 1980s. White-collar workers faced a greater rate of attrition, losing 41.5 percent of its work force between 1982 and 1991, while blue-collar

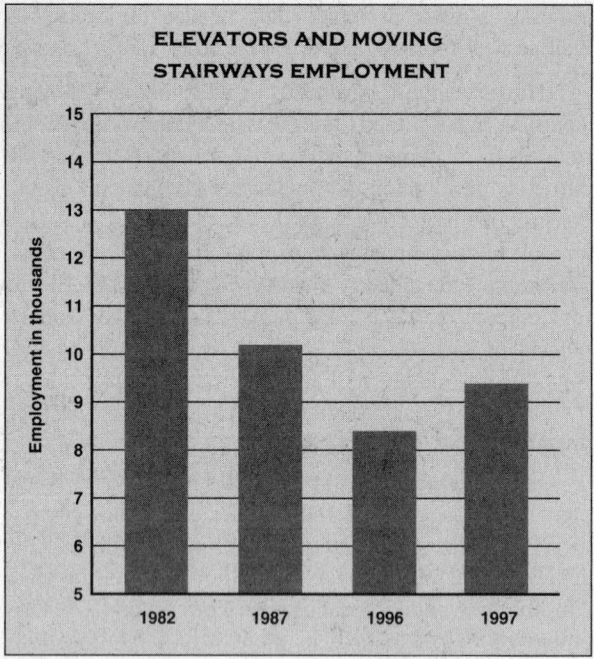

ELEVATORS AND MOVING STAIRWAYS EMPLOYMENT

at the expense of several left waiting somewhere else. This innovative system by Otis, first installed in Japan in 1993, encountered some problems, but it held great potential for the future of the industry.

In 1996, Otis introduced the Odyssey, a multi-directional system of transistor elevator cabs, which could take a person from parking lot to penthouse, even in structures more than 1,000 meters high.

FURTHER READING

Darnay, Arsen J., ed. *Manufacturing USA*. Detroit: Gale Research, 1996.

Brown, Randy. "Need a Lift?" *Buildings,* December 1996.

"Schindler's Lift: Elevators." *The Economist,* 16 March 1996.

U.S. Census Bureau. "Elevators and Moving Stairway." Available from http://www.census.gov/prod/ec97/97m3314c.pdf. October 1999.

"World of Otis—Who Are We?" Available from http://www.nao.otis.com/whoweare.htm.

positions were reduced by only 25 percent during the same period. On average, production workers in this industry earned $14.64 per hour during a 40 hour week.

As elevator and moving stairway establishments continued to downsize their work forces to accommodate the shift towards modernization and renovation and away from the manufacturing of new units, the education requirements for working in the industry promised to change as well. As evidenced by the NAEC's early campaign to improve the training of field personnel and recruit more people with computer experience, the industry's introduction of more sophisticated computerized technology demanded a larger percentage of workers with a strong college or trade school background in computers.

RESEARCH AND TECHNOLOGY

While the Japanese centered their efforts on the production of faster elevators during the 1990s, U.S. companies focused on making them run "smarter," or more efficiently, in relation to the needs of their patrons. One of the most promising developments in domestic elevator technology came in Otis's introduction of a new type of computer software that used "fuzzy logic" to decide upon the best way to accommodate the various traffic needs of a modern office building. This type of artificial intelligence software distinguished itself from the standard computer logic governing conventional modern elevators by its ability to process uncertainties of information more efficiently. Rather than simply sending the closest elevator when a patron signaled, fuzzy logic took into account the number of people waiting for elevators throughout the building, hoping to avoid the common problem of sending an elevator to service one individual

SIC 3535

CONVEYORS AND CONVEYING EQUIPMENT

This category covers establishments primarily engaged in manufacturing conveyors and conveying equipment for installation in factories, warehouses, mines, and other industrial and commercial establishments. Establishments primarily engaged in manufacturing farm elevators and conveyors are classified in **SIC 3523: Farm Machinery and Equipment;** those manufacturing passenger or freight elevators, dumbwaiters, and moving stairways are classified in **SIC 3534: Elevators and Moving Stairways;** and those manufacturing overhead traveling cranes and monorail systems are classified in **SIC 3536: Overhead Traveling Cranes, Hoists, and Monorail Systems.**

NAICS CODE(S)

333922 (Conveyor and Conveying Equipment Manufacturing)

INDUSTRY SNAPSHOT

Conveying systems have been an integral part of mining operations for nearly a century, but manufacturing industries have also become dependent on them. Regulations mandated by the Occupational Safety and Health Administration (OSHA) limited human exposure to certain harmful materials, requiring more extensive machine automation. With increased automation, conveying systems became an absolutely necessary part of operating a manufacturing plant.

Global competition has forced business owners to look for ways to cut costs and improve productivity. In industrial firms, again, automating production processes are a way to help reach their goal. While ways to do this vary with the type of business and the degree to which production processes are repeatable, most manufacturing firms looked at material handling systems as a possible answer. It is for these reasons that material handling systems manufacturers experienced considerable growth during the profit-driven 1980s and the cost-cutting 1990s.

However, as with most mining and manufacturing support industries, builders of conveyors and conveying equipment were limited by industry-related economic cycles. Senior management officials, who were directly accountable to stockholders, heavily scrutinized the installation of non-value added equipment. Such investment was often viewed as an unnecessary expense, especially when the company's financial health was in question. Therefore, the conveying system industry was reliant on a company's willingness to invest in itself.

ORGANIZATION AND STRUCTURE

The conveying system industry is highly specialized, and therefore almost totally self-contained. While the industry relies heavily on suppliers for many of the materials consumed, the design and assembly of the systems is usually performed at one facility. Armed with design engineers and production facilities, the industry is capable of meeting individual material movement challenges in industries ranging from mining to heavy manufacturing to the airline industry. Standard equipment is produced in the pre-engineered sector of the industry.

About 50 percent of the manufactured products in this industry were dedicated to unit handling conveyors and conveying systems, with an additional 4 percent dedicated to these systems' parts, attachments, and accessories. Another 27 percent of the product share was dedicated to bulk material handling conveyors and conveying systems, with about 10.5 additional percent dedicated to these systems' parts, attachments, and accessories. The remainder of the industry (approximately 8.5 percent) was allotted to miscellaneous conveyors and conveying equipment.

BACKGROUND AND DEVELOPMENT

The first conveying systems were developed to draw water from wells in the ground. This method was used in various applications over the centuries, but conveying systems really gained importance with the development of the mining industry. In the beginning, mine cars were used as buckets to haul coal or other ores to the earth's surface. Mine cars have been replaced with continuous

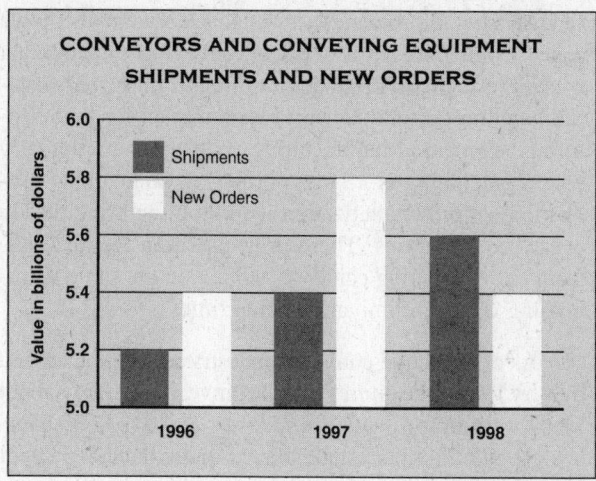

conveying systems such as belt conveyors, steel-apron conveyors, and chain-conveyors, which are used to haul as much as 5,000 tons per hour on lower-grade slopes and 1,300 tons per hour on steep slopes. Since wages accounted for most of the production costs in the mining industry, mechanization was necessary. Likewise, as the government began to regulate worker safety and workers' compensation claims, the initial expense of installing a mechanized system seemed like a good investment because the systems could minimize workers' contact with hazardous materials and reduce physical strain.

Although mining has long been the greatest force in the conveying system industry, the growing presence of production lines since Henry Ford's development of the assembly line has expanded the industry and brought new challenges. As machines were created to perform at higher capacities, the conveying systems delivering the materials to the machines had to meet these capacities. For example, in some beverage industries today, conveying systems are required to maintain a flow of up to 1,600 units per minute.

The worldwide recession of the late 1980s and early 1990s affected the mining industry significantly. In countries where commodity prices fell, some mining operations ceased due to production costs exceeding the market value of the extracted raw materials. Capital expenditures in this area fell as well, with investment in conveying systems being an unjustifiable expenditure.

As one component of the greater material handling industry, conveyers found new importance in the flexible manufacturing systems (FMS) methodology during the 1980s. However, as this theoretical approach was moving in one direction, manufacturers were concentrating more on productivity in terms of cost reduction. The installation of FMS was often cost prohibitive and limiting to companies reliant on reacting quickly to changing market needs. Yet, in terms of lowering costs through increased quality and efficiency to increase profitability, the material handling improvements through FMS were justifiable costs. Companies with existing conveying systems that wished to increase productivity through improved material handling techniques provided a market for the retrofitting segment. Manufacturing industries, particularly where machining is a large portion of value-added production, employ palletization work-holding principles in everyday operations. These principles transfer materials from one machining center to another on the same work-holding device, eliminating setup time.

As of 1994, the conveyor industry was characterized by very low expenditures for plant investment, only about $89.4 million for the entire industry and $123,683 average expenditures per establishment (more than 60 percent below the total manufacturing industries average).

CURRENT CONDITIONS

The late 1990s brought record results industrywide in shipments and new orders, according to the Conveyor Equipment Manufacturers Association (CEMA). Both shipments and new orders set records in 1996, at $5.2 billion and $5.4 billion, respectively. 1997 results broke both these records, with shipments of $5.4 billion and new orders of $5.8 billion. Shipments continued to rise in 1998, increasing by 2 percent to set a new record of $5.6 billion. New orders in 1998, on the other hand, decreased by 8 percent, falling to $5.4 billion. For the first 6 months of 1999, shipments amounted to $2.8 billion, and new orders reached $3.4 billion. Extrapolating these rates, full-year 1999 shipments would equal the 1998 record, and new orders would climb to a record $6.8 billion. Industry executives attributed these strong results to the capital investment trend that improved the flow of work and speeded the processing of orders.

INDUSTRY LEADERS

Atlanta-based Siemens Energy and Automation Inc. led the industry with $1.8 billion in sales for the fiscal year ended September 30, 1997, the most recent results available on Infotrac. Heil Co. of Chattanooga, Tennessee came in second with 1998 sales of $1.4 billion. Nesco Inc. of Mayfield Heights, Ohio, followed with 1998 sales of $1.1 billion. Joy Mining Co. of Warrendale, Pennsylvania generated $930.0 million for its fiscal year ended October 31, 1997. FKI Industries Inc. of Fairfield, Connecticut, rounded out the top 5 with $790.0 million in sales for its fiscal year ended March 31, 1999.

WORKFORCE

Employment levels in this industry were dropping as automation increased. In 1982 employment was 36,400 nationwide, falling to 30,600 by 1993. While this figure rose to 33,100 in 1994.

With average earnings of $12.78 per hour in 1994, employees were paid 6 percent over the average reported by all other forms of manufacturing in the nation. However, workers were spending 4 percent more time on the job than most other manufacturing workers, which implies overtime compensation was granted.

The strongest employment opportunities in the industry in future years will most likely be found in the fields of service and technical support rather than in the production of new units. While employment of machine assemblers in the general construction and related machinery industry was expected to increase by almost two-thirds by 2005, significant cuts were expected in almost all other areas, particularly machine builders and operators and clerical staff.

In 1997 the industry's 868 establishments employed 38,840 people, nearly 23,000 of whom were production workers. The average hourly wage for production workers was $14.14.

AMERICA AND THE WORLD

The Commonwealth of Independent States (CIS) did not implement conveying systems in mining operations until the early 1990s. Rather, inefficient trucks remained the material handling equipment of choice at mining pits and quarries. Demand for conveying technology increased in response to increased demand for fuel efficiency. Various combinations of dead-end and lateral-field conveyors were being used for maximum fuel efficiency. The industry in the former Soviet Union also enjoyed productivity increases of between 11 and 25 percent, which were accomplished by implementing a material storage location midway through the conveying system. Other benefits enjoyed were increased worker safety by the automated equipment and decreased labor costs.

Conveying systems were used extensively by the Japanese, who invested heavily in automation. Japan's use of high-tech systems caught the attention of U.S. manufacturers, who by the mid- to late 1980s started experimenting with new approaches to material handling. One application that became a buzzword in manufacturing is "palletization." In automated systems, material is transported on a pallet through a conveying system. When pallets are designed as work-holding devices, personnel and machining resources are maximized and productivity increases. Leaving the machine operator free to set up machines, the material flow is refined because both horizontal and vertical machining centers can interface with palletized work-holding devices.

While the economy provides one set of influences on making business decisions, the U.S. government provides another. OSHA continues to impose regulations concerning worker safety. In applications where hazardous waste or dangerous fumes are employed, robotics and automated machining centers are the only solution for meeting government regulations.

While the Europeans and Asians do not regulate worker safety to the same degree as the United States, they do investigate ways to increase quality and productivity at minimal costs. The Japanese government provides programs for funding robot application development, education, tax credits, and loans to purchase the equipment.

RESEARCH AND TECHNOLOGY

The food and beverage industries employ conveying systems primarily for their labor savings. Speed, reliability, and performance are emphasized as top priorities of beverage production lines. Production machines are continually being improved to perform at faster rates. However, the production rate of a machine is meaningless unless the conveyor system can deliver the containers on time. Because bottling companies are demanding higher production rates from machines, in some cases as much as 1,600 units per minute or more, material handling equipment manufacturers have had to redesign their products to meet the higher speeds. Computerized process flows have made the industry more sophisticated, allowing for variable speed control through ''intelligent'' software that accepts feedback from key points in the system.

Although conveyor manufacturers often specialize in designing and installing specialized conveying systems, some companies choose to build the system with internal engineering staff, using pre-engineered components. One such company is Richards-Wilcox Manufacturing Company, a builder of file and shelving products. In March 1993, Richards-Wilcox announced that it built a monorail conveyor system that was proving to be cost effective. The system, called the ZIG-ZAG, is used specifically for heavy components, sometimes weighing as much as a human is allowed to lift by law. The ZIG-ZAG is a continuous loop system that automatically loads and transports the file and shelving components through a final coating process at a rate of 22 feet per minute. At the end of the cycle, the system unloads the components. The system features an overhead transport and assembly system, which saves shop floor space.

Despite the tight world economy, some mining companies have chosen to invest in better conveying systems in light of the potential operational cost-savings. Due to many problems in the early 1970s, Neyveli Lignite Corporation, in India, tried this approach in 1974. As a result Neyveli was very successful through the 1980s. Again faced with problems common to the lignite mining industry, Neyveli announced in 1993 that it had installed a sophisticated system of belt conveyors that operate 24 hours a day. Through this system, Neyveli reported increased production capability, which improved its financial outlook.

Another mining advancement in recent years is Butterley Engineering's Moving Car Bunker system. The system keeps coal mine conveyor belts running at a constant rate through surge control technology. The surge control system is activated when the trunk belt becomes overloaded and coal starts to build up. This is an alternative to conventional design, in which trunk belts respond to peak tonnage. The bunker is designed with open-bottom storage units, coupled together. Each of these units is capable of hauling as much as 3,000 tons of coal.

The Conveyor Equipment Manufacturers Association released a standard for unit-handling conveyors in 1996. Technological developments of particular significance in the later 1990s include faster and quieter belt conveyors, such as the ''European'' or monofilament belt; self-powered conveyors, dividing the line into smaller zones, without the traditional belts, pulleys, and chains; ''intelligent conveyors'' being used by AT&T for computer assembly, which refill empty locations on the conveyor automatically; distributed logic control systems, which are used by NCR Corporation to allow assembly of specialized computer models; and more durable modular plastic and stainless steel designs that eliminate rubber belts.

FURTHER READING

''AT&T Relies Upon Intelligent Conveyors for PC Assembly.'' *Assembly,* April 1996.

Conveyors Equipment Manufacturers Association. ''Conveyor Industry Reports Favorable Mid-Year Results.'' 1 October 1999. Available from http://www.cemanet.org (visited 20 January 2000).

———. ''Another Record Year for Conveyor Shipments.'' 17 March 1999. Available from http://www.cemanet.org (visited 20 January 2000).

———. ''Conveyor Industry—Another Record Year in 1997.'' 16 March 1998. Available from http://www.cemanet .org (visited 20 January 2000).

''Conveyor Maker Joins With Detroit Company.'' *Kansas City Star,* 18 August 1995.

Darnay, Arsen J., ed. *Manufacturing USA: Industry Analysis, Statistics, and Leading Companies,* 5th ed. Detroit: Gale Research, 1996.

Gyorki, John. ''Conveyor Controls Computer Manufacturing Mix.'' *Machine Design,* 12 September 1996.

Infotrac Company Profiles. Available from http://web4.infotrac .galegroup.com (visited I20 January 1999).

''Interlake Corp. Reports Earnings for Quarter to Dec. 31.'' *New York Times,* 28 January 1997.

Knill, Bernie. ''Less Noise and More Speed in Belt Conveyors.'' *Material Handling Engineering,* February 1996.

Mancini, Leticia. "Movin' on Down the Line; Conveying Equipment." *Chilton's Food Engineering,* 17 July 1996.

"Prab Reports Record Profits in 1996." *Business Wire,* 23 January 1997.

"Self-powered Conveyors Get Smart." *Machine Design,* 18 April 1996.

U.S. Census Bureau. *Survey of Manufacturers.* 10 February 2000. Available from http://www.census.gov/prod/www/abs/97ecmani.html.

SIC 3536

OVERHEAD TRAVELING CRANES, HOISTS, AND MONORAIL SYSTEMS

This classification comprises establishments primarily engaged in manufacturing overhead traveling cranes, hoists, and monorail systems for installation in factories, warehouses, marinas, and other industrial and commercial establishments. Excluded from this classification are establishments primarily engaged in manufacturing cranes except industrial types, automobile wrecker hoists, and aerial work platforms, which are classified in **SIC 3531: Construction Machinery.** Also excluded from this industry are those manufacturing aircraft loading hoists, which are classified in **SIC 3537: Industrial Trucks, Tractors, Trailers, and Stackers.**

NAICS CODE(S)

333923 (Overhead Traveling Crane, Hoist, and Monorail System Manufacturing)

INDUSTRY SNAPSHOT

The overhead traveling crane, hoist, and monorail system industry includes a diverse assortment of products that fit within a narrowly defined segment of the materials handling equipment industry. Not to be confused with various types of mobile cranes used in construction projects, overhead cranes are variously structured machines that "travel" along a runway structure or pair of tracks located above the work floor of a plant or factory. They are further characterized by the presence of a fixed or trolley-mounted hoisting system that is connected to the tracks by a bridge structure, which consists of either a single or double girder.

The industry manufactures three basic kinds of overhead traveling cranes that accommodate the vast majority of materials handling needs. The first type is the overhead bridge crane, which is fixed to an overhead beam running the length of the building. Generally regarded as the most rugged of all overhead traveling cranes, this class of crane is noted for its ability to cover the entire width and length of a plant. The jib crane is the second variety of crane produced by the industry. It is usually mounted to a wall or pillar and is used to service a smaller area of a plant, usually the area of a single workstation. Gantry cranes, which are mounted overhead and are able to service a particular bay or workstation, comprise the third category.

While overhead traveling cranes are sometimes operated manually, they are usually powered by electricity and can be interfaced with automatic guided vehicles, stacker cranes, and monorails for increased efficiency. Accordingly, hoists and monorails, the other major segments of this industry classification, are often manufactured for use in conjunction with overhead traveling cranes. Employed mainly in an industrial capacity, products in this industry are also employed in stone and concrete pre-casting yards, steel fabricating shops, and storage facilities.

ORGANIZATION AND STRUCTURE

Geographically, the greatest concentration of hoist, crane, and monorail manufacturing takes place in the five-state region of Ohio, Michigan, Pennsylvania, Illinois, and Wisconsin, where more than a third of all the industry's establishments are located and 3,300 of its 7,900 employees work. California, with only 300 employees, has the most establishments (19). Ohio, the state employing the most people in the industry (1,000), has 17 establishments, as does Michigan (with 600 employees). Texas (600 employees) and Pennsylvania (500 employees) each have 15 establishments.

As a whole, the industry spent over $500 million on raw materials in 1994, which translates to about $3 million per establishment, roughly 40 percent below the average for all construction and related machinery manufacturing establishments. New capital expenditures, just over $59,000 per establishment, also fell far below the larger industry group average of $321,000.

BACKGROUND AND DEVELOPMENT

While various types of jib cranes and other lifting devices were installed in foundries during the late eighteenth century, and the overhead traveling bridge crane existed as early as 1860, materials handling systems were not widely used in the United States until its entrance into World War II in 1941. During the 1940s, however, firms that had previously been hesitant to make the large capital investment necessary for implementing an extensive materials handling system were forced to do so in order to meet the production demands of war materials contracts. The fact that the implementation of materials handling systems actually lowered production costs in many cases was only a by-product of the more pressing concern of supplying the military with the necessary weaponry and machinery for winning the war.

New levels of production volume and efficiency demonstrated during the war through the use of materials handling systems led to a phenomenal increase in the use of various types of overhead traveling cranes, hoists, and monorails in the years immediately after. Having demonstrated its potential for lowering production costs during the war, materials handling emerged as the most effective tool for offsetting the rising costs of labor and materials. During this period materials handling research and development efforts evolved into an integral segment of industrial management and engineering education programs as well, legitimizing the discipline of materials handling within both academic and industrial settings.

As technology—especially in the field of electronics—progressed during the 1950s and 1960s, gradual improvements were made in overhead traveling cranes, hoists, and monorail systems, enabling the industry to carve a profitable niche in the larger spectrum of materials handling equipment. As industries were being pressured to increase production while employing the same amount of floor space, equipment that could move materials overhead offered several advantages over its competitors in the broadly defined materials handling industry. While most types of conveyor systems, for instance, occupied a considerable amount of floor space, overhead cranes kept this space free for other production activities. Offering this ergonomic advantage, the hoist, crane, and monorail industry grew into a $500 million a year business by the early 1970s, employing over 16,000 people, according to Census of Manufactures statistics.

As the 1970s progressed, the introduction of computer technology revolutionized the field. While the development of solid-state logic had signaled the end of many of the bulky relay-type controls of earlier years in storage-retrieval systems, the same technology could not be applied to complex one-of-a-kind systems without a relatively high capital investment. The widespread availability of microcomputers, however, solved this problem, enabling cranes to be regulated by programmable controllers. Rather than investing large amounts of capital to perform specialized tasks requiring automation, companies were often able to use existing hardware for a variety of tasks, changing only the computer software to accommodate the desired new function. Largely through the improvements in efficiency engendered by these technological advances, the overhead traveling crane, hoist, and monorail industry more than doubled the value of its annual shipments by the end of the decade, while increasing its production work force by only 7 percent.

Although the 1981 passage of the Economic Recovery Tax—which offered incentives to companies that invested in the modernization and expansion of production facilities—held promise for a strong decade for the materials handling business as a whole, such expectations

did not hold true for most segments of the broad industry group. While the conveyor and conveying equipment industry enjoyed steady increases in revenues during the early and mid-1980s, the hoist, crane, and monorail industry lagged behind, suffering nearly a 50 percent decrease in revenue between 1981—the industry's best year of production, with over $1.4 billion in shipping—and 1987, according to Census of Manufactures information. The increased use of robotics, the fastest growing segment of the materials handling industry in the 1980s, was partially responsible for this decline. Revenues for the hoist, crane, and monorail industry steadily improved during the late 1980s, however, as the nation's economy grew, enabling businesses to purchase materials handling equipment they had put off buying earlier in the decade.

The volume of materials handling equipment is generally thought to be closely correlated to the condition of the U.S. economy as a whole. Accordingly, the recessive conditions of the early 1990s resulted in sluggish patterns of growth for all segments of the materials handling market during this period. Lacking the cash flow to justify new purchases of equipment, most companies relied on existing machinery to handle materials handling needs. The hoist, crane, and monorail industry, however, went against this general trend. While shipments for the industry's counterparts in the conveyor and conveying equipment and industrial truck and tractors industries fell 5 and nearly 12 percent, respectively, manufacturers of hoists, cranes, and monorails enjoyed a 20 percent increase in shipments between 1990 and 1991, according to the Annual Survey of Manufactures.

According to Manufacturing USA, 168 establishments, employing 7,900 people, were engaged in the manufacturing of hoists, overhead cranes, and monorail systems in 1994. These companies combined produced $1.07 billion in industry shipments that year, a drop from 1991's $1.21 billion, but a slight improvement over 1992 and 1993. The manufacturing of overhead traveling cranes and monorail systems accounted for about 47 percent of total shipments, as did the production of various types of hoists. Miscellaneous hoist, crane, and monorail products made up the remaining 6 percent.

Many companies made heavy purchases of materials handling equipment in the late 1980s and so made minimal capital investments in the early 1990s. As equipment aged and the economy continued to improve, capital investment rose in the late 1990s. However, much of this investment was in retrofitting of existing equipment, rather than new equipment purchases. Orders increased within the industry in early 1996, rising almost 6 percent in the first quarter over the last quarter of 1995. The renewed health of the U.S. automobile manufacturing industry also translated into an improved financial outlook for the overhead crane, hoist, and monorail industry.

CURRENT CONDITIONS

The industry experienced growth throughout the late 1990s due to favorable interest rates, which fueled the construction equipment market. Congress passed a new U.S. highway bill to increase infrastructure spending, which bolstered spending on this industry. Abroad, select European markets improved, spelling good fortune for this industry. However, at least one company began to feel the effects of a tightening economy in January 2000. Facing declining quarterly earnings from $20 million to $15 million and a 25 percent reduction in production due to decreased orders, Terex Corporation of Westport, Connecticut, laid off 20 of its 103 employees in its Conway, South Carolina, plant and took similar action at its 16 other plants throughout the country. Industrywide shipments totaled $1.33 billion in 1997.

INDUSTRY LEADERS

Weatherford International Inc., an integrated oil drilling company, led the industry with net revenues of $2 billion in 1998. Its Artificial Lift Systems division, with 1998 revenues of $329 million, received important new projects in early 1999 for YPF in Argentina and for Mobil's Cerro Negro project in Venezuela. Terex generated sales of $1.2 billion in 1998, up $391 million (a 46 percent increase) from 1997 sales. The Terex Lifting division generated 1998 sales of $771 million, up $223 million (a 41 percent increase) from 1997.

Amherst, New York-based Columbus McKinnon Corp. generated sales of $735.4 million in its fiscal year ended March 31, 1999. In May 1999 Columbus McKinnon acquired overhead crane manufacturer Washington Equipment Co. of Eureka, Illinois, which had $16.5 million in sales for fiscal 1998. In February 1998 Columbus McKinnon acquired Univeyor A/S of Arden, Denmark, which manufactures crane systems, among other products. Dover Industries Inc. of Elgin, Illinois, created sales of $718 million in 1997, according to the most recent information available on Infotrac. Manitowoc Company Inc. of Manitowoc, Wisconsin, the world leader in manufacturing lattice-boom crawler cranes for heavy construction and equipment rental markets, garnered 1998 sales of $694.8 million.

WORKFORCE

Total employment in the hoist, crane, and monorail industry declined sharply in the early and mid-1980s, climbed to 8,400 in 1991, fell again in 1992 and 1993, and then rose back to 7,900 in 1994. Of the 7,900 employees of hoist, crane, and monorail establishments in 1994, 4,500 were classified as production workers, while the remaining 3,400 were engaged in technical, managerial, or administrative duties.

The pattern of decline established in the 1980s proved to have lasting damage for the blue-collar work force, whose wages in 1994 (an average of $12.83 per hour) remained well below their 1991 level ($13.45), although they still were well above the total industry sector average of $12.09. In 1994 the average number of employees per establishment in the hoist, crane, and monorail industry was slightly lower than the average for all establishments engaged in the manufacturing of industrial machinery and equipment, according to *Manufacturing USA* statistics. The average establishment in this sector employed 47 people. In 1997 the industry's 217 establishments employed 7,679 people, 60 percent of whom were production workers who earned an average hourly wage of $16.02.

While the recovery of the U.S. economy signaled better times for the materials handling work force as a whole in the late 1990s, blue-collar employment prospects in the hoist, crane, and monorail industry may suffer from the very durability of the products they manufacture. With a life span of 30 years or more, cranes installed in the 1980s may not need to be replaced until well into the 21st century. As they face the need for new materials handling functions, companies in the future are expected to "retrofit," or modernize, older model equipment to cut costs.

Consequently, the strongest employment opportunities in the industry in future years will be found, most likely, in the fields of service and technical support rather than in the production of new units. While employment of machine assemblers in the general construction and related machinery industry is expected to increase by almost two-thirds by 2005, significant cuts are expected in almost all other areas, particularly machine builders and operators and clerical staff.

RESEARCH AND TECHNOLOGY

For an industry whose fundamental hardware components originated more than a century ago, new developments in product technology have, for the most part, occurred gradually over a number of years as the country's material handling needs have changed. According to Clyde E. Witt, senior editor for *Material Handling Engineering,* "Crane technology has been stimulated through innovative thinking and creative efforts of manufacturers as well as users. Mechanical and technological advances have been a process of evolution, not revolution or major breakthroughs." This is not to say, however, that significant technological innovations have not been made in this segment of the materials handling industry.

The most significant of these changes in recent years occurred, similarly to other manufacturing industries, as a result of the development and advancement of solid state logic and computer technology. Whereas overhead traveling cranes of the past were controlled by bulky relay-type systems, models developed since the 1970s were regulated by highly developed solid-state logic and computer regulated control systems. Although older control systems were sufficient for simple storage and retrieval tasks, they were less successful when applied to production functions, which often required the crane to perform a variety of precise movements by several different components. The development of these new forms of technology enabled overhead cranes to perform these complex production tasks more efficiently by reducing the size of control system hardware and improving its flexibility and durability.

In the 1980s and 1990s control mechanisms for overhead traveling cranes and other types of equipment within this industrial classification were further refined and modernized to accommodate the changing needs of their users. The major developments in this period involved the increased efficiency and wider range of applications for automated cranes regulated by programmable controllers or other computers. Such improvements brought forth the introduction of automated cranes to a wide range of manufacturing environments, servicing locations as varied as an aerospace plant and a textile factory. The widespread acceptance of automated control systems also facilitated a variety of interfacing applications, linking overhead cranes with other types of materials handling equipment, such as monorails, robots, and automated guided vehicles. Promising technological developments of special note in the late 1990s included more sophisticated radio programmable logic controllers, self-propelled floor cranes, cordless and infrared control technology, and retrofitting innovations.

FURTHER READING

"Columbus McKinnon acquires Danish firm." *Modern Materials Handling,* February 1998.

Darnay, Arsen J., ed. *Manufacturing USA: Industry Analysis, Statistics, and Leading Companies,* 5th ed. Detroit: Gale Research, 1996.

Delano, Daryl. "Demand for Materials Handlings Systems, Equipment Strengthens." *Modern Materials Handling,* July 1996.

"Infotrac Company Profiles," 20 January 1999. Available from http://web4.infotrac.galegroup.com.

Laughlin, Tom. "What's New in Cranes, Remote Controls, and Magnets." *Metal Center News,* May 1995.

"Manitowoc." *The Business Journal-Milwaukee,* 12 December 1997.

"New York Firm Buys Eureka, Ill.-Based Maker of Overhead Cranes." *Knight-Ridder/Tribune Business News,* 11 May 1999.

"Radio Control System Handles Ten Hoists on Monorail." *Material Handling Engineering,* January 1997.

Semling, Harold V. "Commerce Predicts Good MH Sales Year." *Material Handling Engineering,* March 1982.

"Sun News, Myrtle Beach, S.C., Business Briefs Column." *Knight-Ridder/Tribune Business News,* 5 January 2000.

"Terex Corporation Reports 1998 Net Income of $72.8 Million, or $3.25 Per Share, On Revenues of $1.23 Billion." 2 March 1999. Available from http://www.corporate-ir.net.

U.S. Census Bureau. *Survey of Manufacturing,* 10 February 2000. Available from http://www.census.gov/prod/www/abs/97ecmani.html.

"Weatherford Reports Results for the 1998 Fourth Quarter and Full Year." 18 February 1999. Available from http://www.weatherford.com.

SIC 3537

INDUSTRIAL TRUCKS, TRACTORS, TRAILERS, AND STACKERS

This classification comprises establishments primarily engaged in manufacturing industrial trucks, tractors, trailers, stackers (truck type), and related equipment used for handling materials on floors and paved surfaces in and around industrial and commercial plants, depots, docks, airports, and terminals. Excluded from this classification are establishments primarily involved in manufacturing motor vehicles and motor vehicle type trailers, which are classified in **SIC 3710: Motor Vehicles and Motor Vehicle Equipment,** and those manufacturing farm type wheel tractors, which are classified in **SIC 3523: Farm Machinery & Equipment.** Also excluded from this industry are establishments primarily engaged in manufacturing tractor shovel loaders and track laying tractors, which are classified in **SIC 3531: Construction Machinery and Equipment,** and those manufacturing wood pallets and skids, which are classified in **SIC 2448: Wood Pallets and Skids.**

NAICS CODE(S)

333924 (Industrial Truck, Tractor, Trailer, and Stacker Machinery System Manufacturing)

332999 (All Other Miscellaneous Fabricated Metal Product Manufacturing)

332439 (Other Metal Container Manufacturing)

INDUSTRY SNAPSHOT

The industrial truck and tractor industry includes a narrowly defined yet diverse assortment of products that are part of a larger industrial classification commonly known as the material handling equipment industry. Equipment within the smaller industrial truck and tractor category is utilized to move, package, and store both finished products and raw materials used to manufacture finished products. Accordingly, industrial truck and tractor products are used in nearly every industrial setting, from supermarkets to missile manufacturing installations.

ORGANIZATION AND STRUCTURE

The average staff size of establishments in the truck and tractor industry was about 10 percent lower than that of all other manufacturing industries. The industry was predominately comprised of establishments employing less than 20 people. Of the 447 establishments in operation in 1996, only 161 employed 20 or more workers.

Geographically, the greatest concentration of industrial truck and tractor manufacturing establishments were in California, Michigan, Ohio, and Illinois, followed by New York and Pennsylvania. The 42 establishments in California represented the greatest number of industry establishments located in one state, followed by 31 in Michigan, 29 in Ohio, and 25 in Illinois. In the Northeast, New York had 29 establishments, followed by Pennsylvania with 23. Ohio led the industry in shipment value—totaling $399.8 billion, or 15.4 percent of the U.S. total—and had 2,700 employees. Illinois followed, with shipments valued at $293.2 million and 1,100 employees. While North Carolina had only 10 establishments, it employed 1,400 workers and accounted for $249.8 million in sales, the third highest after Ohio and Illinois.

In 1994, the average amount paid for raw manufacturing materials per establishment was somewhat higher than the average recorded by all other manufacturing industries. A typical firm in the truck and tractor industry spent $5.9 million on these materials, while firms in all other manufacturing industries spent an average of $5.0 million. Likewise, the average amount spent on manufacturing machinery and production retooling for an industrial truck and tractor establishment was considerably lower than the average recorded by all other manufacturing industries. In 1994, the average investment per establishment in the industrial truck and tractor industry was $158,215, less than half the average of $321,011 spent by firms in all other manufacturing industries.

BACKGROUND AND DEVELOPMENT

America's entrance into World War II in 1941 signaled the beginning of a four-year surge in business activity that defined the future of many U.S. industries. The frenetic pace of production required to support the country's war efforts rejuvenated some industries, sparked the genesis of others, and launched many more toward exponentially higher production and sales volumes. For the industrial truck and tractor industry, the dramatically increased demand for manufactured goods created a commensurately heightened demand for material handling equipment; as the country manufactured more products, there was a growing need to move, stack, and store them quickly and efficiently. Consequently, the industrial truck and tractor industry was swept up into the expansion of U.S. industry as a whole, benefiting from the increased business activity enjoyed by the individual companies it served.

Augmenting this demand from the industry's traditional industrial customers was a vast government market that opened up during the war, as industrial truck and tractor manufacturers answered the sundry material handling needs of the military. The combination of these two factors fostered a rapid growth rate for the industry, amplifying the importance of industrial truck and tractor products in the successful operation of any manufacturing plant or military installation. During this period, truck and tractor products enabled manufacturers to approach production and sales volumes proportionate to levels recorded 50 years later, in the 1990s. Though its foundation was established before the war, the industry's modern structure was not fully defined until the 1950s and 1960s, when industrial establishments nationwide were transformed by the trend toward automation.

The robust growth experienced as a result of the war, and the increased applications for the industry's products prompted by the automation of U.S. industry following the war, prompted years of growth for the industry, a period during which industrial truck and tractor manufacturing companies began to record production and sales levels that distinguished the industry from other segments within the material handling equipment industry.

In the early 1960s, the sale of industrial trucks and tractors and related products accounted for approximately $389 million of the nearly $1 billion generated by the material handling equipment industry. The leading manufacturers involved in the industry at this time were primarily publicly held companies engaged in the manufacture of other products included in the material handling industry, such as conveyor and monorail systems, but derived the majority of their revenue from the sale of industrial truck and tractor equipment, particularly from the sale of forklifts. Clark Equipment Co., the largest of these manufacturers, posted annual sales of approximately $200 million in the late 1950s and early 1960s, far exceeding the sales volumes of its nearest competitors. These competitors, however, compensated for their more diminutive size by developing industrial truck and tractor equipment for more diverse applications, focusing on manufacturing equipment that increased efficiency in the industrial workplace.

Initially, the pace of the industry's growth was largely determined by the amount other businesses were spending on capital expansion, but by the early 1960s, U.S. industry as a whole began to focus on increasing the efficiency of manufacturing facilities. Manufacturers realized that industrial truck and tractor equipment could help them make great strides toward this goal. Decreasing the turning radius of a forklift, for example, allowed a manufacturer to reduce the distance between storage aisles and therefore increase inventory space without realizing any increase in land costs. Accordingly, many manufacturers, both large and small, were developing industrial truck and tractor products during the early 1960s that would eventually become integral components of modern manufacturing establishments.

Despite its relatively unimpressive revenue total of $49 million in 1960, Hyster Co. of Portland, Oregon, was, nevertheless, contributing to the industry's technological advancement by designing prototypes of forklifts that automatically weighed loads to be lifted and adjusted their operating speed accordingly. If a load was light, this sensing system enabled the forklift to operate at a higher speed than was normally achieved by earlier forklifts that operated at set speeds, regardless of load weight. Similar advancements were being made by other manufacturers. For instance, Barrett-Cravens Co.'s "Guide-o-matic" system controlled industrial tractors by a buried wire, enabling them to function without an operator.

The popularity of innovative products such as these fueled the industry's growth during the 1960s, as manufacturers increasingly began to look toward the industrial truck and tractor industry for solutions to problems associated with moving, stacking, and storing their manufactured products, and to aid in their move toward automated operation. This represented a significant shift in the nature of the needs that this industry's products filled. Instead of supplying equipment solely to manufacturers expanding the size of their plants, industrial truck and tractor manufacturing companies now could rely on business from companies that were streamlining their operations or automating their production processes.

Along with its move toward manufacturing more sophisticated products and designing complete material handling systems, the industry was enjoying increased demand for its newly developed large steel and aluminum containers. "Containerization," or the utilization of trailer-sized steel and aluminum containers for shipping purposes, was, in the early 1960s, one of the relatively recent innovations developed by the industry to help its customers cut costs. These containers, sometimes referred to as "ambulatory vaults," had been used by an increasing number of manufacturers in the 1950s because they reduced handling costs and allowed for quicker delivery.

Two developments in the early 1960s ensured that manufacturers could continue to rely on large containers to generate additional business. In early 1961, industry-wide standards were established for the production of containers, specifying that all containers in the future must be 8 feet in width and height and either 10, 20, or 40 feet in length. Following the establishment of these speci-

fications, the Federal Maritime Board ordered that only ships built to accommodate these new, standardized containers would be eligible for government subsidies or government-insured mortgages.

By the mid-1960s the industry's annual value of shipments had surpassed $500 million, making it the largest segment within the overall material handling industry. Growth continued to be spurred by the industry's development of innovative products, which persuaded some of its customers to apportion a larger percentage of their capital investment budget toward material handling needs, and others to scrap their existing machinery and invest in more sophisticated equipment. A considerable amount of the industry's growth, however, came through capital expansion programs initiated by its customers. While this presented no problem to industrial truck and tractor manufacturers when economic conditions were particularly favorable, this dependency on the health of the U.S. economy in general made the industry vulnerable to general economic downturns.

By the close of the decade, however, the overall U.S. economy had proven strong enough to support the continued growth of the industrial truck and tractor industry. Revenues exceeded $1 billion by 1970, representing an average annual growth rate of greater than 11 percent during the previous decade. While no single dramatic technological advancement launched the industry toward higher revenues, each year customer demands were stimulated by new products that incorporated innovative designs and functions.

Over the course of the next several years, as the nation's economy spiraled downward in reaction to a shortage of oil and petroleum products, the industrial truck and tractor industry's performance began to flag. The industrial sector of the U.S. economy operated below capacity throughout the recession, causing the cancellation or postponement of many manufacturers' expansion plans. Because these investments represented a major source of industrial truck and tractor manufacturers' revenues, business faltered, demonstrating the volatility of the industry's market. With the industrial sector of the nation's economy operating at 70 percent of its capacity, the industrial truck and tractor industry's revenues dropped from $1.53 billion in 1974 to $1.30 billion in 1975.

The industry slowly recovered from the losses of the early and mid-1970s, generating revenues of $1.91 billion in 1977, and by the end of the decade, revenues skyrocketed to nearly $3 billion. This growth, however, masked the emergence of a pernicious force that threatened to derail the industry's leading companies from their meteoric recovery.

For years, industrial truck and tractor manufacturers' command of the U.S. market was virtually unassailable;

foreign manufacturers were relegated to producing inexpensive equipment and left the manufacturing of higher-priced, more sophisticated equipment—which was by far the more lucrative segment of the global industrial truck and tractor market—to American companies. But by the late 1970s, domestic manufactures had become lulled into complacency by decades of dominance, and foreign manufacturers, particularly the Japanese, began to woo customers away from U.S. manufacturers. Ironically, the reason for this rise in demand for Japanese products was attributed largely to the success domestic manufacturers enjoyed for the previous several decades. Each year new designs and features were incorporated into U.S.-produced equipment, creating an assortment of highly-sophisticated equipment by the late 1970s. The incremental advances in technology had, by this time, spawned equipment too advanced and too costly for the basic material handling needs of U.S. industries. Concurrently, an increasing number of industrial truck and tractor customers found the cheaper Japanese equipment suitable for their basic material handling tasks, a revelation that led to reduced operating costs for customers and to an erosion of U.S. industrial truck and tractor manufacturers' market share. American truck and trucking equipment had simply become too sophisticated for the needs of its average customer.

By the early 1980s, the price advantage afforded to purchasers of Japanese industrial truck and tractor equipment widened to as much as 30 percent. Still, in the face of this trend toward more inexpensive, less sophisticated equipment, U.S. manufacturers were slow to respond. As conditions worsened, domestic manufacturers attempted to stave off mounting foreign competition by designing even more sophisticated products, which further aggravated their losses. Clark Equipment Co., for example, spent $25 million on the design of a high-technology lift truck equipped with oil-cooled brakes that failed miserably when it was introduced in 1982.

When the U.S. forklift market plummeted in 1982 and 1983, many domestic manufacturers were poorly positioned to sustain further losses. Caterpillar Inc., bereft of its once commanding lead over the industry, sought cheaper manufacturing sites for its production of industrial trucks and tractors, and, in 1983, the company moved the majority of its lift truck production to Korea under the aegis of a South Korean company, Daewoo Heavy Industries Ltd. Similarly, Clark Equipment relocated from Michigan to more inexpensive Kentucky, and, in 1986, Clark eventually followed Caterpillar's lead by signing a ten-year production accord with Samsung Group in Korea.

Among the industry's leaders, Hyster Co. was the one notable exception to domestic manufacturers' disregard toward the shifting market demands. Introducing an inexpensive "XL" line of forklifts in 1981, which matched the Japanese in terms of price and accounted for $44 million in sales in 18 months, Hyster avoided the debilitating losses suffered by its largest competitors. Moreover, Hyster revamped its design, engineering, and manufacturing methods to emulate the cross-functional and more efficient style of Japanese production, enabling the company to manufacture as many industrial truck and tractor products by the end of the 1980s as it had ten years earlier, with half as many employees. Consequently, Hyster was the only U.S. industrial truck and tractor manufacturer among the industry's three largest producers to remain profitable during the 1980s, further underscoring the imprudence of Clark Equipment's and Caterpillar's continued focus on producing technologically advanced equipment in the early 1980s.

The relocation of key manufacturing responsibilities to Korea by Clark Equipment Co. and Caterpillar failed to arrest the plunge of their integral fork lift operations. Korean wages tripled during the 1980s, erasing any benefits that would have been otherwise realized by relocating, and the dollar declined 24 percent against the Korean won between 1986 and 1989, further increasing the severity of their losses. By the early 1990s, the cumulative effect of the previous decade's failures forced Clark Equipment and Caterpillar Inc. to divest their core industrial truck and tractor businesses. In 1992, Clark Equipment sold its forklift operations to Terex Corp. for $95 million. Later that year, Caterpillar signed a joint venture agreement with Mitsubishi Heavy Industries Ltd. that ceded 80 percent of its fork lift business to the Japanese company.

The industrial truck and tractor industry adjusted slowly to the changing needs of its customers as it entered the mid-1990s. Sparked by the recessive economic conditions of the early 1990s, the U.S. industry as a whole experienced changes, and many businesses reduced their work force and streamlined their operations, leading to greater operating efficiencies.

The concerted movement toward manufacturing a proportionately higher number of electric lift trucks, initiated by the Japanese in 1992, prompted a parallel response by U.S. manufacturers. These electrically powered lift trucks were more profitable for industrial truck and tractor manufacturers than gas-powered lift trucks and became the industry's most popular product in the mid-1990s.

Forklift manufacturers also made changes. According to Beverage World, the forklift companies compete fiercely with each other. Consequently the electric forklift was in a constant state of flux, and each manufacturer regularly improved and updated its products, creating a "quality through competition" mentality for forklift manufacturers. This continuing trend ensures better products and greater customer satisfaction.

In 1992-93, the worldwide lift truck market grew by approximately 30 percent, or 100,000 units, but the market softened in 1996; the North American market declined by an estimated 13,000 units, 8 percent, that year. An estimated 447 companies in the United States were involved in manufacturing industrial trucks and tractors in 1996. These companies generated $3.7 billion in revenues for products included in this classification. This figure represents an aggregate value of shipments largely derived from the production of forklift trucks and other work trucks fitted with lifting or handling equipment machines—the largest product group within the industry. Industrial trucks, tractors, mobile straddle carriers and cranes, and automatic stacking machines accounted for 67.1 percent of the value of the industry's total shipments. Of these, self-propelled, electric-powered fork lift work trucks accounted for 27.2 percent, and liquid petroleum gas motor-powered accounted for 16.8 percent. Self-propelled nonriding forklift and other work trucks fitted with lifting or handling equipment accounted for 10.4 percent. The other primary product group was comprised of parts and attachments for industrial trucks and tractors, which composed 21.7 percent of the industry's total shipments.

CURRENT CONDITIONS

In 1997, the 483 establishments in this industry employed 26,214 people and shipped $5.57 billion worth of products. Of this total, $5.53 billion was from the production of industrial trucks, while the remaining $40 million was from the production of metal pallets and metal air cargo containers.

INDUSTRY LEADERS

Ford Motor Co. of Dearborn, Michigan, led the industry with overall sales of $144 billion for 1998 (though most of these sales were concentrated in Ford's other markets). Of the companies that focused their efforts within this industry, Caterpillar Inc. of Mossville, Illinois, led the pack with $21 billion in 1998 sales. Arch-rival Deere and Co. of Moline, Illinois, generated $14 billion in sales for its fiscal year ended October 31, 1998. Deere long dominated the farm machinery and equipment market with its John Deere tractors, but Caterpillar broke into that market in the late 1980s to contend head-to-head with Deere. Deere responded by breaking into the construction machinery and equipment market, which traditionally belonged to Caterpillar. This rivalry also played itself out in the industrial truck and tractor industry.

In 1996, Caterpillar launched a new line of 24-volt narrow aisle reach trucks with 3,000-, 3,500-, and 4,000-pound capacity. The new line of trucks were ergonomically designed around an original ''CAT Command Center,'' which puts all controls within easy reach. The truck was controlled by Caterpillar's ''Micro Command,'' an advanced microprocessor control system. In 1995 Caterpillar introduced its E-series, a new line of articulated trucks, which offered operators added comfort and serviceability. The trucks were capable of any earthmoving function and were ideal to be used in distances between 0.5 km and 5.0 km.

Other industry leaders included CSX Corp. of Richmond, Virginia, which garnered $10 billion in 1998 sales. CSX suffered a bit in 1999 due to declines in its Sea-Land container-shipping business and due to the rail congestion affecting it through its acquisition of a part of Conrail in June. Analysts estimated that 1999 earnings could fall 65 percent under earlier projections. PACCAR Inc. of Bellevue, Washington, generated record sales of $8 billion in 1998. PACCAR achieved such success due to its marketing of its Class 8 heavy trucks in Europe as well as in North America. The company improved its European presence by purchasing the Dutch truck builder DAF for $550 million in 1996 and the British truck builder Leyland Trucks Ltd. in 1998, for an undisclosed sum.

WORKFORCE

Total employment in the industrial trucks and tractors industry declined during the 1980s and 1990s, slipping from 24,000 in 1982 to a low of 17,300 in 1991, recovering to 19,800 in 1994. While employment swelled through the late 1990s, decreases were predicted for the industry as it entered the 21st century.

Of the approximately 26,000 people employed by the industry in 1997, 18,756 were production workers, while the remaining employees performed technical, managerial, or administrative duties. Executive and managerial positions suffered a high rate of attrition through the early 1990s.

Typically, production workers were employed on a full-time basis, averaging 2,060 hours annually in 1994, almost the same as the 2,056 hours averaged by production workers employed in all other manufacturing industries. Average hourly wages of workers in the industrial truck and tractor industry were slightly higher than those of workers in all other manufacturing industries. In 1997, production workers in the industrial truck and tractor industry earned an average hourly wage of $13.62.

Prospects in the industry's work force remain bleak, according to U.S. Bureau of Labor projections. Between 1994 and 2005, positions for general manufacturing assemblers and fabricators, welders, cutters, and machinists employed by the construction and related machinery industry, of which the industrial truck and tractor industry is a subdivision, were expected to decline 9.1 percent. Predicted to be even more hard hit were positions for drilling and boring machine tool workers, which were expected to drop 54.6 percent. Other job categories projected to decline by more than 20 percent were machine builders, drafters, and machine tool cutting operators.

Non-production workers including bookkeepers, accountants, and general office clerks were also expected to experience declines of more than 20 percent.

AMERICA AND THE WORLD

As U.S. manufacturers of industrial trucks and tractors entered the mid-1990s, competition from foreign manufacturers posed the greatest threat to the industry's future. For years, U.S. manufacturers held the domestic market largely to themselves; businesses in need of industrial truck and tractor equipment generally shied away from purchasing products manufactured abroad, fearing a lack of spare parts and service. By 1970, imports accounted for a mere $13 million of the $1 billion U.S. industrial truck and tractor market. Moreover, the $13 million recorded by foreign manufacturers in 1970 reflected a 72 percent increase from the total posted two years earlier. Likewise, U.S. manufacturers explored profit potentials overseas. By 1970, the value of U.S. exports neared $100 million a year, with parts and complete trucks and tractors being shipped to Europe, South America, and Asia.

By the end of the 1970s, however, the commanding position that U.S. manufacturers held over foreign manufacturers was reversed, largely due to the gains achieved by Japanese manufacturers. By concentrating on supplying inexpensive yet sturdy industrial truck and tractor products, the Japanese were able to secure a formidable presence in the U.S. market. Competition became fierce, leading one of the few large U.S. manufacturers of industrial truck and tractor products that fared well during the 1980s, Hyster Co., to petition the International Trade Commission in 1986, charging that Japan was selling equipment in the United States at prices below the cost of production. Two years later, the International Trade Commission ruled in Hyster's favor and applied import duties of up to 51.3 percent to Japanese products entering the U.S. market. Although these import duties provided a much needed respite from increasing Japanese competition, Japanese manufacturers began establishing assembly plants in the United States soon after the ruling to circumvent the tariff payments. Entering the 1990s, the Japanese continued to maintain a roughly 50 percent share of the U.S. market.

FURTHER READING

"Caterpillar Is Offering Versatile Narrow Aisle Reach Trucks." *Vending Times*, 25 March 1996, 188.

"Clark Plant Gears Up for New Models." *Modern Materials Handling*, February 1996, 15.

"CSX Earnings Warning." *Chemical Week*, 5 January 2000.

Darnay, Arsen J., ed. *Manufacturing USA*. 5th ed. Detroit: Gale Research, 1996.

Infotrac Company Profiles. Available from http://web5.infotrac .galegroup.com, 1/20/99.

MacLachlan, Claudia. "Cat Claws Deere Over Army Contract: But GAO Upholds Approval of Bid from Moline Firm." *Crain's Chicago Business*, 9 November 1998.

"NACCO Materials Handling Group." *NACCO Industries, Inc. 1996 Annual Report*, December 1996, 9-11.

"New Engine Options For Navistar Cabovers." *Diesel Progress Engines & Drives*, Oct. 1995, 8.

"Our Friend the Forklift." *Beverage World*, April 1995, 24.

"Record Sales Spur Paccar Earnings Surge." *Refrigerated Transporter*, May 1999.

Wilhelm, Steve. "Freightliner Rival Paccar Just Keeps Rolling Along." *Business Journal-Portland*, 6 November 1998.

SIC 3541

MACHINE TOOLS, METAL CUTTING TYPES

This industry details establishments primarily engaged in manufacturing metal cutting type machine tools, not supported in the hands of an operator when in use, that shape metal by cutting or use of electrical techniques; the rebuilding of such machine tools; and the manufacture of replacement parts for them. Also included in this industry are metalworking machine tools designed primarily for home workshops. Establishments primarily engaged in the manufacture of electrical and gas welding and soldering equipment are classified in **SIC 3548: Electric and Gas Welding and Soldering Equipment**; those establishments manufacturing portable power-driven handtools are classified in **SIC 3546: Power-Driven Handtools.**

NAICS CODE(S)

333512 (Machine Tool (Metal Cutting Type) Manufacturing)

INDUSTRY SNAPSHOT

The metal cutting industry is concerned with the removal of metal from a larger piece of metal to create a desired shape. Metal cutting, also referred to as machining, is performed on most manufactured items. The uses range from low-precision machining, such as grinding undesired protrusions from a rough casting, to high-precision machining, which involves working tolerances of less than half the thickness of a human hair (0.0001 inch). Classic metal cutting produces scrap pieces, called chips, that are relatively useless and generally cannot be reused through remelting or pressing. Both the environmental and economic consequences of such waste has created new processes referred to as chipless machining. General machining processes include turning, shaping, milling, drilling, sawing, abrasive machining, and broaching.

The machine tool industry as a whole is closely tied to national and world economic conditions. The total shipments of metal cutting machine tools dropped sharply between 1982 to 1983 from $4.5 billion to below $3 billion. From that point, shipments recovered somewhat, but remained greatly reduced. The world-wide recession of the late 1980s and early 1990s created a trough in machine tool-related sales. Shipments between 1990 and 1994 varied only slightly, hovering around $3.5 billion. By 1997, shipments had recovered and climbed to $5.33 billion. Nearly 370 establishments participated in this industry in 1997.

The prices for metal cutting machine tools ranged from under $100,000 to several million dollars, depending on the sophistication and purpose of the tool. Multiple machining centers, capable of performing several metal cutting processes, were becoming more popular with larger companies interested in decreasing the amount of time handling materials between machining stations.

As worldwide competition increases in areas of quality and precision, U.S. machine shops will be forced to update or totally replace machine tools with those that possess higher levels of technical innovation. However, a significant downward trend in employment levels continued through the 1990s as machine tool manufacturers cut direct labor costs. This trend, a disheartening one for those seeking employment in this industry, has come about due to higher levels of automation throughout all related industries and the continued drive to manufacture still more automated machine tools.

Half of the machine tool market is concentrated within the automotive industry, one-quarter within non-mechanical industries, and the remainder within aerospace, defense, and other industries.

ORGANIZATION AND STRUCTURE

Four major categories comprise this industry: classic machine tools; automated machine tools; expendable tools; and machine tool repair. Classic metal cutting machine tools are characterized by manually operated, power driven (usually electric) stationary machines. These machines are operated by skilled machinists with relatively good trigonometry skills. The demand for these machines has dropped, giving way to the use of automated machine tools.

Automated machine tools are more commonly known as numerically controlled (NC) machine tools. NC machines use a generated program of coordinate values (numerics) to move machine parts quickly, with consistency and precision. Downtime between tool changes is minimized, compared to classic machining

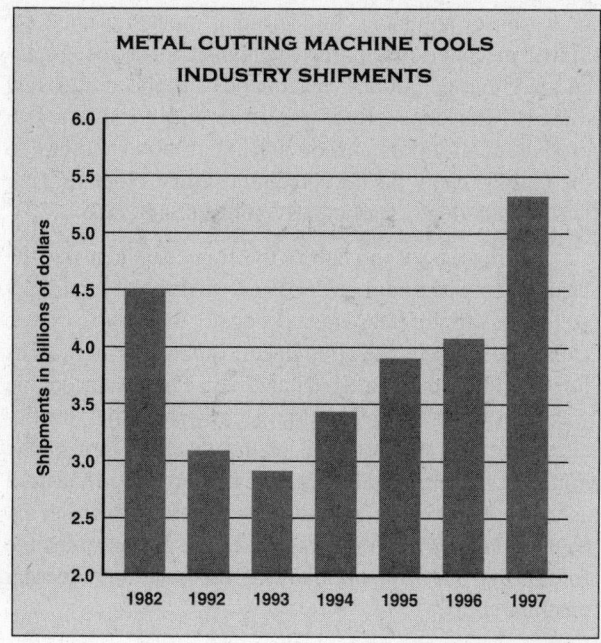

methods. The information is loaded into the machine by punched tape, punched cards, or magnetic tape that has been generated by a computer program written by an NC programmer. The NC machines have given way to computer numerically controlled (CNC) machines due to the affordability of microcomputers. The next wave of NC machines is expected to include downloadable numerically controlled (DNC) machines, which are network-based CNC machines. This technology reduces the steps between design engineering and manufacturing. All NC machines created a large market for manufacturers of machine controls, and increased microcomputer markets. Chipless machining processes implement some form of NC capabilities to the various machine configurations.

Expendable tools are the actual cutting pieces that wear as a result of use. Therefore, this segment of the industry is closely tied to client industry levels of activity. Although many of these tools can be resharpened and reused, many machine shops find it more economical to replace the tool once it is worn. When industry success is high, this segment of the industry experiences increased sales.

Machine tool repair has become a more specialized segment due to the increased popularity of NC machines. The nature of this business category requires that repair technicians have adequate computer hardware/software trouble-shooting skills. Machine tool repair in the late 1990s was thus closely related to computer electronics as well as mechanics.

BACKGROUND AND DEVELOPMENT

Various machine tools have been crafted through the centuries to address man's specific needs, but it was the invention of the clock in 1364 that created a need for higher precision machining methods. Clocks require accurately turned arbors, machine-cut gears, and screw threads. The concepts of precision and consistency in product quality thus pushed machine tool technology to the point that, by the seventeenth century, clock making was regarded as a particularly painstaking craft.

During the second half of the eighteenth century, the barriers between pure science and workshop technology were dissolving. Scientists began interacting more closely with mechanical engineers, spawning new ideas for improved machining techniques. The steam engine was born from this interaction, an invention that drastically increased the potential of the machine tool in the minds of the industrial leaders of the day. The industrial age was afoot. This period was greatly influenced by Henry Maudslay, who is known as the man responsible for the introduction of many of the early engineering machine tools.

Maudslay introduced the concept of precision to heavy machinery, which before that time had been only the concern of watch and scientific instrument makers. In the early 1800s he made the first screw-cutting lathe, a device that remains the standard even today. His second great contribution was the creation of a method of finishing a plane surface with a surface plate, marking compound, and hand scraper. Maudslay also constructed a micrometer in 1805 that enabled machinists to measure work to one ten-thousandths of an inch. Maudslay's successors furthered his craft and assisted in the evolution of machine tools, thus encouraging the industrial revolution.

Today, metal cutting tools remain very similar to those used in the nineteenth century. The implementation of computers has increased the precision and time efficiency of the metal cutting tools, but the basic processes have not changed significantly. However, new metal cutting advances are gaining acceptance and applicability in industry, whereby metal is eroded by chemical discharges, electric discharges, water jets, and laser beams. These advances could again bring significant changes to the methods employed to cut metal to achieve a desired shape.

In the early 1990s, the industries placing the most orders with metal cutting machine tool manufacturers had limited orders due to large financial losses, as exhibited by the poor performance during that time of some American auto makers. Decreases in spending by farming and construction industries in the late 1980s and early 1990s were offset by the aerospace industry. However, this industry also suffered due to the financial instability of various airline companies, as well as military spending cutbacks. The condition of the industry was attributed to three factors: high sensitivity of the industry to the overall health of the economy; a lag time of a year between economic improvements and growth in machine tool shipments; and long-term decline in machine tool demand.

CURRENT CONDITIONS

The incremental gains made by the metal-cutting machine tool industry were reversed in 1997 with the collapse of Asian economies—an essential market for U.S. manufacturers' machine tools. Shipments plummeted 6 percent between 1997 and 1998, with the contraction continuing in 1999. As Asian currencies rapidly devalued, the construction and automotive industries in once-expanding economies such as China curtailed spending. A market analyst explained the effect on the metal-cutting machine tool industry to *Manufacturing Automation* by saying that "the sudden drop in purchases by Asian economies caused a supply glut and an overcapacity in manufacturing." Moreover, a widespread strike by General Motors workers eroded demand for machine tools from U.S. car companies.

Despite the difficulties of 1998 and 1999, the metal-cutting machine tool industry was expected to rebound in 2000, largely on the strength of an anticipated increase in domestic demand rather than any major recovery in foreign markets. Many U.S. companies relied on outdated and underperforming metal cutting machine tools, which was expected to lead to a spate of replacement orders in the early 2000s. As a result, the overall domestic machine tool industry was forecast to grow at between 1 and 2 percent in 2000 and 2001.

INDUSTRY LEADERS

In 1998, Giddings & Lewis, a subsidiary of Thyssen Krup AG, was the largest manufacturer of industrial automation products and machine tools in the United States. With operations in over 70 countries, Giddings & Lewis sold its tools under brand names such as Cordax, Fadal, and Giddings & Lewis. The company's key clients included the automotive industry—especially the Ford Motor Company—as well as firms in the aerospace, construction, and defense sectors. In 1998, the Fond du Lac, Wisconsin-based company employed 3,100 workers.

Milacron Inc. had maintained a rare position in the early 1990s by reporting profits at a time when other metal cutting machine tool manufacturers were suffering losses. These salubrious results were largely due to the company's diversified interests outside of the machine tool industry, including plastics machinery, computer controls, measurement and inspection equipment, and grinding wheels. In 1996 Milacron reported record sales of $1.73 billion, with machine tool sales remaining level with 1995 at about $372 million. However, in 1998, the company reported falling sales because of weakened Asian demand for its products, as well as the General Motors strike that temporarily closed GM factories. 1998 sales were $1.5 billion, while employment levels declined slightly to 11,855.

Ingersoll International Inc., of Rockford, Illinois, was another leading company in the metal cutting machine tools industry. Ingersoll produced machine tools, manufacturing systems, and metal-cutting told to a number of businesses in the transportation, construction, and agricultural sectors. With 1998 sales topping $611 million, Ingersoll manufactured 40 percent of its products in Germany, and the remaining 60 percent in the United States.

Bridgeport Machines Inc., a subsidiary of Goldman Industrial Group, reported 1999 sales of $179 million. With its 934 employees, the company manufactured manual milling machines, machining centers, and CNS controlled manual tool change milling machines. Well-aware of the technological changes sweeping the industry, Bridgeport also created software for machine control and computer assisted manufacturing. Based in Bridgeport, Connecticut, the company sold its products to small job shops worldwide.

The industry leaders in NC machine tools are General Electric and Allen-Bradley, both of which primarily manufacture control systems. Expendable tools, such as drills, taps, chucks, and reamers are produced by TRW Geometric Tools, Acme-Cleveland, and National Twist Drill, among others.

WORKFORCE

A total of 29,371 workers were employed in the metal cutting machine tool industry in 1997. 57 percent were production workers, who earned an average wage of $17.83 per hour—well-above the national average for manufacturing jobs. Most people employed by this industry reside in the Great Lakes region and the northeastern United States (Michigan, Ohio, Illinois, Wisconsin, and New York), as well as in California. In 1997, 89 hundred metal cutting-related establishments and 5,761 employees called Michigan home, with 21 percent of all American machine tool shipments originating in that state. With its 46 companies and 4,382 employees, Ohio accounted for 16 percent of the industry's total shipments in 1997.

AMERICA AND THE WORLD

Throughout the 1980s, the Japanese provided stiff competition for American manufacturers of metal cutting tools. In 1974, the United States enjoyed a machine tool trade surplus relative to the Japanese. In 1991 that surplus had been transformed into a $1 billion trade deficit. As a result, seven of the world's largest machine tool companies were based in Japan in the early 1990s. An increasing German presence also threatened the U.S. metal cutting industry, as German companies produced some of the leading specialty CNC machines. German metal cut-

ting machine tool manufacturers had a successful 1998, in which the overall tool market grew 21 percent. Exports were an important facet of these good fortunes. In 1998, German exports rose 9 percent, with the United States named as a major export market, according to *Industry Sector Analysis.*

Between 1992 and 1997, imports of machine tools rose dramatically at an average annual rate of 18.2 percent. In 1995, import penetration had reached 39 percent. Nevertheless, American metal cutting machine tool manufacturers saw their exports rise during this period, as well. According to *Manufacturing Automation,* exports increased at an average annual rate of 10.5 percent. The economic crisis that buffeted the economies of Asia and Latin America in 1997 reversed this trend, however, as export markets eroded and foreign producers achieved significant cost advantages due to favorable exchange rates. As a result, the level of exports in 1998 stagnated while imports increased an additional 11.5 percent.

RESEARCH AND TECHNOLOGY

Due to the limitations and adverse side-effects of traditional machining, chipless machining processes have been developed. These processes are primarily concerned with chemical, electrochemical, electrodischarge, water jet, and laser machining techniques. Intricate parts require non-traditional machining methods and the advent of the computer age have hastened the research and development of chipless machining processes. As NC controls become more sophisticated, environmental laws grow more stringent, and technology advances, the need for chipless machining processes is expected to increase. Promising technological developments in the later 1990s included robotized waterjet cutting systems (developed by Ingersoll-Rand Company of Woodcliff Lake, New Jersey, and a Swedish partner) and sophisticated laser cutting systems.

FURTHER READING

''Giddings & Lewis, Inc.'' *Hoover's Company Capsules,*1997. Available from http://www.hoovers.com/.

''Domestic Machine Tool Demand Should Moderate After Peaking in 1995.'' *Manufacturing Automation,* 1 March 1996.

''Industrial Laser Shipments Shine Through Third Quarter.'' *Manufacturing Automation,* 1 March 1997.

''Machine and Plant Floor News.'' *Manufacturing Automation,* 1 September 1999.

''Machine Tool Market by End Use.'' *Market Share Reporter.* 7th ed. Detroit: Gale Research Inc., 1997.

''Milacron Reports Record Orders, Sales and Earnings in 1996.'' *PR Newswire,* 7 February 1997.

U.S. Census Bureau. ''Machine Tool (Metal Cutting Types) Manufacturing,'' October 1999. Available from http://www.census.gov.

"Waterjet Cutting Now Available for Fully Automated Production Lines." *Manufacturing Automation,* 1 February 1997.

Weydman, Ulrich. "Germany: Metalworking Machine Tools market." *Industry Sector Analysis,* 25 May 1999.

Young, David. "Mammoth Machines Get Fitting Showcase." *Chicago Tribune,* 4 September 1996.

SIC 3542

MACHINE TOOLS, METAL FORMING TYPES

This industry covers establishments primarily engaged in manufacturing metal forming machine tools, independent from the hands of an human operator, for pressing, hammering, extruding, shearing, die-casting, or otherwise forming metal into shape. This industry also includes the rebuilding of such machine tools and the manufacture of repair parts for them. Establishments primarily engaged in the manufacture of electric and gas welding equipment and soldering equipment are classified in **SIC 3548: Electric and Gas Welding and Soldering Equipment;** those manufacturing portable, power-driven handtools are classified in **SIC 3546: Power-Driven Handtools;** those manufacturing rolling mill machinery and equipment are detailed in **SIC 3547: Rolling Mill Machinery and Equipment.**

NAICS CODE(S)

333513 (Machine Tool (Metal Forming Types) Manufacturing)

According to the U.S. Census Bureau's *1997 Economic Census—Manufacturing,* 225 establishments operated in this category for part or all of 1997. Industry-wide employment totaled 14,185 workers receiving a payroll of almost $599 million. Of these employees, 9,118 worked in production, putting in almost 19 million hours to earn wages of almost $346 million. Overall shipments for the industry were valued at almost $2.3 billion.

According to the most recent results available on Infotrac databases, Boston-based Connell L.P. led the industry in 1997 with sales of more than $811 million. Blount Inc. of Montgomery, Alabama followed with 1997 sales of $717 million. Ingersoll International Inc. of Rockford, Illinois generated sales of $611 million for its fiscal year ended November 30, 1998. Gleason Corp. of Rochester, New York garnered 1998 sales of $409 million. Hans Automation Inc. rounded out the top five industry leaders with 1998 sales of $327 million.

The metal forming machine tool industry is closely related to the metal cutting industry. Many machine shops employ both types of machine tools. The primary difference between metal cutting and metal forming concerns the way in which the finished product is removed from the raw metal. Metal forming is a process by which a piece of metal, generally a flat sheet stock or a rod, is forced into another shape by means of pressing the material beyond its present yield strength condition. Because most metals can be formed in this way, the metal forming industry is significant to many major industries throughout the United States. According to Standard & Poor's *Industry Surveys,* "The automotive industry is the largest single market for metal-forming machinery."

Since the metal forming industry is linked so closely to the automotive industry, growth in the industry is closely linked to the health of domestic car manufacturers. Consequently, the metal forming machine tool industry did not enjoy extraordinary success in the 1970s and 1980s. Public demand for American-made products, however, has encouraged automakers, even those held by Japanese firms operating in the United States, to purchase American-made tooling whenever possible. Metal forming equipment manufacturers in the United States hope to benefit from this movement.

Most metal forming companies are concentrated around the Great Lakes region and some northeastern states. Another smaller concentration of metal forming interests lies along the West Coast and Alaska. Thirty-one establishments are located in Ohio; they ship a total of $345.8 million worth of metal forming equipment. Illinois is home to 32 such establishments, which ship $341 million domestically and internationally. Michigan also claims 27 establishments, shipping $173.3 million.

At the conclusion of the 1980s, the average worker in the metal forming tool industry was earning more than $13 per hour. At that time, approximately 14,600 people were employed in this industry. Machinists and tool and die makers accounted for 25 percent of the entire labor force. In 1994, the industry had 13,100 employees making $16 per hour. Machinists and tool and die makers accounted for about 22 percent of the industry's work force. In 1998, the number of employees was estimated to be 10,500 people earning about $18 per hour.

The number of domestic shipments outweighed foreign shipments of complete metal forming tools. Foreign competitors have rallied for a share of the metal cutting tool market rather than the metal forming tool market. In 1994, U.S. machine tool production—cutting and forming—was valued at $3.7 billion, Japan's production was valued at $6.7 billion, and Germany's was valued at $5.3 billion.

In 1995 the shipment value of both metal cutting and metal forming machines was about $6.427 billion. The value of shipments of metal forming machine tools in

1995 was approximately $1.742 billion. By 1998, the shipment value was expected to be $1.840 billion.

FURTHER READING

Central Intelligence Agency. *Handbook of International Economic Statistics, 1996.*

Darnay, Arsen J., ed. *Manufacturing USA.* 5th ed. Detroit: Gale Research, 1996.

Infotrac Company Profiles. Available from http://web6.infotrac .galegroup.com (2/12/99).

Nugent, Thomas M., ed. "Steel and Heavy Machinery: Basic Analysis." *Standard & Poor's Industry Surveys,* 24 December 1992.

U.S. Census Bureau. *1997 Economic Census—Manufacturing.* Available from http://www.census.gov/prod/ec97/97m3335c .pdf (2/14/00).

U.S. Department of Commerce. "Value of Product Shipments." *1995 Annual Survey of Manufactures.* Washington: GPO, January 1997.

U.S. Department of Commerce. *Statistical Abstract of the United States.* Washington: GPO, October 1996.

SIC 3543

INDUSTRIAL PATTERNS

This category covers establishments primarily engaged in manufacturing industrial patterns.

NAICS CODE(S)

332997 (Industrial Pattern Manufacturing)

Industrial patternmaking companies make patterns for forming and molding metal. These patterns are used by other companies to produce metal ornaments, tools, automobile parts, cutlery, and other goods. The largest consumer of industrial patterns was the architectural metalworking industry, which consumed more than 20 percent of industry output in the early 1990s. Producers of pipes, valves, and fittings represented roughly 12 percent of the market. Miscellaneous repair shops purchased 27 percent of output. Other specialized industries purchased patterns to make engineering and scientific apparatus, prefabricated structural metal, car parts, railroad equipment, and other metal products.

Industrial patterns are often used in foundries to create molds and dies for iron, steel, and other metals. Foundries typically melt scrap in an electric furnace. The liquid is then poured into a mold, which is usually formed from sand, metal, or ceramic material. The metal cools and solidifies into any number of complicated shapes, such as an engine block, a turbine blade, or a surgical instrument.

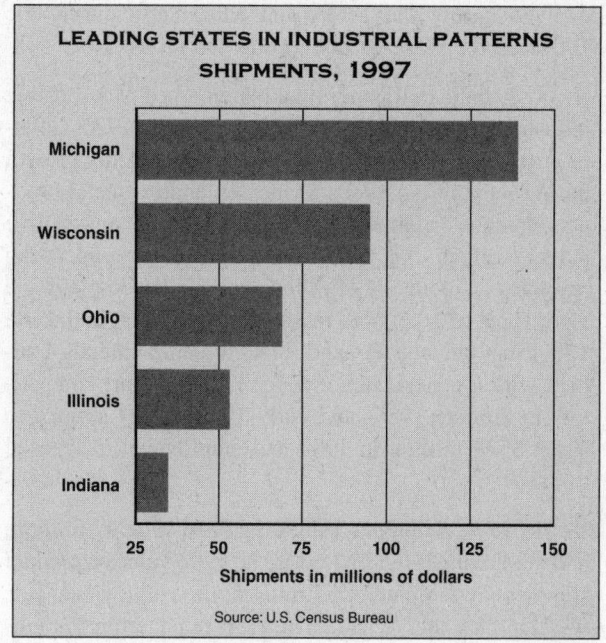

LEADING STATES IN INDUSTRIAL PATTERNS SHIPMENTS, 1997

Shipments in millions of dollars

Source: U.S. Census Bureau

According to the U.S. Census Bureau's *1997 Economic Census—Manufacturing,* 672 establishments operated in this category for some or all of 1997. Industrywide employment totaled 7,891 workers receiving a payroll of almost $282 million. Of these employees 6,464 worked in production, putting in more than 12 million hours to earn wages of almost $216 million. Overall shipments for the industry were valued at more than $618 billion.

Citation Corp., which merged with RSJ Acquisition Co. of New York City-based Kelso & Co. in late 1999, led the industry with sales of $724 million for its fiscal year ended September 30, 1998. Bodine Aluminum Inc. of Overland, Missouri, generated sales of $165.6 million for its fiscal year ended September 30, 1998. Two companies from Neenah, Wisconsin, followed: Hartley Controls, Corp., which specialized in green sand applications for molding of patterns to create $165.4 million in sales for its fiscal year ended September 30, 1997; and Neenah Foundry Co., with sales of $112 million for its fiscal year ended September 30, 1998. Alabama Ductile Castings of Brewton, Alabama, rounded out the top 5 industry leaders with sales of $106 million for its fiscal year ended September 30, 1997.

Copper was the first material that metallurgists learned to melt and form. By 4000 B.C. smiths had developed sophisticated smelting (melting and molding) techniques. Iron ore was first smelted in 1500 B.C. to make utensils and weapons. The advancement of the blast furnace, which was invented in 1323, was hastened by the industrial revolution in eighteenth-century England. Advanced metallurgical and patternmaking techniques evolved during the 1800s and particularly during the 1900s, in the wake of both world wars.

U.S. industrial patternmaking emerged as a separate industry from the 1950s through the 1970s. Patternmakers continued to enjoy relatively healthy growth during most of the 1980s as the demand for metal products, such as architectural metalwork and automotive parts, swelled. By 1988, the industry was generating revenues of about $719 million per year and employing a work force of 10,500. A real estate depression in the late 1980s that reduced demand for architectural metals, coupled with a general nationwide recession, hurt competitors in the late 1980s and early 1990s. Sales slipped to about $530 million in 1990 and employment decreased to 8,100.

In 1994, shipment values declined to $597 million, and employment fell to 7,600. The 1995 value of product shipments was about $552 million; the employment rate was approximately 7,200. The average patternmaker employed 12 workers in the late 1980s and garnered revenues of about $750,000. In the mid-1990s, the average number of employees per establishment was 11. The industry consisted of approximately 625 companies, most of which were privately owned and located in the Midwest. Michigan and Ohio each had 94 establishments and Wisconsin had 59.

Despite an economic boost going into the mid-1990s, the long term employment outlook for the overall metalworking industry is dismal. Jobs for most laborers are expected to decline 20-30 percent between 1990 and 2005, according to the Bureau of Labor Statistics. For example, the demand for machine tool cutting operators was expected to plummet about 27 percent by 2005. Jobs for machine tool cutting and forming workers were expected to fall by about 19 percent. Positions for engineers and sales professionals, in contrast, should rise 10-20 percent. The average patternmaking industry employee earned about 14 percent more than the average U.S. manufacturing worker in the early 1990s. In the late 1990s, the average hourly wage for the industry was about $17 per hour.

FURTHER READING

"Citation Corp." *The Business Journal—Milwaukee,* 17 December 1999.

Darnay, Arsen J., ed. *Manufacturing USA.* 5th ed. Detroit: Gale Research, 1996.

U.S. Census Bureau. *1997 Economic Census—Manufacturing.* Available from http://www.census.gov/prod/ec97/97m3329k .pdf (visited 2/14/00).

U.S. Department of Commerce. "Value of Product Shipments." *1995 Annual Survey of Manufactures.* Washington, D.C.: GPO, 1997.

SIC 3544

SPECIAL DIES AND TOOLS, DIE SETS, JIGS AND FIXTURES, AND INDUSTRIAL MOLDS

This classification includes establishments commonly known as contract tool and die shops primarily engaged in manufacturing, on a job or order basis, special tools and fixtures for use with machine tools, hammers, die-casting machines, and presses. The products of establishments classified in this industry include a wide variety of special tooling, such as dies; punches; die sets and components, and sub-presses; jigs and fixtures; and special checking devices. Establishments primarily engaged in manufacturing molds for die-casting and foundry casting; metal molds for plaster working, rubber working, plastics working, and glass working and similar machinery are also included. Establishments primarily engaged in manufacturing molds for heavy steel ingots are classified in **SIC 3321: Gray and Ductile Iron Foundries,** and those manufacturing cutting dies, except metal cutting, are classified in **SIC 3423: Hand and Edge Tools, Except Machine Tools and Handsaws.**

NAICS CODE(S)

333514 (Special Die and Tool, Die Set, Jig, and Fixture Manufacturing)
333511 (Industrial Mold Manufacturing)

INDUSTRY SNAPSHOT

U.S. Census Bureau's *1997 Economic Census-Manufacturing* split this industry between 2 NAICS (North American Industry Classification System) codes: industrial mold manufacturing and special dies, tools, jigs, & fixtures. Between these two categories, 7,270 establishments operated in this category for some or all of 1997. Industry-wide employment totaled 126,459 workers receiving a payroll of more than $5.3 billion. Of these employees, 100,547 worked in production, putting in almost 221 million hours to earn wages of more than $3.7 billion. Overall shipments for the industry were valued at more than $13.0 billion in 1997.

ORGANIZATION AND STRUCTURE

In the mid-1990s, the states ranking in the industry top ten by value of shipments were, in order of descending value, Michigan, Ohio, Illinois, Pennsylvania, California, Indiana, Wisconsin, New York, New Jersey, and Minnesota. Together these ten states accounted for 81 percent of total shipments and 79 percent of total employment for the industry. Of the top 15 firms in the industry, five were located in Michigan, reflecting the firms' proximity to centers of automotive design and production. The automobile industry has long provided tool and die producers with one of their most important markets.

The industry is served by the National Tooling and Machining Association of Fort Washington, Maryland, known as the National Tool and Die Manufacturers Association until 1960 and the National Tool, Die and Precision Machining Association until 1980. The Association was founded in 1943 and had 3,100 members and a staff of 40 in 1996, making it among the largest trade associations in the United States. Among the Association's publications were the annual *Buyers Guide of Special Tooling and Precision Machining Services, Basic Diemaking,* and *Advanced Diemaking.* The Association organizes an annual convention and semi-annual conferences. The industry was also served by the Tooling and Manufacturing Association of Chicago and the Michigan Tooling Association of Dearborn. The latter Association of 715 members was founded in 1933 and published the periodical *Tool Talk.* Other industry journals included *Tooling and Production, Modern Machine Shop, Precision Toolmaker,* and *American Machinist.*

Union workers in this industry are represented by the International Union of Tool, Die and Mold Makers, founded in 1972 and based in Rahway, New Jersey. The Union absorbed the Tool, Die and Mold Makers Guild in 1975.

BACKGROUND AND DEVELOPMENT

There are essentially two types of dies, pressworking dies and molding dies. Pressworking dies (also called stamping dies) are used to cut and shape sheet metals with electrical or hydraulic presses ranging in size from bench presses to the three-story-high giants used to stamp automotive body parts. A pressworking die set consists of two components, the upper part attached to the press ram, called a punch, and the lower part attached to the press bed, called a die (though die sets are often simply referred to as dies). Molding dies are used to form both metals and plastics. The most common type consists of two units that when closed form a cavity into which molten material is poured.

The development of the tool and die industry was central to the development of interchangeable parts and mass production technologies in manufacturing. As the *U.S. Industrial Outlook 1994* reported, ''Nearly every manufacturer that mass produces a product relies to some degree on contract manufacturing support provided by the small business companies that make up the special tooling and machining industry in the United States.'' A key historical figure in the industry was Eli Whitney, who used jigs and fixtures to assure the uniformity and thus interchangeability of component parts of firearms used during the War of 1812.

The rapid growth of mass production technologies after the late nineteenth century led to the development of a great number of tool and die shops, most of them small independent contractors. The number of tool and die producing establishments increased from 5,209 in 1954 to 6,616 in 1972 and 6,983 in 1989. Of the total number of establishments in 1989, 1,665 had 20 or more employees. By 1996 the number of establishments increased to an estimated 7,924—1,740 these had 20 or more employees.

In their book *The Tool and Die Industry,* Harold E. Arnett and Donald N. Smith described the special characteristics of the tool and die industry. They wrote: ''While mass production is made possible by tooling, the principal tools themselves cannot be mass produced. Tool making, and especially mold and diemaking, is one of the few activities connected with modern large-scale industry in which there has not been a general substitution of machinery for basic skills. These tools are custom-made, one-at-a-time by skilled artisans who patiently and precisely machine, finish, and construct the complicated devices. Only one die, or set of dies, is needed for the manufacture of many thousands, and sometimes millions, of automobile fenders or hoods of a given design.''

There was substantial evidence that the characteristics of tool and die production as described by Arnett and Smith were undergoing significant change in the 1980s and 1990s. While the output of the industry increased by 14 percent in real terms from 1987 to 1993, the employment of production workers increased by only 1.3 percent. Such labor displacement was partially the result of computerized production technologies. The flexibility of these technologies also enabled tool and die producers to undertake a broader range of operations. A number of industry observers predicted the consolidation of tool and die firms, resulting in fewer and larger firms.

In the wake of the North American Free Trade Agreement (NAFTA), a number of U.S. tool and die producers looked to export markets for growth. These producers hoped to serve both Mexican and Canadian manufacturers and also to benefit from the expanded export sales of U.S. manufacturers.

A number of large manufacturing firms were reducing or eliminating their in-house tool and die operations during the 1990s, creating new possibilities for independent producers. Among these was General Motors, which announced in 1993 that it expected to eliminate four of its 11 tool and die shops.

The value of shipments in the tool and die industry in 1995 was over $13.5 billion, up from $10.2 billion in 1992. Over 50 percent of these shipments ($7.5 billion) consisted of special dies and tools, die sets, jigs, and fixtures. Industrial molds and mold boxes comprised over 35 percent of all shipments ($4.7 billion); the remainder of shipments, over $1.1 billion, were not specified by kind. The number of establishments in the industry increased by over 3 percent since 1990, to approximately 7,280 in 1995.

The tool and die industry employed an estimated 161,000 employees in 1995, an increase of about 9 percent since 1990. There were about 123,000 production workers in 1995, up from 114,300 in 1990. Production workers accounted for about 77 percent of all employees in 1995, which was approximately the same percentage as in 1990. In 1995, production workers' average weekly hours were 44.1; hourly wages were $14.55. The 1995 averages for all production workers in manufacturing industries were 41.6 weekly hours and $12.37 in hourly wages.

INDUSTRY LEADERS

O'Neal Steel Inc. of Birmingham, Alabama led the industry with almost $1.8 billion in sales for its fiscal year ended June 30, 1997. MTD Products Inc. of Valley City, Ohio, followed with 1998 sales of almost $1.3 billion. La-Z-Boy Inc. of Monroe, Michigan generated more than $1.1 billion in sales for its fiscal year ended April 25, 1998. Prince Corp. of Holland, Michigan garnered sales of $875.0 million for its fiscal year ended September 30, 1997. Boston-based Connell L.P. rounded out the top 5 industry leaders with 1997 sales of more than $811.0 million. Other industry leaders included Pittsburgh-based Cable Design Technologies Inc., Dayton Progress Corp. of Dayton, Ohio, and Progressive Tool and Industries Co./Wisne Design of Southfield, Michigan.

RESEARCH AND TECHNOLOGY

The key area of research and technical change in the tool and die industry in the 1990s involved CAD/CAM technologies. The journal *Plastics Technology* surveyed 700 producers of industrial molds regarding their use of CAD. These producers used CAD for 10 percent of their tooling in 1992 and aimed to increase this to 40 to 50 percent. In 1993, Solingen Incorporated of Northridge, California, introduced a manufacturing process called direct shell production casting, which enabled the casting of metal parts directly from a three-dimensional image on a computer screen. Among the leading producers of software for the industry were the Roland Digital Group and Delcam International PLC.

FURTHER READING

Arnett, Harold, and Donald Smith. *The Tool and Die Industry: Problems and Prospects.* Ann Arbor, MI: University of Michigan School of Business Administration, 1975.

Darnay, Arsen J., Ed. *Manufacturing USA.* 5th ed. Detroit: Gale Research, 1996.

Infotrac Company Profiles. Available from http://web6.infotrac.galegroup.com, 2/14/99.

U.S. Census Bureau. *1997 Economic Census-Manufacturing.* Available from http://www.census.gov/prod/ec97/97m3335d.pdf and http://www.census.gov/prod/ec97/97m3335a.pdf, 2/14/00.

U.S. Department of Commerce. *1995 Annual Survey of Manufactures.* Washington: GPO, 1997.

SIC 3545

CUTTING TOOLS, MACHINE TOOL ACCESSORIES, AND MACHINIST'S PRECISION MEASURING DEVICES

This category covers establishments primarily engaged in manufacturing cutting tools, machinists' precision measuring tools, and attachments and accessories for machine tools and for other metalworking machinery, not elsewhere classified. Establishments primarily engaged in manufacturing hand tools, except power-driven types, are classified in the cutlery, hand tools, and general hardware industries.

NAICS CODE(S)

333515   (Cutting Tool and Machine Tool Accessory Manufacturing)

332212   (Hand and Edge Tool Manufacturing)

333991   (Power-Driven Hand Tool Manufacturing)

INDUSTRY SNAPSHOT

In 1997, the industry's 2,096 establishments shipped $6.0 billion worth of goods, a 17 percent increase over 1995. Of the total shipments, $5.3 billion came from cutting tool and machine tool accessory manufacturing, while $680.0 million came from hand and edge tools.

The cutting tools, machine tool accessories, and precision measuring devices industry is facing transition. Increased global competition in all aspects of manufacturing have created demand for better, longer lasting tools and accessories. Extensive development of tougher cutting tool materials and coatings has been the driving force of change in this industry, along with improved cutting tool design that lends extended performance. Increased emphasis on quality control is affecting the measuring device segment through demand for electronic gauges that link to statistical process control software packages. Modular tooling designs have affected the accessories segment.

Ironically, while this industry has paced itself to match industry demand for productivity improvements, it also has met with its own problems. The influx of foreign competitors to this market has been staggering, forcing cutting tool and measuring device manufacturers to look introspectively at their own operations. Process improvements and increased development became commonplace practices to remain profitable.

A downturn in the machine tool industry does not necessarily correlate to the health of the cutting tool industry. Generally, cutting tool sales are viewed as an economic indicator of the nation's manufacturing productivity level. The difference primarily is capital expense. A corporation may decide to purchase a used machine tool over a new one in recessionary times. However, if a company is cutting metal, the cutting tools wear or break and must be sharpened or replaced with new cutting tools. Therefore, the productivity of a metal cutting company generally is directly related to the purchasing levels of machine tools. However, longer lasting cutting tools are being manufactured with specialized coatings that extend the wear life of the tool—sometimes as much as four times the normal wear. With improved cutting tool materials and geometry, the volume of machine tool sales will inevitably drop because the tools are designed to reduce the frequency of replacement. Likewise, improved engineering design of metal castings intentionally reduce the amount of removable machine stock, requiring less cutting tool activity.

BACKGROUND AND DEVELOPMENT

The background and development of cutting tools, accessories, and measuring devices is closely tied to the history of machine tool development. The first gear-cutting mechanism was designed by Leonardo da Vinci. However, no evidence indicates that it was ever built. Through the clock making industry, the demand for precision gears and precision measuring devices grew. As time-keeping devices became more popular, production techniques were developed to meet the increasing demand. Metal removing devices were available with very small teeth, which served more as rotary files than chip-forming, cutting tools. Yet, it was not until the mid-1800s that the first cutting tool was developed.

The Phoenix Iron Works of Hartford, Connecticut, created the first tool to really form a metal chip, thereby cutting the metal. The tool had 56 teeth placed around its nearly 3-inch diameter. The teeth were chipped by a hammer and chisel. While effective, the tool required too much labor when it needed sharpening. In 1864, the Brown & Sharpe Co., later the Brown & Sharpe Manufacturing Co., developed the first cutter that could be sharpened by grinding the face without altering its shape. To date, the elements of this design are still in use.

In the mid-1990s, there were about 1,900 establishments in the industry, an increase of about 9 percent over 1990. In 1995, the industry shipped $4.8 billion in products; more than half ($2.6 billion) consisted of small

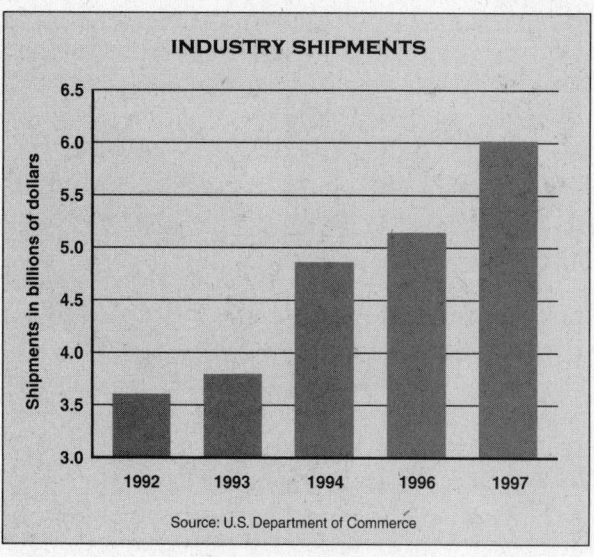

INDUSTRY SHIPMENTS

Source: U.S. Department of Commerce

cutting tools for machine tools and metalworking machinery; 22 percent ($1.1 billion) consisted of precision measuring tools.

CURRENT CONDITIONS

In the late 1990s, Worcester, Massachusetts-based Norton Co. developed the AVOS (Allows View of Surface) design, whereby it punched holes in the cutting blades to view through. The company also triangulated the rotating blades to improve vision as well as for brief breaks in the cutting process where the blade loses contact with the surface, allowing it to "breathe," as airflow swarfed out the grinding zone. This reduced heat and friction by 25 percent, improved the finish, and increased the life of the tool.

End mill design is evolving into more specialized geometries for certain material applications. For example, when milling aluminum, a standard, two-flute, high speed, steel end mill was used. However, studies show that using a three-flute end mill on aluminum grants ample space for chip formation while allowing a feed rate increase of up to 50 percent. This tool design change increases productivity by allowing aluminum to be machined faster without increased tool breakage.

New tool coatings also improve performance. Cubic boron nitride coated tooling inserts are gaining ground on carbide and ceramic inserts in areas like high production milling of cast iron. Polycrystalline diamond (PCD) coated inserts also are expected to gain acceptance, largely due to research and development efforts in PCD film technology. PCD is especially suited for ultrahard cutting applications. Titanium nitride coatings also can provide significant benefits—including lower machining cost per part, longer tool life, higher feeds and speeds, improved finished part quality, and reduced tool deflection.

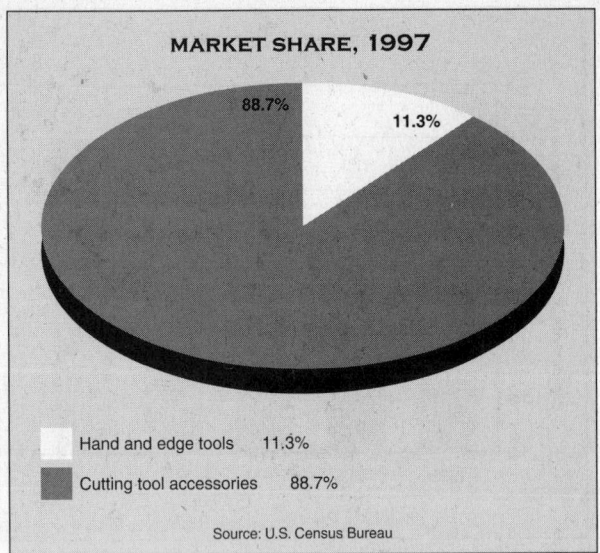

MARKET SHARE, 1997

88.7%

11.3%

Hand and edge tools   11.3%

Cutting tool accessories   88.7%

Source: U.S. Census Bureau

Another example of improved tool wear through coating is polycrystalline cubic boron nitride (PCBN). This innovation, when applied to turning inserts, threatens to replace many grinding operations. Used to machine hardened steel, PCBN turning inserts have no equal. Referred to as hard turning, the insert comes within or surpasses the accuracy and surface finish once reserved for grinding operations. The surface is improved because hard turning burnishes the surface, ending in a cleaner, rust- and crack-inhibitive surface.

Quick change and modular tools are making inroads. Flexibility and adaptability, which these tooling configurations offer, have been emphasized by customers over the years. Rapid precise tool changes save downtime and enable the tailoring of production schedules, thus using personnel and machine tools more efficiently. Modular tooling systems standardize spindle-to-tool interface connections, offering reduced hardware inventories. According to Charles R. Brown, Kennametal Inc.'s application engineering systems manager, "These systems move a process that for centuries has been manual into the age of automation. It's a quantum leap."

Statistical process control (SPC) is taking a new turn through increased use of electronic gauges on the shop floor. Wired to a computer, the gauges show digital readout of the measurement. This reading is input to the SPC software, which creates process control charts. The operator/inspector no longer shuffles through paperwork and calculations, and the readings are much more accurate. Such real-time information is beneficial in seeing trends, such as tool wear, before any parts are scrapped. The major trend in SPC today is moving measuring devices from the quality assurance department to the shop floor. Coordinate measuring machines and computer-linked electronic gauges are two examples of measurement equipment moving to the source to gain better control

through improving response time when a problem arises on the SPC charts. The biggest drawback to implementing use of electronic gauges is the initial cost involved. Purchasing the computer equipment and special gauges, training employees in the use of the software and hardware, and specialized calibration require such an outlay of money that many machine shops are intimidated—while remaining skeptical of any additional cost savings. Mitutoyo/MTI Corp. studied the level of electronic gauge use in industries in 1989. It found 61 percent of the surveyed machine shops used both dial and electronic gauges, while 31 percent did not use electronic gauges at all. Only 1.5 percent of the machine shops surveyed were totally committed to electronic gauge use.

INDUSTRY LEADERS

Washington, D.C.-based Deneher Corp. led the industry with 1998 sales of $2.9 billion. Norton followed closely with $2.6 billion in 1997. Latrobe, Pennsylvania-based Kennametal generated $1.7 billion in sales for the fiscal year ended June 30, 1998. Milacron Inc. of Cincinnati garnered 1998 sales of $1.5 billion before it sold its machine tooling business to Unova of Beverly Hills for $178 million. Global Industrial Technologies of Dallas, Texas, generated 1998 sales of $1.3 billion.

WORKFORCE

In 1997, there were 53,863 employees in the machine tool accessories industry. The 38,283 production workers in the industry earned an average of $14.86 per hour.

Many occupations in this industry will be reduced as the country moves toward the next century. Those facing the most significant reductions (more than 10 percent) include tool cutting operators, assemblers and fabricators, secretaries, machine builders, precision inspectors, and metal forming operators. Small increases in a few occupations are expected; these include industrial production managers, mechanical engineers, combination machine tool operators, numerically controlled machine operators, and machinists.

AMERICA AND THE WORLD

Competition and cost were the battle cries of the 1990s. Global competition is fierce, and only those who master cost savings measures will beat the competition. Nowhere is this more evident than in the auto industry. Although the Americans have experienced difficulty in the marketplace where Japanese cars reign supreme, the Europeans face greater challenges. Nissan's plant in Sunderland, England, lags one hour behind normal production time in Nissan's Japanese plants—18 man-hours versus 17 man-hours per car. However, European plants, on the average, produce a car in 30 to 35 man-hours. German automakers generally require 40 man-hours per car. In terms of cost cutting, it has been estimated that 150,000 jobs too many exist as a result of this inefficiency. Although work ethics differ between the cultures, so does the level of sophisticated machine tools and cutting tools. In order to bridge this gap, European manufacturers may order higher standard machine tools, cutting tools, and accessories and increase the order quantities.

The advent of International Organization for Standardization (ISO 9000) certification brought global uniformity to quality standards. Most European countries have adopted ISO 9000 regulations as official. When business is viewed in a global perspective, the ISO certifications are becoming increasingly necessary to obtain. In the United States, many of the larger companies and organizations—such as Caterpillar, York International, and American Petroleum Institute—have developed their own quality standards. Once a company becomes a potential supplier for the larger company, a quality audit is performed at the potential supplier's facility. Depending on the customer-supplier base, it would be possible for a company to hold several quality certifications, each with its own unique requirements. The benefit to obtaining ISO certification is to achieve a quality level that is understood throughout the world. The ISO certification is reviewed and reaudited every six months. While this is relatively new and fairly controversial in the United States, more than 15,000 certifications are held in Britain alone. The cost of compliance is one of the major obstacles to applying for certification—$15,000 to $20,000 for average sized companies. However, the cost of non-compliance in the future could mean fewer business opportunities, as ISO could become a general requirement for contract awards both domestically and internationally.

RESEARCH AND TECHNOLOGY

Cryogenic treatment, or the deep freezing of cutting tools, is currently a relatively unexplored process. There is little technical data available to support the successes in increased tool life as a result of the process. For years, one small tooling and die company in Arcadia, Ohio, experimented with dropping several materials, like metals and nylon, to 320 degrees below zero Fahrenheit, or 77 degrees Kelvin. The results have been outstanding. Carbide inserts seem to last 2 to 8 times longer than untreated inserts. Blades for cutting abrasive rubber are lasting up to 37 times longer. Carbide dies stay in service for months, rather than weeks, before needing to be sharpened. Even nylon stockings seem better able to resist runners better. The National Science Foundation has approved a research grant for the company to investigate the effect of cryogenic treatment on the wear life and microstructure of steel. If the research leads to significant findings, deep freezing may become another significant option for the improvement of tool life.

FURTHER READING

"Better Vision of the Work Surface: Abrasives." *Industry Week,* 17 February 1997.

Frazier, Mya. "New Milacron Looks to Turn Corner." *Business Courier Serving Cincinnati—Northern Kentucky,* 12 November 1999.

"Hoover's Online." Austin, TX: Hoover's Inc., 1997. Available from http://www.hoovers.com.

U.S. Census Bureau. *1997 Economic Census—Manufacturing.* Washington, D.C.: GPO, 1999.

U.S. Department of Commerce. *1995 Annual Survey of Manufactures.* Washington, D.C.: GPO, 1997.

Woodbury, Robert S. *Studies in the History of Machine Tools.* Cambridge, MA: The MIT Press, 1972.

SIC 3546

HANDTOOLS

This industry includes establishments primarily engaged in manufacturing power-driven handtools, such as drills and drilling tools, battery-powered (cordless) handtools, pneumatic and snagging grinders, and electric hammers. Establishments primarily engaged in manufacturing metal cutting type and metal forming type machines (including home workshop tools), which are not supported in the hands of an operator are classified in **SIC 3541: Machine Tools, Metal Cutting Types** and **SIC 3542: Machine Tools, Metal Forming Types;** and those primarily manufacturing power-driven heavy construction or mining handtools are classified in a range of construction machinery and equipment industries.

NAICS CODE(S)

333991 (Power-Driven Hand Tool Manufacturing)

INDUSTRY SNAPSHOT

The U.S. power-driven handtool industry includes professional and nonprofessional tools such as electric drills, portable chain saws, portable electric sanders, and pneumatic hammers. According to the Census Bureau, battery-powered (cordless) handtools, which include driver/drills and other tools, accounted for 15 percent of total shipments in 1997, while electric power-driven handtools represented approximately 46 percent of total shipments. When combined, battery-powered and electric handtools represented 61 percent of the industry's total shipments. This emphasizes the success of the non-professional consumer handtool market, which represented 50 percent of the industry's shipments in the early 1990s. Pneumatic, hydraulic, and powder-actuated handtools, which are produced for industrial and professional

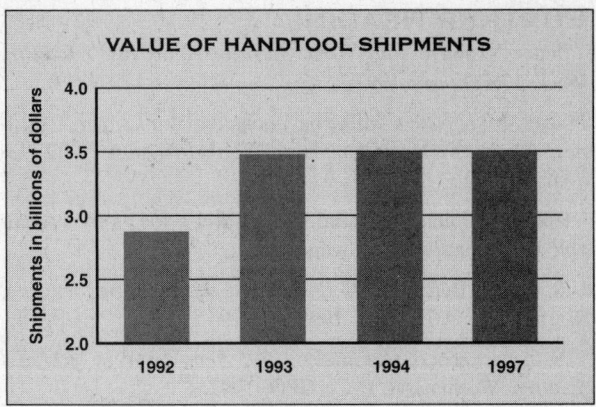

VALUE OF HANDTOOL SHIPMENTS

customers, represented 29 percent of total shipments in 1997, while internal combustion power-driven handtools and unspecified handtools represented the remaining 10 percent of total shipments.

The handtool industry is closely linked with the residential and commercial construction and home repair and renovation industries. The strong economy of the mid- to late 1990s contributed to the industry's health, as did advances in ergonomics and battery power technology—especially appealing to the do-it-yourself consumer.

According to the U.S. Census Bureau, 214 establishments manufactured goods in this category in 1997. They shipped $3.5 billion worth of merchandise, spent $1.6 billion on materials, and invested $119 million in buildings and other structures, machinery, and equipment. About 29 percent of the establishments in this category employed at least 20 people. California, Ohio, and Illinois had the largest concentrations of operations in this classification.

ORGANIZATION AND STRUCTURE

Success for the power-driven handtool industry depends on a variety of economic factors influencing industrial and consumer spending. Capital spending by business and industry directly affects power-driven handtool manufacturers, particularly in their manufacture of pneumatic power tools.

Pneumatic handtools operate by forcing compressed air through rotor blades. They are lightweight, durable, high performance tools used in demanding industrial applications. Examples of pneumatic products include: drills, grinders (metalworking machinery), pneumatic chip removal guns, hammers, ratchet wrenches, and sanders.

According to the 1996 edition of *Manufacturing USA,* retail sales to the do-it-yourself consumer sector accounted for 57 percent of the industry's total shipments in 1992 and have become a major influence on the success of the industry. Industry leader Black and Decker Corp., for example, received $1.826 million, or 39 percent, of its revenues from its power tool division by the end of 1995, largely a result of do-it-yourself retail sales

at home improvement stores such as The Home Depot. Because of this success, Black and Decker planned to introduce an assortment of new products for do-it-yourself customers in 1996. This sales strategy emphasizes the industry's sensitivity to spending trends for home improvement, maintenance, and repair. Electric power handtools dominated these sectors because they were generally less expensive than pneumatic tools. The cordless battery-powered handtool market also gave the industry a boost in the early 1990s and continued its success through the 1990s. Examples of electric power handtools include: buffing machines, chipping hammers, drills, grinders, hammers, polishers, sanders, saws, shears, screwdrivers, and wrenches.

The power-driven handtool industry also includes gasoline-powered chain saws. This product class is directly tied to the success of the timber industry. Lower timber harvests, due in part to environmental concerns, became a serious problem for chain saw manufacturers in the early 1990s and continued to effect sales in through the end of the century. Moreover, lower consumer purchases—due to a declining use of firewood for home heating—contributed to a decade of flat sales. Gasoline powered chain saws comprised an estimated 11 percent of the industry's total shipments in 1992, but all internal combustion tools together accounted for less than 10 percent of shipments in 1997.

BACKGROUND AND DEVELOPMENT

The power-driven handtool industry developed in conjunction with the rest of the United States' industrial growth. U.S. manufacturers often started as small operations producing specific power tools for local markets. As the United States grew into a world economic leader, the power-driven handtool industry likewise expanded internationally.

For example, Black and Decker (founded in 1910 in Baltimore, Maryland) first began manufacturing candy dippers and capping machines for milk bottles. By 1917 Black and Decker patented the first pistol grip, trigger switch electric drill. The company's success enabled it to begin international operations by 1918. Black and Decker products helped define the power tool industry. For example, the company introduced the first portable screwdriver in 1923, the first electric hammer in 1936, and the first portable electric drill for consumer use in 1946. In 1999 Black and Decker was the world's leading power-driven handtool manufacturer.

Another industry leader, Danaher Corp., was organized in 1969 originally as a Massachusetts real estate investment trust known as DMG, Inc. In 1989 the corporation entered the handtool market by merging with Easco Handtools, Inc., and by the mid-1990s handtools made up approximately half of Danaher's total sales. By opening its doors to this market, Danaher achieved sales of $897 million in 1992, the best year in the company's history for per share earnings. A year later, the company's international sales rose to more than 10 percent of total sales.

According to *U.S. Industrial Outlook,* the recession seriously hurt the handtool industry in 1990 and 1991 when overall shipments dropped by $163 million (6.9 percent). The industry recovered by 1994 when the value of shipments reached $3.5 billion, up from $2.9 billion in 1992.

During the early to mid-1990s, automation played a major role in reducing the number of workers employed by the industry. The falling employment rate had not affected the industry's continued status as a net importer by 1992, however, when imports comprised 27 percent and exports represented 14 percent of total shipments.

The proliferation of large home centers, such as The Home Depot and Lowe's, gave manufacturers additional markets in which to sell their products. Technology also boosted the power-driven handtool industry by opening new markets for cordless tools, which accounted for 15 percent of the industry's shipments in 1997.

Industry growth depends upon increased expenditures in the home improvement, home repair and maintenance, and residential and commercial construction sectors. In addition, new battery technology has helped the industry expand the market for advanced cordless tools.

CURRENT CONDITIONS

Companies continued to introduce new products to generate consumer demand in this category. For example, new products accounted for about a third of Black and Decker's sales. In 1999 the firm began marketing a new version of its Mouse, a small, hand-held sander and polisher priced at $60. The original Mouse had been launched with great success in the previous year. In 1999 the company also introduced a powerful hammer drill (priced at $72) , a jig saw with a contoured two-finger trigger (priced at $45), a Pivot Driver cordless screwdriver (priced at $36) with a pistol grip that made it easier to drive screws into corners, and the Sandstorm 2-in-1 sander (priced at $48) with a palm grip designed to allow the consumer to use the tool on various projects.

Ergonomics—the engineering of tools for maximum comfort and minimal hazard to the human body—was an increasingly popular consideration for this industry. In 1999 Stanley Works redesigned the handles of many of its tools to better fit the human hand and to reduce the likelihood of injury from vibration and other stresses. For instance, the company incorporated a carbon-steel shank into its AntiVibe framing hammer to absorb the shock that traditional hammers transmitted to the human arm. Stanley Works also offered an ergonomic screwdriver with a diamond-textured handle made of soft elastomer

and a layer of hard polypropylene, so that consumers could grasp the tool firmly without needing to squeeze hard enough to hurt their hands.

INDUSTRY LEADERS

With 21,800 employees and sales of $4.6 billion in 1998, Black and Decker Corp. (Towson, Maryland) retained its place as the largest company that made primarily power-driven handtools. Subsidiary North American Power Tools and Accessories had 2,000 employees and estimated sales of $428 million that year. By the early 1990s Black and Decker had become an international company that carried the seventh most recognized brand name in the United States. Its brand recognition was also among the top 20 in Europe. In 1995 the company had expanded this international presence by beginning joint operations in India and China and introducing DeWALT power tools to Europe and Latin America.

The second largest U.S. power-driven handtool manufacturer was Danaher Corp. (Washington, DC), with 18,000 employees and sales of $2.9 billion in 1998. Founded in 1984 as a holding company, Danaher expanded by merging with Chicago Pneumatic Tool Company, Acme-Cleveland Corporation, Pacific Scientific Co., and Joslyn Corp. According to *International Directory of Company Histories,* in 1994 Danaher Corporation was recognized as the world's largest producer of drill chucks, the country's largest producer and marketer of Swiss screw machine components, and the leading automotive tools supplier to the National Automotive Parts Association (NAPA) and Sears.

SPX Corp. (Muskegon, Michigan) had 14,000 employees and sales of $1.8 billion. Previously known as Sealed Power Corp., it had merged with Signal Corp. Another industry leader, Milwaukee Electric Tool Corp. (Brookfield, Wisconsin) had 2,200 employees and estimated sales of $430 million. Stihl Inc. (a subsidiary of Firma Andreas Stihl based in Virginia Beach, Virginia) had 600 employees and estimated sales of $57 million. Sioux Tools Inc. (a subsidiary of Snap-On Inc. based in Sioux City, Iowa) had 250 employees and sales of $50 million.

Other diversified firms that also competed in this category included Ingersoll-Rand Co. (Woodcliff Lake, New Jersey); Illinois Tool Works Inc. (Glenview, Illinois); Stanley Works (New Britain, Connecticut); Snap-On Inc. (Kenosha, Wisconsin); and Applied Power Inc. (Butler, Wisconsin).

WORKFORCE

The U.S. power-driven handtool industry employed 16,436 people in 1997, compared to 15,600 in 1994 and 17,100 in 1990. This included 12,173 production workers who earned an average hourly wage of $12.95. The 6,880 production workers who made electric power-driven

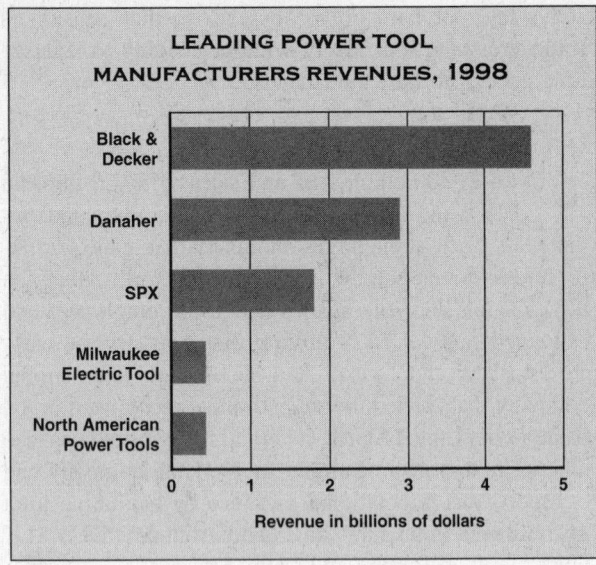

LEADING POWER TOOL MANUFACTURERS REVENUES, 1998

Revenue in billions of dollars

handtools (not battery-powered) earned an average hourly wage of $10.68. Total payroll for the industry was $512 million. Some of the occupations in the power-driven handtool industry include tool and die makers, machinists, mechanical engineers, drafters, blue collar worker supervisors, inspectors, industrial production managers, and stock clerks.

AMERICA AND THE WORLD

The United States is a world leader in the manufacture of power-driven handtools, although in the early 1990s the nation imported more goods in this category than it exported. This was part of a trend reflected in other industries as well. In 1994 the U.S. trade deficit was $108.1 billion compared with $75.7 billion in 1993. Nevertheless, most U.S. manufacturers were significant exporters in the mid- to late-1990s. Black and Decker, for example, had total export sales (for all products) of $1.956 billion in 1996, or 37 percent of its total sales revenues.

Major U.S. competitors included Germany, Japan, and Great Britain. The Robert Bosch Company, with its headquarters in Stuttgart, Germany, had total sales of $33.6 billion in 1991 and employed 181,498 people. Another large German power tool manufacturer was Stihl Andreas Co., which manufactured chain saws, hand saws, and replacement parts. The company had total sales of $1.15 billion in 1991 and employed 5,666 people.

In 1992 Sumitomo Electric Industries LTD of Osaka, Japan, exported $126.113 million worth of goods. The company had sales of $1.157 billion and 14,833 employees.

In Great Britain, Dobson Park Industries exported shipments worth $73,600 to the United States in 1992. Its power tool sales were $19,849, totaling 9 percent of the company's revenues.

Other large power-driven handtool manufacturers included Hitachi Koki Co. (Japan), Makita Corp. (Japan), Shibaura Engineering Works Co. (Japan), Hilti Ag Co. (Switzerland), Johnson Electric Holdings Ltd. (Hong Kong), and Kanematsu-Nnk Corp. (Japan).

RESEARCH AND TECHNOLOGY

Most research in the power-driven handtool industry in the 1990s was directed toward ergonomics and portability. Ergonomic designs create tools that are more comfortable and efficient for the user. Long term use of poorly designed power-driven handtools can have serious consequences to workers' health and safety. Constant exposure to noise and vibrations can cause such injuries as hearing loss, carpal tunnel syndrome, and hand-arm vibration syndrome (HAVS). Injuries of this type cost companies an estimated $100 billion annually. For example, according to the Manufacturing Information Resource Center (MIRC) home page on the Internet, Pratt & Whitney reported 1,500 claims in 1994 averaging approximately $5,000 each, costing the company more than $5 million in claims that year. As a result, Pratt & Whitney made plans to reduce its cumulative trauma disorder (CTD) claims related to the use of power handtools by 10 to 15 percent, which would save the company $500,000 to $750,000 a year.

Improved ergonomic designs can significantly reduce injuries caused by long-term use of power-driven handtools. In the mid-1990s Stanley Tools presented a new line of ergonomically designed tools that help the user maximize job performance, enhance work quality, and minimize physical stress and fatigue. Stanley Contractor Grade tools, for example, featured cushioned, dual-durometer grips that improved user comfort and reduced the likelihood of the tool slipping in the user's hand. The tools lowered the number of repetitive motions needed to execute a given task and reduced the occurrence of CTDs.

The power-driven handtool industry has also changed due to the development of cordless, battery-operated tools. According to *Business Week,* the key advantages of cordless tools are indoor safety and outdoor convenience. Cordless tools were an expanding area for power-driven handtool manufacturers through the 1990s: in 1992, they accounted for 12 percent of the industry's total shipments, and increased 3 percent by 1997.

FURTHER READING

"Dun's Marketing Services." *Dun's Business Rankings, 1996.* Dun & Bradstreet, Inc., 1996.

Guagenti, Toni. "Italian Maker of Parts for Power Tools Plans Virginia Beach, Va., Plant." *Knight-Ridder/Tribune Business News,* 17 November 1999.

Hughlett, Roger. "New Products Power B&D's 1999 Rebound: Keeping Customers Excited is Crucial to Tool Company's Revamping Efforts." *Baltimore Business Journal,* 28 May 1999.

Industry Surveys. New York: Standard & Poor's Corporation, 1997.

International Trade Administration. *Executive Summary.* Washington: U.S. Department of Commerce, 1997. Available from http://www.ita.doc.gov.

————. *1996 Report on U.S. Trade Deficit and World Economic Conditions.* Washington: U.S. Department of Commerce, 1996.

Manufacturing Information Resource Center (MIRC), 1997. Available from http://www.ncms.org/mirc/index.html.

Singer, Sherri. "A Better Grip on Ergonomic Design." *Machine Digest,* 5 August 1999.

Spain, Patrick J., and James R. Talbot, eds. *Hoover's Handbook of American Business 1997.* Austin, TX: Hoover's, Inc., 1996.

Strickland, Amanda. "Stihl Unit Powers Up Orange Office Park." *Triangle Business Journal,* 26 November 1999.

U.S. Department of Commerce. Census Bureau. *1997 Economic Census.* Washington, D.C.: GPO, 1999. Available from http://www.census.gov/prod/ec97/97m3339h.pdf.

Weston, Randy. "Black & Decker Turns to New Tools." *Computerworld,* 1 December 1997.

SIC 3547

ROLLING MILL MACHINERY

This category covers establishments primarily engaged in manufacturing rolling mill machinery and processing equipment for metal production, such as cold forming mills, structural mills, and finishing equipment.

NAICS CODE(S)

333516 (Rolling Mill Machinery and Equipment Manufacturing)

According to the U.S. Census Bureau's *1997 Economic Census—Manufacturing,* 100 establishments operated in this category for some or all of 1997. Industry-wide employment totaled 4,149 workers receiving a payroll of more than $167 million. Of these employees, 2,210 worked in production, putting in almost 5 million hours to earn wages of more than $75 million. Overall shipments for the industry were valued at more than $700 million.

The U.S. government divides rolling mill machinery into four classifications: hot rolling mill machinery (except tube rolling), cold rolling mill machinery, other roll milling machinery (including tube mill machinery), and rolling mill machinery that is not classified elsewhere. In 1995, the value of shipments for these four classifications was $621 million. The most valuable classification was "other rolling mill machinery" with a product shipment value of $244.5 million.

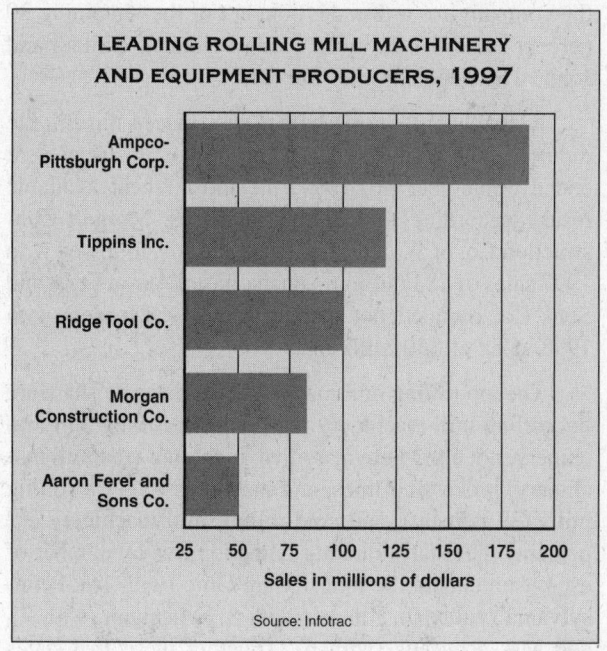

LEADING ROLLING MILL MACHINERY AND EQUIPMENT PRODUCERS, 1997

Sales in millions of dollars

Source: Infotrac

The combined 105 establishments in the rolling mill machinery industry generated a total value of shipments of $521 million in 1994. Forty percent of these establishments had 20 or more employees that year. Two years before, the rolling mill machinery industry employed a peak of 5,400 production workers. Average firm size as measured by the number of production workers per establishment was 19 percent smaller than that for the manufacturing sector as a whole. Annual capital investments were $9.9 million in 1994, and approximately $9.8 million in 1997.

The industry is relatively labor-intensive, having 30 percent as much investment per production worker as that for the manufacturing sector as a whole. Annual hours worked by production workers in the industry were 9 percent higher on average than those worked in the manufacturing sector at large, and hourly wages, at approximately $15 per hour, were 18 percent higher. By 2005, machinist jobs are expected to decrease 17.4 percent. Tool and die makers' jobs are expected to decrease 15.3 percent. A 37.7 percent increase is expected for combination machine tool operators.

The capital requirements for the industry are relatively low, with average investment per establishment at 25 percent of that for the manufacturing sector as a whole. In 1997, capital investment for the industry was about $9.8 million.

Two Pittsburgh-based firms—Ampco-Pittsburgh Corp. and Pippins Inc.—led the industry with 1998 sales of almost $188 million and $120 million, respectively. The former employed 1,332, the latter 300. Tippins ended 75 years of familial ownership in 1998 when president and CEO John Thomas, who held a 40 percent stake in the company for a decade, bought out the remaining 30 percent stakes of the two remaining heirs, William and John, who pursued other interests.

Ridge Tool Co. of Elyria, Ohio, placed third in the industry with sales of $100 million for its fiscal year ended September 30, 1997, the most recent available results according to Infotrac databases. Morgan Construction Co. of Worcester, Massachusetts, followed with 1997 sales of $83 million. Omaha-based Aaron Ferer and Sons Co. rounded out the top 5 industry leaders with 1998 sales of $50 million.

The top rolling mill machinery products by share are hot rolling mill machinery (47 percent); rolling mill machinery, not elsewhere classified, including tube mill machinery, processing lines, and machined rolls for rolling mills (37 percent); and cold rolling mill machinery (12 percent). The states ranking in the top five by number of establishments in the industry are Ohio (with 16), Pennsylvania (with 10), Illinois (with 8), Michigan (with 7), and Massachusetts (with 6). Together these five states account for 79 percent of total employment for the industry in the United States. Ohio by itself accounts for about 31 percent of total employment in the industry.

The top five industries and sectors buying the outputs of the industry are: gross fixed private investment, with a 75.4 percent share; exports, with a 17.8 percent share; change in business inventories, with a 3.7 percent share; rolling mill machinery, with a 2.6 percent share; and federal government purchases, for national defense, with a 0.1 percent share.

FURTHER READING

Boselovic, Len. "Tippins Family Ends 75 Years of Ownership at Etna, Pa., Steel Equipment Firm." *Knight-Ridder/Tribune Business News,* 25 August 1998.

Darnay, Arsen J., ed. *Manufacturing USA.* 5th ed. Detroit: Gale Research, 1996.

U.S. Census Bureau. *1997 Economic Census—Manufacturing.* Available from http://www.census.gov/prod.

U.S. Department of Commerce. "Value of Product Shipments." *Annual Survey of Manufactures.* Washington, D.C.: GPO, 1997.

SIC 3548

ELECTRIC AND GAS WELDING AND SOLDERING EQUIPMENT

This industry includes establishments primarily engaged in manufacturing electric and gas welding and soldering equipment and accessories. Also included are establishments primarily engaged in coating welding wire from purchased wire or from wire drawn in the same establishment. Establishments primarily engaged in manufacturing hand-held soldering irons are classified in **SIC 3423: Hand and Edge Tools, Except Machine Tools and Handsaws,** and those manufacturing electron beam, ultrasonic, and laser welding equipment are classified in **SIC 3699: Electrical Machinery, Equipment, and Supplies, Not Elsewhere Classified.**

NAICS CODE(S)

333992 (Welding and Soldering Equipment Manufacturing)

335311 (Power, Distribution, and Specialty Transformer Manufacturing)

According to the U.S. Census Bureau's *1997 Economic Census—Manufacturing,* 243 establishments operated in this category for part or all of 1997. Industry-wide employment totaled 22,011 workers receiving a combined payroll of almost $900 million. Of these employees, 14,307 worked in production, putting in almost 29 million hours to earn wages of almost $476 million. Overall shipments for the industry were valued at almost $4.4 billion.

Welding and soldering equipment manufacturers, as a whole, experienced a more than $2 billion increase in shipments between 1987 and 1996. In that year, the industry employed an estimated 19,000 people and paid significantly higher wages than other forms of manufacturing. In 1994 the average compensation for an hourly worker in this sector was $15.28, compared to the entire manufacturing sector's average of $12.09 per hour. There were 246 establishments in 1996, mostly concentrated in the Great Lakes region and supporting the automotive industry. Michigan claimed the most establishments, followed by Ohio.

Approximately 31 percent of the industry's manufacturers produced arc welding machines and their components and accessories, while another 27 percent made arc welding electrodes. The rest of the industry was split between manufacturing resistance welders, gas welding and cutting equipment, welding apparatus, and miscellaneous welding equipment.

Liburdi-Dimetrics Corp. of Davidson, North Carolina, a computer peripherals and electronics components manufacturer, led the industry with 1998 sales of almost $2.4 billion. Lincoln Electric Holdings Inc. of Euclid, Ohio fell by more than $100 million from 1998 sales of almost $1.2 billion to 1999 sales of almost $1.1 billion. Inco United States followed up with sales of almost $1.2 billion in 1997, according to the most recent results available on Infotrac databases. Cleveland-based Premier Industrial Corp. generated sales of more than $818 million for its fiscal year ended May 31, 1998. NCH Corp. of

Irving, Texas rounded out the top five industry leaders with sales of more than $784 million for its fiscal year ended April 30, 1998.

Lincoln Electric's unique pay structure and bonus-incentive plans have created a source of study for management researchers and motivational theorists. Lincoln has an open-door policy to encourage communication between various employee levels. Rather than resorting to layoffs as the only course of downsizing, Lincoln practices hiring freezes and voluntary layoffs. Lincoln credits its outstanding production volumes to this type of management-worker relationship.

FURTHER READING

Carey, Christopher. "Color Them Red LBOs, Losses Leave Firms Deep in Debt." *St. Louis Post Dispatch.* 13 May 1996.

Darnay, Arsen J., ed. *Manufacturing USA: Industry Analyses, Statistics, and Leading Companies.* Detroit: Gale Research, Inc., 1996.

Infotrac Company Profiles. Available from http://web6.infotrac.galegroup.com (visited 2/15/99).

Lazich, Robert S., ed. *Market Share Reporter.* Detroit: Gale Research, 1997.

"Lincoln Electric Reports Improved Fourth-Quarter, Year-End Results and Key Strategic Acquisitions." *PR Newswire,* 3 February 2000.

"Thermodyne Holdings Corp." *Market Guide: Company Snapshot,* 1997. Available from http://www.marketguide.com/MGI/SNAP/A0EA0-CS.ohtml.

U.S. Census Bureau. *1997 Economic Census-Manufacturing.* Available from http://www.census.gov/prod/ec97/97m3339i.pdf (visited 2/15/00).

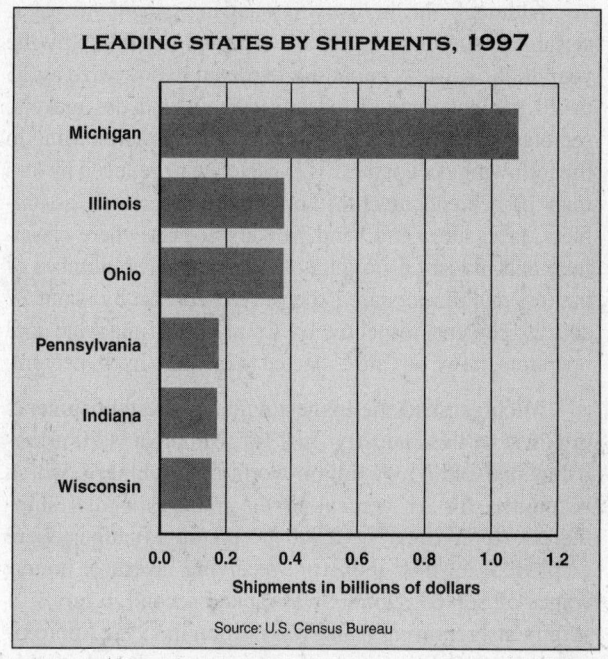

LEADING STATES BY SHIPMENTS, 1997

Shipments in billions of dollars

Source: U.S. Census Bureau

SIC 3549

METALWORKING MACHINERY, NOT ELSEWHERE CLASSIFIED

This classification covers establishments primarily engaged in manufacturing metalworking machinery, not elsewhere classified. Establishments primarily engaged in manufacturing automotive maintenance equipment are classified in **SIC 3559: Special Industry Machinery, Not Elsewhere Classified.**

NAICS CODE(S)

333518 (Other Metalworking Machinery Manufacturing)

According to the U.S. Census Bureau's *1997 Economic Census—Manufacturing,* 474 establishments op-erated in this category for part or all of 1997. Industry-wide employment totaled 19,023 workers receiving a payroll of more than $857 million. Of these employees, 11,314 worked in production, putting in more than 25 million hours to earn wages of almost $441 million. Overall shipments for the industry were valued at almost $3.5 billion.

This industry includes special purpose machinery such as robotics machinery, which alone encompasses a growing trend in manufacturing. As the industry continues to automate repetitive and often dangerous tasks, the use of assembly machines is expected to increase. The growth in this industrial classification during the early to mid-1980s was a testament to this trend, and it is still growing in the late 1990s.

In 1998 New York City-based Dover Corp. led the industry with sales just shy of $4 billion. In that same year, Cincinnati-based Milacron Inc. followed with sales of more than $1.5 billion, and Giddings and Lewis Inc. of Fond du Lac, Wisconsin posted sales of $763 million. Thermadyne Holdings Corp. of Clayton, Missouri, which was bought out by New York City-based Donald, Lufkin & Jenrette Merchant Banking in 1998, generated sales that year of almost $533 million. West Bend Mutual Insurance Co. of West Bend, Wisconsin rounded out the top five industry leaders with 1997 sales of $488 million.

The product share of this classification is split between assembly machinery with 55 percent; coiling, cut-to-length, and slitting line metalworking machinery with 31 percent; and miscellaneous metalworking machinery with 12 percent. In 1995 total sales in this industry were $2.67 billion.

Although the industry is showing growth in sales, certain employment levels are expected to decline by the year 2005. Those occupations expected to downsize by 15 to 20 percent include machinists, tool and die makers, secretaries, and blue collar worker supervisors. Staffing in the following occupations is expected to be reduced by less than 10 percent: machine tool cutting operators, assemblers, fabricators and hand workers not elsewhere classified, and industrial production managers. The number of janitors and drafters are expected to decrease by about 27 and 29 percent, respectively. Combination machine tool operators, however, are expected to increase by 38 percent.

Michigan had the highest number of establishments involved in this industry. In 1997, Michigan's 90 establishments sold $1.08 billion worth of machinery, which accounted for 31 percent of the industry's total shipments. Approximately 2,700 people in Michigan were employed in this industry, receiving average hourly wages of $16.63. Illinois was ranked second in terms of shipments, reporting over $378 million in 1997. Approximately 1,000 Illinois residents were employed in this industry at an average wage of $17.37 per hour. Connecticut was the highest paying state in this industry in 1997. Reporting about $96 million in sales and employing 428 people, Connecticut's establishments paid workers an average hourly wage of $21.42.

FURTHER READING

Darnay, Arsen J., ed. *Manufacturing USA*. 5th Ed. Detroit: Gale Research, 1996.

Infotrac Company Profiles. Available at http://web6.infotrac .galegroup.com (visited 2/15/99).

"Thermadyne Holding Corp. gets $25 million loan." *St. Louis Business Journal,* 17 January 2000.

U.S. Census Bureau. *1997 Economic Census-Manufacturing.* Available at http://www.census.gov/prod/ec97/97m3335g.pdf (2/15/2000).

U.S. Department of Commerce. "Value of Product Shipments." *Annual Survey of Manufactures.* Washington: GPO, 1997.

Ward's Business Directory of U.S. Private and Public Companies. Detroit: Gale Research, 1997.

SIC 3552

TEXTILE MACHINERY

This industry deals with establishments primarily engaged in manufacturing machinery for the textile industries, including parts, attachments, and accessories. Establishments primarily engaged in manufacturing industrial sewing machines are classified in **SIC 3559:** **Special Industry Machinery, Not Elsewhere Classified,** and those manufacturing household sewing machines are classified in **SIC 3639: Household Appliances, Not Elsewhere Classified.**

NAICS CODE(S)

333292 (Textile Machinery Manufacturing)

INDUSTRY SNAPSHOT

The textile machinery industry is closely tied with American consumer demand for textile products, including clothing and home furnishing fabrics. With the steady growth of the economy during the 1990s, the textile machinery industry remained healthy, driven by consumer spending and a booming market for higher quality products.

According to the U.S. Census Bureau, 477 establishments made products in this classification in 1997. They shipped $1.8 billion worth of merchandise that year, compared to $1.9 billion in 1994 and $1.5 billion in 1990. These businesses spent $745 million on materials in 1997, and they invested $55 million in buildings and other structures, machinery, and equipment. The largest concentrations of facilities in this industry were in North Carolina, South Carolina, and Georgia. About two-thirds of the establishments in this category had fewer than 20 employees.

ORGANIZATION AND STRUCTURE

The textile machinery industry encompasses all machinery used from the start of the yarn-making process through weaving the cloth, final treatments, and dyeing. Most fabrics produced by weaving or knitting must undergo a number of further processing treatments before they are ready for sale. In the finishing operations the fabric is subjected to mechanical and chemical treatment, whereby its appearance and quality are improved and its commercial value is enhanced. Each of these processes requires different machinery, thus the scope of textile machinery is very broad.

The term "finishing" or "dressing" is collectively applied to the various finishing treatments required for each type of fabric. For example, textiles produced from vegetable fibers require different treatment—raising, singeing, dyeing, printing—than those produced from animal or synthetic fibers. These procedures require mechanical treatment and processing by chemicals to improve the glaze, shape-retaining properties, crease resistance, smoothness, and drape of the material. Additionally, depending on the kind of material and the purpose for which it is to be used, a textile can be made shrink-proof, water-repellent, supple, soft, or heavy. Mechanical finishing treatments may consist of mangling, pressing, rolling, milling, shearing, calendering, raising, and singeing. Before undergoing these treatments, the material is passed through liquid baths or steam baths in which various substances, such as starch, vegetable gums, glues, gelatins, and mucilages are added to the fabric.

Of the 500 U.S. textile machinery establishments operating in the mid-1990s, fewer than 200 made complete machines. Although a number of textile machinery manufacturers made assorted products, original-equipment manufacturers tended to concentrate production on one or two types of machines.

Revenues derived from the sale of parts and accessories accounted for approximately 36 percent of the industry's annual sales in the mid-1990s. Fiber-to-fabric textile machinery accounted for 9 percent of the product share. Fabric machinery for weaving, knitting, embroidering, braiding, tufting, and lace making accounted for 6 percent. Finishing machinery accounted for 5 percent. Machines used for bleaching, mercerizing, and dyeing accounted for 5.5 percent. Machinery for drying stocks, yarns, cloth, carpet, and other non-woven materials accounted for 4.2 percent. Non-specific machinery and machinery not elsewhere classified accounted for the remaining 34.3 percent.

BACKGROUND AND DEVELOPMENT

The first hand weaving looms are thought to date back to 4000 B.C. Although the East is credited with the first horizontally arranged weaving plane, its date of origin is unknown. A shedding mechanism, which originated in China, was not introduced in Europe until the third or fourth century A.D. Only minor advances were made with the hand loom over the next millennium. The first major development occurred in 1733, when the flying shuttle was introduced. Designed by an Englishman, the shuttle came equipped with wheels, which reduced resistance as the shuttle passed through the fibers. This considerably decreased the time constraints of producing woven fabrics and expanded the capabilities of the hand loom.

Several blueprints for power looms were developed during the sixteenth, seventeenth, and eighteenth centuries. Circa 1500, Leonardo da Vinci sketched a hydraulic-driven power loom. This idea was repeated in 1678 and later in 1745; however, none of these were built. It was not until 1784 that an English parson designed the first manufacturable and functional power loom, which was able to produce a limited number of fabrics. In 1796 an automatic loom stopping system, called the "shuttle stop motion," was developed. In 1822 an English engineer made further improvements to the power loom, which prompted the manufacture of the first large series of power looms.

The oldest known patterning device is drawn in a Chinese book dating back to the twelfth century A.D. In 1725 a punched cardboard card served as the first dobby, a device used for creating unusual weaves. J. M. Jacquard created the first patterning machine in 1805, and variations

of this machine still bear his name. Another significant advance occurred in 1835, when a shuttle was developed that enabled different thread colors to be inserted into the fabric weave.

Textile manufacturers of the early- to mid-1990s were secure in a potentially growing market. The development of machinery to support this industry mirrors the outlook of the entire retail industry. Likewise, technological developments in machinery that offer textile manufacturers a competitive edge in terms of cost savings, increased productivity, and better quality, also stimulate the machinery side of the textile industry.

Due to higher sales volumes and increased efficiencies from capital investment in machinery, profits in the textiles industry exploded in the early 1990s. Record profits of $1.9 billion were reported in 1992, rising from $882 million in 1991 and $433 million in 1990. However, industry profits had dropped to $832 million by the end of 1996, despite predictions that the industry's explosive growth would continue.

Continued investment in textile machinery climbed in the mid-1990s, reflecting textile manufacturers' optimism toward the industry's future. Buyer demands for higher quality apparel and home furnishings at lower prices encouraged capital investment. Manufacturers also shifted to automated processes in lieu of labor intensive operations that could increase costs.

Inventories grew significantly between 1985 and 1993, rising from a value of nearly $4.5 billion to $6.0 billion. During the mid-1990s, most companies in the machinery industry reduced costs to compete more effectively in the global marketplace. They upgraded plants and equipment, reduced employment, increased inventory turnover, and sold marginal businesses. Many also acquired other firms, consolidating operations to further reduce costs.

CURRENT CONDITIONS

According to the Census Bureau, textile machinery represented nearly two-thirds of the sales in this classification in 1997. This was primarily from sales of cleaning and opening fiber-to-fabric machinery, carding and combing fiber-to-fabric frames, and other fiber-to-fabric yarn preparing machines, which accounted for about 30 percent of the industry's shipments. By far the largest value of product shipments in this segment originated in North Carolina and South Carolina, trailed by Georgia, Illinois, and New York. The 157 establishments whose primary products fell within this segment shipped $1.2 billion worth of merchandise and spent $523 million on materials.

Parts and attachments for textile machinery made up the remaining one-third of the industry's sales. This was primarily from parts and attachments for weaving ma-

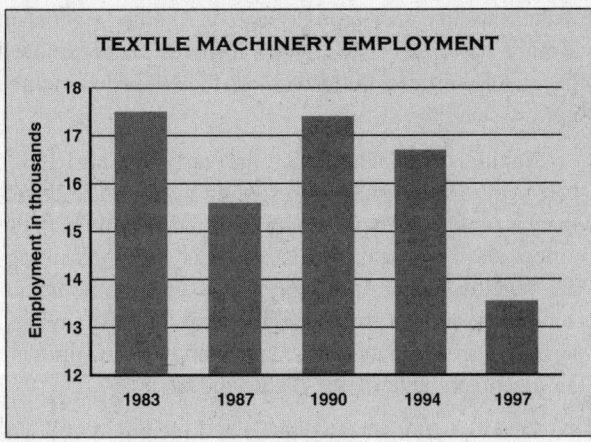

TEXTILE MACHINERY EMPLOYMENT

(Employment in thousands — bar chart showing values for 1983, 1987, 1990, 1994, and 1997)

chines (about 6 percent of sales) and fiber-to-fabric card clothing machinery (also 6 percent). By far the largest value of product shipments in this segment originated in North Carolina and South Carolina, with Connecticut and Georgia a distant third and fourth. The 91 establishments whose primary products fell within this segment shipped $473 million worth of merchandise and spent $174 million on materials.

INDUSTRY LEADERS

Among companies whose primary products fell within this classification, Hirsch International Corp. (Hauppauge, New York) was the largest with 365 employees and sales of $127 million in 1998. Speizman Industries Inc. (Charlotte, North Carolina) had 231 employees and sales of $90.9 million. Saco Lowell Inc. (a subsidiary of CT Enterprises based in Easly, South Carolina) had 200 employees and estimated sales of $30 million. Morrison Textile Machinery Co. (Fort Lawn, South Carolina) had 200 employees and estimated sales of $29 million, and Eastman Machine Co. (Buffalo, New York) had 210 employees and estimated sales of $25.7 million.

WORKFORCE

Employment in the textile machinery industry dropped from 17,500 people in 1983 to 15,600 in 1987, then rose to 17,400 in 1990. Employment dropped again to 16,700 in 1994, and dropped further to 13,551 in 1997. The industry's 8,536 production workers earned an average hourly wage of $13.88 in 1997. At plants that made primarily textile machinery but not parts, attachments, and accessories, the average hourly wage for production workers was $14.40. At plants that made primarily parts and attachments for those machines, the average hourly wage for production workers was $13.13.

Certain occupations in this industry were expected to be cut back significantly by the year 2005, including secretaries; drafters; engineering, mathematical, and science managers; bookkeeping, accounting, and auditing clerks; welding machine setters and operators; machine tool cutting operators (except in North Carolina); general office clerks; and stock clerks. However, job opportunities for machine builders and North Carolina machine tool operators were expected to increase by at least 10 percent. Industrial machinery mechanics positions were expected to increase by about 8 percent.

AMERICA AND THE WORLD

The textile machinery industry is ultimately driven by the retail buying habits of American shoppers. In 1992 sales profits hit a record high of $1.9 billion, but by 1994, those profits had plunged 55 percent to $832 million. Lagging consumer confidence was cited as the main reason for this trend. However, such factors as decreasing leisure time and increased bargain shopping also contributed to the decline in retail sales. Consequently, the industry suffered from decreasing domestic demand through the mid-1990s.

Ratification of the North American Free Trade Agreement (NAFTA) opened new markets, expanded sales, and increased production for the textile industry. In the mid-1990s Canada and Mexico were the two largest export markets for U.S. textile and apparel products. U.S. exports to Canada had grown an average of 19 percent per year since 1986, reaching $2.5 billion in 1994 and resulting in a trade surplus in the sector of $892 million. U.S. exports to Mexico had increased by 25 percent on average each year since 1986, reaching $2.3 billion in 1994. U.S. imports from Mexico exceeded sector exports by $7 million in 1994, largely reflecting the increased use of offshore production, where cut fabric parts were exported to Mexico for assembly into apparel and then re-exported to the United States. NAFTA contains a "rule of origin" clause that will gradually enable Canada, Mexico, and the United States to waive duties and quotas on products made from raw materials that were produced in one of the three nations. Tariffs will be phased out in a maximum of ten years for products manufactured in North America that meet NAFTA rules of origin. In time, this will give U.S., Mexican, and Canadian manufacturers a competitive advantage over textile producers in other countries.

The dramatic political and economic changes in Europe and the former Soviet Union have also created new markets for textile machinery. While many machinery suppliers exist within Europe, their technology is inferior to that of the West and Japan. Consequently, textile producers in these European countries may look to U.S. manufacturers to help modernize their facilities.

With nearly half of its production exported, the U.S. textile machinery industry markets its equipment aggressively in many foreign markets. The major markets are China, Canada, Japan, Mexico, Germany, Thailand, and Italy.

RESEARCH AND TECHNOLOGY

One industry leader in technical innovation, Muratech Textile Machinery, has developed an automatic transportation system for synthetic fibers. This system can automate every aspect of a synthetic textile plant, from package transportation to package inspection. The company also developed an automatic transportation system for spun yarn, which does everything from transporting bobbins to inspecting packages. These automation systems enhance quality and production control, improve working environments, and save labor.

Hollingsworth Saco Lowell Corporation has developed an automatic bale opening system, the Rotomix. Its counter-rotating heads blend the top, middle, and bottom of the bales to achieve a superior blend over other bale mixing equipment. The Rotomix can open three different bale sizes and boasts a maximum production speed of 1,500 kilograms per hour.

In the early 1990s another innovative company, Marshall & Williams, developed a dye pen that operates in a vertical orientation. The pen offers the control and accuracy normally reserved for horizontally orientated pens, while achieving efficiency characteristic of vertically oriented pens. Made of heat-treated, powdered steel alloy components, the pen is durable and stable, and it provides a superior pen line. Its close-return design features an offset for the return track and reduces nozzle-to-cloth distance. The company also developed an internal incineration system in which small incinerators are placed in several oven zones. Oven exhaust air is drawn into the incinerators, where it is heated to between 1,000 and 1,500 degrees Fahrenheit until all volatile organic compounds in the exhaust have been destroyed. The clean exhaust is passed through a heat exchanger before it is released from the oven. Demand for this system is expected to grow dramatically as manufacturers strive to meet increasingly strict regulations imposed by the Environmental Protection Agency.

FURTHER READING

Darnay, Arsen J., ed. *Manufacturing USA.* 5th ed. Detroit: Gale Research, 1996.

Dun's Business Rankings, 1996. Bethlehem, PA: Dun & Brandstreet, Inc., 1996.

International Trade Administration. *Executive Summary.* U.S. Department of Commerce, 1997. Available from http://www.ita.doc.gov.

Standard & Poor's Industry Surveys. New York: Standard & Poor's Corporation, 1997.

"The Industry." American Textile Machinery Association, 1997. Available from http://www.webmasters.net/atma/.

Troester, David. "Eastman on Cutting Edge as Machine Sales Expand." *Business First of Buffalo,* 28 December 1998.

U.S. Department of Commerce. Census Bureau. *1997 Economic Census.* Washington, D.C.: GPO, 1999. Available from http://www.census.gov/prod/.

SIC 3553

WOODWORKING MACHINERY

This category includes establishments primarily engaged in manufacturing machinery for sawmills, for making particleboard and similar products, and for otherwise working or producing wood products. Establishments primarily engaged in manufacturing hand tools are classified in cutlery, handtools, and general hardware manufacturing industries, while those engaged in manufacturing portable power-driven hand tools are classified in **SIC 3546: Power-Driven Handtools.**

NAICS CODE(S)

333210 (Sawmill and Woodworking Machinery Manufacturing)

According to the U.S. Census Bureau's *1997 Economic Census—Manufacturing,* 327 establishments operated in this category for some or all of 1997. Industrywide employment totaled 9,117 workers receiving a payroll of more than $302 million. Of these employees, 5,793 worked in production, putting in almost 12 million hours to earn wages of almost $160 million. Overall shipments for the industry were valued at more than $1.3 billion.

One dilemma the industry faced in the late 1990s was a shortage of qualified and trained workers. Technical schools were not graduating students knowledgeable in woodworking, threatening the future of the industry. To correct this, the Woodworking Machinery Industry Association sent an interactive CD-ROM recruitment kit to high school students and guidance counselors, educating them about the benefits of working in this industry.

In 1995, according to the *1995 Annual Census of Manufactures,* this industry employed 9,800 workers, an increase of about 36 percent over the 7,200 workers reported in 1992. The figure also was about 10 percent above the 8,900 workers reported in the previous census of 1987. In 1995 the industry shipped goods to the value of about $1.48 billion, an increase of about 23 percent over the $1.2 billion reported in 1994. In 1992, Oregon, Tennessee, Mississippi and Indiana accounted for 39 percent of all workers employed in the industry. In 1997 North Carolina, Ohio, Indiana, Minnesota, and Tennessee were the leading states. Equipment made by the industry included machinery used in cutting, shaping, sanding, gluing, laminating and finishing wood products.

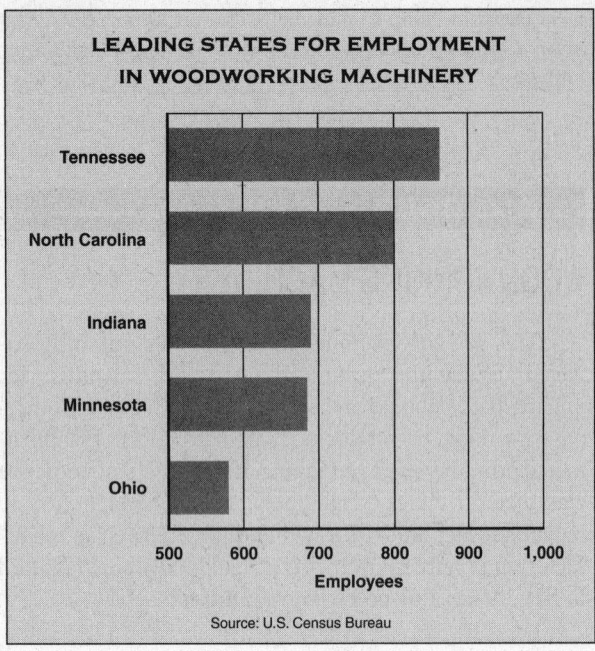

LEADING STATES FOR EMPLOYMENT IN WOODWORKING MACHINERY

Source: U.S. Census Bureau

In the 1980s, the woodworking machinery industry was affected by a slowdown in the housing industry and a general recession in the U.S. economy. In the early 1990s, the industry was further affected by cutting limits imposed on the logging industry in the Pacific Northwest. However, in 1992, George Delaney, then president of the Wood Machinery Manufacturers of America (WMMA), which represented more than 100 companies in the industry, said the number one issue facing the organization's membership was product liability reform legislation. Woodworking machinery manufacturers often paid as much as 10 percent of their annual sales for liability insurance, a cost that foreign competitors did not face.

In the early 1990s, the woodworking machinery industry benefitted from legislation that required woodworking companies to reduce the amount of dust in the air of their factories. Several companies in the industry increased their revenues by manufacturing dust-reduction equipment. Environmental concerns over logging also prompted production of new machinery. With stricter limits on logging, the forest products industry was buying updated equipment that reduced the amount of waste in manufacturing wood products.

The Coe Manufacturing Co., founded in 1852, was one of the first companies to manufacture computerized woodworking machinery, introducing a computer-controlled veneer lathe in 1977. The company operates manufacturing facilities in Tigard, Oregon, and Painesville, Ohio, where its headquarters are located. In 1992, Coe, a privately held company, employed approximately 760 workers and had revenues of $80 million. Most of Coe's woodworking machinery is sold to plywood manufacturers.

Norton Co. of Worcester, Massachusetts, led the industry with sales of almost $2.6 million in 1997, according to the most recent results available on Infotrac databases. Pentair Inc. of St. Paul, Minnesota, followed with 1998 sales of more than $1.9 billion. Katy Industries Inc. of Englewood, Colorado, placed third in the industry with 1998 sales of more than $342 million. Smurfit Newsprint Corp. of Oregon City, Oregon, generated 1997 sales of $270 million, and St. Louis-based Mitek Industries Inc. rounded out the top 5 industry leaders with 1997 sales of $180 million.

FURTHER READING

U.S. Bureau of the Census. *1995 Annual Survey of Manufactures.* Washington, D.C.: GPO, 1997.

U.S. Census Bureau. *1997 Economic Census—Manufacturing.* Available from http://www.census.gov/prod/ec97/97m3332a .pdf (visited 2/15/00).

''Woodworking Machinery Industry Assn.'' *Wood & Wood Products,* December 1998.

SIC 3554

PAPER INDUSTRIES MACHINERY

This category covers establishments primarily engaged in manufacturing machinery used in the pulp, paper, and paper products industries. Establishments primarily engaged in manufacturing printing trades machinery are classified in **SIC 3555: Printing Trades Machinery and Equipment.**

NAICS CODE(S)

333291 (Paper Industry Machinery Manufacturing)

INDUSTRY SNAPSHOT

The United States is the world's leading producer of paper-making machinery. According to the U.S. Census Bureau's *1997 Economic Census,* 365 establishments operated in this category for some or all of 1997. Industry-wide employment totaled 18,349 workers receiving a payroll of almost $762.0 million. Of those workers, 10,124 worked in production, putting in almost 21 million hours to earn wages of almost $365.0 million. Overall 1997 shipments for the industry were valued at almost $3.4 billion.

BACKGROUND AND DEVELOPMENT

The first machines used for making paper were invented in France in the late 18th century. In 1799, Frenchman Nicholas Louis Robert received a patent on a machine that could produce a continuous roll of paper. Several years later, London stationers Henry and Sealy

Fourdrinier financed improvements for Robert's paper-making machine, which eventually came to bear their name. Manufacturers began using the Fourdrinier machine for the commercial production of paper in England in 1812. Eventually, the Fourdrinier machine became the foundation of the paper-making industry.

The first Fourdrinier machine used in the United States was imported from England in 1827 and put into operation at a paper mill in Saugerties, New York. However, by 1829, an American company, Phelps & Spafford, began manufacturing Fourdrinier machines, the first of which was installed at Norwich, Connecticut. Phelps & Spafford reorganized after the recession of 1837 as Smith and Winchester, and continued to operate into the 20th century.

Pulping. Until the mid-1800s, paper was made principally from rags rather than wood. Between 1840 and 1860, several mechanical processes were developed that produced wood pulp suitable for making rough-grained paper. One of these pulp grinders was known as the Jordan refiner. Invented in 1858 by two Americans, Joseph Jordan and Thomas Eustace, the Jordan refiner was the principal pulping machine until it was replaced in the early 20th century by disk refiners. In 1867, American chemist Benjamin Tilghman found that pulp could also be produced by dissolving wood in a solution of sulfuric acid. A German chemist, Carl Dahl, perfected chemical pulping in the late 1880s. Mechanical pulping was extremely efficient, converting as much as 90 percent of the basic raw material into usable pulp. Although chemical pulping was considerably less efficient, the pulp generated by this process could be used to produce a higher grade of paper. Newsprint was generally a blend of about 25 percent mechanical pulp and 75 percent chemical pulp. Top quality stationery was still made from rag pulp. Many of the machines manufactured by the paper machinery industry during this period, such as barkers, chippers, and refiners, were used for the pulping processes.

One of the most capital-intensive manufacturing industries in the nation, the paper industry hasn't always been able to invest in new mills or upgrade existing mills during demand shortages. In 1994, paper demand shot up in the United States, Japan, and Europe as economies improved. Lacking the capacity to match the demand, many mills were running at 98 percent capacity, so they were unable to slow production down enough even to oil their machinery.

CURRENT CONDITIONS

In 1994, the industry had a shipment value of $2.8 billion and consisted of more than 300 companies with 17,400 employees. The U.S. Department of Commerce estimated that shipments peaked at $2.8 billion in 1990, after five years of steady growth, but subsequently de-

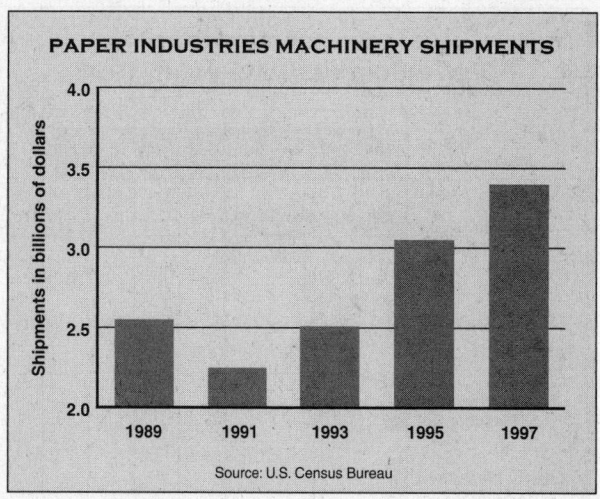

PAPER INDUSTRIES MACHINERY SHIPMENTS

Source: U.S. Census Bureau

clined by 7 percent during the global recession of the early 1990s. That period represented the paper industry's worst financial slump since the Great Depression. Shipments returned to $2.8 billion by 1994, when supply and demand drove paper costs up dramatically, and reached $3.4 billion in 1997.

The growth of the free market in Eastern Europe also resulted in a 25 percent increase in the export of U.S. paper products in 1991, further increasing demand for new or rebuilt paper industry machinery at home. According to industry figures, parts for rebuilt machines accounted for as much as 70 percent of the paper-making machinery market. There also was a growing market for used machinery, particularly in the specialties paper industry.

INDUSTRY LEADERS

Thermo Electron Corp. of Waltham, Massachusetts, led the industry with sales of almost $3.9 billion for its fiscal year ended January 30, 1999. Milwaukee-based Harnischfeger Industries Inc. followed with sales of just more than $2 billion for its fiscal year ended October 31, 1998. Harnischfeger had led the industry in 1996 with $2.2 billion in sales.

Beloit Corp. of Deerfield, Illinois, acquired by Harnischfeger Industries in 1986, was the third-largest U.S. producer of machinery for the paper industry, with sales of $750 million for its fiscal year ended October 31, 1998. Omega Papier of Wernshausen, Germany, contracted Beloit to assemble its 3.45 meter-wide paper mill capable of processing fully ink-free fiber into tissues and hand towels at speeds of up to 1,600 meters per minute. Paper Converting Machine Co. of Green Bay, Wisconsin, generated $267.0 million in sales for its fiscal year ended October 31, 1997. Minneapolis-based Liberty Diversified Industries Inc. rounded out the top 5 industry leaders with 1997 sales of $250 million.

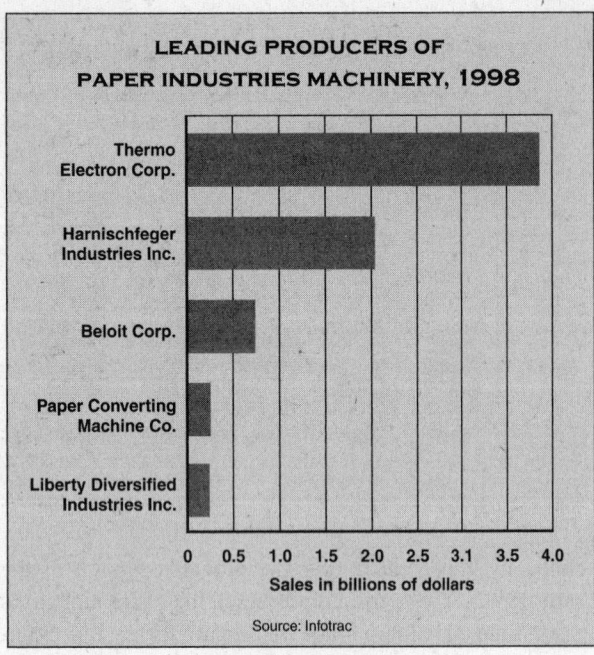

**LEADING PRODUCERS OF
PAPER INDUSTRIES MACHINERY, 1998**

Sales in billions of dollars

Source: Infotrac

AMERICA AND THE WORLD

Historically, the United States has been a net exporter of paper industries machinery, with Canada, the United Kingdom, Mexico and Australia being its most important foreign markets. However, imports began growing in relation to exports during the 1970s, and in 1979 the balance tipped in favor of imports. Before the rise of imports, nearly 90 percent of all new paper-making machines installed in the United States came from U.S.-based manufacturers. By the early 1980s, however, 50 percent of the new machines came from foreign manufacturers. There was a brief recovery in 1982, when exports exceeded imports by about $110 million. However, the downward trend returned in 1983, and by 1987 the industry's trade deficit had grown to almost $300 million. Much of the imported machinery came from Germany, the leading exporter of paper industries machinery in the world. Finland, Sweden, Switzerland, and Japan have also sold significant amounts of paper-making machinery in the U.S. market.

Exports began to improve in the late 1980s and early 1990s, with imports accounting for 25.8 percent of total shipments and exports comprising 19.7 percent. The Department of Commerce estimated that the U.S. industry would again be a net exporter by 1993.

FURTHER READING

Darnay, Arsen J., ed. *Manufacturing USA. 5th Ed. 1996.* Detroit: Gale Research, 1996.

Dun's Business Rankings, 1996. Bethlehem, PA: Dun & Bradstreet, Inc., 1996.

Infotrac Company Profiles. Available from http://web6.infotrac.galegroup.com (visited 2/15/00).

International Trade Administration. *Executive Summary.* U.S. Department of Commerce, 1997. Available from http://www.ita.doc.gov.

"Omega to install new German PM." *Pulp & Paper,* September 1999.

Pagano, Elizabeth. "Paper Prices Pinch Printers, Publishers." *Nashville (Tennessee) Banner,* 29 January 1996.

Standard & Poor's Industry Surveys. New York: Standard & Poor's Corporation, 1997.

U.S. Census Bureau. *1997 Economic Census.* Washington, DC: GPO, 1999. Available from http://www.census.gov/prod/ec97/97m3332c.pdf.

SIC 3555

PRINTING TRADES MACHINERY AND EQUIPMENT

This category covers establishments primarily engaged in manufacturing machinery and equipment used by the printing and bookbinding trades, including printing presses, bookbinding machines, typesetting and photoengraving equipment, and a variety of specialized tools for the printing trades.

NAICS CODE(S)

333293 (Printing Machinery and Equipment Manufacturing)

INDUSTRY SNAPSHOT

According to the U.S. Census Bureau's *1997 Economic Census,* 546 establishments operated in this category for some or all of 1997. This figure reflects steady growth from 430 in 1990 to approximately 525 in 1995. Industry-wide employment totaled 21,000 workers receiving a payroll of almost $853.0 million. Of those workers, 11,483 worked in production, putting in almost 24 million hours to earn wages of almost $404.0 million. Overall shipments for the industry were valued at more than $3.5 billion in 1997, up from $3.0 billion in 1995.

ORGANIZATION AND STRUCTURE

Leading members of the printing equipment industry banded together in 1910 to form the Printing Press Manufacturers Association (PPMA), with the purpose of convincing Congress to pass laws protecting the industry from foreign imports.

In 1933, the National Printing Equipment Association was founded, hoping to help the industry recover from the Great Depression. Industry codes enforcing fair competition proposed by the NPEA were accepted by President Franklin Roosevelt's National Recovery Administration (NRA) in 1934, but in 1935, a unanimous U.S. Supreme Court ruled that the National Industrial Recovery Act, under which the NRA was formed, was unconstitutional. Although the NPEA code of fair competition was invalidated, the organization voted to continue as a source of information and education for the printing equipment industry.

The name of NPEA was changed to the National Printing Equipment and Supply Association in 1978, and changed again in 1991 to the Association for Suppliers of Printing and Publishing Technologies (NPES). In 1996, NPES had more than 300 members, which included computer manufacturers and software companies, as well as traditional printing machinery manufacturers. NPES conducted market research and promotes international trade on behalf of its members.

BACKGROUND AND DEVELOPMENT

Letterpress printing, using raised images to print on paper, was an ancient art developed by the Babylonians as early as 2000 B.C. for producing playing cards. The first printing presses, however, were derived from machines used to press grapes and cheese and were not invented until the early 15th century, more than 3,000 years later. The modern printing industry is generally considered to date from the mid-15th century with the invention of moveable type by German printer Johannes Gutenberg. The Gutenberg press used a flat wooden plate, or platen, to press a single sheet of soft paper against a form containing letters cast in metal from clay molds.

The printing press changed very little over the next 400 years. When Stephen Daye established the first publishing house in the American Colonies in 1639, his English-made press was not significantly different from Gutenberg's. Christopher Sauer Jr. of Cambridge, Massachusetts, also followed the Gutenberg model when he manufactured the first press built in the American Colonies in 1750. However, printing machinery technology began to change radically in the early 1800s, with many of the advancements developed by American manufacturers. Among the most important U.S. contributions to printing machinery were the development of the Columbian press, the rotary press, the Linotype machine, and the offset press. The United States was the leading manufacturer of printing presses from the mid-1800s until after World War II, when Germany began to challenge U.S. dominance.

Columbian Press. In 1813, George Clymer, a printer in Philadelphia, replaced the cumbersome screw mechanism of the Gutenberg press with a much faster system of levers that allowed press operators to achieve sufficient pressure for printing. The elaborate system had a long handle known in the printing trades as "the devil's tail." Clymer's Columbian press was cast from iron and was

noted for its intricate metal work, which included dolphins, flowers, and an intimidating American eagle perched on top. However, due to the Western expansion of the United States, many American printers preferred lighter wooden presses that could be transported more easily. Clymer moved to England in 1817, where Clymer & Company manufactured presses until 1851.

Rotary Press. The rotary press was an American adaptation of the cylinder press. Friedrich Koenig, a German clockmaker who emigrated to England, developed the first practical cylinder press about 1811. Koenig replaced the flat platen with a cylinder that allowed press operators to maintain a uniform pressure as the type bed was moved horizontally. The first Koenig press, which could print about 1,100 sheets per hour, was installed at *The Times of London* in 1816. Koenig later returned to Germany, where he established the first printing press factory. The Koenig press, however, cost about 10 times as much as other presses and never became popular.

Richard March Hoe, a New York City manufacturer, built the first cylinder press in the United States in 1830. Hoe also realized that the greatest limitation to Koenig's press was the time it took to move the massive type bed back and forth. In 1846, R. Hoe & Company developed the first rotary press. Instead of using a flat type bed, Hoe mounted type around the outside of a huge cylinder. This cylinder was surrounded by four smaller platen cylinders. Instead of the back and forth motion of the Koenig press, the Hoe type cylinder revolved in a continuous motion. Each of the four hand-fed platen cylinders could print about 2,000 sheets per hour. This gave the Hoe rotary press a capacity of 8,000 copies per hour. The speed was later increased to 20,000 sheets. The first Hoe rotary press was installed at *The Philadelphia Public Ledger*. Hoe & Co. continued to manufacture presses and other printing machinery until 1968, when it declared bankruptcy.

William Bullock, a Philadelphia printer, perfected the first rotary press able to print on both sides of the paper. In 1880, he also developed the first high-speed press to print from a continuous roll of paper. The Goss Printing Company, founded in Chicago in 1885, was the first company to combine multiple high-speed rotary presses into a single machine that could print entire newspapers in one press run. In 1889, Goss installed a set of six presses for *The New York Herald* that could print 72,000 newspapers per hour.

Typesetting. For 400 years after Gutenberg invented moveable type, printers composed lines of type by hand, one letter at a time. When the printing was completed, the letters were returned to a type case. It was a tedious process, and one that resisted all attempts at mechanization. *American History Illustrated* once called it "the century's most perplexing invention problem." By one account, more than 200 inventors attempted to solve the enormous engineering problem posed by typesetting. Most ended up frustrated, and many went bankrupt. Mark Twain lost most of his fortune backing the Paige Compositor, which turned out to be an impractical failure. An examiner in the U.S. Patent Office reportedly went insane trying to cope with the technical complexity of the many patents filed on mechanical typesetters in the late 1880s.

In 1884, Ottmar Mergenthaler, an immigrant German clockmaker working for a scientific instruments company in Baltimore, invented a machine he named the Linotype. The Linotype allowed an operator sitting at a keyboard to compose lines of type from brass molds, or matrices. Separate lines of type were then cast in metal and slid into galleys for printing. The brass matrices returned to their original position until they were needed again. After printing, the type was melted down and the metal could be reused.

The Linotype, which Thomas Edison called "the eighth wonder of the world," solved several critical problems. First, because the brass matrices were immediately reusable, there was no need for a large precast supply of type. Since every line of type was newly cast from an alloy of lead, tin, and antimony, printers always received a quality impression. The Linotype also justified each line of type automatically by sliding wedge-shaped pieces of metal between each word. The first 12 Linotypes were installed at *The New York Tribune* in 1886. Within 10 years, there were Linotypes in use throughout the United States and Europe.

The Monotype, a machine similar to the Linotype, was invented in 1887 by an American, Tolbert Lanston. The Monotype cast individual letters from brass matrices and was especially popular with book publishers because it could cast special symbols or non-Latin alphabets. Additionally, corrections could be made by changing a single letter rather than an entire line of type.

The first photo typesetting machines were patented about 1880, but did not become practical until after World War II when the graphic arts industry began to grow. Linotype and Monotype typesetters were used almost universally by commercial printers until photo typesetting machines began to replace them in the 1970s. By the mid-1980s, most major newspapers had switched from "hot lead" to "cold type."

In 1992, *The Wall Street Journal* printed a story about "The Last Yiddish Linotype in America." Linotype machine No. 23,211 was one of nine made for the *Jewish Daily Forward* in New York in 1918. Outfitted with Hebrew letters and converted to compose type right to left, this machine was in operation until 1991, when the 3,000 pound machine, and a host of other equipment, was replaced by a single desktop computer.

Other American developments in printing machinery included offset printing. This process is often attributed to an American printer named Ira Rubel. Offset lithography had been used since the 1880s to print labels directly on tin containers. In 1905, Rubel was operating a rotary press when he unintentionally transferred an image onto the rubber impression cylinders. When he then fed paper through the press he noticed that the images left by the rubber cylinders were much sharper than the direct image left by the raised type. For many years, offset printing was used for high-quality work. In the 1970s, offset presses also began to replace letter presses for projects requiring high speed, such as newspapers.

New York World's Fair. In 1939, more than 100,000 people visited a display of printing machinery technology at the New York World's Fair, including the original Stephen Daye Press, then owned by the Vermont Historical Society. More than 200 companies participated in the exhibition, which covered 50,000 square feet in the Grand Central Palace. Mayor Fiorello LaGuárdia declared the last week in September to be "Printing Industry Week," and the U.S. Post Office issued a 3-cent stamp commemorating the 300th anniversary of printing in the United States.

World War II. Rationing of critical supplies such as steel and rubber nearly shut down the printing machinery industry during World War II. Many manufacturers compensated by accepting government contracts to build weapons. As early as 1939, even before the United States entered the war, the Goss Printing Company turned down a major contract with the *St. Louis Post Dispatch* because the newspaper was unwilling to accept a clause excusing Goss if the war prevented it from fulfilling the contract. Goss did negotiate a contract with the U.S. Navy to build gun mounts, sighting mechanisms, and other weapons machinery.

After the United States entered the war, the War Production Board (WPB) halted the manufacture of all printing equipment for civilian use. By July 1942, nearly the entire industry had been converted to the production of war material. Industry leaders, including Goss, R. Hoe & Company, and the ATF-Webendorfer Company, were building recoil mechanisms for anti-aircraft guns. Mergenthaler Linotype Company was making fire control instruments, F.P. Rosback Company was making parts for anti-aircraft guns and wing tips for P-38 airplanes, and the Miehle Printing Press & Manufacturing Company was making shell casing and naval ordnance.

Eventually, the WPB allocated some material to manufacture spare parts for printing equipment, but between 1943 and 1945 the printing machinery industry nearly quadrupled its pre-war output—and more than 80 percent was for the war effort. The WPB later reported, "No other segment of the metal-working industry showed a higher degree of conversion to war work." According to the Board, 22 printing machinery manufacturers were awarded the Army-Navy "E" for production excellence, including every manufacturer of printing presses.

Xerography. In 1938, Chester F. Carlson, a patent attorney in New York with a degree in physics, invented a process for transferring images he called "electrophotography." The Battelle Memorial Institute, a nonprofit research organization, and the Haloid Co., a producer of photo supplies founded in 1906, later renamed the process "xerography." In 1961, Haloid became the Xerox Corporation. Xerography began replacing job presses for many printing functions in the 1970s.

The printing machinery industry began undergoing tremendous change in the 1970s as computer technology replaced or significantly changed the type of machinery used by the printing trades. This included developments in photo typesetting and photocomposition, and greater automation of traditional printing press operations.

With the development of photo typesetting, photocomposition, and non-impact printing, the printing trades were evolving from a craft to a high-technology industry. Consequently, the printing machinery industry evolved as well. In the early 1990s, there was still a need for the massive presses that dominated the industry and the equipment necessary to run them. However, just as Linotypes gave way to computer typesetters, industry leaders were predicting that non-impact printing would someday replace the huge presses. In 1992, AM International Inc., a Chicago-based manufacturer of printing machinery, unveiled the Electrobook Press, a non-impact press based on electrostatic imaging. The Electrobook Press was developed jointly by AM International, publisher McGraw-Hill, Inc., and commercial printer R.R. Donnelly & Sons. McGraw-Hill expected to use the new press to publish customized textbooks for university professors.

INDUSTRY LEADERS

Rockwell International Corp. of Costa Mesa, California, led the industry with sales of almost $6.8 billion for its fiscal year ended September 30, 1998. New York City-based Volt Information Sciences Inc. placed second in the industry with sales of more than $2.1 billion for its fiscal year ended October 29, 1999. RICOH Corp. followed with sales of $1.6 billion for its fiscal year ended March 31,1998. General Binding Corp. of Northbrook, Illinois, generated 1998 sales of more than $922.0 million. Rounding out the top 5 industry leaders was Goss Graphic Systems Inc. of Westmont, Illinois, with sales of $769.0 for its fiscal year ended September 30, 1998.

In January 2000, Goss supplied Phoenix Newspapers with a 22-unit Universal press. The publisher, which also prints the 475,000-daily-circulation *Arizona Republic,* deemed it the best press to meet the challenge of printing the national edition of the *New York Times* for regional distribution. The press won the assignment on the basis of its high-quality graphics, its ability to make 45,000 copies per hour, and its flexibility to accommodate 7 daily editions.

WORKFORCE

Employment in the printing machinery industry remained near 22,000 in 1995, close to 1990 employment levels. Within that time period, there were significant fluctuations, the greatest between 1990 and 1991, when the figure decreased by 23 percent from 24,000 to about 19,000. In 1995, slightly more than 50 percent of all employees in the industry were production workers, about the same as in 1990. Production workers' average hourly earnings increased from about $14 in 1990 to $15 in 1995.

FURTHER READING

Angrist, Stanley W. "The Last Yiddish Linotype." *The Wall Street Journal,* 5 March 1992.

"Phoenix Newspapers Chooses Goss to Print The New York Times." *PR Newswire,* 28 January 2000.

U.S. Census Bureau. *1995 Annual Survey of Manufactures.* Washington: GPO, 1997.

———. *1997 Economic Census.* Washington, DC: GPO, 1999. Available from http://www.census.gov/prod/ec97/97m3332e.pdf.

U.S. Department of Labor. Bureau of Labor Statistics. *Employment, Hours, and Earnings, United States, 1988-96.* Washington: GPO, 1996.

SIC 3556

FOOD PRODUCTS MACHINERY

This industry covers establishments primarily engaged in manufacturing machinery for use by the food products and beverage manufacturing industries and similar machinery for use in manufacturing animal foods. Establishments primarily engaged in manufacturing food packaging machinery are classified in **SIC 3565: Packaging Machinery;** those manufacturing industrial refrigeration machinery are classified in **SIC 3585: Air-Conditioning and Warm Air Heating Equipment and Commercial and Industrial Refrigeration Equipment.**

NAICS CODE(S)

333294 (Food Product Machinery Manufacturing)

INDUSTRY SNAPSHOT

The food products machinery industry and the processed food industry enjoy a very close relationship. This is illustrated by the presence of engineering departments within large food processing corporations. For their own specialized applications, many of which may be considered proprietary, patents may be obtained. Often, the level of this cooperation depends on the sophistication of the processing operations and the equipment required to carry out those steps.

In 1997, 587 establishments were engaged in the U.S. food processing machinery industry, employing 18,401 people and shipping almost $2.8 billion of equipment that year. The machinery industry as a whole was stable and growing in certain segments. The presence of foreign-made machinery, however, showed increase beginning in the early 1990s.

ORGANIZATION AND STRUCTURE

Food products machinery and packaging equipment were included in the same industrial code until 1987, and much of the literature and data from the 1970s and 1980s combines the two industries into one category. The 1987 classification split the two types of businesses into separate categories, recognizing that the industries were serving divergent business niches.

According to a United Nations report, the industrial production of food processing machinery in North America was characterized by the following features: (1) a still large, but declining, part of manufacturing takes place in small and medium sized independent firms; (2) production is usually based on orders received; (3) the markets for many types of machines are restricted; (4) equipment production is heterogeneous; (5) production series are relatively small; (6) concentration similar to that in food industries is taking place; and (7) internationalization is accelerating. In the United States, over 500 establishments shipped processing equipment, which had total value of nearly $2.8 billion in 1997. The smaller, specialized equipment manufacturers produced nearly 80 percent of all food processing equipment in the United States, while the 12 largest companies in the industry supplied the remaining 20 percent.

CURRENT CONDITIONS

The American trend toward healthier food consumption patterns has had a direct impact on this industry. For example, demand for lower fat meats such as poultry and seafood increased, while annual per capita beef consumption dropped significantly. Likewise, changing demographics radically effected the entire food industry. The most significant demographic change that influenced the food industry in the early 1980s was the increasing number of women in the work force. Double income families have

driven consumer demand for foods that can be prepared quickly and easily. However, U.S. Department of Commerce studies show that the number of women joining the work force showed a moderate decline in the early 1990s. As a result, sales of at-home food products improved.

The steadily growing economy of the 1990s provided optimistic news for the food and beverage industry in general. Even during the recession of the late 1980s and early 1990s, the food industries did not suffer heavy losses. Price stability—a direct impact of the recession on the cost side of the industry—provided constant prices for consumers and steady wages for employees. The wage increases across the food industry were comparable to inflation, at about 5 percent. As long as food stocks such as agricultural commodities and meat production remain strong, the entire food industry is expected to remain healthy.

In developed countries, demographic trends determine the focus of the food industry. According to a UN report, longer lives, earlier marriages, more divorces, and fewer children are giving rise to new population patterns, where more one- and two-person households are establishing new consumer patterns, such as eating out more often. A new structure in age distribution—more people in the over 60 group—leads to new demand patterns, as the requirements from aged people differ from those of younger individuals. For example, elderly people eat smaller portions but need a higher concentration of essential proteins and vitamins in those portions. Market forecasters are keenly aware of this trend as the baby boomer generation reaches middle age and develops altered consumption patterns.

The increasing number of women in the work force is perhaps the most important of the demographic trends affecting the industry, as women have been the traditional food preparers in the family unit. Working women have less time to fix meals for their families and consequently purchase food that requires little preparation. The effects of this trend can be seen especially in meat processing, where secondary operations are employed in response to consumer eating habits. Both the processing and packaging industries have been influenced by the trend because meats in the fresh chilled form, already marinated, skinned, and sectioned, are growing in availability. There is also an increasing variety of frozen foods available.

Technological home innovations, such as microwave ovens, have also led to new consumption patterns. These differences directly influenced the development and design of food processing equipment, especially where secondary operations may be employed.

INDUSTRY LEADERS

In 1997, the highest concentration of shipments originated from California's 85 food processing machinery establishments. California' s shipments, valued at $243.4 million, represented about 9 percent of the nation's total shipments. Illinois' 40 establishments shipped $370.4 million worth of equipment, claiming 13 percent of the nation's total shipments. Ohio, which had 77 establishments engaged in this industry, controlled a 10.6 percent share of the market with $298.3 million in shipments.

In 1998, Premark International Inc., located in Deerfield, Illinois, was the industry leader with sales of $2.73 billion and a work force of 19,300. Now a subsidiary of Illinois Tool Works, Premark manufactured commercial kitchen equipment, which was sold under its Hobart brand name. Premark is a relatively new company; it was created in 1986 after the failed Dart & Kraft merger. Kraft, feeling that its earnings were being stifled by the Dart interests, returned alone to its primary concern, food products. The Dart companies formed Premark, which consisted of Tupperware products, Ralph Wilson Plastics, and West Bend. Premark also obtained Hobart, which was acquired by the Dart & Kraft group. The Tupperware operation lost $57.9 million for Premark in its first year and continued to lose money until 1994, when demand for Tupperware in Europe and Latin America increased. In 1992, Premark announced it would close the Tennessee factory that makes Tupperware products and, in 1996, sold its Tupperware division as part of an extensive re-engineering plan.

The Hobart line was the core of Premark's food equipment group. Hobart was acquired by Dart & Kraft in 1981 after a hostile takeover attempt by Canadian Pacific Enterprises failed. Canadian Pacific offered a reported $300 million for Hobart's operations, but Hobart, preferring independence, declined. Congressmen supported Hobart and appealed to U.S. Treasury Secretary Donald Regan to prohibit the takeover on grounds of breaching national security. Hobart finally sold out to Dart & Kraft for $460 million, having realized it probably did not have the strength to battle future takeover attempts alone.

Americans' changing lifestyles and eating habits boosted Premark's food equipment sales. Fast food menus began changing in the mid-1980s and required new equipment—such as catalytic chicken fryers and grooved griddles for fajitas. Take-home foods, such as bakery products from grocery stores, were more readily available for consumers as 2,500 in-store bakeries were built in 1987. These bakeries generally cost $130,000 to equip with the necessary machinery, although some cost as much as $300,000. International lifestyles and eating habits were changing too, as the English started eating more pizza, and the Japanese started eating more hamburgers. Improved sales of these foods helped the food equipment group to contribute $57.8 million to Premark's profits.

WORKFORCE

While the industry's stock of machinery and equipment grew in the late 1980s and early 1990s, the number of production worker man-hours has decreased steadily. Increased competition from imports were a motivating force, as was consumer demand for a broader range of food products. Of the industry's 18,401 employees, over 60 percent were production workers in 1997. On average, these production workers earned $15.65 per hour during a 37 hour work week.

As previously mentioned, the employment outlook for the industry is expected to decrease in the twenty-first century. Significant staff reductions of greater than 17 percent are expected in occupations such as machine builders, assemblers, secretaries, precision inspectors, welding machine setters, and machine assemblers. Increases of greater than 10 percent are expected for sales workers, production managers, machinery mechanics, and engineers.

FURTHER READING

Bohman, Jim. ''Hobart Corp: Oakwood Resident to Head U.S. Group.'' *Dayton Daily News,* 20 August 1996.

Darnay, Arsen J., ed. *Manufacturing USA.* 5th ed. Detroit: Gale Research, 1996.

Dempsey, Dale. ''Business: PMI to Cut 301 Workers at Troy Plant.'' *Dayton Daily News,* 12 June 1996.

''Premark International Inc.'' *Chicago Tribune,* 2 June 1996.

U.S. Census Bureau. Available from http://www.census.gov. October 1999.

SIC 3559

SPECIAL INDUSTRY MACHINERY, NOT ELSEWHERE CLASSIFIED

This classification covers establishments primarily engaged in manufacturing special industry machinery, not elsewhere classified, such as equipment for smelting and refining, cement making, clay working, glass making, incandescent lamp making, leather working, paint making, printed circuit boards, semiconductors, rubber working, cigar and cigarette making, tobacco working, shoe making, stone working machinery, industrial sewing machines, and automotive maintenance machinery and equipment. In the past, cotton ginning machinery was also included. Under the new NAICS codes, farm equipment and machinery (**SIC 3523**) is included in this classification. Cotton ginning machines are not included in that subclassificiation; this issue will be rectified by 2002 when the SIC-to-NAICS conversion is expected to be complete.

NAICS CODE(S)

333220 (Rubber and Plastics Industry Machinery Manufacturing)

333319 (Other Commercial and Service Industry Machinery Manufacturing)

333295 (Semiconductor Manufacturing Machinery)

INDUSTRY SNAPSHOT

As of the late 1990s, the special industry machinery, not elsewhere classified classification was comprised of companies that manufactured a wide variety of miscellaneous machines used to produce goods in other industries. Numerous product offerings ranged from broom making contraptions to zipper makers, although semiconductor manufacturing equipment accounted for the largest portion of the classification's output.

Employment figures peaked for this industry at 103,500 in 1996. They fell about 5 percent the following year, but then began rising slowly. Estimated 1999 employment figures stood at around 99,700. The total value of shipments for establishments was estimated at $23.4 billion in 1999, a figure that was expected to rise to $24.8 billion in 2000. The leading states in industry employment, according to figures from the 1990s, were California, Ohio, Michigan and Massachusetts, accounting for about 39 percent of total employment. The total cost of materials, services, fuels, and energy used by establishments in this category was estimated at $10.5 billion in 1999.

The number and production volume of machines classified in this industry increased substantially during the industrial revolution, particularly after World War II. By the early 1980s, about $5.0 billion in annual U.S. machinery sales were attributed to this SIC. Although overall U.S. industrial machinery sales growth slowed during the 1980s, a surging demand for high-tech semiconductor manufacturing equipment doubled industry revenues to about $10.0 billion in 1989.

While a U.S. recession in the late 1980s and early 1990s depressed many industrial machinery segments, semiconductor machine sales continued to grow. Renewed U.S. competitiveness in high-tech equipment manufacturing allowed domestic competitors to thwart their Japanese rivals. In addition, increased semiconductor demand from industries such as telecommunications augmented growth. Output expanded throughout the mid- to late-1990s, though the cyclical nature of the industry did drive output down in 1997.

Despite being affected by business cycles in the chip making industry, the long-term prospects for semiconductor equipment manufacturing appeared strong. In the mid- to late-1990s, there were several powerful trends behind the growing demand for silicon wafer fabrication systems. A global increase in PC sales drove increased demand for semiconductors of all kinds, plus new chips being produced required more memory. For example, Intel's first Pentium chip required at least 16 megabytes of memory, almost double that of 486-based PCs. Also, the rapid growth of telecommunications and the use of electronics in automobiles increased semiconductor sales. The lightning-fast changes in the computer industry have rendered the first Pentium chip something of a dinosaur even to casual computer users, and there seems to be little evidence that changes will not continue on their rapid course.

ORGANIZATION AND STRUCTURE

The special industry machinery industry encompassed a plethora of devices as of the late-1990s, including: tire retreading machinery, stone tumblers, tile making equipment, automotive frame straighteners, lumber drying kilns, cork cutters, brick makers, shoe repair equipment, leather-working devices, and plastic molding machines.

Semiconductor manufacturing equipment was the leading segment in this industry, and it saw spectacular growth in the 1990s. For example, in 1987, shipments from this segment were valued at just $1.01 billion, but by 1992 had more than doubled to $2.27 billion, or 21.6 percent of the total industry's output. By 1995, that total had ballooned even more, reaching $6.80 billion, and the latest figures from the U.S. Census Bureau list the value of shipments in 1997 at $11.20 billion.

Other groups that fell onto this category include plastics and rubber industry manufacturing (with 1997 shipments valued at $3.8 billion); power boiler and heat exchange manufacturing (with 1997 shipments valued at $3.8 billion); other commercial and service industry machinery (with 1997 value of shipments listed at $9.3 billion); and all other industrial machinery (with 1997 shipments valued at $8.7 billion).

Semiconductor equipment was expected to remain the largest and fastest growing sector of the industry throughout the 1990s. As of the mid-1990s, semiconductor production involved a sequence of more than 200 steps using numerous machines. Although the manufacturing process varies depending on the type of chip produced, four basic functions are typically performed to complete a semiconductor wafer, or circuit: 1) deposition of thin film on the (usually silicon) wafer; 2) impurity doping, when selected impurities are introduced that controlled conductivity; 3) lithographic patterning, which determines the geometric features and layout of the circuit; and 4) etching, which removes coating material to reveal the structure patterned in the lithographic process. These steps are repeated sequentially until the semiconductor wafer is complete. After the semiconductor is created using "front-end" fabrication equipment, "back-end" machines are used to test and assemble the chips. Back-end devices include three categories of machines: material handling, process diagnostics and testing, and assembly.

Semiconductor Equipment Markets. According to the U.S. Census Bureau, the equipment market for semiconductor manufacturing equipment is divided into four categories: wafer processing equipment, assembly and packaging equipment, parts for semiconductor manufacturing equipment, and all other equipment.

The wafer manufacturing category is the largest, accounting for 60 percent of product shipment values. The product categories included thin layer deposition equipment, which accounted for over $1.0 billion in product shipments in 1997; etch and strip equipment ($658 million); microlithography ($430 million); ion implantation ($867.5 million); and other wafer processing equipment ($1.9 billion).

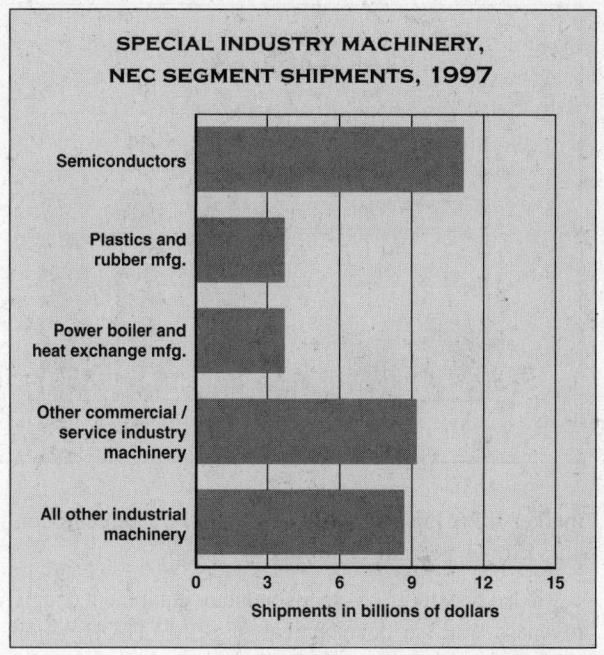

SPECIAL INDUSTRY MACHINERY, NEC SEGMENT SHIPMENTS, 1997

BACKGROUND AND DEVELOPMENT

The history of miscellaneous special industry machinery varied by product group. One of the earliest and most renowned machines in this industry was the cotton gin, which Eli Whitney invented in 1793. The gin removed seed from cotton by pulling the fiber through a set of wire teeth mounted on a revolving cylinder. Because the device could be powered by man, animal, or water, it received immediate and widespread acceptance and made cotton a staple of nineteenth century southern life.

The development and widespread dissemination of electric power during the late-nineteenth and early-twentieth century resulted in the introduction of a multitude of machinery for miscellaneous industries. Likewise, postwar U.S. economic expansion propelled product introductions and sales throughout the mid-1900s. A pivotal breakthrough was Bell Laboratories' introduction in 1947 of the solid-state transistor, which utilized semiconductors. By the 1960s a market for semiconductor manufacturing equipment began to emerge.

Spurred by important chip advances such as Intel Corporation's 1971 introduction of the memory integrated circuit, U.S. producers took the early lead in producing semiconductor manufacturing equipment. The mass production of chips allowed by these high-tech machines resulted in dramatic semiconductor price reductions. As a result, the demand for chips surged as semiconductors were integrated into all types of electronic consumer and business devices. Importantly, the use of semiconductors in personal computers caused chip manufacturing equipment sales to balloon during much of the 1980s.

The 1980s. Although domestic manufacturers took the early lead, Japanese semiconductor machinery makers successfully captured much of the global market during the 1980s. The Japanese particularly excelled at delivering equipment for high-volume commodity chips. To combat Japanese strengths, U.S. semiconductor producers restructured, increased their manufacturing efficiency, and concentrated on developing new technologies during the mid-1980s. As the U.S. chip industry made a transition from commodity to proprietary chip production, it ceded a 45 percent share of the global semiconductor equipment market to Japanese producers.

Despite a loss of market share, chip machinery makers increased sales substantially during the 1980s. However, most other special industry machinery producers suffered. Capital spending on new equipment by other industries declined or grew at a slow pace in comparison to pre-1980 expenditures. Spending on new equipment by the transportation industry stagnated, for example, as did equipment purchases by the important petroleum and coal sector. Nevertheless, growth of semiconductor equipment demand helped double industry revenues to more than $10 billion by 1990.

The 1990s. Strategies adopted by U.S. semiconductor manufacturers in the 1980s began to pay off in the early 1990s. Aided by a weak dollar and a recession in Japan, U.S. producers boosted revenues to $5.8 billion in 1991. Although sales dropped 3 percent in 1992, shipments climbed an impressive 18 percent in 1993 to about $6.0 billion. Assisted by a technological lead in growing product segments and new-found productivity, U.S. manufacturers were able to recover a 4 percent share of the global

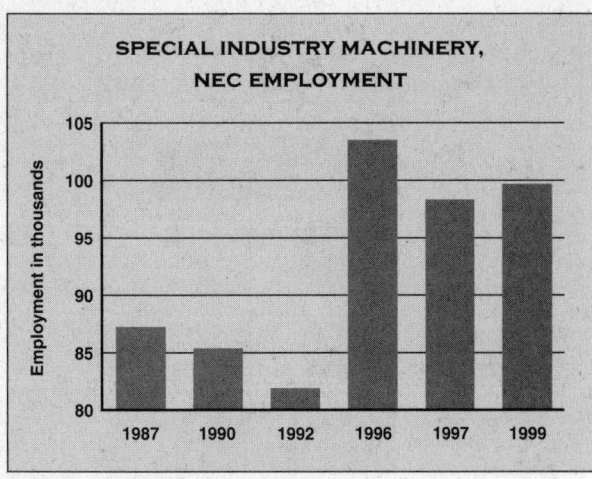

SPECIAL INDUSTRY MACHINERY,
NEC EMPLOYMENT

market from Japan. In 1993 they held 51 percent, compared to 41 percent controlled by Japan.

Also boosting U.S. semiconductor equipment competitiveness was the development of SEMATECH, a joint private sector/government funded research and development consortium. SEMATECH was formed in 1987 to combat increasingly competitive Japanese semiconductor producers. In addition, industry participants on both sides of the Pacific benefited from technology exchanges and partnerships with foreign and domestic competitors. Indeed, U.S. firms learned from the Japanese that traditional methods of developing and producing manufacturing technology in isolation from competitors were no longer feasible. While government funding for SEMATECH was reduced sharply in the mid-1990s, the organization restructured, increased dues, and remained a viable organization.

CURRENT CONDITIONS

Front-end equipment sales led industry growth going into the mid-1990s. Most importantly, shipments of deposition equipment rose 17 percent in 1993. U.S. producers held the lead in deposition technology, and benefited from a proliferating trend toward smaller, more integrated chips that required more complex deposition. A shift toward the production of high-profit, application-specific, integrated circuits (ASIC) also boosted sales of U.S. front-end manufacturing devices. In contrast, sales of lithographic machinery, of which the U.S. supplied only a 16 percent global share in 1993, plummeted in the early 1990s.

Back-end equipment sales also rose at a steady clip. Global shipments of test equipment gained 14 percent in 1993, and sales of material handling and diagnostic machines increased about 13 percent. Production of assembly devices, of which the U.S. made 30 percent globally, jumped 15 percent.

The market for semiconductors has traditionally been very cyclical, and as a result the market for semicon-

ductor equipment is cyclical as well. For example, in 1994 and 1995, semiconductor equipment firms enjoyed a booming market. A study conducted by VLSI Research on the 10 largest global semiconductor equipment suppliers showed that they sold $14.2 billion of equipment in 1995, a 74.4 increase over their net sales for 1994. However, in 1996 this strong growth rate slowed to 12 percent and semiconductor manufacturing equipment suppliers such as Applied Materials Inc., Lam Research Corp., and Varian Associates Inc. cut back on production and laid off workers. Conditions worsened in 1997 and 1998, but the industry turned around in 1999.

Some industry observers had predicted an upsurge in sales of semiconductor manufacturing equipment during 1997 due to a major change in the manufacturing process for dynamic random access memory (DRAM) chips. As manufacturers moved to produce higher memory chips (for example, from 16MB DRAM to 64MB DRAM), it was expected that they would change from using 200 mm wafers to 300 mm wafers. This would have created the need for a major retooling of manufacturing capacity. However, release of the 300 mm chip was delayed when industry changes made it impossible to make the 300 mm chip available in 1998 or even 1999.

Overall global semiconductor industry sales reached an all-time high of $149.0 billion, up nearly 19 percent from the previous year. Experts in the industry expected sales to rise even more in 2000, given the growing demand.

Markets for other kinds of equipment in this industry were down in 1996. For example, total shipments of domestically produced plastic injection molding machinery decreased by about 15 percent in 1996 after strong growth in 1995. Capital investment in equipment was expected to decline throughout all of 1996 due to the decline in injection molding resin sales.

INDUSTRY LEADERS

Over 2,000 companies participated in the special industry machinery industry in the 1990s. Semiconductor equipment manufacturers dominated the top spots. The top U.S. companies in 1999 included Applied Materials, with sales of $5.5 billion; Teradyne, with sales of $1.2 billion; KLA-Tencor, with $1.1 billion in sales; and Advantest, with sales of $955.0 million.

WORKFORCE

Despite expectations of healthy growth in production, employment in the special industry machinery business was relatively static in the late 1990s. After employment figures peaked at 103,500 in 1996, they fell about 5 percent the following year. Since then they have been rising slowly; 1999 estimates stood at around 99,700. When this industry's production more than doubled in the 1980s, the work force grew by only about 10 percent, and in the 1990s the work force grew hardly at all while the value of shipments continued to rise. Continued restructuring and the movement of some manufacturing activities to low-cost countries were expected to curtail increases in U.S. employment.

AMERICA AND THE WORLD

Of the top 10 semiconductor equipment manufacturers in 1999, four were based in the United States, five in Japan, and one in the Netherlands. The rivalry between the United States and Japan has continued, but a growing level of cooperation, spurred in part by market softness in 1997 and 1998, has obviously been viewed as beneficial by all parties, as illustrated by the change in membership at SEMATECH (see below).

RESEARCH AND TECHNOLOGY

Semiconductor equipment manufacturers were heavily dependent upon research and technology to sustain competitiveness. Applied Materials, for example, injected about 10 percent of its total revenues into capital investments in the early 1990s. For comparison, the average capital investment for all U.S. manufacturers was closer to 4 percent of gross sales. In contrast, capital spending by other firms in the special industry machinery industry were much lower than even the national average.

U.S. semiconductor machinery makers invested heavily in productivity, quality, customer service programs, and new plants and equipment during the 1980s and 1990s. Most importantly, though, research and development outlays allowed them to sharpen their competitive edge in the development of high-tech, value-added machinery. They especially advanced in the fast-growing market for chemical and physical vapor deposition equipment, which was expected to lead industry growth throughout the mid-1990s. They also stretched their lead in automatic test equipment technology.

In the latter half of the 1990s, development efforts were expected to emphasize, among other technologies, machinery for advanced multichip modules, which mounted multiple integrated circuits on one unit. The Advanced Research Projects Agency (ARPA), a high-tech consortium, already provided funding for this research in the early 1990s. Equipment for manufacturing liquid crystal displays (LCDs) should also be a priority. LCDs were used for flat-panel displays on portable computers, and were manufactured using a process similar to that used to make chips. The U.S. Display Consortium, which included ARPA and several equipment and display providers, was formed in 1993 to further LCD manufacturing technology.

While its government funding was reduced dramatically in the mid-1990s, Sematech continued to be an important force for research and development in the semiconductor equipment manufacturing industry in the late 1990s. In response to the cuts in government funding, SEMATECH members raised their dues and cut back on staffing to keep the group viable. The group launched International SEMATECH in April 1998, which included the 10 U.S. companies, plus two from Asia and three from Europe. According to SEMATECH president and CEO Mark Melliar-Smith, "Precompetitive cooperation has proven to be a cost-effective way to share the risks of semiconductor manufacturing research. Because of the growing financial burden and increasing complexity of this research, sharing resources internationally is the best way to address it."

FURTHER READING

Banks, Howard. "Made in the U.S.A." Forbes, 11 September 1995, 37.

Barrett, Larry. "Reversal of Fortunes Not Likely Anytime Soon for Chip Makers." The Business Journal, 30 December 1996, 16.

Darnay, Arsen J., ed. Manufacturing USA. 6th ed. Detroit: The Gale Group, 1999.

"Equipment Makers Chase Mercosur Outlets." ChemicalWeek, 12 March 1997, S14.

Morris, Kathleen. "The Alpha Principle: No Guts, No Glory. That's How Applied Materials Plays the Game. Take Notes." Financial World, 21 November 1995, 30.

Jareaux, Robin. "Winning Through Cooperation: An Interview with William Spencer." Technology Review, January 1997, 22.

Pollack, Andrew. "Japan Aims to Regain Semiconductor Leadership." New York Times, 18 November 1996, C1.

SEMATECH 1998 Annual Report. Available at http://www.sematech.org.

Semiconductor Capital Equipment Industry Report. New York: PaineWebber Inc., 21 January 1997.

VLSI Research, "1999 Top Ten Equipment Suppliers to the Semiconductor Industry." February 11, 2000. Available at http://www.semiconductoronline.com.

Wood, Bill. "Machinery Demand Will Shrink in 1996." Plastics World, December 1995, 73.

SIC 3561

PUMPS AND PUMPING EQUIPMENT

This category covers firms primarily engaged in manufacturing pumps and related equipment for general industrial, commercial or household use, including domestic water and sump pump manufacturers. It does not cover manufacturers of fluid power pumps or motors (**SIC 3594: Fluid Power Pumps & Motors**); manufacturers of measuring and dispensing pumps for gasoline service stations (**SIC 3586: Measuring and Dispensing Pumps**); non-laboratory-use vacuum pumps (**SIC 3563: Air and Gas Compressors**); laboratory vacuum pumps (**SIC 3821: Laboratory Apparatus and Furniture**); or motor vehicle pumps (**SIC 3714: Motor Vehicle Parts and Accessories**).

NAICS CODE(S)

333911 (Pump and Pumping Equipment Manufacturing)

INDUSTRY SNAPSHOT

Because pumps are one of the most common machines used by industry, second only to electric motors, the health of the pump manufacturing industry depends to a great extent on the general health of industrial America. Particularly important are the petrochemical and the pulp and paper industries, but steel making, electric power generation, sewage system construction, general housing and commercial construction, and oil and gas wells, fields, and pipelines also depend on special purpose pumps.

Such pumps, which can be abrasive by nature themselves, often wear quickly because they frequently move materials contaminated with abrasives in challenging climates and environments. This requires frequent replacement or repair, making the replacement parts segment of the industry particularly important. The U.S. pump industry is considered mature, and the bulk of growth is expected to be tied to replacement purchases.

ORGANIZATION AND STRUCTURE

Some 613 establishments manufactured pumps and pump equipment in 1977, an increase of 10 percent over the 1972 census figures. However, this number dropped to 528 by 1987 and an administrative redistribution of SIC codes left the industry with only 405 establishments at the end of 1987. The other 123 establishments were reclassified into **SIC 3594: Fluid Power Pumps and Motors.** The 1990s saw a small rally in the industry, though, and 489 establishments existed by 1997.

At 55 percent of output, industrial pumps constituted the largest product class in the business in 1997. Replacement parts and accessories generated the next-largest share of sales, at about 19 percent, followed by domestic water systems and sump pump (9 percent) and oil and oil field pumps (7 percent). Other miscellaneous pumps made up the remaining 10 percent.

Historically, manufacturing in this industry has been heavily concentrated; in 1977 more than half the industry's employees worked in the four largest facilities, and 79 percent of all facilities employed fewer than 100 workers. By 1987 this had changed slightly with 75 percent of all facilities employing fewer than 100 work-

ers, but diffusion was more evident in the larger firms. The 1987 Census showed the largest 41 firms employing 52.6 percent of all workers. In 1997 about half of the industry's establishments had at least 20 employees, and 20 percent had at least 100 employees.

BACKGROUND AND DEVELOPMENT

The world's first pump was probably the force or air pump built by Ktesibios of Alexandria about 270 B.C. He used a cylinder and plunger arrangement to pump air through pipes of various lengths, creating the first water organ. The water was used to maintain a steady air pressure in the system. Simple pumps became common fairly quickly for domestic use and as fire extinguishers. Roman ruins yield examples of pumps used for fire control and for lifting water in wells. The famed Roman aqueducts were probably not fed with pumps, but rather used water wheels to lift water from reservoirs directly to the piping system.

A major advancement in pumping technology came in 1698 with the issuing of a British patent to Thomas Savery for a steam powered pump for use in coal mines. The device was later adapted to provide water to some country houses. This pump was effectively replaced by the Newcomen engine, patented in 1712, which placed the steam boilers and piston assembly at the top of the mine shaft instead of at the bottom. The concept introduced the now familiar working or balance beam to transfer power to the pump mechanism in the mine.

The industrial revolution found many uses for the powered pump, including industrial processing and domestic distribution of water. However, the twentieth century introduced a new refinement, electrification. The first American factory to replace its central steam plant and its maze-like system of pulleys and belts with electric motors was a cotton mill in 1894. All new factories used the new technology.

Economic and technological expansion in the 1960s stimulated pump production and encouraged the adoption of new manufacturing techniques. The industry adopted specially designed milling machines and combination machines that could perform milling, radial drilling, and facing (smoothing) in one operation. Automatic tool changing devices, operated by numerical control tape programs, increased production efficiency.

In general the pump industry manufactures large specialty items to meet a client's specific needs. To accommodate such a need for flexibility, the industry quickly adopted numerically controlled machine tools and computer numerical controls. This shifted the center of production control to the firm's engineering department and away from the craftsmen on the shop floor. Computer assisted drafting and modeling programs have further increased design efficiency.

The general industrial slowdown of the 1980s hit the pump industry hard. Major clients such as the nuclear power industry, the oil well and pipeline industry, and the construction industry cut back on orders for new equipment and idled existing components. A strong U.S. dollar made American products uncompetitive in foreign markets.

By 1988 this began to change. A weakening dollar increased exports and a general pickup in the manufacturing climate sparked new domestic orders in almost all sectors. The industry continued to modernize production by consolidating facilities and adopting sophisticated CAD/CAM systems and metalworking and casting technologies. New materials and designs were explored to extend the life of components in corrosive environments and to increase reliability.

The most important markets served by the pump industry have been the steel, oil, construction, and chemical industries.

Steel mills and blast furnaces used industrial pumps to move liquid fuels and water for coolant. The move in the steel industry away from open-hearth furnaces to oxygen and electric furnaces and to continuous casting instead of slabbing mills necessitated larger, more powerful pumps to provide higher volumes of coolant water. This meant the development of higher-output centrifugal pumps.

The oil well and pipeline industries also purchased a large number of pumps. Demand in this sector dropped off dramatically in the 1960s but recovered after that. This industry bought reciprocal pumps for mud circulation, submersible centrifugal units for lifting crude oil, and standard centrifugal pumps to maintain pressure with water flooding. Pipelines required high-horsepower centrifugal pumps. In the 1960s the average pipeline diameter was enlarged by 33 percent, requiring much larger pumps to move the higher volumes of petroleum products.

The construction industry used centrifugal pumps and trash pumps, which could accommodate up to 25 percent small solids in the pumped liquid. New sewage plant construction to accommodate increasingly stringent environmental regulations was expected to increase the demand for pumps. Infrastructure replacement and upgrading was expected to do the same through the end of the twentieth century and into the 2000s.

Another important user of pumps was the chemical industry. Pumps for this market used special materials such as fiberglass, plastics, and stainless steel to accommodate salt solutions, acids, and chlorine.

CURRENT CONDITIONS

The U.S. Census Bureau reported that in 1997 this industry shipped $6.8 billion worth of goods, spent $3.4

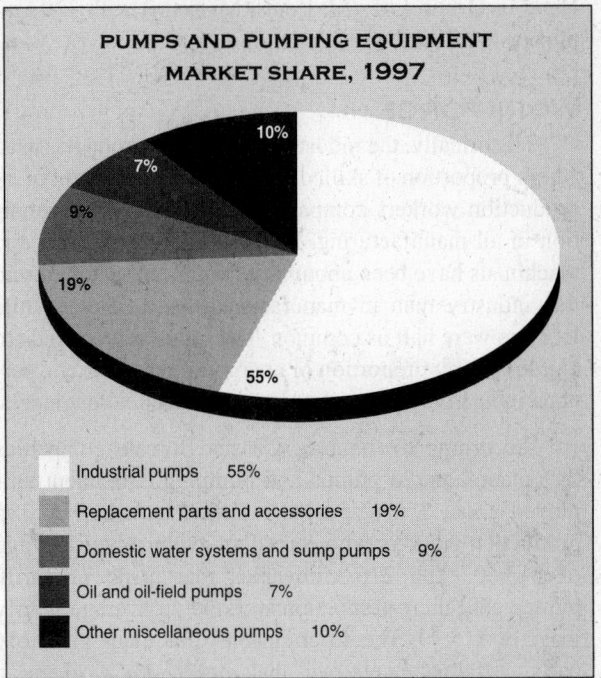

PUMPS AND PUMPING EQUIPMENT MARKET SHARE, 1997

10%
7%
9%
19%
55%

- Industrial pumps   55%
- Replacement parts and accessories   19%
- Domestic water systems and sump pumps   9%
- Oil and oil-field pumps   7%
- Other miscellaneous pumps   10%

billion on materials, and invested $190 million in capital expenditures. The 216 establishments that made primarily pumps shipped $5.5 billion worth of merchandise. The 43 companies that made primarily parts and attachments shipped $964 million worth of merchandise. Texas, California, Illinois, Ohio, Oklahoma, and Florida had the highest concentrations of establishments in this category.

The pumps and pumping equipment industry remains closely linked to the state of American industry in general. Focus in the 21st century will be on producing technologically advanced, highly customized pumps and equipment.

INDUSTRY LEADERS

Of companies whose primary products were in this classification, Dover Resources Inc. (a subsidiary of Dover Corp. based in Tulsa, Oklahoma) had 3,600 employees and estimated sales of $3.9 billion in 1998. Ingersoll-Dresser Pump Co. (Liberty Corner, New Jersey) had 6,000 employees and estimated sales of $800 million. Goulds Pumps Inc. (a subsidiary of ITT Industries Inc. based in Seneca Falls, New York) had 5,250 employees and sales of $774 million. Commercial Intertech Corp. (Youngstown, Ohio) had 3,904 employees and sales of $576 million. BW/IP Inc. (Long Beach, California) had 3002 employees and sales of $492 million.

Diversified companies also competing in this category included Orion Research Inc. (a subsidiary of Thermo Electron Corp. based in Beverly, Massachusetts) with 20,000 employees and sales of $3 billion; and

Harbour Group Ltd. (St. Louis, Missouri) with 300 employees and sales of $750 million.

WORKFORCE

Historically, the industrial machinery group has used a high proportion of skilled trades, about 30 percent of all production workers compared to the 26 percent proportion in all manufacturing. Metal working craftsmen and machinists have been about three times more common in this industry than in manufacturing as a whole, while laborers were half as common. The industry also tends to employ a high proportion of nonproduction workers, perhaps indicative of its reliance on mechanical engineers.

According to the U.S. Census Bureau, companies that manufactured pumps and pumping equipment employed about 37,042 people in 1997, including 21,335 production workers who earned an average hourly wage of $15.60. The 216 companies that made primarily pumps paid their production workers an average hourly wage of $15.39. The 43 companies that made primarily parts and attachments paid their production workers an average hourly wage of $17.02.

AMERICA AND THE WORLD

Pumps and pumping equipment were manufactured to international standards, allowing American manufacturers to compete in the international market. These same standards, however, also made the United States vulnerable to foreign competition, particularly with regard to price and quality. During the early half of the 1980s, the strong American dollar made such competition particularly difficult, undermining an already weak industrial climate in American manufacturing. As a result, the U.S. merchandise trade deficit quadrupled between 1982 and 1984, reaching $145 billion. This effect showed up in the pump manufacturing industry but was delayed. In 1985 the industry showed a trade surplus, but by 1987 this had become a $1.9 billion deficit. The drop of the value of the U.S. dollar in 1985 provided new impetus for the pump industry. By 1987 the average export price expressed in foreign currency of pumps and other machinery had fallen 23.1 percent. By 1990, even though domestic prices increased an average of 5 percent each year, the foreign currency price of pumps and components had dropped more than 11 percent. This made American operations more profitable, increased export volumes, and discouraged imports. It also encouraged foreign firms to establish manufacturing and assembly facilities in the United States.

By 1990 exports approached $1.1 billion while imports exceeded $700 million. By mid-decade, *Purchasing* magazine estimated foreign purchases at 45 percent of overall demand. This share was expected to decline as companies set up overseas manufacturing operations.

Major markets for American products included Canada, Mexico, the United Kingdom, Saudi Arabia, West Germany, Venezuela, and Japan. The top importers included Japan, West Germany, Canada, and the United Kingdom. Emerging markets included Latin America, Africa, the Mideast, and Asia, especially China.

Goulds Pumps, an industry leader, was particularly focused on international sales. By 1995, 45 percent of its revenues were generated overseas, with 29 percent of its total sales coming from Europe. The company expected most of its future growth to be concentrated in the Asia-Pacific region. China appeared an especially appealing target. In 1985 Bingham-Willamette (based in Portland, Oregon) sold the country six pumps valued at $600,000 and expected to increase that to 200 pumps per year, but the business dwindled within two years. In 1998 Goulds signed a joint-venture agreement with Nanjing Deep Well Company to produce 600 pump units for four petrochemical plants, a deal worth several million dollars at each plant.

RESEARCH AND TECHNOLOGY

Most pumps are made to a client's specific requirements for use in complex applications where the failure of the pump could be disastrous. Consequently, manufacturing innovation has stressed flexibility and reliability. Major innovations included the adoption of numerical and computer control manufacturing systems and the reliance on engineering expertise, assisted by computer modeling software, to custom design components for short run production. New corrosion resistant materials have been developed and refinements to old processes adopted. Specially designed metal-forming machines were created for the industry, including combination milling, radial drilling and facing machines, variable setting grinders which automatically form tapered shafts, and automatic tool changing devices controlled by NC tapes or computer software. Foundry operations for production of pump casings and core-making have advanced with rapid-cycle machinery, synchronous fabricating machinery, and a no-bake molding process using a resin binder and catalyst. Closer tolerances were achieved in components by replacing wooden molds and cores with ceramic.

Demands for higher-efficiency pumps meant an industry shift from fixed displacement pumps to variable displacement because they do not waste energy by venting excess pumped material through a relief valve. A variable displacement pump adjusts its own flow rate to match demand.

Ongoing research concerns include noise and leakage reduction, increased efficiency, corrosion-resistance, and development of oil-free and self-lubricating models.

FURTHER READING

Darnay, Arsen J., ed. *Manufacturing USA: Industry Analyses, Statistics, and Leading Companies.* Detroit: Gale Research, 1996.

U.S. Department of Commerce, Census Bureau. *1997 Economic Census.* Washington, DC: GPO, 1999. Available from http://www.census.gov.

SIC 3562

BALL AND ROLLER BEARINGS

This industry covers establishments primarily engaged in manufacturing ball and roller bearings (including ball or roller bearing pillow block, flange, takeup cartridge, and hangar units) and parts. Establishments primarily engaged in manufacturing plain bearings are classified in **SIC 3568: Mechanical Power Transmission Equipment, Not Elsewhere Classified.**

NAICS CODE(S)

332991 (Ball and Roller Bearing Manufacturing)

INDUSTRY SNAPSHOT

The ball and roller bearing industry is very large, but mature. It affects everything from the production space shuttles to household appliances, automobiles, dentist drills, roller skates, and computer disk drives. In 1997 there were 184 establishments involved in ball and roller bearing manufacturing with a total employment of nearly 36,800.

The issues facing the bearing industry are both numerous and complex. As a secondary steel product manufacturing industry, it is in the middle of the production chain; however, policies favoring the steel industry may not be in the best interest of the bearing industry, and vice versa. Because bearings are essential components of military and civilian machinery and equipment, the federal government has historically been a major customer of the industry. Nonetheless, high labor and production costs have caused the bearing industry to lose business to foreign competitors who have been able to sell bearings of equal quality at lower prices. U.S. bearing companies have also had to contend with illegal dumping practices by foreign competitors. Found guilty of these practices, many perpetrators then turned around and either opened plants in the United States or bought plants to supply their American customers. In the late 1990s, American manufacturers were especially confronted with competition from Asian countries, most notably China.

ORGANIZATION AND STRUCTURE

The ball and roller bearing business is unusual because it is strictly a component manufacturing industry. The industry accommodates its markets by selling loose or packaged bearings; these packaged bearings are installed in races that allow manufacturers to interchange complete bearing components. The industry has continued to evolve by developing new materials and lubricants and searching for alternative uses for bearings. Bearings have been found to have almost limitless applications and are expected to be in demand as long as machines are manufactured.

Ball bearings are spherical in shape, while roller bearings are cylindrical and may be tapered on one end or flattened to resemble needles. Generally, a ball bearing is used when speed is important; a roller bearing is used more often when load is most important. The manufacture of antifriction bearings starts from rod or wire. In a typical production process, pieces of wire are cut off in a press, placed between dies, and pressed into the shape of a ball or roller. Large rollers are produced by machining turning processes. The fin of surplus material that forms in the pressing process is removed between rotating file discs, and the diameter of the bearings is reduced through grinding and tumbling processes. Roundness specifications and surface finish improvements are also attained during grinding and tumbling. The bearings are then hardened, tempered, and given a high polish by further tumbling with a polishing agent. Finally, the elements are graded according to diameter.

Ball and roller bearings are used in anything that slides, glides, or rolls and, in some cases, are as large as 15 meters in diameter. Two general classes of bearings exist: commodity and precision. Commodity bearings are used in rotating elements that have relatively low revolutions per minute and do not face extreme stresses. Precision bearings, on the other hand, are highly accurate in terms of material quality, consistency of finish and diameter, and repeatability of tolerance levels. These bearings go through rigorous tests that check internal structure for failure tendencies and measure diameters to within one-millionth of an inch. Because the bearing industry has achieved such high product standards, it is widely respected for its ability to ensure an extraordinarily high level of quality control.

The value of shipments of complete antifriction bearings and components, including balls and rollers, was $5.7 billion in 1997, representing an increase of 5 percent over 1996 shipments of $5.4 billion. The industry's product share is divided into many different categories. In 1997, the industry produced complete ball bearings valued at $2.1 billion; completed tapered roller bearing and roller bearing parts (except rollers) valued at $1.4 billion; mounted bearings (except plain) valued at $426 million;

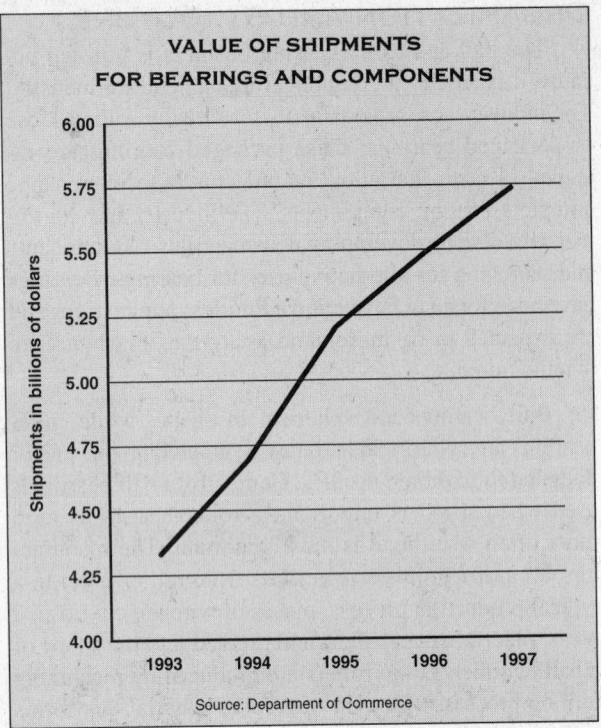

VALUE OF SHIPMENTS FOR BEARINGS AND COMPONENTS

Shipments in billions of dollars

Source: Department of Commerce

and parts and components of ball and roller bearings valued at $656 million.

The primary materials consumed by the industry include alloy steel mill shapes. Cold steel and iron forgings, however, are also widely used in the bearing industry. Other materials and devices used by the industry include raw and composite ceramics, electric motors, machine cutting tools, grinding wheels, powdered metals, copper wire, stainless steel sheets, carbon steel bars, and iron, steel, and copper scrap.

The delivered cost of materials consumed by kind by the bearing industry in 1997 was as follows: metal bolts, nuts, screws, washers, rivets, and other screw machine products were valued at $18.4 million; balls, rollers, cages, collars, races, and other anti-friction bearing components and parts were valued at $601.5 million; miscellaneous materials, component parts, containers and supplies were valued at $424.8 million; other iron and steel forgings were valued at $239 million; steel bars, bar shapes, and plates (except castings, forgings, and fabricated metal products) were valued at $186.8 million; and all other steel shapes and forms (except castings, forgings, and fabricated metal products) were valued at $182 million.

Traditionally, manufacturers of motor vehicles and their parts and accessories are the largest consumer of U.S. bearing industry output, often accounting for over 15 percent of production. The next four leading sectors for the industry are exports at about 10 percent; ball and roller bearings at about 7 percent; telephone and tele-

graph communications at about 6 percent; and blast furnaces and steel mills at about 4 percent. The mining, oil drilling, and metalworking industries are also heavy consumers of antifriction bearings. Additionally, bearings of various types and sizes are widely used in refrigeration and heating equipment, motors and generators, aircraft and related parts, and railroad equipment.

Antifriction bearings offer several advantages to machine designers. The friction placed on the bearings due to loads exerted is much lower than for other types of bearings. It is the lack of bearing friction that prevents excessive wear and abrasions on machines that start and stop while loads are applied. Automobile parts are examples of elements that benefit from less friction and wear. Roller bearings, in particular, are easily lubricated, can carry heavy loads relative to their size, and remain accurately aligned over extended periods of use. For these reasons, the huge market for antifriction bearings is stable and nearly recession proof.

BACKGROUND AND DEVELOPMENT

Since the invention of the wheel, the theory of bearing movement has been understood as a powerful phenomenon. The transfer of power to a rolling element has allowed societies to develop increasingly sophisticated structures and innovative machinery. As engines became more advanced and technology and production techniques improved, bearing manufacturing itself became a high-precision trade. Because virtually anything that rolls or spins uses bearings, the performance of the moving part is directly related to the bearing component. As such sophisticated machinery as military and commercial aircraft and nuclear-powered submarines have demanded increasingly high levels of precision and performance, bearing technology has evolved as a science and industry of its own.

Beginning in the mid-1980s and continuing through the mid-1990s, American bearing manufacturers were subjected to dumping by foreign bearing manufacturers and various tactics designed to circumvent subsequent anti-dumping regulations. Dumping is a strategy that involves selling products in foreign countries at prices lower than the cost of manufacture in the parent country. The strategy is designed to allow a manufacturer to gain market share in a foreign country by providing a product at a price that is too low for competitors to match. Eventually competitors will be forced out of business, and the foreign competitor can command much higher prices because the competition has died.

Between 1968 and 1986, market share of imported bearings in the United States rose from 30 percent to 64 percent. After experiencing significant market share losses, Timken Company and the Anti-Friction Bearing Manufacturers Association (AFBMA, now known as the

American Bearing Manufacturers Association) petitioned the Department of Commerce in 1987 to conduct an investigation of import practices.

The Trade Expansion Act of 1962 makes provisions for such investigations if the industry has been eroded to the point that it cannot compete internationally and if the nation's security is at risk. Because bearings are used in missile guidance systems, aircraft engines, tanks, and machine guns, dependence on foreign suppliers could leave production of this military equipment vulnerable. Moreover, because U.S. equipment manufacturers do not have control over the production schedules of foreign companies they could be limited in their response to a surge in production demands during a military emergency.

Timken and the AFBMA eventually prevailed and the Department of Commerce instructed U.S. Customs to collect duties on shipments of bearings and related parts from Great Britain, Sweden, Italy, France, West Germany, Japan, Romania, Singapore, and Thailand. The Defense Department supported domestic manufacturers by issuing a "buy-American" policy for all antifriction bearing purchases.

These actions resulted in a rise in bearing prices and bearing purchasers soon became incensed. Although the decision to impose duties only affected imported antifriction bearings, distributors took this as an opportunity to implement across-the-board increases. By 1989, a coalition of original equipment manufacturers called the American Manufacturers for Trade in Bearings (AMTB) took a stand against the duties on imported bearings. The AMTB represented manufacturers that collectively purchased over 200 million products annually. This amounted to two-thirds the consumption of commodity ball bearings and double the amount produced by U.S. bearing manufacturers. The AMTB claimed that domestic bearing manufacturers had been unable to meet U.S. demand for commodity ball bearings since the early 1980s and argued that the imports made up for this shortfall.

The specific bearings the AMTB was fighting for were commodity ball bearings, which have specific applications. The five most popular models in this line collectively account for more than 50 percent of the commodity bearings sold in the United States. Their primary applications are in power tools, appliances, automobiles, office equipment, and computer components. According to the director of commodities purchasing at Black & Decker, an AMTB member, only three companies in the United States were capable of producing commodity ball bearings at the time of this decision.

The legal battle between foreign and domestic bearing manufacturers continued past the 1980s. In 1990 Ingersoll-Rand, then America's leading bearing manufacturer, prevailed in convincing the U.S. International

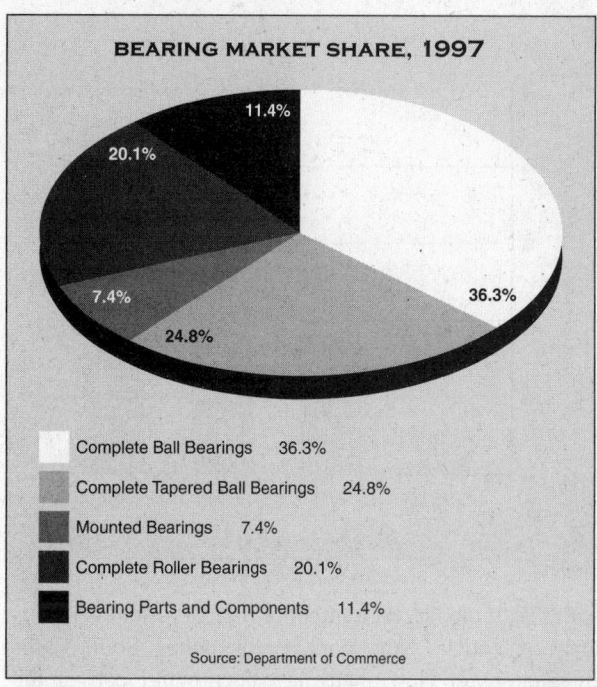

BEARING MARKET SHARE, 1997

- Complete Ball Bearings — 36.3%
- Complete Tapered Ball Bearings — 24.8%
- Mounted Bearings — 7.4%
- Complete Roller Bearings — 20.1%
- Bearing Parts and Components — 11.4%

Source: Department of Commerce

Trade Commission to raise duties on ball bearings from nine foreign nations that were selling bearings in the United States for sometimes as little as one-third of their home market price. In 1994 the Japanese bearing manufacturer NTN Corp. announced that bearing production at its U.S. subsidiary, NTN Bauer, would increase by 150 percent. Simultaneously, 50 percent of production at its Okayama factory would be shifted to its facilities in Alabama and Illinois. Production was shifted to the United States to counter dumping allegations aimed at NTN exports, which already had a dumping tariff levied against them. In the early 1990s, the United States had begun to more broadly define "cylindrical roller bearings," which were dutiable. Subsequently, in 1995, Nippon Thompson Co., Ltd. began shipping a new needle roller bearing to the United States that was specifically designed to circumvent U.S. anti-dumping duties. Needle roller bearings, which previously fell outside the boundaries of dutiable goods, had begun to be included in the new broader classification. NTN's new bearing was specifically designed to challenge this reclassification.

CURRENT CONDITIONS

In 1997 there were 184 establishments in the U.S. ball and roller bearing industry. It is predicted that this figure will increase to 197 by 2000. These establishments manufacture a diverse product line of ball bearings, roller bearings, mounted bearings and various related parts. Although there are a number of small- and medium-size establishments, the industry trend has been towards consolidation via mergers and acquisitions. Of these establishments, 89 had 100 or more employees, 40 had between 20 and 99, and 55 had 19 or fewer employees. The

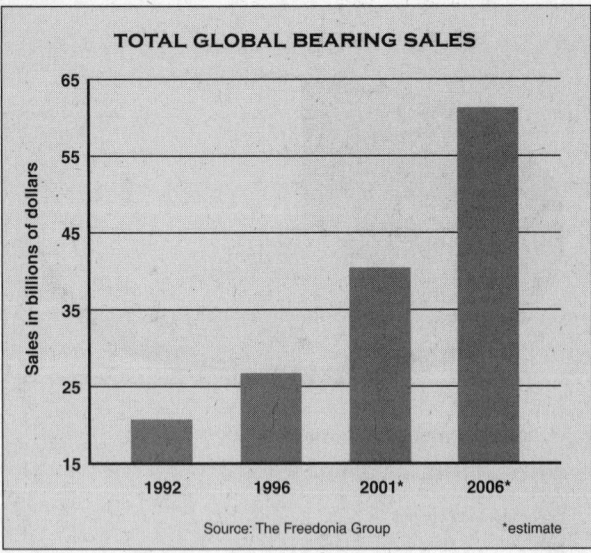

TOTAL GLOBAL BEARING SALES

Source: The Freedonia Group   *estimate

states with the largest number of industry establishments are Connecticut, New York, Pennsylvania, South Carolina, and Ohio. New plants have been built mostly in the south so as to take advantage of lower labor costs. Older plants have either been refurbished or their production capacity has been increased.

Because bearings are vital components of machinery, the industry is relatively recession proof. World ball and roller bearing production is estimated to be around $25.0 billion. According to the U.S. Department of Commerce, in 1995 the value of U.S. industry shipments was $5.2 billion. After showing a slight decline in 1996, this figure was predicted to reach $5.6 billion by 1999 and nearly $5.8 billion in 2000. An early 1999 survey of the industry by *Purchasing*, however, quotes a more optimistic forecast by the Freedonia Group which shows U.S. bearing sales of $8.3 billion in 2001 and $11.0 billion in 2006.

While industry shipments are expected to remain high some analysts predicted flat or slightly falling prices for much of 1999. "The cost increase in material, consumables, and wages can only be partially offset by productivity changes and or design changes. A modest increase in aftermarket prices for select product groups is possible in 1999. However, original equipment prices have been flat," according to David Gridley, executive director, marketing services at the Torrington Company. Laura Grondin, vice president and general manager for Hartford Bearing concurs, "Prices will either stay the same or fall by 2 to 3 percent. The industry is still extremely competitive, and it will get worse." Much of this pessimism is due to overcapacity and softening demand. "There is overcapacity domestically," Grondin concludes.

According to Gridley demand has softened in the agricultural equipment, steel, paper, oil field, and aircraft sectors. In the automotive industry, however, demand for bearings for both light and heavy trucks rose significantly, according to the U.S. Department of Commerce. Industry insiders also predicted bearing orders to be up in the overall 1999 automotive sector. "The automotive industry is booming and the demand for product has been very strong and will continue," says Grondin.

INDUSTRY LEADERS

Ingersoll-Rand has consistently led the U.S. industry in sales. Based in Woodcliff, New Jersey, Ingersoll boasted total 1997 sales of $7.1 billion, up from $6.7 billion in 1996. In 1997 the company had 46,600 employees. At its beginning in 1905, Ingersoll-Rand was primarily an engineering products firm that specialized in coal mining equipment and air compressors. By the 1960s, however, the company was searching for diversified product lines that would complement existing products. In 1968 Ingersoll-Rand entered the bearing industry through the acquisition of the Torrington Company. This placed Ingersoll-Rand in the business of making needle and roller bearings as well as knitting needles, metal-forming machines, universal joints, and roller clutches. This investment turned out to be extremely beneficial to Ingersoll-Rand, as it protected the company from the cyclical economic downturns.

Timken has been perfecting its tapered roller bearings since 1898, and, by the early 1990s, the company offered 26,000 different bearing combinations. Promoting itself as the world's largest tapered roller bearing producer, Timken attributes part of this success to international trade. After establishing a sales office in Japan in 1974 in an effort to serve Asian distributors, Timken finally made inroads with Japanese automobile manufacturers in 1987. The currency exchange rate and political climates contributed to the company's success in 1987, but the company received an important image boost, primarily by maintaining a good reputation for quality when other U.S. goods were perceived as being inferior to Japanese products. While price competitiveness was not possible, technical expertise from Timken's side won praise from Japanese design engineers who started specifying tapered roller bearings for their products. With patience and expertise, Timken started supplying Nissan Motor Company and Mazda Motor Corporation with wheel bearings. Generally about 20 percent of Timken's sales comes from the export market and bearings represent about two-thirds of Timken's total sales. In 1997 Timken had sales of over $2.6 billion, up from $2.4 billion in 1996. Timken has operations in 25 countries and employs nearly 21,000. Its subsidiary, MPB Corp., manufactures precision bearings for various specialty markets.

In late 1999, Timken announced a reorganization that will focus on four basic industries rather than geographic areas. "This reorganization is designed to cut across geographic boundaries. It will allow us to work more like our customers do," said Elaine Reolfi, Timken's manager of corporate and marketing communications. The new business lines are automotive, industrial, aerospace, and rail. "This is a more efficient and logical organization for the company that will help facilitate additional growth," according to Reolfi.

The Torrington Co. of Torrington, Connecticut was founded in 1866 as a manufacturer of sewing needles. Since 1968, it has been a subsidiary of Ingersoll-Rand and part of its Engineered Products Segment. Torrington markets the Kilian, Argosy, and Kilrol brands of bearings. Torrington had sales of $1.2 billion in 1998 and employed 11,400.

Sweden-based SKF, which was incorporated in 1907, is the acknowledged leader of the world's roller bearing industry. In 1988, SKF controlled 20 percent of the world market in bearings, which was more than twice the market share held by its closest competitors. The company's entrance into the bearings market was motivated by its frustration with the poor quality and high cost of other bearings. The parent company, Gamlestadens Fabriker, a textile manufacturer, granted funds for research into producing bearings. Subsequently, the founder of SKF, Sven Wingquist, went on to develop the double row, self-aligning ball bearing that introduced SKF as a leader and innovator in the industry. From the onset, SKF aligned itself with the automotive industry and pushed its operations into France and the United Kingdom in order to compete directly with German manufacturers. In 1909 SKF established a New York subsidiary which acted as a sales office for products manufactured in Sweden. In 1916 the SKF Administrative Company was formed in New York, and in 1918 a manufacturing plant was established in Hartford, Connecticut. SKF quickly acquired two other manufacturing plants in Philadelphia. Also in 1916 the company acquired another Swedish ball bearing producer as well as a steel works company to increase its steel supply for bearings. During the 1920s, SKF furthered its reputation for innovation when it introduced spherical and taper roller bearings.

SKF USA is the American subsidiary of SKF. Headquartered in Norristown, Pennsylvania, it employs 5,000 and had 1998 sales of $1.1 billion.

WORKFORCE

In 1997 the 184 establishments involved in the U.S. ball and roller bearing industry employed 36,788, with a total payroll of nearly $1.4 billion. Just over 30,000 were classified as production workers with a payroll of just over $1.0 billion. The average hourly wage in 1997 for the industry was estimated to be $16.33. For 2000, the total number of industry employees was predicted to be 32,000, with nearly 27,000 being production workers. Total payroll compensation was predicted to be $1.3 billion with the average hourly wage being $17.55.

The technical side of the bearings industry offers employment for such job classifications as engineers and metallurgists as well as skilled and semi-skilled workers. The U.S. Bureau of Labor Statistics generally predicts that employment opportunities for mechanical engineers will grow about as fast as the average for all occupations. The outlook for metallurgists is slightly pessimistic with a forecast for employment opportunities to increase more slowly than the average for all occupations. Because relatively few students choose to go into metallurgy, however, all graduates are expected to be able to find employment. The outlook for skilled and semi-skilled workers in such occupational classifications as assemblers, inspectors, machine tool cutting operators, welders, and the like is generally expected to decline through 2006. Much of the decline in these occupational classifications is due to increased automation.

AMERICA AND THE WORLD

The largest bearing producing countries are the United States, Japan, and Germany. These three countries also represent the three largest markets for bearings in spite of growing demand in other European and Asian countries. In the United States, about 24 percent of bearing consumption comes from imports. U.S. bearing imports increased 5 percent in 1997 and were expected to increase 7 percent in 1998. Japan had a 34 percent share of the U.S. market in 1997 down from 40 percent in 1995. Canada, Germany, and China have market shares of 12 percent, 11 percent, and 9 percent respectively. U.S. imports of bearings have grown an average of 10 percent annually between 1992 and 1997.

U.S. bearing manufacturers increased their exports by 9 percent in 1997 and this figure was expected to increase to 8 percent in 1998. Canada was the primary market accounting for 45 percent of U.S. bearing exports worth $449 million. Canada was followed by Mexico, which took in 12 percent of industry exports valued at $123 million. The other three major importing countries were Germany (4.6 percent, $46 million), the United Kingdom (4.3 percent $42 million), and Japan (3.6 percent, 36 million.)

The Asian economic crisis of 1997 and 1998 was still influencing the U.S. bearing industry in 1999. The crisis resulted in a rise of low-priced imports that in turn created more competition and pressure for domestic manufacturers according to David Gridley of the Torrington Company. "Capacity utilization is at 90 percent and falling. Many segments, such as standard radial ball bearings, have unused capacity due to rising low priced imports and falling industrial demand in North America and worldwide due to the Asian crisis.'' ''The general economy for bearings has weakened in the last six months,'' Gridley said in early 1999.

In order to meet demand in developing countries it is expected that the world's major bearing manufacturers will build facilities in these regions to take advantage of cheap labor and lower production costs. Advantages in labor costs are, however, somewhat offset by a shortage of skilled workers.

RESEARCH AND TECHNOLOGY

The production of ball and roller bearings is a mature industry and the basic technology for it has been in place for decades. Technological innovations in the industry in the late 1990s focused on the use of new and sometimes exotic materials, more efficient bearings, and bearings specifically designed for more narrow market applications.

Traditionally, steel was the major component of ball bearings because of its strength and existing technology for its production and machining. By the late 1990s, however, many bearing manufacturers were looking towards the use of other materials for their bearings. The use of exotic materials in bearings, often called hybrid bearings, was becoming more and more the norm. Hybrid bearings using such materials as silicon nitride ceramics were being produced and tested for improved performance. Wausau Paper Mills estimated savings of $40,000 per year by using self-lubricating graphite alloy bearings in their stock tank agitators. These agitators have a propensity to destroy bearing lubricants and Wausau found that the original equipment bronze bushings would frequently fail between the recommended six-month preventative maintenance inspections. The graphite alloy bearings have lasted 12 to 24 months of service without showing wear.

Silicon nitride ceramic hybrid bearings and even all ceramic self-lubricating bearings are finding increasing applications in the semiconductor industry. Sulfuric acid and other corrosives, which are used to etch silicon wafers, also have a corrosive effect on steel roller bearings. The traditional lubricants used with steel bearings also tend to become gaseous in vacuum systems thus contaminating the ultra-clean environment required by the semiconductor industry. The answer is silicon nitride hybrid bearings. The industry is also awaiting development of all ceramic bearings.

The EGC Corp. has developed a new material for high-load bushing and bearing applications called XC-2L. The PEEK (polyetheretherketone) carbon-fiber reinforced material incorporates a lubricant compound, making it ideal for applications where more common materials cannot be used because of media incompatibil-

ity, dry running, high PV, high temperature requirements, or contact with abrasive mediums. In comparative testing XC-2L outperformed traditional materials such as steel and bronze.

Duralon composite bearings are being produced by the Rexnord Corp. for special applications, especially in the textile industry. The bearings are made of a self-lubricating, low friction composite, consisting of a Teflon/Dacron fabric liner bonded to a supporting shell of filament-wound, high strength fiber glass and epoxy resin. These bearings have a low friction coefficient and require no lubrication. Because they need no lubrication, there is no danger of them ''running dry,'' and they are thus well suited for machinery locations where accessibility is difficult. The absence of grease or oil lubricants also makes them ideal for the textile industry because there is no danger of lubricant stains on fibers or fabrics. They also do not suffer from fretting corrosion or brinelling that is common in other bearings because of the high cyclic rate of mechanisms used in weaving machinery.

Aiming at industries concerned with machine tool precision, accuracy, and part-surface quality NSK of Ann Arbor has introduced their Ultra bearing. This new bearing combines high-speed capability with low internal heat generation. The low heat generation is attributed to design features of the bearing and a lightweight phenolic cage. Also aiming at a particular market niche, Torrington is developing camshaft supports that use needle instead of slide bearings. The use of needle bearings for this application is expected to lower friction, boost fuel economy, and eliminate valve train durability concerns.

FURTHER READING

American Bearing Manufacturers Association. *American Bearing Manufacturers Association.* Washington: American Bearing Manufacturers Association, 1999. Available from: http://www.abma-dc.org.

Castonguay, Larry. ''Graphite Alloy Bearings Withstand Run-Dry Conditions, Extend Life.'' *Pulp & Paper.* July 1999.

Cento, Pete, and Don W. Dareing. ''Ceramic Materials in Hybrid Ball Bearings.'' *Tribology Transactions.* October 1999.

Ciancarelli, Agatha. ''Price Remain Flat with Downward Pressure.'' *Purchasing.* 14 January 1999.

D & B Million Dollar Directory: America's Leading Public & Private Companies. Bethlehem, Pennsylvania: Dun & Bradstreet, 1999.

Darney, Arsen J. ed. *Manufacturing USA: Industry Analyses, Statistics, and Leading Companies.* 6th ed. Detroit: Gale, 1998.

''Greaseless Bearings for Harsh Environments.'' *Machine Design.* 7 October 1999.

Harris, Bernard. ''Composite Bearings Come Clean in Textile Industry.'' *Textile Maintenance & Engineering.* May 1999, 89-91.

"High Speed Spindle Bearing (NSK)." *Manufacturing Engineering.* September 1999.

Hoover's Masterlist of Major U.S. Companies 1998-1999. Austin, Texas: Hoover's Business Press, 1998.

Kobe, Gerry. "Torrington Needle Bearing Cam-Support Lowers Friction." *Automotive Industries.* July 1997.

Lubove, Seth. "Cat and Mouse Game (U.S. imports of ball bearings)." *Forbes.* 28 May 1990.

"Lubricated PEEK Composite for Bushings, Bearings." *Plastics Engineering.* September 1999.

"Nippon Thompson Designs New Bearing to Avoid US Anti-Dumping Duties." *Nikkan Kogyo Shimbun.* 2 May 1995.

"Timken Co. is Reorganizing Its Business." *American Metal Market.* 22 November 1999.

"Timken Co. Will Reorganize." *Akron Beacon Journal* 19 November 1999.

"Timken (US), a Bearings Manufacturer is Pursuing Global Expansion and Plant Innovation." *Engineer.* 30 April 1999.

U.S. Bureau of Labor Statistics. *1998-99 Occupational Outlook Handbook.* Washington: GPO, 1998. Available from: http://stats.bls.gov/ocohome.htm.

U.S. Bureau of the Census. *Ball and Roller Bearing Manufacturing. 1997 Economic Census: Manufacturing, Industry Series.* Washington: GPO, 1999. Available from: http://www.census.gov/prod/ec97/97m3329e.pdf.

U.S. Dept. of Commerce. *Current Industrial Reports: Antifriction Bearings - 1997.* Washington: U.S. Bureau of the Census, 1999. Available from: http://www.census.gov/industry/ma35q97.txt.

SIC 3563

AIR AND GAS COMPRESSORS

This category covers firms primarily engaged in manufacturing air and gas compressors for general industrial use, and non-agricultural spraying and dusting equipment. It does not include manufacturers of refrigeration and air-conditioning compressors, which are classified in **SIC 3585: Air-Conditioning and Warm Air Heating Equipment and Commercial and Industrial Refrigeration Equipment;** pneumatic pumps and motors for fluid power transmission, classified in **SIC 3594: Fluid Power Pumps and Motor;** agricultural spraying and dusting equipment, classified in **SIC 3523: Farm Machinery and Equipment;** or laboratory vacuum pumps, classified in **SIC 3821: Laboratory Apparatus and Furniture.**

NAICS CODE(S)

333912 (Air and Gas Compressor Manufacturing)

INDUSTRY SNAPSHOT

Although air and gas compressors are vital to scores of commercial and industrial products and activities, compressor manufacturing is a small and mature industry within the industrial machinery sector. Products from this $5 billion industry are used in the chemical industry, steel mills and blast furnaces, energy-related extraction industries, pipelines and well-drilling, and general construction. Despite slow and often cyclical business, several of the industry's top producers have managed to turn a healthy profit, especially on newer technology and aftermarket parts.

In 1997 some 269 U.S. companies manufactured air and gas compressors and related devices. They employed almost 25,000 workers, including 14,800 production workers, and had a collective payroll of $940 million. The vast majority of air compressor makers operated small facilities with fewer than 100 employees, but a relatively low number of larger facilities supplied the lion's share of output.

ORGANIZATION AND STRUCTURE

The number of U.S. establishments manufacturing air and gas compressors grew during the 1990s, reaching 314 in 1997, up from 254 just five years earlier. Historically, manufacturing in this industry has been heavily concentrated; in 1977 more than half the industry's employees worked in the four largest facilities, and 79 percent of all facilities employed fewer than 100 workers. By 1992 this had changed somewhat—while 79 percent of all facilities still employed fewer than 100 workers, diffusion was more evident in the larger firms. The 56 firms that had more than 100 employees accounted for 81 percent of all workers.

The use of compressed air and gas can be divided into three major categories, according to the *Compressed Air and Gas Handbook:* compressed air and gas for process services, compressed air for power, and compressed air for general industrial applications.

Process services include chemical alterations like combustion, nitrogen fixation, polymerization, hydrogenation and alkylation, and change of state operations like quenching, drying, and atomization. Products that result from these types of procedures include liquid fuels, plastics, synthetic rubber, ammonia, and fertilizers.

Power uses utilize the potential energy of stored compressed air to directly perform work. The tools and devices powered by compressed air are termed pneumatic. They generally perform more slowly than electric tools but are faster than hydraulic and provide smooth power application. The energy potential can be translated into rotation and torque with the use of rotary air motors, vanes, or air turbines. Reciprocating motion and direct force provide easily controllable presses, clamps, and feeding devices. Air pressure can be used to accelerate a mass such as a pile driver or pavement breaker. Blowguns use the air pressure stream directly to move materials such as chips, debris, and paint. Air can displace fluids, semi-fluids, and solids to drive materials through pipelines. When air and liquid are mixed, the resulting bubbling action provides agitation, mixing, and aeration.

Industry uses of compressed air include plant maintenance and the powering of pneumatic tools for production line work. This has been especially important for automation of thread-tightening, pressing, hammering, feeding, positioning, and safety-control sensors.

BACKGROUND AND DEVELOPMENT

The world's first pump was probably the force or air pump built by Ktesibios of Alexandria about 270 B.C. He used a cylinder and plunger arrangement to pump air through pipes of various lengths, creating the first water organ. The water was used to maintain a steady air pressure in the system. Simple air pumps and bellows provided low-pressure compressed air for such devices as organs and blacksmith furnaces, but major advancements in compressor technology had to wait until the arrival of the Industrial Revolution.

Generally the term compressor was applied to any blower that produced compressed air in excess of 40 psi. Below that pressure, the device is simply called a blower or industrial fan. With new industrial processes came new demands for flexibility of power sources. Coupling the air pump to a steam engine showed the potential of air power. By 1900, the stationary air compressor was a common tool for industry, albeit a massive one requiring bulky, space-consuming foundations. In 1900, the portable compressor made its debut by the simple expedient of placing wheels under some of the smaller stationary engines. Until 1910, the most common power for such compressors was the steam engine or an oil engine. The main application for the devices was for rock drilling. The invention of a lightweight air drill spurred development of the portable compressor.

Major advances came in the 1930s, when the two-stage, air-cooled compressor appeared, followed by multi-speed regulation by the end of the decade. The 1950s saw the introduction of the rotary-screw compressor in the United States, which allowed for considerably higher operating speeds in smaller, lighter units. Continued improvements made possible the now common truck-mounted diesel-powered units used by utilities and construction companies as a completely portable and flexible power source.

One industry that especially benefited from the new technology was oil exploration and drilling. In 1938 some oil companies began experimenting with air-powered drills. The technique used a rotating bit and pumped either mud or air through holes in the bit to clear the cutting face. New booster compressors producing 1,500 psi were developed specifically for the industry. By the end of World War II, portable drilling rigs were quickly and efficiently boring shallow wells.

The construction industry borrowed the technology for its blast-hole drillers in 1946. In 1954 it developed its own bottom-hole tool, which used 100 psi compressed air to rotate a carbide-tipped tool. Water-well drills used 250 psi air to clear water from the hole while drilling.

The two most common types of compressors are the positive-displacement and the velocity or dynamic. Positive-displacement machines trap air in a confined space and then reduce the volume of that space to increase the pressure. The bicycle pump is a familiar example of this type of compressor. It need not use a piston assembly, a rotating gear, or a screw mechanism. Such compressors can be powered by electric motors, oil or gas engines, and steam engines or turbines. The most common applications for these compressors are off-shore oil drilling, construction applications, locomotives, ships, mining, and smaller units in machine shops, bakeries, dry cleaning plants, food processing plants, furniture factories, printing plants, textile mills, automotive service shops, and other industrial and commercial applications using compressed air.

The dynamic system uses a fan or turbine mechanism to force the air or gas against the casing by centrifugal force. Such systems often use several stages or series of compression to achieve high pressures. The systems can be either axial, expelling gas along the line of its impeller axis, or radial, expelling gas against the casing by centrifugal force. The most common applications for these devices are in refineries, petrochemical plants, steel mills, ammonia plants, sewage aeration, pipeline boosters, wind tunnels, and supercharging diesel engines.

By the early 1980s, the chemical industry had become one of the largest users of compressors. According to the *Monthly Labor Review,* in 1982 the chemical industry was using about 10 percent of the compressor industry's output. In comparison, steel mills and blast furnaces took about 7 percent of output. The oil-well and pipeline industries purchased 18 percent of output. Demand in this sector dropped off dramatically in the 1960s but steadily recovered. Compressors are used in both oil drilling and oil field maintenance operations, particularly for secondary recovery efforts. Construction took 18 percent of output. Particularly important in this market category were the sales of portable compressors used to drive pneumatic tools on the construction site where other sources of energy might be restricted.

The general industrial slowdown of the 1980s hit the compressor industry hard. Major clients like the nuclear power industry, oil well and pipeline industry, and the construction industry cut back on orders for new equipment and left existing components idle. A strong U.S. dollar made American products noncompetitive in foreign markets.

By 1988, this started to change. A weakening dollar spurred exports and a general pickup in the manufacturing climate sparked new domestic orders in almost all sectors. The industry continued to modernize production by consolidating facilities and adopting sophisticated CAD/CAM systems and metalworking and casting technologies. New materials and designs were explored to extend the life of components in corrosive environments and to increase reliability.

CURRENT CONDITIONS

Market conditions for compressors and related equipment vary widely by application and region, but in general the industry has struggled with limited growth opportunities. In the late 1990s, most markets—domestic and foreign—were tough, characterized by slack demand and rising international competition. For much of the 1990s the oil and natural gas markets were especially disappointing, as low oil prices made energy companies leery of investing in new equipment. Indeed, for many compressor makers, selling aftermarket parts and accessories became significantly more profitable than selling new compressors. Some industry firms also attempted to cope with sluggish growth by developing economies of scope, such as offering leasing and maintenance services for compressor equipment.

Portable air compressors, ones that have wheels and can be taken from site to site, have proven one of the industry's fastest-growing lines. In 1997, according to Census Bureau figures, the U.S. industry shipped some 2.99 million compressors. Almost three-quarters of these, 2.20 million, were portable models. Whereas overall unit output remained nearly flat from 1994 to 1997, portable compressor production jumped 28 percent over that period. As much as 90 percent of portable units were sold to equipment rental services.

INDUSTRY LEADERS

Ingersoll-Rand Company has long been one of the top U.S. air-compressor manufacturers. By some estimates it was the largest U.S. producer and the world's second-largest. In 1998 its Air and Temperature Control division, which made air compressors and refrigeration equipment, recorded sales of $2.2 billion. With profit margins above 10 percent, the compressor line was considered one of Ingersoll's stronger segments. Based in Woodcliff Lake, New Jersey, the firm brought in a

substantial amount of its sales from overseas and thus is particularly sensitive to international economic conditions.

Another important player, Thomas Industries of Louisville, Kentucky, made small custom compressors and vacuum pumps as components for other devices, including printing equipment, vending machines, transportation equipment, and medical and laboratory equipment. Medical applications like oxygen concentrators represented more than a third of Thomas' $177.0 million in 1998 sales. Earnings of $30.7 million that year made for a robust 17 percent net margin. However, the company's profits have slumped in the price-sensitive medical equipment market; Thomas sought out new product niches to sustain its earnings. Like Ingersoll-Rand, Thomas Industries was also heavily dependent on international sales, which made up as much as 40 percent of its revenue in the late 1990s.

Serving a much different market, Cooper Cameron Corp. sold compressors and other pressure-control machinery to oil and gas mining concerns. The Houston-based manufacturer also made general industrial compressor systems through its turbocompressor unit. In 1998 revenues from Cooper Cameron's two compressor-producing units totaled $577.0 million. Net income for the two units that year skidded more than 50 percent to $33.2 million, for a 5.7 percent net margin. The company's exposure to international markets and the cyclical energy business were to blame. In 1999 Cooper sold its flagging rotating compressor business to Rolls Royce.

WORKFORCE

Industrial machinery industries employ a high proportion of skilled trades—about 30 percent of all production workers compared to 26 percent in manufacturing in general. Metal-working craftsmen and machinists are three times more common in this industry than in manufacturing as a whole, while laborers are half as common. The industry's production workers in 1999 earned an average of more than $14.50 an hour, slightly ahead of the manufacturing average of $13.91. The industry also employs a high proportion of nonproduction workers, indicating a reliance on mechanical engineers. More than 40 percent of the compressor industry's workforce is located in New York, Ohio, Pennsylvania, and Texas.

AMERICA AND THE WORLD

The United States typically incurs a deficit in compressor trade with other nations. In 1997, U.S. firms imported $683 million worth of compressors and vacuum pumps, while exports trailed at $309 million. In 2000 the global market was estimated at $10 to $12 billion.

These numbers, however, don't reflect the global character of many of the industry's leading companies.

They have plants and offices around the world and increasingly hunt for opportunities outside the overfed markets of the United States and Europe.

Sweden's Atlas Copco AB is a case in point. The world's largest compressor maker, with an estimated 20 percent share, Atlas Copco manufactures compressor gear in seven countries, including the United States. It has separate assembly plants in seven countries as well. Perhaps most notable, though, is that Atlas Copco decided in the late 1990s to stop making many of its own components and instead import them from cheaper competitors in developing economies. In the late 1990s, Atlas was reportedly behind half of all compressor imports into the United States.

RESEARCH AND TECHNOLOGY

The majority of compressors manufactured are custom made to a client's specific requirements for use in complex applications where the failure of the compressor could be disastrous. Consequently, manufacturing innovation has stressed flexibility and reliability. As in many traditional manufacturing fields, emphasis has been on efficient, short-run, just-in-time manufacturing processes that allow rapid customization for changing market needs.

New corrosion resistant materials were developed and refinements to old processes adopted. Specially designed metal-forming machines were created for the industry, including combination milling, radial drilling, and facing machines; variable setting grinders that automatically form tapered shafts; and automatic tool changing devices controlled by NC tapes or computer software. Foundry operations for production of compressor casings and core making advanced with rapid-cycle machinery, synchronous fabricating machinery, and a no-bake molding process using a resin binder and catalyst. Closer tolerances were achieved in components by replacing wooden molds and cores with ceramic. Increasing concern over energy efficiency dictated more advanced compressor designs with larger displacements.

FURTHER READING

Compressed Air and Gas Handbook. New York: Compressed Air and Gas Institute, 1973.

U.S. Census Bureau. *1996 Annual Survey of Manufactures: Value of Product Shipments.* Washington, D.C.: Department of Commerce, 1998.

———. *1997 Census of Manufactures.* Washington, D.C.: Department of Commerce, 1999.

———. ''Industrial Equipment.'' *1997 Manufacturing Profiles.* Washington, D.C.: Department of Commerce, 1999.

Yengst, Charles R. ''Portable Air Compressor Market More Than Just a Lot of Air.'' *Diesel Progress North American Edition,* November 1997.

INDUSTRIAL AND COMMERCIAL FANS AND BLOWERS AND AIR PURIFICATION EQUIPMENT

This category covers firms primarily engaged in manufacturing blowers for general industrial and commercial use, and commercial exhaust fans, ventilating fans and attic fans. Also included are manufacturers of duct collection equipment and other air purification equipment for heating and air conditioning systems and equipment for industrial gas cleaning systems. It does not include manufacturers of refrigeration and air-conditioning components, which are covered under **SIC 3585: Refrigeration and Heating Equipment.** Small household fans, kitchen and bath ventilation fans, or other domestic fan components are included in **SIC 3634: Electric Housewares and Fans.**

NAICS CODE(S)

333411 (Air Purification Equipment Manufacturing)
333412 (Industrial and Commercial Fan and Blower Manufacturing)

INDUSTRY SNAPSHOT

U.S. industry depends on the low-pressure, high-volume movement of air. Without it, much industrial and commercial activity would quickly suffocate. Consequently, the fan can be found in applications as diverse as huge blowers used to bubble air through sewage water and industrial waste, to street cleaners and industrial leaf blowers. In modern shopping centers and commercial/industrial strip malls, unnoticed roof ventilators silently exchange contaminated air for fresh; the attic fan performs the same function for residential buildings. Heating and air conditioning systems depend on fans to move heat away from coils and heat exchangers and into the structure, and to feed the fossil fuel combustion processes with large quantities of oxygen-bearing air. Exhaust systems push the products of this combustion outside the structure or extract grease and heat from commercial cooking appliances and industrial ovens.

Estimated 1996 U.S. shipments of products within the blowers, fans, and air cleaners industry were valued at $4.1 billion. This figure fluctuated during the 1990s but was projected to remain between $3.5 and $4.2 billion through the year 2000.

More than 500 companies manufactured fans and blowers at roughly 600 locations in the mid-1990s. This figure grew gradually since the 1980s, when there were around 450 companies and 500 facilities. Industry employment figures rose slightly in the early to mid-1990s compared to the low rates of the late 1980s. However, this rate was expected to decline steadily from 31,400 in 1996 to 28,100 in 2000. Ohio, Illinois, California, and North Carolina were the leading states in employment, employing approximately 33 percent of the total industry workers.

The fan's ability to move large quantities of air makes it the base component of the rapidly expanding air pollution control industry. Starting with the plant, the device has been harnessed to help contain and remove pollutants like dust and metal particles, carbon monoxide, nitrous oxides, sulfur dioxide, sulfuric acid, and hydrocarbon solvents in a variety of filters and traps.

Fans and blowers belong to the same family of devices as compressors and pumps. A pump moves liquids, while the others move gases. A compressor will provide a means of increasing the pressure of the gas to more than 40 pounds per square inch (psi). That gas can then either be delivered directly to the application or stored for metered use. A blower can also increase the pressure of the gas to as much as 40 psi, but delivers it directly to the application through an area of high resistance such as a pipeline. Fans provide large volumes of uncompressed gas and operate in low-resistance environments that could also include ducting systems. Technically, an increase in gas density of less than 7 percent between inlet and outlet defines the gas as uncompressed.

The two most common types of fans and blowers are the axial and the centrifugal, which together account for about 45 percent of the industry's output. Axial fans are used in applications that produce low resistance to airflow. The gas is moved in the same direction as the fan's axis of rotation, much as a water wheel on a classic mill or paddle steamer. In the centrifugal fan, the gas moves perpendicular to the fan's axis of rotation. Most domestic fans use angled and curved blades to produce the centrifugal effect at low pressure. Centrifugal blowers and fans are used in relatively high resistance applications and usually provide quieter operation than axial units.

The main uses of fans and blowers, according to the *Compressed Air and Gas Handbook,* are for process services (including chemical alterations like combustion, nitrogen fixation, polymerization, hydrogenation, and alkylation), and for change-of-state operations (including quenching, drying, and atomization). Products that result from these types of procedures include liquid fuels, plastics, synthetic rubber, ammonia, and fertilizers.

BACKGROUND AND DEVELOPMENT

The world's first pump was probably the force or air pump built by Ktesibios of Alexandria about 270 B.C. He used a cylinder and plunger arrangement to pump air through pipes of various lengths, creating the first water organ. The water was used to maintain a steady air

pressure in the system. Simple air pumps and bellows provided low-pressure "compressed" air for such devices as organs and blacksmith furnaces, but major advancements in fan technology had to wait until the arrival of the Industrial Revolution.

As large-scale manufacturing emerged in the late nineteenth and early twentieth centuries, fans became an integral part of factory and commercial building infrastructure in the United States. The fan and blower industry's successes have been largely tied to the health of commercial and industrial construction and renovation.

The general industrial slowdown of the 1980s hit the fan and blower industry hard. Major clients like the petrochemical industry, the construction industry, and the heating, ventilation and air conditioning industry cut back on orders for new equipment and left existing components idle. A strong U.S. dollar made American products uncompetitive in foreign markets.

By 1988, this started to change. A weakening dollar stimulated exports and a general pickup in the manufacturing climate sparked new domestic orders in almost all sectors. The industry continued to modernize production by consolidating facilities and adopting sophisticated CAD/CAM systems and metalworking and casting technologies. New materials and designs were explored to extend the life of components in corrosive environments and to increase reliability.

New environmental regulations like the Clean Air Act Amendments of 1990 and their counterparts in other countries spurred the development and sale of air pollution abatement equipment. Two major products in this category were particle emission collectors, with shipments of $513 million in 1990, and gaseous emission control units, with sales of $220 million that year. In 1990, the major clients for such products were steam electric power generators, industrial steam plants, pulp and paper mills, chemical and fertilizer producers, and petroleum refiners.

CURRENT CONDITIONS

In 1996, shipments in this industry were valued at $4.1 billion, an increase from $3.6 billion the previous year. This figure was expected to remain between $3.8 and $4.2 billion through the year 2000. Dust collection and air purification equipment represented the largest segment of the industry in the 1990s, followed closely by centrifugal blowers and fans, and propeller fans and accessories.

The industry benefitted in the mid- and late 1990s from the Clean Air Act Amendments of 1990, because they imposed time limits on the reduction of specified hazardous industrial air pollutants. Compliance generated significant capital investment into this industry's products.

The success of this industry tends to coincide with the seasons of the year and with allergy seasons. Changes in weather conditions prompt consumers to buy products such as fans at certain times of the year. Air purification equipment tends to be more popular during allergy seasons.

INDUSTRY LEADERS

The top selling company in this industry in the late 1990s was Eagle Industries, Inc., of Chicago, Illinois. Founded in 1961, Eagle Industries reported total annual sales of $9.9 million and employed 7,000 people at the end of the decade. In addition to ventilation systems, Eagle Industries manufactures toilet bowls and tanks, urinals, plastic plumbing fixtures, commercial refrigeration equipment and electrical power distribution equipment.

Other top sellers in the industry included Fasco Motors Group of Chesterfield, Missouri, with $4.7 million in sales and 4,000 employees, and Air and Water Technologies Corp of Somerville, New Jersey, with $4.5 million in sales and 2,900 employees.

WORKFORCE

Total employment for the industry was 31,400 in 1996, an increase over the 29,000 employed in 1995. However, employment in the industry was expected to decrease through 2000, dropping to 28,100. Of the 31,400 industry workers employed in 1996, 21,000 were production workers earning an average of $11.17 per hour. By the year 2000, 19,100 production workers were expected to make an average of $12.41 per hour.

The Bureau of Labor Statistics projected declines for most occupations within this industry through 2005. Significant growth was expected, however, for machine builders, machine tool operators, and welders and cutters.

AMERICA AND THE WORLD

Blowers and fans and the increasingly important air pollution abatement equipment are manufactured to international standards, allowing American manufacturers to compete effectively on the international market. These same standards, however, also make the United States vulnerable to foreign competition, particularly on price and quality.

Globalization is particularly important in the air pollution abatement equipment (APC) sector. U.S. and European multinationals use direct investment, cross-border mergers, acquisitions, joint ventures, and foreign collaboration to gain entry to each other's markets and to other markets around the world. The main target markets for such equipment have been Asia, Eastern Europe, and Latin America, since the industry already faces significant competition from domestic producers in major trading partners like Japan, Germany, and France. Mexico is also a potentially significant market for U.S. fan and blower products. Many firms prefer to license to foreign manufacturers instead of competing directly, creating a brisk trade in environmental technology. Unlike the industry in general, this segment posted a trade surplus in the 1990s.

RESEARCH AND TECHNOLOGY

New and more stringent environmental regulations in the United States and around the world encouraged research into new air pollution abatement technology. This was especially true since some regulations called for pollution limitations in excess of what was technically possible at the time.

However, the industry also found ways of applying old technologies in new ways. Some major areas of research included electrostatic precipitators with the addition of high-voltage direct-current pulses to capture fly-ash; filter bags treated with microporous films or membranes to keep dust cake out of the filter material; conditioning flue gas streams with sulfur trioxide or ammonia before filtering to improve the life of the filter; the development of sulfur trioxide generators to convert flue gases without the need of adding chemicals; new plastic materials to extend the concept of flue gas cooling with water beyond the wood products industry; and sorbent injection of such materials as carbon, char, and sodium sulfide to capture heavy metals like mercury.

The end of the 1990s saw new products, especially in the area of air cleaning and purification, being introduced by various leaders in this industry. In 1999, Lentek International added several new products to its Sila line of air purifiers, including a purifier/deodorizer, a personal air supply device, and a coat and closet purifier. Also in 1999, Clairion introduced a new line of decorative fans that are both energy efficient and excellent air cleaners.

FURTHER READING

"1999 Appliance Statistical Forecast: Comfort and Conditioning Appliances." *Appliance,* January 1999.

3564, General Statistics. Detroit: Gale Group, 1999.

3564, Occupations Employed by SIC 356. Detroit: Gale Group, 1999.

3564, Product Share Details. Detroit: Gale Group, 1999.

"Airing It Out." *HFN,* 02 August 1999.

"Clairion to Debut Air Cleaner/Ceiling Fan Combo." *HFN,* 14 December 1998.

Compressed Air and Gas Handbook. New York: Compressed Air and Gas Institute, 1973.

Darnay, Arsen J., ed. *Manufacturing USA,* 5th ed. Detroit: Gale Research, 1996.

Eagle Industries, Inc. Detroit: Gale Group, 1999.

U.S. Bureau of the Census. *1992 Annual Survey of Manufacturers.* Washington: GPO, Updated 1996. Available from www .census.gov/epcd/ec92/mc92ht35.html.

Ward's Business Directory of U.S. Private and Public Companies, Volume 5. Detroit: Gale Group, 1999.

''Will a Good Year End Up In the Record Books?'' *Appliance,* January 1998.

Zaczkiewicz, Arthur. ''Season for Sales Opportunity.'' *HFN,* 28 August 1999.

SIC 3565

PACKAGING MACHINERY

Firms in this industry manufacture machinery used in packaging, wrapping and bottling. In 1987 the classification code was changed to combine two 1972 categories, SIC 35514: Food Packaging and Bottling Machinery and SIC 35691: Non-food Packaging and Bottling, along with parts of the two general categories: **SIC3551: Food Products Machinery** and **SIC 3569: General Industry Machinery.** The 1972 category numbered **SIC 3565: Industrial Patterns** was renumbered as **SIC 3543.**

NAICS CODE(S)

333993 (Packaging Machinery Manufacturing)

In 1997 the industry shipped $4.82 billion worth of products, a 32.8 percent increase since 1995. Employment in the industry increased to 31,227 in 1997, an increase of 11.5 percent from 28,000 only two years earlier.

The industry found itself challenged to change and innovate in the late 1980s and early 1990s, as industry shifted to leaner production methods requiring just-in-time (JIT) inventory management and as consumers rebelled against excessive and expensive product packaging. This meant new technology to manufacture smaller, more flexible machinery and more packaging options for manufacturers.

To meet the demand, the industry introduced programmable logic controllers, robotics, self-diagnostic systems, microprocessor controls, automated testing, vision inspection systems, and built-in fault correction devices. Hydraulic and pneumatic actuators reduced clamping time and sped line changeover rates. Modern lines could shift from producing one part to an entirely different component in minutes instead of the previously common hours.

Illinois, Wisconsin, California, and Ohio led the country in employment in the production of packaging equipment in 1997. These states accounted for nearly 42 percent of the nation's total employment in the industry.

Major players in the packaging machinery industry included Bemis Company Inc., 3M/Packaging Systems Division, and Signode Packaging Systems. Headquartered in Minneapolis, Bemis not only produces packaging machinery but also turns out a broad range of packaging materials itself. With more than 9,000 employees, Bemis reported 1998 revenue of $1.85 billion. Based in nearby St. Paul, Minnesota, 3M/Packaging Systems Division employed more than 5,000 in late 1999 and generated sales of more than $500 million. Signode, an operating unit of Illinois Tool Works Inc., is based in Baltimore. Although specific financial details of Signode's operations were unavailable, it is known that its parent company employed more than 25,000 employees as of 1999 and reported 1998 sales of $5.6 billion.

Exports formed an important part of the industry's market with roughly 15 percent of its 1997 production shipped to about 140 foreign countries. This represented $723 million in sales. The largest purchaser of American equipment was Canada followed by Europe, the Asia-Pacific region, and Central and South America. *U.S. Industrial Outlook 1997* identified five exceptional growth markets: Japan, South Korea, Taiwan, Germany, and France.

The industry faced major challenges by environmental and energy concerns both in the United States and in foreign countries, especially Europe. The demands for recyclable and reusable materials and containers prompted more than 500 legislative proposals in 50 states to control solid waste. Other countries instituted their own measures. Concerns over conflicting regulations prompted interest in such measures as the ISO 9000 international machinery standard, which define the rules of manufacture and prevent such national or state standards from becoming non-tariff barriers to trade.

At the same time, industry was demanding lighter materials both in the actual packaging and the machinery, to reduce energy costs in transportation. Responding to the JIT philosophies, packaging equipment companies were beginning to use air freight to speed delivery time.

FURTHER READING

''3M/Packaging Systems Division.'' *CorpTech,* 14 January 2000. Available from http://www.corptech.com/ ResearchAreas/CompanyProfile.cfm?URI=10N6PZ15.

''Bemis Company Inc.'' *Hoover's Online,* 14 January 2000. Available from http://research.web.aol.com/data/hoovers/bios/ b/bms.htm.

Darnay, Arsen J. *Manufacturing USA.* Detroit: Gale Group, 1998.

''Fluid Power in Action: Packaging Equipment.'' *Hydraulics & Pneumatics,* September 1991.

"Signode Packaging Systems." *CorpTech*, 14 January 2000. Available from http://www.corptech.com/ResearchAreas/CompanyProfile.cfm?URI = 10J64E.

U.S. Bureau of the Census. *1997 Economic Census.* Washington: GPO, 1999.

U.S. Department of Commerce. International Trade Administration. *U.S. Industrial Outlook 1999,* Washington: GPO, 1999.

SIC 3566

SPEED CHANGERS, INDUSTRIAL HIGH-SPEED DRIVES, AND GEARS

Firms in this industry manufacture speed changers, industrial high-speed drives, and gears. Hydrostatic drives are classified under **SIC 3594: Fluid Power Pumps and Motors**; automatic transmissions are in **SIC 3714: Motor Vehicle Parts and Accessories**; and aircraft power-transmission devices are found in **SIC 3728: Aircraft Parts and Auxiliary Equipment, Not Elsewhere Classified.**

NAICS CODE(S)

336120 (Speed Changers, Industrial High-Speed Drive, and Gear Manufacturing)

INDUSTRY SNAPSHOT

The industry provides basic mechanical power transmission components used in most industrial machinery. It demonstrated slow but steady growth throughout the 1990s, with the value of shipments increasing from $1.82 billion in 1992 to $2.4 billion in 1997. Companies in this industry downsized during the 1990s; the total number of employees, and the number of production workers, decreased consistently between 1988 and 1997. Over a quarter of the industry's shipments were generated by only four establishments.

Trends affecting this industry during the 1990s included automation production technology and government restrictions on industrial waste.

BACKGROUND AND DEVELOPMENT

Typical manufacturing includes metal grinding, cutting, degreasing, and surface finishing (including hardening). Such metalworking includes basic metal-shaping, heat treatment, and metallurgic modifications using chemicals during processing.

The origin of the gear concept remains uncertain. It was not one of the basic five "simple machines" defined by Hero of Alexandria (the wheel and axle, the lever, the pulley, the wedge, and the screw), but it probably evolved from the screw. Until the Industrial Revolu-

tion, craftsmen used the gear primarily in small mechanisms like clocks, or to guide and locate machinery components. The idea of using it to transmit power in larger machines did not gain prevalence until the 19th century in England.

In America, the technology and the expertise of local artisans to produce quality gears lagged behind Europe until near the end of that century. In 1896, F.W. Fellows patented a gear-shaping machine that could turn out a wide variety of gears quickly and cheaply. The rise of the "American system" of mass manufacturing on an assembly line made such tools quickly popular, displacing the traditional hand-chiseled and filed gears of Europe. These two machine concepts became the dominant technology used in the manufacture of almost all gears in the United States and elsewhere.

By the 1990s, however, the advantages of mass production faded in the face of demands for more flexibility in the design and delivery of individual part orders. Gear manufacturers shifted to heavily automated production systems using Statistical Process Control (SPC), Computerized Numerical Control (CNC), and Just-In-Time (JIT) philosophies. These systems allowed greater precision and faster production shifts. Three-dimensional, computer-digitized master components maintain closer tolerances than can be achieved even with a skilled craftsman, and allow the same master to be used as a benchmark at production facilities around the globe.

In 1995, industry shipments reached $2.13 billion, according to the U.S. Department of Commerce's *Annual Survey of Manufactures,* up from the 1992 value of $1.82 billion. In 1992 there were 256 companies in this industry, with the largest four companies accounting for 28 percent of the total value of shipments. In 1995, firms in this industry averaged 142 employees per establishment, although the largest four establishments (by sales) each had 900 employees or more.

Since the industrial process of making large quantities of gears produces large amounts of waste by-products, the Environmental Protection Agency (EPA) targeted the industry as a waste minimization opportunity in 1992. In particular, it noted that the use of trichloroethane as a degreasing agent would eventually need to be replaced with other chemical solvents or a more advanced technology like ultrasonics. Trichloroethane is one of 17 chemicals listed by the EPA as an industrial toxin. International agencies have identified trichloroethane as an ozone-depleting substance contributing to global warming. For this reason, production of trichloroethane for emissive uses was banned in 1995 under amendments to the Clean Air Act of 1992. Chemical manufacturers have attempted to preserve sales by offering alternative chlorinated solvents as replacements to trichloroethane.

CURRENT CONDITIONS

According to the U.S. Census Bureau's *1997 Economic Census- Manufacturing,* 266 establishments operated in this category for some or all of 1997. Industry-wide employment totaled 16,203 workers receiving a payroll of more than $596 million. Of this number, 11,243 employees worked in production, putting in almost 23 million hours to earn wages of almost $363 million. Overall shipments for the industry in 1997 were valued at almost $2.4 billion.

INDUSTRY LEADERS

Nashville-based MagneTek Inc. Lighting and Electronics Div. led the industry with sales of $860 million for its fiscal year ended June 30, 1997. Dayco Products Inc. of Dayton, Ohio, followed with $850 million in sales for its fiscal year ended February 28, 1998. Baldor Electric Co. of Forth Smith, Arkansas, placed third in the industry with 1998 sales of more than $589 million. Fasco Motors Group of Chesterfield, Missouri, generated $470 million in 1997 sales. Gleason Corp. of Rochester, New York, filled out the top 5 industry leaders with 1998 sales of $409 million.

WORKFORCE

Employment in this industry peaked in 1974 at 27,000, then dropped to 17,400 in 1986 before recovering to 19,300 by 1988. Employment has steadily fallen since that time, however. By 1995, the industry employed 16,900 people, with 12,100 production workers. The average hourly wage in this industry in 1991 was $12.84. The *1992 Census of Manufactures* found that the leading states in employment were Illinois, Indiana, New York, and Wisconsin, compared to 1987, when Wisconsin, Illinois, Indiana, and Pennsylvania were the leaders in employment.

FURTHER READING

Darnay, Arsen J., ed. *Manufacturing USA.* 5th ed. Detroit: Gale Research, 1996.

Hoffman, John. ''Chlorinated Solvents on a Phaseout Course.'' *Chemical Marketing Reporter,* 25 September 1995.

Infotrac Company Profiles, 17 February 2000. Available from http://web4.infotrac.galegroup.com.

Moody's Industrial Manual, New York: Investors Service, Inc., 1996.

Standard & Poor's Register of Corporations, Directors and Executives. New York: McGraw-Hill, 1996.

U.S. Census Bureau. *1995 Annual Survey of Manufactures.* Washington: GPO, 1996.

U.S. Census Bureau. *1997 Economic Census,* 17 February 2000. Washington, D.C.: GPO, 1999. Available from http://www.census.gov/prod/ec97/97m3336b.pdf.

INDUSTRIAL PROCESS FURNACES AND OVENS

Firms in this industry are primarily engaged in manufacturing industrial process furnaces, ovens, induction and dielectric heating equipment and related devices. Products not included in the classification include bakery ovens **SIC 3556: Food Products Machinery**); cement, wood and chemical kilns (**SIC 3559: Special Industry Machinery, Not Elsewhere Classified**); cremating ovens (**SIC 3569: General Industrial Machinery and Equipment, Not Elsewhere Classified**); and laboratory furnaces and ovens (**SIC 3821: Laboratory Apparatus and Furniture**).

NAICS CODE(S)

333994 (Industrial Process Furnace and Oven Manufacturing)

Between 1992 and 1995, the industry showed steady growth in both production and employment with shipments rising from $1.8 billion to $2.65 billion—an increase of 47 percent—and employment increasing from 17,000 to 18,700, an increase of 10 percent. The 1995 figures also represent a 4 percent increase over the 18,000 workers listed in the 1994 census, and an increase of about 20 percent over the $2.2 billion in shipments listed the same year.

In 1997, shipments increased to over $2.8 billion but with a drop in employment to 17,382. The average hourly wage was $12.35 of the same year. Employment is concentrated in the Midwest, with Michigan, Missouri, Illinois, Ohio, and Wisconsin each employing over 1,000 people. California is another leading state, with over 2,057. The remaining 78 percent of the 400 plus establishments in this industry employ 20 or less.

The concept of using heat to modify a material in some desirable manner originated very early in human history. Its application gave us names for eras like the Bronze Age and the Iron Age, as scientific advancement combined furnace design and fuels to achieve higher and more controllable temperatures and chemical reactions within the combustion or heating chambers. The Industrial Revolution brought the biggest advancements and launched the Steel Age as industry abandoned charcoal as the most common fuel and adopted coal and coke. By the end of the twentieth century natural gas and electricity were displacing much solid fuel use.

Near the end of the twentieth century, though, many of the industry's prime customers did not utilize the new technologies. For instance, the steel industry used the Bessemer process, which involved blowing large volumes of heated air through molten iron in a furnace. The American steel industry began using the process in the 1860s. The open hearth method, developed in the same decade, produced larger volumes of steel over longer periods of time, allowing for better quality control. By 1907, the open hearth method was more popular than the Bessemer was. In the 1950s, however, furnace designers found they could improve the performance of the Bessemer furnace by using oxygen instead of air and the Bessemer furnace once again took the lead. By 1990, U.S. steel producers were using the Bessemer oxygen furnace for 59.7 percent of production, the open hearth method for 3.5 percent, and electric furnaces had grabbed 36.8 percent of the market, according to *Market Share Reporter*.

This was only after more efficient foreign competition forced U.S. steel manufacturers to close out-dated smelters and blast furnaces across the country. The area around Pittsburgh once supported 80,000 steel manufacturing jobs, but by 1990 fewer than 4,000 remained as the industry shut down and shifted production to newer mini-mill facilities.

In the 1990s, concern over air quality prompted passage of the Clean Air Act, which mandated reductions of nitrous oxide emissions from such facilities as smelters and blast furnaces and designated such facilities as prime areas of concern. The legislation required special operating permits and monitoring provisions.

According to the Industrial Heating Equipment Association, total domestic and foreign orders for industrial heating equipment (as reported by 20 companies) dropped by 6 percent to about $112 million during the first quarter of 1999, compared to the previous year. Domestic orders also dropped by 8 percent to roughly $98 million for the same period. Domestic industrial furnace and oven orders dropped by 1 percent to about $49 million. Despite these decreases, Leading Edge Reports, an affiliate of Business Trend Analysts, Inc., forecast an average annual growth of 6.9 percent by 2002 for the entire industry.

Three of the largest firms by sales volume in the industry were Inductotherm Industries Inc. of Rancocas, New Jersey at $440 million; Wiegand Industrial Div. of Pittsburgh, Pennsylvania, at $200 million; and Watlow Electric Manufacturing Co. of St. Louis, Missouri, at $150 million.

Both U.S. exports and imports decreased in 1998, compared to 1997. In 1998, exports dropped slightly from $672.08 to $662.29 but the imports saw a even larger decrease to $370,508 from $434,373 in the same year. Asia remained the largest export market in 1998, followed by Western Europe at 43 percent and 19 percent, respectively. Though Asia was the highest importer in 1997, followed by Western Europe, the latter took over the lead in 1998.

FURTHER READING

Darnay, Arsen J., ed. *Manufacturing USA*. 5th ed. Detroit: Gale Research, 1996.

Industrial Heating Equipment Association News August 1999.

"Leading Edge Publishes Report on Industrial Furnaces, Kilns, and Ovens." *Press Release, Business Trend Analysis,* 1 December 1999. Available from http://www.businesstrendanalysts.com/PRFurnKilnOv.shtml

"NAICS 333994" *Manufacturing-Industry Series,* U.S. Census Bureau, 1997 Economic Census, 20 September 1999.

U.S. Bureau of the Census. *1995 Annual Survey of Manufactures.* Washington: GPO, 1997.

SIC 3568

MECHANICAL POWER TRANSMISSION EQUIPMENT, NOT ELSEWHERE CLASSIFIED

The Mechanical Power Transmission Equipment, Not Elsewhere Classified, Industry is comprised of companies that manufacture mechanical power transmission equipment and parts for industrial machinery. Products include ball joints, pulleys, bearings, drive chains, sprockets, shafts, couplings, and other parts. Companies that make transmission devices for vehicles and aircraft are classified in **SIC 3714: Motor Vehicle Parts and Accessories** and **SIC 3728: Aircraft Parts and Auxiliary Equipment, Not Elsewhere Classified,** respectively.

NAICS CODE(S)

333613 (Mechanical Power Transmission Equipment Manufacturing)

The market for miscellaneous transmission equipment is fragmented. Motor vehicle manufacturers were the largest buying sector, accounting for 9.2 percent of industry revenues in the late 1990s. Tanks and tank components accounted for another 5.2 percent of sales, while iron and steel foundries took 4.3 percent. Blast furnaces and steel mills purchased 4 percent of the industry's sales, and the logging industry took another 3 percent. The construction and farm machinery industries consumed 2.9 percent and 2.8 percent, respectively, of output. Motorcycle and bicycle makers purchased about 2 percent of production. Other significant markets for transmission equipment included shipbuilders, lawn and garden equipment manufacturers, nonferrous metals refiners, and the missile industry. About 10.5 percent of production were exported.

Power transmission refers to the transfer of power through mechanical devices. The invention of the steam engine by James Watt in 1765 and the development of the internal combustion engine during the mid-1800s greatly expanded applications for power transmission equipment and played an important role in the industrial revolution. The industry realized its greatest growth during the U.S. economic expansion of the post-World War II era. Indeed, by the early 1980s, makers of miscellaneous transmission equipment were shipping about $2 billion worth of goods annually.

The effects of global competition seriously cut into the profits of U.S. manufacturers during the 1980s. In an effort to sustain profitability, miscellaneous transmission manufacturers increased productivity through automation and restructuring. As real output rose, the industry work force shrank more than 13 percent during the decade, from over 27,000 to about 24,000. Employment continued to drop, falling to 21,800 in 1992. With the recovery of the economy in the mid-1990s, however, employment figures began to rise. By 1995, employment in the industry had climbed back to 22,700—a 4 percent increase over the 1992 figures—although still almost 6 percent below the employment figures at the end of the previous decade. However, during the second half of the decade the sector's workforce once again resumed its downward trend, falling to 21,400 in 1997. Further shrinkage of the workforce was projected through the year 2000.

Despite efficiency gains, a recession in the late 1980s and early 1990s reduced profits for many competitors. Sales dropped about 2.5 percent in 1992. In that year, the industry shipped goods worth $2.4 billion. By 1994, the total value of goods shipped reached $2.79 billion—an increase of 16.4 percent—and in 1995, that total had risen to $2.89 billion, a further increase of 3.5 percent. Shipments of $3.25 billion in 1997 represented a jump of 12.5 percent over the industry's showing in 1995.

Among the leaders in the industry in the late 1990s was Funk Manufacturing Co., a subsidiary of Deere and Co. Headquartered in Coffeyville, Kansas, Funk employed a workforce of about 500 and reported 1998 sales of close to $100 million. About 300 companies competed in the industry in the late 1990s, but only the top 10 reached sales over $30 million.

Future employment prospects are dim. Productivity gains and the movement of some production facilities across U.S. borders has resulted in continued work force reductions. Most labor opportunities have declined and will continue declining by about 20 percent to 30 percent by the year 2005, according to the Bureau of Labor Statistics—although the *1995 Annual Survey of Manufactures* reports that the number of jobs remained constant from 1994 to 1995. Even jobs for managers will decline significantly. Sales and marketing positions, however, will likely increase slightly.

FURTHER READING
Darnay, Arsen J., ed. *Manufacturing USA*. Detroit: Gale Research, 1998.

U.S. Bureau of the Census. *1997 Economic Census*. Washington: GPO 1997.

SIC 3569

GENERAL INDUSTRIAL MACHINERY AND EQUIPMENT, NOT ELSEWHERE CLASSIFIED

This category covers establishments primarily engaged in manufacturing machinery, equipment, and components for general industrial use, and for which no special classification is provided. Machine shops primarily engaged in producing machine and equipment parts, usually on a job or order basis, are classified in **SIC 3599: Industrial and Commercial Machinery and Equipment, Not Elsewhere Classified.**

NAICS CODE(S)
333999 (All Other General Purpose Machinery Manufacturing)

Companies in this industry produce miscellaneous manufacturing equipment. The plethora of industry offerings includes items such as altitude testing chambers, hydraulic bridge machinery, industrial centrifuges, cremating ovens, industrial fluid filters, swimming pool heaters, fire hoses, hydraulic jacks, and fire sprinkler systems.

The general industrial machinery and equipment industry is heavily dependent upon sales to other manufacturing businesses and to construction industries. In addition, about 30 percent of revenues are derived from exports. Intense capital investments during the U.S. industrial boom of the mid-1900s resulted in steady growth in demand for all types of industrial machinery. By the early 1980s, in fact, domestic producers of miscellaneous industrial machines were shipping about $4.5 billion worth of products each year and employing a work force of about 65,000.

Rampant growth in U.S. capital spending slowed in the 1980s, as foreign-manufactured goods reduced U.S. producers' share of capital goods markets. Machinery purchases by transportation industries were particularly slow. As a result, sales of miscellaneous machinery stagnated. Industry revenues lagged as a result of inflation and climbed at an average rate of about 2 percent per year during the 1980s to about $5.36 billion. Recessed commercial and residential construction markets added

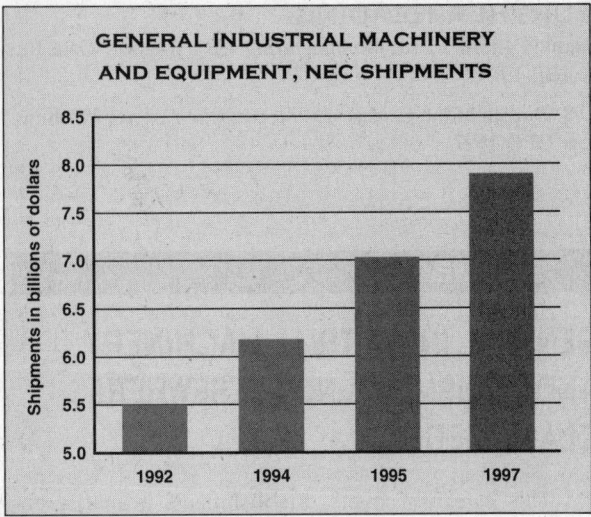

GENERAL INDUSTRIAL MACHINERY
AND EQUIPMENT, NEC SHIPMENTS

to industry woes in the late 1980s and early 1990s. Ailing manufacturers scrambled to sustain profitability by raising productivity, cutting their work force, and merging with or acquiring competitors.

Going into the mid-1990s, producers of miscellaneous machinery hoped to benefit from increased capital spending by the Clinton administration, an uptick in capital equipment replacements, and a devalued dollar, which was boosting exports. In addition, sales of machinery to some sectors showed signs of increasing. Construction equipment sales, for example, rose about 3 percent. However, spending on new manufacturing facilities and infrastructure was expected to remain flat at least through the mid-1990s.

The industry began a slow recovery after the recession ended in the mid-1990s. In 1995, according to the *1995 Annual Survey of Manufactures,* the industry employed 46,200 workers, a decrease of about 46 percent. However, this figure was 11.3 percent above the 41,500 workers in the industry reported in the 1992 census, and 13.8 percent above the 40,600 workers in the 1987 census. Industry productivity continued to rise as well, with $7.03 billion in value of goods reportedly shipped in 1995. This was 13.75 percent above the $6.18 billion worth of goods shipped in 1994 and 27.8 percent above the $5.5 billion shipped in 1992. By 1997, sales had reached almost $8 billion.

The industry is primarily run by numerous specialty manufacturers. Despite industry consolidation, over 1,000 companies competed going into the 1990s. In 1997, there were over 1,200 establishments employing almost 50,000 workers. Of the top 75 competitors, over half had sales of less than $40 million and employed fewer than 300 workers. One of the top leaders, according to *Ward's Business Directory 2000,* was ABB Flexible Automation Inc. of Michigan, which had sales of $6.4 billion and employed 800 people. Grinnell Corp. of New Hampshire,

had revenues of $3.08 billion and 24,000 employees. Other major manufacturers of miscellaneous industrial machinery included Nordson Corp. of Ohio with revenues of $661 million and 4,500 employees; Nesco Inc. of Ohio with estimated revenues of $420 million and 3,400 employees; and FANUC Robotics Corp. of Michigan with $412 million and 1,100 employees.

As companies continue to automate production facilities and move manufacturing operations across U.S. borders, the Bureau of Labor Statistics suggests that general industrial machinery industry employment will continue to decline. Jobs for assemblers and fabricators, which make up over 10 percent of the work force, will likely decline 32 percent by 2005, as will positions for machinists. Management opportunities will also deteriorate significantly. Sales and marketing positions, on the other hand, may increase slightly.

FURTHER READING

1995 Annual Survey of Manufactures. Washington: Bureau of the Census, 1997.

Darnay, Arsen J., ed. *Manufacturing USA; Industry Analyses, Statistics, and Leading Companies,* Detroit: Gale Research, 1993.

''NAICS 333999.'' *Manufacturing-Industry Series* U.S. Census Bureau, 1997 Economic Census, 17 November 1999.

U.S. Industrial Outlook 1993. Washington: U.S. Department of Commerce, January 1993.

Ward's Business Directory of U.S. Private and Public Companies, 2000. Detroit: Gale Group, 2000.

SIC 3571

ELECTRONIC COMPUTERS

The industry encompasses companies primarily engaged in manufacturing electronic computers. By definition, this includes machines that:

- Store the processing program or programs and the data immediately necessary for execution of the program;
- Can be freely programmed in accordance with the requirements of the user;
- Perform arithmetical computations specified by the user; and
- Execute, without human intervention, a processing program which requires them to modify their execution by logical decision during the processing run.

Included in this industry are digital computers, analog computers, and hybrid digital/analog computers. Establishments primarily engaged in manufacturing machinery or equipment that incorporate computers or a central processing unit for the purpose of performing functions such as measuring, displaying, or controlling process variables are classified based on the manufactured end product.

NAICS CODE(S)

334111 (Electronic Computer Manufacturing)

INDUSTRY SNAPSHOT

Led by swift sales of personal computers, the computer industry closed out the 1990s with broadly based growth but shrinking profits. In 1999 PC shipments worldwide exceeded many analysts' expectations, jumping more than 20 percent to reach about 113 million units, according to two separate estimates. PC revenue growth, however, lagged at 11 percent as ardent competition and mounting price sensitivity continued to erode prices. International Data Corp. valued PC shipments in 1999 at $189 billion globally; combined with sales of workstations, servers, and other computers, the world computer industry had revenues of more than $200 billion that year.

Global competition among computer makers has favored nimble, low-cost producers, and many of these are U.S. firms. In fact, according to a Dataquest analysis of 1999 results, the six largest U.S. owned computer makers—Compaq, Dell, IBM, Hewlett-Packard, Gateway, and Apple—controlled almost 45 percent of world PC shipments, up slightly from about 43 percent a year earlier. Dell emerged in 1999 as a particularly potent competitor by wresting the U.S. market lead from Compaq and pushing IBM to third place both in the United States and worldwide. Compaq, though bruised by financial troubles and a resulting management shakeup, prevailed as the world's largest PC manufacturer in 1999, but it ceded market share to the likes of Dell and Hewlett-Packard.

Despite all the computer industry's bounty in the 1990s, many foresee a slowdown is inevitable. Already higher-end segments of the business, such as mainframes, servers, and workstations, have turned in performances that are much less consistent and robust than PC sales. With falling prices chipping away at profits, too, most of the leading manufacturers have embraced other lines of business—often services—for fiscal sustenance in leaner times. International markets like Latin America and Asia are expected to be increasingly important, as well, because they are less saturated and offer faster growth.

ORGANIZATION AND STRUCTURE

The computer industry is segmented by product category. Different kinds of computers contain differing components, varying performance and price levels, and, to a certain extent, service different functions and markets.

At the most fundamental level, electronic computers can be categorized as either analog or digital. Analog computers are electromechanical devices whose operation is based on continuously variable quantities such as lengths, weights, or voltages. Digital computers, by contrast, operate by processing discrete quantities of digits or characters and offer greater flexibility in programming. Thus, almost all computers today are digital, and analogs represent a very small portion of industry production and sales. For this discussion, the term ''computer'' will refer to digital devices unless noted otherwise.

General-purpose computers are traditionally categorized by size, function, and processing power. These main categories are supercomputers, mainframes, midrange systems and servers, and microcomputers (PCs and workstations). While some have advanced formal definitions of each category, in practice the boundaries between each class are vague and, for example, there may be little or no difference between a low-end server and a high-end microcomputer.

Supercomputers. Supercomputers are high-speed number crunchers that allow scientists, engineers, and government researchers to process and manipulate massive amounts of data very quickly. Their performance is typically measured in terms of billions of floating point operations per second, or gigaflops, as opposed to millions of instructions per second (MIPS) assigned to most other types of computers. The fastest supercomputers reach processing speeds in the teraflops, or trillions of floating point operations per second. These technological taskmasters are used to complete complex feats, such as forecasting weather, designing ships and automobiles, conducting nuclear research, and carrying out advanced simulations. Supercomputers under development by IBM in the early 2000s were predicted to surpass the 1,000 teraflops threshold, entering the realm of petaflops, or quadrillion floating point operations per second.

An important distinction exists between traditional high-powered ''vector,'' and low-powered ''parallel'' supercomputers. The newer parallel devices join as many as tens of thousands of cheap microprocessors to accomplish what vector systems achieve with a handful of more expensive processors. Though usually less expensive, systems that use Massively Parallel Processing (MPP) technology can perform many tasks faster than traditional vector systems.

Because supercomputers are such specialized devices—and usually regulated by the U.S. government—they are mostly used in defense and limited academic research settings. In the late 1990s, supercomputer sales represented less than half of one percent of industry revenues.

Mainframes. Mainframe computers generally offer less raw computational power than supercomputers and are most often used to handle large volumes of large enterprise or institutional applications. Mainframes are also used by large Internet and e-commerce companies to meet the high-volume, high-reliability requirements of such firms. Traditionally, users accessed mainframes through satellite terminals, but mainframes are now commonly accessed by a variety of different devices over corporate networks. Some mainframes also offer add-on features that make them competitive with low-end supercomputers. In 2000, mainframe processing speeds ranged from approximately 50 MIPS to upwards of 3,000 MIPS.

Midrange Systems. Midrange computers, also called minicomputers and servers, serve anywhere from a few to several hundred users, either locally or at remote locations. Small to medium-sized businesses, company departments, and manufacturing facilities commonly use midrange systems for communications processing, automation, reporting, and networking. Midrange systems often employ vendor-developed proprietary applications that are tailored to the organization's needs. Newer ''open systems,'' though, allow the use of standardized operating systems and applications. Midrange computers can range in price from $10,000 to approximately $1 million.

Midrange systems include the diverse array of servers that are used in local area networks (LANs) and other networking arrangements. These servers are similar to midrange or mainframe computers in function, by serving multiple users with shared data, yet may be more similar to personal computers in structure, by being based on microprocessors. In fact, the lowest-end servers are merely high-end personal computers or workstations configured with the necessary software and telecommunications hardware. High-end servers often contain multiple microprocessors and have cut into the market traditionally served by computers based on more advanced processors.

Microcomputers. By far the industry's largest product segment, microcomputers, divided between personal computers (PCs) and workstations, are single-user, self-contained units. They offer the least raw computing power of any segment of the industry but provide the greatest amount of flexibility, diversity, and portability. This segment includes laptop and notebook computers.

Workstations are a special class of high-powered microcomputers. Many workstations are capable of performing intensive research, engineering, and graphics tasks that allow them to compete with low-end supercomputers and mainframes. High-performance microprocessors allow many workstations to employ high-resolution or 3-D graphic interfaces, sophisticated multi-task software, and advanced communication capabilities. Work-

station prices can range from $3,000 to more than $100,000. The traditional definition of workstations are microcomputers based on RISC (reduced instruction set computing) microprocessor design, but the distinction between workstations and personal computers is becoming increasingly blurred.

BACKGROUND AND DEVELOPMENT

The first mechanical calculating devices were built in Europe in the seventeenth century. The English mathematician Charles Babbage carried that concept a step further in the nineteenth century with the design of the Analytical Engine, the first digital computer. The Engine design showed how programs could be stored on punched cards similar to those used by French looms. Although the Analytical Engine was never built, it influenced the first digital mechanical computers and helped pave the way for the computer revolution that changed the world.

The few computers in existence in the 1940s were primarily used to grind out tables of complex mathematical functions. Researchers that understood the potential of more advanced devices, however, were successful in securing sizable U.S. government and military grants to fund further development. The first general-purpose electronic computer, ENIAC, was completed in 1946. ENIAC, which stands for electronic numerical integrator and calculator, required partial rewiring in order to program it for different tasks. The first operational stored-program electronic digital computer, similar in function to computers of today, was completed in 1949 at the University of Cambridge. Although various analog devices were also developed and tested in the 1930s and 1940s, analog computers played a relatively minor role in the development of the industry.

The electromechanical computers of the mid-1940s had already been replaced by the early 1950s with more powerful and flexible electronic versions. The UNIVAC system, developed for the U.S. Bureau of the Census, and a similar system, used by the General Electric Company, were two of the first commercially viable electronic computers put into use. By the end of the 1950s, business, government, and scientific communities began to view the computer as a dependable and potentially effective tool for an enormous variety of tasks.

Timesharing systems, pioneered at the Massachusetts Institute of Technology, allowed public and private entities to gain extensive access to large, expensive mainframe computer systems in the 1960s. Timesharing allowed several users at remote locations to simultaneously use a single machine. Users were charged for the amount of time that they were actually connected to the computer by cables or telephone lines. Although timeshare technology was first used primarily for scientific and technical endeavors, business and industry participants soon learned that they, too, could benefit from access to centralized processors.

By the end of the 1960s the computer industry was poised for rapid growth. Computers in the 1960s were already up to 100 times faster than their counterparts of the 1950s—and computer memory and speed continued to rise at an increasing rate. Furthermore, the first minicomputer was installed in 1965, breaking ground for an entirely new segment of the industry. The number of digital computers had increased from less than 15 in 1950 to more than 40,000 by the late 1960s. Going into the 1970s, though, all sectors of society were beginning to seek the computational power offered by supercomputers and mainframes to handle labor-intensive tasks. In addition, industry leaders were continually striving to expand their market by increasing computer access to end-users, rather than only trained computer professionals.

Development of the microprocessor in 1971 allowed the entire central processor of a computer to be placed on a single silicon chip. It was this development that led to subsequent rapid expansion and transformation of the industry. In addition to the proliferation of supercomputers, mainframes, and midrange systems that took advantage of new chip technology, workstations and PC devices began to emerge. By the early 1980s, more than 500,000 general-purpose computers had been installed in North America. Furthermore, the market was growing at an annual rate of about 20 percent.

In the early 1980s, the computer industry consisted of several niches, each dominated by one or two manufacturers that had been the first to successfully exploit an opening in the market. International Business Machines (IBM), Sperry, Wang, Unisys, and Digital Equipment Corporation (DEC) were among the many companies that generated immense revenues during the decade. For the most part, these companies succeeded by developing proprietary hardware and operating systems that effectively prohibited customers from switching to a competitor's product.

Manufacturers often enjoyed profit margins of 70 to 90 percent on sales of various mainframe and minicomputer installations. Demand ballooned throughout the decade as business, industry, and the public sector invested billions of dollars to computerize and automate information management, manufacturing, computationally-intensive research, and other activities. As many mainframe companies settled into their respective niches, however, the rapid advancement of microprocessor technology caused a market shift that took many industry leaders by surprise.

Many industry participants failed to foresee the dominance of PCs, workstations, and some midrange systems. Within a period of a few years, in fact, technologi-

cal innovations turned the slow and limited microcomputer of the early 1980s into a relatively low-cost, powerful, and speedy contender. Furthermore, by networking these smaller devices, users were able to develop cost-effective systems that could handle tasks that were previously performed only by mainframes and powerful minicomputers.

Although the demand for mainframe and supercomputer sales advanced throughout most of the decade, manufacturers that focused solely on those products and failed to respond to the inevitable dominance of workstations and PCs found themselves in serious financial trouble in the mid-1980s. The number of PCs purchased by Americans rose from fewer than 500,000 PCs in 1980 to approximately 7 million in 1984. By 1989, annual PC sales approached 10 million. Sales of RISC workstations grew at a rate of more than 110 percent annually between 1986 and 1988. As PCs increased their share of the entire computer-related market revenues from 10.6 percent in 1987 to 15.2 percent in 1991, the share of the market held by large-scale systems fell from 12.6 percent to 9.5 percent.

Many companies that led the computer industry in the 1980s suffered massive financial losses in the early 1990s, as they either retrenched or shifted their focus. Wang Laboratories, for instance, declared bankruptcy after posting an $11 million loss on $1.2 billion in sales and has since restructured itself as a software company. IBM accrued more losses in 1992 than most industry leaders generated in sales revenue.

Strong growth and solid profits enjoyed by most computer manufacturers during the 1980s faded in the early 1990s, as the industry realized a serious reduction in the overall growth of domestic demand. Several factors contributed to the downturn. In addition to the global recession of the early 1990s, manufacturers were beginning to confront the fact that the U.S. computer market was becoming saturated. Also, the shift from high-profit, large-scale proprietary systems to low-margin, open architecture, desktop computers was reducing profit opportunities.

Indeed, inexpensive personal systems that offered computing power similar to that offered by the mainframes of the early 1980s were now viewed as a commodity by many consumers. Rather than purchasing a PC system from a retail outlet at a price of $4,000 or $5,000, many customers in the early 1990s began purchasing more advanced systems through the mail or at discount warehouses for approximately $1,000 to $2,000. This trend only accelerated in the mid- and late 1990s with the explosive growth of Internet shopping (often direct from manufacturers) and the advent of sub-$1,000 PCs.

CURRENT CONDITIONS

By most measures, the computer industry had a phenomenal run in the 1990s. Based on estimates by Interna-

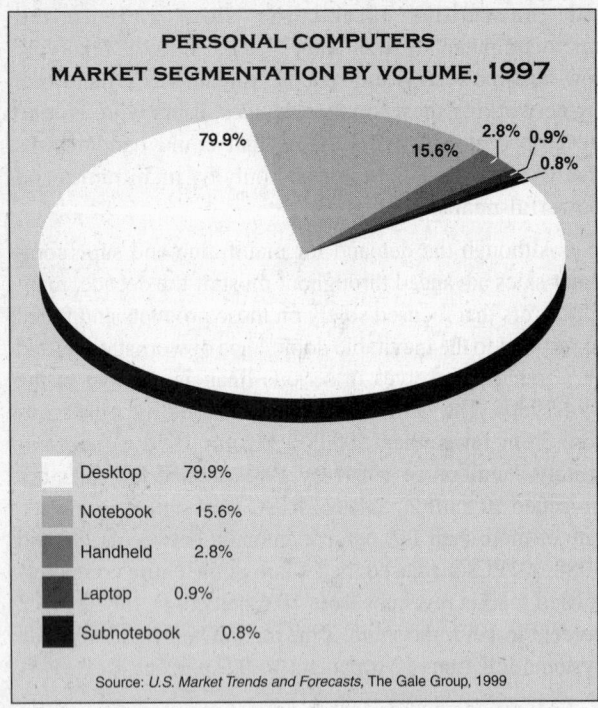

PERSONAL COMPUTERS
MARKET SEGMENTATION BY VOLUME, 1997

79.9% 15.6% 2.8% 0.9% 0.8%

Desktop	79.9%
Notebook	15.6%
Handheld	2.8%
Laptop	0.9%
Subnotebook	0.8%

Source: *U.S. Market Trends and Forecasts*, The Gale Group, 1999

tional Data Corp. (IDC), between 1992 and 1999 annual PC shipments worldwide skyrocketed 280 percent, including a 295 percent leap in U.S. shipments. Although global unit growth slipped to single-digit percentage gains in the early 1990s, the late 1990s saw consecutive years of 15 percent or greater increases, culminating in a torrid 20 percent unit rise during 1999.

Still, the financial picture was less triumphant. U.S. industry revenues stalled in the $50 to $55 billion range in the mid- and late 1990s as price cuts all but washed out gains in unit volume. In 1998, for example, U.S. shipments rose about 14 percent, but revenue only treaded water with a 1 percent uptick, according to a published assessment by Forrester Research.

Although price pressures eased somewhat in parts of 1999 and 2000, when a shortage of chips left PC makers struggling to keep up with demand and gave an opportunity to firm up prices, in the longer term further price erosion is likely. Indeed, a variety of free PC promotions have been mounted by different parties, notably Free-PC, Inc. This trend wasn't expected to affect the industry much—in 1999 Free-PC was bought out and its free program abolished—but it suggests how unstable the industry's pricing climate has been. From 1998 to 2000, reported IDC, average PC prices worldwide skidded 18 percent, to $1,543 a machine. Averages in the consumer market were already much lower, at $844 in late 1999.

Aside from pricing worries, in the longer term the PC segment faces a potential slowdown, particularly in the United States, as the market for conventional PCs grows saturated and as other kinds of devices like wireless

Internet appliances gain favor. Although a large portion of the U.S. consumer population doesn't yet own a computer, reaching that market may only yield diminishing returns. In the home market, replacement PCs and second or third PCs for existing users may prove more fertile, but again other, more specialized devices are likely to encroach on PCs in these areas. Meanwhile, in the larger corporate market, research suggests that companies are spending a declining share of their technology dollars on PCs, instead devoting those funds to developing efficiencies through e-commerce.

All of this, of course, doesn't portend the demise of the computer business. In 2000, for example, IDC predicted another buoyant year for PC shipments, which were expected to swell 18 percent to 132 million units. Still, evidence points to a more fragmented market in the early 2000s, forcing computer makers to contend with handheld computing devices like the Palm Pilot as well as Internet-enabled phones from companies like Qualcomm and Nokia. Such gadgets tend not only to be cheaper than PCs, but also simpler and more user-friendly. To this end, most of the PC titans, including Compaq, Hewlett-Packard, and Gateway, were expected to unveil a widening line of simpler computers in 2000 and 2001.

Mainframes. In the early to mid-1990s, mainframes were roundly derided as archaic beasts, but by 1996 these high-powered creatures found redemption. For one thing, mainframe makers like IBM labored to bring prices down. In the early 1990s mainframe power cost a steep $100,000 per MIPS of processing power. By 1997 prices were drastically lower, around $10,000 per MIPS, and by 2000 they had plunged to $2,270. At least one analyst believed mainframes could dip to $400 per MIPS by 2003.

As prices spiraled downward, steady demand sustained manufacturers. IBM, the U.S. mainframe leader, experienced as much as 60 percent annual growth during the late 1990s in mainframe demand as measured in MIPS—but this barely kept sales level amid tumbling prices. Driving the growth, as companies rushed into e-commerce and other Internet activities, they found they needed mainframes' vast processing speed, storage capacity, and reliability more than ever. As a result of e-commerce and growth in the more traditional corporate application hosting market, the broader mainframe hardware market was expected to rise by a brisk 30 percent a year in the early 2000s.

Servers. Much larger than mainframes in terms of revenue, servers are also one of the industry's most diverse categories. By various definitions, anything from a $3,000 souped-up PC to a $1-million mainframe can qualify as a server, depending on how it's marketed and used. Low-end servers, used to power small LANs and low-volume Internet sites, have been the fastest-growing segment, with sales up 10 percent in 1999. The low end has also been battered less by price cuts. Sales of higher-end servers, though, were weaker in the late 1990s in part because of preparations for the Y2K date transition. Low-end machines were expected to continue leading server growth in the early 2000s.

INDUSTRY LEADERS

Compaq. Compaq Computer Corp., which introduced its first IBM-compatible PC in 1982, managed to pull ahead of the competition through a strong capital base and superior marketing. By the late 1990s, Compaq, based in Houston, Texas, became the largest PC maker in the world, surpassing IBM. Its 13.2 percent stake in the global PC market was the dominant share, but its lead was narrowing because of stiff competition from Dell and Hewlett-Packard. Compaq has traditionally focused sales through dealers and distributors, but in face of rising competition, in 1997 it began expanding its direct sales efforts.

Compaq produces computers in the desktop, laptop/notebook, and server categories. The company's mid-range and low-end server lines have proven highly competitive with those of IBM and others, and in 1999 Compaq became the dominant maker of entry-level servers. Compaq also greatly strengthened its place in the high-end hardware and services market with its 1998 acquisition of Digital Equipment Corp. (DEC).

In 1999 Compaq's revenue from all hardware products, including PCs, workstations, servers, and storage systems, totaled $31.9 billion, marking a 16.5 percent gain for those segments. Net income that year also improved after a dismal 1998, when Compaq posted a net loss for the year because of merger costs and revenue shortfalls. In early 1999 Compaq dismissed its longtime CEO Eckhard Pfeiffer because of the company's poor showing both on its income statement and in the stock market.

IBM. Though it has trailed Compaq in some segments, IBM Corp., of Armonk, New York, remains a mammoth in the global computer hardware, software, and services industries. The company, founded in 1910 as Calculating-Tabulating-Recording (CTR), got its start by producing punch-card tabulating machines. IBM grew quickly by stressing large-scale, custom-built systems, and by leasing, rather than selling, its products to most of its customers. Government contracts were largely responsible for the company's rapid growth during the 1940s. It was during this period that IBM developed the Mark I, the first computer capable of retaining a set of rules that could be applied to information that was input at a later time.

By the mid-1960s, IBM owned 65 percent of the U.S. computer market. IBM's mainframe models, the S/360 and S/370, generated massive profits for the company during the 1970s. Although IBM continued to grow

through the mid-1980s, the company began to lose focus, and its hesitation in taking the PC market seriously was only belatedly seen as a miscalculation. Between 1985 and 1992, IBM dismissed 100,000 employees and restructured its operations several times.

After a period of losses in the early 1990s, when breakup rumors were rampant and its mainframe business was thought dead, IBM staged a turnaround in the mid-1990s under its new chief executive, Louis V. Gerstner, Jr. It branched further into software, high-end consulting, and systems management services to diversify its revenues. Moreover, it made all of its hardware businesses—from mainframes to PCs—more competitive on price and features. In the late 1990s its strategy also included aggressive courting of Internet and e-commerce customers, offering Web-oriented servers, like the Netfinity model, and e-commerce services to help other companies build and manage their sites.

Though it lost market share to Compaq and others in the lower-end hardware markets, IBM still had a commanding presence in the mainframe and server markets with its S/390, RS/6000, and AS/400 models. In 1999 IBM ranked third in worldwide PC sales, behind Compaq and Dell. Hardware of all kinds made up 42.3 percent of IBM's $87.5 billion in 1999 revenues. IBM's high-end hardware lines suffered a weak 1999, however, with server revenue dropping 17.9 percent on the year. The company attributed much of the shortfall to Y2K technology freezes by many of its large corporate clients.

Dell. Dell Computer Corp., of Round Rock, Texas, first gained its place in the computer industry as a direct seller of discounted IBM-compatible PCs to businesses. By the late 1990s, Dell had started to embrace the consumer market as well, vigorously pushing its Web site as a convenient way for companies and individuals to order the exact system they wanted. In addition to desktop models, Dell makes notebooks and lower-end servers, and more recently, it has begun to offer Internet hosting and related services, which carry higher profit margins than some of its hardware lines.

Legendary for its efficient inventory and production systems, Dell climbed its way from being the world's seventh-largest PC maker in 1992 to the number-two producer, with 9.8 percent of the market, by 1999. That year the company's unit shipments surged 50 percent and revenue jumped 38 percent, to $25.3 billion. Reflecting tighter margins, however, Dell's net income in 1999 only rose 27 percent.

Hewlett-Packard. Hewlett-Packard (HP), founded in 1938 and based in Palo Alto, California, is a leading company in PCs, workstations, servers, notebooks, and handheld computers, in addition to being the leading U.S. manufacturer of computer printers. The company also produces scientific and medical instrumentation, but computers and peripherals account for 80 percent of its revenues. HP is a leader in Unix operating system-based workstations and computers in general, for which it has designed its own microprocessor chips and developed a version of the Unix software.

In 1999 HP ranked as the world's fourth-largest PC maker, with 6.4 percent of the market, and the world's second-biggest manufacturer of midrange servers, behind IBM. Computer systems revenue at HP reached $18.4 billion in fiscal 1999, up less than 4 percent from the year before because of lower prices. Despite its negligible improvement in revenue, HP's computer unit shipments grew 34.4 percent during the calendar year, driven by particularly strong results in the consumer market.

Apple. Apple Computer is well known for being the most visible dissenter to the Windows/Intel standards that dominate the PC business. Apple, based in Cupertino, California, was a pioneer in PC technology when it was founded in 1977 and, after several short-lived models, introduced its immensely successful Macintosh line of computers in 1984. From the beginning, Apple's marketing efforts were aimed at the school, college, and home markets. It was never as successful in the business market. By the 1990s, the position of the rival PCs based on Intel microprocessors and DOS/Windows operating systems had become solidly entrenched, and Apple's market share began to decline.

Apple finally decided to license its MacOS operating system in 1995 to spur the development of Macintosh clones, but the move failed to reverse the company's bad fortune. The computer maker's turning point came in 1997 when co-founder Steve Jobs was brought back as interim chief executive. Jobs halted Mac clone licensing, narrowed the company's sprawling product lines, revamped product marketing, and endorsed new product initiatives like the iMac.

By its fiscal 1998 Apple was turning an annual profit once again and riding on the success of the iMac. The popular model, which featured a simple, colorful design aimed at the consumer and education markets, sold about 1.8 million units in the company's fiscal 1999, almost half of all Apple's unit sales. For calendar 1999, Apple was rated the world's seventh-largest PC maker, with a 3.4 percent share of the market. Sales in its fiscal year, which ended 25 September 1999, reached $6.1 billion and net income topped $600 million. While its monetary sales growth was lackluster that year, unit shipments were up 34 percent and profits were at record levels.

Sun. Sun Microsystems Inc., based in Mountain View, California, became the leader of the workstation industry segment only five years after the company was founded

in 1982 and only six years after the first workstations appeared on the market.

Sun pioneered the open system, Unix-based workstation, as opposed to those that ran only proprietary software. Open standards allow the sharing of software and hardware components among competing workstation manufacturers. Sun has also been a leader in developing computers based on the RISC microprocessor chip architecture. It developed its own improved version of RISC called SPARC (scalable performance architecture) and it licenses the technology to chip manufacturers. Sun's SPARCstation workstation computer, introduced first in 1989 and based on the SPARC technology, became the most popular workstation model.

As growth in the workstation market began to slow in the early 1990s, Sun began to focus more on developing Unix servers and storage systems and became an important contender in those segments as well. In 1999 Sun's revenues totaled $11.7 billion, up almost 20 percent from 1998 because of solid demand for its enterprise and workgroup servers. Meanwhile, its traditional workstation business suffered setbacks as businesses opted for servers or lower-end PCs instead. Hardware sales accounted for 86 percent of its revenues.

WORKFORCE

The computer industry employs large numbers of electrical engineers, programmers, assemblers, and technicians. In fact, these occupations represent about 30 percent of the industry total. Companies also hire large numbers of people for miscellaneous management, sales, and clerical positions.

Despite the sharp uptrend in the industry's output, U.S. employment in computer manufacturing has been declining since its peak in 1984. Between 1984 and 1995, the computer manufacturing industry lost 32 percent of its workforce, an average annual rate of 3 percent. The computer industry is one of the more highly automated manufacturing industries, and many manual assembly jobs have been eliminated. Other manufacturing and assembly work has been relocated overseas.

As of 1999, computer manufacturing employed 182,400 U.S. workers, about 40 percent of whom were production workers. This reflects a dramatic decrease from earlier years. In 1990, for example, the industry employed as many as 278,500 people, with production workers making up just 25 percent.

Given the ongoing pressure on computer makers' revenues and profits, companies are expected to continue to introduce labor-saving automation and to outsource manufacturing activities to low-cost foreign producers. Furthermore, corporate alliances should moderate the demand for research and development professionals.

While the demand for programmers in the industry was expected to rise slightly, the demand for other occupations will likely fall, according to the Bureau of Labor Statistics. The demand for engineers, for instance, will slip about 3.5 percent by 2005. Likewise, technician and engineering management jobs will fall by 2 to 5 percent. Manufacturing jobs, especially, will disappear. The demand for electrical and electronic assemblers, for example, will likely plummet 55 percent by 2005. Analysts project that assemblers and fabricator positions will decline by about 37 percent, while the demand for production planning professionals will fall more than 20 percent.

Management executive positions are expected to decrease as well—by an estimated 22 percent. Even the number of lower level management jobs is expected to fall by about 20 percent by 2005. The one bright spot in the job picture is an expected 47 percent increase in the demand for systems analysts and computer scientists. This group currently accounts for only about 2.4 percent of employment in the computer and office equipment industries.

Professionals with bachelor's degrees in computer engineering (BSCE) were in high demand in the mid-1990s. Computer and business-equipment manufacturers planned to hire almost 66 percent more graduates in 1997 than in 1996. Graduates with BSCE degrees could expect starting salaries on average of $37,301 in 1997, up 5.9 percent over 1996. Many of these new employees were not be directly involved in computer manufacturing, however, rather in services. Most of the biggest computing companies have extensive and growing service and consulting divisions, which hire hundreds of new graduates every year.

AMERICA AND THE WORLD

U.S. computer companies solidified their lead in the global computer industry in the 1990s, aided by aggressive marketing, a strong U.S. economy, and weakness in parts of Asia and Latin America. In the PC segment, the top six U.S. manufacturers held a combined 44.8 percent share of the world market, according to estimates by Dataquest.

U.S. Export Trends. Nonetheless, for some of the same reasons, U.S. computer exports weakened in the late 1990s while imports were up sharply. In 1999 U.S. computer exports fell to $8.35 billion, down 1.5 percent from 1998. Economic turmoil in Asia, including a protracted recession in Japan, diminished demand for U.S. exports in affected countries. In addition, U.S. manufacturers continued to seek cost savings on labor and other production expenses, and relocating operations in other countries—or simply importing components from other countries—has been a key strategy to keep costs down. As a result, although the production may be attributed to, say, Compaq on a corporate basis, on a trade basis, foreign-made computers and components are recorded as imports.

Europe continued to be the largest regional market for the U.S. computer industry in the late 1990s. Europe accounted for $7.7 billion, or 36 percent, of all U.S. computer, computer peripheral, and computer part exports in 1999. That percentage was consistent with previous years, but the dollar value was down by as much as 50 percent since the mid-1990s.

Asia was the second biggest buyer of U.S. computer equipment in 1999, with $6.1 billion (28 percent) of U.S. exports. Japan accounted for one-third of U.S. exports to Asia.

U.S. Import Trends. Imports of computers into the United States have been on a steady incline. In 1999 they totaled $10.22 billion, jumping almost 38 percent from the year before. Asia has long been the greatest source of U.S. imports, supplying 79 percent in 1999. Japan, Singapore, Taiwan, China, and Malaysia are the biggest Asian sources. Outside Asia, the United States also imports significant amounts of computer equipment from Mexico, Ireland, and most recently, Hungary.

Leading International Markets. Despite economic and currency troubles scattered throughout parts of Asia and Latin America in the late 1990s, by 1999 some of those areas were beginning to recover. International Data Corp. estimated 1999 PC shipments in Latin America at 5.9 million, for a total market value of $7.4 billion. Unit sales for the region that year grew a healthy 15 percent. Mexico, with almost 24 percent of the Latin American market, was especially strong, with shipments nearly doubling in 1999. IDC reported that Chile was another fast-moving market for PCs in 1999, while Brazil and Argentina were more subdued but stable. Strong consumer sales were a major factor. Among U.S. manufacturers, Compaq and IBM were best poised to capitalize on Latin American growth.

Western Europe has been another bastion of relative stability and growth for PC makers. The market as whole grew some 17-18 percent in 1999, led by gains in large countries like Germany, France, and the United Kingdom, as well as emerging growth in places like Spain and Greece. Dataquest estimated Western European shipments in 1999 at almost 30 million units. The consumer market, which made up 28 percent of Western European demand, proved particularly buoyant, growing 32 percent on the year. Compaq had a sizable lead in Western Europe, with 15.6 percent of the market as of 1999, but Fujitsu Siemens and Dell were closing in on its lead.

RESEARCH AND TECHNOLOGY

The computer industry has historically benefited from considerable government funds in research and development. This was especially the case during the Cold War. More recently government funding of research in high technology industries has declined, and, according to a study by the Institute for the Future, the industry's own investments in research have not been as great to make up the difference. Furthermore, in the early and mid-1990s computer companies actually decreased the percentage of their revenues that they invest in R&D. Computer companies still invest considerable resources in new product research and development, but this is mostly for the short term. Long-term basic research in entirely new technologies is not funded as well as it was in the past. Shorter product life cycles and a commoditization of the computer industry have contributed to this trend.

Nevertheless, the computer industry remains very technology-driven. Many of the technological innovations that impact the computer industry are being developed in other, related industries, however. These include faster and more powerful microprocessors developed by the semiconductor industry, the capacity for more memory storage developed by the computer storage device industry, the support of more detailed graphic and video developed by manufacturers of computer monitors and displays, faster communications capabilities between computers developed by the telecommunications equipment industry, and more robust operating systems and sophisticated applications developed by the computer software industry. A trend toward smaller, faster, cheaper machines with greater memory will continue.

One continuing trend that is common among all these aspects of computers and related devices is miniaturization. Beginning with the invention of the microprocessor chip in 1971, and followed by the ability to store more data on smaller data storage media, the development of flat-panel displays, and computer system designs that better conserve space, computers have been getting smaller while retaining or increasing their processing power.

Another trend in computers is the integration of communications and processing equipment technologies that allow computers to act as telephones, answering machines, video-conferencing devices, and television sets. Still cameras, video cameras, and video players may also be attached. Eventually, some argue, the distinction between television sets and computers will be blurred.

FURTHER READING

"Brining Mainframe Might to PC Servers." *Business Week,* 5 July 1999.

Burrows, Peter. "Computers and Chips." *Business Week,* 10 January 2000.

"Californians' Online Spending Highest in U.S." *Newsbytes,* 28 February 2000.

Churbuck, David, and Gary Samuels. "Can IBM Keep It Up?" *Forbes,* 3 June 1996.

"Compaq Results Rise In 4Q, Year." *Electronic News,* 27 January 1997.

"Computers - Major." *Moody's Industry Review,* 4 October 1996.

Damore, Kelley, and Deborah Gage. "Servers." *Computer Reseller News,* 3 June 1996.

DePompa, Barbara. "Hitachi's Big Win." *InformationWeek,* 24 February 1997.

Dicarlo, Lisa. "Big Blue Outlines Power Plays." *PC Week,* 20 December 1999.

Doyle, T.C. "What Makes HP Tick." *VARbusiness,* 1 May 1996.

Hoffman, Thomas. "Vendors Face Y2K Spending Freeze." *Computerworld,* 9 November 1998.

Howard, Bill. "Looking Forward: Technology on the Way." *PC Magazine,* 25 March 1997.

Johnston, Stuart J. "The PC is Alive and Well." *InformationWeek,* 3 June 1996.

Kirkpatrick, David. "Why Compaq Envies Dell: The Leading Maker Alters Course." *Fortune,* 17 February 1997.

Korzeniowski, Paul. "Manufacturers Debate Platform Futures." *Software Magazine,* August 1995.

Linden, Dana Wechsler, and Bruce Upjohn. "Top Corporate Performance of 1995: Boy Scouts on a Rampage." *Forbes,* 1 January 1996.

Marcus, Mary Brophy, et al. "Personal Tech—Low PC Prices No Longer Compute." *U.S. News & World Report,* 6 March 2000.

McWilliams, Gary. "A Healthy Economy Spurs Recent Price Hikes in PCs." *Wall Street Journal,* 13 January 2000.

"Personal Computers: Are the Glory Days Over?" *Business Week,* 14 February 2000.

Ramo, Joshua Cooper. "Act Two for Big Blue." *Time,* 4 November 1996.

Reinhardt, Andy. "Computers and Chips." *Business Week,* 11 January 1999.

Rodriguez, Karen. "HP Servers to Battle IBM Mainframes." *The Business Journal,* 13 August 1999.

Schlosberg, Jeremy. "Independence Day." *PC Week,* 24 June 1996.

"Strong Industry Demand Fuels Transpacific Flow of Computer Parts, Finished Goods to Pacific Rim." *Traffic World,* 3 June 1996.

"Survey: Mainframe to Remain in Mainstream Beyond the Year 2000." *EDGE: Work-Group Computing Report,* 2 October 1995.

Thibodeau, Patrick. "Trade Pact Could Boost Computer Sales." *Computerworld,* 16 December 1996.

U.S. Department of Commerce. International Trade Administration. Office of Computers and Business Equipment. "Electronic Computer Equipment Trade Summary: 1999." Washington, D.C.: GPO, 14 March 2000. Available from www.ita.doc.gov.

Vijayan, Jaikumar. "Outrageous Fortune?" *Computerworld,* 10 January 2000.

Ward, Judy. "How Bright is Sun's Future? Sun Microsystems is Stronger Than Ever, But So Is the Competition." *Financial World,* 5 December 1995.

"Will PC Demand Diminish in the Fourth Quarter?" *Purchasing,* 17 June 1999.

SIC 3572

COMPUTER STORAGE DEVICES

This classification covers establishments primarily engaged in manufacturing computer storage devices.

NAICS CODE(S)

334112 (Computer Storage Device Manufacturing)

INDUSTRY SNAPSHOT

The computer storage industry manufactures tape, magnetic, and optical storage and retrieval devices for computer systems. These products range from the common floppy and hard disk drives built into desktop computers to stand-alone storage management systems used in large enterprise networks.

Demand for storage capacity and performance has risen sharply as microprocessors have grown faster, software applications have become more resource-intensive, and network computing has become more pervasive. Attempts to harness processing power and offer users more features have made the typical new software application require vastly more storage space than earlier versions. On personal computers, storage needs have further evolved and multiplied because of expanding multimedia features and content such as DVD movies and downloadable music on the Internet. Meanwhile, corporate systems have had to cope with escalating storage and processing needs from internal users as well as from the Internet.

In 1999 the industry shipped worldwide an estimated 168 million hard disk drives, the industry's largest product segment by revenue, and 260 million optical and removable drives, according to research published by Disk/Trend, Inc. U.S. companies hold a dominant share of the world market.

Despite the myriad forces stimulating demand for storage devices, the industry, like other computer hardware segments, has been hurt by fierce price competition. In the late 1990s this eroded both revenues and profits—even while unit shipments climbed. Such pressures have prompted significant consolidation within the industry and have brought cost-cutting to the fore at several storage device companies.

While unit growth was expected to remain strong and prices were expected to stabilize, the industry in the early 2000s also faced new challenges and opportunities associated with storage outsourcing services, or so-called storage service providers (SSPs). Such Internet-based services offer storage space and management tools that clients can simply connect to and use, enabling companies to avoid purchasing and maintaining storage hardware and software themselves. The nascent SSP field had potential to alter how storage devices are used and marketed; it also created an opportunity for makers of storage equipment to branch into services.

ORGANIZATION AND STRUCTURE

Most computer memory storage devices can be classified as either optical or magnetic. In 1997, about 135 million magnetic devices were sold by U.S. manufacturers, up from 107 million in 1996. Optical components and other storage devices were being shipped at a rate of about 6.3 billion units per year. In addition to optical and magnetic storage, semiconductor memory chips that store data and programs in the form of digital impulses had gained recognition as a viable new technology by the early 1990s.

Magnetic Storage. Magnetic devices record information in the form of magnetized spots that represent a binary code—a series of digits represented by either 1 or 0. A magnetized head suspended slightly above the surface of a medium reads and writes information on the disk. To record information, electrical charges that register a pattern on the surface of the magnetically sensitive medium are delivered through the head. To read data, the same head detects and converts spots into electrical impulses. The data can be retained indefinitely, or erased and replaced with new magnetic spots.

The three primary classes of magnetic storage devices are hard disk drives, floppy disk drives, and magnetic tape machines. Magnetic tapes, which were once the most widely used method of computer memory storage, store data on 4-inch-wide or 8 millimeter tape coated with a magnetically sensitive compound. Tape units typically read and write at a rate of 183 to 722 kilobytes per second and can store more than 270 gigabytes. Some units, called autoloaders, combine several tape cartridges to maximize speed and capacity.

The advantage of magnetic tape storage is that massive quantities of information can be stored in a relatively compact space. Furthermore, tape devices have historically been the fastest method of reading and writing large amounts of data. The drawback of tape systems, however, is that the tape must be read from one end to the other in order to retrieve and store information. For this reason, magnetic tape is most often used to copy, or backup, large amounts of data stored on a network or mainframe system (or for other purposes in which stored data can be sequentially accessed). In 1995, about 3.5 million magnetic tape storage components were sold by U.S. manufacturers.

Floppy diskette drives read and write information to a single rotating disk that can be removed from the drive. They are used to transfer and temporarily store information on 3.5-inch or 5.25-inch diskettes. Floppy drive technology is essentially the same as that used in hard disk drives, but floppy disks are made of coated synthetic material rather than metal. Although some U.S. manufacturers produce floppy drives, the domestic magnetic drive industry emphasizes hard drive production.

A hard disk magnetic storage device resembles a stack of small metal plates that rotate at a constant speed. Between each plate, a magnetic head is positioned on an arm that sweeps across the disk's surface. Each plate is coated on both sides with a magnetically sensitive compound on which a head can read or write information. Every bit of information stored on the disks is accessible by the heads each time the stack rotates.

The advantage of hard drives is that they can quickly retrieve information nonsequentially. Furthermore, because they are compact they make excellent storage devices for microcomputers. Of the more than 1 billion hard drives sold in 1995, most held a gigabyte or more of information. According to Disk/Trend Inc., a California market research firm, leading-edge disk drives in 1997 had a density of 1.36 billion bits per square inch. Disk drives with greater capacities were commonly used in workstations, minicomputers, local area networks (LANs), and mainframes.

Hard drives for larger computer systems are generally 14-inch, 10-inch, or 8-inch drives. Microcomputers typically have 5.25-inch, 3.5-inch, 2.5-inch, or 1.8-inch drives. Smaller disks usually hold one to two megabytes of information. In 1994, hard disk drives sold 33 percent more units—67.2 million—than in 1993, with revenues totaling $16.9 billion. In 1995, 2.8 million 3.5-inch drives were sold by U.S. firms. Sales of older 5.25-inch drives lagged at about 91,000 units. Sales of 2.5-inch drives had sales of about 5.7 million in 1992, and approximately 300,000 1.8-inch drives were sold in 1992.

Computers communicate, or interface, with disk drives through a controller. Most drives comply with high-performance interface standards such as the Enhanced Small Drive Interface (ESDI), or the Small Computer Systems Interface (SCSI). SCSI drives are more easily integrated into other manufacturers' products; consequently, they are the most common type of drive.

Optical Storage. Compact Disc-Read Only Memory (CD-ROM) drives use laser beams to read information on a rotating synthetic disk. Most consumer disks are composed of three layers: an overcoat that protects the information on the disk; the dye layer, where the information is recorded as digital bits of information; and a mirrored base that reflects the laser back to its source.

CD-Write Once Read Many (CD-WORM) drives and discs also allow users to store their own information on a disc, though that data cannot be erased and replaced with new information. CD-Recordable (CD-R) is a write-once technology like the CD-WORM that has become one of the first of such devices to be priced within the consumer/small business market. In 1996 the cost of the technology ranged from $800 to $1,000 for the drives and $6 to $8 per disc. CD-R drive prices were expected to drop to about $300 within a few years, with disc prices dropping to $3. Another optical storage option available in the late 1990s was the "erasable CD-ROM," which had the capability to rewrite or replace existing data. Finally, another optical storage device gaining popularity in the late 1990s was the DVD, or high-density compact disc. The drives and discs have more capacity to handle video with storage levels of 4.7 to 17 gigabytes. Conventional CD-ROMs used in most PCs have a capacity of roughly 650 megabytes.

The advantage of optical storage is that comparatively massive amounts of information can be inexpensively stored on a small, portable medium. Because a single CD can store up to 300,000 pages of information, CD-ROM is often used for storing such memory intensive applications as information databases or programs with elaborate graphics. The name and phone number of every household in the United States, for instance, was available on three CDs in 1997 for less than $100.

The disadvantage of CD-ROM is that information retrieval is significantly slower than that of magnetic devices. Also, optical storage is relatively inflexible because it does not allow users to easily write and erase information. In 1995, U.S. firms shipped 38.7 million CD-ROM drives, a 130 percent increase over 1994. About 250,000 CD-WORM drives were shipped in 1992.

Semiconductor Memory. Manufacturers in the early 1990s were also delivering computer storage on innovative new semiconductor memory chips called flash cards. Flash memory stores programs and data in the form of digital impulses. Data can be easily read, written, and erased on cards that hold two to four megabytes of data. The cards can be inserted and removed from a flash card slot just like a floppy diskette. Flash cards perform much faster than magnetic devices and require much less power to operate.

Because flash memory is nonvolatile and requires no moving parts, a user can turn off his computer, turn it back on later, and find himself at the same place he was when he powered down. Because of its advantages, flash memory technology is popular with manufacturers of notebook, pen-based, and hand-held computers. The Personal Computer Memory Card International Association (PCMCIA) represents the interests of this industry segment and strives to maintain manufacturing standards.

Competitive Structure. A multitude of different organizational structures are represented in the computer memory storage industry. The industry is highly fragmented and is characterized by technological volatility. Firms that do not develop and produce breakthrough products are often forced to compete in a high-volume, low-margin, commodity-like market environment. Leading firms, in contrast, can reap huge short-term profits as a result of innovation. These firms, though, must often risk large research and development expenditures to generate new technology for rapidly shifting, unpredictable markets.

Original equipment manufacturers, such as IBM, Compaq (including the former Digital Equipment Corp.), and Hewlett-Packard, produce or purchase devices that are integrated into their own computers. Other large vendors, such as Seagate Technologies and Conner Peripherals, produce devices that are installed in, or used with, other computer manufacturers' products. These companies tend to purchase few of their components from other companies. In contrast to the more vertically integrated companies just described, several companies utilize foreign manufacturers to produce their drives or to manufacture many of the components that go into their storage devices.

BACKGROUND AND DEVELOPMENT

The punch card, the first storage mechanism used with a mechanical computer, was introduced by Herman Hollerith in 1886 to help the U.S. Bureau of the Census calculate demographic data. The punch card concept was actually developed by Charles Babbage and was demonstrated in his 1833 design of the Analytical Engine. Although Babbage's engine was never built, it provided a model for Hollerith and others. Punch cards allowed computer operators to automatically repeat arithmetic operations on numbers that were represented by holes punched into successive cards.

In 1944, IBM developed the first large-scale automatic digital computer, which was conceived by Howard H. Aiken of Harvard University. The Automatic Sequence Controlled Calculator (nicknamed the Mark I) utilized more than 750,000 parts and relied on punched cards and punched tape to store data. The device was used to compute ballistic data for defense purposes and could calculate three additions per second. In 1946, Bell Telephone Laboratories developed a similar computer that stored and read sequences of instructions on loops of paper tape.

The Electronic Numerical Integrator and Calculator (ENIAC), which was completed in 1945, stored numbers and computing instructions entirely by electronic circuits containing more than 18,000 vacuum tubes. Although ENIAC still used punched cards for input and output data, the computer could electronically store 20 numbers. The computer had to be programmed by tedious rewiring in order to accomplish different tasks. Despite its limitations, the computer was used until 1956.

During the mid-1940s researchers realized that a major hurdle in the advancement of computer technology was a lack of adequate resident memory storage capacity. During the 1940s and 1950s, four storage techniques were developed: acoustic delay lines, magnetic drums, electrostatic devices, and magnetic cores. Mathematician John von Neumann was one of the most influential developers of storage technology during this era.

The first magnetic core computer, the Whirlwind, was developed at the Massachusetts Institute of Technology in 1953. By the mid-1950s magnetic core memory had become the principal storage system. At this point, many companies realized that computer production and design had the potential to be a viable industry. IBM, Sperry, Rand, Burroughs, RCA, General Electric, and other companies quickly began introducing computers for a variety of commercial and institutional applications. By 1960, in fact, approximately 5,000 stored-program computers were operating in the United States. Throughout the 1960s this number doubled every two to three years.

As the computer industry expanded during the 1960s and 1970s, the need for mass memory storage devices that could hold programs and backup data drove the development of a variety of mechanisms. Some of the most successful storage devices used magnetic "Winchester" technology. These devices, which were developed by IBM in 1956, evolved into what is now the magnetic hard disk drive.

The 1980s. During the 1980s the use of Winchester drives began to dominate the memory storage industry. Prior to disk storage, magnetic tape was the industry's primary information storage medium. Advancements in disk technology, though, quickly outpaced the speed and efficiency of tape systems—resulting in the obsolescence of tape for most applications.

Augmenting growth of both hard disk and floppy disk drives in the 1980s was the proliferation of the microcomputer. Throughout the 1980s these personal computers (PCs) relied solely on magnetic disk technology for memory storage. Sales of PCs skyrocketed from less than 500,000 per year in 1980 to 10 million in 1990; the demand for disk storage devices soared. Growth in workstations, microcomputers, and mainframes also spurred demand. By 1990, manufacturers were shipping more than 26 million Winchester hard drives and about 40 million floppy drives per year.

Despite the decline of market share attributable to magnetic tape drives, this segment experienced steady growth during the 1980s and early 1990s. By 1989, manufacturers were shipping about 1.6 million tape drives per year, most of which were being used to backup hard disks and network systems. Furthermore, tape drive sales were expected to grow at an annual rate of approximately 8 percent in the early 1990s.

As computer memory storage device manufacturers entered the 1990s, new storage technology was beginning to gain widespread attention by the industry and consumers. Optical memory, which had been viewed essentially as an experimental or specialty technology during the late 1980s, was beginning to establish itself in mainstream business and consumer markets. There was also an increasing interest in semiconductor memory.

The 1990s. Magnetic disk drives continued to dominate industry offerings in the 1990s. The number of hard drives sold, for instance, climbed steadily to 31 million in 1991 and to 37 million by 1992. Floppy drive sales volume also climbed, much as it had during the 1980s, to about 45 million per year by 1993. Despite a massive shakeout in the PC market, which was placing severe downward pressure on PC prices, many storage device producers enjoyed solid profit growth in the early 1990s. This was partly a result of PC industry price wars that were boosting PC unit shipments.

Still, disk drive prices continued to drop for all but the latest models. While the most advanced drives still provided comfortable profit margins, mainstream technology grew ever cheaper and less profitable. Between February and June of 1993, for example, disk drive prices dropped 25 percent.

To counter the shift toward commoditization, storage device makers in the mid-1990s tried to expand their development and production of technologically superior products that offered higher profit margins. Some firms focused on 2.5-inch and 1.8-inch hard drives for notebook computers to stimulate sales. Many of the weaker competitors were bought out.

By 1995, several companies had expanded the marketing and manufacturing of removable media, both tapes and disks, into the home computer market. Companies such as Iomega and SyQuest developed affordable tape drives and removable disks available for $150 to $200, with cartridges and disks costing between $20 and $25 each. These removable units could hold between 100 megabytes and 2 gigabytes of information to backup or enhance hard drive capacity.

Around the same time, CD-ROM drives became standard accessories on most new computers. CD-ROM drives were originally targeted at libraries and research organizations because CD-ROMs' capacity was so much greater than anything used in the consumer market. However, the popularity of games and multimedia software, along with the mushrooming size of general applications, made CD-ROMs a requisite feature, lest home users and corporate administrators be forced to juggle dozens of floppy disks in order to install a single program. The speed of CD-ROM drives rapidly increased as the technology reached mainstream status. By the late 1990s, recordable CD drives and the newer Digital Versatile Disc (DVD) technology, geared toward reproducing full-length movies and holding other storage-intensive applications, were also increasingly common.

Although they accounted for only a small portion of industry sales, magneto-optical (MO) drives gained popularity in the mid- to late 1990s. These storage devices combined the ease and portability of a floppy disk with the capacity and speed of a hard disk. The systems use both magnetic and optical technology. The drive reads and writes the disk with a read/write head assisted with a pulse-modulated laser beam. In 1996, MO drives came in two sizes, 5.25-inch and 3.5-inch, and could store between 128 megabytes and 1.3 gigabytes of data.

Corporate storage and reliability needs fueled vigorous demand for redundant arrays of inexpensive disks (RAID), which were first introduced in 1987. RAID storage systems allow several hard drives to work in concert as a single, high capacity, relatively inexpensive, and dependable memory backup device. Applications include backup storage for mainframes, networks, and other high-end systems. Sales of RAID units skyrocketed from just 16,000 in 1991 to well over a million units by 1998. RAID product revenue also grew tenfold from 1992 to 1998, from $1.2 billion to more than $12 billion.

Flash memory cards, first developed in the early 1990s, were another growth vehicle for the industry by the mid- and late 1990s. The compact, energy-efficient, high-capacity devices proved to be weighty contenders in the bid to serve the rapidly expanding notebook and pen-based computer markets.

CURRENT CONDITIONS

The computer storage industry still contends with the market paradox of unprecedented demand by computer users for storage capacity and versatility, yet unwillingness to pay commensurately more for storage devices. According to the 1999 Disk/Trend Report, the price per megabyte of hard disk space was expected to continue to tumble, falling from 4.3 cents in 1998 to a projected 0.3 cents in 2002. By comparison, hard drives cost an average of $11.54 a megabyte back in 1988.

Hard disk drives remain the industry's bread and butter in terms of revenue. Disk/Trend forecast that in 2000 the industry would ship 194 million hard drives of all sizes valued at $36 billion worldwide. By 2002 the respective numbers were projected to reach 253 million units and $50 billion, with 40 to 80 gigabyte drives becoming the largest revenue category. More than 85 percent of all hard drives sold are 3.5-inch models. Sales of smaller-format drives were expected to continue rising, more than offsetting the decline of 5.25-inch drives, which were expected to fall obsolete in the early 2000s.

The business market has provided solid demand for RAID systems, and increasingly, more network-oriented storage systems like storage-area networks (SANs) and network-attached storage (NAS) devices. SANs combine multiple disk arrays with controller hardware and software to create stand-alone and interdependent storage systems for large networks and heavy-traffic distributed environments. NASs, on the other hand, provide supplemental storage capacity to smaller networks without taxing existing servers.

Tape drive sales have been mixed, with sluggish performance from devices aimed at individual PCs but better results from drives aimed at servers. Newer tape automation systems have gained popularity because they can reduce the workload associated with managing tape backups. In the late 1990s tape drive manufacturers hoped to secure better footing in the network storage arena by offering higher-capacity formats, including the new Linear Tape Open (LTO) standard backed by three of the industry's biggest participants—Hewlett-Packard, IBM, and Seagate. A key selling point for tape technology is its low price compared to disk drives.

Meanwhile, removable and optical storage has been, and will likely continue to be, one of the industry's slowest segments as far as revenue growth. The main growth technologies have been DVD-ROM drives and writable CD and DVD drives, whereas revenues from floppy drives and cartridge drives have stagnated and aren't expected to stage any significant recovery.

INDUSTRY LEADERS

The storage industry consists of both integrated and independent manufacturers. Among the largest integrated players are IBM and Hewlett-Packard, which dominate certain product segments of the business, especially in technologies geared toward large companies.

Seagate Technologies Inc., of Scotts Valley, California, is the largest independent producer of storage devices. Despite its stature in the industry, shipping an estimated 20.5 percent of the world's hard drives as of 1998, Seagate has been bruised by the market's unfavorable pricing climate. In its fiscal 1999, Seagate sold $6.1 billion worth of hard drives, which accounted for 90 percent of its corporate revenue. The company achieved its dominant position in part through acquisitions, the biggest of which was its 1999 purchase of Conner Peripherals, its closest competitor. Conner Peripherals had led

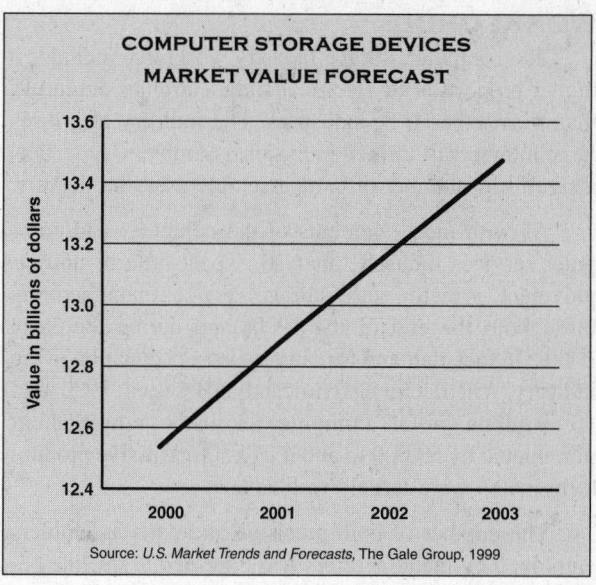

COMPUTER STORAGE DEVICES MARKET VALUE FORECAST

Source: *U.S. Market Trends and Forecasts*, The Gale Group, 1999

the market in 3.5-inch hard drives. Seagate remains one of the most vertically integrated firms in the industry; it manufactures most of the parts that go into its drives. The company's weakness, however, has been its dependence on low-margin drives and absence from the more lucrative value-added storage systems for large businesses.

Quantum Corp. of Milpitas, California, was the second-largest independent in the late 1990s, with 17.4 percent of the hard drive market in 1998. Like Seagate, Quantum has relied on strategic acquisitions to expand its business, most notably the takeover of the former Digital Equipment Corp.'s storage device business (the rest of DEC was later bought by Compaq). Quantum is also a major vendor of tape drives, particularly those using the Digital Linear Tape (DLT) format, which represent more than a quarter of its revenue. The company reported $4.9 billion in disk and tape revenues in its fiscal 1999.

EMC Corp. of Hopkinton, Massachusetts, led the fast-growing market for high-end network storage subsystems in the late 1990s. By some estimates it controlled more than 30 percent of the enterprise storage system market at that time. The company has established itself as the premier provider of top-of-the-line storage systems, software, and services to major corporations. Estimates by the SG Cowen investment bank projected EMC's enterprise systems revenues to more than double between 1998 and 2001, although it faces vigorous challenges in that market from the likes of Compaq, IBM, Hewlett-Packard, and Sun Microsystems.

Other industry leaders include Western Digital Corp. of California, with $2.8 billion in fiscal 1999 revenues; Maxtor, with $2.5 billion; Storage Technology Corp. (StorageTek) of Colorado, with $2.4 billion; and Iomega of Utah, with $1.5 billion.

WORKFORCE

The computer storage industry workforce includes a higher proportion of electrical and electronics engineers than most other U.S. industries. The industry also hires large numbers of trained precision assemblers, as well as a significant number of parts assemblers and fabricators.

As with most segments of the computer and computer services industry, analysts expect little or no employment growth with storage device manufacturers throughout the end of the 1990s and during the early 2000s. In fact, demand for almost every occupation in the industry will decline significantly. Between 1990 and 1993 alone, total computer industry employment plummeted by 50,000 to about 214,500. Massive productivity gains were largely to blame.

The number of both precision and parts assemblers employed by manufacturers was expected to decline between 40 and 55 percent from 1990 to 2005. Automation, as well as outsourcing of labor tasks to foreign countries, will account for much of this loss. Clerical positions will also decline drastically, by about 30 percent. Even the demand for engineers will fall by 1 or 2 percent by 2005, as companies form corporate alliances that allow them to reduce overlapping research and development expenditures.

On the bright side, the demand for systems analysts and computer scientists is expected to increase by about 40 percent between 1990 and 2005. Furthermore, opportunities will become available to professionals who can help develop cutting edge technologies, particularly for optical and semiconductor products.

AMERICA AND THE WORLD

U.S. computer storage device makers have long dominated the world industry. U.S. firms served 75 percent of the $24 billion global hard drive market in 1993, while Japan only held about 15 percent. Japanese firms, though, played an important role in the hard drive sector by supplying most of the spindle motors, bearings, and other parts that U.S. firms incorporate into the drives that they build.

Japanese firms dominated the world floppy drive market, though U.S. companies manufactured about 44 percent of the floppy diskettes used worldwide. Japanese firms have invested heavily in American companies that produce drives and diskettes. Japan also maintains a technological lead in the burgeoning CD-ROM market, with Sony, Hitachi, and Toshiba leading industry advancements. Philips NV, a Netherlands competitor, was also a major force in this segment. Intel, however, garnered the dominant share of the semiconductor market for America in the mid-1990s.

One factor thwarting global progress for American exporters was the inaccessibility of one of the largest computer storage device markets in the world—Japan. Despite relatively open U.S. markets, shrewd Japanese trading tactics were succeeding in leaving U.S. producers out of many segments of that market. Japan accounted for about 20 percent of the global demand for all computer equipment and services in 1993.

Europe participated in the growth of optical storage devices by 1997. Sales of CD-ROM drives in Europe were expected to climb 12 percent annually to sales of about 16 million drives in the year 2001. In 1996, consumer sales accounted for 79 percent of total sales, but sales were expected to shift to European business and education. Consumer sales were forecast to drop to 72 percent of the total CD-ROM drive sales by 2001.

RESEARCH AND TECHNOLOGY

Industry research and development will increasingly result both from strategic alliances and from government initiatives. For example, General Electric, AT&T, Honeywell, and IBM established the Optoelectronic Technology Consortium (OTC) in July 1992 to advance domestic optical technology. Consortium members will share research already completed on their own and will release their combined findings to other U.S. computer and semiconductor firms. The OTC was scheduled to continue for 30 months and was backed by $8 million in initial funding. Half of the funding for the OTC was supplied by the federal Defense Advanced Research Projects Agency (DARPA).

In addition to the OTC, the Microelectronics and Computer Technology Corp. (MCC), also an industry consortium, began a five-year research project on holographic mass-storage subsystems. This effort was backed by $10.3 million in federal grants and $12.7 million from consortium members. A similar government/private enterprise effort was underway in California that involved the National Institute of Standards and Technology and several universities. Its purpose was to integrate optical technology into a prototype computer that might eventually lead to a desktop supercomputer.

In 1995, the U.S. Department of Commerce's National Institute of Standards and Technology sponsored research projects at 3M Co. of Minnesota, Seagate Tape Technology of California, and Advanced Research Corp. of Minnesota. The goal of the projects was to develop a high-performance, variable-data-rate, multimedia magnetic tape recorder that would have the ability to accommodate the high-data capacity, transmission, and acquisition rates needed for applications such as teleconferencing and satellite-based television.

With more immediate results, in the late 1990s the industry was in the midst of a transition to giant magnetoresistive (GMR) heads in disk drives. This technology, necessary to continue the ongoing miniaturization of storage components, held the potential to read as much as 10 gigabits per square inch of disk space, or twice the capacity of standard magnetoresistive (MR) heads. The adoption of GMR was expected to continue into the early 2000s. Further research promised to deliver heads approaching 35-gigabit capacity.

The Future. Memory storage devices will continue to play a leading role in the advancement of computer technology, as they have since the birth of the computer industry. The role of the memory storage device industry will become increasingly blurred, however, as the computer, telecommunications, consumer electronics, information, and entertainment industries converge into a massive multimedia industry that interconnects various technologies and services. Multimedia, by its most basic definition, will combine data, audio, and video signals into one digital stream.

The dominant technologies that will drive this metamorphosis are data processing, storage, interface, fiber optics, wireless, compression, and digital broadband switching. As a result, companies from many industries will find themselves competing and cooperating with firms in completely separate industries. Firms that once delivered memory storage solely for the computer industry will be selling their technology to a wide range of markets. The advancement of flash memory technology provides evidence of this trend. Semiconductor and disk storage companies have cooperated to develop flash memory storage products not only for computers, but also for digital cameras, telephones, automobiles, and other devices.

Optical memory will likely play an integral role in the future of multimedia because of its capacity to store text, images, animation, and video. Virtual reality products represent another area in which optical technology can be applied.

FURTHER READING

Aragon, Lawrence. "Driving Out of a Rut." *PC Week,* 26 August 1996.

Byers, T.J. "All About Removable Media Drives." *Electronics Now,* September 1996.

Chu, R.S. "EMC Corporation." New York: SG Cowen Securities Corp., 5 November 1999.

Disk/Trend, Inc. *1999 Disk/Trend Report.* Mountain View, CA, 1999. Available from www.disktrend.com.

International Disk Drive Equipment and Materials Association. *Welcome to IDEMA.* Santa Clara, CA: 2000. Available from www.idema.org.

Moore, Fred. "Storage 2000." *Computer Technology Review,* December 1999.

Neil, Stephanie. "Storage Cellars." *PC Week,* 26 July 1999.

O'Regan, Rob. "In Enterprise Storage Arena, EMC Sets the Standard." *PC Week,* 26 July 1999.

Rigney, Steve. "Better Ways to Serve and Protect." *PC Magazine,* 25 May 1999.

SIC 3575

COMPUTER TERMINALS

Companies primarily engaged in manufacturing computer terminals, teleprinters, and multistation cathode ray tubes (CRTs) make up the computer terminal industry. Personal computers, workstations, minicomputers, and other systems that contain central processing units (CPUs) are classified in the electronic computer industry. Establishments primarily engaged in manufacturing point-of-sale, funds transfer, and automatic teller machines are classified in **SIC 3578: Calculating and Accounting Machines, Except Electronic Computers.**

NAICS CODE(S)

334113 (Computer Terminal Manufacturing)

A form of so-called thin-client computing, a computer terminal acts as an interface between a user and a system server that has a CPU and storage capacity. Typically, a network of terminals is attached to the server. While some network systems allow terminals to have unimpeded access to the server, most systems require users to share the processor. As a result, such "timeshare" servers can operate more slowly as more users access the processor. Advanced software on terminal systems can help maintain a minimum standard of service, though, and can even provide a more stable working environment than some PCs. According to one late 1990s estimate, there were 30 million traditional, non-PC computer terminals in operation worldwide.

Terminals were first used to access large mainframe and minicomputer systems that became popular in the 1970s. As the speed and memory capacity of computers increased and prices of desktop computers fell during the 1980s, however, the popularity of systems that used terminals declined. By the mid-1990s the market for traditional terminals without CPUs appeared moribund, with demand channeled toward PCs and other devices.

Terminal sales lagged as corporations began looking to PC-oriented networks to replace so-called dumb terminals. Contrary to the rapid growth most computer hardware companies enjoyed, terminal manufacturers' shipments fell from $2.3 billion in 1988 to about $1.9 billion in the early 1990s. By 1997 the value of terminal shipments languished below $1.5 billion. Meanwhile, industry employment had fallen from about 18,000 in 1988 to less than 5,800 in 1997. But these numbers belied a resurgence taking shape in the business under the mantle of thin-client computing and terminals that embraced Windows and other popular operating systems.

Despite their limitations, terminals offer several advantages over stand-alone workstations, which are known in a network environment as thick clients. For instance, microcomputers and workstations run applications locally and therefore require more memory and an operating system. When working on a network, thick clients can require large amounts of bandwidth because they transfer data back and forth for processing. Terminals, on the other hand, run only the display part of a computer application locally and rely on the server to handle data processing and storage. For large companies, this can greatly reduce the cost of owning and maintaining a system over time. Thus, depending on how they're deployed, terminals can offer advantages in costs, centralized control, and security.

X-Terminals. During the mid-1990s, terminal manufacturers increased revenues with new products, such as X-terminals and Windows terminals. X-terminals contain internal software and therefore allow the interaction of concurrent applications running in the popular Windows environment. In addition, X-terminals cost nearly 50 percent less than PCs in 1996. X-terminals also offered higher resolution, larger screens, and greater networking capabilities than many desktop and workstation computers. However, the disadvantages of X-terminals included slower running applications and slower Internet access than that of PCs.

Sales of X-terminals grew in the early 1990s due to concerns about system and information security in companies, as well as budget and staff cutbacks in system support departments. X-terminals also reduced the need for hardware upgrades with the introduction of new software. With uneven growth, shipments of X-terminals rose from about 178,000 in 1994 to approximately 269,400 in 1997.

Network Computers. A hybrid that straddles the PC and terminal designations is the network computer (NC). These scaled-back PCs were first promoted in the mid-1990s by companies like Sun Microsystems and Oracle Corp. as solutions to the costs, complexities, and inefficiencies of using thick clients in large networked environments. Although they come in many configurations, NCs are in essence networked PCs without disk drives for local storage. Instead, they download applications and files from a server and store all their data on the server. But they still have their own processors and memory for running applications locally. Many of those applications are intended to be Internet-related, such as Web browsers, or portable, system-independent applications created in the Java programming language.

NCs, which aren't terminals but are sometimes seen as competition to terminals, never took off as their backers hoped. Critics, especially those in the terminal industry, complain that NCs aren't true thin clients because of all the data the devices must download and upload in order to function. Terminals, by contrast, only transmit basic input and output data and don't perform any kind of application downloading or processing. A dearth of Java software and standards for NCs likewise has made them hard to market, whereas terminals can display almost any kind of software that the server can run, including popular programs like Windows NT and Windows 2000.

Windows-Based Terminals. Holding perhaps the key to the industry's future, meanwhile, Wyse Technology Inc. led the introduction of Windows-based terminals in 1995. These terminals give users the ability to access Windows-, mainframe-, or Unix-based applications. Unlike traditional terminals, they can display the full range of color graphics familiar to PC users. In fact, the only processing power in a Windows-based terminal is for displaying graphics, as application processing and memory is generally left to the server. Still, to the end user, the terminal may look and feel much like a PC, complete with a mouse and a local printer hook-up. Some Windows terminals have the operating system, a Web browser, and emulation programs embedded as firmware.

Wyse, which also makes the more traditional monochrome terminals, emerged in the latter part of the 1990s as a dominant force in the business. Its 1999 sales of $160 million, while modest for an industry leader, represented approximately one-tenth of industry sales. More important, in the late 1990s Wyse found itself holding 65 percent of the fast-growing Windows-based terminal market. In the broader thin-client market, Wyse's share was estimated at 39 percent of unit shipments. Indeed, Windows-based terminals helped bring double-digit growth back to a flagging industry. According to the market research firm International Data Corp., thin-client unit sales were expected to nearly double from 1999 to 2000, rising from 690,000 to 1.2 million devices. Windows-based terminals were expected to lead this growth.

Other important manufacturers of Windows-based terminals and similar thin-client devices include Acute Technologies Inc., Addonics Communications Inc., Boundless Corp., Hewlett-Packard, IBM, Network Computing Devices Inc., and Sun Microsystems. Outside the United States, Asia is an important and growing source of terminal hardware.

FURTHER READING

Bank, David, and Don Clark. ''Network Computers Fall Short in Contest Against Cheap PCs.'' *Wall Street Journal,* 3 April 1998.

Caton, Michael. "Sun Plays Right Card with Sun Ray Terminal." *PC Week,* 24 January 2000.

Deckmyn, Dominique. "Thin Clients To Get Win 2K Boost." *Computerworld,* 14 February 2000.

Kirchner, Jake. "When No News Is Good News." *PC Magazine,* 25 March 1997.

Rice, Valerie. "The Disposable Alternative to the PC." *PC Week,* 18 October 1999.

Valigra, Lori. "X Terminals: Cheap and Easy." *Datamation,* 15 April 1996.

Wyse Technology Inc. "Thin Clients, Windows-Based Terminals, NCs: What's the Difference?" San Jose, CA, 1999. Available from www.wyse.com.

SIC 3577

COMPUTER PERIPHERAL EQUIPMENT, NOT ELSEWHERE CLASSIFIED

The computer peripheral equipment, not elsewhere classified, industry includes establishments that manufacture miscellaneous computer accessories supporting the activities of a computer's central processing unit (CPU). Companies in this industry manufacture a variety of products, including printers, input devices, plotters, graphic displays (monitors), and optical scanners. Not included in this industry segment are computer terminals, storage devices, modems and other communications devices, or computer-driven office machines. For information on computer peripheral equipment classified elsewhere, see **SIC 3571: Electronic Computers, SIC 3572: Computer Storage Devices, SIC 3575: Computer Terminals,** and **SIC 3579: Office Machines, Not Elsewhere Classified.**

NAICS CODE(S)

334119 (Other Computer Peripheral Equipment Manufacturing)

INDUSTRY SNAPSHOT

Rising unit sales and falling prices have pervaded the computer peripherals business, making for tight competition in the markets for mainstream or lower-end technology. At the same time, leading peripherals manufacturers look to high-end and emerging technologies to provide comfortable profit margins, and if they're lucky, give them market supremacy if the technology becomes mainstream.

Demand for peripheral equipment thrived in the late 1990s as new computer sales remained strong and as users replaced their older devices. In the printer segment, color ink-jet printers enjoyed the most robust sales overall, aided by performance improvements in newer models and by intense price competition between ink-jet vendors. Color laser printers also gained a small following, but their high cost and lower market awareness thus far relegated them to a minor share of the market. Multifunction printers—those that can act as copy machines, scanners, or fax machines in addition to ordinary printing—were another of the fastest-growing categories. Meanwhile, sales of standard monochrome laser printers decelerated as these other technologies diverted demand.

Computer monitor sales were also buoyant, led by trends toward larger viewing areas, higher resolutions, and thin display technology that takes up less space on a desk. Conventional cathode-ray tube (CRT) displays still made up the bulk of industry shipments—as much as 95 percent in 1999—but flat-panel LCD screens and flatter CRT models were expected to win a growing share of the market.

Optical scanners, the third major segment of the peripherals market, likewise achieved double-digit growth in the late 1990s. Again, inexpensive, mass-oriented devices and improving technology, particularly with flatbed models, have fueled strong demand among both consumers and businesses. Although the market for traditional handheld scanners had been soft, a new generation of fast, easy-to-use pen scanners, or digital highlighters, was expected to experience swift growth in the early 2000s, according to market research published by International Data Corp.

Performance in the industry's smaller segments, such as keyboards, pointing devices, and specialty input and output devices, has been mostly subdued. For standard mass-market devices, there have been few innovations and thus upgrade and replacement sales are minimal; most of these commodity peripherals are sold bundled with new computer systems. New product lines like wireless keyboards and mice have so far failed to ignite significant new sales.

ORGANIZATION AND STRUCTURE

Facilitating communication with a computer's processor, peripheral equipment is used on nearly all types of computers, ranging from home PCs to supercomputers. The three largest categories of peripherals are graphic displays, printers, and scanners. In addition to the major peripheral categories, numerous miscellaneous products include computer input devices (keyboards and mice), computer sound systems, magnetic-ink recognition devices, graphic and technical plotters, graphics production equipment, and various multimedia devices.

Two main markets exist for peripherals: (1) devices shipped as part of original equipment manufacturers' (OEM) computer systems and (2) aftermarket upgrades, add-ons, and replacements that are bought separately from computer systems. Some peripherals manufacturers exclusively serve the OEM market, typically providing peripheral equipment on contract to a large computer maker like Compaq, Dell, or Gateway. OEM contractors often make customized versions of their products for specific customers. For example, Lexmark International Group Inc., a major player in the printer market under its own nameplate, manufactures a series of printers that are branded as Compaq printers to go with Compaq computer systems. Key Tronic Corp., as another example, produces keyboards for Gateway and other OEMs.

Peripheral manufacturers like Lexmark and Key Tronic often also serve the aftermarket. They can do so through several channels, including wholesalers and distributors, retailers, or direct sales. Some peripheral makers sell only to the aftermarket. This route can be more profitable, but depending on the kind of device, it can also be smaller than the OEM market as well as more volatile.

Graphic Displays. The most popular types of graphic displays are traditional cathode-ray tube (CRT) monitors and flat-panel liquid crystal displays (LCDs). Although some displays are built into computer terminals, most are offered as peripheral devices that attach to a computer's video port. A video card interfaces between the monitor and the CPU, allowing compatibility for specific monitors and computer systems.

CRTs provide either monochrome or color graphics and deliver varying degrees of flexibility, performance, resolution quality, and size. Low resolution monitors, for instance, display 640 x 480 pixels per inch, while higher resolution CRTs can deliver 1,280 x 1,024; 1,600 x 1,200; or more pixels per inch. Most CRTs measure between 15 inches and 19 inches diagonally. CRT prices ranged from $50 for monochrome displays to several thousand dollars for large, high-definition color monitors. As of 1999, CRTs accounted for around 95 percent of all monitor sales.

Liquid crystal displays (LCDs) are among the fastest growing and most dynamic segments of the graphic display market. Because LCD technology allows for much flatter displays than CRT devices, LCDs originally caught on as monitors for notebook computers. LCDs also tend to weigh less than CRTs, consume less power, and flicker less, potentially reducing eye strain. By the late 1990s, stand-alone flat-panel LCDs were being sold as high-end displays for desktop computers. As such, LCDs have tended to be more profitable for manufacturers than CRTs. Originally most color LCDs sold were passive-matrix displays, also called super-twisted nematic (STN). Active-matrix displays, also called thin-film transistors (TFTs), which provide higher graphic quality, grew quickly in the mid- and late 1990s to become the dominant format.

Input Devices. Common input devices for personal computers include keyboards, mice, joysticks, touch screens, microphones, and optical scanners. Specialized hardware for commercial applications includes magnetic-ink reading devices, bar-code scanners, and magnetic card readers.

Printers. The three principal printer types are dot-matrix, ink-jet, and laser. Dot-matrix printers were one of the first responses to demands by computer users for an output device that offered more flexibility than impact character printers. Dot-matrix devices dominated the printer market in the early 1990s, accounting for more than 50 percent of unit sales, but offered poor resolution, particularly for graphics. By the mid-1990s, the dot-matrix printer was largely being replaced since it offered smaller profit margins and appealed to consumers less than newer technology.

Ink-jet printers offer much higher resolution and flexibility than dot-matrix technology. Ink-jets in the late 1990s commonly offered resolution of 600 or more dots per inch (dpi) and allowed users to print text and graphics in color.

Laser printers are often seen as providing the highest quality printing short of professional printing machinery, although some of the better ink-jet models increasingly compete with lasers on quality. Laser printers typically offer 600 to 1,200 dpi resolution. Laser printers are likewise often faster than ink-jets and usually have a greater paper-handling capacity. Color laser machines are also an increasingly affordable option.

Multifunction printers, often based on laser technology, emerged in the second half of the 1990s as a popular and viable alternative. These models (which double as fax machines, scanners, or copiers) appeal particularly to small businesses and home workers, who tend to have occasional need for the various functions but don't use them enough to warrant buying separate machines.

Scanners. Peripheral scanners are used to translate images and text into electronic signals. Able to recognize characters, line art, gray-scale, and color images, scanners use photosensitive arrays that reflect light to digitize printed information. The three types of scanners common in the 1990s were handheld, flatbed, and drum. Drum scanners are not considered peripheral equipment, however, because they were a high-end tool used primarily in the printing industry.

Flatbed, or desktop, scanners are the most common form. Using optical character recognition (OCR) technology, these scanners can be used to translate printed pages into a document that could be viewed, searched, and manipulated using a word processor. Particularly for home users, Web developers, and graphic artists, desktop scanners are also frequently used to input and manipulate photographs and other graphic images. Typical flatbed scanners have a resolution of 600 to 1,200 dpi.

Handheld scanners are usually priced much lower than flatbeds and are more useful for scanning small graphics. They tend to deliver lower resolution than flatbeds and have limited OCR capability; as a result, sales for general use markets have been sluggish and far fewer models of handheld scanners were offered in the late 1990s than just a few years earlier. Handheld devices remain popular, though, for certain commercial and industrial applications like scanning bar codes. Moreover, a revival of small, reliable handheld devices called pen scanners (also digital highlighters) held promise in the early 2000s to expand handhelds' usefulness for general computing applications.

BACKGROUND AND DEVELOPMENT

The peripherals industry emerged from the commercial computer industry in the 1970s. Not until the creation and subsequent widespread acceptance of desktop and personal computers (PCs) in the 1980s, however, did the industry capture a significant share of all computer-related expenditures. PCs extended the market for peripherals to the consumer market and generated demand for numerous add-on products.

Some of the early peripherals included card punching and sorting machines, microfilm output units, plotter controls, tabulators, tape cleaners, and tape print units. During the 1980s, however, scanners, printers, and displays that complemented PCs, workstations, and network systems grew to dominate the market. As the speed and memory storage capacity of desktop computers increased, so did the capabilities of peripherals. By the mid-1980s, peripherals accounted for 20 percent of all computer industry revenues.

Global computer equipment and services sales escalated from $243 billion in 1988 to about $280 billion in 1990. Despite an overall slowdown in computer industry growth in the early 1990s, revenues from peripherals continued their spiral to $290 billion in 1991, reaching nearly $320 billion in 1992. Throughout this period the market for peripherals, including storage devices as well as some other peripherals classified under other industries, maintained about a 20 percent share of the total market.

The rapid shift toward graphic user interfaces, multimedia computing, and Internet computing in the mid-1990s gave a solid boost to peripheral sales. However, net revenues and profits in some peripherals categories were sluggish as prices fell faster than unit sales rose. As computer prices trended downward and many PCs were selling at or below $1,000, peripherals makers felt pressure to lower prices. In some OEM arrangements, large computer manufacturers required their peripherals ven-

dors to cut costs by a target percentage. In order to reach the goal, peripheral makers sometimes had to skimp on quality and sacrifice their own profitability. Manufacturing was done increasingly outside the United States where it was cheaper.

Nonetheless, new computer shipments in the United States and worldwide continued to boom into the late 1990s, with unit sales rising more than 20 percent a year. Peripheral sales rose in tandem. Economic crises in Asia and Latin America, however, deflated sales in those regions.

CURRENT CONDITIONS

The major peripheral product segments experienced solid growth in the late 1990s and this trend was expected to continue in the early 2000s. Aside from premium products, downward pressure on prices was expected to continue for most classes of peripherals.

The peripherals business is, and will continue to be, highly internationalized. Asian firms, especially in China and southeast Asia, are involved in a disproportionate share of the manufacturing and assembly work. It's therefore important to distinguish between what products are actually made in a country, say the United States, and what products are made elsewhere by affiliates or contractors to the company whose name goes on the products. In addition, a considerable share of the brand-name peripheral companies are headquartered in Asia, and some of these own factories in the United States.

Printers. Worldwide, according to Lyra Research of Newton, Massachusetts, 75 million printers of all types were shipped in 1999, a better than 13 percent increase in volume. Global printer revenue, however, was flat with the year before, at $32 billion, due to lower prices. Manufacturers located in the United States produced less than 20 percent of the world's printers, although that percentage doesn't include output by foreign factories owned by U.S. firms. Still, the United States remains the world's largest printer market, representing almost half of global demand by volume, according to estimates based on census and trade data. Consequently, the United States imports nearly twice as many monitors as it produces domestically.

By printer type, ink-jets dominated two-thirds of world volume, driven by their popularity as low-cost consumer devices. Monochrome laser and multifunction printers weighed in with 13 percent each. The rest of the market consisted of impact printers, thermal printers, and the fast-growing color laser segment. Because of tightening profit margins on printers, though, some printer manufacturers are actually more dependent on sales of printer supplies like toner and ink cartridges for their profits than they are on the hardware that requires those supplies.

Lyra Research forecast global printer demand to approach 100 million units by 2003. Revenue, on the other hand, was expected to stay flat as prices continued to creep downward. Ink-jets and multifunction printers were forecast to be the dominant technologies, while standard monochrome laser sales were projected to be flat or receding slightly.

Graphic Displays. In 1999 peripheral manufacturers shipped about 100 million graphic displays, according to various estimates. Most—up to 96 percent—used cathode-ray tube (CRT) technology; the remainder employed LCD screens. The United States manufactured less than 3 percent of the world's monitors, and thus depended dearly on imports for as much as 94 percent of all new monitors purchased that year. The value of world monitor shipments in 1999 was estimated at $20 billion, although International Data Corp. reckoned monitor revenues at closer to $33 billion.

Taiwanese firms are the biggest in the monitor segment based on volume, according to statistics released by the Taiwanese government. Although only about 11 percent of the world's monitors in 1999 were assembled on Taiwan's soil, Taiwanese companies such as Acer and Mitac laid claim to a startling 59 percent stake in global unit production. Taiwanese affiliates in China supplied the largest share, equal to about a quarter of the world market.

LCD displays in the late 1990s remained on average several hundred dollars more than a typical CRT display—many flat-panel LCDs cost more than the popular sub-$1,000 PCs. Indeed, LCD prices actually rose somewhat because of new features. As prices ease, LCD flat-panel monitors are expected to continue to steal market share from traditional CRT devices, through both the OEM and replacement channels. According to a DisplaySearch market report, a third of LCDs in 1999 were shipped with new computer systems; the rest were sold in the aftermarket. Within the LCD category, thin-film transistor (TFT) devices were expected to continue to edge out competing technologies, making up 70 percent of the product mix by 2002.

LCDs will compete, however, with a newer breed of slimmer CRTs, which have been positioned as a less expensive alternative to LCDs. These so-called shortneck CRTs are being offered with larger viewing areas and take up somewhat less space depthwise on a desk. The shift toward larger format CRTs will help sustain demand for that technology well into the 2000s. In fact, one research firm, Stanford Resources of San Jose, California, predicted that demand for CRT displays would grow almost 50 percent between 1999 and 2005.

Separately, the industry is undergoing a transition to digital signal transmission under the digital visual inter-face (DVI) standard. DVI is being implemented in both CRT and LCD models.

Scanners. Demand for optical scanners has also welled because of sharply falling prices and rapid improvements in the technology. In 1998 manufacturers around the world shipped 13.9 million scanners of all types, according to estimates by International Data Corp. (IDC). With color depth pushing 36 bits and prices slipping below $100 in some models, color flatbeds have been the most widely sought, displacing drum scanners in the high-end market as well as usurping share from the low end. The introduction of contact image sensor (CIS) technology in the late 1990s to replace the older charged-coupled device (CCD) standard also significantly deflated prices of CCD-based machines. Assuming more of the same, IDC projected global shipments of color flatbeds to approach 39 million units in 2003. Handheld units, particularly for bar-code reading and other specialized functions, weren't selling as well as expected in the late 1990s, but unit shipments were still growing at a low double-digit clip.

INDUSTRY LEADERS

Because of the industry's diverse product segments, many of its estimated 1,000 U.S. companies specialize in a relatively narrow range of technologies, such as printers only or input devices only, although a few larger companies compete across several segments. A number of the top participants, both in the U.S. market and the world market, are based outside the United States—particularly in Asia, and to a lesser extent, in Europe.

In the printer segment, leaders include Hewlett-Packard (HP), Seiko Epson, Canon, Lexmark, NEC Corp., and Xerox. Hewlett-Packard has led the U.S. market in most of the mainstream printer categories, especially laser printers, but it faces a stiff challenge from Epson, Canon, and Lexmark in the low-cost ink-jet arena, which already caused HP to lose market share. Xerox entered the higher-end printer market in 1999 with its acquisition of the Tektronix printer line.

Leading display manufacturers include NEC, Sony, Fujitsu, Samsung, IBM, Acer, Mitsubishi, and Viewsonic. A large number of the monitors sold with new computers in the United States are branded under the names of computer makers like Compaq, Dell, and Gateway; many of these are actually produced by other companies, often abroad.

Important names in the comparatively small keyboard and input device market include Key Tronic, NMB Technologies, Mitsumi Electronics, and Seijin.

RESEARCH AND TECHNOLOGY

U.S. firms were on the leading edge of almost every peripheral technology in the industry in the mid-1990s. At least two efforts were underway during this time to advance the role of U.S. firms in the production of the rapidly growing color LCD market. One was a joint venture between Motorola Inc. and In Focus Systems, called Motif. Motif sought to develop high-quality LCDs that could be manufactured inexpensively. The other effort was initiated by the Defense Advanced Research Projects Agency (DARPA). DARPA planned to provide $15 million in seed money for a consortium of large and small companies that would assemble the framework necessary to effectively compete in the color LCD market.

Scanner and printer manufacturers were striving toward similar technological and productivity goals. The demand for higher resolution, faster input and output, lower production costs, and greater flexibility were driving investment and development in printer technologies.

Advances in the input devices market focused on ease and multifunctions. In 1995, Other 90 Percent Technologies of California was working on a mouse that controls action by reading the electromagnetic signals within the user's skin.

In the future, the computer peripheral industry will likely become increasingly integrated with complementary industries, as data processing, interface, storage, fiber optics, wireless, and digital broadband switching technologies converge into a massive multimedia industry. Scanners, printers, and displays would also likely be used in conjunction with other communications and information equipment.

FURTHER READING

Amadio, Jill. "Key Players." *Entrepreneur,* June 1996.

Hayes, Frank. "Flat-Panel Displays." *Computerworld,* 29 November 1999.

Kay, Russell. "Flat or Fat?" *Computerworld,* 3 May 1999.

Klein, Alec. "As Cheap Printers Take Off, H-P Is Forced to Play Catch-Up." *Wall Street Journal,* 21 April 1999.

Lyra Research, Inc. "As the Century Closes, Vendors Mull over the Industry's Future." *The Hard Copy Observer,* January 2000.

Perenson, Melissa J. "Printer and Scanner Prices: Is $100 Too Low?" *Home Office Computing,* April 1999.

Poor, Alfred. "DVI: An Interface for All Displays." *PC Magazine,* 14 December 1999.

———. "LCD Monitors Near Perfection." *PC Magazine,* 7 March 2000.

Sharples, Hadley. "Changing of the Guard." *Graphic Arts Monthly,* December 1998.

U.S. Bureau of the Census. "Computer and Office Accounting Machines." *Current Industrial Reports.* Washington, D.C.: 1999. Available from www.census.gov.

CALCULATING AND ACCOUNTING MACHINES, EXCEPT ELECTRONIC COMPUTERS

This industry covers establishments primarily engaged in manufacturing point-of-sale devices, fund transfer devices, and other calculating and accounting machines, except electronic computers. Included are electronic calculating and accounting machines that must be paced by operator intervention, even when augmented by attachments. These machines may include program control or have input/output capabilities.

NAICS CODE(S)

334119 (Other Computer Peripheral Equipment Manufacturing)
333313 (Office Machinery Manufacturing)

Charles Xavier Thomas, of France, is credited with starting the calculating and accounting machines industry when he introduced the arithmometer in the 1870s. Frank Baldwin and William S. Burroughs were also major innovators in early calculating machine technology. During the industrial revolution and until the mid-1900s, mechanical and electrical adding machines dominated industry offerings. The invention of the hand-held calculator in 1948 and the integrated circuit in the late 1960s, however, initiated the demise of traditional adding machines.

Producers of desk-top and hand-held calculators shipped goods worth a total of $1.4 billion in the late 1990s. Both products had essentially become commodity items by that time. Electronic cash registers, an offshoot of calculating machines, offered higher profit margins for manufacturers. Scanning technology and the demand for related inventory tracking systems in the 1980s and early 1990s spurred the development of new "high-tech" cash registers that buoyed profits for some prior producers of traditional calculating machines. Other competitors exited the market or shifted to production of other equipment.

Automatic Teller Machines (ATMs) and Point of Service (POS) devices, which were added to industry offerings in the 1980s, quickly escalated sales of cash registers and adding machines. Sales of ATMs, which store cash and are used primarily by bank customers to conduct account transactions, skyrocketed past a total of 90,000 units by 1993. Less expensive POS devices, which allow consumers to conduct electronic account transactions from a purchase point such as a gas station or supermarket, numbered about 300,000 in 1993.

By the early 1990s, the market for ATMs was becoming saturated in comparison to the 1980s. Manufacturers' earnings were expected to rise as industry analysts projected a growing demand for replacement machines and a 20 percent rise in the number of ATM installations between 1993 and 1997. The number of POS devices sold, on the other hand, was expected to increase to more than 1.1 million by 1997 as a growing number of retailers adopted this method of accepting payment.

In 1999 there were four top companies in this industry. GTECH Holdings Corporation, of Greenwich, Rhode Island, posted sales of $973 million and employed 4,800 people. Diebold Inc., of North Canton, Ohio, posted $825 million in sales and had 6,700 employees. VeriFone Inc., of Santa Clara, California, had sales of $500 million and 3,600 employees. Finally, Powerhouse Technologies Inc., of Bozeman, Montana, reported $201 million in sales and employed 1,400 people. Most companies in the industry, however, were small. Only the top few competitors, for example, employed more than 100 people or generated more than $15 million in revenues. Most workers earned an average of $13.90 per hour and worked 41.9 hours per week.

Manufacturers hoped to increase ATM sales by integrating video-conferencing and imaging capabilities into their products. Some banks were also experimenting with selling mutual fund shares through ATMs. Cash register manufacturers were striving to jump-start lagging sales by integrating advanced inventory tracking and information systems technology into new product offerings.

Despite the popularity of ATMs and POS devices in the United States, the technology has been slow to catch on overseas. Only about 40,000 ATMs, for example, have been installed outside the United States. Spain and the United Kingdom combined have approximately 10,000 ATMs, while Austria, Denmark, Germany, Ireland, Norway, and Sweden have none. ATMs in Japan are available for use only during daylight hours.

FURTHER READING

Bureau of the Census. *1995 Annual Survey of Manufactures.* Washington, D.C.: GPO, 1997.

Bureau of Labor Statistics. *Employment Statistics.* Washington, D.C.: GPO, 2000. Available from http://www.bls.gov.

Ward's Business Directory of U.S. Private and Public Companies. Detroit: Gale Group, 1999.

SIC 3579

OFFICE MACHINES, NOT ELSEWHERE CLASSIFIED

Companies principally engaged in manufacturing miscellaneous office machines and devices comprise this industry classification. Such devices include typewriting,

mailroom, and dictation machines. In addition, a multitude of companies in the industry produce specialty products, such as paper shredders, envelope stuffing machines, ticket counters, and coin wrapping machines. Establishments primarily engaged in manufacturing modems, facsimile machines, and other communications interface equipment are classified in **SIC 3661: Telephone and Telegraph Apparatus.**

NAICS CODE(S)

339942 (Lead Pencil and Art Good Manufacturing)
334518 (Watch, Clock, and Part Manufacturing)
333313 (Office Machinery Manufacturing)

INDUSTRY SNAPSHOT

Sales of miscellaneous office machines fluctuated throughout the 1990s. The value of shipments declined drastically in the first part of the decade, averaging about $3.5 billion per year, compared to a high of $5 billion in 1985. Although the figures increased slightly in the mid-1990s, reaching $3.8 billion in 1996, they were expected to decrease again through the year 2000. The main reasons for this decrease include an increased use of computers, foreign competition, increased productivity, reduced corporate spending, and U.S. demographic changes.

The number of establishments in the office machines industry has also fluctuated throughout the 1990s, but the general trend was decline. The 202 establishments in existence in 1990 decreased to 154 in 1996; this number was projected to drop to 129 in 2000.

Manufacturers responded to the more competitive environment of the 1990s by integrating the latest technology into new product offerings, infiltrating new channels of distribution and targeting home offices. Sustaining the industry through the 1990s were record numbers of new business starts; all of the new businesses required office equipment and supplies.

ORGANIZATION AND STRUCTURE

Typewriters. Typewriters and word processing machines accounted for a large segment of the miscellaneous business machines industry in the 1990s. While most of the units sold were electronic typewriters, some companies were still marketing electromechanical typewriters, which resemble traditional manual typewriters, but use electricity to reduce the effort required by the typist and to increase the quality of type.

Electronic typewriters take the electromechanical concept a step further by reducing the number of moving parts and featuring advanced capabilities. For instance, many electronic typewriters can recall a series of pressed keys and then delete those characters from a sheet of paper on command. Some units also allow the typist to store a word or phrase in the machine's memory, which automatically recalls and prints on command.

A third model of typewriter is the personal word processor (PWP). PWPs allow the typist to view text on a screen before it is actually transferred to paper, much like a personal computer (PC). Most PWPs are simply an electronic typewriter with a liquid crystal display and a central processing unit attached. Unlike PCs, PWPs usually offer access only to internally stored proprietary software programs. Many PWPs are also equipped with spreadsheet software, and some advanced units offered disk drives, DOS compatibility, and hand-held scanners.

Typewriters and PWPs were less expensive and typically regarded as easier to use than most PCs. Even so, they continued to lag far behind PCs in popularity, despite efforts by major manufacturers to catch up. In 1996, Olympia, a home office company based in Dallas, launched a major effort to market its electronic typewriters as viable alternatives to PCs for performing simple word processing tasks without the hassle of booting up a computer. In 2000, Smith Corona Corp. announced its intentions to launch a series of new typewriters and supplies and to step up its marketing efforts with the goal of increasing typewriter sales. Despite these efforts, consumers are still expected to continue to choose the PC's versatility over the typewriter's simplicity in the new century.

Mailroom Equipment. Another major segment of the industry consisted of mailroom equipment. Designed to meter, sort, and track mail, such machines were used by the postal service as well as private organizations. While sorting machines could mean an initial cost of anywhere from $5,000 to $500,000, they greatly reduced the cost of sorting mail manually from $35 per thousand to less than $3 per thousand pieces of mail. The most advanced sorters utilized optical character recognition (OCR) to read addresses and U.S. Postal Service bar codes.

Shredders. Shredders, used to destroy internal printed documents, accounted for a slim segment of the market. In the mid-1990s, personal shredders used by small companies and professional practices ranged widely in options and prices. The more advanced models featured conveyer belts and were capable of shredding boxes, metal binders, and entire wastebaskets. Simple model paper shredders represented the fastest growing segment of the miscellaneous office products industry in the mid-1990s, mainly due to their increased popularity for home use. Consumers began buying shredders in increasing numbers because of privacy concerns and because the prices of these devices had decreased to the point that they were now affordable for the average consumer.

Other Products. Making up the remaining portion of the miscellaneous office machines industry were a variety of specialty devices. Dictation machines, for instance, have been used by professionals and executives, for whom certain jobs require the recording of their voices for later transcription.

BACKGROUND AND DEVELOPMENT

The business machine industry emerged from the industrial revolution in the latter part of the nineteenth century. As the need to record and manage business information grew, several products, including the typewriter, were developed to meet demands. Although the typewriter was invented in 1714 by London engineer Henry Mill, the most famous devices were developed in the late 1800s. The Remington typewriter, first offered to the public in 1874, was one of the more popular early machines.

The first electromechanical typewriter was invented by Thomas Edison in 1872, although practical application of this device did not occur until the twentieth century. One of the first electric models, the Electromatic, was purchased by International Business Machines in 1933; after World War II, several other companies introduced electric typewriters. During the post-war era, the business machine industry flourished. A booming economy and new technology soon prompted the development of a plethora of labor-saving devices.

While dictation machines also gained widespread public acceptance during the mid-1900s, the invention of the integrated circuit in the 1960s brought hand-held recording devices into the professional mainstream. Dictaphones remained the primary means of recording information for doctors, lawyers, and business executives throughout the 1970s and much of the 1980s. The advent of personal computers, notebook computers, and cellular telephone technology adversely affected sales of dictation equipment in the 1980s, and by the early 1990s, dictation machines were largely being replaced with machines featuring alternative technologies.

As increasingly inexpensive computer and cellular technology was rendering Dictaphones and typewriters obsolete, many business machine companies struggled to adapt to evolving market demands. Nevertheless, technological advances were opening new markets for other miscellaneous business machines—particularly postal equipment—in demand due to increased postal volume and new postal requirements for addresses.

Shipments of miscellaneous business machines peaked in 1985 at over $5 billion. After that time, however, several factors combined to deflate revenues and profit margins for manufacturers. Most importantly, the popularity of superior computer technology was affecting revenues from industry staples such as typewriters and dictation equipment. Although business machine manufacturers countered with PWPs and other low-cost, higher technology products, computers threatened to eventually deplete the market for even those items.

At the same time that computers and cellular phones were making industry waves, the U.S. business machine market experienced an economic recession in the late 1980s. Revenues from miscellaneous business machines fell to about $3.2 billion in 1987. Although sales picked up in 1988 and 1989, shipments only reached $3.5 to $4 billion per year before slumping again in the early 1990s. Sales figures then increased slightly in the mid-1990s to $3.8 billion but were expected to decrease again through 2000.

In addition to alternative technologies and the economic recession, manufacturers were also facing a more competitive market in the 1980s and early 1990s. Many products, such as typewriters, had become low-cost commodity items that offered slim profit margins. In response to price competition from both domestic and foreign manufacturers, many U.S. companies moved their production operations overseas or increased automation in domestic facilities. The number of establishments in the industry dropped 23 percent from 1990 to 1996. As a result, industry employment in the United States plummeted from about 45,000 in 1982 to about 30,000 in the early 1990s.

CURRENT CONDITIONS

According to government figures, both the value of shipments and the number of establishments within the industry were expected to continue their downward slope through the end of the 1990s until the year 2000, when sales were expected to drop to $3.1 billion and the number of establishments were predicted to be as low as 129. As a result of this downward trend, employment in the industry was predicted to plummet below 20,000.

Industry Response. In response to these declining figures, manufacturers scrambled to buoy profits and remain competitive. Besides diverting investments into competing industries, such as computer-related office products, producers tailored product offerings to appeal to the growth market of the 1990s—small businesses.

By the mid-1990s about 40 million home offices had emerged. Because the average home office spent $40 to $50 per week on business supplies, manufacturers increasingly catered to this segment. In an effort to reach small businesses and home office buyers, manufacturers also adjusted their marketing and distribution strategies in the mid-1990s. While producers once sold products primarily through dedicated office device resellers, many companies were using 50 or more different types of retailers to move their equipment in the 1990s.

One of the fastest growing distribution channels during this time was the discount superstore and business center, such as Wal-Mart, Office Depot, and K-Mart. In the mid-1990s, manufacturers distributed an estimated 7 to 10 percent of their shipments through these retail chains, and some industry participants suggested that this figure would eventually exceed 20 or 30 percent. By 1997, there were more than 1,600 superstores in the North American market with a potential for more than 3,000 stores, according to some industry analysts.

Manufacturers also boosted sales by emphasizing distribution through equipment leasing companies. Many businesses favored the lease agreement in order to take advantage of changing technology and certain tax benefits. In addition, leasing allowed companies to reduce their capital equipment investment—an important point in the capital-starved environment of the 1990s.

Some manufacturers looked forward to increased sales in Mexico as a result of the North American Free Trade Agreement (NAFTA), which was expected to increase capital spending in that nation. Furthermore, some competitors hoped to shore up their bottom line by moving manufacturing facilities south, where they could take advantage of inexpensive labor and a loosely regulated manufacturing environment.

INDUSTRY LEADERS

The largest supplier of miscellaneous office equipment in the United States in the late 1990s was Canon USA, Inc., headquartered in New Hyde Park, New York. Canon manufactured copiers, computer printers, video cameras and fax machines, with sales for 1997 totaling $7 billion. Because Canon manufactures such a variety of products, it is difficult to discern how much of that total was the result of sales in the miscellaneous office equipment industry. Canon was established in 1955, and in 1997, the company employed 8,700 people.

Other leaders in the industry included Pitney Bowes of Stamford, Connecticut, with $3.5 billion in sales and 28,600 employees; and Harris Corp. of Melbourne, Florida, with $3.7 billion in sales and 28,700 employees. Both companies are involved in other industries along with the miscellaneous office equipment industry.

WORKFORCE

Employment by miscellaneous business equipment manufacturers, like employment in most other business equipment and computer-related industries, was expected to drastically decline during the 1990s and into the next century. Contributing to this decline will be advances in productivity and automation, outsourcing of manufacturing activities to foreign firms, and stagnation in demand for traditional equipment such as typewriters.

Electrical and electronic equipment assemblers made up the largest percentage of workers in this industry in 1996, 12.7 percent, but one quarter of these jobs were expected to be eliminated by 2006. A variety of other occupations were employed by the computer and office equipment industry at that time, including computer engineers, sales personnel, general assemblers, and managers. Of these occupations, only the highly technical ones such as computer engineers and systems analysts were expected to increase in number.

In 1996, the miscellaneous office machine industry employed a total of 29,800 workers, a slight increase over 1995. The figure was expected to decline, however, to 19,500 by the year 2000. Of the 29,800 people employed in the industry in 1996, 8,900 of them were production workers making an average of $17.60 per hour. By 2000, the number of production workers was expected to drop to 3,400.

RESEARCH AND TECHNOLOGY

Manufacturers sought to retain market share and revenues by delivering new products and technology in the 1990s. PWPs represented efforts by typewriter companies to combat the dominance of PCs. Smith Corona introduced a new selection of typewriters and related equipment in an effort to boost the company's lagging sales. Olympia also expanded its line of electronic typewriters and other office equipment.

Competitors were also improving other office products such as shredders and digital voice recorders. In 1998, Alleghany Paper Shredders Corp introduced two automated high-volume shredders designed to cut labor costs by allowing one operator to do the work of two or three. In 1999, Olympus began offering a digital voice recorder that could record thoughts and memos on a flash memory card to be edited and/or converted to text. In 2000, Royal announced the introduction of several new office products, including a computer-based time clock and four new crosscut shredders with all the latest features.

FURTHER READING

''Alleghany Paper Shredders Corp.'' *Waste News,* 3 August 1998.

''Beam Me Up Scottie!'' *Stationary Trade Review,* December 1999.

Canon U.S.A. Inc. Detroit: Gale Group, 1999.

''CEMA 1996-97 Home Office, Computer Media Sales Outlook.'' *Twice,* 20 January 1997.

''Clack, Clack. The Typewriter's Back?'' *Wall Street Journal,* 14 January 2000.

Gilroy, Amy. ''Royal to Display Linux-Equipped PDA at CES.'' *Twice,* 6 January 2000.

Ryan, Ken. ''Typewriters Alive, If Small.'' *HFN,* 01 January 1996.

''Shred It.'' *USA Today,* 22 October 1998.

AUTOMATIC VENDING MACHINES

This industry consists of establishments primarily engaged in manufacturing automatic vending machines and coin-operated mechanisms for such machines.

NAICS CODE(S)

333311 (Automatic Vending Machine Manufacturing)

INDUSTRY SNAPSHOT

The vending machine industry generated U.S. sales of about $22.1 billion in 1998. With significant advances in technology and innovation, the vending machine industry served numerous markets. In 1996, the last year for which vending machine industry information was available from the United States Department of Commerce, shipments of coin-operated vending machines by manufacturers totaled $815.1 million, up from $767.0 million in 1995. The late 1990s saw improvements in vending machine sales, though the market had its ups and downs in the early and mid-1990s. Machine manufacturers shipped a total of 787,517 coin-operated vending machines in 1996. The largest percentage were machines that dispensed beverages.

The industry segments itself by the kind of service provided by the vending operator. Some of the major categories include: the 4 C's, which include coffee, club soda, candy, and cigarettes; full-line vending, which includes hot food, canned soda, and diary and frozen food; specialty vending, which encompasses such special products as pizza or french fries; OCS, or office coffee service; bulk vending, focusing on such unpackaged items as gum or nuts; and street vending, which includes music machines, video games, and other vending machines used in public places.

ORGANIZATION AND STRUCTURE

Vending is essentially a three-step process involving three separate industries: manufacturing companies, distributors, and vending machine operators. This industry group (SIC 3581) primarily covers the manufacturing step in this multi-stage industrial sequence.

About 90 U.S. companies produced automatic vending machines or parts for them in the 1990s. Although a vast majority of vending machines were manufactured by large companies, the industry did sustain quite a few smaller firms. The merchandise vending industry is essentially part of the small business community.

The U.S. Department of Commerce reported that 45 companies were engaged in manufacturing coin-operated vending machines in 1996. Thirty-five of the companies produced beverage machines, 27 were involved in manufacturing machines that sold food and confections, and 31 manufactured other types of vending machines, including those selling cigarettes, water, and postage stamps. As the numbers indicate, many of the companies manufacture machines for several segments. Canned and bottled soft drink machines made up by far the largest share of beverage machines manufactured in 1996, totaling 316,362 units. Among confection and food vending machines, those that sold bulk confections and charms predominated, totaling 158,039, while bagged snacks and confections made up another significant share at 88,271.

The National Automatic Merchandising Association (NAMA) has been the most important trade organization in the vending industry in the 1990s. NAMA represents companies involved in every facet of vending, from machine manufacturers to suppliers of vended products. Founded in 1936, NAMA compiles a broad range of statistics and produces several periodicals, including a regular industry newsletter, a review of pertinent state legislation, and a labor issues bulletin.

The National Bulk Vendors Association (NBVA) concentrates specifically on the manufacture and operation of bulk vending equipment. The NBVA was founded in 1949 and is based in Chicago.

BACKGROUND AND DEVELOPMENT

The earliest recorded "vending machine" was in 215 B.C. when the mathematician Hero described and illustrated a number of inventions conceived by himself and his teacher, Tesibius, in a book called Pneumatika. Included in the book was the plan for a completely automatic, coin-operated machine that dispensed a small amount of sacrificial water when a five-drachma coin was deposited. It is unlikely that the machine was used on a large scale, and there is no evidence to suggest that anything was sold automatically again for centuries.

Coin-operated machines that sold snuff and tobacco appeared in English taverns around 1615. These machines were actually cruder than Hero's device and required the proprietor to shut the lid after each use. Usually made of brass, the machines were portable and were carried from customer to customer.

In the nineteenth century, vending machines began to appear in much greater variety and quantity. An early incarnation of the newspaper machine appeared in England in 1822. The device was the brainchild of Richard Carlile, a bookseller trying to avoid arrest for peddling copies of banned works such as Thomas Paine's *The Age of Reason*. While his machine worked, his plan to avoid arrest didn't.

The first known patent for a vending machine was issued in 1857 to Simeon Denham for a penny postage stamp device. Over the next couple of decades, inventors

began showing up at patent offices all over the world with coin-operated machines that sold candy, cigarettes, handkerchiefs, and other small items. In 1884, the first U.S. vending machine patent was issued to W.H. Fruen for a contraption remarkably similar to Hero's holy water machine.

The American vending machine industry was truly born in 1888, when Thomas Adams of the Adams Gum Company began selling his Tutti-Frutti gum out of machines on the platforms of New York's elevated rail system. These machines were an immediate success, and toward the end of the century, postage stamp machines also became more common. The Automatic Machine Company of Buffalo, New York, was the first company to sell stamps automatically on a large scale, beginning in 1891. Bulk vending machines began to appear around the turn of the century. The Mills Novelty Company introduced the first of these, which sold a pre-set amount of peanuts for a penny, at the Pan American Exposition in 1901. The following year, the Horn & Hardart Baking Company revolutionized vending in the United States by opening is first Automat restaurant in Philadelphia.

Prior to 1908, beverage vending machines dispensed only the beverages themselves, which the customer then drank out of a common cup. That year, with public awareness of sanitation growing, the Public Cup Vendor Company of New York (later to become the Dixie Cup Company) unveiled a machine that dispensed water in individual paper cups.

By the 1920s, the vending industry had been divided into manufacturers and operators. The Doehler Die Casting Company, for example, developed machines for vending a diverse range of products that included Life Savers, lighter fluid, and sanitary napkins. Another industry revolution took place in 1925, when three new machines were developed, all of which sold cigarettes. Candy machines offering customers a choice of products began to spread in the 1930s. Nathaniel Leverone, the founder of the Canteen Company, was a pioneer in the development of this type of machine.

The manufacture of vending machines was suspended during World War II, but at the war's conclusion the industry regained its momentum. Among the machines that appeared during this time were the first hot coffee vendors and a hot dog machine. In the first decade after World War II, hundreds of small manufacturing companies entered the vending machine arena, and vast improvements were made in design—especially in the area of coin mechanisms. In 1960, paper money changers came into widespread use. When machines for vending canned soft drinks were introduced in 1961, vending sales soared.

Since that time the vending machine industry has been consolidating to a great degree. Manufacturing has become increasingly dominated by large companies. At the same time, advances in electronic components, which first appeared in vending machines in 1980, have made machines "smarter," enabling them to keep records and diagnose glitches. The variety of products vended automatically has continued to grow explosively, as items specifically created for machine vending, such as microwave popcorn, have made their appearances.

In the early 1990s, vending machine manufacturing appeared to be entering a new era. The emergence of "smart" machines was certain to affect every part of the industry. The availability of full-service machines that could handle a variety of products and perform their own record keeping was enabling bottling companies to take over many of the chores that were previously handed over to third-party operators. This represented the reversal of a trend that began in the 1950s, when bottlers began to remove themselves from the day-to-day servicing of machines. In addition, the replacement of moving parts by electronic components was expected to contribute to a further concentration of manufacturing companies, since the demand for spare parts was sure to decline sharply.

The new generation of smart vending machines was also expected to give manufacturers a healthy boost. Since the beginning of the 1990s, the slumping U.S. economy had led operators to seek ways to hold their costs in check. Frequently, this meant refurbishing old machines rather than purchasing new ones. Dixie-Narco Inc., for example, saw its sales drop by about 18 percent in 1990, while its parts business was actually more active than usual. The improved security and record keeping capabilities offered by newer machines, and their potential to save operators money in the long run, might provide operators an incentive to invest in the latest equipment.

Inflation in the 1990s affected the vending industry adversely as well. The convenience of dropping coins into a machine in exchange for merchandise disappeared when the price of an item exceeded the amount of change reasonably accommodated in a pocket. Manufacturers reacted to this problem in two ways. One involved the introduction of debit cards, first introduced in 1985. Debit cards eliminated the need to carry change, enabling regular users of a vending area to pre-pay for several dollars worth of merchandise at a time. Mechanized dollar bill acceptors, notoriously fussy and uncooperative, had also improved somewhat by the mid to late 1990s.

CURRENT CONDITIONS

Several significant changes were taking place in the vending industry in the 1990s. Some resulted from new technology, while others stemmed more directly from general societal changes. New machines developed during this time were capable of vending food of much higher quality than was previously possible. This ability

was having a particularly noticeable effect in the work place, as corporate downsizing necessitated the replacement of many company cafeterias with vending areas. With a new emphasis on hot, nutritious foods, the major manufacturers began producing machines that sold items such as french fries, fresh pizza, and a much broader line of microwaveable frozen foods.

According to the "State of The Vending Industry Report," published by *Automatic Merchandiser*, the automatic merchandising industry grew 5.6 percent in 1998, to $23.3 billion. The jump represented the largest one-year increase in the 1990s. All product categories enjoyed increases with the exception of cigarettes, a segment that accounted for less than 1 percent of the total in 1998. The beverage category was especially enthusiastic about vending machines, and about 1.2 billion cases of soft drinks were traded via vending machines in the U.S. in 1998. One reason soft drink companies invested in vending machines was because vending machine drink prices were less subject to the discounting and extreme competition affecting beverage brands in supermarkets.

With coffee shops springing up all over the United States, flavored and specialty coffee sales soared. This was also true for vending machines that sold flavored coffee and even ground their own beans. Still, the majority of coffee vending machines in the late 1990s continued to use pre-ground coffee beans, according to *Automatic Merchandiser*. In 1998 about 49.4 percent of coffee vending machines were of the freshly brewed, preground type. About 32 percent used whole beans that were ground upon machine activation.

Other trends in the late 1990s included the increase of plastic beverage bottles in vending machines. As soft drink manufacturers turned to larger, plastic bottles, vending machine manufacturers developed machines that accommodated not only the larger sized bottles but different sizes of bottles as well. Other innovative machines accepted credit cards, debit cards, and coupons. Glass-front cold beverage machines that showcased the enclosed drinks gained in popularity, and insulated machines that allowed candy machines to be placed outdoors were developed.

The sharp decline in cigarette smoking the United States throughout the 1990s has had a dramatic impact on the vending industry. Once a huge seller as one the four Cs of vending, cigarettes only generated a small portion of the vending operator's revenue compared to the considerable percentage of revenue cigarettes generated in the 1960s (at 45.5 percent).

One of the most significant issues affecting the vending machine industry in the late 1990s was the introduction of new currency. When new $20 bills were released in the U.S. in 1998, many vending machine manufacturers were unprepared. As a result, about 250,000 vending machines that normally accepted $20 bills, including bill changers and fare card machines, were unable to take the newly designed bills. New $5 and $10 bills were scheduled for release in 2000, and the Bureau of Engraving and Printing, the printers of U.S. currency, worked closely with the vending machine industry to make sure machines would be prepared. The adaptation of the new machines was estimated to be a $100 million project. As the vending machine industry was rooted largely in coin-operated machines, the release of a dollar coin in 2000 was greatly anticipated.

INDUSTRY LEADERS

Dixie-Narco, Inc., a division of Maytag Corporation, was one of the nation's leading manufacturers of automatic vending machines. Other major companies in the industry included Multiplex Co., Inc., and Automatic Products International Inc. About 40 percent of Multiplex's sales were from overseas sales.

AMERICA AND THE WORLD

The United States was not alone in its obsession with the convenience offered by vending machines. Industry leader Dixie-Narco, for example, was selling a complete line of models in over 30 countries by 1990. The company began to emphasize exports, tailoring machines for the specific needs of its foreign markets rather than merely making small adjustments in existing models.

The popularity of the vending machine proved even stronger in Japan. Half of Japan's retail soft drink sales in the early 1990s came through vending machines, and this market share is expected to increase. In Japan, the machines lined the sidewalks, playing music and offering a wide variety of merchandise, including beer, sushi, and panty hose. One advantage that vending operators in Japan had over their American counterparts was that vandalism was almost unheard of in that country in the 1990s.

The enthusiasm for vended goods was not global, however. Although American manufacturers sold machines successfully in Europe for years, the machines were not always welcome. Cafe proprietors in Bordeaux, France, for example, refused to serve Coca Cola for a period in 1990 in protest of the placement of Coke machines on public sidewalks in their city, an offense to both their sense of good taste and fair competition.

RESEARCH AND TECHNOLOGY

Flexibility and security were two areas in which engineers in the vending industry made great strides in the 1990s. The Merlin 2000 series developed by a company called InterBev in 1989 provided a good example of the flexibility built into the new generation of vending machines. The Merlin 2000 machines could sell both sodas

and juice from a single machine, with an improved mechanism for adjusting prices from one selection to the next.

Furthermore, electronic bill and coin changing mechanisms made fraud more difficult. A common form of vandalism, injecting salt water into the coin mechanisms, and putting the machine in "jackpot" mode by shorting out the electronic parts was circumvented by improved shielding of electronic components. Programmable security code devices were also installed on many new machines to prevent unauthorized individuals from tampering with pricing and removing money or merchandise.

Other innovations in the 1990s included a new vending technology that provided computerized capabilities of the machines to record their own vending statistics. In 1999 Coca-Cola Company began testing a new vending machine that was capable of raising beverage prices as the outdoor temperature increased. Though the company would not reveal the technology behind the machine, it was believed a computer chip and temperature sensor were responsible for regulating the prices.

FURTHER READING

"About Vending." Chicago: National Automatic Merchandising Association, 1996. Available from http://www.vending .org/about.htm.

Hays, Constance L. "Variable-Price Coke Machine Being Tested." *New York Times,* 28 October 1999.

Hill, Raven. "Vending Machines Have a Big Surprise." *Deseret News,* 31 October 1999.

Maras, Elliot. "Thriving economy creates growing base of small customer locations; sales reach $23.3 billion." *Automatic Merchandiser,* August 1999. Available from http://www .amonline.com.

McMahan, Thomas E. "Vending Machines Keep Up with Change." *Chicago Sun-Times,* 4 December 1999.

Postlewaite, Kimbra. "Changing of the Guard." *Beverage Industry,* 1 May 1999.

U.S. Department of Commerce. Economic and Statistical Administration. Bureau of the Census. "Vending Machines (Coin-Operated)." Washington, DC: Current Industrial Reports, 25 July 1997. Available from http://www.census.gove/industry/ ma35u96.txt.

"Vending Machines Offering Healthier Choices." *Beloit Daily News,* 11 September 1996.

SIC 3582

COMMERCIAL LAUNDRY EQUIPMENT

The commercial laundry, dry cleaning, and pressing machine industry encompasses companies primarily engaged in manufacturing nonresidential laundry equipment. Coin-operated machines are classified in **SIC 3633: Household Laundry Equipment.**

NAICS CODE(S)

333312 (Commercial Laundry, Drycleaning, and Pressing Machine Manufacturing)

The largest product group in this industry is washers and extractors, which account for almost 40 percent of sales. Commercial dryers and presses make up about 16 and 11 percent of output, respectively. Dry cleaning equipment accounts for an additional 11 percent of production, while parts, attachments, and miscellaneous equipment represent the remainder of sales.

Hotels, hospitals, and contract laundry services that serve commercial and institutional customers were the biggest consumers of commercial laundry equipment in the early 1990s. Dry cleaners represented about 17 percent of the market. Government institutions, including the armed services, prisons, schools, and hospitals, bought about 11 percent of industry output; and 12 percent of production was exported.

Maytag Corporation introduced the first electric washing machine in 1907. Not until the 1950s, however, did commercial laundry equipment producers achieve widespread market penetration. The proliferation of hotels, hospitals, and government institutions during the post-World War II economic boom pushed industry revenues to almost $300 million per year by the end of the 1970s. Continued growth in demand during the 1980s, particularly in hotel and hospital markets, increased sales to $587 million by 1988.

The commercial laundry industry faltered in the late 1980s and early 1990s as recession gripped the U.S. economy. Sales plummeted to $480 million during 1989 and bobbed up to only $526 million in 1990. Although commercial construction markets remained sluggish in the early and mid-1990s, increased sales to institutional consumers helped some manufacturers stabilize their earnings. An increase in new construction in 1993 and 1994, moreover, partially renewed industry optimism. In 1997, the industry employed 4,523 people and had $605 million in shipments.

Manufacturers in the mid-1990s were striving to boost profits by building machines that were more energy efficient, conserved water, and offered more features. Pellerin Milnor Corp., for example, introduced a valve that allowed commercial washing machines to reuse water. Speed Queen designed a line of commercial laundry machines that took more time, effort, and noise to steal. The machines also increased dryer airflow and allowed easier loading and servicing.

In 1997, most of the businesses in this classification were medium-sized. There were 35 companies that gen-

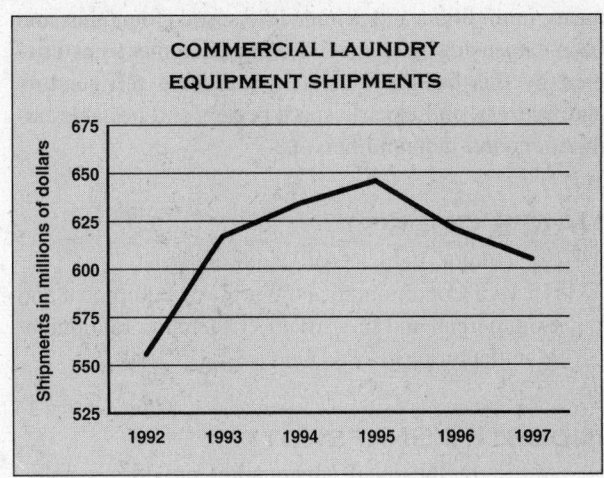

erated sales between $250,000 and $499,000, and 45 companies that had sales between $1.0 million and $4.9 million. The smallest groupings were at the two extremes, with two firms reporting sales below $49,000, and six reporting sales over $5.0 million.

The largest U.S. company primarily engaged in the production of commercial laundry equipment in the late-1990s was Pellerin Milnor Corp. of Kenner Louisiana, with sales of $91 million and employed 900 workers. Unimac was second with sales of $40 million and employed 700 workers. Cissell Manufacturing Company of Louisville, Kentucky, was third. It boasted revenues of about $40 million and had 400 employees. Other major players included American Dryer Corporation of Massachusetts and Hotsy Corporation of Colorado.

FURTHER READING

Darnay, Arsen J., ed. *Manufacturing USA.* 5th ed. Detroit: Gale Research, 1996.

U.S. Bureau of the Census. *1995 Annual Survey of Manufactures.* Washington: GPO, 1997.

Dun's Census of American Business 1997. Parsippany, NJ: Dun & Bradstreet, 1997.

Ward's Business Directory of U.S. Private and Public Companies, 1999. Detroit: Gale Group, 1999.

SIC 3585

REFRIGERATION AND HEATING EQUIPMENT

This category includes establishments primarily engaged in the manufacture of commercial or industrial refrigeration equipment or domestic, commercial, or industrial air-conditioning units. Other equipment manufactured under this classification includes warm air furnaces, humidifiers and dehumidifiers, soda fountains, and beer dispensing machines. Similar equipment not covered by this category includes household refrigerators and freezers, and electric space heaters and portable humidifiers and dehumidifiers.

NAICS CODE(S)

336391 (Motor Vehicle Air Conditioning)

333415 (Air Conditioning and Warm Air Equipment and Commercial and Industrial Refrigeration Equipment Manufacturing)

INDUSTRY SNAPSHOT

A trip to the local supermarket provides graphic evidence of the importance of the heating, refrigeration, and air-conditioning industry (HVAC) to modern American society. Many of the products found in the air-conditioned aisles, like fresh fruits or live fish, could never have been transported without cooling technology. The Air Conditioning and Refrigeration Institute (ARI) estimates that more than three-fourths of all foods consumed by Americans have been produced, packaged, shipped, stored, or preserved by refrigeration. Temperature control systems have also become common in shopping malls, commercial office buildings, and hospitals.

New building construction has always been and remains an extremely important market sector for the HVAC industry. In 1992 for instance, 77 percent of all new houses in the U.S. were built with central air-conditioning. The HVAC industry is affected by the cyclical nature of the building industry. For example, overall demand for new home construction in the early 1990s was flat because of high interest rates and a sluggish economy. This slowdown in construction subsequently softened the demand for new heating, refrigeration, and air-conditioning equipment, but did spur some repairs and up-grade replacements. Much of the housing built in the 1950s, 1960s, and 1970s needed such up-grade replacements or equipment repairs since the average domestic furnace or air conditioner has a useful life of about twenty years.

The demand for air-conditioning systems and room air conditioners is often dependent on the state of the nation's economy and the vagaries of the weather. The 1990s, for instance, were never able to match industry shipments of over 5 million room air conditioners in 1989. Through 1998 the highest number of unit shipments was recorded in 1996 with just over 4.8 million. The lowest number of unit shipments was in 1991 with just over 2.8 million. In 1998, the last year for which figures are available, there were just over 4.4 million room air conditioners shipped. According to an *Appliance* article on air quality, the HVAC industry shipped

more than 6 million heat pumps and air conditioners in 1998, a 16 percent increase over 1997.

The total value of HVAC industry shipments in 1997 was $22.94 billion, according to the U.S. Census Bureau. The 799 establishments involved in the industry employed a total of 120,341 employees. 91,845 of these employees were production workers. The total payroll for the industry was just over $3.6 billion with $2.3 billion representing wages. The largest number of industry establishments are in Texas followed by California, Florida, Ohio, and Illinois.

BACKGROUND AND DEVELOPMENT

Until the industrial revolution, refrigeration depended on the natural mediums of ice, snow, and water. The early Chinese harvested winter ice and packed it in dried straw for use in the summer. The Egyptians used porous earthenware jugs placed on their rooftops at night to cool their liquid contents by the natural process of evaporation. Since changing a liquid to a gas requires a considerable amount of heat energy, the liquid remaining in the containers became much cooler by morning. During colonial times, the ice hut was a familiar part of the landscape. It used the Chinese concept of harvesting ice to preserve food during the summer. Well into the 1800s, Americans sold ice to foreign countries as a natural refrigerant. The periodic home deliveries of ice were a commonplace experience for most Americans during the early part of the twentieth century.

The first attempts to find an industrial method to duplicate and improve on nature came in 1748 from Dr. William Cullen of Scotland. In 1851, Dr. John Gorrie, director of the U.S. Marine Hospital at Apalachicola, Florida, built the first commercial machine, receiving U.S. Patent 8080 for it. By 1880, the fledgling industry had developed reciprocating compressors which made possible such things as commercial ice making, brewing, meat-packing and fish processing. In 1904, 70 of the industry pioneers formed the American Society of Refrigeration Engineers , officially creating a new profession.

In 1911, Willis H. Carrier presented the mathematical bases for the now-standard psychometric charts, which define the theoretical properties of heat transfer through air. His work earned Carrier the title of "the father of air-conditioning." In 1922, he invented the centrifugal refrigeration compressor. During World War II, he contributed to the building of a 10 million cubic foot wind tunnel that could be cooled to -67 degrees Fahrenheit. The most notable use of the new air-conditioning technology was in the motion picture theaters of the 1920s. New York City theaters, including the Rivoli, Paramount, Roxy, and Lowe's in Times Square, lead the innovation. By the end of the decade hundreds of theaters across the country offered a controlled climate along with their feature film.

The heating industry refined the early concept of the open fire by enclosing the fire with brick or stone structures equipped with chimneys. These dirty and inefficient first efforts generally heated only the room they occupied, but could also be used for cooking and provided a central focus to the household. Throughout the nineteenth century, developments in metallurgy and forging promoted the use of remote water boilers attached to radiators by metal piping. These sturdy contrivances often used layers of asbestos to retain the heat in the water.

The warm-air furnace reduced the cost of heating, making the concept of central heating more available. Early systems were usually coal-fired, cast-iron machines that filled whole basements. They distributed the heat by means of ''gravity'' through large metal ducts attached to ornate grills in floors and walls. Like any other material when heated, air becomes lighter and tends to be pushed upwards by the cooler air surrounding it. The gravity is actually ''working'' on the cooler air, pushing it down to displace the lighter warm air. Later, electric fans attached to the heaters created the first forced-air systems. Cast-iron heaters have been replaced by compact sheet-metal cabinets, which contain burner, blower, and filter.

Burning Alternatives. A more integral change occurred in the fuel being burned. The early machines used coal or even wood or charcoal. Such material required large storage areas and considerable labor in feeding the furnace and cleaning out the burnt residue of cinders and ash. The fire produced great amounts of air pollution in the form of sooty smoke and smog. London's famous pea-soup fogs of Victorian days disappeared when the British parliament banned the burning of coal within the city limits.

The first technological revolution in modern heating fuel technology came with the use of fuel oil as a replacement for coal. The Gilbert and Barker company claims to have produced the first industrial oil burner in North America in 1889, but patents for several burners were not issued until 1892. These early machines were often called range burners because they were primarily used for the kitchen stove. New heat resistant metals made the use of fuel oil as a furnace fuel both practical and desirable by the late 1920s. That began a shift in consumer fuel preference which virtually eliminated coal as a domestic fuel by the late 1950s. A second fuel revolution came with the OPEC oil embargoes of the 1970s. Once cheap and plentiful, fuel oil quickly rose in price and scientists began predicting a world-wide oil shortage and depletion of reserves by the year 2000. To compensate, the industry shifted to domestically-available natural gas and, to some extent, electricity. By 1992, with the cost of generating electricity escalating,

natural gas became the clear preference of most American consumers, reaching a market penetration of 65 percent, according to the *Detroit Free Press*.

Modern refrigeration and air-conditioning work on essentially the same principle. Both collect heat from one area and transfer it to another where it dissipates into some medium. The basic system consists of a compressor driven by an electric motor and two coils. In the first coil, called the condenser, the refrigerant gas is compressed into a liquid, discharging heat as it changes state. In the second coil, called the evaporator, the refrigerant becomes a gas again, absorbing heat from outside the coil. The essential ingredient is the refrigerant gas. Early refrigerant materials included air, water, butane, propane, ether, ammonia, sulfur dioxide and methyl chloride. Some, like ammonia, continue to be used in large commercial applications like skating rinks and ice factories. Many of these materials were highly toxic, corrosive, and flammable.

In 1930, Thomas Midgely of the DuPont Company developed the first fluorocarbon refrigerant and demonstrated his faith in its safety at a company press conference by inhaling a stream of the gas and blowing out a candle with it. In 1956, the industry adopted DuPont's numbering system for all fluorocarbon refrigerants. The most common used in the 1990s were the chlorofluorocarbons R-12 for automotive and appliance applications and R-502 for commercial and industrial applications. A second generation of refrigerant compound displaced CFCs in many applications. The hydrochlorofluorocarbon (HCFC) R-22 dominated the domestic central air-conditioning market and was gaining popularity for some commercial applications.

Until 1953, water remained the most common cooling medium for air conditioning and refrigeration. Systems of that day used municipal water supplies or cooling towers, making the technology difficult for most domestic applications. The introduction of air-cooled systems in 1953, followed by the now-familiar split-system, launched the concept of controlled cooling into national acceptance. By 1973, 75 percent of industry sales were residential units. The development of electrically activated refrigerant reversing valves allowed cooling systems to be used for heating as well. The heat pump concept pioneered in the 1960s exchanged the functions of the two coils, as the evaporator became the condenser and the condenser acted as an evaporator. The systems scavenged usable heat out of the fall and winter air and pumped it into the building. Early models operated inefficiently in unsuitable climates, earning the technology a bad reputation with consumers. In 1960, only 28 percent of new homes were installed with central air-conditioning, but by 1992, the technology was included in 77 percent of new homes.

The technology sparked development of the commercial rooftop combination heating and cooling unit. Placing the heating and cooling equipment in a single box on the roof freed up valuable commercial space and simplified servicing and installation. In addition, improvements in compressor design, particularly the hermetic or sealed compressor, allowed the size and capacity of industrial refrigeration machines to increase and spurred the advancement of the chiller systems that dominated the large building and industrial markets.

The 1990s marked a decade of revolutionary change for the HVAC industry. The Centers for Disease Control and Prevention reported 1,604 cases of Legionnaires' disease in the United States for 1994, but epidemiologist believed the total to range between 10,000 and 100,000 cases. Office building operators across the country were reporting cases of "sick-building syndrome," in which workers developed debilitating symptoms from a build-up of pollution levels in sealed, air-conditioned buildings. In 1993, Congress passed a new energy bill that mandated higher efficiency standards for heating and air-conditioning appliances and promised to make the requirements stricter in 1998. But the most devastating event to the HVAC industry was the discovery of a 7 million square kilometer hole in the ozone layer above the South Pole, and the scientific evidence which linked that phenomenon to the release of chlorofluorocarbons (CFCs) into the atmosphere. That revelation threatened the basic component of the HVAC industry. Midgley's supposedly safe refrigerant, around which the industry was designed, had become an unacceptable pollutant.

Global Warming and Ozone Depletion. The first rumblings of environmental damage were initiated by the British scientist, James Lovelock. In 1973, Lovelock wrote that carbon dioxide and CFCs in the atmosphere created a "greenhouse" effect by trapping heat in the lower atmosphere. Although few scientists argued the physics, the expected warming did not materialize as predicted. Other factors intervened, making it clear that the atmosphere and its energy transmission characteristics were too complicated to be fully understood as of yet. In 1995, the Nobel Prize in Chemistry was awarded to Paul Crutzen, who identified the chemical reactions that destroy the ozone layer, and F. Sherwood Rowland and Mario Molina who determined that chlorofluorocarbons, CFC's were responsible for triggering ozone depletion. The essential problem is the chlorine component of the CFC. The chlorine atom destroys ozone molecules in the high atmosphere through a complicated series of chemical reactions. Each chlorine atom destroys one ozone molecule every minute for about one year.

In 1973, the industrial world was dumping almost one megaton of CFCs into the atmosphere every year. CFC production was a $2 billion a year business. Its leaders resisted the scientific theories, calling for extensive studies and time to develop replacement materials. Eventually Sweden, Norway, and Canada banned CFCs used in aerosol cans, but nothing further happened until the British Antarctic Survey discovered a hole in the ozone layer half the size of Antarctica. In 1987, 24 industrialized countries signed the Montreal Protocol, calling for a 50-percent reduction in CFC production by the year 2000.

The Clean Air Act of 1990, which introduced extensive air-quality standards and the incremental reduction and eventual banning of chlorofluorocarbons (CFCs) by the year 2000, challenged the industry to improve its technology. This challenge caused uncertainty in the industry as new systems were developed, using chemicals which were not compatible with the old refrigerants. In the early 1990s, the fear of products becoming obsolete caused the industry to stagnate, while alternative refrigerants were researched.

In June 1990, the protocol timetable was amended. CFC production in developed nations was banned by the year 2000 but developing nations could continue to produce them until 2010. As a temporary replacement refrigerant, hydrochlorofluorocarbons (HCFC) were scheduled for phase-out in 2030. This answered a concern by developing nations that the ban would work to the advantage of European and American firms who had the money to invest in alternative refrigerant technology. Manufacturers in those two regions produced two-thirds of the world's CFCs at that time.

Also in 1990, the refrigeration industry petitioned the Environmental Protection Agency to develop and issue uniform national recycling standards and requirements in anticipation of the large quantities of old refrigerant which would need to be removed from refurbished machinery. In 1992, ARI estimated the existing stock of refrigeration and air-conditioning equipment in the United States exceeded $135 billion. In February 1992, President George Bush reset the Montreal Protocol timetable, moving its requirements ahead by four years and calling for other nations to follow suit. On January 1, 1996, the production of chlorofluorocarbons was banned in the United States and other developed countries. Hydrofluorocarbon blends were already being used as refrigerants since they were legal until 2010 and these could be used to service old HCFC equipment until 2020.

The problem for the industry revolved around finding a suitable replacement refrigerant which could be produced quickly enough to meet the phase-out schedule. To make the ban effective, that technology would have to be shared with developing nations in order to persuade them not to continue building their own CFC industry. Refrigerant engineers looked for chemical combinations that were not flammable, corrosive, or toxic and which would operate reasonably well in existing equipment. The lubricants in the old systems had to be compatible with the new gases and in some cases new lubricants had to be found. In addition, the new designs had to meet the higher energy efficiency standards of 1993. Most of the new chemicals worked reasonably well but not as efficiently as CFCs, therefore, equipment redesigns were necessary to meet the efficiency ratings. The research and new technology added to the cost of the machinery at a time when sales of refrigeration equipment were at best stagnant. Another round of higher energy requirements was slated to go into effect in 1998, but the industry could not build towards that higher target because the standard was still being developed.

The process of replacing CFCs required a shift to HCFC-22, which was the only proven substitute for CFC refrigerants in 1993. In 1996, AlliedSignal Inc. introduced Genetron AZ-20 (R-410a) as a new alternate refrigerant. This non-ozone depleting replacement for HCFC-22 was quickly adopted by Carrier Corporation for use in their air conditioning units. Genetron AZ-20 is a patented azetropic blend of HFC-125 and HFC-32 and demonstrated a 7.5 percent higher energy efficiency rating (EER) over HCFC-22. At the same time, equipment manufacturers were redesigning compressors to match the characteristics of the new gases.

In the 1990s, modern HVAC systems were designed to isolate the indoor environment from an increasingly polluted urban world. With the rising cost of energy after the OPEC oil shocks, consumers sought to minimize consumption through energy conservation. The first and most obvious method was to tighten homes and buildings to prevent heat loss through the use of insulation and thermal window glass. In some cases, overzealous efforts had deadly consequences when the structures became too tight and the heating equipment burned up all the available oxygen. Instead of air, the occupants found they were breathing high concentrations of carbon dioxide or, even more deadly, carbon monoxide. In 1986, the Consumer Products Safety Commission reported that more than 200 Americans died each year from carbon monoxide poisoning in their homes. To combat this problem the industry promoted sealed combustion appliances, high-efficiency, chimney-less furnaces and outside-air-intake devices called make-up-air units.

In large buildings the problem surfaced as the "sick-building syndrome," first noted in the 1970s. Workers complained of fatigue, headaches, eye and respiratory-tract irritations, excessive colds, and dry, itchy skin. Investigators discovered air-borne asbestos particles, bacteria, chemicals, carcinogenic tobacco residues in the forced air systems. The EPA reported the presence of asbestos in 733,000 public and commercial buildings in 1988. Legionnaires' disease developed from bacteria carried by aerosols in ventilation systems. As with the atmospheric environment, the building micro-environment was a complicated system requiring careful scientific evaluation and monitoring to keep it safe for human occupation.

CURRENT CONDITIONS

Unlike the rather steady market for room air conditioners throughout the 1990s, demand for unitary systems dropped after 1989 which saw shipments of 3.5 million units, but began rising in 1994 with nearly 3.9 million units. The years between 1995 and 1998 were good for this market sector with 4 million, 4.5 million, 4.3 million and 4.9 million units shipped respectively. Unitary systems are matched cooling components in factory fabricated assemblies, of which there are three basic types: single package systems which are usually rooftop horizontal units applicable to single story buildings such as motels and bowling alleys; split systems which consist of interconnected indoor and outdoor sections and are used in small retail and office buildings and restaurants; and packaged terminal air conditioners which are designed for through-the-wall single room or zone applications and are often used in office buildings, condominiums, and metered multi-story buildings. The Air Conditioning and Refrigeration Institute, as reported in *HPAC Heating/ Piping/Air Conditioning* in 1999, released the following decade-long rising figures representing the dollar total of installed non-residential air-conditioning units: 1995— $19,900,000; 1996—$22,600,000; 1997—$23,320,000; 1998—$24,600,000; 1999—$25,584,000 (1998 and 1999 figures are *HPAC* estimates.) These figures include both unitary and field engineered units.

Contractor predicted that 6.2 million unitary air-conditioning units were shipped in 1998. They also predicted that 1998 would be a record year and produce unit shipments that won't be seen for years—or at least through 2004. *Contractor's* predictions for shipments of unitary air-conditioning units through 2004 are: 1999— 5.8 million; 2000—5.6 million; 2001 5.6 million; 2002—5.1 million; 2003 5.7 million; and 2004—5.7 million

Contractor also quotes the Gas Appliance Manufacturers Association as expecting a slowdown in gas furnace shipments in 1999. Shipments of gas furnaces are predicted to be around 2.9 million units or a drop of 50,000 units over 1998.

What is driving the HVAC industry is a nearly recession proof replacement market. "We're becoming more and more replacement, repair, and maintenance oriented," GroupMac vice president Russel Bay told *Contractor* in a 1999 interview. Trane Co. vice president Tom Mikulina concurs. "Equipment reaches the end of its useful life and it's scheduled for replacement or it's a reactive investment

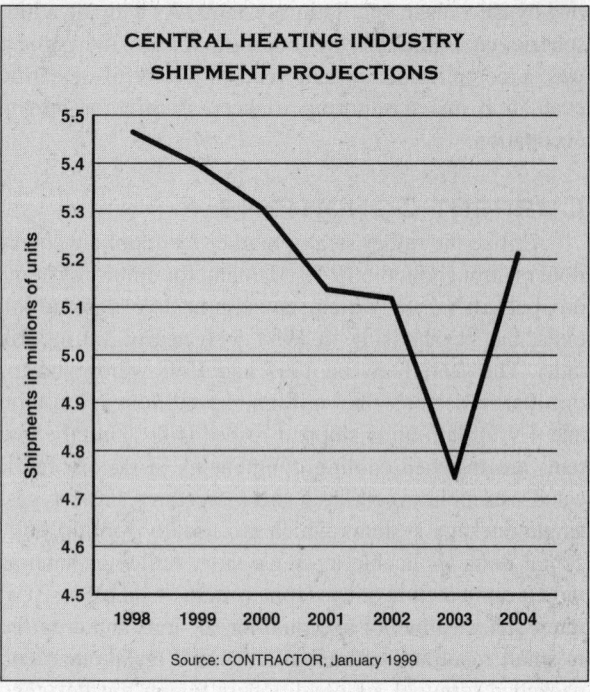

CENTRAL HEATING INDUSTRY
SHIPMENT PROJECTIONS

Source: CONTRACTOR, January 1999

the building owner makes to keep tenants. You put all of these issues together and it isn't susceptible to recession like the new construction market,'' he says. Replacement air-conditioning and gas furnace units can account for up to 55 percent of the annual market.

The 1990s showed mixed demand for furnaces. For the popular warm air gas furnaces the decade high (through 1998) was nearly 3 million units shipped in 1998. The decade low was 1990 when 1.9 million units were shipped. This figure generally remained high for the years 1993 through 1997 with shipments of 2.5 million, 2.7 million, 2.6 million, 2.8 million, and 2.7 million units respectively.

HPAC estimates that 82 percent of the new homes built between January and May 1998 had central air-conditioning units. Homeowners also had enough discretionary income to either add air-conditioning to existing homes or buy new replacement units. Quoting figures generated by the American Refrigeration Institute *HPAC* maintains that the strong 1998 U.S. economy and early summer heat waves were responsible for the shipment of 837,682 shipments of central air conditioners and air-source heat pumps for the month of June. This figure easily eclipsed the previous record of 730,692 units shipped in June of 1996. According to *HPAC* manufacturers shipped 3,432,914 units during the first six months of 1998 up 11 percent over the same period for 1997. Shipments of central air-conditioning units have, except for a slight dip in 1997, risen consistently each year since 1992 when shipments stood at 3.7 million units. 5.7 million units were shipped in 1996, 5.4 million in 1997, and it is estimated that 6.2 million units were shipped in 1998.

The HVAC industry is a large consumer of various metal products and assembled pieces of machinery. Dollar values of material consumed by kind in 1997(except for miscellaneous materials and supplies) were: steel sheet and strip—$724.6 million; Copper and copper based alloy pipes and tubes—$535.1 million; refrigerator compressors, compressor units, condensing units, and other heat transfer equipment—$1.7 billion; steel bars, bar shapes, and plates—$288.9 million; automatic temperature controls—$362.0 million; integral horse power electric motors and generators (more than 1 horse) $792.

Industry and Primary Class Specialization statistics for the 1997 HVAC industry are: heat transfer equipment, mechanically refrigerated and self-contained—$5.4 billion; commercial refrigeration related equipment—$3.1 billion; refrigeration condensing units (all refrigerants except ammonia)—$135.0 million; room air-conditioning units and dehumidifiers (except portable dehumidifiers)—$1.0 billion; refrigeration and air-conditioning equipment—$772.2 million; compressors and compressing units (except automotive)—$3.3 billion; warm air furnaces including duct furnaces, humidifiers, and electric comfort heating equipment—$1.7 billion; parts and accessories for air-conditioning and heat transfer equipment—$979.6 million; unitary air conditioners except air source heat pumps—$6.0 billion; air source heat pumps except room air conditioners—$36.3 million; and ground and ground water source heat pumps—$67.4 million.

INDUSTRY LEADERS

At the close of World War II, America's clear leader in the HVAC industry was the Carrier Corp. of Farmington, Connecticut. At that time Carrier controlled about 90 percent of the American market. By the 1990s Carrier had become a subsidiary of the giant United Technologies Corporation but nonetheless it lost its hold on a stable industry lead. In 1991, as a result of poor quality control, under-investment in research and development, inconsistent dealer relations, and poor marketing decisions, Carrier's market share had dropped to 37 percent. In 1992, however, the company began replacing its product line with high-tech innovations, spending tens of millions of dollars in research and development, and selling off business ventures unrelated to HVAC. In 1996 Carrier had sales of $5.9 billion which represented about 25 percent of the total sales of United Technologies. In 1998 carrier had sales of $7 billion up from $6 billion in 1997. 52 percent of Carrier's 1998 revenues came from U.S. exports and international operations. Carrier employs about 27,000. In early 1999 Carrier announced a restructuring which would eliminate 400 salaried workers or about 6 percent of Carrier's U.S. salaried workforce. In 1999 Carrier also acquired the refrigeration business of Electrolux for $145 million.

American Standard of Piscataway, New Jersey manufactures air-conditioning products and home comfort systems under a variety of names with American Standard and Trane being the most well known. In 1998 American Standard had total sales revenues of $6.7 billion. $3.9 billion of these revenues were from the sale of air-conditioning products up 10 percent from 1997. 50 percent of revenues came from overseas markets. It is also estimated that 65 percent of sales are for replacements and repairs because due to the maturity of the U.S. and European market. 59 percent of American Standard's revenues come from air-conditioning products with 25 percent coming from plumbing products and 16 percent from automotive products. In 1997 American Standard had about 51,000 employees.

York International of York, Pennsylvania is the third largest manufacturer (after Carrier and American Standard) of heating, ventilation, air-conditioning, and refrigeration equipment. In 1998 York had $3.2 billion in revenues from manufacturing operations in 15 countries and employed about 25,000. In 1998, 13 percent of revenues came from refrigeration products, 44 percent from unitary products, and 43 percent from engineered systems. York is also the supplier of snowmaking equipment for the 2002 Winter Olympics to be held in Salt Lake City. The company will also supply ice-making equipment and heating, ventilation, and cooling equipment for indoor venues. York manufactures heating and cooling equipment for a wide variety of commercial and industrial applications as well as hermetic compressors and split-unit central air-conditioning and heating systems for residential applications.

To the man on the street, Lennox is perhaps one of the most recognizable names in the HVAC industry. The company traces its roots to 1895 and a riveted steel furnace built by Dave Lennox in Marshalltown, Iowa. In 1904 Lennox sold his company to a group of investors led by D.W. Norris, a Marshalltown businessman. In 1978 the company moved to Dallas. By the end of the 1990s, the company had three manufacturing sites in North America and was marketing its products through 6,000 independent dealers. Lennox has four operating companies: Lennox Industries, Inc., Armstrong Air Conditioning, Inc., Heatcraft, Inc., and Lennox Global Ltd. In 1998 Lennox had earnings of $52 million on $1.8 billion in sales with about 14,000 employees. Lennox was a privately held company until 1999 when it launched a $141.4 million initial public offering. The Norris family will, however, retain ownership of 70 percent of the company's stock.

WORKFORCE

Traditionally, the heating, refrigeration and air-conditioning manufacturing industry has been highly lab-or intensive. In 1996, the average number of production workers at an establishment in the industry was 146, compared to the average number of 49 workers in all manufacturing establishments. Employment in the industry was predicted to remain flat but stable between the years 1997 and 2000 with total industry employment staying at about 131,000. Average hourly wages were predicted to increase slowly from $14.69 in 1997 to $15.68 in 2000.

Much of the assembly work was done by hand fitting many small parts and cutting metal shapes with the use of templates. By the mid-1980s, the industry was shifting towards more automated production with the use of numerical control machining tools and welding robots. Eventually computerized control led to automated plants conditioning facility. Consequently employment in the industry was expected to remain relatively stable at around 131,000 for the years 1995—2000.

Of these 131,000 employees approximately 100,000 were expected to be wage earners. Employment of heating, air-conditioning and refrigeration technicians and mechanics is expected to grow about as fast as the average for all U.S. workers through 2006. Employment for those involved in the maintenance and repair of heating and cooling units is expected to generally remain stable. Installers of new equipment, however, may experience cyclic employment as a result of ups and downs relating to the level of new construction. The average salary for workers in these areas is $535 a week, with lows of about $285 and highs of $885. Future employment for these job classifications will be affected by regulations prohibiting the discharge of CFC and HCFC refrigerants as well as a market emphasis on better energy management, indoor air quality and a rising demand for frozen or refrigerated convenience foods.

AMERICA AND THE WORLD

Like the American HVAC market, the global HVAC market is driven by new building construction and weather conditions. Mild weather generally contributes to a reduced demand for air conditioners and air-source heat pumps. Unseasonably mild weather in 1997, for instance, contributed to a global slowdown for unitary equipment (factory assembled units) resulting in a fall in demand for the first time since 1994 and a 6 percent drop from 1996 when a record 5.7 million units were shipped. Canada, however, remains a strong market accounting for 29 percent of U.S. industry exports in 1997. The Asian economic crisis of 1997 and 1998 affected the U.S. HVAC industry and caused U.S. exports to fall 27 percent in 1997 compared to 1996. In 1997 Asia accounted for 24 percent of U.S. industry exports. Early 1998 figures showed the decline continuing. Total exports for 1997 increased, however, largely due to a 34 percent increase in exports to Latin America worth $540 million. The top five countries for U.S. industry exports in 1997 were: Canada—$1.5 billion; Mexico—$551 million; South Korea—$249 million; Saudi Arabia—$247 million; and Hong Kong—$193 million. The largest region for U.S. exports in 1997 were the NAFTA trading partners at over $2 billion. The top five countries for U.S. imports in 1997 were: Mexico—$711 million; Japan—$539 million; Canada—$307 million; Brazil—$199 million; and Singapore—$134 million. The largest region for U.S. imports in 1997 was likewise the NAFTA trading partners at just over $1 billion.

1998 was predicted to be a down year for the HVAC industry by the U.S. Department of Commerce and 1999 was predicted to be only slightly better. These predictions were based on anticipated slowdowns in new housing and weather. The effects of the El Niño weather pattern caused a 15 percent drop in shipments of heat pumps in the first quarter of 1998, compared to the first quarter of 1997.

Demographic shifts in the U.S. population, however, are having a positive effect on the HVAC industry. In 1991, 75 percent of new houses were built with central air-conditioning. By 1996, this figure had increased to 81 percent of new homes. Much of this increase is attributable to population growth in southern states where 98 percent of new homes are built with central air-conditioning.

RESEARCH AND TECHNOLOGY

There are many global issues facing the American HVAC industry as it enters the new century. Topping the list would be energy efficiency, quality indoor air, and the concurrent issues of global warming and ozone depletion. Chillers, for instance, are mechanical devices used in commercial cooling applications and are major energy consumers. Newer chillers that use HFC-134a and HCFC-123 as alternative refrigerants are able to increase efficiency by more than 44 percent when compared to the CFC chillers that were used in the 1970s. According to Robert Ratcliffe of the American Refrigeration Institute, however, conversion to the new refrigerants has been slower than expected and needs to be speeded up. "It will take until the year 2000 for 44 percent of the CFC chillers to be replaced or converted to non-CFC refrigerants," Ratcliffe told *HPAC*. Ratcliffe went on to say that chillers that have been converted or replaced are conserving 7 billion kilowatt hours of electricity annually at a savings of $480 million. However, 64 percent of the 80,000 CFC chillers that were in service in 1992 were still expected to be in service in 1999.

The HVAC industry is also looking towards advanced software in pursuit of energy efficiency. The so-called "intelligent buildings" of the 21st century will employ "neural networks" and "fuzzy logic" and other ". . . software intensive, artificial intelligence-based technologies," according to a 1999 *HPAC* roundtable. Sensors and actuators will be integrated so as to monitor and control the formation of regional and even national "central stations." All of these innovations will save operator time while increasing system performance, reducing costs and eliminating system redundancies.

Indoor air quality is another issue demanding technological innovations by the HVAC industry. Due to shifting attitudes towards indoor air quality, especially in the workplace, the 1990s saw many litigious claims from workers claiming that workplace air had made them "sick" and they were thus due compensation for their illness. Subsequently there has been increasing pressure on building designers and owners to assure clean air in the workplace. "More and more, indoor air quality is becoming the driving issue in our industry, especially as we learn more about the impact comfort has on employee productivity [and] the dramatic increase in health problems that are possibly due to indoor air quality," according to George Jerkins , president of the American Society of Heating, Refrigeration, and Air Conditioning Engineers in a 1999 *Appliance* article. "Experts estimate that one million buildings in the U.S. have poor indoor air quality, with an annual cost to U.S. business of $60 billion, mostly in lost productivity," Jerkins says.

Smoking in public places is another major issue related to air quality. The hospitality industry, which includes bars, restaurants, and other similar businesses, serves many patrons who feel they have a right to smoke when patronizing these establishments. As a result the hospitality industry has been particularly susceptible to issues of air quality and many have striven via air filtering systems to accommodate the needs and desires of all patrons—those who smoke and those who need or prefer a smoke-free environment. A 1999 *HPAC* roundtable on smoking and the hospitality industry quoted a 1995 study which showed smokers spending an estimated $50 billion annually in restaurants alone. Another study quoted by the roundtable claims that if smoking were banned in all U.S. restaurants, the hospitality industry would have lost $18.2 billion in 1994 or about 6 percent of sales. In response to the hospitality industry's concerns about accommodating both smokers and non-smokers, the American Society of Heating, Refrigeration, and Air Conditioning Engineers first published its "Ventilation for Acceptable Indoor Air Quality" in 1989. The society has updated the publication periodically in response to evolving technology. The HVAC industry is addressing indoor air quality issues with more efficient and more effective air filtering and air control systems that make use of existing technology.

In the 1970s the so-called "oil crisis" or "energy crisis" was a major factor in motivating the HVAC industry to produce more efficient products. The major industry issue of the 1990s has been ozone depletion caused by chlorofluorocarbon (CFC) refrigerants being released into the atmosphere. Early air-conditioning systems relied exclusively on CFC refrigerants. This global problem resulted in the U.S. Clean Air Act amendments of 1990, numerous Environmental Protection Agency regulations, and the development of alternate refrigerants such as HFC-134a, HFC-410A, HCFC-123, and HCFC-22. With these new refrigerants available the HVAC industry has worked to set up compliance and training programs which necessitate sizable capital investments. Service technicians, for instance, must have the tools and know-how to recover CFC refrigerants since they can no longer be vented into the atmosphere. "Only EPA-certified technicians can open and service equipment using CFCs and HCFCs, and they must follow scrupulous rules or face potential fines," according to Clifford Rees, Jr., president of the Air-Conditioning and Refrigeration Institute. These fines may reach $27,500 per day for violations.

Concurrent with the concern over ozone depletion is concern over global warming, which has generally been attributed to carbon dioxide emissions but also to emissions of certain refrigerants and methane. A U.S. global action plan was written in relation to Title XVI of the Energy Policy Act of 1992. The plan calls for a switch from high carbon fuels, such as coal and oil, to low carbon fuels such as natural gas. The plans also call for more fuel-efficient energy using equipment. A potential global agreement tentatively called the Kyoto Protocol has set a goal of reducing emissions by 7 percent from 1990 levels between 2008 and 2012. It has been determined that to meet this goal, a 33 percent reduction in energy consumption will be necessary.

FURTHER READING

Air Conditioning and Refrigeration Institute. *ARI Cool Net: Air-Conditioning and Refrigeration Institute.* Arlington, VA: Air-Conditioning and Refrigeration Institute, 1999. Available from: http://www.ari.org.

American Society of Heating, Refrigeration, and Air-Conditioning Engineers. *Welcome to ASHRAE Online.* Atlanta: American Society of Heating, Refrigeration, and Air Conditioning Engineers, 1999. Available from http://www.ashrae.org.

American Standard Companies, Inc. *Welcome to American Standard.* Piscataway, New Jersey: American Standard Companies, Inc., 1999. Available from: http://www.americanstandard.com.

Career Information Center. 7th ed. New York: Macmillan Reference USA, 1998.

Carrier Corp. *Carrier: World Leader in Air Conditioning, Heating, and Refrigeration Systems.* Hartford, CN: United Technologies, Inc., 1999. Available from: http://www.carrier.com.

"Carrier Corp. Completes Restructuring." *American Metal Market.* 11 October 1999.

"Carrier Restructures." *Appliance.* September 1999.

Darnay, Arsen J. *Manufacturing U.S.A.* 6th ed. Detroit: Gale, 1998.

"Electrolux to Sell Its Refrigeration Business to Carrier Corp." *New York Times,* 20 November 1999.

Ivanovich, Michael. "'99 Economic Forecast: The Health of the Industry." *HPAC Heating/Piping/Air Conditioning,* January 1999.

Ivanovich, Michael and Dale Gustavson. "Intelligent Building Roundtable." *HPAC Heating/Piping/Air Conditioning.* May 1999.

Johnson, Robert. "Refrigerant Management and Regulations Compliance." *HPAC Heating/Piping/Air Conditioning.* December 1999.

Knoth, Janmarie. "New HVAC/R Equipment: AHR Exposition Review." *HPAC Heating/Piping/Air Conditioning.* April 1999.

"Lennox Acquires Most Ducane Assets." *Contractor.* December 1999.

"Lennox Buys Service Experts." *Contractor.* December 1999.

Lennox Inc. *Welcome to Lennox.* Dallas: Lennox, Inc., 1999. Available from: http://www.lennox.com.

"Lennox International to Launch $141.4 mil. Initial Public Offering." *Dallas Morning News.* 29 July 1999.

Mader, Robert P. and Kelly Falloon. "HVAC Market Looks For Second Best Year on Record." *Contractor.* January 1999, 3+.

Marino, Allyson and Michael Ivanovich. "Accommodating Smoking in the Hospitality Industry." *HPAC Heating/Piping/Air Conditioning.* October 1999.

Mollohan, Gary. "A Breath of Fresh Air." *Appliance.* April 1999.

"A Practical Guide to Ventilation Practices and Systems for Existing Buildings." *HPAC Heating/Piping/Air Conditioning April/May 1999 Supplement.*

"Service Experts Inc. to Sell Rolf Heating and Air Conditioning to Lennox International." *Fort-Wayne News Sentinel.* 1 November 1999.

"Statistical Review: Appliance Shipments Are Charted By product category for 10 Years Through 1998." *Appliance.* April 1999, 51-56.

Tardiff, Joseph C. ed. *U.S. Industry Profiles: The Leading 100.* 2nd. Ed. Detroit: Gale, 1998.

U.S. Bureau of Labor Statistics. *1998-99 Occupational Outlook Handbook.* Washington D.C.: G.P.O., 1998. Available from: http://www.bls.gov/oco/ocos192.htm.

U.S. Census Bureau. *Air Conditioning and Warm Air Heating Equipment and Commercial and Industrial Refrigeration Equipment Manufacturing: 1997 Economic Census, Manufacturing, Industry Series.* Washington: G.P.O., 1999. Available from: http://www.census.gov/prod/ec97/97m3334d.pdf.

U.S. Industry & Trade Outlook '99. New York: DRMI/McGraw-Hill: Standard & Poor's; Washington D.C.: U.S. Department of Commerce/International Trade Administration, 1999.

York International Corporation. *York International Corporation*. York, Pennsylvania: York International Corporation, 1999. Available from: http://www.york.com.

MEASURING AND DISPENSING PUMPS

The measuring and dispensing pumps industry is comprised of establishments primarily engaged in manufacturing pumps used in service stations for dispensing gas, oil, and grease. This category also includes grease guns. Industrial pumps are classified in **SIC 3561: Pumps and Pumping Equipment.**

NAICS CODE(S)

333913 (Measuring and Dispensing Pump Manufacturing)

In the 1990s, multi-pump units, which offer several grades of gasoline from the same pump, accounted for about 22 percent of industry sales. More traditional single-pump units still held a 19 percent share of the market. Lubricating oil pumps represented about 4 percent of output, and grease guns made up 3 percent of sales. Approximately 30 percent of industry revenues were made from the sale of parts and attachments, such as vapor recovery systems and replacement hoses.

Non-industrial gas, oil, and grease pumps were a corollary of the proliferation of cars and trucks during the early and mid-1900s. As American society became increasingly mobile, markets for service station pumps expanded rapidly. Indeed, by the late 1970s the service station pump industry was shipping more than $600 million worth of products per year and employing about 8,000 workers.

Despite an oil shortage in the United States in the late 1970s and a recession in the early 1980s, industry revenues climbed sporadically to $1.14 billion by 1988. Although growth of demand for new gas, oil, and grease pumps waned in comparison to growth in previous decades, other product segments prospered. Importantly, environmental regulations forced service stations in many states to equip their pumps with costly new vapor recovery systems and safety devices.

A U.S. economic recession in the late 1980s and early 1990s suppressed pump sales to about $1.03 billion per year in the early 1990s. As sales faltered, industry employment plummeted from a high of 9,400 in 1987 to about 8,000 by 1990. Figures for 1992 showed that employment levels were at 6,500 workers, 31 percent below 1987 levels, while the value of goods shipped slipped to $896.3 million. In 1993, however, the economy began to improve, and the industry responded. In 1997, the industry reported 6,824 employees and shipment of goods worth $1.3 billion.

In the mid-1990s, pump manufacturers scrambled to revive profits by introducing new gas pump systems, focusing on the multi-pump market, and incorporating computer technology into their machines. New pumps with point-of-sale credit card devices, for example, allowed customers to fill a vehicle with gas and pay without leaving their car, thus reducing labor costs. Likewise, to help service stations comply with Federal ''Stage II'' vapor recovery guidelines, producers of vapor recovery pumps and attachments were introducing a variety of new systems and designs.

The largest U.S. company primarily engaged in the production of service station pumps and equipment in 1999 was Graco Inc. of Minneapolis, Minnesota. Graco boasted sales of $432 million and had 2,100 employees. Second was Tokheim Corporation, of Fort Wayne, Indiana, with $386 million in sales and 2,900 employees. Gilbarco Inc. of Greensboro, North Carolina, placed third, with $344 million in sales and 1,500 employees. Fourth was Wayne Division of Austin, Texas, with sales of $283 million and 900 employees. In all, about 71 companies were classified in the industry in 1999.

Industry participants were able to increase production yet keep a lid on employment growth during the 1980s—primarily through productivity gains. The movement of some manufacturing activities overseas also reduced work force gains. The future of employment in this industry was uncertain for the twenty-first century, having decreased in employee count from 1995 to 1997. However, the outlook for job growth in the overall service machinery sector was generally positive through 2005, according to the U.S. Bureau of Labor Statistics.

FURTHER READING

Darnay, Arsen J., ed. *Manufacturing USA*. 5th ed. Detroit: Gale Research, 1996.

U.S. Bureau of the Census. *1997 Economic Census*. Washington, D.C.: GPO, 2000. Available from http://www.census.gov.

Ward's Business Directory of U.S. Private and Public Companies. Detroit: Gale Group, 1999.

SERVICE INDUSTRY MACHINERY, NOT ELSEWHERE CLASSIFIED

Companies in this classification are principally engaged in manufacturing miscellaneous equipment for use in service businesses. Examples of industry products are floor sanding machines, cafeteria food warmers, commercial fryers, sludge processors, sewage treatment equipment, mop wringers, and commercial corn poppers. Household appliances and machinery are classified in **3630: Household Appliances.** For more information on the history and structure of U.S. machinery industries, see **SIC 3552: Textile Machinery** through **SIC 3559: Special Industry Machinery, Not Elsewhere Classified.**

NAICS CODE(S)

333319 (Other Commercial and Service Industry Machinery Manufacturing)

One of the larger segments of the miscellaneous service machine industry is food service equipment, which accounted for about 20 percent of total industry shipments in 1997. Commercial ranges, stoves, and broilers made up the bulk of that group. Commercial and industrial vacuum cleaners, including parts and attachments, accounted for another 5.4 percent of the market. The biggest single category was miscellaneous machinery products, which included an array of products ranging from commercial car washing machinery to service industry water heaters. This miscellaneous category alone accounted for nearly half of all industry shipments in 1997.

General industry expansion between 1950 and 1980 resulted in aggregate shipments of more than $2.5 billion by the early 1980s. Steady growth of service industries during the 1980s, particularly food services, resulted in rapid growth. Sales went from about $2.6 billion in 1983 to $3.4 billion by 1986, and to $4.9 billion by 1990. The 1990s witnessed even more dramatic growth as industry shipments jumped just over 90 percent to $9.3 billion by 1997. As the industry's revenues grew steadily through the 1980s and 1990s, employment jumped from 31,000 in the early 1980s to nearly 57,000 by 1997.

Despite U.S. economic malaise in the early 1990s, most service machinery manufacturers performed well into the second half of the decade. Sales of commercial food service equipment, for example, grew 38.4 percent from $1.3 billion in 1992 to $1.8 billion in 1997. Shipments of commercial and industrial vacuum cleaners, including parts and attachments, jumped 66.9 percent from $319.5 million in 1992 to $533.2 million in 1997.

The miscellaneous service machinery industry is extremely fragmented and is dominated by relatively small, specialty manufacturers. The average industry participant employed only 45 workers in 1997, compared to an average of 49 for all other U.S. manufacturers. The total number of companies active in the industry in 1997 was 1,269. These companies operated a total of 1,347 establishments and employed 56,658 workers, of which 32,435 were engaged in production. One of the largest

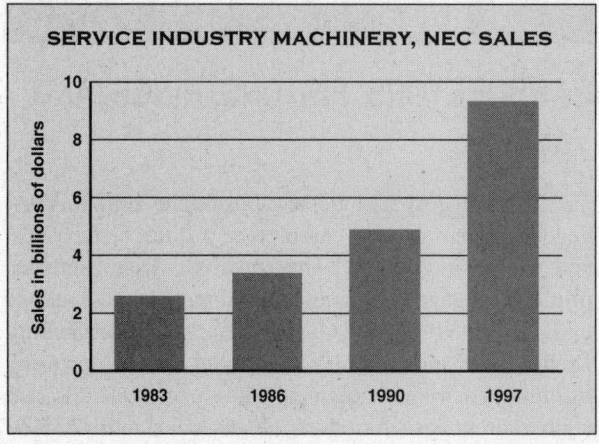

SERVICE INDUSTRY MACHINERY, NEC SALES

companies in the industry was Welbilt Corp., a subsidiary of Berisford PLC based in Stamford, Connecticut. The late 1990s saw a flurry of acquisitions that further strengthened Welbilt's position as a leader in the food service equipment market.

Other players in the miscellaneous service machinery industry were Hoover Co. of North Canton, Ohio, a leading manufacturer of floor care and vacuuming equipment; Tennant Co. of Minneapolis, Minnesota, also involved in floor care; and Ionics Inc., a supplier of water treatment equipment. Tennant, with more than 2,100 employees, posted 1998 sales of $389.4 million, up 4.6 percent from 1997. Ionics, headquartered in Watertown, Massachusetts, employed 2,200 as of late 1998 and reported 1998 sales of $351.3 million, off 0.3 percent from the previous year.

Despite continued productivity increases and the movement of some manufacturing facilities to foreign countries, employment prospects for the overall service machinery industry were positive. Opportunities for most occupations were expected to swell by 10 to 20 percent between 1990 and 2005, according to the U.S. Bureau of Labor Statistics. Jobs for assemblers and fabricators, which account for about 25 percent of the work force, will likely decline slightly; however, the number of labor positions should grow. Openings for some workers, such as sales and marketing professionals, will likely increase by as much as 50 percent.

FURTHER READING

Darnay, Arsen J., ed. *Manufacturing USA.* 6th ed. Detroit: Gale Research, 1998.

"Ionics Incorporated." Hoover' Online, 1999. Available from http://www.hoovers.com/co/capsule/1/0,2163,12061,00.html.

"Tennant Company." Hoover's Online, 1999. Available from http://www.hoovers.com/co/capsule/3/0,2163,14903,00.html.

U.S. Bureau of Census. *1997 Economic Census.* Washington: GPO, 1999.

SIC 3592

CARBURETORS, PISTONS, RINGS, AND VALVES

This category includes establishments primarily engaged in manufacturing carburetors, pistons, piston rings, and engine intake and exhaust valves. Establishments primarily engaged in manufacturing metallic packing are classified in **SIC 3053: Gaskets, Packing, and Sealing Devices,** and those primarily engaged in manufacturing machine repair and equipment parts (except electric), on a job or order basis for others, are classified in **SIC 3599: Industrial and Commercial Machinery and Equipment, Not Elsewhere Classified.**

NAICS CODE(S)

336311 (Carburetor, Piston, Piston Ring, and Valve Manufacturing)

INDUSTRY SNAPSHOT

Carburetors, pistons, intake and exhaust valves, and piston rings account for a relatively small and declining portion of the broader automotive and machine engine parts industries, which together are valued at more than $150 billion. The industry's fortunes have declined significantly since the 1980s; shipments peaked at $3.1 billion in 1984. In 1997, the value of industry shipments was just over $2.8 billion. This figure is expected to decline to $2.4 billion by 2000. Employment in the industry has declined by nearly 50 percent since the mid-1980s. In 1997 the industry employed 16,226 people, 15,117 of which were production workers. In 2000, this figure is expected to decline to 11,200 employees, 9,500 of which would be production workers. The greatest factors contributing to this long decline are technological changes and greater competition from foreign manufacturers and suppliers. Despite this decline, workers in this industry were expected to average $16.43 an hour in 2000. In 1996 the average hourly wage was $14.70, compared to the average of $12.68 for all other manufacturing industries. The total payroll for the industry in 2000 was expected to be nearly $549 million.

ORGANIZATION AND STRUCTURE

This industry supplies engine parts as original equipment and as aftermarket replacement parts. Dominated by mid-sized and large companies, the industry employed an average of 151 workers per establishment in 1996. In 1997 the industry claimed 142 establishments, predominantly in California, Indiana, Michigan, Ohio, Wisconsin, Texas, and Pennsylvania.

The total auto parts industry, according to Standard & Poor's, is very fragmented and consists of thousands of suppliers, ranging from small specialty shops to multinational corporations. According to 1999 reports from the U.S. Department of Commerce, there were about 5,000 American firms and about 500 foreign firms producing parts for the U.S. market, with about 100 large dominant firms. In general, this industry sector is comprised of four lines of business: original equipment, replacement parts, distribution, and rubber fabrication. Original equipment is manufactured and sold to the automobile companies for installation in new vehicles. The replacement sector produces parts and equipment for either replacement or supplementation. Replacement and supplemental parts are sold primarily to retail outlets and fleet owners. In 1997 U.S. shipments from the automotive parts industry accounted for just over 4 percent of total U.S. manufacturing shipments and represented nearly 4 percent of U.S. manufacturing jobs.

The industry's product share is divided into three major categories, each with several subcategories. In 1997 the industry produced carburetors, both new and re-built, valued at $1.28 billion; pistons, piston rings, and piston pins valued at $992.6 million; and engine intake and exhaust valves valued at $496.7 million. In each industry sector the largest share of parts was manufactured for use in motor vehicle engines. Miscellaneous non-motor vehicle internal combustion engines and farm machinery made up the second and third largest uses of this industry's products.

The materials consumed by the industry cover most of the materials used in manufacturing: ferrous and nonferrous stock, ceramics, rubber, and plastic. The industry supplies carburetors, pistons, rings, and valves either as original equipment for manufacturers of new products or as replacement parts for older products. In 1997 the five largest categories of materials consumed by kind by the industry were aluminum and aluminum based alloy castings ($259.7 million); miscellaneous materials, components, parts, and supplies ($231.7 million); steel shapes and forms ($127.3 million); iron and steel castings ($77.3 million); and metal bolts, nuts, screws, washers, rivets, and other screw machine products ($62.2 million).

CURRENT CONDITIONS

In the late 1990s, the industry continued to be affected by foreign competition and changing technology. Especially in the motor vehicle sector, developments in technology meant that some products needed to be replaced less frequently or were on the verge of obsolescence. In the automotive market, for instance, the traditional carburetor has largely been supplanted by fuel injection, which is more precise and fuel-efficient. After-factory rebuilding and replacement of existing carburetors constitutes the extent of this declining market. Motorcycles and heavy trucks typically still use carburetors, as do other types of non-automotive engines, such as those produced by Briggs & Stratton and Tecumseh. Among all industry products, demand for more reliable components has led to longer-lasting parts that require servicing and replacement less often than in the past. The industry's pistons, rings, and valves are still viable components for the automotive market.

In attempt to curtail prices U.S. vehicle manufacturers demanded increased quality and lower prices from auto parts manufacturers. This pressure started in the mid-1980s due to competition from Japan and continued through the 1990s. By 1993, the quality of automobile parts had measurably improved and productivity had risen by over 2 percent. Ford and Chrysler, however, sought further price cuts hovering around 5 percent or savings equal to 5 percent of suppliers sales. Large-volume parts suppliers such as TRW and Dana were generally able to comply, but diminishing returns to smaller suppliers forced them into a spate of mergers and acquisitions. Between 1993 and 1996, for instance, Dana was involved in 24 purchases or joint ventures. Ford and General Motors also spun off their parts operations—Visteon and Delphi, respectively—into independent suppliers who must compete in the marketplace for contracts with their previous parent companies.

Because half of its revenues came from automotive applications, the industry was largely dependent on sales of motor vehicles in general, and automobiles and light trucks in particular. While U.S. automakers posted a modest recovery in the mid-1990s from their early 1990s slump, growth had been tempered by slim margins and had been uneven across different segments. By the late 1990s, however, truck and automobiles sales had reached unprecedented levels. Writing for *Automotive Manufacturing & Production*, Michael Robinet predicted total sales for the 1999 North American automotive market would "eclipse 18 million units, an all-time record by over 4 percent from the previous best." NAFTA light vehicle production was expected to register 16.7 million units. Strong demand was expected to extend into the first quarter of 2000, with the rest of the year seeing a slight decline. Total production for 2000 was expected to decline about 4 percent. These nonetheless optimistic figures included a strong and continuing demand for light trucks. "By 2001, light truck production will pass the 8 million mark and the annual light-truck share of the total North American [market] will exceed 50 percent by 2002," according to Christopher Benko of *Automotive Industries*.

AMERICA AND THE WORLD

U.S. suppliers of auto parts are facing increasing competition from foreign suppliers. Between 1995 and 1998, the U.S. automotive trade deficit widened because of imports from NAFTA partners Mexico and Canada

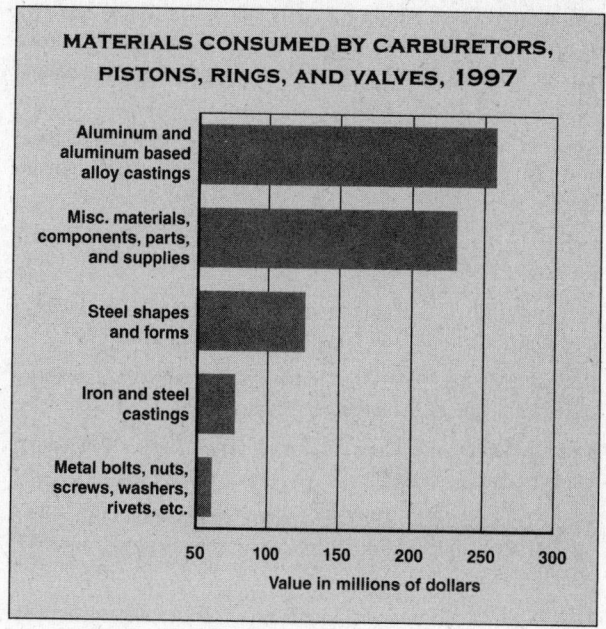

MATERIALS CONSUMED BY CARBURETORS, PISTONS, RINGS, AND VALVES, 1997

and increased competition from the Chinese Economic Area (Taiwan, China, and Hong Kong). Japan showed a decrease in automotive parts exports, largely because of increased Japanese production in the United States and increased outsourcing to American companies. Most gains in exports of American automotive parts came from shipments to American plants in Canada, Mexico, Brazil, and Argentina. Exports to Asia were adversely affected by the Asian economic crisis.

RESEARCH AND TECHNOLOGY

According to the U.S. Department of Commerce, expansion of the U.S. automotive parts industry will only come by responding to demands for improved technology and products—technology that will produce a lighter, fuel-efficient, and environmentally friendly vehicle. In response to the Clean Air Act of 1990 and other legislation, composite materials—plastics, carbon fibers, and other substrates—are being developed by the industry. The main goal of the government's Partnership for a New Generation of Vehicles is an affordable mid-size passenger vehicle able to travel 80 miles on a gallon of gas. Attaining this goal will mean new technologies for the vehicle's power plant, drive train, and chassis. The industry will have to respond with lighter materials and newer fuel delivery and exhaust systems.

FURTHER READING

Automotive Aftermarket Industry Association. *AAIA Online: Automotive Aftermarket Industry Association.* Bethesda, Maryland: Automotive Aftermarket Industry Association, 1999. Available from http://www.aftermarket.org.

Automotive Aftermarket Industry Association. *1999 Aftermarket Factbook & Mini-Monitor.* Bethesda, Maryland: Automotive Aftermarket Industry Association, 1999.

Automotive Service Industry Association. *The Shape and Size of the USA Motor Vehicle Aftermarket: A Profile.* Elk Grove Village, Illinois: Automotive Service Industry Association, 1998.

Benko, Christopher J., and Marjorie Sorge. "'99 U.S. Market Forecast: It's Rock and Roll." *Automotive Industries.* January 1999.

Darnay, Arsen J., ed. *Manufacturing USA.* 6th ed. Detroit: Gale Research, 1999.

McGraw-Hill. U.S. Department of Commerce. *U.S. Industry and Trade Outlook '99.* New York: McGraw-Hill, 1999.

Robinet, Michael E. "Big Demand—For Now." *Automotive Manufacturing & Production.* October 1999.

Standard & Poor's Corp. *Autos & Auto Parts.* New York: Industry Surveys, 1999.

U.S. Census Bureau. *1997 Economic.* Washington D.C.: GPO, 1999. Available from http://www.census.gov/prod/ec97/97m3363a.pdf.

U.S. Dept. of Commerce. International Trade Administration. *Welcome to the International Trade Administration.* Washington D.C.: International Trade Administration, 1999. Available from http://www.ita.doc.gov.

SIC 3593

FLUID POWER CYLINDERS AND ACTUATORS

This classification covers establishments primarily engaged in manufacturing hydraulic and pneumatic cylinders and actuators for use in fluid power systems.

NAICS CODE(S)

333995 (Fluid Power and Actuator Manufacturing)

According to the U.S. Census Bureau's *1997 Economic Census,* 320 establishments operated in this category for some or all of 1997. Industry-wide employment totaled 23,062 workers receiving a payroll of more than $900 million. Of those workers, 15,106 worked in production, putting in more than 31 million hours to earn wages of $526 million. Overall shipments for the industry were valued at almost $3.4 billion in 1997.

Companies in the fluid power cylinders and actuators industry manufacture hydraulic and pneumatic cylinders used in various devices, such as jacks, lifters, and machine tools. These devices are used to exert massive amounts of force in a controlled manner. One of the simplest machines that uses a fluid power cylinder is the hydraulic press, which is used, for example, to press plastics into forms. Important markets for this industry included the aerospace industry and the defense industry.

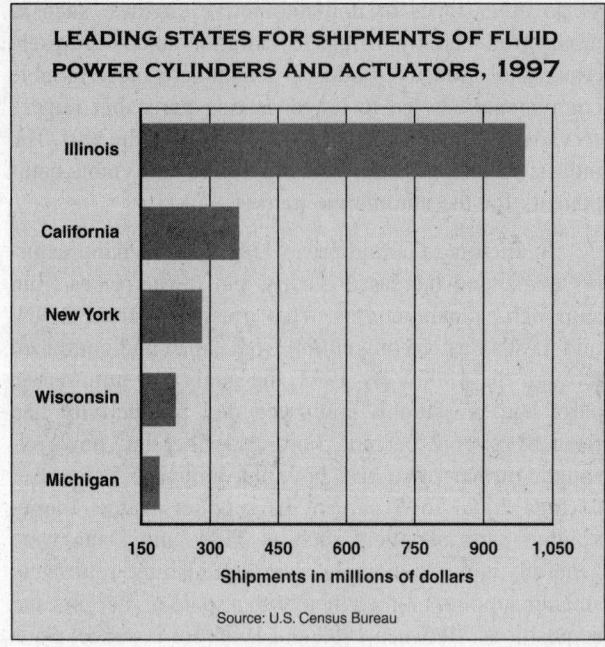

LEADING STATES FOR SHIPMENTS OF FLUID POWER CYLINDERS AND ACTUATORS, 1997

Shipments in millions of dollars

Source: U.S. Census Bureau

The three primary types of modern hydraulic cylinders are single-acting, double-acting, and differential. Single-acting devices consist of a large plunger, or piston, into which oil (or air in a pneumatic cylinder) is pumped. A valve keeps the oil from backing up into the pump and allows a controlled release of the pressure. Double-acting cylinders work similarly, but oil is pushed against one side of the cylinder, thus allowing a push or pull motion; these cylinders are used in construction machinery such as cranes and earth-moving machines. A differential cylinder has a large piston that requires a greater amount of oil to displace the cylinder, thus allowing greater uniformity of force than a typical single-acting cylinder.

Although hydraulic pumps for powering hydraulic cylinders were developed in the 19th century, it was not until the 20th century that fluid power devices became a widespread means of energy transmission. By 1987, the first year in which this industry was classified separately by the federal government, fluid power cylinder manufacturers were generating sales of about $1.9 billion. Although receipts rose to more than $2.2 billion by 1989, a recession in the late 1980s and early 1990s reduced demand from industrial sectors such that sales slipped below $2 billion annually during the early 1990s.

Industry participants in the mid-1990s benefited from a gradual U.S. economic recovery. The total value of product shipments in the industry was $2.56 billion in 1995, up 42 percent from 1992. Although growth was flat in the aerospace industry in the early 1990s, steady recovery was projected for this market through the end of the decade. However, continued slack demand from the defense industry and a slumping commercial airline industry boded poorly for overall industry growth. As domestic market growth was uncertain, manufacturers were looking to exports and advanced technology to boost sales.

Soon after the turn of the millennium, the United States Navy supported this industry's top 2 leaders by awarding them lucrative contracts. Industry leader Curtiss-Wright Corp. of Lyndhurst, New Jersey, which garnered 1999 sales of over $293 billion, won a contract to manufacture shuttle assemblies to replace worn ones in aircraft catapult propulsion systems mounted aboard all naval aircraft carriers. ITT Industries Inc. of West Harrison, New York, which placed third in the industry with 1998 sales of almost $4.5 billion, landed a $13.7 million radar refurbishment contract with the Naval Sea System Command in Arlington, Virginia, in early 2000.

The other industry leaders included second-place Parker Hannifin Corp., which generated sales of almost $5 billion for its fiscal year ended June 30, 1999; fourth-place Aeroquip-Vickers Inc. of Maumee, Ohio, with 1997 sales of more than $2.1 billion; and fifth-place Flowserved Corp. of Dayton, Ohio, which garnered 1997 sales of almost $1.2 million.

FURTHER READING

"Curtiss-Wright Receives Contracts to Supply Key Components for the United States Navy." *PR Newswire,* 20 January 2000.

Darnay, Arsen J., ed. *Manufacturing USA,* 5th ed. Detroit: Gale Research, 1996.

Infotrac Company Profiles, 17 February 2000. Available from http://web4.infotrac.galegroup.com.

"ITT Industries Awarded $13.7 Million Contract by the U.S. Navy." *PR Newswire,* 2 February 2000.

U.S. Census Bureau. *1995 Annual Survey of Manufactures.* Washington, D.C.: GPO, 1997. Available from http://www.census.gov/prod/www/titles.html#mm.

U.S. Census Bureau. *1997 Economic Census,* 17 February 2000. Washington, D.C.: GPO, 1999. Available from http://www.census.gov/prod/ec97/97m3339l.pdf.

SIC 3594

FLUID POWER PUMPS AND MOTORS

This classification covers establishments primarily engaged in manufacturing hydraulic and pneumatic fluid power pumps and motors, including hydrostatic transmissions. Establishments primarily engaged in manufacturing pumps for motor vehicles are classified in **SIC 3714: Motor Vehicle Parts and Accessories.**

NAICS CODE(S)

333996 (Fluid Power Pump and Motor Manufacturing)

Manufacturers in this industry produce pumps and drives for hydraulic and pneumatic power mechanisms, primarily for use in industrial and aerospace applications. Because fluid power devices can exert massive mounts of controlled pressure, they are commonly utilized to power aircraft landing gear, industrial presses and lifts, heavy earth-moving equipment, and other heavy-duty equipment. They are also often integrated into smaller machines that require precise power transfer.

Fluid power systems combine cylinders, couplings, valves, and pumps and motors. A positive displacement hydraulic pump, such as a piston pump, is the part of the system that delivers the oil required to drive or control hydraulic machinery. It creates pressure in a series of short bursts. In contrast, impulse pumps, such as the centrifugal pump, deliver steady, continuous oil pressure with less vibration. Hydraulic motors typically operate in conjunction with pumps and are often used to precisely vary the rotational speed of various machines.

Pascal's law, which states that pressure exerted upon a liquid is evenly transmitted in all directions, was posited in the mid-1600s. However, pumps that could efficiently deliver high and controlled pressure were not introduced until the 1800s. Not until the mid-1900s, in fact, did hydraulic pumps and motors become a common means of power transfer. By 1987, the first year in which this industry was separately classified by the U.S. government, sales of fluid power pumps and motors approached $1.5 billion. Although industry revenues increased to nearly $1.8 billion by 1990, a recession halted sales and earnings growth for most competitors throughout the early 1990s.

Industry participants in the mid-1990s benefitted from a moderate upturn in the United States and global economy that boosted pump and motor demand in the industrial sector. Unfortunately, vital aerospace and defense markets remained depressed and offered little hope for gains in the near future. The most successful competitors countered market malaise with productivity gains and the introduction of cutting edge, high-performance equipment. Many also looked to increased demand in overseas markets for high-tech U.S. pumps and motors. The industry experienced rapid growth in 1995, as the value of all product shipments increased 14 percent from 1994 figures, to $2 billion, and up 36 percent from $1.4 billion in 1992.

In 1997, sales reached $2.64 billion. Total employment was slightly over 15,000 with almost 70 percent involved with production. The average wage was $16 per hour. The states of Illinois, Michigan, and Ohio were the leading employers. Almost 73 percent of all establishments had 20 or fewer employees. Of total sales, 41 percent went to reciprocating pumps used in non-aerospace applications; only 12 percent went to pumps and motors used in the aerospace industry.

According to the National Fluid Power Association, the U.S. market for all fluid power products grew by 3 percent in 1998 to $13.5 billion. The fluid power industry grew 58 percent from 1992 to 1997, with exports of such products reaching almost $1.3 billion in 1997. Though the industry did not experience as much growth in 1998 as 1997, some manufacturers expect continued growth due to strong global demand in consumer products, as well as demand for capital equipment in Eastern Europe and South America.

About half of the fluid power market goes to hydraulic power components, according to Frost & Sullivan. This market was worth $6.4 billion in 1997 and is expected to continue growing through 2004 as a result of end-user capital spending and product replacement. Consolidation of the industry is increasing as acquisitions continue. In 1999, Eaton Corp. of Ohio acquired Aeroquip-Vickers, Inc., which had 1998 sales of $2.1 billion. Other challenges facing the industry include product standardization, a demand for higher product quality and faster product delivery, the lack of qualified workers, environmental concerns, leakage problems, and successful integration of electronic controls.

About 150 companies served this industry in 1997, totaling 169 establishments. Mannesmann Corp., of New York, was one of the leaders with $3.3 billion in sales and 1,000 employees. ITT Fluid Technology Corp., a subsidiary of ITT Industries, Inc., logged over $1.7 billion in net sales. The parent company employs 13,000 workers. Emerson Power Transmission Corp. of New York had sales of over half a billion and employed 900 employees. The majority of the top 50 companies, however, generated sales of less than $15 million and employed fewer than 50 workers.

The average salary for production workers in the industry was $31,300, which is considerably higher than the average for all manufacturing. Although in the mid-1990s the industry employed about 11,500 Americans, long-term employment prospects were bleak, according to the U.S. Bureau of Labor Statistics. Increased foreign competition and continued productivity gains, through automation and restructuring, were projected to be factors in work force reduction, for labor and white-collar workers alike.

The Hydraulic Institute and the McIlvaine Company predict the global pump market will reach over $30 billion in 2003, an increase of 20 percent from 1999. Sales of parts and drivers will add another $17 billion. Sealless pumps are expected to have the highest growth rate at 10 percent, as chemical process industries make the switch to these pumps.

The pump market in Asia is expected to have the fastest growth rate (8 percent versus 4 percent overall), as new water and wastewater treatment plants are built. The United States will retain the largest market share, at $6.2 billion. About 800 pump companies control 90 percent of global sales, with 20 percent of this market shared by the top three pump manufacturers (ITT, Ebara and KSB).

FURTHER READING

Brunelli, Mark. "Expect Stable But Slower Growth" *Purchasing* 21 October 1999, p 89.

Crabb, Charlene and Shelley, Suzanne. "World Pump Demand Spurred by Environmental Mandates." *Chemical Engineering,* February 1999.

Darnay, Arsen J., ed. *Manufacturing USA.* 5th ed. Detroit: Gale Research, 1996.

"Eaton Completes Acquisition of Aeroquip-Vickers, Inc." Company Press Release, 12 April 1999. Available from: http://www.theautochannel.com.

"Growth Continues in Hydraulic Power Component Industry as Participants Employ New Market-Based Strategies to Meet End-User Demands." PR Newswire, 27 April 1998. Available from: http://www.frost.com/verity/press/industrial/pr575417 .htm.

Heney, Paul J. "Fluid Power: 2000 and Beyond-A Blueprint for the Future." *Hydraulics & Pneumatics,* 1 March 1998, p 68-75.

"NAICS 333996." *Manufacturing-Industry Series,* U.S. Census Bureau, 1997 Economic Census, 30 November 1999.

Soltis, Dan. "Report Shows Pump Market at $22 Billion by 2003." *Water Engineering & Management,* March 1999, p 10.

U.S. Bureau of the Census. *1995 Annual Survey of Manufactures.* Washington: GPO, 1997. Available from http://www .census.gov/prod/www/titles.html#mm.

Ward's Business Directory of U.S. Private and Public Companies 2000 The Gale Group, 2000.

SIC 3596

SCALES AND BALANCES, EXCEPT LABORATORY

This industry is made up of establishments primarily engaged in manufacturing weighing and force-measuring machines and devices, except those regarded as scientific apparatus for laboratory work, which are classified under **SIC 3821: Laboratory Apparatus and Furniture.**

NAICS CODE(S)

333997 (Scale and Balance (except Laboratory) Manufacturing)

Vehicle and industrial scales, which are used primarily in factories and truck weighing stations to measure amounts of goods to be packaged or delivered, comprise the largest segment of the industry, accounting for roughly 42 percent of U.S. shipments. Retail, commercial, and milling scales form the second-largest category at approximately 31 percent and include household scales, scales in grocery stores and delicatessens, and postal scales. Parts and accessories total 22 percent of shipments, and miscellaneous balance and scale equipment make up the remaining 5 percent.

In 1995, manufacturers in this category shipped $642.8 million in products, a 3.8 percent increase over 1994 before inflation. Scales and balances alone, however, sold $590.3 million in 1995, which was less than half of 1 percent greater than in 1994. The industry spent $12.4 million in capital expenditures in 1995. Real growth in the industry has been largely flat to negative since the 1980s, when the industry posted record sales. New business for the industry is often dependent upon external factors, such as postal rate changes and other government regulations that require the industry's customers to upgrade their weighing systems.

The estimated 110 establishments in the U.S. scale and balance industry are geographically concentrated, with California and the Midwest employing roughly half of the industry's workforce. The industry's production labor force in late 1999 earned an average of $14.60 per hour for an average work week of 42 hours, with an average of 5.1 overtime hours. Major occupations within the industry include machinists, machine tool operators, assemblers, and product inspectors. The outlook for many of this industry's occupations, however, is limited as the U.S. Bureau of Labor Statistics forecast declines of 5 to 15 percent for most of the industry's job titles.

In the late 1990s Signature Brands, USA, Inc., was the industry leader, with 1998 earnings of $276 million and 1,000 employees. Mettler-Toledo International Inc. was also one of the top manufacturers of industrial scales in 1998. Mettler's operations generated approximately $936 million in sales, of which an estimated $175 million was from its weighing devices.

FURTHER READING

Average Hours and Earnings of Production and Nonsupervisory Workers on Private Nonfarm Payrolls. Bureau of Labor Statistics, 1999. Available from http://www.bls.gov.

"Hoover's Company Capsules." *Hoover's Online: The Business Network,* 1999. Available from http://www.hoovers.com.

U.S. Bureau of the Census. *1995 Annual Survey of Manufactures.* Washington, D.C.: GPO, 1997. Available from http://www.census.gov/prod/www/titles.html.

SIC 3599

INDUSTRIAL AND COMMERCIAL MACHINERY AND EQUIPMENT, NOT ELSEWHERE CLASSIFIED

This industry is made up of firms that manufacture miscellaneous machinery and equipment not elsewhere classified. It also encompasses establishments primarily engaged in producing or repairing machinery and equipment on a job or order basis for other companies. Examples of industry output include carnival amusement rides, catapults, sludge tables, flexible tubes and hoses, weather vanes, and non-vehicle engine filters. Motor vehicle engine filter manufacturers are classified separately in SIC **3714: Motor Vehicle Parts and Accessories** and those manufacturing coin-operated amusement machines are classified in SIC **3999: Manufacturing Industries, Not Elsewhere Classified.**

NAICS CODE(S)

336399 (All Other Motor Vehicle Part Manufacturing)

The industry is highly fragmented. According to the U.S. Census Bureau's *1997 Economic Census,* 833 establishments operated in this category for part or all of 1997. Industry-wide employment totaled 10,858 workers receiving a payroll of almost $353 million. Of those workers, 7,910 worked in production, putting in almost 15 million hours to earn wages of more than $228 million. Overall 1997 shipments for the industry were valued at more than $1.1 billion.

New York City-based Siemens Corp. led the industry with sales of more than $11.0 billion for its fiscal year ended September 30, 1998. Van Dusen and Meyer of Shelton, Connecticut followed with sales of more than $7.0 billion for its fiscal year ended March 31, 1999. NCR Corp. of Dayton, Ohio placed third with 1998 sales of $6.5 billion. General Dynamics Corp. of Falls Church, Virginia generated 1998 sales of almost $5.0 billion, and Chicago-based FMC Corp. rounded out the top five industry leaders with 1998 sales of almost $4.4 billion. In contrast to the industry leaders, the majority of companies in this highly fragmented category generated revenues of less than $100 million. Typically, small to mid-sized machine shop receipts account for as much as 70 percent of industry revenues.

A slowdown in capital spending by durable goods manufacturers during the 1980s dampened sales and profit growth in comparison to the 1960s and 1970s. Revenue growth averaged only 4 percent annually between 1982 and 1990, mirroring capital spending increases. New capital expenditures for all manufacturing were up roughly 14 percent in 1995, contributing to the relative health of this industry. In 1995, the value of products in this category totaled $26.9 billion; this was a 19 percent increase from 1994. Strong U.S. economic performance in the mid- to late 1990s and recovering foreign markets, notably in Europe and East Asia, were expected to produce continued prosperity for the industry.

In the mid-1990s, capital investment by domestic industry accounted for approximately 55 percent of miscellaneous industrial machinery purchases. About 30 percent of the industry's mid-1990's sales were exports; the remaining 15 percent of production was consumed by numerous market niches. The armed forces, for example, purchased about 2 percent of output, and communication service industries made up slightly less than 1 percent of the market.

The industry's labor force numbered 319,000 in 1995, 77 percent of whom were engaged in production work. The average hourly production wage of $12.33 was slightly below average for manufacturing in general. According to the U.S. Bureau of Labor Statistics, opportunities for most workers were expected to decline significantly between 1990 and 2005, including positions for such primary occupations as machinists and assemblers.

FURTHER READING

Darnay, Arsen J., ed. *Manufacturing USA*. 5th ed. Detroit: Gale Research, 1996.

Infotrac Company Profiles. Available at http://web4.infotrac .galegroup.com. (2/17/00).

Reimer, David M. "Machinery Industry." *Value Line Investment Survey*. 9th ed. New York: Value Line Publishing Inc., 1997.

U.S. Census Bureau. *1997 Economic Census*. Washington, D.C.: GPO, 1999. Available at http://www.census.gov/prod/ec97/97m3339o.pdf.

Electronic & Other Electrical Equipment & Components, Except Computer Equipment

POWER, DISTRIBUTION, AND SPECIALTY TRANSFORMERS

This category covers establishments primarily engaged in manufacturing power, distribution, instrument, and specialty transformers. Radio frequency or voice frequency electronic transformers, coils, and chokes are classified in **SIC 3677: Electronic Coils, Transformers, and Other Inductors**, and resistance welder transformers are part of **SIC 3548: Electric and Gas Welding and Soldering Equipment.**

NAICS CODE(S)

335311 (Power, Distribution, and Specialty Transformer Manufacturing)

A transformer is used to reduce or increase the voltage, or electromotive force, of electricity traveling through a wire. It accomplishes this by transferring electric energy from one coil or winding to another coil through electromagnetic induction. Electric-generating plants use generator transformers to ''step-up,'' or increase, voltage that is transferred through power lines. When the high voltage electricity reaches a community, a ''step-down'' transformer reduces its power. A distribution transformer makes a final step-down in voltage by diminishing the force of the electricity to a level usable in homes and businesses. Some electrical devices, such as doorbells and small appliances, use additional step-down transformers to decrease voltage.

A typical transformer has two windings, or coils of wire, that are insulated from each other. The two coils are wound on a common magnetic circuit of laminated sheet metal, called the core. Each end of the primary coil is connected to the incoming alternating current (AC) power source. Each end of the secondary coil, which receives the energy, is connected to the outgoing power line. The ratio between the number of windings in each coil determines whether the voltage will be boosted or diminished.

There are two types of transformers: core and shell. In core-type equipment the windings surround the laminated metal core. In shell-type transformers the metal surrounds the windings. Distribution transformers are usually core-type, while more advanced high-voltage devices are often shell-type. Transformers can also be classified according to the type of cooling system they use; smaller transformers are usually cooled by air and larger equipment is liquid-cooled. Finally, transformers are either single-phase or polyphase. Polyphase devices typically have a three-legged core that can produce at least three different voltages.

The majority of apparatus manufactured in this industry are power and distribution transformers purchased by electric utilities. These devices accounted for about 50 percent of industry shipments in 1997. Because most transformers are simple and rugged, they often last as long as 40 years. Therefore, producers are largely dependent on purchases by utilities that are expanding service. Shipments of distribution transformers, for instance, are closely linked to new housing starts. Demand is also influenced by conversion to more efficient or aesthetically pleasing transformers.

The other 51 percent of the transformer market was primarily comprised of step-down equipment integrated into individual electrical devices. Fluorescent lamp ballasts, for instance, represented approximately 18 percent of production in 1997. Various specialty transformers, such as machine tool and high-intensity light trans-

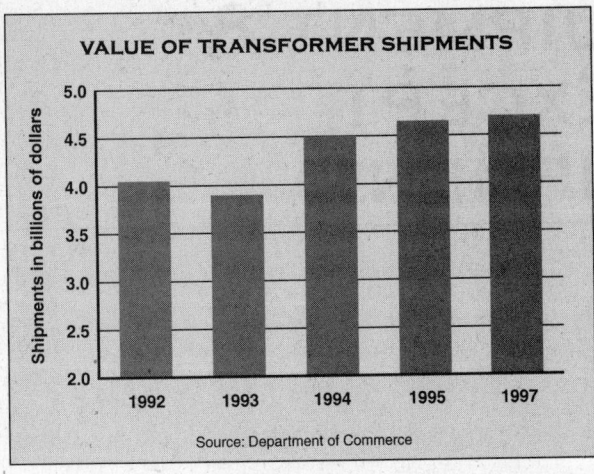

VALUE OF TRANSFORMER SHIPMENTS

Source: Department of Commerce

formers, accounted for 12 percent of sales. Other popular industry offerings include transformers for electric furnaces, rectifiers, ignition systems, consumer electronics, and toys.

BACKGROUND AND DEVELOPMENT

Transformer operation is based on a principle discovered in 1830 by Joseph Henry that electrical energy can be moved efficiently from one coil to another through electromagnetic induction. Michael Faraday and Henry independently observed in 1831 that a magnet moved through a closed coil of wire induces a current. When Faraday replaced the magnet with a charged electromagnet, he had built the first transformer. The value of the transformer was not fully understood until later in the nineteenth century, when devices that used alternating current became popular.

As the demand for electricity swelled during the late 1800s and early twentieth century, the need for electrical transforming devices emerged. As the United States built its massive electrical distribution infrastructure during the early part of the century, transformer sales ballooned. During the post-World War II economic expansion, moreover, the industry benefitted from aggressive government attempts to bring electricity to every American home. The Rural Electrification Administration, established in 1935, was charged with distributing power to even the most remote regions and communities of the nation. In addition, electricity demand swelled during the mid-1900s as new applications for electricity, such as air-conditioning, became popular.

By the early 1980s the transformer industry was shipping about $3 billion worth of equipment annually and employing a workforce of 40,000. Growth slowed throughout the 1980s as the demand for new infrastructure equipment leveled. Total U.S. electric utility capacity rose roughly 20 percent between 1978 and 1991—tepid growth in comparison to the increases of the 1950s and 1960s. However, manufacturers were aided by

healthy housing starts during the mid-1980s and the development of more efficient transformers that boosted replacement demand. Industry revenues climbed at an average annual rate of six percent between 1983 and 1990, to about $4.2 billion.

Low housing starts and a general U.S. recession stalled transformer demand in the early 1990s. Sales slipped to about $4.1 billion in 1991 and $3.9 billion in 1993, then rose to $4.5 billion in 1994. While demand for the largest transformers increased, shipments of most industry offerings declined.

Demand for transformers in the mid-1990s remained relatively stable. Of the high-voltage and distribution transformers already in service, many were scheduled for replacement during the 1990s and early 2000s. In addition, many utilities were replacing good units with newer, more efficient designs. Almost all transformer manufacturers focused on products that integrated advanced silicon low-loss steel or amorphous metal cores and offered greater serviceability. Likewise, the market for overhead transformers, which are typically mounted on poles, was being displaced by newer ground units.

U.S. producers also faced an influx of transformer imports from Mexico. International competition traditionally had made a minimal impact on this industry because of the high weight-to-value ratio of larger transformers and the propensity of some utilities to purchase American products. However, in the mid-1990s the North American Free Trade Agreement (NAFTA) boosted imports from nearby Mexico, which was already the largest industry importer. In 1994, $325 million worth of transformers were imported from Mexico. U.S. manufacturers in this industry exported $384 million worth of goods in 1995, mostly to Mexico and Canada.

Deregulation. As a result of the 1992 Federal Energy Policy Act (FEP), electric utilities, which had traditionally been regulated at the state and national level, began converting to open market competition and adopting market-based pricing instead of regulatory rate structures. Companies that owned high-voltage transmission lines were required to make them available to distribution companies wanting to rent their capacity to "wheel" energy over them. As a result, it had been predicted that the industry would undergo massive restructuring and be affected at many levels, including the manufacturing sector. In the mid-1990s electric utility deregulation was still only beginning to take effect, but as of 1996, legislation in four states required deregulation by 1997-98. Similar legislation was being drafted in 43 other states. Deregulation caused widespread mergers and a downsized workforce. Opponents of deregulation predicted that mergers would create monopolies in many regions, and that the consistency and quality of electric service would suffer. Proponents said deregulation would lower rates for consumers and increase quality through competition.

CURRENT CONDITIONS

The U.S. Census Bureau reported that in 1997 there were 318 establishments manufacturing products in this classification. They shipped $4.7 billion worth of goods, spent $2.2 billion on materials, and invested $131 million in buildings and other structures, machinery, and equipment. About 47 percent of those establishments employed at least 20 people.

The largest concentrations of operations in this industry were in California, Texas, Illinois, New Jersey, Florida, and New York. There were 56 establishments that primarily made power and distribution transformers, except parts. The largest value of product shipments in this segment originated in Mississippi, followed by Wisconsin and Virginia. There were 15 establishments that primarily made fluorescent lamp ballasts. The largest value of product shipments in this segment originated in Illinois.

INDUSTRY LEADERS

Of companies whose primary products were in this classification, Cooper Industries Inc. (Houston, Texas) was one of the largest with 28,100 employees and sales of $3.7 billion in 1998. Siemens Energy and Automation Inc. (a subsidiary of Siemens AG based in Alpharetta, Georgia) had 9,500 employees and sales of $1.8 billion.

Other diversified companies that also competed in this category included General Electric Company PLC (London, United Kingdom) with 71,963 employees and sales of $18.6 billion; Eaton Corp. (Cleveland, Ohio) with 49,500 employees and sales of $6.6 billion; and MagneTek Inc. (Nashville, Tennessee) with 14,900 employees and sales of $1.2 billion.

WORKFORCE

The long-term employment outlook for manufacturers of transformers and related equipment is poor. The workforce had already shriveled 25 percent during the 1980s, to about 30,000 by 1992, and it dropped to 26,644 by 1997. Increased productivity, through automation and management restructuring, were responsible for work force reductions. The U.S. Bureau of Labor Statistics estimated that jobs in this sector for assemblers and fabricators, which accounted for roughly 20 percent of the electric distribution equipment workforce, would plummet by nearly 50 percent between 1990 and 2005. Other labor positions were expected to decline similarly. However, opportunities for sales professionals, engineers, and industrial production managers were anticipated to expand about 15 percent by the year 2005.

In 1997 the industry's 19,918 production workers earned an average hourly wage of $12.52. Those employed by companies that primarily made power and distribution transformers earned an average hourly wage of $14.30. The average wage was $8.83 at companies that mostly made fluorescent lamp ballasts and $9.72 at companies whose main products were other specialty transformers.

RESEARCH AND TECHNOLOGY

Technical innovations in the early 1990s included new transformer test equipment that allowed operators to select and apply test voltage to any leg of a transformer winding, thereby eliminating the need to disconnect the leads. Also, new insulating materials allowed companies to refurbish old transformers and boost their efficiency, a development that was anticipated to reduce demand for new, more efficient replacement units. Another threat to industry growth was inventions such as semiconductors and microprocessors, which can increase the capacity of existing transmission lines, reducing demand for new distribution equipment.

In the mid-1990s the consequence of controversial electromagnetic fields (EMFs) was still undetermined. The EPA's 1990 finding that EMFs are a "probable" cause of cancer had not yet had a tangible impact on the transformer industry. However, as an environmental protection measure, the EPA had restricted the use of polychlorinated biphenyls (PCBs) as a cooling medium for liquid-filled transformers, due to the flammability and toxicity of the fluid. Less flammable replacements such as polydimethyl siloxane and fire-resistant hydrocarbon fluids were phasing out the use of PCBs.

FURTHER READING

Darnay, Arsen J., ed. *Manufacturing USA*. 5th ed. Detroit: Gale Research, 1996.

"Executive Summary, U.S. Transformers." *MarketLine U.S. Snapshots OnDisc*. London: MarketLine International, 1996.

Hillesiand, Glen. "Effects of Electric Utility Deregulation on Manufacturers." *CIRAS News* vol. 30, no. 2 (winter 1996).

U.S. Department of Commerce. Bureau of the Census. *1995 Annual Survey of Manufactures*. Washington: GPO, 1997. Available from http://www.census.gov.

U.S. Department of Commerce. U.S. Census Bureau. *1997 Economic Census*. Washington, DC: GPO, 1999. Available from http://www.census.gov.

SIC 3613

SWITCHGEAR AND SWITCHBOARD APPARATUS

This category covers establishments primarily engaged in manufacturing switchgear and switchboard apparatus. Important products of this industry include power switches, circuit breakers, power switching equipment, and similar switchgear for general industrial application; also, switchboards and cubicles, control and metering panels, fuses and fuse mountings, and similar switchboard apparatus and supplies. Relays and switches in electronic devices and industrial controls are classified elsewhere. This industry was reclassified in 1987, thus figures from prior years include additional product categories.

NAICS CODE(S)

335313 (Switchgear and Switchboard Apparatus Manufacturing)

A switchgear is used to interrupt or reestablish the flow of electricity in a circuit. It is generally used in combination with metering, protective, and regulating equipment to protect and control motors, generators, transformers, and transmission and distribution lines. A switchboard is comprised of one or more panels with various switches and indicators that are used to route electricity and operate circuits.

Switchgears are typically concentrated at points where electrical systems make significant changes in power, current, or routing, such as electrical supply substations and control centers. Switchgear assemblies range in size from smaller, ground-mounted units to large walk-in installations and can be classified as outdoor or indoor units. Commercial and industrial assemblies are usually indoors, while utilities and cogeneration facilities are more likely to have outdoor gear. Manufactured for a variety of functions and power levels, all switchgear conforms to standards set by the Institute of Electrical and Electronic Engineers (IEEE), the American National Standards Institute (ANSI), or the National Electrical Manufacturers Association (NEMA).

Metal-clad switchgear assemblies are the most common devices used in electricity distribution. They usually contain: circuit breakers, which can be deactivated; primary circuits, such as transformers; insulating materials; interlocks, which ensure that circuit breakers can be safely inserted into and removed from the assembly; and, instrument panels that control the assembly. Metal-clad power center switchgear is used to regulate and route power in high-voltage applications. Similarly, medium-voltage vac-clad switchgear is used in circuits involving transmission and distribution lines and motors. Other common types of assemblies used in electrical distribution include metal-clad interrupter, low voltage, and station-type cubicle switchgear.

Low voltage panelboards and distribution boards represented about 30 percent of industry revenues in 1995, and circuit breakers made up about 26 percent of sales. Switchgear units and fuses accounted for about 26 percent

and 8 percent of shipments, respectively. Miscellaneous parts and apparatus comprised the remainder of output.

The market for switchgear and related apparatus is highly fragmented. Approximately 21 percent of purchases in the mid-1990s were classified as fixed capital investments, mostly by utilities and power generation companies. Six percent of industry output was used in office buildings, and industrial building applications consumed approximately five percent of production. Other significant market segments included refrigeration and heating equipment manufacturers, residential home builders, and communications industries. About 7 percent of production was exported. In 1997, total value of shipments was $7.6 billion.

BACKGROUND AND DEVELOPMENT

Power transformation technology was conceived as early as 1830 by Michael Faraday and Joseph Henry, who discovered the theory of electromagnetic induction. But the first commercially practical manual switching systems emerged during the late 1800s to service the flourishing telephone industry. By the late 1880s, shortly after Alexander Graham Bell's invention of the telephone in 1876, the telephone switchboard had evolved to a state where thousands of calls could be switched and connected at the same time. The first automatic switching system was introduced at the 1881 Paris Electrical Exposition, and a workable system had been patented by 1889. A similar device was installed in New Jersey in 1914. Using electrical impulses, it raised and rotated a shaft in a series of movements to make a contact.

The need for gear that would protect and control high-power electric circuits, which constitutes most of the equipment in this industry, resulted from advances in electricity during the early 1900s. Lee De Forest's 1906 invention of the electron tube and a plethora of subsequent breakthroughs spawned a huge demand for electricity in the United States. As the country built its massive electrical power infrastructure, sales of fuses, control panels, and all types of switchgear soared. Notably, the Rural Electrification Administration, which was established in 1935, and other government initiatives expended massive funds to try to bring electricity into every American home.

Electricity demand swelled during the mid-1900s as new applications for electric power, such as air-conditioning and television, became popular. In addition, post-World War II U.S. economic growth resulted in a great demand from industry for circuit control and protection apparatus. Equipment also improved as manufacturers developed means of reducing arcing (damaging sparks that occur when switches are activated), and integrated circuits were applied to switchboards and control devices. By the late 1970s, manufacturers of switchgear and switchboard equipment were shipping about $5 billion worth of goods annually and employing a workforce of more than 66,000.

Industry sales effectively stagnated during the 1980s, continuing a trend started in the 1970s. Indeed, the rampant expansion of the U.S. electric power infrastructure had subsided. Total U.S. electric utility capacity increased a modest 20 percent between 1978 and 1990—pitiful in comparison to growth during the 1950s and 1960s. Industry revenue growth was well below inflation rates during the early 1980s, rising to only $5.5 billion by 1986. Official industry content was changed in 1987, reducing sales volume to about $4.9 billion. Sales continued to slightly increase at an annual rate of less than 2 percent during the late 1980s, to about $5.5 billion by 1990.

Slack demand for new electric power infrastructure, recessed construction sectors, weak industrial demand, and a generally despondent U.S. economy hindered many industry participants in the early 1990s. Sales slipped in 1991 and fell again in 1992 by one percent in inflation-adjusted terms. Likewise, in 1993 shipments rose only 4.5 percent before inflation, despite an overall U.S. economic recovery and a surge in new construction. Furthermore, the long term industry outlook was lamentable going into the mid-1990s. Domestic demand for new switchgear was expected to likely decline further, or stagnate, and because most switchgear was rugged and durable, replacement activity offered limited profit opportunities.

CURRENT CONDITIONS

Product shipments showed mixed returns entering the late 1990s. In 1995 shipments grew 12.5 percent in current dollars to $6.6 billion. That year represented the highest growth the industry had enjoyed since the 1980s. In 1997 the value of shipments jumped again to $7.6 billion. Modest growth was expected to continue at 1 to 2 percent annually through 2002. Demand was expected to be concentrated on electronic switchgear.

Opportunities for savvy U.S. exporters remained strong in the early and mid-1990s, particularly in Mexico and East Asia. Export activity was 18 percent in early 1992, bolstered by a weak dollar and a growing demand by developing countries for reputable U.S. equipment. It was expected that broadening technology and overseas acquisitions would increase the market on into the next century. In 1997, sales to Canada represented 20 percent of the market, 15 percent for Mexico, 11 percent to the Dominican Republic, and 7 percent to Japan. Exports were expected to increase 6 percent annually through 2002. The United States imported most switchgear industry products in 1997 from Mexico.

INDUSTRY LEADERS

There were roughly 583 establishments manufacturing switchgear in the late 1990s. Despite growth there

has been steady corporate consolidation in the industry as companies merged with and acquired rivals in an effort to boost capital and take advantage of other economies of scale.

The biggest manufacturer of switchgear and switchboard equipment in 1999 was Liebert Corp., of Columbus, Ohio, with $500 million in sales. Second was Micro Switch Division, of Freeport, Illinois, with $440 million in sales. Third was Schlumberger Inc., of Norcross, Georgia, with $370 million in sales.

WORKFORCE

Approximately 44,600 workers served this industry in 1999. In addition to slack demand, productivity gains contributed to workforce reductions during the 1980s and early 1990s. Specifically, factory automation and advanced information systems allowed many manufacturers to boost international competitiveness and retain profits in spite of stagnant markets. Likewise, the long term employment outlook for makers of switchgear was generally poor. The number of jobs for assemblers and fabricators, which make up almost 30 percent of the work force, was expected to decline by more than 40 percent between 1990 and 2005, according to the Bureau of Labor Statistics. Most labor positions were expected to fall 10 to 30 percent. Opportunities for engineers and sales professionals, on the other hand, were expanding and an increase by approximately 15 percent by 2005 was expected.

In 1999 the average work week was 43 hours with 5.3 of overtime. The average compensation was $13.70 per hour.

RESEARCH AND TECHNOLOGY

The switchgear and switchboard industry invests relatively little in research and development. In the early 1990s, for example, companies invested an average of $2,720 per employee back into their business, compared to about $5,520 spent by the average U.S. manufacturer. One of the most important areas of technological advancement in the early 1990s was switchgear that integrated sulfur hexafloride gas (SF6). SF6 has insulation and arc-quenching properties that could be used to reduce damage caused by arcing. The newer switches are safer, more reliable and require less maintenance than conventional switchgear.

FURTHER READING

Darnay, Arsen J., ed. *Manufacturing USA*. 5th ed. Detroit: Gale Research, 1996.

Economic Census 1997. Bureau of the Census. 2000. Available from http://www.census.gov.

Employment Statistics Bureau of Labor Statistics. 2000. Available from http://www.bls.gov.

U.S. Bureau of the Census. *1995 Annual Survey of Manufactures*. Washington: GPO, 1997.

U. S. Industry and Trade Outlook '99. The McGraw-Hill Companies, 1999.

Ward's Business Directory of U.S. Private and Public Companies. Detroit: Gale Group, 1999.

SIC 3621

MOTORS AND GENERATORS

This classification comprises establishments primarily engaged in manufacturing power generators, motor generator sets, and electric motors, excluding engine-starting motors. Also covered in this classification are establishments primarily involved in manufacturing railway motors and control equipment, as well as motors, generators, and control equipment for gasoline, electric, and oil-electric buses and trucks.

Establishments primarily engaged in manufacturing turbo generators are classified in **SIC 3511: Steam, Gas, and Hydraulic Turbines, and Turbine Generator Set Units** and those manufacturing starting motors and battery-charging generators for internal combustion engines are grouped in **SIC 3694: Electric Equipment for Internal Combustion Engines.** Establishments primarily engaged in manufacturing generators for welding equipment are classified in **SIC 3548: Electric and Gas Welding and Soldering Equipment.**

NAICS CODE(S)

335312 (Motor and Generator Manufacturing)

INDUSTRY SNAPSHOT

Approximately 529 establishments in the United States were involved in manufacturing motors and generators in 1997. These companies recorded more than $11.8 billion in sales for the industry's products, which consisted of four primary product groups: fractional horsepower motors, integral horsepower motors and generators, land prime mover generator sets, and parts and supplies for motors and generators. Other products manufactured by the industry included land transportation motors and fractional and integral motor generator sets. Of these products, fractional horsepower motors represented nearly 47 percent of the industry's shipments, followed by integral horsepower motors and generators, which accounted for 18.5 percent. Prime mover generator sets accounted for another 13.7 percent of the industry's shipments, while parts and supplies for motors and generators represented nearly 6 percent. These figures reflect a slight decrease from 1995 in the fractional horsepower motors

and parts sectors of the industry, and a slight increase in prime mover generators.

Motor and generator manufacturers are heavily dependent on the health of several industrial markets to sustain their growth. Fractional horsepower motors are used in various household appliances, including refrigerators, freezers, air conditioners, automatic dishwashers, and microwave ovens, as well as other products requiring a small horsepower motor, such as computer disk drives. Falling prices in electronics and stable economic conditions for consumers were a boon for this sector in the late 1990s. Total revenues for fractional horsepower motors in 1998 were $5.1 billion, with increases expected up through 2004.

Integral horsepower motors are best suited for industrial uses, where greater horsepower is required. Integral motor power vehicles are used in large construction projects and provide the necessary power for many different types of manufacturing facilities. Any significant changes in nonresidential construction activity or capital expenditures in the industrial sector generally have parallel affects on integral motor production. Again, a strong economy helped bring about a 25 percent increase for this sector between 1992 and 1997. The integral motor production market saw revenues of $2.9 billion in 1998, with continued growth expected.

In addition to these market dependencies, motor and generator sales are affected by the vacillating costs of raw materials. Steel—an essential element in the production of motors, generators, and their related parts and supplies—is subject to pernicious price swings that could impinge on the industry's profit margin. Other materials, such as wire and brushes used in the manufacturing of motors and generators, also demonstrate a propensity for erratic jumps in price that have an appreciable affect on the motor and generator industry. Government regulations requiring premium efficiency motors, rapid technological advancements, and intense foreign competition were also major factors affecting the motor and generator industry in the late 1990s.

ORGANIZATION AND STRUCTURE

The motor and generator industry is predominantly populated by medium and large sized companies employing more than 20 people. In 1998, the 75 largest establishments employed a total of 587,200 people. Of this number, however, 239,000 were employed by the combined divisions of General Electric Co.; 3,000 were employed by GE Motors. On average, a motor and generator establishment in 1996 employed 160 people, more than three times the average number of people employed in a typical manufacturing facility for all other U.S. industries.

Geographically, motor and generator production occurred throughout much of the nation, according to the

1997 Economic Census, but was particularly concentrated in Wisconsin, Tennessee, Arkansas, and New York.

The costs involved in establishing and operating a motor and generator manufacturing facility are substantially higher than the average manufacturing facility. In 1996, the average cost per establishment was $12.5 million in the motor and generator industry, compared to $4.54 million for the average of all manufacturing industries. The average investment per establishment was $839,797 in the motor and generator industry—nearly 50 percent higher than the average for other industries.

The relatively expensive nature of conducting business in the motor and generator industry tends to discourage the entry of small manufacturing companies. Manufacturers frequently encounter expensive retooling costs—when a particular product becomes obsolete and is replaced by a new product, for example, or when a significant technological advancement dictates the implementation of a new production process. As a result many companies manufacture a diverse line of products, some of which are excluded from the boundaries of the SIC 3621 classification. This diversity helps to insulate companies from potentially deleterious financial conditions affecting the motor and generator industry.

BACKGROUND AND DEVELOPMENT

The principle of the electric motor was first developed by Michael Faraday in 1821, but a diverse group of scientists and lay innovators quickly followed Faraday's lead and began experimenting with amended designs. Improvements on Faraday's design followed in quick succession, as inventors of the nineteenth century were swept up by the inspiring and momentous technological advancements that characterized the era. This work helped pave the way toward developing the type of electric motor that became an integral component in twentieth century factories, stores, and homes.

Sixteen years after Faraday first announced his discovery, Thomas Davenport, a blacksmith from Vermont, developed a motor that successfully powered a printing press. This invention marked one of the earliest uses of the electric motor for commercial purposes, and Davenport was granted Patent No. 132 for it. Not to be outdone, Moses Farmer, another Yankee pioneer in the development of the electric motor, created a miniature electric railway as an exhibit for country fairs. Charles G. Page used this application of the electric motor on a larger scale in 1857 when he made an experimental run with a full sized locomotive from Washington to Baltimore.

While these developments were encouraging and marked significant technological advancements, the design of these early motors limited the ways in which they could be used. Since they derived energy from large, expensive batteries, these early versions were essentially suitable only for demonstration purposes—to utilize them in a commercial or industrial setting on a daily basis was still impractical. But this shortcoming disappeared with the advent of practical dynamos, or direct-current generators. No longer fettered by cumbersome batteries, early models of these smaller, cheaper to operate motors appeared at the Electrical Exhibition and National Conference of Electricians in Philadelphia in 1884. These were electrically driven rather than battery powered motors, and their development greatly increased the potential applications for the electric motor. By 1887, there were already 15 well known manufacturers of small electric motors in the United States, and more than 10,000 electric motors of 15 horsepower or less had been produced.

The development of direct-current generators greatly enhanced the economic feasibility of electric motors in the workplace and the home. But, while the technology was in place, the fledgling industry's growth suffered from the shortsightedness of some business leaders. The individuals spearheading the movement towards electrification focused their efforts on employing electricity to generate light rather than on the vast industrial and commercial applications for the electric motor. In fact, the majority of early electric utilities were established as lighting businesses. As a result, other uses for electric motors were lost in the rush. But the incorporation of the first practical dynamo into the operation of the electric motor slowly drew the attention of more than a few enterprising individuals, and the industry formally began to experience a substantial demand for its products.

As the nation entered a new century, two companies became established as pioneers in the industrial and commercial development of electric motors. General Electric Company (GE), created to market and manufacture the innovations developed by Thomas Edison, entered into the electric motor field through mergers and acquisitions. Emerson Electric Manufacturing Company, formed to explore applications for the newly developed alternating current electric motor, entered the market with manufacturing processes it had developed specifically to use electrically driven motors.

Growing from a storied past, GE became one of the handful of behemoth corporations dictating the health of the national economy. In fact, GE's history charted some of the most significant technological discoveries and advancements of the twentieth century. From Thomas Edison's development of the light bulb to advances in turbine engines, to the refinement of nuclear power production processes, GE has stood as a pioneer in the engineering and manufacturing world for over 100 years.

Emerson Electric also figured prominently throughout the course of the industry's history and helped catapult the use of electric motors and generators toward the pervasive levels of the 1990s. Founded in 1890 in St. Louis, Missouri, by Judge John Wesley Emerson, Emerson Electric at first engaged in the production of alternating current electric motors. The company enjoyed considerable success well into the twentieth century incorporating electric motors into sundry household appliances.

Emerson and GE were joined by many other manufacturers of motors and generators during these pre-World War II decades, as the relatively new technology beckoned entrepreneurs into the market and expanded the size of the industry. Rural Electrification Administration crews were constantly stringing transmission wire, convincing observers that electrification of the entire nation was inevitable. For those contemplating a foray into the electric motor and generator industry, this development translated into encouraging prospects for the future. Manufacturing facilities mechanized their processes to be powered by electricity, if they had not already done so, and appliances used in the home increasingly depended on electricity for power.

The nation slowly became electrified during the first half of the twentieth century. It took until the 1950s for certain segments of the country to install the necessary electrical wire to enable the transmission of electricity. GE manufactured a broad assortment of electric motors and generators to run cement, paper, and steel manufacturing facilities and also spent considerable effort on developing electric powered locomotive engines. Emerson, meanwhile, concentrated on producing electric motors for use in home appliances such as sewing machines, water pumps, and fans and also carved a niche in the growing market for electric motors within products intended for business offices.

When the postwar economic boom of the 1950s exponentially increased consumer spending and invigorated both residential and nonresidential construction, the motor and generator industry gained a solid foundation. Every American home aspired to own at least two modern appliances, which marked the dawn of a new era and infused motor and generator manufacturers with increased business. Manufacturing activity in general increased as well, with electrically driven production lines becoming the norm.

The lucrative conditions characterizing the market attracted more and more manufacturers, and by the end of the decade competition became intense within the industry. In addition, the nature of the competition changed during this period, as the smattering of smaller companies that had proliferated before World War II began consolidating into large conglomerates.

In the 1960s, Emerson and GE competed for market share against such manufacturers as Reliance Electric & Engineering Co., Wagner Electric Co., and Westinghouse Electric Corp. This competition resulted in a significant decline in the price of fractional horsepower motors, the primary product within the motor and generator industry. Exacerbating the effect of the shrinking profit margins was the increasing cost of raw materials used in the production of fractional motors, particularly of magnetic wire. By the middle of the decade, a majority of the leading companies raised their prices for fractional motors in an attempt to stave off the debilitating effects of rising raw material expenditures.

At this time, there were approximately 325 companies competing in the industry, operating more than 400 establishments and employing slightly more than 100,000 workers. Despite the shrinking profit margins and other problems associated with the rapid pace at which the industry was maturing, the demand for electric motors continued to increase, attracting more and more competitors. Growth of the industry primarily stemmed from demand for fractional motors, which far outpaced other motor and generator products in terms of proportional representation of industry shipments. Fractional motors accounted for over 36 percent of total industry shipments by the mid-1960s—up from less than 30 percent in the 1950s—and this percentage would increase in the coming years. The reasons for this growth were as numerous as the different types of household items and appliances that were sold to consumers. Fractional motors were used in such diverse items as electric lawn mowers and hedge trimmers, electric toothbrushes, refrigerators, and washing machines.

Other products classified in the motor and generator industry recorded respectable sales figures, but their growth was less dramatic than the growth for fractional motors. Products such as small generating sets powered by diesel and other internal-combustion engines benefitted from stable demand from the farming and transportation industries, while shipments of integral horsepower motors spiraled downward during the late 1950s and early 1960s. Integral motors could be reconditioned, whereas fractional motors were rarely rebuilt. This in part accounted for an increasing disparity between fractional and integral motor shipments. In 1958 the value of shipments for fractional and integral motors was approximately even at $430 million. Six years later the value of shipments of fractional motors had soared to nearly $600 million, while integral motor shipments had fallen to roughly $375 million.

This period in the history of the motor and generator industry also witnessed the increasing encroachment of foreign manufacturers into the U.S. market. In 1963, 5 million motor and generator units were imported into the United States, but this figure nearly quintupled four years later when more than 23 million imported units were sold. This growth in total imports was occasioned by significant increases in the value of shipments recorded by two countries—the United Kingdom and Japan. The United Kingdom increased motor and generator product shipments to the United States from $1.5 million in 1963 to $18.4 million by 1967. But this was a one-time surge for U.K. producers: five years later shipments dropped to $12.6 million, and by the end of the 1970s U.K. imports slipped below $10 million. Japan, on the other hand, went from negligible shipments in 1963 to over $15 million worth four years later, and this continued to increase to $27.8 million by 1972 and $67 million by the end of the decade.

High inflation in the early 1970s negatively affected manufacturers of motors and generators, as residential and nonresidential construction declined and many consumers delayed appliance purchases. The total value of industry shipments declined by five percent between 1974 and 1975 to $3.12 billion, while production worker employment within the industry decreased from 77,700 to 60,600. Hoping to escape the rising costs of materials and supplies occurring at this time, many manufacturers overstocked their inventories. This led to a later downward adjustment in production, further eroding the industry's profit margins. Once consumer appliance purchases returned to normal levels and construction picked up in the late 1970s however, the industry again exhibited robust growth. Shipment values increased by 12 percent between 1977 and 1978 to $5 billion and approached $6 billion by the beginning of the 1980s.

Entering the 1980s however, high inflation continued to inflict damage on the motor and generator industry, particularly due to reduced capital expenditure programs initiated by other industries. In the absence of vigorous, nationwide plant expansion and the consequent orders for motors and generators, the industry was forced to look elsewhere for money. Since major retooling of production machinery was prohibitively expensive, many manufacturers streamlined their operations, relying on more efficient production procedures to help them withstand the decline in business. Part of this effort to economize resulted in a reduction of the industry's labor force. From 1981 to 1982, employment of production workers dropped from 93,400 to 84,100—the latest of a series of significant declines from the 107,000 high recorded in 1979.

In the meantime, the value of import shipments entering the United States continued to increase dramatically during the 1970s, and by the early 1980s foreign competition stood as a formidable force. The value of all import shipments classified in the motor and generator industry in 1972 was $181 million, but this figure ballooned to $801 million 10 years later. U.S. manufacturers, however, had simultaneously intensified their efforts to increase exports in order to combat escalating material costs and declining business. Consequently domestic exports, a majority of which were shipped to Canada and Mexico, also grew

substantially. Between 1979 and 1981, the value of export shipments increased from $887 million to nearly $1.4 billion, maintaining a favorable trade balance for U.S. manufacturers.

A recession in the early 1990s led to flagging consumer spending and a decline in housing and industrial construction, which compounded the existing difficulties associated with foreign competition, excess industry capacity, and cascading prices. Escalating energy costs, coupled with federal regulations requiring new energy efficiency standards, made the development of new technology and manufacturing processes intrinsic to any manufacturer's future profitability. The motor and generator industry made progress in this direction during the 1980s, including the development of a highly efficient fractional motor in 1985 that enabled appliances to operate more quietly and at lower cost. However, the industry needed further advances in the 1990s to ensure its viability.

CURRENT CONDITIONS

In the late 1990s, due to slowing growth rates in the motor and generator industries, mergers and acquisitions became a crucial means for individual manufacturers to maintain profitability and market share. A case in point was Pennsylvania-based AMETEK Inc., which in 1997 purchased Rotron Inc. for $103 million, bringing it into the top tier of motor and generator manufacturers. The movement of production units into Mexico, Canada, and Brazil also put pressure on U.S. makers to stay competitive by increasing operating margins or by offering greater customer service. For example in all areas of the motor and generator market, manufacturers were pre-engineering motors for specific applications, according to the needs of a particular user.

According to Energy User News, "between 30 percent to 40 percent of all fossil fuels burned are used to generate electricity; two-thirds of that electricity goes to run motors." Those statistics helped drive the passage of the 1997 Energy Policy Act (often referred to as EPACT), which affected nearly 70 percent of the integral horsepower motor market, according to analysts at Frost and Sullivan. The act set a minimum energy efficiency rating for all squirrel-caged, T-frame polyphase induction motors with 1 to 200 hp. Analysts predicted that in the long run manufacturers with limited funds for research and development would be most affected.

The late 1990s saw the emergence of the linear motor as a competitor for market share. The estimated market for linear motors in 2002 was expected to be $108 million, which reflects a greater than 100 percent increase over 1999 figures. While this was a comparatively small segment of the market compared to multibillion dollar shares for fractional and integral horsepower motors, growth was expected to continue at a rapid pace, as

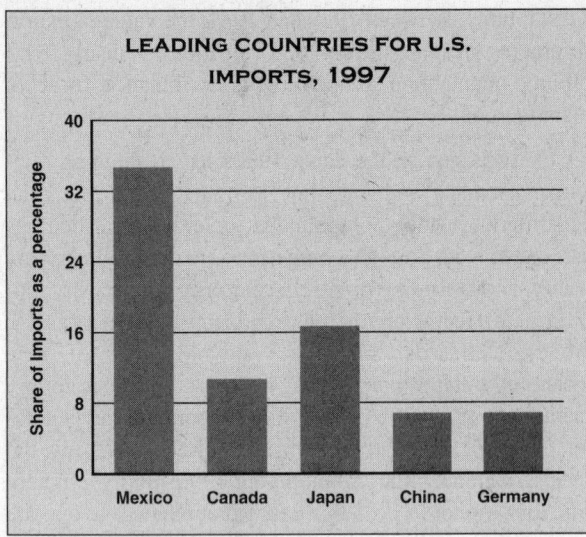

LEADING COUNTRIES FOR U.S. IMPORTS, 1997

Share of Imports as a percentage

| Mexico | Canada | Japan | China | Germany |

applications for the motor began to catch up with the technology. In addition, the price of linear motors dropped at a rate of 30 to 40 percent per year, making them a more viable alternative to traditional rotary motors. In a February 1999 report in *Design News*, Mark Sabine listed the benefits of such a motor: "Obviously speed is one main advantage. The technology is ideal for applications that require high position accuracy and repeatability. Using linear motors, designers can also gain more travel in the same envelope—they can even have two different motors go to the same area." Major manufacturers who have developed linear motors include General Electric Co., Baldor Electric Co., Krollmorgen Corp., and Ingersoll-Rand.

INDUSTRY LEADERS

Ranked according to sales volume, the two largest companies engaged in the motor and generator industry in 1998 were General Electric Company and Emerson Electric Company. These companies began competing for market share before the turn of the century and have managed to lead the motor and generator industry through much of its history.

Emerson Electric, with about 86,400 employees, reported $14.27 billion in sales in 1999, a 6 percent increase from 1998. The company reported an 11 percent compound annual growth rate over the five-year period from 1994 to 1999.

Following the Great Depression in the 1930s—when sales plummeted, stock dividend payments were halted, and hotly contested labor disputes threatened to bankrupt the company—Emerson Electric's financial condition was buoyed by military contracts obtained during World War II. The company manufactured a variety of war-related products, including gun turrets installed in Air Force bombers such as the B-17, B-25, and B-26. Com-

bined with its other contributions toward the war effort, these products infused the company with $100 million annually.

Defense-related work continued to support Emerson Electric following the war, although during the immediate postwar years military contracts dropped to as low as $1.5 million. But defense-related work picked up again in the 1950s when the Air Force modernized its bomber fleet, elevating sales from military contracts to 30 percent of the company's total. To supplement its armament production, company management also decided to branch out into the engineering and development of electronics and avionics.

By the end of the 1950s however, Emerson Electric's management grew fearful of the company's dependence on the military for such a considerable portion of its revenues. To address this, they began an aggressive acquisition program in the 1960s, averaging one acquisition per year throughout the decade. Acquisitions and diversification continued into the 1970s and 1980s, as Emerson Electric became a leader in both consumer and industrial markets. By the 1990s, Emerson Electric's products were sold to commercial and industrial businesses involved in a wide assortment of factory automation and process control enterprises.

General Electric posted a record $112 billion in sales in 1999, reflecting an 11 percent increase from the previous year. While its impressive past elevated the company into the upper echelon of international businesses, GE's more recent achievements, especially in the motor and generator industry, have been comparatively dismal. During the 1970s and 1980s, the company suffered increasing losses from foreign competition, labor disputes, and "indirect imports" (finished products that were assembled with electric motors already included). These mounting difficulties forced GE to close several motor and generator manufacturing plants in the late 1980s and to lay off a considerable percentage of its workforce. Harder hit by these market-wide developments than rival Emerson Electric, GE began to slip from its almost unassailable position atop the motor and generator industry in the late 1980s and early 1990s. While still a leader in the industry in 1999, motors were not one of its high-profile business, which included NBC and GE Capital Services, a financial concern.

WORKFORCE

Total employment in the motor and generator industry decreased through much of the 1980s. This trend continued into the 1990s as a nationwide recession weakened the motor and generator market. Beyond the negative effects of market fluctuations, manufacturing industries as a whole continued to streamline their operations by eliminating layers of managerial staff and altering production processes to reduce the number of workers required to perform certain tasks. This general movement toward fewer employees per manufacturing facility made future reductions of the motor and generator industry employment base likely. This trend may have bottomed out in 1992, when employment in the industry reached a low of 67,900. By 1995, the number of workers was back up to 77,300, then down to 74,720 by 1997. Modest declines were again expected through the year 2000, with decreases focused in machine operator positions, but were not expected to reach 1992 levels at that time.

Of the 75,200 total people employed in the motor and generator industry in 1996, 59,900 were production workers. Managerial, administrative, and technical employees composed the remainder of the industry's work force. Wages for production workers in 1996 were slightly lower than average for all manufacturing industries, at $12.21 per hour compared to $12.68 per hour overall. Wages were expected to dip slightly in 1997, then continue to rise through the year 2000.

AMERICA AND THE WORLD

The trade gap between U. S. manufacturers of motors and generators and their foreign competitors widened throughout the 1990s. Exports from the United States totaled $2.2 billion in 1991, $15 million greater than the import total. In 1996, that gap was calculated at $717 million. Leading importers include Mexico, Japan, Canada, Germany, and China. Although in 1997 Mexico was by far the import leader, with 34.7 percent of the U.S. import market, China has been the fastest growing, with exports increasing annually by 32 percent from 1992 to 1997. Japan had a 16.7 percent share of the U.S. import market, Canada 10.7 percent, and both Germany and China had 6.8 percent.

The primary markets for motors and generators manufactured in the United States were Mexico, Canada, Asia, Western Europe, and Latin America. Mexico represented a 23.3 percent share, Canada a 19.5 percent share, China a 3.8 percent share, Japan a 3.5 percent share, other parts of Asia an 11.5 percent share, and the United Kingdom a 3.2 percent share. The United States exported over 25 percent of its motors and generators in 1996.

FURTHER READING

"AC IHP Motor Participants Face Challenges as Government Regulations Change Competitive Environment," 8 April, 1999. Available from http://www.frost.com/pdf/reports/industrial/rp557617.pdf.

Darnay, Arsen J., ed. *Manufacturing USA*. 6th ed. Detroit: Gale Research, 1998.

Emerson Electric. *1999 Annual Report*. Available from http://www.emersonelectric.com.

"Fractional Horsepower Motor Manufacturers Grab Market Share Through Competitor Acquisition," 24 December, 1998. Available from http://www.frost.com/pdf/reports/industrial/rp557617.pdf.

General Electric Co. *1998 Annual Report*. Available from http://www.ge.com/annual98.

"GE Reports Record Results," 20 January, 2000. Available from http://www.ge.com.

Gorenstein, Nathan. "Pennsylvania—Based Ametek to Buy Electric Motor Maker." *Philadelphia Inquirer,* 30 December, 1997.

"Linear Motors Come Into Their Own." *Design News,* 18 May, 1998.

Sabine, Mark. "Linear Motor Shootout." *Design News,* 15 February, 1999.

Schiff, Debra. "A Horse of a Different Power." *Electronic Design,* 3 February, 1997.

Stebbins, Wayne. "Motor Management Strategies." *Energy User News,* June 1998.

"U.S. AC Integral Horsepower Motor Markets," 8 April, 1999. Available from http://www.frost.com/pdf/reports/industrial/rp557617.pdf.

U.S. Bureau of the Census. *1997 Current Industrial Report.* Available from http://www.census.gov/industry/ma36h97.txt.

U.S. Department of Commerce. *1997 Economic Census.* Washington: GPO, 1999.

U.S. Department of Commerce.*U.S. Industry and Trade Outlook, 1999.* McGraw-Hill, 1999.

"U.S. Fractional Horsepower Motor Markets," 24 December, 1998. Available from http://www.frost.com/pdf/reports/industrial/rp532917.pdf.

SIC 3624

CARBON AND GRAPHITE PRODUCTS

This category covers establishments primarily engaged in manufacturing carbon, graphite, and metal-graphite brushes and brush stock; carbon or graphite electrodes for thermal and electrolytic uses; carbon and graphite fibers; and other carbon, graphite, and metal-graphite products.

NAICS CODE(S)

335991 (Carbon and Graphite Product Manufacturing)

INDUSTRY SNAPSHOT

Carbon and graphite products manufacturing establishments were responsible for shipments worth approximately $2.3 billion in 1997. Total value of shipments during the 1990s reached a peak with the 1997 amount;

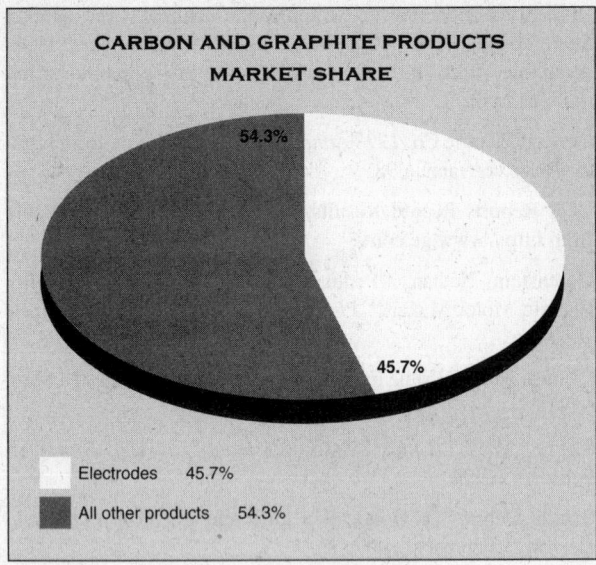

CARBON AND GRAPHITE PRODUCTS
MARKET SHARE

54.3%

45.7%

Electrodes   45.7%

All other products   54.3%

the lowest total value for the decade was $1.16 billion in 1990.

The lackluster performance of the industry in the 1980s and until the late 1990s was attributed to the effect of several economic forces that created product oversupply and excess capacity in the industry. One of the main causes cited for almost two decades of industry stagnation was the decline of the steel industry, a prime market for the industry's products. In addition, world demand for carbon and graphite electrodes plummeted, due to the development of more efficient electrode performance in steel production. This decline in demand for carbon and graphite electrodes for use in steel production, coupled with the strength of the dollar in the 1980s and early 1990, allowed rival foreign producers to increase their profitability in the U.S. market, which adversely affected the industry's output and profitability.

On the positive side, structural changes in the industry led to a rebound in the 1990s, including growth in some export markets. Although the industry was a perennial net importer of carbon and graphite products, the volume of carbon and graphite exports continued to increase steadily throughout the 1990s.

ORGANIZATION AND STRUCTURE

In 1997, approximately 99 establishments were engaged in the production of carbon and graphite products. These establishments employed approximately 110 workers each, 80 of which were employed as production workers. For the same year, the average value added per production worker was more than $120,000. This figure showed significant improvement over the 1994 figure for the industry which was about $84,500.

In 1997, the product share was split between two product classes—electrodes, which claimed 45.7 percent

of the market, and all other graphite and carbon products, which claimed the remaining 54.3 percent. Graphite electrodes for use in electrolytic cells and electric furnaces represented the largest portion of the electrode product share.

Geographically, the greatest number of establishments producing carbon and graphite products in 1997 were located in the steel production region in the Northeast and in the South. Ranked by the number of establishments per state, Pennsylvania ranked first with 18, followed by Pennsylvania with 15, California with 12, New York with 7, Connecticut with 6, and Alabama with 5.

The bulk of the industry's revenue was garnered by a limited number of manufacturers. The leading three companies accounted for almost 90 percent of the total industry's output in 1996. It was estimated that UCAR International Inc., with sales of $947 million, accounted for more than 50 percent of industry sales in 1998. The other two dominant companies in the carbon and graphite products industry were: Keystone Consolidated Industries Inc. of Dallas, with $370 million in sales and 2,100 employees in 1998; and Carbide/Graphite Group Inc. of Pittsburgh, with $240.1 million in sales and 965 employees in 1999. The remaining market was controlled by about 20 companies. All of the top companies in the industry are private concerns.

BACKGROUND AND DEVELOPMENT

The products composing the carbon and graphite products industry were mostly carbon products of a very high carbon content, including both natural and synthetic graphites. Carbon's hardest form is known as diamond; graphite is its softest form. Graphite appears naturally in three forms: amorphous, which is the last stage of the coalification process; crystalline flake, which is used in brake linings and pencils; and lump, used mostly in batteries and found primarily in Sri Lanka.

Synthetic carbon and graphite comes in three basic product categories. Electrodes composed the industry's largest product category. Making up more than half of the industry's products, electrodes are used in all types of electric furnaces. Graphite fibers are the second largest category of graphite products. Synthetic powder, made from scraps that are pulverized into a powder, make up the bulk of the remainder of synthetic products.

Industrial uses of graphite and carbon began in the early 1800s. In 1800, Sir Humphry Davy (1778-1829) used carbon in the electric arc, which used an electrode made out of charcoal. By 1857, after seven years of experiments with new electrodes yielding a purer carbon, De Grasses B. Fowler patented the process of making carbon plates by mixing ground coke with tar and shaping the mixture under pressure in molds. Soon after, in 1877, Charles F. Brush and Washington H. Laurence of Cleveland began to experiment with carbon electrodes, and by 1878, Brush was manufacturing electrodes.

In 1896, E.G. Atcheson patented a process that transformed amorphous carbon to synthetic graphite by heat treatment, which laid the foundation for the modern graphite industry. A succession of inventions followed in the electrothermal field, all of which required electrodes of carbon or graphite for their applications. For example, in 1896, H.Y. Castner patented a process that involved heating carbon electrodes with electricity so that a graphite-like form of carbon was produced. By 1899, the Atcheson Graphite Company was formed in Niagara Falls, New York, producing electrodes for Castner's electrochemical processes, with most of the production being exported to Europe, which was the center of the industry at the time.

In 1906, the first steel made with electric power was manufactured in the United States by the Holcomb Steel Company in Syracuse, New York, using German electrodes. As the industry progressed, larger and larger electrodes were needed. By 1914, there was a vast expansion in electric furnace capacity and in the electrochemical industry, leading to a rise in the demand for electrodes of all varieties. The 30-inch carbon electrode was produced in 1927 and the 40-inch carbon electrode followed a year later. Graphite electrodes progressed similarly, but at a slightly slower pace, with the 14-inch electrode introduced between 1914 and 1918. By 1937, the size of graphite electrodes reached 20 inches. At that time, Germany, England, France, Italy, and Sweden made graphite and amorphous electrodes. Carbon products were made in most countries including Europe and Japan.

By 1959, many new products followed. Filamentary carbon was made into graphite cloth and eventually carbon and graphite cloth, felt, yarn, tape, and fibers were to follow. These products had the desirable properties of not melting at high temperatures or under high pressures. Such applications for carbon and graphite increased exponentially, with many new firms capitalizing on the thermal stability, electrical conductivity, thermal conductivity, and corrosion resistance of carbon and graphite fibers.

By the early 1980s, world demand began to collapse because of the decline in consumption of graphite electrodes, particularly by the steel industry. This decline was attributed to improved electrode performance as well as lower priced electrode imports. By 1985, leading producer Union Carbide suspended production at its Clarksville, Tennessee, plant. A lower cost of production at the company's facilities in Yabucoa, Puerto Rico, and Columbia, Tennessee, attributed to this closure. It reopened the Clarksville facility in 1987.

At that time, costs were rising and carbon products firms were experiencing poor profitability. Union Carbide was not the only firm experiencing poor profitability

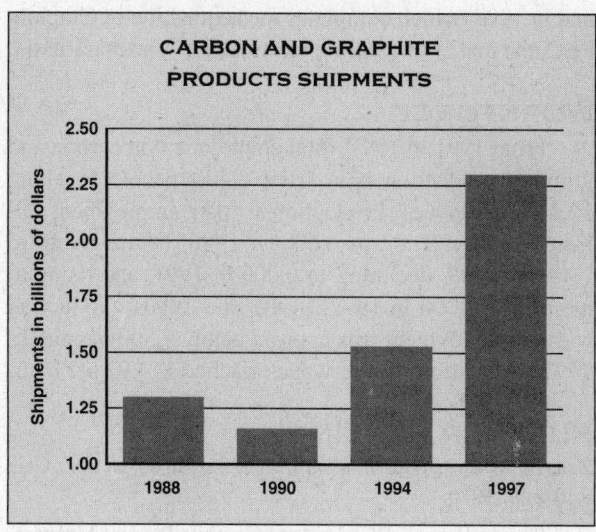

CARBON AND GRAPHITE PRODUCTS SHIPMENTS

and excess capacity. Fierce domestic and foreign competition was making it hard to meet rising costs in new carbon electrode plants. Declining demand led to overcapacity in electrodes, due mostly to low operating rates in steel mills. Coupled with this was the decline in the U.S. steel industry caused by heightened competition from foreign producers. Another key factor was the increased costs of fuels, such as natural gas used to carbonize coal to make carbon and graphite. Foreign competition was strengthened further by the strength of the U.S. dollar at the time, which increased prices of U.S. goods in proportion to foreign goods, and enabled consumers to purchase lower priced products from rival producers, predominantly the Italian and Japanese companies. Lastly, alternative products (titanium diboride electrodes were substituted for carbon or graphite) provided a 25-percent savings on electrical energy, which is a major expense in aluminum smelting. Accordingly, key aluminum producers, such as Kaiser Aluminum, Alcoa, and Alcan, began using titanium diboride instead of carbon or graphite.

CURRENT CONDITIONS

Toward the end of the 1990s, UCAR International Inc., the largest manufacturer of carbon and graphite electrodes, was positioned for future growth in this market. In 1996, UCAR Chairman and CEO Robert Krass indicated that more than 78 million metric tons of new capacity in the electric steel making industry had been planned for installation between 1996 and 1999. This should maintain a constant demand of 1 to 2 percent per year for the carbon and graphite electrodes consumed in this manufacturing process. Furthermore, electrode pricing has remained favorable and there is no expected change in their global market. UCAR also announced the purchase of the graphite electrode business of Elektrokohle Lichtenberg AG in Berlin, Germany, in 1996 and in 1997, which completes the acquisition of Graphite PLC, the maker of graphite electrodes in Viazma, Russia.

WORKFORCE

From 1991 to 1997, total employment in carbon and graphite production rose from 8,400 people to about 10,900 employees. Production worker employment fell from 8,500 in 1982 to 6,600 in 1986, before rising to 7,400 in 1988, declining to 6,000 in 1991, and rising to more than 8,000 in 1997. In the mid-1990s, production worker employment was approximately 7,300 people. In 1997, production worker wages reached $14.92 per hour.

FURTHER READING

Darnay, Arsen J., ed. *Manufacturing USA,* 5th ed. Detroit: Gale Research, 1996.

U.S. Census Bureau. ''Carbon and Graphite Product Manufacturing.'' *1997 Economic Census: Manufacturing Industry Series.* June 1999.

SIC 3625

RELAYS AND INDUSTRIAL CONTROLS

This category covers establishments primarily engaged in manufacturing electronic relays and industrial controls used for starting, regulating, stopping, and protecting circuits and electric motors. Mechanical switches and relays are classified elsewhere.

NAICS CODE(S)

335314 (Relay and Industrial Control Manufacturing)

INDUSTRY SNAPSHOT

The industry encompasses two major categories: electronic relays and industrial controls. Electronic relays are used in circuitry for computers, communications equipment, and a multitude of other electronic devices. A relay is basically a switch that is used to open or close a circuit. It controls the flow of electricity to create a desired result. Most industrial controls are essentially switches, but of a more complex nature. They are usually associated with the control of electric motors and systems. Industrial controls include devices such as motor starters, contactors, control centers, and programmable logic controllers.

A conventional electronic relay contains a solenoid, which is a coil of wire with an enclosed, fixed iron core. When electricity passes through the wire a magnetic field is created that energizes the core. An armature connected to the core allows it to move and activate, or trip, the relay. Smaller relays used in transistorized equipment work similarly, but are much smaller and require a fraction of the power consumed by electromechanical relays.

The tiny reed relay, for example, is made with two flat magnetic strips. The separated strips are sealed in a capsule filled with an inert gas (to prevent corrosion), which sits inside a coil. When electricity is applied to the coil the two magnetic strips are drawn to each other, thus completing a circuit. Finally, miniaturized solid-state relays are not magnetically activated, but are instead triggered by electrical pulses.

ORGANIZATION AND STRUCTURE

Two standards for industrial controls are administered by the International Electrotechnical Commission (IEC)and the National Electrical Manufacturers Association (NEMA). IEC-approved controls conform to standards which have brought them a reputation for compactness and affordability. Controls rated by NEMA, while considered less streamlined, are generally perceived by users to be more reliable and serviceable for heavy industrial uses. Parts, accessories, and miscellaneous related items make up the remaining share of industry products.

The largest consumer of relays and industrial controls in the 1990s was the computer equipment industry, which purchased 14 percent of production. Most of the remaining output was consumed by various manufacturing industries, particularly those producing electrical and electronic equipment. Machine tool producers, for example, made up about three percent of the market, and manufacturers of heating and air-conditioning equipment represented two percent of industry revenues. Other consumers of industrial controls included producers of mining machinery, automobiles, railroad equipment, aircraft, and construction equipment.

BACKGROUND AND DEVELOPMENT

One of the first practical applications of electrical relay technology was the telegraph, which was patented by Samuel F.B. Morse in 1844. Relays that were used to operate electronic devices were not developed on a significant scale until late in the nineteenth century, following Thomas Edison's work with the electronic vacuum tube. As the demand for lighting, phonograph, and other electrical devices flourished during the early 1900s, the need for relays surged. Importantly, U.S. investments in electronics research during World War II spawned significant advancements in all types of electronic components.

When integrated circuits were introduced in 1958, many manufacturers of relays and other electromechanical devices feared that the new solid-state components would make some conventional products obsolete. But the development of miniaturized relays served to expand the breadth of the industry and culminated in demand growth for both traditional and new devices during the 1960s and 1970s. Demand for relays boomed as a result of expanding consumer electronics, business machine, computer, and communications markets. Likewise, industrial controls evolved from relatively simple relay and switch devices used to start and control motors into complex, high-tech mechanisms used to regulate speed, pressure, timing, and other mechanical characteristics.

Overall demand for electronic components grew during the 1980s, bolstered by the proliferation of personal computers and peripherals, telecommunications equipment, and the integration of electronics into industrial and consumer products. Worldwide sales of integrated circuits, for example, jumped 464 percent during the decade. Shipments of many conventional relay products stagnated or declined, largely as a result of foreign competition. But the demand for new high-tech industrial controls, as well as some types of relays, thrived. By 1987, the peak of the 1980s economic expansion, industry sales reached $6.1 billion and employment topped 66,000.

While the United States slumped into a recession during the late 1980s and early 1990s, sales of relays and industrial controls continued to climb at a healthy pace until 1991, when sales dipped by about 6 percent. Entering the mid-1990s, sales in 1995 climbed to more than $9.5 billion. In addition to strong demand, manufacturers benefitted from industry consolidation and increased efficiency which had characterized electrical component manufacturers during the 1980s. Indeed, as shipments grew producers continued to reduce employment through automation and restructuring.

The relays and industrial controls industry began to feel the pinch of recession in the early 1990s. Conventional relay shipments, which had already dropped 2.7 percent in 1991, were hit hardest. Nevertheless, overall sales climbed about three percent in both 1992 and 1993, and growth in some segments remained strong.

Three factors contributed to the success of relay and industrial control makers in the mid-1990s:

- The recovery of industries that purchased their products.
- Increased global competitiveness, which was the result of productivity gains and a devalued U.S. dollar.
- Technological advances that broadened the market for industrial controls.

Long term industry gains will partially depend on U.S. export growth. While exports accounted for only about 6 percent of sales in the early 1990s, they made up the fastest growing market segment and offered lucrative long term potential for sales of high-tech industrial controls. Canada and Mexico were the largest foreign consumers of U.S. exports and represented about 30 percent of cross-border revenues. European nations also consumed 30 percent of U.S. exports. But East Asian markets, which purchased 14 percent of exports in the early

1990s, showed the fastest growth. The United States imported a total of $650 billion worth of relays and controls annually in the early 1990s, more than 40 percent of which came from Japan.

CURRENT CONDITIONS

According to a recent study conducted by the Venture Development Corporation of Natick, Massachusetts, growth in the North American relay market is expected to increase from the 3 percent annual growth charted during the mid-1990s to 4.5 percent by 2003. Experts say that strong market economies will lead to increased profit levels for end user and OEMs, which will, in turn, lead to increased demand for components and parts.

Continuous improvement in technology and product quality, a greater variety of product offerings, and improved customer relations are other factors that will contribute to the growth of the relay market. Another is the growing trend toward consolidation of smaller companies into large conglomerates, which may be better equipped to offer expanded product lines and to make maximum use of improved technology.

Similar growth is expected in the industrial controls market, according to the Freedonia Group, a leading industrial study provider. A six percent annual gain is expected to be fueled by a healthy maintenance/repair/operations (MRO) aftermarket as repair and maintenance needs increase. Technological advances such as computer-based factory automation will also contribute to the growth of the industrial controls industry.

INDUSTRY LEADERS

Despite steady consolidation in electronics components industries during the 1980s and 1990s, the relay and industrial controls industry remained relatively fragmented in the late-1990s with about 1,200 competitors. Most companies built industrial controls and specialized in a specific industry niche.

Based on sales, the top three companies in the relays and industrial controls industry in 1999 were Rockwell Automation, of Milwaukee, Wisconsin, Allen-Bradley Company, also of Milwaukee, and Crouse-Hinds, a division of Cooper Industries. If broken down by category, the industry leaders in the relay market included Siemans, Aromat, Omron, CII, Hella, and CP Clare. These six companies combined accounted for 52 percent of the relay market in the late 1990s. Significant forces in the industrial controls industry included, among others, Robert Bosch, Dana, General Electric, Honeywell, and Rockwell International.

WORKFORCE

Despite a generally positive outlook for most companies in this industry, long term job prospects are less pleasant. The industry employed 62,500 workers in 1996, down from 63,400 in 1995. Productivity gains and imports of some commodity-like relays and controls will continue to diminish opportunities, particularly for laborers. Jobs for assemblers and fabricators, which account for about 25 percent of the U.S. electrical apparatus work force, were predicted to decline by 30 to 50 percent between 1990 and 2005, according to the Bureau of Labor Statistics. Positions for white collar managers and top executives are expected to be cut by about ten percent. Jobs for sales professionals and engineers are expected to increase, though slightly.

RESEARCH AND TECHNOLOGY

One of the most significant industry trends in the mid-1990s was the integration of fuzzy-logic into control systems. Fuzzy-logic employs the chaos theory, which holds that there are identifiable tendencies of movement amid apparently random patterns. Fuzzy-logic industrial controls are particularly well-suited for complex systems that are heavily dependent on human supervision. In addition to U.S. initiatives, Siemens and several Japanese firms were investing heavily in this new technology.

To keep pace with the demand from increasingly sophisticated consumers, new product products are being developed and introduced in this industry continuously. For example, in 1999, Aromat Corporation, of New Providence, N.J. Introduced a new high-sensitivity Relay designed to provide low-level switching capacity for measuring Instruments and other applications. Also, in 1999, Eaton Corporation, of Pittsburgh, introduced a new protection relay, designed to maximize motor operation while protecting against excessive heating and overload conditions.

In this ever-changing industry, experts predict that those companies that can continue to explore advanced technologies and to expand their product lines will be the survivors of the future.

FURTHER READING

Darnay, Arsen J., ed. *Manufacturing USA*. 5th ed. Detroit: Gale Research, 1996.

U.S. Bureau of the Census. *1995 Annual Survey of Manufactures*. Washington: GPO, 1997.

SIC 3629

ELECTRICAL INDUSTRIAL APPARATUS, NOT ELSEWHERE CLASSIFIED

This category covers companies that primarily make industrial and commercial electric apparatus, such as fixed and variable capacitors and rectifiers for industrial applications.

Product examples in the miscellaneous electrical industrial apparatus industry include battery chargers, non-electronic condensers, non-electric rectifiers, surge suppressors, and thermoelectric generators. Companies that make capacitors and rectifiers are classified elsewhere.

NAICS CODE(S)

335999 (All Other Miscellaneous Electrical Equipment and Component Manufacturing)

Nonelectric rectifying apparatus used to convert alternating current to direct current accounted for about 50 percent of industry output in the early 1990s. Nonelectric capacitor equipment made up about 12 percent of revenues. Other major product groups included coil windings (3.65 percent of sales), solenoids (2.53 percent), and cathodic protection equipment (1.7 percent). About 50 percent of output was sold to other manufacturing industries, and 30 percent was made for the U.S. military. Federal nondefense purchases contributed 10 percent of revenues. The remaining output went to other sectors, such as the automotive repair and communications industries.

According to the U.S. Census Bureau's *1997 Economic Census-Manufacturing*, 411 establishments operated in this category for some or all of 1997. Industry-wide employment totaled 18,682 workers receiving a payroll of more than $565.0 million. Production employees totaled 12,689, putting in almost 25 million hours to earn wages of almost $280.0 million. Overall shipments for the industry were valued at more than $2.8 billion.

The beginning of practical electronics applications was marked by American Lee DeForest's patent of an electrical vacuum tube in 1906, based on a design by Thomas Edison. Technological breakthroughs during both world wars also broadened the scope of the electronics industry. As electrical apparatus sales surged during the U.S. economic boom after World War II, miscellaneous electrical industrial apparatus shipments swelled. By the beginning of the 1980s, the industry was generating revenues of about $1.1 billion per year and employing a work force of more than 16,000.

Industry growth lagged during the 1980s, due in part to foreign imports. Also, more popular solid state components reduced demand for traditional electromechanical equipment produced by this industry. Even greater U.S. defense spending did not bring much growth. Sales increased to just $1.5 billion by 1990, reflecting a decline in inflation-adjusted revenues since 1980.

The industry emerged from a U.S. recession in the mid-1990s with a healthy forecast. Industry shipments for 1995 totaled $2.7 billion, up from $2.4 billion in 1994. Employment totaled 17,500 in 1995, 12,200 of which were in production. The total payroll for 1995 was $514.6 million, with $252.6 million of that devoted to production workers.

The largest player in the industry was New York City based Siemens Corp. with more than $11.0 million in sales for its fiscal year ending September 30, 1998. Motorola Inc. Automotive, Component, Computer and Energy Sector of Northbrook, Illinois generated $2.5 billion in 1997 sales, according to Infotrac databases. Computer Power Inc. of High Bridge, New Jersey was third in the industry with 1998 sales of more than $2 billion.

Job prospects for this industry, at least for production workers, was projected to decline. Automation, restructuring, and foreign labor could reduce positions for U.S. production workers such as electrical assemblers, machine operators, and coil winders. There could be, however, more industry jobs for engineers, sales people, and technical support staff.

FURTHER READING

Darnay, Arsen J., ed. *Manufacturing USA*. 5th ed. Detroit: Gale Research, 1996.

Infotrac Company Profiles. 2000. Available from http://web4 .infotrac.galegroup.com.

U.S. Census Bureau. 2000. *1997 Economic Census-Manufacturing*. Available from http://www.census.gov/prod/ec97/ 97m3359h.pdf.

U.S. Department of Commerce. *1995 Annual Survey of Manufactures*. Washington, DC: GPO, 1997.

SIC 3631

HOUSEHOLD COOKING EQUIPMENT

This category covers establishments primarily engaged in manufacturing household electric and nonelectric cooking equipment, such as stoves, ranges, and ovens, except portable electric appliances. This industry includes establishments primarily engaged in manufacturing microwave and convection ovens, including portable. Establishments primarily engaged in manufacturing other electric household cooking appliances, such as portable ovens, hot plates, grills, percolators, and toasters, are classified in **SIC 3634: Electric Housewares and Fans.** Establishments primarily engaged in manufacturing commercial cooking equipment are classified in **SIC 3589: Service Industry Machinery, Not Elsewhere Classified.**

NAICS CODE(S)

335221 (Household Cooking Appliance Manufacturing)

INDUSTRY SNAPSHOT

The U.S. Census Bureau reported that in 1997 the 84 establishments in this classification shipped $3.5 billion worth of merchandise, spent $1.8 billion on materials, and invested $121 million in capital expenditures. About 55 percent of these operations employed at least 20 people, and about 35 percent had at least 100 employees. The largest concentrations of operations in this industry were in California and Tennessee.

ORGANIZATION AND STRUCTURE

Household cooking equipment was part of the appliance market that included washing machines, refrigerators, and other long-term appliances. Most appliances were purchased for new housing, replacement, or remodeling. Because people bought household cooking equipment to furnish their homes, housing slumps sometimes hurt the industry severely. By the 1990s this was a mature industry, with much consolidation occurring among the major appliance manufacturers. Replacement of old and worn-out appliances drove the market, since most major appliances lasted 10-15 years.

Five major corporations dominated the household appliance industry during the 1990s. Many of the main appliance manufacturers attempted to expand their markets globally, often by opening factories in Europe and Asia.

In the mid-1990s about 98 percent of all major appliances, except microwave ovens, were American-made. Smaller appliances, such as coffee makers, food processors, and toasters, were often imported from Europe.

BACKGROUND AND DEVELOPMENT

Before the advent of the Franklin stove (invented by Ben Franklin), food was typically cooked in a fireplace or potbellied stove. Franklin's invention was only a slight improvement over open-hearth cooking, since his stove was only an iron box with flues.

During the nineteenth century, cast iron ranges that burned coal or wood were developed, but food still had to be monitored constantly because these heat sources were unpredictable. While these stoves enabled a variety of foods to be cooked at once, they were dirty and a fire hazard.

Gas burning stoves were also developed in the nineteenth century. They concentrated heat at the cooking source and ensured that food was cooked more evenly and all the way through. The transition to gas cooking, however, required a major plumbing overhaul as pipes had to be hooked up to a stove. Middle- and upper-class housewives used the first gas stoves. Thermostatically controlled gas ovens began appearing in 1915 and essentially freed cooks from the kitchen, since food could be left unattended for brief periods of time.

The 1893 Columbian Exhibition at Chicago featured a "Model Electric Kitchen." Attempts to use electricity in home cooking occurred as early as the late nineteenth century. In 1905 the "General Electric Range" was introduced. Equipped with its own switchboard, it sat on metal legs with the oven well above the cooking surface. Until 1912 most electric ranges were converted gas cookers made of cast-iron and some insulation. In this type of range all the heating elements were sealed in airtight containers to prevent them from burning out. Electric cookers relied on the "Bastian heater," or a wire spiral contained inside a quartz tube. An improvement on this theme, the Dowsing Electric Fire with sausage lamps, featured resistance wires of nickel and chromium that heated without oxidization. Early electric cooking overloaded circuits and was not made efficient until power companies were able to supply more electricity to homes.

Eventually, tabletops, cabinets, and drawers were added to gas burning stoves, which transformed the devices into "kitchen furniture." Because of the gas stove, cooking utensils evolved from wood to heavy cast iron and tin, to lightweight aluminum, tempered glass, and ceramic. By the 1920s gas ranges were made of white porcelain enamel. Within a decade they were produced in decorative colors to match other kitchen appliances and cabinetry. Gas ranges helped revolutionize cooking, making it more sanitary and time saving.

Some consumers favored gas ranges over electric ovens because food could be cooked faster on a gas range, and gas ovens did not interfere with other electrical appliances. A gas range also left no residual heat. On the other hand, an electric range did not need to be lit, and they offered features such as automatic oven timers.

In 1945 Percy L. Spencer, a researcher at Raytheon Co., invented the microwave oven. Spencer looked for a way to cook by radio waves. It wasn't until he was working around a magnetron that he discovered that a candy bar melted in his pocket even though he had not felt any heat. He placed Indian corn in front of the magnetron and witnessed kernels popping.

Spencer later added a cabinet with trays to the machine and created the first "radar range." Microwave ovens were used commercially before entering the home cooking market. Raytheon and Litton Industries Inc., both defense contractors, tried to sell microwave ovens in the United States without much success. Most consumers thought it was unnecessary to use a microwave in addition to a gas or electric range.

The Japanese were among the first big manufacturers of microwave ovens, in part because the appliances fit the Japanese lifestyle. Japanese cooking required reheating, and since most Japanese houses and kitchens were small, microwave ovens were the perfect space savers. Japan exported microwaves to the United States in the 1970s, and within five years, the market had swelled to 2.2 million microwaves. American appliance manufacturers began promoting microwave ovens again in the late 1970s, but by that time the Japanese controlled 25 percent of the market.

Samsung and other Korean manufacturers entered the American market during the early 1980s by supplying merchandisers such as J.C. Penney Company, Inc. with inexpensive microwave ovens. Eventually U.S. manufacturers began producing microwave ovens that would compete directly with imported models.

Americans soon began to perceive microwave ovens as an adjunct to the kitchen. Microwave ovens could reheat leftover food and frozen items quickly, cleanly, and conveniently. However, studies in the late 1980s showed that gas or electric convection ovens were still used to prepare the main meal or to cook meals from scratch. By the mid-1990s more than 90 percent of American households had a microwave, and nearly 9 million microwave ovens were being shipped annually.

Sales of major appliances peaked in 1987 with 38 million units sold, but the industry endured a slowdown during the early 1990s. Overall product shipments of appliances grew 3 percent in 1993 to $17.7 billion, while housing starts only increased about 4 percent during the same period of time, according to the *1994 U.S. Industrial Outlook*. Household cooking equipment represented an estimated $3.3 million worth of shipments or about 20 million units in 1993.

In the mid-1990s cooking appliance trends continued to emphasize cleanability, convenience, and sophisticated design, with a growing concern for energy efficiency. Major manufacturers focused on improving the overall product with new engineering. Consumers were becoming interested in convection cooking appliances such as wall ovens. Improvements in technology were helping gas ranges compete with electric ranges and microwave ovens. Also, glass "cook tops" that covered burners and electric coil eyelets became popular, as well as microwave and conventional oven combinations that saved space and were more energy efficient than separate units.

CURRENT CONDITIONS

The Census Bureau reported that in 1997, of household cooking equipment shipped by the entire industry, gas appliances constituted about 17 percent, and electric appliances constituted about 51 percent. The electric appliances included ranges, ovens, surface cooking units, and equipment (48 percent); and parts and accessories for ranges and ovens such as burners, oven racks, and broiler pans (2 percent).

There were 24 establishments whose primary product was electric household cooking equipment, including microwave ranges, ovens, and surface cooking units. This segment shipped $2 billion worth of merchandise, spent $999 million on materials, and invested $66 million in capital expenditures. It employed 9,106 people and had a payroll of $269 million. The largest value of shipments in this segment originated in Tennessee.

There were 10 establishments whose primary product was gas household ranges, ovens, surface cooking units, and equipment, including parts and accessories. This segment shipped $394 million worth of merchandise, spent $264 million on materials, and invested $19 million in capital expenditures. It employed 2,980 people and had a payroll of $69 million. The largest value of shipments in this segment originated in Tennessee.

There were 35 companies whose primary product was other types of household ranges and cooking equipment. This segment shipped $1.1 billion worth of merchandise, spent $489 million on materials, and invested $33 million in capital expenditures. It employed 5,140 people and had a payroll of $128 million. The largest value of shipments in this segment originated in Illinois, followed by Tennessee and California.

As more companies conducted business via the Internet, some appliance manufacturers tailored their sites to provide information to customers without undermining the dealers who sold those appliances at retail outlets. For example, Whirlpool Corp. set up more than 3,000 customized pages on the World Wide Web for the use of its dealers. In 1999 Whirlpool launched an interactive site on the Internet (http://www.whirlpool.com/virtualkitchen) where visitors could experiment with the company's products in a virtual, three-dimensional kitchen, design kitchens with a selection of Whirlpool appliances and customized floorplans, and research technical information about the company's merchandise. During the late 1990s consumers tended to conduct research, often on the Internet, before they invested in major appliances.

In another innovative Internet venture, Whirlpool owned a 37 percent interest in Brandwise.com, a site where consumers could search a vast database to determine which appliances and prices best suited their needs. The site was unusual because it provided consumers with information about appliances made by various companies, not only Whirlpool, and it also offered the data for sale to Whirlpool's competitors. By sponsoring the service, Whirlpool gained access to valuable marketing data about people who visited the site, allowing it to design products better suited to the needs of its customers.

INDUSTRY LEADERS

As the world's largest manufacturer of various major appliances, Whirlpool (Benton Harbor, Michigan) dominated the household cooking equipment industry. In 1998 the company had 59,000 employees and sales of $10.3 billion. It was the primary supplier of household cooking ranges to be sold under the Kenmore brand name at retail outlets of Sears, Roebuck & Co. Whirlpool also made household cooking equipment under the Whirlpool and KitchenAid brand names. The company's marketing strategy has been to produce specific appliances to serve a widening global consumer base. For example, in Africa it sold a 42-inch oven large enough to cook a whole sheep or goat.

General Electric Co. sold household cooking equipment under the GE, Hotpoint, and RCA brand names. Its GE Appliances subsidiary (Louisville, Kentucky) had 22,000 employees and sales of $5.6 billion in 1998. In 1997 GE introduced a double wall oven that featured both convection and conventional heat sources. Priced at about $1,200 to $2,200, convection ovens usually sold for about twice as much as gas and electric ovens. In 1999 GE launched its Advantium oven, which could cook food four times faster than conventional ovens and could also function as a microwave oven. It used halogen lights to cook the food from both sides at the same time. Cooking instructions for more than 80 dishes were programmed into the appliance.

Maytag Corp. (Newton, Iowa) had 20,595 employees and sales of $4.1 billion in 1998. It sold ranges under the Maytag, Magic Chef, Admiral, Hardwick, and Jenn-Air brand names. Its Jenn-Air Co. subsidiary, also known as Jenn-Air and Magic Chef Products (Indianapolis, Indiana), had 1,340 employees and sales of $190 million. In 1999 Maytag introduced its Gemini electric range, which featured two ovens that allowed consumers to cook foods at two different temperatures at the same time. The ovens could also keep food warm at a steady 145 or 170 degrees, and they operated on the standard 220 volts and 30 amperes that other ranges used. Maytag's marketing strategy emphasized its product features and their benefits to consumers.

In 1997 Raytheon sold its Amana Appliance subsidiary (Amana, Iowa) to Goodman Holding Company L.P. Amana had 5,500 employees and estimated sales of $590 million in 1998. In 1997 Amana introduced a miniature oven that used halogen lights to cook food from the inside out, like a microwave unit.

United States Stove Company Inc. (South Pittsburg, Tennessee) had 150 employees and estimated sales of $26 million in 1998.

Other leading manufacturers of household cooking equipment during the 1990s included White Consolidated Industries, Inc. (the American subsidiary of the Swedish company AB Electrolux); Sony Electronics, Inc.; Sharp Electronics Corp.; and Sunbeam-Oster Company, Inc.

WORKFORCE

The Census Bureau estimated that 17,630 people were employed in the manufacturing of household cooking appliances in 1997. This included 14,427 production workers who earned an average hourly wage of $11.02. Total payroll for the category was $481 million.

AMERICA AND THE WORLD

Many appliances were American-made, but others were imported from countries such as Japan, South Korea, Mexico, China, and Taiwan. In the early 1990s, according to the *1994 U.S. Industrial Outlook,* imports were increasing at an annual rate of about 7 percent while exports were increasing at about 6 percent.

American appliance manufacturers such as General Electric formed joint partnerships with foreign companies to make stoves and microwave ovens overseas for the American market. Many of these foreign-made appliances were then sold under an American label. The *U.S. Industrial Outlook* stated that "Mexico is expected to increase its lead regardless of the fate of the North American Free Trade Agreement, because of the growing integration of its appliance industry with that of the United States." Countries with traditionally lower wages, such as South Korea and China, were expected to continue as major suppliers of small appliances. Microwave ovens still represented the majority of imported appliances, but demand for microwaves had begun to taper off.

Competing for a leadership position in the global marketplace, Whirlpool owned stakes in Inglis of Canada and in an Italian company. Whirlpool also developed joint ventures with companies in India, Mexico, and the Netherlands. The leading markets for American appliances were Canada, Mexico, Japan, Germany, and Saudi Arabia, respectively. The lowering of tariffs in the early 1990s led to significant increases in exports to Canada and Mexico.

RESEARCH AND TECHNOLOGY

This industry experienced a substantial increase in technological innovations during the 1990s. This was due in part to national efficiency standards for major household appliances, including kitchen ranges and ovens, that the U.S. Department of Energy published in 1994. The standards were scheduled to become effective by the end of 1997.

Features such as induction, halogen, sealed burners, solid black glass and ceramic cooktops, and downdraft and radiant heating techniques were also introduced during the 1990s. The new technologies made ovens "self-cleaning," more fuel and energy efficient, safer, and streamlined for decorative purposes. A consumer could reheat, thaw, barbecue, broil, grill, griddle, bake, boil, and poach food at the same time, on the same appliance, and in less time.

FURTHER READING

Babyak, Richard J. "Technology Backs Design: Appliance Makers Displayed More Than Just New Looks, They Showed New Ways to Get the Job Done." *Appliance Manufacturer,* April 1997, 19.

Beatty, Gerry. "Consumer Advertising Expenditures Continue to Climb." *HFN The Weekly Newspaper for the Home Furnishing Network,* 11 October 1999, 87.

———. "Maytag Unveils 2-Oven Range." *HFN The Weekly Newspaper for the Home Furnishing Network,* 29 March 1999, 1.

"Big Business Meets the E-World: Sears? Whirlpool? Now Even These Guys Want to Create E-Businesses. It's Weird, It's Awkward, but It's Also Absolutely Necessary." *Fortune,* 8 November 1999, 88.

Lazich, Robert S. *Market Share Reporter 1996.* Detroit: Gale Research, 1996.

———. *Market Share Reporter 1997.* Detroit: Gale Research, 1997.

Lowe, Linda. "High-Style Kitchen Appliances." *Builder,* May 1997, 260.

"Product Roundup." *HFN The Weekly Newspaper for the Home Furnishing Network,* 4 October 1999, 69.

U.S. Department of Commerce. Census Bureau. *1997 Economic Census.* Washington, DC: GPO, 1999. Available from http://www.census.gov/prod/ec97/97m3352c.pdf.

SIC 3632

HOUSEHOLD REFRIGERATORS AND HOME AND FARM FREEZERS

This category covers establishments primarily engaged in manufacturing household refrigerators and home and farm freezers. Establishments primarily engaged in manufacturing commercial and industrial refrigeration equipment, packaged room coolers, and all refrigeration compression and condenser units are classified in **SIC 3585: Air-Conditioning and Warm Air Heating Equipment and Commercial and Industrial Refrigeration Equipment**, and those manufacturing portable room dehumidifiers are classified in **SIC 3634: Electric Housewares and Fans.**

NAICS CODE(S)

335222 (Household Refrigerator and Home and Farm Freezer Manufacturing)

INDUSTRY SNAPSHOT

Shipment of refrigerators represented the largest share of the appliance industry. The industry was considered one of the most efficient in the country, leaving little room for foreign products to take any significant market share as they had in the car and electronics industries. In addition, prices of American refrigerators and freezers remained reasonable. Several stylish European appliances found a small market in the United States, but they were unlikely to take any significant market share because of their expense.

By the beginning of the 1990s decades of consolidation had left the industry with little room for domestic growth. The market was dominated by a handful of large corporations, and there were no smaller companies left to buy. According to *Appliance* magazine, the industry was mature with 99.9 percent of American households possessing refrigerators and about 40 percent of homes contained a freezer.

Manufacturers achieved growth in a low-growth industry by expanding their profit margin (either by raising prices or cutting production costs and operating expenses) and by increasing sales abroad. The refrigerator industry enjoyed a steady market for replacements and units for new homes. According to *Standard and Poor's* industry survey, brand loyalty was strong in the replacement appliance market, and although percentages shifted from year to year, it was unlikely that any manufacturer would take a serious bite out of another manufacturers' market shares.

In the 1990s U.S. manufacturers were under serious environmental pressure to increase recyclability of refrigerators, reduce energy consumption, and eliminate chlorofluorocarbons as the refrigerant in refrigerators and freezers.

ORGANIZATION AND STRUCTURE

Both refrigerator manufacturers and appliance distributors consolidated in the 1970s and 1980s. As distributors became larger, they wanted more pricing and service concessions. This put pressure on manufacturers to accept smaller profit margins. As a result manufacturers consolidated, which enabled them to produce more efficiently and maintain tight profit margins despite large volume discounts to giant distributors and mega-retailers.

This trend towards selling directly to mass merchandisers hurt many distributors who had exclusive contracts with particular manufacturers. Many smaller distributors were driven out of business because they depended heavily upon a particular manufacturer for most of their inventory, or they depended upon a few large retailers who suddenly decided to deal directly with the manufacturer for most of their sales. Meanwhile, small retailers were concerned that they were too small to have much clout dealing directly with the manufacturer and needed distributors to represent them.

The manufacturer's suppliers—especially the steel industry—improved processes and offered more finished and flexible products in the 1990s which helped increase profits. Gains in such technology as powder painting and custom steel cutting made for faster turn-around and less costly manufacturing.

Home Furnishings Daily indicated that 10 retailers handled more than 44 percent of the appliance market in 1992. The largest was Sears, Roebuck and Co. with 29 percent of the market. The large retailers dealt directly with the manufacturers rather than distributors, to streamline marketing and distribution.

Some manufacturers were also becoming disenchanted with marketing directly to large retailers, finding that brand loyalty and profits were declining, and loyal distributors and dealers were going out of business. Some companies let their dealers electronically tap into the company's production schedules and place direct orders with a guarantee of two-day delivery.

Traditionally, dealers maintained large inventories of products. However this trend was changing, and there was some speculation that retail outlets would become showrooms, and products would be shipped directly from the manufacturer to the customer. In response, manufacturers would have to guarantee delivery of appliances within a two- or three-day period. Manufacturers were also restructuring their sales departments to offer greater exposure of their entire product lines to more distributors and retailers. In the mid-1990s manufacturers had friendly "showrooms" on the Internet designed to speak directly to the consumer. These sites were packed not only with a catalog of merchandise, but also with tips on how to choose an appliance of the most appropriate size, the proper way to move a refrigerator, and other practical advice.

In the mid-1990s about 75 percent of all appliance sales were for replacements due to serious repairs, redecorating, or moving. Market saturation for refrigerators was estimated at 99.9 percent in 1996, which meant that most sales were in the new development and replacement markets. For freezers, saturation was at 41 percent in 1996. Compression refrigerators built in the previous few decades had an average life span of about 16 years, and refrigerators and freezers built in the 1990s had an average life expectancy of 15 and 12 years, respectively.

About 25 percent of appliance sales were linked to new construction of houses and apartment buildings. However, because they were frequently replaced, refrigerators were less dependent than other appliances upon housing starts.

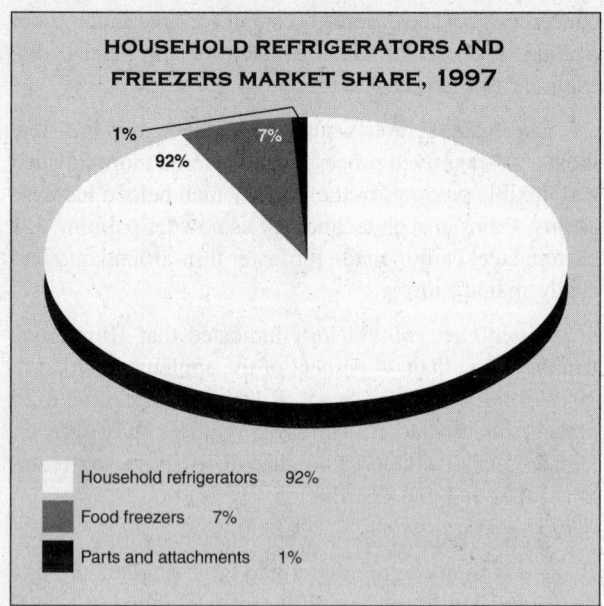

HOUSEHOLD REFRIGERATORS AND FREEZERS MARKET SHARE, 1997

Household refrigerators	92%
Food freezers	7%
Parts and attachments	1%

BACKGROUND AND DEVELOPMENT

The history of electric refrigerators is relatively short. In the 1920s few American households had refrigerators. Ice and ice boxes (insulated boxes or cabinets in which a block of ice was set) were the norm for keeping items cold. The ice could keep for several days if the box was well insulated and well sealed. Every few days, the ice had to be replaced.

During the nineteenth century, many inventors patented mechanical refrigerating machines that could make ice and others that could keep things cool in a large compartment. In the Northeast natural ice was available during the winter months; however, selling manufactured ice became a big business in the southeastern United States by the 1890s, and a few years later in the North as well. Breweries all over the country adopted refrigeration. Cold storage buildings became common in cities, meat packers were using refrigeration units, and even railroad cars and ships provided refrigerated transportation. But home refrigeration would wait several decades because refrigeration required a bulky cooling system that was not practical for home use.

The quest for an effective mechanical refrigeration system for the home was widespread. Large companies as well as individual inventors could see how popular home refrigerators would be. People working to develop a refrigerator were often backed by large manufacturers who knew that if their inventors were successful, the invention would be worth millions of dollars since the market was so vast. Cities in the United States and abroad were expanding, and people lived farther and farther from the places where food was produced. They needed to keep more supplies on hand, but they needed a place to

preserve them. Use of ice boxes was widespread, but a refrigerator would be more convenient.

A home refrigerator needed many qualities that commercial units lacked. The home unit had to be small enough to fit easily into the house. It had to be automatic and not require an operator as the commercial units did. It also had to use safer chemicals than the highly toxic or flammable ones used in commercial units. And the unit had to be affordable, which meant mass-production.

Early in the twentieth century two avenues of development were being pursued—compression technology and absorption technology. Compression required electricity to power a pump called a compressor. Absorption required gas power and did not even need a motor. The first functional household refrigerator, the Domelre, was produced in Chicago in 1912. Six years later, American Nathaniel Wales designed a unit called the Kelvinator, which employed compression technology. The Kelvinator became the first mass-produced home refrigerator. In 1919 General Motors bought a small refrigerator company called Frigidaire, which also made compression refrigerators. By 1920 about 75,000 homes had refrigerators.

Since gas was the most widely used energy source, the absorption refrigerator might have seemed a better choice than compression. Yet dozens of companies were involved in refrigerator development, and the few that had substantial corporate backing were working on compression machines.

General Electric Co. (GE) had been developing commercial and household refrigerators for many years, but it wasn't until 1923 that it put substantial resources into developing the home version. Since refrigerators on the market had not yet been perfected, whoever solved some of the early problems could dominate the market. For one thing, refrigerators had dropped in price but still cost $450 for the most inexpensive model, a great deal of money in a time when most people had annual incomes of less than $2,000. These early compression models used the refrigerants ammonia, sulfur dioxide, or methyl chloride, which could explode and were toxic if leaked. The refrigerators also had a short life since these refrigerants were corrosive.

The first home refrigerators were also noisy and needed servicing every few months. The noisy motor was separate from the cooling box and could be put in the basement or elsewhere, but the separation of the two parts also forced the compressor to work harder to pump the refrigerant to the cooling box in the kitchen.

Considering that government requirements in the 1990s called for refrigerators that would run on less electricity, it is ironic that in the 1920s a compelling reason to pursue compression technology was that it required electricity 24 hours a day and would use a lot of power. The use of electricity was in its infancy, but GE was betting that electricity would become more popular than gas. General Electric was also watching out for the interests of the electric utility companies, their main customers.

In 1927 General Electric began marketing the first refrigerator with a hermetically sealed motor and an attached cooling box. It was called the "Monitor Top," because the motor was in a circular box on top of the cooling compartment. By 1929 the company had sold an astonishing 50,000 Monitor Tops. That same year, GE replaced the wood cabinet with steel and brought out its first all-steel refrigerators. In 1931 GE produced its one millionth Monitor Top refrigerator.

In the 1930s General Motors' Frigidaire company developed the first use of chlorofluorocarbons as a refrigerant. This technology became the standard for decades and essentially eliminated the danger of fire and poisoning. In 1939 GE produced the first refrigerator with a freezer compartment as well as a cooling compartment.

The absorption unit was not completely out of the picture, however. Inventors were still working on improved versions, and once perfected they would have offered many advantages over the compression machines. They were not as noisy, they had few movable parts, and in many places gas was cheaper than electricity. But slowly the companies developing these machines went out of business; they received very little development or promotional capital from the gas companies or other corporations. Between 1926 and 1957 only one large company, Servel, manufactured and marketed absorption refrigerators. By 1940 there were four major manufacturers of compression refrigerators, and each was associated with a large corporation: General Electric, Westinghouse, American Motors' Kelvinator, and General Motors' Frigidaire.

Ice boxes remained common during the 1930s and even into the 1940s, but refrigerators were becoming a large industry by the 1930s, despite the Great Depression. Prices came down with improved mass production, and consumers could also buy the appliance on an installment plan. The industry grew as refrigerator motors and refrigerant systems were made smaller and safer for home use. The refrigerator was constantly being improved, with features such as automatic defrost, ice makers, and redesigned interior shelving.

A similar appliance, the freezer, has not been nearly as successful as the refrigerator. The process for quick-freezing food began to gain popularity during the 1920s, when families bought frozen food to keep in their new freezers. In the 1940s and 1950s freezers and the convenience of frozen food were in their heyday; families

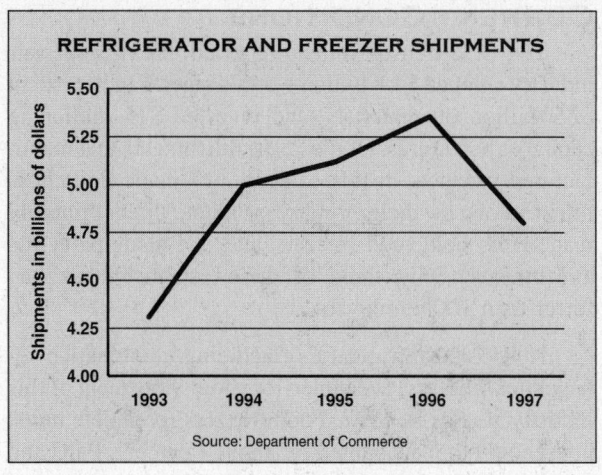

REFRIGERATOR AND FREEZER SHIPMENTS

Shipments in billions of dollars

Source: Department of Commerce

saved money by purchasing meat, frozen vegetables, and other items in large quantities. However, freezers were expensive to run, which offset any savings from bulk purchases of food.

Until the early 1980s, there were 15 to 30 domestic appliance manufacturers. Consolidation whittled them down to five major companies. Some of the most familiar names in U.S. refrigerators and freezers—Frigidaire, Kelvinator, White-Westinghouse, Gibson, and Tappan—were owned by a Swedish company, AB Electrolux. Between 1970 and 1985, Electrolux bought more than 300 companies in 40 countries. In 1987 Electrolux greatly expanded its presence in the United States by acquiring White Consolidated Industries.

Raytheon, an aerospace company, joined the appliance business through its acquisition of Amana in 1965 and produced refrigerators and other products under that established brand name. Amana was a cooperatively owned company run by the Amana Society, a German religious sect that had emigrated to Iowa. The society had begun making refrigerators in 1934. By the 1990s Raytheon also owned the brand names Caloric, Speed Queen, Unimac, and Heubsch.

The top refrigerator in the mid-1990s was Whirlpool's Kenmore (sold by Sears, Roebuck and Co.) with 20.1 percent of the market. It was followed by GE's Profile line with 19.6 percent, Whirlpool's own brand with 11.5 percent, and Amana with 8.5 percent. Other brands with small fractional ratings included Hotpoint, Roper, Maytag, Admiral, and White-Westinghouse.

Among leading freezer brands, according to the May 1996 edition of *Dealerscope,* Tappan held the lead in 1995 in a fragmented market with 5.25 percent, and Amana followed with 4.2 percent. That year, a total of 4.87 million refrigerators and freezers were sold, according to *Appliance* magazine.

CURRENT CONDITIONS

The U.S. Census Bureau reported that in 1997 this industry shipped $4.8 billion worth of merchandise, spent $2.9 billion on materials, and invested $75 million in capital expenditures. Of the 25 establishments that manufactured products in this category, 17 made household refrigerators as their primary product, three primarily made household food freezers, and one made parts and attachments. Only three of these establishments had fewer than 100 employees.

Household refrigerators (including combination refrigerator-freezers) accounted for about 92 percent of this industry's sales in 1997. Food freezers (complete units, household type) accounted for about 7 percent. Parts and attachments for household refrigerators and freezers (excluding compressors, condensing units, and ice making machines) accounted for about 1 percent.

INDUSTRY LEADERS

During most of the 1990s, the U.S. household refrigerator and freezer industry and the appliance industry in general were dominated by five companies: Whirlpool Corp.; General Electric Co. (GE); Maytag Corp; Raytheon; and White Consolidated Industries Inc. (the U.S. subsidiary of Electrolux, which owned Frigidaire, Kelvinator, and other familiar brand names). Most of these companies sold appliances under many brand names that had been around since home refrigeration became feasible in the late 1920s.

In 1997 Raytheon sold its Amana subsidiary to Goodman Holding Company L.P. By 1998 Whirlpool was the nation's leading appliance maker, GE was in second place, and Maytag was third.

In 1998 Whirlpool (Benton Harbor, Michigan) had 59,000 employees and sales of $10.3 billion, up from $8.69 billion in 1996, $6.8 billion in 1991, and $2.4 billion in 1981. It owned the Whirlpool, KitchenAid, Roper, Coolerator, and Speen Queen brand names, and many of its appliances were sold under the Kenmore name through Sears, Roebuck and Co. The company had started out making only washing machines but became a full-line appliance manufacturer in the 1950s and 1960s. At that time it also became the principal supplier of the Sears Kenmore brand. Sears had accounted for about 19 percent of Whirlpool's revenues in 1991.

In 1986 Whirlpool had acquired KitchenAid, a high-end producer of appliances, and in 1991 it also acquired Philips, the second largest appliance company in Europe. Philips also had partners in Eastern Europe, Brazil, Argentina, Mexico, Italy, and India. The Philips acquisition boosted Whirlpool's global presence and made Whirlpool one of the top two appliance makers in the world, along with Electrolux.

In second place, General Electric's GE Appliances subsidiary had 22,000 employees and sales of $5.6 billion in 1998. General Electric, a huge American conglomerate that competed in various industries, had expanded its European presence in the mid-1990s by purchasing a 50 percent share in a British appliance company. It had also made a landmark agreement with Japan's Kojima to distribute products directly through the 160-store Japanese retailer.

Maytag (Newton, Iowa) was in third place in 1998 with 20,595 employees and sales of $4.1 billion. It made refrigerators under the Maytag, Jenn-Air, and Magic Chef brand names. In the early 1980s Maytag had been a small company making top-of-the-line washers and dryers. With the decade of consolidation beginning, Maytag saw that it either had to expand its product line or risk being taken over. By the 1990s Maytag was making refrigerators, freezers, stoves, washers, dryers, microwaves, and even soft-drink vending machines and dollar-bill changers. It had plants in eight states and eight foreign countries. Maytag's acquisition of Hoover had given the company an instant presence overseas. In the United States Hoover was known as a vacuum cleaner company, but overseas it also made refrigerators, washers, dryers, and dishwashers.

In 1998 Amana Appliance (Amana, Iowa) remained one of the leading refrigerator manufacturers with 5,500 employees and estimated sales of $590 million. Frigidaire Refrigerator Products (Greenville, Michigan) had 2,000 employees and sales of $260 million. Sub Zero Freezer Co. (Madison, Wisconsin), a firm known for its innovative household compression refrigerators and freezers, had 500 employees and estimated sales of $75 million.

WORKFORCE

The Census Bureau reported that this industry employed 24,385 people in 1997, including 21,371 production workers who earned an average hourly wage of $15.76. Total payroll for this industry was $794 million.

General Electric employed about 30,000 people at 12 domestic appliance plants in the early 1990s. The company was at the forefront of innovative workplace programs. With its "Work-Out" program, teams of 50 to 60 people, including suppliers, customers, production workers, engineers, and marketing and sales people, met to come up with recommendations to the business staff.

Whirlpool was involving workers with an incentive program at one of its appliance plants. Improved productivity translated into an extra $2,700 in annual pay, raising average annual wages for production workers to $26,400 in 1991. The more productive the plant, the larger the pool of money for the workers to share. The improvements in productivity reduced costs for the company and boosted profits; quality also improved at the plant, with fewer mistakes or bad parts. The plant also opened a new training center. As part of its program to involve production workers more in the total process, the company offered workers the opportunity to see how the components made were used in the finished appliance. Other Whirlpool plants were also achieving higher productivity and lower costs.

Maytag established focus groups to improve its manufacturing productivity. All products in a category were to be produced at one plant; therefore, all refrigerators in all price ranges would be developed in one plant to improve design and efficiency.

AMERICA AND THE WORLD

The leading export markets for U.S. appliances were Canada, Mexico, Taiwan, Germany, and Saudi Arabia. Exports to Canada increased during the 1990s after tariffs were removed on appliances sold to that country.

In 1991 Europe accounted for about a third of Whirlpool's sales and 15 percent of Maytag's sales. In 1996 Whirlpool's European profits fell, but the company posted record earnings in 1997, due largely to stronger markets in North America and Latin America.

GE especially looked overseas in the mid-1990s to increase profits and invest for long-term growth. Since European demands differed from American demands in appliances (European appliances tended to be smaller and more stylish), GE redesigned the distinctive Profile line of appliances in 1996 to appeal to the European eye. In 1996 GE also struck a deal with Japan, allowing GE products to be retailed directly to Japanese consumers. Southeast Asia was a tough market that U.S. makers for the most part had left alone, since it was dominated by three Japanese businesses: Matsushita, Hitachi, and Toshiba.

RESEARCH AND TECHNOLOGY

During the 1990s, Congressional bills called for manufacturers to recycle both packaging and the products themselves. The bills stipulated that new products had to be easier to disassemble for recycling and that some packaging had to be reusable.

In addition, refrigerator and freezer makers faced strict new guidelines from the Department of Energy for 1993. The guidelines required higher efficiency standards, and manufacturers were making small changes to meet the energy-use goals, such as improving insulation, compressors, motors, and door gaskets. Interior dimensions on some machines were to be smaller to allow for thicker walls and doors.

For the typical home of the early 1990s, a frost-free refrigerator or freezer was the second most expensive home appliance to operate besides the water heater. Appliance makers were required to include labels listing an estimate of the annual cost of running each appliance so consumers could compare costs and energy usage.

A typical 15-year old refrigerator consumed about 1,700 kilowatts of electricity, for an average annual cost of $136 based on a cost of eight cents a kilowatt-hour. That meant a consumer would pay five or six times the price of the refrigerator in energy costs over the refrigerator's lifetime. More recent models consumed less than half as much, generally about 700 kilowatts annually, and many state-of-the-art refrigerators consumed 350 to 525 kilowatts. According to the Environmental Protection Agency (EPA), that represented an annual savings for American consumers of half a billion dollars or more in electric bills. This reduction in energy use would in turn reduce the need for coal, oil, and nuclear materials that generate electricity. The EPA estimated that widespread adoption of the new refrigerators would save the country 3 to 6 billion kilowatt-hours a year, which would require from 5 to 10 million barrels of oil to generate. According to utility companies, refrigerators and freezers consumed 20 percent of the electricity used in a home. Development of more efficient refrigerators would even curtail the need for new power plants.

The refrigerator and freezer industry was also under pressure to find an alternative coolant to chlorofluorocarbons (CFCs), which were believed to cause depletion of the ozone layer that protects the planet from dangerous cancer-causing ultraviolet rays. A compression refrigerator works by pumping refrigerant, a liquid chemical, through tubes in the cooling cabinet. The refrigerant evaporates there and pulls heat from the air. The gas is pumped out of the cabinet and into the compressor and condenser where the heat is expelled into the room. The evaporator chemical becomes liquid again and is pumped back into the food area.

Chemical companies as well as refrigerator makers and environmentalists were involved in development of alternative refrigerants. One of the alternative refrigerants suggested was a hydro fluorocarbon (HFC). Use of an alternate substance such as this would allow refrigerator makers to retain the current technology of the vapor-compressor refrigerator. One of the other proposed refrigerants was said to be dangerous because it posed a risk of fire or toxic fumes. Environmentalists claimed that another posed an environmental threat because, although it was not harmful to the ozone layer of the atmosphere, it might contribute to the "greenhouse effect," an atmospheric condition thought to contribute to global warming. Furthermore, because chlorofluorocarbons (CFCs) were also used in refrigerator insulation, several possible replacements would require new liner materials.

Another approach was represented by the work of U.S. physicist Steven L. Garrett, who was developing a thermo-acoustic refrigerator that used sound instead of CFCs to transfer heat. This technology, which was first designed for military satellites, would be less harmful to the environment than any substance in a vapor-compressor refrigerator. Even so, thermo-acoustics would require big changes by manufacturers to retool their facilities or send their production workers back to school to learn a new technology. Alternative refrigerants would not require these changes.

Researchers financed in part by the EPA built demonstration CFC-free refrigerators that were 8 percent to 16 percent more energy-efficient than existing refrigerators cooled by CFCs. These test refrigerators also cooled freezer and refrigerator sections separately instead of using the same air to cool both sections, as traditional models did.

German scientists were working on a refrigerator that used a mixture of propane and butane in place of CFCs. The unit they were developing, however, had no freezer compartment and used more electricity than a typical refrigerator cooled by CFC vapor compression. Italian scientists used the same vapor-compression technology that is found in CFC-refrigerators, but they substituted a hydro fluorocarbon, HFC-134a. The refrigerator had two modules for refrigeration and one for freezing; the modules were made from polystyrene and made recycling and manufacture easier. The power pack was easily removable for recycling or repairs.

FURTHER READING

Business Rankings Annual 1997. Detroit: Gale Research, 1997.

Conley, Thomas P. "Combating the Slow Growth Scenario for Housewares." *Appliance.* January 1997.

Koenig, Peter. "If Europe's Dead, Why Is GE Investing Billions There?" *Fortune.* 9 September 1996.

Lazich, Robert S., ed. *Market Share Reporter.* Detroit: Gale Research, 1997.

Le Blanc, Jenny. "1997: Slow Growth Ahead." *Appliance,* January 1997.

"The Man Who Fixed Maytag: Len Hadley has Refocused the Appliance Maker and Cut Overseas Operations." *Money,* November 1998.

Milano, Mike, and Gerry Beatty. "Sub-Zero: A Chilling Effect." *HFN, The Weekly Newspaper for the Home Furnishings Network,* 14 June 1999.

"Portrait of the U.S. Appliance Industry." *Appliance,* September 1996.

"Process and Product Design." *Appliance,* September 1996.

U.S. Department of Commerce. Census Bureau. *1997 Economic Census.* Washington, DC: GPO, 1999. Available from http://www.census.gov.

HOUSEHOLD LAUNDRY EQUIPMENT

This classification covers establishments primarily engaged in manufacturing laundry equipment, such as washing machines, dryers, and ironers, for household use, including coin-operated equipment. Establishments primarily engaged in manufacturing commercial laundry equipment are classified in **SIC 3582: Commercial Laundry, Drycleaning, and Pressing Machines,** while those manufacturing portable electric irons are classified in **SIC 3634: Electric Housewares and Fans.**

NAICS CODE(S)

335224 (Household Laundry Equipment Manufacturing)

INDUSTRY SNAPSHOT

Although mechanical washing contraptions existed before the start of the twentieth century, only since the 1950s has gas and electric-powered laundry equipment achieved widespread use. By the early 1990s, over 70 percent of all U.S. homes had both a washer and a dryer. In 1997, there were 17 establishments in this industry. Whirlpool Corporation, General Electric Appliances, and Maytag Corporation led the industry in 1999.

In 1996, 6.92 million washers and 5.24 million dryers (both electric and gas) were shipped. Laundry equipment was the second largest home appliance market, following refrigeration. In 1997, shipments totaled nearly $3.6 billion.

ORGANIZATION AND STRUCTURE

Household laundry equipment represented about 17 percent of the overall U.S. household appliance industry in the 1990s. Although ironers and mangles, or pressing machines, account for a small portion of industry sales, washers and dryers made up the lion's share of production.

Nearly 80 percent of all household laundry equipment is purchased by individuals for home use. An additional 6 percent of industry output is consumed by laundromats, dry cleaners, and other services that use domestic laundry equipment. The remainder of the U.S. market is comprised of state, local, and federal government institutions, such as the armed forces and prisons.

The market for first-time purchasers of washers and dryers is relatively saturated. As a result, the industry is highly dependent upon sales of replacement appliances. Most laundry equipment has a life span of 10 to 12 years. However, several factors may influence the replacement rate of washers and dryers. An increase in sales of existing homes, for example, boosts replacements because new occupants are more likely to buy new appliances. Likewise, heightened remodeling activity also spurs replacements.

Changes in home trends may also spawn premature replacements. For instance, as laundry equipment was increasingly moved out of basements and closer to living areas in the 1980s, the need for quieter and more attractive washers and dryers caused an influx of consumers to upgrade. Increases in repair costs in relation to price of new units can also shorten replacement cycles. Finally, because appliances are discretionary purchases that can be postponed, industry revenues are closely tied to the health of the overall economy.

Types of Products. The three major household laundry product categories were electric washing machines, electric dryers, and gas dryers. Washers are of two types: top-load and front-load. Top-load washers have an agitator in the center of the wash tub that thrashes the water and the fabric. Front-load, or tumble-type, washers lift and drop the laundry into the wash water as the tub spins. Both washer types wring out excess water by spinning.

Although many top-loading machines are easier to access, tumble-type washers require less water and detergent to clean a load of laundry. Both types of washers are differentiated primarily by their features, which include washing actions, capacity, water temperature combinations, water levels, and noise levels. Most top-load washers range in price from $400 to $550, while front-load machines usually cost an additional $100.

Dryers are basically revolving drums which tumble clothes through heated air. Different features and product quality result in a price range of $400 to $800. More expensive dryers offer as many as three different heating cycles, extended tumble cycles, wrinkle-remove features, and sturdier construction, such as porcelain coated drums and tops. Although gas dryers are typically more expensive to purchase initially, they are often significantly cheaper to operate.

BACKGROUND AND DEVELOPMENT

Numerous washer and dryer devices, ranging from washboards to hand-cranked wringers, were used to clean laundry prior to the twentieth century. The first electric washing machine was introduced in 1907 by the Maytag Company. But not until after World War II, during the post-war U.S. economic expansion, did electric washing machines, and later dryers, realize mainstream acceptance. As the demand for all types of appliances proliferated during the 1950s, 1960s, and 1970s, the laundry equipment industry grew rapidly. The introduction of fully automatic washers and dryers in the mid-1960s rocketed the industry to prominence during the following decade, as washers and dryers became standard household amenities.

By the early 1980s the laundry equipment industry was shipping over $2 billion worth of goods annually and employing over 16,000 workers. Well over 50 percent of U.S. households had both a washer and a dryer. Strong home construction and appliance replacement markets, moreover, allowed producers to enjoy solid gains throughout the 1980s. Indeed, industry revenues grew at an average annual rate of over five percent between 1982 and 1990, despite an economic slowdown in the late 1980s. Sales surged past $3.2 billion in 1990, stagnated in 1991, and grew about 3 percent in 1992.

An important dynamic which characterized the laundry equipment industry during the 1980s was consolidation. As the vigorous growth of the late 1960s, 1970s, and early 1980s waned, producers tried to achieve economies of scale though merger and acquisition. By the end of the 1980s only 16 competitors remained, compared to over 25 at the start of the decade. In fact, the top two companies controlled nearly 70 percent of the market, and the top four manufacturers accounted for about 80 percent of sales. Antitrust laws enacted during the 1980s succeeded in slowing the rate of consolidation by the early 1990s.

Positive demographic trends and healthy housing starts helped boost household laundry equipment sales by more than 50 percent between 1980 and 1990. Although industry participants suffered the effects of recessed construction markets and economic malaise in the early 1990s, sales were rebounding going into the mid-1990s and analysts predicted that shipments would continue to grow at a rate of 1 percent to 3 percent through the end of the decade. By 1997, shipments were valued at $3.7 billion.

To boost sales and profits in 1994, washer and dryer manufacturers were striving to develop new and better appliances which would spur replacement sales, while also scrambling to comply with new federal environmental regulations. In addition, most were seeking growth outside the United States in regions such as Asia and Mexico.

Manufacturers were able to boost unit shipments faster than revenues and retain profit growth through productivity gains. Indeed, hefty capital investments in automation and information systems during the 1980s helped the appliance industry become one of the most efficient businesses in the United States. As the value of washer and dryer shipments grew 50 percent during the 1980s, unit prices remained stable in real dollars and unit volume soared. Despite a huge surge in real output, industry employment actually declined slightly during the decade. Efficiency gains contributed to the industry's dominance of the domestic market, of which it controlled a whopping 85 percent.

In addition to short term economic factors and production efficiencies, laundry equipment manufacturers in the mid-1990s also benefited from long-term demographic factors and buying patterns. Importantly, the baby boom generation, aged 35 to 54 years, was becoming wealthier and was investing a greater share of its income in home-related goods. Because this important market segment was also spending an increasing amount of time working and having children, analysts expected boomers to begin spending a greater proportion of their income on conveniences, such as washers and dryers.

Augmenting renewed sales were new distribution and customer service programs, which manufacturers were initiating. Many producers, for example, were strengthening their support for retailers with training and service programs. Likewise, customer relationship initiatives were helping manufacturers cultivate consumer loyalty. Whirlpool, for example, announced early in 1994 that it was going to replace its system of independent distributors with factory-direct distribution.

Laundry industry sales grew about 2 percent per year from 1990 to 1997. Unit volume grew annually at a steady 2 to 3 percent. Increased sales were largely the result of an increase in housing starts and escalating consumer expenditures following the recession. The replacement market for washers and dryers was a constant; for example, in 1996, 3.4 million washing machines were replaced.

CURRENT CONDITIONS

Federal Regulation. New U.S. Department of Energy Standards (DOE) initiatives, which took effect in May of 1994, required machine makers to lower rinse-water temperatures, reduce water consumption, and install energy-efficient motors and insulation. In a 1996 study conducted by a Maytag R&D team, it was discovered that a high-efficiency washer can save from 3,500 to 6,000 gallons of water per household per year. In the mid-1990s, manufacturers strove to meet the challenge. They started using solid concrete weights in washers to steady the machine during the spin cycle. Previously, energy-intensive iron casts weighted laundry machines. New washers also offered wash programming, to allow the user to program the washing machine to start the wash during nonpeak electric hours. New methods also included recycling the dirty wash water into clean rinse water, increasing the use of enzymatic detergents and reducing foaming detergents, and spray rinse cycles instead of deep rinse.

Manufacturers were also under pressure to increase the recyclability of their machines. Two Congressional bills that failed to pass in 1992 would have mandated product material content, recycling rates, and packaging. In anticipation of new laws, some producers were striving to improve the recyclability of their machines by making them out of components that could be recovered, restored, and reused.

Future Growth. Besides baby-boom patterns, overall U.S. household formations rose during the 1990s. This resulted in steady growth of first-time appliance buyers. Furthermore, because a large percentage of existing washers and dryers were purchased in the early 1980s, some observers expected replacement sales to increase in the latter part of the 1990s as old machines wear. The industry was also expected to benefit from low interest rates, a reduction in inventories in 1994, more strategic inventory management in the future, and export growth. Greater demand for compact washers and dryers that suit smaller living spaces will offer a small, high-growth niche. In 1996 *Appliance* magazine cited five technologies that would help define the laundry manufacturer's path to the millennium: increasing water extraction to improve clothes care; using low-sudsing detergents and creating technologies that use those kinds of detergents effectively; faster spin cycles; and electronic sensing and process of the wash.

INDUSTRY LEADERS

Whirlpool overtook General Electric in 1993 to become the largest appliance manufacturer, with 1999 revenues of $10 billion and employment of 59,000. Leading edge production techniques and improved product quality helped Whirlpool achieve a record $205 million profit in 1992 from $6.3 billion in sales. After realizing growth of 14 percent annually during the 1980s, Whirlpool was concentrating on global expansion in the 1990s, and was investing heavily in Asian and European markets. General Electric Appliances came in second in the industry, with 1998 sales of $5 billion and 50,000 employees.

Maytag Corporation is credited with giving birth to the industry, and has a proven reputation for supplying high quality washers and dryers. Maytag began by selling farm equipment, but invented electric laundry machines in the early 1900s. In 1966 Maytag introduced fully automatic washers, and in 1976 brought out a complimentary line of dryers. It maintained a focused product line until the 1980s, when it acquired Hardwick Stove in 1981, Jenn-Air in 1982, and Magic Chef in 1986. In an effort to expand its overseas operations, Maytag formed a strategic alliance with Germany's Bosch-Siemens in 1993. Maytag and Siemens shared design and process technologies. Maytag's total sales in 1999 were $4.3 billion, and total employment exceeded 20,000.

WORKFORCE

Although the top four laundry equipment producers expected to increase production, many analysts expected industry employment in the United States to decline. Heightened campaigns for greater productivity, the likely movement of some manufacturing activities to Mexico, and continued management restructuring may diminish opportunities for workers in the industry.

In 1999, 18,400 workers were employed by this industry. Assemblers and fabricator positions, which accounted for about 40 percent of the entire workforce, will plummet by as much as 37 percent between 1990 and 2005, according to the Bureau of Labor Statistics. Other blue-collar jobs in this industry will drop by 15 percent to 50 percent. Management and support opportunities are expected to decline as well. In fact, only jobs for sales and marketing workers were expected to increase. The average wage for production workers in 1999 was $13.39 per hour.

AMERICA AND THE WORLD

U.S. washer and dryer makers supplied about 30 percent of global demand going in the 1990s. Although they exported less than 10 percent of total production, domestic producers were avidly seeking to capture a greater share of the world export market. Overall appliance exports grew, continuing a trend started in the 1980s. The leading foreign markets were Canada, Mexico, Taiwan, Germany, and Saudi Arabia.

In the early 1990s a weak U.S. dollar boosted exports, particularly to Europe and Japan. In addition, exports to Mexico grew a healthy 18 percent, though imports from that country soared an estimated 40 percent as U.S.-Mexican joint ventures proliferated. While U.S. producers were benefitting from cheap Mexican labor, low-cost appliance manufacturers in other emerging regions, especially in Asia, posed a threat to future U.S. export growth.

Whirlpool, which derived about one-third of its revenues from overseas sales, had been the most successful U.S. exporter. It maintained substantial interests in South American countries, such as Brazil and Argentina, and was working hard at penetrating the European market. Maytag also advanced in Europe in the 1990s, and garnered about 15 percent of its revenues from foreign operations. U.S. manufacturers have enjoyed less success in the Asian arena, which was dominated by three major Japanese appliance conglomerates.

Although U.S. washer and dryer makers held a stranglehold on domestic markets, their dominance was expected to wane in the wake of increased imports from Mexico. Passage of the North American Free Trade Agreement (NAFTA) in 1994 was expected to accelerate the movement of production facilities across U.S. borders—a trend which analysts expected would increase corporate earnings and reduce domestic employment and payrolls.

RESEARCH AND TECHNOLOGY

Due to increased environmental concern, innovation from the late 1990s into the early part of the next century was expected to focus on ''greener'' products and disposal methods. Designed to cut electricity, water, and gas usage, laundry products were incorporating greater technology in the manufacturing process.

Capital investments during the mid-1990s were used to develop more efficient production and distribution methods and to achieve compliance with environmental regulations and pressures. They were also used to create better and less-expensive products. For example, control software that was being incorporated into machines optimized wash and dry cycles for different types of laundry, adjusted temperature and water levels during a cycle, and allowed machines to talk to users. These microprocessors also made possible many advanced features, such as self-diagnostic systems, delayed-start timers, and touch controls with cycle programming. New features were designed to maximize energy efficiency—an improvement which would expedite replacement sales.

One of the most advanced innovations under development in the 1990s involved the study of washing machines that can use ''fuzzy-logic.'' In 1993 South Korea's Goldstar Co. claimed to have invented the first consumer product that exploited the chaos theory, which holds that there are identifiable tendencies of movement amid the apparent randomness of patterns. Goldstar analyzed the movements of water in a standard washing machine, identified those that produced cleaner and less-tangled clothes, and then designed a washing machine that mimicked the movements. Whirlpool was integrating similar technology into some of its models. In the mid-1990s, machines appeared that could use Dialogic, a new term coined by Merloni Elttrodomestici, an Italian manufacturer. The machine only needs to be loaded, and told what is the most delicate garment in the wash. It then evaluates other wash factors to create the ''perfect'' wash—lowest possible noise, cleanest rinse, appropriate detergent, and appropriate water usage. ''Smart'' dryers sense the clothes' dampness, when to shut off, and what temperatures at which to dry. In 1999, laundry appliances were starting to include digital signal processors (DSP) to select wash programs and monitor the machines.

Following the trend toward electronic business, companies like Whirlpool Corporation were looking into so-called e-business in 1999. Whirlpool, which sells to retailers rather than directly to customers, hoped to work more with individual consumers via the Internet.

FURTHER READING

Ashley, Steven. ''Energy-Efficient Appliances.'' *Mechanical Engineering—CIME*. March 1998.

''Big Business Meets the E-world.'' *Forbes*. November 8, 1999.

Bureau of the Census. *Economic Census 1997*, 2000. Available from http://www.census.gov.

Bureau of Labor Statistics. *Employment Statistics,* 2000. Available from http://www.bls.gov.

Conley, Thomas P. "Combating the Slow Growth Scenario for Housewares." *Appliance.* January 1997, p. 68.

Darnay, Arsen J., ed. *Manufacturing USA.* Detroit: Gale Research, 1996.

General Electric Company. *1995 Annual Report.* Fairfield, CT, 1996. Available from http://www.ge.com/annual95/ibb6a18 .htm.

Hoover's Company Capsules. *Hoover's Online,* 2000. Available from http://www.hoovers.com.

LaPat, Kimberly L. "Clothes Encounters." *Appliance.* September 1996.

Le Blanc, Jenny. "1997: Slow Growth Ahead." *Appliance.* January 1997, 38.

Market Share Reporter. Detroit: Gale Research, 1997.

Murray, Aengus. "DSP Motor Control Boosts Efficiency in Home Appliances." *Electronic Design.* 25 May 1998.

"Portrait of the U.S. Appliance Industry." *Appliance.* September 1996.

"Whirlpool Earnings Rise 21 Percent." *Reuters,* 16 April 1997.

SIC 3634

ELECTRIC HOUSEWARES AND FANS

This category includes establishments primarily engaged in manufacturing electric housewares for heating, cooking, and other purposes; and electric household fans, except attic fans. Important products of this industry include household-type ventilation and exhaust fans; portable household cooking appliances, except convection and microwave ovens; electric space heaters; electrically heated bed coverings; electric scissors; and portable humidifiers and dehumidifiers. Establishments primarily engaged in manufacturing attic fans and industrial and commercial exhaust and ventilation fans are classified in **SIC 3564: Industrial and Commercial Fans and Blowers and Air Purification Equipment;** and those manufacturing room air-conditioners and humidifying and dehumidifying equipment, except portable, are classified in **SIC 3585: Air-Conditioning and Warm Air Heating Equipment and Commercial and Industrial Refrigeration Equipment.**

NAICS CODE(S)

335211 (Electric Houseware and Fan Manufacturing)
333414 (Heating Equipment (except Electric and Warm Air Furnaces) Manufacturing)

INDUSTRY SNAPSHOT

Electric housewares and fans comprise a major portion of the widely diverse products of the general housewares category, ranking third in shipments—refrigeration is first and laundry equipment second. In 1997 the industry shipped an estimated 16 billion units, totaling $3 billion worth of product, and employed 20,000 workers. Average earnings for production workers in the industry in 1998 were $12.43 per hour, according to U.S. Census Bureau figures. Like the other sectors of the housewares industry, the economic success of this industry is tied to the health of the housing industry and to general consumer confidence levels.

By the 1990s little product was sold directly from the manufacturer to the consumer. Instead, manufacturers sold to mass distribution networks on a wholesale basis, using account representatives who not only knew the company's product line but also the best way to market the products. These account representatives replaced the door-to-door salesmen employed during the industry's early years. At first, these sales representatives were company employees working directly for the manufacturing firm but, in the early 1990s, some firms started to contract out the sales function to independent marketing firms that specialized in product promotion.

Manufacturers engaged in national advertising and promotion campaigns, headlining the product and directing customers to major retail chains. One very successful advertising medium for the industry was the infomercial. Manufacturers discovered that by packaging advertising material as a television talk show and featuring celebrity guest appearances, they could capture consumer attention and dramatically raise awareness of new products. Consumers seemed to like the option of getting detailed information on a product without the pressure of dealing directly with a salesperson. Infomercials were used to target specific television audiences as a direct sales pitch or to supplement national advertising campaigns. They also appeared in the stores as part of point-of-purchase displays.

In the late 1990s, manufacturers developed extensive Internet sites primarily to market to the Generation-X audience. Sites like Sunbeam's offered a virtual home that the cyberconsumer could tour, "touching" and eliciting information about a variety of products. Another example is the InterCenter Company, which opened an Internet shopping center that allowed consumers to cybershop for everything from skillets to blenders and gourmet coffee supplies.

BACKGROUND AND DEVELOPMENT

Housewares evolved with the changing needs of the modernizing kitchen and the growing demand for more efficient, less labor-intensive work spaces and appliances.

In *The Housewares Story: A History of the American Housewares Industry,* Earl Lifshey described the transition from wasteful disorder to luxurious convenience. An important part of this progress was the advent of the first electric houseware, the electric iron. The first iron patent was issued on June 6, 1882, but the power needed to run it was not available until 1890. Power generating companies had to first be convinced to keep generators on during the day. A more successful iron followed in 1905 when Earl Richardson, an electric company plant supervisor and meter reader, developed the first iron with the heating element concentrated at the point. He marketed the new concept, developed with input from homemakers, under the brand name "Hotpoint."

Many of the early housewares designs met with manufacturer resistance. What the inventors needed was a marketing network, and the most logical one was the power companies themselves. Inventors would give some of their products away to homeowners for them to try out the products; then the inventors took these field test results to the utilities as proof of the existence of a market and the product's quality. Eventually, utilities realized the market potential of electric housewares and bought into the concept of load building as a way to increase profitability. They began offering appliances directly to homeowners, allowing them to finance their purchases through their utility bills.

Some major electric appliance developments were Landers, Frary & Clark's 1908 introduction of the "universal" coffee Percolator; General Electric's and Westinghouse's 1909 marketing of the first electric toaster; Westinghouse's first electric frying pan in 1911; Landers, Frary & Clark's 1918 introduction of an electric waffle iron that plugged into a light socket; and A. F. Dormeyer's 1927 introduction of an electric household beater that featured a detachable motor for cleaning purposes.

The proliferation of products in the industry prompted retailers to consider the future of electric appliances. The first to adopt a marketing strategy to promote them was Wanamaker's in New York. In 1906 it opened its "Electro-Domestic Science" exposition. The department store placed the display in its basement—the poorly-lit, badly-ventilated, unevenly-heated space that had become associated with housewares. However, it was not long before the housewares department found itself displaced upwards by the "bargain basement" concept and into the mainstream of department store marketing. Other marketers, such as hardware and drug stores and discount and wholesale outlets, quickly entered the arena, but with the poor transportation facilities of the day, they serviced essentially local and somewhat isolated markets. To grow into a mass production industry, electric housewares needed a mass distribution system. The "drummer" or traveling salesman, so named because of the huge drums of product he carried around, could only begin to tap the potential of this market.

The mail order catalog was already a success by the turn of the nineteenth century. Mail order companies provided an excellent alternative to traveling salesmen because they bought large volumes of goods cheaply and distributed them by means of the mail system. By 1972, mail order accounted for $261 million worth of the retail sale of general housewares.

During the mid- to late 1980s, many long-time industry giants were beginning to falter or fail. In 1985 the biggest name in the industry, General Electric Company, sold its housewares division to The Black & Decker Corporation. That was only one of many deals throughout the 1980s that rearranged the list of major players in the industry. Much of the activity was driven by a shift from traditional mass production and inventory systems to more time-sensitive "just-in-time" production. Some poorly capitalized corporations could not handle the erratic production schedules of the latter method to provide reliable product delivery. The result was a concentration of production in fewer, larger companies using modern production techniques. Between 1972 and 1987 the number of establishments manufacturing electric housewares dropped from 299 to 230. At the same time, automation and more efficient production techniques reduced the number of production workers from 41,000 to 19,300.

In 1988 the leading firm in the electric housewares industry, Allegheny International (AI), filed for Chapter 11 bankruptcy and began a long series of maneuvers to recapitalize. At one point, AI accepted an offer from Black and Decker that would have given that company 63 percent of the iron market, 59 percent of hand-held mixers, and almost 40 percent of food processors. That seemed to be too much concentration for the industry, and a campaign of determined opposition scuttled the deal. AI eventually emerged from Chapter 11 in 1990 as Sunbeam-Oster Corp. and in 1996 achieved stature as the most profitable publicly held appliance manufacturer— ahead of even such behemoths as Whirlpool and Black & Decker.

As the economy began to pick up in the early 1990s, consumer confidence buoyed industry production, but the consolidation trend continued. By 1992 three of the largest firms—the revitalized Sunbeam-Oster Inc., Rival Co., and Toastmaster Inc.—had each successfully floated large initial public offerings and intended to spend at least some of that capital on corporate acquisitions. They targeted firms with less than $10 million in sales, since those companies would be having difficulty meeting the increasingly demanding shipment requirements of the major retailing chains. Some of the $299 million raised was to be used to erase debt incurred during the 1980s and some was earmarked for new product development.

New product may have been the real driving force of the electric housewares industry in the early 1990s. At this time baby boomers began to cocoon, retreating into their homes and looking for ways to optimize comfort and style. Sunbeam estimated that 24 percent of its 1992 sales came from products introduced for the first time within the preceding four years.

One area that came of age in the 1990s was the fan portion of the electric housewares industry. The Vornado fan, with its modernistic styling and quiet but high-volume air moving capabilities, revitalized the domestic circulation fan business for many retailers. At the same time, the ceiling fan, most popular in the southern United States, changed from the functional, low-priced favorite of the mass merchandiser to an up-scale designer product. Style and color (as well as quiet, efficient, and variable operation) became important selling features. Sixty percent of the 17 million fans sold in 1996 included some type of light fixture, and many of those were of the chandelier style, incorporating French glass, lead cut crystal, and solid Italian brass.

In 1996 *Appliance* magazine analyzed manufacturers of blenders, can openers, coffee makers, food processors, hand mixers, irons, toaster ovens, and toasters to determine market share rankings of small household appliance manufacturers. Hamilton Beach/Proctor-Silex held 27.9 percent of the market; Black and Decker, 18.5 percent; Oster/Sunbeam, 9.2 percent; and the rest of the market was divided between Toastmaster, Rival, HPA/Betty Crocker, Braun, and others.

CURRENT CONDITIONS

According to the U.S. Census Bureau, in 1997 the value of shipments for electric fans decreased 8 percent to $486.8 million, compared to 1996 shipments totaling $527.3 million. The value of small household appliance shipments in 1997 totaled $1.8 billion, an increase of 5.8 percent over the 1996 total of $1.7 billion.

Appliance color and shape became important criteria as consumers demanded innovation in form as well as function. Other important appliance features were multiple functions (e.g., a handheld mixer with kneading, whisking, and drink-blending attachments), smaller size, and speed. Such products included the "Robochef," which used microprocessor technology to computerize food preparation from raw ingredients to finished meal; West Bend's "Chip Factory," which automatically prepared and dispensed customized potato chips for the home consumer; and completely automatic bread makers that also prepared dough for cookies, pies, and pasta.

FURTHER READING

"Healthy Home Relations." *Appliance,* 1997. Available from http://www.appliance.com/app/cover.story.

Jiambalvo, John R. "The Skinny On Small Appliances." *Appliance,* January 1997.

Lifshey, Earl. *The Housewares Story: A History of the American Housewares Industry.* Chicago: National Housewares Manufacturers Association, 1973.

Magid, Lawrence J. "Home, Sweet, Automated Home." *Los Angeles Times Syndicate,* 1997. Available from http://www.msnbc.com/news/6966.asp.

"A Portrait of the U.S. Appliance Industry." *Appliance,* September 1996.

Rees, Clifford, Jr. "Good Year to Follow Great Leap Forward." *Appliance,* January 1997.

"Small Electric Appliances." *InterCenter Company Web Site,* 1997. Available from http://www.intercenter.com.

"Sunbeam Acquires Three Companies." *Appliance,* March 1998. Available from http://www.appliancemagazine.com.

U.S. Census Bureau. *Current Industrial Report Manufacturing Profiles 1997.* Washington, D.C.: GPO, August 1999. Available from http://www.census.gov.

SIC 3635

HOUSEHOLD VACUUM CLEANERS

This classification covers establishments primarily engaged in manufacturing vacuum cleaners for household use. Establishments primarily engaged in manufacturing vacuum cleaners for industrial use are classified in **SIC 3589: Service Industry Machinery, Not Elsewhere Classified.** Establishments primarily engaged in installation of central vacuum cleaner systems are classified in **SIC 1796: Installation or Erection of Building Equipment, Not Elsewhere Classified.**

NAICS CODE(S)

335212 (Household Vacuum Cleaner Manufacturing)

Vacuums remove 80 percent of soil from carpet, making them essential for carpet care. Vacuums are more effective if they have a rotating brush, beater bar, and powerful suction capabilities. Even with these features, they must be adjusted to carpet height, bags must be changed when full, and belts and brushes must be maintained.

The four primary categories of household vacuums are upright, canister, stick, and handheld models. The upright vacuum cleaner, which was the first vacuum to gain widespread acceptance in the United States, descended from the manual carpet sweeper. Uprights come in two styles: those with a vertically mounted soft collector bag and those with an exterior plastic shell that contains the bag. Because they have a rotating brush, uprights are usually better at cleaning carpets. Their limited suction makes them less efficient at cleaning upholstery and bare surfaces, however. According to the U.S. Census Bureau, the value of shipments for household vacuum cleaners (including parts and attachments) was $2.34 billion in 1996, up from 1992 totals of $1.81 billion.

Canister vacuums have more suction and are easier to use on stairs. But they are generally difficult to store, have a small collector bag, and require the user to pull the canister along the floor behind the nozzle. About 1.8 million canister vacuums were shipped in 1993, down from more than 2.0 million in 1992. *Appliance* magazine predicted this downward trend would continue.

Stick vacuums are similar to upright cleaners, but they usually lack a rotating brush and are less adept at cleaning than either canister or uprights. Stick vacuums, though, are usually lightweight, easy to store, and inexpensive. About 1.6 million stick vacuums were sold by U.S. producers in 1993, up from 1.5 million in 1992.

The two types of handheld vacuums are electric and rechargeable. About 3.3 million electric and nearly 2.2 million rechargeable units were shipped in 1993, according to *Appliance*. These figures mark a slippage in shipments from 1992, when 3.6 million electric and 2.7 million rechargeable units were sold.

Following solid industry growth during the 1960s and 1970s, the household vacuum cleaner industry experienced steady expansion during the 1980s. Prodded by new product introductions and positive demographic trends, vacuum cleaner sales rocketed from $775 million in 1982 to $1.87 billion in 1990, reflecting an average annual growth rate of more than 10 percent. Stick and handheld vacuums were the fastest-growing product segments during this period. An economic recession, however, sent industry revenues tumbling below $1.7 billion in the early 1990s. The industry recovered entering the mid-1990s, which buoyed earnings and promised to revive struggling manufacturers. Overall unit shipments were forecast by some observers to rise as much as 4 percent in 1994, with stick and upright vacuums leading industry growth. According to *Appliance* January 1998, the number of full-size units sold in 1997 was expected to be over 15 million, and experts predicted sales of over 16 million units in 1998. A 3 to 5 percent increase for industry unit sales of full-size portable vacuums was expected for 1999, according to the Vacuum Cleaner Manufacturers Association *Appliance* magazine industry forecast for 1999.

Appliance manufacturers in general found that 1995 sales were not as spectacular as they had expected, but 1996 was estimated to be healthy. The 1997 economy was expected to be relatively stable, so sales were expected to be stable also; that year, the value of shipments was over $2.3 billion. The number of establishments also increased from 40 in 1993 to about 45 in 1997.

In the mid-1990s the largest vacuum manufacturer was the subsidiary Hoover Co., of Ohio, generating sales of an estimated $1.5 billion and employing over 10,000 workers. According to the December 1998 issue of *Appliance* magazine, Hoover expanded its El Paso, Texas plant in 1997 with a $47 million capital investment, aiding production of its Wind Tunnel upright vacuum and opening a major distribution center—doubling the size of the plant and creating 220 new jobs. Other industry leaders included Eureka Co., of Illinois, and Kirby Co., of Ohio. Ohio also had the greatest number of establishments in the United States.

In the mid-1990s, vacuum makers were trying to boost sales with new high-tech products. In order to make filtration systems more desirable, vacuum manufacturers wanted consumers to be alerted to the damage caused by fine dusts. Eureka, for example, introduced a line of environmentally friendly vacuums that were designed to filter out 99 percent of the dust and dirt that entered the vacuum. Philips Home Products Corp. brought out Blue Magic, a high-tech vacuum with a turbo-compressor that operated by fuzzy logic. Blue Magic also had a silencing mechanism and could be operated with a remote control. Another technological highlight included new polymers, which allowed vacuum manufacturers to reduce unit costs and weight and improve quality.

Trying to guage consumer interest in the concept of automatic vacuums at the 1999 International Housewares Show, Eureka unveiled a prototype robotic vacuum cleaner, according to *Appliance*, January 1999. With cordless operation, sonar, and an onboard microprocessor to detect and avoid obstacles, the robot vac could operate for one hour before needing to be recharged.

FURTHER READING

"1999: The New Optimism." *Appliance,* Available from http://www.appliancemagazine.com/mm/focus/html/industry_forecasts_p1.html.

Darnay, Arsen J., ed. *Manufacturing USA.* 5th ed. Detroit: Gale Research, 1996.

"Eureka Unveils Robot Vacuum." *Appliance,* January 1999. Available from http://www.appliancemagazine.com/mm/indup/html/01-99.html.

Gornick, Tina. "Emphasis on Housewares." *Appliance,* January 1998. Available from http://www.appliancemagazine.com/mm/focus98/html/forecasts_01-98_p_5.html.

Hepworth Air Filtration. "Effective Filtration for Domestic and Industrial Cleaners." Available from http://www.hepair.com/nf_ap_v.html.

"Hoover Wins Star Award." *Appliance,* December 1998. Available from http://www.appliancemagazine.com/mm/indup/html/12-98.html.

Remich, Norman C., Jr. "Clean Comfort." *Appliance Manufacturer,* June 1993.

Somheil, Timothy. "1994: The Key Word Is Improvement." *Appliance*, January 1994.

U.S. Census Bureau. *Value of Shipments for Product Classes: 1992 to 1996.* Available from http://www.census.gov/prod/3/98pubs/m96-as2.pdf.

SIC 3639

HOUSEHOLD APPLIANCES, NOT ELSEWHERE CLASSIFIED

This industry includes establishments primarily engaged in manufacturing household appliances, not elsewhere classified, such as water heaters, dishwashers, food waste disposal units, and household sewing machines. Major product groups include water heaters, dishwashers, food disposers, trash compactors, floor waxers, and sewing machines. Laundry equipment, refrigerators, and other major household goods are classified separately, as are commercial appliances.

NAICS CODE(S)

335212 (Household Vacuum Cleaner Manufacturing)
333298 (All Other Industrial Machinery Manufacturing)
335228 (Other Household Appliance Manufacturing)

INDUSTRY SNAPSHOT

A uniquely American innovation, electric and gas household appliances became commonplace in U.S. homes during the postwar economic expansion of the 1950s, 1960s, and 1970s. By the early 1980s, miscellaneous appliance makers in the United States were shipping about $1.5 billion worth of goods each year and employing a work force of more than 14,000. Continued rapid growth in the 1980s pushed industry sales past $3.2 billion by the early 1990s. In the late 1990s, industry shipments were valued at $3.7 billion. In 1997, combined sales were approximately $2.9 billion for just the water heater, dishwashing machine, floor-care machine, food waste disposal, and household trash compactor industry segments.

Although limited due to manufacturing consolidation, intense competition, and market maturity, growth in this industry seems assured as the economy stays strong and demographics change.

ORGANIZATION AND STRUCTURE

The largest segment of this household appliances category is water heater manufacturing, which accounts for roughly 40 percent of industry sales. Dishwashers, the second largest product category, are trailed by trash com-

pactors, disposers, floor waxers, sewing machines, and related supplies and attachments.

Appliance sales are driven primarily by three factors: replacement sales; product market penetration, particularly in the case of completely new appliances; and new construction, which generates demand by builders that perform first-time installations. Because most product categories have achieved almost full market penetration, miscellaneous appliance sales are highly dependent upon replacement sales and new construction, and are closely linked to housing starts and economic growth.

Pricing is very competitive. According to Standard & Poor's, "To gain or simply maintain market share, domestic appliance manufacturers have endeavored over the past few years to offer consumers more product at a lower price, to improve relationships with the strongest distributors, and to keep operating costs down." Manufacturers attempt to keep costs down by more efficient manufacturing and through restructurings, and work to build brand loyalty, especially in the replacement market.

The appliance industry can be differentiated from other manufacturing sectors by its production characteristics. Appliance manufacturing is essentially an assembly-line process whereby ready-made components are assembled. Because it has low fixed costs and is labor intensive, appliance production offers abundant opportunities for manufacturing efficiency gains. This characteristic contributes to a high weight-to-value ratio that limits overseas appliance imports into the United States, and has caused prices to remain effectively fixed during the 1980s and 1990s.

Appliances are mainly sold through retail outlets, which have trained workers. Manufacturers usually ship products to warehouses from which they are distributed to retailers. However, some large retailers, such as Sears, Roebuck & Co., establish agreements with manufacturers for shipments directly to their warehouses. While manufacturers generally use the Internet only for providing product information to consumers, retailers, including Sears, are beginning to offer products online.

Products. The two main types of water heaters are electric- and gas-powered. Gas heaters made up nearly 55 percent of all residential water heater sales in the first two months of 1998. Although electric heaters are often priced lower, gas heaters usually operate less expensively. Most water heaters consist of a tank that is made of galvanized iron or aluminum alloys and holds between 20 and 140 gallons. A glass or plastic liner is used to reduce corrosion inside the tank. Water temperature can be adjusted between 100 and 200 degrees Fahrenheit. In 1997 U.S. producers sold about 9.1 million water heaters.

The two main categories of household dishwashers are portable and built-in. Of the estimated 4.8 million dishwashers shipped in 1997, only about 210,000 were portable units. Manufacturers shipped a total of 5.14 million dishwashers in 1998. Most dishwashers use pumps and impellers to throw the same water against dishes over and over to clean them. Fresh rinse water is then used. The cycle is typically completed by heat-drying the dishes. About 50 percent of all U.S. homes had a dishwasher in the early 1990s, up from 45 percent in 1980. However, in the late 1990s, dishwashers still were not considered a must-have appliance by homeowners, and they had a low market saturation in comparison to other major appliances.

Garbage disposal units are motor-operated grinders that are installed in kitchen sinks. These devices allow food to be washed down the drain. Approximately 50 percent of all U.S. homes were equipped with a disposal unit in the early 1990s, and nearly 4 million units were sold in 1993. In 1998, 4.9 million units were shipped, an increase of 6.9 percent over the 1997 level of 4.6 million. Trash compactors represent a negligible share of the appliance market. In 1989, manufacturers shipped 207,000 compactors. Except for a spike of 130,000 units in 1994, the category slipped to just 97,000 units in 1995 and 1996 before increasing to 103,000 in 1997 and 106,000 in 1998. Floor polishers and sewing machines also account for a meager share of U.S. miscellaneous appliance output. Manufacturers exported 49,000 floor polishers in 1997, while 13,200 units were imported. Most sewing machines are manufactured in Japan. In 1997, 1.56 million household sewing machines, with a value of $232 million, were imported; 50,000 machines, with a value of $14 million, were exported.

BACKGROUND AND DEVELOPMENT

Many of the appliances classified in this industry have existed for centuries. Not until the twentieth century, however, did self-contained electric- and gas-powered household appliances appear. A primary impetus for the development of such tools was the almost total disappearance of full-time domestic servants.

Appliances available in the early 1900s included electric clothes washers, water heaters, refrigerators, and sewing machines. In the second half of the century, during rapid postwar U.S. economic growth, a demand emerged for dishwashers, clothes dryers, food disposers, floor polishers, and similar devices of convenience. A rise in discretionary income, growth in the number of U.S. households, and a desire for more recreational time were major factors contributing to the rise of the miscellaneous appliance industry from the 1950s to the 1970s.

By the early 1980s, miscellaneous appliance manufacturers were shipping about $1.5 billion worth of goods each year, and employing over 14,000 workers. Strong industry growth continued during the 1980s as housing starts surged and growing home renovation markets spurred replacement sales. In addition, an increase in the number of working women boosted market penetration by some products.

Although industry revenues shot up over 100 percent between 1982 and 1990, to about $3.3 billion, unit shipments grew at an even faster rate and industry profits climbed. Manufacturers were able to achieve such growth through economies-of-scale and productivity gains. Indeed, as revenues and shipments more than doubled during the 1980s, industry employment remained steady. Hefty investments in automation and information systems permitted these efficiency gains.

Economies of scale were attained primarily through mergers and acquisitions, which characterized almost all appliance sectors throughout the 1980s and early 1990s. As manufacturers joined forces to increase investment capital and reduce research and production expenditures, the number of competitors in the miscellaneous appliances industry lessened. Antitrust legislation enacted during the 1980s slowed the rate of consolidation by the early 1990s.

Sluggish economic conditions, which suppressed housing starts and replacement sales, battered manufacturers of miscellaneous appliances in 1990. Home building and consumer expenditures picked up in 1992, though, prodded by low interest rates and pent-up demand. After plunging to $3.1 billion in 1990, industry revenues climbed to $3.3 billion in 1991 and grew about 4 percent annually during 1992 and 1993. Unit sales volume climbed even faster. Dishwasher shipments, for example, jumped almost 8 percent in 1993, and water heater orders increased by about 6 percent. Export growth augmented the domestic recovery and promised to provide an avenue for long-term expansion.

About 26 percent of industry revenues in the early 1990s was garnered from individual consumer purchases. Residential builders consumed about 20 percent of aggregate output, while commercial and institutional developers made up approximately 24 percent of the market. Roughly 5 percent of production was exported. The remaining 25 percent of sales were made to the armed forces, state and local governments, mobile home builders, and other sectors.

Although appliance makers lacked major new product offerings that could broaden their industry, they were having some success enticing new buyers to the market by adding new features to established products. Manufacturers were also benefitting from generally positive demographic trends. For instance, aging baby-boomers were investing an increasing proportion of their income into their homes, reflecting a desire for products that make the lives of two-income families more convenient and more comfortable. In addition, large numbers of appliances sold in the early 1980s were rapidly approaching replacement age. In an effort to exceed forecasts of modest growth, producers in the mid-1990s strove to accelerate replacement sales by developing more energy-efficient, convenient, and versatile machines.

New government environmental regulations were one of the greatest hurdles facing appliance makers in the mid-1990s. The Department of Energy's (DOE's) National Appliance Energy Conservation Act of 1987, for example, set new standards that limit energy consumption by new appliances. The act requires manufacturers to cut energy consumption by their products by 25 percent every five years. DOE mandates that became effective in May 1994 also required dishwasher manufacturers to build machines that use less water and make more efficient use of electric energy. Likewise, new regulations that were expected to be published by the DOE in late 1999 encompass water heaters. Other regulatory initiatives were aimed at making appliances more recyclable.

Most industry participants expected to achieve compliance with all regulations on schedule, and some manufacturers even hoped to boost sales with environmentally friendly products. Nevertheless, some appliance makers resented the new regulations, citing the capital investments required to meet the stipulations of such legislation. The industry was able to develop products that met the first energy efficiency standard, but was given until 2001 to meet a second standard requiring an additional 30 percent improvement in efficiency.

While opportunities prevailed in rapidly unfurling Asian markets, U.S. producers were largely avoiding that region in the early 1990s. Three successful Japanese conglomerates—Hitachi, Toshiba, and Matsushita—had established a strong grip on much of the Asian market and posed formidable entry barriers to even the most savvy American competitors. Likewise, Japanese producers were avoiding North American markets for fear of their U.S. counterparts, which maintained a lead in production efficiency, distribution, and marketing know-how—U.S. producers supplied over 75 percent of domestic demand for all types of appliances in 1993. Japanese companies had succeeded in penetrating the sewing machine market, though, and were supplying over 70 percent of global demand going into 1994.

U.S. appliance exports jumped 16 percent in 1992. Canada and Mexico consumed about 46 percent of those shipments, while the European Community purchased about 15 percent. East Asian and South American consumers accounted for 12 percent and 6 percent of U.S. exports, respectively. In the short term, Canada and Mexico will continue to offer strong growth opportunities, particularly in the wake of the North American Free Trade Agreement (NAFTA) that Congress passed in 1994. Exports to Mexico jumped 18 percent in 1993, while shipments to Canada ballooned 20 percent following a 1992 reduction in tariffs.

As domestic appliance makers continued to boost exports, imports surged. Imports increased by an uncharacteristically high 28 percent in 1992, despite a weak U.S. dollar, and imports were forecast to rise steadily during the 1990s and early 2000s. The main reason for import growth was the proliferation of U.S.-owned manufacturing plants in foreign countries. U.S. producers were shifting production to low-cost countries, such as Mexico and China, that offered cheap labor and materials. Imports from Mexico, for example, grew by 40 percent in 1993 and were expected to expand further with the passage of NAFTA.

CURRENT CONDITIONS

Several trends were contributing to favorable conditions for the industry at the close of the twentieth century. The pool of likely buyers was increasing as a large segment of the population was reaching their peak spending years. Because employment was high, more consumers had disposable income. In addition, available credit and lower interest rates spurred housing activity and remodeling, and thus, appliance sales. Home ownership reached a record level of 66 percent. Homeowners purchased appliances to furnish new houses, to replace those in houses new to their buyers, to replace worn-out appliances, and to renovate their kitchens with modern appliances. Four or five appliance units are bought for each new housing start. Replacement sales were expected to be strong in the next decade as appliances bought in the 1980s come to the end of their 10- to 15-year life spans. Approximately three-quarters of all appliance sales are to replace broken or worn-out appliances.

Product shipments in this industry were forecast at $3.34 billion in 1999, compared to an estimated $3.30 billion in 1998. Shipments were worth $2.92 billion in 1996. Because the market for appliances is mature and 1980s consolidation concentrated manufacturing, the industry is expected to grow at an annual rate less than the overall economy. Product shipments of appliances are forecast to increase only about 1.5 percent annually into the 2000s. Contributing to the increase will be an annual increase of 1 percent of households and the trend toward two-income families. Companies will also seek growth overseas where the market is not yet saturated, either by taking market share away from smaller companies or by acquiring competitors.

The appliance industry was globalizing as many countries lowered their tariffs, thus enabling appliance imports and exports to increase about 6 percent between 1996 and 1997. Also, appliance companies invested in foreign companies through acquisitions and joint ventures, particularly in the former communist countries and in industrializing countries in Asia and Latin America. China, Mexico, Canada, Taiwan, and South Korea accounted for 66 percent of imports in 1997. Mexico and Canada were benefitting from NAFTA and the U.S.-Canada Free Trade Agreement; China was benefitting from low labor costs. In 1998, imports caused U.S. appliance producer prices to decline. Fifty-three percent of U.S. appliance exports went to Canada, Mexico, the United Kingdom, Japan, and South Korea. Exports were expected to increase at a higher rate than imports. Foreign competition was not expected to be a threat.

INDUSTRY LEADERS

The appliance industry is highly consolidated; five major firms supply over 98 percent of all U.S. appliances. The biggest players in the miscellaneous appliance market are Whirlpool, General Electric (GE) Appliances, and Maytag. Whirlpool, the number one major home appliance producer in the United States and number two in the world, markets its products under the Kenmore, KitchenAid, Whirlpool, and other brand names. Products include dishwashers and compactors. GE is the number two producer of major household appliances. Its products include dishwashers, disposals, and compactors. Number three Maytag sells Maytag, Jenn-Air, Performa, and Magic Chef dishwashers, and Hoover floor polishers.

Some smaller product segments, however, are dominated by niche firms. In-Sink-Erator is the largest food waste disposer manufacturer in the world, followed by Anaheim Manufacturing Co. Anaheim's brands include Waste King, Sinkmaster, and Whirlaway. The Singer Company, founded in the United States and now headquartered in Netherlands Antilles, is the world's leading producer of sewing machines. Its brands are Singer and Pfaff. Water heater manufacturers include State Industries, Inc., which produces more than 2.3 million units per year, including Maytag brand, and A.O. Smith Corporation.

AMERICA AND THE WORLD

The United States is the largest consumer and producer of appliances in the world. It maintains the highest level of market saturation in virtually every major line of appliances. Generally low penetration of major appliances in comparison to the United States reflects higher energy costs, less space, and lower living standards characteristic of other countries.

Because manufacturers have achieved close to maximum market penetration with most miscellaneous appliances in the United States, they increasingly focused their expansion efforts in the 1990s on foreign markets that offered a greater potential for growth. Europe posed the greatest prospects for profits. Appliance industries on that continent were still fragmented, leaving the market open

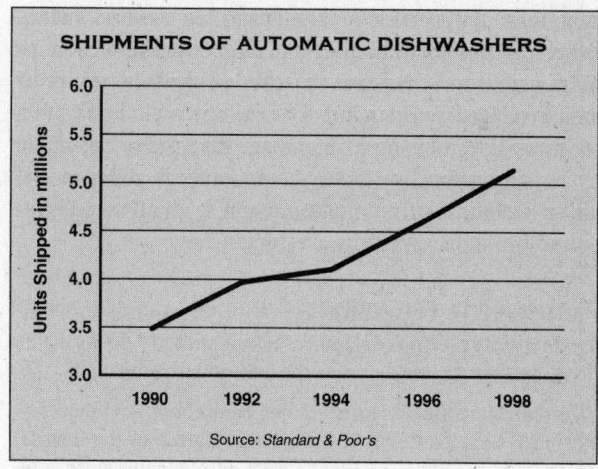

SHIPMENTS OF AUTOMATIC DISHWASHERS

Source: *Standard & Poor's*

for massive U.S. conglomerates to take market share or make company acquisitions. The Latin American market was also fragmented, with about 65 manufacturers. However, by 1998, Whirlpool and its affiliates had already garnered a 25 percent share. Asia promises to be the world's largest market in the twenty-first century. According to Standard & Poor's, "it could consume as many appliances as North America and Western Europe combined." Whirlpool has entered this market through joint ventures in China and as a major distributor to India, Pakistan, and other nations. Maytag also has entered into a partnership in China.

Although imports have risen, exports were expected to increase at a higher rate.

RESEARCH AND TECHNOLOGY

Technological advancements in the mid-1990s centered around compliance with environmental regulations and the development of more efficient appliances. Producers were striving to retain the cleansing power of dishwashers, for example, while reducing water usage. Meanwhile, water heater manufacturers continued to search for more efficient heating, insulation, and distribution technology.

European manufacturers were involved in producing a noise-free dishwasher in the early 1990s. Although the cleansing power of such machines was not yet acceptable to U.S. consumers, manufacturers from all continents were trying to develop a soundless machine. Frigidaire, for example, was offering three sound-blanketing packages with its dishwashers which incorporated vinyl-backed fiberglass, quilted foil-backed fiberglass, and asphaltic sound-damping materials. Manufacturers were also experimenting with quieter motors and noise-cancellation frequency generators.

Advances related to all types of appliances were being achieved through the increased use of plastics. New thermoplastics, for example, were being used to reduce heat loss that occurs in appliances encased in metal. Other plastics were helping manufacturers reduce shipping weight and increase the strength and durability of their products. Waste King, for example, switched from a stainless steel housing on a garbage disposal to one made of an engineered polymer compound. It reduced the unit's weight by five ounces, made it smaller, and decreased its noise level by five decibels.

FURTHER READING

Appliance Manufacturer shipment information, 1999. Available from http://www.ammagazine.com/pdfiles/02shipment.pdf.

"Current Industrial Reports: Major Household Appliances—1997." U.S. Department of Commerce. Bureau of the Census, 23 September 1998. Available from http://www.census.gov/pub/industry/1/ma36a97.pdf.

Hoover's Online Company Capsules. Available from http://www.hoovers.com/.

"Household Durables." *Standard & Poor's Industry Surveys,* October 1999.

Jancsurak, Joe. *Marketing Power Supplement,* November 1996.

U.S. Industry and Trade Outlook '99. McGraw-Hill and U.S. Department of Commerce, 1999.

SIC 3641

ELECTRIC LAMP BULBS AND TUBES

This industry classification covers establishments primarily engaged in manufacturing electric bulbs, tubes, and related light sources. Important products of this industry include incandescent filament lamps, vapor and fluorescent lamps, photoflash and photoflood lamps, and electrotherapeutic lamp units for ultraviolet and infrared radiation. Establishments primarily engaged in manufacturing glass blanks for bulbs are classified in **SIC 3229: Pressed and Blown Glass and Glassware, Not Elsewhere Classified.**

NAICS CODE(S)

335110 (Electric Lamp Bulb and Part Manufacturing)

INDUSTRY SNAPSHOT

The electric lamp bulbs and tubes industry in the late 1990s was characterized by intensive competition but was also aided by a strong U.S. economy that lead to increased housing starts and a long-awaited resurgence in commercial office building construction. While technological innovations remained the heart of the competitive atmosphere, major manufacturers were focusing ever more heavily on strategic marketing campaigns to ease customer confusion and showcase their products in a crowded market. Moreover, customer perception of lighting products in general were targeted to promote electric lamp bulbs and lighting as a decorative item rather than a commodity.

About 53 companies were engaged in the manufacture of electric lamp bulbs and tubes in 1997, generating shipments of $3.3 billion. This represented a 14 percent increase from 1995, though the 1997 total was below expectations of a few years earlier, largely as a result of the increasing presence of foreign competition. The number of employees, meanwhile, fell from 26,200 to 15,800 over that period as firms downsized to streamline costs and boost efficiency. Due to the high maturation of many market segments, manufacturers were looking to boost profits with high-tech lamps and bulbs that could burn longer, brighter, and more efficiently. The implementation of laws prohibiting the continued manufacture of more than 45 electric lamps that didn't meet newly established energy standards will certainly create additional changes in the market in the years to come.

ORGANIZATION AND STRUCTURE

The light bulb and electric lamp industry provides a practical means of converting electric energy into usable light. In the late 1990s just under one-fourth of all the electricity sold in the United States was used for lighting. Besides illuminating businesses, schools, and homes, light bulbs are used in a plethora of applications and products—including automobiles, flashlights, sports fields, medical equipment, airport runways, and emergency exit signs.

The industry produces thousands of different bulbs, tubes, strobes, and flashes. But the three primary products sold by U.S. electric lamp manufacturers are incandescent, fluorescent, and electric-discharge lights and bulbs.

Incandescent bulbs produce light by heating a filament to a high temperature. The filament, which is usually composed of tungsten, emits a yellowish glow as electricity flows through it. The bulb is filled with an inert gas, such as argon, to keep the filament from melting and evaporating. Most incandescent bulbs are designed to operate at between 30 and 150 watts of power and at 120 volts of electricity. They typically produce between 750 and 2,500 lumens of light (a lumen is the amount of light that falls on each square foot of a 1-foot radius sphere when a candle is placed at the center).

One reason incandescent bulbs are popular is because they are inexpensive to purchase. A standard 60-watt bulb usually costs about $1.99 and provides about 750 to 1,000 hours of light. Incandescent bulbs are also relatively compact, operate well at low temperatures, and offer a high degree of optical control. The primary disadvantage of this type of lamp, however, is low efficiency. A typical 100 watt bulb, for example, dissipates about 95 percent of its electric current as heat. Less than 5 percent is actually converted to light, resulting in high operating temperatures and superfluous energy consumption.

A second type of incandescent bulb is the halogen lamp, which became popular during the 1980s. Halogen bulbs are filled with iodine or bromine gas, which prolongs the filament's life by reducing tungsten evaporation. A standard halogen bulb lasts about 3,000 hours at 25 lumens-per-watt. Some halogen lamps also consume less energy. Because these bulbs emit ultraviolet radiation and can get extremely hot, however, they are often encased in a heat resistant material, like quartz, within the outer bulb. For this and other reasons, halogen lamps cost as much as five or even ten times more than traditional tungsten bulbs.

The second major category of electric bulbs is the fluorescent bulb and tube sector, which serves as the primary electric light source in the United States. Most fluorescent lamps are tube shaped, have a tungsten filament or tungsten coils, and are filled with mercury vapor and argon gas. When electricity is applied to the lamp, an electrode at one end emits electrons that travel through the bulb, react with the mercury, and emit ultraviolet radiation. The radiation reacts with a phosphor coating on the inside of the bulb to produce visible light. Fluorescent lamps are usually tubular, but also come in compact rod, ring, and globe shapes.

Although they are larger than incandescent bulbs and cost more to produce, fluorescent lamps are more energy efficient and have a longer life. Compact florescent lamps that can be substituted for standard incandescent bulbs, for example, produce between 80 and 100 lumens-per-watt. Incandescent bulbs, in contrast, deliver only 14 to 18 lumens-per-watt. Compact fluorescents also consume about 75 percent less energy than a standard incandescent and can burn for up to 6,000 hours. These lamps tend to sell at retail for about $19 to $24. The only drawback of compact fluorescent bulbs is that retailers usually have limited supplies available, and there is not as much variety as with conventional incandescent fixtures.

Electric-discharge lamps, the third major industry category, produce light through a gas or a metallic vapor. The color and intensity of the light can be altered by using different types of gas and varying the pressure in the bulb. Gases such as neon, argon, krypton, mercury, and xenon allow electric-discharge lamps to be used in a variety of applications. Mercury lamps, which deliver an efficient 65 lumens-per-watt, are widely used to light industrial spaces and roadways. Although electric-discharge lamps are expensive, slow-starting, and usually produce an unappealing bluish-greenish glow, they are long lasting, energy efficient, and compact. Recent developments have brought neon lamps into the home sector with the development of microelectronic transformers—

necessary for the operation of neon lamps—which are now smaller than a pack of cigarettes.

Markets. Approximately half of light bulb industry revenues in the late 1990s were derived from sales to individual consumers. State and local governments, including schools, hotels, and hospitals accounted for small percentages of revenues. The remainder of the market was highly fragmented. Motor vehicle manufacturers and electric utilities consumed small portions of total production units.

BACKGROUND AND DEVELOPMENT

Oil lamps were used for illumination in the earliest known civilizations and were a common artificial light source for more than 6,000 years. Gas lamps became popular early in the nineteenth century, particularly in Europe. Neither gas nor oil lamps, however, were sufficient to light entire rooms or mimic daylight.

The first incandescent electric lamp was produced in 1802 by Humphrey Davy, an English chemist. Davy heated strips of platinum in the open air using an electric current. The strips soon burned up, and the lack of a satisfactory source of electric power made the concept impracticable. Similar efforts during the succeeding 70 years caused some scientists to declare the development of a long burning electric lamp impossible.

Good vacuum pumps that removed air from glass bulbs made the creation of the first commercially viable incandescent lamps possible. Joseph Wilson Swan, of England, and Thomas Edison, of the United States, separately invented the first successful light bulbs in 1878. Both lamps used carbon filaments in evacuated glass bulbs. Edison received most of the credit for the invention, however, because he subsequently invented much of the equipment needed to implement his lamp in a practical lighting system.

Edison's first lamp provided the same amount of light as 16 candles and produced about 1.4 lumens-per-watt. But technological advancements soon improved Edison's original bulb. Notably, in 1911 tungsten was introduced as a filament. In 1913 filaments were coiled for the first time, and bulbs were filled with inert gas. Beginning in 1925, bulbs were frosted on the inside to emit a diffused glow instead of a glaring brightness. Improvements in energy flow and bulb pressure helped boost standard 40 watt bulbs to 1,000 hours of life and 14 lumens-per-watt by the early 1960s. Incandescent lamps with more power had developed by the 1960s as well.

The first electric arc lamp was patented in 1845 by Thomas Wright. Wright's carbon-arc lamp led to the development in the late 1800s of electric-discharge bulbs that could produce ten times the light emitted by carbon-filament incandescent lamps. These early bulbs were largely limited to use as heavy-duty street lights, however, because they had to be continuously fed with carbon rods. The mercury-arc lamp, developed in 1901, eliminated many drawbacks of early electric-discharge bulbs. Likewise, the introduction of neon tubes in 1920 led to the popularization of electric-discharge lamps for advertising signs. Sodium lamps developed during the 1930s became popular for various outdoor and industrial applications.

The fluorescent lamp was invented by Frenchman Alexandre Edmond Becquerel in 1859, but it was not introduced commercially in the United States until 1938. By the early 1950s, though, fluorescent lamps had overtaken incandescent bulbs as the primary source of artificial light in the United States. Superior efficiency, long life, and greater light output drove the growth of this important industry segment. By the 1960s, in fact, manufacturers were offering more than 50 shapes and sizes of fluorescent lamps ranging from four to 240 watts in power.

Booms in residential, commercial, and institutional construction from the 1950s to the 1970s vastly expanded U.S. light bulb markets. By the early 1980s, in fact, about 60 U.S. producers were shipping $2 billion worth of various electric lamps and were employing more than 22,000 workers. Following a development lull in the late 1970s and early 1980s, renewed demand pressed industry sales past an impressive $2.8 billion per year by 1986. This figure reflected average annual growth of nearly 10 percent between 1982 and 1986. Although sales increased at a more tepid pace through 1988—to about $3.2 billion—a U.S. recession in the late 1980s and early 1990s depressed industry revenues back below $3 billion.

Going into the late 1990s, U.S. electric lamp manufacturers were hoping to benefit from slowly strengthening commercial and residential construction industries. Nevertheless, demand from builders was expected to remain suppressed as contractors reeled from the building glut of the mid- and late 1980s. Instead, bulb makers were focusing on increasing profits through sales of advanced lamps that could reduce energy consumption, improve lighting, boost longevity, and minimize adverse environmental impacts. Compact fluorescent and halogen bulbs, particularly, offered solid growth potential.

The National Energy Security Act of 1992 effectively mandated the use of such advanced bulbs. The act sought to prevent the sale of inefficient fluorescent light bulbs beginning in 1994, and other energy-inefficient bulbs by 1995. It banned most standard four-and eight-foot fluorescent light tubes, some incandescent reflector lamps, and many types of flood lamps. Likewise, the Environmental Protection Agency's (EPA's) "Green Lights" voluntary conservation program was designed to encourage corporations to install new lighting. Full national participation, according to the EPA, could reduce total U.S. electric consumption by 10 percent and slash lighting electricity requirements by 50 percent, resulting in an annual $18.6 billion savings. By mid-1998, consumers were having to pay approximately 9 percent more for their bulbs, in no small part due to the implementation of the act.

CURRENT CONDITIONS

In efforts to maintain a competitive edge in the mature light bulb market, the grounds for competition were rapidly shifting to the marketing arena. Manufacturers, aware that most customers purchase bulbs at discount retail stores whose shelves were stocked full of bulbs of all different sorts, actively wanted to save off the kind of consumer anxiety in the face of such an array of choices that would lead individuals to simply purchase whatever bulb was cheapest, failing to scrutinize for the intricate variations manufacturers have worked so hard to develop. As a result, creative packaging and marketing has become a primary industry priority. By color-coding similar product lines and advertising lamps with different duration and features from a more utilitarian standpoint, manufacturers enable customers to mentally narrow down their choices and make more informed purchasing decisions. In addition, industry players have placed a premium on delivering elaborate, user-friendly marketing displays to retail outlets, the logic being that such displays can feature the range of company products together while showcasing and explaining standard wattage variations for regular incandescents as well as the company's more expensive and decorative feature products. Most such in-store displays were fairly costly to ship due to their bulk and fragility; thus, they were placed primarily by the larger manufacturers who maintained the financial leverage to manufacture and ship them. In other efforts, bulbs have increasingly been manufactured to fit the same type of socket across a broad range of product lines, while product-differentiation advertising campaigns have flourished.

Incandescent bulbs remained the anchor of the industry, accounting for about 90 percent of all bulb sales in 1998. But sales of incandescents have remained flat throughout the mid- and late 1990s, as sales of advanced high-margin lamps accelerated. Longer-lasting and more costly halogen lamps faced down some negative publicity in the 1990s, including the revelation that these lamps were responsible for more than 100 fires since 1992. Nonetheless, sales of halogen lamps rose 8 percent in 1998, benefiting largely from an industry-wide effort to push lighting as a decorative item. Analysts expect that the trend toward high-value decorative lighting is fairly commensurate with the overall strength of the U.S. economy and was thus expected to cool somewhat in the early 2000s. Nonetheless, all manufacturers expect that more efficient and longer-lasting compact fluorescent and halogen lamps will take on increasing prominence in the light bulb industry.

Energy-conservation efforts intensified during this period in response to heightened consumer demand for environmentally sound products. In 1999, the U.S. EPA modified its Subtitle C hazardous waste rules, specifically targeting fluorescent lamps containing the toxic pollutant mercury. The ruling maintains the federal ban on high-mercury-volume products and standardizes at the federal level a potpourri of often-confusing and conflicting rules enforced at the state level and, as such, should help manufacturers systematize their disposal and recycling procedures. While the ruling reduces the costs to manufacturers for recycling mercury-based lamps, the new classification of these bulbs as "universal waste" demands that they be labeled as such, a development that worries some manufacturers who fear that such labeling will discourage consumers. The EPA estimated that the move would increase the rate at which mercury-filled lamps were recycled to 50 to 70 percent by the early 2000s. In the late 1990s, some 1 billion fluorescent lamps were discarded annually.

INDUSTRY LEADERS

General Electric Lighting is widely acknowledged as the industry leader, a position it has maintained for years. The firm sells about 500 million standard incandescent bulbs and 10 million compact fluorescent bulbs annually. General Electric commanded an estimated market share of 20 percent in 1999. By the late 1990s, the company was focusing increasingly on its decorative products, heavily marketing its Enrich light bulb line, which features a glass casing designed to filter out some colors to enhance the contrasts between surrounding colors. General Electric does not release financial information on its subsidiaries to the public.

Philips Lighting Company employed more than 6,000 workers in the United States in 1998. Philips focused its business on its line of longer-life, higher margin halogen lamps and generated sales of more than $1 billion.

Osram Sylvania, the Boston-based North American subsidiary of Germany's Osram GmBH, rounds out the big three. In 1998, Osram Sylvania maintained a payroll of 13,000 employees in the United States and Canada and brought in revenues of $1.74 billion.

MagneTek, Inc., an electronics and electrical products firm specializing in lighting, was another industry leader, employing 8,700 workers and posting sales of $678.9 million in 1998.

WORKFORCE

Although sales and production volume increased for most industry participants during the 1980s, aggregate

employment actually dropped about 12 percent to less than 25,000 in the early 1990s. Manufacturing productivity gains and management restructuring were the primary culprits of recessed employment figures. After registering a brief upswing in the mid-1990s, employment figures spiraled downward to 15,800 in 1997. Production workers accounted for 13,363 of this total, earning an average of $16.59 per hour. Falling employment trends are likely to continue well into the next decade.

AMERICA AND THE WORLD

Besides domestic sales, many manufacturers were also striving to take advantage of growth opportunities overseas. Global electric lamp sales were estimated at about $11 billion in 1998 and were expected to increase to about $12 billion by 2001. U.S. producers accounted for just under one-third of global industry sales and hoped to further boost their global market share. Although low-cost foreign manufacturers posed significant obstacles to exporters of traditional, commodity-like incandescent bulbs, U.S. manufacturers maintained a decided advantage in markets for high-tech lamps. Thus U.S. manufacturers will try to fill an open niche market for high-efficiency bulbs in the ripe Asian and European markets.

RESEARCH AND TECHNOLOGY

As light bulb producers labored to develop new, high-tech lamps that could increase their market share and boost profit margins, a steady stream of technological advancements greeted consumers in the mid- and late 1990s. Most bulbs offered superior lighting characteristics, greater efficiency, and improved longevity. Other advances were making bulbs more environmentally safe for disposal; this is a particularly relevant development in the case of fluorescent bulbs, which contain mercury.

White LED (light emitting diode) lamps were expected to achieve dramatic growth in market share in the early 2000s as a replacement for automotive, halogen, incandescent, and fluorescent bulbs. White LEDs were especially attractive for their durability, which, at 100,000 hours, is 100 times that of standard incandescents. The biggest issues preventing LED bulbs from taking over the lighting market, according to analysts, was the continuing challenge to developers to increase the brightness capacity while managing to keep costs under control.

Perhaps the most unique innovation in the late 1990s was the digital light bulb developed by Color Kinetics in Boston. The digital bulb incorporates a tiny chip that enables consumers to generate varying hues through LED bulbs. The digital microchip is programmed by software that allows users to actually program their light bulbs to perform whatever coloration functions they desire, such as gradually changing the light's color over time. This development comes at a convenient time for the light bulb industry, focused as it is on promoting the decorative qualities of lighting.

FURTHER READING

"Boston-Based Company Has Bright Idea in Digital Light Bulb." *Boston Globe,* 12 November 1999.

"Consumers Willing to Pay More." *MMR,* 12 July 1999.

"Hot Product: Softer Halogen Lamps." *National Home Center News,* 8 March 1999.

"Hot Product: The Bulb Fluorescent Light." *National Home Center News,* 23 March 1999.

Howell, Debbie. "Diversity Sidelines Soft White." *Discount Store News,* 5 April 1999.

Johnson, Jim. "New Rules Target Fluorescent Light Bulbs." *Waste Management News,* 5 July 1998.

"Light Bulbs." *MMR,* 20 September 1999.

"Lightbulbs." *Supermarket News,* 17 May 1999.

"Packaging, Merchandising Clarify Choices, Spark Trade-Ups in Lighting." *Drug Store News,* 1 March 1999.

"Prospects Dim for Hot, Costly Halogens." *Wall Street Journal,* 10 March 1997.

U.S. Department of Commerce. Bureau of the Census. *1997 Census of Manufacturers.* Washington, D.C.: GPO, 19 May 1999.

U.S. Department of Commerce. International Trade Administration. *U.S. Industry and Trade Outlook 1999.* New York: The McGraw Hill Companies, 1999.

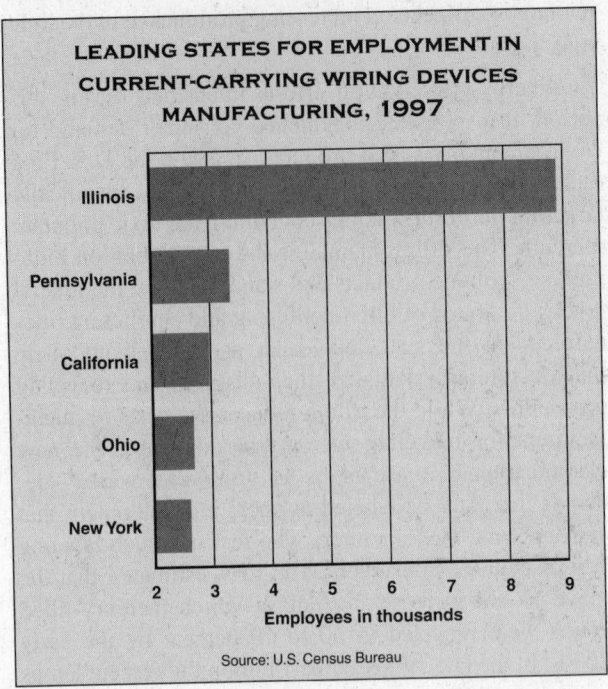

LEADING STATES FOR EMPLOYMENT IN CURRENT-CARRYING WIRING DEVICES MANUFACTURING, 1997

Employees in thousands

Source: U.S. Census Bureau

SIC 3643

CURRENT-CARRYING WIRING DEVICES

The current-carrying wiring devices industry is comprised of establishments principally engaged in manufacturing current-carrying wiring devices, primarily interior electrical components used to connect equipment to a power source.

The industry is divided into six major categories: switches, wire connectors, convenience and power outlets, lampholders, metal contacts, and other devices such as plug caps and connector bodies. Miscellaneous products encompass items such as trolley line materials, lightning protectors, and fluorescent starters.

NAICS CODE(S)

335931 (Current-Carrying wiring Device Manufacturing)

According to the U.S. Census Bureau's *1997 Economic Census—Manufacturing,* 519 establishments operated in this category for some or all of 1997. Industry-wide employment totaled 44,907 workers, who received a payroll of almost $1.3 billion. Of that number, 32,867 employees worked in production, putting in more than 63.0 million hours to earn wages of more than $754.0 million. Overall shipments for the industry were valued at almost $5.9 billion in 1997.

The basic technology for this industry was discovered in 1729, when Stephen Gray, an English physicist, found that some substances could carry electricity from one location to another. These substances were called conductors. In 1820, Danish physicist Hans Christian Oersted found that a metal wire carrying a current of electricity would cause a compass needle to change direction. Georg Simon Ohm is credited with developing the theory of electric circuits in 1825. Subsequent advances gave birth to manufactured current-carrying wiring devices.

Rapid development of residential, commercial, and institutional structures in the United States between 1945 and 1980 propelled industry revenues past $2.5 billion per year. Strong development during most of the 1980s resulted in average annual growth of about 8 percent. By 1989, sales of current-carrying devices had surged to about $4.4 billion. Economic recess in 1990 stalled industry growth, as sales dropped nearly 2 percent. Stagnant construction markets repressed growth throughout the early 1990s, although an increase in housing starts and general economic improvement in 1993 boosted shipments 2 percent, to about $4.5 billion. The value of all industry shipments in 1995 was about $4.8 billion.

To compensate for slow domestic sales, some industry participants capitalized on expanding export demand, which rose as a result of a weak U.S. dollar. Exports gained 14 percent in 1991, reaching a record $1.4 billion, or nearly 30 percent of total shipments, but growth of exports was flat through 1995. In combination with slow export growth, imports increased significantly in the mid-1990s, adding to the deficit trend that began in the early 1990s. Major importers into the United States were Japan, Mexico, Taiwan, and Germany. Imports from Mexico were expected to continue growing in the mid-1990s, particularly in light of the North American Free Trade Agreement (NAFTA), which was initiated in 1994.

In the mid-1990s, wiring device manufacturers benefited from steady residential construction markets and an upsurge in home renovations. In addition, new government building regulations mandated the use of certain wiring products. The National Electrical Code (NEC) that was implemented in 1993, for example, required the installation of special ground-fault circuit interrupters (GFCIs) that detect ground faults and shut off power to protected circuits. The revised 1996 NEC code augmented GFCI requirements. The sale of these and other devices were expected to bolster industry growth.

The industry is extremely fragmented. The largest competitor was Nashville-based Northern Telecom Inc., which boasted sales of more than $11.0 billion for its fiscal year ended July 1, 1998. Cleveland-based Eaton Corp. followed with 1999 sales of $8.4 billion. ABB Inc. of Norwalk, Connecticut, placed third in the industry with 1998 sales of $6.0 billion. 3Com Corp. of Santa Clara, California, generated sales of almost $5.8 billion for its fiscal year ended May 31, 1999. AMP Inc. of Harrisburg, Pennsylvania, rounded out the top 5 industry leaders with almost $5.5 billion in 1998 sales.

Prospects for most occupations in this industry were expected to be weak throughout 2005, according to the U.S. Bureau of Labor Statistics. Aggregate industry employment fell slightly during the 1980s, despite output growth. Continued productivity gains were expected to contribute to a decline of 15 to 35 percent for many labor positions between 1995 and 2005. Some positions, such as those for sales and marketing professionals, were forecast to grow as much as 38 percent.

FURTHER READING

Darnay, Arsen J., ed. Manufacturing USA. 5th ed. Detroit: Gale Research, 1996.

Infotrac Company Profiles. Available from http://web4.infotrac.galegroup.com. (visited 2/18/00).

U.S. Census Bureau. 1995 Annual Survey of Manufactures. Washington, DC: GPO, 1997. Available from http://www.census.gov/prod/www/titles.html#mm.

U.S. Census Bureau. 1997 Economic Census. Washington, DC: GPO, 1999. Available from http://www.census.gov/prod/ec97/97m3359e.pdf.

U.S. Department of Commerce. Bureau of the Census. Current Industrial Reports, Wiring Devices and Supplies, 1995. Washington, 1996. Available from http://www.census.gov/industry/ma36k95.txt.

SIC 3644

NONCURRENT-CARRYING WIRING DEVICES

The noncurrent-carrying wiring devices industry is made up of companies that primarily manufacture hardware used to support electrical systems. Popular products include electrical conduits and fittings, boxes for outlets, switches, and fuses, and pole and transmission line devices. Insulators are also included in this industry, with the exception of those made from glass or ceramics. For information about the history of electrical systems, see **SIC 3641: Electric Lamp Bulbs and Tubes** and **SIC 3643: Current-Carrying Wiring Devices.**

NAICS CODE(S)

335932 (Noncurrent-Carrying Wire Device Manufacturing)

According to the U.S. Census Bureau's 1997 Economic Census-Manufacturing, 220 establishments operated in this category for some or all of 1997. Industry-wide employment totaled 23,221 workers receiving a payroll of almost $777.0 million. 16,975 of these employees worked in production, putting in more than 36 million hours to earn wages of almost $480.0 million. Overall shipments for the industry were valued at almost $4.5 billion.

Most noncurrent-carrying wiring products are consumed by the nonresidential construction sector. A leading 51 percent of industry output in the mid-1990s was attributed to electrical conduit and fittings, which includes conduit, connectors, junction boxes and related products. Pole and transmission line hardware, which was purchased by cable television and utility companies, comprised about 17 percent of production. The remainder of the market was highly fragmented. Store and restaurant construction, for example, accounted for about 1 percent of sales, as did construction related to mobile homes. Other industry outputs included highway and street construction, sewer system development, industrial controls, and lawn and garden equipment.

Rampant infrastructure growth and commercial development following World War II helped the industry attain revenues of $2 billion by the late 1970s. Steady market growth during the 1980s moreover, generated average annual revenue growth of about 4.5 percent. By

LEADING STATE BY EMPLOYMENT
FOR NONCURRENT-CARRYING
WIRING DEVICES MANUFACTURING

Illinois

Connecticut

New York

California

Ohio

1.25   1.50   1.75   2.00   2.25   2.50

Employees in thousands

Source: U.S. Census Bureau

1989, industry participants were shipping about $3.4 billion worth of goods per year.

A severe depression in commercial development and stagnant institutional construction markets contributed to industry decline in the early 1990s. Sales slipped by about 2.5 percent in 1990 and continued to fade approximately 1.5 percent per year through 1993. Although sales reached nearly $4.0 billion in 1994, growth in 1995 was nearly flat, with revenues increasing only 2 percent.

The total value of shipments in 1995 reached $4.0 billion, and the total value of exported shipments was about $1.0 billion. About 200 companies competed in the noncurrent-carrying wiring device industry in the mid-1990s, with about 17,000 employees. The majority of the top 50 producers had sales of less than $20.0 million and employed fewer than 200 workers, and there were only seven establishments with more than 500 employees in 1994. The average annual salary for production workers was $24,654 in 1996.

EGS Electrical Group L.L.C. of Skokie, Illinois led the industry with sales of $653.0 million for its fiscal year ending September 30, 1997, according to Infotrac databases. Panduit Corp. of Tinley Park, Illinois followed with 1998 sales of $600.0 million. LTV Steel Tubular Products Co. was third in the industry with 1998 sales of $300.0 million. MacLean-Fogg Co. of Mundelein, Illinois generated 1998 sales of $280.0 million, and Chicago-based Allied Products Corp. rounded out the top 5 industry leaders with 1998 sales of $274 million.

Prospects for employment in this industry were relatively poor. Although output increased during the 1980s, employment declined from about 26,000 in the early 1980s

to around 22,000 a decade later. There were 16,700 employees in the industry in 1996, 75 percent of which were classified as production workers. Productivity gains, management restructuring, and the movement of some manufacturing activities to foreign countries were the primary reasons for work force reductions. Although the Bureau of Labor Statistics predicts many labor positions will be eliminated between 1996 and 2005, jobs for sales and marketing professionals are expected to increase.

FURTHER READING

Darnay, Arsen J., ed. *Manufacturing USA.* 5th ed. Detroit: Gale Research, 1996.

Infotrac Company Profiles. 2000. Available from http://web4 .infotrac.galegroup.com.

U.S. Census Bureau. 2000.*1997 Economic Census-Manufacturing.* Available from http://www.census.gov/prod/ec97/ 97m3359f.pdf.

U.S. Department of Commerce. Bureau of the Census. ''Wiring Devices and Supplies, 1995.'' *Current Industrial Reports.* Washington, DC: 1996. Available from http://www.census.gov/ industry/ma36k95.txt.

U.S. Department of Commerce. Economics and Statistics Administration. Bureau of the Census. *1995 Annual Survey of Manufactures; Value of Product Shipments.* Washington, DC: GPO, 1997. Available from http://www.census.gov/prod/www/ titles.html#mm.

SIC 3645

RESIDENTIAL ELECTRIC LIGHTING FIXTURES

The residential electric lighting fixtures industry encompasses manufacturers that produce a variety of equipment and components for home use. Popular offerings include chandeliers, desk and floor lamps, glass and metal lamp shades, yard lights, and wall-mounted lighting fixtures. Light bulbs, cloth and plastic lamp shades, flashlights, and lanterns are classified in other industries.

NAICS CODE(S)

335121 (Residential Electric Lighting Fixture Manufacturing)

About 50 percent of industry revenues in the mid-1990s were derived from stationary, or mounted, fixtures, such as ceiling and wall lamps. Portable lamps, like movable desk and floor lamps, accounted for about 36 percent of shipments. The remainder of revenues were garnered from the sale of lamp shades and various types of parts and accessories. The total value of shipments in 1997 was $2.25 billion.

The first lighting apparatus pre-dates the light bulb—in 1650, German Otto von Guericke produced a luminous glow from a spinning globe of sulfur. However, the evolution of modern day lamps and fixtures parallels the popularization of the electric light bulb, which Thomas Edison invented in 1879. Rapid demand for all types of lighting devices helped the residential lighting fixture industry grow to a $1.4 billion business by the early 1980s.

Industry revenues grew sluggishly during the 1980s, despite healthy residential construction markets. Increased foreign competition was a primary reason for stagnant sales. Although revenues reached about $1.8 billion by 1988, the industry suffered a severe commercial development depression and stalled housing starts in the late 1980s and early 1990s. Sales plummeted about 16 percent between 1988 and 1990 to $1.56 billion.

New home construction buoyed sales to about $1.6 billion in 1992 and to $1.8 billion by 1993. In the mid-1990s, the industry benefited from the passage of nationwide energy initiatives and legislation. The National Energy Security Act of 1992 mandated the use of new energy-saving bulbs, and the EPA's "Green Lights" program encouraged companies to install new energy-efficient lighting fixtures and related products. Many U.S. residential lighting fixture producers rejuvenated lagging margins with sales of the new energy-saving lighting equipment, while others sought profit growth through mergers and acquisitions. The number of companies dwindled from about 650 in the early 1980s to 498 in 1994, as companies combined forces to survive withering demand.

Despite consolidation, the residential lighting fixture industry remained fragmented in the mid-1990s. The majority of the top 50 competitors had sales of less than $25 million in the mid-1990s and employed fewer than 400 workers. The largest producer was Genlyte Group Inc. of New Jersey, which had sales of $456 million from its diversified operations and employed about 2,600 workers. The Genlyte Group Incorporated reported 1998 sales of $664.1 million and had 3,490 employees according to Hoover's Online. The Genlyte Group, Inc. and Thomas Industries, Inc. entered into a joint venture in 1998 creating Genlyte Thomas Group LLC, a top lighting fixture manufacturer in North America. Thomas Industries, Inc. owns a 32 percent interest and Genlyte owns 68 percent in the joint venture, according to Thomas Industries Inc., 1998 Annual Report. Other top competitors in the residential lighting fixture industry include Catalina Lighting, Inc. and Cooper Lighting, a division of Cooper Industries, Incorporated. Catalina Lighting reported 1999 sales of $176.6 million and had 2,815 employees in 1998. Catalina Lighting fixtures are sold under the names Illuminada, Dana, Catalina and Westinghouse. Product lines include functional and decorative lamps and lighting fixtures. Cooper Lighting manufactures recessed, track, fluorescent, and emergency lighting fixtures. Brand names include Halo, Metalux, Sure-Lites, Lumière and Optiance.

Industry trends show that job growth for most occupations in this industry will remain stagnant through the year 2000. Aggregate employment fell from about 22,000 in the early 1980s to about 19,000 in 1995—the result of workforce reductions and manufacturing productivity gains. The number of production workers was expected to decrease by almost 20 percent from 1995 to 1998, according to the Bureau of Labor Statistics, but selected positions such as those for sales professionals and machinists were expected to increase in number.

FURTHER READING

Darnay, Arsen J., ed. Manufacturing USA. 5th ed. Detroit: Gale Research, 1996.

Cooper Industries. Cooper Lighting/Brands. January 2000. Available from http://www.cooperlighting.com/brands.

Hoover's Online. Catalina Lighting, Inc. December 1999. Available from http://www.hovers.com/co/capsule/7/0,2163,11807,00.html.

Hoover's Online. The Genlyte Group Incorporated. December 1999. Available from http://www.hovers.com/co/capsule/7/0,2163,13557,00.html.

Thomas Industries, Inc. Thomas Industries Inc. 1998 Annual Report. December 1999. Available from http://www.thomasind.com/annual98/text2/report.html.

U.S. Bureau of the Census. 1995 Annual Survey of Manufactures. Washington, DC: GPO, 1997. Available from http://www.census.gov/prod/www/titles.html#mm.

U.S. Bureau of the Census. Residential Electric Lighting Fixture Manufacturing 1997. September 1999. Available from http://www.census.gov/prod/ec97/97m3351b.pdf.

SIC 3646

COMMERCIAL, INDUSTRIAL, AND INSTITUTIONAL ELECTRIC LIGHTING FIXTURES

The commercial lighting fixture industry is comprised of establishments primarily engaged in manufacturing electric lighting fixtures for commercial, industrial, and institutional customers. Popular industry offerings include hotel and restaurant chandeliers, desk and floor lamps for offices, luminous ceiling panels, and industrial fluorescent lighting fixtures.

NAICS CODE(S)

335122 (Commercial, Industrial, and Institutional Electric Lighting Fixture Manufacturing)

INDUSTRY SNAPSHOT

About 80 percent of industry output in 1997 was used for commercial and institutional purposes, while 15 percent was utilized in industrial applications. Approximately 4 percent of production was exported. The largest single market for commercial lighting devices was in office buildings, which purchased about 9 percent of all fixtures produced by both residential and commercial fixture manufacturers; hospitals and parking garages both consumed about 1 percent of production. The remainder of the market was highly fragmented.

BACKGROUND AND DEVELOPMENT

Following Thomas Edison's invention of the light bulb in 1879, the use of lighting fixtures in commercial applications gradually became widespread. During the industrial revolution of the late 1880s and early 1900s, electric light fixtures became common in factories, hospitals, hotels, and other commercial structures. Fixtures for fluorescent bulbs, which were introduced in 1938 and were more energy-efficient than previous bulbs, became the emphasis of the industry by the 1950s. The steady market growth precipitated by the post-World War II U.S. economic expansion pushed sales of commercial fixtures past $1.5 billion by the early 1980s.

Healthy commercial development throughout most of the 1980s resulted in an average annual revenue growth of nearly 8 percent for the commercial fixture industry, and, by 1990, sales topped $3.0 billion per year. Despite a severe downturn in commercial development in the late 1980s and early 1990s, sales dipped only 1 percent in 1991 before rising an encouraging 4 percent in 1992. Healthy institutional demand and sales of fixtures for new energy-saving bulbs continued to buoy earnings in 1994 and 1995, as industry revenues climbed to around $3.5 billion, up more than 16 percent from 1992. In 1997 the value of shipments reached a little over $4.0 billion.

In the mid-1990s U.S. commercial lighting fixture producers benefited from government initiatives that encouraged businesses to replace existing lamps and fixtures with new energy-saving devices, which gradually phased out the old equipment. The new devices and lamps produced more light per watt, so less electricity was needed to power the fixture. Companies also boosted profits through cost-cutting programs and productivity gains, which traditionally meant reductions in the work force. In light of increasing foreign competition, as well as the introduction of the North American Free Trade Agreement (NAFTA), many manufacturers were forming joint ventures with overseas producers and moving production facilities outside the United States. Shipments by both residential and commercial fixture producers were expected to grow at a rate of between 3 and 5 percent annually through the end of the decade.

CURRENT CONDITIONS

According to Frost & Sullivan, the North American lighting equipment market will reach $15.2 billion in total revenue by 2005, up from $10.3 billion in 1998. Consolidation is a major trend, as large companies acquire smaller ones. Moreover, manufacturers are targeting the institutional and commercial segments. Another report from the Freedonia group expects U.S. lamp demand to reach 6.3 billion units in 2001, a direct result of an increase in the need for commercial and industrial retrofit lighting.

INDUSTRY LEADERS

About 320 U.S. companies competed in the commercial lighting fixture industry in 1997, with about half of all establishments employing 20 or more workers. The majority of the top 50 competitors reported less than $50.0 million in sales and had fewer than 200 employees. The industry's largest participant was National Service Industries Inc., of Georgia, which had sales of about $2.0 billion and 16,100 employees throughout its diversified operations. Other industry leaders included Lithonia Lighting Co., with $764.0 million in sales and 4,500 employees, and Cooper Lighting, with $475.0 million in sales and 5,000 employees.

WORKFORCE

Although industry employment rose from 19,000 in the early 1980s to 23,000 by the early 1990s, the total number of employees dropped slightly in 1997 to 22,818 workers, over 70 percent employed in production. These production workers earned about $11 per hour. The leading states in number of employees were California (3,053), New York (1,654), Massachusetts (1,259), Ohio (1,070), and Pennsylvania (1,019).

Future employment prospects in this industry are not encouraging. According to the Bureau of Labor Statistics, many manufacturing positions were expected to decline significantly between 1990 and 2005, in the wake of productivity gains and the movement of production facilities overseas. Sales positions and some specialized machinist occupations, however, which account for a relatively small share of this industry's workforce, will probably increase.

AMERICA AND THE WORLD

The global market for all lighting products (including lamps, lighting fixtures and fittings/control equipment) was estimated at $26.0 billion in 1996, according to Frost & Sullivan. Through 2000, the market was expected to grow by 5.1 percent to $28.0 billion. Metal halide lamps and compact fluorescent lamps are two of the fastest growing segments. The European professional lighting equipment market was estimated at almost $7.0

billion in 1999, which Frost & Sullivan predicted would to rise to over $8.0 billion by 2006. The majority of total sales are comprised of interior products for the commercial sector. Over 100 small- to medium-sized manufacturers make up the industry, led by Philips and Osram.

Because Asian imports are pushing down U.S. prices, American and European manufacturers are expanding into the Chinese market. The two European leaders, Philips and Thorn, established either joint ventures or separate facilities during 1998. Cooper Lighting and Thomas Industries, both based in the United States, also established several joint ventures. Japanese manufacturers are following their example with at least one joint venture and a major contract at the Capital Airport.

FURTHER READING

Darnay, Arsen J., ed. *Manufacturing USA.* 5th ed. Detroit: Gale Research, 1996.

"Frost & Sullivan Sheds Light on North American Lighting Equipment Market" Press Release. Available from http://www.frost.com/verity/press/environment_energy/pr576314.htm.

Lamps to 2001. The Freedonia Group, December 1997.

"Major Foreign Lamp Producers Edge into Chinese Market." *Asia Pulse,* 19 September 1998.

U.S. Department of Commerce. International Trade Administration. *U.S. Industrial Outlook 1994.* Washington: GPO, 1994.

U.S. Bureau of the Census. Economics and Statistics Administration. *1995 Annual Survey of Manufactures; Value of Product Shipments.* Washington: GPO, 1997. Available from http://www.census.gov.

SIC 3647

VEHICULAR LIGHTING EQUIPMENT

This category includes establishments primarily engaged in manufacturing vehicular lighting equipment. Establishments primarily engaged in manufacturing sealed-beam lamps are classified in **SIC 3641: Electric Light Bulbs and Tubes.**

NAICS CODE(S)

336321 (Vehicular Lighting Equipment Manufacturing)

The world has come a long way since the first driver of a horseless carriage attached two kerosene lamps to his vehicle to light his way at night. Aftermarket electric lighting systems were available for vehicles as early as the turn of the nineteenth century, and acetylene headlamps started appearing on cars around 1905. It was not until 1912 that Cadillac featured electric lights as standard equipment on its cars. Lights for airplanes were also an afterthought, first appearing some years after the

Wright Brothers flew their aircraft at Kitty Hawk. Vehicular lighting is now standard equipment on aircraft, automobiles, boats, bikes, motorcycles, and locomotives, and it is even used on roller skates and baby buggies. Vehicular lights flash, flicker, and give signals; their messages have become an integral part of our daily lives.

Companies that manufacture vehicular lighting equipment generally do so for a wide range of vehicles, including automobiles, airplanes, trains, boats, bicycles, motorcycles, and amusement rides. Also, companies frequently work together on the same lighting project, often on a contractor-subcontractor basis. According to the *1995 Annual Survey of Manufactures,* the vehicular lighting equipment industry ships goods valued at approximately $3 billion and employs approximately 17,400 people.

In 1999 the two leading companies in the vehicular lighting equipment industry were North American Lighting Inc. and Peterson Manufacturing Company. North American Lighting's sales were $293 million in 1999 and it had 1,900 employees. Peterson—a leading manufacturer of vehicle lights, reflectors, and mirrors for the automotive and trucking industry—had sales of about $137 million and employed 2,300 people. Another industry leader, Truck-Lite Company, Inc., of Falconer, New York, had sales of more than $100 million.

Through the middle of the 1990s, the United States was expected to import more automotive parts and accessories, including vehicular lighting equipment, than it exports. This trade imbalance was due chiefly to increased shipments from Japan. Overall, however, U.S. parts exports were expected to increase slowly. Some U.S. companies were looking to Mexico for increased export business, mainly because of the North American Free Trade Agreement (NAFTA). Others, including Allied-Signal and Federal-Mogul Corp., were exploring joint ventures with foreign manufacturers and acquiring overseas manufacturing facilities. Foreign investment in the U.S. parts industry was also expected to grow slowly.

Industry leaders were looking to electronic data transfer to decrease production time and innovations such as Truck-Lite's electronic cooling system that would allow the industry to stay technologically current into the twenty-first century.

FURTHER READING

"Hoover's Company Capsules." *Hoover's Online: The Business Network,* 1999. Available from http://www.hoovers.com.

"Innovative Cooling Water Management." *The Protector,* 1999. Available from http://www.dep.state.pa.us.

"North American Lighting Selects e-Parcel for CAD Data Delivery." *The Auto Channel,* 1999. Available from http://www.theautochannel.com.

U.S. Bureau of the Census. *1995 Annual Survey of Manufactures.* Washington, D.C.: GPO, 1997.

SIC 3648

LIGHTING EQUIPMENT, NOT ELSEWHERE CLASSIFIED

This classification covers establishments primarily engaged in manufacturing miscellaneous lighting fixtures and equipment, electric and non-electric, not elsewhere classified. Examples of such products include flashlights and similar portable lamps, searchlights, ultraviolet lamp fixtures, and infrared lamp fixtures. Establishments primarily engaged in manufacturing electric light bulbs, tubes, and related light sources are classified in **SIC 3641: Electric Lamp Bulbs and Tubes.** Those establishments producing glassware for lighting fixtures are classified in various glass manufacturing industries. Those establishments manufacturing traffic signals are classified in **SIC 3669: Communications Equipment, Not Elsewhere Classified.**

NAICS CODE(S)

335129 (Other Lighting Equipment Manufacturing)

INDUSTRY SNAPSHOT

The two major groupings in the industry are outdoor lighting equipment, which constituted 57 percent of industry output in the mid-1990s, and electric and nonelectric equipment not elsewhere classified, which represented 35 percent of industry production. The majority of products in this category are handheld, portable lighting equipment, such as flashlights and lanterns. The remainder of the market is highly fragmented among various electric and nonelectric devices. Personal consumption expenditures represented about 16 percent of total consumption, while 4 percent of the industry's output was exported. Institutional and commercial sectors accounted for the majority of sales.

BACKGROUND AND DEVELOPMENT

Late 1980's revenues of over $1.8 billion per year for the miscellaneous lighting equipment industry (approximately 20 to 25 percent of total lighting equipment industry total) represented an average annual growth rate of more than 8 percent between 1982 and 1988, when sales were about $1.0 billion. Strong commercial and residential construction markets boosted shipments through the late 1980s, but growth faltered in the early 1990s, as economic malaise and depressed construction sectors pinched profits. Recovering residential building and re-

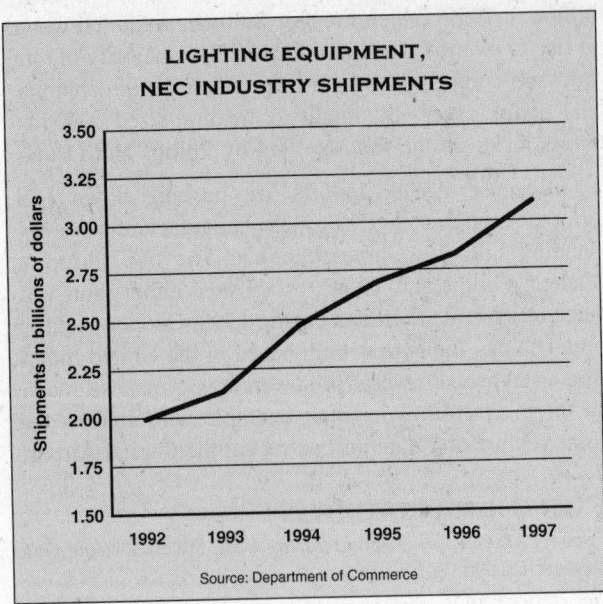

LIGHTING EQUIPMENT, NEC INDUSTRY SHIPMENTS

Shipments in billions of dollars

Source: Department of Commerce

modeling markets rejuvenated demand in 1992 and 1993, however, and these markets continued to improve through the mid-1990s.

Miscellaneous lighting equipment manufacturers hoped to overcome analysts' predictions of slow 1990's growth by introducing new and better fixtures. Much of the emphasis was on devices that could reduce energy consumption and accommodate new high-tech bulbs. The National Energy Security Act of 1992 even mandated the use of more efficient bulbs and equipment. In addition, the Environmental Protection Agency's voluntary "Green Light" conservation program encouraged corporations to install new energy-efficient equipment and fixtures. Even in this changing environment, growth through the mid-1990s was stable, as the total value of shipments increased 22 percent from 1992 to reach $2.4 billion in 1994. Despite this trend, there was no increase in the value of shipments in 1995. The industry exported about $540.0 million in goods.

In 1997 the value of shipments grew to about $3.1 billion. There were over 300 establishments in the industry, employing 18,252 workers, almost 70 percent of whom were in production; about half of these establishments employed 20 employees or more. California employed the most, followed by Ohio, Texas and Wisconsin. According to the Freedonia Group, increased road work and public safety concerns would help increase demand for small outdoor lighting through 2001.

Overall, the North American lighting equipment market was worth over $10.0 billion in 1998, according to Frost & Sullivan. Furthermore, increased demand for outdoor lighting in the next millenium is expected to vault the market's value to over $15.0 billion by 2005.

INDUSTRY LEADERS

The largest company in this industry, according to Ward's Business Directory 2000, was Coleman Company Inc. This Kansas-based outfit generated sales of $1.2 billion from its operations and had about 6,000 employees. Another major competitor was Juno-Lighting, based in Illinois, with $140 million in sales and 1100 employees. Other leaders included Stabler Company, Mag Instrument Inc., and Valley Forge Corp.

WORKFORCE

Although industry employment grew from about 8,500 to more than 9,500 during the 1980s, the outlook for employment growth was bleak from the mid-1990s through the end of the decade. Productivity gains and the transfer of some manufacturing activities to low-cost foreign producers are expected to contribute to job losses for several occupations. Positions for assemblers and fabricators, which account for over 16 percent of the workforce, were expected to decline by 7 percent between 1994 and 2005, and positions for machine operators were projected to drop as much as 35 percent, according to the Bureau of Labor Statistics. While most blue-collar opportunities will wane, jobs for such specialized groups like industrial machinery mechanics were projected to rise significantly in the new millenium. Prospects were also good for sales and marketing positions through 2005.

FURTHER READING

Darnay, Arsen J., ed. *Manufacturing USA*. 5th ed. Detroit: Gale Research, 1996.

"Energy Act Sets New Lightbulb Standards." *Hardware Age*, December 1992.

"Frost & Sullivan Sheds Light on North American Lighting Equipment Market"Press Release. Available from: http://www .frost.com/verity/press/environment_energy/pr576314.htm.

"How the New Energy Law Affects the Lighting Buy." *Purchasing*, 1 April 1993.

Lamps to 2001. The Freedonia Group, December 1997.

"NAICS 335129." *Manufacturing-Iindustry Series*. U.S. Census Bureau, 1997 Economic Census, 5 August 1999.

U.S. Department of Commerce. International Trade Administration. *U.S. Industrial Outlook 1994*. Washington: GPO, 1994.

SIC 3651

HOUSEHOLD AUDIO AND VIDEO EQUIPMENT

This category includes establishments primarily engaged in manufacturing electronic audio and video equipment for use at home or in automobiles, such as televisions, video recorders and players, radio receivers and amplifiers, phonographs, cassette tape players, and compact disc (CD) players. This industry also includes companies that manufacture microphones, speakers, and public address systems.

NAICS CODE(S)

334310 (Audio and Video Equipment Manufacturing)

INDUSTRY SNAPSHOT

The household audio and video equipment industry faced a number of challenges in the late 1990s, which was nothing new for this often-bruised category. In 1998, manufacturers generated sales of $8.4 billion, marking a 22 percent decline from the 1996 total of $10.8 billion. This was an exceptionally mature market in the United States, with household penetration for products in this category around 95 percent, while technological innovations have, with some notable exceptions, been few. Consumers in the market for home electronic equipment in the late 1990s were devoting their disposable income more often to personal computers and related equipment. Meanwhile, Internet-based audio and video software was expanding the capacities of personal computers in a manner detrimental to the household audio and video equipment market. Moreover, the rate of obsolescence among products in this category is fairly slow, particularly in comparison to computer products; thus, the large numbers of Americans who already possess such equipment have fewer reasons to upgrade.

Manufacturers were moving steadily toward an almost entirely digital market, including digital radio, cameras, television, and audio and video recording equipment. Industry players hoped that this long-awaited technological revolution will lift the industry out its malaise and get customers excited about new audio and video equipment.

The industry employed 31,000 workers—including approximately 21,000 production workers. U.S. manufacturers were focused almost exclusively on producing audio speakers and advanced technology televisions. Virtually all other consumer electronic components sold in the United States were manufactured abroad or manufactured in the United States by foreign-owned companies.

ORGANIZATION AND STRUCTURE

The U.S. household audio and video manufacturing industry was dominated in the 1990s by American subsidiaries of Japanese companies who used technologies developed by American companies. These subsidiaries assembled color televisions and high fidelity audio equipment from components imported from Japan or from Japanese-owned manufacturing facilities in other countries. The exception was speaker systems, where U.S.

owned companies were recognized as market leaders worldwide. The Zenith Electronics Corporation in Glenview, Illinois, was the only major U.S. owned company still manufacturing color televisions in 1999, rebounding after having filed for bankruptcy a few years earlier. Zenith controlled about 10.9 percent of the U.S. market. Bose Corporation of the United States supplies nearly one-fourth of the speakers purchased in the country—more than twice the amount as the next leading competitor. More than one-third of all U.S. establishments employed fewer than five workers.

BACKGROUND AND DEVELOPMENT

U.S. manufacturers dominated the household audio and video industry from the first experimental radio and television broadcasts until the 1980s, when many U.S. owned companies were forced out of manufacturing by foreign competition. The first radios to be mass manufactured were developed by RCA in the 1920s, which also pioneered television manufacturing in the 1930s. For years, American manufacturers like RCA, Westinghouse, General Electric, Motorola, Philco, and Zenith dominated the industry.

Television Manufacturing. Although the nature of television manufacturing in the United States began to change in the late 1960s, the stage was set more than a decade earlier when several major Japanese manufacturers formed the Home Electronic Appliance Market Stabilization Council. Despite opposition from the Japanese Fair Trade Commission, this cartel successfully lobbied the Japanese government to establish tariffs and other trade barriers that protected the manufacturers from foreign competition. This allowed the cartel to establish minimum prices and control their domestic market. In addition, U.S. companies locked out of the Japanese market began to license advanced technology to the Japanese. In 1962, RCA Corporation became the first company to license color technology to the Japanese manufacturers.

In 1963, the Japanese manufacturers began to export televisions to the United States—using the profits from their protected domestic market to subsidized below cost sales in the United States, in violation of U.S. trade laws. In addition, a Department of Justice investigation later revealed that the Japanese gave American importers, including Sears, Roebuck & Co., illegal rebates on every Japanese television they sold in the United States. Sales of Japanese-made televisions soared while U.S. companies suffered.

The United States Electronic Industry Association filed a complaint about the illegal "dumping" in 1968. However, Japanese manufacturers stonewalled the investigation for more than three years. In addition, the U.S. government was not eager to upset trade negotiations with Japan and proceeded with the investigation reluctantly. In 1971, the Treasury Department ruled that the Japanese companies had violated U.S. law and owed millions of dollars in antidumping levies. Nine years passed before a settlement was reached, however, and the Japanese paid about one-tenth of what they owed. The damage to U.S. television manufacturers was irreversible.

In 1968, there were 28 U.S. owned companies manufacturing televisions in this country. By 1976, there were only six. More than 20,000 jobs were eliminated. Several financially strapped U.S. companies were purchased by Japanese or European competitors, while others simply went out of business. Matsushita Electric Industrial Company, the largest consumer electronics company in the world, purchased Motorola's Consumer Products Division. Magnavox was purchased by N.V. Philips, S.A., a Dutch manufacturer. Among the brand names to disappear were Admiral and Dumont. In addition, dozens of smaller manufacturers making parts for U.S. made televisions also failed.

In 1977, the Japanese manufacturers signed an Orderly Marketing Agreement limiting exports to the United States to 1.5 million sets annually. However, the agreement allowed the Japanese to manufacture televisions in the United States in excess of the quotas. Three of the five largest Japanese companies—Matsushita, the Sony Corporation, and Sanyo Electric Company—had already established manufacturing facilities in the United States, and Hitachi and Tokyo Shibaura Electric soon followed suit. The Japanese also established manufacturing facilities in other countries with abundant, low cost labor such as Mexico and Argentina to circumvent the limits on imports from Japan. In addition, Taiwan and South Korea began exporting televisions to the United States. Taiwanese imports more than doubled in 1977, increasing that country's share of the U.S. market from 7 to 14 percent.

An investigation later revealed that Robert Strauss, the former Democratic Party chairman who had been appointed by President Carter as special trade representative to Japan, signed a secret agreement in which he promised that the United States would settle financial claims against the Japanese manufacturers "expeditiously" and would limit an International Trade Commission investigation into further allegations of illegal dumping. Strauss also promised that the Carter Administration would appeal a ruling court decision in favor of Zenith, who had won a $400 million predatory pricing suit against Matsushita. The award would have been tripled under U.S. antitrust law to $1.2 billion. Finally, Strauss agreed to ignore official Japanese government policies that prevented U.S. companies from competing in the protected Japanese home electronics market.

Congress did not learn of the secret agreement until 1979, but nevertheless agreed to honor the commitment.

Under the Strauss agreement, the Japanese eventually paid about $66 million of the $500 million the Treasury Department said they owed for illegal dumping; the antitrust suit filed by Zenith was eventually dismissed by the Supreme Court. Meanwhile, the Japanese solidified their hold on the U.S. television market.

At least one U.S. company, however, blamed irrational cost cutting by U.S. market leaders as much as the Japanese for the decline of U.S. manufacturing. Robert J. O'Neil, then president of GTE Consumer Electronics Co., told *Business Week* in 1978 that "RCA and Zenith are the biggest problem in the industry." At the time, RCA and Zenith were battling each other for the number one position in U.S. sales of color televisions. According to O'Neil, cost cutting by RCA and Zenith forced other U.S. companies to lower their prices to unprofitable levels. In dismissing the antitrust suit against Matsushita, the Supreme Court noted that Zenith and RCA were still the leading television makers in the United States, with more than 40 percent of the market between them, despite 20 years of Japanese competition. GTE eventually sold its consumer electronics company, including the Sylvania and Philco brand names, to the Dutch company that purchased Magnavox, N.V. Philips.

Among the last major U.S. owned companies to manufacture televisions were the General Electric Corporation and the RCA Corporation, which together accounted for about 45 percent of all color television sets sold in the United States in 1980. General Electric quit manufacturing televisions in 1984 and began importing sets made by Matsushita with the GE brand name. In 1985, General Electric temporarily re-entered the market when it purchased RCA. However, despite a 23 percent share of the market for color televisions in the United States and 17 percent of the market for VCRs, the RCA consumer electronics division was losing money. In 1986, General Electric sold the RCA consumer products division to Thomson, S.A., a French electronics corporation second only to Matsushita in size. The sale left the United States without a single American-owned firm manufacturing VCRs.

Audio Equipment. The experience of the audio equipment manufacturing industry in the United States was similar to that of television manufacturers. Until the mid-1960s, most of the leading manufacturers in the world were U.S. owned companies with such well known brand names as Fisher, Bose, Sherwood, and Marantz. The first Japanese brand to appear in the annual *Stereo/Hi-Fi Directory and Buyers Guide* was Kenwood, in 1965. However, over the next five years, the number of Japanese brands sold in the United States increased dramatically. Sony, Pioneer, and Sansui were introduced in 1968; JVC was introduced in 1970.

By 1980, most U.S. owned companies had either moved their manufacturing facilities offshore to take advantage of cheap labor or had licensed their brand names to Japanese companies and become distributors for foreign manufacturers. Many Japanese companies eventually built manufacturing facilities in the United States. It soon became difficult to distinguish U.S.-made from foreign-made products. Or, as William Livingstone, then editor-in-chief of *Stereo Review Magazine,* wrote in 1986, "Do you give more support to the labor force and overall economy of the United States by buying a component manufactured in Hong Kong for an American company or by buying one made by American hands in a Japanese-owned factory in California or Tennessee?"

VCRs, Camcorders, and CD Players. With the exception of RCA, major American manufacturers disdained entering the market for VCRs, camcorders, and CD players as those technologies were developed in the 1980s. In many cases, U.S. companies apparently underestimated the tremendous markets that developed. But economist Pat Choate, writing in the *Washington Post,* pointed out that the loss of U.S. television manufacturing also hamstrung U.S. manufacturers' ability to enter these new fields by undermining the companies that produced high technology components. U.S. companies were relegated to a marketing role, rather than manufacturing, which helped create a huge trade deficit in consumer electronics in the 1980s.

The 1980s and 1990s. Increased competition from Korean and Taiwanese manufacturers continued to affect the U.S. consumer electronics manufacturing in the mid-1980s. Reminiscent of Japan's entry into the U.S. market, Goldstar Electronics, a leading Korean television manufacturer, was found guilty in 1984 of selling its televisions in the United States for 20 percent less than those same sets were sold for in Korea. To avoid paying a 20 percent antidumping tariff, Goldstar began beefing up production at a plant it opened in Alabama in 1981.

In the early lingering recession was also affecting the industry. Ironically, many of the same Japanese companies that established U.S. manufacturing facilities in the 1970s to avoid restrictions on imports were beginning to move their operations to Mexico, where labor costs were considerably lower. Televisions made in Mexico by foreign companies went almost exclusively into the U.S. market. The North American Free Trade Agreement (NAFTA), endorsed by President Clinton in 1993, was expected to hasten this movement to Mexico.

In 1993, several major corporations, including Zenith and General Instruments, were waiting for the Federal Communications Commission (FCC) to set technological protocols for High Definition Television (HDTV) in the United States. These companies—and a third partnership led by Thomson, Philips, and NBC—were hopeful that HDTV would help revitalize the U.S. electronics manufacturing industry. However, after considerable activity in the late 1980s, interest in HDTV appeared to be waning. Meanwhile, to maximize profits, U.S. based manufacturers were beginning to concentrate on large-screen televisions and home-theater units, leaving low-margin color televisions to be manufactured elsewhere.

CURRENT CONDITIONS

The mature television market remains the industry's center of gravity. With a 98 percent market penetration and intense competition for market share anchoring prices and demanding bulk shipments to procure profits, the television market was stuck in a malaise that has placed many companies in a precarious position. Digital television (DTV) technology was widely expected to become the new lifeline of the industry, a hope upon which some firms have staked their fortunes.

DTV technology involves the digital transmission of data signals to produce a TV picture. There, however, the consensus ends. There were nearly twenty different formats that fall under the definition of DTV technology, primarily distinguishing themselves by the technique by which pictures are scanned or by the resolution of the picture. The Consumer Electronics Association (CEA) has been working to establish a clear definition of DTVs so as to launch a concentrated marketing campaign, but squabbling continues among manufacturers over the nature of the standard. Despite the animosity and continued consumer confusion about digital television products, the CEA expected the technology to take firm hold in coming years, reaching a 30 percent market share by 2006.

Standards for high-definition televisions (HDTVs) have been no less controversial. When, in 1999, the CEA approved their standard for HDTV, they effectively excluded several high-level sets manufactured by companies such as Toshiba and Hitachi, who both refused to recognize the vote and continued to market the televisions in question under the HDTV label. While the Toshiba and Hitachi models were digital in format and met the resolution requirements, they were in the traditional square-screen style, while the CEA standard defines HDTVs as fitting the movie-theater style wide-screen format. Cable operators, meanwhile, have not been as quick to adopt the HDTV format into their programming schedules as manufacturers had hoped. The uncertain future of HDTV may be spurring much of this hesitation. In its first year on the market, HDTVs shipped a mere 100,000 units.

Compatibility between various technological capabilities was becoming a primary and frustrating concern to the home audio and video equipment industry in the late 1990s. Direct broadcast satellite (DBS) systems, for example, experienced a swift decline in sales as a result of consumer dissatisfaction with their inability to receive many local broadcasts or integrate surround-sound audio technology. While these problems have been attended to by industry players such as Thomson, sales in this category have yet to recover to their mid-1990s peak. Meanwhile, manufacturers were scrambling to integrate their products' capabilities with those of personal computers in a move toward "convergence." Convergence technologies refer to equipment that can record and playback signals transmitted electronically via Internet connections.

Digital video disc (DVD) players, meanwhile, sold 3.9 million units in 1999, greatly exceeding expectations and signaling that analysts' predictions claiming that DVD's would steadily supercede traditional video tapes may prove accurate. Aiding growth in this market sector was the increasing number of personal computer manufactured with DVD drives. Observers expected DVD players to have achieved a 10 percent household penetration rate by the end of 2000; that figure is generally viewed as a benchmark figure for this category, signaling the product's arrival as a market force.

Although consumers tend to replace video cassette recorders (VCRs) more quickly than televisions, due to declining prices, including a 30 percent drop between 1995 and 1997, this category has hardly consoled industry players. Compact disc (CD) players, likewise, have registered increasing unit sales while dollar sales remain flat as prices continue to fall for this market staple.

Until cutting-edge technologies are fully developed and immersed in consumer markets, they continue to play a somewhat dubious role within the industry. Because consumers remain relatively ignorant of the new technologies, the products have generally helped flatten overall sales as they sit on shelves and older, lower margin products continue to make up the sales.

INDUSTRY LEADERS

The leading makers of household audio and video equipment in the United States were generally subsidiaries of foreign-owned companies, including Matsushita Electric Industrial Co., with 10 percent of the global television market and revenues of $28 billion; Harman International Industries, the world's largest speaker producer with sales of $1.5 billion, though Harman's 14 percent market share trailed Bose Corporation's 22 percent; Zenith Electronics Corporation with 11.3 percent of the television market and revenues of $1.17 billion in 1998; and Philips Consumer Electronics Company, one component on Philips Electronics' $8 billion U.S. electronics business.

WORKFORCE

The workforce in this classification continues to decline, due mostly to the fact that American companies are increasingly getting out of the business due to foreign companies' domination. The industry's 20,700 production workers earned an average of $11.75 per hour in 1997.

RESEARCH AND TECHNOLOGY

The next hot digital product in the home video product industry was the digital video recorder (DVR). In early 1994, the HG Digital Conference—a committee representing 50 electronics companies in Europe, Asia, and the United States—agreed on a proposed standard for VCRs that will use digital technology. The agreement was reached in part to avoid future format battles such as the one that took place in the 1980s between Beta and VHS systems. This new technology, which is expected to provide manufacturers with the ability to increase image quality, involves storing tape images with ones and zeroes of binary computer codes rather than the current wave-like form. These new VCRs are expected to use video tapes that are one-quarter inch wide—one-half the width of existing VHS tapes. The technology will allow greater "personalization" from television viewers by committing their preferences to memory. In addition, DVRs can be paused and played back during the recording process, affording the user enhanced editing capabilities.

Also in development were personal video recorders (PVRs), which dispense with tapes altogether. PVRs do away with rewinding and storing by storing information digitally on a hard drive. They can also be programmed to regularly store programs and even remember the user's preferred kinds of shows, film stars, or sports teams, and can even record shows automatically based on previous viewing habits as long as disk space is available.

One of the most important innovations in the industry, as far as potential market exposure is concerned, revolves around the production of Internet TV equipment, which began in late 1996. Industry sources believe that sales of software/Internet TV equipment will increase from $2.3 billion in 1995 to more than $25 billion by 2002, when an estimated 33 percent of all American households will own such devices. Internet TVs and set top units will allow television users to access the Internet without having to use a personal computer. Among the potential drawbacks of Internet TV is that the average American views television from 8-12 feet away, making script on the screen difficult to see. Increasing the size of the text would mean less information would be available on each screen, meaning more scrolling up and down. The market potential for this technology appears to be tremendous, since about 60 percent of American homes are not currently connected to the Internet.

FURTHER READING

Doman, Matthew. "Little Demand for Digital TV, Int'l Study Says." *Hollywood Reporter*, 27 September 1999.

"DVD Killed Video's Star." *New York Times*, 7 January 2000.

"DVD Players Set Records in Electronics Sales." *Salt Lake Tribune*, 30 November 1999.

"DVD: The Story So Far." *Screen Digest*, November 1998.

Knibbs, Robert. "VHS Under DVD's Shadow." *One to One*, September 1998.

"Loudspeaker Envy." *Forbes*, 9 August 1998.

"Markets for Recordable CDs Spin Briskly Along." *Journal of the Electronics Industry*, December 1999.

"New Rule on High-Definition TV Roils Toshiba and Hitachi." *New York Times*, 18 December 1999.

"Sales of Ordinary Tube TVs Rise 0.2 Percent While Big-Screen Models Jump 16 Percent." *Wall Street Journal*, 10 August 1999.

"Sony Claims Top Spot in TV, DVD." *Twice*, 7 June 1999.

Stern, Christopher. "Slow Sales Hamper High-Def." *Variety*, 3 January 2000.

Symons, Allene. "Into the Future with Home Entertainment." *Supermarket News*, 13 December 1999.

U.S. Department of Commerce. Bureau of the Census. *1997 Census of Manufacturers*. Washington, D.C.: GPO, 20 August 1998.

U.S. Department of Commerce. International Trade Administration. *U.S. Industry and Trade Outlook 1999*. New York: The McGraw Hill Companies, 1999.

SIC 3652

PHONOGRAPH RECORDS AND PRERECORDED AUDIO TAPES AND DISKS

This category includes establishments primarily engaged in manufacturing phonograph records and prerecorded audio tapes and disks. Establishments primarily engaged in the design, development, and production of prepackaged computer software are classified in Computer Programming, Data Processing, and Other Computer Related Services; and those reproducing prerecorded video tape cassettes and disks are classified in the Motion Picture industries.

NAICS CODE(S)

334612 (Prerecorded Compact Disc (Except Software), Tape and Record Reproducing)
512220 (Integrated Record Production/Distribution)

INDUSTRY SNAPSHOT

"When Thomas Edison invented practical phonograph recording in 1877, he could hardly have anticipated the powerful mass entertainment medium it would become,'' wrote Michael Fink in *Inside the Music Business*. After a rocky start in the first decades of the twentieth century, the business of recording and selling music has grown into an international industry worth billions of dollars. Analysts from the International Federation of the Phonographic Industry (IFPF) estimated that, in 1990, international record sales, a category that includes audiotapes and disks, grossed $24.1 billion. Though five major companies dominate the industry, the nature of the music business has always guaranteed a place for the small record company attuned to new forms of popular music and specialized interests. The twenty-first century is expected to make the Internet a major player in the recorded music industry, and the home-based music lover will be able to use recordable compact discs to compile unique collections of music from online and prerecorded sources. In 1997, the industry shipped $3.9 billion worth of goods.

ORGANIZATION AND STRUCTURE

The business of producing recorded music is like digging for gold—a record company has to pan many streams before it hits the jackpot. The principal work of each recording company consists of locating promising musical acts, producing them in the most commercial way, promoting them to fit into a rapidly changing market, producing the physical, recorded product, and providing efficient distribution. Record companies lose money on recordings that do not sell as well as anticipated, but those that become ''hits'' provide such immense profits that they make up for the failures.

Industry Organization. Although the Recording Industry Association of America (RIAA) claims 220 members, five of those corporations account for over 90 percent of the market. In November of 1992, *Music and Media* reported that PolyGram held 27 percent of the market, Sony Music Entertainment Inc. held 17.8 percent, Time Warner and Thorn/EMI both held 16.7 percent, and the Bertelsmann Music Group (BMG) held 15.3 percent. The smaller companies, called independent labels, together accounted for only 6.5 percent of the market.

Recording companies are often referred to as ''labels,'' though that term became less accurate when large companies began marketing music under several different labels or brands. Originally, the label was synonymous with the company, for each recording company had one label that identified its records. During the years, however, big companies have bought little companies, and single firms have acquired several smaller companies and their labels. When CBS bought the American Record Corporation in 1938, for example, they acquired both the Brunswick and Vocalion labels. After the very large corporate mergers and buyouts of the late 1980s and early

1990s, each one of the five companies that dominated the market owned many labels: PolyGram had 27 and Sony had 25. These companies are known as the major labels, or simply ''the majors.'' Many of the individual labels owned by a large corporation retain their own staff, which enables the large companies to maintain better and more personal relations with the artists, who record on only one label. Independent record companies are usually still identified with a single label and are referred to as ''the independents'' or ''the indies''.

Single labels often produce only one kind of music. For example, Deutche Grammophon is a classical music label, Mercury carries country-western music, and Motown is a rhythm and blues (R&B) label; all are owned by PolyGram. Occasionally, a major label will create, rather than buy, a new label to produce one specific genre, as when Warner launched Warner Western in 1992. On the other hand, not all labels are thus limited. Koch International, an independent label, produces classical, country, pop, and jazz.

Company Organization. The first job of any recording company is to sign up musicians. This job is handled by the Artists and Repertoire (A&R) department, which scouts for and signs contracts with new talents, finds them songs if they do not write their own, and finds the right producer to oversee their records. In the first few decades of the industry, the A&R department hired singers, found new songs for these singers to perform, and produced the record. These functions made the A&R department one of the largest and most powerful in any recording company.

Rock and roll music changed much of the music industry and affected A&R departments more than any other type of music. Rock musicians often wrote their own songs and found their own producers. As Steve Chapple and Reebee Garofalo explain in *Rock 'n' Roll Is Here to Pay: The History and Politics of the Music Industry*, ''In the 1950s, the bulk of music was produced with staff producers who were assigned by the all-powerful A&R heads to record several of a company's acts. But these men often did not understand the new music. What's more, because many new groups wrote their own material, an A&R person was not needed to bring publisher and performer together. As conflicts between staff producers and groups increased, and as company A&R men proved for the most part unable to recognize underground talent, record companies turned to independent producers.'' The role of the A&R department became much more limited, and relied heavily on the independent producer for the sound of the final product.

The producer of a record, as the name implies, oversees the production of the master recording. The producer serves as the artistic director and business manager for the recording. The record company, through the A&R department, contracts with the artist and producer and provides the advance money for both. The producer then handles the main business aspects of recording the record. This includes budgeting for the project, arranging the copyright licenses when necessary, booking the recording studio, and hiring any extra musicians and equipment as needed. While recording companies frequently own studios, independent studios are also used for a variety of reasons, including the local musical styles of an area. Most records are still made in one of the three major musical cities—Los Angeles, New York, and Nashville—but the studios of smaller cities with unique musical roots are often hired for their unique sounds.

The producer also oversees the rehearsing, recording, and mixing of the musical tracks. Depending on the musicians involved, the producer sometimes has an enormous artistic role in the recording. The producer may hire out or write an arrangement, choosing how the accompaniment will sound. Working with the musicians in rehearsal, the producer frequently contributes to the musical interpretation. "My job is to help writers," Chris Thomas, rock star Elton John's producer, told *Billboard* in 1993. "That's the reason you're there: to help them get their song realized in recorded form." Thomas defines producing as "filling in the colors of a picture." No matter the size of the group, each instrument and voice is recorded separately on its own track. The producer oversees the mixdown of the tracks, combining the individual instruments into the final ensemble sound. "Recording basic tracks is a game. It's fun. It's easy," said Thomas. "Mixing is much harder because you can't always fix it tomorrow. . . . You've got to balance it very carefully." The final balance of instruments and voices, as well as the use of different electronic effects such as tone-quality filters, reverberation, delay, and echo, are determined by the producer. Musicians who want complete control over their own artistic productions will sometimes produce their own work, but many recordings are still governed by producers who are trained in sound engineering.

After the master recording is made and delivered to the record company, the production and promotion departments take over. The production department makes the physical items that the consumers will buy, both the recording and, just as importantly, the packaging. Both the producer and the promotion department may have roles in the artwork for the packaging. A given music video (music videos are a major form of promotion on music television networks) may have the same producer as the recording.

Because the ultimate goal of record companies is to sell a record, the marketing department is frequently the largest and most important. In this intensely competitive industry, promotion and marketing play a large part in the final success of any recording. Marketing departments use two primary avenues of publicity: radio promotion and media advertising.

Airplay is the most effective form of promotion for any popular recording, whether it be on radio or television, and having a new record programmed onto the playlist is the goal of all promoters. While there are several thousand music-format radio stations across the United States, only several hundred are important. Record promoters may send promotional copies to all stations, but they concentrate their personal efforts on the important few—the stations that determine the poll lists in the trade publications, such as Billboard's Top Ten. Most radio stations, however, usually play less than 40 songs in rotation in a week. Because the recording industry produces several hundred new recordings each week, the competition for these spots is fierce. Since the early 1960s, "payola," or money paid to radio stations to play music, has been outlawed, but legal giveaways to radio station program directors and other personnel include records, T-shirts, concert tickets, and invitations to press parties. Music television works much the same way. To become a hit, a song now must not only be played on the radio, but also be shown in video format on television.

Since 1957, when Dick Clark introduced hit after hit on his dance show, American Bandstand, television has been an effective promotional tool to supplement radio. In 1981, Warner Amex Cable Communications, which has since become Time Warner, introduced rock music programming to cable television in the form of MTV, and music videos revolutionized the industry. During the first few years, when not every pop musician made videos, MTV provided an avenue for new artists to reach audiences. By the middle of the 1980s, however, MTV became as play-list oriented as radio, and competition to have a video shown became as fierce as on any top-40 radio station. Other channels have also shown music videos, including VH-1, the adult-oriented MTV spin-off; Video Music Channel; Country Music TV; the Nashville Network; and NBC's Friday Night Videos. Videos have become essential to music promotion, and, as Michael Fink wrote in his 1989 book on the music industry, "any new record/tape release with aspirations to be a hit must have a music video clip to accompany it."

Publicity and advertising departments also cultivate the popular music press when releasing records. Press kits for new artists include carefully prepared biographies presenting the most profitable image for the artist. Established and beginning artists alike go on publicity tours, although the rising costs of concert tours have kept record companies from providing full financial support for this element of publicity. In the late 1980s, retail outlets started sponsoring in-house concerts of relatively unknown artists as part of the promotional package. National and local radio and television interviews help to publicize new releases; music critics receive advance copies of the new records with the hopes that favorable reviews will sell disks. Music trade publications carry much advertising for artists and their recent releases.

Large companies distribute their records through branch distributors, independent distributors, and mail-order record clubs. In major musical cities, branch offices of the recording company distribute their recordings locally in conjunction with local promoters and advertising specialists. In smaller areas not covered by branch offices, record companies use the services of independent distributors, one-stops, and rack jobbers, who deal with many different record companies and distribute to record stores, department stores, and other record outlets (see **SIC 5735: Record and Prerecorded Tape Stores**). While retailing is considered a different industry altogether, some of the major labels own retail outlets; they do not limit their distribution to these stores, of course.

The first company foray into record-company-owned retail was the formation of the record club, pioneered by Columbia Records when they formed Columbia House in the mid 1950s. RCA soon followed, and both have remained the biggest sponsors of direct-mail distribution. Because direct mail avoids middle-man costs, the companies can make more profit while still giving consumers a discounted price. From their inception, record clubs have proved profitable for the majors. Shortly after Sony bought CBS Records in the late 1980s, they entered into an agreement with Time Warner, owners of Warner Records, to jointly operate Columbia House Records. In 1993, the two conglomerates announced a new joint ownership and operation of two other direct-mail operations, Warner's Music Sound Exchange for the U.S. market, and Sony's Music $More in Germany.

Corporate Structure of Independents. Independent labels, while varying greatly in size and complexity, generally have few of the administrative capabilities of the major labels. Their strong point is signing and producing new or special interest music, and they often contract out other elements of their business. The small companies, like the rap-music label Flavor Unit Records, which released its first recording in December of 1992, have a skeletal administrative and production staff. Major label Epic Records agreed to promote and distribute Flavor Units' records. The small company's benefit from such an arrangement is access to the publicity power of a major label; the larger company reaps the benefits of an expanding market without much company investment. "Epic hasn't ventured that deep into rap," Epic executive vice-president Richard Griffith told *Billboard*. "We've been looking for people to be our partners as experts." Small labels that do not connect with major labels often hire out for such services, contracting with independent public relations firms, distributors, studios, and disk factories.

BACKGROUND AND DEVELOPMENT

A few years after Thomas Edison invented phonograph recording using wax cylinders in 1877, Emile Berliner developed the disk format of recording. These two formats competed in popularity for a few years, but by the beginning of the twentieth century, the disk format had won. The earliest music recorded was classical, opera, popular tin-pan alley music, and Broadway songs. In 1917, the first jazz recordings were made, and in 1920, the first blues were recorded. These recordings signaled the industry's discovery of music performed by and for African-Americans, which influenced the industry and American popular music greatly throughout the century. By the 1940s, the genre was universally known as "rhythm and blues."

From the outset, the industry has been dominated by a few large companies. The two earliest recording companies have remained among the majors throughout the century. The Victor Talking Machine Company, formed as an offshoot of the English Gramophone and Typewriter Company in 1901, eventually became RCA records; the Columbia Gramophone Company became Columbia Records in the late 1930s. Together, RCA and Columbia have shared the majority of the market for decades. Although by the early 1990s they were owned by different corporations, they still belong to the majors. The industry grew rapidly after 1900, peaking in 1921 with sales of $106 million. By 1922, however, radio had destroyed the market with the free music it offered over the airwaves. Sales fell throughout the entire decade and when the stock market crashed in 1929, most of the smaller companies either went out of business or were bought by the two larger companies.

Although radio almost destroyed the industry in the 1920s, it saved the industry in the 1930s. The two rival radio networks, Radio Corporation of America and Columbia Broadcasting System, bought the rival record firms, Victor and Columbia Gramophone, respectively. The large profits from the radio industry financed recorded music. New technologies developed for radio, such as the electronic microphone, enhanced music recording as well. Record stars became radio stars and radio became the main promotional tool for selling records. In the mid-1930s when Jack Kapp—of the newly-formed independent label Decca—reduced the price of records from 75 cents to 35 cents, people could afford to buy them again, and the demand for recordings began to pick up. Music popular in the late thirties and early forties included big-band jazz and popular Broadway and movie songs, and (in limited but growing regional markets) country music and rhythm and blues. The record format during these early years was the shellac disk playing at 78 rotations per minute (rpm) with only one song on each side (singles).

The social and economic changes accompanying World War II created changes in the music world that would impact the industry forever. Because of war-induced shortages of shellac, RCA and CBS limited their record production to mainstream popular music, leaving a hole in the R&B and country market. Small independent labels grew to fill the gap left by the majors.

Radio also filled this gap between supply and demand. Some stations began programming R&B between the pop music programs, some began to program country music, and new stations formed to play only R&B or country. While both R&B and country records had previously sold only in small and isolated areas of the country, both could now be heard everywhere on radio. A few companies, like Capitol Records, continued to produce both R&B and country and succeeded in spreading this music into the pop market. Young people, mostly teenagers, began buying all three: R&B, country, and pop. Thus, the market was diversifying. Record formats changed from the 78 rpm single to the 45 rpm single with better sound, and the 33-1/3 rpm Long Playing album (nicknamed the "vinyl") started gaining popularity as well, especially for classical music.

The kids who listened to a variety of popular music in the 1940s became the musicians of the 1950s who played a new kind of music that synthesized all three: rock and roll. Elvis Presley's "Heart Break Hotel," an early rock and roll hit, topped pop, R&B, and country charts. This new music drew even bigger teenage audiences, who were, in the affluence of the 1950s, able to spend more on luxuries like records than their predecessors. Sales soared. The new music, with its stronger rhythms and stronger lyrics than Broadway pop tunes, scandalized conservative critics and frightened the major labels. Independent labels, growing more numerous and larger than ever before, cashed in on the new music while the majors tried to control the market by making records of their contracted popular crooners singing the new hits. By the end of the decade, the frenzy for the new music had subsided, and the majors were moving back onto the charts with watered-down versions of the rock songs, thanks in part to Dick Clark and his dance show, American Bandstand, which captivated thousands of teenagers by bringing the recording stars into their homes through the medium of television.

The arrival of The Beatles in the early 1960s injected a new fever of activity into the industry, benefiting both the independents and majors. Independent producers, who seemed to understand the new music better than the staff producers of the major companies, became the "wizards" of the industry, discovering and recording the

new talents that fed the business. Sales patterns began to change as well. Albums started replacing singles as the dominant format. A wide spectrum of popular musical styles flourished, and FM radio grew in popularity as it played and promoted the different types of rock and pop.

Even with the economic recession of the 1970s, which slowed record sales and bankrupted many of the smallest independents, the market has continued to grow since the advent of rock and roll. In an effort to produce something for everyone at great profits, record companies have expanded the types of popular music available. As Michael Fink wrote in *Inside the Music Business*, "American taste and the U.S. market for records and tapes have splintered and broadened to an extreme degree in the 1980s. A 1984 report issued by the Recording Industry Association of America (RIAA), covering the years 1979-1983, identified no fewer than ten distinct 'music types': rock, country, pop/easy listening, dance, gospel, classical, show/soundtracks, jazz, children's, and other (ethnic, nostalgia, folk, Latin, and so forth)." As the decade progressed, some of these categories splintered further; dance includes rap and hiphop, while rock includes acid, punk, techno, and fusion, just to name a few.

The introduction of the compact disc (CD), with its greater durability and much higher fidelity, brought new profits to the industries. Sales jumped as consumers began to replace their vinyl collections with the better sounding product, and new markets for older records opened up as companies began reissuing older albums in the new format. By the end of the 1980s, sales of vinyl records had almost completely died out, and most companies stopped producing the older format completely in the early 1990s.

The late 1980s and early 1990s saw the absorption of the biggest independent companies into huge conglomerates, as large electronics firms bought up record labels. Sony Corporation started the trend in 1987 when it bought CBS Records for $2.0 billion, an unheard of figure. Two years later, EMI, Philips, and Bertelsmann Music Group led bidding wars for the largest independent labels like A&M and Motown, which eventually went to Philips' PolyGram division. By 1996, six conglomerates controlled all the major labels—Time Warner Inc., Sony Corporation, Philips N.V., Thorn/EMI, Bertelsmann A.G., and Seagram (MCA).

After several years of sluggish sales due to economic recession, 1992 record industry sales figures began to recover. While unit sales were down 7.5 percent in 1991, they bounced back up 6.7 percent in 1992, with total gross income up 11 percent—the strongest gain since 1987. Strong growth continued through 1993 and 1994, with sales in 1994 leaping by more than 17 percent over 1993 figures. Industry euphoria was short-lived, however. U.S. music sales in 1995 totaled an estimated $11.0

billion, up slightly from 1994 sales. Time Warner's labels including Warner Brothers, Elektra, and Atlantic) grabbed the lion's share of the market, taking 21.6 percent, followed by Sony Music with 13.9 percent, and PolyGram with 13.5 percent. German-based Bertelsmann A.G.'s Columbia Records came fourth with 12.4 percent, followed by Thorn/EMI with 9.8 percent and MCA's UNI with 9.7 percent.

CURRENT CONDITIONS

Overall, music sales growth was expected to slow between 1995 and 2000. The anticipated slowdown was predicated on two factors: overexpansion of the retail sector and the maturing of the CD format. Much of the growth of the previous decade had come as the result of consumers replacing their libraries of vinyl and cassette albums with high-priced CD versions. Though CDs were the dominant recorded medium in 1995 and 1996, accounting for an estimated 70 percent of total industry revenues—the number of CDs sold in 1995 was up 11 percent over 1994, while the volume of prerecorded cassettes dropped by about 16 percent—some analysts feared the high retail cost of CDs was limiting sales to younger consumers. As the CD market became more dependent on sales of current releases in the latter part of the decade, this price factor was expected to start hurting the industry.

Another threat to new CD sales came from the fast-growing used CD market. Because of the CD's durability and high price tag in relation to previous records and cassettes, several of the largest music retail chains in the United States began selling used CDs. Previously, only small locally owned stores sold used products. Rather than lowering the prices on CDs, which retailers had been requesting for years, the industry leaders fought back by withholding cooperative advertising dollars. They thought this would be effective because distributors and retailers share some publicity costs at the local level. Artists began to get involved in the fray. For example, country music superstar Garth Brooks declared that he would refuse to distribute his albums, the best-selling country albums at the time, to any store selling used CDs. Such tactics had little effect. Independent record retailers responded by filing lawsuits against the four major distributors that instituted the punitive policies; this occurred at roughly the same time the Federal Trade Commission announced it was launching an investigation into the policies. The distributors quickly retreated from their hard line stance, putting an end to the confrontation.

Growth in sales of both CD singles and music videos was expected to accelerate. The price of a CD single dropped to just over $5 in 1995, putting it well within the budget of the younger consumer; sales increased by more than 84 percent. A decline in the price of music videos also prompted a surge in sales.

In 1997, the industry as a whole shipped $3.9 billion worth of goods. Total employment reached 25,553 people. The nearly 20,000 production workers included in this number earned an average hourly wage of $12.77.

INDUSTRY LEADERS

Today the industry is dominated by six huge conglomerates called "the majors". Each owns many different record labels, and each produces hundreds of new potential "hit" records each month.

Technically, Warner Communications Inc. is the only American-owned conglomerate in the majors, though the purchase of MCA by Canada's Seagram Company put another major label in the hands of a North American company. The Warner brothers—Jack, Albert, Harry, and Sam—established a successful film production and distribution company in the 1910s. The company remained strong well into the 1950s, when television began to change consumer entertainment patterns and cut into the film market. In 1966, the last Warner brother sold the company to Seven Arts Productions, which was more interested in selling television rights to old movies than making new movies, and the company continued to decline.

Warner Brothers-Seven Arts first got into the record business in 1969, when they bought the large independent Atlantic Records. In 1971, after being purchased by Stephen Ross, the company was renamed Warner Communications. Under the new director, the company once again flourished and began buying up smaller record labels and launching new ones. They acquired contracts for many of the hottest musical acts in the business and became a prominent force in the industry.

In 1989, Warner was purchased by Time Inc., and became Time Warner Inc., one of the largest media conglomerates in the world. By 1992, when record sales for Time Warner reached the $3.0 billion mark, the company owned some of the most profitable labels, including Atlantic, Elektra, Warner Bros., and Giant/Reprise. The company has continued to grow by creating new labels for new markets, such as Warner Western. By 1995, with a market share of 21.6 percent, the company had taken over the top spot in the record business from Sony Music.

Sony Corp., one of the best known names in consumer electronics, was established shortly after World War II. Their early products, tape recorders and transistor radios, sold well. In the 1960s, they led the international electronics industry with their miniaturized products based on the transistor. After faltering sales growth in the mid-1970s due to increasing competition, Sony once again came to dominate the market in 1978 with their introduction of the portable stereo system, the Walkman. Within another three years, they broke new ground again when they developed and introduced the CD in conjunction with the Dutch electronics firm, Philips.

In January 2000, Time Warner, Inc., and the Internet giant America On Line (AOL) shocked the communications world with announcement of their merger. The merger buys Time Warner a huge audience on the worldwide web, and AOL benefits from Time Warner's extensive news, movie, and audio resources. The full impact of this merger may take years to mature and be analyzed, but other mergers between Internet services and communications resources are sure to follow.

Bertelsmann A.G. and AOL Europe also tentatively announced a joint venture in January 2000. Bertelsmann representatives state that their objective is to make Bertelsmann a larger player in world audio sales, and they intend to accomplish this in part through AOL Europe, the Lycos search engine, and their own e-commerce site.

Sony established itself as the largest record producer when it formed its subsidiary, Sony Music Entertainment International, and bought CBS Records in 1987. Sony wanted to gain better control over the sales of new formats by producing both the hardware (equipment) and the software (recordings). The Columbia Broadcasting System, which had been formed in the late 1920s as a separate entity from Columbia Phonograph, entered the record business in 1938 when it purchased the American Record Corporation; their new record division then became Columbia Recording Corporation, or Columbia Records. The record group remained a profitable arm of CBS, and a major presence in the industry for decades. In the 1980s, when CBS began faltering in the television ratings and losing revenues, they sacrificed their record group to Sony Corporation, despite the fact they were the best selling U.S. record company.

The third largest distributor in 1995 was PolyGram N.V. Owned by Dutch electronics giant, Philips N.V., PolyGram's labels included A&M, Island, Mercury, Motown, and Polydor. PolyGram was also the leading supplier of classical music through labels such as Deutche Grammophon, as well as being one of the largest music publishers.

AMERICA AND THE WORLD

While American music enjoys wide-spread popularity even in non-English speaking countries, America no longer dominated the industry after the large electronic conglomerates bought out the major and independent labels. While most of the labels were still American, the biggest of the majors were European and Japanese. Sony, the firm that bought CBS records and owns over 20 labels, is a Japanese electronics conglomerate. Philips N.V., a Dutch electronics firm, owns 80 percent of PolyGram, which carries the American labels Motown and A&M, and also owns European labels like Deutche Grammophon. Thorn/EMI of England owns Capitol, an American label. The German Bertelsmann Music Group

bought RCA and Arista in 1986, and the Japanese company Matsushita, bought MCA in 1991, then sold it a few years later to beverage giant Seagram. All companies, of course, have international distribution.

In Japan in 1998, American and other foreign music logged a drop of 6 percent from the previous year's sales. For Dublin, Ireland, 1997 and 1998 were landmark years because the city became firmly established as a world music capital that is the home not only of Celtic musicians but many pop groups who record in Dublin. The city is also the host of many independent labels and companies making compilation CDs.

In 1998, American album sales rose to 711.0 million units, a 9.1 percent increase over 1997. Single sales, however, declined by 18 percent to 110.0 million; the labels themselves are responsible for not releasing more top-selling and top-playing music in single format. Country music is the largest seller by type and is preferred by 15 percent of record buyers, according to a 1998 survey. Rock'n'roll and R&B are second and third with nearly 13 percent and 10 percent of the market, respectively. Seventy-nine percent of all music sales in the United States were in the CD format and amounted to $9.9 billion in 1996. Worldwide sales of recorded music totaled $39.8 billion, also in 1996, according to the International Federation of the Phonographic Industry. The U.S. sells about 50 percent of all music worldwide.

RESEARCH AND TECHNOLOGY

Because the industry is highly reliant on electronics technology, research and technological development in the electronics industry has a large impact on the recording industry. The developments with the greatest impact have been newer electronic formats with greater sound fidelity.

In the early 1990s, two new formats were introduced, the mini disc and the digital compact cassette (DCC). Both of these formats brought CD quality fidelity to home recording. Industry analysts in 1992 claimed the new formats would benefit long-term growth prospects, encouraging customers once again to replace their older recordings in the new format. The new formats worried many in the industry, however, and artists and companies alike feared the loss of copyright revenues from home recordings; piracy has always been the major form of income loss. In 1992 however, the consumer electronics industry worked out compromise legislation with government and industry leaders which provides compensation for prospective copies done on the digital machines by imposing royalty fees on the equipment sales. By early 1993, both formats had been released. Due to high initial equipment costs, sales started slowly, but analysts agreed that, once prices come down, both formats would do well. While many agreed that one format would eventually dominate over the other, none could predict which format would win.

As it turned out, such speculation turned out to be moot. Consumers once again confounded the experts by failing to show any interest in the new formats. As with the earlier digital audio tape format (DAT), sales languished and consumer enthusiasm was lukewarm at best. The failure of DCC in particular came as a surprise, because this format at least offered backward compatibility with conventional analog cassettes, allowing users to play their old tapes on their new digital decks. Nevertheless, consumers seemed far more interested in convenience and affordability than in improved quality, staying away from the new formats in droves. The failure of these formats was puzzling to many in the industry, given the success of CDs. The success of the CD, however, probably had as much to do with its convenient small size and durability as with its improved sound quality. In fact, many audiophiles still insisted that analog sound (as represented by vinyl records) was superior to digital sound.

In 2000 and beyond, the home computer operator can easily become his or her own independent label thanks to recordable and erasable CDs. Recordable CDs (called CD-Rs) and recording units were first widely marketed in 1996, although the recorders take some experience to operate because they depend heavily on the type of source material. Assuming the source has digital optical output, it can be recorded as input and dubbed much like an audio tape. Erasable CDs first appeared on the market in 1997 but were initially too expensive for the average individual. Erasable CDs (called CD-Es) are useful for data storage because old data can be erased and overwritten; in music applications, similarly, yesterday's "hit parade" can be erased and replaced with the hottest tunes. High-density CD-Rs and CD-Es are being developed as are High Definition Compatible Digitals or HDCDs.

FURTHER READING

"CD-E: The Future of Compact Disc Technology," *The CD Erasable Page* (nd). Available from http://home.cdarchive .com/info/cd_erasable.htm.

Christman, Ed. "Black and Red are the Colors in this Year-End Report Card." *Billboard,* 23 December 1995.

Christman, Ed. "U.S. music industry marks strong rebound in yr." *Billboard* 16 January 1999.

Clark-Meade, Jeff. "CD Still Drives 14 Percent Global Sales Growth." *Billboard,* 28 October 1995.

Jeffrey, Don. "Country Is No. 1 Genre, But Its Fans Aren't Big Buyers: Buying Trends" *Billboard* 5 September 1998.

Jeffrey, Don. "Music Sales Growth Seen Slowing From 1995-2000." *Billboard,* 31 August 1996.

McClure, Steve. "Foreign music hits a record low in Japan." *Billboard* 16 January 1999.

"Pre-Recorded Music." *Standard and Poor's Industry Surveys.* New York: McGraw Hill, January, 1997.

Reuters Limited. "AOL/Time Warner merger a hit for digital music distribution," 13 January 2000. Available from http:// dailynews.yahoo.com/h/nm/20000113/en/music-timewarner_1 .html.

Reuters Limited. "Bertelsmann, AOL plan to float AOL Europe-paper," 12 January 2000. Available from http://biz.yahoo .com/rf/000112/b4.html.

Stewart, Ken. "Europe's City of the Moment." *Billboard* 5 September 1998.

U.S. Census Bureau. *1997 Economic Census—Manufacturing.* Washington DC: 1998.

U.S. Department of Commerce. *U.S. Industry and Trade Outlook 1998.* Washington, DC: GPO, 1998.

Vizard, Frank. "Recording CDs," *Popular Science,* November 1997.

SIC 3661

TELEPHONE AND TELEGRAPH APPARATUS

This industry covers establishments primarily engaged in manufacturing wire telephone and telegraph equipment. Included are establishments manufacturing modems and other telephone and telegraph interface equipment. Establishments primarily engaged in manufacturing cellular radio telephones are classified in **SIC 3663: Radio and Television Broadcasting and Communications Equipment.**

NAICS CODE(S)

334210 (Telephone Apparatus Manufacturing)

334416 (Electronic Coil, Transformer, and Other Inductor Manufacturing)

334220 (Radio and Television Broadcasting and Wireless Communications Equipment Manufacturing)

INDUSTRY SNAPSHOT

The telecommunications equipment manufacturing industry at the end of the 1990s was strong and growing. Global revenues reached $179 billion in 1998, according to *Data Communications* magazine, and were expected to reach $217 billion in 1999. In the United States, revenues for 1999 were predicted to hit $123 billion, up 16 percent from 1998 levels. Growth was especially expected in equipment for high speed data communications and expansion of the Internet, while sales of equipment for older technologies were expected to decline.

The industry was also changing in response to advances in technology and in the deregulation of the telecom services industry. The shift from analog transmission to digital was virtually complete and the next phase in the evolution of communication networks, the shift from separate networks for voice and data to a single network for both, was underway. This prompted the leading companies in the industry, formerly focused on only one kind of network, to move to establish themselves as capable for the coming converged network. The deregulation of the telecommunications services industry enabled the service giants such as AT&T to diversify their offerings as well, expanding the market for equipment. Moreover, the explosive growth of the Internet created demand for further advances in equipment, and the industry was eagerly responding.

ORGANIZATION AND STRUCTURE

The telephone and telegraph equipment manufacturing industry can be divided into two broad categories: service carrier network equipment manufacturers, who sell telephone switching and switchboard equipment primarily to local and long distance phone companies; and end-user or enterprise equipment manufacturers, who sell data and voice communications equipment, facsimile equipment, call/voice processing equipment, consumer communications electronics, private branch exchanges (PBX), and videoconferencing equipment to both businesses and residential users alike. At the end of the 1990s, however, significant changes were taking place in the telecommunications industry that tended to blur such distinctions. Technological changes made possible the convergence of voice communication networks and data networks. In addition, some consolidation was taking place as industry leaders acquired or established partnerships with smaller companies that had particular technological or marketing strengths. The result was that the industry leaders began manufacturing equipment for all segments of the telecommunications market. Small start-up companies, created around a particular advance in technology, were also an important part of the industry because they were the source of important innovation. Such companies were often the target of acquisition by a larger company in the industry.

BACKGROUND AND DEVELOPMENT

American Samuel F.B. Morse introduced the first commercially successful telegraph in 1844. "What hath God wrought?" was the first message to be transmitted on the 37-mile pole line between Baltimore, Maryland, and Washington, DC. Under Morse licenses, open-wire pole lines were soon erected all over the United States and Canada.

Alexander Graham Bell patented the telephone in 1876, beating Elisha Gray by a matter of hours. The technology was immediately put to use in telephone systems by the National Bell Telephone Company (originally the Bell Telephone Company). Western Union Telegraph Company also began offering phone service, using technology developed partly by Gray and Thomas Edison. But as a result of an out-of-court settlement in a patent dispute, Western Union sold its phone operations to Bell in 1879. Bell also purchased its manufacturing arm, which became the Western Electric Company.

Bell's phone service was immediately popular. By March of 1880, there were over 30,000 U.S. telephone subscribers and 138 telephone exchanges. By 1887, just ten years after the commercial introduction of the telephone, there were over 150,000 subscribers and about 146,000 miles of wire. In addition, nearly 100,000 people had phone service in Europe and Russia.

Developments in the switching equipment was necessary to make this growth possible. The first switchboard was installed in Boston in 1877. Before, this one telephone had to be directly connected to another in order to make a call; 1,000 connections were necessary for 50 telephones to call each other. In 1891, American Almon B. Strowger patented the first automatic switchboard. As telephone services proliferated, a demand for long-distance services arose, and Bell established the American Telephone and Telegraph Company in 1885 as its long-distance subsidiary. Important equipment and wire advances allowed commercial service to be implemented between Boston, Massachusetts, and Providence, Rhode Island, by the 1890s. Distances gradually increased with the introduction of new equipment, such as relays, loading coils, amplifiers, and repeaters. Radiotelephone service to Europe was established in 1927, but large-scale wireline telecommunications were not available until 1956 when the first transatlantic cable was completed.

Broad patent rights enabled the National Bell Telephone Company, which became the American Bell Telephone Company in 1878, to completely dominate the telephone service and equipment industry. Bell built a nationwide network by licensing local operating companies to deliver service for five to ten years. Bell received $20 per phone each year and reserved the right to buy the local network at contract expiration. Although Bell's patent rights terminated in 1894, only a few independent companies emerged as competitors. By 1899, Bell maintained a network of 800,000 lines.

AT&T became the parent company of the Bell system in 1899, and grew steadily through the first half of the century. Demand surged during the 1950s and 1960s, with an influx of new products, services, and technological breakthroughs. Despite pressure by anti-trust regulators to cede its market dominance, AT&T continued to grow during the 1960s and 1970s, becoming the largest company in the world. In 1974, however, anti-trust suits filed separately by MCI (now MCI WorldCom) and the Justice Department signaled an end to the company's unfettered reign. Ten years later the monopoly was finally broken when AT&T was divided into eight pieces.

Prior to the 1980s, business telecommunications were more or less a straightforward matter. Services were provided by AT&T with its undisputed monopoly as the carrier of voice, data, and text communications. Large business users had private branch exchanges (PBXs), for internal and external voice traffic, telex machines for instantaneous transmission of text, and dedicated data lines for communications with mainframe computers. Small businesses used key telephone systems and facsimile machines.

Progress in microelectronics and the deregulation of the telecommunications structure in the United States changed all that. The boundaries between computing and telecommunications became blurred. With the advent of the Integrated Service Digital Network (ISDN), the telecommunications network no longer had to separate voice, text, data, and image traffic. Everything could go over the wire or fiber optic cable in bits. There could be a uniform ISDN plug for telephones, computers, and fax machines. Personal computers not only became more powerful, they also had the potential to double as telex and data communications terminals, as fax machines, and as telephones and telephone answering machines. Electronic data interchange (EDI) could eventually do away with forms completed in duplicate and triplicate. Videophones would bring the person at the other end of the line right into the office.

Changes in telecommunications regulations since the early 1980s also transformed the way telecommunications developed. Competition in network provision improved the quality of traditional services. Waiting lists for business and residential voice and data lines fell dramatically. Telecommunication and equipment prices also declined. New telecommunication based services sprang up, bringing revenue not only to telecommunication operators and the information providers, but also generally enhancing the value of business operations. Even domestic users with touch tone telephones were beginning to avail themselves of network-based facilities that ten years ago only users with sophisticated communications equipment could afford.

Central Office Switching Systems. When large scale integrated circuits were perfected in the 1970s, it became technically feasible to develop a digital-switching network to replace the electronic network in central offices. Modern central office technology had a digital switching network controlled by a programmable central processor. Switching systems route calls between themselves and selected terminating stations by addressing. Station addresses in the United States consist of a three-digit area code and a seven-digit telephone number. From overseas locations, a country code is added.

Centrex. Before the arrival of microelectronics and PBXs, large companies were reluctant to place switching systems on the premises to provide private branch exchange service. Centrex is a PBX-like service furnished by the local telephone company through equipment located in the central office. Centrex features allow direct inward dialing (DID) to a telephone number and direct outward dialing (DOD) from a number without operator intervention. For calls into the Centrex, the service is equivalent to individual line service. Outgoing calls differ from individual line service only in the requirement that the caller dials an individual access code (usually 9). Calls between stations in the Centrex group require four or five digits instead of the seven digits required for ordinary calls. An attendant position located on the customer's premises is linked to the central office over a separate circuit. Centrex service provides PBX features without locating a switching system on the user's premises.

Customer Premise Equipment. This category includes all the equipment that makes up the customer's network, which may be as simple as a telephone handset or as complicated as a network of thousands of phones, computers, fax machines, and other terminal equipment as well as all the wires, cables, routers and switches that connect them.

Key Telephone Systems. Key Telephone Systems (KTS) are not high-technology products compared to radio, satellite, and fiber optics, and they don't have the technical appeal of a PBX, but they are the workhorses of American business. Like other customer premise products, KTSs have evolved from wired logic and electromechanical operation to stored program or firmware control. In the process, they adopted many features that were once the exclusive province of PBX. The Electronic Key Telephone System offers most of the features of a PBX, especially the hybrid version, which is a cross between a PBX and a Key System. The distinction between the KTSs and PBXs is becoming more blurred as technology brings more intelligence to the KTS. Further blurring the trend between Key Systems and PBXs is the propensity of some manufacturers to make Key Telephone instrument lines compatible with PBX lines, allowing a company to grow out of its KTS and into a larger more sophisticated PBX.

Private Branch Exchanges. Many organizations operate private telecommunications systems. These systems range in size from the federal telephone system, which is larger than the telecommunications systems in many countries, to small private branch exchanges (PBXs). Nearly every business with more than 30 to 100 stations is in the market for a PBX, or its central office counterpart, Centrex. PBXs are economical for some very small businesses in need of features that most key systems do not provide, such as restriction and least cost routing. They are also economical for very large businesses that have PBXs using central office switching systems of a size that rivals many metropolitan public networks. Most PBXs can be mounted in a cabinet on the business user's premises and can operate without air conditioning in an ordinary office environment.

The office PBX increasingly controls private voice networks. As the network evolves into all-digital, so does the PBX in all but the low end systems of 100 stations or fewer, which remain analog. The advent of the T-1 carrier as the preferred transmission medium is the principle force driving the evolution of the PBX. The long distance carriers make it increasingly attractive for business users to bypass the local central office with T-1 trunks directly to the long distance carrier's central office. The cost of T-1 service for PBX lines is particularly advantageous when data transmission facilities parallel the route of voice. The integration of voice and data reduces the cost of access lines to the outside world.

Call/Voice Processing Equipment. Several converging forces have increased the importance of incoming call management systems. First, there is the increasing use of telemarketing. A telemarketing center typically has banks of 800-numbers with different numbers associated with different product lines or promotions, and different agents with access to various databases to handle callers' questions. A caller distribution system is needed in this case to direct incoming calls to the appropriate agent. Secondly, most incoming 800-calls are delivered via T-1 technology. With this technology, calls need to be routed to the appropriate party when they reach the customer premise. Finally, call distribution technology has advanced to the point where it is basically a merger of telephone and computer operations. Any organization with more than a few answering positions finds that the cost of some machine-controlled call distribution pays for itself quickly.

A uniform call distribution system (UCD), a standard feature of many PBXs, often significantly improves call handling. The stand-alone counterpart of a UCD is the call sequencer. This device may work with a PBX or key telephone system, or it may be connected directly to incoming lines. Unlike the UCD, a call sequencer does not direct calls, but alerts agents to the presence of incoming calls. The most sophisticated device is an automatic call distributor (ACD), which can either stand alone or integrate with a PBX. An ACD directs calls to the least busy agent to equalize the work load. The ACD administrator typically has a video display terminal that presents call statistics in real time, and has many management tools that monitor and improve service and measure the agent's effectiveness. Any organization that has a large number of incoming calls targeted for service posi-

tions is a potential ACD user. This includes departments that handle mail orders, literary delivery, inquiries, field service, credit, and collections.

Modems. Like other types of telecommunications equipment, modems have become faster, cheaper, and smarter. The ready availability of inexpensive personal computers has expanded the demand for modems, and basically two types of modems exist in the market: dial-up modems and private line modems. Dial-up modems either plug into a personal computer slot, or are self contained devices that plug into the computer's serial port. Many of the modem's features are designed to emulate a telephone. These features include: dial tone recognition, automatic tone and pulse dialing, monitoring call progress tones such as busy and reorder, automatic answer, and call termination. These items are priced on a commodity type basis and use the public network for the transmission of information. Private line modems work exclusively with voice and data private lines, and although it has the same functions as a dial-up modem, they are not as popular.

Many data applications, by nature, are incapable of fully using a data circuit. Rather than flowing in a steady stream, data usually flows in short bursts with idle periods intervening. To make use of this idle capacity, data multiplexers are employed to collect data from multiple stations and create a single, high-speed bit stream. Data multiplexers come in two types: time division multiplexers (TDM) and statistical multiplexers (statmux). In a TDM, each station is assigned a time slot, and the multiplexer collects data from each station in turn. If a station has no data to send, its time slot goes unused. A statmux makes use of the idle time periods in a data circuit by assigning time slots to pairs of stations according to the amount of traffic they have to send. The multiplexer collects data from the terminal and sends it to the distant end, with the address of the receiving terminal minimizing idle times between transactions.

Analog or frequency division multiplexers are also available to divide a voice channel into multiple segments for data transmission. Their primary use is to connect multiple, slow-speed data terminals over voice channels. A concentrator is similar to a multiplexer except that it is usually a single-ended device that connects directly to a host computer. The primary application for multiplexers is in data networks that use asynchronous terminals. Since many of these items cannot be addressed and have no error correction capability, they are of limited use by themselves in remote locations. The multiplexer provides end-to-end error checking and correction, and circuit sharing to support multiple terminals.

Facsimile Equipment. In the 1990s facsimile equipment (FAX) became an indispensable business machine essential to the every day transactions of most businesses. The FAX machine works by scanning the printed page, encoding it, and transmitting a facsimile of the images in shades of black and white without identifying individual characters. Facsimile can convey both text and graphic information, source documents can be retransmitted without rekeying, and facsimile transmission is affected less by transmission errors than other types of data communication. Facsimile is also fast. Some facsimile machines double as printers and copiers.

Telephones. The market offered two categories of telephone sets: general purpose sets or corded phones and special purpose telephones, such as coin operated telephones. The price of general purpose sets is often a clue to quality. Many inexpensive instruments provide poor transmission quality and fail when dropped. At the high end of the scale, price usually is a function of features or looks. Single-line phone sets will be replaced by feature phones with many more characteristics and capabilities than existing models. In recent years, cordless telephones have gained wide consumer acceptance with an estimated 40 percent household penetration in the United States. These instruments use a low-powered radio link between a base unit and the portable telephone. Answering machines were still popular home equipment, but technological innovation was replacing the traditional stand-alone telephone answering machine connected to a telephone with integrated telephone answering devices. These units include telephone answering devices incorporated into every piece of communications equipment from basic telephones to cordless integrated answering telephone devices and personal computer systems.

Coin Telephones. The advent of the customer-owned coin operated telephone (COCOT) is another by-product of divestiture that is confusing to many users. In the first few years following the dissolution of the Bell System, many private companies saw COCOTs as a potentially lucrative business. The companies that ventured into this market with less than adequate equipment, however, quickly discovered what the local exchange companies or LECs have long understood: the risks and administrative costs of coin telephones are high, and the companies that enter this market without understanding the hazards can lose large amounts. The two major risks are fraud and vandalism.

CURRENT CONDITIONS

A major development at the end of the 1990s was the growing convergence of voice and data networks. Advances in technology, of which ISDN was the first evidence, created the possibility for voice traffic to be inexpensively carried over data networks. A standard voice network is circuit-switched, meaning a circuit is established and dedicated to the call as long as it lasts. A data network, on the other hand, is packet-switched, meaning the data is bundled into packets that are transmitted separately, which enables the system to eliminate silence in the transmission and allows great flexibility in routing the information. As a result, as many as five to eight simultaneous Internet Protocol (IP) connections can be established on every traditional telephone circuit. A major issue in sending voice over data in 1999 was the voice quality provided by the system, but rapid improvement had been made and was expected to continue. Furthermore, not all customers required the same voice quality.

Deploying one network to handle voice, data traffic, and Internet access had great appeal, although companies with an extensive pre-existing infrastructure did not rush to replace it. According to a 1999 study by Information Week Research, 72 percent of companies operated separate networks for voice, data, and video while 19 percent had a single network combining voice and data. Only nine percent had a fully converged network for voice, data, and video. However, 23 percent of the companies contacted for this study said they planned to use a single network for all three types of traffic within twelve months. A study by Phillips Group-InfoTech reported that nearly 90 percent of companies with multiple sites would begin switching to voice traffic using Internet Protocol over their local area networks (LANs). This report predicted an average growth in this segment of the industry of 138 percent each year for the five years after 1998, creating a $1.9 billion industry by 2004. The Yankee Group, another marketing research organization, was even more optimistic, projecting a voice- and fax-over IP services market of $3.6 billion in 2002.

Accompanying the convergence of voice and data was the development of alternatives to the traditional PBX, called PC-PBXs. Instead of using what in effect was a custom-built computer that required custom software and could only be used with specific peripheral equipment and enhancements, PC-PBXs were designed to be regular PC servers. This more open approach allowed for greater flexibility and potentially lower costs. One factor slowing this innovation was the pace of development of accepted standards. A greater problem was the issue of reliability. Telephone customers, especially business customers, were accustomed to "five nine" reliability, that is, 99.999 percent uptime. Such capability had been developed over decades of refinement of PBX technology, but the new PC-based alternatives had not yet reached that level. At the end of the 1990s, the new systems were being aimed at small and mid-sized organizations and branch offices of large organizations.

According to the Multimedia Association, a telecommunications industry trade group, nearly 70 million PBX lines were in use in 1998. During that year more than 7.5 million had been added, and more than $7.5 billion had been spent on new PBX systems, a clear indication that the PBX was far from dead. Nevertheless, according to a study by the marketing research firm Data-quest, 11,503 PC-PBX systems were shipped in 1998, and 20,941 were projected for 1999. That number was expected to more than triple by 2002.

The phenomenal growth in the popularity and business importance of the Internet contributed greatly to the continually growing demand for bandwidth, that is, the volume of traffic carried at one time and the speed at which it was transmitted. New technologies had been developed that pushed ISDN, a technology never fully exploited in the United States, into the background. The most common type of access used by business at the end of the 1990s was called T1, which provided much greater bandwidth than ISDN, though at a much higher cost. A newer technology, which promised bandwidth equivalent to that of T1 but at a cost like that of ISDN or lower, was Digital Subscriber Line (DSL). A number of variants of DSL were being used in 1999, but set standards were being developed. ISDNs still remained for customers that were more than three miles from a telephone company's central office, beyond the range of DSL.

In general, the telecommunications equipment manufacturing industry at the end of the 1990s was very strong despite weakness in world markets caused by the economic crisis in Asia. The Telecommunications Industry Association reported that U.S. spending in 1998 totaled $121 billion, an increase of 10 percent over the previous year. This was despite a drop of one percent in exports. Imports rose 19 percent, primarily from Canada and Mexico. The Data Comm 1999 Market Forecast, put out by *Data Communications* magazine, projected growth of 16 percent in U.S. telecommunications products and services, stronger in some areas than in others. IP tools, Web servers and software, network security, cable services equipment, and DSL equipment were some of the categories expected to experience the greatest growth.

INDUSTRY LEADERS

Of the six leading telecommunications manufacturers in the world at the end of the 1990s, two were U.S. companies—Lucent and Cisco. A third—Nortel Networks—was Canadian, but did more than half its business in the United States. The remaining three were European—Alcatel, Siemens, and Ericsson. Lucent and Nortel traditionally focused on equipment for telephone systems while Cisco was the giant of the enterprise network and Internet markets. The advancing convergence of voice and data networks, however, and the explosive growth of data transmission, led all these companies to develop products for the converged network, often by buying companies with the products or expertise it lacked.

Lucent Technologies Inc. traces its roots to the very beginning of the telecommunications industry as the manufacturing arm of first Western Union and then the Bell system. The R & D unit, Bell Laboratories, was credited with many technological advances, most importantly, the transistor; its inventors received the Nobel Prize in 1956 for this achievement. In 1996, AT&T spun Western Electric and Bell Labs off as Lucent Technologies. In 1998, Lucent's market value surpassed that of AT&T. In 1999, it reported revenue of $38.3 billion, an increase of 27.1 percent over 1998.

Cisco Systems was the number one supplier of computer networking products, with about 85 percent of the market for routers and network switches. It was also a growing force in the telephone industry as well; one third of its sales were to telephone companies. Its 1999 revenue was over $12.1 billion, an increase of 43.7 percent over 1998.

Nortel Networks began life as the manufacturing arm of Bell Canada, but by the 1950s a majority of its shares were owned by Western Electric, subsidiary of AT&T. Bell Canada purchased most of those shares when the U.S. Justice Department forced Western Electric to divest. Northern Electric, as it was named then, was wholly owned by Bell Canada until 1973. In 1976 it changed its name to Northern Telecom, and in the same year introduced the first digital switch, which fired its growth into the 1980s. The company went through hard times in the early 1990s, including a loss of $900 million in 1993. Its 1998 sales were about $17.6 billion, 13.8 percent above 1997. In 1999 it changed its name to Nortel Networks. Sales that year reached $22.2 billion, a 26.4 percent increase over 1998.

AMERICA AND THE WORLD

Historically, the United States has been the leader in telecommunications equipment technology and innovation. This factor was due primarily to the monopoly that AT&T (the Bell System) had on the nations' telephone system for the first 100 years of its existence. The breakup of the Bell System in 1984 created a new playing field for telecommunication equipment manufacturers worldwide. Since telephone technology is not drastically different from computer technology, and in fact, many of the same components and techniques are used in both, the race to compete in this market became a global endeavor. This factor coupled with the regulatory barriers harnessing the former Bell Operating Companies resulted in the United States losing this 100 year advantage almost overnight.

Between the years 1983 to 1989, the United States export of telecommunication equipment increased at a compound annual rate of 15 percent. During this same period, imports of telecommunication equipment grew by

30 percent. In 1989, the U.S. telecommunication equipment industry had a trade deficit of $2.7 billion, which improved 15 percent in 1990 to $2.4 billion. Low-technology terminal equipment (i.e., telephones) accounted for the largest component of foreign imports. Foreign producers in the Far East were able to capture this market through lower manufacturing costs. China, Malaysia, and Thailand contributed the most to this market. The U.S. Senate, in response to these developments, passed the Telecommunications Equipment Research and Manufacturing Act of 1991 in an attempt make the market more competitive.

Although the United States was no longer the dominant manufacturer in the telecommunications equipment market as it had been at one time, it was reestablishing itself as an international force during the later 1990s. Despite an enormous overall trade deficit with Japan and other Far Eastern suppliers, the United States did not have a deficit in telecommunications gear. In 1998, U.S. exports of telecommunications equipment totaled $20. 7 billion, a drop of one percent from 1997 levels. On the other hand, imports increased by 19 percent, to $17.9 billion. Canada and Mexico were the dominant trading partners for both imports and exports.

FURTHER READING

Benson, Woody. "PBX's Demise Has Been Greatly Exaggerated." *Business Communications Review,* April 1999.

Beyda, William J. *Basic Data Communications—A Comprehensive Overview.* Englewood Cliffs, NJ: Prentice-Hall, 1989.

Brewster, R.L. *Communication Systems and Computer Networks.* New York: John Wiley & Sons, 1989.

Brown, Dave. "Branch-Office: ISDN Routers." *Network Computing,* 19 October 1999.

CTI Futures Committee. "Vision: The Future of Computer-Telephony." *MultiMedia Telecommunications Association,* March 1999. Available from http://www.mmta.org/pubs/frame5.html

Dordick, H.S. *Understanding Modern Telecommunications.* New York: McGraw-Hill, 1986.

Duffy, Jim. "Cisco Bringing Convergence to Small Offices." *Network World,* 9 August 1999.

Henricks, Mark. "Selecting a Phone System." *Office Systems,* September 1999.

Jessup, Toby. "Porting the PBX." *Data Communications,* July 1999.

Korzeniowski, Paul. "PC-PBX Systems Build Momentum." *Information Week,* 8 November 1999.

Leibowitz, Ed. "The Great Dumb Switch Debate-Part One: Dumb Switches and Intelligent Switches; An OAI Focus." *Teleconnect,* July 1992.

Levitt, Jason. "DSL Comes Together." *Informationweek,* 26 April 1999.

McNamara, Thomas F., and Khaled Nassoura. "Voice over Data." *Consulting-Specifying Engineer,* September 1999.

Noll, A. Michael. *Introduction to Telephones and Telephone Systems.* Norwood, MA: Artech House, 1988.

O'Connell, Brian. "IPTelephony over LAN a New Industry." *Newsbytes News Network,* 23 September 1999.

———. "New Comms Platforms Take Dead Aim at PBX." *Newsbytes News Network,* 3 August 1999.

"Recession Proof?" *Data Communications,* December 1998.

Sulkin, Allan. "Centrex Providers Discover that Small Can Be Beautiful." *Business Communications Review,* April 1992.

———. "Changes Coming to PBX Technology." *Business Communications Review,* September 1999.

———. "PBX Alternatives: How Far Have They Come?" *Business Communications Review,* August 1999.

"Survey—Financial Times Telecoms—1 and 2: Quick Entry Rings Some Alarm Bells." *Financial Times Surveys Edition,* 30 September 1999.

"Telecommunications Report: 1998 Economic Report." *TIA Online.* 1999. Available from http://www.tiaonline.org.

Thyfault, Mary E. "Enterprise Networks - Merge Ahead." *Information Week,* 1 February 1999.

"Vanguard's Voice Processing Industry Temperature Check." *Voice Technology News,* 6 April 1993.

Waite, Andrew, J. *The Inbound Telephone Call Center.* New York: Telecom Library, 1989.

"Who Has the Winning Strategy?" *Telecommunications Americas Edition,* April 1999.

SIC 3663

RADIO AND TELEVISION BROADCASTING AND COMMUNICATIONS EQUIPMENT

This industry manufactures radio and television broadcasting and communications equipment. Important products of this industry are closed-circuit and cable television equipment; studio audio and video equipment; light communications equipment; transmitters, transceivers, and receivers (except household and automotive); cellular radio telephones; fiber optics equipment; communication antennas; receivers; RF power amplifiers; satellite communications systems (space and ground segments); and fixed and mobile radio systems. Establishments primarily engaged in manufacturing household audio and communications equipment are classified in **SIC 3651: Household Audio and Video Equipment;** those manufacturing intercommunications equipment are classified in **SIC 3669: Communications**

Equipment, Not Elsewhere Classified; and those manufacturing consumer radio and television receiving antennas are classified in **SIC 3679: Electronic Components, Not Elsewhere Classified.**

NAICS CODE(S)

334220 (Radio and Television Broadcasting and Wireless Communications Equipment Manufacturing)

INDUSTRY SNAPSHOT

This industry covers a range of interrelated and sometimes competing communications systems, continually reinventing itself as its individual segments grow. The emerging structure is being shaped by consumer trends, regulations, technological advances, and corporate decisions. The electromagnetic spectrum, through which the wireless communications companies of this industry transmit signals, is controlled by the federal government, which has exerted profound influence over this industry in recent years with new regulations and legislation.

Because communications systems are rapidly being transformed by the demand for customized, interconnected, and wireless services, products leading growth in this industry include wireless communication systems (pagers, cellular phones, personal communications systems) mobile communications equipment, and satellite communications devices.

ORGANIZATION AND STRUCTURE

This category contains several different types of communications' technologies. Connectivity between these technologies is increasing, resulting in hybrid products and systems. This is reflected by the diversity of the players in this industry, which includes cable television, cellular, electronics, telephone, computer, and satellite communications companies. Wireless communications services include cellular, paging, and specialized mobile radio. Cellular and paging, the largest segments of this market, generated over $20 billion in service fees in the late 1990s.

Typically, high-technology consumer electronics equipment becomes less expensive in the years after introduction. This has been true of many products offered by this industry, and it has helped drive growth by attracting new consumer markets. In 1999, the price for cellular phones fell nearly 15 percent across United States.

Pagers. The early to mid-1990s saw significant growth in the paging industry due to increasingly sophisticated and lower-priced products and services. Despite this growth, however, the vast majority of the leaders in the field of paging had been losing money steadily during the latter half of the that decade due to heavy competition in the industry, which was brought about by fierce price cutting schemes. The number of paging subscribers in the United States reached approximately 50 million by 1999, up from 14 million at the beginning of 1993. Some of this growth can be attributed to a trend toward non-business use. When pagers first appeared on the market in the early 1980s, they were most commonly found on doctors and other busy professionals ''on call.'' They are now likely to be found on parents trying to contact their children, or waiters who need to know when orders are ready.

Consumers gravitated to pagers because of a new generation of models that offered new services like two-way paging, verbal messages, portable e-mail, readers, customized stock prices, news flashes, and sports scores. There is also a developing consumer trend toward integrating and customizing communications services that contributes to growth and reduces imputation among different communication services. For example, about 20 percent of cellular subscribers use paging in conjunction with cellular service to mediate costs, because being paged is less expensive than receiving an incoming call on a cellular phone.

Cellular Telephones. Cellular telephones get their name from the small regions (cells) into which service areas are divided. Each cell contains a base station with a low-power transmitter/receiver. Base stations are connected to mobile telephone switching offices (MTSOs), either by telephone wire or microwave transmission. A computer at the switching office coordinates calls for the service area and monitors a call's signal strength. When the signal loses strength because the caller is exiting the cell, the MTSO switches the call to the next cell. Cells sometimes overlap one another or have gaps between them because of topographical obstructions.

The number of cellular subscribers reached over 80 billion in 1999, which amounted to nearly one-third of the population in the United States. Subscribers were drawn by enhancements such as improved capacity, seamless networking, and personal 800 service. Cumulative capital investment and revenues from cellular services were expected to continue increasing through the 1990s. Equipment sales were expected to rise, to the benefit of companies in this category, as operators replaced their analog technology with digital technology. This transition was viewed as critical to the cellular industry's competitiveness. A digital cellular system transmits a caller's voice by converting the sound waves into a numerical code, rather than a wave pattern, as in analog systems. Calling capacity was expected to increase by a factor of three or more with digital cell sites. In addition to increased capacity, the conversion to digital offers other advantages: lower unit costs; better quality; increased privacy; and the promise of advanced services and data transmission.

Business users still account for the majority of cellular users, but much of the growth in cellular, as with paging, has come from the consumer market since the equipment has become more affordable. A decrease in prices may drive down average revenues per consumer but should not hamper overall growth, because of increased volume and product innovations. Technological innovations in electronic circuitry and in the intelligence built into the cellular network have resulted in new features that make cellular more attractive. Short messaging can be displayed on an alphanumeric display, for example. Some companies have introduced cellular phones that can also handle regular wired calls, faxes, or modems.

Another development affecting the structure of the cellular industry is the creation by Independent Telecommunications Network, Inc. (ITN) of a nationwide Signaling System 7 backbone network to transport cellular calls between cell sites. Signaling System 7 is an advanced network protocol that manages traffic flow through a telephone network. This is a significant development because it will eliminate charges related to ''roaming'' agreements between operators and special access codes that now complicate the use of a cellular phones outside of home service regions. Cellular carriers are trying to capitalize on the increasing mobility of business people by moving into data transmission. In 1992, nine major cellular carriers teamed up with IBM to provide a data network called CelluPlan II over existing analog cellular networks. Their competition comes primarily from two major providers of mobile data services: Ardis, a joint venture between IBM and Motorola, and RAM Mobile Data, a creation of BellSouth and RAM Broadcasting. These networks are independent of the cellular network and serve businesses only via radio waves.

The involvement of BellSouth, a long-distance wireline telephone company, in a cellular venture is not unusual. Several major long-distance wireline telephone companies have staked a claim in the cellular market by buying cellular companies; AT&T acquired McCaw Cellular, while MCIWorldcom Inc. was in the process of purchasing Sprint in 1999. In addition to giving the wireline companies the chance to join rather than compete with wireless services, this gives the cellular companies access to the huge marketing resources of the parent companies.

Personal Communications Services. Personal communications networks, or services, (PCS) describes low-powered microcellular technology that operates in the 900 MHz band. Although available to consumers in Europe they are becoming more widely available in the United States. PCS enables a person, carrying a pocket-sized phone, to be contacted at the same number no matter where the person goes. They transmit calls via radio waves to base stations clustered in many service areas. The system is digital and is expected to be cheaper

than existing cellular once widely available to consumers. Some analysts believe that it would be ideally suited for telecommuters because digital technology allows PCS to provide data and video services as well as voice, and will give employees the ability to hook up to office computers or fax machines while traveling.

On September 23, 1993 the Federal Communications Commission (FCC) authorized 160 MHz of spectrum for PCS. Starting in 1994, the FCC began auctioning PCS licenses, which generated billions for the federal government and stimulated the creation of a new generation of wireless services and products. Hundreds of companies applied to the FCC to operate PCS systems. Carriers invested in new transceivers, and consumers purchased feature-rich new phones and wireless portable devices.

The FCC enforces anticollusion rules upon business contracts between broadband licensees, auction winners, and eligible participants in ongoing broadband block auctions. These rules ''place significant limitations on an auction participant's ability to pursue business opportunities involving services in the geographic area in which it has applied for a license,'' according to the FCC. The anticollusion rules were intended to ensure competitiveness in the auction process and in the post-auction market structure, according to a public notice issued by the FCC on August 28, 1996.

Microwave and Satellite Systems. This is one of the more mature technologies in this category. Microwave transmission can be achieved via terrestrial or satellite systems. Terrestrial, or ground, systems work by sending very high frequency signals from transmitters to repeater stations and back to receivers. For these systems to work, there must be no obstructions, such as mountains, between stations. Satellite transmission works similarly but the repeater station is placed in orbit, usually with the region it serves. Because satellites lack the geographic constraints of terrestrial systems, they are better suited for long-distance, point-to-multipoint transmissions such as television broadcasts. Microwave and satellite systems can also be used to transmit audio, video, and data.

Microwave systems can be categorized as long-haul (transmission distances greater than five miles) or short-haul applications. Long-haul microwave equipment is used by common carriers, oil companies, electric utilities, broadcast and cable television operators, pipeline industries, and government agencies. Almost 90 percent of public and private television stations transmit signals via satellite. Short haul customers include universities, institutions, corporations, hotel chains, hospitals, local area networks, cellular phone networks, and local governments. According to the FCC, the majority of users of the 36,538 existing private microwave networks are industrial. Public services hold about 22 percent of private microwave network licenses.

Throughout the first half of the 1990s, the United States saw an explosion in global positioning system (GPS) units. The GPS marks the beginning of a technological revolution in navigational aids. Originally developed by the U.S. Department of Defense as an alternative to traditional radio navigation, the GPS uses a system of 24 satellites to triangulate the position of a receiver. The signals can identify a receiver's position within a range of about 100 meters. New products that use the GPS for military, aviation, marine, survey and mapping purposes, and tracking and car navigation come onto the market about every 18 months.

The United States is a global leader in sales of GPS equipment and technology, producing more than twice as many units per month as Japan, the next largest producer. As GPS technology becomes more affordable, the technology will come within reach of millions of consumers. According to James Brandon in *Industry, Trade, and Technology Review,* by 2000 GPS systems are projected to net $8 billion in sales, with U.S. products accounting for about $4 billion.

BACKGROUND AND DEVELOPMENT

This industry has developed by continually shedding its old identity as new technologies come along. For example, Motorola, one of the giants in the industry, began in the car radio business. The company sold Handie-Talkies to the Army in World War II and later installed radios in police cars. Many of the companies in this category have been defense contractors.

In the early 1980s, when cellular phones were introduced, AT&T predicted that by 2000 about 900,000 mobile phones would be in use in the United States. By 1993, that number had already been exceeded a dozen times. In the early 1990s, cordless phones began to outsell corded phones. Much of this activity would have been inconceivable before the U.S. Justice Department filed suit against AT&T, and the Bell monopoly was subsequently broken up in the early 1980s. Until 1957, when the courts ruled that telephone customers had the right to use non-AT&T telephone equipment as long as it didn't interfere with the public network, everyone used AT&T equipment and service. AT&T's dominant position as the primary U.S. carrier was finally challenged in 1969 by a company using newly developed microwave technology. That company would become MCI Communications Corporation. The industry did not undergo complete restructuring, however, until the Justice Department officially broke the monopoly in 1984, making way for new communications technologies, equipment, and services.

The accelerating development of wireless personal communications services will continue to fuel the demand for radio base station equipment, antennas, low earth orbit satellite systems, and wireless equipment. Because there has been no decision on which of two rival digital standards—time division multiple access (TDMA) and code division multiple access (CDMA) will be the industry standard—there is currently a market for products that support multiple interfaces. Generic base station transceivers that handle calls using all modulation standards, including U.S. and foreign, analog and digital, voice and data, may also be available for use with a variety of wireless networks, including paging and PCS.

Some industry observers believe the shift from wireline to wireless communications could be as profound as the shift from gaslight to electric light bulbs. After first underestimating the market for wireless communications, major communications, computers, electronics, and data companies have begun investing heavily in it. AT&T's deal to pay $12.6 billion for McCaw Cellular is one of many examples. A highly publicized health scare in 1993, in which a Florida widower claimed that cellular phone use caused his wife's brain cancer, has spurred research into a possible cellular cancer link. Long-term impact on the growth of the market will be negligible unless a viable link is found. The FCC decision to reallocate 200 MHz of spectrum to make way for emerging PCS technologies is vital to the development of the industry and will likely be considered a landmark decision in the future.

CURRENT CONDITIONS

The current status of this industry is both innovative and dynamic. Because of excitement surrounding the idea of a national "information superhighway" and growth in new communications technologies, companies in this industry are keenly watched by Wall Street. The Clinton administration's technology-friendly position fostered industry growth throughout the 1990s. Clinton proposed a broad 10-year plan to force the Pentagon and other federal agencies to cede control of a big block of the nation's airwaves and make them available for new commercial technologies. This comes in addition to the FCC's 1993 decision to reallocate the public airwaves. Even the older, less cutting-edge areas of this industry are profitable. While the biggest revenues are anticipated in wireless communications services, rather than in equipment, some analysts predicted a hardware market with sales of nearly $2 billion by 2000.

Technological advances like cellular digital packet data (CPCD) for cellular service were introduced to help analog cellular systems compete with new digital systems. CPCD has been adopted by companies with analog systems to make them more competitive with digital systems. The FCC decision regarding the reallocation of spectrum is powerful for this industry because it means companies have a chance at gaining more transmission access. Ultimately, it will translate into money. As a result of the FCC decision green-lighting PCS, the formulation of strategic alliances, the valuation of desired PCN territories, and the sale and purchase of cellular holdings will occur furiously as companies try to maneuver into the emerging PCS market.

The FCC decision to reallocate 220 MHz of spectrum previously occupied by fixed microwave users will boost microwave equipment sales by allowing fixed microwave users to relocate to higher frequencies, and by freeing 200 MHz of formerly government-occupied spectrum for private sector use.

The late 1990s, saw the birth of smart phones—digital cellular phones with paging devices incorporated in them. They allowed the user to receive and send e-mails, along with connecting to corporate intranets and the Internet. Business people were no longer tied to the computer to keep abreast of the latest in news, and transactions in the global arena.

The wireless application protocol (WAP), a technical standard, which linked cellular phones and hand held computers to the Internet, was agreed upon in the late 1990s. It was hoped that the WAP based mini-browser would help the industry grow and flourish in much the same way that MOSAIC, the first computer browser, had helped the computer industry grow in the early 1990s.

Pager innovations have included two-way paging, where e-mails can be sent and received from the pager which was equipped with a tiny keyboard, and what has been called a mobile answering machine, which allows the sender to leave a voice message for the receiver. In 1999, stocks began to be traded via these new smart pagers.

By the end of 2000, pagers will be able to surf the Internet and a company's intranet site. They will also be able to obtain materials from databases, e-commerce sites, and participate in a global positioning system. There will even be the potential to upgrade wireless systems by downloading the necessary software in less than ten years.

The Telecommunications Competition and Deregulation Act of 1996 has also had a strong impact on the radio and electronics field. It eliminated monopolies in cable television and telephone companies, opening fields traditionally regulated as public utilities to competition. Perhaps the most controversial part of the law, however, was the introduction of the so-called "v-chip"—a programmable microchip that interprets an encoded program rating transmitted as part of the television signal. The v-chip is intended to allow parents to block programs whose content ratings are deemed unacceptable. It has been perceived by some as a veiled form of censorship.

Its impact on the radio and television industry, however, has yet to be determined.

INDUSTRY LEADERS

The massive capital requirements of building unique telecommunications systems guarantees that the companies involved will be large and powerful. The biggest players in the computer, communications, and information industries are all maneuvering for the anticipated wireless revolution. Nokia is the leader in this industry with almost $16 billion in sales and nearly 45,000 employees. Between 1997 and 1998, Nokia's sales grew by 60 percent, with digital phone sales accounting for 80 percent of their revenue. Motorola, the industry leader during the first half of the 1990s, was in second place by decade's end with a 40 percent share of the cellular market and company-wide sales of over $29 billion. Motorola had a broad product line compatible with most standards and long-standing experience in radio electronics. It is the world's leading supplier of pagers, two-way radios, and dispatch systems for commercial fleets. Motorola has the largest segment of the global cellular telephone market, according to U.S. International Trade Commission (ITC) reports. In addition to its strong position on the equipment side, it is buying radio frequencies around the world. Motorola was instrumental in the development of the Iridium project, a $4 billion system, which will use 66 small satellites in low earth orbit to connect calls around the world. By 2001, companies were expected "to spend up to $50 billion to build and launch new satellites—and twice that for antennas, phones, switches, and other gear to support their birds aloft," according to William J. Cook in *U.S. News & World Report*. The third major player in the cellular industry was Ericcson, with 30 percent of the market and sales of almost $23 billion in 1998. This was an increase of over 7 percent since 1997.

WORKFORCE

The top three companies in this industry employed over 281,000 people in 1998. Mergers and consolidations among manufacturers, as well as improved productivity and technology, may mean employment declines in the future. However, this effect may be countered by the growing demand in certain segments of the industry.

AMERICA AND THE WORLD

This industry is positioned to take advantage of demand from developing markets abroad, such as Eastern Europe, Central and South America, and China. American companies are increasingly linking up with overseas competitors to create global partnerships.

The U.S. cellular industry is highly competitive in cellular licenses awarded to foreign operators. About 70 percent of the total licenses to operate cellular systems abroad have been awarded to U.S. firms. American companies will continue to dominate international cellular operations, however, the lack of a common digital standard has hindered sales of U.S. cellular network equipment abroad.

RESEARCH AND TECHNOLOGY

Because of the technological orientation of this industry, research and technology are a continual, high priority concern. Most of the research and technology is intended to achieve one of several goals: to maximize an existing technology, such as CDPD; to combine existing technologies for enhanced competitiveness across technologies, such as PCS; and to improve technology in existing products to attract consumers with next-generation models, like a new generation of pagers.

FURTHER READING

Bounds, Jeff. "Two Way Paging Might Rescue Ailing Industry." *Dallas Business Journal,* September 25, 1998.

Brandon, James. "The Global Positioning System Advances Toward Universal Acceptance." *Industry, Trade, and Technology Review,* July, 1996.

Business Week. "Close to Perfect Pocket E-Mail." 3 May 1999.

Business Wire. "AirTouch Launches All-Digital Mobile Internet Service." 4 November 1999.

Business Wire. "Iridium North America Offers New Maritime Equipment Options." 3 November 1999.

Business Wire. "SBC Communications Announces Wireless Expansion Into New Orleans, Southern Louisiana and Northern Michigan." 3 November 1999.

Cohen, Robert. "New Telecommunications Technologies." *Business Economics,* April, 1998.

Cook, William J. "1997: A New Space Odyssey." *U.S. News & World Report,* 3 March 1997.

Day, Rebecca. "Pagers Get Smart." *Popular Mechanics,* February, 1999.

Economist. "The Conquest of Location." October 9, 1999.

Federal Communications Commission. *Wireless Telecommunications Bureau Provides Guidance on the Anti-Collusion Rule for D, E and F Block Bidders.* Washington, 1996. Available from http://www.fcc.gov/wtb/auctions/def/da961460.txt.

Florida Times-Union. "Competetion Drives Costs Down for Cellular-Telephone Users." 31 October 1999.

Folkers, Richard. "Answer This." *U.S. News & World Report,* 15 December 1997.

Fortune. "A Pager That Talks: Motorola's Voice-Mail Pager is a Boon to Road Warriors Tired of Trying to Decipher Alphanumeric Messages." 11 May 1998.

Hoover Online, 9 November 1999. Available from http://www.hoovers.com.

Masie, Elliott. "Two-Way Pagers to the Rescue." *Meetings and Conventions,* July, 1999.

O'Malley, Chris. "Blueprint for a Revolution." *Popular Science,* July, 1996.

PR Newswire. "First Personalized Portal WAP and Internet Phones Launched by SmartRay Network 'Internet Phone' Users Will be Able to Access and Customize." 3 November 1999.

Quittner, Joshua. "Beeping Back: Two-Way Pagers are Supposed to Bail Out the Industry. But What Can They do for You." *Time,* 7 September 1998.

Toth, Simone. "Cell Phones, TVs Spark the Electronics Industry." *San Diego Business Journal,* 29 September 1997.

SIC 3669

COMMUNICATIONS EQUIPMENT, NOT ELSEWHERE CLASSIFIED

This classification covers companies primarily engaged in manufacturing communications and related equipment, not elsewhere classified. Important products of this industry include intercommunication equipment, traffic signaling equipment, and fire and burglar alarm apparatus. In 1997 there were about 500 companies employing over 25,000 workers with total shipments valued over $4.2 billion. Establishments that provide security systems monitoring and maintenance are discussed in **SIC 7382: Security Systems Services.**

NAICS CODE(S)

334290 (Other Communication Equipment Manufacturing)

While this miscellaneous communications equipment industry includes a number of visible and important products, such as railroad signaling devices and various traffic control equipment, the revenue accrued in this industry originates primarily from the sale of security and smoke/fire alarm systems (about 63 percent). Traffic control equipment makes up about 25 percent, followed by intercommunications' systems at a distant 4 percent. The Freedonia Group estimated security equipment sales (alarms, electronic article surveillance systems, closed circuit television, etc.) at $4.5 billion in 1997, and this total was expected to reach $6.6 billion in 2002. Conversely, alarms' share is projected to drop from 65 percent to 59 percent during that period.

Alarm Systems. The United States has long dominated the alarm manufacturing and alarm monitoring industries worldwide. A myriad of alarm manufacturers have been able to establish themselves over the years: in 1997 the National Burglar and Fire Alarm Association estimated that an average of 13,100 local installation companies were operating in America. The number of alarm systems installed grew from 2.1 million in 1994 to 2.4 million in

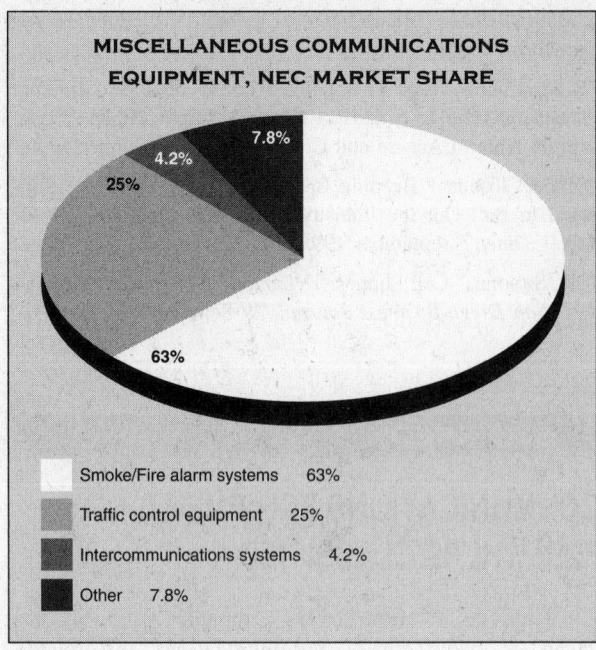

MISCELLANEOUS COMMUNICATIONS EQUIPMENT, NEC MARKET SHARE

7.8%
4.2%
25%
63%

Smoke/Fire alarm systems   63%

Traffic control equipment   25%

Intercommunications systems   4.2%

Other   7.8%

1997, while total industry revenues grew from $9.8 billion to $13.9 billion, respectively.

STAT Resources Inc. estimated that by the end of 1998 more than one in five homes would be electronically protected. From 1995 to 1998, consumers spent more than $33.0 billion on home security installations and monitoring. In 1997, Americans spent around $14.8 billion on professionally installed security products and services, up from $10.2 billion in 1995. Spending is expected to continue at an estimated rate of 4.3 percent per year. Long term factors that drive security system sales are economic conditions, crime, sales and marketing prowess, disposable consumer income, and capital spending by businesses.

Security Distributing & Marketing reported that the total number of new residential installations by the top 100 companies rose 22 percent in 1998, representing combined revenues of $120.0 million. Total revenue for these companies (including installation and service) was nearly $3.8 billion with a workforce near 40,000. A greater number of firms reported shrinking revenues compared to 1997, after several years of growth through acquisitions (a total of 142 in 1998). Consistent with the other trends in this weakening market, the workforce grew only 2 percent.

Three major trends drove the growth of the security systems market in the mid-1990s: growing public concern about crime, reluctance on the part of the U.S. Government to increase public safety expenditures, and a combination of technological advances and intensified price competition that made home security systems more affordable. By the middle of the decade, a basic home security system could be had for $200 or $300—down

from about $1500 only a few years earlier. The increasing use of personal computers in American homes also opened a new and exploitable market niche for manufacturers of security systems. In the late 1990s, for example, security systems' manufacturers began to develop software that integrated equipment from various providers or allowed for future upgrades.

Manufacturers of alarm systems generally produce two kinds of component systems: perimeter and interior alarms. Perimeter systems typically consist of magnetic contacts that detect the opening of doors and windows, detectors that pick up the cutting and breaking of glass, and alarm screens that allow windows to be opened for fresh air, but activate an alarm if the screen is tampered with. Interior systems usually provide infrared motion detectors located in strategic areas, fire alarms, panic buttons that can be operated manually to alert the monitoring station, and an electronic keypad that both accesses and operates the system.

In the late 1990s, manufacturers created new alarm systems capable of operating in concert with other home automation features so that homeowners could manipulate their surveillance system along with their entertainment systems and heating and cooling systems. The determination of prices is based on several factors, such as the size of the area being defended, the number of apertures that need to be protected, and the quantity and nature of the devices installed. The average family home can be protected for between $800 and $1500. The average price of a security system has dropped from $1,509 in 1990 to $1,200 in 1998.

Fire Systems. There are two smoke-sensing technologies commonly used in residential smoke detectors: photoelectric and ionization. Both are available in 9-volt battery and 110-volt house current models. Photoelectric detectors are more sensitive to slow, smoldering fires, while ionization detectors respond to fast burning fires like stove grease flare-ups or burning newspapers. The top smoke detector makers in 1997, based on shipments of 16,650,000 units, were First Alert, which controlled 60 percent of the market, and Jameson (Maple Chase), which controlled 32 percent.

According to Ward's Business Directory 2000, Tyco International of New Hampshire led the way in the communications equipment industry, with $12.3 billion in sales and 87,000 employees worldwide. Pittway Corporation of Chicago, Illinois is a $1.4 billion holding company that owns several firms in the fire alarm/security industry and has 7,800 employees. This company is a leader in the smoke alarm manufacturing arena via its Ademco Security Group, which had sales around $400.0 million in the late 1990s. Pittway's System Technology Group is the leading manufacturer of automatic fire alarm control systems. Pittway's Notifier Engineered Systems Company (NESCO) subsidiary provides systems' design, training, and marketing services to distributors of its fire alarm systems. Another subsidiary, Fire-Lite/NOTIFIER firm has steady sales in 32 countries and does half of its business outside of the United States.

FURTHER READING

Hoover's Company Capsules. Austin, TX: Hoover's Inc., 1997.

Bowman, Eric J. "Security Tools Up For the Future." *Security Management,* January 1996.

Coombs, Joe. "North Branford, Conn.-Based Firm's Fire Alarms Keep Businesses Safe." *Waterbury Republican-American.* Knight-Ridder/Tribune Business News, 14 August 1999.

"NAICS 334290." *Manufacturing-Industry Series.* U.S. Census Bureau, 1997 Economic Census, 10 September 1999.

"Quick Facts & Stats about the Electronic Security Industry"The National Burglar & Fire Alarm Association, April 1999. Available from http://www.nbfaa.org/consumer/quick .htm.

Schulman, Robert. "All About Home Alarm Systems: Burglar, Fire, Flood—Name It, You Can Guard Against It." *New York Times,* 10 January 1993.

"1999 SDM 100 Stat Sheet." *Security and Distribution Magazine.* Cahners Business Information, 1999. Available from http:/ /www.sdmmag.com/stats.asp.

"Security Equipment Sales, 1997 and 2002." *Security Management,* December 1998.

"Top Smoke Detector Makers, 1997." *Appliance,* September 1998.

SIC 3671

ELECTRON TUBES

This category covers establishments primarily engaged in manufacturing electron tubes and tube parts. Establishments primarily engaged in manufacturing X-ray tubes and parts are classified in **SIC 3844: X-Ray Apparatus and Tubes and Related Irradiation Apparatus;** those manufacturing liquid crystal displays (LCDs) are classified in **SIC 3679: Electronic Components, Not Elsewhere Classified;** those manufacturing computer terminals are classified in **SIC 3575: Computer Terminals.**

NAICS CODE(S)

334411 (Electron Tube Manufacturing)

INDUSTRY SNAPSHOT

Companies engaged in this industry in 1997 were down by 15 percent from the number of firms in 1992.

Yet, in 1997, 158 industry establishments generated just over $3.8 billion in shipments, a 19 percent increase over 1992. The industry employed nearly the same number of employees, 21,699, but increased productivity. Over three-fourths (76 percent) of the value of industry revenues in 1997 was derived from the production of new and rebuilt receiving-type electron tubes such as TV and cathode-ray tubes, up from only 61 percent in 1992. The second major product group, accounting for 17 percent of the value of total 1997 shipments, consisted of transmittal, industrial, and special-purpose electron tubes (except X-ray tubes). This represented a decline from 31 percent of total industry revenues in 1992.

ORGANIZATION AND STRUCTURE

The two most recognizable types of electron tubes were the ordinary television and computer tube and the once common vacuum tube traditionally used in radios and other electronic equipment. Generally speaking, electron tubes were sealed glass, enamel, or metallic tubes of varying sizes into which electrons were fired for the purpose of displaying images or conducting, transmitting, or multiplying light for nondisplay purposes. Although television tubes and computer displays were the most common products, industry firms also manufactured camera tubes, microwave tubes, Geiger counters, radar screens, and such specialized devices as electron beam (beta ray) generator tubes, klystron tubes, magnetron tubes, planar triode tubes, and tubes for operating above the X-ray spectrum.

Electron tubes varied according to the extent to which they were "evacuated," or emptied, of gases and vapors; by the capability and type of the electron source; and by the number and configuration of electrodes they contained. The amount of power used in electron tubes ranged from milliwatts to hundreds of megawatts, and the frequency of operation ranged between zero and ten-to-the-eleventh-power Hertz depending on the type of tube. In general, CRTs operated by playing a beam of electrons of varying intensities over a display surface such as a phosphor screen, which formed patterns of light that took the form of characters or images. The three basic components of a CRT were the envelope, the electron gun, and the phosphor screen. The envelope, which was usually made of glass, was a funnel-shaped element through which the electrons were fired toward the faceplate on the broad end of the envelope. The electron gun was the source of the electrons, which, when heated and formed into a beam, were directed to differing parts of the screen by magnetic fields surrounding the envelope. The phosphor screen itself consisted of a layer of phosphor dots that coated the inner surface of the CRT's faceplate. Color CRTs used a screen made up of red, green, and blue phosphors, with an electron gun for each color; monochrome CRT screens employed one electron gun.

In the everyday family "direct view" TV, the face of the picture tube on which the electrons are projected is the same as the screen the viewer sees. In rear-projection TV sets, which became increasingly common in the 1980s, a translucent screen was used against which images were projected indirectly from three small CRTS (one each for the colors red, green, and blue) through a series of mirrors. In the mid-1990s projection TV tube manufacturers were using compact CRTs and lenses with shorter focal lengths to reduce the amount of space taken up by the television box, reducing the size of the once bulky rear projection sets by a third. In contrast to the 4:3 aspect ratio of the standard television tube, wide screen TVs employed a 16:9 ratio that resembled the wide ratio of movie theater screens and were therefore marketed as the precursor to the so- called high-definition television (HDTV) technology that Japanese TV makers trumpeted throughout the 1990s. With the advent of advanced data streaming technology, computer CRTs were increasingly used to display downloaded and/or Digital Video Disk (DVD) movies and multimedia entertainment.

Despite its continued popularity in the 1990s, the CRT was by no means a perfect piece of technology. In a world increasingly permeated by digital solid state electronics technology, the CRT remained the last holdover of the old analog glass vacuum tube, which in fact it essentially was. The CRT was bulky, hot, and heavy, used large amounts of power, and was prone to disruptions of glare and magnetic and electrical fields. By the mid-1990s, in fact, few experts doubted that for mainstream computer and TV uses the CRT's days were numbered. In their place, came the advent of high definition liquid crystal display (LCD) screens for computers. These displays utilized an active matrix view panel. Display resolution often surpassed the capabilities of traditional CRT displays. While such technology was often far more expensive, the promise of ever-decreasing manufacturing costs and higher consumer demand marked LCD technology as the heir-apparent to traditional CRT use for computer displays.

The second largest industry product group, transmittal, industrial, and special-purpose electron tubes, included electro optical tubes and miscellaneous special-purpose tubes. The electro optical tube segment included everything from camera tubes and photo cells to other photo-conductive and photo-emissive tubes, most notably the airport bomb detector picture tube, the largest market of the electro optical tube segment.

Microwave tubes were primarily used in high and ultrahigh frequency applications such as radars, telecommunications equipment, military communication and control systems, high-frequency microwave ovens, scientific research equipment, FM radio transmitters, and industrial heating equipment. Traveling wave tubes, which were divided into forward and backward wave electron tubes, accounted for a majority of the microwave electron tubes produced. Microwave tubes as a whole comprised a majority of the power and special-purpose tube market. Gas tubes were used primarily in industrial applications because of their efficiency and ability to handle high levels of power or current at generally low frequency levels. Product types included diodes, rectifiers, control-type industrial triodes, hydrogen and nonhydrogen thyratons, and other gas and vapor tubes. High-power tubes were also used in broadcasting transmitters. Vacuum tubes, once the primary element in electrical circuits, were primarily used in applications where low noise and high frequency were involved.

BACKGROUND AND DEVELOPMENT

Electron tubes were the principal components of almost all electronic circuits and equipment until semiconductors were developed and began to replace them in the late 1940s and 1950s. The first application of CRT technology was for an oscilloscope in 1897, and the first television using a CRT was developed in the late 1920s. Commercial production of monochrome television picture tubes began in the late 1940s. After World War II, U.S. electron tube manufacturers found a diverse and lucrative market in defense applications, ranging from radar to communication and control equipment.

By the mid-1990s, the fastest-growing segment of the TV picture tube market was big-screen TVs, those providing from 31 to 58 inches of viewable screen image. Despite the fact that by the mid-1990s nearly every U.S. home had at least one TV, there were 22.9 million direct-view TVs sold in 1999. In 1994 over 26 million color TVs were sold in the United States. Spurred on by a demand estimated to reach $20 billion by the turn of the century, industry firms were making significant strides in improving CRT's resolution, brilliance, size, energy usage, and cost. Television tubes and computer monitors were becoming flatter and bigger (the standard 14-inch PC monitor, for example, was giving way to 17- and even 20-inch models), digital circuits were being used to enhance picture quality, and advances in nonelectron tube technology were coming on so quickly that the CRT itself seemed destined for only niche uses in specialized applications.

CURRENT CONDITIONS

In the 1990s the CRT sector of the electron tube industry continued to establish itself as the sector's primary revenue machine, accounting for 61 percent of the value of the industry's total shipments in 1992. Despite a drop-off in government spending for military-related CRT display technologies, the consumer computer CRT and television tube markets were promising to provide more than enough demand to fuel the industry's continuing growth. Between 1994 and 1999, the value of PC system sales (which included a CRT monitor) grew by almost 77 percent. Concurrent expansion occurred in the number of systems sold, which increased over the same period by 121 percent. A total of 90.5 million CRTs were sold in 1998 and generated a $17.2 billion market share of the electron tube industry. Monitor Market Trends (twelfth edition) projected an increase to 134.7 units sold by 2004, but due to a decline in per unit cost, revenues would only increase to $18.9 billion.

In the mid-1990s the battle between the computer CRT and the flat panel display (FPD) intensified. Developed in America but later co-opted by Japanese firms, the FPD encompassed several display technologies, from active- and passive-matrix liquid-crystal displays (LCDs) to field-emission, micromirror, diamond emission, and neon- or xenon-based gas plasma displays. Between 1989 and 1995, demand for LCD FPDs alone grew from $1 billion to $10 billion.

By the mid-1990s, FPD manufacturers had overcome hurdles in FPD design complexity and subsequent high cost and the technology's high power requirements. At one time, the only CRT markets immediately threatened by FPDs were point-of-sale terminals, medical imaging applications, and displays for instrumentation and factory automation. However, when the twentieth century ended, manufacturers had broken out of the laptop and avionics display markets into the television tube and PC monitor markets, the electron tube's home turf.

Flat panel display technology began to find application in a wide variety of uses at the close of the 1990s. According to the U.S. Display Consortium (USDC), innovative uses included analytical equipment, conference-room equipment, marine instruments, hand-held devices, electronic books, passenger entertainment systems, and home appliances. So-called "cutting-edge" technology also included filed-emission displays (FEDs). According to *Electronic Business*, total revenues from flat panel display sales at the end of 1999 were estimated at $11 billion.

Throughout the 1990s high-resolution HDTV was marketed as the next great advance in television technology. Because its superiority was only noticeable in 40-inch screens, the resulting increases in TV tube size spelled more trouble for the electron CRT's future. As the resolution of television screens increased, the brightness of the traditional CRT fell and the FPD became no more expensive than a comparably sized CRT, but 75 percent thinner. Indeed, in the mid-1990s, one producer, Photonic Imaging, had already tested a thirty-inch plasma FPD television that was only a few inches thick but whose image was virtually indistinguishable from a standard thirty-inch CRT television. Finally, in the mid-1990s the distinction between the television tube and the computer monitor threatened to vanish. By using a combined link, "Web TV" technologies like Zenith's "NetVision" al-

lowed consumers to watch TV or surf the World Wide Web from the same screen.

INDUSTRY LEADERS

Among the leading firms in the electron tube industry in the 1990s were Zenith Electronics Corporation, Philips Display Components Company, Hitachi Electronic Devices, and Toshiba Westinghouse Electronic. Other major industry players included GM Hughes Electronics Corporation, Hewlett-Packard Co., ITT Corporation, Litton Industries Inc., Electron Devices Division, Philips Electronics North America, and Raytheon Electronic Components. The pace of change in the electron tube industry was frenetic in the mid-1990s. In 1994, Display Technologies Inc., a joint venture of International Business Machines Corporation (IBM Corp.)and Japan's Toshiba Corporation, continued to develop IBM's flat-screen CRT product line. The same year, Fluke Corporation sold off its CRT operation, and in 1995, Advanced Technology Materials Inc. and Silicon Video Corporation agreed to market a new generation of thin CRT flat panel displays. Varian Associates Inc., once an industry leader, sold its electron devices operations to Leonard Green & Partners L.P. for $200 million in 1995. In 1996 Japan's Sony Corp. and the U.S. firm Tektronix Inc. unveiled a big-screen "Plasmatron" television line that offered consumers a 25-inch flat-screen television (about four inches thick), with 40- and 50-inch flat TVs to follow.

With LCD/FPD technology establishing a strong foothold in the market for displays and TVs, upcoming leaders in the industry were often a result of joint ventures among recognized, historical leaders. One of the most active of these collaborations was Display Technologies Inc., which was the result of a venture between IBM Corp. and Toshiba Corp. Other LCD/FPD leaders at the end of the 1990s included TEAC, Epson America Inc. (the U.S. affiliate of Japan's Seiko Epson Corp.), Fujitsu Microelectronics Inc., Hitachi, and NEC Electronics Inc. Leaders in the newest of flat panel technologies, thin-film-transistor (TFT) displays (most notably used for huge multimedia displays for rock concerts and sporting/recreational events) were Hitachi and Sharp Electronics Corp.

RESEARCH AND TECHNOLOGY

The growing demand for computer monitors for use in homes and offices starting in the 1980s forced industry firms to develop more user-friendly monitor designs, such as the "flat square CRT," in which the curvature of the CRT's screen was greatly reduced. CRT display technology also continued to evolve in the areas of unit price and color display capabilities.

The application of multifunctional CRT displays in the instrument panels of military and to a lesser degree commercial aircraft also continued in the 1990s. However, the inherent disadvantages of CRTs—limited screen size, unwieldy shape, high power requirements, and fragility— led manufacturers to investigate alternatives to CRT technology, such as light-emitting diodes, FPDs, and LCDs. Improvements in LCDs, which were thinner and lighter than CRTs, enabled them to compete in price with CRT-based, large-screen, video-data projectors while offering roughly 2 to 4 times their brightness. In aircraft cockpit applications in particular—where limited space and high levels of glare diminished the usefulness of CRTs—flat panel displays increasingly emerged as the favored display technology. Another emergent technology, the field emission display, was structurally less complex than LCDs and even thinner in size and further threatened to unseat the electron CRT. In general terms, field emission displays were based on vacuum microelectronics and combined the advantages of the old vacuum tube technology with the benefits of digital computer chips. Advances in research and technology also continued in non-CRT product categories in the 1990s. Direct broadcast satellites for noncable, HDTV transmissions (among other uses) were developed that used electron tubes, such as traveling wave tubes, for satellite tubes and uplink stations with tube lifetimes of up to 15 years.

As the twenty-first century began, electron tube technology continued to evolve. In addition to well-known applications such as CRTs for television and computers, advances in the way electron tubes were configured opened up new applications and markets. Using technology developed in 1997 by Lawrence Livermore National Laboratory researchers Booth Myers, Hao-Lin Chen, Glenn Meyer, and Dino Ciarlo, new designs eliminated the need for vacuum systems used in conventional electron beam equipment. The new, sealed electron tube reduced cost tenfold, were smaller and easier to use, and (in high-risk applications for X-rays and high electrical voltages) reduced worker exposure. This technology made possible applications as diverse as processing inks, adhesives, paints with greatly-reduced pollutants, processing floppy disks for computers, and medical supplies.

FURTHER READING

"ATMI, SVC Expand CRT Partnership." *Electronic News* 41, no. 2062, 24 April 1995, 4.

Barry, James. "Big Screen Bonanza." *Stereo Review* 60, no. 4, April 1995, 53+.

"Beyond Laptops." *Electronic Business*, January 1999.

Britt, Russ. "One-for-all, all-in-one." *Electronic Business*, December 1999.

Cataldo, Anthony. "CRTs Are Solid Fixtures but FPDs Keep Pressing On." *Electronic News* 41, no. 2070, 19 June 1995, 68.

Churbuck, David C. "The Last Picture Tube." *Forbes* 155, no. 10, 8 May 1995, 136+.

"Commerce Department/The McGraw-Hill Companies Forecast Continued Economic Growth." *Business Wire*, 21 November 1997.

"CRT Monitors Continue to Fend Off Flat Panel Challenge; Market Will Top $17 Billion in 1998." *Business Wire*, 19 October 1998.

Delano, Daryl. "Solid Growth for Consumer Electronics." *Electronic Business*, February, 1999.

"Extra: Top Component Suppliers: Displays." *Electronic Buyer News*, 3 November 1997.

"Information Impact." *Fortune* (technology guide supplement), Winter 1997, 93+.

Lawrence Livermore National Laboratory. "Livermore Researchers Garner Three Awards for Successful Projects with U.S. Businesses." U.S. Department of Energy Information Locator, 1998. Available from http://gils.doe.gov:1782/cgi-bin/w3vdkhgw?qryMGACldAU_;doecrawl-028326/.

"Preparing for Prime Time," *Economist* 340, no. 7980, 24 August 1996, 49.

U.S. Department of Commerce. "Electron Tube Manufacturing." *1997 Economic Census, Manufacturing Industry Series*. Washington: GPO, 1999.

"Varian Sells Off Electron Devices." *Electronic News* 41, no. 2081, 4 September 1995, 40.

SIC 3672

PRINTED CIRCUIT BOARDS

This category includes establishments primarily engaged in the manufacture of printed circuit boards, sometimes referred to as printed wiring boards.

A printed circuit board (PCB) is a thin piece of insulating material onto which tiny electrical wiring pathways or "traces" have been printed, usually by a photoengraving process. PCBs provide the physical structure for mounting electronic components, such as semiconductors. The printed traces then serve to interconnect the components, forming an electronic system. PCBs are used in a wide range of electronic products, including computers, telecommunications equipment, electronic instruments, and automobiles.

NAICS CODE(S)

334412 (Printed Circuit Board Manufacturing)

INDUSTRY SNAPSHOT

U.S. PCB production reached $5.3 billion in 1991, according to the Institute of Interconnecting and Packaging Electronic Circuits (IPC); and worldwide sales of PCBs reached $20 billion in 1997, according to the Electronic Outlook Corporation. In 1997, there were more than 1,300 U.S. facilities that shipped printed circuit boards worth $9.6 billion. Total value of the industry, including bare boards, components, and various activities involved in the assembly of boards, was estimated at $60 billion in the early 1990s.

ORGANIZATION AND STRUCTURE

According to the IPC, approximately 650 independent companies produced PCBs in the United States in 1997, accounting for 90 percent of the entire market. So-called ''captive'' PCB-makers, primarily large original equipment manufacturers (OEMs) that make their own boards, comprised the remaining 10 percent. Though the largest market for OEM boards was in computer applications, captive board makers also served a large number of communications and government/military users as well.

Computer makers were the major consumers of independently produced PCBs in 1991, when over 43 percent of overall independent board production went to computer companies. Communications constituted the second major market for independently produced PCBs, using more than 17 percent of the industry's output. The role of independent PCB manufacturers has increased steadily over the years. Though more than 90 percent of independent PCB-makers reported annual sales of less than $10 million in 1991, OEMs were increasingly relying on them to supply boards for their products, and industry observers expect this trend to continue.

BACKGROUND AND DEVELOPMENT

Printed circuit board assembly companies (PCBAs) comprised a growing, specialized segment of the PCB industry. More than just contract assemblers, PCBAs provided design, global procurement, cost reduction services, and access to advanced technology. The early 1990s saw a dramatic growth in the use of PCBAs, and industry observers expected that trend to continue because of the cost-savings measures these companies provided. There were nearly 800 PCBAs in operation in the United States in 1992, with an estimated total value of $5.9 billion. PCBAs employed approximately 80,000 workers in 1991, while independent board makers employed about 70,000.

At the start of the 1990s PCB makers were adapting to two important industry trends: first, the increasing use of smaller circuitry products and, second, a greater demand for surface mount technology. The drive among electronics firms toward smaller components had been cited as one reason for the decline in PCB usage from 1988 to 1991. Smaller components required smaller or fewer boards and less space on the PCB.

Spurred by demand, the industry moved quickly toward surface mount technology. Surface mounting involves the soldering of components directly onto the surface of a board, which in turn allows components to be mounted closer together and even on both sides of a board. In 1989, however, less than 12 percent of boards included surface mounted components. By 1992 more than half of all PCBs were assembled with one or more surface-mounted components.

Through 1997, contract manufacturers continued to invest heavily in conventional surface mount technology (SMT) equipment rather than in new technologies such as chip on board (COB) and ball grid arrays (BGA). The manufacturers were slow in adopting the new technologies; about 25 percent of them, however, focused on BGA as their next generation packing technology. By mid-1996, copper-clad printed circuit board materials were used increasingly in the electronics industry because of their excellent electrical and thermal properties.

In the mid- to late 1990s, one of the most popular trends in the industry was the reuse of the vast amount of waste generated each year. More than 10 million pounds of trim and rejected boards were being generated each year.

In June of 1998, the Environmental Protection Agency (EPA) issued guidelines for PCB disposal. Proler International Corporation launched a new circuit board recycling operation—Proler Recycling, in Coolidge, Arizona—where they started processing recycled boards in the summer of 1995. According to *American Metal Market,* in 1995 Proler Recycling was the only company in the United States that recovered all three metal components (tin, copper, and lead) from circuit boards and successfully converted them to high purity metals. At the time, the other companies were typically recovering only one of the metals from the circuit boards.

In 1996, Daimler Benz was using a four-stage process for recycling circuit boards. The technology, which was in the pilot plant stage in Germany, involved Benz's customized version of first shredding the electronic scrap and then using various techniques to separate out and clean the various scrap elements. According to Benz, the recycling technique cost them about $198.48 to $338.80 per metric ton of circuit board scrap and gave them a return of $529.28 to $1,984.80 per ton depending on gold content.

New ''via'' technologies capable of addressing complex capability requirements were also becoming important in the mid-1990s. The 1996 IPC Printed Circuits Expo showcased several of these technologies. According to *Electronic Design* magazine, DuPont Advanced Fiber Systems demonstrated a method of producing high speed micro-vias in dimensionally stable, non-woven Aramid reinforced laminates using laser-ablation technology. Mommers Print Service B.V. demonstrated a cheaper but more complex technique that also

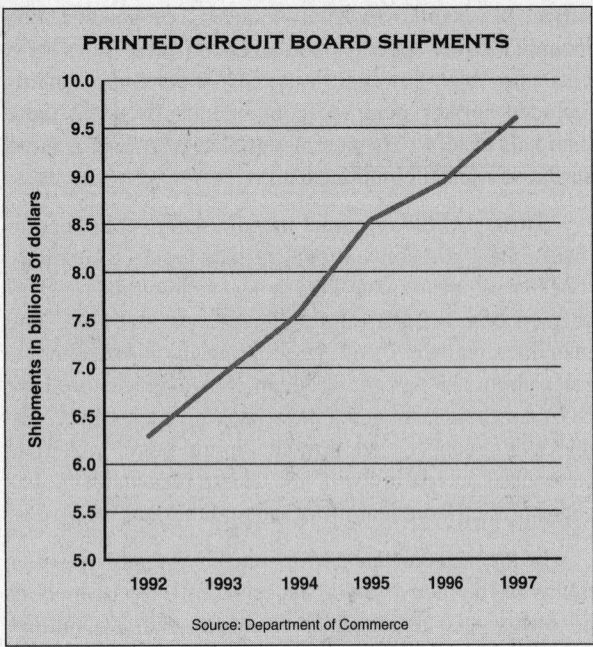

PRINTED CIRCUIT BOARD SHIPMENTS

Shipments in billions of dollars

Source: Department of Commerce

involved laser formation of micro-vias. As circuit board makers scrambled to stay on technology's cutting edge, the need for greater interconnect density on printed circuit boards seemed to be the next step for circuit board manufacturers.

Although the domestic PCB industry continued to remain globally competitive in its utilization of advanced manufacturing technologies, increasing overseas production resulted in a significant decrease in the U.S. share of the world PCB market from 40 percent in 1980 to 29 percent in 1990. In 1991, Japan ranked first in worldwide production of rigid PCBs with 33.8 percent of the market; the United States ranked second with 26.9 percent. Germany, Taiwan, the United Kingdom, and Hong Kong ranked third through sixth, respectively.

CURRENT CONDITIONS

Due to rapidly changing technology, PCB manufacturers were constantly modifying their products to adapt and grow. Surface mount components were rapidly becoming the norm; copper baths were being replaced by direct metallization; and the need for adhesives was being phased out through the use of thermocouple probes that measured and adjusted temperature. Research was being performed to manufacture PCBs with smaller holes to allow more space on the boards and accommodate changes in semiconductors. The trend toward less space-consuming units was seen in smaller digital frequency units that required only one PCB rather than multiple boards.

Another popular trend of the mid- to late 1990s was the increased use of signal analysis tools to design printed

circuit boards capable of operating at high frequency levels. These tools were used to accurately analyze the signal integrity of printed circuit board designs with respect to several circuit parameters, such as crosstalk, ground bounce, resonance, and dispersion.

In 1997, shipment values reached nearly $9.6 billion and were expected to continue climbing into 2002, bolstered by new technology and expanding markets. Foreign competition was expected to pick up as well in order to help meet growing demand, with Asian countries providing the strongest competition in the U. S. market. It was predicted that more companies would consolidate and merge by the year 2002 and beyond, because of the cost and increased need for technological advances.

INDUSTRY LEADERS

In 1997 there were 1,389 establishments employing 75,091 workers. In 1999, Solectron Corporation of Milpitas, California was the industry leader with nearly $5.3 billion in sales and 24,900 employees. The second largest company was Hadco Corporation of Salem, New Hampshire with $649 million in sales and 6,100 employees.

FURTHER READING

"An IFM Receiver on a Single PCB." *Microwave Journal,* January 1998.

Economic Census 1997. *Bureau of the Census.* 2000. Available from http://www.census.gov.

"EPA Issues New PCB Disposal Procedures." *Pesticide and Toxic Chemical News,* July 8,1999.

Haystead, John. "Look Before You Leap." *Electronic Business Today,* January 1997, 67.

"Instability May Stay." *Electronic News,* November 16, 1998.

LaRue, Gloria T. "Daimler-Benz Develops Circuit Board Process." *American Metal Market,* 13 November 1996.

Maliniak, David. "Solving Inner-layer Via Problems." *Electronic Design,* 1 May 1996.

Maliniak, Lisa. "Signal Analysis: A Must For PCB Design Success." *Electronic Design,* 18 Sept 1995.

Pease, Robert A. "What's All This Copper Clad Stuff, Anyhow?" *Electronic Design,* 19 August 1996.

"Profiling Technique Improves PCB Assembly." *Design News,* April 6, 1998.

"Proler Set to Start Circuit Boar Unit." *American Metal Market,* 25 May 1995.

U. S. Industry and Trade Outlook '99. The McGraw-Hill Companies, 1999.

Ward's Business Directory of U.S. Private and Public Companies. Detroit: Gale Research, 1999.

SIC 3674

SEMICONDUCTORS AND RELATED DEVICES

This category covers establishments primarily engaged in manufacturing semiconductors and related solid-state devices. Important products of this industry are semiconductor diodes and stacks, including rectifiers, integrated microcircuits (semiconductor networks), transistors, solar cells, and light sensing and emitting semiconductor (solid-state) devices.

NAICS CODE(S)

334413 (Semiconductor and Related Device Manufacturing)

INDUSTRY SNAPSHOT

No longer wholly dependent on personal computer sales, the U.S. semiconductor industry provides components for a wide range of consumer and industrial electronics. Computers still account for about 50 percent of the industry's sales, however, with the growing field of data and telecommunications accounting for nearly 25 percent. The industry is notoriously cyclical. After worldwide semiconductor sales grew 40 percent in 1995 to nearly $150.0 billion, sales dropped in 1996 and were flat through 1998. A rebound in sales for 1999—forecast to reach $144.0 billion level—promised the beginning of another cycle of growth in the semiconductor industry.

The semiconductor industry was one of the fastest growing sectors in the U.S. economy between 1987 and 1996, when it grew from the seventeenth largest industry in the United States to the largest as measured by its contribution to the U.S. gross domestic product. In 1996 semiconductor manufacturers contributed $41.6 billion to the U.S. economy. Entering the twenty-first century, the information technology sector accounted for 11 percent of the U.S. gross domestic product and one-fourth of the U.S. manufacturing output.

ORGANIZATION AND STRUCTURE

Sometimes referred to as "the crude oil of the information age," semiconductors are a pervasive but generally unseen aspect of everyday life. The tiny electronic circuits etched on chips of silicon are critical to the operation of virtually all electronics, from automatic coffee makers and antilock braking systems to cellular phones and supercomputers.

The computer industry is by far the largest market for semiconductors. In the late 1990s, sales to computer manufacturers and related enterprises accounted for 50 percent of overall sales of semiconductors in this country.

Consumer electronics and the automotive industry were also important users of semiconductors and related products. The fastest growing market for semiconductors was related to communications, which accounted for 23 percent of sales in 1998, reflecting the rise of a global networked economy that relied on the electronic transfer of data.

Semiconductor chips are manufactured in "clean rooms," free of contaminating dust. In those facilities, thin, round silicon wafers are processed in batches. Chipmakers buy polished blank wafers from companies that specialize in growing silicon crystals, from which the wafers are cut. Each wafer is about half a millimeter thick. Microelectronics circuits are built up on the wafer layer by layer.

Circuit patterns—the collection of transistors, capacitors, and associated components and their interconnections—are inscribed on large glass plates called photomasks. The photomasks are later reduced and photolithographically projected onto the silicon wafers. Each mask comprises a total integrated circuit design.

Semiconductor companies design and manufacture primarily two types of products: integrated circuits (ICs) and discrete devices. A discrete semiconductor is an individual circuit that performs a single function affecting the flow of electrical current. For example, a transistor, one of the most common types of discrete devices, amplifies electrical signals; rectifiers and diodes generally convert alternating current into direct current; capacitors block the flow of alternating current at controlled levels; and resistors limit current flow and divide or drop current.

Integrated Circuits.   Also called chips, integrated circuits are a collection of microminiaturized electronic components, such as transistors and capacitors, placed on a tiny rectangle of silicon. A single integrated circuit can perform the functions of thousands of discrete transistors, diodes, capacitors, and resistors. There are three basic types of integrated circuits currently produced by American semiconductor manufacturers: memory components, which are used to store data or computer programs; logic devices, which perform such operations as mathematical calculations; and components that combine the two. This latter category of integrated circuit is the most sophisticated and includes microprocessors, the computer "brain" that manipulates a wide range of data, and microcontrollers, which perform repetitive tasks.

The two largest selling types of memory integrated circuits are DRAMs and SRAMs. A DRAM (dynamic random access memories; pronounced DEE-ram) stores digital information and provides high-speed storage and retrieval of data. It is called a "dynamic" circuit because the data is stored in a temporary medium that allows it to fade, and so must be constantly refreshed electronically.

SRAMs (static random access memories; pronounced ESS-rams) perform many of the same functions as DRAMs, but at higher speeds. Unlike DRAMs, they do not require constant electronic refreshing, hence the term "static." They also contain more electronic circuitry and are more expensive to produce than DRAMs.

Both of these integrated circuit products are manufactured in large quantities, and so are considered to be "process drivers." That is, the manufacturing processes used to produce them are constantly being refined, and those refinements often affect manufacturing processes of other products.

Two other important semiconductor memory products are EPROMs (erasable programmable read-only memories) and EEPROMs (electrically erasable read-only memories). EPROMs are used to store computer programs. Unlike older read-only memories (ROMs), which carried fixed programs, EPROMs are programmed by the customer. EEPROMs are easier and faster to update than EPROMs because they are programmed using electricity. While EPROMs are usually programmed only once, EEPROMs can be reprogrammed without removing them from their applications, so they can be updated virtually anytime.

ASICS. Most logic semiconductors are now customized products tailored to the specific needs of each customer. In fact, ASICS (application-specific integrated circuits) have become the most commonly manufactured non-microcomponent logic semiconductors.

There are four basic classes of ASICs; each class has a different degree of customization of the chip. Full-custom ASICs are designed from scratch; standard cells are designed by combining modular cells from a cell library; semi-custom chips are customized in only one or two areas; and programmable logic devices are programmed by blowing fuses in a device to alter the logic function. Because of high design costs and the often limited quantities produced, ASICs tend to be more expensive than integrated circuits built from off-the-shelf components. But because they combine several specialized functions on a single chip, they offer some important advantages: they are smaller, simpler, and fewer of them are needed; they allow for a greater degree of integration, which leads to more efficient use of circuitry; and, since they contain less circuitry, fewer interconnections are needed and overall performance is enhanced.

Microprocessors and Controllers. Microprocessors (MPUs) are the central processing units in all microcomputer-based systems. These products perform a variety of tasks by manipulating data within a system and controlling input, output, peripherals, and memory devices.

The two major types of MPUs are CISCs (complex instruction set computing) and RISCs (reduced instruc-

tion set computing). Though CISCs used to be the basis for all MPU operations, RISCs became increasingly popular in the 1990s because of their faster operating speeds, their ability to run more sophisticated software, and their ability to deliver better graphics. MPUs are used in local area networks (linked personal computers and workstations; called LANs) and satellites. The latest generation of these circuits operate at speeds of from 40 to 50 million cycles per second.

Microcontrollers (MCUs), which combine a microprocessor, memory circuits, and input/output circuitry, are used as embedded controllers in virtually every electronic product. They perform such repetitive tasks as controlling the antilock brake systems in automobiles.

BACKGROUND AND DEVELOPMENT

Semiconductors were invented in the United States in the late 1950s, but the invention that truly began the electronics revolution appeared nearly 50 years earlier. The three-element vacuum tube was invented by Lee de Forest in Palo Alto, California, in 1906. Called the audion, the tube was used as a sound amplifier and generator of electromagnetic waves; its invention laid the foundation for the development of radio, television, radar, computers and many other ground-breaking electronic devices. These early tubes, however, were bulky and fragile. For example, ENIAC (Electronic Numerical Integrator and Computer), the world's first large electronic computer, ran on 18,000 vacuum tubes and was the size of a house.

The tubes also played a vital role in the development of early telephone communications networks. But as those networks expanded across the United States, the unreliability of the tubes became intolerable. Consequently, the main push for a replacement for the vacuum tube came from researchers at AT&T Bell Laboratories in New Jersey.

For a number of years, the company had been studying potential uses of solid materials that were poor conductors of electricity, primarily silicon and germanium. Silicon, one of the world's most plentiful elements, is found in the earth's crust as silica and silicate and is the principal component of sand, quartz, and glass. In its pure form, silicon is a very poor conductor, but Bell Lab researchers found that it could be treated, or "doped," with other materials to act as a conductor under some conditions and an insulator under others.

These new "semiconductors" allowed for the development in 1947 of the transistor, which marked the beginning of the age of solid-state electronics. In 1956, William Shockley, John Bardeen, and Walter H. Brattain—the Bell Labs research team responsible for the development and refinement of the transistor—received the Nobel Prize for their invention. The same year he was awarded the Nobel Prize, Shockley returned to his boyhood home of Palo Alto, California, and established his own semiconductor manufacturing operation. To staff his new company, Shockley recruited many of the country's brightest young scientists and engineers.

Disagreements eventually led seven of Shockley's recruits to set out on their own. The company they founded, Fairchild Semiconductor, would become "the mother of semiconductor companies." According to the Semiconductor Industry Association, more than 23 semiconductor and related enterprises can trace their origins back to Fairchild. Among them were such important and well-known companies as Intel, Advanced Micro Devices, and National Semiconductor.

Probably the most important technological development to come out of Fairchild was the integrated circuit or "chip." Both the head of Fairchild, MIT graduate Robert N. Noyce, and Texas Instruments researcher Jack Kilby are credited with inventing the integrated circuit almost simultaneously in 1958. The original Texas Instruments version of the chip required the soldering of tiny gold wires on the outside to connect the components. The Fairchild version, on the other hand, relied on a thin layer of metal conducting film, which was sprayed onto the chip like paint. Roadways were then cut by lithography into this metallic layer to create the desired pattern of connections between elements of the circuit. This version of the chip was more readily manufacturable, and Fairchild soon emerged as the early leader of the semiconductor industry.

Noyce left Fairchild in 1968, along with Gordon E. Moore, a respected physical chemist. Together, they formed Intel Corporation and set out to manufacture a computer memory chip. Intel eventually came to dominate the industry as the undisputed leader in semiconductor technology. In addition to the first memory chips, Intel was responsible for pioneering the development of the microprocessor, the so-called "computer-on-a-chip."

U.S. manufacturers continued to dominate the semiconductor industry until the 1980s, when foreign industrial targeting and illegal dumping practices combined to erode U.S. worldwide market share. This "blood bath," as it was referred to in industry publications at the time, drove Intel, Motorola, National Semiconductor, Advanced Micro Devices, and Mostek out of the dynamic random access memory (DRAM) market altogether. Japanese manufacturers, however, who utilized investment cost advantages to conquer the DRAM market, saw that market plunge at the onset of the 1990s. As *Forbes* noted in 1991, DRAM sales in 1990 "contracted instead of growing, plunging 24 percent—or roughly $2 billion in annual revenues."

Consequently, U.S. semiconductor manufacturers began to refocus their efforts on proprietary products during the early 1990s, capitalizing on their well-known strengths in design and innovation, and moving away from commodity products. According to industry observers, two Congressional actions were instrumental in paving the way for this development.

The first was the establishment in 1982 of the U.S. Court of Appeals for the Federal Circuit in Washington, D.C., a court specifically formed to hear patent cases. Previously, patent cases had been tried in federal district courts, where an estimated 70 percent of patents were successfully challenged. With the new court, however, that statistic was reversed, with about two-thirds of patents upheld.

The second was the Semiconductor Chip Protection Act, passed by Congress in 1984. The new law specifically protected semiconductor design, or "mask work," for up to 10 years. As electronics firms began to exercise their rights, the courts continued to provide stronger legal protection for proprietary chip designs. In 1991, Congress extended the Act through 1995.

The U.S. semiconductor industry experienced generally sluggish conditions during the mid-1980s, but entered a period of renewed growth in the early 1990s. Worldwide sales of semiconductors and semiconductor products grew dramatically from 1991 through 1995, from around $50.0 billion to $150.0 billion. The health of the semiconductor industry, though, is dependent on other historically cyclical industries, notably computers, automobiles, and consumer electronics. Consequently, the industry has a history of erratic earnings. As an international industry, it is also affected by economic conditions around the world.

The early 1990s also saw the continuation of the trend toward strategic alliances and corporate partnering among semiconductor companies. This trend was fast becoming an important competitive tool, allowing individual firms to share the ever-increasing costs of production. Entering the mid-1990s, U.S. semiconductor manufacturers were shifting their attention from commodity products to the development of innovative proprietary products, which they have begun vigorously protecting with the help of new patent legislation.

Two additional factors were expected to contribute to the continued growth of the semiconductor industry: overall increases in worldwide sales of electronic equipment, and the increasing semiconductor content of electronic products. This growth was driven by the increasingly sophisticated nature of consumer electronics. Manufacturers of fax machines, notebook computers, and camcorders, for example, used semiconductors in these products to perform increasingly complex operations.

The continuing development of Integrated Services Digital Network (ISDN) technology was expected to

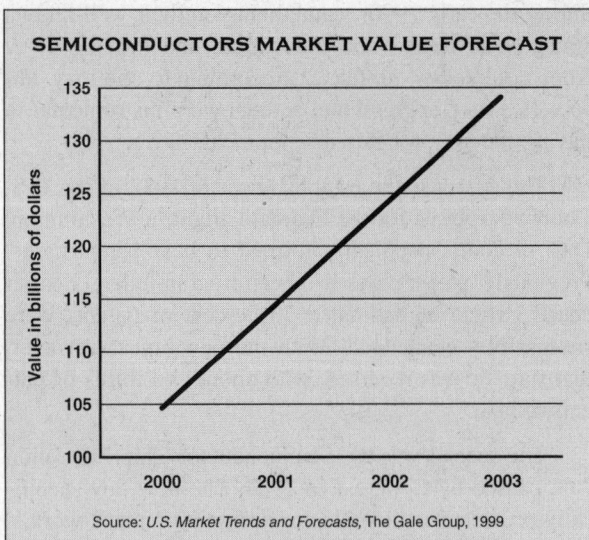

SEMICONDUCTORS MARKET VALUE FORECAST

Source: *U.S. Market Trends and Forecasts*, The Gale Group, 1999

provide an important new market for chipmakers in the future. The ISDN is a high-speed digital communications network capable of carrying voice, data, and video signals simultaneously over existing telephone lines. The network, which was first commercially introduced in the early 1990s, requires large numbers of semiconductors.

Another factor in the industry is the shrinking number of production options available to players in the field. Many companies that have emerged in recent years in this realm have farmed out production to other facilities with spare capacity in their wafer fabrication plants. As *Business Week* noted, by using these facilities, "U.S. entrepreneurs avoided the main hurdle for a chip start-up: the tens or hundreds of millions in wafer-fabrication costs. A new venture could thus devote its resources to innovative designs . . . By pioneering these cutting-edge products, fabless companies grew faster and earned higher returns than established chipmakers. However, excess capacity disappears in times of high demand, and companies without their own production facilities faced possibly substantial investment to secure guaranteed access to production facilities."

By the mid-1990s the semiconductor industry had become one of the most explosive segments of the economy as worldwide sales surged from around $100.0 billion in 1994 to nearly $150.0 billion in 1995. The history of the semiconductor industry was cyclical, though, with semiconductor products having short life cycles caused primarily by rapid technological innovations and resulting in pricing pressures. Overexpansion of fabrication facilities in times of strong demand also contributed to the cyclicality of the industry.

The demand for chips was driven not only by the increasing sales of PCs but also by the use of chips in consumer electronics, telecommunications, and networking. As inventory exceeded demand in late 1995,

DRAM prices started plummeting, creating an overall impact on the global chip market. Worldwide sales declined in 1996, with DRAM prices remaining low and worldwide sales staying flat through 1998.

CURRENT CONDITIONS

Worldwide semiconductor sales for 1999 were projected to rise to $144 billion, according to the Semiconductor Industry Association (SIA). Analysts hoped a strong 1999 would signal a growth phase for the industry, as the Asia/Pacific region and Japan began to show signs of strength following the Asian financial crisis of 1998. The SIA projected sustained growth for the industry, with sales increasing 21 percent in 2000 to $174 billion and 20 percent growth for 2001 to $209 billion in sales. By 2002, excess capacity was expected to bring semiconductor industry growth to a halt.

The growth of a global, networked economy—and the resulting demand from data and telecommunications markets—has begun to result in incremental growth in the semiconductor industry. Demand in the communications market stems from the need for greater bandwidth and faster transmission of data as well as from the growth of the Internet and wireless communication and the resulting buildup of a communications network infrastructure. One analyst predicted that the market in communications for integrated circuits would double between 1997 and 2002.

Despite the growth afforded by demand from the communications sector, PC sales remain an important factor in the growth of the semiconductor industry. PC sales from early 1998 to early 1999 showed strong growth. It remained to be seen what effect Y2K would have on PC sales, as many consumers and businesses were expected to delay major PC purchases until after January 1, 2000.

However, the head of National Semiconductor Corp. noted in November 1999 that "The PC is no longer the dominant driving force for semiconductor consumption." Rather, demand for semiconductors was expected to surge due to a proliferation of wired and wireless information appliances, a market that was projected to grow by 76 percent between 1997 and 2002. Also supporting strong semiconductor demand was the growing cellular handset market, projected to increase 49 percent between 1996 and 2003.

Following three years of flat sales and declining prices for DRAM chips, semiconductor manufacturers cut their capital spending budgets in 1998 by 21 percent. As demand began to rebound in 1999, chipmakers began utilizing more capacity, causing a tightening supply situation. That prompted some of the major manufacturers, such as Texas Instruments in the United States and others in the Pacific Rim, to expand their capital budgets.

INDUSTRY LEADERS

The semiconductor industry is truly international, with major manufacturers located in Japan, Korea, and Europe as well as the United States. The top three U.S. manufacturers in 1998 were Intel Corporation, with sales of $26.3 billion and the number one chip manufacturer in the world; Motorola Inc., with overall sales of $29.4 billion and estimated semiconductor revenues of $7.3 billion; and Texas Instruments Inc., with sales of $8.5 billion.

Intel Corporation was ranked the leader in the electronics and electrical equipment industry by *Fortune.* Also ranked as one of the 10 most admired companies in the United States by *Fortune,* Intel Corporation held a more than 90 percent share of the microprocessors market because of the success of its Pentium chip. Intel was founded in what would become California's Silicon Valley in 1968 by industry pioneers Robert N. Noyce, Gordon E. Moore, and Andrew S. Grove. Starting with 12 employees, Intel pursued research that led to the development of the first computer chip. The company also played an instrumental role in the development of metal oxide semiconductor (MOS) technology.

Originally a supplier of semiconductor memory for mainframe computers and mini-computers, Intel eventually became a leading supplier of microcomputers. The company sells its microcomputer components, modules, and systems directly to companies that incorporate them into their products. These are primarily computer systems manufacturers, but also include makers of automobiles and a wide range of industrial and telecommunications equipment. The company also sells personal computer enhancements and networking products through distributors, resellers, and retail stores worldwide. The company sells supercomputers directly to end users. Intel has design, development, production, and administration facilities throughout the Western United States, Europe, and Asia.

Motorola Corporation was ranked the third leader in the electronics and electrical equipment industry by *Fortune.* Motorola was also among the 40 largest industrial companies in the United States ranked by total sales.

Motorola was founded in 1928 in Chicago, Illinois, by Paul V. Galvin. As the Galvin Manufacturing Corp., the company's first product was a "battery eliminator" that allowed consumers to operate radios directly from household current instead of the batteries supplied with early models. In the 1930s the company successfully commercialized car radios under the brand name "Motorola." The company's name was changed to Motorola, Inc., in 1947, the same year it began research into solid-state electronics.

The company's semiconductor division designs and produces a broad line of discrete semiconductors and integrated circuits, including microprocessors, micro-

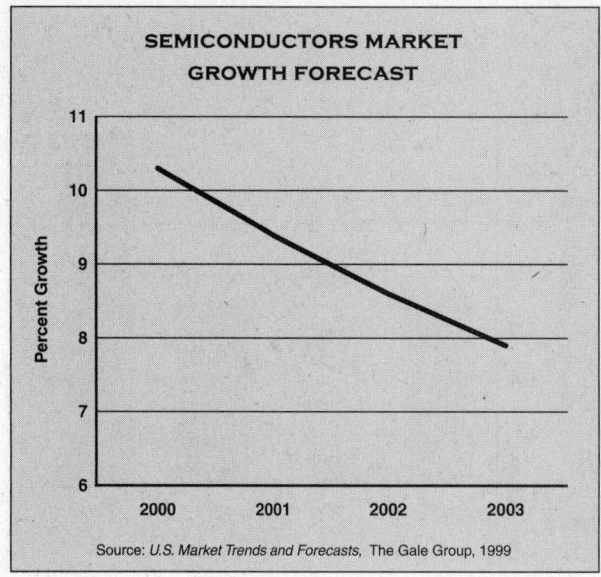

SEMICONDUCTORS MARKET GROWTH FORECAST

Source: *U.S. Market Trends and Forecasts,* The Gale Group, 1999

computers, and memory products. These products are sold to computer, consumer, automotive, industrial, federal government/military and telecommunications markets. In addition to being one of the world's leading providers of semiconductor technology, Motorola also provides wireless communication and advanced electronics equipment and services to worldwide markets. The company maintains sales and service offices around the world.

Texas Instruments was ranked the fifth leader in the electronics and electrical equipment industry by *Fortune.* Headquartered in Dallas, Texas, the company has manufacturing facilities in 18 countries and marketing or engineering services in more than 30 countries.

The company was founded in 1930 as the "Geophysical Service" by J. Clarence "Doc" Karcher and Eugene McDermott. It was the first independent contractor to specialize in reflection seismograph methods of exploration. The firm's name was changed to Texas Instruments, better known as TI, in 1951. The company entered the semiconductor business in 1952 with the purchase of a license from Western Electric Company to manufacture transistors.

In addition to semiconductors, TI products and services include defense electronics systems, software productivity tools, computer and peripheral products, custom engineering and manufacturing services, electrical controls, metallurgical materials, and consumer electronics products.

WORKFORCE

Semiconductor jobs more than doubled from 115,200 workers in 1972 to 258,500 workers in 1996. According to the U.S. Department of Labor, the all-time high of almost 300,000 semiconductor workers in 1985 was reached amidst a robust economy. However, from

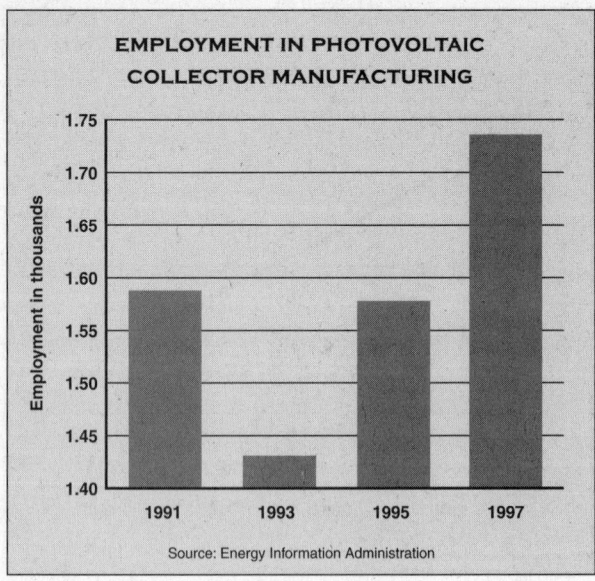

EMPLOYMENT IN PHOTOVOLTAIC
COLLECTOR MANUFACTURING

Source: Energy Information Administration

1985 to 1993 employment levels declined, in spite of a brief upsurge in 1988. U.S. firms employed about half of their workforce in facilities abroad, according to the Semiconductor Industry Association.

Semiconductor manufacturing jobs in the United States are concentrated in four states. In 1996 California had the most jobs (62,878), followed by Texas (46,514), Arizona (34,458), and Oregon (19,947). However, new manufacturing jobs in the industry were being added at a faster rate in Oregon, Texas, and Arizona, than in California, where property was becoming too expensive and the labor market too tight.

Within the United States, average hourly earnings for production workers in the semiconductor industry were $14.59 in 1995, 18 percent above the average for all manufacturing. According to the U.S. Department of Labor, this reflected in part, the higher skill and value added associated with the capital intensive processing steps and research and development activities performed by U.S. semiconductor workers.

AMERICA AND THE WORLD

In terms of semiconductor consumption, the Americas form the world's largest market, accounting for approximately one-third of chip revenues worldwide, and it was projected to remain the largest market through 2002. The second largest market is Asia and the Pacific Rim, followed by Europe. Japan, affected by a lengthy recession during the 1990s, is experiencing declining semiconductor consumption, from 40 percent of worldwide consumption in 1991 to an estimated 20 percent by 2002.

Of projected 1999 sales of $144 billion, the Americas were expected to account for some $49 billion;

Japan, $27 billion; Europe, $34 billion; and Asia/Pacific excluding Japan, $33 billion.

The international DRAM market changed dramatically in the late 1990s. After international DRAM sales peaked in 1995 at $41 billion, they declined sharply to $14 billion in 1998. Japan, which once accounted for 80 percent of the world's market share in DRAMs, saw its market share decline to 37 percent in 1997, when it was surpassed by Korea as the leading DRAM producer. Japan's NEC Corporation lost $290 million in DRAM chips in fiscal 1998, while Hitachi Ltd. attributed half of its $830 million loss in fiscal 1999 (ending March 31) to DRAMs. As a result, the two leading Japanese chipmakers decided to forge an alliance in 1999 to develop the next generation of DRAM chips to cut costs, accelerate development, and increase their global marketing clout. NEC and Hitachi together controlled about 16 percent of the $14 billion DRAM market, behind leaders Samsung and Hyundai of South Korea and Micron Technology of the United States.

The United States has had a trade deficit in semiconductors throughout the 1990s. In 1995 the deficit amounted to some $16 billion, with U.S. imports valued at $38 billion and exports at $22 billion.

In 1986, the United States and Japan entered into an agreement called the U.S.-Japan Semiconductor Arrangement, which was designed to eliminate dumping of Japanese products in world markets and to increase market access for foreign semiconductor manufacturers in the Japanese market. In 1991 the follow-on agreement to the 1986 agreement went into effect. The new agreement reflected U.S. expectations that more than 20 percent share of the Japanese market could be captured by foreign suppliers by 1992 through the efforts of government and industry. By 1999 foreign chips accounted for about one-third of the Japanese market, up from only 8 percent in 1986.

Normal trade relations with China remain important to the semiconductor industry. The SIA estimated China to be an $8 billion semiconductor market in 1999, and experts believe that the market potential in China for American semiconductor companies could double by 2002.

U.S. chipmakers began facing export restrictions on some advanced semiconductors in 1999. The U.S. Department of Commerce uses MTOP (million theoretical operations per second) as a measure to determine whether chips can be exported to a short list of potentially hostile countries, including the former Soviet states and China. Intel's Pentium III chip, introduced in 1999, runs at 1,200 MTOPs, the exact limit at which export control regulations take effect for microprocessors. Other devices, including the K7 microprocessor of Advanced Micro Devices Inc. and some of Texas Instruments' digital signal processors (DSPs) could also feel the effect of trade restrictions. Also affected are supercomputers exceeding 2,000 MTOPs, a limit which was reached in computers running two Pentium III chips. To alleviate the problem for exporters in the short term, the U.S. Department of Commerce has been raising the limit at which export regulations take effect.

RESEARCH AND TECHNOLOGY

According to Dataquest, about one-third of U.S. semiconductor industry revenues is spent on technology development and capital; 14 percent of revenues is spent on research and development alone. Costs for new semiconductor fabrication facilities are a major capital consideration for many companies. High-end DRAM wafer-fabrication facilities, for example, can cost more than $1.5 billion.

High Definition Television.   One emerging technology that could trigger a boom in semiconductor sales is high definition television (HDTV). HDTV produces pictures that are four to five times clearer than the standard television picture. In addition to commercial broadcast television, the first of which were expected by the mid-1990s, HDTV technology could also find applications in areas such as medical imaging and computer graphics. Since the sets require a huge number of semiconductors, they are expected to be a major new market for chipmakers.

Fuzzy Logic.   Another emerging semiconductor technology expected to create important future markets was called "fuzzy logic." As *Standard & Poor's Industry Surveys* noted, "Currently led by Japanese manufacturers, fuzzy logic allows microcontrollers to create gray areas between the yes/no, on/off choices of the binary world. The result is that engineers can design microprocessors that allow machinery to operate with gradual refinements."

With the unprecedented growth in the mid- to late 1990s, some believe the industry faces a slowdown due to the eventual breakdown of Moore's Law, according to *The Wall Street Journal*. Moore's Law named after Intel's co-founder Gordon Moore, referred to the accumulation of transistors on microchip, doubling the computing capabilities on a single chip the same size every 18 months. Moore's Law was seen to reach its limits due to barriers imposed by quantum physics. According to *The Wall Street Journal*, the end of continued progress within the semiconductor industry was slated for the year 2010 by the U.S. Semiconductor Industry Association. This prompted American companies to initiate new research projects.

Still, Moore's law still seemed to be in effect in the late 1990s, as chips continued to double in power every 18 months or so. In 1999 Intel introduced the Pentium III, with a 550-megahertz (MHz) version, to be followed by a 600-MHz version.

Not all chips are made from silicon. The profitable development of gallium arsenide (GaAs) chips in the 1990s was made possible by the growing data and telecommunications market, which demanded greater bandwidth and higher transmission speeds. GaAs chips can handle transmissions up to 10 Gb/s (gigabits per second). The performance advantages of GaAs over silicon were based on the fact that electrons travel five to six times faster in GaAs than silicon. One of the leading GaAs chip manufacturers is Vitesse Semiconductor Corporation, which pioneered the volume manufacturing of GaAs and eventually produced competitively priced ICs that offered superior price and performance over silicon devices. In 1997 and 1998 Vitesse had the highest one-year and five-year compound growth rate in operating revenues of any semiconductor manufacturer, as revenues increased from $66 million in 1996 to $175 million in 1998. While Vitesse's revenues are quite small compared to the industry leaders, GaAs chips represent a profitable and growing niche in the semiconductor industry.

FURTHER READING

Ascierto, Jerry. "A New Rising Sun?: Japan's Chipmakers Seek the Dawn," *Electronic News*, 16 August 1999.

Ascierto, Jerry. "SIA: Sustained Growth into the Next Millennium," *Electronic News*, 1 November 1999.

Business Rankings Annual 2000. Farmington Hills, MI: Gale Group, 1999.

Bylinksky, Gene. "Halcyon Days for Chipmakers, But How Long Will They Last?" *Fortune*, 16 October 1995.

Cassell, Jonathan. "Dealing with the ODT," *Electronic News*, 1 November 1999.

Cohen, Warren. "Why the Chip Is Still the Economy's Champ." *U.S. News and World Report*, 25 March 1996.

Delano, Daryl. "Economic Growth Exceeds Expectations," *Electronic Business*, July 1999.

"The Dragons Bulk Up," *Business Week*, 12 July 1999.

"Expect Renewal of Semiconductor Deal with Japan by End of July," *Purchasing*, 17 June 1999.

Gawel, Richard. "Load Up! Semiconductors Moving up in 1999," *Electronic Design*, April 1999.

Grossman, Steven. "Today's Global Chip Supplier," *Electronic News*, 29 November 1999.

Hamilton, David P., and Takahashi, Dean. "Scientists Are Battling to Surmount Barriers in Microchip Advances." *The Wall Street Journal*, 10 December 1996.

Harbert, Tam. "Busted Barriers," *Electronic Business*, June 1999.

Harbert, Tam. "High-Tech Runs into an Export Control Wall," *Electronic News*, 29 March 1999.

Harbert, Tam. "The Little Company that Could," *Electronic Business*, April 1999.

Hills, Leonard. *Competitive Strategies Semiconductor Almanac 1997.* San Jose, CA: Competitive Strategies, 1997.

Hof, Robert D. and Port, Otis. "Silicon Goes from Peak to Peak." *Business Week,* 8 January 1996.

"IC Industry is Mending," *Purchasing,* 16 September 1999.

McGrath, Dylan. "High-Tech Jobs Moving from California," *Electronic News,* 15 June 1998.

Moris, Francisco A. "Semiconductors: The Building Blocks of the Information Revolution," *Monthly Labor Review,* August 1996.

Morrison, Gale, and Tam Harbert. "SIA Lauds China Ruling," *Electronic News,* 7 June 1999.

"Rambo Rambus." *The Economist,* 8 February 1997.

Robinson, Edward A. "America's Most Admired Companies." *Fortune,* 3 March 1997.

Rosch, Winn L. "The Evolution of the PC Microprocessor." *PC Magazine,* 31 January 1989.

"Squeeze, Gently: Intel and Microchips." *The Economist,* 30 November 1996.

Standard & Poor's Industry Surveys: Semiconductors. New York: Standard & Poor's Corporation, 14 October 1999.

"Where Companies Rank in Their Own Industries." *Fortune,* 3 March 1997.

Yu, Albert. *Creating the Digital Future: The Secrets of Consistent Innovation at Intel.* New York: Simon & Schuster, 1998.

SIC 3675

ELECTRONIC CAPACITORS

This category covers establishments primarily engaged in manufacturing electronic capacitors. Establishments primarily engaged in manufacturing electrical capacitors are classified in **SIC 3629: Electrical Industrial Apparatus, Not Elsewhere Classified.**

NAICS CODE(S)

334414 (Electronic Capacitor Manufacturing)

INDUSTRY SNAPSHOT

The value of shipments in the electronic capacitors industry in 1997 was slightly over $2.4 billion, up from roughly $1.4 billion in 1992. There were about 128 establishments in the industry in 1997, three-fourths of which had 20 or more employees. Average firm size as measured by the number of production workers per establishment was over three times as large as that for the manufacturing sector as a whole.

Employment of production workers in the industry increased from 13,500 in 1991 to 21,200 by 1995, but dropped to 18,770 in 1997. The industry was relatively labor intensive, having 44 percent as much investment per production worker as that for the manufacturing sector as a whole. Annual hours worked by production workers in the industry were slightly lower on average than those worked in the manufacturing sector at large, and hourly wages were 23 percent lower. Production workers earned an average of about $11 per hour in 1997.

ORGANIZATION AND STRUCTURE

The U.S. capacitor market was still dominated by foreign-owned subsidiaries, and consolidation continued in the late 1990s. Two of the leading firms in the industry, the AVX Corporation and Murata Electronics North America Inc., were owned by Japanese firms.

Ranked according to employment, the top six states in the electronic capacitor industry in 1997 were, in order of descent, California, New York, Massachusetts, Florida, North Carolina, and New Jersey. Together, these six states accounted for 33 percent of total employment, over 26 percent of total shipments, and about 48 percent of all establishments for the industry in the United States. The top two firms by sales in the industry, AVX and the Kemet Electronics Corp., were both based in South Carolina.

The top four types of capacitors by product share in 1997 were those made from ceramic, at 48 percent; tantalum, at 26 percent; paper and film, at 16 percent; and aluminum, at 9 percent. The share of ceramic capacitors increased from 39 percent in 1983, whereas the share of paper and film and aluminum capacitors declined from 19 and 13 percent, respectively. The share of tantalum capacitors held steadily during the 1990s.

Among the largest of the several trade organizations serving the industry were the Electronic Industries Alliance (EIA) of Arlington, Virginia and the American Electronics Association (AEA) of Santa Clara, California. EIA was founded in 1924 and had 2,100 members, a staff of 150, and an annual budget of $26 million during the late 1990s. The group produced a number of publications, cataloged in its semiannual *EIA Publications Index.* AEA was founded in 1943, and had 3,500 members and a staff of 140. In addition to organizing an annual convention, AEA published the monthly *American Electronics Association Update* (with a circulation of 35,000), as well as a number of handbooks.

BACKGROUND AND DEVELOPMENT

In his *Basic Electricity and Electronics,* Delton T. Horn defined capacitors and capacitance: "A capacitor is a device capable of storing charge in a circuit, and typically consists of two metal plates separated by an insulator, called a *dielectric.* Capacitance is directly proportional to the area of the plates and the dielectric constant of the insulator and is inversely proportional to the distance between the plates." Capacitors can store charges from voltage sources for a wide range of time, to be released as needed. The classification of capacitor types by material such as paper, ceramic, or tantalum refers to the insulating dielectric. Electronic capacitors are part of a class of electronic components called passive components. They differ from active components, such as vacuum tubes and transistors, in that they can neither distinguish voltage polarity nor amplify a signal.

The first capacitor was the Leyden jar, invented independently in the mid-1740s by both Ewald Georg von Kleist and Pieter van Musschenbroek. A glass jar acted as the insulating material. M. Bauer developed the mica capacitor in Germany in 1874. Mica had advantages over glass because it could better withstand shocks and could produce the same capacitance as a smaller capacitor. D.G. Fitzgerald was the first to patent the paper capacitor, in 1876; later, L. Lombardi produced the first ceramic capacitor, in Italy. Ceramic capacitors can withstand extreme temperatures and are highly stable. The tubular glass capacitor was produced in 1904 by I. Moscicki in the United Kingdom. It was this capacitor that Guglielmo Marconi used in his early experiments with radio communication.

World War I provided an important catalyst for technical change in electronic communications, during which new radio tubes and circuits were developed. The interwar years saw the rapid growth of radio, and, on the eve of World War II, millions of radios were in use worldwide. Paper dielectric capacitors enclosed in cardboard tubes and Bakelite-enclosed stacked mica capacitors most commonly used during the interwar period.

During the World War II years, substantial developments were made in communications electronics, radio astronomy, xerography, and radar and computer technology, as well as in miniaturization and the improvement of the energy efficiency of components. The harsh conditions and importance of reliability imposed by the war led to the development of metal-cased and metalized paper dielectric capacitors, as well improvements in ceramic capacitors. The tantalum capacitor was produced in 1956 by D. McLean and F. Power of the United States, after which it became among the most widely used capacitor types.

Among the most significant developments in electronic components in the postwar period were the transistor and integrated circuit. Transistors are based on solid-state technology, serving as substitutes for the older triode vacuum tube active components, developed by Lee De Forest in 1906. In 1948, Bell Laboratories developed the transistor (whose name derives from transferred resistor), which enabled electronic equipment to be produced in increasingly smaller sizes. The first integrated circuit was produced by Texas Instruments in 1959. This device made use of transistors and other components mounted on a semiconductor chip to form an entire electronic

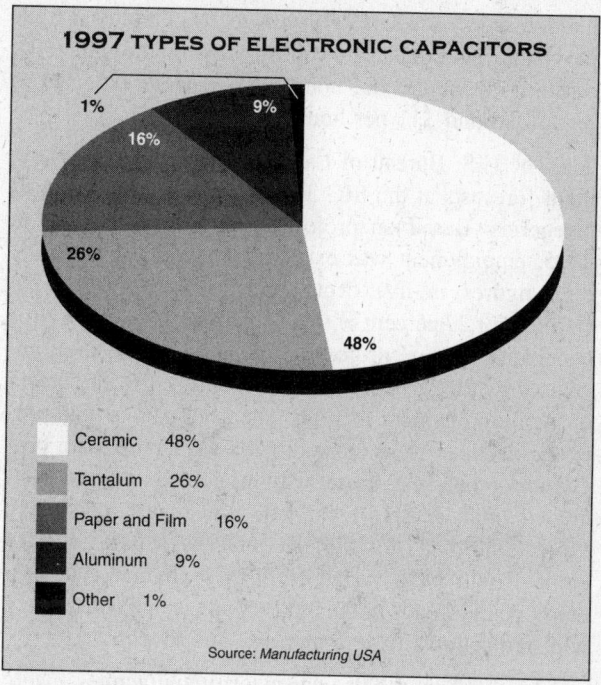

1997 TYPES OF ELECTRONIC CAPACITORS

Ceramic	48%
Tantalum	26%
Paper and Film	16%
Aluminum	9%
Other	1%

Source: *Manufacturing USA*

circuit. Prior to the development of integrated circuits, electronic circuits were made exclusively of discreet and separable components—combinations of vacuum tubes or transistors and passive components. Since capacitors with high capacitance values were relatively large, they were generally not produced within an integrated circuit but rather added externally.

Chip capacitors are surface-mounted to circuit boards, in contrast to traditional capacitors with wire leads. Although chip capacitors are generally higher priced than those with leads, the price gap decreased in the 1990s. Also during this time, chip capacitors came into increasing use, especially in equipment such as portable phones, video cameras, and electronic notebooks, items for which space constraints were a prime consideration. Demand for surface mounting and miniaturization continued in the late 1990s, along with higher capacitance and integrated devices.

CURRENT CONDITIONS

The value of shipments in the U.S. electronic capacitor industry declined from $1.7 billion in 1988 to $1.5 billion in 1990. This pattern reversed itself in the 1990s, with $1.6 billion in shipments in 1992, nearly $1.8 billion in 1995, and slightly over $2.4 billion in 1997. Annual capital investments were $95 million in 1988, $52 million in 1990, $57 million in 1995, and $124 million in 1997. Sales and investments were forecast to remain relatively flat through 2000.

Employment of production workers declined from 18,100 in 1988 to 14,200 in 1991, but rebounded to 18,770 in 1997. The peak year for employment of production workers was 1984, with 25,100 employed. Employment was expected to continue to drop through 2000, reaching about 14,000; hourly wages were expected to remain around $11 per hour.

The U.S. Bureau of Labor Statistics made employment forecasts at the SIC 367 level for 20 occupational categories. Based on projected changes from 1990 to 2005, employment was expected to decline by double-digit figures in five occupations, which together accounted for 27 percent of total employment in 1990. Nine occupations were projected to show double-digit increases by 2005, occupations accounting for 23 percent of total employment in 1990. The occupations with projected declines were those directly associated with production processes; those with projected increases included managerial, technical, and sales personnel. Projections made for the electronic capacitors industry alone would have varied from these figures, but past employment trends in the industry suggested consistency with projections made at the SIC 367 level.

In the late 1990s, capacitor manufacturers were faced with declining prices. According to the Paumanok Group of Apex, North Carolina, overall prices dropped almost 9 percent in 1998. Some manufacturers reported price drops of as much as 15 percent. Prices of ceramic capacitors fell by 3 to 5 percent. In response, companies were partnering with customers to develop new high-margin products. They were also establishing joint ventures overseas; Vishay Intertechnology Inc. was working with the Chinese government in the area of tantalum capacitors. Kemet established a joint venture with Tokyo-based Showa Denko KK to develop solid conductive polymer aluminum surface-mount capacitors. Kemet also had a joint venture with NEC Corp. involving tantalum capacitors.

The U.S. ceramic capacitor market was expected to grow from about $1 billion in 1998 to $1.3 billion in 2002, according to the Freedonia Group. Demand was being driven by the computer, telecommunications, consumer electronics and automotive industries. Since multilayer ceramic capacitors could be surface mounted, they came to account for 90 percent of all ceramic types. Excess ceramic capacity, especially from Japan, continued to put pressure on prices in 1999. Therefore, competition from Japanese exports to the United States was expected to continue until domestic Japanese demand improved.

Globally, the market for fixed capacitors reached $9.5 billion in 1998, a drop of 4.2 percent from the previous year. Unit shipments rose by 5.9 percent. Aluminum capacitors shared 31 percent of this market in value, followed by multilayer at 29 percent, tantalum at 18 percent, DC film at 15 percent, and single-layer capacitors at 7 percent. Tantalum capacitors were starting to compete more with aluminum types; likewise, ceramic surface-mount capacitors could take market share from tantalum ones as prices became similar.

The global market for capacitors was expected to reach over $10 billion in 1999, according to Frost & Sullivan. From 1997 to 2000, a compound annual growth rate of 13.3 percent was expected, reaching almost $12 billion in 2000. Unit sales were forecast to increase from about 194 billion in 1997 to slightly over 390 billion in 2000.

INDUSTRY LEADERS

The top five firms in the U.S. electronic capacitor industry, according to *Ward's Business Directory, 2000,* were the AVX Corp. of Myrtle Beach, South Carolina; the Kemet Electronics Corp. of Greenville, South Carolina; Aerovox Inc. of New Bedford, Massachusetts; Vitramon Inc. of Bridgeport, Connecticut; and Murata Electronics North American Inc. of State College, Pennsylvania. The Tantalum Capacitor Division of the Sprague Electric Co. of Sanford, Maine, followed closely behind.

AVX was founded in 1972 and had roughly $1.3 billion in sales and 13,500 employees in 1997. The firm produced ceramic and tantalum capacitors. As a result of a 1990 merger, the firm became a subsidiary of Kyocera America Inc. of San Diego, with ultimate ownership held by the Kyocera Corp. of Japan (previously the Kyoto Ceramic Co.). Their customers included leading original equipment manufacturers (OEMs) in the telecommunications, computer, medical device, aerospace, and consumer electronics industries. AVX acquired Thomson-CSF, a manufacturer of film and ceramic capacitors and other components, and introduced a low-inductance ceramic capacitor in 1998.

Kemet Electronics, a privately held firm, was founded in 1954 and had $677.5 million in sales and 11,000 employees in 1997. Kemet introduced around 80 new products in 1997 and established an agreement with NEC Corp. to develop ceramic and tantalum capacitors. The two companies were codeveloping a conductive-polymer tantalum capacitor. Kemet also continued to expand in Mexico, building its eighth plant in 1998.

Aerovox manufactured film, paper, and aluminum electrolytic capacitors for worldwide markets. The company's products were used in air conditioners, fluorescent and high-intensity discharge lighting, microwave ovens, defibrillators, lasers, phone switching systems, heat pumps, ventilator fans, garbage disposals, washing machines, dimmer controls, motors, power supplies, photocopiers, telecommunications equipment, computers, medical instrumentation, industrial electrical systems, and other appliances and electrical equipment. Aerovox sold primarily to OEMs of electrical and electronic products. They employed 1,428 people and posted sales of $116 million in 1998.

Murata Electronics North America's State College Division had annual sales over $90 million and employed around 1,100. Sprague's Tantalum Capacitor Division had $90 million in sales and 900 employees in 1998. In 1992, this division was bought out by publicly held Vishay Intertechnology of Malvern, Pennsylvania. Sprague represented part of Vishay's strategy of acquiring electronic components producers around the world and selling components under their original brand names.

According to *Electronic Buyer News,* the top ceramic capacitor suppliers in the world in 1997 were Murata, AVX, TDK, Kemet, Philips Components, and Vishay. For tantalum, the leaders were AVX, Kemet, NEC, Vishay, and Panasonic. AVX and Kemet tied for first place in this category. Panasonic, Nissei-Arcotronics, Wilhelm Westermann, Vishay, and Philips Components were the top companies in DC film capacitors. Aluminum capacitor leaders were Nippon, Chemi-Con, Nichicon, Rubycon Corp., Elna Co. Ltd., and Panasonic.

AMERICA AND THE WORLD

In the early 1990s, the United States experienced a trade surplus in capacitors. Mexico was the largest export market for U.S. capacitors, accounting for 61 percent of total 1997 exports. Canada was the second largest at 7 percent, followed by Singapore at 6 percent. The European Union was another large export market, at 11 percent. Germany and the United Kingdom had the largest shares among European countries.

Imports continued to challenge U.S. manufacturers. Import penetration was particularly strong from Japan: Japanese capacitors made up 39 percent of total U.S. imports in 1997, a slight drop from 41 percent in 1992. The United States, on the other hand, exported only 3 percent of its capacitors to Japan. Other major importers of passive components (including capacitors) were Mexico, China, Taiwan, and Canada.

Asian competitors continued to cut capacitor prices. Newcomers from China and South Korea entered the market, which was expected to affect pricing significantly once again. The U.S. industry was also being hurt by the Information Technology Agreement, which phased out U.S. tariffs that protected capacitor manufacturers. Japan was expected to continue to dominate the world chip capacitor market, regardless of the increased production of the United States and other Asian countries.

RESEARCH AND TECHNOLOGY

Among the key technical developments in the electronic capacitor industry in the 1990s was the use of new insulating, or dielectric, materials in response to the miniaturization demand. Materials included Teflon, a combination of polyester and metal foil, other organics, and glass-based materials. Other emerging technologies could change the capacitor market: for instance, AVX planned to introduce a line of double-layer supercapacitors in mid-1999.

Near the end of the decade, the trend to higher capacitance and smaller devices continued. AVX expected to have reached 100 microfarads by the end of 1999. Sizes continued to drop, from formats three to four times smaller than previous models. Philips planned to introduce one of the smallest surface-mount capacitors in the third quarter of 1999.

Increased integration and the use of alternative materials also continued. The rising cost of palladium, an electrode material, forced many ceramic capacitor manufacturers to switch to such base metals as nickel or copper. Palladium's price almost doubled during the first half of 1997 and reached $300 per troy ounce in 1998. Murata Electronics North America of Smyrna, Georgia, converted about 70 percent of its products to nickel and expected to reach 90 percent by 2000.

Integrated passive devices (IPDs), which contain capacitors, resistors, inductors, and other components on a printed-circuit board, were under investigation in order to reduce board size and the cost of component packaging. AVX introduced a discrete impedance-matching series resistor/capacitor chip in 1999. Avex Electronics Inc., California Micro Devices, and Flip Chip Technologies were also jointly developing a flip-chip package of integrated passive components. Kemet and Murata were also developing IPDs.

FURTHER READING

Costlow, Terry. "Product Week: Integrated Passives Gain Momentum." *Electronic Engineering Times,* 27 July 1998.

Darnay, Arsen J., ed. *Manufacturing USA.* Detroit: Gale Research, 1998.

"Extra: Resistors & Capacitors: Industry Pioneer Analyzes Constants and Variables." *Electronic Buyer News,* 1 December 1997.

"Extra: Resistors & Capacitors: The Year in Review." *Electronic Buyer News,* 30 November 1998.

"Extra: Resistors & Capacitors: Top Component Suppliers." *Electronic Buyer News,* 14 September 1998 and 30 November 1998.

Hassenberg, Mark. "Business & Finance—Quarterly Financial Review: Passive Components Still Face Tough Market." *Electronic Buyer News,* 8 February 1999.

Horn, Delton T. *Basic Electricity and Electronics.* Westerville, OH: Glencoe Division, 1993.

Marcoux, Phil. "Product Week: New Passive Development Benefit All." *Electronic Engineering Times,* 26 October 1998.

McKeefry, Hailey. "Supply-Chain Management: Modest Rise in Passives Sales Foreseen." *Electronic Buyer News,* 26 July 1999.

"Technology Focus: Capacitors: Pointing the Spotlight on Customer Needs." *Electronic Buyer News,* 4 January 1999.

Richtmyer, Richard. "Kemet Building Ties with Japan." *Electronic Buyer News,* 19 July 1999.

"Passives: Kemet, NEC Team Up on Caps." *Electronic Buyer News,* 12 July 1999.

"Steady Growth Ahead for Ceramic Capacitor Market." *Purchasing,* 17 June 1999.

U.S. Census Bureau. *Manufacturing—Industry Series,* 1999.

Annual Survey of Manufacturers. Washington, DC: GPO, 1996.

U.S. Department of Commerce. International Trade Administration. *U.S. Industry & Trade Outlook '99.* U.S. Department of Commerce/International Trade Administration and McGraw-Hill, 1999.

SIC 3676

ELECTRONIC RESISTORS

This category covers establishments primarily engaged in manufacturing electronic resistors. Establishments primarily engaged in manufacturing resistors for telephone and telegraph apparatus are classified in **SIC 3661: Telephone and Telegraph Apparatus.**

NAICS CODE(S)

334415 (Electronic Resistor Manufacturing)

INDUSTRY SNAPSHOT

The value of shipments in the electronic resistors industry in 1997 was almost $1.3 billion, up from $1 billion in 1996. The number of establishments and the percentage with more than 20 employees was stable throughout the 1980s. During the 1990s, there was a steady consolidation of workers in larger firms. Average firm size as measured by the number of production workers per establishment was over three times as large as for the manufacturing sector as a whole. In 1997, there were 118 establishments in the industry, 71 percent of which had 20 or more employees.

Employment of production workers in the industry declined from 12,400 in 1982 to 6,900 in 1995. But an increasingly robust U.S. economy, especially in technology sectors, accounted for an increase to 8,640 by 1997. The industry is relatively labor intensive, having 60 percent as much investment per production worker as that for the manufacturing sector as a whole. Annual hours for production workers were 10 percent lower on average than those worked in the manufacturing sector at large; hourly wages were also 31 percent lower.

ORGANIZATION AND STRUCTURE

In terms of employment, the states that have the most firms in the electronic resistors industry are California (with 1,522 employees), Florida (1,201), Pennsylvania (948), Texas (663), Massachusetts (382), and New Jersey (374). Together these states account for about half of total employment and for about half of all industry establishments in the United States.

Some of the top ten industries and sectors buying the outputs of the electronic components and accessories industries are: radio and TV communication equipment; exports; telephone and telegraph apparatus; electronic computing equipment; electronic components, not elsewhere classified; radio and TV receiving sets; guided missiles and space vehicles; personal consumption expenditures; X-ray apparatus and tubes; and aircraft.

There are three basic classes of resistors: fixed resistors, variable resistors, and resistor networks. Fixed resistors had a 34 percent product share in 1991, followed by variable resistors, with 27 percent, and resistor networks, with 21 percent. Fixed resistors grew by product share from 1990 to 1991 at the expense of variable resistors, while the share of resistor networks remained stable.

Within the class of fixed resistors, the four types by product share were metal and other film, at 64 percent; wirewound, at 9 percent; chip, at 21 percent; and carbon composition and carbon film, at 6 percent. Metal and other film and chip fixed resistors almost doubled in product share from 1990 to 1996 at the expense of wirewound and carbon composition and carbon film fixed resistors. By the middle of the 1990s, the total number of fixed resistor units sold dropped by 16 percent from the beginning of the decade; however, revenues increased by an equivalent percentage (from $247.8 million to $288.3 million).

Within the class of variable resistors, the share of wirewound devices remained relatively stable. By contrast, nonwirewound resistors posted an increase of just over 20 percent in units sold and revenues. Within the class of resistor networks, the top three types by product share were single in-line package (SIP), at 44 percent; surface mount, also at 44 percent; and dual in-line package (DIP), at 9 percent. Profit per unit peaked in 1995 for all classes of resistors; but total revenues dipped back to 1994 levels. Although fixed resistor output showed a dramatic 20 percent increase between 1995 and 1996, variable resistors and resistor networks posted declining numbers.

One of the largest trade organizations serving the industry is the Electronic Industries Alliance, founded in

1924 (then known as the Radio Manufacturers Association); it has 1,200 members, a staff of 150, and an annual budget of $26 million. Another large trade organization serving the industry is the American Electronics Association of Santa Clara, California, founded in 1943; it has 3,500 members and a staff of 140.

BACKGROUND AND DEVELOPMENT

In his *Basic Electricity and Electronics,* Delton T. Horn defined resistors and resistance: "A resistor is a device which opposes current in a dc (direct current) circuit; a measure of this opposition is called *resistance,* measured in ohms. . . . Ohms's Law, the relationship between voltage, current, and resistance, states that current is directly proportional to voltage and inversely proportional to resistance in a circuit." Resistance is one of the three variables of Ohm's Law, and is thus a necessary precondition for any functioning circuit. Resistors are either fixed, with a designated ohm value, or variable, with a designated range of ohm values. Variable resistors are either potentiometers, which control voltage, or rheostats, which directly control resistance. Electronic transistors are part of a class of electronic components called passive components. They differ from active components, such as vacuum tubes and transistors, in that they can neither distinguish voltage polarity nor amplify a signal.

The first electronic resistor was patented in the United Kingdom by C.S. Bradley in 1885. This was a molded carbon composition resistor made of a carbon-rubber mixture. The earliest carbon film resistor was produced in the United Kingdom by T.E. Gambrell and A.F. Harris in 1897. As with the carbon composition resistor, this device preceded the development of broadcasting by a number of years. The first thin metal film resistor was developed in the United Kingdom by W.F. Swann in 1913. The first high-resistance metal film resistor was produced in Germany by F. Kruger in 1919.

The first cracked carbon resistor was produced by Germans Siemens and Halske in 1925. Siemens produced so many of these resistors that they became commonly referred to as "Siemens resistors." The first sprayed metal film resistor was developed in Germany by S. Loewe in 1926. This was produced by spraying an atomized solution of platinum impregnated with resin, after which the sprayed form was heated. In his *Electronic Inventions and Discoveries,* G.W.A. Dummer described developments in the industry around this time: "It might be considered that this period (the early 1920s) saw the birth of the components industry. Resistors were produced in large quantities and used as grid leaks, anode loads, etc., and consisted of carbon compositions of many kinds compressed into tubular containers and fitted with end caps. . . . Cracked-carbon film-type resistors were introduced from Germany . . . and by 1934 were being manufactured in quantity in the United Kingdom." The rapidly expanding use of radio and other forms of electronic communication provided an ever-growing market for resistors and other electronic components in the period between the World Wars.

During the early 1950s, electronic engineers realized that the working portion of a resistor was only a small fraction of the total volume. For plastic-molded carbon film resistors, for example, only 3.6 percent of the total volume was actually used. This realization led to the development of early thick film and thin film circuits. One of the most important of these was the nickel-chromium (or nichrome) thin film resistor, produced in the United Kingdom by R.H. Alderton and F. Ashworth in 1957. This became the most widely used type of thin film resistor. It was also in the 1950s that automation techniques were developed for attaching traditional electronic components with wire leads to circuit boards. These processes could produce up to 10,000 finished circuit boards per day. A key development in the production of thick film resistors was the use of lasers for trimming in the late 1960s.

The first integrated circuit was produced by Texas Instruments in 1959. This device made use of components mounted on a semiconductor chip to form an entire electronic circuit. Prior to the development of integrated circuits, electronic circuits were made exclusively of discreet and separable components—combinations of vacuum or transistors and passive components. In *Electronic Inventions and Discoveries,* Dummer wrote, "The present explosion of integrated circuits in the form of VLSI (very large-scale integration) and VHSIC (very high-speed integrated circuit) has been the most important development in the history of electronics."

The mass production and widespread commercial viability of integrated circuits was made possible by the planar process of production, developed in the United States in 1959 by Jean Hoerni, a Swiss physicist, and Robert Noyce, an American physicist. Chip resistors are surface-mounted to circuit boards, in contrast to traditional resistors with wire leads running through circuit boards. Surface mount resistor types became even more important in the 1990s.

CURRENT CONDITIONS

Though technical change remained dynamic in the electronic resistors industry, growth prospects did not appear promising until 1994. The value of shipments in the electronic capacitor industry increased from $869 million in 1994 to $1.3 billion in 1997. Employment of production workers declined from 11,700 in 1989 to 9,700 in 1995. The peak year for employment of production workers was 1984, with 13,000. However, by 1997, employment rose again to 11,850.

Overall, the U.S. resistor industry is mature, and profit margins are slim. The December 12, 1991, issue of *Electronic News* noted the effects of consolidation on suppliers of electronic components as the decade opened: "So much consolidation could expectedly be accompanied by a feverish degree of franchise shuffling as suppliers attempted to shore up their distributor networks against a persistent recessionary climate." Later in the decade, as the U.S. economy operated with increasing robustness, such consolidation failed to inflate prices and pricing remained competitive between competing firms.

INDUSTRY LEADERS

Leading firms, by sales, in the electronic resistors industry were Bourns Inc. of Riverside, California; Dale Electronic Inc. of Columbus, Nebraska; and CTS Resistor Network of Berne, Indiana. Bourns Inc. is a privately held firm founded in 1946 with $300 million in sales and 4,000 employees in 1998. The firm's products are distributed across North America and in 12 European countries by the ITT Corporation's Electronic Components Distribution unit. Bourns underwent a streamlining operation in 1991, which resulted in the elimination of a number of managerial positions. The firm entered into a cooperative agreement with number four producer IRC Inc. in early 1992. By mid-1992, between 50,000 and 100,000 thin-film precision resistor networks were being produced each month under the agreement. Bourns announced in 1992 that it was diversifying into the production of miniature electronic switches **SIC 3679: Electronic Components, Not Elsewhere Classified.**

Dale Electronics Inc. was founded in 1951 and reported $110 million in sales and 2,100 employees in 1997. In addition to electronic resistors, the firm also produced electronic capacitors **SIC 3675: Electronic Capacitors** and nonelectronic power transformers **SIC 3612: Power, Distribution, and Specialty Transformers.** Dale Electronics is a subsidiary of Dale Holdings Inc., itself a subsidiary of Vishay Intertechnology Inc. of Malvern, Pennsylvania. Vishay Intertechnology is a manufacturer of resistor-based stress measurement sensors **SIC 3829: Measuring and Controlling Devices, Not Elsewhere Classified,** inductors **SIC 3677: Electronic Coils, Transformers, and Other Inductors,** and specialized connectors **SIC 3678: Electronic Connectors.** Dale Electronics represented part of Vishay's strategy of acquiring electronic components producers around the world and selling components under their original brand names.

CTS Corporation commanded a significant portion of the market by 1999 with a reported $677 million in sales achieved by an employee force of 4,000. The firm is a subsidiary of the Murata Manufacturing Co. Ltd. of Japan, and in addition to producing electronic resistors produces electronic capacitors. Once known as CTS Resistor Network, the CTS Corporation moved dramatically from the number five position in 1996 with 500 employees and $30 million in sales. No doubt their meteoric rise in the resistor industry can be attributed to competitive success in major resistor markets with leaders within those market; for example a significant third of sales were made to General Motors, Compaq, and Seagate Technology. Additionally, CTS' success as a major player in the resistor manufacture market also resulted from international expansion into European telecommunications markets and domestic acquisition of aerospace and defense contracts with the U.S. government.

AMERICA AND THE WORLD

Exports of electronic resistors produced in the United States more than doubled between 1992 and 1998, from $242.5 million to $522.2 million. Chip resistors experienced rapid export growth throughout the 1990s. The three largest export markets for resistors produced in the United States were Mexico, Canada, and Japan. Mexico and Canada by themselves accounted for 45 percent of all U.S. resistor exports in 1992. Reflecting an increasing dependence on overseas manufacturers that required resistors, the most rapidly growing export markets for U.S. resistors were in East Asia and Latin America, with growth rates between 1996 and 1998 of 26 and 50 percent, respectively.

Imports of electronic resistors into the United States peaked in the mid-1990s from $411 million in 1992 to $666 million in 1995. Yet by 1998, imports remained relatively flat at $623.2 million. Imports from Mexico accounted for 33 percent of this total, and from Japan, 17 percent.

In early 1997, the Components Group of the Electronic Industries Association (EIA) described to officials of the United States Trade Representative, the catastrophic effects upon the U.S. capacitor and resistor industry, if the Information Technology Agreement (ITA) was implemented and no follow-up action taken to remove nontariff trade barriers in existence in markets outside of North America.

The Information Technology Agreement would eliminate all tariffs on information technology products by the year 2000. Negotiations on the ITA among the United States, Japan, Canada, and the European Union were completed at the inaugural ministerial meeting of the World Trade Organization (WTO) held in December 1996. Products covered by this agreement include semiconductors, computer hardware, and telecommunications equipment. Also included in the coverage are electronic components such as resistors and capacitors.

RESEARCH AND TECHNOLOGY

The Electronic Industries Association's *1993 Edition Electronic Market Data Book* described technical developments in the electronic resistors industry: "The move to surface mount resistor chips is the dominant technology trend in the resistor industry. A strong link is developing between the expansion of the automotive industry's use of printed circuit boards (PCBs) and the increased use of surface mounted resistor chips. Product development trends in resistors are primarily toward thin- and thick-film resistor networks." Resistor networks combine a set of electronic components, such as integrated circuits and resistors, to carry out coordinated functions. These networks have come to replace individual resistors, a trend that was expected to continue.

As of 1992, approximately 10 percent of trimming potentiometers, variable resistors used in high-volume PCB applications, were surface mounted types. A marketing manager at Bourns Inc., the industry's largest producer, expected this share to reach 25 to 30 percent by the late 1990s. Trimming potentiometers were the most important class of potentiometers. In 1992, Ohmtek Inc., a division of Vishay Intertechnology Inc., announced the development of its Quick-Net program, which reduced lead times for the production and delivery of resistor network prototypes to two weeks. Previously, it typically took 10 to 12 weeks for a firm to complete this process.

By the end of the century, demand for smaller resistors continued to accelerate despite technical problems associated with miniaturization of electronic devices. Consumer demand for ever smaller, easily portable electronics products such as compact cellular phones, lightweight laptop computers, and personal digital assistants drove market research towards miniaturization of electronics components such as resistors. Such miniaturization heralded increasing integration of resistors, capacitors, inductors, and logic circuitry into chip products via thin-film-on-silicon technology. Industry executives expected that devices based on that technology would account for a 20 percent compound annual growth rate through 2005. By comparison, (discrete) resistor sales were projected to increase by 13 percent during the same time period.

FURTHER READING

Company Intelligence Database. Detroit: Gale Research, 2000.

Electronic Market Data Book. Arlington, VA: Electronic Industries Alliance, 1998.

Haystead, John. "The Big Squeeze." *Electronic Business,* June 1997.

Levine, Sy. *Annual Survey of Manufactures.* Washington: GPO, 1996.

————. *Current Industrial Report.* Washington: GPO, 1996.

U.S. Department of Commerce. "Electronic Resistor Manufacturing." *1997 Economic Census, Manufacturing, Industry Series.* Washington: GPO, 1999.

U.S. Department of Commerce. "U.S. Exports of Electronic Resistors (SIC 3676), 1992-1998." *Microelectronics Web Site,* 2000. Available from http://www.ita.doc.gov.

U.S. Department of Commerce. "U.S. Imports of Electronic Resistors (SIC 3676), 1992-1998." *Microelectronics Web Site,* 2000. Available from http://www.ita.doc.gov.

SIC 3677

ELECTRONIC COILS, TRANSFORMERS, AND OTHER INDUCTORS

This industry classification includes establishments primarily engaged in manufacturing electronic coils, transformers, and inductors. Establishments primarily engaged in manufacturing electrical transformers are classified in **SIC 3612: Power, Distribution, and Specialty Transformers;** those manufacturing transformers and inductors for telephone and telegraph apparatus are classified in **SIC 3661: Telephone and Telegraph Apparatus;** and those manufacturing semiconductors and related devices are classified in **SIC 3674: Semiconductors and Related Devices.**

NAICS CODE(S)

334416 (Electronic Coil, Transformer, and Other Inductor Manufacturing)

INDUSTRY SNAPSHOT

According to the Electronic Industries Alliance (EIA), a trade group of 2,100 member organizations representing 80 percent of the $550 billion overall U.S. electronics industry, 1999 first-quarter U.S. factory sales of electronics equipment, components, and related products rose to almost $126 billion, a 7.4 percent increase compared to first-quarter 1998 sales. Sales of electronic components, the segment containing electronic coils, transformers, and other inductors, rose 5.5 percent, from $33.4 billion in the first quarter of 1998 to $38.4 billion in the first quarter of 1999. Factory sales reached $244 million in the first half of 1999, rising by 9 percent over the first half of 1998. Component sales accounted for $72.5 billion in sales for the first half of 1999, pushing up this segment's already high volume.

BACKGROUND AND DEVELOPMENT

The pioneering figure in the industry was English chemist and physicist Michael Faraday (1791-1867): credited with discovering the phenomenon of electromagnetic induction in 1831, he was also the first person to use a magnetic circuit to connect two electric circuits. In his experiments with induction, Faraday developed an early version of the transformer. The earliest patent for a power transformer was granted to C. Zipernowski, O. Blathy, and M. Deri of Budapest in 1885. Deri also received the first patent for a distribution transformer in 1885.

"Inductor" is a generic term for an electronic coil, sometimes referred to as an electronic choke. Inductors either filter or select certain frequencies within AC or pulsating DC circuits. In his *Basic Electricity and Electronics,* Delton T. Horn defined inductors and inductance as follows: "An inductor is a device capable of storing magnetic energy in a circuit. Typically it consists of a coil of wire around some type of core, which may be magnetic or nonmagnetic. Inductance is directly proportional to the square of the number of turns (of wire). An inductor opposes changes in current. It also opposes current, and this opposition increases as the frequency of the signal increases." Coil wire must be coated with an insulating material (usually varnish, lacquer, or enamel) to prevent turns of wire from coming into electrical contact. The greater the ferrous content of the core, the greater the coil's inductance. Coils with nonferrous cores are referred to as "air core" inductors.

In his *Basic Concepts and Passive Components,* Sy Levine defined a transformer as: "A component consisting of a group of separate and unconnected lengths of wire wound around a common core. Its purpose is to provide an efficient transfer of electrical power between circuits connected to its various sections while maintaining electrical isolation between them. This transfer of power is accomplished magnetically." Transformers serve a number of functions, and transformer types are defined by their function. Among the most important of these types are power transformers, output transformers, radio frequency (RF) transformers, and pulse transformers. Power transformers convert distribution voltages (typically 110-220 volts AC) to other levels required by electrical and electronic devices. Output transformers function to transfer signals from an audio amplifier to a loudspeaker. RF transformers function to transfer signals between stages of radio frequency amplification circuits. Pulse transformers function to transfer signals between stages of digital electronic systems.

"The chief end uses of coils and transformers are in stereos and other home entertainment equipment, computers, telecommunications equipment, and industrial and control instruments," according to the *U.S. Industrial Outlook.* As with other electronic components, the growth of the coil and transformer industry was tied up with the growth of radio broadcasting after World War I. Stringent demands were made on all electronic components during World War II. This led to a large number of technological improvements, among them standardization, energy efficiency, miniaturization, ease of maintenance, and reliability—especially in the face of mechanical shocks, vibration, temperature extremes, humidity,

and high altitude. During these years, resin-encased transformers were developed, as were oil-filled transformers sealed in metal housings.

Electronic coils and transformers are part of a class of electronic components called passive components. They differ from active components, such as vacuum tubes and transistors, in that they can neither distinguish voltage polarity nor amplify a signal. In 1995, the top nine types of coils and transformers according to product share were, in descending order, pulse transformers, computer, and other (15.5 percent); plate and filament transformers (13.5 percent); toroidal windings (10.7 percent); audio transformers (9.2 percent); radio frequency coils (4.8 percent); radio frequency chokes (4.7 percent); low frequency chokes (3.9 percent); IF transformers (2.2 percent); and television transformers and reactors (2.2 percent). (The "other" category accounted for 33.2 percent of product share in 1991, up from 22.9 percent in 1982.)

Employment of production workers declined from 19,100 in 1988 to 16,600 in 1991, but grew to 21,300 by 1995. The U.S. Bureau of Labor Statistics made employment forecasts at the SIC 367 level for 20 occupational categories. Based on projected changes from 1990 to 2005, employment was expected to level off in five occupations, whereas nine occupations were projected to show double-digit increases by 2005—occupations accounting for 23 percent of total employment in 1990. The occupations with projected declines were those directly associated with production processes; those with projected increases included managerial, technical, and sales personnel. Projections made for the electronic capacitors industry alone would have varied from these figures, but past employment trends in the industry suggested consistency with projections made at the SIC 367 level.

Employment of production workers in the industry was 17,000 in 1995, continuing a declining trend from a peak of 21,200 in 1983. Employment of production workers was lower in 1994 than in all years of the prior decade. The industry was highly labor intensive, having only 20 percent as much investment per production worker as that for the manufacturing sector as a whole. Annual hours worked by production workers in the industry were 7 percent lower on average than those worked in the manufacturing sector at large, and hourly wages were 34 percent lower.

In the 1993 edition of their *Electronic Market Data Book,* the Electronic Industries Alliance (EIA) published their forecast for sales of defense-related electronics for years 1993-2002. EIA summarized their forecast as follows: "Despite the forecast of a flat budget for defense procurement, there will be increasing purchases of electronic equipment, with contractors the winners. Production will be limited to the most advanced weapon systems and high technology will be inserted into existing equipment through modifications and upgrades. In addition, a majority of the research and development investment will be in electronics. Suppliers of state-of-the-art electronic systems can therefore expect modest growth in their defense market.''

The value of shipments in the electronic coils and transformers industry declined every year from 1988 to 1991. This pattern appeared to breakdown in the mid-1990s, however, with the estimated value of shipments growing to $1.56 billion in 1995, up from $1.38 billion in 1994. The *U.S. Industrial Outlook* noted that export growth could play an important role for the industry. It reported that ''Since the primary end market for coils and transformers are consumer electronic products, such as television sets, U.S. exports will grow in conjunction with increased production in the major consumer electronics (industries) in Mexico, Japan, Singapore, Hong Kong, and Taiwan. China is expected to be a strong long-term growth market for U.S. exports.'' Annual capital investments showed consecutive declines between 1989 and 1991. Annual capital investments exceeded $30 million in 1982 and 1983 but in no year thereafter up to 1991 (all values in current dollars).

The United States had a trade surplus in electronic coils and transformers of $101 million in 1992, compared to a deficit of $3.11 billion for all passive components for that year. Exports of electronic resistors produced in the United States increased by 8 percent in 1992, reaching $501 million. Mexico was by far the largest export market for electronic coils and transformers produced in the United States, accounting for 67 percent of U.S. exports in 1992. The United States ran a $140 million surplus with Mexico in electronic coils and transformers in that year. Other important export markets included Canada, Singapore, Taiwan, Hong Kong, and Japan.

Imports of electronic coils and transformers into the United States increased by 23 percent in the first half of 1993. The three largest importers of electronic coils and transformers into the United States were, in order of descent, Mexico, Japan, and Taiwan. In the first half of 1993, imports from Japan increased by 39 percent, whereas imports from Taiwan decreased by 18 percent.

The most important trends in coil and transformer production were continued miniaturization and weight reduction, as well as surface mounting. Surface-mounted devices, or SMDs, offered a number of advantages over traditional components with wire leads inserted through holes in printed circuit boards. Since SMDs could be placed on both sides of a circuit board, they optimized space and thus reduced cost. SMDs were lighter than components with wire leads and enabled automated assembly techniques. SMDs made possible shorter distances between components, which reduced circuit capacitance and resistance and minimized interference. As a result of size constraints, coils with high levels of inductance were very difficult to produce in integrated circuits. Integrated coils were generally produced by forming flat spirals of metal on the face of a circuit.

INDUSTRY LEADERS

Industry leaders included Valor Electronics Inc. of San Diego, California; American Precision Industries Inc. (API) of Buffalo, New York; Products Unlimited Corp. of Stirling, Illinois; and Midcom Inc. of Watertown, South Dakota. API, founded in 1946, generated net sales of $58.1 million in the third quarter of 1999, an increase of 5.6 percent over 1998 third quarter sales of $55.0 million. API earnings of $2.0 million for the third quarter of 1999 represented an increase of 6 percent over 1998 third-quarter earnings of $1.9 million. The publicly held firm's secondary activities included the manufacture of heat transfer products, electromagnetic clutches, and brakes used in rotary control applications. Products Unlimited, a privately held firm founded in 1978, purchased a line of electrical contactors from Cooper Industries in 1992. Midcom was a privately held firm operating since 1968. It had total employment of 2,210 in 1997. It built additional factories in Huron, South Dakota in 1992; Aberdeen, South Dakota in 1994; Waverly, Iowa in 1995; and Nogales, Mexico in 1996.

RESEARCH AND TECHNOLOGY

There was a considerable amount of new product development in the electronic coil and transformer industry in the 1990s. Beta Transformer Technology introduced a series of surface-mount transformers that were only 0.13 inch thick. The J.R. Miller Division of Bell Industries began the production of four new series of surface-mount inductors. Schaffer EMC announced the development of a new series of toroidal inductors. Ohmite Manufacturing, primarily a producer of electronic resistors, began production of miniature high-current radio-frequency inductors. The Signal Transformer Co. announced its development of a high-power transformer that was the first in its class to meet international certification standards.

Significant developments were made in the production of thermoplastic encapsulated coils, which the May 1993 issue of *Appliance* described as follows: ''Recent developments include the first successful encapsulation of integrated circuit chips in an electrical device; further increases in the production of thermoplastic-encapsulated solenoids, sensors, transformers, motor components and other coil devices; new wire-friendly nylon resins that minimize magnet wire corrosion; and direct encapsulation of components with crimped connections as a low-cost alternative to the potting of complex circuits.'' Thermoplastic encapsulated coils were one of the more promising products the industry had to offer, and demand for these devices was rising.

The U.S. Department of Energy's Argonne National Laboratory and the Intermagnetics General Corp. announced the development in 1993 of a superconducting coil with a magnetic field 50 thousand times as strong as that produced by Earth. The American Superconductor Co. received a $1.9 million, three-year contract from the U.S. Department of Commerce in 1992 to manufacture superconducting magnetic coils.

FURTHER READING

American Precision Industries. "API Reports Solid Third Quarter Results with Record Level of Bookings." Available from http://www.apicorporate.compr/pr_3qy99.html. 10 December 1999.

"Appliance Coil Winding: Advances in Thermoplastic Encapsulation of Transformers and Small Wound Coils." *Appliance,* May 1993.

Electronic Industries Alliance. "Factory Sales of Electronics 9 Percent First Half of 1999, Reaching $244 Billion." Available from http://www.eia.org/PAD/PRESS/FILES/99-38.html. 10 December 1999.

———. "First Quarter 1999 U.S. Electronics Sales Reach Nearly $126 Billion, Up 7.4 Percent over 1998." Available from http://www.eia.org/PAD/PRESS/FILES/99-25.htm. 10 December 1999.

Horn, Delton T. *Basic Electricity and Electronics.* Westerville, OH: Glencoe Division, 1993.

Levine, Sy. *Basic Concepts and Passive Components.* Plainview, NY: Electro-Horizons Publications, 1986.

U.S. Census Bureau. *Annual Survey of Manufacturers.* Washington, DC: GPO, 1995.

U.S. Department of Commerce. International Trade Administration. *U.S. Industrial Outlook 1994.* Washington, DC: GPO, 1994.

SIC 3678

ELECTRONIC CONNECTORS

This industry is comprised of manufacturers of electronic connectors, e.g. coaxial, cylindrical, rack and panel, and printed circuit connectors. Establishments primarily engaged in manufacturing electrical connectors are classified in **SIC 3643: Current-Carrying Wiring Devices;** those manufacturing electronic capacitors are classified in **SIC 3675: Electronic Capacitors;** and those manufacturing electronic coils, transformers, and other inductors are classified in **SIC 3677: Electronic Coils, Transformers, and Other Inductors.**

NAICS CODE(S)

334417 (Electronic Connector Manufacturing)

INDUSTRY SNAPSHOT

The health of the electronic connectors industry is tied to that of electronic equipment and other finished-product (e.g., automobile) manufacturers. A cutback in military spending and substantial reductions in the price of personal computers (PCs) has reduced the number of connector manufacturers through closures and mergers. The most successful companies, such as AMP Inc. and Molex, have traditionally invested heavily in research and development, effectively differentiating their products in a competitive environment.

ORGANIZATION AND STRUCTURE

Makers of electronic connectors and other passive electronic components must rely on manufacturers of finished products to maintain favorable prices and provide a market for their goods. As is the case in most components industries, military markets generally require the most advanced products, which are usually the most expensive. When an industry such as the PC industry slows or is forced to reduce its prices (the case worldwide in the late 1980s and early 1990s) or when PC prices permanently drop from the pressure of intense competition (as was the case during the mid-1990s), connector manufacturers have difficulty maintaining profits.

Throughout the 1980s and 1990s, the connector industry was overcrowded, with approximately 800 manufacturers worldwide. However, consolidations and mergers considerably reduced the number of players in the United States as the 1990s came to a close. According to *Electronic Business* the number of connector manufacturers dwindled to an estimated 347 establishments in 1997. A total of 37,330 workers were employed in the manufacture of electronic connectors, about 75 percent of whom were classified as "direct production workers."

BACKGROUND AND DEVELOPMENT

The beginnings of the electronic connectors industry can be traced to products such as the solderless electrical connectors AMP Inc. manufactured for use in aircraft and boats in the 1940s, and the introduction of the printed wiring board in 1936 by Dr. Paul Eisner. The increased use of electronic components, particularly in military applications in the 1980s, was ironically foreshadowed by growth in demand for electrical components in military ships and aircraft during World War II. At the end of the War, contract terminations eliminated many shops. However, the postwar explosion of the semiconductor-related industries eventually made the connectors field more attractive, so that by the early 1990s, the number of connector manufacturers had risen to approximately 800.

Challenging operational environments of industry and the military continued to provide a demand for specialized connectors. In 1991, Ocean Design Inc. introduced an oil-filled, pressurized connector for military and petroleum industry use underseas and in damp conditions. This connector could be mated underwater without shutting off power. The design relied on a thin layer of a specially engineered thermoplastic to strengthen its protective epoxy layer. Another specialized connector with military applications was the BetaFlex circuit board connector. This connector was developed to meet a need for very fast data transmission in the high vibration environment of avionics. At the core of this design was a nickel-titanium memory alloy. Pave Technology Co. introduced a radiation-resistant "push-through" connector, allowing workers to replace its connection without entering a sealed chamber.

Not content with the connector's status as the weak link in the signal chain, coaxial connector-and-cable assemblies were developed in which the connectors as well as the cable were shielded, preventing signal loss of as much as 30 percent. In addition, such connector assemblies featured a four-beam contact, providing more surface area than the standard two-beam contact. In 1992 AMP Inc. introduced another important innovation within the industry, a hybrid called the Active Eurocard Connector. It was a high speed connector that featured a small printed circuit board on which microchips could be placed, freeing motherboard space. The design was said to allow space to be utilized more efficiently and to dramatically increase bus speed. Highly controlled impedance was a feature of all such high-density connectors.

Providing standards for the vast number of new technologies remained a problem going into the mid-1990s, although some manufacturers preferred proprietary standards, forcing customers to purchase many different components from one source. Concurrently, with the push for proprietary standards, a trend developed in which suppliers worked closely with clientele to develop customized connectors; the result accounted for somewhat higher profit margins but only in specialized applications (such as for military use). Increased consumer demand for inexpensive products that utilized electronic connectors and increased competition among producers of electronic connectors continued to whittle down the number of manufacturers within the industry.

CURRENT CONDITIONS

A promising long-term trend was the proliferation of electronics in such varied industries as industrial connector applications in data communications, commercial aircraft, medical technology, automobiles, and telecommunications. Mobile phones also offered a greatly expanding market potential; world production grew from 12 million mobile phones in 1993 to 64 million by 1994, with projections of 140 million by 2000.

In 1996 the United States produced an estimated $12.6 billion worth of connectors. Revenues grew to $13.4 billion in 1997 (according to Fleck Research). Mirroring growth in the whole of the electronic components industries sector, the electronic industry continues to consolidate and fewer manufacturers produced connectors. Interestingly, revenues leapfrogged. Total production was up 44 percent in 1999.

INDUSTRY LEADERS

The worldwide connector industry had been dominated by AMP Inc. of Harrisburg, Pennsylvania, with Thomas and Betts Corp. a distant second. Notable competitors included Molex Inc., Amphenol Corp., and Berg Electronics Corp. AMP had sales of $5.2 billion in the mid-1990s, and a market-share of about 18 percent. The company employed 40,000 workers in 43 countries.

AMP, originally known as Aircraft Marine Products, was founded by Uncas A. Whitaker in 1941. Initially the domestic leader in the U.S. electrical connector industry, AMP succumbed by the end of the century in a merger with a larger, international manufacturing concern, Tyco International Ltd. Emblematic of trends in the ever-increasing globalization of the market for electronic connectors, AMP was expected to greatly increase market share of (the parent) Tyco's electrical and electronic components group. Tyco's justification for the merger reflected a growing intersect of technologies within electronic components, particularly in communications technologies; the expectation was that AMP's fiber optics and backplane assembly technologies would aptly mesh with connector technology to increase Tyco's competitiveness in marketing fiber optic communications cable, precision printed circuit boards, and backplanes.

AMERICA AND THE WORLD

In 1998, imports of electronic connectors were valued at over $1.3 billion, well over double the imports in 1993. Over the same time frame, the value of overseas shipments almost tripled to over $1.1 billion in 1998. Interestingly, the primary export markets for U.S.-made electronic connectors remained in the North American hemisphere and accounted for almost half of total exports. Mexico ($306 million) and Canada ($229 million) were leading importers. Most of the rest of exports went to Singapore, the United Kingdom, and Germany, which tripled their consumption over a scant 6 years (1992 to 1998). However, the once-largest overseas importer, Japan, barely doubled shipments of electronic connectors during the same time frame.

RESEARCH AND TECHNOLOGY

About one-third of electronic connectors sold in the United States are printed circuit boards. Cylindrical, rack and panel, planar hermetic sealed, and fiber optic connectors divide the rest of the electronic connector market, with fiber optic connectors showing a strong potential for growth. The demand for increasing miniaturization will drive technological advances in the future. Specialized military and commercial applications will also fuel research.

Citing the failure of solder joints under fatigue as a causative factor in avionics failures, Westinghouse introduced Solder Free Interconnects, secured by cantilever spring clips, and Lockheed Sanders introduced folding printed circuit boards with flexible printed wiring. Although some aspects of the emerging technology made manufacturing less labor-intensive, others, particularly the small size of the components, required heavy investments in specialized machines able to handle the process.

The data communications market remained one of the largest users of electronic connectors during the 1990s. In particular, private networks in commercial buildings accounted for a significant increase in use of multimode fiber-optic connectors. In an effort to address difficulties during installation of extensive networks (which accounted for a significant amount of the expense when using fiber-optics), traditional epoxy and hot-melt connectors were supplanted by crimp-style connectors. Moreover, at the close of the decade, manufacturers were investigating the possibility of using (nonglass) plastic and copper fibers to further reduce cost.

Market demand, especially over local area networks (LAN), required connection bandwidth for high-speed serial data connectors in such applications. In fact, while demand for high-speed connectors required 3.2 billion leads/contacts in 1997, projections (that year) estimated an almost nine-fold increase to 27 billion leads/contacts by 2002. Computer hardware (e.g., hardware for graphic workstations, servers, wireless interfaces, telecom hubs, and military programs) had been engineered to reach speeds of 500 to 800 MHz, pulse rise times from 50 to 120 picoseconds, and transmission speeds greater than 580 Mbits per second. Yet, because over shorter distances (no greater than 30 meters) the benefits of fiber optics were not significantly appreciable, connector technology continued to focus on developing technologies that were compatible with copper fiber channel cabling.

The drive for miniaturization was also fueled by the laptop computer industry, which required in 1994 high density interconnections for such next-generation components as miniaturized memory cards and 1.8-inch disk drives, and connectors for linking the laptops with networks and desk-based PCs. Two-millimeter to 0/8-millimeter connectors were developed for use in the smallest of computers and electronic devices, such as pagers. However, newer designs were required as applications for electronic components demanded smaller, conveniently sized and weighted apparatus. Traditional manufacturing processes were based in traditional engineering schemes that utilized mated pairs (a receptacle and plug). Newer designs, first intended for use in the telecommunications handset market, featured connectors that did not require a receptacle.

Another concern, as electronic devices grew increasingly smaller, was the drain on available power attributable to electronic connectors. Resistance factors in connectors and attendant power consumption accounted for approximately 10 percent of power usage in small devices such as pocket electronic personal organizers. However, as electronic devices became smaller, were more powerful, and used miniaturized batteries, such power drain became unacceptable.

By 1997, standard-contact connectors had resistance of about 3 ohms; more costly gold contacts were about 1 ohm. Future applications, however, demanded connector resistance in the range of micro ohms. In an effort to meet demand for low-cost, miniature, low-resistance connectors, engineers began to create designs that used new materials such as flowable polymers that potentially allowed for wall thicknesses of 0.005 inch. Designers could put mating contacts on the thin-cut edges instead of wider, stamped sides of electronic components. In this manner, the width of connector pins was reduced and an attendant drop in resistance was achieved.

Another concern brought on by miniaturization of electronic devices was the need to reduce the number of pins required to make connectors but, at the same time, increase the flow of data that would go through those connectors. As the twentieth century ended, engineers conceived interconnection designs, called MicroElectro-Mechanical Systems (MEMS), which utilized a system similar to the one used in integrated circuit fabrication. MEMS devices enabled inclusion of microminiature motors, pumps, switches, actuators, sensors, and mirrors by exploiting the mechanical and electrical properties of silicon. Thus, connectors and circuitry would be integrated onto a single chip.

In addition to MEMS-based design, more radical research and development was underway before the twenty-first century began. Rather than basing technology on silicon, engineers and scientists began to explore the possibilities presented by carbon-based materials. This would make possible electronic and mechanical components on a molecular scale. Such designs depended on the effective development of a corm of carbon comprised of 60 atoms arranged in a spherical latticework and configured in hexagonal faces. Researchers thought that the molecular structure known as ''fullerene'' had mechanical properties similar to those that MEMS made possible but on an infinitesimally smaller magnitude.

FURTHER READING

DeMeis, Rick. "Connectors Tread New Ground." *Design News Online,* 15 December 1997. Available from http://www.manufacturing.net/magazine/dn/archives/1997/dn1215.97/25f1538.htm/.

"Economic Census Data for Electronics." *Electronic Business,* October 1999. Analysis, 2000. Available from http://209.67.253.150/eb-mag/issues/1999/9910/1099out.asp/.

Hailey, Lynne M. "Technology Focus: Connectors: Markets Drive Connector Development." *Electronic Buyer News,* 15 December 1997, 56.

"Industrial Production Analysis and Forecast." *Electronic Business.* Electronic Components (SIC 367), 1999. Available from http://www.eb-mag.com/eb-mag/exclusive/research/prodctn/index.asp#4.

Shames, Germaine W. "Master Every Peak." *Success,* March 1996, 30-31.

"Tyco International Announces Merger Agreement with Amp Incorporated Valued at $11.3 Billion." General News Release, 2000. Available from http://www.tycoint.com/.

"U.S. Exports of Electronic Connectors (SIC 3678), 1992-1998". The International Trade Commission, 2000. Available from http://www.ita.doc.gov/td/industry/ommi/3678.htm/.

SIC 3679

ELECTRONICS COMPONENTS, NOT ELSEWHERE CLASSIFIED

The Electronic Components, Not Elsewhere Classified industry segment is comprised of firms primarily engaged in manufacturing a multitude of miscellaneous electronic devices. Examples of more popular industry offerings include automobile antennas, oscillators, mechanical rectifiers, solenoids, quartz crystals, and electronic switches. For information on semiconductors, resistors, capacitors, connectors, and coils, see related electronic component industries.

NAICS CODE(S)

334220 (Radio and Television Broadcasting and Wireless Communications Equipment Manufacturing)
334418 (Printed Circuit/Electronics Assembly Manufacturing)
336322 (Other Motor Vehicle Electrical And Electronic Equipment Manufacturing)
334419 (Other Electronic Component Manufacturing)

INDUSTRY SNAPSHOT

Miscellaneous electronic component manufacturers supply products for five broad areas: communications, such as radios, televisions, and satellite systems; comput-ers and calculators; scientific instruments; military applications, particularly missile and radar systems; and power control and manufacturing equipment, such as machine controllers and industrial robots.

The single largest market for electronic components in the early 1990s was radio and television transmission equipment producers, which consumed about 14 percent of industry output. Telephone and telegraph communications equipment makers purchased about 10 percent of shipments, and computer manufacturers represented 9 percent of the market.

Other major market segments included: radio and television receiving equipment (which made up 6 percent of sales); guided missiles, space, and aircraft components (7 percent); X-ray apparatus (3 percent); and individual consumers (5 percent). Ten percent of production was exported, and the remainder of output was used in numerous niche markets, such as musical instruments, surgical equipment, children's toys, and surveillance devices.

Products. Most miscellaneous electronic components are used to accomplish or support the primary electronic functions of rectification, amplification, oscillation, and switching and timing. In addition, this industry encompasses several peripheral products, such as headphones and phonograph needles. Finally, some unrelated odds and ends are lumped into this industry, such as hermetic seals for equipment, record cutting styli, and video triggers (except those on remote control devices).

In comparison to the leading edge semiconductors and circuits manufactured in other electronic sectors, the majority of components classified in this industry are low-tech, commodity-like products. The major product groups listed below, for example, were developed during the birth of the electronics industry and remain similar in function to their earliest predecessors. For example, rectifiers, which are used to convert alternating current (AC) to direct current (DC), were one of the first electronic components developed.

Piezoelectric devices, like oscillators, are used in clocks, pressure gauges, communications equipment, and other contraptions. They utilize materials, such as slivers of quartz that can convert high-frequency AC into ultrasonic waves of the same frequency. They can also change a mechanical vibration into an electrical signal. Properly cut quartz crystals, for instance, are used as frequency controls in radios and televisions.

Switches and relays are devices that open and close electronic and electrical circuits. Common switches, which are manually operated, include push-button, rotary, slide, and toggle mechanisms. Types of relays, which are triggered electronically, are timing, electromechanical, and reed. Solid state relays are excluded from this industry. Relays are often activated by a solenoid, which is a uniformly wound coil of wire in the form of a cylinder. Passage of DC through the wire creates a magnetic field that moves a metal (usually iron) core that actuates the relay.

BACKGROUND AND DEVELOPMENT

Thomas Edison gave birth to the electronics industry in 1883, ten years after he invented the light bulb, when he induced electrons to jump from a carbon filament to a metal plate inside a vacuum tube. Edison did not exploit this discovery. Lee De Forest, another American, patented a tube based on Edison's concept in 1906. De Forest's discovery marked the beginning of practical applications in electronics.

Many of the products in the miscellaneous components industry, such as piezoelectric devices, relays, and rectifiers, were developed during the initial stages of the electronics revolution. Wireless communication systems, for example, were pioneered by the British Marconi Company. The National Electric Signaling Company of the U.S. General Electric Company, which was formed by Edison interests, led the development of lighting, phonograph, and other electrical equipment. Later, Westinghouse and the Radio Corporation of America made significant contributions to component advancements.

Intense development efforts during World War I spurred electronic component improvements. Piezoelectricity, for example, had been discovered in 1880. Not until World War I however, was it applied—piezoelectric devices were used to produce underwater acoustic waves in an early form of submarine-detecting sonar, and later as control devices in radios.

The popularization of the radio after World War I, combined with the proliferation of commercial broadcasting, generated huge demand by the general public for radio components during the 1920s and 1930s. Although television was invented during the late 1920s and 1930s, World War II delayed the expansion of television broadcasting. But World War II spawned huge advancements in electronic components such as radar, as electronic research expenditures reached $1.5 billion per year.

Integrated circuits that were introduced in 1958, as well as other advanced semiconductors that were popularized during the 1960s and 1970s, threatened to displace some components that were electromechanical or moved electrons by heat. Instead, these devices served to expand the breadth of the electronics industry, resulting in demand growth for most traditional electronic components.

The proliferation of military electronics, particularly during the Korean War, and of consumer electronics during the 1950s resulted in massive industry expansion. Likewise, the introduction of microwave communications, computers, electronic scientific apparatus, and

aerospace equipment during the 1960s and 1970s resulted in huge new markets for all types of switches, rectifiers, piezoelectric devices, and other miscellaneous components. Indeed, as new applications for electronic components mushroomed, industry revenues surged to about $13 billion by the late 1970s.

The 1980s and 1990s. Demand for all electronic components surged during the 1980s, ramrodded by the global explosion of personal computers and peripherals, telecommunications equipment, and the introduction of electronics into a broad range of industrial and consumer products. Worldwide sales of integrated circuits, for example, swelled 464 percent during the decade. U.S. shipment growth of the miscellaneous electronic components in this classification, however, stagnated. Industry revenues climbed at a meager pace of less than 2 percent per year during the 1980s to about $17 billion, not even keeping up with inflation. The industry fared better than many analysts predicted it would, though, in the face of falling prices and fierce foreign competition from low-cost producers. Industry revenues surged as high as $19 billion in 1984, but then waffled between $15 and $17 billion throughout the remainder of the decade and into the early 1990s.

Realizing that profit opportunities from traditional miscellaneous components were dwindling, many U.S. manufacturers simply abandoned the industry or switched their emphasis to related growing segments of the electronics industry. Other producers maintained profitability through vast manufacturing productivity gains. Importantly, many makers of traditional components maintained a resilient market presence by developing and introducing miniaturized products with greater reliability.

The dominant feature of this industry during the 1980s was consolidation. In an effort to maximize efficiency, take advantage of new manufacturing processes, and increase capital, companies rapidly merged with or acquired their competitors. In fact, the number of industry participants plummeted from over 3,700 in the early 1980s to less than 2,500 by the late 1980s.

Industry employment peaked in 1984 at 243,000. Productivity gains, company consolidation, and the movement of some manufacturing activities outside the United States contributed to significant work force reductions after that year, though. Employment plummeted to about 160,000 by the late 1980s, a decline of about 35 percent, and was stable going into the early 1990s.

Miscellaneous electronic component producers enjoyed encouraging revenue gains of between 3 and 5 percent per year between 1988 and 1990. Economic recession caught up with the industry in 1991 however, when sales rose a tepid 2.2 percent. Shipments of filter devices, for example, increased 2.2 percent, as did piezoelectric components. Sales of piezoelectric mechanisms, though, had fallen dramatically from a peak of $295 million in 1987 to about $238 million in 1991. Bucking analysts' predictions, relay sales declined only 2.7 percent in 1991, to $495 million, as solid state devices encroached on their market dominance.

As domestic sales of miscellaneous devices continued to sputter in the early 1990s, manufacturers increasingly looked to exports to buoy thinning profit margins. Export growth had been consistently strong since 1989, and cross-border sales had grown to more than $2 billion by the early 1990s. The strongest export markets were Canada, Mexico, Japan, and the United Kingdom. The largest importers to the United States, which were increasingly grasping domestic market share, were Japan, Taiwan, Singapore, Mexico, and Canada. Japan dominated U.S. miscellaneous component imports with a staggering 53 percent share.

In the mid-1990s, economic recovery in the United States and abroad was expected to boost worldwide demand for passive components. In 1995 the value of industry shipments totaled $31.07 billion, and the number of employees grew to 20,300. Although integrated circuits and other advanced devices will continue to cannibalize miscellaneous component market share, slow expansion through the mid-1990s will be fueled by strengthening computer, telecommunications, and automotive industries.

Exports offered growth opportunities, as well, boosted by the weak dollar and the passage of the North American Free Trade Agreement (NAFTA) in 1994. Imports, though, may rise significantly as U.S. manufacturers move production to low-cost production regions, particularly Mexico and the Pacific Rim.

U.S. miscellaneous electronic component manufacturers were struggling to overcome intense competition from low-cost foreign producers in the mid-1990s. Makers of many traditional products were also striving to retain market share in the face of increasingly popular solid state components. Nevertheless, rising exports and gains in selected product lines were predicted to allow participants in this industry to maintain growth of 2 percent per year throughout the decade.

CURRENT CONDITIONS

In this industry filled with miscellaneous low-tech products, one segment displayed promising growth in the late 1990s. Liquid crystal display (LCD) production snowballed as this technology became ubiquitous in the digital revolution of the 1990s. The display market alone generated 1998 sales of $38 billion, with flat-panel displays accounting for about $12 billion in sales. Experts projected that flat-panel displays would fuel growth in the industry, accounting for over half of the projected $75 billion in sales by 2005.

Another technology poised for potential growth was organic light-emitting diode (OLED) displays, which offered energy-efficiency, high color fidelity, and thumbnail-to-wall size flexibility. FED Corporation of Hopewell Junction, NY, pioneered this technology and continued to tweak it, most significantly developing the ability to graft OLEDs with silicon components. Whereas Thomas Edison's light bulb was essentially a heat-generating device that emitted some light, the OLED display was essentially a light-generating device that emitted some heat; this reversal in the efficiency quotient represented a kind of maturation for this industry.

Production jobs in the overall electronic components industry was forecast to fall considerably between 1990 and 2005, according to the U.S. Bureau of Labor Statistics. Past trends indicated that sales of miscellaneous components would decline at a much faster rate, however. Jobs for electrical assemblers, which comprise 20 percent of the overall electronic component workforce, will likely decline by about 40 percent by 2005. However, employment prospects for management and sales professionals and engineers were less discouraging.

INDUSTRY LEADERS

Because of the breadth and diversity of its offerings, the miscellaneous electronic component industry was still fragmented, despite consolidation. Most all high-tech companies, such as silicon valley's Hewlett-Packard Co. and Tokyo-based Toshiba Corp., NEC Corp. and Fujitsu Corp., participated in the industry to some degree. However, the industry leaders tended to be smaller concerns; most of the top 75 firms in the industry had less than $100 million in sales and fewer than 1,000 workers in the 1990s. Some companies, such as FEI Microwave, Inc. and Electro-Scan, Inc., specialized in producing a few niche proprietary products. Companies like Texas Instruments and Motorola, which were primarily engaged in producing products in other electronics segments, manufactured miscellaneous components to support other product lines. Other companies produced high-volume commodity components for sale to other manufacturers, like automakers and appliance manufacturers.

One of the industry leaders, Oak Industries, Inc. of Massachusetts, implemented an exemplary strategy to stave off shrinking profits and growth in 1989. Oak divested its cable box business, dumped entertainment investments, and focused its resources on its core businesses of controls, solenoids, and switches. It slashed its work force by 25 percent (to 1,500) and cut its corporate staff from 47 to 22. Oak also acquired components-maker Gilbert Engineering Co. to help it attain an advantage over smaller industrial controls producers. In 1991, Oak Industries was ranked 24th by revenues. By 1993, the company had more than doubled its sales per employee and had boosted annual revenues to over $200 million. Net sales jumped over the next four years, from $231 million in 1994 to $348 million in 1998.

The industry leader in the 1990s was the Harris Corporation of Melbourne, Florida. Harris generated 1995 revenues of more than $3.65 billion from its diversified operations, and employed 26,600 workers. However, Harris experienced the opposite effect of the rest of the industry: instead of consolidating, Harris shed divisions as its revenues fell. Fiscal 1998 sales had decreased to $1.9 billion, so Harris divested both its semiconductor division as well as Lanier Worldwide Inc., its electronic office products division, further decreasing sales to $1.7 billion for fiscal 1999. Other industry leaders included SCI Systems Inc. of Huntsville, Alabama, with $6.8 billion in 1999 sales and 22,324 employees and ITT Industries, Inc., of West Harrison, New York, with 1999 sales of $4.5 billion with 33,000 employees.

FURTHER READING

Darnay, Arsen J., ed. *Manufacturing USA*. Detroit: Gale Research, 1996.

Davis, Andrew W. "FED takes OLEDs on-chip to market: organic displays are looking up." *Advanced Imaging*. May 1999.

Harris Corporation. 1999. "Harris Corporation Reports Lower Sales and Earnings for Fiscal 1999." Available from http://www.harris.com/harris/whats_new/4th-qtr-99.html.

Oak Industries. 1999. "Financial Highlights."

SIC 3691

STORAGE BATTERIES

This category is comprised of establishments primarily engaged in manufacturing storage batteries, including alkaline cell storage batteries, rechargeable batteries, lead acid storage batteries, nickel cadmium storage batteries, and other types of storage batteries.

NAICS CODE(S)

335911 (Storage Battery Manufacturing)

INDUSTRY SNAPSHOT

The storage battery industry is driven by industry needs for small, long-lasting, cost-effective storage, or rechargeable, batteries. Batteries have been named as the limiting factor in the design of products ranging from laptop computers to electric automobiles. They are important in supplying starting and lighting power for conventionally fueled vehicles; supplying emergency power for various applications; for load-leveling or supplying additional power during peak demand as part of electrical utility systems; and as a supplement to solar, wave, or wind power. Uninterruptable power supply systems, usually designed to combat drops in power for personal computers (PCs), have created a new market for storage batteries. In all of these applications, the main feature of the storage battery is that it can retain energy supplied from an external electrical charge, whereas the electrochemical reaction within primary batteries cannot be reversed.

ORGANIZATION AND STRUCTURE

Approximately 133 major U.S. establishments competed in the $4.0 billion storage battery industry in 1996, with 84 having more than 20 employees. According to one accounting, regional producers accounted for about 13 percent of sales of automotive and specialized storage batteries. The overall market was dominated by large manufacturers such as Duracell International and Rayovac Corp., and by companies specializing in SLI (starting, lighting, and ignition) and industrial storage batteries, such as Exide Corp. and Gates Energy Products. These latter companies gained market share through acquisitions of related manufacturers since the earliest days of the industry.

BACKGROUND AND DEVELOPMENT

Credit for the invention of the first true storage battery has been given to Gaston Plant, for a lead-acid battery he developed in 1859. It was made of two coiled lead strips separated by a cloth. However, his storage battery required charging by primary cells, a process taking months to years. The introduction of the French "Faure Electric Accumulator" two decades later generated excitement in Europe, Great Britain, and the United States. It was conceived that the devices would be delivered to homes and businesses daily, like milk deliveries. Demand for electric, rather than gas, streetlights was strong from the beginning, and electrical lighting in the home gradually became a status symbol. However, similar designs of batteries patented by Faure, a Frenchman, and Charles Brush, an American, resulted in patent litigation, which paralyzed American storage battery manufacturers for four years.

Electricity was not readily available on a large scale until the 1880s. This gave impetus to the development of storage batteries, used for over 35 years while alternating current systems were being developed and perfected. The batteries used were large enough to power over 2 million homes for an hour. Although AC power began to carry more of the load, storage batteries continued to be used in the operation of electrical switches in the power networks. The appearance of "horseless carriages" in the 1890s also fueled demand for storage batteries.

In the early days of the automobile, storage batteries were seriously considered as an alternative to horses and internal combustion engines. Storage batteries powered racing horseless carriages and electric cabs. However, the batteries could not compete in long distance travel and use declined with an increase in better roads. However, they continued to be well-suited for town travel; gasoline vehicles of the day had to be hand-cranked, a risky prospect. Storage batteries helped provide a solution for this difficulty, thereby relegating the electric passenger car to obsolescence. The first automobile to use an electric starter as standard equipment was the 1912 Cadillac.

The use of electric street trucks continued into the 1930s. By this time, storage batteries powered household appliances, boats, and the first submarines. In World War II they also powered torpedoes, aircraft radios, and commercial broadcast stations. In addition, they were used to power local telephone exchanges and intercontinental repeater stations. Storage batteries excelled in other industrial uses, such as powering electric shuttles in mines and battery-powered trains, which became quite popular in Germany. Golf carts provided an important market for the batteries as well.

The market for automotive, commercial, and industrial storage batteries had long been considered mature and highly competitive by the 1990s. This competition drove many smaller manufacturers out of business as prices fell because of excess capacity. Successful producers of these types of batteries sought to maximize economies of scale; new technologies were often quite expensive to introduce. Replacement batteries made up over 80 percent of the automotive battery market. An emphasis on technological improvement was most evident with suppliers for military and space programs, electric vehicles, laptop computers and cellular phones, and power management accessories.

Environmental legislation has driven carmakers to develop electric vehicles. Laws were introduced in various states requiring carmakers to sell a certain number of emissionless vehicles. The limiting factor in efforts to create such vehicles was the creation of storage batteries that were light and powerful, yet cost effective. Recycling efforts were another important theme in the storage battery industry, as many metals (e.g. cadmium) used posed health and environmental risks. The recycled metals also form an important part of commodity supplies, particularly recovered lead.

CURRENT CONDITIONS

A key indicator of the competitive nature of the storage battery industry in the late 1990s was the Ralston Purina Co.'s decision to spin off its Eveready Battery Co. in June 1999. The battery division had been experiencing hard times: Duracell International Inc., which claimed a 50 percent share of the U.S. battery market, sued Eveready, which claimed a 19 percent market share, over the latter's advertising of superiority for its Energizer

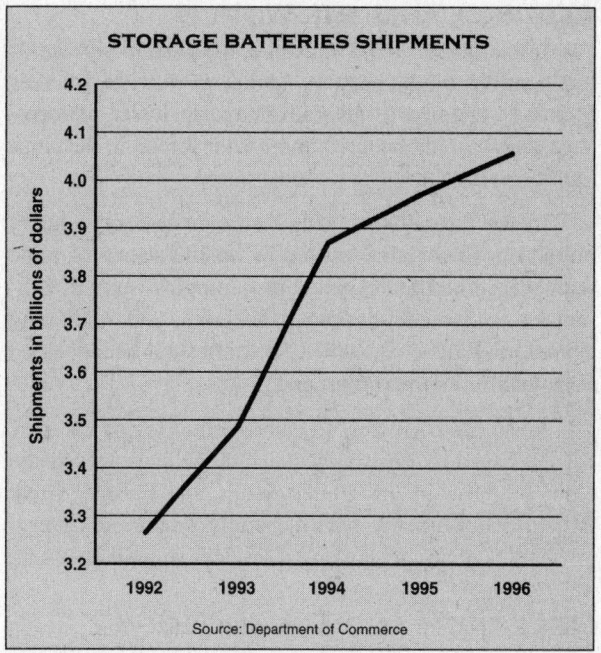

STORAGE BATTERIES SHIPMENTS

(vertical axis: Shipments in billions of dollars; values 3.2 to 4.2)
(horizontal axis: 1992 1993 1994 1995 1996)

Source: Department of Commerce

batteries. Moreover, Eveready backed out of the rechargable battery business in the face of stiff competition from Asian battery manufacturers. In November 1999 Ralston Purina finalized its sales of its Energizer Power Systems Original Equipment Manufacturer rechargable battery business to Tucson-based Moltech Corporation.

INDUSTRY LEADERS

Exide Corporation of Bloomfield Hills, Michigan, generated $2.4 billion in sales for the fiscal year ending March 31, 1998; Exide employed 16,300 workers. Duracell (bought in 1996 by Gillette Co. for over $7.0 billion), reported sales of $2.3 billion for the fiscal year ending June 30, 1996, according to the most recent information available on Infotrac. Duracell reported 9,600 employees. Eveready's sales reached $2.1 billion for the fiscal year ending September 30, 1998, with 18,000 employees. Motorola Inc. Energy Products Div. of Lawrenceville, Georgia, garnered $555.0 million in sales for the fiscal year ending December 31, 1997, with 4,000 employees. Rayovac Corp. of Madison, Wisconsin, employed 2,300 workers and generated sales of $432.0 million for the fiscal year ending September 30, 1997.

WORKFORCE

The top 500 industry competitors employed about 26,300 workers in 1995. In the mid-1990s, Exide employed 1,501 salaried employees and 3,791 hourly employees. It reported that 40 percent of its salaried employees were engaged in sales, service, and marketing, and 30 percent were engaged in engineering and manufacturing. Of its hourly employees, 32 percent were represented by unions, with whom the company claimed good relations.

AMERICA AND THE WORLD

In the mid-1990s, Duracell controlled 40 percent of the lucrative alkaline battery market worldwide, whereas Eveready claimed a sales advantage in lower performance zinc-carbide batteries more widespread in developing countries.

In the mid-1990s, Japan's storage battery industry pulled out of a slump caused by an imbalance of trade with the United States. New technologies, such as lithium-ion and nickel-hydrogen batteries, and marketing geared toward the consumer electronics market appeared responsible for the turnaround.

Japan has been slow to embrace the electric car, perhaps because its environmental lobbies have lacked the clout of those in the United States and Europe. Great Britain and Germany have generally embraced battery-powered vehicles, where postal services were likely users.

RESEARCH AND TECHNOLOGY

Most SLI batteries have been of the lead-acid variety developed in the late nineteenth century. They are an excellent potential power supply for other applications because of their low cost and availability. They are also easy to recycle. Specialized military and aviation-related applications have called for nickel-cadmium cells, which were popularized through portable radios and other consumer devices. Their cost remained prohibitive for automotive use, however, due to the high cost of cadmium. As used in vehicles, they offer somewhat higher performance than lead-acid batteries but are equally as heavy and much more difficult to recycle.

A similar type of battery to the nickel-cadmium, the iron-nickel oxide alkaline battery was invented by Thomas Edison and patented in the United States in 1901—the same year as Jungner's nickel-cadmium battery. Due to poor performance, the iron-nickel oxide batteries did not meet with the same success as the nicads.

Nickel hydrogen batteries have been introduced as an alternative to nicads. They possess a greater capacity and boast environmental benefits since they do not contain cadmium. Sanyo Electric has been the leader in developing and producing these cells, used in portable telephones, laptop computers, and camcorders, in the early 1990s. Other types of secondary cells invented at the end of the nineteenth century included those utilizing zinc as an electrode. These have been used in satellites, military aircraft, submarines, and assorted military equipment. On satellites, they have generally been used in conjunction with solar power.

Sony introduced a lithium ion secondary storage battery for use in portable telephones and camcorders. It featured twice the capacity of a hydrogen storage cell and one-third the weight. An innovation among consumer battery manufacturers was announced by Rayovac in 1993: reusable alkaline batteries, a concept traditionally thought unworkable. The company claimed its batteries could hold a charge for up to five years, compared to three months for nicads. In 1993, toy manufacturer SLM International introduced a controversial recharger for ordinary alkaline batteries. In 1994, Duracell Inc. announced its Advanced Battery-Pack Interconnect for nickel-metal-hydride connections, which featured an automatic battery contact cleaner and other refinements. The number of competing designs among manufacturers, in addition to the higher initial cost for rechargeables, seemed to slow this segment's growth.

Nickel-metal-hydride (NiMH) batteries showed great promise in the 1990s for applications involving laptop computers. However, both nickel-cadmium and nickel-metal-hydride (NiMH) batteries deteriorate if they are overcharged. A strategy to combat this has been to install integrated circuits capable of monitoring battery voltage, charge/discharge current, and cell case temperature. The goal in the mid-1990s was to recharge a typical laptop battery in 15 minutes. Several automobile manufacturers, including General Motors, Honda, and Toyota, gambled that NiMH would become the next generation fuel source for electric vehicles. Other research tested nicad, sodium sulfur, zinc-air, and lithum technologies as possible alternatives to lead-acid batteries.

Consumer demand, environmental legislation, and other factors made electric car research a high priority in the last quarter of the twentieth century. Electric utility companies supported research in electric cars, partially to encourage the more consistent electricity use that would occur from the vehicles being charged at night, during off-peak hours. Vehicle traction batteries, the kind used to drive vehicles, have been produced in various configurations. Lead-acid batteries were not powerful enough or light enough for the task.

Other more complex electric vehicle options included hybrid systems involving a battery in addition to an internal combustion engine. The hope was that a practical vehicle of this type would also allow increased efficiency by means such as regenerative braking. Hybrid battery types, including a lead-acid battery for acceleration and a zinc-oxide battery for cruising, were also considered.

Other technological innovations included gauges to indicate the remaining life on individual alkaline batteries. Both Duracell and Eveready used these to market their batteries in the mid-1990s. In addition, at least one company was investigating insulation as a means of maintaining the performance of lead-acid batteries in cold weather.

FURTHER READING

Bottoms, David. "Rechargeable Batteries: The Quest for More Power." *Industry Week,* 3 June 1996.

Bulkeley, William M. "Duracell Pact Gives Gillette an Added Source of Power." *The Wall Street Journal,* 13 September 1996.

Infotrac Company Profiles, 21 December 1999. Available at http://web7.infotrac.galegroup.com.

Lowentstein, Roger. "Intrinsic Value: Blades, Batteries, and a Fifth of Gillette." *The Wall Street Journal,* 19 September 1996, C1.

Naj, Amal Kumar. "Latest Version of Zinc-Air Batteries Promises to Show Long-Lasting Results." *The Wall Street Journal,* 10 November 1995.

"Ralston Completes Sale of Rechargable Battery Business." *PR Newswire,* 1 November 1999.

Reda, Susan. "Cost, Standardization Issues Plague Rechargeable Market." *Stores,* June 1996.

Stroud, Jerri. "Ralston Plans to Spin Off Eveready." *St. Louis Post-Dispatch,* 11 June 1999.

Vincent, Colin A., Bruno Scrosati, Mario Lazzari, and Franco Bonino. "You Can Buy Yourself an Electric Car, But It Isn't Going to Take You Very Far." *The Wall Street Journal,* 15 May 1996.

Yuasa, Teruhisa. "Storage Battery Industry Sees Revival." *Japan 21st,* October 1996, 41.

SIC 3692

PRIMARY BATTERIES, DRY AND WET

This industry covers establishments primarily engaged in manufacturing primary batteries, dry or wet.

INDUSTRY SNAPSHOT

In the mid-1990s, demand for primary (disposable, nonrechargeable) batteries remained healthy because of the ever-expanding use of portable electronic products. Longer-lasting alkaline batteries, introduced in the 1980s, continued to expand their share of the U.S. retail (household) market, which was growing at a rate of 6 to 8 percent per year. The industry also had met the challenge of producing a mercury-free battery that satisfied environmental concerns. The two major primary battery manufacturers, Duracell and Eveready, were faced with some competition from the rechargeable sector, where significant strides in research and development had been made. Given their relative convenience and low initial cost, however, disposable batteries remained dominant in the household sector at least to the year 2000.

In 1997, the industry's 135 establishments employed 23,227 people. Of this number, 18,654 were production workers who earned an average hourly income of $15.66.

NAICS CODE(S)

335912 (Dry and Wet Primary Battery Manufacturing)

ORGANIZATION AND STRUCTURE

Duracell (which became a division of Gillette in 1996), Eveready Battery (a division of Ralston-Purina), and Rayovac are considered the "Big Three" of disposable batteries, representing about 90 percent of U.S. sales. The total value of shipments in this industry was reported at $2.3 billion in 1997. Both Duracell and Eveready are powerful players in the European and other international markets.

Other companies have tried to wedge into the battery business, but they've generally been unsuccessful. In 1986, for example, Eastman Kodak Co. entered the alkaline market. But even with its powerful brand name, gold-tipped batteries, and flashy commercials featuring Stevie Wonder, Kodak was unable to become a strong contender. In 1995, Kodak had less than 1 percent of the U.S. alkaline market.

BACKGROUND AND DEVELOPMENT

Around the start of the nineteenth century, the first battery was constructed by Alessandro Volta. The Leclanch cell, developed by the French engineer Georges Leclanch in 1866, immediately became a commercial success in large sizes because its component materials were easily available. Until fairly recently, however, the major use for primary batteries in the home was in flashlights. The strong growth in primary battery sales began to accelerate in the 1950s, with expanding demand for transistor radios. The continuing introduction of new electronic products—including pagers, hand-held video games, cellular phones, and portable CD players—and the increasing desire for portability has fueled the growth in sales for primary batteries. Zinc chloride batteries, which are similar to Leclanch cells but produce more energy, were dominant in the U.S. market in the 1970s and the early 1980s, when longer-lasting alkalines began to overtake them. Alkalines now represent the dominant share of the U.S. consumer battery market.

Other important primary batteries include silver oxide-zinc cells, which are used in watches, hearing aids, and cameras. Lithium cells have attracted the most research in recent years; they are particularly suited for such applications as personal paging systems, heart pacers, and automated cameras.

CURRENT CONDITIONS

Throughout the 1990s, the retail market for battery sales in the United States was characterized by constant growth. In 1992 total shipments were valued at $1.9 billion; within five years, the market had increased 20 percent to $2.4 billion in 1997. A majority of sales consisted of round and prismatic battery cells for the consumer market—almost $2.2 billion of total shipments were for these kinds of batteries.

In 1993, Rayovac introduced a rechargeable alkaline battery named Renewal, in the standard AAA, AA, C, and D sizes, putting it in direct competition with disposable alkaline products. At the beginning of 1995, no other firm produced a rechargeable primary cell. According to *Machine Design,* "the basic chemistry was alkaline, but the anode construction (which differs from primary cells) allowed recharging the battery with a special power supply." By the end of the decade, however, Rayovac no longer held the lead in rechargeable batteries. Battery manufacturers uniformly made rechargeable batteries out of nickel metal hydride and lithium ion.

Nevertheless, throwaways will not soon be obsolete, or even lose their dominant position in many consumer markets. Most consumers still preferred the convenience of throwaways, even if they could ultimately save a few dollars by consistently using rechargeables.

Some of the supposed environmental benefits of rechargeables also were open to question, since primary batteries, while numerous, represented less than 1 percent of all municipal solid waste. Battery makers have been making additional efforts to cut their waste products. Panasonic, for example, designed new packaging for its batteries that was made of high-density polyethylene and was therefore recyclable through 6,000 service centers nationwide.

Another argument for rechargeables had been that the throwaways contained relatively high levels of mercury, which is said to damage the nervous system and increase the risk of cancer when ingested in even small quantities. The Mercury-Containing and Rechargeable Battery Management Act of 1996 banned the practice of adding mercury to almost all alkaline and zinc carbon batteries. But the aspects of this law pertaining to mercury usage, as well as similar legislation passed by many states, were actually moot—battery makers already had solved the problem. According to the U.S. Bureau of the Mines, the battery industry reduced the use of mercury by 99 percent between 1984 and 1994.

The top three battery companies battle fiercely for the consumer's dollar, especially at Christmas time, when batteries are needed for toys, games, and other electronic gifts. Historically, some 35 to 40 percent of all household battery sales are made in the final quarter of the year, while less than 20 percent take place in the first quarter. To distinguish their brands and maintain or expand share, the major firms spend huge sums on advertising. For example, in 1999 Duracell spent $60 million—a strategy which paid off with an increase of market share to almost 50 percent. Such heavy expenditures create a significant

barrier to entry for new companies. They also make advertising characters like Eveready's Energizer Bunny familiar to almost every American who owns a TV.

Besides advertising, the big firms continue to find innovations to gain the consumer's attention. In the spring of 1996, for instance, both Duracell and Eveready introduced on-cell battery testers. Both batteries use similar technology that measures the power based on the amount of heat generated in the tester. The Duracell battery gives a graduated reading; the Eveready Energizer, in contrast, reads "Good" at full power, but remains black when less than 25 percent power remains.

The two companies have spent millions on research for these products, and their market research indicated that up to 90 percent of consumers liked the testers after they had tried them. Nevertheless, according to retailers, neither product has sparked much consumer interest or affected sales. As Nelson Rodenmayer, a marketing director for Winn-Dixie Stores, told *Supermarket News,* "While a new technological innovation may be a nice novelty for consumers, I don't know if they're going to make a difference in terms of sales. In my experience, it's been a nonissue."

As the century closed, battery manufacturers strove to maintain a robust market by developing improved-technology alkaline batteries. In addition to increasing the potency of interactive elements to create long-lasting cells, batteries also incorporated designs that facilitated electric flow. Longer-lasting batteries and improved flow resulted in faster, more robust performance of battery-powered devices.

Besides struggling to gain the consumer's interest, the companies also jockey for shelf space in consumer outlets—particularly near the checkout counter, where last-minute purchases are made. Indeed, Duracell has attributed much of its growth to increased distribution at mass merchandisers and warehouse clubs. The manufacturers walk a fine line as they try to gain new distributors without offending old ones.

INDUSTRY LEADERS

In 1988, a leveraged buyout (LBO) led by Kohlberg Kravis Roberts (KKR) took Duracell private. While some LBOs have come under attack for weakening strong companies by saddling them with debt, Duracell's LBO was generally judged a success. The company completed an initial public offering in 1991 that reduced its $1.6 billion of debt by one-third, and it once again became profitable in fiscal 1992.

In 1996, Duracell once again changed hands when Gillette bought the company for $7.1 billion in stock. Most analysts were pleased with the combination, since they believed Gillette's international marketing muscle would help Duracell overseas. The company already held a solid lead in the global alkaline market, with a 42 percent share compared with 24 percent for Eveready. Since only 20 percent of Duracell sales came from outside North America and Western Europe, Gillette management believed the company offered excellent opportunities for international expansion.

Worldwide, batteries made by Duracell have been marketed under the Duracell trademark. That gave it an advantage in Europe over Eveready, which initially marketed its alkalines under local brand names in Europe. As the new millennium approached, Duracells' worldwide sales of its copper-topped battery product line out performed all other manufacturers of alkaline batteries. Duracell also continued to be a leading producer of lithium batteries for consumer applications and zinc air batteries, most of which are so-called button cells used in hearing aids and medical equipment.

Eveready is one of the oldest battery companies, dating back to the nineteenth century. Eveready was sold by Union Carbide in 1986 to Ralston-Purina, which also markets pet foods and other consumer and agricultural products. At the time of merger, the once-named Energizer Battery Co. became known simply as Energizer Holdings. According to one estimate, its U.S. market share in 1996 was 37 percent, versus 44 percent for Duracell; nonetheless, in certain market sectors, specifically dry cell batteries and flashlights, Eveready laid claim to being the world's largest manufacturer in 1999. While Eveready is a leading manufacturer of alkaline batteries, it also continues to make zinc carbon brands in huge numbers. While zinc carbon usage is declining worldwide, these batteries remain good moneymakers: because they are cheaper to produce, zinc carbon batteries' margins of profit are generally higher than those of alkalines.

Eveready's overall margins, however, have been below those of Duracell. As noted earlier, Eveready initially elected to keep the many brand names of the companies it bought in Europe, rather than consolidating them under the Eveready name. The strategy proved unworkable, and in the mid-1990s Eveready was busy trying to consolidate all of its alkaline brands under the Energizer name. Moreover, by the end of the decade, competition from Asia forced Energizer to seek a buyer for its rechargeable battery division. Despite the anticipated sale of its rechargeable business, Eveready achieved sales greater than $500 million in 1998.

In 1996, Boston financier Thomas Lee bought an 80 percent interest in Rayovac Corp., the firm accounting for the third largest amount of sales in the battery business. Despite a $20 million advertising campaign featuring Michael Jordan in 1996, its Renewal alkaline rechargeable line had yet to catch on with American consumers.

While the company had some success selling low-cost alkalines, its overall share in dollar volume remained steady through the end of the 1990s at about 10 percent of total market share.

AMERICA AND THE WORLD

Overall, the worldwide disposable battery market totals about 20 billion units annually. The widespread diffusion of portable electronic products in Europe and Asia has, as in the United States, been accompanied by strong sales of batteries to operate them. And again, as in the United States, there has been a move toward more-powerful alkaline batteries from zinc-chloride cells; still, non-alkaline batteries predominate. According to one estimate, in 1996 only one-third of all batteries sold worldwide were alkalines.

In 1996, the overseas market that had battery manufacturers most excited was China. Duracell was selling alkalines in all but one of China's provinces. It also was finishing construction of a $60 million alkaline plant. The plant was expected to give Duracell a huge cost advantage, since the heavy tariffs ordinarily imposed on imported batteries would be eliminated by producing locally. Also, the first two years of Duracell's profits in China were tax-exempt. Duracell expected that China would be its third largest market, after the United States and Italy, by the year 2000. In fact, by 1999 the industry's focus on China eventually manifested greatly increased sales in Asia. As reported by the U.S. Department of Commerce, most notable were increases in export sales to the Hong Kong market from $33 million in 1998 to more than $143 million in 1999—an increase of more than 400 percent.

RESEARCH AND TECHNOLOGY

One major focus of research and development in the early 1990s was the effort to produce mercury-free alkaline batteries. By 1994, researchers had been able to reduce mercury levels that had at one time been as high as 6 to 8 percent to merely trace elements. With the goal of mercury-free batteries largely accomplished, manufacturers have been able to concentrate on producing lighter, more powerful, and longer-lasting batteries. As electronics makers produced ever-smaller and smarter products, traditional batteries account for an increasing proportion of total weight. Thus, the development of lithium batteries has been emphasized, since these cells have the advantages of extremely high-energy density and long shelf life. In addition to their widespread use in consumer products, lithium primary batteries had become the power source of choice for a range of medical implants by 1996.

As the millennium approached, battery manufacturers continued improvement of battery design. One important strategy first introduced by Duracell and later embraced by the industry involved improved cell designs which improved efficiency and maximized output. Changing consumer needs necessitated better designs for alkaline batteries due to increased power needs of products such as digital assistants, digital cameras, handheld computers, and wireless peripheral devices.

FURTHER READING

"A Call for More Action." *Supermarket Business,* May 1996.

Bailey, Steve, and Steven Syre. "Battery Market Sparks Bostonians' Interests." *The Boston Globe,* 13 September 1996.

Capell, Kerry. "How Gillette Wowed Wall Street." *Business Week,* 30 September 1996.

Dan, Pnina. "Recent Advances in Rechargeable Batteries." *Electronic Design,* 3 February 1997.

"Duracell Makes Best Alkaline Battery Better with Duracell Ultra 3 Design." Duracell; News Bureau; Press Materials, 2000. Available from http://www.duracell.com/News_Bureau/index.html/.

Duracell; Our Company; Corporate Background, 2000. Available from http://www.duracell.com/Our_Company/index.html.

Elson, Joel. "Charging Batteries." *Supermarket News,* 1 April 1996.

Eveready Battery Co. "Company Information." Eveready, 1999. Available from http://www.energizer.com/companyinfo/.

Gillette Annual Report and 10-K, 1996. Boston: Gillette, 1996.

Hoover's Inc. "Duracell Global Business Management Group Company Capsule." Austin, TX: Hoover's Online, 1999. Available from http://www.hoovers.com/co/capsule/6/0,2163,60116,00.html/.

Hoover's Inc. "Energizer Holdings, Inc. Company Capsule." Austin, TX: Hoover's Online, 1999. Available from http://www.hoovers.com/co/capsule/4/0,2163,14674,00.html/.

Hoover's Inc. "Rayovac Corporation Company Capsule." Austin, TX: Hoover's Online, 1999. Available from http://www.hoovers.com/co/capsule/0/0,2163,41410,00.html/.

Lamonica, Paul R. "Battling Batteries: Why Duracell and Eveready Are Neck and Neck in Market Share, But Not Brand Value." *Financial World,* 30 January 1996.

"Major Device Manufacturers Recommend New Duracell Ultra as the Best Battery Battery to Power their Sophisticated Electronics." Duracell; News Bureau; Press Materials, 1999. Available from http://www.duracell.com/News_Bureau/index.html/.

Murphy, Elena Epatko. "New Markets Charge Ups Sales and Recycling Efforts." *Purchasing,* 15 August 1996.

Radice, Carol. "Batteries: Specialty Batteries Recharge Category." *Progressive Grocer,* March 1996.

Ralston-Purina Annual Report and 10-K, 1996. St. Louis: Ralston-Purina, 1996.

Rayovac. "Srong Sales Drive Record Market Shares, Sales and Earnings." Rayovac, 2000. Available from http://www.prnewswire.com/cgi-bin/micro_stories.pl?ACCT=742563&TICK=ROV&STORY=/www/story/01-25-2000/0001123463&EDATE=Jan+25,+2000/.

"Reviving Primary Cells." *Machine Design,* 9 March 1995.

Siskin, Jonathan. "Testing the Charge: Shoppers Appear to be Attracted to Competitive Price Points in Batteries Rather than to a Built-In Added Value." *Supermarket News,* 10 February 1997.

U.S. Department of Commerce. "Top 25 U.S. Destinations for Primary Batteries, SIC 3692 U.S. Domestic Exports." Washington, DC: International Trade Administration, 1999. Available from http://www.ita.doc.gov/td/ocg/exp3692.htm/.

U.S. Department of Commerce. "1997 Economic Census Manufacturing Industry Series." *Primary Battery Manufacturing, 1997.* Washington, DC: GPO, 1999.

Vincent, Colin. "Recent Developments in Battery Technology." *Chemistry and Industry,* 16 September 1996.

U.S. Census Bureau. *1997 Economic Census Report—Manufacturing.* GPO: Washington 1999.

SIC 3694

ELECTRICAL EQUIPMENT FOR INTERNAL COMBUSTION ENGINES

This classification covers establishments primarily engaged in manufacturing electrical equipment for internal combustion engines. Important products of this industry include armatures, starting motors, alternators, and generators for automobiles and aircraft, and ignition apparatus for internal combustion engines, including spark plugs, magnetos, coils, and distributors.

NAICS CODE(S)

336322 (Other Motor Vehicle Electrical and Electronic Equipment Manufacturing)

INDUSTRY SNAPSHOT

The automotive electronics sector grew rapidly at the turn of the twenty-first century, with an estimated 22 percent of average vehicle cost attributed to electronics, according to a 1999 report in *Automotive News.* Industry shipments for 1997 totaled over $9 billion.

Electronic parts and components met increasing consumer demand for safety, environmental, and convenience features. As electronic engine controls increased in sophistication, the dollar-value content of these systems in new vehicles continued to rise. In the midst of widespread industry consolidation by the auto parts manufacturers—incited by increased outsourcing from automobile manufacturers—the electrical parts sector shifted gradually into the market domain of the electronic industry. A general restructuring of the auto sector occurred in the 1990s when the Big Three automakers—Ford, Chrysler, and General Motors—cut the number of suppliers they dealt with and concentrated their business on a select group of component manufacturers. Consolidation among the parts industry ensued. The Big Three also shed their noncore parts operations and purchased more parts assemblies from outside vendors, thereby avoiding the overhead costs for plant operations and materials necessary for in-house manufacture and assembly. There was also a movement toward standardization of parts across disparate car model lines, which presented the opportunity for parts manufacturers to diversify into design work in order to develop universal parts.

The aftermarket segment of the electrical auto parts business, devoted to replacement parts for used automobiles, presented a mixed picture as car owners kept their vehicles longer. The average age of cars on the road escalated to 8.9 years by the end of the 1990s, compared with 7.4 years in 1986, a circumstance that boosted sales of replacement parts. Some of the increase was offset, however, by the development of longer-lasting and better-made parts, which in turn decreased the need for replacements. Other offsets occurred due to the significant percentage of imported vehicles, since the share of the business for foreign vehicles remained relatively small. Additionally, the do-it-yourself (DIY) segment was tempered by consumer wariness of doing any work on the increasingly sophisticated electrical systems in new vehicles. In the face of these negatives, sales of items like spark plugs held up remarkably well throughout the 1990s. A push for increasingly tougher auto emission regulations and the resultant equipment necessary for compliance also augured well for the future.

ORGANIZATION AND STRUCTURE

The automotive electronics industry can essentially be divided into two parts: original equipment manufacturing (OEM) and the automotive aftermarket. OEM manufacturing is for new autos; the aftermarket is for used ones. In both segments, the manufacturers comprise the components groups or affiliates of the large automakers, and independent parts makers, which themselves may be divisions of much larger industrial entities. As Japanese companies took an increasing share of the U.S. market, Japanese-affiliated suppliers began to open local branches; by 1993, almost 300 such companies were located in the United States.

BACKGROUND AND DEVELOPMENT

The application of electronic systems into automobiles evolved to increasing levels of sophistication since commercial production of the automobile began in the early 20th century. The first electric starter appeared on a 1912 model and, by the 1930s, six-volt electrical systems were standard. Electrical requirements grew as engines became larger and additional features—for example, radios and multi-speed windshield wipers—were added. By the late 1950s, 12-volt systems had replaced six-volt systems as a requirement. In the 1970s, electrical, or transistorized, ignition systems, which required less maintenance and were more reliable than mechanical breaker-point systems, were introduced.

The OEM parts industry entered a depression cycle in 1989, but revived in 1992 and continued strong into the mid-1990s. Tremendous financial pressure assailed the Big Three automakers during the early 1990s, and caused them to rethink their business practices. They gave their top suppliers greater responsibility for design and engineering in the process. In return for taking on these greater burdens, suppliers received long-range contracts—often for the life of a car model rather than for one to three years as was at the common practice. According to one estimate, the number of auto parts makers in the United States fell from 3,000 to 2,000 during the years from 1983 to 1992. Yet the Big Three sought additional reduction in the proportion of auto parts that they manufactured themselves. In order to reduce further the number of suppliers they dealt with, automakers began awarding contracts for entire components or subassemblies to so-called Tier 1 suppliers. In 1994, General Motors spun off Delco Remy, its automotive engine parts subsidiary, to a group of investors headed by a former auto executive. Also in 1994, Chrysler sold a large portion of its Acustar parts-making subsidiary to Yamazaki of Japan, including eight plants in Mexico that made electrical wiring systems for cars and trucks.

Growth in demand for engine and drive-train electronics increased further in response to the mandates of the Clean Air Act. Other factors being equal, older cars—especially those with more than 100,000 miles—pollute more than new vehicles because exhaust gases become dirtier as spark timing and other factors begin to vary. Environmental regulations requiring ignition designers to build more efficient combustion systems led engineers to scrap the traditional rotor-based distributor and develop a distributorless, all-electronic ignition system (DIS). General Motors introduced the first DIS in 1984, and the systems gained popularity in the 1990s. Rather than distributors, DIS utilized small ignition coils for each spark plug; an ignition computer triggered each coil individually, using engine sensors to time the pulses correctly. DIS systems eliminated the small variations in spark timing that resulted from mechanical wear of the distributor. The DIS compensated for plug misfires by signaling corrections in the fuel-air mixture and in the microprocessor-controlled timing mechanism. While DIS eliminated the distributor, it added one coil for each pair of cylinders; the improved gas mileage and reduced exhaust emissions offset the expense of additional coils and semiconductors. Throughout the decade of the 1990s increasing numbers of new cars operated without distributors; analysts expected that number to rise steadily to 100 percent.

Aftermarket. In the aftermarket segment of the industry, business trends remained subject to a variety of influences. On the positive side, the number of cars on the road increased steadily; according to one estimate, in 1996 there were 101 million vehicles on American roads that were three to seven years old. Those were the cars on which most repairs were performed, and because fuel prices generally remained low, the number of miles driven increased dramatically. Additionally, by 1996, all new vehicles had to meet On-Board Diagnostics Series II emission rules (OBD II), and compliance often required additional equipment or repairs. Finally, sales in the key spark plugs segment rose to $806.0 million in 1995, which was $66.0 million higher than in 1994 and a $105.0 million than in 1993.

Counterfeiting of parts posed a challenge for the aftermarket industry in the 1980s. General Motors contended that it and its suppliers were losing $1.2 billion annually to counterfeits; among the parts most copied were electronic ignition modules. Although Congress attempted to deal with the problem in 1984 by passing the Trademark Counterfeiting Act, the counterfeiting business continued to thrive. In 1993, the Federal Trade Commission estimated that auto parts counterfeiting was a $3-billion-a-year business in the United States.

CURRENT CONDITIONS

Estimates of the dollar volume of electronic engine systems are difficult to evaluate, since they can be calculated in several different ways. As Derrick Kuzak, Ford Motor's director of electric/electronics systems engineering, told *Purchasing,* ''Rather than having a number of stand-alone modules—like processors—that are controlling individual features of a car, there is a trend toward functional integration with more control in fewer, larger modules.'' At the threshold of the 21st century, the automotive electronic parts industry totaled $54.4 billion in North America, Japan, and Europe combined, with increasing emphasis on electronic systems. According to interpolations of a survey performed by *Ward's Auto World,* the per vehicle total of engine electronics by the year 2000 was forecast at $720-900—based on 6 percent per year growth rate in electronics content per vehicle between 1994 and 2000, with 40-50 percent of electronics devoted to engine and drive-train applications.

Consolidation. An ongoing outsourcing of component manufacturing functions bridged from the 1990s and into the 21st century. According to a report in *Economist,* by mid-1998 only 4,060 auto part suppliers survived worldwide, a dramatic decrease from 30,000 suppliers 10 years earlier. *Economist* quoted International Business devel-

opment consultant Donna Parolini saying that as few as 26 global firms might survive the first decade of the 21st century. Indeed, U.S. carmakers decreased their relationships with suppliers by an estimated 80 percent in the late 1990s. Ford Motor Company, in its North American operations alone, reduced its supplier count from 2,400 in 1980 to 1,400 in 1993, with projections for a continued decrease to 1,000 suppliers by the year 2000. Tier 1 companies gained the added responsibility of dealing with smaller sub-contractors that had previously provided goods and services directly to the automakers. As smaller suppliers closed shop, larger suppliers grew and expanded into new functional arenas. Some parts makers huddled in negotiations to purchase design firms, in order to increase their functionality potential in the outsourcing industry. At least one parts maker, Valmet of Finland, produced completely assembled vehicles by 1998.

The consolidation movement led automakers to embrace greater standardization of parts and components across model lines. Rather than customizing each component for a specific car or truck, auto manufacturers accepted common designs for a variety of models. Hidden ''under the hood,'' electronics assemblies did not serve to distinguish one car model from another in the perception of the consumer, making electrical components readily adaptable to standardization. Suppliers might amortize research and development costs and expenses connected to tooling over larger volumes, and might also reduce inventory levels of the wide variety of low-volume parts. Japanese automakers, Toyota and Nissan in particular, initiated this consolidation trend. By 1998 each had outsourced a reported 75 percent of engineering functions.

Emissions Control. The legislative environment of the 1990s proved a boon to replacement part companies, since tougher emission standards related to the Clean Air Act of 1990 and other environmental legislation increased consumer demand for aftermarket parts. Efforts by several states to enhance their emission inspection programs were expected to contribute to improved vehicle-maintenance practices. The Environmental Protection Agency estimated that the 20 percent of all vehicles that fail emission tests are responsible for some 60 percent of all toxic emissions. The cost of bringing those vehicles up to prescribed standards was estimated to run into billions of dollars, much of which flowed to parts companies.

Some technological advances, in contrast, affected the aftermarket sector adversely because parts and components were built with extended life-expectancies—electronically driven systems in particular proved to be very reliable and consequently needed less maintenance. Just as the introduction of electronic ignition systems erased demand for points and condensers, the advent of the distributorless ignition system (DIS) resulted in a shrinking market for distributor caps and rotors. The introduction of the emission-reducing catalytic converter also tended to prolong the life of spark plugs because of its requirement of unleaded fuel. By 1997, spark plugs that could last 100,000 miles were commonplace.

In addition, small, four-cylinder engines, which require fewer plugs than their six- and eight-cylinder counterparts, became more prevalent. Likewise the compact engine departments of many newer vehicles tended to discourage plug changing, which some contend now require the abilities of a contortionist. New technologies superannuated much traditional auto maintenance: few cars needed such items as breaker points, and the annual tune-up became a relic of the past. The number of service stations declined, and there were fewer outlets performing preventive maintenance. For some engine parts, quality had so improved that, barring an automobile accident, they would never be replaced during the auto's lifetime.

The incursion of foreign cars into the U.S. auto market also had a negative impact on U.S. parts makers in the aftermarket. Some professional installers and do-it-yourselfers working on import vehicles continued to feel that, at least in certain applications, it was better to use original equipment version (OEV) products than the aftermarket offerings of U.S. parts manufacturers. In addition, some potential DIYers were reluctant to work on their imported vehicles and opted instead to bring their cars to dealer service departments that used OEV parts. Some observers also commented that, as in other consumer products, brand loyalty was declining among many auto owners who were more concerned with buying quality parts at a competitive price. Despite these limitations, however, since the early 1980s—when sales for imported vehicles accounted for only 1 percent of revenue—domestic parts-makers have made important strides in supplying the import aftermarket.

INDUSTRY LEADERS

In a highly anticipated move in February of 1999 General Motors Corporation spun off its Delphi Automotive Systems parts manufacturing business, with an initial public offering of 100 million shares. Delphi, a subsidiary of General Motors for 90 years prior to the IPO, ranked immediately as the largest independent maker of auto parts worldwide, with sales of $28.5 billion. Also prominent were Dana, with $13.0 billion in sales, and TRW Incorporated, which reported $14.0 billion in annual sales. TRW's revenues were boosted by the purchase of Lucas Varity PLC (of Britain) for $7.0 billion in 1999. The Delphi IPO in fact sparked merger and acquisition negotiations throughout the industry as parts manufacturers rushed to compete.

WORKFORCE

At the close of the 1990s, pay levels in auto parts manufacturing varied widely for basically the same type of work. Wage disparities were attributed primarily to the union contract factor. In unionized plants employees earned approximately $50,000 per year—approximately double the earnings of non-union workers.

In 1999 the United Auto Workers (UAW) Union estimated that the unionization rate at parts manufacturing plants had declined from 20 percent to 10 percent over a three-year period beginning in 1996, and that the overall auto parts industry employed 400,000 non-unionized workers. The growth of spin-off parts companies, many of which were previously owned by one of the Big Three automakers, contributed significantly to the size of the non-unionized population among auto workers. Union leaders, apprehensive of wage erosion among the union ranks, increased recruiting efforts at non-union establishments and further initiated negotiations for non-unionized parts workers to receive wages equivalent to unionized employees of the Big Three car makers. In the spring of 1999 the UAW openly approached the Big Three for cooperation in pressuring suppliers to cease opposition to union activity at parts assembly and manufacturing plants. The UAW' appeal to the big carmakers met with limited success, as many complex issues remained to be resolved into the year 2000.

In 1997, the industry employed nearly 42,000 production workers who earned an average hourly wage of $14.66.

AMERICA AND THE WORLD

The OEM segment benefited from a steady shift of production from Japan to the United States during the 1990s. For many years, U.S. parts makers struggled unsuccessfully to sell their products to Japanese-based automakers producing in the United States. Because of trade friction, many Japanese companies promised to increase their buys of U.S. parts substantially. The U.S. trade deficit with Japan in the overall auto sector was more than $60.0 billion in 1995, and auto parts accounted for perhaps $10.0 billion or more of the total. Nevertheless, there were signs that American manufacturers could expect increasing sales to North American assembly sites (although a more powerful dollar in 1997 made domestic sourcing less attractive). Increasing export sales to plants in Japan, however, was still expected to be a step-by-step battle.

Globalization of the auto parts industry accelerated into the 21st century. Trade relationships expanded between Mexico, Canada, and the United States as a result of the North American Free Trade Agreement (NAFTA), while new auto-producing nations emerged in Asia. That combination of circumstances, in the wake of ongoing consolidation, led to the increasing presence of Tier 1 suppliers at the international level, a growing presence that spurred competition among suppliers worldwide. The rapid consolidation of the parts industry overall, combined with the increased involvement of electronics firms—including an overwhelming majority of Japanese-based firms—afforded a critical edge to Japanese contenders in the parts arena. In that regard, the Japanese industrial model held relevance for all. Tim Moran in an *Automotive News* commentary, extolled the need for all suppliers to streamline operations in order to compete. He cited the success of the Japanese model and noted Japan's "high art of lean production—namely Toyota Motor Corporation." According to Moran, "That automaker's Toyota Production System has become the largely unacknowledged inspiration for lean-manufacturing practices at . . . countless other producers."

RESEARCH AND TECHNOLOGY

Government regulations requiring reductions in auto emissions helped to drive trends in research and technology for the industry. The three government-regulated auto pollutants are hydrocarbon, carbon monoxide, and oxides of nitrogen exhaust emissions. The catalysts that break them down in the exhaust stream must have a carefully balanced chemistry to work properly. Essential to this process are electronically controlled fuel injection and ignition systems with feedback from various sensors. Research efforts in diesel engine electronics were undertaken in anticipation of updated federal and state emissions regulations scheduled for implementation in 2004. The innovative systems incorporated "brain box" technology, featuring electronic control modules (ECMs). ECMs afford centralized control of both fuel emissions and fuel consumption, and provide control of engine pressures and fluid levels as well. ECM technology affords greater fuel efficiency and lower maintenance, as well as reduced emission hazard. In the fall of 1999, Siemens Diesel Systems Technology L.L.C. embarked on a joint venture with Navistar International Transportation Corporation to manufacture components of the electronically controlled systems, with implementation scheduled for the year 2002.

Other developments in emissions controls included Motorola's MPC555 microcontroller chip. In 1999, researchers at Motorola earned for the company the Premier Automotive Suppliers' Contributions to Excellence (PACE) award for the chip, which contained 6.7 million transistorized switches and promised to provide optimized control of electronic emissions and powertrain systems. Later that same year, Hewlett-Packard introduced the TS-4500 Series II test platform for rapid diagnosis of ECM systems.

Siemens's Automotive developed the "Keyless Go" integrated circuit, featuring built-in Identification Friend or Foe (IFF) security encryption. IFF was designed to impede vehicle theft by disabling the engine ignition function in the absence of the chip carried on a key chain or elsewhere on the driver's person. Initial implementations of similar systems resulted in 82 percent theft reduction. The commercial release of programmable fingerprint-recognition technology for ignition security was the predicted follow-up to smart-key technology.

Also new for the 21st century was a programmable electronic sensor, developed by Ab Elektronik GmbH of Germany, which when located on a car's accelerator pedal simulated the function of a mechanical accelerator to control engine speed.

FURTHER READING

Adler, Alan. "General Motors Announces Breakup of Hughes Electronics Subsidiary." *Knight Ridder/Tribune Business News,* 17 January 1997.

Adler, Alan. "General Motors Faces Labor Strike at Another Supplier." *Knight Ridder/Tribune Business News,* 22 March 1997.

Ambrosini, Al. "Diesel engine maintenance is changing." *Auto & Truck International,* September-October 1999.

"Autoparts Report Homepage." *The Autoparts Report,* 16 February 2000. Available from http://www.autopartsreport.com/aprhome.htm.

Couretas, John. "Electronics' role to surge, study says." *Automotive News,* 10 January 2000.

"Delphi Focuses on Emerging Markets." *Ward's Automotive Reports,* 3 March 1997.

"Keyless car ignition." *Design News,* 6 December 1999.

Galuszka, Peter. "Autos: Big Dents in Auto Parts." *Business Week,* 12 April 1999.

Geer, John F. Jr. "Parting Company: Why Echlin's Top Management Needed Fixing." *Financial World,* 15 April 1997.

Gonzalez, Jean Young. "Sensor assembly." *Design News,* 4 October 1999.

Gonzalez, Jean Young. "Test platform." *Design News,* 4 October 1999.

"Growth on Track for Automotive Electronics." *Ward's Auto World,* October 1994.

"Joint venture helps engine customers." *Auto & Truck International.* September-October 1999.

Jost, Kevin. "The Continuing Evolution of the Spark Plug." *Automotive Engineering,* February 1996.

Keenan, Tim. "Bosch Raises the Bar: Microelectronics Advances Keep Company on Cutting Edge." *Ward's Auto World,* November 1996.

Lowell, Jon. "Is the Party Over (Automotive Electronics Growth)." *Automotive Industries,* August 1995.

Koenig, Bill. "Delco Electronics Looks Hopefully Upon GM Spin-Off Fever." *Knight Ridder/Tribune Business News,* 23 June 1996.

Moran, Tim. "Suppliers Lag in Race To Get Lean, Expert Says." *Automotive News,* 21 June 1999.

Reitman, Valerie. "Toyota to Sell Hybrid Gas-Electric Car." *Wall Street Journal,* 26 March 1997.

Schofield, Julie Anne. "PowerPC-based chip wins award." *Design News,* 17 May 1999.

"The Wide World of Auto Parts." *S&P Industry Surveys,* 13 June 1996.

1996 Ward's Automotive Yearbook. Southfield, MI: Ward's Communications, 1996.

"Whoever Said Plugs Lost Their Spark Was Wrong." *Aftermarket Business,* 1 April 1996.

SIC 3695

MAGNETIC AND OPTICAL RECORDING MEDIA

This classification comprises establishments primarily engaged in manufacturing blank tape, disk, or cassette magnetic or optical recording media for use in recording audio, video, or other signals. Excluded from this classification are establishments primarily engaged in manufacturing blank or recorded records and prerecorded audio tapes, which are included within the scope of **SIC 3652: Prerecorded Records & Tapes.** Also excluded are establishments primarily engaged in manufacturing prepackaged computer software and those establishments manufacturing prerecorded video tape cassettes and disks. The former are classified in **SIC 7372: Prepackaged Software** and the latter are classified in **Industry Group 78: Motion Pictures.**

NAICS CODE(S)

334613 (Magnetic and Optical Recording Media Manufacturing)

INDUSTRY SNAPSHOT

The magnetic and optical recording media industry manufactures blank audio and video recording tape, computer tape, and both rigid and floppy computer disks, utilizing either magnetic or optical recording technology. To an extent, the magnetic and optical methods of recording data, images, and sound are competing technologies: the magnetic method offers the user quick retrieval of recorded material, while the optical method benefits those with large storage requirements. Consumers and businesses must choose between the two according to their needs.

Before 1987, the U.S. Census Bureau did not recognize manufacturers of blank audio and video tapes, and floppy and rigid computer disk manufacturers, as composing a distinct industry. Instead, these manufacturers were grouped together with manufacturers of such products as phonograph needles, radio headphones, and mi-

crowave components. In 1987 the U.S. Census Bureau began separately tracking the recording media manufacturing industry, which had emerged as a significant force, generating $3.5 billion in revenue and comprising 181 manufacturing companies scattered throughout the United States. Annual industry revenues increased by 70 percent within 10 years, surpassing $5.9 billion.

The industry's growth from 1987 through the end of the twentieth century was founded not in sales volume, which was modest, but in technological progress. With announcements of improvements in both the production of data storage products and the production of audio and video tape occurring almost monthly during the final decade of the century, the industry as a result underwent repeated periods of flux. The introduction of new high-density writable optical formats in the mid-1990s launched a dramatic upsurge in the volume of optical media sold while projections for sales of magnetic media turned flat. Manufacturers of magnetic and optical recording media poised themselves to garner an appreciable share of the revenue realized from the enormous popularity of home audio and video entertainment and the increasing use of computers for both professional and personal needs.

Conflicting forecasts pelted the industry. Some called for its collapse in anticipation of competing technology that would render magnetic and optical recording technology obsolete, while others promised a meteoric rise in sales. Without question, financial success in the industry is predicated on a manufacturer's continued ability to remain at the forefront of technology, to consistently develop new products to stimulate public interest, and to keep pace with the evolving sophistication of audio, video, and computer equipment. It is an industry characterized by frenetically evolving technologies that, some have argued, are still in their infancy. Thus, manufacturers in the industry throughout the 1990s were challenged by, not only an undetermined future, but also often by an undecided present.

ORGANIZATION AND STRUCTURE

Approximately 241 companies in the United States were involved primarily or exclusively in the manufacture of magnetic and optical recording media in 1997. These companies recorded $4.72 billion in revenue that year. This sales volume represented an increase of $69 million from the total of $4.03 billion generated in 1990.

The average number of employees per establishment was 85.5 people; less than half of the establishments employed 20 or more workers. The majority of the industry's manufacturers, approximately 183 companies, employed fewer than 25 workers and garnered a total of $170 million in collective earnings. The top five companies, ranked according to employee count, averaged more than $200 million in annual revenue ($1.04 billion collectively).

In the early 1990s, the greatest geographic concentration of magnetic and optical recording media manufacturing establishments was in California. California, with 89 manufacturing establishments, produced 48 percent of the industry's total shipments, employed 48 percent of the industry's total work force, and generated $2.27 billion in revenue. The next greatest concentrations of manufacturing establishments were found in Massachusetts, and New York. The two states together contained 28 manufacturing establishments. Over one-half of the total number of establishments were concentrated into these and three other states: Georgia and Oregon, with eight each; and Virginia with six.

BACKGROUND AND DEVELOPMENT

The magnetic and optical recording media industry is a modern phenomenon, its emergence stemming from technological advancements that began following World War II. First, came dictating and audio recording machines, which required blank audio tapes. Next, computers and video tape recorders created a need for tape recording information. As equipment relying on magnetic media became more advanced, magnetic media evolved as well, with improvements in both sound, image, and data recording capabilities occurring alongside advances in the way the tape itself was housed: first on reels, then inside cassettes and cartridges. Eventually, during the 1970s, magnetic recording technology advanced to disks, a response to the advent of personal computers.

Just as the pursuit of better ways to manufacture magnetic media created entirely new forms of magnetic media, the push for progress also led to the discovery of an entirely new method of recording and storing data, images, and sounds: optical recording. Emerging during the 1970s, but experiencing its most appreciable growth during the 1980s, optical recording technology promised to greatly increase recording and storage possibilities for the industry and enrich manufacturers along the way.

The origin of magnetic recording technology dates back more than 50 years before magnetic media became a commercially viable product in the 1950s. The principle of magnetic recording was first developed in 1893 by a Danish inventor named Valdemar Poulsen. Poulsen's encouraging discovery led to the formation of a U.S.-based company 12 years later called the American Telegraphon Company, organized especially to manufacture Poulsen's recording machines. This initial attempt to employ magnetic recording technology failed, largely because the wire Poulsen's design used had a tendency to become twisted, which produced unsatisfactory and irregular results.

For the next 50 years, magnetic recording development remained at a relative standstill, at least in the United States. In Germany, however, experiments continued, particularly during the two decades bridging World War I and World War II, when Karl Bauer and A. Nasavischwily designed a machine called the "Magnetophone," a recording machine that used magnetized plastic tape.

Toward the end of World War II, U.S. soldiers discovered the German Magnetophones and brought them back to the United States, recognizing that the German recording machines were capable of much higher fidelity than the wire recorders used in the United States. Once the German tape recorders became the property of the U.S. Government, they were given to the Brush Development Company to begin production of the far superior tape recorders. Brush Development began marketing tape recorders in 1946, which, obviously, created a need for magnetic tape, a need first filled by Minnesota Mining & Manufacturing (3M) one year later, when the company introduced its Scotch brand magnetic recording tape.

The production of magnetic recording tape by 3M, formally launched the magnetic media industry in the United States. Other manufacturers soon entered the market. Within three years of 3M's initial manufacture of magnetic tape, the industry ranks grew to encompass four manufacturers who led the industry for approximately ten years and produced virtually all magnetic tape sold in the United States. These four manufacturers were Reeves Soundcraft Corporation, which started producing magnetic tape in 1950; Audio Devices, Incorporated; Reeves Soundcraft, of Orradio Industries, whose president, Herbert Orr, was one of the military officers who discovered the Magnetophones in Germany; and, finally, the industry's pioneer, 3M. As these manufacturers entered the 1950s, a decade of exponential growth, the magnetic tape market represented a $500,000 a year business.

In the early years of the magnetic tape industry, the many and varied applications for the media became quickly apparent. Initially, its use as instrumentation tape overshadowed its use in sound recording applications; manufacturers of enormous room-size computers, missiles, satellites, and aircraft purchased magnetic tape to monitor the production and performance of their products. The petroleum industry used magnetic tape in geophysical exploration equipment; telephone companies used tape to record toll calls; and a host of diverse industries used magnetic tape in automation equipment. In addition to these instrumentation uses, magnetic tape was used to record radio programs, and consumers purchased the tapes for use with their audio equipment.

The market for magnetic tape increased steadily during the early 1950s, but new manufacturers failed to materialize within the industry. Audio Devices, Reeves Soundcraft, 3M, and Orradio Industries continued as the sole producers of virtually all of the tape in the United States. In terms of sales volume, the industry's annual revenues soared from $500,000 in 1950 to nearly $15 million by the middle of the decade. The growth was largely a result of the increasing number of applications for magnetic tape in industrial settings. The rise in popularity of home stereo systems and recorders contributed further to the growth. More than 3 million home audio units were in use by then, and unit sales of the equipment increased at a rate of more than 500,000 annually. This provided blank audio tape manufacturers with a burgeoning customer base as music connoisseurs discovered that magnetic tape offered better sound quality than phonograph records. Perhaps the most significant development occurred in 1957, when Ampex Corporation, a manufacturer of recorders and instrumentation machines and 25 percent owner of Orradio Industries, developed the first practical video tape recorder.

The discovery by Ampex ignited demand for blank video tape and created an explosive new market for tape manufacturers. While television producers explored the possibilities of taping television programs, the industry demonstrated a robust vitality throughout the late 1950s and early 1960s, with revenue increases of 35 to 40 percent annually. By the mid-1960s, the magnetic tape industry represented a $100 million business, which now included blank video tape as one of its primary products, in addition to audio and instrumentation tape. Television had switched from live to taped broadcasts, creating a nearly insatiable demand for blank video tape, while automobiles outfitted with cassette decks spurred the sales of blank audio tapes. Competition for this lucrative market had intensified after the 1950s. Approximately 30 manufacturers entered the arena and vied for market share, while 3M retained a commanding lead. After controlling approximately 50 percent of the market during the 1950s, 3M continued to account for one-half of the industry's sales during the 1960s as a result of its early lead in both the blank video and audio tape production markets.

Despite the greater number of manufacturers in the industry, its leading companies, with a few exceptions, were the same companies that led the industry in the early 1950s. Reeves Soundcraft still ranked among the industry's top five manufacturers, as did Audio Devices, and, of course, 3M. Ampex Corporation, by virtue of its partial ownership of Orradio Industries, and its development of the video recorder, now ranked as the second largest manufacturer, while a relatively new player, Memorex Corporation, quickly ascended to the upper echelons of the industry. Memorex, founded in 1961, was formed by a group of former 3M and Ampex employees, and owed its rise to concentrating on computer tape production, which by now accounted for the largest segment of the magnetic tape market. The lucrative magnetic tape market also attracted much larger manufacturers, such as Radio Corporation of America, and Eastman Kodak, but these companies did not derive enough revenue directly from the manufacture of magnetic tape to rank as industry leaders.

As these manufacturers entered the 1970s, they kept pace with the growing sophistication of audio and video equipment by producing higher quality tape and offering consumers various types of blank tape. In addition to choices in tape length, consumers could now opt for low noise or high noise tape, high energy or low energy tape, or ferri-chrome tape—a selection process many found confusing. This problem continued to plague manufacturers into the 1990s, but the industry's sales volume swelled regardless, climbing to approximately $350 million by the early 1970s.

In 1975, North American Philips Corporation, through its subsidiary Magnavox Company, embarked on a joint venture with MCA and its subsidiary MCA Disco-Vision Incorporated to unveil an optical video-disk system for the home consumer market. The new system employed a light beam rather than a needle or stylus to transmit images and sounds from a disk to a television screen. Although it would be several years before optical disk production represented an appreciable portion of industry shipments, the advent of optical media broadened the industry's scope and introduced a new area of competition.

As the industry entered the 1980s, the prospects for further growth were encouraging. Personal desktop computers began to emerge as a popular product, creating a need for magnetic media disks, and the blank video tape market exploded. Blank audio tape, now almost entirely sold in cassette form, also realized exponential growth fueled primarily by the popularity of automobile stereo systems. Consumers continued to be confused by the array of audio tapes from which to choose, a problem now shared by blank video tape manufacturers, who produced tapes for either Beta or VHS video equipment in addition to low-bias and high-bias tape. To combat the confusion, manufacturers began color-coding their products, but assisting consumers in their selection was not of paramount importance during the early 1980s, particularly for blank video tape manufacturers, as the most pressing problem facing consumers was simply locating tape. Blank video tape sales to duplicators, who then sold cassettes of prerecorded programs, were growing as fast as sales to consumers during the early 1980s, creating a shortage of blank tape at the retail level. The market continued to expand at an accelerated rate throughout the decade as the sales of video cassette recorders increased.

The strong steady growth of the blank audio and video tape markets, however, did not overshadow equally encouraging developments in another segment of the magnetic and optical recording media industry, a segment that promised to greatly increase financial rewards. In 1973, IBM developed the Winchester computer drive, a magnetic disk housed in an airtight container. Earlier computer drives were housed in containers that could open and shut to allow the removal of a disk, but the Winchester was permanently sealed in its container, free from dust particles. The air pressure inside the container kept the lightweight recording and writing head a fraction of a millimeter above the spinning disk, enabling the drive that held the head in place to manipulate the magnetic field on the disk's surface with unprecedented precision. The development of the Winchester was a historic event, allowing computer users to store far more data than had been possible with data tape; manufacturers now stood to benefit enormously from the fledgling personal computer market.

Evolution of Data Storage. The late 1980s and early 1990s witnessed the emergence of several new forms of magnetic and optical recording media, particularly in response to the rise of digital technology for both playback and recording. Manufacturers, put in the position of predicting which products would fuel the industry's growth 5 or 10 years into the future, gambled to a certain extent on the development of particular technologies and products, hoping to gain an early lead. Each year new products utilizing innovative technology led some observers to state that advances in optical recording technology would make magnetic media obsolete, while others announced that optical recording technology would never match magnetic media's importance in the industry. Finally, others foresaw a confluence of the two technologies into hybrid products utilizing both magnetic and optical recording technologies.

As recording media manufacturers charted their course through the late 1980s, the computer market came to the fore, making the production of computer diskettes a fiercely contested and lucrative segment of the industry. The increasing number of personal (desktop) computers spurred the sale of 5.25-inch floppy diskettes, at first onesided, then double-sided and high density. Likewise the growth in desktop computer sales had a matching effect on the sale of 3.5-inch (rigidly encased) diskettes, developed after the introduction of 5.25-inch diskettes. In the latter part of the decade, 3.5-inch diskettes eclipsed 5.25-inch diskettes as the industry's biggest seller, while the price of personal computers continued a decade-long price decline, causing more and more consumers to become diskette consumers. Subsequent improvements in optical disk storage during the 1990s gave optical systems a decided advantage over magnetic (tape, disk, and diskette) systems for high-volume, graphics-intensive tasks, such as searching databases of fingerprints to solve criminal cases. However, optical disk storage was unsuited to many other tasks and needed further refinement before gaining widespread usage.

Three advanced audio recording formats developed in the late 1980s and early 1990s provided a glimpse of the market's future when the industry spawned Digital Audio Tape (DAT), Digital Compact Cassette (DCC), and MiniDisc (MD). Each product was still in its infancy during the early 1990s, both in terms of consumer product awareness and the manufacturers' marketing efforts, and, consequently, represented only a small part of the blank audio tape market. However, each was predicted to play a more significant role as the decade progressed. DAT was developed to provide sound quality equal to the high quality of compact disks, but on a medium that could record as well as play back. DAT was also adapted for use with computers, proving to be an ideal medium to back up large capacity hard disk drives.

Against this backdrop, the industry demonstrated vitality and pursued a course of enviable growth in the early 1990s despite recessive economic conditions elsewhere. The trend in video tape production during the early 1990s imitated the audio tape trend during the 1980s, as manufacturers sought to increase their market share by producing longer-playing tapes. BASF Corporation, the industry's leading company in the early 1990s, marketed the first 9-hour video cassette in 1991, then introduced a 10-hour cassette the following year, paving the way for other manufacturers to follow. Although long-playing tapes represented a relatively small portion of the video tape market, sales grew steadily in 1994 and 1995 and increased their proportional representation in the video tape market. Blank VHS (video) tape cassette shipments in the United States surpassed 431 million units in 1994, or 25 percent of the world market. Regardless, this growth did not translate into increased profits. The retail price of video cassettes plunged during the 1980s, dropping from nearly $25 per cassette in the late 1970s, to below $2 per cassette by the beginning of the 1990s. As a result, the dollar volume of U.S. VHS tape shipments which peaked in 1986 at $1.25 billion was reduced to less than $684 million—a decline of more than 45 percent in dollar volume—when unit shipments peaked in 1994.

As the industry entered the mid-1990s, Sony and Philips were pitted against each other. According to the industry's trade organization, the International Association of Magnetic and Optical Media Manufacturers and Related Industries, the competition between Sony's audio MD and Philips's DCC could likely determine the future success of each product. In 1993, nearly every manufacturer participating in the blank audio tape market had plans to market DCC or MD products, roughly a year and a half after BASF became the first independent blank media company to engage in large-scale DCC tape production. MD products entered the market in early 1993 through Sony's Recording Media division, which, later in the year, adapted the 2.5-inch audio disk for use as computer data storage, much like the adaptation of DAT technology.

CURRENT CONDITIONS

The U.S. Census Bureau reported that the magnetic and optical blank media industry earned revenues in excess of $5.9 billion in 1997. Establishments that specialized exclusively in the manufacture of magnetic and optical recording media generated $4.72 billion of the total revenues.

Optical Media.   IRMA reported a 75 percent increase in shipments of all writable optical disk media in 1996 over 1995. With 31.8 million units sold, the industry totaled $250.2 million that year. Included in the gains were shipments of 30 million CD-R (one-time recordable) media in 1996. The new blank CD-R discs entered the market primarily as a digital data storage media and by 1998 sales grew to 600 million units, an excess of 295 million units over original projections for that year. Amid predictions of falling CD-R prices and increased use of the discs for audio recording, forecasters anticipated $1.5 billion in CD-R sales by the year 2000 based on projected shipments of 1.3 billion disks.

In November of 1996, Sanyo-Verbatim CD Company announced the onset of Digital Versatile Disc (DVD) production in the first quarter of 1997. DVD, with the potential to store seven times the capacity of a CD-ROM, offered the options of 4.7 GB capacity (single side, single layer) and 8.5 GB capacity, (single side, dual layer) disc. A dramatic illustration of the storage advantage of DVD is its capacity to contain a full-length feature movie video on a single disc. New DVD-ROMs, when used for data storage, replace CD-ROM capacity by a ratio of 1 to 3. In direct competition with the new DVD technology, Terastor announced in early 1997 its developmental 4.75-inch disk capable of storing 20 gigabytes on one side—the equivalent of four feature-length movies. Also at that time, IBM developers designed prototype holographic storage devices known as volumetric holographic storage. The holographic technology employs light and three-dimensional space to store digital information.

Magnetic Disk Media.   Mounting foreign competition in the global computer disk market, particularly from China, dampened the otherwise encouraging developments in the early 1990s. With more than 60 factories manufacturing computer disks, China's growing prominence threatened to wrest market share from U.S. manufacturers in an industry already dominated by foreign manufacturers. Although disks made in China were inferior to those made in the United States during the mid-1990s, their effect on domestic disk prices was an unpleasant development for U.S. manufacturers after 1996. U.S. shipments of floppy diskettes that year reached a record high, with 1.86 billion units shipped, including 1.82 billion 3.5-inch media. The figures paralleled an event that occurred when shipments of 5.25-inch diskettes peaked at 650 million units ($318 million) in 1988.

Shipments declined steadily thereafter. Similarly, sales of 3.5-inch diskettes peaked in 1996, and accounted for over 96 percent of units shipped that year. By 1997 total diskette sales were down by 36.5 percent. The dollar volume of diskettes dropped from $557 million to $345 million.

Tape Media.   The blank tape industry as a whole suffered from setback as the 1990s drew to a close. The dollar volume of VHS tape shipments in the United States declined to $501 million by 1997 in the wake of an earlier decline in video tape prices at the retail level in the mid-1990s. The price cuts posed a formidable obstacle to future profit growth in the video tape market, despite a $2.2 billion market worldwide for blank VHS tape cassettes. Larger manufacturers with financial interests in businesses unrelated to blank video tape production successfully maneuvered the decline in profit margin with their larger cash reserves. The presence of these larger manufacturers intensified the competition, and they easily usurped market share from smaller, less diverse manufacturers who depended wholly on blank video tape production for revenue.

In 1998 the unit shipments of all types of blank tapes were in decline except 8mm video tapes which increased by 8 percent in 1997. The dollar volumes—even for 8mm—were down in all segments of the tape industry. According to a report by the International Recording Media Association (IRMA) the dollar volume of blank VHS cassettes were down by 10 percent, reflecting a 5 percent reduction in unit shipments. VHS pancake (large reel) sales declined in dollar value by 21 percent, reflecting a 2 percent decline in unit shipments, and 8mm tapes lost 4 percent in dollar volume. Audio tapes declined by 13 percent in dollar volume and 10 percent in unit sales. The entire blank tape segment of the industry declined to $1.19 billion, a 13.5 percent drop in 1997 alone. Analysts projected subsequent annual declines of 5 percent for audio tapes, accompanied by a flat market for video cassettes and camcorder tapes. Industry observers' appraisal of the potential market for the newer DATs—initially developed for audio playback and recording—led to predictions that the DAT segment of the recording tape market might expand rapidly. Projections called for sales of DATs to quadruple, from 5 million units sold in 1992 to 20 million units by 1996.

INDUSTRY LEADERS

TDK Corporation.   TDK Corporation, based in Tokyo, Japan, was the largest producer of blank media worldwide in 1999. Recording media sales accounted for 22 percent, or $1.31 billion, of TDK's total sales revenues of $5.89 billion. The figures reflected a 0.7 percent drop in sales, and TDK cited a highly competitive recording media market for decline.

Komag, Incorporated. Komag is the largest of the U.S.-based producers. Komag posted $328.9 million in revenues in 1998, primarily from the production of thin magnetic film disks. Unlike TDK, Komag's revenues are derived exclusively from the production of blank media. The company, based in San Jose, California, suffered from price erosion in the disk media market subsequent to 1997 when Komag sales topped $631 million. Komag, with factories in the United States and Asia, employed a workforce of 4,000 in 1998.

BASF Corporation. BASF Corporation of Mount Olive, New Jersey gained prominence in the magnetic and optical recording media industry by pioneering long-playing audio and video tapes. BASF Corporation is the U.S. subsidiary of BASF Group, a German conglomerate based in Ludwigshaafen. BASF maintains interests in pharmaceuticals, chemicals, cosmetics, and electronics. It was due to the backing and financial resources of the larger German parent corporation that BASF Corporation withstood the dramatic decline in retail prices of blank video tapes during the 1980s, even as smaller manufacturers ceded market share. BASF Corporation posted $7.52 billion in sales in 1998. BASF Information Systems is BASF Corporation's media manufacturing subsidiary.

WORKFORCE

The U.S. magnetic and optical recording media industry employed 21,291 people in 1997, representing a decrease of 3,409 from 1995. This decline was consistent with predictions by the U.S. Bureau of Labor in the early 1990s for the future of the industry's workforce. Forecasters maintained optimism overall, but identified several occupations that faced potentially severe declines in their proportional representation. From 1990 to 2005, the number of electronic assemblers and precision electronic equipment assemblers were expected to decline by 40 percent and 41 percent, respectively. Occupations that were anticipated to experience the greatest proportional growth were electronic engineers, salespeople, and electronic technicians, each of which were expected to increase by more than 29 percent. Of the 21,291 people employed in 1997, most were production workers; in 1997, there were 14,730 production workers employed in the blank recording media industry. The remainder of the industry's work force was composed of 6,651 salaried employees, or those performing managerial, technical, or administrative duties.

Typically, production workers are employed on a full-time basis; they average 3 percent fewer hours per year than production workers employed by other manufacturing industries. Production workers in the magnetic and optical recording media industry earned an average $13.75 per hour in 1997, a decline of 43 cents per hour from 1995. Salaried employees in 1997 averaged $60,643, nearly double the amount reported in 1990.

FURTHER READING

Dunn, Ashley. "The Quest for Surplus Memory." *New York Times,* 9 October 1996.

Fisher, Lawrence R. "3M Chases Dream of Building Better Disk." *The New York Times,* 11 March 1996.

Johnson, Ian, "Guilty Until Proven Innocent: Groups Representing Artists Are Pushing to Tax Blank Recording Media . . . ," *Computer Dealer News,* 30 November 1998.

"Komage Incorporated." *Hoover's Online,* 6 January 2000. Available at http://www.hoovers.com/co/capsule/2/0,2163,13912,00.html.

Nee, Eric. "Trillions of Bytes." *Forbes,* 24 March 1997.

Poland, Carrie A., "Product Profile: Audio Recording Media: Analog, Digital or Both?" *World Broadcast News,* 1 September 1998.

Statistics, 7 January 2000. Available at http://www.recordingmedia.com/statblank.html.

Statistics, 7 January 2000. Available at http://www.recordingmedia.com/statfloppy.html.

Statistics, 7 January 2000. Available at http://www.recordingmedia.com/cdrstat.html.

Statistics, 7 January 2000. Available at http://www.recordingmedia.com/marketOPfact.html.

"TDK Corporation." *Hoover's Online,* 6 January 2000. Available at http://www.hoovers.com/co/capsule/8/0,2163,54088,00.html.

U.S. Bureau of the Census. *Statistical Abstract of the United States: 1993.* Washington: GPO, 1996.

U.S. Department of Commerce. *Magnetic and Optical Recording Media Manufacturing 1997,* October 1999.

Ward's Business Directory. Detroit: Gale Research, 1997.

SIC 3699

ELECTRICAL MACHINERY, EQUIPMENT, AND SUPPLIES, NOT ELSEWHERE CLASSIFIED

This classification comprises establishments primarily engaged in manufacturing electrical machinery, equipment, and supplies, not elsewhere classified, including high-energy particle acceleration systems and equipment, electronic simulators, appliance and extension cords, bells and chimes, and insect traps.

NAICS CODE(S)

333319 (Other Commercial and Service Industry Machinery Manufacturing)

333618 (Other Engine Equipment Manufacturing)

334119 (Other Computer Peripheral Equipment Manufacturing)

INDUSTRY SNAPSHOT

Industries classified in the *Standard Industrial Classification Manual* as including products "not elsewhere classified" produce miscellaneous products that share a broadly defined similarity but rarely are produced by the same type of manufacturers. These "not elsewhere" classifications (usually abbreviated as NEC) are created to retain the integrity or homogeneity of other industry classifications, which otherwise would become muddled by the inclusion of products that are instead consigned to NEC industries. Consequently, NEC industries frequently include distinctly separate types of manufacturers, competing in entirely different markets, and manufacturing a diverse assortment of products.

SIC 3699: Electrical Machinery, Equipment, and Supplies, Not Elsewhere Classified includes various types of amplifiers, such as magnetic and pulse amplifiers, maser amplifiers, DC amplifiers, and differential and facsimile amplifiers, but excludes audio or video amplifiers. This category also includes various types of particle accelerators (also known as atom smashers), automatic garage door openers, scientific electronic equipment, electronic kits to be assembled by purchaser, and consumer electronic equipment. In the mid-1990s, this segment accounted for roughly 24 percent of the industry's shipments.

The products within the electronic teaching machines, teaching aids, trainers, and simulators category represented approximately 26 percent of the industry's shipments, primarily through the manufacture of electronic trainers and simulators. According to 1992 U.S. Census Bureau figures, electronic trainers and simulators accounted for $1.3 billion of the $4.9 billion generated by the entire product category, or 26 percent, a total largely derived from the manufacture of flight simulators.

The laser systems and equipment, except communication, product category includes laser designator/ranging equipment, laser instrumentation equipment such as laboratory alignment devices and surveying equipment, industrial laser equipment, and medical laser equipment. In the mid-1990s, this category accounted for roughly 16 percent of the industry's shipments.

The electrical products, NEC category includes a host of diverse products such as electric gongs, bells, and chimes; electric Christmas tree lighting sets; electric insect killers; electric fence chargers; and electric outboard motors for boats. The category represented approximately 11 percent of the industry's shipments.

The apparatus wire and cordage product category includes appliance cords manufactured primarily from purchased insulated wire for various household appliances, including electric irons, grills, and waffle irons. This category accounted for approximately 6 percent of the industry's shipments.

The smallest product category within the industry, ultrasonic equipment, except for medical and dental use, includes ultrasonic equipment manufactured for industrial applications, such as ultrasonic cleaners, drills, welders, and solderers. This category accounted for roughly 3 percent of the industry's shipments in the mid-1990s.

Although this classification includes a multitude of diverse products, the industry's core businesses—those products that generate the greatest amount of revenue for manufacturers—are the primary products from the three largest product categories. Accordingly, the miscellaneous electrical machinery, equipment, and supplies industry essentially includes manufacturers of consumer electronic products, particle accelerators, flight simulators, and laser equipment.

The majority of the products that constitute the industry's core businesses were added to its classification in 1987, when **SIC 3699: Electrical Machinery, Equipment, and Supplies, Not Elsewhere Classified** was reclassified. Added to the industry's classification were particle accelerators, flight simulators, laser equipment, and ultrasonic equipment, as well as other less significant products. The effect of this reclassification on the industry's revenue total was enormous. In 1986, the miscellaneous electrical equipment and supplies industry represented a $1.8 billion business. The following year, after reclassification, it represented a $5.1 billion business, and according to estimated figures, the value in 2000 will rise to $5.8 billion.

ORGANIZATION AND STRUCTURE

The miscellaneous electrical equipment and supplies industry became a much more densely populated industry following its reclassification in 1987. Prior to that year, approximately 700 companies in the United States were involved in manufacturing products ascribed to the industry. Once reclassified, the industry's roster nearly doubled to include 1,324 manufacturers and 1,379 individual manufacturing establishments, more than twice as many individual, separate manufacturing establishments as were in operation the previous year. From 1987 into the 1990s, however, the number of manufacturers in the industry declined, falling to 1,185 in 1990 and 912 by 1993. The downward trend was predicted to continue; 1999 estimates indicated approximately 500 existing companies in 1999.

During the 1980s the industry's sales volume rose steadily before and after the reclassification, but realized a greater rate of growth before being reclassified. From

1982 to 1986 aggregate revenue increased nearly 30 percent, more than twice as much as the percentage increase from 1987 to 1990. In 1990 the industry's sales volume reached $5.8 billion, an increase of $792.0 million from the total recorded in 1987. By 1994, however, the value of industry shipments had fallen to $5.1 billion.

In the mid-1990s individual manufacturing establishments in the industry averaged $6.2 million in annual revenue, about 65 percent of the sales volume generated by the typical manufacturing establishment in industries overall. Although generating less revenue than the industrywide average, electrical equipment and supply manufacturing plants had an investment per establishment in 1994 that was only 48 percent of that found in other industries. This highlighted the labor-intensive nature of the work and the relative ease of entry into the market for potential manufacturers. Despite this, the number of establishments in the industry dropped from over 1,300 in 1987 to about 800 in 1994; that number was predicted to drop again by half by the turn of the century.

Geographically, according to the most recent available figures, the bulk of the industry's manufacturing activity took place in California, which employed 19 percent of the industry's workforce and accounted for 22 percent of the industry's sales volume. With 158 manufacturing establishments, California contained the most manufacturing establishments of any one state, distantly followed by Florida, which contained 62 facilities. The third-greatest concentration of manufacturing establishments in the mid-1990s was in New York, with 59 facilities. Production facilities were located throughout the United States in the 1990s, with 36 states containing manufacturing establishments.

BACKGROUND AND DEVELOPMENT

Each product segment composing the miscellaneous electrical machinery and equipment industry possesses a history distinct from the other products grouped into this classification. For the most part, the manufacturers of these disparate product categories have little in common with each other and rarely compete in the same market. Manufacturers of flight simulators, for example, have little in common with manufacturers of automatic garage door openers and compete for market share in entirely different markets. Essentially then, the miscellaneous electrical machinery and equipment industry includes six smaller, subsidiary industries—three of lesser importance and three of greater importance—each of which has experienced different paths of development.

These subsidiary industries, however, do share one common thread; their products depend on electricity and a branch of science and engineering closely related to the science of electricity, electronics. Some of the products within the industry rely solely on electricity to operate, but generally these products are of lesser importance to the growth of the industry as a whole. Rather, many of the more important products that contribute significantly to the industry's growth rely on electronic technology, particularly those products added to the industry after the 1987 reclassification. Accordingly, without electrical power and, perhaps more important, without the emergence of electronics, the miscellaneous electrical equipment and supplies industry would not exist.

Before the electrical machinery industry could emerge as representing an appreciable portion of all manufacturing activity in the United States, sufficient electrical power capacity had to be developed. By the beginning of the twentieth century enough electrical power—2.2 billion kilowatt hours in 1902—was being generated in the United States to engender the electrical machinery industry as a viable sector of U.S. manufacturing. At that time, the electrical machinery industry accounted for roughly 1 percent of the total manufacturing activity in the country, a proportion that would increase to 4.5 percent by 1929 and reach 6.6 percent by the beginning of the 1960s. During those six decades of growth, the electrical machinery industry expanded more than six times as rapidly as did American industry as a whole, and the level of technological sophistication in the country increased sufficiently to encourage the production of electronic products in earnest.

In 1907 American inventor Lee De Forest ushered in the electronic age with his development of a three-electrode vacuum tube, which he called an "audion," making it possible to amplify weak radio signals and transmit them over long distances, a capability earlier vacuum tubes failed to provide. From this discovery, the world was introduced to the radio, creating a small but lucrative market for a new breed of manufacturer: the radio maker. These manufacturers flourished during the 1920s and 1930s, but their numbers began to dwindle as the United States neared involvement in World War II. Infused with orders from the U.S. government for electronic equipment to aid in the war effort, the electronic industry was buoyed for several years during the war, but at its conclusion the small group of electronics manufacturers still represented only slightly more than a fledgling industry, employing relatively few people, contributing a comparatively small amount to the national economy, and amounting to little more than $500.0 million at the factory level.

The industry's growth during its first 40 years of existence only appeared lackluster in retrospect, however, for in the 10 years following the war the industry expanded at a tremendous pace, becoming the fifth-largest industrial segment of the national economy by the late 1950s, employing more than one million people, and comprising more than 2,500 large and small manufacturers. By 1957 the industry's annual sales volume at the manufacturer level had increased 14 times in the previous 10 years, reaching $7.0 billion, considered at the time to be the most prolific growth rate in the shortest time span of any industry in U.S. history. This prodigious growth witnessed the development of many innovative electronic applications, which inspired a host of sophisticated products for commercial, industrial, and consumer use, including the primary products in the miscellaneous electrical machinery and equipment industry. During this decade, flight simulators, an assortment of consumer electronic products, particle accelerators, and lasers each emerged as substantial, revenue-generating products.

Two U.S. physicists, Arthur L. Schawlow and Charles H. Townes, first propounded the theory of the laser (an acronym for "light amplification by stimulated emission of radiation") in 1958, which was based on Townes' development of the maser ("microwave amplification by stimulated emission of radiation") roughly eight years earlier, when the electronics industry was beginning to expand exponentially. Two years after the idea was born, the first laser, a ruby laser, was constructed by Theodore H. Maiman in 1960. Particle accelerators, first developed by John D. Cockcroft and Ernest T.S. Walton in 1932, did not become commercially viable products until the 1950s, their evolution largely attributable to the work of Robert J. Van de Graaff and the company he helped found in 1946, High Voltage Engineering Corporation. During the 1950s a decade of enormous growth in the electronics industry, flight simulators also appeared as a commercially viable product, although they had been in existence for a number of years. Receiving a significant boost from their military applications during World War II, flight simulators gained the attention of the burgeoning commercial airline industry, creating an incentive for electronics manufacturers to convert their facilities to the production of simulators.

From the 1950s forward, the major product categories of the miscellaneous electrical machinery industry were generating appreciable amounts of revenue, albeit from different markets. By the late 1950s, there were eight manufacturers worldwide producing particle accelerators. The largest of these, Van de Graaff's High Voltage Engineering Corporation, controlled 40 percent of the $20 million global market. Although it was still a comparatively small market, industry pundits foresaw the market for particle accelerators increasing to nearly $80.0 million dollars by the mid-1960s. Their optimism stemmed from the various and remarkable industrial applications for particle accelerators, which were then beginning to overshadow their scientific contributions, or at least command more of the limelight.

Functioning as a machine that synthetically produced radiation energy, particle accelerators were used in various production processes, from sterilizing surgical sutures after they had been packaged to irradiating wire and cable insulation used in missiles and jet aircraft as well as other electronic gear exposed to high temperatures. Particle accelerators also could perform other feats, such as converting sawdust into digestible feed for livestock, transforming sugar into acid, and waterproofing shoe leather.

The main obstacle facing particle accelerator manufacturers as they entered the 1960s was the expensive nature of their business and the high price of their products. Some units sold for up to $150.0 million each, limiting the manufacturers' clientele to those businesses for which the high price tag and operating costs of accelerators were offset by their ability to perform a task that otherwise could not be completed. Consequently, there were only 250 particle accelerators in the world by the beginning of the 1960s, but prices were coming down rapidly as manufacturers augmented the world supply by producing 40 to 45 units per year.

As the push toward reducing the manufacturing cost and operating cost of particle accelerators progressed—the cost per kilowatt hour, for example, was cut in third in just two years—scientists also sought to construct bigger units. The bigger the accelerator, the greater the speed at which particles could be slammed against each other, providing scientists with more information about the basic laws of matter with each incremental increase in size and power. Particle accelerator power, measured by the number of electron volts produced by the accelerated particles, increased throughout the 1960s and 1970s, standing at 30.0 billion electron volts at the beginning of the 1960s, then increasing to 500.0 billion electron volts by the beginning of the 1970s. These and further advances in power and research broadened the particle accelerator's applicability for industrial and medical use, particularly in the form of powerful x-ray machines used to detect hidden flaws in metal castings, in the production of semiconductors, and to diagnose and treat cancer.

From the first primitive trainers manufactured in the 1940s by Singer-Link to the early 1990s, the market for flight simulators, marine simulators, and other electronic training devices remained a vital component of the miscellaneous electrical machinery and equipment industry, despite being heavily dependent on military spending, which has fluctuated dramatically since the emergence of simulators. Military sales, both to the U.S. government and to other countries, essentially created the industry during World War II and fueled its growth into the 1950s. The growth of the civilian aircraft industry and the airline industry during the 1950s added to this business. Yet another market segment for flight simulator manufacturers emerged during that decade, when the Soviet Union launched the world's first space satellite in 1957 and formally christened the Space Age. Thus, in quick succession three primary markets for the flight simulator industry were created, inducing a growing number of simulator manufacturers to replicate as best they could the rapid technological advancements taking place in the burgeoning aerospace industry.

The bulk of flight simulator manufacturers' space simulation business came soon after the Soviets launched their satellite, when the frenetic race to reach the moon began. In the early 1960s the U.S. government earmarked $65.0 billion to be spent over a seven-year period to win the race, $300.0 million of which simulator manufacturers could expect to garner. Initially, more 200 space simulators were ordered, as NASA sought to simulate each stage of a moon voyage.

While space simulators were intended to provide training for hypothetical equipment traveling in a hypothetical environment, flight simulators for military and civilian aircraft replicated existing aircraft and would prove to be the linchpin of simulator manufacturers' financial stability in the years to come. As the costs of operating aircraft increased dramatically, simulating the flight without having to pay for fuel and ground support— or risking the destruction of the plane— became a desirable alternative. Consequently, any significant decline in military spending usually had an insignificant effect on simulator manufacturers, since their products could be construed as cost-saving purchases. For the industry's commercial clientele, the same rationale held true, particularly during the energy crises in the early and mid-1970s. With the rising cost of fuel, many airlines opted for simulators to augment their traditional pilot and crew training. To be sure, simulator manufacturers were negatively affected by the usual economic exigencies, and their market was comparatively small, but their business was not affected as severely when economic conditions soured as were other manufacturers dependent on the aerospace industry.

Simulator manufacturers' role in the civilian aircraft industry received a tremendous boost in 1981, when the Federal Aviation Administration authorized the training of pilots by Braniff Airlines without its pilots recording any actual flight time. Instead, pilots trained in a 747 simulator manufactured by U.K.-based Rediffusion. With this edict, the simulator industry reached "total realism," spurring the industry's growth for the decade.

CURRENT CONDITIONS

As the 1990s neared its close, one product category that had been a traditional leader in the industry overall was predicted to fall behind in product shipments. Electronic teaching machines and trainers, which composed 27 percent of the industry as recently as 1992, were expected to fall behind electronic systems and equipment, NEC (including automatic garage door openers), and laser systems and equipment. The U.S. Census Bu-

reau predicted that by the late 1990s, electronic systems and equipment, NEC would be 28 percent of the industry; laser systems, 20 percent; and teaching machines and trainers would account for only about 17 percent.

Particle acceleration scientists and their allied industry got a boost in the late 1990s as the Large Hadron Collider appeared on track to be fully operational by the year 2005, three years ahead of schedule. The collider, which will represent a total cost of $6.0 billion by its completion, was predicted to be the most powerful accelerator ever built. Constructed at CERN, the European Organization for Nuclear Research, at their particle physics center near Geneva, the collider was to be funded by 19 member nations, including the United States.

The development of the Large Hadron Collider was some consolation to U.S. industry participants disappointed in the abandonment of the 54-mile-long particle accelerator known as the Superconducting Supercollider. Due to ballooning cost estimates, Congress voted to cancel the project in 1993—after more than $2.0 billion dollars had been spent to finish roughly 20 percent of the accelerator—and allotted $615.0 million to formally terminate construction.

Prognostications for flight simulator manufacturers generally were encouraging as the industry emerged from the economic recession of the early 1990s. Increases were predicted in the size of the world's aircraft transport fleet through the year 2005, which led industry observers to project a nearly 150 percent increase in the demand for full-flight simulators. In Asia and the Pacific regions, aircraft operators during this period were expected to require 200 percent more simulators than they possessed in 1992, while Western European aircraft operators were predicted to require 155 percent more simulators. Similar percentage increases were predicted by North American and Latin American operators. Driving this increased demand, which promised to expand the size of the simulator industry greatly, was a projected growth in demand for very-long-range aircraft, or those aircraft designed to fly distances greater than 5,500 nautical miles.

That scenario was not embraced wholly by the U.S. Census Bureau, however. It tracked an erosion of the market share of trainers and simulators as the 1990s progressed. That erosion was due at least partly to the growing strength of two other industry segments, electronic systems and equipment, NEC, and laser systems and equipment. Even discounting the gains of those segments, however, the trainer and simulator segment exhibited real declines in the 1990s. Its 1992 value of product shipments was $1.2 billion, about 27 percent of the entire industry's shipments. The segment's shipments dropped to $932.0 million in 1993, and to $840.0 million in 1994, about 18 percent of the total. The segment's $874.0 million value of 1995 shipments represented a resurgence, however, driven by new aircraft technologies requiring new simulators.

INDUSTRY LEADERS

To give an idea of the diversity of the industry, some of its leaders include the Stanley Works, Raychem, Coherent, Inc., Diebold, Inc., and Leviton Manufacturing Co., Inc. The Stanley Works, a $2.7 billion company best known for its tools, has an Air Tools Division, located in Mayfield Village, Ohio, which manufactures a variety of electric hand tools; the division has annual sales between $50.0 million and 100.0 million. Diebold, best known for its automated teller machines, is a leading manufacturer of "smart cards" that can be used, for example, on college campuses by students for a vaiety of transactions. The company, based in North Canton, Ohio, had annual sales in 1999 of $1.1 billion.

Raychem Corporation's Electronics Division, based in Menlo Park, California, manufactures resettable fuses as well as a variety of protective tubing and similar devises for electrical and electronic systems. The division accounts for $250.0-500.0 million in sales; the company's overall 1998 sales were $1.8 billion. Coherent, Inc., based in Santa Clara, California, manufactures lasers for medical, industrial, and scientific use. In fact, Coherent produces more than 150 types of lasers, for everything from drilling holes in printed circuit boards to delicate eye surgery to tattoo removal. The company had 1999 sales of $469.0 million.

Family-owned Leviton, based in Little Neck, New York, is best known as a manufacturer of electric light switches; it would be hard to find a home that does not contain several Leviton switches and plugs. The company, with estimated annual sales of around $800 million, also makes wiring, cable, and adapters.

WORKFORCE

In 1986, 24,700 people were employed by the industry, the majority of whom were employed as production workers. One year later, after the reclassification, the industry's payroll swelled to include 60,300 employees and comprised nearly as many salaried employees as production workers. Before the reclassification, approximately 75 percent of the industry's work force were employed as production workers, while the remaining 25 percent were employed as salaried workers performing administrative, technical, or managerial duties. After the inclusion of manufacturers involved in producing sophisticated, high-technology products the following year, the composition of the industry's work force was nearly evenly divided between the two types of employees, with 47 percent working as salaried employees and 53 percent employed in production.

Following the reclassification, which more than doubled the size of the industry's workforce, total employment declined, dropping to almost 40,000 in the mid-1980s. Production workers bore the brunt of the decline, as more than 12,000 lost their jobs by 1994. Estimates for 1999 indicate a workforce of 30,400 people, with only half that number in production.

Generally, production workers are employed on a full-time basis, working, in the mid-1990s, 6 percent fewer hours per year than the typical production worker, while earning slightly more per hour than the typical production worker. In 1989 production workers employed by all other manufacturing industries averaged $10.49 per hour, compared to the $10.50 per hour averaged by production workers employed by the miscellaneous electrical equipment and supplies industry. This hourly wage fell to $10.37 in 1994, compared to $12.09 industrywide. By 1999, according to estimates, the hourly wage was $11.81.

RESEARCH AND TECHNOLOGY

Some of the most striking research being done in the industry was in the area of particle physics. As the abandonment of the Superconducting Supercollider and the costs of the Large Hadron Collider made clear, advancements in atom smashing in the 1990s were stymied by the astronomical funding and expansive open spaces required to hurl atomic particles quickly enough through a tunnel. Eliminating the need for huge tunnels and their attendant cost occupied a number of researchers, who sought to create what essentially was a tabletop atom smasher. Researchers at the University of Michigan Center for Ultrafast Optical Science were able to generate and manipulate short, powerful laser pulses, which strip electrons from atoms to create a plasma of charged particles. The electric fields created focused the electrons into a tight beam. Using different methods, researchers at the University of California, Los Angeles, the University of Texas, and Argonne National Laboratory worked to achieve similar results.

Such focused beams that could be manipulated by users were predicted to make possible compact, relatively inexpensive devices, to replace or at least supplement their elephantine counterparts. However, the energy generated by the smaller prototypes in the late 1990s was far short of that generated by large supercolliders. At that time, smaller, less expensive accelerators found their abilities best suited to medical uses rather than to studying the nature of matter itself.

FURTHER READING

"Biggest Atom Smasher Rises on Illinois Prairie." *Engineering News-Record,* 6 August 1970.

Byrne, Harlan S. "Broadening Its Niche: Core Industries." *Barron's,* 6 May 1996.

Darnay, Arsen J., ed. *Manufacturing USA: Industry Analysis, Statistics, and Leading Companies,* 5th ed. Detroit: Gale Research, 1996.

Electronics Manufacturers Directory. Twinsburg, OH: Harris Publishing, 1994.

"Extra Zip for Atom Smashers." *Business Week,* 27 March 1981.

"First Industrial Laser Retired to Smithsonian." *Iron Age,* 24 September 1979.

Gutman, Walter K. "Atomic Alchemy." *Barron's,* 19 October 1959.

Hellemans, Alexander. "CERN Sets Sights on an Early LHC." *Science,* 3 January 1997.

"Hurrah for Second Thoughts." *The Economist,* 27 June 1970.

Kolcum, Edward H. "Gulf War Training Deficiencies to Dictate Future of Simulation." *Aviation Week & Space Technology,* 16-23 December 1991.

Macilwain, Colin. "Laboratories Collide Over Rival Tritium Scheme." *Nature,* 13 June 1996.

McKenna, James T. "Very-Long-Range Aircraft Seen Driving 150 Percent Rise in Simulator Demand." *Aviation Week & Space Technology,* 20 July 1992.

Moorman, Robert W. "From the Beginning." *Air Transport World,* August 1992.

Nordwall, Bruce D. "Airline Demand for Flight Simulators to Outstrip Growth in Transport Fleets." *Aviation Week & Space Technology,* 3 August 1992.

Peterson, Ivars. "Surfing a Laser Wave: Toward a Tabletop Particle Accelerator." *Science News,* 10 February 1996.

"Push for Biggest Atom Smasher." *Business Week,* 8 April 1961.

"Radiation for Industry." *Chemical Week,* 5 May 1962.

"Simulator Market to Stay Strong Despite Budget Cuts." *Aviation Week & Space Technology,* 12 November 1990.

"Tunnel Visions: Particle Physics." *The Economist,* 16 March 1996.

"Wanted: Bigger Atom Smashers." *Business Week,* 10 September 1960.

Whitehead, Ross. "Rapid Growth Ahead for Industrial Lasers." *Industry Week,* 28 April 1980.

TRANSPORTATION EQUIPMENT

SIC 3711

MOTOR VEHICLES AND PASSENGER CAR BODIES

This industry classification is comprised of establishments primarily engaged in manufacturing or assembling complete automobiles, trucks, commercial vehicles, and buses, as well as specialty motor vehicles intended for highway use such as ambulances, armored cars, hearses, fire department vehicles, snow plows, and tow trucks. This classification also includes establishments involved in manufacturing passenger car bodies and all types of vehicle chassis. Although some establishments within the industry also manufacture motor vehicle parts, establishments primarily involved in manufacturing motor vehicle parts (other than chassis and passenger car bodies) are classified in **SIC 3714: Motor Vehicle Parts and Accessories.**

Establishments primarily engaged in the manufacture of truck and bus bodies or in the assembly of completed trucks and buses on purchased chassis are classified in **SIC 3713: Truck and Bus Bodies.** Establishments primarily engaged in the manufacture of truck trailers are classified in **SIC 3715: Truck Trailers.** Other motor vehicle classifications include motor homes assembled on purchased chassis (**SIC 3716: Motor Homes**), motorcycles (**SIC 3751: Motorcycles, Bicycles, and Parts**), off-highway tractors (**SIC 3523: Farm Machinery and Equipment**), industrial tractors (**SIC 3537: Industrial Trucks, Tractors, Trailers, and Stackers**), combat tanks (**SIC 3795: Tanks and Tank Components**), and stamped passenger car body parts (**SIC 3465: Automotive Stampings**).

NAICS CODE(S)

336111 (Automobile Manufacturing)

336112 (Light Truck and Utility Vehicle Manufacturing)
336120 (Heavy Duty Truck Manufacturing)
336211 (Motor Vehicle Body Manufacturing)
336992 (Military Armored Vehicle, Tank, and Tank Component Manufacturing)

INDUSTRY SNAPSHOT

The motor vehicle industry represents one of the largest segments within the U.S. economy and forms the core of the nation's industrial strength. In 1998 an estimated 205 million vehicles were on U.S. roads. The U.S. motor vehicle manufacturing industry consisted of three American, two German affiliated, and seven Japanese affiliated manufacturers of light vehicles (LV) plus five large and approximately 100 medium and smaller assemblers of commercial vehicles. Collectively, the industry produced nearly 16 million vehicles in 1998.

On average, the industry generated one-sixth of all U.S. manufacturers' shipments of durable goods and consumed 30 percent of all iron, 15 percent of all steel, 25 percent of all aluminum, and 75 percent of all natural rubber purchased by U.S. industries. According to the U.S. Department of Commerce, on average, every dollar of manufacturing input in the United States allocated to producing motor vehicles added two and one-half dollars to the economy.

At the retail level in 1998, sales of motor vehicles exceeded $300 billion, or 3.5 percent of the nation's gross domestic product—the broadest measure of the nation's economic output. In 1997, sales totaled $293 billion. Through the third quarter of 1999, retail sales continued to be strong and were heading for record breaking levels.

ORGANIZATION AND STRUCTURE

Nine automakers formed a new trade association named *Alliance of Automobile Manufacturers.* The mem-

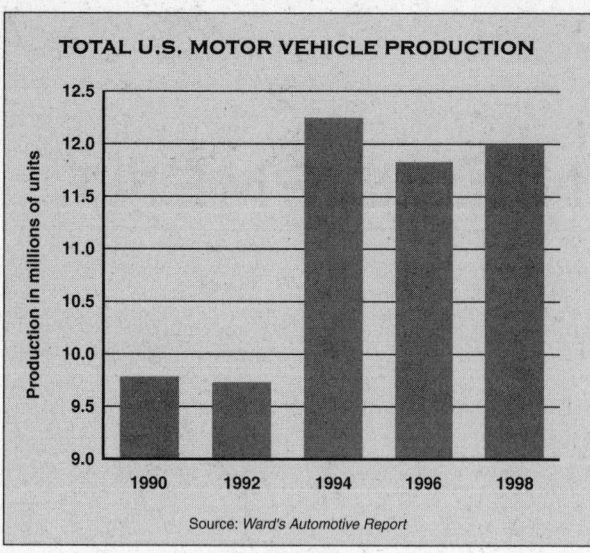

TOTAL U.S. MOTOR VEHICLE PRODUCTION

Source: Ward's Automotive Report

bers were General Motors Corporation and Ford Motor Company of the United States; DaimlerChrysler A.G., BMW A.G., and Volkswagen A.G. of Germany; A.B. Volvo of Sweden; and the Toyota Motor Corporation, the Mazda Motor Corporation and the Nissan Motor Company of Japan. This organization replaced the American Automobile Manufacturers Association (AAMA), which previously represented only American manufacturers. The goals of the group were to work together on public policy matters of common interest to provide credible industry information and data and seek consistent global regulatory standards.

Globalization of the automobile industry gave rise to the Alliance, which replaced the AAMA. The AAMA, formerly the Motor Vehicle Manufacturers Association (MVMA), was originally founded as the National Automobile Chamber of Commerce in 1915. Its purpose was to administer the cross licensing of patents, and during the 1930s, the organization established a code of fair competition.

BACKGROUND AND DEVELOPMENT

History of the Automobile. The modern automobile was not invented by one person. Many people in many nations contributed the ideas, inventions, and innovations required to assemble useful motor vehicles. Roger Bacon, the thirteenth-century English philosopher and scientist, prophesied its development. Leonardo da Vinci envisioned plans for its construction. Nicholas Joseph Cugnot constructed the first functioning self-propelled unit; Cugnot's vehicle, built in 1769, had three wheels and was powered with a steam engine. The first U.S. patent for a self-propelled vehicle was awarded to Oliver Evans by the state of Maryland in 1787. The newly organized Federal Patent Office awarded its first patent for a self-propelled landcarriage to Nathan Read in 1791. By 1891

the country had seen more than 100 renderings of motorized vehicles.

The first internal combustion engine was developed by the Belgian inventor, Etienne Lenoir. He used it to power a car during a demonstration in Paris in 1862. Nicholas Otto, a German inventor, developed a quieter, four-stroke, coal-gas engine in 1878. The first gasoline vehicles were developed in 1885 by two Germans working independently—Karl Benz and Gottlieb Daimler. The world's first motor vehicles built for commercial sale were offered in France by Armand Peugeot in 1889 and Panhard and Levassor in 1890. The French are also credited with coining the term "automobile," formed from two Latin words meaning self-moving.

During the early 1890s, many people in the United States were working separately on producing better "horseless carriages." According to some accounts two brothers—Charles and Frank Duryea of Springfield, Massachusetts—developed the first successful American gasoline automobile. The Duryea model was based on Benz's work as reported in *Scientific American*. Other contenders for the honor of producing the first American motor-car included Gottfried Schloemer of Milwaukee, Wisconsin; Henry Nadig of Allentown, Pennsylvania; Charles H. Black of Indianapolis, Indiana; and John W. Lambert of Ohio City, Ohio.

The 1890s brought commercial automobile production to the United States. Elwood Haynes and Edgar and Elmer Apperson were among the first entrepreneurs of the new technology. They built Haynes-Apperson vehicles in a machine shop located in Kokomo, Indiana. By 1899, 30 motor vehicle producers were offering electric, steam, and gasoline powered vehicles. The 1900 U.S. Census listed motor vehicle manufacturers under "Miscellaneous Manufactures."

Among the long list of early automotive pioneers, the best remembered is undoubtedly Henry Ford. Henry Ford built his first car, called a "quadricycle," in 1896. He established the Detroit Automobile Company in 1899—the venture failed. Ford's second company, the Henry Ford Company, founded in 1901, also failed. He finally achieved success with his third organization, the Ford Motor Company, officially founded on June 10, 1903.

Many other popularly known names in automotive history entered the industry during the last decade of the nineteenth century and the first decades of the twentieth century. Studebaker, originally a manufacturer of wagons, carriages, and horse-drawn vehicles, entered the automotive industry in 1897. Packard Motor Company was founded in 1899 and produced its first car in 1900. Ransom Eli Olds established the Olds Motor Vehicle Company in 1897; the company was later reorganized to form the Olds Motor Works, and by 1904 Olds was producing 5,000

"Olds-mobiles" annually. Cadillac Motor Car was established in 1902 with the help of financial backers who abandoned Henry Ford's earlier efforts. Buick Motor Car Company was founded by David D. Buick in 1903 and was later sold to William Durant, the founder of General Motors. Louis Chevrolet, born in Switzerland, came to the United States in 1905 and began his automotive career as a race car driver for Buick. Walter P. Chrysler purchased his first car in 1908. Following a career at Buick Motor Car Company, he assumed the presidency of the Chrysler Corporation, formed from the remnants of the Maxwell Motor Car Company on June 6, 1925.

Industry Growth. Throughout the early decades of the twentieth century, Henry Ford dominated the industry. He achieved nearly legendary status by introducing the automotive industry to the benefits of automated production and by providing an automobile at a price that most people could afford. In 1908, Ford decided to focus his company's efforts on the construction of only one model—the Model T. To help lower costs and speed production, he began moving toward assembly line production.

In 1913 a moving belt was installed in Ford's magneto department. (A magneto was a part that provided the electric current required for ignition.) After its installation, the moving belt enabled each worker to perform a single task rather than assemble a completed magneto. Production experienced a four-fold increase, and Ford transferred moving assembly lines to other parts of the plant. In its first complete year of assembly line production, the company built 248,000 cars—compared with 78,000 the previous year. In 1915, Ford's annual production reached 500,000 and prices fell. The 1912 Model T sold for $600, the 1914 Model T cost $490, a 1915 touring car cost $440, and the price of the 1925 model dropped to $290. By 1920, an estimated three-fifths of U.S. cars and 50 percent of all the cars in the world were Model Ts. Although its sales diminished as consumers turned to more modern offerings, the Model T earned its place in history. When Model T production was halted in 1927, an estimated 11 of every 20 cars on American roads were Model Ts; fifteen million units had been sold. No other single model surpassed Model T sales until the 1960s, when the record went to the Volkswagen Beetle.

During the mid-1920s, the automobile market became saturated. To bolster sales, auto manufacturers aimed their marketing efforts at creating two-car families. To help families make purchases more quickly, they offered financing, and an estimated 75 percent of all new cars were purchased on installment in 1925. By 1929 motor vehicles had been driven a total of 198 billion miles, and the average motorist logged 7,500 miles per year.

Auto sales dropped in 1929—an indication of the coming Depression. As the 1930s opened, auto output was down 37 percent. Production in 1931 tumbled 30 percent. The auto industry fell from first place, as measured according to the value of products sold, to fourth in the national economy, and its decline created a ripple effect throughout the nation's entire economic infrastructure. Auto makers, however, were among the first to emerge from the Depression years. By 1936, for example, General Motors was close to its pre-Depression profits.

The late 1930s brought technical innovations to the automotive industry. Automatic transmissions became common, increased precision enabled manufacturers to produce better cars, and attention to styling and aerodynamics improved stability and fuel efficiency. Post-Depression era work projects also improved the nation's highway system, and the mileage of paved roads more than doubled between 1933 and 1941. The Pennsylvania Turnpike opened in 1940, and although initial estimates projected the toll road would carry 715 vehicles per day, within two weeks 26,000 vehicles were using the new roadway each day.

Post World War II Period. When World War II arrived, the nation refocused its attention on producing items for the war effort; civilian car production stopped in 1942. One of the most popular cars developed for military use was the "Jeep." Although not all historians agree, some contend that the name "Jeep" was coined from the initials GP—taken from the military lexicon where the "General Purpose Vehicle" had become a "GP." After the war's end, the Jeep was redesigned for civilian use and designated a "Civilian Jeep" or "CJ" model.

American auto makers found an eager market in the post-war years. One-half of the nation's 25.8 million registered cars were ten or more years old, and people were ready to purchase new cars. Between 1946 and 1950, 21.4 million new cars were sold. Production in 1949 topped the five million mark for the first time since the pre-Depression era. The dominance of car and truck transportation was further assured in 1958 when the National Highway Act was passed. This legislation provided funds for significant construction to improve the nation's highway system.

During the 1950s a car's appearance assumed greater importance. Car buyers preferred big and powerful vehicles, which resulted in advertising that emphasized engine horsepower. Ornamental tail fins, inspired by aircraft fuselages, were first incorporated into a Cadillac design and came to symbolize cars of the era. Technical developments included power steering, power brakes, and improvements in automatic transmissions—all necessary to help control large cars.

Modernization of the Motor Vehicle Industry. By the 1960s the new car market was saturated. Manufacturers relied on promotions and annual model changes to boost sales. The market was dominated by the "Big Three" (Chrysler, Ford, and General Motors) and American Motors Corporation, which had been formed following the merger of two independent producers—Hudson and Nash—in the post-war years. Imported cars, led by the Volkswagen Beetle, began to make an impact on the American market during this period. In 1968, 10 percent of all auto sales were captured by foreign manufacturers. The two largest Japanese manufacturers, Toyota and Nissan (Datsun), had entered the U.S. market during the late 1950s and saw rapid growth during the 1960s. By 1970 Toyota was the nation's number two import; Datsun was number three. That year imports accounted for 15 percent of the U.S. passenger car market.

In addition to increased competition, the 1960s brought rising criticism to the auto industry. Ralph Nadar's *Unsafe at Any Speed: The Designed-in Dangers of the American Automobile* was published in 1965 and inaugurated a crusade for safer cars. In 1966 Congress passed the National Traffic and Motor Vehicle Safety Act, which mandated improvements in passenger safety, driver visibility, and braking. The Act also required public announcement of recalls to correct safety defects. During the first ten years of regulation, 52 million cars and trucks were recalled. Safety was not the only arena for critics; cars were also identified as a source of air pollution. In 1965 Congress passed the Vehicle Air Pollution and Control Act setting mandatory pollution standards. The 1970s opened with another anti-pollution effort—Congress passed the Clean Air Act, which mandated a 90 percent reduction in auto emissions within six years.

Concerns about fuel efficiency dominated the 1970s. In 1973, General Motors' cars averaged less than 12 miles per gallon, and other domestic car makers offerings were only slightly better. Two oil crises during the decade brought the nation increased gas prices, local shortages, a 55 miles per hour speed limit, and federally mandated fuel efficiency. The Energy Policy and Conservation Act, passed in 1975, specified that car manufacturers must meet a sales weighted "Corporate Average Fuel Economy" (CAFE) standard of 20 miles per gallon by the 1980 model year and 27.5 miles per gallon by the 1985 model year.

During the early 1980s, domestic auto makers found themselves unprepared for the sudden surge in the small car market, and as a result, they lost substantial ground to imports. A growing sense that the products coming out of Detroit were inferior to those of imports further exacerbated the slide of the domestic automotive manufacturers. Chrysler wavered on the brink of bankruptcy and secured a federal loan guarantee of $1.5 billion to survive. A resurgence during the middle of the decade failed to provide long term stability. The auto industry achieved record sales of 16.3 million units in 1986, but new light

vehicle sales fell in four out of the five years between 1986 and 1991. In 1990 the Big Three reported combined losses of $1.1 billion, and General Motors was in particularly bad shape. During 1991 U.S. production facilities operated at only 60 to 65 percent of their capacity. In 1991, sales of cars and trucks totaled $189 billion, representing 3.3 percent of the nation's gross domestic product (GDP).

U.S. auto makers' profitability suffered during the economic slowdown of the late 1980s and early 1990s, but vehicle sales during 1992 and 1993 indicated that the industry was rebounding. In the fall of 1993, *Fortune* reported that domestic production was up 6 percent. Lower costs and improved productivity helped bolster the industry's profit picture. Cars were manufactured more efficiently, and manufacturing processes had less environmental impact.

Environmental concerns, however, continued to influence the industry. California introduced stringent clean air standards in 1990. The legislation required auto makers to begin offering Zero Emission Vehicles (ZEV) in 1998. The regulations also called for incremental increases in the percentage of ZEV cars sold—beginning with 2 percent in 1998, moving to 5 percent in 2001, and expanding to 10 percent by 2003. Other states were considering adopting California-style legislation. Moreover, the federal government continued to insist on compliance with the CAFE standards previously established by the Energy Policy and Conservation Act.

New passenger cars were required to average 27.5 miles per gallon, and light trucks needed to average 20.2 miles per gallon. Non-compliance by a manufacturer brought penalties of as much as $7,700 per vehicle. According to Environmental Protection Agency (EPA) statistics, the U.S. passenger car fleet averaged 26.9 miles per gallon in 1992; U.S. light trucks averaged 20.4 miles per gallon. Imported passenger cars averaged 29 miles per gallon, and imported light trucks averaged 22.4 miles per gallon.

Some critics in the industry charged that fuel efficiency standards were contradictory to safety requirements. The Coalition for Vehicle Choice (CVC) was formed to counter legislative attempts to increase CAFE requirements to 40 miles per gallon. The CVC argued that high CAFE standards reduced the availability of family-sized vehicles and impeded efforts aimed at enhancing auto safety. To speed efforts at increasing vehicle safety, Congress passed the Intermodal Surface Transportation Efficiency Act in 1992. Its requirements included the installation of driver and front seat air bags in passenger cars by 1998 and in trucks, minivans, and sport/utility vehicles by 1999. The legislation also established rules concerning rollovers, brakes, child booster seats, head injury protection, and side impact protection.

Another issue facing domestic auto makers during the early 1990s was the continued impact of foreign competition. Entering the mid-1990s, however, the Japanese manufacturers were on the defensive. "Why are the Big Three suddenly so hot?," asked *Business Week* in 1993. "'One reason is that the yen has risen sky-high,' notes Chrysler Corp. President Robert A. Lutz, 'and exchange rates are really working against Japanese companies big time.' Quality of the domestic fleet is also way up, Buy American sentiment is strong, and slumping profits are forcing the Japanese to raise prices to boost margins." The magazine also noted that, contrary to past recoveries, the Big Three are showing restraint in their pricing strategies. Another factor is that "major new product launches should keep customer interest high." In 1994, *Fortune* noted that General Motors, Ford, and Chrysler all introduced new small and intermediate size cars.

Still another reason for the success enjoyed by General Motors, Ford, and Chrysler was in the realm of truck sales. As *Automotive Industries* observed in May 1994, "trucks are the single biggest reason the Big Three are re-capturing market share. The numbers tell the story. While car sales increased 312,000 units in 1993, truck sales shot up by 725,000 units—more than twice as much. And the Japanese automakers collectively sell less than 10 percent of the trucks sold in America." While the quality of the American products is one reason for their success, America's 25 percent tariff on imported trucks was another important factor.

In 1993 General Motors, Ford, and Chrysler sold 14.2 million cars and trucks—the most since 1989 and a figure indicative of the turnaround the three Detroit-based automakers have enjoyed in the early 1990s. By the first quarter of 1994, Chrysler was posting a profit per vehicle sold in North America of $1,203, while Ford tallied $656 of profit for every vehicle sold, and General Motors posted $355 of profit for every car sold.

Minivan sales represented one of the fastest growing market segments in the United States and Europe. *Business Week* estimated U.S. minivan sales at 1.1 million units. Annual sales were forecast to increase substantially. Offering affordability to the public with price ranges of $14,000 to $28,000, the manufacturers realized increased profit margins.

CURRENT CONDITIONS

The end of the century saw abundant activity involving automotive company mergers. The era of the U.S. "Big Three" ended on November 12, 1998. Germany's Daimler-Benz A.G. and Chrysler Corporation merged to form DaimlerChrysler A.G., the largest foreign takeover of a U.S. firm in history. The merger created the world's third-largest automaker in terms of revenue.

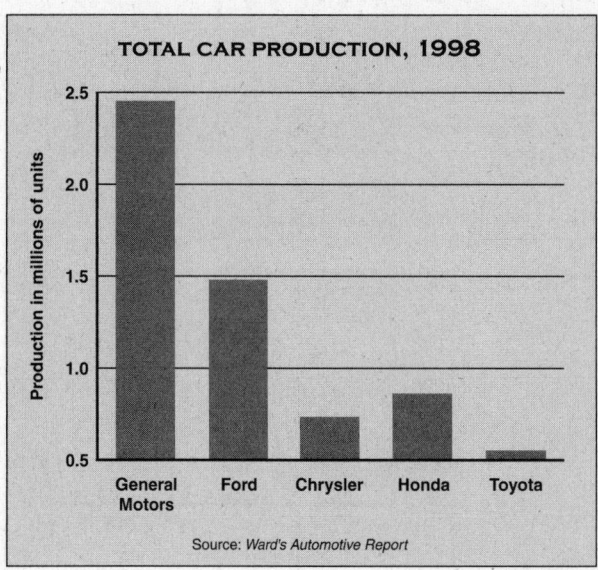

TOTAL CAR PRODUCTION, 1998

Source: *Ward's Automotive Report*

In March 1999, Ford Motor Company purchased Volvo's car operation, adding nearly 400,000 units to Ford's car volume. This acquisition, along with their outright ownership of the British line of Aston Martin and Jaguar and 33.4 percent ownership of Mazda, strengthened Ford's presence.

General Motors took a 50 percent share of the Swedish manufacturer Saab Automobiles A.B., adding it to the 49 percent it held of Isuzu Japan, and its full ownership of Opel, which demonstrated the automaker's focus on global markets.

In 1998, car and light truck sales totaled 15.55 million units. The totals comprised of cars, sport utility vehicles (SUVs), pickup trucks, and vans were an increase of 2.8 percent over 1997 levels. Light truck sales rose 8.1 percent for 1998, while car sales fell 1.6 percent for the same period.

Market share of light trucks in the United States was approaching parity with cars' share. The transition of the light truck from a business and commercial product to a model designed for personal transportation helped to increase its popularity in the U.S. market. Automakers themselves increased attention toward truck projects. With lower CAFE (Corporate Average Fuel Economy) requirements on those vehicles, they produced more V-8 powered trucks and benefited from the high profit margins of $5,000 to $15,000 per truck.

The late 1990s experienced the beginning of changes in the way automakers looked to manufacture cars and trucks. Depending on big suppliers to provide larger and more complete chunks of each vehicle, instead of hundreds of pieces that need to be bolted together, automakers will be changing the process of assembly in plants. Changes in this procedure indicated that the automakers were on track to reach productivity gains in the assembly plants.

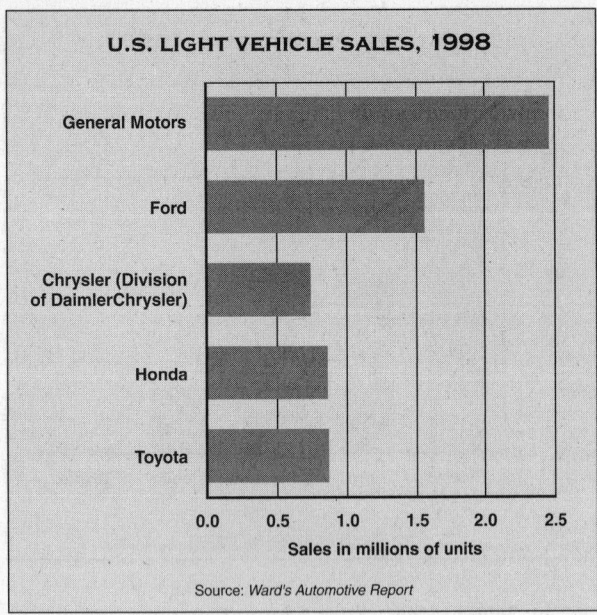

U.S. LIGHT VEHICLE SALES, 1998

General Motors

Ford

Chrysler (Division of DaimlerChrysler)

Honda

Toyota

0.0   0.5   1.0   1.5   2.0   2.5

Sales in millions of units

Source: *Ward's Automotive Report*

In 1998 GM reported revenues of $161.3 billion. Its sale of 2,458,688 cars took a 30.2 percent share of the U.S. market and its sale of 2,116,153 light trucks held a 28.6 percent share of the market.

Ford Motor Company. The second largest auto manufacturer in the United States and in the world in the late 1990s was the Ford Motor Company. In 1998 Ford sold 1,559,190 cars for a 19.2 percent market share and 2,301,077 light trucks for a 31.1 percent market share. Taurus has been one of the best selling cars in the United States, and the Ford F150 pickup has been the best selling truck. Ford represented the corporation's largest division over the Lincoln and Mercury lines. In 1998 the company reported revenues of $144.4 billion.

The Ford Motor Company was established in 1903 by Henry Ford, whose early models bore alphabetic designations. His first offering, the Model A, was introduced in 1903, and the company introduced the Model C the following year. Looking for a car with mass appeal that could be produced at a low cost, Ford continued making innovations. The Model N was introduced for the 1906 and 1907 season and boasted speeds up to 45 miles per hour and a fuel economy of 20 miles per gallon. It sold for $600. The Model N was followed by an upgraded Model R and a refined Model S. Arguably the most famous car in automotive history, Ford's Model T was introduced for the 1908 and 1909 season. Ford's ninth model in six years, the Model T achieved nearly legendary status and dominated the industry for 18 years.

DaimlerChrysler A.G. Formed by Chrysler's acquisition of Germany's Daimler-Benz in 1998, DaimlerChrysler is the number three car maker with 1998 sales of $15.46 billion. Their brands include Dodge, Eagle, Jeep, and Plymouth. Daimler was best known for luxury sedans. The company employed 441,500 people in 1998.

Another area still in its infancy at the close of the twentieth century was the use of the Internet. Eighty-one percent of online shoppers, while using the Internet to gather information, preferred hands-on contact when purchasing an automobile. Only 8 percent indicated that they would buy a vehicle unseen. At that time, the retail purchase of an automobile over the Internet was not the most preferred method.

In 2000, General Motors planned to offer limited Internet access to some of their car lines. Through software and the optional *On-Star* security system, motorists could receive electronic messages and sports, news, and weather information from the system.

Ford Motor Company and Oracle Corporation formed a joint venture (*Auto Exchange*) in November 1999 that would create an Internet network with suppliers. A first in the automotive industry, the venture would be the largest business to business electronic network in the world.

INDUSTRY LEADERS

General Motors. In 1998, the world's largest full line vehicle manufacturer was General Motors Corporation (GM). GM offered domestic automobiles under the nameplates Chevrolet, Pontiac, Oldsmobile, Buick, Cadillac, GMC Truck, and Saturn. International products included Opel, Vauxhall, Saab, Lotus, and Isuzu.

General Motors was incorporated in 1908 by William C. Durant. Its first components were Oldsmobile and Buick. The company acquired two more manufacturers in 1909—Oakland and Cadillac—and between 1910 and 1920, Durant obtained more than 30 companies. The unit that would go on to become GM's largest division, Chevrolet, was acquired in 1918.

WORKFORCE

Strong growth in the light truck market helped to stabilize employment in the late 1990s. Another factor was fluctuations in currency, which encouraged foreign manufacturers to move their production to North America.

Efforts by the automakers to control costs had them looking to productivity gains. Agreements with the unions guaranteed a reduction to the workforce. Auto companies were only required to hire one employee for every two that retired. As the move to make suppliers responsible for large sections of autos takes shape, the need for the number of workers to assemble them declines.

Employment in the auto industry was predicted to remain stable through the early years of the new century with an increase in hiring in 2003, providing that there is not a recession in the economy.

Unions in the Automotive Industry. The United Auto Workers (UAW) union represents many employees within the automotive industry. In 1999 there were 770,000 active and nearly 1.5 million retired union members. The largest employer of UAW members was General Motors. Organization of auto workers began in the post-Depression era. During the Depression, growing labor unrest resulted as companies cut workers' pay, shortened work weeks, fired people irrespective of their seniority, and rehired only younger workers. Workers also expressed job dissatisfaction as companies increased the pressure to speed productivity. In 1933 Congress passed the National Industrial Recovery Act, which gave labor the right to organize and bargain collectively. Although the act was declared unconstitutional in 1935, the rights to bargain collectively and insure union elections were again secured when Congress passed the Wagner-Connery Act (Wagner Act), establishing the National Labor Relations Board.

In 1936, the American Federation of Labor (AFL) granted the United Automobile Workers of America its charter. The union later became the United Automobile, Aerospace and Agricultural Implement Workers (UAW) and was affiliated with the Committee for Industrial Organizations (CIO). Ford was the last of the major auto producers to bargain with the UAW. Elections were held at the Ford Rouge plant in 1941 following years of sometimes violent conflict between union organizers and anti-union forces. Union activity increased following World War II as auto production resumed. Workers joined together to maintain pay levels achieved during the war. Walter Reuther, the UAW's leader, fought for wage packages with a cost of living index and pension plans.

Current Contracts. The year 1999 brought on new contract negotiations that ended with new pacts. The agreements were for four years, one year longer than the traditional three-year pacts. Workers were to receive annual raises of three percent for three years and a signing bonus of $1,350. The 1999 base pay of assembly line workers was $20.69 per hour, including cost of living allowance.

As was in previous contract years, an automaker is chosen and their deal is used as a pattern for negotiations with the other automakers. DaimlerChrysler was the first to reach an agreement with the UAW in 1999. A clause in that contract barring auto companies from spinning off or selling divisions was expected to be a major problem with the Ford negotiations.

In early 1999, General Motors had made announcements about upgrading various plants and building new ones in the United States. Those announcements ended union complaints that General Motors would rather invest overseas. GM reached agreement with the UAW

shortly after the DaimlerChrysler accord. Both agreements allowed for a reduction in the workforce. General Motors was required to replace only one of every two workers retiring until levels reached 80 percent of a preset number. Due to this, General Motors would be able to delay mass hiring until 2002 or 2003—after a large wave of retirement of current workers.

The biggest obstacle in the 1999 negotiations were the differences in the auto companies' spinning off or selling divisions. Ford wanted to reduce the work it does itself in making vehicles. Work done at Ford factories accounts for about 38 percent of the value of its vehicles, more than 33 percent at General Motors and DaimlerChrysler A.G., and 25 percent at Honda Motor Company and the Toyota Corporation.

The key compromise at Ford was when the two sides signed off on a spin-off of the company's Visteon parts unit. The union agreed to the spin-off of Visteon as an independent under the condition that the UAW members at the plants remain Ford employees.

AMERICA AND THE WORLD

In 1991 the U.S. Department of Commerce estimated that 54.4 million motor vehicles were produced worldwide, an indication of its presence in all corners of the world. Indeed, the automobile industry, almost from its inception, has been international in scope. Ford began assembly in Britain in 1911 and by 1914 was the largest British producer. General Motors established an export company in 1911 to sell the company's products overseas. Following World War I, Ford built assembly plants in Denmark, France, Germany, Italy, Spain, and Sweden. General Motors purchased existing corporations such as Vauxhall in Britain and Opel in Germany. Ford and General Motors entered the Japanese market in 1925 and 1927 respectively. And Chrysler established Chrysler de Mexico in 1938 to import and distribute Chrysler products.

The first foreign companies to sell products in the United States offered luxury and sport models such as Rolls-Royce, Mercedes, Jaguar, and Porsche. In 1950, import sales totaled less than 50 percent of total car sales. The first foreign car to penetrate the mainstream market with a small family car was the Volkswagen Beetle. By 1968, Volkswagen accounted for 62 percent of all imports, but the German manufacturer began losing ground to Japanese producers.

At the same time, Japanese manufacturers were battling difficult exchange rates in their efforts to sell cars and trucks in America. The result was a decreased U.S. market share for Japanese companies in the early 1990s. "In 1993, for the second straight year, their share of the U.S. market for cars and light trucks fell—this time to 23.2 percent, off 2.6 points since 1991," noted *Business Week*. "Beleaguered by the strong yen and deep slumps in the Japanese and European auto markets, Japan's car companies are sounding ever more content to back off the market-share race.'' Japanese manufacturers have nonetheless attempted to address the mid-1990s environment, cut into overhead costs, introduce new models in areas of traditional weakness such as minivans, and shift production increasingly to facilities in America, where production costs are lower.

The strategy of Japanese automakers to produce locally high-volume, lower cost vehicles has had a direct effect on the steady decline of U.S. vehicles imported from Japan. In 1996 imports totaled 1.2 million units and 1997 levels increased to 1.4 million—worth $23.6 billion. Even with the 15 percent increase over 1996 levels, the amount was well below the peak of 3.6 million units in 1986. Retail sales of cars imported from Japan increased 9 percent in 1997, and imported light trucks saw retail sales grow by 33 percent.

German manufacturers began production in the United States in 1995. BMW, Bayerische Motoren Werke A.G., produced 11,877 cars its first year at the Spartanburg, South Carolina, plant. Production for 1996 increased to 50,278 and 1997 saw a 25 percent gain over the previous year to 62,943 vehicles. Mercedes-Benz's production of light trucks at its Vance, Alabama, plant began with 1997 production of 19,462 units. Production at the plant was geared for 65,000 units in 1998 to 80,000 in 1999.

United States-Japan Automotive Framework Agreement. In August 1995 the United States-Japan Automotive Framework Agreement came into being. The five year agreement, which culminated two years of intensive negotiations, was crafted to increase U.S. and other foreign access to the Japanese motor vehicle and parts market. According to the U.S. Department of Commerce, the three main goals of the Agreement were: improved access to Japan's motor vehicle distribution system; increased purchases of U.S. parts by Japanese automakers; and deregulation of Japan's $60 billion replacement parts market.

Initially, 1996 sales of Big Three vehicles in Japan increased, though they were still short of U.S. automaker's goals. U.S. exports to Japan dropped more than 14 percent in 1997 to $1.6 billion. The economic crisis in Asia plummeted the U.S. domestic automakers' exports even more in 1998.

NAFTA. Within the U.S. market, analysts expected increased exports for the revitalized domestic producers, in part because of the passage of the North American Free Trade Agreement (NAFTA), which in its first few months pushed a dramatic surge in U.S. car sales to Mexico. In keeping with the Clinton Administration's policy to open foreign markets for the U.S. automotive industry, NAFTA was signed in 1993 and implemented on January

1, 1994. Increased market access for U.S. automotive products in Mexico was imperative, especially since trade in motor vehicles was essentially one way—from Mexico into the United States. In the years since the implementation of NAFTA, the U.S. automotive industry experienced significant benefits. In 1994, U.S. passenger car and light truck exports tripled pre-NAFTA levels. In 1995, U.S. exports of motor vehicles were more than twice their pre-NAFTA levels, despite the severe economic crisis in Mexico.

Shipments to Mexico in 1996 increased more than 225 percent for the year—totaling nearly $1.3 billion; in 1997 the value of shipments grew to almost $2 billion. The effect of NAFTA on U.S. and Canadian trade was not significant due to the fact that trade between both countries had already been very open with little or no tariffs.

Korea's Memorandum of Understanding. In 1993, the U.S. automotive industry requested assistance from the Clinton Administration to open the Korean auto market to U.S. automobiles. In September 1995, the Korean government signed a Memorandum of Understanding (MOU) with the United States, under which it explicitly committed to increase access for U.S. and other foreign passenger vehicles. On October 20, 1998 negotiators from the Department of Commerce and the White House Office of U.S. Trade reached an agreement with South Korea that substantially improved on the previous agreement. In addition to passenger cars, coverage was extended to minivans and sport utility vehicles. Burdensome South Korean standards and procedures were reduced along with the tax on motor vehicles. It also introduced a system of secured financing to facilitate the purchase of U.S. vehicles and committed the South Korean government to a publicity campaign to improve perceptions of foreign automobiles.

According to *The Detroit News,* Korean car manufacturers were in turn increasing their presence in the U.S. market. Following Hyundai's entrance, Kia was the other car company to lead a wave of Korean car makers including Daewoo Motor, which planned to enter the U.S. market in the fall of 1997; Samsung Group, which was just entering the auto manufacturing arena and had plans to enter the U.S. market by the turn of the century; and Ssang Yong Business Group, parent of Ssang Yong Motor, which had planned to enter the U.S. market in 1998 with a sports utility vehicle. These South Korean vehicles performed well in the U.S. market even though their designs were for their home market and were smaller than the majority of vehicles in the United States.

GATT. In 1994, the Clinton Administration passed the Uruguay Round of the General Agreement on Tariffs and Trade (GATT). According to the U.S. Department of Commerce, the Agreement greatly enhanced the export potential of the U.S. automotive industry by improving access to both major and developing markets by achieving a 27 percent reduction in the motor vehicle tariffs of major markets, a 58 percent reduction in the automotive parts tariffs of major markets, and the "binding" of automotive tariffs in many developing countries—including Brazil, Argentina, India, and Indonesia. The U.S. automotive industry experienced positive export results since the January 1995 implementation of the Uruguay Round, especially with developing markets. The Asian monetary crisis stunted any potential growth in the latter 1990s, but automakers continued to eye these markets for the twenty-first century.

Agreement on Global Technical Regulations. In March 1998 negotiators agreed on a global means for governments to develop and harmonize regulations on motor vehicles' design and performance. While offering an opportunity for the cooperative development of safety and environmental regulations (through globally uniform governmental technical regulations), it provided a predictable framework for a global automotive industry. Established under the auspices of the United Nations Economic Commission, the negotiators had consisted of representatives from the United States, Japan, and the European Community.

RESEARCH AND TECHNOLOGY

In the fierce competitive environment of the international automotive industry, any edge in design, engineering, or technology assumes tremendous importance and can result in shifts of market share worth millions of dollars. Timely research and swift technological adaptation are vital in a wide array of automotive niche markets.

A typical example of this dynamic can be seen through an examination of the diesel pickup truck market. Until recently, Ford enjoyed a huge edge in market share in diesel pickups—approximately 12 percent of the total sales of pickups in the United States. Ford's position, however, fell from a commanding 75 percent stake to around 40 percent in 1994. As the *Detroit Free Press* noted, "Ford owned the market for most of the '80s. General Motors had developed a lousy reputation for diesel engines when it tried to convert gasoline engines into diesels for passenger cars during the late '70s. And Chrysler only became a player in the diesel market in 1987 when it began buying diesel engines from Cummins. With the much-revered Cummins engine under the hood, Dodge quickly began taking diesel market share from Ford. Its penetration peaked at 36 percent in 1991, just as GM came back with a new turbo-charged 6.5-liter engine for its diesel trucks. . . . Now Ford, having stood by while its lead all but evaporated, is out with the latest advancement, a massive 7.3-liter turbo-charged, direct-injection diesel from Navistar that gives it a competitive edge in horsepower, hauling and

fuel economy." Thus, the search for the competitive advantage in technology and design remains a central bulwark of the industry mentality.

As the automotive industry entered the 1990s, private industrial research and government funded research focused on improving fuel efficiency, developing alternative fuels, reducing vehicle emissions, developing environmentally friendly manufacturing processes, and recycling junked vehicles. Alternative fuels, such as ethanol and methanol mixtures, liquid natural gas (LNG), and liquid petroleum gas (LPG) were under investigation as clean burning energy sources. Researchers were also working on developing a viable electric car.

The U.S. Advanced Battery Consortium (USABC) was developed by the Big Three and the U.S. Department of Energy to work on new battery technology. Battery Types, other than conventional lead acid batteries, included nickel cadmium, sodium sulfur, zinc air, nickel hydride, lithium polymer, and hydrogen fuel cells. Nickel cadmium batteries were preferred by Japanese manufacturers, although some critics claimed that they were unsuitable for mass production since cadmium was a scarce, highly toxic mineral.

Solar Car Corporation in Melbourne, Florida, was one of the country's pioneering organizations in the construction of hybrid solar/electric vehicles. Hybrid vehicles contained a small auxiliary engine powered by gasoline or other alternative fuel to assist in recharging batteries or extending a vehicle's range. Solar panels helped supplement the battery and extended its life from two to three years to five to six years. According to company statements, its electric vehicles were capable of attaining top speeds of 75 miles per hour and able to travel 50 to 80 miles before recharging.

Another type of alternate vehicle under development by the automotive industry was fueled by natural gas. According to the American Gas Association, an estimated 30,000 natural gas vehicles (NGVs) were operating in the United States in 1993. Some projections anticipated as many as 500,000 NGVs in the United States by the year 2000. In 1993 an estimated 700,000 were in use worldwide. Natural gas proponents cite several advantages the fuel holds over conventional gasoline—it costs 25 to 30 percent less than gasoline, produces 90 percent less carbon monoxide and 50 percent less hydrocarbons, and spurs increased engine efficiency. In addition, because of deep domestic reserves, natural gas holds the potential to help the United States reduce its dependence on imported oil.

Researchers within the automotive industry were also working on creating safer ways to manage traffic. To help further the advancement of traffic management, reduce traffic congestion, and lessen the number of accidents in congested urban regions, Congress appropriated $660 million to be spent during fiscal years 1992 through 1997 on a study of Intelligent Vehicle Highway Systems (IVHS). Potential IVHS technologies included radar, microwave, ultrasonics, and video. Its aim was to assist with driving tasks such as visibility and navigational assistance. Necessary ingredients included anti-lock brakes, better traction control, improved steering responses, refined suspension systems, and the ability to monitor tire pressure.

Fuel cell technology became one of the automakers' top pursuits in the late 1990s to produce zero emissions while achieving 80 miles per gallon fuel standards. Fueled with hydrogen and powered by electricity, fuel-cell vehicles looked promising as the next generation automobile.

A fuel cell is essentially a hydrogen-powered battery that creates electricity by passing hydrogen atoms through a membrane to trip away the electrons that become electric current to power an electric motor. The electrons then rejoin the protons, which they were stripped away from, and air molecules to form water vapor for the tailpipe.

On April 20, 1999, Ford Motor Company and DaimlerChrysler A.G. announced a partnership that would produce a demonstration fleet for California roads of approximately 50 vehicles powered by fuel cells. The partnership also included the California state government, three major oil companies, and a Canadian fuel cell maker, Ballard Power Systems Inc. Regulations for California require that by the year 2003, car company sales must be comprised of a minimum of 10 percent of zero-emissions vehicles.

Partnership for a New Generation of Vehicles. Partnership for a New Generation of Vehicles (PNGV) was established in September 1993 to develop technologies for a new generation of affordable, mid-size passenger vehicles that would travel the equivalent of 80 miles per gallon—three times greater than the average achieved in 1994—while at the same time producing much lower emissions. PNGV was coordinated by the Commerce Department, from the government side, and on the industry side, it was coordinated by USCAR, the pre-competitive research venture established by Chrysler, Ford, and General Motors. In addition, PNGV included research from more than 350 automotive suppliers and universities. Research to develop new power plant, drive train, and chassis technologies were being studied, along with more economically efficient and environmentally safe ways of employing the manufacturing processes. According to the U.S. Department of Commerce, by the year 2000 each car company would have a PNGV concept car, followed by PNGV production prototypes in 2003.

A frequently overlooked goal of the PNGV was implementing new technologies on conventional vehicles. The Plymouth Prowler was a good example of this technology; aluminum and magnesium were used to reduce weight of the conventional design by 25 percent.

PNGV technology developed a standardized code that contained a "library" of computer models that allowed engineers to learn one code instead of several. This approach enabled automakers to substantially reduce the time it takes from concept to introduction saving millions of dollars.

New fuel systems in 1998 for Pontiac Firebirds and Chevrolet Camaros reduced hydrocarbon emissions. Additionally, Ford reduced emissions in the Windstar and their sport utility vehicles for 1999.

FURTHER READING

Askari, Emilia. "Auto Show's Green Theme is Subtle." *The Detroit Free Press,* 14 January 1999.

"The Big Three: Hearty Cheers In Detroit As Japan Renews Earlier Goals." *New York Times,* 29 June 1995.

Bloomberg News Service. "DaimlerChrysler Says Fuel Cells Are Five Years Away." *Automotive News,* 11 January 1999.

Bradsher, Keith. "Auto Industry Finds Surprises at the End of a Rainbow Year." *New York Times,* 7 January 1999.

———. "GM and Union are Near Deal on New Plants." *New York Times,* 8 January 1999.

Bureau of Economic Analysis. "Gross Domestic Product by Industry 1992-1997." Available from http://www.bea.doc.gov/bea/dn2/gpoc.htm.

Chappell, Lindsay. "Bigger and Fewer." *Auto News,* 11 January 1999.

Eldridge, Earle. "Blistering Auto Sales on Track for Record." *USA Today,* 4 August 1999.

———. "DaimlerChrysler Deal Includes Pay Raises, Bonus." *USA Today,* 17 September 1999.

Evanoff, Ted. "OnStar to be Available to Other Manufacturers." *The Detroit Free Press,* 3 November 1999.

"Fortune's 20 Largest U.S. Corporations." *Fortune Magazine,* 26 April 1999.

General Motors. "About Our Company," 20 January 1999. Available from http://www.gm.com/about/investor/financials/quarterly.

Klayman, Ben. "Ford, Oracle to Create Online Supply Network." *Reuters,* 3 November 1999.

Lippert, John. "Ford, UAW Reach Tentative Agreement on Four-Year Pact." *Bloomberg News,* 10 October 1999.

Morris, Ralph W. "Motor Vehicles, Model Year 1998." *Survey of Current Business,* November 1998.

Nikkel, Cathy. "Halfway to the Future." *Motor Trend,* November 1998.

Schroeder, Mary. "The DaimlerChrysler Composite Concept Vehicle." *The Detroit Free Press,* 2 November 1999.

UAW. ''Portrait of a New Union,'' 1999. Available from http://www.uaw.org/publications/wash-report/.

U.S. Department of Commerce. ''Motor Vehicles.'' *U.S. Global Trade Outlook: 1995-2000.* Washington, D.C.: GPO, 1995.

U.S. Department of Commerce. Office of Automotive Affairs. ''The Road Ahead.'' Washington, D.C.: GPO, February 1997.

Ward's Automotive. ''U.S. Sales Surge to 11th Straight Increase,'' 11 August 1999. Available from http://www.wardsauto.com/v3/article/php3.

SIC 3713

TRUCK AND BUS BODIES

This industry is comprised of establishments primarily involved in the manufacture of truck and bus bodies. Some establishments also provide complete vehicles by assembling the bodies they make onto purchased chassis. Establishments engaged in the manufacture of vehicle chassis are classified in **SIC 3711: Motor Vehicles and Passenger Car Bodies.** Establishments primarily engaged in the manufacture of truck trailers and demountable cargo containers are classified in **SIC 3715: Truck Trailers.**

Other related motor vehicle classifications include establishments primarily engaged in the assembly of motor homes on purchased chassis **SIC 3716: Motor Homes,** stamped body parts for trucks and buses **SIC 3465: Automotive Stampings,** cabs for agricultural tractors **SIC 3523: Farm Machinery and Equipment,** cabs for industrial tractors **SIC 3537: Industrial Trucks, Tractors, Trailers, and Stackers,** and cabs for off-highway construction tractors **SIC 3531: Construction Machinery and Equipment.**

NAICS CODE(S)

336211 (Motor Vehicle Body Manufacturing)

INDUSTRY SNAPSHOT

The truck and bus bodies industry had sales of 421,000 medium and heavy duty trucks in 1998 because of the stability of the U.S. economy. Truck sales tended to be volatile because they were subject to cyclical changes in the overall economy. The nation's industrial sector created the largest portion of freight tonnage, and changes in the volume of industrial freight shipments led to parallel shifts in total truck sales. Interest rates and fuel costs also impacted the industry.

Government forecasters and industry watchers predicted continued stability into the new millenium. Although initial orders showed faster growth within the heavy duty truck segment, some analysts expected long term demand for medium duty trucks to outpace the heavier vehicles. Reasons cited included a growing number of service industries and ''just-in-time'' inventory practices. Service industries typically required smaller vehicles than manufacturing industries, and ''just-in-time'' inventory practices required smaller, more frequent deliveries, making the lighter trucks more economical.

ORGANIZATION AND STRUCTURE

Established guidelines in the United States categorized on-road trucks and buses into one of eight classes according to their gross vehicle weight. As a group, Classes 1 through 3 were referred to as light duty trucks; Classes 4 through 7 were referred to as medium duty trucks; and Class 8 vehicles were referred to as heavy duty trucks. Light duty trucks included personal pickups, minivans, and sport/utility vehicles. Class 1 vehicles were those weighing up to 6,000 pounds; Class 2 vehicles weighed between 6,001 and 10,000 pounds; and Class 3 vehicles weighed between 10,001 and 14,000 pounds. Medium duty trucks included service or local delivery vehicles, some types of construction vehicles, school buses, and refuse collection vehicles. Class 4 vehicles weighed between 14,001 and 16,000 pounds; Class 5 vehicles weighed between 16,001 and 19,500 pounds; Class 6 vehicles weighed between 19,501 and 26,000 pounds; and Class 7 vehicles weighed between 26,001 and 33,000 pounds. (Purchasers of medium duty trucks tended to be small to medium sized businesses.) Heavy duty trucks, listed as Class 8, were the largest type of on-road vehicle sold in the United States. Class 8 vehicles weighed more than 33,000 pounds and were primarily purchased by large industrial manufacturers and interstate fleet operators.

Trucks and buses were made up of three primary parts—the chassis, the body, and the engine. The chassis contained the wheels, axles, and fuel tank, as well as all the structural elements necessary to provide support to the body and engine. Manufacturers often used one single chassis style with many different body types.

Truck and bus body makers provided a variety of body styles to meet different hauling requirements. Van bodies were used to transport enclosed cargo, and types of vans varied. For example, refrigerated vans were air tight, while livestock vans featured vents to allow for air flow. Tank bodies were used to transport liquids. Hoppers were a special type of tank used to carry chemicals, salt, wheat, and cement. Flat bed truck bodies were designed to carry large, heavy loads such as machinery, steel beams, and telephone poles.

Other factors also distinguished different types of trucks. ''Straight'' or ''rigid'' trucks were mounted on a single chassis, with their cab and load areas forming one unit. "Semi" or "tractor trailer" trucks were mounted on two chassis, with their cab and load areas forming two separate units. The units were attached with a device located behind the cab on the tractor called a "fifth wheel."

Straight trucks, semi-trucks, and buses were available in two basic configurations termed "conventional" and "cab-over." In conventional designs, the vehicle's engine was located under a traditional hood in front of the driver cab. In cab-over designs, the driver cab was mounted directly over the engine. The cab-over design permitted manufacturers to make shorter cabs. In areas where total vehicle length was limited by law, cab-over tractors permitted drivers to pull longer cargo trailers.

Another type of truck designation, based on numerical references, was used to describe how many wheels a vehicle possessed and how many of its wheels were powered by the engine. For example, a 4 x 2 truck was one with four wheels, two of which were drive wheels. A 4 x 4 vehicle had four wheels and all four were drive wheels. A 6 x 4 truck had a total of six wheels and four of them were drive wheels.

BACKGROUND AND DEVELOPMENT

In the United States, many truck engines differed from automobile engines because they ran on diesel fuel rather than gasoline. Diesel engines, invented by Rudolf Diesel in 1897, were a type of internal combustion engine powered by the controlled explosion of fuel sprayed into a cylinder under pressure. Diesel engine design was simpler than gasoline engine design and required no spark plug. Diesel fuel also cost less than gasoline and did not burn as readily if spilled. Diesel engines, however, were more expensive to construct because they required heavier gears to accommodate a more powerful stroke. Because diesel engines were especially suited for heavy duty hauling and long distance running, they gained popularity in cartage vehicles in the United States.

Trucks developed in response to the need to transport goods. John B. Rae, automotive historian and author of *The American Automobile Industry,* wrote, "At the beginning of the nineteenth century the cost of moving goods thirty miles inland by road in the United States was as great as the cost of carrying the same goods across the Atlantic." Although steam locomotives helped provide alternatives to animal power during the mid- and late 1800s, railroads could not offer "door-to-door" service.

As the emerging automotive industry began to supply people with self-propelled vehicles for personal transportation, enterprising innovators began to apply the technology toward the development of commercial vehicles. The popular Model T chassis, introduced in 1908, found itself used in a variety of applications. Ford Motor Company offered it as an ice cream truck, an urban delivery truck, and a farm vehicle.

One of the first types of specialty trucks was the twin boom wrecker, designed by Ernest Holmes in 1914. The truck's twin booms featured cables powered by the vehicle's engine. One cable could be deployed to rescue or lift a disabled vehicle; the other cable could be hooked to a tree to provide additional support. Other truck innovations made during the early decades of the twentieth century included four wheel drive, four wheel steering, and an improved clutch system.

With the coming of World War I, unfavorable front line driving conditions compelled truck designers to make other improvements and refinements. One popular truck developed during the war era was the Mack AC. The Mack AC earned itself the nickname "Bulldog" because of its blunt nose and reputation for toughness. To help it perform in mud, the Bulldog's engine was connected to the vehicle's rear wheels with a drive train, and the truck's solid rubber tires were puncture proof. The Mack Truck Company honored the Bulldog by incorporating the image of a bulldog in the organization's official logo.

During the period between World War I and World War II, truck makers increasingly turned to pneumatic tires. Pneumatic tires were filled with air and provided a smoother ride. Truck designers made larger vehicles capable of carrying heavier loads, making additional wheels necessary to distribute their weight more evenly and avoid damaging tires and road surfaces.

During the 1920s, semi-truck designs were introduced. Semi-trucks featured a tractor front end, which was used to pull a trailer section behind. Semi-trucks were better able to turn tight corners, and they replaced large, rigid, single section trucks. In addition to the improved maneuverability, semi construction provided for more efficient tractor use. Because the trailer could be detached for cargo loading and unloading, the tractor was freed for other tasks.

The 1920s also saw the introduction of modern motor buses. In 1923, two brothers, Frank P. and William B. Fageol, organized the Twin Coach Company. Twin Motor Coach buses were the first to offer underneath engines.

By 1930, the number of trucks on American roads had grown to 3.6 million, up from 1.1 million in 1920. An estimated 1 in 4 were farm-owned, and the era saw vast improvements in farm to market roadways. Although many pioneering truck manufacturers were also involved in making automobiles, the different economies of scale involved in producing the two types of vehicles resulted in a different mix of major manufacturers. Passenger car makers relied on capital-intensive mass production technology. This led to industry consolidation and the emergence of the Big Three automobile companies—Ford,

Chrysler, and General Motors. Truck makers, however, built a variety of vehicles, each type customized to perform a special task. As a result, a greater number of smaller companies were able to compete. During the 1930s the nation's principle truck manufacturers were the White Motor Company, Mack International, Autocar Company, and International Harvester.

During World War II, auto makers and truck makers focused their energies on providing military vehicles. Special task trucks, missile carriers, troop transports, and cargo haulers were all necessary to the war effort. Manufacturers, working under government contract, intensified research and development projects aimed at building better, more reliable trucks. Following the war, the knowledge gained was transferred to civilian undertakings, and the 1950s saw tremendous expansion in the trucking industry.

Improvements in the nation's highway system also played a role. In 1956, Congress passed the Interstate Highway Act, which authorized the construction of 41,000 miles of interstate highways and offered to fund 90 percent of the project with money from the Highway Trust Fund. As the nation's infrastructure improved, long distance trucking became more feasible. Prior to the 1950s, most of the nation's long distance freight shipments were made by rail, and trucks were used primarily to provide local delivery to and from rail stations. Unloading and reloading cargo for rail to truck transfers increased the cost of moving goods and provided an economic incentive for shippers to switch to long distance, over-the-road transport. The percentage of freight deliveries made by truck increased from about 17 percent of all deliveries in 1950 to almost 25 percent by the end of the decade.

Another national phenomenon, suburban growth, increased the importance of trucks to American life. Decentralized, suburban lifestyles required the kind of flexible freight transport trucks provided. Trucks made suburban development possible, and suburban development increased the demand for trucks. Trucks served the construction industry as it built suburbs; trucks carried household possessions as families moved into the suburbs. Trucks also served the businesses that moved from the central city to outlying areas.

During the 1960s and 1970s, the increased presence of large trucks on American roads led to increased concern about their safety. Semi-trucks were notorious for their tendency to jackknife under adverse braking conditions. When the trailer's wheels locked during breaking, it pushed the trailer forward causing the vehicle's two parts to bend into a jackknife position and skid. To help prevent jackknifing, anti-lock brake systems were investigated. The Federal Motor Vehicle Safety Standard 121, enacted in 1975, set performance standards for vehicles

with air brakes and mandated the use of anti-lock braking systems through its stipulation of minimum stopping distances. Unfortunately, available technology was not able to meet the standard.

Anti-lock brakes worked by modulating the amount of air applied to the brakes. When a sensor indicated that a wheel was in danger of locking, it applied air pressure in a pulsing manner. The pulsing pressure enabled the wheel to keep rolling and prevented it from skidding. During the 1970s, however, available computer technology was too slow to immediately interpret sensor input. The resulting time lag caused brake failure. In April 1978, the 9th U.S. Circuit Court of Appeals struck down the ''no-lock'' and minimum stopping distance requirements.

The 1980s brought renewed efforts at making trucks safer. A study done by AAA of Michigan found that in car-truck accidents, motorists sustained a higher percentage of fatalities because trucks were becoming longer, wider, and heavier, while cars were getting smaller and lighter. Researchers investigated ways of preventing small vehicles from underriding trucks during crashes. Congress mandated a study of truck brake systems, and legislators enacted regulations establishing national standards for licensing truck drivers and sharing driver information among the 50 states.

According to figures reported by the U.S. Department of Commerce, the truck and bus bodies industry shipped products valued at $4.6 billion in 1987. Of this total, $4.2 billion represented products considered primary to the industry. Secondary products were valued at $184.7 million, and $222.9 million represented miscellaneous transactions. These figures yielded a specialization ratio of 96 percent, an increase from the 93 percent reported in 1982.

Medium and heavy duty truck makers marked their most productive year in 1988 when the industry sold 334,000 units. Sales tumbled in subsequent years, however. In 1991, heavy duty truck makers recorded their worst year since 1983. An improving national economy helped sales begin to rebound in 1992. During that year, combined heavy duty and medium duty truck sales rose 11 percent over 1991, reaching 246,000 units.

During the late 1980s and early 1990s, truck manufacturers suffered the effects of a nationwide economic slow down. In 1992, however, sales and orders began to show improvement. According to the *1993 Ward's Automotive Yearbook,* overall truck sales in 1992 were 12.8 percent higher than those for 1991. Medium duty trucks in Classes 4 through 7 posted a 6.5 percent gain, and heavy duty Class 8 truck sales increased 20.6 percent.

The recovery extended into 1993. In January 1993, Class 8 sales were 44.7 percent higher than those for January 1992. Production continued to be high during the early months of the year, and industry watchers estimated that Class 8 factory sales would hit 160,000 by the year's end. Although increases in medium duty truck sales lagged behind heavy duty sales in the early months of 1993, the medium duty segment began to catch up during the middle of the year.

According to a report in *Automotive News,* the truck market was expected to continue improving through 1994. The rebound was attributed to a better economic climate and the effect of an aging national truck fleet. Another factor bolstering expectations among truck makers was a government announcement of plans to spend $15 billion to upgrade the nation's infrastructure. Planners predicted an increased demand for vehicles such as dumpers, haulers, and mixers needed to construct and repair road surfaces.

Within the motor coach segment of the industry, manufacturers placed an ever increasing emphasis on luxury. Motor coaches offered amenities such as VCRs, kitchens, and larger bathroom facilities. Buses were also available in a wide variety of vehicle sizes—ranging from small 20 seat mini buses to vehicles capable of seating 76 passengers.

One segment of the industry unique to Canada and the United States was the manufacture of school buses for student transport. School bus models, however, because they were simpler and less expensive than other types of buses, were a common export item. In developing countries such as Costa Rica, Nicaragua, Columbia, Venezuela, and Bolivia, they were used to provide community transportation.

Safety issues continued to be a primary concern within the industry. The 1990s brought a newly designed anti-lock braking system based on digital computer technology. Advanced computer capabilities helped anti-lock brakes overcome some of the problems associated with earlier systems. The National Highway Traffic Safety Administration (NHTSA) began studying the new anti-lock brake Systems.

Underride regulations were also forthcoming. In an effort to reduce traffic fatalities resulting from cars striking the rear ends of trucks and truck trailers, NHTSA was considering mandating design modifications. One possible future alteration was a change in bumper heights. Some researchers argued that if collisions occurred at the car's frame elevation, occupants would be better protected by the controlled crush design features of the automobile.

In environmental matters, truck makers were preparing to meet newer, more stringent emission standards. Many medium and heavy duty trucks burned diesel fuel. Diesel exhaust contained pollutants such as nitrogen oxides, hydrocarbons, carbon monoxide, and particulate matter visible as black smoke. Between 1988 and 1991,

emissions of nitrogen oxides had been cut by more than one-half. New emission standards were scheduled to begin in 1994 and 1998. The 1994 standards required that levels of particulates be cut by more than 50 percent; the 1998 standards required a further 25 percent cut in emissions of nitrogen oxide.

According to the American Automobile Manufacturers Association in Detroit, all U.S. heavy truck makers set a monthly production record in June 1994—17,247 vehicles. According to the *Puget Sound Business Journal,* the key factor driving the industry upswing was the growing U.S. economy, which directly affected the need for transportation equipment to move parts and finished products. The other factors for the demand were the age of the truck fleets, which were about eight years old in 1993, relatively low interest rates, and competition for trucking firms among customers.

Another reason for the high demand was the federal government's deregulation of the trucking industry during the 1980s, which heightened competition and forced weaker carriers out of business and caused most of the rest of the carriers to economize and delay truck purchases, says the *Oregonian.*

Analysts predicted that the Class 8 truck demand was expected to be robust through 1997. This proved to be wrong when 1996 truck sales slumped 25 percent from 1995. According to *Forbes,* the business was in a serious recession; one of the key reasons was that freight sales were off; hence, there was no rush to buy additional or even replace equipment. The other reason was that the average age of trucks—which was eight years—had been reduced to five because of the increased buying in the last few years, which meant that the truck fleet was fairly modern.

CURRENT CONDITIONS

Ford, Freightliner, and Navistar were the leading medium and heavy duty truck manufacturers in the United States at the turn of the century. Ford, having abandoned class 6 through 8 trucks, sold that division to Freightliner in 1997. Sterling Truck Corporation, the name Freightliner gave this new acquisition, began production in 1999.

U.S. demand was expected to remain steady from the late 1990s into 2002. In fact, with the average 3 percent economic growth being experienced in the United States at century's end, heavy truck sales were predicted to increase ten percent every three years. The strong economy being experienced in the United States since 1997 was reflected in the need for more trucks to carry freight.

The truck makers were also under enormous pressure to improve productivity and efficiency and to become suppliers of high quality, low cost service. While trucking firms and carriers were struggling to attract drivers by providing creature comforts offered by new generation trucks, the truck manufacturers were also under pressure to provide amenities for drivers in their newer models to increase sales.

INDUSTRY LEADERS

Perhaps one of the best known names within the truck-making industry was Mack Trucks, Inc. Mack Trucks celebrated its fifth straight year of increased profits and sixth straight year for U.S. market growth in 1998. The company shared 12.8 percent of the U.S. market for heavy duty trucks by delivery 26,801 units. Mack was the only U.S. truck maker to experience consistent growth from 1993-1999. The company held the third position in the American market. Exports for the company were up almost 15 percent in 1998 with 3,269 units shipped, giving Mack a 25.4 percent share of the foreign market.

During the mid-1990s, Mack introduced new features to its customer support program. Their "Vision By Mack" program kept company staff a toll-free phone call away, ready to provide any assistance an operator might need. Their "Mackmart" was a quarterly flyer highlighting special promotions that was sent to the company's parts dealers. By revitalizing their fleet credit program called "Mackcharge," the company saw transactions jump nine-fold for the first half of 1999. By branching out into the "all-makes" market, more than 150 supplied components were available at their six distribution centers in the United States and Canada and would soon include more fleet product supplies. Barcoding was also implemented to increase accuracy and efficiency at their warehouses. Also in 1999, Mack was in the stages of planning a computer network for their parts dealers featuring catalogs, cross-referencing, pricing, and billing.

In the worldwide market, Mack's heavy duty and medium duty diesel products were sold in more than 65 countries with more than 860 sales, parts, and service centers. Although Mack Trucks had a long history of truck making in the United States, the company was not U.S. owned. In 1979, the French Renault Vehicles Industriels SA began purchasing an interest in Mack. Renault's ownership totaled 46 percent in 1985, and in 1990 the French firm purchased the remainder, acquiring complete ownership.

Navistar, located in Chicago, Illinois, has led the market for 18 consecutive years. At the end of the century, the company's products encompassed heavy trucks, medium trucks, severe service trucks, school buses, engine and foundry, parts, and Navistar Financial Corporation. The company's diesel powered products were marketed under the "International" brand.

Navistar was also the nation's leading supplier of school bus chassis—a position it had held for more than two decades. Navistar sold bus chassis to body manufacturers who completed the buses and delivered them to end consumers. In addition, the company manufactured chassis for small capacity buses such as those operated to provide service to disabled students. American Transportation Corporation, maker of Ward brand school bus bodies, was partly owned by Navistar.

Navistar's roots can be traced back to the first decade of the twentieth century. The company was built on a foundation laid by International Harvester. International Harvester was founded in 1907 and played a leading role in the development of the industry through the early decades of the 1900s. By 1999 Navistar employed 17,000 people in more than 40 locations around the world. The company ranked near the top 200 on the Fortune 500 listing. Navistar was forecast to experience a 25 percent market share for the year 2003.

Both Kenworth and Peterbilt trucks were divisons of the Paccar Manufacturing Company in 1999. Paccar recorded sales of $7.6 billion in 1998 delivery of 93,800 trucks worldwide, a five percent increase over 1997. Through many upgrades at their factories, the company increased production by 30 percent in 1998. Peterbilt's new aerodynamic Model 387 set new standards for luxury, performance, and efficiency in 1999.

Oshkosh Truck Corporation, located in Oshkosh, Wisconsin, reported fourth quarter fiscal 1999 growth in sales of $314 million. The growth in sales was led by the company's commercial truck division. Oshkosh showed tremendous growth with the 1998 acquisition of McNeilus, increasing sales in the construction and refuse markets. Their defense sales accounted for 25 percent of the 1999 totals. By century's end, Oshkosh was a leading U.S. manufacturer in the construction, fire and emergency, refuse, defense, and snow removal markets.

Oshkosh Truck traced its beginnings back to two inventors, William R. Besserdich and Bernhard A. Mosling. Besserdich and Mosling held patents for innovations necessary to produce four wheel drive vehicles. One patent was for a method of transferring the engine's power to all four vehicle wheels using an automatic locking differential. A differential enabled the wheels on the axle to go around corners at different speeds. The other patent improved the front axle's steering and drive abilities. In 1915, Besserdich and Mosling approached several major car manufacturers but were turned away. They incorporated their own company, Wisconsin Duplex Auto Company, in 1917. Wisconsin Duplex later moved to Oshkosh and became Oshkosh Truck. The company's first vehicle, nicknamed "Old Betsy," had a three speed transmission, one ton hauling capacity, and weighed 3,280 pounds.

U.S. car manufacturers also had subsidiaries manu-facturing heavy trucks. One of the largest truck makers was Ford Truck Operations, a division of Ford Motor Company. Ford Truck, with headquarters in Dearborn, Michigan, was the number one producer of medium duty trucks. In 1997, Ford reported sales of 77,228 units, giving them 21 percent of the market. Ford is forecast to retain this 21 percent share through 2003.

Another truck maker was GM Truck and Bus, a division of General Motors. GM's North American Truck Platforms subsidiary was ranked third in the industry with sales of 34,102 units in 1997, giving them a nine percent market share. GM is forecast to retain its position in the industry through 2003.

GM's involvement in Class 8 trucks changed in 1988 with the establishment of Volvo GM Heavy Truck Corpo-ration. Volvo GM was formed as a joint venture between GM and the heavy truck divisions of the Swedish firm Volvo—White Motor Trucks and Autocar. Volvo GM held 5 percent of the market in 1997 with 17,622 units sold.

WORKFORCE

According to government statistics, the truck and bus body industry employed 40,952 workers in 1997. Top states in employment were Pennsylvania, Indiana, North Carolina, and California. Single establishment companies with 20 or fewer employees accounted for 14 percent of shipments as measured by value.

AMERICA AND THE WORLD

American exports of medium and heavy duty trucks were projected to decline from 1998 through 2002. This decline was expected to represent a nearly 26 percent drop in the market. New growth in production from countries in Latin America and Asia were expected to play a major role in this reduction.

The biggest U.S. trading partner in heavy and me-dium duty trucks continued to be Canada. Some analysts also expected Mexico to be the fastest growing market for U.S. medium and heavy duty trucks. Other growing over-seas markets included South and Central America, east-ern Europe, and nations formed following the break up of the former Soviet Union.

U.S. exports to Mexico were expected to grow stead-ily over the turn of the century. The signing of the North American Free Trade Agreement (NAFTA) provided for Mexico's adoption of U.S. safety standards for trucking and elimination of all restrictions on U.S. exports of me-dium and heavy duty trucks, buses, and special purpose motor vehicles to Mexico by January 1, 1999, among other provisions. In addition, analysts foresaw growing demand for U.S. built medium and heavy duty trucks, buses, and special purpose vehicles during the mid- to late 1990s as Mexico replaced its aging trucking fleet. New production

of some of these vehicles in Mexico were also expected to utilize U.S. parts and components—another bonus for exports of U.S. after-market parts.

Unfortunately, with the Mexican recession, produc-tion decreased significantly during the mid-1990s, but recovery is expected by 2002 with shipments equaling nearly 30,000 with 12,000-15,000 of these units being produced at U.S. plants.

The Kenworth Mexican plant was founded in 1959. By 1995 Paccar owned the factory outright and devel-oped an aggressive export program to help recover the low employment levels felt from the Mexican recession of the mid-1990s. By 1998 the company had its products selling in Chile, Russia, Columbia, Ghana, Canada, the United States, and Puerto Rico. The company achieved employment levels of 1,930 people in 1999, versus the 445 employees of 1995.

Entering 1999, the Mack Truck Company had al-ready increased its share of the export market by 15 percent, totaling 3,269 units in 1998. Mack kept its stronghold as America's number two truck exporter. Both Mack's Canadian and Australian subsidiaries also had increased retail sales for 1998.

Because trucks dominate the cross-border trade be-tween the United States and Canada and the United States and Mexico, the demand for these vehicles was expected to remain stable through the opening of the twenty-first century.

RESEARCH AND TECHNOLOGY

During the early 1990s, truck and bus makers were facing many challenges to improve their environmental and safety records. Research toward improving the indus-try's environmental impact focused on reducing vehicle emissions, improving fuel economy, and developing al-ternative fuels.

The Clean Air Act Amendments of 1990 imposed increasing reductions in vehicle emissions, creating a need for expanded research in clean-burning diesel tech-nology. Efforts were also underway to make vehicles with increased fuel economy. Designers worked toward making lighter trucks with smaller dimensions, better aerodynamic styling, and improved engine performance. In a similar vein, some groups were advocating the development of alternate fuels. One of the most promis-ing alternate fuels was natural gas. Many environmental groups favored natural gas over gasoline and diesel fuels because it emitted 90 percent less carbon monoxide and 50 percent less hydrocarbons.

Safety issues under investigation included searches for innovative designs offering improved driver visibil-ity, better braking systems, and the development of colli-sion avoidance technologies. Greyhound Lines, Inc.

planned to provide radar collision avoidance on buses by the middle of the 1990s. The system under development used a light and buzzer to alert drivers when other vehicles got too close.

Other changes were also being studied. Manufacturers investigated possible alterations to improve driving and sleeping accommodations for truck operators. They were also developing advanced drive trains to permit the construction of trailers capable of carrying more cargo.

Roll Stability Control was a new safety feature developed by Freightliner in 1999. This system would alert the driver to potentially hazardous driving behaviors and/ or would automatically slow the truck down, thus helping to prevent a rollover accident. The system has a data log unit that should help fleet managers maintain a safe driver base for their company.

The industry was taking significant steps at the turn of the century to upgrade its information technology. By use of the Internet, Paccar, for one, was setting a standard for e-commerce in the truck manufacturing industry. By investing in new product development, the company was able to upgrade the quality of their product while lowering operating costs.

FURTHER READING

Bradley, Peter. "Medium Trucks: Safe, Lean, Clean Machines." *Purchasing,* 18 February 1993.

Brooke, Greg. "International Helps Used Truck Buyers Go the Distance," 29 September 1999. Available from http://www .navistar.com.

Flint, Jerry. "In Good Times, Prepare For Bad." *Forbes,* 1 July 1996.

"Freightliner Unveils Technology That Guards Against Rollover," 1 November 1999. Available from http://www .freightliner.com

"Kenworth Mexicana Company History," 1999. Available from http://www.kenworth.com.

Kenworth. "Meeting Difficult Challenges," 1999. Available from http://www.kenworth.com.

Mack Trucks, Inc. "Mack News," 10 March 1999. Available from http://www.macktrucks.com.

"Oshkosh Truck Corporation." *Oshkosh Truck Reports Record Net Income for Fiscal 1999,* 25 October 1999. Available from http:www.oshkosh.com

Paccar. "Annual Report 1998," 26 February 1999. Available from http://www.kenworth.com.

Peterbilt. "The History of Peterbilt," 1999. Available from http://www.kenworth.com.

U.S. Bureau of the Census. *1997 Census of Manufactures.* Washington, D.C.: GPO, 1197.

U.S. Department of Commerce. "U.S. Automotive Industry Sector Report." Office of Automotive Affairs. Washington, D.C.: GPO, 17 September 1996.

U.S. Department of Commerce. Office of Automotive Affairs. "The Road Ahead." Washington, D.C.: GPO, February 1997.

Ward's Automotive Yearbook, "Medium & Heavy Trucks," 1998.

SIC 3714

MOTOR VEHICLE PARTS AND ACCESSORIES

This industry includes establishments primarily engaged in manufacturing motor vehicle parts and accessories but not engaged in manufacturing complete motor vehicles or passenger car bodies. Establishments primarily engaged in manufacturing or assembling complete automobiles and trucks are classified in **SIC 3711: Motor Vehicles and Passenger Car Bodies;** those manufacturing tires and inner tubes are classified in **SIC 3011: Tires and Inner Tubes;** those manufacturing automobile stampings are classified in **SIC 3465: Automotive Stampings;** those manufacturing vehicular lighting equipment are classified in **SIC 3647: Vehicular Lighting Equipment;** those manufacturing ignition systems are classified in **SIC 3694;** those manufacturing storage batteries are classified in **SIC 3691;** and those manufacturing carburetors, pistons, piston rings, and engine intake and exhaust valves are classified in **SIC 2592: Carburetors, Pistons, Piston Rings, and Valves.**

NAICS CODE(S)

336211 (Motor Vehicle Body Manufacturing)

336312 (Gasoline Engine and Engine Parts Manufacturing)

336322 (Other Motor Vehicle Electrical and Electronic Equipment Manufacturing)

336330 (Motor Vehicle Steering and Suspension Components (except Spring) Manufacturing)

336340 (Motor Vehicle Brake System Manufacturing)

336350 (Motor Vehicle Transmission and Power Train Part Manufacturing)

336399 (All Other Motor Vehicle Parts Manufacturing)

INDUSTRY SNAPSHOT

An estimated 15,000 parts and accessories are used in the production of motor vehicles. These parts represent the principle products of about 5,000 companies and a portion of the output of thousands of others. The annual U.S. production of motor vehicle parts and accessories is valued at more than $90 billion. The Motor Equipment Manufacturers Association (MEMA) is the leading industry trade organization, and it compiles industry statistics.

ORGANIZATION AND STRUCTURE

The auto parts industry is divided into two principle segments: original equipment (OE) suppliers and aftermarket suppliers.

Original Equipment Suppliers. Original equipment suppliers sell parts and components directly to automobile manufacturers for the production of new vehicles. Consequently, sales in the OE market depend on the number, size, and complexity of new vehicles produced. Primary products include wheels, frames, axles, transmissions, transaxles, bearings, springs, bumpers, brake systems, fuel injectors, seats, seat belts, airbags, cushioning, and safety padding materials. For many large suppliers, OE parts provide the majority of sales, although most suppliers also produce parts for aftermarket sales. Companies that supply both OE and aftermarket parts can generally cover development and tooling costs on the OE sales volume and supply the aftermarket at higher volumes than pure aftermarket suppliers.

Furthermore, spreading research, development, and tool and die outlays over several contracts with different manufacturers provides OE suppliers a cost advantage over the in-house parts divisions of vehicle manufacturers. OE suppliers typically concentrate on a few components and systems requiring a high degree of technological skill and manufacturing efficiency. By supplying parts for new vehicles, OE manufacturers are generally on the leading edge of technology, and vehicle manufactures have started turning to suppliers for increased engineering and development responsibilities. Auto makers also look to leading suppliers for financing and services related to inventory management, logistics, and tooling.

Aftermarket Suppliers. Aftermarket parts suppliers manufacture and sell replacement products for used vehicles. Primary products include spark plugs, shock absorbers, struts, springs, brakes pads, rotors, filters, wiper blades, and exhaust systems. Aftermarket parts are distributed through a few major parts distributors and thousands of small jobbers and local firms; they are for sale by auto dealers, service stations, repair shops, auto parts stores, tire stores, department stores, discount stores, and home and do-it-yourself stores. Aftermarket sales tend to be more stable than OE sales, particularly during recessionary times. As owners put off the purchase of new autos, they tend to extend the life of their current vehicles through increased maintenance and parts replacement.

With industry restructuring and realignment, the auto industry's supplier and original equipment manufacturer (OEM) roles were expected to change dramatically. Automakers and suppliers were expected to forge long-term agreements that focused on quality rather than price. Three layers of suppliers were expected—the system integrator, the direct supplier, and the indirect supplier. The ratios of these types of suppliers were also expected to change with system integrators growing to include 35 percent of suppliers—a 13 percent increase—and the indirect suppliers decreasing from 70 percent to 40 percent.

BACKGROUND AND DEVELOPMENT

The automotive parts industry began with the development of the automobile at the turn of the century, and the growth in the parts industry followed that of the automotive industry. By 1970, automobiles were manufactured in long production runs of few vehicle models. The vehicle population consisted of a fairly homogenous group of cars—known to be not particularly well made. Automobiles of the era were easy to repair, and, with nearly all of the 225,000 service stations in operation providing repair services, mechanics were abundant. Parts suppliers found it easy to predict the demand for a relatively narrow range of parts and profited from their manufacture.

Beginning in the 1970s, several trends in the U.S. automobile industry started to affect domestic parts producers. The number of vehicle models produced began to expand, buoyed mostly by the increased sales of Japanese automobiles in the U.S. market. The continued proliferation of models and the shortening of model lives increased the number of parts required for vehicle manufacture and repair while lowering the volume of individual part production. Lowered economies of scale began to dampen the profits of parts suppliers while growing product lines increased the number of niche suppliers.

During the 1980s, small trucks began to sell more rapidly than passenger cars—requiring an increased production of parts for the truck population. During this time, the increasing market share gained by foreign vehicle manufacturers—whose OE and replacement parts were principally supplied by foreign parts producers—resulted in a decrease in the overall market for domestic parts.

Responding to this global competition, U.S. vehicle manufacturers placed a stronger emphasis on quality and reliability. However, more reliable new cars led to fewer repairs, slowing growth in aftermarket parts sales. In addition, the increased technical complexity of newer vehicles made performing repairs more difficult. Of the roughly 130,000 service stations in existence in 1990, only about 50 percent still performed repair services; dealers and independent service facilities were gaining a share of repair services.

The increased cost of repairing more complex systems, the inability of do-it-yourselfers to perform their own repairs, and the decreased number of service stations performing routine checks led to an underperformance of maintenance and repair. To a limited extent, these effects were counteracted by the aging automobile population.

While the number of cars under three years old remained relatively constant between 1970 and 1991, the number of cars greater than three years old increased significantly; thus, the aging vehicle population provided a growing market for vehicle repair and parts replacement.

In the late 1980s and early 1990s, parts manufacturers were forced to respond to major changes in technological advances, relationships with vehicle manufacturers, and the impact of Japanese auto makers.

Technology. Parts makers worked to meet the increased technological sophistication of new automobiles. Protective airbags were installed in 51 percent of 1992 model year cars compared to almost none in 1989. With regulations requiring the use of passive restraints, airbags were expected to be standard equipment on almost all cars and light trucks by 1998. Anti-lock braking systems were installed on 32 percent of new automobiles in the 1992 model year, and traction control systems and innovative suspensions gained popularity.

Additional developments were underway to increase the use of lighter-weight materials throughout new vehicles. While increasing research and development costs, the use of complex and expensive components and systems improved opportunities for revenue and profit increases for parts suppliers. Further opportunities were provided by new clean air regulations. More stringent regulations increased the complexity of engine control and emissions systems, and a required increase in inspection programs led to more repair and parts replacement opportunities for aftermarket suppliers.

Relationship with the Auto Makers. With an influx of auto makers, the United States evolved into the most competitive automotive market in the world. To meet the demands of increased competition, the Big Three U.S. auto makers—General Motors, Ford, and Chrysler—focused efforts on quality improvement, cost reduction, and strategic sourcing, thus reducing the number of primary suppliers while increasing their responsibilities. These efforts had tremendous impact on parts manufacturers. Although in the past OE parts were sold largely on annual contracts covering the model year, in a move to improve supplier relationships, vehicle manufacturers began to award contracts for the life of a vehicle model.

In addition, auto makers reduced the number of suppliers they dealt with directly, awarding primary suppliers more responsibility for the design and development of entire systems and sub-assemblies. Primary suppliers were expected to integrate and coordinate the purchase of parts from smaller secondary and tertiary suppliers, and suppliers of all levels were urged to raise their quality standards while reducing costs. In response, many parts suppliers reduced the number of vendors they dealt with. Large parts suppliers who were able to increase the ser-

vices they offered to vehicle manufacturers benefited most from these trends.

Each of the Big Three auto makers initiated programs for supplier management. Between 1980 and 1991, Ford reduced its worldwide supplier base by 50 percent and, in 1991, it began a restructuring plan that included increased supplier reductions. The company also asked suppliers to cut costs by 1 percent annually until 1997 and opened up its bidding system so that outside suppliers competed evenly against Ford Automotive Components Group, which supplied about 50 percent of the company's parts in the early 1990s.

Chrysler implemented its Supplier Cost-Reduction Effort (SCORE) program, urging suppliers to come up with ideas for improvements and cost savings in manufacturing, scheduling, inventory, and shipping. Chrysler attempted to establish long-term relationships with suppliers by naming suppliers for specific commodities. The company had fewer than 2,500 suppliers in 1992—down from more than 3,000 in the late 1980s—and it had a goal of eventually reducing the number of suppliers to 750. The company's 1993 LH model used 170 suppliers, compared to 600 to 800 suppliers for cars of earlier model years.

General Motors initiated the industry's most controversial supplier management plan with its Purchased Input Concept Optimization with Suppliers (PICOS) program, which demanded significant price reductions from suppliers given long-term contracts. Under the program, GM sent teams of engineers, designers, and purchasing cost accountants to meet with parts suppliers at their plants to investigate production inefficiencies and propose solutions leading to cost reductions. The program also allowed GM to accept unsolicited bids from worldwide suppliers for contracts it had already negotiated for future models, and it stripped away advantages to GM's Automotive Components Group. In addition, the company offered suppliers the opportunity to lease factory space in GM plants and a supply of labor from idled workers.

In 1992, the Big Three announced plans to develop a standardized quality assessment program for suppliers. Such a move, which would reduce the time and paperwork required in undergoing several quality audits by different auto makers, was expected to eventually save suppliers $160 million annually. A first step toward a common standard was taken by eliminating a major source of redundancy in quality auditing.

Previously, first-tier suppliers were required to audit second- and third-tier suppliers from whom they purchased parts. However, because many companies acting as second- and third-tier suppliers also sold parts directly to one of the Big Three, they were already required to be audited under either the Ford Q101, Chrysler Supplier Quality Assessment, or GM Target for Excellence quality program. With the new arrangement, suppliers that were already qualified through one of the Big Three were no longer required to be audited by a primary supplier. The agreement was expected to save the supplier industry $500,000 a year.

The Impact of Japanese Auto Makers. Increased sales of Japanese automobiles affected the operations of both OE and aftermarket parts manufacturers. Because most Japanese aftermarket parts were furnished by Japanese OE suppliers, the volumes of replacement parts for domestic parts suppliers dropped as Japanese vehicles increased their market share in the United States. Domestic parts suppliers started increasing their offerings of replacement parts for Japanese vehicles but, at the same time, Japanese suppliers started seeking higher profit margins through the supply of aftermarket parts for U.S. vehicles.

While Japanese manufacturers increased their production of cars within the United States, the move had not significantly improved the opportunities for domestic parts manufacturers. Foreign vehicles manufactured in the United States had significantly fewer domestic suppliers than Big Three cars. Domestic OE suppliers argued that the Japanese plants in the United States continued to purchase parts from suppliers based in Japan and the growing number of Japanese suppliers operating in the United States. Furthermore, with the increased capacity of many American factories manufacturing Japanese cars, Japanese suppliers started competing for OE contracts with the Big Three. Some suppliers believed that their industry could be permanently suppressed by these developments.

Some domestic parts suppliers claimed they were hampered by the Japanese *keiretsu* system—the close relationship between auto makers and their suppliers—arguing that the system impinged on their ability to supply parts to Japanese vehicle manufacturers in North America and Japan. At the request of U.S. suppliers, the Federal Trade Commission (FTC) began an investigation of alleged antitrust violations by Japanese auto producers in the United States.

Japanese producers argued that they purchased from suppliers meeting their needs and, so far, the FTC had concluded that there was no clear evidence of collusion among Japanese companies. During President Bush's 1992 trade mission to Japan, Japanese auto makers pledged to purchase $19 billion worth of U.S. auto parts annually by 1995. During 1992 and 1993, Japanese purchases of U.S. auto parts began to increase. The rising value of the yen relative to the dollar made shipments of parts from Japan more expensive, encouraging Japanese transplant manufacturers to purchase more U.S. parts.

The automobile industry continued to buy an increasing number of automotive parts from outside suppliers through the 1990s because it reduced costs, provided

more flexibility, and allowed for a greater specialization of technology according to an article in *Fortune* magazine. During the mid-1990s, the U.S. automotive parts industry comprised some 5,000 firms—including about 500 Japanese, European, and Canadian manufacturers—that supplied either the original equipment (OE) market, the replacement parts market, or both. According to the U.S. Department of Commerce, industry production hit an all-time high in 1994, reaching $134 billion. The following year, output fell slightly to $131 billion, mirroring the slight decline in motor vehicle production. However, the motor vehicle parts industry represented a 25 percent growth since 1992.

The U.S. industry was dominated by 50 large manufacturers that accounted for the large majority of sales. From 1992 to 1995, North American sales by these top 50 suppliers increased by almost 50 percent, growing from $68 billion to $101 billion according to U.S. Department of Commerce reports. The United States was home to the world's sales leader, Delphi Automotive Systems, with 1995 global sales of over $26 billion, $10 billion more than its nearest foreign competitor.

In the mid-1990s, the fight was on among automotive parts manufacturers to dominate the growing *Smart Car* parts market. With the establishment of the Partnership for a New Generation of Vehicles (PNGV) by President Clinton in 1993, auto manufacturers were competing to produce new generation concept cars. The ripple effect of this affected the automotive parts industry. High-tech console gadgetry was being produced by most large auto manufacturers.

''Competition for space on your dashboard is looming, as TRW, Texas Instruments, and Eaton, among others, race to recast their battlefield products for the U.S. car market,'' reported a *Fortune* article. Competition for this market was global. Smart car products already available and in the works included satellite navigation and mayday systems, radar intelligent cruise control, and night vision.

With the restructuring of the automotive parts industry, the U.S. automotive industry was expected to be challenged by foreign competition and customer demands for continued cost cuts and quality improvements. The global automotive parts market was expected to total about $519 billion by the year 2000. According to the *U.S. Global Trade Outlook,* growth in major markets was expected to average less than 2 percent annually; hence, the biggest opportunities for U.S. exporters were expected to be in the fast growing Asian and Latin American markets.

CURRENT CONDITIONS

In the late 1990s, automakers put great pressure on their parts suppliers to reduce costs. Suppliers initiated programs to increase productivity and improve efficiency. As the manufacturers tried to streamline assembly plants, they looked to the parts suppliers to provide the systems that would reduce the number of parts assembled at the plant. Acquiring a company meant adding parts to the systems and modules.

Consolidations and mergers were taking place in the industry, enabling suppliers to continue offering savings to the automobile manufacturers. The mergers and acquisitions were the means used to provide more modules and systems to the automakers.

General Motors Corporation and Ford Motor Company made announcements in 1999 that they were moving all of their annual purchases of materials and components onto the Internet. Suppliers were virtually forced into e- business. The automakers looked to the Internet to simplify supplier links and eliminate costly paperwork related to bids, billings, orders, and shipments.

INDUSTRY LEADERS

Delphi Automotive Systems was the number one OEM parts supplier to North America in 1998. North American parts sales totaled $20.6 billion, up from 1997 totals of $19.9 billion. Products for sale were steering, chassis, electrical, energy and engine management, thermal management, and interiors.

Visteon Automotive Systems was the number two supplier with parts sales of $14.4 billion in 1998, an increase of $39 million from 1997. Visteon products included chassis, climate control, electronic, exterior and interior systems, and powertrain controls.

Johnson Controls, Inc. was ranked third with sales of $5.59 billion, Dana Corporation was fourth with $5.54 billion, and Lear Corporation was fifth with sales of $5.3 billion.

WORKFORCE

Vehicle manufacturers generally have higher labor costs than parts suppliers, who are able to employ more non-union workers. In 1997, the Bureau of Labor Statistics reported that 691,000 people were employed in the U.S. motor vehicle parts industry.

Problems arose between General Motors and the United Auto Workers (UAW) over outsourcing. In June 1998 the union workers went on strike at GM parts facilities over cost cutting issues. GM pushed for higher production and claimed that union rules prohibited efficiency. The UAW stand was that workers were endangered when production was sped up to increase productivity. Problems also surfaced in 1996 at GM's Delphi brake plant with a 17-day strike over outsourcing. Negotiations led to a contract that guaranteed that the

automakers would maintain a 95 percent workforce while the manufacturers kept the right to outsource.

AMERICA AND THE WORLD

U.S. parts manufacturers have been forced to match the growth in global operations of domestic auto makers to maintain their primary supply relationships. Additionally, international growth has been spurred by the desire to gain supply contracts with overseas vehicle manufacturers. Most leading domestic producers have established manufacturing facilities in the principle auto producing regions of the world—including Canada, Europe, and Mexico. In Europe alone, seven leading U.S. parts manufacturers have combined annual sales exceeding $1 billion. The global integration of the auto industry has led many suppliers to develop joint ventures with foreign parts producers. As the industry continues to globalize, increased U.S. supplier investments are expected in Mexico, Asia, and Europe.

The United States has posted a trade deficit in automotive parts since 1983, primarily due to a large deficit with Japan. Between 1989 and 1992, the parts trade deficit with Japan remained between $9 billion and $10 billion, accounting for one-fifth of the overall trade deficit with Japan. Canada is the only major nation with which the United States has maintained a trade surplus, and Canada remains the leading trading partner of U.S. firms. Between 1985 and 1991, Canada received more than 60 percent of total U.S. parts exports and supplied one third of total imports.

The number of foreign firms producing parts in the United States increased dramatically throughout the 1980s and early 1990s. In the early 1990s, approximately 350 wholly-owned foreign part plants and more than 120 joint ventures operated in the United States. Japanese suppliers owned 167 U.S. parts plants and were part of 123 joint ventures. European firms, led by German manufacturers, owned 168 plants in the United States, and Canadian firms owned 17, with one joint venture. While fairly well established in Europe and Canada, U.S. penetration of the Japanese domestic market remained weak. In 1992, one wholly owned U.S. parts plant—and a few joint ventures—were operating in Japan.

Continued consolidation and increasing global competition are forecast for the automotive parts industry. The future prospects for large domestic producers are likely to depend on their ability to obtain contracts with Japanese transplant manufacturers as well as to retain contracts with the Big Three against competition from Japanese suppliers. For smaller second- and third-tier suppliers, the key is likely to be establishing strong relationships with primary suppliers.

U.S. Automotive Parts Exports. During the late 1980s and early 1990s, exports had become more vital to the

U.S. automotive parts industry, growing from 15 percent of production in 1986 to 30 percent of output in 1995. The Clinton Administration's trade policy efforts to open closed markets made the U.S. automotive parts industry one of the leading exporters. From 1992 to 1995, U.S. exports of automotive parts grew at an average annual rate of 12 percent, rising from $28 billion to $40 billion according to the Office of Automotive Affairs, U.S. Department of Commerce.

Expanded efforts by the industry, backed by the Clinton Administration's work to increase U.S. access to the Japanese automotive parts market, resulted in a 58 percent increase in exports to Japan—growing from $1 billion in 1992 to $1.6 billion in 1995. Japanese car manufacturers purchased $19.9 billion worth of U.S. made automotive parts and materials in the 1994 fiscal year. Approximately 75 percent was spent to transplant Japanese manufacturing operations in the United States, while the remaining 25 percent was spent on exports to Japan. Exports to Mexico and Canada benefited from the passage of the North American Free Trade Agreement (NAFTA)—growing from $26 billion in 1993 to $29 billion in 1995.

In 1997, U.S. imports of automotive parts increased 4.8 percent over 1996 to $50.7 billion. Fifty-three percent of the imports were from NAFTA countries. Automotive parts imports from Japan accounted for 23 percent of the shipments.

In 1997, 73 percent of U.S. exports of automotive parts were to NAFTA countries. The European Union received 9 percent. U.S. penetrations increased in the Asian and Latin American markets but were stymied by the Asian currency crisis. U.S. exports of automotive parts totaled $47 billion in 1997.

FURTHER READING

Automotive News. "Top 150 OEM parts suppliers to North America." *1998 Market Data Book,* 1998.

"GM to Pressure Suppliers to Use New Web Site," 5 November 1999. Available from http://www.auto.com/reutersl.htm.

Hoffman, Gary. "Suppliers Seek Bigger Chunk of Inside Jobs." *The Detroit News,* 19 July 1996.

"Japanese Increase Auto Purchases." *Ward's Automotive Reports,* 17 July 1995.

Moran, Tim. "Automakers Cut the Old Connections to Suppliers." *Automotive News,* 13 September 1999.

Office of Automotive Affairs. U.S. Department of Commerce. "Automotive Parts." *U.S. Global Trade Outlook: 1995-2000.* Washington, D.C.: GPO, March 1995.

Office of Automotive Affairs. U.S. Department of Commerce. "The Road Ahead." Washington, D.C.: GPO, February 1997.

Office of Automotive Affairs. "U.S. Automotive Industry Sector Report." Washington, D.C.: GPO, 17 September 1996.

Robinson, Edward A., and Hillary Margolis. "Soon Your Dashboard Will Do Everything (Except Steer)." *Fortune,* 22 July 1996.

Standard and Poor's Industry Surveys. New York: Standard & Poor's, 1999.

"Supplier Pushed into E-business." *Automotive News,* 1 December 1999. Available from http://www.auto.com.

"The Next Supplier Evolution." *Automotive Industries,* 1 January 1996.

SIC 3715

TRUCK TRAILERS

This industry covers establishments primarily engaged in manufacturing truck trailers, truck trailer chassis for sale separately, detachable trailer bodies (cargo containers) for sale separately, and detachable trailer (cargo container) chassis for sale separately.

NAICS CODE(S)

336212 (Truck Trailer Manufacturing)

INDUSTRY SNAPSHOT

Shipments for this industry increased through the 1980s and 90s, reaching $5.5 billion in 1997. Demand was driven by changes in shipping methods and, in the 1990s, by a booming U.S. economy.

Design innovations in the industry focused on increasing payloads and improving safety, particularly in braking systems. Manufacturers also used different materials including aluminum and plastics—in addition to steel—to make increasingly lightweight trailers.

ORGANIZATION AND STRUCTURE

Like heavy trucks, truck trailers are purchased for specific applications and are therefore manufactured in a variety of styles and types. Van, container chassis, and flatbed trailers comprise the majority of trailer shipments, while the remainder consists of a small number of more specialized trailer types. Both the number of axles and length of trailers vary, with the most popular trailers having two axles, followed by single-axle designs and trailers with three or more axles. Popular trailer lengths are 48 feet and 28 feet.

Trailers are used singly or in combinations of three, as in triple "pups." Pups are 28-foot trailers that have limited use in 16 states. Sometimes three of these trailers are attached to a truck tractor to form triple pups, which together span about 104 feet. Trucking firms have urged Congress to expand the use of triples. Even though the triple pups save trucking firms millions of dollars, The

Citizens for Reliable and Safe Highways, a not-for-profit organization, fought to keep larger trucks off the roads.

Truck trailers were manufactured in most of the 50 states. In 1999, Texas, California, and Pennsylvania led the nation in the number of manufacturing establishments per state.

BACKGROUND AND DEVELOPMENT

In the early 1980s, in response to an increase in intermodal shipments of goods—a system using two or more methods of transport, including trucks, trains, and ships—container chassis trailer shipments increased. The demand for a variety of trailer types, including custom designs, prompted the establishment of several original equipment manufacturers (OEMs) in the trailer industry. Furthermore, increased competition arose from deregulation of the industry in 1980, making manufacturers leaner and more efficient. Many trailer manufacturers were small businesses serving local areas, often employing 50 or fewer workers.

In 1984 approximately 400 truck trailer manufacturers were operating in the United States, employing almost 28,000 workers. Approximately 214,000 trailers were shipped that year, for total sales of $3.31 billion. In 1995, an improvement in the economy brought the industry work force up to 38,700 workers, of which 31,700 were production workers. Trailer shipments totaled 187,000 units in 1992, and total industry sales were estimated at $3.47 billion. The industry was operating below capacity during the early 1990s.

The market for exporting truck trailers was expected to expand throughout the 1990s. The United States maintained a trade surplus in truck trailers, and in 1991 the value of exports for the truck trailer industry was $175 million, while the value of imports was only $23.9 million.

CURRENT CONDITIONS

In mid-1990 the demand for truck trailers reached an all-time high. Projections for 1994 put the total order for truck trailers at approximately 211,500 units, just short of the record 214,000 truck trailers set in 1984. Stronger U.S. economic growth drove the demand, as a sharp rise in freight shipments spurred higher spending by truckers.

The record highs for the demand for truck trailers continued to rise through the late 1990s. The increase in trailer shipments was expected to parallel that of tractor production as a result of record improvement in the truck tractor industry. In 1997, the truck trailer manufacturing industry totaled $5.5 billion in shipments.

The industry employed a total of 30,644 people in 1997, 83.7 percent of whom were production workers. The average hourly wage for production workers during

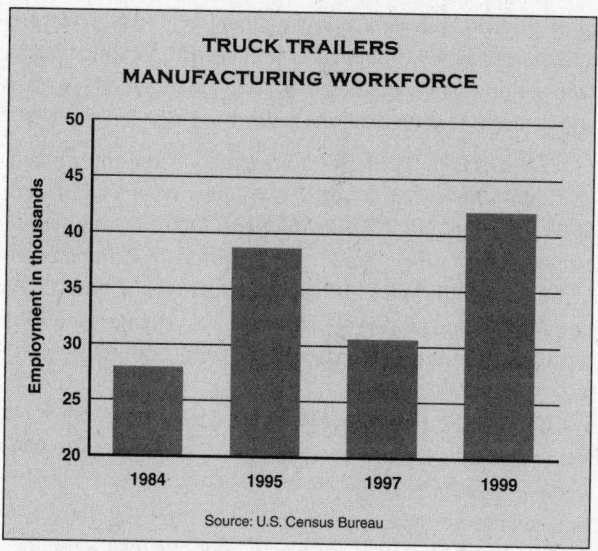

this time was $11.45. In late 1999, the Bureau of Labor Statistics noted a work force of 42,100 workers

A host of new truck trailer models rolled off assembly lines in 1996. The emphasis was on ease, safety, lightness, and stable frame-designs capable of hauling heavier payloads. The trailers were easier to attach, had lower load angles, and were made of lighter but stronger steel to make heavier loads possible.

One of the safety-related additions to new truck models was the implementation of anti-lock brakes in truck trailers. The new anti-lock braking system (ABS), designed especially for truck trailers, was expected to result in substantial savings for motor carriers by providing controlled braking, enhanced vehicle stability, increased driver control, and stable stopping during emergency brake situations. Rockwell WABCO Vehicle Control Systems' Easy-Stop (TM) was one of the first innovators of ABS for truck trailers.

Another innovation, pioneered by Raven-Trailers of England in 1999, allows trailer pins and brakes to be locked in seconds by the driver from the cab, eliminating the time-consuming manual locking system.

INDUSTRY LEADERS

Out of about 134 operating companies in this industry, Wabash National Corporation was the industry leader. The company posted 1998 sales of nearly $1.29 billion, having grown over 52 percent from the previous year. Based in Lafayette, Indiana, Wabash had about 5,300 employees.

In 1997, Wabash National bought out Fruehauf Trailer Corporation, the former industry leader, after the company suffered huge financial wounds due to Chapter 11 filing. Wabash was also an industry leader in advanced trailer designs, including aluminum-plate trailers that don't require plywood interiors, allowing them to hold more cargo, and their patented, lightweight trailers with flexible plastic walls. Forecasters predicted trailer manufacturers would adopt these new innovations industry-wide.

Great Dane Trailers of Savannah, Georgia, ranked second in the industry with 1998 sales revenue estimated at $1.0 billion and 4,700 employees. Other leading companies were Utility Trailer Manufacturing Company of California, with $584 million in sales revenue and 2,600 employees, and Dorsey Trailers Inc., of Atlanta, Georgia, with $150.3 million in sales and over 1,000 employees.

FURTHER READING

Berman, Phyllis. "The Wabash Way." *Forbes*, 6 April 1999, 78.

Bureau of Labor Statistics. "Employment—National, Not Seasonally Adjusted." 1999. Available from http://www.bls.org.

"Custom Cylinder Improves Trailer Locking" *Design News* 16 August 1999.

Gruebnau, Pam. "Today's Trailers Work to Make Hauling Easier." *Construction Equipment,* October 1996.

"Hoover's Industry Snapshots." *Hoover's Online: The Business Network,* 1999. Available from http://www.hoovers.com.

Isidore, Chris. "Triple 'Pups' Not Everyone's Best Friends." *Journal of Commerce and Commercial,* 26 November 1996.

SIC 3716

MOTOR HOMES

This category covers establishments primarily engaged in manufacturing self-contained motor homes on purchased chassis. Establishments engaged in manufacturing self-contained motor homes on chassis manufactured in the same establishment are classified in **SIC 3711: Motor Vehicles and Passenger Car Bodies.** Establishments primarily engaged in manufacturing mobile homes are classified in **SIC 2451: Mobile Homes;** and those manufacturing travel trailers and pickup campers are classified in **SIC 3792: Travel Trailers and Campers.** Establishments primarily engaged in van conversion on a custom basis are classified in **SIC 7532: Top, Body, and Upholstery Repair Shops and Paint Shops.**

NAICS CODE(S)

336213 (Motor Home Manufacturing)

INDUSTRY SNAPSHOT

Going into the twenty-first century, the U.S. motor home industry was seeing some growth. Factors contributing to this were a good economy, the aging of the American population increasing the size of the industry's core

market, and the prospect of younger Americans with more disposable income becoming motor home customers.

ORGANIZATION AND STRUCTURE

The recreational vehicle (RV) industry can be divided into two groups: towables, which include conventional and fifth-wheel travel trailers, folding camping trailers, and truck campers; and motorized vehicles, which include motor homes and van conversions. However, the only segment of the industry that is covered in this essay is motor homes that are built on purchased chassis. The overwhelming majority of motor homes sold in the United States are built on chassis that have been purchased from an outside manufacturer. The two key manufacturers of gasoline-powered chassis for motor homes are General Motors Corp. and Ford Motor Co.

Motor homes are classified as either Class A, B, or C models. Class A vehicles are probably what most people think of when they hear the term "motor home." It is a living unit entirely constructed on a bare, specially designed motor vehicle chassis, and the driver sits within the vehicle itself. Class A models have been the most popular type of motor home. In 1995 they represented about 62 percent of all motor homes shipped (and more in terms of the dollar value of shipments). Class B motor homes, also called van campers, are defined by the Recreational Vehicle Industry Association (RVIA) as "a panel-type truck to which the RV manufacturer adds any two of the following conveniences: sleeping, kitchen, and toilet facilities." Class B vehicles represented about 7 percent of 1995 shipments. Class C models are smaller than Class A, and the driver usually sits inside a separate cab; they accounted for about 31 percent of unit shipments in 1995.

The two largest manufacturers in the industry, Fleetwood Enterprises and Winnebago Industries Inc., held about 44 percent of the motor home market in 1995. Together, the 10 largest makers accounted for more than 85 percent of total industry sales.

BACKGROUND AND DEVELOPMENT

According to one source, the first motor home in the United States was built to take tourists out West for the San Francisco Exposition of 1915. Although its promoters claimed that it had all the advantages of an ocean cruiser—with hot, running water and electric lights—testimony confirming the comfort of the journey does not appear in any historical record. Wealthy industrialists, notably Henry Ford and Thomas Edison, were among the pioneers of the motor home industry; they built relatively luxurious caravans with amenities like leather swivel chairs and refrigerators. The well-to-do were imitated by the middle class, who bolted boxes to the backs of Model Ts and fastened a bed and dresser inside to create what was then called a "house car." American individualism soon made itself felt, and by the late 1920s one could see house cars that looked like log cabins, miniature mansions, and even airplanes.

The early motor home travelers stayed overnight at farms and ranches, but eventually large campgrounds were built that could hold more than 1,000 vehicles. The sites were often overcrowded and unsanitary, and a far cry from the outdoor life these early RV users sought. Driving the first professionally built motor homes was not much fun either. They were made with heavy materials that overtaxed the chassis and gave poor weight distribution. Insulation was poor and the vehicles were not suited to the roads of the time. Thus, until the 1960s, the towable trailer was the more popular form of RV.

In the mid-1950s some small companies began to build what might be called motorized trailers. While they represented a significant improvement, they were still overweight and underpowered. A few years later, however, Winnebago Industries began to introduce its innovative products, which became popular in the late 1960s and early 1970s. The company developed a special wall construction called Thermo-Panel that had the required structural strength and offered good insulation; at the same time, it was light enough to increase gas mileage and engine performance. Moreover, once Winnebago introduced assembly line production, it was able to make its motor homes a lot cheaper than the competition could.

Nevertheless, buying a motor home represented a major financial commitment—in 1994 the average price of a Class A motor home was more than $62,000. According to a survey conducted by the RVIA in 1993, about 69 percent of motor home purchasers had a gross income between $50,000 and $100,000 a year, while 59 percent had been in the same job or the same industry for ten years or more. Hence, older, more financially secure Americans were the industry's key customers.

A notable trend in the industry was toward larger vehicles with more equipment. A corollary was the increasing popularity of slideouts—roll-out room extensions that allowed manufacturers to increase the size of floor plans. Although slideouts posed problems for campground and resort operators, consumers wanted them and, by the mid-1990s, slideouts held about 30 percent of the market.

CURRENT CONDITIONS

In 1997 industry participants were optimistic about the industry's long-term prospects. The essential economic ingredients appeared to be in place—expanding economy, low interest rates, and low unemployment— while demographic trends were on the industry's side. The prime buyers of motor homes were people 50 years of age or older, and this market was expanding with the aging of the U.S. population. At the same time, those between the ages of 30 and 49 were entering the RV market in significant numbers. While they tended to buy inexpensive towables, their purchases signaled that they liked the RV lifestyle and perhaps would be willing to trade up to a motor home when they had more leisure time and more money. Some also believed that the growing preference of consumers for "car substitutes" like light trucks and sport utility vehicles would make the prospect of tooling around in a 40-foot Class A motor home less formidable.

In 1997 a joint promotional campaign was launched by recreational vehicle manufacturers, suppliers, dealers, and campgrounds promoting the lifestyle and experience of owning a recreational vehicle. Those efforts were rewarded in 1998 with the best year the industry had enjoyed in twenty years. Calendar year 1998 showed shipments of recreational vehicles totaling 292,700, an increase of 15 percent from 1997. The growth rate was equally shared by both industry sectors, with motor homes up 15 percent with 63,500 units and towables up 14.9 percent with 229,200 units. Type C mini-motor homes and conventional travel trailers had the largest increases, at 25.1 percent with 98,600 units and 25 percent with 17,000 units, respectively. Type A motor home shipments increased by 14.1 percent to 42,900 units. The best total in nearly 25 years was seen by folding camping trailers, at 9.9 percent and 63,300 units. The total for truck campers rose 4.9 percent with 10,800 units, and an all-time record was set for fifth-wheel travel trailers, with a 7 percent increase and 56,500 units shipped. The retail value of these shipments reached $8.4 billion.

David J. Humphreys, president of the Recreation Vehicle Industry Association (RVIA), has stated that the industry was benefiting from the baby boomers entering the recreational vehicle market in the late 1990s. The customer profile was no longer only that of the over-55 "empty nester," but also of younger families with more disposable income.

According to a research study conducted by the University of Michigan in 1999, one in four households headed by 35- to 54-year-olds indicated that they intended to purchase a recreational vehicle sometime in the future.

INDUSTRY LEADERS

Fleetwood Enterprises is the largest U.S. motor home manufacturer, with about 28 percent of the market. The company is headquartered in Riverside, California, and employs nearly 21,000 people throughout the United States and Canada. Fleetwood also manufactures factory-built homes and has become a leader in that industry, too.

Winnebago Industries, Inc., headquartered in Forest City, Iowa, is the industry's second-largest company. Winnebago celebrated its fortieth year in the industry in

1998. Net revenues for fiscal year 1998 were $525 million. The brand name ''Winnebago'' is often used interchangeably with the term ''motor home'' in the vocabulary of many Americans.

Founded in 1958 by John K. Hanson, who died in 1996 at the age of 83, Winnebago posted increasingly strong sales and profits in the late 1960s and early 1970s. Afterward, however, recessions, gas shortages, and, some say, poor management cost the company market share and hurt profitability. Between 1989 and 1992 the company lost money each year. In fiscal 1993, however, Winnebago benefited from a new line of motor homes that was well received, as well as reduced costs and greater automation of production. These factors, coupled with the improved economy and low interest rates, continued to support the company's profitable performance.

AMERICA AND THE WORLD

European motor home markets differ substantially from those in the United States. While European RVs can be as sophisticated as American models, their campgrounds lag notably behind. The campgrounds often lack the amenities of U.S. sites, such as dumping stations and full hookups. European RVs tend to be smaller because of higher gasoline prices and licensing rules that limit motor homes to about 6,000 pounds. Certainly Europe offers attractive demographics, with an affluent workforce that gets four to six weeks of vacation each year. Thus far, however, the experience of U.S. motor home makers in Europe has been less than overwhelming. Indeed, the industry's participation in European markets took a step back in 1996 when Fleetwood sold its German subsidiary, Niesmann and Bischoff.

U.S. makers have made some inroads into the Japanese market. The focus there has been on Class B models because Japanese motorists can operate them with regular driver licenses. Since Japanese roads tend to be narrower, compact motor homes that can also be used for everyday driving are popular. American makers have modified their designs for the special needs of the Japanese market. For instance, kitchen sinks are made one-foot deep so they can accommodate a rice cooker.

RESEARCH AND TECHNOLOGY

As with many industries, the growth of the Internet is having an impact on the motor home industry. By 1997 significant numbers of manufacturers and dealers had created Web sites to advertise their product lines and supply customers with information. The Internet is particularly useful for motor home rentals. People from all over the world can now conveniently reserve vehicles online at a low cost to the dealer.

While the Internet is affecting marketing, new technology is changing manufacturing. Motor home produ-

cers are seeking to incorporate lightweight materials that are nonetheless strong and resilient. In some instances, aluminum is replacing rubber in roofs and fiberglass in sidewall paneling. Winnebago is using a combination of aluminum and steel to eliminate wood framework.

Moreover, manufacturers are investing more capital in the production process to make it less labor intensive. For example, Winnebago has moved to a flexible manufacturing system in its metal-stamping operations. As Ron Buckmeier, director of engineering, told *RV Business,* ''There's some labor savings, but the real advantage is quality improvement and the variability to do mixed-model manufacturing.''

FURTHER READING

'''95 Adjusted Shipments Show Decline Over '94.'' *RV Business,* March 1996.

Fleetwood Enterprises, Inc., Web Site, 1999. Available from http://www.fleetwood.com.

Kurowski, Jeff. ''Tokyo Show Targets New RVers with U.S., International Imports.'' *RV Business,* May 1996.

''November Shipments Impacted by Lagging Conversion Market.'' *RV Business,* February 1997.

''Research Reveals Larger, Younger RV Market.'' *RVIA Web Site,* 1999. Available from http://www.RVIA.com.

Sullaway, John. ''Creating Coaches for the Physically Challenged.'' *RV Business,* June 1996.

Thompson, John. ''Selling in Cyberspace.'' *RV Business,* February 1997.

Winnebago Industries Annual Report, 1999. Available from http://www.winnebagoind.com.

SIC 3721

AIRCRAFT

This category includes establishments primarily engaged in manufacturing or assembling complete aircraft. This industry also includes establishments owned by aircraft manufacturers and primarily engaged in research and development on aircraft, whether from enterprise funds or on a contract or fee basis. Also included are establishments engaged in repairing and rebuilding aircraft on a factory basis. Establishments primarily engaged in manufacturing engines and other aircraft parts and auxiliary equipment are classified in **SIC 3724: Aircraft Engines and Engine Parts** and **SIC 3728: Aircraft Parts and Auxiliary Equipment, Not Elsewhere Classified.** Establishments primarily engaged in the repair of aircraft, except on a factory basis, are classified in **SIC 4581: Airports, Flying Fields, and Airport Terminal Services;** and research and development on aircraft by establishments not owned by aircraft manufacturers are classified in **SIC 8731: Commercial Physical and Biological Research.**

NAICS CODE(S)

336411 (Aircraft Manufacturing)

INDUSTRY SNAPSHOT

The aerospace industry consists of space vehicles, space propulsion parts, guided missiles, aircraft, aircraft engines, and aircraft parts. The value of all products and services of the aircraft industry alone is nearly one-half that of the aerospace industry total. The production and sale of aircraft further constitutes about 50 percent of the total aircraft industry's value.

The Aerospace Industries Association of America (AIAA), forecasted that manufacturers would ship 2,925 units of civilian (transports, general aviation, and rotocraft) aircraft valued at $44.0 billion in 1999. A total of 580 aircraft would be accepted by U.S. military agencies in 1999 at a flyaway value of $15.4 billion. The Teal Group predicted 25,537 aircraft valued at $655.5 billion will be built throughout the world during the decade 1997-2006.

Commercial aircraft deliveries are expected to rise to over 700 by the year 2000. The commercial jet fleet was estimated to be 23,600 by the year 2016, 7,000 of which were expected to be Boeing aircraft. Aircraft deliveries are expected to crest in the year 2000.

Industry earnings celebrated a milestone in 1997 when commercial and foreign customer sales matched sales to the U.S. Government Military, the first time since 1934. The U.S. Aerospace industry saw new orders grow 14.8 percent in the first eight months of 1998.

By August 1997 there were three major manufacturers in the United States because of mergers and acquisitions—The Boeing Company, Lockheed Martin Corporation, and Raytheon Company, in size respectively. In July 1998 Lockheed Martin announced the termination of a proposed merger with Northrop Grumman because the U.S. Department of Justice questioned the merger giving too much market leverage to the merged company in the defense industry.

ORGANIZATION AND STRUCTURE

American aircraft companies provide airplanes for three distinct markets: the military, commercial aviation, and general aviation, which includes business aviation. From the end of World War II until the collapse of the Soviet threat in 1989, the American military services had a voracious appetite for sophisticated aircraft, which American firms sought to satisfy. This 49-year boom in military spending not only guaranteed the health of many manufacturers, but it also allowed those manufacturers to devote resources to research and development, ensuring

that American aircraft would be the most technologically advanced in the world. The end of the Cold War, which reduced military spending in the United States and around the world, provided the greatest challenge for American aircraft manufacturers, who had grown accustomed to lucrative Department of Defense contracts. As a result, the military aircraft industry appears to be shrinking. Although the U.S. government has sought to guarantee its technological dominance through continued funding of research and development, funds are declining.

The development of commercial aircraft poses far greater risks than that of military aircraft. The development process for a passenger airliner capable of carrying several hundred people is both lengthy and costly, requiring manufacturers to anticipate the needs of airlines far in advance and to gamble vast amounts of money on the product's success. This is the main reason why Boeing canceled its development of the super jumbo aircraft. Manufacturers have usually designed new or modified aircraft in response to the demands of carriers, who have typically asked for more fuel efficiency and more seating rather than major redesigns. The *Economist* estimated that a new medium-sized airliner costs over $2.0 billion to develop, with engines costing another $1.5 billion, and noted that "aerospace companies bet their futures on each product."

As a result of the risks involved, commercial aircraft manufacturers have been rather conservative, pursuing modifications on existing airframes rather than reinventing complete aircraft, and most existing commercial airliners have changed little in recent history. However, some exciting new aircraft developments are taking place in the areas of speed, range, capacity, and efficiency. Given the tremendous financial risks associated with developing new aircraft, many manufacturers today work cooperatively, jointly developing a design and dividing work among partners if the design is successful. The development of a new aircraft might involve many dozens of companies, each contributing some portion of a plane that they have perfected. The merger of the two dominate aircraft companies, The Boeing Company of Seattle, Washington, and the McDonnell Douglas Company of St. Louis, Missouri, will result in economies of operation that could allow more funds for development. In a calculated risk, Boeing canceled its plans to develop a super jumbo jet and concentrated instead on long range, fuel efficient planes with a modestly higher passenger capacity, citing the ratio of development costs to demand as justification. Airbus was still pursuing the super jumbo concept.

Though military and commercial aircraft manufacturers dominate the industry, American companies also produce a number of aircraft for the general aviation and the helicopter market segments, which include fixed wing aircraft and rotorcraft for business transportation, regional airline service, recreation, specialized uses such as ambulance service and agricultural spraying, and training. American manufacturers have historically produced about 60 percent of the world's general aviation aircraft and 30 percent of the helicopters. Major U.S. manufacturers of general aviation aircraft include the Beech Aircraft Corp., the Fairchild Aircraft Corp., the Cessna Aircraft Co., Gulfstream Aerospace, and the Learjet Corp.

Most aircraft manufacturers derive a significant proportion of their profits from the production of replacement and upgrade parts for their airplanes. Since large commercial jets represent such a large investment—a new twin-engine passenger jet may cost several hundred million dollars—airlines try to keep them in the air for many years. Moreover, the Federal Aviation Administration (FAA) sets stringent guidelines on repair and replacement procedures for passenger aircraft. Manufacturers provide parts through a network of suppliers and subcontractors, which comprise **SIC 3728: Aircraft Parts, Not Elsewhere Classified.**

BACKGROUND AND DEVELOPMENT

The American aircraft manufacturing industry traces its origin to one of the seminal events of the twentieth century: the Wright brothers' first powered flight in 1903. While many others had flown with gliders, balloons and dirigibles, Wilbur and Orville Wright marked a tremendous breakthrough with powered flight, because they proved the dynamics of flying a wing. In cross section, a wing is flat on the bottom but curved on top. As a wing moves through the air, air passing over the wing is forced to travel a greater distance than air passing under the wing. This causes a pocket of low pressure that literally sucks the wing up into the air. In order to work, the wing must be driven forward, or powered. These principles were described years before the Wrights' flight by Samuel P. Langley, a luckless professor whose aviation experiments were either ignored or a failure.

The Wrights originally hoped to sell airplanes to the United States Army as battlefield reconnaissance devices. The idea of employing aircraft to attack or drop bombs had not yet occurred to anyone. One of those on hand to witness the Wright brothers' first demonstration for the Army was a young conscript named Donald Douglas. Despite several impressive flights, Army officials were unmoved. The Wrights took their show to Europe, where they flew for the German, French and British armies. In the process, they prompted interest with such European aviation pioneers as Louis Blériot, Willy Messerschmidt, Anthony Fokker and Marcel Dassault.

Aviation was immediately embraced in Europe as a powerful new force in warfare, but it also made for good entertainment. Blériot and others such as Louis Paulhan built their own airplanes and began touring flying circuses. During 1910 and 1911, these European aviators toured the United States, flying before garage tinkerers like Glenn Martin, Clyde Cessna, Glenn Curtiss and Bill Boeing. Curtiss, a motorcycle repairman, was immediately drawn to flight, and he had access to the lightweight engines needed to power aircraft. Curtiss was one of the first to mount a propeller on the front of the aircraft in a "tractor" design. Until that time, propellers had been rear-mounted "pusher" models which are still found on some aircraft today, particularly amphibians.

After several of the Army's Wright planes crashed, killing the pilots, the Army found a new supplier in Curtiss, who escaped the enforcement of the Wrights' patents by incorporating the first ailerons. Curtiss thus emerged as the nation's leading aircraft manufacturer and the new supplier of choice to the Army.

Wilbur Wright died in 1912, leaving his brother in charge of their company. A poor manager, Orville Wright naively sold the company and its patents to a group of financiers led by William Boyce Thompson.

With the outbreak of war in Europe in 1914, Germany and France were quick to apply aviation to the battlefield, producing the world's first aces, Roland Garros and Manfred von Richtofen. The United States Army embraced air power in 1914 by creating an aviation group within the Signal Corps. One of its first members was Donald Douglas. Douglas, an engineering graduate of the Massachusetts Institute of Technology, was briefly employed by Glenn Martin, who had experimented with gliders since 1905. He built his first powered aircraft near Los Angeles about 1909, having been bankrolled by another aviation enthusiast, inventor Alexander Graham Bell. Douglas helped Martin develop his first production aircraft, the TT trainer, before he was dispatched to Washington to oversee the government's aviation program. Thompson's group later purchased Martin's company to form an aircraft combine called the Wright-Martin Company.

By 1918, the government had shown its interest in aviation through expansion of an air squadron and active intervention in the industry. Having seen the effect of air power in Europe during World War I, it was determined not to see American air power stunted by legal wrangling or patent hoarders. What emerged was a loosely policed competition for government contracts, primarily military and later air mail business. Hundreds of airplane builders emerged from garages and warehouses.

Automobile executives were chosen to head the government's ambitious 22,000-plane military aeronautics program. Favored for their ability to turn out huge quantities of a standardized product, these executives openly conspired to keep aircraft builders out of the industry. But Douglas, a member of the government board, fed information on the aeronautics program to other aircraft designers. Finally, upset with the performance of the

Army's air squadron, and disgusted with government bureaucracy, Douglas resigned in 1919 and moved to Los Angeles to start his own company.

In 1919, automotive interests led by Delco persuaded Orville Wright to lend his name to another venture called Dayton-Wright. Wright was retained only for his venerable name and its ability to draw investment dollars. As an automotive venture, Dayton-Wright built only aircraft engines, and later fell under the control of General Motors. At the close of World War I, the government canceled 90 percent of the aircraft it had ordered, forcing many airplane builders to close. An investigation later revealed criminal collusion and widespread scandal among those who were empowered to grant contracts. However, virtually all involved escaped without prosecution.

Having briefly regained the services of Donald Douglas, Glenn Martin abandoned Thompson's company and struck up an important relationship with General Billy Mitchell, the Army's most powerful advocate of air power. With Mitchell's backing, Martin won a contract to build twenty MB-2 bombers, which Mitchell subsequently used in a spectacular demonstration off the Virginia Capes, sinking the supposedly unsinkable captured German battleship *Ostfriesland.*

A separate aircraft concern was established in 1914 by Allan and Malcolm Loughead. The brothers built their first aircraft in a small garage in San Francisco with financial backing from Max Mamlock and his Alco Cab company. After crashing it and scaring away Mamlock and his money, the brothers began flying exhibitions and sold Curtiss airplanes to raise money. The Lougheads, intent on military applications for aircraft, embarked on the construction of a large bomber at a site near Santa Barbara. There they met a young builder with an understanding of mathematics named Jack Northrop, whom they asked to join the company as chief engineer.

President Coolidge appointed Dwight Morrow to devise a government program for measured development of the industry in 1925. The resulting Air Commerce Act of 1926 set annual procurement levels for 2,600 military aircraft. Loughead and Northrop, who had drifted for six years, suddenly regained their market and managed to secure financial backing from a Los Angeles venture capitalist named Fred Keeler. As a condition, however, Keeler demanded that Loughead change the spelling of his Scotch-Irish name to accurately match its proper pronunciation. Apparently tired of being addressed as "Mr. Lug Head," Allan relented, and the new company was called Lockheed. The company later completed an all-metal, single-skin model called the Vega. This model, based on a design by Holland's Anthony Fokker, was developed by Northrop, who then left the company to work for Donald Douglas.

Douglas, whose business was growing on the strength of government sales, had been approached by David R. Davis, who offered to invest $40,000 for a transcontinental airliner. With Northrop's help, Douglas produced the Cloudster, of which the government ordered several hundred for military use. Davis, fearing the risk, bailed out immediately. The Cloudster, however, led Douglas to a series of successful designs, including the DT series torpedo planes and Douglas World Cruiser. Between 1921 and 1928, Douglas' annual production grew from six aircraft to more than 300.

The growing aircraft industry received a tremendous boost in 1927 when Charles Lindbergh completed the first successful trans-Atlantic flight using a modified Ryan Aeronautical tri-motor. Lindbergh's daring and nearly suicidal stunt so strongly revived interest in aviation that investors began pumping millions of dollars into aircraft companies. The following year, Martin relocated to Baltimore to be closer to his customers in Washington. Building bombers, he purchased the engine business of Louis Chevrolet, whose automobile business had been acquired by General Motors.

United Aircraft was the creation of Bill Boeing, a rich Seattle forester who purchased his first plane in 1910 from Glenn Martin and took flying lessons from the builder himself. Boeing and his partner Conrad Westerveldt built a number of early floatplane models for maritime postal delivery. After producing aircraft for the military during World War I, Boeing was persuaded by a customer named Ed Hubbard to form an airline service. In 1920, Boeing won a contract to haul mail between Chicago and Seattle. For the job, he developed a new design, the Model 40, fitted with a Pratt & Whitney engine. Boeing's association with Pratt & Whitney brought him the acquaintance of that company's president, Frederick Rentschler.

The Kelly Airmail Act of 1925 returned airmail service to private bidders after a series of bloody crashes by the government's own air service. Postmaster William Folger Brown actively encouraged the formation of large airline companies by carefully awarding profitable air mail contracts. Boeing acquired numerous private airmail companies and their lucrative contract rights, and in 1928 banded them together to form the National Air Transport Company. The following year, Boeing and Rentschler merged their airframe and engine businesses to form the United Aircraft & Transportation Company. By the end of 1929 the company had taken over two propeller makers as well as Northrop's Avion company, and laid out an air transportation network that later became United Air Lines.

In August of 1929, Allan Loughead (who retained his own name) and Fred Keeler sold the Lockheed company to a group of automotive investors organized as the Detroit Aircraft company. The company drew tremendous investor interest after aviatrix Amelia Earhart crossed the Atlantic with one of the company's Vegas. Only one month later, world financial markets were buffeted by a stock market crash that plunged the nation into the Great Depression. Aviation company stocks, valued at more than $1.0 billion on total earnings of more than $9.0 billion, were decimated.

Detroit Aircraft, whose share price had tumbled from $15.0 to 12.5 cents, failed in 1932. The Lockheed operation was purchased out of receivership for $40,000 by Robert and Courtlandt Gross. The acquisition included an important new design, the Orion. Meanwhile, Allan Loughead had returned to his original real estate business. Jack Northrop, however, returned to Douglas, where he established yet another company as a subsidiary of the Douglas enterprise.

Douglas was associated with an aviation combine similar to Boeing's, called North American Aviation, which controlled Eastern Airlines and TWA. As a result of this relationship, Douglas, who had grown rich on military contracts, was now called upon to develop commercial airliners for his parent company. The first of these, the Douglas Commercial One, or DC-1, emerged during the worst years of the Depression. In February of 1934, the government reduced its subsidy to airmail carriers, creating a sudden demand for faster, more efficient aircraft. Douglas refined his DC design to meet this demand, and in 1935 produced the DC-3, an extremely versatile craft that nearly rendered competitors such as Boeing's 247 obsolete. The Gross Brothers and their Lockheed company likewise improved upon earlier designs and emerged with the Electra.

Even Glenn Martin, spurned by the War Department, was brought into the commercial market. The devout Republican was forced to mortgage his plant under a Democratic New Deal program. Desperate for business, Martin built a luxurious flying boat, called the China Clipper, for Pan American's trans-Pacific routes. But when Martin only managed to sell three Clippers, the government was forced to support his business by purchasing the company's newly developed B-10 bomber.

The Depression would have destroyed the aircraft industry were it not for government support. It became official policy to award contracts to an increasingly privileged club of manufacturers, so that their expertise could be preserved and developed for military purposes. This policy hardened the cycle of concentration promoted by Brown. American aviation was controlled by three huge vertical monopolies, each maintaining huge airframe and engine manufacturing facilities and airline services.

In 1934, Senator Hugo Black completed an investigation of improprieties in these aviation investment trusts, which included United Aircraft, North American Aviation,

and a third group called the Aviation Corporation of the Americas, or Avco. Several magnates were called to testify at hearings, including Bill Boeing, Donald Douglas and Glenn Martin. All admitted huge profiteering from aviation activities but, due to the absence of laws against these practices, no prosecution could result. Boeing, however, was so incensed by the nature of the investigation that he sold all his aviation interests and retired.

The combines were eventually dissolved on antitrust grounds, creating an enduring line of business restriction in American aviation. Airframe, engine and airline companies could not now be associated in any way. Boeing's conglomerate was divided into The Boeing Company in Seattle, United Aircraft in Connecticut, and United Air Lines, headquartered in Chicago. Likewise, North American Aviation lost its association with TWA and Eastern Airlines, and Avco lost American Airlines and Pan Am. Martin and Lockheed remained intact, as did Consolidated Aircraft, a company whose growth sprung from its acquisition of the defunct Dayton-Wright's designs.

By 1937, the emergence of the DC-3 and Electra enabled airlines to make money from passenger services alone, ending the reliance on airmail. The efficiency of these aircraft was recognized by belligerents in the small wars being fought in Europe and Asia. Unbeknownst to them, Lockheed, Douglas and Martin frequently sold aircraft to fictional airline companies and other front organizations for the Japanese and German armed forces. The discovery of this led to neutrality laws, which prescribed an aircraft embargo to any belligerent. But the demand for aircraft, particularly from Britain and France, was so great that the Roosevelt Administration created loopholes designed to allow the export of aircraft to American allies. This enabled the industry to fund development of new designs from large, lucrative export orders.

Much of this development was highly experimental. Northrop, whose subsidiary had been consolidated by Douglas in 1937, formed another company in 1939 with backing from LaMotte Cohu. After raiding Douglas of dozens of engineers, he resumed work on his radical flying wing project. Lockheed produced an equally strange design, a triple-hull fighter called the P-38 Lightning, while Boeing began work on its large B-17 bomber.

Several other smaller manufacturers gained admission to the defense industry club during this time. Grumman, a company established in 1929 to build naval aircraft, grew quickly after winning a contract to supply folding-wing F4F Wildcats to the Navy. By 1941 the company, established by Leroy Grumman and Leon Swirbul, had become the primary supplier to the Navy, overtaking even Martin. McDonnell Aircraft began building aircraft on a large scale in 1939, producing fighters for the Army Air Force. Meanwhile, Consolidated merged with the Vultee Company, forming a huge manufacturing operation in Texas called Convair.

While military preparations were stepped up in 1940 and 1941, the event that sparked tremendous growth in the aircraft industry was the Japanese attack on Pearl Harbor. Huge amounts of government money were poured into engineering and production facilities. President Roosevelt ordered 60,000 aircraft in 1942, and 125,000 the year after. Douglas converted its DC-3 into military cargo planes and bombers, more than 10,000 of which were built. Other manufacturers were suddenly able to complete new designs. Convair produced the B-24 Liberator, and Martin the B-26 and A-30 Baltimore bombers and 70-ton Mars freighter. North American turned out the B-25 Mitchell bomber and the P-51 Mustang, while Douglas added the A-20 Havoc and SBD Dauntless dive bomber. The newly reconstituted Curtiss company returned with its C-46 cargo craft. Grumman provided the Navy with its Widgeon, TBF Avenger and F6F Hellcat.

Boeing, which at one point turned out 16 bombers every day, went into production on its B-29 Super Fortress. Even Ford, which exited the aircraft business during the Depression, was pressed into service, building B-24s. Northrop got his flying wing, the B-49, to fly. With every surface of the craft devoted to creating lift, it was capable of tremendous payloads. The Army, however, refused to develop the boomerang-shaped bomber, fearing possible instability in flight and the use of electronic, rather than cable, controls.

Small airplane builders, such as Beech Aircraft, Cessna and Piper, also participated in the war effort. But due to their limited manufacturing facilities and lack of advanced engineering talent, they were relegated to building support aircraft and parts for other manufacturers. Employment in the industry peaked at 1.3 million people in 1943, as every manufacturer participated in some way in the war effort.

The war completely changed the aircraft industry. In addition to demonstrating the power and strategic importance of aerial combat, it established the parallel relationship between investment and technological development. The war allowed the perfection of strategic bombing tactics, carpet bombing, dogfighting, naval attack bombing and, in the last days of the war, atomic bombing. Wars that were previously fought with tanks and battleships were now waged from above. By the end of the war, work had begun on a new generation of aircraft: jets. Larry Bell's Bell Aircraft Company, Lockheed and McDonnell were the first to experiment with jet power, having gained volumes of captured German jet airframe research.

While the military threat from Germany and Japan had been vanquished, a new adversary emerged in the form of the Soviet Union and became the focus of continued government investment in aviation. The development that began during World War II was scaled down, but concentrated in promising new technologies. Development centered on long-range strategic bombers for delivering nuclear bombs to targets in the Soviet Union and speedy fighters to intercept a similar threat from Soviet bombers.

Transition to a peacetime economy was considerably better managed than after World War I, due to the Contract Settlement Act of 1944. Still, the entire industry was forced to choose between commercial and military manufacturing. North American, Grumman, McDonnell, Northrop and Vought chose to develop only military craft, while Douglas pursued commercial designs. Boeing, Martin, Lockheed and Convair elected to develop commercial as well as military designs.

The most important postwar commercial entries were the four-engine Douglas DC-4, the Boeing 377 Stratocruiser and the triple-finned Lockheed Constellation, designed by Howard Hughes for TWA. Having emerged from the war with tremendous manufacturing capacity and engineering talent, these three companies dominated the commercial aircraft industry. Competitors, including Curtiss, Martin and Convair, were forced to exit the market in rapid succession, taking refuge in the more secure military businesses. Hughes Aircraft, famed for its massive Spruce Goose amphibian freighter, failed to break into the production market. After building a few experimental designs, it became the plaything of its owner, the difficult millionaire Howard Hughes. Hughes Aircraft later retreated into the missile and aviation controls business.

Boeing and Lockheed also became leading defense suppliers after the war. Lockheed extended its lead in jet fighter designs during the Korean War with its F-94 interceptor and, later, F-104 Starfighter. Boeing developed a family of huge intercontinental bombers, including the B-57, B-50 and B-52. Meanwhile, Convair introduced its B-36, with six pusher propellers, and supersonic B-58 Hustler.

On the recommendations of the Finletter Air Policy Commission, the government made air power the crux of its military establishment. While tremendous competition existed for seemingly open-ended military contracts, manufacturers found new ways to commercialize military designs. Boeing was the first to develop an entirely new passenger aircraft with technologies gained from a jet bomber. Boeing requested permission to use government-funded technologies from its successful eight-engine B-52 to develop a new four-engine jetliner called the 707. Eager to prevent a European monopoly in passenger jets—DeHavilland had just introduced its sleek Comet—the government agreed.

Soon after the 707 flew in 1954, American Airlines, a good Douglas customer, announced plans to buy 30 of

Boeing's new jets. Douglas, which had put off introduction of a jet in favor of its DC-6s and DC-7s, was forced to rush a similar design into production or risk following Curtiss and Martin into oblivion. Douglas emerged the following year with highly similar jet design called the DC-8. Ironically, United Air Lines, historically associated with Boeing, placed the first order for the DC-8. Boeing, however, had eclipsed Douglas as the premier American aircraft builder.

Two new jet designs emerged from Europe during the early 1960s, the Sud Aviation Caravelle and Hawker Siddeley Trident. These jetliners featured engines tucked onto the rear of the fuselage, rather than under the wings. At the request of Eastern Airlines, Boeing pursued a three-engine 727, delivered in 1964, while Douglas built a more economical two-engine DC-9, delivered in 1965. Boeing introduced a smaller twin-engine jetliner, the 737, in 1967.

Tremendous consolidation occurred in the aircraft industry during this period. Convair was acquired by General Dynamics in 1952. Martin, which had abandoned aircraft production during the 1950s to concentrate on missiles and aircraft parts, was acquired by the American Marietta Corporation in 1961. North American, a builder of Air Force fighters, was thrown into deep disarray in 1967 after a fire destroyed one of its Apollo space capsules, killing three astronauts. The company was taken over that year by the machinery manufacturer Rockwell Standard. Also that year, financial difficulties resulting from the DC-8 and DC-9 finally caught up with Douglas. Unable to keep up with the demand for its aircraft, Douglas neared bankruptcy. Eventually, McDonnell Aircraft, a manufacturer of fighter jets and space capsules, prevailed in its bid to acquire Douglas.

The 1960s were a period of feverish development in military aviation, due to continued investments by the Defense Department in new technologies and academic programs, and the creation of the National Aeronautics and Space Administration (NASA). Some of the major accomplishments of this period were in the development of supersonic and rocket-powered aircraft. North American built a six-engine, triple sonic delta wing bomber called the B-70. Obsolete before its first flight, this aircraft evolved into the B-1 Bomber a dozen years later. Lockheed marked two great achievements, with its ultra high-altitude U-2 and triplesonic SR-71 spy planes. Developed in 1964 at Lockheed's super-secret "skunk works," this aircraft remains the fastest jet ever to fly in the American arsenal.

After abandoning research on a revolutionary nuclear-powered bomber, General Dynamics' Convair group became involved in the development of a multi-use fighter/bomber called the F-111 and the F-16 fighter. During the 1960s, McDonnell, Douglas, Martin, Boeing, Grumman and Convair became major participants in the space program. Other manufacturers were reduced to production of single-mission aircraft, such as Vought, with its A-7 Corsair, and Fairchild, with its A-10 Warthog. Northrop began work mainly as a subcontractor to McDonnell Douglas, building the F-18.

A postwar boom in private aviation greatly expanded the fortunes of small aircraft manufacturers such as Cessna, Beech and Piper. General aviation accounted for 17,811 or 90 percent of all U.S. aircraft by 1978. A wave of personal injury law suits precipitated by one pilot's suit against Piper Aircraft brought general aviation aircraft manufacturers to their knees. Manufacture of the most popular single-engine propeller plane in the world was halted in 1986.

In 1969 aviation engineer Bill Lear introduced the first private jet, which Cessna and Beech later imitated. Fairchild and Beech Aircraft became active in the small airliner market, defined as nineteen seats or less. Fairchild, which built the Fokker 27 under contract, developed the Metro airliner. Beech introduced its King Air, followed some years later by its Model 1900. These craft were operated on small airline "feeder" routes.

In commercial circles, a new market was emerging for larger 300 to 400 passenger jumbo jets. Boeing and McDonnell Douglas, eager to maintain their passenger jet franchises, began the extremely costly development of their 747 and DC-10, respectively. Surprisingly, Lockheed re-entered the market after 20 years, building a three-engine jumbo called the L-1011 Tristar. Boeing was nearly ruined by its four-engine behemoth, and at one point was forced to lay off two-thirds of its work force. McDonnell Douglas fared little better, and Lockheed, mired in huge cost overruns from its massive C-5 Galaxy military cargo plane, required a federal loan guarantee to remain solvent.

The 747 and Tristar hit the market in 1970, and the DC-10 followed in 1971. These aircraft revolutionized air travel by offering airlines the capability to move as many as 400 passengers over distances of up to 5,000 miles. While sales of the DC-10 gained slowly, the 747 soon dominated the skies.

The Airline Deregulation Act, meanwhile, was signed in 1978. This legislation had a tremendous impact on airlines across the country, and plane manufacturers soon felt its repercussions as well. Major national carriers were unprepared for the newly competitive environment created by the Act and found themselves with fleets of Boeing 707s and McDonnell Douglas DC-8s that, because of fuel costs, become prohibitively expensive. In the meantime, new regional carriers utilized fuel-efficient aircraft that fit their needs. The national trunks were forced to examine their fleet configurations and make significant new purchases. Even then, however, analysts charge that the carriers were sluggish in responding. In many cases orders for new aircraft were not made to Boeing or McDonnell Douglas or any other manufacturers until well into the 1980s. The backlog of orders subsequently reached all-time high levels, with waiting periods for delivery of new aircraft ranging as long as seven years by 1986.

Efforts to build a supersonic transport, or SST, were abandoned by Lockheed and Boeing in 1970 after the market evaporated and the government refused to cover skyrocketing development costs. A European consortium succeeded in building a jet capable of breaking the speed of sound, but the plane proved so costly to build and operate, and its sonic boom so disruptive, that flights were severely curtailed and the planes operated at a loss.

On the success of its F-4 Phantom in Vietnam, McDonnell Douglas developed a family of new military aircraft during the 1970s, including the F-15 Eagle and A-4 Skyhawk. Boeing developed its venerable 707 into tankers and powerful AWACs airborne radar platforms, while Lockheed built large new military cargo craft, such as the C-130 and the Galaxy. Northrop remained a strong player in the military market with aging entries such as its F-5, and failed designs such as the export-intended F-20 Tigershark. Grumman did extremely well in the 1970s with its F-14 Tomcat and a smaller version of the AWACs, the E-2C Hawkeye.

The American military aircraft arsenal gained a huge boost in 1980. The industry, starved for investment since Vietnam, was the primary beneficiary of a massive armament program started by President Carter and trebled by President Reagan. Reagan resurrected Rockwell's $200 million B-1 bomber, canceled by Carter in 1977, and ordered development of a range of new radar-evading aircraft. Pentagon funding poured into these super secret "black projects." One of the beneficiaries was Lockheed, whose success with the SR-71 won it the right to develop the tiny diamond-shaped F-117 Stealth Fighter. Another was not revealed until 1988, when Northrop unveiled its sinister-looking B-2 Stealth Bomber. A flying wing, the B-2 represented the culmination of the late Jack Northrop's life-long dream. It also emerged, along with the B-1, as the replacement for the elderly but still devastating B-52 and the versatile F-111.

The flood of investment into military aircraft resulted in a series of scandals unrivaled since World War I. Several companies were investigated for vastly overcharging the Pentagon and misappropriating funds. In response, the government began shifting contracts away from offenders and forcing them to compete for business they had earlier taken for granted. In one of the few signs of growth, a consortium of Lockheed, Boeing and General Dynamics was chosen to develop the Advanced Tactical Fighter. In a period of decline for the

defense industry, the ATF was one of the few large military projects remaining.

Significant activity also occurred in the commercial airliner market during the 1980s. Boeing introduced several upgraded versions of its hugely profitable 747, and a new series of economical, large twin-engine aircraft, the 757 and widebody 767. These aircraft finished off Lockheed's otherwise excellent L-1011 which, with three engines and a larger crew, was discontinued in 1981. Unable to design entirely new aircraft, McDonnell Douglas upgraded its DC-9 into the MD-80 series, and offered a similarly improved DC-10, called the MD-11.

The late 1980s and early 1990s saw manufacturers seeking partnerships to develop commercial aircraft. McDonnell Douglas failed to establish a limited merger with Taiwan Aerospace in 1990, and was seeking a partner to share development costs of a new four-engine MD-12 jetliner. Boeing, meanwhile, investigated a partnership with Deutsche Airbus, the disaffected German member of Boeing's arch rival, Airbus. Similarly, Boeing was seeking a partner for a planned 1000-passenger super jumbo craft. Boeing eventually dropped this project due to the billions of dollars necessary to develop a new jet. Airbus remained committed to this questionable project.

The combination of the long-term impact of the hub concept, the increasing concerns of passengers, greater concern for reduced operating costs on the part of the airlines, and rapid technological developments especially in the area of GPS (Global Position Satellite) are affecting the industry. GPS navigational devices will allow more direct flights from airport to airport. Historically, pilots have relied on VOR (VHF Omnidirectional Range) transmitters which emitted a distinct radio signal for each degree of the 360 degrees from magnetic North. For tracking purposes pilots routinely fly from one VOR at a fixed location to another via established routes, which at lower altitudes is not necessarily a straight line. Pilots using GPS navigational systems can now fly in a straight line from airport to airport and even fly an instrument approach using GPS navigational systems (precise within 50 feet), thus reducing actual mileage necessitated by the fixed location of VORs. This could reduce both travel time and fuel costs, especially for regional airlines. The growing number of regional jets has the potential for allowing for the return of more direct flights. Newer, more fuel efficient planes with longer ranges, such as the Boeing 777, will also impact the airlines.

Aircraft industry analysts expect that the 1990s will see a period of great change in aircraft manufacturing. For years the industry had been propelled by ever-increasing military budgets and ever-increasing numbers of commercial airline passengers, but both of those stimuli changed in the 1990s. Government military expenditures peaked in 1987, when aircraft manufacturers supplied over 1,200 planes. In 1994, U.S. manufacturers shipped only 755 military aircraft or $7.9 billion in sales, approximately two-thirds the number shipped in 1987. By 1995 the number of military aircraft had dropped to 410 although the value had risen to $11.0 billion, generally reflecting budget cuts with corresponding reductions in employment by military aircraft manufacturers. During 1992, McDonnell Douglas, General Dynamics, Northrop, Lockheed, Rockwell, and Grumman cut over 29,000 jobs and were expected to cut another 20,000 jobs during the following two years. The increased competition for scarce military dollars is expected to reduce the number of military aircraft providers or possibly force industry consolidation. Deputy Defense Secretary William Perry told *Interavia* that the ''DOD budget will not come back. . . . The companies that succeed are those that will plan accordingly in accepting the new reality despite the hardships it will cost to downsize.''

''While procurement of aircraft has declined significantly,'' noted *U.S. Industrial Outlook 1993*, ''research, development, testing, and evaluation funding has remained somewhat stable, providing some haven for U.S. providers of advanced military aircraft technologies.'' In 1993, the Clinton Administration took steps to protect the U.S. aerospace industry's long-held technological superiority, increasing NASA's research and development budget, maintaining the DOD's research and development budget, and creating the National Commission to Ensure a Strong, Competitive Airline Industry, which has attempted to challenge the subsidies provided by European Community countries to their aircraft manufacturers. Such efforts are expected to maintain the technological superiority of the American aircraft manufacturing base even while the number of manufacturers shrinks.

Much of the ordering activity for new planes was from leasing companies. British Aerospace Asset Management's jet and turboprop divisions manage and lease more than 500 planes with $700 million in revenues. Another leader is GE Capital Aviation Services, which ordered 45 Airbus jet transports with options on another 45, with delivery beginning in 1997 and continuing at the rate of 15 to 20 per year until the order is complete. Leasing is the primary means by which the global air industry will acquire new aircraft in 1997-99 and beyond.

While military aircraft manufacturers struggled to adjust to changing military budgets, commercial aircraft manufacturers had to adjust to declining demand for aircraft by major carriers, production overcapacity, and government-supported foreign competition in the first half of the 1990s. These challenges were made all the more pressing in 1991, when for the first time in history, the number of passengers riding on commercial airlines declined. This drop in air travel prompted many airlines to cancel or postpone orders for aircraft, leaving manufacturers with an excess of inventory. U.S. manufacturers shipped 408 large

transport aircraft valued at $26 billion in 1993, down from their peak of 610 aircraft valued at $30 billion in 1992. Both Boeing and McDonnell Douglas had to reduce production and lay off nearly 10,000 employees each. Fortunately, by 1996 the industry had begun to recover.

According to *Interavia* contributor John Crampton, ''Aerospace manufacturers are learning to live with a whole new set of rules brought about by the industry-wide recession and the peace dividend.'' Manufacturers were adjusting to this changed marketplace in a number of ways. Most notable was been a trend toward industry consolidation and cooperation. Many of the smaller manufacturers in the industry were eliminated by the recession, and those that have survived have increasingly banded together to share the risk of developing new products. For both Boeing and McDonnell Douglas, this has meant teaming with Asian manufacturers in order to better penetrate the rapidly expanding Asian market. Industry analysts believe that those manufacturers best able to form working partnerships will be the ones to succeed in the 1990s. In 1996 there were many mergers, primarily precipitated by the effects of deregulation and the decline in military contracts. In order to remain competitive, aircraft manufacturers must also reduce costs by as much as 30 percent, concluded Crampton. Technological advances will pave the way for some cost reduction, as manufacturers increasingly turn to computer-assisted design mock-ups and paperless workplaces as ways of reducing costly experimentation and excess paperwork exemplified by Boeing's 777.

In an effort to lock-in its customers, Boeing has recently established an ''exclusive supplier'' relationship with several airline companies. Its twenty-year agreement with American Airlines gives the airline more flexibility in aircraft selection types and delivery dates than previous arrangements did.

In April 1997, the new F-22 Raptor single seat fighter—a joint effort of Lockheed, Boeing, and Pratt Whitney (United Technology Corp.)—was unveiled and scheduled to make its debut flight in May 1997. At $70 million per unit, this fighter was designed to secure dominance over any adversary aircraft. Original plans for the U.S. military to purchase 438 of these planes at more than $71 billion, however, may not survive the budget cuts of 1997.

CURRENT CONDITIONS

Both major U.S. aircraft manufacturers, Boeing and Airbus, were affected by the Asian crisis during the late 1990s. Although net orders for that period were up 9.7 percent year to year, it was a marked deceleration from the 139 percent gain in the second quarter of 1997 for commercial jet orders. About one-fifth of Boeing's and Airbus' back orders were from Asian airlines, many such orders were being deferred or canceled. Despite the decline Boeing forecast the production of 550 airplanes in 1998, Airbus' planned production was set at 230, up 182 units from 1997. As of June 1, 1998 Boeing had 20 completed wide-body planes in storage waiting for Asian delivery.

The competition between Boeing and Airbus also cut into industry profits. Boeing has tried to maintain its 65 percent market share while Airbus has strived to gain a 50 percent market, which caused both manufacturers to cut sale prices by as much as 30 percent.

Another factor that played a part in the decline in sales is the current decline in air travel, again affected by the Asian economic crisis. The International Air Transport Association (IATA), a Geneva-based international airline industry association, reduced its forecast of Asian air traffic growth from an annualized rate of 7.7 percent down to 3.7 percent from 1999 through 2004. The publication *Economist* reported the 3.7 percent forecast as optimistic. Airbus predicted U.S. air traffic growth to slow to an annualized rate of 3.5 percent from 5 percent in the first decade of the new century.

British Airways, the first commercial airline to foresee the decline in the early 1990s, trimmed its capacity growth rate from 9 percent to less than 3 percent in late 1999.

According to its 1998 *Current Market Outlook*, Boeing's projected worldwide passenger and cargo traffic to grow at an annualized rate of 5 percent and 6 percent respectively through 2007. This projection would mean 7,600 commercial aircraft would need to be produced from 1997 through 2007. This estimate would comprise a market worth $520 billion. About two-thirds of these aircraft would be purchased in markets outside the United States.

Larger, longer-range jets are expected to be in greater demand because of increased air travel. But Boeing and Airbus disagree on the future needs of the industry. Boeing has canceled plans to develop a larger capacity 747 jumbo jet, while Airbus is designing their new super-jumbo jet with seating to accommodate 500-1000 people.

Along with growth, many airliners will be forced into retirement due to the noise regulations set by the International Civil Aviation Organization (ICAO), a trade association with members comprised of most of the world's air transport regulatory authorities. A deadline of 2002 has been agreed upon for all aircraft with a Stage Two designation to be retired. By the year 2000, the Federal Aviation Administration (FAA) has implemented the ruling that all aircraft flying over U.S. soil must meet the more stringent Stage Three limits. Most aircraft designated Stage Two are 15-20 years old and are less efficient.

In 1999 there were about 3,600 Stage Two planes in operation throughout the world, 2,090 of them in the

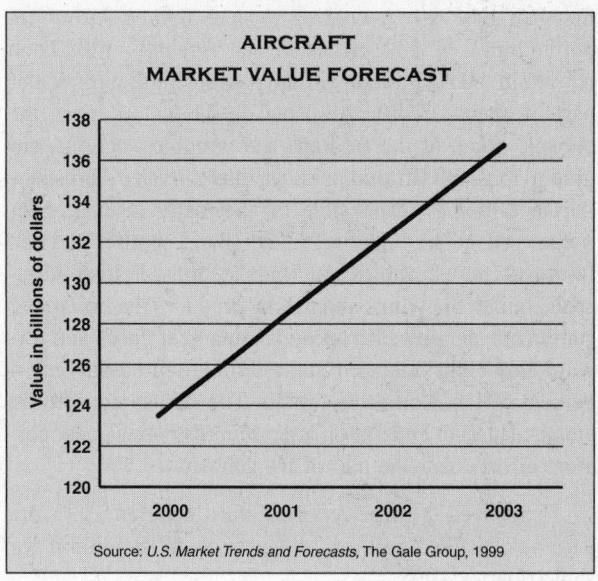

AIRCRAFT MARKET VALUE FORECAST

Source: *U.S. Market Trends and Forecasts,* The Gale Group, 1999

United States. Because of the costs and reduction in efficiency, it is expected that more than 50 percent of these Stage Two aircraft will be replaced rather than retrofitted with ''hushkits'' on their engines.

Since the cargo market is expected to more than triple in the first twenty years of 2000, it is predicted that many of these old aircraft would be used for freight transport. Boeing also projected the need for an additional 620 new aircraft for cargo in this time period to carry the forecasted revenue ton kilometers expected to grow from approximately 100 billion to about 350 billion revenue ton kilometers. Some 1,500 converted used aircraft sold by the commercial airlines will also provide those airlines with financial support to purchase their new aircraft.

INDUSTRY LEADERS

The Boeing Company acquired the defense and space units of Rockwell International in 1996 and merged with McDonnell Douglas in 1997 making Boeing the world's largest manufacturer of commercial jetliners, military aircraft, and NASA's leading contractor. The company employed more than 200,000 people in 1999 in more than 60 countries worldwide. Company revenues reached $56.2 billion in 1998. Boeing reported first quarter 1999 profits up 55 percent due to improved efficiency of commercial aircraft and cost reductions in business and research. Unfortunately, production problems have plagued Boeing since 1997 and as a result the company lost orders for aircraft from large companies such as British Airways, United Parcel Service, and Boulhoun Aviation Services to Airbus Industries costing Boeing millions of dollars and threatened its standing as the number one manufacturer.

Because of Boeing's production problems, Airbus Industries was able to move ahead of Boeing in orders for the first half of 1999. According to sales figures Airbus reported sales of 234 planes versus Boeing's 120. Each partner in the Airbus consortium manufactures a particular part of their aircraft. Aerospatiale Matra produces the cockpit, some of the fuselage and wingbox sections, engine pylons and lift dumpers. DaimlerChrysler Aerospace Airbus Gmbh is responsible for the major fuselage Sections, vertical tail, tail cone, rudder, flaps, spoilers and flap fairings, and assembles the wing sections. British Aerospace builds the wings and CASA produces the horizontal stabilizers and elevators, nose landing gear doors and forward cabin entry doors. Final assembly represents only 4 percent of labor on each aircraft. The Airbus consortium and the Russian Federation aircraft industry began cooperative efforts near the end of the century.

Lockheed Martin reported third quarter 1999 net earnings of $217 million, down from $318 million for same quarter 1998.

Northrop Grumman, based in Los Angeles, California, employs 49,600 people responsible for the design, development, and manufacture of aircraft, aircraft subassemblies, and electronic systems for the military. The company also designs, develops, operates and supports computer systems. Net sales rose 2 percent from January to September 1999 reaching $6.5 billion.

Bombardier the Montreal-based manufacturer received an order from Northwest Airlines in February 1999 for 54 50-passenger CRJ jet models totaling $1.9 billion Canadian to be delivered from 2000-2005. Bombardier fought and won a World Trade lawsuit against Brazilian Embraer, a rival company, because Embraer was benefiting from government subsidies allowing them to sell planes abroad at artificially low prices. As of late 1999 the company was considering the manufacture of a 90-seat jetliner because of the increase air travel. The company also manufactures railroad cars and recreational vehicles.

Eurocopter has four plants, two in France and two in Germany. The company also has 46 offices worldwide. Eurocopter has served 1,740 customers in 132 countries from December 1998 through November 1999. The company employs a workforce of 9,506 people producing 42 percent of the civil market, 25 percent of the military (excluding the United States) and 17 percent of the U.S. military market. As of December 31, 1998 Eurocopter had 8,414 helicopters in operation.

WORKFORCE

The total aircraft industry employment was 204,401 in 1997, with 98,552 employed as production workers at an average wage of close to $21.31 per hour. With the backlog of orders at several manufacturers, the potential for employment remained good through the year 2000.

AMERICA AND THE WORLD

Because of the Asian economic crisis that began in 1997 causing the Asian currencies to devalue, Alan Mulally, president for commercial aircraft at Boeing announced that his company, as well as the entire industry, would be Down 30-40 percent in 1999. However, he was optimistic orders would rise again in the year 2000. Prior to 1998, Japanese banks funded at least 25 percent of new equipment financing for the world's airlines. By 1998 there were few commitments made by these banks for aircraft. Although China did not suffer as greatly from the crisis, there was a significant Drop in airline traffic through the 1998 first quarter.

These reductions of U.S., Western European, Asian, and military orders the industry began looking to Latin American countries for sales. Argentina, Brazil, Chile, Mexico, Columbia and Venezuela were the major Latin markets in the late 1990s and into the year 2000.

Changes were also being made in Europe during the late 1990s. The political leaders of France, Germany, and England requested that the Airbus Industries consortium to restructure Europe's aerospace and defense Industries by December 1999. The Airbus consortium consisted of four Partner companies—British Aerospace PLC, Aerospatiale SA of France, Daimler-Benz Aerospace AG of Germany and Construcciones Aeronauticas SA of Spain. The goal is for a single unified European aerospace and defense Company to build aircraft, helicopters, missiles, launchers, and defense systems.

RESEARCH AND TECHNOLOGY

Augmented reality, a variation of virtual reality, lets the user see the world as an overlay of information so that it appears attached to a work piece, and has been installed in Boeing's wire shop. It assists workers by highlighting drilling locations. Airbus Industries was experimenting with a thin-film skin of nearly imperceptible ridges developed by 3M. By reducing surface turbulence, this skin could cut fuel burn by 1 percent. Northrup Grumman used advanced laser-based technology to reduce manufacturing and scheduling costs in its efforts to establish a digital airframe factory using a laser tracking system.

Research continued to develop new combustion chambers to further reduce exhaust emissions from aircraft. BMW Rolls-Royce's tests in November 1999 showed their new chamber significantly reduced emissions.

FURTHER READING

Aboulafia, Richard. "Flat Market for Business Aircraft." *Aviation & Space Week Technology,* 13 January 1997.

———. "Helo Makers: Decisions Pending." *Aviation & Space Week Technology,* 13 January 1997.

————. "Uncertain Upturn Challenges Commercial Transport Makers." *Aviation & Space Week Technology*, 13 January 1997.

Aerospace Industries Association. "Military Aircraft Accepted by U.S. Military Agencies: Number and Flyaway Value: Calendar Years 1981-1995." *Aerospace Facts and Figures 1996/1997*.

"Air China Orders Five Boeing 777s." Available from http://biz.yahoo.com/finance/97/03/24/ba_seattl_1.html.

Aibus Industrie. "Company History," 19 November 1999. Available from http://www.airbus.com

"Airbus See Exclusive Pacts as Bad for Business." Available from http://biz.yahoo.com/finance.

"An-70 Set to Fly." *Aviation Week & Space Technology*, 13 January 1997.

"BAE Australia Wins Exports." *Aviation Week & Space Technology*, 3 March 1997.

"Boeing 777 Breaks Speed and Distance Records." Available from http://biz.yahoo.com/finance/97/04/02/ba_y0002_1.html.

"Boeing Co. to Discuss Production in Turkey." Available from http://biz.yahoo.com/finance.

The Boeing Company. "Company History." November 19, 1999 Available from http://www.boeing.com.

"Boeing Creates Enterprise Unit." *Aviation Week & Space Technology*, 3 February 1997.

"Boeing Projects Healthy Airplane Demand Over Next 20 Years." Available from http://biz.yahoo.com/prnews/97/03/04/ba_y0002_1.html.

"Boeing Reports First Quarter Deliveries." Available from http://biz.yahoo.com/prnews/97/04/07/ba_y0001_1.html.

Byrne, Harlan S. "Borne Winners." *Barron's 1997*, 17 February 1997.

————. "Gaining Altitude." *Barron's 1999*, 3 May 1999.

Crock, Stan. "Aviation & Defense." *Business Week*, 13 January 1997.

Dahl, Robert V. "Air Freight Market is Expanding." *Aviation & Space Week Technology*, 13 January 1997.

Darlin, Darmin. "Aerospace & Defense." *Forbes*, 13 January 1997.

"Deflating the Jumbo." *Economist*, 25 January 1997.

Donoghue, J.A. "AE-100 at Center Stage." *Air Transport World*, January 1997.

————. "Boeing's Afternoon Delight." *Air Transport World*, February 1997.

Egan, Mark. "Gulfstream Looking for Revenues to Soar." Available from http://biz.yahoo.com/finance/97/04/08/ba_gacge_1.html.

Edmundson, Gail. "Europe Can't Delay any Longer." *Business Week*, 13 January 1997.

Flint, Perry. "Business as Usual." *Air Transport World*, February 1997.

Friedman, Matthew. "How Bombardier Created Sleek Global Express." *Computing Canada*, 3 February 1997.

Fulghum, David A. "Chile Agrees to First Foreign T-6A JPATS Sale." *Aviation Week & Space Technology*, 13 January 1997.

"GAMA Reports Record Billings." *Aviation Week & Space Technology*, 17 February 1997.

"Industry Awaits Impact of Boeing Merger." *Industrial Distribution*, February 1997.

InterPlane. "Airline Fleet Management News." 19 November 1999. Available from: http://www.inter-plane.com/newsfr.htm

Krumenaker, Larry. "Virtual Assembly." *Technology Review*, February/March 1997.

Langfield, Martin. "U.S. Military Unveils New 'Raptor' Stealth Fighter." Available from http://biz.yahoo.com/finance/97/04/09/ba_lmt_utx_2.html.

"Lockheed Martin Corp Boeing Co. Get Hellfire Work." Available from http://biz.yahoo.com/finance/97/04/07/ba_lmt_1.html.

Lockheed Martin Corporation. "Company History." 11/19/99 Available from: http://www.lockheedmartin.com

Northrop Grumman. "Company Statistics." 11/19/99 Available from: http://www.biz.yahoo.com/p/n/noc.html

Nundy, Julian. "Orders for Airplanes Dive Mainly Because of Asia." USA Today, June 14, 1999.

Proctor, Paul. "Boeing Balks, Airbus Talks——Big." *Aviation Week & Space Technology*, 27 January 1997.

————. "First Flight of Updated 737 Rejuvenates Narrow-Body Line." *Aviation Week & Space Technology*, 17 February 1997.

————. "Helicopter Sales Buoyed by Strong Economics." *Aviation Week & Space Technology*, 3 February 1997.

Shifrin, Carole A. "A Big Win for Airbus in North America." *Aviation & Space Week Technology*, 13 January 1997.

————. "Atlantic Southeast Plans Order of CJRs." *Aviation Week & Space Technology*, 13 January 1997.

————. "Derivatives of 777 and 767 Take Shape at Boeing." *Aviation Week & Space Technology*, 17 February 1997.

Sparaco, Pierre. "Airbus Plows Ahead with A3XX Plans." *Aviation Week & Space Technology*, 27 January 1997.

————. "Eurocopter Forecasts Modest Market Upturn." *Aviation Week & Space Technology*, 3 February 1997.

————. "French Merger Makes Progress." *Aviation & Space Week Technology*, 13 January 1997.

Standard and Poor's Industry Survey. "Aerospace." 1999.

Symonds, Willam C. "Bombardier Is Doing Barrel Rolls." *Business Week*, 3 March 1997.

"Teal Group Predicts 25,537 Aircraft Valued at $655.5 Billion Will be Built Throughout the World in the 1997-2006 Decade." Available from http://biz.yahoo.com/prnews/97/02/14/ba_md_y00_1.html.

U.S. Department of Commerce. Economics and Statistics Administration. Bureau of the Census. *Statistical Abstract of the United States 1997.* Washington: GPO, 1997.

U.S. Department of Commerce. International Trade Administration. *U.S. Industrial Outlook 1997.* Washington: GPO, 1997. Available from http://www.ita.gov

U.S. Department of Labor. Bureau of Labor Statistics. *Employment, Hours, and Earnings, United States, 1988-96.* Washington: GPO, 1996.

Occupational Outlook Handbook: 1996-97. Washington: GPO, 1996.

"Jumbo Market Too Slim for Two Manufacturers." *Aviation & Space Week Technology,* 27 January 1997.

Whitford, David. "Sale of the Century." *Fortune,* 17 February 1997.

Wolk, Martin. "Boeing Considers Move into Airline Maintenance." Available from http://biz.yahoo.com/finance/97/04/11/ba_brka_md_1.html.

Zuckerman, Lawrence. "An Order for Airbus Hits Its Rival, Boeing, Close To Home." New York Times, January 7, 1999.

SIC 3724

AIRCRAFT ENGINES AND ENGINE PARTS

This industry includes establishments primarily engaged in manufacturing aircraft engines and engine parts. This industry also includes establishments owned by aircraft engine manufacturers and primarily engaged in research and development on aircraft engines and engine parts, whether from enterprise funds or on a contract or fee basis. Also included are establishments engaged in repairing and rebuilding aircraft engines on a factory basis. Establishments primarily engaged in manufacturing guided missile and space vehicle propulsion units and parts are classified in **SIC 3764: Guided Missile and Space Vehicle Propulsion Units and Propulsion Unit Parts;** those manufacturing aircraft intake and exhaust valves and pistons are classified in **SIC 3592: Carburetors, Pistons, Piston Rings, and Valves;** and those manufacturing aircraft internal combustion engine filters are classified in **SIC 3714: Motor Vehicle Parts and Accessories.** Establishments primarily engaged in the repair of aircraft engines, except on a factory basis, are classified in **SIC 4581: Airports, Flying Fields, and Airport Terminal Services;** and research and development on aircraft engines on a contract or fee basis by establishments not owned by aircraft engine manufacturers are classified in **SIC 8731: Commercial Physical and Biological Research.**

NAICS CODE(S)

336412 (Aircraft Engine and Engine Parts Manufacturing)

INDUSTRY SNAPSHOT

The total value of aircraft engines and engine parts was $22.6 billion in 1997 according to the U.S. International Trade Administration. While the overall value of shipments decreased from a high of $25.3 billion in 1990, the positive balance of trade (exports over imports) continued through 1997. The consumption of aircraft engines is obviously a function of aircraft production and usually a multiple function due to the fact that many aircraft have several engines. The health of the aircraft industry is well-documented under **SIC 3721,** and projected growth on aircraft orders should bode well for the future of engine manufacturers as long as the aircraft industry continues to improve.

The world aircraft engine industry is dominated by three companies: General Electric (GE); Pratt & Whitney, which is a division of United Technologies Corporation; and Rolls-Royce. Each of these companies achieved their leading role through the successful development of jet engine models for commercial aircraft, though GE and Pratt & Whitney maintained significant interest in the development of engines for military aircraft. The big three offered jet engines in nearly every thrust range and competed with each other for use on commercial aircraft produced by Boeing, McDonnell Douglas, and Airbus Industries. Several other engine manufacturers, including Allison, Garrett, and Lycoming, were involved primarily with small jet turbines and piston engines, which power propeller-driven aircraft.

Aircraft engine manufacturers enjoyed a long period of industry growth from the end of World War II until the first years of the 1990s, when changes in military spending and changing commercial air travel patterns caused dramatic shifts in industry planning and expectations. Industry analysts predicted that engine manufacturers would struggle to adjust to an industry-wide recession throughout the mid-1990s when a revitalized commercial air travel market would increase orders for aircraft engines. The future of the aircraft engine market seemed likely to depend on the development of big engines with a thrust of 60,000 pounds or more, according to *Interavia.* Each of the leading engine manufacturers is expected to take steps to develop engines to compete in this market category, which is expected to generate $210 billion in sales of engines and parts through 2012.

ORGANIZATION AND STRUCTURE

The manufacture of aircraft engines was once controlled by the same companies assembling aircraft and operating airlines, but industry regulation initiated in

1934 forced aircraft engine manufacturers to work independently of aircraft manufacturers. This antitrust legislation is partly responsible for the intense competition that characterizes the aircraft engine industry in which each of the leading engine makers seeks to provide engines to fit the requirements of a wide range of aircraft. Engine companies are typically chosen to design an engine at the concept stage of a new aircraft. Once the engine is developed, the engine builder may try to adapt the design for other aircraft. In fact, it is common to find the same engine on a variety of competing aircraft. Engine manufacturers rarely develop an engine that is not capable of multiple applications.

For decades following the end of World War II, military funding supplied much of the research and development money that allowed U.S. manufacturers to continually upgrade their engines. Technical breakthroughs achieved on military projects found their way into commercial engine applications, thus allowing engine manufacturers to achieve substantial profits from commercial engine sales. This arrangement has changed significantly since the end of the Cold War when the U.S. military budget decreased dramatically. Though the Clinton Administration has promised to continue providing research and development funding to the aerospace industry, engine manufacturers are increasingly faced with incorporating the cost of research and development spending into the price of their engines. Bob Leduc, director of strategic planning at Pratt & Whitney, told *Interavia* that his company will need to spend close to $6 billion in development to compete for the large engine market—costs that will require the manufacturer to recover $1.3 million per engine just to cover engineering and development costs. Such prohibitive costs may force manufacturers to remove themselves from competition in some market segments.

All of the American aircraft engine manufacturers are divisions of larger corporations. Pratt & Whitney is a division of United Technologies, GE Aircraft Engines is a unit of General Electric, Allison is owned by General Motors, Garrett is a part of AlliedSignal, and Lycoming is part of Textron. Pratt & Whitney and GE are thought to possess an advantage over their British competitor, Rolls-Royce, because of their corporate support, which allows them to better weather industry cycles. While the Pratt & Whitney Power Group contributes approximately 32 percent of United Technologies' revenue and GE Aircraft Engines supplies 12 percent of GE's revenue, the aircraft engine portion of Rolls-Royce totals 60 percent of that company's revenue.

BACKGROUND AND DEVELOPMENT

The development of powered aviation, which began with the Wright Brothers in 1903, fell mainly to those who understood engines, rather than those who understood flight. In fact, aeronautical scientists—such as Samuel P. Langley, who was perhaps the first to describe the dynamics of lift over a wing—had very little to do with powered aircraft. Instead, a pair of bicycle mechanics, Wilbur and Orville Wright, and a motorcycle mechanic named Glenn Curtiss, were the first to demonstrate propeller-driven aircraft. In fact, Curtiss gained an early lead over the Wrights and a third aviator, Glenn Martin, precisely because he knew how to build lighter, more powerful motors. The first 10 years of motorized flight was pioneered by eccentric inventors working out of their garages by night and flying in air shows by day. These barnstormers relied on show earnings to pay for their building efforts, and many died in the process.

Industrial support for aviation did not materialize until European aviators demonstrated the strategic use of aircraft in World War I. Major industrial involvement in the United States occurred only after the U.S. Army requested funding for aviation projects. Financiers and industrial magnates were drawn to the industry not by their love of aviation, but by the opportunity to enrich themselves with government contracts. Some of the earliest investors in aircraft ventures were automobile manufacturers and automobile fleet owners. They sponsored specific aircraft builders and later pulled dishonest financial stunts to take control of aircraft builders' fledgling companies.

Edward Deeds, founder of Delco and the first to commercialize an electric starter, formed a one-sided partnership with the well-known Orville Wright called the Dayton-Wright Company. The company built engines, but no aircraft. The company was later acquired by William Boyce Thompson, who established the first American aircraft combine. Thompson acquired the patents owned by Wright and later Martin; he bought the rights to a light, European-designed engine called the Hispano-Suiza, and he acquired the facilities of the Simplex Automobile Company to build his engines. Shut out from the management of the company by Thompson and unhappy at only building engines, Wright retired and Martin started another company.

Unwilling to allow any single group of financiers to corner the aviation industry, U.S. government officials created the Aircraft Production Board to oversee the development of the American aviation industry. This Board was soon dominated by the automobile industry, which assembled an industrial federation called the Manufacturers Aircraft Association. Auto manufacturers, led by the Packard and Hall-Scott Motor Car companies, convinced the Aircraft Production Board to support the mass production of a single type of aircraft motor—a 400-horsepower, 8-cylinder model called the "Liberty." As evidence of the industry's widespread complicity, this huge water-cooled engine featured an unnecessary electronic ignition system supplied by Delco. Completely inappropriate for use on existing aircraft designs, the monstrosity was better suited for a truck or a boat than an aircraft.

Under pressure from auto manufacturers, the government ordered the production of 11,000 Libertys. This so infuriated Donald Douglas, the leading aircraft designer on the board, that he resigned his position and returned to making airplanes for Glenn Martin. Confident of the program's failure, he, like many other aircraft manufacturers, simply ignored the Liberty. Despite problems with Delco's starter and with the reconfiguration of the Liberty into an even larger 12-cylinder engine, the government remained perfectly comfortable entrusting the future of aviation to such experienced transportation pioneers as Packard, Hudson, Nash, and Ford.

An Indianapolis, Indiana, engine builder named Jim Allison recognized the futility of placing the huge Liberty motor in the light aircraft of the day and decided to build a light engine of his own. As he pursued the development of lighter engines, he stumbled across a variety of high-quality manufacturing techniques. Engines, he discovered, ran most efficiently at about 30,000 rotations per minute while propellers generated the greatest amount of thrust at about 2,000 rotations. What was required was a precisely-machined reduction gear. Allison was the first major manufacturer to perfect an engine and clutch mechanism with acceptable tolerances. His lead in this area greatly advanced the Allison reputation and provided the company with hundreds of profitable orders.

Another engine builder of the day was Frederick Rentschler, one of the original founders of Wright Aeronautical. Rentschler grew increasingly weary of managerial interference from automobile magnates, whom he thought were interested only in short-term profit. The development of engines required years of expensive and often fruitless experimentation. Rentschler resigned from Wright in 1924 and began searching for a factory and financial backing to develop better engines. Like Douglas and Allison, Rentschler knew the Liberty design was a failure. He learned from a naval officer that the service would soon announce a competition for a powerful, lightweight, air-cooled design.

In 1925, Rentschler acquired the Pratt & Whitney company, a small machine tool manufacturer in Hartford, Connecticut. Rentschler raided the Wright company of its best engineering talent and enlisted the help of Chance Vought, an aircraft builder. By Christmas of that year, Pratt & Whitney completed its first air-cooled radial engine, the 425-horsepower Wasp. The radial design meant that the cylinders were arranged in a circular fashion around the prop shaft, rather than being lined up along the shaft as in an automobile. This allowed the cylinders to be directly exposed to the thrust of air generated by the propeller. As a result, there was no need

for a bulky radiator or heavy liquid coolant, as in the Liberty. Barely one year old, the Pratt & Whitney company secured an order from the Navy for 200 Wasps. This provided the capital needed to develop an even larger, 525-horsepower engine, the Hornet.

In 1929, automotive interests organized yet another company, Curtiss-Wright, bearing the name of aviation's first pioneers. While neither Glenn Curtiss nor Orville Wright were active in the company, it did manage to turn out a successful product, the Cyclone radial engine. General Motors made the switch to air-cooled engines when its Dutch designer, Anthony Fokker, chose Pratt & Whitney's Wasp engine for his aircraft. Ford, meanwhile, dropped out of the aircraft business to concentrate on automobiles. The Lycoming Foundry and Machine Shop, established in Williamsport, Pennsylvania in 1908, began building aircraft engines during the late 1920s. Its position in the industry was secured by the success of its nine-cylinder R-680 radial engine, which was standard on many aircraft.

Pratt & Whitney gained dominance in the industry when it gained the attention of Bill Boeing, an aircraft builder in Seattle, Washington. Boeing, too, was looking for a replacement for the Liberty and considered the Wasp to be the perfect engine for his fighters and mail planes. When Boeing married the Wasp to his Model 40 mail plane, he discovered the craft could carry an additional 500 pounds of mail, or even passengers, making it extremely profitable. Boeing, Rentschler and Vought later merged their companies into what became America's most powerful aeronautical combine. The new company, called United Aircraft & Transportation, acquired the amphibious airplane builder Sikorsky, the light aircraft manufacturer Stearman, Jack Northrop's Avion experimental aircraft company, propeller makers Hamilton and Standard Steel, and a combination of small airline companies.

United Aircraft grew at an extremely fast pace. While the Great Depression virtually destroyed the industry, United Aircraft continued to expand, taking over the routes of defunct airline companies and providing a stream of exclusive Pratt & Whitney-driven aircraft for the military. In 1934, Senator Hugo Black led an investigation of the industry that resulted in legislation that broke up the aircraft combines. The Boeing Company was separated from United Aircraft, as were the airline services, which were reincorporated as United Airlines in Chicago. Pratt & Whitney, however, remained a division of United Aircraft.

The importance of efficient, powerful engines was well understood by manufacturers in Germany and Japan, who embraced aviation as an instrument of warfare during the mid-1930s. Companies such as Daimler-Benz and Mitsubishi closely studied the advancements in American engine designs and were heavily sponsored by their governments. As a result, during the years leading up to World War II, Japanese and German aircraft advanced beyond the capabilities of American designs. By 1940, however, with the war raging in Europe, the U.S. government began a massive mobilization of its war industries.

Pratt & Whitney, which had developed a 2,000-horsepower Double Wasp engine, was required to vastly expand its production capacity. Still unable to meet the demand for nearly 8,000 of these engines, Pratt & Whitney licensed production of its designs to Ford, Buick, Chevrolet, and Nash-Kelvinator. By the end of the war, Pratt & Whitney and its licensees produced a staggering 363,619 aircraft engines, representing half of all the horsepower used by the U.S. military during the war.

Meanwhile, Curtiss-Wright's R1820 Cyclone was used to power the Boeing B-17 bomber, the Douglas Dauntless dive bomber, and a number of DC-3s. A second design, the R3350, powered Boeing's B-29 bomber and, later, Lockheed's Constellation airliner. Curtiss-Wright provided 35 percent of American wartime horsepower. Allison occupied a special position during the war, producing 70,000 of its V1710 engines for aircraft such as the Lockheed P-38 and Curtiss P-40 Tomahawk. Lycoming, now a division of Avco, built only smaller engines—one of which powered Sikorsky's first helicopter in 1939.

Another manufacturer, the Garrett Corporation, was drawn into engine manufacture during the war. Garrett entered the market first by building intercoolers and turbochargers, devices that heated and concentrated the mix of oxygen and fuel in the combustion chamber for higher engine performance. Garrett turbochargers were fitted to existing engines on American aircraft, vastly improving their performance. Garrett also was active in the production of air conditioning systems and flight controls. Established in 1935 by Cliff Garrett, the company emerged from the war with an excellent reputation among airframe builders and later launched an aggressive diversification that included the development of engines. Garrett's first engine design was the 575-horsepower Model 331 gas turbine, intended for use on helicopters and light aircraft. This engine was later used to power the Beechcraft 18, Aero Commander, and Mitsubishi models.

Curtiss-Wright emerged from the war as the number two engine builder in the industry—a position it did not hold for long. Rather than plow its substantial earnings back into product development, Curtiss-Wright chose to invest its profits in other businesses, thus ceding its position to more enlightened competitors such as Pratt & Whitney and General Electric.

During the war, government war procurement officials had designated Pratt & Whitney, Curtiss-Wright, and Allison to produce only piston-driven engines. Meanwhile, the development of jet engines was given to Allis Chalmers, General Electric, and Westinghouse, since they were experienced with steam turbines. The introduction of the jet engine was the most significant development in aviation since the Wright Brothers' first flight. Existing engines used fuel to drive pistons down, turning a shaft while driving other pistons up for another firing. Jet engines used an entirely different principle: air was scooped into a chamber and compressed by a series of turbine blades. Behind these blades, a highly refined fuel was sprayed into the compressed air and ignited. The resulting blast was channeled out the rear of the engine, where it drove a second turbine that powered the intake compressors. With their enormous thrust, jet engines could propel an aircraft at much greater speeds than conventional propellers.

The first jet engines were successfully built in Germany and England. Britain's Rolls-Royce held a strong lead in jet engine technology, due to the work of the inventor Frank Whittle. It was several years before American companies assumed leadership in jet technology, using Whittle's designs. General Electric, whose experience in turbine technology originated with steam-driven electrical generators, was given a government contract to develop Whittle's engine for a new jet, the Bell Aircraft XP-59A, which first flew in 1942. A practical jet engine emerged only after the war, however, with the J33 and J35, which were used to power the Boeing B-47 and Northrop B-49 flying wing. GE turned over its licenses for these designs to Allison in 1946.

Westinghouse scored an early coup in jet technology by building the first axial flow engine; earlier models used less efficient centrifugal compression. But Westinghouse lost its early lead in jet technology when the Navy changed its weight specifications for the engines and canceled millions of dollars worth of orders for Westinghouse engines. Unable to adapt quickly, Westinghouse simply abandoned the jet engine market.

Pratt & Whitney was first introduced to jet engines as a subcontractor to Westinghouse. Later, because American law required that foreign designs for military craft be manufactured domestically, Pratt & Whitney built versions of Rolls-Royce's Nene and Tay jet engines, which saw action during the Korean War. Pratt & Whitney's future was secured when it achieved a major engineering breakthrough. General Electric had been planning engines with up to 7,000 pounds of thrust, but Pratt & Whitney decided to leapfrog other competitors by building an engine that would produce 10,000 pounds of thrust. The result, the J57/JT3, was used to power the F-100, F-101, and F-102 fighters while eight of the engines were used on Boeing's massive new B-52 bomber. Thus the continuing battle for ever-increasing amounts of jet thrust was born.

General Motors' Allison division, initially paralyzed by postwar labor action, pursued jet engine development with GE's J33 design. Allison manufactured 15,525 of these engines for a variety of fighter aircraft, and secured its position in the postwar engine market. Lycoming capitalized on its involvement with helicopters after the war. Under the direction of Dr. Anselm Franz, the company built the T53, the first jet engine designed specifically for helicopters. Nearly 20,000 were produced.

Following World War II, government-led industry coordination ended and free market competition, fueled by Cold War military budgets, began. As a result GE terminated its technological partnership with Allison and began work on the J47, which drove the North American F-86 in combat over Korea. A later model, the high-performance J79, powered Convair's B-58, the Lockheed F-104 and McDonnell F-4 Phantom. As in the airframe industry, many of the advancements earned from wartime engine development were applied to commercial markets. Thousands of airliners were retrofitted with more efficient turbo-powered engines.

The advent of jet-powered bombers gave aircraft builders the experience necessary to create jet airliners. After Britain's DeHavilland built the first commercial jet, the Comet, Boeing, Douglas and Convair scrambled to develop their own jetliners. When Boeing's 707 was introduced in 1954, it was powered by four Pratt & Whitney JT3s. Douglas' DC-8, which took to the air in 1955, used the same engine. A commercial version of GE's J79 powered Convair's short-lived 880 and 990 jetliners.

While jet engine companies had successfully converted military engines to civilian uses, the Defense Department continued to press for even greater advancements in propulsion technology. The leading manufacturers began testing ramjets, engines that were designed for such high-speed flight that they required no compressor fans. General Electric was given a contract to build a nuclear-powered jet engine, and Pratt & Whitney was asked to develop liquid hydrogen-fueled rocket motors. Allison built a counter-rotating propeller engine for Convair's vertical takeoff and landing "Pogo Stick" airplane. All the projects were successful, though only the rocket technology was developed.

Within the conventional jet engine arena, General Electric built a massive new J93 engine in 1963. This boron-fueled engine, rated at 30,000 pounds thrust, was developed for North American's brilliant but obsolete Mach-3 B-70 bomber. Pratt & Whitney had better luck in triplesonic flight, developing the J58 engine for Lockheed's SR-71. Capable of crossing the United States in only 68 minutes, the SR-71 established numerous performance records. Pratt & Whitney also built the J75 for Lockheed's high altitude U-2 spy plane. The J52, how-

ever, was the company's military mainstay. In production for 30 years, the J52 powered a long line of naval aircraft.

Among the smaller manufacturers, Curtiss-Wright's sales were declining rapidly by 1960. In 1963, as part of a scheme to bolster its position in the market and acquire a staff of talented engineers, Curtiss-Wright launched a hostile takeover bid for Garrett. Garrett's management remained deeply suspicious of its suitor, however, and enlisted the support of Signal Oil & Gas, a company with the financial resources to thwart Curtiss-Wright's bid. Signal acquired Garrett in 1964, permitting the company to operate autonomously. Garrett was firmly established as a manufacturer of auxiliary power units, small engines that are used to provide power to start main engines. Garrett built this business into a series of successful small propulsion engines, principally the TFE731, which powered the Learjet 25, Cessna Citation, and Hawker Siddeley 125 business jets.

Lycoming regained its position in the fixed wing market in the mid-1960s, after developing its own small turbofan. This design evolved into the ALF502 which, like Garrett's design, was popular with a variety of business jets. The engine was chosen to power the Hawker Siddeley 146, which eventually emerged as the popular British Aerospace BAe 146 commuter jet.

In the airliner market, Allison briefly extended the life of turboprops by developing a T56 powerplant for a family of Convair airliners, the 440, 540, and 580. Meanwhile Boeing was developing a new medium-range trijet called the 727 and asked for an engine similar to Rolls-Royce's Spey. Allison formed a partnership with Rolls-Royce, but lost the 727 business to Pratt & Whitney, whose JT8D became a best-seller in the industry. In addition to the 727, the versatile engine was used on four twinjets: the Boeing 737, Douglas DC-9, Sud Aviation Caravelle, and Dassault Mercure.

While Pratt & Whitney and its JT8D dominated the commercial market, General Electric's J79 derivative declined with the increasingly unpopular Convair jetliners. But General Electric expanded its market for jet engines well beyond the aircraft industry. Variations on the company's engines powered missiles, helicopters, hovercraft, speedboats, and even electrical power generators. GE's J85 series became a favorite among the growing ranks of private jet manufacturers. The company scored a major coup in 1965 when it was chosen to develop the engines for Lockheed's super transport, the C-5 Galaxy. To lift the massive freighter into the sky, GE had to develop a more efficient high-bypass "turbofan" engine.

With early turbofans, about half the air taken into an engine passed concentrically around its combustion chamber, providing additional thrust and allowing the engine to operate more efficiently. GE's high-bypass design, the

TF39, increased the bypass ratio to eight to one. Four of the engines, which generated 41,100 pounds of thrust, would enable the C-5 to carry 132 tons of cargo. Airline companies immediately embraced the quieter, more fuel-efficient turbofan, which was perfectly suited for subsonic passenger aircraft. But because the engines were considerably fatter, it was impossible to retrofit the thousands of existing aircraft that were designed for the long, skinny JT8D turbojet. Instead, turbofans were reserved for the new line of jumbo jets. The TF39 gave GE the lead in engines for large passenger aircraft such as Boeing's 747, McDonnell Douglas' DC-10 and Lockheed's L-1011. A commercial version of the high-bypass turbofan, the CF6, was developed for the DC-10 in 1971 and Airbus' A300 in 1974.

Pratt & Whitney began development of its own high-bypass engine in 1960. The company's TF30 was used aboard General Dynamics' F-111 and Grumman F-14 and led to a civilian version, the JT9D, which could generate more than 43,000 pounds of thrust. The JT9D entered service with the 747 in 1969 and was the only 747 powerplant until 1975, when GE developed a CF6 for the jumbo jet.

Meanwhile, Lockheed's L-1011 Tristar, a competitor to the DC-10 and 747, was powered by RB211 engines from Rolls-Royce. Allison, Rolls-Royce's American partner, wisely elected to steer clear of the RB211, sure that its pricing was flawed. When problems later arose with the engine, Allison avoided the brush with bankruptcy that nearly ruined Rolls-Royce and Lockheed. Allison did, however, convert its production of Rolls-Royce's Spey into its own TF41, which went on to power Vought's A-7 Corsair. In addition, Allison's T56 turboprop was chosen for the Lockheed C-130 transport, Grumman E-2C, and Lockheed Orion.

During the late 1960s, GE was asked to apply its experience with the J93 toward the development of an engine for Boeing's supersonic transport. The resulting design, the GE4, generated nearly 70,000 pounds of thrust. Four of these engines would enable the SST to reach 1,800 miles per hour. However, Boeing canceled the program after airlines lost interest in the SST.

General Electric was awarded a contract to develop a new engine for Rockwell's B-1 bomber in 1970. Unlike the B-52, which the bomber would replace, the B-1 was fitted with afterburners. A common feature of fighter jets, the afterburner was a mechanism that detonated a second spray of fuel into an engine's exhaust thrust. The resulting blast could add as much as 50 percent more power to an engine. The B-1, and the F101 engine GE developed for it, were canceled in 1977. But the engine went back into production when the B-1 program was revived in 1981.

Engine manufacturers benefited greatly from drastically increased defense spending under the Reagan admin-

istration. But the heavy investment in defense industries during those years led to several scandal-ridden cases of overcharging and non-performance. While few of these cases involved engine manufacturers, the laws put in place to correct the abuses still applied to them. These laws were meant to extract more economical and responsible development by mandating strict competitions for government business, particularly between General Electric and Pratt & Whitney.

General Electric's F404 engine, developed for McDonnell Douglas' F-18 fighter, was fitted to Grumman's X-29, an experimental high-maneuverability aircraft with forward swept wings. The engine was later used for Lockheed's F-117 Stealth fighter—which flew secretly as early as 1981—and SAAB's Gripen fighter.

Pratt & Whitney developed the F100 in 1970 for McDonnell Douglas' F-15. The engine, which could send an F-15 to 98,000 feet in only three minutes, was later fitted to General Dynamics' F-16. However, turbine wear on the F100 took years to correct, enabling General Electric to step in with an alternative. GE combined the finest elements of the F101 and F404 to produce the versatile F110. This engine powered all of America's leading fighter jets, including the F-15, F-16 and F-14. Eventually, GE's F110 gained 75 percent of the F100's market.

The loss convinced Pratt & Whitney to pay closer attention to the Pentagon's needs. The company developed variants with special new capabilities and by 1990 had won back a quarter of the government's Fighter Engine Competition business. Meanwhile, Pratt & Whitney developed a second derivative of its F101, the F118, which was chosen to power Northrop's B-2 Stealth bomber.

Strong growth in airline traffic during the 1970s led aircraft manufacturers to create a new family of airliners to replace the aging DC-8, DC-9, and 727. Boeing designed two large twin-jets, the 757 and 767. The European Airbus consortium introduced a new line of A310, A320, and A330 aircraft. McDonnell Douglas, however, elected to update its existing models. The DC-9 became the MD-80, and the DC-10 became the MD-11. Development centered on improved avionics and control functions, but the greatest advancement occurred with engines, which were now quieter and far more fuel-efficient.

Pratt & Whitney's position in the commercial markets started to wane in the 1980s. The company was reviled for its growing arrogance and lack of customer focus, and had rested too long on the laurels of its successful JT8D. General Electric's deliveries surpassed Pratt & Whitney's in 1986. General Electric captured a large portion of the new market through its CF6 series and a partnership with the French engine manufacturer SNECMA called CFM International. The company's

CFM56 was used to re-engine the old fuel-guzzling DC-8 and military versions of the 707, and was the standard engine on Airbus' A320. In 1987, GE formed a second partnership with Garrett called the CFE Company. This company developed the CFE738, a 6,000 pound thrust turbofan for the small jet market, specifically the Dassault Falcon 2000 business jet.

Eager to remain in the game, Pratt & Whitney established its own international partnership with the German Motoren und Turbinen Union and Italy's Fiat Avianzione. The company developed the PW2037 for Boeing's 757, and the PW4000—designed specifically to compete with the CF6—for the 747. The PW2037 caused General Electric to abandon its entry for the 757, but Pratt & Whitney still faced competition from a modified version of Rolls-Royce's RB211. Pratt & Whitney later formed a second consortium, called International Aero Engines, with MTU, Fiat, Rolls-Royce, and Japanese Aero Engines. The company's V2500 engine was used to power Airbus' A320. The partnerships helped preserve Pratt & Whitney's position in the industry until it could mend its relations with airline companies and aircraft manufacturers.

While manufacturers were often able to convert military engines into commercial versions, the two markets held fundamentally different requirements. Airline companies wanted highly reliable, fuel-efficient engines that were quiet and did not pollute. The military, on the other hand, wanted powerful lightweight engines that remained cool enough to avoid detection by enemy tracking. During the mid-1980s, demand grew for a new type of commercial engine with little or no use for the military. Conventional high-bypass jet engines burned too much fuel for the increasingly cost-conscious airline industry, which requested development of a new hybrid propjet.

General Electric and Pratt & Whitney immediately began work on elaborate jet engines whose turbines drove two rear-mounted counter-rotating propellers with crescent-shaped blades. This "propfan," while slightly slower than conventional engines, was twice as fuel efficient as turbofans. The propfan was an unducted pusher propeller design, intended for installation on the rear fuselage of aircraft. Accordingly, Boeing and McDonnell Douglas tested propfans on a 727 and MD-80, and began development of two new twin-propfan designs, the 7J7 and MD-91. In England, Rolls-Royce began work on a ducted propfan, with its blades enclosed within a large shell, called the contrafan. Such a propfan would be suitable for the thousands of aircraft whose engines were wing-mounted.

During the late 1980s, a vicious cycle of competition drove airlines into near bankruptcy while fuel prices dropped. Airline companies canceled orders for hundreds of new aircraft, choosing instead to squeeze a few more years of service out of their existing fleets. As a result, airframe and engine manufacturers were forced to shelve

the propfan indefinitely. Despite this, Boeing began planning a larger super twinjet, the 777, intended to compete with the MD-11. Pratt & Whitney's PW4000 was chosen as the launch customer for the 777.

After the worst recession in over a decade, the turbine engine was slowly rebounding in 1996. Airframes manufacturers and engine producing counterparts had a successful year in 1996. Intense competition threatened profitability in the recent past but also led to the development of products. General Electric and Pratt & Whitney teamed to help reduce the threat of competitiveness to earnings.

Fundamental forces have reshaped the jet engine market. Solutions to the challenges posed by developing near perfect engines and competition have resulted in alliances between competitors, new pricing mechanisms, increased participation in aftermarket, and a reduction in the number of engine types per platform.

Cooperative ventures are being forced because of competition. Two rivals—GE Aircraft Engines and Pratt & Whitney—had joined together to develop a power plant for the Boeing 747-500X primarily in reaction to GEAE, Rolls-Royce, and Pratt's price competition for the Boeing 777. Boeing subsequently decided to cancel the 747X program. Airbus remains committed to the super jumbo, however. Several joint ventures such as GE Aircraft and Pratt & Whitney, Rolls Royce and Pratt & Whitney, and GEAE and Snecma have had varying degrees of success. In the past several have fallen apart over strategies or details.

The early 1990s saw one of the biggest shakeups in aerospace industry history, as military budgets shrank and fewer people chose to fly. Commercial airlines canceled or postponed their orders for airplanes, and aircraft manufacturers, in turn, canceled their orders for aircraft engines. The industry recession proved particularly challenging for the aircraft engine industry, which was in the process of developing a number of engines for the expected orders of large jet-powered aircraft. General Electric, which had been pouring money into the development of its GE90 engine for the Boeing 777 aircraft, was the most severely affected of the big three engine manufacturers, but all three companies faced dismal short-term prospects.

Industry analysts wondered if the intense competition that had characterized the aircraft engine industry through the 1980s could continue through the 1990s. *Air Transport World* contributor J.A. Donoghue noted that "all three major manufacturers say they are committed to a battle across a broad front; the trend is for competitive offerings to increase as the defense market continues its decline. Airlines undoubtedly are the beneficiaries of these aggressive competitive matchups virtually across the board. The key question is whether this level of competitiveness is sustainable.'' The biggest drain on the competitors is likely to be research and development costs, which, following the end of the Cold War, are no longer boosted by Department of Defense dollars.

One difficulty, according to *Interavia* is that "engine manufacturers live in a world where the time unit is not the year, but the decade." Dozens of years are needed to develop an engine and expand it across a wide range of aircraft, and dozens more to realize that engine's impact on the market. Luckily, engine manufacturers are rewarded for successful development by a lucrative spare parts and upgrade market. Since aircraft engines represent such a large investment for airlines, those airlines seek to extend engine life up to 25 years through frequent maintenance and upgrading. According to *Interavia,* "Pratt & Whitney derives about 40 percent of its pre-tax earnings from commercial engine spares sales," a figure characteristic of the industry.

Leasing engines is becoming increasingly popular as airlines seek to obtain totally predictable engine costs and to avoid stocking inventories of back-up engines and spare parts. Leasing is packaged with fixed maintenance service costs. However, Steve Forbes argued against recent IRS decisions not to allow regional carriers to expense the cost of inspecting aircraft engines and a proposed technical change regarding leasing rules that could cost the industry millions of dollars. Willis Lease Finance Corporation was leasing 35 engines in October 1996 and expected to increase this number to 40 by the end of 1996 with additional increases in 1997.

CURRENT CONDITIONS

By 1998, the total value of aircraft engines and parts had risen 20 percent from 1997; an increase of approximately 3 percent was expected for 1999. The industry was expected to continue a 3 to 4 percent annual increase through 2003. Exports accounted for nearly 40 percent of 1996 shipments, increased 25 percent in 1997, and had a forecasted increase of 20 percent for 1998.

Boeing and General Electric, as well as other original engine and parts manufacturers (OEMs) of aircraft engines, formed their own independent service centers. Outsourcing was becoming more popular by the major airlines to help reduce costs. The U.S. government also saw this as a means for savings by shifting civilian and military personnel from non-combatant support to warfighting aircraft only.

Industry forecasts are much more optimistic when they are extended into the twenty-first century. "Forecasters estimate that between 1992 and 2012, about $330 billion in engines and spare parts will be sold to commercial carriers outside of the former Soviet Union, with $200 billion of the quantity directly attributable to engine sales," according to *Aviation Week & Space Technology.*

According to estimates, 54 percent of this money will be spent on engines with thrust greater than 45,000 pounds, 32 percent on engines with thrust less than 30,000 pounds, and the remainder on mid-range engines. The anticipated boom in engine sales is expected to begin after 1995 and continue for at least a decade as airlines retire their older aircraft and trade up to larger aircraft capable of carrying more than 200 passengers.

Meanwhile, in the military arena, the Pentagon is sponsoring a competition for a new Advanced Tactical Fighter, or ATF, between Northrop and Lockheed. Similarly, General Electric and Pratt & Whitney were asked to compete for the engine to drive the ATF. In this test, Pratt & Whitney's F119 would challenge GE's F120. The successful model could be worth more than 1 billion dollars to the winner.

INDUSTRY LEADERS

As manufacturer of the first jet engine, General Electric still held the title as the world's leading manufacturer of military and commercial aircraft jet engines. The company also produced, as well as serviced, small jet engines for airlines, charter and leasing companies, and the military.

GE Aircraft Engines reported $10.3 billion in revenue for 1998 and expected further growth through their life-cycle engineering and maintenance service to their customers. In 1999 General Electric received orders for more than 1,000 CFM56 engines for the third consecutive year. GE's CF6-80C2 engine is used to power Air Force One, the 747 airplane used by America's president. General Electric Services, the world's leading integrated engine maintenance resource, had revenues exceeding $5 billion in 1999.

BMW Rolls-Royce acquired Indiana's Allison Engine Company in 1995 and became Rolls-Royce Allison. The Rolls-Royce companies developed and produced the new BR700 engine family for corporate jets and transport craft. The BMW Rolls-Royce division was responsible for development, production, and repair/overhaul of small gas turbines and components for civil and military engines. For almost 30 years, BMW Rolls-Royce had been manufacturing engine parts for the German military at its Oberursel facility in Germany.

Pratt & Whitney, a division of United Technologies, had supplied the engines to more than 50 percent of the world's commercial airliners. Pratt & Whitney Canada was the world's number one supplier of engines for corporate jets, commuter planes, and helicopters. Pratt & Whitney partnered with General Electric in the late 1990s to create The GE-P&W Engine Alliance. This program was designed to upgrade the performance of the GP7000 series of engines for Airbus A3XX and the Boeing Growth 747.

Textron Lycoming and Detroit Diesel joined forces in 1998 to design, develop, certify, and manufacture aerodiesel engines for aircraft. Because jet fuel was readily available throughout the world (as were the new lighter alloys to build lighter, more efficient engines) it was believed these new engines would be successful especially in remote areas of the world.

WORKFORCE

In November 1997 there were 82,892 employees in the aircraft engine industry, 48,212 of which were specifically engaged in production. These employees were averaging eight hours in overtime per week and earned an average of $19.59 per hour. If the aircraft industry is able to replace losses in military orders with civilian orders, employment in the industry should be steady.

AMERICA AND THE WORLD

CFM International, a joint company of General Electric, created a 50-50 company with SNECMA of France to become the world's leading supplier of mid-size commercial engines. SNECMA had also supplied the French military with most of their aircraft engines. This new company received orders from American Airlines, Continental Airlines, Delta Air Lines, Iberia Airlines, Korean Airlines, Lufthansa German Airlines, Sabena Belgian Airlines, Southwest Airlines, and VARIG. In 1998 the new Boeing 777 was being delivered to Saudi Arabian Airlines. CFM also created GE VARIG Engine Services in Brazil to expand their worldwide market. A joint venture maintenance contract with EVA Airways and an expanded On-Wing SupportSM maintenance network in China also helped to broaden their scope.

Pratt & Whitney signed a 10-year maintenance contract with Japan Air System in November 1999. The value of this contract to service 63 JT8D-200 engines at their Columbus, Georgia, facility was estimated to be worth $150 million. Pratt & Whitney owned major overhaul centers in Connecticut, Georgia, and Singapore and repair facilities throughout the United States, Europe, and Asia.

RESEARCH AND TECHNOLOGY

Research was underway to develop an unleaded avgas to replace the 100 low lead (LL) avgas used for aircraft near the end of the century. The American Society of Testing and Materials (ASTM) was to conduct the research. There were many issues facing this program. Among them were the environment, cost, and the segregation of avgas from all other fuels, the system maintenance of the lead-contaminated fuels, and the world's political climate.

The FAA's Technical Center was addressing such issues as engine detonation, material compatibility, volatility (vapor lock), engine performance, storage stability,

water reactions, emissions, changes in fuel consumption, and engine durability.

BMW Rolls-Royce developed the engine for the "Future Large Aircraft" (FLA), a military transporter, which meets the air force requirements of Belgium, France, Germany, Italy, Portugal, Spain, Turkey, and the United Kingdom. This turboprop engine will meet maximum take-off weight, operate from short unpaved runways, and will have good low speed and high cruise speed flight. The FLA is scheduled to be in service by 2006.

FURTHER READING

Aboulafia, Richard. "Turbine Market Slowly Rebounds." *Aviation Week & Space Technology,* 13 January 1997.

BMW Rolls-Royce. *BMW Rolls-Royce,* 1999. Available from http://www.airforce-technology.com/contractors/engines.

"Boeing 777, Powered by Pratt & Whitney Engines, Receives Certification," 28 February 1997. Available from http://biz.yahoo.com/prnews/97/02/28/ba_y0002_2.html.

"BR710 is Certified." *Air Transport World,* October 1996.

Davidson, Lesia. "Business Watch." *Aviation Week & Space Technology,* 26 October 1998.

"Engine Makers Persevere in Face of Boeing Challenge." *Aviation Week & Space Technology,* 27 January 1997.

"F119 Versatility Challenged by JSF Requirements." *Aviation Week & Space Technology,* 25 November 1996.

Forbes, Steve. "Ground These Changes." *Forbes,* 2 December 1996.

"GE Tests Japanese Engine Aimed at Future SSTs." *Aviation Week & Space Technology,* 20 January 1997.

General Electric Aircraft Engines. *History,* 1999. Available from http://www.ge.com/aircraftengines.

"General Electric Tests Improved GE90 System." *Aviation Week & Space Technology,* 21 October 1996.

Hui, Yang. "A Artificial Intelligence System of Trouble Diagnosis for Aircraft Engines." *Computers & Industrial Engineering,* December 1996.

Mecham, Michael. "Two Chinese Carriers Named to A320 List." *Aviation Week & Space Technology,* 11 November 1996.

"NTSB Targets JT8D Cracks." *Aviation Week & Space Technology,* 3 February 1997.

Phillips, Edward H. "Cracks Focus of FAA Airworthiness Directives." *Aviation Week & Space Technology,* 14 October 1996.

"Reduced-Signature Nozzle Tested by GE." *Aviation Week & Space Technology,* 17 February 1997.

Sparaco, Pierre. "Airbus Plows Ahead with A3XX Plans." *Aviation Week & Space Technology,* 27 January 1997.

U.S. Department of Commerce. Bureau of the Census. "Aircraft Engines & Engine Parts," 1997.

U.S. Industry and Trade Outlook 1999. McGraw-Hill, 1999.

Woolsey, James P. "Riding the '96 Buying Surge." *Air Transport World,* January 1997.

SIC 3728

AIRCRAFT PARTS AND AUXILIARY EQUIPMENT, NOT ELSEWHERE CLASSIFIED

This category includes establishments primarily engaged in manufacturing aircraft parts and auxiliary equipment, not elsewhere classified. This industry also includes establishments owned by manufacturers of aircraft parts and auxiliary equipment and primarily engaged in research and development on aircraft parts, whether from enterprise funds or on a contract or fee basis. Establishments primarily engaged in manufacturing or assembling complete aircraft are classified in **SIC 3721: Aircraft;** those manufacturing aircraft engines and parts are classified in **SIC 3724: Aircraft Engines and Engine Parts;** those manufacturing aeronautical instruments are classified in **SIC 3812: Search, Detection, Navigation, Guidance, Aeronautical, and Nautical Systems and Instruments;** those manufacturing aircraft engine electrical equipment are classified in **SIC 3694: Electrical Equipment for Internal Combustion Engines;** and those manufacturing guided missile and space vehicle parts and auxiliary equipment are classified in **SIC 3769: Guided Missile and Space Vehicle Parts and Auxiliary Equipment, Not Elsewhere Classified.** Establishments not owned by manufacturers of aircraft parts but primarily engaged in research and development on aircraft parts on a contract or fee basis are classified in **SIC 8731: Commercial and Biological Research.**

NAICS CODE(S)

332912 (Fluid Power Valve and Hose Fitting Manufacturing)
336413 (Other Aircraft Part and Auxiliary Equipment Manufacturing)

INDUSTRY SNAPSHOT

The total value of shipments of aircraft parts and equipment (products and services) for 1998 was expected to be $25.2 billion. Estimated exports of $15.7 billion were forecast to exceed imports of $5.5 billion by century's end.

The American aircraft industry may be divided into four segments. In one segment, manufacturers such as Boeing-McDonnell Douglas and Lockheed build the wings and fuselages that comprise the airframe. Meanwhile, companies such as General Electric and Pratt & Whitney manufacture the engines that propel aircraft.

The third segment covers flight instrumentation, an area where the most profound advances in aviation have taken place. But the fourth segment, broadly defined by industrial classification as "aircraft parts not otherwise classified," includes manufacturers of surface control and cabin pressurization systems, landing gear, lighting, galley equipment, and general use products such as nuts and bolts. This highly diversified industry generated shipments in 1996 of $20.2 million and regularly was running a $6 million trade surplus at that time, contributing significantly to the greater aerospace industry, which ranked sixth in the United States in overall value of shipments and first in exports.

ORGANIZATION AND STRUCTURE

Aircraft manufacturers rely on a broad base of suppliers to provide the thousands of subsystems and parts that make up their products. There are more than 4,000 suppliers contributing parts to the aerospace industry, including rubber companies, refrigerator makers, appliance manufacturers, and general electronics enterprises. This diversity is necessary because in most cases it is simply uneconomical for an aircraft manufacturer to establish, for example, its own landing light operation. The internal demand for such a specialized product is insufficient to justify the creation of an independent manufacturing division.

Aircraft manufacturers have found it cheaper and more efficient to purchase secondary products from other manufacturers, who may sell similar products to other aircraft companies, as well as automotive manufacturers, railroad signal makers, locomotive and ship builders, and a variety of other customers. For example, an airplane builder such as Boeing, Grumman, or Beech is likely to purchase landing lights from a light bulb maker such as General Electric. Such subcontractors supply a surprisingly large portion of the entire aircraft. On the typical commercial aircraft, a lead manufacturer such as McDonnell Douglas may actually manufacture less than half of the aircraft, though it is responsible for the design and assembly of the final product.

When a major manufacturer discontinues an aircraft design, as Lockheed did with its L-1011 Tristar, a ripple effect is caused that affects every manufacturer that supplied parts for that aircraft. Therefore, parts suppliers strive to diversify their customer base to ensure that the decline of one manufacturer will be tempered by continued sales to others. Given the unstable nature of the industry, parts manufacturers also attempt to find customers outside of the aircraft business as well.

BACKGROUND AND DEVELOPMENT

Aircraft parts manufacturing may be said to predate the invention of powered aircraft. The Wright Brothers' first airplane, little more than a propeller-driven kite, was equipped with cables, chains, and an engine that were built by others. In the purest sense, Orville and Wilbur Wright merely designed and assembled their aircraft from existing parts. The same was true of innovator Glenn Curtiss, a motorcycle repairman from upstate New York. While Curtiss had access to the lightweight engines required for flight, he began to experiment with flight controls and invented the aileron, a movable surface on the trailing edge of a wing that revolutionized handling characteristics. The Wrights had clearly invented the airplane, but Curtiss had undoubtedly developed a key control mechanism that made flight practical.

American aviation remained the province of tinkerers from the Wrights' first flight in 1903 until 1916, when European combatants in World War I demonstrated the utility of aircraft as strategic battlefield weapons. The government hastily created an aviation program within the Army Signal Corps and held a competition for the right to supply more than 20,000 aircraft. Hundreds of amateur flyers, including Glenn Martin, Bill Boeing, Donald Douglas, and Allan and Malcolm Loughead, rushed into the business. Limited in their resources and working out of garages, these pioneers were forced to incorporate whatever parts they could find into their aircraft. The designs of these aircraft were simple, often consisting of fabric stretched over a wooden frame and manipulated with cables and hinges. But the most important part of these aircraft was the engine.

At the time, automobile manufacturers held a virtual monopoly on advanced engine designs. They also had the manufacturing capacity to mass produce the thousands of aircraft the government wanted. As a result, automobile executives easily muscled their way into control of the nation's aviation industry. While this arrangement bred only bad designs and corruption, it established an enduring organizational structure in the aviation industry. General Motors, Ford, Nash, and Packard had long subcontracted manufacturing of parts for its automobiles to independent manufacturers. Unwilling to build manufacturing facilities for something as speculative as aircraft, these manufacturers simply turned to the established automotive supply network for items such as glass, wheels, instrumentation, and seats.

As quickly as they had entered, automobile companies abandoned aviation after the government canceled its 20,000-plane order at the end of World War I. Aircraft designers were once again in charge of their destinies as manufacturers. But they continued to be supplied by the very same parts network that served the automobile industry. Aviation enterprises floundered until 1927, when Charles Lindbergh's daring cross-Atlantic flight inspired tremendous investment in the industry. This growth was choked off after 1929, however, as the nation sunk into the depths of the Great Depression. Traumatized by

changes in the industry, aviation companies continued to make small advances on the strength of military sales and a growing air mail business. Eventually this led to the formation of three enormous aviation combines, the largest of which, United Aircraft, might one day have rivaled General Motors in size.

United Aircraft consisted of four airframe builders, Boeing, Vought, Northrop, and Stearman, the engine maker Pratt & Whitney, and a series of airline companies that later became United Air Lines. This powerful organization took over two propeller makers and numerous other manufacturers and began manufacturing a greater proportion of its own parts. The other two monopolies, North American Aviation and the Aviation Corporation of the Americas, were in the process of building similar organizations when, in 1934, the government stepped in with antitrust investigation that broke up the combines and decentralized aircraft manufacturing.

This breakup provided new growth opportunities for a wide variety of potential suppliers. Companies that had previously never even considered the aircraft parts business suddenly discovered the viability of extending their product line into aviation. The driving force behind this expansion was technology. Where aviators were once limited to day flight, lighting and instruments enabled them to fly in darkness. Where navigation had once required visual landmarks, such as railroad tracks, now there were radio and gyroscopes. And where flying was once limited to lower elevations, now there were cabin pressurization systems and oxygen supplements.

The greatest advances in aviation took place during World War II. Heavy government investment in the industry enabled new technologies to be developed that enabled aircraft to fly higher, faster, and with more agility than ever before. This placed new stresses on conventional parts and encouraged the development of specialized engineering. Jet aircraft, first tested in 1942, provide the best example of this. While airframes had to be fundamentally redesigned to handle the rigors of jet flight, so too did items such as terminal wiring, indicator lamps, pumps, and fluid systems. Repeated exposure to vibration and powerful G-forces caused many conventional parts to break apart. As a result, the development of high-performance aircraft was hampered as much by weak light bulb filaments and rivets as by weak airframes.

The specialized engineering required for postwar aviation necessitated tremendous research funding and elevated manufacturing occupations to fine sciences. Companies that were ill-prepared for this new type of work were forced out of the market or into consolidation with other, stronger manufacturers. Aircraft contractors necessarily became fewer, and the prices of their products grew higher.

Generally, navigation and communications systems were handled by companies that specialized in instrumentation, such as Sperry, Lear, and Motorola. Meanwhile, with a few notable exceptions, heating, hydraulics, and pressurization systems were handled by engine manufacturers such as Pratt & Whitney, Curtiss-Wright, Allison and General Electric. Manufacturers such as Garrett, Teledyne, Litton, and Dowty manufactured adjunct systems that provided compressed air, temperature regulation, cabin pressurization, and hydraulic pressure. Other companies historically associated with the automotive industry, such as BF Goodrich, Bendix, and Cleveland Pneumatic, provided products such as wheel assemblies, pumps, hoses, gaskets, and even window seals.

A large constituent in the industry consisted of companies that were already associated with aviation, including United Aircraft, Boeing, Lockheed, and McDonnell Douglas. Other smaller manufacturers, such as Cessna and Beech, also found a place in the market as suppliers of specialized parts. As a result of bad management, Curtiss-Wright was slowly forced out of engine manufacturing during the 1950s. But the company managed to maintain a leading position in the parts industry, particularly with propellers and a series of wing actuator systems.

Heavy government investment in aviation, primarily through military programs and a budding space agency, continued to result in ever more advanced aircraft. North American Aviation's B-70 bomber and Lockheed's SR-71 reconnaissance jet established new triplesonic speed records, while a variety of other craft managed to climb to more than 100,000 feet. Such planes required paint that exhibited special heat deflection properties. Even landing tires required coating with aluminum paints and inflation with lithium. Windshields were required to withstand tremendous impacts, such as collision with a bird at 2,200 miles per hour. In each case, aircraft parts suppliers never led development of new aircraft. Instead, lead manufacturers conceived of new designs and issued required specifications, and parts manufacturers filled their requirements.

While the Cold War confrontation with the Soviet Union provided the justification for new weapons, American involvement in Vietnam often provided the testing ground. New military designs enabled aircraft manufacturers to develop a further variety of new aircraft, including a supersonic passenger transport, jumbo jets, and huge freighters. Advances funded by military dollars helped lower the costs of commercial flight and allowed airline companies to offer passengers more sophisticated in-flight services, including radio headphone entertainment and movies. In addition, galley service became more efficient, incorporating microwave as well as convection heat sources and complex food storage conveyors and dumbwaiters. As aircraft became ever more complex, the aircraft parts industry grew proportionally, until it numbered almost 11,000 suppliers.

The entire aerospace industry had enjoyed nearly fifty years of growth following the end of World War II, but an industry recession beginning in the late 1980s and early 1990s caused major shifts in the industry. Military spending peaked in 1987 and dropped precipitously following the end of Cold War tensions in 1989, forcing many military-oriented parts suppliers to leave the market. According to *U.S. Industrial Outlook 1993,* about 15,000 suppliers left the aerospace defense market between 1982 and 1987, a decrease that continued into the 1990s, though at a slower rate. A similar decrease occurred in the commercial aircraft parts industry, as the supplier base dropped from 11,000 to 4,000, driven by aircraft manufacturer's demands for greater efficiency. ''For parts suppliers, this streamlining has meant that only the most efficient and highest quality manufacturers have been able to stay in this market,'' noted *U.S. Industrial Outlook 1993.*

Exacerbating the effects of industry streamlining has been the increasing competition from foreign parts suppliers. In order to penetrate international markets, U.S. aircraft and aircraft engine makers have entered into international teaming agreements that specify that a certain proportion of parts are purchased from overseas suppliers. Such agreements have helped foster advances in the aerospace industries of many countries, particularly in the Far East, but have contributed to the shrinkage of the U.S. aircraft parts industry. Employment fell 13 percent between 1990 and 1992, and an additional 6 percent decline was expected in 1993. Total employment numbered 166,000 people in 1993. According to *U.S. Industrial Outlook 1993,* ''long-term prospects are for continued declines on the military side, and stabilizing employment on the commercial side.''

The late 1980s saw a rash of problems associated with the manufacture of faulty and inadequate parts. The Federal Aviation Administration sets guidelines for the quality and precision of airline parts and certifies the acceptability of manufacturers, but prior to the appearance of bogus parts in the late 1980s it had no measures in place to enforce conformity with these standards. When aircraft mechanics discovered that parts of inferior quality had infiltrated the spare parts marketplace, several task forces set about to establish more stringent means of identifying and monitoring parts. Such guidelines are expected to be in place by 1994. According to *Aviation Week & Space Technology,* most of the manufacturers of defective parts are ''small companies, in the $3-10 million range. The companies have been immediately suspended from doing business with the government, and could be debarred for three to five years.''

CURRENT CONDITIONS

The problem of bogus parts continued to plague the industry in the late 1990s. The cause of a ValuJet engine explosion on the ground at Atlanta in June 1996 was determined to be an engine that had been overhauled by a repair station in Turkey that lacked Federal Aviation Administration (FAA) approval. The engine contained a crackled and corroded compressor disk. The National Transportation Safety Board (NTSB) uses the term "unapproved parts" in its official accident reports. A three-month investigation by *Business Week* revealed that bogus parts, including fakes, used parts sold as new, and new parts sold for unapproved purposes have found their way into the inventory of every major airline in the country. In 1996 some fire extinguishers intended for Air Force One were found to be falsely certified by a repair station. While bogus parts are not routinely causing accidents, the problem of substandard parts has grown substantially in the past five years. One supplier mislabeled spacers with fake Pratt & Whitney labels, but was caught by an astute airline mechanic. Clearly, parts are not labeled as bogus by the suppliers, but are laundered from used, stolen or substandard parts, or are incorrectly specified as meeting standards via a number of means. Parts brokers adding false paperwork sell to unsuspecting brokers which sell to an unwitting FAA approved facility or airline. The FAA regulates manufacturers, repair facilities, and aircraft operators, but it is more difficult to regulate parts brokers. Although there have been 164 indictments and 130 convictions in the past decade, the airlines rely primarily on sharp-eyed mechanics to spot counterfeit parts.

A further concern of the FAA involved revisions requiring helicopters that were type-certified after 1989 meet stricter seat load standards to improve the chance of survival of passengers and crew. The changes were a result of military pilots suffering from back injuries in crashes where the occupants were unable to exit the aircraft. These energy-absorbing seats are produced in the United States, U.K., Germany, and Israel, and are optional to buyers of the helicopters certified previous to 1989.

As of 1999 ejection seats, which are an important factor in saving the lives of military fighters, may no longer be produced in the United States. At the time the United States had only one active producer of these important components. Major reductions in U.S. defense procurement of new combat aircraft within the past 10 years had severely eroded the market, and prospects for expanding this market between 1998-2003 were not very encouraging. The future market of the ejection seats will be given to foreign countries unless industry-government action steps in.

INDUSTRY LEADERS

The major manufacturers are Sundstrand Corp., BF Goodrich who merged with Coltec Industries and Coltec Holdings, Aero and Industrial Technology Limited, for-

merly Lucas Aerospace, Fairchild, Boeing, and Textron Aerostructures.

The largest supplier of aircraft parts is Sundstrand, a Rockford, Illinois-based defense electronics company that broke into the aviation market during World War II. The company established a leading position in hydraulics and generators that paved the way for its involvement in jet aircraft technologies during the 1960s. Sundstrand's aviation supply operations expanded rapidly after 1967, due to an aggressive acquisition campaign that gave it the ability to manufacture instrumentation, entertainment systems, temperature controls, and gear drives.

The company's earnings from aircraft parts grew rapidly during the 1980s as a result of generous defense budgets. Sundstrand acquired several more aviation supply companies that broadened its position as a military contractor and provided new opportunities in civilian aviation. Accused of fraud in 1988, Sundstrand was fined and temporarily suspended from bidding on government contracts. The company later endured reverses from a rapid decline in defense spending. However, Sundstrand managed to realign its operations toward more stable civilian work, supplying products to Boeing, Airbus, McDonnell Douglas, and other customers. Sundstrand is the largest parts manufacturer, comprising 9 percent of the segment's total sales.

As of 1999 Sundstrand Corporation announced record year-end results. Full year net earnings for 1998 increased 26 percent to $227 million. In 1998 Sundstrand's aerospace group made two small "bolt-on" acquisitions which helped give immediate entrance into the relatively new commercial space launch business with light-weight propellant tanks, pressure tanks, and domes for commercial satellites and launch vehicles.

In November 1998 Coltec merged with the BF Goodrich Company to create a corporation with approximately $6 billion in annual revenues. The combined company, headquartered in Charlotte, North Carolina, had leading market positions in aerospace systems, performance materials, and industrial products.

Lucas Aerospace became Aero and Industrial Technology Limited (AIT) in the 1990s. As Lucas Aerospace this company gained its expertise in aviation products early, adapting its core automotive parts line for British aircraft manufacturers during World War I. Lucas was introduced to American aviation in the 1930s through a partnership with Bendix called Rotax. Rotax was closely involved with jet engine technologies, and manufactured a variety of electronic and fuel control systems in the post-World War II period. Rotax became Lucas Aerospace in 1971, and prospered from its parent company's involvement with British Aerospace and the Airbus consortium. Due to the fact that Lucas is foreign-controlled, its sales are mainly confined to the civilian aircraft market. Lucas has moved away from the traditional job shop mode into a just-in-time production and integrated disparate manufacturing and business systems using CONTROL, an enterprise resources planning software system from Cincom Systems.

BF Goodrich, began as a supplier in 1909, providing the wheels for Glenn Curtiss' early designs. The company subsequently branched into de-icing systems, flight suits, self-sealing fuel tanks, and later inflatable aircraft evacuation slides. BF Goodrich sold its tire operations to Michelin in 1986 specifically to concentrate on the aircraft supply market. Through a series of acquisitions, the company expanded into engine and fuel systems, test equipment, and flight instruments. In 1993 BF Goodrich took over Cleveland Pneumatic, a supplier of landing gear for the 747, 767, MD-11, and B-2 bomber. Fairchild remains active in the market through its association with the now defunct Republic Aircraft company. Allied-Signal also plays a major role, stemming from its acquisition of Garrett, as does Boeing, by virtue of its leading role in the airframe industry.

In November 1998 the BF Goodrich Company and Coltec Industries agreed to a strategic merger. The combined company, headquartered in Charlotte, had leading market positions in aerospace systems, performance materials and industrial products and generated approximately $6 billion in annual revenues. In 1998 net income went up to $226.5 million from $178.2 million in 1997. Between 1997 and 1998 the company's Aerospace Equipment Segment had a 48 percent increase of operating income.

In the late 1990s Boeing had been a world leader in commercial flight for over 40 years with extensive global operations in 27 states, employees in more than 60 countries and customers in over 140 countries. It's main commercial products consisted of the 717 (formerly the Md-95), 737, 747, 757, 767, and 777 families of jetliners, the MD-80, MD-90, MD-11, and Boeing Business Jet. In total, the corporation had more than 10,000 commercial jetliners in service worldwide. Boeing was also responsible for a substantial number of military aircraft and defense-system products and programs and was NASA's leading contractor. Throughout the late 1990s, Boeing enjoyed a steady increase of revenues. In 1999 the company earned approximately $58 billion in revenues compared with $22.7 billion in 1996.

Boeing Commercial Airplane Group and Concentra Corporation were developing a strategic electrical-configuration application that would reduce the cycle time for routing aircraft wire harnesses. Boeing was also charged with integrating avionics, sensors, and vehicle management systems with cockpit controls and displays for the F-22 scheduled to be come airborne in mid-1997.

In the area of commercial space, Boeing teamed up with Teledesic Corporation to create a satellite network. This "Internet-in-the-sky" brought affordable fiber-quality access to even the most remote areas of the planet. By building the first 40 Global Positioning System Satellites, Boeing revolutionized precision navigation. It obtained a contract to build 33 next-generation Global Positioning Satellites and teamed with partners from Russia, Ukraine, and Norway on the Sea Launch joint venture, which launched satellites from a mobile platform in the Pacific (the first of which took place in October 1999).

Commercial aerospace vendors have developed a new generation of cabin equipment that reduces operating costs, enhances passenger comfort, is lighter and more reliable, and requires less maintenance. Envirovac introduced a new glide rinse valve for toilets that ended the failure connected with wet solenoid rinse valves. Boeing enhanced this product with a device that allows the flush cycle to be independently adjusted in the front and the rear of the aircraft to reduce unnecessary noise.

By the end of 1997, 300 planes will be retrofitted with EmPower, a standard interface for in- flight power mounted in the armrest of the seat. This device will free portable computers from dependence on batteries during long flights.

A new in-flight financial services terminal to accommodate the need for foreign exchange, estimated to be $20 billion in currencies a year, is needed by passengers who travel on long-range wide-body planes. The developer, Aero-Design Technology, has also sold more than 1,000 galley trash compactors to over 40 airlines.

The new National Route Program and ensuing transition to Free Flight is posing a cockpit challenge that is being met with new electronics equipment. In the Fall of 1997 the Boeing 737-700 carried this new crystal display cockpit.

In August 1996 Motorola announced a two-way messaging device that lets users send and receive e-mail unobtrusively and access the Internet. Transmission is via Sky Tel's network of ground transmitters.

Using FANS-I, the Future Air Navigation System's suite of the Global Positioning System (GPS), and satellite data link communication, United Air Lines was permitted to fly from Chicago to Hong Kong through Chinese and Siberian airspace. Clearance through this airspace was made available only to planes with this equipment and clearance was on a flight by flight basis. By the end of 1997 certified FANS packages was available for new installation or retrofitting on most of the major aircraft types. Rockwell Collins Air Transport Division expects use will continue to grow, especially in India, as more Required Navigation Performance routes are established. The sole in-service FANS equipment as of September 1996 was on 747-400s which used the Honeywell equipment. The Boeing 777 includes FANS as standard equipment with its Increased weight aircraft. It is optional on 757/767 planes. Over 650 HT9100 units were sold in 1996. Airbus is also constructing its own FANS package.

By the year 2000, the GPS market was expected to reach $8.4 billion compared to $1.9 billion in 1996. Prices have been dropping at the rate of 20 percent a year. Applications are endless.

WORKFORCE

A total of 120,800 persons were employed in the aircraft parts and equipment industry in December 1996 (an increase of 9,100 or nearly 9 percent over December 1995) with 75,800 in production alone. Average hourly earnings were $16.68 in December 1996.

AMERICA AND THE WORLD

Because of the 1998-1999 financial crisis of eastern Asia, that region's aerospace industry as well as it's airlines had been greatly effected. The crisis could deplete $2.5 billion world airline's operating profits and lessen the demand for international passengers through 2003—a warning issued by the International Air Transport Association (IATA). As a result, IATA revised the forecast for passenger traffic downward for 1997-2001. The prospected average international growth went from 6.6 percent to 5.5 percent.

A further consequence for the aerospace parts industry from the situation in eastern Asia was the reduction of capacity for funding since Japanese banks were among the most important of these equipment funders. From 1988-1997 Japanese banks provided some 25 percent of the financing needed for equipment raised from the world's airlines. As of February 1998 Japanese banks had made almost no new funding commitments. Other countries, notably Germany, had become more active in this area, although not nearly enough to pick up the slack left by the Japanese. The International Monetary Fund (IMF) noted in their report, however, that the United States and the European Union in 1998-99 would continue experiencing solid growth despite this "Asian flu."

Beginning in October 1998 and continuing to 2001, South Korea's Samsung Aerospace Industries Ltd. was scheduled to provide U.S.-based Boeing with $13 million worth of plane wing frameworks for Boeing's 767 series airplanes. From 2002-2006 the company will sell Boeing $17 million worth of frameworks.

Also in 1999 Taiwan's Aero Industry Development Center (AIDC), a manufacturing company, was looking to privatize, supplying parts to larger, more established companies and entering partnership programs for various types of aircraft and their components.

Singapore Technologies Aerospace (STA) joined with European manufacturers such as Airbus Industries and Eurocopter (the Franco-German helicopter manufacturer) to produce parts and emphasize regional maintenance of European aircraft.

RESEARCH AND TECHNOLOGY

A structural foam was developed by researchers at MER Corporation of Tucson, Arizona and the U.S. Air Force Research Laboratories Materials and Manufacturing Directorate. They successfully produced a one-foot long test sample of graphite foam. As a replacement for aluminum and graphite honeycomb core and for use in aircraft structures, this development showed promise. The many advantages to this structural foam included high three-directional strength, net shape molding and integral bonding, and co-curing to face sheet composite fabric without adhesive on intermediate steps, according to James Withers, CEO of MER Corporation.

A further development in the industry dealt with a Millennium piston engine rebuild program in association with overhaul companies. Superior Air Parts of Dallas, Texas developed rebuilds for the most popular Lycoming and Continental piston engine models which perform to more exacting standards than the factory overhauled engines. The rebuilds also came with a 5-year parts and labor warranty and included Superior's investment-cast Millennium cylinders. Montrose, Colorado's Western Skyways was the first engine overhaul facility certified to perform Millennium rebuilds. As of 1999, a network of 10 centers was expected to be implemented.

In the late 1990s research had also been done by the U.S. Air Force (USAF) about seats which enhance the survivability of an aircraft's occupants, notably ejection seats. Ejection seats enhance national security by saving the lives and operation experience of pilot fighters and thus were studied extensively.

FURTHER READING

"Aerospace." *Business Africa,* August 1996.

"Aircraft Repair Station Speeds Turnaround." *Adhesives Age,* May 1996.

AIT Ltd. *AIT Ltd.* 1999. Available from http://www.ait.ac .psiweb.com

BF Goodrich. *BF Goodrich Reports Significantly Increased Earnings for Fourth Quarter and Full Year 1998.* 1999. Available from http://www.prnewswire.com/cnoc/exec/menu

Boeing. *Company History.* 1999. Available from http://www .boeing.com

Coltec. *From Debt Reduction to Growth.* 1999. Available from http://www.coltecindustries.com

Donoghue, J. A. "Equipping for FANS." *Air Transport World,* September 1996.

Flint, Perry. "I Want Pilots, Not Monitors." *Air Transport World,* October 1996.

"Flying High." *Manufacturing Systems. Supplement for Makers of Highly Engineered Products Supplement,* May 1996.

"Foreign Exchange Goes Airborne." *Air Transport World,* November 1996.

"Ion-Based Treatment Fills Microcracks." *Manufacturing Equipment,* July 1996.

Klass, Philip J. "New Device Cuts Cost of Fiber-Optic Gyros." *Aviation Week & Space Technology,* 11 November 1996.

McKenna, James T. "A Team of Engineers from Boeing." *Aviation Week & Space Technology,* 12 August 1996.

Nordwall, Bruce D. "Chicago-Hong Kong: First Direct FANS-1 Flight." *Aviation Week & Space Technology,* 12 August 1996.

———. "Collins Pro Line 21 Features Adaptive Flight Displays." *Aviation Week & Space Technology,* 18 November 1996.

———. "Optimism Grows for GPS/Glonass." *Aviation Week & Space Technology,* 14 October 1996.

Patterson, Lee. "A Mode Less Traveled." *Forbes,* ASAP Supplement, 24 February 1997.

Proctor, Paul. "F-22 Components Underway at Boeing." *Aviation Week & Space Technology,* 10 June 1996.

———. "Rebuild Networking." *Aviation Week & Space Technology.* 8 November 1999.

———. "Low-Level Collision Avoidance Tested." *Aviation Week & Space Technology,* 3 February 1997.

Scott, William B. "Composite Parts Will Pay Dividends in Future Engines." *Aviation Week & Space Technology,* 26 August 1996.

Schwartz, Ephriam. "In-Flight Power on the Way." *InfoWorld,* 10 March 1997.

Stern, Willy. "Warning! Bogus Parts Have Turned Up in Commercial Jets." *Business Week,* June 1996.

Sundstrand Corporation. *Sundstrand Reports record Fourth Quarter and Full Year Results.* 1999. Available from http://www.snds.com.

Sykes, Rebecca. "Motorola's Tango Offers Wireless E-mail." *InfoWorld,* 26 August 1996.

U.S. Industry & Trade Outlook 99. Aircraft Parts & Equipment n.e.c. 1999.

U.S. International Trade Administration. "No. 11495. Recent Trends in Aircraft and Aircraft Engines & Engine Parts." Available from http://www.ita.doc.gov/industry/otea/usio/95s1495.txt.

Velocci, Anthony L. "Operating Costs Drive Cabin Product Design." *Aviation Week & Space Technology,* 5 September 1996.

———. "Raytheon Pursues Double Acquisition." *Aviation Week & Space Technology,* 13 January 1997.

SHIP BUILDING AND REPAIRING

This category covers establishments primarily engaged in building and repairing ships, barges, and lighters, whether self-propelled or towed by other craft. This industry also includes the conversion and alteration of ships, the manufacture of offshore oil and gas, well drilling and production platforms (whether or not self-propelled). Establishments primarily engaged in fabricating structural assemblies or components for ships, or subcontractors engaged in ship painting, joinery, carpentry work, and electrical wiring installation are classified in other industries. Boat building and repairing are excluded as they are in a separate category, **SIC 3732: Boat Building and Repairing.**

NAICS CODE(S)

336611 (Ship Building and Repairing)

INDUSTRY SNAPSHOT

The U.S. commercial shipbuilding and repair industry entered the last half of the 1990s with the brightest prospects it has had in decades. The dramatic turnaround, according to former Maritime Administrator Adm. Albert Herberger, is due in large part to President Clinton's five-point national shipbuilding initiative.

Speaking in the spring of 1996 at the first American International Shipping Exposition (AISE) in New Orleans, Admiral Herberger credited the recovery to determination by shipbuilders and the president's support of the industry. Clinton's five-point plan calls for his administration to negotiate for the elimination of foreign shipbuilding subsidies, improve competitiveness, deregulate existing programs, enhance private sector financing of shipbuilding with federal loan guarantees, and expand international marketing activities. As of April 1996, Admiral Herberger said, 15 oceangoing ships were under construction in American shipyards, the largest number in more than a decade. Even more encouraging were the first U.S. exports of commercial vessels in 30 years.

Until this startling turnaround during the mid-1990s, virtually all merchant tonnage built in American shipyards was destined for domestic customers under a subsidy program or under the protection of the Merchant Marine Act of 1920, the Jones Act, which specifies that all inter-coastal traffic must move in U.S.-built vessels. The U.S. Navy in recent years has been the largest customer of the industry. As a result, American yards have a greater capability to build one-of-a-kind sophisticated ships than to mass-produce less complex large merchant vessels.

U.S. shipyards build about 1.1 percent of world commercial deadweight tonnage annually (deadweight tons is a measure of ship carrying capacity), which is well below that produced by Japan, Korea, China, and several other countries. An illustration of the decline of the United States in the world shipping market can be measured as a percentage of world vessel tonnage under order.

With the end of the Cold War, the U.S. military industrial base began shrinking dramatically, as did the nation's shipbuilding industry, dependent as it was on defense orders. This made it all the more imperative that a means was found to get the U.S. industry moving in another direction. In January of 1990, an American shipbuilding concern received the first order for a commercial oceangoing vessel since 1984. Ship owners, including American companies, favored foreign shipyards because of cheaper prices and faster order turn-around time. Government subsidies in Japan, Korea, and Germany ranged from 20 percent to 30 percent of the cost of the ship, enabling these builders to capture almost all of the commercial shipbuilding business.

It became very clear that unless foreign shipbuilding and repair subsidies were eliminated, it would be difficult for U.S. shipbuilders to fully participate in the forecasted replacement of the world's aging merchant fleet during the 1990s. With the downsizing of the U.S. Naval fleet and the lockout of U.S. shipbuilders from the commercial market in the face of government-subsidized competition, the future of the U.S. shipbuilding and repair industry was looking bleak. The industry was facing massive layoffs and yard closures in this noncompetitive market.

One of the biggest obstacles to U.S. shipbuilding competitiveness was high state-sponsored shipbuilding subsidies, which were enjoyed by shipyards in a number of other countries. In early 1997, an international agreement to end such subsidies, thus leveling the playing field for U.S. shipyards, was pending before Congress. A continuing recovery for the U.S. shipbuilding industry depended heavily on the successful passage of such measures.

ORGANIZATION AND STRUCTURE

The United States has four shipbuilding regions: the Atlantic Coast, Gulf Coast, Pacific Coast, and Great Lakes. All four have capabilities to construct commercial and military ships. The Great Lakes yards, however, can only export ships that fit within the constraints of the Welland Canal and the St. Lawrence Seaway. For this reason, Great Lakes shipbuilding employment is only a small percentage of the industry total in the United States. Peterson Builders Inc. was the last major shipbuilder in the area with less than 5 percent of the shipbuilding industry's work force. The Atlantic Coast has the largest percentage of total employment, followed by the Gulf Coast, with the Pacific Coast third.

In the United States, most major shipbuilding yards are owned by conglomerates or large corporations. The Bethlehem Steel Corporation is an example of this type of entity—BethShip is its shipbuilding unit and is located in Port Arthur, Texas, and Sparrows Point, Maryland. One of the problems with this type of alignment is that it places the shipbuilding division in competition with other divisions of the corporation for investment dollars for expansion, modernization, or other purposes. With an average return on equity of 6 percent in the shipbuilding industry, shipbuilding divisions have been losing the fight for corporate resources. An argument in behalf of this structure is that the parent corporation may have more success in obtaining favorable financing than a relatively small subdivision would have if it operated independently.

The shipbuilding and repair industry is a capital-intensive business requiring extensive initial capital to enter the industry and meet subsequent outfitting and technological requirements. These factors provide substantial barriers to entry, especially since the industry is not very profitable. The protection of the Shipping Act of 1916 is important to the survival of industry members because it helps them consistently attract sufficient cargo to cover initial outlays and fixed costs. The conference system was created to help protect this Act. Through agreements enforced among the member groups, the conference system stabilized freight rates and the production of new commercial vessels. The stability of this system is necessary for individual shipbuilders to establish a cost structure and pricing policy.

As compared with the shipbuilding industry overseas, there has been relatively little cooperation among the yards in the United States. In Norway and Sweden for example, research is sponsored jointly by the major shipyards. Other shipbuilding and shipping organizations abroad jointly sponsor computer programming and economic studies for the common benefit. U.S. shipyards operate independently as they seek contracts competitively. Limited though these exchanges may be, they have stimulated programs of research, ship computer programming, and ship construction techniques.

Despite the strong government ties to the industry of the Maritime Administration and Navy-supported programs, until very recently there was little government intervention in industry-wide planning, quotas, and other programs. This restraint reflects policies of antitrust legislation as well as the traditions of free, competitive enterprise. Unfortunately, U.S. shipyards have been denied many benefits they could acquire from cooperation, such as the use of standard parts and components (as employed profitably by Japanese shipbuilders). Benefits could also be gained from exchanges of engineering and other technical information. Hopefully, President Clinton's MARITECH program will go a long way toward addressing some of these problems in the U.S. shipbuilding and repair industry.

MARITECH is a key component of the Clinton administration's program to strengthen U.S. shipyards by assisting efforts to make the transition from the military to the commercial market. This program will keep the industrial defense base healthy by helping U.S. shipyards become commercially competitive in the international market.

The MARITECH program is an industry-led five-year campaign funded and managed by the Department of Defense's Advanced Research Projects Agency in consultation with the Maritime Administration. In addition, MARITECH is being executed in full partnership with the Navy through the Office of Naval Research. Total government funding for the 1994-1999 MARITECH program is $220 million. The MARITECH program will award matching federal funds to develop and implement technologies and advances processes for the competitive design, marketing, production, and support of commercial ships.

The basic production facilities of the industry are the shipbuilding positions, either shipways or docks, along with work areas, essential supporting shops, and engineering and design capability. Heavy-duty equipment is used for bending, rolling, forming, cutting, and welding plates and shapes; for forming pipe and sheet metal; and for performing a wide range of machining operations. In addition, shipyards require storage facilities—open areas for steel, piping, subassemblies, and other items requiring minimal protection; and shelters for machinery, equipment, stores, outfits, and other items requiring protection from rain, sun, or pilferage. Facilities for the assembly of heavy steel include large cranes and handling and conveying equipment. The shipyard must also have piers where the ships can be outfitted after launching. These piers are equipped completely with service facilities such as fire mains, electrical power supply, compressed air, and fresh water.

Ship Repair. Ship repair is a sustaining element in the maritime industry. It has enabled many shipbuilders to ride the storm in a capital-intensive and cyclical industry. Selection of a repair facility depends upon the magnitude and type of work, the preference of the ship or boat owners, and the proximity of the repair facility to the ship or boat. Periodic and emergency maintenance and repair work is essential to keep vessels operable. A report by the Ocean Shipping Consultants, an industry trade group, predicts a positive outlook for the repair industry throughout the 1990s. This trend can be attributed to the aging fleet of operational ships and the decision by ship owners to extend their useful life.

Repair crews are also called into action when it becomes necessary to break out mothballed merchant and naval ships from the reserve fleets located strategically on Atlantic, Gulf, and Pacific coasts. All vessels must also undergo special surveys every five years in addition to regular repairs to remain seaworthy. Economically, many ship owners have found it more profitable to increase the life of their existing fleet due to the high building costs of a new vessel. The results are increased surveys and repair work for the yards. Finally, environmental issues arising as a result of accidents and oil spills have put pressure on ship owners to improve maintenance standards.

A critical requirement for a successful repair yard is its ability to meet schedules and complete work rapidly and satisfactorily. Many shipbuilding facilities have repair yards capable of dry-docking vessels of 400 feet or more. These firms handle a majority of the repair dollar volume, with the rest going to smaller docks or pier facilities. The balances are shops that do special or limited repairs, transporting labor or material to the work site. Repair firms without dry docking facilities do not work on such underwater parts as the hull and the propeller. An integrated repair yard uses extensive waterfront acreage with facilities capable of dry-docking and berthing large ships. These integrated yards, as well as smaller repair facilities, cluster around active ports.

Repair yards also require a heavy financial investment. Dry docks are expensive, and most integrated yards have two or more piers, about 1,000 feet long and 40 feet wide. These features are in addition to the cranes, electrical, and mechanical facilities. All such yards have warehouses to stock and shops to process raw materials. In addition, each must have a wider variety of tools than shipbuilders require, since each repair job can be unique. Ship repair yards do not need to invest as heavily in capital as shipbuilding yards. Most of the investments are directly connected with the prospect of using these facilities for ship construction. This long-range planning will help the shipbuilder manage the business when shipbuilding demands have abated.

The Shipbuilders Council of America, the one industry body that functions for private yards as a group, is the basic source of industry planning. This organization's membership covers most but not all of the major shipbuilding and repair yards and major segments of allied industries that supply materials and equipment. As a trade association, the council informs and appropriately presents the views of its members concerning pertinent legislative, executive, and judicial government actions and worldwide industrial and economic trends as they affect the private shipbuilding industry.

BACKGROUND AND DEVELOPMENT

The colonists came to North America with strong maritime backgrounds. Shipping and shipbuilding, since colonial days, have exerted a powerful influence on the development of the United States. The transport of people and commodities until late in the nineteenth century was accomplished most easily and expeditiously by water, and with few exceptions, populations clustered at seaports or river ports. During its early history, moreover, the country imported many of its finished goods and industrial products from Europe and exported raw materials and agricultural products. The coastal forests provided an apparently inexhaustible supply of inexpensive virgin timber for the construction of the many ships the colonists needed.

Legislation by the first Congress of the United States was similar in intent to modern maritime subsidies. The first tariff, enacted in 1789, stipulated a 10 percent reduction in custom duties for goods imported in American vessels and a tonnage tax in favor of American shipping. The first literal subsidy by the government was paid in 1845, when Congress authorized the Postmaster General to award mail subsidies, with preference to steamships that could be converted into vessels of war. These subsidies were discontinued in 1858 as an unnecessary drain on the Treasury.

Infant maritime industries continued to flourish. By 1850, American clipper ships were showing the flag in most ports of the world and were widely considered to be the world's best sailing vessels at that time. The American merchant marine was second in size only to England's. Although coastwise shipping was protected from foreign flag competition by the Navigation Act of 1817, the American merchant fleet received little more in the way of government assistance before 1845 than discriminatory duties or taxes and periodic contracts for mail. Essentially, throughout this successful era, the maritime industries of the United States were strictly private enterprises.

The Civil War began the decline of the American foreign-trade merchant fleet. As vessels were lost as prizes, American vessels shifted to foreign registry to lessen the risk of capture and to avoid exorbitant insurance rates. Vessels so transferred were not permitted to return to the U.S. registry. Even more far-reaching in its effects than the war itself was the development of steel-hull, steam-propelled ships. The advanced technology of England and of other European countries gave foreign builders a considerable advantage in the cost of building iron vessels. Since it was prohibited by law to register foreign-built ships under U.S. documentation, the high cost of domestically built ships demanded a heavier capital investment for American-flag ships than for ships built abroad. The capital costs reduced potential earnings in foreign trade to a point where investment in American transoceanic shipping was unattractive. Under these conditions, private capital was not attracted to the highly competitive field of shipping. The American merchant marine declined from its once prominent position to a

level in 1914 where only 9 percent of the value of foreign commerce, imports and exports, was carried in American bottoms.

Awareness of the inadequacy of the U.S. merchant fleet led to attempts to reduce shipbuilding costs by removing tariffs from imported materials, but these measures were ineffective. Between 1900 and 1914 Congress made several attempts to expand and strengthen the U.S. merchant marine fleet by enacting various subsidy programs and establishing a Merchant Marine Commission in 1904. All of these efforts failed as U.S. merchant tonnage fell to an historic low as a percentage of foreign-flag tonnage.

The outbreak of war in Europe in 1914 finally aroused the country to correct this imbalance in its merchant fleet as American ports were glutted with cargo for export with nowhere to go. That year emergency legislation permitted foreign-built vessels of any age to be documented by the United States for use in foreign trade. The Shipping Act of 1916 was enacted, which established a Shipping Board of Commissioners to oversee the acquisition of vessels by purchase, to regulate the use of these vessels through liner and conference agreements, and to provide general instructions for the sale or disposal of vessels to U.S. citizens. The Act was modified in 1918 to prohibit the sale or lease of ships, shipyards, or dry docks to a foreigner in time of national emergency. It provided further that no U.S. shipyard could build for a foreign account. This was the first piece of comprehensive maritime legislation of the twentieth century and it remains current law in the U.S. shipping industry.

Under the Act, the United States embarked upon its largest shipbuilding program up to that time to yield 2,300 vessels. The American merchant fleet grew from 6.8 percent of the world total in gross tons in 1914 to 22.2 percent in 1920. The Merchant Marine Act of 1920 was established after the Shipping Act to facilitate the disposal of surplus government owned vessels, to settle claims among carriers, to provide assistance to the U.S. merchant marine, and to regulate foreign commerce. The goal of the United States was to establish a merchant marine fleet that could meet all of the country's commerce and military needs. Congress ultimately wanted this fleet to be owned and operated privately by U.S. citizens and enacted provisions such as tax savings and subsidy assistance to stimulate the transfer of the government-owned fleet to private firms. Disposal of the ships to private citizens under the Act of 1916 and later under the Act of 1920 progressed slowly, and most of the fleet operated under the direction of the Shipping Board.

The disposal of ships to the private sector fluctuated from year to year, with most of the surplus ships sold at prices below cost. At the same time, the opening of the Panama Canal expanded the development of inter-coastal shipping. Availability of ships at low prices, fluctuations in the volume of foreign commerce, and the inability of the U.S. ships built under wartime conditions to compete with swift, modern foreign-flag tonnage resulted in a decline in foreign trade for the United States. This backdrop, combined with congressional dissatisfaction with mail-contract payments to the industry, resulted in the passage of the Merchant Marine Act of 1936. This Act set the congressional foundation on which modern-day maritime policy rests and was the first attempt to set down a comprehensive maritime policy in the post-1916 Act period.

The Merchant Marine Act of 1936 provided subsidies to private U.S. ship owners on essential foreign trade routes. It also provided for the payment of subsidies to cover differentials in construction costs of foreign and domestic builders of vessels ordered for private operators for use on these routes. In addition, the Act authorized the government to build and charter vessels for operation on trade routes when private enterprise was unwilling to fill this role. Other provisions of the Act required subsidized lines to establish special funds to replace older vessels and to provide for loans and mortgage insurance, established citizen requirement for crews, required the establishment of manning scales and conditions for living and working on subsidized vessels, and authorized the establishment of a training program.

Under this Act, a building program of 50 ships a year over a ten-year period was planned to rehabilitate the dry-cargo tonnage of the merchant marine. This program turned out to be of inestimable value. At the outbreak of World War II, a substantial number of ships under construction provided an impetus to the required expansion of the shipbuilding industry with high-quality ships of proven design and performance for wartime service. The U.S. shipbuilding industry reached a peak of ship production by the end of World War II, having built 5,700 vessels during the war. Fifty-seven major private shipyards were in operation—23 on the Atlantic Coast, 22 on the Pacific Coast, and 12 on the Gulf Coast. In addition to achieving high production levels, these yards were innovative and brought new concepts to the industry, including multiple production of standardized designs, a switch from riveted to welded shipbuilding, and techniques for fabricating large subassemblies.

When it became apparent that World War II was drawing to a close in March of 1946, the Ship Sales Act was passed. The objective of the Ship Sales Act was to dispose of surplus tonnage of ocean vessels while promoting the national policy of maintaining a merchant marine owned and operated by private citizens of the United States and to avoid some of the mistakes of the past. It provided for the sale, over a limited period of time, of war-built vessels to citizens and foreigners alike on a fixed-price basis. Charter of war-built vessels to foreigners was not permitted, but U.S. citizens could charter vessels on a short-term basis.

The postwar period began the decline of the U.S. shipbuilding industry. The downturn was interrupted by four spurts of orders. The first program began in the late 1940s and carried into 1950. It grew primarily out of the need for replacement tonnage that could not be met sufficiently by foreign yards, in part because the German and Japanese yards and component manufacturers could not operate on or near capacity. The second program was sparked by the Korean conflict and continued into 1954. The third program began in 1956 with the Suez crisis, and the fourth began in 1961 with the beginning of deliveries under the Maritime Administration cargo vessel replacement program. Wide fluctuation in demand over the postwar period, coupled with ambitious spending plans by U.S. shipyards to increase automation and an increasingly competitive environment, resulted in the decline of the U.S. shipbuilding industry.

In an effort to maintain the operation of a certain number of shipyards, the U.S. Government parceled out orders among several yards, rather then giving a single yard the run of a specific ship. In effect, this put shipbuilders in the position of contractors, building small numbers of ships to individual specifications, rather than that of manufacturers producing large quantities of identical items. Shipbuilders were unable to profit from learning curve benefits that accrue with long runs, and although the government's intentions were good, its actions killed the incentive of shipbuilders to diversify, and they lost their competitive edge. Government subsidies that supported the industry and paid for a small number of expensive vessels discouraged capital investment among the shipbuilders and expansion of their yards. The resulting shipyards had a high ratio of labor to capital, making the industry labor-intensive and cost prohibitive. The industry became dependent on government subsidies and Naval construction for its survival.

The industry has been hurt by over-capacity since the 1970s, which was driven by the lack of linkage between supply and demand. Shipping companies, which were not forced to suspend operations, moved to U.S. trades to attract high-value cargo. As a result of the influx of carriers, U.S.-flag shipping was hit especially hard. A more recent threat posed by open conferences is the entry of state-controlled carriers in world trade. These carriers do not operate in pursuit of profit. Rather, they exist to promote their country's national shipping policies and to earn foreign exchange. The subsidies provided in many of these countries created an artificially high supply of ships that were later sold at low prices. In addition, the rates charged by these carriers were substantially lower than conference rates and resulted in foreign carriers siphoning off high-rated freight. The U.S. shipbuilding industry had not made the conversion from the military to civilian markets and was effectively shut out of this area because of the foreign subsidies. Even if there were a curb on foreign subsidies, it is still uncertain whether U.S. shipyards could make the transition to the civilian markets. The industry structured shipyards around the complexity of the Navy projects, and they were not prepared for the simplicity of design, speed of delivery, and low-cost requirements of the commercial sector.

In the early 1980s, the Reagan administration eliminated the direct federal subsidies of about $200 million each year that made U.S. shipyards competitive with foreign manufacturers. Almost all commercial shipbuilding moved overseas. At the same time, however, the president called for a 25 percent expansion in the Navy to increase the fleet to 600 ships. The defense buildup was enough to insulate the shipbuilding industry for the time being, but the industry was working from a much smaller base. In 1979, U.S. shipyards employed 150,000 workers and had 166 oceangoing vessels under construction, 67 of which were commercial ships. In the last ten years, employment has dropped to 72,000 workers and 45 yards have closed, leaving only 17 yards capable of building oceangoing vessels. In 1990, 96 Navy ships and one commercial vessel were under construction at American shipyards. The shipbuilders that survived relied on the Naval building program; which increased its fleet from roughly 450 ships in 1980 to more than 580. In 1990, 95 percent of the business in the shipbuilding industry was Navy construction, overhaul, and repair, with ship repairs accounting for the remaining 5 percent.

After the Cold War, the U.S. military-industrial base began shrinking dramatically, as did the nation's shipbuilding industry. In January of 1990, an American shipbuilding concern received the first order for a commercial oceangoing vessel since 1984. This was despite the fact that cabotage laws remain in effect that require that containerships serving only U.S. ports must be manufactured in a domestic yard. Shippers, including American companies, have favored foreign shipyards because of cheaper prices and faster order turnaround time. Government subsidies in Japan, Korea, and Germany range from 20 to 30 percent of the cost of the ship, enabling those builders to capture almost all of the business. In 1989 the Bush administration failed in a year-long effort to persuade foreigners to end their subsidies. As of early 1997, an international accord to phase out shipbuilding subsidies worldwide was pending before Congress. Giving additional hope for the U.S. shipbuilding industry was the Clinton administration's plan to help shipyard become competitive in the international market. However, its success remains to be seen.

The shipbuilding down cycle of the 1980s was unusually severe because it was preceded by a period of massive speculative overbuilding. During the early part of that decade, governments of most shipbuilding countries made decisions to pour money into commercial shipyards. The lone exception was the United States, which terminated its shipbuilding subsidies instead. This decision by the Reagan administration, coupled with the "Section 615" waivers that encouraged American shipbuilders to buy overseas, devastated commercial shipbuilding in the United States. These yards then became dependent on the U.S. defense budget for survival. Because of cuts in the defense budget and reduced requirements for Navy ships for the remainder of the 1990s, the Shipbuilders Council of America estimated that most of the private shipyards in the United States would have to close. The transition to competitive commercial shipbuilding by U.S. shipbuilders was the goal of the Clinton administration's five-point national shipbuilding initiative. The fate of the U.S. shipbuilding industry rested in large measure upon the success of this and similar programs that could follow, as well as on the elimination of shipbuilding subsidies worldwide.

Although the world shipbuilding market began to turn around in 1988, foreign yards continued to depend on government support to capture contracts and build ships. They received government payments to modernize facilities through restructuring and investment aid, indirectly benefited from government-supported ship financing provided to domestic customers from export and home credits, and realized special tax benefits. In addition, many of these foreign yards were awarded government grants to capture shipbuilding and repair contracts, and benefited from government-aided research and development of advanced manufacturing technology. During this same period, U.S. shipyards received none of these advantages.

Throughout most of the 1980s, the justification for foreign shipbuilding subsidies was low demand. In the 1990s, however, the reluctance of many foreign shipbuilders to let go of government subsidies was caused by the desire to capture as many contracts as possible while demand was high, and while denying market access to U.S. shipyards. The U.S. shipyards have been losing the battle with the international commercial shipbuilding market during the last ten years as measured in the number of new merchant vessels under construction or on order at U.S. private shipyards.

CURRENT CONDITIONS

The National Shipbuilding and Conversion Act of 1993 continued to help the U.S. shipbuilding industry re-emerge in the commercial marketplace. In a Report issued by the U.S. Major Shipbuilding Base (MSB) dated January 1, 1998 there were 18 major shipbuilding facilities in America.

Through federal assistance programs such as MARAD and MARITECH, the U.S. government continued to assist the shipbuilding industry with both short- and long-term objectives throughout the 1990s. MARITECH, for example, had 27 ongoing projects ranging from design to research technology including nine projected projects totaling $79.8 million with government funding of $36.6 million for fiscal year 1997. Additional orders for shuttle tankers were also expected in that time period. American shipbuilders had no construction or conversions projects for major commercial cruise ships scheduled.

The shipbuilding industry had received orders for eight tankers and three ferries by April 1, 1998 with original contract values of approximately $777.9 million. Six of these eleven vessels were covered by Title XI with values of $239.3 millions—MARAD providing $209.9 million.

The Navy's orders in the same time period had declined significantly, dropping from 88 vessels in 1988 to 51 in 1998. Fiscal Years 1998-2003 of the Navy's budget included new construction totaling 32 vessels, 13 conversion or major overhaul projects, and work on three T-AKR military sea-lift vessels. Going into the new millennium all major full-service shipyards will continue to depend on the Navy as their primary source of employment.

The last decade of the century also saw the U.S. Navy closing four of its eight shipyards. Several commercial ventures acquired these properties for redevelopment. Braswell Services Group, Inc. and Detyens Shipyard, Inc. leased facilities at Charleston Naval Shipyards for the purpose of repairing ships. Another company, Kvaerner Philadelphia Shipyard USA owned by Kvaerner Masa, a Norwegian shipbuilder, acquired a portion of the former Philadelphia Naval Shipyard. Kvaerner received an estimated $480 million in local, state, and federal funding for design, improvement, and retraining 1,000 local employees. In return, the company agreed to purchase the first three containerships it constructed, the first to be completed in 2001.

By the beginning of the century, approximately 40 percent of the world's tanker fleet would have been in service for 25 years or more. Because of this, both U.S. and foreign shipyards were beginning to see new orders for double-hulled tankers in the late 1990s. New orders for commercial vessels were also expected due to the rise in sea-borne trade for oil and dry bulk cargo.

INDUSTRY LEADERS

The leading shipbuilders in the United States are: Newport News Shipbuilding located in Newport News, Virginia; Ingalls Shipbuilding Corp., headquartered in Pascagoula, Mississippi; Bath Iron Works Corporation in Bath, Maine; and Avondale Industries Inc., based in New Orleans, Louisiana. The remaining major U.S. shipyards are clustered on the Atlantic, Pacific, and Gulf coasts. Peterson Builders, Inc. is the last major shipbuilder serving the Midwest region. Eastern Shipbuilding Group, located in Panama City, Florida, was fast becoming one of the leading innovators in marine construction and repair by the late 1990s.

Newport News Shipbuilding is the largest privately owned, most diversified shipyard in the United States. It is strategically located in Newport News, Virginia, with deepwater access to major shipping lines served by all major airlines and rail transportation. It has the resources to accommodate major overhaul and repair work, new construction, conversion, and routine maintenance work. Newport News Shipbuilding is the only ship builder that can build Nimitz-class nuclear powered aircraft carriers and only one of two manufacturing nuclear-powered submarines. In addition, its Sperry Marine subsidiary develops, designs, and markets marine instrumentation and communication systems. An announcement by Newport News Shipbuilding in March 1997 stated that it would discontinue commercial shipbuilding by mid 1999, and canceled the construction of three tankers.

Ingalls Shipbuilding, the second largest American shipbuilder, is a division of Litton Industries and is headquartered in Pascagoula on the Gulf Coast of Mississippi. Ingalls is one of the nation's leading systems companies for the design, engineering, construction, life cycle and fleet support, and repair and modernization of advanced surface combatant ships for the U.S. Navy and international navies, as well as for commercial marine structures of all types. In 1999 Ingalls was constructing the first large, luxury cruise ship in America in 40 years. In continuous operation since 1938, Ingalls is Mississippi's largest private employer with 10,700 employees.

The shipyard of Bath Iron Works Corporation, located in Bath, Maine, is on the Kennebec River 15 miles from the Gulf of Maine, and its fabrication facility is located eight miles west in Brunswick. Bath Iron works is renowned for its design and construction of the Arleigh Burke Class guided missile destroyer but is also capable of building high technology commercial vessels.

Avondale Shipyards, a division of Avondale Industries, Inc., is located on the Gulf Coast in Avondale, Louisiana. The shipyard uses computer-aided design and modern series and modular construction methods to build a variety of military and complex commercial vessels.

Peterson Builders Inc. was founded in 1907 by Martin Peterson in Sturgeon Bay, Wisconsin and in 1999 remains a family owned business. Along with shipbuilding, the company also provides spare and repair parts for a variety of weapons platforms used by U.S. and foreign military commands.

WORKFORCE

The shipbuilding and repair industry employed 96,524 workers in 1997, down nearly 2 percent from 118,300 in 1992. Many of these workers have special skills such as welding, cutting, assembling and fabricating, blue collar supervising, shipfitting, and a host of other important trades necessary for the completion of shipbuilding tasks. Most of the major yards are also active in repair and conversion. The balance of the industry is engaged in the construction or repair of small ships, drill rigs, and small, specialized commercial craft.

Basic skill requirements for the repair industry are generally higher than those required for shipbuilding. In yards that do both construction and repair, it is common practice to assign the same workers either to building or repair as the workload shifts. These floating assignments help maintain the continuity of employment at a stable level. Other workers may migrate between shipbuilding yards and repair yards. Although supervisory and planning skills for repair and construction differ distinctly, both sets of skills may be learned and used by the same person.

Industry Problems. The first and foremost problem of a shipbuilder is that of utilizing the resources at his command to produce a reasonable return on investment. Within this context, as with any commercial enterprise, the shipbuilder has the problem of maintaining an adequate orderbook, obtaining necessary financing, obtaining and retaining competent personnel, establishing and maintaining suitable facilities, obtaining and utilizing the proper materials, and maintaining an organization that will use these resources properly and efficiently.

One of the most difficult and important problems is the maintenance of a stable orderbook. All of the foregoing considerations, from finance through organization, are strongly supported by stability in the orderbook and suffer severely from instability. The beneficial effects and the efficiency of the enterprise are materially enhanced if the orders are repetitive, to permit series production. The need for an assured market, of course, is implicit throughout all considerations.

In the United States, the problem of obtaining series production has been more difficult than in countries where the government, consortia, and individual yards by mutual agreement can allocate particular types of construction to specific yards. Antitrust provisions prevent this type of rationalization in the United States. U.S. yards therefore have to compete with each other for series production and attempt to obtain series production and develop special capabilities for the types of vessels they prefer to build. The industry's reliance on Naval orders has put them at a competitive disadvantage because they are building smaller numbers of ships to individual specifications, rather then producing large quantities of identical items.

Finance for needed expansion has not been difficult to obtain in the past. However, massive demands on the capital markets for other needs of the industry during the mid-1990s may pose future restrictive problems. This factor, coupled with past overbuilding trends in the industry and the current competitive climate facing U.S. shipbuilders, has resulted in a lack of capital available to shipbuilders.

The matter of obtaining and retaining competent personnel has also been a difficult problem for most shipyards. This problem is chiefly due to the cyclic nature of the orderbooks and the workflow. Compounding the problem is the work availability in the construction industry at higher levels of pay. A workload with a reasonable promise of continuing stability is the most significant factor in the attraction and retention of competent personnel.

The establishment and the upgrading of facilities to improve operating efficiency are always under consideration by a shipbuilder. Again, such commitments are only practical with reasonable assurance or high expectation of a market sufficient to produce an adequate return on investment. The cost and availability of material similarly is always important to a shipbuilder, since material constitutes about half the cost of the usual commercial vessel. The small demand for material and equipment from the shipbuilding industry leaves the shipbuilder with little bargaining power to improve prices and delivery.

AMERICA AND THE WORLD

The building of oceangoing ships is practiced throughout the world. All nations engaged in major shipbuilding participate heavily in world trade. Many build ships as a significant export commodity and their economies are closely tied to the success of this industry. The areas responsible for most of ship production are grouped broadly into three sectors: the United States, the Far East, and Europe. European membership is represented by the Association of Western European Shipbuilders and includes Belgium, Denmark, Finland, France, Germany, Italy, the Netherlands, Norway, Spain, Sweden, and the United Kingdom. The industry has been dominated by the Far East sector with Japan and South Korea controlling over 50 percent of the orders of commercial vessel tonnage. Although American shipyards were once again beginning to build for foreign customers, U.S. yards were not a significant factor in international competition with only 1 percent of the commercial tonnage under construction at U.S. shipyards in 1999.

Globally, the military market will demand more ships throughout the first 15-20 years of the new century, the Asian military expected to have the highest demand.

Western Europe, the Middle East, eastern Europe, and Latin America to follow with a forecasted total amounting to 180 destroyers, frigates, and corvettes.

RESEARCH AND TECHNOLOGY

The National Oceanic and Atmospheric Administration (NOAA) began plans for two new classes of fisheries research vessels (FRA) in the late 1990s. These vessels will be equipped with new technology and design to better evaluate research while accommodating a crew of 38 for 30-40 day voyages. Along with the plans for the two new vessels, NOAA solicited funding for their ship *Miller Freeman*, which conducted fishery research in the Bering Sea and the Gulf of Alaska. The U.S. Navy also budgeted a new oceanic research ship in their Fiscal Year 1999 budget.

Energy Research Corporation (ERC) and Advanced Technology, a division of Bath Iron Works, partnered in 1999 to develop technology for advanced marine power systems.

A deadline of February 1, 1999 saw the compulsory Global Maritime Distress and Safety System, a new satellite-based communication system, replace the Morse code equipment signaling the end of an era in the world's shipping industry. The Global Maritime Distress and Safety System enables any person aboard a ship to simply press a button to send a distress call containing all pertinent information needed for rescue.

FURTHER READING

Lazich, Robert S., ed. *Market Share Reporter 1996*. Detroit: Gale Research, 1996.

Litton Avondale Industries. "Litton Avondale Industries Delivers Icebreaking Research Ship USCGC," 1999. Available from http://www.avondale.com.

Litton Ingalls Shipbuilding. "Building Freedom One Great Ship at a Time," 1999. Available from http://www.Ingalls.com.

U.S. Department of Transportation. "Maritime Administrator Lauds Reemerging U.S. Shipbuilding Industry." Available from http://www.dot.gov/affairs/mar0496.htm.

U.S. Industry and Trade Outlook '99. "Shipbuilding." McGraw-Hill, 1999.

SIC 3732

BOAT BUILDING AND REPAIRING

This industry consists of establishments primarily engaged in building and repairing boats. Establishments primarily engaged in operating marinas and that perform incidental boat repair are classified in **SIC 4493: Marinas.** Membership yacht clubs are classified under **SIC**

7997: Membership Sports and Recreation Clubs; and outboard motor repair is classified under **SIC 7699: Repair Shops and Related Services, Not Elsewhere Classified.**

NAICS CODE(S)

811490 (Other Personal Household Goods Repair and Maintenance)
336612 (Boat Building)

INDUSTRY SNAPSHOT

In the second half of the 1990s, the recreational boating industry in the United States was continuing to recover from a devastating industry-wide slump that began in the late 1980s and continued into the early 1990s. During the industry recession, stretching from 1988 through 1992, constant-dollar product shipments declined at a compound annual rate of approximately 15 percent. The turnaround began in 1993, when the industry cut its decline in shipments to less than 1 percent. In 1996 an unseasonably cool, damp summer in much of the United States cast something of a chill over the domestic market for pleasure boats. But market observers and U.S. boat builders were optimistic that many of these sales would occur during a bulge in 1997 sales of recreational boats.

Forecasted total shipments of boats by U.S. manufacturers was expected to reach $6.2 billion in 1999, which included forecasted U.S. consumer consumption at $5.9 billion.

According to the National Marine Manufacturers Association (NMMA), total U.S. boat registrations at the beginning of 1995 were 11.4 million, an increase of 1.3 percent from registrations of 11.3 million at the beginning of 1994.

The outlook for the recreational boating industry in 1997 was reasonably bright, according to the marine equipment economist of the Commerce Department's International Trade Administration. Among the factors cited for this cautious optimism were the Environmental Protection Agency's new emissions standards. The standards don't take full force until 2005, but they are being phased in gradually. ITA's economist said many consumers might have postponed purchases because they want to see what this new technology is and how it will affect them. In 1994 the government projected real annual growth of 3 percent for the period through the end of the decade.

ORGANIZATION AND STRUCTURE

Repairs account for only about a 4 percent share of the boat building and repairing industry's revenue. In 1987, in the thick of the industry's boom period, 151 of the 2,176 establishments in this classification were engaged primarily in repairing boats. These establishments employed 3,500 workers and generated $223.0 million in shipment value. There was some evidence that slow sales of new boats in recent years have provided a bit of a spark to the repair business. In the early 1990s boat yards specializing in refurbishing older boats charged in the range of $50 to $60 an hour for semiskilled labor on repairs.

Types of Boats Manufactured. Outboard boats make up the largest category of boats built in the United States, accounting for approximately 47 percent of all pleasure boats owned. In 1992 about 192,000 outboard boats were sold, a slight drop from the previous year and a 40-year low. Nearly 150 companies specialized in the manufacture of outboard boats in 1987. The value of outboard boats shipped that year was $1.2 million. About 8 million of these boats were currently owned in the United States in the mid-1990s. Boats in this category include runabouts, bass boats, utility boats, offshore fishboats, and pontoons. Aluminum and fiberglass are the most common materials used in the construction of these boats.

Inboard/outdrive (I/O) boats, also known as sterndrive boats, account for nearly 11 percent of U.S. pleasure boats. More than 90 companies specialized in I/O boats in 1987. Larger, higher-priced sterndrive boats were among those that suffered particularly harsh sales declines since the late 1980s. As a result of this decline, manufacturers attempted to attract buyers with significantly lower prices. This resulted in a 2,000-unit increase in sales of sterndrive boats in 1992.

Inboard boats include mainly cabin cruisers and sportboats. The inboard cruiser business was hit hard by the recession and the 10 percent excise tax on luxury boats that took effect in 1991 (but was repealed by the Clinton administration in 1993). Largely due to the tax, inboard cruiser sales were cut in half in 1991, and had yet to recover in 1997. Ski boats accounted for 88 percent of the inboard sportboats manufactured. Other inboard sportboats include runabouts, which represent about 9 percent of the market, and inboard fishing boats (under 25 feet).

Of the boats owned in the United States (about 1.4 million units), 8 percent are sailboats. This includes both nonpowered sailboats (1.3 million) and auxiliary-powered craft (70,000). Altogether, sailboats represent about 4 percent of boats manufactured. The vast majority of sailboats built were in the 12 to 19 foot range. From 1991 through 1993 sales of larger sailboats plummeted, largely attributable to the excise tax on luxury boats. In 1994, even after the repeal of the excise tax on luxury boats, large sailing craft's percentage of total sailboat production continued to be quite small. Of the 13,000 sailboats produced that year about two-thirds were in the 12 to 19 foot class. Another 20 percent were sailboats ranging from 20 feet to 29 feet in length. Sailboats of 41 feet or more in length accounted for a mere 2.9 percent of total production.

One of the fastest-growing segments of the U.S. recreational boating market in 1997 was personal watercraft, sales of which have almost doubled, from 1993's 107,000 units with a retail value of $618.0 million to sales in 1995 of 200,000 units with a value of $1.1 billion. Personal watercraft are small in-board engine boats powered by a jet propulsion unit and operated by a person or persons sitting, standing, or kneeling on it.

Until fairly recently this segment of the market was supplied very heavily by imports, with the three leading producers being Canada's Bombardier and Japan's Kawasaki and Yamaha. The Japanese companies have since established extensive U.S. manufacturing facilities, and in 1993, traditional U.S. boat manufacturers Sea Ray Boats and Boston Whaler Inc. began producing personal watercraft.

Other types of boats include unregistered small craft (canoes, rowboats, dinghies, etc.), open-deck boats (deck-style monohull runabouts and aluminum pontoons), and houseboats.

Markets. In 1994 sales of boats, motors, trailers, and marine accessories were highest in Florida, which took more than 21 percent of total sales, followed by Michigan and Texas, each accounting for slightly more than 12.5 percent of total sales. Californians bought the next highest share of boating equipment, accounting for 10.8 percent of total U.S. sales. Minnesota and New York followed, with shares of 8.7 and 8.6 percent, respectively.

Establishment Distribution and Size. Boats are built primarily where there is a lot of water. Geographically, Florida and California dominate the boat building and repairing industry. More than $1.0 billion in product shipments, about 21 percent of the U.S. total, originate in Florida, where over 400 establishments are located. California is home to about 250 establishments in this industry. Washington and Tennessee, the latter of which has extensive recreational boating waters (though it is landlocked), round out the top four states in the manufacture of pleasure boats.

Boat building and repairing concerns can vary dramatically in size. About half of the more than 2,000 establishments in the industry employ only one to four people. The largest share of revenue, however, is generated by more sizable operations, especially the approximately 100 companies with between 100 and 500 employees. This group accounts for about half of the dollar value of the industry's shipments.

BACKGROUND AND DEVELOPMENT

Prior to the mid-nineteenth century, boats in the United States were built primarily by the people who used them. Most were workboats designed for specific uses. These included whaling boats for the Arctic seas, dories for the Grand Banks, log canoes used by oystermen, and a huge variety of skiffs and other small craft. Eventually boats became more versatile. The Whitehall was a pulling boat first used in New York harbor as sort of a water taxi. A classic rowing boat, the Whitehall was found to be well suited as a sailing vessel as well, and it began to appear in other harbors on both coasts, both with and without sails, and was sometimes used for fishing.

Around 1850 recreational boating began to grow significantly in the United States. Boat builders throughout the Northeast, previously makers of workboats, were in demand for the production of leisure boats for weekend amateurs. This led to a proliferation of Whitehalls, guide boats, and Saint Lawrence skiffs on lakes from New England to the Midwest. The popularity of row boats dropped when the gasoline engine appeared in the United States in 1878. Fishermen, both professional and recreational, began using boats with motors instead.

Some of the companies that entered the early motorboat industry were automobile manufacturers. One such company was the Lozier Motor Company, which began building boats around the turn of the century. Another important company in the early 1900s was the Electric Boat Company of Bayonne, New Jersey, which manufactured a wide variety of boats, including tiny launches and huge luxury cruisers by the time of the company's demise around 1950. Chris-Craft Boats was another important powerboat manufacturer by 1930. By the middle of the twentieth century, there was a renaissance of classic boat designs. New boats modeled on the vessels of the past were constructed using fiberglass and other modern materials. To an extent, this trend has continued.

In the 1950s the number of recreational boats owned in the United States more than doubled, reaching over 7 million by 1961. This number has climbed slowly and steadily for the most part since then. In the mid-1980s, the pleasure boat industry boomed, with product shipments growing at an average rate of 13 percent a year. In 1989, however, the economy soured, sending boat manufacturing into a tailspin from which it has yet to emerge. The industry's problems were compounded in 1991 when a 10 percent federal tax on boats retailing for over $100,000 was enacted. Largely as a result of the tax, the share of the pleasure boat market by dollar value accounted for by boats in that high-price bracket slipped from 33 percent to 25 percent in one year.

Three factors contributed to the major drop in the demand for boats in the United States between 1989 and 1991. One was the reluctance on the part of consumers to take on additional debt on top of that incurred during the industry's boom years of 1982 through 1988. Another factor was the overall decline in the economy during this period. As disposable personal income declines, pleasure boats, being large and unnecessary (or "luxury") purchases, are among the first items deleted from shopping lists during economic downturns. A third factor was the 10 percent federal luxury tax on pleasure boats with price tags over $100,000. The tax, which was repealed in 1993, has generally taken the blame for the departure of several luxury boat builders from the market, and the loss of thousands of industry jobs.

Signs of Recovery. The earliest signs of a recovery emerged in 1992. The 1993 repeal of the luxury tax appears to be helping complete the recovery. Part of the increase in orders that took place was to rebuild dealers' inventories, which had reached the lowest levels in history by the beginning of 1992. Nevertheless, most manufacturers reported improving conditions, and some began rehiring laid-off workers. Viking Yacht Co. (a maker of high-end vessels), for example, began rehiring after seeing its work force plunge to 65 employees from its 1990 level of 1,500. Industry analysts expect the recovery to continue at a modest pace through the end of the 1990s. In order to affect the expected recovery, the boating industry must meet the challenge of restoring consumer demand. Manufacturers are hopeful that the rapidly growing 35- to 54-year-old age group will live up to its demographic billing as big spenders on leisure activities such as boating.

CURRENT CONDITIONS

The U.S. boat manufacturers enjoy the largest market in the world making up 40 percent of the global pleasure boat market. Florida led the nation in 1997 with 203 boat manufacturers. By 1999 used boats accounted for almost two thirds of all boat sales cutting into the industries production.

Due to the lagging sales in the late 1990s, the Marine Design Resource Alliance, a non-profit organization made up of seven suppliers, developed a plan to help increase sales of pleasure craft. The cornerstone of this program was the concept boats program. Under this program, Marine Design Resource Alliance would supply a manufacturer with 50 percent of the cost as well as free design talent to produce a half-scale concept model to showcase at nationwide boat shows. By using this approach Peter Granata, president of Marine Design Resource Alliance, believed that consumer reaction to these models would help the industry address the desires of the consumer—thus boosting sales.

The boating industry moved into the 21st century facing many issues that would have a significant impact. All of these issues—U.S. Environmental Protection Agency standards, operator licensing, marine wildlife protection laws, various new or increased user fees and taxes, and consumer debt—will play a major role in determining the U.S. market for pleasure craft.

INDUSTRY LEADERS

The world's leading manufacturer of pleasure boats and motors in the mid-1990s was Brunswick Corporation, based in Lake Forest, Illinois. By 1999 Brunswick was number one boat building with $8.2 million in the global retail market. In addition to its boat and boating motor product lines, Brunswick is a leading manufacturer of bowling and bicycling equipment. Among the boat brands Brunswick builds are Sea Ray, Bayliner, Maxum, Baja, Boston Whaler, and Robalo. Brunswick also manufactures Mercury, Mariner, and Force outboard engines.

Brunswick was founded in 1845, and for much of its history was principally a maker of billiards and bowling equipment. In the early 1960s, the popularity of bowling declined, and the company diversified. By the following decade, Brunswick was building boats on a large scale. In 1986, Brunswick bought two important boat companies, Bayliner and Ray Industries.

The number two major player in the boat building industry is Genmar Industries Inc., which is headquartered in Minneapolis but builds recreational powerboats in Florida, Minnesota, Wisconsin, North Carolina, Louisiana, and Arkansas. Genmar's boat brands include Trojan, Crestliner, Glastron, Aquasport, Cajun, Wellcraft, Carver, Logic, Lund, Nova, and Ranger. In addition to its U.S. facilities, Genmar builds boats at a plant in the Canadian province of Manitoba. Genmar's worldwide employees total approximately 5,000.

Genmar is dedicated to developing research and technology that will not only change the recreational boat industry, but will also improve and establish new standards in manufacturing. Robotics is just one example of the work they are doing.

WORKFORCE

There were 40,890 people in the United States employed in the boat building and repairing industry in 1997, about 8 percent less than the 44,500 employees reported in 1992. Production workers, who made up 80 percent of the total industry employment, earned an average of $11.00 an hour in 1997.

AMERICA AND THE WORLD

In 1997 U.S. imports of pleasure boats dropped 18 percent from 1996. Canada, being the number one foreign supplier to the United States experienced a 28 percent decline in shipments to America. Despite the drop in Canada's declining market, Italy saw a 45 percent increase in shipments to the United States in 1997. The United Kingdom became the third largest supplier to the United States in 1997 with imports equaling $68.0 million. Taiwan's boat imports were up 9 percent and in the first 5 to 10 years of the next century, Taiwan could become a major source of production.

By 1999 U.S. boat manufacturers were still considered to be the best, making them the number one supplier of pleasure boats worldwide. The largest exporters of boats, after the United States are, Canada, Japan, Netherlands, Germany, United Kingdom, and Australia, respectively. Italy and the Bahamas were two growing markets for these manufacturers in the late 1990s.

In the first quarter of 1998 exports to Japan, Singapore, Hong Kong, and Malasia were down 23 percent, 48 percent, 66 percent, and 97 percent, respectively. This was due to the Asian Economic Crisis. As foreign exchange rates improve, however, U.S. boat manufacturers expect to see these exports rise in number again.

RESEARCH AND TECHNOLOGY

For over 40 years fiberglass was the most common material used to build small watercraft. But in 1999, a new process called Advanced Composite Process (ACP) incorporated a vacuum-formed outer shell reinforced by a central foam core with inner bi-directional fabric for added strength, making the hulls of boats five times stronger against impact and exposure. Along with enhanced quality, this is an automated process which cuts man hours in the production of the boat hulls versus the more labor intensive fiberglass product.

Along with the technology for creating stronger, lighter boats, the late 1990s brought about a new add-on feature to the pleasure boat industry. Boats were now being offered with large swim platforms 15 to 20 percent larger than conventional designs in years past without compromising performance.

Some of the most impressive innovations in the boat industry in recent years have been in electronics. VHF (very high frequency) radios, among the most common pieces of boating equipment, have evolved from heavy, permanently installed instruments to hand held, portable devices. Advances have also been made in atmosphere sensor technology, including equipment for detecting carbon monoxide. Another major technological development in boating was the Global Positioning System (GPS), a satellite-based navigational system. GPS was originally developed by the Defense Department for use in deploying weapons. The system, which is available to the public in a semi-crippled form, can be used for navigating on land and in the air as well as at sea.

The boat repair industry has also benefited from technological advances of recent years. Computer-based inventory systems have enabled companies to keep their inventories smaller, while at the same time improving the efficiency of parts delivery.

FURTHER READING

Amerman, Don. "Cool Summer Dampens Pleasure Boat Sales." *The Journal of Commerce,* 23 September 1996.

Brunswick Corporation. "History," 1999. Available from http://www.brunswickcorp.com

Genmar. "Virtual Engineered Composites," 1999. Available from http://genmar.com/html.

Gromer, Cliff. *Popular Mechanics.* "Dream Boat," April 1999.

Janssen, Peter A. *Motor Boating and Sailing.* "At the Helm - A Lot of Changes." January 1999.

Linskey, Tom. *Sail Magazine.* "Brave New Boating," July 1998.

U.S. Bureau of the Census. "1997 Economic Census: Boat Building," 1997.

SIC 3743

RAILROAD EQUIPMENT

This classification covers establishments primarily engaged in building and rebuilding locomotives (including frames and parts not elsewhere classified) of any type or gauge; and railroad, street, and rapid transit cars and car equipment for operations on rails for freight and passenger service. Establishments primarily engaged in manufacturing mining cars are classified in **SIC 3532: Mining Machinery and Equipment, Except Oil and Gas Field Machinery and Equipment.** Repair shops owned and operated by railroads or local transit companies that repair locomotives or cars for their own use are classified in various transportation industries. Establishments primarily engaged in repairing railroad cars on a contract or fee basis are classified in **SIC 4789: Transportation Services, Not Elsewhere Classified;** and those repairing locomotive engines on a contract or fee basis are classified in **SIC 7699: Repair Shops and Related Services, Not Elsewhere Classified.**

NAICS CODE(S)

333911 (Pump and Pumping Equipment Manufacturing)
336510 (Railroad Rolling Stock)

INDUSTRY SNAPSHOT

In 1998 the railroad equipment industry reported total shipments of approximately $5.0 billion to the nation's rail systems. In 1997 the industry employed 31,464 persons, that figure was down by nearly 14,000 employees working in 1996. Leading states in railroad equipment industry employment were Pennsylvania, Illinois, and Texas in 1998.

The railroad equipment manufacturers that supply the nation's railroads with cars and track are slowly recovering from several extremely difficult decades. Despite new light-rail projects across the nation and an increase in federal money targeted toward mass transit projects, do-

mestic demand was not regarded as a strong enough motive to attract new American manufacturers to the business until the mid-1990s. As part of an effort to shore up the industry, the U.S. Department of Transportation promulgated a "Buy America" program that required rail passenger vehicles purchased with federal funds from foreign companies to have a "domestic content" of 60 percent. Also of great import to the manufacturers of rail equipment was the improved financial performance of several major rail carriers during the early 1990s.

The need for high-speed ground transportation (HSGT) prompted the Department of Transportation Federal Railroad Administration (FRA) to finance the upgrade of existing railroads to magnetically levitated vehicles. One such contract was awarded to Morrison Knudsen July 1999 to provide the technical and support services for future deployment of the first magnetic levitation (Maglev) high-speed-rail service in the United States.

ORGANIZATION AND STRUCTURE

The nation's freight railroads carry more than one-third of all intercity ton-miles of freight. Their rails are used for all commuter rail traffic and for Amtrak's long-distance passenger traffic, except for the Northeast corridor, which Amtrak owns. The railroads rely upon suppliers to provide equipment, supplies, many services, and the research and development required to help them improve productivity.

Railroad equipment manufacturers sell products not only to the railroads, but also to leasing companies, manufacturing concerns, farmers, and other entities that use the rails for the transportation of their commodities.

Unlike flatcars and boxcars, which are purchased or leased by the railroads, rail tankcars are owned primarily by chemical manufacturers and other manufacturers, such as food and fabricated metal products/machinery companies, who use the rails to transport goods on a regular basis. Recent proposals by the U.S. Department of Transportation (DOT) requiring more expensive better protected cars for the transportation of hazardous waste have caused concern among the nation's railroad carriers, who worry that forcing shippers to pay for these more expensive cars will force them to use trucks as the first choice of transport. Rail market share has already suffered attrition at the hands of the trucking industry and other transportation sectors. Since 1945, the railroads' share of the freight business has fallen almost in half to 37 percent, while the truckers' share has climbed from 5 percent to more than 25 percent.

The rail industry is the transport method of choice for commodities that are not "time-sensitive," such as perishable products, and for goods that need to be transported over distances greater than 500 miles. For short-haul food shipments, trucks have captured most of the traffic in the freight market. Recently, there has been an increase in intermodal transportation where manufacturers use the railways to transport their goods for a leg of the journey via trailers and containers and then switch to another form of transport such as trucks or ships. Intermodal loading has almost doubled in capacity since 1980.

Industry Representation. The Railway Progress Institute (RPI), originally founded as the Railway Business Association in 1908, is the international trade association of suppliers to the nation's freight railroads and rail passenger systems. Headquartered in Alexandria, Virginia, it has more than 100 members. The association's objectives are threefold: to support and promote a strong nationwide free enterprise system of railroads for the United States; to support and promote rail rapid transit and light rail systems in major metropolitan areas; and to represent and further RPI members' interests.

In 1992 the Rail Supply and Service Coalition (RSSC) was formed to act as a lobbying group to Washington and state governments. The group consists of the National Railroad Construction and Maintenance Association, the Railway Engineering-Maintenance Suppliers Association, the Railway Supply Association, and Railway Systems Suppliers, Inc. The coalition actively represents the interests of its member groups to further their bargaining position on federal and state issues affecting the industry.

BACKGROUND AND DEVELOPMENT

The railroads were one of the nation's first big businesses. With their intricate network of lines, these companies gave inland points access to navigable waters and joined these waters to the seaboard, linked farms and villages to the rising industrial cities, opened millions of acres of land to cultivation, provided the means to ship raw materials and finished goods quickly and cheaply, and created billions of dollars in capital for reinvestment in the nation's economy.

At the outset of the 1830s the steam locomotive made its arrival. On Christmas Day, 1830 the *Best Friend of Charleston,* the first locomotive built for sale in the United States, made its maiden run. The nation's rail system grew rapidly during the next several decades. The lines largely served cities along the Atlantic coast; New England and the mid-Atlantic states had over 50 percent of the total track mileage in the United States. American railroads, however, did not have a uniform track gauge (distance between the rails). This confusion of gauges necessitated expensive and inefficient transshipment of goods where lines of different gauges intersected.

Early Advances. Throughout this time period, the companies constantly improved tracking and rolling equipment. The first railroads were built on tracks of iron straps or bars fastened to wooden rails that were attached to

blocks of stone embedded in the earth. The iron straps often broke loose under the weight of the passing trains and damaged the bottom of the cars. In response to this, the iron T-rail was developed and wooden ties replaced the stone underneath the rails. A roadbed surface covered with crushed stone or gravel supported the track. Originally most of the engines were imported from England, but Philadelphia jewelry manufacturer Matthias Baldwin entered the business in the 1830s, and soon thereafter other locomotive builders emerged in the Northeast. Passenger cars that were once nothing more than stagecoaches with railroad wheels quickly evolved into more spacious, comfortable accommodations. Diminutive four-wheeled freight cars were replaced by longer and heavier eight-wheeled cars with greater carrying capacity. Thus the railways spawned auxiliary enterprises in T-rail manufacturing, locomotive works, and car and wheel shops, and gave impetus to the lumber industry that furnished the wooden ties.

During the 1840s and 1850s there was a proliferation of railroad construction. By 1860 many of the shorter railway lines were consolidated through the merger of regional railroad companies. The federal government supported this expansion through land grants and other forms of financial incentives to railroad companies. Land grants became the major form of financial assistance offered to railroad companies to encourage the development of railroads to the West in advance of settlement. Revelations of corruption and bribery caused public opinion to demand that such assistance be ended. By the 1870s, most direct federal aid to the railroads had terminated, and most state and local support was stopped within the next decade. But government aid, in any case, was relatively small in comparison to investment by private capital in the form of stocks and bonds in rail companies. With the continued growth of the railway industry, companies that provided needed equipment to that industry remained prosperous.

By 1880 carriers had standardized their gauge to 4 feet 8 1/2 inches as the railroads established transcontinental operations. To further facilitate the interchange of railroad traffic, railroad companies required standardized coupling devices, car trucks, bills of lading, and classification of products. Larger locomotives and freight cars with increased carrying capacities required that steel rails be implemented in place of the iron rails. The steel rails provided a smoother, safer, and faster track and lasted much longer than wrought iron, saving the railroads significant maintenance costs. The link-and-pin couplers, long utilized to engage railcars together, had over the years cost thousands of men their fingers; these were replaced by more effective automatic safety couplers. Similarly, the hand brake system that required men to run along the top of cars to set the devices was replaced by an air brake system mandated by federal law in 1893.

The railroad industry continued as the primary transportation mode throughout the first half of the twentieth century in America. Throughout the 1920s and 1930s, the railroads generally improved and modernized their operations. New steam locomotive designs were introduced by the major builders—Baldwin, Lima, and the American Locomotive Company. These designs increased efficiency, raised average speeds for passenger and freight trains, and reduced the need for double-headed trains and pusher locomotives in mountainous terrain. Capital improvement programs were begun that increased freight car capacities, length of freight trains, and the net tonnage capable of being carried by the average train. Many of the infrastructure systems installed at this time remained for many years as well. The rise of the automobile and air transportation, however, dramatically impacted on the fortunes of rail lines and affiliated industries.

By 1940 the heyday for railroads was over and many of the railroads were in receivership. Industries that had long had the railroad companies as their primary clients suffered accordingly. The Railroad Credit Corporation was created to aid the carriers, but the problems surpassed this emergency type of legislation. The entry of the United States into World War II temporarily alleviated this problem and brought much needed liquidity to the railroads. During this time frame, the Offices of Defense Transportation coordinated the operations of the railroads. Between 1942 and 1945, the railroads moved more freight each year than they had since 1918, although they did so with fewer freight and passenger cars, locomotives, and employees. The vast increase in traffic produced record profits for the railroads and allowed them to reduce their debts and establish financial health.

Rise of the Diesel. By 1945 many of the carriers had dieselized locomotive fleets. The Electro-Motive Division of General Motors developed separate locomotive units for freight service that was adopted by several railroads. Diesel locomotives cost far more than steam power locomotives to acquire, but operational savings came quickly. The diesels did not need the vast amounts of water that steam locomotives required, a significant factor in parts of the West where water was scarce. Diesels also required far less maintenance, had a high level of availability, were fuel efficient, and could operate for many miles without servicing. The diesel also was less harmful to railroad tracks than the steam engine and when placed in reverse could act as a dynamic braking system. This saved the railroad millions of dollars in freight car brake shoes. By 1955 carriers had spent $3.3 billion for 21,000 diesel locomotives from Electro-Motive, American Locomotive Company, Fairbanks-Morse, and Baldwin Locomotive Works. These manufacturers provided the carriers with a wide range of diesel products to choose from for passenger and freight service.

The revolution in transportation opportunities available to the general public, however, made these railroad advancements seem insignificant. The internal combustion engine placed the automobile in the hands of virtually every family. As a result, the long-distance passenger train almost died. The diverse railroad-reliant industries also suffered from the emergence of airlines, which provided speedy service between major cities. Pipelines, barges, trucks, and intercoastal shipping companies carried a large percentage of commodity products as well.

By the 1960s the rail industry as a whole was in a state of decline. In 1971 Congress created the National Railroad Passenger Corporation, known as Amtrak, to operate virtually all of the nation's remaining rail passenger services. In 1976 the federal government created the Consolidated Rail Corporation (Conrail) to salvage Penn Central and other bankrupt lines in the Northeast. Several carriers prospered by focusing on long-haul freight lines and piggyback trailer traffic.

The railroads survived by scrambling for market share, often establishing services for special product niches. Carriers introduced unit trains dedicated to one cargo—coal, wheat, sulfur, or chemicals that moved in continuous runs from the production site to docks, generators, or factories. The unit trains often utilized specially designed equipment to accommodate the transport of different commodities such as grain or liquid chemicals, resulting in reduced freight rates. Railroads also established "run through trains" that stopped only for crew changes and retained the locomotives of the original carriers. To succeed, the carriers acquired pipelines, barge lines, and trucking companies and invested in airfreight forwarding to obtain a total intermodal position.

Dieselization, the utilization of new technologies, the introduction of new services, the renewed emphasis on marketing, and the end of money losing passenger business failed to prevent a massive restructuring of the nation's railroads. The Staggers Act of 1980 provided significant relief for the railroads in rate development as the federal government moved into an era of deregulation. This brought giant mergers, massive line abandonments, and shrinking locomotive and equipment fleets. Railway managers in an era of deregulation continued line rationalization, sought new technologies, and placed a major emphasis on marketing transportation.

The railroad equipment manufacturers that supply the nations' railroads with cars and track and other equipment were slowly recovering from the lean decade of the 1980s. Capital expenditures by the railroads for equipment contracted went from $2.3 billion in 1980 to $995.0 million in 1990 for a total decline of 58 percent. Moreover, carriers were not purchasing new locomotives; 70 percent of locomotives in operation in 1990 were more than 15 years old, with another 15 percent constructed prior to 1984. The number of freight cars in service dropped as well, falling almost 30 percent between 1980 and 1990 from 1.7 million to 1.2 million.

Looking ahead as 1997 began, James J. Unger, chairman of the Railway Progress Institute, assured his membership that RPI had on its agenda several legislative issues crucial to the railway supply industry. "You can be sure that the Railway Progress Institute and its staff will diligently work at 'tracking the issues' on behalf of you and your company," Mr. Unger wrote in his annual letter to members. "RPI activities undertaken in 1997 will be handled by a staff with almost one hundred years of cumulative experience working with Congress, the Department of Transportation, and the railroad and railway supply industries."

RPI's chairman said the organization marked 1996 as a successful year for the rail supply industry. "We knew back in 1995 when Congress began calling for fiscal responsibility and budget cuts that it would mean cuts in transportation, so we were prepared. We are fortunate to have fared as well as we have."

In 1996, RPI worked with Transportation Secretary Frederico Peña to recognize the supply industry's issues as DOT began working on legislation reauthorizing the Intermodal Surface Transportation Efficiency Act (ISTEA). During the year RPI monitored several congressional hearings on this subject.

Mr. Unger noted that the 1996 national elections had brought changes to the Clinton Administration and Congress, where there were many new members and new staff who needed to be introduced to the rail supply industry's issues. He wrote that 1997 was likely to be an extremely busy year for the railway supply industry with the reauthorization of ISTEA being on top of the agenda.

The railways' steady return to health has helped equipment manufacturers supporting the industry climb out of a prolonged slump, although it will be difficult for the industry to reach 1980 levels of production, when more than 93,000 railcars were built. Carbuilders' deliveries, considered a benchmark of the industry's health, climbed to 35,000 new freight cars in 1993, up from 25,000 in 1992.

CURRENT CONDITIONS

A major problem facing the railroad industry as we move into the new century will be designing equipment able to handle larger payloads more efficiently. The American Railway Car Institute reported that builders delivered 75,704 new cars in 1998, the most delivered since the 1980s. The average cost per car was $63,000 putting the freight car market at a value of almost $5 billion. High level production continued through 1999 because of utilization of the new technologies, new ser-

vices, renewed emphasis on marketing, and the restructuring of the nation's railroads.

The Economic Planning Associates predicted that the years 2000-2005 will see production levels between 55,000-60,000 cars each year. This stability is a welcome change from the inconsistent cycles of the early 1990s.

The increase in production has seen existing companies merge and new companies begin. One such merger is that of Motive Power Industries, Inc. and Westinghouse Air Brake Company in 1999. This merger was called a "merger of equals" creating a "one-stop shop" for locomotive and freight car components and services. First quarter net sales for 1999 were $107.3 million for Motive Power Industries, Inc. and $191.2 million for Westinghouse Air Brake Company.

A new company named Clinton County Economic Partnership began making container cars for bulk commodities and waste products in 1999. The company also manufactures mill gondolas in their plant, a former freight car manufacturing facility in Renovo, Pennsylvania.

The upturn in equipment manufacturing is more reflected in subtle design changes to existing technology, as well as car types that provide the shipper with rapid loading and unloading capabilities, sanitary cleanout, and a large carrying capacity. The three major types of cars in demand are covered hopper cars, intermodal cars, and tankcars. Most of the design changes in the last several years have occurred in the tankcar-manufacturing arena, and were brought about by concerns about environmental safety and product liability. Changes in the tankcar design include sloping bottoms, improved heater systems, better gates and hatches, new kinds of insulation, and better interior coating. These changes help to protect the product from contamination while also serving to insulate the tanker from corrosion.

INDUSTRY LEADERS

Trinity Industries, Inc., based in Dallas, Texas, continued to lead the railroad equipment industry at the end of the century. Trinity produces a wide range of railcars, including railroad tankcars, gondola cars, intermodal cars, and hopper cars. The initial cost of their composite-body box car is somewhat higher in price, but Trinity is looking to increase the market volume for frozen foods and other commodities requiring cooling or heating. Trinity is involved in a wide variety of other metal product manufacturing, including marine products, such as tugboats, ferries, barges, and construction products, including airport conveyor systems and highway guardrails.

Johnstown America Industries Inc., headquartered in Chicago, Illinois, has designed a new, more efficient two-platform car. These lightweight Articulated Bulk Containers can carry a total weight capacity up to

354,000 pounds of structural steel, timber, and other non-hazardous products.

Electro-Motive of GM Corporation, a division of General Motors Corporation, was the originator of diesel-electric motive power for locomotives. The company is headquartered in LaGrange, Illinois. Electro-Motive's onboard locomotive management systems along with the introduction of new models and technology made 1999 a "banner year" for the company.

Thrall Car Manufacturing Company of Chicago Heights, Illinois, is the leading manufacturer of freight cars including intermodal equipment, auto racks, aluminum coal cars, centerbeams, coiled steel, pressured differential, plastics, and woodchip cars. Thrall Car's new Q2 motor vehicle carrier is designed to carry all sizes of cars except the larger trucks and SUVs. Two prototypes were tested with Union Pacific in 1999.

WORKFORCE

Projected employment for the railroad equipment industry by the year 2005 is expected to include 35,000 employees. That number is up 4,000 from 1993. The railroad equipment industry consists of less than 2 percent of the total railroad industry's workforce.

AMERICA AND THE WORLD

Overseas, European and Japanese manufacturers have developed extensive rail lines using high-speed rail technology. This thriving domestic market has provided these countries with an industrial base that they have used to expand internationally. This manufacturing base enabled these countries to capture a large percentage of the U.S. freight and passenger car market. In North American, for instance, the Canadian Bombardier Corporation has had a virtual monopoly on the U.S. passenger railcar business. An example of this is Bombardier's 1999 contract with MTA Long Island Rail Road valued at $515.0 million by November 1999 for 192 electric multiple-units. This contract supplies the Long Island Rail Road with the design, manufacture, and delivery of new M-7 cars and could total 808 units by contract end.

With the assistance from the High Speed Ground Transportation Administration (HSGTA), Amtrak is expected to be self-sufficient by the year 2002. The end of the 20th century is perfect timing for Amtrak to seek federal assistance to improve its infrastructure to sway travelers from the already over-burdened airline industry.

Union Pacific, North America's largest railroad, faced many lawsuits because of service problems related to The North American Free Trade Agreement (NAFTA). These problems have cost the U.S. Economy almost $2.0 billion in lost production when over 5,000 rail cars awaited entry into Mexico in 1997. As a result of this, the rail line hired more than 1,000 workers, pur-

chased new locomotives, and improved their infrastructure in the late 1990s.

Compliance with U.S. EPA emissions regulations will be a major challenge facing locomotive manufacturers at the beginning of the 21st century. The three-tier program begins in 2001 and will be completed by 2005.

RESEARCH AND TECHNOLOGY

The U.S. intermodal rail system was undergoing significant change through the use of information technology. Carriers were going high-tech with innovative electronics equipment and computers designed to improve tracking of shipments and make the railroads increasingly user friendly for commodity transfer. Information technology changes were proposed for nearly every aspect of the railroad industry as follows:

Automated Equipment Identification. This program mandates that all railroad equipment be outfitted with electronic identification tags that allow each freight container to be identified by a trackside laser scanner. This system will track freight container shipments among multiple carriers and eliminate the need for railroad staff to visually identify containers and manually type in shipment information.

Computer Systems. Railroads are working together to create a single computer hardware package that allows customers to communicate with all their carriers. In addition, railroad locomotives are being outfitted with computers that communicate via wireless technology with the railroad's mainframe or central computer. It's hoped that data radio technology will improve shipment information and increase operational efficiency and productivity.

On-Board Locomotive Diagnostics. Electro-Motive Division's FIRE (Functionally Integrated Railroad Electronics) and GE's IHUB (Integration Hub) support multiple systems from multiple vendors to help standardize the industry.

EPA Emissions. Electro-Motive Division and GE Transportation Systems are working to develop equipment to meet EPA standards without affecting fuel efficiency and horsepower on locomotives.

In addition to innovations in information technology, changes in the industry's traditional hardware such as locomotives, freight cars, air brakes, and couplers have taken place or are undergoing redesign. For example, high strength, lightweight materials are providing the industry with the ability to ship more product at one time. Locomotives are bigger and faster.

FURTHER READING

Challenges Accepted-The Story of Railroading. Association of American Railroads, n.d.

Cremeans, John E., editor. *Handbook of North American Industry: NAFTA and the Economics of its Member Nations,* 1998.

Longman, Phillip J., "Rail Crisis Imperils NAFTA Trade." *U.S. News and World Reports,* April 6 1999.

Railway Age. "Supply Side", July 1999.

———. "Motive Power Industries and Westinghouse Air Brake Company Will Merge", July 1999.

Standard and Poor's Industry Surveys, 1999.

U.S. Bureau of the Census. "Description of Industries and Summary of Findings: Industry 3743, Railroad Equipment." Available from http://www.census.gov/mcd/mancen.

Vantuono, William C. "Cars and Locomotives: Building for Bigger Capacity". *Railway Age.* September 1999. Available from http://www.railwayage.com

SIC 3751

MOTORCYCLES, BICYCLES, AND PARTS

This category includes establishments primarily engaged in manufacturing motorcycles, bicycles, and similar equipment, and parts. Establishments primarily engaged in manufacturing children's vehicles, except bicycles, are classified in **SIC 3944: Games, Toys, and Children's Vehicles, Except Dolls and Bicycles.** Establishments primarily engaged in manufacturing golf carts and other similar personnel carriers are classified in **SIC 3799: Transportation Equipment, Not Elsewhere Classified.**

NAICS CODE(S)

336991 (Motorcycle, Bicycle, and Parts Manufacturing)

INDUSTRY SNAPSHOT

In one form or another, the two-wheeled personal vehicle has played an important role in U.S. transportation systems. Bicycling, as reported by the National Sporting Goods Association, fell from third to fourth place in sporting activity popularity in 1998. This drop could be attributed to the rising popularity of in-line skating. Many U.S. manufacturers closed plants because of this decline. Despite the slip in popularity, bicycle sales did reach $3.4 billion in 1997.

In spite of the slow growth of entry-level and off-road motorcycles in the previous years, the 1990s may be called the decade of the luxury or big bike for the motorcycle industry. The popularity of heavyweight motorcycles with engines larger than 800 cubic centimeters (cc) held an estimated 45 percent of the market. As baby boomers grew older and their incomes increased, they traded up for the larger, more customized motorcycles. By catering to baby boomers' nostalgia with safe, reliable replicas of older

models, Harley-Davidson continued to dominate the U.S. market late into the 1990s. Known in the industry as "RUBs" (Rich Urban Bikers), these consumers of the larger motorcycles were predicted to be marketing targets well into the next century. Annual sales of heavyweight cycles reached $1.8 billion dollars in 1998.

ORGANIZATION AND STRUCTURE

Harley-Davidson Inc. of Milwaukee, Wisconsin, the only remaining major U.S. motorcycle manufacturer, knows it is selling more than "bikes." The image of the Harley as America's motorcycle has become integral to its marketing success. Its extensive national dealer network sells motorcycles, parts, and service, and it also promotes Harley-Davidson's own line of "Motorclothes" in "designer stores." The company sponsors a motorcycle enthusiast club, the Harley Owners Group (HOG), and organizes rallies and product demonstrations.

The Asian financial crisis affecting the mid-1990s allowed Japanese motorcycle manufacturers to lower prices because of the favorable exchange rates. The lower prices, in turn, increased production at two Japanese motorcycle makers—Honda and Kawasaki—who have facilities in Ohio and Nebraska respectively. Like other Japanese and European motorcycle manufacturers, these manufacturers maintain their own dealer networks and generally enjoy a price advantage over comparable Harley models. Even so, the effectiveness of the Harley-Davidson lifestyle marketing campaign has made the "Hog," as the Harley-Davidson is affectionately known, a desirable status symbol in the biking world. In the late-1990s, used Harleys routinely sold for more than their original price.

The bicycle segment of the industry also sells much of its product through specialized dealer networks. These dealer networks generally carry the sophisticated, higher-priced models for the cycling enthusiast. Bikes in this category, like Schwinn's Paramount line, can sell for more than $5,000. Cutthroat competition and rapid innovation in the bicycle segment of the industry forced many firms out of the market. Chicago, once the world's bike manufacturing capital with more than 90 manufacturers, only has Schwinn left, and that in name only. Schwinn, established in 1895, sold 25 percent of America's bikes during the 1960s, earning it the reputation as America's bicycle manufacturer, although it was never the largest. A 1981 labor dispute prompted Schwinn to phase out its U.S. manufacturing operations in favor of overseas facilities. That move created a new competitor, Giant Bicycles of Taiwan, which eventually drove Schwinn out of the market after supplying 70 percent of Schwinn's product in 1984. In 1991, Schwinn filed for bankruptcy. Scott USA of Ketchum, Idaho, bought its remaining assets, including the Schwinn trademark, for $41 million in

1993. Schwinn reported 1999 sales of approximately $200 million. Many of the U.S. bicycle manufacturers now outsource to China or Mexico.

BACKGROUND AND DEVELOPMENT

Bicycles. The bicycle originated in France when Paris carriage maker Pierre Michaux fitted cranks to the front wheel of the German designed draisienne, or hobby horse. By 1867, a bicycle craze was sweeping Europe. According to David A. Hounshell, author of *From the American System to Mass Production: 1800-1932,* the Boston merchant Albert A. Pope deserves credit for introducing the device to America. Pope began importing the British High-Wheel, also known as the ''Penny-Farthing,'' in 1876. By 1878, he was producing his own version at the Weed Sewing Machine plant in Hartford, Connecticut.

The new product tapped a growing demand in America for increased mobility and provided work for the idling American arms industry. Much of the industrial expertise developed for the weapons industry during the Civil War found useful employment in the production of bicycle components. In 1890, 27 bicycle manufacturers produced 40,000 ''safety'' bicycles, featuring two equal sized wheels.

By 1897 production increased to 1.2 million bicycles annually. Demand evaporated, though, as the horseless carriage began to make its impact felt. Auto manufacturer Hiram Percy Maxim noted that the bicycle revealed the advantage of quicker personal transportation but failed to answer the challenge. According to Maxim, the bicycle created the demand for the automobile and provided the technology needed to mass produce it.

Bicycles retained a steady but small popularity through the first half of the twentieth century; it was the baby boomer generation that fueled the resurgence of the bicycle starting in the 1950s. The single-speed child's bike gave way to multiple speed versions and, eventually, the popular light-weight 10-speed. Throughout the 1970s, the 10-speed dominated the market with a market share of 56 percent. However, an American innovation, the mountain bike, changed everything. Initially designed for climbing the scrubby hills north of San Francisco, mountain bikes and all-terrain bikes sported fat tires, sturdy frames, and multiple gears. By 1991 they boomed in popularity even in areas miles from any mountain and commandeered a 50 percent market share.

Many traditional companies like Schwinn and Murray failed to react quickly enough to the popularity of the mountain bike, leaving the door open for small innovators to carve out a niche and for large foreign firms like Taiwan's Giant and China's CBC to gain control of trademarks. The showroom models still sport familiar brand names, but many are foreign-made while others use components no longer made in America. Those firms that did react, like Trek and Cannondale, are enjoying great success in the export market, especially in Europe and Japan. In 1998 Cannondale was the leading manufacturer of aluminum bicycles with combined sales of more than $171 million for their bicycles, accessories, apparel, and components.

The phenomenon of the mountain bike may be dwindling in importance, as the sales of these bikes decreased in 1996 for the first time in ten years (from $1.6 billion in 1995 to $1.5 billion in 1996). Once again, the baby boomer market may be fertile, as shown by the introduction of expensive ''nostalgia'' bicycles by companies such as Schwinn. Some automobile manufacturers started producing bicycles under their own logos, hoping to appeal to customers who want to lead an active lifestyle (or at least to project that image); these companies include Mercedes-Benz, Volkswagen, BMW, and Jeep. Bicycles also are being used more frequently by non-recreational riders such as commuters, couriers, and police officers.

Motorcycles. The motorcycle represented a first step from the bicycle to the automobile. The simple expedient of attaching a gasoline-powered engine to a bicycle frame produced a device that was at once exotic and affordable. During the early 1900s, more than 100 companies began manufacturing motorcycles, including Harley-Davidson, Indian, Orient, Excelsior, Cyclone, Henderson, and Marsh. By 1915, they produced models that could exceed 100 mph. The 1915 Cyclone, designed specifically for racing, could reach speeds of 124 mph, but had no throttle and no brakes. Harley-Davidson began production of its first model, the Silent Grey Fellow, in 1903, the same year Henry Ford unveiled the Model A. When Ford introduced his mass-produced Model T in 1913 and sold it for $500, most motorcycle manufacturers could not compete. After World War I, only Harley-Davidson, Indian, and Excelsior remained. By 1953 Harley-Davidson was the lone American producer.

With the OPEC oil embargo of the early 1970s, motorcycles became popular for commuting—but not the Harley. Consumers wanted cheap, reliable, bikes, and those came from Japan. In 1973, sales of motorcycles reached an all-time high of 1.5 million. In 1983, Harley-Davidson sought and received tariff protection from the Reagan Administration to help it battle Japanese competition. Even with the 45 percent tariff protection, the company was almost bankrupt by 1985 due to poor quality and inefficient production. By applying Japanese management techniques, Harley-Davidson finally reversed its situation and asked for the tariff to be removed one year before it was due to expire. Meanwhile, Honda miscalculated the heavyweight motorcycle market, concentrating instead on small bikes and high-priced, high-tech super-bikes. Honda's market share dropped from 44 percent in 1985 to 32 percent in 1989.

There was a new surprise for the industry in 1994 when Polaris introduced their heavyweight Victory V92C cycle, the largest V-twin engine on a cruiser-style cycle. Polaris is the first new U.S. motorcycle manufacturer since 1960. The Victory V92C was chosen Best Cruiser of the Year by *Cycle World*.

The motorcycle sector of the industry will be competing with the bicycle sector as it targets much of the same audience, playing on that group's high level of physical activity. Increased pressure to use bicycles for environmentally friendly commuting in congested cities may also continue to push the domestic market.

CURRENT CONDITIONS

Bicycles. In 1997 a reported 45 million active bicyclists were in the United States. That report showed a 15 percent decline from the previous year. High demand for American mountain bikes overseas accounted for an estimated 17 percent increase in exports in 1998. Improved quality without significant price increases have occurred because of the competition's ability to mass produce their product.

Electric bicycle technology was at the forefront in 1999. Schwinn's partnering with Currie Technologies had the two companies hoping to be the worldwide frontrunners in the electric bike market in the new millenium.

Motorcycles. The average motorcycle rider at the turn of the century looks little like the stereotypical biker depicted in popular movies like *Easy Rider*. A biker is more likely to be an aging baby boomer who bought an expensive, heavy-duty "cruising bike," most commonly a Harley-Davidson. While the median age of a Harley rider was 34 in the mid-1980s, the age rose to the 55-64 group as the fastest growing and ages 45-54 the second fastest. Those age groups were expected to increase 4 percent and 3 percent annually from 1998 through the year 2003. Many Harley buyers are professionals who spend weekends and vacations on their bikes. Harley-Davidson reported a $214 million profit for 1998. In the late 1990s, the smaller, faster sport bikes were being marketed to the ever popular baby boomers with their greater disposable income. This is evidenced by Buell Motorcycle sales reaching $40 million in 1998. The bicycle manufacturer Cannondale announced in February 1998 that it planned to manufacture and market its own motorcross, off-road motorcycles.

According to the Motorcycle Safety Foundation, rider education programs helped reduce the accident rate. This improvement in safety enhanced the appeal of motorcycles for many potential riders.

The 1990s have seen domestic production relying much more on exports—although Harley-Davidson continued to have difficulty meeting those demands. But, improvement in the Asian financial situation near the end of 1999 was expected to help economic growth for the major motorcycle manufacturers. According to the Consumer Expenditure Survey, baby boomers will continue to play a major factor in the growth of the motorcycle industry since they will be at their highest level of discretionary income.

INDUSTRY LEADERS

In 1999 Cannondale remained the bicycle industry's leader in aluminum bicycles. The company offered 55 models and had total sales in excess of $171 million for fiscal year 1998 for their bicycles, apparel, accessories, and components. In 1998 Cannondale began plans to manufacture and market its first off-road (motorcross) motorcycles and unveiled the MX400 at the International Powersports Expo in Indianapolis, Indiana, in 1999. The company plans to be as innovative with their line of motorcycles as they have been with their bicycles in the past.

In 1998 Schwinn signed an agreement with Currie Technologies, giving Schwinn Cycling and Fitness exclusive license to the electric bicycle technology Currie Technologies has developed. This new electric bicycle was available in 1998. It is lightweight and frictionless, can be operated in inclement weather and be serviced at traditional bike shops, and delivers state-of-the-art performance. Maximized production efficiency by Curry Technologies has made this electric bike affordable to the public. Schwinn also launched a full line helmet program for the safety of adults and children in June 1998.

Huffy Corporation, the world's largest bicycle seller, announced net sales of $112.8 million, down 6.1 percent from the same period 1998. At the end of 1999, the company's planned transformation from a single-brand to a multi-brand bicycle design manufacturer was complete. These changes were projected to increase the company's earnings significantly in the year 2000 and continue through the first decade of the new century.

The undisputed leader in the U.S. motorcycle industry is Harley-Davidson of Milwaukee, Wisconsin, which maintained a 67 percent share of the domestic motorcycle market in 1997. The company's net sales rose to $2,063,956 in 1998, and the company increased its production target in 1999 to 175,000 units. Harley-Davidson increased its production target for 2000 to 193,000 units because of the positive reaction from motorcycle press, dealers, and customers, as well as the continued strength of the heavyweight motorcycle worldwide. Seven new models were introduced by Harley-Davidson in the third quarter of 1999, all having the new Twin Cam 88B counterbalanced engine. Also, third quarter sales for Harley-Davidson apparel rose 22.2 percent—totaling $40.9 million. Buell Motorcycle, a division of Harley-Davidson making smaller, sportier motorcycles, had sales totaling $16.7 million—an increase of $7.5 million from 1998.

Polaris Industries, Inc. reported a 9 percent increase in net income for the first six months of 1999 and a 16 percent increase in sales totaling a little more than $562 million. This growth was attributed to a 26 percent increase in all-terrain vehicle (ATV) sales, which continue to grow at more than 20 percent industry-wide.

WORKFORCE

Harley-Davidson reported a workforce of 6,200 employees for 1998—a 3 percent increase over 1995. In 1997 the United States motorcycle, bicycle, and parts manufacturing industry reported 17,074 employees working in its 387 establishments.

AMERICA AND THE WORLD

The expansion of exports in both bicycles and motorcycles throughout the late 1980s and the late 1990s has been steadily growing. U.S. exports of motorcycles has grown steadily from 1987 to 1997 at an annual rate of 18 percent. The apparent consumption totaled $2.4 billion in 1998, a 10 percent increase. Harley-Davidson now exports 30 percent of its motorcycles, which could be higher if they could meet production demands. By contrast, imports of motorcycles and parts decreased 3 percent to an estimated $1.3 billion in 1998. Harley-Davidson maintains 55 percent of the total U.S. market, far more than all Japanese manufacturers combined.

American companies are seizing new market opportunities in countries such as China, which traditionally have been controlled by domestic manufacturers. In early 1997 ZAP Power Systems of Sebastopol, California, received a grant from the U.S. Environmental Protection Agency (EPA) to promote sales of its electric-powered bicycles in China. This grant came on the heels of Shanghai's ban on the licensing of new gas mopeds and bicycles and its plans to replace 80 percent of the 470,000 gas vehicles in the city with cleaner vehicles.

RESEARCH AND TECHNOLOGY

The mountain bike continued the technological revolution started with the 10-speed bicycle by reducing cost and increasing comfort levels. Innovators in bicycle design use new materials and electronic gadgets to bring the century-old "safety" bicycle into the computer age. The molded carbon fiber metals that made stronger, lighter frames possible, for example, came from missile technology, while Special Bicycle Components' three-spoke wheel (which combines carbon fiber, epoxy resin, Kevlar, and aluminum) was designed on the Cray Super-

computer. In addition, hydraulic brakes are replacing the familiar cable systems, and electronic shifters make changing gears a snap. Some manufacturers are investigating a new enclosed automatic transmission system, which could banish "gear fear" forever. The most visible innovation in bicycling may be a completely new design. The new recumbent bicycle places the rider in a sitting position with the pedals in front, thus providing a low center of gravity, which improves cornering and pedaling efficiency.

Foreign manufacturers are changing the way they do things, as well. National Bicycle Industrial Co., a subsidiary of Matsushita, builds its bikes one at a time. Using robots and computer tracking, its 20 employees custom manufacture the product from the individual customer's order. From a base of 18 models of racing, road, and mountain bikes, they can build 11,231,862 variations in 199 color patterns.

The manufacturing expertise of Harley-Davidson has grown steadily since its first 1903 model, which used a tomato can for a carburetor. Faced with sophisticated competition from Japanese manufactures in the 1980s, the company adopted modern Just-In-Time inventory management and computerized information systems. It retrained its production workers to use statistical monitoring methods, and re-educated managers to work as team leaders instead of bosses. New production line techniques included a state-of-the-art robot assembly system and a $23-million paint center at York, Pennsylvania. The result was the vastly improved quality and productivity needed to overcome Harley-Davidson's reputation as unreliable and expensive.

FURTHER READING

"About the Motorcycle Safety Foundation." Irvine, CA: Motorcycle Safety Foundation, 1997. Available from http://www.tiac.net/users/emax/MSFaboutMSF.html.

Brown, Don J. "Systemic Change: 1986-1996; Motorcycle Industry." Dealernews, January 1997.

Celente, Gerald. "Americans Finding Happiness Outdoors." Trends in the News, 19 June 1995.

Doyle, Rob. "No Saddlebags on This Screamer." Business Week, 21 October 1996.

Drake, Geoff. "Toy Story: Workaday Role of the Bicycle." Bicycling, January 1997.

"Electric Bike Firm Receives EPA Grant to Expand Market in China." Business Wire, 18 March 1997.

Fauber, John. "Bike Helmets Found to Cut Risk of Head Injury by 69 Percent." Milwaukee Journal Sentinel, 6 January 1997.

"GT Bicycles Reports Record Fourth Quarter and Full-Year 1996 Results." Business Wire, 19 February 1997.

Harley-Davidson, The Art & Science of Harley-Davidson— 1998 Annual Report, 1999. Available from http://www.harley-davidson.com.

Jesitus, John. "On the Road Again; New Top Management Uses a Teamwork Approach to Put Schwinn Back Into the Bicycle-Industry Race." *Industry Week,* 4 November 1996.

Kinsler, Christen. "Two-Wheeling-and-Dealing; Automakers Beginning to Make, Sell Bicycles." *Ward's Auto World,* September 1996.

La Franco, Robert. "The Battle of the Bikes." *Forbes,* 26 August 1996.

Lafee, Scott. "Relive Your Childhood—For $3,000." *Business Week,* 18 March 1996.

Melcher, Richard A. "Tune-up for Harley." *Business Week,* 8 April 1996.

"Mountain Bikes' Demographics Are Broader Than Gen X." *The Public Pulse,* July 1995.

Schonfeld, Erick. "Betting on the Boomers." *Fortune,* 25 December 1995.

U.S. Department of Commerce. Bureau of the Census. International Trade Administration. "Recent Trends in Motorcycles, Bicycles, and Parts." Washington, D.C.: GPO, 1995.

"Welcome to Trek Bikes Online." Waterloo, WI: Trek Bicycle Corp., 1997. Available from http://www.trekbikes.com.

SIC 3761

MANUFACTURERS OF GUIDED MISSILES AND SPACE VEHICLES

This category covers establishments primarily engaged in manufacturing guided missiles and space vehicles. This industry also includes establishments owned by guided missile and space vehicle manufacturers and primarily engaged in research and development on these products, whether from enterprise funds or on a contract or fee basis. Establishments primarily engaged in manufacturing guided missile and space vehicle propulsion units and propulsion unit parts are classified in **SIC 3764: Guided Missile and Space Vehicle Propulsion Units and Propulsion Unit Parts;** those manufacturing space satellites are classified in **SIC 3669: Communications Equipment, Not Elsewhere Classified;** those manufacturing guided missile and space vehicle airborne and ground guidance, checkout, and launch electronic systems and components are classified in **SIC 3812: Search, Detection, Navigation, Guidance, Aeronautical, and Nautical Systems and Instruments;** and those manufacturing guided missile and space vehicle airframes, nose cones, and space capsules are classified in **SIC 3769: Guided Missile and Space Vehicle Parts and Auxiliary Equipment, Not Elsewhere Classified.** Research and development on guided missiles and space vehicles, on a contract or fee basis, by establishments not owned by guided missile or space vehicle manufacturers are classified in **SIC 8731: Commercial Physical and Biological Research.**

NAICS CODE(S)

336414 (Guided Missile and Space Vehicle Manufacturing)

INDUSTRY SNAPSHOT

In 1997, this industry shipped $14.8 billion worth of goods. In 1996, the United States had approximately 50 establishments in this industry, with total gross sales totaling slightly more than $15 billion, down $4 billion from 1992. Of the total value of net new orders, about 16 percent of this industry's production was for complete guided missiles and space vehicles; 12 percent was for other aircraft, space vehicle, and missile activities; 8 percent was for research and development of guided missiles and space vehicles; and 16 percent went toward services on these products. The military accounted for 61 percent of net sales, with the U.S. government purchasing 52 percent and other governments purchasing 9 percent. Of the 39 percent of nonmilitary sales, the U.S. government accounted for 6 percent and other customers accounted for 33 percent.

The industry's largest customer had long been the U.S. government. However, the government's market share started to decrease in the late 1980s with the end of the Cold War, which reduced defense needs, and a rapidly growing commercial market dominated by foreign-owned companies. Military spending dropped to $36.1 billion in 1997, down about 6 percent from 1996 levels. In constant dollars, that figure represented less than half of the 1987 spending peak.

While the end of the Cold War initiated cuts in defense spending, the view that the United States needed to retain its technological base in defense caused an increase in funding for research and development. This trend was expected to continue, with 57 percent of procurement going toward research and development in 1997, compared with 30 percent in 1985. New products were being manufactured only as a limited number of prototypes and were taken to full-scale production on the basis of need and available funding. Recent trends in aerospace saw decreases in total employment, imports, and exports. In order to meet the challenges posed by military downsizing, major defense companies merged in 1996 and shifted some of their resources toward nonmilitary commercial enterprises, such as designing medical laboratory equipment and software for the communications field.

The end of the twentieth century also saw a new phase in the space vehicles segment of the industry. As a result of the 1986 *Challenger* space shuttle disaster and other highly publicized space failures, Congress reduced

NASA's budget. NASA subsequently launched fewer flights annually, but used larger and more expensive payloads, thereby producing greater financial risks. Meanwhile, space vehicle manufacturers moved away from government projects and into the commercial market. According to Otis Port of *Business Week,* "Thanks mainly to advances in technology, aerospace companies and some in Washington think they see a chance to make space travel an airline-type business." The focus shifted to funding space projects with greater relevance to living on Earth. The orbiting of communications satellites and the construction of the *Freedom* space station were new priorities for the U.S. space program.

ORGANIZATION AND STRUCTURE

This industry classification comprises a large part of the aerospace industry, which is made up of roughly 4,000 companies. The production of missiles accounted for 5 percent of sales in the aerospace industry, and space vehicles (along with related equipment) accounted for 25 percent of sales.

Of the companies in the aerospace industry, only 60 were primary contractors, mostly in the guided missile and space vehicle sectors. These establishments regularly hire subcontractors in other sectors of the aerospace industry. Due to the size and technical scope of aerospace programs, a company that acts as the primary contractor on one project may be a subcontractor on another project.

This industry is subdivided by the type of manufacturing workload an establishment undertakes. Basically, three types of manufacturing establishments exist in this industry: manufacturers of conventional, battlefield, and short- to medium-range guided missiles; producers of strategic ballistic, antiballistic, and long-range missiles; and manufacturers of space vehicles.

Establishments rely on state-of-the-art systems management in which a subcontractor, often the major computer hardware supplier, supervises hundreds of companies at one time. The development of systems management in the United States has been credited to this industry.

BACKGROUND AND DEVELOPMENT

The history of this industry is characterized by the world political climate and technological developments. In the United States, wars and foreign policy directly affected the production of guided missiles, while the space race with the Soviet Union prompted U.S. production of space vehicles. Two major technological developments also have advanced the growth of this industry: the gas turbine engine, developed in the late 1940s for supersonic speed, and the ballistic missile, first developed in the late 1950s for long-range capabilities in war and space exploration.

The aerospace industry emerged from the aftermath of World War II, which introduced jet rockets and atomic weaponry. These developments added to the already growing aviation industry. Aviation became established in the late 1920s, with the success of Charles Lindbergh's flight across the Atlantic. Many companies that were in the aviation business later made the transition into aerospace technology by manufacturing missiles for the U.S. military during World War II.

Space vehicles developed into an industry during the mid-1950s, when the U.S. became engaged in the "space race" against the Soviet Union. Initially, space vehicles explored the earth's upper atmosphere and the moon. Man's first trip to the moon sparked new interest in space technology—that interest peaking in the late 1960s.

The 1960s also marked tremendous growth in the development of guided missiles. Missiles manufactured in the United States were sold to parties in conflict in the Middle East and to other troubled areas of the world. The production of both missiles and space vehicles decreased during the mid- to late 1970s because of the end of the Vietnam War and the economic recession.

During the 1980s the guided missile portion of this industry hit its all-time peak as a result of renewed defense spending by the Reagan administration. During this *arms race,* missile sales escalated from slightly more than $10 billion in 1983 to nearly $14 billion in 1988, according to the Electronic Industries Association. President Reagan also proposed the development of antiballistic strategic defenses, commonly known as the *Star Wars* initiative, to counter possible Soviet missile attacks.

However, by the end of the 1980s, yet another dramatic shift occurred in this industry. With the fall of the Iron Curtain bringing about the dismantling of the Soviet Union's satellite empire in eastern Europe, and the subsequent dissolution of the Soviet Union itself, U.S. defense spending was greatly reduced. From 1987 to 1994, U.S. Defense Department outlays for aircraft dropped from more than $30 billion to slightly more than $19 billion. Similarly, the government budget for research and development in defense and space technology dropped significantly. This also was due to the explosion of the *Challenger* space shuttle, in which 7 astronauts perished.

Missiles. Among the types of guided missiles are antitank and assault, antiship, air-to-surface, air-to-air, and surface-to-air. Antitank and assault missiles were developed in the United States after World War II (although some accounts have Germany developing these missiles near the end of the war). These missiles were first installed on light trucks and helicopters and were equipped with warheads to penetrate armor. In early models, tracking was visual, with commands controlled by a hand-operated system transmitted by wire. Later, antitank missiles transmitted commands by radio, laser and infrared homing techniques. By the 1980s, optical fibers had become the standard guidance device for these missiles.

Antiship missiles were designed to fight against the heavy armor of warships. These types of guided missiles received little attention by U.S. manufacturers after World War II until the Soviet Union developed some. The United States countered with turbojet-powered missiles such as the Harpoon, which weighed about 1,200 pounds and carried a warhead weighing 420 pounds. Later, the U.S. Navy Tomahawk introduced a new type of antiship missile—a long-range cruise missile intended for strategic nuclear defense. Its antiship version carried a modified Harpoon guidance system. By the 1980s, antiship missiles were developed for stealth aircraft with visual, infrared, and radar tracking.

Air-to-surface missiles became standard in U.S. combat by the late 1950s with the AGM-12 Bullpup, a rocket-powered tracking missile with visual tracking and radio transmitted commands. After several variations of the AGM-type missiles were employed during the Vietnam War, the Bullpup was replaced by the AGM-64/65 Maverick group of rocket-powered missiles, which first used television tracking and later used infrared devices.

Air-to-air missiles were first developed in the United States in the late 1940s with the subsonic Firebird, a radar-guided missile. However, this particular missile became obsolete within a few years, being replaced by supersonic missiles, such as the Falcon, the Sidewinder, and the Sparrow. The Sidewinder became the most used of these missile types; later versions of this missile had highly sensitive emission seekers. Tactical demands brought about improvements in air-to-air technology, which resulted in long-range air-interception missiles and missiles with higher maneuverability.

Surface-to-air missiles were first introduced by the Germans during World War II, but they were not widely used until the 1950s and 1960s. The most important American-produced surface-to-air missile was the Hawk; this missile was extremely effective in targeting low-flying aircraft. In the mid-1980s the Hawk was replaced by the Patriot, which gained popularity as a result of the Persian Gulf War.

Missiles are classified as either conventional or strategic. Strategic missiles refer to long-range missiles, especially those with nuclear warheads, and include ballistic and cruise missiles. Ballistic missiles are rocket-propelled systems that are launched either from land or sea and move by the launch rocket momentum. Cruise missiles are powered continuously by air-breathing jet engines. These types of missiles are aided by guidance systems and early warning devices on satellites.

Space Vehicles. There are three basic types of space vehicles: space capsules with rocket boosters, reentry vehicles, and satellites. Satellites are classified under **SIC 3669: Communications Equipment, Not Elsewhere Classified.** Space vehicles are made of two basic components—the launch vehicle and the spacecraft, also referred to as the payload. The spacecraft is unpowered; it relies on the initial velocity provided by the launch vehicle so that it can either enter an orbit around the earth or continue to a further destination.

Space capsules with rocket boosters were first designed and tested in the United States in the mid-1950s with the intent of sending a man into outer space. These capsules are environmentally controlled containers for living organisms. The rockets attached to the space capsule are used for launching the capsule and later separate from it.

Reentry vehicles, such as space shuttles, were first launched by the United States in 1981. These space vehicles were designed to go into the Earth's orbit, drop off a payload such as a satellite, and return to earth by making a gliding landing. Shuttles are made of three basic components: a winged orbiter that houses crew and cargo, an external tank containing fuel and liquid oxygen, and booster rockets, which separate from the space craft and return to earth. By 1990 the United States had used four shuttles, many on repeated missions but also with much difficulty. Technical and design problems frequently delayed launches and also were responsible for the explosion of the *Challenger* space shuttle in 1986.

Satellites, classified under **SIC 3669: Communications Equipment, Not Elsewhere Classified,** are spacecraft that revolve around planets and are used for communications, weather forecasting, scientific research, and military reconnaissance. The first satellite was launched in 1957 by the Soviet Union. By the end of the 1980s there were hundreds of satellites orbiting the Earth and nearby planets. In the early 1990s an estimated $3 billion annually went into the manufacturing of communications satellites in the United States alone. The estimated figure for 1995 was almost $8 billion.

This industry was further affected by the signing of the Strategic Arms Reduction Treaty (START) in July 1991. According to the treaty, guided missiles with nuclear warheads would no longer be produced, while 30 percent of existing ones would be destroyed.

CURRENT CONDITIONS

By the end of the century, both national and international manufacturers were partnering in order to stay competitive in the industry. The merger between Boeing and McDonnell Douglas brought about the launching of the new American-built rockets, Delta 2 and Delta 3. The company's new Delta 4 rockets, able to carry heavier payloads, won 19 launches worth $1.37 billion for missions scheduled between fiscal years 2002-2006. Boeing is hopeful that the EELV program will help to elevate the company into a leading launch provider. Boeing also partnered with Ukranine's Yuzhnoye, Russia's Khrunichev, and Norway's Kvaerner for the Sea Launch project, of which the first launch took place from a mobile platform in the Pacific Ocean, near the equator, in October 1999. Hughes Space and Communications purchased 13 of the 18 launch slots in the belief that the satellites will have a longer life span by being launched at the low latitude near the equator. By 1999 more than 30 major systems in the construction of the International Space Station (ISS), and more than 50 percent of the major tests, were completed on the module. The station, a joint ISS venture between the United States and Russia, was scheduled to be completed by 2005-2006.

Reusable launch vehicles (RLVs) were being developed in the late 1990s. Florida and Texas were the frontrunners vying for the futuristic "spaceports" in a market expected to be worth more than $120 billion by 2010. Fred Welch, executive director of Brazoria County Partnership, developed a plan to build a spaceport in Freeport, Texas. There also were plans underway by partners Andy Pole and William Dettmer for a similar spaceport to be erected in New Mexico. Because of the high demand for Internet and cellular telephone service worldwide, hundreds of satellites were needed in orbit as quickly and as inexpensively as possible. Spaceports were seen as the answer. Lockheed Martin's VentureStar would be able to transport cargo into space at one tenth of the current expense and would be able to fly every 2 or 3 days. NASA showed interest in the VentureStar as a means to replace the Space Shuttle and become the courier to the International Space Station. Testing was scheduled to begin in 2000 and projected operation to begin in 2005. NASA put up a significant part of the initial funding for the VentureStar prototype.

Lockheed Martin launched heavy payloads from Cape Canaveral, Florida, Vandenburg Air Force Base in California, and Baikonur Cosmodrome in Kazakhstan, Russia. These international partnerships had 49 confirmed launches set as of May 1998 and a backlog of international sales. ILS, as the partnering was called, planned 1.6 launches per month through 1999.

Orbital Sciences Corp. had 8 launches scheduled for 1998, including an experimental launch in February of the Teledesic LEO communications system. LMC had 6 launches scheduled for its small launch vehicles called Athenas in 1998 and three more for 1999.

New construction began during 1999 at Cape Canaveral and at the NASA Kennedy Space Center for a major new launch facility. Plans included a facility to support the RLV development and flight testing as well as several $100 million worth of Evolved Expendable Launch Vehi-

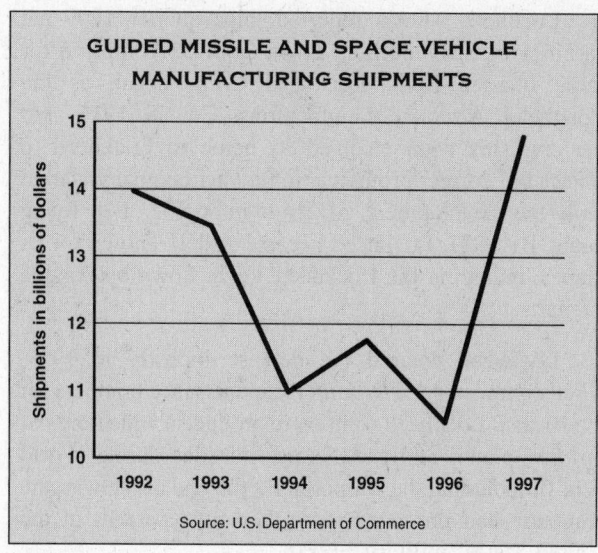

GUIDED MISSILE AND SPACE VEHICLE MANUFACTURING SHIPMENTS

Source: U.S. Department of Commerce

cles sponsored by both Boeing and Lockheed Martin. Launch pad construction at Complex 37 was underway but construction at Complex 41 was delayed because of a Titan 4 failure in August 1999.

More than 1,700 new satellites were being constructed in 1999 for launchings scheduled in the first decade of 2000. New manufacturers also came on the scene in the 1990s due to the high growth in the space launch industry. However, this growth rate is expected to level off after about 2003. Despite the leveling off, service providers should continue to grow due to the maintenance factor of both the LEO satellite communications system and the replacement of the GEO telecommunications system.

INDUSTRY LEADERS

The Boeing Co. acquired the defense and space units of Rockwell International in 1996 and merged with McDonnell Douglas in 1997, making Boeing the world's largest manufacturer of commercial jetliners, military aircraft, and NASA's leading contractor. The company employed more than 200,000 people in 1999 in more than 60 countries worldwide. Company revenues reached $56.2 billion in 1998. Boeing reported first quarter 1999 profits up 55 percent due to improved efficiency of commercial aircraft and cost reductions in business and research. Moving into the new millennium, Boeing will continue to increase its technologies in fields of space flight and exploration, as well as commercial space applications. The International Space Station, a joint venture with 16 nations, is being led by a team of Boeing engineers.

The satellite network known as Internet-in-the-sky was developed through the teamwork of Boeing and Teledesic Corp. Boeing also is contracted to build 33 next-generation global positioning satellites. Along with international partnering for the Sea Launch joint venture, the company also makes expendable launch vehicles.

Lockheed Martin reported third quarter 1999 net earnings of $217 million, down from $318 million for same quarter 1998. Lockheed Corp. began as the Loughead Aircraft Manufacturing Co. in 1916 (but the company soon changed its name to Lockheed to reflect the correct pronunciation). This company started with the development of its twin-engine, F-1 flying boats. By 1927, Lockheed became widely known for its planes, including the Lockheed Vega, flown by Amelia Earhart.

Lockheed entered the defense industry in 1938, when commissioned to build reconnaissance bombers for the British. Lockheed went on to produce a wide range of military planes and early cruise missiles during World War II, including the Harpoon. By the end of the war, the company had produced more than nine percent of the United States' military aircraft.

After the war, Lockheed established its missile and space division, starting with submarine launched missiles. During the Cold War, Lockheed developed guided missiles for the Pentagon, including its U-2 spy plane, which had notable success during the Cuban missile crisis in 1962. In addition to military contracts, Lockheed stayed in the commercial aircraft business, manufacturing jetliners; however, this division nearly placed the company into bankruptcy by the early 1970s. The company finally gained some success in jetliners in the foreign market—at the expense of being involved in an international scandal. Lockheed was implicated in accepting bribes from several countries, including Iran and Japan.

During the 1980s, Lockheed led the industry in government defense contracts, primarily in building F-19 stealth bombers and Trident II missiles, as well as in servicing NASA's space shuttles. During the early 1990s, the company remained successful in defense technology, with its stealth fighters being used in the Persian Gulf War. After an unsuccessful expansion of its commercial divisions, Lockheed reversed course to attempt to become the nation's largest defense contractor. In the mid-1990s, the company employed 81,300 workers and predicted a 10 percent annual increase in its earnings.

In March 1995, Lockheed merged with Martin Marietta Corp. which, like other industry leaders, had its origins in airplane production in the early days of aviation. Martin Marietta remained closely aligned with U.S. military projects from bomber production in World War II, rockets and missiles in the 1960s, to space vehicles from the 1970s to the present. In April 1996, Lockheed Martin bought Loral Corp., emerging as the largest defense contractor in the United States. The company had $25.5 billion in sales for 1999 and employed approximately 165,000 people.

Raytheon Co. is divided into four segments: electronics, aircraft, engineering and construction, and appliances. Its electronics segment ranked Raytheon number six nationwide. Listed among its products are Patriot missiles. Raytheon employed 108,200 people in 1999, a decrease of 5 percent from 1997. The company showed a profit of more than $860 million in 1998.

Other key companies in the manufacture of guided missile systems and space vehicles included Tracor Inc., Loral Space & Communications Ltd., and ITT Defense and Electronics.

Tracor, one of the fastest growing defense electronics and information technology companies in the United States, announced that first quarter sales for 1997 showed a 30 percent increase over first quarter 1996. Based in Austin, Texas, Tracor was listed as one of the 15 largest defense electronic firms in the United States. The company provided sophisticated electronic and information technology products, systems, and services to its customers in the U.S. Department of Defense, as well as to nondefense U.S. government agencies, other governments, and the commercial marketplace. In 1997, Lockheed Martin, Tracor, and TRW planned to form a joint venture to bid for all work related to national missile defense.

Loral Space & Communications Ltd. has as its primary operations the manufacture of satellites and satellite-based telecommunications systems. The company was formed by the remains of Loral Corp., the bulk of which was acquired by Lockheed Martin.

ITT Defense and Electronics (ITTD&E), a unit of ITT Industries Inc., has been selected by NASA as its sole supplier of meteorological instruments for the newest members of the NOAA's Geostationary Operational Environmental Satellite (GOES). The company has been a leading supplier of high technology commercial and defense electronic systems and services.

WORKFORCE

By 1997, this industry employed 52,158 people. Of this total, 18,722 were production workers who earned an average hourly wage of $22.59. Nearly 60 percent of the workforce lived in California.

For both production and research and development, the main occupations needed for this industry are engineers, scientists, and technicians. Engineers usually have specialized as either aeronautical engineers working with aircraft, or as astronautical engineers working with space vehicles. Technicians working in this industry include laboratory technicians, electrical technicians, and draftsmen. Other occupations required by this industry include technical writers, machinists, assembly workers, system managers, worker supervisors, computer programmers, and various clerical workers.

AMERICA AND THE WORLD

The production of strategic missiles, given their nuclear capabilities, was originally restricted to the United States and the Soviet Union. However, since the end of the Cold War, there has been worldwide concern that the superpowers would sell their stockpile of weapons—and possibly new weapons—to third world countries. Other countries that developed missile technology became somewhat successful in ballistic missiles, but less so with cruise missiles. Ballistic missiles do not require the sophisticated guidance system of cruise missiles and adapt to chemical weaponry more easily.

The end of the Cold War, coupled with worldwide economic recession, gave rise to change in the international market for space programs in the 1990s. An industry first monopolized by the United States and the former Soviet Union entered into competition with the European Space Agency, the People's Republic of China, and Japan. The new political and economic climate allowed for more cooperative efforts in space. NASA considered Russian contributions to the U.S. *Freedom* space station and other ventures.

The United States also imported guided missiles and space vehicles, but only on a small scale and mostly for research and development. In the mid-1990s, U.S. imports in this industry totaled approximately $1.6 million.

Arianespace, the European consortium, was the global leader in the guided missile and space vehicle industry by 1999. Like in the United States, the European missile programs have been plagued with budget problems through the late 1990s. Germany partnered with Canada, Greece, Italy, Norway, Sweden, and the Netherlands to develop the IRIS-T short-range air-to-air missile. The United Kingdom was developing larger, more powerful missiles at that time. Israel was exporting smaller missiles to Chile, China, Thailand, and South Africa. However, the United States continued to produce the best beyond-visual-range missiles throughout the world.

Japan scheduled the first launch of its commercial vehicle, the H-2A, for 2001. A new agreement with the Japanese fisherman led the way for Japan to update and enlarge the infrastructure at Tanegashima. This agreement also allows Japan to use the launch site for a longer duration of the year.

RESEARCH AND TECHNOLOGY

Engineers at NASA's Marshall Space Flight Center in Huntsville, Alabama, partnered with industry leaders to develop new graphite epoxy technology. This new material would create lightweight cryogenic fuel lines for such vehicles as NASA's X-33 Advanced Technology Demonstrator. This new system would not only create a fuel line that is lighter and stronger than metal, but the materials do not expand or contract as much as metal in extreme temperatures.

FURTHER READING

Anselmo, Joseph C. "EELV Win Boosts Boeing Launch Plans." *Aviation Week & Space Technology,* 26 October 1998.

———. "Launchers See Nothing But Blue Skies Ahead." *Aviation Week & Space Technology,* 7 April 1997.

The Associated Press. "Spaceport Competitors See New Era of Industry in Stars." *USA Today,* 27 April 1999.

Banks, Howard. "McDonnell Douglas' Last Flight?" *Forbes,* 16 December 1996. Available from http://www.forbes.com.

Crock, Stan. "Does Firepower=Earning Power?" *Business Week,* 6 May 1996.

Darlin, Damon. "Aerospace & Defense." *Forbes,* 13 January 1997. Available from http://www.forbes.com.

"Fortune." *Industry Snapshot,* 1999. Available from http://www.fortune.com.

"Frost & Sullivan—Defense Industry Faced with a Reality Check: Adapting and Surviving in This Critical Period of Rapid Change," 22 April 1997.

"Global State of the Industry." *Aerospace,* 1996. Available from http://www.oregonbusiness.com/ae-global.html.

"Hoover's Company Capsules." Austin, TX: Hoovers's, Inc., 1999. Available from http://www.hoovers.com.

"Lockheed Martin to Link Headquarters Operating Budgets Worldwide Using Comshare's Commander Budget Plus," 23 April 1997.

"Next Generation Space Shuttle, the X-33 Will Exploit Veda Systems Technology," 23 April 1997.

"New Materials May Make Vehicles Lighter, Cheaper." *Design News,* 15 February 1999.

"Reusable Rocket Flies Again." *USA Today Nation,* 8 June 1996. Available from http://www.usatoday.com/news.

Scott, William B. "Lockheed Martin, Energomash Development of RD-180 on Track." *Aviation Week & Space Technology,* 7 April 1997.

Smith, Bruce A. "Construction Plans." *Aviation Week and Space Technology,* 1 January 1999.

"The Space Industry Vying for Stardom." *The Economist,* 17 July 1999.

"Space Vehicles." *Design News,* 15 February 1999.

Spiegel, Peter. "Free Launch." *Forbes,* 24 February 1997. Available from http://www.forbes.com/forbes.

U.S. Census Bureau. *1997 Economic Census—Manufacturing.* Washington, D.C.: GPO, 1999.

SIC 3764

GUIDED MISSILE AND SPACE VEHICLE PROPULSION UNITS AND PROPULSION UNIT PARTS

This industry consists of establishments primarily engaged in manufacturing guided missile propulsion units and propulsion unit parts. This industry also includes establishments owned by manufacturers of guided missile and space vehicle propulsion units and parts and primarily engaged in research and development on such products, whether from enterprise funds or on a contract or fee basis. Research and development on guided missile and space propulsion units, on a contract or fee basis by establishments not owned by manufacturers of guided missile and space vehicle propulsion units and parts are classified in **SIC 8731: Commercial Physical and Biological Research.**

NAICS CODE(S)

336415 (Guided Missile and Space Vehicle Propulsion Unit and Propulsion Unit Parts Manufacturing)

INDUSTRY SNAPSHOT

In 1995 American manufacturers of propulsion units, jet engines, and propulsion unit parts for guided missiles and space vehicles recorded $2.4 billion in gross sales. The number was roughly split 50-50 between military and nonmilitary markets; $1.1 billion accounted for military markets, $1.3 billion accounted for civilian markets. The end of year backlog was $6.1 billion; with $792.0 million for the military, and $5.3 billion for non-military. Industry shipments reached $3.2 billion in 1997.

In the 1990s there were two basic types of propulsion systems used for guided missiles and space vehicles—solid-fueled and liquid-fueled engines. Solid-fueled engines were more commonly used because liquid fuels require storage at very low temperatures. Other rockets produced by this industry included hybrid rockets, which use a combination of solid and liquid fuel systems, small propellant rockets for adjusting the altitude of space vehicles, and rockets for track-borne research sheds. By the end of the century the industry was seeking a method to propel vehicles for longer and further space exploration. Nuclear fission, sun laser/solar sails, and anti-matter were just a few methods being researched.

ORGANIZATION AND STRUCTURE

Establishments in this industry were generally subcontractors for producers of complete guided missiles and space vehicles. Primary contractors and subcontractors were hired by a single customer. In 1995 net sales for

the entire industry (complete aircraft, space vehicles, missiles, and selected parts) was $101 billion, with $52 billion military related, and $49 billion nonmilitary. Of the nonmilitary sales, $7 billion went to the U.S. government. The industry's shipments manufactured under government contracts were primarily for the U.S. Department of Defense and NASA. The balance of the industry's shipments manufactured for private sector companies were used in producing propulsion and engine systems to launch commercial satellites.

BACKGROUND AND DEVELOPMENT

Propulsion units and engines were often referred to as "rockets." Rockets were believed to have originated in China during the thirteenth century, soon after the invention of gunpowder. Rockets appeared in Europe in the early fourteenth century, but did not see regular military use until the War of 1812 and the Napoleonic Wars. Rockets during this period still used some form of gunpowder for propulsion. It was not until the late nineteenth and early twentieth century that modern rocketry, using stored fuels, was first developed.

World War II witnessed the first guided missiles and military aircraft powered by propulsion systems. During the war, only the Germans used propulsion guided missiles, though other countries possessed the technological capabilities. It was not until after the war that other countries, including the United States, developed these systems.

The development of the propulsion units used in ballistic missiles enabled the launching of the first space vehicles into orbit by the end of the 1950s. Another significant development in propulsion systems came in the 1970s, concurrent with the first designs for space shuttles. These engines were built with propulsion units that either jettisoned off the spacecraft, or were permanently fixed and reusable.

Rockets using nuclear and solar fuel sources were also tested for space missions. Nuclear propulsion was first developed in the 1960s, and was considered 20 years later for missions to Mars, but concerns about space debris kept this system in the experimental stages. Solar propulsion appeared promising for its ability to run an engine at tremendous cost savings.

Entering the 1990s, the guided missile and space vehicle propulsion industry, like other aerospace industries, was downsizing operations while trying to retain a strong research and development base. With the end of the Cold War, new propulsion systems for military and space exploration programs were limited to prototypes, which were then taken to full-scale production on the basis of need and available funding.

With federal cut-backs, a number of fixed-price contracts created losses for companies in the late 1980s and early 1990s. In the late 1980s, the U.S. Air Force proposed development of the Titan 4 Launcher through the "SRMU stabilization program," but did not fund the program. Both the contractor, Martin Marietta Corp., and the subcontractor, Hercules, Inc., invested substantially, and both ended up suing each other over contract terms. In 1993 the U.S. government agreed to appropriate funds for some of the losses.

CURRENT CONDITIONS

The end of the twentieth century was the beginning of a new phase in the production of space vehicles. Production was geared toward low-cost rather than high-cost systems. U.S. export forecasts for guided missiles and space vehicle parts were $5.9 million for 1999 as compared to $5.6 million in 1998. Import forecasts from foreign countries were $39.0 million in 1999 as compared to $37.0 million in 1998. The largest foreign supplier to the U.S. aerospace market in 1999 was France.

Like other industries in aerospace, the guided missile and space vehicle propulsion industry was expected to undergo restructuring as a result of federal defense budget cuts. According to industry leaders, by the end of the century the industry was expected to be smaller, with many individual companies having a larger market share than in the mid-1980s. While the aerospace industry was smaller in 1999 than it was in the early 1990s, conditions were on an upswing.

INDUSTRY LEADERS

In 1998, the three leaders of the guided missile and space vehicle propulsion industry were GenCorp, Inc. who reported $673.0 million in net sales; Cordant Technologies owner of Thiokol Propulsion, recorded $2.5 billion in combined sales; and Alliant Techsystems, with net sales of $1.1 billion, and a backlog totaling $1.7 billion.

Alliant is a relative newcomer to the industry, having purchased the aerospace component for $300.0 million in March 1995 from Hercules, Inc., a Delaware-based company and diversified worldwide producer of chemicals and related products. Alliant Techsystems, Inc. became a business entity of its own following a spinoff from Honeywell, Inc., in October 1990. Alliant gained access to new markets in 1997 when it purchased Motorola's military fuse business. Headquartered in Hopkins, Minnesota, Alliant employed a workforce of approximately 6,300 employees. Alliant Techsystems supplied aerospace technologies to the United States and its allies. Alliant Aerospace Company designed, developed and manufactured solid rocket propulsion systems throughout the 1990s and into the new century.

GenCorp, Inc. was established in 1915 as General Rubber Manufacturing Co. In 1996 GenCorp had 8,950 employees and Aerojet, the company's aerospace and defense division, accounted for nearly one third of GenCorp's total sales. In addition to producing solid and liquid propulsion systems and their related parts, Aerojet manufactured sensors, warheads, and munitions used in the aerospace industry. Aerojet was most widely known for its Titan IV engines and its second stage Delta engines, which allowed spacecraft to maneuver in orbit. The U.S. Army recently awarded Aerojet with a $43.8 million product improvement contract for the Sense and Destroy Armor Program. The contract's value may increase to over $150 million if all options are exercised. Aerojet played a major role in the Space-Based Infrared System (SBIRS) in 1999. SBIRS was predicted to generate $780 million in sales while in the developmental stage and generate further income for decades.

Thiokol Corp. was established in 1969 as Morton-Norwich Products, Inc., and changed its name later that year to Morton Thiokol, Inc. Thiokol was the nation's leading supplier of solid rocket propulsion systems for space launch vehicles since the inception of manned space flight. In 1992, 96 percent of the company's sales came from government contracts, including propulsion units for NASA's space shuttle programs and the military's Trident and Patriot missiles. During 1996 space systems remained Thiokol's largest and most profitable business, with 46 percent of fiscal 1996 sales. Approximately 95 percent of space systems sales came from Thiokol's support of NASA as the exclusive builder and refurbisher of reusable solid rocket motors used in the Space Shuttle program. In 1992 Thiokol employed over 11,000 workers. In 1996 they downsized to 5,900 employees, restructured their defense and non-shuttle space activities, and closed their Huntsville, Alabama, plant.

Thiokol Propulsion was a subsidiary of Cordent Technologies in 1999. Cordent Technology employs a total workforce of 17,000 people worldwide with annual sales estimated at $2.5 billion. Cordent Technologies' Thiokol Propulsion is the industry leader in solid propulsion systems. Huck International, also a subsidiary of Cordent, produces high performance aerospace and industrial fastener systems. James R. Wilson, chairman and chief executive officer, announced in February 1999 that the strength of Cordent Technologies' industrial segment would offset any losses suffered from the decline in the commercial aerospace segment. However, propulsion systems had a 27 percent increase in 1998 over 1997.

WORKFORCE

In 1995 the guided missile and space vehicle propulsion industry employed roughly 20,500 workers in the United States. Of these, an estimated 25 percent were engineers, mainly aeronautical, astronautical, electronic, and industrial. Other occupations needed in the manufacturing of guided missile and space vehicle propulsion systems included systems analysts, computer scientists, specialized technicians, production managers, and machinists.

The industry employed 18,540 people in 1997. The 8,264 production workers earned an average hourly wage of $24.65 that year, well above the manufacturing average.

Overall employment in this industry was expected to drop considerably by the year 2005. The largest decline was expected to be in jobs related to the inspection and testing of products. Computer scientists however, were expected to increase their representation in this industry to facilitate the development of computerized prototypes to replace full-scale testing of new products. Overall employment in the aerospace industry has declined; direct employment related to aircraft, missiles, and space vehicle manufacture declined more than 35 percent from 905,100 in 1989 to 586,800 in 1994. The Aerospace Research Center predicts that some employment growth in the defense sector may occur by the end of the decade, but any significant upturn in aerospace jobs will come from the commercial sector.

AMERICA AND THE WORLD

Manufacturers of guided missile and space vehicle propulsion and engine systems were affected by developments in foreign countries. Entering the 1990s, France and Great Britain were leading competitors with America in the production of missiles. By the mid-1990s, the United States and former Soviet Union no longer competed solely between themselves for the defense and space related business of smaller nations. Other nations, such as France, Great Britain, Australia, Canada, China, Germany, and Japan entered this market. The European conglomerate, Arianespace, was the world leader in the production of commercial satellites.

The change in America's relationship with the former Soviet Union also helped to create a highly competitive international market for commercially operated communication satellites and low-budget commercial satellites.

RESEARCH AND TECHNOLOGY

There were nearly 60 worldwide launch failures in the 1990s—five of which occurred from August 1998 through March 1999. It was feared these failures would have a fatal impact on the U.S. industry's efforts to recapture a larger percentage of the worldwide market. Therefore, ongoing studies were being performed to determine the cause of the many failures.

Technology for deep space exploration would be implemented through NASA's "New Millennium Program." The Deep Space 1 mission was developed to focus on new technologies and concepts, but at the same time, reduce time and costs involved with each launch.

By the end of 1999 Deep Space 1 had completed 100 percent of the testing to validate the new technologies. Deep Space 1 would visit asteroid 1992 KD among other solar bodies during its mission.

NASA's Advanced Space Transportation Program (ASTP) was actively researching new methods of propulsion for both manned and unmanned spacecraft. Chemical propellants did not have the capability to boost a vehicle beyond the speed of light. Three of the methods being researched were nuclear fission, laser and solar sails, and anti-matter. Two of these concepts had drawbacks. Nuclear fission was cleaner, but raised environmental concerns. Sun laser and solar sails were not developed to a point of accuracy and their performance would be diminished due to the lack of solar light outside the solar system. Studies done in the late 1990s indicated that anti-matter might offer the greatest specific impulse needed for the longer space missions.

FURTHER READING

The Aerospace Research Center. "Aerospace Employment Trends, 1962-1995." May 1995. Available from http://www.access.digex.net.

"Gencorp Aerojet Receives $43.8 Million Product Improvement Contract for SADARM." *PR Newswire.* Available from http://www.prnewswire.com/cgi-bin/stories.pl?ACC.

"GenCorp Announces Improved Fourth Quarter Results." *PR Newswire.* Available from http://www.prnewswire.com/cgi-bin/stories.pl?ACC.

Rayman Ph.D., Marc D. "Entering the New Millennium with Cutting-Edge Technology. 1999" Available from http://www.nmp.jpl.nasa.gov/ds1.

Scott, William B. "Launch Failures Cripple U.S. Space Prowess." *Aviation Week and Space Technology* 3 May 1999.

Standard & Poor's. "Industry Survey: Aerospace 1998." 1999.

Thiokol Propulsion. "Company History. 1999" Available from http://www.thiokol.com.

U.S. Securities and Exchange Commission. "Annual and Quarterly Reports." Available from http://www.sec.gov/cgi-bin/srch-edgar.

SIC 3769

SPACE VEHICLE EQUIPMENT, NOT ELSEWHERE CLASSIFIED

This category covers establishments primarily engaged in manufacturing guided missile and space vehicle parts and auxiliary equipment, not elsewhere classified. This industry also includes establishments owned by manufacturers of guided missile and space vehicle parts and auxiliary equipment, not elsewhere classified, and primarily engaged in research and development on such products, whether from enterprise funds or on a contract or fee basis. Establishments primarily engaged in manufacturing navigational and guidance systems are classified in **SIC 3812: Search, Detection, Navigation, Guidance, Aeronautical, and Nautical Systems and Instruments.** Research and development on guided missile and space vehicle parts, on a contract or fee basis by establishments not owned by manufacturers of such products, are classified in **SIC 8731: Commercial Physical and Biological Research.**

NAICS CODE(S)

336419 (Other Guided Missile and Space Vehicle Parts and Auxiliary Equipment Manufacturing)

Products manufactured by this industry are mostly airframe assemblies for guided missiles, castings for missiles and missile components, nose cones for guided missiles, and space capsules for space vehicles. In the early 1990s, roughly 70 percent of this industry's production went towards manufacturing these types of products, while the remaining 30 percent went towards research and development. By 1997, research and development made up less than 12 percent of industry production, and manufacturing made up more than 87 percent.

According to the *1997 Economic Census,* the value of product shipments for guided missile and space vehicle parts and auxiliary equipment fell by approximately 48 percent between 1992 and 1997. In 1992, this industry's shipments were valued at $4.18 billion, a drop from 1998's total at the height of the aerospace industry as a whole. In 1997, shipments were valued at $2.81 billion. The sector of the industry showing the biggest decline was production for U.S. government military customers—not including manufacture of airframes and space capsules. Shipment values in 1997 were just 33 percent higher than 1992 levels. Nonetheless, the industry saw slight gains in shipments to nonmilitary government customers and commercial customers—between 1992 and 1997, those sectors combined jumped 36 percent.

The number of workers in this industry has fallen dramatically since a high in 1985 of 33,700. Smaller peaks occurred in 1988 and 1992, when the number of workers was 19,400 and 17,200, respectively. Employment in 1996 was at 8,100, another significant drop, and was expected to fall as low as 2,500 by the year 2000. Wages increased considerably throughout the 1990s, and in 1996 workers in this industry enjoyed earnings of nearly 70 percent more than the average of all manufacturing industries.

Jobs most affected by the decline in employment have included precision assemblers, inspectors, secretarial and clerical workers, and machinists. Other areas were expected to increase through the first decade of the

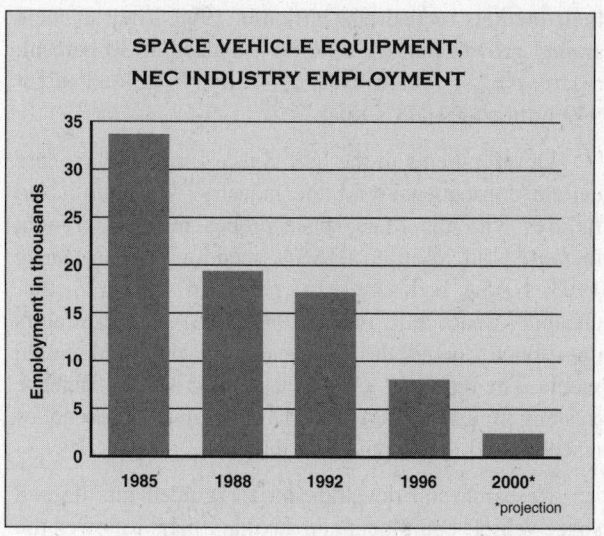

twenty-first century, particularly electrical engineers and systems analysts. By contrast, jobs for aeronautical and astronautical engineers, which made up 8.4 percent of the industry work force in 1996, were expected to decline by over 11 percent by the year 2006.

Like other sectors of the aerospace industry, U.S. space vehicle equipment exports far exceed imports. In 1997, this industry exported over $690 million in equipment, compared to $109 million in imports. The value of imports has held fairly steady since 1992 ($103 million), while the value of exports has decreased overall. Although forecasts for 1999 exports were as high as $730 million, that was nonetheless a 5 percent decline from 1992 levels.

Industry leaders in 1998 included Intercontinental Manufacturing, with sales of $58 million; Engineering Group Inc., with sales of $54 million; and Aerotherm Corp, with sales of $47 million. Sales for individual companies continued to plummet during the late 1990s as government contracts continued to shrink. This, combined with the constant dismantling of missiles and reduced spending on space missions, has been detrimental for the health of the industry.

The growth and stability of this industry are dependent on manufacturers of complete guided missiles and space vehicles, **SIC 3761: Manufacturers of Guided Missiles and Space Vehicles**, who act as primary contractors in the manufacturing of these products. Both industries rely largely on the world political situation that dictates military needs, and on the competitiveness of the world market for space exploration and commercial space ventures, mainly in launching communications satellites.

Positive indicators for the industry include a thriving market in satellite services that is expected to continue at least until 2005. In 1999, Richard Gawel reported in *Flight International,* "The commercial space manufacture and services industries are booming.... Worldwide, their markets totaled $68 billion in 1998. Their average annual growth rate (AAGR) is projected at 30 percent, reaching $251 billion by 2003. The U.S. accounted for $39 billion of 1998's total.''

Developments in the U.S. Space Program have less certain consequences for the industry. Well-publicized failures with the Mars space probes in 1999 brought increased attention to NASA spending habits. Since 1993, NASA had adopted a policy of ''faster, better, cheaper'' spacecraft, but in 1999 NASA administrators questioned whether the low spending levels could remain viable. The failure of a test of a planned Missile Defense System in early 2000 may have signaled the end of research and development in that area.

Research and development for guided missile and space vehicle equipment and auxiliary parts followed the trend of the aerospace industry as a whole in its focus on reduced-cost reusable products. Early in 1999, Rotary Rocket Co. claimed success in building the first reusable prototype ''that would actually fly,'' according to *Fortune* magazine; several other major space vehicle manufacturers were close behind. The rockets were targeted for use in the growing market of small communications satellites, with an eye toward space tourism in the future.

FURTHER READING

Darnay, Arsen J., ed. *Manufacturing USA.* 6th ed. Detroit: Gale Research, 1998.

Gawel, Richards. ''Commercial Space Industry Ready to Blast Off.'' *Flight International,* 15 Dec., 1999.

Kelly, Emma. ''Mission failure leaves Mars exploration in disarray.'' *Electronic Design,* 31 May, 1999.

''Little rockets, cheap.'' *U.S. News and World Report,* 15 March 1999.

U.S. Department of Commerce. *1997 Economic Census,* Washington: GPO, 1999.

U.S. Industry and Trade Outlook, 1999, McGraw-Hill, 1999.

SIC 3792

TRAVEL TRAILERS AND CAMPERS

This industry consists of establishments primarily engaged in the manufacture of travel trailers and chassis and campers for attachment to motor vehicles, pick-up coaches and caps, covers and canopies for mounting on pick-up trucks, and tent camping trailers. This classification includes travel trailers of up to 35 feet long and 8 feet wide (with storage facilities for waste and water), but excludes mobile home manufacturers. Mobile home manufacturers are classified in **SIC 3716: Motor Homes.**

NAICS CODE(S)

336214 (Travel Trailer and Camper Manufacturing)

INDUSTRY SNAPSHOT

In 1999 there were approximately 806 U.S. establishments in this industry. Most were private subsidiaries of companies that manufacture a range of recreational vehicles. Manufacturers of trailers and campers often incorporate chassis made elsewhere into their products; these chassis are produced by large automakers such as Ford Motor Co. and General Motors.

Several factors contributed to the steady sale of travel trailers and campers, resulting in a modest growth at the end of the twentieth century. The popularity of outdoor recreation, particularly with the baby boomer generation as they approached retirement age, boosted recreational vehicle sales. The strong economy and booming stock market of the late 1990s sparked the industry's growth, as well.

BACKGROUND AND DEVELOPMENT

Travel trailers and pick-up cabs were introduced in the early 1930s, with camper attachments entering the market in the late 1940s. The emergence of mobile homes, also in the late 1940s, shifted manufacturers' emphasis away from travel trailers and camper attachments. While mobile homes dominated the recreational vehicle market in the 1950s and 1960s, the market for travel trailers and camper attachments continued to grow.

The economic recessions of the 1970s and 1980s dramatically reduced sales and manufacturing in this industry. Also during that time, some travel trailer and chassis producers were negatively effected by recalls of their products; at one point, over 10,000 units of small mobile homes attached to Toyota pick-up truck chassis were recalled.

Because the recreational vehicle field was increasingly competitive and crowded, the future for the industry was uncertain. Some analysts felt that the continued development of other types of recreational vehicles boded ill for this segment of the transportation manufacturing industry. Richard Rescigno of *Barron's,* however, predicted that sales of small campers and travel trailers might actually improve through the 1990s, since such products were at the inexpensive end of the recreational vehicle market. Rescigno reasoned that such products would appeal to the growing number of retirees on limited incomes.

Just as Rescigno had predicted, motor home sales rose sharply: retail figures went up by 19.4 percent from September 1992. Recreational vehicle (RV) trailers also posted a 15.0 percent gain in overall sales for September 1993. RV shipments increased by 2.7 percent from May

1993 to May 1994. The growth trend continued into the mid-1990s, with sales of RV trailers growing by 18.8 percent to 13,962 units for the first half of 1994. The continued growth trend was attributed to strong sales in the east north central and west north central regions of the United States.

By the mid-1990s the state of Indiana had the distinction of being the RV capital of the world, producing 49.8 percent of all RVs in the country. According to the *Tribune Business Weekly,* the total retail value of the industry nationwide was $9.5 billion during that period, with $4.5 billion being generated from the production in Indiana.

CURRENT CONDITIONS

America's increasing demand for travel trailers and motor homes continued into the late 1990s. This growth was attributed to the nation's aging population of baby boomers. People between the ages of 55 and 65 accounted for much the industry sales, which were expected to grow over the next 10 years. In 1997, shipments were reported at $4.3 billion.

In June 1995, the Recreational Vehicle Industry Association (RVIA) gave its final approval to a RV weight-labeling requirement. Motor homes, travel trailers, fifth wheels, and folding camping trailers would be required to comply; truck campers and conversion vehicles were exempted from this requirement.

INDUSTRY LEADERS

Employing around 21,000 people, Fleetwood Enterprises Inc. of Riverside, California led the industry with sales revenues of $3.5 billion in 1999. Known as the "Big Guy" in the industry, Fleetwood was the only Fortune 500 company in Riverside and rolled out 250 RV models from its California plants.

Thor Industries of Ohio was second in the industry, with 1999 sales of $805 million and 3,350 employees. Other leaders included Holiday Rambler LLC, Winnebago Industries Inc., Coachmen Industries Inc., and Safari Motor Coaches Inc.

WORKFORCE

By 1999, 23,200 workers were employed by this industry. Most worked just over 40 hours a week for an average wage of $13.20 per hour.

FURTHER READING

Bureau of the Census. *Economic Census 1997,* 2000. Available from http://www.census.gov.

Bureau of Labor Statistics. *Employment Statistics,* 2000. Available from http://www.bls.gov.

"Hoover's Company Capsules." *Hoover's Online,* 2000. Available from http://www.hoovers.com.

Longsdorf Jr., Robert. "RVIA Board OK's Labeling, Market Expansion Plan." *RV Business,* August 1995.

Ward's Business Directory of U S. Private and Public Companies. Detroit: Gale Research, 2000.

SIC 3795

TANKS AND TANK COMPONENTS

This category covers establishments primarily engaged in manufacturing complete tanks, specialized components for tanks, and self-propelled weapons. Establishments primarily engaged in manufacturing military vehicles, except tanks and self propelled weapons, are classified in **SIC 3710: Motor Vehicles and Motor Vehicle Equipment,** and those manufacturing tank engines are classified in **SIC 3510: International Combustion Engines, Not Elsewhere Classified.**

NAICS CODE(S)

336992 (Military Armored Vehicle, Tank, and Tank Component Manufacturing)

INDUSTRY SNAPSHOT

The end of the Cold War has reduced U.S. tank production to almost nothing. From a peak of about 900 new tanks produced each year in 1987-88, no new tanks were being built in the United States at the end of the century. The only work being done was upgrading of older tanks with new equipment at the rate of about 120 tanks per year. Although orders were anticipated in the post-2000 era from Denmark, Turkey, and Greece, no tank production was underway in the mid- to late 1990s for any of America's allies. This drop in production has resulted in the consolidation and closure of many defense-related manufacturers and subcontractors with further structural adjustments needed to accommodate the proposed cutbacks.

The largest U.S. tank manufacturers, General Dynamics Corporation of Virginia and Raytheon Defense Systems, headquartered in Tucson, Arizona, have adopted different corporate strategies to survive in this uncertain environment. General Dynamics has continued to focus its business on defense contracting, filling such key niches as nuclear submarines for the Navy and a new amphibious vehicle for the Marine Corps.

ORGANIZATION AND STRUCTURE

The tank manufacturing and component industry has relied mostly on government procurement trends to fund both the development and production of military armor. With few exceptions, defense manufacturers are privately held. Most of the contracts issued by the U.S. Department of Defense are fixed-price contracts that cover both the research/development and production of armored vehicles. These contracts have been problematic for manufacturers because they require considerable investment during the development stage. Traditionally, even though many of these contracts are multi-year and provide compensation if cancelled, such payments usually do not cover the price of new machinery and plants. As a result, there has been a consolidation of players in the defense industry, with many manufacturers having to shed facilities and workers to remain competitive in an uncertain defense-spending environment.

Plants that manufacture tanks and tank components vary between those that are contractor owned and others that are government owned and contractor operated. In the latter case, a plant may close but the facilities remain for possible future mobilization. It is extremely expensive, however, to mothball such facilities and then reopen them.

The only tank production plant still active in the United States during the mid-1990s was the General Dynamics facility in Lima, Ohio, operated by the company's Land Systems Division. General Dynamics closed its other tank facility, in Sterling Heights, Michigan, in December 1996. By the time the Detroit facility closed, manufacturing employment there had shrunk to fewer than 100 workers, from a high of about 2,500 a decade earlier. The Lima plant was capable of assembling completed tanks as well as producing tank components. While the Lima plant was responsible for the assembly of the M1A1 and M1A2 tanks, it relied on countless subcontractors across the United States to supply it with key components in the tank assembly process. By 1997, the plant in Lima was upgrading about 120 older tanks a year for the U.S. Army, the sole tank production work being done at that time. Long-range plans to develop the next-generation Block III tank were scrapped for budgetary reasons in the early '90s. Some long-range planning was underway but no completely new tanks were expected to be produced until after the year 2010 at the earliest.

BACKGROUND AND DEVELOPMENT

The tank, a British invention from World War I, had the mission of advancing on the static German defense lines in northern France. It was developed to flatten thick coils of barbed wire, fend off machine-gun fire, and to rumble over previously inviolable trenches. In short, the tank was to do what great waves of infantry men had failed to do—break the stalemate of trench warfare.

The tank performed as required during World War I, but was viewed by most strategists as merely a precursor to infantry attack. That sentiment was ultimately put to rest by the German *blitzkrieg* into Poland in September of 1939, when a Polish brigade of cavalry vainly attacked an onrushing wedge of German tanks.

In June of 1920, the U.S. National Defense Act was passed into law. This act disbanded the army's tank corps, a unit created three years previously, and placed all tanks under the command of the infantry branch. Further, the act stipulated that no new branch of the army, such as a revived tank corps, could be created without congressional approval. This decision was based on the army's conclusion that the tank corps had failed to provide either a doctrine or a justification for itself as an independent arm of the American war effort.

The early perception was that the tank-based armies of the twentieth century were slower then the foot soldier's marching rate of a century before. This speculation concerning tank warfare inhibited its role as a support weapon for the infantry for years.

Following World War I, the most plausible threat to U.S. security was a naval war in the Pacific against Japan. In the following decade, Congress reduced the military budget. Senior officers cut costs by halting production and maintenance of equipment. Inevitably, tanks suffered from this policy, and the U.S. Army had no large tank formations during this inter-war period.

The beginning of the mechanization of the U.S. Army began in 1928 after Secretary of War Dwight D. Davies observed the British Army's Experimental Mechanical Armed Force. In response, the United States developed the Christie, complete with a modern suspension system and capable of speeds approaching 40 miles per hour. It was during this period that the war department recognized that the development of future armies depended on the proliferation of a mechanized force. The tank was, for the first time, perceived as an offensive power in its own right.

In the spring of 1939, America's main battle tanks were still the M1917 and the Mark VIII of World War I vintage. In the previous several years the army had produced several hundred tanks, the majority being experimental models of light tanks armored with only machine guns. Although some effort had been made to keep the United States abreast of mechanized warfare, until the outbreak of World War II the American experience of armor hardly existed.

Following the collapse of France in June of 1940, Congress passed a munitions program to provide material for an army of 1.2 million. Supplemental defense appropriations acts authorized $5.0 billion for armed forces expenditure. By the end of 1940, the country had produced only 331 tanks. By the end of 1941, it had outproduced Germany with 4,052 tanks. Tank production for the next two years was 24,997 and 29,497 tanks respectively. By the end of the war in Europe, American industry had produced 88,410 tanks, of which 57,027 were medium tanks. More than 8,000 subcontractors working in some 850 different towns and cities throughout the United States had a hand in the production of these tanks.

By 1943, the U.S. Army had created 16 armored divisions and 65 independent tank battalions. Each of these armored divisions consisted of 10,937 men and 2,650 vehicles, of which 248 were tanks. Tanks were used as a highly mobile force for pursuit, exploitation, and disruption of unarmored forces, rather than as an arm of attack against other armored formations. This doctrine had important consequences for American tank design and development. The first of the wartime tanks, the M3 Stuart light tank and M3 Grant/Lee medium tank, were developed from pre-war designs. The main American battle tank of the war, the M4 Sherman, was first planned in March of 1941 and produced a year later. Weighing approximately 33 tons and equipped with a 75mm dual-purpose gun, it was highly maneuverable and reliable and boasted a road speed of just under 30 miles per hour (mph).

The U.S. responded to Germany's Panther and Tiger tanks by producing the M26 Pershing. This tank held a 90mm gun, weighed 42.5 tons, and had a top speed of 25 mph. This tank, however, played a relatively small role in the war because it had less speed and maneuverability than the M4 Sherman and because tactical air power was generally used to halt the German armored thrust. By 1947, due to the success of air power and the invention of atomic weapons, the role of the tank had again come into question.

During the Korean War, American tanks proved less than perfect. The M26 Pershing was underpowered for Korea's mountainous terrain, and the army at first was compelled to rely upon its Shermans. The army eventually added the more powerful M46 and M47 Patton tanks to its lineup. In fact, the Korean War confirmed the tank's role as an essential part of the U.S. fighting forces. The heavier armor developed during this conflict changed the tank's principal role to fighting and destroying other tanks.

Throughout the 1950s and early 1960s, the U.S. Army continued to regard its armored forces as central to its fighting doctrine. When U.S. forces were committed to Vietnam in 1965, however, armor had a reduced role. Still, the M48 tanks' firepower and mobility were valuable assets in creating quick reaction teams for preventing infiltration by enemy units. But to work well, the teams had to be part of an all-arms formation; without helicopters, air and artillery support, and infantry, the armored units could be unwieldy, noisy, and less then effective. Tank battalions successfully carried out roles such as route security, convoy escort, and border protection.

There were no major developments in the tanks industry during the 1970s. The anti-war movement of the late 1960s and early 1970s—coupled with the perception that the United States had fought a losing battle—resulted in the redeployment of government resources into domestic endeavors. In 1980, however, President Reagan vowed to rearm America with an unprecedented $1.6 trillion defense spending program over the next six years. The Defense Department's renewed interest in planning and multi-year funding of contracts boosted the sagging defense industry. The tanks and tank component sector of the defense industry was expected to grow by 12.6 percent over this period with nondefense growth hovering at 4.5 percent.

The army's M-1 tank benefited greatly from the increased defense expenditures. A heavy tank with a combat load of 54.5 tons, the M-1 was able to carry a crew of four and had a maximum speed of 45 mph on the road and 30 mph cross country. The tank's road range stood at 275 miles and its main armament was a 105mm gun. The M-1 tank was criticized for transmission malfunctions and the need for frequent maintenance of other components during the test process. In addition, the M-1 was found to be incapable of digging itself into a hull-down battle position without the assistance of bulldozers. Nonetheless, the Defense Department budgeted for 7,058 M-1s at a cost of roughly $19 billion.

By 1986, defense budget outlays had grown to $200 million annually. These high levels of defense spending stimulated many U.S. industries. In 1986, 75 sectors of the economy produced at least 5 percent of output for defense purposes and 13 sectors produced at least 30 percent of output for delivery to the U.S. Department of Defense. The passage of the Gramm-Rudman deficit reduction bill, as well as reduced government research and development budgets, however, resulted in declines in defense production throughout the remainder of the 1980s.

The multi-year structure of rearmature programs from the 1980s temporarily insulated the defense industry from budget cuts. In the wake of reduced defense expenditures, many manufacturers began to look to foreign markets to maintain and expand their production base.

Significant events in the 1990s that had a major impact on defense forces and their supporting industries included: the departure of Soviet forces from Eastern Europe; the dismantling of the Warsaw Pact; the reunification of East and West Germany; the successful eviction of Iraq from Kuwait by the Allied coalition forces; and various United Nations peace-keeping efforts. The very success of Operation Desert Storm prompted questioning in the U.S. legislature about the rationale behind developing new, costly weapons systems. (The ground war lasted just 100 hours with little loss of life or equipment on the Allied Coalition side while Iraqi forces suffered massive losses in both men and equipment.)

CURRENT CONDITIONS

For the first time in 13 years, President Clinton authorized an increase in defense procurement spending for the year 2000. The U.S. Army was in the third year of a 1996 contract with General Dynamics to upgrade 600 M1A2s. The digital command and control capabilities, new infrared gunner systems, and upgraded commander thermal sights were part of the ongoing Systems Enhancement Package (SEP). Further improvements in the upgrade included under-armor auxiliary power units, a new computer mass memory unit and color display and maps. There were also ongoing fielding of M1A2 tanks to both Fort Hood, Texas and Fort Carson, Florida in 1999.

The trend toward private venture projects and cooperative agreements with foreign countries is necessary for the survival of U.S. defense manufacturers. General Dynamics, for example, expects to build between 500 and 1,000 tanks for Turkey between 2000 and 2010. This joint venture operation will see the tanks designed here but both components and final assembly taking place jointly in both countries. General Dynamics also expects to produce between 200 and 500 tanks for Greece in the period after 1999.

The Land Systems unit of General Dynamics estimated delivery of 240 M1A2 Systems Enhancement Packages to the U.S. Army at a rate of 10 per month, beginning August 1999. An extension of that multi-year contract included refurbishing additional tanks through the year 2005.

Raytheon Company received a $13.3 million contract for the development of the Tank Extended Range Munition (TERM) for the Army's M1A2 tanks in 1999. This program is divided into two segments. Phase 2 will provide a multi-mode seeker and chemical energy warhead. Phase 2A, to begin in 2002, will fabricate the multi-mode seeker components, develop software and fusion algorithms and integrate hardware.

INDUSTRY LEADERS

General Dynamics Corporation, the Falls Church, Virginia-based company is among the nation's largest defense contractors and produces a wide range of major weapons systems for all branches of the armed forces. In 1998 the company had approximately $10.0 billion in annualized sales and third quarter 1999 ended with a funded backlog of $10.5 billion and total backlog of $17.9 billion. By the late-1990s, the company had concentrated its work in a few key areas: shipbuilding and marine systems, land and amphibious combat systems, information systems, and business aviation. The company's Land Systems division produced the upgraded M1A2 battle tank, radios for the army, and was working on the Advanced Amphibious Assault Vehicle for the Marine Corps.

Raytheon Systems Company, a global leader in defense electronics, was made up of five divisions: Defense Systems, Sensors and Electrical Systems, Command Control, Communications and Information Systems, Aircraft Integration Systems, and Training and Services. Raytheon Defense Systems Segment (DSS), headquartered in Tucson, Arizona, consisted of three business divisions that focused on total mission solutions in the areas of Combat Ground, Combat Air, Undersea Warfare, Air Defense and Surface Navy. Raytheon Defense Systems Segment had revenues of more than $5.0 billion dollars in 1999 with employment exceeding 20,000 people.

Subcontractors make up the remainder of the industry players in the tank and tank components industry. This group includes not only many of the top ten defense manufacturers, but also hundreds of smaller entities that produce more specialized and highly sophisticated subsystem equipment.

WORKFORCE

In the tank and tank components industry, approximately 25 percent of the plant labor force is directly engaged in production, while the remaining 75 percent is engaged in management and support functions.

AMERICA AND THE WORLD

The United States' tank and tank components industry is the largest and most technically advanced in the world. The health of the industry is closely tied to its ability to forge international cooperative agreements with larger arms-producing countries such as Russia, Germany, Britain, France, and China and to increase foreign military sales of tanks and tank conversion kits. The reduction in the U.S. military budget has had a direct impact on the ability of defense manufacturers to compete in foreign markets. Foreign sales of tank and tank components are an essential element in the survival of U.S. tank production facilities. In order to achieve this goal, the industry requires a sound and profitable production base to invest in the future and to maintain current cost/pricing levels. By protecting the industrial base, the United States will be able to honor pricing levels in completed foreign tank sales contracts and to assure foreigners of the U.S. manufacturers' ability to meet future demand at competitive pricing levels.

International sales of the Abrams M1A1 kits and M1A2 tanks had been strong in the Middle East near the century's end. Egypt, Greece, Turkey, Saudi Arabia, and Qatar expressed interest in the M1 tanks, therefore, the U.S. Army and General Dynamics combined efforts to upgrade the tanks for sales to these countries. These opportunities abroad represent a market potential of more than $5 billion.

RESEARCH AND TECHNOLOGY

Research and development funding in the tank industry has suffered along with production as defense spending dwindled. That which continues focuses on upgrades of systems dealing with targeting and night vision. Much of the production in the defense industries is inherently inefficient because high volume, mass production techniques are not applicable. Except for the turret and hull components of a tank, most of the production involves small batch processing of relatively complex items with frequent modifications or changes in design. In this type of low volume manufacturing, specialized equipment is under utilized and inventories are relatively high.

Although computer-aided automation has moved slowly into the tank production process, computer-controlled machine tools are standard fixtures in machining operations. Examples of these processes include automated spray systems used for coating metals; automated inspection and optical measuring systems; and computer-aided manufacturing applications used for forging and electron beam welding in tank production. Other areas of the production process which have been computerized consist of process modeling, performance measurement, and on-line production information systems.

Many of the technological changes that have taken place in tank manufacturing involve metalworking. Automated metal cutting systems are in place that use computer-controlled laser machining techniques. Computer-integrated welding systems are in place that make use of sensory process controls. The technology is available to transform the manufacturing system of tank production facilities into a totally computer-integrated process, but the economies of scale associated with expensive outlays in plant and equipment have deterred the manufacturers from pursuing this option.

In the mid-1990s, main battle tanks possessed nuclear, biological, and chemical (NBC) systems that regulate the environment within the tank in case of this type of warfare. The Department of Defense has made land navigational systems a priority for improvement and installation in all tank subsystems. In the wake of Operation Desert Storm, more emphasis was placed in the development of friend or foe devices to reduce friendly fire causalities. Such technology would become a part of the tank's vehicle protection system, which already includes threat displays, sensors, and decoy launchers.

Other areas of research include ways to construct smaller and lighter main battle tanks, armored turrets to protect the vulnerable top of the tank, development of more powerful cannons, experimentation into a common chassis for futuristic combat vehicles, guns that will utilize electromagnetic and electrothermal cannons. Electromagnetic guns use electric currents as their power source and can power a round farther and faster than a conventional cannon. Electrothermal guns use hot gases and a high-energy charge to propel artillery with comparable results.

By 1999 the Abrams tank contained many of the aforementioned upgrades making it superior on the battlefield. The upgraded guns combined with 1,500 horsepower turbine engine and special armor made the tank suitable for both attack and defense. The tanks featured increased armor protection, suspension improvements, nuclear, biological and chemical protection, a Commander's Thermal Viewer and improved weapon station, data and power architecture, embedded diagnostic system and an upgraded fire control system. The new radio interface was compatible anywhere on the battlefield.

FURTHER READING

General Dynamics. "Land Systems - M1A2." 1999. Available from http://www.gdls.com/.

———. "Press Releases." 1999. Available from http://www.gdls.com/.

Raytheon. "Defense Briefing - Land Combat." 30 August 1999. Available from http://www.defensebriefing.com.

U.S. Army. *Technology.* 1999. Available from http://www.army-technology.com/.

U.S. Bureau of Census. *Military tank and tank component manufacturing.* 1997.

SIC 3799

TRANSPORTATION EQUIPMENT, NOT ELSEWHERE CLASSIFIED

This industry consists of establishments primarily engaged in manufacturing transportation equipment, not elsewhere classified. The transportation equipment classified under this industry includes specialty vehicles and all-terrain vehicles for military, industrial, and agricultural purposes; towing bars and systems and trailers for transporting animals; recreational vehicles, such as snowmobiles, water jet-skis, golf carts and recreational all-terrain vehicles; boat trailers; and wheelbarrows. Associated establishments involved in manufacturing industrial vehicles are discussed in **SIC 3537:Industrial Trucks, Tractors, Trailers, and Stackers.**

NAICS CODE(S)

336214 (Travel Trailer and Camper Manufacturing)
332212 (Hand and Edge Tool Manufacturing)
336999 (All Other Transportation Equipment Manufacturing)

Shipments of all-terrain vehicles (ATVs), snowmobiles, golf carts, and personal watercraft totaled more than $4.5 billion in 1997. This was a sharp increase from the industry's level of shipments only five years earlier and, in several categories, represented gains of 100 percent or better. Shipments of gasoline- or electric-powered ATVs, for example, climbed from a level of $341 million in 1992 to $934 million in 1997. Sale of self-propelled golf carts more than doubled from $382 million in 1992 to $768 million in 1997.

In the latter half of the 1990s, most of the leading establishments in this field had interests in different segments within the industry. Polaris Industries Inc., the world's largest manufacturer of snowmobiles and number two producer of ATVs, was the undisputed leader of the industry in the United States. Based in Minneapolis, Minnesota, Polaris employed a workforce of more than 3,000 and reported 1998 sales of $1.18 billion. Another major player in the U.S. industry was Arctic Cat Inc., also headquartered in Minnesota. Arctic Cat, which markets both snowmobiles and ATVs, reported sales of $480 million for fiscal 1999.

This market is heavily influenced by foreign competition, coming largely from Japanese and Canadian firms, some of which have U.S. subsidiaries. Playing a major role in this market from north of the border is Canada's Bombardier, manufacturer of the popular Ski-Doo brand snowmobile and Sea-Doo personal watercraft. Headquartered in Montreal, Quebec, Bombardier first entered the ATV market in 1998 with its utility model called the Traxter. For 2000, the company plans to expand distribution of the Traxter from 13 states to all 50 and will also introduce a new sport ATV.

Japanese companies active in the U.S. transportation equipment market include Suzuki Motor Corp., which markets the QuadRunner ATV; Yamaha Motor Company Ltd., producer of the WaveRunner personal watercraft and the Kodiak line of ATVs; Honda Motor Company Ltd., the world's largest manufacturer of ATVs; and Kawasaki Heavy Industries Ltd., producer of the Mule line of ATVs and the Jet Ski personal watercraft.

All-terrain vehicles, built with wide tires for driving over difficult terrain and road conditions, originally were produced primarily for military purposes. For this reason, the prosperity and growth of this segment of the industry was for so long dependent on government defense spending. With the decreases in defense spending during the 1990s, manufacturers of all-terrain vehicles began to diversify.

The biggest sector in the $4.5 billion transportation equipment market in 1998 was the category including snowmobiles and personal watercraft, totaling about $1.47 billion in revenue, or 32.7 percent of the overall market. Gasoline- and electric-powered all-terrain vehicles and parts accounted for roughly 21.4 percent of the total transportation equipment market, while self-propelled golf carts and industrial in-plant personnel carriers and parts made up approximately 17 percent of the market.

In 1954, Polaris Industries became the first American manufacturer to produce snowmobiles. In the United States, snowmobile sales reached their peak in 1971, having over 500,000 sold. In the late 1970s and early 1980s, snowmobile sales decreased dramatically, the "victims of higher energy costs, recessions, a few snowless winters, and a serious rash of overbuilding by manufacturers," said *Forbes.* By 1983 only 87,000 snowmobiles were sold in the United States. At the beginning of the 1990s, however, sales figures and profits began to increase again, with Polaris' revenues almost doubling between 1994 and 1996.

FURTHER READING

Byrne, Harlan S. "Oshkosh Truck Corp.: A Bright Outlook Despite Pentagon Cutbacks." *Barron's,* 20 January 1992.

Darnay, Arsen J., ed. *Manufacturing USA.* 6th ed. Detroit: Gale Research, 1998.

Harris, John. "Noisemakers." *Forbes,* 29 October 1990.

Hoover's Online, 1999. "Arctic Cat Inc." Available from http://www.hoovers.com/co/capsule/6/0,2163,13346,00.html.

———, 1999. "Polaris Industries Inc." Available from http://www.hoovers.com/co/capsule/6/0,2163,12246,00.html.

Lawton, Kurt. "Work Horses." *Farm Industry News,* 1 October 1999.

U.S. Bureau of the Census. *1997 Economic Census.* Washington: GPO, 1999.

MEASURING, ANALYZING & CONTROLLING INSTRUMENTS

SIC 3812

SEARCH, DETECTION, NAVIGATION, GUIDANCE, AERONAUTICAL, AND NAUTICAL SYSTEMS AND INSTRUMENTS

This category includes establishments primarily engaged in manufacturing search, detection, navigation, guidance, aeronautical, and nautical systems and instruments. Important products of this industry are radar systems and equipment; sonar systems and equipment; navigation systems and equipment; countermeasures equipment; aircraft and missile control systems and equipment; flight and navigation sensors, transmitters, and displays; gyroscopes; airframe equipment instruments; and speed, pitch, and roll navigational instruments and systems. Establishments primarily engaged in manufacturing aircraft engine instruments or meteorological systems and equipment, including weather tracking equipment, are classified in **SIC 3829: Measuring and Controlling Devices, Not Elsewhere Classified.**

NAICS CODE(S)

334511 (Search, Detection, Navigation, Guidance, Aeronautical, and Nautical System and Instrument Manufacturing)

INDUSTRY SNAPSHOT

In 1997, more than 577 companies in the United States were involved in the manufacture of search and navigation systems and instruments. Together these companies shipped $32.5 billion worth of these goods while employing 185,888 people in the process.

While 1997 marked an upturn in business for the search and navigation industry, such years were rare throughout the 1990s. Decreased defense budgets, the end of the Cold War, and diminished commercial aircraft industry purchases all contributed to annual declines. Sharp reductions in the military-related expenditures that formed the backbone of industry profits led to a flurry of acquisition and merger activity among many of the major companies in the field. The consolidation within the industry led to a reduction of its production workforce at an annual rate of ten percent throughout much of the decade. Although the pace of workforce reduction showed signs of slowing, the forecast for the first few years of the twenty-first century was that the overall decline would continue.

Nevertheless, the United States was expected to continue leading the world in new technology in this market for years to come. Much of the new technology will aim at reaching the civilian sector. Especially important will be those instruments relating to Global Positioning Systems (GPS) and innovative automobile navigation and safety systems. The United States will also continue to be the leading exporter of search and navigation equipment, as other countries seek to upgrade their air safety and NATO allies continue to procure the latest defense technology.

ORGANIZATION AND STRUCTURE

With few exceptions, the principle suppliers of search and navigation equipment are the same contractors who comprise the larger U.S. aerospace and defense industry. Search and navigation equipment contributed significantly to the larger $140 billion industry. Although not necessarily the most prolific producers of search and navigation instruments, many of the largest and most recognizable corporations in the United States had their hands in the business, including AT&T, Boeing, General Electric, General Motors, and IBM.

Along with such aerospace sectors as the business and commercial jet, helicopter, aircraft maintenance, and spare parts industries, the search and navigation industry comprises a so-called "niche segment" of the larger aerospace manufacturing group. A substantial majority of the industry's product types fall into the avionics (aviation electronics) product classification, which includes aeronautic radar systems, air traffic control systems, weaponry sighting and fire control systems, and autopilots. Product groups traditionally associated with the avionics industry but excluded from the search and navigation industry include flight trainers and simulators, which are included in **SIC 3699: Electrical Machinery, Equipment, and Supplies, Not Elsewhere Classified;** and radio communications equipment and telemetry systems and equipment, which is classified under **SIC 3663: Radio and Television Broad casting and Communications Equipment.** Conversely, product groups classified as search and navigation industry products but excluded from the avionics industry's product mix include such nautical instruments as fathometers, hydrophones, sonabuoys, marine sextants, sonar fish finders and other sonar systems, and taffrail logs (torpedo-shaped instruments dragged behind ships to determine distance traveled or speed).

Historically, the primary customer for industry products has been the U.S. government—in particular the Department of Defense, Federal Aviation Administration, and National Aeronautics and Space Administration. Industry sales to commercial establishments adhere to the traditional terms and conditions of the business marketplace, and products are evaluated in terms of competitive value for technical superiority, reputation, price, delivery schedule, financing, and reliability. Sales to the federal government, however, tend to follow a highly specialized and structured set of procedures.

Government Procurement. Funds for government search and navigation equipment contracts are authorized by Congress based on budget requests submitted by the executive branch for the agency or department requiring the equipment. Congress appropriates specific funding for programs on an annual basis, which often means that programs originally approved for development over several years are subject to adjustments or outright cancellation on a yearly basis. Contractors submit bids to government officials at bidding conferences attended by "prime" contractors—firms or consortia who submit the final integrated system directly to the end-user agency—and subcontractors who attend the conferences to seek out prime contractors with whom to team.

Contracts may be awarded to a single contractor in a "winner-take-all" competition or divided among several contractors or consortia as a percentage of the total awarded contract. Contracts may cover specific phases of the product development process: the concept/design or project definition stage, the prototype or demonstration/validation stage, or the execution or large-scale production stage. Government contracts are also awarded according to the method by which the contractor is paid. In cost reimbursement contracts, the contractor is paid for allowable or "allocable" costs such as engineering and manufacturing expenses, special tooling and test equipment costs, marketing and administrative expenditures, and the cost of the bid proposal itself. Cost plus fixed fee contracts involve payments to the contractor by the government of a preestablished fee regardless of the firm's actual final costs. Such contracts award contractors who deliver systems below the contracted price and penalize contractors who experience cost overruns. In cost plus incentive fee contracts, the government reimburses the contractor based on the firm's ability to meet certain targets such as cost guidelines, "mission success" parameters, and delivery time constraints. The average industry "win rate"—the ratio of contracts awarded to total contracts bid on—is about 25 percent in the aerospace, and thus the search and navigation, industry as a whole. Some firms, however, achieve win rates nearly twice as high.

Contractors are generally paid through periodic "progress payments" for work performed with a final payment for remaining costs paid upon delivery of the product. Contracts may be extended through "replenishment" and "follow on" orders by the government customer and may be terminated without cause at the sole discretion of the government. Disputes regarding unpaid or overpaid amounts are handled by a Defense Contract Management District Termination Contracting Officer to whom settlement proposals are submitted by the contractor for claimed expenses and "termination costs." The contracting officer may award the contractor funds for work performed prior to the contract's termination or may require that the contractor reimburse funds paid out for canceled work.

The "monopsonic"—or single customer—nature of the government procurement market has led to a unique division of operations in the search and navigation industry: one set of rules and procedures for commercial clients and a second, completely segregated set of rules and procedures for government contracts. The purpose of the complex government procurement apparatus is to protect the government's interest in fair and reasonable prices, to eliminate contractor fraud, to ensure equal access by all bidders, and to guarantee that federal funds appropriated for government contracts reflect the economic and social priorities of the government. As a result, the process of bidding on federal contracts entails separate data collection and accounting procedures, conformance to supplier network requirements, adherence to hiring and personnel guidelines, and the disclosure of the contractor's corporate financial information to government auditors. These and other requirements regarding contractor certification and auditing and oversight conformance have resulted in historical labor costs for the industry three times higher for federal contracts (as a percentage of sales) than for equivalent commercial contracts.

Procurement Agencies. Several government agencies perform oversight and other procurement-related functions that directly affect search and navigation industry activities. The Defense Contract Audit Agency oversees expense, scheduling, and product performance reviews of industry contractors and specifies guidelines for planning and implementing federal contracts. The Government Accounting Office (GAO) and Office of Federal Procurement Policy of the Office of Management and Budget perform watchdog reviews of government contracts. ''First tier'' contractors—firms whose products are delivered directly to a prime contractor—may experience as many as 100 government audits in a single year for pricing, quality, and safety reviews. Similarly, an ''operational readiness review'' administered by a defense department branch can involve as many as 50 auditors assigned to a single contractor plant at one time.

Contractors may be temporarily suspended or permanently debarred from bidding on government contracts if they are found to be in violation of employment practice laws, standard accounting procedures, or product pricing guidelines. A contractor, for example, who falsely claims that a delivered product has passed more tests than it actually has may be given a ''not a responsible contractor'' designation and debarred from government bids. Improper enhancement of a product's capabilities in order to inflate the contractor's bill is termed ''goldplating'' and represents another significant area of potential abuse that government procurement oversight agencies monitor.

Other agencies, such as the Navy's Operational Test and Evaluation Force and the Department of Defense's Operational Test and Evaluation Office, perform the tests that gauge the delivered system's adherence to contracted performance specifications. Federal projects like the Army's Contractor Performance Certification Program recognize contractors who consistently deliver quality products, and the NASA-funded National Technology Transfer Center serves as a medium for sharing federal research project advances with firms in the industry.

Prime Contractors vs. Subcontractors. The Competition in Contracting Act of 1984 attempted to make government contracts equally available to all potential contractors. Still, major prime contractors continued to dominate the defense market, and thus the search and navigation industry. The consolidation among these contractors as the defense budget dwindled throughout the 1990s had a drastic effect on subcontractors. For instance, AlliedSignal, a major prime contractor, which

merged with Honeywell in 1999, planned even before the merger to reduce its number of suppliers from 3,750 in 1997 to 1,200 by 2000. Smaller companies also suffered from Defense Department policies that called for a smaller base of contractors with larger resources than before, giving companies working for the Pentagon special leniency in Justice Department reviews of their acquisitions and mergers. With these larger, more diversified contractors, the Defense Department then began to contract with a single company for an entire system instead of having two share the responsibility as previously.

Business Environment. The unique nature of the government procurement environment entails business trends uncommon in other U.S. industries. Although this industry's profit rates as a percentage of sales have historically been less than for other industries, profits measured in terms of rate of return on investment are comparable to rates enjoyed by other manufacturing sectors. Search and navigation firms, like other defense sector businesses, may invest in plants and equipment at half the rate of firms in other industries because government contracts often reimburse firms for aging or obsolescent equipment, make available government-owned plants and equipment to the contractor, and offer no guarantee that the plant or equipment utilized for the procured product will ever be contracted for again.

The Defense Department also motivates cost consciousness by writing incentives into contracts, basing payments and penalties on the producer's performance. In return for these cost restrictions, the Pentagon only specifies what the product should do, not how it should be built. This allows the contractors to use more components that are readily available than in previous times, when they would have to create components according to Pentagon instructions. Like members of other defense industries, search and navigation contractors require less working capital because they can rely on regular government progress payments instead of depending on unpredictable commercial revenues.

The search and navigation industry is subject to business risks not shared by other American industries. These include unusually high costs for obtaining skilled employees, intense domestic and international competition, continual need to retrain employees and retool facilities, inevitable cost overruns resulting from untried technologie advanced designs, and instability in the price of rials and supplies. Because defense-relate driven by the requirement of conti improvement and superiority, th industry products is much h dictable than in other Ame

Product Groups. Search an divided into two broad divisions

1210

Search and detection systems and navigation and guidance systems and equipment ($26.60 billion worth of shipments in 1997) constitute 91 percent of the total search and navigation market and include the following product groups: light reconnaissance and surveillance systems; identification-friend-or-foe equipment; proximity fuses; radar systems and equipment; sonar search, detection, tracking, and communications equipment; specialized command and control data processing and display equipment; electronic warfare systems and equipment; and navigation systems and equipment, including navigational aids for aircraft, ships, and navigation applications.

The remaining 9 percent of the industry's market ($2.54 billion worth of shipments in 1997) consists of aeronautical, nautical, and navigational instruments (excluding aircraft engine instruments) and includes the following product groups: flight and navigation sensors, transmitters, and displays; gyroscopes; airframe equipment instruments; thermocouple and thermocouple lead wire; nautical instruments; other aerospace flight instruments; and parts and components.

Light Reconnaissance and Surveillance Systems. This product group includes infrared, ultraviolet, and visible light reconnaissance systems excluding radar systems such as bomber-defense equipment, weapon fire control equipment, infrared fuses, infrared detection and warning systems, and such night vision equipment as sniper scopes, snooper scopes, and night driving equipment.

Radar Systems and Equipment. This category includes airborne, ship-based, and ground-based radar systems such as early warning radar, air defense and fighter control radar, harbor control radar, meteorological radar, highway speed control radar, bomber navigational radar, space satellite tracking radar, precision approach radar, and other forms of tracking radar technology.

Sonar Systems. This product group consists of airborne, surface ship, and submarine-based sonar systems including depth-finding equipment, guidance hydrophones, sonabuoys, sonar fish finders, navigation and mapping sonar, and anti-submarine sonar equipment.

Electronic Warfare Equipment. Electronic warfare systems include such missile-borne and non-missile-borne "countermeasures" equipment as radar jamming devices, underwater countermeasures technology, beam-riders, infrared homing systems, specialized signal processing and intelligence equipment, and other "active" countermeasures equipment (excluding such passive systems as chaff and windows).

Navigation Systems and Equipment. Included in this category are such navigational aids as beacons, transmitters, collision warning systems, inertial navigation radio compasses and direction-finders, auto-

pilots, data systems/flight recorders, distance measuring equipment, pilots' "head-up" instrument displays (HUD), aircraft proximity warning systems, flight directors/situation displays, and ship and submarine navigational systems.

Flight and Navigation Sensors, Transmitters, and Displays. This product group includes altimeters; compasses; artificial horizon instruments; and airspeed, acceleration, rate-of-climb, angle-of-attack, and bank and turn indicators.

Airframe Equipment Instruments. This category includes position indicators for landing gear and cowl flaps, hydraulic systems for liquid level and temperature indicators, and cabin environmental instruments such as air conditioning, cabin pressure, oxygen, and heating.

BACKGROUND AND DEVELOPMENT

Before the invention of the floating gimball gyroscope in the first years of the twentieth century, sea navigators had relied on celestial azimuths, star tables, the sextant, timekeeping instruments, and dead reckoning (a type of inferential estimation) with a magnetic compass.

Rudimentary radio direction-finders consisting of large manually-rotated loop antennas for receiving the homing signals of coastal radio beacons came into wide use in the years before World War I. With the discovery that radio waves striking seagoing vessels produced measurable echoes, radar technology became possible and, by the 1930s, the first on-board VHF radars were installed on ocean liners and naval vessels. By the close of World War II, every capital ship in the U.S. fleet was equipped with a radar unit.

The invention of radar, however, had its greatest impact in air operations and immediately began to play a critical role in the European and Pacific theaters. Prior to its invention, pilots navigated using magnetic compasses, airspeed instruments, and direction-finding gyros. Radio beacons that enabled pilots to plot their position relative to intercepted radio signals came into use in the late 1920s. These early developments were followed by advances in flight control technology, including General Electric's first light control system in 1931 and Honeywell Inc.'s first electric autopilot in 1941.

During World War II, radar proved most effective as a fighter-interceptor tool, a strategic early warning device, an anti-submarine weapon, and as a navigation resource for bombardiers approaching enemy targets. Raytheon Company emerged as the leading producer of radar tubes and systems during the war, and General Electric Company produced more than 50 different types of radar for the U.S. armed services. A precursor of Texas Instruments developed the first anti-submarine detection system in 1941.

Sonar, which was based on the principal that transmitted sound waves deflecting against underwater objects could be used for detection and identification purposes, had been invented by the U.S. Navy in 1922 and by World War II became a strategic weapon for airborne, surface ship, and underwater surveillance. Electronic warfare and countermeasures technology grew out of the discovery that radars could be "spoofed" or "jammed" into misinterpreting returning signals. Strips of aluminum foil called "chaff" or "windows" proved to be effective anti-radar measures and led scientists to modify radar technology to overcome such obstacles. Most major radar technology breakthroughs since World War II, such as pulse and phased array, have been attempts to overcome existing or anticipated jamming or countermeasure technologies.

The development of search and navigation systems in the post-War years was driven by revolutionary advances in jet aircraft, missile technology, satellite systems, digital computers, miniaturization of electronic components, and the specialized needs of the space program. The 1950s witnessed the emergence of the first inertial guidance systems for missiles and submarines. By 1958, the submarine Nautilus was able to successfully navigate underwater to the North Pole using inertial guidance systems modified from Air Force cruise missiles. In 1955, a tactical air navigation system (TACAN) had been introduced, and one year later the first efforts at developing an air collision avoidance system began.

In 1960, Litton Industries introduced an inertial navigation system using a central integrated digital computer for attack aircraft. Four years later, the Navy's Navigational Satellite System became operational with the launching of the Transit satellite. In the 1960s, sonar technology evolved beyond surface ship and submarine applications to networks of fixed sonar systems capable of identifying and tracking vessels from the ocean floor. The decade also saw the emergence of the modern automatic flight control system for aircraft. General Electric's systems for the F-105, F-111, and F-4 used sensors and computerized components that issued automatic commands to the aircraft's flight control surfaces for stabilization and control. In 1967, the first automatic landing using guidance systems designed for low visibility landing approaches was made at JFK Airport, and Texas Instruments developed the first solid state radar using semiconducting materials and components. Two years later, Texas Instruments delivered its first laser-guided missile systems to the U.S. Air Force.

During the 1970s, the Global Positioning System satellite network first came under development. Inertial navigators using digital computers also became common on civil and military aircraft. In the early part of the decade, Sundstrand Corporation developed a multimode radar for mapping terrain and seeking airborne targets. The late

1970s and early 1980s saw the emergence of radical new "stealth" or radar-evading "low observable" technologies in the form of the B-1, F-117, and B-2 aircraft. Using radar absorbing materials, innovative airframe shapes, and a variety of other design techniques, the radar "signature" of the B-2 bomber on enemy radar screens was estimated to be the equivalent of a large insect. The emergence of stealth technology and the likelihood that eventually it would become available to potentially hostile nations compelled search and navigation manufacturers to investigate alternative radar detection technologies (like infrared, ultraviolet, and electro-optical detection) and to search for new, more sensitive radar technologies capable of counteracting stealth "invisibility."

Space programs begun by NASA in the 1960s generated new navigation technologies for satellites, interplanetary probes, lunar landing and "roving" vehicles, and, in the 1980s, the space shuttle. In 1985, Texas Instruments developed a new phased array radar technology that offered greater sensitivity and versatility over previous radar systems and, in the latter part of the decade, land navigation systems for automobiles, emergency vehicles, and rental cars began to be developed for complex urban environments. In 1989, the first five Global Positioning System satellites were launched, offering unprecedented accuracy up to a few yards to system users.

The Gulf War between Iraq and a coalition of international forces demonstrated the degree to which search and navigation industry products could influence the outcome of military conflicts. The so-called "Microchip War" was the first conflict fought directly with real-time support from satellite surveillance and communications systems, and Raytheon's Patriot missile—a ground-to-air defensive missile system employing advanced seeking technology—proved itself as a reliable and effective weapon system.

CURRENT CONDITIONS

The search and navigation instrument industry shipped $32.5 billion worth of equipment in 1997 and employed almost 186,000 people. While the value of shipments marked the second consecutive year of growth after the industry had declined throughout the 1990s, the employment figures indicated only a stabilization in the size of the workforce. Previously, employment had been dwindling at an annual rate of 10 percent. Both trends indicated that the mergers and acquisitions that occurred after the end of the Cold War had begun to pay dividends, increasing the value of goods produced while reducing labor costs.

INDUSTRY LEADERS

Many of the largest search and navigation industry firms are prominent Fortune 500 multinational corporations whose highly diversified corporate activities cover a wide range of industry groups including heavy construction equipment, engineering services, electronic components, business credit services, office furniture, ship construction, oil and gas services, semiconductors, computers, and radio and television equipment. Additionally, many of the major firms in this industry reached their status through mergers and acquisitions, often attempting to increase their competitiveness by creating the economy of scale that comes with large, diversified corporations. This strategy also presented the challenge of bringing together the varied practices and atmospheres of previously separate companies into one larger organization.

Lockheed Martin led the way in aerospace mergers, bringing together Lockheed and Martin Marietta in 1995. These two companies were already heavily involved in guidance and navigation equipment, as Martin Marietta had previously purchased General Electric Aerospace in 1992. The combined companies went on to acquire another leading company in the field, Loral Defense Systems, in 1996. Lockheed Martin produces navigation instruments for land, sea, and air use.

Raytheon is another company that increased its size through acquisitions, purchasing six other large corporations or divisions of corporations throughout the 1990s. Overall sales for Raytheon grew from around $8.8 billion in 1989 to $19.5 billion in 1998. The acquisitions of Texas Instruments' missile and defense operations and the defense operations of Hughes Electronics not only made Raytheon a large company, but also made it one of the most significant ones in navigation equipment. Its electronics division, which includes its radar and guidance equipment, brings in 60 percent of the company's sales.

The company known as Honeywell was actually acquired by and combined with AlliedSignal in 1999. Although each company had to sell off some of its search and navigation lines in order to comply with Justice Department guidelines to avoid monopoly, what remained was expected to account for $7.5 billion of the anticipated $25 billion in revenues for the new entity in 1999.

WORKFORCE

Employment in the search and navigation industry declined steadily through much of the 1990s. From 253,000 employees in 1992, industry employment fell to 185,000 in 1997. This latter figure represented a decrease of only 1,000 form the previous year. Still, mergers and acquisitions among the firms in this industry are expected to keep diminishing the workforce. The Bureau of Labor Statistics has projected that only 109,500 people will be employed in the search and navigation instrument industry by 2006.

In 1997, approximately 35 percent of the industry's employees were classified as production workers, whose average pay was $20.62 per hour. For all employees, the annual salary averaged $50,687, up from $43,328 five years earlier. Because of the number of jobs eliminated in the meantime, though, total payrolls dropped by $1.5 million during that period, in spite of rising salaries. In 1997 the industry product groups with the highest concentration of employers were light reconnaissance and surveillance systems and equipment, with 37 companies; missile-borne and space vehicle systems and equipment, with 35 companies; and specialized electronic and communication equipment, with 32 companies. A total of 34 companies also employed workers in the production of ship and ground navigational systems, but this group shipped less than $400,000 worth of goods, compared to at least $2 billion for each of the other groups mentioned.

Occupational categories employed in the industry included production workers such as machinists and assemblers, administrative support staff, administrators and executives, and engineers and other technical personnel. The industry employed a wide variety of engineering professionals—from aeronautical, civil, electrical, mechanical, quality assurance, and manufacturing engineers to computer and digital systems, hardware, software, logistical, and algorithm systems engineers.

Because the search and navigation industry historically has been dependent on multi-million dollar, large-scale, limited duration government contracts, fluctuations in employment can be severe. The streamlining effect of mergers and acquisitions has exacerbated this effect. The Honeywell-AlliedSignal merger, for instance, was expected to eliminate 4,500 jobs during the first 18 months of the new entity's existence.

AMERICA AND THE WORLD

The United States continues to lead the world in developing and manufacturing search and navigation instruments and systems. This global dominance is reflected in U.S. export and import superiority relative to other leading nations. In 1997, the search and navigation industry exported about $2.5 billion in shipments, a 23 percent increase from 1996. By contrast, Canada, the next leading exporting nation, shipped $382 million worth of goods, followed by Japan ($306 million in shipments), the United Kingdom ($203 million), and France ($158 million). Similarly, while U.S. imports of search and navigation instruments and systems rose to $1.3 billion in 1997, America's closest foreign competitors imported $302 million (Canada), $177 million (the United Kingdom), and $129 million (Japan) that same year.

Historically, the U.S. search and navigation industry has experienced trade surpluses reflecting its advantage in developing advanced technology. Imports increased, though, throughout the 1990s, reaching $1.3 billion by 1997, a 22 percent increase over the previous year; this figure represented a jump in the trend that had been showing a 6 percent increase in such imports over the previous few years.

Foreign Markets. Radar apparatus and parts have traditionally had the largest export market for U.S. search and navigation equipment, and these items led the way in the increased export market of 1997. Altogether $833 million worth of these items were sold to other countries. New purchases by Saudi Arabia and Kuwait helped drive the market, purchasing 44 percent of the radar apparatus. Other potential markets include NATO nations, which will need to upgrade search and navigation systems to meet the requirements of the organization's Security Investment Program.

Air traffic control systems represented another significant opportunity for U.S. search and navigation firms to expand their export market. U.S. search and navigation firms began to undertake upgrades of aging overseas air facilities, with Raytheon and Lockheed Martin both providing air traffic control systems for Chinese airports. Russia has announced plans to upgrade its air traffic control center in Moscow, another lucrative opportunity for U.S. firms. Other countries in Latin America, the Middle East, and Africa also announced plans to upgrade their systems.

Joint Ventures. The globalization of the search and navigation market offered the potential for enhanced efficiency, improved market access, and increased worldwide competition. Rationalization, standardization, and interoperability of technology and the growing number of international business arrangements resulted from an increasingly interlinked global marketplace for search and navigation equipment. Joint ventures, in which a technologically superior U.S. manufacturer typically teams up with a less advanced foreign partner firm, are the most common industry business arrangement and often hinge on the U.S. firm's willingness to surrender technology to the foreign producer in exchange for cheaper labor costs, larger markets, or some other "sweetener." In offset agreements, an exporter agrees to obtain domestic markets for the products of the purchaser, and in some cases the exporter is obliged to buy products within the purchasing nation equal to a certain percentage of the contract's value. Offset agreements may also require the production of the product in the purchasing country or some form of co-production under a licensing arrangement.

Government Intervention. Some domestic aerospace and defense contractors have claimed that the historical unwillingness of the U.S. government to imitate foreign governments by actively intervening to aid exporting companies has weakened U.S. competitiveness. Competitive financing of exports by government bodies (such as the U.S. Export Import Bank), federal funding of

"blended" commercial/military foreign sales, or government guarantees of commercial financing for military products are among the remedies advocated by some industry leaders to increase the U.S. position internationally in search and navigation and other defense sectors.

In 1993, the Clinton administration signed into law a National Cooperative Production Amendments Act that modifies U.S. antitrust law so that penalties imposed on U.S. firms for engaging in joint ventures are reduced. The legislation also includes provisions allowing industry firms to share technology, pool resources, and share the burden of risks associated with equipment and research and development costs. The act also enables foreign firms to engage in joint ventures with U.S. firms if equal treatment to U.S. firms is extended by their home country.

RESEARCH AND TECHNOLOGY

Research and development (R&D) costs for new technology in the search and navigation industry are assumed by both the federal government and industry contractors. Most government funding comes from the Department of Defense and the Department of Transportation. The two departments integrated their goals and defined their responsibilities for R&D in a joint report, the *1996 Federal Radionavigation Plan*. In spite of this plan, funding for research in this field continued its downward trend into the twenty-first century. Both departments received significantly lower funding than they had requested for the development of GPS-related technologies in 2000. Developments such as these have caused industry firms either to begin replacing that support with company funds or to reduce their R&D investment.

Long-term R&D contracts made by industry firms with the federal government are often undertaken with no expectation of immediate profit. These so-called "loss contracts" sometimes involve the granting of exclusive data or technical rights to the contractor, which enable the firm to become the sole producer of the technology should it eventually reach a production phase.

The search and navigation industry is one of the most technologically sophisticated sectors of American industry. Major advances in virtually every product group continue to occur at a rapid rate because unlike many other industries, search and navigation and other defense sectors are driven not only by intrinsic market competition but by a government-sponsored national security mandate to produce technologies superior to future projected threats as well as existing ones.

New Technologies. Overall trends in search and navigation systems include increased reliability, "fault-tolerance" (i.e., ability to operate through system failures), and reduced size, cost, weight, and power consumption of system components. Specific innovations now operational or under development in the area of flight control and guidance include night-vision helmets for pilots in which flight instrument data are displayed on a visor; "three-dimensional" synthesized cockpit voices that help pilots visualize threats surrounding the aircraft; aircraft optical sensors that can imitate the processes of the human optic nerve for increased sensitivity and responsiveness to external threats; and windshear warning systems that can give pilots up to 90 seconds advance notice of dangerous conditions. Other advances include moving map displays projected onto the cockpit windscreen for navigation, voice-controlled avionics that respond to pilots' verbal commands, and on-board "Stormscope" systems that can detect lightning threatening commercial aircraft.

The major technological development in the field of search and navigation instruments is the growth of Global Positioning Systems (GPS) for the commercial, and especially for the consumer, market. GPS originated with the U.S. Air Force and was used by all branches of the military as guidance systems for troops, vehicles, and weapons. The system is dependent on 24 U.S. government-supported satellites in six separate orbits around the earth. A GPS receiver measures the time interval between a satellite's high-frequency radio signal and its reception by the receiver on the ground. With this data the user can instantly acquire the latitude, longitude, and altitude of the receiver via electronic triangulation. Depending on a number of factors, accuracy can range from 100 meters to less than a centimeter. By 1989 the civilian market for GPS instruments was $40 million but it quickly leaped to $1.2 billion by 1995 and was expected to top $8 billion by the end of the century. Although GPS systems are used by marine and air vehicles, the greatest growth is predicted for the automobile market, which is expected to be worth $1 billion in 2001, compared to $246 million in 1996.

By late 1996, American automobile makers were offering GPS systems as an option on select vehicles. Like other GPS systems, automobile navigators rely on satellite signals to plot the car's position and direction on an electronic road map stored in a computer memory. In 1996 one million GPS systems were built for cars, a number that was predicted to grow to 7.7 million by 2001. Japan has led the world market, making GPS a common option on most new vehicle models.

Costs for automobile navigation systems in 1996 began at around $900 for a basic no-frills unit from Delco Electronics to $3,000 for a state of the art system from Rockwell International. Designed for delivery fleets, the Rockwell system offers real time vehicle location on an electronic road map as well as route and destination location. In the United States, Hertz and Avis began to offer navigation systems in select areas on their rental units. By 1997 General Motors had made its OnStar navigation system available to purchasers of 24 of its car and truck

models. The company was able to keep the price of the system down by integrating telephone and emergency service with GPS location and mapping.

Other electronic systems being adapted for automobile applications are radar, intelligent cruise control, and night vision. Intelligent cruise control automatically decreases the automobile's speed as it approaches a slower moving vehicle. This system became available on a limited number of high-end European cars in the 2000 model year. The price for this equipment remained high, adding $2,300 to the cost of a Jaguar XKR coupe in England. Also being developed are radar systems that will monitor a vehicle's blind spots for approaching automobiles and provide a visual warning signal in the side and rear view mirrors. An introductory date for these crash protection radar systems has not been announced, but the price for the consumer is expected to be under $1000.

The National Highway and Traffic Safety Administration, however, was leery of many of these devices. The concern is that a plethora of electronic devices may prove distracting to a driver and cause more accidents than they are intended to prevent. A study focusing just on the advantages of instruments providing rear-end, blind-spot, and lane-departure warnings showed, though, that if all cars had such devices, highway crashes would decrease by 15 percent. More sophisticated features, such as collision-warning devices that would alert a driver in a precarious situation, posed a daunting task for programmers trying to make such a system sensitive without creating false alarms. Other industry insiders fear that the high cost of these systems will scare away the consumer. One approach involves integrating the features the consumers most desire into one unit. Research showed that emergency services, traffic updates, navigation, and the ability to track a stolen vehicle were most important GPS-related features for consumers. The industry goal is to provide these systems in the price range of $100 to $600, a threshold price for common acceptance of new vehicle features.

The second largest market for GPS devices after the automobile market is the consumer/cellular or hand-held GPS receivers. These instruments are about the same size as TV remote controls and are used by outdoor enthusiasts intent on not getting lost. Sold by major retailers such as Wal-Mart and L.L. Bean, these devices sold for around $3,000 in 1989 but the mid-1990s saw the price drop to a few hundred dollars. By 2000 this market segment is expected to grow to $2 billion in annual sales, a tenfold increase over just five years. Similar devices are currently being used for everything from keeping track of rare tortoises to locating oil wells in New Guinea. In early 1996, the U.S. Office of Science and Technology recommended continued support via the defense budget for the GPS satellite system and world wide availability of free C/A-code (commercial use) satellite signals.

Advances in nautical and marine search and detection technology include new mine-hunting sonar systems, vessel alert systems for oil tanker navigation in dangerous seas, sonar fish finders that project live-action sonar images onto display screens, and digital sonar systems that can see through large ocean-bottom objects to detect severed cables or an aircraft's submerged black box. The U.S. National Oceanic and Atmospheric Administration, which is part of the Department of Commerce, is also using search and navigation instrumentation to make America's waterways safer for commercial ships and recreational boaters. Automated nautical charts, a Differential Global Positioning System, and a Real-Time Tide and Current System are part of this agencies' innovative approach to maritime safety.

FURTHER READING

1996 Federal Navigation Plan. Washington, D.C.: U.S. Department of Defense and U.S. Department of Transportation, 1997.

Content, Thomas. "Radar-aided Cruise Control: Avenue to Safer Roads." *USA Today,* 23 November 1999.

Cremeans, John E., ed. *Handbook of North American Industry.* Washington: Bernan Press, 1999.

Current Industrial Reports: Selected Instruments and Related Products. Washington, D.C.: U.S. Department of Commerce, 1997.

"DOT and DOD Budgets Suffer GPS, Augmentation Systems Cuts." *Global Positioning and Navigation News,* 20 October 1999.

Hoover's Company Profiles. Austin, TX: Hoover's, 1999. Available from http://www.hoovers.com.

Kelly, Emma. "US Sets Honeywell Merger Rules." *Flight International,* 13 October 1999.

Martin, Norman. "Bright Future for Nav Systems." *Automotive Industries,* June 1998.

Robinson, Edward A. "Soon Your Dashboard Will Do Everything Except Steer." *Fortune,* 22 July 1996.

Safe Passage into the 21st Century: Modernizing NOAA's Navigational Services. Washington: U.S. Department of Commerce, National Oceanic and Atmospheric Administration, 1995.

"Search, Detection, Navigation, Guidance, Aeronautical, and Nautical System and Instrument Manufacturing." *1997 Economic Census, Manufacturing Industry Series.* Washington, D.C.: U. S. Department of Commerce, 1999.

Sedgwick, David. "Navigators Try to Locate Serious Market Niche." *Automotive News,* 29 January 1996.

U.S. Industry & Trade Outlook '99. New York: McGraw-Hill, 1999.

Velocci, Anthony L., Jr. "Competitive Advances of Scale Could Elude Aerospace Giants." *Aviation Week and Space Technology,* 10 February 1997.

Velocci, Anthony L., Jr. "Industry Posts Solid Revenue, Profit Gains." *Aviation Week and Space Technology,* 5 May 1997.

LABORATORY APPARATUS AND FURNITURE

Establishments in this industry are primarily engaged in manufacturing laboratory apparatus and furniture. The main products of this industry include baths and melting point apparatus, laboratory furniture such as furnaces and ovens, component parts and accessories for instruments, and centrifuges.

NAICS CODE(S)

339111 (Laboratory Apparatus and Furniture Manufacturing)

The laboratory apparatus and furniture industry in the United States is stable domestically, with a small but growing market for international trade. In 1996 this industry was valued at $2.3 billion, an 8 percent increase over its value in 1991, and a 3 percent increase over its 1995 value. This increase has been attributed to growth in exports, which totaled $243 million in 1994, and to an increase in medical and scientific research.

In 1997, a major jump in mergers and acquisitions of laboratory equipment and analytical instrument companies occurred, more than doubling the previous year's value of transactions from $2.2 billion to more than $5.5 billion. Other driving forces behind this trend included technology, geographic expansion, and diversification of product range, among others.

The export market for this industry has not been dominated by any one customer, though Canada, Mexico, and Japan remained the strongest trading partners. Those three countries were almost even in the amount they imported in 1995, each accounting for roughly 25 percent of export dollars. Europe and Asia accounted for another 25 percent, and the rest of the world divided up the remaining slim percentage. Imports in this industry, meanwhile, were estimated at $148 million in 1995, which was a hefty 17 percent increase over the 1993 figure.

Research and development (R&D) spending, both by industry and the federal government, drives this market. Industrial R&D spending was expected to increase by 5 percent in 1999, followed by a 3 percent increase in governmental R&D. Environmental applications are also expected to spur growth. Of the total laboratory instruments and apparatus market, instruments make up 76 percent, followed by laboratory apparatus at 24 percent. The laboratory instrument and apparatus market accounted for over 25 percent of the total industrial and analytical instrument market in 1998.

In the United States, an estimated 358 establishments, employing roughly 16,700 workers, provided laboratory furniture and apparatus manufacturing services in 1996. Establishments were generally small in both size and sales volume when compared to the entire manufacturing industry. Of the top 20 companies within the industry, for example, only six had more than 500 employees, and only three had revenues of more than $100 million. Of the 358 establishments, less than half (140) employed more than 20 people. The manufacturing industry as a whole employed 34 production workers per establishment, whereas laboratory apparatus manufacturers employed just 26. That number is projected to decrease by 2005, with the industry employment rate projected to shrink by 1.2 percent.

The industry leaders, according to Ward's Business Directory 2000, are Newport Corp., with $133 million in sales and 800 employees; BOC Edwards, with an estimated $122 million in sales and 1000 employees; and Fisher Hamilton Inc., with an estimated $120 million in sales and 900 employees. Barnstead Thermolyne Corp. and Helena Laboratories follow, with sales of $100 million and $88 million, respectively, and 500 and 700 employees, respectively.

In 1999, exports were expected to account for 45 percent of total laboratory instrument and apparatus shipments. The top five export countries in 1997 were Japan, Germany, Canada, United Kingdom and South Korea. Regionally, Western Europe and Asia/Japan shared the lead in exports. Japan/Asia had a slight lead over Western Europe in imports.

Technological Advances. New apparatus needs, along with a concurrent need to make laboratory costs more efficient, have increased several product lines in this industry. Autosamplers, which separate chemicals within a liquid sample, have been in high demand as environmental, pharmaceutical, and biological applications have increased. According to *Research and Development,* most manufacturers of autosamplers developed these apparatus for use with their own analytical instruments and are making the apparatus more useable to laboratory personnel without formal training. For medical labs, I-STAT developed a hand-held blood analyzer that could perform many common blood tests with just a few drops of blood in less than two minutes, keeping the labs efficient and reducing the number of resources used to conduct the tests.

The effort to control laboratory costs has resulted in numerous product developments, which are also better for the environment. Heto Lab Equipment of Denmark, for instance, designed several new lines of equipment for laboratory use, including a vacuum pump that recirculates water, saving up to five tons of water daily.

FURTHER READING

Darnay, Arsen J. *Manufacturing USA.* 5th ed. Detroit: Gale Research, 1996.

"Making Your Lab Greener." *Research and Development,* April 1992.

"Merger/Acquisition Announcements at Pittcon '98." *Ceramic Industry,* June 1998.

U.S. Department of Commerce. *U.S. Foreign Trade Highlights 1995.* Washington, D.C.: GPO, 1995. Available from http://www.ita.doc.gov/industry/otea/usfth/tabcon.html.

U.S. Industry & Trade Outlook '99. U.S. Department of Commerce/International Trade Administration and McGraw-Hill, 1999.

SIC 3822

AUTOMATIC CONTROLS FOR REGULATING RESIDENTIAL AND COMMERCIAL ENVIRONMENTS AND APPLIANCES

Establishments in this industry are primarily engaged in manufacturing temperature and related controls for heating and air-conditioning installations and refrigeration applications, which are electrically, electronically, or pneumatically actuated, and which measure and control variables such as temperature and humidity; also included are automatic regulators used as components of household appliances. Automatic controls for regulating residential and commercial environments include heating, ventilating, air-conditioning (HVAC) unit controls and building monitoring controls for temperature and humidity modulation. Automatic controls for appliances include oven temperature controls, dryness controls for clothes dryers, controls for gas burners, and refrigeration thermostats and pressure controls. Establishments primarily engaged in manufacturing industrial process controls are classified in **SIC 3823: Industrial Instruments for Measurement, Display, and Control of Process Variables; and Related Products**; those manufacturing motor control switches are classified in **SIC 3625: Relays and Industrial Controls**; those manufacturing switches for household appliances are classified in **SIC 3643: Current-Carrying Wiring Devices**; and those manufacturing appliance timers are classified in **SIC 3873: Watches, Clocks, Clockwork Operated Devices, and Parts.**

NAICS CODE(S)

334512 (Automatic Environmental Control Manufacturing for Regulating Residential, Commercial, and Appliance Use)

INDUSTRY SNAPSHOT

The total value of shipments in this industry decreased slightly in the early 1990s, but it has been gradually rising since then. The total for 1997 was about

$2.9 billion; this figure was projected to increase to $3.5 billion by 2000.

Customers for these products are primarily equipment and appliance manufacturers, electrical contractors, and large industrial users. The market for environmental controls is principally affected by activity in residential and commercial construction. In addition, the market for American manufacturers is greatly affected by foreign competition, which has been rising since the 1980s.

ORGANIZATION AND STRUCTURE

This industry is composed of two groups: manufacturers of automatic controls used in residential and commercial HVAC units and manufacturers of automatic controls used in household appliances and industrial equipment. Manufacturers of automatic controls for HVAC units primarily distribute their products to suppliers for building construction and contracting firms. For industrial upgrades of HVAC systems, the controls are also sold directly to end users. Manufacturers of automatic controls for household appliances and industrial equipment are typically subsidiaries or divisions of large establishments, where other subsidiaries or divisions of the same establishment use the controls to assemble appliances and equipment.

BACKGROUND AND DEVELOPMENT

Major Products. HVAC unit controls are the industry's major product. These controls are produced for residential and commercial buildings and come in a variety of styles to meet industrial needs. Factories using temperature and humidity-sensitive chemicals and materials require highly sophisticated environmental controlling systems. Computerized HVAC monitoring and controlling have made some printing plants more efficient; such systems provide information for facility operators to electrically monitor HVAC operations from a central location and independently provide cooling and heating of water pumps in ways that save energy.

Another major product line for this industry is automatic igniters and thermostats for appliances and equipment. These controls include gas-fired igniters used for water heaters and gas stoves in the food-service industry; thermostats used in office equipment, such as photocopiers; and custom-designed thermostats for medical equipment, such as blood analyzers and respiratory humidifiers, and kitchen appliances for the home.

As environmental control equipment has grown in size and sophistication, basic designs of automatic controls have undergone considerable changes. Heavy wiring and cables have been replaced by hydraulic systems and low-voltage ignition starters. Electrical controls have also been used increasingly for their high sensitivity and fast response capabilities. In laboratories and factories, pneumatic controls used in exhaust and ventilating systems have been replaced by digital controls, which are basically electronic versions of the original pneumatic devices.

Environmental and Energy Concerns. Concerns about the environment and the resulting legislation have helped this industry to grow. Environmental issues created an increased demand for systems that control air quality and conserve energy. In the 1990s, for example, companies in the United States invested significant capital on devices to lower air, water, and solid waste pollution. Factories from a variety of industries are continuing to monitor and control pollution through the purchase and implementation of highly sensitive control systems.

Along with energy conservation, energy management systems (EMS) have also kept this industry active in redesigning and improving their products; energy management systems are computerized control systems implemented mostly by the utility industry, but also by large manufacturers with their own power stations. Automatic controls have been altered and redesigned for energy efficiency to work within these systems and for the HVAC units in the buildings in which they are stored. Computerized energy management systems, on a smaller scale, are also being installed in commercial buildings as a result of the Comprehensive National Energy Policy Act of 1993. These systems combine monitoring and controlling of HVAC units with security, lighting, and fire safety systems.

Hotels, department stores, and grocery stores, all large users of energy, began implementing energy management systems in the 1980s. In hotels, for instance, automatic controls on heating and air-conditioning units are regulated by sensors in individual rooms that detect whether the rooms are occupied; the controls are also linked to the hotel's front desk in order to respond to check-ins and check-outs. For hotel owners, these systems cost an average of $120,000 in 1991, but their energy-cost savings were estimated at $30,000 annually. Similarly, energy management systems have saved energy and money for department and grocery stores. In these cases, computerized systems are monitored for a chain of stores by a centralized network. According to Steve Thompson of McRae's department stores, "(the) automated system has not only maintained the chain's standards for temperature and humidity, but has also strengthened them."

CURRENT CONDITIONS

This industry entered the 1990s experiencing small growth following the decline in construction of residential and commercial buildings. This modest growth, along with small sales margins, limited research and development in new technologies and investment in new facilities. In addition, as a result of the weak economy at the

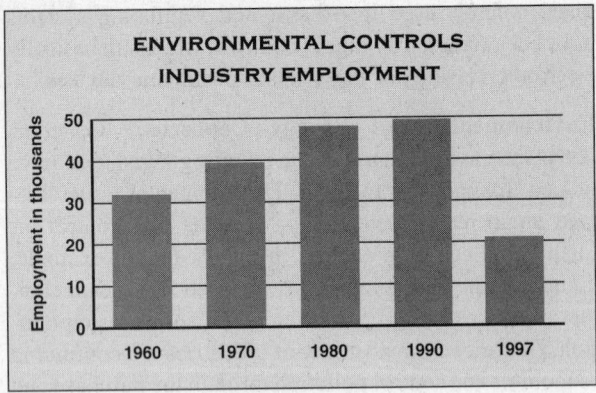

ENVIRONMENTAL CONTROLS INDUSTRY EMPLOYMENT

time, many companies chose to upgrade their existing HVAC systems. Upgrading increased commercial repair and maintenance, while sales of new HVAC systems dropped by 3 percent in 1991 and 1992. Sales rebounded to $4.5 billion in 1998, however, and were anticipated to exceed $6.4 billion by 2005, helped along by technological advances and improved service.

In 2000 the industry was dominated by a few large companies that continued to compete in a saturated market by increasing efficiency in their products, such as improving circulation control, compressor design, and network automation. Products became increasingly standardized, causing companies to differentiate themselves by other means, such as expansion into the global market. Deregulation of electricity was expected to be a significant factor in the HVAC industry's future.

INDUSTRY LEADERS

The industry's largest establishment, Honeywell of Minneapolis, Minnesota, reported $23.7 billion in total sales in 1997, employing more than 120,000 people worldwide. Honeywell is a global company operating in more than 95 countries and generating a large percentage of its revenues outside the United States. Honeywell manufactures products for three segments within this industry: homes and buildings, industry, and space and aviation. For homes and buildings, Honeywell makes thermostats, gas valves, and other residential heating and cooling controls. For industry, the company provides HVAC controls and digital control systems for use with computerized energy management systems. The company's space and aviation segment manufactures environmental controls and guidance system controls.

Other industry leaders included Watsco Inc. of Cocount Grove, Florida, with 1998 sales of about $1 billion and 3,000 employees. Robertshaw Controls Company of Long Beach, California, had about $500 million in sales worldwide in 1997 with more than 5,500 employees. Therm-O-Disc, Inc. of Mansfield, Ohio, had over $338 million in sales in 1997 and more than 5,500 employees.

WORKFORCE

In the early 1990s, more than 49,000 workers were employed in this industry. Nearly 60 percent of these were production workers, including electricians and assembly line workers; their wages were $9.50 per hour. The remaining 40 percent were employed in administration and management and sales capacities; their salaries, unlike those of production workers, varied greatly.

The 1997 level of employment was estimated at 21,040 people receiving hourly wages of about $12.50. The number of people employed in this industry dropped sharply since 1987, with less than half as many people employed in 1997 than in 1987.

AMERICA AND THE WORLD

In 1996 the United States had a trade deficit in the environmental controls industry segment, importing $381 million of products and services while exporting $242 million. The value of exports by the entire measuring and controlling instruments industry, however, was $5.4 billion while imports were almost $4.0 billion.

China was especially important to this industry in the 1990s. In the 1980s China resembled the United States of the 1950s by building new cities, electric power systems, immense factories, and a much improved highway system. Consumerism was also growing and being fueled by democratic capitalism. In the 1990s, as it narrowed the gap between itself and global competitors, China appeared more like the United States of the 1960s, 1970s, and even the 1980s. High-tech companies have been incredibly important to the economic emergence of this nation and will continue to be necessary into the twenty-first century.

RESEARCH AND TECHNOLOGY

With the downturn in the real estate market in the late 1980s and early 1990s, building owners and developers became interested in automated building systems as a way of cutting overhead costs and as a marketing device to showcase cost savings and modernization. Technology in these systems included management-regulated HVAC controls to lower energy costs.

Automated building systems have also been developed for in-home use, combining heating and air-conditioning control with security and fire and smoke detector systems. Honeywell's TotalHome, an automated home control system, uses a remote control to program room temperature, appliances, lights and locks. More research is expected in this area as consumer interest in these systems increases.

Continued research is also predicted for automatic controls within energy management systems. Some of these projects involve the use of artificial intelligence and complex information systems.

In early 2000, Quantum Group of San Diego, California announced a carbon monoxide sensor system able to detect and respond to small changes of carbon monoxide within seconds, regardless of humidity. A joint venture among emWare, Motorola, GE, Sunbeam, and AT&T produced a system for networking smart, non-PC devices such as home appliances, business products, and security, lighting, and heating systems. At the same time, a similar line of smart appliances was introduced by Sunbeam: these appliances "talk" to each other when plugged in to coordinate tasks. They included a coffeemaker, electric blanket, smoke detector, stand mixer, bathroom scale, alarm clock, and kitchen console.

FURTHER READING

Bonsignore, Michael. "Balancing Risk and Reward in China." *Chief Executive (U.S.),* December 1996, 34.

Darnay, Arsen, J., ed. *Manufacturing USA: Industry Analyses, Statistics, and Leading Companies.* 5th ed. Detroit: Gale Research, 1996.

"emWare, Invensys, Motorola, GE, Sunbeam and AT&T Team To Deliver Networked Devices for Homes and Businesses." *Appliance Manufacturer,* January 2000.

Frost and Sullivan. *Heating, Venting, and Air Conditioning in Commercial and Institutional Markets Report: 5469—19,* January 2000.

International Trade Administration. "U.S. Aggregate Foreign Trade Data." *U.S. Foreign Trade Highlights.* Available from http://www.ita.doc.gov/tradestats/.

"Introducing World's Fastest Solid State Carbon Monoxide Sensor." *Appliance Manufacturer,* January 2000.

"Time for Smart Talk is Over; Sunbeam Trumps Small Appliance Industry With Smart Appliance Debut." *Appliance Manufacturer,* January 2000.

U.S. Bureau of the Census. *1997 Economic Census—Manufacturing.* Washington: GPO, 1997. Available from http://www.census.gov.

SIC 3823

INDUSTRIAL INSTRUMENTS FOR MEASUREMENT, DISPLAY, AND CONTROL OF PROCESS VARIABLES, AND RELATED PRODUCTS

This category includes establishments primarily engaged in manufacturing industrial instruments and related products for measuring, displaying (indicating and/or recording), transmitting, and controlling process variables in manufacturing, energy conversion, and public service utilities. These instruments operate mechanically, pneumatically, electronically, or electrically to measure process variables such as temperature, humidity, pressure, vacuum, combustion, flow, level, viscosity, density, acidity, alkalinity, specific gravity, gas and liquid concentration, sequence, time interval, mechanical motion, and rotation.

Establishments primarily engaged in manufacturing electrical integrating meters are classified in **SIC 3825: Instruments for Measuring and Testing of Electricity and Electrical Signals;** those manufacturing residential and commercial comfort controls are classified in **SIC 3822: Automatic Controls for Regulating Residential and Commercial Environments and Appliances;** those manufacturing all liquid-in-glass and bimetal thermometers and glass hydrometers are classified in **SIC 3829: Measuring and Controlling Devices, Not Elsewhere Classified;** those manufacturing recorder charts are classified in the Commercial Printing industries; and those manufacturing analytical and optical instruments are classified in **SIC 3826: Laboratory Analytical Instruments** and **SIC 3827: Optical Instruments and Lenses.**

NAICS CODE(S)

334513 (Instruments and Related Product Manufacturing for Measuring, Displaying, and Controlling Industrial Process Variables)

INDUSTRY SNAPSHOT

More than 1,000 U.S. companies manufactured process control instruments (PCIs) in 1997, and the value of all industry shipments that year was nearly $8 billion. Because of the industry's technology-intensive products, variety of product types, and the tendency of end-user industries to continue to invest in process improvements even during recessions, PCI manufacturers were expected to experience solid growth through the turn of the century. The global sensor industry as a whole (of which the PCI industry was only one segment) was dominated by small ($10 million in sales or less) firms in the mid-1990s. The U.S. PCI industry was expected to generate more than $8 billion in shipments in 1998. As computerized advanced process control techniques continued to become the norm in American industry, PCI end-users increasingly demanded more accurate sensing devices and process control computers (or "controllers") capable of providing real-time direction of a sophisticated range of manufacturing process operations.

Shipments of general industrial process display/control instruments and temperature measuring instruments—the two fastest-growing product groups—grew at an estimated annual rate of 13.6 and 10.8 percent, respectively, between 1987 and 1995. Intense competition from foreign PCI manufacturers challenged U.S. producers at home; at the same time, growing markets in

Asia, Eastern Europe, and the former Soviet Union offered U.S. producers opportunities to expand their leading role in the international PCI marketplace.

ORGANIZATION AND STRUCTURE

At the heart of industrial process control is the measurement of certain variables, such as temperature and pressure, used in manufacturing processes to transform raw materials into finished products. Measurements made by sensors, meters, or other measuring instruments on the manufacturing process line are sent by a transmitting device to an indicator or recorder for display and/or to a controller (by the 1990s, to a computer) where the data is compared to a preestablished set of parameters. The controller calculates the difference between the measured data and the programmed "setpoint" values and, if necessary, adjusts the process variables to conform to the desired parameters. This feedback-and-response cycle is called a loop, and continuous, repeating loops are performed during the industrial process to ensure product quality, efficient use of raw materials, and process safety. Processes typically involving control include reacting, heating and cooling, distilling, petroleum refining, and pulp and paper manufacturing.

PCI End-Users. The PCI industry is tightly linked to its end-user industries and to the process or so-called "wet" industries in particular. Capital expenditures by these industries on plant and process improvements have a direct effect on the profits of PCI manufacturers. The process industries use raw materials in fluid or bulk solid form for product manufacture and include the chemical, petroleum, petrochemical, pharmaceutical, pulp and paper, food processing, plastics, and municipal water and waste treatment industries.

Historically, the process industries have accounted for almost two-thirds of all PCI purchases. The chemical industry alone traditionally purchases 25 percent of all PCI shipments, followed by the petroleum (19 percent), pulp and paper (11 percent), and food processing industries (7 percent). Other important purchasers include nonprocess or discrete-piece manufacturing industries, which manufacture iron, steel, and nonferrous metals (such as aluminum and copper), glass and ceramic products, textiles, and machine tools; mining industries; and electric and gas utilities.

Competitive Structure. In spite of historically strong growth performance and high technology product groups, the PCI industry has traditionally been undervalued by the financial community. This sometimes prevented PCI companies from attracting the capital necessary to maintain growth and made firms in the industry ideal targets for acquisition by foreign and domestic companies. Although changes in the PCI industry's structure challenged the traditional hold of the largest companies in the 1990s,

such major producers as Thermo Electron Corporation, ABB Automation, Rosemount Inc., and Foxboro Co. dominated the industry and were the leaders in sales and employment in the late 1990s. Due to advances in digital technology, however, PCI system integratibility and product compatibility increased considerably in recent years. As a result, manufacturers who formerly dominated the industry now face competition from firms whose products can be tied into larger manufacturers' systems, thereby allowing these smaller firms to penetrate closed markets.

An increasing number of end-user manufacturers sought out PCI vendors who could provide them with complete integrated systems for their process control applications. Instrument manufacturers who formerly produced only components were thus forced to broaden their product lines. Despite increasing system compatibility, PCI vendors still competed in the areas of price, quality, added features, delivery, reputation, reliability, and service.

Legislation. Antipollution regulations by the Environmental Protection Agency (EPA)—the largest single regulatory influence on the PCI industry—required manufacturers to purchase instruments to monitor and control their industrial waste levels. Mandated spending to comply with Occupational Safety and Health Administration (OSHA) plant safety regulations was the next largest regulatory action affecting PCI purchases in the 1990s. PCI producers were also affected by Food and Drug Administration (FDA) policies regulating the manufacture of pharmaceuticals. While government regulation stimulated the sale of antipollution-related PCI products, it also reduced the capital available for new projects that would increase sales of PCIs.

Product Groups. The products of the PCI industry can be divided into several broad groups: general-purpose control system instruments (1991 shipments, $1.5 billion); flow and level instruments ($871.5 million); pressure instruments ($411.3 million); temperature and primary temperature instruments ($547.8 million); gas and liquid analyzers ($362.3 million); humidity instruments ($21.2 million); instruments for process variables such as speed, weight, density, and specific gravity ($105.2 million); and other PCI instruments and spare parts, supplies, accessories, and related products ($950.9 million).

General Purpose Control System Instruments. The biggest-selling PCIs, general purpose control system instruments, included multifunction computer control systems as well as general instruments for measuring, displaying, transmitting, and controlling process variables. General-purpose measuring instruments operate electronically or pneumatically to register and quantify process variable conditions in the manufacturing process. In the mid-1990s sensor products were available for measuring more than 40 different physical properties, from wind to acceleration, and roughly 75 different sensing technologies (for example, acoustic or zirconium oxide) were in use worldwide. The sensor's measurement or reading is transformed into a signal that is displayed or sent to the controller for comparison with process variable setpoints.

Indicators receive the data gathered by the measuring sensor and present it to the operator in digital or analog form. Digital indicators represent process variable data in discrete numerical or alphanumerical form on a liquid-crystal or light-emitting diode display or through a computer screen. Recorders are used for graphing or permanently storing process variable measurements. Early recorders used pen-and-ink mechanisms to mark rolled strips of paper or circular charts. Computer technology has enabled measurements to be recorded digitally in computer memory for later display in printed form or on computer graphics programs. Controllers receive data signals remotely or directly from measuring or transmitting instruments and send instructions or error signals to actuating valves or other components on the process line if the signals indicate that the process variables are diverging from desired conditions.

Flow and Level Instruments. Flowmeters have historically constituted one of the largest sources of industry revenue. Although there are over 100 types of meters, the most common are differential-pressure, turbine, mass-flow, variable-area, magnetic, and positive-displacement meters. Flowmeters are used to measure the rates of flow of fluid chemicals, gases, liquids containing particulate matter (slurries), water, sewage, and gas, among other applications. Level instruments can be used to determine the amount of raw materials available for production purposes or the number of items manufactured by the process. They are typically installed in tanks, bins, hoppers, or other storage devices to monitor levels of materials such as gasoline, milk, solvents, plastic granules, coal, or oil.

Pressure Instruments. The vast majority of products manufactured by industry firms are the result of processes that use pressure to perform work. Punch presses and boilers are typical pressure-based industrial process machines. Pressure-measuring instruments such as gauges and pressure transmitters operate hydraulically, pneumatically, or electronically to measure pressure, absolute pressure, vacuum pressure, or draft pressure. The two most common types of pressure gauges are liquid-filled columns or tubes (similar to household barometers) and elastic pressure elements, which operate on spring-action, diaphragm, or bellows principles.

Temperature and Primary Temperature Instruments. More than half of all measured process variables undergo some form of temperature measurement during the manufacturing process. Accurate temperature mea-

surements are important in many industrial processes but are critical in processes like rubber curing, food processing, and medical sterilization, where slight temperature variances can destroy final product quality. The four basic temperature-measuring instrument types are thermocouples, resistance thermometers, thermal radiation meters, and nonglass filled systems, such as industrial mercury-filled thermometers. Primary temperature instruments are the sensors that receive and measure the initial temperature data in the process control loop.

Gas and Liquid Analyzers. Analyzers of gas and liquid in continuous on-stream industrial processes are often classified according to the nature of the interaction between the gas and liquid to be measured and an external source of energy. Analyzers allow molecular-level measurement of process materials without interruption of the process for sample extraction. Analyzers are used to measure industrial effluents and waste products, viscosity of liquids used in mixing processes and food processing, the acidity or alkalinity of process materials, and the octane number in petroleum refining, among other applications. In addition to gas and liquid analyzers, the most common instrument types are oxygen, chromatographic, infrared, and pH analyzers.

Humidity Instruments. Instruments such as hygrometers and psychrometers measure the water vapor content of air in such industrial applications as test chambers, pharmaceutical and food packaging, heat treating, and industrial drying. Wet-bulb/dry-bulb humidity, relative humidity, vapor pressure, and dew point are the most common types of measurements performed by industrial humidity instruments.

Other Process Control Instruments. This category includes instruments for measuring such process variables as specific gravity, density, viscosity, weight, or force. Instruments in this category are used in such specialized applications as determining the "freeness" of pulp and paper products, the size of particulate solids in slurries, or the boiling point in petroleum refining.

BACKGROUND AND DEVELOPMENT

The modern process controls industry grew out of three historical developments: the emergence of mass production technology, the evolution of instruments for measuring and analyzing process variables, and the development of computer technology in process control applications.

Eli Whitney's invention of the interchangeable part in 1800 represented an important early milestone in the evolution of mass production manufacturing techniques. In the early 1800s, Oliver Evans developed the principle of the automatic manufacturing sequence, which was followed later in the century by advances in machine tooling and the gradual transition from rudimentary assembly-line manufacturing methods to true industrial mechanization.

In the nineteenth century there was fundamental progress in the measurement of properties like temperature, pressure, and fluid flow. In 1822, Thomas J. Seebeck's development of the principle of continuous electrical current flow across metals of differing temperatures laid the foundation for the modern industrial thermocouple. Contemporary thermistor technology grew out of Michael Faraday's discovery of the principles of temperature resistance in the 1830s. E. Bourdon's invention in 1852 of a method for measuring pressure based on the effect of internal pressure variations on the closed end of a curved tube remains a common pressure instrument technology, and the production of the first commercial venture tube flowmeter in 1887 marked a major advance in fluid meter technology that was still in wide use in the 1990s.

The first commercial industrial controller using newly developed computational procedures, or algorithms, for regulating processes was marketed in 1936. The earliest form of process control was performed solely by the operator who read data from a measuring gauge on the process line, determined whether the measurement varied from some desired setpoint value, and turned a valve if the process variable required adjusting. Later controllers were pneumatically or electrically powered devices designed to maintain constant, hard-wired setpoints and sometimes contained both the component for measuring process variables and the component for actuating the regulating valves.

The earliest computer-based control systems appeared in the mid-1950s. Computer technology allowed controllers to communicate with other PCIs (such as measuring sensors) as well as a central control room computer. These controllers contained a computer-driven version of a control algorithm for indicating, controlling, and actuating control components. In addition to allowing process setpoints to be altered remotely and automatically through a computer terminal, computerized controllers offered lower cost, greater control speed, and increased reliability in comparison to earlier analog systems.

The first automated industrial process plants were constructed in the 1950s, and by 1965 over 1,000 industrial plants worldwide were computer controlled to some extent. The evolution of computer operation—from vacuum tubes to transistors, then from integrated circuits to microchips—led to the introduction of faster and smaller microprocessing computers in the 1970s and 1980s. Identical microprocessor-based controllers located at different points on the process line—so-called distributed control systems—quickly began to replace centralized stand-alone control computers. This generation of high-powered, reprogrammable controllers gave operators direct control over more process loops and also enabled them to reconfigure control programs for new processes or applications.

INDUSTRY LEADERS

The largest firms in the U.S. PCI industry in 1998 were Thermo Electron Corporation ($4.0 billion in sales, 26,000 employees), ABB Automation ($1.3 billion in sales for its ICP products), Rosemount Inc. ($527 million, 11,000 employees), and Foxboro Company ($250 to $500 million, 5,500 employees). Thermo Electron was founded in 1956 in Massachusetts by a professor of mechanical engineering who had a vision of creating a "technology-driven" company that produced new technologies to meet emerging social needs. Since its inception, Thermo Electron has spun off no fewer than 18 publicly traded companies. Among its PCI-related operations, the company's Thermo Instrument Controls division manufactured PCIs and systems, from gas analysis to flow automation, for the chemical, petrochemical, refining, oil and gas, and mining industries. Incorporated in 1947, EG&G provides engineering and scientific services to customers such as the National Aeronautics and Space Administration (NASA) and the U.S. auto industry. It also manufactures mechanical aerospace components, optoelectronic sensors and imaging systems, process control sensing and analysis hardware and software (amounting to 21 percent of its sales) for such applications as oil refining, petrochemical and food processing, and wood, cement, and coal production.

Like Thermo Electron, Rosemount was founded in 1956 and initially built up its business through government aerospace contracts until it diversified into PCIs in the mid-1960s. After gaining a reputation for manufacturing reliable pressure and temperature transmitters, Rosemount merged with Emerson Electric in 1976 and, in 1993, acquired Fisher Controls International to form Fisher-Rosemount, one of the world's largest manufacturers of PCI equipment. Other leading industry firms in the late 1990s included Schneider Automation Inc., Barber-Colman Co., and Analogic Corporation. The industry was also represented by the PCI divisions of several well-known major instrument and/or computer giants, including Texas Instruments Inc., Rockwell International Corp., and Hewlett-Packard Co.

WORKFORCE

Although the number of establishments in the U.S. PCI industry has been growing steadily since 1972 (more than 1,000 establishments in operation during 1997 compared to 175 in 1972), the size of the industry's work force has declined since its peak in 1989. In 1997, the PCI industry employed approximately 49,000 people, with a further decrease projected to 47,600 in 2000. The average hourly wage was slightly above $13.

Production positions accounted for more than half of the industry's employment in 1996. The production positions most representative of the industry included machinists, precision electrical and electronic assemblers, and instrument makers. Workers in these categories built and integrated the components that constituted the industry's product groups and, in some applications, fabricated instruments requiring accuracies of one ten-millionth of an inch. Engineers—from electrical and electronics engineers to mechanical and computer engineers—comprised another significant segment of the industry's employment. Only electrical and electronics engineers and computer engineers were expected to see significant employment growth to 2005.

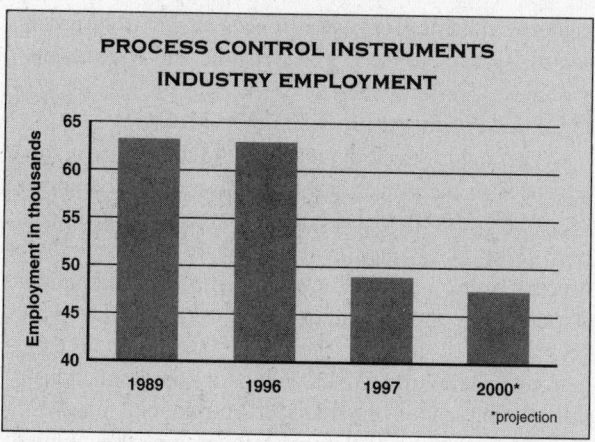

AMERICA AND THE WORLD

U.S. companies have played a leading role in the worldwide PCI marketplace. Nonetheless, foreign PCI industries—led by Germany, Japan, and the United Kingdom—have made significant inroads into the U.S. domestic and overseas markets. Between 1989 and 1995, for example, PCI imports more than doubled, fueled by comparatively lower foreign labor costs, foreign government subsidies of overseas PCI manufacturers, and the ability of some foreign manufacturers to bring research breakthroughs to commercial use sooner than U.S. firms. Moreover, some foreign PCI manufacturers responded to the focus placed by many U.S. companies on quarter-to-quarter profits by adopting long-term market penetration strategies, which allowed them to absorb short-term losses. In 1996, however, the value of imports dropped from slightly over $2 billion to an even $2 billion. From 1989 to 1996, the value of PCI exports rose from $1.50 billion to $2.85 billion.

Although the United States continued to lead the world in new PCI technology in the 1990s, American engineers focused on revolutionary breakthroughs in technology, while foreign research concentrated on gradual, evolutionary innovation. At the same time, foreign manufacturers' readiness to embrace new technologies enabled them to market PCI innovations sooner than more cautious U.S. producers. While U.S. funding of industrial research and development has focused on product development almost twice as much as improvements in industrial processes, the emphasis of Japanese funding has been the reverse, thus contributing in part to Japan's competitiveness in new PCI technology. Foreign firms looking for acquisition targets have been drawn to PCI industry firms because of the industry's history of continual growth, its high technology base, and its generally undervalued stocks and book value.

Exports and Free Trade. Despite the success of foreign companies in penetrating the U.S. market, the United States continued to show a trade surplus in PCIs,

aided by continuing U.S. advances in new technology and the weakness of the dollar overseas. Historically, one-fifth to one-quarter of U.S. PCI shipments have gone to the export market, with the highest concentrations in high technology products like computer controllers and process analyzers. Because of its high labor costs, European firms (especially those in France, Germany, and Switzerland) turned increasingly to PCI technology to streamline their manufacturing processes in the mid-1990s. Moreover, improved European process data acquisition products—that allowed process engineers to monitor and control process machines, security and access, and process variables remotely—also fueled the growth of Europe's PCI industry.

In 1994, the market for sensors (which included many products not produced in the PCI industry) in the United States, western Europe, and Japan combined was estimated at roughly $24.3 billion, with western Europe accounting for about 40 percent of the demand. The annual growth rate for the European PCI industry was expected to be roughly 4 percent between 1994 and 2001. Process sensors, transmitters, and converters were expected to account for 45 to 46 percent of the total European PCI market between 1997 and 2001; followed by distributed control systems (23 to 24 percent); programmable logic controllers (10 percent); stand-alone controllers (5 percent); and indicators, recorders, and displays (about 4 percent).

Efforts to ease international trade barriers and open foreign markets—such as the General Agreement on Tariffs and Trade (GATT)—promised to offer U.S. PCI producers potential new opportunities overseas in the 1990s. The North American Free Trade Agreement (NAFTA) in particular was projected to substantially expand the markets for U.S. PCIs in Mexico and Canada, which ranked first and third, respectively, in imports of U.S. PCIs in 1992. Other leading foreign markets for U.S. PCIs included the European Community nations, eastern Europe (especially Poland), Asia (especially China), and South America. In the mid-1990s, for example, U.S. PCI firms Westinghouse Electric Corp. and Honeywell Inc. sold process control systems to the Czech Republic and Kazakhstan.

RESEARCH AND TECHNOLOGY

The major developments in PCI technology involve advances in the power and usefulness of the computers used in process control applications, the continued evolution of artificial intelligence software applications for process control, and the development of an international standard for communicating between components in process control systems. In the mid-1990s, the rapid emergence of the World Wide Web as a source of industry information and a medium for commercial marketing also allowed small PCI firms to overcome their limited marketing budgets and to sell their products globally.

PCI Computer Hardware. The PCI industry is the most computer-automated segment of the combined measuring and control industry. As was true throughout U.S. industry in general, the computers used in industrial process control continued to fall in price and increase in power, speed, and memory in the mid-1990s. Advances in microchip technology allowed PCI producers to offer a wider range of functions in smaller, lighter, and cheaper instrument packages. Personal computers were increasingly used as process monitors, as workstations for configuring control systems, and as a means for gathering process data and coordinating controllers. Microchip technology also resulted in microprocessor-based "smart" instruments with self-learning and self-tuning capabilities.

PCI Computer Software. Many of the research advances benefiting the PCI industry involve artificial intelligence software used in experimentation, analysis, design, and prototyping of process control systems. Computer graphics modeling or simulation software programs allowed designers of process control systems to simulate complex manufacturing processes before they were actually created. Because they could also predict the final properties of raw material mixtures, these systems could also be used in the formulation of new products. Some programs also permitted simulated process system models to be tested through online interaction with the sensors and actuators that measure and control the variables in the manufacturing process. Self-diagnosing systems are capable of analyzing their own operation, anticipating future conditions, and making changes before problems arise.

Knowledge-based or expert systems used alogical, inductive reasoning and pattern recognition techniques to simulate the imprecise and unpredictable nature of manufacturing processes. These and related "fuzzy logic" programs learn from process events, make qualitative instead of purely logical adjustments to process conditions, and can evaluate and compensate for faults in the process design. In addition to optimizing efficient use of process variables, such software programs allow end-

users to more accurately predict the final properties of process mixtures. Because expert systems are programmed to learn and "think" independently, they are able to make instantaneous changes in the quantity and quality of the raw materials introduced into the process without the intervention of human operators.

Communication Standards. Although long delayed, so-called fieldbus communications, an international protocol for linking all data communications between process control components regardless of design or manufacturer, was expected to eventually have a profound effect on the structure of the process controls industry. Fieldbus would allow the immediate conversion of data from traditionally analog-operating process sensors into digital signals, thus greatly expanding the integratibility or interoperability of PCIs. It represented a trend toward open or "transparent" system architectures that would allow end-users to mix and match system components, resulting in less expensive system expansion, improved performance, and enhanced reliability. Because of protracted debate over which fieldbus standard should be the international norm, full implementation of fieldbus communications was not expected until the turn of the century.

FURTHER READING

Adrian, Peter. "From the Editor: U.S. Sensor Companies Benefit from Strategically Exploiting European Markets." *Sensor Business Digest,* 1 April 1997.

Industrial Computing. Instrument Society of America. Available from http://www.isa.org.

Instrument Society of America. Available from http://www.isa .org.

International Trade Administration. "U.S. Aggregate Foreign Trade Data." *U.S. Foreign Trade Highlights.* Available from http://www.ita.doc.gov/tradestats/.

InTech: The International Journal of Measurement and Control. Instrument Society of America. Available from http://www .isa.org.

Motion Control. Instrument Society of America. Available from http://www.isa.org.

U.S. Bureau of the Census. *1997 Economic Census—Manufacturing.* Washington: GPO, 1997. Available from http://www.census.gov.

SIC 3824

TOTALIZING FLUID METERS AND COUNTING DEVICES

This category includes establishments primarily engaged in manufacturing meters for registering or tallying quantities of fluids, motor vehicle measuring instruments, and instruments for counting the frequency of items or events. This category includes establishments that manufacture domestic, commercial, and industrial gas and water meters; meters for measuring speed, distance traveled, and other variables for the motor vehicle industry; and counters and timers for quantifying production rates in industrial processes. Establishments primarily engaged in manufacturing electricity integrating meters and electronic frequency counters are classified in **SIC 3825: Instruments for Measuring and Testing of Electricity and Electrical Signals.** Establishments primarily engaged in manufacturing flow meters for industrial process control and other industrial process instruments are classified in **SIC 3823: Industrial Instruments for Measurement, Display, and Control of Process Variables; and Related Products.**

NAICS CODE(S)

334514 (Totalizing Fluid Meter and Counting Devices Manufacturing)

Approximately 223 U.S. establishments manufactured totalizing fluid meters and counting devices in 1997. These establishments employed over 17,426 people and generated over $3.77 billion in sales. In 1997, the industry shipped integrating and totalizing fluid meters for gas and liquids valued at $1.78 billion, and other totalizing fluid meters and counting devices valued at $171 million. "Residential construction is the most important factor that underlies the growth of this market," according to *U.S. Industry & Trade Outlook '99.*

Totalizing fluid meters measure fluids in quantity terms (such as gallons or cubic feet) and indicate total fluid volume rather than the rates of flow indicated by the flow meters used in industrial process control. The most common type of totalizing fluid meter is the positive-displacement meter, which operates by allowing the fluid to enter a chamber where the force of fluid motion causes a diaphragm, disk, vane, or other element to move or rotate. Each cycle of the rotating or moving element generates a signal that is sent to the registering component of the meter, which tallies or indicates the total fluid quantity.

Small positive-displacement meters used for registering consumption of water in households or businesses have traditionally been the largest product type in the integrating and totalizing fluid meter segment, followed by meters for registering residential gas consumption. Other significant product groups in this segment include registering or totalizing gas meters for commercial or industrial use, impeller meters and consumption-registering rotary and turbine gas meters, gauges for computing pressure and temperature corrections in industrial processes, and liquid meters used in industrial bulk plants and pipelines.

Fuelled by the needs of the process control industry beginning in the 1980s, fluid meter technology began to

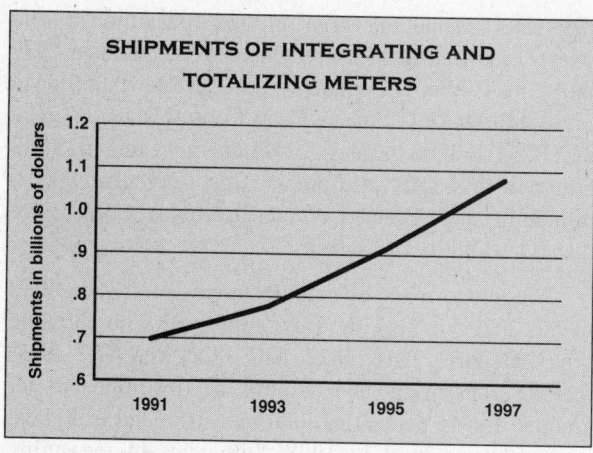

evolve at a dramatic pace, offering enormous improvements in reliability, accuracy, and range of measurable flow rates. Among the most important new flow measurement technologies most likely to have an impact on the totalizing fluid meter industry were the use of "nonintrusive" measuring devices that do not change the characteristics of the fluids they measure; improved meter maintenance performance through advanced diagnostic techniques; a trend toward solid-state meters with no moving parts; and perhaps even the eventual replacement of the traditional meter itself by pipes that contain their own measuring sensors.

In 1997, the largest percentage of the value of the industry's shipments, or $2.32 billion, was derived from the motor vehicle instrument sector, which produced speedometers, tachometers, odometers, fuel level gauges, water temperature gauges, ammeters, oil pressure gauges, and other motor vehicle instruments. Most of these products are installed in new vehicles. Customers dealing with this segment of the industry often are large automotive suppliers that provide vehicle manufacturers with subassemblies (such as dashboards complete with instruments) ready for installation. The motor vehicle instruments segment is expected to grow in accordance with the increases in the worldwide demand for vehicles and with the development of integrated electronic digital controls.

Counters and timers are used in a wide variety of manufacturing applications and typically indicate how many items have been fed into a machine, how fast a machine is operating, how many items have been produced, how long it will take to perform a process, or what time a specific event will occur. In 1997, these nonautomotive counters and timers accounted for almost $428 million of the value of the industry's shipments.

Firms in five states—California, Illinois, Ohio, Pennsylvania, and Texas—accounted for 28 percent of the value of all industry shipments in 1997. Companies in this industry include American Meter Co. (more than $100.0 million in sales), Badger Meter, Inc. ($143.8 million in

1998 sales), Daniel Industries, Inc. ($283.2 million in 1998 sales), Engineering Measurements ($9.7 million in 1999 sales), the Foxboro Company (more than $250.0 million in sales), Milton Roy Company/Flow Control Division (more than $25.0 million in sales), Schlumberger Limited ($11.8 billion in 1998 sales), Rosemount, Inc. (more than $500.0 million in sales), Stewart Warner Instrument Corp. (more than $25.0 million in sales)

Shipments made by manufacturers of totalizing fluid meters and counting devices, combined with those in other categories (SIC 3822, SIC 3823, and SIC 3829) making measuring and controlling instruments, accounted for 44 percent of total industrial and analytical instrument products in 1998. Shipments of measuring and controlling instruments are projected to grow 3 percent annually through 2003. Motor vehicle instruments and integrating fluid meters and counting devices will be among the higher-growth segments. Estimates for 1999 forecasted 33 percent of product shipments would be exported, while 25 percent of U.S. demand would be imported. The top five export markets in 1997 were Canada, Mexico, Japan, United Kingdom, and Germany, and the top five import countries were Mexico, Japan, Canada, United Kingdom, and Germany.

FURTHER READING

Blickley, George J. "Flowmeter Selection Isn't Easy, But Tools Are Here." *Control Engineering,* 1 November 1996.

"Current Industrial Reports: Totalizing Fluid Meter and Counting Device Manufacturing—1997." U.S. Department of Commerce. Bureau of the Census. September 1999. Available from http://www.census.gov/prod/ec97/97m3345e.pdf.

Furness, Richard. "Future Flow Measurement Has Digital Influence." *Control Engineering,* 1 October 1996.

Hoover's Online Company Capsules. Available from http://www.hoovers.com.

U.S. Industry and Trade Outlook '99. McGraw-Hill and U.S. Department of Commerce, 1999.

SIC 3825

INSTRUMENTS FOR MEASURING AND TESTING OF ELECTRICITY AND ELECTRICAL SIGNALS

This industry is made up of companies that manufacture a multitude of analytical devices. Examples of industry output include voltmeters, ammeters, wattmeters, watt-hour meters, semiconductor test equipment, and circuit testers. Establishments that produce monitoring and testing equipment for navigational, radar, and sonar sys-

tems are described in **SIC 3812: Search, Detection, Navigation, Guidance, Aeronautical, and Nautical Systems and Instruments.**

NAICS CODE(S)

334416 (Electronic Coil, Transformer, and Other Inductor Manufacturing)

334515 (Instrument Manufacturing for Measuring and Testing Electricity and Electrical Signals)

INDUSTRY SNAPSHOT

Shipments of instruments to measure electricity have increased in value every year from 1991 to 1997. This industry did not suffer as badly as many did in the recession of the early 1990s. Many establishments came into operation in the 1980s, and employment for this industry was highest in 1984. In the late 1980s, U.S. companies were shipping over $7 billion worth of goods per year, employing around 90,000 workers, and exporting equipment valued at about $2 billion annually. While shipments were 73 percent greater in 1996 than in 1987, the number of people employed (62,000) was 35 percent less than the record high of 95,800 employed in 1984. The average hourly wage in 1996 was $15.53.

Growth in the mid-1990s was due to demand for Automatic Test Equipment (ATE), a devalued U.S. dollar, and shipments of high-tech devices to telecommunications industries. Despite increased foreign competition, the United States widened its trade surplus to $2.6 billion in 1996 and poised itself for steady global expansion into the twenty-first century.

ORGANIZATION AND STRUCTURE

The electrical Testing and Measuring (T&M) instruments industry encompasses eight major product groups. ATE, the largest industry segment, includes T&M instruments for semiconductors, circuit boards, and computer disk drives. Communications test equipment, the second-ranked product group, includes T&M devices for landline, wireless, and fiber-optic communications gear.

Other major industry categories include signal generators, electrical integrating instruments, multimeters, oscilloscopes, and spectrum analyzers. Each of these product groups is comprised of many different devices. In addition, more than half of industry revenues are garnered from a wide range of miscellaneous T&M instruments, such as tube testers, impedance measurers, frequency meters, battery testers, stroboscopes, tachometers, reflectometers, ammeters, and ohmmeters.

Ohmmeters, a common and traditional product of the industry, are used to measure the amount of electrical resistance in a circuit. Likewise, watt-hour meters are most often used to measure the amount of power that is used by a utility customer, and are mounted on an outside wall of most homes and buildings. Potentiometers are used to precisely measure direct current or voltage, as are voltmeters and ammeters. The galvanometer, another indicating instrument, indicates extremely small currents. Reflectometers measure the amount of light or energy reflected from a surface. An oscilloscope converts electron motion into a visual display on a cathode-ray tube.

Nearly one-third of the companies in the industry, representing almost 25 percent of total sales, were located in California in the 1990s due to the large defense, semiconductor, and telecommunications industries in that state.

BACKGROUND AND DEVELOPMENT

In 1833, Englishman Carl Friedrich Gauss was the first to show that magnetic quantities could be measured in terms of mechanical units. Wilhelm Weber, also of England, defined a system of electrical units in 1851 that foreshadowed the development of the ohm (1864), a measure of electrical resistance. The ampere, a unit used to measure electrical current, soon followed. The United States made the ohm and ampere legal units of electrical measurement in 1894.

Early measuring devices were functional, though generally unreliable for precise readings. The earliest device that would deliver a standard for voltage (electromotive force) for measuring instruments was built in 1836 and was reproducible only to about 1 percent accuracy. The Clark Cell of 1872, which was used to establish a standard voltage measurement, also proved unreliable. The Weston Cell, introduced in 1892, became the first device to successfully provide a standard for electrical measuring.

Following the development of electrical units and credible standards, numerous electricity measuring devices emerged during the early 1900s. Among the first devices were instruments used to measure electrical resistance, such as ohmmeters. In addition, power meters, or wattmeters, became industry mainstays. One of the largest classes of early devices was indicating instruments, such as voltmeters and ammeters.

Many of the first indicating instruments were iron-vane devices, which utilized a plate of steel, a spring pointer, and a damper to form the vane, or moving elements of the meter. As electricity passed through a magnetic coil, the vane tipped to provide a reading. These rugged instruments remained the primary indicating devices for much of the twentieth century, despite the development of more advanced meters. Electrodynamic instruments, which were much more precise than iron-vane mechanisms, were also developed in the early part of the twentieth century. These indicating instruments utilized two sets of coils and became popular for laboratory applications.

The development of the transistor in 1947 by Bell Telephone Laboratories led to the introduction of a profusion of extremely accurate electrical T&M equipment during the latter half of the century. Tube-type and electromechanical instruments were soon replaced by devices accurate to within one-millionth of a unit. As the number of applications for solid-state electronics ballooned, the demand for various T&M equipment flourished throughout the 1950s, 1960s, and 1970s.

By the end of the 1970s, electrical T&M equipment manufacturers were shipping about $6 billion worth of goods per year. Although industry growth decelerated during the previous decade, shipments continued to increase and U.S. manufacturers maintained a significant technological lead over their global counterparts. In 1982 the industry had sales of $6.1 billion and a workforce of 90,000 employees.

As the T&M industry recovered from a major recession in the late 1970s and early 1980s, revenues jumped to $6.5 billion in 1983 and then to $7.8 billion a year later. Increased defense spending, growth in telecommunications, and a general proliferation in computers and other electronic devices also contributed to growth. In 1986, total sales fell 10 percent from the previous year, from $7.7 billion to $6.9 billion. Then, in 1987, the industry recovered, generating sales of $7.7 billion.

In an effort to maintain profitability, U.S. T&M instrument companies initiated aggressive productivity programs during the 1980s and focused on research and development efforts in high-tech fields. As a result, industry employment dropped to 81,000 by 1989 and to 63,000 by 1997. Still, the United States retained its significant technological lead in high-profit T&M devices, such as ATE and telecommunications testing equipment.

The low value of the U.S. dollar and a resurgence in domestic semiconductor manufacturing spurred electrical T&M device receipts to increase by 6 percent in 1990, to $8.4 billion. Although a global recession pushed sales down 1 percent in 1991, revenues struggled upward 6 percent in 1992 and rose to $9.2 billion in 1993. The value of shipments was $9.5 billion in 1994, $9.6 billion in 1995, and $12.8 billion by 1997.

In addition to healthy demand, producers enjoyed the benefits of massive productivity gains achieved during the 1980s and 1990s. Despite shipment growth, industry employment continued to decline. Improved efficiency was allowing some domestic producers to compete in markets for low-priced, traditional equipment. At the same time, however, many companies were striving to move their low-tech production facilities overseas.

Exports also raised the profit margin, as foreign demand for price-competitive, high-tech equipment rose. Overseas shipments were up 4 percent in 1993, 11 per-

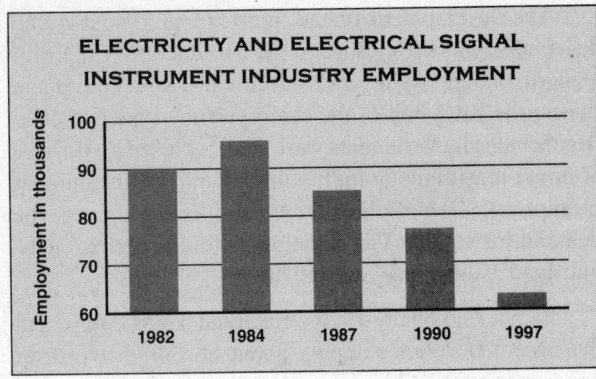

ELECTRICITY AND ELECTRICAL SIGNAL INSTRUMENT INDUSTRY EMPLOYMENT

cent in 1994, 23 percent in 1995, and 17 percent in 1996. At the same time, import growth was significantly lower than exports from 1993 through 1996 as U.S. firms pelted their competition with efficiency gains and advanced product introductions. In 1996, the United States had a healthy surplus of $2.6 billion.

CURRENT CONDITIONS

The value of shipments for 1997 was $12.8 billion, up from $9.55 billion in 1995. Capital investment in the industry was on the decline, falling to $672 million in 1996. Many analysts were surprised at the impressive performance of this industry in the early 1990s, particularly because of drastically reduced spending in the defense sector and the recession. But sales of advanced T&M devices were rising fast enough to make up for slower traditional markets. Shipments of digital oscilloscopes and multimeters that were priced to compete with similar analog devices, for instance, offered significant profit opportunities. Likewise, new products related to wireless communications displayed excellent growth.

Automatic Test Equipment was the fastest growing sector of the electrical T&M device industry in the 1990s. After ceding market share to Japanese semiconductor manufacturers in the previous decade, U.S. chip producers were turning the tables by dominating the market for a new generation of high-speed semiconductors (called application specific integrated circuits). T&M device makers benefited as U.S. semiconductor shipments from the top four semiconductor companies alone (Intel, NEC, Motorola, Texas Instruments) totaled $47.3 billion in 1997. All this semiconductor production required increased ATE production.

INDUSTRY LEADERS

The giant of the electrical T&M industry is Hewlett-Packard Company of California, with 1999 revenues of $42.4 billion ($19 billion in the United States) and about 83,200 employees worldwide. It was founded in 1938 by William Hewlett and David Packard, graduates of Stanford University's electrical engineering program. With $538 in startup funds, the two entrepreneurs developed an

audio-testing oscillator that was used by one of their first customers, Walt Disney, for the classic movie *Fantasia*.

Hewlett-Packard realized steady growth during and after World War II by developing and selling various electrical T&M equipment. Their first major breakthrough was the HP-524A. Introduced in 1951, this device reduced the time required to measure radio frequencies from 10 minutes to about 2 seconds.

The current leader in the industry of instruments to measure electricity is Tektronix Incorporated of Beaverton, Oregon. Tektronix had total 1999 sales of $1.9 billion and employed 7,600 people. The company, founded in 1946, holds more than 1,500 patents worldwide and receives nearly 60 per year. In 1999, Tektronix decided to sell off its color printer operations and focus exclusively on test and measurement equipment.

The second largest company, and gaining on Tektronix, is Teradyne Incorporated of Boston, Massachusetts, with 1999 sales of $1.8 billion and 7,500 employees worldwide. Founded in 1960 by Alex d'Arbeloff and Nick DeWolf, Teradyne produced its first product, the D133 diode tester, in 1961. In 1999 it introduced the AWG2400 10-bit Waveform Generator, claimed to be the highest arbitrary waveform generator in the ATE industry.

These companies are followed by KLA-Tencor, formed by the 1997 merger of KLA Instruments and Tencor Instruments (both founded in 1976). Headquartered in San Jose, California and garnering $843 million in sales behind the strength of 4,800 employees in 1999, KLA-Tencor derives more than half its revenues from outside the United States.

WORKFORCE

Despite rising sales, employment prospects in the electrical T&M device business were stagnant in the mid-1990s. Continued productivity gains and the movement of manufacturing facilities overseas resulted in diminished opportunities for virtually every occupation in the industry. In 1982 there were about 90,000 workers employed; in 1984 the number jumped to 95,800. But the total workforce was down to 85,200 in 1987, 77,100 in 1990, 59,600 in 1993, and 55,400 for 1996. In 1997, however, total U.S. employment increased slightly to 63,300.

Overall, jobs for most production workers were expected to decline from 20 to 50 percent between 1995 and 2005, according to the Bureau of Labor Statistics. Jobs for general managers and executives are expected to drop 20 percent. Even positions for research engineers and technicians will decrease by 1 to 3 percent by 2005.

AMERICA AND THE WORLD

U.S. electrical T&M device manufacturers are the most technologically advanced in the world, as evidenced by their strong trade surplus. Their primary competitive advantage is their ability to develop and manufacture high-tech, high-profit devices, such as ATE and telecommunications instruments. In contrast, many firms have licensed their low-end technology to regions such as China and India, where production costs are lower than in the United States.

Japan was by far the leading importer of U.S. T&M instruments, accounting for more than 16 percent, or about $430 million, of U.S. overseas sales in 1993. Canada and the United Kingdom each represented 8.0 percent of the U.S. export market. Germany and Mexico purchased 7.0 and 5.5 percent, respectively, of U.S. exports. The European Community took 36.0 percent of overseas shipments, and East Asia (not including China) purchased 22.0 percent. Japan was also the largest exporter of T&M to the United States, exporting about $175 million worth of equipment to this country in 1993. In 1996 the total value of imports was $2.3 billion, and the total value of exports was $4.9 billion.

Although competition was increasing in the mid-1990s, particularly from Europe and Japan, U.S. manufacturers in this industry expected to maintain their technological lead into the twenty-first century. Sales to the viable domestic semiconductor industry will be augmented by strong growth in demand from new wireless telecommunications industries, in which the United States also maintained a technological edge.

RESEARCH AND TECHNOLOGY

In the mid-1990s, U.S. electrical T&M producers were ardently pursuing technological advances that would allow them to sharpen their competitive edge at home and abroad. Several emerging industry segments, such as wireless data communications and digital transmission, offered solid growth opportunities for companies on the cutting edge. Thin film transistor liquid crystal displays (LCDs), commonly used on portable computers, was one of the fastest growing fields that required new types of T&M instruments. Although Japan dominated LCD markets, several U.S. producers were developing T&M devices and were communicating with Japanese LCD manufacturers.

Virtual instruments were another emerging industry technology. These are T&M instruments that combine computer software and instrumentation hardware. The instrument appears on a personal computer screen and provides readings as would a T&M device. In fact, an exact graphic replica of the device is displayed on the computer screen, complete with tuning knobs, meters, and digital readout. Instrumentation hardware is used to take readings that are fed into the computer, analyzed by the software, and displayed on the screen. An important advantage of virtual instruments is that they are easily upgraded with new software, as opposed to T&M devices that become obsolete and must be scrapped.

A multitude of other advances in the mid-1990s included miniature, battery-powered, hand-held oscilloscopes. These devices were being used by automotive technicians, for example, to easily monitor electronic modules in cars and trucks. Similarly, Sentech Systems Incorporated of Pennsylvania introduced a device in 1993 that employs laser-based optics to measure the distortion of a turbine shaft. The technology held promise for like applications in the power generation industry. Also in 1993, Motorola, Inc., of Illinois introduced a sensor that monitors a vehicle's intake manifold to compute the amount of fuel required for each cylinder.

In 1997, digital multimeters (DMMs) were greatly improved to provide users with more accuracy and better display resolution; true root mean squared AC measurements; and upgraded capabilities, including graphical waveform displays, time-stamping of minimum/maximum values, dual-measurement displays, and trend plotting.

Hewlett-Packard, the industry leader, introduced a voice-controlled oscilloscope in 1999, allowing hands-free adjustment of all functions via voice commands in plain English. At the same time, Gage Applied Sciences brought out what it called the deep-memory oscilloscope (DMO), able to retain 1 gigabyte of scope measurements. Tektronix developed mid-priced digital-phosphor scopes that can display, store, and analyze complex waveforms using three dimensions of signal information, similar to their high-end counterparts.

FURTHER READING

Bradley, Gale. ''Teradyne Shows Muscle at Semicon/Korea Show.'' *Electronic News (1991),* 10 February 1997.

Darnay, Arsen J., ed. *Manufacturing USA.* 5th ed., Detroit: Gale Research, 1996.

''Electronic Products 1999 Editors' Roundup: Oscilloscopes and Computer Boards.'' *Electronic Products,* January 2000.

''Global Chip Sales in '97 Up 5.5 Percent.'' *Investor's Business Daily,* 6 January 1998.

Hunt, Jim. ''You May Not Recognize Today's DMMs.'' *Quality,* February 1997.

International Trade Administration. ''U.S. Aggregate Foreign Trade Data.'' *U.S. Foreign Trade Highlights.* Available from http://www.ita.doc.gov/tradestats/.

''Tek Pins Growth Rate on New Scopes.'' *Electronic News (1991),* 2 September 1996.

U.S. Bureau of the Census. *1997 Economic Census— Manufacturing.* Washington: GPO, 1997. Available from http://www.census.gov.

SIC 3826

LABORATORY ANALYTICAL INSTRUMENTS

This group covers establishments primarily engaged in manufacturing laboratory instruments and instrument-ation systems for chemical or physical analysis of the composition or concentration of samples of solid, fluid, gaseous, or composite material. Establishments primarily engaged in manufacturing instruments for monitoring and analyzing continuous samples from medical patients are classified in **SIC 3845: Electromedical and Electro-therapeutic Apparatus;** and from industrial process streams are classified in **SIC 3823: Industrial Instru-ments for Measurement, Display, and Control of Pro-cess Variables; and Related Products.**

NAICS CODE(S)

334516 (Analytical Laboratory Instrument Manufactur-ing)

INDUSTRY SNAPSHOT

Laboratory analytical instruments manufactured by this industry were used to conduct physical and chemical analyses. Major product groups included clinical labora-tory, chromatographic, and spectrophotometric instru-ments, and mass spectrometers. In the early 1990s, this high-technology sector exported 30 percent of its output, which contributed to a $1 billion trade surplus. By 1997, industry shipments were worth almost $7 billion, and the industry's workforce numbered 37,718 employees.

Devices used to measure the purity of gold date back to the fourth century B.C. The term "analysis," in the chemical sense, was first posited in the 1660s. A series of breakthroughs in chemical measuring methods occurred during the 1800s that preceded the development of more advanced analytic instruments later in the nineteenth cen-tury. But not until the twentieth century did the industry begin to resemble the state it achieved in the 1990s.

From about $3.5 billion in 1987, the first year in which this industry was recognized as a separate indus-trial classification, sales of laboratory analytical instru-ments increased to nearly $6.8 billion by 1995, and many expect this growth to continue into the twenty-first cen-tury. U.S. technological superiority and increasing de-mand for analytical instruments make this an important growth industry.

One of the largest product segments in this industry is mass spectrometry instrumentation, which represented 25 percent of industry shipments in 1997. This type of equipment analyzes chemicals by sorting gaseous ions in electric and magnetic fields. The two major types of mass spectroscopes are spectrographs, which use nonelectric means to detect the sorted ions, and spectrometers, which measure ions electrically.

Chromatographic equipment is used to separate chemical substances to determine their content, or to prepare them for further testing. Chromatography instru-ments are applied in oil refineries and on space vehicles to analyze atmospheres on other planets. This segment accounted for 14 percent of industry sales in 1997.

Spectrophotometric instruments represented 11 per-cent of the industry's shipments in 1997. These devices are used to view, meter, and record spectrums of light or forms of radiated energy. Spectrochemical analysis usu-ally involves the examination of the emission of radiation by molecules that have been heated or excited by some other form of energy, or the absorption of radiation of particular wavelengths by certain molecules.

In addition to the three major product segments, 50 percent of industry sales were derived from many other devices, including a wide range of instruments made for clinical laboratories, individual parts and accessories, and other specialized instruments. Examples of specialized instruments are titrimeters, which measure the concentra-tion of a substance in a solution; densitometers, which gauge the optical density of a material; coulometric ana-lyzers, which detect the amount of a substance released during electrolysis; and turbidimeters, which measure the scattering of a light beam through a solution that contains suspended particulate matter.

ORGANIZATION AND STRUCTURE

The laboratory analytical instruments industry is an international business dominated by large, innovative companies. In addition, numerous small firms compete by forming alliances or operating in niche markets. The industry is characterized by high profits, an emphasis on advanced technology, and sporadic growth. Companies typically sell their products directly to research laborato-ries in pharmaceutical firms, food companies, hospitals, and other establishments that work with chemicals or analyze substances.

BACKGROUND AND DEVELOPMENT

Rudimentary analytical instruments and measuring devices predate the birth of Christ. Naturalist Robert Boyle of England was credited with introducing the term "analysis," in the chemical sense, in his book *The Sceptical Chymist,* published in 1661. In 1669, Isaac Newton conducted light spectrum experiments that even-tually lead to the development of the spectroscope. Also in the seventeenth century, the first precise gravimetric analysis equipment (used to measure specific gravity) was believed to have been created by Friedreich Hoff-man, a German physician and chemist. Numerous key inventions and discoveries during the eighteenth century included the flame test for alkali metals, qualitative analysis techniques, and titrimetric analysis.

Most instruments and methods before the eighteenth century yielded qualitative analyses. In the nineteenth century, however, French chemist Antoine-Laurent Lavoisier ushered in quantitative analysis, or the determination of the amounts and proportions of chemicals or elements in a substance or gas. Major breakthroughs in analytical instruments and methods during the 1800s included electrochemical analysis methods and gas analysis. In addition, German chemists Gustav Robert Kirchoff and Robert Bunsen introduced the first practical spectroscope in 1859. This important development lead to the discovery of new elements. Spectrographic equipment improved greatly during the late 1800s and early 1900s with the introduction of mass spectrography, in 1920; flame photometry, in 1928; and radiochemical methods developed after World War II.

Perhaps the greatest innovations in the history of this industry related to the development of chromatography. Although first conceived in 1903, workable chromatography equipment was not built until the early 1940s. Gas chromatography and other advanced techniques that emerged during the 1950s significantly expanded the breadth of the analytical instrument industry. These pivotal innovations, combined with steady market growth during the post-World War II economic expansion, resulted in healthy revenue gains for instrument manufacturers. The United States assumed a global technological lead that it enjoyed throughout the 1960s and 1970s.

Although shipments of all types of U.S. laboratory equipment surged during the 1980s, not until 1987 did the U.S. government classify analytical instruments as a separate industry. By that time, sales of goods in this sector had grown to about $3.5 billion and were rising rapidly compared to most laboratory equipment industries. Indeed, sales jumped 11.5 percent in both 1988 and 1989, and, in 1990, as the U.S. economy slumped into a recession, shipments grew 14 percent to almost $5.0 billion, then increased more slowly to $5.8 billion in 1995. In addition to steady growth in domestic demand, U.S. producers reaped the benefits of a global interest in their high-technology products. U.S. exports soared from $1.3 billion in 1989 to nearly $2.7 billion in 1996, while imports climbed more slowly, from $654 million to only $1.3 billion during the same period.

CURRENT CONDITIONS

The laboratory analytical instruments industry prospered during the 1990s because of four key factors: (1) the increased concern over the spread of viruses, such as acquired immune deficiency syndrome (AIDS); (2) an intensified quest for new drugs by pharmaceutical com-

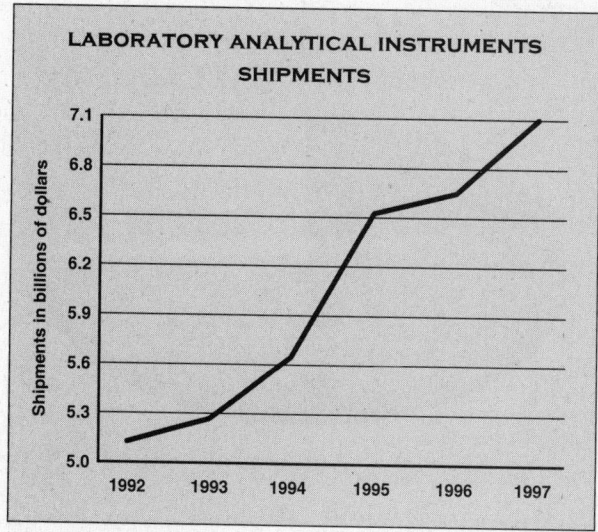

LABORATORY ANALYTICAL INSTRUMENTS SHIPMENTS

panies; (3) a proliferation of environmental concerns and regulations, and; (4) strong demand overseas for high-technology, high-profit instruments. As a result, industry shipments rose approximately 22 percent between 1990 and 1995 to over $6.0 billion. Furthermore, exports grew about 6 percent in 1996 to nearly $2.7 billion.

During the same time that manufacturers in this industry were boosting sales and profit margins on high-technology items, many were also increasing their profits through gains in productivity. Increased automation, advanced information systems, and management restructuring allowed many competitors to cut costs. Thus, for the average industry participant the amount of value added during the manufacturing process increased over 34 percent between 1989 and 1995 to $6 billion. At the same time, the size of the workforce grew less than 13 percent, from 68,400 to approximately 77,000, about 46 percent of which, or 35,300, were production workers. Gains in productivity were partly offset by higher research and development costs.

In the mid-1990s, manufacturers focused on product quality and customer service to help them regain the rampant growth they enjoyed during the late 1980s. They also emphasized new product introductions. Environmental and pharmaceutical markets offered the strongest growth domestically. But demand from food processing, biotechnology, and chemical industries remained relatively healthy.

In the long term, makers of laboratory analytical instruments were predicted to become increasingly dependent on sales of advanced technology products utilized by highly industrialized nations. Gas chromatography and mass spectrometry equipment were anticipated to be major growth segments, as were several newer niche product groups, such as capillary electrophoresis devices. Markets for low-technology products were ex-

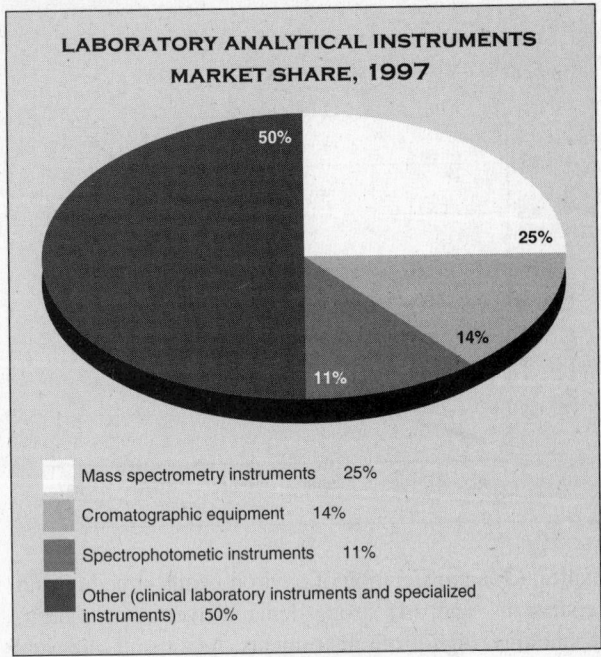

LABORATORY ANALYTICAL INSTRUMENTS MARKET SHARE, 1997

50%

25%

14%

11%

Mass spectrometry instruments   25%

Cromatographic equipment   14%

Spectrophotometic instruments   11%

Other (clinical laboratory instruments and specialized instruments)   50%

pected to be controlled by low-cost producers in emerging regions, such as Mexico and East Asia.

INDUSTRY LEADERS

Market share in the laboratory analytical instruments industry is concentrated, with a few industry leaders controlling the market. High start-up costs and rigid technological requirements discourage new entrants. Beckman Coulter, headquartered in Fullerton, California, is the largest manufacturer, attaining its status through the acquisition of Coulter by Beckman Instruments in 1997. In 1998, its sales reached $1.7 billion and its workforce nearly 10,000 employees worldwide.

Thermo Instruments Systems, Inc. (Waltham, Massachusetts), a subsidiary of Thermo Electron Corporation, had 1998 sales of $1.6 billion and 9,700 employees. The company has several subsidiaries that produce measurement instruments for a range of industries, including industrial production, food and beverage production, life sciences research, and medical diagnostics.

PerkinElmer Corporation, (formerly EG&G) of Wellesley, Massachusetts, generated $1.4 billion in 1998 sales while employing 13,000 people. About 60 percent of PerkinElmer's sales come from outside the United States.

Close behind is PE Corporation, which sold its Perkin-Elmer name to EG&G in 1999. The company develops, markets, and supports systems consisting of instruments, reagents, and software used in basic life science research, pharmaceutical research and development, diagnostics, forensics, and food testing. PE Corporation had 1999 sales of $1.2 billion and 3,800 employees.

WORKFORCE

Despite expectations for market growth, future employment opportunities in this industry are questionable. The number of employees was slightly less in 1997 than in 1995, with most labor positions expected to decline 15 to 50 percent between 1995 and 2005, according to the U.S. Bureau of Labor.

Positions for managers, engineers, and sales professionals are expected to diminish about 10 percent. Although workers in the laboratory analytical instruments business will probably fare better than their counterparts in related industries, continued productivity gains, consolidation, and the movement of some manufacturing activities overseas will likely thwart long-term job growth.

AMERICA AND THE WORLD

The U.S. laboratory analytical industry is the most advanced and productive in the world. Despite lower sales to Canada and western Europe, total exports, which constitute 11 percent of product shipments, grew 5 percent, reaching $178 million in current dollars. Much of this growth came from healthy sales in East Asia. In Japan, U.S. producers achieved an impressive $170 million annual surplus by 1991. Foreign demand for advanced proprietary gear remained strong going into the mid-1990s. Japan, with significant research and development in process, replaced Canada as the major U.S. export market. U.S. exports to Europe dropped in the mid-1990s, because of competition and Europe's economic problems. U.S. imports nearly doubled, but exports more than doubled and so did the trade surplus, going from $618 million to $1.4 billion.

The export market for U.S. goods is extremely fragmented, suggesting solid long-term growth potential. Product categories realizing the greatest overseas demand in the mid-1990s included chromatographs and electrophoresis instruments, general chemical instruments, and viscosity measuring devices.

Demand is expected to increase with the growing biotechnology field, more stringent requirements for environmental testing, and increased capital spending by the pollution control, semiconductor, paper, automotive, and food industries. Development of new foods and flavors has increased both demand and sales of laboratory equipment for assessing moisture content, quality, and shelf life. U.S. sales to Europe were not expected to increase noticeably, because of their slow economic recovery. Exports to East Asia and Mexico are expected to grow, however, with imports remaining relatively flat in comparison.

Many competitors in the mid-1990s felt that a global industry presence was a necessity in light of rising development costs and maturing domestic markets.

RESEARCH AND TECHNOLOGY

Major technological trends in the mid-1990s included the proliferation of combined equipment, such as single units that integrated both chromatograph and spectrometer functions; smaller instruments, particularly portable environmental field equipment; increased quality and precision; and growth in information systems and robotics. The growth in information systems and robotics was evidenced by rising installations of laboratory information management systems (LIMS), as well as a growing demand for automated sample preparation systems for bio-pharmaceutical applications. A new system introduced in 1993, for example, handled multiple-sample preparation tasks and was operated by Windows-based personal computer software for easy use. Several other automation and robotics systems, offered by companies such as CRS Plus Inc. and Zymark Inc., were aimed at relatively inexperienced users that wanted to conduct complex sample preparations and analyses.

Similarly, manufacturers were also introducing easier-to-use chromatography and mass spectrometry devices. Advanced systems automatically optimized and tuned themselves during operation, thereby eliminating much of the practice and guesswork associated with conventional instruments. In addition, many newer instruments combined up to three major functions into one unit. While these high-technology workhorses were regularly priced at more than $200,000, they were typically easier to operate and less expensive than two or more side-by-side units with commensurate capabilities.

In early 1997, MEMS, also known as micro-electromechanical systems, began to make their appearance with the promise of an impact as profound as the microchip. Many small American companies are bringing new MEMS applications to the market.

In December 1999, Beckman Coulter and Third Wave Technologies announced a high-throughput automation platform that provides researchers access to an automated nucleic acid analysis platform for SNP (single nucleotide polymorphism). SNPs are differences in genetic codes that account for variations among people and are believed to determine susceptibility to many diseases and individual responsiveness to treatments. This analysis tool is expected to make it possible to cost-effectively develop and use tens of thousands of individual pharmacogenetic assays that will be required for drug development, clinical trials, patient profiling, and personalized medicine.

FURTHER READING

International Trade Administration. "U.S. Aggregate Foreign Trade Data." *U.S. Foreign Trade Highlights.* Available from http://www.ita.doc.gov/tradestats/.

Markoff, John. "New Wave in High-Tech: Deus Ex(Tiny) Machina." *The New York Times,* 27 January 1997.

"Third Wave Technologies and and Beckman Coulter Team-Up for Automation of High Throughput SNP Studies." Beckman Coulter Press Release, 21 December, 1999.

U.S. Bureau of the Census. *1997 Economic Census—Manufacturing.* Washington: GPO, 1997. Available from http://www.census.gov.

U.S. Bureau of the Census. *Annual Survey of Manufactures.* Washington: GPO, 1996.

U.S. Bureau of the Census. *Current Industrial Reports: MA38B.* Washington: GPO, 21 October 1998. Available from http://www.census.gov/industry/ma38b97.txt.

Current Industrial Report. Washington: GPO, 1996.

SIC 3827

OPTICAL INSTRUMENTS AND LENSES

This category covers establishments primarily engaged in manufacturing instruments and apparatus that measure an optical property and optically project, measure, or magnify an image, such as binoculars, microscopes, prisms, and lenses. Included are establishments primarily engaged in manufacturing optical sighting and fire control equipment. Establishments engaged in manufacturing contact lenses and eyeglass frames and lenses are classified under **SIC 3851: Ophthalmic Goods.**

NAICS CODE(S)

333314 (Optical Instrument and Lens Manufacturing)

INDUSTRY SNAPSHOT

Companies in this industry manufacture a plethora of devices, including weapon-firing control mechanisms, optical laser-sighting systems, binoculars, borescopes, camera lenses, contour projection apparatus, gun sights, opera glasses, interferometers, microscopes, telescopes, periscopes, and spyglasses. Most devices in this industry use lenses. Some products, however, do not utilize lenses, such as rifle-aiming circles and some types of surveying equipment; they simply help users to align or measure objects. Electronic optical devices that do not use glass or plastic lenses, like the electron microscope, are classified elsewhere.

Long-term growth in the industry will depend on the ability of U.S. companies to continue to introduce new optical technologies and improve on existing ones, such as advanced laser-optics, new liquid-crystal devices, and scanning equipment. The latter, used for business, home, security, and banking purposes, has been one of the most promising areas for the optical industry. Infotrends Research Group Inc. predicted that 8 million scanners would be sold by the year 2000.

ORGANIZATION AND STRUCTURE

The largest segment of this industry—about one-third of industry sales—is sighting, tracking, and fire control equipment, much of which is used in missile systems, combat aircraft, and other defense applications. Optical test and inspection equipment, which makes up about 7 percent of sales, includes a variety of mechanisms. Much of it is used by other industries, like automobiles and steel, for quality control and other purposes. About 4 percent of industry output is in the form of binoculars and astronomical instruments, and about 3 percent consists of microscopes. About half of the industry's sales are garnered from miscellaneous devices.

Most products in the industry use compound (more than one) lens systems. A series of several convex and/or concave lenses often is used to magnify light reflected from an image. Although a single convex lens theoretically will focus incoming light, such a system typically suffers from defects that cause blurring and distortion. Therefore, many lens systems, such as those in cameras, use eight or more lenses in series or cemented together to reduce aberration, coma (blurring), and distortion.

Lenses typically are manufactured from glass in a process called grinding. First, the glass is cast in blocks, strips, panes, and rods, or it may be molded into a rough lens form. Then it is cut and rough-ground using a diamond abrasive on a grinding wheel. Fine grinding is accomplished using a silicon carbide or emery abrasive. For fine optical instruments, final polishing may take several hours using a precise lapping tool. Finally, the edge of the lens is ground so that its axis is centered precisely. Sometimes the lens is coated with a substance that reduces distortion. In addition to glass, transparent plastics also are used for lenses. They are simply molded, rather than ground.

BACKGROUND AND DEVELOPMENT

Modification of simple glass lenses has been practiced since ancient times, but the development of compound lens devices did not occur until 1600. That year, Dutch lensmaker Hans Jannsen and his son, Zacharias, mounted sliding lenses in a tube to form the first simple microscope. In 1611, a compound lens system that used a convex lens in the microscope's eyepiece was built by Johannes Kepler.

Historians often credit Hans Lippershey of Holland with inventing the telescope in 1608, when he accidentally aligned two lenses of opposite curvature and different focal length. The concept, however, may have been first understood in the thirteenth century by friar Roger Bacon. Galileo Galilei developed the first lens, or refracting, astronomical telescope in 1609. Christian Huygens improved Galileo's design soon afterward, with a telescope that reduced aberration. While these simple devices suffered a variety of defects, they achieved useful results.

During the remainder of the seventeenth century, compound optical instruments were vastly improved to increase magnifying power and reduce distortion. Important developments included Isaac Newton's design of a reflecting telescope that used mirrors to reduce aberration in 1668. Innovations during the eighteenth century largely reduced aberration and distortion in both telescopes and microscopes, resulting in apparatus that closely resembled the instruments commonly used during most of the twentieth century.

Early in the twentieth century, optical apparatus manufacturers focused on increasing power, or magnification. New lens manufacturing and mounting techniques allowed significant gains in this area. Conventional glass lens magnifying technology, however, was approaching its limit. Large refracting lenses suffered from distortion caused by sagging under their own weight. After World War II, scientists began searching for optical instruments that used alternatives to glass lenses, such as radio waves and magnetic lenses, to improve microscope and telescope devices.

In addition to the development of optical devices that did not use glass lenses, new types of optical devices emerged during the mid-1900s. Optical apparatus that could be used to control laser beams, for example, became an important industry offering. And the creation of new electro-optical devices opened up entirely new markets in other industries. By the 1980s, electro-optical equipment was being used to analyze and control manufacturing processes, guide missiles, operate audio-visual systems, and perform many other functions. Optical interferometers, for example, were developed to measure wavelengths, and optical metallographs were created to study the structure of metals and their compounds.

CURRENT CONDITIONS

According to the U.S. Census Bureau, there were at least 500 companies engaged in the manufacturing of optical instruments and lenses in 1997. The industry employed approximately 20,300 persons, and generated about $3.08 billion in revenues. States with the most establishments in the industry were California, Massachusetts, and New York. The industry could be divided into two major product classes: more than two-thirds of revenues came from companies manufacturing optical lenses and equipment (such as binoculars, camera and microscope lenses, and astronomical instruments), while the remaining segment of the industry produced optical sighting, tracking, and fire-control equipment.

RESEARCH AND TECHNOLOGY

In the late 1990s, several new optical products appeared on the market, keeping industry leaders in keen competition. On the verge of widespread product application were "switchable optical elements" (SOEs)—new devices that combined diffractive structures with electro-optical components. Potential commercial applications of SOEs included reading glasses that changed magnification degrees electronically, windows that redirected sunlight to the ceiling for more diffuse room light, camera lenses that zoomed from wide-angle to telescopic without moving parts, and sunglasses with lenses that darkened with the flip of a small switch located in the frame.

With much of the demand coming from the military and law enforcement sectors, a rapid increase in commercial applications was expected in the night-vision optical device market (including night-vision goggles and scopes), which had grown to $404 million by 1997.

In 1999 scientists optically recorded the most volatile cosmic eruption ever detected—capturing a gamma ray burst from 9 billion light-years away. The images were taken at the Los Alamos National Laboratory with a telephoto camera having the acronym of ROTSE-1 (Robotic Optical Transient Search Experiment 1). The system incorporated space satellites that, upon detecting bursts, alerted ground telescopes that in turn scanned the sky in the identified region.

On the forefront of telescopic technology was the linear tracking of stellar/heavenly bodies, replacing traditional tape encoders. In 1998 the first Heidenhain LIDA 105C exposed linear encoder was supplied to an 8m Gemini telescope on the top of Mauna Kea, Hawaii; the second was to be added to another 8m Gemini in Cerro Pachon, Chile, after its completion at the TELAS/NFM factory in France in the year 2000. These systems allowed telescopes to pinpoint specific areas of the sky with extreme accuracy.

FURTHER READING

Aguirre, Edwin L. "Imaging Totality." *Sky & Telescope,* July 1999, 136.

Cowen, R. "Catching a Burst's Visible Glow." *Science News,* 30 January 1999, 70.

Darnay, Arsen J., ed. *Manufacturing USA,* 5th ed. Detroit: Gale Research, 1996.

Dorminey, Bruce. "Into Infinity." *The Financial Times,* 10 September 1996.

Dykeman, John. "A Scanner at Your Desk?" *Managing Office Technology,* March 1996.

Farhi, Paul. "Vision III's Depth-Defining Feat." *Washington Post,* 4 March 1996, WB15.

Konish, Nancy, and Richard Gawel. "Lethal Lenses Make a Move to Mainstream Markets." 22 March 1999. Available from http://www.searchnet.com.

McEvoy, Christopher. "SGB Survey: Optics '97." *Sporting Goods Business,* December 1996.

McRae, Bill. "Focus on Quality." *Outdoor Life,* August 1999.

"New Products." *Science,* 22 January 1999, 559.

Parker, Bill. "Switchable Optical Elements Merge Optics and Electronics." *Laser Focus World,* March 1999.

Tejada, Carlos. "Scanners Finally Find a Place in Homes." *The Wall Street Journal,* 20 May 1996.

Tracy, Brian. "Wachovia Moves Into Check Imaging Elite." *American Banker,* 3 April 1995.

U.S. Census Bureau. *1997 Economic Census.* Washington: GPO, 1999.

Ward's Business Directory of U.S. Private and Public Companies. Detroit: Gale Research, 1996.

Warren, Susan. "Souped-Up Shades." *The Wall Street Journal,* 14 June 1999, B1.

"Way to the Stars With Optical Tracking." *Design Engineering,* February 1999.

Zimmerman, Denise. "Star Market to Install Self-Scanning Stations in One Unit." *Supermarket News,* 12 February 1996.

SIC 3829

MEASURING AND CONTROLLING DEVICES, NOT ELSEWHERE CLASSIFIED

This industry is comprised of companies primarily engaged in manufacturing a multitude of miscellaneous monitoring instruments. Major industry product segments include aircraft engine instruments; nuclear radiation detection and monitoring instruments; commercial, geophysical, meteorological, and general-purpose instruments and equipment; and physical properties testing and inspection equipment. This industry also encompasses companies that produce selected surveying and drafting supplies, such as transits, slide rules, and T-squares, as well as other measuring and controlling devices. For more information on the history of measuring devices, see other entries in SIC group 382.

NAICS CODE(S)

339112 (Surgical and Medical Instrument Manufacturing)
334519 (Other Measuring and Controlling Device Manufacturing)

The main customers of the aircraft engine instruments segment are General Electric (GE), United Technologies, Rolls Royce, and other aircraft manufacturers. The sector shipped temperature, pressure, vacuum, fuel and oil flow-rate sensors, and other measuring devices valued at $511 million in 1997. Growth in this market is linked to aircraft production.

Most of the $490 million in products shipped by the nuclear radiation detection and monitoring segment were shipped to the U.S. Department of Energy, U.S. Department of Defense, and nuclear power plants. These products included radiation detection instruments, radiation dosage monitoring instruments, pulse analyzers, and nuclear spectrometers. The segment's growth hinges on defense R&D spending.

Commercial, geophysical, meteorological, and general-purpose instruments and equipment is the second largest segment in the measuring and controlling devices industry. Valued at more than $1.5 billion, product shipments include weather forecasting and other meteorological instruments, seismic detection, petroleum exploration, and other geophysical instruments. This segment's growth is affected by the nation's economy.

Physical properties testing and inspection equipment, with product shipments valued at some $1.6 billion, is the industry's largest segment. R&D investment by durable goods manufacturers spurs demand for the physical properties testing instruments, physical properties inspection equipment, and kinematic testing equipment produced by this segment.

Construction activity affects growth in the surveying and drafting instruments and apparatus segment. Surveying equipment comprises 80 percent of the $345 million in product shipments. Shipments of another industry segment, other measuring and controlling devices, have a value of $570 million.

After 1950, rising demand for measuring and controlling devices by aerospace, nuclear, and petroleum industries pushed industry revenues to about $2 billion by the end of the 1970s. Likewise, increased defense spending and general U.S. economic growth, combined with steady export gains, almost doubled revenues during the 1980s. Indeed, as aerospace and nuclear device sales proliferated, overall industry sales grew at an average rate of 7 percent between 1982 and 1990, to more than $4 billion. Exports represented 40 percent of total shipments.

Although industry employment remained steady during the 1980s—at about 37,000 workers—increased automation and the movement of some manufacturing activities overseas resulted in work force cutbacks during the 1990s. In fact, by 1996 the work force as a whole had dropped 17 percent from 1990, and production workers fell 11 percent since 1992.

Sharp cutbacks in defense spending and the virtual cessation of new nuclear facility construction in the United States rattled industry participants in the early 1990s. Despite some domestic setbacks, the demand for meteorological measuring devices continued to grow, and exports surged. Sales in physical properties testing took up the rest of the slack in the industry, passing up

meteorological measuring in 1995 as the biggest division within the industry in terms of sales dollars. Total value of shipments in 1995 was $4.6 billion, with physical properties accounting for $1.5 billion of that total, and meteorological measuring devices accounting for $1.4 billion. Although imports increased, exports still held a commanding 40 percent of sales, thus bringing the trade surplus down to $1.1 billion.

The industry was fragmented in comparison to other U.S. manufacturing sectors, with an estimated 908 companies competing in the late 1990s. The average industry participant employed only 38 workers in 1994, compared to 49 for all other U.S. manufacturing firms. Most firms were specialized, and only two of the top 20 companies made above $500 million in revenue. A large number of the firms were small, though the larger ones continued to grow. In the early 1990s, most top firms employed less than 400 people. Through 1996, each of the top 20 companies employed more than 700 people. By 1997, the number of establishments operating in this industry had dropped to 853, employing 33,904 workers, and shipping products valued at $5.1 billion.

The top suppliers in the industry include AMETEK, Inc., with 1998 corporate-wide sales of $927.5 million; National Instruments Corporation, with 1998 corporate-wide sales of $274.2 million; and MTS Systems Corp., whose Sensors Division had sales between $10 and $25 million.

Through 2003, the miscellaneous measuring and controlling devices industry is projected to grow at an annual rate of 3 percent. Aircraft engine instruments is predicted to be one of the industry's faster growing segments. Furthermore, the addition of software and services will contribute to overall industry growth, as will further expansion into overseas markets. The top five export markets in 1997 were Canada, Mexico, Japan, United Kingdom, and Germany; these five countries were also the top import countries that year. 1999 estimates forecasted 33 percent of measuring and controlling instruments product shipments would be exported, while 25 percent of U.S. production would be imported.

FURTHER READING

"Current Industrial Reports: Other Measuring and Controlling Device Manufacturing - 1997." U.S. Department of Commerce. Bureau of the Census. November 1999. Available from http://www.census.gov/prod/ec97/97m3345j.pdf.

Darnay, Arsen J., ed. Manufacturing USA; Industry Analyses, Statistics, and Leading Companies. Detroit: Gale Research Inc., 1996.

"Financial News." Vishay Intertechnology, Inc., 4 April 1997. Available from http://vishay.com/vishay/news/freleases/FourthQ.html.

Hoover's Online Company Capsules. Available from http://www.hoovers.com/.

U.S. Industry and Trade Outlook '99. McGraw-Hill and U.S. Department of Commerce, 1999.

SIC 3841

SURGICAL AND MEDICAL INSTRUMENTS AND APPARATUS

This category covers establishments primarily engaged in manufacturing medical, surgical, ophthalmic, and veterinary instruments and apparatus. Establishments primarily engaged in manufacturing surgical and orthopedic appliances are classified in **SIC 3842: Orthopedic, Prosthetic, and Surgical Appliances and Supplies;** those manufacturing electrotherapeutic and electromedical apparatus are classified in **SIC 3845: Electromedical and Electrotherapeutic Apparatus;** and those manufacturing X-ray apparatus are classified in **SIC 3844: X-ray Apparatus and Tubes and Related Irradiation Apparatus.**

NAICS CODE(S)

339112 (Surgical and Medical Instrument Manufacturing)

INDUSTRY SNAPSHOT

The first medical instruments of precision were used in the seventeenth century. Not until the eighteenth century was surgery recognized as a specific science. Rapid technological advances in the twentieth century have given the United States the most advanced surgical device industry in the world. In addition to serving a critical role in the care of Americans, the medical and surgical instrument business has the added benefit of being a nonpolluting industry that employs more than 100,000 individuals.

ORGANIZATION AND STRUCTURE

Major consumers of industry output in order of market size, include foreign consumers, the federal government, medical and health services, doctors and dentists, hospitals, individual consumers, and drug companies.

Like other knowledge-based businesses, the medical and surgical products industry is growing rapidly. However, unlike many technology businesses, barriers to entry are significant. Companies often must incur huge start-up costs to cover research and product development. Furthermore, acute technical expertise typically is needed to develop proprietary knowledge necessary to differentiate products from others in the marketplace and to obtain approvals and patents. Companies that overcome these hurdles, however, can reap large profits if their products succeed.

Products. The industry encompasses a plethora of nonelectric diagnostic and therapeutic surgical devices. "Diagnostic" equipment is used to identify physical problems based on signs and symptoms. Therapeutic devices treat ailments and illnesses. Some of the largest general categories of equipment are hand instruments, monitoring equipment, intravenous apparatus, syringes, and catheters.

Examples of hand instruments include forceps, knives, saws, retractors, clamps, bone drills, and other products. Forceps are used to grasp, pull, and hold objects during delicate operations. Several monitoring devices also exist. Gastroscopes, for instance, are used to view the interior of the stomach. Cystoscopes provide a view of the interior of the bladder. Likewise, a laryngoscope is used to study the larynx and vocal cords. Ophthalmoscopes permit inspection of the retina, and stethoscopes are used to listen to internal organs, particularly the heart and lungs. Intravenous equipment basically consists of IV transfusion apparatus, which transfer blood or other fluids into the body.

Catheters, an important industry segment, are tubes that are inserted into various body cavities to drain liquids or remove material. Cardiac catheterization involves introducing a small catheter into a vein and then passing it into the heart. This procedure allows doctors to get accurate diagnostic measurements or to clear blocked arteries. A more advanced procedure, angioplasty, incorporates a tiny balloon into the procedure. As an ultra-thin catheter is slipped into an artery, the balloon is inflated, widening clogged arteries. Catheters are also used to drain urine and other bodily fluids.

Other devices produced in the industry include tonometers, speculums, skin grafting equipment, sphygmomanometers, silt lamps, hypodermic rifles, surgical probes, operating tables, needle holders, inhalators, and bone plates and screws.

Federal Regulation. An important dynamic influencing the industry's production and profitability is Food and Drug Administration (FDA) regulation. The FDA is responsible for insuring that all products sold in the industry comply with federal safety standards. The FDA possesses the authority to recall products, temporarily suspend devices it deems high-risk, and impose monetary penalties for violations.

The 1990 Safe Medical Devices Act (SMDA), which defined procedures for bringing medical products to the market, is one of the most significant pieces of legislation governing producers. Among other stipulations, the SMDA requires certain manufacturers to track patients that should be notified in case of product failure; submit follow-up reviews for certain implants and devices; and, when applying for pre-market clearance, provide a summary of safety and effectiveness data for each device.

One practice presently under FDA review is the reuse of disposable medical instruments approved for one-time use only. Without much federal oversight and against devise maker's advice, hospitals often take intrusive medical devices, apply toxic chemicals and then sterilize at high temperatures. Prompted by the cost-cutting pressures demanded by managed care, this little-known practice has spawned a "reprocessing" industry with revenues in excess of $40.0 million.

Every year, nearly 2.0 million patients become sick and 90,000 die from infections contracted while in the hospital. There is no hard data at present linking infection with the reuse of disposable medical equipment, but the savings resulting from recycling are easy to calculate. For example, an argon beam plasma coagulation probe used to stop bleeding in the gastrointestinal tract costs $190. If used 10 times it would cost $24 per procedure, even when the cost of cleaning and sterilizing is added.

Hospital administrators and the reprocessing companies on whom they increasingly depend say equipment manufacturers are raising false claims to protect sales. But the Association of Disposable Device Manufacturers says patient safety, not corporate profits, is the real issue.

BACKGROUND AND DEVELOPMENT

In the early 1600s, an Italian professor named Sanctorious was the first doctor to employ diagnostic instruments of precision in the practice of medicine. Using a pendulum made from a cord and a weight, he was able to measure a pulse rate by adjusting the weight until it swung at an even tempo with the patient's pulse. Sanctorious later implemented a type of thermometer that could measure a patient's weight and temperature. Both inventions were influenced by his friend Galileo.

The seventeenth and eighteenth centuries produced several advancements in surgical and anatomical knowledge. Noted physicians such as Englishmen William Harvey, John Monro, Robert Sibbald, and Archibald Pitcairne contributed to the science and helped establish some of the first formal educational institutions for doctors. Microscopes, injection needles, and instruments of dissection were a few of the tools that allowed researchers of that period to gain a comprehensive understanding of the internal human structure, as well as of physiological processes.

The most important American contribution to the advancement of surgery came in the mid-1800s when doctors Crawford Long, Gardner Colton, and Horace Wells perfected the use of ether and nitrous oxide anesthetics. The nineteenth century also brought important inventions such as the ophthalmoscope, the sphygmomanometer (for measuring blood pressure), and the stethoscope. Invented in 1816, the first stethoscope consisted of a perforated wooden cylinder that transmitted sounds from the patient's chest to the doctor's ear. Perhaps more important than new instruments, though, was a gradual understanding of germs. This evolution led to the use of antiseptics, as well as surgical caps, masks, and rubber gloves in the 1890s.

While surgical tools and techniques advanced throughout the eighteenth and nineteenth centuries, surgery remained a relatively crude science up until the early 1900s. Despite their knowledge of germs, most surgeons before 1910 continued to operate without gloves, masks, or caps. They commonly wore the same smock until it was caked with blood from several surgeries and would continue using instruments that had been dropped on the floor. Surgery was usually performed in a theater-type setting before an audience as the patient lay on a narrow wooden table. Instruments were usually forged steel and had wooden or ivory handles. Because amputation was one of the most common procedures, the saw was a favored tool.

Better anesthetics, specialized surgeons, and X-ray machines prompted a transition to more scientific surgery and the demand for more sophisticated instruments. New materials, such as stainless steel and plastics, broadened the scope of the device and apparatus industry. New equipment such as catheters, suction devices, intravenous infusion apparatus, and various mechanical and electrical diagnostic devices opened up new surgical specialties, such as neurosurgery and cardiac and urinary tract surgery.

Instruments and apparatus introduced in the postwar period were numerous. Inert metals, such as vitalium and tantalum, were used to create wire and mesh devices that could be left inside the body. Nylon thread and special plastics revolutionized heart surgery. Orlon tubes became arteries, while plastic sponges patched heart defects.

By 1980, the medical instrument and apparatus industry shipped nearly $4.0 billion worth of products each year. Such dynamic sales growth since the 1960s was attributable to several factors. Employer-sponsored health care systems developed after World War II offered few incentives for providers to control costs. As a result, expenditures on instruments and apparatus, as well as other health care products and services, ballooned. In fact, throughout the 1970s and 1980s, U.S. health care expenditures rose at a rate of more than 10 percent per year.

During the 1970s and 1980s, one factor attributable to growth in health care expenditures was increased demand for health care. Largely, the development of more advanced procedures and equipment spurred growth by enabling the health care industry to deliver more comprehensive and higher quality care. Indeed, U.S. expenditures on health care jumped from 6 percent to more than 15 percent of the gross domestic product (GDP). Some of the fastest growing segments included instruments for angioplasty, cardiac catheterization, and orthopedic operations.

As expenditures leapt during the 1980s, development and sales of instruments and apparatus blossomed. While manufacturers made massive investments in product research and development, yearly expenditures on industry products often jumped to more than 10 percent between 1980 and 1990. Furthermore, exports continued to grow as foreign markets looked to the United States as a source of state-of-the-art surgical instruments and apparatus. Throughout the 1980s, in fact, U.S. firms dominated more than 50 percent of the world market for surgical supplies.

By 1990, the medical instrument and apparatus industry was generating more than $10.0 billion worth of products each year. Stellar sales growth was attributable to several factors, the main one being employer-sponsored health care systems developed after World War II that offered few incentives for providers to control costs. As a result, expenditures on instruments and apparatus, as well as other health care products, grew at an annual rate of 10 percent throughout the latter decades of the twentieth century.

Despite strong growth and optimism, competitors were facing significant obstacles to continued profitability as they entered the mid-1990s. Growing regulatory costs and barriers, decreased access to investment capital, and increased competition in the health care industry all posed formidable challenges. Furthermore, some large segments of market sales (such as catheters) appeared to be entering a stage of maturity; the result meant slower growth and reduced profit margins.

According to the 1993 *MDDI* survey that polled industry executives, inadequate funding for growth and research and development was a primary concern. Although a traditionally significant source of medical device research and development funding, declining venture capital was a major reason for the shortfall. As FDA regulations increased, venture capitalists viewed new projects as riskier.

FDA Stymies New Products. Besides a capital shortage and the threat of nationalized health care, the most prolific problem facing manufacturers in the early 1990s was a slowdown in FDA product approvals. In 1993 producers were still scrambling to learn how to comply with stringent new product standards imposed by the 1990 Safe Medical Devices Act (SMDA). After the FDA's initiation of the SMDA, approvals for new products fell dramatically. Although the FDA received 5,000 applications for new de-

vices resembling products on the market in 1991 and 1992, the number of approved products slipped from 3,000 in 1991 to 2,500 in 1992. Furthermore, in mid-1993 the FDA had a backlog of 1,400 applications that had been pending for more than three months (historically, the norm was closer to 20). Product Marketing Applications (PMAs) showed even greater declines. Usually submitted at a rate of 60 to 70 per year, PMA approvals fell from 47 in 1990 to 27 in 1991, and to only 12 in 1992. The FDA was also under Congressional order to review 130 products that went on sale before 1976. FDA approval for new medical devices in 1996 took an average of 2.2 years, which was twice the amount of time the same process took in 1992.

In an effort to speed the process, the medical device industry began supporting proposed user fees. Under the proposal, firms were required to pay a fee for each application processed by the FDA. A similar fee system implemented in 1993 for pharmaceutical firms was costing that industry approximately $36 million per year. However, the FDA had reason for caution. It came under fire in the 1980s and 1990s for approving a heart valve connected with 300 deaths and for permitting the sale of silicone breast implants.

In response to FDA initiatives, the Medical Device Manufacturers Association (MDMA) was formed in November 1992. It succeeded the Small Manufacturers Medical Device Association that was established in 1980. The organization's focus was to ensure that FDA regulations did not adversely affect the industry, particularly smaller manufacturers.

Congress ultimately loosened the collar on the FDA's regulations of the surgical and medical instruments industry in 1996. U.S. companies no longer needed FDA approval for products intended solely for export. The provision ensured that Europe became the industry testing ground for U.S. companies.

By the close of the twentieth century, the medical and surgical equipment business had become one of America's leading export industries. It entered the new century with export sales of more than $4.5 billion. (When sales from opthomological devices are added in, export revenues jump to nearly $14.4 billion.) Ironically, Japan, America's leading competitor in this market sector, was also the biggest consumer, accounting for exports worth $731.4 million according to the U.S. Department of Commerce.

CURRENT CONDITIONS

Industry growth in sales during the 1990s was attributable to a promising new sphere of "minimally invasive" surgical instruments. These devices allowed surgeons to conduct complex operations without the pain, time, and expense associated with conventional procedures. Laparoscopic and endoscopic devices, for instance, involved the insertion of narrow tubes, called trocars, into a patient's abdomen. A laparoscope inserted into the tube is used to take pictures of the patient's inner organs, and miniature devices sent through the tube are used to perform complex surgical procedures. The market for minimally invasive devices was expected to explode in the 2000s.

Indeed, because of the changing dynamics of the health care market, cost-containment pressures were driving the growth of money-saving procedures like angioplasty and laparoscopy. As purchasing decisions in the 1980s and 1990s shifted from physicians to hospitals and managed care facilities, producers were being forced to demonstrate the cost effectiveness of their products. Devices that could reduce hospital stays, increase labor productivity, and facilitate patient care in less expensive settings had become the dominant growth market by the mid-1990s.

With the dawn of the new millennium came a promising new generation of ''minimally invasive'' surgical instruments. Many of these new devices originated in the lucrative field of sports medicine.

When San Francisco 49ers tight end Brent Jones dislocated his shoulder, he normally would have had to have surgery followed by six months or more of rehabilitation. Instead the 49ers team surgeon turned to a company called Oratex that made a slim probe only 2.3 millimeters wide. Inserting the probe through a puncture the size of a pencil point, doctors were able to tighten Jones's distended ligaments by bombarding the ligament's collagen with radio waves. Instead of being out for the season, Jones returned to the field in five weeks.

Often called ''electronic scalpels'', tiny probes were being used to treat damaged spinal disks in ways that would have been impossible with cut-and-sew surgery. Traditionally, back pain only can be eliminated by removing the damaged disk or fusing vertebrae with plates or rods. By the late 1990s, more than 700,000 people a year elected to have this surgery in the United States. Using a probe was much less invasive. Instead of slicing open the chest, a wire-like probe was inserted into a patient under local anesthetic. Inched into the gel-filled center of a damaged disk, the probe released a burst of radiation that shrank the stretched rings of collagen and cauterized inflamed blood vessels and nerves that had intruded into the damaged area.

The cost containment pressures flowing from managed healthcare, and the growing need for procedures like angioplasty and laparoscopy promoted increased use of probes which have been proven to reduce hospital stays, increase labor productivity, and facilitate patient care in less expensive settings.

An aging population requiring more health care will augment overall growth. In addition, U.S. firms were well positioned to take advantage of emerging foreign markets. Increased efficiency of the FDA approval process should diminish industry costs, though the high rate of investment in research and development is expected to continue.

INDUSTRY LEADERS

One of the largest manufacturers of surgical and medical instruments and apparatus is Baxter International Inc. and its subsidiary, Baxter Healthcare Corp. The Deerfield, Illinois, industry giant had $6.6 billion in sales in 1998.

Siemens Medical Systems, Inc. of New Jersey, a subsidiary of Siemens in Germany, employed 4,500 people in the United States during 1998 and had $1.7 billion in sales.

Other companies with significant international sales are Medtronic of Minneapolis, Minnesota, ($4.1 billion in 1998 sales); Becton, Dickinson & Co. of Franklin Lakes, New Jersey ($3.1 billion); Boston Scientific Corp. ($2.2 billion); and United States Surgical Corp. ($1.2 billion in 1997).

Despite the dominance of a few massive competitors, such as Baxter and Siemens, the industry remains relatively unconcentrated. Like most growth industries, revenues are spread among many niche firms that have developed proprietary products or production techniques, or excel at marketing or distribution.

One of the most active is Colorado MEDtech of Boulder, Colorado, which makes medical equipment ranging from catheters and respiratory equipment to radio frequency amplifiers used in magnetic resonance imaging systems. In 1999, *Forbes* magazine named it one of the 200 best small companies in America based on $65.0 million in annual sales and a 36.1 percent return on equity. One other small company admired by analysts is Priority Healthcare of Altamonte Springs, Florida. It distributes specialty pharmaceuticals and medical supplies to oncologists, outpatient dialysis centers and home care markets.

WORKFORCE

Difficulties gaining FDA approval have caused some U.S. companies in this industry to focus their attention overseas when introducing products. One study conducted by the Wilkerson Group for the Health Industry Manufacturers Association showed that roughly 10,000 industry jobs with average salaries of $50,000 are being exported yearly. But the flow of jobs, and to a lesser extent investment, is expected to decline as America's population continues to age.

More than 21,000 companies employing well over 100,000 people are licensed to produce medical devices in the United States. Assemblers and fabricators comprise 14 percent of the industry's workforce. Inspectors, testers, and graders accounted for 3.4 percent, and manufacturing supervisors made up 3.3 percent. Other blue-collar manufacturing positions represent an additional 60 percent of the workforce. Sales personnel accounted for 6 percent of nonlabor workers, while secretaries and clerical staff accounted for about 5 percent. Relatively high-paying engineering positions accounted for over 6 percent of the workforce, while white-collar managers and executives represented about 3.3 percent. Each job category is expected to grow, especially those in engineering, management and sales.

AMERICA AND THE WORLD

With roughly one-half ($2.7 billion) of Baxter International's 1996 sales coming from outside the United States, this industry giant more than doubled the 1993 surgical and medical instruments export figures of all U.S. companies ($2.6 billion). Although the U.S. share of the global medical device market fell from 60 percent in 1980 to about 50 percent in 1993, rapid expansion of global markets allowed domestic producers to sustain record export growth throughout that period. America's share of the world market was expected to decline to 40 percent by 2000, though export sales volume should rise steadily, even outpacing domestic growth.

As the century closed, the United States remained the world leader in medical device technology and maintained an especially dominant role in medical and dental instruments and supplies. But U.S. dominance did not go unchallenged. Japan and Germany made significant strides in some market segments, such as high-tech electromedical equipment and some diagnostic machines. Furthermore, Japan planned to increase its investment in medical device research and development to catch up with capital expenditures made by its U.S. and German counterparts.

Although Japan had the second largest market for medical devices in the world, it was hard to enter because of protectionist barriers. The Asian recession of the late 1990s also affected sales adversely. But as Japan's population continues to age, sales of U.S. made medical equipment was expected to increase. Other leading export markets remained the European Union, Canada, Mexico and Southeast Asia. The largest buyer of U.S. goods was Canada, followed closely by Japan and Germany. Those three countries, combined with France and Mexico, consumed around 50 percent of all industry exports.

RESEARCH AND TECHNOLOGY

Besides new product development, manufacturers were also concentrating on increased productivity going into the mid-1990s. A number of new flexible computer-integrated manufacturing techniques were being implemented. These techniques promised to synthesize manufacturing operations and promote international production standards. New information software had been developed, for instance, that helped device manufacturers integrate and manage software development, design changes, and testing data. The primary goal of such techniques was to reduce labor costs and increase productivity. Other companies were experimenting with cost-saving approaches like cellular manufacturing. By assigning a cell, or team, of workers responsibility for production of each product, some companies had increased productivity by 25 percent and improved product quality.

The medical and surgical device and apparatus industry is heavily driven by technological advances. For manufacturers that devised new and better devices to help remedy ailments and illnesses, care providers were afforded an enthusiastic market. Life-saving procedures that were unheard of before 1970, such as angioplasty and coronary bypass, were commonplace when the new millennium began. Industry profits boomed, partially as a result of the increased demand for these procedures.

New procedures accompanied new products. Shape-memory polymers, for instance, are polyurethane-based polymers that can undergo and retain dramatic changes in hardness, flexibility, elasticity, and vapor permeability when exposed to heat. Among other uses, the resins could be used to form catheters that remain stiff until inserted into the body. Similarly, new plastic springs offered an alternative to metal components in operations requiring resistance to corrosion and static charges.

Silicone balloon cuffs that could be made through extrusion, rather than molding, offered producers of laparoscopic and other devices the advantage of reduced production costs. Likewise, new injection-molded components provided more efficient prototyping of new instruments and devices. Other new or improved products included miniature cables, high-tensile wire, heat-shrinking tubing, and a variety of minimally invasive instruments.

FURTHER READING

Gianturco, Michael. "A Play on Catheterization." *Forbes,* 30 December 1996, 146.

Lane, Randall. "It's a Start." *Forbes,* 3 June 1996, 97-98.

Standard & Poor's Register CD. New York: McGraw-Hill Companies, Inc., 1997.

Kolata, Gina. "Single Use Medical Devices are Often Used Several Times." *New York Times,* 10 November 1999.

Weinberg, Neil. "Blood Money." *Forbes,* 22 March 1999.

McHugh, Josh. "The Electromagnetic Scalpel." *Forbes,* 5 October 1998.

SIC 3842

ORTHOPEDIC, PROSTHETIC, AND SURGICAL APPLIANCES AND SUPPLIES

This classification covers establishments primarily engaged in manufacturing orthopedic, prosthetic, and surgical appliances and supplies; arch supports and other foot appliances; fracture appliances, elastic hosiery, abdominal supporters, braces, and trusses; bandages; surgical gauze and dressings; sutures; adhesive tapes and medicated plasters; and personal safety appliances and equipment. Establishments primarily engaged in manufacturing surgical and medical instruments are classified in **SIC 3841: Surgical and Medical Instruments and Apparatus.** Establishments primarily engaged in manufacturing orthopedic or prosthetic appliances and in the personal fitting to the individual prescription by a physician are classified in **SIC 5999: Miscellaneous Retail Stores, Not Elsewhere Classified.**

NAICS CODE(S)

339113 (Surgical Appliances and Supplies Manufacturing)

INDUSTRY SNAPSHOT

During the 20th century, rapid medical advances spawned a huge market for all types of surgical and medical appliances and supplies. By the early 1990s, makers of devices classified in this industry were generating over $13 billion in annual sales and employing over 90,000 workers. They also maintained a nearly $1 billion trade surplus.

In the mid-1990s, surgical appliance and supplies manufacturers hoped to benefit from solid market growth that had characterized the industry for over two decades. However, several issues clouded the industry's future: slow product approvals from the Food and Drug Administration, the potential overhaul of the U.S. health care industry, and reduced availability of outside investment capital. In addition, several major players in the industry agreed to pay a total of $4.7 billion to as many as two million women who have experienced breast implant-related illnesses. Demographic factors and export opportunities, however, are regarded as sources of optimism for the industry.

ORGANIZATION AND STRUCTURE

The entire medical device industry, which is divided into six sub-industries, shipped about $42 billion worth of products in 1993. The surgical appliances industry described in this classification is the largest of those divisions, accounting for about 33 percent, or approximately $14.0 billion, of total medical product sales in 1995. In 1997 the industry shipped $14.7 billion worth of products.

The top five states by number of manufacturers for 1997 were California, with 238 establishments; Florida, with 113 establishments; Texas, with 111 establishments; New York, with 102 establishments; and Pennsylvania, with 86 establishments.

The industry experienced overall growth, large capital investment, and high profit margins in the early 1990s—often indicators that an industry has not yet reached maturity. While high-tech devices accounted for most revenue and profit, other segments offered limited opportunities. For example, personal safety equipment and some appliances, such as wheelchairs and crutches, represented sectors of modest growth.

Personal consumption expenditures accounted for about 22 percent of industry sales in the 1980s. Government purchases, including purchases through health care facilities and hospitals, consumed about 15 percent of industry output. Hospitals represented an additional 14 percent of the market, and doctors and dentists purchased about 4 percent of manufacturers goods. Approximately 14 percent of sales were attributable to exports, and 12 percent of industry revenues were classified as gross private-fixed investment in the early 1990s. Miscellaneous consumers, which accounted for the remaining 19 percent of sales, included child care services, construction industries, correctional and educational institutions, the U.S. Department of Defense, and police departments.

Products. Surgical, orthopedic, and therapeutic appliances and supplies accounted for over 88 percent of industry output in the late 1980s, with orthopedic and prosthetic appliances comprising the largest share. Orthopedic equipment refers to devices used in the preservation, restoration, and development of the form and function of the extremities and spine. The term ''prosthetic appliances'' in this industry refers to devices related to artificial limbs and joints. Popular hip and knee replacement devices, for instance, reduce pain and allow patients to regain mobility.

Prosthetic and orthopedic appliances represented approximately 20 percent of industry sales in the late 1980s. Artificial joints, the largest single segment, accounted for about 6.5 percent of total sales, while artificial limbs made up less than 0.5 percent of shipments. Electronic hearing aids represented over 3 percent of revenues, and elastic braces and supports represented about 1.2 percent of shipments. Additionally, arch supports accounted for 1.5 percent of sales, and replacement and add-on parts for orthopedic and prosthetic devices accounted for 12 percent of industry shipments. This industry segment also includes the following products: bone plates, screws, and nails; mechanical braces; elastic stockings; surgical corsets; splints and trusses; and intraocular lenses, or lens implants.

Therapeutic appliances and related supplies include a wide array of surgical dressings and devices. Surgical dressings, which include elastic bandages, plaster, gauze, and cotton swabs, represented nearly 13 percent of total industry sales in the late 1980s. Bed pads, adult diapers, and incontinent pads constituted an additional 6 percent share, and wheelchairs and other patient transport appliances accounted for about 2.5 percent of shipments. Examples of other products in this category are surgical kits, tongue depressors, breathing devices, and therapeutic whirlpool baths.

In addition to the 88 percent of the market represented by the products described above, this industry also encompasses a variety of personal and industrial safety equipment, which includes protective clothing, welders' hoods, motorcycle and racing helmets, fire-fighting suits and breathing apparatus, safety gloves, bullet-proof vests, ear and nose plugs, safety goggles, and space suits.

BACKGROUND AND DEVELOPMENT

Prosthetics date back to 600 B.C. during the Roman Empire, when artificial legs were used to help amputees regain mobility. It was not until the 16th century, through the efforts of French surgeon Ambroise Pare, that prosthetics became a science. His work lead to the development, during the 16th and 17th centuries, of replacements for upper extremities. Metal hands, some of which contained moving parts and springs, became popular prosthetics in Europe during the 1600s. They were replaced in the 1700s by two innovations: a single hook, or a leather-covered, nonfunctioning hand attached to the forearm by a leather or wooden shell.

Public acceptance of prostheses, as well as improvements in design, paralleled major wars during the 18th, 19th, and 20th centuries. In particular, World War I and World War II boosted the use of prosthetics, which benefited from the integration of new lightweight metals and better mechanical joints. Advances in materials and mechanical design proliferated during the post-World War II era, when the development of indwelling materials, such as coated steel, inactive metals, and durable synthetics, gave specialists new ways to replace or mend body joints and parts. New materials and mechanisms also made possible the creation of artificial limbs that more closely mimicked the natural body.

The term "orthopedics" was given to that specialty in 1741 by Nicholas Andre, a Frenchman. Orthopedic surgery originally applied only to the prevention and care of deformities in children. However, the branch soon grew to encompass treatment of extremities, the spine, and associated structures of all humans. The first institute dedicated to the treatment of skeletal deformities was established in Switzerland in the 18th century. One of the first notable devices introduced by the industry was the

Thomas Splint, which was used for leg fractures. An important U.S. leader in the development of therapeutic orthopedic devices was F.H. Albee (1876-1945), who developed the motor bone saw in 1909.

Rapid advances in medical technology caused a shift in orthopedic treatment during the 20th century from the use of braces, splints, and other mechanical devices, to surgical procedures. Such procedures incorporated implants and devices that helped surgeons perform such advanced operations as spinal reconstruction, skin grafts, tendon transplants, limb lengthening, restoration of shattered bones and joints, and bone grafts.

Surgical advances in the 20th century, which paralleled both orthopedic and prosthetic breakthroughs, greatly increased the demand for procedures and treatments that required apparatus developed and manufactured by the surgical appliance industry. In addition, generous employer-sponsored health care plans made large sums of insurance money available for such equipment. Indeed, as a result of overall increased U.S. expenditures on health care during the 1950s, 1960s, and 1970s, sales of orthopedic and prosthetic appliances skyrocketed. Sellers of surgical dressings and other supplies realized similar gains.

The 1980s. By 1980, the surgical appliance and supply business had grown into a $5.0 billion industry that employed over 40,000 workers. This growth epitomized the immense proliferation of U.S. health care expenditures, which rose at an annual rate of more than 15 percent throughout most of the 1960s and 1970s. By the early 1980s, in fact, Americans were spending more than 10 percent of their gross domestic product on health care. The demand for surgical appliances and supplies continued to balloon throughout the 1980s, as money spent on health care soared. Between 1982 and 1990, industry revenues grew an average of 8.6 percent annually. Moreover, despite manufacturing productivity gains, industry employment increased more than 25 percent during the same period, to exceed 85,000.

Driving revenue and profit growth during the decade was the development of high-tech, high-cost prosthetic and orthopedic devices. Better and stronger artificial joints, limbs, and associated devices allowed specialists to deliver treatments unheard of just a few years earlier. As surgical procedures in general increased, the demand for surgical dressings, drapes, and other supplies grew as well. Exports, too, provided significant profit opportunities.

Silicone Implant Settlement. In 1994 eight companies that manufactured silicone breast implants agreed to contribute nearly $4.7 billion to a fund for two million women worldwide who have had breast implants. The agreement marked the single largest product liability settlement in U.S. history. The fund was expected to cover routine testing, medical care, and surgery (including implant removal), for the next 30 years. As the *Detroit Free Press* noted, "the settlement attempts to resolve two and a half years of bitter controversy and one of the stormiest chapters in U.S. medical history." Companies making the largest contributions to the settlement were Bristol-Myers Squibb Co., Baxter Healthcare Corp., and Dow Corning Corp., once the country's foremost producer of implants.

Healthcare Recoveries, Baxter Healthcare, Bristol-Myers Squibb, McGhan Medical, 3M, and Union Carbide all participated in the $50 million silicon breast implant settlement, which originated in 1992. This was one of the first instances in which health care payers received medical expenses on a large scale involving a personal injury class-act suit. Dow Corning declined their original contribution and filed for bankruptcy protection in Michigan.

CURRENT CONDITIONS

Notwithstanding a U.S. economic downturn, surgical appliance and supply manufacturers continued to post solid gains in the early 1990s, although growth appeared to be slowing in comparison to the 1980s. Employment grew by roughly 3 percent between 1990 and 1995, to around 94,000. By 1997, however, employment in this industry had dropped 8.7 percent to around 81,800 workers.

Despite strong markets, medical device manufacturers faced several hurdles to continued success. Concerns emerged about a lack of outside investment capital necessary to fund research and development of new products, as analysts pointed to the uncertainties associated with various health care reform initiatives.

Industry participants were also suffering from cost-containment pressures, which particularly affected low-tech items such as surgical dressings, drapes, and sutures. Increasingly cost-conscious hospitals were working to ensure that prices of conventional supplies remained near the overall inflation rate. At the same time, domestic sales of personal and industrial safety equipment were down—a result of recessed construction and manufacturing activity in the early 1990s. Cost-containment pressures also hindered makers of orthopedic and prosthetic supplies. The average orthopedic implant, for instance, cost more than $2,400 in 1993.

Industry Regulations. Many manufacturers of such high-tech products were even more concerned with a slowdown in FDA new product approvals. New stringent approval requirements were keeping some new products out of the market and diminishing outside investment in new product development. FDA restrictions were expected to loosen, however, as a result of congressional pressures to quicken the FDA's new medical product review process.

As a result of product-use-related deaths and injuries—discussed at the AAMI/FDA's Human Factors in Medical Devices Conference in 1995—the FDA was to begin reviewing how medical devices are designed to prevent human error.

A 1996 California Supreme Court ruling addressed insufficient warnings on device labels. As a result of *Carlin v. The Superior Court of Sutter Court,* medical product makers now have to furnish adequate warnings of any possible risks that were known or "reasonably scientifically knowable." The Health Insurance Portability & Accountability Act of 1996 included additional clauses to prevent fraud, which could affect device and drug manufacturers.

The Future. A rise in services and procedures provided in outpatient settings will stimulate demand, as will an aging U.S. and world population. The home health care market, which includes kidney dialysis items that can be used in outpatient settings, implantable infusion pumps, and nutritional therapy products, was expected to realize significant profits as a result of the U.S. Congress's passage of the North American Free Trade Agreement (NAFTA).

INDUSTRY LEADERS

After the early 1990s, buyouts increased within the medical equipment supply industry because of increased demand for cost reduction and quality medical care, combined with a decrease in inpatient hospital usage and increase in outpatient care (outpatient surgery, home health care, and rehabilitation).

Merger and acquisition activity was also on the rise. In 1995, for example, Johnson & Johnson acquired Cordis, a top manufacturer of angioplasty and angiographic equipment, for $1.8 billion in stock. The largest infection control company, Steris Corporation, purchased Amsco International in 1996. These two companies had combined earnings of $45 million on $545 million in revenues for 1995 and combined assets worth approximately $450 million.

St. Jude Medical Incorporated acquired Cyberonics Incorporated (maker of implantable devices for epileptic seizure prevention) for $72 million in 1996. Medex Inc. was bought by Furon Co., California, for $160 million in 1996. Medex, a leader in plastic components, had sales of over $99 million in 1996. Its new company, Furon, makes silicones, thermoplastics elastomers, and thermoplastic polyurethanes, which were expected to help Medex expand its product line.

Tyco International Ltd.'s Healthcare Products Group was one of the largest suppliers in this industry, with sales of approximately $1.5 billion. Tyco International's growth was in part spurred by the purchase of Kendall

International Inc. of Massachusetts in 1994. In second place was St. Jude Medical Inc. of Minnesota, with approximately $1 billion in sales for 1998. Third, with approximately $500 million in sales, was Ethicon Endo-Surgery, Inc., a subsidiary of Johnson and Johnson.

WORKFORCE

The 1,634 companies primarily engaged in the industry employed 81,881 workers in 1997, representing a jump from less than 70,000 in the early 1980s. About 65 percent of the workforce—or 52,000 workers—held production jobs in 1997, up 3.7 percent from 1991. Production workers received an average hourly wage of $12.52. Assemblers and fabricators comprised about 15 percent of production positions. Positions in sales and marketing accounted for 7 percent of industry employment, and white collar administration jobs accounted for less than 3 percent.

A 1998 survey of 140 companies in this industry reported that 76 of these companies had increased their workforce by 10.4 percent. Of those, 26 had increased their workforce by 40.4 percent in the previous 12 month period.

The industry's workforce was expected to grow through the year 2000 and beyond. Manufacturing positions, for example, were expected to rise by 10 to 50 percent between 1990 and 2005, according to the Bureau of Labor Statistics. A few positions, however, such as electrical and electronic assemblers, were expected to fall by over 25 percent. Jobs in sales and marketing were likely to rise by more than 70 percent, and positions related to engineering, math, and science were expected to increase by 50 percent to 65 percent.

In 1997, California, had the largest number of surgical appliances and supplies employees, with 11,994 jobs. New Jersey had 6,521 employees, and Indiana had 6,384 employees.

AMERICA AND THE WORLD

As domestic prices and market growth declined in the early 1990s, manufacturers were increasingly looking overseas to boost profits. In 1989, surgical appliance and supplies producers exported less than 10 percent of their output, but then the rapid growth of foreign markets and the demand for high-tech implanted devices led a surge of export growth. Because U.S. medical equipment producers offered the most advanced products in the world, they controlled approximately 50 percent of the world export market in 1990. Between 1990 and 1993, the industry increased exports by an average of 18.3 percent annually. By 1993, the industry shipped nearly 14 percent, or $1.87 billion, of its total production overseas, with Canada, Mexico, and Germany having purchased about 50 percent of all U.S. exports. In contrast, im-

porters served less than 7 percent of the U.S. market in 1993. In 1997, other factors favoring U.S. sales were the absence of customs duties levied on medical surgical devices and no other major trade restrictions.

By 1998, the industry exported 29 percent of its output valued at approximately $4 billion overseas. Japan, Canada, the Netherlands, France and Mexico purchased the majority of these exports.

Rapid export growth was expected to continue through the early 2000s. Standardization of European Community (EC) medical device regulations was expected to stimulate sales in that region, which already consumed 36 percent of U.S. exports in 1992. Popular export items to the EC include respiratory products, orthopedic equipment and supplies, and artificial joints. In particular, the European market for orthopedic products increased from $1.44 billion in 1995 to a projected $1.89 billion in 2001. Hip implants dominated the European market, with increased demand also for renal supplies and peritoneal dialysis, which both facilitate at-home care.

Japan entered the nursing care product market because of the government's drug price reductions and decreased medical supply profits from other markets. Imports were expected to grow at an approximate 5 to 8 percent annual increase in 1997 and beyond, with the imports of U.S. industry products growing at an estimated 5 to 10 percent.

Other parts of Asia and Latin America presented new inroads for industry growth as well. The overall medical device market for Asia and Latin America grew two to four times more than Japan, Europe, and the United States, according to a Health Industry Manufacturers Association (HIMA) study released in 1996. Countries showing potential as growth markets included Brazil, China, India, Korea, Mexico, and Taiwan.

For example, infection control devices experienced increasing demand in the late 1990s in China and India. Steris Corp., a manufacturer of such items, expanded international operations to accommodate the demand.

RESEARCH AND TECHNOLOGY

Many surgical appliance and supply manufacturers relied heavily on development of new technology to create high-profit products and to increase market share—particularly for orthopedic and prosthetic devices.

Johnson and Johnson was among the industry leaders in developing new products. In 1995, besides the One Touch Profil System, an advanced home blood glucose monitoring system, the company introduced the Endopath Optiview Optical Surgical Obturator, giving physicians the ability to see multilevels of tissue while operating; Fibracol Collagen-Alginate Dressing, an advanced surgical dressing; the EZ45 Thoracic Linear Cutter, which allows a videoscopic approach to surgery; and Ortho Summit Processor, which automates blood virus testing.

The first over-the-counter HIV test was made available in 1996 and was nationally available in 1997. The introduction of this product may have an effect on laboratory equipment sales.

In the late 1990s and 2000s, research was expected to emphasize development of better metals and plastics, new non-metallic plastic and ceramic products, and new synthetics that could be used to create implants. Although outside investment capital for new product development waned in the early 1990s, various government partnering programs promised to boost research and development funding. For instance, the Clinton administration backed programs such as the Defense Technology Conversion Council to transfer military and other public technology to the private sector.

FURTHER READING

"'96 Mantra: Let's Make a Deal." *Crain's Cleveland Business,* 6 January 1997.

Anstett, Patricia. "3 Breast Implant Firms Settle." *Detroit Free Press,* 24 March 1994.

"Breast Implant Manufacturers Settle Medical Subrogation Suit." *Business Insurance,* 2 December 1996.

"Business Briefs: U.S. Court Trims Judgement in Patent-Infringement." *The Wall Street Journal,* 8 August 1996.

"California Has Twice as Many Medical Mfgrs as Any Other State." *Biomedical Market Newsletter,* August 1996.

"European Rehabilitation Products Market to Reach $1.5 Billion." *Medical Devices Business News,* October 1996.

"FDA Clears Steris Corp. Acquisition." *Plain Dealer,* 8 January 1997.

"5 More Implant Makers Join Settlement." *Detroit Free Press,* 25 March 1994.

"Healthdyne Recommends Rejection of Invacare Offer." *New York Times,* 1 February 1997.

"Hip Implants Dominate European Orthopedic Market." *Medical Device Business News,* July 1996.

"Insufficient Warnings on Device Labels Are Now Against the Law." *Biomedical Market Newsletter,* 30 September 1996.

"Invacare Is Acquiring Frohock-Stewart." *Chain Drug Review,* 26 February 1996,.

"Invacare Broadens Its Base." *Plain Dealer,* 21 April 1996.

"Invacare Offers to Buy Healthdyne Technologies." *New York Times,* 11 January 1997.

"Japanese Domestic Market for Nursing Care Products, Inc." *Medical Device Business News,* November 1996.

"Johnson & Johnson Band-Aid Brand Adhesive Bandages with Antibacterial Ointment." *Product Alert,* 8 April 1996.

"Johnson & Johnson's Acquisition of Florida's Cordis." *Miami Herald,* 23 January 1996.

"Johnson & Johnson's Pharmaceutical Pipeline: 1995 Research and Development Expenditure: $1.63 Billion." *PharmaBusiness,* November 1996.

"LifeCell Raising $12.4M." *Private Equity Week,* 25 November 1996.

"Medical Disposables Market in Mexico Is Growing Rapidly." *Biomedical Market Newsletter,* March 1996.

"New Business For Old." *Chemist and Druggist,* 5 October 1996.

"Pacific Dunlop Is to Sell Telectronics to St. Jude Medical for $135 Million." *Medical Device Business News,* November 1996.

"Protein Polymer Technologies Raises $4.8M with Private Placement." *Private Equity Week,* 20 January 1997.

"Purchase Boosts Furon's Presence." *Rubber & Plastics News,* 2 December 1996.

"St. Jude Medical's Acquisition," *The Wall Street Journal,* 24 July 1996.

"Seprafilm Wins FDA Approval." *Boston Globe,* 14 August 1996.

"Steris Adds to Growing Stable of Infection-Control Businesses." *Plain Dealer,* 28 November 1996.

"Topsy-Turvy Industry Posts Merger Record." *Modern Healthcare,* 23 December 1996.

SIC 3843

DENTAL EQUIPMENT AND SUPPLIES

This classification comprises establishments primarily engaged in manufacturing artificial teeth, dental metals, alloys, and amalgams, as well as a wide variety of equipment, instruments, and supplies used by dentists, dental laboratories, and dental colleges. Excluded from this classification are dental laboratories that construct artificial dentures, bridges, inlays, and other dental restorations on specifications from dentists; these are classified in **SIC 8072: Dental Laboratories.**

NAICS CODE(S)

339114 (Dental Equipment and Supplies Manufacturing)

INDUSTRY SNAPSHOT

Essential to the practice of dentistry, the dental equipment and supply industry represents a modestly sized market and, in terms of sales, is considered to be one of the smallest industries, compared to the other medical supply and equipment industries. It is also an industry of expected growth due to increases in the cost of dental care, baby boomers taking better care of both their teeth and their children's teeth, and technological advances in dental equipment such as advanced root canal procedure machines, less expensive oral cameras, and the Food and Drug Administration's (FDA) approval of Perioglass, a surface-active, bone-grafting material.

Dental equipment and dental supplies are regarded as separate markets, with some companies manufacturing only supplies; some manufacturing only equipment; and others, generally the larger companies (with a diverse mix of medical products), manufacturing both equipment and supplies. These products are then sold to dentists, dental laboratories, and dental colleges.

Products manufactured by industry participants include dental chairs, dental hand instruments, and drills, which are considered equipment; and plaster, amalgams (alloyed metals used for filling cavities), and cements, which are considered supplies. Other products, more than 25,000 of them, include abrasive points, wheels, and disks; dental cabinets; denture materials; orthodontic appliances; and artificial teeth, which are not made in dental laboratories. Dental accessories, which include dental picks, dental floss, dental stimulators, mouth mirrors, and other items, accounted for $35 million in sales in 1995 and were expected to grow at a 5 to 10 percent increase per year, according to Eric Happell, director of retail marketing, at John O. Butler Company. Niche products have been developed and are expected to become increasingly popular. Examples include premixed temporary fillings (DenTek's Tempenol), reusable toothpicks, and plastic dental cleaning equipment for those who are "metal sensitive." These products are mostly sold through drugstores. In 1995, 41 percent of all dental floss sales were at drugstores.

ORGANIZATION AND STRUCTURE

In the early 1990s, approximately 500 companies in the United States were manufacturing dental equipment and supplies as their primary business. The majority of these manufacturers were small- and medium-sized companies, with only 25 percent of the total employing 20 or more employees. The typical dental equipment and supply manufacturing establishment was half the size of the typical establishment in all other U.S. manufacturing industries, employing 26 people compared to the national standard of 54 employees per establishment.

By the mid- to late nineties, larger medical supply companies also started to include dental products in their portfolios and changed the market from exclusive type manufacturers (small to medium sized companies) to multi-manufacturers (larger companies). Mergers and acquisitions became more common among medical companies to enhance the current product line for greater profits, and to share research and development costs of new dental products and supplies.

The bulk of the industry's manufacturing establishments were located in California, which contained 124

facilities in the early 1990s, leading all other states in dental equipment and supply production. New York was a distant second, with 48 manufacturing establishments; Illinois followed, with 39 facilities. Aside from the concentration of facilities on the West Coast, in the Northeast, and in the Great Lakes region, dental equipment and supply production was scattered throughout the country, with 25 states containing manufacturing establishments.

BACKGROUND AND DEVELOPMENT

Manufacturers of dental equipment and dental supplies first emerged as an appreciable component of American industry in the 1890s, although the first manufacturers of such products undoubtedly originated much earlier, appearing during the genesis of the nation itself, when the practice of dentistry first began in the United States. In fact, the earliest progenitors of the dental equipment and supply industry were the dentists themselves, who made their own equipment in workshops adjoining their public offices. Over the ensuing decades, as the nation's population grew and the magnitude of the country's commerce increased, the production of dental equipment and supplies became distinct from the practice of dentistry, leading to the emergence of small, independent dental manufacturing companies by the latter half of the nineteenth century.

Once the manufacture of dental equipment and supplies became a distinct segment of the dental industry, characterized by small, frequently family-owned businesses—many of which appeared in the decade leading up to the turn of the twentieth century—the dental equipment and supply industry was truly born. During the next half century, the industry remained small, comprised of companies that generated a negligible amount of revenue. The modern version of the dental equipment and supply industry, which began to assume the characteristics of the industry in existence during the 1990s, would not emerge until the 1960s, when a combination of developments engendered a new breed of dental equipment and supply manufacturers.

By the 1960s, the scope of the dental equipment and supply industry widened considerably, and its market matured significantly, drawing the attention of would-be manufacturers and investors. The shift toward preventive dentistry altered the complexion of the dental equipment and supply industry, but it had not significantly changed the composition of the industry. Still primarily comprised of small, independent manufacturing companies, roughly 500 of them in the early 1960s, the industry continued in many ways to resemble itself 50 years earlier. Its sales volume still represented a modest sum, amounting to roughly $150 million per year as the movement toward preventive dentistry gained momentum. Still, it had not yet attracted large manufacturing concerns; its largest manufacturer, S.S. White Dental Manufacturing Co., generated $40 million in sales in 1961. The optimism pervading the industry, therefore, was not so much attributable to a dramatic transformation of the industry, but rather stemmed from the expectation of a future transformation.

During the early 1960s, American families on average were spending twice as much per year on dental care as they had 10 years earlier—the natural extension of a society growing increasingly more affluent—while the number of prepaid dental plans multiplied during the same period, covering approximately 700,000 Americans. These prepaid plans, coming from either private insurance plans or union-employer agreements, would grow exponentially throughout the decade and into the 1970s, fueling much of the optimism articulated by manufacturers and industry pundits during this 20-year period. Union-sponsored dental care plans proliferated after the landmark agreement reached between the International Longshoremen's & Warehousemen's Union and the Washington State Dental Association in 1954, when the first such program was initiated.

By the mid-1960s, thanks in large part to the growth of union dental care plans, the number of Americans provided with an opportunity for dental care increased to 3 million from the 700,000 covered roughly 5 years earlier. Also, Medicare, a U.S. government health insurance program for those over 65 years of age, and Medicaid, a program that provided medical care to those who could not pay for it, both came into existence in 1965, and promised to extend dental coverage throughout the country. By the end of the decade, the number of Americans covered by dental care plans doubled again in a five-year period and included more than 6 million people.

The increase in the number of potential dental care customers that sparked so much interest in the dental equipment and supply industry during the 1960s persuaded larger, conglomerate manufacturing companies with no previous vested interest in the dental field to begin dental equipment production. Many of the smaller, independent manufacturing concerns were absorbed by the incursion of these larger companies, altering the composition of the industry. Meanwhile, those manufacturers already in the industry were diversifying, applying the same technology used in the production of dental equipment to the manufacture of nondental products. Consequently, as this period of mergers and diversification occurred into the late 1960s, the typical manufacturer in the industry changed from a small, independent company, almost entirely devoted to the production of dental-related products, to a larger, more diversified manufacturer.

This transformation did not, however, have an equally significant effect on the industry's sales volume. From the $150 million generated by U.S. manufacturers at the beginning of the decade, the industry's sales volume only increased to roughly $280 million by the beginning of the 1970s, a total that seemed to belie the industry's growth in other areas over the course of the decade. Dental equipment manufacturers supplied two revolutionary pieces of equipment during the dental industry's emergence as a more visible sector of the health care field: the air-driven, high-speed drill and the reclining dentist's chair.

By the mid-1970s, approximately 30 million Americans were covered under some sort of dental care plan, which represented a tremendous increase during the previous 15 years. When this figure was analyzed to reflect the number of those who actually visited dentists, rather than the number who were provided the opportunity to visit a dentist, the reason for the industry's laggard growth in sales volume became readily apparent. Of all the people receiving dental care in the United States, only 15 percent were covered by dental insurance, compared to more than 90 percent for health care. Since a large proportion of the people covered by dental insurance opted not to receive dental care, the number of people insured in the country, which over the past 20 years had inspired much of the optimism within the dental equipment and supply industry, proved to be a misleading figure: the more people covered did not necessarily translate into an increase in the industry's sales volume.

Once this misleading measure of the industry's potential growth was removed, a clearer estimate of its true position within the larger health care field showed a relatively small industry, generating roughly $670 million in revenue in 1975.

As the industry progressed past the mid-1970s, when it was mired for several years in a global recession, its growth during the 1980s continued at a moderate rate. By 1982, the industry's sales volume increased to $1.11 billion, having eclipsed the $1 billion mark three years earlier. In the face of a sharp decline in the number of labor contract agreements that included dental care coverage, the industry's sales volume increased only marginally by the end of the decade, reaching $1.27 billion.

Ambiguity about U.S. health care reform and its effect on dentistry coupled with deleterious economic conditions during the early 1990s stunted the dental equipment and supply industry's growth in 1995, causing the value of its shipments to increase by only 2 percent to $2.39 billion, compared to the 14 percent growth recorded between 1993 and 1994. Projections for the industry's growth called for a 3 percent increase in aggregate revenue from 1995 to 1998, fueled in part by the growth of certain fledgling areas of dentistry, such as periodontal surgery, treatment with lasers, and cosmetic dentistry.

Dental products and accessories have become more specialized and targeted to end users: adults, children, and infants. Dental floss and dental picks, products for healthier gums, and premixed fillings are all examples of these niche products. The biggest product changes have occurred in children's dentistry. Various manufacturers added specialty-type products for children, including brighter colors, different packaging, timers to help children know when to brush, and smaller sizes.

During the 1990s manufacturers focused on gum care. Dental supply and equipment manufacturers built relationships within the community of 140,000 dentists by conducting research on dental care and publishing the results in various studies. For example, Bausch & Lomb conducted one of the largest ongoing studies on plaque removal by using different brushes on implant wearers to remove plaque.

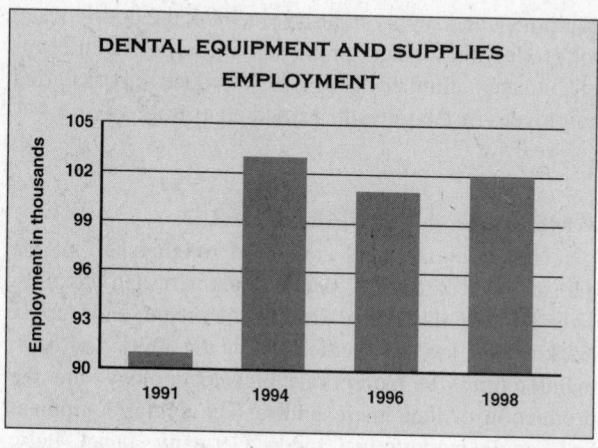

CURRENT CONDITIONS

From 1995 to 1997, the dental care industry offered advanced toothbrushes that enabled users to decrease the plaque formation around the gumline (for adults and children), and dental floss with fluoride, mint-taste, whitening abilities, and a special feature called nonshredding, which prevents breakage of the floss. New ways of flossing were introduced that allowed users greater precision and control to reach plaque in between teeth by using specially designed prongs.

Other introductions in the dental equipment industry that are expected to increase sales to dentists are oral cancer tests, digital radiography (which decreases radiation exposure to the patient by 90 percent), "Save-A-Tooth" program developed by 3M, oral cameras that allow dentists an easier option for root canals, and more consumer-related dental products to increase patients' awareness of the importance of self-care.

INDUSTRY LEADERS

Sybron Corporation, based in Milwaukee, Wisconsin, led the industry with sales of $960.7 million for the fiscal year ending September 30, 1998; Sybron employed 7,900 workers. The company's total unadjusted net sales for fiscal 1999 amounted to $1.1 billion. The company made six acquisitions during the year, requiring restructuring of its financial statements.

Block Drug Company, Inc., based in Jersey City, New Jersey, generated $821.1 million in sales during its fiscal year ending March 31, 1999. For the next six months (ending September 30, 1999), Block reported sales of $415.8 million, an 11.4 percent increase over the same period in 1998, after taking into account the effects of currency and the selling of its household products businesses. Block capitalized on this strength in December 1999 by approving a repurchase of 500,000 shares of its Class A Common Stock. Block is perhaps best known as the marketer of Polident, a widely popular brand name most closely tied to denture care products.

The industry's highest-ranking privately owned manufacturer, Dentsply International Inc. of York, Pennsylvania, posted sales of $795.1 million for its fiscal year ended December 31, 1998. Industry observers attributed the growth of Dentsply to acquisitions, baby boomer demand for dental care, and the improvement of dental care in developing countries. Only half of Dentsply's sales are domestic.

Braun, Sonicare, and Interplak, which were recently purchased by Conair, were the major players in the dental accessory market. These three companies all introduced rotary type toothbrushes that cleaned in between teeth. Rowenta introduced two new interdental brushes, Dentacontrol for adults ($80 retail) and Dentiphant for children ($25 retail). Glide led the industry in tooth floss sales, though it was a premium product at $4 per unit. Procter & Gamble marketed the best-selling denture adhesive, Fixodent. Block's Poli-Grip competed by growing its product line to include Poli Grip Free, Super Poli-Grip, and Ultimate Hold Poli-Grip.

WORKFORCE

In 1991, with a total of 100 companies employing 20 or more people, the work force numbered around 91,000. The number of companies remained fairly stable, and the number of employees increased to 103,000 in 1994 and declined to 101,000 in 1996. Only slight increases were expected through 1998 to around 102,000 total employees in the dental equipment and supply industry. Payroll for 1994 was around $103 million; this figure increased to $111 million in 1996, and was expected to increase to $114 million by 1998. The average number of employees per company was 49 in 1994 with an average wage per hour of $13.09.

Production workers in the dental equipment and supply industry generally earned slightly less than the national standard for production workers employed by manufacturing industries. In 1989, the typical production worker earned $10.49 per hour compared to the $10.31 per hour averaged by production workers in the dental equipment and supply industry. In 1994, the hourly wage for production workers in the dental equipment and supply industry climbed to $11.43, at which time salaried employees in the industry earned an average of $43,441 per year.

AMERICA AND THE WORLD

U.S. manufacturers controlled roughly half of the international market for dental equipment and supplies. This lead in the global dental equipment and supply market was largely predicated on the ability of U.S. manufacturers to incorporate high technology into the production of their merchandise. The dental equipment and supply markets in Canada, Germany, Japan, Italy, and France proved to be the strongest export destinations for U.S. manufacturers, while manufacturers in Germany, Japan, Switzerland, Italy, and France posed the greatest threat to the overwhelming lead of U.S. manufacturers in the global market.

Fluctuations in foreign exchange rates tend to work for the U.S. import market. In 1994 the United States had 62.3 percent of the import market, and further growth was expected. No customs duty was levied on medical, surgical, and dental instruments and supplies, which also had a favorable effect on U.S. dental supply and accessory sales.

China imported $737,000 or 30,910 kilograms of dental cements, dental fillings, and bone reconstruction cements in the first three quarters of 1996. Japan's imports of medical and dental equipment were expected to rise steadily from $3.33 billion in 1994. Imports from the United States accounted for 62.3 percent of the import market, totaling $3.51 billion in 1995 and $3.86 billion in 1996. Japan's expected introduction of social insurance for long-term care, improvement of government relations during the past decade, and U.S.-Japan agreement on government procurement, all provided more opportunities for U.S. suppliers of health care products.

FURTHER READING

"Best-selling Denture Adhesives." *Chain Drug Review,* 6 January 1997, 19.

"Block Drug Company Approves Stock Repurchase." *PR Newswire,* 7 December 1999.

CorpTech Technology Industry Growth Forecaster, January 1997.

Darnay, Arsen J., ed. *Manufacturing USA.* 5th ed. Detroit: Gale Research, 1996.

"Dental Tech Firm Bites Into Sales." *Crain's Small Business-New York,* May 1996, 3.

"Dentsply to Buy New Image." *Wall Street Journal,* 26 December 1996, 125.

Infotrac Company Profiles, 21 December 1999. Available at http://web7.infotrac.galegroup.com.

"Inside Industry: USBiomaterials." *Genetic Engineering News,* 1 November 1996, 16.

"Japan Medical and Dental Equipment & Supplies Markets Are Steadily Increasing." *Biomedical Market Newsletter,* 30 September 1996, 6.

"Mergers and Acquisitions." *Med Ad News,* February 1996, 15.

"New Flosses from Colgate." *News Brief Journal,* 2 December 1996, 46.

"A Next Step for Rowenta." *HFN,* 30 September 1996, 70

"Putting Teeth In Relationships." *HFN,* 8 April 1996, 70.

"Save-A-Tooth is Unveiled at Retail by 3M." *Chain Drug Review,* 20 May 1996, 18.

Schifrin, Matthew and Christopher Helman. "Streetwalker" *Forbes,* 27 December 1999.

"Shiseki-Ya Kun Teeth Cleaner and Mirror." *International Product Alert,* 19 February 1996, 13.

"Statistics: China Chemical Import & Export Data From January to October 1996, Part 80." *China Chemical Reporter,* 26 December 1996.

"Super Poli-Grip Denture Adhesive Cream." *Product Alert,* 9 September 1996, 26.

"Sybron International Announces Fourth Quarter Record Sales and Earnings." *PR Newswire,* 16 November 1999.

"Zila Inc. to Absorb Bio-Dental Technologies Corp." *Denver Post,* 4 June 1996.

SIC 3844

X-RAY APPARATUS AND X-RAY TUBES

Firms in this industry engage primarily in manufacturing irradiation apparatus and tubes for applications such as medical diagnostic, medical therapeutic, industrial, research and scientific evaluation.

NAICS CODE(S)

334517 (Irradiation Apparatus Manufacturing)

INDUSTRY SNAPSHOT

Nearly a decade of growth made X-ray apparatus and tubes one of America's fastest growing industries in the 1990s. Its 1997 shipments reached $3.8 billion—almost 60 percent more than 1992's total of $2.4 billion. Much of this success came from the growing sophistication and portability of X-ray products. The massive machines of hospital X-ray departments still had their place, but now miniaturized versions found every-day use in doctors' and dentists' offices nationwide. In addition, the industry discovered new uses for the non-destructive technology that both increased efficiency and quality of manufacturing processes. With the fall of communism and the relaxation of U.S. technology bans, the industry found a number of new and expanding markets in Eastern Europe and portions of the former Soviet Union.

The U.S. sales volume for 1996 was estimated to be $369.8 million for conventional X-ray and fluoroscopy equipment and $36 million for radiation detection equipment. The U.S. sales volume for 1997 was estimated to be $550 million for X-ray apparatus and tubes.

Among medical services, lab tests and X-rays ranked as the fifth category in terms of consumer usage behind physician's services, dental services, eye care services, and service by someone other than a physician. For 1995 (in 1988 dollars), the average expenditure on X-rays for 100.3 million households was $2.7 billion out of a total of $135.1 billion aggregate health care expenditure. On average in 1997, X-ray services were performed in 9.4 percent of all combined visits to physicians (office, outpatient departments, and emergency departments). The largest consumer dollar amount was spent on X-rays for individuals between the ages of 35-74. The projected figure for the year 2000 was $2.9 billion based on 105.9 million households with aggregate expenditures of $141.5 billion. The highest consumer expenditure for 2000 was expected to be between the ages of 35 and 74.

ORGANIZATION AND STRUCTURE

Approximately one-half of all sales in this industry went to hospital end-users, with the medical profession in general making up the majority of all shipments. Other demands for X-ray equipment have evolved with the need for increased security measures at airports in the late 1990s. Research facilities provided another avenue for sales of major pieces of often experimental equipment. However, the industry was growing increasingly interested in the non-destructive and non-intrusive nature of the imaging technologies.

The 1997 Economic Census reported 154 establishments for the irradiation apparatus industry, an increase of 17 percent from 1992. Total revenues were reported at approximately $3.8 billion. These establishments employed 13,659 people, a decrease of 9.5 percent from 1992.

The medical industry, which also includes dental, electromedical, surgical, and ophthalmic goods, ranked sixth out of 17 major technological manufacturers of various equipment. Out of 189 firms surveyed, a 4.1 percent growth rate was expected for 1999. The greatest growth in employees was expected in the Eastern Lakes region of the United States. The Northwest region placed second with a 10 percent projected growth rate and the southwestern U.S. was third with 7.0 percent projected growth.

BACKGROUND AND DEVELOPMENT

The discovery of the X-ray was an accident. In 1895, Wilhelm Conrad Roentgen, experimenting with electrical discharges in an evacuated tube called a Crookes' tube, discovered that the invisible rays given off from his experiment could penetrate a human hand and project a skeletal image onto a florescent screen. Later, he substituted photographic film to make a permanent record. Since then, scientists have discovered that X-rays are a type of electromagnetic radiation. An X-ray's wavelength of 0.01 to 300 angstroms is shorter than visible light, lying between and partially over the ultraviolet and gamma-ray segments of the electromagnetic spectrum. They are produced by the collision of high-energy particles with other charged particles.

American scientist, William D. Coolidge, developed the first efficient X-ray tube, called a Coolidge tube, in 1913. Modern tubes fire electrons from a tungsten filament cathode at a target anode, usually made of tungsten, molybdenum, or copper and coated with a thin film of gold.

The speed of passage of the x-radiation through a body depends on density. Relatively dense material, like bone, yielded white images, while less-dense material like lungs appeared black. Doctors found the phenomenon invaluable for accurately diagnosing such things as tuberculosis, miners' black lung, and broken bones. However, it only provided a two-dimensional image of the problem area, superimposing layers of body components one on top of another without any indication of depth. One solution to that problem was to use a contrast medium like liquid barium to highlight the esophagus, stomach, and intestine. By using a fluoroscope, which produces real-time images on a video screen, the physician tracked the medium through the digestive system, pinpointing any problem areas.

The late 1960s saw a major advancement in the effective use of X-rays for medical diagnosis. By linking the computer to a moving X-ray emitter inside a doughnut-shaped machine, Geoffrey Hounsfield of EMI produced a three-dimensional image of an entire object. Instead of a few X-ray photographs, the computer-aided-tomograph (CAT) took hundreds of thousands of carefully directed, slice-like images which the computer reassembled. Tomograph comes from the Greek word for slice. The results, startlingly clear, could be manipulated to highlight specific areas. CAT scans could locate bleeding inside a brain, find and measure tumors, or help to evaluate injuries anywhere in the body.

Concerns over the amount of radiation a patient would be exposed to and the cost and sheer physical immensity of the equipment led to the development of ultrasound tomograph which did not use X-rays. By the mid-1980s, the ultrasound systems were beginning to gain popularity. Ultrasound systems are classified under **SIC 3845: Electromedical Apparatus.**

Magnetic Resonance Imaging (MRI) uses a powerful magnet to align the hydrogen atoms in a patient's body.

When the magnetic field is released, the atoms return to their original orientation, but different tissues realign at different rates. By using a computer to clock the relative rates of change, physicians can map joints, tumors, post-surgical changes in the chest, abdomen, pelvis, brain, and spinal cord.

The safety and effectiveness of all medical devices became the responsibility of the Food and Drug Administration in 1938. Radiation emitting devices were specifically targeted in 1968 by the Radiation Control for Health and Safety Act and, in 1976, by the Medical Device Amendments to the Food, Drug, and Cosmetic Act.

In the late 1990s, the continued concern for radiation exposure to patients led to further advances in X-ray equipment development and technological advances. One of the technological advances in 1997, called a "soft" X-ray, was a new technology that used long wavelengths to decrease radiation.

CURRENT CONDITIONS

Even though other, safer technologies were displacing X-rays by the 1990s in their traditional medical applications, radiation proved useful in unique ways. The fluoroscope could show movement within the body like the operation of the heart and the intestines. It facilitated angioplasty, providing the physician with a real-time way of guiding a balloon-tipped catheter down a blood vessel to the point where the balloon insert could be expanded with the greatest effect. Radiation oncology used X-rays or gamma-rays to attack cancerous tumors without damaging surrounding tissue. With this technique a linear accelerator, betatron, or cobalt machine is used to direct a beam of radiation from outside the patient's body at the pinpointed tumor.

Initial investigations of the radiation in the research laboratory led to many useful applications for the non-visible light energy. X-ray crystallography led to X-ray microscopes. Crystal structures direct and control X-rays much as lenses do with normal light energy. Using this principle, researchers were able to delve ever-deeper into the structure of crystals. The fact that X-rays are absorbed by material led to absorption spectroscopy, which studies metals in living systems. The industry began using lithography to produce densely packed computer chips. Holography made it possible to glimpse the world within a living cell.

Scientists also used the radiation to look beyond this world. By launching satellites equipped with X-ray detectors, they were able to observe and theorize about the structure of the universe. The first such satellite, UHURU, was launched from a site near Kenya in 1970 and was followed by an international series of successors. Gamma-ray astronomy extended the reach of X-ray as-tronomy, making visible the processes of the destruction and creation of chemical elements throughout the universe.

Archeology and paleontology also benefited from the use of X-ray technology. Previously, the study of such ancient artifacts as mummies and fossilized bones required the systematic destruction or at least the disassembly of the scientific treasures. Using a CAT scan, often tied to a supercomputer, researchers could get clear three-dimensional images without reducing the artifact to dust. Such scans often revealed surprising facts about the subject giving a glimpse of what life, society, disease, nutrition, and intrigue was like in historically distant times.

X-rays also proved invaluable in probing modern-day intrigues. In the 1980s and 1990s, plane hijackings and bombings brought terror to the skies, and advances in weapons technology threatened to make conventional X-ray scanners ineffective in preventing them. Although metals show up clearly on an X-ray scan, lighter materials like plastics do not. Plastic explosives and the mostly-plastic handgun, the Glock 17, could be smuggled through security inspections undetected. Specially designed innovations like American Science & Engineering Inc.'s Model Z scanner sought ways to tighten security. The Z-scanner concentrates a high intensity beam of X-rays onto the carry-on luggage to compensate for the low absorption rate of softer materials. It then displays both the normal X-ray image which would pick up metals and the Z-image which catches plastics. In 1991, France extended that technology for use in its massive cargo inspection facility at Paris's Charles de Gaulle airport. Their building-size X-ray machine examines entire pallet loads of luggage or entire vehicles at once, producing a sophisticated, easily read image.

By increasing the power and size of the X-ray equipment, industry businesses were able to probe through several feet of metal to map interior details. Defense subcontractors used CAT scans to inspect MX missiles and Saturn rockets looking for cracks, poor material bonds, migration of fuel or coolants, integrity of castings, and gaps in insulation. In traditional CAT scans, the object to be probed sits within the doughnut shaped emitter ring, but in the late 1980s industry leaders developed a new innovation on the technology, backscatter imaging tomography (BIT). By capturing only the portion of the beams which are reflected back, BIT machinery allowed operators to probe objects even if they could only access one side.

The process provided an efficient method for checking the quality of manufactured parts and allowed inspectors to certify and document such critical items as pipe welds in nuclear reactors. X-rays have also been used to examine the nation's highways by detecting early signs of failure and allowing preventative maintenance in place of major periodic rebuilding.

Mergers and acquisitions of X-ray apparatus and tubes companies became popular in the mid- to late 1990s to match the trend in hospitals downsizing, physician's offices combining, changes in managed care, and decreases in insurance availability for medical services.

The estimated 1996 U.S. sales volume for conventional fluoroscopy was $369.8 million and $36 million for radiation detection equipment, according to the March 1996, Biomedical Marker Newsletter. Bone density scanning tests were more popular among research centers, hospitals, and physicians. Until the mid 1990s osteoporosis was usually detected by breaking bones. In 1996, normal X-rays were no longer considered acceptable to detect bone loss. The bone density scan tests costs around $220 per patient and the demand for this testing equipment is expected to increase as patients use Fosamax and wish to have their results and condition monitored.

INDUSTRY LEADERS

Siemens Medical/Nuclear Medicine Group, Illinois, with a total of 925 employees, was ranked number one out of 10 companies that in 1997 were considered to be the largest emerging operating units. In 1997, Ward's Business Directory of U.S. Private and Public Companies ranked Siemens Medical Systems Inc. Nuclear Medicine Group, Illinois, as the largest X-ray apparatus equipment company with and estimated $110 million in sales. OEC Medical Systems-Inc., Utah, had $102 million in revenues and Fischer Imaging Corporation, Ohio, had $77 million in sales. In 1998, Siemens reported sales of approximately $11 billion; OEC Medical Systems, Inc. reported sales of $188.7 million, and Fischer Imaging Corporation reported sales of $59.8 million.

The German conglomerate Siemens Aktiengesellschaft wanted to buy a company, Diasonics in 1980, but early market conquests by that company put it beyond reach. In 1990, Siemens formed Siemens-Gammasonics as a subsidiary of Siemens Medical Systems Inc. The company had sales between $50 million and $100 million through the 1990s.

A 1996 cooperative alliance was formed between Siemens Medical System's Inc. Oncology Care Systems Group and Intraop Medical Inc. to deliver Intraop's cancer treatment, the first of its kind, a mobile and self-shielded electron beam system that treats cancer using intraoperative radiotherapy.

Sony Corp. (Japan) and the National Institute of Radiological Sciences developed a computerized sectional radiograph that has the ability to take 3-dimensional images of human anatomy parts. This device, introduced in 1996, can take up to 360 photographs in 12 seconds. A drug which became popular during the discovery of treatment for osteoporosis (a bone thinning disease), Fosamax, increased the demand for Hologic's Acclaim

series, a line of X-ray machines, by 50 percent. Hologic shipped around 700 to 750 units per year with sales of $43.5 million in 1995. Schick Technologies, which began producing digital radiography machines in 1995, generated $45.6 million in 1999 sales—a dramatic increase from 1995's $7.0 million. Intraoral cameras were also expected to become more popular to help dentists examine and diagnose their patients more accurately.

X-ray Corp., Georgia and Chesapeake X-ray Corp. were acquired by Physician Sales & Service, Inc., Florida for $18 million in stock and another $6.8 million of debt in 1996.

A buyout of Diagnostic Imaging (which had 1995 sales of $58 million), for $19.2 million of stock and debt took place in 1996 by Physician Sales and Service, a medical supply, equipment and pharmaceutical distributor that reported $236.2 million in sales.

Other manufacturers of note include Acuson Corporation, reporting sales of $475.9 million for 1999 and Trex Medical Corporation, reporting sales of $241.6 million.

WORKFORCE

X-ray equipment manufacturing facilities tend to be large, high-tech facilities. In 1988, the average establishment employed 117 compared to the manufacturing average of 57. Wages accordingly ran about 20 percent higher than average reaching $12.49 per hour in 1988 compared to the average hourly wage in all manufacturing firms of $10.66. Total employment in the industry increased throughout the late 1980s and early 1990s reaching 13,740 in 1992 according to U.S. Industrial Outlook. Production workers made up 51.7 percent of the industry's workforce. The users of X-ray equipment are radiologists. In the United States, they must take four-to-seven years of specialized training after graduating from medical school.

The number of establishments continued to grow throughout the 1990s with a total of 103 for 1993, up to 154 in 1997. Out of the 103 establishments, 92 of them had over 20 employees. Correspondingly, in 1997, 73 of the 154 establishments had over 20 employees.

Employment decreased from a total of 14,253 in 1992 to 13,659 in 1997 with production workers equaling 50 percent in 1992 and 41 percent in 1997. Average hourly wages for production workers increased during this time period as well, going from $14.79 to $16.69.

The medical equipment and services 1997 workforce that includes X-ray and irradiation apparatus, ranked California as number one with 3,960 jobs, Massachusetts second with 1,901 employees, and Illinois third with 1,354 employees.

AMERICA AND THE WORLD

Foreign imports of X-ray equipment accounted for 42 percent of industry sales in 1992 according to *U.S. Industrial Outlook,* higher than any other segment of the medical industry group. America's largest competitors were Japan and Germany, contributing 60 percent. Overall, the American X-ray industry ran a trade deficit with 1992 imports of $1.1 billion compared to exports of $783 million.

However, imports declined 2.7 percent that year, the first decline since 1987. The main export markets for American products were Japan, Germany, and Canada but exports to Eastern Europe tripled their 1991 level reaching $8 million and making that region a prime future growth area.

In 1996, the diagnostic imaging equipment accounted for $331 million of the $443 million Italian electromedical market. In 1997, Hong Kong's Chek Lap Kok Airport and Kuala Lumpur International Airport in Malaysia were supplied by a $19 million contract with Vivid Technologies to supply explosive screenings equipment. A European hospital was the first in 1996 to integrate their clinical and administrative systems with a digital medical imaging system. The system allowed physicians to have access to patient's X-ray images anywhere on the hospital network. Electronic imaging has been of benefit to the medical industry by providing greater diagnostic accuracy, better resource utilization and increased productivity. A Japanese device, Compact X 3720A was developed and can detect up to 10 chemical elements using wavelength-distribution optics. This device, which became available in 1996, can show 20 times better resolution than traditional type energy-distribution optics. It is manufactured by Rigaku Industrial Co. Ltd. Siemens Medical Systems assisted Kazanskij Optiko-Mekhanicheckij Zavod, a former defense industry, in producing X-ray medical complexes. Annually, up to 250 units were expected to be produced starting in 1997.

RESEARCH AND TECHNOLOGY

The uses of X-ray technology and its spin-offs continued to grow throughout the 1990s. Medical advancements included such procedures as mammograms, which allowed physicians to detect cancerous tumors in women's breasts, before they became apparent by traditional methods. Even so, the technology had its limitations. In 1993, a Canadian study revealed that mammograms were ineffective in predicting breast cancer for women younger than 50. The relatively dense tissue in younger women's breasts hid developing tumors resulting in no difference in diagnosis rates for women who received mammograms and those who did not. At the close of the century, there still remained a strong amount of controversy as to when women should be tested for breast cancer and how often they should be checked with a mammogram.

Tomography has also found its way into agriculture to observe harvesting techniques for fruits and vegetables and find out when and why crop damage occurred. The rays showed distribution patterns of pesticides and rates of water absorption by different types of roots and different soil-seed combinations.

Micro-tomography opened the miniature world of ceramics and plastics to the researcher and quality control inspector. By using high-energy sources like synchrotron radiation, industry researchers could analyze the internal structures of rocks and minerals like coal and oil-bearing shales, aiding companies like Exxon in their search for new oil and coal fields. Synchrotron radiation is produced by accelerating particles like electrons to nearly the speed of light within a magnetic field. The result is an intense white light. By channeling that light, researchers can create pencil-thick concentrated beams of x-radiation, ultraviolet, and infrared radiation.

This tunable radiation source could map chemical elements within an object. Exxon has used the technology to map other elements found within copper, nickel, and iron. Biomedical researchers have used the technology to study calcium to gain more knowledge of the makeup of human bones. Intense X-rays could look within the walls of living cells to study their structure and watch the movements of elements like calcium within a body; however, the individual cells targeted by the X-rays would be killed.

A gamma-ray version of the CAT scan—Positron-emission-topography (PET)—measured brain activity. Areas of the brain engaged in thought processes absorbed glucose tagged with positron radiation. Decaying positrons gave off gamma-rays which receptors picked up and translated into a light-and-dark image of the brain. Brains which showed higher IQ levels in standard tests showed less activity than those which scored lower. Researchers theorized that the more intelligent brain was "wired" more efficiently and so used less of its capacity to solve a problem. PET was also used for diagnosing cancer and Alzheimer's disease and in evaluating epileptic patients. In the mid-to-late nineties, scientists have also been able to test the areas of the brain for depression, aggression, gender differences and memory loss using the PET scan.

Another recent advance also used gamma-rays. The single photon emission computed tomograph (SPECT) also tracked radioactive isotopes through the body and used a computer to build an image of a metabolic function. It was particularly useful for monitoring heart functions.

Researchers used the technology to examine the internal structure of the earth and to test the "Global

Warming'' hypothesis. Using seismic waves, rather than X-rays, they mapped the boundary between the earth's core and its mantle. In 1991, researchers began sending a series of sound waves from Heard Island in Antarctica through the naturally stable environment of deep ocean water. Scientists will need to continue this research for several years in order to obtain accurate and meaningful information. American Science & Engineering Inc, MA was interested in using its screen equipment technology for airports to screen cargo and mail. Because of the expense of the equipment—ballet scanners cost around $1.2 to $1.5 million—and level of skill needed to operate the machinery, the company president doubts airlines will purchase the equipment anytime soon.

The 60-year-old gamma camera that uses vacuum tube technology, was replaced by a gamma camera called Notebook Imager that uses a cadmium-zinc-telluride, solid-state detector array. It was a leading product of Digirad Corporation.

A 1996 study done on rats examined the ability of X-rays to help restore paralyzed limbs to partial use, if applied at the right moment with the right dosage.

Universal Plastics Corp., and Eastman Kodak Scientific Imaging Division worked cooperatively in 1996 to develop a sequencing device to identify strands of DNA. Kodak also indicated they would replace X-ray film used to capture the images of the strands with a digital imaging capability.

Shimadzu developed a X-ray machine that measures X-rays as digital input. The data can be sent to physicians all over the world as a image because it is stored on optical and magnetic disks. The Japanese manufacturer expected to make it available in 1997 and will retail for 60 million yen.

In 1999, Hitachi won the Medical Design Excellence Award for their AIRIS II open magnetic resonance imaging system. The unit features an open air design that is open on four sides, offering greater comfort and access for the patient. 650 of these systems are installed in the United States, and 1,700 are installed worldwide. Hitachi has joined with the University of Cincinnati Medical Center to develop and explore other indications for use of this equipment.

FURTHER READING

"Airline Baggage Inspection Systems Developer Eyes IPO Market," *The IPO Reporter,* 28 October 1996, 20.

"AS&E's Cargo Scanners," *Traffic World,* 16 December 1996, 248.

"Coming to an X-ray Room Near You: 3-D Anatomy," *Nikkei Weekly,* 22 April 1996, 34.

"Demand for Drug Lifts Hologic X-ray Product," *Boston Globe,* 3 April 1996.

"Dental Tech Firm Develops an Alternative to X-rays," *Crain's New York Business,* 1 April 1996.

Dorminey, Bruce. "Technology: A Source of High Energy: 'Soft' X-ray Advances Have a Variety of Medical and Dental Applications." *Financial Times London Edition,* 28 January 1997.

Drew, Glen. "Medical devices: A Primer on Medical Device Regulation." *FDA Consumer* (May, 1986): 24-7.

"Eastman, Universal Device Charts DNA," *Plastics News,* 10 June 1996, 8.

"Fischer Imaging Corp.," Department of Defense News Release, 12 September 1996. (DDNR 96)

"Fluroscan Imaging Systems Inc.," *Crain's Chicago Business,* 29 July 1996, 19.

"Gamma Camera Developer Raises $6M," *Private Equity Week,* 28 October 1996, 3.

"Hologic Agrees to Merge With Fluorscan," *New York Times,* National Edition, 20 July 1996.

Hoover's Company Capsule, 20 March 2000. Available from http://www.hoovers.com.

"Industry News (Joint Venture) Alliance Formed to Distribute Products to Treat Cancer," *Cancer Weekly Plus,* 7 October 1996.

"Italy Diagnostic Industry Shows Modest Growth in 1995," *Medical Device Business News,* July 1996.

"Italy: Medical Diagnostic Imaging Equipment," *Journal of Commerce,* 18 December 1996, 410.

Leitch, Andrew. "Leave Them Bones Alone." *Discover* (March, 1992).

Lenorovitz, Jeffrey M. "France Nears Service Introduction of X-ray-Based Cargo Inspection System." *Aviation Week & Space Technology* 134 (March 25, 1991): 64.

"New Questions about Mammograms." *Newsweek* (March 8, 1993).

"Physician Sales and Service," *Modern Healthcare,* 23 September 1996, 26.

"Physician Sales and Service," *New York Times,* National Edition, 20 November 1996.

"Rigaku Industrial Develops X-ray Device that Analyzes Magnetic Disks Thickness and Chemical Composition of Magnetic Disks," *Nikkei Sangyo Shimbun,* 22 August 1996.

"Shimadzu Develops Digital X-ray Machine," *Nihon Keizi Shimbun,* 12 January 1996.

"SMS Clinical Imaging System," *Medical Device Business News,* October 1996

U.S. Census Bureau. *1997 Economic Census—Manufacturing,* 20 March 2000. Available from http://www.census.gov.

"Varian Signs Supply Deal with Toshiba for X-ray Tubes." *Biomedical Market Newsletter,* April 1996.

"Vivid Technologies Inc." *New York Times,* 8 January 1997

Weiss, Rick. "You Say Tomato, They Say Tomography." *Science News* 132 (Sept 12, 1987).

"X-rays May Help to Repair Spine Damage, Study Suggests," *New York Times,* National Edition, 1 October 1996.

SIC 3845

ELECTROMEDICAL AND ELECTROTHERAPEUTIC APPARATUS

This classification comprises establishments primarily engaged in manufacturing electromedical and electrotherapeutic apparatus, such as magnetic resonance imaging equipment, medical ultrasound equipment, pacemakers, hearing aids, electrocardiographs and electromedical endoscopic equipment. Establishments primarily engaged in manufacturing electrotherapeutic lamp units for ultraviolet and infrared radiation are classified in **SIC 3641: Electric Lamp Bulbs and Tubes.**

NAICS CODE(S)

334517 (Irradiation Apparatus Manufacturing)
334510 (Electromedical and Electrotherapeutic Apparatus Manufacturing)

INDUSTRY SNAPSHOT

In 1997, the electromedical and electrotherapeutic apparatus industry had 458 establishments. These establishments shipped $10.5 billion worth of goods, 67 percent more than 1992's totals, and 50 percent more than 1995.

Born from the rapid technological advances that occurred in the electronics field following the war, specifically from the technological achievements that spawned the semiconductor and computer industries, the list of products manufactured by companies within the electromedical industry comprises a host of medical devices regarded in the 1990s as indispensable to the practice of medicine. These products include pacemakers, heart defibrillators, magnetic resonance imaging (MRI) devices, ultrasonic scanning devices, computerized axial tomography (CAT) scanners, and cardiographs, as well as a number of other medical devices equally essential to the diagnosis and treatment of diseases.

ORGANIZATION AND STRUCTURE

Approximately 400 companies in the United States manufactured electromedical or electrotherapeutic devices as their primary business in the late 1990s. Of the approximately 450 manufacturing establishments operated by the industry's manufacturers, roughly 200 employed 20 or more workers. Compared to the typical size of a manufacturing facility in the United States, the electromedical industry exceeded the national standard, employing nearly 100 workers per establishment.

California led all other states in electromedical device production, manufacturing 19 percent of the industry's total shipments and employing 15 percent of the industry's total workforce. With its 90 manufacturing facilities, California contained more than twice as many facilities as the second and third ranking states, Minnesota and Florida.

Although classified as a distinct industry by the U.S. Government's *Standard Industrial Classification Manual* in the early 1990s, the electromedical industry was not always regarded as such, functioning for roughly the first 25 years of its existence in an ancillary position to the then-larger X-ray apparatus and tubes industry. From the early 1960s to 1987, electromedical industry statistics were combined with those of the X-ray apparatus and tubes industry. During that time, the electromedical industry evolved from a group of manufacturers representing a modestly sized market into a genuine industry of it own. The classification "X-Ray Apparatus and Tubes; Electromedical and Electrotherapeutic Apparatus," initially was a logical combination of what became two separate industries, primarily because the X-ray apparatus segment overshadowed the smaller electromedical segment, generating the bulk of the industry's revenue and representing a more formidable economic force.

In 1987, when many industries were reclassified to more accurately reflect the true nature of American industry, the X-ray apparatus and tubes segment of the classification "X-Ray Apparatus and Tubes; Electromedical and Electrotherapeutic Apparatus," became **SIC 3844: X-ray Apparatus and Tubes and Related Irradiation Apparatus,** while the electromedical segment, by then a larger industry than the X-ray apparatus industry, became **SIC 3845: Electromedical and Electrotherapeutic Apparatus.** This reclassification by the *Standard Industrial Classification Manual,* however, came more than a decade after the electromedical industry had eclipsed the X-ray apparatus industry in magnitude, serving as a somewhat belated recognition of the electromedical industry's force. Consequently, during the electromedical industry's prolific rise to the fore in the 1970s, all of the statistics that tell the story of its growth are somewhat inflated due to the inclusion of the statistical information generated by X-ray apparatus manufacturers.

BACKGROUND AND DEVELOPMENT

In the half century following World War II, the electromedical industry recorded greater growth than the four other industries composing the medical and dental industrial category, outpacing the revenue growth of the surgical and medical instruments industry, the surgical appliances and supplies industry, the dental equipment and supplies industry, and the X-ray apparatus and tubes industry. The rise of the electromedical industry to a position of prominence within the medical and dental category was attributable primarily to the revolutionary nature of the products manufactured under its purview, a diverse selection of technologically sophisticated medical devices that greatly ameliorated the art of medicine not only in the United States, but throughout the world.

Truly a product of a technologically modern society, the electromedical industry owes its emergence largely to research and development conducted in the 1950s by scientists and manufacturers in the then-nascent semiconductor and computer industries. From these two technological staging grounds, combined with advancements in the electronic field resulting from the enormous effort put forth by the nation's space program, the process by which electronic technology developed was greatly accelerated. The knowledge gained from these three components of American industry, each heavily dependent on electronic technology, proved to be a boon to other industries as well, strengthening some, while enabling the outright creation of others. Such was the case with the electromedical industry, which emerged during the 1960s.

To be sure, there were precursors to electromedical devices before the 1960s. Electrical pulsing as means to treat a variety of ailments had been employed since before the turn of the twentieth century, but these early devices were more curiosities than representative of a genuine industry. Instead, perhaps the first piece of equipment that could justify prognostications for the emergence of a future electromedical industry appeared in the late 1950s, when Earl Bakken, chairman of a biomedical company named Medtronic, and cardiologists from the University of Minnesota developed one of the first workable cardiac pacemakers.

Nothing more than an automobile battery resting on a dolly and attached to the patient's chest through wire cables, this first pacemaker was rather primitive, but led to further advancements and the emergence of much smaller versions that soon were regarded as viable medical devices suitable for implantation. As improvements were made in pacemakers, additional products that would later compose the electromedical industry, such as ultrasonic medical equipment and cardiographs, were developed as well. Their development would take time, but the developmental challenges, though formidable, were not the major obstacles barring the appearance of the electromedical industry. Instead, marketing these new products posed the greatest challenge to the fledgling electromedical manufacturers, as industry participants found it difficult to convince the medical community that electromedical devices provided in many cases a preferable alternative to extant medical equipment. This took time as well, but eventually doctors and hospital administrators embraced the new electronic equipment, and by the end of the 1960s, the industry began to emerge as a recognizable economic force.

For electromedical manufacturers, the rewards were worth the wait. The industry quickly flourished, its growth fueled by the widespread acceptance of all kinds of electromedical equipment throughout U.S. health care institutions. Sales amounted to a modest $233 million in 1967, particularly small considering electromedical manufacturers were responsible for generating only a fraction of the total, overshadowed by their larger cousins, X-ray apparatus manufacturers. But the electromedical industry would not be cast in this supportive role for long, and indeed from this point forward, growth of the electromedical industry would outpace that of the X-ray apparatus industry and thereby fuel the growth of the industry as whole. When, five years later, total sales climbed to $429 million, the leap was even more pronounced for electromedical manufacturers, having started from much below the $233 million figure in 1967, yet accounting for a large part of the nearly $200 million increase.

By 1974, the electromedical industry had closed the gap separating its revenue production with that of the X-ray apparatus industry and drew even, with each segment accounting for half of the $650 million in sales recorded that year. With slightly less than 100 X-ray apparatus and electromedical device manufacturers in the country at that time, the number of manufacturers would swell to nearly 240 in two years, a dramatic increase once again reflective mainly of the electromedical industry's rapid rate of growth. From 1974 to the end of the decade, the electromedical industry's revenue volume skyrocketed at a compound annual rate of 31 percent, an increase that dropped to a less prolific 16.4 percent when adjusted for inflation, yet still representative of robust vitality.

Still benefiting from further improvements and from the continued acceptance of their products, which by the mid-1970s had firmly established the electromedical industry as a major player in the broadly defined medical industry, electromedical manufacturers had made great strides since the first awkward and rudimentary pacemaker appeared in the late 1950s. No longer attached via cable or measuring as large as a hat box, pacemakers were now roughly the size of a fingertip and enjoyed widespread demand. In 1970, 53,000 pacemakers were implanted, and by 1976 the yearly implants had increased to 175,000, representing a quarter of a billion dollars in sales. At this time, the prospects for further sales appeared almost guaranteed, as a development of great significance augured a dramatic increase in the number of pacemakers installed each year. Powered by mercury-zinc batteries, pacemakers typically needed to be replaced at least three times during a patient's life span, but the use of lithium-powered batteries, a development that promised to reshape the market for pacemakers, reduced the average replacement expectation of pacemakers to one per patient. Although the switch to lithium-powered batteries would sharply reduce the industry's replacement sales, the prospect of undergoing fewer surgical procedures induced more patients to opt for pacemaker implants, which drove sales upward.

By 1976, the electromedical and X-ray apparatus industry's aggregate revenue neared the $1 billion mark, then shot past it the following year, increasing 86 percent to reach $1.88 billion. Underpinned by strong pacemaker sales and even stronger ultrasonic equipment sales, which were increasing 18 percent annually, the electromedical industry approached the end of its decade of prodigious growth nearing $2.5 billion in sales. Success came slower in the early 1980s, but only in contrast to the dramatic growth of the 1970s. Sales eclipsed $5 billion in 1984, then began to suffer in the ensuing years, falling 2.7 percent in 1985 and increasing only marginally thereafter, as flat demand, a buildup of inventories, and strong competition from imports combined to arrest the industry's expansion.

In 1987, the electromedical industry was separated at last from the X-ray apparatus industry, their respective statistics no longer pooled together. In the last year of their combination, total sales were estimated to be $5 billion; their separation gave, for the first time, a clear indication of their individual magnitude. The electromedical industry emerged as a $3.57 billion industry, employing 29,200 workers, while the X-ray apparatus industry's value of shipments amounted to $1.55 billion and its workforce totaled 8,700.

As the electromedical industry entered the late 1980s, manufacturers attempted to effect a recovery from the mid-1980s, a downturn that was exacerbated by the increasingly cost-conscious health care industry. By 1989, price increases at the manufacturer level averaged only 3 percent in the previous four years, as increased competition and production overcapacity limited the manufacturers' ability to raise prices. Profits suffered as a result, but revenue continued to grow, sending many manufacturers overseas to forge joint ventures with other companies to lessen the financial constraints of a capital-intensive business.

After recording double-digit growth between 1987 and 1990, the electromedical industry entered the early 1990s watching its inspiring growth shudder to a stop, particularly in 1993, when sales were flat. In 1994, the industry's revenue total was an estimated $6.23 billion. The industry-wide stagnation of the early 1990s was attributable largely to a sharp decline in MRI shipments, which plummeted nearly 20 percent compared to shipment increases of pacemakers and ultrasonic scanning devices of 3 and 5 percent, respectively. The decline in MRI shipments, more capital-intensive than pacemakers or ultrasonic scanning devices, was attributed primarily to recessive economic conditions during the early 1990s, coupled with uncertainty regarding the future of health care as a result of President Bill Clinton's health care reforms.

Looking forward from the mid-1990s, prognostications for the electromedical industry were predicated on the further technological development of MRIs, and generally on advancements emanating from the diagnostic side of the electromedical industry. With improved imaging systems, operating at significantly higher speeds, this type of electromedical equipment provided the industry's best answer to the health care industry's need for cost-cutting, more efficient equipment in the 1990s.

Tattoo removal was also becoming a larger market for the electromedical industry. A dermatological laser distributed only by Laser Photonics, Florida, signed a 1996, three-year deal for $5.4 million to provide medical lasers for removing tattoos, pigmented skin, and unwanted hair to American Laser Corp.

CURRENT CONDITIONS

A solid U.S. economy, growing at a slow and steady pace throughout the 1990s has apparently benefited this industry. In 1997, there were 542 establishments engaged in producing electromedical and electrotherapeutic apparatus, employing 53,680 persons. Revenues for 1997 were $11.36 billion, almost doubling the revenues of 1994. This growth is projected to continue. CorpTech, in October, 1999 surveyed 52 of these establishments. Over half of the establishments surveyed indicated that they planned to increase their workforce during the next year by an average of 12.3 percent. More than one company in six projected growth of over 25 percent.

As of the close of the century, medical device manufacturers can be subject to product-liability claims in state court. The U.S. Supreme Court found Medtronic Inc., the world's largest pacemaker manufacturer, liable for design defects, a ruling that could influence the 11 million people in the United States with such implanted medical devices as pacemakers, silicone breast implants, hearing aids, penile implants, hip replacements, and knee replacements. The company had 1999 sales of $4.1 billion and employed 21,794 people.

INDUSTRY LEADERS

The largest manufacturer in the electromedical industry during the 1990s, General Electric's Medical Systems Group based in Milwaukee, Wisconsin, stood as a classic example of the electromedical industry's efforts to further penetrate the international electromedical market and reduce the production costs of its products. With joint ventures scattered across Asia, General Electric's Medical Systems Group entered into a joint venture with a personal computer manufacturer, Wipro Ltd., in India in 1990 to produce and sell a wide variety of ultrasound devices. By forging such ties, the Medical Systems Group became one of General Electric's most profitable divisions in the mid-1990s, recording more than $5 billion in sales in 1993. In 1998, the Medical Systems Group recorded sales of $4.8 billion, an increase of $0.5 billion over 1997. In December, 1999, General Electric purchased OEC Medical Systems, Inc. This company had 1998 sales of $188.7 million, and further strengthened General Electric's place at the industry's forefront.

Other important manufacturers in the electromedical industry include Marconi Medical Systems (formerly Picker International Inc.), based in Cleveland, Ohio, and St. Jude Medical, Inc., based in St. Paul, Minnesota. Marconi Medical Systems reported revenues of $1.5 billion in sales and employed approximately 5,000 person in 1999. St. Jude Medical, Inc., a heart valve manufacturer, acquired Ventritex, a leading heart defibrillator company, for $501 million in 1997. St. Jude Medical is the world's leading manufacturer of mechanical heart valves. This company recorded sales of $1.1 billion in 1999, employing approximately 4,000 people. In December, 1999, St. Jude Medical announced the first implants of the Photon DR Dual—Chamber Implantable Cardioverter Defibrillator.

WORKFORCE

Total employment during the electromedical industry's history generally paralleled its pattern of revenue growth, climbing while sales increased and leveling off when revenue growth became less prolific. In 1974, when the industry already was experiencing a phenomenal surge of growth and its total employment included employees involved in the production of X-ray apparatus, there were 13,000 employees composing its workforce. Two years later, total employment vaulted to 30,900, largely due to the growth of the electromedical segment of the industry. This figure continued to increase, reaching 41,500 by 1981, then climbing to 48,800 by 1984, at which time total employment in the industry began to record successive annual declines as manufacturers streamlined their operations. By 1988, total employment had fallen to 31,400, then began to increase once again, rising to 34,400 by 1991.

Of the 34,400 people employed by the electromedical industry in 1991, less than half were production workers, an atypical ratio of production workers to salaried employees in American manufacturing industry. The greater proportional representation of salaried employees, those performing managerial, administrative, or technical duties, was primarily due to the technological sophistication of the products manufactured by the industry, which, as the level of sophistication increased over the course of the industry's existence, winnowed the ranks of production workers in the industry. These trends have continued into 1998, when 46,416 people were employed in this industry with less than half being production workers.

Generally, production workers were employed on a full-time basis during the 1990s, averaging 4 percent more hours per year than the typical production worker employed by other manufacturing industries. Production workers in the electromedical industry generally earned more per hour than their counterparts as well, averaging $10.91 per hour in 1989, compared to the national average of $10.49 per hour. In 1996, this average hourly wage increased to $12.90, and in 1997, the wage increased to $14.28.

Of the 458 establishments in the electromedical industry, the majority of them are located in California. Other states with significant concentrations of establishments in this industry include Minnesota, Florida, and Massachusetts.

AMERICA AND THE WORLD

Historically, the electromedical industry's international presence has been a major source of its strength, providing manufacturers with ample room to market their highly sophisticated products in markets bereft of similar equipment. In 1993, this presence continued to support the industry at a time when domestic conditions had soured. In that year, U.S. exports of electromedical equipment increased 8 percent to $2.4 billion, giving U.S. manufacturers a $1.1 billion trade surplus. Much of this business was attributable to the strong sales performance of electrodiagnostic devices, ultrasonic scanners, and patient monitoring systems. These products were sold chiefly to European Community countries, Japan, and Canada. In 1997, exports totaled $2.6 billion.

RESEARCH AND DEVELOPMENT

Recent technological advances have led to the improvement of current instruments. One such device, a smaller, lighter, defibrillator, restores the heartbeat of cardiac arrest victims more quickly than the older version. Since it improves the survival rate of these patients, sales of the instrument are expected to reach $150 million per year by 2000.

New diagnostic tools and surgical devices are expected to benefit the industry and patients alike. In-body blood and tissue surveillance systems sales approximated $360 million in 1996, and the industry anticipates sales of $630 million by the year 2000. A non-evasive, 15-minute cancer test, approved in 1997, was expected to reduce the number of biopsies and increase early detection of the disease.

FURTHER READING

American Journal of Emergency Medicine, January 1995, 13.

"Americas: FDA Tightens Manufacturing Quality Standards." *Medical Device Business News,* October 1996.

"Asahi Glass Engineering: Electrolysis Water Generator Approved by Ministry of Health and Welfare." *Nikkan Kogyo Shimbun,* 8 January 1997.

"Automation, Resolution & Speed Mark Capillary Electrophoresis Trends." *Genetic Engineering News,* 15 January 1997, 17.

"Breast Disease (Screening) Adjunctive Screening Device Enhances Early Detection." *Cancer Weekly Plus,* 11 November 1996.

"Brit, Dr. Reddy's Lab in Technical Collaboration." *Business Line,* 10 July 1996.

Chiu, Yvonne. "California Couple Markets Reusable Fertility Test Device." *Sacramento Bee,* 12 April 1996.

"Circon Expected To Seek White Knight." *Mergers & Acquisitions Report,* 19 August 1996, 9.

"Court Allows State Litigation in Medical Device Lawsuits." *Plastics News,* 1 July 1996, 8.

Darnay, Arsen J., ed. *Manufacturing USA.* 5th edition, Detroit: Gale Research, 1996.

"Diagnosis by Videophone-Teledoc From NEC." *Newsbytes News Network,* 23 February 1996.

Engardio, Pete. "An Ultrasound Foothold in Asia." *Business Week,* 8 November 1993, 68.

"Expanding the Pie." *HFN,* 8 April 1996, 70.

"FDA OKs Device to Remove Lesions." *Household & Personal Products Industry.* August 1996, 33.

"FDA Panel Backs Pacemaker Device." *Chicago Tribune,* 16 July 1996.

"Financing Business." *Wall Street Journal,* 7 October 1996.

"Florida's Laser Photronics Signs Deal with Utah's American Laser Corp." *Orlando Sentinel,* 19 July 1996.

"Heartsteram, Physio-Control Vie to Arrest Cardiac Arrest." *Seattle Times,* 26 September 1996.

"Hitachi Setting Up R&D Group." *Plain Dealer,* 26 May 1996.

"Hologic Announces $59M Plan to Merge with Fluroscan." *Boston Globe,* 20 July 1996.

Hoover's Company Capsules, 20 March 2000. Available from http://www.hoovers.com.

"ISG Technologies." *Globe & Mail,* 23 July 1996.

"Italy: Medical Diagnostic Imaging and Equipment." *Journal of Commerce,* 18 December 1996, 410.

"LG Industrial Systems Launches R&D Centers Worldwide." *Korea Economic Daily,* 14 August 1996.

"Medical Device Makers Face State Court Suits." *Chicago Tribune,* 27 June 1996.

"Medtronic." *Modern Healthcare,* 29 April 1996, 26.

"Now Surgeons Can Nip and Tuck in 3-D." *Business Week,* 3 February 1997.

"Outlook Brightens for Ultrasound Firm Advanced Technology Labs." *Seattle Times,* 9 May 1996.

"Quorum Sells ISG Stake." *Globe & Mail,* 19 December 1996.

"Roche Bioscience Deal with Affymetrix." *Marketletter,* 20 January 1997.

"St. Jude Medical Agrees to Acquire Ventritex." *Wall Street Journal,* 24 October 1996.

"Ultrasound Market in Emerging Countries." *Biomedical Market Newsletter,* 31 October 1996, p. 6.

U.S. Census Bureau. *1997 Economic Census—Manufacturing.* GPO: Washington 1999.

U.S. Department of Commerce. International Trade Administration. *U.S. Industrial Outlook.* Washington: GPO, 1993.

"U.S. Sales of Electronics up 11 Percent." *Newsbytes News Network,* 2 August 1996.

SIC 3851

OPHTHALMIC GOODS

This classification includes establishments primarily engaged in manufacturing ophthalmic frames, lenses, contact lenses, and sunglass lenses. Establishments involved in manufacturing molded glass blanks are included in **SIC 3229: Pressed and blown glass and glassware, Not Elsewhere Classified;** and businesses engaged in grinding lenses and fitting glasses to prescriptions are classified in **SIC 5995: Optical Goods Stores.**

NAICS CODE(S)

339115 (Ophthalmic Goods Manufacturing)

INDUSTRY SNAPSHOT

The ophthalmic goods industry was marked by intense competition among its major players in the late 1990s, not surprisingly considering the potential market to be conquered. About 159 million people in the United States require some type of vision correction. By 2005, 20 percent of the population will be between the ages of 55 and 74, about 95 percent of which will consume ophthalmic goods. Meanwhile, industry players hoped to develop long-term relationships with younger customers, unleashing an expansive advertising effort in the mid- and late 1990s.

About 520 companies in the United States, including 26,366 employees and 17,936 production workers, were involved in manufacturing ophthalmic goods, according the 1997 Census of Manufacturers. These companies generated about $3.6 billion in 1997 shipment values for products covered in this industry classification. This figure represented an aggregate value of shipments largely derived from the production of the four primary products in the ophthalmic goods industry: ophthalmic lenses and frames, sunglasses, industrial eyewear, and contact lenses. Contact lenses, by far the dominant ophthalmic goods product in the 1990s, accounted for more than 43 percent of the total shipments delivered by the industry, with soft contact lenses representing 95 percent of the contact lens product share. Plastic ophthalmic focus lenses accounted for approximately 18.3 percent of the industry's shipments while ophthalmic frames and industrial eyewear each accounted for 3.6 percent of the product share. Non-prescription sunglasses represented four percent of the total shipments delivered by the industry. Other products within the ophthalmic goods industry include underwater goggles, reading and simple magnifiers, and a ophthalmic lens coating.

The ophthalmic goods industry has retained solid growth for nearly two decades. In 1990, shipments of ophthalmic goods totaled $2.27 billion, having risen from $1.28 billion in 1982, though with a slight downturn in the mid-1980s. Through the 1990s, sales have continuously improved, attributable in part to the increasing popularity of designer sunglasses and to technological innovations in the development of contact lenses. Especially in the late 1990s, growth-hungry U.S. manufacturers sought markets overseas with less penetration than mature U.S. markets—in which rising consumer prosperity was reaching levels attractive to U.S. manufacturers.

ORGANIZATION AND STRUCTURE

The ophthalmic goods industry was predominantly populated by relatively small manufacturing operations. Of the 575 establishments involved in producing ophthalmic goods, nearly 75 percent employed fewer than 20 people and more than a third had less than 5 employees. Typically, the larger companies do not solely manufacture ophthalmic goods but manufacture a diverse line of products to generate sales. For example, the leading company in the industry, Bausch & Lomb Inc., garnered more than two-thirds of its sales in 1999 from healthcare products.

The industry relies heavily on consumer advertising for retail sales, spending $517 million on such advertising in 1998, up eight percent from 1997. Indicative of the vigorously competitive atmosphere, much of this advertising is price-driven, whereby companies broadcast their products' cost-savings to consumers.

In the distribution sector, optical chains have gained a significant foothold, with $5.2 billion in retail sales in 1998, a five percent increase over 1997, due in large part to consolidation. Mass retailers, like Wal-Mart, were also aggressively moving into the ophthalmic-goods distribution market during the 1990s. Meanwhile, retail sales were somewhat curtailed by the explosion of electronic commerce. To try to minimize the costs involved in trying to secure distributors, manufacturers made great efforts to expand their relationships with various dispensers, which include opthamologists and optometrists, optical chains, mass retailers, and HMO practices.

During the 1980s, the cost of conducting business in the ophthalmic goods industry rose sharply, far outpacing the increase in sales during the decade. In 1982, the industry recorded $1.28 billion in sales and spent $41 million on capital investment. By 1990, sales had climbed to $2.27 billion, but capital investment had more than tripled to $137 million. In 1997, capital investment reached $2.38 billion against sales of $3.6 billion. The average investment required to operate an ophthalmic facility in 1989 was $282,398, a figure that totaled $414,325 by 1997. The average cost for facilities operating in the ophthalmic goods industry reached $2.7 million in 1997, up from $1.3 million in 1989.

BACKGROUND AND DEVELOPMENT

Until the 1960s, growth in the ophthalmic goods industry had occurred at a steady, predictable rate, largely dictated by the rate of population growth in the United States. During the 1960s, however, an increased demand for ophthalmic products elevated the production and sales levels of manufacturers to an unprecedented high. A combination of several factors prompted this remarkable surge in growth, including a dramatic rise in the nation's population and an increase in the availability of eye examinations. The advent of contact lenses in the 1950s as a genuine alternative to conventional corrective eyewear, however, contributed most significantly to the growth of the ophthalmic goods industry.

Although extraordinary gains were achieved by contact lens manufacturers and retailers during the first years of quantifiable production in the 1950s, certain difficulties associated with the early development of contact lenses slowed the public's acceptance of the new product. On average, a pair of contact lenses sold for $200, an exceedingly high price to pay for many consumers, and the discomfort caused by wearing the hard, hydrophobic lenses, which initially covered most of the exposed eyeball, dissuaded a considerable percentage of consumers from making a long-term conversion to contact lenses. According to industry estimates, roughly half of the people who began fittings for contact lenses reverted back to conventional corrective eyewear, a rate of attrition that continued to plague contact lens manufacturers into the 1970s.

Despite the high cost of these lenses and the discomfort they often caused, consumers purchased enough contact lenses to push annual sales from $2 million in 1950 to $60 million by 1959. The number of contact lens manufacturers, the majority of which were small, privately-owned companies, also increased at a commensurate rate during the decade, climbing from 20 in 1950 to more than 400 by 1960. This proliferation of contact lens manufacturers led to a rash of deceptive advertising complaints issued by the Federal Trade Commission (FTC) and sparked several fiercely contested patent disputes, as the excitement generated by the creation of a new, potentially lucrative market within the ophthalmic goods industry attracted increased competition. Complaints filed by the FTC, 15 of which were recorded in 1961 compared to only four prior to 1960, and patent disputes, along with issues such as whether only ophthalmologists and oculists should be allowed to prescribe and fit contact lenses, caused the sales of contact lenses to stagnate at the close of the decade. But these were problems generally associated with the nascence of the market and, as such, inflicted only a temporary setback on the burgeoning industry.

By the mid-1960s, improvements had been made in contact lenses, although their cost still hovered around $200 a pair. The thickness of the plastic used to manufacture the lenses had been reduced, alleviating some of the irritation experienced when a contact lens wearer's eyelid passed over the lens, and the diameter of the lenses had also been reduced so that they only covered the iris and the pupil, rather than the entire exposed eyeball. Shortly before these improvements were made, however, a discovery of lasting importance for the future of the contact lens market overshadowed the technological strides made by the industry in hard contact lens design—although it would be years before its impact would be felt by manufacturers and retailers. In 1965, two Czechoslovakian scientists, Otto Wichterle and Drahoslav Lim, were awarded a patent for their invention, five years earlier, of a soft plastic suitable for body implants that could also be used to produce contact lenses. Marking the beginning of soft contact lenses, which would eventually account for an overwhelming percentage of contact lens sales, the pliable, hydrophilic material absorbed tears rather than shedding them, as did hard contact lenses, and virtually eliminated any sensation of the eyelid passing over the lens.

Concurrent with the encouraging development of soft contact lenses, the rest of the ophthalmic goods industry was expanding at a robust rate, exceeding the rate of growth in the nation's population. From 1955 to 1965, the population over the age of five increased 18.4 percent, while the number of corrective eyewear users rose by 30 percent. This growth was primarily attributable to a greater portion of the population undergoing complete eye examinations, a trend facilitated by Medicare and Medicaid health programs, increased screening for vision acuity in public school systems, and states requiring mandatory eye examinations for people applying for driving licenses. The increasing number of union optical plans, coupled with a greater number of corrective lens wearers purchasing more than one pair of ophthalmic lenses and frames, also fueled the expansion of the ophthalmic market in the 1960s.

New product developments in the conventional corrective eyewear field also contributed to the gains achieved by the ophthalmic industry in the 1960s. One of the four leading publicly-held companies engaged in the ophthalmic goods industry at the time, American Optical Corporation, introduced a new single vision lens that provided increased visual sharpness and less distortion from peripheral angles of view. Another leader in the industry, Univis, developed bifocal lenses in 1964 without a visible line separating each half of the lens. Plastic, shatterproof, and lightweight lenses also made their debut in the 1960s. Accounting for only 5 percent of the total corrective lens sales by the mid-1960s, plastic lens sales, nevertheless, had been growing faster than the industry itself during the decade.

Sunglasses also experienced a surge in sales during the 1960s, further accelerating the rapid pace at which the ophthalmic goods industry was expanding. During the 1960s, sunglasses became fashionable accessories worn throughout the year and were no longer considered seasonal products. As the product in the ophthalmic goods industry most sensitive to fashion trends, sunglasses quickly became a lucrative product to manufacture and sell, as unit sales rose from 60 million pairs in 1960 to 175 million pairs in 1966. By the end of the decade, the sunglasses market had leapt 70 percent from the sales volume recorded in 1965—to approximately $200 million.

Conspicuously absent from the contact lens market during the 1960s were the leading manufacturers in the ophthalmic goods industry. American Optical Company and Bausch & Lomb Inc., which together controlled more than 90 percent of the conventional eyeglass market, had eschewed entrance into the contact lens market primarily because the directors of the companies perceived the competition to be too intense. Moreover, neither company felt it had developed a technological innovation in the product encouraging enough to warrant a foray into the market. In 1966, however, Bausch & Lomb acquired the exclusive rights to manufacture and sell the soft, hydrophilic lenses developed by the two Czechoslovakian scientists and, by 1972, the company started distributing soft contact lenses nationwide.

In the 1970s, the ophthalmic goods industry continued to benefit from the population growth, as the prodigious sales increases of the 1960s continued. Wholesale billings for the optical industry as a whole increased from $400 million in 1959 to $900 million by 1969 then doubled to nearly $2 billion by the end of the 1970s. The success of the industry attracted the attention of the FTC once again, in 1974, when it began investigating restraints on price advertising in the optical industry. In the course of its investigation, the FTC found a significant discrepancy in the price of eyewear throughout the nation, with the average price of eyewear running 25 percent higher in states where advertising was illegal and varying by as much as 300 percent within the same state. In 1978, the same year in which eyeglass coverage became mandatory under Medicaid, the FTC lifted the restrictions on advertising with the hope of saving consumers as much as $400 million annually. Consequently, competition within the ophthalmic goods industry intensified as pricing strategies became of paramount importance.

Along with this transformation of the retail side of the optical industry, ophthalmic goods manufacturers continued to experience growth, engendered in part by the expansion of the sunglasses market. In the early 1980s, sunglasses sales dropped, with unit demand slipping 15 percent in 1981 and 1982, but sales began rising as the decade progressed. Indicative of the product's dependency on fashion trends, the increase in sales was partly attributable to the popularity of several films during the early 1980s that featured well-known actors wearing sunglasses. For example, perhaps the greatest boost from the motion picture industry came when a pair of Bausch & Lomb's Ray-Ban Wayfarer sunglasses were prominently featured in *Risky Business*. In 1981, 18,000 pairs of the Wayfarer sunglasses were sold; however, after the film was released in 1983, unit sales ballooned to 330,000 pairs. Retail sales in the sunglasses market rose from $361 million in 1985 to $1.5 billion by the end of the decade, reflecting a 100 percent increase from 1980.

Although the number of contact lens wearers in the United States tapered off at approximately 24 million in the four or five years prior to 1992, the dynamics within this segment of the ophthalmic goods industry were rapidly changing in the early 1990s. Disposable soft contact lenses, first marketed by Johnson & Johnson in 1988, grabbed the attention of consumers during the product's first years of availability and were expected to woo many contact lens wearers away from conventional contact lenses.

CURRENT CONDITIONS

By 1999 the number of people wearing contact lenses in the United States had grown for seven consecutive years. That year, about thirty million people in the United States wore contact lenses, creating a $2.5-billion market. The largest market was for soft lenses, with 27.6 million wearers, while rigid gas permeable lenses accounted for 5.6 million wearers. In addition, the market for disposable lenses skyrocketed throughout the 1990s; two-thirds of soft lens wearers now use these lenses.

Retail margins began to flatten somewhat in the late 1990s amidst competition from mail-order providers and online lens sales. Ten percent of contact lens wearers purchase lenses through the mail, a figure that doubles for disposable lens wearers. As a result, prices were driven downward, forcing ophthalmic goods manufacturers to streamline their production processes in order to maintain solid margins. Optometrists and manufacturers joined together against mail-order outlets and, to a lesser degree, other discount outlets, who have garnered an increasing share of the market in recent years. Many manufacturers,

including the giants of the industry, refuse to sell lenses to mail-order companies or discount outlets that don't have eye-care professionals on-site. Nonetheless, these distribution outlets continue to gain popularity.

Manufacturers have thus invested extensively to build brand equity, especially among younger customers with whom they hope to develop lifelong relationships, a primary focus of the recent advertising blitz. These trends, furthermore, helped spur the emerging specialty lens market, particularly among the industry's top players, who hope to realize higher margins. One of the most notable niche markets was for colored contact lenses, which have started to place contact lenses, like eyeglass frames, as fashion items. Colored contact lenses generated sales of $200 million in 1998, primarily of blue-tinted lenses. Another emerging niche market was for intraocular lenses, which replace the natural lens that is removed during cataract surgery. Cataracts occur in half of all 65- to 75-year-olds in the United States; thus, the aging of the population constitutes a prime factor driving future sales expectations in this market category.

Among the most notable developments in contact lens manufacturing was the development in the late 1990s of lenses that treat colorblindness. ColorMax Technologies, a California-based firm, received U.S. Food and Drug Administration (FDA) approval in 1999 to sell lenses that enable a colorblind wearer to distinguish between colors that would normally appear similar. The technology functions by altering the wavelength of colors as they meet the eye. These lenses were to be customized for the particular patient's form of colorblindness. Whereas similar technologies were already in existence, they failed to account for variations is the type or severity of customers' afflictions.

The industry was challenged in the late 1990s by the sharp increase in the number of customers foregoing corrective lenses altogether in favor of laser eye surgery. Analysts expect this market to grow exponentially in the early 2000s, which will likely force many players out of the ophthalmic goods industry. However, some of the larger firms such as Bausch & Lomb were able to capitalize on this growing market by diversifying and incorporating surgery into their business.

This competitive atmosphere of the ophthalmic goods industry was marked in 1999 by a false-advertising complaint to the FDA lodged by Johnson & Johnson against its chief competitor Bausch & Lomb. The controversy began when Bausch & Lomb ran an advertisement, which the FDA described as "false and misleading," that claimed their Pure Vision contact lenses were superior to Johnson & Johnson's AcuVue brand. The ad claimed that Pure Vision lenses caused the eye to swell only 4.1 percent, compared with AcuVue's 9.1 percent, due to the greater level of oxygen infiltration afforded by Pure Vision lenses. It went on to boast that consumers prefer Pure Vision to AcuVue at a rate of 69 percent. Johnson & Johnson cried foul, claiming that such declarations were not clinically substantiated. A warning letter from the FDA citing lack of adequate proof for such claims forced Bausch & Lomb to retract the advertisement.

As the population ages, continued sales are more or less assured, especially in the bifocal and multifocal lens sectors that target age-related prebyopia. Meanwhile, lighter and thinner ophthalmic lens technology, along with growing style-consciousness, portends a healthy future for eyeglasses, even as contact lenses further penetrate the market.

In 1998, sales of sunglasses equaled $1.9 billion, with mass retailers accounting for $262 million, optical outlets $406 million, and sunglasses specialty stores $495 million. The most robust area of the sunglasses market was for designer sunglasses. These glasses, marketed as fashion wear, exploded beginning in the mid-1980s and became a particularly high-priority market sector in the late 1990s. The average price of sunglasses rose 50 percent between 1990 and 1997, when a pair cost $23.06, largely on the strength of name-brand varieties. About 44 percent of all sunglasses carry designer logos.

In addition to heightened emphasis on designer sunglasses as fashion, sunglasses sales were aided by consumer concern about the protection of their eyes from ultraviolet rays on a year-round basis. Indeed, one of the most promising trends in this sector involved polarized lenses designed specifically to protect the eye from ultraviolet rays. Another innovation was bendable plastic frames for sports-related sunglasses.

Severely affected by the global recession in the early 1990s, the sunglasses market, especially sensitive to the health of the national economy, also suffered from its robust growth during the 1980s, as the proliferation of sunglasses manufacturers exacerbated the effect of the stagnant economy and saturated the market. The surfeit of manufacturers entering the U.S. market from both the domestic and international fronts does not bode well for the immediate future of sunglasses sales.

Additionally, pending legislation regarding the restructuring of the nation's healthcare system will undoubtedly affect individuals' ophthalmology coverage, which will in turn have a significant impact on ophthalmic goods manufacturers. Doubts concerning what provisions will be included for the optical industry, which ranks below the medical and dental industries in terms of size and political clout, characterized the industry's anxiety the last time national health care legislation was seriously considered in the early and mid-1970s. These same concerns were revisited as the industry entered the 2000s.

INDUSTRY LEADERS

With manufacturing or marketing operations in 26 countries, Bausch & Lomb is the dominant company operating in the ophthalmic goods industry. An industry leader since its inception in 1853, Bausch & Lomb secured a lasting foothold in the optical field by developing the first rubber eyeglass frames, contributing significantly to the advancement of microscope and telescope technology, and through the creation of Aviator-style Ray-Ban sunglasses. The acquisition of the rights to manufacture and sell soft contact lenses in 1966 and the subsequent FDA approval to market the lenses in 1971, coupled with the company's diversification in the early 1980s into health care and biomedical business lines, contributed most appreciably to the company's success in the 1980s and 1990s. Bausch & Lomb posted overall sales of $1.8 billion in 1999, while maintaining a payroll of about 12,000 workers. The company reacted to tough competition in the contact lens market by cutting about 850 jobs in 1999. Bausch & Lomb accounts for 16 percent of the contact lens market to place third in that sector; its business includes soft and rigid gas permeable contact lens and lens-care products. In the late 1990s the firm sold its sunglasses business, including the popular Ray Ban line, to Luxottica, and delved into refractive laser eye surgery.

Johnson & Johnson led the contact lens market with a 24 percent share in 1998. The firm's Viskaton unit is the leader in contact lens fits, and achieved sales of $850 million in 1998.

Allergan, Inc. manufacturers and markets of contact lenses and a broad assortment of other ophthalmic products not included in this industry classification. Allergan employed 5,972 people and garnered $1,39 billion in sales in 1999.

Among the other leading companies in 1999 were Sola International, which designs and manufactures plastic and glass eyeglass lenses, with 7,450 employees and $542.2 million in sales in 1999.

The largest specialty retailer of sunglasses was Sunglass Hut International Inc., established in the early 1970s. In 1999, the company maintained 1,401 stores in the U.S. employing 3,678 individuals.

WORKFORCE

The ophthalmic goods industry employed 26,366 people in 1997, 18,000 of whom were production workers, with the remaining workers performing administrative, technical, or managerial duties. By 1998, the employment rate was expected to reach 31,000. Employment within the industry shrank during the mid-1980s to a low of 21,700 people but rebounded by the end of the decade to surpass levels established during the early 1980s.

Typically, production workers in the ophthalmic goods industry are employed on a full-time basis, averaging 2 percent more hours per year than the average of production workers employed by other U.S. industries. By 1997, the average hourly wage for production workers was $12.55, up from $10.09 in 1994.

FURTHER READING

"Alas, Better Focus." *Forbes,* 11 January 1999.

"Bausch & Lomb Retracts Ad Claims For Contact Lens." *Wall Street Journal,* 4 May 1999.

"Boomers Want Style in Reading Glasses." *MMR,* 7 September 1999.

"Eye Strain." *Forbes,* 4 October 1999.

"FDA Approves Sales of Tustin, Calif.-Based Lenses for Color-Blind." *Orange County Register,* 7 December 1999.

"Ophthalmic Devices—Contact Lenses—Market Dynamics." *Medical & Healthcare Marketplace Guide,* 1999.

"Ophthalmic Devices—Intraocular Lenses." *Medical & Healthcare Marketplace Guide,* 1999.

"Ophthalmic Devices—Overview." *Medical & Healthcare Marketplace Guide,* 1999.

"Ophthalmic Devices—Spectacles." *Medical & Healthcare Marketplace Guide,* 1999.

"Optical Retailing." *Medical & Healthcare Marketplace Guide,* 1999.

"Power Shift." *Accessories,* October 1999.

SIC 3861

PHOTOGRAPHIC EQUIPMENT AND SUPPLIES

This classification includes establishments primarily engaged in manufacturing photographic apparatus, equipment, parts, attachments, and accessories utilized in both still and motion photography. Also covered in this classification are establishments primarily involved in manufacturing photocopy and microfilm equipment, blueprinting and diazotype (white printing) apparatus and equipment, sensitized film, paper, cloth, and plates, and prepared photographic chemicals.

Those establishments involved in manufacturing products that are related to the photographic industry, but are not grouped in the photographic equipment and supplies classification, include manufacturers of unsensitized photographic paper stock, and paper mats, mounts, easels, and folders utilized for photographic purposes. These establishments are classified within the paper and allied products industry. Photographic lens manufacturers are classified in **SIC 3827: Optical Instruments and**

Lenses, and manufacturers of photographic glass are delineated in the stone, clay, glass, and concrete products industry. Also excluded are manufacturers of chemicals produced for technical purposes that are not specifically prepared and packaged for use in photography and those manufacturing photographic flash, flood, enlarger, and projection lamp bulbs. The former are classified within chemicals and allied products, and the latter are classified in **SIC 3641: Electric Lamp Bulbs and Tubes.**

NAICS CODE(S)

333315 (Photographic and Photocopying Equipment Manufacturing)

INDUSTRY SNAPSHOT

The U.S. Census Bureau estimated that there were 428 establishments manufacturing photographic and photocopying equipment in 1997. They shipped $8.4 billion worth of merchandise, spent $3.8 billion on materials, and invested $289 million in buildings and other structures, machinery, and equipment. About 31 percent of these establishments employed at least 20 people. The largest concentrations of facilities in this classification were in California, Illinois, New Jersey, and Pennsylvania.

There were 310 establishments manufacturing photographic film, paper, plate, and chemicals in 1997. They shipped $12.8 billion worth of merchandise, spent $5.0 billion on materials, and invested $567 million in capital expenditures. About 35 percent of these establishments employed at least 20 people. The largest concentrations of facilities in this classification were in California, Illinois, Texas, and New Jersey.

Growth in the photographic equipment and supplies industry was usually fueled by the introduction of new products that featured innovative technology. In addition, when people bought still and motion camera equipment, they also tended to buy film and related supplies. Since most photographic equipment and supplies were considered leisure or nonessential goods, the industry was particularly sensitive to economic conditions. The industry produced such a broad range of goods, however, that it was somewhat insulated from market fluctuations. For example, still picture film and photocopying equipment typically sold consistently despite economic downturns.

ORGANIZATION AND STRUCTURE

The photographic equipment and supplies industry was comprised mostly of small manufacturing operations. In the late 1980s, most of the facilities had been concentrated in the mid-Atlantic states, but by the early 1990s the industry was beginning to spread out across the country.

The operating costs associated with a photographic equipment and supplies facility, at $7.1 million per year in 1992, were much higher than at the typical manufacturing facility, where the average was only $1.7 million. This gap was expected to widen as electronic imaging products, which required more expensive equipment to manufacture than conventional photographic products, gained popularity and caused more manufacturers to convert their facilities.

BACKGROUND AND DEVELOPMENT

Although photographic equipment and supplies first became available to consumers in the 1880s, it was not until the 1950s that the industry's sales grew rapidly. This was a defining decade for the photographic industry, characterized by a significant increase in consumers' disposable income, the emergence of photocopying and microfilming products as lucrative components within the industry, and the development of still cameras that were easy to operate.

Many of the technological achievements that eventually led to this growth surge were accomplished by Eastman Kodak Company. In the late 1870s, Kodak's founder, George Eastman, had adapted a photographic process that replaced wet-plate developing chemicals and equipment with a dry-plate process. Cleaner to operate and generally easier to use than wet-plate cameras, Eastman's dry-plate system was the first step toward making photographic equipment available to all consumers. Eastman said he intended to make the camera affordable and "as convenient as the pencil". Next, Eastman began widespread marketing of roll film, a product that had been developed by film and camera manufacturer Reverend Hannibal Goodwin.

To interest consumers in photography, manufacturers of this era improved the performance of cameras and the quality of film. A giant leap toward this goal was taken in 1900 when Kodak introduced the first model of its popular, inexpensive, and easy-to-operate Brownie line of cameras. Retailing for $1, the first Brownie signaled the beginning of affordable cameras with mass-market appeal. Kodak later developed products to diversify the applications of photographic equipment. The first 8 mm motion picture system designed for the amateur photographer entered the market in 1932, followed by color film three years later.

Additional products that were intended to spark interest in amateur photography soon emerged, but, after World War II, they were overshadowed by the introduction of film that could be developed instantly. The inventor of this new film-development process was Dr. Edwin H. Land, the founder of Polaroid Corporation. Launched in 1947, the first instant camera and film marked the beginning of Polaroid's rise toward multibillion dollar sales.

Meanwhile, manufacturers improved their products, consumers grew accustomed to using photographic equipment, and the economic and population boom of the 1950s ignited photographic sales. According to industry estimates, purchases of photographic products more than doubled during the decade, jumping from less than $500 million in 1950 to $1.2 billion by 1960. This was partly attributable to the robust national economy following the war, which provided consumers with more money to spend on photography. The high birth rate was also a factor, since parents often purchased cameras and film to photograph their children—the subject of approximately 55 percent of the 2.2 billion photographs taken in 1960.

Kodak held a virtual monopoly of the photographic industry from the turn of the century through this period, perennially controlling roughly 90 percent of the film market and an overwhelming share of the camera market. In the early 1950s, the federal government filed an antitrust suit against Kodak that resulted in a consent decree in 1954. Part of Kodak's dominance before the decree was attributable to a film-processing fee that was automatically included with every Kodak film purchase. By including a built-in processing fee, Kodak in effect cornered the processing end of the industry and consequently discouraged any competition for its film manufacturing business, since the dearth of alternative processing facilities inhibited film sales by other manufacturers. This practice ended in 1954, however, when Kodak agreed to sell film without a processing charge and to license other processing companies to develop Kodak film and prints. Although Kodak maintained its grip on the industry, other companies began to enter a market that had been essentially closed to competition.

Meanwhile, competitors were scurrying to secure a foothold in the fledgling photocopying market, which also promised to be a lucrative enterprise. Although photocopying sales did not exceed $100 million until 1958, revenues increased rapidly when a product was developed for office use. Photocopiers were primarily targeted toward industrial users during the 1950s, but new technology enabled manufacturers to make smaller machines suitable for the business community. Each of the market leaders manufactured photocopiers that operated on a different photocopying process. Controlling roughly one-third of the market each, Minnesota Mining and Manufacturing and Kodak used Thermofax and Verifax processes, respectively. American Photocopy Equipment Company, the third-largest manufacturer, used a diffusion transfer process. In the end, however, these types proved inferior to the process marketed by Xerox Corporation. Xerography featured electrostatic dry copying that replaced the chemicals used in the other photocopying machines with a cleaner process that required no specially manufactured paper.

Photocopiers that used xerography grew from 1 percent of Xerox's total sales in 1950 to more than 60 percent in 1960, causing exponential growth throughout the industry. Other companies that followed Xerox's lead into electrostatic copying included American Photocopy, Charles Bruning, BBM Photocopy, and Smith Corona Corporation. The pace of this growth quickened with the introduction of the Xerox 914 office copier in 1960, which enabled rapid duplication of documents for business offices, a task that previously had to be completed manually. Within three years Xerox's sales more than tripled, and annual sales for the industry as a whole soared to $500 million. By this time the market was heavily contested among more than 100 competitors. Many were still not convinced of xerography's merits and continued to manufacture wet-type machines. This issue was soon settled by the response of the industry's business customers, and photocopiers rapidly became an indispensable accessory for nearly every office in the United States.

Meanwhile in the photographic market, another innovative product emerged—the Instamatic camera. First marketed by Kodak in 1963, the Instamatic camera and film formed an integrated system that made photography simpler for consumers. A film cartridge popped into the camera's back, eliminating the task of threading film into the camera. The camera featured a rapid-action lever that advanced the film and automatically positioned it for each exposure, eliminating the inaccurate and awkward winding knob found on earlier cameras. Some innovations of the camera and film had been developed as far back as the 1940s, but never before had so many convenient features been combined into a single product.

Mysteriously named Project 13, the development of Kodak's Instamatic was shrouded in secrecy, catching all of its competitors by surprise and heightening the camera's popularity. Within two years approximately 7.5 million Instamatics were sold. Kodak estimated that the average camera owner purchased four rolls of film a year, but with the easy-to-use Instamatic, consumers increased their purchases to eight rolls a year.

During this time, the photographic industry also experienced a considerable boost from industrial and government purchases. As photographic technology advanced, the useful applications of photographic equipment in factories and for high technology purposes broadened, making the development of more sophisticated products almost as lucrative as the development of simple products. Equipment that could take as many as 5,000 photographs per second was used to identify product inconsistencies occurring along production lines and to improve the design of industrial products. Cameras were also used inside missiles to photograph foreign countries for military purposes, inside layer cakes to improve leavening agents manufactured by chemical companies, and aboard rockets to record details of the moon's

surface. Sales to industries and government organizations increased from $360 million in 1959 to $630 million in 1964, which represented nearly half of the $1.4 billion photographic industry's revenues for that year.

By the 1970s, photocopying had become a $1 billion a year business, with Xerox in the lead. In 1963 Xerox followed the 914 model with a smaller version, the 813, and subsequent models entered the market throughout the rest of the decade. Photocopying technology advanced rapidly during these years, increasing the production output of the machines and reducing their size, which heightened the popularity of photocopiers in business and government offices.

In 1970 Xerox began marketing the Model 4000 photocopier, which churned out 45 copies a minute, or 2,700 an hour, compared to the approximately 1,000 copies the 914 could produce in a day. Its two paper trays could hold different sizes and types of paper, and it could automatically copy to both sides of a sheet of paper. Xerox was not the only pioneer in the photocopying equipment market, however, and consumer demand increased as other manufacturers developed attractive features for their machines. This meant more revenue for industry participants and more competition from companies in related businesses. Competition intensified for the remainder of the decade, and Xerox began to cede a large portion of its commanding lead to domestic and foreign competitors.

The microfilm market also expanded during the early 1970s, fueled by the growing popularity of computers in business and government. Computers became capable of storing massive amounts of data. One reel of magnetic computer tape stored enough information to fill 3,500 pages of paper, a task that took impact printers nearly four hours to complete. This new technology proved a perfect match for micrographic technology's ability to reduce documents to a fraction of their original size, since the same amount of information could be placed on microfilm in 12 minutes. This process, a fusion of micrographics and computer technology known as computer-output microfilm (COM), eventually boosted the microfilm market considerably. Sales were sluggish until Minnesota Mining and Manufacturing and Kodak, two of the leading companies in the microfilm market, opened a successful network of regional COM centers in 1971.

Micropublishing was another area in which microfilming equipment performed well during the 1970s, although this segment generated revenues of only $50 million a year at the start of the decade. The nation was producing and storing documents at an accelerating rate. Bank checks were microfilmed, newspapers and periodicals were microfilmed for storage in libraries, and many businesses needed to consolidate the plethora of documents they produced each year. In the early 1970s, the microfilm market grew at a rate of 18 percent annually and evolved into a $500 million a year business. This decade established the foundation for future growth as computer usage became more pervasive and the nation moved into the information age. By early 1997, most companies involved in microfilm were moving into CD-ROM. Instead of putting information onto microfilm, they would scan it into digital format to be placed onto a CD-ROM. This allowed consumers to store more information on a disk and to access and print it faster with a personal computer.

Entering the 1980s, manufacturers of conventional film, paper, and cameras began to suffer the effects of a saturated market and foreign competition. Nearly every industry leader reorganized extensively to capitalize on the trend toward electronic imaging products. Several products that featured the new technology emerged in the mid-1980s, including Sony Corporation's electronic still camera called the Mavica, Canon Incorporated's Xapshot, and Fuji Photo Film Company's Fujix, but sales were disappointing. One product that did sell well, however, was the camcorder, which was introduced in 1983. Within two years 500,000 units were sold, a remarkable success, considering that each unit cost an average of $1,000. By 1990, unit sales exceeded 3 million.

By the mid-1990s electronic imaging was dramatically changing the photographic equipment and supplies industry. This new technology used semiconductor sensors instead of film to record images and then displayed the images on television screens or computer monitors rather than paper. While some people worried that the new format would entirely supplant conventional photographic equipment and supplies, others predicted that electronic imaging would merely augment the existing market. Initially, electronic imaging products were prohibitively expensive, and the quality of images was far inferior to what could be achieved with film, but by the late 1990s the digital field began to explode. Digital point-and-shoot cameras were being sold at prices as low as $300 to $500, compared to $20,000 for the professional style cameras that had previously been the only type available. The new hand-held digital cameras had relatively poor resolution but gained popularity quickly, with sales of digital equipment doubling annually. In 1995, 500,000 digital cameras were sold. That number jumped to 1.2 million in 1996.

With new digital imaging printers, copiers, cameras, software, and film, other industries were making the move into digital. Throughout much of 1996 and 1997, the photocopier industry was also beginning to incorporate digital technology. Some copiers used digital scanners with conventional toners. Most companies had designed digital lenses and optics into standard copiers, making them more efficient and higher quality, using less

toner and sometimes appearing even sharper than the original document. Xerox developed a high-end copier that mixed digital sensors with standard printing. It could print up to 135 copies per minute. The photocopying industry experienced record sales in 1996. Copier sales increased 31 percent at Canon, Inc., and 57 percent at Oce-Van der Grinten. After years in second or third place, Xerox became the leader in this segment.

Advanced Photo Systems. In 1996, five companies that had been working together on a new film format released the Advanced Photo System (APS). Kodak, Fujifilm, Canon, Nikon Corp., and Minolta Corp. had spent billions of dollars in research, with $500 million contributed by Kodak alone. These companies had interviewed more than 22,000 people in 11 countries. Customers had been given a camera-size wooden block and told to place features where they thought they would be easiest and most efficient to operate, with fewer mistakes.

The goal was to develop a new format that would be easier to operate, create better pictures, and use some of the new digital technology to augment standard film formats instead of competing with them. The traditional silver-based emulsion technology was combined with digital input and output devices to create the APS film and cameras. A durable, higher resolution emulsion was developed with a magnetic covering. The camera could read information from this magnetic strip on the film, and the film could also interact with the camera, sharing and storing information in a constant dialogue.

The new film had a stronger emulsion to withstand the tight winding as it moved in and out of the compact canister in which it was stored. The size of APS film was 24mm, smaller than the 35mm film that had previously dominated the industry. Despite its size, the new film had a higher resolution, with only one-half to one-third the grain size of standard 35mm film. Even with the added magnetic strip, the emulsion was flatter, allowing longer strips of film to be stored in a smaller area. It was also more durable, making it less susceptible to everyday damage.

In addition, the APS camera could take pictures in three sizes. Once exposed, the film stored information such as camera settings, format, time, date, exposure number, and even personal information provided by the consumer, such as a title or names to be printed on the back of the photograph. With new APS lab equipment, photofinishers used the information on the film to make the best possible print. For example, if the subject was washed out and the background was too dark, the printer could read the camera settings used in that picture and adjust printing to darken the subject and brighten the background.

In a follow-up survey of APS customers, 90 percent felt the new system was better, and 70 percent believed they would take better pictures. Companies saw amazing growth in 1996 as the new system began to take hold. During December, when 30 percent of camera buying occurs, APS cameras accounted for as much as 60 percent of non-SLR cameras sold and 30 percent of all cameras sold. More than 5 percent of the more than two billion rolls of film sold in 1996 were APS. Kodak's goal was for APS to account for 20 percent of all film sales and 80 percent of all camera sales by the year 2000. That goal had almost been reached by 1997.

Kodak's overall sales jumped 5 percent by the end of 1996, despite the loss of Office Imaging, a division that manufactured and marketed photocopiers, which was sold during 1996. The company's sales for the fourth quarter alone jumped from $275 million in 1995 to $395 million in 1996, including the loss from the Office Imaging division, which was 13 percent of sales. Fujifilm's sales also surged from $5.4 billion in 1995 to $10.2 billion in 1996. The company's fourth quarter sales more than doubled between 1995 and 1996.

Approximately 800 companies were involved in manufacturing photographic equipment and supplies in the United States in the mid-1990s. These companies together recorded an estimated $24.4 billion in shipments for products included in the classification. The aggregate value of shipments predominantly derived from the industry's six primary product groups: sensitized photographic film, paper, and plates; photocopy equipment; prepared photographic chemicals; still picture equipment; microfilming equipment; and motion picture equipment. Of the various products, still picture equipment had the highest share of the market in 1995 with 43.9 percent of sales, and sensitized photographic film accounted for 24.3 percent of sales. Photocopy equipment accounted for 23.2 percent of industry sales, and prepared photographic chemicals, microfilming equipment, and motion picture equipment together totaled 8.6 percent of industry sales.

CURRENT CONDITIONS

The Census Bureau estimated that in 1997 there were 62 establishments whose main product was still picture photographic equipment. These facilities shipped $2.5 billion worth of merchandise, spent $1.7 billion on materials, invested $187 million in capital expenditures, and employed 11,931 people. There were 23 establishments that made primarily motion picture equipment; 13 that made primarily photocopying equipment; and 13 that made primarily microfilming, blueprinting, and whiteprinting equipment.

Among shipments of photographic and photocopying equipment in 1997, still picture photographic equipment accounted for about 15 percent. The largest value of shipments in this segment originated in New York and Massachusetts. Microfilming, blueprinting, and white-

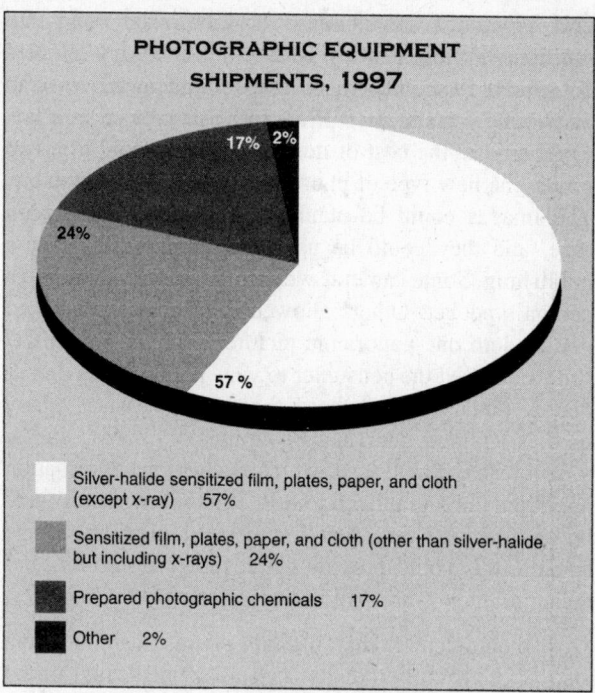

PHOTOGRAPHIC EQUIPMENT
SHIPMENTS, 1997

Silver-halide sensitized film, plates, paper, and cloth (except x-ray)   57%

Sensitized film, plates, paper, and cloth (other than silver-halide but including x-rays)   24%

Prepared photographic chemicals   17%

Other   2%

printing equipment accounted for 2 percent. The largest value of shipments in this segment originated in Wisconsin.

There were 25 establishments whose primary products were silver-halide sensitized film, plates, paper, and cloth (except for X-rays). These facilities shipped $9.0 billion worth of merchandise, spent $3.6 billion on materials, invested $410 million on capital expenditures, and employed 28,727 people. There were 46 establishments whose primary products were sensitized photographic film, plates, paper, and cloth (other than silver-halide but including products for X-rays). These facilities shipped $2.4 billion worth of merchandise and employed 5,958 people. There were 45 establishments whose primary product was prepared photographic chemicals. They shipped $1.3 billion worth of merchandise and employed 3,097 people.

Silver-halide sensitized film, plates, paper, and cloth (except X-ray) accounted for about 57 percent of this category's shipments in 1997. The largest value of shipments in this segment originated in Missouri. Sensitized film, plates, paper, and cloth (other than silver-halide but including products for X-rays) accounted for 24 percent. The largest value of shipments in this segment originated in South Carolina and New York. Prepared photographic chemicals accounted for 17 percent. The largest value of shipments in this segment originated in New York and California.

In the late 1990s, manufacturers introduced new digital cameras and related products to meet continuing demand as consumers sent electronic images to their acquaintances via e-mail, posted them on their World Wide Web sites, used computers to incorporate them into business brochures and mailings, and designed them into multimedia presentations. The new technology allowed consumers to see their photographs immediately instead of waiting for slides or prints to be developed at a lab. Compared to the cost of developing traditional film and prints, the new type of photograph was more affordable. The images could be manipulated and improved with ease, and they could be used conveniently in desktop publishing. Some cameras were small enough to fit into a person's pocket. Others allowed the user to merge two images into one panoramic picture. Cameras with LCD panels allowed the consumer to view photographs immediately and eliminate those they did not want. Many models featured interchangeable memory cards, similar to solid-state disk drives, which could store information about the photographs. By early 1998 zoom lenses were being sold for a few digital cameras, a great advantage because this could provide better image resolution, but these products were still not common.

To complement their digital cameras, manufacturers also offered new products such as sophisticated photo printers that could transfer images to media such as glossy paper, postcards, labels, and stickers. Some were ink-jet printers, and others used dye sublimation technology involving print ribbons. Some models could also operate as scanners, converting printed photographs into digital images. These products were often priced affordably. In 1999 the Kodak Personal Picture Maker PM1000 by Lexmark cost $150 after the consumer was sent a rebate, and the Canon BJC-8200 Color Bubble Jet Photo Printer cost $400.

INDUSTRY LEADERS

Eastman Kodak Co. (Rochester, New York) reported sales of $13.4 billion in 1998, down 8 percent from $14.5 billion in 1997. Minolta Corp. Business Products Group (a subsidiary of Minolta Camera Company Ltd. based in Ramsey, New Jersey) had 500 employees and estimated sales of $3.3 billion. Its products included photocopy and facsimile machines, micrographic equipment, and color graphic and imaging systems. Polaroid Corp. had 9,274 employees and sales of $1.8 billion.

Several firms based in Japan were among the leading companies that marketed photographic equipment and supplies in the United States. These included Canon Inc. and Nikon Corp. Fuji Medical Systems USA Inc. (a subsidiary of Fuji Photo Film Company Ltd. based in Stamford, Connecticut) had 300 employees and estimated sales of $200 million in 1998. It marketed X-ray and industrial film. During the late 1990s, Fuji Photo Film became one of the leaders in the U.S. photographic film market.

Incorporated in 1889, Kodak had led the industry throughout much of the twentieth century; however, the industry giant struggled with the growing popularity of electronic imaging, restructuring its organization on four separate occasions in the 1980s and early 1990s. Entering the electronic imaging market in 1992, Kodak unveiled its Photo CD system, which enabled purchasers to transfer images captured on conventional film to a digital disk for display on a television screen or computer. Kodak offered 20 new products in early 1993, the largest number introduced at one time in the company's history. The products were designed and marketed primarily for children and elderly people, with the hope of expanding what Kodak perceived as a saturated market in the 25- to 40-year-old age group.

Photocopiers were consistent losers for Kodak in the late 1980s and early 1990s, a situation that was exacerbated as the company fell behind its competition technologically. A pressing concern for Kodak was the successful development of a digital color copier that would enable the company to respond to the significant trend in that direction. During the last quarter of 1996, Kodak sold its Office Imaging division, because it was constantly trailing in the photocopying industry. Despite these problems, Kodak maintained a considerable lead over its competitors, controlling 70 percent of the market for film and photographic paper in both the United States and worldwide in 1995.

Polaroid Corporation was the world's leading manufacturer of instant cameras and film during the 1990s. The company was established in 1923 by Edwin H. Land, who left college after beginning the research that eventually led to the development of the first synthetic light polarizing material. Polaroid experienced its first considerable growth spurt during World War II, when sales skyrocketed from $1 million in 1941 to $15 million in 1945. Since this exponential leap in sales was primarily attributable to the company's work for the military, which used Land's discovery for various purposes, sales returned to their prewar levels afterward, falling to $1.5 million in 1947. In that same year Land introduced his first instant picture camera and sales ballooned once again.

After enjoying considerable success with subsequent instant developing film and camera models, Polaroid's revenues declined in the early 1970s due to unexpectedly low demand for its SX-70 camera. The company's sales were revived in 1975 with the introduction of its inexpensive Pronto camera. Six million units were sold in the first year. After rival Kodak introduced an array of instant cameras that year, Polaroid filed a patent infringement lawsuit, touching off a hotly contested and long drawn out legal battle.

Polaroid's sales plummeted once again during the 1980s, while the company streamlined its operations to invigorate profits and forestall a hostile takeover attempt by Shamrock Holdings. The company's Spectra camera and film, introduced in 1986, provided a much-needed boost to revenues and brightened what was generally a disappointing decade of performance. The company began manufacturing conventional film for the first time in 1989, and two years later it finally received $873 million from the patent infringement lawsuit it had filed against Kodak 16 years earlier.

WORKFORCE

Employment in the photographic equipment and supplies industry declined during the 1980s, a time of corporate restructuring, consolidations, and layoffs. Employment in the category dropped from more than 130,000 in 1980 to 70,500 in 1994.

The Census Bureau reported that, in 1997, the 428 establishments engaged in manufacturing photographic and photocopying equipment employed 24,706 people, including 14,767 production workers who earned an average hourly wage of $18.55. Among those, the production workers employed by companies that made primarily microfilming, blueprinting, and whiteprinting equipment earned an average hourly wage of $11.49.

The 310 establishments engaged in manufacturing photographic film, paper, plate, and chemicals employed 39,032 people in 1997, including 21,858 production workers who earned an average hourly wage of $16.81. Pay for production workers in this category was lowest ($15.37 per hour) at facilities whose primary business was prepared photographic chemicals.

AMERICA AND THE WORLD

Historically, foreign manufacturers of photographic equipment and supplies have enjoyed considerable success competing in the U.S. market. This tradition continued in the early 1990s, as a global recession exacerbated the competition for flagging consumer spending and retarded the sale of U.S. products overseas. Exports of domestic photographic products were flat in 1992 at an estimated $3.8 billion, after a 10 percent increase in 1991. In 1993, after slumping for so long, exports began to rise again to $4.6 billion in 1995, a 12 percent growth between 1994 and 1995. The rise was partially attributable to Japan's own economic slump, which decreased the competition. During the first six months of 1996, exports increased 10 percent over the same period of 1995 to $2.3 billion. Sensitized film, paper, and plates accounted for 47 percent of the export total and had the fastest growth rate at 17 percent. Photocopying equipment and photographic chemicals both increased about 8 percent. Still picture equipment increased by 2 percent. Motion picture equipment continued to decline, down 14 percent from 1995.

The largest export market for U.S. manufacturers, the European Union, accounted for $1.4 billion of all domestic photographic sales overseas in 1995. Sales to

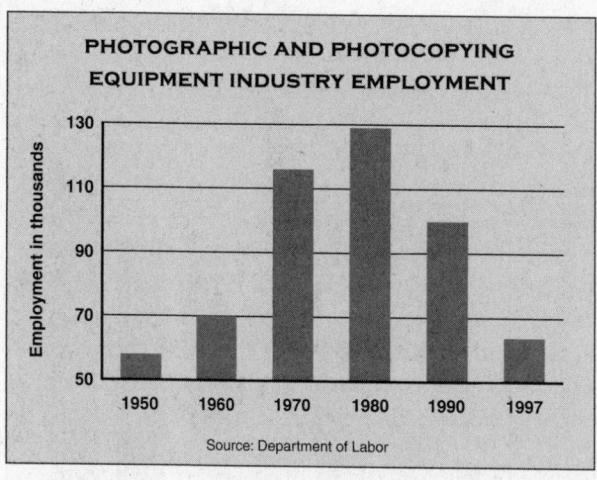

PHOTOGRAPHIC AND PHOTOCOPYING EQUIPMENT INDUSTRY EMPLOYMENT

Source: Department of Labor

Eastern Europe declined in 1992 after demonstrating encouraging results the previous year, especially in photocopying equipment sales. Exports to eastern and western Europe combined fell 2 percent in 1992, following a 6 percent increase in 1991. North America, mainly Canada and Mexico, was second at $1.2 billion, followed by the rest of the Americas with $715 million. Exports to Japan rose to $522 million for 1995.

Imports of photographic equipment and supplies to the United States increased in 1995 to $8.8 billion, the highest it had been in years. Through the first six months of 1996, however, it dipped again, dropping to an estimated $8.1 billion by the end of 1996. Imported motion picture equipment and copying equipment rose while everything else was decreasing. Motion picture equipment went up by over 33.0 percent, and copying equipment rose 2.6 percent. Imports of still picture equipment dropped 6.9 percent, sensitized film dropped 1.6 percent, and photo chemicals went down by 8.5 percent through the first half of 1996. Despite motion picture equipment's rise, overall imports had decreased by a little more than 1 percent.

The majority of U.S. imports were manufactured in Japan, which had continually increased its international presence since supplanting West Germany in 1962 as the world's second largest exporter. Japanese manufacturers attained their commanding position in the international photographic industry by producing inexpensive, reliable photographic equipment that employed the latest technological advancements. Japan had used these two marketing and manufacturing strategies to increase its share of the international photographic market since the early 1960s and gained a solid position as the main rival of U.S. manufacturers. In 1995 Japan accounted for $5.1 billion of the import total of $8.8 billion in the United States. The European Union followed with $1.5 billion, and North America accounted for $581 million.

As exports continued to grow and imports continued to shrink, the trade balance had been narrowing. The hope

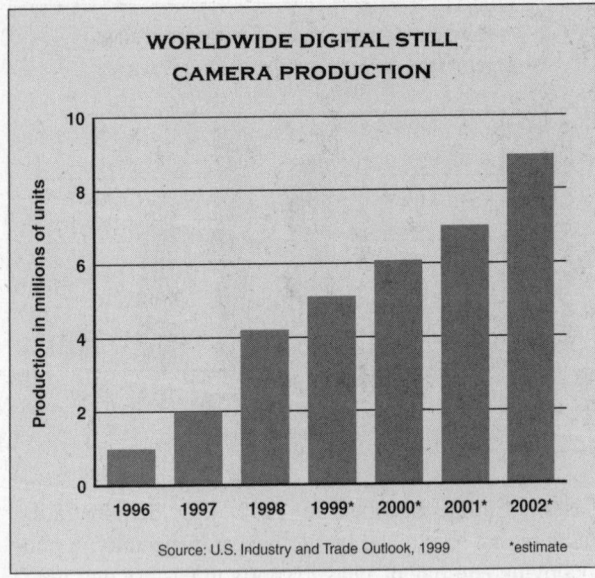

WORLDWIDE DIGITAL STILL
CAMERA PRODUCTION

Source: U.S. Industry and Trade Outlook, 1999   *estimate

was that the expected economic recovery of international markets, particularly in Europe, and reduced tariffs and trade barriers among European Community countries would ameliorate overseas sales—especially considering the low saturation level of photographic equipment in Eastern Europe and the European Community. The economic slump in Japan throughout the mid-1990s, the worst since the late 1970s, continued to affect the trade balance as exports to Japan dropped steadily through 1994, however.

During the 1990s, the North American Free Trade Agreement (NAFTA) reduced tariffs on photographic products being marketed among Mexico, Canada, and the United States, an arrangement that promised to benefit photographic equipment and supplies manufacturers in the United States. By 1995 the United States was exporting about $555 million more in photographic products than it was importing from countries participating in NAFTA. (Those exports totaled $1.14 billion that year, compared to $581 million in imports.) The trade balance had been improving overall as consumers in the United States purchased fewer still-picture products made in other countries. For the first half of 1995 the trade deficit was $1.9 billion, but it declined to $1.7 billion for the same period of 1996.

FURTHER READING

Brown, Bruce, and Marge Brown. "Picture-Perfect Printers: Three New Photo Ink Jet Printers Vary in Featuers and Price, but All of Them Produce Great-Looking Prints." *PC Magazine,* 14 December 1999, 45.

———. "Dye-Sub Snapshot Printers." *PC Magazine,* 14 December 1999, 45.

Darnay, Arsen J. ed. *Manufacturing USA.* 5th ed. Detroit: Gale Research, 1996.

"Digital Darkrooms." *PC Magazine,* 15 May 1998, 9.

Gair, Cristina. "Sneak Peeks." *Home Office Computing,* February 1999, 27.

"Infotrends Study Shows Digital Camera Market Is Doubling Annually." *Business Wire,* 10 February 1997. Available from http://www.businesswire.com.

Lazich, Robert S., ed. *Market Share Reporter.* Detroit: Gale Research, 1997.

McLellan, Charles. "Canon PowerShot A5." *PC Magazine (UK),* August 1998, 62.

Menendez, Arthur. "High Tech and the Internet." *SwissWORLD,* April-May 1999, 33.

Morgenstern, Steve. "Digital Cameras." *Home Office Computing,* January 1998, 81.

"Small Copiers/Big Advantage." *PRNewswire,* 24 February 1997. Available from http://www.prnewswire.com.

U.S. Department of Commerce. Census Bureau. *1997 Economic Census.* Washington, DC: GPO, 1999. Available from http://www.census.gov/prod/ec97/97m3333e.pdf and http://www.census.gov/prod/ec97/97m3259d.pdf.

White, Larry. "APS . . . It's Finally Here! The Advanced Photo System: Will It Change Photography Forever?"*Hyperzine,* 10 February 1997. Available from http://www.hyperzine.com.

SIC 3873

WATCHES, CLOCKS, CLOCKWORK OPERATED DEVICES, AND PARTS

This segment covers establishments primarily engaged in manufacturing clocks, watches, watchcases, mechanisms for clockwork operated devices, and clock and watch parts. This industry includes establishments primarily engaged in assembling clocks and watches from purchased movements and cases. Establishments primarily engaged in manufacturing time clocks are classified in **SIC 3579: Office Machines, Not Elsewhere Classified;** those manufacturing glass crystals are classified in **SIC 3231: Glass Products, Made of Purchased Glass;** and those manufacturing plastic crystals are classified in **SIC 3089: Plastics Products, Not Elsewhere Classified.**

NAICS CODE(S)

334518 (Watch, Clock, and Part Manufacturing)

INDUSTRY SNAPSHOT

The watch and clock industry has always been small compared to other industries, and, since the late 1980s and early 1990s, the number of manufacturers has declined. This is due in large part to the movement, begun in the 1970s, of watch parts manufacture from the continental United States to offshore facilities. The popularity of quartz watches, which are produced primarily in mainland Asia as well as in Japan, have prompted the shift to offshore facilities.

BACKGROUND AND DEVELOPMENT

Although the clock industry has existed in the United States since pre-Revolutionary days, it did not begin to flourish until the early 1800s when such companies as Ingraham Clock Co. and Chelsea Clock Co. were established. The first clocks manufactured for home use were pendulum clocks that, despite their excellent timekeeping, were rather cumbersome. Whether a huge mantle clock or a floor clock, the instrument had to be set perfectly plumb to keep time accurately. Such clocks were handmade, and their cost was prohibitive. A clock was considered an investment and bought with the understanding that it would be passed from generation to generation. With the advent of the Industrial Revolution, new technologies were developed, clocks became less cumbersome and expensive, and, subsequently, watch manufacturing began.

Prior to the 1920s, almost all watches were carried in the pocket or purse. Some women's watches were designed as pieces of jewelry in the form of brooches or integrated into necklaces. The first watches were analog—the time was displayed via hands pointing at markers or numerals. In addition, the watches were mechanical, powered by a coiled mainspring that required manual winding.

The industry grew as further technological advances were made. In the 1950s, the first battery powered watch was introduced, ushering in the electronic age in personal timekeepers. The spring mechanism was replaced by vibrating quartz crystals that contained a battery-powered silicon chip, and the use of integrated circuits led to the development of the digital watch.

The first digital watch, the Pulsar by Hamilton, was launched in the 1970s. Two types of digital watches were introduced—the Liquid Crystal Display (LCD), which required light to read the numerals and the Light Emitting Diode (LED), which required the wearer to push a button to light it and read the time. Neither gained true acceptance because the LCD was not practical at night, and the LED battery was short lived. The main reason digital watches did not become popular, however, was the reluctance of consumers to accept them. People felt more comfortable with a more traditional watch that gave a visual indication of the time remaining until a meeting or appointment, for example.

The digital clock fared much better than the digital watch. The clock companies solved the problems with LCD and LED displays by designing a digital clock run by an electronic chip that called for a light to plug directly into the line cord, stay lit, and give a constant display. The result is that approximately 40 percent of all bedside alarm clocks have digital readouts.

While the digital watch was not a success, the quartz watch was. During the 1980s, the production of the mechanical watch fell, and watches with quartz chip movements became popular. The vanguard of the industry was the analog quartz watch; more than half are sold in North America, western Europe, and Japan.

Although the components of the watches are mainly manufactured overseas, assembly takes place in plants in the United States. Although the number of people employed in the U.S. watch and clock industry has been steadily declining since 1970, wages have been growing. Production workers were earning $8.69 per hour in 1990, compared to figures from the previous year showing hourly wages at $8.06.

In 1991, according to the U.S. Department of Commerce, watchcases, watch straps, bands, bracelets, and movements were increasingly imported from Switzerland, Japan, Hong Kong, Thailand, and several other countries. Still, the trend in the industry was toward having both the manufacture of the parts and the assembly of the watches done overseas. Most of the major clock companies still produce their parts domestically.

The clock industry expected production to remain steady. Bedside alarm clocks, especially digital ones, continued to be strong-selling items, and sales of fine clocks were rising. One explanation for the increase was the growing consumer interest in home fashion and decorating. More and more clocks are being considered accessories for the home.

Watch companies registered impressive sales in 1994 and repeated their robust performance a year later. The biggest factor behind the surge in sales was the revival of interest in fashion watches. Another factor partly responsible was the strong marketing campaign for both the newer and the established brands. The moderately priced watches recorded the highest sales during this period.

Swatch USA launched a new line of metal watches in 1995, known as the Irony Line. The line, which was the company's first venture into traditional design, featured 12 new varieties with leather wristbands. In 1996 the major growth areas for clock manufacturers were consolidation and licensing.

In 1996, massive print and television advertising campaigns drove sales. Fashion trends, fostering growing interest in watches that complement clothing, also continued to boost watch sales. In 1996 there were about 88 U.S. companies operating in this industry.

CURRENT CONDITIONS

The biggest trends in watches in the late 1990s, according to a September 1998 survey of jewelers conducted by Jewelers Circular Keystone magazine, were colored components (dials, straps, bezels, and gemstones), diamonds (even on moderately priced models), and unusual shapes (such as oval, rectangular, and tonneau). This survey also identified watches as items that enhanced the image and prestige of jewelers: 60 percent of the respondents believed that carrying watches attracted customers to their stores, and 40 percent believed that watches added prestige to their image. These respondents reported that watches accounted for 15 percent of their annual sales, and 77 percent of the respondents projected good-to-excellent watch sales for the coming year.

INDUSTRY LEADERS

Timex Corp. of Middlebury, Connecticut was the industry leader, with estimated sales of $850 million for the fiscal year ending December 1997; the company employed about 7,500 people. The Seiko Corporation of America of Mahwah, New Jersey, a subsidiary of the international industry leader Seiko Epson Corporation of Nagano, Japan, garnered estimated sales of $389 million for the fiscal year ending March 1998; they had 700 employees. Fossil Inc. of Richardson, Texas generated $305 million in sales for the fiscal year ending December 1998, with 828 employees.

The Movado Group Inc. of New Jersey ranked fourth, with 855 employees and $278 million in sales revenues for the fiscal year ending January 1998. Next came Intermatic Inc. of Spring Grove, Illinois, with $200 million in sales revenue behind the strength of 1100 employees. SMH (US) Inc., a subsidiary of the Swiss company that makes Swatch watches, tied Intermatic with $200 million in sales for the fiscal year ending December 1997; they employed 400 people. Bulova Corp. of Woodside, New York employed 445 workers and generated $129 million in sales for the fiscal year ending December 1998. General Time Corp. of Norcross, Georgia acquired one of its main competitors, Spartacus Corp. of Stamford, Connecticut, in 1996.

This industry included not only watchmakers but also components makers. Time Delay, a company founded by the expert watch repairman Bob McQuirk in 1978, created a niche market as an accessories supplier by providing diamond bezels, dials, and bands for watches.

AMERICA AND THE WORLD

In the 1980s, there was a profound change in the industry. The Swiss watch industry had hit hard times; production was down. A turnaround occurred in 1983,

however, when Nicolas G. Hayek, chairman of SMH Group, introduced the Swatch watch. This inexpensive, trendy watch in a plastic case was a deviation from the traditional high-priced luxury watch usually associated with the Swiss industry. The Swatch was an immediate success and sparked a continuing interest in inexpensive fashion watches.

The analog quartz watch, once the industry weakling, had become its mainstay—more than 500 million were produced in 1992. Despite its impact, the Swatch did not reestablish Switzerland as the leading watch producer. For the past decade Japan has led the field in production with Hong Kong second, and Switzerland third. Figures from 1992 indicated Japan's production accounted for roughly 44 percent of total global output, Hong Kong was responsible for about 20 percent, and Switzerland contributed approximately 17 percent. U.S. production had little impact on total global figures.

The United States, the biggest single market for this industry, had a large trade deficit in watches; 1991 exports totaled $73.4 million compared to imports of 1.8 billion.

In the area of watch and clock parts, 1990 statistics showed imports of clock movements valued at $22.1 billion; watch movement imports totaled $13.2 billion; imports of watch straps, bands, and bracelets reached $43.2 billion; and $26.7 billion of watch cases were imported. Overall growth in the watch market has slowed from double-digit to single-digit figures. Nonetheless, production is expected to reach the 1 billion mark by the end of the 1990s, aided by such nations as China, India, and Thailand.

During the 1990s, the global watch industry began to assess its ecological impact, and in 1992 watchmakers pledged to support and aid environmental efforts. Among the steps taken were the development of watch batteries with life spans of 10 to 20 years and the use of recycled, biodegradable materials for packaging, catalogs, press material, and publications.

Sports sponsorship continued to boost watch sales worldwide. Watches have been linked to many high profile sports and sports stars. Citizen's sponsorship of the U.S. Open Tennis Tournaments, and Seiko's deal with figure skater Nancy Kerrigan were some of the more prominent efforts of watchmakers.

Luxury watches was another sector of this industry that was growing worldwide. The U.K. market for luxury watches alone was forecast to grow 22 percent between 1996 and 2000. The 1995 market for luxury watches in the United Kingdom was valued at £250 million.

One of the biggest problems for watch manufacturers in the mid-1990s was counterfeiters, who were becoming increasingly ambitious and producing high quality products. The 1995 sales of counterfeit watches accounted for about 10 percent of the value of world wristwatch trade. Ties, fragrances, and other consumer goods were also branded with names of prominent world watch manufacturers. The 1994 Uruguay Round Agreement confirmed the role of intellectual property rights to reduce counterfeiting.

FURTHER READING

Balfour, Michael. "Fakers' Time is Running Out." *The Financial Times,* 18 April 1996.

"Keeping watch on today's market." *Jewelers Circular Keystone,* vol. 169, no. 9, September 1998.

"Luxury Watches." *Market Intelligence,* July 1996, 1B.

"Sports Events Help Promote Watches." *Jewelers Circular Keystone,* Vol. 166, no. 1, January 1995, 183.

"Swatch's New Irony Aimed at Jewelers." *Jewelers Circular Keystone,* Vol. 166, no. 1, January 1995, 107.

Thompson, Michael. "Fashion and Marketing to Boost Watch Sales." *Jewelers Circular Keystone,* Vol. 166, no.1, January 1995, 90.

"Time On Your Side." *Jewelers Circular Keystone,* Vol. 167, no. 1 January 1996, 77.

Werner, Holly M. "Keeping Clocks Ticking." *HFN The Weekly Newspaper for the Home Furnishings Network,* Vol. 71, no. 3, 20 January 1997, 38.

MISCELLANEOUS MANUFACTURING INDUSTRIES

SIC 3911

JEWELRY, PRECIOUS METAL

This category encompasses those establishments primarily engaged in Manufacturing jewelry and other articles worn on or carried about the person, made of precious metals such as platinum, gold, and silver (including base metals clad or rolled with precious metals), with or without stones. In addition to personal jewelry, products of this industry include cigarette cases and lighters, vanity cases and compacts; trimmings for umbrellas and canes; and jewel settings and mountings. Establishments primarily engaged in manufacturing costume jewelry from non-precious metals and other materials are classified in **SIC 3961: Costume Jewelry and Costume Novelties, Except Precious Metal.**

NAICS CODE(S)

339911 (Jewelry (Including Precious Metal) Manufacturing)

In 1990, the U.S. Department of Commerce identified 2,147 manufacturers of precious metal in the United States. The industry employed approximately 38,000 people in 1990. By 1996 the employment rate had fallen to 36,000, and in 1997 it continued to decline to 34,717. In 1997 the U.S. Census Bureau identified 2,293 companies which employed 34,717 people; New York, California, Rhode Island, and Texas accounted for the majority of employment in the industry.

Despite the lingering recessionary conditions of the early 1990s and fierce international competition, the industry managed to grow slightly. The estimated value of precious metal jewelry shipments in 1992 was $3.7 million, an increase of 0.9 percent from the 1991 figures.

Nonetheless, some retailers experienced sales decreases because of lowered consumer confidence and decreased discretionary income. Expectations of an improved economy, and the hope that customers would begin indulging in long-deferred purchases, led to an optimistic view of the industry's future. The demand for jewelry is largely affected by the amount of disposable income people have. Therefore, the increasing number of affluent individuals, working women, double-income households, and fashion-conscious men in the latter part of 1999 kept jewelry sales strong at the close of the century.

The precious metal jewelry industry encompasses retailers, wholesalers, manufacturers, and suppliers, including lapidaries, refiners, stone dealers, findings manufacturers (manufacturers of the small parts used in making jewelry, such as clasps and other items), and subcontractors who provide services such as polishing and electroplating. Manufacturing firms in the precious metal jewelry industry tend to be small establishments and are concentrated in the New York City area. The industry's major expenses are the costs of raw materials and highly skilled workers.

Two major issues of concern to the precious metal jewelry industry are the 10 percent luxury tax imposed on jewelry sales exceeding $10,000 and environmental regulations related to manufacturing processes. Regulations concerning the removal of toxic levels of metals used in electroplating have added financial burdens to many manufacturers and subcontractors. Beginning in May 1993, products that were made with ozone-depleting chemicals were required to carry identifying labels.

Despite the falling value of the U.S. dollar abroad, the United States maintained an unfavorable trade balance in 1992. Italy, one of the United States' major competitors, supplied 40 percent of all precious metal

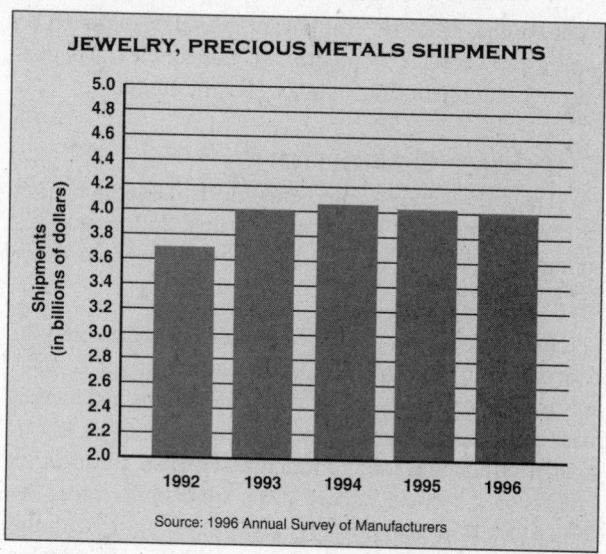

JEWELRY, PRECIOUS METALS SHIPMENTS

Shipments (in billions of dollars)

Source: 1996 Annual Survey of Manufacturers

jewelry imports in 1992. Thailand, Israel, and Hong Kong were also key suppliers. Thailand and Israel both benefited from the Generalized System of Preferences (GSP), a program that permits developing countries to export some products to the United States duty-free.

The main markets for U.S. exports of precious metal jewelry were Switzerland, Japan, and Thailand. In 1997 the United States was Japan's fourth largest overseas supplier of jewelry, with 15.3 percent of it's import market, following Hong Kong (23.1 percent), Italy (18.8 percent), and Thailand (17.1 percent), and leading France (8.6 percent). Exports to Mexico were expected to increase after ratification of the North American Free Trade Agreement, which enables American goods to enter Mexico duty-free. Most Mexican goods already enter the United States duty-free under the GSP; tariffs between Canada and the United States were already being eliminated under the U.S.-Canada Free Trade Agreement. Some industry experts also hoped that the establishment of product standards for the European Community would benefit the United States. The year-to-date total for jewelry imports in September 1999 was $5.9 billion while total jewelry exports were $1.7 billion.

On October 13, 1999, in a speech to the Democratic Leadership Council, President Bill Clinton outlined his agenda for the new round of World Trade Organization negotiations. This included Immediate Tariff Cuts, which would phase out tariffs in eight areas, including the jewelry industry. Dropping these tariffs would create new opportunities for growth.

Technology, in the form of various computerized systems, is beginning to affect the jewelry industry. Some Manufacturing firms use CAD/CAM (computer-aided design and manufacturing) to design and automate some steps in mold and model making. Use of such systems should increase in the future as they become more afford-

able to smaller companies. Some jewelers use computers to design and create customized pieces according to their customers' wishes. With the aid of computers, customers visualize different combination of styles, cuts, shanks, and stones to create their own pieces.

FURTHER READING

Bureau of Labor Statistics. *Jewelers,* 1999. Available from http://stats.bls.gov.

"The Clinton Administration Agenda For The Seattle WTO: November 24, 1999." Office of the Secretary, November 1999. Available from http://www.pub.whitehouse.gov.

Frankovich, George R. *The Jewelry Industry,* Providence, RI: Manufacturing Jewelers and Silversmiths of America.

"Precious Metal Jewelry: Japan, 1998." *Exporthotline.com,* 2000. Available from http://exporthotline.com.

U.S. Bureau of the Census. *1995 Annual Survey of Manufactures.* Washington, D.C.: GPO, 1997.

SIC 3914

SILVERWARE, PLATED WARE, AND STAINLESS STEEL WARE

This category includes businesses whose primary activities consist of manufacturing flatware (including knives, forks, and spoons), hollowware, ecclesiastical ware, trophies, trays, and related products made of sterling silver; metal plated with silver, gold, or other metal; nickel silver; pewter; or stainless steel. The category also includes establishments primarily engaged in manufacturing table flatware with blades and handles of metal. Establishments primarily engaged in manufacturing other metal cutlery are classified in **SIC 3421: Cutlery,** and those manufacturing metal trophies, trays, and toilet ware made of metals other than silver, nickel silver, pewter, stainless steel, and plated, are classified in **SIC 3499: Fabricated Metal Products, Not Elsewhere Classified.**

NAICS CODE(S)

332211 (Cutlery and Flatware (except Precious) Manufacturing)
339912 (Silverware and Plated Ware Manufacturing)

INDUSTRY SNAPSHOT

The flatware industry was dominated by stainless steel in the mid-1990s. The dominance was expected to continue as a result of consumers seeking to bridge the gap between low-end flatware and silverware. Stainless steel flatware's affordability, attractiveness, and durability has made it the most popular. Although the principal manufacturers of flatware also produce silver or silver-plated jewelry or decorative products such as bowls and goblets, flatware is typically the mainstay of the business.

In 1997 the value of shipments was an estimated $904.2 million. Hollowware (including toiletware, ecclesiastical ware, novelties, trophies, baby goods, and other plated ware) had 26 percent of the product share. Flatware, including all knives, forks, spoons, and carving sets made wholly of metal, accounted for 69 percent. Moreover, in 1997 total exports of silverware, plated ware, and jewelry came to $4.1 billion, while imports were $13 billion.

BACKGROUND AND DEVELOPMENT

Sterling silver is a term used by the U.S. government to describe a silver alloy consisting of 92.5 percent silver and 7.5 percent of another metal, such as copper. The baser metal is used to add strength to silver, which in its pure state is too soft to be practical. Silverplate, which also includes hollowware or hotelware, refers to products made from silver bonded onto a baser metal, such as brass or copper. Silverplating creates a material which is far cheaper to produce than sterling silver and yet gives a similar appearance. It is not, however, as durable as sterling silver, since the plating will eventually wear off. Stainless steel consists of steel alloyed to another metal such as chromium to produce a strong, rust-resistant, and easy-care metal.

The early 1990s found the industry still struggling to counter the effects of a lingering recession and changes in consumer preferences, which particularly affected the sterling silver segment of the industry. While manufacturers and retailers hoped to improve sales of sterling silver through aggressive advertising campaigns, many producers of sterling were also introducing new stainless steel lines to augment their business.

During the early 1990s, American manufacturers were producing approximately 20 percent of the world's silverware. Other major producers included Japan, Korea, France, and Italy.

Department stores were the most common points of sale for products in this industry, accounting for 28 percent of flatware sales and 30 percent of dinnerware sales in 1991.

The trend towards casual dinnerware and flatware was apparent in the mid-1990s. Increasingly casual lifestyles were changing the face of the industry. Alternative metal products contributed to the industry's growth in 1994. The key trends in 1995 were widespread acquisitions, changes in management, and tough competition from companies entering the housewares market.

Importers of tabletop and giftware products had an extreme year in 1996. While some reported record-breaking profits, others barely made it. Many unsuccessful firms left the industry, thereby increasing the overall profit of the industry. Tableware makers continued to exploit the growing popularity of collectibles and giftware by manufacturing holiday specific items.

CURRENT CONDITIONS

The total value of shipments for the tabletop market in 1997 reached $649.9 million. Of this, hollowware accounted for $305.4 million and flatware accounted for $312.8 million.

In 1998, Jeffrey Herman, founder of the Society of American Goldsmiths, predicted that big silver companies would focus less on custom work and instead market mass-produced designs. Designing would thus be left to smaller companies and contractors. He also stated in an address to the Society that, in the silversmith trade, the ability to restore and conserve old pieces, along with the knowledge to create new designs, would pave the way for success in the new century.

INDUSTRY LEADERS

All the leading suppliers of flatware in the United States offered flatware patterns in both sterling silver and flatware, although Gorham and Wallace were better known for their sterling. Oneida is best known for its silver-plated products and for its stainless steel flatware.

Oneida Ltd. was the undisputed leader in the industry with sales of $465.9 million and 5,010 employees. The company used its brand image to move into additional tabletop categories. Having introduced cutlery in January 1996, Oneida planned an extensive array of tabletop products for 1997 and 1998. From 1996 through 1998, the company purchased businesses in China, Italy, Australia, and Germany. Oneida reported net sales of $465.9 million in 1998.

In 1998, the three other top American manufacturers in the industry were Syratech Corp., which had $290.4 million in sales; Celar Shield National Inc., which reported sales of $80 million; and Wallace Sliversmiths, Inc., with $75 million in sales.

FURTHER READING

Andreoli, Teresa. "Holiday Tableware Presents Whole Packages." *Discount Store News,* 19 February 1996.

"Jeffrey Herman, The 21st Century Silversmith." Society of American Silversmiths, 1998. Available from http://www.silversmithing.com/1century.htm/.

Kehoe, Ann Margret. "Alternative Metals' Tabletop Sales Glow." *HFN The Weekly Newspaper for the Home Furnishing Network,* 20 February 1995.

———. "1995 a Tumultuous Year." *HFN The Weekly Newspaper for the Home Furnishing Network,* 15 January 1996.

Libbey Inc. Annual Report (SEC form 10-k), 1999. Available from http://biz.yahoo.com/e/990331/lby.html/.

Oneida Ltd. "About Oneida," 1999. Available from http://www.oneida.com.

U.S. Census Bureau. *Jewelry (Except Costume) Manufacturing.* Washington, D.C.: GPO, 1999.

SIC 3915

JEWELERS' FINDINGS AND MATERIALS, AND LAPIDARY WORK

This category covers establishments primarily engaged in manufacturing unassembled jewelry parts and stock jewelers' materials such as wire, tubing, and sheeting; and establishments of lapidaries primarily engaged in cutting, slabbing, tumbling, carving, engraving, polishing, or faceting stones from natural or manmade precious or semiprecious gem raw materials, either for sale or on a contract basis for the trade; in recutting, repolishing, and setting gem stones; or in drilling, cutting, or otherwise preparing jewels for instruments, dies, watches, chronometers, and other industrial uses. This industry includes the drilling, sawing, and peeling of real or cultured pearls. Establishments primarily engaged in manufacturing synthetic stones for gem stones and industrial uses are classified **SIC 3299: Nonmetallic Mineral Products, Not Elsewhere Classified,** and those manufacturing artificial pearls are classified in **SIC 3961: Costume Jewelry and Costume Novelties, Except Precious Metal.**

NAICS CODE(S)

339913 (Jeweler's Material and Lapidary Work Manufacturing)

ORGANIZATION AND STRUCTURE

The approximately 400 establishments in this industry produced roughly $900 million worth of products in 1995. More than half of these revenues came from precious metal findings.

Production in this industry is centered in New England. The six main states producing jewelers' findings and lapidary work were Rhode Island, Massachusetts, New Jersey, California, New York, and Florida. Together, these states accounted for roughly 50 percent of total U.S. output in this industry.

BACKGROUND AND DEVELOPMENT

The largest diamond in existence is the Cullinan, which was discovered in 1905. The Cullinan weighed 3,106 carats (about 1.4 pounds) before it was cut into 105 distinct gems totaling almost 1,100 carats. The Star of Africa (named for the Cullinan's place of discovery, the Premier Mine in Transvaal State in South Africa) was given to King Edward VII of Great Britain and set in the Royal Scepter, one of the British Crown Jewels. The Star of Africa weighs 530.2 carats. The Great Mogul diamond of 240 carats has vanished since its existence was originally reported in 1665; the Kohinoor Diamond (106 carats and also a part of the British Crown Jewels) may have been part of the Mogul. Other famous single diamonds are the Vargas diamond found in Brazil in 1938 and the Jonker and Lesotho diamonds, also products of African mines.

Diamond cutting takes careful planning and entails a certain amount of risk. Shape and surface problems mean choosing between the largest cut diamond with flaws or the second largest but perfectly finished diamond. Marvin Samuels of Premier Gem Corp. of New York spent four years planning the cutting of what could have been the largest finished diamond in the world, topping the Cullinan. Samuels chose perfect cutting over size, finishing the cutting in early 1988 with a stone weighing 407.43 carats.

The jewelry industry in general suffered with the economic downturn of the late 1980s. One-carat diamonds once valued at $60,000 sold for $12,000. Bankruptcies, closings, and reorganizations sent shock waves through the industry. Many unsecured manufacturers and suppliers in the findings and lapidary segment toppled. That trend was aggravated by a 10 percent federal luxury tax on jewelry over $10,000, though the tax affected only a small portion of the industry. This luxury tax was repealed in 1993.

The worldwide downturn depressed prices on many gems along with gold and silver, but the DeBeers' Central Selling Organization restricted the supply of diamonds along with sapphires, emeralds, and rubies to keep prices up. By 1986, it was supporting diamond sales in the United States with a $35 million advertising campaign. Even so, worldwide downsizing continued. In Antwerp, where diamonds make up 6 percent of Belgium's imports and exports, the number of diamond workers dropped from more than 19,000 in the 1970s to around 7,500 by 1986. Much of the polishing and grinding business traditionally commanded by Antwerp went to lower cost shops in Bombay, India.

CURRENT CONDITIONS

By 1999, manufacturers were anticipating the beginning of the twenty-first century as the time when baby boomers would reach their mature years and spend more of their discretionary income on jewelry and gemstones. Jewelry retailing grew by 6 to 7 percent per year in the late 1990s, and the manufacturing end of the trade was naturally closely related. According to a 1996 survey, diamonds were 61 percent of all gemstones sold; emeralds, sapphires, and rubies were next, in that order. Figures from 1998 show that U.S. consumers lead the world by purchasing half of the diamonds sold annually.

In the late 1990s, light-colored gemstones like tanzanite grew in popularity. The interest in the possible healing and life-enhancing effects of various semiprecious stones and crystals is stimulating growth in sales of gemstone bracelets, pins, and pendants, and is also increasing many hobbyists' interest in lapidary work. Shows sponsored by the Lapidary Dealers' Association and the American Gem Trade Association are experiencing record attendance as hobbyists and small dealers seek new enhancements, treatments, and findings and unique gems, synthetic or otherwise. Ancient Roman glass has become a popular ''gem'' because of its brilliant colors. Popular trends in gemstones include the following: spessartite gems, which are bright yellow to orange garnets from Namibia; vivid green stones of chrome diopside (mined in Siberia) and demantoid (also from Russia and Mexico); rhodolites mined in Tanzania that range in color from browns to reds and purples; and Oregon sunstone, in which carving enhances the luster of the metallic red stones. Synthetic rubies, sapphires, citrines, ametrines, amethysts, and chemical synthetics like cubic zirconia are popular among individual buyers but are causing alarm among wholesalers because large-scale substitutions have been discovered among some wholesale lots.

Eighty percent of the world's diamonds are produced in the countries of Botswana, Russia, South Africa, Angola, Namibia, Australia, and Zaire (in descending order). Botswana boasts the world's largest diamond mine, but Canada is positioned to become a world leader because of the BHP-Dai Met joint venture mine that will generate 3 million carats of diamonds annually after the deposit is fully explored and functioning as a mine. Only 21 operating mines produce all of the world's diamonds (1998 figures), with many other deposits under development. Australia and Russia are the countries with the largest reserves of diamonds, although Russian exports have been heavily hampered by the country's evolving economic system and government operations. Almazy Rossii-Sakha is Russia's largest producer, and it provides the South African giant De Beers with $550 million in rough diamonds per year through an agreement extended to the end of 2001.

INDUSTRY LEADERS

The Central Selling Organization (CSO) of De Beers Consolidated Mines, Ltd., markets over 70 percent of the rough-cut diamonds in the world, as of 1998. The CSO ships rough-cut diamonds to diamond-cutting centers in New York, Antwerp, Tel Aviv, and Bombay. Bombay has remained the cutting capital of the world since the 1980s because of the low labor costs. Economic conditions in Asia in 1997-1998 caused sales of diamonds to decline, which resulted in an oversupply. CSO's diamond

sales for the first half of 1998 totaled only $1.7 billion, a drop of 41 percent from the first half of 1997 and the lowest half-year total in 10 years. De Beers' marketing of diamonds as gifts worthy of commemorating the millennium was calculated to increase worldwide diamond demand. De Beers is considering adding minute identification numbers on its gemstones by laser drilling to boost consumer confidence in real diamonds over cubic zirconium or moissanite substitutes.

FURTHER READING

Darnay, Arsen J., ed. *Manufacturing USA*. 5th ed. Detroit: Gale Research, 1996.

Roskin, Gary. ''New & Hot in Tucson.'' *Jewelers Circular Keystone,* April 1998.

U.S. Bureau of the Census. *1992 Census of Manufactures.* Washington: GPO, 1995.

———. *1995 Annual Survey of Manufactures.* Washington: GPO, 1997.

Zimmerman, R., et al. ''Jewelry Sector Update.'' *The Jewelry Industry Report,* Janney Montgomery Scott, Inc., 25 August 1999.

SIC 3931

MUSICAL INSTRUMENTS

This category covers establishments primarily engaged in manufacturing musical instruments and parts and accessories for musical instruments. The primary products in this category are pianos, with or without player attachments, and organs. This industry also includes string, fretted, wind, percussion, and electronic instruments.

NAICS CODE(S)

339992 (Musical Instrument Manufacturing)

INDUSTRY SNAPSHOT

At one time, the ability to play a musical instrument was considered an essential part of a person's basic education. During the later half of the twentieth century, however, electronic advances like video games and music-playback machines combined with increasingly hectic lifestyles to make the effort of mastering a musical instrument somewhat less appealing. Nevertheless, in 1994 there were more than 62 million musicians in the United States. According to *U.S. Industry & Trade Outlook '99,* musical instrument manufacturers shipped $1.28 billion worth of product in 1998.

As part of the personal consumer durables category, musical instrument purchases depend greatly on consumer confidence. Such purchases are made with disposable personal income. In addition, in times of recession, discretionary spending for school bands and orchestras, personal music lessons, and high-end instruments become the first casualties of austere budgets. Reflecting a strong economy and low unemployment, production of acoustic pianos and school instruments increased in 1997.

ORGANIZATION AND STRUCTURE

While dominated by a few large manufacturers, the musical instruments industry of the 1990s remained rather fragmented. In 1998 the top five companies commanded more than 50 percent of total industry sales, but there remained hundreds of small shops with annual revenues of less than $10 million. Traditionally, the musical instruments industry has been dominated by the production of pianos, player pianos, organs (including electronic), and parts for those products. In 1997 production of acoustic pianos climbed after years of decline; the segment claimed 11.7 percent of market share on sales of $713.8 million. Production of school instruments also improved due to a good economy. Sales of school music products were $628.3 million. Keyboard instruments, which accounted for an estimated one-third of the industry's sales in the mid-1990s, as well as home organs, had lackluster sales in the late 1990s. According to *U.S. Industry & Trade Outlook '99,* consumers perceived portable keyboards as low quality and home organs as old-fashioned. In 1997, the industry sold $710.8 million of fretted instruments, $322.8 million of electronic music products, and $311.7 of percussion products.

While some automation had been introduced to the manufacture of musical instruments, the processes generally remained labor and materials intensive. The cost of building quality pianos soared during the later half of the twentieth century. A good piano used more than 8,000 moving parts, many of which required rare super-quality materials like ten-grain-per-inch spruce and highest-grade wool. Foreign competitors pushed into the market with innovative man-made materials and mass-production techniques that dramatically lowered the cost and increased the flexibility of the instruments.

A convergence of demographic and competitive factors that had shrunk the musical instruments industry in the 1980s continued in the 1990s. Business failures and consolidations were expected to reduce the number of industry firms from the 1987 level of 400. Similarly, across-the-board employment levels were forecast to continue their multi-decade decline.

BACKGROUND AND DEVELOPMENT

The Victorian era (1830-1880) saw the enthroning of music, especially piano music, as an essential stabilizing element of society and, particularly, the family. In 1881, the *Chambers' Journal* reported: "In every house there is

an altar devoted to Saint Cecilia, and all are taught to serve her to the best of their ability. The altar is the pianoforte."

The expected devotees of music were mainly women. In 1922, the Music Teachers National Conference noted that 75 percent of all concert audiences were women and 85 percent of music students were female. In 1978, 57 percent of all music students were female and 79 percent of all piano students were as well. As early as 1840, the American "piano girl" was a recognizable stereotype; at the time, musical ability was thought to enhance a woman's social prestige.

The piano brought families together to play and listen, becoming the centerpiece of the Victorian family and an avidly sought after item in the growing industrialization of hectic post-World War I America. The musical instruments industry sought to capitalize on that interest and place a piano in every parlor in the nation.

Before 1800, all pianos were grand pianos that required a lot of space, but that year saw the development of the John Hawkins' Portable Grand Piano, the precursor of the now-familiar upright piano. That innovation allowed the piano into the parlors of the middle class, a development paralleled by the refinement of the music box, particularly after 1815. This device provided good quality music without the needed effort of the piano or other instruments. These two trends in musical instruments continued throughout the century, with the appeal of passive listening becoming more important in twentieth century America. The first electromechanical piano, the Telharmonium by Thaddeus Cahill, appeared around 1896.

Playing a piano well required effort and practice. Few could develop the talent to any great degree, a fact that prompted piano manufacturers to look seriously at self-playing pianos. These devices held the promise of combining the social values associated with piano ownership with the pleasures of passive listening. The French led the way in 1863 with a patent on music rolls but, like the German versions, they never worked well. The American Angelus player piano of 1897 achieved the first commercial success, followed by the Pianola in 1898 and the Apollo in 1900. By 1918 it was estimated that more than 800,000 player pianos were in operation in America east of the Mississippi alone, and 75,000 piano rolls were sold every month in Philadelphia. Most played popular ragtime pieces, but many delivered concert-quality renditions of classics "recorded" on cylinder by famous concert pianists from America and Europe. More than 100,000 coin-operated electric pianos produced by Wurlitzer and the J.P Seeburg Piano Company were distributed throughout the country, and automatic self-playing pianos became common in many movie houses.

Despite manufacturer claims that anyone could play a player piano, even a child, proper operation required careful and consistent operation of the foot pedals. By 1923, player-piano sales peaked at 56 percent of all pianos sold. The automated devices could not compete with the growing popularity of radios and phonographs, however, which provided simple, reliable listening and took up far less room in the family parlor.

Faced with the evaporation of its market, the industry reversed itself, promoting active piano playing with National Music Week, which encouraged awareness of music in general and music lessons in public schools. In 1928, 358 schools provided piano lessons; that figure jumped to 2,004 by 1930. The National Piano Manufacturers Association, founded in 1901, stressed the joys of active piano playing and encouraged group instruction.

The industry also had to fight an image problem, as mass production techniques led to marketing abuses. The American industrial system of mass production and standardized parts, coupled with the expansion of the railroad transportation system near the end of the nineteenth century, sparked a realignment of the traditional piano craft shop. The corporation became the common business structure, and manufacturers often bought components to assemble a finished product without the need of a manufacturing facility at all. This was a similar development to what was happening in the automotive industry, with small firms becoming adept at supplying specific component elements to an assembly and marketing firm. The result, according to Frank L. Wing of Wing & Sons Piano Company, was the manufacture of the world's best pianos as well as the world's worst. Wing & Sons produced three distinct grades of pianos: professional instruments bought by wealthy middle class clients for about $600 in 1916, commercial pianos that provided reasonable sound quality and durability for $400, and the low-grade "assembled" piano that sold for about $200. Many of the latter category were "stencil" pianos that did not carry the name of the manufacturer or assembler anywhere on the instrument. Dealers usually stenciled their own names onto the casings after delivery and often used names similar to those found on top quality instruments, such as "Baldin" for "Baldwin."

A major innovation in the production of the American piano was the introduction of the console piano in 1935. This smaller, more streamlined instrument fit better with modern American architecture, blending with the living room decor instead of dominating it. The console piano and the new electronic organ formed a major part of the rising postwar demand of the mid-1940s.

In 1969 Baldwin Piano executive Morley Thompson predicted piano sales would double by 1980, but instead they dropped by 30 percent, reflecting a nearly one-third decline in the birth rate from 1965 to 1975. The resulting decline in school-age children decimated the industry's core market. At the same time, high interest rates and rising raw materials costs accelerated the decline of the market. Competition, both from other leisure and entertainment categories and from foreign manufacturers, whittled away at the domestic producers' share of the market. By 1986, imports had captured 43 percent of the U.S. acoustic piano market. In the late 1990s, things began to turn around for the segment, and Baldwin's sales increased 23 percent in 1997.

The electronic revolution had a great effect on the musical instrument industry. Between 1981 and 1986, the price of an acoustic piano doubled because of increasing labor and material costs, while unit sales dropped from 282,172 in 1978 to 166,555 in 1986. Compare that with a 40 percent increase in the sales of electronic keyboard instruments between 1985 and 1986. In fact, Americans bought twice as many keyboards in 1986 (206 million) than in 1985 and more than four times as many as in 1984. Sales of synthesizers jumped from 220,000 in 1985 to 350,000 in 1986. All that was driven by the increased power and flexibility of computer-assisted music production and a drop in the price of such electronic equipment. However, by the late 1990s, the segment had softened because consumers perceived that portable keyboards were of low quality. In 1999, Yamaha attempted to change that perception by introducing a moderately priced keyboard with such professional features as automatic accompaniment and sampled sounds.

Robert Moog introduced the synthesizer concept in 1964, but his company folded in 1977 and Moog moved to Kurzweil Music Systems Incorporated. The company's Kurzweil 250 used computer memory to reproduce the sounds of any musical instrument. The real breakthrough, however, came in 1983 with the musical instrument digital interface (MIDI), which allowed musicians and composers to connect synthesizers, instruments, and even computers together and have electronic signals successfully pass between them. Computer hardware and accompanying MIDI software sales jumped to $500 million in 1987. The computerized equipment allows composers and musicians to master new instruments quickly and to develop new music faster and more efficiently. They can also incorporate other, non-musical sounds into their compositions and performances. The system breaks down the barriers between composer, performer, music printer, and instrument builder, allowing the musician full control of the creative process.

The technology, however, brought a new set of problems. It allowed a musician to "sample" sounds from anywhere and anyone and then modify the sound to fit the need. Entire orchestras can be synthesized by one person, and other performers can be used to computer-produce totally new performances. This has led to copyright battles and fears of lack of work for live-performance musicians. In addition, the old fear that plagued the piano industry during the heyday of player pianos—that the technology will displace the art—has returned.

Introduced in the United States in 1989, acoustic/digital pianos offered the best of both worlds—for a price. The equivalent of a digital age "player piano," these instruments combined the traditional, full sound of a grand or upright piano with computer-driven options like automatic playback of famous performances, self-recording, and headphones for silent practice.

Another advancement in musical technology was the use of virtual reality. Peter Williams of Virtual S of London experimented with a virtual-reality keyboard in the shape of a checkerboard and bouncing ball. Each square could be a specific instrument or effect controlled by filters and other electronic controllers. The effect is a random music piece accompanied by the visual representation of the bouncing ball on the checkerboard. "This is one class of music programming that you couldn't do in the real world," said Williams in *New Scientist*. "We're not trying to replace violins and other instruments; this is a different way of doing it."

Other developments in the industry included a new process for making a plastic clarinet, which was developed by an English clarinetist and teacher along with an industrial designer. By fusing two molded halves instead of injection-molding a single piece, they eliminated the traditional tone problems of earlier plastic clarinets. Traditionally, clarinets are made from African hardwoods usually found in endangered rainforests. Consequently, the price of such wooden instruments was skyrocketing. The inventors hoped to begin using the same molding technique in the production of saxophones.

CURRENT CONDITIONS

Demographics and a strong economy held out some promise for the musical instruments industry of the late 1990s and early 2000s, with growth projected at 2 percent annually. Many of the school students in the "echo boom" were being given the opportunity to learn to play a musical instrument and were potential buyers of instruments. The baby-boomer generation entered the 35-to-54 age group during the 1990s, bringing with it considerable purchasing power and an interest in improved products. The instruments of choice for this generation were the acoustic guitar and similar instruments.

INDUSTRY LEADERS

At the beginning of the twentieth century, the American musical instruments industry was dominated by a few big names like Baldwin, Steinway, Aeolian, American, Kimball, Wurlitzer, Steger, and Kohler. By the mid-1990s, after a century of reorganization, merger, take-over, and bankruptcies, many of these once-famous names had disappeared.

Baldwin Piano and Organ Co. of Loveland, Ohio, survived dropping sales and rising interest rates by getting into the finance business: it bought and sold loan agreements on its pianos and organs. Dwight Hamilton Baldwin, a retail dealer of pianos and organs in Cincinnati, established the company in 1862. Its later success resulted from the takeover of many small piano manufacturers and the development of a consignment-based dealership contract arrangement. The system, actually begun by the W.W. Kimball Co. of Chicago, put pianos in showrooms across the country without major investments from the dealer and made pianos available to consumers on monthly payment terms. By the late 1930s, innovative marketing and quality products had established Baldwin as the industry leader. Hoping to capitalize on its decades of experience in consumer financing, the company diversified into financial services in the 1970s. By the early 1980s, the piano business was a mere 3 percent of the holding company's $3 billion operation. When parent company Baldwin-United went bankrupt in 1983, it spun off its piano interests in a management-led leveraged buyout. Faced with intense foreign competition, heavy debt, and a shrinking customer base, the company struggled to achieve consistent profitability in the 1990s. Sales rose from $110.1 million in 1992 to $122.6 million in 1995. Net income slid from a high of $5.9 million in 1992 to just $345,000 in 1994, rebounding to just under $4 million in 1995. Sales increased to $154 million in 1997. Baldwin has the largest market share of grand pianos in the United States. Since 1988, it has manufactured Wurlitzer pianos, and since 1995, Chickering grand pianos.

Steinway Musical Instruments, Inc. has two divisions: Selmer and Steinway. Founded before the turn of the twentieth century, for most of its history Selmer Co. concentrated primarily on wind instruments—clarinets, trumpets, and saxophones—as well as violins. Leveraged buyouts in 1988 and 1993 put the company in private hands. In 1994, the company acquired Steinway Musical Properties, Inc. for $101.5 million. Steinway had also built a reputation as a maker of quality instruments. Established in 1853 in New York, the firm eschewed price competition, instead cultivating a top-quality image via international endorsements by concert pianists, sponsorship of national concert tours, and with award-winning national advertising campaigns. According to a corporate profile, "More than 90 percent of all concert piano performances are on Steinway grand pianos." It also states that "Selmer is the leading domestic manufacturer of band and orchestral instruments" and that "over 60 percent of professional musicians and performing amateurs" use instruments with a Steinway Musical Instruments brand. Steinway Musical Instruments had sales of $277.8 million in 1997.

Leaders of the guitar segment of the industry included Fender Musical Instruments Corp. and Gibson Guitar Corp. Headquartered in Scottsdale, Arizona, privately-held Fender was acquired by CBS Inc. in 1981 and taken private in 1985. New management reinvigorated the company such that by 1995, the company boasted almost 50 percent of the guitar market. Fender had 1997 sales of $193 million, while Gibson had sales of $120.1 million. Nashville-based Gibson can be traced to the 1870s, when company namesake Orville Gibson opened a mandolin shop in Kalamazoo, Michigan. C.F. Martin & Co., founded in 1833, is a leader in the high-end guitar market. The company's earnings rose 10 percent a year for four years, generating revenues of $53 million in 1998. In 1999, Martin moved into the under-$800 segment.

The founding of United Musical Instruments U.S.A., Inc. (UMI) in 1985 allied the famous musical instrument names of Armstrong, Artley, Benge, Conn, and King. Brands encompass wind and brass instruments. Armstrong, Artley, and Benge began manufacturing in the 1930s. Conn, the oldest continuously produced brand name brass instrument in the United States, was founded in 1875, while King instruments have been manufactured since 1893. UMI also imports and distributes instruments from overseas. The company had 1998 sales of $20 million.

AMERICA AND THE WORLD

The United States imports and exports musical instruments in all categories. The main imports are pianos, guitars, and electric instruments. Japan, Korea, Taiwan, and China are the main suppliers and account for some two-thirds of imports. Chief musical instrument exports are parts (about one-third of total), high-quality guitars, and electric instruments. Half of U.S. musical instrument exports in 1997 went to Japan, Canada, the United Kingdom, and Germany.

RESEARCH AND TECHNOLOGY

An ongoing problem for novice musicians is how to learn to play an instrument without disturbing others or embarrassing themselves. Yamaha tackled this problem by introducing a whole of line of "silent" instruments for practice sessions. By 1999 the line included the violin, drum, cello, and a brass collection. For people who wanted to pretend to be playing, QRS Music, maker of a wide selection of self-playing instruments, introduced the world's first self-playing violin.

Developed by Virtual DSP Corp. in the late 1990s, the MidiAxe guitar contains a circuit board embedded in the back. Competitors' guitar MIDI systems, such as those from market leader Roland Corp., required a sensor to be attached to the guitar—something musicians balked at doing to their expensive instruments. Notes George Erb in *Puget Sound Business Journal*, "Because of that

board, players can plug a MidiAxe directly into a computer and use the instrument to create a wide array of digital sounds."

FURTHER READING

Brown, Ed. "Sing Me a Song, Mr. Piano Man . . . Excuse Me, Orchestra." *Fortune,* 15 March 1999.

Cummings, James. "Yamaha's Affordable, Easy-to-Use Keyboard in High Demand." *Kinght-Ridder/Tribune Business News,* 8 July 1999.

Darnay, Arsen J., ed. *Market Share Reporter.* Detroit: Gale Research, 1998.

———. *Manufacturing USA.* 6th ed. Detroit: Gale Research, 1998.

Erb, George. "Plenty of Pluck." *Puget Sound Business Journal,* 9 April 1999.

Feibelman, Adam. "The Good Wizard: He Saved Gibson Guitars From Being a Firm That Sold Seconds." *Memphis Business Journal,* 14 October 1996.

Fitch, Stephanie. "Stringin Them Along." *Forbes,* 26 July 1999.

Grument, Tobey. "Silence Is Golden." *Popular Mechanics,* April 1999.

Lim, Paul. "How You Can Get a High-Tech Piano That's Truly Grand." *Money,* February 1997.

Matzer, Marla. "Playing Solo." *Forbes,* 25 March 1996.

Smith, David. "Conway Plant Builds 2,200 Baldwin Pianos a Year." *Arkansas Business,* 6 April 1998.

U.S. Industry & Trade Outlook '99. McGraw-Hill and U.S. Department of Commerce, 1999.

Watson, Bruce. "How to Take on an Ailing Company and Make It Hum." *Smithsonian,* July 1996.

SIC 3942

DOLLS AND STUFFED TOYS

This category covers establishments primarily engaged in manufacturing dolls, doll parts, and doll clothing, except doll wigs. Establishments primarily engaged in manufacturing stuffed toys are also included in this industry. Doll wigs are classified under **SIC 3999: Manufacturing Industries, Not Elsewhere Classified.**

NAICS CODE(S)

339931 (Doll and Stuffed Toy Manufacturing)

In 1998, according to the New York-based trade group Toy Manufacturers of America, toy industry shipments of dolls were $2.085 billion—a drop of 32 percent over 1997. Shipments of stuffed toys were $1.614 billion. To counter the market decline attributed to competition from computer and electronic games targeted to girls, manufacturers brought out more interactive dolls and updated their current products in 1999—though traditional baby dolls were the top seller in the year's first quarter.

To contain labor costs, many companies imported branded products or used parts made in developing countries. Mattel, Inc. was among several retailers that came under scrutiny in the mid-1990s, when it was alleged that young Chinese workers earned less than China's minimum wage of $1.99 a day making Barbie dolls. Still, in the late 1990s it was expected that imports would continue to displace domestic production. China, Japan, and Taiwan were major suppliers. Exports were being helped by an increased interest in products made in the United States and the lifting of trade barriers.

The biggest name in doll manufacturing is Mattel, Inc., maker of Barbie, the number one brand targeted toward girls aged three to seven. Two Barbies are sold every second. It has been estimated that, on average, young females in the United States own eight Barbie dolls, and 95 percent of all young females have at least one. Barbie dolls had worldwide annual sales of $1.7 billion in 1998. According to Donna Leccese of *Playthings,* "Barbie accounts for more than half of all doll sales"—despite shipments decreasing 14 percent in 1998. Market saturation and new competition may have contributed to the decline.

Since her creation in 1959 as a teenage fashion model, Barbie has engaged in various professional roles and has been joined by friends and family. In 1965 she gained her first ethnic friend and, in 1997, a disabled friend. Recognizing some serious competition from a growing collection of ethnic dolls, Mattel introduced an African-American Barbie in 1980, but only the coloring—not the doll's features—was modified. The company later introduced other ethnic dolls, but these only imitated products already being marketed by minority entrepreneurs. Barbie underwent a makeover in 1998 in response to complaints that she was a "self-esteem destroyer;" her figure was given more realistic proportions and her makeup was toned down. Also in 1998, Mattel launched a Web site that let girls design and order their own "Friend of Barbie" doll by choosing from some 15,000 feature combinations (but no shape choices).

In the late 1990s, smaller manufacturers challenged the norm set by Barbie by introducing more life-like dolls. Get Set Club Inc. produced five ethnically diverse dolls that were fully poseable and had naturally shaped bodies, while GP Toys introduced Walking Tanya, which had a human stride.

Barbie is not the only cause of Mattel's strength in this industry. Through licensing agreements and acquisi-

tions, Mattel has brought under its umbrella such hit dolls and stuffed toys as Cabbage Patch Kids, Tickle Me Elmo, Winnie-the-Pooh, and the American Girls Collection. Targeted to girls aged seven to twelve, the American Girls line of historical dolls was the second largest girl's brand in the world in 1999, having sold some four million units between 1986 and 1998. The line's acquisition anchored Mattel's position in the girl's consumer brand market.

Mattel's closest competitor in the dolls and stuffed toys industry is Hasbro, Inc., many of whose products are geared towards boys. Hasbro had sales of $3.3 billion in 1998, compared to Mattel's sales of $4.7 billion. Hasbro sells a doll perhaps equally as famous as Barbie—G.I. Joe, who turned 35 in 1999. Like Mattel, Hasbro has numerous licensing agreements that allow it to offer a variety of brands, including action figures under the Starting Lineup, Star Wars, Batman, Superman, and Pokemon names. In the late 1990s, the company's divisions sold three of the industry's hottest product lines: Teletubbies, Furby, and Pokemon. The Teletubbies plush were offered in many sizes and forms, including an interactive version. The interactive Furby plush toy speaks "Furbish" and other languages and reacts to different conditions. Although Pokemon's most popular product is trading cards, the plush "pocket monsters" are highly demanded as well.

Another strong industry player is Ty Inc., maker of Beanie Babies. These plush-like collectibles have been on the market since 1993, ranging from $6 to hundreds of dollars for "retireds." In September 1999, Ty announced that all Beanies would be retired as of December 31, 1999. Ty reported 1998 estimated sales of $1 billion.

Several smaller manufacturers produced interactive dolls in the 1990s. DSI Toys produced a doll that recited a bedtime prayer. Irwin Toy Ltd. implanted moisture-sensitive switches in its Kissy Kissy Baby doll that activated when kissed, causing the doll to kiss and giggle.

Traditional dolls—especially those in the collectible segment—gave interactive dolls competition. Sometimes dolls extended across segments. By giving its collectible Gene doll a bended knee, Bradford Exchange made it popular as a play doll, too. Many manufacturers, such as Alexander Doll Company, Lee Middleton, and Gotz, benefited by serving specialty, or collector, markets.

FURTHER READING

About Mattel Company History, 1999. Available from http://www.mattel.com/corporate/company/about/.

Baldwin, Kristen. "A Doll's Life: Four Decades Ago, A New Starlet Broke the Mold. Here's Her Story." *Entertainment Weekly,* 5 March 1999.

Bilzi, Jane. "Beyond the Silicon 'Valley of the Dolls'." *Playthings,* April 1999.

Bryant, June Smith. "More Dolls of Color." *Black Enterprise*, December 1991.

Chmielewski, Dawn C. "Mattel's New Web Site Lets Girls Design, Order Own Barbie Dolls." *Knight-Ridder/Tribune Business News*, 26 October 1998.

Cole, Wendy. "Doll With a Past." *Time*, 19 October 1998.

Doll and Stuffed Toy Manufacturing: 1997 Economic Census. Washington, DC: U.S. Census Bureau, 1999.

Hasbro Corporate Information, 1999. Available from http://www.hasbro.com.

Hayden, Thomas. "Fun! Fearless! Furby! (Furby Electronic Doll Could Be Christmas Craze)." *Newsweek*, 19 October 1998.

Holstein, William J. "Santa's Sweatshop." *U.S. News & World Report*, 16 December 1996.

Leccese, Donna. "Imitation of Life." *Playthings*, April 1999.

Miller, Cyndee. "Toy Companies Release 'Ethnically Correct' Dolls." *Marketing News*, 30 September 1991.

Toy Manufacturers of America, Inc. Research, 1999. Available from http://www.toy-tma.com/industry/news.

U.S. Industry and Trade Outlook '99. McGraw-Hill and U.S. Department of Commerce, 1999.

SIC 3944

GAMES, TOYS, AND CHILDREN'S VEHICLES

This entry consists of establishments primarily engaged in manufacturing games and game sets for adults and children and mechanical and non-mechanical toys. Important industry products include games; toy furniture; doll carriages and carts; construction sets; mechanical trains; toy guns and rifles; baby carriages and strollers; children's tricycles, coaster wagons, play cars, sleds and other children's outdoor wheel goods and vehicles, except bicycles. Also included are establishments primarily engaged in manufacturing electronic board games; electronic toys; and electronic game machines, except coin-operated. Establishments primarily involved in manufacturing dolls and stuffed toys are included in **SIC 3942: Dolls and Stuffed Toys.**

NAICS CODE(S)

336991 (Motorcycle, Bicycle, and Parts Manufacturing)

339932 (Game, Toy, and Children's Vehicle Manufacturing)

INDUSTRY SNAPSHOT

The U.S. toy industry is a fast-paced industry. Product-driven, it rides the crest of a fad until the next fad happens through a combination of product merit, marketing, and luck. Although the classics such as Monopoly, Scrabble, and Slinky have demonstrated strong, long-term sales performance, few toys or games stay on the shelves for more than a year or two. The early 1990s were healthy years for the toy industry, although the fortunes of various companies have swung wildly. Several factors make the toy industry a risky business, including boom-or-bust sales patterns, short product life, and only one major selling season, Christmas, which historically has accounted for 50 to 60 percent of annual sales. In 1992, total annual sales were $15.3 billion, up 19 percent from the year before. In 1998, the figure was $21 billion.

Game makers think of themselves as publishers more than toy makers because many games have a longer sales life than most toys and sell at a fairly predictable level. But game publishers are subject to the same instability of the market, with some games failing and others, such as Trivial Pursuit and Pictionary, experiencing unpredictable success. The game segment was formerly a relatively staid component within the toy industry until Trivial Pursuit's sudden success tipped the market upside down and showed that games were not just products for children. Soon, other companies were also looking for the key to success in the adult game market. Manufacturers looked to expand the market in the late 1990s by offering computer and Internet versions of their board games.

ORGANIZATION AND STRUCTURE

Because the industry is heavily dependent on capricious trends, miscalculation or misjudgment at times can result in enormous losses. The life span of even the most successful toys is often brief, with sales dropping as quickly as they rise. Typically, companies count themselves among the fortunate if they have one product that sells well for a year. Even if a product remains popular after its debut year, it is likely to be copied, since toy manufacturers often attempt to replicate each other's successful products.

The Toy Manufacturers of America (TMA), the industry's trade organization, was founded shortly after the United States entered World War I, when toy makers faced severe shortages of materials, and Congress was considering an embargo on the buying and selling of Christmas presents to conserve materials needed for the war. TMA was formed and successfully lobbied Congress to continue producing toys for America's children despite the war. A few years later, TMA convinced representatives to impose large tariffs on toy imports to protect the American toy industry. TMA continued to lobby and compile information and statistics for the toy industry in the 1990s.

Ideas for games and toys may originate in-house, but the industry also relies heavily on the ideas of freelance inventors. A company may pour thousands, even hundreds of thousands of dollars into market testing before committing to production. Toy development is risky and speculative. During the course of its development, a concept may change drastically. Most toy manufacturers also subscribe to *Toy Retail Sales Tracing Service* for quantitative market research that reveals trends, product performance, and competition. Qualitative market research involves product testing, usually with small focus groups of children. Until it is officially previewed at the annual American International Toy Fair, a project can be aborted at any stage if it does not meet expectations or if buyers do not express much interest.

Historically, distributors and wholesalers were the toy manufacturers' biggest customers, but in the early 1990s large retail chains began ordering directly from the toy makers. Smaller toy stores looked to regional distributors, but for the most part distributors were a dying breed.

While the big box merchandiser Toys "R" Us accounted for as much as 25 percent of the retail toy market in the United States in 1994, by 1998 Wal-Mart, with 17.4 percent of the market share, held a narrow edge as the top toy retailer. The rest of the toy market was comprised of national and regional toy store chains, mass merchandisers, wholesalers, catalog showrooms, warehouse clubs, variety stores, discount stores, department stores, drugstores, local chains, and independent toy stores. There were also "jobbers" who bought closeout merchandise from toy makers to sell to retailers. Mass merchandisers, such as Kmart Corp. and Target, did not carry as wide a range of merchandise as the large toy stores, but these retailers had tremendous clout with toy makers. The national distribution and volume buying that these stores and others, such as Sears, Roebuck & Co. and J.C. Penney, offered helped them negotiate beneficial deals with toy makers. Although the warehouse clubs mostly sold toy products during the holiday season, in 1997 a federal court ruled Toys "R" Us pressured manufacturers to not sell popular toys to the clubs. In the late 1990s, catalog and Internet shopping were increasing. In 1998 Toys "R" Us started selling on the Internet, and the eToys company acquired Toys.com, while other companies also developed sites on the Web to sell toys.

Although the law prohibits manufacturers from selling merchandise to different customers at different prices, in reality, the larger the customer, the larger the volume discount. The purchasing power of the customer also affects many other negotiable terms, including credit against future sales and extra merchandise from the manufacturer. These discounts and special terms result in widely varying retail prices. Powerful customers also are able to receive markdown money from manufacturers of products that failed so badly retailers were forced to sell them below cost. However, what smaller retailers lack in price breaks often is made up in convenience, service, and unique products. In the late 1990s, it was the small retailers that offered the extremely popular Beanie Babies, and chains specializing in educational toys were growing.

BACKGROUND AND DEVELOPMENT

The first U.S. toy manufacturer was established in the 1830s. Tower Toy Company produced doll furniture, toy tools, and toy boats. In 1860, Milton Bradley Co. established a publishing and lithography business, but as financial problems plagued the company, Bradley diversified by inventing and publishing The Checkered Game of Life, the precursor of The Game of Life, still popular in the late 1990s. The Civil War slowed the toy industry somewhat, although toy guns were popular, as were Milton Bradley's portable editions of chess, checkers, and dominoes.

In 1883, 16 year-old George S. Parker started his own game company. When his brothers joined him, the company became Parker Brothers & Company Inc. It became the publisher of many games still popular in the late 1990s, including the perennial number one-selling board game, Monopoly, as well as Sorry!, Risk, and Clue.

Around the turn of the century, the "Golden Age of Toys" brought walking and talking dolls, toy pianos, friction motorized vehicles, steam-powered toys, the Erector Set, the Flexible Flyer sled, Lionel toy trains, and Crayola crayons. In 1906, the Teddy bear craze began with the stuffed animals named for Teddy Roosevelt because he refused to shoot a trapped bear cub during a hunting trip. Between 1900 and 1910, American toy production doubled. During the next decade, it grew 500 percent, largely because World War I had halted the import of European toys. In 1923, Hasbro Inc. brought out its classic real estate game, Monopoly, and Milton Bradley introduced Easy Money—games that allowed players to imagine being rich by making deals with play dollars. In 1930, Herman G. Fisher and Irving R. Price established the very successful Fisher-Price, Inc., which in the early 1990s was the biggest name in infant and preschool toys and merchandise. Fisher-Price merged with Mattel, Inc. in 1993.

World War II slowed the toy industry's growth because of labor and material shortages, but the post-war years brought prosperity to the entire country; the toy industry reaped the benefits as well. Following World War II, the toy world was revolutionized with the introduction of plastic.

Television Advertising. In 1955, an advertising move by Mattel, Inc. changed the way toys and games were marketed and also launched the promotional toy business. The nascent American Broadcasting Company (ABC) television network approached Mattel about weekly national advertising on its new show, Walt Disney Co.'s "The Mickey Mouse Club," beginning in November, just as the Christmas shopping season opened. To the surprise of many, Mattel took a big financial risk and paid half a million dollars to become a sponsor. Before this bold move, most advertising money was spent on catalogs and trade ads during the Christmas season and an occasional local TV ad to promote the most promising items. With this advertising agreement between Mattel and ABC, Mattel's famous slogan was born ("You can tell it's Mattel, it's swell") and the power of weekly advertising to kids was launched. The product Mattel had advertised, the Burp Gun, sold out, and the promotional toy business was on its way.

Promotional toys were products advertised on television directly to the consumers—the kids. Television became the number one advertising force in the toy industry. With the line between advertising and entertainment blurred in the late 1980s and early 1990s, entire shows became based on the exploits of a line of characters invented or promoted by a toy company. In 1969, Mattel underwrote a program based on its very successful Hot Wheels line. When a competitor complained, the Federal Communications Commission (FCC) banned it, calling it a "program-length commercial." In 1983, the FCC ruled that the marketplace should determine programming. This change of policy cleared the way for toy-based programming. By the 1986-1987 season, more than 40 toy-based programs were on the air.

According to Sydney Stern and Ted Schoenhaus in *Toyland, The High Stakes Game of the Toy Industry,* television changed the very nature of toys by allowing the toy industry to sell toys that they could never sell before because they could now demonstrate the features of the product. Products that could do something—walk, talk, move, crash—had existed for a long time, but now they came to life on television and soon dominated the market. Advertising even began to dictate product development. Products were developed on the basis of how well they would lend themselves to television commercials. Television also allowed the toy makers to create a fantasy around the product, so that children were not only demanding a toy, they were buying into the fantasy that made that particular toy unique. By the 1980s, the commercial became more important than the product itself because it was the commercial that created the concept, while the product actually did little on its own. Retailers, trying to anticipate what toys kids would want, paid close attention to the manufacturers' ads and ad budgets in making their purchasing decisions during the early 1990s. At toy fairs for buyers, toy manufacturers previewed the commercials as well as the toys.

By the late 1990s, companies sought to increase market share by engaging in cross-marketing. These activities included product tie-ins with movies and various sports, such as NASCAR. The success of these tie-ins was unpredictable. Despite heavy marketing, sales of products associated with the *Star Wars* trilogy, *The Hunchback of Notre Dame, Godzilla,* and other movies were disappointing. Yet, Danish manufacturer Lego signed its first licensing agreement for products tied to the *Star Wars* prequels.

The Advent of Video Games. A second "revolution" in toy making began with the first video games. In 1972, Nolan Bushnell and a friend invested $250 each to found Atari Corp. and produce Pong, a simple video table tennis game. It became a coin-operated hit in bars and arcades and, in 1975, Bushnell began marketing a home version to compete with Odyssey, a video game system being produced by Magnavox Co. Atari was sold to Warner Communications Inc. in 1976. Mattel followed with Intellivision in late 1979 and Coleco Industries Inc. brought out ColecoVision in 1983.

Soon, the industry was licensing the most popular arcade games for home video systems. Video games were bringing in hundreds of millions of dollars. Many new companies formed just to manufacture and sell cartridges for Atari and other game systems, thus taking valuable profits from the systems' developers. Large and small toy companies rushed to produce their own video systems. In a few short years, however, the video game and cartridge fad ran out of steam. Warner lost $539 million on its consumer electronics segment in 1983, and it ended up burying truckloads of game cartridges. Warner, Mattel, and Coleco sold their video game businesses during the next two years.

Nintendo Co., Ltd., a Japanese electronics company, learned from the mistakes of its predecessors. In the late 1980s, Nintendo was generating sales of more than $1 billion in the United States alone. It was making this money at the expense of other traditional toys and games, taking market share from industry leaders Hasbro Inc. and Mattel. Nintendo controlled licensing and sales of all game cartridges so that it would not meet the same fate as Atari.

Sega Enterprises Co., Ltd., another Japanese company, challenged Nintendo in the United States during the early 1990s. In 1991, Sega introduced its Genesis system, and Nintendo responded with Super Nintendo. The battle continued throughout the 1990s, with Sega launching a major market offensive with its high-performance, CD-based Saturn game system. During this period, a number of other companies entered the fray—most notably a U.S. company, 3D Co., and the Japanese electronic giant Sony Corp. While Sony's PlayStation managed to establish itself in the market, 3D's game player eventually fell by the wayside, largely as a result of being priced too high for the average consumer. In late 1996, Nintendo struck back with Nintendo 64. Boasting high-resolution, 64-bit, 3D graphics, Nintendo 64 delivered processing power exceeding that of many personal computers, and its eagerly awaited introduction led to long waiting lists, high-priced black marketing, and even theft. Sega countered with the introduction of its 128-bit Dreamcast machine in 1999.

CURRENT CONDITIONS

Because toy manufacturers sell to children, their ads are designed to appeal to children, thus generating much controversy about ethics in children's advertising. Children are easily exploited, children's advocates contend; they lack the experience to discern poorly made products or recognize that a commercial has presented a fantasy world rather than the reality of a particular toy. Action for Children's Television unsuccessfully tried to convince the FCC that toy-based shows were 30-minute commercials and should be purchased as advertising time. Critics of children's television and its ads also continued to protest the promotion of violence through toy-based shows and the weaponry toys advertised, as well as gender stereotyping reflected in many shows and advertised toys.

In the 1980s, television networks ABC, the National Broadcasting Company Inc. (NBC), and CBS Inc. required the last five seconds of a toy commercial to show the product all alone so that children could see what they are really getting. The networks also limited animation within the ad to one-third of the total ad time. Independent stations, however, had no such restrictions, and with the growth of cable, the independents became important advertising channels for toy makers during the 1990s. Bandai America produced numerous toys based on top-rated children's television series on Fox Kids Network.

Video games continued to present a threat to the traditional toy market in the 1990s. Nintendo and Sega were the video leaders, and unlike other toy trends, which soared briefly and then saw sales drop dramatically, this generation of electronic games remained popular, with sales expected to keep rising. Sony also was a player in this segment. During the early 1990s, traditional toy makers were considering whether to compete for market share with traditional, non-video toys, or to enter the video market themselves.

By the mid-1990s, another threat challenged both traditional toy makers and the electronic game giants. This threat came in the form of computer games. Long the poor cousin of the video game, computer games increased their market share rapidly with the advent of the CD-ROM and continued reductions in the cost of personal computers equipped with multimedia capabilities. With more than half of U.S. households owning computers, manufacturers saw an emerging market and began developing CD-ROM

products based on their toy and game lines. In 1996, Mattel introduced "Fashion Designer Barbie," for designing Barbie doll outfits on the computer, and Hasbro released its first Tonka CD-ROM, for building construction projects. Since then, these companies and others have released numerous CD-ROM titles that extend their toy brands, as well as interactive versions of board games. Mattel was the leader in children's CD-ROM sales in the late 1990s, and with its merger with The Learning Company, an educational software publisher, Mattel had attained interactive sales of $1 billion.

The toy industry turned to more intensive brand management during the 1990s, focusing on either extending existing lines of products, spending more money marketing the "classics," or entering into licensing agreements. For example, Hasbro added new products to the Nerf line of foam sports toys (including Nerf Turbo Football and Nerf Bow 'n' Arrow), augmented its Monopoly line of products with the introduction of Monopoly Junior, and dominated the top 15 selling toys introduced in 1999 with licensed products. Hasbro was Nintendo's worldwide master licensee of hot-selling Pokemon toys and games—products that included action figures, trading card games, electronic plush, and Pokemon Monopoly. Hasbro also had agreements with baseball greats Mark McGwire and Sammy Sosa, Universal Studios, and NASCAR.

Demand for toys in the United States declined slightly in the late 1990s as the population of children declined, yet it was estimated that $350 on toys was spent on each child in 1998. The industry also saw an increase in year-round sales, believed to be due to movie tie-ins, new releases of Beanie Babies and Tamagotchis, and more toy givers per child. Imports accounted for 75 percent of consumption in 1996 and were expected to increase because of lower production costs offshore. American companies sought to expand sales and profits by aggressively marketing abroad, working to open markets in Asia, South America, and the Middle East. Exports were expected to maintain a 6 percent annual growth rate. Most of this growth would be in higher-end products, educational software, computer games, and electronic toys.

Although the industry was dominated by several giants, small companies also had opportunities for success. Some smaller companies acquired rights to products that the big companies had retired, such as Erector Sets and Creepy Crawlers, or launched their own new products. The toy and game industry was attractive to small businesses because start-up costs remained low when manufacturing was subcontracted. Smaller companies could be more innovative since they did not have the layers of bureaucracy associated with the larger companies, and they did not have to generate as much income.

Consolidation also reduced the likelihood that a large company would take a chance on an item able to generate only $1 or $2 million. By the early 1990s, large manufacturers needed $10 million in product sales to justify spending their advertising dollars. Advertising costs continued increasing into the 2000s.

INDUSTRY LEADERS

The toy industry underwent extensive consolidation after the video game era began. Some of the most familiar brands lost their independence and became part of the world's two largest toy corporations, Mattel and Hasbro. Still, there were some 752 companies in this category in 1997.

Mattel, Inc. held the top spot among toy manufacturers in 1997, with sales of approximately $4.8 billion. In the 1990s, the company merged with Fisher-Price (infant and preschool toys) and Tyco Toys (Matchbox cars, View-Master, Magna Doodle, "Sesame Street" toys) and acquired International Games (UNO and Skip-Bo card games), Power Wheels (ride-on vehicles), J.W. Spear (Scrabble), and the Pleasant Company (the "American Girl" brand). Mattel signed a multiyear agreement with Walt Disney Co., guaranteeing it worldwide toy rights for all Disney television and film properties. The company also had licensing rights to characters on Nickelodeon, Cabbage Patch Kids, and Polly Pocket. Convinced that children everywhere like the same toys, the company made no effort to modify its products for different markets. Instead, it designed products with universal appeal and marketed them globally. In 1999, it operated in 36 countries and marketed its products in more than 150 countries.

Hasbro Inc., a small company in the early 1980s, became the largest U.S. toy manufacturer in 1985 by eschewing the video market and benefiting from widely popular products such as G.I. Joe, Transformers, and My Little Pony. In 1984, Hasbro bought Playskool, as well as the Milton Bradley company, the fourth largest company in the toy industry. With Milton Bradley came the rights to The Game of Life, Twister, and other solid-selling games. By 1988, Milton Bradley accounted for 20 percent of Hasbro's sales. Hasbro also acquired Coleco and Tonka just as each was headed for bankruptcy. Tonka had owned Kenner Products and Parker Brothers, so the acquisition of Tonka also brought a second most-famous game company into the Hasbro empire. Hasbro also acquired Larami (1995); OddzOn Products and Cap Toys (1997); Tiger Electronics, MicroProse and Galoob (1998); and Europress and Wizards of the Coast (1999). Brands included Furby, Mr. Potato Head, and Play-Doh, and partnership brands included Pokemon, Star Wars, Batman, Teletubbies, and Superman. Though Mattel eclipsed Hasbro's position in the 1990s, the company

nevertheless finished a strong second with 1998 revenues of $3.3 billion and projected growth in interactive and electronic games and toys and in license and alliance opportunities.

Bandai America Incorporated is a subsidiary of Bandai Co., Ltd. of Japan, the world's third largest toy company. In 1997, Bandai produced the hottest toy of the year—Tamagotchi, the original "virtual pet." The company is the master toy licensee of Power Rangers, Xber 9, Digimon, and Big Guy and Rusty action figures.

Two surviving independents are Little Tikes, a division of Rubbermaid, and Ty, the maker of Beanie Babies. In 1999, in collaboration with IBM and Edmark software, Little Tikes began producing the Young Explorer computer for 3- to 7-year-olds.

FURTHER READING

Annicelli, Cliff. "Tackling a New Year." *Playthings,* January 1995.

Hoover's Company Capsules. Austin, TX: Hoover's Inc., 1997.

Leccese, Donna. "Searching for Innovation." *Playthings,* January 1996.

———. "Year-Round Sales: Myth or Reality?" *Playthings,* August 1998.

Liebeck, Laura. "Brand Extensions Heat Up as Vendors Get Creative." *Discount Store News,* 8 March 1999.

Reysen, Frank Jr. "U.S. Toy Market Expected to Grow 6 Percent in 1996." *Playthings,* April 1996.

Sheff, David. *Game Over: How Nintendo Zapped an American Industry, Captured Your Dollars, and Enslaved Your Children.* New York: Random House, 1993.

U.S. Census Bureau. *Game, Toy, and Children's Vehicle Manufacturing: 1997 Economic Census.* Washington, D.C.: GPO, 1999.

SIC 3949

SPORTING AND ATHLETIC GOODS, NOT ELSEWHERE CLASSIFIED

This industry covers establishments primarily engaged in manufacturing sporting and athletic goods not elsewhere classified, such as fishing tackle; golf and tennis goods; baseball, football, basketball, and boxing equipment; roller skates and ice skates; gymnasium and playground equipment; billiard and pool tables; and bowling alleys and equipment. Establishments primarily engaged in manufacturing athletic apparel are classified in the major group for apparel and other finished products made from fabrics and similar materials; those manufacturing athletic footwear are classified in **SIC 3021: Rub-**

ber and Plastics Footwear and SIC 3149: Footwear, Except Rubber, Not Elsewhere Classified; those manufacturing small arms ammunition are classified in SIC 3482: Small Arms Ammunition; and those manufacturing small arms are classified in SIC 3484: Small Arms.

NAICS CODE(S)

339920 (Sporting and Athletic Good Manufacturing)

INDUSTRY SNAPSHOT

Like other sectors of the U.S. economy, the sporting goods industry was undergoing substantial change in the mid- to late 1990s. Computer technology linked sports equipment manufacturers more closely to retailers. Super sporting goods stores oversaturated the market and squeezed out smaller chains. The trends of globalization and restructuring transformed the organization of sporting goods companies. Sports equipment makers began to exploit the stunning growth of the Internet. In 1998, a large percentage of companies used the Internet to post company or product information for consumers, while 7 percent used it to sell to consumers; 92 percent planned to use it by 2000. Additionally, changing demographics and lifestyles affected the popularity of individual sports and pastimes.

Overall, the industry shared in the general prosperity of the U.S. economy. From 1989 to 1997, U.S. personal consumption of sporting goods increased 6 percent annually, while disposable income increased only 3 percent annually. In 1998, however, according to the Sporting Goods Manufacturers Association (SGMA), the industry underperformed the economy for the first time since 1990, and growth was projected to be low in most segments. Although the American population was aging, much of the postwar baby-boom generation remained committed to staying fit. Frequent participation by individuals over 55 in sports and fitness increased 25 percent between 1987 and 1997. In addition, growing numbers of women were becoming sports enthusiasts, and manufacturers were designing offerings specifically for their needs (rather than simply painting existing products in pastels). In general, companies were creating new demand by appealing to specific market segments (e.g., basketballs and backboards especially designed for children). However, the industry was concerned about a decline among youngsters in sports and fitness activities. Overseas markets were a source of new demand because of expanding economies and liberalized trade regulations, although the Asian financial crisis was spurring imports.

Performance among the industry's numerous segments continued to vary significantly in the late 1990s as a sport's popularity waxed or waned depending on demographics, economics, marketing skill, and fads. The golf (though hurt by product oversaturation) and fitness segments were doing well because of technologically im-

proved products and new adherents among an older population. After several years of spectacular growth, the in-line skating segment contracted significantly in 1996 and continued to decline in 1999. Archery and tennis also were declining. Camping, water sports, soccer, bowling, and billiard sales were projected to grow modestly.

ORGANIZATION AND STRUCTURE

The sporting goods industry encompasses a wide variety of businesses and products with hundreds of participants. Within a specific segment, however, a few large companies may dominate. In the 1990s, ownership of many sporting goods companies changed hands through acquisitions or mergers. Most notably, in 1996 Kohlberg Kravis Roberts & Co. acquired Spalding Sports Worldwide in a deal estimated at $1 billion. That record deal was eclipsed in 1998 when Sunbeam Corporation acquired The Coleman Company for $2.1 billion. Other companies, like Wilson Sporting Goods, owned by Amer Group PLC, consolidated and restructured operations.

The sporting goods sector offers stunning success stories as a new or substantially improved product, or even an entirely new sport, can capture the public's fancy and produce spectacular returns for the originator. But for every Rollerblade, Inc. (a company that rode the in-line skating boom), there are dozens of failures.

BACKGROUND AND DEVELOPMENT

Albert G. Spalding, the man often misidentified as the inventor of baseball, was actually one of the pioneers of the sporting goods industry. After pitching his team, the Boston Red Stockings, to victory in three consecutive National Professional Association pennant races in the early 1870s, Spalding helped found the National League in 1876. In 1878 he opened a sporting goods store with his brother in Chicago. The company expanded from 2 to 14 stores within two years and soon afterwards began selling products it manufactured directly to other retail dealers. Spalding is given much of the credit for introducing gloves to baseball; after developing a sore arm from pitching, he switched to first base in 1877 and started wearing highly visible black gloves. Cynics have suggested, however, that Spalding's interest in wearing gloves was not unrelated to his desire to sell them.

Spalding also figures prominently in the history of basketball. James Naismith, the inventor of the game, commissioned him to create the world's first basketball in 1892. In 1999, Spalding balls were still the official standard of the National Basketball Association (NBA), as well as of the Women's National Basketball Association (WNBA).

Another important sporting goods company with a colorful history is Wilson. The firm was originally known as the Ashland Manufacturing Company and was a subsidiary of a meatpacking firm. It sold violin strings, surgical sutures, and strings for tennis products, all by-products of animal gut. In 1914 the company was forced into receivership and taken over by New York bankers. They picked Thomas Wilson to manage the company, partly because of his name—President Woodrow Wilson was then at the height of his popularity, and the owners hoped to capitalize on the association in the consumer's mind. The new firm became Wilson & Company. The firm soon expanded into tennis rackets, hunting and camping equipment, and fishing tackle. It continued to be one of the top manufacturers in the 1990s with a full line of sports equipment.

A more modern, but already legendary, figure in the history of sports equipment is Scott Olson. Olson was a 19-year-old goaltender with a minor league hockey team in 1980 when he found a pair of roller skates on which the wheels were arranged in a single row. While the skates felt slow and clumsy, they gave him the sense of skating on ice that traditional roller skates did not. Olson contacted the manufacturer, who had stopped making the line, and bought up the back stock. He put the blades on good skate boots and began selling them out of his house. In 1983 he quit pro hockey, bought up the existing patents, and started the company that would eventually become Rollerblade, Inc. While Olson was forced out of the business in 1985, he continued to design and develop new products, including a lightweight golf bag with wheels and a built-in pull handle.

CURRENT CONDITIONS

According to the annual survey of the SGMA, sales of sporting goods equipment increased just 1.7 percent throughout 1997 to total $17.5 billion. Low growth was projected to continue due to oversaturation of some products and weakness in some market segments. The economy was doing well in the late 1990s, demographic trends and healthy lifestyles were boosting demand in the over-40 age group, more women were playing sports, and the North American Free Trade Agreement (NAFTA) and other pacts liberalizing trade augured well for overseas business. Nevertheless, export sales growth dropped from 29 percent in 1997 to 18 percent in 1998, while imports grew from 2 percent in 1997 to 11 percent in 1998.

The industry faced several challenges, including how to increase participation levels. Many sports were not attracting significant numbers of new enthusiasts but instead were competing against each other for participants. The industry was seeking to boost interest in sports and fitness activities among youngsters to counter a decline in that market. Teens participated 18 percent less often in such activities in 1997 than in 1987.

For individual companies, however, the environment in its particular segment often overshadows the positives and negatives of the industry as a whole. The following

paragraphs discuss business conditions in important sporting areas.

Golf. According to *U.S. Industry & Trade Outlook '99*, 1997 shipments of golfing equipment rose 5 percent from 1996 totals to an estimated $2.5 billion. Although imports increased 23 percent, compared to 5 percent for exports, at $804 million, the value of exports still exceeded that of imports. From 1993 to 1998, the golf equipment industry grew some 9 percent. Sales increased due to increased participation in the sport—there were 26.5 million players in 1998 (though still down from 27.8 million in 1990)—and to increased demand for the latest in clubs, balls, shoes, and gloves. Golfers tend to be affluent with the means to buy technologically improved products, such as titanium clubs and balls and spikeless shoes. At Callaway, demand for Big Bertha metal oversized woods produced truly astonishing growth, as sales rose from $132 million in 1992 to $678 million in 1996.

Whether better clubs have actually helped the golfer's game is questioned by some observers, but there was little doubt they've done wonders for investors in golf club stocks. Manufacturers of smaller club brands have gone bankrupt or been consolidated. In January 1996, conglomerate American Brands bought Cobra Golf, makers of the King Cobra Titanium club that duels with Callaway's Big Bertha for the golfer's dollar. American paid $715 million for a company that had just $152 million in sales for the nine months ended September 30, 1995. In 1997, Spalding acquired Ben Hogan. In 1999 there were just four major golf ball manufacturers.

Manufacturers were developing products made out of new materials, such as ceramics, hoping to start a trend. Still, the market for golf equipment was expected to decline.

Tennis. Tennis made a small comeback in 1996 but declined the following two years. Tennis associations sponsored programs across the country to promote the game, but participation still slid 8.1 percent between 1996 and 1997. Sales of equipment dropped from $318.7 million in 1997 to $313.2 million in 1998.

In-Line Skating. The growth of in-line skating has been truly astonishing. According to one estimate, in-line skating participation grew 634 percent from 1987 to 1995. In 1997, 29.1 million Americans went skating at least once a year. By 1998 there was a 22 percent household penetration. Naturally, the surge in popularity catapulted sales, which rose from nearly nothing to $725 million in 1995.

In 1998, however, the industry had a bad fall, as sales declined 18 percent to $435 million. Overall, the market declined 66 percent between 1995 and 1998. Some of the reasons offered for the industry's decline were overloaded inventories at the retail level and the entrance of several new companies. The market was expected to continue to decline, although new products were being developed to keep participants interested. The market contains the recreation/fitness, aggressive skating, and in-line hockey categories.

Fitness Equipment. The desire of an aging American population to keep fit has conveniently supported sales of the fitness equipment segment. According to the SGMA survey, sales of fitness products totaled an estimated $2.68 billion in 1997, up from $2.07 billion in 1996 and compared with just $680 million in 1986. Cardiovascular machines and strength equipment were the largest categories of sales. Approximately one-third of American households owned and used exercise equipment. The most popular home exercise equipment was free weights, treadmills, and stationary bikes. Sales for home use slowed in 1998 after a decade, but sales to institutions and overseas were on the upswing. Exports increased 9 percent, while imports declined 15 percent.

So-called "infomercials" and television shopping networks have also given a big boost to sales of fitness equipment. Sales of the abdominal exerciser reached more than $200 million in 1996, although some observers think that the popularity of these machines has crested and also contributed to the decline in imports. The aero rider/glider was another product whose sales were propelled by the infomercial.

Basketball. Basketball has benefited from increasing participation by women, spurred by the formation of professional women's leagues and the success of the women's team at the 1996 Olympics. Moreover, Title IX and other gender equity programs have encouraged more women to take up the game. Meanwhile, men aged 35-44 are playing the game in growing numbers. According to the SGMA, "Basketball [is] . . . the largest participation team sport in the country." Innovations include smaller balls, adjustable height baskets, portable basketball systems, and a composite ball. Sales dipped to $184.6 million in 1998 from $185.6 million in 1997, but they were estimated to reach $190.1 million in 1999.

Baseball and Softball. Sales in the baseball and softball segment have been lackluster as participation rates stay flat or decline. Few adults played baseball, and most of the youth playing baseball were in tee ball programs. However, interest in baseball was spurred in 1998 by Mark McGuire's and Sammy Sosa's pursuit of the home run record. Consequently, participation in the game went up 12.1 percent. Manufacturers faced flat sales in 1999, as well as uncertainty over the effects of proposed equipment. Softball has declined steadily since its heyday in the 1970s as an adult male-dominated sport; participation dropped 4.6 percent in 1998 and by 10.4 million from 1990 to 1997. One bright spot was women's fast pitch,

whose image was enhanced by the excellent performance by the U.S. team in the 1996 Olympics and whose participation has increased at the high school and college levels since 1990. Combined sales of baseball and softball equipment were $303.1 million in 1998.

Bowling. More than 53.3 million people aged six or older bowled at least once in 1997, making it the sport with the largest number of participants. But league play, the traditional segment of the business, has been falling since the 1970s and the number of bowling centers has been shrinking. Indeed, the decline in league play gained notoriety in 1995 when Harvard professor Robert Putnam linked it to a general drop in participation of all kinds of neighborhood- and community-level groups. Calling the syndrome "Bowling Alone," Putnam blamed it for the collapse of the democratic process. According to the SGMA survey, sales of bowling products in 1998 were estimated at $215 million, virtually unchanged from 1995 and not projected to grow in 1999. Industry leaders were updating bowling centers, building new centers, and offering "cosmic" bowling as well as other entertainment to bolster interest. Through a series of acquisitions, AMF Bowling became the largest operator of bowling centers in 1998.

Fishing Tackle and Equipment. Sales of fishing tackle increased from $1.89 million in 1997 to $1.90 million in 1998. Due to the Asian financial crisis, imports (which came mostly from South Korea, Japan, and China) declined in 1997. U.S. exports of fishing tackle also declined. The market is expected to grow 2 to 3 percent as baby boomers engage more in the sport.

Soccer. Participation in soccer grew 18.4 percent from 1987 to 1997, with some 18.2 million Americans playing the game at least one day in 1997. It is the top team sport for children under 10 years old and has increased participation by adults. With the 1999 Women's World Cup win by the U.S. team, development of a professional league, and increased television exposure, participation in the sport and sales of soccer equipment are expected to increase modestly.

Volleyball. According to the SGMA survey, volleyball ranks "second to basketball in team sport popularity, with an estimated 29 million people playing indoor or beach volleyball." Once dominated by Americans, beach volleyball is now played worldwide. Volleyball teams may be coed or composed of one gender. At the high school level, girls far outnumber boys on interscholastic teams. Volleyball also is a popular women's intercollegiate sport. Major matches are televised; both indoor and beach volleyball will be played at the 2000 Olympic Games.

Billiards. In 1998, some 44.5 million players made billiards one of the fastest growing sporting goods sectors. Billiards play ranks fifth in participation overall. There have been double-digit increases in play by female players, casual players, and baby boomers. Sales of billiards/pool products increased from $248.8 million in 1997 to $251.2 million in 1998, and sales were projected to reach $258.8 million in 1999. The growth of the sport was attributed to increased media coverage, upscale billiard parlors, and families adding recreation rooms to their homes.

INDUSTRY LEADERS

AMF Bowling is the largest operator of bowling centers in the world. It supplies bowling goods and equipment, builds Michael Jordan Golf practice ranges, and makes Renaissance and PlayMaster billiard tables.

Brunswick Corporation is among the largest sporting goods companies. The company is a leading name in bowling, and the products of its Zebco division are well known to fishermen. The firm also makes billiard tables, fitness equipment, and camping equipment. In total, the company's so-called recreation segment accounted for about 26 percent of the firm's sales of $2.9 billion in 1995. The balance of the company's revenues mostly came from sales of boats and outboard motors.

The sporting goods brands of Amer Group PLC of Finland include Wilson golf, racquet, and team sports equipment; Atomic, Dynamic, and Koflach skiing equipment; and Oxygen and Shockz snowboards and in-line skates. In February 1997, Amer completed the sale of its MacGregor Golf division. Amer's Wilson Sporting Goods, based in Chicago, was founded in 1914 and is one of the oldest names in American sporting goods. In 1999, the company had more than 3,000 employees worldwide. Wilson has been selected as the Official Football of the NFL (since 1941); Official Football of College Football USA; Official Softball of the NCAA Softball Championships; Official Volleyball of the AVP; and Official Ball Glove of Major League Baseball.

Spalding, one of the most famous names in sporting equipment, makes a complete line of golf and team sports equipment. Founded in the 1870s by Boston Red Stockings pitcher Albert Goodwill Spalding, the company grew from a small sporting goods store to a global manufacturer of sporting goods. The company claims a long list of firsts, including first Major League baseball (1876); first American-made football (1887); first official basketball (1894); and first American-made golf club (1894), among many others. In 1996 Kohlberg Kravis Roberts & Co. acquired Spalding for an estimated $1 billion. Brands include Top-Flite and Ben Hogan golf balls and equipment, Etonic golf shoes, Spalding basketballs, and Dudley softball bats and gloves.

Rawlings Sporting Goods Company manufactures baseball, softball, football, basketball, hockey, and volleyball equipment, gear, and apparel. More than 50 percent of its sales are in baseball and softball equipment. Rawlings equipment is used in all Major League Baseball games.

Riddell Sports Inc. makes football protective equipment, including the brand of football helmet worn by most NFL players and high school and college players. The company also produces baseball and soccer gear.

AMERICA AND THE WORLD

In 1997, U.S. imports and exports of sporting goods grew about 2 percent. In 1998, imports were projected to increase 11 percent, due to the Asian financial crisis, and exports only 1 percent. The estimated value of imports in 1998 was $3.9 million and the value of exports was $2.4 million. The top export markets were Japan, Canada, Mexico, the United Kingdom, and China. The top import markets were China, Taiwan, Canada, Mexico, and South Korea. In 1997, much interest centered on China, where entire industries can spring up almost overnight. For example, bowling has surged in popularity, and 90 percent of U.S. sports equipment exported to China was bowling equipment.

The broad penetration of U.S. culture overseas has been a boon to the sporting goods industry. Often there is a dynamic interplay between the popularity of the American lifestyle, the star-quality of American athletes, and the marketing savvy of American industry. For example, the growing popularity of basketball among kids in Europe has been linked to the NBA's Shaquille O'Neal, whom they know solely through watching Pepsi commercials. U.S. sporting goods products are thus valued in some countries simply because they are made in the United States. Consumers believe that they are participating in the American lifestyle by purchasing them. The perception that U.S. sporting goods are of unusually high quality in certain product categories has also spurred sales.

U.S. manufacturers were also eyeing South American markets. The restoration of democracy to many Latin American governments was accompanied by better economic conditions, giving consumers more spending power. Moreover, the trend toward freer trade has been marked, as Argentina and Brazil have sharply reduced trade barriers to overseas goods. While Latin Americans have always been passionate about soccer, they have started to take up typically American sports like basketball and in-line skating, where U.S. companies hold an edge.

The manufacture of many sporting goods is labor-intensive, so U.S. companies have shifted much production to east Asia, where wage rates are generally lower. High-tech computer systems enable companies to institute global manufacturing programs that maximize efficiency. The move toward more open markets and reduced tariffs also accelerates the trend toward globalization. Thus companies can produce wherever efficiencies are greatest. *U.S.*

Industry & Trade Outlook '99 reported that in 1997, 33 percent of all sporting goods emanated from China.

RESEARCH AND TECHNOLOGY

New technology plays a vital role in the sports market. Consumers are often driven to buy new equipment because of the real or perceived advantages of product introductions. On the other hand, tradition also has a hallowed place in sports, and participants need to feel comfortable that their equipment is in the historical spirit of the game. Additionally, innovative manufacturers can create substantially new sports through their products.

In some sports there have been revolutionary changes in equipment throughout the past 20 or 30 years. The traditional wooden tennis racket had basically stayed the same until the 1960s, when manufacturers began to redesign it in an effort to improve performance and ease of play. The introduction of durable metal and fiber-reinforced-composite rackets was followed by oversized and wide body models. More recently, finely balanced rackets that have shock- and vibration-damping handles and new string bed patterns for greater accuracy have been introduced. Compared with the classic wooden model that weighed 14 ounces and had a hitting area of 68 square inches, rackets sold in the early 1990s were 35 to 40 percent lighter, with the weight redistributed for better performance, and had a hitting area of 120 square inches.

In 1997, softball bats also received an upgrade. A division of Spalding was set to introduce the Fusion bat; a composite of aluminum and graphite, it was supposed to provide a lighter, faster swing. The SZ1-C from Easton Sports, on the other hand, is made from a rare material used in Soviet MiG fighter jets. Meanwhile, Worth Inc. was expected to offer a new line of cryogenic bats, which are first heated, then chilled to temperatures as low as −310 degrees.

Intriguingly, engineers have also had stunning successes in overhauling the humble bowling ball. Several new urethane and reactive resin bowling ball shells and complex inner core configurations—designed to vary the ball's rotation as it goes down the lane—have substantially altered the ball's hook as it approaches the pocket. According to some observers, the sharp rise in the number of perfect games—17,654 during the 1992-93 season versus 14,889 during the prior year—is closely related to the improvements in ball designs.

Smart entrepreneurs have also developed innovative products for niche markets. Passengers on cruise ships used to drive thousands of regulation golf balls into the sea. But in 1990 the International Maritime Organization banned the practice as part of its effort to protect sea life. Responding to opportunity, Patrick Kane of Bonita, California, developed a golf ball that flies almost as well as a traditional ball but is made of materials that decompose quickly and can be consumed safely by fish and other marine life. He told the *New York Times* that "It's basically fish food . . . you can market on the basis of sympathy for the environmentalists."

The sporting goods industry was also improving its technology in the more mundane, but nonetheless important, areas of inventory and delivery systems. Better information systems allowed manufacturers to keep retailers stocked in goods that were selling well and reduce their own inventories of slow-moving items. Manufacturers could also alert stores to overall sales patterns so that retailers could better react to market trends. Sporting goods companies have also worked to develop packaging that is more environmentally friendly.

FURTHER READING

"1999 State-of-the-Industry Report." Sporting Goods Manufacturers Association, 1999. Available from http://www.sportlink.com/research/1999_research/99soti/.

Broida, Rebecca. "In-Line Market Going Soft." *STN,* March 1997.

Dolbow, Sandra. "Holding Court (Tennis Equipment Industry)." *Sporting Goods Business,* February 1996.

Geer, Carolyn. "Gold Mine or Sand Trap: If Golf is Such a Great Business, How Come the Number of Players and Rounds Has Been Dropping?" *Forbes,* 12 August 1996.

"Growing Stars: Major League Soccer." *The Economist,* 13 April 1996.

Hyman, Mark. "The New Bats of Summer." *Business Week,* 21 April 1997.

Leivenberg, Richard. "Tennis, Anyone?" *Sporting Goods Business,* February 1995.

Murphy, Ian. "Bowling Industry Rolls Out Unified Marketing Plan." *Marketing News,* 20 January 1997.

"Super Show Exercises Options; Flood of Innovations Try to Appeal to the Time Pressed." *Discount Store News,* 3 March 1997.

U.S. Industry and Trade Outlook '99. McGraw-Hill and U.S. Department of Commerce, 1999.

SIC 3951

PENS, MECHANICAL PENCILS AND PARTS

This industry contains establishments primarily engaged in manufacturing pens (including ball point pens), refill cartridges, mechanical pencils, fine and broad tipped markers, and parts.

NAICS CODE(S)

339941 (Pen and Mechanical Pencil Manufacturing)

INDUSTRY SNAPSHOT

According to 1992 *Economic Census* data, annual sales of all pens, mechanical pencils, markers, and parts totaled $1.2 billion. In 1997, pens alone generated $1.7 billion in annual sales, according to the Writing Instrument Manufacturers Association.

Nearly 50 U.S. companies manufacture writing instruments that are sold in the United States and throughout the world. The ball point pen, introduced to the U.S. market in 1945, continues to dominate writing instrument sales. Combined sales of markers/highlighters, roller ball pens, and mechanical pencils represent about the same market share as ball point pens alone.

ORGANIZATION AND STRUCTURE

Manufacturers and suppliers of pens and other writing instruments traditionally have been large public companies, such as BIC Corp., and conglomerates, like the Gillette Co., which sell writing instruments and other non-writing related products.

Writing instruments are sold to wholesalers and retailers and then are resold to consumers through fine jewelry stores, stationery and office supply stores, department stores, discounters, mass merchandisers, catalog showrooms, and specialty stores. Pen manufacturers not only produce writing instruments but also are responsible for marketing and selling these products to retailers and consumers.

BACKGROUND AND DEVELOPMENT

The Pen. The earliest writing instruments were developed during the ancient civilizations of China, Greece, Egypt, and Mesopotamia nearly 5,000 years ago. Mesopotamians used wooden styluses to impress their characters on wet clay tablets. The Egyptians used hollow reeds to apply ink on sheets of papyrus, while the Chinese drew ideograms with brushes made from animal hair.

The Europeans began to use goose quills as ink pens in the sixth century, and this practice grew rapidly during the Middle Ages. Flocks of geese were specifically bred for their feathers as quill production became an important industry throughout Europe. For nearly 1,000 years the quill pen remained the most popular writing instrument.

In the nineteenth century, however, the steel pen replaced the quill. The steel pen point, or nib, first appeared in England sometime between 1790 and 1803, but this product was not manufactured efficiently or economically until the 1830s. In another 50 years American inventor Lewis Edmon Waterman created the fountain pen, which features its own self-contained ink supply.

Waterman's product ushered in a new generation of writing instruments that dominated the first half of the twentieth century. His basic design, which includes a metal nib, a built-in ink supply, and an outer shell, are still the main components of fountain pens today.

Fountain pens experienced a resurgence in popularity at the end of the twentieth century. According to retailers, most fountain pens were purchased by individuals or corporations for use as business gifts or promotional items. Two reasons for the fountain pen's popularity were its association as a status symbol and its improved technology, most notably replacement ink cartridges.

Ball Point Pens. The ball point pen also dates back to the late nineteenth century. This type of pen consists of a metal ball that is housed in a socket and rotates freely. The ball, constantly covered in ink from a reservoir, rolls across a writing surface.

Commercial models of ball point pens appeared in 1895 and the first satisfactory model was patented in Argentina by the Hungarian Lazlo Biro. His ball point pen, commonly called the "biro," soon became popular in Great Britain during the late 1930s and 1940s. The ball point pen was introduced to the U.S. market in 1945. U.S. manufacturers quickly adopted the new design and soon dominated worldwide production in the ball point pen industry. By the late 1990s more than 3 billion ball point pens were manufactured each year in a variety of styles, point sizes, and colors, with prices ranging from no-frills disposables selling for $1.00 a dozen to state-of-the-art, solid gold retractables costing hundreds of dollars.

Felt-Tip Pens. In 1964 the porous-point or "felt-tip" pen was developed in Japan. Papermate's Flair model was among the first felt-tip pens to hit the U.S. market in the 1960s, and it has been the leader ever since. Following their initial success with felt-tips, manufacturers branched out with a variety of fiber-tipped instruments, including highlighters.

Roller Ball Pens. The most recent large-scale innovation in the writing instrument industry is the roller ball pen, which was introduced in the early 1980s. Unlike the thick ink used in a conventional ball point, roller ball pens employ a mobile ball and liquid ink to produce a smoother line. Technological advances achieved during the late 1980s and early 1990s have greatly improved the roller ball's overall performance.

CURRENT CONDITIONS

The industry's 112 establishments shipped $1.59 billion worth of goods in 1997, a 21 percent increase from the $1.31 billion shipped in 1995. The country's leading production states are Tennessee with shipments worth

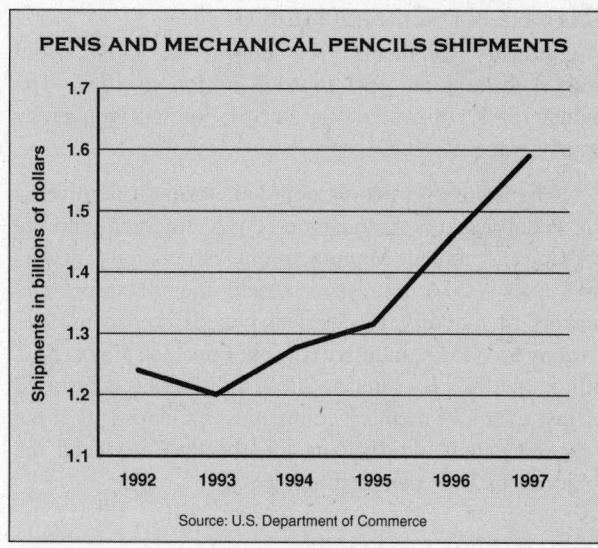

PENS AND MECHANICAL PENCILS SHIPMENTS

Source: U.S. Department of Commerce

$312 million, Rhode Island with $146 million, and Wisconsin with $120 million.

INDUSTRY LEADERS

BIC Corp. Connecticut-based BIC Corp. is one of the largest manufacturers and distributors of ball point pens in North America. BIC ball point pens are available in non-retractable, non-refillable models and retractable, refillable models, as well as in various ink and barrel colors and point sizes. BIC also manufactures highlighting markers and roller pens and distributes mechanical pencils.

Gillette Co. More commonly associated with men's shaving products, Boston-based Gillette has become a leader in the writing instruments industry. With the low-price Papermate, mid-price Parker, and high-end Waterman franchises, Gillette has established a strong position in the industry at all price levels, distribution channels, and geographic areas.

Gillette built its leadership position in the writing instruments market through the acquisition of Waterman in 1987 and Parker Pen Holdings Ltd. in 1993. After its purchase, Gillette soon began to sell Waterman fountain pens at discount outlets in the United States. Francine Gomez, then chief executive of Waterman S.A. and a third-generation family operator, was displeased with this decision. Although sales increased 40 percent since the Gillette takeover, Gomez argued that the company's marketing strategy in the United States devalued the luxury image of Waterman in France. Gomez resigned from the company in 1988.

A. T. Cross Co. Based in Lincoln, Rhode Island, A. T. Cross Co. has been a major international manufacturer of fine writing instruments sold to the consumer gift market through stores worldwide and to the business market via a

network of companies specializing in recognition and awards programs. Cross products include ball point pens, mechanical pencils, rolling ball/porous-point pens, and fountain pens.

Other major U.S. companies in this industry are Illinois-based Sanford Corp., Philadelphia's Hunt Corp., and Tennessee-based Berol Corp.

WORKFORCE

The industry employed a total of 8,394 people in 1997, 29 percent of whom worked in Tennessee and Rhode Island. The 6,000 production workers who manufactured pens and mechanical pencils earned an average hourly wage of $13.17.

FURTHER READING

Darnay, Arsen J., ed. *Manufacturing USA*, 6th edition. Detroit: Gale Group, 1998.

———. *Market Share Reporter*. Detroit: Gale Group, 1999.

Hessen, Wendy. "The Signature of a Fine Pen." *WWD*, 8 May 1995.

Tooher, Nora Lockwood. "A. T. Cross Expects to Report 50 Percent Earnings Drop for 1996." *Knight-Ridder/Tribune Business News*, 11 December 1996.

U.S. Census Bureau. *1997 Economic Census—Manufacturing*. Washington, D.C.: GPO, 1997.

SIC 3952

LEAD PENCILS, CRAYONS AND ARTISTS' MATERIALS

This category includes establishments primarily engaged in manufacturing lead pencils, pencil leads, and crayons, and materials and equipment for artwork, such as airbrushes, drawing tables and boards, palettes, sketch boxes, pantographs, artists colors and waxes, pyrography goods, drawing inks, and drafting materials. Establishments primarily engaged in manufacturing mechanical pencils are classified in **SIC 3951: Pens, Mechanical Pencils, and Parts,** and those manufacturing drafting instruments are classified in **SIC 3829: Measuring and Controlling Devices, Not Elsewhere Classified.**

NAICS CODE(S)

337127 (Institutional Furniture Manufacturing)
325998 (All Other Miscellaneous Chemical Product Manufacturing)
339942 (Lead Pencil and Art Good Manufacturing)

INDUSTRY SNAPSHOT

According to the U.S. Census Bureau, there were 172 establishments primarily producing pencils and art supplies in the latter part of the 1990s. A work force of 6,189 generated the industry's $1.2 billion in shipments in 1997. General-use pencils, in particular, serve a mature and possibly declining market as computers and other electronic devices continue to serve such traditional school and office functions as test taking and mathematical calculation.

The majority of the industry's sales, about 57 percent in 1997, came from blackboards. Lead pencils and art goods made up an additional 19 percent, artists equipment made up 14 percent, and the remaining 10 percent of sales came from miscellaneous related goods.

BACKGROUND AND DEVELOPMENT

The Smithsonian Institution estimated that America's 100 billionth pencil was produced in 1976, and by the early 1990s, U.S. companies produced the seven-inch-long, two-for-a-quarter writing utensils at the rate of 2.5 billion per year.

The image of pencils was tarnished in 1971, when a child who chewed pencils was found to have lead poisoning, and the media blamed the pencil "lead." Even though pencils were made with graphite, not lead, the story pushed the industry to start a product certification program open to any pencil manufacturer.

In 1988, Congress passed the Labeling of Hazardous Art Materials Act, which required that all art materials be reviewed to determine the potential for causing a chronic hazard and that appropriate warning labels be placed on those materials. The artists materials law was finalized in 1992 with the U.S. Consumer Product Safety Commission's issuance of definitions of chronic toxicity and the codification of ASTM D-4238 as a mandatory regulation.

When the lead in crayons became an issue in the industry in 1994, the problem was easily solved. Hazardous amounts of lead were found in the yellow and orange color crayons imported from China by Concord Enterprises. In 1994, when the U.S. Consumer Product Safety Commission and Concord Enterprises announced the recall of the crayons, parents were instructed to buy only crayons and childrens art materials labeled with "Conforms to ASTM D-4236," indicating that the materials had been approved by a toxicologist and labeled appropriately.

A recall of a different sort occurred in August 1991, when two importers, the Brandy Trading Corp. and Mirage Imports, announced they would no longer sell novelty pencils that resembled hypodermic syringes. The Taiwan-made "Gold Doctor" pencils were sending the wrong message to schoolchildren, parents and teachers complained.

CURRENT CONDITIONS

Industry shipments grew during the 1990s, from $648.3 million in 1992 to $1.2 billion in 1997. The industry's 4,678 production workers earned an average hourly wage of $9.72.

The industry trade association, formerly known as the Pencil Makers Association (PMA), merged with the Writing Instruments Manufacturers Association (WIMA) in 1994. WIMA represents pencil manufacturers and makers of markers, mechanical pencils, and pens. According to WIMA, industry revenues reached almost $2.2 billion in 1997. By January 2000, WIMA was comprised of just over 140 member companies, including 30 in the pen and pencil industry; its membership produced the majority of U.S. pencil shipments.

INDUSTRY LEADERS

The largest U.S. concern in this industry is Newell Co., a diversified manufacturer of home and office products. In the early and mid-1990s, Newell acquired three top U.S. pencil and art goods companies: Sanford Corporation, Faber-Castell Corporation, and Empire-Berol Corporation. All three were integrated into Newell's Sanford division, which also includes the art materials brand M. Grumbacher. In 1996 Newell's combined office products sales, which include products outside of this industry, reached $742.0 million. In 1998, the company purchased the Rotring Group, a manufacturer and supplier of writing instruments, drawing instruments, art materials, and color cosmetic products in Germany. The writing and drawing instruments division of Rotring operates as part of the company's Sanford International division. The art materials division of Rotring operates as part of the company's Sanford North America division. Newell Co. completed a merger with Rubbermaid Incorporated in 1999, and Rubbermaid became a wholly owned subsidiary of Newell. With the merger, Newell changed its name to Newell Rubbermaid Inc. Net sales for Newell and all its subsidiaries for the nine months ending September 30, 1999, totaled $4.7 billion.

Another leading firm in the late 1990s was Binney & Smith of Easton, Pennsylvania, the maker of Crayola crayons and a subsidiary of Hallmark Cards, with estimated sales of $300.0 million.

AMERICA AND THE WORLD

The United States imported $156.0 million in pencils, crayons, and artists supplies in 1995 and $1.1 billion in 1997, compared to exports of only $62 million and $887.0 million respectively. Major trading partners include Thailand and China, which are both sources of low-priced imports in this category. Imports of pencils from these two nations have grown substantially since the 1980s. The U.S. industry has not competed well against the imports, which has led to the shutdown of several domestic manufacturers.

RESEARCH AND TECHNOLOGY

Responding to rising environmental consciousness on the part of the pencil consumer, Faber-Castell Corporation introduced a pencil made of recycled materials in 1992. Instead of the traditional wood casing, Faber-Castell said its American EcoWriter would offer a pencil shaft made from reprocessed newspapers and cardboard boxes. The project involved developing a material that could be sharpened as easily as a wood pencil. Faber developed the material with Lydall Inc., the company that reprocesses the paper into slats used by Faber in manufacturing. The EcoWriter was Faber-Castell's second environmental contribution, following the American Natural, which was introduced to highlight Faber's use of ''sustained yield'' cedar supplies (which meant that no more wood would be harvested for Faber products than could be replaced by new planting).

FURTHER READING

''Amid Furor, Importers Drop Syringe Pencil.'' *New York Times,* 11 August, 1991.

FreeEdgarOnline. Newell Company Filings, 1999. Available from www.freeedgar.com.

Newell Co. *Annual Report.* Freeport, IL: Newell Co., 1997.

U.S. Census Bureau. *1995 Annual Survey of Manufactures.* Washington, DC: GPO, 1997.

———. *Lead Pencil and Art Goods Manufacturing.* Washington, DC: GPO, 1999.

WIMA. ''Industry Statistical Info.'' WIMA—Writing Instrument Manufacturers Association, 2000. Available from www.wima.org.

SIC 3953

MARKING DEVICES

This category covers establishments primarily engaged in manufacturing stencils for use in painting or marking; or the production of steel letters and figures, rubber and metal hand-stamps, dies, and seals. Establishments primarily engaged in manufacturing felt tip markers are covered in **SIC 3951: Pens, Mechanical Pencils, and Parts.**

NAICS CODE(S)

339943 (Marking Device Manufacturing)

As of 1996, leaders in this category were: Weber Marking Systems Inc. of Arlington Heights, Illinois; Diagraph Corp. of Earth City, Missouri; Cosco Industries Inc.; GM Nameplate Inc. of Seattle, Washington; Pannier Corp. of Pittsburgh, Pennsylvania; and Marsh Co. of Belleville, Illinois.

According to the U.S. Census Bureau's *1997 Economic Census*, there were 634 companies employing 7,831 people in the marking device industry with a total annual payroll of $185.3 million. All but 75 of these companies employed less than 20 people and were situated in 12 states.

The design for several of the devices in this category date from antiquity and have changed very little over the centuries, even though technological innovations have made a key difference in some cases. The introduction of the mass-production automobile assembly line, for instance, led to notable advances in die-casting technology and to the very precise formation of even the tiniest metal parts.

The introduction of stenciling has been dated to eighth century China, and this technique of reproducing designs has long been deemed well-suited for metal or cardboard cuts to produce simple shapes. Only with the introduction of silk-screen printing, however, was it possible to overcome the inherent limitations of stencils' great simplicity. The stencil, for instance, does not permit the reproduction of one design enclosing another (as in the case of a figure eight), unless it is halved to prevent the necessarily unattached central sections from dropping out. The fine meshes used in silk screen printing were substantial enough to support the unattached elements of a stencil, without posing a barrier to the passage of the dye or paint being forced through a water-soluble glue into the desired design. A variant to this blockout-stencil or glue-cut-out-stencil method was the film-stencil method, whereby designs were cut into a colored lacquer laminated to a sheet of glassine paper, so that the whole assemblage could be mounted on a screen before the removal of the uncut paper backing and subsequent printing.

The technological advances made by computers transformed many features of office life in the United States at the end of the twentieth century, including the use of certain numbering and lettering devices. Even though the modern office had no use for certain types of marking devices, such age-old implements as hand presses, stamps, and seals, however, were still widely used as a means of officially marking paperwork of various sorts. Indeed, the increasing automation of offices gave a new lease on life to such marking devices. Highly sophisticated photocopying machines, for instance, reproduced documents with such great accuracy that forgeries were easily made in the absence of a physical impression left by the impact of a notary public's or government official's seal, for example.

FURTHER READING

Rothman, Raymond C. *Notary Public Practices & Glossary.* Woodland Hills, CA: National Notary Association, 1978.

Seals and Other Devices in Use at the Government Printing Office. Washington, D.C.: U.S. Government Printing Office, n.d.

U.S. Census Bureau. *1997 Economic Census, Manufacturing—Industry Series.* Washington, D.C.: U.S. GPO, 1998.

SIC 3955

CARBON PAPER AND INKED RIBBONS

This industry contains establishments primarily engaged in manufacturing carbon paper, spirit or gelatin process and other stencil paper, and inked or carbon ribbons for business machines.

NAICS CODE(S)

339944 (Carbon Paper and Inked Ribbon Manufacturing)

The value of industry shipments of carbon paper and inked ribbons was $820 million in 1997; this represented a slight increase over 1992's total. Shipments of carbon paper, however, decreased from $148 million to $84 million during the same time period. There were approximately 119 establishments in the industry in 1997; 49 of these establishments had 20 or more employees. Only a year earlier, however, there were 137 companies employing 20 or more people. Annual capital expenditures were $17 million in 1997, down from a peak of $23 million invested in 1982. The cost of purchased fuels and electric energy for the industry in 1995 was $9.3 million.

According to the U.S. Census Bureau, the carbon paper and inked ribbons industry employed a total of 5,923 employees in 1997; of these, 4,332 were involved in production. They worked 8.3 million annual hours, and their total wages were $91.3 million, accounting for an average hourly wage of $11.00.

Private independents accounted for 77 percent of the top 30 firms in the industry. The capital requirements for the industry were relatively low: the average investment per establishment was only 59 percent of that for the manufacturing sector as a whole.

In the late 1990s, the top firms in the carbon paper and inked ribbons industry were Nu-Kote Holding Inc. of Dallas, Texas; Nashua Corporation of Nashua, New Hampshire; and Daisytek International Corporation of Plano, Texas. In 1998, Nu-Kote Holding reported $295 million in sales and approximately 2,300 employees, while the Nashua Corporation had $167 million in sales and about 725 employees.

The states with the highest number of establishments in the industry in 1997 were California with 14; New York with 10; New Jersey, Pennsylvania, and Ohio with 10; Texas with 7; and Georgia with 6. Together these seven states accounted for more than 47 percent of total employment in the industry.

The top industries and sectors buying the products of the carbon paper and inked ribbons industry included businesses buying manifold business forms, state and local government purchases for education and hospitals, exports, banking, and the retail trade.

FURTHER READING

U.S. Department of Commerce. *U.S. Industrial Outlook 1994.* Washington: GPO, January 1994.

U.S. Census Bureau. *1997 Economic Census* Washington, D.C.: U.S. GPO, 1998.

SIC 3961

COSTUME JEWELRY AND COSTUME NOVELTIES, EXCEPT PRECIOUS METALS

This category encompasses businesses primarily engaged in manufacturing costume jewelry, costume novelties, and ornaments made of all materials, except precious metal, precious or semiprecious stones, and rolled gold paste and gold-filled materials. The products manufactured within this category include such items as necklaces, rings, artificial pearls, compacts, cuff links, and rosaries. Businesses primarily engaged in manufacturing jewelry of precious and semiprecious material are classified in **SIC 3911: Jewelry, Precious Metal;** those manufacturing leather compacts and vanity cases are classified in **SIC 3172: Personal Leather Goods, Except Women's Handbags and Purses;** and those manufacturing synthetic stones for gem stone and industrial use are classified in **SIC 3299: Nonmetallic Mineral Products, Not Elsewhere Classified.**

NAICS CODE(S)

339914 (Costume Jewelry and Novelty Manufacturing)

INDUSTRY SNAPSHOT

There were slightly more than 900 firms actively manufacturing costume jewelry in the United States in the late 1990s. Many of the older companies were still based in Rhode Island (which hosts more than 270 of the firms in this industry). According to the U.S. Department of Conmmerce's *1997 Economic Census*, total product shipments for 1997 were valued $1.2 billion. This was down from the combined value of all goods produced by these companies in 1996, which totaled $1.6 billion. Only about 8 percent of the industry's total production was exported to other countries, including Canada, Japan, and Korea, the top three importers of American-made costume jewelry. Some of the firms were only involved in the manufacture of pieces using purchased components. The items were then sold to costume jewelry retailers, especially department stores. Other firms, however, both fabricate and market their own product lines.

The government was beginning to play an increasingly significant role in the industry. Costume jewelry manufacturers found it necessary to upgrade facilities in order to comply with environmental legislation. While such measures meant increased costs, the industry remained healthy and was expected to benefit from free trade arrangements that recently were signed by the government.

ORGANIZATION AND STRUCTURE

American costume jewelry companies manufacture products in various ways, primarily using base metals like tin and lead to fashion such findings as clasps and pin-backs—the basic components of a finished piece. One manufacturing process used is stamping, a labor-intensive method that produces a finer, more polished piece of metal. The more typical method in the shaping of metal for costume jewelry, however, is casting, which involves pouring molten metal into a mold. This process lends itself more readily to mass production of the jewelry. Manufacturers also utilize relatively recent methods of centrifugal casting and injection molding of plastic. The findings produced from these processes are then used to fabricate finished pieces or are sold to individual costume jewelry houses. Another integral function is electroplating, the electrolytic process of coating base metals with a small amount of a precious metal to give the jewelry its gold or silver appearance.

Most large costume jewelry companies sell their wares through department stores, an innovative marketing strategy that evolved during the 1950s. Earrings are one of the biggest sellers, followed in volume by necklaces and pins. One-third of all costume jewelry purchased in the United States is purchased as a gift—Christmas, Mother's Day, and Valentine's Day are the peak selling seasons. Two-thirds are purchased for individual use. Costume jewelry also is a popular product on home-shopping networks found on cable channels both in the United States and, increasingly, abroad.

BACKGROUND AND DEVELOPMENT

The industry is centered in the city of Providence, Rhode Island, which originally attracted fine jewelry arti-

sans in the eighteenth century. A craftsperson by the name of Nehemiah Dodge introduced gold-plating technology to the area in the late 1700s. The costume jewelry industry benefited from the nineteenth century's great advances in industrial technology, including the development of new machinery that allowed inexpensive jewelry to be mass-produced; by 1900, these items had found a significant domestic market. Portuguese immigrants skilled in the necessary handiwork accounted for a large part of the labor pool and proved influential in the rise of Rhode Island as a base for costume jewelry manufacturers.

The term "costume jewelry" was first used in a 1933 article in the *New Yorker*. The development of the modern industry was directly influenced by such European fashion designers as Elsa Schiaparelli and Coco Chanel. These designers commissioned original pieces that clearly were not real, and the sole purpose of which was to complement the sartorial ensemble. Many of the early examples of costume jewelry were larger-than-life imitations of fine jewelry, but the burgeoning industry soon spawned innovative artisans who experimented with a variety of shapes, materials, and color palettes. Designers of costume jewelry then, as now, were often allowed by the disposable nature of the product to experiment wildly and inject a good dose of imagination into their work, an attitude not often encouraged within the realm of more traditional fine jewelry.

In the early decades of the twentieth century, costume jewelry manufacturers primarily used cut-glass stones, imitation pearls, and enamel. Costume jewelry became overwhelmingly popular during the social upheavals of the 1920s, and the materials of choice for fashionable flappers were the glass materials of jet and crystal. The Great Depression that choked the American economy during the 1930s brought many new customers to the costume jewelry market, as those who lost fortunes could no longer afford fine jewelry. White metal became the most common material in inexpensive metal jewelry, but World War II restrictions on the use of metals was manifested in the proliferation of gold- and silver-plated pieces. In addition, the war caused American manufacturers to be cut off from their Czechoslovakian and Japanese suppliers of cut glass and pearls.

The popularity of ornate gilt pieces and the continued use of crystal, jet, and inexpensive stones grew during the 1950s. An important court decision at that time was instrumental in solidifying the respectability of the creators and manufacturers of costume jewelry. When First Lady Mamie Eisenhower wore Trifari pieces to both presidential inaugural balls in 1952 and 1956, the much-publicized act spawned legions of copycat pieces. Trifari successfully filed suit to protect the copyright of their designs.

Innovative uses of materials and forms were the hallmark of costume jewelry styles in the 1960s. After the profitable synthetics industry burgeoned in the aftermath of World War II, molded plastics such as Perspex became commonplace as a material for inexpensive jewelry that could be easily transformed into daring shapes and colors complementing the outrageous fashions of the decade. In 1971 the U.S. gold market was deregulated, which set off waves of sizable price increases over the next decade that raised the cost of fine jewelry. This had a beneficial effect upon costume jewelry manufacturers, as more consumers turned to higher-end costume pieces from upscale designers, including Kenneth Jay Lane and Robert Lee Morris, rather than purchasing the genuine article from fine jewelers. Sterling silver also became a popular material during the late 1960s and early 1970s.

Even the British punk movement of the late 1970s exerted its influence on costume jewelry trends of the 1980s, as the "creative salvage" look, utilizing leather and rubber, became popular. The legions of women that began entering the work force in the 1970s also were influential in the development of costume jewelry styles. The working woman's choice of clothing often was restricted to conservative styles that fit into a business environment, and thus costume jewelry became a way of personalizing a wardrobe. In the 1990s, an interest in multiculturalism was evident in the use of motifs and materials inspired by indigenous cultures and natural elements, a prime example of which was the popularity of faux-ivory materials. By the mid-1990s, one of the most popular new looks in costume jewelry was the cubic zirconia, a simulated diamond. It can be made transparent to resemble a diamond, or colored to simulate precious stones, and is used primarily in rings, earrings, bracelets, and necklaces.

CURRENT CONDITIONS

Costume jewelry sales in the early 1990s were noteworthy, as consumers hit hard by the recession of the late 1980s became less likely to purchase fine jewelry. Indeed, some of the largest U.S. fine jewelry firms suffered severe financial setbacks in the early 1990s, a fate that did not befall costume jewelry companies at that time. A newly popular niche in the market was the "fakes" category that marketed relatively inexpensive pieces that look amazingly similar to the genuine article. Industry analysts noted that the economic downturn of the mid- to late 1990s, while affecting overall consumer spending, had relatively little effect on the overall health of the industry.

Legislation regarding environmental issues had an adverse effect on the industry, however. Clean air and water laws enacted in the 1990s presented challenges to manufacturers, particularly those firms involved in electroplating, causing the cost of the process to increase significantly. Generally, such establishments were required to have wastewater treatment facilities that removed harmful chemicals and metals from discharge water, and some manufacturers also were required to install air scrubbers to clean exhaust.

Although the projected forecast for the future of the industry was positive, this prediction proved to be false. The industry took a downturn after 1993, and costume jewelry sales continued to languish into 1995. One sign of recovery was seen when the Jewelry Manufacturers Association reported increased attendance at their 1995 exhibition by overseas companies, including buyers from South America, Japan, Ireland, the Czech Republic, and Romania.

Beginning in 1995, the costume jewelry industry began to pick up again. According to Amanda Meadus and Wendy Hessen of *WWD*, "designer-manufacturers" were in the best position for a comeback. The largest of those companies were Carolee Designs and Erwin Pearl.

In 1997, this industry's 826 establishments shipped $1.2 billion, a sharp decrease from the more than $1.6 billion shipped in each of the three previous years.

INDUSTRY LEADERS

The top company involved in the costume jewelry industry in 1995 in the United States was Illinois-based Artra Group, a publicly held conglomerate founded in 1933. Artra held many subsidiaries, including the number-two firm, Lori Corp. Lori Corp.'s 1995 sales totaled approximately $160 million. Third in line was the Napa Co., with origins dating back to 1875, making it the oldest costume jewelry manufacturer in the United States. Its 1995 sales totaled approximately $70 million. The New York City-based firm of Trifari Krussman and Fischel Inc. was fourth in production and sales, with origins that date back to the early 1920s and sales totaling around $63 million. Industry leaders in the Rhode Island area included Victoria Creations Inc. ($43 million), Swarovski Jewelry U.S. Ltd. ($50 million), and Monet Jewelers ($7 million).

WORKFORCE

Employment figures for the costume jewelry industry rose from a five-year low of 166,000 by the close of 1992 to 180,000 by 1995. The boon in costume jewelry, however, soon waned and, by 1996, the industry employed 166,000 workers. Employment was expected to remain flat into the new millennium. Hourly wages for production workers in the field also remained relatively flat. On a more positive note, the increase in public awareness of such repetitive-injury afflictions as carpal-tunnel syndrome resulted in improved working conditions for costume jewelry industry employees.

In 1997, this industry employed 13,975 people, 72 percent of whom worked in production. They earned an average hourly wage $9.10.

FURTHER READING

Hessen, Wendy. "Providence: Where's the New Stuff?" *WWD,* 19 June 1995.

Meadus, Amanda and Wendy Hessen. "Designer-makers in Driver's Seat." *WWD,* 21 February 1995. Available from http://sbweb2.med.iacnet.com.

"Statistics—SIC Code 3961." *Gale Business Resources (Integrated).* Detroit: Gale Group, 1999.

U.S. Census Bureau. Industry Quick Reports; 31-33 : Manufacturing; 339 : Miscellaneous Mfg; 3399: Other Miscellaneous Mfg; 33991: Jewelry & Silverware Mfg; 339914: Costume Jewelry & Novelty Mfg; View Report/Create.

U.S. Census Bureau, American Fact Finder, 1999. Available from http://factfinder.census.gov/java_prod/dads.ui.homePage.HomePage.

U.S. Department of Commerce. "Costume Jewelry And Novelty Manufacturing." *U.S. Census Bureau, 1997 Economic Census.* Washington DC: GPO, 1999.

U.S. Census Bureau. *1997 Economic Census Report—Manufacturing.* GPO: Washington 1999.

SIC 3965

FASTENERS, BUTTONS, NEEDLES, AND PINS

This industry includes companies that make notions, such as slide and snap fasteners and zippers, machine and hand needles, pins, hooks and eyes, buckles, buttons, button parts, and button blanks. Companies that make these items from precious metals or from precious or semiprecious stones are classified in **SIC 3911: Jewelry, Precious Metals.**

NAICS CODE(S)

339993 (Fastener, Button, Needle and Pin Manufacturing)

Needles, pins, and fasteners—made from metals and both natural and manmade fibers—comprised the largest share of industry output. Zippers, slide fasteners, buttons, and button parts—made from both plastics and metals—were less dominant but notable types of industry products. Nearly 90 percent of industry output re-entered as components for other manufacturing industries. Of these, apparel, shoes, knitting mills, and household furniture makers were most prominent. Items sold directly to consumers made up the remainder.

In 1990 this industry had 237 companies; by 1997, this number rose to 573. Most of the companies in this category were small: 162 establishments employed less than five people, while 118 had between five and nine

employees. The remainder of the companies were fairly evenly distributed, with 71 reporting between 10 and 14 employees, 30 reporting between 15 and 19, and 90 reporting between 20 and 49. Fifty-eight companies employed between 50 and 99, while 57 had 100 or more employees.

In general, the mid- to large companies had the largest range of sales, with 148 reporting sales of $1 million to $4.9 million, 83 garnering sales of $500,000 to $999,000, and 80 reporting sales over $5 million. The smallest grouping were those with sales below $49,000: only 11 companies reported sales within that range.

In 1995, the total value of goods shipped was $856.9 million. During the 1990s, manufacturers of fasteners, buttons, needles, and pins were primarily located in the eastern United States. New York, with 82 establishments, and Connecticut, with 25, led the nation in the number of establishments per state. The industry leader in 1997 continues to be Coats Crafts North America of Greenville, South Carolina, with $200 million in annual sales and 2,000 employees. Second place in the industry was occupied by YYY (USA), Inc., of Lyndhurst, NJ, with over 1,000 employees. Another industry leader in this category was Scovill Fasteners, Inc. of Clarkesville, Georgia, with $65 million in annual sales and 600 employees.

FURTHER READING

Darnay, Arsen J., ed. *Manufacturing USA.* 5th ed. Detroit: Gale Research, 1996.

Textile Highlights. Washington: American Textile Manufacturers Institute, March 1997.

U.S. Department of Commerce. *1995 Annual Survey of Manufactures.* Washington, D.C.: GPO, 1997.

Dun's Census of American Business 1997. Parsippany, NJ: Dun & Bradstreet, 1997.

SIC 3991

BROOMS AND BRUSHES

This category covers establishments primarily engaged in manufacturing household, industrial, and street sweeping brooms; and brushes, such as paintbrushes, toothbrushes, toilet brushes, and household and industrial brushes.

NAICS CODE(S)

339994 (Broom, Brush and Mop Manufacturing)

U.S. manufacturers generated approximately $2.0 billion in broom and brush shipments in 1997, up from $1.3 billion in 1995. The industry employed some 17,000 people in 1997, three-quarters of whom were engaged in production labor.

Manufacturers range from small, family-owned businesses to large corporations for whom broom or brush manufacture is one of many interests. The 1980s and early 1990s were characterized by a series of acquisitions of smaller firms by larger corporations. Empire Brush Company of Greenville, North Carolina, acquired six companies in that period and reported a 100 percent increase in sales. Two of the largest makers of "stick goods," O-Cedar and Vining Industries, merged in 1993. This proved to be a profitable merger as the Ohio-based company boosted its home state as the leading brush and broom producer in the United States by 1997.

The vast majority of companies are privately owned. The industry is most heavily concentrated in the Midwest, with Ohio, Illinois, and Wisconsin responsible for more than 30 percent of shipments.

Until the mid-twentieth century, brushes were made of natural materials such as hog bristles, horsehairs, and Tampico fibers. Brooms were made of birch and willow twigs until replaced in the early 1800s by broomcorn straw (actually a type of sorghum). In 1906, the entire brush industry generated $19 million in sales. The innovative sales techniques of the Fuller Brush Company helped revitalize the industry, so when founder Alfred Fuller turned operations over to his son Howard in 1946, Fuller Brush alone earned $41 million. Fuller Brush, a division of the Sara Lee Corporation, saw its importance as an industry leader diminish from 1968 through 1989.

The replacement of original materials with longer-lasting synthetic fibers and metal alloys caused a major change in the industry. This, combined with advances in mass production techniques following World War II, decreased production costs and allowed for greater profit margins. Broom making was also affected by mass production. Plastic brooms became more common, although more than 50 percent of all brooms are still made of broomcorn.

Industry growth in the 1980s continued slightly but steadily. Profit margins in the early 1990s were above average compared to other manufacturing industries, due largely to increased sales caused by new designs. Oral-B Laboratories of Redwood City, California, led the nation in the development of new toothbrush designs.

Broom manufacturers in particular became concerned with the potential threat caused by the North American Free Trade Agreement (NAFTA). Before NAFTA, the American industry was protected by a 32 percent tariff on imports, due to phase out over an 11-year period. Mexico, already the largest supplier of brooms, was expected to benefit from the elimination of tariffs. The fears were unrealized, however, as the U.S.

brush and broom industry saw a 65 percent increase in sales between 1995 and 1997.

Leading industry publications include *Brushware,* published by 12/Twelve Media and *Broom, Brush and Mop,* published by Rankin Publishing. The American Broom Manufacturers Association (ABMA), based out of Philadelphia, Pennsylvania, is a membership trade organization representing broom, brush, and mop manufacturers. According to ABMA, most industry statistics, including the data collected by the association, are closely guarded.

FURTHER READING

Huyser-Honig, Joan. "A Bounteous Crop of Broom." *Americana,* October 1991.

Muirhead, Greg. "Brush Strokes: New Toothbrushes Designed to Promote Better Hygiene Are Creating Opportunities for Growth." *Supermarket News,* 16 November 1992.

"Sweeping Sales: Brushes Produce Better than Average Margins." *Industrial Distribution,* February 1993.

U.S. Census Bureau. U.S. Department of Commerce. *1997 Economic Census.* Washington, D.C.: GPO, 1999. Available from http://www.census.gov.

SIC 3993

SIGNS AND ADVERTISING SPECIALTIES

This category covers establishments primarily engaged in manufacturing electrical, mechanical, cutout, or plate signs and advertising displays, including neon signs and advertising specialties. Sign painting shops doing business on a custom basis are classified in **SIC 7389: Business Services, Not Elsewhere Classified.** Establishments primarily engaged in manufacturing electric signal equipment are classified in **SIC 3669: Communications Equipment, Not Elsewhere Classified,** and those manufacturing commercial lighting fixtures are classified in **SIC 3646: Commercial, Industrial, and Institutional Electric Lighting Fixtures.**

NAICS CODE(S)

339950 (Sign Manufacturing)

INDUSTRY SNAPSHOT

More than 5,743 establishments were engaged in the manufacture of signs and advertising displays in 1997, producing industry shipments of $7.9 billion. The largest portion of sales in this market was attributable to sign sales of $7.1 billion. The industry grew at a healthy pace throughout the 1980s, spurred largely by developments in computer technology. In 1990 and 1991, it followed the national economic downturn with consecutive 8 percent decreases in sales volume, but rebounded with a 4 percent increase in 1992 and continued to increase slowly throughout the 1990s.

In 1997, nonelectric signs accounted for 34 percent of all specified types of signs, while electric signs made up 28 percent. Of those, 28 percent of electric signs used fluorescent lamps, 20 percent used luminous tubing (such as neon, argon and hydrogen), and almost 50 percent used incandescent bulbs. The most common materials used in making signs (10 percent of the total materials consumed) were polymers and plastics (including vinyl), followed by fabricated metal/metal products and paper/paperboard products. Advertising specialties accounted for less than 15 percent of the total output.

Throughout its history, and especially in recent years, the industry had fought against perceptions of signs as visual pollutants, which must be controlled or even banned except when conveying "vital information." These perceptions often were countered with new stylistic designs and aggressive government lobbying.

ORGANIZATION AND STRUCTURE

A sign shop is an establishment that manufactures signs and advertising specialties. Sign shops are located throughout the country, with the greatest number of establishments located in California (about 580 in 1997). In general, though, the largest amount of shipments and the greatest number of employees are clustered in the Midwest and eastern seaboard states. In 1997, with fewer than half the number of firms in California, Illinois' 224 establishments accounted for almost the same dollar amount in shipments—$631 million (8 percent of the U.S. total). Shipments from California, Illinois, New York, Ohio, Texas, and Wisconsin made up 40 percent of the 1997 U.S. total, and 38 percent of the industry's employees worked in those states. A 1992 state-of-the-industry survey reported a significant increase in the percentage of shops doing business in the Midwest, as well as in the nation's central, southern and eastern regions. Furthermore, many sign shops expanded operations to serve a wider geographic base. This expansion was probably the result of a trend toward larger shops, whose greater output quantities and increased sales forces allow them to serve larger areas.

The largest buyer of signs and advertising specialties was the gross private fixed investment industry. The next largest were highway and street construction, eating and drinking places, and wholesale trade.

In 1998, the size of establishments ranged from single-person sign shops to such industry giants as Everbrite Inc. and Signmark, each with sales estimated at more than $110 million. An estimated 75 percent of sales volume in 1992 was generated by less than 10 percent of all sign

shops. This top-heaviness may continue due to the increased volume of signs and the prevalence of quantity orders over custom or finely crafted work. The development of computer technology decreases the need for specialized skills and gives rise to rapid-sign franchises, which facilitate same-day construction of signs. According to the 1997 Economic Census, moderately sized sign shops (those with between 20 and 100 employees) accounted for almost 42 percent of total shipments (approximately $3.3 billion).

The *1997 Economic Census* showed that the electric and non-electric sign industries continued to experience great expansion and had a combined, all-time high of $7.1 billion in sales in 1997, up from 4.9 billion in 1992. This represents an average increase of nearly 9 percent each year. In the entire industry (including advertising specialties), the average sales per employee totaled $95,526. This represented a 6 percent upswing in profitability compared to 1995, when average sales per employee totaled $90,046.

A 1996 *Signs of the Times* state-of-the-industry survey reported that about 64 percent of respondents outsourced less than 10 percent of sales in 1995, up from 62 percent in 1994. A total of 23 percent outsourced between 10 percent and 24 percent of their sales, and 13 percent outsourced more than 25 percent of sales. Generally, as indicated in the survey, companies that outsourced more than 10 percent of their business showed higher sales-per-employee figures.

BACKGROUND AND DEVELOPMENT

In the nineteenth century, signs and advertising displays were a common sight in both residential neighborhoods and commercial areas. Since electronic media was not yet developed, outdoor advertisements played a more crucial role in name recognition than they do today. Advertisements were often painted on empty brick walls, storefronts, or barns. The growth of cities reduced the amount and visibility of available space and necessitated free-hanging signs made of wood or metal. The advent of the automobile also increased the amount of road and traffic signs.

The public perception of advertising signs as eyesores was slow to develop. If it existed at all in the first half of the twentieth century, it was certainly not evidenced by the popularity of such cultural icons as the Burma Shave signs. With the ascendancy of television, the use of signs as part of nationwide advertising campaigns diminished.

Regulation and zoning have been recurring trends throughout the latter part of the century. Long considered the province of local governments, limitation of signs became a federal issue during the Johnson administration, with the passage of the 1965 Highway Beautification Act. And, in 1990, the introduction of the Visual Pollution Control Act by Republican Senator John H. Chafee of Rhode Island, which made it easier for governments to compensate owners, reflected a national desire to remove many highway signs. Under this legislation, funds earmarked for highway construction and maintenance were to be used for sign removal. Up to $428 million was allocated to the Federal Highway Administration to compensate sign owners who had erected signs before laws were passed that made them illegal. Federal regulation of sign display has been opposed by active lobbying, as well as by publications such as the *Wall Street Journal.* For the most part, control of sign proliferation has remained on the community level. The potential negative impact to the industry caused by the reduction of advertising signs has been offset by an increased demand for signs of other types.

Electric Signs and Luminous Tubing. At the end of the nineteenth century, luminous signs were a new phenomenon. The hazardous and expensive gaslit method of lighting quickly gave way to electricity. In 1898, Sir William Ramsay and Morris William Travers discovered neon. In 1910, French physicist Georges Claude experimented with sending an electric discharge through a neon-filled tube. The charge produced a bright red light whose color and luminosity could be modified by altering the current. The subsequent development of luminous tubing using inert gases provided a relatively safe method of lighting. Though too expensive for general purposes, its brightness made it ideal for advertising and other special uses. Increased production of hydroelectric power under the Roosevelt administration lowered the cost involved in electric sign manufacture and use and expanded the use of neon as an advertising tool; and as an art form. Two of the best-known neon-using locales, Las Vegas and the Times Square area of New York, were developed during this neon heyday of the 1930s and 1940s. Artkraft Strauss Co., the original manufacturer of virtually all of Broadway's electric signs, continues to be the major supplier for the area. The company also redevelops and renovates signs that are now considered historic landmarks (such as Times Square's famous Coca-Cola sign).

Neon reached the peak of its popularity in the 1950s. Regarded as an example of the opulent decadence of the previous generation, it gave way to inexpensive plastics as the advertising medium of choice during the 1960s. Electric signs in general, however, continued to thrive. Electric advertising displays with moving mechanical parts proved to be attention-getting, point-of-purchase devices. Computer software also allowed for the programming of changeable messages on road signs, advertisements, and architectural signs.

The industry also has been spurred by changes in signs on roadways and other public places. As travel becomes easier and tourism from non-English-speaking countries grows, a trend toward universal symbols to replace or augment public signs has increased demand. The National Park Service was at the forefront of a movement to make recreational signs easier to read.

CURRENT CONDITIONS

The most important development in the industry since the early 1980s was the introduction of computer technology into the manufacture of signs and displays. The ability to program sign design and manufacture through software greatly reduced turnaround time, often to less than a day. It also increased quantitative capabilities and reduced the amount of craftsmanship necessary in production.

At the same time, however, there was a resurgence of hand craftsmanship in sign making (perhaps in response to the stylistic standardization caused by computer technology). Major consumers such as Disney and MGM ordered signs made of ornately hand carved gold leaf. In addition, neon had regained much of its former popularity.

According to *Entrepreneur,* Sign Biz Inc., a computer-aided sign network, had attained a measure of distinction by providing its franchisees with good support without charging royalties. Store owners were given turnkey equipment and training material for $72,500.

Another important industry development was the response to the Americans With Disabilities Act (ADA). Its enactment in 1992 required that all public buildings display architectural signs (including exit signs, emergency instructions, and elevator signs) that are readable by disabled persons, including the blind and visually impaired. In practice, this entailed creating signs with raised characters at least three inches high that were accessible by touch. Since many architectural signs were originally engraved, replacing them with raised-letter signs necessitated complete retooling.

The expected increase in sales caused by the ADA had not occurred by the end of 1993. Consumers were slow to enact the required changes, and the federal government was slow to enforce them. In the absence of a test case, the government was unwilling to provide its own interpretation of the act, so businesses, building managers, and architectural firms were uncertain as to exactly what changes were required. By 2000 the industry still had no clear-cut direction from the federal government, as many cases were still being mediated.

The ratio of sales to payroll costs increased by 3 percent from 1992 to 1997. The average sales volume per sign shop in 1997 was $1.38 million, an increase since 1992 ($1.21 million) of 14 percent.

According to *Forbes,* Whiteco Industries (Merrillville, Indiana) was the largest private business in the billboard industry as of October 1996, occupying a 7 percent share. Averaging $850 per month for highway signs and $3,500 monthly in large markets, it had a yearly cash flow of about $60 million. In 1998, however, Whiteco's outdoor unit was purchased by the Chancellor Media Corp., which was in turn acquired by the Lamar Advertising Co. in 1999. Lamar's 1998 sales totaled $289 million, making it the largest player in the outdoor advertising business. The company also markets interstate logo signs and transit-related displays on buses and bus shelters.

In the mid-1990s, television broadcasters and cable networks began showing electronic sponsorship signs on the playing fields during the broadcasting of sports events. The effect that virtual signs would have on sports enthusiasts had not really been discerned by 1997.

One continuing trend was electric and/or architectural sign companies diversifying or merging their operations. A total of 91 percent of surveyed companies in *The State of the Industry Report* made at least some custom electric signs (as compared to 86 percent in the previous year) and about 82 percent (as compared to 76 percent in the previous year) maintained and repaired electric signs and/or lighting. In July 1996, Outdoor Systems of Phoenix contracted to purchase Gannett Outdoor for $690 million in order to merge their industry strengths.

The Internet greatly influenced the signs and advertising industry in the mid-1990s. In particular, the vinyl type of signshop demonstrated much enthusiasm for the Web. According to *Signs of the Times,* the most useful Web site for the industry in the mid-1990s was at http://www.sign.web.com. Originally planned as a ''mall'' for the sign industry, by 1997 it typically received as many as 10,000 hits on some days.

In the mid-1990s, fiber optics (FO) turned up as an option to neon and other lighting. In *Signs of the Times,* corporate sales director Fritz Mayne Jr. of Orlando, Florida-based SuperVision, enumerated some of FO's advantages over neon: FO does not require electrical permits, and as a material poses no fire threats; with FO, users can alter the cable's color at any time, with a diachronic color wheel; and FO requires very little maintenance, just lamp replacement and illuminator cleaning.

In January 2000, Sign Business Inc. reported that the largest LED video display in the world was near completion in Times Square. The display is the NASDAQ Stock Market's new headquarters and will consist of an LED screen 120 feet high by 90 feet wide. Stock price updates and video content will be shown on the screen.

Despite the changing conditions of the sign industry, vinyl was still of paramount importance to the business; in fact, in a 1996 survey, it was revealed that more than 75 percent of all signs manufactured by responding shops employed at least some vinyl in their products. Of the electric shops that took part in the survey, only 31 percent used vinyl at all. About 80 percent of respondents, however, said they used more vinyl on individual signs in 1996 than in 1994.

WORKFORCE

The industry as a whole experienced reductions in total number of employees, payroll, and production workers in the early 1990s. On the other hand, sales per employee reached an all-time high of $97,700 in 1991, which indicated that many companies were focusing on streamlining their work force. In 1996, signs and advertising specialties manufacturers employed about 82,246 workers, 53,516 of which were production workers. This was up from 72,000 workers (46,200 production workers) in 1994. Total 1997 payroll of roughly $2.3 billion was up from $1.8 billion in 1994. In 1997, the industry's production workers earned an average hourly wage of $11.70.

By far the largest production group employed by the industry consisted of assemblers and fabricators. These workers made up 14.9 percent of the entire work force in 1996, but was down from 17.0 percent in 1994. The next largest groups were production supervisors at 4.0 percent, sales workers at 3.9 percent, and general managers and top executives at 3.9 percent. The Bureau of Labor Statistics estimates that by the year 2005, the number of assemblers, fabricators, machine operators, and hand workers as a percentage of the total work force will be reduced by 18.7 percent. Automation may be chiefly responsible for this decline. During the same time span, the sales force was expected to increase by 30.1 percent. This may be explained by the expanded size and geographical client base of the average sign shop. Precision workers, sheet metal workers, and duct installers were predicted to increase by 16.2 percent.

RESEARCH AND TECHNOLOGY

American industry started the revolution in computer-aided sign making in 1983. The most important innovation gave an operator the ability to key instructions to a CAD-based knife plotter, an instrument that cuts a pressure-sensitive design (such as a logo or lettering) from a sheet of perforated vinyl. This vinyl substrate (the material on which the actual sign information is contained) can then be attached to a signboard or directly to another surface, such as a store window or truck door.

Most large and mid-sized sign companies had computerized systems, and it was estimated that up to 90 percent of hand lettering jobs had been taken over by computers. Startup costs for computer systems range from $6,000 to $35,000, but the increased speed of production reduces turnaround time and employee hours. Orders that previously took six weeks to complete were now done in a single day. The demand for quickly made signs had spawned a number of rapid-sign franchises. Fastsigns, a national vinyl-graphics chain, had 165 stores nationwide by mid-1992. By 2000, it had expanded into the Industry's leading quicksign and graphics franchise with 420 stores in the United States and abroad, including the United Kingdom, Canada, Mexico, Argentina, Brazil, and Columbia. In Australia, the company was known as Signwave.

Another computer-based innovation is the electronic message sign programmable through software. Traffic signs benefit from this innovation, as do supermarkets and retail stores. In 1989, Videocart introduced a video screen mounted on the handle of a shopping cart. As the cart passes electronic sensors placed in the store, a message appears on screen relating to a specific item or promotion. At the checkout counter the screen displays news and entertainment features. The Videocart and other electronic merchandising, such as electronic coupon machines, were slow to gain acceptance in the marketplace in the early 1990s, however. *Progressive Grocer* reported that only 12 percent of chain groceries used electronic media in 1990 and 1991.

Although Norway, Germany, and Japan added important contributions to computer-aided sign making, America was still the leader in the field at the end of 1993. Calcomp, Xerox, and Hewlett Packard pioneered four-color imaging, a process which produces a color image directly onto the substrate by a method similar to that of a laser printer. This technique will bring more color and versatility to computerized sign design.

Advances in the area of luminous sign manufacture have served primarily to increase safety. A solid-state transformer has been developed to replace the core-and-coil construction previously used in neon lighting.

In response to a growing public concern over the rights of disabled people, a "talking sign" has been developed which may satisfy the requirements of the Americans with Disabilities Act. This small, hand-held device, when pointed in the direction of a sign, would activate a sensor that converts the sign's information to a voiced message. The talking sign's limitation is that it only works with signs equipped with the sensors; however, it has applications in public arenas, government offices, rapid rail systems, and other large venues.

FURTHER READING

County Business Patterns. *U.S. Census Bureau* Available from http://www.census.gov/pub/epcd/cbp/view/us97.txt.

Darnay, Arsen J., ed. *Manufacturing USA.* 5th ed. Detroit: Gale Research, 1996.

Dundas, Bill. "Fiber Optics on the Fast Track." *Signs of the Times,* March 1997.

Hudis, Mark. "All the Signs Point Up." *Mediaweek,* 15 July 1996.

Industry News from Sign Business. Available from http://www.nbm.com/signbusiness.news.shtm.

Lefton, Terry. "The New Sign Age." *Brandweek,* 27 January 1997.

Samuelson, James. "You Can't Zap It." *Forbes,* 21 October 1996.

"Statistics-SIC Code 3993." *Gale Business Resources (Integrated).* Detroit: Gale Group, 1999.

"A Sure Sign." *Entrepreneur,* January 1997.

"The 1996 State-of-the-Industry Report." *Signs of the Times,* July 1996.

Tymoski, John. "Sign Making on the Internet Goes Mainstream." *Signs of the Times,* June 1996.

U.S. Department of Commerce. "Sign Manufacturing." *U.S. Census Bureau, 1997 Economic Census.* Washington DC: GPO, 1999.

"Vinyl Usage; The Signshops Speak." *Signs of the Times,* January 1996.

SIC 3995

BURIAL CASKETS

This industry includes companies primarily engaged in manufacturing burial caskets, vaults, and cases, including shipping cases, of wood, metal, fiberglass, or other material except concrete.

NAICS CODE(S)

339995 (Burial Casket Manufacturing)

INDUSTRY SNAPSHOT

High overhead and limited market potential have limited the number of participants in this industry. The complete set of dies necessary to manufacture a metal casket shell is estimated to cost as much as $1 million, not including the cost of the stamping machines in which the dies are used. The Casket & Funeral Supply Association (CFSA) estimated in 1997 that fewer than 325 companies were involved in the various aspects of casket manufacturing in the United States.

The *Nationwide Summary Estimate of Sales to Funeral Directors* for the fiscal year ending March 1999 totaled the value of industry shipments at $1.1 billion. For the same period, shipped metal caskets comprised approximately 68 percent of the total dollar value of caskets shipped, with wood comprising 27 percent and alternative materials such as fiberglass, cardboard, and composite materials making up the final 5 percent. By comparison, in 1995 metals comprised 64.3 percent of industry shipments; wood, 23.7 percent; and alternative materials, 12 percent.

ORGANIZATION AND STRUCTURE

Caskets are generally made of two types of material, wood and metal. Wooden caskets are available in both soft and hardwood. Because they do not generally have a sealing mechanism, wooden caskets are known as nonprotective caskets. Nonprotective caskets are not designed to prevent the entrance of air or moisture. Metal caskets are available in carbon steel, copper, bronze, and stainless steel. Carbon steel caskets are available in different gauges, ranging from 20 gauge (the thinnest) to 16 gauge (the thickest). Bronze and copper caskets are available in 32 and 48 ounces of material per square foot. The majority of metal caskets are protective caskets, meaning that they use some type of sealing mechanism, usually a natural rubber gasket, to prevent the entrance of air or moisture into the casket. There are also lower-end metal caskets that are nonprotective. Although alternative materials, such as fiberglass or plastics, are also Used in casket manufacturing, none of the major U.S. casket manufacturers employ these materials in their shell production.

Casket costs vary according to the type of material the casket is made of, the quality of the construction, and the type of interior used. Also, the most expensive material used to make a casket, bronze, is considered by the industry to be the material most suitable for casket construction due to its strength and natural ability to resist rust. Copper is comparable to bronze, but is a less expensive material. Stainless steel has a higher tensile strength than either bronze or copper and is also a naturally rust resistant material; it is not used as a primary material for shell construction by any major manufacturer other than the Aurora Casket Company of Aurora, Illinois.

In the past, consumer selection of wooden caskets over metal caskets has been governed by regional preferences, with rural areas being more likely to purchase wooden caskets—a material with which the consumer is more familiar. Urban areas have traditionally had higher sales of metal caskets. Marketing wood as a natural and renewable material has contributed to a steady increase in wooden casket sales.

Materials consumed by the casket manufacturing industry include steel and nonferrous metals, in various shapes and forms, and rough and dressed lumber for outer shell construction. The outer shells are typically finished with paints, stains, lacquers and applied fabric coverings made of wool or felt. Casket hardware consists of cast and forged metals and formed plastics. Interior materials are usually cotton, satin, velvet, or other manmade fabrics.

BACKGROUND AND DEVELOPMENT

The U.S. casket industry has its origins in the 1800s. Merchants operating furniture stores were called upon by the community to supply a casket at the time of a death. As time passed, casket manufacturing developed into an industry separate from furniture manufacturing, and the selling moved from the furniture store to the newly emerging funeral parlor.

By the early 1950s, more than 700 casket manufacturing companies existed in the United States, with more than half of the units sold being cloth-covered caskets. (Cloth-covered caskets are generally softwood, composite wood, or high strength cardboard covered in felt.) Availability of sheet steel grew after the end of the Korean War, allowing casket manufacturers to increase production of steel units. As a result of this, by the mid- to late 1970s, almost two-thirds of all caskets were made of metal, with cloth-covered caskets being relegated to the role of inexpensive alternatives.

CURRENT CONDITIONS

The casket manufacturing industry is faced with a unique obstacle to growth that other industries rarely, if ever, face. Annual casket sales are dependent on several variables, the most obvious being the number of deaths for that year. The low U.S. death rate—projected to grow 1 percent annually through 2010—and an increasing number of noncasketed cremations have created a stable to declining market for the last 15 years.

With the rate of cremations projected to increase over the coming years, the major casket manufacturers have needed to position themselves for further changes in the industry. Looking to offset a market with little or no growth, casket manufacturers have started entering market areas formerly left to other vendors. Cremation urns and specialized cremation caskets are being both manufactured and aggressively marketed by companies who had traditionally limited themselves to casket manufacturing and sales. Industry analyst Steven Saltzman sees this trend continuing, with markers and vaults being added to the types of products supplied.

Traditionally, funeral homes have been the only source of caskets for the retail consumer. But due to the 1994 Federal Trade Commission (FTC) ruling prohibiting funeral homes from charging casket handling fees for caskets purchased from a source other than the funeral home, retail casket stores have started appearing across the United States. These retailers sell their caskets from display rooms, catalogs, and the Internet. Claiming to offer caskets at 40 to 60 percent less than funeral homes, these casket "stores" have become a source of competition for the funeral home industry. While not directly having an adverse effect on the casket manufacturing industry, there is potential for loss of funeral home showroom space for manufacturers that sell to casket stores; funeral homes have been reluctant to carry stock available on the retail market. Batesville Casket Company, the largest firm in the industry, is so aware of This potential that it does not sell its products to anyone other than a licensed funeral director. According to the International Cemetery & Funeral Management's (ICFM) 1999 informal survey of Internet store fronts, virtual casket stores have had lower than expected sales, with the exception of Casket Royale of Hampton Falls, New Jersey. Casket Royale does not sell directly to the public, however, limiting its sales to third party marketing centers. Funeral homes have also started offering more discount packages, which often offset any savings from third party purchases.

Increasing manufacturing cost and stagnant market growth seem to indicate that consolidation of the smaller companies is necessary for the continued survival in an industry dominated by Batesville, Aurora, and the York companies. Inventive marketing techniques and product support will be essential to the growth of the casket manufacturing industry. In 1998, The York Group lost sales revenue from Service Corporation International (SCI) when SCI signed a supplier contract with Batesville Casket. However, any loss of revenue from SCI-owned funeral homes is predicted to be offset by an increase in sales to independently-owned funeral homes lashing out at Batesville's deal. Aurora casket, the smallest of the Big Three, has started targeting independents for special discounts to pick up new customers from the Batesville backlash. SCI also tied up the high end of the wood casket supply by purchasing Marsellus Casket. Though not a large company, Marsellus caskets are considered the "Rolls Royce" of wood caskets, being spotlighted at former President Richard Nixon's funeral.

INDUSTRY LEADERS

In 1996 there were only seven companies producing all of the necessary components for metal caskets. According to the CFSA, of the more than 30 companies that assemble metal caskets, 90 percent are produced by around a dozen companies. Hardwood casket manufacturing is believed to be limited to another dozen companies, with the manufacturing of both metal and hardwood caskets being limited to a very small number of companies as well.

Hillenbrand Industries—located in Batesville, Indiana, and parent company of Batesville Casket—reported revenues of $1.5 million as of October 1999, up 3 percent from 1998 reports. Batesville Casket Company is the largest manufacturer of caskets in the United States. The York Group, Inc. of Houston, Texas, commanded a 15 percent share of the market. The publicly held York had sales of $104,782 as of June 30, 1999, down from the $115,834 reported for the first half of 1998. The third largest manufacturer was privately held Aurora Casket Company of Aurora, Indiana.

FURTHER READING

Acorn, Linda. "Online Casket Sales: Boom or Bust?" *ICFM*, July 1999.

"Has a Casket Store Opened in Your Neighborhood Yet?" *Batesville Source,* March 1997.

"Industry Statistics." *American Funeral Director,* June 1999.

Saltzman, Steven. "Death Care Industry Still Riding Consolidation Wave." *American Funeral Director,* June 1998.

"York Announces 1st Quarter Results; Closes Aiken Bronze Plant." *CFSA Newsletter,* June 1999.

"Your Casket Discount Survey Report" *Funeral Service Insider,* May 1998.

SIC 3996

LINOLEUM, ASPHALTED-FELT-BASE, AND OTHER HARD SURFACE FLOOR COVERINGS, NOT ELSEWHERE CLASSIFIED

This category covers establishments primarily engaged in manufacturing linoleum, asphalted-felt-base, and other hard surface floor coverings, not elsewhere classified. Establishments primarily engaged in manufacturing rubber floor coverings are classified in **SIC 3069: Fabricated Rubber Products, Not Elsewhere Classified,** and those manufacturing cork floor and wall tile are classified in **SIC 2499: Wood Products, Not Elsewhere Classified.**

NAICS CODE(S)

326192 (Resilient Floor Covering Manufacturing)

Companies in the $1.8 billion hard surface floor coverings industry supply flooring primarily for residential homes, which accounted for almost 60 percent of the market in the 1990s. Coverings used in apartment buildings represented 10 percent of industry sales. Other major consumers of hard surface flooring, in order of industry purchases, include office buildings, mobile homes, hospitals, industrial facilities, hotels and motels, stores, and restaurants.

Linoleum, a traditionally popular industry offering, is made in sheets by pressing a mixture of heated linseed oil, rosin, powdered cork, and pigments onto a textile backing, such as burlap or canvas. Synthetic coverings similar to linoleum are created with mixtures of resins, elastomers, and plasticizers. Typically, these newer types of flooring are more moisture resistant, durable, and workable than linoleum.

Englishman Frederick Walton invented the linoleum production process in 1860. The use of linoleum and similar floor coverings expanded greatly during the 1920s. Asphalt tiles were developed in 1930, and vinyl

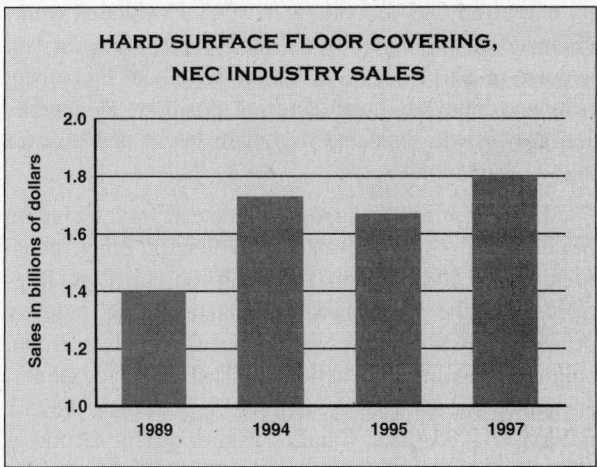

HARD SURFACE FLOOR COVERING, NEC INDUSTRY SALES

floor was invented in 1945. But it was not until the 1960s, when flat concrete subsurfaces became standard in U.S. homes, that hard surface coverings exploded in popularity. A profusion of synthetic flooring products during the 1960s and 1970s sharply increased industry sales. By the early 1980s, manufacturers were shipping about $600 million worth of flooring each year and employing about 3,000 workers.

Steady market growth and the development of new and better floor coverings more than doubled industry revenues during the 1980s. Advanced polymer technology and new plasticizers allowed the introduction of less expensive materials with higher performance. By 1989, industry participants were enjoying sales of $1.4 billion. The industry exhibited a mixed performance in the 1990s: showing only modest gains in the early 1990s, industry sales hit $1.73 billion in 1994 but then drew back to $1.67 billion in 1995, when manufacturers reported sluggish retail sales. By 1997, sales were back up to $1.8 billion. Continued strength in new housing starts in 1999, as well as general U.S. economic strength, was expected to contribute to growth in hard surface flooring.

The hard surface flooring industry is extremely consolidated—only about 34 companies made up the industry in 1997, according to the U.S. Census Bureau. The largest producer was Armstrong World Industries, Inc., of Pennsylvania, which had 1998 company-wide sales of approximately $2.7 billion and employed 18,900 workers in its operations worldwide. Other industry leaders included Mannington Mills Inc., of Salem, New Jersey, and National Floor Products Company, Inc., of Florence, Alabama.

Increased manufacturing efficiency, achieved through automation and restructuring, will inhibit employment growth in this industry in the long term. Increased demand for new synthetic coverings, however, will create opportunities for some occupations. The number of sales positions, for example, is expected to rise 30 percent for the miscella-

neous manufacturing sector between 1990 and 2005, according to the Bureau of Labor Statistics. A total of about 5,840 workers made up the industry in 1997. The average production wage was about $18.36 per hour in the mid-1990s, which was well above the $12.37 hourly average for all other U.S. manufacturing industries.

FURTHER READING

Armstrong World Industries, Inc. *Annual Report.* Lancaster, PA, 1997.

Darnay, Arsen J., ed. *Manufacturing USA.* 5th ed. Detroit: Gale Research, 1996.

Hoover's Company Capsules. Hoover's Online, 2000. Available from http://www.hoovers.com.

U.S. Census Bureau. *1995 Annual Survey of Manufactures.* Washington: GPO, 1997.

U.S. Census Bureau. *Economic Census 1997.* 2000. Available from http://www.census.gov.

U.S. Census Bureau. Manufacturing and Construction Division. *Construction Reports, Series C20, Housing Starts.* Washington: GPO, 1997.

Ward's Business Directory of U. S. Private and Public Companies. Detroit: Gale Research, 1999.

SIC 3999

MANUFACTURING INDUSTRIES, NOT ELSEWHERE CLASSIFIED

This category covers establishments primarily engaged in manufacturing miscellaneous fabricated products, including beauty shop and barber shop equipment; hair work; tobacco pipes and cigarette holders; coin-operated amusement machines; matches; candles; lamp shades; feathers; artificial trees and flowers made from all materials, except glass; dressed and dyed furs; umbrellas, parasols, and canes; and other articles, not elsewhere classified.

NAICS CODE(S)

337127 (Institutional Furniture Manufacturing)
321999 (All Other Miscellaneous Wood Product Manufacturing)
316110 (Leather and Hide Tanning and Finishing)
335121 (Residential Electric Lighting Fixture Manufacturing)
325998 (All Other Miscellaneous Chemical Product Manufacturing)
332999 (All Other Miscellaneous Fabricated Metal Product Manufacturing)
326199 (All Other Plastics Product Manufacturing)
323112 (Commercial Flexographic Printing)

323111 (Commercial Gravure Printing)
323110 (Commercial Lithographic Printing)
323113 (Commercial Screen Printing)
323119 (Other Commercial Printing)
322212 (Hand and Edge Tool Manufacturing)
339999 (All Other Miscellaneous Manufacturing)

This fragmented category accounts for all U.S. manufacturing activities not included under other headings. CCL Custom Manufacturing Inc. of Niles, Illinois, led the industry with 1998 sales of $406.5 million. Caffco International of Cranford, New Jersey, followed with 1998 sales of almost $71.7 million. Exeter, New Hampshire-based Tyco International Inc. placed third in the industry with sales of almost $22.5 million. San Francisco-based McKesson HBOC Inc. generated sales of almost $20.9 million for its fiscal year ended March 31, 1999. Rennoc Corp. of Vineland, New Jersey, rounded out the top 5 industry leaders with 1998 sales of more than $20.3 million.

In the late 1990s, the profile of miscellaneous manufactured goods consumers mirrored that of the manufacturing sector at large in the early 1990s. About 45 percent of industry consumption was classified as private fixed investment (for use in other for-profit businesses). Personal consumption expenditures made up about 15 percent of sales. Four percent of output was exported, and state and local governments received about 3.5 percent of shipments. The remainder of the market was highly fragmented.

The industry's approximately 3,000 establishments were predominately small and mid-sized companies, but there were several larger corporations as well. The industry employed 68,600 workers in 1995. Production workers made up 69 percent of the labor force and earned an average of $9.11 per hour, which was about 25 percent below average for manufacturing positions in general. Job growth was expected to remain flat or decrease for many occupations.

In 1995 products shipped in this category, including those made by firms primarily involved in other industries, totaled $6.04 billion. Despite its obscurity and fragmentation, the miscellaneous manufacturing industry produces a few well-known items. By product group, coin-operated amusement devices, such as arcade games, accounted for the largest share, 13.7 percent, at $825.8 million in 1995 sales. Candles were a distant second at $494.6 million, or about 8.2 percent; chemical fire extinguishers were a close third with $470.9 million in sales and a 7.8 percent share of industry shipments. All other products made up less than 3 percent each—although they accounted for 70 percent of the industry total collectively. These small segments included such diverse items as wigs and barber and beauty shop equipment; artificial Christmas trees and nonglass, nonelectric Christmas ornaments; artificial flowers and plants; matches; umbrellas; potpourri; and lamp shades.

FURTHER READING

Darnay, Arsen J., ed. *Manufacturing USA*. 5th ed. Detroit: Gale Research, 1996.

U.S. Census Bureau. *1995 Annual Survey of Manufactures*. Washington, D.C.: GPO, 1997.

U.S. Department of Labor. Bureau of Labor Statistics. *Occupational Outlook Handbook, 1996-97 Edition*. Washington, D.C.: GPO, 1996.

CONTRIBUTOR NOTES

Adams, Mary Alice: Coordinator of Telecommunicated Instruction at Troy State University, Montgomery, Alabama; freelance writer, researcher, and editor for various publications including *Business Leaders for Students, Notable Black American Men,* and *Encyclopedia of World Biographies.*

Alberts, Daniel J: Technical writer based in Sterling Heights, Michigan; author of computer software and hardware operations manuals; a recognized member of the Society for Technical Communication.

Alexanian, Christine: Freelance copyeditor based in Spokane, Washington; B.A. in English and a Publishing Certificate from the University of Denver's Publishing Institute; does work for the State University of New York Press and the University of Pennsylvania Press, as well as the Gale Group.

Amato, Sara: Electronic Services and Web Development Librarian at Bowdoin College; degrees in library sciences and change management; has written for publications in the area of Internet organization, use, and research.

Amerman, Don: Freelance writer, editor, and owner of A&M Editorial Services based in Saylorsburg, Pennsylvania; has written extensively for *The Journal of Commerce;* work for the Gale Group includes *Encyclopedia of Emerging Industries, Women in World History, Notable Hispanic-American Women,* and *The African-American Almanac.*

Armstrong, Robin: Freelance writer; contributor to *Contemporary Musicians, Contemporary Black Biography,* and *International Dictionary of Opera.*

Azzata, Gerry: Freelance writer and researcher based in Medford, Massachusetts; former academic reference librarian with graduate degrees in law and Library Science; has written numerous materials in the areas of law, business, health, and online research.

Baker, Sandy: Freelance writer, researcher, and editor from Normal, Illinois; work experience in employee communications, university public relations, textbook publishing, and newspaper reporting.

Baker, Suzanne: Freelance writer; MBA, University of Michigan, Ann Arbor.

Balch, Trudy: Freelance writer.

Ballard, Andrew: Freelance writer.

Banks, Leslie: Freelance writer and publicist based in Chicago, Illinois; experienced in public relations, Web site content development, and business writing.

Barduson, Thomas: MBA and freelance writer and researcher.

Barnett, Kris: Freelance writer based in Portland, Connecticut; adjunct English instructor at the University of New Haven.

Baue, William D: Freelance writer who has published articles on William Faulkner and Toni Morrison, as well as on business topics, such as work apprenticeships; has taught writing and literature to both college and high school students.

Beard, James L: Freelance writer and essay author; CPA and MBA candidate, Oral Roberts University, Tulsa, Oklahoma.

Bellenir, Karen: Freelance writer and editor.

Bennett, Bill: Business writer and researcher; MBA, University of Oregon.

Berger, Percy Lee: J.D. and MBA candidate, University of Michigan, Ann Arbor; associate editor, *Michigan Journal of International Law;* freelance writer.

Berry, Pamela: Freelance writer and editor.

Bianco, David P: Freelance writer, editor, and publishing consultant; editor of several reference books; graduate degrees in business and English.

Bilas, Wendy Johnson: Freelance writer; MBA in marketing, Wake Forest University; director of marketing for the Charlotte Symphony Orchestra.

Black, Virginia Mayo: Freelance reporter and editor based in Madison, Wisconsin; writer for newspapers and magazines covering business and general news topics.

Blumenfield, Steven: MBA candidate, University of Chicago; managing editor, *Chicago Business.*

Bodine, Paul S: Freelance writer and editor based in Milwaukee, Wisconsin; has edited for McGraw-Hill Professional Publishing, New York University Press, and the University of Michigan Press; his work has appeared in the *Milwaukee Journal* and the *Baltimore Sun.*

Boyer, Dean: Former newspaper reporter; freelance writer in Seattle area.

Brennan, Carol: Freelance writer and regular contributor to numerous Gale Group titles, as well as *Hour Detroit.*

Briggs, Karen: Freelance writer and editor based in Toronto, Ontario; has written for more than 20 general-interest magazines in Canada, the United States, Great Britain, and Bermuda.

Brinker, Kaye: Freelance writer based in Brooklyn Heights, New York; former advertising copywriter; contributor to *Discount Merchandiser, Advertising Career Directory,* and *Bank Security Report.*

Brooke, Bob: Freelance writer and author of six books; writes weekly for the *Philadelphia Business Journal* and has also been published in *Business Traveler (US/UK), Mexico Business, The Rotarian, Delta Sky,* and the Rand McNally *Guide to World Business.*

Brooks, Jeanette: Technical writer and editor specializing in technical training and manufacturing.

Brown, Susan: Freelance writer.

Broyles, Michael J: Ph.D. ABD working on his thesis at the University of Western Ontario; has also written for the *Encyclopedia of Latin American History.*

Brussel, Marika: Freelance writer and editor, specializing in food and dance articles, based in Santa Fe, New Mexico.

Burke, Andrew: Freelance writer.

Burnett-Balga, Beth: Freelance writer and full-time communications manager based in Atlanta, Georgia; has published articles in *Resource, American City and County,* and *World Wastes* magazines.

Burton-Faulkner, Kimberly: Freelance writer and editor based in Ann Arbor, Michigan; has written for the *Detroit Free Press Magazine;* masters candidate, University of Michigan, Ann Arbor.

Calhoun, Lisa: Freelance writer based in San Antonio, Texas; has written for a range of magazines on subjects from new media to Russian mafia; degree in professional writing from Baylor University, Waco, Texas.

Casey, Jim: Freelance technical writer based in Galveston, Texas; systems operator of CompuServe forums; former computer programmer and electrical engineer.

Chittick, Paul: Freelance writer; M.D. candidate at Wayne State University, Detroit, Michigan.

Clark, Margaret: Freelance writer.

Cohen, Kerstan B: Freelance writer and French translator; editor for *Letter-Ex* poetry review.

Cohen, Paula Hartman: Freelance writer.

Cohn, Lynne M: Writer, poet, and editor; has written for *New York Newsday, Michigan Living,* and *Woman's Own,* as well as publishing her own poetry.

Collins, Cheryl: Freelance writer and researcher.

Cook, Allan R: Freelance writer and journalist; graduate student in English, Oakland University, Rochester, Michigan.

Cooksey, Gloria: Freelance writer; earned a certificate in programming and operations from Data Control Institute and is certified as a network engineer; holds associate degrees in electronic communications and computer electronics and is licensed by the FCC to repair aircraft and marine communications equipment.

Costilow, Donald R: Graphic artist/illustrator, Monongahela Power Company; instructor of business, Fairmont State College, Fairmont, West Virginia.

Covell, Jeffrey L: Freelance writer and corporate history contractor.

Creighton, Kevin: Freelance writer; MBA, University of Michigan, Ann Arbor.

Cuene, Jim: Freelance writer; graduate student in American Studies, Purdue University, West Lafayette, Indiana.

Daily, Kristine: Freelance writer; MBA candidate, Boston College.

Daniels, Garth K: Business consultant in corporate strategy and new venture development; adjunct faculty member, Westminster College, Salt Lake City, Utah.

Day, Holly L: Freelance writer and editor living in Minneapolis, Minnesota; her fiction and nonfiction writing has appeared in more than 800 publications internationally.

Dee, James P: Freelance writer based in Pittsburgh, Pennsylvania; specialist in business and legal writing, editing, and project management.

DeShantz-Cook, Lisa: Freelance writer and editor.

Distelzweig, Howard: Freelance writer and researcher based in Ann Arbor, Michigan; former educator currently working in Quality Assurance Documentation; has written numerous materials in the areas of business, industry, and technology.

Dorman, Evelyn: Freelance journalist, as well as French teacher, tutor, and graduate student; Contributor to *Brides Today, Lerner-Pulitzer* newspapers, the *Chicago Sun Times,* and the *International Directory of Company Histories.*

Dougal, April S: Archivist and freelance writer specializing in business and social history in Cleveland, Ohio.

Eigo, Tim: Freelance business and law writer based in Phoenix, Arizona; M.A. from the University of Notre Dame and J.D. from the University of California, Hastings College of Law.

Estioco, Rose M: Freelance writer and editor based in Detroit, Michigan, with writing experience on a variety of subjects including health care, science, aging, and business.

Evans, Ken: Doctoral candidate in Economics, University of Michigan, Ann Arbor.

Fagan, Dave: Business and technical writer and freelance journalist in Seattle, Washington; writes regularly for *Downtown Source,* a weekly newspaper owned by *The Seattle Times;* his professional honors include writing awards from the Society of Professional Journalists in 1995 and 1996.

Fee, Joe: Freelance writer.

Fishel, Larry: Freelance writer and chemist based in East Lansing, MI.

Fisher, Rogene M: Freelance writer and editor.

Frick, Lisa: Freelance writer based in Columbia, Missouri; former newspaper reporter, copyeditor, and research assistant for the *Missouri Historical Review;* contributor to *Marketing Missouri History;* specializes in writing business features for the *Columbia Daily Tribune.*

Fujinaka, Marika: Freelance writer and editor living in the central coast region of California.

Gallagher, Elizabeth A: Freelance writer.

Gallagher, John: Freelance writer.

Gallman, Jason: Freelance writer; graduate student in literature, Purdue University, West Lafayette, Indiana.

Gasbarre, April Dougal: Freelance writer specializing in business and social history in Cleveland, Ohio.

Genaway, David C: Library Director Emeritus, Youngstown State University, Ohio; president of Genaway & Associates, Inc. based in Canfield, Ohio; founded the national Conference on Integrated Online Library Systems, editor/compiler/publisher of the proceedings of seven national conferences; author of several books and articles; Ph.D., University of Minnesota.

Giglierano, Joan: Independent information professional and former business librarian based in Columbus, Ohio.

Glover, Beaird: Freelance writer.

Gluskin, Lisa: Writer and editor based in San Francisco; editor of *And . . .* arts and culture magazine.

Goldfarb, Kathie: Freelance writer; librarian and Webmaster at Florida State University Libraries.

Grant, Tina: Freelance writer and editor.

Grensing-Pophal, Lin: Business author and consultant in Chippewa Falls, Wisconsin; B.A. in psychology and M.A. in organizational management; author of four books on employee management and marketing issues; frequent contributor to business and trade publications.

Griffin, Attrices Dean: Freelance researcher and writer; former owner of research and technical writing firm.

Gundersen, Linda: Freelance editor and writer based in Doylestown, Pennsylvania; contributor to *The Strategic Healthcare Atlas,* freelancer for Aetna/U.S. Healthcare and Springhouse Corp., a publisher of nursing textbooks.

Gustafson, Randy: Freelance writer; MBA, University of Michigan, Ann Arbor.

Haas, Leslie M: Head of General Reference Department at the Marriott Library at the University of Utah; has written several articles on the subject of business research and products.

Hammond, Nancy: Freelance writer and researcher working in the Detroit, Michigan area.

Harding, Lauri: Freelance writer and editor.

Harris, Lisa: Graduate student in business, Chattanooga, Tennessee.

Harrison, Susan R: Writer and educator.

Harvey, Dan: Freelance writer and editor based in Wilmington, Delaware; former newspaper and magazine editor specializing in news and features on business, medicine, and health.

Hedden, Heather: Senior staff writer, *Middle East Times,* Cairo Bureau, 1991-92.

Heil, Karl: Freelance writer; M.A. in linguistics, Eastern Michigan University, Ypsilanti, Michigan.

Hemingway, Lloyd: Freelance writer.

Henderson, Tona: Freelance consultant, Internet trainer, and business researcher; business librarian at Pennsylvania State University, University Park, Pennsylvania.

Hernandez, Rolando: Computer systems analyst, project leader, and knowledge engineer.

Hillstrom, Laurie Collier: Freelance writer and editor; MBA, University of Michigan, Ann Arbor; former editor of *Authors and Artists for Young Adults,* and *Major Authors and Illustrators for Young Children and Young Adults.*

Hillyer, Richard: Freelance writer and editor, poet, and part-time English teacher; Ph.D. in English, University of Michigan, Ann Arbor.

Hogan, Beatrice: Freelance writer based in New York City.

Holm, Catherine Dybiec: Freelance writer, researcher, and editor based in Cook, Minnesota; former planner with degrees in natural resource management; areas of writing and publication include: business, career development, trade and industry, trends, sociology, fiction, and fantasy.

Holmes, Gillian S: Freelance writer and engineer in Hayward, California.

Hornbeck, Diane M: Co-owner of Home Based Data Services, Inc., offering services to the publishing industry; graduate of Wayne State University, Detroit, Michigan, with a degree in mass communications.

Hoyt, Douglas: Freelance writer.

Huerster, Paricia G: Freelance writer and editor.

Hunt, Christopher: Freelance writer and editor; former advertising copyeditor in Japan; contributor to *Mainichi Daily News, The Japan Times, Canadian Biker, Exile,* and *Intertext.*

Ingram, Frederick: Freelance writer based in Sumter, South Carolina; contributor to *Encyclopedia of Business, Encyclopedia of Consumer Brands,* and *The Disaster Planning Handbook.*

Isaacs, McAllister III: Freelance writer and editor of *Textile World.*

Jaffe, Roger: Received a bachelor's degree in mathematics from UCLA and a master's in statistics from San Diego State University; has been involved in the real estate development industry; currently teaches middle- and high-school mathematics in San Diego, California.

Jacobson, Robert R: Freelance writer and musician.

Jeffrey, Tim: Playwright, short story writer, and freelance writer based in Detroit, Michigan.

Jochnowitz, Marinell: Writer and editor based in San Francisco, California.

Jones, Allison: Freelance writer.

Jones, J. Jacob: Graduate student in American history, Purdue University, West Lafayette, Indiana.

Joseph, Leslie: Freelance writer and editor based in Birmingham, Michigan; worked on *Lifetime Book of Money Management, Chronology of 20th Century Eastern European History,* and *Contemporary Heroes and Heroines, Book II* as an editor for Gale Research.

Kalfatovic, Mary C: Freelance writer and librarian in the Washington, DC area; has written on film, theater, and entertainment for a variety of publications and is the author of *Montgomery Clift: A Bio-bibliography.*

Karl, Lisa: Editor at LifeServ.com, a life-events software and Internet company in Chicago, Illinois; freelance writer and editor in business, parenting, and sports; has written for numerous regional newspapers and magazines, sports teams, reference publishers, and national magazines.

Kaufman, Scott: Freelance writer.

Kelley, Christine: Freelance writer.

King, Brett Allan: Freelance writer.

King, Daniel: Freelance writer; doctoral candidate in economics, New School for Social Research, New York, New York.

King, Susan Wood: Freelance writer and communications specialist based in Research Triangle Park, North Carolina.

Kirchner, Joseph: Freelance writer based in Alexandria, Virginia.

Kirn, Kathy: Freelance writer and owner of KMK Communications based in Baltimore, Maryland; experienced in corporate communications, public relations, and technical writing.

Kiser, Helene: Graduate of Purdue University's and Warren Wilson College's writing programs; freelance writer and former teacher of learning disabled children and college students.

Kitsuse, Alicia: Freelance writer and editor based in Boulder, Colorado.

Kleiman, Robert T., Ph.D: Professor of finance at Oakland University, Rochester, Michigan, and a nationally known consultant; frequently used as a source in such publications as *Money* magazine and the *Wall Street Journal.*

Kline, Trish: Freelance writer experienced in business script writing, public relations and advertising/marketing; author of children's books, teacher's guides, and educational software.

Knes, Michael E: Freelance writer.

Knight, Judson: Freelance writer and editor; partner in the Knight Agency, specializing in literary representation.

Kody, John: Freelance writer.

Kolberg, Sharyn: Freelance writer and editor based in New York, New York; has written and ghostwritten dozens of non-fiction books, articles, and audio tapes.

Koserowski, Laurette: Freelance writer and assistant editor of *Traditional Quilter* magazine.

Kucera, David: Ph.D. candidate in economics, New School for Social Research, New York, New York.

Kuhn, Karyn Bober: Freelance writer and editor.

Lawrie, Laura: Freelance writer, editor, and publishing consultant based in Arizona; has worked on *The Association of MBAs Guide to Business Schools, The New Grove Dictionary of Opera,* and *The Macmillian Dictionary of Art.* Currently the managing editor of *American Behavioral Scientist.*

Leahy, Norman W: Writer and researcher living in Richmond, Virginia; his work has appeared in such publications as the *Christian Science Monitor, USA Today, The San Diego Union-Tribune,* and the *Washington Times;* M.A. in writing from Johns Hopkins University, Baltimore, Maryland.

Leotta, Joan: Freelance business and travel writer and storyteller in Burke, Virginia; published a book on writing techniques for hotel managers; writes poetry, fiction, and nonfiction for children.

Levine, David: Freelance writer based in New York City specializing in gay, lesbian, and medical topics.

Levine, Kathie: Attorney and freelance writer; contributing editor for *California Employer Advisor;* contributor to *San Francisco Business Times* and *Marin Independent Journal.*

Lewis, Scott M: Freelance writer and editor; contributing editor, *Option;* staff editor, *Security, Distributing and Marketing,* 1989-90.

MacFarlane, K. Thomas: Freelance writer.

Malkin, Shula: Freelance writer.

Mandeville, Gertrude: Freelance writer.

Marshall, Mary: Publications editor for a trade association in Fairfax, Virginia; has worked in publishing, researching, writing, and editing for more than 10 years; former project editor at *Congressional Quarterly* in Washington, DC.

Maschinot, Michael: Freelance writer.

Mason, Todd: Manager of Information Systems at Michigan Credit Union League and freelance writer/computer consultant.

Maxfield, Doris: Freelance editor, writer, and owner of Max's Word Services, an editorial services business based in Linden, Michigan; has contributed to numerous reference publications in diverse fields and has extensive experience editing grant proposals.

McDonald, Avril: Freelance writer.

McInerney, Merry: Freelance writer.

McKelvey, Paul S: Principal, McKelvey & Associates, Slidell, Louisiana; extensive writing on international commerce, inland waterways and ports, and shipbuilding; member of New Orleans Press Club, International Association of Business Communicators, Public Relations Society of America, and Society for Technical Communication.

McNulty, Mary: Freelance writer and editor based in Chicago, Illinois; regular Gale contributor since 1988 whose work has also appeared in the *Chicago Tribune.*

Meyer, Bruce: Senior Editor for *Rubber & Plastics News,* Akron, Ohio.

Milite, George A: Philadelphia-based independent writer and editor specializing in business management issues; longtime contributing editor with the American Management Association; past president of the Editorial Freelancers Association.

Mogelonsky, Marcia: Freelance writer.

Mogul, Jonathan: Freelance writer based in Washington DC; Ph.D. in history from the University of Michigan, Ann Arbor.

Moncada, Patricia: Freelance editor based in Burke, Virginia; M.A. in English and American Literature from Southern Illinois University at Edwardsville.

Mote, Dave: Freelance writer and editor based in Indianapolis, Indiana; president of information retrieval company Performance Database.

Mote, Michelle: Freelance writer and professional educator.

Motta, Paolo: Freelance writer.

Mumma, Lisa: Freelance writer based in Raleigh, North Carolina; experienced in corporate communications and public relations.

Nash, Margo: Freelance writer.

Neilson, Susan: Business reference librarian at the Charleston County Library, Charleston, South Carolina.

Nelson, Roxanne: Freelance writer based in San Francisco, California; regular contributor to *Living Healthy;* currently writing a book on sleep disorders.

Neubauer, Joan R: Owner, Word Wright International, Houston, Texas; public speaker, teacher, author of *Tell Them Like it Really Was: The Five Step Method to Writing Your Story,* and publisher of *The Last Word.*

Norman, Bill: Former newspaper reporter and editor based in northern Illinois.

O'Donnell, Sondra E: University of Michigan graduate; translates from the Spanish language and freelance writes from her home in Ann Arbor, Michigan.

Oleck, Joan: Freelance writer in Brooklyn, New York; contributor to *New York Times, New Woman, Washington Journalism Review,* and business publications.

Opdycke, Betty: Freelance writer.

Ossip, Kathleen: Freelance writer.

Paulson, Linda: Graduate of Columbia University Graduate School of Journalism, New York, New York; currently a contributor for numerous regional and national publications on a variety of topics.

Peck, Matthew C: M.A., Wayne State University, Detroit, Michigan; faculty member at the University of North Alabama, Florence.

Pederson, Jay P: Freelance writer and editor.

Pendergast, Sara: Freelance writer and copyeditor.

Pendergast, Tom: Freelance writer and editor; graduate student in American studies, Purdue University, West Lafayette, Indiana.

Pennie, Ariel: Freelance writer.

Pennington-Boyce, Amy: Consultant, researcher, and freelance business writer based in Ypsilanti, Michigan; provides services to profit and nonprofit organizations and to individuals regarding commercial and philanthropic development in the former Soviet Union, international business, healthcare, and public relations.

Pitts, Lee: Executive editor, *Livestock Market Digest;* author of several books and a syndicated humor column.

Plamondon, Scott: Freelance writer.

Poss, Andrew: Freelance writer based in Buffalo, New York; Ph.D. in chemistry from the University of Rochester, New York.

Powell, Tami L: Freelance writer based in La Crescent, Minnesota; specializing in technical writing and editing, including computer software manuals.

Przybylo, Christine: Freelance writer and researcher based in Dearborn, Michigan.

Quagliana, Catherine A: Freelance writer and editor based in Austin, Texas.

Ratcliffe, Mary: Freelance writer and editor; author of brochures, newsletters, press releases, and advertising copy.

Rhodes, Scott: Freelance writer and funeral director based in Burlington, North Carolina.

Risland, Susan: Writer whose work experience has appeared in *Ferguson's Guide to Apprenticeship Programs, Exploring Tech Careers,* and other publications; is an associate editor for the *Missouri River Basin,* and was once co-owner and editor of an equine magazine.

Rooks, Alan: Freelance writer.

Ross-Flanigan, Nancy: Freelance writer based in Belleville, Michigan; has written for *Technology Review, The Dallas Morning News, The Harley-Davidson Enthusiast,* and other national publications; former science writer for the *Detroit Free Press.*

Rothman, Howard: Book author, magazine writer, and Web content provider based in Colorado; books include *RX Inc.: The Small Business Handbook for Building a Healthier Workforce, Companies with a Conscience: Intimate Portraits of Twelve Firms That Make a Difference,* and *All That Once Was Good: Inside America's National Pastime.*

Roy, Soumya: Freelance writer; MBA candidate, Temple University, Philadelphia, Pennsylvania.

Salamie, Dave: Co-owner of InfoWorks Development Group, a reference publication development and editorial services company; contributor to such reference works as *International Directory of Company Histories* and *International Dictionary of Films and Filmmakers.*

Saporito, Kathy: Freelance writer based in Warren, Michigan, specializing in technical writing and corporate communications; has more than 12 years of experience in the communications field and has written for various forms of media including reference materials, user manuals, newsletters, newspapers, videos, and online help.

Sarich, John A: Freelance writer and editor; graduate student in economics, New School for Social Research, New York, New York.

Schneider, Bob: Freelance writer and Japanese translator; CPA, MBA, and New York Stock Exchange supervisory analyst.

Scott, Paula Pyzik: Freelance writer and video producer based in Ada, Ohio; contributed to numerous reference publications including *Contemporary Authors, Native American Tribes,* and *Newsmakers.*

Seablom, Kathy: Freelance writer.

Sharp, Arthur G: Business faculty member of Naugatuck Valley Community/Technical College, Waterbury, Connecticut.

Sharp, Kim: Freelance writer and information developer based in Houston, Texas; academic medical librarian with a graduate degree in library and information science; has published book reviews, articles, and presented papers in the area of medical library science.

Sheil, Richard: Freelance writer, MBA candidate, University of Wisconsin—Madison.

Sheldon, AnnaMarie: Freelance writer.

Shelton, Sonya: Freelance writer and editor based in Seattle, Washington; former editor of *RadioActive, Screamer,* and *Image* magazines; has written for various consumer and business magazines, corporate marketing, and reference books for more than 12 years.

Shepherd, Kenneth R: Freelance writer based in Detroit, Michigan; history teacher at Henry Ford Community College, Dearborn.

Sheppard, Laurel: Freelance writer and owner of Lash Publications International, based in Hilliard, Ohio; has an engineering background and writes for a variety of trade and association publications including *SWE Magazine* (Society of Women Engineers), *Software Strategies, Refractories Applications, Photonics Spectra,* and *Ceramic Industry;* also contributes to Gale's *How Products Are Made* and *Notable Women Scientists.*

Sherman, Fran Shonfeld: Freelance writer and editor; former contributor to *Compton's Encyclopedia* and *Britannica Book of the Year;* has worked on the online version of *Compton's Interactive Encyclopedia.*

Shostak, Elizabeth: Freelance writer.

Shugg, Elizabeth P: Freelance writer and editor specializing in corporate communications literature and feature writing for magazines and newspapers; she writes for regional newspapers in North Carolina as well as national magazines such as *Coastal Living* and *Web-Guide.*

Slick, Scott: Freelance writer and attorney from Lakeville, Minnesota; practiced for four years as public defender in Minnesota's Third Judicial District; writes a monthly column for "Beyond the Bar;" frequent contributor to Gale Group publications.

Spencer, Dorothy: Freelance writer and editor.

Sprinkle, David: Freelance writer and editor.

Stanfel, Rebecca: Freelance writer living in Helena, Montana; her work has appeared in several other business-oriented texts, including the *Encyclopedia of Major Marketing Campaigns.*

Stanley, Jill: Freelance writer.

Stansell, Christina: Freelance writer and editor based in Farmington Hills, Michigan; experienced in business writing and online research.

Steward, Celeste: Reference librarian for Contra Costa County Library, Pinole, California; former news reporter and contributor to *What Do I Read Next* CD-ROM.

Stong, Jennifer: Freelance writer.

Straub, Deborah: Freelance writer and editor based near Grand Rapids, Michigan; has compiled several reference works published by Gale, including *Voices of Multicultural America* and *Contemporary Heroes and Heroines.*

Strohmer, Shaun: Freelance writer and editor based in Minneapolis, Minnesota; former instructor at the University of Michigan with a doctoral degree in English; author of numerous essays and articles on literature, theatre, music, education, biography, business, and science.

Sturzenacker, Gloria: Freelance writer and editor based in New York, New York; former editor of the New York City Fire Department training magazine and local government reporter in public radio; editor of a variety of consumer and trade magazines.

Summers, Shannon: Freelance writer.

Sunder, Aaron: Freelance writer; MBA, University of Michigan, Ann Arbor.

Swartz, Mark: Manuscript editor for the journals division of the University of Chicago Press.

Theodoroff, Mike: Freelance writer.

Thor, Angela: Information specialist based in Syracuse, New York; indexed *Higher & Higher* magazine and several historical books.

Thuermer, Karen: Editor and writer on international topics for 16 years; former editor of *Global Trade Magazine;* currently contributes to *International Business, Journal of Commerce,* and *World Trade* among others; masters degree in journalism form Pennsylvania State University, Hershey, Pennsylvania.

Tilak, Visi: Freelance writer based in Detroit, Michigan.

Trimarco, Paola: Freelance business and health writer based in Washington, DC; Ph.D., University of Edinburgh, Scotland.

Untener, Deborah J: Freelance writer and editor based in Broomfield, Colorado; eight years of experience with reference products, including directories, encyclopedias, and essay collections.

Urbiel, Martha: Librarian based in Hillsdale, New Jersey; regular contributor to Gale Group publications including *Children's Book Review Index.*

Vecchiolla, Richard R: Freelance writer and researcher focusing on shareholders rights and total quality management issues; J.D. candidate, Georgetown University, Washington, DC.

Viswanathan, Shoba: Freelance writer and editor currently working as a senior editor in an electronic publishing company based in the San Francisco Bay area, California.

Von Heitman, Khatanga: Freelance writer.

Vyn, Kathleen: Freelance writer based in Chicago, Illinois; M.A. in creative writing from San Francisco State University, California; has written two nonfiction books and had articles published in the *Chicago Tribune,* the *San Francisco Examiner, American Health, Omni,* and other publications.

Waters, John K: Freelance writer and editor based in California; author of *Silicon Valley: Inventing the Future* and *The Bay Area: California Gateway to the Future;* contributor to *San Jose Magazine, South Bay Accent,* and *The Silicon Valley Insider.*

Wagner, Katherine: Freelance writer and editor based in Chicago, Illinois; correspondent for a variety of general-interest and business publications and has edited catalogs, brochures, and travel guides.

Weaver, Danialle: Professional business and technology writer in Port Orange, Florida; has covered the energy and electricity industries since 1986 for publications such as *The Electric Daily, The Energy Daily,* and *Warfield's Business & Technology.*

Weber, Nathan: Freelance writer.

Weisman, Charlotte: Freelance writer and editor located in Wayne, Pennsylvania; has worked on various publications in Miami and Philadelphia.

Wellner, Margot: Freelance writer.

Westbrook, M. David: Freelance writer.

Wilson, Valerie: Freelance writer.

Wingett, Jeffery T: Freelance writer; MBA from California Polytechnic State University, San Luis Obispo.

Winters, Elaine: Award winning writer whose work has appeared in print and online; currently based in Berkeley, California; has also worked in Asia and the South Pacific.

Withem, Karen: Freelance writer.

Wolf, Gillian: Freelance writer based in Evanston, Illinois; ten years of experience in history, corporate history, and biography.

Wolfe, Joanne: Freelance writer, editor, and desktop publishing service provider based in Springfield, Oregon.

Woodward, Angela: Freelance writer.

Woodward, Nancy Hatch: Freelance writer based in Chattanooga, Tennessee; contributes regularly to several business- and health-oriented publications.

Yocca, Beth: Freelance writer.

York, Leslee: Freelance writer.

Yu, Simone: Assistant Bibliographer and Research Librarian at the Graduate School of Business, Stanford University.

Zrinsky, Christine M: Freelance writer and editor; director of individual gifts, Chicago Symphony Orchestra.

NAICS to SIC Conversion Guide

The following guide cross-references six-digit 1997 North American Industry Classification System (NAICS) codes with four-digit 1987 Standard Industrial Classification (SIC) codes. Because the systems differ in specificity, some NAICS categories correspond to more than one SIC category. Please refer to the **Introduction** under "About Industry Classification" for more information.

AGRICULTURE, FORESTRY, FISHING, & HUNTING

111110 Soybean Farming *see* SIC 0116: Soybeans

111120 Oilseed (except Soybean) Farming *see* SIC 0119: Cash Grains, NEC

111130 Dry Pea and Bean Farming *see* SIC 0119: Cash Grains, NEC

111140 Wheat Farming *see* SIC 0111: Wheat

111150 Corn Farming *see* SIC 0115: Corn

111150 Corn Farming *see* SIC 0119: Cash Grains, NEC

111160 Rice Farming *see* SIC 0112: Rice

111191 Oilseed and Grain Combination Farming *see* SIC 0119: Cash Grains, NEC

111199 All Other Grain Farming *see* SIC 0119: Cash Grains, NEC

111211 Potato Farming *see* SIC 0134: Irish Potatoes

111219 Other Vegetable (except Potato) and Melon Farming *see* SIC 0139: Field Crops, Except Cash Grains, NEC; SIC 0161: Vegetables and Melons

111310 Orange Groves *see* SIC 0174: Citrus Fruits

111320 Citrus (except Orange) Groves *see* SIC 0174: Citrus Fruits

111331 Apple Orchards *see* SIC 0175: Deciduous Tree Fruits

111332 Grape Vineyards *see* SIC 0172: Grapes

111333 Strawberry Farming *see* SIC 0171: Berry Crops

111334 Berry (except Strawberry) Farming *see* SIC 0171: Berry Crops

111335 Tree Nut Farming *see* SIC 0173: Tree Nuts

111336 Fruit and Tree Nut Combination Farming *see* SIC 0179: Fruits and Tree Nuts, NEC

111339 Other Noncitrus Fruit Farming *see* SIC 0175: Deciduous Tree Fruits; SIC 0179: Fruits and Tree Nuts, NEC

111411 Mushroom Production *see* SIC 0182: Food Crops Grown Under Cover

111419 Other Food Crops Grown Under Cover *see* SIC 0182: Food Crops Grown Under Cover

111421 Nursery and Tree Production *see* SIC 0181: Ornamental Floriculture and Nursery Products; SIC 0811: Timber Tracts

111422 Floriculture Production *see* SIC 0181: Ornamental Floriculture and Nursery Products

111910 Tobacco Farming *see* SIC 0132: Tobacco

111920 Cotton farming *see* SIC 0131: Cotton

111930 Sugarcane Farming *see* SIC 0133: Sugarcane and Sugar Beets

111940 Hay Farming *see* SIC 0139: Field Crops, Except Cash Grains, NEC

111991 Sugar Beet Farming *see* SIC 0133: Sugarcane and Sugar Beets

111992 Peanut Farming *see* SIC 0139: Field Crops, Except Cash Grains, NEC

111998 All Other Miscellaneous Crop Farming *see* SIC 0139: Field Crops, Except Cash Grains, NEC; SIC 0191: General Farms, Primarily Crop; SIC 0831: Forest Nurseries and Gathering of Forest Products; SIC 0919: Miscellaneous Marine Products; SIC 2099: Food Preparations, NEC

112111 Beef Cattle Ranching and Farming *see* SIC 0212: Beef Cattle, Except Feedlots; SIC 0241: Dairy Farms

112112 Cattle Feedlots *see* SIC 0211: Beef Cattle Feedlots

112120 Dairy Cattle and Milk Production *see* SIC 0241: Dairy Farms

112210 Hog and Pig Farming *see* SIC 0213: Hogs

112310 Chicken Egg Production *see* SIC 0252: Chicken Eggs

112320 Broilers and Other Meat-Type Chicken Production *see* SIC 0251: Broiler, Fryers, and Roaster Chickens

112330 Turkey Production *see* SIC 0253: Turkey and Turkey Eggs

112340 Poultry Hatcheries *see* SIC 0254: Poultry Hatcheries

112390 Other Poultry Production *see* SIC 0259: Poultry and Eggs, NEC

112410 Sheep Farming *see* SIC 0214: Sheep and Goats

112420 Goat Farming *see* SIC 0214: Sheep and Goats

112511 Finfish Farming and Fish Hatcheries *see* SIC 0273: Animal Aquaculture; SIC 0921: Fish Hatcheries and Preserves

112512 Shellfish Farming *see* SIC 0273: Animal Aquaculture; SIC 0921: Fish Hatcheries and Preserves

112519 Other Animal Aquaculture *see* SIC 0273: Animal Aquaculture

112910 Apiculture *see* SIC 0279: Animal Specialties, NEC

112920 Horse and Other Equine Production *see* SIC 0272: Horses and Other Equines

112930 Fur-bearing Animal and Rabbit Production *see* SIC 0271: Fur-Bearing Animals and Rabbits

112990 All Other Animal Production *see* SIC 0219: General Livestock, Except Dairy and Poultry; SIC 0279: Animal Specialties, NEC; SIC 0291: General Farms, Primarily Livestock and Animal Specialties

113110 Timber Tract Operations *see* SIC 0811: Timber Tracts

113210 Forest Nurseries and Gathering of Forest Products *see* SIC 0831: Forest Nurseries and Gathering of Forest Products

113310 Logging *see* SIC 2411: Logging

114111 Finfish Fishing *see* SIC 0912: Finfish

114112 Shellfish Fishing *see* SIC 0913: Shellfish

114119 Other Marine Fishing *see* SIC 0919: Miscellaneous Marine Products

114210 Hunting and Trapping *see* SIC 0971: Hunting, Trapping, and Game Propagation

115111 Cotton Ginning *see* SIC 0724: Cotton Ginning

115112 Soil Preparation, Planting and Cultivating *see* SIC 0711: Soil Preparation Services; SIC 0721: Crop Planting, Cultivating and Protecting

115113 Crop Harvesting, Primarily By Machine *see* SIC 0722: Crop Harvesting, Primarily by Machine

115114 Postharvest Crop Activities (except Cotton Ginning) *see* SIC 0723: Crop Preparation Services For Market, except Cotton Ginning

115115 Farm Labor Contractors and Crew Leaders *see* SIC 0761: Farm Labor Contractors and Crew Leaders

115116 Farm Management Services *see* SIC 0762: Farm Management Services

115210 Support Activities for Animal Production *see* SIC 0751: Livestock Services, Except Veterinary; SIC 0752: Animal Specialty Services, Except Veterinary; SIC 7699: Repair Shops and Related Services, NEC

115310 Support Activities for Forestry *see* SIC 0851: Forestry Services

MINING

211111 Crude Petroleum and Natural Gas Extraction *see* SIC 1311: Crude Petroleum and Natural Gas

211112 Natural Gas Liquid Extraction *see* SIC 1321: Natural Gas Liquids

212111 Bituminous Coal and Lignite Surface Mining *see* SIC 1221: Bituminous Coal and Lignite Surface Mining

212112 Bituminous Coal Underground Mining *see* SIC 1222: Bituminous Coal Underground Mining

212113 Anthracite Mining *see* SIC 1231: Anthracite Mining

212210 Iron Ore Mining *see* SIC 1011: Iron Ores

212221 Gold Ore Mining *see* SIC 1041: Gold Ores

212222 Silver Ore Mining *see* SIC 1044: Silver Ores

212231 Lead Ore and Zinc Ore Mining *see* SIC 1031: Lead and Zinc Ores

212234 Copper Ore and Nickel Ore Mining *see* SIC 1021: Copper Ores; SIC 1061: Ferroalloy Ores, Except Vanadium

212291 Uranium-Radium-Vanadium Ore Mining *see* SIC 1094: Uranium-Radium-Vanadium Ores

212299 Other Metal Ore Mining *see* SIC 1061: Ferroalloy Ores, Except Vanadium; SIC 1099: Miscellaneous Metal Ores, NEC

212311 Dimension Stone Mining and Quarry *see* SIC 1411: Dimension Stone

212312 Crushed and Broken Limestone Mining and Quarrying *see* SIC 1422: Crushed and Broken Limestone

212313 Crushed and Broken Granite Mining and Quarrying *see* SIC 1423: Crushed and Broken Granite

212319 Other Crushed and Broken Stone Mining and Quarrying *see* SIC 1429: Crushed and Broken Stone, NEC; SIC 1499: Miscellaneous Nonmetallic Minerals, Except Fuels

212321 Construction Sand and Gravel Mining *see* SIC 1442: Construction Sand and Gravel

212322 Industrial Sand Mining *see* SIC 1446: Industrial Sand

212324 Kaolin and Ball Clay Mining *see* SIC 1455: Kaolin and Ball Clay

212325 Clay and Ceramic and Refractory Minerals Mining *see* SIC 1459: Clay, Ceramic, and Refractory Minerals, NEC

212391 Potash, Soda, and Borate Mineral Mining *see* SIC 1474: Potash, Soda, and Borate Minerals

212392 Phosphate Rock Mining *see* SIC 1475: Phosphate Rock

212393 Other Chemical and Fertilizer Mineral Mining *see* SIC 1479: Chemical and Fertilizer Mineral Mining, NEC

212399 All Other Non-Metallic Mineral Mining *see* SIC 1499: Miscellaneous Nonmetallic Minerals, Except Fuels

213111 Drilling Oil and Gas Wells *see* SIC 1381: Drilling Oil and Gas Wells

213112 Support Activities for Oil and Gas Field Exploration *see* SIC 1382: Oil and Gas Field Exploration Services; SIC 1389: Oil and Gas Field Services, NEC

213113 Support Activities for Coal Mining *see* SIC 1241: Coal Mining Services

213114 Support Activities for Metal Mining *see* SIC 1081: Metal Mining Services

213115 Support Activities for Non-metallic Minerals, (except Fuels) *see* SIC 1481: Nonmetallic Minerals Services Except Fuels

UTILITIES

221111 Hydroelectric Power Generation *see* SIC 4911: Electric Services; SIC 4931: Electric and Other Services Combined; SIC 4939: Combination Utilities, NEC

221112 Fossil Fuel Electric Power Generation *see* SIC 4911: Electric Services; SIC 4931: Electric and Other Services Combined; SIC 4939: Combination Utilities, NEC

221113 Nuclear Electric Power Generation *see* SIC 4911: Electric Services; SIC 4931: Electric and Other Services Combined; SIC 4939: Combination Utilities, NEC

221119 Other Electric Power Generation *see* SIC 4911: Electric Services; SIC 4931: Electric and Other Services Combined; SIC 4939: Combination Utilities, NEC

221121 Electric Bulk Power Transmission and Control *see* SIC 4911: Electric Services; SIC 4931: Electric and Other Services Combined; SIC 4939: Combination Utilities, NEC

221122 Electric Power Distribution *see* SIC 4911: Electric Services; SIC 4931: Electric and Other Services Combined; SIC 4939: Combination Utilities, NEC

221210 Natural Gas Distribution *see* SIC 4923: Natural Gas Transmission and Distribution; SIC 4924: Natural Gas Distribution; SIC 4925: Mixed, Manufactured, or Liquefied Petroleum Gas Production and/or Distribution; SIC 4931: Electric and Other Services Combined; SIC 4932: Gas and Other Services Combined; SIC 4939: Combination Utilities, NEC

221310 Water Supply and Irrigation Systems *see* SIC 4941: Water Supply; SIC 4971: Irrigation Systems

221320 Sewage Treatment Facilities *see* SIC 4952: Sewerage Systems

221330 Steam and Air-Conditioning Supply *see* SIC 4961: Steam and Air-Conditioning Supply

CONSTRUCTION

233110 Land Subdivision and Land Development *see* SIC 6552: Land Subdividers and Developers, Except Cemeteries; SIC 1521: General Contractors-Single-Family Houses; SIC 1531: Operative Builders

233220 Multi-Family Housing Construction *see* SIC 1522: General Contractors-Residential Buildings, Other Than Single-Family; SIC 1531: Operative Builders

233310 Manufacturing and Light Industrial Building Construction *see* SIC 1531: Operative Builders; SIC 1541: General Contractors-Industrial Buildings and Warehouses

233320 Commercial and Institutional Building Construction *see* SIC 1522: General Contractors-Residential Buildings, Other Than Single-Family; SIC 1531: Operative Builders; SIC 1541: General Contractors-Industrial Buildings and Warehouses; SIC 1542: General Contractors-Nonresidential Buildings, Other than Industrial Buildings and Warehouses

234110 Highway and Street Construction *see* SIC 1611: Highway and Street Construction, Except Elevated Highways

234120 Bridge and Tunnel Construction *see* SIC 1622: Bridge, Tunnel, and Elevated Highway Construction

234910 Water, Sewer and Pipeline Construction *see* SIC 1623: Water, Sewer, Pipeline, and Communications and Power Line Construction

234920 Power and Communication Transmission Line Construction *see* SIC 1623: Water, Sewer, Pipeline, and Communications and Power Line Construction

234930 Industrial Nonbuilding Structure Construction *see* SIC 1629: Heavy Construction, NEC

234990 All Other Heavy Construction *see* SIC 1629: Heavy Construction, NEC; SIC 7353: Heavy Construction Equipment Rental and Leasing

235110 Plumbing, Heating and Air-Conditioning Contractors *see* SIC 1711: Plumbing, Heating, and Air-Conditioning

235210 Painting and Wall Covering Contractors *see* SIC 1721: Painting and Paper Hanging; SIC 1799: Special Trade Contractors, NEC

235310 Electrical Contractors *see* SIC 1731: Electrical Work

235410 Masonry and Stone Contractors *see* SIC 1741: Masonry, Stone Setting and Other Stone Work

235420 Drywall, Plastering, Acoustical, and Insulation Contractors *see* SIC 1742: Plastering, Drywall, Acoustical and Insulation Work; SIC 1743: Terrazzo, Tile, Marble, and Mosaic Work; SIC 1771: Concrete Work

235430 Tile, Marble, Terrazzo and Mosaic Contractors *see* SIC 1743: Terrazzo, Tile, Marble, and Mosaic Work

235510 Carpentry Contractors *see* SIC 1751: Carpentry Work

235520 Floor Laying and Other Floor Contractors *see* SIC 1752: Floor Laying and Other Floor Work, NEC

235610 Roofing, Siding, and Sheet Metal Contractors *see* SIC 1761: Roofing, Siding, and Sheet Metal Work

235710 Concrete Contractors *see* SIC 1771: Concrete Work

235810 Water Well Drilling Contractors *see* SIC 1781: Water Well Drilling

235910 Structural Steel Erection Contractors *see* SIC 1791: Structural Steel Erection

235920 Glass and Glazing Contractors *see* SIC 1793: Glass and Glazing Work; SIC 1799: Special Trade Contractors, NEC

235930 Excavation Contractors *see* SIC 1794: Excavation Work

235940 Wrecking and Demolition Contractors *see* SIC 1795: Wrecking and Demolition Work

235950 Building Equipment and Other Machinery Installation Contractors *see* SIC 1796: Installation or Erection of Building Equipment, NEC

235990 All Other Special Trade Contractors *see* SIC 1799: Special Trade Contractors, NEC

FOOD MANUFACTURING

311111 Dog and Cat Food Manufacturing *see* SIC 2047: Dog and Cat Food

311119 Other Animal Food Manufacturing *see* SIC 2048: Prepared Feed and Feed Ingredients for Animals and Fowls, Except Dogs and Cats

311211 Flour Milling *see* SIC 2034: Dried and Dehydrated Fruits, Vegetables, and Soup Mixes; SIC 2041: Flour and Other Grain Mill Products

311212 Rice Milling *see* SIC 2044: Rice Milling

311213 Malt Manufacturing *see* SIC 2083: Malt

311221 Wet Corn Milling *see* SIC 2046: Wet Corn Milling

311222 Soybean Processing *see* SIC 2075: Soybean Oil Mills; SIC 2079: Shortening, Table Oils, Margarine, and Other Edible Fats and Oils, NEC

311223 Other Oilseed Processing *see* SIC 2074: Cottonseed Oil Mills; SIC 2076: Vegetable Oil Mills, Except Corn, Cottonseed, and Soybeans; SIC 2079: Shortening, Table Oils, Margarine, and Other Edible Fats and Oils, NEC

311225 Fats and Oils Refining and Blending *see* SIC 2074: Cottonseed Oil Mills; SIC 2075: Soybean Oil Mills; SIC 2076: Vegetable Oil Mills, Except Corn, Cottonseed, and Soybeans; SIC 2077: Animal and Marine Fats and Oils; SIC 2079: Shortening, Table Oils, Margarine, and Other Edible Fats and Oils, NEC

311230 Breakfast Cereal Manufacturing *see* SIC 2043: Cereal Breakfast Foods

311311 Sugarcane Mills *see* SIC 2061: Cane Sugar, Except Refining

311312 Cane Sugar Refining *see* SIC 2062: Cane Sugar Refining

311313 Beet Sugar Manufacturing *see* SIC 2063: Beet Sugar

311320 Chocolate and Confectionery Manufacturing from Cacao Beans *see* SIC 2066: Chocolate and Cocoa Products

311330 Confectionery Manufacturing from Purchased Chocolate *see* SIC 2064: Candy and Other Confectionery Products

311340 Non-Chocolate Confectionery Manufacturing *see* SIC 2064: Candy and Other Confectionery Products; SIC 2067: Chewing Gum; SIC 2099: Food Preparations, NEC

311411 Frozen Fruit, Juice, and Vegetable Processing *see* SIC 2037: Frozen Fruits, Fruit Juices, and Vegetables

311412 Frozen Specialty Food Manufacturing *see* SIC 2038: Frozen Specialties, NEC

311421 Fruit and Vegetable Canning *see* SIC 2033: Canned Fruits, Vegetables, Preserves, Jams, and Jellies; SIC 2035: Pickled Fruits and Vegetables, Vegetables Sauces and Seasonings, and Salad Dressings

311422 Specialty Canning *see* SIC 2032: Canned Specialties

311423 Dried and Dehydrated Food Manufacturing *see* SIC 2034: Dried and Dehydrated Fruits, Vegetables, and Soup Mixes; SIC 2099: Food Preparations, NEC

311511 Fluid Milk Manufacturing *see* SIC 2026: Fluid Milk

311512 Creamery Butter Manufacturing *see* SIC 2021: Creamery Butter

311513 Cheese Manufacturing *see* SIC 2022: Natural, Processed, and Imitation Cheese

311514 Dry, Condensed, and Evaporated Dairy Product Manufacturing *see* SIC 2023: Dry, Condensed, and Evaporated Dairy Products

311520 Ice Cream and Frozen Dessert Manufacturing *see* SIC 2024: Ice Cream and Frozen Desserts

311611 Animal (except Poultry) Slaughtering *see* SIC 0751: Livestock Services, Except Veterinary; SIC 2011: Meat Packing Plants; SIC 2048: Prepared Feed and Feed Ingredients for Animals and Fowls, Except Dogs and Cats

311612 Meat Processed From Carcasses *see* SIC 2013: Sausages and Other Prepared Meats; SIC 5147: Meats and Meat Products

311613 Rendering and Meat By-product Processing *see* SIC 2077: Animal and Marine Fats and Oils

311615 Poultry Processing *see* SIC 2015: Poultry Slaughtering and Processing

311711 Seafood Canning *see* SIC 2077: Animal and Marine Fats and Oils; SIC 2091: Canned and Cured Fish and Seafood

311712 Fresh and Frozen Seafood Processing *see* SIC 2077: Animal and Marine Fats and Oils; SIC 2092: Prepared Fresh or Frozen Fish and Seafoods

311811 Retail Bakeries *see* SIC 5461: Retail Bakeries

311812 Commercial Bakeries *see* SIC 2051: Bread and Other Bakery Products, Except Cookies and Crackers; SIC 2052: Cookies and Crackers

311813 Frozen Bakery Product Manufacturing *see* SIC 2053: Frozen Bakery Products, Except Bread

311821 Cookie and Cracker Manufacturing *see* SIC 2052: Cookies and Crackers

311822 Flour Mixes and Dough Manufacturing from Purchased Flour *see* SIC 2045: Prepared Flour Mixes and Doughs

311823 Pasta Manufacturing *see* SIC 2098: Macaroni, Spaghetti, Vermicelli, and Noodles

311830 Tortilla Manufacturing *see* SIC 2099: Food Preparations, NEC

311911 Roasted Nuts and Peanut Butter Manufacturing *see* SIC 2068: Salted and Roasted Nuts and Seeds; SIC 2099: Food Preparations, NEC

311919 Other Snack Food Manufacturing *see* SIC 2052: Cookies and Crackers; SIC 2096: Potato Chips, Corn Chips, and Similar Snacks

311920 Coffee and Tea Manufacturing *see* SIC 2043: Cereal Breakfast Foods; SIC 2095: Roasted Coffee; SIC 2099: Food Preparations, NEC

311930 Flavoring Syrup and Concentrate Manufacturing *see* SIC 2087: Flavoring Extracts and Flavoring Syrups NEC

311941 Mayonnaise, Dressing, and Other Prepared Sauce Manufacturing *see* SIC 2035: Pickled Fruits and Vegetables, Vegetables Sauces and Seasonings, and Salad Dressings; SIC 2099: Food Preparations, NEC

311942 Spice and Extract Manufacturing *see* SIC 2087: Flavoring Extracts and Flavoring Syrups NEC; SIC 2095: Roasted Coffee; SIC 2099: Food Preparations, NEC; SIC 2899: Chemicals and Chemical Preparations, NEC

311991 Perishable Prepared Food Manufacturing *see* SIC 2099: Food Preparations, NEC

311999 All Other Miscellaneous Food Manufacturing *see* SIC 2015: Poultry Slaughtering and Processing; SIC 2032: Canned Specialties; SIC 2087: Flavoring Extracts and Flavoring Syrups NEC; SIC 2099: Food Preparations, NEC

BEVERAGE & TOBACCO PRODUCT MANUFACTURING

312111 Soft Drink Manufacturing *see* SIC 2086: Bottled and Canned Soft Drinks and Carbonated Waters

312112 Bottled Water Manufacturing *see* SIC 2086: Bottled and Canned Soft Drinks and Carbonated Waters

312113 Ice Manufacturing *see* SIC 2097: Manufactured Ice

312120 Breweries *see* SIC 2082: Malt Beverages

312130 Wineries *see* SIC 2084: Wines, Brandy, and Brandy Spirits

312140 Distilleries *see* SIC 2085: Distilled and Blended Liquors

312210 Tobacco Stemming and Redrying *see* SIC 2141: Tobacco Stemming and Redrying

312221 Cigarette Manufacturing *see* SIC 2111: Cigarettes

312229 Other Tobacco Product Manufacturing *see* SIC 2121: Cigars; SIC 2131: Chewing and Smoking Tobacco and Snuff; SIC 2141: Tobacco Stemming and Redrying

TEXTILE MILLS

313111 Yarn Spinning Mills *see* SIC 2281: Yarn Spinning Mills; SIC 2299: Textile Goods, NEC

313112 Yarn Texturing, Throwing and Twisting Mills *see* SIC 2282: Yarn Texturizing, Throwing, Twisting, and Winding Mills

313113 Thread Mills *see* SIC 2284: Thread Mills; SIC 2299: Textile Goods, NEC

313210 Broadwoven Fabric Mills *see* SIC 2211: Broadwoven Fabric Mills, Cotton; SIC 2221: Broadwoven Fabric

Mills, Manmade Fiber and Silk; SIC 2231: Broadwoven Fabric Mills, Wool (Including Dyeing and Finishing); SIC 2299: Textile Goods, NEC

313221 Narrow Fabric Mills *see* SIC 2241: Narrow Fabric and Other Smallware Mills: Cotton, Wool, Silk, and Manmade Fiber; SIC 2299: Textile Goods, NEC

313222 Schiffli Machine Embroidery *see* SIC 2397: Schiffli Machine Embroideries

313230 Nonwoven Fabric Mills *see* SIC 2297: Nonwoven Fabrics; SIC 2299: Textile Goods, NEC

313241 Weft Knit Fabric Mills *see* SIC 2257: Weft Knit Fabric Mills; SIC 2259: Knitting Mills, NEC

313249 Other Knit Fabric and Lace Mills *see* SIC 2258: Lace and Warp Knit Fabric Mills; SIC 2259: Knitting Mills, NEC

313311 Broadwoven Fabric Finishing Mills *see* SIC 2231: Broadwoven Fabric Mills, Wool (Including Dyeing and Finishing); SIC 2261: Finishers of Broadwoven Fabrics of Cotton; SIC 2262: Finishers of Broadwoven Fabrics of Manmade Fiber and Silk; SIC 2269: Finishers of Textiles, NEC; SIC 5131: Piece Goods, Notions, and Other Dry Goods

313312 Textile and Fabric Finishing (except Broadwoven Fabric) Mills *see* SIC 2231: Broadwoven Fabric Mills, Wool (Including Dyeing and Finishing); SIC 2257: Weft Knit Fabric Mills; SIC 2258: Lace and Warp Knit Fabric Mills; SIC 2269: Finishers of Textiles, NEC; SIC 2282: Yarn Texturizing, Throwing, Twisting, and Winding Mills; SIC 2284: Thread Mills; SIC 2299: Textile Goods, NEC; SIC 5131: Piece Goods, Notions, and Other Dry Goods

313320 Fabric Coating Mills *see* SIC 2295: Coated Fabrics, Not Rubberized; SIC 3069: Fabricated Rubber Products, NEC

TEXTILE PRODUCT MILLS

314110 Carpet and Rug Mills *see* SIC 2273: Carpets and Rugs

314121 Curtain and Drapery Mills *see* SIC 2391: Curtains and Draperies; SIC 5714: Drapery, Curtain, and Upholstery Stores

314129 Other Household Textile Product Mills *see* SIC 2392: Housefurnishings, Except Curtains and Draperies

314911 Textile Bag Mills *see* SIC 2392: Housefurnishings, Except Curtains and Draperies; SIC 2393: Textile Bags

314912 Canvas and Related Product Mills *see* SIC 2394: Canvas and Related Products

314991 Rope, Cordage and Twine Mills *see* SIC 2298: Cordage and Twine

314992 Tire Cord and Tire Fabric Mills *see* SIC 2296: Tire Cord and Fabrics

314999 All Other Miscellaneous Textile Product Mills *see* SIC 2299: Textile Goods, NEC; SIC 2395: Pleating, Decorative and Novelty Stitching, and Tucking for the Trade; SIC 2396: Automotive Trimmings, Apparel Findings, and Related Products; SIC 2399: Fabricated Textile Products, NEC

APPAREL MANUFACTURING

315111 Sheer Hosiery Mills *see* SIC 2251: Women's Full-Length and Knee-Length Hosiery, Except Socks; SIC 2252: Hosiery, NEC

315119 Other Hosiery and Sock Mills *see* SIC 2252: ,Hosiery, NEC

315191 Outerwear Knitting Mills *see* SIC 2253: Knit Outerwear Mills; SIC 2259: Knitting Mills, NEC

315192 Underwear and Nightwear Knitting Mills *see* SIC 2254: Knit Underwear and Nightwear Mills; SIC 2259: Knitting Mills, NEC

315211 Men's and Boys' Cut and Sew Apparel Contractors *see* SIC 2311: Men's and Boys' Suits, Coats and Overcoats; SIC 2321: Men's and Boys' Shirts, Except Work Shirts; SIC 2322: Men's and Boys' Underwear and Nightwear; SIC 2325: Men's and Boys' Trousers and Slacks; SIC 2326: Men's and Boys' Work Clothing; SIC 2329: Men's and Boys' Clothing, NEC; SIC 2341: Women's, Misses, Children's, and Infants' Underwear and Nightwear; SIC 2361: Girls', Children's and Infants' Dresses, Blouses and Shirts; SIC 2369: Girls', Children's and Infants' Outerwear, NEC; SIC 2384: Robes and Dressing Gowns; SIC 2385: Waterproof Outerwear; SIC 2389: Apparel and Accessories, NEC; SIC 2395: Pleating, Decorative and Novelty Stitching, and Tucking for the Trade

315212 Women's and Girls' Cut and Sew Apparel Contractors *see* SIC 2331: Women's, Misses', and Juniors' Blouses and Shirts; SIC 2335: Women's, Misses', and Junior's Dresses; SIC 2337: Women's, Misses', and Juniors' Suits, Skirts and Coats; SIC 2339: Women's, Misses', and Juniors' Outerwear, NEC; SIC 2341: Women's, Misses, Children's, and Infants' Underwear and Nightwear; SIC 2342: Brassieres, Girdles, and Allied Garments; SIC 2361: Girls', Children's, and Infants' Dresses, Blouses, and Shirts; SIC 2369: Girls', Children's, and Infants' Outerwear, NEC; SIC 2384: Robes and Dressing Gowns; SIC 2385: Waterproof Outerwear; SIC 2389: Apparel and Accessories, NEC; SIC 2395: Pleating, Decorative and Novelty Stitching, and Tucking for the Trade

315221 Men's and Boys' Cut and Sew Underwear and Nightwear Manufacturing *see* SIC 2322: Men's and Boys' Underwear and Nightwear; SIC 2341: Women's, Misses, Children's, and Infants' Underwear and Nightwear; SIC 2369: Girls', Children's and Infants' Outerwear, NEC; SIC 2384: Robes and Dressing Gowns

315222 Men's and Boys' Cut and Sew Suit, Coat, and Overcoat Manufacturing *see* SIC 2311: Men's and Boys' Suits, Coats and Overcoats; SIC 2369: Girls', Children's and Infants' Outerwear, NEC; SIC 2385: Waterproof Outerwear

315223 Men's and Boys' Cut and Sew Shirt, (except Work Shirt) Manufacturing *see* SIC 2321: Men's and Boys' Shirts, Except Work Shirts; SIC 2361: Girls', Children's and Infants' Dresses, Blouses and Shirts

315224 Men's and Boys' Cut And Sew Trouser, Slack, And Jean Manufacturing *see* SIC 2325: Men's and Boys' Trousers and Slacks; SIC 2369: Girls', Children's and Infants' Outerwear, NEC

315225 Men's and Boys' Cut and Sew Work Clothing Manufacturing *see* SIC 2326: Men's and Boys' Work Clothing

315228 Men's and Boys' Cut and Sew Other Outerwear Manufacturing *see* SIC 2329: Men's and Boys' Clothing, NEC; SIC 2369: Girls', Children's and Infants' Outerwear, NEC; SIC 2385: Waterproof Outerwear

315231 Women's and Girls' Cut and Sew Lingerie, Loungewear, and Nightwear Manufacturing *see* SIC

2341: Women's, Misses, Children's, and Infants' Underwear and Nightwear; SIC 2342: Brassieres, Girdles, and Allied Garments; SIC 2369: Girls', Children's and Infants' Outerwear, NEC; SIC 2384: Robes and Dressing Gowns; SIC 2389: Apparel and Accessories, NEC

315232 Women's and Girls' Cut and Sew Blouse and Shirt Manufacturing *see* SIC 2331: Women's, Misses', and Juniors' Blouses and Shirts; SIC 2361: Girls', Children's and Infants' Dresses, Blouses and Shirts

315233 Women's and Girls' Cut and Sew Dress Manufacturing *see* SIC 2335: Women's, Misses' and Junior's Dresses; SIC 2361: Girls', Children's and Infants' Dresses, Blouses and Shirts

315234 Women's and Girls' Cut and Sew Suit, Coat, Tailored Jacket, and Skirt Manufacturing *see* SIC 2337: Women's, Misses' and Juniors' Suits, Skirts and Coats; SIC 2369: Girls', Children's and Infants' Outerwear, NEC; SIC 2385: Waterproof Outerwear

315238 Women's and Girls' Cut and Sew Other Outerwear Manufacturing *see* SIC 2339: Women's, Misses' and Juniors' Outerwear, NEC; SIC 2369: Girls', Children's and Infants' Outerwear, NEC; SIC 2385: Waterproof Outerwear

315291 Infants' Cut and Sew Apparel Manufacturing *see* SIC 2341: Women's, Misses, Children's, and Infants' Underwear and Nightwear; SIC 2361: Girls', Children's and Infants' Dresses, Blouses and Shirts; SIC 2369: Girls', Children's and Infants' Outerwear, NEC; SIC 2385: Waterproof Outerwear

315292 Fur and Leather Apparel Manufacturing *see* SIC 2371: Fur Goods; SIC 2386: Leather and Sheep-Lined Clothing

315299 All Other Cut and Sew Apparel Manufacturing *see* SIC 2329: Men's and Boys' Clothing, NEC; SIC 2339: Women's, Misses' and Juniors' Outerwear, NEC; SIC 2389: Apparel and Accessories, NEC

315991 Hat, Cap, and Millinery Manufacturing *see* SIC 2353: Hats, Caps, and Millinery

315992 Glove and Mitten Manufacturing *see* SIC 2381: Dress and Work Gloves, Except Knit and All-Leather; SIC 3151: Leather Gloves and Mittens

315993 Men's and Boys' Neckwear Manufacturing *see* SIC 2323: Men's and Boys' Neckwear

315999 Other Apparel Accessories and Other Apparel Manufacturing *see* SIC 2339: Women's, Misses' and Juniors' Outerwear, NEC; SIC 2385: Waterproof Outerwear; SIC 2387: Apparel Belts; SIC 2389: Apparel and Accessories, NEC; SIC 2396: Automotive Trimmings, Apparel Findings, and Related Products; SIC 2399: Fabricated Textile Products, NEC

LEATHER & ALLIED PRODUCT MANUFACTURING

316110 Leather and Hide Tanning and Finishing *see* SIC 3111: Leather Tanning and Finishing; SIC 3999: Manufacturing Industries, NEC

316211 Rubber and Plastics Footwear Manufacturing *see* SIC 3021: Rubber and Plastics Footwear

316212 House Slipper Manufacturing *see* SIC 3142: House Slippers

316213 Men's Footwear (except Athletic) Manufacturing *see* SIC 3143: Men's Footwear, Except Athletic

316214 Women's Footwear (except Athletic) Manufacturing *see* SIC 3144: Women's Footwear, Except Athletic

316219 Other Footwear Manufacturing *see* SIC 3149: Footwear, Except Rubber, NEC

316991 Luggage Manufacturing *see* SIC 3161: Luggage

316992 Women's Handbag and Purse Manufacturing *see* SIC 3171: Women's Handbags and Purses

316993 Personal Leather Good (except Women's Handbag and Purse) Manufacturing *see* SIC 3172: Personal Leather Goods, Except Women's Handbags and Purses

316999 All Other Leather Good Manufacturing *see* SIC 3131: Boot and Shoe Cut Stock and Findings; SIC 3199: Leather Goods, NEC

WOOD PRODUCT MANUFACTURING

321113 Sawmills *see* SIC 2421: Sawmills and Planing Mills, General; SIC 2429: Special Product Sawmills, NEC

321114 Wood Preservation *see* SIC 2491: Wood Preserving

321211 Hardwood Veneer and Plywood Manufacturing *see* SIC 2435: Hardwood Veneer and Plywood

321212 Softwood Veneer and Plywood Manufacturing *see* SIC 2436: Softwood Veneer and Plywood

321213 Engineered Wood Member (except Truss) Manufacturing *see* SIC 2439: Structural Wood Members, NEC

321214 Truss Manufacturing *see* SIC 2439: Structural Wood Members, NEC

321219 Reconstituted Wood Product Manufacturing *see* SIC 2493: Reconstituted Wood Products

321911 Wood Window and Door Manufacturing *see* SIC 2431: Millwork

321912 Cut Stock, Resawing Lumber, and Planing *see* SIC 2421: Sawmills and Planing Mills, General; SIC 2426: Hardwood Dimension and Flooring Mills; SIC 2429: Special Product Sawmills, NEC; SIC 2439: Structural Wood Members, NEC

321918 Other Millwork (including Flooring) *see* SIC 2421: Sawmills and Planing Mills, General; SIC 2426: Hardwood Dimension and Flooring Mills; SIC 2431: Millwork

321920 Wood Container and Pallet Manufacturing *see* SIC 2441: Nailed and Lock Corner Wood Boxes and Shook; SIC 2448: Wood Pallets and Skids; SIC 2449: Wood Containers, NEC; SIC 2499: Wood Products, NEC

321991 Manufactured Home (Mobile Home) Manufacturing *see* SIC 2451: Mobile Homes

321992 Prefabricated Wood Building Manufacturing *see* SIC 2452: Prefabricated Wood Buildings and Components

321999 All Other Miscellaneous Wood Product Manufacturing *see* SIC 2421: Sawmills and Planing Mills, General; SIC 2426: Hardwood Dimension and Flooring Mills; SIC 2429: Special Product Sawmills, NEC; SIC 2499: Wood Products, NEC; SIC 3131: Boot and Shoe Cut Stock and Findings; SIC 3999: Manufacturing Industries, NEC

PAPER MANUFACTURING

322110 Pulp Mills *see* SIC 2611: Pulp Mills

322121 Paper (except Newsprint) Mills *see* SIC 2611: Pulp Mills

322121 Paper (except Newsprint) Mills *see* SIC 2621: Paper Mills

322122 Newsprint Mills *see* SIC 2621: Paper Mills

322130 Paperboard Mills *see* SIC 2611: Pulp Mills

322130 Paperboard Mills *see* SIC 2631: Paperboard Mills

322211 Corrugated and Solid Fiber Box Manufacturing *see* SIC 2653: Corrugated and Solid Fiber Boxes

322212 Folding Paperboard Box Manufacturing *see* SIC 2657: Folding Paperboard Boxes, Including Sanitary

322213 Setup Paperboard Box Manufacturing *see* SIC 2652: Setup Paperboard Boxes

322214 Fiber Can, Tube, Drum, and Similar Products Manufacturing *see* SIC 2655: Fiber Cans, Tubes, Drums, and Similar Products

322215 Non-Folding Sanitary Food Container Manufacturing *see* SIC 2656: Sanitary Food Containers, Except Folding; SIC 2679: Converted Paper and Paperboard Products, NEC

322221 Coated and Laminated Packaging Paper and Plastics Film Manufacturing *see* SIC 2671: Packaging Paper and Plastics Film, Coated and Laminated

322222 Coated and Laminated Paper Manufacturing *see* SIC 2672: Coated and Laminated Paper, NEC; SIC 2679: Converted Paper and Paperboard Products, NEC

322223 Plastics, Foil, and Coated Paper Bag Manufacturing *see* SIC 2673: Plastics, Foil, and Coated Paper Bags

322224 Uncoated Paper and Multiwall Bag Manufacturing *see* SIC 2674: Uncoated Paper and Multiwall Bags

322225 Laminated Aluminum Foil Manufacturing for Flexible Packaging Uses *see* SIC 3497: Metal Foil and Leaf

322231 Die-Cut Paper and Paperboard Office Supplies Manufacturing *see* SIC 2675: Die-Cut Paper and Paperboard and Cardboard; SIC 2679: Converted Paper and Paperboard Products, NEC

322232 Envelope Manufacturing *see* SIC 2677: Envelopes

322233 Stationery, Tablet, and Related Product Manufacturing *see* SIC 2678: Stationery, Tablets, and Related Products

322291 Sanitary Paper Product Manufacturing *see* SIC 2676: Sanitary Paper Products

322292 Surface-Coated Paperboard Manufacturing *see* SIC 2675: Die-Cut Paper and Paperboard and Cardboard

322298 All Other Converted Paper Product Manufacturing *see* SIC 2675: Die-Cut Paper and Paperboard and Cardboard; SIC 2679: Converted Paper and Paperboard Products, NEC

PRINTING & RELATED SUPPORT ACTIVITIES

323110 Commercial Lithographic Printing *see* SIC 2752: Commercial Printing, Lithographic; SIC 2771: Greeting Cards; SIC 2782: Blankbooks, Loose-leaf Binders and Devices; SIC 3999: Manufacturing Industries, NEC

323111 Commercial Gravure Printing *see* SIC 2754: Commercial Printing, Gravure; SIC 2771: Greeting Cards; SIC 2782: Blankbooks, Loose-leaf Binders and Devices; SIC 3999: Manufacturing Industries, NEC

323112 Commercial Flexographic Printing *see* SIC 2759: Commercial Printing, NEC; SIC 2771: Greeting Cards; SIC 2782: Blankbooks, Loose-leaf Binders and Devices

323112 Commercial Flexographic Printing *see* SIC 3999: Manufacturing Industries, NEC

323113 Commercial Screen Printing *see* SIC 2396: Automotive Trimmings, Apparel Findings, and Related Products;

SIC 2759: Commercial Printing, NEC; SIC 2771: Greeting Cards; SIC 2782: Blankbooks, Loose-leaf Binders and Devices; SIC 3999: Manufacturing Industries, NEC

323114 Quick Printing *see* SIC 2752: Commercial Printing, Lithographic; SIC 2759: Commercial Printing, NEC

323115 Digital Printing *see* SIC 2759: Commercial Printing, NEC

323116 Manifold Business Form Printing *see* SIC 2761: Manifold Business Forms

323117 Book Printing *see* SIC 2732: Book Printing

323118 Blankbook, Loose-leaf Binder and Device Manufacturing *see* SIC 2782: Blankbooks, Loose-leaf Binders and Devices

323119 Other Commercial Printing *see* SIC 2759: Commercial Printing, NEC; SIC 2771: Greeting Cards; SIC 2782: Blankbooks, Loose-leaf Binders and Devices; SIC 3999: Manufacturing Industries, NEC

323121 Tradebinding and Related Work *see* SIC 2789: Bookbinding and Related Work

323122 Prepress Services *see* SIC 2791: Typesetting; SIC 2796: Platemaking and Related Services

PETROLEUM & COAL PRODUCTS MANUFACTURING

324110 Petroleum Refineries *see* SIC 2911: Petroleum Refining

324121 Asphalt Paving Mixture and Block Manufacturing *see* SIC 2951: Asphalt Paving Mixtures and Blocks

324122 Asphalt Shingle and Coating Materials Manufacturing *see* SIC 2952: Asphalt Felts and Coatings

324191 Petroleum Lubricating Oil and Grease Manufacturing *see* SIC 2992: Lubricating Oils and Greases

324199 All Other Petroleum and Coal Products Manufacturing *see* SIC 2999: Products of Petroleum and Coal, NEC; SIC 3312: Steel Works, Blast Furnaces (Including Coke Ovens), and Rolling Mills

CHEMICAL MANUFACTURING

325110 Petrochemical Manufacturing *see* SIC 2865: Cyclic Organic Crudes and Intermediates, and Organic Dyes and Pigments; SIC 2869: Industrial Organic Chemicals, NEC

325120 Industrial Gas Manufacturing *see* SIC 2813: Industrial Gases; SIC 2869: Industrial Organic Chemicals, NEC

325131 Inorganic Dye and Pigment Manufacturing *see* SIC 2816: Inorganic Pigments; SIC 2819: Industrial Inorganic Chemicals, NEC

325132 Organic Dye and Pigment Manufacturing *see* SIC 2865: Cyclic Organic Crudes and Intermediates, and Organic Dyes and Pigments

325181 Alkalies and Chlorine Manufacturing *see* SIC 2812: Alkalies and Chlorine

325182 Carbon Black Manufacturing *see* SIC 2816: Inorganic Pigments; SIC 2895: Carbon Black

325188 All Other Inorganic Chemical Manufacturing *see* SIC 2819: Industrial Inorganic Chemicals, NEC; SIC 2869: Industrial Organic Chemicals, NEC

325191 Gum and Wood Chemical Manufacturing *see* SIC 2861: Gum and Wood Chemicals

325192 Cyclic Crude and Intermediate Manufacturing *see* SIC 2865: Cyclic Organic Crudes and Intermediates, and Organic Dyes and Pigments

325193 Ethyl Alcohol Manufacturing *see* SIC 2869: Industrial Organic Chemicals, NEC

325199 All Other Basic Organic Chemical Manufacturing *see* SIC 2869: Industrial Organic Chemicals, NEC; SIC 2899: Chemicals and Chemical Preparations, NEC

325211 Plastics Material and Resin Manufacturing *see* SIC 2821: Plastics Material Synthetic Resins, and Nonvulcanizable Elastomers

325212 Synthetic Rubber Manufacturing *see* SIC 2822: Synthetic Rubber

325221 Cellulosic Manmade Fiber Manufacturing *see* SIC 2823: Cellulosic Manmade Fibers

325222 Noncellulosic Organic Fiber Manufacturing *see* SIC 2824: Manmade Organic Fibers, Except Cellulosic

325311 Nitrogenous Fertilizer Manufacturing *see* SIC 2873: Nitrogenous Fertilizers

325312 Phosphatic Fertilizer Manufacturing *see* SIC 2874: Phosphatic Fertilizers

325314 Fertilizer (Mixing Only) Manufacturing *see* SIC 2875: Fertilizers, Mixing Only

325320 Pesticide and Other Agricultural Chemical Manufacturing *see* SIC 2879: Pesticides and Agricultural Chemicals, NEC

325411 Medicinal and Botanical Manufacturing *see* SIC 2833: Medicinal Chemicals and Botanical Products

325412 Pharmaceutical Preparation Manufacturing *see* SIC 2834: Pharmaceutical Preparations; SIC 2835: In Vitro and In Vivo Diagnostic Substances

325413 In-Vitro Diagnostic Substance Manufacturing *see* SIC 2835: In Vitro and In Vivo Diagnostic Substances

325414 Biological Product (except Diagnostic) Manufacturing *see* SIC 2836: Biological Products, Except Diagnostic Substances

325510 Paint and Coating Manufacturing *see* SIC 2851: Paints, Varnishes, Lacquers, Enamels, and Allied Products; SIC 2899: Chemicals and Chemical Preparations, NEC

325520 Adhesive and Sealant Manufacturing *see* SIC 2891: Adhesives and Sealants

325611 Soap and Other Detergent Manufacturing *see* SIC 2841: Soaps and Other Detergents, Except Specialty Cleaners; SIC 2844: Perfumes, Cosmetics, and Other Toilet Preparations

325612 Polish and Other Sanitation Good Manufacturing *see* SIC 2842: Specialty Cleaning, Polishing, and Sanitary Preparations

325613 Surface Active Agent Manufacturing *see* SIC 2843: Surface Active Agents, Finishing Agents, Sulfonated Oils, and Assistants

325620 Toilet Preparation Manufacturing *see* SIC 2844: Perfumes, Cosmetics, and Other Toilet Preparations

325910 Printing Ink Manufacturing *see* SIC 2893: Printing Ink

325920 Explosives Manufacturing *see* SIC 2892: Explosives

325991 Custom Compounding of Purchased Resin *see* SIC 3087: Custom Compounding of Purchased Plastics Resins

325992 Photographic Film, Paper, Plate and Chemical Manufacturing *see* SIC 3861: Photographic Equipment and Supplies

325998 All Other Miscellaneous Chemical Product Manufacturing *see* SIC 2819: Industrial Inorganic Chemicals, NEC; SIC 2899: Chemicals and Chemical Preparations, NEC;

SIC 3952: Lead Pencils, Crayons, and Artist's Materials; SIC 3999: Manufacturing Industries, NEC

PLASTICS & RUBBER PRODUCTS MANUFACTURING

326111 Unsupported Plastics Bag Manufacturing *see* SIC 2673: Plastics, Foil, and Coated Paper Bags

326112 Unsupported Plastics Packaging Film and Sheet Manufacturing *see* SIC 2671: Packaging Paper and Plastics Film, Coated and Laminated

326113 Unsupported Plastics Film and Sheet (except Packaging) Manufacturing *see* SIC 3081: Unsupported Plastics Film and Sheet

326121 Unsupported Plastics Profile Shape Manufacturing *see* SIC 3082: Unsupported Plastics Profile Shapes; SIC 3089: Plastics Products, NEC

326122 Plastics Pipe and Pipe Fitting Manufacturing *see* SIC 3084: Plastic Pipe; SIC 3089: Plastics Products, NEC

326130 Laminated Plastics Plate, Sheet, and Shape Manufacturing *see* SIC 3083: Laminated Plastics Plate, Sheet, and Profile Shapes

326140 Polystyrene Foam Product Manufacturing *see* SIC 3086: Plastics Foam Products

326150 Urethane and Other Foam Product (except Polystyrene) Manufacturing *see* SIC 3086: Plastics Foam Products

326160 Plastics Bottle Manufacturing *see* SIC 3085: Plastics Bottles

326191 Plastics Plumbing Fixtures Manufacturing *see* SIC 3088: Plastics Plumbing Fixtures

326192 Resilient Floor Covering Manufacturing *see* SIC 3069: Fabricated Rubber Products, NEC; SIC 3996: Linoleum, Asphalted-Felt-Base, and Other Hard Surface Floor Coverings, NEC

326199 All Other Plastics Product Manufacturing *see* SIC 3089: Plastics Products, NEC; SIC 3999: Manufacturing Industries, NEC

326211 Tire Manufacturing (except Retreading) *see* SIC 3011: Tires and Inner Tubes

326212 Tire Retreading *see* SIC 7534: Tire Retreading and Repair Shops

326220 Rubber and Plastics Hoses and Belting Manufacturing *see* SIC 3052: Rubber and Plastics Hose and Belting

326291 Rubber Product Manufacturing for Mechanical Use *see* SIC 3061: Molded, Extruded, and Lathe-Cut Mechanical Rubber Products

326299 All Other Rubber Product Manufacturing *see* SIC 3069: Fabricated Rubber Products, NEC

NONMETALLIC MINERAL PRODUCT MANUFACTURING

327111 Vitreous China Plumbing Fixture and China and Earthenware Fitting and Bathroom Accessories Manufacturing *see* SIC 3261: Vitreous China Plumbing Fixtures and China and Earthenware Fittings and Bathroom Accessories

327112 Vitreous China, Fine Earthenware and Other Pottery Product Manufacturing *see* SIC 3262: Vitreous China Table and Kitchen Articles; SIC 3263: Fine Earthenware (Whiteware) Table and Kitchen Articles; SIC 3269: Pottery Products, NEC

327113 Porcelain Electrical Supply Manufacturing *see* SIC 3264: Porcelain Electrical Supplies

327121 Brick and Structural Clay Tile Manufacturing *see* SIC 3251: Brick and Structural Clay Tile

327122 Ceramic Wall and Floor Tile Manufacturing *see* SIC 3253: Ceramic Wall and Floor Tile

327123 Other Structural Clay Product Manufacturing *see* SIC 3259: Structural Clay Products, NEC

327124 Clay Refractory Manufacturing *see* SIC 3255: Clay Refractories

327125 Nonclay Refractory Manufacturing *see* SIC 3297: Nonclay Refractories

327211 Flat Glass Manufacturing *see* SIC 3211: Flat Glass

327212 Other Pressed and Blown Glass and Glassware Manufacturing *see* SIC 3229: Pressed and Blown Glass and Glassware, NEC

327213 Glass Container Manufacturing *see* SIC 3221: Glass Containers

327215 Glass Product Manufacturing Made of Purchased Glass *see* SIC 3231: Glass Products, Made of Purchased Glass

327310 Cement Manufacturing *see* SIC 3241: Cement, Hydraulic

327320 Ready-Mix Concrete Manufacturing *see* SIC 3273: Ready-Mixed Concrete

327331 Concrete Block and Brick Manufacturing *see* SIC 3271: Concrete Block and Brick

327332 Concrete Pipe Manufacturing *see* SIC 3272: Concrete Products, Except Block and Brick

327390 Other Concrete Product Manufacturing *see* SIC 3272: Concrete Products, Except Block and Brick

327410 Lime Manufacturing *see* SIC 3274: Lime

327420 Gypsum and Gypsum Product Manufacturing *see* SIC 3275: Gypsum Products; SIC 3299: Nonmetallic Mineral Products, NEC

327910 Abrasive Product Manufacturing *see* SIC 3291: Abrasive Products

327991 Cut Stone and Stone Product Manufacturing *see* SIC 3281: Cut Stone and Stone Products

327992 Ground or Treated Mineral and Earth Manufacturing *see* SIC 3295: Minerals and Earths, Ground or Otherwise Treated

327993 Mineral Wool Manufacturing *see* SIC 3296: Mineral Wool

327999 All Other Miscellaneous Nonmetallic Mineral Product Manufacturing *see* SIC 3272: Concrete Products, Except Block and Brick; SIC 3292: Asbestos Products; SIC 3299: Nonmetallic Mineral Products, NEC

PRIMARY METAL MANUFACTURING

331111 Iron and Steel Mills *see* SIC 3312: Steel Works, Blast Furnaces (Including Coke Ovens), and Rolling Mills; SIC 3399: Primary Metal Products, NEC

331112 Electrometallurgical Ferroalloy Product Manufacturing *see* SIC 3313: Electrometallurgical Products, Except Steel

331210 Iron and Steel Pipes and Tubes Manufacturing from Purchased Steel *see* SIC 3317: Steel Pipe and Tubes

331221 Cold-Rolled Steel Shape Manufacturing *see* SIC 3316: Cold-Rolled Steel Sheet, Strip, and Bars

331222 Steel Wire Drawing *see* SIC 3315: Steel Wiredrawing and Steel Nails and Spikes

331311 Aluminum Refining *see* SIC 2819: Industrial Inorganic Chemicals, NEC

331312 Primary Aluminum Production *see* SIC 3334: Primary Production of Aluminum

331314 Secondary Smelting and Alloying of Aluminum *see* SIC 3341: Secondary Smelting and Refining of Nonferrous Metals; SIC 3399: Primary Metal Products, NEC

331315 Aluminum Sheet, Plate, and Foil Manufacturing *see* SIC 3353: Aluminum Sheet, Plate, and Foil

331316 Aluminum Extruded Product Manufacturing *see* SIC 3354: Aluminum Extruded Products

331319 Other Aluminum Rolling and Drawing, *see* SIC 3355: Aluminum Rolling and Drawing, NEC; SIC 3357: Drawing and Insulating of Nonferrous Wire

331411 Primary Smelting and Refining of Copper *see* SIC 3331: Primary Smelting and Refining of Copper

331419 Primary Smelting and Refining of Nonferrous Metals (except Copper and Aluminum) *see* SIC 3339: Primary Smelting and Refining of Nonferrous Metals, Except Copper and Aluminum

331421 Copper (except Wire) Rolling, Drawing, and Extruding *see* SIC 3351: Rolling, Drawing, and Extruding of Copper

331422 Copper Wire Drawing *see* SIC 3357: Drawing and Insulating of Nonferrous Wire

331423 Secondary Smelting, Refining, and Alloying of Copper *see* SIC 3341: Secondary Smelting and Refining of Nonferrous Metals; SIC 3399: Primary Metal Products, NEC

331491 Nonferrous Metal (except Copper and Aluminum) Rolling. Drawing, and Extruding *see* SIC 3356: Rolling, Drawing, and Extruding of Nonferrous Metals, Except Copper and Aluminum; SIC 3357: Drawing and Insulating of Nonferrous Wire

331492 Secondary Smelting, Refining, and Alloying of Nonferrous Metals (except Copper and Aluminum) *see* SIC 3313: Electrometallurgical Products, Except Steel; SIC 3341: Secondary Smelting and Refining of Nonferrous Metals; SIC 3399: Primary Metal Products, NEC

331511 Iron Foundries *see* SIC 3321: Gray and Ductile Iron Foundries; SIC 3322: Malleable Iron Foundries

331512 Steel Investment Foundries *see* SIC 3324: Steel Investment Foundries

331513 Steel Foundries (except Investment) *see* SIC 3325: Steel Foundries, NEC

331521 Aluminum Die-Castings *see* SIC 3363: Aluminum Die-Castings

331522 Nonferrous (except Aluminum) Die-Castings *see* SIC 3364: Nonferrous Die-Castings, Except Aluminum

331524 Aluminum Foundries *see* SIC 3365: Aluminum Foundries

331525 Copper Foundries *see* SIC 3366: Copper Foundries

331528 Other Nonferrous Foundries *see* SIC 3369: Nonferrous Foundries, Except Aluminum and Copper

FABRICATED METAL PRODUCT MANUFACTURING

332111 Iron and Steel Forging *see* SIC 3462: Iron and Steel Forgings

332112 Nonferrous Forging *see* SIC 3463: Nonferrous Forgings

332114 Custom Roll Forming *see* SIC 3449: Miscellaneous Structural Metal Work

332115 Crown and Closure Manufacturing *see* SIC 3466: Crowns and Closures

332116 Metal Stamping *see* SIC 3469: Metal Stamping, NEC

332117 Powder Metallurgy Part Manufacturing *see* SIC 3499: Fabricated Metal Products, NEC

332211 Cutlery and Flatware (except Precious) Manufacturing *see* SIC 3421: Cutlery; SIC 3914: Silverware, Plated Ware, and Stainless Steel Ware

332212 Hand and Edge Tool Manufacturing *see* SIC 3423: Hand and Edge Tools, Except Machine Tools and Handsaws; SIC 3523: Farm Machinery and Equipment; SIC 3524: Lawn and Garden Tractors and Home Lawn and Garden Equipment; SIC 3545: Cutting Tools, Machine Tool Accessories, and Machinists' Precision Measuring Devices; SIC 3799: Transportation Equipment, NEC; SIC 3999: Manufacturing Industries, NEC

332213 Saw Blade and Handsaw Manufacturing *see* SIC 3425: Saw Blades and Handsaws

332214 Kitchen Utensil, Pot and Pan Manufacturing *see* SIC 3469: Metal Stamping, NEC

332311 Prefabricated Metal Building and Component Manufacturing *see* SIC 3448: Prefabricated Metal Buildings and Components

332312 Fabricated Structural Metal Manufacturing *see* SIC 3441: Fabricated Structural Metal; SIC 3449: Miscellaneous Structural Metal Work

332313 Plate Work Manufacturing *see* SIC 3443: Fabricated Plate Work (Boiler Shops)

332321 Metal Window and Door Manufacturing *see* SIC 3442: Metal Doors, Sash, Frames, Molding, and Trim Manufacturing; SIC 3449: Miscellaneous Structural Metal Work

332322 Sheet Metal Work Manufacturing *see* SIC 3444: Sheet Metal Work

332323 Ornamental and Architectural Metal Work Manufacturing *see* SIC 3446: Architectural and Ornamental Metal Work; SIC 3449: Miscellaneous Structural Metal Work; SIC 3523: Farm Machinery and Equipment

332410 Power Boiler and Heat Exchanger Manufacturing *see* SIC 3443: Fabricated Plate Work (Boiler Shops)

332420 Metal Tank (Heavy Gauge) Manufacturing *see* SIC 3443: Fabricated Plate Work (Boiler Shops)

332431 Metal Can Manufacturing *see* SIC 3411: Metal Cans

332439 Other Metal Container Manufacturing *see* SIC 3412: Metal Shipping Barrels, Drums, Kegs and Pails; SIC 3429: Hardware, NEC; SIC 3444: Sheet Metal Work; SIC 3499: Fabricated Metal Products, NEC; SIC 3537: Industrial Trucks, Tractors, Trailers, and Stackers

332510 Hardware Manufacturing *see* SIC 3429: Hardware, NEC; SIC 3499: Fabricated Metal Products, NEC

332611 Steel Spring (except Wire) Manufacturing *see* SIC 3493: Steel Springs, Except Wire

332612 Wire Spring Manufacturing *see* SIC 3495: Wire Springs

332618 Other Fabricated Wire Product Manufacturing *see* SIC 3315: Steel Wiredrawing and Steel Nails and Spikes; SIC 3399: Primary Metal Products, NEC; SIC 3496: Miscellaneous Fabricated Wire Products

332710 Machine Shops *see* SIC 3599: Industrial and Commercial Machinery and Equipment, NEC

332721 Precision Turned Product Manufacturing *see* SIC 3451: Screw Machine Products

332722 Bolt, Nut, Screw, Rivet, and Washer Manufacturing *see* SIC 3452: Bolts, Nuts, Screws, Rivets, and Washers

332811 Metal Heat Treating *see* SIC 3398: Metal Heat Treating

332812 Metal Coating, Engraving, and Allied Services (except Jewelry and Silverware) to Manufacturing *see* SIC 3479: Coating, Engraving, and Allied Services, NEC

332813 Electroplating, Plating, Polishing, Anodizing, and Coloring *see* SIC 3399: Primary Metal Products, NEC; SIC 3471: Electroplating, Plating, Polishing, Anodizing, and Coloring

332911 Industrial Valve Manufacturing *see* SIC 3491: Industrial Valves

332912 Fluid Power Valve and Hose Fitting Manufacturing *see* SIC 3492: Fluid Power Valves and Hose Fittings; SIC 3728: Aircraft Parts and Auxiliary Equipment, NEC

332913 Plumbing Fixture Fitting and Trim Manufacturing *see* SIC 3432: Plumbing Fixture Fittings and Trim

332919 Other Metal Valve and Pipe Fitting Manufacturing *see* SIC 3429: Hardware, NEC; SIC 3494: Valves and Pipe Fittings, NEC; SIC 3499: Fabricated Metal Products, NEC

332991 Ball and Roller Bearing Manufacturing *see* SIC 3562: Ball and Roller Bearings

332992 Small Arms Ammunition Manufacturing *see* SIC 3482: Small Arms Ammunition

332993 Ammunition (except Small Arms) Manufacturing *see* SIC 3483: Ammunition, Except for Small Arms

332994 Small Arms Manufacturing *see* SIC 3484: Small Arms

332995 Other Ordnance and Accessories Manufacturing *see* SIC 3489: Ordnance and Accessories, NEC

332996 Fabricated Pipe and Pipe Fitting Manufacturing *see* SIC 3498: Fabricated Pipe and Pipe Fittings

332997 Industrial Pattern Manufacturing *see* SIC 3543: Industrial Patterns

332998 Enameled Iron and Metal Sanitary Ware Manufacturing *see* SIC 3431: Enameled Iron and Metal Sanitary Ware

332999 All Other Miscellaneous Fabricated Metal Product Manufacturing *see* SIC 3291: Abrasive Products; SIC 3432: Plumbing Fixture Fittings and Trim; SIC 3494: Valves and Pipe Fittings, NEC; SIC 3497: Metal Foil and Leaf; SIC 3499: Fabricated Metal Products, NEC; SIC 3537: Industrial Trucks, Tractors, Trailers, and Stackers; SIC 3599: Industrial and Commercial Machinery and Equipment, NEC; SIC 3999: Manufacturing Industries, NEC

MACHINERY MANUFACTURING

333111 Farm Machinery and Equipment Manufacturing *see* SIC 3523: Farm Machinery and Equipment

333112 Lawn and Garden Tractor and Home Lawn and Garden Equipment Manufacturing *see* SIC 3524: Lawn and Garden Tractors and Home Lawn and Garden Equipment

333120 Construction Machinery Manufacturing *see* SIC 3531: Construction Machinery and Equipment

333131 Mining Machinery and Equipment Manufacturing *see* SIC 3532: Mining Machinery and Equipment, Except Oil and Gas Field Machinery and Equipment

333132 Oil and Gas Field Machinery and Equipment Manufacturing *see* SIC 3533: Oil and Gas Field Machinery and Equipment

333210 Sawmill and Woodworking Machinery Manufacturing *see* SIC 3553: Woodworking Machinery

333220 Rubber and Plastics Industry Machinery Manufacturing *see* SIC 3559: Special Industry Machinery, NEC

333291 Paper Industry Machinery Manufacturing *see* SIC 3554: Paper Industries Machinery

333292 Textile Machinery Manufacturing *see* SIC 3552: Textile Machinery

333293 Printing Machinery and Equipment Manufacturing *see* SIC 3555: Printing Trades Machinery and Equipment

333294 Food Product Machinery Manufacturing *see* SIC 3556: Food Products Machinery

333295 Semiconductor Manufacturing Machinery *see* SIC 3559: Special Industry Machinery, NEC

333298 All Other Industrial Machinery Manufacturing *see* SIC 3559: Special Industry Machinery, NEC; SIC 3639: Household Appliances, NEC

333311 Automatic Vending Machine Manufacturing *see* SIC 3581: Automatic Vending Machines

333312 Commercial Laundry, Drycleaning, and Pressing Machine Manufacturing *see* SIC 3582: Commercial Laundry, Drycleaning, and Pressing Machines

333313 Office Machinery Manufacturing *see* SIC 3578: Calculating and Accounting Machines, Except Electronic Computers; SIC 3579: Office Machines, NEC

333314 Optical Instrument and Lens Manufacturing *see* SIC 3827: Optical Instruments and Lenses

333315 Photographic and Photocopying Equipment Manufacturing *see* SIC 3861: Photographic Equipment and Supplies

333319 Other Commercial and Service Industry Machinery Manufacturing *see* SIC 3559: Special Industry Machinery, NEC; SIC 3589: Service Industry Machinery, NEC; SIC 3599: Industrial and Commercial Machinery and Equipment, NEC; SIC 3699: Electrical Machinery, Equipment, and Supplies, NEC

333411 Air Purification Equipment Manufacturing *see* SIC 3564: Industrial and Commercial Fans and Blowers and Air Purification Equipment

333412 Industrial and Commercial Fan and Blower Manufacturing *see* SIC 3564: Industrial and Commercial Fans and Blowers and Air Purification Equipment

333414 Heating Equipment (except Electric and Warm Air Furnaces) Manufacturing *see* SIC 3433: Heating Equipment, Except Electric and Warm Air Furnaces; SIC 3634: Electric Housewares and Fans

333415 Air-Conditioning and Warm Air Heating Equipment and Commercial and Industrial Refrigeration Equipment Manufacturing *see* SIC 3443: Fabricated Plate Work (Boiler Shops); SIC 3585: Air-Conditioning and Warm Air Heating Equipment and Commercial and Industrial Refrigeration Equipment

333511 Industrial Mold Manufacturing *see* SIC 3544: Special Dies and Tools, Die Sets, Jigs and Fixtures, and Industrial Molds

333512 Machine Tool (Metal Cutting Types) Manufacturing *see* SIC 3541: Machine Tools, Metal Cutting Type

333513 Machine Tool (Metal Forming Types) Manufacturing *see* SIC 3542: Machine Tools, Metal Forming Type

333514 Special Die and Tool, Die Set, Jig, and Fixture Manufacturing *see* SIC 3544: Special Dies and Tools, Die Sets, Jigs and Fixtures, and Industrial Molds

333515 Cutting Tool and Machine Tool Accessory Manufacturing *see* SIC 3545: Cutting Tools, Machine Tool Accessories, and Machinists' Precision Measuring Devices

333516 Rolling Mill Machinery and Equipment Manufacturing *see* SIC 3547: Rolling Mill Machinery and Equipment

333518 Other Metalworking Machinery Manufacturing *see* SIC 3549: Metalworking Machinery, NEC

333611 Turbine and Turbine Generator Set Unit Manufacturing *see* SIC 3511: Steam, Gas, and Hydraulic Turbines, and Turbine Generator Set Units

333612 Speed Changer, Industrial High-Speed Drive, and Gear Manufacturing *see* SIC 3566: Speed Changers, Industrial High-Speed Drives, and Gears

333613 Mechanical Power Transmission Equipment Manufacturing *see* SIC 3568: Mechanical Power Transmission Equipment, NEC

333618 Other Engine Equipment Manufacturing *see* SIC 3519: Internal Combustion Engines, NEC; SIC 3699: Electrical Machinery, Equipment, and Supplies, NEC

333911 Pump and Pumping Equipment Manufacturing *see* SIC 3561: Pumps and Pumping Equipment; SIC 3743: Railroad Equipment

333912 Air and Gas Compressor Manufacturing *see* SIC 3563: Air and Gas Compressors

333913 Measuring and Dispensing Pump Manufacturing *see* SIC 3586: Measuring and Dispensing Pumps

333921 Elevator and Moving Stairway Manufacturing *see* SIC 3534: Elevators and Moving Stairways

333922 Conveyor and Conveying Equipment Manufacturing *see* SIC 3523: Farm Machinery and Equipment; SIC 3535: Conveyors and Conveying Equipment

333923 Overhead Traveling Crane, Hoist, and Monorail System Manufacturing *see* SIC 3531: Construction Machinery and Equipment; SIC 3536: Overhead Traveling Cranes, Hoists and Monorail Systems

333924 Industrial Truck, Tractor, Trailer, and Stacker Machinery Manufacturing *see* SIC 3537: Industrial Trucks, Tractors, Trailers, and Stackers

333991 Power-Driven Hand Tool Manufacturing *see* SIC 3546: Power-Driven Handtools

333992 Welding and Soldering Equipment Manufacturing *see* SIC 3548: Electric and Gas Welding and Soldering Equipment

333993 Packaging Machinery Manufacturing *see* SIC 3565: Packaging Machinery

333994 Industrial Process Furnace and Oven Manufacturing *see* SIC 3567: Industrial Process Furnaces and Ovens

333995 Fluid Power Cylinder and Actuator Manufacturing *see* SIC 3593: Fluid Power Cylinders and Actuators

333996 Fluid Power Pump and Motor Manufacturing *see* SIC 3594: Fluid Power Pumps and Motors

333997 Scale and Balance (except Laboratory) Manufacturing *see* SIC 3596: Scales and Balances, Except Laboratory

333999 All Other General Purpose Machinery Manufacturing *see* SIC 3569: General Industrial Machinery and Equipment, NEC; SIC 3599: Industrial and Commercial Machinery and Equipment, NEC

COMPUTER & ELECTRONIC PRODUCT MANUFACTURING

334111 Electronic Computer Manufacturing *see* SIC 3571: Electronic Computers

334112 Computer Storage Device Manufacturing *see* SIC 3572: Computer Storage Devices

334113 Computer Terminal Manufacturing *see* SIC 3575: Computer Terminals

334119 Other Computer Peripheral Equipment Manufacturing *see* SIC 3577: Computer Peripheral Equipment, NEC; SIC 3578: Calculating and Accounting Machines, Except Electronic Computers; SIC 3699: Electrical Machinery, Equipment, and Supplies, NEC

334210 Telephone Apparatus Manufacturing *see* SIC 3661: Telephone and Telegraph Apparatus

334220 Radio and Television Broadcasting and Wireless Communications Equipment Manufacturing *see* SIC 3663: Radio and Television Broadcasting and Communication Equipment; SIC 3679: Electronic Components, NEC

334290 Other Communication Equipment Manufacturing *see* SIC 3669: Communications Equipment, NEC

334310 Audio and Video Equipment Manufacturing *see* SIC 3651: Household Audio and Video Equipment

334411 Electron Tube Manufacturing *see* SIC 3671: Electron Tubes

334412 Printed Circuit Board Manufacturing *see* SIC 3672: Printed Circuit Boards

334413 Semiconductor and Related Device Manufacturing *see* SIC 3674: Semiconductors and Related Devices

334414 Electronic Capacitor Manufacturing *see* SIC 3675: Electronic Capacitors

334415 Electronic Resistor Manufacturing *see* SIC 3676: Electronic Resistors

334416 Electronic Coil, Transformer, and Other Inductor Manufacturing *see* SIC 3661: Telephone and Telegraph Apparatus; SIC 3677: Electronic Coils, Transformers, and Other Inductors; SIC 3825: Instruments for Measuring and Testing of Electricity and Electrical Signals

334417 Electronic Connector Manufacturing *see* SIC 3678: Electronic Connectors

334418 Printed Circuit/Electronics Assembly Manufacturing *see* SIC 3661: Telephone and Telegraph Apparatus; SIC 3679: Electronic Components, NEC

334419 Other Electronic Component Manufacturing *see* SIC 3679: Electronic Components, NEC

334510 Electromedical and Electrotherapeutic Apparatus Manufacturing *see* SIC 3842: Orthopedic, Prosthetic, and Surgical Appliances and Supplies; SIC 3845: Electromedical and Electrotherapeutic Apparatus

334511 Search, Detection, Navigation, Guidance, Aeronautical, and Nautical System and Instrument Manufacturing *see* SIC 3812: Search, Detection, Navigation, Guidance, Aeronautical, and Nautical Systems and Instruments

334512 Automatic Environmental Control Manufacturing for Regulating Residential, Commercial, and Appliance Use *see* SIC 3822: Automatic Controls for Regulating Residential and Commercial Environments and Appliances

334513 Instruments and Related Product Manufacturing for Measuring Displaying, and Controlling Industrial Process Variables *see* SIC 3823: Industrial Instruments for Measurement, Display, and Control of Process Variables; and Related Products

334514 Totalizing Fluid Meter and Counting Device Manufacturing *see* SIC 3824: Totalizing Fluid Meters and Counting Devices

334515 Instrument Manufacturing for Measuring and Testing Electricity and Electrical Signals *see* SIC 3825: Instruments for Measuring and Testing of Electricity and Electrical Signals

334516 Analytical Laboratory Instrument Manufacturing *see* SIC 3826: Laboratory Analytical Instruments

334517 Irradiation Apparatus Manufacturing *see* SIC 3844: X-Ray Apparatus and Tubes and Related Irradiation Apparatus; SIC 3845: Electromedical and Electrotherapeutic Apparatus

334518 Watch, Clock, and Part Manufacturing *see* SIC 3495: Wire Springs; SIC 3579: Office Machines, NEC; SIC 3873: Watches, Clocks, Clockwork Operated Devices and Parts

334519 Other Measuring and Controlling Device Manufacturing *see* SIC 3829: Measuring and Controlling Devices, NEC

334611 Software Reproducing *see* SIC 7372: Prepackaged Software

334612 Prerecorded Compact Disc (Except Software), Tape and Record Reproducing *see* SIC 3652: Phonograph Records and Prerecorded Audio Tapes and Disks; SIC 7819: Services Allied to Motion Picture Production

334613 Magnetic and Optical Recording Media Manufacturing *see* SIC 3695: Magnetic and Optical Recording Media

ELECTRICAL EQUIPMENT, APPLIANCE, & COMPONENT MANUFACTURING

335110 Electric Lamp Bulb and Part Manufacturing *see* SIC 3641: Electric Lamp Bulbs and Tubes

335121 Residential Electric Lighting Fixture Manufacturing *see* SIC 3645: Residential Electric Lighting Fixtures; SIC 3999: Manufacturing Industries, NEC

335122 Commercial, Industrial, and Institutional Electric Lighting Fixture Manufacturing *see* SIC 3646: Commercial, Industrial, and Institutional Electric Lighting Fixtures

335129 Other Lighting Equipment Manufacturing *see* SIC 3648: Lighting Equipment, NEC; SIC 3699: Electrical Machinery, Equipment, and Supplies, NEC

335211 Electric Houseware and Fan Manufacturing *see* SIC 3634: Electric Housewares and Fans

335212 Household Vacuum Cleaner Manufacturing *see* SIC 3635: Household Vacuum Cleaners; SIC 3639: Household Appliances, NEC

335221 Household Cooking Appliance Manufacturing *see* SIC 3631: Household Cooking Equipment

335222 Household Refrigerator and Home and Farm Freezer Manufacturing *see* SIC 3632: Household Refrigerators and Home and Farm Freezers

335224 Household Laundry Equipment Manufacturing *see* SIC 3633: Household Laundry Equipment

335228 Other Household Appliance Manufacturing *see* SIC 3639: Household Appliances, NEC

335311 Power, Distribution, and Specialty Transformer Manufacturing *see* SIC 3548: Electric and Gas Welding and Soldering Equipment; SIC 3612: Power, Distribution, and Specialty Transformers

335312 Motor and Generator Manufacturing *see* SIC 3621: Motors and Generators; SIC 7694: Armature Rewinding Shops

335313 Switchgear and Switchboard Apparatus Manufacturing *see* SIC 3613: Switchgear and Switchboard Apparatus

335314 Relay and Industrial Control Manufacturing *see* SIC 3625: Relays and Industrial Controls

335911 Storage Battery Manufacturing *see* SIC 3691: Storage Batteries

335912 Dry and Wet Primary Battery Manufacturing *see* SIC 3692: Primary Batteries, Dry and Wet

335921 Fiber Optic Cable Manufacturing *see* SIC 3357: Drawing and Insulating of Nonferrous Wire

335929 Other Communication and Energy Wire Manufacturing *see* SIC 3357: Drawing and Insulating of Nonferrous Wire

335931 Current-Carrying Wiring Device Manufacturing *see* SIC 3643: Current-Carrying Wiring Devices

335932 Noncurrent-Carrying Wiring Device Manufacturing *see* SIC 3644: Noncurrent-Carrying Wiring Devices

335991 Carbon and Graphite Product Manufacturing *see* SIC 3624: Carbon and Graphite Products

335999 All Other Miscellaneous Electrical Equipment and Component Manufacturing *see* SIC 3629: Electrical Industrial Apparatus, NEC; SIC 3699: Electrical Machinery, Equipment, and Supplies, NEC

TRANSPORTATION EQUIPMENT MANUFACTURING

336111 Automobile Manufacturing *see* SIC 3711: Motor Vehicles and Passenger Car Bodies

336112 Light Truck and Utility Vehicle Manufacturing *see* SIC 3711: Motor Vehicles and Passenger Car Bodies

336120 Heavy Duty Truck Manufacturing *see* SIC 3711: Motor Vehicles and Passenger Car Bodies

336211 Motor Vehicle Body Manufacturing *see* SIC 3711: Motor Vehicles and Passenger Car Bodies; SIC 3713: Truck and Bus Bodies; SIC 3714: Motor Vehicle Parts and Accessories

336212 Truck Trailer Manufacturing *see* SIC 3715: Truck Trailers

336213 Motor Home Manufacturing *see* SIC 3716: Motor Homes

336214 Travel Trailer and Camper Manufacturing *see* SIC 3792: Travel Trailers and Campers; SIC 3799: Transportation Equipment, NEC

336311 Carburetor, Piston, Piston Ring and Valve Manufacturing *see* SIC 3592: Carburetors, Pistons, Piston Rings and Valves

336312 Gasoline Engine and Engine Parts Manufacturing *see* SIC 3714: Motor Vehicle Parts and Accessories

336321 Vehicular Lighting Equipment Manufacturing *see* SIC 3647: Vehicular Lighting Equipment

336322 Other Motor Vehicle Electrical and Electronic Equipment Manufacturing *see* SIC 3679: Electronic Components, NEC; SIC 3694: Electrical Equipment for Internal Combustion Engines; SIC 3714: Motor Vehicle Parts and Accessories

336330 Motor Vehicle Steering and Suspension Components (except Spring) Manufacturing *see* SIC 3714: Motor Vehicle Parts and Accessories

336340 Motor Vehicle Brake System Manufacturing *see* SIC 3292: Asbestos Products; SIC 3714: Motor Vehicle Parts and Accessories

336350 Motor Vehicle Transmission and Power Train Part Manufacturing *see* SIC 3714: Motor Vehicle Parts and Accessories

336360 Motor Vehicle Fabric Accessories and Seat Manufacturing *see* SIC 2396: Automotive Trimmings, Apparel Findings, and Related Products; SIC 2399: Fabricated Textile Products, NEC; SIC 2531: Public Building and Related Furniture

336370 Motor Vehicle Metal Stamping *see* SIC 3465: Automotive Stamping

336391 Motor Vehicle Air Conditioning Manufacturing *see* SIC 3585: Air-Conditioning and Warm Air Heating Equipment and Commercial and Industrial Refrigeration Equipment

336399 All Other Motor Vehicle Parts Manufacturing *see* SIC 3519: Internal Combustion Engines, NEC; SIC 3599: Industrial and Commercial Machinery and Equipment, NEC; SIC 3714: Motor Vehicle Parts and Accessories

336411 Aircraft Manufacturing *see* SIC 3721: Aircraft

336412 Aircraft Engine and Engine Parts Manufacturing *see* SIC 3724: Aircraft Engines and Engine Parts

336413 Other Aircraft Part and Auxiliary Equipment Manufacturing *see* SIC 3728: Aircraft Parts and Auxiliary Equipment, NEC

336414 Guided Missile and Space Vehicle Manufacturing *see* SIC 3761: Guided Missiles and Space Vehicles

336415 Guided Missile and Space Vehicle Propulsion Unit and Propulsion Unit Parts Manufacturing *see* SIC 3764: Guided Missile and Space Vehicle Propulsion Units and Propulsion Unit Parts

336419 Other Guided Missile and Space Vehicle Parts and Auxiliary Equipment Manufacturing *see* SIC 3769: Guided Missile Space Vehicle Parts and Auxiliary Equipment, NEC

336510 Railroad Rolling Stock Manufacturing *see* SIC 3531: Construction Machinery and Equipment; SIC 3743: Railroad Equipment

336611 Ship Building and Repairing *see* SIC 3731: Ship Building and Repairing

336612 Boat Building *see* SIC 3732: Boat Building and Repairing

336991 Motorcycle, Bicycle, and Parts Manufacturing *see* SIC 3751: Motorcycles, Bicycles, and Parts; SIC 3944: Games, Toys, and Children's Vehicles, Except Dolls and Bicycles

336992 Military Armored Vehicle, Tank, and Tank Component Manufacturing *see* SIC 3711: Motor Vehicles and Passenger Car Bodies; SIC 3795: Tanks and Tank Components

336999 All Other Transportation Equipment Manufacturing *see* SIC 3799: Transportation Equipment, NEC

FURNITURE & RELATED PRODUCT MANUFACTURING

337110 Wood Kitchen Cabinet and Counter Top Manufacturing *see* SIC 2434: Wood Kitchen Cabinets; SIC 2541: Wood Office and Store Fixtures, Partitions, Shelving, and Lockers; SIC 5712: Furniture Stores

337121 Upholstered Wood Household Furniture Manufacturing *see* SIC 2512: Wood Household Furniture, Upholstered; SIC 2515: Mattresses, Foundations, and Convertible Beds; SIC 5712: Furniture Stores

337122 Nonupholstered Wood Household Furniture Manufacturing *see* SIC 2511: Wood Household Furniture, Except Upholstered; SIC 5712: Furniture Stores

337124 Metal Household Furniture Manufacturing *see* SIC 2514: Metal Household Furniture

337125 Household Furniture (except Wood and Metal) Manufacturing *see* SIC 2519: Household Furniture, NEC

337127 Institutional Furniture Manufacturing *see* SIC 2531: Public Building and Related Furniture; SIC 2599: Furniture and Fixtures, NEC; SIC 3952: Lead Pencils, Crayons, and Artist's Materials; SIC 3999: Manufacturing Industries, NEC

337129 Wood Television, Radio, and Sewing Machine Cabinet Manufacturing *see* SIC 2517: Wood Television, Radio, Phonograph and Sewing Machine Cabinets

337211 Wood Office Furniture Manufacturing *see* SIC 2521: Wood Office Furniture

337212 Custom Architectural Woodwork, Millwork, and Fixtures *see* SIC 2541: Wood Office and Store Fixtures, Partitions, Shelving, and Lockers

337214 Nonwood Office Furniture Manufacturing *see* SIC 2522: Office Furniture, Except Wood

337215 Showcase, Partition, Shelving, and Locker Manufacturing *see* SIC 2426: Hardwood Dimension and Flooring Mills; SIC 2541: Wood Office and Store Fixtures, Partitions, Shelving, and Lockers; SIC 2542: Office and Store Fixtures, Partitions Shelving, and Lockers, Except Wood; SIC 3499: Fabricated Metal Products, NEC

337910 Mattress Manufacturing *see* SIC 2515: Mattresses, Foundations, and Convertible Beds

337920 Blind and Shade Manufacturing *see* SIC 2591: Drapery Hardware and Window Blinds and Shades

MISCELLANEOUS MANUFACTURING

339111 Laboratory Apparatus and Furniture Manufacturing *see* SIC 3821: Laboratory Apparatus and Furniture

339112 Surgical and Medical Instrument Manufacturing *see* SIC 3829: Measuring and Controlling Devices, NEC; SIC 3841: Surgical and Medical Instruments and Apparatus

339113 Surgical Appliance and Supplies Manufacturing *see* SIC 2599: Furniture and Fixtures, NEC; SIC 3842: Orthopedic, Prosthetic, and Surgical Appliances and Supplies

339114 Dental Equipment and Supplies Manufacturing *see* SIC 3843: Dental Equipment and Supplies

339115 Ophthalmic Goods Manufacturing *see* SIC 3851: Ophthalmic Goods; SIC 5995: Optical Goods Stores

339116 Dental Laboratories *see* SIC 8072: Dental Laboratories

339911 Jewelry (including Precious Metal) Manufacturing, *see* SIC 3469: Metal Stamping, NEC; SIC 3479: Coating, Engraving, and Allied Services, NEC; SIC 3911: Jewelry, Precious Metal

339912 Silverware and Plated Ware Manufacturing *see* SIC 3479: Coating, Engraving, and Allied Services, NEC; SIC 3914: Silverware, Plated Ware, and Stainless Steel Ware

339913 Jewelers' Material and Lapidary Work Manufacturing *see* SIC 3915: Jewelers' Findings and Materials, and Lapidary Work

339914 Costume Jewelry and Novelty Manufacturing *see* SIC 3479: Coating, Engraving, and Allied Services, NEC; SIC 3499: Fabricated Metal Products, NEC; SIC 3961: Costume Jewelry and Costume Novelties, Except Precious Metals

339920 Sporting and Athletic Good Manufacturing *see* SIC 3949: Sporting and Athletic Goods, NEC

339931 Doll and Stuffed Toy Manufacturing *see* SIC 3942: Dolls and Stuffed Toys

339932 Game, Toy, and Children's Vehicle Manufacturing *see* SIC 3944: Games, Toys, and Children's Vehicles, Except Dolls and Bicycles

339941 Pen and Mechanical Pencil Manufacturing *see* SIC 3951: Pens, Mechanical Pencils and Parts

339942 Lead Pencil and Art Good Manufacturing *see* SIC 2531: Public Building and Related Furniture; SIC 3579: Office Machines, NEC; SIC 3952: Lead Pencils, Crayons, and Artist's Materials

339943 Marking Device Manufacturing *see* SIC 3953: Marking Devices

339944 Carbon Paper and Inked Ribbon Manufacturing *see* SIC 3955: Carbon Paper and Inked Ribbons

339950 Sign Manufacturing *see* SIC 3993: Signs and Advertising Specialties

339991 Gasket, Packing, and Sealing Device Manufacturing *see* SIC 3053: Gaskets, Packing, and Sealing Devices

339992 Musical Instrument Manufacturing *see* SIC 3931: Musical Instruments

339993 Fastener, Button, Needle, and Pin Manufacturing *see* SIC 3131: Boot and Shoe Cut Stock and Findings; SIC 3965: Fasteners, Buttons, Needles, and Pins

339994 Broom, Brush and Mop Manufacturing *see* SIC 2392: Housefurnishings, Except Curtains and Draperies; SIC 3991: Brooms and Brushes

339995 Burial Casket Manufacturing *see* SIC 3995: Burial Caskets

339999 All Other Miscellaneous Manufacturing *see* SIC 2499: Wood Products, NEC; SIC 3999: Manufacturing Industries, NEC

WHOLESALE TRADE

421110 Automobile and Other Motor Vehicle Wholesalers *see* SIC 5012: Automobiles and Other Motor Vehicles; SIC 5013: Motor Vehicle Supplies and New Parts

421130 Tire and Tube Wholesalers *see* SIC 5014: Tires and Tubes

421140 Motor Vehicle Part (Used) Wholesalers *see* SIC 5015: Motor Vehicle Parts, Used

421210 Furniture Wholesalers *see* SIC 5021: Furniture

421220 Home Furnishing Wholesalers *see* SIC 5023: Home Furnishings

421310 Lumber, Plywood, Millwork, and Wood Panel Wholesalers *see* SIC 5031: Lumber, Plywood, Millwork, and Wood Panels; SIC 5211: Lumber and Other Building Materials Dealers

421320 Brick, Stone and Related Construction Material Wholesalers *see* SIC 5032: Brick, Stone and Related Construction Materials

421330 Roofing, Siding, and Insulation Material Wholesalers *see* SIC 5033: Roofing, Siding, and Insulation Materials

421390 Other Construction Material Wholesalers *see* SIC 5039: Construction Materials, NEC

421410 Photographic Equipment and Supplies Wholesalers *see* SIC 5043: Photographic Equipment and Supplies

421420 Office Equipment Wholesalers *see* SIC 5044: Office Equipment

421430 Computer and Computer Peripheral Equipment and Software Wholesalers *see* SIC 5045: Computers and Computer Peripheral Equipment and Software

421440 Other Commercial Equipment Wholesalers *see* SIC 5046: Commercial Equipment, NEC

421450 Medical, Dental and Hospital Equipment and Supplies Wholesalers *see* SIC 5047: Medical, Dental, and Hospital Equipment and Supplies

421460 Ophthalmic Goods Wholesalers *see* SIC 5048: Ophthalmic Goods

421490 Other Professional Equipment and Supplies Wholesalers *see* SIC 5049: Professional Equipment and Supplies, NEC

421510 Metals Service Centers and Offices *see* SIC 5051: Metals Service Centers and Offices

421520 Coal and Other Mineral and Ore Wholesalers *see* SIC 5052: Coal and Other Minerals and Ores

421610 Electrical Apparatus and Equipment, Wiring Supplies and Construction Material Wholesalers *see* SIC 5063: Electrical Apparatus and Equipment Wiring Supplies, and Construction Materials

421620 Electrical Appliance, Television and Radio Set Wholesalers *see* SIC 5064: Electrical Appliances, Television and Radio Sets

421690 Other Electronic Parts and Equipment Wholesalers *see* SIC 5065: Electronic Parts and Equipment, Not Elsewhere Classified

421710 Hardware Wholesalers *see* SIC 5072: Hardware

421720 Plumbing and Heating Equipment and Supplies (Hydronics) Wholesalers *see* SIC 5074: Plumbing and Heating Equipment and Supplies (Hydronics)

421730 Warm Air Heating and Air-Conditioning Equipment and Supplies Wholesalers *see* SIC 5075: Warm Air Heating and Air-Conditioning Equipment and Supplies

421740 Refrigeration Equipment and Supplies Wholesalers *see* SIC 5078: Refrigeration Equipment and Supplies

421810 Construction and Mining (except Petroleum) Machinery and Equipment Wholesalers *see* SIC 5082: Construction and Mining (Except Petroleum) Machinery and Equipment

421820 Farm and Garden Machinery and Equipment Wholesalers *see* SIC 5083: Farm and Garden Machinery and Equipment

421830 Industrial Machinery and Equipment Wholesalers *see* SIC 5084: Industrial Machinery and Equipment; SIC 5085: Industrial Supplies

421840 Industrial Supplies Wholesalers *see* SIC 5085: Industrial Supplies

421850 Service Establishment Equipment and Supplies Wholesalers *see* SIC 5087: Service Establishment Equipment and Supplies

421860 Transportation Equipment and Supplies (except Motor Vehicles) Wholesalers *see* SIC 5088: Transportation Equipment and Supplies, Except Motor Vehicles

421910 Sporting and Recreational Goods and Supplies Wholesalers *see* SIC 5091: Sporting and Recreational Goods and Supplies

421920 Toy and Hobby Goods and Supplies Wholesalers *see* SIC 5092: Toys and Hobby Goods and Supplies

421930 Recyclable Material Wholesalers *see* SIC 5093: Scrap and Waste Materials

421940 Jewelry, Watch , Precious Stone, and Precious Metal Wholesalers *see* SIC 5094: Jewelry, Watches, Precious Stones, and Precious Metals

421990 Other Miscellaneous Durable Goods Wholesalers *see* SIC 5099: Durable Goods, NEC; SIC 7822: Motion Picture and Video Tape Distribution

422110 Printing and Writing Paper Wholesalers *see* SIC 5111: Printing and Writing Paper

422120 Stationery and Office Supplies Wholesalers *see* SIC 5112: Stationery and Office Supplies

422130 Industrial and Personal Service Paper Wholesalers *see* SIC 5113: Industrial and Personal Service Paper

422210 Drugs, Drug Proprietaries, and Druggists' Sundries Wholesalers *see* SIC 5122: Drugs, Drug Proprietaries, and Druggists' Sundries

422310 Piece Goods, Notions, and Other Dry Goods Wholesalers *see* SIC 5131: Piece Goods, Notions, and Other Dry Goods

422320 Men's and Boys' Clothing and Furnishings Wholesalers *see* SIC 5136: Men's and Boys' Clothing and Furnishings

422330 Women's, Children's, and Infants' Clothing and Accessories Wholesalers *see* SIC 5137: Women's Children's and Infants' Clothing and Accessories

422340 Footwear Wholesalers *see* SIC 5139: Footwear

422410 General Line Grocery Wholesalers *see* SIC 5141: Groceries, General Line

422420 Packaged Frozen Food Wholesalers *see* SIC 5142: Packaged Frozen Foods

422430 Dairy Products (except Dried or Canned) Wholesalers *see* SIC 5143: Dairy Products, Except Dried or Canned

422440 Poultry and Poultry Product Wholesalers *see* SIC 5144: Poultry and Poultry Products

422450 Confectionery Wholesalers *see* SIC 5145: Confectionery

422460 Fish and Seafood Wholesalers *see* SIC 5146: Fish and Seafoods

422470 Meat and Meat Product Wholesalers *see* SIC 5147: Meats and Meat Products

422480 Fresh Fruit and Vegetable Wholesalers *see* SIC 5148: Fresh Fruits and Vegetables

422490 Other Grocery and Related Product Wholesalers *see* SIC 5149: Groceries and Related Products, NEC

422510 Grain and Field Bean Wholesalers *see* SIC 5153: Grain and Field Beans

422520 Livestock Wholesalers *see* SIC 5154: Livestock

422590 Other Farm Product Raw Material Wholesalers *see* SIC 5159: Farm-Product Raw Materials, NEC

422610 Plastics Materials and Basic Forms and Shapes Wholesalers *see* SIC 5162: Plastics Materials and Basic Forms and Shapes

422690 Other Chemical and Allied Products Wholesalers *see* SIC 5169: Chemicals and Allied Products, NEC

422710 Petroleum Bulk Stations and Terminals *see* SIC 5171: Petroleum Bulk Stations and Terminals

422720 Petroleum and Petroleum Products Wholesalers (except Bulk Stations and Terminals) *see* SIC 5172: Petroleum and Petroleum Products Wholesalers, Except Bulk Stations and Terminals

422810 Beer and Ale Wholesalers *see* SIC 5181: Beer and Ale

422820 Wine and Distilled Alcoholic Beverage Wholesalers *see* SIC 5182: Wine and Distilled Alcoholic Beverages

422910 Farm Supplies Wholesalers *see* SIC 5191: Farm Supplies

422920 Book, Periodical and Newspaper Wholesalers *see* SIC 5192: Books, Periodicals, and Newspapers

422930 Flower, Nursery Stock and Florists' Supplies Wholesalers *see* SIC 5193: Flowers, Nursery Stock, and Florists' Supplies

422940 Tobacco and Tobacco Product Wholesalers *see* SIC 5194: Tobacco and Tobacco Products

422950 Paint, Varnish and Supplies Wholesalers *see* SIC 5198: Paint, Varnishes, and Supplies; SIC 5231: Paint, Glass, and Wallpaper Stores

422990 Other Miscellaneous Nondurable Goods Wholesalers *see* SIC 5199: Nondurable Goods, NEC

RETAIL TRADE

441110 New Car Dealers *see* SIC 5511: Motor Vehicle Dealers (New and Used)

441120 Used Car Dealers *see* SIC 5521: Motor Vehicle Dealers (Used Only)

441210 Recreational Vehicle Dealers *see* SIC 5561: Recreational Vehicle Dealers

441221 Motorcycle Dealers *see* SIC 5571: Motorcycle Dealers

441222 Boat Dealers *see* SIC 5551: Boat Dealers

441229 All Other Motor Vehicle Dealers *see* SIC 5599: Automotive Dealers, NEC

441310 Automotive Parts and Accessories Stores *see* SIC 5013: Motor Vehicle Supplies and New Parts; SIC 5531: Auto and Home Supply Stores

441310 Automotive Parts and Accessories Stores *see* SIC 5731: Radio, Television, and Consumer Electronics Stores

441320 Tire Dealers *see* SIC 5014: Tires and Tubes; SIC 5531: Auto and Home Supply Stores

442110 Furniture Stores *see* SIC 5021: Furniture; SIC 5712: Furniture Stores

442210 Floor Covering Stores *see* SIC 5023: Home Furnishings; SIC 5713: Floor Covering Stores

442291 Window Treatment Stores *see* SIC 5714: Drapery, Curtain, and Upholstery Stores; SIC 5719: Miscellaneous Homefurnishings Stores

442299 All Other Home Furnishings Stores *see* SIC 5719: Miscellaneous Homefurnishings Stores; SIC 5722: Household Appliance Stores

443111 Household Appliance Stores *see* SIC 5999: Miscellaneous Retail Stores, NEC; SIC 7623: Refrigeration and Air-Conditioning Services and Repair Shops; SIC 7629: Electrical and Electronic Repair Shops, NEC

443112 Radio, Television, and Other Electronics Stores *see* SIC 5731: Radio, Television, and Consumer Electronics Stores; SIC 5999: Miscellaneous Retail Stores, NEC; SIC 7622: Radio and Television Repair Shops

443120 Computer and Software Stores *see* SIC 5045: Computers and Computer Peripheral Equipment and Software; SIC 5734: Computer and Computer Software Stores; SIC 7378: Computer Maintenance and Repair

443130 Camera and Photographic Supplies Stores *see* SIC 5946: Camera and Photographic Supply Stores

444110 Home Centers *see* SIC 5211: Lumber and Other Building Materials Dealers

444120 Paint and Wallpaper Stores *see* SIC 5198: Paint, Varnishes, and Supplies; SIC 5231: Paint, Glass, and Wallpaper Stores

444130 Hardware Stores *see* SIC 5251: Hardware Stores

444190 Other Building Material Dealers *see* SIC 5031: Lumber, Plywood, Millwork, and Wood Panels; SIC 5032: Brick, Stone and Related Construction Materials; SIC 5039: Construction Materials, NEC; SIC 5063: Electrical Apparatus and Equipment Wiring Supplies, and Construction Materials; SIC 5074: Plumbing and Heating Equipment and Supplies (Hydronics); SIC 5211: Lumber and Other Building Materials Dealers; SIC 5231: Paint, Glass, and Wallpaper Stores

444210 Outdoor Power Equipment Stores *see* SIC 5083: Farm and Garden Machinery and Equipment; SIC 5261: Retail Nurseries, Lawn and Garden Supply Stores

444220 Nursery and Garden Centers *see* SIC 5191: Farm Supplies; SIC 5193: Flowers, Nursery Stock, and Florists' Supplies; SIC 5261: Retail Nurseries, Lawn and Garden Supply Stores

445110 Supermarkets and Other Grocery (except Convenience) Stores *see* SIC 5411: Grocery Stores

445120 Convenience Stores *see* SIC 5411: Grocery Stores

445210 Meat Markets *see* SIC 5421: Meat and Fish (Seafood) Markets, Including Freezer Provisioners; SIC 5499: Miscellaneous Food Stores

445220 Fish and Seafood Markets *see* SIC 5421: Meat and Fish (Seafood) Markets, Including Freezer Provisioners

445230 Fruit and Vegetable Markets *see* SIC 5431: Fruit and Vegetable Markets

445291 Baked Goods Stores *see* SIC 5461: Retail Bakeries

445292 Confectionery and Nut Stores *see* SIC 5441: Candy, Nut, and Confectionery Stores

445299 All Other Specialty Food Stores *see* SIC 5451: Dairy Products Stores; SIC 5499: Miscellaneous Food Stores

445310 Beer, Wine and Liquor Stores *see* SIC 5921: Liquor Stores

446110 Pharmacies and Drug Stores *see* SIC 5912: Drug Stores and Proprietary Stores

446120 Cosmetics, Beauty Supplies, and Perfume Stores *see* SIC 5087: Service Establishment Equipment and Supplies

446120 Cosmetics, Beauty Supplies, and Perfume Stores *see* SIC 5999: Miscellaneous Retail Stores, NEC

446130 Optical Goods Stores *see* SIC 5995: Optical Goods Stores

446191 Food (Health) Supplement Stores *see* SIC 5499: Miscellaneous Food Stores

446199 All Other Health and Personal Care Stores *see* SIC 5047: Medical, Dental, and Hospital Equipment and Supplies; SIC 5999: Miscellaneous Retail Stores, NEC

447110 Gasoline Stations with Convenience Stores *see* SIC 5411: Grocery Stores; SIC 5541: Gasoline Service Stations

447190 Other Gasoline Stations *see* SIC 5541: Gasoline Service Stations

448110 Men's Clothing Stores *see* SIC 5611: Men's and Boys' Clothing and Accessory Stores

448120 Women's Clothing Stores *see* SIC 5621: Women's Clothing Stores

448130 Children's and Infants' Clothing Stores *see* SIC 5641: Children's and Infants' Wear Stores

448140 Family Clothing Stores *see* SIC 5651: Family Clothing Stores

448150 Clothing Accessories Stores *see* SIC 5611: Men's and Boys' Clothing and Accessory Stores; SIC 5632: Women's Accessory and Specialty Stores; SIC 5699: Miscellaneous Apparel and Accessory Stores

448190 Other Clothing Stores *see* SIC 5632: Women's Accessory and Specialty Stores; SIC 5699: Miscellaneous Apparel and Accessory Stores

448210 Shoe Stores *see* SIC 5661: Shoe Stores

448310 Jewelry Stores *see* SIC 5944: Jewelry Stores; SIC 5999: Miscellaneous Retail Stores, NEC

448320 Luggage and Leather Goods Stores *see* SIC 5948: Luggage and Leather Goods Stores

451110 Sporting Goods Stores *see* SIC 5941: Sporting Goods Stores and Bicycle Shops; SIC 7699: Repair Shops and Related Services, NEC

451120 Hobby, Toy and Game Stores *see* SIC 5945: Hobby, Toy, and Game Shops

451130 Sewing, Needlework and Piece Goods Stores *see* SIC 5714: Drapery, Curtain, and Upholstery Stores; SIC 5949: Sewing, Needlework, and Piece Goods Stores

451140 Musical Instrument and Supplies Stores *see* SIC 5736: Musical Instrument Stores

451211 Book Stores *see* SIC 5942: Book Stores

451212 News Dealers and Newsstands *see* SIC 5994: News Dealers and Newsstands

451220 Prerecorded Tape, Compact Disc and Record Stores *see* SIC 5735: Record and Prerecorded Tape Stores

452110 Department Stores *see* SIC 5311: Department Stores

452910 Warehouse Clubs and Superstores *see* SIC 5399: Miscellaneous General Merchandise Stores; SIC 5411: Grocery Stores

452990 All Other General Merchandise Stores *see* SIC 5331: Variety Stores; SIC 5399: Miscellaneous General Merchandise Stores

453110 Florists *see* SIC 5992: Florists

453210 Office Supplies and Stationery Stores *see* SIC 5049: Professional Equipment and Supplies, NEC; SIC 5112: Stationery and Office Supplies; SIC 5943: Stationery Stores

453220 Gift, Novelty and Souvenir Stores *see* SIC 5947: Gift, Novelty, and Souvenir Shops

453310 Used Merchandise Stores *see* SIC 5932: Used Merchandise Stores

453910 Pet and Pet Supplies Stores *see* SIC 5999: Miscellaneous Retail Stores, NEC

453920 Art Dealers *see* SIC 5999: Miscellaneous Retail Stores, NEC

453930 Manufactured (Mobile) Home Dealers *see* SIC 5271: Mobile Home Dealers

453991 Tobacco Stores *see* SIC 5993: Tobacco Stores and Stands

453998 All Other Miscellaneous Store Retailers (except Tobacco Stores) *see* SIC 5261: Retail Nurseries, Lawn and Garden Supply Stores; SIC 5999: Miscellaneous Retail Stores, NEC

454110 Electronic Shopping and Mail-Order Houses *see* SIC 5961: Catalog and Mail-Order Houses

454210 Vending Machine Operators *see* SIC 5962: Automatic Merchandising Machine Operator

454311 Heating Oil Dealers *see* SIC 5171: Petroleum Bulk Stations and Terminals; SIC 5983: Fuel Oil Dealers

454312 Liquefied Petroleum Gas (Bottled Gas) Dealers *see* SIC 5171: Petroleum Bulk Stations and Terminals; SIC 5984: Liquefied Petroleum Gas (Bottled Gas) Dealers

454319 Other Fuel Dealers *see* SIC 5989: Fuel Dealers, NEC

454390 Other Direct Selling Establishments *see* SIC 5421: Meat and Fish (Seafood) Markets, Including Freezer Provisioners; SIC 5963: Direct Selling Establishments

TRANSPORTATION & WAREHOUSING

481111 Scheduled Passenger Air Transportation *see* SIC 4512: Air Transportation, Scheduled

481112 Scheduled Freight Air Transportation *see* SIC 4512: Air Transportation, Scheduled

481211 Nonscheduled Chartered Passenger Air Transportation *see* SIC 4522: Air Transportation, Nonscheduled

481212 Nonscheduled Chartered Freight Air Transportation *see* SIC 4522: Air Transportation, Nonscheduled

481219 Other Nonscheduled Air Transportation *see* SIC 0721: Crop Planting, Cultivating and Protecting; SIC 7319: Advertising, NEC; SIC 7335: Commercial Photography

482111 Line-Haul Railroads *see* SIC 4011: Railroads, Line-haul Operating

482112 Short Line Railroads *see* SIC 4013: Railroad Switching and Terminal Establishments

483111 Deep Sea Freight Transportation *see* SIC 4412: Deep Sea Foreign Transportation of Freight

483112 Deep Sea Passenger Transportation *see* SIC 4481: Deep Sea Transportation of Passengers, Except by Ferry

483113 Coastal and Great Lakes Freight Transportation *see* SIC 4424: Deep Sea Domestic Transportation of Freight; SIC 4432: Freight Transportation on the Great Lakes-St. Lawrence Seaway; SIC 4492: Towing and Tugboat Services

483114 Coastal and Great Lakes Passenger Transportation *see* SIC 4481: Deep Sea Transportation of Passengers, Except by Ferry; SIC 4482: Ferries

483211 Inland Water Freight Transportation *see* SIC 4449: Water Transportation of Freight, NEC; SIC 4492: Towing and Tugboat Services

483212 Inland Water Passenger Transportation *see* SIC 4482: Ferries; SIC 4489: Water Transportation of Passengers, NEC

484110 General Freight Trucking, Local *see* SIC 4212: Local Trucking Without Storage; SIC 4214: Local Trucking with Storage

484121 General Freight Trucking, Long-Distance, Truckload *see* SIC 4213: Trucking, Except Local

484122 General Freight Trucking, Long-Distance, Less Than Truckload *see* SIC 4213: Trucking, Except Local

484210 Used Household and Office Goods Moving *see* SIC 4212: Local Trucking Without Storage; SIC 4213: Trucking, Except Local; SIC 4214: Local Trucking with Storage

484220 Specialized Freight (except Used Goods) Trucking, Local *see* SIC 4212: Local Trucking Without Storage; SIC 4214: Local Trucking with Storage

484230 Specialized Freight (except Used Goods) Trucking, Long-Distance *see* SIC 4213: Trucking, Except Local

485111 Mixed Mode Transit Systems *see* SIC 4111: Local and Suburban Transit

485112 Commuter Rail Systems *see* SIC 4111: Local and Suburban Transit

485113 Bus and Motor Vehicle Transit Systems *see* SIC 4111: Local and Suburban Transit

485119 Other Urban Transit Systems *see* SIC 4111: Local and Suburban Transit

485210 Interurban and Rural Bus Lines *see* SIC 4131: Intercity and Rural Bus Transportation

485310 Taxi Service *see* SIC 4121: Taxicabs

485320 Limousine Service *see* SIC 4119: Local Passenger Transportation, NEC

485410 School and Employee Bus Industry *see* SIC 4119: Local Passenger Transportation, NEC; SIC 4151: School Buses

485510 Charter Bus Industry *see* SIC 4141: Local Bus Charter Service; SIC 4142: Bus Charter Service, Except Local

485991 Special Needs Transportation *see* SIC 4119: Local Passenger Transportation, NEC

485999 All Other Transit and Ground Passenger Transportation *see* SIC 4111: Local and Suburban Transit; SIC 4119: Local Passenger Transportation, NEC

486110 Pipeline Transportation of Crude Oil *see* SIC 4612: Crude Petroleum Pipelines

486210 Pipeline Transportation of Natural Gas *see* SIC 4922: Natural Gas Transmission; SIC 4923: Natural Gas Transmission and Distribution

486910 Pipeline Transportation of Refined Petroleum Products *see* SIC 4613: Refined Petroleum Pipelines

486990 All Other Pipeline Transportation *see* SIC 4619: Pipelines, NEC

487110 Scenic and Sightseeing Transportation, Land *see* SIC 4119: Local Passenger Transportation, NEC; SIC 4789: Transportation Services, NEC; SIC 7999: Amusement and Recreation Services, NEC

487210 Scenic and Sightseeing Transportation, Water *see* SIC 4489: Water Transportation of Passengers, NEC; SIC 7999: Amusement and Recreation Services, NEC

487990 Scenic and Sightseeing Transportation, Other *see* SIC 4522: Air Transportation, Nonscheduled; SIC 7999: Amusement and Recreation Services, NEC

488111 Air Traffic Control *see* SIC 4581: Airports, Flying Fields, and Airport Terminal Services; SIC 9621: Regulations and Administration of Transportation Programs

488119 Other Airport Operations *see* SIC 4581: Airports, Flying Fields, and Airport Terminal Services; SIC 4959: Sanitary Services, NEC

488190 Other Support Activities for Air Transportation *see* SIC 4581: Airports, Flying Fields, and Airport Terminal Services

488210 Support Activities for Rail Transportation *see* SIC 4013: Railroad Switching and Terminal Establishments; SIC 4741: Rental of Railroad Cars; SIC 4789: Transportation Services, NEC

488310 Port and Harbor Operations *see* SIC 4491: Marine Cargo Handling; SIC 4499: Water Transportation Services, NEC

488320 Marine Cargo Handling *see* SIC 4491: Marine Cargo Handling

488330 Navigational Services to Shipping *see* SIC 4492: Towing and Tugboat Services; SIC 4499: Water Transportation Services, NEC

488390 Other Support Activities for Water Transportation *see* SIC 4499: Water Transportation Services, NEC; SIC 4785: Fixed Facilities and Inspection and Weighing Services for Motor Vehicle Transportation; SIC 7699: Repair Shops and Related Services, NEC

488410 Motor Vehicle Towing *see* SIC 7549: Automotive Services, Except Repair and Carwashes

488490 Other Support Activities for Road Transportation *see* SIC 4173: Terminal and Service Facilities for Motor Vehicle Passenger Transportation; SIC 4231: Terminal and Joint Terminal Maintenance Facilities for Motor Freight Transportation; SIC 4785: Fixed Facilities and Inspection and Weighing Services for Motor Vehicle Transportation

488510 Freight Transportation Arrangement *see* SIC 4731: Arrangement of Transportation of Freight and Cargo

488991 Packing and Crating *see* SIC 4783: Packing and Crating

488999 All Other Support Activities for Transportation *see* SIC 4729: Arrangement of Passenger Transportation, NEC; SIC 4789: Transportation Services, NEC

491110 Postal Service *see* SIC 4311: United States Postal Service

492110 Couriers *see* SIC 4215: Couriers Services Except by Air; SIC 4513: Air Courier Services

492210 Local Messengers and Local Delivery *see* SIC 4215: Couriers Services Except by Air

493110 General Warehousing and Storage Facilities *see* SIC 4225: General Warehousing and Storage; SIC 4226: Special Warehousing and Storage, NEC

493120 Refrigerated Storage Facilities *see* SIC 4222: Refrigerated Warehousing and Storage; SIC 4226: Special Warehousing and Storage, NEC

493130 Farm Product Storage Facilities *see* SIC 4221: Farm Product Warehousing and Storage

493190 All Other Warehousing and Storage Facilities *see* SIC 4226: Special Warehousing and Storage, NEC

INFORMATION

511110 Newspaper Publishers *see* SIC 2711: Newspapers: Publishing, or Publishing and Printing

511120 Periodical Publishers *see* SIC 2721: Periodicals: Publishing, or Publishing and Printing

511130 Book Publishers *see* SIC 2731: Books: Publishing, or Publishing and Printing

511140 Database and Directory Publishers *see* SIC 2741: Miscellaneous Publishing

511191 Greeting Card Publishers *see* SIC 2771: Greeting Cards

511199 All Other Publishers *see* SIC 2741: Miscellaneous Publishing

511210 Software Publishers *see* SIC 7372: Prepackaged Software

512110 Motion Picture and Video Production *see* SIC 7812: Motion Picture and Video Tape Production

512120 Motion Picture and Video Distribution *see* SIC 7822: Motion Picture and Video Tape Distribution; SIC 7829: Services Allied to Motion Picture Distribution

512131 Motion Picture Theaters, Except Drive-In *see* SIC 7832: Motion Picture Theaters, Except Drive-In

512132 Drive-In Motion Picture Theaters *see* SIC 7833: Drive-In Motion Picture Theaters

512191 Teleproduction and Other Post-Production Services *see* SIC 7819: Services Allied to Motion Picture Production

512199 Other Motion Picture and Video Industries *see* SIC 7819: Services Allied to Motion Picture Production; SIC 7829: Services Allied to Motion Picture Distribution

512210 Record Production *see* SIC 8999: Services, NEC

512220 Integrated Record Production/Distribution *see* SIC 3652: Phonograph Records and Prerecorded Audio Tapes and Disks

512230 Music Publishers *see* SIC 2731: Books: Publishing, or Publishing and Printing; SIC 2741: Miscellaneous Publishing; SIC 8999: Services, NEC

512240 Sound Recording Studios *see* SIC 7389: Business Services, NEC

512290 Other Sound Recording Industries *see* SIC 7389: Business Services, NEC; SIC 7922: Theatrical Producers (Except Motion Picture) and Miscellaneous Theatrical Services

513111 Radio Networks *see* SIC 4832: Radio Broadcasting Stations

513112 Radio Stations *see* SIC 4832: Radio Broadcasting Stations

513120 Television Broadcasting *see* SIC 4833: Television Broadcasting Stations

513210 Cable Networks *see* SIC 4841: Cable and Other Pay Television Services

513220 Cable and Other Program Distribution *see* SIC 4841: Cable and Other Pay Television Services

513310 Wired Telecommunications Carriers *see* SIC 4813: Telephone Communications, Except Radiotelephone; SIC 4822: Telegraph and Other Message Communications

513321 Paging *see* SIC 4812: Radiotelephone Communications

513322 Cellular and Other Wireless Telecommunications *see* SIC 4812: Radiotelephone Communications; SIC 4899: Communications Services, NEC

513330 Telecommunications Resellers *see* SIC 4812: Radiotelephone Communications; SIC 4813: Telephone Communications, Except Radiotelephone

513340 Satellite Telecommunications *see* SIC 4899: Communications Services, NEC

513390 Other Telecommunications *see* SIC 4899: Communications Services, NEC

514110 New Syndicates *see* SIC 7383: News Syndicates

514120 Libraries and Archives *see* SIC 8231: Libraries

514191 On-Line Information Services *see* SIC 7375: Information Retrieval Services

514199 All Other Information Services *see* SIC 8999: Services, NEC

514210 Data Processing Services *see* SIC 7374: Computer Processing and Data Preparation and Processing Services

FINANCE & INSURANCE

521110 Monetary Authorities-Central Banks *see* SIC 6011: Federal Reserve Banks

522110 Commercial Banking *see* SIC 6021: National Commercial Banks; SIC 6022: State Commercial Banks; SIC 6029: Commercial Banks, NEC; SIC 6081: Branches and Agencies of Foreign Banks

522120 Savings Institutions *see* SIC 6035: Savings Institutions, Federally Chartered; SIC 6036: Savings institutions, Not Federally Chartered

522130 Credit Unions *see* SIC 6061: Credit Unions, Federally Chartered; SIC 6062: Credit Unions, Not Federally Chartered

522190 Other Depository Intermediation *see* SIC 6022: State Commercial Banks

522210 Credit Card Issuing *see* SIC 6021: National Commercial Banks; SIC 6022: State Commercial Banks; SIC 6141: Personal Credit Institutions

522220 Sales Financing *see* SIC 6141: Personal Credit Institutions; SIC 6153: Short-Term Business Credit Institutions, Except Agricultural; SIC 6159: Miscellaneous Business Credit Institutions

522291 Consumer Lending *see* SIC 6141: Personal Credit Institutions

522292 Real Estate Credit *see* SIC 6162: Mortgage Bankers and Loan Correspondents

522293 International Trade Financing *see* SIC 6081: Branches and Agencies of Foreign Banks; SIC 6082: Foreign Trade and International Banking Institutions; SIC 6111: Federal and Federally Sponsored Credit Agencies; SIC 6159: Miscellaneous Business Credit Institutions

522294 Secondary Market Financing *see* SIC 6111: Federal and Federally Sponsored Credit Agencies

522298 All Other Non-Depository Credit Intermediation *see* SIC 5932: Used Merchandise Stores; SIC 6081: Branches and Agencies of Foreign Banks; SIC 6111: Federal and Federally Sponsored Credit Agencies; SIC 6153: Short-Term Business Credit Institutions, Except Agricultural; SIC 6159: Miscellaneous Business Credit Institutions

522310 Mortgage and Other Loan Brokers *see* SIC 6163: Loan Brokers

522320 Financial Transactions Processing, Reserve, and Clearing House Activities *see* SIC 6019: Central Reserve Depository Institutions, NEC; SIC 6099: Functions Related to Deposit Banking, NEC; SIC 6153: Short-Term Business Credit Institutions, Except Agricultural; SIC 7389: Business Services, NEC

522390 Other Activities Related to Credit Intermediation *see* SIC 6099: Functions Related to Deposit Banking, NEC; SIC 6162: Mortgage Bankers and Loan Correspondents

523110 Investment Banking and Securities Dealing *see* SIC 6211: Security Brokers, Dealers, and Flotation Companies

523120 Securities Brokerage *see* SIC 6211: Security Brokers, Dealers, and Flotation Companies

523130 Commodity Contracts Dealing *see* SIC 6099: Functions Related to Deposit Banking, NEC; SIC 6221: Commodity Contracts Brokers and Dealers; SIC 6799: Investors, NEC

523140 Commodity Brokerage *see* SIC 6221: Commodity Contracts Brokers and Dealers

523210 Securities and Commodity Exchanges *see* SIC 6231: Security and Commodity Exchanges

523910 Miscellaneous Intermediation *see* SIC 6211: Security Brokers, Dealers, and Flotation Companies; SIC 6799: Investors, NEC

523920 Portfolio Management *see* SIC 6282: Investment Advice; SIC 6371: Pension, Health, and Welfare Funds; SIC 6733: Trusts, Except Educational, Religious, and Charitable; SIC 6799: Investors, NEC

523930 Investment Advice *see* SIC 6282: Investment Advice

523991 Trust, Fiduciary and Custody Activities *see* SIC 6021: National Commercial Banks; SIC 6022: State Commercial Banks; SIC 6091: Nondeposit Trust Facilities; SIC 6099: Functions Related to Deposit Banking, NEC; SIC 6289: Services Allied With the Exchange of Securities or Commodities, NEC; SIC 6733: Trusts, Except Educational, Religious, and Charitable

523999 Miscellaneous Financial Investment Activities *see* SIC 6099: Functions Related to Deposit Banking, NEC; SIC 6211: Security Brokers, Dealers, and Flotation Companies; SIC 6289: Services Allied With the Exchange of Securities or Commodities, NEC; SIC 6792: Oil Royalty Traders; SIC 6799: Investors, NEC

524113 Direct Life Insurance Carriers *see* SIC 6311: Life Insurance

524114 Direct Health and Medical Insurance Carriers *see* SIC 6321: Accident and Health Insurance; SIC 6324: Hospital and Medical Service Plans

524126 Direct Property and Casualty Insurance Carriers *see* SIC 6331: Fire, Marine, and Casualty Insurance; SIC 6351: Surety Insurance

524127 Direct Title Insurance Carriers *see* SIC 6361: Title Insurance

524128 Other Direct Insurance Carriers (except Life, Health, and Medical) *see* SIC 6399: Insurance Carriers, NEC

524130 Reinsurance Carriers *see* SIC 6311: Life Insurance; SIC 6321: Accident and Health Insurance; SIC 6324: Hospital and Medical Service Plans; SIC 6331: Fire, Marine, and Casualty Insurance; SIC 6351: Surety Insurance; SIC 6361: Title Insurance

524210 Insurance Agencies and Brokerages *see* SIC 6411: Insurance Agents, Brokers, and Service

524291 Claims Adjusters *see* SIC 6411: Insurance Agents, Brokers, and Service

524292 Third Party Administration for Insurance and Pension Funds *see* SIC 6371: Pension, Health, and Welfare Funds; SIC 6411: Insurance Agents, Brokers, and Service

524298 All Other Insurance Related Activities *see* SIC 6411: Insurance Agents, Brokers, and Service

525110 Pension Funds *see* SIC 6371: Pension, Health, and Welfare Funds

525120 Health and Welfare Funds *see* SIC 6371: Pension, Health, and Welfare Funds

525190 Other Insurance and Employee Benefit Funds *see* SIC 6321: Accident and Health Insurance; SIC 6324: Hospital and Medical Service Plans; SIC 6331: Fire, Marine, and Casualty Insurance; SIC 6733: Trusts, Except Educational, Religious, and Charitable

525910 Open-End Investment Funds *see* SIC 6722: Management Investment Offices, Open-End

525920 Trusts, Estates, and Agency Accounts *see* SIC 6733: Trusts, Except Educational, Religious, and Charitable

525930 Real Estate Investment Trusts *see* SIC 6798: Real Estate Investment Trusts

525990 Other Financial Vehicles *see* SIC 6726: Unit Investment Trusts, Face-Amount Certificate Offices, and Closed-End Management Investment Offices

REAL ESTATE & RENTAL & LEASING

531110 Lessors of Residential Buildings and Dwellings *see* SIC 6513: Operators of Apartment Buildings; SIC 6514: Operators of Dwellings Other Than Apartment Buildings

531120 Lessors of Nonresidential Buildings (except Mini-warehouses) *see* SIC 6512: Operators of Nonresidential Buildings

531130 Lessors of Mini-warehouses and Self Storage Units *see* SIC 4225: General Warehousing and Storage

531190 Lessors of Other Real Estate Property *see* SIC 6515: Operators of Residential Mobile Home Sites; SIC 6517:

Lessors of Railroad Property; SIC 6519: Lessors of Real Property, NEC

531210 Offices of Real Estate Agents and Brokers *see* SIC 6531: Real Estate Agents and Managers

531311 Residential Property Managers *see* SIC 6531: Real Estate Agents and Managers

531312 Nonresidential Property Managers *see* SIC 6531: Real Estate Agents and Managers

531320 Offices of Real Estate Appraisers *see* SIC 6531: Real Estate Agents and Managers

531390 Other Activities Related to Real Estate *see* SIC 6531: Real Estate Agents and Managers

532111 Passenger Cars Rental *see* SIC 7514: Passenger Car Rental

532112 Passenger Cars Leasing *see* SIC 7515: Passenger Car Leasing

532120 Truck, Utility Trailer and RV (Recreational Vehicle) Rental and Leasing *see* SIC 7513: Truck Rental and Leasing, Without Drivers; SIC 7519: Utility Trailer and Recreational Vehicle Rental

532210 Consumer Electronics and Appliances Rental *see* SIC 7359: Equipment Rental and Leasing, NEC

532220 Formal Wear and Costumes Rental *see* SIC 7299: Miscellaneous Personal Services, NEC; SIC 7819: Services Allied to Motion Picture Production

532230 Video Tapes and Disc Rental *see* SIC 7841: Video Tape Rental

532291 Home Health Equipment Rental *see* SIC 7352: Medical Equipment Rental and Leasing

532292 Recreational Goods Rental *see* SIC 7999: Amusement and Recreation Services, NEC

532299 All Other Consumer Goods Rental *see* SIC 7359: Equipment Rental and Leasing, NEC

532310 General Rental Centers *see* SIC 7359: Equipment Rental and Leasing, NEC

532411 Commercial Air, Rail, and Water Transportation Equipment Rental and Leasing *see* SIC 4499: Water Transportation Services, NEC; SIC 4741: Rental of Railroad Cars; SIC 7359: Equipment Rental and Leasing, NEC

532412 Construction, Mining and Forestry Machinery and Equipment Rental and Leasing *see* SIC 7353: Heavy Construction Equipment Rental and Leasing; SIC 7359: Equipment Rental and Leasing, NEC

532420 Office Machinery and Equipment Rental and Leasing *see* SIC 7359: Equipment Rental and Leasing, NEC; SIC 7377: Computer Rental and Leasing

532490 Other Commercial and Industrial Machinery and Equipment Rental and Leasing *see* SIC 7352: Medical Equipment Rental and Leasing; SIC 7359: Equipment Rental and Leasing, NEC; SIC 7819: Services Allied to Motion Picture Production; SIC 7922: Theatrical Producers (Except Motion Picture) and Miscellaneous Theatrical Services

533110 Owners and Lessors of Other Non-Financial Assets *see* SIC 6792: Oil Royalty Traders; SIC 6794: Patent Owners and Lessors

PROFESSIONAL, SCIENTIFIC, & TECHNICAL SERVICES

541110 Offices of Lawyers *see* SIC 8111: Legal Services

541191 Title Abstract and Settlement Offices *see* SIC 6541: Title Abstract Offices

541199 Other Legal Services *see* SIC 7389: Business Services, NEC

541211 Offices of Certified Public Accountants *see* SIC 8721: Accounting, Auditing, and Bookkeeping Services

541213 Tax Preparation Services *see* SIC 7291: Tax Return Preparation Services

541214 Payroll Services *see* SIC 7819: Services Allied to Motion Picture Production; SIC 8721: Accounting, Auditing, and Bookkeeping Services

541219 Other Accounting Services *see* SIC 8721: Accounting, Auditing, and Bookkeeping Services

541310 Architectural Services *see* SIC 8712: Architectural Services

541320 Landscape Architectural Services *see* SIC 0781: Landscape Counseling and Planning

541330 Engineering Services *see* SIC 8711: Engineering Services

541340 Drafting Services *see* SIC 7389: Business Services, NEC

541350 Building Inspection Services *see* SIC 7389: Business Services, NEC

541360 Geophysical Surveying and Mapping Services *see* SIC 1081: Metal Mining Services; SIC 1382: Oil and Gas Field Exploration Services; SIC 1481: Nonmetallic Minerals Services Except Fuels; SIC 8713: Surveying Services

541370 Surveying and Mapping (except Geophysical) Services *see* SIC 7389: Business Services, NEC; SIC 8713: Surveying Services

541380 Testing Laboratories *see* SIC 8734: Testing Laboratories

541410 Interior Design Services *see* SIC 7389: Business Services, NEC

541420 Industrial Design Services *see* SIC 7389: Business Services, NEC

541430 Graphic Design Services *see* SIC 7336: Commercial Art and Graphic Design; SIC 8099: Health and Allied Services, NEC

541490 Other Specialized Design Services *see* SIC 7389: Business Services, NEC

541511 Custom Computer Programming Services *see* SIC 7371: Computer Programming Services

541512 Computer Systems Design Services *see* SIC 7373: Computer Integrated Systems Design; SIC 7379: Computer Related Services, NEC

541513 Computer Facilities Management Services *see* SIC 7376: Computer Facilities Management Services

541519 Other Computer Related Services *see* SIC 7379: Computer Related Services, NEC

541611 Administrative Management and General Management Consulting Services *see* SIC 8742: Management Consulting Services

541612 Human Resources and Executive Search Consulting Services *see* SIC 7361: Employment Agencies; SIC 8742: Management Consulting Services; SIC 8999: Services, NEC

541613 Marketing Consulting Services *see* SIC 8742: Management Consulting Services

541614 Process, Physical, Distribution and Logistics Consulting *see* SIC 8742: Management Consulting Services

541618 Other Management Consulting Services *see* SIC 4731: Arrangement of Transportation of Freight and Cargo; SIC 8748: Business Consulting Services, NEC

541620 Environmental Consulting Services *see* SIC 8999: Services, NEC

541690 Other Scientific and Technical Consulting Services *see* SIC 0781: Landscape Counseling and Planning; SIC

8748: Business Consulting Services, NEC; SIC 8999: Services, NEC

541710 Research and Development in the Physical Sciences and Engineering Sciences *see* SIC 8731: Commercial Physical and Biological Research; SIC 8733: Noncommercial Research Organizations

541720 Research and Development in the Life Sciences *see* SIC 8731: Commercial Physical and Biological Research; SIC 8733: Noncommercial Research Organizations

541730 Research and Development in the Social Sciences and Humanities *see* SIC 8732: Commercial Economic, Sociological, and Educational Research; SIC 8733: Noncommercial Research Organizations

541810 Advertising Agencies *see* SIC 7311: Advertising Agencies

541820 Public Relations Services *see* SIC 8743: Public Relations Services

541830 Media Buying Agencies *see* SIC 7319: Advertising, NEC

541840 Media Representatives *see* SIC 7313: Radio, Television, and Publishers' Advertising Representatives

541850 Display Advertising *see* SIC 7312: Outdoor Advertising Services; SIC 7319: Advertising, NEC

541860 Direct Mail Advertising *see* SIC 7331: Direct Mail Advertising Services

541870 Advertising Material Distribution Services *see* SIC 7319: Advertising, NEC

541890 Other Services Related to Advertising *see* SIC 5199: Nondurable Goods, NEC; SIC 7319: Advertising, NEC; SIC 7389: Business Services, NEC

541910 Marketing Research and Public Opinion Polling *see* SIC 8732: Commercial Economic, Sociological, and Educational Research

541921 Photographic Studios, Portrait *see* SIC 7221: Photographic Studios, Portrait

541922 Commercial Photography *see* SIC 7335: Commercial Photography; SIC 8099: Health and Allied Services, NEC

541930 Translation and Interpretation Services *see* SIC 7389: Business Services, NEC

541940 Veterinary Services *see* SIC 0741: Veterinary Service For Livestock; SIC 0742: Veterinary Services for Animal Specialties; SIC 8734: Testing Laboratories

541990 All Other Professional, Scientific and Technical Services *see* SIC 7389: Business Services, NEC

MANAGEMENT OF COMPANIES & ENTERPRISES

551111 Offices of Bank Holding Companies *see* SIC 6712: Offices of Bank Holding Companies

551112 Offices of Other Holding Companies *see* SIC 6719: Offices of Holding Companies, NEC

ADMINISTRATIVE & SUPPORT, WASTE MANAGEMENT & REMEDIATION SERVICES

561110 Office Administrative Services *see* SIC 8741: Management Services (Except Construction Management Services)

561210 Facilities Support Services *see* SIC 8744: Facilities Support Management Services

561310 Employment Placement Agencies *see* SIC 7361: Employment Agencies; SIC 7819: Services Allied to Motion Picture Production; SIC 7922: Theatrical Producers (Except Motion Picture) and Miscellaneous Theatrical Services

561320 Temporary Help Services *see* SIC 7363: Help Supply Services

561330 Employee Leasing Services *see* SIC 7363: Help Supply Services

561410 Document Preparation Services *see* SIC 7338: Secretarial and Court Reporting Services

561421 Telephone Answering Services *see* SIC 7389: Business Services, NEC

561422 Telemarketing Bureaus *see* SIC 7389: Business Services, NEC

561431 Other Business Service Centers (including Copy Shops) *see* SIC 7389: Business Services, NEC; SIC 7334: Photocopying and Duplicating Services

561439 Private Mail Centers *see* SIC 7389: Business Services, NEC

561440 Collection Agencies *see* SIC 7322: Adjustment and Collection Services

561450 Credit Bureaus *see* SIC 7323: Credit Reporting Services

561491 Repossession Services *see* SIC 7322: Adjustment and Collection Services; SIC 7389: Business Services, NEC

561492 Court Reporting and Stenotype Services *see* SIC 7338: Secretarial and Court Reporting Services

561499 All Other Business Support Services *see* SIC 7389: Business Services, NEC

561510 Travel Agencies *see* SIC 4724: Travel Agencies

561520 Tour Operators *see* SIC 4725: Tour Operators

561591 Convention and Visitors Bureaus *see* SIC 7389: Business Services, NEC

561599 All Other Travel Arrangement and Reservation Services *see* SIC 4729: Arrangement of Passenger Transportation, NEC; SIC 7389: Business Services, NEC; SIC 7999: Amusement and Recreation Services, NEC; SIC 8699: Membership Organizations, NEC

561611 Investigation Services *see* SIC 7381: Detective, Guard, and Armored Car Services

561612 Security Guards and Patrol Services *see* SIC 7381: Detective, Guard, and Armored Car Services

561613 Armored Car Services *see* SIC 7381: Detective, Guard, and Armored Car Services

561621 Security Systems Services (except Locksmiths) *see* SIC 1731: Electrical Work; SIC 7382: Security Systems Services

561622 Locksmiths *see* SIC 7699: Repair Shops and Related Services, NEC

561710 Exterminating and Pest Control Services *see* SIC 4959: Sanitary Services, NEC; SIC 7342: Disinfecting and Pest Control Services

561720 Janitorial Services *see* SIC 4581: Airports, Flying Fields, and Airport Terminal Services; SIC 7342: Disinfecting and Pest Control Services; SIC 7349: Building Cleaning and Maintenance Services, NEC

561730 Landscaping Services *see* SIC 0782: Lawn and Garden Services; SIC 0783: Ornamental Shrub and Tree Services

561740 Carpet and Upholstery Cleaning Services *see* SIC 7217: Carpet and Upholstery Cleaning

561790 Other Services to Buildings and Dwellings *see* SIC 7389: Business Services, NEC; SIC 7699: Repair Shops and Related Services, NEC

561910 Packaging and Labeling Services *see* SIC 7389: Business Services, NEC

561920 Convention and Trade Show Organizers *see* SIC 7389: Business Services, NEC

561990 All Other Support Services *see* SIC 7389: Business Services, NEC

562111 Solid Waste Collection *see* SIC 4212: Local Trucking Without Storage; SIC 4953: Refuse Systems

562112 Hazardous Waste Collection *see* SIC 4212: Local Trucking Without Storage; SIC 4953: Refuse Systems

562119 Other Waste Collection *see* SIC 4212: Local Trucking Without Storage; SIC 4953: Refuse Systems

562211 Hazardous Waste Treatment and Disposal *see* SIC 4953: Refuse Systems

562212 Solid Waste Landfills *see* SIC 4953: Refuse Systems

562213 Solid Waste Combustors and Incinerators *see* SIC 4953: Refuse Systems

562219 Other Nonhazardous Waste Treatment and Disposal *see* SIC 4953: Refuse Systems

562910 Remediation Services *see* SIC 1799: Special Trade Contractors, NEC; SIC 4959: Sanitary Services, NEC

562920 Materials Recovery Facilities *see* SIC 4953: Refuse Systems

562991 Septic Tank and Related Services *see* SIC 7359: Equipment Rental and Leasing, NEC; SIC 7699: Repair Shops and Related Services, NEC

562998 All Other Miscellaneous Waste Management *see* SIC 4959: Sanitary Services, NEC

EDUCATIONAL SERVICES

611110 Elementary and Secondary Schools *see* SIC 8211: Elementary and Secondary Schools

611210 Junior Colleges *see* SIC 8222: Junior Colleges and Technical Institutes

611310 Colleges, Universities and Professional Schools *see* SIC 8221: Colleges, Universities, and Professional Schools

611410 Business and Secretarial Schools *see* SIC 8244: Business and Secretarial Schools

611420 Computer Training *see* SIC 8243: Data Processing Schools

611430 Professional and Management Development Training Schools *see* SIC 8299: Schools and Educational Services, NEC

611511 Cosmetology and Barber Schools *see* SIC 7231: Beauty Shops; SIC 7241: Barber Shops

611512 Flight Training *see* SIC 8249: Vocational Schools, NEC; SIC 8299: Schools and Educational Services, NEC

611513 Apprenticeship Training *see* SIC 8249: Vocational Schools, NEC

611519 Other Technical and Trade Schools *see* SIC 8243: Data Processing Schools; SIC 8249: Vocational Schools, NEC

611610 Fine Arts Schools *see* SIC 7911: Dance Studios, Schools, and Halls; SIC 8299: Schools and Educational Services, NEC

611620 Sports and Recreation Instruction *see* SIC 7999: Amusement and Recreation Services, NEC

611630 Language Schools *see* SIC 8299: Schools and Educational Services, NEC

611691 Exam Preparation and Tutoring *see* SIC 8299: Schools and Educational Services, NEC

611692 Automobile Driving Schools *see* SIC 8299: Schools and Educational Services, NEC

611699 All Other Miscellaneous Schools and Instruction *see* SIC 8299: Schools and Educational Services, NEC

611710 Educational Support Services *see* SIC 8299: Schools and Educational Services, NEC; SIC 8748: Business Consulting Services, NEC

HEALTH CARE & SOCIAL ASSISTANCE

621111 Offices of Physicians (except Mental Health Specialists) *see* SIC 8011: Offices and Clinics of Doctors of Medicine; SIC 8031: Offices and Clinics of Doctors of Osteopathy

621112 Offices of Physicians, Mental Health Specialists *see* SIC 8011: Offices and Clinics of Doctors of Medicine; SIC 8031: Offices and Clinics of Doctors of Osteopathy

621210 Offices of Dentists *see* SIC 8021: Offices and Clinics of Dentists

621310 Offices of Chiropractors *see* SIC 8041: Offices and Clinics of Chiropractors

621320 Offices of Optometrists *see* SIC 8042: Offices and Clinics of Optometrists

621330 Offices of Mental Health Practitioners (except Physicians) *see* SIC 8049: Offices and Clinics of Health Practitioners, NEC

621340 Offices of Physical, Occupational, and Speech Therapists and Audiologists *see* SIC 8049: Offices and Clinics of Health Practitioners, NEC

621391 Offices of Podiatrists *see* SIC 8043: Offices and Clinics of Podiatrists

621399 Offices of All Other Miscellaneous Health Practitioners *see* SIC 8049: Offices and Clinics of Health Practitioners, NEC

621410 Family Planning Centers *see* SIC 8093: Specialty Outpatient Facilities, NEC; SIC 8099: Health and Allied Services, NEC

621420 Outpatient Mental Health and Substance Abuse Centers *see* SIC 8093: Specialty Outpatient Facilities, NEC

621491 HMO Medical Centers *see* SIC 8011: Offices and Clinics of Doctors of Medicine

621492 Kidney Dialysis Centers *see* SIC 8092: Kidney Dialysis Centers

621493 Freestanding Ambulatory Surgical and Emergency Centers *see* SIC 8011: Offices and Clinics of Doctors of Medicine

621498 All Other Outpatient Care Facilities *see* SIC 8093: Specialty Outpatient Facilities, NEC

621511 Medical Laboratories *see* SIC 8071: Medical Laboratories

621512 Diagnostic Imaging Centers *see* SIC 8071: Medical Laboratories

621610 Home Health Care Services *see* SIC 8082: Home Health Care Services

621910 Ambulance Service *see* SIC 4119: Local Passenger Transportation, NEC; SIC 4522: Air Transportation, Nonscheduled

621991 Blood and Organ Banks *see* SIC 8099: Health and Allied Services, NEC

621999 All Other Miscellaneous Ambulatory Health Care Services *see* SIC 8099: Health and Allied Services, NEC

622110 General Medical and Surgical Hospitals *see* SIC 8062: General Medical and Surgical Hospitals; SIC 8069: Specialty Hospitals, Except Psychiatric

622210 Psychiatric and Substance Abuse Hospitals *see* SIC 8063: Psychiatric Hospitals; SIC 8069: Specialty Hospitals, Except Psychiatric

622310 Specialty (except Psychiatric and Substance Abuse) Hospitals *see* SIC 8069: Specialty Hospitals, Except Psychiatric

623110 Nursing Care Facilities *see* SIC 8051: Skilled Nursing Care Facilities; SIC 8052: Intermediate Care Facilities; SIC 8059: Nursing and Personal Care Facilities, NEC

623210 Residential Mental Retardation Facilities *see* SIC 8052: Intermediate Care Facilities

623220 Residential Mental Health and Substance Abuse Facilities *see* SIC 8361: Residential Care

623311 Continuing Care Retirement Communities *see* SIC 8051: Skilled Nursing Care Facilities; SIC 8052: Intermediate Care Facilities; SIC 8059: Nursing and Personal Care Facilities, NEC

623312 Homes for the Elderly *see* SIC 8361: Residential Care

623990 Other Residential Care Facilities *see* SIC 8361: Residential Care

624110 Child and Youth Services *see* SIC 8322: Individual and Family Social Services; SIC 8641: Civic, Social, and Fraternal Associations

624120 Services for the Elderly and Persons with Disabilities *see* SIC 8322: Individual and Family Social Services

624190 Other Individual and Family Services *see* SIC 8322: Individual and Family Social Services

624210 Community Food Services *see* SIC 8322: Individual and Family Social Services

624221 Temporary Shelter *see* SIC 8322: Individual and Family Social Services

624229 Other Community Housing Services *see* SIC 8322: Individual and Family Social Services

624230 Emergency and Other Relief Services *see* SIC 8322: Individual and Family Social Services

624310 Vocational Rehabilitation Services *see* SIC 8331: Job Training and Vocational Rehabilitation Services

624410 Child Day Care Services *see* SIC 7299: Miscellaneous Personal Services, NEC; SIC 8351: Child Day Care Services

ARTS, ENTERTAINMENT, & RECREATION

711110 Theater Companies and Dinner Theaters *see* SIC 5812: Eating and Drinking Places; SIC 7922: Theatrical Producers (Except Motion Picture) and Miscellaneous Theatrical Services

711120 Dance Companies *see* SIC 7922: Theatrical Producers (Except Motion Picture) and Miscellaneous Theatrical Services

711130 Musical Groups and Artists *see* SIC 7929: Bands, Orchestras, Actors, and Other Entertainers and Entertainment Groups

711190 Other Performing Arts Companies *see* SIC 7929: Bands, Orchestras, Actors, and Other Entertainers and Entertainment Groups; SIC 7999: Amusement and Recreation Services, NEC

711211 Sports Teams and Clubs *see* SIC 7941: Professional Sports Clubs and Promoters

711212 Race Tracks *see* SIC 7948: Racing, Including Track Operations

711219 Other Spectator Sports *see* SIC 7941: Professional Sports Clubs and Promoters; SIC 7948: Racing, Including Track Operations; SIC 7999: Amusement and Recreation Services, NEC

711310 Promoters of Performing Arts, Sports, and Similar Events with Facilities *see* SIC 6512: Operators of Nonresidential Buildings; SIC 7922: Theatrical Producers (Except Motion Picture) and Miscellaneous Theatrical Services; SIC 7941: Professional Sports Clubs and Promoters

711320 Promoters of Performing Arts, Sports, and Similar Events without Facilities *see* SIC 7922: Theatrical Producers (Except Motion Picture) and Miscellaneous Theatrical Services; SIC 7941: Professional Sports Clubs and Promoters

711410 Agents and Managers for Artists, Athletes, Entertainers and Other Public Figures *see* SIC 7389: Business Services, NEC; SIC 7922: Theatrical Producers (Except Motion Picture) and Miscellaneous Theatrical Services; SIC 7941: Professional Sports Clubs and Promoters

711510 Independent Artists, Writers, and Performers *see* SIC 7819: Services Allied to Motion Picture Production; SIC 7929: Bands, Orchestras, Actors, and Other Entertainers and Entertainment Groups; SIC 8999: Services, NEC

712110 Museums *see* SIC 8412: Museums and Art Galleries

712120 Historical Sites *see* SIC 8412: Museums and Art Galleries

712130 Zoos and Botanical Gardens *see* SIC 8422: Arboreta and Botanical or Zoological Gardens

712190 Nature Parks and Other Similar Institutions *see* SIC 7999: Amusement and Recreation Services, NEC; SIC 8422: Arboreta and Botanical or Zoological Gardens

713110 Amusement and Theme Parks *see* SIC 7996: Amusement Parks

713120 Amusement Arcades *see* SIC 7993: Coin Operated Amusement Devices

713210 Casinos (except Casino Hotels) *see* SIC 7999: Amusement and Recreation Services, NEC

713290 Other Gambling Industries *see* SIC 7993: Coin Operated Amusement Devices; SIC 7999: Amusement and Recreation Services, NEC

713910 Golf Courses and Country Clubs *see* SIC 7992: Public Golf Courses; SIC 7997: Membership Sports and Recreation Clubs

713920 Skiing Facilities *see* SIC 7999: Amusement and Recreation Services, NEC

713930 Marinas *see* SIC 4493: Marinas

713940 Fitness and Recreational Sports Centers *see* SIC 7991: Physical Fitness Facilities; SIC 7997: Membership Sports and Recreation Clubs; SIC 7999: Amusement and Recreation Services, NEC

713950 Bowling Centers *see* SIC 7933: Bowling Centers

713990 All Other Amusement and Recreation Industries *see* SIC 7911: Dance Studios, Schools, and Halls; SIC 7993: Coin Operated Amusement Devices; SIC 7997: Membership Sports and Recreation Clubs; SIC 7999: Amusement and Recreation Services, NEC

ACCOMODATION & FOODSERVICES

721110 Hotels (except Casino Hotels) and Motels *see* SIC 7011: Hotels and Motels; SIC 7041: Organization Hotels and Lodging Houses, on Membership Basis

721120 Casino Hotels *see* SIC 7011: Hotels and Motels

721191 Bed and Breakfast Inns *see* SIC 7011: Hotels and Motels

721199 All Other Traveler Accommodations *see* SIC 7011: Hotels and Motels

721211 RV (Recreational Vehicle) Parks and Campgrounds *see* SIC 7033: Recreational Vehicle Parks and Campsites

721214 Recreational and Vacation Camps *see* SIC 7032: Sporting and Recreational Camps

721310 Rooming and Boarding Houses *see* SIC 7021: Rooming and Boarding Houses; SIC 7041: Organization Hotels and Lodging Houses, on Membership Basis

722110 Full-Service Restaurants *see* SIC 5812: Eating and Drinking Places

722211 Limited-Service Restaurants *see* SIC 5499: Miscellaneous Food Stores; SIC 5812: Eating and Drinking Places

722212 Cafeterias *see* SIC 5812: Eating and Drinking Places

722213 Snack and Nonalcoholic Beverage Bars *see* SIC 5461: Retail Bakeries; SIC 5812: Eating and Drinking Places

722310 Foodservice Contractors *see* SIC 5812: Eating and Drinking Places

722320 Caterers *see* SIC 5812: Eating and Drinking Places

722330 Mobile Caterers *see* SIC 5963: Direct Selling Establishments

722410 Drinking Places (Alcoholic Beverages) *see* SIC 5813: Drinking Places (Alcoholic Beverages)

OTHER SERVICES

811111 General Automotive Repair *see* SIC 7538: General Automotive Repair Shops

811112 Automotive Exhaust System Repair *see* SIC 7533: Automotive Exhaust System Repair Shops

811113 Automotive Transmission Repair *see* SIC 7537: Automotive Transmission Repair Shops

811118 Other Automotive Mechanical and Electrical Repair and Maintenance *see* SIC 7539: Automotive Repair Shops, NEC

811121 Automotive Body, Paint, and Upholstery Repair and Maintenance *see* SIC 7532: Top, Body, and Upholstery Repair Shops and Paint Shops

811122 Automotive Glass Replacement Shops *see* SIC 7536: Automotive Glass Replacement Shops

811191 Automotive Oil Change and Lubrication Shops *see* SIC 7549: Automotive Services, Except Repair and Carwashes

811192 Car Washes *see* SIC 7542: Carwashes

811198 All Other Automotive Repair and Maintenance *see* SIC 7534: Tire Retreading and Repair Shops; SIC 7549: Automotive Services, Except Repair and Carwashes

811211 Consumer Electronics Repair and Maintenance *see* SIC 7622: Radio and Television Repair Shops; SIC 7629: Electrical and Electronic Repair Shops, NEC

811212 Computer and Office Machine Repair and Maintenance *see* SIC 7378: Computer Maintenance and Repair; SIC 7629: Electrical and Electronic Repair Shops, NEC; SIC 7699: Repair Shops and Related Services, NEC

811213 Communication Equipment Repair and Maintenance *see* SIC 7622: Radio and Television Repair Shops; SIC 7629: Electrical and Electronic Repair Shops, NEC

811219 Other Electronic and Precision Equipment Repair and Maintenance *see* SIC 7629: Electrical and Electronic Repair Shops, NEC; SIC 7699: Repair Shops and Related Services, NEC

811310 Commercial and Industrial Machinery and Equipment (except Automotive and Electronic) Repair and Maintenance *see* SIC 7623: Refrigeration and Air-Conditioning Services and Repair Shops; SIC 7694: Armature Rewinding Shops; SIC 7699: Repair Shops and Related Services, NEC

811411 Home and Garden Equipment Repair and Maintenance *see* SIC 7699: Repair Shops and Related Services, NEC

811412 Appliance Repair and Maintenance *see* SIC 7623: Refrigeration and Air-Conditioning Services and Repair Shops; SIC 7629: Electrical and Electronic Repair Shops, NEC; SIC 7699: Repair Shops and Related Services, NEC

811420 Reupholstery and Furniture Repair *see* SIC 7641: Reupholster and Furniture Repair

811430 Footwear and Leather Goods Repair *see* SIC 7251: Shoe Repair Shops and Shoeshine Parlors; SIC 7699: Repair Shops and Related Services, NEC

811490 Other Personal and Household Goods Repair and Maintenance *see* SIC 3732: Boat Building and Repairing; SIC 7219: Laundry and Garment Services, NEC; SIC 7631: Watch, Clock, and Jewelry Repair; SIC 7692: Welding Repair; SIC 7699: Repair Shops and Related Services, NEC

812111 Barber Shops *see* SIC 7241: Barber Shops

812112 Beauty Salons *see* SIC 7231: Beauty Shops

812113 Nail Salons *see* SIC 7231: Beauty Shops

812191 Diet and Weight Reducing Centers *see* SIC 7299: Miscellaneous Personal Services, NEC

812199 Other Personal Care Services *see* SIC 7299: Miscellaneous Personal Services, NEC

812210 Funeral Homes *see* SIC 7261: Funeral Services and Crematories

812220 Cemeteries and Crematories *see* SIC 6531: Real Estate Agents and Managers; SIC 6553: Cemetery Subdividers and Developers

812220 Cemeteries and Crematories *see* SIC 7261: Funeral Services and Crematories

812310 Coin-Operated Laundries and Drycleaners *see* SIC 7215: Coin-Operated Laundry and Drycleaning

812321 Laundries, Family and Commercial *see* SIC 7211: Power Laundries, Family and Commercial

812322 Drycleaning Plants *see* SIC 7216: Drycleaning Plants, Except Rug Cleaning

812331 Linen Supply *see* SIC 7213: Linen Supply; SIC 7219: Laundry and Garment Services, NEC

812332 Industrial Launderers *see* SIC 7218: Industrial Launderers

812391 Garment Pressing and Agents for Laundries *see* SIC 7212: Garment Pressing, and Agents for Laundries

812399 All Other Laundry Services *see* SIC 7219: Laundry and Garment Services, NEC

812910 Pet Care (except Veterinary) Services *see* SIC 0752: Animal Specialty Services, Except Veterinary

812921 Photo Finishing Laboratories (except One-Hour) *see* SIC 7384: Photofinishing Laboratories

812922 One-Hour Photo Finishing *see* SIC 7384: Photofinishing Laboratories

812930 Parking Lots and Garages *see* SIC 7521: Automobile Parking

812990 All Other Personal Services *see* SIC 7299: Miscellaneous Personal Services, NEC; SIC 7389: Business Services, NEC

813110 Religious Organizations *see* SIC 8661: Religious Organizations

813211 Grantmaking Foundations *see* SIC 6732: Education, Religious, and Charitable Trusts

813212 Voluntary Health Organizations *see* SIC 8399: Social Services, NEC

813219 Other Grantmaking and Giving Services *see* SIC 8399: Social Services, NEC

813311 Human Rights Organizations *see* SIC 8399: Social Services, NEC

813312 Environment, Conservation and Wildlife Organizations *see* SIC 8399: Social Services, NEC; SIC 8699: Membership Organizations, NEC

813319 Other Social Advocacy Organizations *see* SIC 8399: Social Services, NEC

813410 Civic and Social Organizations *see* SIC 8641: Civic, Social, and Fraternal Associations; SIC 8699: Membership Organizations, NEC

813910 Business Associations *see* SIC 8611: Business Associations; SIC 8699: Membership Organizations, NEC

813920 Professional Organizations *see* SIC 8621: Professional Membership Organizations

813930 Labor Unions and Similar Labor Organizations *see* SIC 8631: Labor Unions and Similar Labor Organizations

813940 Political Organizations *see* SIC 8651: Political Organizations

813990 Other Similar Organizations *see* SIC 6531: Real Estate Agents and Managers; SIC 8641: Civic, Social, and Fraternal Associations; SIC 8699: Membership Organizations, NEC

814110 Private Households *see* SIC 8811: Private Households

PUBLIC ADMINISTRATION

921110 Executive Offices *see* SIC 9111: Executive Offices

921120 Legislative Bodies *see* SIC 9121: Legislative Bodies

921130 Public Finance *see* SIC 9311: Public Finance, Taxation, and Monetary Policy

921140 Executive and Legislative Offices, Combined *see* SIC 9131: Executive and Legislative Offices, Combined

921150 American Indian and Alaska Native Tribal Governments *see* SIC 8641: Civic, Social, and Fraternal Associations

921190 All Other General Government *see* SIC 9199: General Government, NEC

922110 Courts *see* SIC 9211: Courts

922120 Police Protection *see* SIC 9221: Police Protection

922130 Legal Counsel and Prosecution *see* SIC 9222: Legal Counsel and Prosecution

922140 Correctional Institutions *see* SIC 9223: Correctional Institutions

922150 Parole Offices and Probation Offices *see* SIC 8322: Individual and Family Social Services

922160 Fire Protection *see* SIC 9224: Fire Protection

922190 All Other Justice, Public Order, and Safety *see* SIC 9229: Public Order and Safety, NEC

923110 Administration of Education Programs *see* SIC 9411: Administration of Educational Programs

923120 Administration of Public Health Programs *see* SIC 9431: Administration of Public Health Programs

923130 Administration of Social, Human Resource and Income Maintenance Programs *see* SIC 9441: Administration of Social, Human Resource and Income Maintenance Programs

923140 Administration of Veteran's Affairs *see* SIC 9451: Administration of Veteran's Affairs, Except Health Insurance

924110 Air and Water Resource and Solid Waste Management *see* SIC 9511: Air and Water Resource and Solid Waste Management

924120 Land, Mineral, Wildlife, and Forest Conservation *see* SIC 9512: Land, Mineral, Wildlife, and Forest Conservation

925110 Administration of Housing Programs *see* SIC 9531: Administration of Housing Programs

925120 Administration of Urban Planning and Community and Rural Development *see* SIC 9532: Administration of Urban Planning and Community and Rural Development

926110 Administration of General Economic Programs *see* SIC 9611: Administration of General Economic Programs

926120 Regulation and Administration of Transportation Programs *see* SIC 9621: Regulations and Administration of Transportation Programs

926130 Regulation and Administration of Communications, Electric, Gas, and Other Utilities *see* SIC 9631: Regulation and Administration of Communications, Electric, Gas, and Other Utilities

926140 Regulation of Agricultural Marketing and Commodities *see* SIC 9641: Regulation of Agricultural Marketing and Commodities

926150 Regulation, Licensing, and Inspection of Miscellaneous Commercial Sectors *see* SIC 9651: Regulation, Licensing, and Inspection of Miscellaneous Commercial Sectors

927110 Space Research and Technology *see* SIC 9661: Space Research and Technology

928110 National Security *see* SIC 9711: National Security

928120 International Affairs *see* SIC 9721: International Affairs

999990 Unclassified Establishments *see* SIC 9999: Nonclassified Establishments

SIC TO NAICS CONVERSION GUIDE

*The following guide cross-references four-digit 1987 Standard Industrial Classification (SIC) codes with six-digit 1997 North American Industry Classification System (NAICS) codes. Because the systems differ in specificity, some SIC categories correspond to more than one NAICS category. Please refer to the **Introduction** under "About Industry Classification" for more information.*

AGRICULTURE, FORESTRY & FISHING

0111   Wheat *see* NAICS 111140: Wheat Farming

0112   Rice *see* NAICS 111160: Rice Farming

0115   Corn *see* NAICS 111150: Corn Farming

0116   Soybeans *see* NAICS 111110: Soybean Farming

0119   Cash Grains, NEC *see* NAICS 111130: Dry Pea and Bean Farming; NAICS 111120: Oilseed (except Soybean) Farming; NAICS 111150: Corn Farming; NAICS 111191: Oilseed and Grain Combination Farming; NAICS 111199: All Other Grain Farming

0131   Cotton *see* NAICS 111920: Cotton Farming

0132   Tobacco *see* NAICS 111910: Tobacco Farming

0133   Sugarcane and Sugar Beets *see* NAICS 111991: Sugar Beet Farming; NAICS 111930: Sugarcane Farming

0134   Irish Potatoes *see* NAICS 111211: Potato Farming

0139   Field Crops, Except Cash Grains, NEC *see* NAICS 111940: Hay Farming; NAICS 111992: Peanut Farming; NAICS 111219: Other Vegetable (except Potato) and Melon Farming; NAICS 111998: All Other Miscellaneous Crop Farming

0161   Vegetables and Melons *see* NAICS 111219: Other Vegetable (except Potato) and Melon Farming

0171   Berry Crops *see* NAICS 111333: Strawberry Farming; NAICS 111334: Berry (except Strawberry) Farming

0172   Grapes *see* NAICS 111332: Grape Vineyards

0173   Tree Nuts *see* NAICS 111335: Tree Nut Farming

0174   Citrus Fruits *see* NAICS 111310: Orange Groves; NAICS 111320: Citrus (except Orange) Groves

0175   Deciduous Tree Fruits *see* NAICS 111331: Apple Orchards; NAICS 111339: Other Noncitrus Fruit Farming

0179   Fruits and Tree Nuts, NEC *see* NAICS 111336: Fruit and Tree Nut Combination Farming; NAICS 111339: Other Noncitrus Fruit Farming

0181   Ornamental Floriculture and Nursery Products *see* NAICS 111422: Floriculture Production; NAICS 111421: Nursery and Tree Production

0182   Food Crops Grown Under Cover *see* NAICS 111411: Mushroom Production; NAICS 111419: Other Food Crops Grown Under Cover

0191   General Farms, Primarily Crop *see* NAICS 111998: All Other Miscellaneous Crop Farming

0211   Beef Cattle Feedlots *see* NAICS 112112: Cattle Feedlots

0212   Beef Cattle, Except Feedlots *see* NAICS 112111: Beef Cattle Ranching and Farming

0213   Hogs *see* NAICS 112210: Hog and Pig Farming

0214   Sheep and Goats *see* NAICS 112410: Sheep Farming; NAICS 112420: Goat Farming

0219   General Livestock, Except Dairy and Poultry *see* NAICS 112990: All Other Animal Production

0241   Dairy Farms *see* NAICS 112111: Beef Cattle Ranching and Farming; NAICS 112120: Dairy Cattle and Milk Production

0251   Broiler, Fryers, and Roaster Chickens *see* NAICS 112320: Broilers and Other Meat-Type Chicken Production

0252   Chicken Eggs *see* NAICS 112310: Chicken Egg Production

0253   Turkey and Turkey Eggs *see* NAICS 112330: Turkey Production

0254   Poultry Hatcheries *see* NAICS 112340: Poultry Hatcheries

0259   Poultry and Eggs, NEC *see* NAICS 112390: Other Poultry Production

0271   Fur-Bearing Animals and Rabbits *see* NAICS 112930: Fur-bearing Animal and Rabbit Production

0272   Horses and Other Equines *see* NAICS 112920: Horse and Other Equine Production

0273　Animal Aquaculture *see* NAICS 112511: Finfish Farming and Fish Hatcheries; NAICS 112512: Shellfish Farming; NAICS 112519: Other Animal Aquaculture

0279　Animal Specialties, NEC *see* NAICS 112910: Apiculture; NAICS 112990: All Other Animal Production

0291　General Farms, Primarily Livestock and Animal Specialties *see* NAICS 112990: All Other Animal Production

0711　Soil Preparation Services *see* NAICS 115112: Soil Preparation, Planting and Cultivating

0721　Crop Planting, Cultivating and Protecting; NAICS 481219: Other Nonscheduled Air Transportation; NAICS 115112: Soil Preparation, Planting, and Cultivating

0722　Crop Harvesting, Primarily by Machine *see* NAICS 115113: Crop Harvesting, Primarily By Machine

0723　Crop Preparation Services For Market, except Cotton Ginning *see* NAICS 115114: Postharvest Crop Activities (except Cotton Ginning)

0724　Cotton Ginning *see* NAICS 115111: Cotton Ginning

0741　Veterinary Service For Livestock *see* NAICS 541940: Veterinary Services

0742　Veterinary Services for Animal Specialties *see* NAICS 541940: Veterinary Services

0751　Livestock Services, Except Veterinary *see* NAICS 311611: Animal (except Poultry) Slaughtering NAICS 115210: Support Activities for Animal Production

0752　Animal Specialty Services, Except Veterinary; NAICS 115210: Support Activities for Animal Production; NAICS 812910: Pet Care (except Veterinary) Services

0761　Farm Labor Contractors and Crew Leaders *see* NAICS 115115: Farm Labor Contractors and Crew Leaders

0762　Farm Management Services *see* NAICS 115116: Farm Management Services

0781　Landscape Counseling and Planning *see* NAICS 541690: Other Scientific and Technical Consulting Services; NAICS 541320: Landscape Architectural Services

0782　Lawn and Garden Services *see* NAICS 561730: Landscaping Services

0783　Ornamental Shrub and Tree Services *see* NAICS 561730: Landscaping Services

0811　Timber Tracts *see* NAICS 111421: Nursery and Tree Production; NAICS 113110: Timber Tract Operations

0831　Forest Nurseries and Gathering of Forest Products; NAICS 111998: All Other Miscellaneous Crop Farming; NAICS 113210: Forest Nurseries and Gathering of Forest Products

0851　Forestry Services *see* NAICS 115310: Support Activities for Forestry

0912　Finfish *see* NAICS 114111: Finfish Fishing

0913　Shellfish *see* NAICS 114112: Shellfish Fishing

0919　Miscellaneous Marine Products *see* NAICS 114119: Other Marine Fishing; NAICS 111998: All Other Miscellaneous Crop Farming

0921　Fish Hatcheries and Preserves *see* NAICS 112511: Finfish Farming and Fish Hatcheries; NAICS 112512: Shellfish Farming

0971　Hunting, Trapping, and Game Propagation *see* NAICS 114210: Hunting and Trapping

MINING INDUSTRIES

1011　Iron Ores *see* NAICS 212210: Iron Ore Mining

1021　Copper Ores *see* NAICS 212234: Copper Ore and Nickel Ore Mining

1031　Lead and Zinc Ores *see* NAICS 212231: Lead Ore and Zinc Ore Mining

1041　Gold Ores *see* NAICS 212221: Gold Ore Mining

1044　Silver Ores *see* NAICS 212222: Silver Ore Mining

1061　Ferroalloy Ores, Except Vanadium *see* NAICS 212234: Copper Ore and Nickel Ore Mining; NAICS 212299: Other Metal Ore Mining

1081　Metal Mining Services *see* NAICS 213114: Support Activities for Metal Mining; NAICS 541360: Geophysical Surveying and Mapping Services

1094　Uranium-Radium-Vanadium Ores *see* NAICS 212291: Uranium-Radium-Vanadium Ore Mining

1099　Miscellaneous Metal Ores, NEC *see* NAICS 212299: Other Metal Ore Mining

1221　Bituminous Coal and Lignite Surface Mining *see* NAICS 212111: Bituminous Coal and Lignite Surface Mining

1222　Bituminous Coal Underground Mining *see* NAICS 212112: Bituminous Coal Underground Mining

1231　Anthracite Mining *see* NAICS 212113: Anthracite Mining

1241　Coal Mining Services *see* NAICS 213113: Support Activities for Coal Mining

1311　Crude Petroleum and Natural Gas *see* NAICS 211111: Crude Petroleum and Natural Gas Extraction

1321　Natural Gas Liquids *see* NAICS 211112: Natural Gas Liquid Extraction

1381　Drilling Oil and Gas Wells *see* NAICS 213111: Drilling Oil and Gas Wells

1382　Oil and Gas Field Exploration Services *see* NAICS 541360: Geophysical Surveying and Mapping Services; NAICS 213112: Support Activities for Oil and Gas Field Exploration

1389　Oil and Gas Field Services, NEC *see* NAICS 213112: Support Activities for Oil and Gas Field Exploration

1411　Dimension Stone *see* NAICS 212311: Dimension Stone Mining and Quarry

1422　Crushed and Broken Limestone *see* NAICS 212312: Crushed and Broken Limestone Mining and Quarrying

1423　Crushed and Broken Granite *see* NAICS 212313: Crushed and Broken Granite Mining and Quarrying

1429　Crushed and Broken Stone, NEC *see* NAICS 212319: Other Crushed and Broken Stone Mining and Quarrying

1442　Construction Sand and Gravel *see* NAICS 212321: Construction Sand and Gravel Mining

1446　Industrial Sand *see* NAICS 212322: Industrial Sand Mining

1455　Kaolin and Ball Clay *see* NAICS 212324: Kaolin and Ball Clay Mining

1459　Clay, Ceramic, and Refractory Minerals, NEC *see* NAICS 212325: Clay and Ceramic and Refractory Minerals Mining

1474　Potash, Soda, and Borate Minerals *see* NAICS 212391: Potash, Soda, and Borate Mineral Mining

1475　Phosphate Rock *see* NAICS 212392: Phosphate Rock Mining

---

1479 Chemical and Fertilizer Mineral Mining, NEC *see* NAICS 212393: Other Chemical and Fertilizer Mineral Mining

1481 Nonmetallic Minerals Services Except Fuels *see* NAICS 213115: Support Activities for Non-metallic Minerals, (except Fuels); NAICS 541360: Geophysical Surveying and Mapping Services

1499 Miscellaneous Nonmetallic Minerals, Except Fuels *see* NAICS 212319: Other Crushed and Broken Stone Mining and Quarrying; NAICS 212399: All Other Non-Metallic Mineral Mining

CONSTRUCTION INDUSTRIES

1521 General Contractors-Single-Family Houses *see* NAICS 233210: Single-Family Housing Construction

1522 General Contractors-Residential Buildings *see* NAICS 233320: Commercial and Institutional Building Construction; NAICS 233220: Multi-Family Housing Construction

1531 Operative Builders *see* NAICS 233210: Single-Family Housing Construction; NAICS 233220: Multi-Family Housing Construction; NAICS 233310: Manufacturing and Light Industrial Building Construction; NAICS 233320: Commercial and Institutional Building Construction

1541 General Contractors-Industrial Buildings and Warehouses *see* NAICS 233320: Commercial and Institutional Building Construction; NAICS 233310: Manufacturing and Light Industrial Building Construction

1542 General Contractors-Nonresidential Buildings, Other than Industrial Buildings and Warehouses *see* NAICS 233320: Commercial and Institutional Building Construction

1611 Highway and Street Construction, Except Elevated Highways *see* NAICS 234110: Highway and Street Construction

1622 Bridge, Tunnel, and Elevated Highway Construction *see* NAICS 234120: Bridge and Tunnel Construction

1623 Water, Sewer, Pipeline, and Communications and Power Line Construction *see* NAICS 234910: Water, Sewer and Pipeline Construction; NAICS 234920: Power and Communication Transmission Line Construction

1629 Heavy Construction, NEC *see* NAICS 234930: Industrial Nonbuilding Structure Construction; NAICS 234990: All Other Heavy Construction

1711 Plumbing, Heating, and Air-Conditioning *see* NAICS 235110: Plumbing, Heating and Air-Conditioning Contractors

1721 Painting and Paper Hanging *see* NAICS 235210: Painting and Wall Covering Contractors

1731 Electrical Work *see* NAICS 561621: Security Systems Services (except Locksmiths); NAICS 235310: Electrical Contractors

1741 Masonry, Stone Setting and Other Stone Work *see* NAICS 235410: Masonry and Stone Contractors

1742 Plastering, Drywall, Acoustical and Insulation Work *see* NAICS 235420: Drywall, Plastering, Acoustical and Insulation Contractors

1743 Terrazzo, Tile, Marble, and Mosaic Work *see* NAICS 235420: Drywall, Plastering, Acoustical and Insulation Contractors; NAICS 235430: Tile, Marble, Terrazzo and Mosaic Contractors

1751 Carpentry Work *see* NAICS 235510: Carpentry Contractors

1752 Floor Laying and Other Floor Work, NEC *see* NAICS 235520: Floor Laying and Other Floor Contractors

1761 Roofing, Siding, and Sheet Metal Work *see* NAICS 235610: Roofing, Siding, and Sheet Metal Contractors

1771 Concrete Work *see* NAICS 235420: Drywall, Plastering, Acoustical and Insulation Contractors; NAICS 235710: Concrete Contractors

1781 Water Well Drilling *see* NAICS 235810: Water Well Drilling Contractors

1791 Structural Steel Erection *see* NAICS 235910: Structural Steel Erection Contractors

1793 Glass and Glazing Work *see* NAICS 235920: Glass and Glazing Contractors

1794 Excavation Work *see* NAICS 235930: Excavation Contractors

1795 Wrecking and Demolition Work *see* NAICS 235940: Wrecking and Demolition Contractors

1796 Installation or Erection of Building Equipment, NEC *see* NAICS 235950: Building Equipment and Other Machinery Installation Contractors

1799 Special Trade Contractors, NEC *see* NAICS 235210: Painting and Wall Covering Contractors; NAICS 235920: Glass and Glazing Contractors; NAICS 562910: Remediation Services; NAICS 235990: All Other Special Trade Contractors

FOOD & KINDRED PRODUCTS

2011 Meat Packing Plants *see* NAICS 311611: Animal (except Poultry) Slaughtering

2013 Sausages and Other Prepared Meats *see* NAICS 311612: Meat Processed From Carcasses

2015 Poultry Slaughtering and Processing *see* NAICS 311615: Poultry Processing; NAICS 311999: All Other Miscellaneous Food Manufacturing

2021 Creamery Butter *see* NAICS 311512: Creamery Butter Manufacturing

2022 Natural, Processed, and Imitation Cheese *see* NAICS 311513: Cheese Manufacturing

2023 Dry, Condensed, and Evaporated Dairy Products *see* NAICS 311514: Dry, Condensed, and Evaporated Dairy Product Manufacturing

2024 Ice Cream and Frozen Desserts *see* NAICS 311520: Ice Cream and Frozen Dessert Manufacturing

2026 Fluid Milk *see* NAICS 311511: Fluid Milk Manufacturing

2032 Canned Specialties *see* NAICS 311422: Specialty Canning; NAICS 311999: All Other Miscellaneous Food Manufacturing

2033 Canned Fruits, Vegetables, Preserves, Jams, and Jellies *see* NAICS 311421: Fruit and Vegetable Canning

2034 Dried and Dehydrated Fruits, Vegetables, and Soup Mixes *see* NAICS 311423: Dried and Dehydrated Food Manufacturing; NAICS 311211: Flour Milling

2035 Pickled Fruits and Vegetables, Vegetables Sauces and Seasonings, and Salad Dressings *see* NAICS 311421: Fruit and Vegetable Canning; NAICS 311941: Mayonnaise, Dressing, and Other Prepared Sauce Manufacturing

2037 Frozen Fruits, Fruit Juices, and Vegetables *see* NAICS 311411: Frozen Fruit, Juice, and Vegetable Processing

2038 Frozen Specialties, NEC *see* NAICS 311412: Frozen Specialty Food Manufacturing

2041 Flour and Other Grain Mill Products *see* NAICS 311211: Flour Milling

2043 Cereal Breakfast Foods *see* NAICS 311920: Coffee and Tea Manufacturing; NAICS 311230: Breakfast Cereal Manufacturing

2044 Rice Milling *see* NAICS 311212: Rice Milling

2045 Prepared Flour Mixes and Doughs *see* NAICS 311822: Flour Mixes and Dough Manufacturing from Purchased Flour

2046 Wet Corn Milling *see* NAICS 311221: Wet Corn Milling

2047 Dog and Cat Food *see* NAICS 311111: Dog and Cat Food Manufacturing

2048 Prepared Feed and Feed Ingredients for Animals and Fowls, Except Dogs and Cats *see* NAICS 311611: Animal (except Poultry) Slaughtering; NAICS 311119: Other Animal Food Manufacturing

2051 Bread and Other Bakery Products, Except Cookies and Crackers *see* NAICS 311812: Commercial Bakeries

2052 Cookies and Crackers *see* NAICS 311821: Cookie and Cracker Manufacturing; NAICS 311919: Other Snack Food Manufacturing; NAICS 311812: Commercial Bakeries

2053 Frozen Bakery Products, Except Bread *see* NAICS 311813: Frozen Bakery Product Manufacturing

2061 Cane Sugar, Except Refining *see* NAICS 311311: Sugarcane Mills

2062 Cane Sugar Refining *see* NAICS 311312: Cane Sugar Refining

2063 Beet Sugar *see* NAICS 311313: Beet Sugar Manufacturing

2064 Candy and Other Confectionery Products *see* NAICS 311330: Confectionery Manufacturing from Purchased Chocolate; NAICS 311340: Non-Chocolate Confectionery Manufacturing

2066 Chocolate and Cocoa Products *see* NAICS 311320: Chocolate and Confectionery Manufacturing from Cacao Beans

2067 Chewing Gum *see* NAICS 311340: Non-Chocolate Confectionery Manufacturing

2068 Salted and Roasted Nuts and Seeds *see* NAICS 311911: Roasted Nuts and Peanut Butter Manufacturing

2074 Cottonseed Oil Mills *see* NAICS 311223: Other Oilseed Processing; NAICS 311225: Fats and Oils Refining and Blending

2075 Soybean Oil Mills *see* NAICS 311222: Soybean Processing; NAICS 311225: Fats and Oils Refining and Blending

2076 Vegetable Oil Mills, Except Corn, Cottonseed, and Soybeans *see* NAICS 311223: Other Oilseed Processing; NAICS 311225: Fats and Oils Refining and Blending

2077 Animal and Marine Fats and Oils *see* NAICS 311613: Rendering and Meat By-product Processing; NAICS 311711: Seafood Canning; NAICS 311712: Fresh and Frozen Seafood Processing; NAICS 311225: Fats and Oils Refining and Blending

2079 Shortening, Table Oils, Margarine, and Other Edible Fats and Oils, NEC *see* NAICS 311225: Fats and Oils Refining and Blending; NAICS 311222: Soybean Processing; NAICS 311223: Other Oilseed Processing

2082 Malt Beverages *see* NAICS 312120: Breweries

2083 Malt *see* NAICS 311213: Malt Manufacturing

2084 Wines, Brandy, and Brandy Spirits *see* NAICS 312130: Wineries

2085 Distilled and Blended Liquors *see* NAICS 312140: Distilleries

2086 Bottled and Canned Soft Drinks and Carbonated Waters *see* NAICS 312111: Soft Drink Manufacturing; NAICS 312112: Bottled Water Manufacturing

2087 Flavoring Extracts and Flavoring Syrups NEC *see* NAICS 311930: Flavoring Syrup and Concentrate Manufacturing; NAICS 311942: Spice and Extract Manufacturing; NAICS 311999: All Other Miscellaneous Food Manufacturing

2091 Canned and Cured Fish and Seafood *see* NAICS 311711: Seafood Canning

2092 Prepared Fresh or Frozen Fish and Seafoods *see* NAICS 311712: Fresh and Frozen Seafood Processing

2095 Roasted Coffee *see* NAICS 311920: Coffee and Tea Manufacturing; NAICS 311942: Spice and Extract Manufacturing

2096 Potato Chips, Corn Chips, and Similar Snacks *see* NAICS 311919: Other Snack Food Manufacturing

2097 Manufactured Ice *see* NAICS 312113: Ice Manufacturing

2098 Macaroni, Spaghetti, Vermicelli, and Noodles *see* NAICS 311823: Pasta Manufacturing

2099 Food Preparations, NEC *see* NAICS 311423: Dried and Dehydrated Food Manufacturing; NAICS 111998: All Other Miscellaneous Crop Farming; NAICS 311340: Non-Chocolate Confectionery Manufacturing; NAICS 311911: Roasted Nuts and Peanut Butter Manufacturing; NAICS 311991: Perishable Prepared Food Manufacturing; NAICS 311830: Tortilla Manufacturing; NAICS 311920: Coffee and Tea Manufacturing; NAICS 311941: Mayonnaise, Dressing, and Other Prepared Sauce Manufacturing; NAICS 311942: Spice and Extract Manufacturing; NAICS 311999: All Other Miscellaneous Food Manufacturing

TOBACCO PRODUCTS

2111 Cigarettes *see* NAICS 312221: Cigarette Manufacturing

2121 Cigars *see* NAICS 312229: Other Tobacco Product Manufacturing

2131 Chewing and Smoking Tobacco and Snuff *see* NAICS 312229: Other Tobacco Product Manufacturing

2141 Tobacco Stemming and Redrying *see* NAICS 312229: Other Tobacco Product Manufacturing; NAICS 312210: Tobacco Stemming and Redrying

TEXTILE MILL PRODUCTS

2211 Broadwoven Fabric Mills, Cotton *see* NAICS 313210: Broadwoven Fabric Mills

2221 Broadwoven Fabric Mills, Manmade Fiber and Silk *see* NAICS 313210: Broadwoven Fabric Mills

2231 Broadwoven Fabric Mills, Wool (Including Dyeing and Finishing) *see* NAICS 313210: Broadwoven Fabric Mills; NAICS 313311: Broadwoven Fabric Finishing Mills; NAICS 313312: Textile and Fabric Finishing (except Broadwoven Fabric) Mills

2241 Narrow Fabric and Other Smallware Mills: Cotton, Wool, Silk, and Manmade Fiber *see* NAICS 313221: Narrow Fabric Mills

2251   Women's Full-Length and Knee-Length Hosiery, Except Socks *see* NAICS 315111: Sheer Hosiery Mills

2252   Hosiery, NEC *see* NAICS 315111: Sheer Hosiery Mills; NAICS 315119: Other Hosiery and Sock Mills

2253   Knit Outerwear Mills *see* NAICS 315191: Outerwear Knitting Mills

2254   Knit Underwear and Nightwear Mills *see* NAICS 315192: Underwear and Nightwear Knitting Mills

2257   Weft Knit Fabric Mills *see* NAICS 313241: Weft Knit Fabric Mills; NAICS 313312: Textile and Fabric Finishing (except Broadwoven Fabric) Mills

2258   Lace and Warp Knit Fabric Mills *see* NAICS 313249: Other Knit Fabric and Lace Mills; NAICS 313312: Textile and Fabric Finishing (except Broadwoven Fabric) Mills

2259   Knitting Mills, NEC *see* NAICS 315191: Outerwear Knitting Mills; NAICS 315192: Underwear and Nightwear Knitting Mills; NAICS 313241: Weft Knit Fabric Mills; NAICS 313249: Other Knit Fabric and Lace Mills

2261   Finishers of Broadwoven Fabrics of Cotton *see* NAICS 313311: Broadwoven Fabric Finishing Mills

2262   Finishers of Broadwoven Fabrics of Manmade Fiber and Silk *see* NAICS 313311: Broadwoven Fabric Finishing Mills

2269   Finishers of Textiles, NEC *see* NAICS 313311: Broadwoven Fabric Finishing Mills; NAICS 313312: Textile and Fabric Finishing (except Broadwoven Fabric) Mills

2273   Carpets and Rugs *see* NAICS 314110: Carpet and Rug Mills

2281   Yarn Spinning Mills *see* NAICS 313111: Yarn Spinning Mills

2282   Yarn Texturizing, Throwing, Twisting, and Winding Mills *see* NAICS 313112: Yarn Texturing, Throwing and Twisting Mills; NAICS 313312: Textile and Fabric Finishing (except Broadwoven Fabric) Mills

2284   Thread Mills *see* NAICS 313113: Thread Mills; NAICS 313312: Textile and Fabric Finishing (except Broadwoven Fabric) Mills

2295   Coated Fabrics, Not Rubberized *see* NAICS 313320: Fabric Coating Mills

2296   Tire Cord and Fabrics *see* NAICS 314992: Tire Cord and Tire Fabric Mills

2297   Nonwoven Fabrics *see* NAICS 313230: Nonwoven Fabric Mills

2298   Cordage and Twine *see* NAICS 314991: Rope, Cordage and Twine Mills

2299   Textile Goods, NEC *see* NAICS 313210: Broadwoven Fabric Mills; NAICS 313230: Nonwoven Fabric Mills; NAICS 313312: Textile and Fabric Finishing (except Broadwoven Fabric) Mills; NAICS 313221: Narrow Fabric Mills; NAICS 313113: Thread Mills; NAICS 313111: Yarn Spinning Mills; NAICS 314999: All Other Miscellaneous Textile Product Mills

APPAREL & OTHER FINISHED PRODUCTS MADE FROM FABRICS & SIMILAR MATERIALS

2311   Men's and Boys' Suits, Coats and Overcoats *see* NAICS 315211: Men's and Boys' Cut and Sew Apparel Contractors; NAICS 315222: Men's and Boys' Cut and Sew Suit, Coat, and Overcoat Manufacturing

2321   Men's and Boys' Shirts, Except Work Shirts *see* NAICS 315211: Men's and Boys' Cut and Sew Apparel Contractors; NAICS 315223: Men's and Boys' Cut and Sew Shirt, (except Work Shirt) Manufacturing

2322   Men's and Boys' Underwear and Nightwear *see* NAICS 315211: Men's and Boys' Cut and Sew Apparel Contractors; NAICS 315221: Men's and Boys' Cut and Sew Underwear and Nightwear Manufacturing

2323   Men's and Boys' Neckwear *see* NAICS 315993: Men's and Boys' Neckwear Manufacturing

2325   Men's and Boys' Trousers and Slacks *see* NAICS 315211: Men's and Boys' Cut and Sew Apparel Contractors; NAICS 315224: Men's and Boys' Cut And Sew Trouser, Slack, And Jean Manufacturing

2326   Men's and Boys' Work Clothing *see* NAICS 315211: Men's and Boys' Cut and Sew Apparel Contractors; NAICS 315225: Men's and Boys' Cut and Sew Work Clothing Manufacturing

2329   Men's and Boys' Clothing, NEC *see* NAICS 315211: Men's and Boys' Cut and Sew Apparel Contractors; NAICS 315228: Men's and Boys' Cut and Sew Other Outerwear Manufacturing; NAICS 315299: All Other Cut and Sew Apparel Manufacturing

2331   Women's, Misses', and Juniors' Blouses and Shirts *see* NAICS 315212: Women's and Girls' Cut and Sew Apparel Contractors; NAICS 315232: Women's and Girls' Cut and Sew Blouse and Shirt Manufacturing

2335   Women's, Misses' and Junior's Dresses *see* NAICS 315212: Women's and Girls' Cut and Sew Apparel Contractors; NAICS 315233: Women's and Girls' Cut and Sew Dress Manufacturing

2337   Women's, Misses' and Juniors' Suits, Skirts and Coats *see* NAICS 315212: Women's and Girls' Cut and Sew Apparel Contractors; NAICS 315234: Women's and Girls' Cut and Sew Suit, Coat, Tailored Jacket, and Skirt Manufacturing

2339   Women's, Misses' and Juniors' Outerwear, NEC *see* NAICS 315999: Other Apparel Accessories and Other Apparel Manufacturing; NAICS 315212: Women's and Girls' Cut and Sew Apparel Contractors; NAICS 315299: All Other Cut and Sew Apparel Manufacturing; NAICS 315238: Women's and Girls' Cut and Sew Other Outerwear Manufacturing

2341   Women's, Misses, Children's, and Infants' Underwear and Nightwear *see* NAICS 315212: Women's and Girls' Cut and Sew Apparel Contractors; NAICS 315211: Men's and Boys' Cut and Sew Apparel Contractors; NAICS 315231: Women's and Girls' Cut and Sew Lingerie, Loungewear, and Nightwear Manufacturing; NAICS 315221: Men's and Boys' Cut and Sew Underwear and Nightwear Manufacturing; NAICS 315291: Infants' Cut and Sew Apparel Manufacturing

2342   Brassieres, Girdles, and Allied Garments *see* NAICS 315212: Women's and Girls' Cut and Sew Apparel Contractors; NAICS 315231: Women's and Girls' Cut and Sew Lingerie, Loungewear, and Nightwear Manufacturing

2353   Hats, Caps, and Millinery *see* NAICS 315991: Hat, Cap, and Millinery Manufacturing

2361   Girls', Children's and Infants' Dresses, Blouses and Shirts *see* NAICS 315291: Infants' Cut and Sew Apparel Manufacturing; NAICS 315223: Men's and Boys' Cut and Sew Shirt (except Work Shirt) Manufacturing;

NAICS 315211: Men's and Boys' Cut and Sew Apparel Contractors; NAICS 315232: Women's and Girls' Cut and Sew Blouse and Shirt Manufacturing; NAICS 315233: Women's and Girls' Cut and Sew Dress Manufacturing; NAICS 315212: Women's and Girls' Cut and Sew Apparel Contractors

2369   Girls', Children's and Infants' Outerwear, NEC *see* NAICS 315291: Infants' Cut and Sew Apparel Manufacturing; NAICS 315222: Men's and Boys' Cut and Sew Suit, Coat, and Overcoat Manufacturing; NAICS 315224: Men's and Boys' Cut and Sew Trouser, Slack, and Jean Manufacturing; NAICS 315228: Men's and Boys' Cut and Sew Other Outerwear Manufacturing; NAICS 315221: Men's and Boys' Cut and Sew Underwear and Nightwear Manufacturing; NAICS 315211: Men's and Boys' Cut and Sew Apparel Contractors; NAICS 315234: Women's and Girls' Cut and Sew Suit, Coat, Tailored Jacket, and Skirt Manufacturing; NAICS 315238: Women's and Girls' Cut and Sew Other Outerwear Manufacturing; NAICS 315231: Women's and Girls' Cut and Sew Lingerie, Loungewear, and Nightwear Manufacturing; NAICS 315212: Women's and Girls' Cut and Sew Apparel Contractors

2371   Fur Goods *see* NAICS 315292: Fur and Leather Apparel Manufacturing

2381   Dress and Work Gloves, Except Knit and All-Leather *see* NAICS 315992: Glove and Mitten Manufacturing

2384   Robes and Dressing Gowns *see* NAICS 315231: Women's and Girls' Cut and Sew Lingerie, Loungewear, and Nightwear Manufacturing; NAICS 315221: Men's and Boys' Cut and Sew Underwear and Nightwear Manufacturing; NAICS 315211: Men's and Boys' Cut and Sew Apparel Contractors; NAICS 315212: Women's and Girls' Cut and Sew Apparel Contractors

2385   Waterproof Outerwear *see* NAICS 315222: Men's and Boys' Cut and Sew Suit, Coat, and Overcoat Manufacturing; NAICS 315234: Women's and Girls' Cut and Sew Suit, Coat, Tailored Jacket, and Skirt Manufacturing; NAICS 315228: Men's and Boys' Cut and Sew Other Outerwear Manufacturing; NAICS 315238: Women's and Girls' Cut and Sew Other Outerwear Manufacturing; NAICS 315291: Infants' Cut and Sew Apparel Manufacturing; NAICS 315999: Other Apparel Accessories and Other Apparel Manufacturing; NAICS 315211: Men's and Boys' Cut and Sew Apparel Contractors; NAICS 315212: Women's and Girls' Cut and Sew Apparel Contractors

2386   Leather and Sheep-Lined Clothing *see* NAICS 315292: Fur and Leather Apparel Manufacturing

2387   Apparel Belts *see* NAICS 315999: Other Apparel Accessories and Other Apparel Manufacturing

2389   Apparel and Accessories, NEC *see* NAICS 315999: Other Apparel Accessories and Other Apparel Manufacturing; NAICS 315299: All Other Cut and Sew Apparel Manufacturing; NAICS 315231: Women's and Girls' Cut and Sew Lingerie, Loungewear, and Nightwear Manufacturing; NAICS 315212: Women's and Girls' Cut and Sew Apparel Contractors; NAICS 315211: Men's and Boys' Cut and Sew Apparel Contractors

2391   Curtains and Draperies *see* NAICS 314121: Curtain and Drapery Mills

2392   Housefurnishings, Except Curtains and Draperies *see* NAICS 314911: Textile Bag Mills; NAICS 339994:

Broom, Brush and Mop Manufacturing; NAICS 314129: Other Household Textile Product Mills

2393   Textile Bags *see* NAICS 314911: Textile Bag Mills

2394   Canvas and Related Products *see* NAICS 314912: Canvas and Related Product Mills

2395   Pleating, Decorative and Novelty Stitching, and Tucking for the Trade *see* NAICS 314999: All Other Miscellaneous Textile Product Mills; NAICS 315211: Men's and Boys' Cut and Sew Apparel Contractors; NAICS 315212: Women's and Girls' Cut and Sew Apparel Contractors

2396   Automotive Trimmings, Apparel Findings, and Related Products *see* NAICS 336360: Motor Vehicle Fabric Accessories and Seat Manufacturing; NAICS 315999: Other Apparel Accessories, and Other Apparel Manufacturing; NAICS 323113: Commercial Screen Printing; NAICS 314999: All Other Miscellaneous Textile Product Mills

2397   Schiffli Machine Embroideries *see* NAICS 313222: Schiffli Machine Embroidery

2399   Fabricated Textile Products, NEC *see* NAICS 336360: Motor Vehicle Fabric Accessories and Seat Manufacturing; NAICS 315999: Other Apparel Accessories and Other Apparel Manufacturing; NAICS 314999: All Other Miscellaneous Textile Product Mills

LUMBER & WOOD PRODUCTS, EXCEPT FURNITURE

2411   Logging *see* NAICS 113310: Logging

2421   Sawmills and Planing Mills, General *see* NAICS 321912: Cut Stock, Resawing Lumber, and Planing; NAICS 321113: Sawmills; NAICS 321918: Other Millwork (including Flooring); NAICS 321999: All Other Miscellaneous Wood Product Manufacturing

2426   Hardwood Dimension and Flooring Mills *see* NAICS 321918: Other Millwork (including Flooring); NAICS 321999: All Other Miscellaneous Wood Product Manufacturing; NAICS 337215: Showcase, Partition, Shelving, and Locker Manufacturing; NAICS 321912: Cut Stock, Resawing Lumber, and Planing

2429   Special Product Sawmills, NEC *see* NAICS 321113: Sawmills; NAICS 321912: Cut Stock, Resawing Lumber, and Planing; NAICS 321999: All Other Miscellaneous Wood Product Manufacturing

2431   Millwork *see* NAICS 321911: Wood Window and Door Manufacturing; NAICS 321918: Other Millwork (including Flooring)

2434   Wood Kitchen Cabinets *see* NAICS 337110: Wood Kitchen Cabinet and Counter Top Manufacturing

2435   Hardwood Veneer and Plywood *see* NAICS 321211: Hardwood Veneer and Plywood Manufacturing

2436   Softwood Veneer and Plywood *see* NAICS 321212: Softwood Veneer and Plywood Manufacturing

2439   Structural Wood Members, NEC *see* NAICS 321912: Cut Stock, Resawing Lumber, and Planing; NAICS 321214: Truss Manufacturing; NAICS 321213: Engineered Wood Member (except Truss) Manufacturing

2441   Nailed and Lock Corner Wood Boxes and Shook *see* NAICS 321920: Wood Container and Pallet Manufacturing

2448   Wood Pallets and Skids *see* NAICS 321920: Wood Container and Pallet Manufacturing

2449   Wood Containers, NEC *see* NAICS 321920: Wood Container and Pallet Manufacturing

2451   Mobile Homes *see* NAICS 321991: Manufactured Home (Mobile Home) Manufacturing

2452   Prefabricated Wood Buildings and Components *see* NAICS 321992: Prefabricated Wood Building Manufacturing

2491   Wood Preserving *see* NAICS 321114: Wood Preservation

2493   Reconstituted Wood Products *see* NAICS 321219: Reconstituted Wood Product Manufacturing

2499   Wood Products, NEC *see* NAICS 339999: All Other Miscellaneous Manufacturing; NAICS 321920: Wood Container and Pallet Manufacturing; NAICS 321999: All Other Miscellaneous Wood Product Manufacturing

FURNITURE & FIXTURES

2511   Wood Household Furniture, Except Upholstered *see* NAICS 337122: Nonupholstered Wood Household Furniture Manufacturing

2512   Wood Household Furniture, Upholstered *see* NAICS 337121: Upholstered Wood Household Furniture Manufacturing

2514   Metal Household Furniture *see* NAICS 337124: Metal Household Furniture Manufacturing

2515   Mattresses, Foundations, and Convertible Beds *see* NAICS 337910: Mattress Manufacturing; NAICS 337121: Upholstered Wood Household Furniture Manufacturing

2517   Wood Television, Radio, Phonograph and Sewing Machine Cabinets *see* NAICS 337129: Wood Television, Radio, and Sewing Machine Cabinet Manufacturing

2519   Household Furniture, NEC *see* NAICS 337125: Household Furniture (except Wood and Metal) Manufacturing

2521   Wood Office Furniture *see* NAICS 337211: Wood Office Furniture Manufacturing

2522   Office Furniture, Except Wood *see* NAICS 337214: Nonwood Office Furniture Manufacturing

2531   Public Building and Related Furniture *see* NAICS 336360: Motor Vehicle Fabric Accessories and Seat Manufacturing; NAICS 337127: Institutional Furniture Manufacturing; NAICS 339942: Lead Pencil and Art Good Manufacturing

2541   Wood Office and Store Fixtures, Partitions, Shelving, and Lockers *see* NAICS 337110: Wood Kitchen Cabinet and Counter Top Manufacturing; NAICS 337212: Custom Architectural Woodwork, Millwork, and Fixtures; NAICS 337215: Showcase, Partition, Shelving, and Locker Manufacturing

2542   Office and Store Fixtures, Partitions Shelving, and Lockers, Except Wood *see* NAICS 337215: Showcase, Partition, Shelving, and Locker Manufacturing

2591   Drapery Hardware and Window Blinds and Shades *see* NAICS 337920: Blind and Shade Manufacturing

2599   Furniture and Fixtures, NEC *see* NAICS 339113: Surgical Appliance and Supplies Manufacturing; NAICS 337127: Institutional Furniture Manufacturing

PAPER & ALLIED PRODUCTS

2611   Pulp Mills *see* NAICS 322110: Pulp Mills; NAICS 322121: Paper (except Newsprint) Mills; NAICS 322130: Paperboard Mills

2621   Paper Mills *see* NAICS 322121: Paper (except Newsprint) Mills; NAICS 322122: Newsprint Mills

2631   Paperboard Mills *see* NAICS 322130: Paperboard Mills

2652   Setup Paperboard Boxes *see* NAICS 322213: Setup Paperboard Box Manufacturing

2653   Corrugated and Solid Fiber Boxes *see* NAICS 322211: Corrugated and Solid Fiber Box Manufacturing

2655   Fiber Cans, Tubes, Drums, and Similar Products *see* NAICS 322214: Fiber Can, Tube, Drum, and Similar Products Manufacturing

2656   Sanitary Food Containers, Except Folding *see* NAICS 322215: Non-Folding Sanitary Food Container Manufacturing

2657   Folding Paperboard Boxes, Including Sanitary *see* NAICS 322212: Folding Paperboard Box Manufacturing

2671   Packaging Paper and Plastics Film *see* NAICS 322221: Coated and Laminated Packaging Paper and Plastics Film Manufacturing; NAICS 326112: Unsupported Plastics Packaging Film and Sheet Manufacturing

2672   Coated and Laminated Paper, NEC *see* NAICS 322222: Coated and Laminated Paper Manufacturing

2673   Plastics, Foil, and Coated Paper Bags *see* NAICS 322223: Plastics, Foil, and Coated Paper Bag Manufacturing; NAICS 326111: Unsupported Plastics Bag Manufacturing

2674   Uncoated Paper and Multiwall Bags *see* NAICS 322224: Uncoated Paper and Multiwall Bag Manufacturing

2675   Die-Cut Paper and Paperboard and Cardboard *see* NAICS 322231: Die-Cut Paper and Paperboard Office Supplies Manufacturing; NAICS 322292: Surface-Coated Paperboard Manufacturing; NAICS 322298: All Other Converted Paper Product Manufacturing

2676   Sanitary Paper Products *see* NAICS 322291: Sanitary Paper Product Manufacturing

2677   Envelopes *see* NAICS 322232: Envelope Manufacturing

2678   Stationery, Tablets, and Related Products *see* NAICS 322233: Stationery, Tablet, and Related Product Manufacturing

2679   Converted Paper and Paperboard Products, NEC *see* NAICS 322215: Non-Folding Sanitary Food Container Manufacturing; NAICS 322222: Coated and Laminated Paper Manufacturing; NAICS 322231: Die-Cut Paper and Paperboard Office Supplies Manufacturing; NAICS 322298: All Other Converted Paper Product Manufacturing

PRINTING, PUBLISHING, & ALLIED INDUSTRIES

2711   Newspapers: Publishing, or Publishing and Printing *see* NAICS 511110: Newspaper Publishers

2721   Periodicals: Publishing, or Publishing and Printing *see* NAICS 511120: Periodical Publishers

2731   Books: Publishing, or Publishing and Printing *see* NAICS 512230: Music Publishers; NAICS 511130: Book Publishers

2732   Book Printing *see* NAICS 323117: Book Printing

2741   Miscellaneous Publishing *see* NAICS 511140: Database and Directory Publishers; NAICS 512230: Music Publishers; NAICS 511199: All Other Publishers

2752   Commercial Printing, Lithographic *see* NAICS 323114: Quick Printing; NAICS 323110: Commercial Lithographic Printing

2754   Commercial Printing, Gravure *see* NAICS 323111: Commercial Gravure Printing

2759   Commercial Printing, NEC *see* NAICS 323113: Commercial Screen Printing; NAICS 323112: Commercial Flexographic Printing; NAICS 323114: Quick Printing; NAICS 323115: Digital Printing; NAICS 323119: Other Commercial Printing

2761   Manifold Business Forms *see* NAICS 323116: Manifold Business Form Printing

2771   Greeting Cards *see* NAICS 323110: Commercial Lithographic Printing; NAICS 323111: Commercial Gravure Printing; NAICS 323112: Commercial Flexographic Printing; NAICS 323113: Commercial Screen Printing; NAICS 323119: Other Commercial Printing; NAICS 511191: Greeting Card Publishers

2782   Blankbooks, Loose-leaf Binders and Devices *see* NAICS 323110: Commercial Lithographic Printing; NAICS 323111: Commercial Gravure Printing; NAICS 323112: Commercial Flexographic Printing; NAICS 323113: Commercial Screen Printing; NAICS 323119: Other Commercial Printing; NAICS 323118: Blankbook, Loose-leaf Binder and Device Manufacturing

2789   Bookbinding and Related Work *see* NAICS 323121: Tradebinding and Related Work

2791   Typesetting *see* NAICS 323122: Prepress Services

2796   Platemaking and Related Services *see* NAICS 323122: Prepress Services

CHEMICALS & ALLIED PRODUCTS

2812   Alkalies and Chlorine *see* NAICS 325181: Alkalies and Chlorine Manufacturing

2813   Industrial Gases *see* NAICS 325120: Industrial Gas Manufacturing

2816   Inorganic Pigments *see* NAICS 325131: Inorganic Dye and Pigment Manufacturing; NAICS 325182: Carbon Black Manufacturing

2819   Industrial Inorganic Chemicals, NEC *see* NAICS 325998: All Other Miscellaneous Chemical Product Manufacturing; NAICS 331311: Aluminum Refining; NAICS 325131: Inorganic Dye and Pigment Manufacturing; NAICS 325188: All Other Inorganic Chemical Manufacturing

2821   Plastics Material Synthetic Resins, and Nonvulcanizable Elastomers *see* NAICS 325211: Plastics Material and Resin Manufacturing

2822   Synthetic Rubber *see* NAICS 325212: Synthetic Rubber Manufacturing

2823   Cellulosic Manmade Fibers *see* NAICS 325221: Cellulosic Manmade Fiber Manufacturing

2824   Manmade Organic Fibers, Except Cellulosic *see* NAICS 325222: Noncellulosic Organic Fiber Manufacturing

2833   Medicinal Chemicals and Botanical Products *see* NAICS 325411: Medicinal and Botanical Manufacturing

2834   Pharmaceutical Preparations *see* NAICS 325412: Pharmaceutical Preparation Manufacturing

2835   In Vitro and In Vivo Diagnostic Substances *see* NAICS 325412: Pharmaceutical Preparation Manufacturing; NAICS 325413: In-Vitro Diagnostic Substance Manufacturing

2836   Biological Products, Except Diagnostic Substances *see* NAICS 325414: Biological Product (except Diagnostic) Manufacturing

2841   Soaps and Other Detergents, Except Specialty Cleaners *see* NAICS 325611: Soap and Other Detergent Manufacturing

2842   Specialty Cleaning, Polishing, and Sanitary Preparations *see* NAICS 325612: Polish and Other Sanitation Good Manufacturing

2843   Surface Active Agents, Finishing Agents, Sulfonated Oils, and Assistants *see* NAICS 325613: Surface Active Agent Manufacturing

2844   Perfumes, Cosmetics, and Other Toilet Preparations *see* NAICS 325620: Toilet Preparation Manufacturing; NAICS 325611: Soap and Other Detergent Manufacturing

2851   Paints, Varnishes, Lacquers, Enamels, and Allied Products *see* NAICS 325510: Paint and Coating Manufacturing

2861   Gum and Wood Chemicals *see* NAICS 325191: Gum and Wood Chemical Manufacturing

2865   Cyclic Organic Crudes and Intermediates, and Organic Dyes and Pigments *see* NAICS 325110: Petrochemical Manufacturing; NAICS 325132: Organic Dye and Pigment Manufacturing; NAICS 325192: Cyclic Crude and Intermediate Manufacturing

2869   Industrial Organic Chemicals, NEC *see* NAICS 325110: Petrochemical Manufacturing; NAICS 325188: All Other Inorganic Chemical Manufacturing; NAICS 325193: Ethyl Alcohol Manufacturing; NAICS 325120: Industrial Gas Manufacturing; NAICS 325199: All Other Basic Organic Chemical Manufacturing

2873   Nitrogenous Fertilizers *see* NAICS 325311: Nitrogenous Fertilizer Manufacturing

2874   Phosphatic Fertilizers *see* NAICS 325312: Phosphatic Fertilizer Manufacturing

2875   Fertilizers, Mixing Only *see* NAICS 325314: Fertilizer (Mixing Only) Manufacturing

2879   Pesticides and Agricultural Chemicals, NEC *see* NAICS 325320: Pesticide and Other Agricultural Chemical Manufacturing

2891   Adhesives and Sealants *see* NAICS 325520: Adhesive and Sealant Manufacturing

2892   Explosives *see* NAICS 325920: Explosives Manufacturing

2893   Printing Ink *see* NAICS 325910: Printing Ink Manufacturing

2895   Carbon Black *see* NAICS 325182: Carbon Black Manufacturing

2899   Chemicals and Chemical Preparations, NEC *see* NAICS 325510: Paint and Coating Manufacturing; NAICS 311942: Spice and Extract Manufacturing; NAICS 325199: All Other Basic Organic Chemical Manufacturing; NAICS 325998: All Other Miscellaneous Chemical Product Manufacturing

PETROLEUM REFINING & RELATED INDUSTRIES

2911   Petroleum Refining *see* NAICS 324110: Petroleum Refineries

2951   Asphalt Paving Mixtures and Blocks *see* NAICS 324121: Asphalt Paving Mixture and Block Manufacturing

2952   Asphalt Felts and Coatings *see* NAICS 324122: Asphalt Shingle and Coating Materials Manufacturing

2992   Lubricating Oils and Greases *see* NAICS 324191: Petroleum Lubricating Oil and Grease Manufacturing

2999 Products of Petroleum and Coal, NEC *see* NAICS 324199: All Other Petroleum and Coal Products Manufacturing

RUBBER & MISCELLANEOUS PLASTICS PRODUCTS

3011 Tires and Inner Tubes *see* NAICS 326211: Tire Manufacturing (except Retreading)

3021 Rubber and Plastics Footwear *see* NAICS 316211: Rubber and Plastics Footwear Manufacturing

3052 Rubber and Plastics Hose and Belting *see* NAICS 326220: Rubber and Plastics Hoses and Belting Manufacturing

3053 Gaskets, Packing, and Sealing Devices *see* NAICS 339991: Gasket, Packing, and Sealing Device Manufacturing

3061 Molded, Extruded, and Lathe-Cut Mechanical Rubber Products *see* NAICS 326291: Rubber Product Manufacturing for Mechanical Use

3069 Fabricated Rubber Products, NEC *see* NAICS 313320: Fabric Coating Mills; NAICS 326192: Resilient Floor Covering Manufacturing; NAICS 326299: All Other Rubber Product Manufacturing

3081 Unsupported Plastics Film and Sheet *see* NAICS 326113: Unsupported Plastics Film and Sheet (except Packaging) Manufacturing

3082 Unsupported Plastics Profile Shapes *see* NAICS 326121: Unsupported Plastics Profile Shape Manufacturing

3083 Laminated Plastics Plate, Sheet, and Profile Shapes *see* NAICS 326130: Laminated Plastics Plate, Sheet, and Shape Manufacturing

3084 Plastic Pipe *see* NAICS 326122: Plastics Pipe and Pipe Fitting Manufacturing

3085 Plastics Bottles *see* NAICS 326160: Plastics Bottle Manufacturing

3086 Plastics Foam Products *see* NAICS 326150: Urethane and Other Foam Product (except Polystyrene) Manufacturing; NAICS 326140: Polystyrene Foam Product Manufacturing

3087 Custom Compounding of Purchased Plastics Resins *see* NAICS 325991: Custom Compounding of Purchased Resin

3088 Plastics Plumbing Fixtures *see* NAICS 326191: Plastics Plumbing Fixtures Manufacturing

3089 Plastics Products, NEC *see* NAICS 326122: Plastics Pipe and Pipe Fitting Manufacturing; NAICS 326121: Unsupported Plastics Profile Shape Manufacturing; NAICS 326199: All Other Plastics Product Manufacturing

LEATHER & LEATHER PRODUCTS

3111 Leather Tanning and Finishing *see* NAICS 316110: Leather and Hide Tanning and Finishing

3131 Boot and Shoe Cut Stock and Findings *see* NAICS 321999: All Other Miscellaneous Wood Product Manufacturing; NAICS 339993: Fastener, Button, Needle, and Pin Manufacturing; NAICS 316999: All Other Leather Good Manufacturing

3142 House Slippers *see* NAICS 316212: House Slipper Manufacturing

3143 Men's Footwear, Except Athletic *see* NAICS 316213: Men's Footwear (except Athletic) Manufacturing

3144 Women's Footwear, Except Athletic *see* NAICS 316214: Women's Footwear (except Athletic) Manufacturing

3149 Footwear, Except Rubber, NEC *see* NAICS 316219: Other Footwear Manufacturing

3151 Leather Gloves and Mittens *see* NAICS 315992: Glove and Mitten Manufacturing

3161 Luggage *see* NAICS 316991: Luggage Manufacturing

3171 Women's Handbags and Purses *see* NAICS 316992: Women's Handbag and Purse Manufacturing

3172 Personal Leather Goods, Except Women's Handbags and Purses *see* NAICS 316993: Personal Leather Good (except Women's Handbag and Purse) Manufacturing

3199 Leather Goods, NEC *see* NAICS 316999: All Other Leather Good Manufacturing

STONE, CLAY, GLASS, & CONCRETE PRODUCTS

3211 Flat Glass *see* NAICS 327211: Flat Glass Manufacturing

3221 Glass Containers *see* NAICS 327213: Glass Container Manufacturing

3229 Pressed and Blown Glass and Glassware, NEC *see* NAICS 327212: Other Pressed and Blown Glass and Glassware Manufacturing

3231 Glass Products, Made of Purchased Glass *see* NAICS 327215: Glass Product Manufacturing Made of Purchased Glass

3241 Cement, Hydraulic *see* NAICS 327310: Cement Manufacturing

3251 Brick and Structural Clay Tile *see* NAICS 327121: Brick and Structural Clay Tile Manufacturing

3253 Ceramic Wall and Floor Tile *see* NAICS 327122: Ceramic Wall and Floor Tile Manufacturing

3255 Clay Refractories *see* NAICS 327124: Clay Refractory Manufacturing

3259 Structural Clay Products, NEC *see* NAICS 327123: Other Structural Clay Product Manufacturing

3261 Vitreous China Plumbing Fixtures and China and Earthenware Fittings and Bathroom Accessories *see* NAICS 327111: Vitreous China Plumbing Fixture and China and Earthenware Fitting and Bathroom Accessories Manufacturing

3262 Vitreous China Table and Kitchen Articles *see* NAICS 327112: Vitreous China, Fine Earthenware and Other Pottery Product Manufacturing

3263 Fine Earthenware (Whiteware) Table and Kitchen Articles *see* NAICS 327112: Vitreous China, Fine Earthenware and Other Pottery Product Manufacturing

3264 Porcelain Electrical Supplies *see* NAICS 327113: Porcelain Electrical Supply Manufacturing

3269 Pottery Products, NEC *see* NAICS 327112: Vitreous China, Fine Earthenware, and Other Pottery Product Manufacturing

3271 Concrete Block and Brick *see* NAICS 327331: Concrete Block and Brick Manufacturing

3272 Concrete Products, Except Block and Brick *see* NAICS 327999: All Other Miscellaneous Nonmetallic Mineral Product Manufacturing; NAICS 327332: Concrete Pipe Manufacturing; NAICS 327390: Other Concrete Product Manufacturing

3273 Ready-Mixed Concrete *see* NAICS 327320: Ready-Mix Concrete Manufacturing

3274 Lime *see* NAICS 327410: Lime Manufacturing

3275 Gypsum Products *see* NAICS 327420: Gypsum and Gypsum Product Manufacturing

3281 Cut Stone and Stone Products *see* NAICS 327991: Cut Stone and Stone Product Manufacturing

3291 Abrasive Products *see* NAICS 332999: All Other Miscellaneous Fabricated Metal Product Manufacturing; NAICS 327910: Abrasive Product Manufacturing

3292 Asbestos Products *see* NAICS 336340: Motor Vehicle Brake System Manufacturing; NAICS 327999: All Other Miscellaneous Nonmetallic Mineral Product Manufacturing

3295 Minerals and Earths, Ground or Otherwise Treated *see* NAICS 327992: Ground or Treated Mineral and Earth Manufacturing

3296 Mineral Wool *see* NAICS 327993: Mineral Wool Manufacturing

3297 Nonclay Refractories *see* NAICS 327125: Nonclay Refractory Manufacturing

3299 Nonmetallic Mineral Products, NEC *see* NAICS 327420: Gypsum and Gypsum Product Manufacturing; NAICS 327999: All Other Miscellaneous Nonmetallic Mineral Product Manufacturing

PRIMARY METALS INDUSTRIES

3312 Steel Works, Blast Furnaces (Including Coke Ovens), and Rolling Mills *see* NAICS 324199: All Other Petroleum and Coal Products Manufacturing; NAICS 331111: Iron and Steel Mills

3313 Electrometallurgical Products, Except Steel *see* NAICS 331112: Electrometallurgical Ferroalloy Product Manufacturing; NAICS 331492: Secondary Smelting, Refining, and Alloying of Nonferrous Metals (except Copper and Aluminum)

3315 Steel Wiredrawing and Steel Nails and Spikes *see* NAICS 331222: Steel Wire Drawing; NAICS 332618: Other Fabricated Wire Product Manufacturing

3316 Cold-Rolled Steel Sheet, Strip, and Bars *see* NAICS 331221: Cold-Rolled Steel Shape Manufacturing

3317 Steel Pipe and Tubes *see* NAICS 331210: Iron and Steel Pipes and Tubes Manufacturing from Purchased Steel

3321 Gray and Ductile Iron Foundries *see* NAICS 331511: Iron Foundries

3322 Malleable Iron Foundries *see* NAICS 331511: Iron Foundries

3324 Steel Investment Foundries *see* NAICS 331512: Steel Investment Foundries

3325 Steel Foundries, NEC *see* NAICS 331513: Steel Foundries (except Investment)

3331 Primary Smelting and Refining of Copper *see* NAICS 331411: Primary Smelting and Refining of Copper

3334 Primary Production of Aluminum *see* NAICS 331312: Primary Aluminum Production

3339 Primary Smelting and Refining of Nonferrous Metals, Except Copper and Aluminum *see* NAICS 331419: Primary Smelting and Refining of Nonferrous Metals (except Copper and Aluminum)

3341 Secondary Smelting and Refining of Nonferrous Metals *see* NAICS 331314: Secondary Smelting and Alloying of Aluminum; NAICS 331423: Secondary Smelting, Refining, and Alloying of Copper; NAICS 331492: Secondary Smelting, Refining, and Alloying of Nonferrous Metals (except Copper and Aluminum)

3351 Rolling, Drawing, and Extruding of Copper *see* NAICS 331421: Copper (except Wire) Rolling, Drawing, and Extruding

3353 Aluminum Sheet, Plate, and Foil *see* NAICS 331315: Aluminum Sheet, Plate, and Foil Manufacturing

3354 Aluminum Extruded Products *see* NAICS 331316: Aluminum Extruded Product Manufacturing

3355 Aluminum Rolling and Drawing, NEC *see* NAICS 331319: Other Aluminum Rolling and Drawing

3356 Rolling, Drawing, and Extruding of Nonferrous Metals, Except Copper and Aluminum *see* NAICS 331491: Nonferrous Metal (except Copper and Aluminum) Rolling, Drawing, and Extruding

3357 Drawing and Insulating of Nonferrous Wire *see* NAICS 331319: Other Aluminum Rolling and Drawing; NAICS 331422: Copper Wire Drawing; NAICS 331491: Nonferrous Metal (except Copper and Aluminum) Rolling, Drawing, and Extruding; NAICS 335921: Fiber Optic Cable Manufacturing; NAICS 335929: Other Communication and Energy Wire Manufacturing

3363 Aluminum Die-Castings *see* NAICS 331521: Aluminum Die-Castings

3364 Nonferrous Die-Castings, Except Aluminum *see* NAICS 331522: Nonferrous (except Aluminum) Die-Castings

3365 Aluminum Foundries *see* NAICS 331524: Aluminum Foundries

3366 Copper Foundries *see* NAICS 331525: Copper Foundries

3369 Nonferrous Foundries, Except Aluminum and Copper *see* NAICS 331528: Other Nonferrous Foundries

3398 Metal Heat Treating *see* NAICS 332811: Metal Heat Treating

3399 Primary Metal Products, NEC *see* NAICS 331111: Iron and Steel Mills; NAICS 331314: Secondary Smelting and Alloying of Aluminum; NAICS 331423: Secondary Smelting, Refining and Alloying of Copper; NAICS 331492: Secondary Smelting, Refining, and Alloying of Nonferrous Metals (except Copper and Aluminum); NAICS 332618: Other Fabricated Wire Product Manufacturing; NAICS 332813: Electroplating, Plating, Polishing, Anodizing, and Coloring

FABRICATED METAL PRODUCTS, EXCEPT MACHINERY & TRANSPORTATION EQUIPMENT

3411 Metal Cans *see* NAICS 332431: Metal Can Manufacturing

3412 Metal Shipping Barrels, Drums, Kegs and Pails *see* NAICS 332439: Other Metal Container Manufacturing

3421 Cutlery *see* NAICS 332211: Cutlery and Flatware (except Precious) Manufacturing

3423 Hand and Edge Tools, Except Machine Tools and Handsaws *see* NAICS 332212: Hand and Edge Tool Manufacturing

3425 Saw Blades and Handsaws *see* NAICS 332213: Saw Blade and Handsaw Manufacturing

SIC TO NAICS CONVERSION GUIDE

3429   Hardware, NEC *see* NAICS 332439: Other Metal Container Manufacturing; NAICS 332919: Other Metal Valve and Pipe Fitting Manufacturing; NAICS 332510: Hardware Manufacturing

3431   Enameled Iron and Metal Sanitary Ware *see* NAICS 332998: Enameled Iron and Metal Sanitary Ware Manufacturing

3432   Plumbing Fixture Fittings and Trim *see* NAICS 332913: Plumbing Fixture Fitting and Trim Manufacturing; NAICS 332999: All Other Miscellaneous Fabricated Metal Product Manufacturing

3433   Heating Equipment, Except Electric and Warm Air Furnaces *see* NAICS 333414: Heating Equipment (except Electric and Warm Air Furnaces) Manufacturing

3441   Fabricated Structural Metal *see* NAICS 332312: Fabricated Structural Metal Manufacturing

3442   Metal Doors, Sash, Frames, Molding, and Trim Manufacturing *see* NAICS 332321: Metal Window and Door Manufacturing

3443   Fabricated Plate Work (Boiler Shops) *see* NAICS 332313: Plate Work Manufacturing; NAICS 332410: Power Boiler and Heat Exchanger Manufacturing; NAICS 332420: Metal Tank (Heavy Gauge) Manufacturing; NAICS 333415: Air-Conditioning and Warm Air Heating Equipment and Commercial and Industrial Refrigeration Equipment Manufacturing

3444   Sheet Metal Work *see* NAICS 332322: Sheet Metal Work Manufacturing; NAICS 332439: Other Metal Container Manufacturing

3446   Architectural and Ornamental Metal Work *see* NAICS 332323: Ornamental and Architectural Metal Work Manufacturing

3448   Prefabricated Metal Buildings and Components *see* NAICS 332311: Prefabricated Metal Building and Component Manufacturing

3449   Miscellaneous Structural Metal Work *see* NAICS 332114: Custom Roll Forming; NAICS 332312: Fabricated Structural Metal Manufacturing; NAICS 332321: Metal Window and Door Manufacturing; NAICS 332323: Ornamental and Architectural Metal Work Manufacturing

3451   Screw Machine Products *see* NAICS 332721: Precision Turned Product Manufacturing

3452   Bolts, Nuts, Screws, Rivets, and Washers *see* NAICS 332722: Bolt, Nut, Screw, Rivet, and Washer Manufacturing

3462   Iron and Steel Forgings *see* NAICS 332111: Iron and Steel Forging

3463   Nonferrous Forgings *see* NAICS 332112: Nonferrous Forging

3465   Automotive Stamping *see* NAICS 336370: Motor Vehicle Metal Stamping

3466   Crowns and Closures *see* NAICS 332115: Crown and Closure Manufacturing

3469   Metal Stamping, NEC *see* NAICS 339911: Jewelry (including Precious Metal) Manufacturing; NAICS 332116: Metal Stamping; NAICS 332214: Kitchen Utensil, Pot, and Pan Manufacturing

3471   Electroplating, Plating, Polishing, Anodizing, and Coloring *see* NAICS 332813: Electroplating, Plating, Polishing, Anodizing, and Coloring

3479   Coating, Engraving, and Allied Services, NEC *see* NAICS 339914: Costume Jewelry and Novelty Manufacturing; NAICS 339911: Jewelry (including Precious Metal) Manufacturing; NAICS 339912: Silverware and Plated Ware Manufacturing; NAICS 332812: Metal Coating, Engraving, and Allied Services (except Jewelry and Silverware) to Manufacturing

3482   Small Arms Ammunition *see* NAICS 332992: Small Arms Ammunition Manufacturing

3483   Ammunition, Except for Small Arms *see* NAICS 332993: Ammunition (except Small Arms) Manufacturing

3484   Small Arms *see* NAICS 332994: Small Arms Manufacturing

3489   Ordnance and Accessories, NEC *see* NAICS 332995: Other Ordnance and Accessories Manufacturing

3491   Industrial Valves *see* NAICS 332911: Industrial Valve Manufacturing

3492   Fluid Power Valves and Hose Fittings *see* NAICS 332912: Fluid Power Valve and Hose Fitting Manufacturing

3493   Steel Springs, Except Wire *see* NAICS 332611: Steel Spring (except Wire) Manufacturing

3494   Valves and Pipe Fittings, NEC *see* NAICS 332919: Other Metal Valve and Pipe Fitting Manufacturing; NAICS 332999: All Other Miscellaneous Fabricated Metal Product Manufacturing

3495   Wire Springs *see* NAICS 332612: Wire Spring Manufacturing; NAICS 334518: Watch, Clock, and Part Manufacturing

3496   Miscellaneous Fabricated Wire Products *see* NAICS 332618: Other Fabricated Wire Product Manufacturing

3497   Metal Foil and Leaf *see* NAICS 322225: Laminated Aluminum Foil Manufacturing for Flexible Packaging Uses; NAICS 332999: All Other Miscellaneous Fabricated Metal Product Manufacturing

3498   Fabricated Pipe and Pipe Fittings *see* NAICS 332996: Fabricated Pipe and Pipe Fitting Manufacturing

3499   Fabricated Metal Products, NEC *see* NAICS 337215: Showcase, Partition, Shelving, and Locker Manufacturing; NAICS 332117: Powder Metallurgy Part Manufacturing; NAICS 332439: Other Metal Container Manufacturing; NAICS 332510: Hardware Manufacturing; NAICS 332919: Other Metal Valve and Pipe Fitting Manufacturing; NAICS 339914: Costume Jewelry and Novelty Manufacturing; NAICS 332999: All Other Miscellaneous Fabricated Metal Product Manufacturing

INDUSTRIAL & COMMERCIAL MACHINERY & COMPUTER EQUIPMENT

3511   Steam, Gas, and Hydraulic Turbines, and Turbine Generator Set Units *see* NAICS 333611: Turbine and Turbine Generator Set Unit Manufacturing

3519   Internal Combustion Engines, NEC *see* NAICS 336399: All Other Motor Vehicle Parts Manufacturing; NAICS 333618: Other Engine Equipment Manufacturing

3523   Farm Machinery and Equipment *see* NAICS 333111: Farm Machinery and Equipment Manufacturing; NAICS 332323: Ornamental and Architectural Metal Work Manufacturing; NAICS 332212: Hand and Edge Tool Manufacturing; NAICS 333922: Conveyor and Conveying Equipment Manufacturing

3524   Lawn and Garden Tractors and Home Lawn and Garden Equipment *see* NAICS 333112: Lawn and Garden Tractor and Home Lawn and Garden Equipment Manufacturing; NAICS 332212: Hand and Edge Tool Manufacturing

3531   Construction Machinery and Equipment *see* NAICS 336510: Railroad Rolling Stock Manufacturing; NAICS 333923: Overhead Traveling Crane, Hoist, and Monorail System Manufacturing; NAICS 333120: Construction Machinery Manufacturing

3532   Mining Machinery and Equipment, Except Oil and Gas Field Machinery and Equipment *see* NAICS 333131: Mining Machinery and Equipment Manufacturing

3533   Oil and Gas Field Machinery and Equipment *see* NAICS 333132: Oil and Gas Field Machinery and Equipment Manufacturing

3534   Elevators and Moving Stairways *see* NAICS 333921: Elevator and Moving Stairway Manufacturing

3535   Conveyors and Conveying Equipment *see* NAICS 333922: Conveyor and Conveying Equipment Manufacturing

3536   Overhead Traveling Cranes, Hoists, and Monorail Systems *see* NAICS 333923: Overhead Traveling Crane, Hoist, and Monorail System Manufacturing

3537   Industrial Trucks, Tractors, Trailers, and Stackers *see* NAICS 333924: Industrial Truck, Tractor, Trailer, and Stacker Machinery Manufacturing; NAICS 332999: All Other Miscellaneous Fabricated Metal Product Manufacturing; NAICS 332439: Other Metal Container Manufacturing

3541   Machine Tools, Metal Cutting Type *see* NAICS 333512: Machine Tool (Metal Cutting Types) Manufacturing

3542   Machine Tools, Metal Forming Type *see* NAICS 333513: Machine Tool (Metal Forming Types) Manufacturing

3543   Industrial Patterns *see* NAICS 332997: Industrial Pattern Manufacturing

3544   Special Dies and Tools, Die Sets, Jigs and Fixtures, and Industrial Molds *see* NAICS 333514: Special Die and Tool, Die Set, Jig, and Fixture Manufacturing; NAICS 333511: Industrial Mold Manufacturing

3545   Cutting Tools, Machine Tool Accessories, and Machinists' Precision Measuring Devices *see* NAICS 333515: Cutting Tool and Machine Tool Accessory Manufacturing; NAICS 332212: Hand and Edge Tool Manufacturing

3546   Power-Driven Handtools *see* NAICS 333991: Power-Driven Hand Tool Manufacturing

3547   Rolling Mill Machinery and Equipment *see* NAICS 333516: Rolling Mill Machinery and Equipment Manufacturing

3548   Electric and Gas Welding and Soldering Equipment *see* NAICS 333992: Welding and Soldering Equipment Manufacturing; NAICS 335311: Power, Distribution, and Specialty Transformer Manufacturing

3549   Metalworking Machinery, NEC *see* NAICS 333518: Other Metalworking Machinery Manufacturing

3552   Textile Machinery *see* NAICS 333292: Textile Machinery Manufacturing

3553   Woodworking Machinery *see* NAICS 333210: Sawmill and Woodworking Machinery Manufacturing

3554   Paper Industries Machinery *see* NAICS 333291: Paper Industry Machinery Manufacturing

3555   Printing Trades Machinery and Equipment *see* NAICS 333293: Printing Machinery and Equipment Manufacturing

3556   Food Products Machinery *see* NAICS 333294: Food Product Machinery Manufacturing

3559   Special Industry Machinery, NEC *see* NAICS 333220: Rubber and Plastics Industry Machinery Manufacturing; NAICS 333319: Other Commercial and Service Industry Machinery Manufacturing; NAICS 333295: Semiconductor Manufacturing Machinery; NAICS 333298: All Other Industrial Machinery Manufacturing

3561   Pumps and Pumping Equipment *see* NAICS 333911: Pump and Pumping Equipment Manufacturing

3562   Ball and Roller Bearings *see* NAICS 332991: Ball and Roller Bearing Manufacturing

3563   Air and Gas Compressors *see* NAICS 333912: Air and Gas Compressor Manufacturing

3564   Industrial and Commercial Fans and Blowers and Air Purification Equipment *see* NAICS 333411: Air Purification Equipment Manufacturing; NAICS 333412: Industrial and Commercial Fan and Blower Manufacturing

3565   Packaging Machinery *see* NAICS 333993: Packaging Machinery Manufacturing

3566   Speed Changers, Industrial High-Speed Drives, and Gears *see* NAICS 333612: Speed Changer, Industrial High-Speed Drive, and Gear Manufacturing

3567   Industrial Process Furnaces and Ovens *see* NAICS 333994: Industrial Process Furnace and Oven Manufacturing

3568   Mechanical Power Transmission Equipment, NEC *see* NAICS 333613: Mechanical Power Transmission Equipment Manufacturing

3569   General Industrial Machinery and Equipment, NEC *see* NAICS 333999: All Other General Purpose Machinery Manufacturing

3571   Electronic Computers *see* NAICS 334111: Electronic Computer Manufacturing

3572   Computer Storage Devices *see* NAICS 334112: Computer Storage Device Manufacturing

3575   Computer Terminals *see* NAICS 334113: Computer Terminal Manufacturing

3577   Computer Peripheral Equipment, NEC *see* NAICS 334119: Other Computer Peripheral Equipment Manufacturing

3578   Calculating and Accounting Machines, Except Electronic Computers *see* NAICS 334119: Other Computer Peripheral Equipment Manufacturing; NAICS 333313: Office Machinery Manufacturing

3579   Office Machines, NEC *see* NAICS 339942: Lead Pencil and Art Good Manufacturing; NAICS 334518: Watch, Clock, and Part Manufacturing; NAICS 333313: Office Machinery Manufacturing

3581   Automatic Vending Machines *see* NAICS 333311: Automatic Vending Machine Manufacturing

3582   Commercial Laundry, Drycleaning, and Pressing Machines *see* NAICS 333312: Commercial Laundry, Drycleaning, and Pressing Machine Manufacturing

3585   Air-Conditioning and Warm Air Heating Equipment and Commercial and Industrial Refrigeration Equipment *see* NAICS 336391: Motor Vehicle Air Conditioning Manufacturing; NAICS 333415: Air Conditioning and Warm Air Heating Equipment and Commercial and Industrial Refrigeration Equipment Manufacturing

3586   Measuring and Dispensing Pumps *see* NAICS 333913: Measuring and Dispensing Pump Manufacturing

3589 Service Industry Machinery, NEC *see* NAICS 333319: Other Commercial and Service Industry Machinery Manufacturing

3592 Carburetors, Pistons, Piston Rings and Valves *see* NAICS 336311: Carburetor, Piston, Piston Ring and Valve Manufacturing

3593 Fluid Power Cylinders and Actuators *see* NAICS 333995: Fluid Power Cylinder and Actuator Manufacturing

3594 Fluid Power Pumps and Motors *see* NAICS 333996: Fluid Power Pump and Motor Manufacturing

3596 Scales and Balances, Except Laboratory *see* NAICS 333997: Scale and Balance (except Laboratory) Manufacturing

3599 Industrial and Commercial Machinery and Equipment, NEC *see* NAICS 336399: All Other Motor Vehicle Part Manufacturing; NAICS 332999: All Other Miscellaneous Fabricated Metal Product Manufacturing; NAICS 333319: Other Commercial and Service Industry Machinery Manufacturing; NAICS 332710: Machine Shops; NAICS 333999: All Other General Purpose Machinery Manufacturing

ELECTRONIC & OTHER ELECTRICAL EQUIPMENT & COMPONENTS, EXCEPT COMPUTER EQUIPMENT

3612 Power, Distribution, and Specialty Transformers *see* NAICS 335311: Power, Distribution, and Specialty Transformer Manufacturing

3613 Switchgear and Switchboard Apparatus *see* NAICS 335313: Switchgear and Switchboard Apparatus Manufacturing

3621 Motors and Generators *see* NAICS 335312: Motor and Generator Manufacturing

3624 Carbon and Graphite Products *see* NAICS 335991: Carbon and Graphite Product Manufacturing

3625 Relays and Industrial Controls *see* NAICS 335314: Relay and Industrial Control Manufacturing

3629 Electrical Industrial Apparatus, NEC *see* NAICS 335999: All Other Miscellaneous Electrical Equipment and Component Manufacturing

3631 Household Cooking Equipment *see* NAICS 335221: Household Cooking Appliance Manufacturing

3632 Household Refrigerators and Home and Farm Freezers *see* NAICS 335222: Household Refrigerator and Home and Farm Freezer Manufacturing

3633 Household Laundry Equipment *see* NAICS 335224: Household Laundry Equipment Manufacturing

3634 Electric Housewares and Fans *see* NAICS 335211: Electric Houseware and Fan Manufacturing; NAICS 333414: Heating Equipment (except Electric and Warm Air Furnaces) Manufacturing

3635 Household Vacuum Cleaners *see* NAICS 335212: Household Vacuum Cleaner Manufacturing

3639 Household Appliances, NEC *see* NAICS 335212: Household Vacuum Cleaner Manufacturing; NAICS 333298: All Other Industrial Machinery Manufacturing; NAICS 335228: Other Household Appliance Manufacturing

3641 Electric Lamp Bulbs and Tubes *see* NAICS 335110: Electric Lamp Bulb and Part Manufacturing

3643 Current-Carrying Wiring Devices *see* NAICS 335931: Current-Carrying Wiring Device Manufacturing

3644 Noncurrent-Carrying Wiring Devices *see* NAICS 335932: Noncurrent-Carrying Wiring Device Manufacturing

3645 Residential Electric Lighting Fixtures *see* NAICS 335121: Residential Electric Lighting Fixture Manufacturing

3646 Commercial, Industrial, and Institutional Electric Lighting Fixtures *see* NAICS 335122: Commercial, Industrial, and Institutional Electric Lighting Fixture Manufacturing

3647 Vehicular Lighting Equipment *see* NAICS 336321: Vehicular Lighting Equipment Manufacturing

3648 Lighting Equipment, NEC *see* NAICS 335129: Other Lighting Equipment Manufacturing

3651 Household Audio and Video Equipment *see* NAICS 334310: Audio and Video Equipment Manufacturing

3652 Phonograph Records and Prerecorded Audio Tapes and Disks *see* NAICS 334612: Prerecorded Compact Disc (Except Software), Tape and Record Reproducing; NAICS 512220: Integrated Record Production/Distribution

3661 Telephone and Telegraph Apparatus *see* NAICS 334210: Telephone Apparatus Manufacturing; NAICS 334416: Electronic Coil, Transformer, and Other Inductor Manufacturing; NAICS 334418: Printed Circuit/Electronics Assembly Manufacturing

3663 Radio and Television Broadcasting and Communication Equipment *see* NAICS 334220: Radio and Television Broadcasting and Wireless Communications Equipment Manufacturing

3669 Communications Equipment, NEC *see* NAICS 334290: Other Communication Equipment Manufacturing

3671 Electron Tubes *see* NAICS 334411: Electron Tube Manufacturing

3672 Printed Circuit Boards *see* NAICS 334412: Printed Circuit Board Manufacturing

3674 Semiconductors and Related Devices *see* NAICS 334413: Semiconductor and Related Device Manufacturing

3675 Electronic Capacitors *see* NAICS 334414: Electronic Capacitor Manufacturing

3676 Electronic Resistors *see* NAICS 334415: Electronic Resistor Manufacturing

3677 Electronic Coils, Transformers, and Other Inductors *see* NAICS 334416: Electronic Coil, Transformer, and Other Inductor Manufacturing

3678 Electronic Connectors *see* NAICS 334417: Electronic Connector Manufacturing

3679 Electronic Components, NEC *see* NAICS 334220: Radio and Television Broadcasting and Wireless Communications Equipment Manufacturing; NAICS 334418: Printed Circuit/Electronics Assembly Manufacturing; NAICS 336322: Other Motor Vehicle Electrical and Electronic Equipment Manufacturing; NAICS 334419: Other Electronic Component Manufacturing

3691 Storage Batteries *see* NAICS 335911: Storage Battery Manufacturing

3692 Primary Batteries, Dry and Wet *see* NAICS 335912: Dry and Wet Primary Battery Manufacturing

3694 Electrical Equipment for Internal Combustion Engines *see* NAICS 336322: Other Motor Vehicle Electrical and Electronic Equipment Manufacturing

3695　Magnetic and Optical Recording Media *see* NAICS 334613: Magnetic and Optical Recording Media Manufacturing

3699　Electrical Machinery, Equipment, and Supplies, NEC *see* NAICS 333319: Other Commercial and Service Industry Machinery Manufacturing; NAICS 333618: Other Engine Equipment Manufacturing; NAICS 334119: Other Computer Peripheral Equipment Manufacturing; NAICS 335129: Other Lighting Equipment Manufacturing; NAICS 335999: All Other Miscellaneous Electrical Equipment and Component Manufacturing

TRANSPORTATION EQUIPMENT

3711　Motor Vehicles and Passenger Car Bodies *see* NAICS 336111: Automobile Manufacturing; NAICS 336112: Light Truck and Utility Vehicle Manufacturing; NAICS 336120: Heavy Duty Truck Manufacturing; NAICS 336211: Motor Vehicle Body Manufacturing; NAICS 336992: Military Armored Vehicle, Tank, and Tank Component Manufacturing

3713　Truck and Bus Bodies *see* NAICS 336211: Motor Vehicle Body Manufacturing

3714　Motor Vehicle Parts and Accessories *see* NAICS 336211: Motor Vehicle Body Manufacturing; NAICS 336312: Gasoline Engine and Engine Parts Manufacturing; NAICS 336322: Other Motor Vehicle Electrical and Electronic Equipment Manufacturing; NAICS 336330: Motor Vehicle Steering and Suspension Components (except Spring) Manufacturing; NAICS 336340: Motor Vehicle Brake System Manufacturing; NAICS 336350: Motor Vehicle Transmission and Power Train Part Manufacturing; NAICS 336399: All Other Motor Vehicle Parts Manufacturing

3715　Truck Trailers *see* NAICS 336212: Truck Trailer Manufacturing

3716　Motor Homes *see* NAICS 336213: Motor Home Manufacturing

3721　Aircraft *see* NAICS 336411: Aircraft Manufacturing

3724　Aircraft Engines and Engine Parts *see* NAICS 336412: Aircraft Engine and Engine Parts Manufacturing

3728　Aircraft Parts and Auxiliary Equipment, NEC *see* NAICS 332912: Fluid Power Valve and Hose Fitting Manufacturing; NAICS 336413: Other Aircraft Part and Auxiliary Equipment Manufacturing

3731　Ship Building and Repairing *see* NAICS 336611: Ship Building and Repairing

3732　Boat Building and Repairing *see* NAICS 811490: Other Personal and Household Goods Repair and Maintenance; NAICS 336612: Boat Building

3743　Railroad Equipment *see* NAICS 333911: Pump and Pumping Equipment Manufacturing; NAICS 336510: Railroad Rolling Stock Manufacturing

3751　Motorcycles, Bicycles, and Parts *see* NAICS 336991: Motorcycle, Bicycle, and Parts Manufacturing

3761　Guided Missiles and Space Vehicles *see* NAICS 336414: Guided Missile and Space Vehicle Manufacturing

3764　Guided Missile and Space Vehicle Propulsion Units and Propulsion Unit Parts *see* NAICS 336415: Guided Missile and Space Vehicle Propulsion Unit and Propulsion Unit Parts Manufacturing

3769　Guided Missile Space Vehicle Parts and Auxiliary Equipment, NEC *see* NAICS 336419: Other Guided Missile and Space Vehicle Parts and Auxiliary Equipment Manufacturing

3792　Travel Trailers and Campers *see* NAICS 336214: Travel Trailer and Camper Manufacturing

3795　Tanks and Tank Components *see* NAICS 336992: Military Armored Vehicle, Tank, and Tank Component Manufacturing

3799　Transportation Equipment, NEC *see* NAICS 336214: Travel Trailer and Camper Manufacturing; NAICS 332212: Hand and Edge Tool Manufacturing; NAICS 336999: All Other Transportation Equipment Manufacturing

MEASURING, ANALYZING, & CONTROLLING INSTRUMENTS

3812　Search, Detection, Navigation, Guidance, Aeronautical, and Nautical Systems and Instruments *see* NAICS 334511: Search, Detection, Navigation, Guidance, Aeronautical, and Nautical System and Instrument Manufacturing

3821　Laboratory Apparatus and Furniture *see* NAICS 339111: Laboratory Apparatus and Furniture Manufacturing

3822　Automatic Controls for Regulating Residential and Commercial Environments and Appliances *see* NAICS 334512: Automatic Environmental Control Manufacturing for Regulating Residential, Commercial, and Appliance Use

3823　Industrial Instruments for Measurement, Display, and Control of Process Variables; and Related Products *see* NAICS 334513: Instruments and Related Product Manufacturing for Measuring Displaying, and Controlling Industrial Process Variables

3824　Totalizing Fluid Meters and Counting Devices *see* NAICS 334514: Totalizing Fluid Meter and Counting Device Manufacturing

3825　Instruments for Measuring and Testing of Electricity and Electrical Signals *see* NAICS 334416: Electronic Coil, Transformer, and Other Inductor Manufacturing; NAICS 334515: Instrument Manufacturing for Measuring and Testing Electricity and Electrical Signals

3826　Laboratory Analytical Instruments *see* NAICS 334516: Analytical Laboratory Instrument Manufacturing

3827　Optical Instruments and Lenses *see* NAICS 333314: Optical Instrument and Lens Manufacturing

3829　Measuring and Controlling Devices, NEC *see* NAICS 339112: Surgical and Medical Instrument Manufacturing; NAICS 334519: Other Measuring and Controlling Device Manufacturing

3841　Surgical and Medical Instruments and Apparatus *see* NAICS 339112: Surgical and Medical Instrument Manufacturing

3842　Orthopedic, Prosthetic, and Surgical Appliances and Supplies *see* NAICS 339113: Surgical Appliance and Supplies Manufacturing; NAICS 334510: Electromedical and Electrotherapeutic Apparatus Manufacturing

3843　Dental Equipment and Supplies *see* NAICS 339114: Dental Equipment and Supplies Manufacturing

3844　X-Ray Apparatus and Tubes and Related Irradiation Apparatus *see* NAICS 334517: Irradiation Apparatus Manufacturing

3845　Electromedical and Electrotherapeutic Apparatus *see* NAICS 334517: Irradiation Apparatus Manufacturing;

NAICS 334510: Electromedical and Electrotherapeutic Apparatus Manufacturing

3851   Ophthalmic Goods *see* NAICS 339115: Ophthalmic Goods Manufacturing

3861   Photographic Equipment and Supplies *see* NAICS 333315: Photographic and Photocopying Equipment Manufacturing; NAICS 325992: Photographic Film, Paper, Plate and Chemical Manufacturing

3873   Watches, Clocks, Clockwork Operated Devices and Parts *see* NAICS 334518: Watch, Clock, and Part Manufacturing

MISCELLANEOUS MANUFACTURING INDUSTRIES

3911   Jewelry, Precious Metal *see* NAICS 339911: Jewelry (Including Precious Metal) Manufacturing

3914   Silverware, Plated Ware, and Stainless Steel Ware *see* NAICS 332211: Cutlery and Flatware (except Precious) Manufacturing; NAICS 339912: Silverware and Plated Ware Manufacturing

3915   Jewelers' Findings and Materials, and Lapidary Work *see* NAICS 339913: Jewelers' Material and Lapidary Work Manufacturing

3931   Musical Instruments *see* NAICS 339992: Musical Instrument Manufacturing

3942   Dolls and Stuffed Toys *see* NAICS 339931: Doll and Stuffed Toy Manufacturing

3944   Games, Toys, and Children's Vehicles, Except Dolls and Bicycles *see* NAICS 336991: Motorcycle, Bicycle, and Parts Manufacturing; NAICS 339932: Game, Toy, and Children's Vehicle Manufacturing

3949   Sporting and Athletic Goods, NEC *see* NAICS 339920: Sporting and Athletic Good Manufacturing

3951   Pens, Mechanical Pencils, and Parts *see* NAICS 339941: Pen and Mechanical Pencil Manufacturing

3952   Lead Pencils, Crayons, and Artist's Materials *see* NAICS 337127: Institutional Furniture Manufacturing; NAICS 325998: All Other Miscellaneous Chemical Product Manufacturing; NAICS 339942: Lead Pencil and Art Good Manufacturing

3953   Marking Devices *see* NAICS 339943: Marking Device Manufacturing

3955   Carbon Paper and Inked Ribbons *see* NAICS 339944: Carbon Paper and Inked Ribbon Manufacturing

3961   Costume Jewelry and Costume Novelties, Except Precious Metals *see* NAICS 339914: Costume Jewelry and Novelty Manufacturing

3965   Fasteners, Buttons, Needles, and Pins *see* NAICS 339993: Fastener, Button, Needle and Pin Manufacturing

3991   Brooms and Brushes *see* NAICS 339994: Broom, Brush and Mop Manufacturing

3993   Signs and Advertising Specialties *see* NAICS 339950: Sign Manufacturing

3995   Burial Caskets *see* NAICS 339995: Burial Casket Manufacturing

3996   Linoleum, Asphalted-Felt-Base, and Other Hard Surface Floor Coverings, NEC *see* NAICS 326192: Resilient Floor Covering Manufacturing

3999   Manufacturing Industries, NEC *see* NAICS 337127: Institutional Furniture Manufacturing; NAICS 321999: All

Other Miscellaneous Wood Product Manufacturing; NAICS 316110: Leather and Hide Tanning and Finishing; NAICS 335121: Residential Electric Lighting Fixture Manufacturing; NAICS 325998: All Other Miscellaneous Chemical Product Manufacturing; NAICS 332999: All Other Miscellaneous Fabricated Metal Product Manufacturing; NAICS 326199: All Other Plastics Product Manufacturing; NAICS 323112: Commercial Flexographic Printing; NAICS 323111: Commercial Gravure Printing; NAICS 323110: Commercial Lithographic Printing; NAICS 323113: Commercial Screen Printing; NAICS 323119: Other Commercial Printing; NAICS 332212: Hand and Edge Tool Manufacturing; NAICS 339999: All Other Miscellaneous Manufacturing

TRANSPORTATION, COMMUNICATIONS, ELECTRIC, GAS, & SANITARY SERVICES

4011   Railroads, Line-haul Operating *see* NAICS 482111: Line-Haul Railroads

4013   Railroad Switching and Terminal Establishments *see* NAICS 482112: Short Line Railroads; NAICS 488210: Support Activities for Rail Transportation

4111   Local and Suburban Transit *see* NAICS 485111: Mixed Mode Transit Systems; NAICS 485112: Commuter Rail Systems; NAICS 485113: Bus and Motor Vehicle Transit Systems; NAICS 485119: Other Urban Transit Systems; NAICS 485999: All Other Transit and Ground Passenger Transportation

4119   Local Passenger Transportation, NEC *see* NAICS 621910: Ambulance Service; NAICS 485410: School and Employee Bus Industry; NAICS 487110: Scenic and Sightseeing Transportation; NAICS 485991: Special Needs Transportation; NAICS 485999: All Other Transit and Ground Passenger Transportation; NAICS 485320: Limousine Service

4121   Taxicabs *see* NAICS 485310: Taxi Service

4131   Intercity and Rural Bus Transportation *see* NAICS 485210: Interurban and Rural Bus Lines

4141   Local Bus Charter Service *see* NAICS 485510: Charter Bus Industry

4142   Bus Charter Service, Except Local *see* NAICS 485510: Charter Bus Industry

4151   School Buses *see* NAICS 485410: School and Employee Bus Industry

4173   Terminal and Service Facilities for Motor Vehicle Passenger Transportation *see* NAICS 488490: Other Support Activities for Road Transportation

4212   Local Trucking Without Storage *see* NAICS 562111: Solid Waste Collection; NAICS 562112: Hazardous Waste Collection; NAICS 562119: Other Waste Collection; NAICS 484110: General Freight Trucking, Local; NAICS 484210: Used Household and Office Goods Moving; NAICS 484220: Specialized Freight (except Used Goods) Trucking, Local

4213   Trucking, Except Local *see* NAICS 484121: General Freight Trucking, Long-Distance, Truckload; NAICS 484122: General Freight Trucking, Long-Distance, Less Than Truckload; NAICS 484210: Used Household and Office Goods Moving; NAICS 484230: Specialized Freight (except Used Goods) Trucking, Long-Distance

4214   Local Trucking with Storage *see* NAICS 484110: General Freight Trucking, Local; NAICS 484210: Used Household and Office Goods Moving; NAICS 484220: Specialized Freight (except Used Goods) Trucking, Local

4215   Couriers Services Except by Air *see* NAICS 492110: Couriers; NAICS 492210: Local Messengers and Local Delivery

4221   Farm Product Warehousing and Storage *see* NAICS 493130: Farm Product Storage Facilities

4222   Refrigerated Warehousing and Storage *see* NAICS 493120: Refrigerated Storage Facilities

4225   General Warehousing and Storage *see* NAICS 493110: General Warehousing and Storage Facilities; NAICS 531130: Lessors of Mini-warehouses and Self Storage Units

4226   Special Warehousing and Storage, NEC *see* NAICS 493120: Refrigerated Storage Facilities; NAICS 493110: General Warehousing and Storage Facilities; NAICS 493190: All Other Warehousing and Storage Facilities

4231   Terminal and Joint Terminal Maintenance Facilities for Motor Freight Transportation *see* NAICS 488490: Other Support Activities for Road Transportation

4311   United States Postal Service *see* NAICS 491110: Postal Service

4412   Deep Sea Foreign Transportation of Freight *see* NAICS 483111: Deep Sea Freight Transportation

4424   Deep Sea Domestic Transportation of Freight *see* NAICS 483113: Coastal and Great Lakes Freight Transportation

4432   Freight Transportation on the Great Lakes-St. Lawrence Seaway *see* NAICS 483113: Coastal and Great Lakes Freight Transportation

4449   Water Transportation of Freight, NEC *see* NAICS 483211: Inland Water Freight Transportation

4481   Deep Sea Transportation of Passengers, Except by Ferry *see* NAICS 483112: Deep Sea Passenger Transportation; NAICS 483114: Coastal and Great Lakes Passenger Transportation

4482   Ferries *see* NAICS 483114: Coastal and Great Lakes Passenger Transportation; NAICS 483212: Inland Water Passenger Transportation

4489   Water Transportation of Passengers, NEC *see* NAICS 483212: Inland Water Passenger Transportation; NAICS 487210: Scenic and Sightseeing Transportation, Water

4491   Marine Cargo Handling *see* NAICS 488310: Port and Harbor Operations; NAICS 488320: Marine Cargo Handling

4492   Towing and Tugboat Services *see* NAICS 483113: Coastal and Great Lakes Freight Transportation; NAICS 483211: Inland Water Freight Transportation; NAICS 488330: Navigational Services to Shipping

4493   Marinas *see* NAICS 713930: Marinas

4499   Water Transportation Services, NEC *see* NAICS 532411: Commercial Air, Rail, and Water Transportation Equipment Rental and Leasing; NAICS 488310: Port and Harbor Operations; NAICS 488330: Navigational Services to Shipping; NAICS 488390: Other Support Activities for Water Transportation

4512   Air Transportation, Scheduled *see* NAICS 481111: Scheduled Passenger Air Transportation; NAICS 481112: Scheduled Freight Air Transportation

4513   Air Courier Services *see* NAICS 492110: Couriers

4522   Air Transportation, Nonscheduled *see* NAICS 621910: Ambulance Services; NAICS 481212: Nonscheduled Chartered Freight Air Transportation; NAICS 481211: Nonscheduled Chartered Passenger Air Transportation; NAICS 487990: Scenic and Sightseeing Transportation

4581   Airports, Flying Fields, and Airport Terminal Services *see* NAICS 488111: Air Traffic Control; NAICS 488119: Other Airport Operations; NAICS 561720: Janitorial Services; NAICS 488190: Other Support Activities for Air Transportation

4612   Crude Petroleum Pipelines *see* NAICS 486110: Pipeline Transportation of Crude Oil

4613   Refined Petroleum Pipelines *see* NAICS 486910: Pipeline Transportation of Refined Petroleum Products

4619   Pipelines, NEC *see* NAICS 486990: All Other Pipeline Transportation

4724   Travel Agencies *see* NAICS 561510: Travel Agencies

4725   Tour Operators *see* NAICS 561520: Tour Operators

4729   Arrangement of Passenger Transportation, NEC *see* NAICS 488999: All Other Support Activities for Transportation; NAICS 561599: All Other Travel Arrangement and Reservation Services

4731   Arrangement of Transportation of Freight and Cargo *see* NAICS 541618: Other Management Consulting Services; NAICS 488510: Freight Transportation Arrangement

4741   Rental of Railroad Cars *see* NAICS 532411: Commercial Air, Rail, and Water Transportation Equipment Rental and Leasing; NAICS 488210: Support Activities for Rail Transportation

4783   Packing and Crating *see* NAICS 488991: Packing and Crating

4785   Fixed Facilities and Inspection and Weighing Services for Motor Vehicle Transportation *see* NAICS 488390: Other Support Activities for Water Transportation; NAICS 488490: Other Support Activities for Road Transportation

4789   Transportation Services, NEC *see* NAICS 488999: All Other Support Activities for Transportation *see* NAICS 487110: Scenic and Sightseeing Transportation, Land; NAICS 488210: Support Activities for Rail Transportation

4812   Radiotelephone Communications *see* NAICS 513321: Paging; NAICS 513322: Cellular and Other Wireless Telecommunications; NAICS 513330: Telecommunications Resellers

4813   Telephone Communications, Except Radiotelephone *see* NAICS 513310: Wired Telecommunications Carriers; NAICS 513330: Telecommunications Resellers

4822   Telegraph and Other Message Communications *see* NAICS 513310: Wired Telecommunications Carriers

4832   Radio Broadcasting Stations *see* NAICS 513111: Radio Networks; NAICS 513112: Radio Stations

4833   Television Broadcasting Stations *see* NAICS 513120: Television Broadcasting

4841   Cable and Other Pay Television Services *see* NAICS 513210: Cable Networks; NAICS 513220: Cable and Other Program Distribution

4899   Communications Services, NEC *see* NAICS 513322: Cellular and Other Wireless Telecommunications; NAICS 513340: Satellite Telecommunications; NAICS 513390: Other Telecommunications

4911   Electric Services *see* NAICS 221111: Hydroelectric Power Generation; NAICS 221112: Fossil Fuel Electric Power Generation; NAICS 221113: Nuclear Electric Power Generation; NAICS 221119: Other Electric Power Generation; NAICS 221121: Electric Bulk Power Transmission and Control; NAICS 221122: Electric Power Distribution

4922   Natural Gas Transmission *see* NAICS 486210: Pipeline Transportation of Natural Gas

4923   Natural Gas Transmission and Distribution *see* NAICS 221210: Natural Gas Distribution; NAICS 486210: Pipeline Transportation of Natural Gas

4924   Natural Gas Distribution *see* NAICS 221210: Natural Gas Distribution

4925   Mixed, Manufactured, or Liquefied Petroleum Gas Production and/or Distribution *see* NAICS 221210: Natural Gas Distribution

4931   Electric and Other Services Combined *see* NAICS 221111: Hydroelectric Power Generation; NAICS 221112: Fossil Fuel Electric Power Generation; NAICS 221113: Nuclear Electric Power Generation; NAICS 221119: Other Electric Power Generation; NAICS 221121: Electric Bulk Power Transmission and Control; NAICS 221122: Electric Power Distribution; NAICS 221210: Natural Gas Distribution

4932   Gas and Other Services Combined *see* NAICS 221210: Natural Gas Distribution

4939   Combination Utilities, NEC *see* NAICS 221111: Hydroelectric Power Generation; NAICS 221112: Fossil Fuel Electric Power Generation; NAICS 221113: Nuclear Electric Power Generation; NAICS 221119: Other Electric Power Generation; NAICS 221121: Electric Bulk Power Transmission and Control; NAICS 221122: Electric Power Distribution; NAICS 221210: Natural Gas Distribution

4941   Water Supply *see* NAICS 221310: Water Supply and Irrigation Systems

4952   Sewerage Systems *see* NAICS 221320: Sewage Treatment Facilities

4953   Refuse Systems *see* NAICS 562111: Solid Waste Collection; NAICS 562112: Hazardous Waste Collection; NAICS 562920: Materials Recovery Facilities; NAICS 562119: Other Waste Collection; NAICS 562211: Hazardous Waste Treatment and Disposal; NAICS 562212: Solid Waste Landfills; NAICS 562213: Solid Waste Combustors and Incinerators; NAICS 562219: Other Nonhazardous Waste Treatment and Disposal

4959   Sanitary Services, NEC *see* NAICS 488119: Other Airport Operations; NAICS 562910: Remediation Services; NAICS 561710: Exterminating and Pest Control Services; NAICS 562998: All Other Miscellaneous Waste Management

4961   Steam and Air-Conditioning Supply *see* NAICS 221330: Steam and Air-Conditioning Supply

4971   Irrigation Systems *see* NAICS 221310: Water Supply and Irrigation Systems

WHOLESALE TRADE

5012   Automobiles and Other Motor Vehicles *see* NAICS 421110: Automobile and Other Motor Vehicle Wholesalers

5013   Motor Vehicle Supplies and New Parts *see* NAICS 441310: Automotive Parts and Accessories Stores; NAICS 421120: Motor Vehicle Supplies and New Part Wholesalers

5014   Tires and Tubes *see* NAICS 441320: Tire Dealers; NAICS 421130: Tire and Tube Wholesalers

5015   Motor Vehicle Parts, Used *see* NAICS 421140: Motor Vehicle Part (Used) Wholesalers

5021   Furniture *see* NAICS 442110: Furniture Stores; NAICS 421210: Furniture Wholesalers

5023   Home Furnishings *see* NAICS 442210: Floor Covering Stores; NAICS 421220: Home Furnishing Wholesalers

5031   Lumber, Plywood, Millwork, and Wood Panels *see* NAICS 444190: Other Building Material Dealers; NAICS 421310: Lumber, Plywood, Millwork, and Wood Panel Wholesalers

5032   Brick, Stone and Related Construction Materials *see* NAICS 444190: Other Building Material Dealers; NAICS 421320: Brick, Stone and Related Construction Material Wholesalers

5033   Roofing, Siding, and Insulation Materials *see* NAICS 421330: Roofing, Siding, and Insulation Material Wholesalers

5039   Construction Materials, NEC *see* NAICS 444190: Other Building Material Dealers; NAICS 421390: Other Construction Material Wholesalers

5043   Photographic Equipment and Supplies *see* NAICS 421410: Photographic Equipment and Supplies Wholesalers

5044   Office Equipment *see* NAICS 421420: Office Equipment Wholesalers

5045   Computers and Computer Peripheral Equipment and Software *see* NAICS 421430: Computer and Computer Peripheral Equipment and Software Wholesalers; NAICS 443120: Computer and Software Stores

5046   Commercial Equipment, NEC *see* NAICS 421440: Other Commercial Equipment Wholesalers

5047   Medical, Dental, and Hospital Equipment and Supplies *see* NAICS 421450: Medical, Dental and Hospital Equipment and Supplies Wholesalers; NAICS 446199: All Other Health and Personal Care Stores

5048   Ophthalmic Goods *see* NAICS 421460: Ophthalmic Goods Wholesalers

5049   Professional Equipment and Supplies, NEC *see* NAICS 421490: Other Professional Equipment and Supplies Wholesalers; NAICS 453210: Office Supplies and Stationery Stores

5051   Metals Service Centers and Offices *see* NAICS 421510: Metals Service Centers and Offices

5052   Coal and Other Minerals and Ores *see* NAICS 421520: Coal and Other Mineral and Ore Wholesalers

5063   Electrical Apparatus and Equipment Wiring Supplies, and Construction Materials *see* NAICS 444190: Other Building Material Dealers; NAICS 421610: Electrical Apparatus and Equipment, Wiring Supplies and Construction Material Wholesalers

5064   Electrical Appliances, Television and Radio Sets *see* NAICS 421620: Electrical Appliance, Television and Radio Set Wholesalers

5065   Electronic Parts and Equipment, Not Elsewhere Classified *see* NAICS 421690: Other Electronic Parts and Equipment Wholesalers

5072   Hardware *see* NAICS 421710: Hardware Wholesalers

5074 Plumbing and Heating Equipment and Supplies (Hydronics) *see* NAICS 444190: Other Building Material Dealers; NAICS 421720: Plumbing and Heating Equipment and Supplies (Hydronics) Wholesalers

5075 Warm Air Heating and Air-Conditioning Equipment and Supplies *see* NAICS 421730: Warm Air Heating and Air-Conditioning Equipment and Supplies Wholesalers

5078 Refrigeration Equipment and Supplies *see* NAICS 421740: Refrigeration Equipment and Supplies Wholesalers

5082 Construction and Mining (Except Petroleum) Machinery and Equipment *see* NAICS 421810: Construction and Mining (except Petroleum) Machinery and Equipment Wholesalers

5083 Farm and Garden Machinery and Equipment *see* NAICS 421820: Farm and Garden Machinery and Equipment Wholesalers; NAICS 444210: Outdoor Power Equipment Stores

5084 Industrial Machinery and Equipment *see* NAICS 421830: Industrial Machinery and Equipment Wholesalers

5085 Industrial Supplies *see* NAICS 421830: Industrial Machinery and Equipment Wholesalers; NAICS 421840: Industrial Supplies Wholesalers

5087 Service Establishment Equipment and Supplies *see* NAICS 421850: Service Establishment Equipment and Supplies Wholesalers; NAICS 446120: Cosmetics, Beauty Supplies, and Perfume Stores

5088 Transportation Equipment and Supplies, Except Motor Vehicles *see* NAICS 421860: Transportation Equipment and Supplies (except Motor Vehicles) Wholesalers

5091 Sporting and Recreational Goods and Supplies *see* NAICS 421910: Sporting and Recreational Goods and Supplies Wholesalers

5092 Toys and Hobby Goods and Supplies *see* NAICS 421920: Toy and Hobby Goods and Supplies Wholesalers

5093 Scrap and Waste Materials *see* NAICS 421930: Recyclable Material Wholesalers

5094 Jewelry, Watches, Precious Stones, and Precious Metals *see* NAICS 421940: Jewelry, Watch, Precious Stone, and Precious Metal Wholesalers

5099 Durable Goods, NEC *see* NAICS 421990: Other Miscellaneous Durable Goods Wholesalers

5111 Printing and Writing Paper *see* NAICS 422110: Printing and Writing Paper Wholesalers

5112 Stationery and Office Supplies *see* NAICS 453210: Office Supplies and Stationery Stores; NAICS 422120: Stationery and Office Supplies Wholesalers

5113 Industrial and Personal Service Paper *see* NAICS 422130: Industrial and Personal Service Paper Wholesalers

5122 Drugs, Drug Proprietaries, and Druggists' Sundries *see* NAICS 422210: Drugs, Drug Proprietaries, and Druggists' Sundries Wholesalers

5131 Piece Goods, Notions, and Other Dry Goods *see* NAICS 313311: Broadwoven Fabric Finishing Mills; NAICS 313312: Textile and Fabric Finishing (except Broadwoven Fabric) Mills; NAICS 422310: Piece Goods, Notions, and Other Dry Goods Wholesalers

5136 Men's and Boys' Clothing and Furnishings *see* NAICS 422320: Men's and Boys' Clothing and Furnishings Wholesalers

5137 Women's Children's and Infants' Clothing and Accessories *see* NAICS 422330: Women's, Children's, and Infants' Clothing and Accessories Wholesalers

5139 Footwear *see* NAICS 422340: Footwear Wholesalers

5141 Groceries, General Line *see* NAICS 422410: General Line Grocery Wholesalers

5142 Packaged Frozen Foods *see* NAICS 422420: Packaged Frozen Food Wholesalers

5143 Dairy Products, Except Dried or Canned *see* NAICS 422430: Dairy Products (except Dried or Canned) Wholesalers

5144 Poultry and Poultry Products *see* NAICS 422440: Poultry and Poultry Product Wholesalers

5145 Confectionery *see* NAICS 422450: Confectionery Wholesalers

5146 Fish and Seafoods *see* NAICS 422460: Fish and Seafood Wholesalers

5147 Meats and Meat Products *see* NAICS 311612: Meat Processed from Carcasses; NAICS 422470: Meat and Meat Product Wholesalers

5148 Fresh Fruits and Vegetables *see* NAICS 422480: Fresh Fruit and Vegetable Wholesalers

5149 Groceries and Related Products, NEC *see* NAICS 422490: Other Grocery and Related Product Wholesalers

5153 Grain and Field Beans *see* NAICS 422510: Grain and Field Bean Wholesalers

5154 Livestock *see* NAICS 422520: Livestock Wholesalers

5159 Farm-Product Raw Materials, NEC *see* NAICS 422590: Other Farm Product Raw Material Wholesalers

5162 Plastics Materials and Basic Forms and Shapes *see* NAICS 422610: Plastics Materials and Basic Forms and Shapes Wholesalers

5169 Chemicals and Allied Products, NEC *see* NAICS 422690: Other Chemical and Allied Products Wholesalers

5171 Petroleum Bulk Stations and Terminals *see* NAICS 454311: Heating Oil Dealers; NAICS 454312: Liquefied Petroleum Gas (Bottled Gas) Dealers; NAICS 422710: Petroleum Bulk Stations and Terminals

5172 Petroleum and Petroleum Products Wholesalers, Except Bulk Stations and Terminals *see* NAICS 422720: Petroleum and Petroleum Products Wholesalers (except Bulk Stations and Terminals)

5181 Beer and Ale *see* NAICS 422810: Beer and Ale Wholesalers

5182 Wine and Distilled Alcoholic Beverages *see* NAICS 422820: Wine and Distilled Alcoholic Beverage Wholesalers

5191 Farm Supplies *see* NAICS 444220: Nursery and Garden Centers; NAICS 422910: Farm Supplies Wholesalers

5192 Books, Periodicals, and Newspapers *see* NAICS 422920: Book, Periodical and Newspaper Wholesalers

5193 Flowers, Nursery Stock, and Florists' Supplies *see* NAICS 422930: Flower, Nursery Stock and Florists' Supplies Wholesalers; NAICS 444220: Nursery and Garden Centers

5194 Tobacco and Tobacco Products *see* NAICS 422940: Tobacco and Tobacco Product Wholesalers

5198 Paint, Varnishes, and Supplies *see* NAICS 422950: Paint, Varnish and Supplies Wholesalers; NAICS 444120: Paint and Wallpaper Stores

5199   Nondurable Goods, NEC *see* NAICS 541890: Other Services Related to Advertising; NAICS 422990: Other Miscellaneous Nondurable Goods Wholesalers

RETAIL TRADE

5211   Lumber and Other Building Materials Dealers *see* NAICS 444110: Home Centers; NAICS 421310: Lumber, Plywood, Millwork, and Wood Panel Wholesalers; NAICS 444190: Other Building Material Dealers

5231   Paint, Glass, and Wallpaper Stores *see* NAICS 422950: Paint, Varnish, and Supplies Wholesalers; NAICS 444190: Other Building Material Dealers; NAICS 444120: Paint and Wallpaper Stores

5251   Hardware Stores *see* NAICS 444130: Hardware Stores

5261   Retail Nurseries *see* NAICS 444220: Nursery and Garden Centers; NAICS 453998: All Other Miscellaneous Store Retailers (except Tobacco Stores); NAICS 444210: Outdoor Power Equipment Stores

5271   Mobile Home Dealers *see* NAICS 453930: Manufactured (Mobile) Home Dealers

5311   Department Stores *see* NAICS 452110: Department Stores

5331   Variety Stores *see* NAICS 452990: All Other General Merchandise Stores

5399   Miscellaneous General Merchandise Stores *see* NAICS 452910: Warehouse Clubs and Superstores; NAICS 452990: All Other General Merchandise Stores

5411   Grocery Stores *see* NAICS 447110: Gasoline Stations with Convenience Stores; NAICS 445110: Supermarkets and Other Grocery (except Convenience) Stores; NAICS 452910: Warehouse Clubs and Superstores; NAICS 445120: Convenience Stores

5421   Meat and Fish (Seafood) Markets, Including Freezer Provisioners *see* NAICS 454390: Other Direct Selling Establishments; NAICS 445210: Meat Markets; NAICS 445220: Fish and Seafood Markets

5431   Fruit and Vegetable Markets *see* NAICS 445230: Fruit and Vegetable Markets

5441   Candy, Nut, and Confectionery Stores *see* NAICS 445292: Confectionery and Nut Stores

5451   Dairy Products Stores *see* NAICS 445299: All Other Specialty Food Stores

5461   Retail Bakeries *see* NAICS 722213: Snack and Nonalcoholic Beverage Bars; NAICS 311811: Retail Bakeries; NAICS 445291: Baked Goods Stores

5499   Miscellaneous Food Stores *see* NAICS 445210: Meat Markets; NAICS 722211: Limited-Service Restaurants; NAICS 446191: Food (Health) Supplement Stores; NAICS 445299: All Other Specialty Food Stores

5511   Motor Vehicle Dealers (New and Used) *see* NAICS 441110: New Car Dealers

5521   Motor Vehicle Dealers (Used Only) *see* NAICS 441120: Used Car Dealers

5531   Auto and Home Supply Stores *see* NAICS 441320: Tire Dealers; NAICS 441310: Automotive Parts and Accessories Stores

5541   Gasoline Service Stations *see* NAICS 447110: Gasoline Stations with Convenience Stores; NAICS 447190: Other Gasoline Stations

5551   Boat Dealers *see* NAICS 441222: Boat Dealers

5561   Recreational Vehicle Dealers *see* NAICS 441210: Recreational Vehicle Dealers

5571   Motorcycle Dealers *see* NAICS 441221: Motorcycle Dealers

5599   Automotive Dealers, NEC *see* NAICS 441229: All Other Motor Vehicle Dealers

5611   Men's and Boys' Clothing and Accessory Stores *see* NAICS 448110: Men's Clothing Stores; NAICS 448150: Clothing Accessories Stores

5621   Women's Clothing Stores *see* NAICS 448120: Women's Clothing Stores

5632   Women's Accessory and Specialty Stores *see* NAICS 448190: Other Clothing Stores; NAICS 448150: Clothing Accessories Stores

5641   Children's and Infants' Wear Stores *see* NAICS 448130: Children's and Infants' Clothing Stores

5651   Family Clothing Stores *see* NAICS 448140: Family Clothing Stores

5661   Shoe Stores *see* NAICS 448210: Shoe Stores

5699   Miscellaneous Apparel and Accessory Stores *see* NAICS 448190: Other Clothing Stores; NAICS 448150: Clothing Accessories Stores

5712   Furniture Stores *see* NAICS 337122: Nonupholstered Wood Household Furniture Manufacturing; NAICS 337110: Wood Kitchen Cabinet and Counter Top Manufacturing; NAICS 337121: Upholstered Wood Household Furniture Manufacturing; NAICS 442110: Furniture Stores

5713   Floor Covering Stores *see* NAICS 442210: Floor Covering Stores

5714   Drapery, Curtain, and Upholstery Stores *see* NAICS 442291: Window Treatment Stores; NAICS 451130: Sewing, Needlework, and Piece Goods Stores; NAICS 314121: Curtain and Drapery Mills

5719   Miscellaneous Homefurnishings Stores *see* NAICS 442291: Window Treatment Stores; NAICS 442299: All Other Home Furnishings Stores

5722   Household Appliance Stores *see* NAICS 443111: Household Appliance Stores

5731   Radio, Television, and Consumer Electronics Stores *see* NAICS 443112: Radio, Television, and Other Electronics Stores; NAICS 441310: Automotive Parts and Accessories Stores

5734   Computer and Computer Software Stores *see* NAICS 443120: Computer and Software Stores

5735   Record and Prerecorded Tape Stores *see* NAICS 451220: Prerecorded Tape, Compact Disc, and Record Stores

5736   Musical Instrument Stores *see* NAICS 451140: Musical Instrument and Supplies Stores

5812   Eating and Drinking Places *see* NAICS 722110: Full-Service Restaurants; NAICS 722211: Limited-Service Restaurants; NAICS 722212: Cafeterias; NAICS 722213: Snack and Nonalcoholic Beverage Bars; NAICS 722310: Foodservice Contractors; NAICS 722320: Caterers; NAICS 711110: Theater Companies and Dinner Theaters

5813   Drinking Places (Alcoholic Beverages) *see* NAICS 722410: Drinking Places (Alcoholic Beverages)

5912   Drug Stores and Proprietary Stores *see* NAICS 446110: Pharmacies and Drug Stores

5921   Liquor Stores *see* NAICS 445310: Beer, Wine and Liquor Stores

5932 Used Merchandise Stores *see* NAICS 522298: All Other Non-Depository Credit Intermediation; NAICS 453310: Used Merchandise Stores

5941 Sporting Goods Stores and Bicycle Shops *see* NAICS 451110: Sporting Goods Stores

5942 Book Stores *see* NAICS 451211: Book Stores

5943 Stationery Stores *see* NAICS 453210: Office Supplies and Stationery Stores

5944 Jewelry Stores *see* NAICS 448310: Jewelry Stores

5945 Hobby, Toy, and Game Shops *see* NAICS 451120: Hobby, Toy and Game Stores

5946 Camera and Photographic Supply Stores *see* NAICS 443130: Camera and Photographic Supplies Stores

5947 Gift, Novelty, and Souvenir Shops *see* NAICS 453220: Gift, Novelty, and Souvenir Stores

5948 Luggage and Leather Goods Stores *see* NAICS 448320: Luggage and Leather Goods Stores

5949 Sewing, Needlework, and Piece Goods Stores *see* NAICS 451130: Sewing, Needlework, and Piece Goods Stores

5961 Catalog and Mail-Order Houses *see* NAICS 454110: Electronic Shopping and Mail-Order Houses

5962 Automatic Merchandising Machine Operator *see* NAICS 454210: Vending Machine Operators

5963 Direct Selling Establishments *see* NAICS 722330: Mobile Caterers; NAICS 454390: Other Direct Selling Establishments

5983 Fuel Oil Dealers *see* NAICS 454311: Heating Oil Dealers

5984 Liquefied Petroleum Gas (Bottled Gas) Dealers *see* NAICS 454312: Liquefied Petroleum Gas (Bottled Gas) Dealers

5989 Fuel Dealers, NEC *see* NAICS 454319: Other Fuel Dealers

5992 Florists *see* NAICS 453110: Florists

5993 Tobacco Stores and Stands *see* NAICS 453991: Tobacco Stores

5994 News Dealers and Newsstands *see* NAICS 451212: News Dealers and Newsstands

5995 Optical Goods Stores *see* NAICS 339115: Ophthalmic Goods Manufacturing; NAICS 446130: Optical Goods Stores

5999 Miscellaneous Retail Stores, NEC *see* NAICS 446120: Cosmetics, Beauty Supplies, and Perfume Stores; NAICS 446199: All Other Health and Personal Care Stores; NAICS 453910: Pet and Pet Supplies Stores; NAICS 453920: Art Dealers; NAICS 443111: Household Appliance Stores; NAICS 443112: Radio, Television, and Other Electronics Stores; NAICS 448310: Jewelry Stores; NAICS 453998: All Other Miscellaneous Store Retailers (except Tobacco Stores)

FINANCE, INSURANCE, & REAL ESTATE

6011 Federal Reserve Banks *see* NAICS 521110: Monetary Authorities-Central Banks

6019 Central Reserve Depository Institutions, NEC *see* NAICS 522320: Financial Transactions Processing, Reserve, and Clearing House Activities

6021 National Commercial Banks *see* NAICS 522110: Commercial Banking; NAICS 522210: Credit Card Issuing; NAICS 523991: Trust, Fiduciary, and Custody Activities

6022 State Commercial Banks *see* NAICS 522110: Commercial Banking; NAICS 522210: Credit Card Issuing; NAICS 522190: Other Depository Intermediation; NAICS 523991: Trust, Fiduciary, and Custody Activities

6029 Commercial Banks, NEC *see* NAICS 522110: Commercial Banking

6035 Savings Institutions, Federally Chartered *see* NAICS 522120: Savings Institutions

6036 Savings institutions, Not Federally Chartered *see* NAICS 522120: Savings Institutions

6061 Credit Unions, Federally Chartered *see* NAICS 522130: Credit Unions

6062 Credit Unions, Not Federally Chartered *see* NAICS 522130: Credit Unions

6081 Branches and Agencies of Foreign Banks *see* NAICS 522293: International Trade Financing; NAICS 522110: Commercial Banking; NAICS 522298: All Other Non-Depository Credit Intermediation

6082 Foreign Trade and International Banking Institutions *see* NAICS 522293: International Trade Financing

6091 Nondeposit Trust Facilities *see* NAICS 523991: Trust, Fiduciary, and Custody Activities

6099 Functions Related to Deposit Banking, NEC *see* NAICS 522320: Financial Transactions Processing, Reserve, and Clearing House Activities; NAICS 523130: Commodity Contracts Dealing; NAICS 523991: Trust, Fiduciary, and Custody Activities; NAICS 523999: Miscellaneous Financial Investment Activities; NAICS 522390: Other Activities Related to Credit Intermediation

6111 Federal and Federally Sponsored Credit Agencies *see* NAICS 522293: International Trade Financing; NAICS 522294: Secondary Market Financing; NAICS 522298: All Other Non-Depository Credit Intermediation

6141 Personal Credit Institutions *see* NAICS 522210: Credit Card Issuing; NAICS 522220: Sales Financing; NAICS 522291: Consumer Lending

6153 Short-Term Business Credit Institutions, Except Agricultural *see* NAICS 522220: Sales Financing; NAICS 522320: Financial Transactions Processing, Reserve, and Clearing House Activities; NAICS 522298: All Other Non-Depository Credit Intermediation

6159 Miscellaneous Business Credit Institutions *see* NAICS 522220: Sales Financing; NAICS 522293: International Trade Financing; NAICS 522298: All Other Non-Depository Credit Intermediation

6162 Mortgage Bankers and Loan Correspondents *see* NAICS 522292: Real Estate Credit; NAICS 522390: Other Activities Related to Credit Intermediation

6163 Loan Brokers *see* NAICS 522310: Mortgage and Other Loan Brokers

6211 Security Brokers, Dealers, and Flotation Companies *see* NAICS 523110: Investment Banking and Securities Dealing; NAICS 523120: Securities Brokerage; NAICS 523910: Miscellaneous Intermediation; NAICS 523999: Miscellaneous Financial Investment Activities

6221 Commodity Contracts Brokers and Dealers *see* NAICS 523130: Commodity Contracts Dealing; NAICS 523140: Commodity Brokerage

6231 Security and Commodity Exchanges *see* NAICS 523210: Securities and Commodity Exchanges

6282 Investment Advice *see* NAICS 523920: Portfolio Management; NAICS 523930: Investment Advice

6289   Services Allied With the Exchange of Securities or Commodities, NEC *see* NAICS 523991: Trust, Fiduciary, and Custody Activities; NAICS 523999: Miscellaneous Financial Investment Activities

6311   Life Insurance *see* NAICS 524113: Direct Life Insurance Carriers; NAICS 524130: Reinsurance Carriers

6321   Accident and Health Insurance *see* NAICS 524114: Direct Health and Medical Insurance Carriers; NAICS 525190: Other Insurance and Employee Benefit Funds; NAICS 524130: Reinsurance Carriers

6324   Hospital and Medical Service Plans *see* NAICS 524114: Direct Health and Medical Insurance Carriers; NAICS 525190: Other Insurance and Employee Benefit Funds; NAICS 524130: Reinsurance Carriers

6331   Fire, Marine, and Casualty Insurance *see* NAICS 524126: Direct Property and Casualty Insurance Carriers; NAICS 525190: Other Insurance and Employee Benefit Funds; NAICS 524130: Reinsurance Carriers

6351   Surety Insurance *see* NAICS 524126: Direct Property and Casualty Insurance Carriers; NAICS 524130: Reinsurance Carriers

6361   Title Insurance *see* NAICS 524127: Direct Title Insurance Carriers; NAICS 524130: Reinsurance Carriers

6371   Pension, Health, and Welfare Funds *see* NAICS 523920: Portfolio Management; NAICS 524292: Third Party Administration for Insurance and Pension Funds; NAICS 525110: Pension Funds; NAICS 525120: Health and Welfare Funds

6399   Insurance Carriers, NEC *see* NAICS 524128: Other Direct Insurance Carriers (except Life, Health, and Medical)

6411   Insurance Agents, Brokers, and Service *see* NAICS 524210: Insurance Agencies and Brokerages; NAICS 524291: Claims Adjusters; NAICS 524292: Third Party Administrators for Insurance and Pension Funds; NAICS 524298: All Other Insurance Related Activities

6512   Operators of Nonresidential Buildings *see* NAICS 711310: Promoters of Performing Arts, Sports and Similar Events with Facilities; NAICS 531120: Lessors of Nonresidential Buildings (except Mini-warehouses)

6513   Operators of Apartment Buildings *see* NAICS 531110: Lessors of Residential Buildings and Dwellings

6514   Operators of Dwellings Other Than Apartment Buildings *see* NAICS 531110: Lessors of Residential Buildings and Dwellings

6515   Operators of Residential Mobile Home Sites *see* NAICS 531190: Lessors of Other Real Estate Property

6517   Lessors of Railroad Property *see* NAICS 531190: Lessors of Other Real Estate Property

6519   Lessors of Real Property, NEC *see* NAICS 531190: Lessors of Other Real Estate Property

6531   Real Estate Agents and Managers *see* NAICS 531210: Offices of Real Estate Agents and Brokers; NAICS 813990: Other Similar Organizations; NAICS 531311: Residential Property Managers; NAICS 531312: Nonresidential Property Managers; NAICS 531320: Offices of Real Estate Appraisers; NAICS 812220: Cemeteries and Crematories; NAICS 531390: Other Activities Related to Real Estate

6541   Title Abstract Offices *see* NAICS 541191: Title Abstract and Settlement Offices

6552   Land Subdividers and Developers, Except Cemeteries *see* NAICS 233110: Land Subdivision and Land Development

6553   Cemetery Subdividers and Developers *see* NAICS 812220: Cemeteries and Crematories

6712   Offices of Bank Holding Companies *see* NAICS 551111: Offices of Bank Holding Companies

6719   Offices of Holding Companies, NEC *see* NAICS 551112: Offices of Other Holding Companies

6722   Management Investment Offices, Open-End *see* NAICS 525910: Open-End Investment Funds

6726   Unit Investment Trusts, Face-Amount Certificate Offices, and Closed-End Management Investment Offices *see* NAICS 525990: Other Financial Vehicles

6732   Education, Religious, and Charitable Trusts *see* NAICS 813211: Grantmaking Foundations

6733   Trusts, Except Educational, Religious, and Charitable *see* NAICS 523920: Portfolio Management; NAICS 523991: Trust, Fiduciary, and Custody Services; NAICS 525190: Other Insurance and Employee Benefit Funds; NAICS 525920: Trusts, Estates, and Agency Accounts

6792   Oil Royalty Traders *see* NAICS 523999: Miscellaneous Financial Investment Activities; NAICS 533110: Owners and Lessors of Other Non-Financial Assets

6794   Patent Owners and Lessors *see* NAICS 533110: Owners and Lessors of Other Non-Financial Assets

6798   Real Estate Investment Trusts *see* NAICS 525930: Real Estate Investment Trusts

6799   Investors, NEC *see* NAICS 523910: Miscellaneous Intermediation; NAICS 523920: Portfolio Management; NAICS 523130: Commodity Contracts Dealing; NAICS 523999: Miscellaneous Financial Investment Activities

SERVICE INDUSTRIES

7011   Hotels and Motels *see* NAICS 721110: Hotels (except Casino Hotels) and Motels; NAICS 721120: Casino Hotels; NAICS 721191: Bed and Breakfast Inns; NAICS 721199: All Other Traveler Accommodations

7021   Rooming and Boarding Houses *see* NAICS 721310: Rooming and Boarding Houses

7032   Sporting and Recreational Camps *see* NAICS 721214: Recreational and Vacation Camps

7033   Recreational Vehicle Parks and Campsites *see* NAICS 721211: RV (Recreational Vehicle) Parks and Campgrounds

7041   Organization Hotels and Lodging Houses, on Membership Basis *see* NAICS 721110: Hotels (except Casino Hotels) and Motels; NAICS 721310: Rooming and Boarding Houses

7211   Power Laundries, Family and Commercial *see* NAICS 812321: Laundries, Family and Commercial

7212   Garment Pressing, and Agents for Laundries *see* NAICS 812391: Garment Pressing and Agents for Laundries

7213   Linen Supply *see* NAICS 812331: Linen Supply

7215   Coin-Operated Laundry and Drycleaning *see* NAICS 812310: Coin-Operated Laundries and Drycleaners

7216   Drycleaning Plants, Except Rug Cleaning *see* NAICS 812322: Drycleaning Plants

7217   Carpet and Upholstery Cleaning *see* NAICS 561740: Carpet and Upholstery Cleaning Services

7218   Industrial Launderers *see* NAICS 812332: Industrial Launderers

7219   Laundry and Garment Services, NEC *see* NAICS 812331: Linen Supply; NAICS 811490: Other Personal and Household Goods Repair and Maintenance; NAICS 812399: All Other Laundry Services

7221   Photographic Studios, Portrait *see* NAICS 541921: Photographic Studios, Portrait

7231   Beauty Shops *see* NAICS 812112: Beauty Salons; NAICS 812113: Nail Salons; NAICS 611511: Cosmetology and Barber Schools

7241   Barber Shops *see* NAICS 812111: Barber Shops; NAICS 611511: Cosmetology and Barber Schools

7251   Shoe Repair Shops and Shoeshine Parlors *see* NAICS 811430: Footwear and Leather Goods Repair

7261   Funeral Services and Crematories *see* NAICS 812210: Funeral Homes; NAICS 812220: Cemeteries and Crematories

7291   Tax Return Preparation Services *see* NAICS 541213: Tax Preparation Services

7299   Miscellaneous Personal Services, NEC *see* NAICS 624410: Child Day Care Services; NAICS 812191: Diet and Weight Reducing Centers; NAICS 532220: Formal Wear and Costumes Rental; NAICS 812199: Other Personal Care Services; NAICS 812990: All Other Personal Services

7311   Advertising Agencies *see* NAICS 541810: Advertising Agencies

7312   Outdoor Advertising Services *see* NAICS 541850: Display Advertising

7313   Radio, Television, and Publishers' Advertising Representatives *see* NAICS 541840: Media Representatives

7319   Advertising, NEC *see* NAICS 481219: Other Nonscheduled Air Transportation; NAICS 541830: Media Buying Agencies; NAICS 541850: Display Advertising; NAICS 541870: Advertising Material Distribution Services; NAICS 541890: Other Services Related to Advertising

7322   Adjustment and Collection Services *see* NAICS 561440: Collection Agencies; NAICS 561491: Repossession Services

7323   Credit Reporting Services *see* NAICS 561450: Credit Bureaus

7331   Direct Mail Advertising Services *see* NAICS 541860: Direct Mail Advertising

7334   Photocopying and Duplicating Services *see* NAICS 561431: Other Business Service Centers (including Copy Shops)

7335   Commercial Photography *see* NAICS 481219: Other Nonscheduled Air Transportation; NAICS 541922: Commercial Photography

7336   Commercial Art and Graphic Design *see* NAICS 541430: Graphic Design Services

7338   Secretarial and Court Reporting Services *see* NAICS 561410: Document Preparation Services; NAICS 561492: Court Reporting and Stenotype Services

7342   Disinfecting and Pest Control Services *see* NAICS 561720: Janitorial Services; NAICS 561710: Exterminating and Pest Control Services

7349   Building Cleaning and Maintenance Services, NEC *see* NAICS 561720: Janitorial Services

7352   Medical Equipment Rental and Leasing *see* NAICS 532291: Home Health Equipment Rental; NAICS 532490: Other Commercial and Industrial Machinery and Equipment Rental and Leasing

7353   Heavy Construction Equipment Rental and Leasing *see* NAICS 234990: All Other Heavy Construction; NAICS 532412: Construction, Mining and Forestry Machinery and Equipment Rental and Leasing

7359   Equipment Rental and Leasing, NEC *see* NAICS 532210: Consumer Electronics and Appliances Rental; NAICS 532310: General Rental Centers; NAICS 532299: All Other Consumer Goods Rental; NAICS 532412: Construction, Mining and Forestry Machinery and Equipment Rental and Leasing; NAICS 532411: Commercial Air, Rail, and Water Transportation Equipment Rental and Leasing; NAICS 562991: Septic Tank and Related Services; NAICS 532420: Office Machinery and Equipment Rental and Leasing; NAICS 532490: Other Commercial and Industrial Machinery and Equipment Rental and Leasing

7361   Employment Agencies *see* NAICS 541612: Human Resources and Executive Search Consulting Services; NAICS 561310: Employment Placement Agencies

7363   Help Supply Services *see* NAICS 561320: Temporary Help Services; NAICS 561330: Employee Leasing Services

7371   Computer Programming Services *see* NAICS 541511: Custom Computer Programming Services

7372   Prepackaged Software *see* NAICS 511210: Software Publishers; NAICS 334611: Software Reproducing

7373   Computer Integrated Systems Design *see* NAICS 541512: Computer Systems Design Services

7374   Computer Processing and Data Preparation and Processing Services *see* NAICS 514210: Data Processing Services

7375   Information Retrieval Services *see* NAICS 514191: On-Line Information Services

7376   Computer Facilities Management Services *see* NAICS 541513: Computer Facilities Management Services

7377   Computer Rental and Leasing *see* NAICS 532420: Office Machinery and Equipment Rental and Leasing

7378   Computer Maintenance and Repair *see* NAICS 443120: Computer and Software Stores; NAICS 811212: Computer and Office Machine Repair and Maintenance

7379   Computer Related Services, NEC *see* NAICS 541512: Computer Systems Design Services; NAICS 541519: Other Computer Related Services

7381   Detective, Guard, and Armored Car Services *see* NAICS 561611: Investigation Services; NAICS 561612: Security Guards and Patrol Services; NAICS 561613: Armored Car Services

7382   Security Systems Services *see* NAICS 561621: Security Systems Services (except Locksmiths)

7383   News Syndicates *see* NAICS 514110: New Syndicates

7384   Photofinishing Laboratories *see* NAICS 812921: Photo Finishing Laboratories (except One-Hour); NAICS 812922: One-Hour Photo Finishing

7389   Business Services, NEC *see* NAICS 512240: Sound Recording Studios; NAICS 512290: Other Sound Recording Industries; NAICS 541199: Other Legal Services; NAICS 812990: All Other Personal Services; NAICS 541370: Surveying and Mapping (except Geophysical) Services; NAICS 541410: Interior Design Services; NAICS 541420: Industrial Design Services; NAICS 541340: Drafting Services; NAICS 541490: Other Specialized Design Services; NAICS 541890: Other Services Related to Advertising; NAICS 541930: Translation and Interpretation Services; NAICS 541350: Building Inspection Services; NAICS 541990: All Other

Professional, Scientific and Technical Services; NAICS 711410: Agents and Managers for Artists, Athletes, Entertainers and Other Public Figures; NAICS 561421: Telephone Answering Services; NAICS 561422: Telemarketing Bureaus; NAICS 561439: Private Mail Centers; NAICS 561431: Other Business Service Centers (including Copy Shops); NAICS 561491: Repossession Services; NAICS 561910: Packaging and Labeling Services; NAICS 561790: Other Services to Buildings and Dwellings; NAICS 561599: All Other Travel Arrangement and Reservation Services; NAICS 561920: Convention and Trade Show Organizers; NAICS 561591: Convention and Visitors Bureaus; NAICS 522320: Financial Transactions, Processing, Reserve and Clearing House Activities; NAICS 561499: All Other Business Support Services; NAICS 561990: All Other Support Services

7513　Truck Rental and Leasing, Without Drivers *see* NAICS 532120: Truck, Utility Trailer and RV (Recreational Vehicle) Rental and Leasing

7514　Passenger Car Rental *see* NAICS 532111: Passenger Cars Rental

7515　Passenger Car Leasing *see* NAICS 532112: Passenger Cars Leasing

7519　Utility Trailer and Recreational Vehicle Rental *see* NAICS 532120: Truck, Utility Trailer and RV (Recreational Vehicles) Rental and Leasing

7521　Automobile Parking *see* NAICS 812930: Parking Lots and Garages

7532　Top, Body, and Upholstery Repair Shops and Paint Shops *see* NAICS 811121: Automotive Body, Paint, and Upholstery Repair and Maintenance

7533　Automotive Exhaust System Repair Shops *see* NAICS 811112: Automotive Exhaust System Repair

7534　Tire Retreading and Repair Shops *see* NAICS 326212: Tire Retreading; NAICS 811198: All Other Automotive Repair and Maintenance

7536　Automotive Glass Replacement Shops *see* NAICS 811122: Automotive Glass Replacement Shops

7537　Automotive Transmission Repair Shops *see* NAICS 811113: Automotive Transmission Repair

7538　General Automotive Repair Shops *see* NAICS 811111: General Automotive Repair

7539　Automotive Repair Shops, NEC *see* NAICS 811118: Other Automotive Mechanical and Electrical Repair and Maintenance

7542　Carwashes *see* NAICS 811192: Car Washes

7549　Automotive Services, Except Repair and Carwashes *see* NAICS 811191: Automotive Oil Change and Lubrication Shops; NAICS 488410: Motor Vehicle Towing; NAICS 811198: All Other Automotive Repair and Maintenance

7622　Radio and Television Repair Shops *see* NAICS 811211: Consumer Electronics Repair and Maintenance; NAICS 811213: Communication Equipment Repair and Maintenance; NAICS 443112: Radio, Television and Other Electronics Stores

7623　Refrigeration and Air-Conditioning Services and Repair Shops *see* NAICS 443111: Household Appliance Stores; NAICS 811310: Commercial and Industrial Machinery and Equipment (except Automotive and Electronic) Repair and Maintenance; NAICS 811412: Appliance Repair and Maintenance

7629　Electrical and Electronic Repair Shops, NEC *see* NAICS 443111: Household Appliance Stores; NAICS 811212: Computer and Office Machine Repair and Maintenance; *see* NAICS 811213: Communication Equipment Repair and Maintenance; NAICS 811219: Other Electronic and Precision Equipment Repair and Maintenance; NAICS 811412: Appliance Repair and Maintenance; NAICS 811211: Consumer Electronics Repair and Maintenance

7631　Watch, Clock, and Jewelry Repair *see* NAICS 811490: Other Personal and Household Goods Repair and Maintenance

7641　Reupholster and Furniture Repair *see* NAICS 811420: Reupholstery and Furniture Repair

7692　Welding Repair *see* NAICS 811490: Other Personal and Household Goods Repair and Maintenance

7694　Armature Rewinding Shops *see* NAICS 811310: Commercial and Industrial Machinery and Equipment (except Automotive and Electronic) Repair and Maintenance; NAICS 335312: Motor and Generator Manufacturing

7699　Repair Shops and Related Services, NEC *see* NAICS 561622: Locksmiths; NAICS 562991: Septic Tank and Related Services; NAICS 561790: Other Services to Buildings and Dwellings; NAICS 488390: Other Support Activities for Water Transportation; NAICS 451110: Sporting Goods Stores; NAICS 811310: Commercial and Industrial Machinery and Equipment (except Automotive and Electronic) Repair and Maintenance; NAICS 115210: Support Activities for Animal Production; NAICS 811212: Computer and Office Machine Repair and Maintenance; NAICS 811219: Other Electronic and Precision Equipment Repair and Maintenance; NAICS 811411: Home and Garden Equipment Repair and Maintenance; NAICS 811412: Appliance Repair and Maintenance; NAICS 811430: Footwear and Leather Goods Repair; NAICS 811490: Other Personal and Household Goods Repair and Maintenance

7812　Motion Picture and Video Tape Production *see* NAICS 512110: Motion Picture and Video Production

7819　Services Allied to Motion Picture Production *see* NAICS 512191: Teleproduction and Other Post-Production Services; NAICS 561310: Employment Placement Agencies; NAICS 532220: Formal Wear and Costumes Rental; NAICS 532490: Other Commercial and Industrial Machinery and Equipment Rental and Leasing; NAICS 541214: Payroll Services; NAICS 711510: Independent Artists, Writers, and Performers; NAICS 334612: Prerecorded Compact Disc (Except Software), Tape, and Record Manufacturing; NAICS 512199: Other Motion Picture and Video Industries

7822　Motion Picture and Video Tape Distribution *see* NAICS 421990: Other Miscellaneous Durable Goods Wholesalers; NAICS 512120: Motion Picture and Video Distribution

7829　Services Allied to Motion Picture Distribution *see* NAICS 512199: Other Motion Picture and Video Industries; NAICS 512120: Motion Picture and Video Distribution

7832　Motion Picture Theaters, Except Drive-In *see* NAICS 512131: Motion Picture Theaters, Except Drive-In

7833　Drive-In Motion Picture Theaters *see* NAICS 512132: Drive-In Motion Picture Theaters

7841　Video Tape Rental *see* NAICS 532230: Video Tapes and Disc Rental

7911   Dance Studios, Schools, and Halls *see* NAICS 713990: All Other Amusement and Recreation Industries; NAICS 611610: Fine Arts Schools

7922   Theatrical Producers (Except Motion Picture) and Miscellaneous Theatrical Services *see* NAICS 561310: Employment Placement Agencies; NAICS 711110: Theater Companies and Dinner Theaters; NAICS 711410: Agents and Managers for Artists, Athletes, Entertainers and Other Public Figures; NAICS 711120: Dance Companies; NAICS 711310: Promoters of Performing Arts, Sports, and Similar Events with Facilities; NAICS 711320: Promoters of Performing Arts, Sports, and Similar Events without Facilities; NAICS 512290: Other Sound Recording Industries; NAICS 532490: Other Commercial and Industrial Machinery and Equipment Rental and Leasing

7929   Bands, Orchestras, Actors, and Other Entertainers and Entertainment Groups *see* NAICS 711130: Musical Groups and Artists; NAICS 711510: Independent Artists, Writers, and Performers; NAICS 711190: Other Performing Arts Companies

7933   Bowling Centers *see* NAICS 713950: Bowling Centers

7941   Professional Sports Clubs and Promoters *see* NAICS 711211: Sports Teams and Clubs; NAICS 711410: Agents and Managers for Artists, Athletes, Entertainers, and Other Public Figures; NAICS 711320: Promoters of Performing Arts, Sports, and Similar Events without Facilities; NAICS 711310: Promoters of Performing Arts, Sports, and Similar Events with Facilities; NAICS 711219: Other Spectator Sports

7948   Racing, Including Track Operations *see* NAICS 711212: Race Tracks; NAICS 711219: Other Spectator Sports

7991   Physical Fitness Facilities *see* NAICS 713940: Fitness and Recreational Sports Centers

7992   Public Golf Courses *see* NAICS 713910: Golf Courses and Country Clubs

7993   Coin Operated Amusement Devices *see* NAICS 713120: Amusement Arcades; NAICS 713290: Other Gambling Industries; NAICS 713990: All Other Amusement and Recreation Industries

7996   Amusement Parks *see* NAICS 713110: Amusement and Theme Parks

7997   Membership Sports and Recreation Clubs *see* NAICS 713910: Golf Courses and Country Clubs; NAICS 713940: Fitness and Recreational Sports Centers; NAICS 713990: All Other Amusement and Recreation Industries

7999   Amusement and Recreation Services, NEC *see* NAICS 561599: All Other Travel Arrangement and Reservation Services; NAICS 487990: Scenic and Sightseeing Transportation, Other; NAICS 711190: Other Performing Arts Companies; NAICS 711219: Other Spectator Sports; NAICS 713920: Skiing Facilities; NAICS 713940: Fitness and Recreational Sports Centers; NAICS 713210: Casinos (except Casino Hotels); NAICS 713290: Other Gambling Industries; NAICS 712190: Nature Parks and Other Similar Institutions; NAICS 611620: Sports and Recreation Instruction; NAICS 532292: Recreational Goods Rental; NAICS 487110: Scenic and Sightseeing Transportation, Land; NAICS 487210: Scenic and Sightseeing Transportation, Water; NAICS 713990: All Other Amusement and Recreation Industries

8011   Offices and Clinics of Doctors of Medicine *see* NAICS 621493: Freestanding Ambulatory Surgical and Emergency Centers; NAICS 621491: HMO Medical Centers; NAICS 621112: Offices of Physicians; NAICS 621111: Offices of Physicians (except Mental Health Specialists)

8021   Offices and Clinics of Dentists *see* NAICS 621210: Offices of Dentists

8031   Offices and Clinics of Doctors of Osteopathy *see* NAICS 621111: Offices of Physicians (except Mental Health Specialists); NAICS 621112: Offices of Physicians, Mental Health Specialists

8041   Offices and Clinics of Chiropractors *see* NAICS 621310: Offices of Chiropractors

8042   Offices and Clinics of Optometrists *see* NAICS 621320: Offices of Optometrists

8043   Offices and Clinics of Podiatrists *see* NAICS 621391: Offices of Podiatrists

8049   Offices and Clinics of Health Practitioners, NEC *see* NAICS 621330: Offices of Mental Health Practitioners (except Physicians); NAICS 621340: Offices of Physical, Occupational, and Speech Therapists and Audiologists; NAICS 621399: Offices of All Other Miscellaneous Health Practitioners

8051   Skilled Nursing Care Facilities *see* NAICS 623311: Continuing Care Retirement Communities; NAICS 623110: Nursing Care Facilities

8052   Intermediate Care Facilities *see* NAICS 623311: Continuing Care Retirement Communities; NAICS 623210: Residential Mental Retardation Facilities; NAICS 623110: Nursing Care Facilities

8059   Nursing and Personal Care Facilities, NEC *see* NAICS 623311: Continuing Care Retirement Communities; NAICS 623110: Nursing Care Facilities

8062   General Medical and Surgical Hospitals *see* NAICS 622110: General Medical and Surgical Hospitals

8063   Psychiatric Hospitals *see* NAICS 622210: Psychiatric and Substance Abuse Hospitals

8069   Specialty Hospitals, Except Psychiatric *see* NAICS 622110: General Medical and Surgical Hospitals; NAICS 622210: Psychiatric and Substance Abuse Hospitals; NAICS 622310: Specialty (except Psychiatric and Substance Abuse) Hospitals

8071   Medical Laboratories *see* NAICS 621512: Diagnostic Imaging Centers; NAICS 621511: Medical Laboratories

8072   Dental Laboratories *see* NAICS 339116: Dental Laboratories

8082   Home Health Care Services *see* NAICS 621610: Home Health Care Services

8092   Kidney Dialysis Centers *see* NAICS 621492: Kidney Dialysis Centers

8093   Specialty Outpatient Facilities, NEC *see* NAICS 621410: Family Planning Centers; NAICS 621420: Outpatient Mental Health and Substance Abuse Centers; NAICS 621498: All Other Outpatient Care Facilities

8099   Health and Allied Services, NEC *see* NAICS 621991: Blood and Organ Banks; NAICS 541430: Graphic Design Services; NAICS 541922: Commercial Photography; NAICS 621410: Family Planning Centers; NAICS 621999: All Other Miscellaneous Ambulatory Health Care Services

8111   Legal Services *see* NAICS 541110: Offices of Lawyers

8211   Elementary and Secondary Schools *see* NAICS 611110: Elementary and Secondary Schools

8221   Colleges, Universities, and Professional Schools *see* NAICS 611310: Colleges, Universities, and Professional Schools

8222 Junior Colleges and Technical Institutes *see* NAICS 611210: Junior Colleges

8231 Libraries *see* NAICS 514120: Libraries and Archives

8243 Data Processing Schools *see* NAICS 611519: Other Technical and Trade Schools; NAICS 611420: Computer Training

8244 Business and Secretarial Schools *see* NAICS 611410: Business and Secretarial Schools

8249 Vocational Schools, NEC *see* NAICS 611513: Apprenticeship Training; NAICS 611512: Flight Training; NAICS 611519: Other Technical and Trade Schools

8299 Schools and Educational Services, NEC *see* NAICS 611512: Flight Training; NAICS 611692: Automobile Driving Schools; NAICS 611710: Educational Support Services; NAICS 611691: Exam Preparation and Tutoring; NAICS 611610: Fine Arts Schools; NAICS 611630: Language Schools; NAICS 611430: Professional and Management Development Training Schools; NAICS 611699: All Other Miscellaneous Schools and Instruction

8322 Individual and Family Social Services *see* NAICS 624110: Child and Youth Services; NAICS 624210: Community Food Services; NAICS 624229: Other Community Housing Services; NAICS 624230: Emergency and Other Relief Services; NAICS 624120: Services for the Elderly and Persons with Disabilities; NAICS 624221: Temporary Shelter; NAICS 922150: Parole Offices and Probation Offices; NAICS 624190: Other Individual and Family Services

8331 Job Training and Vocational Rehabilitation Services *see* NAICS 624310: Vocational Rehabilitation Services

8351 Child Day Care Services *see* NAICS 624410: Child Day Care Services

8361 Residential Care *see* NAICS 623312: Homes for the Elderly; NAICS 623220: Residential Mental Health and Substance Abuse Facilities; NAICS 623990: Other Residential Care Facilities

8399 Social Services, NEC *see* NAICS 813212: Voluntary Health Organizations; NAICS 813219: Other Grantmaking and Giving Services; NAICS 813311: Human Rights Organizations; NAICS 813312: Environment, Conservation and Wildlife Organizations; NAICS 813319: Other Social Advocacy Organizations

8412 Museums and Art Galleries *see* NAICS 712110: Museums; NAICS 712120: Historical Sites

8422 Arboreta and Botanical or Zoological Gardens *see* NAICS 712130: Zoos and Botanical Gardens; NAICS 712190: Nature Parks and Other Similar Institutions

8611 Business Associations *see* NAICS 813910: Business Associations

8621 Professional Membership Organizations *see* NAICS 813920: Professional Organizations

8631 Labor Unions and Similar Labor Organizations *see* NAICS 813930: Labor Unions and Similar Labor Organizations

8641 Civic, Social, and Fraternal Associations *see* NAICS 813410: Civic and Social Organizations; NAICS 813990: Other Similar Organizations; NAICS 921150: American Indian and Alaska Native Tribal Governments; NAICS 624110: Child and Youth Services

8651 Political Organizations *see* NAICS 813940: Political Organizations

8661 Religious Organizations *see* NAICS 813110: Religious Organizations

8699 Membership Organizations, NEC *see* NAICS 813410: Civic and Social Organizations; NAICS 813910: Business Associations; NAICS 813312: Environment, Conservation, and Wildlife Organizations; NAICS 561599: All Other Travel Arrangement and Reservation Services; NAICS 813990: Other Similar Organizations

8711 Engineering Services *see* NAICS 541330: Engineering Services

8712 Architectural Services *see* NAICS 541310: Architectural Services

8713 Surveying Services *see* NAICS 541360: Geophysical Surveying and Mapping Services; NAICS 541370: Surveying and Mapping (except Geophysical) Services

8721 Accounting, Auditing, and Bookkeeping Services *see* NAICS 541211: Offices of Certified Public Accountants; NAICS 541214: Payroll Services; NAICS 541219: Other Accounting Services

8731 Commercial Physical and Biological Research *see* NAICS 541710: Research and Development in the Physical Sciences and Engineering Sciences; NAICS 541720: Research and Development in the Life Sciences

8732 Commercial Economic, Sociological, and Educational Research *see* NAICS 541730: Research and Development in the Social Sciences and Humanities; NAICS 541910: Marketing Research and Public Opinion Polling

8733 Noncommercial Research Organizations *see* NAICS 541710: Research and Development in the Physical Sciences and Engineering Sciences; NAICS 541720: Research and Development in the Life Sciences; NAICS 541730: Research and Development in the Social Sciences and Humanities

8734 Testing Laboratories *see* NAICS 541940: Veterinary Services; NAICS 541380: Testing Laboratories

8741 Management Services *see* NAICS 561110: Office Administrative Services

8742 Management Consulting Services *see* NAICS 541611: Administrative Management and General Management Consulting Services; NAICS 541612: Human Resources and Executive Search Consulting Services; NAICS 541613: Marketing Consulting Services; NAICS 541614: Process, Physical, Distribution, and Logistics Consulting

8743 Public Relations Services *see* NAICS 541820: Public Relations Services

8744 Facilities Support Management Services *see* NAICS 561210: Facilities Support Services

8748 Business Consulting Services, NEC *see* NAICS 611710: Educational Support Services; NAICS 541618: Other Management Consulting Services; NAICS 541690: Other Scientific and Technical Consulting Services

8811 Private Households *see* NAICS 814110: Private Households

8999 Services, NEC *see* NAICS 711510: Independent Artists, Writers, and Performers; NAICS 512210: Record Production; NAICS 541690: Other Scientific and Technical Consulting Services; NAICS 512230: Music Publishers; NAICS 541612: Human Resources and Executive Search Consulting Services; NAICS 514199: All Other Information Services; NAICS 541620: Environmental Consulting Services

PUBLIC ADMINISTRATION

9111   Executive Offices *see* NAICS 921110: Executive Offices

9121   Legislative Bodies *see* NAICS 921120: Legislative Bodies

9131   Executive and Legislative Offices, Combined *see* NAICS 921140: Executive and Legislative Offices, Combined

9199   General Government, NEC *see* NAICS 921190: All Other General Government

9211   Courts *see* NAICS 922110: Courts

9221   Police Protection *see* NAICS 922120: Police Protection

9222   Legal Counsel and Prosecution *see* NAICS 922130: Legal Counsel and Prosecution

9223   Correctional Institutions *see* NAICS 922140: Correctional Institutions

9224   Fire Protection *see* NAICS 922160: Fire Protection

9229   Public Order and Safety, NEC *see* NAICS 922190: All Other Justice, Public Order, and Safety

9311   Public Finance, Taxation, and Monetary Policy *see* NAICS 921130: Public Finance

9411   Administration of Educational Programs *see* NAICS 923110: Administration of Education Programs

9431   Administration of Public Health Programs *see* NAICS 923120: Administration of Public Health Programs

9441   Administration of Social, Human Resource, and Income Maintenance Programs *see* NAICS 923130: Administration of Social, Human Resource, and Income Maintenance Programs

9451   Administration of Veteran's Affairs, Except Health Insurance *see* NAICS 923140: Administration of Veteran's Affairs

9511   Air and Water Resource and Solid Waste Management *see* NAICS 924110: Air and Water Resource and Solid Waste Management

9512   Land, Mineral, Wildlife, and Forest Conservation *see* NAICS 924120: Land, Mineral, Wildlife, and Forest Conservation

9531   Administration of Housing Programs *see* NAICS 925110: Administration of Housing Programs

9532   Administration of Urban Planning and Community and Rural Development *see* NAICS 925120: Administration of Urban Planning and Community and Rural Development

9611   Administration of General Economic Programs *see* NAICS 926110: Administration of General Economic Programs

9621   Regulations and Administration of Transportation Programs *see* NAICS 488111: Air Traffic Control; NAICS 926120: Regulation and Administration of Transportation Programs

9631   Regulation and Administration of Communications, Electric, Gas, and Other Utilities *see* NAICS 926130: Regulation and Administration of Communications, Electric, Gas, and Other Utilities

9641   Regulation of Agricultural Marketing and Commodities *see* NAICS 926140: Regulation of Agricultural Marketing and Commodities

9651   Regulation, Licensing, and Inspection of Miscellaneous Commercial Sectors *see* NAICS 926150: Regulation, Licensing, and Inspection of Miscellaneous Commercial Sectors

9661   Space Research and Technology *see* NAICS 927110: Space Research and Technology

9711   National Security *see* NAICS 928110: National Security

9721   International Affairs *see* NAICS 928120: International Affairs

9999   Nonclassified Establishments *see* NAICS 999990: Unclassified Establishments

INDEX

Citations in this index are followed by the volume number and page number(s) in which the indexed term is referenced.

Acoustical Board, **1:** 686, 687
Acoustical Technology
  in emissions, **1:** 794
  in fish detection, **2:** 121
  in insulation, **2:** 281
Acquired Immunodeficiency Syndrome. *See* AIDS (Disease)
Acquisitions and Mergers
  in advertising, **2:** 1022–1023
  in aerospace industry, **1:** 1190, 1192–1193, 1211–1212
  in agriculture, **2:** 40, 68
  in aircraft industry, **1:** 1143, 1146, 1148, 1149
  in airline industry, **2:** 398
  in aluminum production, **1:** 724–725, 737, 740, 742, 744
  in art materials, **1:** 1298
  in automotive industry, **1:** 1121, 1122, **2:** 659
    lease and rental services, **2:** 1134, 1135, 1136, 1138
    parts and suppliers, **1:** 1102, 1137, **2:** 668
    parts suppliers, **1:** 987
  in banking, **2:** 808, 828, 841, 956, 958
    commercial, **2:** 804, 809–810
  in battery manufacturing, **1:** 1098
  in biotechnology industry, **1:** 490, 502
  in broom and brush manufacturing, **1:** 1304
  in carpet and rug manufacturers, **1:** 181, 183–184
  in catalog sales companies, **2:** 778–779
  in chemical industry, **1:** 475, 482, 538–539, 545–546,
    549–550, 553
  in clothing industry, **1:** 221, **2:** 692
  in computer services, **2:** 1117
  in concrete industry, **1:** 675
  in construction, **2:** 238
  in consulting services, **2:** 1430–1431
  in courier services, **2:** 335, 337
  in credit unions, **2:** 825
  in cruise lines, **2:** 373
  in defense industry, **1:** 1143
  in department stores, **2:** 631, 632
  in distilleries, **1:** 107
  in door and window manufacturing, **1:** 788
  in drug stores, **2:** 743
  in financial institutions, **2:** 818, 823, 828, 860, 883, 918
  in food industry
    baked products, **1:** 60, 66
    candy manufacturing, **1:** 77
    dairies, **2:** 589
    flavoring extract manufacturing, **1:** 118
    flour mills, **1:** 46
    grocery stores, **2:** 647
    machinery, **1:** 921
    meat packing plants, **1:** 5
    poultry and egg processing, **1:** 12
    soft drink manufacturing, **1:** 110, 112, 114
    sugar production, **1:** 74
  in footwear manufacturing, **1:** 625
  in furniture industry, **1:** 315
  in gasket and seal manufacturing, **1:** 584
  in health care
    home health care, **2:** 1303
    hospitals, **2:** 1283, 1285, 1294
    managed care, **2:** 898
  holding companies and, **2:** 811, 961
  in household appliance manufacturing, **1:** 1015, 1019, 1023,
    1027
  in industrial gas production, **1:** 447
  in insurance, **2:** 889, 905, 908, 925–926, 929
  in investment management, **2:** 883

  in lighting fixture manufacturing, **1:** 1038
  in lumber and building materials dealers, **2:** 617
  in medical equipment manufacturing, **1:** 1244, 1247, 1253
  in merchant shipping, **2:** 353
  in metal working, **1:** 765, 793, 796
  in mining, **2:** 132–133, 140, 141, 166, 171–172, 214, 226
  in mortgage companies, **2:** 860
  in motion picture production, **2:** 1172, 1174, 1177, 1178,
    1183
  in motor and generator manufacturing, **1:** 1001
  in music recording, **1:** 1046, 1049, 1050, 1051
  in natural gas transmission, **2:** 493
  in office supply stores, **2:** 762
  in paint and varnish industry, **1:** 520, 522, 523, 524, 525
  in paper industry, **1:** 346, **2:** 579
  in petroleum industry, **1:** 558, 560, 564, **2:** 180–181,
    184–185, 193–194, 201
    exploration services, **2:** 196, 197, 198
    oil field machinery manufacturers, **1:** 872
    pipelines, **2:** 422
  in pharmaceutical industry, **1:** 494–495, 497
  in photographic equipment and supplies wholesalers, **2:** 539
  in plastics industry, **1:** 468
  in printing industry, **1:** 410, 421, 425
  in publishing, **1:** 390, 396, 402, 403, 404, 405
  in radio broadcasting, **2:** 460, 462–463
  in railroad industry, **2:** 302–303
  in real estate, **2:** 945
  in search and navigation systems, **1:** 1209, 1212
  in securities trading, **2:** 870, 871
  in security systems services, **2:** 1122
  in shipping, **2:** 369
  in sporting goods, **1:** 1291, 1292
  in steel industry, **1:** 695
  in telecommunications, **2:** 448, 452, 454, 457, 1519
  in telephone service, **2:** 454, 457, 458
  in television, **2:** 465–466, 467, 468, 471, 473–474
  in textile industry, **1:** 162, 166, 173
  in tire industry, **1:** 571, 572, 573, 574, 576
  in tool manufacturing, **1:** 905
  in toy manufacturing, **1:** 1290
  in toy stores, **2:** 568
  in transformer manufacturing, **1:** 994
  in travel services, **2:** 425
  in wholesalers, **2:** 565
  in wine companies, **1:** 101, 102
  in wood products, **2:** 111
ACR Group Inc., **2:** 557
Acreage Reduction Programs, **2:** 2, 9
Acrylates, **1:** 593
Acrylic
  bathtubs, **1:** 609
  carpets and rugs, **1:** 182
  demand for, **1:** 482
  development of, **1:** 481
  glass coatings, **1:** 647
  paint, **2:** 1144–1145
  in textiles, **1:** 160, 173
  underwear, **1:** 236
  uses of, **1:** 481, 610
  yarn, **1:** 186, 187
Acrylonitrile Butadiene, **1:** 595
Acrylonitrile-Butadiene-Styrene, **1:** 610, 819
Acta Diurna, **1:** 389
Activase, **1:** 502
Active Eurocard Connectors, **1:** 1089

Active Ingredient Suppliers, **1:** 485–489
Active Wear, **1:** 171, 186, 198, 201. *See also* Clothing
  brassieres, **1:** 240, 241, 242
  coats, **1:** 218
  shirts, **1:** 201
Actors, 2: 1210–1212
Actuarial Firms, **2:** 1444. *See also* Insurance
Actuators, hydraulic and pneumatic, **1:** 941, 988–989
Acupuncture, **2:** 1259, 1263
Acuson Corporation, **1:** 1250
ACX Technologies Inc., **1:** 665, 752
AD Sutton and Sons, **1:** 634
Adams, Elwood, **2:** 622
Adams, John Quincy, **2:** 1366
Adams, Steve, **1:** 300
Adams, Thomas, **1:** 972
Adams Express Company, **2:** 970
Adams Gum Company, **1:** 972
Adams-Millis Division, **1:** 169
Adchem Inc., **1:** 606
Adderley, Terence, **2:** 1070
Addison, Eric, **2:** 1504, 1505
Addison-Wesley, **1:** 404, 405
Adecco SA, **2:** 1070, 1078
ADEM (Advanced Diesel Engine Management), **1:** 858
Ademco Security Group, **1:** 1064, 1065
Adesa Corporation, **2:** 527
Adhesives, 1: 547–551
  in bookbinding, **1:** 438, 439
  in carpets, **1:** 185
  in corrugated boxes, **1:** 357
  in electronics, **1:** 548
  in envelopes, **1:** 382
  in fiber drums, **1:** 360
  in furniture manufacturing, **1:** 316, 321
  hot-melt, **1:** 548–549
  natural base, **1:** 548
  pressure-sensitive, **1:** 548
  reactive, **1:** 548
  in reconstituted wood products, **1:** 303
  soybean-based, **1:** 550
  synthetic rubber-based, **1:** 472
Adidas, **1:** 578, 626
Adjustment Services, 2: 848, 1031–1034
ADM Malting Division, **1:** 96
Administration
  of community and rural development, 2: 1507–1512
  of educational programs, 2: 1469–1474
  of general economic programs, 2: 1507, 1512–1514
  of housing programs, 2: 1502–1507
  of public health programs, 2: 1474–1481
  **of social, human resource and income maintenance
      programs, 2:** 1481–1485
  of transportation programs, 2: 1514–1516
  of urban planning, 2: 1507–1512
  of utilities, 2: 1516–1520
  of veterans affairs, 2: 1485–1490
Administration for Children and Families, **2:** 1481
Adobe Systems Inc., **2:** 1089
Adolph Coors Company, **1:** 94–95, 665, 765, **2:** 606. *See also*
  Coors Brewing Company
Adoption Information Exchange, **2:** 1363
Adoption Services, **2:** 1347–1348
ADSL. *See* DSL
ADT Security Services, Inc., **2:** 1123
Adult Education Act, **2:** 1470

Advance Holdings Corporation, **2:** 668, 669
Advance Publications Inc., **1:** 397
Advanced Drainage Systems, **1:** 597
Advanced Encryption Standard, **2:** 803
Advanced Glass Treatment Systems, **1:** 647
Advanced Photo Systems, **1:** 1268, **2:** 538, 768–769
Advanced Research Corporation, **1:** 960
Advanced Research Projects Agency
  in computer display development, **1:** 967
  in computer storage devices, **1:** 960
  in semiconductor development, **1:** 925
  in weapons systems, **2:** 1536, 1537
Advanced Technology Materials Inc., **1:** 1067, 1177
Advanced Train Control Systems (ATCS), **2:** 305–306, 307
Advancetech Monitor, **1:** 490
Advanstar Communications, **1:** 398
Advantest, **1:** 924
Adventure Tours, **2:** 433
Adverse Drug Reactions, **1:** 493
Advertising, 2: 1019–1024, 1030–1031. *See also* Infomercials;
    Marketing
  acquisitions and mergers in, **2:** 1022–1023
  aerial, **2:** 1030–1031
  alcoholic beverages, **2:** 1024, 1026
  by associations, **2:** 1376
  athletic shoes, **1:** 624, 626, **2:** 704
  automobile, **1:** 394, 396, **2:** 1026
  brand-name products, **1:** 210, **2:** 1021
  candy, **1:** 77, 78
  cereal, **1:** 50
  chewing gum, **1:** 83
  chewing tobacco, **1:** 153
  children's products, **1:** 246, 249, 1288, 1289, **2:** 699
  cigarettes, **1:** 147, 394
  classified, **1:** 389
  clothing, **2:** 683, 699
  consumer controlled, **2:** 1046
  contact lenses, **1:** 1261, 1262, 1263
  cooperatives, **2:** 27
  cotton fabrics, **1:** 161
  by dentists, **2:** 1247
  direct mail, **2:** 1038–1046
  displays, **1:** 1304–1308, **2:** 1024–1027
  on electronic mail systems, **2:** 1039, 1043
  entertainment industry, **1:** 394
  ethics in, **1:** 1289
  eyeglasses, **1:** 1262
  by financial institutions, **1:** 396, **2:** 1026
  fruit, **2:** 27
  furniture, **1:** 313
  groceries, **2:** 647
  health care, **1:** 396, **2:** 792, 1240, 1247
  history of, **2:** 1020–1022, 1025–1026
  home furnishings, **1:** 396
  by hotels and motels, **2:** 1026
  household appliances, **1:** 1022
  insurance, **1:** 396, **2:** 1026
  international commerce in, **2:** 1023–1024
  Internet, **2:** 1022, 1030
  lead generation, **2:** 1039–1040
  in newspapers, **1:** 388, 389, 390, 392, **2:** 1022, 1028, 1029
  outdoor, 2: 1024–1027
  in periodicals, **1:** 393–394, 395, 396, **2:** 1022, 1028, 1029
  pharmaceutical, **1:** 493
  by physicians, **2:** 792, 1240
  postage costs in, **1:** 383

American Society of Heating, Refrigeration and Air Conditioning Engineers, **1:** 640

American Society of Landscape Architects, **2:** 102, 103

American Society of Mechanical Engineers, **1:** 789, 791, 793, 846–847, **2:** 1398

American Society of Plastic and Reconstructive Surgeons, **2:** 1240

American Society of Plumbing Engineers, **1:** 661

American Society of Refrigeration Engineers, **1:** 976, 982

American Society of Travel Agents, **2:** 426, 430, 437

American Soda LLP, Inc., **2:** 224

American Soybean Association, **2:** 12–13

American Specialty Toy Retailers Association, **2:** 765

American Speech-Language-Hearing Association, **2:** 1259

American Speedy, **2:** 1048

American Sports Data, Inc., **2:** 566

American Staffing Association, **2:** 1076

American Standard Inc., **1:** 660, 661, 779, 981

American Standards Association, **2:** 1151

American Steamship Company, **2:** 364

American Steel Foundries, **1:** 843

American Steel Institute, **1:** 35

American Stock Exchange, **2:** 869, 879, 968

American Stores Company, **2:** 647, 648

American Street Railway Association, **2:** 310

American Suffolk Sheep Society, **2:** 96

American Sugar Alliance, **1:** 72

American Surety Corporation, **2:** 910

American Telephone and Telegraph. *See* AT&T Corporation

American Textile Manufacturing Institute, **1:** 162, 179
  on GATT, **1:** 158, 176
  on NAFTA, **1:** 260, 265

American Textile Partnership, **1:** 162, 171, 177, 180, 187

American Tobacco Company, **1:** 146–147, 150

American Tourister, **1:** 632, 633

American Trans Air, **2:** 410, 411

American Transit Association, **2:** 309

American Transportation Corporation, **1:** 1131

American Tree Farm System, **2:** 114

American Trucking Association, **2:** 325, 329

American Veterinary Medical Association, **2:** 98

American Warehouse Association, **2:** 341, 342

American Watchmakers Institute, **2:** 1168

American Water Works, **2:** 509, 510

American Waterways Operators, **2:** 369

American Wilderness Experience, **2:** 430

American Woodmark Corporation, **1:** 282

American Yarn Spinners Association, **1:** 186

American Zoo and Aquarium Association, **2:** 1368

American's Lucky Stores, **2:** 649

Americans with Disabilities Act
  cost of implementation, **2:** 932
  on fitness centers, **2:** 1229
  office furniture for, **1:** 322
  renovations for, **1:** 609, 798, **2:** 544, 1407
  on signs, **1:** 1306, 1308
  training and, **2:** 1350

America's Blood Centers, **2:** 1311

America's Community Bankers, **2:** 819

Americold Logistics, **2:** 340

Americorps, **2:** 1473

Americus Dental Labs LP, **2:** 1301

AmeriGas Partners, LP, **2:** 605, 785

Ameriserve, **2:** 588

AmeriSource, **2:** 581

Ameritech Corporation, **1:** 418, **2:** 918

merger of, **2:** 457, 458, 1519

Ameritrade, **2:** 871, 885

Ameron International Corporation, **1:** 705

Ames, John, **2:** 622

Ames Department Stores, **2:** 641

Ames Research Center, **2:** 1525

AMETEK Inc., **1:** 1001, 1236

AMEX. *See* American Stock Exchange

AMF Bowling Centers, **1:** 1293, 1294, **2:** 1213–1214

AMFM Inc., **2:** 461, 462, 463, 1029

Amico, Gregory D., **1:** 429

Amino Acid Supplements, **1:** 488

Ammeters, **1:** 1125, 1126

Ammonia, **1:** 510
  anhydrous, **1:** 540

Ammoniacal Copper, **1:** 302

Ammonium Nitrate, **1:** 540, 551

Ammunition, 1: 824–830
  exports of, **1:** 825
  history of, **1:** 825–827, 829–830
  imports of, **1:** 826
  phosphorous in, **1:** 460

Ammunition Boxes, **1:** 853

Amniotic Fluid, **1:** 516

Amoco Corporation, **1:** 558, 563
  in cyclic crudes and intermediates, **1:** 531, 532
  history of, **2:** 185
  merger of, **1:** 539, 563, **2:** 198, 419, 918
  multi-franchising by, **2:** 672
  in petroleum exploration, **2:** 196
  in pipelines, **2:** 420
  in plastics, **1:** 468

AMP Inc., **1:** 1035, 1088, 1089

Ampad Corporation, **1:** 385

Ampco-Pittsburgh Corporation, **1:** 907

Ampex Corporation, **1:** 1107

Amphenol Corporation, **1:** 1089

Amphetamines, **1:** 492

Amphibious Vehicles, **1:** 1201, 1204

AMPI Southern Region, **2:** 589

Amplifiers, **1:** 1111

Ampolex Ltd., **2:** 197

Amputation, **1:** 1243

AMR Services Corporation, **2:** 416

Amrak, **2:** 300

AMRCombs, **2:** 411

Amsco International, **1:** 1244

AMSTAT Corporation, **2:** 680

AMSTED Industries Inc., **1:** 707

Amtech Elevator Services, **1:** 879

Amtrak, **1:** 1181, 1183, **2:** 303–304, 306, 307, 317

Amtrak Reauthorization Act, **2:** 303

Amtrak Reform Council, **2:** 303

Amtralease, **2:** 1130

Amtram, **2:** 412

Amurol Confections Company, **1:** 83

Amusement Machines, Coin-Operated, 1: 1311, 1312, **2:** 1232–1233

Amusement Parks, 1: 301, **2:** 1233–1234

Amusement Rides, **1:** 991

Amusement Services, 2: 1235–1237. *See also* Entertainment

Amway Corporation, **1:** 509

Anaheim Manufacturing Company, **1:** 1029

Analgesics, development of, **1:** 490

Analog Computers, **1:** 946, 947, **2:** 455

Analogic Corporation, **1:** 1222

Automobiles. *See* Cars
Automotive Bodies
    repair services, 2: 1143–1146
    truck and bus, 1: 1117–1126, 1127–1133
Automotive Dealers. *See* Motor Vehicle Dealers
Automotive Fuels. *See* Fuels
Automotive Industry, 1: 654–673, 1117–1138. *See also* Cars;
    Transportation
    acquisitions and mergers in, **1:** 1121, 1122, **2:** 659
        lease and rental services, **2:** 1134, 1135, 1136, 1138
        parts suppliers, **1:** 1102, 1137
    aftermarket suppliers and, **1:** 1134
    in aircraft engine manufacturing, **1:** 1155–1156, 1164
    assembly lines in, **1:** 1119, **2:** 1143, 1144
    automobile loans by, **2:** 846
    in bicycle manufacturing, **1:** 1187
    dealers (*See* Motor Vehicle Dealers)
    general services, **2:** 1161–1162
    glass replacement shops, 2: 1150–1153
    history of, **1:** 1118–1121, **2:** 525–527, 655–659, 666–668
    international competition in, **1:** 902–903, 1137–1147
    Japanese, **1:** 1136
    just-in-time manufacturing in, **1:** 585, 813, 814
    labor unions and, **1:** 894, 1103
    lease and rental services (*See* Automobile Leasing;
        Automobile Rentals)
    machine tools for, **1:** 893, 894, 896, 902–903
    original equipment suppliers in, **1:** 1134
    parts (*See* Automotive Parts)
    projected sales for, **1:** 987
    repair shops (*See* Automotive Repair Shops)
    supply stores, 2: 664–669
    technological changes in, **1:** 815, 1125–1126
    textile products for, **1:** 263–264, 265–266
    tire industry and, **1:** 572
    value of, **2:** 524
    wholesalers, 2: 524–528
    workforce in, **1:** 1122–1123, 1139, **2:** 1162
        automotive stampings, **1:** 812, 813, 815
        parts suppliers, **1:** 1103, 1137
        trailer trucks, **1:** 1138, 1139
        truck and bus, **1:** 888, 891, 1132
Automotive Insurance, **2:** 902
Automotive Parts, 1: 986–988, 1133–1138
    acquisitions and mergers in, **1:** 987, 1102
    aftermarket suppliers in, **1:** 1134
    automakers and, **1:** 1135–1136
    automotive trimmings, 1: 263–264
    counterfeit, **1:** 1102
    in dealerships, **2:** 658
    exports of, **1:** 1136, 1137–1138
    foreign suppliers of, **1:** 987, 1134
    history of, **1:** 1134–1135, **2:** 666–668
    imports of, **1:** 1103, 1137, 1138
    Japanese, **1:** 1136
    online shopping for, **2:** 669
    original equipment suppliers in, **1:** 1134
    outsourcing, **1:** 814, 1137
    retail stores for, 2: 664–669
    sales of, **1:** 1136, **2:** 660
    superstores for, **2:** 668
    wholesalers
        new, 2: 528–529
        used, 2: 530–531
    workforce in, **1:** 1103, 1137
Automotive Recyclers Association, **2:** 530, 570

Automotive Repair Shops, 2: 1155–1159
    for bodies, 2: 1143–1146
    chains of, **2:** 1155, 1156, 1157, 1158
    in dealerships, **2:** 1155, 1156, 1157
    for exhaust system, 2: 1146–1149
    for glass, **2:** 1150–1153
    paint, 2: 1143–1146
    for transmissions, 2: 1153–1155
    for upholstery, 2: 1143–1146
    workforce in, **2:** 1145, 1152, 1157, 1158
Automotive Service Association, **2:** 1157
Automotive Stampings, 1: 812–815
Automotive Trimmings, 1: 263–264
AutoNation, Inc., **2:** 660, 663
Autopilots, **1:** 1208, 1210, 1211
Autotronics System, **1:** 878
AutoZone Inc., **2:** 668, 669
Avalon Properties Inc., **2:** 936
Avco, **1:** 1146
Avery, Stanton, **1:** 368
Avex Electronics Inc., **1:** 1081
Aviation Corporation of the Americas, **1:** 1164, **2:** 397, 400
Aviation Industry. *See* Aircraft Industry
Avion Company, **1:** 1145, 1156
Avionics Research Corporation, **2:** 1055
Avirex Ltd., **1:** 255
Avis, Warren, **2:** 1132, 1135
Avis Rent A Car, Inc., **2:** 1132–1136, 1139, 1140
Avnet Incorporated, **2:** 555
Avocados, **2:** 36, 37
Avon Books, **1:** 404
Avon Products Inc., **2:** 782
Avondale Industries Inc., **1:** 1175
AVOS (Allows View of Surface) System, **1:** 901
AVRE Plasma, **2:** 1312
AVX Corporation, **1:** 1078, 1080, 1081
AWACS. *See* Airborne Warning & Control System
Awnings, **1:** 261, 795
Axciom Corporation, **2:** 1116
Axes, **1:** 771
Axiom Real Estate Management Inc., **2:** 1439
Azimuths, **1:** 1210
Azinphos-Methyl, **1:** 545
Azumaya, Inc., **1:** 141

B

Babbage, Charles, **1:** 948, 957
Babbitt, Bruce, **2:** 1500, 1501
Babcock, Barry, **2:** 473
Babcock, George Herman, **1:** 793
Babcock, S.M., **1:** 27
Babcock and Wilcox Company, **1:** 705, 793
Babies' Clothing. *See* Infants' Clothing
Babson School of Executive Training, **2:** 1341
Baby Bells, **2:** 456–457, 458
Baby Diaper Service Inc., **2:** 1007
Baby Foods, **1:** 32, 33, 34
Baby Sitting Bureaus, **2:** 1019
BabyGap, **2:** 702
BAC Amendment, **1:** 107
Baca Ranch, **2:** 1501
Back Pain, **1:** 280, 1240, **2:** 1252
Backhoes, **1:** 866, 868
Backscatter Imaging Tomography, **1:** 1252
Backstreet Boys, **2:** 1210

Brandt, George, **1:** 460
Brandt Color Coat Process, **1:** 647
Brandwise.Com, **1:** 1011
Brandy. *See* Wine
Brandy Trading Corporation, **1:** 1298
Braniff Airlines, **1:** 1114, **2:** 401
Bransom, H.O., **1:** 116
Bras, **1:** 239–242
Brass
    forgings, **1:** 811
    mills, **1:** 758
    ornamental fixtures, **1:** 797
    plating, **1:** 819
    plumbing fixtures, **1:** 777
Brass Mills, **1:** 733–735
Brassieres, 1: 239–242. *See also* Underwear
Braswell Services Group, **1:** 1175
Bratt, Rachel G., **2:** 1503
Brattain, Walter H., **1:** 1072
Braum's Dairy Farms, **2:** 66
Braun, **1:** 1024, 1249
Braun, Karl, **2:** 1163
Brazilian Pine, **1:** 302
Bread Machines, **1:** 1024
Breads and Cakes, 1: 60–65
    consumption of, **1:** 62, 64
    enriched, **1:** 60, 61, 64
    fat content of, **1:** 63
    French, **1:** 62
    frozen, **1:** 69–70
    history of, **1:** 60–64
    mixes, **1:** 54
    rye, **1:** 62
    as snacks, **1:** 62–63, 64
    wheat for, **2:** 1
    whole wheat, **1:** 62, 63
    wholesalers of, **2:** 595
    yeast, **1:** 60–61, 62
Breakfast Foods, **1:** 48–52, 69–70, 76
Brearely, Harold, **1:** 460
Breast Cancer Drugs, **1:** 495
Breast Implants, **1:** 1243–1244
Breathing Assistance Devices, **1:** 1243
Breeding
    associations, **2:** 96
    cats, **2:** 98
    cattle, **2:** 52, 53, 56, 96–97, 598
    dogs, **2:** 98, 99
    hogs, **2:** 58, 96
    horses, **2:** 76–77, 79, 99
    livestock, **2:** 93, 96
    pets, **2:** 81
    poultry, **2:** 93, 96, 97
    services, **2:** 98, 99
    sheep, **2:** 96
Breedlove Dehydration Foods, **1:** 38
Breuer, Marcel, **1:** 309
Breweries, **1:** 91–96, **2:** 607. *See also* Beer
Brewpub Beer. *See* Microbreweries
Breyer's Ice Cream Company, **1:** 24
Brick
    common, **1:** 653–654
    concrete, **1:** 668–669
    extruded, **1:** 654, 657
    face, **1:** 654
    firebrick, **1:** 657

glazed, **1:** 654
handmade, **1:** 654
recycled, **1:** 654
refractory, **1:** 657, 688, **2:** 216
reinforced, **2:** 277
sales of, **2:** 535
silica, **2:** 216, 217
tile, 1: 653–655
wholesalers of, 2: 534
Brick Industry Association, **1:** 654
Bridge Construction, 1: 671, **2:** 257–264
    government funding of, **2:** 258, 260–261
    joint ventures in, **2:** 258, 261
    machinery for, **1:** 867
    workforce in, **2:** 261–262
Bridge Information Systems, Inc., **2:** 1103
Bridgeport Machines Inc., **1:** 895
Bridges (Structures), **1:** 867
    aluminum for, **1:** 744, **2:** 263
    cable-stayed, **2:** 263
    construction of (*See* Bridge Construction)
    double-swing, **2:** 260
    engineering of, **2:** 1398
    fabricated structural metal for, **1:** 785, 786
    history of, **2:** 259–260, 293–294
    hydraulic systems for, **1:** 945
    repairs to, **2:** 254, 260, 294
    steel for, **2:** 294
    suspension, **2:** 259
    toll, **2:** 259, 447
Bridgestone/Firestone, Inc., **1:** 573, 574, 575–576, **2:** 1384
Briefcases, **1:** 632
Briggs Industries Inc., **1:** 661
Bright Horizons, **2:** 1356
Brighteners, in Cleaning Products, **1:** 504, 511
Brinker International, **2:** 735
Brink's, Inc., **2:** 1120, 1123
Brins Oxygen Company, **1:** 454
Brinson Partners, **2:** 883
Briquettes, **1:** 569, 570
Bristol, William, **1:** 496
Bristol Myers-Squibb Company, **1:** 496
    history of, **1:** 487
    in infant formula, **1:** 20
    in penicillin, **1:** 492
    research by, **1:** 492, 497
    in silicone implants, **1:** 1243–1244
Briston, John, **1:** 591
Brithinee Electric, **2:** 1170
British Aerospace PLC, **1:** 1151, 1152
British Airways, **1:** 1151
British American Tobacco PLC, **1:** 151
British Car Auction Group, **2:** 527
British Columbia Packers, **1:** 122
British Cutlery and Silverware Association, **1:** 770
British Glaxo, **1:** 497
British Inman Lime, **2:** 371
British Petroleum Company PLC, **1:** 558, 563. *See also* BP
    AMOCO
British Telecommunications, **1:** 419
Britt, Wayne, **2:** 68
Brittan, David, **2:** 1399
Brix Maritime Company, **2:** 391
Broaching, **2:** 206
Broadband Transmission, Wireless, **1:** 750
Broadcast Partners Holdings LP, **2:** 463

Broadcasting. *See* Radio Broadcasting; Television Broadcasting
Broadway Books, **1:** 404
Broadway Productions, **2:** 1206–1207, 1209, 1211
Broadwoven Fabric Mills
   cotton, **1:** 157–159, 175–178
   manmade fiber and silk, 1: 159–163, 478
   wool, **1:** 163–166
Brock Associates, **2:** 57
Brock Enterprises, **2:** 275
Broilers (Chicken), 2: 67–70. *See also* Poultry
Broken Hill Proprietary Company, **1:** 759, **2:** 132
Broker Booth Support System, **2:** 880
Brokers
   commodities, **2:** 874–875, 879, 885–886, 892, 984–986
   customs, **2:** 439–440, 441–442
   discount, **2:** 871, 877
   employment (*See* Employment Agencies)
   independent, **2:** 872, 873, 875
   information (*See* Information Retrieval Services)
   insurance (*See* Insurance, Agents and Brokers)
   mortgage, **2:** 861–867
   patient, **2:** 1291
   planned community, **2:** 245
   regional, **2:** 872
   stock (*See* Security Brokers)
Bromine, **1:** 460, 461
Bronfman, Sam, II, **1:** 102
Bronner, Slosberg, and Humphrey, **2:** 1044
Bronze
   caskets, **1:** 1309
   discovery of, **1:** 798
   forgings, **1:** 811
   plumbing fixtures, **1:** 777
Brook Street Bureau, **2:** 1340
Brookings Institute, **2:** 747
Brooklyn Union Gas Company, **2:** 495
Brooks, Garth, **2:** 639, 1210
Brooks Brothers, **1:** 196, 210, **2:** 682, 684
Broomcorn, **1:** 1304
Brooms, 1: 1303–1304, **2:** 712–713
Browder Tours Inc., **2:** 320
Brower, Abraham, **2:** 310
Brown, Charles R., **1:** 902
Brown, George W., **1:** 107, 860
Brown, Jesse, **2:** 1489
Brown, Kevein, **2:** 1215
Brown, Linda, **2:** 78
Brown, Nathaniel, **2:** 682
Brown, Walter, **2:** 397
Brown, William Folger, **1:** 1145
Brown & Sharpe Manufacturing Company, **1:** 802, 901
Brown & Williamson Tobacco Corporation, **1:** 145, 149, 151, 153, 156
Brown and Root International Inc., **1:** 156, **2:** 203
Brown Brothers Harrisman, **2:** 814
Brown-Forman Corporation, **1:** 102, 107, 292, 663, 667
Brown Group, Inc., **1:** 629, **2:** 704, 705
Brown Lung, **1:** 186
Brown Rental Equipment Company Inc., **2:** 1062
Brown Shoe Company, **2:** 584, 704
Brown V. Board of Education, **2:** 1320, 1472
Browne, David, **2:** 729
Browner, Carol, **1:** 462, **2:** 1491, 1496
Browning, John M., **1:** 832–833
Browning-Ferris Industries, Inc., **2:** 518
Broxterman, Bill, **1:** 549

Bruning, Charles, **1:** 1267
Brunswick Corporation, **1:** 858, 1180, 1294
Brunswick Recreation Centers, **2:** 1214
Brunswick Worsted Mills, **1:** 187
Brush, Charles F., **1:** 1004
Brush Development Company, **1:** 1106
Brush Electric Light and Power Company, **1:** 790, 793
Brush Wellman Inc., **1:** 665, 759
Brushes, 1: 1303–1304, **2:** 712–713
   graphite, **1:** 1003–1006
Bryant Universal Roofing Inc., **2:** 289
Brynestad, Atle, **2:** 374
BSC Group, Inc., **2:** 1413
BSMG Worldwide, **2:** 1435
B.T. Miller, **2:** 763
BT Mancini Company Inc., **2:** 285
Bubble Gum, **1:** 82, 83, 84
Buck Knives, **1:** 770
Buckeye Pipe Line Company, LP, **2:** 420
Buckeye Technologies Inc., **1:** 479
Buckley, James, **2:** 1391
Buckmeier, Ron, **1:** 1142
Buckwheat, **2:** 13
Bucyrus International, **1:** 871
Bud Hatfield Printers, **2:** 1049
Budd, Edward, **1:** 813
Budd Company, **1:** 759, 814, 815
Budget Group, **2:** 1129, 1131, 1135, 1136–1137
Budget Rent-A-Car Corporation, **2:** 1133–1134, 1137
Budget Truck Rentals, **2:** 1129
Buell Motorcycle, **1:** 1183
Buena Vista Home Video, **2:** 1185, 1188, 1202
Buffalo China, **1:** 663
Buffalo Statler, **2:** 989
Buffing Wheels, **1:** 681
Buffs-N-Puffs Ltd., **2:** 1161
Buick, David D., **1:** 1118
Buick Motor Car Company, **1:** 1118
Builders Square, Inc., **2:** 623, 624
Building. *See* Construction
Building Codes
   for electrical work, **2:** 276
   for glass, **1:** 641
   for lumber *vs.* steel, **1:** 274
   for masonry work, **2:** 276
   for structural members, **1:** 289
Building Contractors Association, **2:** 1058
Building Maintenance Services, 2: 1057–1059
Building Materials
   dealers, **2:** 238, 615–618
   wholesalers, **2:** 533–537
Building Officials and Code Administrators International, **1:** 639
Building One Services Corporation, **1:** 277, 278
Building Owners and Managers Association International, **2:** 931
Building Societies, **2:** 816
Buildings. *See also* Housing; Nonresidential Construction; Residential Construction
   apartment (*See* Apartment Houses)
   automatic controls for, **1:** 1218
   farm, **1:** 799
   high-rise, **1:** 671, 878, **2:** 277, 294
   intelligent, **1:** 982
   manufactured (*See* Manufactured Homes)
   office (*See* Office Buildings)
   operators of nonresidential, **2:** 930–935
   panelized, **1:** 299, 300

Buildings *(cont'd)*
  portable, **1:** 799
  prefabricated, **1:** 298–302, 799–800, **2:** 536
Buker, Robert H., Jr., **1:** 72
Bulbs
  flower, **2:** 38
  light, **1:** 649, 1030–1033, 1040, 1164
Bulgur Wheat, **1:** 45
Bulk Lift International Inc., **1:** 261
Bulldozers, **1:** 866, 868
Bullet-Proof Vests, **1:** 826, 1243
Bullets. *See* Ammunition
Bullock, William, **1:** 917
Bulova Corporation, **1:** 1274, **2:** 573
Bumble Bee Seafoods, **1:** 121
Bundle System, in Clothing Manufacturing, **1:** 199, 212
Bunge Corporation, **2:** 597, 875
Bunsen, Robert, **1:** 460, 1231
Buracell International Inc., **1:** 1095
Bureau of Alcohol, Tobacco and Firearms
  on explosives, **1:** 552
  on firearms records, **2:** 567
  role of, **1:** 91, 98, 103, **2:** 1457, 1468, 1523–1524
Bureau of Apprenticeship and Training, **2:** 1145
Bureau of Biological Survey, **2:** 1497
Bureau of Chemistry, **1:** 459
Bureau of Commercial Fisheries, **2:** 119, 1497
Bureau of Economic Analysis, **2:** 1081
Bureau of Export Administration, **2:** 1467
Bureau of Federal Credit Unions, **2:** 825
Bureau of Fisheries, **2:** 1497
Bureau of Forestry, **2:** 113
Bureau of Home Economics, **2:** 1509
Bureau of Indian Affairs, **2:** 1478, 1497, 1501
Bureau of Justice Statistics, **2:** 1465–1466
Bureau of Labor Statistics
  on ammunition manufacturing, **1:** 828
  on armature winding, **2:** 1170
  on automotive services, **2:** 660, 1162
  on banks, **2:** 959
  on bearings, **1:** 933
  on beer production, **1:** 95
  on bus services, **2:** 319
  on capacitor manufacturing, **1:** 1080
  on carbon black manufacturing, **1:** 555
  on cellulosic fiber manufacturing, **1:** 479
  on chief executives and legislators, **2:** 1447
  on clothing manufacturing, **1:** 238
  on commercial art, **2:** 1055
  on commercial banks, **2:** 819
  on computer maintenance and repair, **2:** 1113
  on computer programming, **2:** 1081
  on cookies and crackers, **1:** 67
  on court reporters, **2:** 1056
  on direct mail, **2:** 1045
  on domestic workers, **2:** 1443
  on eldercare, **2:** 1347
  on electrical wiring devices, **1:** 1035, 1036
  on electricians, **2:** 278
  on electronic components, **1:** 1093
  on electronics repairs, **2:** 1167
  on employment, **2:** 1066
  on employment agencies, **2:** 1076
  on engineering, **2:** 1397
  on equipment rentals, **2:** 1063
  on facilities support services, **2:** 1439

  on fire departments, **2:** 1464
  on floor covering manufacturing, **1:** 1311
  on fluid power equipment manufacturing, **1:** 990
  on furniture manufacturing and repair, **1:** 311, **2:** 1169
  on hat manufacturing, **1:** 241
  on home care, **2:** 1304
  on hotels and lodging, **2:** 1001
  on industrial machinery, **1:** 946
  on industrial machinery manufacturing, **1:** 992
  on insurance services, **2:** 922
  on janitorial services, **2:** 1059
  on lime manufacturers, **1:** 677
  on lithographic printing, **1:** 423
  on management services, **2:** 1426
  on mortgage brokers, **2:** 866
  on nonmineral product manufacturers, **1:** 689
  on periodical publishing, **1:** 398
  on personal services, **2:** 1019
  on petroleum royalties, **2:** 978
  on photography, **2:** 1051
  on plastic production, **1:** 603, 608
  on podiatry, **2:** 1257
  on power transmission equipment, **1:** 945
  on prisons, **2:** 1463
  on public relations, **2:** 1436
  on real estate, **2:** 934, 942
  on reconstituted wood products, **1:** 304
  on restaurants, **2:** 737
  on retail employment, **2:** 702
  on rubber manufacturing, **1:** 476
  on secondary metals, **1:** 732
  on the service industries, **2:** 1444
  on service industry equipment, **1:** 985
  on shirt manufacturing, **1:** 202
  on shoe repair shops, **2:** 1013
  on steel foundries, **1:** 715
  on sugar production, **1:** 73
  on surveying, **2:** 1414
  on trailer manufacturing, **1:** 1139
  on truck manufacturing, **1:** 891
  on wholesalers, **2:** 553
  on work clothes manufacturing, **1:** 216
Bureau of Land Management
  campgrounds, **2:** 998
  on coal resources, **2:** 171
  on forest fires, **2:** 114, 115
  on grazing, **2:** 54
  on logging, **1:** 269
  on mining, **2:** 148
  role of, **2:** 1498
Bureau of Mines, **1:** 1098, **2:** 136, 161, 164, 489, 1499
Bureau of Pensions, **2:** 1486, 1487
Bureau of Reclamation, **2:** 268, 1498–1499
Bureau of Sport Fisheries and Wildlife, **2:** 1497
Bureau of Transportation, **2:** 316, 351
Bureau of War Risk Insurance, **2:** 1487
Burford, Anne. *See* Gorush, Anne M.
Burger King, **1:** 373, **2:** 672, 736
Burglar Alarms. *See* Alarm Systems
Burial Caskets, 1: 1308–1310
Burke Mills Inc., **1:** 187
Burlap Bags. *See* Textile Goods, bags
Burley Tobacco Growers Cooperative, **2:** 789
Burlington Air Express, **2:** 403–404, 407
Burlington Industries, **1:** 163, 175, 186
Burlington Northern Santa Fe Railroad, **2:** 300, 303, 304, 306

Casting (Metal) *(cont'd)*
  iron (*See* Cast Iron)
  jewelry, **1:** 1301
  magnesium, **1:** 753, 760
  nickel, **1:** 760
  permanent mold, **1:** 755
  plaster mold, **1:** 755
  in pump manufacturing, **1:** 927
  sand, **1:** 754, 757, **2:** 216
  services for, **2:** 1181, 1182
  shell mold, **1:** 755
  slip, **1:** 658
  steel (*See* Steel Investment Foundries)
  titanium, **1:** 753, 760
  zinc, **1:** 760
Casting Society of America, **2:** 1182
Castle Neckwear Inc., **1:** 208
Castner, H.Y., **1:** 1005
Casual Wear, **1:** 218
  for children, **2:** 694–695
  development of, **1:** 201
  footwear, **1:** 617, 620, 622, 628, **2:** 583–585
  jeans, **2:** 701
  men's and boys', **2:** 680
  in offices, **1:** 197
  sales of, **1:** 218
Casualty Insurance. *See* Property and Casualty Insurance
Caswell-Massey, **1:** 515
CAT Command Center, **1:** 891
Cat Fancier Association, **2:** 98
Cat Food, 1: 55–57
CAT Scan. *See* Computed Tomography Scan
Catalina Channel Express, Inc., **2:** 381
Catalina Lighting, Inc., **1:** 1037
Catalog and Mail-Order Houses, 2: 775–781, 1044
  acquisitions and mergers in, **2:** 778–779
  for chewing tobacco, **1:** 153
  for children's clothing, **2:** 698–699
  for cigars, **1:** 152
  for computers, **2:** 723, 724, 726
  consumer information and, **2:** 780–781, 1039, 1040–1041
  department stores as, **2:** 635–636
  direct selling and, **2:** 782–783
  envelopes for, **1:** 382–383
  for furniture, **1:** 313
  history of, **2:** 776–778, 1041–1042
  for household appliances, **1:** 1023
  international, **2:** 780
  Internet based (*See* Electronic Shopping)
  for lingerie, **1:** 241, **2:** 692
  magazine hybrids, **2:** 779
  manufactures, **1:** 230
  for ophthalmic goods, **1:** 1263
  for pharmaceuticals, **2:** 742–743
  for photofinishing, **2:** 1125–1126
  printing for, **1:** 420, 424, 426, 427
  publishing for, **1:** 415, 418, 419
  for recorded music, **1:** 1048
  sales by, **2:** 775, 1042, 1044
  specialty, **2:** 777–778
  taxes and, **2:** 777
  for work clothes, **1:** 215
  workforce in, **2:** 780
Catalog City, **2:** 781
Catalog Showroom Stores, **2:** 642–643
Catalyst Group, **1:** 468

Catalytic Converters, **2:** 1146, 1147, 1149
Catapults, **1:** 991
Catazines, **2:** 779
Catello Tile, **2:** 283
Catellus Development Corporation, **2:** 950
CaterAire, **2:** 414
Caterers, **2:** 414, 732
Caterpillar Financial Services, **2:** 854
Caterpillar Inc.
  autonomous truck control system, **1:** 871
  in construction machinery, **1:** 867–868, **2:** 560, 1061
  engines, **1:** 858
  in industrial trucks, **1:** 890, 891
  yellow paint for, **1:** 457
Catfish, **1:** 124–125, **2:** 80, 81
Catheters, **1:** 1237
Cathode Protection Equipment, **1:** 1008, **2:** 263
Cathode Ray Tubes, **1:** 961, 963, 964, 966, 1065–1068
Catholic Church, **2:** 1394
Cats, as pets, **2:** 95, 98
Cattle. *See also* Beef
  alfalfa for, **2:** 24
  artificial insemination of, **1:** 27, **2:** 56, 97
  auctions, **2:** 52, 598, 600
  breeding, **2:** 52, 53, 56, 96–97, 598
  computer identification systems for, **2:** 56
  custom feeding of, **2:** 599
  farms, **2:** 51–57, 63, 84
  feed for, **1:** 58–59, 75, **2:** 48, 49
  feedlots for, **2:** 47–51
  genetic engineering of, **2:** 56
  hides, **1:** 612, 613
  manure, **1:** 303
  sales of, **2:** 51
  services for, **2:** 96–98
  sheep and, **2:** 63
  slaughtering, **1:** 1, 2
  veterinary services for, **2:** 92–93
  wholesalers of, 2: 597–601
Cattle-Fax, **2:** 600
Cattle Feeders, **2:** 50
Cattleman's Inc., **2:** 650
Caustic Soda. *See* Sodium Hydroxide
Cavco Industries, **1:** 301, **2:** 246, 536
Cavin, Bram, **2:** 786
Caxton, William, **2:** 1025
C.B. Jackson, **2:** 650
C-Band Satellites, **2:** 478
CB Radio. *See* Citizens Band Radios
CBC Bicycles, **1:** 1187
CBOE. *See* Chicago Board Options Exchange
CBOT. *See* Chicago Board of Trade
C. Brewer & Company, **2:** 32
CBR-HCI Construction Materials Inc., **1:** 653
CBS Corporation, **2:** 463, 465, 466–467, 468
  advertising revenues of, **2:** 467
  in cable television, **2:** 472
  history of, **2:** 466
  merger of, **2:** 463, 468
  in radio, **2:** 463
  in recorded music, **1:** 1046, 1048, 1049, 1051
CCL Manufacturing Inc., **1:** 1312
CD Radio, **2:** 463
CD-ROM. *See also* Electronic Publishing; Optical Storage
  Devices
  books, **1:** 406

Copper *(cont'd)*
  treated wood, **1:** 302
  uses of, **1:** 716, 718, 719, 728, 733–734, **2:** 131–132
  wire, **1:** 733, 735, **2:** 131
  workforce in, **1:** 718, 736, **2:** 133
  in x-ray tubes, **1:** 1251
Copper and Brass Sales Inc., **1:** 759
Copper Development Association, **1:** 718, 734, 758, **2:** 131
Copper Foundries, 1: 757–759
Copper Ores, 2: 130–133
  pipelines for, **2:** 424
Copperfield, David, **2:** 1211
Copperplate Engraving, **1:** 424
Coppola, Francis Ford, **2:** 1188
Copps Supermarkets, **1:** 434
Cops-in-Shops Program, **2:** 748
Copy Shops. *See* Photocopying and Duplicating Services
Copying Machines. *See* Photocopiers
Copyright Law, **2:** 978–980
  on artistic works, **2:** 1054
  on databases, **2:** 1102
  on electronic publishing, **1:** 399, 406, **2:** 1338
  exports and, **1:** 427
  foreign printers and, **1:** 412
  on jewelry designs, **1:** 1301
  libraries and, **2:** 1338
  on motion pictures, **2:** 1191
  on music, **1:** 1057, **2:** 554, 979, 1205–1206
  overseas publishers and, **1:** 406
  on Swiss Army knives, **1:** 771
  video piracy and, **2:** 1177, 1189, 1201, 1204
Copyright Owners and Lessors, 2: 978–980
Cora-Texas Manufacturing, **1:** 73
Coram Healthcare Corporation, **2:** 1277, 1304
Cordage and Twine, 1: 186, 193–194
  tire, **1:** 190–191
Cordant Technologies Inc., **1:** 837, 1197
Cordials, **1:** 79, 80, 105, 108
Cordis, **1:** 1244
Cordura Plus, **1:** 161
Core Materials Corporation, **1:** 608
Cork, in linoleum, **1:** 1310
Corn, 2: 8–11, 46
  in alternative fuels, **2:** 11, 312
  in animal feed, **2:** 8, 9, 10
  canned, **1:** 34, 35, 37
  cereal, **1:** 49
  detasseling, **2:** 87
  exports of, **2:** 8, 10
  fertilizer for, **1:** 541
  frozen, **1:** 42
  genetically engineered, **2:** 11, 44, 68
  harvesting, **2:** 8, 9, 89
  history of, **2:** 9–10
  hybrid, **2:** 11
  mill products, **1:** 44
  oil, **1:** 54, 55, **2:** 10
  planting equipment, **1:** 860, **2:** 9
  production of, **1:** 55, **2:** 8, 10, 89
  puffs, **1:** 133
  reserves of, **2:** 9
  sales of, **2:** 40
  silage, **2:** 8
  starch, **1:** 54, 55, **2:** 11
  sweeteners, **1:** 54, 55
  syrup, **1:** 72, 74, **2:** 10

  uses of, **2:** 8, 11
  wet milled, 1: 54–55
Corn Chips, 1: 129–135
Corn Products International Inc., **1:** 55
Corn Refiners Association, **1:** 55
Cornelius, Adam E., Sr., **2:** 364
Cornerstone Construction and Materials, Inc., **2:** 214
Cornerstone Propane Partners, L.P., **2:** 785
Cornices, **1:** 795
Corning Consumer Products Company, **1:** 649
Corning Glass Works. *See* Corning Incorporated
Corning Incorporated, **1:** 648, 649
  in catalytic converters, **2:** 1149
  in fiber optics, **1:** 747
  in metal stampings, **1:** 817
  in vitreous china manufacturing, **1:** 663
Cornish Game Hens, **1:** 11
Corona Corporation, **2:** 140
Corporacion Nacional del Cobre de Chile, **2:** 148
Corporate Average Fuel Economy Standard, **1:** 706, 720, 755, 1120
Corporate Educational Services, **2:** 1341, 1343, 1344
Corporate Express, **2:** 335
Corporate Family Solutions, **2:** 1356
Corporate Income Tax, **2:** 1469
Corporate Property Investors, **2:** 950
Corporate Publishing Services, **1:** 413
Corporate Restructuring Consultants, **2:** 1427
CorpTech, **1:** 1258, **2:** 1401
Correctional Homes, **2:** 1358–1361
Correctional Institutions, 2: 1460–1463
  city and county, **2:** 1461
  cost of, **2:** 1460
  federal, **2:** 1461
  furniture manufacturing in, **1:** 316, 321
  history of, **2:** 1461–1462
  management of, **2:** 1438
  prefabricated, **1:** 299, 301
  privatization of, **2:** 1462
  state, **2:** 1461
  women in, **2:** 1462
Corrective Lens, **1:** 1260–1264
Correspondence Courses, **2:** 1341–1343
Corrosion Resistance
  plating for, **1:** 820
  zinc for, **2:** 134, 135
Corrugated Products
  envelopes, **1:** 382
  manufacturing of, 1: 290, 356–360
  paperboard, **1:** 345, 351, 352, 353
Corsets, **1:** 239, 240
Cort, Stanton G., **1:** 838, 839
CORT Business Services, **2:** 1065
Cortaid, **1:** 497
Cortez, Hernando, **2:** 59
Corundum, **1:** 681
Cosby, William, **1:** 389
Cosco Industries Inc., **1:** 1299
Cose, Ellis, **1:** 388
Coslett, Thomas Watts, **1:** 822
Cosmetic, Toiletry and Fragrance Association, **1:** 514, 515, 518, 519
Cosmetic Act, **2:** 1423
Cosmetic Ingredient Review, **1:** 515
Cosmetic Surgery, **1:** 519, **2:** 1240
Cosmetics. *See* Perfumes and Cosmetics

Cosmetologists, **2:** 1010, 1011
Cost Plus, **2:** 748
Costle, Douglas M., **2:** 1494
Costume Jewelry, 1: 1300–1302, **2:** 692
Costumes
    manufacturing of, **1:** 257
    for motion pictures, **2:** 1181, 1182
    rental of, **2:** 1019
Cottage Cheese, **1:** 25, 26, 28
Cotter & Company, **2:** 556, 621, 622, 623
Cotton, 2: 15–16, 46
    advertising, **1:** 161
    Amer-Pima, **2:** 15
    American upland, **2:** 15
    beaching, **1:** 446
    blended, **2:** 16
    brassieres, **1:** 239
    breeding, **1:** 162
    broadwoven, **1:** 157–159, 161, 175–178, 199, 204, 208, 215
    consumer preferences for, **1:** 161
    cordage, **1:** 193
    dust, **1:** 186, **2:** 92
    embroidery, **1:** 264
    exports of, **2:** 15, 46
    flame-retardant, **1:** 157
    gloves, **1:** 252–253
    history of, **2:** 15–16, 41
    hosiery, **1:** 168
    improvements in, **2:** 602
    narrow fabric and smallwares, **1:** 166–167
    nonwoven fabrics, **1:** 192
    organic, **2:** 16
    Pima, **2:** 91
    pricing, **1:** 158
    shirts, **1:** 200
    socks, **1:** 168
    subsidies, **2:** 16
    thread, **1:** 189
    underwear, **1:** 172, 236
    wash-and-wear, **1:** 176, 200, 211
    water repellent, **1:** 176, 254
    wholesalers of, 2: 601
    wrinkle resistant, **1:** 157, 161
    yarn, **1:** 170, 186, 187
Cotton Ginning, 2: 91–92
Cotton Gins, **1:** 923, **2:** 15, 41, 91
Cotton Growers Association, **1:** 176
Cotton Incorporated, **1:** 161, 176, 177, 233, **2:** 16
Cotton Technology International, **1:** 171
Cottonseed, **1:** 86–87, **2:** 15–16, 40
Cottonseed Oil Mills, 1: 86–87
Council of Better Business Bureaus, **2:** 766, 1372
Council of Consulting Organizations, **2:** 1425, 1440
Council of Economic Advisors, **2:** 1467
Council of Hygiene and Public Health, **2:** 1476
Council on Environmental Quality, **2:** 1492, 1493
Countermeasures, **1:** 1207, 1210, 1211
Counting Devices, 1: 1224–1226
Country Clubs, **2:** 1234–1235
Country Poultry, Inc., **2:** 69
Countrywide Funding Corporation, **2:** 866
Countrywide Home Loans, Inc., **2:** 845, 860
County Business Patterns, on School Buses, **2:** 322
Couper, A.D., **2:** 383
Couplers
    automatic safety, **1:** 1182

    link-and-pin, **1:** 1182
    manufacturing, **1:** 773, 944
Coupons. *See* Discount Coupons
Courier Dispatch Group, **2:** 337
Courier Services, 2: 324, 334–338
    acquisitions and mergers of, **2:** 335, 337
    air freight, **2:** 335, 336, 403–409
    for bakery products, **1:** 68
    competition in, **2:** 335
    computer systems for, **2:** 337–338, 408
    envelopes for, **1:** 382
    history of, **2:** 335
    international, **2:** 335, 337, 407
    labor unions in, **2:** 335, 336
    mobile communication systems for, **2:** 337
    for motion pictures, **2:** 1191–1192
    workforce in, **2:** 407
Court of Appeals, **2:** 1454
Court Reporters, 2: 1055–1056
Courtaulds Coatings, Inc., **1:** 521
Courtaulds Fibers Inc., **1:** 160, 479
Courtaulds United States Inc., **1:** 603
Courtoid, Bernard, **1:** 460
Courts, 2: 1453–1456
Covance Research Products Inc., **2:** 82
Cowboy Hats, **1:** 243
Cowboys, **2:** 55–56
Cowpeas, **2:** 13
Cows. *See* Cattle
Cox, Archibald, **2:** 1495
Cox Enterprises, **2:** 471
Cox Radio, **2:** 463
Coyotes, **2:** 126
CP Clare, **1:** 1007
CPC Baking, Inc., **1:** 63
CPC International, Inc., **1:** 39
CPI Corporation, **2:** 1127
CPI Graphics, Inc., **1:** 439
CPI Photo, **2:** 1127
C.R. England and Sons, **2:** 331
Crabmeat, **1:** 123, **2:** 122
Crabtree and Evelyn, **1:** 504
Cracker Barrel, **2:** 769
Cracker Meal, **1:** 66
Crackers. *See* Cookies and Crackers
Craft and Hobby Supplies, 2: 568
    retail stores for, 2: 765–768, 772
Craft Beer. *See* Microbreweries
Craft Unions, **2:** 1379, 1380, 1381
Crafted with Pride in U.S.A. Council, **1:** 226
Craig, Charles, **2:** 1070
Crain, Jim, **1:** 842
Crampton, John, **1:** 1150
Cranberries, **2:** 27–28
    juice from, **1:** 35, 37
Crane, Cornelius, **1:** 77
Crane Company, **1:** 845
Crane Plastics Company L.P., **1:** 593
Crane Stationary, **2:** 762
Crane Valves, **1:** 839
Cranes and Hoists
    bridge, **1:** 884
    for containerized freight, **2:** 384
    for forest management, **2:** 116
    gantry, **1:** 884
    jib, **1:** 884

Delphi Automotive Systems, **1:** 1103, 1136, 1137, **2:** 529
Delphi Energy and Engine Management Systems, **1:** 844
Delphi Interior and Lighting Systems, **1:** 773
Delta Air Lines, **2:** 396, 398, 400
Delta Employees Credit Union, **2:** 827
Delta Queen Steamship Company, **2:** 382
Deluxe Corporation, **1:** 430
Deluxe Homes, **1:** 301
Demand Activated Manufacturing Architecture Project, **1:** 171, 176, 177, 178, 179, 187
Demantoid, **1:** 1280
Demco Inc., **1:** 385
Demichele, Robert M., **2:** 905, 926
Demolition Work, 2: 296–297
Den Corp/Information and Engineering Technology, **2:** 1441
Deneher Corporation, **1:** 902
Denham, Simeon, **1:** 972
Denig, Tom, **2:** 286
DeNike, Edward, **2:** 385
Dennis, Martin, **1:** 613
Densitometers, in Lithography, **1:** 423
Dental Arts Laboratory Inc., **2:** 1301
Dental Assistants Association, **2:** 1246
Dental Equipment and Supplies, 1: 1246–1250
   wholesalers of, 2: 544–546
Dental Hygienists, **2:** 1248, 1260, 1263
Dental Insurance, **1:** 1245, 1247, 1248
Dental Laboratories, 2: 1299–1300
Dental Laboratory Institute, **2:** 1300
Dental Maintenance Organizations, **2:** 1245, 1247
Dentalcare Partners Inc., **2:** 1301
Dentistry
   fraud in, **2:** 1247
   history of, **2:** 1245–1247, 1300
   wages and salaries in, **2:** 1248
Dentists, 2: 1245–1249
   advertising by, **2:** 1247
   veterinary, **2:** 92–93
Dentsply International Inc., **1:** 1249
Dentyne, **1:** 82
Deodorants, **1:** 516
Department of Agriculture
   on alcoholic beverages, **2:** 746
   on animal damage, **2:** 98
   on aquaculture, **2:** 80, 81
   on avocados, **2:** 37
   on baked goods, **1:** 62
   on barley, **1:** 96
   on beef, **2:** 54, 600
   on butter production, **1:** 14
   on canned food, **1:** 35
   on chemical safety, **1:** 459
   on Christmas trees, **2:** 108
   on citrus, **2:** 33
   on coffee, **1:** 127
   in community development, **2:** 1507
   on corn, **2:** 10, 46
   on cotton, **2:** 46, 92
   on dairy products, **1:** 29, **2:** 64
   environmental horticulture, **2:** 105
   on factory farms, **2:** 84
   on farm cooperatives, **2:** 609
   on farm debt, **2:** 845
   on farm machinery, **1:** 863
   on farm profits, **2:** 42
   on fertilizer manufacturing, **1:** 542

   on floriculture, **2:** 38
   on food expenditures, **2:** 643
   in food safety, **2:** 1465
   on frozen foods, **1:** 42
   on fruit, **1:** 41, **2:** 35, 36
   funding for, **2:** 1469, 1521–1522
   on genetically engineered food, **2:** 26
   on goats, **2:** 62
   on grains, **1:** 50, **2:** 13
   history of, **2:** 41–42, 1521
   on hog farms, **2:** 57, 60
   on horses, **2:** 78
   in housing, **2:** 1503
   on livestock feed, **1:** 58, 59
   on livestock sales, **1:** 1–2, **2:** 598
   on mad cow disease, **2:** 54, 84
   on meat consumption, **1:** 3, 6
   on meat exports, **1:** 10
   in meat inspection, **1:** 1–2, 2–3
   on milk prices, **1:** 27, **2:** 63, 65
   on mushrooms, **2:** 39
   on nuts, **2:** 31
   on pesticides, **1:** 544, **2:** 1493
   on pet food, **1:** 56
   on photo-mapping, **2:** 47
   on pork safety, **2:** 60
   on potatoes, **2:** 23
   on poultry, **2:** 68, 591
   on poultry and egg processing, **1:** 10, 11–12, **2:** 75
   on poultry inspections, **2:** 68
   on rail stockyards, **2:** 447–448
   in resource management, **2:** 1490
   on rice, **1:** 53
   role of, **2:** 1520
   on sheep, **2:** 61
   on soybeans, **1:** 88, **2:** 46
   on spices, **1:** 142
   on strawberries, **2:** 28
   on sugar production, **1:** 70, 72, **2:** 22
   on testing labs, **2:** 1423
   on tobacco, **1:** 155, **2:** 19
   on turkeys, **2:** 73
   on vegetables, **1:** 34, **2:** 26
   on veterinary services, **2:** 93, 95
   on wetlands, **2:** 44
   on wheat, **2:** 1, 2–3, 4–5, 6
Department of Commerce. *See also* U.S. Census Bureau
   on automobile manufacturing, **1:** 1123, 1126
   on automotive parts, **1:** 986, 987, 1136, 1137
   on bearings, **1:** 931, 932
   on beer, **1:** 92
   on biological products, **1:** 500
   on boating, **1:** 1178
   on book publishing, **1:** 405
   on bridge and tunnel construction, **2:** 262
   on bridge construction, **1:** 786
   on cereals, **1:** 49
   on chemical sales, **1:** 461
   on chlorine production, **1:** 449
   on cleaning products, **1:** 513
   on clothing manufacturing, **1:** 220–223, 226, 234
   on coal mining, **2:** 178
   on commercial printing, **1:** 421
   on computer services, **2:** 1114, 1117
   in computer storage devices, **1:** 960
   on concrete dumping, **1:** 675

Department of Justice *(cont'd)*
  on psychiatric hospitals, **2:** 1291
  on radio stations, **2:** 462
  on student loans, **2:** 1033
  on telephone service, **2:** 456
  on television dumping, **1:** 1042
  on water pollution, **2:** 1493
Department of Labor
  on airport workers, **2:** 416
  on chemical workers, **1:** 464
  on clothing stores, **2:** 688
  on day care, **2:** 1357
  on embroidery workers, **1:** 264
  on farm workers, **2:** 100
  on food production, **1:** 114
  funding for, **2:** 1469
  on furniture and fixture manufacturing, **1:** 328
  on glass manufacturing, **1:** 642
  on independent contractors, **2:** 1115
  on lab technicians, **2:** 1301
  on maintenance personnel, **2:** 1171
  on men's and boys clothing, **2:** 685
  on millwork, **1:** 278, 280
  on plywood manufacturing, **1:** 285
  on restaurants, **2:** 737, 738
  on retail employment, **2:** 751–752
  on retail sales, **2:** 632, 635
  on road construction, **2:** 251
  on tilesetters, **2:** 282
  on vocational training, **2:** 1351
  on well drilling, **2:** 292
Department of State, **2:** 1537, 1539
  on engineering, **2:** 1403
Department of the Interior
  history of, **2:** 1499–1500
  on logging, **1:** 270
  in resource management, **2:** 1490, 1497
  on water pollution, **2:** 1492
Department of the Treasury, **2:** 1467, 1468
  on banking, **2:** 806–807
  in customs brokerage, **2:** 439–440
  funding for, **2:** 1469
  in law enforcement, **2:** 1457
  on television dumping, **1:** 1042
  on thrifts, **2:** 815
Department of Transportation
  on airlines, **2:** 396–397, 398, 401
  on airports, **2:** 415
  on bus transportation, **2:** 316, 323
  on charter airlines, **2:** 410
  Chlorine Institute and, **1:** 446
  the Coast Guard and, **2:** 1533
  on highway and bridge safety, **2:** 260
  on inspection and weighing, **2:** 446–447
  on intermodal transit, **2:** 346
  on liquefied petroleum gas, **2:** 499
  on motor carriers, **2:** 325
  on pipelines, **2:** 417, 419
  on railroads, **1:** 1181, **2:** 307, 941
  on road construction, **2:** 252
  role of, **2:** 1465, 1514–1515
  search and navigation systems for, **1:** 1213
  on shipping containers, **1:** 767
  on tire retreads, **2:** 1150
  on travel agencies, **2:** 431

Department of Veterans Affairs, **2:** 1271, 1477, 1485, 1489–1490
Department Stores, 2: 629–637, 642–643
  acquisitions and mergers in, **2:** 631, 632
  appliances in, **2:** 714
  children's clothing in, **2:** 694, 695, 699
  discount stores *vs.,* **2:** 631
  in electronic shopping, **2:** 636
  energy management systems for, **1:** 1217
  handbags in, **1:** 634
  history of, **2:** 630–632
  in international commerce, **2:** 635–636
  in mail order, **2:** 635–636
  market share of, **1:** 202
  point-of-sale systems in, **2:** 636
  sales in, **2:** 629
  superstores *vs.,* **2:** 630
  women's clothing in, **2:** 687
Dependent Pension Act, **2:** 1487
DepoNet, **2:** 1056
Depository Institutions Deregulation and Monetary Control Act, **2:** 816, 822, 825, 956
Depository Insurance, **2:** 821
Depression Glassware, **1:** 649
Depression Medication, **1:** 496
Depth Charges, **1:** 829–830
Depth-Finding Equipment, **1:** 1210, **2:** 121
Deregulation
  of the aircraft industry, **1:** 1148
  of airlines, **2:** 398, 404, 435–436
  of bank holding companies, **2:** 955, 957
  of banks, **2:** 806, 807, 810–811, 816, 956, 958
  of bus services, **2:** 318
  of cable television, **2:** 1519
  of electric utilities, **1:** 994, **2:** 270, 278, 484, 1519
  of natural gas transmission, **2:** 489–490, 492, 497, 503, 1519
  of ports, **2:** 385
  of public utilities, **2:** 1516, 1518–1519, 1520
  of radio broadcasting, **2:** 462
  of railroads, **2:** 302
  of securities trading, **2:** 870, 873
  of taxi service, **2:** 314
  of thrift institutions, **2:** 816, 822
  of travel agencies, **2:** 428
  of trucking, **2:** 325, 327, 328, 346, 440
Deri, M., **1:** 1086
Derwinski, Edward J., **2:** 1489
Desalination, **2:** 270, 510, 523
Desert Land Act, **2:** 42
Designated Order Turnaround, **2:** 873
Designed Genetic Change. *See* Genetic Engineering
Designers, Fashion. *See* Fashion
DesiLu Productions, **2:** 1176
Desk Sets, **1:** 637
Deskey, Donald, **1:** 309
Desktop Graphics Inc., **2:** 1055
Desktop Publishing
  in book publishing, **1:** 405, 407, 410
  in commercial art, **2:** 1053
  by photocopy services, **2:** 1050
  typesetting and, **1:** 408, 440, 441
DeSoto Mills Inc., **1:** 169
DeSoto Paints, **1:** 524
Desrosier, Norman W., **1:** 126
Desserts, Frozen, 1: 21–25
Destect Energy Inc., **2:** 172

INDEX

Dow Jones & Company, Inc., **1:** 392, 418, **2:** 1125
Dow Jones Industrial Average, **2:** 736, 885, 1469
Dow Plastic and Advanced Environmental Recycling
    Technologies, **1:** 592
Down Clothing, **1:** 217
Down Syndrome, **2:** 1481
Downsizing
  in aerospace industry, **1:** 1190
  in aircraft industry, **1:** 1149, 1150
  in beef cattle industry, **2:** 49
  in chemical industry, **1:** 537
  in clothing manufacturing, **1:** 201, 202, 209, 212, 237
  in cutlery industry, **1:** 769
  in defense industry, **1:** 1202
  in metal can production, **1:** 765
  in newspaper publishing, **1:** 388
  in paint and varnish industry, **1:** 523
  in paper industry, **1:** 344
  in periodical publishing, **1:** 397
  in petroleum industry, **2:** 199
  in search and navigation systems, **1:** 1212
  in securities trading, **2:** 872
  in steel industry, **1:** 715
  storage services and, **2:** 342–343
  in tire industry, **1:** 576
  in transformers, **1:** 994
Downspouts, **2:** 288
Downy Refill, **1:** 511
Dowsing Electric Fire, **1:** 1010
Dr. Pepper, **1:** 114, 644
Drafting Materials, **1:** 1235, 1297
Drafting Tables, **1:** 333
Drains, **1:** 659, 777
Drake, Edwin L., **1:** 560, **2:** 181, 192, 196, 418, 492
DRAM. *See* Dynamic Random Access Memory
Drama Schools, **2:** 1343, 1344
Draper Corporation, **1:** 191
Draperies, 1: 258–259
  hardware for, 1: 330–333
  retail stores for, 2: 709–711
Drapery Exchange, Inc., **2:** 711
Dravo Corporation, **1:** 677
Drawing of Nonferrous Wire, 1: 748–750
Dreamcast Machine, **1:** 1288
DRECO, **2:** 194
Dredging
  environmental impact of, **2:** 364, 384
  equipment for, **1:** 866, **2:** 211, 215, 269, 395
  services for, **2:** 395
Dreft, **1:** 504
Dress Codes, **1:** 197, 208
Dress Gloves, 1: 174, 252–253, 630
Dresser Industries Inc., **2:** 562
Dresser Wheatley, **1:** 873, 875
Dresses
  children's and infants', 1: 246–248
  sheath, **1:** 240
  women's, 1: 224–228
Dressing Gowns, 1: 253–254
Drew Industries Inc., **1:** 798
Drew Pearson, **1:** 241
Drexel Burnham Lambert Inc., **2:** 870
Dreyer's Grand Ice Cream, **1:** 24
Dreyfus, **2:** 883
DRG Funding, **2:** 1511
DRGs. *See* Diagnostic Related Groups

Dried Fruits and Vegetables, 1: 38–39, **2:** 28, 36
Drilling Oil and Gas Wells, 2: 189–195. *See also* Crude Oil
    and Natural Gas Extraction; Oil Field Machinery
  cable-tool, **2:** 192
  coiled-tubing, **2:** 195
  directional, **2:** 186–187
  environmental impact of, **2:** 192
  horizontal, **2:** 195
  joint ventures in, **2:** 193
  neural networks in, **2:** 195
  offshore, **2:** 182, 191, 192
  redrilling, **2:** 189, 191
  rotary, **2:** 191
  seismic technology in, **2:** 195
  slim-hole, **2:** 195
  spudding, **2:** 191
Drills
  air, **1:** 936
  blast-hole, **1:** 871, 936
  cable-tool, **2:** 192
  coiled-tubing, **2:** 195
  dental, **1:** 1247
  hammer, **1:** 905
  hand, **1:** 903, 904
  mining, **2:** 149, 150
  oil, **1:** 872
  quarrying, **2:** 206
  rock, **1:** 868, 869
  rotary, **2:** 191, 192, 202
  slim-hole, **2:** 195
Drinking Places (Alcoholic Beverages). *See* Bars (Drinking
    Establishments)
Drinking Water
  bottled, **1:** 109–116
  chloroform in, **2:** 516
  safety of, **2:** 509–510
  sources of (*See* Water Supply)
  standards for, **2:** 1494
Drive Chains, **1:** 944
Drive-in Motion Picture Theaters, 2: 1198–1200
Drive-In Theater Fanatic Fan Club, **2:** 1200
Drivers, Licensing, **2:** 255, 1514–1516
Drives, Industrial, **1:** 942–943
Driving While Intoxicated (DWI), **2:** 748
Droxies, **1:** 67
Drug Abuse, **2:** 1321. *See also* Substance Abuse Programs
Drug Delivery Systems, **1:** 490, 498
Drug Enforcement Agency, **2:** 1457
Drug Industry. *See* Pharmaceutical Industry
Drug Price Competition and Patent Term Restoration Act, **1:**
  494
Drug Rehabilitation Facilities, **2:** 1359
Druggists, 1: 486, 487
Drugs. *See* Pharmaceutical Preparations
Drugstores, 2: 741–746
  in photofinishing, **2:** 1126
  tobacco sales in, **2:** 789
Drums
  fiber, **1:** 360–361
  shipping, **1:** 766–767
Dry Branch Kaolin Company, **2:** 220
Dry Cleaning, 2: 563, 1002–1006
  coin operated, **2:** 1004–1005
  equipment, **1:** 974–975
Dry Cleaning Fluids, **1:** 512
  chlorine in, **1:** 447, 450

environmental impact of, **2:** 1002–1003, 1005

Dry Color Manufacturers Association, **1:** 456

Dry Dairy Products, 1: 18–21

Dry Docks, **1:** 1171

Dry Goods, 2: 581

   retail stores for, 2: 771–775

Dry Press Systems

   in ceramic electrical supplies, **1:** 665

   in vitreous china manufacturing, **1:** 663, 668

Dryclean USA, **2:** 1005

Dryers

   clothes, **1:** 974–975, 1018–1021, 1216, **2:** 554

   textile, **1:** 178

Drysdale, Don, **2:** 1217

Drywall Installation, 2: 281–282

DSC Logistics, **2:** 344

DSI Toys, **1:** 1285

DSL (Digital Subscriber Lines), **1:** 1057, **2:** 458

DSP. *See* Digital Signal Processors

Du Pont Company. *See* E.I. DuPont de Nemours and Company

Duales System Seutschland, **1:** 601

DuBridge, Lee A., **2:** 1492

Duchossois Industries Inc., **1:** 829

Ducker Research Company, **1:** 713

Duckling Council, **1:** 11

Ducks, **1:** 11

Ductile Iron. *See* Cast Iron

Duda and Sons Inc., **2:** 34

Dudley, Sumner, **2:** 995

Duett, **1:** 331

Duferco Energy Group, Inc., **2:** 562

Duffle Bags, **1:** 631

Duffy, James E., **2:** 1155

Duke, James, **1:** 146

Duke Energy, **2:** 494, 503

Duke Power, **2:** 503

Dumb Terminals. *See* Computer Terminals

Dumbwaiters, **1:** 877, **2:** 297

Dumont Television, **2:** 466

Dump Trucks, **1:** 868, **2:** 324

Dumping

   aluminum, **1:** 725

   ball and roller bearings, **1:** 929, 930

   carpets, **1:** 184

   concrete, **1:** 675

   industrial trucks, **1:** 892

   pasta, **1:** 139

   sewage, **2:** 511

   steel, **1:** 693, 694, 700, 705

   televisions, **1:** 1042–1043

Dun, R.G., **2:** 1037

Dun & Bradstreet Inc., **1:** 418, **2:** 1037, 1044, 1168

Dun & Bradstreet Information Services, **2:** 1034, 1035, 1037

Dunbar, Jim L., **2:** 1119

Duncan Foods, **1:** 110, 114

Dundee Mills Inc., **1:** 265

Dune Buggies, **2:** 679

Dunham's Athleisure Corporation, **2:** 754

Dunleavy, M.P., **1:** 402

Dunlop, John Boyd, **1:** 572

Dunlop Commission, **2:** 1383

Dunn, William, **2:** 1472

Dunn Edwards Corporation, **2:** 620

Dunstan, Paul, **2:** 387

Dunster, Henry, **1:** 409

Duplicating Services. *See* Photocopying and Duplicating Services

DuPont Advanced Fiber Systems, **1:** 1069

DuPont Agricultural Products, **1:** 545–546

DuPont Company. *See* E.I. DuPont de Nemours and Company

DuPont Industrial Diamond Division, **2:** 232

DuPont Performance Coatings, **1:** 512

DuPont Pharmaceutical Company, **1:** 495

DuPont Printing and Publishing, **1:** 439

Duquesne Light Company, **1:** 791

Durable Goods

   boxes for, **1:** 358

   sales of, **2:** 574

   wholesalers, 2: 552–553, 574–575

   workforce in, **2:** 575

Durable Press, **1:** 179

Duracell Inc., **1:** 1096, 1097, 1098–1099

Duraglas XLT, **1:** 647

Durand, Karen, **1:** 434

Durand, Peter, **1:** 32, 34, 764

Durant, William C., **1:** 1118, **2:** 655

Durham-Humphrey Amendment, **1:** 492

Durham Transportation Inc., **2:** 322

Duriron, **1:** 839

Duro Bag Manufacturing Company, **1:** 373, 374

Duryea, Charles, **1:** 560, 1118

Duryea, Frank, **1:** 560, 1118

Dust

   in cotton ginning, **1:** 186, **2:** 92

   in flour mills, **1:** 48

   in plywood production, **1:** 284

   reduction equipment, **1:** 914, 938, 939, 940, **2:** 297

Dutch-Boy Paints, **1:** 524

Dutton Publishing, **1:** 404

DVD. *See* Digital Video Disk

Dwarfism, Human Growth Hormone for, **1:** 501

DWI. *See* Driving While Intoxicated

Dyckerhoff, **1:** 674

Dye Pens, **1:** 913

Dyeing

   services, **2:** 1005–1006

   textiles, **1:** 165, 175, 178, 180

   yarn, **1:** 180

Dyersburg Corporation, **1:** 170, 173

Dyes

   alum in, **1:** 460

   demand for, **1:** 532

   history of, **1:** 530, 536

   imports of, **1:** 531

   natural, **1:** 528–534

   organic, 1: 529–534

   vs. pigments, **1:** 455

   synthetic, **1:** 461, 536

Dynacast Inc., **1:** 753

DynAir. *See* DynCorp Commercial Aviation Services Group

Dynamic Random Access Memory, **1:** 1071–1072, 1072–1074

Dynamite, **1:** 551. *See also* Explosives

DynCorp Commercial Aviation Services Group, **2:** 415

Dyno Nobel, Inc., **1:** 551

E

E.A. Miller, **2:** 594

Eagle Garden & Hardware, **1:** 788

Eagle Industries, Inc., **1:** 608, 940

Eagle-Picher Industries Inc., **1:** 685, 686

F

INDEX

INDEX

General Accounting Office *(cont'd)*
  on sugar production, **2:** 22
General Agreement on Tariffs and Trade. *See also* Uruguay
    Round (GATT)
  on automobile manufacturing, **1:** 1124–1125
  on book publishing, **1:** 406
  on clothing manufacturing, **1:** 209, 220, 223, 227–228
  on computer services, **2:** 1081, 1117
  on copper, **1:** 718
  on industrial instruments, **1:** 1223
  on meat products, **1:** 9, **2:** 60
  on plastics, **1:** 608
  on real estate, **2:** 934
  on service industries, **2:** 1410–1411
  on textiles, **1:** 158, 162, 174, 179, 223
  World Trade Organization and, **2:** 1540
  on yarns, **1:** 186
General American Investors Company, **2:** 969, 970
General American Transportation, **2:** 444
General Arrangements to Borrow, **2:** 835
General Automotive Repair Shops, 2: 1155–1158
General Aviation, **1:** 1143, 1148
General Aviation Manufacturers Association, **1:** 806–807
General Binding Corporation, **1:** 919
General Cable Corporation, **1:** 747
General Cigar Holdings Inc., **1:** 152
General Cinema Corporation, **2:** 1198
General Contractors
  bridge and tunnel, **1:** 867, **2:** 257–264
  carpentry, **2:** 283–286
  communication with, **2:** 247
  concrete work, **2:** 289–292
  drywall, **2:** 281–282
  electrical, **2:** 275–279
  excavation, **2:** 295–296
  general, **2:** 234–243
  industrial, 2: 247–249
  masonry, **2:** 279–281
  miscellaneous, **2:** 297–298
  nonresidential, 2: 249–250
  operative builders, **2:** 243–246
  painting and paper hanging, **2:** 274–275
  plumbing, heating and air conditioning, **2:** 273–274
  residential, 2: 240–243
  road *(See* Highway Construction)
  roofing, **2:** 288–289
  sheet metal, **2:** 288–289
  single-family housing, 2: 234–240
  special trade, 2: 298–299
  tilesetting, **2:** 282–283
  water, sewer and utility lines, **2:** 264–266
General Dynamics Convair, **1:** 1148
General Dynamics Corporation, **1:** 991, 1149, 1201, 1202, 1204,
    2: 917
General Electric Aircraft Engines, **1:** 1155, 1157, 1159, 1160,
    1161
  ATF development, **1:** 1161
  in cooperative ventures, **1:** 1160
  jet engines, **1:** 1157, 1158, 1159
General Electric Capital Corporation, **2:** 527, 1034
General Electric Capital Fleet Services, **2:** 1138, 1139
General Electric Capital Information Technology Solutions, **2:**
    1111
General Electric Capital Mortgage, **2:** 1019
General Electric Capital Railcar Services, **2:** 444, 941
General Electric Capital Services, **2:** 854

General Electric Company
  in adhesives and sealants, **1:** 549
  in aircraft instruments, **1:** 1164
  in appliances, **1:** 1011, 1014–1015, 1016, 1017–1018, 1020,
    1023, 1029
  in automatic controls, **1:** 1219
  in car leasing, **2:** 1138
  in computer development, **1:** 948
  in computer storage devices, **1:** 960
  in electric motors, **1:** 998, 1001, 1002
  in electromedical equipment, **1:** 1258
  history of, **1:** 999–1000, 1210
  in lighting fixtures, **1:** 1033
  in machine tools, **1:** 895
  in measuring and control devices, **1:** 1235
  in motors, **1:** 996, 1000, 1002
  in nuclear power, **2:** 485
  in plastics, **1:** 595, **2:** 603
  in power generation, **2:** 503
  in stoves, **1:** 1010
  in superabrasives, **2:** 232
  in synthetic diamonds, **1:** 682
  in televisions, **1:** 1043, **2:** 468
  in turbine generators, **1:** 855, 856
General Electric Company PLC, **1:** 995
General Electric Credit Corporation, **2:** 1139
General Elevator Company, Inc., **2:** 298
General Foods Corporation, **1:** 65, 150, **2:** 734
General Growth Properties Inc., **2:** 933
General Housewares Corporation, **1:** 756
General Land Office, **2:** 114
General Merchandise Stores, 2: 642–643. *See also* Department
    Stores
General Mills, Inc., **1:** 46, 48, 49, 50, 51, 52, 143
General Motors Acceptance Corporation, **2:** 846, 849, 851, 854,
    860
General Motors Corporation
  acquisitions by, **1:** 1121, 1122
  advertising by, **1:** 394
  in aircraft engines, **1:** 1155, 1158, 1164
  in Alliance of Automobile Manufacturers, **1:** 1117
  aluminum auto parts for, **1:** 743
  in appliances, **1:** 1014, 1015
  in automobile exhaust repair, **2:** 1148
  in car leasing and rentals, **2:** 1134, 1136, 1138
  on counterfeit parts, **1:** 1102
  diesel engines, **1:** 1125
  fuel efficiency and, **1:** 1120
  history of, **1:** 1120, **2:** 656
  labor unions and, **1:** 894, 1123, 1137, **2:** 1384
  motor homes, **1:** 1140
  in navigation systems, **1:** 1214
  one-price policy, **2:** 659
  online sales by, **1:** 1122
  paint for, **2:** 1145
  parts suppliers and, **1:** 987, 1135, 1137
  pension fund, **2:** 918
  Pulsat satellite network, **2:** 661
  in railroad equipment, **1:** 1185
  sales by, **1:** 1121, 1123, **2:** 526, 660
  steel purchases by, **1:** 760
  suppliers for, **1:** 1103
  in television, **2:** 473, 474
  on tool and die manufacturing, **1:** 899
  trimmings for, **1:** 264
  trucks and buses, **1:** 1132

Gillette Company *(cont'd)*
in batteries, **1:** 1098–1099
employee health clinics and, **2:** 1240
in pens and pencils, **1:** 1296
in razors, **1:** 514, 519
Gilsonite, **2:** 424
Gin, **1:** 105, 106, 108
Ginnie Mae. *See* Government National Mortgage Association
Ginseng, **2:** 109, 110
Gioa, Paul, **2:** 1516, 1518
Giovannucci, Edward, **2:** 26
Girdles, 1: 239–242
Girl Scouts of America, **1:** 68, **2:** 1396
Girls' Clothing, 1: 246–248. *See also* **Children's Clothing;**
Clothing
dresses, 1: 246–248
history of, **1:** 225, 229–230, **2:** 687
imports of, **1:** 221, 222–223, 227–228, 231, 232, 233
outerwear, 1: 248–251, 254–255
sales of, **2:** 686, 699
GIS. *See* Geographic Information Systems
Gitano Handbags, **1:** 634
Givaudan-Roure Corporation, **1:** 118
Glad Bags, **1:** 370
Glands, Extracts From, **1:** 486
Glascock, David, **2:** 1113
Glasgow Inc., **2:** 296
Glass, 1: 638–652, **2:** 294–295. *See also* **Glassware**
automotive, **2:** 1150–1153
blown, **1:** 648–650, 651
bullet-proof, **2:** 295
ceramic, **1:** 641, 649
coatings, **1:** 639, 647
colored, **1:** 649
in costume jewelry, **1:** 1301
enameling, **1:** 651
energy efficient, **1:** 639, 640, 642, **2:** 295
exports, **1:** 638, 642
fiber, **1:** 160, 648, 650
filaments from, **1:** 481
fire-resistant, **1:** 640–641
flat, 1: 638–643
float, **1:** 639, 650
handmade, **1:** 648
history of, **1:** 639–640, 645, 648–649, **2:** 295
laminated, **1:** 638, 641, 651, **2:** 1151
liquid crystal, **1:** 642
low-e, **1:** 642
metal fusion, **1:** 788
in millwork, **1:** 278
ornamental, **1:** 651
vs. polycarbonates, **2:** 1152
pressed, 1: 648–650, 651
products of purchased glass, 1: 650–652
Pyrex, **1:** 460
recycling, **1:** 647
retail stores for, 2: 618–621
safety, **1:** 638–641, 651, **2:** 295
sand for, **1:** 650, **2:** 215, 216, 217
sheet, **1:** 650
stained, **1:** 651
tempered, **1:** 639, 641, **2:** 1151, 1152
walls, **1:** 640
wholesalers of, 2: 536
wired, **1:** 638–641
wool, **1:** 686

Glass and Glazing Work, 2: 294–295
Glass Container Manufacturing, 1: 643–648. *See also*
Glassware
Glass Molders, Pottery, Plastics and Allied Workers
International Union, **1:** 661, 667
Glass Packaging Institute, **1:** 644, 645, 646
Glass-Steagall Act, **2:** 801, 807, 824, 870, 956
Glass Stores, **2:** 618–621
Glassware, 1: 648–650
for beverages, **1:** 650, 764
collectible, **1:** 644, 649
commemorative, **1:** 644
depression, **1:** 649
designing, **1:** 644–645
history of, **1:** 645
laboratory, **1:** 651
vs. metal, **1:** 764
narrow neck, **1:** 644, 645
vs. plastic, **1:** 599
for radioactive materials, **1:** 647
recycling, **1:** 645, 646, 647
single-serve, **1:** 645
for soft drinks, **1:** 112
wholesalers, 2: 533
wide mouth, **1:** 644, 645
Glazer, Howard, **2:** 1248
Glazer's Wholesale Drug Company, **2:** 608, 609
Glazing. *See* Glass and Glazing Work
Glazing Industry Code Committee, **1:** 639
Gleason Corporation, **1:** 896, 943
Glemby International, **2:** 1010
Glen-Gery Corporation, **1:** 669
Glen Raven Mills Inc., **1:** 168
Glenn, Owen G., **2:** 386
Glickman, Arthur P., **2:** 1154, 1156
Glickman, Dan, **2:** 591
Glidden, Joseph, **1:** 849
Glidden Company, **1:** 521, 524, 525, 527
Global Alcoholic Beverage Drinks Study, **1:** 106
Global Change Research Program, **2:** 117
Global Economy. *See* International Commerce
Global Environment Facility, **2:** 1501
Global Health Care Partners, **2:** 82
Global Industrial Technologies, **1:** 902, **2:** 220
Global Marine, **2:** 195
Global Maritime Distress and Safety System, **1:** 1177
Global Positioning Systems, **1:** 1061, 1207, 1213, 1214
in boats, **1:** 1180
in crop dusting, **2:** 87
development of, **1:** 1149, 1167–1168, 1211
differential, **1:** 1215
in farming, **2:** 102
in fish detection, **2:** 121
in forest management, **2:** 118
handheld, **1:** 1214, **2:** 118
in inland waterway navigation, **2:** 369
in landscape architecture, **2:** 103
market for, **1:** 1167
in mining, **2:** 214
in surveying, **2:** 1414
Global Warming
carbon dioxide and, **2:** 117
chlorofluorocarbons and, **1:** 978, **2:** 1165
reforestation for, **2:** 117
x-ray technology for, **1:** 1255
Globalization. *See* International Commerce

Globalstar, **2:** 451, 479
Globe Business Furniture, **1:** 320
Globe Business Resources Inc., **2: 1065**
Globe Manufacturing Company, **1: 160**
Globe Metallurgical Incorporated, **1: 691, 692**
Globe Works, **1:** 770
Globes, **1:** 416
GLOBEX System, **2:** 877, **985–986**
Globulins, **1:** 502
Glonass, **2:** 479
Gloria Jean's Coffee, **1:** 128
Glover, Jose, **1:** 409
Gloves, 1: 174–175, 252–253, **630**
   baseball, **1:** 1291
   cotton, **1:** 252–253
   dress, 1: 252–253, 630
   industrial, **1:** 252–253
   latex, **1:** 589
   leather, 1: 253, 630
   linen, **1:** 253
   rubber, **1:** 588–589
   silk, **1:** 253
   specialty, **1:** 252–253
   wool, **1:** 252–253
   work, 1: 174, 252–253, 630
Glues. *See* Adhesives
Glulam Products, **1:** 287, 288
Gluten, **1:** 61, **2:** 1
GM Nameplate Inc., **1:** 1299
GML Inc., **2:** 1055
Go Camping America Program, **2: 998**
Go-Karts, **2:** 679, 680
Goals 2000, **2:** 1470, 1472–1473
   Educate America Act, **2: 1322–1323**
Goats, 2: 60–62, 84
   services for, **2:** 96–98
   veterinary services for, **2:** 92–93
   wholesalers of, 2: 597–601
Godchaux, Auguste, **1:** 424
Goddard, Robert H., **2:** 1527
Goddard, William, **2:** 348
Goddard Space Flight Center, **2: 1526**
Godiva Chocolatier, Inc., **1:** 24
Goggles
   safety, **1:** 1243
   underwater, **1:** 1261
Golany, Gideon S., **2:** 1409
Gold
   analysis of, **1:** 1230, **2:** 140
   currency and, **2:** 137, 138
   grading, **2:** 140
   history of, **2:** 138–139
   international commerce in, **2: 140, 141**
   jewelry, **1:** 1276–1277
   mining, **2:** 136, 138–141, 150
   ornamental metal work, **1:** 798
   plate, **1:** 819, 821, 1277
   prices, **2:** 137–138, 141, 573
   refining, **2:** 139
   sales of, **2:** 140–141
   in x-ray tubes, **1:** 1251
Gold Fields Mining Company, **2:** 141
Gold Institute, **2:** 138
Gold Kist Inc., **1:** 12, **2:** 68, 69, 75
Gold Ores, 2: 136–141
Gold Rush of 1848, **1:** 215

Golden 1 Credit Union, **2:** 827
Golden Care, **2:** 1270
Golden Hope Berhad, **2:** 951
Golden Lady, **1:** 169
Golden Peanut Company, **2:** 90
Golden Rule stores, **2:** 634
Golden State Foods Corporation, **2:** 614
Golden West Homes, **1:** 298
Goldman, Emanuel, **1:** 93
Goldman, Jonathan, **2:** 1279, 1280
Goldman Sachs Company, **2:** 859, 875
Goldstar Electronics, **1:** 1021, 1043
Goldwyn Pictures Corporation, **2:** 1175
Golf Courses, 2: 1231–1232, 1234–1235
Golf Equipment, **1:** 1291, 1292, 1294
   carts, **1:** 1205, 1206, **2:** 679
   clubs, **1:** 747, 1290, **2:** 1235
   decomposable balls, **1:** 1295
   footwear, **1:** 619
   sales of, **1:** 1292, **2:** 566, 753
Golf Trust of America, **2:** 1235
Goman, Carol Kinsey, **2:** 1373
Gomez, Fancine, **1:** 1297
Gomez Advisors, **2:** 877
Gompers, Samuel, **2:** 1379, 1380, 1385
Good Manufacturing Practices, **1:** 493
Goodman Holding Company L.P., **1:** 1011, 1016
Goodwill Industries International, Inc., **2:** 751, 1350, 1351
Goodwin, Hannibal, **1:** 1266
Goodwin & Company, **1:** 146
Goodworks International Group, **1:** 577
Goodwrench Service Centers, **2:** 660
Goody, Sam, **2:** 729
Goodyear, Amasa, **2:** 714
Goodyear, Charles, **1:** 473, 572, 574
Goodyear Tire & Rubber Company, **1:** 575–576, 589, **2:** 1240
Goody's Family Clothing Stores, **2:** 699
Gordon, Charles, **2:** 769
Gordon, Jeff, **1:** 113
Gordon Brothers Group LLC, **2:** 794
Gordon Food Service Inc., **2:** 544
Gore, Al, **2:** 115
Gore, George, **1:** 460
Gore Report on Reinventing Government, **2: 1506**
Gorrie, John, **1:** 976, **2:** 1165
Gorton's Seafood, **1:** 124
Gorush, Anne M., **2:** 1495
Goss Graphic Systems Inc., **1:** 919
Goss Printing Company, **1:** 918
Gossard, **1:** 241
Gottstein Foods Company, **2:** 748
Gotz Toys, **1:** 1285
Gould, Jay, **2:** 310
Gould Electronics, **1:** 852
Goulds Pumps Inc., **1:** 927, 928
Government
   executive offices, **2:** 1445–1447, 1451
   general, 2: 1451–1453
   lawyers, **2:** 1460
   legislative bodies, **2:** 1447–1451
   workforce in, **2:** 1447
Government Accounting Office, **1:** 1208
Government Agencies
   in agricultural administration, **2:** 1520–1522
   in business regulation and inspection, **2:** 1522–1524
   in economic administration, **2:** 1512–1514

Highway Construction *(cont'd)*
trucks and, **1:** 1129
workforce in, **2:** 251, 256
Highway Industries Association, **2:** 253
Highway Trust Fund, **1:** 1129, **2:** 214, 253, 254
Highways
elevated, **2:** 257–264
interstate, **2:** 253, 259
toll, **2:** 251, 259, 311
Highways Beautification Act, **2:** 1025
Higonnet, RenQ, **1:** 429
Hilfiger, Tommy, **1:** 622
Hill, James J., **2:** 302
Hill and Knowlton Inc., **2:** 1435
Hill-Rom Inc., **1:** 334
Hillblom, L., **2:** 407
Hillenbrand Industries Inc., **1:** 334, 1310
Hills Brothers Coffee, **1:** 126
Hill's Pet Nutrition, **2:** 94
Hillshire Farms, **1:** 8
Hilti Ag Company, **1:** 906
Hilton Hotels, **2:** 1237
Hines, Frank T., **2:** 1487, 1488
Hines Horticulture, Inc., **2:** 38
Hirotec Corporation, **1:** 814
Hirsch International Corporation, **1:** 912
Hispanic Broadcasting Corporation, **2:** 463
Hispanics
in clothing industry, **1:** 217, 222, 238, 245
clothing sales to, **1:** 233
mortgages for, **2:** 860
radio stations for, **2:** 463
Hispano-Suiza, **1:** 1155
Historic American Engineering Record, **2:** 1399
Historic Preservation Fund, **2:** 1498
Historic Sites, **2:** 1364–1367, 1497
Hitachi Electronic Devices, **1:** 960, 1028, 1042, 1067, 1250
Hitachi Koki Company, **1:** 906
HitecASA, **1:** 873
HIV. *See* AIDS (Disease)
H.J. Heinz Company
in canned foods, **1:** 33, 37, 39, 121, 122
in frozen foods, **1:** 40, 43
in pet food, **1:** 57
Hjerstedt, Bud, **2:** 1051
H.M. Gousha, **1:** 418
H&M Food Systems, **1:** 4
HMK Enterprises, **1:** 321
HMOs. *See* Health Maintenance Organizations
Hobart Brand Foods, **1:** 921
Hobby, Oveta Culp, **2:** 1478
Hobby Goods, 2: 567–569
Hobby Industries of America, **2:** 568
Hobby Industry Association, **2:** 772, 773
Hobby Shops, 2: 765–768
Hobby Shops, Inc., **2:** 765
Hock, Julius, **1:** 560
Hockey Equipment, **1:** 1292, 1294, **2:** 565
Hockey Teams, **2:** 1215–1216, 1221–1222
Hocking Glass Company, **1:** 649
Hoe, Richard March, **1:** 429, 917, **2:** 756
Hoerni, Jean, **1:** 1083
Hoeschst Celanese Corporation
in carpets, **1:** 185
founding of, **1:** 461
in pharmaceuticals, **1:** 491, 494

in synthetic fibers, **1:** 484
in textiles, **1:** 160
in yarns, **1:** 186
Hoffa, James P., **2:** 1385
Hoffman, Friedreich, **1:** 1230
Hoffman Engineering Company, **1:** 329
Hoffman-La Roche, Inc.
ingredient suppliers for, **1:** 485
price fixing by, **1:** 488
in vitamins, **1:** 487
Hoffman Laces Ltd., **1:** 173
Hogs, 2: 57–60. *See also* Pork
artificial insemination of, **2:** 58, 97
breeding, **2:** 58, 96
farms for, **2:** 63, 83
feed for, **1:** 58, **2:** 58
services for, **2:** 96–98
slaughtering, **1:** 1, 2
veterinary services for, **2:** 92–93
wholesalers of, 2: 597–601
Hoists. *See* Cranes and Hoists
Holberg Industries Inc., **2:** 589
Holcomb Steel Company, **1:** 1005
Holding Companies, 2: 807, 960–961
bank owned, **2:** 811, 833, 953–960
deregulation of, **2:** 955, 957
government regulation of, **2:** 954–955, 957–958
history of, **2:** 954–958
investment, **2:** 960–961
multibank, **2:** 953–960
personal, **2:** 960–961
public utility, **2:** 960–961
Holiday Fair, **1:** 635
Holiday Inn Worldwide, **2:** 991
Holiday Rambler LLC, **1:** 1201
Holland America Lines, **2:** 373, 374
Hollerith, Herman, **1:** 957
Hollinghead, Richard Milton, **2:** 1198–1199
Hollinghead Industries Inc., **2:** 1161
Hollingsworth Saco Lowell Corporation, **1:** 913
Hollow Metal Door, **1:** 788
Holloway Company, **1:** 77
Hollowware, **1:** 1277–1278
Holly Farms, **2:** 68
Hollywood Entertainment Corporation, **2:** 1203
Hollywood Marine, **2:** 369
Hollywood Park Inc., **2:** 1225, 1226
Hollywood Studios. *See* Motion Picture Production
Hollywood Video, **2:** 1203
Holmes, Ernest, **1:** 1128
Holmes, Hodgen, **2:** 91
Holnam Inc., **1:** 653, 673, 674
Hologic Acclaim Series, **1:** 1249
Holographic Data Storage System, **1:** 960, 1252
Holography, **1:** 430, 960, 1252
Holson Burnes Group, Inc., **1:** 437
Holstein, William J., **2:** 767
Holsters, **1:** 637
Holt, Rinehart & Winston, **1:** 406
Home Baking Company, **1:** 64
Home Box Office, **2:** 1173, 1177, 1201–1202
Home Centers, **2:** 615–618
hardware sales in, **2:** 621, 623
paint sales in, **1:** 523, **2:** 618
Home Control Systems, **1:** 1218
Home Depot, Inc., **2:** 617, 623, 624

Hydro Conduit Corporation, **1:** 671
Hydrocarbons, **1:** 470
Hydrochloric Acid Toxicity, **1:** 464
Hydrochlorofluorocarbons, **1:** 604, 978, 979
Hydroelectric Power, **2:** 268, 271, 482, 485
Hydrofluoric Acid, **1:** 462
Hydrofluorocarbons, **1:** 1018, **2:** 672
Hydrogen, **1:** 451–454
   automobile fuel, **1:** 1125–1126
   pipelines for, **2:** 424
   rocket fuel, **1:** 1158
Hydrogen Peroxide
   bleaches, **1:** 447, 459
   vs. chlorine, **1:** 450
   demand for, **1:** 462, 463
   in textile finishes, **1:** 178
Hydronics Wholesalers, 2: 556–557
Hydrophones, **1:** 1208, 1210
Hydrostatic Pressing, **1:** 658
Hydrostatic Transmissions, **1:** 872
Hydrotherapy, **1:** 775, 780, 1243
Hydrox Cookies, **1:** 67
Hygienic Laboratory, **1:** 492, **2:** 1477, 1478
Hyland Therapeutics, **2:** 1312
Hyperion Treatment Facility, **2:** 514
Hypermarkets, **2:** 721
Hypertension Drugs, **1:** 493, 496
Hypnosis, **2:** 1263
Hypoallergenic Products, **1:** 516
Hypocausts, **1:** 782–783
Hyster Company, **1:** 889, 890
Hyundai, **1:** 1124

I

I-Beams, **1:** 288, **2:** 293
I Do-I Do, **2:** 750
I-Joists, **1:** 287, 288
I-STAT, **1:** 1216
IATSE. *See* International Alliance of Theatrical Stage
   Employees
Iberia Sugar Coop Inc., **1:** 73
IBM Corporation, **1:** 951, **2:** 1088
   CeluPlan II, **1:** 1060
   in computer development, **1:** 949, 957, 1107–1108
   in computer storage devices, **1:** 959, 960
   in CRTs, **1:** 1067
   in data processing services, **2:** 1096
   dress code, **1:** 197
   in expert systems, **2:** 913
   history of, **2:** 1084, 1085, 1107
   in intelligent neighborhoods, **2:** 951–952
   in leasing, **2:** 1110
   in mainframes, **1:** 950
   in office machines, **1:** 969
   in personal computers, **2:** 725
   retail sales by, **2:** 1044
   sales by, **1:** 947
   in wholesale distribution, **2:** 543
IBM Credit Corporation, **2:** 854
IBM Global Financing, **2:** 1111
IBM Global Services, **2:** 1080, 1093–1094
IBP, Inc., **1:** 3, 4, 5, 9, **2:** 600
Ice Boxes, **1:** 1014, 1015
Ice Cream, 1: 21–25
   fat content of, **1:** 23, 24

   mixes, **1:** 18
   wholesalers of, 2: 590
Ice Cream Partners USA, **1:** 24
Ice Manufacturing, 1: 135, **2:** 559
Ice Milk, **1:** 18
Ice Skates, **1:** 1290
Icebreakers, **2:** 363
Iced Tea, **1:** 111, 141
ICFS, 2: 1274–1278
ICI Paints, **1:** 521, 525
Icicle Seafood International Inc., **1:** 122, 124
ICO Global Communications, **2:** 451, 479
ICON Health and Fitness Inc., **1:** 593
ICS Learning Systems, **2:** 1343
Ida Cuber House, **2:** 1280
IDEA-the Association for Fitness Professionals, **2:** 1230
IDEA Wizard, **1:** 69
IDEXX Laboratories, **1:** 499
IDG, **1:** 398
IEC. *See* International Electrotechnical Commission
IEEE. *See* Institute of Electrical and Electronic Engineers
IFCO Systems, **1:** 291
IFilms.Com, **2:** 1204
IFPF. *See* International Federation of the Phonographic Industry
IG Farben, **1:** 461
IGA Stores. *See* Independent Grocers Alliance
Ignition Systems, **1:** 1101–1102, 1102–1103
   automatic, **1:** 1217
IHS. *See* Indian Health Service
IHUB (Integrated Hub), **1:** 1185
IIC Industries Inc., **2:** 561
IKON Office Solutions, **2:** 541
Illegal Immigrants, **2:** 100, 1442, 1443, 1540
Illegal Immigration Reform and Immigrant Responsibility Act,
   2: 1540
Illinois Agricultural Association, **2:** 610
Illinois Central Railroad, **2:** 303, 307
Illinois Steel Company, **1:** 692
Illinois Tool Works, **1:** 807, 905, 921, 941
Illinois Waterway, **2:** 366
Illiteracy. *See* Literacy
Illustration, Medical, **2:** 1311, 1313
Ilmenite Pigments, **1:** 457
I.M. Singer & Co., **1:** 196
Ima Fashions Inc., **1:** 634
Imaging Systems. *See also* Digital Imaging
   for banks, **2:** 960, 974
   for charitable trusts, **2:** 974
   for checks, **2:** 802
   four-color, **1:** 1308
   history of, **1:** 1268
   in motion picture production, **2:** 1184
   satellites for, **2:** 480
   thermal, **1:** 1204, 1205
Imax Corporation, **2:** 1197
IMC-Agrico Company, **1:** 541, **2:** 226
IMC Global Inc., **1:** 541, **2:** 224, 225, 226, 228, 229
IMC Kalium, **1:** 541
IMCO Recycling Inc., **2:** 570
IMDM. *See* Intelligent Mobile Data Network (IMDM)
IMETAL SA, **2:** 208, 220
Immesote, Philip L., **1:** 3
Immigrants
   in clothing industry, **1:** 196, 225
   computer programming by, **2:** 1081
   illegal, **2:** 100, 1442, 1443, 1540

Jewelry Stores, 2: 764–765
J.F. Shea, **2:** 260
Jiffy Lube International, Inc., **2:** 1157
Jig Saws, **1:** 905
Jigs, 1: 898–900
Jim Beam Brands Company, **1:** 107, 108
J&J Flock Products Inc., **1:** 179
J.L. Hammett Company, **2:** 763
J.L. Turner and Son, Inc., **2:** 712
J&L Specialty, **1:** 703
JLN Inc., **1:** 634
JM Huber Corporation, **1:** 555, **2:** 218, 220
JMJ Fleet Services, **2:** 1139
Jo-Ann Stores, Inc., **2:** 772, 773–774
Job Placement Agencies. *See* Employment Agencies
Job Training, 2: 1349–1352
Jobs, Steve, **1:** 952
Jockey Club, **2:** 77
Jockey International Inc., **1:** 169, 172
Joe Boxer Corporation, **1:** 205
Johansson Kurt, **1:** 581
John B. Sanfilippo & Son Inc., **1:** 86
John Crane Inc., **1:** 584
John Deere Company. *See* Deere and Company
John Morrell, **1:** 3, 4
John Nuveen Company, **2:** 970
John O. Butler Company, **1:** 1247
Johns-Manville Corporation, **1:** 684–685
Johnson, Donald, **2:** 1489
Johnson, Jimmy, **2:** 1228
Johnson, Lyndon, **2:** 1510
Johnson, Robert Wood, **1:** 496
Johnson, William, **1:** 630
Johnson & Johnson, **1:** 490, 497
    in contact lenses, **1:** 1263, 1264
    in cosmetics and toiletries, **1:** 518
    in diagnostic substances, **1:** 499
    in orthopedic and surgical equipment, **1:** 1244, 1245
    in pharmaceuticals, **1:** 493, 495, 496
Johnson Brothers Wholesale Liquor, **2:** 609
Johnson Controls Inc., **1:** 265, 324–325, 601, 1137
Johnson Electric Holdings Ltd., **1:** 906
Johnson Group Management, **2:** 1005
Johnson Space Center, **2:** 1526, 1531
Johnstown America Industries Inc., **1:** 1184
Joint Chiefs of Staff, **2:** 1533
Joint Economic Committee, **2:** 1468
Joint Taxation Committee, **2:** 1468
Joint Ventures
    in aerospace industry, **1:** 1194, **2:** 1532
    in aircraft industry, **1:** 1160
    in airline industry, **2:** 399
    in aluminum production, **1:** 722, 741
    in appliance manufacturing, **1:** 1021, 1029
    in automatic control manufacturing, **1:** 1219
    in biotechnology industry, **1:** 490, 500
    in book and magazine wholesaling, **2:** 611
    in bridge and tunnel construction, **2:** 258–259, 261
    in capacitor manufacturing, **1:** 1080
    in carwashes, **2:** 1159
    in cast iron foundries, **1:** 712
    in cereal production, **1:** 52
    in cogeneration, **2:** 521
    in colleges and universities, **2:** 1329
    in communication satellites, **2:** 480
    in computer storage devices, **1:** 960

    in cruise lines, **2:** 375
    in defense industry, **1:** 1204
    in discount stores, **2:** 641
    in electric lighting, **1:** 1037
    in electromedical equipment, **1:** 1258
    in farm machinery manufacturing, **1:** 863
    in fishing, **2:** 121
    in hand tool manufacturing, **1:** 905
    in hose and belt manufacturing, **1:** 581
    by hotels, **2:** 989
    in household appliances, **1:** 1012
    in ice cream manufacturing, **1:** 24
    in industrial truck manufacturing, **1:** 890
    in intermodal transit, **2:** 326, 327, 328
    in investment management, **2:** 884
    in life insurance, **2:** 889
    in lighting fixture manufacturing, **1:** 1038, 1039
    by museums, **2:** 1367
    in music recording, **1:** 1051
    in natural gas transmission, **2:** 494, 495
    in newspaper industry, **1:** 390
    in petroleum industry, **2:** 186, 193, 199
    in pharmaceutical industry, **1:** 488, 490, 495, 497
    in photographic film, **1:** 1268
    in pipelines, **2:** 419, 422
    in plastics industry, **1:** 468, 597
    by port authorities, **2:** 385
    public-private, **2:** 258–259
    in public transportation, **2:** 311
    in pump manufacturing, **1:** 928
    in railroad shipping, **2:** 305
    in rubber products manufacturing, **1:** 587
    in search and navigation system manufacturing, **1:** 1213
    in semiconductor manufacturing equipment, **1:** 924, 925
    in ship building, **1:** 1170
    in soft drink manufacturing, **1:** 111
    in steel industry, **1:** 695
    in tea production, **1:** 142
    in telecommunications, **2:** 457
    in utility construction, **2:** 272
    in wholesaling, **2:** 553
Joints, Artificial, **1:** 1242, 1243
Joists
    bar, **1:** 800
    metal, **1:** 785
    series, **1:** 288
Jonabell Farm Inc., **2:** 79
Jones, Brent, **1:** 1240
Jones, Malcolm, **1:** 401
Jones & Laughlin, **1:** 695
Jones Act, **2:** 362, 363
Jones Apparel Group, **1:** 227, 621, 622
Jones Chemical, **1:** 448
Jone's Wood, **2:** 1233
Jordan, Joseph, **1:** 915
Jordan, Michael, **2:** 1215
The Jordan Refiner, **1:** 915
Jos. A. Bank Clothiers Inc., **1:** 218, **2:** 684
Joseph Gallo Farms, **2:** 66
Joseph Seagram & Sons, Inc., **1:** 106, 107
Joshua Tree National Park, **2:** 1501
Joslyn, M.A., **1:** 40
Joslyn Corporation, **1:** 905
Jossey-Bass, **1:** 404
Jostens, Inc., **1:** 418
Journal Des Scavans, **1:** 394

Kelly Services, **2:** 1070, 1077–1078
Kelso & Company, **1:** 897
Kelvinator, **1:** 1014, 1015
Kemet Electronics Corporation, **1: 1080, 1081**
Kemp, Jack, **2:** 1505
Kemper Insurance Company, **2:** 870
Kenco Group, **2:** 344
Kendall, Bonnie L., **2:** 1300
Kendall, Donald M., **1:** 114
Kendall International Inc., **1:** 1244
Kenetch, **1:** 856
Kenmore Brand, **1:** 1011, 1015, 1029
Kennametal Inc., **1:** 902
Kennecott Corporation, **2:** 148
Kennecott Energy Company, **2:** 166, 171, 172, **549**
Kennecott Utah Copper Corporation, **2: 133**
Kennedy, John F., **2:** 1528
Kennedy Information Research Group, **2: 1430**
Kennedy Space Center, **2:** 1526
Kennels, **2:** 98, 99
Kenneth Cole Productions Inc., **1:** 622
Kenneth Fox Supply Company, **1:** 261
Kenny Construction, **2:** 260
Kent, Jerry, **2:** 473
Kentucky Derby Hosiery Company Inc., **1: 169**
Kentucky Fried Chicken. *See* KFC
Kenworth Trucks, **1:** 1131, 1132
Kenyon Industries Inc., **1:** 179
Kepler, Johannes, **1:** 1234
Keratin, **1:** 466, 605, 607
Kerber, Ron, **2:** 717
Keremedjiev, George, **1:** 843–844
Kerkorian, Kirk, **2:** 1177
Kernite, **2:** 225
Kernstock, Nicholas, **2:** 411
Kerosene
    history of, **2:** 181, 182
    lamps, **1:** 560
    pipelines for, **2:** 420
    refining, **1:** 558, 559
Kerr Drug Stores, **2:** 634
Kerr Group Inc., **1:** 647, 816
Kerr-McGee Coal Company, **1:** 456, **2:** 171, **549**
Kerrville Bus Company Inc., **2:** 321
Kessler, David, **1:** 148
Ketchum Communications Holdings, **2: 1022**
Ketchup, **1:** 37
Kevlar, **1:** 160
Key Cases, **1:** 636
Key Tronic Corporation, **1:** 964
Keyboard Instruments, **1:** 1282, 1283
Keyboards (Computer), **1:** 963–967
Keyes Fibre Company, **1:** 362
Keystone Consolidated Industries Inc., **1: 1004**
Keystone Flight Services, **2:** 411
Keystone International, **1:** 839
Keystone Steel & Wire Company, **1: 701, 787**
KFC, **2:** 736
Khrunichev, **1:** 1192
Kia, **1:** 1124
Kibbe, Richard R., **1:** 805
Kiddie Parks, **2:** 1233–1234
Kidney Dialysis Centers, **2:** 1305–1308
Kidney Transplantation, **1:** 501
Kids Kabs, **2:** 313
Kids 'R Us, **2:** 694, 696

Kidwell, Claudia B., **1:** 196
Kiewet Construction Group, Inc., **2:** 255, 260, 262
Kiewit Pacific, **2:** 258
Kilby, Jack, **1:** 1073
Killian, James, **2:** 1528
Killian's Irish Red, **1:** 92
Kilns, **1:** 451, 664, 667, **2:** 267
    hazardous waste burning, **1:** 671, 675
    high-volume tunnel, **1:** 665
    tire burning, **1:** 671, 675
Kilowatt Hours, **2:** 481
Kimball International Inc., **1:** 315, 334
Kimberly-Clark Corporation
    disposable diapers by, **1:** 378
    merger of, **1:** 346
    paper production by, **1:** 348, **2:** 108
    sales by, **2:** 109
    sanitary paper products by, **1:** 375, 377, 378, 380, 381
    tree sales by, **2:** 108
Kimberly Quality Care, **2:** 1303
Kimco Realty Corporation, **2:** 933
KinderCare Learning Centers, **2:** 1353–1354, 1356–1357
Kindill Mining, **2:** 171
Kinetic Concepts Inc., **1:** 333, 334
Kinetoscopes, **2:** 1173
King Graphics Inc., **2:** 1055
King Ranch, **2:** 55
Kinko's, Inc., **2:** 1048, 1049
Kinnear, E.L., **2:** 757
Kinney National Services, **2:** 1177
Kinney Shoe Corporation, **1:** 626
Kinney Tobacco Company, **1:** 146
Kinyuon, Joseph J., **2:** 1476
Kiosks, in banks, **2:** 820
Kirby Company, **1:** 1025
Kirby Lines, **2:** 369
Kirchoff, Gustav Robert, **1:** 1231
Kirin, **1:** 95
Kirsch, **1:** 332
Kit Kat, **1:** 78
Kitchen Cabinet Manufacturers Association, **1:** 282
Kitchen Cabinets, 1: 282–283
Kitchen Equipment, Commercial, **1:** 921
Kitchen Housewares. *See* Cooking Equipment; Housewares
Kitchen Sinks, **1:** 775
KitchenAid, **1:** 1016, 1029
Kits Cameras, Inc., **2:** 769
Kiwi Fruit, **2:** 36
Kizer, Kenneth, **2:** 1490
K-Lath Division, **2:** 283
KLA-Tencor, **1:** 924, 1128
Kleenex, **1:** 377, 381
Kleider, Liz, **2:** 538, 539
Klein, Joel I., **1:** 488
Klein, Robert, **2:** 1488
Kline and Company Inc., **1:** 488
KLM Royal Dutch Airlines, **2:** 402
Klochner Capital Corporation, **1:** 595
Kloster Cruise, Ltd., **2:** 375
Kmart Corporation, **2:** 637, 639–640
    in automobile repair, **2:** 1156
    bags for, **1:** 372
    in book sales, **2:** 760
    in children's clothing, **2:** 695
    in footwear, **1:** 622
    in handbags, **1:** 634

L

L and W Supply Corporation, **2:** 537
L.A. Darling Company, **1:** 329
L.A. Gear, **1:** 622, 626
La Petite Academy, **2:** 1356
La Salle, Sieur De, **2:** 359
La-Z-Boy Inc., **1:** 900
Label Manufactures Association, **1:** 129
Label Printing Industries of America, **1:** 408
Labeling of Hazardous Art Materials Act, **1:** 1298
Labels
   on canned food, **1:** 32, 36
   on clothing, **2:** 1005
   on cosmetics and toiletries, **1:** 516
   on dairy products, **1:** 15, 22, 23, 29
   digital technology for, **1:** 369
   fabric for, **1:** 166
   on genetically engineered products, **2:** 12
   gummed, **1:** 367
   in-mold, **1:** 369
   on livestock feed, **1:** 59
   market for, **1:** 369
   on meat products, **1:** 7, 9
   nutritional, **2:** 1481
   on paints, **1:** 526
   on pasta, **1:** 137
   on pet food, **1:** 56
   on poultry products, **1:** 12
   pressure sensitive, **1:** 367, 368
   printing, **1:** 420
   shrink sleeve, **1:** 369
   warning (*See* Warning Labels)
   wet glue, **1:** 367
Labinal Inc., **1:** 753
LabOne Inc., **2:** 1424
Labor, Child. *See* Child Labor
Labor Force, **2:** 1143–1146
   in abrasive products, **1:** 682
   in accounting services, **2:** 1418
   in advertising, **2:** 1026
   in aerospace industry, **1:** 1194, 1197–1198, 1199
   in agriculture, **2:** 45–46
      agricultural services, **2:** 90, 96
      beef cattle, **2:** 55–56
      contractors, **2:** 100–101
      diary farms, **2:** 66
      farm supplies, **2:** 610
      fertilizer manufacturing, **1:** 540
      poultry farms, **2:** 69, 72, 75
      wheat, **2:** 5
   in aircraft industry, **1:** 1152, 1162, **1165**, **1168**
   in airline industry, **2:** 400–401
   in airports, **2:** 416
   in aluminum production, **1:** 725, 740, 744, **751–752**, **754**, **756**
   in ammunition manufacturing, **1:** 828
   in appliance manufacturing, **1:** 1012, **1020–1021, 1022**
   in architectural services, **2:** 1409–1410
   in armature rewinding, **2:** 1170
   in armed forces, **2:** 1535–1536
   in art materials, **1:** 1298
   in asphalt products, **1:** 565, 566, 567
   in associations, **2:** 1377
   in audio and video equipment manufacturing, **1:** 1041, 1044
   in automobile dealerships, **2:** 660
   in automobile repair shops, **2:** 1145, 1152, 1157, 1158
   in automotive manufacturing, **1:** 1122–1123, **2:** 1162

      automotive stampings, **1:** 812, 813, 815
      parts suppliers, **1:** 986, 1103, 1137
      trailer trucks, **1:** 1138, 1139
      truck and bus, **1:** 888, 891, 1132
   in automotive parts stores, **2:** 669
   in ball and roller bearings, **1:** 933
   in banking, **2:** 809, 958–959
   in battery manufacturing, **1:** 1095
   in beauty salons, **2:** 1010, 1011
   in bicycle manufacturing, **1:** 1189
   in boat building and repairing, **1:** 1178, 1180
   in cabinetry, **1:** 312
   in camps, **2:** 997
   in carbon and graphite products, **1:** 1004, 1006
   in cast iron foundries, **1:** 711
   in charitable trusts, **2:** 973
   in chemical manufacturing, **1:** 464, 546, 557
      carbon black, **1:** 555
      cellulosic fibers, **1:** 479
      cyclic crudes and intermediates, **1:** 529, 531, 532
      organics, **1:** 534, 537, 538, 539
      pigments, **1:** 457
      synthetic fibers, **1:** 480, 483–484
      synthetic rubber, **1:** 472, 476
      wood chemicals, **1:** 528, 529
   in chewing gum production, **1:** 82
   in cleaning product manufacturing, **1:** 509, 513
   in clock and watch manufacturing, **1:** 1273
   in clothing industry, **1:** 238, 257, 258, 262, 263
      belts, **1:** 256, 257
      children's, **1:** 247, 248, 249, 250
      dresses, **1:** 227
      embroidery, **1:** 264–265
      furs, **1:** 252
      gloves, **1:** 253, 630
      hats, caps and millinery, **1:** 243, 245
      hosiery, **1:** 168
      menswear, **1:** 198, 218–219
      neckwear, **1:** 208
      rainwear, **1:** 255
      retail stores, **2:** 685, 688–689
      robes and dressing gowns, **1:** 253, 254
      shirts, **1:** 199, 202
      trousers, **1:** 213
      underwear, **1:** 205, 235, 238
      women's and girls', **1:** 222, 224, 226, 228, 231, 234, 235
      work clothes, **1:** 214, 215, 216–217
   in commercial art, **2:** 1054, 1055
   in compressor manufacturing, **1:** 935, 937
   in computer manufacturing, **1:** 952–953, 960, 1075–1076
   in computer programming, **2:** 1081
   in computer services, **2:** 1094, 1103–1104, 1108, 1111, 1113, 1116–1117
   in computer software, **2:** 1089
   in concrete products, **1:** 670, 671
   in construction
      bridge and tunnel, **2:** 261–262
      carpentry work, **2:** 285, 286
      cement and concrete work, **2:** 290, 291
      drywall, **2:** 281
      electrical work, **2:** 275–276, 278
      excavation, **2:** 296
      flooring, **2:** 287
      heavy, **2:** 271
      land subdivision and development, **2:** 950–951
      masonry work, **2:** 276–277

Logistics Services, **2:** 342, 344, 345
Logo &, **1:** 241
Logos
for cotton fabrics, **1:** 161
on hats, **1:** 242–243, 244–245
for luggage, **1:** 633
Logs, Exports of, **1:** 281
LoManto, Lisa, **2:** 1134
Lombardi, L., **1:** 1079
London Fog, **1:** 255
London International, **1:** 589
London International Financial Futures **& Options Exchange, 2:** 877
London Metal Exchange, **1:** 727, 735, **740, 759, 2: 131,** 146–147
London School of Economics, **2:** 1341
London Stock Exchange, **2:** 879
London Zoo, **2:** 1369
Londontown Corporation, **1:** 255
Lone Star Industries Inc., **1:** 674, 675
Long, Crawford, **1:** 1238
Long-Distance Telephone Service, **2: 454–455, 457**
Long Painting Company, **2:** 275
Long Term Care. *See* Nursing Homes; **Residential Care** Facilities
Longaberger Company, **1:** 305
Longman Publishing, **1:** 404
Longmont Foods, **2:** 69
Longshoremen, **2:** 383, 384, 386
Longview Fibre Company, **1:** 373, 767
Look (Magazine), **1:** 395
Looms. *See also* Weaving Machines
history of, **1:** 911
hydraulic, **1:** 911
industrial, **1:** 910–912
power-driven, **1:** 181, 911
Looseleaf Binders, 1: 437
Lopid, **1:** 493
Loral Space & Communications Ltd., **1: 1194, 2: 480**
Lorenzi, Neal, **2:** 1047
Loreto Y Pena Paper Company, **1:** 380
Lori Corporation, **1:** 1302
Los Angeles Lakers, **2:** 1223
Los Angeles Times, **1:** 388, 391, 392
Los Angeles Turf Club, Inc., **2:** 1226
Loss Control (Insurance), **2:** 928
Lost Arrow, Inc., **2:** 706
Lotteries, Video Terminals for, **2:** 1232
Lotus Development Corporation, **2: 1084**
Loughead, Allan, **1:** 1145–1146
Loughead, Malcolm, **1:** 1145
Loughead Aircraft Manufacturing **Company, 1: 1194**
Louima, Abner, **2:** 1458
Louis Harris and Associates, **2:** 999
Louis Rich Meat Products, **1:** 9
Louisiana-Pacific Corporation, **1:** 284, **303**
Louisiana Sugar Cane, **1:** 73
Love Box Company Inc., **1:** 291
Love Canal, **2:** 1494
Lovelock, James, **1:** 978
Low-Cost Housing, **1:** 296
Low-Fat Food
bakery goods, **1:** 63, 66
benefits of, **1:** 131–132
candy, **1:** 76, 78, 79
cheese, **1:** 17–18

chips, **1:** 129, 132, 134
chocolate, **1:** 80
cookies and crackers, **1:** 66–67
frozen, **1:** 43
ice cream, **1:** 23, 24
meat, **1:** 8
milk, **1:** 26, 28, 29, **2:** 589
Low-Income Housing, **2:** 242, 1504, 1510
Lowe, Don, **2:** 1048
Lowe Lintas & Partners Worldwide, **2:** 1022
Lowell, Francis Cabot, **2:** 1508
Lowell Inc., **2:** 912
Lowenstein, Joanna, **2:** 1044
Lowe's Companies Inc., **1:** 523, 788, **2:** 534, 556, 617, 623–624, 709
Lozier Corporation, **1:** 328, 329
Lozier Motor Company, **1:** 1179
LPG. *See* Liquefied Petroleum Gas
L.S. Starrett Company, **1:** 772
LTV Corporation, **1:** 695, 703, 760, 853, **2:** 562
LTV Steel Company Inc., **1:** 703, 705, 823, 1036, **2:** 501, 521
Lubacks and Company, **2:** 531
Lubricating Oils and Greases, 1: 558, 568–569
industrial, **1:** 569
for metal forgings, **1:** 809
pipelines for, **2:** 420
pumps for, **1:** 984
synthetic, **1:** 568, 809
vegetable-oil, **1:** 568
Lucas, George, **2:** 1182
Lucas Aerospace, **1:** 1166–1167
Lucas Spindletop Wells, **1:** 874
Lucas Variety PLC, **1:** 1103
Lucent Technologies, **2:** 464, 1057
Luciano, Lani, **2:** 1238
Lucier, Richard L., **1:** 126
Luck Stone Corporation, **2:** 210
Lucky Friday Mine, **2:** 145
Lucky Stores, **1:** 30
Ludlow Corporation, **1:** 190
Lufkin, Donals, **2:** 414
Lufkin Industries Inc., **1:** 711
Lugar, Richard, **2:** 19
Luggage, 1: 631–633
carry-on, **2:** 771
designer, **1:** 631–632
nylon, **1:** 631, 633
plastic, **1:** 631
retail stores for, 2: 771
soft, **1:** 631
Luggage and Leather Goods Manufacturers of America, **2:** 771
Lumber. *See also* Logging; Sawmills; Wood Products
alternatives to, **2:** 286
clear, **1:** 274
dealers, 2: 238, 615–618
demand for, **2:** 108
exports of, **1:** 268, 273, 274
hardwood (*See* Hardwood Lumber)
housing starts and, **1:** 268, 269, 270
imports of, **1:** 268, 273, 281
laminated veneer, **1:** 288
oriented strand, **1:** 283, 286, 303, 304
parallel strand, **1:** 288
pricing, **1:** 273, 274, **2:** 283, 284–285
production of, **1:** 267
sales of, **1:** 346, **2:** 534

merger of, **1:** 468, 538, **2:** 180, 184, **198, 419**
in neural networks, **2:** 195
in oil exploration, **2:** 199
in sulfur production, **2:** 227
Mobil Pipeline Company, **2:** 417, 419
Mobil Road Atlas, **1:** 418
Mobile Communication Systems, **2:** 448–453
in courier services, **2:** 337
satellites for, **2:** 476, 477–478
switching offices for, **2:** 448, 449
Mobile Computers. *See* Portable Computers
Mobile Homes, 1: 293–298, 722
cost of, **2:** 938
history of, **2:** 938–940
loans on, **2:** 938, 940
parks of, **1:** 296, **2:** 937–940
wholesalers of, 2: 536
Mobile Radio Systems. *See* **Mobile Communication Systems**
Model Cities Administration, **2:** 1510
Model Communities, **2:** 1509
Model Consumer Finance Act, **2:** 849
Modell, John, **2:** 992
Modems, **1:** 1055
cable, **2:** 475
video-on-demand and, **2:** 475
Modern Fibers Inc., **1:** 187
Modtech, **1:** 300
Modular Buildings, **1:** 299, 300, **2:** 277
Modular Furniture, **1:** 314, 316
Modular Production Systems, in clothing **industry, 1:** 201, 212, 254
Moen Inc., **1:** 776
Moffet, James, **2:** 229
Mohair, 1: 165, 186, 187
goats for, **2:** 62
hosiery, **1:** 168
subsidies, **2:** 62
wholesalers of, 2: 601
Mohawk Industries, Inc., **1:** 184
Mohican Mills Inc., **1:** 174
Mohl Fur Company, Inc., **1:** 252
Mohrfeld Inc., **2:** 784
Moison, David, **1:** 741
Moissanite, **1:** 1280
Moisson, Henri, **1:** 460
Mokhiber, Russell, **2:** 185
Molasses, **1:** 74, 75
Molasses Act, **2:** 740
Molded Mechanical Rubber Goods, 1: 585–588
Molding
blow, **1:** 600, 601, 609
compression, **1:** 585, 586
dies, **1:** 899
green sand, **1:** 897
industrial, **1:** 898–900
injection, **1:** 586, 587, 602, 609
metal-clad, **1:** 787–789
plastics, **1:** 606
sand for, **2:** 215–216
transfer, **1:** 586
Molds (Fungi), Pharmaceuticals From, **1: 486**
Molex Inc., **1:** 1089
Molina, Mario, **1:** 978
Mollusks, **1:** 119, **2:** 122–123
Molnycke, **1:** 380
Moltech Corporation, **1:** 1095

Molybdenum
alloys, **1:** 698, 727
demand for, **1:** 698
mining, **2:** 148
shaping, **1:** 746
vs. vanadium, **2:** 152
in x-ray tubes, **1:** 1251
Mommers Print Service B.V., **1:** 1069–1070
Monarch Design Systems, **1:** 171
Monarch Knitting Machine Corporation, **1:** 170
Mondavi, Robert, **1:** 102
Monet Jewelers, **1:** 1302
Monetary Control Act, **2:** 825, 832
Monetary Policy, 2: 797, 1466, 1467, 1468
Money Laundering, **2:** 828
Money Market Funds, **2:** 869, 957, 963–965
Money Orders, **2:** 840
Money Supply, Gold and, **2:** 137
Monfort, Inc., **2:** 594, 600
Monier, Joseph, **2:** 290
Monistat 7, **1:** 496
Monitor Top, **1:** 1015
Monitors. *See* Displays (Computer)
Monk-Austin Inc., **1:** 156
Monoclonal Antibodies, **1:** 500, 501, 502
Monofilaments Fibers, **1:** 480–481
Monopolies. *See also* Antitrust Law
in aircraft industry, **1:** 1164
in dairy products, **1:** 27–28
in photographic equipment and supplies, **1:** 1266
in railroad industry, **2:** 302
in telephone service, **2:** 456
Monorail Systems, 1: 883, 884–887
Monotype Machines, **1:** 410, 429, 918
Monro, **2:** 1146
Monro Muffler Brake Inc., **2:** 1148, 1158
Monroe, James, **2:** 1486
Monroney Act, **2:** 657
Monrovia Nursery Company, **2:** 38
Monsanto Corporation
in acrylic fibers, **1:** 160
in bovine growth hormones, **1:** 15, 31
in cyclic crudes and intermediates, **1:** 533
in floriculture, **2:** 38
in genetic engineering, **1:** 546
in organic chemicals, **1:** 539
in plastics, **1:** 468
in rubber, **1:** 475
Montana Resources Inc., **2:** 148
Montana Tunnels Mine, **2:** 145
Monterey Bay National Marine Sanctuary, **2:** 1368
Monterey Mushrooms, Inc., **2:** 39
Montessori, Maria, **2:** 1320
Montgomery Ward and Company, **2:** 631, 708, 715, 776, 778
Montreal Protocol. *See* Protocol on Substances **That Deplete the** Ozone Layer
Monumental Investment Corporation, **2:** 274
Monuments, Granite, **1:** 679
Moody's Investors Service, **1:** 418
Moog, Robert, **1:** 1282
Moonlight Products, **2:** 546
Moore, Gordon E., **1:** 1073, 1075
Moore, J. Stuart, **2:** 1251
Mopeds, **2:** 676–677, 678
Moran, Tim, **1:** 1104
Moran Towing Corporation, **2:** 391

Moto Photo, **2:** 1127
Motor and Equipment Manufacturers Association, **2: 660**
Motor Carrier Act, **2:** 328, 447
Motor Carrier Safety Assistance Program, **2: 329**
Motor Carriers. *See* Trucking
Motor Equipment Manufacturers Association, **1: 1133**
Motor Homes, 1: 1140–1142, 1200, **2: 674**
  self-contained, **2:** 675, 676
Motor Oil, **2:** 784
Motor Scooters, **2:** 676–677, 678
Motor Transit Corporation, **2:** 317
Motor Vehicle Air Pollution Control Act, **2: 1491**
Motor Vehicle Dealers, 2: 654–661, 679–680
  advertising by, **2:** 1026
  floorplan loans for, **2:** 846, 851, 853
  franchises for, **2:** 656, 657, 659
  government regulation of, **2:** 657
  history of, **2:** 655–659, 666
  one-price policies of, **2:** 659
  parts and suppliers, **2:** 658
  profit margins of, **2:** 658
  repair services by, **2:** 658, 660, 1155, **1156, 1157**
  used car auctions and, **2:** 527
  used only, 2: 661–664
  web site development for, **2:** 1118
  workforce in, **2:** 524, 660
Motor Vehicle Manufacturers Association, **1: 1118**
Motor Vehicle Parts. *See* Automotive Parts
Motor Vehicles. *See also* Cars; Transportation; **Trucks**
  all-terrain, **1:** 1189, 1205–1206
  amphibious, **1:** 1201, 1204
  auctions of, **2:** 525
  bodies, 1: 1117–1126, **2:** 217, 1143–1146
  children's, **1:** 1286–1290
  electric, **1:** 738, 1125, **2:** 314
  electrical equipment for, **1:** 1100–1105
  government administration of, **2:** 1514–1516
  inspection facilities, **2:** 446–447
  instruments for, **1:** 1224–1226
  lighting equipment for, 1: 1039–1040
  maintenance facilities for, **2:** 345–346
  motors and generators for, **1:** 998
  per household, **2:** 526
  sales of, **1:** 1117, **2:** 654–655
  weighing facilities, **2:** 446–447
  wholesalers of, 2: 524–528
  zero emission, **1:** 1120, 1125
Motorcycle Dealers, 2: 676–679
Motorcycle Industry Council, **2:** 677
Motorcycle Safety Foundation, **1:** 1183, **2: 679**
Motorcycles
  carburetors for, **1:** 986–987
Motorcycles, 1: 1186–1187
  buyer profile for, **1:** 1188
  exports of, **1:** 1188, 1189
  franchises for, **2:** 677, 679
  heavyweight, **1:** 1186
  history of, **1:** 1187–1188, **2:** 677–678
  imports of, **1:** 1187
  Japanese, **2:** 677–678
  off-road, **1:** 1186
  power transmission equipment for, **1: 944**
  racing, **2:** 1223, 1224
  safety of, **2:** 679
  sales of, **2:** 677, 679
  in traffic accidents, **1:** 1188

  women and, **2:** 679
Motoren and Turbinen Union, **1:** 1160
Motorola Inc.
  in aircraft instruments, **1:** 1164, 1167
  in automatic controls, **1:** 1219
  in batteries, **1:** 1095
  in cellular networks, **1:** 1060
  in computer displays, **1:** 967
  in electrical test equipment, **1:** 1129
  in industrial electrical apparatus, **1:** 1009
  in semiconductors, **1:** 1075
  in smart cards, **2:** 312
  in telecommunications, **1:** 1062
  in television manufacturing, **1:** 1042
Motors, 1: 998–1003. *See also* Electric Motors; Generators
  fluid power, **1:** 989–990
MotorVac Technologies Inc., **1:** 513
Motown Records, **1:** 1046, 1049
Motrin IB, **1:** 497
Mott, Stewart, **2:** 1391
Mount Isa Mines, **2:** 149
Mountain Bicycles, **1:** 1187, 1188, 1189
Mountaineer Mine, **2:** 170
Mouse (Computer), **1:** 967
Mouth Cancer, From Tobacco, **1:** 153
Movado Group Inc., **1:** 1274
Movie Gallery, **2:** 1203
Movie Star Inc., **1:** 253
Movie Theaters. *See* Motion Picture Theaters
Moving Car Bunker System, **1:** 883
Moving Picture Machine Operators of the United States and
    Canada, **2:** 1182
Moving Services. *See* Household Moving Services
Moving Stairways. *See* Elevators and Moving Stairways
Mowers, Lawn. *See* Lawn Mowers
Mowry, J. Kelly, **1:** 820
Moynihan, Daniel Patrick, **1:** 826
Moyroud, Louis, **1:** 429
MP3 Technology, **2:** 554
MPB Corporation, **1:** 932
Mrs. Field's Cookies, **1:** 66
Mrs. Smith's, **1:** 70
MSB. *See* Major Shipbuilding Base
MSE Corporation, **2:** 1413
MTA Long Island Rail Road, **1:** 1185
MTBE. *See* Methyl Tertiary Butyl Ether
MTD Products Inc., **1:** 900
MTS Systems Corporation, **1:** 1236
MTV, **1:** 1047, **2:** 1178
Mubarak, Mohamed Hosni, **2:** 1373
Mueller Industries Inc., **1:** 707, 735
Mufflers, **1:** 206, **2:** 1146, 1149
Muir, John, **2:** 1499
Mulally, Alan, **1:** 1152
Mulch
  bark, **2:** 110
  plastic, **1:** 591
  tillage system, **2:** 85
Muldoon, P.J., **2:** 714, 715
Mules, **2:** 76
Muller, Karen, **2:** 1338
Muller Martini Trendbinder, **1:** 438
Mullins, Peter J., **2:** 1152
Multi-Laser Imagesetter, **1:** 431
Multi-Tools, **1:** 770
Multibank Holding Companies, **2:** 953–960

Multichannel Multipoint Distribution Systems, **2:** 457, 458
Multifiber Arrangement
   impact of, **1:** 162, 168, 227, 237
     on suits and coats, **1:** 198, 227, 228
     on women's and girls shirts, **1:** 223
     on work clothes, **1:** 216
Multifoods Specialty Distribution, **2:** 589
Multifunction Computer Peripherals, **1:** 963, 964, **2:** 1050
Multilateral Investment Guarantee Agency, **2:** 928
Multilevel Marketing, **2:** 783
Multimedia Technology, **1:** 405, 961
Multimeters, **1:** 1129, 1226
Multiplex Co., Inc., **1:** 974
Multipoint Multichannel Distribution Service, **2:** 470, 475
Multistate Tax Commission, **2:** 1062
Multiwall Bags, 1: 371–374
Mumm, Cliff, **2:** 286
Muncy Building Enterprises, **1:** 301
Munecas Y Juguetas Ensueno S.A., **2:** 569
Municipal Government
   in community development, **2:** 1508, 1509
   courts of, **2:** 1454
   executive offices of, **2:** 1445–1446
   jails, **2:** 1461
   marinas and, **2:** 393
   in refuse disposal, **2:** 516, 569
   segregation and, **2:** 1509
   in sewage treatment, **2:** 512, 513
   utilities administration, **2:** 1516
Municipal Water Supply. *See* Water Supply
Munn V. Illinois, **2:** 301
Murals, **1:** 418
Murata Electronics North America Inc., **1:** 1078, 1081
Muratech Textile Machinery, **1:** 913
Murdoch, Rupert, **2:** 468
Murdoch Magazines, **2:** 778
Murdock, William, **2:** 499
Murphy, Gerry E., **2:** 740
Murray, **1:** 1187
Murray, Arthur, **2:** 1205
Murry's Inc., **2:** 650
Museum Shop, **2:** 769
Museums, 2: 1364–1367
Mushrooms, **2:** 39
Music
   copyright law and, **1:** 1057, **2:** 554, 979, 1205–1206
   country, **2:** 1210
   digital, **2:** 554
   Internet access to, **1:** 1046, **2:** 727
   libraries, **2:** 1183
   pop, **2:** 1210–1211
   recorded (*See* Sound Recordings)
   rock and roll, **1:** 1046, 1049
   schools, **2:** 1343, 1344
   sheet, **1:** 415, 418, 419, **2:** 732, 979
   videos, **1:** 1047, **2:** 1177–1178, 1189
Music and Recording Superstores, **2:** 732
Music $More, **1:** 1048
Music Sound Exchange, **1:** 1048
Music Stores, 2: 718–722
Music Teachers National Conference, **1:** 1281
Musical Groups and Artists, **1:** 1046, **2:** 1210–1212
Musical Instrument Digital Interface (MIDI), **1:** 1282
Musical Instrument Stores, 2: 732
Musical Instruments, 1: 1280–1284
   plastic, **1:** 1283

   self-playing, **1:** 1284
   silent, **1:** 1284
   virtual reality technology in, **1:** 1283
   wholesalers of, 2: 574–575
Musicland Group, **2:** 728, 730, 731
Muskie, Edmund, **2:** 1492
Muskrat, **2:** 126
Mussels, **1:** 550, **2:** 81, 122
Mustard Seeds, **2:** 13
Mutton, **2:** 61
Mutual Benefit Associations, **2:** 848
Mutual Funds, **2:** 881–882, 961–967. *See also* Money Market
   Funds
   acquisitions and mergers of, **2:** 883
   assets in, **2:** 872, 881, 883, 884, 957, 962, 963
   balanced, **2:** 962–963
   banks in, **2:** 957
   costs of, **2:** 884
   foreign, **2:** 966–967
   government regulation of, **2:** 963
   growth of, **2:** 962
   history of, **2:** 963–965
   load, **2:** 962
   long-term *vs.* short term, **2:** 965
   non-load, **2:** 962
   open-end, **2:** 961–967, 970
Mutual Mortgage Insurance, **2:** 1506
Mutual Series, **2:** 883
MW Kellog Company, **2:** 270
Myers, Booth, **1:** 1068
Myers, Charles, **1:** 613, 614, **2:** 1340
Myers, John, **1:** 496
Mylar OL, **1:** 592

N

NAACP. *See* National Association for the Advancement of
   Colored People
Nabisco Brands, Inc., **1:** 66, 67–68, 150
Nabisco Group Holdings Corporation, **1:** 68, 143
   in candy, **1:** 78, 79
   in chewing gum, **1:** 84
   in nuts, **1:** 86
NACCO, **2:** 180
Nader, Ralph, **1:** 27, 864, 1120
Nadig, Henry, **1:** 1118
NAFTA. *See* North American Free Trade Agreement
Nail Guns, **1:** 290
Nailed Wood Boxes, 1: 289–291
Nails
   copper, **1:** 716, 734
   development of, **1:** 805
   nonferrous, **1:** 761
   steel, 1: 699–701
NAISE. *See* National Institute for Automotive Service
   Excellence
Naismith, James, **1:** 1291, **2:** 1220
Nance, Chris, **1:** 279
Nanjing Deep Well Company, **1:** 928
Nannies, **2:** 1442, 1443
NAP Inc., **1:** 253
NAPA Auto Parts Group, **2:** 530
Napa Company, **1:** 1302
NAPCORE, **1:** 601
Naphtha Gas, **2:** 498–499
Naphthenate Wood Treatment, **1:** 302

New York City Board of Education, **2:** 996
New York City School Construction Authority, **1:** 300
New York Daily News, **1:** 391
New York Envelope, **1:** 384
New York Futures Exchange, **2:** 985
New York Knicks, **2:** 1223
New York Life Group, **2:** 893
New York Life Insurance and Trust Company, **2:** 887, 889, 890
New York Mercantile Exchange, **2:** 877, 879, 985
New York Public Library, **2:** 1337, 1338
New York Racing Association, **2:** 1225, 1226
New York Rangers, **2:** 1223
New York State Common, **2:** 918
New York State Teachers Fund, **2:** 918
New York Stock Exchange, **2:** 869, 873, 878
  closed-end funds on, **2:** 968
  history of, **2:** 876, 877, 878, 879
  in online trading, **2:** 880
  volume of, **2:** 867
New York Times, **1:** 391, 392
New York Times Company, **1:** 388, 389, 392
New York Tribune, **1:** 389–390
New York Yankees, **2:** 1223
Newark Group, **1:** 354
Newcomb Spring Corporation, **1:** 847
Newcomen, Thomas, **1:** 839
Newell Rubbermaid Inc., **1:** 329, 332, 648, 649, 1298
Newmont Gold, **2:** 150
Newmont Gold Company, **2:** 141
Newmont Mining, **2:** 140
Newmont Mining Corporation, **2:** 150
Newnham, Robert, **1:** 771
Newport Corporation, **1:** 1216
Newport News Shipbuilding, **1:** 1175
News Corporation, **1:** 396, 404, **2:** 468
News Dealers, 2: 790–792
News Syndicates, 2: 1124–1125
Newsletters, **1:** 414, 415, 419
Newspaper Association of America, **1:** 388
Newspaper Preservation Act, **1:** 390
Newspaper Publishing and Printing, 1: 388–393, 420
Newspapers, 1: 388–393, 420
  advertising in, **1:** 388, 389, 390, 392, **2:** 1022, 1028, 1029
  chains of, **1:** 388
  circulation of, **1:** 388, 392, **2:** 1029
  community, **1:** 389
  dailies, **1:** 389, 390
  foreign, **2:** 790
  full-color, **1:** 429
  gatefold, **1:** 389
  history of, **1:** 388, 389–390
  magazine sections, **1:** 425, 426
  national, **1:** 391
  online, **1:** 391, 392, **2:** 1104
  publishing of (*See* Newspaper Publishing and Printing)
  retail dealers of, 2: 790–792
  tabloid, **1:** 389, 390
  vending machines for, **1:** 972
  weeklies, **1:** 389
  wholesalers of, 2: 610–611
Newsprint, **1:** 343, 345, 347, 915
  cost of, **1:** 389
  growth of, **1:** 349
  recycled, **1:** 346, 349
Newsreels, **1:** 390
Newsstands, 2: 790–792

Newton, Isaac, **1:** 1230, 1234
NEXTEA. *See* National Economic Crossroads Transportation
    Efficiency Act
Nextel Communications, **2:** 452
NFC PLC, **2:** 337
NFO Research, **2:** 672
NHK Spring Company Ltd., **1:** 844
Niantic Seal Inc., **1:** 584
Nichols, Jeffrey A., **2:** 140
Nickel
  alloys, **1:** 698, 727
  castings, **1:** 760
  demand for, **1:** 727
  discovery of, **1:** 460
  mining, **2:** 148
  plating, **1:** 819, 821
  price of, **1:** 698, 727, 747
  resistors, **1:** 1083
  silver, **1:** 1277
  superalloys, **1:** 698
Nickel Antimony Titanate, **1:** 455
Nickel-Cadmium Batteries, **1:** 1125
Nickel Solution Trust, **1:** 643–644
Nicor, **2:** 498
Nicotine, **1:** 148, **2:** 19
Nieder, Norm, **1:** 739
Nielsen, Louis, **1:** 607
Nielsen Media Research, **2:** 466. *See also* AC Nielsen
Nielson, James, **1:** 493
Niesmann and Bischoff, **1:** 1142
Nieto, Augie, **2:** 1230
Night Vision Devices, **1:** 1210, 1213, 1214, 1235
Nightwear, 1: 171–172
  children's, 1: 234–239
  history of, **1:** 204
  mens and boys', 1: 203–206
  robes and dressing gowns, 1: 253–254
  women's, 1: 234–239
Nike Inc., **1:** 578, 626, 627, 629, **2:** 584
  history of, **2:** 703
  influence of, **2:** 583
  layoffs by, **2:** 565
  overseas operations of, **1:** 577, **2:** 584
  in sports clothing, **1:** 241
Nike Securities, **2:** 970
Nikon Corporation, **1:** 1268, 1270, **2:** 538
Nine West Accessories Inc., **1:** 634
Nine West Group Inc., **1:** 621–622, 629
Nintendo Company, Ltd., **1:** 1289
Niobium, **2:** 149
Nipco-L-Flex Calendaring System, **1:** 180
Nippon Kaiji Kyokai, **2:** 395
Nippon Thompson Company, Ltd., **1:** 931
NIPSCO Industries, **2:** 521
NiSource Inc., **2:** 501, 521
Nissan Motor Co., Ltd., **1:** 161, 932, 1117, 1119
Nissho Iwai America Corporation, **2:** 534
Nitches, Inc., **2:** 583
Nitrates, in water, **2:** 43, 85–86
Nitric Acid, **1:** 421, 451
Nitrile
  hydrogenated, **1:** 477
  rubber, **1:** 472, 474
Nitrobenzene, **1:** 530
Nitrogen, **1:** 451–454
  alloy, **1:** 727

Occupational Safety and Health Administration *(cont'd)*
  on paints, **1:** 526
  on poultry processing, **2:** 68
  on silica, **2:** 217
Occupational Therapists, **2:** 1261, 1263, 1264
Oce-Van Der Grinten, **1:** 1268
Ocean Beauty Seafoods, **1:** 120
Ocean Chemical Carriers, **2:** 354
Ocean Chemical Transport, **2:** 354
Ocean Design Inc., **1:** 1089
Ocean Liners, **2:** 369–376
Ocean Shipping Consultants, **1:** 1171
Ocean Shipping Reform Act, **2:** 353, 357, 385
Ocean Spray Cranberries, Inc., **1:** 37, 111, 644, **2:** 27
Oceanic Research Ships, **1:** 1177
Oceanic Steam Navigation Company, **2:** 371
Ocher Pigments, **1:** 455
Ochs, Adolph, **1:** 392
OCI Chemical Corporation, **1:** 447, **2:** 224
O'Connell, Lloyd T., **1:** 740
O'Connor, Daniel, **1:** 313, 595
OCR. *See* Optical Character Recognition
October Studio, **2:** 1187
Odometers, **1:** 1125
OEC Medical Systems Inc., **1:** 1249
Oehser, Paul H., **2:** 1366
Oersted, Hans Christian, **1:** 1034
Oexhsner, Marynell, **2:** 115
O.F. Mossberg & Sons, Inc., **1:** 834
Off-Broadway Productions, **2:** 1207–1208
Office Buildings. *See also* Offices
  construction of, **2:** 244, 249, 298
  demolition of, **2:** 297
  elevators for, **1:** 879
  fixtures for, **1:** 326–330, 1038
  glass for, **2:** 295
  growth of, **2:** 246
  modular, **1:** 300
  operation and leasing of, **2:** 930–935
Office Depot, Inc., **1:** 385, **2:** 532, 763
  attempted merger of, **2:** 762
  in catalog sales, **2:** 778
  in furniture sales, **2:** 708
  sales by, **2:** 761, 1044
Office Equipment Wholesalers, 2: 540–542
Office for Civil Rights, **2:** 1482
Office Furniture, 1: 314–323
  ergonomics of, **1:** 315, 318, 321
  exports of, **1:** 322
  for home workers, **1:** 310, 313, 315, 317, 318, 320, 322
  imports of, **1:** 318, 322
  metal, **1:** 310, 315, 319–323
  modular, **1:** 319
  multifunction, **1:** 321
  nonwood, **1:** 319–323
  partitions, **1:** 317, 320, 326–328
  ready-to-assemble, **1:** 316, 317, 318, 320, 321
  reconstituted wood products for, **1:** 304
  sales of, **1:** 314, 317, 319, 320, **2:** 532
  wholesalers of, 2: 531–532
  wood, 1: 314–318
  workforce in, **1:** 317, 321–322
Office Machines
  manufacturing, **1:** 967–971
  repair of, **2:** 1166
Office of Computers and Business Equipment, **2:** 722

Office of Defense Transportation, **2:** 1132
Office of Disease Prevention and Health Promotion, **2:** 1480
Office of Economic Opportunity, **2:** 1363, 1510
Office of Environmental Health Sciences, **2:** 1491
Office of Federal Procurement Policy, **1:** 1208
Office of International Aviation, **2:** 401
Office of Malaria Control, **2:** 1478
Office of Management and Budget, **2:** 1467
Office of Personnel Management, **2:** 1452
Office of Price Administration, **2:** 656
Office of Public Roads, **2:** 252
Office of Road Inquiry, **2:** 252
Office of Solid Waste Management, **1:** 730–731
Office of Surface Mining Reclamation and Enforcement, **2:** 1498
Office of Technology Assessment, **1:** 226, **2:** 1349
Office of the Assistant Secretary for Health, **2:** 1475
Office of the Comptroller of the Currency, **2:** 805, 1508
Office of the Inspector General, **2:** 1501
Office of Thrift Supervision, **2:** 815, 817, 818, 821–822, 1508
Office Storage Equipment, 1: 328–330
Office Supplies
  international commerce in, **2:** 577
  mergers in, **2:** 762
  sales of, **2:** 761
  superstores for, **1:** 314, 385, **2:** 541, 577–578, 761–762, 1048
  wholesalers of, 2: 577–579
OfficeMax, Inc., **1:** 385, **2:** 761, 763, 1048
Officer Candidate School, **2:** 1536
Offices
  clothing for, **1:** 197, 208, 218, 224, 230
  design of, **1:** 319, 320
  fixtures for, **1:** 326–330
Official All-Star Cafe, **2:** 735
Offset Printing, **1:** 409, 420, 442, 443, 552
Offshore Data Services, **1:** 874
Offshore Drilling, **2:** 182, 191, 198. *See also* Crude Oil and
    Natural Gas Extraction; Oil Field Machinery
  history of, **2:** 192
  for natural gas, **2:** 488
Offshore Manufacturing
  of athletic shoes, **1:** 577, **2:** 584
  of automobiles, **1:** 1123
  of automotive parts and trimmings, **1:** 264, 1137
  of cigarettes, **1:** 150
  of clothing, **1:** 231–232
    children's, **1:** 247–248, 250
    leather, **1:** 255
    shirts, **1:** 201
    suits and coats, **1:** 195
    trousers, **1:** 211, 213
    underwear, **1:** 205, 237
    women's and girls', **1:** 222, 228, 229
  of cyclic crudes and intermediates, **1:** 533
  of footwear, **1:** 621, 622–623, 624
  of heating systems, **1:** 784
  of industrial trucks, **1:** 890
  of leather goods, **1:** 614
  of pharmaceuticals, **1:** 497
  of printed material, **1:** 411
  of sporting goods, **1:** 1294
  of synthetic fibers, **1:** 482, 483
  of toys, **1:** 1285, **2:** 767
Ogallala Aqufer, **2:** 509
Ogden Aviation Services, **2:** 415
Ogden Corporation, **2:** 386, 1439
Ogee, Joe, **2:** 377

Philadelphia Stock Exchange, **2:** 878
Philadelphia Suburban Water, **2:** 510
Philanthropy, **2:** 1209, 1366
Philharmonic Society of Orange County, **2:** 1211
Philip Carey Corporation, **1:** 685
Philip Morris & Company Ltd., **1:** 145, 147, 150–151
    in coffee, **1:** 127
    General Foods Corporation and, **1:** 150
    litigation against, **2:** 19
    market share of, **1:** 149
    in meat products, **1:** 8, 9
    merger of, **1:** 65
    periodical advertising by, **1:** 394
    in tobacco processing, **1:** 156
Philip Morris Capital Corporation, **2:** 854
Philips CD-Interactive, **1:** 406
Philips Display Components Company, **1:** 1067
Philips Electronics, **1:** 1044, 1107, 1108
Philips Home Products Corporation, **1:** 1016, 1025
Philips Lighting Company, **1:** 1033, 1039
Philips N.V., **1:** 960, 1049, 1050, 1051
Phillips Chemical Company, **1:** 597
Phillips Fibers Corporation, **1:** 160
Phillips Group-Info Tech, **1:** 1056
Phillips Petroleum Company, **2:** 189, 494
Phillips Van Heusen Corporation, **1:** 202
PHLX. *See* Philadelphia Stock Exchange
Phoenix Iron Works, **1:** 901
Phoenix Suns, **2:** 1223
Phone Companies. *See* Telephone Companies
Phonograph Cabinets, **1:** 311–312
Phonograph Records. *See* Sound Recordings
Phosphate Rock, 2: 225–226, 229
    pipelines for, **2:** 423, 424
    in soaps and detergents, **1:** 505–506, 507, 509, **2:** 1492
Phosphates, in detergents, **2:** 1002, 1492
Phosphatic Fertilizers, 1: 459, 463, 541–542, **2:** 225
Phosphine, **1:** 47
Phosphor Scopes, Digital, **1:** 1129
Phosphorous, **1:** 460
Phosphorus Pollution, **2:** 44
Photo CD Technology, **2:** 768
Photo Finishers Association of America, **2:** 768
Photo Marketing Association International, **2:** 538, 768, 1009, 1126
Photocomposition, **1:** 439, 440, 919
Photocopiers, 1: 1265–1272
    controls for, **1:** 1217
    digital, **1:** 1268, **2:** 540–542
    high quality, **1:** 423
    high speed, **2:** 1048
    wholesalers of, 2: 540–542
Photocopying and Duplicating Services, 2: 1046–1051
Photoengraving Equipment, **1:** 916
Photofinishing Laboratories, 2: 1125–1128
Photoflash and Photoflood Lamps, **1:** 1030
Photogrammetry, **2:** 1412–1415
Photographers
    commercial, **2:** 1051
    passport, **2:** 1008
    school, **2:** 1008, 1009
    sports, **2:** 1009
    video, **2:** 1008
    wedding, **2:** 1009
Photographic Equipment and Supplies, 1: 1265–1272. *See also* Photographic Film

exports of, **1:** 1271, 1272, **2:** 537
history of, **1:** 1266–1270
imports of, **1:** 1271–1272
retail stores for, 2: 768–769, 1125, 1127
sales of, **1:** 1265, 1269
wholesalers, 2: 537–539
Photographic Film, 1: 1265–1272
    advanced photo system (APS), **2:** 538
    developing and printing, **2:** 1125–1128
    digital, **1:** 1268
    disc, **2:** 1127
    joint ventures in, **1:** 1268
    microlabs for, **2:** 1127–1128
    minilabs for, **2:** 1125, 1126, 1127
    retail stores for, 2: 768–769
    sales of, **2:** 1126, 1127
    silver-bromide, **1:** 460
    silver-free, **2:** 144–145
    silver-halide, **1:** 1269, **2:** 144–145
Photographic Studios, Portrait, 2: 1008–1009
Photographs, CD-ROM Storage of, **2:** 1052
Photography
    history of, **2:** 1008–1009
    medical, **2:** 1311
Photolithography, **1:** 420
Photophone System, **2:** 1175
Phototypesetting, **1:** 439, 440–441
PhotoWorks, **2:** 1127
PhyAmerica Physician Group Inc., **2:** 1242–1243
PhyCor Inc., **2:** 1242–1243
Phylloxera, **1:** 98, **2:** 30
Physical Fitness Equipment. *See* Exercise Equipment
Physical Fitness Facilities, 2: 566, 1227–1231
Physical Research, 2: 1419–1420
Physical Sciences Research, **2:** 1419–1420
Physical Therapists, **2:** 1262, 1264
Physician Assistants, **2:** 1243, 1287–1288
Physician-Hospital Associations, **2:** 1238–1239
Physician Practice Management, **2:** 1242–1243
Physician Sales and Service, **1:** 1250
Physicians. *See also* Health Care; Medicine
    advertising by, **2:** 792, 1240
    hospital-based, **2:** 1288
    naturopathic, **2:** 1260–1261
    number of, **2:** 1238
    offices of, 2: 1237–1244
    osteopathic, 2: 1249–1250
    primary care, **2:** 1239
    for rural areas, **2:** 1242, 1250
    salaries of, **2:** 1239, 1244, 1288
    self-referrals by, **2:** 1241, 1296, 1312
    surplus of, **2:** 1244
Physiologic Monitoring Equipment, **1:** 1237
Pi Sheng, **1:** 438
Pianos, **1:** 773, 1280–1284
    acoustic/digital, **1:** 1283
    console, **1:** 1282
    player, **1:** 1281–1282
    upright, **1:** 1281
Picker International Inc., **1:** 1259
Pickle, Kirby, **2:** 458
Pickle Packers International, Inc., **1:** 39
Pickled Fish, **1:** 120
Pickled Fruits and Vegetables, 1: 39
Pickwick Transportation Lines, **2:** 317
Picture Frames, **1:** 281, 305

Q

R

Recycled Products (cont'd)
  in furniture, **1:** 306
  lead, **1:** 728, 731, 732, 733
  linerboard, **1:** 357
  in metal sanitary ware, **1:** 775
  newsprint, **1:** 346
  paper, **1:** 346–347, 349, 368, 373, 386, **434, 2: 579**
  paperboard, **1:** 351, 352, 356–357, 360, **363, 364**
  plastic, **1:** 592, 595, 596, 598, 604, 610, **611**
  plastic bottles, **1:** 600, 601
  polyurethane, **1:** 604
  precious metals, **1:** 728
  in road construction, **1:** 566, **2:** 257
  sanitary paper products, **1:** 376, 379
  silver, **2:** 143
  textiles, **1:** 194
  zinc, **1:** 728, 731, 733
Recycling
  asphalt products, **1:** 566, 568
  automobiles, **1:** 738, 1125
  books, **1:** 407
  carpets and rugs, **1:** 484
  copper, **1:** 719
  corrugated boxes, **1:** 356–357, 360
  crowns and closures, **1:** 817
  glass, **1:** 645, 646, 647
  greeting cards, **1:** 434
  history of, **1:** 345, 730, **2:** 516, 517
  household appliances, **1:** 1013, 1017, **1028**
  nonferrous metals, **1:** 727–733
  nylon, **1:** 484
  packaging materials, **1:** 366, 941
  pallets, **1:** 292
  paper, **1:** 338–339, 345, 346–347, 350, **361–362, 368**
  paperboard, **1:** 354, 363, 364
  pencils, **1:** 1299
  plastic containers, **1:** 517
  polyester, **1:** 484
  profit margins in, **2:** 517
  refrigerators and freezers, **1:** 1013, 1017
  sand, **2:** 218
  sewage sludge, **2:** 1496
  soap and detergent packaging, **1:** 507
  soft drink containers, **1:** 112
  solid waste, **2:** 516
  in solid waste management, **2:** 518
  steel, **1:** 701
  surgical and medical instruments, **1:** 1238
  thermoplastics, **1:** 477
  thermosetting plastics, **1:** 477
  tires, **1:** 475, 477, 573, 576
  washers and dryers, **1:** 1020
  waste from, **1:** 339, 346
  wholesalers, 2: 569–570
Red Cedar
  log homes, **1:** 300
  shingles and shakes, **1:** 277
Red Cross, **2:** 1311, 1347
Red Kap Industries, **1:** 215
Red Lobster Restaurants, **2:** 736
Red Snapper, **2:** 122
Red Star Yeast, **1:** 143
Red Tide, **2:** 123
Red Wing Shoe Company, **1:** 629
Redenbacher, Orville, **1:** 130
Redford, Robert, **2:** 1188

Redhook Ale Brewery, **1:** 92
Rediffusion Company, **1:** 1114
Redland PLC, **2:** 214
Redland Stone Products Company, **2:** 209
Redman Industries, **1:** 298
Redmanol Company, **1:** 595
Reebok International Ltd.
  athletic shoes, **1:** 626, 629
  children's shoes, **1:** 627
  in clothing, **1:** 218
  influence of, **2:** 583
  layoffs by, **2:** 565
  men's shoes, **1:** 619
  overseas operations of, **2:** 584
  shoe sales by, **1:** 578, **2:** 584
  women's shoes, **1:** 621
Reed, Bruce, **2:** 1505
Reed, Jacob, **1:** 210
Reed Elsevier PLC, **1:** 397, 404, **2:** 1102
Reed International P.L.C., **1:** 397
Reed Tool Company, **1:** 874
Reeds, **1:** 304, 312–314
Reel.Com, **2:** 1203
Reemay Inc., **1:** 193
Reengineering Consultants, **2:** 1427, 1429
Reentry Vehicles, **1:** 1192
Rees, Clifford, Jr., **1:** 983
Reese's Peanut Butter Cups, **1:** 77, 78
Reeves Brothers Inc., **1:** 190
Reeves Soundcraft, **1:** 1106, 1107
Reference Books, **1:** 406, 414–415
Refineries. *See* Petroleum Refining
Reflectometers, **1:** 1226
Reforestation, **2:** 108, 110–111, 113, 116
  aerial seeding in, **2:** 117
  for carbon dioxide emissions, **2:** 117
  for global warming, **2:** 117
  management of, **2:** 112
  pulp mills and, **1:** 339
Reform Act, **2:** 113
Refractories, Nonclay, 1: 688
Refractory Materials, 2: 220–223
  alumina-fused, **1:** 688
  bauxite, **1:** 688
  brick, **1:** 657, 688, **2:** 216
  carbon, **1:** 688–689
  cement, **1:** 657, 688
  clay, 1: 657–658
  extruded, **1:** 657
  fusion casting, **1:** 658
  graphite, **1:** 688
  hydrostatic pressing, **1:** 658
  minerals, **1:** 685, **2:** 220–223
  monolithic, **1:** 688–689
  nonclay, **1:** 658, 688
  nonfiring, **1:** 688–689
  plastics in, **1:** 658
  sand for, **2:** 216
  silica, **1:** 658, 688–689
  slip casting, **1:** 658
  for the steel industry, **1:** 657, 658
  tiles, **1:** 657
Refrigerants, **2:** 558, 559. *See also* Chlorofluorocarbons
  alternative, **1:** 982, 983
  development of, **1:** 977
  hydrofluorocarbons as, **2:** 672, 1018

Scanners *(cont'd)*
  demand for, **1:** 1233
  equipment-ballet, **1:** 1255
  for explosives, **1:** 1254
  in grocery stores, **2:** 649, 650
  handheld, **1:** 965
  for printing, **1:** 429
  for railroad equipment, **1:** 1185
  in sawmills, **1:** 275
  in typesetting, **1:** 441
Scarves, **1:** 206–209
Scenic Tours, **2:** 381–382
Schaffer EMC, **1:** 1087
Schawlow, Arthur L., **1:** 1113
Scheele, Carl Wilhelm, **1:** 446, 453
Scheid, Alfred G., **2:** 29
Scheid Vineyards Inc., **2:** 29
Scheinfeld, Aaron, **2:** 1073
Scheuer, James, **2:** 1495
Schiaparelli, Elsa, **1:** 1301
Schick Technologies, **1:** 1249
Schiffenhaus Industries Inc., **1:** 356
Schiffli Machine Embroideries, 1: 264–265
Schiffrin, Andre, **1:** 402
Schindel, Joan, **2:** 751
Schindler Elevator Corporation, **1:** 879
Schiner, Johann, **1:** 416
Schloemer, Gottfied, **1:** 1118
Schlumberger, Conrad, **2:** 203
Schlumberger, Marcel, **2:** 203
Schlumberger Electronic Transactions, **2:** 201
Schlumberger Inc., **1:** 873, 875, 997
Schlumberger Integrated Project Management, **2:** 200
Schlumberger Limited, **1:** 570, 1125, **2:** 193, 200, 201, 203
Schluter, Ed, **2:** 389
Schneider, Richard, **1:** 842
Schneider Automation Inc., **1:** 1222
Schneider National Inc., **2:** 324, 327, 329
Schoen, Armund, **2:** 1138
Schoen, L.S., **2:** 1131, 1140–1141
Schoenhaus, Ted, **1:** 1288, **2:** 568
Schoffer, Peter, **1:** 408
Scholarships, **2:** 1469
School Buses, 1: 1130, 1131, **2:** 319, 321–323
School Districts, **2:** 1319, 1323
School Libraries, **2:** 1335, 1336
School Supplies and Equipment, **1:** 385, **2:** 577
  furniture, **1:** 310, 323
School Supplies and Equipment
  wholesalers of, 2: 547
Schools, 2: 1343. *See also* Education; Universities and Colleges
  alternative, **2:** 1319
  architectural services for, **2:** 1405
  attendance at, **2:** 1318
  for beauticians, **2:** 1010
  books for, **1:** 401, 405
  business and secretarial, **2:** 1340–1341
  charter, **2:** 1322, 1323–1324
  choice of, **2:** 1324
  construction of, **2:** 250
  dance, 2: 1204–1206
  data processing, 2: 1339–1340
  drama, **2:** 1343, 1344
  drug abuse in, **2:** 1321
  elementary, 2: 1318–1325
  for-profit, **2:** 1323

  funding for, **1:** 403
  for handicapped students, **2:** 1318, 1319, 1321
  history of, **2:** 1319–1321, 1333–1334
  home, **2:** 1324
  integration of, **2:** 1320
  Internet access for, **2:** 1323
  land grant, **2:** 5, 1471
  language, **2:** 1343, 1344
  magnet, **2:** 1324
  military, **2:** 1533–1534
  music, **2:** 1343, 1344
  for native Americans, **2:** 1470, 1501
  official drinks of, **2:** 1323
  performance tests and, **2:** 1473
  photographers for, **2:** 1008, 1009
  prefabricated, **1:** 299, 300
  preparatory, **2:** 1343–1344
  private, **2:** 1470
  professional, **2:** 1325–1332
  public, **2:** 1319
  religious, **2:** 1318, 1319
  secondary, 2: 1318–1325
  segregation in, **2:** 1472
  trade, **2:** 1328
  violence in, **1:** 830, **2:** 1321, 1324
  vouchers for, **2:** 1470, 1473
  workforce in, **2:** 1324–1325
  yearbooks for, **1:** 418
Schooners, Great Lakes, **2:** 360
Schottenstein Bernstein Capital Group, **2:** 794
Schramyr, Ernest, **1:** 202
Schuff Steel Company, **2:** 294
Schulman, Milt, **2:** 767
Schultz, August, **1:** 613
Schulze-Delitzsche, Hermann, **2:** 825
Schumann, Patrick, **1:** 50
Schuster, M. Lincoln, **1:** 405
Schutx, Susan Polis, **1:** 436
Schutz, Stephen, **1:** 436
Schuylkill Navigation Company, **2:** 175
Schwab, Charles, **1:** 692
Schwab Investments, **2:** 885
Schwabe, Louise, **1:** 481
Schwarzkopf, Norman, **2:** 1536
Schwinn Cycling and Fitness, **1:** 1181, 1183, 1187, **2:** 565, 754
SCI Systems Inc., **1:** 1094
Science
  education, **2:** 1322, 1325
  research, **2:** 1419–1420
Science Applications International Corporation, **2:** 1420
Scientists, **2:** 1444
Scissors, **1:** 767, 770
  electric, **1:** 1022
SCM Corporation, **1:** 525
Scoria, **2:** 210
Scotchgard, **1:** 200, 207
Scott, Debbie, **1:** 50
Scott Fetzer Company, **1:** 770
Scott Mills Inc., **1:** 175
Scott Paper Company, **1:** 346, 377, 378, 380
Scott USA, **1:** 1181
Scotts Company, **1:** 540, 545, **2:** 38
Scoular Company, **2:** 597
Scovill Fasteners, Inc., **1:** 1303
SCP Pool Corporation, **2:** 566

INDEX

Stationers Distributing, **2:** 578
Stationery, 1: 384–385, 915
  retail stores, 2: 761–764
  wholesalers, 2: 577–579
Statistical Process Control, **1:** 813, 902, 942
Statler, E.M., **2:** 989
Staves, **1:** 292
Stealth Technology, **1:** 1149, 1211, **2:** 1537
Steam and Air Conditioning Supply, 2: 521–522
Steam Condensers, **1:** 793
Steam Heating Systems, **1:** 781–782
Steam Power
  boilers for, **1:** 789
  coal for, **2:** 163, 302
  for ferries, **2:** 378, 382
  history of, **1:** 790–792, **2:** 1397
  locomotives, **2:** 301
  for pumps, **1:** 926
  for sawmills, **1:** 273
  for ships, **1:** 1172
  turbines, **2:** 482
Steam Turbines, 1: 855–857, **2:** 482
Steamers
  high-temperature pressure, **1:** 178
  roller, **1:** 178
Steel, 1: 690–697, 699–705
  alloys, **1:** 691, 696, 697–699, 712, 809, 813, **2:** 152
  vs. aluminum, **1:** 722, 739
  aluminum hybrids, **1:** 801
  bars, **1:** 702
  bridges, **2:** 294
  cable, **1:** 700
  cans, **1:** 35, 763–766
  carbon, **1:** 691
  vs. cast iron, **1:** 708
  chairs, **1:** 310
  closures, **1:** 816
  coatings, **1:** 696
  cold finishing of, 1: 701–704
  in concrete products, **1:** 671
  crucible, **1:** 768
  cryogenic treatment of, **1:** 903
  for cutlery, **1:** 768
  demand for, **1:** 694
  doors, **1:** 278, 279
  dumping, **1:** 693, 694, 700, 705
  electrogalvanized, **1:** 819
  enameled sanitary ware, **1:** 774
  exports of, **1:** 696
  fasteners, **1:** 805
  ferroalloys in, **2:** 146
  flooring, **1:** 797
  foundries, 1: 712–716
  high-strength low alloy, **1:** 691
  in housing, **1:** 269
  I-beams, **1:** 288
  imports of, **1:** 693, 694, 696, 700, 800, **2:** 128–129
    cold-rolled, **1:** 702, 704
    stainless, **1:** 700
    wire, **1:** 700–701
  iron ores for, **2:** 127–129
  manufacturing techniques
    basic oxygen furnaces, **1:** 691, 693
    Bessemer process, **1:** 692
    continuous casting, **1:** 691, 693
    direct-process, **1:** 695

    electric arc, **1:** 691, 693, 696
    electromagnetic braking, **1:** 696
    investment castings, **1:** 712–715
    Siemens-Martin open-hearth, **1:** 692, 693
    thin-slab casting, **1:** 695, 696
  nails and spikes, 1: 699–701
  office furniture, **1:** 315, 319
  online shopping for, **1:** 696, 760–761
  pens, **1:** 1296
  pipelines, **2:** 418
  pipes and tubes, 1: 598, 704–705
  prefabricated buildings, **1:** 799
  price fixing of, **1:** 699, 843–844
  prices of, **1:** 694, 703
  production of, **1:** 690
  in recreational vehicles, **1:** 1142
  recycling, **1:** 701
  refractory materials, **1:** 657, 658
  sales of, **1:** 690, 695, 703, 705, 712
  scrap, **1:** 690, **2:** 570
  seamless tubular, **1:** 310
  service centers for, **2:** 547–549
  sheets, **1:** 702, 703
  springs, 1: 843–844
  stainless (*See* Stainless Steel)
  steel, **1:** 712–715
  strips, **1:** 702
  structural, **1:** 785–787, **2:** 293–294
  substitutes for, **1:** 693, 694, 704
  tire cords, **1:** 190
  tool, **1:** 691
  wire, **1:** 573, 699, 700–701, 849
  wood replacements, **1:** 274
Steel Dynamics Inc., **1:** 696, 760, 786
Steel Forgings, 1: 808–810
Steel Industry
  acquisitions and mergers in, **1:** 695
  antitrust law and, **1:** 699
  coal for, **2:** 163, 164, 168, 170
  corporate restructuring in, **1:** 693, 694
  downsizing in, **1:** 715
  history of, **1:** 692–694, 702–703, 943–944
  information technology in, **1:** 696
  integrated manufacturers in, **1:** 691, 694
  joint ventures in, **1:** 695
  labor unions in, **1:** 691, 692, 800
  minimills in, **1:** 691–692, 693, 694, 695, **2:** 129
  pollution from, **1:** 694, **2:** 1493
  price fixing in, **1:** 699, 703
  workforce in, **1:** 696, 699, 700, 715
    cast products, **1:** 714
    cold-rolled products, **1:** 703
    pipes, **1:** 705
    wire products, **1:** 701
Steel Investment Foundries, 1: 712–715
Steel of West Virginia, **1:** 692
Steel Service Center Institute, **2:** 548
Steel Tubular Products Company, **1:** 705
Steel Works, 1: 690–697
Steelcase Inc.
  consulting by, **1:** 321
  distribution system, **1:** 320
  in metal furniture, **1:** 310
  in nonwood furniture, **1:** 319, 321
  unionization of, **1:** 322
  in wood furniture, **1:** 314, 316, 317

Strikes *(cont'd)*
  airline, **2:** 399, 401
  automobile industry, **1:** 894
  baseball, **2:** 1217
  bus line, **2:** 317
  coal mine, **2:** 175–176
  construction machinery plant, **1:** 867–868
  firearms manufacturing, **1:** 833
  football, **2:** 1219
  grocery store, **2:** 649
  meat packing plant, **1:** 5
  mine, **1:** 735, **2:** 135
  paper industry, **1:** 349
  pharmaceutical industry, **1:** 497
  railroad, **2:** 302
  replacement workers and, **2:** 1383
  steel industry, **1:** 800
  tire manufacturing, **1:** 575
String Instruments, **1:** 1280–1284
String Trimmers, **1:** 864, 865
Strip Flooring, **1:** 276
Strip Malls. *See* Shopping Malls
Strip Mining, **2:** 161, 162, 164, 174, 214, 230
Stroh Brewery Company, **1:** 92, 93
Strontium, **1:** 460
  mining, **2:** 227, 228
Structural
  clay, 1: 653–655, 659
  lumber members, 1: 287–289
  metal, 1: 785–787, 800–801, 907
Structural Board Association, **1:** 288, 289
Structural Panels, **1:** 287, **2:** 286
Structural Steel Erection, 2: 293–294
Stuart Medical, **2:** 545
Studebaker, **1:** 1118
Student Loan Marketing Association, **2:** 844
Student Loans, **2:** 844, 1033, 1344, 1472, 1473
Students
  college and university, **2:** 1330
  foreign, **2:** 1331–1332
  gifted, **2:** 1324
  handicapped, **2:** 1318, 1319, 1321
  minority, **2:** 1322, 1326
Stuffed Toys, 1: 1284–1285
Sturn, Ruger & Company, **1:** 830
Styrene
  demand for, **1:** 529, 531
  production of, **1:** 530
  rubber pipe, **1:** 598
Styrene-Butadiene, **1:** 466
  rubber, **1:** 472, 473, 474
Styrene Copolymer, **1:** 593
Sub-Presses, **1:** 898
Sub Zero Freezer Company, **1:** 1016
Submachine Guns. *See* Small Arms
Submarines, Nuclear Powered, **1:** 1175
Submerged Lands Act, **2:** 182
Subscriptions
  online, **1:** 406
  periodical, **1:** 393–394, 398
Subsidies. *See also* Government Funding
  airplane, **1:** 1150
  bus, **2:** 318
  corn, **2:** 8–9
  cotton, **2:** 16
  farm, **1:** 861, **2:** 42, 43

  housing, **2:** 1504
  merchant marine, **2:** 352
  milk, **2:** 63, 64
  railroad, **1:** 1182
  rent, **2:** 1504
  ship building, **1:** 1169, 1170, 1172–1173, 1174
  sugar, **1:** 71, 72, 74, 75, **2:** 21–22
  vegetable oil, **1:** 88
  wheat, **2:** 2
  wool, **2:** 62
Subsistence Homestead Division, **2:** 1510
Substance Abuse and Mental Health Services Administration, **2:** 1475
Substance Abuse Programs
  hospital-based, **2:** 1288–1292, 1292–1296
  outpatient, **2:** 1308–1310
  residential, **2:** 1359
Subtitle Services, **2:** 1183
Suburban Areas
  development of, **2:** 237, 1509
  housing for, **2:** 1503
  landscape services for, **2:** 104
  manufactured homes in, **1:** 294
  transit in, **2:** 308–312
  trucks and, **1:** 1129
Suburban Propane Partners, L.P., **2:** 785
Subway Restaurants, **2:** 672
Subways, **2:** 267, 310, 311
Sud Aviation Caravell, **1:** 1148
Suede
  Nubuck, **1:** 256
  rainwear, **1:** 254
Suez Lyonnaise Des Eaux, **2:** 266
Sugar, **1:** 70–75, **2:** 21–22, 89. *See also* Cane Sugar
  acquisitions and mergers in, **1:** 74
  beet, **1:** 74, 75–76, **2:** 21–22
  brown, **1:** 74
  for candy, **1:** 74
  consumption of, **2:** 22
  corn, **1:** 54
  government regulation of, **1:** 71, 72
  granulated, **1:** 70, 75
  harvesters, **2:** 21
  history of, **1:** 70, 71, 75, **2:** 21
  imports of, **1:** 71, 72, 74, **2:** 22
  invert, **1:** 75
  prices of, **1:** 72, 74, **2:** 21, 22
  raw, **1:** 70
  subsidies, **1:** 71, 72, 74, 75, **2:** 21–22
  syrup, **1:** 70, 74, 75
  trade barriers on, **1:** 72, 74
  workforce in, **1:** 73, 74, 75
  yield of, **2:** 21
Sugar Act, **1:** 70
Sugar Beets, 1: 74, 75–76, **2:** 21–22, 89
Sugar Cane Growers Cooperative, **1:** 71
Sugar Refineries, **1:** 793
Sugarcane, 2: 21–22, 89
Suitcases. *See* Luggage
Suits
  imports of, **1:** 195, 197, 198
  leisure, **1:** 197
  men's and boys', 1: 195–198, **2:** 682
  ready-to-wear, **1:** 196
  sack, **1:** 196
  sales of, **1:** 230, **2:** 682

INDEX

Surface Transportation Board, **2:** 303, 317, 353, 357
Surface Transportation Board Reauthorization Act, **2:** 308
Surfactants, **1:** 513–514
  anionic, **1:** 511
  cationic, **1:** 511
  in fabric softeners, **1:** 511
  in soaps and detergents, **1:** 504, 505, 513
Surge Protectors, **1:** 1008
Surgeon General
  on chewing tobacco, **1:** 153
  on cigarettes, **1:** 147
  on health insurance, **2:** 1291
  on health promotion, **2:** 1480
  history of, **2:** 1475, 1476, 1479
  on pollution, **2:** 1491
Surgery
  history of, **2:** 1012
  lasers for, **1:** 1263, 1264, **2:** 793
  outpatient, **2:** 1244
  plastic, **2:** 1240
  veterinary, **2:** 92–93
Surgical and Medical Instruments, 1: 1237–1241
  acquisitions and mergers in, **1:** 1244, 1247, 1253
  disposable, **1:** 1238
  electromedical, **1:** 1256–1259
  exports of, **1:** 1239, 1241, 1243, 1246
  gloves, **1:** 588–589
  history of, **1:** 1238–1239
  minimally invasive, **1:** 1239–1240
  orthopedic, **1:** 1242–1246
  recycling, **1:** 1238
  rental and leasing of, **2:** 1059–1060
  sales of, **1:** 1238–1239
  testing laboratories for, **2:** 1423
  wholesalers, **2:** 544–546
  workforce in, **1:** 1237–1238, 1240
Surgical Appliances and Supplies, 1: 1242–1246
Surveillance. *See* Electronic Surveillance
Survey Ordinance, **2:** 1471
Surveying Instruments, **1:** 872, 1235
Surveying Services, 2: 201, 1412–1415
Suspenders, **1:** 257
Susquehanna Broadcasting, **1:** 663
Sustainable Cocoa Program, **1:** 81
Sustainable Development Challenge Grant Program, **2:** 103
Sustainable Development Grants, **2:** 103
Sustendal, Diane, **1:** 631
Sutter Home, **1:** 100
Suzuki Motor Corporation, **1:** 1206
Svedala Industries Inc., **1:** 871
Sverdrup Corporation, **2:** 1409
Svoboda, John, **1:** 713
Swampland Act, **2:** 41
Swan, Joseph Wison, **1:** 478, 1031
Swan Cleaners Inc., **2:** 1005
Swank Inc., **1:** 256
Swarovski Jewelry U.S. Lt., **1:** 1302
Swartz, Herman, **1:** 618
Swartz, Nathan, **1:** 618
Swatch USA, **1:** 1273, 1274
Swathers, **1:** 861
Sweat Shop Labor
  in athletic shoes, **1:** 577
  in clothing industry, **1:** 225, 229, 250
  in toys manufacturing, **2:** 767
Sweatsuits, **1:** 248

Swedish Match, **1:** 153
Sweet, Melinda, **1:** 507
Sweet Factory, Inc., **2:** 652
Sweet Potatoes, **2:** 24
Sweetening Agents. *See also* Sugar
  artificial (*See* Artificial Sweeteners)
  average cost of, **1:** 72
  for beverages, **1:** 72
  corn based, **1:** 54, 55
  in ice cream, **1:** 22
  for soft drinks, **1:** 74
Swell-Wear Inc., **1:** 255
Swift, T. Kevin, **2:** 604
Swift-Eckrich, **1:** 9
Swift Energy Annual Report, **2:** 195
Swimming Pools, **1:** 945, **2:** 298, 1236
Swimwear, **1:** 218, 248
Swine Flu, **2:** 1480
Swirburl, Leon, **1:** 1146
Swisher International Group Inc., **1:** 152, 153
Swiss Army Brands, Inc., **2:** 573
Swiss Army Knives, **1:** 770
Swiss Bank, **2:** 883
Switched Multimegabit Data Service, **2:** 458
Switches, **1:** 1034, 1035
  electronic, **1:** 1091–1092
  exports of, **1:** 996
  industrial, **1:** 1006
  optical element, **1:** 1234
  power, **1:** 995
  railroad (*See* Railroad Switching and Terminal Establishments)
  solid state pressure, **1:** 842
  sulfur hexafluoride gas in, **1:** 997
Switchgear and Switchboard Apparatus, 1: 995–997
  central office, **1:** 1054
  electronic, **1:** 997
  telephone, **1:** 995, 996
  wholesalers of, **2:** 550
Sybron Corporation, **1:** 1249
Sylvan Learning Systems, **2:** 1339, 1343, 1344
Sylvanite, **2:** 138
Symix Systems Inc., **2:** 1111
Symonds, William C., **1:** 833
Symons Corporation, **1:** 796
Symphony Orchestras, **2:** 1211
Synchrotron Radiation, **1:** 1254
Synthesizers, **1:** 1282
Synthetic Fibers, **1:** 479–485
  in brooms and brushes, **1:** 1304
  in clothing, **1:** 480
  for the defense industry, **1:** 481
  exports of, **1:** 482, 483
  in floor coverings, **1:** 480
  history of, **1:** 481–482
  in home furnishings, **1:** 480
  imports of, **1:** 482, 483
  machinery for, **1:** 913
  microfibers, **1:** 484
  vs. natural fibers, **1:** 480
  offshore manufacturing of, **1:** 482, 483
  organic chemicals for, **1:** 530
  in space technology, **1:** 481
  in textiles, **1:** 200, 204
  wages in, **1:** 484
Synthetic Rubber, 1: 471–478, 587

Tariffs *(cont'd)*
  on ships, **1:** 1172
  on steel, **1:** 704
  on sugar, **1:** 72
  on televisions, **1:** 1043
  on textiles, **1:** 158, 162, 176
  on uranium, **2:** 155
  on wine, **1:** 102
Tarmac American Inc., **1:** 671
Tarpaulins, **1:** 261
Tarrant, Stephen, **2:** 389
Tate and Lyle North American Sugars, **1:** 70, 71
Tattoo Removal, **1:** 1258
Taverns. *See* Bars (Drinking Establishments)
Tax Credits, for Horses, **2:** 77
Tax Deductions, for Restaurant Meals, **2:** 741
Tax Equity and Fiscal Responsibility Act, **2:** 870
Tax Reform Act
  on construction, **2:** 244, 265, 1406
  on insurance, **2:** 888
  on investment taxes, **2:** 1110
  on marinas, **2:** 393
  on pension funds, **2:** 916
  on real estate, **2:** 948
  on REITs, **2:** 982
  on rentals, **2:** 1061–1062, 1065
  on trusts, **2:** 972, 975
Tax Return Preparation Services, 2: 1017–1019
Taxes
  administration of, 2: 1466–1469
  on alcoholic beverages, **1:** 107
  capital gains, **2:** 617
  on catalog sales, **2:** 777
  on cigarettes, **1:** 145, 147, 148, 149, **2:** 19
  on cigars, **1:** 152
  corporate, **2:** 1469
  on gasoline, **2:** 254
  generation-skipping transfer, **2:** 972–973
  income, **2:** 1469
  on Internet sales, **2:** 749
  on life insurance, **2:** 888
  revenue from, **2:** 1469
Taxi and Limousine Commission, **2:** 315
Taxicabs, 2: 314–316
Taxpayer Relief Act, **2:** 303, 976
Taylor, Frank W., **2:** 1430
Taylor, Frederick W., **2:** 1440
Taylor, Stephanie, **2:** 1457
Taylor, Zachary, **1:** 832
Taylor Grazing Act, **2:** 1499
Taylor Publishing Company, **1:** 418
TBC Corporation, **2:** 530
TCI. *See* Telecommunications Inc.
TDI Worldwide, **2:** 1026
TDK Corporation, **1:** 1109–1110
TDR International, **2:** 148
Tea, 1: 141, 142
  decaffeinated, **1:** 141
  green, **1:** 141
  herbal, **1:** 141
  iced, **1:** 111, 141
  instant, **1:** 141
  juice mixes, **1:** 141
  retail stores for, 2: 653
TEA-21. *See* Transportation Equity Act
Teaberries, **2:** 109

Teachers Insurance Annuity Association, **2:** 890
Teaching Machines, Electronic, **1:** 1111, 1113
Teal Group, **1:** 1143
Teamsters Union. *See* International Brotherhood of Teamsters
Tech Data Corporation, **2:** 543
Technical and Miscellaneous Revenue Act, **2:** 888, 982
Technical Association of the Pulp and Paper Industry, **1:** 345
Technical Institutes, 2: 1332–1335
Technical Manuals, Publishing, **1:** 419
Technical Writers, **2:** 1444
Technicar Inc., **2:** 1163
Technicolor Entertainment Services, **2:** 1188
Technomic Inc., **1:** 40
TechnoTrim Inc., **1:** 265
Techtronic, Inc., **1:** 43
Teck and Joinville Neckwear, **1:** 206
Tectrix, **2:** 565
Teddy Bears, **1:** 1284–1285
Teenform, **1:** 236
Teeth, Artificial, **1:** 1247, **2:** 1300
Teflon, **1:** 581, 934
Tejada, Carlos, **1:** 293
Tektronix Incorporated, **1:** 1067, 1128, 1129
TELAS/NFM, **1:** 1235
Tele-Communications Inc., **2:** 472, 1044, 1519
Telecommunications Act
  on directories, **1:** 417
  on media representation, **2:** 1028
  on radio broadcasting, **2:** 460, 462
  on telephone service, **2:** 454, 456
  on television, **2:** 469, 471
  on wireless communications, **2:** 449
Telecommunications Competition and Deregulation Act, **1:** 1062
Telecommunications Equipment, **1:** 1052–1058
  bearings for, **1:** 930
  copper for, **1:** 716
  fieldbus, **1:** 1224
  history of, **1:** 1053–1056, 1061
  international commerce in, **1:** 1057–1058
  online information services and, **2:** 1104–1105
  in public transportation, **2:** 312
  real-time, **1:** 1211
  sales of, **1:** 1052
  test equipment for, **1:** 1126
  wireless (*See* Wireless Communication Systems)
Telecommunications Inc., **2:** 457, 471, 472, 473
Telecommunications Industry
  acquisitions and mergers in, **2:** 448, 452, 454, 457, 1519
  campaign contributions by, **2:** 1392
  government administration of, **2:** 1516–1520
  international commerce in, **2:** 452–453
  joint ventures in, **2:** 457
  newspaper companies in, **1:** 388
  pipeline companies and, **2:** 503, 504
  revenues from, **2:** 454
  trade agreements in, **2:** 1541
Telecommunications Infrastructure, **2:** 277, 278, 448, 454
Telecommunications Reform Act, **2:** 448, 454, 1519
Teledesic Corporation, **1:** 1167, 1193, **2:** 451, 479
Teledyne Inc., **1:** 811, 1164
Telefacsimile. *See* Fax Transmission
Teleflex Inc., **1:** 856
Teleglobe Companies, **2:** 455, 458
Telegraph, 2: 459–460
  apparatus, 1: 1052–1058
  history of, **2:** 455, 459, 1398

3M Corporation *(cont'd)*
  in coated & laminated paper, **1:** 368, 432
  in microfilm, **1:** 1267
  in packaging machinery, **1:** 941
  in photocopiers, **1:** 1266
  Save-A-Tooth program, **1:** 1249
  in silicone implants, **1:** 1244
  in textiles, **1:** 200
Thrift Drug, **2:** 743
Thrift Institutions, **2:** 814–820, 859
  acquisitions and mergers of, **2:** 823
  assets of, **2:** 814, 820
  charter conversions by, **2:** 823
  classification of, **2:** 815
  deregulation of, **2:** 816, 822
  failure of, **2:** 816–817
  government regulation of, **2:** 815–816, 821–822
  loans by, **2:** 817–818
Thrifty Rent-A-Car, **2:** 1134
Thyrogen, **1:** 502
Thyroid Cancer, **1:** 502
Thyroid Diseases, **1:** 499
Thyssen Inc., **2:** 548
Thyssen Krupp AG, **1:** 814, 852, 894
Tibbet & Britten, **2:** 343
TIC United Corporation, **1:** 759
Ticket Sales
  automated distribution machines for, **2:** 425
  online shopping for, **2:** 431
  reservation systems for, **2:** 431
  satellite printers for, **2:** 427–428, 431
Tide and Current Systems, **1:** 1215
Tidewater, Inc., **2:** 390
Tidewater Construction, **2:** 260
Ties, Neck, **1:** 206–209
Tiffany & Company, **2:** 573, 764
Tiffen Manufacturing Corporation, **2:** 539
Tiger Electronics, **1:** 1290
Tilapia, **2:** 81
Tilden Mining Company, **2:** 129
Tiles
  brick, **1:** 653–655
  ceramic, **1:** 653, 655–657
  drain, **1:** 659
  fireproof, **1:** 653
  floor, **1:** 655–657, **2:** 286
  glazed, **1:** 655
  history of, **1:** 655–656, **2:** 282
  machine decorated, **1:** 656
  marble, **2:** 282–283
  mosaic, **1:** 655
  quarry, **1:** 655
  refractory, **1:** 657
  retail stores for, **2:** 709
  roofing, **1:** 655
  setting, **2:** 282–283
  structural, **1:** 653–655
  wall, **1:** 655–657
Tilghman, Benjamin, **1:** 915
Tillage, **2:** 85
  conservation, **2:** 44, 85
  mulch system, **2:** 85
  ridge system, **2:** 85
Tillman Act, **2:** 1391
Timber Company, **1:** 271, **2:** 109, 111
Timber Culture Act, **2:** 113

Timber Culture and Preemption Acts, **2:** 1499
Timber Harvesting. *See* Logging
Timber Tracts, 2: 107–109. *See also* Forests
Timberland Company, **1:** 618, 627–628, 629
Time, Inc., **2:** 1172, 1178
Time Delay, **1:** 1274
Time Division Multiple Access (TDMA), **1:** 1061, **2:** 452
Time Energy Systems Inc., **2:** 557
Time Equities Inc., **2:** 936
Time-Life Books, **1:** 405
Time Service Inc., **2:** 1168
Time Warner Entertainment, **2:** 473
Time Warner Inc., **1:** 396–397, **2:** 1179
  in book publishing, **1:** 404, 405
  in cable television, **2:** 472, 473, 474
  direct mail sales by, **2:** 1044
  inaters, **2:** 1195
  merger of, **2:** 1172
  in music publishing, **1:** 418, 1047, 1048, 1050, 1051
  periodical advertising by, **1:** 394
  in specialty services, **2:** 1128
Timers, **1:** 1224–1226
Times Mirror Center for the People and Press, **1:** 391
Times Mirror Company, **1:** 388, 392
Timeshare Lodging, **2:** 1001
Timeshare Technology, **1:** 948, 961, **2:** 1096
Timex Corporation, **1:** 1274
Timken Company, **1:** 930–931, 932–933
Timothy Grass, **2:** 24
Tin
  cans, **1:** 763, 764
  closures, **1:** 816
  mining, **2:** 159
Tindell, F. Carl, **2:** 617
Tinklepaugh, Bill, **1:** 28
Tinsmithing, **2:** 288
Tire Cord and Fabrics, 1: 190–191
Tire Retread Information Bureau, **2:** 1150
Tires, 1: 571–576
  aircraft, **1:** 1165, **2:** 1150
  all-weather, **1:** 574
  in asphalt paving, **1:** 567
  bias, **1:** 191
  carbon black for, **1:** 554, 555
  cord for, **1:** 190–191
  covers for, **1:** 265
  development of, **1:** 1128
  environmental impact of, **1:** 576
  fiberglass in, **1:** 573
  as fuel, **1:** 671, 675
  high performance, **1:** 191
  history of, **1:** 572–573, **2:** 1149
  imports of, **1:** 573, 575
  long-lasting, **1:** 477
  mini-spares, **2:** 667
  oil for, **2:** 1149
  pneumatic, **1:** 572, 573
  radial, **1:** 191, 474, 573, 574
  recycling, **1:** 475, 477, 573, 576
  repair shops, 2: 1149–1150
  retail stores for, 2: 664
  retreaded, **1:** 573, **2:** 530, 1149–1150
  run-flat, **1:** 575
  sales of, **1:** 571, 573, **2:** 667
  solid rubber, **1:** 572
  synthetic rubber, **1:** 472, 473, 474, 573

INDEX

INDEX

price of, **2:** 662

program cars as, **2:** 658

from rental services, **2:** 1133

sales of, **2:** 658–659

superstores for, **2:** 664

Used Merchandise Stores, 2: 749–750

USG Corporation, **1:** 677, 678

Usher, Hezekiah, **2:** 756

UST Inc., **1:** 156

USTS. *See* United States Travel Service

USX Corporation, **1:** 695, **2:** 1401

USX-U.S. Steel Group, **2:** 1401

Utah Clay Technology, **2:** 223

Utah Kaolin Corporation, **2:** 223

Utica Converters Inc., **1:** 191

Utilities. *See* Public Utilities

Utility Lines, 1: 1035, **2:** 264–266, 500, 505

construction of, **2:** 264–266

leasing, **2:** 448, 454

non-current carrying wiring devices for, **1:** 1035

Utility Poles, Treated, **1:** 302

Utility Trailer Manufacturing Company, **1:** 1140

Utility Trailer Rentals, 2: 1140–1141

V

V-Packings, **1:** 582, 583

VA-HUD Appropriations Act, **2:** 1490

VAC Chemical Corporation, **1:** 546

Vaccination Assistance Act, **2:** 1478

Vaccines, **1:** 500, 501, 502

colibacillosis, **1:** 501

development of, **1:** 490, 492, 503

feline leukemia, **1:** 501

for fish diseases, **2:** 125

genetically engineered, **1:** 495, 501

hepatitis, **1:** 495, 501

needleless, **1:** 502

pertussis, **1:** 501

polio, **2:** 1478

pseudorabies, **1:** 501

rabies, **1:** 501

swine flu, **2:** 1480

tetanum toxoids, **1:** 501

Vacoal, **2:** 693

Vacuum Arc Remelting, **1:** 811

Vacuum Cleaner Manufacturers Association, **1:** 1025

Vacuum Cleaners

canister, **1:** 1025

commercial, **1:** 985

household, 1: 1024–1025

installation of, **2:** 297

lawn, **1:** 864

rechargeable, **1:** 1025

robotic, **1:** 1025

stick, **1:** 1025

upright, **1:** 1024, 1025

Vacuum Coatings, **1:** 823

Vacuum Oil Company, **2:** 184

Vacuum Pumps, **1:** 937, 1216

Vacuum Tubes, **1:** 1008, 1112, **2:** 1398

Vagelos, Roy, **1:** 495

Vail Resorts Inc., **2:** 1235

Valet Parking Services, **2:** 1019

Valins, Martins S., **2:** 1278

Valley Crest Landscape Inc., **2:** 103

Valley Forge Corporation, **1:** 1041

Valley Leasing Company, **2:** 1139

Valley Pride, Inc., **2:** 101

Valley Resources Inc., **2:** 961

Valmont Industries Inc., **1:** 786

Valois, **1:** 816

Valor Electronics Inc., **1:** 1087

Valspar Corporation, **1:** 521, 524

Value-Added Partnering, **1:** 320

Value City Furniture Division, **2:** 532

Value Line Incorporated, **1:** 418

Value Line Investment Survey

on petroleum exploration, **2:** 201

on sheet metal, **1:** 795

on wastewater treatment, **2:** 514

Value Rent-A-Car, **2:** 1134

ValuJet Explosion, **1:** 1165–1166

Valve Closets, **1:** 607

Valve Manufacturers Association, **1:** 838

Valves, 1: 838–845

development of, **1:** 839

fluid power, **1:** 840–843, 872

hydraulic, **1:** 840–843, 872

industrial, 1: 838–840

intake and exhaust, 1: 986–988

metal, **1:** 844–845

miniaturized, **1:** 842

patterns for, **1:** 897

pneumatic, **1:** 840–843

for water treatment, **1:** 446

Valvoline Company, **1:** 569

Van Camp Seafood Company, **1:** 5, 120, 121

Van De Graaff, Robert J., **1:** 1113

Van Den Bergh Food Company, **1:** 36

Van Dusen and Meyer Inc., **1:** 853, 991

Van Heusen, John M., **1:** 200

Van Heusen Shirt Company, **1:** 200, 241

Van Kleeck, Bruce, **2:** 721

Van Museechenbroek, Pieter, **1:** 1079

Van Ommeren, **2:** 386

Van Pool Services Inc., **2:** 313

Vanadium Mining, **2:** 150–157

Vanderbilt, Cornelius, **1:** 130, **2:** 380

Vanderslice, James, **1:** 413

Vanguard Group, Inc., **2:** 884, 966

Vanguard-Supreme, **2:** 170

Vanity Fair Mills Inc., **1:** 239, 241

Vanpools, **2:** 309, 313, 314

Vans, Inc., **1:** 577, 622

Vapor Deposition Equipment, **1:** 925

Varco International, Inc., **2:** 191

Variable-Data-Rate Tape Drives, **1:** 960

Varian Associates Inc., **1:** 924

Variety Stores, 2: 637–642. *See also* Discount Stores

Varlen Corporation, **1:** 707, 752

Varney Airlines, **2:** 399

Varnishes. *See* Paints

Varsity Spirit Corporation, **1:** 258

Vaults (Bank), **1:** 854

Vaults (Burial), **1:** 1308

Vauquelin, Nicolas, **1:** 460

Vaux, Calvert, **2:** 1509

VCR. *See* Video Cassette Recorders

Veal, **1:** 12

Vectura Group, Inc., **2:** 386, 391

Vegetable Fibers, **1:** 681

Volatile Organic Compounds *(cont'd)*
  in automobile manufacturing, **2:** 659
  in cleaning products, **1:** 513
  in cosmetics and toiletries, **1:** 517
  in furniture manufacturing, **1:** 307, 316
  in paints and varnishes, **1:** 523, 527, **2:** 620, 1144, 1145
  in printing, **1:** 421, 427
  in refrigerants, **2:** 1145
  in soil, **2:** 86
Volcanic Repeating Arms Company, **1:** 834, 836
Volcanic Rock, Crushed, **2:** 210
Volfram. *See* Niobium
Volkswagen A.G., **1:** 1117, 1119, 1123, **2:** 343
Volleyball Equipment, **1:** 1293, 1294
Volpe, Justin, **2:** 1458
Volstead Act. *See* Pure Food and Drug Act
Volt Information Sciences Inc., **1:** 919
Volta, Alessandro, **1:** 819, 1097
Voltmeters, **1:** 1126
Voluntary Product Environmental Profile, **1:** 162
Voluntary Restraint Agreements, **1:** 693
Volvo GM, **1:** 1132, **2:** 659
Volvo North America Corporation, **1:** 1121, **2:** 1134
Volvo Truck Corporation, **1:** 858
Volvo-White Motor Trucks and Autocar, **1:** 1132
Von Braun, Werner, **1:** 1527
Von Guericke, Otto, **1:** 1037
Von Kekule, Friedrick. *See* von Stradonitz, Friedrich Kekule
Von Kleist, Ewald Georg, **1:** 1079
Von Neumann, John, **1:** 957
Von Richtofen, Manfred, **1:** 1144
Von Stradonitz, Friedrich Kekule, **1:** 530, 536
Vopalensky's Inc., **2:** 1170
Vornado Fans, **1:** 1024
Voss, William, **2:** 72
Vought, Chance, **1:** 1156
Voyager Emblems Inc., **1:** 264
Voyager Space Probes, **2:** 1530
VPS AG, **1:** 381
VPSI, **2:** 313
Vroom, Jay, **1:** 545
VTT Energy, **2:** 571
Vulcan Materials Company, **1:** 449, 566, 674, **2:** 214
Vulcanizable Elastomers. *See* Synthetic Rubber
Vultee Company, **1:** 1146
VVP America Inc., **2:** 537
VWR Scientific Products Corporation, **2:** 547, 562

W

Wabash Alloys, **1:** 732, 756
Wabash National Corporation, **1:** 1139
Wachner, Linda, **1:** 241
Wackenhut, George R., **2:** 1120
Wackenhut Corporation, **2:** 1119, 1120, 1123
Wackenhut Corrections Corporation, **2:** 1438
Wade & Leverich, **2:** 310
Waferboard, **1:** 303, 304
Waffle Irons, **1:** 1023
Waffles, Frozen, **1:** 70
Wages and Salaries
  in accounting, **2:** 1418
  in aerospace industry, **1:** 1199
  in agriculture, **2:** 45, 55
  in airline industry, **2:** 400
  in aluminum production, **1:** 725, 740, 744, 751–752

  in appliance manufacturing, **1:** 1012, 1021, 1022
  in architectural and ornamental metal work, **1:** 797
  in architectural services, **2:** 1410
  in asphalt products, **1:** 567
  in audio and video equipment, **1:** 1044
  in automatic control manufacturing, **1:** 1218
  in automobile repair shops, **2:** 1157
  in automotive manufacturing, **1:** 986, 1123
  in automotive parts stores, **2:** 669
  in bakeries, **1:** 68
  in ball and roller bearing manufacturing, **1:** 933
  in baseball, **2:** 1217–1218, 1222
  in basketball, **2:** 1221
  in book publishing, **1:** 405
  in bridge and tunnel construction, **2:** 261
  in bus services, **2:** 319, 321, 322
  in carbon and graphite production, **1:** 1006
  in cast iron foundries, **1:** 707–708
  in chemical manufacturing, **1:** 457, 476, 484, 539
  in clock and watch manufacturing, **1:** 1273
  in clothing manufacturing, **1:** 217, 218
  in commercial art, **2:** 1054
  in commercial real estate, **2:** 934
  in compressor manufacturing, **1:** 937
  in computer software, **2:** 1089
  in construction, **1:** 799, **2:** 256, 275, 289, 291
  in copper production, **1:** 736
  in copy shops, **2:** 1049
  in cruise lines, **2:** 375
  in cutlery industry, **1:** 770
  in dairy products, **1:** 30
  in day care centers, **2:** 1357
  in dental equipment manufacturing, **1:** 1249
  in distilleries, **1:** 108
  in durable goods manufacturing, **2:** 575
  in education, **2:** 1331, 1351
  in electrical contracting, **2:** 278
  in electromedical equipment, **1:** 1259
  in electronics repair, **2:** 1167
  in elevator and escalator manufacturing, **1:** 879
  in engineering services, **2:** 1402
  in fabricated metal products, **1:** 786, 794
  in fan and blower manufacturing, **1:** 940
  on farms, **2:** 66, 100
  in fastener manufacturing, **1:** 807
  in fish processing, **1:** 124
  in floor covering manufacturing, **1:** 1311
  in flour mills, **1:** 48
  in fluid power equipment manufacturing, **1:** 990
  in food production, **1:** 33, 143
  in food products machinery, **1:** 921
  in football, **2:** 1220
  in footwear manufacturing, **1:** 577, 616, 619
  in furniture manufacturing, **1:** 306, 317, 322, 325, 328
  in gasket and seal manufacturing, **1:** 584
  in gear manufacturing, **1:** 943
  in hand tool manufacturing, **1:** 771, 905
  in health care, **2:** 1263
    chiropractic, **2:** 1251
    dentistry, **2:** 1248
    hospitals, **2:** 1287–1288
    intermediate care, **2:** 1277
    nursing homes, **2:** 1272
    ophthalmic good manufacturing, **1:** 1264
    optometry, **2:** 1256
    physicians, **2:** 1239

INDEX

in pipelines, **2:** 418

therapeutic, **1:** 1252

X-Ray Corporation, **1:** 1250

X-Terminals, **1:** 962

Xaver Fendt Gmbh & Company, **1:** 863

Xeikon, **1:** 413

Xenon, **1:** 452, 453, 454

Xerographic Plates, **1:** 443

Xerography, **1:** 919, 1266

Xerox Corporation

bookbinding system, **1:** 438

in color imaging, **1:** 1308

history of, **1:** 919, 1266–1267, 1268, **2:** 540

managed care for, **2:** 899–900

in printers, **1:** 966

XM Satellite Radio, **2:** 463

Xpedite Systems Inc., **2:** 460

Xybernaut Corporation, **1:** 565

Xylenes, **1:** 529, 530, 531

XyliFresh, **1:** 83

Xylitol, **1:** 82

Y

Yag Lasers, **1:** 796

Yahoo!Inc, **2:** 1071, 1103

Yamaha Corporation of America, **1:** 1284, **2:** 574

Yamaha Motor Company Ltd., **1:** 1206, **2:** 678

Yamaichi International, **2:** 875

Yamato, **1:** 695

Yams, **2:** 24

Yankee Group, **1:** 1056, **2:** 448

Yard and Garden Equipment. *See* Lawn and Garden Equipment

Yarn, 1: 186–189

abrasion-resistant, **1:** 187

acetate, **1:** 186

acrylic, **1:** 186, 187

animal fiber, **1:** 186, 187

in broadwoven fabrics, **1:** 157

cordage, **1:** 186

cotton, **1:** 170, 186, 187

crafts, **2:** 773

dyeing, **1:** 180

elastic, **1:** 166

fabric covered, **1:** 166

filament, **1:** 160–161, 188

in hosiery, **1:** 168

in knit fabrics, **1:** 170

manmade, **1:** 160–161, 187

mohair, **1:** 186, 187

nylon, **1:** 187

partially oriented filament, **1:** 167, 187

plied, **1:** 188, 193

retail stores for, 2: 771–775

silk, **1:** 186, 187

in tire cord, **1:** 191

wholesalers of, 2: 581

wool, **1:** 163, 165, 186, 187

Yarn Mills

spinning, 1: 186–187, 910, 911

texturizing, 1: 187–189, 910

Ycaipa Companies, **2:** 614

Yearbooks, **1:** 418

Yeast

baking, **1:** 60–61, 62, 139, 143

extracts, **1:** 516

Yellow Book U.S.A., **1:** 418, 419

Yellow Cab Services Corporation, **2:** 315

Yellow Fever Epidemics, **2:** 1476

Yellow Freight, **2:** 329, 331

Yellow Journalism, **1:** 389

Yellow Lead Chromates, **1:** 457

Yellow Pages, **1:** 416

advertising in, **1:** 416, **2:** 1022

Yellow Pages Publishers Association, **1:** 417

Yoder Brothers Inc., **2:** 38

Yogi Bear's Jellystone Park Camp Resorts, **2:** 998

Yogurt, **1:** 25, 26, 28, **2:** 590, 652

frozen, **1:** 21, 23

Yogurt Ventures USA, **2:** 652

Yom Kippur War, **2:** 182–183

York Graphic Services Incorporated, **1:** 441

York Group, Inc., **1:** 1310

York International, **1:** 981

Yoshitomi Pharmaceutical Industries, Ltd., **1:** 502

Young, Andrew, **1:** 577

Young & Rubicam Inc., **2:** 1023

Young American Bowling Alliance, **2:** 1213

Young Men's Christian Association, **2:** 995, 1001, 1389

Young Sales Corporation, **2:** 289

Young Women's Christian Association, **2:** 995, 1396

Young's Market Company, **2:** 609

Youth Hostels Inc., **2:** 1001

Ypsilanti Reed Furniture Company, **1:** 309

Y&S Candies, **1:** 77

Yttrium, **1:** 852, **2:** 159

Yukon Express Service, **2:** 748

Yuzhnoye, **1:** 1192

YYY (USA), Inc., **1:** 1303

Z

Z-Seven Fund, **2:** 969

Zacky Foods, **2:** 591

Zale Corporation, **2:** 572, 573, 764

Zantac, **1:** 494, 497

ZAP Power Systems, **1:** 1184

Zapata Gulf Marine Corporation, **2:** 120, 390

Zapme!Corp., **2:** 1323

Zayre Corporation, **2:** 700

Zbrojovka-Vsetin, **1:** 161

Zebrafish, for Water Treatment, **2:** 510

Zeien, Alfred, **1:** 769

Zeigler Coal Holding Company, **2:** 171, 549

Zell, Sam, **2:** 983

Zeneca, **1:** 546

Zenger, John Peter, **1:** 389

Zenith Electronics Corporation, **1:** 1039, 1044, 1067

Zeolites, **1:** 510

Zerega, Antione, **1:** 136

Zero Emission Vehicles Company, **1:** 1120, **2:** 314

Zero-Inventory Manufacturing, **2:** 328

Ziegler, Karl, **1:** 473

Ziff-Davis, **1:** 396

ZIG-ZAG System, **1:** 883

Zila, Inc., **1:** 488

Zimmer, George, **2:** 685

Zimmerman, Harry, **2:** 642

Zimmerman, Mary, **2:** 642

Zinc

castings, **1:** 760

closures, **1:** 816